UNGER'S
BIBLE
DICTIONARY

By

MERRILL F. UNGER

✠

Drawings by

ROBERT F. RAMEY

MOODY PRESS

CHICAGO

Printed in the United States of America

PREFACE

IN 1900 CHARLES RANDALL BARNES edited a *Bible Encyclopaedia* which was the work of a number of distinguished scholars of that day and appeared in both a two-volume and a three-volume edition. In 1913 this work was issued in a single volume, which was identical in content with the earlier *Encyclopaedia* except that a short archaeological supplement by Melvin Grove Kyle was added. This edition was entitled *The People's Bible Encyclopaedia.*

The present dictionary is based upon this earlier *Bible Encyclopaedia.* However, it has been revised and rewritten in the light of the latest historical, archaeological and linguistic discoveries in Bible lands. Most of the more than 500 photographs, maps and drawings are new and were especially prepared for this volume. The eight splendid maps at the end of the book were prepared by C. S. Hammond & Company, Maplewood, N. J., and have not been previously used in any publication.

Only because of the drastic nature of the revision and rewriting of this earlier work and in acquiescence to the definite desires of the publisher, did the writer consent to the title, *Unger's Bible Dictionary.* In doing so, he has no intention of detracting from the credit due earlier scholars nor does he have any thought of diminishing his great obligation to them. Rather, he fully confesses his deep indebtedness to those whose labors preceded his.

Where new articles of any length have been added or older entries retained but completely revised, they are usually appended by the editor's initials. Large numbers of entries, however, that have to a great extent been rewritten have not been initialed and this is likewise the case with many completely rewritten shorter articles.

In addition to *Barnes' Bible Encyclopaedia* the editor acknowledges his heavy indebtedness to practically all of the standard Bible Dictionaries of the past seventy-five years. Especially useful have been Smith's Bible Dictionary (edited by James Hackett), Peloubet's, Davis', Davis' revised by Gehman, and Harper's.

Useful, too, have been *Encyclopaedia Biblica, The Jewish Encyclopaedia, The International Standard Bible Encyclopaedia,* Hasting's *Encyclopedia of Religion and Ethics,* Hasting's *Dictionary of the Bible* and *The New Schaff-Herzog Encyclopaedia of Religious Knowledge.*

Scientific periodicals have been consulted throughout, particularly the *Biblical Archaeologist, The Bulletin of the American Schools of Oriental Research, The Annual of the American Schools of Oriental Research, The Journal of Biblical Literature, Archiv für Orientforschung, Révue Biblique, The Bulletin of The*

John Rylands Library, *The American Journal of Semitic Languages and Literatures* and *Révue d'Assyriologie*, *Palästina Jahrbuch*, *Zeitschrift für Assyriologie* and *Zeitschrift des Deutschen Palästina-Vereins*.

In the preparation of this work the editor has made extensive use of the labors of contemporary scholars, in particular the published works of the following: Professor William Foxwell Albright, of the John Hopkins University, under whose stimulating guidance the author spent three years of study and research; the late professor James H. Breasted and Professor A. T. Olmstead, both of the University of Chicago; Professor Millar Burrows of Yale University; Dr. G. Ernest Wright of McCormick Seminary, Chicago; Dr. Nelson Glueck of the Hebrew Union College, Cincinnati; Eleazar L. Sukenik of the Museum of Jewish Antiquities, Jerusalem; and Professor H. L. Ginsberg of the Jewish Theological Seminary of New York.

Museums, publications and other agencies that have furnished photographs include the Oriental Institute of the University of Chicago (with special assistance of Miss Jessie Abbott), the Metropolitan Museum of Art, The Wellcome Trust, The British Museum, The Museum of the University of Pennsylvania, Princeton University Department of Art and Archaeology, The Turkish Information Office, The Royal Greek Embassy, The Consulate General of Israel (Chicago), The Department of Antiquities, Jerusalem, Israel, *The Biblical Archaeologist* and *The Bulletin of the American Schools of Oriental Research*. Special thanks is due Zondervan Publishing House and Jack Cochrane, artist, for the use of several illustrations from *Archaeology and the Old Testament*, by Merrill F. Unger.

Individuals furnishing private photographs taken in Bible Lands include Dr. Charles C. Ryrie of Dallas Theological Seminary; Dr. John C. Trever, Morris Harvey College; Dr. E. W. Saunders, Garrett Biblical Institute; Dr. G. Ernest Wright, McCormick Theological Seminary; Dr. André Parrot, the Louvre, Paris; Dr. O. R. Sellers, Santa Fe, N.M.; Dr. Kenneth W. Clark, Duke University; James Henry Breasted, Jr.; Dr. Ernest R. Lacheman, Wellesly College; Dr. Joseph P. Free, Wheaton College, Ill.; Rev. Richard E. Ward, Amman, Jordan; Mr. Fred Visser of the Fred Visser Company; Mrs. Lowell S. Orth, Dallas Bible Institute; Dr. Yigael Yadin, Hebrew University; Dr. James L. Kelso, Pittsburgh-Xenia Theological Seminary, Dr. Nelson Glueck, Hebrew Union College; Dr. William F. Albright, Johns Hopkins University; J. M. Allegro; and E. G. Howland. Mr. Robert Ramey drew practically all of the maps and line drawings used in the text.

While the editor is indebted to many authors and publishers, special thanks is due to The Johns Hopkins Press and the Muhlenberg Press for permission to use brief quotations from the writings of W. F. Albright; the University of Chicago Press for permission to quote from D. B. Luckenbill's *Ancient Records of Assyria and Babylonia*, Vols. I and II; the

Westminster Press for brief quotations from the *Westminster Historical Atlas to the Bible* by George Ernest Wright and Floyd Filson; Harper & Brothers, Publishers, for short references from the *Encyclopaedia of Bible Life,* by Madeline S. Miller and J. Lane Miller, and especially for many adaptations and for lengthy quotations from approximately fifty articles in the *Harper's Bible Dictionary* by Madeline S. Miller and J. Lane Miller; also for adaptations of twenty or more line drawings by Claire Valentine, prepared for *Harper's Bible Dictionary;* Princeton University Press for brief excerpts from Jack Finegan's *Life from the Ancient Past* and J. B. Pritchard's *Ancient Near Eastern Texts;* and Thomas Nelson & Sons and the Division of Christian Education of the National Council of Churches for brief quotations from the *Revised Standard Version.* Special acknowledgment is given Dr. A. Henry Detweiler, President of the American Schools of Oriental Research, for permission to quote briefly from the *Bulletin,* the *Annuals,* and the *Biblical Archaeologist.*

The dictionary, which is actually a one volume Bible Encyclopaedia, has aimed at clarity, conciseness and Biblical relevancy.

To achieve clarity and simplicity, longer articles have been outlined in bold type, so a busy reader can more readily locate what he is looking for without having to read through an entire article. Hebrew and Greek words have been transliterated for the convenience of lay readers, and full pronunciation of all proper names and places given. Mere technical discussions and impractical theorizings have been bypassed.

To achieve conciseness and Biblical relevancy the dictionary has omitted subjects that do not have a direct bearing upon the Bible. The goal has been to provide a readily usable handbook for the help of Bible teachers and Christian workers in general.

Duplication has been avoided by a system of cross references. In addition, consecutive study of particular subjects has been facilitated by subgroupings under general topics—such as, Animals, Dress, False Gods, Festivals, Handicrafts, etc. This arrangement enables the reader with ease to gain a comprehensive knowledge of a particular subject, if he so desires.

Four emphases characterize the dictionary. First, the *archaeological.* The latest contributions of scientific Biblical archaeology have been collated to expand and illustrate Bible backgrounds, customs, and history. Second, *the historical-geographical.* The facts of the history and geography of ancient Near Eastern lands as they bear upon the Bible are copiously drawn upon to make the Old and New Testament live. Third, *the biographical.* Bible characters are presented in consecutive narrative form, and events in their lives connected with the history, geography and archaeology of Palestine and the ancient Near East. Fourth, *the doctrinal.* Important Biblical doctrines are presented—yet not as held by any one group, but as subscribed to by the various segments of the Church as a whole.

In matters of chronology the editor employs an early (*c.* B. C. 1440) date for the Exodus and posits an extended period of *c.* 1400-1020 B. C. for the Period of the Judges. On the other hand, he is fully aware of the present trend of modern scholarship to place the Exodus much later (not before *c.* 1280 B. C.) and thereby practically to telescope the Era of the Judges. The editor feels this practice of late-dating in Israel's early history is so seriously out of focus with Biblical chronology that he has been unable conscientiously to subscribe to it in a work aimed at being not only accurate scientifically but sound theologically and Biblically. However, after the period of Saul (*c.* B. C. 1020), the author follows substantially the results of chronological researches of Albright, Kugler, Vogelstein, Thiele, Begrich and others in a period where archaeological synchronisms are more specific and incontrovertible.

The editor is especially grateful to Dr. Howard Vos, professor at the Moody Bible Institute, Chicago, for invaluable editorial assistance, to Dr. Charles Pfeiffer, also of the Moody Bible Institute, for his careful research in finding appropriate illustrations for the dictionary, and to Mr. Kenneth Taylor and the Moody Press staff for their efficiency in the publication of the work.

MERRILL F. UNGER

Dallas, Texas

TO THE READER

In general, after each entry appears a set of parentheses enclosing the pronunciation, followed by a semicolon and the meaning of the entry in italics. Sometimes, as with such terms as *darkness*, where a pronunciation is not needed, Greek or Hebrew words from which the English is translated are listed and defined. In these instances, and elsewhere throughout the text, Hebrew words are transliterated with full diacritical markings; Greek words are transliterated with only long vowels marked. When words are followed by *q. v.*, more information can be found on the given subject under that heading.

Line drawing maps accompany articles where it is thought they will be of most help to the reader. Full color maps appear at the end of the text.

ABBREVIATIONS

Contributors

S. L. B.   Rev. S. L. Bowman
H. A. B.   Professor H. A. Buttz
W. H.   W. Haskell, Yale University
D. S. M.   Professor D. S. Martin, Barnard College, New York City
E. McC.   Rev. E. McChesney

J. F. McC.   Professor J. F. McCurdy, Toronto, Canada
G. E. P.   George E. Post, M.D., Beirut, Syria
R. W. R.   Professor R. W. Rogers, Assyrian scholar
A. H. T.   Rev. A. H. Tuttle
M. F. U.   Merrill F. Unger

General

A. D.   *anno domini* (in the year of our Lord)
A. U. C.   *ab urbe condita* (from the founding of the city—Rome)
Ant.   *Antiquities of the Jews* by Josephus
art.   article
A. V.   Authorized Version (King James)
B. C.   Before Christ
c.   *circa* (about)
cen.   century
cf.   *confer* (compare)
chap.   chapter
Com.   *Commentary*
e. g.   *exempli gratia* (for example)
et al.   and others
f.   following
Gr.   Greek
Heb.   Hebrew
ibid.   *ibidem* (in the same place)
i. e.   *id est* (that is)

in loc.   *in loco* (used in conjunction with commentaries and signifying that the discussion can be found under the appropriate verse in the commentary)
illus.   illustration
K. & D.   Keil and Delitzsch (commentators)
LXX   *Septuagint* (Greek translation of the Old Testament)
marg.   margin, marginal reading
MS., MSS   manuscript, manuscripts
N. T.   New Testament
op. cit.   *opere citato* (in the work cited)
O. T.   Old Testament
p., pp.   page, pages
pl.   plural
q. v.   *quod vide* (which see)
R. S. V.   Revised Standard Version
R. V.   Revised Version
sing.   singular
sq.   *sequentia* (the following)

KEY TO PRONUNCIATION

ā   as in lāte
å   as in våcation
â   as in câre
ă   as in ădd
ä   as in fäther
à   as in àsk
ē   as in ēve
ê   as in dêpend
ě   as in pět
ẽ   as in portẽr
ī   as in līke

ĭ   as in tĭll
î   as in marîne
ō   as in ōat
ȯ   as in ȯbey
ô   as in lôrd
ǒ   as in nǒt
ōō   as in sōōn
ū   as in fūse
û   as in ûnite
û   as in tûrn
ǔ   as in rǔb

The accent mark (′) shows the syllable receiving the primary stress.

SIDON

TYRE

SYRIA

MEDITERRANEAN SEA

MEROM   HAZOR
           CHORAZIN
              CAPERNAUM
ACHSHAPH   KARNAIM
  SALMONAH
  HELKATH   BETH YERAH
  HAROSHETH
ATHLIT SHEIKH NAZARETH   TELL EL-HAMMEH
         ABREIQ
MEGIDDO   MT TABOR
  TAANACH   AFFULEH
               BETH ALFA
           DOTHAN

Z

                    AJLUN
  SAMARIA   TIRZAH
MT GERIZIM   GERASA
         SHECHEM
APHEK
TELL EL-QASILEH ZEREDAH
TELL EJ-JERISHEH SHUQBAH SHILOH

RIVER JORDAN

         BETHEL
GEZER MIZPAH AI
  EMMAUS GIBEAH
ABU GHOSH JERICHO
         JERUSALEM   TELEILAT EL-GHASSUL
BETH-SHEMESH
   BEIT JEMAL BETHLEHEM   MEDEBA
LIBNAH AZEKAH
ASHKELON
         MORESHETH-GATH
LACHISH ELEUTHEROPOLIS   DIBON
  GAZA MARESHAH BETH-ZUR
BETH-EGLAIM EL-QUBEIBEH MAMRE
  TELL JEMMEH DEBIR
         ZAHARIYEH MASADA
  SHARUHEN   ESHTEMOA   BAB EDH-DHRA
                         ADER
      TELL ABU MATAR

P   DEAD SEA

A

L

E

S

T

I

N

E

TRANSJORDAN

   KHIRBET ET-TANNUR
  AUJA EL-HAFIR
    SUBAITA

EGYPT

SOME OF MANY
EXCAVATION SITES
MAJOR EXCAVATIONS •
MINOR EXCAVATIONS ○
0 5 10 15 20 25 30

PETRA

A

Aaron (ār'ŭn; Heb. derivation uncertain), the son of Amram the Levite and Jochebed (Exod. 6:20) and the first high priest of Israel. He was the brother of Moses and his senior by three years, although he was younger than his sister Miriam (*q. v.*). His wife was Elisheba, the daughter of Amminadab, by whom he had four sons: Nadab, Abihu, Eleazar and Ithamar. (Exod. 6:23). 1. **Moses' Assistant.** He was eloquent of speech and divinely appointed to be Moses' mouthpiece (prophet). God specifically told Moses that Aaron would be his "spokesman unto the people" and that "he shall be to thee a mouth, and thou shalt be to him as God" (Exod. 4:16). Together with Moses he withstood Pharoah and saw the deliverance of the Israelites from Egypt by great signs and miracles. In the battle with Amalek, Aaron and Hur supported Moses' arms, which held the official rod, and the uplifting of which brought victory to Israel. When Moses went up to Mount Sinai to receive the tables of the law (Exod. 24:12), Aaron and his sons, Nadab and Abihu, and the seventy elders accompanied him part of the way, being granted a glimpse of the divine presence (Exod. 24:1-11). While Moses was on the mountain, Aaron in a moment of weakness and under pressure from the people made a golden image of a male calf as a visible symbol of Jehovah (Exod. 32:4). The choice of this animal was doubtless suggested by the vigor and strength symbolized by it and by the people's recollection of bull worship in Egypt. 2. **High Priest.** In the divine institution of the priesthood Aaron was appointed high (Heb. "great") priest, and his sons and descendants priests. The tribe of Levi was consecrated as the sacerdotal caste. After the Tabernacle was erected according to the divine plan and the ritual established (Exod. 24:12-31; 18; 35:1-40:38), Aaron and his sons were solemnly consecrated to their priestly office by Moses (Lev. 8:6) about 1440 B. C. (cf. I Kings 6:1). The elaborate description of the High Priest's garments of "glory and beauty" (Exod. 28:2), including the jewelled ephod, mitre, head tire, is not an anachronistic retrojection from a later period. Archaeology has shown that in the Desert of Sinai at Serabit el-Khadem turquoise and copper were being mined for Egyptian craftsmen at this early period. The "jewels of silver and gold" which the Israelites borrowed from the Egyptians (Exod. 11:2) are illustrated from most ancient times. Artistic gold and jewelled ornaments were recovered from the ruins of Sumerian Ur many centuries before the Mosaic period, and there is nothing in the furnishing of the tabernacle or the clothing of

the high priest that would be out of keeping with the artistic accomplishments of contemporary craftsmen of the period. In his invidious conduct against Moses (Num. 12:1-15) the same weak side of Aaron's character appears as in the incident of the golden calf.

1. Jewish High Priest

In the conspiracy formed against Aaron and Moses led by Korah, a Levite, and Dathan and Abiram, Reubenites, the destruction of the conspirators by the hand of God resulted in the vindication of the Aaronic priesthood (Num. 16). An added attestation of Aaron's divine priestly appointment was the budding of his rod, which was preserved "for a token against the children of rebellion" (Num. 17:10). Aaron shared Moses' sin at Meribeh (Num. 20:8-13, 24) and consequently was not allowed to enter the Promised Land, dying soon after (Num. 20:22-29) on Mount Hor at the borders of Edom. 3. **Type of Christ.** In Scripture typology Aaron is a figure of Christ, our High Priest (Exod. 28:1), who executes His priestly office after the Aaronic pattern (Heb. 9). This type is seen (1) in Aaron's offering sacrifice, (2) in being anointed with oil by *pouring* (Exod. 29:7; Lev. 8:12), prefiguring our Lord's measureless anointing with the Holy Spirit (John 3:34), (3) in bearing the names of the Israelite Tribes upon his breast and shoulders, thus presenting them perpetually before God as our Lord bears our cause before the Father (John 17; Heb. 7:25) in entering into the Holy Place on the Day of Atonement (Lev. 16) as Christ has entered "into heaven itself, now to appear in the presence of God for us" (Heb. 9:24). *M. F. U.*

A'aronite, descendants of Aaron, and therefore priests, who to the number of three thousand seven hundred fighting men under Jehoiada joined David at Hebron (I Chron. 12:27). Later we find that their leader was Zadok (I Chron. 27:17).

Ab (ăb), Babylonian name of the fifth ecclesiastical and the eleventh civil month of the Jewish year. It was introduced after the Babylonian captivity, and is not mentioned in Scripture, in which it is known as the *fifth* month (Num. 33:38).

Ab (ăb; *father*), the first member of several Hebrew compound names, e.g., Absalom, etc.

Abad'don (á-băd'dŏn; Gr. *'Abaddon, destruction*), the angel of the bottomless pit (Rev. 9:11), and corresponding to Apollyon, *destroyer*. The word *abaddon* means destruction (Job 31:12), or the place of destruction, i.e., Hades or the region of the dead (Job. 26:6; 28:22; Prov. 15:11).

Abag'tha (á-băg'thá), one of the seven chief eunuchs of Xerxes, who were commanded by the king to bring Queen Vashti into the royal presence (Esth. 1:10), 486-465 B. C.

Aba'na (á-bá'ná), one of the rivers of Damascus (II Kings 5:12). It is, no doubt, the present *Barada*, and has its source in Anti-Lebanon Mts. and flows through the city of Damascus; thence after fifty miles it is lost in the marshy lake Bahret el-Kibliyeh. It was one of the rivers which Naaman would have washed in rather than the river Jordan (marg. *Amana*). Greek, Chrysorrhoas, "golden river."

Ab'arim (ăb'á-rîm; *regions beyond*), a mountain chain S. E. of the Dead Sea, and of which Pisgah is a part, or Mount Nebo (Deut. 3:27; 32:49). Israel had an encampment in the mountains of Abarim (Num. 33:47, 48).

Ab'ba (ăb'á), a customary title of God in prayer (Mark 14:36; Rom. 8:15; Gal. 4:6). It was in common use in the mixed Aramaic dialect of Palestine, and was used by children in addressing their father. It answers to our *papa*. The right to call God "Father" in a special and appropriative sense pertains to all who have received the testimony of the Spirit to their forgiveness. *See* Adoption.

Ab'da (ăb'dá; *the servant*, i. e., *of God*).
1. The father of Adoniram, which latter was an officer of the tribute under Solomon (I Kings 4:6), B. C. about 960.
2. The son of Shammua, and a Levite of the family of Jeduthun, resident in Jerusalem after the exile (Neh. 11:17), B. C. after 444. Elsewhere (I Chron. 9:16) he is called Obadiah the son of Shemaiah.

Ab'deel (ăb'dĕ-ĕl; *servant of God*), the father of Shelemaiah, which latter was one of those appointed to apprehend Jeremiah (Jer. 36:26), B. C. before 606.

Ab'di (ăb'dĭ; *my servant*).
1. A Levite, and grandfather of Ethan; the latter was one of the singers appointed by David for the sacred service (I Chron. 6:44).
2. A Levite, in the reign of Hezekiah, father of Kish (II Chron. 29:12).
3. One of the sons of Elam, who put away his Gentile wife after the return from Babylon (Ezra 10:26), B. C. 456.

Ab'diel (ăb'dĭ-ĕl; *servant of God*), son of Guni and father of Ahi, one of the Gadites resident in Gilead (I Chron. 5:15).

Ab'don (ăb'dŏn; *servile*).
1. The son of Hillel, a Pirathonite, of the tribe of Ephraim. He ruled Israel for eight years, B. C. about 1120-1112. The only other fact respecting him is that he had forty sons and thirty nephews (marg. sons' sons), who rode on young asses—a mark of their consequence before the introduction of the horse into Israel. Upon his death he was buried in Pirathon (Judg. 12:13-15).
2. A son of Shashak, and one of the chief Benjamites dwelling in Jerusalem (I Chron. 8:23), B. C. before 1200.
3. The firstborn of Gibeon, a Benjamite resident at Jerusalem (I Chron. 8:30; 9:36), ancestor of King Saul.
4. The son of Micah, and one of those sent by King Josiah to Huldah to inquire concerning the recently discovered books (II Chron. 34:20, sq.), B. C. about 624. In II Kings 22:12, he is called Achbor.

Abed'nego (á-bĕd'nĕ-gō; *servant of Nego* or *Nebo*), the Babylonian god of wisdom, connected with the planet Mercury. Abednego was the Aramaic name given to Azariah by the king of Babylon's officer, and was one of the three Jewish youths who, with Daniel, were selected by Ashpenaz (master of the eunuchs) to be educated in the language and wisdom of the Chaldeans (Dan. 1:3, ff). With his two friends, Shadrach and Meshach, he was cast into the fiery furnace for refusing to worship the golden statue set up by Nebuchadnezzar, but was miraculously delivered (Dan. 3) B. C. about 606. The Hebrew name Azariah means "Jehovah has helped." The folly of trying to change inward character by an outward name is hereby illustrated. A tyrant may change the name but not the nature of one true to God. *M. F. U.*

A'bel, 1. (ā'bĕl; Heb. *hĕbĕl*, breath), probably applied to the younger son of Adam and Eve anticipatively because of the brevity of his life, being slain by his elder brother Cain. Abel, a shepherd and a righteous man (Matt. 23:35; I John 3:12), speaks of a regenerate believer. Cain, the farmer, on the other hand, well illustrates the unregenerate natural man, whose worship was destitute of any adequate sense of sin or need of atonement, and who offered the works of his hands instead of faith as a basis of acceptance with God. Abel, by contrast, in bringing "the firstlings of his flock and the fat thereof" (Gen. 4:4), shed atoning blood (Heb. 9:22). By this act he confessed his sense of sin and need of atonement, and exercised faith in the interposition of a coming Substitute (Gen. 3:15; Heb. 11:4), instead of presenting the works of his hands as a ground for acceptance with God. *M. F. U.*

A′bel, 2. (Heb. *'ābēl*; a *grassy place*, or *meadow*.)

1. A word used as a prefix in a number of cases (II Sam. 20:14, 18). *See* Abel-beth-maachah.

2. A great stone (I Sam. 6:18) near Beth-shemesh, upon which the Philistines set the ark when they returned it to Israel.

A′bel-beth-ma′achah (ā′bĕl-bĕth-mā′á-ká; *meadow of the house of oppression*, II Sam. 20:14, 15; I Kings 15:20; II Kings 15:29), a place in the north of Palestine, near the waters of Merom, identified with Abil-el-Kumh. In II Sam. 20:14, 18, it is called simply Abel. It was a place of importance, a metropolis, and called a "mother of Israel" (II Sam. 20:19). It was besieged by Joab, Ben-hadad, and Tiglath-pileser (II Sam. 20:14; I Kings 15:20; II Kings 15:29).

A′bel-ma′im (ā′bĕl-mā′ĭm; *meadow of water*), the name by which Abel-beth-maachah is called in II Chron. 16:4.

A′bel-meho′lah (ā′bĕl-mê-hō′lăh; *meadow of dancing*), a place in the Jordan valley, and the home of Elisha (I Kings 19:16; Judg. 7:22). It was in the tribe of Issachar. Identified by Nelson Glueck with Tell el-Maqlub. (*See, The River Jordan*, Phila., Westminster Press, pp. 166-174.)

A′bel-miz′raim (ā′bĕl-mĭz′rā-ĭm; *meadow*, or *mourning, of Egypt*), the scene of the lament of Egypt over Jacob (Gen. 50:11); the name the Canaanites gave to the "threshing-floor of Atad" in Transjordan.

A′bel-shit′tim (ā′bĕl-shĭt′tĭm; *meadow of acacias*), the last halting place of Israel (Num. 33:49). Identified as Tell el-Hammam in the plains of Moab opposite Jericho. The acacias still fringe the upper terraces of the Jordan with green. Near Mount Peor at Shittim in the shade of the acacia groves, Israel was lured into the licentious rites of Baal worship (Num. 25:1; Josh. 2:1; Mic. 6:5), resulting in the death of twenty-four thousand by plague.

A′bez (ā′bĕz) in A. V., same as Ebez, *tin*, a town in Issachar (Josh. 19:20).

A′bi (ä′bî; *my father*), the daughter of Zachariah and mother of King Hezekiah (II Kings 18:2). The fuller form of the name, Abijah, is given in II Chron. 29:1.

A′bi (ä′bî; an old construct form of *father of*) forms the first part of several Hebrew proper names.

Abi′a (á-bī′á), another form of *Abiah* (*q. v.*).

1. The name given in I Chron. 3:10 to the son of Rehoboam, king of Judah.

2. (Gr. *'Abia*). A priest in the time of David (Luke 1:5), called Abijah (I Chron. 24:10).

Abi′ah (á-bī′á), another mode of anglicizing *Abijah* (*q. v.*).

1. The second son of Samuel, appointed with Joel, his elder brother, judge of Beersheba, by his father. The brothers "turned aside after lucre, and took bribes, and perverted judgment." By reason of their conduct Israel demanded of Samuel a king (I Sam. 8:2, sq.; I Chron. 6:28), B. C. before 1030.

2. The wife of Hezron and mother of Ashur (I Chron. 2:24).

3. One of the sons of Becher, the son of Benjamin (I Chron. 7:8).

A′bi-al′bon (á′bī-ăl′bŏn; *father of strength, valiant*), one of David's mighty men (II Sam. 23:31), called in the parallel passage (II Chron. 11:32), by the equivalent name *Abiel* (*q. v.*).

Abi′asaph (á-bī′ă-săf; *father of gathering*), the last-mentioned (Exod. 6:24) of the sons of Korah, the Levite. His identity with *Ebiasaph* (*q. v.*) (I Chron. 6:23, 37) is a matter of much uncertainty and difference of opinion. The probability is that they are different persons.

Abi′athar (á-bī′á-thär; *father of preeminence*, i.e. *preeminent*), a high priest and fourth in descent from Eli, who alone of the sons of the high priest Ahimelech escaped death when Saul, in revenge for aid given to David, attempted to wipe out this entire line of priests (I Sam. 22). Fleeing to David, Abiathar inquired of the Lord for him in the fierce struggle with Saul (I Sam. 23:9, 10; 30:7), and became his lifelong friend. When he became king, he appointed Abiathar high priest (I Kings 2:26, I Chron. 15:11). David did not depose Zadok, whom Saul had appointed after Ahimelech's decease. Both appointments accordingly stood, and Zadok and Abiathar constituted a double high priesthood (I Kings 4:4). They jointly superintended the transfer of the ark to Jerusalem (I Kings 2:26, I Chron. 15:11). During Absalom's rebellion Abiathar remained loyal to David (II Sam. 15:24). However, he adhered to Adonijah when the latter attempted to gain the royal succession at David's death, while Zadok cast his lot with Solomon (I Kings 1:19). For this unwise move Solomon banished Abiathar to Anathoth, deposing him from his office (I Kings 2:26, 27), and confining the high priestly succession to Zadok of the elder line of Aaron's sons. In this manner the rule of Eli's house terminated in fulfilment of prophecy (I Sam. 2:31-35). **Difficulties.** The reference to Ahimelech, the son of Abiathar, as priest with Zadok (II Sam. 8:17) is most unusual and is regarded by many as a simple copyist's error, in which the names of the father and the son were accidentally transposed. But this solution of the difficulty is unlikely since the references to Ahimelech, the son of Abiathar, as priest are so clear that a mistake is not easily explained (I Chron. 18:16, Septuagint; 24:3, 6, 31). The best explanation seems to be that Abiathar, who was becoming quite old toward the latter part of David's reign, had his eldest son Ahimelech assume the heavy responsibility of the priesthood, and who, accordingly, was actually considered as the functioning high priest in the place of his father. The reference to Abiathar in Mark 2:26 as high priest at Nob (instead of his father Ahimelech, as recounted in I Samuel 21:1) is to be explained under the supposition either that our Lord used the name of the more famous priest of the two, who, though not then actually high priest, was at the tabernacle at the time alluded to, or that the son acted as coadjutor to his father, as Eli's sons apparently did (I Sam. 4:4). *M. F. U.*

A'bib (ā'bĭb; *an ear of corn*), the month the Hebrews were divinely directed to make the first of the year as a memorial of their deliverance from Egypt (Exod. 12:1, 2; 13:4). The passover and the feast of unleavened bread occurred in it, and it marked the beginning of the barley harvest. On the tenth day the passover lamb was selected and on the fourteenth day was slain and eaten. On the fifteenth day the Jews began harvesting by gathering a sheaf of the barley first fruits and on the sixteenth day offered it (Lev. 23:4-14). The slaying of the lamb was typical of the death of Christ, the feast of unleavened bread of the believer's separated walk, while the waving of the sheaf of first fruits spoke of the resurrection of Christ. The Jewish months were lunar, and do not exactly correspond to ours, which are fixed. Abib corresponds to March-April, and its name was changed to Nisan (*q. v.*) after the exile (Neh. 2:1; Esth. 3:7). *M. F. U.*

Abi'da (à-bī'dă; *father of knowledge*, that is, *knowing*), the fourth of the five sons of Midian, the son of Abraham by Keturah (Gen. 25:4; I Chron. 1:33).

Abi'dah (à-bī'dă), a less correct mode of anglicizing Abida (Gen. 25:4).

Abi'dan (à-bī'dăn; *father of judgment*, i. e., *judge*), son of Gideoni, prince of the tribe of Benjamin (Num. 1:11; 2:22; 10:24). *See* Num. 7:60, 65.

A'biel (ā'bĭ-ĕl; *father of strength*, i. e., *strong*).
  1. A Benjamite, son of Zeror (I Sam. 9:1) and father of Ner (I Sam. 14:51), which last was the grandfather of King Saul (I Chron. 8:33, 9:39). In I Sam. 9:1 the phrase "son of Abiel" should be "grandson of Abiel."
  2. One of David's mighty men (I Chron. 11:32). He is the same as Abi-albon, the Arbathite (II Sam. 23:31), B. C. about 1000.

Abie'zer (ā'bĭ-ē'zẽr; *father of help*, i. e., *helpful*).
  1. The second son of Hammoleketh, sister of Gilead and granddaughter of Manasseh (I Chron. 7:17, 18). He was the founder of the family to which Gideon belonged, and which bore his name as a patronymic (Josh. 17:2; Judg. 6:34), B. C. before 1170. He is elsewhere called Jeezer, and his descendants Jeezerites (Num. 26:30).
  2. The Anethothite, one of David's thirty chief warriors (II Sam. 23:27). Abiezer commanded the ninth division of the army (I Chron. 27:12), B. C. 1000.

Abi'ezrite (à-bī'ĕz-rīt; *father of the Ezrite*), a patronymic designation of the descendants of Abiezer (Judg. 6:11, 24; 8:32).

Ab'igail (ăb'ĭ-gāl; *father of joy*, i. e., *exultation*).
  1. The wife of Nabal (*q. v.*), a sheep master of Carmel (I Sam. 25:3), B. C. about 1000. In sheep-shearing time David sent some of his young men to Nabal for a present, which was insolently refused. David was greatly enraged, and set out with four hundred men to avenge the insult. Abigail, having been informed of her husband's conduct and the impending danger, went to meet David with an abundant supply of bread, corn, wine, etc. She prayed David's forbearance, arguing from Nabal's character (v. 25), the leadings of God by which David had been kept from murder by

her coming to meet him, and the fact that God is the avenger of the wicked (v. 26). David was mollified by Abigail's tact and beauty, and he recalled his vow. Returning home, Abigail found her husband intoxicated, and told him nothing of her conduct and his danger until morning. The information produced so great a shock "that his heart died within him, and he became as a stone" (v. 37), and he died about ten days after. Abigail became David's wife, and shared his varying fortunes, dwelling at Gath (I Sam. 27:3), being among the captives taken by the Amalekites from Ziklag (30:5), and accompanying her husband to Hebron when he was anointed king (II Sam. 2:2). She bore David a son named Chileab (3:3), called also Daniel (I Chron. 3:1).
  2. A daughter of Nahash (Jesse) and sister of David, and wife of Jether, or Ithra, an Ishmaelite, by whom she had Amasa (II Sam. 17:25; I Chron. 2:16, 17).

Ab'ihail (ăb'ĭ-hāl; *father of might*, i. e., *mighty*).
  1. The father of Zuriel, which latter was chief of the Levitical family of Merari when Moses numbered the Levites at Sinai (Num. 3:35), B. C. c.1440.
  2. The wife of Abishur (of the family of Jerahmeel) and mother of Ahban and Molid (I Chron. 2:29).
  3. The son of Huri, and one of the chiefs of the family of Gad, who settled in Bashan (I Chron. 5:14).
  4. The daughter, i. e., *descendant*, of Eliab, David's oldest brother, and second wife of Rehoboam. She could hardly have been the daughter of Eliab, as David, his youngest brother, was thirty years old when he began to reign, some eighty years before her marriage (II Chron. 11:18).
  5. The father of Esther and uncle of Mordecai (Esth. 2:15; 9:29), B. C. c. 500.

Abi'hu (à-bī'hū; *father is he*, i. e., *to whom He* (God) *is Father*). One of Aaron's sons, who with his brother Nadab offered "strange fire before the Lord, which he commanded them not" (Lev. 10:1, 2). As a result both priests were struck dead by the divine Presence manifested in fire. The sin of Nadab and Abihu, illustrative of the sin of a believer unto physical death (I Cor. 5:5; I John 5:16) was in acting in the things of God without first seeking the mind of God. It was "will worship" (Col. 2:23). Supernatural fire from the divine Presence had kindled the natural fire which burned upon the altar of burnt-offering. It was the priests' duty to keep this fire burning continuously. No command, however, had been given as to how the incense should be kindled (Lev. 16:12). Not waiting for instruction concerning taking the sacred fire from the brazen altar, but taking common fire which they themselves had kindled, they lighted the incense on the golden altar. This flagrant sacrilege at the commencement of a new dispensation (the legal) had to be divinely punished to serve as a warning, as the sin of Ananias and Sapphira at the beginning of the New Testament Church age was similarly severely dealt with (Acts 5:1-11). Aaron's disobedient sons seem, moreover, to have committed their serious trespass under the influence of wine (cf. Lev. 10:8, 9). The true source of exhilaration in the genuine spiritual priest, is not wine, with its attendant temptations and perils, but the Holy Spirit (Eph. 5:18). *M. F. U.*

Abi'hud (à-bī'hûd; *father of renown*), one of the sons of Bela, the son of Benjamin (I Chron. 8:3).

Abi'jah (à-bī'jà; *whose father God is*).

1. A son of Jeroboam I, king of Israel. On his falling ill Jeroboam sought help secretly from the God whom he had openly forsaken. He sent his wife, disguised and bearing a present of bread and honey, to Ahijah, the prophet, who was at Shiloh. The prophet was blind, but had been warned by God of her coming. He revealed to her that, though the child was to die, yet because there was found in Abijah only, of all the house of Jeroboam, "some good thing toward the Lord," he only, of all that house, should come to his grave in peace, and be mourned in Israel. The queen returned home, and the child expired as she crossed the threshold. "And they buried him; and all Israel mourned for him" (I Kings 14:1-18), B. C. about 922.

2. The second king of the separate kingdom of Judah, the son of Rehoboam and grandson of Solomon (I Chron. 3:10). He is called *Abia* (I Chron. 3:10), *Abijah* (II Chron. 12: 16), and *Abijam* (I Kings 14:31; 15:1-8). Abijah began to reign B. C. 915, in the eighteenth year of Jeroboam, king of Israel, and reigned three years. Considering the separation of the ten tribes of Israel as rebellion, Abijah made a vigorous attempt to bring them back to their allegiance. He marched with four hundred thousand men against Jeroboam, who met him with eight hundred thousand men. In Mount Ephraim he addressed a speech to Jeroboam and the opposing army, in which he advocates a theocratic institution, refers to the beginning of the rebellion, shows the folly of opposing God's kingdom, and concludes with urging Israel not to fight against God. His view of the political position of the ten tribes with respect to Judah, though erroneous, is such as a king of Judah would be likely to take. He gained a signal victory over Jeroboam, who lost five hundred thousand men, and though he did not bring Israel to their former allegiance, he took Beth-el, Jeshanah, and Ephraim, with their dependent towns, from them, and Jeroboam never again warred with him (II Chron. 13:1-20). He imitated his father's sins (I Kings 15:3), and had fourteen wives, by whom he had twenty-two sons and sixteen daughters (II Chron. 13:21). He was succeeded by Asa, his son (II Chron. 14:1).

NOTE.—*The maternity of Abijah.* In I Kings 15:2, we read, "His mother's name was Maachah, the daughter of Abishalom" (comp. II Chron. 11:20, 22); but in II Chron. 13:2, "His mother's name also was Michaiah, the daughter of Uriel of Gibeah." The solution of the difficulty probably is that the mother of Abijah had two names, and that Absalom was her grandfather.

3. One of the descendants of Eleazar, the son of Aaron, and chief of one of the twenty-four courses or orders into which the whole body of the priesthood was divided by David (I Chron. 24:10). Of these the course of Abijah was the eighth, B. C. 1000.

4. The daughter of Zechariah and mother of King Hezekiah (II Chron. 29:1), and, consequently, the wife of Ahaz. She is called Abi (II Kings 18:2), B. C. before 719.

5. One of the priests, probably, who affixed their signatures to the covenant made with God by Nehemiah (Neh. 10:7). He seems to be the same (notwithstanding the great age this implies) who returned from Babylon with Zerubbabel (Neh. 12:4), and who had a son Zichri (Neh. 12:17), B. C. 445.

Abi'jam (à-bī'jăm; *father of the sea*, i. e., *seaman*), the name always given in the Book of Kings to the daughter of Judah (I Kings 14:31; 15:1, 7, 8); elsewhere called Abijah. I Kings 14:1, refers to another person. *Abijam* is probably a clerical error, some manuscripts giving Abijah.

Abile'ne (ăb-ĭ-lē'nē; Gr. *'Abilēnē*, so-called from its capital Abila, which probably in turn was derived from Heb. *'abel, meadow*). A Tetrarchy on the eastern slope of Lebanon, governed in the 15th year of Tiberius by Lysanias (Luke 3:1). Abila lay on the Barada (Abana) about 20 miles N. W. of Damascus, where the modern village of es-Suk now stands. Tradition in naming the spot as the location of the tomb of Abel, the first martyr, is the result of confusing Abel, properly Hebrew *Hebel* with *'abel*, "a meadow." Latin inscriptions found here mentioning repairs to the local road by the *Abileni* and having reference to the 16th legion, identify the place. *M. F. U.*

Abim'ael (à-bĭm'â-ĕl; *father of Mael*), one of the sons of Joktan, in Arabia (Gen. 10:28; I Chron. 1:22). He has been supposed to be the founder of an Arabian tribe called Maël.

Abim'elech (à-bĭm'ĕ-lĕk; *father of the king*, i. e., *royal father*), probably a general title of royalty, as *Pharaoh* among the Egyptians.

1. **The Philistine king of Gerar** in the time of Abraham (Gen. 20:1, sq.), B. C. about 2086. After the destruction of Sodom, Abraham removed into his territory, and remained some time at Gerar. Abimelech took Sarah, whom Abraham had announced to be his sister, into his harem, being either charmed with her beauty or desirous of allying himself with Abraham. God, in a dream, appeared to Abimelech, and threatened him with death on account of Sarah, because she was married. Abimelech, who had not yet come near her, excused himself on the ground that he supposed Sarah to be Abraham's sister. That Abimelech, in taking Sarah, should have supposed that he was acting "in the integrity of heart and purity of hands" is to be accounted for by considering the customs of that day. Abimelech, the next morning, obeyed the divine command, and restored Sarah to Abraham, providing him with a liberal present of cattle and servants, and offered him a settlement in any part of the country. He also gave him a thousand pieces of silver as "a covering of the eyes" for Sarah, i. e., according to some, as an atoning present. Others think that the money was to procure a veil for Sarah to conceal her beauty, that she might not be coveted

for her comeliness. "Thus she was reproved" for not having worn a veil, which as a married woman, according to the custom of the country, she ought to have done. Some years after, Abimelech, accompanied by Pichol, "the chief captain of his host," repaired to Beersheba to make a covenant with Abraham, which is the first league on record. Abimelech restored a well which had been dug by Abraham but seized by the herdsmen of Abimelech without his knowledge (Gen. 21:22-34).

2. Another king of Gerar in the time of Isaac (Gen. 26:1-22), B. C. about 1986. Supposed to have been the son of the preceding. Isaac sought refuge with Abimelech from famine, and dwelt at Gerar. Having the same fear respecting his wife, Rebekah, as his father entertained respecting Sarah, he reported her to be his sister. Abimelech discovered the untruthfulness of Isaac's statement (v. 8), whereupon he reproved him for what he had said, and forbade any of his people to touch Rebekah on pain of death. The agricultural operations of Isaac in Gerar were very successful, returning him in one year a hundredfold. He also claimed his proprietary right to the soil by reopening the wells dug by his father. The digging of wells, according to the custom of those times, gave one a right to the soil. His success made the Philistines envious, so that even Abimelech requested him to depart, fearing his power. Isaac complied, and encamped in the open country ("the valley of Gerar"). In this valley he opened the old wells of Abraham's time, and his people dug three new ones. But Abimelech's herdsmen contended concerning two of these, and the patriarch removed to so great a distance that there was no dispute respecting the third. Afterward Abimelech visited Isaac at Beersheba, and desired to make a covenant of peace with him. Isaac referred to the hostility that the Philistines had shown; to which Abimelech replied that they did not smite him, i. e. drive him away by force, but let him depart in peace, and closed by recognizing Isaac as being one blessed of God. Isaac entertained Abimelech and his companions with a feast, contracted the desired covenant with them, and dismissed them in peace (Gen. 26:26-31).

3. King of Shechem. (1) His conspiracy. After Gideon's death Abimelech formed a conspiracy with his mother's family, who seem to have had considerable influence in Shechem. The argument used was the advantage of the rule of *one* person to that of seventy. He also reminded them that he was one of themselves. Thus influenced, the Shechemites furnished him money out of the treasure of Baal-berith, with which Abimelech hired desperate men, and, repairing to Ophrah with them, slew all his brothers save Jotham, the youngest, who hid himself. (2) **The Bramble King.** At a general assemblage of the men of Shechem and the house of *Millo* (*q. v.*) Abimelech was declared king, B. C. c. 1108-1105. When Jotham was told of the election of Abimelech he went to the top of Mount Gerizim, where the Shechemites were assembled for some public purpose, perhaps to inaugurate Abimelech (Kitto), and rebuked them in his famous

parable of the trees choosing a king (Judg. 9:7-21). (3) **Revolt of Shechem.** Judgment against Abimelech was not long delayed, for in three years "God sent an evil spirit between" him "and the men of Shechem," and they "dealt treacherously with Abimelech." They caused ambuscades to be laid in the mountains, and robbed all that passed. The design was, probably, to bring the government into discredit by allowing such lawlessness, or to waylay Abimelech himself. The insurgents found a leader in *Gaal* (*q. v.*), the son of Ebed, who, while they were cursing Abimelech in the excitement of a village feast to Baal, called upon them to revolt from Abimelech, and declared that he would dethrone him. He then challenged the king to battle (Judg. 9:22-29). (4) **Destroys Shechem.** Zebul, the ruler of Shechem, sent word to Abimelech of the revolt, and requested him to place himself in ambush that night, and be prepared to surprise Gaal in the morning. As was expected, Gaal started out in the morning, was met and defeated by Abimelech, and prevented by Zebul from entering the city. The next day the people went out into the field, possibly to continue their vintage, and Abimelech slew them with two of his companions, while with his other two he seized the city gates. After fighting against the city all day he took it, destroyed it utterly, and strewed it with salt (Judg. 9:30-45). (5) **Destroys the hold.** When the inhabitants of the town of Shechem heard of the fate of the city they betook themselves to the temple of Baal-berith. Their purpose in so doing was evidently not to defend themselves, but to seek safety at the sanctuary of their God from the vengeance of Abimelech. When he heard of this, Abimelech went with his men to Mount Zalmon, and brought from thence branches of trees. These were piled against the building and set on fire. The building was consumed with all its occupants, about one thousand men and women (Judg. 9:46-49). (6) **Abimelech's death.** At last the fate predicted by Jotham (v. 20) overtook Abimelech. He went from Shechem to Thebez, besieged the town, and took it. This town possessed a strong tower, and in this the inhabitants took refuge. When Abimelech approached near the door to set it on fire a woman threw a piece of millstone (the upper millstone) upon him, crushing his skull. Seeing that he was mortally wounded, he called upon his armor-bearer to thrust him through with a sword, lest it should be said, "A woman slew him." After Abimelech's death his army was dissolved. "Thus God rendered the wickedness of Abimelech" upon his head "which he did unto his father, in slaying his seventy brethren" (Judg. 9:50-56).

4. The Son of Abiathar, and high priest in the time of David (I Chron. 18:16). The name is probably an error of transcription for *Ahimelech* (II Sam. 8:17).

5. In the title of Psa. 34 the name Abimelech is interchanged for that of *Achish* (*q. v.*), king of Gath, to whom David fled for refuge from Saul (I Sam. 21:10).

Abin'adab (à-bǐn'a̍-dăb; *father of generosity*, i. e., *liberal*).

1. A Levite of Kirjath-jearim, in whose house the ark was deposited after it was returned by the Philistines (I Sam. 7:1; II Sam. 6:3, 4; I Chron. 13:7), B. C. before 1030.

2. The second of the eight sons of Jesse (I Sam. 17:13; I Chron. 2:13), and one of the three who followed Saul to the campaign against the Philistines in which Goliath defied Israel (I Sam. 17:13).

3. One of the four sons of King Saul (I Chron. 9:39; 10:2). He was slain by the Philistines in the battle of Gilboa (I Sam. 31:2; I Chron. 10:2), c. B. C. 1004. His name appears as Ishui in the list in I Sam 14:49.

4. The father of one of Solomon's purveyors (or, rather, Ben-Abinadab is to be regarded as the name of the purveyor himself), who presided over the district of Dor, and married Taphath, the daughter of Solomon.(I Kings 4:11), B. C. after 960.

Abin'oam (à-bĭn'ō-ăm; *father of pleasantness* or *grace*, i. e., *gracious*), the father of Barak, the judge (Judg. 4:6, 12; 5:1, 12), B. C. about 1190.

Abi'ram (à-bī'ràm; *father of height*, i. e., *lofty*, *proud*).

1. One of the sons of Eliab, a Reubenite, who with his brother Dathan, and with On, of the same tribe, joined Korah, a Levite, in conspiracy against Moses and Aaron, B. C. about 1430, in which he, with the other conspirators, were destroyed by an earthquake (Num. 16:1-33; 26:9, 10; Deut. 11:6). *See* Korah.

2. The eldest son of Hiel, the Beth-elite, who died prematurely (for such is the evident import of the statement) for the presumption or ignorance of his father, in fulfillment of the doom pronounced upon the posterity of him who should undertake to rebuild Jericho (I Kings 16:34). For prophecy, *see* Josh. 6:27.

Ab'ishag (ăb'ĭ-shăg; *father of error*), a beautiful young woman of Shunem, in the tribe of Issachar, who was selected by the servants of David to minister unto him in his old age (I Kings 1:3, 4), B. C. 965. She became his wife, but the marriage was never consummated (I Kings 1:4). Soon after David's death Adonijah sought, through the intercession of Bath-sheba, Solomon's mother, the hand of Abishag. But as the control and possession of the harem of the deceased king was associated with rights and privileges peculiarly regal, Solomon supposed this demand to be part of a conspiracy against the throne. Adonijah was therefore put to death (I Kings 2:17-25). *See* Adonijah.

Abish'ai (à-bĭsh'à-ī; *father of a gift*), a son of Zeruiah, sister of David (by an unknown father), and brother to Joab and Asahel (I Chron. 2:16). The first we learn of Abishai is his volunteering to accompany David to the camp of Saul, B. C. about 1006. The two went down by night and found Saul and his people asleep. Abishai begged of David that he might slay Saul with his spear, which was stuck in the ground near his head (I Sam. 26:6-12). With his brother Joab he pursued after Abner (who had just slain Asahel) until sundown, and until they had reached the hill

of Ammah (II Sam. 2:24), and aided in the treacherous assassination of Abner (II Sam. 3:30). In the war against Hanun, undertaken by David to punish the Ammonites for insulting his messengers, Abishai, as second in command, was opposed to the army of the Ammonites before the gates of Rabbah and drove them headlong into the city (II Sam. 10:10, 14; I Chron. 19:11, 15). The same impetuous zeal and regard for David which he showed in the night adventure to Saul's camp Abishai manifested in his desire to slay Shimei, when the latter abused David (II Sam. 16:9, 11; 19:21). When the king fled beyond Jordan, Abishai remained faithful to David, and was intrusted with the command of one of the three divisions of the army which crushed the rebellion (II Sam. 18:2, 12), B. C. 967.

In the revolt of Sheba, the Benjamite, David ordered Amasa to muster the forces of Judah in three days. His tardiness compelled David again to have recourse to the sons of Zeruiah, and Abishai was appointed to pursue Sheba, which he did (accompanied by Joab), leading the Cherethites, the Pelethites, and all the mighty men (II Sam. 20:6-10). Later, when David's life was imperiled by Ishbi-benob, Abishai came to his help and slew the giant (II Sam. 21:15-17). He was chief of the three "mighties" who performed the chivalrous exploit of breaking through the host of the Philistines, to procure David a draught of water from the well of his native Bethlehem (II Sam. 23:14-17). Among the exploits of this hero it is mentioned (II Sam. 23:18) that he withstood three hundred men and slew them with his spear, but the occasion of this adventure, and the time and manner of his death, are equally unknown.

In II Sam. 8:13, the victory over the Edomites in the valley of Salt is ascribed to David, but in I Chron. 18:12, to Abishai. It is hence probable that the victory was actually gained by Abishai, but is ascribed to David as king and commander.

Abish'alom (à-bĭsh'à-lŏm), a fuller form (I Kings 15:2, 10) of the name *Absalom* (*q. v.*).

Abish'ua (à-bĭsh'ū-à; *father of salvation*).

1. The son of Phineas (grandson of Aaron), and fourth high priest of the Jews (I Chron. 6:4, 5, 50).

2. One of the sons of Bela, the son of Benjamin (I Chron. 8:4); possibly the same as Jerimoth (I Chron. 7:7).

Ab'ishur (ăb'ĭ-shûr; *father of the wall*, i. e., *stronghold*, or perhaps *mason*), the second son of Shammai, of the tribe of Judah. He was the husband of Abihail, and father of two sons, Ahban and Molid (I Chron. 2:28, 29).

Ab'ital (ăb'ĭ-tăl; *father of the dew*, i. e., *fresh*), the fifth wife of David and mother of Shephatiah, who was born in Hebron (II Sam. 3:4; I Chron. 3:3).

Ab'itub (ăb'ĭ-tŭb; *father of goodness*, i. e., *good*), a son of Shaharaim, a Benjamite, by his wife Hushim, in Moab (I Chron. 8:11).

Abi'ud (à-bī'ŭd), A Grecised form (Matt. 1:13) of *Abihud* (*q. v.*), the great-great-grandson of Zerubbabel, and father of Eliakim, among the paternal ancestry of Jesus (Matt.

1:13). He is probably the same with Judah, son of Joanna, and father of Joseph in the maternal line (Luke 3:26), and also with Obadiah, son of Arnan, and father of Shechaniah in I Chron. 3:21.

Ab'ject (Heb. *nēkĕh*; a *smiter*), one smiting with the tongue, i. e., a *railer*, *slanderer* (Psa. 35:15; comp. Jer. 18:18).

Ablution, a ceremonial washing, it might be of the person (or part thereof), clothing, vessels, or furniture, as a symbol of purification.

2. Hand Washing in the East

1. Cleansing from the taint of an inferior condition preparatory to initiation into a higher one. Of this sort was the washing with water of Aaron and his sons before they were invested with the priestly robes and anointed with the holy oil (Exod. 29:4; Lev. 8:6). The same is doubtless true of the ablution of persons and raiment which was required of the Israelites as a preparation to their receiving the law from Sinai (Exod. 19:10-15).

2. Preparation for special act of religious service. The priests before they entered into the service of the tabernacle were required, under penalty of death, to wash their hands and feet. For this purpose a large basin of water always stood in readiness (Exod. 30:18-21; Lev. 16). The Egyptian priests carried the practice to a burdensome extent. Herodotus tells us (ii, 37) that they shaved their bodies every third day, that no insect or other filth might be upon them when they served the gods. The Mohammedan law requires ablution before each of the five daily prayers, permitting it to be performed with sand when water is not to be had, as in the desert.

3. Purification from actual defilement. Eleven species of uncleanness of this nature are recognized by the Mosaic law (Lev. 12-15), the purification for which ceased at the end of a prescribed period, provided the unclean person then washed his body and his clothes. In a few cases, such as leprosy and the defilement caused by touching a dead body, he remained unclean seven days. The Jews afterward introduced many other causes of defilement, being equaled, however, by the Mohammedans.

4. Declaration of freedom from guilt of a particular action. An instance of this is the expiation for the murder of a man by unknown hands, when the elders of the nearest village washed their hands over a slain heifer, saying, "Our hands have not shed this blood, neither have our eyes seen it." (Deut. 21:1-9). The Pharisees carried the practice of ablution to such excess, from the affectation of purity while the heart was left unclean, that our Lord severely rebuked them for their hypocrisy (Matt. 23:25).

All these practices come under the head of purification from uncleanness; the acts involving which was made so numerous that persons of the stricter sect could scarcely move without contracting some involuntary pollution. Therefore, they never entered their houses without ablution, from the strong probability that they had unknowingly contracted some defilement on the streets. They were especially careful never to eat without washing their hands (Mark 7:1-5). A distinction must be made between this ceremonial washing and ordinary cleansing of the hands as a matter of decency. When the charge was made against our Lord's disciples that they "ate with unwashen hands" it was not meant that they did not at all wash their hands, but that they did not do it ceremonially.

These ceremonial washings were prescribed with such minute details as to be not only burdensome, but sometimes impossible. Before the ceremony one must decide the kind of food to be partaken of—whether it was prepared first fruits, common food, or holy, i. e, sacrificial food. "The water was poured on both hands, which must be free from anything covering them, such as gravel, mortar, etc. The hands were lifted up, so as to make the water run to the wrist, in order to insure that the whole hand was washed and that the water polluted by the hand did not again run down the fingers. Similarly, each hand was rubbed with the other (the fist), provided the hand that rubbed had been affused; otherwise the rubbing might be done against the head, or even against a wall. But there was one point on which special stress was laid. In the 'first affusion' which was all that originally was required when the hands were not Levitically 'defiled,' the water had to run down to the wrist. If the water remained short of the wrist, the hands were not clean. Accordingly, the words of St. Mark can only mean that the Pharisees eat not 'except they wash their hands to the wrist.' If the hands were 'defiled' two affusions were required: the first to remove the defilement, and the second to wash away the waters that had contracted the defilement of the hands. Accordingly, on the affusion of the first waters the hands were elevated, and the water made to run down at the wrist, while at the second waters the hands were depressed, so that the water might run off by the finger joints and tips" (Edersheim, *Life and Times of Jesus*, ii, 11).

Ab'ner—1. Name and Family. (ăb'nẽr; *father of light,* i. e., *enlightening*). The son of Ner and uncle of Saul (being the brother of his father, Kish).

2. **Personal History** (1) **Under Saul.** Abner was a renowned warrior, and the commander-in-chief of the army of Saul (I Sam. 14:50), B. C. 1030. He was the person who conducted David into the presence of Saul after the death of Goliath (I Sam. 17:57). He was doubtless held in high esteem by Saul, and with David and Jonathan sat at the king's table (I Sam. 20:25). He accompanied Saul to Hachilah in his pursuit of David, who sarcastically reproached him for not keeping more securely his master (I Sam. 26:1, 5, 15). (2) **Under Ish-bosheth.** After the death of Saul, B. C. 1004, Abner, taking advantage of the feeling entertained in the other tribes against Judah, took Ish-bosheth, a surviving son of Saul, to Mahanaim, and proclaimed him king, and ruled in his name. This happened five years after Saul's death, the intervening time being probably occupied in recovering land from the Philistines and in gaining influence with the other tribes. A sort of desultory warfare was kept up for two years between the armies of David and Ish-bosheth. The only engagement of which we have an account is the battle of Gibeah, Joab and Abner commanding the opposing forces. (3) **Slays Asahel.** Abner was beaten and fled for his life, but was pursued by Asahel (brother of Joab and Abishai). Abner, not wishing to have a blood feud with Joab (for according to usage, Joab would become the avenger of his brother Asahel, in case he was slain), begged Asahel to cease following him and pursue some other one. Asahel refused, and Abner thrust him through with a back stroke of his spear. The pursuit was kept up by Joab and Abishai until sunset, when a parley was held between the leaders, and Joab sounded the trumpet of recall. Abner retired to Mahanaim and Joab to Hebron (II Sam. 2:8-30). (4) **Breaks with Ish-bosheth.** At last Abner took a step which was so presumptuous and significant of his consciousness of power that even the feebler Ish-bosheth protested. It was the exclusive right of the successor to the throne to cohabit with the concubines of the deceased king. Yet Abner took to his own harem Rizpah, one of Saul's concubines. The rebuke of Ish-bosheth so greatly enraged him that he declared his purpose of abandoning the house of Saul and allying himself with David (II Sam. 3:6-9). To excuse his conduct he asserted that he was aware of the divine purpose concerning David. (5) **Joins David.** He made overtures through messengers to David, who required, as a preliminary, the restoration of his wife, Michal, who had been given to Phaltiel by Saul. Abner made a tour among the elders of Israel and Benjamin, advocating the cause of David. He then repaired in person to David, who showed him great attention and respect, giving him and the twenty men accompanying him a feast. In return Abner promised to gather all Israel to the standard of David, and was then dismissed in peace (II Sam. 3:9, sq.). (6) **Slain by Joab.** Joab, returning from Hebron from a military expedition, and fearing the influence of such a man as Abner, resolved to avenge his brother's death. Unknown to the king, but doubtless in his name, he sent messengers after Abner to call him back. Drawing Abner aside under the pretense of private conversation, he smote him under the fifth rib so that he died (II Sam. 3:6-30). Abner was buried at Hebron with the honors due to a prince and chieftain, David himself following the bier (vers. 31, 32). David's lamentation over 'Abner exonerated him in public opinion from any blame, and his declaration to his servants (II Sam. 3:38, 39) showed that he could properly estimate the character even of an enemy, and that he would have punished his murderer had he only the power.

Abomination (Heb. *piggûl, filth,* Lev. 7:18; *shiqqûts, unclean,* Deut. 29:17, etc., *shĕqĕts, rejected,* Lev. 7:21, etc.; *tōēbāh, causing abhorrence,* Gen. 43:32; Gr. *bdelugma,* Matt. 24:15, etc.). This word is used to denote that which is particularly offensive to the moral sense, the religious feeling, or the natural inclination of soul. Israel became an abomination to the Philistines because of the antipathy caused by reverses in war (I Sam. 13:4); David, for his distressed condition, was an abomination to his friends (Psa. 88:8).

The practices of sin—such as the swellings of pride, lips of falsehood, the sacrifices of the wicked, and the foul rites of idolatry—are stigmatized as abominations (Prov. 6:16; 12:22; 15:8; Jer. 6:15, etc.).

There are some peculiar applications of the term, to which attention is called:

1. "The Egyptians might not eat bread with the Hebrews, for that is an abomination (*tōēbāh'*) unto the Egyptians" (Gen. 43:32). The explanation probably is that the Egyptians thought themselves ceremonially defiled if they ate with strangers. The primary reason may have been that the cow was the most sacred animal to the Egyptians, and the eating of it was obnoxious to them; whereas it was eaten and sacrificed by the Jews and most other nations. The Jews themselves, in later times, considered it unlawful to eat or drink with foreigners in their houses, or even to enter their dwellings (John 18:28; Acts 10:28; 11:3).

2. Joseph told his brethren to answer when questioned by Pharaoh, "Thy servants' trade hath been about cattle from our youth even until now, both we, and also our fathers." Joseph adds as a reason for giving this statement, "That ye may dwell in the land of Goshen; for every shepherd is an abomination unto the Egyptians." The origin of this feeling is nowhere given either in sacred or profane history, but the fact is beyond dispute, being amply attested by the evidence of the monuments, on which shepherds are always represented in a low and degrading attitude. It may be that this feeling arose from the subjugation of Lower and Middle Egypt by a tribe of nomad shepherds; or that the Egyptians, as a settled and civilized people, detested the lawless and predatory habits of the wandering shepherd tribes, which then as now bounded the valley of the Nile and occupied the Arabias.

3. When Pharaoh told the Israelites to sacrifice to "your God" without going to the desert, Moses replied, "It is not meet so to do; for we shall sacrifice the abomination of the

Egyptians to the Lord our God: lo, shall we sacrifice the abomination of the Egyptians before their eyes, and will they not stone us?" (Exod. 8:26). Some think the abomination to consist in the sacrifice of the cow. Others (K. and D., *Com., in loco*) think that "the Israelites would not carry out the rigid regulations observed by the Egyptians with regard to the cleanness of the sacrificial animals, and in fact would not observe the sacrificial rites of the Egyptians at all." The Egyptians would, doubtless, consider this a manifestation of contempt for themselves and their gods, and this would so enrage them that they would stone the Israelites.

Abomination of Desolation is interpreted by premillennialists as the idolatrous image to be set up by the final Antichrist (the "beast" or "man of sin" of II Thess. 2:3, 4) in the restored temple at Jerusalem in the latter half of Daniel's seventieth week (Dan. 9:27; 12:11). For the first part of the three and one-half days (years) of the prophetic week of years, the Antichrist keeps his covenant with the Jews. At the beginning of the last half of the week he breaks it (Zech. 11:16, 17) compelling the Jews to worship his image. This is "the abomination (idol) of the desolator" or "the idol that causes desolation," inaugurating the period of "Jacob's trouble" (Jer. 30:5), a time of terrible suffering to Palestinian Jews of the end-time, of which our Lord spoke (Matt. 24:15). In Dan. 11:31 the reference is to the act of Antiochus Epiphanes, prototype of final Antichrist, who, in June, 168 B. C. desecrated the temple at Jerusalem. He built an altar to Jupiter Olympius on the altar of burnt offering, dedicated the temple to this heathen deity, and offered swine's flesh. Premillennialists maintain that neither Antiochus Epiphanes nor the Romans under Titus in 70 A. D. exhausted Daniel's prophecy, which still awaits fulfillment. Amillennial interpretation, however, sees a fulfillment in the advance of the Romans against Jerusalem in 70 A. D. with their image-crowned standards, which were regarded as idols by the Jews. *M. F. U.*

A′braham (ā′brȧ-hăm; *father of a multitude*). Up to Gen. 17:5, also in I Chron. 1:27; Neh. 9:7, he is uniformly called Abram, *high father*. The name of Abram—Abu-ramu, "the exalted father"—is found in early Babylonian contracts.

    1. Family. Abraham was a native of Chaldea, and descendant in the ninth generation from Shem, the son of Noah. His father's name was Terah, and he was born in Ur, B. C. 2161 (Gen. 11:27).

    2. Personal History. The Life of Abraham, from his call to his death, consists of four periods, the commencement of each of which is marked by a divine revelation of sufficient importance to constitute a distinct epoch.

    (1) **The First Period**—*The Call.* (1) *Removal to Haran.* When Abraham was about seventy years of age he, with his father Terah, his nephew Lot, and his wife Sarah, went and abode in Haran (Gen. 11:27-31). The reason for this movement is given in Acts 7:2, 3: "The God of glory appeared unto our father Abraham when he was in Mesopotamia, be-

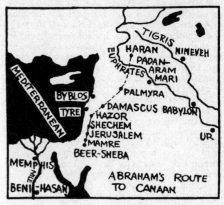

3. The World of Abraham's Day

show thee." (2) *Leaves Haran.* At the death of his father the call to Abraham was renewed. "Now the Lord had said unto Abram, Get thee out of thy country, and from thy kindred, and from thy father's house, unto a land that I will show thee" (Gen. 12:1-3). A condition was annexed to the call that he should separate from his father's house and leave his native land. He left his brother Nahor's family (who had also come to Haran, comp. Gen. 22:20, 23; 24:29, and 27:43) and departed, taking with him Lot, probably regarded as his heir (Josephus, *Ant.*; i, 7, 1), and all his substance, to go "not knowing whither" (Heb. 11:8). (3) *Reaches Canaan.* He traveled until he came into the land of Canaan, and formed his first encampment in the vale of Moreh, between the mountains of Ebal and Gerizim, where his strong faith was rewarded by the *second promise* that his seed should possess this land. Here Abraham built "an altar to the Lord, who appeared unto him." It is probable that the Canaanites were jealous of Abraham, and that he therefore soon removed to the mountainous district between Beth-el and Ai, where he also built an altar to Jehovah. (4) *In Egypt.* He still moved southward until, at length, compelled by a famine, he went into Egypt. Fearing that the beauty of Sarah would tempt the Egyptians and endanger his life, he caused her to pass for his sister, a term used in Hebrew, as in many other languages, for a niece, which she really was. Sarah was taken to the royal harem and Abraham loaded with valuable gifts, that could not be refused without an insult to the king, which he did not deserve. Warned of his mistake, Pharaoh summoned Abraham, and indignantly rebuked him for his subterfuge. He then dismissed Abraham, who went out of Egypt, taking his wife and Lot and his great wealth with him (Gen. 12). (5) *Return to Canaan.* Having reached his former encampment between Beth-el and Ai, he again establishes the worship of Jehovah (Gen. 13:3, 4). The increased wealth of Abraham and Lot became the cause of their separation. The country did not furnish sufficient pasture for the flocks and herds of Abraham and Lot, and dissensions arose between their herdsmen. In order to avoid strife and consequent weakness before their enemies, Abraham proposed that they occupy different districts. He gave the choice of locality to Lot, who selected the plain of Jordan, and went thither and pitched his tent. The childless Abraham was rewarded with a *third blessing*, in which God reiterated his promise to give him the land and a posterity like the dust of the earth for number. Then Abraham removed his tent, and came and dwelt in Mamre near Hebron, and built an altar (Gen. 13). (6) *Rescues Lot.* Lot was now involved in danger. The five cities of the plain had become tributary to Chedorlaomer, king of Elam. In the thirteenth year of their subjection they revolted, and Chedorlaomer marched against them with three allied kings. The kings of Sodom and Gomorrah fell, their cities were spoiled, and Lot and his goods were carried off (Gen. 14:1-12). Word was brought to Abraham, who immediately armed his dependents, three hundred and eighteen men, and with his Amorite allies overtook and defeated them at Dan, near the springs of Jordan. Abraham and his men pursued them as far as the neighborhood of Damascus, and then returned with Lot and all the men and goods that had been taken away. B. C. about 2080. (7) *Meets Melchizedek.* Arriving at Salem on their return, they were met by *Melchizedek* (*q. v.*), king of Salem, and "priest of the most high God," who brought him refreshments. He also blessed Abraham in the name of the most high God, and Abraham presented him with a tenth of the spoils. By strict right, founded on the war usages still subsisting in Arabia, Abraham had a claim to all the recovered goods. The king of Sodom recognized this right, but Abraham refused to accept anything, even from a thread to a shoe latchet, lest any should say, "I have made Abram rich" (Gen. 14:17, ff.).

(2) **The Second Period**—*The promise of a lineal heir and the conclusion of the covenant* (Gen. 15, 16). (1) *Vision of Abraham.* Soon after this Abraham's faith was rewarded and encouraged by a distinct and detailed repetition of former promises, and by a solemn covenant contracted between himself and God. He was told, and he believed, that his seed should be as the stars of heaven for number, and that his posterity should grow up into a nation under foreign bondage, and that after four hundred years they should come up and possess the land in which he sojourned (Gen. 15). (2) *Birth of Ishmael.* Ten years Abraham had dwelt in Canaan, and still he had no child. Sarah, being now seventy-five years of age, and probably despairing of bearing children herself, persuaded Abraham to take Hagar, her Egyptian handmaid, who bore him Ishmael (Gen. 16), B. C. 2076.

(3) **The Third Period**—*The establishment of covenant, change of name, and the appointment of the covenant sign of circumcision* (Gen. 17-21). (1) *Change of Name.* Thirteen years more pass by, and Abraham reached his ninety-ninth year. God appeared to him, and favored him with still more explicit declarations of his pur-

pose. He changed his name from Abram to Abraham, renewed his covenant, and in token thereof commanded that he and his should receive circumcision. Abraham was assured that Sarah, then ninety years old, should a year hence become the mother of Isaac, the heir of the special promises. Abraham wavered in faith and prayed for Ishmael, whom God promised abundantly to bless, but declared that he would establish his covenant with Isaac. (2) *Circumcision.* That very day Abraham, his son Ishmael, and all the males of his household were circumcised (Gen. 17). (3) *Visit of Angels.* Abraham was favored, shortly after, with another interview with God. Sitting in his tent door under the oaks of Mamre he saw three travelers approaching and offered them his hospitality. They assented, and partook of the fare provided, Abraham standing in respectful attendance, according to oriental custom. These three persons were, doubtless, the "Angel of Jehovah" and two attending angels. The promise of a son by Sarah was renewed, and her incredulity rebuked. The strangers continued their journey, Abraham walking some way with them. (4) *Destruction of Sodom.* The Lord revealed to him the coming judgment upon Sodom and Gomorrah; and then followed that wondrous pleading in behalf of the cities (Gen. 18). Abraham rose early the next morning to see the fate of the cities, and saw their smoke rising "up as the smoke of a furnace" (Gen. 19:27-29), B. C. 2063. (5) *Sarah Taken by Abimelech.* After this Abraham journeyed southward, and dwelt between Kadesh and Shur, and sojourned in Gerar. Abimelech, king of Gerar, sent and took Sarah, but was warned of God in a dream, and sent her back the next morning to Abraham, whom he reproved for the deceit he had employed. He was healed in answer to Abraham's prayer (Gen. 20). (6) *Isaac Born.* At length, when Abraham was one hundred years old, and Sarah ninety, the long-promised heir was born, B. C. 2061. The altered position of Ishmael in the family excited the ill will of himself and his mother. This was so apparent in the mocking behavior of Ishmael at the weaning of Isaac, that Sarah insisted that he and Hagar should be sent away, to which Abraham reluctantly consented. Abraham, after settling a dispute concerning a well taken by Abimelech's servants, made a treaty with him (Gen. 21).

(4) **The Fourth Period.** (1) *Abraham's Great Trial* (Gen. 22-25:11), B. C. 2036. When Isaac was nearly grown (twenty-five years old, says Josephus, *Ant.*, i, 13, 2) God subjected Abraham to a terrible trial of his faith and obedience. He commanded him to go to Mount Moriah (perhaps where the temple afterward stood) and there offer up Isaac, whose death would nullify all his hopes and the promises. Probably human sacrifices already existed, and therefore the peculiar trial lay in the singular position of Isaac and the improbability of his being replaced. Abraham decided to obey, "accounting (literally, *reasoning*) that God was able to raise him up, even from the dead" (Heb. 11:19). Assisted by his two servants he made preparations for

the journey, and started early the next morning. On the third day he saw the place, and told his servants that he and his son would proceed on further to worship and return. Upon Isaac's asking, "Where is the lamb for a burnt offering?" Abraham replied, "The Lord will provide himself a lamb." The altar was built and Isaac placed thereon. The uplifted hand of the father was arrested by the angel of Jehovah, and a ram caught in the thicket was substituted for Isaac. Abraham called the name of the place Jehovah-jireh, *"the Lord will provide."* The promises formerly made to Abraham were then confirmed in the most solemn manner. Abraham returned unto his young men, and with them went to Beer-sheba and dwelt there (Gen. 22:1-19). (2) *Death of Sarah.* The next event recorded in Abraham's life is the death of Sarah, aged one hundred and twenty-seven years, at or near Hebron. Abraham purchased, of Ephron the Hittite, the cave of Machpelah, the field in which it stood, and all the trees in the field, and there he buried Sarah (Gen. 23). (3) *Marriage of Isaac.* His next care was to procure a suitable wife for Isaac. He commissioned his eldest servant to go to Haran, where Nahor had settled, and get a wife for his son from his own family. He went, and, directed by God, chose Rebekah, the daughter of Bethuel, son of Nahor. In due time he returned, and Rebekah was installed in Sarah's tent as chief lady of the camp (Gen. 24). Some time after Abraham took another wife, Keturah, by whom he had several children. These, together with Ishmael, seem to have been portioned off by their father in his lifetime, and sent away to the east, that they might not interfere with Isaac. (4) *Death.* Abraham died, aged one hundred and seventy-five years, and was buried, by Isaac and Ishmael, in the cave of Machpelah (Gen. 25), B. C. 1986.

3. Man of Faith. The spiritual experience of Abraham was marked by four far-reaching crises in which his faith was tested, and which, in each case, called forth the surrender of something naturally most dear to him: first, his giving up country and kindred (Gen. 12:1); second, his breaking off with his nephew, Lot, particularly close to Abraham by virtue of kinship as a fellow believer and possible heir (Gen. 13:1-18); third, the abandonment of his own cherished plans for Ishmael and his being called upon to center his hope in the promise of the birth of Isaac (Gen. 17:17-18); fourth, the supreme test of his mature life of faith in his willingness to offer up Isaac, his "only son, Isaac," whom he loved passionately and in whom all his expectations centered (Gen. 22:1-19; Heb. 11:17, 18).

4. Man of Covenant Promise. As a friend of God and a man who implicitly trusted the divine promises, Abraham was the recipient of an important covenant involving not only himself, but his posterity, natural as well as spiritual. The Abrahamic Covenant as originally given (Gen. 12:1-4) and reaffirmed (Gen. 13:14-17; 15:1-7; 17:1-8), contains the following elements (1) "I will make of thee a great nation"—fulfilled (a) in a natural posterity, "as the dust of the earth," the Hebrew people (Gen. 13:16, John 8:37), (b) in a

spiritual progeny "look now toward *heaven* . . . so shall thy seed be" (John 8:39; Rom. 4:16; Gal. 3:6, 7, 29), comprising all men of faith, whether Jew or Gentile, (c) in the descendants of Ishmael (Gen. 17:18-20). (2) "I will bless thee" fulfilled in a double sense (a) temporally (Gen. 13:14-18; 15:18) and (b) spiritually (Gen. 15:6; John 8:56). (3) "And make thy name great." In the three great world religions—Judaism, Mohammedanism and Christianity, Abraham is revered as one of the eminent men of all time. (4) "And thou shalt be a blessing." By his personal example of faith and that faith as manifested in his descendants, Abraham has been a world-wide blessing. (5) "I will bless them that bless thee and curse him that curseth thee." This has been remarkably fulfilled in the Jewish dispersion. Nations who have persecuted the Jews have fared ill and those who have protected them have prospered. Prophecy, both fulfilled and unfulfilled, substantiates this principle (Deut. 30:7; Mic. 5:7-9; Hag. 2:22; Zech. 14:1-3; Matt. 25:40, 45; Jer. 50:11-18; 51:24-36; Ezek. 25:2; 26:2-3). (6) "In thee shall all families of the earth be blessed." This is the great Messianic promise fulfilled in Abraham's Descendant, Christ (Gal. 3:16; John 8:56-58).

5. Abraham and Archaeology. (1) **Life in Ur.** The Biblical chronology would place Abraham's birth in lower Mesopotamia about 2161 B. C. According to one chronology, he lived there under the new Sumero-Akkadian empire of Ur Nammu, the founder of the famous third dynasty of Ur (c. 2135-2035 B. C.), who took the title of "King of Sumer and Akkad," and whose mightiest work was the erection of the great ziggurat (temple tower) at Ur. Abraham quitted "Ur of the Chaldeans" (Gen. 11:31) when it was entering the heyday of its commercial and political prestige. According to the new minimal chronology, Abraham was born in Ur and left it during the period when the hated Guti ruled the land (2180-2070 B. C.). He then left Haran for Canaan about the time Ur entered her golden age (Ur III period). The new chronology dates Ur III 2070-1960 B. C. It was the appearance of "the God of glory" to him "when he was in Mesopotamia, before he dwelled in Haran" (Acts 7:2) that enabled Abraham to quit a famous center of wealth and culture for an unknown destination. In addition to a lucrative woolen trade, Ur was the center of numerous other industries that centered about the worship of the moon-god Sin (Nannar) and his consort Nin-gal. The great temples and ziggurat of this deity made Ur a mecca for thousands of pilgrims. (2) **At Haran.** The town of Haran (Gen. 11:31; 12:5) in northwest Mesopotamia to which Abram migrated on his way to Canaan, is still in existence on the Balikh River sixty miles west of Tell Halaf. It was a flourishing city in the nineteenth and eighteenth centuries B. C., as is known from frequent references to it in cuneiform sources (Assyrian, *Harranu*, "road"). It was on the great east-west trade route, and like Ur, it was the seat of the worship of the moon god. Whether Terah chose Haran as a place to settle because he had not made a clean break with the idolatry of his youth, or perhaps for commercial reasons, can only be surmised. The city of Nahor, which was Rebekah's home (Gen. 24:10) is also attested by the Mari Tablets, discovered in 1935 and belonging to the eighteenth century B. C. Evidence of Hebrew occupation of this region also appears in names of Abraham's forefathers, which correspond to the names of towns near Haran: Serug (Assyrian *Sarugi*) and Terah (*Til Turakhi*, "Mound of Terah,") in Assyrian times. Other immediate ancestors of Abraham listed in Genesis 11:10-30 have left their trace in this territory called Padan-Aram (Aramaic "field or plain of Aram," Gen. 25:20; 26:6, 7). Reu corresponds to later names of towns in the Middle Euphrates Valley and Peleg recalls later Paliga on the Euphrates just above the mouth of the Habur River. (3) **In Canaan.** After the death of Terah, Abraham left Haran and came into Canaan (Gen. 12:4, 5). The hill country was for the most part still unoccupied by sedentary population in the Middle Bronze Age (2000-1500 B. C.), so that the Genesis narratives are "absolutely correct in making the patriarchs wander over the hills of central Palestine and the dry lands of the south, where there was still plenty of room for them." (W. F. Albright "The Old Testament and Archeology" in *Old Testament Commentary*, Philadelphia, 1948, p. 140). The places which appear in connection with the movements of the patriarchs are not the sites of later periods, such as Mizpah or Gibeah, but include Shechem, Bethel, Dothan (now being excavated), Gerar, Jerusalem (Salem) and likely Beersheba—all known by means of exploration and excavation to have been inhabited in the patriarchial age. The five cities of the plain (circle) of the Jordan (Gen. 13) which appear prominently in the story of Abraham and Lot, namely; Sodom, Gomorrah, Admah, Zeboiim and Zoar also belong to this early period (c. 2065 B. C.), being located at the southern end of the Dead Sea. This area "full of slime (asphalt) pits" (Gen. 19:23-28) was overwhelmed by a catastrophe of fire, which with the salt and sulphur of the region, doubtless accompanied by earthquake common in this area of the Arabah, was the natural aspect of the supernatural destruction of the cities of the plain. These cities are now probably under the slowly rising waters at the southern end of the Dead Sea. The account of Lot's wife turned into a pillar of salt is reminiscent of the great salt mass, five miles long, stretching north and south at the S. W. end of the Dead Sea. (4) **Clash With the Mesopotamian Kings.** The 14th chapter of Genesis is the most pivotal passage in the patriarchal narratives from a historical point of view. While archaeology has not yet furnished a link to tie it into the general context of ancient Near-Eastern history, evidence is continually increasing of its historical character, which used to be almost universally denied by critics. A very remarkable fact about this chapter demonstrating its great age and authenticity, is its use of archaic words and place names, often appended with a scribal explanation to make them comprehensible to

a later generation when the name had changed. Examples are "Bela (the same is Zoar)" in verse 2; "the vale of Siddim (the same is the Salt Sea)" in verse 3; Enmishpat (the same is Kadesh)" in verse 7; "the vale of Shaveh (the same is the King's Vale)" in verse 17. Interesting examples of the confirmation of place names occur in the reference to Ashteroth-karnaim and Ham (Gen. 14:15). These two cities, mentioned in the invasion of Chedorlaomer and the kings with him, have both been shown to have been occupied at this early period, as archaeological examination of their sites has demonstrated. Ham was first surmised to be identical with a modern place by the same name in eastern Gilead, and examination of the site by A. Jirku and W. F. Albright (1925 and 1929) disclosed a small but ancient mound going back to the Bronze Age. Thutmose III lists the place among his conquests in the early 15th century B. C. Archaeology has likewise confirmed the general line of march followed by the invading kings, later known as "The King's Highway." (5) **Added Archaeological Light.** The site of Nuzu near modern Kirkuk (excavated between 1925 and 1941) dates from the 15th century B. C. and has yielded several thousand tablets illustrating vividly adoption (cf. Gen. 15:2), marriage laws (cf. Gen. 16:1-16), rights of primogeniture (Gen. 25:27-34), the teraphim (Gen. 31:34) and other customs and practices appearing in the life of Abraham and the Hebrew patriarchs. Also the discoveries at Mari, a site near modern Abou Kemal on the Middle Euphrates, since 1933 have shed a great deal of indirect light on the Age of Abraham. Moreover, the name Abraham (not of course the Biblical character) has been found in Mesopotamia in the second millennium B. C., showing that it was actually a name in use at an early date.—*M. F. U.*

NOTE.—(1) *Sacrifice of Isaac.* Some have found it difficult to reconcile God's command to sacrifice Isaac with his prohibition of human sacrifices (Lev. 18:21; 20:2). We answer, "God's design was not to secure a certain *outward act,* but a certain *state of mind,* a willingness to give up the beloved object to Jehovah" (Haley). "The divine command was given in such a form that Abraham could not understand it in any other way than as requiring an outward burnt offering, because there was no other way in which Abraham could accomplish the complete surrender of Isaac than by an actual preparation for really offering the desired sacrifice" (Keil, *Com.*). *See* Sacrifice, Human. (2) Gen. 12:5, states that Abraham "went forth to go into the land of Canaan," but Heb. 11:8, that "he went out, not knowing whither he went." At first the *name* of the country was not revealed to him. It is designated simply as "a land that I will show thee" (Gen. 12:1). But even if the name "Canaan" had been mentioned at the onset, it might still be true that he went forth "not knowing whither he went." For, in those days of slow transit, imperfect intercommunication, and meager geographical knowledge, the mere name of a country several hundred miles distant would convey almost no idea of the country itself (Haley).

Abraham's Bosom. The phrase "to be in one's bosom" applies to the person who so reclines at the table that his head is brought almost into the bosom of the one sitting next above him. To be in Abraham's bosom signified to occupy the seat next to Abraham, i. e., to enjoy the same felicity with Abraham. Jesus, accommodating his speech to the Jews, describes the condition of Lazarus after death by this figure (Luke 16:22, 23). "Abraham's bosom" is also an expression of the Talmud for the state of bliss after death. Father Abraham was, to the Israelites, in the corrupt times of their later superstitions, almost what the Virgin Mary is to the Roman Church. He is constantly invoked as though he could hear the prayers of his descendants, wherever they are; and he is pictured standing at the gate of paradise to receive and embrace his children as they enter, and the whole family of his faithful descendants is gathered to his arms.

A'bram (ā'brăm; *father of height*, i. e., *high father*), the original name (Gen. 17:5) of Abraham.

Ab'salom—1. Name and Family. (ăb'să-lŏm; *father of peace.*) The third son of David, and his only one by Maacah, the daughter of Talmai, king of Geshur (II Sam. 3:3), born B. C. about 1000.

2. Personal History. (1) Avenges Tamar. Absalom's sister, Tamar, became the object of the lustful desire of Amnon, her half brother, David's eldest son, and was violated by him (II Sam. 13:1-18). According to Eastern notions the duty of avenging his sister's wrong fell upon Absalom. He therefore took Tamar and kept her secluded in his own house, saying nothing to Amnon, "neither good nor bad." After two years had passed he found an opportunity for revenge. He then invited all his brethren, including Amnon, to a great sheepshearing at Baal-hazor, and, to lull suspicion, requested the presence of his father also. Amid the mirth of the feast, while they were warm with wine, the servants of Absalom, at a preconcerted signal, fell upon Amnon and slew him (II Sam. 13:23-29). Absalom fled to his grandfather, Talmai, and remained there three years (vers. 37, 38). **(2) Return to Jerusalem.** David, yearning for his exiled son Absalom (v. 39), yielded easily to the scheme of Joab, and permitted Absalom to return to Jerusalem, but not to appear before him. Absalom dwelt for two whole years in Jerusalem, and then sent for Joab, who refused to see him, until Absalom ordered his servants to burn his (Joab's) barley field. Then Joab secured for him an interview with the king (II Sam. 14). **(3) Preparations for revolt.** But Absalom proved himself false and faithless. He secretly plotted a revolt, propitiating the populace by the beauty of his person and the magnificence of his surroundings, riding in a chariot with fifty outriders. He also fostered the discontent of the people by insinuations against his father's justice. Other causes, doubtless, were favorable for Absalom: the affair of Bath-sheba, the probable disaffection of Judah for being merged in one common Israel, and less attention on the part of David, through age, to individual complaints (II Sam. 15:1-6). **(4) Revolt.** When the plot was ripe, Absalom sought and obtained leave to go to Hebron, to pay a vow which he had made at Geshur in case he should be permitted to return to Jerusalem. He had sent spies throughout all the tribes of Israel, summoning those favorable to his cause to assemble at Hebron, whither he went attended by two hundred unsuspecting adherents (II Sam. 15:7-11). His next step was to send for Ahithophel, David's counselor, and

secure his approval and advice (II Sam. 15:12), he being an oracle in Israel (II Sam. 16:23). **(5) Entry into Jerusalem.** When David heard the sad tidings of revolt he at once prepared for flight, and, leaving Jerusalem, repaired to Mahanaim, beyond Jordan (II Sam. 15:13, sq.). Absalom now entered Jerusalem (II Sam. 15:37), and, through the advice of Ahithophel, publicly took possession of the portion of his father's harem left in the city. The motive in this latter act was the more unreserved support of the people, from the assurance that any reconcilement between Absalom and his father would hereafter be impossible (II Sam. 16:20-22). Absalom had already met Hushai, who had been sent to join him by David, that he might be instrumental in thwarting the counsels of Ahithophel (II Sam. 15:33-37; 16:16-19). A council of war was held to consider the course to be pursued against David. Ahithophel advised the immediate pursuit and death of the king—that one death would close the war. Hushai, to gain time for David, urged his skill and bravery, the number and might of his warriors, the possibility and disastrous consequences of defeat, and advised a general gathering against David, and the total annihilation of him and his followers. The advice was accepted by Absalom. Information was secretly sent to David, who then went beyond Jordan, and there collected a force sufficient to oppose Absalom (II Sam. 17:1-14, 21-24). **(6) Anointed king.** Absalom was formally anointed king (II Sam. 19:10), appointed Amasa captain of his host, and crossed over Jordan in pursuit of his father (II Sam. 17:25, 26). A battle was fought in the wood of Ephraim. The army of Absalom was defeated, twenty thousand were slain, and a still greater number perished in the defiles of the forest. **(7) Death.** Absalom fled on a swift mule, and, riding through the forest, his long locks became entangled in the boughs of a great terebinth (or oak), and he was left suspended. Joab, being informed of this, hastened to the spot and slew him, notwithstanding David's request that he should be spared. The body was taken down and cast into a pit, over which the people raised a great heap of stones as a mark of abhorrence, a burial which the historian contrasts with the splendid monument prepared by Absalom for himself in the "King's Dale" (II Sam. 18:1-18), B. C. about 967. Absalom had three sons and one daughter, the latter named Tamar (II Sam. 14:27), who alone survived him (II Sam. 18:18) and became the mother of Maachah, the wife of Rehoboam (II Chron. 11:20, 21).

NOTE—(1) *Weight of hair.* "At every year's end." Literally, *from the end of days to days;* i.e., from time to time. Though Absalom's hair was doubtless very heavy, and thus was considered beautiful, the weight given, two hundred shekels, is too much. This is evidently a scribal error (Keil, *Com.;* II Sam. 14:26). (2) *After forty years.* This is a scribal error in the text, for David reigned but forty years in all (I Kings 2:11), and he certainly had reigned many years before Absalom's rebellion. The Syriac and Arabic versions read *four years,* and with this agrees Josephus.

Abstinence, a general term signifying to refrain from something or some action. In the ecclesiastical sense it means the refraining from certain kinds of food or drink on certain days.

1. Jewish. The first mention of abstinence in Scripture is found in Gen. 9:4, where the use of blood was forbidden to Noah. The next is in Gen. 32:32: "Therefore the children of Israel eat not of the sinew which shrank, which is upon the hollow of the thigh, unto this day: because he (the angel) touched the hollow of Jacob's thigh in the sinew that shrank." The law confirmed abstinence from blood (Lev. 3:17), and the use even of lawful animals if the manner of their death rendered it likely that they were not properly bled (Exod. 22:31; Deut. 14:21). Whole classes of animals which might not be eaten are given in Lev. 11. *See* Animal; Food. Certain parts of lawful animals, as being sacred to the altar, were forbidden, viz.: the caul (or net covering the liver), the kidneys, and the fat upon them, the fat covering the entrails, also the tail of the "fat-tailed sheep" (Lev. 3:9-11). Everything consecrated to idols was also interdicted (Exod. 34:15). While engaged in their official duties, the priests were commanded to abstain from wine and strong drink (Lev. 10:9), and the Nazarites had to abstain from strong drink and the use of grapes during the whole time of their separation (Num. 6:3). The *Rechabites* (*q. v.*) voluntarily assumed a constant abstinence from wine (Jer. 35:6). The Essenes, a Jewish sect, were very stringent in their abstinence, refusing all pleasant food, eating nothing but coarse bread and drinking only water, while some abstained from all food until evening.

2. Christian. Some among the early Christian converts thought themselves bound by Mosaic regulations respecting food, and abstained from flesh sacrificed to idols, and from animals accounted unclean by the law. Others considered this a weakness, and boasted of the freedom with which Christ had set them free. Paul discusses this matter in Rom. 14:1-3; I Cor. 8, and teaches that everyone was at liberty to act according to his own conscience, but that the stronger should refrain from that which might prove a stumbling-block to his weaker brother. In I Tim. 3:3, 4 he reproves certain persons who should forbid marriage and enjoin abstinence from meats. The council of the apostles at Jerusalem limited enforced abstinence upon the converts to that of "meats offered to idols, blood, and things strangled" (Acts 15:29).

In the early Church catechumens were required, according to Cyril and Jerome, to observe a season of abstinence and prayer for forty days; according to others, twenty days. Superstitious abstinence on the part of the clergy was considered a crime, and if that abstinence arose from the notion that any creature of God was not good they were liable to be deposed from office. Strict observance of the Church fasts was enjoined.

Abyss' (à-bĭs'; Gr. *hē 'abussos*). In the N. T. the abyss is the abode of the imprisoned demons (Rev. 9:1-21). At least many of the demons, whom Jesus expelled in His earthly ministry, were remanded to the abyss (Luke 8:31). But these evil spirits dreaded to go

there before their predetermined time. Myriads of demons will be let loose from thence during the Tribulation Period to energize age-end apostasy and revolt against God and His Christ, but will be shut up again in this prison together with Satan at the Second Advent of Christ to establish his kingdom (Rev. 20:1-3). The abyss is therefore to be distinguished from sheol (hell) or hades (*q. v.*). "The unseen world" is revealed as the place of departed *human* spirits between death and the resurrection (Matt. 11:23; 16:18; Luke 10:15; Rev. 1:18; 20:13, 14). It is also to be distinguished from "tartarus" the "prison abode of fallen angels" (II Pet. 2:4) and "the lake of fire" (Rev. 19:20; 20:10; 21:8) or the eternal abode of all wicked unrepentant creatures, including Satan, angels and men. The LXX renders Hebrew *tehom*, "the primeval ocean" (Gen. 1:2; Psa. 24:2, etc.) as "abyss." In classical Greek the word *abussos* is always an adjective meaning "very deep" ("bottomless") or "unfathomable" ("boundless"). *M. F. U. See* Hell, Tartarus, Lake of Fire.

Ac'cad (ăk'ăd), a very ancient center of Hamitic imperial power founded by Nimrod (Gen. 10:10). *The city* is evidently Agade, which Sargon I brought into great prominence as the capital of his far-flung Semitic empire which dominated the Mesopotamian world from about B. C. 2360-2180. The present site identified as Agade is on the Euphrates a short distance southwest of modern Bagdad. *The Country* was named after its capital and embraces the stoneless alluvial plain of southern Babylonia north of Sumer (*q. v.*). The term "the land of Shinar," in which the world's first imperial power developed embracing "Babel and Erech (Uruk) and Accad and Calneh" (Gen. 10:10) is descriptive of the entire alluvial plain of Babylonia between the Tigris and the Euphrates, in approximately the last 200 miles of the course of these great rivers as they flowed in ancient times. In the cuneiform inscriptions the region is divided into a northern portion called Accad (Akkad), in which Babel (Babylon) and the city of Accad (Agade) were situated; and a southern portion called Sumer, in which Erech (ancient Uruk, modern Warka) was located. At Uruk the first sacred temple tower (Babylonian, ziggurat) was found, as well as evidence of the first cylinder seals (Finegan, *Light from the Ancient Past*, pp. 19-23). The inhabitants of this region were originally non-Semitic Sumerians, who racially must have been of Hamitic origin, according to Gen. 10:8-10 and who were the inventors of cuneiform writing and the cultural precursors of their later conquerors the Babylonian Semites. The city of Accad (Agade) disappeared in ancient times and by Assyrian times was utterly unknown. *M. F. U.*

Accept, Acceptable, Accepted (Heb. *rätzäh, to take pleasure in*; Gr. *dechomai, to take with the hand*, i. e., *to receive with hospitality*). *To accept* is to receive with pleasure and kindness (Gen. 32:20), and is the opposite of *to reject*, which is a direct refusal with disapprobation (Jer. 6:30; 7:29). An *accepted* or *acceptable time* (Psa. 69:13; II Cor. 6:2) is the time of favor, a favorable opportunity. Luke 4:24 means that no prophet is welcomed, appreciated favorably in his own country. "Neither acceptest thou the person," etc. means that Jesus was not a partisan, given to partiality.

Acceptance also means that relation to God in which he is well-pleased with his children, for by children of God only is it enjoyed. In Acts 10:35 we learn that "in every nation he that feareth him and worketh righteousness is *accepted* of him."

The Christian scheme bases acceptance with God on justification. Paul in Eph. 1:6 refers to "the grace" of God, "wherein he hath made us accepted in the beloved." In Christ only are we acceptable to God. Out of him we are sinners and subjects of wrath.

The Calvinist teaches that the sins which are pardoned in justification include all sins, past, present, and future, and that God will not deal with the believer according to his transgressions; whereas the Arminian holds that the state of *acceptance* can be maintained only by perpetually believing in and appropriating to himself the atoning merits of Jesus, and obediently keeping God's holy commandments.

Access to God (Gr. *prosagōgē, act of moving to*), that friendly relation with God whereby we are acceptable to him and have assurance that he is favorably disposed toward us (Rom. 5:2; Eph. 2:18; 3:12). In substance it is not different from the "peace of God," i. e., the peaceful relation of believers toward God, brought about through Christ's death. By the continuous power and efficiency of His atoning act, Jesus is the constant *Bringer* to the Father. Access means the obtaining of a hearing with God, and if a hearing, the securing in some form of an answer to our requests. The Apostle John (I John 5:14, 15) says: "This is the confidence that we have in him, that, if we ask anything according to his will, he heareth us: and if we know that he hear us, whatsoever we ask, we know that we have the petitions that we desired of him." Here we learn that access to God involves asking according to his will. A child has right of access to his father. Such right and privilege are granted to, and should be enjoyed by, every child of God. We must not infer that our access is cut off if we do not realize direct answers to some of our requests, but believe that God heareth his children always and does for them the best things.

Ac'cho (ăc'kō), a town on the Mediterranean coast, thirty miles south of Tyre, and ten from

4. Accho (Acre) viewed across the bay of Accho.

Mount Carmel (Judg. 1:31). It was known to the ancient Greeks and Romans as Ptolemais, from Ptolemy the king of Egypt, who rebuilt it in 100 B. C. During the Middle Ages it was called Acra, and subsequently called St. Jean d'Acre. Paul visited this place (Acts 21:7). *See* Ptolemais.

Accountability is not a Bible word, but an abstract term for that return for his talents and opportunities which every soul must make to God day by day, and especially at the judgment, as we are taught in Matt. 12:36; Rom. 14:10; Heb. 13:17, and I Pet. 4:5. It is a well-established doctrine of holy Scripture, attested to by the human consciousness, that we are free moral agents, entirely dependent upon our Creator for our existence and maintenance, and rightly answerable to him for our conduct; and that God consequently has a right to our perfect obedience and service. It is accordingly easy for us to feel that he is justified in calling us to a strict reckoning for all he has intrusted us with. Disabled by our fall into sin, gracious strength has been provided for us in the atonement, so that we are without excuse if we fail to do God's will.

Accursed. *See* Anathema, Ban, Oath.

Accuser (Heb. *lāshăn, to lick, to use the tongue;* in the New Testament, *katēgoros, prosecutor*).

1. One who has a cause or matter of contention; the accuser, opponent, or plaintiff in any suit (Judg. 12:2; Matt. 5:25; Luke 12:58).

2. In Scripture, in a general sense, an adversary or enemy (Luke 18:3; I Pet. 5:8). In the latter passage reference is made to the old Jewish teaching that Satan was the accuser or calumniator of men before God (Job. 1:6, ff.; Rev. 12:10). *See* Adversary.

Acel'dama (à-sĕl'dà-mà; A. S. V. Akeldama), called at present *Hak ed-damm*. It signifies *field of blood*, once called the "Potter's Field" (Matt. 27:8; Acts 1:18, 19), now at the east end and on the southern slope of the valley of Hinnom. The tradition which fixes this spot reaches back to the age of Jerome. Once the tradition was that the soil of this spot, a deep pit or cellar, was believed to have the power of consuming dead bodies in the space of twenty-four hours, so that whole shiploads of it are said to have been carried away in A. D. 1218, in order to cover the famous Campo Santo in Pisa.

Achai'a (à-kā'ya), the name once applied to the northwest portion of the Peloponnesus. It was afterward applied to the entire Peloponnesus, called now the Morea. It was one of the two provinces, of which Macedonia was the other, into which the Romans divided Greece (140 B. C.). It was under a proconsular government at the time when Luke wrote the Acts of the Apostles, so that the title given to Gallio, "deputy," was proper (Acts 18:12). c. A. D. 51 or 52.

Acha'icus (à-kā'ĭ-kŭs; *an Achaean*), a Christian of Corinth who had rendered Paul personal aid, and by him was kindly commended to the Corinthian church (I Cor. 16:17; c. A. D. 54.

A'chan (ā'kăn; *troublesome*), a son of Carmi, of the tribe of Judah; called also Achar (I Chron. 2:7).

Personal History. (1) Achan's sin. By one incident of his life Achan attained a disgraceful notoriety. Jericho, before it was taken, was put under that awful ban, whereby all the inhabitants (excepting Rahab and her family) were devoted to destruction; all the combustible goods to be burned, and the metals consecrated to God (Deut. 7:16, 23-26; Josh. 6:17-19). After Jericho fell (B. C. 1400) the whole nation kept the vow of devotement, with the exception of Achan. His covetousness made him unfaithful, and, the opportunity presenting, he took a goodly Babylonish garment, two hundred shekels of silver, and an ingot of gold of fifty shekels' weight (Josh. 7:21). **(2) Result of Achan's sin.** Ai had been visited by spies, who declared that it could easily be taken. An expedition of three thousand men, sent against the city, was repulsed, and returned to Joshua, who inquired of the Lord concerning the cause of the disaster. The answer was that "Israel had sinned, . . . for they have even taken of the accursed thing, and have also stolen, and dissembled also, and they have put it even among their own stuff" (Josh. 7:11). This was the reason for Israel's defeat; and Joshua was commanded to sanctify the people, and on the morrow to cast lots for the offender. Achan was chosen, and, being exhorted by Joshua, made a confession of his guilt; which was verified by the finding of the spoil in his tent. **(3) Achan's punishment.** Achan was conveyed, with his family, property, and spoils, to the valley (afterward called Achor, *trouble*), where they "stoned him with stones, and burned them with fire" (Josh. 7:25).

NOTE—(1) Objection has been urged against the use of the lot to discover the guilty party. We answer that the decision by lot, when ordered by God, involved no chance, but was under his special direction, as is evident from the expression, "Which the Lord taketh" (Josh. 7:14); "The lot is cast into the lap, but the whole disposing thereof is of the Lord" (Prov. 16:33). (2) The severity of the punishment of Achan, as regards his family, has excited considerable comment. Some vindicate it by saying that Achan, by his sin had fallen under the ban pronounced against Jericho, and was exposed to the same punishment as a town which had fallen away into idolatry (Deut. 13:16, 17); others believe that the family of Achan were privy to his crime, and therefore were deserving of a share in his punishment (K. and D., *Com.*); others, again, consider it as the result of one of those sudden impulses of indiscriminate popular vengeance to which the Jewish people were exceedingly prone (Kitto). The real explanation is evidently to be found in the fact that the iniquity of the inhabitants of Canaan was now "full" (cf. Gen. 15:16) and God's righteous wrath was outpoured upon them.

A'char (ā'kăr; *trouble*), another form of the name Achan, and given to that person in I Chron. 2:7.

A'chaz (Matt. 1:9), elsewhere *Ahaz* (*q. v.*).

Ach'bor (ăk'bor; *mouse*).

1. The father of Baal-hanan, the seventh Edomite king, mentioned in Gen. 36:38, 39.

2. The son of Michaiah, and one of the courtiers whom Josiah sent to Huldah to inquire the course to be pursued respecting the newly discovered book of the law (II Kings 22:12, 14), B. C. 624. In the parallel passage (II Chron. 34:20) he is called Abdon the son of Micah. He is doubtless the same person whose son, Elnathan, was courtier of Jehoiakim (Jer. 26:22; 36:12).

A'chim (ā'kĭm; perhaps the same word as Jachin, *whom God makes firm*), the son of Sadoc, and father of Eleazar, among the paternal ancestors of Christ (Matt. 1:14), B. C. after 410.

A'chish (ā'kĭsh), probably a general title of royalty, like Abimelech (*q. v.*), another Philistine kingly name, with which, indeed, it is interchanged in the title of Psa. 34.

1. A Philistine king of Gath with whom David sought refuge from Saul (I Sam. 21:10-15). The servants of Achish soon recognized David as the successful champion of Israel against Goliath, and he only escaped by pretending madness, "well knowing that the insane were held inviolable, as smitten but protected by the Deity" (De Rothschild, *Hist. of Israel*). This is undoubtedly the same King Achish, to whom David again repaired. Achish received him kindly, probably considering their common enmity against Saul as a strong bond of union. After living awhile at Gath, David received from Achish the town of Ziklag for a possession (I Sam. 27:2-6). He made numerous forays against the neighboring nomads, which he persuaded Achish were as much in his interest as his own (I Sam. 27:8-12). Achish still had great confidence in David, and he proposed making him chief of his bodyguard (I Sam. 28:1, 2). He took David and his men with him when he went up to the battle which sealed the fate of Saul, but was led to dismiss them by the jealousy and opposition of the Philistine leaders. Thus David was spared from participating in the battle (I Sam. 29:2-11), B. C. about 999.

2. Another king of Gath, the son of Maachah, to whom two servants of Shimei fled. Shimei went to reclaim them, and thus, by leaving Jerusalem, broke his parole and met his death (I Kings 2:39, 40), B. C. 957.

Ach'metha (ăk'mĕ-thà; *a station, fortress*), the capital of northern Media. The classical name is Ecbatana, modern *Hamadân*. Cyrus II, the Great, founder of the Persian Empire (died 530 B. C.) held his court here. It is stated (Ezra 6:2) that here was found in the palace a roll upon which was the decree of Cyrus for the rebuilding of the temple at Jerusalem.

A'chor (ā'kōr; *trouble*), S. W. of Jericho; now identified with Wadi Daber and Wadi Mukelik. Its name resulted from the sin and consequent punishment of Achan (Josh. 7:24-26). The term "valley of Achor" was proverbial, and the expression of the prophet (Hos. 2:15), "the valley of Achor, a door of hope," is still more suggestive of the good results of discipline.

Ach'sa (ăk'sà), a less correct mode (I Chron. 2:49) of anglicizing the name *Achsah* (*q. v.*).

Ach'sah (ăk'sàh; *anklet*), the name of Caleb's daughter (I Chron. 2:49). Caleb offered her in marriage to the man who should capture the city of Debir, B. C. c. 1362. His own nephew, Othniel, won the prize, and on her way to her future home she asked of her father an addition to her dower of lands. She received the valley full of springs situated near to Debir. Her request was probably secured the more readily as it was considered ungracious to refuse a daughter under such circumstances (Josh. 15:16, 17; Judg. 1:12, 13).

Ach′shaph (ăk′shăf; *fascination*). Identified with Tell Kisân. It belonged to Asher (Josh. 19:25).

Ach′zib (ăk′zĭb; *falsehood, deceit*), a town of Asher (Josh. 19:29; Judg. 1:31), identical with es-Zib, about ten miles north of Accho.

The town of the same name in Judah (Josh. 15:44; Mic. 1:14) is probably the same as Chezib (Gen. 38:5).

Acknowledge, Acknowledgement (Gr. *epignōsis, precise and correct knowledge*), used in the New Testament of the knowledge of things ethical and divine; of God, especially the knowledge of his holy will and of the blessings which he has bestowed and constantly bestows through Christ (Eph. 1:17; Col. 1:10; II Pet. 1:2); of Christ, i. e., the true knowledge of Christ's nature, dignity, benefits (Eph. 4:13; II Pet. 1:8; 2:20).

Acre (Heb. *tsemed, a yoke*), is given as the translation of the Hebrew word which is used as a measure of land, i. e., so much as a yoke of oxen can plow in a day (I Sam. 14:14; Isa. 5:10).

5. The Acropolis at Athens.

Acrop′olis (ă-crŏp′ō-lĭs), a fortified hill overlooking many Graeco-Roman cities. The famous Acropolis at Athens rose to a height of 512 feet and was adorned with splendid temples when the Apostle Paul visited the famous center of art and culture. The renowned sculptor, Phidias, who died about 432 B. C., made a colossal statue of Athena Promachos, the goddess who fights in front, which was erected on the Acropolis. Then the magnificent Parthenon was built housing a great gold and ivory statue of Athena by Phidias. Later the stately entrance, the Propylaea, was completed and the beautiful temples, the Erechtheum and the shrine of Athena Nike, the goddess of victory. Of the Parthenon-crowned Acropolis at Athens J. P. Mahaffey in his *Rambles and Studies in Greece*, 1878, p. 83 says: "There is no ruin all the world over which combines so much striking beauty, so distinct a type, so vast a volume of history, so great a pageant of immortal memories. . . . All the Old World's culture culminated in Greece—all Greece in Athens—all Athens in its Acropolis—all the Acropolis in the Parthenon." Paul in his Second Missionary journey visited other cities with a fortified Acropolis, such as Philippi and Corinth. But

at Athens "his spirit was provoked within him as he beheld the city full of idols" (Acts 17:16).
               M. F. U.

Acrostic, an ode in which the first, the first and last, or certain other letters of the lines taken in order, spell a name or sentence. They are not found in this form in the Bible. In the poetical parts of the Old Testament are what may be called alphabetical acrostics: e. g., Psa. 119 has as many stanzas or strophes as there are letters in the Hebrew alphabet. Each strophe has eight lines, each beginning with the same letter, the first eight lines beginning with Aleph, the next with Beth, and so on. Psa. 25 and 34 have one verse to each letter in its order. In others, as Psa. 111, 112, each verse is divided into two parts following the alphabet. The Lamentations of Jeremiah are mostly acrostic, and the last chapter of Proverbs has the initial letters of its last twenty-two verses in alphabetical order. In ecclesiastical history the term acrostic is used to describe a mode of performing the psalmody of the ancient Church. A precentor began a verse and the people joined him at the close. It was then much used for hymns, as follows:

> **J** esus, who for me hast born
> **E** very sorrow, pain, and scorn,
> **S** tanding at man's judgment seat,
> **U** njust judgment there to meet:
> **S** ave me by thy mercy sweet, etc.

The acrostic was also commonly used for epitaphs. But the most famous of all ancient acrostics is the one used by ancient Christians as a secret symbol of faith. This is the Greek word *ichthus, fish,* formed from the initial letters of five titles of our Lord, "Jesus Christ, God's Son, Saviour."

> Ἰ ησοῦς
> Χ ριστὸς
> Θ εὸς
> Υ ἱὸς
> Σ ωτήρ

Acts, Book of, the fifth book of the N. T. **1. The name.** Commonly called the "Acts of the Apostles," a more accurate title would be "The Acts of the Holy Spirit" since He fills the scene. As the presence of the Son, exalting and manifesting the Father, is the central theme of the four Gospels, the presence of the Holy Spirit, who came at Pentecost (Acts 2), magnifying and revealing the Risen and Ascended Son, is the underlying truth of the Acts. **2. The Date** is probably about A. D. 63 or a little later, since the book concludes with the account of Paul's earliest ministry in Rome. **3. The Author** is Luke, the "beloved physician," who also wrote the Gospel of Luke (Acts 1:1). Both the Gospel and the Acts are addressed to "the most excellent Theophilus," who was evidently a distinguished Gentile. The numerous "we" sections (16:10-17; 20:5-21:18; 27:1-28:16) indicate where Luke joined Paul as a fellow traveller. **3. The Theme** is the continuation of the account of Christianity begun in the Gospel of Luke. In the "former treatise" Luke relates what Jesus "began both to do and teach" and catalogues in the Acts what Jesus continued to do and teach through the Holy Spirit sent down from heaven. The book, accordingly, records the ascension and promised return of the Risen Lord (Acts 1); the advent of the Spirit and the first historical occurrence of the baptism of the Spirit (Acts 2; cf. 1:5 with 11:16) with the consequent formation of the Church as the mystical body of Christ (I Cor. 12:13). It also recounts Peter's use of the keys of the kingdom of the heavens in opening gospel opportunity for this age to Jew (Acts 2), Samaritan (Acts 8) and Gentile (Acts 10). It describes Paul's conversion and the extension of Christianity through him to the "uttermost part of the earth." **4. The Content** of the book is arranged about the threefold outline given in 1:8: Part I. The Apostles as Witnesses "in Jerusalem" (1:1-8:3). Part II. "In all Judaea and in Samaria" (8:4-12:24). Part III. Paul As A Witness "Unto the Uttermost part of the earth" (12:25-28:31). **5. Acts and Archaeology.** Recent researches have greatly strengthened the historical credibility of the Acts (see A. T. Robertson, *Luke The Historian In the Light of Historical Research* for detailed account). Besides being accurate in detail, Luke gives a remarkably vivid account of many phases of first-century life in the Mediterranean world, for example, the philosophical inquisitiveness of the Athenians (Acts 17:17, 18) and the commercial monopoly of the silversmiths at the Temple of Diana in Ephesus (Acts 19:24-34). His picture of modes of travel of the day is far clearer than that set forth in the *Odyssey*. Whether on land on foot or horse (Acts 23:24, 32) or chariot (Acts 8:27-38) or on sea by coastal freighter (21:1-3; 27:1-5), Luke's account is filled with local color. The story of the wreck of Paul's ship is the most exciting and dramatic narrative of sea adventure in ancient literature (Acts Chaps. 27 and 28). *M. F. U.*

Ad'adah (ăd'á-dáh; *festival*), a place in Palestine, in the southern part of Judah (Josh. 15:22).

A'dah (ā'dá; *ornament, beauty*).
1. One of the two wives of Lamech, and mother of Jabal and Jubal (Gen. 4:19-23).
2. Daughter of Elon the Hittite, the first of the three wives of Esau, and mother of Eliphaz (Gen. 36:2, 4, 10, 12, 16). She is elsewhere (Gen. 26:34) called Bashemath.

Ada'iah (ăd-ā'yä; *whom Jehovah adorns*).
1. A native of Boscath (Bozkath, in the valley of Judah, Josh. 15:39), and father of Jedidah, the mother of Josiah, king of Judah (II Kings 22:1), the latter born B. C. 632.
2. The son of Ethni and father of Zerah, of the Levitical family of Gershom, in the ancestry of Asaph, the celebrated musician (I Chron. 6:41). Probably the same as Iddo (v. 21).
3. A son of Shimhi, and one of the chief Benjamites resident in Jerusalem before the captivity (I Chron. 8:21), B. C. before 586.
4. A priest, son of Jeroham, who, after the return from Babylon, was employed in the work of the sanctuary (I Chron. 9:12; Neh. 11:12).
5. Father of Maaseiah, who was one of the "captains of hundreds" during the protectorate of Jehoiada (II Chron. 23:1).

6. A "son of Bani," an Israelite who divorced his Gentile wife after the captivity (Ezra 10:29).
7. Another of the sons of Bani (probably not the same Bani as in No. 6) who put away his Gentile wife (Ezra 10:39).
8. Son of Joiarib and father of Hazaiah, of the tribe of Judah (Neh. 11:5), some of whose posterity dwelt in Jerusalem after the captivity, B. C. 445.

Ada'lia (ä-dā'li-a; probably of Persian origin), one of the ten sons of Haman, the enemy of the Jews. He was slain by the Jews under the royal edict at Shushan (Esth. 9:8), B. C. probably 477.

Ad'am. I. *The first man.* **1. Name and Family.** (Heb. *'ädäm, red;* hence *adamah,* the *ground.*) The first man and "son of God" (Luke 3:38) by special creation. The name which God gave him (Gen. 5:2) is founded upon the earthly side of his being: Adam from *'ädämäh,* earth, the earthly element, to guard him from self-exaltation; not from the red color of his body, since this is not a distinctive characteristic of man, but common to him and to many other creatures.

2. Personal History. (1) Creation. In the first nine chapters of Genesis there appear to be three distinct histories relating more or less to the life of Adam. The first (1:1-2:3) records the creation; the second (2:4-4:26) gives an account of paradise, the original sin of man, and the immediate posterity of Adam; the third (5:1-9:29) contains mainly the history of Noah, referring to Adam and his descendants principally in relation to that patriarch. "The Almighty formed man of the dust of the earth, breathed into his nostrils the breath of life, and man became a living soul" (2:7). **(2) In Eden.** He gave him dominion over all the lower creatures (1:26), and placed him in Eden that he might cultivate it and enjoy its fruits (2:15, 16). The beasts of the field and the birds of the air were brought to Adam, who examined them and gave them names. This examination gave him an opportunity of developing his intellectual capacity, and also led to this result, that there was not found a helpmeet for man. **(3) Creation of Eve.** "And the Lord God caused a deep sleep to fall upon Adam, and he slept; and he took one of his ribs, and closed up the flesh instead thereof. And the rib, which the Lord God had taken from man, made he a woman, and brought her unto the man." The design of God in creation of the woman is perceived by Adam when she is brought to him by God, and he said, "This is now bone of my bones, and flesh of my flesh: she shall be called Woman, because she was taken out of man." Thus we find Adam appointed Lord of the earth and its inhabitants, endowed with everything requisite for the development of his nature and the fulfillment of his destiny. In the fruit of the trees he found sustenance; in "the tree of life," preservation from death; in "the tree of knowledge," a positive law for the training of his moral nature; in the care of the garden, exercise of his physical strength; in the animal and vegetable kingdom, a capacious region for the development of his intellect; and in the woman, a suitable companion and help. "The first man was a true man, with the powers of a man and the innocence of a child." (4) **Fall.** But Eve, having been beguiled by the tempter to eat of the forbidden fruit, persuaded her husband to do the same. When called to judgment before God, Adam blamed his wife, who in turn blamed the tempter. God punished the tempter by degradation and dread, the woman by painful travail and submission (*See* Eve), and the man by a life of labor. With the loss of innocence came a feeling of shame, and they sought to hide their nakedness with leaves, but were afterward taught of God to make clothing of the skins of animals. Adam and Eve were expelled from the garden, at the eastern side of which cherubim and a sword of flame turning every way were placed. The object of these was to guard the way of the tree of life (*q. v.*), and prevent Adam's return to it (Gen. 3). (5) **Subsequent history.** It is not known how long Adam lived in Eden, and therefore we cannot determine the length of his life after the expulsion. Shortly after leaving Eden, Eve gave birth to Cain (Gen. 4:1). Scripture gives the names of only three sons of Adam—Cain, Abel, and Seth—but contains an allusion (Gen. 5:4) to "sons and daughters."

3. Figurative. Paul declares that Adam was a type of Christ, "the figure of him that was to come" (Rom. 5:14); hence our Lord is sometimes called the *second Adam.* This typical relation stands sometimes in *likeness*, sometimes in *contrast.* In *likeness*: Adam was formed immediately by God, as was the human nature of Christ; in each the nature was holy; both were invested with dominion over the earth and its creatures (see Psa. 8). In *contrast*: Adam and Christ were each a *federal head* to the whole race of mankind, but the one was the fountain of sin and death, the other of righteousness and life (Rom. 5:14-19); Adam communicated a living soul to all his posterity, Christ is a quickening Spirit to restore life and immortality to them (I Cor. 15:45).

4. Chronology. The opening chapters of the Bible leave both the date of the creation of the world and of man an open question. Gen. 1:1 places the origin of the universe in the dateless past. The appearance of man upon the earth is set forth as the result of a direct creative act of God, which took place at least over 4,000 years B. C. and perhaps as early as seven or ten thousand years B. C. "which is more in the spirit of the Biblical record than either Ussher's compressed chronology or the evolutionist's greatly expanded ages" (Laird Harris, "The Date of the Flood and the Age of Man" in *Bible Today* 37, no. 9, Sept., 1943, p. 570). Byron Nelson, a conservative, argues for a still greater antiquity for man (*Before Abraham, Prehistoric Man in Biblical Light,* 1948, p. 95). In dealing with the genealogies of Genesis chapters 5 to 11 it must be remembered that these lists are symmetrical rather than exhaustive or complete and most certainly are abbreviated. B. B. Warfield demonstrated long ago that there are gaps in Biblical genealogies (Exod. 6:16-24, Ezra 7:1-5, Matt. 1:1-17), see "The Antiquity and Unity of the Human Race" in *Studies in Theology,* New

York, 1932, pp. 235-258). Furthermore Semitic idiom dealing with "beget," "begotten," "father" and "son," etc. differs strikingly from our usage, and "son" may be an actual son, a grandson, or a great grandson, or even, in the case of royalty, no blood relation at all. To employ the genealogical lists of Genesis to calculate the creation of man about 4004 B. C. as Archbiship Ussher has done, is not only unwarranted from the text of Scripture, but is incontrovertibly disproved by the well-attested facts of archaeology. *M. F. U.*

II. A town near the Jordan, and beside Zaretan (Josh. 3:16). Adam is identified with Tell ed-Damieh on the east bank of the river, near the mouth of the Jabbok and 18 miles above Jericho. Here the waters miraculously rose in a heap while the Israelites crossed the river Jordan.

Ad′amah (ăd′ă-mä; *earth, ground*), a fenced city of Naphtali (Josh. 19:36). The modern Tell ed-Damiyeh.

Adamant. *See* Mineral Kingdom.

Ad′ami (ăd′ă-mī; *pertaining to (red) earth, earthy*), a place in Palestine near the border of Naphtali, now identified with Khirbet Damiyeh.

A′dar (ā′där; from Akk. *adaru, addaru,* probably *dark* or *cloudy*), a later name of the twelfth month of the Jewish year borrowed by the Jews from the Babylonian Calendar during the Exile. It extended from the new moon of February to that of March (Ezra 6:15; Esth. 3:7, 13; 9:15). *See* Time.

Ad′beel (ăd′bē-ĕl; *disciplined of God*), the third-named of the twelve sons of Ishmael (Gen. 25:13; I Chron. 1:29).

Ad′dan (ăd′dăn), another form (Ezra 2:59) of the name (Neh. 7:61) *Addon* (*q. v.*).

Ad′dar (ăd′där; *threshing floor,* or *wide, open place*), a son of Bela and grandson of Benjamin (I Chron. 8:3), elsewhere (Gen. 46:21) called Ard.

Ad′der (ăd′dēr), the rendering in the A. V. of four Hebrew words, each of which probably signifies some kind of venomous serpent. *See* Animal Kingdom.

Ad′di (ăd′dī; *ornament*), the son of Cosam and father of Melchi, in the maternal ancestry of Jesus (Luke 3:28).

Ad′don (ăd′dŏn), the name of the second of three persons (Neh. 7:61) who, on returning from the captivity to Palestine, were unable to "show their father's house, nor their seed, whether they were of Israel," B. C. 536. In Ezra 2:59, he is called Addan.

A′der (ā′dēr; *a flock*), a chief Benjamite, son of Beriah, resident at Jerusalem (I Chron. 8:15).

A′diel (ā′dĭ-ĕl; *ornament of God*).
1. One of the family heads of the tribe of Simeon, who seem to have dispossessed the aborigines of Gedor (I Chron. 4:36).
2. A priest, son of Jahzerah and father of Maasiai, which last was very active in reconstructing the temple after the captivity (I Chron. 9:12), B. C. 563.
3. The father of Azmaveth, which latter was treasurer under David (I Chron. 27:25).

A′din (ā′dĭn, *effeminate*).
1. The head of one of the Israelitish families, of which a large number returned with

Zerubbabel to Jerusalem from Babylon, B. C. 536. The number is given in Ezra 2:15, as four hundred and fifty-four; in Neh. 7:20, as six hundred and fifty-five, the discrepancy being occasioned by an error in the hundreds and the including or excluding of himself. Fifty more of the family returned (with Ebed, the son of Jonathan) under Ezra (Ezra 8:6), B. C. 457.

2. One of those who sealed the covenant made by Nehemiah and the people after their return to Jerusalem (Neh. 10:16), B. C. about 445.

Ad′ina (ăd′ĭ-nà; *slender, delicate*), the son of Shiza, a Reubenite, captain of thirty of his tribesmen—one of David's mighty men (I Chron. 11:42), B. C. before 1000.

Ad′ino (ăd′ĭ-nō; *slender*, as a *spear*), the name given in II Sam. 23:8, as one of David's mighty men. Much difference of opinion respecting it exists. Some think the passage has been corrupted. It is clear that these words "Adino the Eznite" are not proper names, although their grammatical construction is not very easy. See also the parallel passage (I Chron. 11:11).

Aditha′im (ăd-ĭ-thă′ĭm), a place in Palestine, but location unknown (Josh. 15:36).

Adjuration (Heb. *'äläh*, in Hiph., *to cause to swear*, in I Kings 8:31; II Chron. 6:22, *shăbă, to make swear*; Gr. *exorkidzō, to exact an oath*).

1. An act or appeal whereby a person in authority imposes upon another the obligation of speaking or acting as if under the solemnity of an oath (I Sam. 14:24; Josh. 6:26, I Kings 22:16; II Chron. 18:15). In the New Testament we have an example of this where the high priest calls upon Jesus to avow his character as the Messiah (Matt. 26:63; compare Mark 5:7). Such an oath, although imposed upon one without his consent, was binding in the highest degree; and when connected with a question, made an answer compulsory.

2. In Acts 19:13, the term occurs with reference to the expulsion of demons.

3. In the Roman Catholic Church, the use of the name of God, or of some holy thing, to induce one to do what is required of him.

Ad′lai (ăd′lā-ĭ), the father of Shaphat, which latter was a chief herdsman under David (I Chron. 27:29), B. C. after 1000.

Ad′mah (ăd′mäh; *red earth*), a city in the vale of Siddim (Gen. 10:19), destroyed with Sodom (Gen. 19:24; Deut. 29:23). Supposed by some to be identical with Adam of Josh. 3:16.

Ad′matha (ăd′mă-thá; perhaps *earthly, dark-colored*), the third-named of the princes or courtiers of Ahasuerus (Esth. 1:14).

Administration (Gr. *diakonia, service*), in the New Testament signifies "to relieve," "to minister," as in II Cor. 9:12.

Ad′na (ăd′nà; *pleasure*).

1. An Israelite of the family of Pahathmoab, who divorced his Gentile wife after the captivity (Ezra 10:30).

2. A chief priest, son of Harim, and contemporary with Joiakim (Neh. 12:15), B. C. about 536.

Ad′nah (ăd′náh; *pleasure*).

1. One of the captains of the tribe of Manasseh who joined David at Ziklag (I Chron. 12:20), B. C. before 1000.

2. A warrior of the tribe of Judah, and principal general under Jehoshaphat (II Chron. 17:14), B. C. about 872-852.

Ado′ni-be′zek (à-dō′nĭ-bē′zĕk; *lord of Bezek*), king or lord of Bezek, a city of the Canaanites. He had subdued seventy of the petty kings around him, and, after having cut off their thumbs and great toes, compelled them to gather their food under his table. At the head of the Canaanites and Perizzites he opposed the men of Judah and Simeon, and, being defeated, was served in the same manner as he had treated his own captives, B. C. about 1375. He died of his wounds at Jerusalem, whither he was carried by his captors. (Judg. 1:5-7).

Adoni′jah (ă-dō-nī′jäh; *my lord is Jehovah*).

1. The fourth son of David and second by Haggith, born in Hebron while his father reigned over Judah only (II Sam. 3:4), B. C. about 1003. According to oriental usages Adonijah might have considered his claim superior to that of his eldest brother, Amnon, who was born while his father was in a private station; but not to that of Absalom, who was not only his elder brother, and born while his father was a king, but was of royal descent on the side of his mother. When Amnon and Absalom were dead, Adonijah became heir apparent to the throne. But this order had been set aside in favor of Solomon, who was born while his father was king over *all* Israel. (**1**) **Anointed King.** Adonijah aspired to the throne, prepared a guard of chariots and horsemen and fifty foot runners, and gained over to his side Joab and Abiathar, the priest. He was also a man of handsome appearance and likely to win the people. Waiting until David seemed to be at the point of death, he called around him his brothers (excepting Solomon) and other influential men, and was proclaimed king at Zoheleth. The plot was defeated by the prompt action of the aged king, who, through the influence of Nathan and Bath-sheba, caused Solomon to be proclaimed king and to be anointed by Zadok, the priest. (**2**) **Pardoned.** Adonijah fled for refuge to the altar, which he refused to leave until pardoned by Solomon. He received pardon, but was told that a future attempt of the same kind would be fatal to him (I Kings 1:5-53). (**3**) **Death.** Some time after David's death he covertly asserted his claim in asking for *Abishag* (*q. v.*) the virgin widow of his father in marriage. Adonijah was immediately put to death by the order of Solomon (I Kings 2:23-25), B. C. about 960. The execution of Adonijah by Solomon must not be judged by the standards of the present day. According to the custom of Eastern princes, a thousand years before Christ, Solomon would probably have slain all his brothers upon ascending the throne, whereas we learn of the death of Adonijah alone, and that only after his second treasonable attempt.

2. One of the Levites sent by King Jehoshaphat to assist in teaching the law to the people of Judah (II Chron. 17:8), B. C. after 875.

3. A chief Israelite after the captivity (Neh.

10:16), probably the same elsewhere (Ezra 2:13; 8:13; Neh. 7:18) called *Adonikam* (*q. v.*).

Adoni′kam, many **Adon′ikam** (ă-dŏn-ī′kăm; *whom the Lord sets up*, or *lord of the enemy*), one whose descendants, to the number of six hundred and sixty-six, returned to Jerusalem with Zerubbabel (Ezra 2:13), B. C. 536. He himself is included in Neh. 7:18. Somewhat later three of his immediate descendants, with sixty male followers, came with Ezra (Ezra 8:13), B. C. 458. He appears (from the identity of the associated names) to have been the Adonijah who joined in the religious covenant of Nehemiah (Neh. 10:16).

Adoni′ram (ă-dŏ-nī′răm; *lord of height*, i. e., *high lord*), the son of Abda, and receiver-general of the imposts in the reigns of David, Solomon, and Rehoboam (I Kings 4:6). During his extended term of office he rendered both himself and the tribute so odious to the people, in sustaining the immense public works of Solomon, that when Rehoboam rashly sent him to enforce the collection of the taxes the exasperated populace rose upon him and stoned him to death. This was the signal for the revolt under Jeroboam (I Kings 12:18), B. C. 922. Adoniram is called, by contraction, Adoram (II Sam. 20:24; I Kings 12:18) and Hadoram (II Chron. 10:18).

Ado′ni-ze′dek (ă-dŏ′nĭ-zĕ′dĕk; *lord of justice*, i. e., *just lord*), the king of Jerusalem when the Israelites invaded Palestine (Josh. 10:1), B. C. 1170. After Jericho and Ai were taken, and the Gibeonites had succeeded in forming a treaty with the Israelites, Adoni-zedek induced the Amorite kings of Hebron, Jarmuth, Lachish, and Eglon to join him in a confederacy against the enemy. They began operations by besieging the Gibeonites, who sent to Joshua for help. Joshua marched all night from Gilgal, and, falling unexpectedly upon the besiegers, put them to utter rout. The five kings took refuge in a cave at Makkedah, but were detected, and the cave's mouth was closed by placing huge stones against it. When the Israelites returned from the pursuit the cave was opened and the kings taken out. The chief men of Israel then set their feet upon the necks of the prostrate monarchs—an ancient mark of triumph. The five kings were then slain, and their bodies hung on trees until evening, when, as the law forbade a longer exposure of the dead (Deut. 21:23), they were taken down and cast into the cave, the mouth of which was filled up with large stones, which remained long after (Josh. 10:1-27). In considering the severe treatment of these kings we must remember that the war was one of extermination, and that the treatment of the Jews was neither better nor worse than those of the people with whom they fought.

Adoption (Gr. *huiothesia*, the *placing* as a *son*), the admission of a person to some or all of the privileges of natural kinship. As the practice of adoption was confined almost exclusively to sons—the case of Esther being an exception —it probably had its origin in the natural desire for male offspring. This would be especially true where force, rather than well-observed laws, decided the possession of estates.

1. Among the Hebrews. Abraham speaks of Eliezer (Gen. 15:3), a houseborn slave, as

his heir, having, probably, adopted him as his son. Jacob adopted his grandsons, Ephraim and Manasseh, to be counted as his sons (Gen. 48:6), thus enabling him to bestow, through them, a double portion upon his favorite son Joseph. Sometimes a man without a son would marry his daughter to a freed slave, the children being accounted her father's; or the husband himself would be adopted as a son (I Chron. 2:34). Most of the early instances of adoption mentioned in the Bible were the acts of women who, because of barrenness, gave their female slaves to their husbands, with the intention of adopting any children they might have. Thus Sarah gave Hagar to Abraham, and the son (Ishmael) was considered as the child of Abraham and Sarah (Gen. 16:1, ff.). The childless Rachel gave her maid, Bilhah, to her husband (Gen. 30:1-7), and was imitated by Leah (Gen. 30:9-13). In such cases the sons were regarded as fully equal in the right of heritage with those by the legitimate wife.

2. Among the Romans. Adoption was a familiar social phenomenon, and its initial ceremonies and incidents occupied a large and important place in their laws. By adoption an entire stranger in blood became a member of the family in a higher sense than some of the family kin, than emancipated sons, or descendants through females. Such a one assumed the family name, engaged in its sacrificial rites, and became, not by sufferance or at will, but to all intents and purposes, a member of the house of his adoption. The tie thus formed could only be broken through the ceremony of emancipation, and formed as complete a barrier to intermarriage as relationship by blood. At Rome there were two kinds of adoption, both requiring the adopter to be a male and childless: *arrogatio* and adoption proper. The former could only take place where the person to be adopted was independent (*sui juris*) and his adopter had no prospect of male offspring. The adopted one became, in the eyes of the law, a new creature. He was born again into a new family. This custom was doubtless referred to by Paul (Rom. 8:14-16).

The *ceremony* of adoption took place in the presence of seven witnesses. The fictitious sale and resale, and the final "vindication" or claim, were accompanied by the legal formula, and might mean the sale of a son into slavery or his adoption into a new family, according to the words used. The touch of the *festuca* or ceremonial wand might be accompanied by the formula, "I claim this man as my son," or "I claim this man as my slave." It was the function of the witnesses, upon occasion, to testify that the transaction was in truth the adoption of the child.

3. Greek. At Athens adoption took place either in the lifetime of the adopter or by will; or if a man died childless and intestate, the state interfered to bring into his house the man next entitled by the Attic law of inheritance, as heir and adopted son. If there were daughters, one of them was usually betrothed to the adopted son. If after that a male heir was born, he and the adopted son had equal rights.

4. The custom of adoption still prevails in the East among the Turks, Greeks, and Armenians. This is done in order to have an heir to the estate, and implies the renouncing of all claim to the child by its parents. Among the Mohammedans the ceremony of adoption is sometimes performed by causing the adopted one to pass through the shirt of the adopter. Something like this may have been the action of Elijah when he threw his mantle on Elisha (I Kings 19:19).

Adoption. *Theological.* This term as used in a theological sense commonly denotes that act of God by which he restores penitent and believing men to their privileges as members of the divine family, and makes them heirs of heaven.

1. Theology owes its use of the word adoption in this way to the apostle Paul. He is the only Scripture writer who employs the term thus translated. The passages in Paul's writings in which the doctrine of adoption is stated in connection with the use of that term are Rom. 8:15-17; Gal. 4:4-6; Eph. 1:5. These are not by any means, however, the only passages in his writings in which the essential thought is plainly declared (II Cor. 6:18). And more generally speaking this may be said to be one of the doctrines upon which the New Testament lays special stress. That we who have forfeited and lost our place and privileges as children of God may be fully reinstated therein was one of the great teachings of Jesus Christ. For that the parable of the prodigal son was spoken.

Adoption, it appears, taking the Scripture teachings as a whole, while not the same as our justification, is necessarily connected therewith, as forgiveness would be empty without restoration to the privileges forfeited by sin. Adoption and regeneration also are two phases of the same fact, regeneration meaning the reproduction of the filial character, and adoption the restoration of the filial privilege. *See* Justification, Regeneration. Adoption is a word of *position* rather than *relationship.* The believer's relation to God as a child results from the new birth (John 1:12, 13), whereas adoption is the divine act whereby one already a child is, through redemption from the law, placed in the position of an *adult son* (Gal. 4:1-5).

2. The word adoption is also used by the apostle Paul with reference to the full and final outcome of salvation, the complete "manifestation of the sons of God" and perfect investiture with all their heavenly privileges, for which Christians must wait. So he writes of waiting "for the manifestation of the sons of God," and "waiting for the adoption, to wit, the redemption of our body" (Rom. 8:19, 23).

3. Another use of this word by the same apostle is in Rom 9:4, where he speaks of the Israelites "to whom pertaineth the adoption." By this is meant the special place that was given to Israel among the nations as the chosen people of God.

Adora'im (ă-dō-rā'ĭm), a town, doubtless in the S. W. of Judah, since it is enumerated among the cities fortified by Rehoboam (II Chron. 11:9). It is met with in I Macc. 13:20

as an Idumean city, *Adora*, and so also frequently in Josephus. It was taken by Hyrcanus. Robinson has identified it with the present Dûra, a village about seven and one-half miles to the westward of Hebron.

Ado'ram (á-dō'răm), an officer in charge of the tribute (II Sam. 20:24; I Kings 12:18), elsewhere called *Adoniram* (*q. v.*).

Adoration, in its true sense, is the act of paying honors to a divine being. In the Scriptures various forms of adoration are mentioned; e. g., putting off the shoes (Exod. 3:5; Josh 5:15), bowing the knee (Gen. 41:43; 43:26; Dan. 2:46), kissing (Psa. 2:12; Luke 7:38). The passage, "If I had beheld the sun when it shined, or the moon walking in brightness; and my heart had been secretly enticed, or my mouth had kissed my hand: this also were an iniquity to be punished by the judge" (Job. 31:26-28), clearly intimates that kissing the hand was considered an overt act of worship in the East. In the same manner respect was shown to kings and other persons of exalted station. "Laying the hand upon the mouth" (Job. 21:5; 29:9; Psa. 39:9) implied the highest degree of reverence and submission.

Adorn (Gr. *kosmeō, to ornament*), to embellish with honor, gain; followed by participle designating the act by which the honor is gained (Tit. 2:10; I Pet. 3:5).

Adram'melech (ă-drăm'měl-ĕk; *splendor of the king*).

1. A son of Sennacherib, King of Assyria. The king was dwelling at Nineveh after his disastrous expedition abainst Hezekiah. While worshiping in the house of Nisroch, his god, Sennacherib was murdered by Adrammelech and his brother Shareza B. C. 681. Having accomplished the crime, the two brothers fled into Armenia (II Kings 19:36, 37; Isa. 37:38).

2. The name of an Avite god (II Kings 17:31). *See* Gods, False.

Adramyt'tium (ă-dră-mĭt'tĭ-ŭm; *the mansion of death*), a seaport of Mysia, in Asia Minor (Acts 27:2-5), whence Paul sailed in an Alexandrian ship to Italy. It now bears the name Adramyti.

A'dria (ā'drĭ-à), called the "sea of Adria" in R. V. (Acts 27:27). It is the modern Gulf of Venice, the *Mare Supernum* of the Romans, as distinguished from the *Mare Inferum* or the Tyrrhenian Sea. It probably derived its name from Adria, a city in Istria.

A'driel (ā'drĭ-ĕl; *flock of God*), a son of Barzillai the Meholathite. Saul gave to him in marriage his daughter Merab, who had been promised to David (I Sam. 18:17-19). His five sons were among the seven descendants of Saul whom David surrendered to the Gibeonites (II Sam. 21:8) in satisfaction for the endeavors of Saul to extirpate them, although a league had been made between them and the Israelites (Josh 9:15). In II Sam. 21:8 the name of *Michal* occurs as the mother of these sons of Adriel. In explanation, *see* Michal.

Adul'lam (á-dŭl'lăm), a town S. W. of Jerusalem about midway to Lachish and 9 miles N. E. of Beit Jibrin; now identified as Tell esh-Sheikh Madhkur. It first appears as the resident city of a Canaanite king (Josh. 12:15; 15:35, but is most famous for its cave in which David hid as a fugitive from Saul. (I Sam. 22:1; II Chron. 11:7).

Adullamite (á-dŭl'lá-mīt) an inhabitant (Gen. 38:1, 12, 20) of *Adullam* (*q. v.*).

Adultery. 1. Defined. (1) Jewish. The willful violation of the marriage contract by either of the parties, through sexual intercourse with a third party. The divine provision was that the husband and wife should become "one flesh," each being held sacred to the other. So taught Jesus: "Have ye not read, that he which made them at the beginning made them male and female. . . . Wherefore they are no more twain, but one flesh." When the Pharisees, with the apparent hope of eliciting some modification in favor of the husband, put the question, "Why did Moses then command to give a writing of divorcement, and to put her away?" Jesus replied, "Moses because of the hardness of your hearts suffered you to put away your wives: but from the beginning it was not so. . . . Whosoever shall put away his wife, except it be for fornication, and shall marry another, committeth adultery," etc. (Matt. 19:3-9). In perfect accord with this also is the teaching of St. Paul (Eph. 5:25-33; I Cor. 7:1-13; I Tim. 3:12). It will be seen that according to the fundamental law it is adultery for the man as well as the woman to have commerce with another person than the legal spouse. In ancient times, however, exception was made among the nations generally in favor of the man. He might have more wives than one, or have intercourse with a person not espoused or married to him, without being considered an adulterer. Adultery was sexual intercourse with the married wife, or what was equivalent, the betrothed bride of another man; for this act exposed the husband to the danger of having a spurious offspring imposed upon him. In the seventh commandment (Exod. 20:14) all manner of lewdness or unchastity in act or thought seems to be meant (Matt. 5:28). **(2) Roman.** The Roman law appears to have made the same distinction as the Hebrew between the unfaithfulness of the husband and wife, by defining adultery to be the violation of another man's bed. The infidelity of the husband did not constitute adultery. The Greeks held substantially the same view.

2. Trial of Adultery. A man suspecting his wife of adultery, not having detected her in the act, or having no witness to prove her supposed guilt, brought her to the priest that she might be submitted to the ordeal prescribed in Num. 5:11-31. *See* Jealousy, Offering of. When adultery ceased to be a capital crime, as it doubtless did, this trial probably fell into disuse. No instance of the ordeal being undergone is given in Scripture, and it appears to have been finally abrogated about forty years before the destruction of Jerusalem. The reason assigned is that the men were at that time so generally adulterous that God would not fulfill the imprecations of the ordeal oath upon the wife.

3. Penalties. (1) Jewish. The Mosaic law assigned the punishment of death to adultery (Lev. 20:10), but did not state the mode of its infliction. From various passages of Scripture (e. g., Ezek. 16:38, 40; John 8:5) we infer that it was by stoning. When the adulteress was a slave the guilty parties were scourged, the blows not to exceed forty; the adulterer to offer a trespass offering (a ram) to be offered by the priest (Lev. 19:20-22). Death does not appear to have been inflicted, perhaps by reason of guilt on the part of those administering the law (John 8:9). We find no record in the Old Testament of a woman taken in adultery being put to death. The usual remedy seems to have been a divorce, in which the woman lost her dower, right of maintenance, etc., thus avoiding public scandal. The expression to "make a public example" (Matt. 1:19), probably means to bring the matter before the local Sanhedrin, the usual course. **(2) Roman,** etc. The Roman civil law looked upon adultery as "the violation of another man's bed," and thus the husband's incontinence could not constitute the offense. The punishment was left to the husband and parents of the adulteress, who under the old law suffered death. The most usual punishment of the man was by mutilation, castration, cutting off the nose and ears. Other punishments were banishment, heavy fines, burning at the stake, drowning. Among the Greeks and other ancient nations the adulterer might lose eye, nose, or ear. Among savage nations of the present time the punishment is generally severe. The Mohammedan code pronounces it a capital offense.

4. Spiritual. In the symbolical language of the Old Testament adultery means idolatry and apostasy from the worship of Jehovah (Jer. 3:8, 9; Ezek. 16:32; 23:37; Rev. 2:22). This figure resulted from the sort of married relationship, the solemn engagement between Jehovah and Israel (Jer. 2:2; 3:14; 13:27; 31:32; Hos. 8:9). Our Lord uses similar language when he charged Israel with being an "adulterous generation" (Matt. 12:39; 16:4; Mark 8:38), meaning a faithless and unholy generation. An "adulterous" means an apostate church or city (Isa. 1:21; Jer. 3:6-9; Ezek. 16:22; 23:7).

5. Ecclesiastical. The following views obtained in the early Church: **(1) The crime.** Under Justinian the wife was regarded as the real criminal, and her paramour as a mere accomplice. This view seems to have been held during the whole early Christian period. Gregory of Nyssa makes a distinction between fornication and adultery. A canon of Basle furnishes this definition: "We name him who cohabits with another woman (not his own wife) an adulterer." Ambrose says: "All unchaste intercourse is adultery; what is illicit for the woman is illicit for the man." Gregory Nazianzen argues that the man should not be left free to sin while the woman is restrained. Chrysostom says: "It is commonly called adultery when a man wrongs a married woman. I, however, affirm it of a married man who sins with the unmarried." Jerome contends that I Cor. 6:16 applies equally to both sexes. **(2) Penalties.** A convicted adulterer cannot receive orders. An adulterer or adulteress must undergo seven years' penance. A presbyter so offending is to be excom-

municated and brought to penance. The layman whose wife is guilty cannot receive orders, and if already ordained must put her away under pain of deprivation. An unchaste wife must be divorced, but not the husband, even if adulterous. The adulterer must undergo fifteen years of penitence, but only seven for incontinence. Two conclusions were drawn by canonists and divines: (*a*) Divorce, except for adultery, is adultery. (*b*) To retain an adulterous wife is adultery. A woman must not leave her husband for blows, waste of dower, incontinence, nor even disbelief (I Cor. 7:16), under penalty of adultery. An offending wife is an adulteress, and must be divorced, but not so the husband. The Catholic Church holds that marriage is not and ought not to be dissolved by the adultery of either party (Council of Trent, sess. xxiv, can. 7). (3) **Constructive adultery.** The following are treated as guilty of actual adultery: A man marrying a betrothed maiden; a girl seduced marrying another than her seducer; consecrated virgins who sin, and their paramours; a Christian marrying a Jew or an idolater.

Adum′mim (à-dŭm′ĭm; *red*, or *bloody*), a place on the road from Jerusalem to Jericho (Josh. 15:7; 18:17), and supposed to be the scene of the good Samaritan's rescue of the man who fell among thieves. It has the modern name of Tal.'at ed-Damm ("ascent of blood").

Advent, Second. *See* Millennium.

Adversary, in its general meaning, is an enemy; as "The Lord will take vengeance upon his adversaries" (Nah. 1:2). Very frequently it is derived from Heb. *tsûr, to bind*; in I Sam. 2:10, *rîb, to strive.* In the New Testament we have *antikeimenos, hupenantios, one who opposes*; and *antidikos, opponent in law.* In Isa. 50:8, the expression *Baal mishpât*, means "he who has a judicial cause or lawsuit against me;" just as in Roman law *dominus lilit* is distinguished from the procurator; i. e., from the person who represents him in court (Delitzsch, *Com.*). Specifically (Heb. *Sätän*), the devil, as the general enemy of mankind (I Pet. 5:8).

Advocate (Gr. *Paraklētos, Paraclete*), one who pleads the cause of another. The term is applied to the Holy Spirit by Jesus (John 14:16; 15:26; 16:7), where it is rendered Comforter; and by John to Christ himself (I John 2:1). The word Advocate (Lat. *advocatus*) might designate a consulting lawyer, or one who presented his client's case in open court; or one who, in times of trial or hardship, sympathized with the afflicted and administered suitable direction and support.

Aene′as (ê-nê′ăs), a paralytic of Lydda cured by Peter (Acts 9:33, 34).

Ae′non (ê′nŏn; *springs*), the place "near Salim" where John baptized (John 3:23). Site uncertain.

Ae′on (ê′ŏn; Gr. *aiōn, age*), a human lifetime, life itself (according to Homer, Herodotus, etc.); an unbroken age, perpetuity of time, eternity. With this signification the Hebrew and Rabbinic idea of the word *'ōläm, concealed*, combines in the biblical and ecclesiastical writers. Hence in the New Testament aeon is used:

1. In the phrases *eis tōn* ... "always"), *forever* (John 6:51, ... 5:6; 6:20, etc.); (Jude 13), ... *never* (John 4:14; 8:51; 10:2... *unto the ages*, i. e., *as long as tim*... (Luke 1:33; Rom. 1:25; 9:5; ... the expression "unto the ages ... (Gal. 1:5; II Tim. 4:18; I Pe... 1:6, 18, etc.) the endless future ... into various periods, the shorter ... comprehended in the longer. "F... is used in the sense of *from the mo*... *from of old* (Luke 1:70; Acts 3:2... **2.** As the Jews distinguished th... the Messiah, and the time after ... so most of the New Testament ... tinguish *this age* (and similar expr... time before the appointed retu... Messianic advent of Christ, and ... *the future age* (Matt. 12:32; Eph... millennium.

3. Figurative. The container is u... contained, and *hoi aiōnes* denotes *the ... universe*, i. e., the aggregate of things ... in time (Heb. 1:2; 11:3).

Affliction (mostly Heb. *'ōnĕ, depr*... *thlĭp′sĭs, pressure*). Other Hebrew a... words are used, and if they were al... rendered we should have iniquity, s... lowered, evil, breach, suffering. This ... expresses its meaning in common ... English word comes from the Latin *a*... striking, as one thing against anothe... grief, distress of body or mind, etc.

Respecting the well-known and oft... passage, "For our light affliction,....wo... us," etc. (II Cor. 4:17), we quote from ... *Com.*, Notes by American Editor: "T... vision of 1881 gives this weighty and i... sive verse in a rendering which is exac... yet faithful to our English idiom. The ... contains the whole philosophy of the Chr... view of affliction. It does not deny the r... of earthly sorrows or underrate their p... as did the Stoics; but after allowing the... their force, calmly says that they dwindle ... insignificance when compared with the ... ceeding and eternal glory to which they l... But this applies only to believers, as appe... by the next verse, 'while we look,' etc. Aff... tions have a salutary operation, provided t... we look at the things which are eternal."

Afternoon (Heb. *nĕtôth hăyyōm, the day's decl*... *ing*, Judg. 19:8), according to the Jewi... reckoning the fifth of the six divisions of t... day. *See* Time.

Ag′abus (ăg′à-bŭs), a prophet, supposed t... have been one of the seventy disciples of Christ ... He with others came from Jerusalem to Anti... och while Paul and Barnabas were there, and ... predicted an approaching famine, which actu... ally occurred the following year. The expres... sion "throughout all the world" was probably ... used in a national sense, and by it Judea was ... doubtless meant, and the words must be un... derstood to apply to that famine which, in the ... fourth year of Claudius, overspread Palestine. ... The poor Jews in general were then relieved ... by the queen of Adiabne, who sent to Egypt ... to purchase corn for them (Josephus, *Ant.*, xx, ... 2, 5; 5, 2). For the relief of the Christians in ...

idea contributions were raised by their rethren in Antioch, and taken to Jerusalem y Paul and Barnabas (Acts 11:28-30). Many ears after, this same Agabus met Paul at :aesarea, and warned him of the sufferings /hich awaited him if he prosecuted his jour-ey to Jerusalem (Acts 21:10-12). Agabus ook the girdle of St. Paul and fastened it ound his own hands and feet, and said, 'Thus saith the Holy Ghost, So shall the 'ews at Jerusalem bind the man that owneth his girdle, and shall deliver him into the ands of the Gentiles."

'gag (ā'găg), probably a common name of all he Amalekite kings, like Pharaoh in Egypt, etc.

1. The king, apparently, of one of the hostile neighboring nations at the time of the Exodus, B. C. 1441. He is referred to by Balaam (Num. 24:7) in a manner implying that the king of the Amalekites was, then at least, a great monarch, and his people a greater people, than is commonly imagined.

2. The king of the Amalekites, who, being taken prisoner by Saul, was spared by him, contrary to the solemn vow of devotement to destruction whereby the nation, as such, had of old precluded itself from giving any quarter to that people (Exod. 17:14; Deut. 25:19). When Samuel came to the camp of Saul he chided him and told him of his rejection, and ordered Agag to be brought to him. Agag came "delicately," i. e., in a joyous state of mind, thinking that his life would still be spared him (K. and D., Com., in loco.). But the prophet ordered him to be cut in pieces; and in the expression which he employed—"As thy sword hath made women childless, so shalt thy mother be childless among women" —indicates that, apart from the obligations of the vow, some such example of retributive justice was intended as had been exercised in the case of Adoni-bezek (q. v.). Perhaps Agag had treated prisoners in the same way he was now treated by Samuel (I Sam. 15:8-33), B. C. about 1020.

A'gagite (ā'gă-gīt), is found (Esth. 3:1, 10; 8:3, 5; 9:24) in connection with Haman, the enemy of Mordecai. Josephus (Ant., xi, 6, 5) explains it as a synonym of Amalek, and so it possibly was.

Ag'ape (ág'à-pē), pl. Agapae (Gr. agapē, love), a simple meal of brotherly love celebrated daily in the apostolic times in connection with the Eucharist, the two being spoken of to-gether as the Lord's Supper. At this meal the Christians, in connection with their common Redeemer, ignored all distinctions of rank, wealth, and culture, and met as members of one family. At the feast the bishop (or pres-byter) presided, the food having been pre-pared at home, or at the place of meeting, according to circumstances. Before eating the guests washed their hands, prayer was offered, and the Scriptures were read. After the meal a collection was taken for widows and orphans, the kiss of charity was given, and communica-tions from other congregations were read and answered.

The Agape was never enjoined by divine command, and gradually, losing its peculiar feature of childlike unity, it led to all sorts of abuses, such as we find rebuked by St. Paul. Another cause for its discontinuance was that the Third Council of Carthage (A. D. 391) decreed that the Eucharist should be taken fasting. Later several councils forbade their being held in the church buildings. Vestiges of the practice remained as late as the Council of Basle, in the 15th century.

A'gar (ā'gár), a Greek form (Gal. 4:24, 25) of the name Hagar (q. v.)

Agate, the name of one of the precious stones in the breastplate of the high priest (Exod. 28:19; 39:12). In Isa. 54:12 and Ezek. 27:16 the word agate is used for another Hebrew word, which modern interpretation is dis-posed to identify with Ruby (q. v.). See Mineral Kingdom.

Ag'ee (ăg'ē; fugitive), a Hararite, father of Shammah, which latter was one of David's chief warriors (II Sam. 23:11).

Agony (Gr. agōnia, struggle), used both in clas-sical and New Testament Greek of severe mental struggles and emotions; our anguish. The word is used in the New Testament only by Luke (22:44) to describe the fearful strug-gle through which our Lord passed in the garden of Gethsemane. The circumstances of this mysterious transaction are recorded in Matt. 26:36-46; Mark 14:32-42; Heb. 5:7, 8. Luke alone notices the agony, the bloody sweat, and the appearance of the strengthen-ing angel. All agree that he prayed for the re-moval of "this cup," and are careful to note that he qualified this petition by a preference of his Father's will to his own. The question is, what did he mean by "this cup?" what was the cause of this sorrow unto death?

For answer we quote Edersheim: "Not fear, either of bodily or mental suffering: but death. Man's nature, created of God immortal, shrinks (by the law of its nature) from the dissolution of the bond that binds body to soul. Yet to fallen man death is not by any means fully death, for he is born with the taste of it in his soul. Not so Christ. It was the unfallen Man dying; it was he, who had no experience of it, tasting death, and that not for himself but for every man, emptying the cup to its bitter dregs. It was the Christ under-going death by man and for man; the incar-nate God, the God-man, submitting himself vicariously to the deepest humiliation, and paying the utmost penalty: death—all death. No one could know what death was (not dying, which men dread, but Christ dreaded not); no one could taste its bitterness as he. His going into death was his final conflict with Satan for man, and on his behalf. By submitting to it he took away the power of death. He disarmed Death by burying his shaft in His own heart. And beyond this lies the deep, unutterable mystery of Christ bearing the penalty due to our sin, bearing our death, bearing the pen-alty of the broken law, the accumulated guilt of humanity, and the holy wrath of the righteous Judge upon them" (Life of Jesus, ii, 538, 539).

Ag'ora (ăg'ŏ-rà), the market place or public square of a Greek city, where men assembled to debate or transact civic business. In the agora at Athens the Apostle Paul met daily and disputed with those who chanced to be

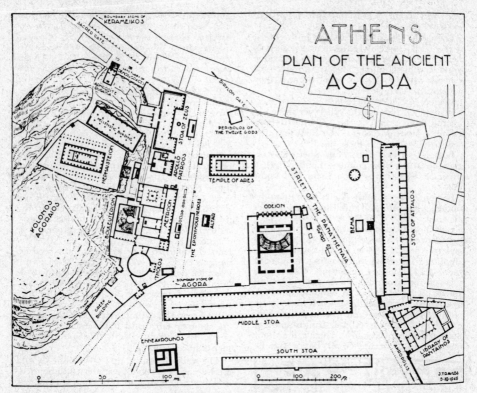

6. Reconstruction of Agora at Athens.

there (Acts 17:17). The Athenian marketplace has been completely excavated by the American School of Classical Studies (in the 1930's and to completion since 1946). Remains of this famous area include the round *Tholos* where standard measures and weights were kept, the *Metroon* where archives were deposited; the *Bouleuterion* or council chamber and a small Temple of Apollo. The entire complex of agora structures was dominated by the temple of Hephaisteion, the god of metal craftsmen. In addition to buildings many small finds have been made such as Mycenean urns (14th century B. C.), ostraca, pottery, jewelry and *objets d'art*. Paul was also familiar with the agora at Corinth and other Greek cities. The Greek agora corresponds to the forum of Roman cities. *M. F. U.*

Agrapha (Gr. *agraphos*; *unwritten*), a term applied to the sayings of our Lord not recorded in the gospels. Naturally, there would be many of these, and such is recorded as the fact (John 21:25). The sources of our knowledge of these sayings are threefold: (*a*) The first and surest is to be found in the books of the New Testament itself. An unquestionable example is given in Acts 20:35: "Remember the words of the Lord Jesus, how he said, It is more blessed to give than to receive." Mayor in his comments on James 1:12, "He shall receive the crown of life, *which the Lord promised* to them that love him," thinks these words a semiquotation of some saying of Christ. (*b*) The next source, both in amount and author-

ity, is supplied by some manuscripts of the New Testament, among them the well-known addition in *Codex Bezae* to Luke 6:4. "On the same day, beholding one working on the Sabbath, he said unto him. *Man, if thou knowest what thou doest, blessed art thou; but if thou knowest not, accursed art thou and a transgressor of the law.*" (*c*) Quotations in early Christian writers and in lost gospels. The quotations of these sayings cease almost entirely after the fourth century, when the current gospel text had won its way to acceptance. Of these unrecorded sayings Resch has collected seventy-four which he regards as genuine, and one hundred and three apocryphal. In the main these sayings neither have historical setting nor affect the truth of our Lord's life. They do, however, often illustrate his teaching, and express it perhaps in a terser, more remarkable form than is found elsewhere. The following are some of the most remarkable of these sayings: "He that is near me is near the fire; he that is far from me is far from the kingdom;" "That which is weak shall be saved by that which is strong." (*d*) "The Logia, or Sayings of our Lord," found in Oxyrhynchus, one hundred and twenty miles south of Cairo, Egypt, by Messrs. B. F. Grenfell and Arthur S. Hunt, 1896.

Logion 1. ". . . and then shalt thou see clearly to cast out the mote that is in the brother's eye."

Logion 2. "Jesus saith, Except ye fast to the world, ye shall in no wise find the kingdom of

God; and except ye keep the sabbath, ye shall not see the Father."

Logion 3. "Jesus saith, I stood in the midst of the world, and in the flesh was I seen of them, and I found all men drunken, and none found I athirst among them; and my soul grieveth over the sons of men, because they are blind in their heart. . . ."

Logion 4. Undecipherable.

Logion 5. "Jesus saith, Wherever there are . . . and there is one . . . alone, I am with him. Raise the stone and there thou shalt find me; cleave the wood, and there am I."

Logion 6. "Jesus saith, A prophet is not acceptable in his own country, neither doth a physician work cures upon them that know him."

Logion 7. "Jesus saith, A city built upon the top of a high hill, and stablished, can neither fall nor be hid."

Logion 8. Undecipherable.

Agriculture. The cultivation of the soil dates back to Adam, to whom God assigned the occupation of dressing and keeping the garden (Gen. 2:15). We are told that "Cain was a tiller of the ground" (Gen. 4:2). The ancestors of the Hebrews in Mesopotamia followed pastoral pursuits, which were kept up by Abraham, Isaac, and Jacob, whose sons settled as shepherds on the fruitful pasture lands of Goshen (Gen. 47). During their four hundred years' residence in Egypt the Is-

7. Agriculture and Grazing Scenes in Egyptian Old Kingdom.

raelites engaged in the pursuit of agriculture (Deut. 11:10), so that they were prepared to make the cultivation of the soil their principal employment, and in this sense the Mosaic state was founded on agriculture. As the soil could not be alienated, but reverted to the owner in the year of jubilee, each family had a stake in the soil, and its culture was held in high esteem (I Sam. 11:5; I Kings 19:19, sq.; II Chron. 26:10). As the pastoral life of Israel had kept it from mixture and local attachment, especially while in Egypt, so agriculture in Canaan tended to check a freebooting and nomad life.

1. Irrigation. In all countries climate and soil have much to do with the methods of agriculture and sorts of crops. In eastern countries, generally, the heat and dryness of the greater portion of the year make irrigation by canals and aqueducts indispensable. This is true to a considerable extent of Palestine, although its rains are more frequent than in Egypt or Assyria. There is reference, however, to natural irrigation by conduits *pălgē-măyim, waterpartings, canals* (Job 38:25; Prov. 21:1). These were well-known to the Israelites in Egypt (Deut. 11:10).

2. Care of Soil. The several portions of the land were carefully marked off (I Sam. 14:14; Prov. 22:28); divided for the various products of the soil (Isa. 28:25); secured against injury from wild animals by hedges and walls (Isa. 5:5; Num. 22:24); and the soil fertilized by manuring (II Kings 9:30; Psa. 83:10). The preparation of manure from straw trodden in the dunghill appears from Isa. 25:10. The dung, the carcasses, and the blood of animals were used to enrich the soil (II Kings 9:37; Psa. 83:10; 8:2; Jer. 9:22). Salt, either by itself or mixed in the dunghill in order to promote putrefaction, is specially mentioned as a compost (Matt. 5:13; Luke 14:34, 35). The land was burned over to destroy the seed of noxious herbs (Prov. 24:31; Isa. 32:13), and was then enriched with ashes. The cultivation of hillsides in terraces cannot be proved from any clear statement of Scripture, but the nature of its soil makes it necessary. Terraces are still seen on the mountain slopes, rising above one another, frequently to the number of sixty or eighty; and on them fields, gardens and plantations.

The soil was broken up by the plow (*q. v.*), a crude affair, probably similar to those used in Egypt. The ground was cleared of stones and thorns (Isa. 5:2), early in the year; sowing or gathering from "among thorns" being a proverb for slovenly husbandry (Job. 5:5; Prov. 24:30, 31). New land was plowed a second time. The plow was followed by men using hoes to break the clods (Isa. 28:24), but in later times a harrow was employed. This appears to have been then as now merely a thick block of wood pressed down by the weight of a stone or a man (Job. 39:10; Isa. 28:24). The seed appears to have been sowed and harrowed at the same time, although sometimes it was plowed in by a cross furrow.

3. Crops. The principal crops of Palestine were, undoubtedly, wheat and barley, from which was derived the common bread of the country. Mention is also made of spelt, millet, lentils, flax, cucumbers, melons, beans, cummin, fennel, etc. Hay was not in use, and, therefore, barley with chopped straw was fed to cattle (Gen. 24:25, 32; Judg. 19:19, sq.).

The sowing began after the Feast of Tabernacles (the end of October and in November), in the time when the autumn rains come gradually, thus leaving the farmer time to sow his wheat and barley. Summer fruits (millet, beans, etc.) were sown in January and February. Harvest began with barley (II Sam. 21:9; Ruth 2:23), which ripens in Palestine from two to three weeks before wheat, and was begun by law on the 16th Nisan with the presentation of the first barley sheaf. Lentils, etc., were ready at the same time as barley. Then came wheat and spelt, so that the chief part of the grain harvest closed about Pentecost.

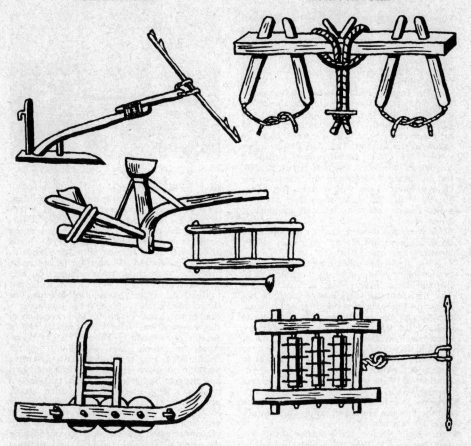

8. Upper left: Ancient Plows, Yoke and Goad. Upper right: Yoke for Pair of Oxen. Lower left: Threshing Sledge (side view). Lower right: Threshing Sledge (top view).

Flax and Cotton. Regarding the cultivation of these the Old Testament gives little information. The Israelites, probably, learned the working of these in Egypt (Exod. 9:31). and they seem to have grown them in Palestine, for according to Hos. 2:9, and Prov. 31:13, flax and wool were to be found in every house. Cotton must have been early cultivated by the Israelites, for in I Chron. 4:21 among the ancient households of Judah is named a family of workers in byssus (linen).

4. Harvest. Grain was cut with the sickle (Deut. 16:9), the reapers living on parched grain and bread dipped in vinegar (Ruth 2:14). It is probable, however, that the modern custom of pulling up by the roots prevailed to a considerable extent in ancient times. This was done to save all the straw, as it grew very short. When cut it was gathered on the arms (Psa. 129:7), bound in sheaves, and laid in heaps (Cant. 7:2; Ruth 3:7) to be threshed. Threshing floors were placed in the open air, leveled and tramped hard, generally on elevated ground, so that in winnowing the wind might carry away the chaff (Hos. 13:3; Jer. 4:11). Threshing was done by oxen driven over the grain to tread out the kernels with their hoofs (Hos. 10:11), by machines made either of planks with stones or bits of iron

fastened to the lower surface to make it rough, and rendered heavy by some weight upon it, or small wagons with low cylindrical wheels like saws (Isa. 28:27; 41:15).

In threshing small quantities of grain, or for tender cereals, flails were used (Ruth 2:17; Isa. 28:27). Winnowing was done with a' broad shovel or wooden fork with bent prongs. The mass of chaff, straw, and grain

⅓SIZE

9. Figs.

was thrown against the wind so that the chaff might be blown away. This was usually done in the evening, when there was generally a breeze (Ruth 3:2; see Jer. 4:11; 51:2). The chaff and stubble were burned (Isa. 5:24; Matt. 3:12). Finally the grain was sifted (Amos 9:9).

Laws. Israel owed Palestine as its possession, and its fertility to Jehovah; hence its cultivation was put under obedience to the Lord's commands. The Sabbath rest was to be observed (Lev. 19:3), the soil was to lie fallow in the sabbatic (25:3 ff.) and jubilee years (25:11). The Israelites were forbidden to yoke an ox and ass together (Deut. 22:10), the one being a clean and the other an unclean animal; to sow with mingled seed (Lev. 19:19; Deut. 22:9), or moistened seed on which the carcass of an unclean animal had fallen (Lev. 11:37, 38). The corners of the fields were not reaped, and the gleanings of the fields were left for the poor (Lev. 19:9; Deut. 24:19; comp. Ruth 2:2).

It was allowed to pluck the heads of ripened grain while passing along in the path left in the field (Deut. 23:25; Matt. 12:1; Luke 6:1). The first fruits of all kinds of planting belonged to Jehovah, in recognition of his being the giver of all good things. The fruit of the orchard the first three years was uncircumcized (unclean), and not to be eaten. All of the fourth year's yield was consecrated to Jehovah; and the first eating by men was to be that of the fifth year (Lev. 19:23). For cultivation of Vine and Olive, see under respective words.

Agrip'pa (à-grĭp'à), the name of two of the members of the Herodian family. *See* Herod.

Ague. *See* Diseases.

A'gur (ā'gŭr; *gathered*), the author of the sayings contained in Prov. 30, which the inscription describes as composed of the precepts delivered by "Agur the son of Jakeh." Beyond this everything that has been stated of him, and of the time in which he lived, is pure conjecture.

Ah- (*brother of*), the former part of many Hebrew words, signifying relationship or property.

A'hab (ā'hăb; *father's brother*).

1. The son of Omri, eighth king of Israel, and second of the dynasty of Omri, succeeded his father in the thirty-eighth year of Asa, king of Judah, and reigned twenty-two years in Samaria, B. C. 869-850. His wife was Jezebel, a heathen princess, daughter of Ethbaal, king of Zidon. (1) **Idolatry.** Jezebel was a decided and energetic character, and soon acquired complete control over her husband, so that she eventually established the worship of the Phoenician idols, and especially of the storm-god Baal-Melcarth. Ahab built him a temple and an altar in Samaria, and made a grove for the impure orgies of the goddess Ashtoreth (I Kings 16:29-33). So strong was the tide of corruption that it appeared as if the knowledge of the true God would be lost among the Israelites. But a man suited to this emergency was raised up in the person of Elijah (I Kings 18), who opposed the royal power, and succeeded in retaining many of his countrymen in the worship of the true

10. Ruins of Ahab's Palace, Samaria.

God. *See* Elijah. Ahab had a taste for splendid architecture, which he indulged by building an ivory house and several cities (I Kings 22:39). He erected his royal residence at Jezreel, in the plain of Esdraelon, still keeping Samaria as capital of his kingdom. (2) **Death of Naboth.** Refused a neighboring vineyard, which he desired to add to his pleasure grounds, Ahab, through the influence of Jezebel, caused its proprietor, Naboth, to be put to death on a false charge of blasphemy. For this crime Elijah prophesied the total extinction of the house of Ahab. The execution of the sentence was delayed in consequence of Ahab's repentance (I Kings 21). (3) **Wars.** Ahab undertook three campaigns against Benhadad I, king of Damascus, two defensive and one offensive. In the first Benhadad had laid siege to Samaria, and Ahab, encouraged by God's prophets, made a sudden attack upon him while at a banquet, and totally routed the Syrians. Benhadad was the next year again defeated by Ahab, who spared his life and released him on condition of restoring the cities of Israel he had held, and allowing Ahab certain commercial and political privileges (I Kings 20:34). For three years Ahab enjoyed peace, when, with Jehoshaphat, King of Judah, he attacked Ramoth in Gilead. Michaiah told Ahab that the expedition would fail. The prophet was imprisoned for giving this warning, but Ahab was so impressed that he took the precaution of disguising himself when he went into battle. (4) **Death.** He was slain by a man who "drew a bow at a venture," and although he stayed up in his chariot for a time he died at even, and his army was dispersed (I Kings 22). When he was brought to be buried in Samaria the dogs licked up his blood as a servant was washing his chariot, thus fulfilling the prophecy of Elijah (I Kings 21:19). (5) **Ahab and Archaeology.** Ahab appears prominently on the Assyrian monuments of the great conqueror Shalmaneser III (859-824 B.C.). The Monolith Inscription, now in the British Museum, recounts the clash of Assyrian arms in 853 B. C. with a Syrian coalition of kings at Karkar north of Hamath, a fortress guarding the approaches to all lower Syria. Conspicuously mentioned among those who successfully withstood Assyria's advance is "Ahab, the Israelite." The Israelite ruler's prominence is indicated by the large number of chariots he is said to have thrown into the battle—2,000 as compared with the next largest number of 1200 supplied by Hadadezer of Damascus. Ahab ran a close race with the Damascene state as heading the foremost power in central and lower Syria in the middle of the 9th century B. C., as is represented by the Bible and proved by the monuments. Revised by *M. F. U.*

2. A false prophet who deceived the Israelites at Babylon, and was threatened by Jeremiah, who foretold that he should be put to death by the king of Babylon, in the presence of those whom he had beguiled; and that in following times it should become a common malediction to say, "The Lord make thee like Zedekiah and like Ahab, whom the king of Babylon roasted in the fire" (Jer. 29:21, 22).

Ahar'ah (à-här'äh), the third son of Benjamin (I Chron. 8:1), elsewhere called Ehi (Gen. 46:21), Ahiram (Num. 26:38), and Aher (I Chron. 7:12).

Ahar'hel (à-här'hĕl), a son of Harum, whose families are named among the lineage of Coz, a descendant of Judah (I Chron. 4:8).

Aha'sai (à-hā'sī; perhaps a prolonged form of *Ahaz, possessor,* or contracted form of *Ahaziah,* whom *Jehovah holds*), a grandson of Immer, and one whose descendants dwelt in Jerusalem after the return from Babylon (Neh. 11:13). Gesenius thinks him the same with *Jahzerah* (*q. v.*), who is made the grandson of Immer (I Chron. 9:12).

Ahas'bai (à-hăs'bī), a Maachathite, father of Eliphelet, one of David's warriors (II Sam. 23:34). In I Chron. 11:35, he is apparently called *Ur* (*q. v.*).

Ahasue'rus (à-hăz-û-ē'rŭs), the Hebrew form of the name representing the Persian Khshayarsha of which the Greek form is Xerxes, and appearing as the title of three Median and Persian monarchs mentioned in the Bible.

1. The Persian king to whom the enemies of the Jews sent an accusation against them, the result of which is not mentioned (Ezra 4:6). He was probably Cambyses, son of Cyrus, who came to the throne B. C. 529, and died after a reign of seven years and five months.

2. The Persian king mentioned in the Book of Esther. He is probably identical with Xerxes, whose regal state and affairs tally with all that is here said of Ahasuerus. His kingdom was very extensive, extending from India even unto Ethiopia (Esth. 1:1). (1) **Divorces Vashti.** In the *third* year of his reign he made a sumptuous banquet for his nobility, and prolonged the feast for one hundred and eighty days. On one occasion, being partially intoxicated, he ordered Vashti, his wife, to be brought before him, that he might exhibit her beauty to his courtiers. She, however, refused to appear; for, in fact, it was contrary to Persian etiquette as well as to female propriety. Thereupon Ahasuerus indignantly divorced her, and published a royal decree asserting the superiority of husbands over their wives. (2) **Marries Esther.** In the *seventh* year of his reign (2:16), he married Esther, the beautiful Jewess, who, however, concealed her parentage. (3) **Haman's plot.** His prime minister, Haman, was enraged with Mordecai, the Jew, because he did not do him reverence; and, in the *twelfth* year of the king's reign, offered him ten thousand talents of

silver for the privilege of ordering a general massacre of the Jews in the kingdom on an appointed day. The king refused the money, but granted the request. Couriers were dispatched to the most distant parts of the realm to order the execution of the decree. Mordecai immediately sent word to Esther of the impending danger, and, through her intercession, the decree was so far annulled as to empower the Jews to defend themselves against their enemies. Ahasuerus disgraced and hanged Haman and his ten sons (7:10; 9-14), and made Mordecai his prime minister (10:3). (4) **Identity.** Xerxes (486-465 B. C.), the son of Darius I the Great is undoubtedly the Ahasuerus of the book of Esther. The third year of his reign in which he held a great feast and assembly at Shushan (Susa), the palace, corresponds identically to the third year of the reign of Xerxes when he arranged the Grecian war. In the seventh year of his reign Xerxes returned defeated from Greece and consoled himself in the pleasures of his palace. It was then that Ahasuerus sought "fair young virgins" and replaced Vashti by marrying Esther. An important historical inscription of Xerxes discovered at Persepolis lists the numerous subject nations over which he ruled, and fully corroborates Esther 1:1 that he ruled "from India to Ethiopia," Revised by *M. F. U.*

3. The father of Darius the Mede (Dan. 9:1). It is generally agreed that the person here referred to is the Astyages of profane history, but some identify him with Cyaxeres.

Aha'va (à-hā'vä), the river or place where was a river at which gathered the Jewish exiles who were to return from Babylon to Jerusalem (Ezra 8:21).

A'haz (ā'hăz; *possessor*).

1. The twelfth king of the separate kingdom of Judah, being the son and successor of Jotham. **Personal History.** He reigned sixteen years (according to some authorities, two years as viceroy), B. C. 735-715. (1) **Wars.** At the time of his accession Pekah, king of Israel, and Rezin, king of Syria, were in league against Judah. They proceeded to lay siege to Jerusalem, intending to place on the throne Ben-Tabeal, probably a Syrian noble (Isa. 7:6). Isaiah hastened to announce to him the destruction of the allied monarchs, who failed in their attack upon Jerusalem, although they inflicted serious damage on him elsewhere. Rezin, king of Syria, captured Elath (II Kings 16:6); Zichri, an Ephraimite, slew the king's son, the governor of his house, and his prime minister; and Pekah, king of Israel, gained a great advantage over him in a battle in Judah, killing one hundred and twenty thousand men, and taking captive two hundred thousand of his people. These, however, were returned through the remonstrance of the prophet Oded (II Chron. 28:3-15). (2) **Becomes a vassal.** In his extremity Ahaz applied to Tiglath-pileser, king of Assyria, for assistance, who freed him from his most formidable enemies by invading Syria, taking Damascus, and killing Rezin. He purchased this help at great cost, becoming tributary to Tiglath-pileser. He sent him the treasures of the temple and of his own palace,

and even appeared before him at Damascus as his vassal. (3) **Idolatry.** While he was there his idolatrous propensities induced him to take the pattern of a heathen altar and have one like it built in Jerusalem. Upon his return he offered upon the altar, closed the temple, removed its sacred utensils, and raised shrines to heathen deities everywhere. (4) **Death.** He died unlamented, and his body was not deposited in the sacred sepulchers (vers. 16-27). (5) **Ahaz and Archaeology.** In an inscription of the famous Assyrian emperor Tiglath-pileser III (744-727 B. C.), referred to as Pul (Pulu) in II Kings 15:19, occurs the name of Ahaz. An account of the payment of tribute by various vassal states of Syria-Palestine including the kings of Hamath, Arvad, Moab, Gaza, Ashkelon, Edom and others, occurs "Iauhazi (Jehoahaz, i. e., Ahaz) of Judah." Tribute is mentioned as consisting of "gold, silver, lead, iron, tin, brightly colored woolen garments, linen, the purple garments of their lands . . . all kinds of costly things, the products of the sea and the dry land . . . the royal treasure, horses, mules, broken to the yoke . . . (D. D. Luckenbill, *Ancient Records of Assyria and Babylonia* Vol. I, sect. 801). Revised by M. F. U.

NOTE—In II Kings 16:2 the age of Ahaz, at his accession, is given as twenty years. This probably refers to some earlier viceroyship, otherwise he would have been only eleven years old at the birth of his son Hezekiah (comp. II Kings 16:2, 20; 18:2). In the latter passage his age is given as 25 years.

2. A great-grandson of Jonathan, son of King Saul, being one of the four sons of Micah, and father of Jehoadah or Jarah (I Chron. 8:35, 36; 9:42).

Ahazi′ah (ā-há-zī′á; *held by Jehovah*).
1. The son of Ahab, king of Israel, whom he succeeded in every sense, being as completely under the control of Jezebel and idolatry as was his father (I Kings 22:51-53). He was the eighth king of Israel, and reigned two years, B. C. 850, 849. The most signal public event of his reign was the revolt of the vassal king of the Moabites, who took the opportunity of the defeat and death of Ahab to discontinue the tribute which he had paid to the Israelites, consisting of one hundred thousand lambs, and as many rams with their wool (II Kings 1:1; 3:4, 5). Ahaziah became a party with Jehoshaphat to revive the maritime traffic of the Red Sea. Because of this alliance God was displeased with Jehoshaphat, the vessels were destroyed, and the enterprise blasted (II Chron. 20:35-37). Soon after Ahaziah was injured by falling from the roof gallery of his palace in Samaria (the "lattice" of the text probably meaning a balustrade to keep persons from falling). He sent to inquire of Baal-zebub, the idol of Ekron, what should be the result of his injury. But the messengers were met and sent back by Elijah, who announced that he should rise no more from the bed upon which he lay. He died shortly after, and was succeeded by his brother Jehoram (II Kings 1:17; 3:1).

2. The son of Jehoram by Athaliah, and sixth king of Judah, B. C. 842. He is also called Jehoahaz (II Chron. 21:17; 25:23) and Azariah (II Chron. 22:6). He followed the ex-

ample of his father-in-law, Ahab, and was given to idolatry (II Kings, 8:25-27; II Chron. 22:1-4). He joined his uncle, Jehoram, of Israel, in an expedition against Hazael, king of Syria, which proved disastrous. The king of Israel was wounded, and Ahaziah visited him in Jezreel. During this visit Jehu was secretly anointed king of Israel, and conspired against Jehoram. The two kings rode out in their several chariots to meet Jehu, and when Jehoram shot through the heart Ahaziah attempted to escape, but was pursued as far as the pass of Gur, and, being there mortally wounded, had only strength to reach Megiddo, where he died. His body was conveyed by his servants to Jerusalem for burial (II Kings 9:1-28).

NOTE—In II Kings 8:26 Ahaziah is aid to have been twenty-two years old when he began to reign; but in II Chron. 22:2 his age is stated to be forty-two years. The former is undoubtedly correct, as in II Chron. 21:5, 20, we see that his father was forty when he died, which would have made him younger than his son. II Chron. 22:7-9 informs us that "the destruction of Ahaziah was of God," since, by fraternizing with the house of Ahab, he was included in the commission given to Jehu to root them out.

Ah′ban (ä′băn; *brother of the wise*), the first named of the two sons of Abishur by Abihail, of the descendants of Judah (I Chron. 2:29).

A′her (ā′hĕr; *after*), a descendant of Benjamin (I Chron. 7:12); probably the same person as Ahiram (Num. 26:38). Some translators consider it as not a proper name at all, and render it literally "another."

A′hi (ā′hī; *brotherly*).
1. A son of Abdiel, and chieftain of the tribe of Gad, resident in Bashan (I Chron. 5:15).
2. The first named of the four sons of Shamer, a chieftain of the tribe of Asher (I Chron. 7:34).

Ahi′ah (á-hī′á; *brother of Jehovah*), another mode of Anglicizing the name Ahijah.
1. The son of Ahitub, and high priest in the reign of Saul (I Sam. 14:3, 18), B. C. about 1020. He is here described as being "the Lord's priest in Shiloh, wearing an ephod." In 14:18 it appears that the ark was under his care. There is some difficulty in reconciling this with the statement (I Chron. 13:3) that they inquired not at the ark in the days of Saul. Some would avoid the difficulty by inserting "ephod" for "ark" (K. and D., *Com.*, *in loco*); others, by interpreting the *ark*, in this case, to mean a chest for carrying the ephod in. Others apply the expression only to all the latter years of the reign of Saul, when we know that the priestly establishment was at Nob, and not at Kirjath-jearim, where the ark was. But probably the last time that Ahiah inquired of the Lord before the ark was on the occasion related in I Sam. 14:36, when Saul marred his victory over the Philistines by his rash oath, which nearly cost Jonathan his life. But God returned no answer in consequence, as it seems, of Saul's rash curse. If, as is commonly supposed, Ahiah is the same person as Ahimelech, this failure to obtain an answer may have led to an estrangement between the king and the high priest, and predisposed him to suspect Ahimelech's loyalty, and to take that terrible re-

venge upon him for his favor to David. Gesenius supposes (*Thes. Heb.*, p. 65) that Ahimelech may have been a brother to Ahiah, and that they officiated simultaneously, the one at Gibeah, or Kirjath-jearim, and the other at Nob.

2. Son of Shisha, and secretary of King Solomon (I Kings 4:3), B. C. about 960.

3. One of the sons of Bela, son of Benjamin (I Chron. 8:7), elsewhere (v. 4) called *Ahoah* (*q. v.*).

Ahi'am (à-hī'ăm; perhaps for *Achiab'*, *father's brother*), a son of Sharar, the Hararite, and one of David's thirty heroes (II Sam. 23:33; I Chron. 11:35), B. C. 1000.

Ahi'an (à-hī'ăn; *brotherly*), the first named of the four sons of Shemidah, of the tribe of Manasseh (I Chron. 7:19).

Ahie'zer (à-hī-ē'zẽr; *brother of help*, i. e., *helpful*).

1. The son of Ammishaddai, and chief of the tribe of Dan when the people were numbered at Sinai (Num. 1:12), B. C. about 1438. He made an offering for the service of the tabernacle, like the other chiefs (Num. 7:66).

2. The chief of the Benjamite warriors who joined David at Ziklag (I Chron. 12:3), B. C. before 1000.

Ahi'hud. 1. (à-hī'hŭd; *brother of renown.*) The son of Shelomi, and prince of the tribe of Asher. He was one of those appointed by Moses to oversee the partition of Canaan (Num. 34:27), B. C. about 1401.

2. (Heb. *brother of a riddle*, i. e., *mysterious.*) The second named of the two later sons of Bela, the son of Benjamin (I Chron. 8:7).

Ahi'jah (à-hī'jäh; *brother of Jehovah*).

1. A prophet of Shiloh (I Kings 14:2), and hence called the Shilomite (ch. 11:29). There are two remarkable prophecies of Ahijah extant. The one in I Kings 11:31-39 is addressed to Jeroboam. B. C. about 940. In this he foretold the rending of the kingdom of Solomon, in punishment for his idolatries, and the transference of ten tribes after his death to Jeroboam. Solomon, hearing of this prophecy, sought to kill Jeroboam, who fled to Shishak, king of Egypt, and remained there until Solomon's death. The other prophecy (I Kings 14:6-16) was delivered to the wife of Jeroboam, who came to him in disguise to inquire concerning the king's son, who was sick. In this he foretold the death of the son, the destruction of Jeroboam's house on account of the images he had set up, and the captivity of Israel. In II Chron. 9:29, reference is made to a record of the events of Solomon's reign contained in the "prophecy of Ahijah the Shilomite."

2. An Israelite of the tribe of Issachar, father of Baasha, king of Israel (I Kings 15:27), B. C. before 911.

3. The last named of the five sons of Jerahmeel by his first wife (I Chron. 2:25).

4. A Pelonite, one of David's famous heroes (I Chron. 11:36), apparently the same called *Eliam* (*q. v.*), the son of Ahithophel the Gilonite in the parallel passage (II Sam. 23:34).

5. A Levite appointed, in the arrangement by David, over the sacred treasure of dedi-

cated things at the temple (I Chron. 26:20), B. C. 1000.

6. One of those who subscribed the covenant, drawn up by Nehemiah, to serve the Lord (Neh. 10:26), B. C. 445.

Ahi'kam (à-hī'kăm; *brother of rising*, i. e., *high;* according to Gesenius, *brother of the enemy*), one of the four persons sent by King Josiah to inquire of the prophetess Huldah concerning the proper course to be pursued in relation to the acknowledged violations of the newly-discovered book of the law (II Kings 22:12-14; II Chron. 34:20), B. C. 624. He afterward protected the prophet Jeremiah from the persecuting fury of Jehoiakim (Jer. 26:24), B. C. about 609. His son, Gedaliah, showed Jeremiah a like kindness (Jer. 39:14). He was the son of Shaphan, and father of Gedaliah, the viceroy of Judea after the capture of Jerusalem by the Babylonians (II Kings 25:22; Jer. 40:5-16).

Ahi'lud (à-hī'lŭd; *brother of one born*), father of Jehoshaphat, recorder under David and Solomon (II Sam. 8:16; 20:24; I Kings 4:3), and also of Baana, one of Solomon's purveyors (I Kings 4:12), B. C. 960.

Ahim'aaz (à-hĭm'à-ăz; *brother of anger*).

1. The father of Ahinoam, wife of King Saul (I Sam. 14:50), B. C. about 1020.

2. The son and successor of Zadok (I Chron. 6:8, 53) in the high priesthood. When Absalom revolted David refused to allow the ark to be removed from Jerusalem, believing that God would bring him back to the city. The high priests, Zadok and Abiathar, necessarily remained in attendance upon it; but their sons, Ahimaaz and Jonathan, concealed themselves outside the city to be in readiness to bear off to David any important movements and designs of Absalom which they might receive from within. When, therefore, Hushai informed the priests that Absalom had preferred his own counsel to that of Ahithophel, they sent word to Ahimaaz and Jonathan by a girl, doubtless to avoid suspicion. A lad saw the transaction and informed Absalom, who dispatched servants after them. They were hid by a woman in a dry well, the mouth of which was covered and strewn over with corn. She told the pursuers that the messengers had passed on in haste, and when all was safe released them, and they made their way to David (II Sam. 15:24-27; 17:15-22), B. C. 967. After the death of Absalom, Ahimaaz prevailed upon Joab to let him run after the Cushite who had been sent to inform David. He outstripped him, being doubtless swift of foot and taking another route, and proceeded to break the news gently to David, telling him at first only of the victory. While speaking the Cushite entered and bluntly revealed the truth. The estimate in which he was held by David is shown in his answer to the watchman who announced his coming: "He is a good man, and cometh with good tidings" (II Sam. 18:19-32).

3. Solomon's purveyor in Naphtali, who married Basmath, daughter of Solomon (I Kings 4:15), B. C. about 950.

Ahi'man (à-hī'măn; *brother of a gift*, i. e., *liberal*).

1. One of the three famous giants of the race of Anak, who dwelt at Hebron when the Hebrew spies explored the land (Num. 13:22), B. C. about 1440, and who (or their descendants) were afterward expelled by Caleb (Josh. 15:14), and eventually slain by the Judaites (Judg. 1:10).

2. A Levite who was one of the porters (wardens) of the temple (I Chron. 9:17).

Ahim′elech (á-hĭm′ê-lĕk; *brother of the king*).

1. High priest of the Jews, son of Ahitub (I Sam. 22:16) and father of Abiathar (v. 20), and probably the same with *Ahiah* (*q. v.*). He was a descendant of the line of Ithamar through Eli (I Chron. 24:3, 6; Josephus, *Ant.*, v, 11, 5; viii, 1, 3). When David fled from Saul (B. C. about 1010) he went to Nob, where the tabernacle then was. His unexpected appearance alarmed Ahimelech, whose anxious inquiry was answered by David's falsehood, "The king hath commanded me a business." Under this pretext Ahimelech was induced to give him bread and the sword of Goliath (I Sam. 21:1-9). A servant of Saul, Doeg, an Edomite, witnessed the transaction, and informed King Saul, who immediately sent for Ahimelech and the other priests then at Nob, and charged them with treason. But they declared their ignorance of any hostile designs on the part of David. This, however, availed them nothing, for the king ordered his guard to slay them. Upon their refusing to do so he commanded Doeg, who slew the priests, eighty-five in number. He then marched to Nob and put to the sword everything it contained (I Sam. 22:9-20). The only priest that escaped was Abiathar, Ahimelech's son, who fled to David, and who afterward became high priest (23:6; 30:7). The names in II Sam. 8:17 and I Chron. 24:6 are commonly regarded as having been transposed by a copyist.

2. A Hittite, one of David's warriors, whom David invited to accompany him at night into the camp of Saul in the wilderness of Ziph; but Abishai seems alone to have gone with him (I Sam. 26:6, 7), B. C. about 1010.

Ahi′moth (á-hī′mŏth; *brother of death*, i. e., *destructive*), one of the sons of Elkanah, a Levite (I Chron. 6:25). In v. 26 he is called Nahath.

Ahin′adab (á-hĭn′á-dăb; *liberal brother*), son of Iddo, and one of the twelve purveyors of Solomon. His district was Mahanaim, the southern half of the region beyond Jordan (I Kings 4:14), B. C. about 950.

Ahin′oam (á-hĭn′ō-ăm; *brother of pleasantness*, i. e., *pleasant*).

1. The daughter of Ahimaaz, and wife of King Saul (I Sam. 14:50), B. C. about 1020.

2. A Jezreelitess, and one of David's wives while he was yet a private person (I Sam. 25:43), B. C. 1004. She and his other wife, Abigail, lived with him at the court of Achish (ch. 27:3), were taken prisoners by the Amalekites when they plundered Ziklag (ch. 30:5), but were rescued by David (v. 18). She went with him to Hebron and resided with him while he remained there as king of Judah (II Sam. 2:2), and was mother of his eldest son, Amnon (3:2).

Ahi′o (á-hī′ō; *brotherly*).

1. One of the sons of the Levite Abinadab, to whom, with his brother, was intrusted the care of the ark when David first attempted to remove it to Jerusalem. Ahio probably guided the oxen, while his brother Uzzah walked by the cart (II Sam. 6:3, 4; I Chron. 13:7), B. C. 992.

2. A Benjamite, one of the sons of Beriah (I Chron. 8:14).

3. One of the sons of Jehiel, a Gibeonite, by Maachah (I Chron. 8:31; 9:37).

Ahi′ra (á-hī′rá; *brother of evil*, i. e., *unlucky*), the son of Enan, and chief of the tribe of Naphtali (Num. 2:29). He was appointed as "head man" of his tribe to assist Moses in numbering the people (ch. 1:15), and made his contribution to the sacred service on the twelfth day of offering (7:78, 83; 10:27), B. C. c. 1440.

Ahi′ram (á-hī′răm). 1. A son of Benjamin (Num. 26:38). 2. A Phoenician king of Gebal (later Byblos) whose magnificent sarcophagus inscribed with Phoenician writing (c. 11th century B. C.) was recovered and forms an important link in the development of the Phoenician alphabet. The sarcophagus and jewels of Ahiram are in the National Museum at Beirut. Ahiram of Byblos, however, is not to be identified with Hiram of Tyre, Solomon's ally, although the names are evidently identical and they lived perhaps contemporaneously. *M. F. U.*

Ahi′ramite (á-hī′rá-mīt), a descendant (Num. 26:38) of the Benjamite *Ahiram* (*q. v.*).

Ahis′amach (á-hĭs′á-măch; *brother of help*), father of one of the famous workers upon the tabernacle, Aholiab, the Danite (Exod. 31:6; 35:34; 38:23), B. C. c.1440.

Ahish′ahar (á-hĭsh′á-här; *brother of the dawn*, i. e., *early*), a warrior, last named of the sons of Bilhan, of the tribe of Benjamin (I Chron. 7:10).

Ahi′shar (á-hī′shär; *brother of song*, or *of the upright*), the officer who was "over the household" of Solomon (I Kings 4:6), i. e., steward, or governor of the palace, a place of great importance and influence in the East, B. C. 960.

Ahith′ophel (á-hĭth′ô-fĕl; *brother of folly*), a counselor of David, whose wisdom was so highly esteemed that his advice had the authority of a divine oracle (II Sam. 16:23). Absalom, when he revolted, sent to Ahithophel, who was at Giloh, his native city, and secured his adhesion. He, perhaps, thought to wield a greater sway under the prince than he had done under David, and also resented David's conduct to his granddaughter, Bathsheba (comp. II Sam. 11:3 with ch. 23:34). When David heard of Ahithophel's defection, he prayed God to turn his counsel to "foolishness" (doubtless alluding to his name), and induced Hushai, his friend, to go over to Absalom to defeat the counsels of this now dangerous enemy (15:31-37). Ahithophel's advice to Absalom was to show that the breach between him and his father was irreparable by publicly taking possession of the royal harem (16:20-23). He also recommended immediate pursuit of David, and would probably have succeeded had not Hushai's plausible advice been accepted by the council. When Ahithophel saw that his counsel was rejected for that of Hushai the far-seeing man gave up the cause of Absalom for lost; and he forthwith returned to his home in Giloh, hanged himself, and was buried in the sepulcher of his father (II Sam. 17), B. C. 967.

Ahi'tub (à-hī'tŭb; *brother of goodness*).

1. The son of Phinehas and grandson of Eli. He probably succeeded the latter in the high priesthood, his father being slain in battle, B. C. 1050. He was succeeded by his son Ahiah, or Ahimelech (I Sam. 14:3; 22:9, 11, 20).

2. The son of Amariah and father of Zadok, who was made high priest by Saul after the death of Ahimelech (II Sam. 8:17; I Chron. 6:8). It is not probable that this Ahitub was ever high priest. The coincidence of the names (I Chron. 6:8, 11, 12) would lead us to infer that by the Ahitub found therein is meant Azariah (II Chron. 31:10). Of the Ahitub mentioned in I Chron. 9:11; Neh. 11:11 nothing definite is known, save that he was "ruler of the house of God."

Ah'lab (äh'lăb; *fatness,* i. e., *fertile*), a town of Asher, whose inhabitants the Israelites were unable to expel (Judg. 1:31). It has not been identified.

Ah'lai (ä'lī; *Oh that! wishful*).

1. The daughter of Sheshan, a descendant of Judah, married to her father's Egyptian slave, *Jarha* (*q. v.*), by whom she had Attai (I Chron. 2:31, 34, 35).

2. The father of one of David's valiant men (I Chron. 11:41), B. C. about 995.

Aho'ah (à-hō'äh; *brotherly*), the son of Bela, the son of Benjamin (I Chron. 8:4); called also Ahiah (v. 7), and perhaps Iri (I Chron. 7:7), B. C. probably about 1600. It is probably he whose descendants are called Ahohites (II Sam. 23:9, 28).

Aho'hite (à-hō'hīt), a patronymic applied to Dodo or Dodai, one of the captains under Solomon (I Chron. 27:4); his son Eleazar, one of David's three chief warriors (II Sam. 23:9; I Chron. 11:12); and Zalmon, or Ilai, another bodyguard (II Sam. 23:18; I Chron. 11:29); probably from their descent from *Ahoah* (*q. v.*).

Aho'lah (à-hō'läh; *her own tent*), the name of a probably imaginary harlot, used by Ezekiel (23:4, 5, 36, 44) as a symbol of the idolatry of Samaria, the apostate branch of Judah being designated by *Aholibah*. The terms indicate respectively that, while the worship of Samaria had been self-invented, and never sanctioned by Jehovah, that at Jerusalem was divinely instituted, but now degraded and abandoned for foreign alliances. They are both graphically described as lewd women, adulteresses, prostituting themselves to the Egyptians and Assyrians, in imitating their abominations and idolatries; wherefore the allegory is an epitome of the history of the Jewish people.

Aho'liab (à-hō'lĭ-ăb; *tent of his father*), the son of Ahisamach, of the tribe of Dan, an expert workman in the precious metals and other materials, and, together with Bezaleel, appointed to superintend the preparation of such articles for the tabernacle (Exod. 31:6; 35:34; 36:1, 2; 38:23), B. C. c. 1440.

Ahol'ibah (à-hōl'ĭ-băh; *my tent is in her*), a symbolical name given to Jerusalem (Ezek. 23:4, 11, 22, 36, 44), under the figure of an adulterous harlot, as having once contained the true worship of Jehovah, and having prostituted herself to foreign idolatries. *See* Aholah.

Aholiba'mah (à-hōl-ĭ-bä'màh; *tent of the height*).

1. The granddaughter of Zibeon the Hivite, and one of the wives of Esau (Gen. 36:2). In the earlier narrative (Gen. 26:34) Aholibamah is called Judith the daughter of Beeri the Hittite. The probable explanation is that her proper name was Judith, and that Aholibamah was the name that she received as the wife of Esau and foundress of the three tribes of his descendants.

2. One of the dukes who sprang from Esau (Gen. 36:41; I Chron. 1:52). The list of names in which this is included is probably of places, and not of persons. This would seem to be evident from the expression in the heading, "*after their places by their names,*" (v. 40) as compared with v. 43 "*according to their habitations in the land of their possession*" (Keil, *in loco*; Smith, *Dictionary, s. v.*).

Ahu'mai (à-hū'mī; *brother of water*), the son of Jahath, a descendant of Judah, and of the family of the Zorathites (I Chron. 4:2).

Ahu'zam (à-hū'zăm; *their possession*), the first named of the four sons of Ashur ("father of Tekoa") by one of his wives, Naarah, of the tribe of Judah (I Chron. 4:6).

Ahuz'zath (à-hŭz'zăth; *possession*), one of the friends (perhaps "favorite") of the Philistine king Abimelech, who accompanied him on his visit to Isaac (Gen. 26:26), B. C. about 2040.

A'i (ā'ī), A. V. Hai ("the Ruin"), a city near Bethel where Abraham sojourned upon his arrival in Canaan (Gen. 12:8) and which the conquering Israelites under Joshua are said to have destroyed (Josh. 7:2-5; 8:1-29). The site is commonly identified with et-Tell, 1½ miles from Bethel and excavated in 1933-35 by Mme. Judith Marquet-Krause. The diggings revealed an occupational gap in the history of the mound from 2200 B. C. till after 1200 B. C., so that if Ai is represented by et-Tell, there was nothing but a ruin there when Joshua and the Israelites are said to have destroyed it. Some critics, like Martin Noth, dismiss the Biblical story as an aetiological legend, which supposedly explains how the place came to be in ruins and to be called "Ruin," the meaning of Ai in Hebrew (*Palaestina Jahrbuch* 1938, pp. 7-20). Others, like W. F. Albright (*Bull. Am. Schs.* 74, pp. 16f.), assume that the narrative of Joshua 8 originally referred to the destruction of Bethel in the 13th century B. C., but that the aetiological interest in the ruins of Ai caused the story to be attached to this site instead of Bethel. But this explanation, besides being objectionable in reflecting upon the historicity of the Biblical account, is extremely unlikely because the Biblical narrative carefully distinguishes between the two cities (Josh. 8:12) and there is not the slightest evidence of any destruction of Bethel at this time (c. 1401 B. C.). More reasonable is the explanation of Hugues Vincent (*Revue Biblique*, 1937, pp. 231-266) that the inhabitants of Ai had merely a military outpost at Ai of such modest proportions and temporary nature that it left no remains to give a clue of its existence to the archaeologist, although the narrative clearly indicates an inhabited city. Whatever the explanation, further research and excavation in the vicinity will doubtless yield the correct solution. It is possible that there was a settlement there in Joshua's day, although no trace of it has yet been found. The Biblical account, in fact, stresses the smallness of the then-existing city (Josh. 7:3). Future research may establish the actual site of the late Bronze Age city, which fell to Joshua, not at et-Tell at all, but somewhere in the general vicinity, and discover that the name of the older city was transferred to it, since as Sir Frederic Kenyon points out "the transference of a name from a ruined or abandoned site to another nearby is a common phenomenon in Palestine" (*The Bible and Archeology* (1940), p. 190). M. F. U.

Ai′ah (ā-ī′áh; *a cry*, often *hawk*).

1. The first named of the two sons of Zibeon the Horite, or rather Hivite (Gen. 36:24, A. V., Ajah; I Chron. 1:40).

2. The father of Rizpah, Saul's concubine (II Sam. 3:7; 21:8, 10, 11), B. C. about 1053.

Ai′ath (ā-ī′áth; Isa. 10:28), another form of the city *Ai* (q. v.).

Ai′ja (ā-ī′já; Neh. 11:31), another form of *Ai* (q. v.).

Ai′jalon, another form of the city *Ajalon* (q. v.).

Ai′jeleth Sha′har occurs in the title of Psa. 22. See Music.

A′in (ā′ēn), literally, an eye, and also, in the simple but vivid imagery of the East, a spring or natural burst of living water, always contradistinguished from the well or tank of artificial formation, and which latter is designated by the words *Beer* and *Bor*. *Ain* oftenest occurs in combination with other words forming the names of definite localities, as En-gedi, Engannim, etc. It occurs alone in two cases:

1. One of the landmarks on the eastern boundary of Palestine, as described by Moses (Num. 34:11). It is probably '*Ain el-'Azy*, the main source of the Orontes, a spring remarkable for its force and magnitude.

2. One of the southernmost cities of Judah (Josh. 15:32), afterward allotted to Simeon (Josh. 19:7; I Chron. 4:32) and given to the priests (Josh. 21:16). In the list of priests' cities in I Chron. 6:59 Ashan takes the place of Ain.

Air (Gr. *aēr; the air*, particularly the lower and denser, as distinguished from the higher and rarer, *hō aithēr, ether*), the atmospheric region (Acts 22:23; I Thess. 4:17; Rev. 9:2, 16:17). In Eph. 2:2 "the ruler of the powers of the air" is the devil, the prince of the demons that fill the realm of the air. It is not to be considered as equivalent to *darkness* (Gr. *skotos*). "To beat the air" (I Cor. 9:26) refers to pugilists who miss their aim, and means "to contend in vain." "To speak into the air" (I Cor. 14:9, i. e., without effect) is used of those who speak what is not understood by their hearers.

A′jah, another form of *Aiah* (q. v.).

Aj′alon (ăj′á-lŏn), or **Ai′jalon** (ā′já-lŏn; *place of deer* or *gazelles*).

1. A Levitical city of Dan (Josh. 19:42);

a city of refuge (Josh. 21:24; I Sam. 14:31; I Chron. 6:69). It was with reference to the valley named after this town that Joshua said, "Sun, stand thou still upon Gibeon; and thou, Moon, in the valley of Ajalon" (Josh. 10:12). Ajalon is the modern Yalo, fourteen miles from Jerusalem, north of the Jaffa road and mentioned as *Aialuna* in the Amarna Letters.

2. A city in the tribe of Zebulun (Judg. 12:12). Elon, the judge, was buried there. The modern site is uncertain.

A′kan (ā′kăn; *twisted*), the last named of the three sons of Ezer, the son of Seir, the Horite (Gen. 36:27), called also (I Chron. 1:42) Jakan.

Ak′kub (ăk′kŭb; *insidious*).

1. The fourth named of the seven sons of Elioenai, or Esli, a descendant of David (I Chron. 3:24).

2. One of the Levitical gatekeepers of the temple after the captivity (I Chron. 9:17; Neh. 11:19; 12:25), B. C. 536. Perhaps the same who assisted Ezra in expounding the law to the people (Neh. 8:7). His descendants appear to have succeeded to the office (Ezra 2:42).

3. The head of one of the families of Nethinim that returned from Babylon (Ezra 2:45), B. C. 536.

Akrab′bim (á-krăb′bĭm; *scorpions*), a place, as the name suggests, which abounded in scorpions, and located where the country ascends from the neighborhood of the southern end of the Dead Sea to the level of Palestine. It is called the ascent of Akrabbim (Num. 34:4).

Alabaster. See Mineral Kingdom.

Al′ameth (ăl′á-měth; less correct form of *Alemeth*, q. v.), the last named of the nine sons of Becher, the son of Benjamin (I Chron. 7:8).

Alam′melech (á-lăm′mě-lěk; *oak of* [the] *king*), a town in the territory of Asher (Josh. 19:26).

Al′amoth (ăl′á′mōth), a musical term (I Chron. 15:20; title Psa. 46).

Alarm (Heb. *těrū″áh, a loud noise or shout*), the peculiar sound of the silver trumpet of the Hebrews, giving them signals while on their journey (Lev. 23:24; 25:9; Num. 10:5, 6; 29:1). In times of peace, when the people or rulers were to be assembled together, the trumpet was blown softly. When the camps were to move forward, or the people march to war, it was sounded with a deeper note. A war note, or call to arms, or other public emergency (Jer. 4:19; 49:2; Zeph. 1:16).

Al′emeth (ăl′ě-měth; *covering*), the first named of the sons of Jehoadah, or Jarah, the son of Ahaz, of the posterity of Saul (I Chron. 8:36; 9:42), B. C. after 1030.

A′leph (ä′lěf; *ox*), the first letter of the Hebrew alphabet, corresponding to Greek *alpha*, cf. English "a." But Hebrew aleph is a consonant and has no representative in English. It is transliterated by the apostrophe (′). This letter heads Psa. 119, each of the first eight verses beginning with aleph in the Hebrew.

Alexan′der (ăl-ĕx-ăn′dēr; *man-defender*).

1. A man, whose father, Simon, a Cyrenian Jew, was compelled to bear the cross of Jesus (Mark 15:21).

2. A kinsman, probably, of the high priest,

and one of the chief men in Jerusalem, present at the examination of Peter and John before the Sanhedrin for the cure of the lame man (Acts 4:6), A. D. 30.

3. A Jew of Ephesus, known only from the part he took in the uproar about Diana, which was raised there by the preaching of Paul (Acts 19:33), A. D. 58. He was probably put forward by the Jews to defend them from any connection with the Christians. His appeal to them for opportunity was in vain, an uproar following for two hours.

4. A coppersmith or brazier, who, with Hymenaeus and others, apostatized (I Tim. 1:20). It is not certain, but not at all improbable, that he is the same person as the one mentioned in II Tim. 4:14, who seems to have opposed and hindered Paul.

Alexan'dria, a celebrated city and seaport of Egypt, situated on a narrow stretch of land between Lake Mareotis and the Mediterranean, fourteen miles from the Canopic mouth of the Nile. It was named for Alexander (*man-defender*), who founded it B. C. 332. The long,

11. Alexandria, Egypt.

narrow island of Pharos was formed into a sort of breakwater to the port, by joining the middle of the island to the mainland by means of a mole, seven stadia in length, and hence called the Hepta-stadium. Upon the island of Pharos was constructed the famous lighthouse, which Alexander called after his friend Hephaestion, but not finished till the reign of Ptolemy Philadelphus, B. C. 284-246.

The most famous of all the public buildings planned by Ptolemy Soter were a library and museum, or college of philosophy, the professors of which were supported out of the public income. The library soon became the largest in the world, numbering seven hundred thousand when the Saracens destroyed it by fire. It was here that the version of the Scriptures called the Septuagint was made.

Alexandria is not named in the Old Testament and only incidentally in the New Testament (Acts 2:10; 6:9; 18:24; 27:6), and yet it is most important in connection with the history of the Jews, and from the foundation of an independent sect of the Jewish religion.

Alexan'drian, an inhabitant of Alexandria in Egypt, specially a Jew resident there (Acts 6:9; 18:24). The Jews, being highly valued as citizens, were encouraged to settle in the city, and were admitted into the first of its three classes of citizens, having equal rights with the Greek inhabitants. In the reign of Tiberius (A. D. 16), the Jews in Alexandria numbered about one third of the population. Notwith-

standing many persecutions and massacres, they continued to form a large proportion of the population, and retained their civil rights till A. D. 415, when forty thousand of them were expelled at the instigation of Cyril, the Christian patriarch. They recovered their strength, and appear to have been very numerous at the time of Mohammedan conquest.

Algum, or Almug. *See* Vegetable Kingdom.

Ali'ah (à-lī'äh), a less correct form of *Alvah* (*q. v.*). The second named of the dukes of Edom, descended from Esau (I Chron. 1:51).

Ali'an (à-lī'ăn), a less correct form of the name *Alvan* (*q. v.*). The first named of the five sons of Shobal, a descendant of Seir (I Chron. 1:40), B. C. about 1853.

Alien (Heb. *gēr*; both *stranger;* Gr. *'allotrios; belonging to another,* i. e., *foreign*), a foreigner, or person born in another country, and thus not entitled to the rights of citizenship in the country in which he lives (Exod. 18:3; Deut. 14:21; Eph. 2:12, etc.). *See* Foreigner.

Allegory (Gr. *'allegoreō*), occurs only once (Gal. 4:24), "Which things are to be allegorized." "To allegorize" means to express or explain one thing under the image of another. "St. Paul is here declaring, under the influence of the Holy Spirit, that the passage he has cited has a second and a deeper meaning than it appears to have: that it has that meaning, then, is a positive, objective, and indisputable truth" (Ellicott, *Com.*). To say that a history is allegorized is quite different from saying that it is allegory itself. "As Hagar bore children to bondage, so does the Sinaitic covenant produce sons under circumcisional bondage to the heavy ritual" (Whedon, *Com.*). Dean Trench says, "The allegory needs not, as the parable, an interpretation to be brought to it from without, since it contains its interpretation within itself." The real object of the allegory is to convey a moral truth. Every allegory is a kind of parable, containing a statement of a few simple facts followed by the explanation or allegorical interpretation (Luke 8:5-15). The allegories found in Scripture are its parabolical representation, such as, in the Old Testament, Canticles, Psalms 45, 80, Isa. 5:1-7, and in the New the parables of our Lord.

In early times there was an allegorical mode of interpreting the historical portions of the Old Testament, which reached its climax in the writings and school of Origen. It assumed a double or threefold sense of the Scriptures, an obvious literal sense, and a hidden spiritual sense, both being intended by the author. Thus the book of Joshua has been treated as an allegory of the soul's victory over sin and self. The allegorical interpretation of the Bible arose among the Alexandrian Jews in their attempt to reconcile the Mosaic account with Greek philosophy. The four rivers of Paradise were Plato's four cardinal virtues. Adam was the lower, sensuous man, etc. The early Christian Church received allegorical interpretation also from the Jews of Alexandria, wishing to reconcile Christianity with Greek thought. Origen taught a threefold sense of Scripture, corresponding to man's body, soul and spirit. As we come to the Middle Ages, four senses were found in Scripture: historical, allegorical, moral, and anagogical; e. g., Jerusalem is, *literally*, a city of Palestine; *allegorically*, the Church; *morally*, the believing soul; *anagogically*, the heavenly Jerusalem.

Swedenborg held that "all and every part of Scripture, even the most minute, not excepting the smallest jot or tittle, signify and involve spiritual and celestial things" (*Arcana Coelestia*, i, 2). This mode of interpreting Scripture is very fascinating and yet dangerous, because there is a temptation to read into the word one's imaginings, and not to be content with its plain and simple teachings.

Alleluia, Allelujah (Gr. *'allēlouia*), a Grecized form (Rev. 19:1, 3, 4, 6) of *Hallelujau* (*q. v.*).

Alliance, the political or social relations formed between nations by treaty. In Scripture such compacts are known as leagues, covenants, treaties, etc. In this article we treat them only as related to the Israelites.

1. Pre-Mosaic. The patriarchs entered into international relations with the peoples of Canaan, for their subsistence in the land of promise, but not yet given in actual possession. Abraham was "confederate" with some of the Canaanite princes (Gen. 14:13), and he also entered into an alliance with Abimelech the Philistine king (Gen. 21:22-24, 32), which was renewed by their sons (Gen. 26:27, sq.).

2. Mosaic. Israel, as the covenant people of Jehovah, was to hold itself aloof from heathen influences and idolaters; and, therefore, when they settled in Palestine, intercourse with such nations was strongly interdicted (Lev. 18:3, 4; 20:22, 23). Their country and their occupation protected them from mixing with peoples which would have endangered their nationality and mission. But it was by no means intended that they should live without any intercourse with other nations; but to cultivate friendly relations with them, and seek their good. The Mosaic legislation taught Israel to love and respect strangers (Exod. 22:20; 23:9; Lev. 19:33, f.; Deut. 10:18, 19). The law commands Israel to root out the nations of Canaan, because of their abominations, and to make no covenant with them (Exod. 23:32, f.; 34:12, f.; Deut. 7:1, f.); also the Amalekites were to be destroyed (Exod. 17:14, 16; Deut. 25:17-19), because of their cruel attack upon the Israelites. Yet it forbade them to make war upon the other peoples, the Edomites, Ammonites, and Moabites, or to conquer their land (Deut. 2:4, f.). The law, therefore, was not opposed to Israel's forming friendly and peaceful relations with other peoples, nor even to maintain peace with them by covenants and treaties.

3. In Later Times. When the commonwealth of Israel was fully established in Canaan, formal alliances sprang up between it and other nations. Thus David entered into friendly relations with Hiram, king of Tyre (II Sam. 5:11), and with King Hanun, the Amorite (II Sam. 10:2); and Solomon made a treaty with Hiram to furnish materials and workmen for the temple (II Kings 5:15 f.). In neither case was their theocratic standing falsified or endangered. Solomon also entered into treaty relations with a Pharaoh, by which he secured the monopoly of trade in horses

and other products (I Kings 10:28, 29). We find Asa, when at war with Baasha, king of Israel, sending an embassy to Ben-hadad, king of Syria, reminding him of a league existing between Israel and Judah (II Chron. 20:35, 36), which ceased in Jehu's reign. When Pekah, king of Israel, with Rezin, king of Syria, laid siege to Jerusalem, Ahaz formed a league with Tiglath-pileser, king of Assyria (II Kings 16:5-7). Later we find the kings of Judah alternately allying themselves with Egypt and Assyria, according as the one or other of these powers was most likely to aid them.

The prophets, however, rightly denounced the treaties by which Israel, distrusting the help of its God, sought to find support from the invasion of nations by allowing themselves to become entangled in idolatrous practices and licentious habits (Ezek. 16:23; Hos. 5).

Respecting the rites by which treaties were ratified, *see* Covenants.

Al'lon (ăl'lŏn; *an oak*).

1. The expression in the A. V. of Josh. 19:33, "from Allon to Zaanannim," is more correctly rendered in the R. V. "from the oak in Zaanannim," which served as a landmark.

2. The son of Jedaiah and father of Shiphi, a chief Simeonite, of the family of those who expelled the Hamites from the valley of Gedor (I Chron. 4:37).

Al'lon-Bach'uth (ăl'lŏn-băk'ŭth; *oak of weeping*), a landmark consisting of a tree marking the spot where Deborah, Rebekah's nurse, was buried (Gen. 35:8).

Almighty, the word used in the Old Testament as the translation of the Hebrew *shaddai*, *mighty*, as, "I am the Almighty God" (Gen. 17:1). In the New Testament it is the word for the Greek *pantokratōr*, *all-powerful*.

Almo'dad (ăl-mō'dăd; meaning unknown), the son of Joktan, of the family of Shem (Gen. 10:26; I Chron. 1:20). He is said to have been the founder of an Arabian tribe, the locality of which is unknown.

Al'mon (ăl'mōn; *hidden*), the last named of the four sacerdotal cities of Benjamin (Josh 21:18; Alemeth, I Chron. 6:60). It is identified with the mound of Khirbet 'Almit between Geba and Anathoth.

Almond. *See* Vegetable Kingdom.

Al'mon-Diblatha'im (ăl'mŏn-dĭb-lä-thä'ĭm), the fifty-first station of the Israelites in the wilderness East of the Dead Sea (Num. 33:46, 47). Perhaps the same with Beth-diblathaim (Jer. 48:22), and Diblath (Ezek 6:14). Identified with Deleilat el-Gharbiyeh, a town commanding three roads, 2½ miles northeast of Libb.

Alms, Almsdeeds (Gr. *eleēmosunē, beneficence*, or *benefaction* itself). In Heb. *tsĕdäqäh, righteousness*, is the usual equivalent for *alms* (Psa. 24:5; Prov. 10:2; 11:4; Mic. 6:5). The word *alms* is not found in the A. V. of the Old Testament, but is met with frequently in the Apocrypha. The great antiquity of almsgiving is shown in Job. 29:13, ff.

1. Jewish Almsgiving. The general distribution of property in Israel, and the precautions taken to prevent the alienation of inheritances on the one hand, as well as the undue accumulation of wealth on the other, with the promised blessing of Jehovah in case of obedience, tended to make extreme poverty very rare. Still, there would arise cases of need. Moses imposed for all time the obligation, "Therefore I command thee, saying, Thou shalt open thine hand wide unto thy brother, to thy poor, and to thy needy, in thy land" (Deut. 15:11). Specific provisions were made for the regular distribution of alms on a large scale among the poorer members of the commonwealth—the Sabbatical year—"that the poor of the people might eat" (Exod. 23:11); the gleanings of field and fruit and the forgotten sheaf (Lev. 23:22; Deut. 24:19-22); the tithings laid up in store every third year for the Levite, the stranger, the fatherless, and the widow (Deut. 14:28, 29); the freeing at Jubilee of the poor (Lev. 25:39-54); the law giving the poor the right to enter a field or vineyard and satisfy hunger (Deut. 23:24, 25); interest forbidden on loans to the poor (Exod. 22:25; Lev. 25:35, 36); the command to entertain at the annual festivals the Levite, stranger, orphan, and poor (Deut. 16:11-14). It is only as we remember these laws that we can understand the expression *righteousness*, which the Old Testament uses to express the idea of charity (Deut. 24:13; Prov. 10:2; 11:14). Literally meaning *right* or *acts of right*, or *justice*, *tsĕdäqäh* came to mean "charity," because according to the Mosaic law the poor had an inalienable right to certain produce of the soil. Hence it does not exactly correspond to our term "alms," but occupies a midway position between deeds of right and love.

Very naturally, almsgiving came to be considered a virtue (Ezek. 18:7; Prov. 19:17), and a violation of the statutes regarding it a heinous sin (Isa. 58:6, 7). Among the later Jews poverty became quite prevalent, owing to foreign dominion and the oppression of wealthy Israelites. The Mosaic statutes were changed to meet the increasing claims upon the charity and benevolence of the community. Two collections were ordered: (1) a daily collection of food (Heb. *tămḥū*, *alms for the dish*), distributed every morning; and (2) a weekly collection of money *qŭppäh*, *alms for the box*), distributed weekly. There was also a chamber in the temple where alms were secretly deposited for the poor of good families who did not wish to receive charity openly.

Almsgiving came to be associated with merit, and was looked upon as a means of conciliating God's favor and warding off evil (Dan. 4:27), and as among the essential virtues of the godly (Isa. 58:4-7; Ezek. 18:7; Amos 2:7). To be reduced to soliciting alms was regarded as a curse from God, and Judaism gave no encouragement to begging as a sacred calling.

2. Christian. Almsgiving was noticed by Jesus in his warning against following the example of those who gave "to be seen of men." He urged his followers to give without ostentation, looking to God alone for reward (Matt. 6:1-4). The Christian spirit of caring for the needy is forcibly expressed (I John 3:17). Christianity does not encourage indolence and consequent poverty (II Thess.

3:10); and yet is very emphatic in insisting upon the general duty of ministering to those in distress (Luke 3:11; 6:30; 12:33; Acts 9:37; 10:2, 4). The disposition of the giver is of more account than the amount of the gift (Mark 12:42; II Cor. 8:12; *see also* Acts 11:29; Rom. 12:13; Eph. 4:28; I Tim. 6:18; Heb. 13:16).

Almug Tree. *See* Vegetable Kingdom.

Aloe, Aloes. *See* Vegetable Kingdom.

A'loth (ā'lŏth; I Kings 4:16). *See* Bealoth.

Al'pha and O'mega (Gr. *'alpha*; *ōmega*), the first and last letters of the Greek alphabet, used to express the eternity of God (Rev. 1:8, 11; 21:6; 22:13; *see also* Isa. 44:6). The early Christians frequently placed the letters A, *alpha*, and Ω, *omega*, on either side of the cruciform monogram, formed from the letters X, *chi*, and P, *rho*, the first two letters of the name Christ in Gr. ΧΡΙΣΤΟΣ.

Alphae'us (ăl-fē'ŭs).

1. The putative father of James the Less (Matt. 10:3; Mark 3:18; Luke 6:15; Acts 1:13), and husband of that Mary who, with the mother of Jesus and others, was standing by the cross during the crucifixion (John 19:25). By comparing John 19:25 with Luke 24:10 and Matt. 10:3 it appears that *Alphaeus* is the Greek, and *Cleophas*, or *Clopas* (*q. v.*), the Hebrew or Syriac, name of the same person.

2. The father of the evangelist Levi, or Matthew (Mark 2:14).

Alphe'us. *See* Alphaeus.

Altar (from Lat. *altus*, *high*; *ara*, *elevation*; Heb. *mĭzbĕäh*; Gr. *thusiastērion*, *place of sacrifice*).

12. Greek Altar.

1. Early. The altar was originally a simple elevation made of earth, rough stones, or turf. The altars for constant use, especially in temple service, were generally of stone, though they might be of other materials. Thus, in Greece, several were built of the ashes of burnt offerings, as that of Zeus at Olympia; and one at Delos made of goats' horns. The probability is that some of the ancient monuments of unhewn stones, usually thought to be Druidical remains, were derived from altars of primitive times, as *cromlechs*, in the form of a table, one large stone being supported in a horizontal position upon other stones.

Another form of altar was a heap of small stones with a large, flat stone placed upon its top. Many of these *cairns* still remain. In some instances, as at Stonehenge, a circle of stones incloses a central one, somewhat similar in construction to those found in Persia. Two pictures discovered at Herculaneum represent sacred Egyptian ceremonies, probably in honor of Isis. The altars in these pictures have at each corner a rising, which continues square to about one half its height, gradually sloping off to an edge or point. These are, no doubt, the "horns of the altar" Exod. 27:2,f.).

Heathen altars generally faced the east, standing one behind the other, and so placed that the images of the gods appeared behind them. Upon them were carved the name of the deity or some appropriate symbols. They were of two kinds, higher and lower: the higher for the celestial gods, and called by the Romans *altaria;* the lower for terrestrial deities, and called *arae.* There was a third kind of altar, *anclabris*, or *enclabris*, a sort of table on which the sacrificial utensils were placed and the entrails of victims laid. The *mensa sacra* was a table on which incense was sometimes presented and offerings not intended to be burned. Some altars, as well as temples, were dedicated to more than one god; we even read of some being dedicated to all the gods.

2. Hebrew. The first altar on record is the one built by Noah after leaving the ark (Gen. 8:20). Mention is made of altars erected by Abraham (Gen. 12:7; 13:4; 22:9), by Isaac (26:25), by Jacob (33:20; 35:1, 3), and by Moses (Exod. 17:15; 20:24-26). In the tabernacle and temple two altars were erected, the one for sacrifices and the other for incense.

1. The Altar of Burnt Offering (Heb. *mĭzbäh hä'öläh*, Exod 30:28; *brazen altar*, *mĭzbäh hännĕhöshĕth*, Exod. 39:39; *table of the Lord*, Mal. 1:7, 12). This altar differed in construction, etc., at different times.

(*a*) *In the Tabernacle* (Exod. 27:38) it was a hollow square, five cubits in length and breadth and three cubits high, and was made of shittim (acacia) wood, overlaid with brass (probably copper). The corners terminated in "horns" (*q.v.*). The altar had a grating, which projected through openings on two sides, and had four rings fastened to it for the poles with which the altar was carried. These poles were made of the same materials as the altar. The priests being forbidden to go up to the altar by steps (Exod. 20:26), the earth was, probably, raised about the altar to enable them to serve easily.

The utensils for the altar (Exod. 27:3), made of brass (copper), were *ash pans*; *shovels*, for cleaning the altar; *basins*, for receiving the blood to be sprinkled on the altar; *flesh hooks*, i. e., large *forks*, to handle the pieces of flesh; *fire pans* (Exod. 38:3), called *censers*, Num. 16:17); *snuff dishes* (Exod. 25:38). According to Lev. 6:13, the fire on this altar was never to be allowed to go out.

(*b*) *In Solomon's Temple.* In adapting the instruments of worship to the larger proportions of the temple, the altar of burnt offering was, naturally, increased in size. It became now a square of twenty cubits, with a height of ten cubits (II Chron. 4:1), made of brass (bronze or copper). This is the altar that was repaired by Asa (II Chron. 15:8), removed by Ahaz, probably to make room for the one erected after a model seen by him in Damascus (II Kings 16:14), "cleansed" by Hezekiah (II Chron. 29:18), and rebuilt by Manasseh (II Chron. 33:16).

(*c*) *In the Second Temple.* This altar was erected before the temple (Ezra 3:3, 6), and on the place occupied by the former (Josephus, *Ant.*, xi, 4, 1). It was probably made of un-hewn stone (Exod. 20:15), for in the account of the temple service by Judas Maccabaeus it is said, "They took whole stones according to the law, and built a new altar according to the former" (I Macc. 4:47).

(*d*) *In Herod's Temple.* According to Josephus, this altar was a square whose sides were fifty cubits each, with a height of fifteen cubits. It had corners like horns, and the passage up to it was by an insensible acclivity from the south. It was formed without any iron tool, nor did any iron tool so much as touch it at any time (*Wars*, v, 5, 6). According to the Mishna, it was a square thirty-two cubits at the base, and decreasing at intervals until it was twenty-four cubits. The Mishna states, according to Josephus, that the stones were unhewn, and whitewashed every year at the Passover and the Feast of Tabernacles. A pipe connected with the S. W. horn conveyed the blood of victims by a subterranean passage to Kedron.

2. Altar of Incense (Heb. *mĭzbäh mĭqtär qĕtörĕth, altar of incensing of incense*, Exod. 30:1; called also the *golden altar, mĭzbäh häzzähäb*, Exod. 39:38; Num. 4:11). (*a*) This would seem to be the "altar of wood," further described as "the table that is before the Lord" (Ezek. 41:22). It was made of shittim wood overlaid with gold, and was one cubit square, with a height of two cubits having horns of the same materials (Lev. 4:7). Running around the sides near the top was a "crown" (border) of gold, beneath which were rings for the staves of shittim wood covered with gold, "to bear it withal" (Exod. 30:1-5). Its place was in front of the veil, midway between the walls (Lev. 16:18; Exod. 30:6). In Exod. 40:5 Moses was commanded to place this altar "before the ark of the testimony," and in Heb. 9:4 it is enumerated among the articles within the second veil, i. e., in the Holy of Holies. The meaning, probably, is that the great typical and symbolical importance of this altar associated it with the Holy of Holies.

(*b*) *In Solomon's Temple* this altar was similar, but made of cedar (I Kings 6:20; 7:48; I Chron. 28:18). Upon this altar incense was burned every morning and evening (Exod. 30:7, 8), and the blood of atonement was sprinkled upon it (v. 10). Being placed immediately before the throne of Jehovah (ark of the covenant), it was the symbol of believing and acceptable prayer.

13. Altar of Incense.

This is the only altar which appears in the heavenly temple (Isa. 6:6; Rev. 8:3, 41). It was the altar at which Zacharias was ministering when the angel appeared to him (Luke 1:11).

3. Mention is made (a) In Isa. 65:3 of "altars of brick," which may have reference to a Babylonish custom of burning incense on bricks covered with magical formulas or cuneiform inscriptions. (b) Of the Assyrian-Damascene altar erected by Ahaz from a model seen by him in Damascus (II Kings 16:10-13). (c) An altar to the "*unknown God*" (Acts 17:23). Reliable authorities assure us that there were several altars in Athens with this inscription. Meyer (*Com., in loco*) says, with reference to the meaning of this inscription, "On important occasions, when the reference to a god known by name was wanting, as in public calamities of which no definite god could be assigned as the author, in order to honor or propitiate the god concerned by sacrifice, without lighting on a wrong one, altars were erected which destined and designated the unknown god."

4. Typology of the Hebrew Altars. The altar of burnt offering (brazen altar) is commonly thought to be a type of the cross upon which Christ, our whole burnt offering (Lev. 1:1-17) offered Himself without spot unto God (Heb. 9:14), the brass speaking of divine judgment as in the brazen serpent (Num. 21:9; John 3:14; 12:31-33). The altar of incense is a type of Christ our Intercessor (John 17:1-16; Heb. 7:25), through whom our prayers and praises ascend to God (Heb. 13:15; Rev. 8:3, 4) and, in turn, pictures the believer-priest's sacrifice of praise and worship (Heb. 13:15).

Al-tas′chith (ăl-tăs′kĭth; more correctly altash′heth), a term found in title of Psalms 57, 58, 59, 75.

A′lush (ā′lŭsh), the place of encampment of Israel in the desert, next to Rephidim, where was no water (Num. 33:13, 14).

Al′vah (ăl′và), the second named of the Edomitish chieftains descended from Esau (Gen. 36:40). The name is translated Aliah in I Chron. 1:51.

Al′van (ăl′văn; *tall*), the first named of the five sons of Shobal, the Horite, of Mount Seir (Gen. 36:23); called also Alian (I Chron. 1:40).

A′mad (ä′măd; *people of duration*), a town near the border of Asher (Josh. 19:26); not identified.

A′mal (ă′măl; *toil*), the last named of the four sons of Helem, of the tribe of Asher (I Chron. 7:35).

Am′alek (ăm′à-lĕk), the son of Eliphaz (the firstborn of Esau) by his concubine, Timma (Gen. 36:12; I Chron. 1:36), and chieftain of an Idumaean tribe (Gen. 36:16). This tribe was probably not the same as the Amalekites so often mentioned in Scriptures, for Moses speaks of the Amalekites long before this Amalek was born (Gen. 14:7). *See* Amalekites.

Am′alekites (ăm′à-lĕk-īts; also *Amalek, Amalekite*), a very ancient race, whose history is thus summed up by Balaam (Num. 24:20): "Amalek was the first of the nations; but his latter end shall be that he perish forever." Although this people is prominent in the O. T., archaeology has as yet revealed nothing concerning them.

In Abraham's time we find the Amalekites S. W. of the Dead Sea (Gen. 14:7). In the time of Moses they occupied all the desert of *et Tih* to the borders of Egypt, and most of the Sinaitic peninsula, with the south country of Palestine. There was also a "mount of the Amalekites" in Ephraim (Judg. 12:15). Two routes lay through the land of Amalek, one by the Isthmus of Suez to Egypt, the other by the Aelanitic arm of the Red Sea (i. e., the Gulf of Akabah). It has been thought that the expedition noted in Gen. 14 may have been connected with the opening of the latter route.

According to the view which we have taken, Amalek, the son of Esau (Gen. 36:12, 16) may have been progenitor of a tribe which was merged with the original Amalekites so as to form part of the great Amalekite race, or he may have taken his name from some connection with the Amalekites, possible as Scipio won his name Africanus, or it may have been a mere coincidence. Historical accounts of Amalekites in southern Arabia will then refer to a time subsequent to their dispossession by the Israelites.

Some have supposed that all the Amalekites were descended from Amalek, son of Esau. In that case the language of Gen. 14:7 would mean what was afterward the country of the Amalekites.

The Amalekites were always bitter foes of Israel, sometimes alone, sometimes in conjunction with other tribes. Their first attack was made in time of distress at Rephidim. They were doomed to utter destruction; but though they suffered heavily, especially at the hands of Saul and David, the sentence was so imperfectly executed that there was a remnant to be smitten in the days of Hezekiah (I Chron. 4:43). This is their last appearance in Bible history. In the Sinaitic peninsula are massive stone buildings averaging seven feet high by eight feet diameter inside, which may perhaps be remains of the Amalekites.

A′mam (ā′măm), a city in the south of Judah (Josh. 15:26), probably in the tract afterward assigned to Simeon (Josh. 19:1-9).

Ama'na (á-mä'nä; *fixed*, i. e., a *covenant*).

1. The marginal reading (II Kings 5:12) of *Abana* (*q. v.*).

2. A mountain (Cant. 4:8), part of Anti-Libanus, from which the waters of Abana flow.

Amaranthine (Gr. *'amarantinos, unfading*), the original of A. V. "that fadeth not away" (I Pet. 5:4; comp. 1:4, Gr. *'amarantos*), and "meaning *composed of amaranth*, a flower so called because it never withers or fades, and when plucked off revives if moistened with water; hence it is a symbol of perpetuity and immortality."

Amari'ah (ăm-ä-rī'ä; *said* (i. e., promised) *by Jehovah*).

1. A person mentioned in I Chron 6:7, 52, in the list of the descendants of Aaron by his eldest son, Eleazer, as the son of Meraioth and father of Ahitub, B. C. 1440. There is no means of determining whether Amariah was ever high priest, but it is probable that he was the last of the high priests of Eleazer's line prior to its transfer to the line of Ithamar in the person of *Eli* (*q. v.*). Josephus calls him Arophaeus, and says he lived in private, the pontificate being at the time in the family of Ithamar.

2. A high priest at a later date (B. C. probably 740), son of another Azariah and father of another Ahitub (I Chron. 6:11; Ezra 7:3).

3. A Levite, second son of Hebron and grandson of Kohath, and of the lineage of Moses (I Chron. 23:19; 24:23).

4. A chief priest active in the reforms instituted by King Jehoshaphat (II Chron 19:11), B. C. c. 873-849.

5. One of the Levites appointed by Hezekiah to superintend the distribution of the temple dues among the sacerdotal cities (II Chron. 31:15), B. C. 726.

6. A Jew, son of Bani, who divorced his Gentile wife, whom he had married after the return from Babylon (Ezra 10:42), B. C. 456.

7. One of the priests who returned from Babylon with Zerubbabel (Neh. 11:4), B. C. 536; and probably the same person who years after (B. C. 445) sealed the covenant with Nehemiah (Neh. 10:3). He appears to have been identical with the chief priest, the father of Jehohanan (Neh. 12:13).

8. The son of Shephatiah and father of Zechariah. His descendant, Athaiah, was one of the Judahite residents in Jerusalem after the captivity (Neh. 11:4), B. C. 445.

9. The great-grandfather of the prophet Zephaniah (Zeph. 1:1).

Amarna, Tell el—("mound of the city of the Horizon"), known also as Akhetaton, located about 200 miles south of present-day Cairo. Here a peasant woman in 1886 accidentally discovered hundreds of clay tablets in Accadian cuneiform, representing the diplomatic correspondence of petty Canaanite princelings with their Egyptian overlords Amenophis III and Amenophis IV (Akhnaton) in the first half of the 14th century B. C. Although many difficulties of interpretation remain, this earliest known international diplomatic correspondence seems to portray the general situation in Palestine resulting from the Israelite invasion under

14. Marsh Life — Fragment of Printed Parchment from Palace of Ikhnaton at Amarna.

Joshua. This is to be expected if the early date of The Exodus (c. 1440) and of the Conquest (c. 1440) is accepted. The Habiru, who appear prominently in the letters of Abdi-Hiba, governor of Jerusalem, to Akhnaton asking for Egyptian troops to stem off these invaders, are likely the actual invading Hebrews under Joshua. At least, the equation Habiru-Hebrew is possible linguistically. This is denied by proponents of later-date theories of the Exodus, but agrees with the underlying chronology of the Pentateuch and Joshua and Judges, as well as with I Kings 6:1. *M. F. U.*

Am'asa (ăm'á-sà; *burden*).

1. The son of Abigail, a sister of King David, by Jether, or *Ithra* (*q. v.*), an Ishmaelite (II Sam. 17:25; I Kings 2:5, 32; I Chron. 2:17). His paternity probably led David to neglect him in comparison with the more honored sons of David's other sister, Zeruiah. He joined Absalom in his rebellion, and was by him appointed commander-in-chief in the place of Joab, by whom he was totally defeated in the forest of Ephraim (II Sam. 18:6, 7). David afterward gave him command of his army in the room of Joab, who had incurred displeasure by his overbearing conduct and his slaying of Absalom (II Sam. 19:13), B. C. after 1000. On the breaking out of Sheba's rebellion, Amasa was so tardy in his movements (probably from the reluctance of the troops to follow him) that David dispatched Abishai with the household troops in pursuit of Sheba, and Joab joined his brother as a volunteer. Amasa overtook them at the great stone of Gibeon, and Joab, while in the act of saluting him, smote him

dead with his sword, thus ridding himself of a dangerous rival. Joab continued the pursuit of Sheba, and, by his popularity with the army, prevented David from removing him from command or calling him to account for his bloody deed (II Sam. 20:4-13). Whether Amasa be identical with the *Amasai* who is mentioned among David's commanders (I Chron. 12:18) is uncertain.

2. A son of Hadlai and chief of Ephraim, who with others vehemently and successfully resisted the retention as prisoners of the persons whom Pekah, king of Israel, had taken captive in a campaign against Ahaz, king of Judah (II Chron. 28:12), B. C. about 735.

Amas'ai (à-măs'ā-ī; *burdensome*).

1. A Levite, son of Elkanah, and father of Mahath, of the ancestry of Samuel (I Chron. 6:25, 35).

2. One of the chief captains of Judah who, with a considerable body of men from Judah and Benjamin, joined David while an outlaw at Ziklag. He with others was made captain of David's band (I Chron. 12:18), B. C. about 1015. This is the Amasai who is supposed by some to be identical with Amasa.

3. One of the priests appointed to precede the ark with blowing of trumpets on its removal from the house of Obed-edom to Jerusalem (I Chron. 15:24).

4. Another Levite, and father of the Mahath who assisted Hezekiah in restoring the worship of God, and was active in cleansing the temple (II Chron. 29:12), B. C. 726.

Amash'ai (à-măsh'ā-ī; probably an incorrect form of the name *Amasai*), the son of Azareel, and one of the priests appointed by Nehemiah to reside at Jerusalem and do the work of the temple (Neh. 11:13), B. C. 445.

Amasi'ah (ăm-à-sī'à; *burden of Jehovah*), the son of Zichri, a chieftain of Judah, who volunteered to assist King Jehoshaphat in his religious reform, with two hundred thousand chosen troops (II Chron. 17:16), B. C. 872.

Amazi'ah (ăm-à-zī'à; *whom Jehovah strengthens*).

1. The son and successor of Jehoash, or Joash, and the ninth king of Judah. He ascended the throne at the age of twenty-five years, and reigned twenty-nine years (II Kings, 14:1, 2; II Chron. 25:1), B. C. c. 800-771. He commenced his reign by slaying the persons who had murdered his father, but spared their children, according to the Mosaic injunction (Deut. 24:16). In the twelfth year of his reign he prepared a great expedition for the recovery of Edom, which had revolted from Jehoram. He raised a large army (three hundred thousand) of his own, and increased it by hiring one hundred thousand Israelites, the first example of a mercenary army that occurs in the history of the Jews. At the command of the prophet he dismissed these mercenaries, who returned in anger and sacked several of the cities of Judah. The obedience of Amaziah was rewarded by a great victory over the Edomites, ten thousand of whom were slain in battle, and ten thousand more dashed to pieces from the rocks of Selah, which Amaziah took, and called Jokteel. Among the spoil which he took were the idols of Mount Seir, in the worship of which

Amaziah suffered himself to be engaged. Then began his disasters. A prophet was sent to reprove him, and he resented his faithful admonition. The prophet then foretold his downfall. Urged by arrogance, or provoked by the conduct of the disbanded mercenaries, he sent a challenge to the king of Israel to meet him in battle. The king returned him a scornful reply through a parable and advised him to remain at home. Amaziah still belligerent, was met by Jehoash, and by him defeated, taken prisoner and brought to Jerusalem, his own metropolis. The north city wall was broken down, the temple and palace despoiled, and hostages taken. Amaziah was allowed to remain upon the throne and survived about fifteen years, when a conspiracy was formed against him, and he was slain at Lachish. His body was brought "upon horses" to Jerusalem and buried in the royal sepulcher (II Kings 14:3-20; II Chron. 25:2-28).

2. The father of Joshah which latter was one of the Simeonite chiefs who expelled the Amalekites from the valley of Gedor in the time of Hezekiah (I Chron. 4:34), B. C. after 726.

3. The son of Hilkiah and father of Hashabiah, a Levite of the ancestry of Ethan, a singer of the temple (I Chron. 6:45), B. C. considerably before 1000.

4. The priest of the golden calves at Beth-el, in the time of Jeroboam II c. 786-746. He complained to the king of Amos's prophecies of coming evil, and urged the prophet to withdraw into the kingdom of Judah and prophesy there. Amos in reply told him of the severe degradation his family should undergo in the approaching captivity of the northern kingdom (Amos 7:10-17), B. C. c. 770.

Ambassador (Heb. *tsîr*, one who goes on an *errand*; *lûts, interpreter*; *măl'āk, messenger*). An isolated position of ancient Israel rendered comparatively unnecessary the employment of ambassadors, although examples are afforded of the employment of such functionaries. They do not seem to have known of "ministers resident" at a foreign court, all the embassies of which we read being "extraordinary." David sent ambassadors to Hanun, king of the Amorites, to congratulate him upon his accession to the throne (II Sam. 10:2), and Hiram sent them to Solomon for a like purpose (I Kings 5:1). Toi, king of Hamath, sent his son Joran to David "to salute him and to bless him" after his victory over Hadadezer (II Sam. 8:10). Ambassadors were also sent to protest against a wrong (Judg. 11:12), to solicit favors (Num. 20:14), and to contract alliances (Josh. 9:3, f.).

Ambassadors were not considered as representing the *person* of the sovereign, according to the present thought, but rather as distinguished and privileged messengers, and their dignity was rather that of heralds (II Sam. 10:1-5). More frequent mention is made of them after Israel came to have relations with Syria, Babylon, etc. They were usually men of high rank. The word occurs once in the new Testament (II Cor. 5:20, Gr. *presbeuō*, to be a *senior*).

Amber. *See* Mineral Kingdom.

Ambush (Heb. *'äräb*, to *lie in wait*), a lying in wait and concealment to attack by surprise. Joshua, at the capture of Ai, shows himself to have been skilled in this method of warfare (Josh. 8). The attempt on the part of Abimelech to surprise Shechem (Judg. 9:30, f.) appears to have been unskillful.

Amen (Heb. *'āmēn*; Gr. *'amēn*, *true*, *faithful*), a word used to affirm and confirm a statement. Strictly an adjective, meaning *firm*, metaphorically *faithful*, it came to be used as an adverb, by which something is asserted or confirmed. Used at the beginning of a sentence it emphasizes what is about to be said. It is frequently so employed by our Lord, and translated "verily." It is often used to confirm the words of another, and adds the wish for success to another's vows and predictions. "The repetition of the word employed by John alone in his gospel (twenty-five times) has the force of a superlative, *most assuredly*" (Grimm, *Gr. Lex.*, *s. v.*).

Its Liturgical Use. Among the Jews this use of the word is illustrated by the response of the woman in the trial by the water of jealousy (Num. 5:22), by that of the people at Mount Ebal (Deut. 27:15-26; comp. Neh. 5:13; see also I Chron. 16:36). It was a custom, which passed over from the synagogues into the Christian assemblies, that when he who had read or discoursed had offered up a solemn prayer to God the others in attendance responded *Amen*, and thus made the substance of what was uttered their own (I Cor. 14:16). Several of the Church fathers refer to this custom, and Jerome says that at the conclusion of public prayer the united voice of the people sounded like the fall of water or the noise of thunder.

Amethyst. *See* Mineral Kingdom.

A'mi (ā'mī), one of the servants of Solomon, whose descendants went up from Babylon (Ezra 2:57). In Neh. 7:59 he is called Amon.

Amiable (Heb. *yĕdîd*, *loved*). This word occurs only in Psa. 84:1, "How amiable are thy tabernacles," etc. In Psa. 127:2 it is rendered "beloved." Its plural form, signifying "delights," is found in the title to Psa. 45, "A song of *loves*."

Amin'adab (ă-mĭn'ä-dăb), a Greek form (Matt. 1:4; Luke 3:33) of *Amminidab* (*q. v.*).

Amit'tai (ă-mĭt'ī; *true*), a native of Gath-hepher, of the tribe of Zebulun, and father of the prophet Jonah (II Kings 14:25; Jonah 1:1), B. C. c. 800.

Am'mah (ăm'mä; Heb. *'ammäh*, a *cubit*), the place reached by Joab and Abishai, in their pursuit of Abner, at sundown (II Sam. 2:24).

Am'mi (ăm'ī; i. e., as explained in the margin of A. V., "my people"), a figurative name applied to the kingdom of Israel in token of God's reconciliation with them, in contrast with the equally significant name Lo-ammi given by the prophet Hosea to his second son by Gomer the daughter of Diblaim (Hos. 2:1). In the same manner Ruhamah contrasts with Lo-ruhamah.

Am'miel (ăm'ī-ĕl; *people of God*).

1. The son of Gemalli, of the tribe of Dan, one of the twelve spies sent by Moses to explore the land of Canaan (Num. 13:12), B. C.

c. 1437. He was, of course, one of the ten who perished by the plague for their "evil report" (Num. 14:37).

2. The father of Machir of Lo-debar, which latter entertained Mephibosheth until he was befriended by David (II Sam. 9:4, 5; 17:27), B. C. before 1000.

3. The father of Bath-sheba, wife of Uriah and afterward of David (I Chron. 3:5), B. C. before 1030. In II Sam. 11:3 he is called *Eliam* (*q. v.*), by the transposition of the first and last syllables.

4. The sixth son of Obed-edom, and one of the doorkeepers of the temple (I Chron. 26:5), B. C. about 955.

Ammi'hud (ăm-mĭ'hŭd; *people of glory*).

1. An Ephraimite, whose son, Elishama, was appointed chief of the tribe at the time of the Exodus (Num. 1:10; 2:18; 7:48, 53; 10:22; I Chron. 7:26), B. C. before 1210.

2. The father of Shemuel, which latter was the Simeonite chief who was appointed for the division of the Promised Land (Num. 34:20), B. C. before 1452.

3. A man of the tribe of Naphtali, whose son, Pedahel, was prince of the tribe, and was appointed for the division of the land (Num. 34:28), B. C. before 1452.

4. The father of Talmai, king of Geshur, to whom Absalom fled after his murder of Amnon (II Sam. 13:37), B. C. before 1030.

5. The son of Omri and descendant of Pharez, and father of Uthai, which last was one of the first to live at Jerusalem on the return from Babylon (I Chron. 9:4), B. C. before 536.

Ammin'adab (ăm-mĭn'ä-dăb; *people of liberality*).

1. Son of Ram, or Aram, and father of Nashon (or Naasson, Matt. 1:4; Luke 3:32), who was prince of the tribe of Judah at the first numbering of Israel in the second year of the Exodus (Num. 1:7; 2:3), B. C. about 1440. He was the fourth in descent from Judah, the sixth in ascent from David (Ruth 4:19, 20; I Chron. 2:10), and one of the ancestors of Jesus Christ (Matt. 1:4; Luke 3:33). He is the same Amminadab, probably whose daughter, Elisheba, was married to Aaron (Exod. 6:23).

2. A son of Kohath, the second son of Levi (I Chron. 6:22). In vers. 2 and 18 he seems to be called *Izhar* (*q. v.*).

3. A Levite of the sons of Uzziel, who, with one hundred and twelve of his brethren, was appointed by David to assist in bringing up the ark to Jerusalem (I Chron. 15:10, 11), B. C. 1000.

Ammin'adib (ăm-mĭn'ä-dĭb; another form of *Amminadab*), a person whose chariots are mentioned as proverbial for their swiftness (Cant. 6:12), from which he appears to have been, like Jehu, one of the most celebrated charioteers of his day.

Ammishad'dai (ăm-mĭ-shăd'dā-ī; *people of the Almighty*), the father of Ahiezer, chief of the tribe of Dan at the time of the Exodus (Num. 1:12, 2:25; 7:66, 71; 10:25), B. C. before 1440.

Ammiz'abad (ăm-mĭz'ä-băd; *people of endowment*), the son and subaltern of Benaiah, which latter was David's captain of the host commanding in the third month (I Chron. 27:6), B. C. 1000.

Am'mon (ăm'mŏn; *inbred*, another form of *Ben-ammi, q. v.*), the son of Lot by his youngest daughter (Gen. 19:38), B. C. about 2000. His descendants were called Ammonites (Deut. 2:20), children of Ammon (Gen. 19:38), and sometimes simply Ammon (Neh. 13:23).

Am'monites (ăm'mŏn-īts), a nomadic race descended from Lot's youngest daughter, as the more civilized Moabites were from the elder one (Gen. 19:36-38). The two tribes were so connected that their names seem sometimes to have been used interchangeably (comp. Deut. 23:4 with Num. 22:2-7; Num. 21:29 with Judg. 11:24; and Judg. 11:13 with Num. 21:26).

Ammon, having dispossessed the Zamzummim (Deut. 2:19-21), dwelt E. and N. of Moab, from the Arnon to the Jabbok; "Sihon king of the Amorites" having just before the Exodus taken the land between these streams from "the former king of Moab" (Num. 21:26), "from the wilderness even unto Jordan" (Judg. 11:22), and thus crowded Ammon eastward into the desert.

Although the Israelites were forbidden to molest the Ammonites, Ammon was often in league with other nations against Israel, as, with Moab (Deut. 23:3, 4); with Moab and Amalek (Judg. 3:13); with the Syrians (II Sam. 10:1-19); with Gebal and Amalek (Psa. 83:7), and was almost always hostile, both before and after the captivity (Neh. 4:3, etc.; see also Judith, chaps. 5-7; I Macc. 6:30-43), till all were swallowed up by Rome. In the time of Justin Martyr (about 150 A. D.) the Ammonites were quite numerous, but in the time of Origen (about 186-254 A. D.) they were merged with the Arabs.

The Ammonites were governed by a king (I Sam. 12:12). The national deity was Molech (I Kings 11:7), often called Milcom (I Kings 11:5, 33.) The capital was Rabbah, or Rabbath Ammon, for a while called Philadelphia, from Ptolemy Philadelphus, but now called *Amman*.

The Ammonites seem to have furnished a small contingent to the Syrian confederacy against Shalmaneser II (854 B. C.), and Budnilu of Ammon was among the twelve kings of the Hatti and of the seacoast who sent ambassadors to Esar-haddon at Nineveh (671 B. C.).

The Ammonite names in the Bible go to show that the language was akin to the Hebrews.

Solomon set an example in marrying Ammonite women. Rehoboam's mother being Naamah, an Ammonitess (I Kings 14:31), which example Israel was too ready to imitate (Neh. 13:23).

The doom of desolation prophesied against Ammon (Ezek. 25:5, 10; Zeph. 2:9) has been literally fulfilled. "Nothing but ruins are found here by the amazed explorer. Not an inhabited village remains, and not an Ammonite exists on the face of the earth" (Thomson, *Land and Book*, iii, 622).

Am'non (ăm'nŏn; *faithful*).

1. The eldest son of David by Ahinoam, the Jezreelitess, born in Hebron (II Sam. 3:2; I Chron. 3:1), B. C. before 1000. By the advice and assistance of Jonadab he violated his half-sister Tamar, which her brother Absalom revenged two years after by causing him to be assassinated (II Sam. 13).

2. The first named of the four sons of Shimon, or Shammai, of the children of Ezra, the descendant of Judah (I Chron. 4:20).

A'mok (ā'mŏk; *deep*), the father of Eber, and a chief among the priests who went up from Babylon with Jerubbabel (Neh. 12:7, 20), B. C. 536.

A'momum (ă'mō-mŭm). The Gr. word *'ammōmon*, occurs only in Rev. 18:13, where it is rendered "odours." It is, however, the name of a plant. *See* Vegetable Kingdom.

A'mon (ā'mŏn; *faithful*).

1. The governor of "the city" (probably Samaria) in the time of Ahab, who was charged to keep Micaiah till the king should return from the siege of Ramoth-gilead (I Kings 22:26; II Chron. 18:25), B. C. c. 850.

2. The fifteenth king of Judah, who succeeded his father Manasseh at the age of twenty-two years (B. C. 642), and reigned two years. He followed Manasseh's idolatries without sharing his repentance. Falling a victim to a court conspiracy, the people avenged his death by slaying the conspirators and placing upon the throne his son Josiah, aged eight years. Amon was buried with his father in the garden of Uzza (II Kings 21:19-26; II Chron. 33:20-25; Jer. 1:2; 25:3; Zeph. 1:1).

3. The head, or ancestor, of one of the families of the Nethinims who returned from Babylon with Zerubbabel after the captivity (Neh. 7:59), B. C. before 536.

4. An Egyptian deity (Egyptian Amun, *the hidden one*). Originally merely a local god of Thebes (Biblical No-amon, the capital of Upper Egypt, Jer. 46:25 R. V., Nahum 3:8 R. V.). With the rapid ascendancy of this city during the strong Middle Kingdom under the Twelfth Egyptian Dynasty (c. 1989-c. 1776 B. C.), the god Amon (Amun) assumed national prominence and was often designated Amon-Re, the sun god. A great temple was erected in his honor at Karnak and it was against the influential priesthood of this deity that the youthful reformer Akhenaton (Akhnaton) revolted when he built a new capital at Amarna where the famous Tell el Amarna Tablets were recovered in 1886. Revised by *M. F. U.*

Am'orites (ăm'ō-rīts; Heb. always singular, used collectively, *hä'ĕmŏrî, the Amorite*), a tribe descended from Canaan (Gen. 10:16), and one of the seven whose lands were given to Israel (Deut. 7:1; comp. Gen. 15:16). "The Amorite" means literally "the high one," whence the name Amorites is very generally supposed to mean "highlanders" (Num. 13:29; Deut. 1:7, 20; Josh. 10:6), or "tall ones" (Amos 2:9; comp. Num. 28:32; Deut. 2:11).

The Amorites were so prominent that their name seems sometimes to be used for Canaanites in general (Josh. 24:8, etc.), and in the Tel-el-Amarna letters *Amurri* is the name for Palestine-Phoenicia.

In Abraham's day they dwelt W. of the Dead Sea, in Hazezon-tamar (Gen. 14:7), "which is Engedi" (II Chron. 20:2), now *Ain Jidi*, and about Hebron (Gen. 14:13, comp. 13:18). The Israelites found E. of Jordan two Amorite kingdoms: that of Sihon, which lay along the Jordan from the Arnon (*Wady Mojib*) to the Jabbok (*Wady Zerka*), and from the Jordan to the Desert (Judg. 11:22); and that of "Og the king of Bashan," from the Jabbok to Mount Hermon (*Jebel esh Sheik*) (Deut. 3:4, 9).

As Sihon and Og attempted to act on the offensive Israel immediately possessed their territories (Deut. 3:8-10). Their next collision with Amorites was with the anti-Gibeonite confederacy of the five Amorite kings of Jerusalem, Hebron, Jarmuth, Lachish, and Eglon (Josh. 10:1-43). Amorites also appear in the northern confederacy which was vanquished near the waters of Merom (Josh. 11:1-14). This was the last hostile stand of the Amorites. In the days of Samuel they were at peace with Israel (I Sam. 7:14). Solomon levied on the remnant of the Amorites and of the other Canaanite nations a tribute of bond service (I Kings 9:20 21). The other notices of the Amorites after Solomon's day are mere historical reminiscences.

The Akkadians called the Amorites *Ammuru* and in the third millennium B. C. Syria-Palestine was called "the land of the Amorites." The First Dynasty of Babylon (c. 1830-c. 1550 B. C.) was Amorite, and its most important king, Hammurabi the Great (1728-1686 B. C.) conquered the Amorite capital Mari (Tell Hariri) on the Middle Euphrates near present-day Abou Kemal. The dynasty of Babylon fell when the Hittites sacked Babylon c. 1550. Thousands of clay tablets from the archives of an Amorite king at Mari are now in the Louvre Museum in Paris as the result of the excavations of that ancient Amorite center since 1933 by André Parrot. From the palace archives of Zimri-Lim, the last king of Mari, over 20,000 tablets were recovered, a large number representing diplomatic correspondence of this king with his own ambassadors and with the great Hammurabi himself. The Mari Letters shed remarkable light on the customs recounted in the patriarchal narratives of Genesis. Revised by *M. F. U.*

A'mos (ā'mŏs; *burden*).

1. One of the twelve minor prophets and a native of Tekoah, a town about six miles S. of Bethlehem. He belonged to the shepherds there, and was not trained in any school of the prophets. And yet, without dedicating himself to the calling of a prophet, he was called by the Lord to prophesy concerning Israel in the reigns of Uzziah, king of Judah, and Jeroboam, King of Israel, B. C. c. 786-746, two years before the earthquake (Amos 1:1), B. C. about 763. The exact date of his appearing, or the length of his ministry, cannot be given. The two kingdoms were at the summit of their prosperity. Idleness, luxury, and oppression were general, and idolatry prevalent. It was at such a time as this that the plain shepherd of Tekoah was sent into Israel and prophesied at Beth-el. This is almost a solitary

instance of a prophet being sent from Judah into Israel, and, doubtless, attracted universal attention. His prophetic utterances were directed against Judah as well as Israel, and close with promises of divine mercy and returning favor to the chosen race. He was charged with a conspiracy against Jeroboam, the king, and threatened by Amaziah, the high priest of Beth-el. After fulfilling his mission he probably returned to Judah. The time and manner of his death are unknown.

2. The ninth in the line of ascent from

15. Amphipolis.

Christ, being the son of Naum and father of Mattathias (Luke 3:25), B. C. about 400.

Amos, Book of. 1. The Time. The second quarter of the 8th century B. C. in which Amos prophesied was one of great wealth and corruption. As a result of Jeroboam II's successes against the Moabites and the Aramaeans, the borders of the Northern Kingdom reached their widest extent since the Solomonic Era (II Kings 14:25; Amos 6:14). Fiery denunciation of the luxurious living, the idolatry and moral depravity of Israel were the subject of the rustic prophet from the mountain top Judaen village of Tekoa. But beyond the warning of judgment and final captivity upon the backslidden people, the prophet catches a magnificent glimpse of the yet-future millennial kingdom (9:11-15). **2. The Contents.** The Book itself falls into three divisions, Part I. Judgments upon surrounding nations—Damascus, Philistia, Phoenicia, Edom, Ammon, Moab (1:1-2:3) and upon Judah (2:4, 5) and Israel herself (2:6-16). Part II. Divine indictment of the whole family of Jacob (3:1-9:10) including three denunciatory sermons (3:1-6:15) and five symbolic visions (7:1-9:10). Part III. Future Kingdom blessing of restored Israel (9:11-15), embracing Messiah's return and the establishment of the earthly Messianic reign (9:11, 12), millennial prosperity (9:13) and a restored Jewish nation (9:14, 15). **3. Authenticity.** The divine authority of the prophecy is corroborated by the New Testament. Stephen in his speech before the Sanhedrin (Acts 7:42, 43) quotes Amos 5:25-27. James, addressing the Jerusalem Council (Acts 15:16), cites Amos 9:11. **4. Criticism.** Practically all critics except the ultra-radical, concede the substantial integrity of the prophecy, except for 1:9, 10; 1:11, 12; 2:4, 5; three doxologies 4:13; 5:8; 9:5, 6 and the Messianic-Millennial passage 9:11-15. The assumptions under which these passages are commonly regarded as later additions (glosses), however, are the result of erroneous theories of the development of Israel's religion. Oesterley and Robinson, for example, regard 9:11-12 as exilic, because it envisions the Tabernacle of David as having fallen (*Intr. to the Books of the O. T.* London, 1934, p. 366). But A. Bentzen (*Introduction II*, 1949, p. 142) is correct in showing that Amos viewed the House of David as fallen "because it had lost the position which it had occupied in David's own time, not as a consequence of the events of 587, which he had not seen." *M. F. U.*

A'moz (ā'mŏz; *strong*), the father of the prophet Isaiah (II Kings 19:2; Isa. 1:1), B. C. before 738. According to rabbinical tradition, he is also the brother of King Amaziah, and a prophet; but of this there is no proof.

Amphip'olis (ăm-fĭp'ô-lĭs; *a city surrounded*, so called because the Strymon flowed round it), a city of Macedonia through which Paul and Silas passed on their way from Philippi to Thessalonica (Acts 17:1). It was about thirty-three miles from Philippi; it is now in ruins, and its site occupied by a village called Neochori.

Am'plias (ăm'plĭ-ăs), a Christian at Rome, and mentioned by Paul as one whom he particularly loved (Rom. 16:8), A. D. 60.

Am'ram (ăm'răm; *high people*).
1. The first named of the sons of Kohath, a Levite. He married his father's sister Jochebed, and by her became the father of Miriam, Aaron, and Moses (Exod. 6:18, 20; Num. 26:59). He died aged one hundred and thirty-seven years, probably before the Exodus.
2. A son of Dishon and descendant of Esau (I Chron. 1:41). In Gen. 36:26 he is called more correctly *Hemdan* (q. v.).
3. One of the sons of Bani, who, after the return from Babylon, separated from his Gentile wife (Ezra 10:34), B. C. 456.

Am'ramites (ăm'răm-īts), descendants (Num. 3:27; I Chron. 26:23) of Amram, No. 1.

Am'raphel (ăm'rà-fĕl), a king of Shinar, the alluvial lowland of southern Babylonia, and an ally of Chedorlaomer in the invasion of the west in the time of Abraham, B. C. c. 2080, and formerly generally identified with Hammurabi the Great of the First Dynasty of Babylon (c. 1728-1689). This Amraphel-Hammurabi equation always was difficult linguistically, but is now also disproved chronologically. *M. F. U.*

Amulet, a supposed preservative against sickness, accident, witchcraft, and evil spirits or demons. Amulets consisted of precious stones, gems, gold, and sometimes of parchment written over with some inscription. They have been widely used from remote antiquity, and are still worn in many parts of the world. They were often worn as earrings (q. v.), as the centerpiece of a necklace, and among the Egyptians frequently consisted of the emblems of various deities. Among the Arabs the figure of an open hand is used, as well as that of a serpent.

The English word Amulet does not occur in Scripture, but the word *lᵉhǎshîm, charms*; Isa. 3:20 (A. V., *earrings*) is now generally understood to have the meaning of amulets. Hence they formed part of the trappings which Jacob commanded his household to put away (Gen. 35:4). The most fanciful and superstitious notions have prevailed respecting the marvelous powers of gems (q. v.). The gem appropriate for a particular month was worn as an amulet during the month, and was supposed to exert mysterious control in reference to beauty, health, riches, etc. One's person and house were thought to be protected from malign influences by holy inscriptions placed upon the door. The existence of such a custom is implied in the attempt of Moses to turn them to a proper use by directing that certain passages of the law should be employed (Exod. 13:9, 16; Deut. 6:9; 11-18), "that they might look upon it, and remember all the command-

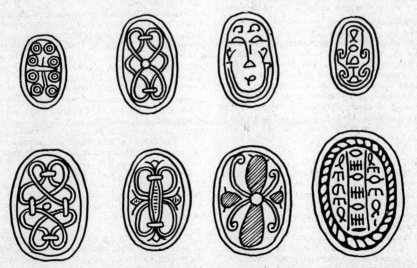

16. Scarabs of the 17th Century B. C. These ornaments or amulets in the form of a beetle (*Scarabaeus sacer*) and bearing the name of a god or king were common among the ancient Egyptians. They were thought to bring protection and good luck.

ments of the Lord, and do them" (Num. 15:38, 39). Such written scrolls afterward degenerated into instruments of superstition among the Jews, so that "There was hardly any people . . . that more used or were more fond of amulets, charms, mutterings, exorcisms, and all kinds of enchantments" (Lightfoot, *Horae Heb.*, Matt. 24:24). These amulets consisted of little roots, parts of animals, or, more commonly, bits of paper or parchment upon which were written words or characters, and were supposed to have magical power; especially to protect from evil spirits or demons. One of the most frequent of the latter was the cabalistic hexagonal figure known as "the shield of David," and "the seal of Solomon."

Many of the Christians of the 1st century wore amulets marked with a fish, as a symbol of the Redeemer, or the pentangle, consisting of three triangles intersected and made of five lines, which may be so set forth with the body of man as to touch and point out the places where our Saviour was wounded. Among the gnostics Abraxas gems were used. At a later period ribbons with sentences of Scripture written on them were hung about the neck. The Council of Trullo ordered the makers of all amulets to be excommunicated, and deemed the wearers of them guilty of heathen superstition. *See* Teraphim.

Am′zi (ăm′zĭ; *strong*).

1. Son of Bani, of the family of Merari, and in the ancestry of Ethan, who was appointed one of the leaders of the temple music (I Chron. 6:46).

2. Son of Zechariah and ancestor of Adaiah, which latter was actively engaged in the building of the second temple (Neh. 11:12), B. C. before 445.

A′nab (ā′năb; *grapes*), a place upon the mountains of Judah, from which Joshua expelled the Anakim (Num. 13:33; Josh. 11:21; 15:50); now bearing the same name *Khirbet 'Anab;* about thirteen miles S. W. of Hebron.

Anagogical (Gr. *anagō, to lead up*), pertaining to the mysterious, spiritual. The older writers on biblical interpretation mention four senses of Scripture—the literal, allegorical, tropical, and *anagogical*. This last is the spiritual sense relating to the eternal glory of the believer up to which its teachings are supposed to lead; thus the rest of the Sabbath, in an *anagogical* sense, signifies the repose of the saints in heaven (Heb. 4:4-11); or the mystery of the union between man and wife, of the union between Christ and the Church (Eph. 5:22-32).

A′nah (ā′năh; *answer*), the son of Zibeon and grandson of Seir. His daughter Aholibamah is the second named of Esau's wives (Gen. 36:2, 14, 25). An Anah is mentioned in Gen. 36:20 as one of the sons of Seir, and head of an Idumaean tribe. Both passages probably refer to the same person, the word "son" being used in v. 20, in the larger sense of descendant. While feeding his father's asses in the desert, he discovered warm springs, from which circumstance he probably obtained the name Beeri, "the man of the wells" (Gen. 26:34).

Ana′harath (ȧ-nā′hȧ-răth; *gorge*), a town on or within Issachar (Josh. 19:19). Now identified with 'En-na'ûrah.

Anai′ah (ȧ-nī′ȧ; *Jah has answered*), one of the persons (probably priests) who stood at the right hand of Ezra, while he read the law to the people (Neh. 8:4), and perhaps the same as one of the chiefs of the people who joined Nehemiah in a sacred covenant (Neh. 10:22), B. C. 445.

A′nak (ā′năk; *long-necked*, i. e., *a giant*), the son of Arba, the founder of Kirjath-arba. He was the progenitor of a race of giants called Anakim. These Anakim were a terror to the children of Israel (Num. 13:22, 28), but were driven out by Caleb, who came into possession of Hebron (Josh. 15:13, 14).

Analogy (Gr. *'analogia, proportion*).

1. As applied to the works of God generally, *analogy* leads to the conclusion that (*a*) a part of a system of which he is the author must, in respect of its leading principles, be similar to the whole of that system; (*b*) the work of an intelligent and moral being must bear in all its lineaments traces of the character of its author; (*c*) the revelation of God in Scriptures is in all respects agreeable to what we know of God from the works of nature and the order of the world.

2. **Analogy of Faith.** This phrase is derived from the words of St. Paul (Rom. 12:6), "Let us prophesy according to the proportion (*analogy*) of faith," and signifies the harmony of the different parts of Scripture. The parts of Scripture must be explained according to the tenor of the whole, not bringing any one part so conspicuously into view as to obscure or contradict others. Thus exaggerated teaching respecting the dignity of the Virgin Mary's relation to our Lord has tended to obscure the doctrines relating to our Lord as the only Mediator. The better to follow the analogy of the faith, one should study the Scriptures with a love of truth for its own sake, and not with the purpose of finding proof for opinions already formed.

An′amim (ăn′ȧ-mĭm), descendants of Mizraim (Gen. 10:13; I Chron. 1:11), and an Egyptian tribe of which nothing is known.

Anam′melech. *See* Gods, False.

A′nan (ā′năn; *a cloud*), one of the chief Israelites that sealed the covenant on the return from Babylon (Neh. 10:26), B. C. 445.

Ana′ni (ȧ-nā′nī; *cloudy*), the last named of the seven sons of Elioenai, a descendant of David, after the captivity (I Chron. 3:24), B. C. about 400.

Anani′ah (ăn-ȧ-nī′ȧ; *protected by Jehovah*).

1. The father of Maaseiah and grandfather of Azariah. The latter repaired a portion of the wall of Jerusalem after the return from exile (Neh. 3:23), B. C. about 445.

2. The name of a town in Benjamin, mentioned as inhabited after the captivity (Neh. 11:32), perhaps Bethany E. of Jerusalem.

Anani′as (ăn-ȧ-nī′ăs; of Heb. *Ananiah, protected by Jehovah*).

1. A member of the early Christian Church at Jerusalem, who, conspiring with his wife, Sapphira, to deceive and defraud the brethren, was overtaken by sudden death, and immediately buried (Acts 5:1, ff.). The members of the Jerusalem Church had a common fund,

which was divided by the apostles among the poor. Those who carried into full effect the principle that "naught of the things which he possessed was his own" sold their lands and houses and laid the price at the apostles' feet. One Joses, surnamed Barnabas, had done this, and, it would seem, had received hearty commendation therefor. Probably incited thereby, and desirous of applause, Ananias, in concert with his wife, Sapphira, sold a possession, and brought the pretended price to the apostle. Either their covetousness or fear of want influenced them to keep back part of the price—an acted lie. Peter was moved by the Spirit to uncover the deceit; and instead of extenuating it because the lie had not been uttered, he passed on all such prevarication the awful sentence, "Thou hast not lied unto men, but unto God." Upon hearing these words Ananias "fell down and gave up the ghost," and was carried out and buried by the young men present. *See* Sapphira. The apparent undue severity of the punishment meted out upon Ananias and Sapphira is to be explained as "a sin unto (physical) death" (I John 5:16). It was an offense which involved being given over to Satan "for the destruction of the flesh, that the spirit may be saved in the day of the Lord Jesus" (I Cor. 5:5). The ushering in of a new era at Pentecost necessitated that offenders against divine dealing in grace might be made a public example, as Nadab and Abihu (Lev. 10:1-10) were made a similar warning when they disregarded God's commands at the beginning of the legal age. Revised by *M. F. U.*

NOTE—"*They had all things common*" (Acts 5:32). By becoming Christians the Jewish converts suffered the loss of all things, unless they had property independent of the will, favor, or patronage of others, and the proportion of these was few. So deep an offense against Jewish prejudices cast them loose from Jewish charities, and involved loss of employment to such as were traders, and dismissal from their employments to such as were workmen and servants, producing a state of destitution which rendered extraordinary exertions necessary on the part of the more prosperous brethren. This is illustrated and proved by what we actually see in operation at this day in Jerusalem. The first Christians did not adopt the fantastical and impracticable theory known in modern times by the name of *communism*, divesting themselves of individual property, and throwing all they had and earned into a common stock. They had a common fund, but that it was not binding upon all to contribute everything thereto is evident from what Peter said to Ananias, that he might have kept the land if he had chosen, or even have used its price after it was sold. The principle universally accepted was, that none should want while any of their brethren had the means of helping them.

2. A devout and honored Christian of Damascus, to whom the Lord appeared in vision and bade him go to a street called Straight and inquire at the house of Judas for Saul of Tarsus. Ananias at first hesitated, because of his knowledge of Saul's former character and conduct. But assured of Saul's conversion and God's purpose concerning him, he consented. He "went his way, and entered into the house; and putting his hands on him said, Brother Saul, the Lord, even Jesus, that appeared unto thee in the way as thou camest, hath sent me, that thou mightest receive thy sight, and be filled with the Holy Ghost. And immediately there fell from his eyes as it

17. Entrance to Straight Street, Damascus.

had been scales;" and, recovering his sight which he had lost when the Lord appeared to him on the way to Damascus, Paul, the new convert, arose, was baptized, and preached Jesus in the synagogues (Acts 9:10-20; 22:12), A. D. 35 or 36. Tradition makes Ananias to have been afterward bishop of Damascus, and to have suffered martyrdom.

3. The high priest before whom Paul was brought previous to being taken to Felix (Acts 23). He was made high priest by Herod, king of Chalcis, who for this purpose removed Joseph, son of Camydus (Josephus, *Ant.*, xx, 1, 3). Being implicated in the quarrels of the Jews and the Samaritans, he with others was sent to Rome to answer for his conduct before Claudius Caesar (Josephus, *Ant.*, xx, 6, 2). The emperor decided in favor of the accused party, and Ananias returned with credit, and remained in office until Agrippa gave it to Ismael (Josephus, *Ant.*, xx, 8, 8). When Paul appeared before Ananias he made the declaration, "I have lived in all good conscience before God until this day." Thereupon the high priest ordered the apostle to be smitten in the face. Paul, indignant at so unprovoked an assault, replied, "God shall smite thee, thou whited wall." Being asked, "Revilest thou God's high priest?" Paul said, "I wist not that he was the high priest," perhaps having overlooked in his warmth the honor due him in his official station. A plot having been formed against Paul, he was sent by Claudius Lysias to Felix, whither he was followed by Ananias (accompanied by the orator Tertullus), who appeared against him. Ananias was deposed shortly before Felix quitted his government, and was finally assassinated (Josephus, *War*, ii, 17, 9), B. C. 67

A'nath (ā'năth; an *answer*, i. e., to prayer).

1. The father of Shamgar, the third of the judges of Israel after the death of Joshua (Judg. 3:31; 5:6). B. C. perhaps 1250.

2. **Anat** (**Anath,** ā'năt), a north Semitic goddess, now well known from the religious epic literature discovered at Ras Shamra (ancient Ugarit) from 1929-1937. Anat was the patroness of sex and war, the paramour of Aliyan Baal. She is to be identified with the "queen of heaven" to whom Jews offered incense in Jeremiah's day (Jer. 44:19). Lewd figurines of the nude goddess have been dug from Palestinian sites at levels dating from the second and first millennia B. C. It was against

the degrading religion of the Canaanites that Moses and Joshua issued such stern warnings to Israel, realizing the utterly debilitating effect of Canaanite cults upon the chaste morality and high spirituality demanded by the worship of Yahweh. Revised by *M. F. U.*

Anathema (Gr. *'anathema,* a *thing laid by*), a votive offering consecrated to a god and hung up in the temple. When used in this general sense, as it often is by classical writers, it is written with a long *ē*, *'anathēma*, Luke 21:5, A. V., "gifts"). The form *'anathema* and its special meaning seem to be peculiar to the Hellenistic dialect, probably from the use made of the word by the Greek Jews. In the Septuagint anathema is generally the translation of the Hebrew word *hĕrĕm,* to *consecrate.* The following are its uses:

1. **Old Testament.** (1) A species of vow (*q. v.*) by which persons and things were irrevocably and irredeemably devoted to the Lord (Lev. 27; Num. 21:2), and in such a way that the persons devoted had to be put to death, while the things fell to the sanctuary or to the priests. But, inasmuch as the deliberate killing of anyone, even a slave, was treated as a punishable offense (Exod. 21:20), it is evident that the pronouncing of the anathema could not be left to the pleasure of any individual, since it might be used for impious purposes. The anathema, being a manifestation of the judicial holiness of God, realizing itself in executing righteous judgment upon men, assumed the character of a theocratic penalty. It could, therefore, be inflicted only by God or by the divinely appointed authorities, acting with a view to the glory of God and the upholding and edifying of his kingdom. (2) It was sometimes a command and not a vow. The only instance in which the anathema is expressly enjoined in the law is the command against those who served other gods (Exod. 22:20), even against whole cities. In such cases the men and cattle were ordered to be put to death by the sword, and the houses with their contents to be burned (Deut. 13:12, sq.). This was carried out, especially in the case of the Canaanites (Deut. 20:17, ff.), but in all its severity against Jericho alone (Josh 6:17, sq.). In the case of the other cities, only that which had life was put to death, the cities themselves being spared (Josh. 10:28, ff.), though often the cattle were spared and with the rest of the spoil divided among the soldiers (Deut. 2:34, ff.; 3:6; Josh. 8:21, ff.; 11:11, ff.). In case anyone retained a part of that which had been anathematized for his own use, he brought upon himself the anathema of death (Josh. 6:18; 7:11, ff.; comp. Deut. 13:17).

2. **Among the later Jews** the ban of the synagogue was the excommunication or exclusion of a Jew (usually for heresy or blasphemy) from the synagogue and the congregation, or from familiar intercourse with other Jews. This modification of the anathema owes its origin to Ezra 10:8, where the *herem* consisted in the anathematizing of the man's whole goods and chattels, and the exclusion of the anathematized individual from the congregation. The later rabbinical writers mention three degrees of *anathema:* (1) *Niddu'i, separation,* a temporary suspension from ecclesiastical privileges, which might be pronounced for twenty-four reasons. It lasted thirty days, and was pronounced without a curse. The person thus anathematized could only enter the temple on the left hand, the usual way of departure; if he died while under anathema there was no mourning for him, and a stone on his coffin denoted that he was separated from his people and deserved stoning. (2) *Herem, curse.* This was pronounced upon the individual who did not repent at the expiration of thirty days, by an assemblage of at least ten persons, and was accompanied with curses. The person so excommunicated was cut off from all social and religious privileges, it being unlawful to eat or drink with him (I Cor. 5:11). The anathema could be removed by three common persons, or one person of dignity. (3) Upon the still impenitent person was inflicted the severer punishment of *shammata', imprecation,* a solemn act of expulsion from the congregation, accompanied with fearful curses, including the giving up of the individual to the judgment of God and to final perdition.

3. **In the New Testament.** From the above we are prepared to find that the *anathema* of the New Testament always implies execration, but do not think that the word was employed in the sense of technical excommunication either from the Jewish or Christian Church. It occurs only five or six times. (*a*) In Acts 23:12 it is recorded that certain Jews "bound themselves under a curse" (literally, anathematized themselves) "that they would neither eat nor drink till they had killed Paul." The probability seems to be that these persons looked upon Paul as unworthy of life, and considered it their religious duty to compass his death. They therefore *anathematized,* i. e., devoted themselves to destruction if they drew back from their purpose. (*b*) When Peter was charged the third time with being a follower of Jesus he began "to *curse* and to swear," etc. (Matt. 26:74, "anathematize." This is thought by some to be a vulgar oath; by others, an imprecation called down upon himself by Peter in case he should be found telling an untruth. (*c*) In Rom. 9:3 Paul writes, "I could wish that myself were accursed (*anathema*) from Christ." We have no means of knowing exactly what the apostle understood by the above expression. From the words "accursed from Christ" we are hardly warranted in believing that he referred to either the Old Testament *anathema* (1) or the ban of the synagogue (2). Nor do they seem to refer to sudden death or a judicial act of the Christian Church. Meyer (*Com., in loc.*) observes, "Paul sees those who belong to the fellowship of his people advancing to ruin through their unbelief; therefore he would fain wish that *he himself* were a curse offering, if by means of this sacrifice of his *own self* he could only save the beloved *brethren.*" Much of the difficulty of understanding this passage would be obviated if we remember that the apostle does not give expression to a decision formally reached, but rather to a sentiment stirred within him by an unutterable sorrow.

He "could wish himself accursed, if the purport of the wish could be realized to the advantage of the Israelites" (Meyer, *Com.*). (*d*) "Let him be anathema" (Gal. 1:8, 9) has the probable meaning of, Let him be execrable and accursed. (*e*) "Calleth Jesus accursed" (anathema, I Cor. 12:3) means, doubtless, the act of any private individual who execrated Christ and accounted him accursed. The thought appears to be that those who speak by the Spirit do not *execrate* Jesus, but *confess Him as Lord*. (*f*) In I Cor. 16:22 we find the expression "Anathema Maran-atha." In this the apostle announces his accord with the will of God, that those who are destitute of love to Jesus should be doomed to final perdition. *Maran-atha* is the Aramaic phrase for *the Lord comes*, and seems to be used in this connection to indicate that the fulfillment of such punishment will be associated with his coming. After "let him be anathema" there should be a full stop.

4. Roman Catholic View. "The Church has used the phrase '*anathema sit*' from the earliest times with reference to those whom she excludes from her communion, either because of moral offenses or because they persist in heresy. In pronouncing anathema against willful heretics the Church does but declare that they are excluded from her communion, and that they must, if they continue obstinate, perish eternally" (*Cath Dict.*).

Anathemata (from '*anatithēmi, to lay up*). In general the term was applied to all kinds of ornaments in churches, these things having been set apart to the service of God. In Luke 21:5 the word is thus used for the gifts and ornaments of the temple. In a stricter sense the word is used to denote memorials of great favors which men had received from God. Very early a custom, still existing, sprang up of anyone receiving a signal cure presenting to the Church what was called his *ectypoma*, or figure of the member cured, in gold or silver. Anathemata is also a term used to designate the coverings of the altar.

An'athoth (ăn'ȧ-thŏth; *answers*, i. e., to prayer).

1. One of the sons of Becher, the son of Benjamin (I Chron. 7:8), B. C.

2. One of the chief Israelites who sealed the covenant after the return from Babylon (Neh. 10:19), B. C. about 445.

3. A town in the tribe of Benjamin, belonging to the priests, also a city of refuge (Josh. 21:18; Jer. 1:1). It is chiefly noted as the birthplace of the prophet Jeremiah, and mostly his residence (Jer. 1:1; 11:21-23; 29:27). It was a walled town of some strength, seated on a broad ridge of hills, overlooking the valley of the Jordan and the northern part of the Dead Sea. It was three miles N. E. of Jerusalem. Modern research identifies the present Anata with Anathoth, distant an hour and a quarter from Jerusalem, containing about one hundred inhabitants. *See* II Sam. 23:27; I Chron. 12:3; Ezra 2:23; Neh. 7:27.

Anchor (Gr. *ankura*). Very naturally the anchor has been in use from the remote ages. In the heroic times of the Greeks large stones called *eunai* were used for anchors. Those used by the Romans were usually of iron, and in shape resembled the modern anchor. The scriptural mention of the use of anchors is in Acts 27:29, 30, 40. From this passage it would seem that anchors were used at both the stern and bow of vessels.

Figurative. In Heb. 6:19 the *anchor* is used metaphorically for a spiritual support in times of trial, in which sense it is still frequently employed. In the early Church it was also used with reference to the persecutions which threatened the ship of the Church. In some cases above the transverse bar of the anchor stands the letter E, probably an abbreviation of *Elpis, hope*. Sometimes the anchor was associated with the *fish*, the symbol of the Saviour, the union of the two symbols expressing "hope in Jesus Christ."

Ancient of Days (Aram. *advanced in days*), an expression applied to Jehovah in a vision of Daniel (7:9, 13, 22). "When Daniel represents the true God as an aged man, he does so not in contrast with the recent gods of the heathen which Antiochus Epiphanes wished to introduce, or specially with reference to new gods; for God is not called the old God, but appears only as an old man, because age inspires veneration and conveys the impression of majesty. This impression is heightened by the robe with which he is covered, and by the appearance of the hair of his head, and also by the flames of fire which are seen to go forth from his throne" (Keil, *Com., in loc.*).

Ancients (Heb. *zāqēn, old*), *aged*, either decrepit or vigorous (Gen. 18:12, 13; 19:31; 24:1, etc.); *elders*, i. e., chief men, magistrats (Isa. 3:14; 24:23; Jer. 19:1; Ezek. 7:26; 8:11, 12, etc.). *See* Elders.

An'drew. 1. Name and Family. (Gr. '*Andreas, manly.*) A native of the city of Bethsaida in Galilee (John 1:44), the son of Jonas (John 21:15) and brother of Simon Peter (Matt. 4:18; 10:2; John 1:40).

2. Personal History. (1) Receives Christ. At first a disciple of John Baptist, Andrew was led to receive Jesus by John pointing him out as "the lamb of God" (John 1:36-40). He then brought his brother Simon to the Master, telling him that he had "found the Messiah" (v. 41). They both returned to their occupation as fishermen on the Sea of Galilee, and there remained until, after John Baptist's imprisonment, they were called by Jesus to follow him (Matt. 4:18, ff.; Mark 1:14-18). (2) **As apostle.** The further mention of him in the gospels is his being ordained as one of the twelve (Matt. 10:2; Mark 3:18; Luke 6:14); his calling the attention of our Lord to the lad with the loaves and fishes at the feeding of the five thousand (John 6:8); his introducing to Jesus certain Greeks who desired to see him (John 12:20-22); and his asking, along with his brother Simon and the two sons of Zebedee, for a further explanation of what the Master had said in reference to the destruction of the temple (Mark 13:3). He was one of those who, after the ascension, continued at Jerusalem in the "upper room" (Acts 1:13). Scripture relates nothing of him beyond these scattered notices. (3) **Traditions.** The traditions about him are various. Eusebius makes him preach in Scythia; Jerome and Theodoret in Achaia (Greece); Nicephorus in Asia Minor and Thrace. It is supposed that he founded a church in Constantinople, and ordained *Stachys* (*q. v.*), named by Paul (Rom. 16:9), as its first bishop. At length, the tradition states, he came to Patrae, a city of Achaia, where Aegeas, the proconsul, enraged at his persisting to preach, commanded him to join in sacrificing to the heathen gods, and upon the apostle's refusal he ordered him to be severely scourged and then crucified. To make his death more lingering, he was fastened to the cross, not with nails, but with cords. Having hung two days, praising God, and exhorting the spectators to embrace, or adhere to, the faith, he is said to have expired on November 30, but in what year is uncertain. The cross is stated to have been of the form called *Crux decussata*, and commonly known as "St. Andrew's cross, **X**." Some ancient writers speak of an apocryphal Acts of Andrew.

Androni'cus (ăn-drŏ-nī'kŭs; *man-conquering*), a Jewish Christian, kinsman and fellow-prisoner of Paul. He was converted before Paul, and was of note among the apostles (Rom. 16:7), A. D. 60. According to Hippolytus, he became bishop of Pannonia; according to Dorotheus, of Spain.

A'nem (ā'nĕm; *two fountains*), a Levitical city in Issachar, assigned to the Gershomites (I Chron. 6:73). It is called En-gannim (Josh. 19:21; 21:29).

A'ner (ā'nẽr).

1. A Canaanitish chief near Hebron who, with Eschol and Mamre, was confederate with Abraham. He joined in pursuit of Chedorlaomer and shared in the spoil, not following the example of Abraham (Gen. 14:13, 24), B. C. about 2060.

2. A Levitical city assigned to the Kohathites, and situated in Manasseh, W. of the Jordan (I Chron. 6:70). It is called Tanach (Josh. 21:25).

An'ethotite (ăn'ĕ-thŏ-tīt), or **Anetothite**, less correct forms of Anglicizing the word *Anathothite*. *See* Anathoth.

Angel (Heb. *măl'äk;* Gr. *'angelos*, both meaning *messenger*). In some cases the word is applied to human beings (Isa. 43:19; Mal. 2:7; Rev. 1:20), or even figuratively to impersonal agents (Exod. 14:19; II Sam. 24:16, 17; Psa. 104:4). The connection must determine its force. In its most common use in Scripture the word nevertheless designates certain spiritual and superhuman beings, who are there introduced to us as messengers of God. There are but few books of the Bible—such as Ruth, Nehemiah, Esther, the epistles of John and James—that make no mention of angels.

With respect to their existence and nature, we find the Scriptures presenting the same progress and development as with many other subjects of revelation. Thus it is that the doctrine of angels becomes more distinct in the later periods of Jewish history, and is more full and significant in the New Testament writings. Angels appear most frequently and conspicuously in connection with the coming and ministry of our Lord. His words concerning the angels are of unmistakable meaning and value. According to his teaching they are personal, sinless, immortal beings, existing in great number, and in close relation not only with individual men, but also with the

history of God's kingdom (Matt. 13:39; 18:10; 22:30; 25:31; 26:53; Luke 15:10; 16:22).

There is harmony between the teachings of our Lord upon this subject and those of the apostles and of the Scripture writers generally. Many questions that may be raised can receive no answer whatever from the Scriptures. Of the history of the angels we can know but little. It is clear Satan and the fallen angels (demons) were created sinless, and later fell (Isa. 14:12-14; Rev. 12:3, 4). Some of their number "kept not their first estate," but fell under divine displeasure, and are reserved "unto the judgment of the great day" (Jude 6).

Aside from the teachings of Scripture there is nothing irrational, but quite the opposite, in believing in the existence of creatures superior to man in intelligence, as there are many inferior. But we depend wholly upon the Scriptures for our knowledge. The denial of the existence of Angels, as that of a personal Devil and demons, springs from the materialistic, unbelieving spirit, which in its most terrible form denies the existence of God.

The revelations of Scripture concerning angels, while they possess a subordinate place, nevertheless have a real value.

1. They furnish a necessary safeguard against narrowness of thought as to the extent and variety of the creations of God.

2. They help us in acquiring the proper conception of Christ, who is above the angels, and the object of angelic worship.

3. They give a wonderfull attractiveness to our conception of that unseen world to which we are hastening.

4. They set before us an example of joyous and perfect fulfillment of God's will. "Thy will be done in earth as it is in heaven," i. e., by the angels.

5. They put to shame the horrible indifference of multitudes of mankind with respect to the great work of conversion. "There is joy among the angels over one sinner that repenteth."

6. They broaden our view of the manifold mercies of God, whose angels are "sent forth to minister for them who shall be heirs of salvation" (Heb. 1:14; comp. 12:22).

7. They remind us of our high rank as human beings, and our exalted destiny as Christians. We, who are "made but little lower than the angels" may become as the angels of God in heaven (Psa. 8:5, R. V., "lower than God;" Matt. 22:30).

Angelic Hymn, the hymn *Gloria in excelsis*, so called because the former part of it was sung by the angels when announcing the birth of Jesus (Luke 2:14). In several oriental liturgies it is used in the earlier part of the service. Before the time of Edward VI it was sung before the collect, epistle, and gospel, but was afterward transferred to the closing part of the office, as a song of thanksgiving after communion.

Angelic Salutation, the greeting extended to the Virgin Mary by the angel when he announced to her that she was to become the mother of Jesus (Luke 1:28). *See* Ave Maria.

Anger, the emotion of instant displeasure, indignation, arising from the feeling of injury done or intended, or from the discovery of offense against law.

The anger attributed to God in the New Testament is that in God which stands opposed to man's disobedience, obstinacy (especially in resisting the Gospel), and sin, and manifests itself in punishing the same.

Anger is not evil *per se*, being, as love, an original susceptibility of our nature. If anger were in itself sinful, how could God himself be angry? Paul commands the Ephesians (Eph. 4:26) that when angry they are not to sin. "Paul does not forbid the being angry in itself, and could not forbid it, because there is a *holy* anger, which is the 'spur to virtue,' as there is also a *divine* anger; . . . but the being angry is to be *without* sin" (Meyer, *Com., in loc.*).

Anger is sinful when it rises too soon, without reflection; when the injury which awakens it is only apparent; when it is disproportionate to the offense; when it is transferred from the guilty to the innocent; when it is too long protracted and becomes revengeful (Matt. 5:22; Eph. 4:26; Col. 3:8).

Angle (Isa. 19:8; Hab. 1:15), mediaeval English for "hook" (Job. 41:1).

Ani'am (à-nī'ăm; *sighing of the people*), the last named of the sons of Shemidah, of the tribe of Manasseh (I Chron. 7:19).

A'nim (ä'nĭm; *fountains*), a city in the mountains of Judah (Josh. 15:50), ten miles S. W. of Hebron, and probably the same as the present *Khirbet Ghuwein.*

Animal, an organized living body, endowed with sensation. In the Hebrew there are several terms rendered "creature," "living thing," "cattle," etc. The animals are in Lev. 11 divided into four classes: (1) Larger terrestrial animals (v. 2); (2) aquatic animals (vers. 9, 10); (3) birds (v. 13); (4) smaller animals (vers. 20, 29, 41, ff.); and these classes were again distinguished into clean, i. e., eatable, and into unclean, whose flesh was not to be eaten (comp. Lev. 11 and Deut. 14:1-20). The larger terrestrial animals were, moreover, in the Old Testament separated into cattle, i. e., tame domestic animals, and into beasts of the field or wild beasts.

Clean and Unclean. The distinction between clean and unclean animals goes back to the time of primeval man (Gen. 7:2; 8:20), but it did not originate in a dualistic view of creation. According to Bible teaching all the creatures of the earth were created good and pure, as creations of the holy God (Gen. 1:31). Impurity entered into creation through man's fall; and the irrational creature, although not affected by sin, suffered under its consequences. From the lists (Lev. 11:1-31, 46; Deut. 14:1-19), the clean animals (i. e., such as could be eaten) were ruminant quadrupeds, which parted the hoof, were cloven-footed, and chewed the cud; aquatic animals with fins and scales; all birds except the nineteen species named; flying insects, having two long legs for leaping, as the grasshopper.

For Sacrifice. Sacrifices were of (*a*) the beeve kind, a cow, bull, or calf; the ox, having been mutilated, could not have been offered

(Lev. 22:24); (*b*) the goat kind—a he-goat, a she-goat, or a kid; (*c*) the sheep kind—an ewe, ram, or lamb. *See* Sacrifice.

These regulations would seem to have been abrogated by our Lord, when he taught that inward purity was the great essential (Matt. 15:11, 17-20). In the vision Peter was taught the essential cleanliness of all God's creatures (Acts 10: 11:16).

Paul speaks decidedly upon this point (Rom. 14; Col. 2:16; Tit. 1:15), and yet the apostolic council at Jerusalem placed "things strangled," and "blood," along with "pollutions of idols and fornication," on the list of things prohibited (Acts 15:20).

ANIMAL KINGDOM

The proportion of animals mentioned in the Bible compared with the total number found in Bible lands is far larger than that which obtains in the case of plants. There are 38 mammals, out of perhaps 130, 34 birds out of about 350, 11 reptiles out of nearly 100, and one amphibian out of a considerable number indigenous in these lands. It is a notable fact that not a single species of fish is mentioned by name. Of insects there are sixteen, out of a number not as yet satisfactorily settled. Scorpions and spiders are mentioned generically. The number of species is considerable. Four only of the large number of mollusks and only one of the worms are specifically named. Coral and sponge are the generic representations of their respective orders. Few even of the mammals, except the domestic animals, are specific. Most of them are generic or family names, to which is often appended, "after his kind." Some, as the *chamois, mole, unicorn*, are mistranslations; others, as the *dragon* and *satyr*, are mythical.

Adder. *See* Serpent.

Ant. There are large numbers of species of ants in the East, and innumerable hosts of them make their nests beside the thrashing floors, and wherever their favorite food is found. In every country in the world the ant is proverbial for *industry*, so there has never been any controversy with regard to the passage in Prov. 6:6, "Go to the ant, thou sluggard." The habits of the ants of cool climates and of those of the tropical and semitropical countries differ so much that considerable controversy has arisen as to the *wisdom* and *foresight* of this insect. Prov. 30:25: "The ants are a people not strong, yet they prepare their meat in the summer." There are, however, certain facts in regard to the ants of the Holy Land which settle this controversy in favor of the rigid accuracy of the author of the Proverbs. They are: (1) The ants of these countries lay up vast stores of grain in their nests. (2) To facilitate this act of providence they place their nests as near as possible to the places where grain is thrashed or stored. (3) They certainly eat this grain during the winter season. (4) They encourage certain insects which secrete sweet juices to consort with them, and collect and store their eggs with their own, that they may have them at hand for future use when they shall have hatched.

In regard to their wisdom, we have abundant evidence of it in their social and military organization, the fact that they take and train slaves, and that they have elaborately constructed nests, with overground and underground roads, and, in some cases, practice a sort of agriculture.

Antelope, an animal referred to in Heb. as *te'ō* in Deut. 14:5 and Isa. 51:20 (both R. V.). In the Greek versions and the Vulgate the word is translated generally oryx (*Antilope leucoryx*). This animal is characterized by long slender cone-shaped horns, and is white with a conspicuous tuft of black hair under its throat. Its habitat is Upper Egypt, Arabia and Syria. The Targums, however, rendered the Hebrew word "wild ox" (so also the R. V.), but probably had in mind the bubale (*Antilope bubalis*) of Arabia and Egypt, classified by Arabs with wild oxen. *M. F. U.*

Apes (Heb. *qōph, monkey*). We have no hint as to the kinds of apes which were brought by the merchant navies of Solomon and Hiram, but it is probable that they were very numerous, as they continue to be to the present day on all the ships coming from the East Indies through the Suez Canal. They are distributed in this way in considerable numbers throughout all the countries bordering on the Mediterranean, though not indigenous in any except the Barbary States and Gibraltar. The Hebrew word *qōph*, derived from Sanskrit *kapi* is rendered ape and probably includes apes which are tailless and monkeys which possess tails. If they came from India, they were a species of tailed monkey, common there and worshipped.

Arrowsnake. *See* Serpent.

Asp. *See* Serpent.

18. Tomb Painting of Semite with His Donkey

Ass (Heb. *hămōr*, the *male ass; 'āthōn, she ass*; Gr. *onos, donkey; hupozugion, under the yoke*). The ass is one of the earliest and most frequently mentioned animals alluded to in the Bible. Asses are spoken of in connection with the history of Pharaoh (Gen. 12:16), Abraham (Gen. 22:3), Jacob (Gen. 32:5), Moses (Exod. 4:20), Balaam (Num. 22:21-33), and in fact most of the notable persons mentioned in the Old Testament. There was nothing in any sense degrading in the idea of riding on an ass, as might perhaps be inferred from Zech. 9:9 (comp. Matt. 21:7). It was the sign of the peaceful mission of Christ. Kings, high priests, judges, and the richest people of ancient and modern times, have ridden on an ass. Many of the asses of Damascus, Bagdad, Aleppo,

Cairo, Cyprus, and other parts of the East are beautiful animals, very easy in gait, and perfectly surefooted. They often cost very high prices, and are adorned with magnificent caparisons.

They have also been used from the remotest antiquity as beasts of burden. Special breeds of them are raised for this purpose. Some of them are very small and cheap, while others are but little smaller than a mule, and carry burdens of greater weight in proportion to their size than any other animal. The pack saddle differs according to the use to which it is put. The familiar crosstree is employed for firewood. Abraham doubtless loaded the wood for the sacrifice in this way (Gen. 22:3). When sheaves of grain are to be loaded a kind of cradle is suspended to this or to the flat saddle. This latter, called in Arabic a *jelâl*, is composed of an under layer of thick felt and an upper of strong haircloth, with a padding between, about six inches in thickness, of straw or sedges. This saddle is flat on top and bent down over each side of the animal, so as to protect his ribs from the pressure of the load. Over such a saddle as this sacks of grain or cut straw are thrown and tied fast by a rope passing under the breast. The sons of Jacob probably used this sort (Gen. 42:26, 27). If sand is to be carried, small panniers are slung over the saddle, and hang down on either side without touching the body. If bread or other provisions, not liable to be injured by pressure, are taken larger panniers are used. In such Jesse and Abigail may have sent their presents (I Sam. 16:20; 25:18). If fruit is to be carried two boxes are slung in similar manner. Children are often carried in this way in larger boxes. Probably Moses's wife sat on a *jelâl*, with her children in boxes on either side of her, when going down to Egypt (Exod. 4:20). Sacks of grain or straw are often slung across the bare back of an ass.

Asses were also used for plowing (Isa. 30:24; 32:20).

It was not allowed to the Israelites to yoke an ox and an ass together (Deut. 22:10). They were not allowed to eat its flesh, yet in the stress of hunger during the siege of Samaria they violated this law (II Kings 6:25).

The *she ass* is the one intended in a number of places not indicated in our translations (Num. 22:21-33; I Sam. 9:3; II Kings 4:22, 24). David had an officer to take care of his she asses (I Chron. 27:30).

Ass colts (Gen. 49:11) are also called *foals* (Gen. 32:15), *young ass* (Isa. 30:6), and *colt* (Job. 11:12). They are all translated from the same Hebrew word, *'ayir*.

Wild asses are frequently mentioned, two Hebrew words (*pĕrĕ', running* wild; *'rōd, lonesome*) being so translated. Both are found together in one parallelism (Job. 39:5), but rendered by the single expression *wild ass*. We have no means of knowing whether they refer to the same or different species. The wild ass is found in the deserts nearest to Palestine.

Badger (Heb. *tăhăsh*). Although the badger is found throughout the Holy Land, its skin is not suited to the outer covering of the tabernacle (Exod. 25:5, etc.) and for sandals (Ezek. 16:10). On the other hand, the Heb. *tăḥash* would seem to be from the cognate Arabic word *tuhas*, which comprehends seals and especially denotes the dugong (*Halicore hemprichii*). This marine animal is nearest allied to mammals of the whale order. It is commonly about 11 feet long, with round head, a fish-like tail, and breasts for suckling young. It reminds one of the fabled mermaid, if indeed it did not give rise to this concept. It abounds on the coral banks of the Red Sea and in tropical waters in general. M. F. U.

Bald Locust. *See* Locust.

Bat (Heb. *'ătălēph*). The Hebrew idea of a bat was "a fowl that creeps, going upon all fours." It was unclean (Lev. 11:19). It is in reality a mammal, and its wings are membranous and destitute of feathers, so that it is in reality not a bird at all. It lives in caverns, tombs, or ruins (Isa. 2:19-21). The bat is a voracious destroyer of fruit, making it necessary for those who try to raise it in the neighborhood of cities to cover the clusters, or even the whole tree, with a net. There are about fifteen species of bats in the Holy Land.

Bear. The bear is now a somewhat rare animal in Syria, being confined to the higher regions of Lebanon, Antilebanon, and Amanus, and found very sparingly in the wilder portions of Bashan, Gilead, and Moab. It is rarely or never seen now in western Palestine. It is known in science as *Ursus Syriacus*, Ehr., and differs from the brown bear of Europe by its grayish fur. It was once abundant in Palestine (I Sam. 17:36; II Kings 2:24). The Scripture alludes to the cunning of the bear (Lam. 3:10), to the ferocity of the she bear robbed of her whelps (II Sam. 17:8; Prov. 17:12; Hos. 13:8), to the danger of the bear to man (I Sam. 17:34, 36; Amos 5:19). The bear feeds principally on roots, fruits, and other vegetable products, but does not fail to avail itself of the chance to devour any animal which may come in its way. Hence the significance of the picture of the peaceful reign of Christ (Isa. 11:7).

Beast. 1. A mammal, not man, as distinguished from creeping things and fowl of the heavens (Gen. 1:29, 30). Wild beasts in Scripture are differentiated from domesticated animals (Lev. 26:22; Isa. 13:21, 22; Jer. 50:39; Mark 1:13). 2. Any of the inferior animals, including birds and reptiles, as differentiated from human beings (Psa. 147:9; Eccl. 3:19; Acts 28:5). 3. Figuratively, a fierce destructive political power, for example, the four successive world powers—Babylon, Media-Persia, Greece and Rome of Daniel 7:1-7. In Revelation 13:1-10 the composite beast represents the final Antichrist, while a Beast with lamb's horns portrays the False Prophet of the end-time (Rev. 13:11-18). Unregenerate man's (i. e. Gentile) civilization and government in its *outward* manifestation is brilliant and dazzling (cf. the shining metallic colossus of Dan. 2:31-45), but internally it is evil and cruel, like so many wild beasts (Dan. 7:1-7). M. F. U.

Bees. In the Holy Land, while bees occasionally make their hives in trees, as in other countries (I Sam. 14:25, 26), they generally resort to clefts in the rocks, usually almost inaccessible to man. There are several allusions to the rocky homes of the bees (Deut. 32:13; Psa. 81:16). They are especially abundant in the wilderness of Judea (Matt. 3:4). They resent with great fury any interference by man with their retreats (Deut. 1:44; Psa. 118:12).

The numbers of wild bees at present in Palestine would not justify the expression "a land flowing with milk and honey." It is, however, probable that they were far more numerous at the time the Israelites entered Canaan. But the number of domesticated bees in the country is enormous, and, added to the wild ones, fully justifies the hyperbole. Among the peasant population they are in almost every house.

Honey is used not only in its separate state, but fruit is preserved in it, and it is used as a sauce for a variety of confections and pastries. It was a standard article of commerce (Ezek. 27:17). Stores of it were collected at Mizpah (Jer. 41:8). It was not allowed to be used in burnt offerings (Lev. 2:11). The honey in the carcass of the lion (Judg. 14:8) is best explained by the rapidity with which a carcass is denuded by wild beasts and ants in this hot climate and then dried in the blazing sun.

According to the author of Proverbs (24:13), it is good to eat honey, but (25:16, 27) not to indulge to surfeit. Other references to honey convey sundry moral lessons (Ezek. 3:3; Psa. 19:10; Prov. 16:24).

Beetle, an insect of the grasshopper kind (Lev. 11:22). *See* Cricket.

Beeves. *See* Cattle, Ox.

Behemoth (bĕ-hē'mŏth; *colossal beast*), the plural of the Hebrew word for beast, used (Job. 40:15-24) of the hippopotamus, *the beast,* only excelled by *leviathan,* with the description of which ends the climax begun in ch. 38, and carried upward until it finds its acme in the "king over all the children of pride" (41:34). The hippopotamus is a pachyderm, the largest except the elephant and the rhinoceros, amphibious in habits, living on vegetable food, and corresponding well with the description in the above passage. It is found in the upper Nile, and was common in the lower in ancient times. It may have been found in the Jordan (40:23), although poetic license would make it quite possible that the mention of that river should have reference only to its aquatic habits and its courage, and not to its geographical range. Indeed, "the river" of the first member of the parallelism can only mean the Nile, and the mention of the Jordan in the second would seem to be simply to strengthen the hyperbole.

Bird. *See* Fowl.

Bittern. *See* Porcupine.

Boar. *See* Swine.

Bull, Bullock. *See* Ox.

Calf. *See* Ox.

Camel (Heb. *gämäl*; Gr. *kamēlos*), one of the most useful of the domestic animals of the East. With the exception of the elephant it is the largest animal used by man. It is often eight feet or more in height, and possessed of great strength and endurance. It has a broad foot, which enables it to walk over sandy wastes without sinking deeply beneath the surface. It has a provision in its stomach for storing water enough to enable it to travel for days together without drinking. It is capable of subsisting on the coarsest and bitterest of herbage, and can take into its horny mouth the most obdurate thorns, which it grinds up with its powerful teeth and digests with its ostrich-like stomach. To offset its great height it is formed to kneel, so that it can be loaded as easily as an ass, and then rise with its burden of five hundred pounds and plod on through the hottest day, and the most inhospitable waste of the deserts, in which it finds its congenial home. The hump on its back is not only a help to retaining its pack saddle, but a storehouse of fat, in reserve against its long fasts. The flesh, although forbidden to the Israelites, is eaten by the Arabs, and sold in the markets of all oriental cities. Its skin is used in making sandals, and its hair in the weaving of the coarse cloth of which their tents and outer garments are made. Its milk, and the products made from it, are a prime element in the diet list of the Bedouin.

The allusions to the camel in the Scripture are so numerous that it is unnecessary to point them out.

Domestication. Archaeological discoveries show the effective domestication of the camel at least as early as 1200-1000 B. C., so that swarms of camel-riding Midianites in Gideon's time (c. 1155-1148 B. C.) as recounted in Judges 6, 7 and later the wealthy camel-caravan of Solomon's royal visitor, the Queen of Sheba (I Kings 10:1, 2), about 950 B. C., offer no difficulties historically. Apparently the earliest yet-known art depiction of a Near-Eastern camel (one-humped) is a late Hurrian work from Tell Halaf, now in the Walters Art Gallery of Baltimore, dating about 1,000 B. C. However, references to domesticated camels in Abraham's time (c. 2000 B. C.) have been set aside by such writers as T. E. Peet, *Egypt and the Old Testament* (1924) p. 60 and R. Pfeiffer, *Intr. to the Old Testament* (1941), p. 154, and others. This however, is presumptuous in the light of such evidence as camel statuettes, bones and other references which appear in archaeological materials beginning about 3,000 B. C. (cf. J. P. Free, "Abraham's Camels" in *Journal of Near Eastern Studies*, July 1944, pp. 187-193). Since wild camels were known from earliest times, there is no credible reason why such an indispensable animal in desert and semi-arid lands should not have been sporadically domesticated in patriarchal times and even earlier. Large scale domestication, however, after the 12th century B. C. greatly expanded desert trade as a result of the great advantages of camel nomadism over ass nomadism, enabling camel traders to travel much greater distances on the animal specially adapted to desert conditions. Revised by *M. F. U.*

Figurative. In the two passages (Matt. 19:24; 23:24) the size of the camel is made the basis of comparison. There is not a particle of evidence in favor of the statement that the needle's eye, in the former passage, refers to the smaller gate cut through the panel of the city gates of the East, or that such a gate is, or ever was, called a needle's eye. The whole force of the comparison in both passages is found in the hyperbole. Moreover, no camel could ever be forced through one of these small gates.

Cankerworm, probably a stage in the development of the *Locust* (*q. v.*).

Cat. The cat is nowhere alluded to in the Bible, excepting in the Apocrypha (Epistle of Jer. 21). It is not mentioned in classical authors, except when treating of Egyptian history. This seems the stranger as there are two species of wild cats in Palestine, and the domestic cat is exceedingly common now all through the East.

Caterpillar. *See* Locust.

Cattle (the rendering of several Hebrew and Greek words) were of prime importance to the Hebrews. Their first employment was the care of flocks and herds. On their arrival in Egypt they were assigned to the land of Goshen, on account of its pastoral facilities. They then became herdsmen and shepherds to Pharaoh. One of the words, *mikneh*, translated *cattle*, signifies *possessions*. In includes horned cattle, horses, asses, sheep, and goats. The specific word for animals of the bovine species, and for sheep and goats, are also occasionally rendered cattle. Also *behêmâh*, which means, primarily, *beast* in general.

Chameleon (Heb. *kŏăḥ*). There is no possibility of determining with certainty the animal intended by this Hebrew word in the list of creeping things (Lev. 11:30). It was probably a lizard, and more likely to have been the *Nile monitor* than the *chameleon*. The R. V. renders it *land crocodile*. The Nile monitor attains a length of five to six feet, and the chamelon four to five. On the authority of the LXX. and the Vulgate the A. V. has rendered it *chameleon*.

On the other hand the R. V. has rendered *tin-shemeth*, at the end of the verse, by *chameleon*, instead of *mole* of the A. V. This is based on the fact that *tinshemeth* is derived from a root signifying *to breathe*, and that the ancients believed that the chameleon *lived on air*. This somewhat fanciful idea is hardly probable enough to do away with the authority of the LXX. and the Vulgate, which render the word *mole*. The reference, however, is not to the true mole, but to the *mole rat*, *Spalax typhlus*, which is abundant in Bible lands. If the above views be correct, chameleon should be dropped from the biblical fauna.

Chamois (Heb. *zĕmĕr*). The chamois of Europe is not found in the Holy Land. The animal referred to by this name (Deut. 14:5) was certainly not one of the domestic animals. It was also certainly known to them by its Hebrew name *zĕmĕr*, and within the reach of the Israelites, as it was spoken of as an animal that they might eat. No animal satisfies the probabilities of the case so well as the *mountain sheep* of Egypt and Arabia, known as the *aoudad* and the *kebsh*. It is probable that it was abundant in Sinai, where it is to be found even now. It is distinguished from the other animals of its group by the long hair on its throat and breast, extending like a ruffle to its foreknee.

Its horns resemble those of the *beden*, or *mountain goat*.

Chicken. See Cock.

Cock. The only mention of domestic fowls in the Old Testament is in connection with the daily provision for Solomon's table (I Kings 4:23). The Hebrew word *bărbūr*, has been rendered *swans geese, guinea fowls, capons*, and *fatted fish*, as well as the *fatted fowl* of the A. V. and the R. V. However, the delicacy referred to is the lark-heeled cuckoo (*Centropus aegyptius Shelley*) a dainty morsel even to the present day in Italy and Greece.

In the New Testament the *cock crowing* is mentioned as a measure of time in connection with Peter's denial of Christ (Matt. 26:34, 74; Mark 14:30; Luke 22:34; John 18:27). Cocks are not regular in their times of crowing, sometimes crowing twice (Mark 13:35), and at other times irregularly through the night or before the dawn.

The *hen* is alluded to but once in the Scripture (Luke 13:34).

Cockatrice. See Serpent.

Colt. See Ass, Horse.

Coney (Heb. *shăphăn*), a small pachydermatous animal, with a dentition and feet resembling those of the hippopotamus. It is as large as a rabbit, but is not to be confused with the coney of England, which is a rabbit. It is the common rock badger, common in Sinai, around the Dead Sea area and in N. Palestine. It has a plump body and very short ears and tail. Its scientific name is *Hyrax Syriacus*. It does not really chew the cud, but has a motion of the jaws which resembles that function. Had it divided the hoof it would undoubtedly have been admitted into the list of animals allowed to the Hebrews for food (Lev. 11:5; Deut. 14:7).

The coney lives in holes and clefts of the rocks (Psa. 104:18) Prov. 30:24, 26). It is found throughout the whole length of Sinai, Palestine, and Lebanon.

Coral (Heb. *ră'măh*, high in value). It is uncertain what substance is intended by the word *rămôth*, rendered *coral* by both the A. V. and the R. V. As coral, however, is a precious commodity, and highly suitable for the requirements of the only two passages in which the word occurs, we may rest contented with this translation (Job. 28:18; Ezek. 27:16). This substance is the skeleton of microscopic zoophytes. It is of a great variety of colors, shapes, and consistency. The most valuable is the red. Many of the branches of coral are extremely beautiful. The Red Sea was probably named so on account of the red coral growing in its waters. The best coral is brought from Persia and the Red Sea, but a very good quality is also found in the Mediterranean. Fine specimens of the best colors may bring fifty dollars the ounce. Coral was much valued among the ancients and the Arabs for making beads and other ornaments.

Cormorant. In the list of unclean birds (Lev. 11:17; Deut. 14:17) the word *cormorant* is probably the correct rendering of the Heb. *shălăk*. It is abundant in the Holy Land. It is a large black bird, living by fishing. Its scientific name is *Phalacrocorax carbo*. In all other places in the A. V. where *cormorant* is used

pelican should be substituted for it, as the true rendering of the original, *gă'răth, vomiting*. See Pelican.

Cow. See Ox.

Crane. The word occurs only twice in the Bible (Isa. 38:14; Jer. 8:7), and in both places should be rendered *twittering*, or *twitterer*, as applied to the swallow or some similar bird. Notwithstanding the opinion of the A. V. and the R. V., we think that the crane ought to be dropped from the list of biblical birds.

Cricket, the rendering of the R. V. and R. S. V. of the Hebrew word *hărgōl* in Lev. 11:22. This is the corrected translation of "beetle" of the A. V. The creature referred to belongs with the locust and the grasshopper, since it is winged and leaps rather than creeps. The chief leaping insects belong to 3 families of *Orthoptera* (the grasshoppers, the locusts, and the crickets). The *hărgōl* undoubtedly belongs to one of the 3, though to which now cannot be determined. The A. V. rendering of *hărgōl* by "beetle," does not take into account that the most typical species of the *Coleoptera* (beetle order) do not leap. *M. F. U.*

Crocodile (marg. Job. 41:1), a well-known saurian, found in ancient times in lower as well as upper Egypt, but now confined to the upper waters of the Nile. It was probably abundant in the Kishon in Bible days. It is said to be still found there. It is the creature intended by "dragon" (Ezek. 29:3) and "whale" (32:2; comp. Jer. 14:6, R. V., marg.). See Leviathan.

Cuckow, a mistranslation of a Hebrew word, *shăhăf*, which is probably generic for bird of the sea gull family. The word occurs only twice (Lev. 11:16; Deut. 14:15, R. V., "seamew"). See Seamew.

Doe (R. V., Prov. 5:19, for *roe*, A. V.) is the female of the *wild goat*. See Goat, Wild.

Dog (Heb. *kĕlĕb*, Gr. *kuōn*, dog). The dog referred to in the Scriptures is invariably the unclean animal, so familiar in the streets of all oriental cities. He is a cowardly, lazy despised creature. He eats garbage, dead animals (Exod. 22:31), human flesh (I Kings 14:11), blood (I Kings 22:38). He is the lowest type of vileness (Eccles. 9:4; II Sam. 3:8; Isa. 66:3). Dogs wander through the streets (Psa. 59:6, 14). With all their cowardice they are treacherous and violent (Psa. 22:16, 20). The only good thing said of them is that they watch the flocks (Job. 30:1; Isa. 56:10). Christ compares the Gentiles to them (Matt. 15:26). Those who are shut out of heaven are called dogs (Rev. 22:15). The price of a dog (Deut. 23:18) probably refers to sodomy. The return of a fool to his folly is compared to one of the most disgusting of the many filthy habits of the dog (Prov. 26:11; II Pet. 2:22).

Doleful Creatures (Heb. *'ŏăh*, a *howler*; Isa. 13:21; A. V., marg., "Ochim") refer to birds or beasts which emit shrieks or howlings or ominous sounds, such as the booming of owls, the wailing cry of jackals, and the dismal howling of wolves. The point of the allusion is the fact that such creatures resort to ruins and deserted dwellings, and indicate the desolation which has overtaken them.

Dove. (Heb. *yōnäh;* Gr. *peristerá*). Four species of wild pigeons are found in Bible lands, the *ring dove*, or *wood pigeon*, the *stock dove*, the *rock dove*, and the *ash-rumped rock dove*. They are all known by the name of *hamâm* in Arabic. They make their nests in the clefts and holes of the rocks (Cant. 2:14; Jer. 48:28; Ezek. 7:16). They also nest in trees. They are unresisting (Matt. 10:16), and therefore suitable for sacrifice (Gen. 15:9; Lev. 12:6-8; Luke 2:24; Mark 11:15; John 2:14-16). They are timid (Hos. 11:11); they fly to great distances in their migrations (Psa. 55:6-8); they are gentle (Cant. 1:15; 4:1, etc.). Therefore a dove was the form in which the Holy Spirit descended on Jesus Christ (Matt. 3:16, etc.). *See* Turtledove. Wild doves are very numerous in some parts of the Holy Land. There are also vast numbers of tame pigeons in all the cities and villages. They have been kept from the earliest times. Being acceptable for sacrifices, they were also clean, and used as food.

Dove's Dung. Several theories have been formulated to explain the difficulty in regard to this material as an article of food (II Kings 6:25): (1) That it was a kind of plant. No plant with this name has been discovered, however, and it is unlikely that any plant would have been found in any quantity in a place in the last extremity of famine. (2) That it was in reality dung, but used as a fertilizer, to promote the quick growth of vegetables for food. This is fanciful, and not supported by the context. (3) That the people, in the depth of their despair and starvation, actually ate this disgusting material. This seems the most probable view, and is supported by the fact that a similar occurrence took place in the English army in 1316.

Dragon (Heb. *tănnîn*). This word is used in the A. V. with several meanings: (1) In connection with desert animals (Isa. 13:22; 34:13, 14, etc.), it is best translated by *wolf*, and not by *jackal*, as in R. V. The feminine form of the Heb. *tănnäh*, is found in Mal. 1:3. (2) *Sea monsters* (Psa. 74:13; 148:7; Isa. 27:1). (3) *Serpents*, even of the smaller sorts (Deut. 32:33; Psa. 91:13). (4) The *crocodile* (Ezek 29:3; 32:2, marg.). (5) In the New Testament (Rev. 12:3, et seq.) it refers to a *mythical monster*, which is variously described and figured in the legends of all nations. This mythical monster is used as a lively figure of Satan (*q. v.*). One of the Hebrew words, usually rendered dragon, is in some places translated *serpents* (Exod. 7:9, 10, 12).

Dromedary (Heb. *rěkěsh*, *swift beast*; *rămmäk*, a brood *mare*). Besides the references to the dromedary in the A. V. (Isa. 60:6; Jer. 2:23) where the word should be rendered *young camel* (Heb. *běqěr*), it is also mentioned in I Kings 4:28 and Esth. 8:10; in the first being an erroneous rendering of a Hebrew word signifying *"swift beasts,"* as in margin, and in the second another word signifying *"mares."* There is no clear and undoubted reference to the dromedary in the Scripture, which is a variety of the Arabian or one-humped camel (*Camelus dromedarius*, fr. Gr. *dromus, running*) bred for swiftness and endurance. It can travel about 125 miles per day.

Eagle. The word eagle in the A. V. includes both the *eagles* proper and the *vultures*. There are no less than four of the former and eight of the latter in the Holy Land. The most common of the vultures are the *griffon* and the *Egyptian vulture*, commonly known as *Pharaoh's chicken*. The commonest of the eagles is the *short-toed eagle*, *Circoetus Gallicus*, Gmel. All of these birds are swift (Deut. 28:49), soar high (Prov. 23:5), nest in inaccessible rocks (Job. 39:27-30), and sight their prey from afar (Job 39:39). Besides the above references the habits of eagles and vultures are alluded to in numerous passages (Num. 24:21; Job 9:26; Prov. 30:17, 19; Jer. 49:16; Ezek 17:3; Obad. 4; Hab. 1:8; Matt. 24:28; Luke 17:37). The tenderness of the eagle to its young is also graphically set forth (Exod. 19:4; Deut. 32:11). Its great age is also noted (Psa. 103:5; Isa. 40:31).

Eggs. *See* Fowl.

Elephant. An animal whose tusks furnished ivory (I Kings 10:22 A. V. margin and II Chron. 9:21 margin). The animal is mentioned in I Macc. 1:17; 3:34 in connection with its later use in war, each beast being manipulated by an Indian driver and supporting on its broad back a tower from which as many as four soldiers fought (I Macc. 6:37, where 32 is obviously erroneous). Before combat, elephants were often inflamed by the smell or taste of wine (I Macc. 6:34; III Macc. 5:2). Two extant species of this huge animal are the *Elephas indicus* (Indian elephant) and the *Elephas africanus* (African variety), with several other types now extinct. *M. F. U.*

Ewe. *See* Sheep.

Falcon. R. V. for A. V. "kite" (Lev 11:14; Deut. 14:13), and A. V. "vulture" (Job. 28:7).

Fallow Deer, a mistranslation of Heb. *yăhmûr*, (Deut. 14:5; I Kings 4:23), which is correctly rendered by R. V. and the R. S. V. "roebuck," (*q. v.*).

Ferret. *See* Gecko.

Fish. The Greek language has over four hundred names of fishes. The Hebrew, as we have it in the Bible, has not even one. Nevertheless fishes are mentioned frequently in the Scriptures. They were classified as *clean*, having fins and scales, and *unclean*, not so furnished. Whales, seals, dugongs, and other creatures, now known to be lung breathers, were regarded by the Hebrews as fish. There are forty-five species in the inland waters and very large numbers in the Mediterranean Sea. Dagon, the god of the Philistines, had a man's body and a fish's tail. There are many allusions to fishing in the Bible.

Flea (Heb. *părōsh*), a most annoying and unfortunately most common insect in the East. David compares himself to a flea in order to discredit Saul (I Sam. 24:14). The similar reference (I Sam. 26:20) is considered by some an error in the text.

Fly (Heb. *z*e*bûb*). The immense number of flies in the East is one of its most striking characteristics. The number of species is also very large. The Heb. *z*e*bûb*, which is part of the name of the god of Ekron, Baal-zebub, is generic, but as the house fly is the most familiar representative it would be most frequently thought of in connection with this name. It is uncertain whether the plague of flies 'ärōb, refers to the swarming of a single species (R. V., Psa. 78:45, "swarms of flies"), or a multiplication of such noxious insects (A. V. "divers sorts of flies"). "Devoured them" can hardly mean ate them up bodily, nor bit them; but destroyed their food, and overwhelmed them with their nastiness.

Foal. *See* Ass, Horse.

19. Egyptians Fowling in Nile Marshes

Fowl. A number of Hebrew words are rendered fowl, as *bărbûr, 'ôf, şĭppōr*. However, the *bărbûr* is the lark-heeled cuckoo, a delicacy served on Solomon's table (I Kings 4:23). *See* Cock. The *'ôf* is a generic word for fowl. The *şĭppōr* is the lowly sparrow.

1. Birds were divided into *clean* and *unclean*, the latter including the carrion birds, fish hunters, and some others, as the hoopoe. Domestic fowls are mentioned, but it nowhere said that they were eaten. It is, nevertheless, extremely probable that they were so used.

2. **Nest.** The allusions to birds' nests in the Bible are frequent and forcible. They were made in the sanctuary (Psa' 84:3), rocks (Job 39:27; comp. Num. 24:21; Jer. 49:16), tress (Psa. 104:17; Jer. 22:23; Ezek. 31:6). Neste are concealed in ruins (Isa. 34:15) and holes (Jer. 48:28). The New Testament nests (Matt. 8:20; Luke 9:58) are mere roosts.

3. **Eggs** are frequently alluded to (Deut. 22:6; Job. 39:14; Isa. 10:14). They were well-known articles of food (Luke 11:13).

4. **Migration** of birds (Cant. 2:11, 12; Jer. 8:7), their singing (Eccles. 12:4; Psa. 104:12), flight (Exod. 19:4), care of young (Deut. 32:11, 12), voracity (Matt. 13:4), and many other characteristics are alluded to.

Fox. In several places it is uncertain whether Heb. *shū'ăl;* Gr. *'alōpēs,* signifies *fox* or *jackal* (Lam. 5:18; Ezek. 13:4; Cant. 2:15). In others it doubtless means *jackals* (Judg. 15:4; Psa. 63:10). The difficulty in regard to the number of jackals which Samson turned loose into the fields of the Philistines disappears if we consider that he probably collected them, doubtless with the aid of his companions, over a wide district of the Philistine plain, and set them loose in pairs, at perhaps as many as a hundred and fifty centers, so as to burn up as much as possible of the "shocks, and also the standing corn, and the vineyards and olives." In only one place is it more probable that fox is intended (Neh. 4:3). *'alōpēs* in the New Testament can mean nothing but *fox.* The Syrian fox is identical with the common European fox, *Vulpes vulgaris,* L.

Frog (Heb. *ş^ephardēăh*). The frog of the Egyptian plague (Exod. 8:2-14) is *Rana esculenta,* L., an amphibian, common everywhere in Egypt and the Holy Land (*see* Wisd. 19:10).

Gazelle, the correct rendering of *şebî* (*beauty*), translated, A. V., *roe* and *roebuck.* It is the smallest of the antelopes in the Holy Land. It is abundant in the wildest portions of the country. Its beauty and speed are often alluded to in sacred and profane poetry. Its scientific name is *Gazella Dorcas,* L.

Gecko (Heb. *'ănăqäh, wail,* R. V., Lev. 11:30, for A. V. "ferret"). This lizard is named from the plaintive wail which it emits. Its scientific name is *Ptyodactylus Hasselquistii,* Schneid. It is frequently found in houses. It runs with great rapidity, and clings to walls and ceilings by the suckers with which its feet are furnished. It is in no way probable that the Hebrew original of this word signifies the *ferret,* which is a weasel-like animal in modern times kept for hunting rabbits and rats.

Gier Eagle, a term in English of indefinite meaning, referring to the soaring of birds of prey. A. V. uses it for Heb. *răḥăm,* which is *Pharaoh's chicken, Neophron percnopterus.* R. V. uses it for *pěrĕs,* which is better rendered *ossifrage.*

Glede, an old name for the kite. If the Hebrew original *rä'äh* (Deut. 14:13) be not the same as *dâ'âh* (Lev. 11:14, A. V., "kite;" R. V., "vulture"), *glede* is as good a rendering as can be given.

Gnat (Gr. *kōnōps*), the wine gnat or midge in fermenting and evaporating wine. Gnats or mosquitoes are most irritating pests in all parts of the East, and are very common in the low-lying marshy lands of Palestine and Egypt. It may refer to any small bloodsucking insect, and the more minute creatures, whether

20. Painting of Geese from an Old Kingdom Tomb at Medûm, Egypt

bloodsuckers or not, which torment man and beast.

Figurative. The custom of filtering wine, among the Jews, was founded on the prohibition of "all flying, creeping things" being used for food, excepting *saltatorii* (see Lev. 11:22, 23). The saying of our Lord, "Blind guides, who strain *out* a gnat and swallow down a camel" (Matt. 23:24), was doubtless taken from this custom. The contrast between the *smallest insect* and the *largest animal* is used to illustrate the inconsistency of those who are superstitiously anxious in avoiding small faults, yet do not scruple to commit the greatest sins.

Goat (Heb. *'äqqō, slender; yä'ēl, climbing*; *'ēz, strong; 'ăttûd, prepared,* and so *leader; sä'îr, shaggy;* Gr. *eriphion, tragos*), an animal often associated with sheep, and mentioned with them in many places in Scripture, once sharply contrasted (Matt. 25:32, 33). Owing to the unlovely disposition of the goat it was less chosen for ordinary sacrifices. Nevertheless it was an allowable victim (Lev. 3:12; 4:24; 9:15; 10:16; ch. 16, passim; Num. 15:27; 28:22, etc.). Goats were only second in importance, as a source and investment of wealth, to sheep.

Figurative. In Matt. 25:32, 33, sheep and goats are used to represent the righteous and the wicked respectively. "The wicked are here conceived of under the figure of *goats*, not on account of the wantonness and stench of the latter (Grotius), or in consequence of their stubbornness (Lange), but generally because these animals were considered to be comparatively worthless (Luke 15:29); and hence, in v. 33, we have the diminutive *ta 'eriphia* for the purpose of expressing contempt" (Meyer, *Com.*, Matt. 25:32, 33).

Goat, Wild, a graceful animal, *Capra Beden,* L., with semicircular horns two and a half to three feet long. It is found in the more inaccessible mountains and deserts. Of the two Hebrew words *ya'alath* and *aqqo* (Deut. 14:5) the first certainly, and the second probably, refers to this species.

Grasshopper. See Locust.

Great Owl. See Owl.

Greyhound, a translation of Heb. *zărzîr mäthnăyim,* "well-girt or well-knit in the loins" (Prov. 30:31). The greyhound, portrayed on Assyrian monuments, may be intended. The word, on the other hand, may denote the "war-horse" (R. V. margin), decorated with trappings around the loins or the starling, as the cognate word in Arab., Syr. and post-Biblical Hebrew suggests. The R. S. V. renders "the strutting cock." *M. F. U.*

Hare (Heb. *'ărnĕbĕth,* Lev. 11:6; Deut. 14:7), a rodent of which there are four species in the Holy Land, of which *Lepus Syriacus,* Hempr. et Ehr., is generally diffused. The others, *L. Sinaiticus,* Hempr. et Ehr., *L Aegyptius,* Geoffr., and *L. Isabellinus,* Rüpp., are desert species.

Hart, *Cervus Dama,* L., an animal once found in Palestine, but now probably extinct S. of Amanus. The Hebrew *'ăyyäl,* and not *yăḥmōr* (Deut. 14:5; I Kings 4:23), is the *fallow deer.* The female is called Hind. *See* Fallow Deer.

Hawk (Heb. *nēṣ,* Lev. 11:16; Deut. 14:15; Job. 39:26; *tăḥmäs,* Lev. 11:16; Deut. 14:15).

There are eighteen species of the hawk "after his kind," ranging in size from the little sparrow hawk to the buzzard. These are exclusive of the kites and gledes.

He Ass. *See* Ass.

Heifer. *See* Ox.

Hen. *See* Cock.

Heron. There are six species of herons in the Holy Land. As the Heb. *'änäphä,* (Lev. 11:19; Deut. 14:18), is associated with the stork, and accompanied by the qualifying phrase "after her kind," it is reasonable to accept "heron," rather than *eagle, parrot, swallow,* or *ibis,* all of which have been suggested in its place.

Hind, the female of *Hart* (*q. v.*).

Hippopotamus. *See* Behemoth.

Honey. *See* Bee.

Hoopoe, probably the correct translation of Heb. *dûkîphăth,* R. V., Lev. 11:19; Deut. 14:18; A. V., "lapwing." It is a migratory bird, *Upupa epops,* L., which spends the summer in the Holy Land and the winter in more southerly districts. Its head is often figured on the Egyptian monuments. If it be the bird intended by *dûkîphăth* it was unclean. It is, however, now freely eaten.

Hornet (Heb. *sîr'ä; stinging*), an insect with a formidable sting. It is found in considerable abundance in the Holy Land. Commentators are at variance as to whether the intention of the passages in which it is mentioned (Exod. 23:28; Deut. 7:20; Josh. 24:12) is literal or figurative. There are several species of hornets in the Holy Land.

Horse. Indo-European nomads east of the Black Sea early domesticated the horse. War horses and horse drawn chariots were introduced in Asia Minor and Syria between 1900 and 1800 B. C. and the patriarchal narratives make mention of horses at the time of Jacob (Gen. 49:17). The horse was found in Egypt where it was introduced by the Hyksos conquerors c. 1776 B. C. When the Exodus took place (c. 1440 B. C.) Pharoah's pursuing army was furnished with horses and chariots (Exod. 14:9; 15:19). Horses were also found in the host of Sisera at the time of Deborah (c. 1195-1155, Judg. 4 and 5.). *M. F. U.*

The Hebrews were at first forbidden to retain the horses they captured (Deut. 17:16), and accordingly houghed most of those which they took (Josh. 11:4-9). But they soon ceased to regard this restriction, and accumulated large studs of cavalry and chariot horses, mostly from Egypt and Assyria. Solomon had twelve thousand cavalry and four thousand chariot horses. Riding a horse was usually a sign of military rank. Many high functionaries, however, rode asses, mules, and camels.

Horseleech (Heb. *'ălûqäh, sucking,* Prov. 30: 15), either one of the leeches, *Hirudo medicinalis,* Sav., or *Hoemopis sanguisorba,* Sav., found in the stagnant waters throughout the land, or a specter like the "night monster."

Hound. *See* Greyhound.

Hyena (Heb. *ṣäbōă', speckled*). The hyena is very common throughout the Holy Land, and would be one of the beasts of the field to devour the carrion (cf. Eccles. 13:18).

Jackal (Heb. *tănnîn, monster*), R. V. Isa. 34:13; Jer. 9:11; 10:22; 51:37; Mic. 1:8, for A. V. "dragon." It would better be rendered *wolf.*

Also R. V., Jer. 14:6, marg., "crocodile;" A. V. "dragons." We believe that this should also be rendered *wolf*. On the other hand, "wild beasts of the islands" should be *jackals*. *Jackal* should in some cases be substituted for *fox*, as the translation of *shû'āl. See* Fox. The jackal is a familiar nocturnal animal, with a peculiar howl, feeding on live prey and carrion.

Kid. *See* Goat.

Kine. *See* Ox.

Kite. A bird of prey belonging to the falcon family with long pointed wings and forked tail. Kites are of various sorts (Deut. 14:13). The black kite appears in Palestine in March and feeds on offal. The word kite in the R. V. renders Hebrew *dā'āh* and *dăyyāh* (Lev. 11:14; Deut. 14:13; Isa. 34:15; in A. V. "vulture") and twice this name is employed in the A. V. to render *'ăyyāh* (Lev. 11:14; Deut. 14:13; in R. V. "falcon"). *M. F. U.*

Lamb. *See* Sheep.

Lapwing. *See* Hoopoe.

Leopard (Heb. *nāmēr, spotted;* Gr. *pardalis, Felis leopardus,* L., a wily, active, ferocious beast (Isa. 11:6; Jer. 5:6; Dan. 7:6; Hab. 1:8; Rev. 13:2). It is next to the bear the largest of the existing carnivora in the Holy Land. It has a beautiful spotted skin (Jer. 13:23), which is highly admired by the people. It is used for rugs, saddle covers, and one is sometimes hung over the back by religious mendicants. The *cheetah,* or *hunting leopard, Felis jubata,* Schreb., is probably included under the Hebrew generic name *nāmēr.*

Leviathan (Heb. *lĭwyäthän*), a word signifying an animal, writhing or gathering itself into folds; used for the *crocodile* (Job. 41:1; and probably 3:8, R. V., "leviathan;" A. V., "their mourning," marg. "leviathan;" also Psa. 74:14); for a *serpent* (Isa. 27:1); for some *sea monster* (Psa. 104:26), possibly the whale. However, leviathan may be purely a mythical concept adapted to Biblical usage (like dragon used to prefigure Satan). Since the discovery of the Ras Shamra religious texts in N. Syria on the site of ancient Ugarit, it has become evident that there is a parallel between the seven-headed Canaanite monster Lotan of prevailing mythology between 1700-1400 B. C. and the Biblical leviathan. Isaiah seems poetically to employ this ancient mythological idea of the destroyed leviathan (27:1) to symbolize the triumphant Judgment Day when God will triumph over the threatening evil of this world system.—*M. F. U.*

Lice. Notwithstanding the authority of R. V. (marg., Exod. 8:16; Psa. 105:31) "sandflies" or "fleas" for Heb. *kēn,* and its derivatives, and the R. S. V. rendering gnats, the weight of evidence is in favor of *lice.* These filthy insects are an endemic pest of the first magnitude in the East. What it must have been when they became universal is beyond the power of our imagination to conceive. The Mohammedans shave their heads, and use means to cause hair to fall out by the roots in other parts of their bodies, to escape this pest. This is the inheritance of an ancient custom of the Egyptian priests, and others of the inhabitants.

Lion, the well-known king of beasts, formerly abundant in Palestine (Judg. 14:5; I Sam. 17:34; II Kings 17:25; Jer. 49:19, etc.), and not extinct there until the end of the 12th century. Seven words, *aryêh, kephîr, gûr, lâbî, layish, shahal,* and *shâhâz,* are used to denote the lion in general, or at different ages and in different states. Four words, *shā'ag, nā'ar, nāham,* and *hâgab,* express his voice in varying moods, as the *roar, yell,* or *growl.* Six words denote his attitudes and movements in quest of prey, *rabaz, shâhah, yâshab, arâb, râmas, zinnêk,* as *prowling, crouching,* and *ambushing.*

Figurative. The Scriptures abound in allusions to the strength, courage, cruelty, and rapacity of this beast. His royal attributes made him an emblem of Christ (Rev. 5:5).

Little Owl. *See* Owl.

Lizard (Heb. *lᵉtā'äh*), a family term, occurring in a list (Lev. 11:30) of six, all of which are rendered in R. V. by names denoting lizards. A considerable number of the lizard family is found in the Holy Land, and several of them are common about houses, especially the *wall lizard, Zootica muralis,* Laur.; the *sand lizard, Lacerta agilis,* L., and the *green lizard, L. viridis,* L. *See* Tortoise, Gecko, Chameleon, Mole.

21. A Locust of Palestine

Locust (Heb. *'ărbĕh,* generic term). The devastations which the locust is capable of producing made it a fitting instrument of one of the ten memorable plagues of Egypt. Two species, *Aedipoda migratoria* and *Acridium peregrinum,* are the most common. They are always to be found in the southeastern deserts, but, from time to time, multiply in vast numbers and spread over the whole country, carrying ruin and despair everywhere. The poetical and prophetical books abound in vivid descriptions of their destructiveness, and the powerlessness of man to resist them. Eight Hebrew words seem to refer to locusts; some of them probably to various stages in their development. It is, however, impossible to determine the exact meaning of each. Locusts were undoubtedly eaten (Matt. 3:4).

The following vivid description of locusts is given by Jahn (*Bib. Arch.,* §23, *s. v.*): "Vast bodies of migrating locusts, called by the orientals the armies of God, lay waste the country. They observe as regular order, when they march, as an army. At evening they descend from their flight, and form, as it were, their camps. In the morning, when the sun has risen considerably, they ascend again, if they do not find food, and fly in the direction of the wind (Prov. 30:27; Nah. 3:16, 17). They go in immense numbers (Jer. 46:23), and occupy a space of ten or twelve miles in length, and four or five in breadth, and are so deep that the sun cannot penetrate through them; so that they convert the day into night, and bring a temporary darkness on the land (Joel 2:2, 10; Exod. 10:15). The sound of their wings is terrible (Joel 2:2). When they descend upon the earth, they cover a vast track a foot and a half high; if the air is cold and moist, or if they be wet with the dew, they remain . . . till they are dried and warmed by the sun (Nah. 3:17). Nothing stops them. They fill the ditches which are dug to stop them with their bodies, and extinguish by their numbers the fires which are kindled. They pass over walls and enter the doors and windows of houses (Joel 2:7-9) They devour everything which is green, strip off the bark of trees, and even break them to pieces by their weight (Exod. 10:12-19; Joel 1:4, 7, 10, 12, 16, 18, 20; 2:3)."

Mice. See Mouse.

Mole. No true mole exists in the Holy Land. The mole rat, *Spalax typhlus*, Pall., may be the animal intended by Heb. *tănshĕmĕth*, (Lev. 11:30, R. V., "chameleoṇ"). Another Hebrew word *hăphŏr*, (Isa. 2:20), is translated "moles." It would perhaps better be translated *burrowing rats* or *mice*, being understood as generic for all the numerous burrowers found in waste places. The mole rat is a rodent, while the mole is one of the insectivora, which comprise the *shrews*, *hedgehogs*, and *moles*.

Moth. Several species of the family *Tineidae* which infest woolen goods and furs. It is almost impossible to guard against them in the eastern climate. The people wrap up their carpets and clothes with pepper grains, tobacco, pride of India leaves, and other substances. The scriptural and apocryphal allusions to moths are very significant of their subtle and noxious agency (Job. 4:19; 27:18; Hos. 5:12; Matt. 6:19, 20; Luke 12:33; Sir. 19:3; 42:13).

Mouse. The number of species of mouselike animals in the Holy Land is about forty. All of them are probably included in the generic prohibition (Lev. 11:29). One species was eaten by the recusant Israelites, along with swine's flesh (Isa. 66:17). We cannot be sure what species it was. It may have been the *hamster*, which is said to be eaten by the Arabs.

Mule. Mules were not allowed according to the Mosaic law (Lev. 19:19). Yet they were used early in the period of the kings (II Sam. 13:29; 18:9; I Kings 1:33, etc.). They were imported from Togarmah (Ezek. 27:14). The Hebrew term *pĕrĕd*, undoubtedly refers to the mule.

Nest. See Fowl.

Night Hawk. The Heb. *tăhmäs*, is uncertain in meaning. Some have rendered it "ostrich," others "owl." As the owl is mentioned in the list (Lev. 11:16; Deut. 14:15), and at least one other word exists for the ostrich, the R. V. has done well in transliterating in the margin "tahmas," with the gloss "of uncertain meaning."

Onycha (ŏn'ĭ-kà), a substance mentioned as an ingredient of the holy perfume (Exod. 30: 34). It is the operculum of shells of Strombi, and is prepared for use by roasting, which evolves an empyreumatic oil, on which its aromatic properties depend.

Ospray (Heb. *ŏznīyäh*; the *fish eagle, Pandion halioetus*, L., an unclean bird (Lev. 11:13; Deut. 14:12), which fishes along the coasts of the Holy Land and in the Hûleh.

Ossifrage (Heb. *pĕrĕs*; the *lamergeier, Gypoetus barbatus*, L., the largest of the vultures of the Holy Land. As it is a familiar bird in Europe its habits are well known. It kills its own prey, but also does not disdain carrion. Hence it was unclean (Lev. 11:13; Deut. 14:12). R. V. renders the Hebrew original *gier eagle*.

Ostrich (Heb. *nŏşäh; flying*, Job. 39:13; elsewhere *yă'ēn*). The A. V. translates this latter in five out of the eight passages in which it occurs by "owl," sometimes with marginal reading "ostrich." R. V. correctly and uniformly renders it "ostrich." The ostrich is a well-known bird, found in the deserts of Africa and Arabia. Its renown for voracity is due to the large size of the pebbles, bits of glass, or other objects which it swallows, as fowls swallow gravel, to assist in the subdivision of their food in the gizzard. The female ostrich makes a shallow nest, and lays so many eggs that some of them are left uncovered and therefore not incubated. She, however, covers most of them with sand, and, while leaving them to the influence of the sun's rays by day, incubates them by night. The ostrich, when pursued, runs against the wind, and in large circles, a fact which enables the hunter to lie in wait for it, and thus partially neutralize the advantage of its great speed. It is not true that it hides its head in the sand on the approach of danger. When compared with some other birds, as the partridge, noted for their cunning in concealing their eggs and young, and escaping from their enemies, the ostrich, which runs away from eggs and chicks, in the frantic desire to escape by its great speed, seems open to the charge of stupidity (Job. 39:14-17).

Ostrich plumes graced ancient royal courts as fans. An ivory-handled fan of King Tutankh-amun still retains its lovely ostrich plumes in the National Museum at Cairo after more than 3,000 years.

Owl in our standard English translations renders some six Hebrew words of which perhaps only two actually refer to this broad-headed, large-eyed bird. (1) Heb. *băth yă'ănäh* (Lev. 11:16 A. V.) is certainly the ostrich. (2) Heb. *lilîth* (Isa. 34:14) is a nocturnal spectre or more precisely a night demon, not a "screech owl" (A. V.). (3) Heb. *qĭppŏz* (Isa. 34:15) is perhaps the dart snake (R. V.). (4) Heb. *tĭnshĕmĕth* (Lev. 11:18) may be a "swan" (A. V. and Vulgate) or "water hen" (R. S. V.). (5) Heb. *yănshûph* (Lev. 11:17; Deut. 14:16; Isa. 34:11) is rendered ibis in the LXX and Vulgate and owl in the Targums and Peshitta. The species may, however, be the Egyptian eagle owl (*Bubo ascalaphus*), living in caves and ruins about Beersheba and Petra. (6) Heb. *kŏs*, "a cup," (Lev. 11:17; Deut. 14:16; Psa. 102.16) probably has reference to the little owl, called *Athene glaux* commonly seen in Palestine at twilight. The Athenians esteemed this bird wise and associated it with their sage Athena, stamping its image on their silver money. *M. F. U.*

Ox. 1. The translation of Heb. *shōr*. The cognate Arab. *thaur*, Gr. *tauros*, Lat. *taurus*, refer to the male. *Shōr*, however, is generic for both sexes and all ages. Though generally translated "ox," it is sometimes rendered "bullock."

22. Oxen with Oxcart

2. **Cow, Kine.** The rendering of Heb. *bäqär*, which is also generic for bovines, *bäqäräh*, with the feminine ending, signifies the *cow*.

3. **Bull, Bullock.** Usually the equivalent of Heb. *pår*, or *pär*. The feminine *pårâh* is once used (Num. 19:2) for heifer. Sometimes the term *abbir*, *strong one*, is used metaphorically for *bull* (Psa. 22:13; Lev. 13; Isa. 34:7), but it is also used in the same sense for the *horse* (Jer. 8:16; 47:3).

4. **Calf, Heifer.** The rendering of Heb. *'ēgĕl*, and *'ĕgläh*. Once "heifer" is the equivalent of *päräh* (Num. 19:2).

5. **Wild Ox**, the translation of Heb. *te'ō* (Deut. 14:5 A. V.). **Wild Bull** is the rendering of Heb. *tō'* (Isa. 51:20 A. V.). The R. V. and R. S. V. correctly render "antelope" (*q. v.*). "Unicorn" of the A. V. is rendered "wild ox" in R. V. (Num. 23:22; 24:8; Job. 39:9, 10; Psa. 29:6; 92:10). *See* Unicorn. *M. F. U.*

Palmerworm (Heb. *gäzäm; devouring*, Joel 1:4; 2:25; Amos 4:9), a destroying larva, possibly a caterpillar, more probably a stage in the development of the locust. Its root signifies to *cut off*. It is impossible to identify it.

Partridge (Heb. *gōrēh*; a *caller*, from its *cry*). There are two species of partridges in the Holy Land, *Caccabis chukar*, C. R. Gray, the *red-legged partridge*, and *Ammoperdix Heyi*, Temm., the *sand partridge*. The former is generally in the middle and upper mountain regions and the Syrian desert. The latter is peculiar to the Dead Sea and Jordan valley. This may be the one alluded to by David (I Sam. 26:20). The passage Jer. 17:11, in which R. V. has adopted A. V. marginal rendering, "gathereth young which she hath not brought forth," is obscure. It may refer to pirating a nest, after the manner of the cuckoo, or decoying away the chicks of another bird. Although no modern authority has witnessed such theft, some of the ancients believed that the partridge was guilty of it.

Peacocks. In one place where A. V. has given "peacock" (Job. 39:13) the original is Heb. *rěh'něn*, which is undoubtedly a name for the ostrich, as in R. V. In the other two passages where "peacocks" occurs in A. V., R. V. and R. S. V. (I Kings 10:22; II Chron. 9:21) the reference is unquestionably to this lordly bird. The Heb. *tŭkkî*, survives in the allied *tokei*, which is the Tamil name of the bird. Since it is now known that the words for the ivory and apes which Solomon imported are of Indian origin, the equation *tŭkkî* = "peacock" may be defended as it finds a satisfactory origin in Malabar *togai*, *toghai* (Old Tamil *tokei*, *togu*) a peacock. The peacock (*Pavo cristatus*) is native to India where it is unmolested and very common. However, another rendering of *tŭkkî* is possible as a result of evidence from Egypt, where it may be equated with *t.ky* (monkey), the letter *t* (feminine particle) indicating two varieties of monkeys. This interpretation would suggest an African origin of the animal as well as an African location for the enigmatic Ophir. Revised by *M. F. U.*

Pelican, probably the correct translation of Heb. *qä'äth*, "the vomiter." It was an unclean bird (Lev. 11:18; Deut. 14:17). It was found in desolate places (Psa. 102:6) and ruins (R. V., Isa. 34:11; Zeph. 2:14, A. V. "cormorant," marg. "pelican"). Two species are found in the Holy Land, *Pelecanus onocrotalus*, L., and *P. crispus*, Brush. The pelican lives on fish, which it catches with its long beak and stores in the capacious pouch beneath it. When gorged with food it flies away to some lonely place, and pressing its pouch against its breast stands in this attitude for hours or days, until it is hungry again, when it resumes its fishing. If *qä'äth* be the pelican, this attitude would well suit the melancholy inactivity to which David alludes in comparing himself with the "pelican in the wilderness."

Pigeon. *See* Dove.

Porcupine. *See* Bittern.

Porpoise. *See* Badger.

Pygarg (Heb. *dishōn, leaper*), probably the *addax, Antilope addax*, Licht., an animal found in the Syrian and Arabian deserts. It is mentioned in only one of the two lists of clean animals (Deut. 14:5). There seems to be no authority for A. V. marg. "bison."

23. A Quail

Quail (Heb. *she'lāw*), a gallinaceous bird, *Coturnix vulgaris*, L., more or less resident in Egypt and the Holy Land, but also passing through them on its migrations northward in March, and southward in September. The quails pass over narrow portions of the sea, but arrive greatly exhausted. Many of them perish in the transit. Those which the Israelites captured (Exod. 16:13; Num. 11:31, 32) were on their way N. Tristram has pointed out their course up the Red Sea, across the mouth of the Gulf of Akabah and Suez, to the Sinaitic peninsula, and so blown by a sea wind over the camp of the Israelites.

Ram. *See* Sheep.

Raven. The raven, *Corvus corax*, L., is the first bird named (Gen. 8:7). It feeds in part on seeds and fruit. To this fact our Saviour alludes (Luke 12:24; Gr. *korax*). It also captures small creatures alive, but it loves carrion (Prov. 30:17), and so was unclean. Orientals, as well as occidentals, look upon it as a bird of evil omen (Isa. 34:11). The Hebrew word '*ōrēb*, of which raven is the translation, doubtless includes the *crows*, *jays*, and *choughs*, as is implied in the expression "after his kind" (Lev. 11:15; Deut. 14:14).

Roe. In one place (A. V., Prov. 5:19; R. V. "doe"; Heb. *yǎ'ǎlǎh*) it should be *wild she-goat;* in all other places, *Gazelle* (*q. v.*).

Roebuck, a mistranslation of the Heb. *ṣᵉbî*, which signifies the *Gazelle* (*q. v.*). The *roebuck*, *Cervus capreolus*, L., is found in the Holy Land, and is the proper translation of Heb. *yǎḥmūr*, (Deut. 14:5; I Kings 4:23; A. V. wrongly "fallow deer"). It must have been very abundant in the days of Solomon. It is now found rarely in northern Galilee and Carmel, and in the woods of Gilead. It is still known in Carmel and E. of the Jordan.

Sand Flies. *See* Lice.

Sand Lizard. *See* Snail and Lizard.

Satyr, the equivalent (Isa. 13:21; 34:14) of *sǎ'îr*, which means a *he-goat*, and is usually so translated. The same word is rendered in A. V. (Lev. 17:7; II Chron. 11:15) "devils," R. V. "he-goats," marg. "satyrs." Grotesque creatures, half man and half goat, figure in the Greek and Roman mythologies under the name of *satyrs* and *fauns*, but the Old Testament representations are rather demonic conceptions.

24. Scorpion

Scorpion, a generic term for about a dozen species of the *Arachnidoe*, which inhabit the Holy Land. The poison is in the sting at the end of the tail. The scropion is an emblem of torture and wrath. Some of the species of southern Palestine are six inches long.

Seal, Seal Skins. *See* Badger.

Seamew (Heb. *shǎḥǎf*), a name of certain birds broad enough to include gulls, terns and petrels, all of which are common on the sea-shore and lakes of Palestine. If a specific bird is meant, the common tern or sea swallow would fit the requirements, being abundant along the shores of Palestine. It was an unclean bird which the A. V. rendered cuckow (cuckoo), perhaps suggesting leanness (Lev. 11:16; Deut. 14:15). *See* Cuckow.

Sea Monster. *See* Dragon, Whale.

Serpent. It is impossible to unravel the tangle in which the translators, ancient and modern, have involved the eight words used in the Hebrew for serpents. Only one of them (Heb. *shᵉphîphōn*), can be identified with any degree of certainty. This is in all probability *Cerastes Hasselquistii*, Strauch, the *horned cerastes* of the desert. It is reasonably probable that *pethen* refers to the *cobra*. *Zepha'* and *ziph'ônì* and *eph'eh* are uncertain. Heb. *tânnîn*, is usually translated *dragon*, and if it refers to a snake in the story of the controversy between Moses and Pharaoh we have no means of guessing the species. Heb. *nāḥāsh*, is a general term, corresponding exactly to the English *serpent* or *snake*. Heb. *sārāf*, means *fiery*, and is therefore only a term to characterize the venomousness of the unknown species intended.

The serpents of Egypt, Sinai, and the Holy Land are numerous. Of the venomous ones the principal are *Daboia zanthina*, Gray, *Cerastes Hasselquistii*, Strauch, *Naja haje*, L., *Echis arenicola*, Boie, *Vipera Euphratica*, Martin, and *V. ammodytes*, L. The English names of snakes mentioned are *adder*, *arrowsnake*, *asp*, *basilisk* (fabulous), *cockatrice* (fabulous), *fiery flying serpent*, *viper*, and the generic term *serpent*. Besides these the following terms are used: *Crooked*, *crossing like a bar*, *fleeing*, *gliding*, *piercing*, *swift*, *winding*, as adjectives to the serpent, but seeming to refer to the *crocodile*, under the name leviathan (Isa. 27:1), (*q. v.*).

Almost all the allusions to the serpent in the Scriptures are to its malignity and venom. Probably the Hebrews regarded most or all snakes as poisonous. Only once (Matt. 10:16) is there a doubtful commendation of the serpent on account of its wisdom. Its habits, even to being oviparous (Isa. 59:5), were minutely noted. The devil is the "old serpent."

Sheep, the rendering of several Hebrew and Greek words. This animal is mentioned about five hundred times in the Bible. The broad-tailed variety is the one which is, and probably has been from ancient times, the one raised in the East. Allusion is made to its fat tail ("rump," A. V.; Exod. 29:22; Lev. 3:9; R. V. "fat tail"). The number of sheep raised in ancient times was prodigious. We read of the tribute of 200,000 fleeces from the king of Moab (II Kings 3:4). Reuben took 250,000 sheep from the children of Ishmael (I Chron. 5:21). Lambs were offered in immense numbers in sacrifice, usually males, in one case a female (Lev. 14:10). Solomon offered 120,000 on occasion of the consecration of the temple (I Kings 8:63). Sheep's milk and wool were and are of immense importance for food and clothing, and as articles of commerce. Ram's skins entered into the structure of the tabernacle.

Shepherds in Bible lands have the same personal knowledge and exhaustive care of their flocks as in ancient times. Their offices were chosen as emblems of those of Christ and his ministers in the care of the believers committed to their charge.

25. An Eastern Sheepfold

The interest of the sheep to Christians culminates in the fact that Christ is the atoning illuminating, lifegiving, reigning Lamb of God.

She Goat. *See* Goat.

Snail. The Hebrew word *hōmĕt*, rendered (A. V., Lev. 11:30) "snail," is generic for *lizard* (R. V., *l. c.*, "sand lizard," which rendering is, however, only conjectural). Another word, *shăblûl*, (Psa. 58:8), is probably generic for *snail*, although neither the LXX. nor Vulgate support the rendering. The surface of rocks, walls, and tree trunks in this land is often covered with a thin pellicle, looking like a film of collodion or gelatine. This is caused by the passing and repassing of snails, which always leave a slimy track behind them. This is the *melting* of the snail, alluded to in the above passage. If a snail remains attached to a place in the hot sun it will dry up and be stuck fast to its resting place by this inspissated mucilaginous fluid. The number of species of snails in Bible lands is large.

Sow. *See* Swine.

Sparrow, one rendering of Heb. *ṣĭppôr*, which, like *'ûsfur* in Arabic, is generic for small birds. Only in one or two instances (Psa. 84:3; 102:7) is it specific for the *house sparrow*. *Ṣĭppôr* is more frequently rendered "bird" and "fowl." The New Testament *strouthion*, probably refers to the house sparrow (Matt. 10:29; Luke 12:6, 7).

Speckled Bird. *See* Hyena.

Spider. Two Hebrew words are translated in A. V. *spider*. 1. *sh*e*māmǐth*, (Prov. 30:28), from a root signifying *to be poisonous*. R. V. gives "lizard." Both the spider and several varieties of lizards frequent houses. 2. *'ăkkābǐsh*, (Job. 8:14; Isa. 59:9, 6), is generic for *spiders*, of which there is a large number in the Holy Land.

Sponge (Gr. *spongos*), a porous body, produced in the sea, composed of tubules and cells, lined with amoeboid substance. The vital action of these protozoa keeps up a steady circulation of water through the channels. Commercial sponges consist only of the skeleton, out of which the lining and investing amoeboid substance has been cleaned. The only mention of the sponge is in connection with the crucifixion of our Saviour (Matt. 27:48, etc.).

Stallion (Sir. 37:8). Unaltered horses are more highly esteemed in the East for all except menial offices. Geldings are seldom seen.

Stork (Heb. *hăsîdäh*). Two species, *Ciconia alba*, L., the *white stork*, and *C. nigra*, L., the *black stork*, are found in the Holy Land. It was an unclean bird. Although its usual nesting place is in ruins, it also, especially the black species, resorts to trees (Psa. 140:17). It is a migratory bird, going to northern Europe in the summer, flying high "in the heaven" (Jer. 8:7), and making a rushing noise ("the wind was in their wings," Zech. 5:9). Their affection for their young is proverbial.

Swallow. The only Hebrew words properly translated swallow are *d*e*rōr* (Psa. 84:3; Prov. 26:2), and *sûs* (Isa. 38:14; Jer. 8:7). *'ăgûr*, in the latter two signifies *twitterer*, instead of "swallow," as in A. V., or "crane," as in R. V. The *swallows*, *swifts* and *martins* are numerous in Bible lands. Their shrill cries, as they skim the ground and sweep through the air with incredible rapidity, are among the most characteristic features of Oriental towns.

Swan. Probably the Heb. *tĭnshĕmĕth* (Lev. 11:18; Deut. 14:16; A. V. "swan," R. V. "horned owl," marg. "swan"), refers to the *purple gallinule*, *Porphyrio coeruleus*, Vandelli, or one of the *ibises*, *Ibis religiosa*, L., or *I. falcinella*, L., and not to the *swan*, which is hardly found in the Holy Land, and would not have been regarded as unclean.

Swine (Heb. *hăzîr*; Gr. *choiros*). The hog is regarded by Mohammedans with no less loathing than by the Jews. Many of the Oriental Christians share this feeling, while others raise swine and freely eat of its flesh. The Jews in Christ's time had come to ignore their own law on this subject (Matt. 8:30, etc.), as had some of their ancestors who ate their flesh (Isa. 66:17).

Tortoise (A. V., Lev. 11:29; R. V. "great lizard"). The Heb. *ṣāb*, is the cognate of the Arab. *dabb*, which is the term applied to the *land monitor*, *Psammosaurus scincus*, an animal often six feet long, and to another lizard, *Uromastyx spinipes*, which attains a length of two feet, and has a short rounded head, and a tail surrounded by rings of spines. Although there are *land* and *sea tortoises* in the Holy Land and its adjacent sea, *ṣāb* does not refer to any of them, and therefore the *tortoise* must be dropped from the list of Scripture animals.

Turtle, Turtledove (Heb. *tōr*), one of the best-known birds of the Holy Land. It was used by the poor for sacrifices (Lev. 5:11, etc.). Its peculiar note and gentle disposition (Psa. 74:19) made it a type of Christ. There are three species in the Holy Land, *Turtur auritus*, L., the *common turtledove*, *T. risorius*, L., the *collared turtledove*, and *T. Senegalensis*, L., the *palm* or *Egyptian turtle*.

Unicorn (R. V., "wild ox," Heb. *r*e*'ēm*), probable *Bos primigenius*, L., the true *auerochs*. This animal is now extinct, but certainly existed in Germany in the time of Caesar, and did not probably become extinct in Europe until the Middle Ages. Caesar describes it as immense in size, of great strength (comp. Num. 23:22; 24:8), speed (Psa. 29:6), and ferocity, untamable (Job. 39:9, 10), associated with bulls (Isa. 34:7; A. V. marg. "rhinoceroses") (*Coes., Bell. Gall.*, iv, 29). It cannot be the Arab. *ri'm*, which is doubtless *Antilope leucoryx* (*see* Antelope), nor *Bison bonasus*, which is called by the modern Germans *auerochs*, but which is an animal with short horns, quite unsuitable for "horns of the unicorn." Still less can it be the intention to speak of a fabulous creature like the traditional *unicorn*, with the single horn springing from the center of the forehead. The *re'ēm* had more than one horn (Deut. 33:17). The Heb. word most certainly denotes the "wild ox" (R. V.), for the cognate word in Akkadian *rimu* has this meaning. Representations of it by ancient Assyrian artists picture it as the aurochs. Tiglath-pilesar I (c. 1115-1102 B. C.) hunted it as game in Hittite country in the Lebanon Mountains. It early became extinct in Syria-Palestine and its name transferred to its descendant, the common ox. But the extinct species was notorious for its flatter forehead, colossal strength and ferocity, and its powerful horns of double curvature. Tristram offered independent corroboration of its previous occurrence in the Lebanon Mountains by recovering its teeth in the bone caves of the region. Revised by *M. F. U.*

Viper. *See* Serpent.

Vulture. Several vultures have already been described. *See* Eagle, Gier Eagle, Ospray, and Ossifrage. The Hebrew words *dā'āh, dayyah*, rendered in A. V. "vulture," should be *kite*, and *'āyyāh*, perhaps (as in R. V., Job. 28:7) "falcon." The word *rāhām*, translated "gier eagle" (Lev. 11:18), should be *vulture*. It refers to *Pharoah's chicken, Neophron Percnopterus,* Sav.

Wasp. The reference in the only passage in which this insect is mentioned (Wis. 12:8) is doubtless to the common *yellow jacket, Vespa vulgaris,* L. It is very common throughout the Holy Land, and is especially so in the vineyards during vintage, and about the grape presses, and the fruit shops in towns.

Weasel (Heb. *hōlĕd*). This is, perhaps, the best translation of *hōlĕd* (Lev. 11:29), notwithstanding the fact that the cognate Arab. *huld* refers to the *mole rat, Spalax typhlus.* The term must be understood in a family sense for all the *Mustelidoe,* as the *marten, ichneumon, genet,* and *polecat.*

Whale (Heb. *tăn,* or *tănnîn;* a *monster*). The "great whales" (A. V., Gen. 1:21; R. V. "sea monsters;" Job 7:12; Ezek. 32:2) are to be understood of all aquatic creatures not considered as fishes. *See* Dragon. Jonah's whale (*kētos,* Matt. 12:40, from the LXX., Jonah 1:17) was a great fish." It might have been a *spermaceti whale,* had one wandered into the Mediterranean, or a *large shark,* of which that sea contains many large enough to have swallowed Jonah.

Wild Ass. *See* Ass.

Wild Beasts. The signification of beasts in many places, and of wild beasts in all, is beasts of prey. The context will always settle

the meaning. There are no more any lions in Syria and Palestine. They were, however, numerous in Bible times. Bears are still found in considerable numbers in Antilebanon, and a few still linger in Lebanon. They become more abundant in Amanus and the Taurus. Wolves are common throughout. Leopards are occasionally met with in Lebanon, and more frequently in Antilebanon and E. of the Jordan, and in the neighborhood of the Dead Sea. Jackals are very common everywhere. Foxes are also very numerous. Hyenas haunt ruins and waste places. Badgers, martens, polecats, ichneumons, and genets are also found. Among the wild beasts which are not carnivorous are the roebuck, the gazelle, the addax, hart, wild ass, the beden (wild goat), swine, and coney.

Hunting, except for roebuck and gazelles, is not common. A few bears are shot every year. Wolves are killed by the shepherds. Foxes are occasionally trapped or shot. Hyenas are caught in steel traps or shot, and rarely a leopard is killed in the more lonely parts of the mountains. Hares are shot in the winter, and brought to the markets of the large cities. The allusions to wild beasts in the Bible are numerous (II Kings 14:9; Job 39: 15; Psa. 80:13; Hos. 13:8, etc.).

Wild Goat. *See* Goat, Wild.

Wild Ox. *See* Ox, Unicorn.

Wolf (Heb. *ze'ēb*; Gr. *lukos*). We believe it also to be the proper rendering of *tănnin*, translated, A. V., "dragons;" R. V., "jackals" Job. 30:29; Psa. 44:19; Isa. 13:22; 34:13; 43:20; Jer. 9:11; 10:22; 14:6; R. V. marg. "the crocodile;" 49:33; 51:37; Mic. 1:8). The wolf is the terror of the sheep, but usually flees from the shepherd. Wolves are very numerous in all the sheep walks of this land. The emblematic reference to the ferocity and bloodthirstiness of the wolf are numerous and forcible.

Worm. The only worms alluded to in Scripture are the *larvae of insects,* as (Isa. 51:8), the *grub of the moth; rĭmmäh,* maggots bred in decaying *vegetable* and *animal* substances (Exod. 16:24; Job. 7:5, etc.), and *tôlâ'îm,* also *maggots* similar to the last. *Tôlâ'* and *tôlâ'ath,* from the same root, refer to the *cochineal insect. Earth worms* are not mentioned in the Bible. The *worms* which devoured Herod (Acts 12:23) were probably also *maggots,* bred in a wound or sore.

Animal, Symbolism of. *See* Symbolism.

Animal, Worship of, is of great antiquity, and its origin is involved in much obscurity. Zoolatria (animal worship) is said to have been introduced into Egypt under the 2nd dynasty (c. 2750 B. C.). The gods of the Egyptian, Indian, Greek, and Teutonic mythologies were the "powers" of nature; and the principal sacred animals and reptiles were worshipped as their incarnations or servants. Many of them were carefully tended while living, and when dead were buried with great pomp. To cause the death of any of these creatures designedly was punishable with death; but if anyone caused the death of a cat, hawk, or ibis, with or without intent, he must die.

The Israelites often degraded themselves

by an imitation of this kind of worship (Exod. 32), for which they were severely punished.

Anise. See Vegetable Kingdom.

Anklet (Heb. *'ĕkĕs*, A. V. "tinkling ornaments"), the ornament mentioned in the description given of female attire (Isa. 3:18). It was a ring of gold, silver, or ivory, worn round the ankles. The anklet was very widely used by the ancients, nor has its use ceased yet in the east. The Egyptian monuments show them to have been worn by both sexes. The practice was forbidden in the Koran (24:31), though the prohibition may refer rather to the small bells worn around the ankles, especially by dancing girls.

An′na (ăn′á), Greek form of *Hannah*, the prophetess, and daughter of Phanuel, of the tribe of Asher. Married in early life, she, after seven years, lost her husband. From that time she devoted herself to attendance upon the temple services, and probably by reason of her great piety was allowed to reside in some one of the chambers of the women's court. Anna was eighty-four years old when the infant Jesus was presented to the Lord. Entering as Simeon was thanking God, Anna also broke forth in praise for the fulfillment of the divine promises (Luke 2:36).

An′nas (ăn′ăs; a contracted form of *Ananias*), a high priest of the Jews. He is called by Josephus *Ananus*, the son of Seth, and was first appointed high priest by Quirinius, proconsul of Syria, about A. D. 7, but was removed after seven years (Kitto says fifteen years) by Valerius Gratus, procurator of Judea (Josephus, *Ant.*, xviii, 2, 1 and 2). Annas is mentioned in Luke 3:2 as being high priest *along with* Caiaphas. Our Lord's first hearing was before Annas (John 18:13), who sent him bound to Caiaphas (v. 24). In Acts 4:6 he is plainly called high priest. He had four sons who filled that office, besides his son-in-law, Caiaphas. There have been several theories advanced to reconcile the application of high priest to Annas and Caiaphas at the same time. Kitto thinks that Annas was regarded as being high priest *jure divino*, and having authority in spiritual matters, while Caiaphas was the pontiff recognized by the government. The probability is that his great age, abilities, and influence, and his being the father-in-law of Caiaphas, made him practically the high priest, although his son-in-law held the office.

Anointing. Anointing the body with oil was a very ancient and widespread custom, being very common among the Egyptians, the Hebrews, and the inhabitants of the far East, as well as among the Greeks and Romans. The purpose was, doubtless, to keep the skin supple, and to moderate the evaporation which is so great in hot climates.

SCRIPTURAL ANOINTING (Heb. usually *māshăḥ*; Gr. *chriō*, to *rub*).

1. **Toilet.** The allusions to anointing as part of the toilet are numerous, both in the Old and New Testaments (Ruth 3:3); as expressive of joy (Psa. 23:5; 45-7; Heb. 1:9); its disuse indicative of grief (II Sam. 14:2; Psa. 92:10; Dan. 10:3). It was reckoned among the civilities extended to guests (Luke 7:46), although the unguents used on such occasions

seem to have been perfumes rather than oils. It was also used medicinally (Isa. 1:6; Mark 6:13; James 5:14). See Oil.

The practice of anointing the bodies of the dead is referred to in Mark 14:8 and Luke 23:56. This ceremony was performed after the washing of the body, and was doubtless intended to check decay. See Embalming.

2. **Consecration.** The first instance of the religious use of oil is the anointing of the stone by Jacob (Gen. 28:18; 35:14), evidently designed to be a formal consecration of the stone, or spot, to a sacred purpose. Under the Mosaic law persons and things set apart for sacred purposes were anointed with the "oil of holy ointment" (Exod. 30:23-26; 29:27). See Priest, Ordination of.

3. **Coronation.** It was a custom among the Jews to anoint with oil those set apart as kings, which custom was adopted by the Christian Church.

4. **Figurative.** The anointing with oil was a symbol of endowment with the Spirit of God (I Sam. 10:1, 6; 16:13; Isa. 61:1) for the duties of the office to which a person was consecrated (Lev. 8). See King, Priest.

Answer (Heb. *'ānäh*, to *testify*; Gr. *'apokrinomai*, to *respond*), has in Scripture other meanings than the usual one of *reply*.

1. Miriam is said to have "answered," i. e., taken up the strain of victory sung by Moses and the men (Exod. 15:21; see I Sam. 18:7; 29:5; comp. Num. 21:17).

2. To respond to requests or entreaties (I Sam. 4:17; Psa. 3:4; 18:41; 27:7); to announce future events (I Sam. 14:37; 28:6).

3. In a forensic sense: of a judge investigating (Acts 17:11), or giving sentence (Exod. 23:2); of a witness answering inquiries of judge, hence *to testify*, *bear witness* (Deut. 19:16; Job. 16:8); to accuse or defend in court (Deut. 31:21; Gen. 30:33; Hos. 5).

4. To "answer" is also used for the commencement of a discourse, when no reply to any question or objection is expected (Job 3:2; Cant. 2:10; Matt. 11:25; 12:38, etc.).

"Answer of a good conscience" (I Pet. 3:21) seems to signify the ability to address God with a conscience free from guilt.

Ant. See Animal Kingdom.

Antediluvians, people who lived before the flood. Of this period we have but little authentic information (Gen. 4:16-6:8), although additional knowledge may be gathered from the history of Noah and the first men after the deluge. In the Bible account we find few indications of savagery among these people, and there need not be the opinion that they civilized themselves.

It is the opinion of some that the antediluvians were acquainted with astronomy, from the fact of the ages of Seth and his descendants being recorded (Gen. 5:6, f.), and they appear to have been familiar with botany, from the mention of the vine, olive, etc. (Gen. 6:14; 8:11), mineralogy (Gen. 2:12), music (Gen. 4:21), architecture, from the fact of Cain having built a city (Gen. 4:17), metallurgy, so far as forging and tempering are concerned (Gen. 4:22). Agriculture was evidently the first employment of Adam (Gen. 2:15; 3-17, 18), afterward of Cain (Gen. 4:2) and of Noah, who planted a vineyard (Gen. 9:20). The slight intimations to be found respecting *government* favor the notion that the particular governments were patriarchal, subject to general theocratic control. Respecting *religion*, sacrifices are mentioned (Gen. 4:4); some think that that the Sabbath was observed; mention is made that "men began to call upon the name of the Lord" (Gen. 4:26). We have here an account of the commencement of that worship of God which consists in prayer, praise, and thanksgiving, or in the acknowledgment and celebration of the mercy and help of Jehovah. Noah seemed to have been familiar with the distinction between clean and unclean beasts (Gen. 7:2).

Anthropopathism (from Gr. *'anthropatheia*, *with human feelings*), the attributing of human emotions, such as anger, grief, joy, etc., to God. Traces of this are found in Scripture (Gen. 6:6; 8:21; 11:5, 6, and many other passages). If we understand such expressions, not as the antipode, but rather the imperfect approximating expression of eternal truth, then they become the means of a better knowledge of God.

Antichrist (Gr. *'antichristos, against Christ*; some, *instead of Christ*), a word used only by the apostle John (Epistles 1 and 2).

1. **Meaning.** The Greek preposition *'anti*, in composition, sometimes denotes substitution, taking the place of another; hence, "false Christ." The connection in which the word is used appears to import opposition, covert rather than avowed, with a professed friendliness.

2. **Antichrists.** St. John seems to make a distinction between "antichrist" and "antichrists" (I John 2:18), for he declares that "even now are there many *antichrists*," but "that *antichrist* shall come. An antichrist is one who opposes Christ, whether he oppose the doctrine of his deity or his humanity; or whether he set himself against him, in respect of his *priestly* office, by substituting other methods of atoning for sin and finding acceptance with God; his *kingly* office, by claiming authority to exact laws in his Church contrary to his laws, or to dispense with his commandments; or his *prophetical* office, by claiming authority to add to, alter, or take away from the revelation which he has given in his holy word This is very agreeable to the description of antichrist (I John 2:22; 4:3; II John 7). In a general sense an antichrist is a person who is opposed to the authority of Christ as the head of the Church and to the supreme head of all creation.

3. **The Antichrist.** From early times the opinion has prevailed that the antichrists referred to were rather the forerunners of an evil than the evil itself. Some individual would arise who, by way of eminence, should be fitly called the Antichrist; and who, before being destroyed by Christ, should utter horrid blasphemies against the Most High, and practice great enormities upon the saints. This view is Scriptural and came from connecting the passages in St. John's epistles with the descriptions in Daniel and the Apocalypse of the great God-opposing power that should persecute the saints of the Most High; and of St.

Paul's "man of sin" (II Thess. 2:3-8). *See* also our Lord's own prediction respecting the last age of the world (Matt. 24:24), and the description of such an Antichrist (Rev. 13:8).

4. **Identification.** Early Christians looked for Antichrist as a person and not a polity or system. The general opinion of those who closely followed the Scriptures was that he would be a man, in whom Satan would dwell utterly and bodily and who would be armed with Satanic and demonic powers. In the O. T. he is prefigured under the "king of Babylon" (Isa. 14:4); "Lucifer" (Isa. 14:12), "the little horn" (Dan. 7:8; 8:9), "the king of fierce countenance" (Dan. 8:23), "Anti-christ" (I John 2:18) and "the Beast" (Rev. 13:1-10). This sinister demon-inspired leader will rise to dominate the world in the end-time, persecute the saints, seek to destroy the Jew and banish the name of God and His Christ from the earth, and thus take over. This would mean the thwarting of God's plan for the Messianic millennial kingdom, involving the restoration of Isarel (Acts 1:6) and universal peace. He is destroyed by the second advent of Christ (Rev. 19:11-16) who sets up the earthly kingdom (Rev. 20:1-3). This is the premillennial view. Amillennialism rejects an earthly kingdom in favor of Christ's ushering in the eternal state, rather than His establishing another era in time. Views which identify the Antichrist with Mohammed (Innocent III in 1213) or with the Papal Church (Protestantism) can scarcely be called Scriptural.

Antichristianism, a convenient term to designate in a collective manner the various forms of hostility to Christianity. It is equivalent to the "spirit of Antichrist" (I John 4:3). It was this which Enoch and Noah denounced in their preaching (Jude 14; II Pet. 2:5-7); that "vexed the righteous soul" of Lot; the "carnal mind" ever opposed to God (Rom. 8:7); the "mystery of iniquity" foreseen by Paul (II Thess. 2:7). It has since the days of persecution been chiefly confined to intellectual modes of opposition, known as Infidelity, Deism, Rationalism, etc.

An'tioch (ăn'tĭ-ŏk), from Antiochus, a Syrian king.

1. In Syria, on the left bank of the Orontes, sixteen and a half miles from the Mediterranean, and three hundred miles N. of Jerusa-

26. A Scene in Modern Antioch on the Orontes

27. Antioch on the Orontes (excavations foreground)

lem, between the Lebanon and Taurus mountain ranges. It was founded about 300 B. C. by Seleucus Nicator, and called Epidaphne (near Daphne), or "on the Orontes," to distinguish it from fifteen other Antiochs. The city was several times destroyed by earthquakes, by one of which, A. D. 526, two hundred and fifty thousand persons were killed. It was luxurious. Its main street, four miles in length, was lined with magnificent mansions. It was highly cultured, but its social life was debased, sensual, and shocking. The Jews formed a large portion of the population, with which class Seleucus Nicator colonized the place. It became the third city in the Roman empire, with a population of five hundred thousand. Pompey made it the seat of the legate of Syria, B. C. 64, and a free city.

Antioch was early associated with Christian effort. Thither fled the persecuted disciples after the death of Stephen (Acts 11:19, 20). The name "Christian," as applied to the followers of Jesus, and the first missionary movement conducted by St. Paul, each had their origin in Antioch. The most flourishing period in the history of the Christian Church in Antioch was in the time of Chrysostom, who was born there in 347. In 635 it was taken by the Saracens, and by the Turks in 1084, captured by Crusaders in 1098. It has been gradually declining under Mohammedan rule since 1268. Six thousand people now comprise its population. The modern name is "Antakia."

Princeton University and the Musées Nationaux de France have excavated at Antioch and many important archaeological findings have been published. Especially sig-

nificant are the mosaic pavements uncovered. These were found in churches, villas and other public buildings of the city which was third in size of the Roman Empire and called "the Queen of the East." More than a score of early Christian churches have been identified from excavated ruins, the most famous being Constantine's 4th century octagonal one. One in the form of a cross was dated A.D. 387. The Martyrion at Seleucia Pierea, the seaport of Antioch, dates from the late 5th century A. D. and is graced with magnificent mosaics of wild life. Revised by *M. F. U.*

2. Antioch in Pisidia, also founded by Seleucus I Nicator (312-280 B. C.), was a commercial center commanding the great trade route between Ephesus and the Cilician Gates. Paul's success here is recounted in Acts 13:14-52, and he revisited this important city on his first missionary tour (Acts 14:21). The ruins of Pisidian Antioch are in the vicinity of the modern Turkish town of Yalovach. Revised by *M. F. U.*

An′tipas (ăn′tĭ-pàs).

1. Herod Antipas was the son of Herod the Great by Malthace, a Samaritan. He inherited of his father's dominions Galilee and Perea, as tetrarch. He was the Herod who executed John the Baptist. *See* Herod.

2. A "faithful martyr" mentioned in Rev. 2:13, A. D. before 100. He is said to have been one of our Saviour's first disciples and a bishop of Pergamus, and to have been put to death in a tumult there by the priests of Aesculapius, who had a celebrated temple in that city. Tradition relates that he was burned in a brazen bull under Domitian.

Antip'atris (ăn-tĭp'à-tris; *instead of* his *father*), a city built by Herod the Great in honor of his father, Antipater. It is the modern Ras-el-Ain. It lay on the road built by the Romans, leading from Caesarea to Jerusalem, thirty-eight miles from the former place. Paul was taken thither a prisoner, and by night (Acts 23:31).

Antitype (Gr. *'antitupon,* a *counterpart* Heb. 9:24; I Pet. 3:21, rendered *figure*), that which is represented or prefigured by a type. The type may be considered a rough draught, while the antitype is the perfect image. The type is a figure, and antitype is the reality which the type prefigured, as Christ is the Antitype of the paschal lamb.

Anto'nia (ăn-tō'nĭ-à), a strong fortress built and named by Herod in honor of Antonius, or Mark Antony, situated to the N. W. of the temple area in Jerusalem, partly surrounded by a deep ditch one hundred and sixty-five feet wide. It was garrisoned with Roman soldiers, whose watchfulness preserved order in the temple courts. Spoken of as the castle (Acts 21:37). Here Paul made an address (Acts 22:1-21). Herod constructed a secret passage from the fortress to the temple.

Antothi'jah (ăn-tō-thī'àh; *answers of Jah*), a Benjamite, one of the sons of Jeroham (I Chron. 8:24).

An'tothite (ăn'tō-thīt), a dweller in Anathoth (I Chron. 11:28; 12:3). *See* Anathoth.

A'nub (ā'nŭb), son of Coz and descendant of Judah through Ashur (I Chron. 4:8).

Anvil (Heb. *pă⁴ăm,* beaten, Isa. 41:7), the utensil employed among the Hebrews, as by other nations, for hammering on.

Ape. *See* Animal Kingdom.

Apel'les (à-pĕl'ēz), a Christian in Rome, whom Paul salutes in his epistle to the church there (Rom. 16:10), and calls "approved in Christ," A. D. 60. According to the old Church traditions, Apelles was one of the seventy disciples, and bishop either of Smyrna or Heracleia. The Greeks observe this festival on October 31.

Aphar'sachites (à-fär'să-kīts, Ezra 5:6; 6:6), or **Aphar'sathchites** (à-fär'săth-kīts, Ezra 4:9), an unknown people, quite probably identical with Assyrian tribes who were settled by Asnapper (Ashurbanipal) (669-626 B. C.) in Samaria.

Aphar'sites (à-fär'sīts, only in Ezra 4:9), an inhabitant of an unknown region of the Assyrian empire, whence colonists had been sent to Samaria after its capture.

A'phek (ā'fĕk; *strength, fortress*).

  1. A city mentioned in Josh. 13:4 apparently north of Sidon, and accordingly commonly identified with *Afqa,* ancient Aphaca some 23 miles north of Beirut.

  2. Aphek (Aphik) an Asherite city not conquered by the Israelites (Josh. 19:30; Judg. 1:31. A. Alt locates it at Tell Kurdaneh about 6 miles S. E. of Accho (Ptolemais).

  3. A town in the plain of Sharon about 11 miles N. E. of Joppa (modern Ras el-'Ain). It was evidently here the Philistines camped on their way to Shiloh to attack Israel at Ebenezer (I Sam. 4:1, 12).

  4. A town beyond Jordan about 4 miles east of the Sea of Galilee on the highway between Damascus and the plain of Esdraelon, fortress city of Bethshan, modern Afik (Fik). Cf. I Kings 20:26, 30: II Kings 13:17. However, another village between Shunem and Jezreel seems required by the narratives of the Philistine wars in I Sam. 28:4; 29:1, 11; 31:3. *M. F. U.*

Aphe'kah (à-fē'käh; *fortress*), a city in the hill country of Judah (Josh. 15:53). Its site has not been discovered.

Aphi'ah (à-fī'à), the father of Bechorath, a Benjamite and ancestor of Saul (I Sam. 9:1).

A'phik. *See* Aphek 2.

A'phrah (Mic. 1:10). *See* Beth-le-aphrah.

Aph'ses (ăph'sēs), the head of the eighteenth sacerdotal family of the twenty-four into which the priests were divided by David (I Chron. 24:15), B. C. 1000.

Apocrypha. The name given by Jerome to a number of books which in the LXX are placed among the canonical books of the Bible but which, for evident reasons, do not belong to the Sacred Canon. The term itself, a Gr. adj, in the neuter pl. (from *apokruphos* "hidden, concealed") denotes strictly "things concealed." But almost certainly the noun *biblia* is understood, so that the real implication of the expression is "apocryphal books" or "writings." *O. T. Apocrypha.* In its *final* quasitechnical meaning of "non canonical," in common use since the Reformation, the term specifically refers to the fourteen books written after the O. T. canon was closed and which being the least remote from the canonical books laid strongest claim to canonicity. The O. T. apocrypha have an unquestioned historical and literary value but have been rejected as inspired for the following reasons:

  1. They abound in historical and geographical inaccuracies and anachronisms.

  2. They teach doctrines which are false and foster practices which are at variance with inspired Scripture.

  3. They resort to literary types and display an artificiality of subject matter and styling out of keeping with inspired Scripture.

  4. They lack the distinctive elements which give genuine Scripture their divine character, such as prophetic power and poetic and religious feeling. The O. T. apocryphal books are fourteen in number, classified as follows:

  a. Didactic or Wisdom Literature (2 books).

  1. *The Wisdom of Solomon.* This pseudepigraph is an ethical treatise in commendation of wisdom and righteousness and a denunciation of iniquity and idolatry, written under the name of Solomon. The writer wrote in Greek and was apparently an Alexandrian Jew who seems to have lived between B. C. 150 and B. C. 50. Swete calls this work "the solitary survival from the wreck of the earlier works of the philosophical school at Alexandria which culminated in Philo, the contemporary of our Lord."

  2. *Ecclesiasticus,* called also *The Wisdom of Jesus, Son of Sirach.* This long and valuable ethical treatise contains a very extensive range of instruction in general morality and practical godliness. It follows the model of Proverbs, Ecclesiastes and Job. It was written originally in Hebrew about B. C. 180 and translated into Gr. about B. C. 132 by a

grandson of the original author. About two-thirds of the Hebrew is now extant.

b. Historical Literature (3 books). 1. *I Esdras*. Esdras is the Gr. for Ezra. The book narrates in Gr. the declension and fall of Judah from Josiah's reign, the destruction of Jerusalem, the Babylonian exile, the return of the exiles and the share taken by Ezra in the restored community. The book consists of an independent and somewhat free version of portions of II Chronicles and Ezra-Nehemiah broken by an extended context which has no parallel in the Hebrew Bible (I Esdras 3:1-5:6). Swete calls this "perhaps the most interesting of the contributions made by the Greek Bible to the legendary history of the captivity and the return." (*Intro. to the O. T. in Gr.*, Cambridge 1902, p. 266). 2. *I Maccabees*. This valuable historical treatise covers a period of about forty years from the accession of Antiochus Epiphanes (B. C. 175) to the death of Simon Maccabees (B. C. 135 or a little later). The book is of first-rate importance as a source for the inter-Biblical period and gives a full and worthy account of the important Maccabean wars and the noble struggle for Jewish independence. 3. *II Maccabees*. This much less historically accurate book covers a part of the same period as the first (B. C. 175-160) but offers a striking contrast to it. Swete (*Opus. cit.*, p. 378) calls it "a partially independent but rhetorical and inaccurate and, to some extent, a mythical panegyric of patriotic revolt."

c. *Religious Romance* (2 books). 1. *Tobit*. This is a tale of a pious Naphtalite, named Tobit, who has a son named Tobias. The father loses his eyesight. The son is dispatched to obtain payment of a debt to a certain Rages in Media. On the way an angel guides him to Ecbatana, where he makes a romantic marriage with a widow who still remained a virgin despite the fact that she had been married to seven husbands, all of whom had been killed by a demon named Asmodeus on their marriage day. Encouraged by the angel to become the 8th husband, Tobias escapes death by burning the inner parts of a fish, the smoke of which exorcises the evil spirit. Thereupon he cures his father's blindness by anointing the sightless eyes with the gall of the fish which had already proved so efficacious. The book was probably written as moral fiction toward the close of the 3rd century B. C. 2. *Judith*. Judith, a rich, beautiful and devout Jewish widow is the heroine of the romance with a pseudo-historical background. At the time of the Babylonian invasion of Judah she disguises herself as a traitoress and succeeds in beguiling and slaying the Babylonian general, Holofernes, thus saving her city. The narrative is apparently intended as religious fiction. It is immoral, since it teaches that the end justifies the means. The book dates from Maccabean times and was almost certainly written in Heb. according to R. H. Ottley (*Handbook to the LXX*, London 1929, p. 138).

d. Prophetic Literature (2 books). 1. *Baruch* (with *The Epistle of Jeremiah*). This consists of prayers and confessions of Jews in exile with promises of restoration reportedly written by Baruch, the scribe, in imitation of Jeremiah's language and style. The first five chapters are made nominally to eminate from Baruch, while the 6th was entitled *The Epistle of Jeremy*, i. e., Jeremiah. While Baruch and the Epistle appear in lists which otherwise rigorously excluded non-canonical books, this work never was included in the Hebrew Scriptures and is unquestionably uncanonical. 2. *II Esdras*. This is a religious treatise, apocalyptic in character. Chapters 3-14 purport to record seven revelations granted to Ezra in Babylon, several of which took the form of visions. The book, according to Ottley, is supposed to have been written about A. D. 100. The R. V. contains 70 additional verses in Chap. 7 which were discovered in 1875.

e. Legendary Additions (5 books). 1. *Prayer of Manasses*. This is supposed to be a deeply penetential prayer of Manasseh, the wicked king of Judah, when he was carried away prisoner to Babylon by the Assyrians. It was thought to follow II Chron. 33:18, 19, which outlines Manasseh's wicked reign and his repentance. Its date is uncertain. 2. *The Rest of Esther*. Composed in Greek, this writing consists of passages which were interpolated throughout the canonical Esther of the LXX in the form of visions, letters and prayers intended to explain supposed difficulties and show the hand of God in the narrative. 3. *Song of the Three Hebrew Children*. This, the first of three unauthenticated additions to the canonical book of Daniel, was inserted after Chapter 3:23 and consists of a petition of Azariah in the furnace and an account of the miraculous deliverance, together with an ode of praise of the three. 4. *The History of Susanna*. This amplification of the book of Daniel is in the form of a religious romance, narrating how the godly wife of a wealthy Jew in Babylon is exonerated of the false charges of two immoral men through the agency of Daniel's wisdom. In the LXX the narrative is placed before Daniel and as Daniel 13 in the Vulgate. 5. *Bel and the Dragon*. This final spurious addition to Daniel in melodramatic fashion tells how Daniel destroys two objects of Babylonian worship, Bel and the Dragon, and his escape from the lion's den.

N. T. Apocrypha. The apocryphal books of the N. T., unlike those of the Old, have never claimed the faith of the Christian Church, excepting in a few and isolated instances. There are over 100 of them, and it is doubtful whether one of them appeared before the 2nd century of our era. Most of them portray a much later date. They are valuable as an indication of the growth of thought and the rise of heresy in the age just subsequent to that of the apostles. None of them ever received the sanction of any ecclesiastical council. *M. F. U.*

Appolo′nia (ăp-ŏ-lō′nĭ-à), Gr. *belonging to Apollo*, the name of several towns in the Mediterranean world, so called in honor of the Greek sun god Apollo. Paul visited the famous Biblical city by this name on his second missionary journey (Acts 17:1). It was located on the well-known Roman road called the Egnatian Way, 28 miles W. of Amphipolis in Macedonia. *M. F. U.*

Apol′los (à-pŏl′lŏs), a learned (or eloquent) Jew of Alexandria, well acquainted with the

Scriptures and the Jewish religion (Acts 18: 24). About A. D. 56 he came to Ephesus, where he began to teach in the synagogue "the things of the Lord, knowing only the baptism of John" (v. 25). Here he met Aquila and Priscilla, who "expounded unto him the way of God more perfectly," and Apollos preached Christ with great zeal and power (v. 26). After this he preached in Achaia, and especially at Corinth (18:27, 28; 19:1), having been recommended by the brethren in Ephesus (v. 27). On his arrival at Corinth he was useful in watering the seed which Paul had sown (I Cor. 3:6). Many of the Corinthians became so much attached to him as to well-nigh produce a schism in the Church, some saying "I am of Paul;" others, "I am of Apollos" (I Cor. 3:4-7). That this party feeling was not encouraged by Apollos is evident from the manner in which Paul speaks of him, and his unwillingness to return to Corinth (I Cor. 16:12). Apollos was, doubtless, at this time with Paul in Ephesus. Paul again mentions Apollos kindly in Tit. 3:13, and recommends him and Zenas, the lawyer, to the attention of Titus, knowing that they designed to visit Crete, where Titus was. Jerome thinks that Apollos remained there until he had heard that the divisions in the Church at Corinth had been healed by Paul's letter, and then returned and became bishop of that city. Other authorities make him bishop of Duras, of Colophon, of Iconium (in Phrygia), of Caesarea.

Apol′lyon (à-pŏl′yŭn; *destroyer*), the Greek equivalent (Rev. 9:11) of *Abaddon* (*q. v.*).

Apostasy, *a falling away.* The common classical use of the word is, a political defection (Gen. 14:4, Sept.; II Chron. 13:6, Sept.; Acts 5:37). In the New Testament its more usual meaning is a religious defection (Acts 21:21; I Tim. 4:1; Heb. 3:12). This is called "apostasy from the faith" (*apostasia a fide*): a secession from the Church, and a disowning of the name of Christ. Some of its peculiar characteristics are mentioned: seducing spirits, doctrines of demons, hypocritical lying, a seared conscience, forbidding of marriage and of meats, a form of godliness without the power (I Tim. 4:1; II Tim. 3:5). The grave nature of apostasy is shown by such passages as Heb. 10:26-29; II Pet. 2:15-21; John 15:22. Apostasy as the act of a professed Christian, who knowingly and deliberately rejects revealed truth regarding the deity of Christ (John 4:1-3) and redemption through his atoning sacrifice (Phil. 3:18; II Pet. 2:1), is different from error, which may be the result of ignorance (Acts 19:1-6), or heresy which may be the result of falling into the snare of Satan (II Tim. 2:25, 26). Both error and heresy may accordingly be consistent with true faith. On the other hand apostasy departs from the faith, but not from the outward profession of it (II Tim. 3:5). Apostasy whether among the angels (Isa. 14:13-14; Ezek. 28:15; Jude 1:6), in Israel (Is. 1:5, 6; 5:5-7) or in the Church (Rev. 3:14-16) is irremediable, and awaits judgment. Mankind's apostasy in Adam (Gen. 3:6, 7) is curable only through the sacrifice of Christ. Apostates apparently can only be professors and not actual possessors of true salva-

tion, otherwise their defection would incur severe chastening, or if this failed to restore them, untimely (physical) death (I Cor. 5:5; 11:32; I John 5:16). Revised by *M. F. U.*

Apostle (Gr. *'apostolos,* a *delegate*).

1. **In General.** One sent with a special message or commission. In this sense the word is used in the Septuagint (I Kings 14:6; Isa. 18:2), and in the New Testament: John 13:16, "Neither is he *who is sent* (apostle) greater than he who sent him;" II Cor. 8:23; Phil. 2:25, where persons deputed by churches on special errands are called their *apostles,* or messengers. In Heb. 3:1 Jesus is called the *Apostle* and High Priest of our profession."

2. **Hebrew.** The Jews, it is said, called the collector of the half-shekel, which every Israelite paid annually to the temple, an *apostle;* also those who carried about encyclical letters from their rulers. Paul may have used the word in this sense when he declares himself "an apostle, not of men, neither by men" (Gal. 1:1), plainly indicating that his commission was directly from Christ. (*See also* Rom. 1:1; I Cor. 15:1.)

3. **Christian.** The official name of those twelve of the disciples chosen by our Lord to be with him during his ministry, and to whom he intrusted the organization of his Church. These he chose early in his ministry, and ordained "that they should be with him." The number *twelve* was, doubtless, with reference to the twelve tribes of Israel, and was fixed, so that the apostles were often called simply "the twelve" (Matt. 26:14, 17; John 6:67; 20:24; I Cor. 15:5). Their names were: 1. Simon Peter (Cephas, Bar-jona); 2. Andrew; 3. John; 4. Philip; 5. James; 6. Bartholomew (perhaps same as Nathanael); 7. Thomas (Didymus); 8. Matthew (Levi); 9. Simon Zelotes; 10. Jude (Lebbaeus, Thaddaeus); 11. James the Less; 12. Judas Iscariot. The original qualification of an apostle, as stated by Peter (Acts 1:21, 22), was that he should have been personally acquainted with our Lord's ministry, from his baptism by John to his ascension. By this close personal intercourse with him they were peculiarly fitted to give testimony to the facts of redemption. Shortly after their ordination "he gave to them power against unclean spirits to cast them out, and to heal all manner of diseases;" "and sent them forth two by two, to preach the kingdom of God" (Mark 3:14; Matt. 10:1-5; Mark 6:7; Luke 6:1, 13; 9:1). They accompanied our Lord on his journeys, saw his wonderful works, heard his discourses to the people (Matt. 5:1; Luke 6:13-49) and those addressed to the learned Jews (Matt. 19:13, sq.; Luke 10:25, sq.). They sometimes worked miracles (Mark 6:13; Luke 9:6), sometimes attempted to do so without success (Matt. 17:16). They recognized Jesus as the Christ of God (Matt. 16:16; Luke 9:20), and ascribed supernatural power to him (Luke 9:54), but did not have a high understanding of his spiritual mission (Matt. 15:16; 16:22; 17:20, 21; Luke 9:54; 24:25; John 16:12), and acknowledged the weakness of their faith (Luke 17:5). Jesus taught them to understand the spiritual meaning of his parables (Mark 4:10, sq.; Luke 8:9, sq.), and yet when he

was removed from the earth their knowledge of his kingdom was very limited (Luke 24:21; John 16:12). Apparently loyal at heart, when he was arrested they all forsook him and fled (Matt. 26:56). Before his death our Lord promised to the apostles the Holy Spirit, to fit them to be founders and rulers of the Christian Church (John 14:16, 17, 26; 15:26, 27; 16:7-15), and after his resurrection he confirmed their call, and commissioned them to "preach the Gospel to every creature" (John 20:21-23; Matt. 28:18-20). Shortly after Christ's ascension they, under divine guidance, chose Matthias to be the successor of Judas Iscariot (Acts 1:26). On the day of Pentecost the Holy Spirit descended upon the Church (Acts 2), and the apostles became altogether different men, testifying with power of the life and death and resurrection of Jesus (Luke 24:48; Acts 1:22; 2:32; 3:15; 5:32; 13:31). Their first work was the building up of the Church in Jerusalem (Acts 3-7), and then they carried the Gospel into Samaria (Acts 8:5-25). With this ends the first period of the apostles' ministry, with its center at Jerusalem, and Peter as its prominent figure. In this age Peter represents Jewish Christianity, Paul Gentile Christianity, and John the union of the two. The center of the second period of the apostolic agency is Antioch, where a Church was soon built up, consisting of Jews and Gentiles. Of this and the subsequent period St. Paul was the central figure, and labored with the other apostles (Acts 11:19-30; 13:1-5). In the third period the twelve almost entirely disappear from the sacred narrative, and we have only bits of personal history, which will be found under their respective names.

4. **The Apostolic Office.** As regards the *apostolic office*, it seems to have been preeminently that of founding the churches, and upholding them by supernatural power specially bestowed for that purpose. It ceased, as a matter of course, with its first holders, all continuation of it, from the very conditions of its existence (comp. I Cor. 9:1), being impossible. The bishops of the ancient Churches coexisted with, and did not in any sense succeed, the apostles; and when it is claimed for bishops or any Church officers that they are their successors it can be understood only chronologically and not officially.

5. In a lower sense the term *apostle* was applied to all the more eminent Christian teachers, e. g., to Adronicus and Junia (Rom. 16:7).

Apostles' Creed. *See* Creed.
Apostolic, Apostolical, belonging or relating to or traceable to the apostles, as apostolical age, apostolical doctrine, etc. The title, as one of honor, and likely also implying authority, has been falsely assumed in various ways. The pretended succession of bishops in some churches is called Apostolical Succession. So the Roman Church calls itself the Apostolical Church, and the see of Rome the Apostolical See, the bishop of Rome styling himself Apostolical Bishop. In the early Church all bishops' sees were called *apostolical*, but at length some of the popes declared that the title "apostolical" was their right as successors of St. Peter, and the Council of Rheims (1049)

declared the pope to be the sole apostolical primate of the universal Church.

Apostolic Age, that period of Church history which covers the time between the day of Pentecost and the death of John, the last apostle. The apostolic age lasted as long as the churches were under the immediate guidance of an apostle. The arrangements made by the apostles can be ascribed to our Lord so far as relates to the principle, but not to the details of execution. The form of worship seems to have been very simple, much being left to the choice of individuals and churches. Its principal features, however, with regard to the Sabbath, church festivals, and the sacraments were fixed. There were many pious customs among these Christians, partly new and partly derived from Judaism. The apostolic age is commonly divided into three periods: 1. From the Pentecost until the second appearance of Paul (about A. D. 41). 2. Until the death of Paul (about 67). 3. The Johannean period (about 100).

Apostolical Council, the assembly of the apostles and elders, held in Jerusalem (A. D. 50), an account of which is given in Acts 15. At Antioch, under the labors of Paul and Barnabas, many uncircumcised persons had been gathered into the Church. Some Jewish Christians on a visit from Jerusalem contended that circumcision was necessary to salvation. Paul and Barnabas, with others, were deputed to lay the matter before a general meeting of the Church in Jerusalem.

A preliminary meeting appears to have been held, at which some converts from among the Pharisees showed such opposition (Acts 15:5, 6; Gal. 2) that it was thought best to submit the matter to the whole body. After much disputation Peter told of his experience with Cornelius, and was followed by Barnabas and Paul, who told of their great success among the Gentiles. Then James, as president of the Council, summed up the debate, and pronounced in favor of releasing Gentile converts from the necessity of circumcision and other observances of the Mosaic ceremonial law. The conclusion being agreed to, a letter was drawn up and sent to Antioch by two delegates chosen to accompany Paul and Barnabas (see Acts 15:22, sq.). The letter when read at Antioch gave great cheer to the Gentile converts.

Apothecary (*rāqăh*, to *perfume*, Exod. 30:25; 37:39; Eccl. 10:1, marg. "perfumer"). A person whose business it was to compound ointments in general was called an apothecary or *perfumer* (Neh. 3:8). The work was sometimes carried on by women "confectionaries" (I Sam. 8:13). Originally the "anointing oil" was prepared by Bezaleel (Exod. 31:11; 37:29), after which it was probably prepared by one of the priests. Not least in importance of the duties of an ancient apothecary was the mixing of medicinal herbs. Babylonia, Egypt and other areas of the Bible world early developed the medical arts. A clay tablet excavated in Nippur in lower Babylonia between the Tigris and the Euphrates gives a formula for a balsam unguent prescribed for a metal worker who lived centuries before Abraham and suffered from burns. Apothecaries also prepared spices for burials (II Chron. 16:14).

Ap'paim (ăp'pă-yĭm; *nostrils*), the second names of the sons of Nadab, and the father of Ishi, of the posterity of Jerahmeel, of the tribe of Judah (I Chron. 2:30).

Apparel (*bĕgĕd, dress*, or some form of Aram. *lᵉbish, clothing*). See Dress.

Appeal (Gr. *'epikaleomai*, to *invoke* for aid, Acts 25:11, 12, 21, 25).

1. **Jewish.** In patriarchal times the head of the tribe, or sheik, administered justice, and, having no superior, there was no appeal from his decisions. In the condemnation of Tamar (Gen. 38:24) Judah exercised the power usual over the women of his family. Had the case been between man and man it would, doubtless, have been referred to Jacob. After the Exodus, Moses at first adjudged all cases himself, but at the suggestion of Jethro he arranged for a number of inferior judges, with evident right of appeal to himself (Exod. 18:13, 26). Later on the judges of the different towns were to bring all difficult cases which they were unable to decide before the Levitical priests and judges at the place of the sanctuary for a final decision (Deut. 17:8-11).

According to the above regulation the appeal lay in the time of the Judges to the judge (Judg. 4:5), and under the monarchy to the king, who appears to have deputed certain persons to inquire into the facts of the case, and record his decision thereon (II Sam. 15:3). Jehoshaphat delegated his judicial authority to a court permanently established for the purpose (II Chron. 19:8). These courts were reestablished by Ezra (Ezra 7:25). After the institution of the Sanhedrin the final appeal lay to them.

2. **Roman.** A Roman citizen under the republic had the right of appealing in criminal cases from the decision of a magistrate to the people; and as the emperor succeeded to the power of the people there was an appeal to him in the last resort. St. Paul, as a Roman citizen, exercised a right of appeal from the jurisdiction of the local court at Jerusalem to the emperor (Acts 25:11). But as no decision had been given there could be no appeal, properly speaking, in his case; the language used (Acts 25:9) implies the right on the part of the accused of electing either to be tried by the provincial magistrate or by the emperor. Since the procedure in the Jewish courts at that period was of a mixed and undefined character, the Roman and Jewish authorities coexisting and carrying on the course of justice between them, Paul availed himself of his undoubted privilege to be tried by the pure Roman law (Smith, *Dict.*, s. v.).

3. **Ecclesiastical.** In the early Church all ecclesiastical matters were determined by the bishop with his court, an appeal being allowed to the provincial synod. Appeal to the pope was first formally recognized by the Council of Sardica (A. D. 343), where it was agreed that a condemned bishop had the right of appeal to the pope, who should either confirm the verdict of the synod or appoint new judges. The decision of the council was not at first generally accepted, yet within the next half century the assumption obtained that in all important cases an appeal could be made not only by a bishop, but by anyone aggrieved. Thus it came to pass that during the mediaeval period the pope became, *ex officio*, the ecclesiastical judge of highest resort for all the nations whose Churches acknowledged obedience to him. The first instance in England of an appeal occurred in the reign of Stephen, but the concession was withdrawn under Henry II when one of the Constitutions of Clarendon decided that no appeals should be made to the pope without the king's consent. In Germany the first reaction against papal usurpation appeared in the "Golden Bull," which forbade appeals to Rome from a civil court. The *Concordatum Constant* (1418), and the decree of the thirty-first sitting of the Council of Basel, determined that appeals to the pope should not be decided in Rome by the *curia*, but by *judices in partubis*, chosen first by provincial or diocesan synods, and afterward by the bishops and chapters. The following is from the *Catholic Dictionary* (s. v.): "*The object* of appeals is the redress of injustice, whether knowingly or ignorantly committed. Appeal can be made from any judge recognizing a superior; thus no appeal is possible in secular matters from the decision of the sovereign power, or the highest secular tribunal, in any country; for these, in such matters, recognize no superior. There can be no appeal from the pope, for he, as the vicar of Christ, recognizes no superior on earth. . . . Nor can an appeal be made from a general council legitimately convened and approved, because it, being in union with the Roman pontiff who approved it, represents the whole Church, from the sentence of which there can be no appeal." In the Methodist, the Presbyterian, and most of the Protestant Churches the right of appeal is recognized and modes of procedure provided for in their several books of Discipline.

Appearance, a term usually applied to the interviews granted to the disciples by Jesus after his resurrection. From the several accounts we see that our Lord's body had undergone a change, having extraordinary powers of locomotion, of becoming invisible and visible at pleasure, while it still retained characteristics of matter, and was capable of taking food in the ordinary way. The following appearances are recorded: To Mary Magdalene (Mark 16:9, 10; John 20:11-18); to other women (Matt. 28:9, 10); to Simon Peter (Luke 24:34; I Cor. 15:5); to the two going to Emmaus (Luke 24:13, s. q.); to ten apostles (Mark 16:14; John 20:19); to apostles, including Thomas (John 20:26, s. q.); to seven disciples at the Sea of Galilee (John 21:1, s. q.); to five hundred (Matt. 28:16-20; Mark 16:15-18; I Cor. 15:6); to James, then then to all apostles, and gives them a commission (Luke 24:44-49; Acts 1:3-8; I Cor. 15:7); at the ascension (Mark 16:19, 20; Luke 24:50-53; Acts 1:9-12).

Appearing of our Lord (I Tim. 6:14; II Tim. 1:10; 4:1, 8, etc.). See Advent, Second.

Apphia (ăf'ĭ-à), the name of a woman affectionately saluted by Paul (A. D. 64) as a Christian at Colosse (Philem. 2), supposed by Chrysostom and Theodoret to have been the wife of Philemon, with whom, according to tradition, she suffered martyrdom. *See* Philemon.

Ap'pii Fo'rum (ăp-ĭ-ī fō'rŭm), the market place of Appius. A town or station located forty miles from Rome, upon the "Appian

28. The Appian Way

Way," over which Paul passed on his way to the capital (Acts 28:15). Three Taverns was a village about ten miles nearer Rome.

Apple. *See* Vegetable Kingdom.

Approve. *See* Glossary.

Apron. *See* Dress.

A'qabah (ä'kȧ-bä), **Gulf of.** The Northern arm of the Red Sea, at the head of which lay Solomon's copper smelting seaport of Eziongeber (I Kings 9:26). This important commercial emporium has been excavated by Nelson Gleuck with the Am. Sch. of Oriental Research, shedding much light on the reign of Solomon and disclosing an important source of his great wealth as a "copper king" and copper exporter.

Aq'uila (ăk'wĭ-lȧ; *eagle*), a Jew and a native of Pontus, and by occupation a tentmaker. Fleeing from Rome in consequence of an order of Claudius commanding all Jews to leave that city, he went to Corinth, where he was living when Paul found him; and, being of the same handicraft, abode with him. Some time after, being opposed by the Jews, and perhaps to remove any obstacle to his acceptance by the Gentiles, Paul left the house of Aquila and dwelt with one Justus. It is not certain when Aquila and his wife, Priscilla, were converted to Christianity, but it was before Paul left Corinth, for they accompanied him to Ephesus. While there they instructed Apollos in "the way of God more perfectly" (Acts 18), and appear to have been zealous promoters of the Christian cause in that city (I Cor. 16:19). At the time of Paul's writing to Corinth, Aquila and his wife were still at Ephesus (I Cor. 16:19), but in Rom. 16:3 we find them again at Rome, and their house a place of assemblage for Christians. Some years after they appear to have returned to Ephesus, for Paul sends salutations to them during his second imprisonment at Rome (II Tim. 4:19), as being with Timothy. Nothing further concerning them is known.

Ar (är; *city*), the same as Ar Moab (Num. 21:15, 28; Deut. 2:9, 18, 29), on the border of the Arnon (22:36).

A'ra (ä'rȧ), the last named of the three sons of Jether, of the tribe of Asher (I Chron. 7:38).

A'rab (ä'răb; *ambush*), a city in the mountains of Judah, and given to that tribe (Josh. 15:52). Modern er-Rabiyeh, a ruin east of Dumah.

Ar'abah (är'ȧ-bäh; *desert*, Josh. 18:18), *the* Arabah (A. V. "the plain"), is applied (Deut.

1:1; 2:8; 3:17; 4:49; Josh. 3:16; 12:1, 3; II Kings 14:25; Amos 6:14) to the great valley between the Dead Sea and the Gulf of Akabah. It may, however, be used as the proper name of the whole valley lying between Mount Hermon and the Red Sea. "By using two of its names which overlap each other we may call it the Jordan-'Arabah valley. From the Lake of Galilee to the S. of the Dead Sea it is called by the Arabs the Ghôr, or Depression." "Toward Jericho, . . . although there is so much fertility, the stretches of sour soil, the unhealthy jungle, the obtrusive marl, and the parched hillsides out of the reach of the streams justify the Hebrew name of the Arabah or Desert. In the New Testament also the valley is called a wilderness (Mark 1:4, 5)." "Robinson (*B. R.*, ii, 490) states that the exact point of division between El Ghor and El 'Arabah is a line of white cliffs which crosses the valley obliquely beyond the flat marshland to the S. of the Dead Sea. From there S. to Akabah is the

29. The Dead Sea and Arabah

'Arabah; but N. to the Lake of Galilee, the Ghôr" (Smith, *Hist. Geog.*, pp. 47, 484, 507, note).

Ara'bia (ȧ-rā'bĭȧ; *desert*). Arabia does not in the Bible denote the whole peninsula between the Red Sea and the Persian Gulf, but only the northern part, contiguous to Palestine (Isa. 21:13; Jer. 25:24; Ezek. 27:21); and in the same manner "the Arabian" (Isa. 13:20; Jer. 3:2) does not denote the Arab in general, but only the inhabitant of the northern prairies and deserts. Only in the later books of the Old Testament, as, for instance, II Chron. 21:16, where the Arabians are spoken of together with the Ethiopians, or in Neh. 2:19; 6:1, and in the New Testament (Acts 2:11; Gal. 1:17; 4:25) the name seems to have obtained a more general signification. Arabia comprises an area of about one million square miles, with about eight million inhabitants (Schaff-Herzog).

It is the world's largest peninsula, consisting of a desert area about one-third the size of the United States. Its ancient divisions were Arabia Petraea (the N. W. section), Arabia

31. Map of Arabia

30. The Treasury, Petra

Felix or Yemen (the S. portion) and Arabia Deserta (the northern part). The large oil-rich kingdom of Saudi Arabia, the small S. W. kingdom known as the Imamate of Yemen, the British protectorates of Aden in in the S. W., adjacent Hadramaut, together with three small Arab kingdoms (Oman, the Bahrein Islands and Kuwair on the E. bordering the Persian Gulf) make up the vast area today.

South Arabia had a very old civilization comprehending the Minaean Kingdom with capital at Karnaw (modern *Ma'in*), roughly from 1300 B. C.-950 B. C. The Sabaean period extends from about 950 B. C. to 115 B. C. About 650 B. C. the Sabaeans succeeded

to the power of the Minaeans with a kingdom whose capital was at Ma'rib. From 1950 on campaigns of excavation in South Arabia have done much to stabilize the chronology of this region from c. 1000 B. C. to the 2nd century A. D. As a result pottery, buildings, inscriptions, etc. can now be dated within at least reasonable time limits. Revised by *M. F. U.*

Arabians. *See* Arabia.

A'rad (ă'răd; *fugitive*).

1. In Num. 21:1 "king Arad" should read "king of Arad." One of the "sons" of Beriah, of the tribe of Benjamin (I Chron. 8:15).

2. A Canaanite city on the southernmost borders of Palestine, whose inhabitants drove back the Israelites while trying to enter Canaan from Kadesh (Num. 21:1; 33:40), but were finally subdued by Joshua (Josh. 12:14; Judg. 1:16). It lay twenty miles S. of Hebron, and is now called Tell Arad.

A'rah (ă'răh; *wayfaring*).

1. The first named of the three sons of Ulla, of the tribe of Asher (I Chron. 7:39).

2. An Israelite, whose posterity (variously stated as seven hundred and seventy-five and six hundred and fifty-two in number) returned from Babylon with Zerubbabel (Ezra 2:5; Neh. 7:10), B. C. 536. He is probably the same as the Arah whose son, Shechaniah, was father-in-law of Tobiah (Neh. 6:18).

A'ram (ă'răm), son of Shem, progenitor of the Aramaean peoples (Gen. 10:22, 23), who spread widely in Syria and Mesopotamia from the Lebanon Mountains to beyond the Euphrates and from the Taurus Range on the north to Damascus and northern Palestine on the south. Contacts of the Aramaeans in the Balikh-Habur region (Paddan-Aram, "the plain of Aram," Gen. 24:10; 28:5) with the Hebrews goes back to the patriarchal age (Gen. 31:47). The maternal ancestry of Jacob's children was Aramaic (Deut. 26:5). During the long period of Israel's sojourn in Egypt, their wanderings in the Sinaitic Wilderness, and the extended period of the Judges in Canaan, the Aramaeans were multiplying and extending in every direction, particularly southward. By the time of Saul (B. C. c. 1020), Aramaic expansion was beginning to clash with Israelite strength and by this time several Aramaean districts appear prominently in the O. T. narratives.

1. **Aram-Naharaim**, "Aram of the (Two) Rivers," was the country between the Tigris and Euphrates (Greek, Mesopotamia) or more probably the territory between the Euphrates and the Habur. This was the region of Haran where the Aramaeans had settled in patriarchal times, where Abraham sojourned, and from which Aramaean power spread.

2. **Aram-Damascus** emerged from a petty south Syrian state when a man named Rezin seized the city at the time David conquered Zobah (I Kings 11:23, 24) and founded a strong Aramaean kingdom there. This power was the inveterate foe of the Northern Kingdom for more than a century and a half under such powerful Aramaean rulers as Hezion, Tabrimmon, the Benhadads, Hazael and Rezin. The Aramaic kingdom of Damascus did not come to an end until destroyed by Assyria in 732 B. C.

3. **Aram-Zobah**, a powerful Aramaean kingdom which flourished north of Hamath and reached its zenith under Saul and the early years of David's reign. David conquered it and incorporated it into his realm (II Sam. 8).

4. **Aram-Maachah** was an Aramean principality which lay east of the Jordan near Mount Hermon (Josh. 12:5; 13:11) and extended at least as far west as the Jordan.

5. **Geshur** was a small Aramaic principality east of the Jordan and the Sea of Galilee and S. of Maachah within Manasseh's territory (Deut. 3:14; II Sam. 15:8 R. V.; 13:37).

6. **Aram-Beth-Rehob** is in the general vicinity of Geshur. If identical with the place mentioned in Num. 13:21 and Judg. 18:28, it was near Maacah and Dan.

7. **Tob** was an Aramaic principality E. of the Jordan and is probably identifiable with et-Taiyibeh, 10 miles south of Gadara. Thither Hanun, king of Ammon, drew soldiers to war against David (II Sam. 10:6 R. V.). David was bound to clash with these Aramaean kingdoms at his back door. He conquered them and incorporated them into his kingdom, making possible the empire of Solomon. *M. F. U.*

Arama'ic (ăr-ȧ-māʹĭk) a northwest Semitic dialect. It was formerly inaccurately called Chaldee (Chaldaic) because spoken by the Chaldeans of the book of Daniel (2:4-7:28). But since the Chaldeans are known to have generally spoken Akkadian, the term Chaldee has been abandoned. Numerous references to the Aramaeans (*Arimi, Ahlâme*) occur in Assyrian records from the 14th century B. C. onward. Monumental inscriptions in Aramaic also are found, such as the votive stela of Benhadad II set up about 850 B. C. and discovered in 1941 just north of Aleppo in Syria. These monuments inscribed in Aramaic extend into the Persian Period, when Aramaic became the lingua franca of all S. W. Asia as the result of the traffic of Aramaean merchants; business documents, weights, measures, etc. are found

in Aramaic dating in the 8th to the 5th century B. C. The main source of Aramaic, however, is the deposit of Aramaic papyri from Elaphantine in Upper Egypt dating from 500-400 B. C. Our Lord spoke Galilean Aramaic, and Aramaic portions of the O. T. include Dan. 2:4-7:28; Ezra 4:8-6; 7:12-26; Jer. 10:11 (gloss?). The Greeks called Aram, Syria; consequently the language is called "Syriac" (Dan. 2:4). This designation is now confined to the Aramaic dialect spoken at Edessa, which became the language of the Christian churches of Syria and Mesopotamia. *M. F. U.*

Ar'arat (ărʹȧ-răt, Gen. 8:4; Jer. 51:27). This name, from being applied to the country between the Tigris and the Caucasus Mountains, known as Armenia, and called in the Assyrian inscription Urarti, came to apply to the mountain range, and especially to the double conical peaks about seven miles apart and respectively fourteen thousand and ten thousand three hundred feet in height above the plain below. The greater height, called by the natives Massis, or Varaz-Baris, and by the Persians Kuhi-Nuh, "the mountain of Noah," has its top covered with perpetual snow. Native traditions locate the resting-place of the ark on the southern slope; Assyrian inscriptions settle upon a peak further S. in the territory E. of ancient Assyria, Mt. Nisi'r, by name, 9,000 feet high and commonly identified with Pir Omar Gudrun. *See* Fig. 30.

Arau'nah (ȧ-rāʹnȧ), a Jebusite who had a threshing floor on Mount Moriah, which he sold to David as a site for an altar to Jehovah. The angel of pestilence, sent to punish King David for taking a census of the people, was stayed in the work of death near the plot of ground belonging to this person. When David desired to purchase it, he liberally offered the ground to him as a free gift. David insisted upon paying Araunah, giving him, according to II Sam. 24:24, fifty shekels of silver, and according to I Chron. 21:25, six hundred shekels of gold.

NOTE—Many efforts have been made to reconcile this difference, some saying that the fifty shekels were given for the oxen, and the six hundred shekels for the land; others, that the fifty shekels were for the thrashing floor and oxen, and the six hundred shekels for additional ground. This land was the site of the temple (II Chron. 3:1). Araunah's name is sometimes written Ornan. See Chronicles.

Ar'ba (ărʹbȧ; *four*), a giant, father of Anak. From him Hebron derived its early name of Kirjath-arba, i. e., *city of Arba* (Gen. 35:27; Josh. 14:15; 15:13; 21:11).

Ar'bathite, The, (ărʹbȧ-thīt), i. e., a native of Beth-arabah in the Ghôr. Abialbon the Arbathite was one of David's mighty men (II Sam. 23:31; I Chron. 11:32).

Ar'bite (ärʹbīt), Paarai the Arbite was one of David's guards (II Sam. 23:35). The word signifies a native of Arab in the hill country of Judah. In I Chron. 11:37 the name is given as Naarai.

Arch (Heb. *'ēläm*), an architectural term in Ezek. 40:16, 22, 26, 29. These terms are very difficult of explanation. By some they are thought to be the same as *'ūläm*, a *vestibule* or *porch*. Keil, following Kliefoth, considers them to be those portions of the inner side walls of

32. American School of Oriental Research, Jerusalem, Jordan (Photo by John C. Trever)

the gateway which projected in the same manner as the two pillars by the porch, viz., the intervening walls between the three guard rooms, and also those portions of the side walls which enclosed the two thresholds on either side (*Com.*, in loc.). In these projecting side walls were the windows mentioned in v. 16. *See* Architecture.

Archaeology (Gr. *archaiologia, science of ancient things*). General archaeology is a study based on the excavation, decipherment and critical evaluation of records of the ancient past.

1. **Biblical Archaeology** is a more restricted field than general archaeology and deals with the excavation, decipherment and critical evaluation of ancient records of the past that touch either directly or indirectly upon the Bible and its message.

(1) **Its Interest and Importance.** Biblical archaeology, shedding light upon the historical background and the contemporary life out of which the Holy Scriptures came, and illuminating and illustrating its pages with its truly remarkable discoveries, borrows much of the great interest that attaches to it from its connection with the Bible. It is accordingly attracting larger and larger numbers of enthusiastic investigators, students and Bible readers in general. In fact, no field of research offers greater challenge and promises than Biblical (particularly O. T. archaeology. This appears from the simple fact that up to about 1800 exceedingly little was known of Old Testament times except what appeared on the pages of the Scriptures themselves or what happened to be preserved in the writings of classical antiquity. This was considerable for the N. T. era, but was practically nil insofar as the O. T. was concerned, since Greek and

Latin historians catalogued sparse information prior to 400 B. C. As a consequence, knowledge of the O. T. period was confined to the Bible itself, and this, from the point of view of contemporary history, was sparse indeed. The result was that before the advent of modern archaeology about 1800, there was practically nothing available to illustrate O. T. history and literature.

(2) **Its Discoveries.** One can imagine the fervor aroused among serious Bible students by illuminating discoveries in Bible lands from about 1800 to the present. Modern archaeology may be said to have had its beginning in 1798 when the rich antiquities of the Nile Valley were opened up to scientific study by Napoleon's expedition. Toward the middle of the next century the treasures of Assyria-Babylonia were uncovered as a result of the work of Paul Botta, A. H. Layard, H. C. Rawlinson and others. With the decipherment of the Rosetta Stone (*q. v.*), which unlocked Egyptian hieroglyphics, and the reading of the Behistun Inscription (*q. v.*), which furnished the key to Assyrian Babylonian cuneiform, a vast mass of material bearing on the O. T. was released. The finding of the Moabite Stone in 1868 created a veritable sensation because of its close connection with O. T. history and aroused widespread enthusiasm in Palestinian excavations.

However, many of the most notable discoveries affecting the Bible (particularly the O. T.) were not made until within approximately the last sixty years, such as the Code of Hammurabi (1901), the Elephantine Papyri (1903), the Hittite Monuments at Boghazkeui (1906), the tomb of Tutankhamun (1922), the sarcophagus of Ahiram of Byblus

(1923), the Ras Shamra religious epic literature (1929-1937), the Mari Letters and the Lachish Ostraca (1935-1938), the Dead Sea Scrolls (1947) and the remarkable mss. finds in Palestine during the past 8 years, particularly as the result of the explorations at Khirbet Qumran and environs in the vicinity of the N. W. shore of the Dead Sea by the Qumran Caves Expedition of March, 1952. (See Bull. of Am. Sch. of Oriental Research 135 (Oct., 1954), pp. 8-13 R. DeVaux, Revue Biblique 60, (1953), pp. 83 sq.; pp. 854 sq.).

(3) **Its Contributions.** Although archaeological findings in the hands of the purely tehnical scholar, who has little proper understanding or appreciation of the unique message and meaning of the Bible, are continually in peril of being misinterpreted and misapplied and made the basis of unsound theories; archaeology in the hands of the scientist who is at the same time a devout believer, yields vast and far-reaching results for good. Legitimately handled, the contributions of archaeology to Biblical studies are tremendous. (a) **Archaeology Authenticates the Bible.** Although this is a real benefit of archaeological research in Bible lands, especially in dealing with extreme liberalism and the many vagaries of higher criticism, yet its subordinate nature appears from several considerations. In the first place, the Bible does not need to be "proved" either by archaeology, geology or any other science. As God's revelation to man, its own message and meaning, its own claims of inspiration and internal evidence, its own fruits and results in the life of humanity are its best proof of authenticity. It demonstrates itself to be what it claims to be to those who *believe* its message. Since God has made the realization of the spiritual life dependent on faith and not sight (II Cor. 5:7; Heb. 11:6), whatever contributions archaeology or any other science might make in at-

testing the reliability of the Bible can never supplant faith. Scientific authentication may act as a help to faith, but God has established simple trust which honors Him as the medium of receiving His salvation and understanding His revealed ways with man. Despite the truth of these facts, archaeology has an important role in authenticating the Bible both generally and specifically. Generally, scientific archaeology has exploded many extreme theories and false assumptions that used to be paraded in scholarly circles as settled facts. But no longer can higher criticism dismiss the Hebrew patriarchs as mere legendary figures or deny that Moses could write, or assert that the Mosaic legislation is completely anachronistic for such an early age. These and other

34. Excavations at Old Testament Jericho

extreme opinions have been proved completely untenable by archaeological research. Other examples of general confirmation of the Bible are the results of excavations at Shiloh, Gibeah of Saul, Megiddo, Samaria and numerous other Palestinian cities. Cases of specific confirmation, while of course less numerous, are very striking. The historicity of Belshazzar (Dan. 5), the authentication of the name Sargon (Isa. 20:1) and the corroboration of Johoiachin's captivity in Babylon (II Kings 25:27-30) by the actual finding of the name of the king on cuneiform tablets there, are but a few examples of specific attestations. (b) **Archaeology Illustrates and Explains the Bible.** This is by far the most important contribution of archaeological research in Bible lands and its ramifications are practically endless. It is no exaggeration to say that insofar as its background is concerned, the Bible is a whole new book as a result of the marvelous contributions of archaeology toward illuminating and illustrating it. Examples are numberless. Whether it is the longevity of the antediluvian patriarchs, the tower of Babel, the "tel" or "mound" of Josh. 11:13, the central sanctuary at Shiloh, the Tabernacle of Moses or the Temple of Solomon, Jeroboam's golden calves at Bethel or Jonah's preaching in Nineveh, or Paul's missionary tours or John's Patmos visions, everywhere archaeology sheds light on the sacred page and makes its message and meaning more understandable to our present day. (c) **Archaeology Supplements the Bible.** The human authors of the Bible, writing under divine inspiration, were not interested in profane history, geography, ethnology and

33. Inside Stairway to Pool at Gibeon, Jordan, 1956 Excavation

other fields of human knowledge, except incidentally as they chanced to touch upon the history of redemption. It is, therefore, natural from the modern scholar's view that there should be great gaps in the Bible in these branches of learning. While from the divine side and insofar as the spiritual comprehension of the divine message is concerned, there was no need of further knowledge of these and kindred subjects. Yet from a human standpoint light from these spheres of research is of incalculable value in extending Biblical horizons, increasing knowledge of Biblical backgrounds, and giving a fuller comprehension of the message of the Bible. Examples of supplementation are numerous, such as the destruction of Shiloh, which is nowhere recounted in Scripture, but assumed by Jeremiah (Jer. 7:12-15; 26:6, 7). Excavations at the site of Israel's ancient sanctuary by the Danish Expedition uncovered pottery and other evidence showing that this destruction took place B. C. 1050, presumably at the hands of the Philistines (see H. Kjaer, *Journal of Palestine Oriental Society* (1930), pp. 87-114). Other examples occur in excavations at Bethshan, the Esdraelon fortress, destroyed not long after Shiloh, and evidently at the hands of David as a punishment for the ignominious treatment of the deceased king Saul. (I Sam. 31:10, 12; II Sam. 21:12). Striking supplementation is common in the Assyrian period. The Israelite kings Omri, Ahab, Jehu, Menahem and Hoshea and the Judean kings Ahaz, Hezekiah, Manasseh, Josiah and Jehoaiachin are all much better known by the supplementary material gleaned from the cuneiform records of the great Assyrian emperors Shalmaneser III, Tiglath-pileser III, Sargon II, Sennacherib, Esarhaddon and Ashurbanipal. Archaeology has thus yielded momentous results up to the present and gives fair promise of even greater contributions in the future as research in Bible lands progresses. *M. F. U.*

Archangel. *See* Michael.

Archela'us (är-kē-lā'ŭs; *ruler of the people*), son of Herod the Great by a Samaritan woman, Malthace (Josephus, *War*, i, 28, 4), and brought up, with his brother Antipas, at Rome (Josephus, *War*, i, 31, 1). Upon his father's death, Caesar divided his kingdom, giving to Archelaus (B. C. 4) Idumea, Judea, and Samaria, with the important cities, Caesarea, Sebaste, Joppa, and Jerusalem. His share of the kingdom brought him a yearly income of six hundred talents. He was made ethnarch, with promise of becoming king if he ruled virtuously (Josephus, *Ant.*, xvii, 11, 4). After Herod's death, and previous to going to Rome to receive the government, Archelaus ordered his soldiers to attack the Jews, who were becoming very tumultuous, at the temple. The attack resulted in the death of about three thousand Jews. On his going to Rome the Jews sent a deputation of the principal citizens protesting against his cruelty, and asking to be permitted to live according to their own laws, under a Roman governor. Some have thought that our Lord alludes to this circumstance in Luke 19:21-27. Archelaus returned to Judea, and, under pretense that he had countenanced the seditions against

him, he deprived Joazar of the high priesthood, and gave that dignity to his brother Eleazar. He governed Judea with so much violence that in the tenth (ninth according to Dio Cassius) year of his reign he was dethroned, deprived of his property, and banished to Vienna, in Gaul (Josephus, *Ant.*, xvii, 13, 2). His cruelty was manifested toward Samaritans as well as Jews. The parents of our Lord turned aside, from fear of him, on their way back from Egypt, and went to Nazareth, in Galilee, in the domain of his gentle brother Antipas (Matt. 2:22). Archelaus illegally married Glaphyra, the wife of his brother Alexander, during the lifetime of the latter.

Archers (Heb. *qǎshshäth, bowman*, Gen. 21:20; *bǎ'ǎl hēṣ, arrow-man*, Gen. 49:23; *'ĕnôsh bǎqqĕshēth, bowman*, I Sam. 31:3; also *shooter with the bow*, I Chron. 10:3; *one bending the bow*, Jer. 51:3). The bow and arrow are weapons of very ancient origin (Gen. 48:22; 49:24; comp. Gen. 9:14, 15). Archers were very numerous among the Hebrews, especially in the tribes of Benjamin and Ephraim (Psa. 76:3; I Chron. 8:40; II Chron. 14:8; 17:17). Archers are frequently found on the Egyptian monuments and Babylon sculptures. Reference is made to the Philistine archers in I Sam. 31:3, and the Persians were famous for their archers (Isa. 13:18; Jer. 49:35; 50:29). *See* Armor.

vites were inhabitants of Erech (*Warka*).

Ar'chevite (är'kĕ-vīt; Ezra 4:9). The Archevites were inhabitants of Erech (*Warka*). Thence came part of the colonists of Samaria after its capture.

Ar'chi (är'kī), a city or district in the neighborhood of Beth-el (Josh. 16:2). *See* Archite.

Archip'pus (är-kĭp'ŭs; *master of the horse*), a Christian minister at Colosse, to whom Paul sends a salutation, calling him "our fellow-soldier" (Philem. 2), and whom he exhorts to increased activity (Col. 4:17), A. D. 61 In the Epistle to Philemon he is addressed jointly with Philemon and Apphia, from which it has been inferred that he was a member of Philemon's family. Tradition states that he was one of Jesus's seventy disciples, and suffered martyrdom at Chonae, near Laodicea.

Ar'chite (är'kīt). The Archites, if we may judge from Josh. 16:2, were a family whose possessions were upon the southern boundary of the tribe of Ephraim, between Beth-el and Ataroth. The term is applied to *Hushai* (*q. v.*), who adhered to David during Absalom's rebellion (II Sam. 15:32; 16:16; 17:5, 14; I Chron. 27:33). Modern 'Ain 'Arik(?).

Architecture. Today hundreds of architectural works built in Bible times and known to Bible characters have been dug up in Bible lands and may be seen. However, the architectural beauty which the Hebrews knew was largely the result of Egyptian, Babylonian, Assyrian, Phoenician, Greek or Roman influence.

1. **Egyptian.** Egyptian art and architecture were splendid almost from the time of Menes of the first Dynasty c. 2900-2700 B. C. Abraham, Jacob and their ancestors gazed upon the gigantic pyramids which were already centuries old by Abraham's time (c. 2000

35. Thutmose IV in Battle with the Syrians (from His Chariot in the Cairo Museum)

B. C.) and belong to the Old Kingdom B. C. (dynasties 3-6) c. 2700-2200 B. C. Djoser, first king of the third Dynasty, had an architect who constructed for him the famous Step Pyramid at Saqqara. Khufu, founder of the fourth Dynasty, built the greatest of the pyramids at Gizeh whose base covers 13 acres, required 2,300,000 2½-ton blocks of yellow limestone to erect and towered originally 481 feet in height. Kafre, the successor of Khufu, built the even more spectacular second pyramid at Gizeh, 447½ feet high. Kafre himself is represented in the head of the Sphinx which stands to the E. of the Second Pyramid, and which was carved out of a spur of natural rock and built up with blocks of stone at the same time the pyramid of Khafre was constructed. Kings of the fifth and sixth Dynasties carved the famous pyramid texts on the walls of the inner chambers of their pyramids. Harvard University with George Reisner, Clarence Fisher and the Boston Museum of Fine Arts excavated and explored the tombs and temples near Mycerinos and studied the great pyramids and the sphinx. Remarkable temples, tombs, etc. were part of Egypt's long and brilliant history. But in the New Kingdom (Dynasties 18-20), c. 1570-c. 1150 B. C., when Egypt ruled the East, many architectural wonders appeared such as the exquisite Mortuary Temple of Queen Hatshepsut (c. 1500 B. C.) at Deir-el-Bahri, near Thebes, a beautiful structure of white limestone built in colonnaded terraces. Two great obelisks of Hatshepsut were also erected at Karnak. Thutmose III (died c. 1450) built magnificently and enlarged the palatial temple of Amun at Karnak (ancient Thebes). The tomb

of his vizier, Rekhmire, is in itself remarkable. Another outstanding builder was Ramesses II (c. 1301-c. 1234 B. C.). His mortuary temple, the Ramesseum at Thebes, is exquisite. Moreover, he added to the temple at Luxor and constructed the enormous hypostyle hall of the Karnak temple, consisting of 134 tremendous columns; this hall was part of the largest temple ever built by man. At Abu Simbel above the First Cataract of the Nile, Ramesses II hewed out a complete temple in the sandstone cliff overlooking the Nile and carved 4 great statues of himself from the rock in front of it.

2. **Mesopotamian.** The O. T. refers a number of times to palaces and other types of Mesopotamian architecture (Isa. 39:7; II Kings 20:18). At Erek (Uruk, Warka, Gen. 10:10) some 50 miles N. W. of Ur the Deutsche Orientgesellschaft under Adolph Koldewey discovered (besides the first cylinder seals and earliest known writing) monumental architecture including temples, remains of the huge mud-brick Tower of Eanna (B. C. c. 2500) and first evidences of the Babylonian stage tower or ziggurat (cf. Gen. 11:1-6). At ancient Ur (Abraham's birthplace) in numerous campaigns Sir Leonard Woolley recovered abundant evidences of Sumerian art, complexes of temples, palaces, city streets and the remains of one of the best preserved ancient ziggurats (cf. Gen. 11:28, 31; 15:7; Neh. 9:7). At Asshur on the Tigris River S. of Nineveh, the German Expedition under Walter Andrae before World War I uncovered an archaic Temple of Ishtar, a fine Temple of Asshur (native god of Assyria), stout city walls, gates and landmarks, reveal-

ing the architectural splendor of the ancient city going back to c. 3000 B. C. At Babylon (Babel) on the Euphrates N. of Kish a German Expedition under Robert Koldewey laid bare the magnificent ancient city of Nebuchadnezzar and an utterly bewildering group of palaces, public buildings, famous streets, including the Processional, masonry temples and a tower identified by many as the Tower of Babel (Gen. 10:10; 11:9, II Kings 17:24, 30, etc.). At Calneh (Calah, Nimrud, Gen. 10:10) some twenty miles S. E. of Nineveh Austin Layard found palaces of Assyrian kings of the 8th century B. C. with man-headed lions and colossal reliefs. At ancient Kish, some 8 miles E. of Babylon, the Oxford University and the Field Museum of Natural History expedition located an ancient palace of the kings of Kish and a Temple of Ishtar. At Nineveh on the Upper Tigris N. of Asshur, A. H. Layard, M. E. Mallowan, H. Rassam and others recovered remains of ornate Assyrian palaces, including the magnificent palace of Sennacherib (c. 704-681 B. C.) containing no less than 71 rooms with almost 10,000 feet of walls lined with sculptured slabs. Besides this, Nineveh yielded the superb library of Asshurbanipal (669-633 B. C.) (cf. Gen. 10:11, 12; II Kings 19:36; Isa. 37:33; Jon. 1:2; Nah. 1:1-3:19; Matt. 12:41). At Khorsabad (Dur Sharrukin) Paul Emile Botta dug up the famous palace of Sargon II (721-705) containing splendid reliefs and enameled tile paintings. At Mari (Tell el Hariri) on the Middle Euphrates near Abou Kemal the Musée du Louvre under André Parrot uncovered a huge palace of Amorite rulers, a temple of Ishtar and a ziggurat. The palace at Mari is most notable, being a tremendous structure covering more than 15 acres, with

royal apartments, offices, school for scribes, etc., besides containing archives yielding 20,000 clay tablets.

3. **Persian.** The most impressive evidence of the height to which Persian art and architecture attained is furnished by the ruins of Persepolis, 25 miles S. W. of Pasargadae. From the latter Darius I the Great (522-486 B. C.) transferred the main capital of Persia to Persepolis. Archaeological excavations at Persepolis by the Oriental Institute of the University of Chicago under the direction of Ernst Herzfeld and Erich Schmidt have uncovered ruins that are mute but eloquent testimony to the splendor that was ancient Persia's. Among the famous buildings are the palace of Darius (known as the Tachara), the Tripylon (reception hall), the Apadana (the huge audience hall of Darius and Xerxes), the Hall of One Hundred Columns, the Gate of Xerxes, with colossal bulls guarding it as in Assyrian palaces, the Harem of Darius and Xerxes, the residence of Xerxes (486-465 B. C.) and the royal treasury which contains fine reliefs of Darius and Xerxes like those in the Tripylon.

Susa (Shushan of the O. T. Neh. 1:1; Esth. 1:2, etc.; Dan. 8:2) in ancient Elam, excavated by a French Expedition under Jacques de Morgan, revealed the palace of Darius I enlarged and beautified by later kings, as its greatest monument of the Persian period. Panels of beautifully colored glazed brick decorated the interior of the palace, many of the designs being executed in relief, including winged bulls, winged griffins, and the famous spearmen of the guard.

4. **Greek.** The architectural glory of Greece is best illustrated at Athens (q. v.). In the 5th century B. C. the ancient hill became a re-

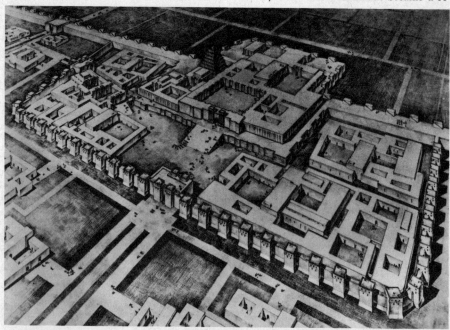

36. Reconstruction Drawing of the Khorsabad Palace of Sargon II of Assyria, by C. B. Altman

37. Temple of Theseus, Athens

ligious center with superb temples, the most important of which were dedicated to Athena, the city's patron goddess. Outstripping all were the world-famous architectural wonders of the Erechtheum, The Parthenon and the Temple of the Wingless Victory. Famous structures located elsewhere in Athens were the Odeion (Music Hall), the Stoa of Eumenes II. The Theseion, The Temple of Zeus and the market place (*see* agora). Besides extensively excavating at Athens, the American School of Classical Studies has conducted 30 seasons of work at Corinth, uncovering a vast agora, a theatre, Temple of Apollo, the Sanctuary of Aesculapius, a Basilica and other buildings. The following Greek orders of architecture appear:

(1) **Doric.** The Doric column consists of (a) the shaft, which increases in diameter almost invisibly up to about one quarter of its height, and diminishes slightly after that point. It has no base, but rests immediately on the stylobate. It is surrounded by semicircular flutings meeting each other at a sharp angle. (b) The capital, consisting of three parts, the *hypotrachelion*, or neck of the column, a continuation of the shaft, but separated by an indentation from the other drums; the *echinus*, a circular molding, or cushion, which widens greatly toward the top; the *abax*, or *abacus*, a square slab supporting the architrave, or *epistylion*. The architrave is the quadrangular stone reaching from pillar to pillar. Above this is the frieze (*zophoros*), surmounted by the cornice.

The style known as the Tuscan is a degenerate form of the Doric. The column has a smooth shaft, tapering up to three quarters of its lower dimensions. Its base consists of two parts, a circular plinth and a cushion of equal height.

(2) **Ionic.** This column is loftier than the Doric; the enlargement of the lower part is less than the Doric; the distance between the columns is greater, and the flutings deeper, and separated by flat surfaces. The Ionic column has a base, consisting of a square slab, and several cushion-like supports separated by grooves. The capital again is more artistically developed, while the architrave is divided into three bands, projecting one above the other, and upon it rises, in an uninterrupted surface, the frieze, adorned with reliefs along its whole length, and, finally, the cornice is composed of different parts.

(3) **Corinthian.** The base and shaft are identical with the Ionic, but the capital takes the form of an open *calix* formed of acanthus leaves, from between which grows stalks with small leaves, rounded into the form of volutes. On this rests a small *abacus* widening toward the top, and on this entablature, borrowed from the Ionic order.

5. **Etruscan and Roman.** The Etruscans united wonderful activity and inventiveness with a passion for covering their buildings with rich ornamental carvings. None of their temples remains, for they built the upper parts of wood; but we have evidences of their activity in *walls* and *tombs*. Some very old gateways, as at Volterra and Perugia, exhibit the true *arch* of wedge-shaped stones. The most imposing monument of ancient Italian arch-building is to be seen in the sewers of Rome, laid in the 6th century B. C.

The Roman architects kept alive the Etruscan method of building the arch, which they developed and completed by the invention of the *cross arch* and the *dome*. With the arch they combined, as a decorative element, the columns of the Greek order. They also introduced building with brick (*see* Pottery). A vigorous advance was made from the opening of the 3rd century B. C., when the Romans began making great military roads and aqueducts.

In the last decades of the republic simplicity gradually disappeared, and a princely pomp was displayed in public and private buildings; witness the first stone theater erected by Pompey as early as 55 B. C. All that had gone before was eclipsed by the works undertaken by Caesar—the theater, the ampitheather, circus, Basilica Iulia, and the Forum Caesaris. These were finished by Augustus, under whom Roman architecture seems to have reached its culminating point. The greatest monument of that age, and one of the loftiest creations of Roman art in general, is the Pantheon, built by Agrippa. Of the luxurious grandeur of private buildings, we have ocular proof in the dwelling houses of Pompeii, a paltry country town in comparison with Rome. The progress made under the Flavian emperors is evidenced by Vespasian's ampitheater (the Coliseum), the mightiest ruin in the world; the baths of Titus, and his triumphal arch. But all previous buildings were surpassed in size and splendor when Trajan's architect, Apollodorus of Damascus, raised the Forum Traianum, with its huge Basilica Ulpia, and the still surviving Column of Trajan.

6. **Hebrew.** The Israelites were shepherds, and by habit, dwellers in tents. They, accordingly, had originally no architecture. It was likely in connection with Egypt that the Hebrews first became builders of cities, being compelled to labor in the vast building enterprises of the pharaohs. From the time of their entrance into Canaan they became dwellers in towns and houses of stone (Lev. 14:34; I Kings 7:10), which, however, in most cases were not built by themselves (Deut. 6:10; Num. 13:19).

(1) **Early Hebrew Architecture.** Hebrew architecture, in the proper sense of the word, did not exist until the time of the kings. Evidently, few if any Israelites before the time of

38. Charles Stevens Reconstruction of Solomon's Temple

Saul had either time or money to indulge in architectural fancies. However, Israel's first king (c. 1020-1000 B. C.) made attempts in this direction as revealed by his fortress city at Gibeah (Tell el Ful), excavated by W. F. Albright (1922 and 1933). But the principal buildings from Saul's era, with massive stone construction and deep walls, were like a dungeon rather than a royal residence in comparison to the Canaanite masonry with which Solomon later graced Jerusalem. "Saul was only a rustic chieftan, as far as architecture and the amenities of life were concerned" (W. G. Albright, *From The Stone Age to Christianity*, Baltimore, 1940, p. 224). Moreover, what was true of Saul was in a general way culturally true of all the Israelite tribes up to the efflorescence of industry and the arts and sciences in the prosperous Davidic-Solomonic era. Israelite poverty and rusticity of life in the premonarchic period have been fully demonstrated by Palestinian excavation.

(2) **Architecture Under David and Solomon.** David as a result of rapid conquest soon had wealth and some leisure to think about building. His first "palace" at Hebron, where he reigned seven years, was perhaps just a flat-roofed stone house, but when he captured the Jebusite stronghold, he built himself "a house of cedar" (I Sam. 7:2) in the S. E. corner of what became Jerusalem. He also began to fortify and build the city itself. But the peaceful reign and vast wealth of his son Solomon gave great impulse to architecture. For his palace and the magnificent temple, which he constructed, Solomon drew heavily upon Phoenician skill. It is now known that the plan of the latter edifice was characteristically Phoenician, which was to be expected, since

it was built by a Tyrian architect (I Kings 7:13-15). Similar ground plans of sanctuaries of the general period B. C. 1200-900 have been excavated in N. Syria at Tell Tainat in 1936, by the University of Chicago, and the findings have demonstrated that the specifications of the Solomonic structure are pre-Greek and authentic for the 10th century B. C. The pillars, Jachin and Boaz (gigantic cressets or fire altars), the proto-Aeolic pilaster, the motifs of lilies, palmettes, cherubim and the cultic furnishings are all authentically early, and show genuine Phoenician or early Semitic genuineness. Archaeological excavations at Megiddo, Hazor and Gezer, give evidence of Solomon's building operations there of "chariot cities" (I Kings 4:26; 10:26) especially the monarch's well-known horse stables at Megiddo.

(3) **Later Hebrew Architecture.** Other kings of Israel and Judah recorded as builders were Asa (I Kings 15:23), Baasha (15:17), Omri (16:24) and Ahab (16:23) (confirmed by the excavations at Samaria), Hezekiah (II Kings 12:11) (confirmed by the Siloam Inscription) (*q. v.*) and Jehoiakim (Jer. 22:14; 36:22). After the captivity, the poverty of the Jewish community made only very modest repairs of walls and construction of a temple possible (Ezra 3:8; 5:8; Neh. 2:8). Later the reigns of Herod and his successor were especially remarkable for their architectural works —the temple (Luke 21:25), Samaria (Sebaste), Caesarea, etc.

7. **Christian.** The early Christians held their services in synagogues, private houses, the fields, the catacombs—indeed, wherever opportunity afforded. As early as in the 3rd century buildings erected by them existed,

but they were neither substantial nor costly. Christian architecture did not become an art until the time of Constantine, when it appeared in two entirely different forms, the *Basilican* and the *Byzantine*.

(1) **Basilican.** When Christianity became the religion of the state and ancient basilicas, or halls of justice, were turned into churches, this style became prevalent throughout the Western countries, and lasted until the 11th century. The lower floor was used by the men, and the galleries reserved for the women. Specimens of this style of architecture still existing and in good repair are S. Paolo fuori le mura. S. Clemente in Rome. S. Apollinaire in Classe in Ravenna, etc.

(2) **Byzantine.** The principal feature of this style is the dome, which was frequently used in Roman tombs. In Persia the problem was first solved by placing the cupola on a square substructure, forming an octagon in the interior of the square by means of a huge pillar in each angle. The Latin cross was abandoned for the Greek cross, whose branches are of equal length. The objection to images obliged the architects to seek some means other than sculpture for enriching the churches, hence the profusion of mosaic work. The masterpieces of this style are St. Mark's at Venice, St. Vitale at Ravenna, and St. Sophia at Constantinople. Still later the Greek cross was combined with the square, and the num-

39. Dome of St. Sophia, Constantinople (Istanbul)

ber of cupolas was increased to nine—one at the end of each arm, one over the crossing, and one in each corner of the square.

(3) **Romanesque.** This resulted from a union of the two previous styles, the basilica and the dome. The ground plan and the interior and exterior of the old basilica were materially changed. A very important feature was the transept, with fixed proportions, the cross being invariably produced by repeating the square, chosen as a unit, three times to the W., and one time respectively to the N., E., and S. Other features were, apses for the side altars; the raised choir, to allow for the crypt; a belfry, first one, and as an independent building, then two, and connected with the western termination of the building; small arched galleries running round parts or the whole of the church within and without; the exterior was covered with numerous well-disposed arches, pilasters, and other ornaments, and the richly decorated doorways and windows drew the eye to the central part of the facade. The result was that the whole external had a dignity not to be found in any other style of church architecture. Among the finest examples of this style are the cathedrals of Pisa, Vercelli, Parma, Modena, and Lucca (in Italy), of Worms, Bonn, Mayence, and St. Gereon and St. Apostoli in Cologne. To this style belong the peculiar churches and round towers of Ireland, and the round tower of Newport, R. I.

(4) **Gothic.** This style retains the ground plan and general arrangement of the Romanesque, but substituted the pointed for the round arch. The pointed arch was probably brought to Europe by the Crusaders from Asia, where it was used by the Saracens. The use of the pointed arch requires, for harmony, a corresponding upward tendency in all parts of the structure, and by obliterating the idea of a mechanical contrivance produces the impression of organic growth. This style arose in the 12th century, reaching its culmination in the 13th, which is known as the "golden period of Gothic architecture." The earliest fully developed example of this style is the cathedral of St. Denis, consecrated in 1144. In northern France it is seen in highest perfection in the cathedrals of Notre Dame (Paris, 1163-1312), Chartres (1195-1260), Rheims (begun 1212) and Amiens (1220-1288). In England examples are seen at Canterbury (1174), Westminster Abbey, London (1245-69), Salisbury (1220-58), and Exeter (1327-69).

(5) **Renaissance.** The Gothic style had never taken such deep root in Italy as in the other countries of Europe. The revival of classic studies resulted in a return to classical forms of architecture. It began with eclecticism, the adoption of the round arch, the cupola, the column in its classical proportions and signification. It ended, however, in servile copying of ancient temples. The chief monument of this style is St. Peter's at Rome.

Respecting modern architecture it can be said that it is marked by no style such as is followed by all builders of the period. Sometimes there is a mixing together of several styles, sometimes a renunciation of style altogether. *M. F. U.*

Arc′turus (ärk′tū-rŭs), a part of the constellation Bootes and one of the three most brilliant stars of the Southern Hemisphere in line with the tail of Ursa Major, "the Great Bear" (Job. 9:9; 38:32).

Ard (ärd; *hump, humpbacked*), named in Gen. 46:21 as a son of Benjamin, and in Num. 26:40 as a son of Bela, and grandson of Benjamin. Both these passages probably refer to the same person, the former mentioning him as a descendant, the latter giving the exact relationship. In I Chron. 8:3 he is called Addar. His descendants were called Ardites.

Ard′ite (ärd′īt), a descendant of Ard, or Addar, the grandson of Benjamin (Num. 26:40).

Ar′don (är′dŏn), the last named of the three sons of Caleb, but whether by Azubah or Jerioth is uncertain (I Chron. 2:18).

Are′li (à-rē′lī), the last named of the seven sons of Gad, and founder of the family of Arelites (Gen. 46:16; Num. 26:17).

Are′lites (à-rē′līts; Heb. same as Areli, Num. 26:17), the descendants of Areli, the last of the seven sons of Gad (Gen. 46:16).

Areop′agite (ăr-ê-ŏp′à-gīt; Acts 17:34), a member of the court of *Areopagus* (*q. v.*).

Areop′agus (ăr-ê-ŏp′à-gŭs), the Hill of Ares, the Greek god of war, equivalent to Roman Mars. Mars' Hill is thus the Latin form of Areopagus. It is the name of a bare rocky place, some 377 feet high, immediately northwest of the Acropolis and separated from it by a narrow declivity. Steps cut in the rock lead to the summit, where benches, rough and rock hewn, can still be seen. In ancient times the Areopagus court assembled at this spot. The word Areopagus in Acts 17:19, 22 may refer either to the hill or to the court which met there. In either case Paul's speech was in all likelihood on this hill as the customary meeting place of the court. This court was composed of city fathers and in early times exercised supreme authority in matters political as well as religious. Although largely a criminal court in the age of Pericles, in Roman times it had reverted once more to interest in matters educational and religious. It is quite understandable therefore that this court "took hold" of Paul and brought him to its judges in session, saying "May we know what this new teaching is, which is spoken by thee?" (Acts 17:19). The Areopagus court, it is true, met at intervals in the Stoa Basileios or Royal Stoa. If this happened to be the case when Paul was in Athens then the famous Apostle gave his address (Acts 17:22-31) in the stoa. This stoa is probably to be connected with the Stoa of Zeus Eleutherios at the northwest corner of the agora (*q. v.*) as now excavated, although future excavations will have to verify this identification. *M. F. U.*

Ar′etas (ăr′ê-tás), a name common to many of the kings of Arabia Petraea, an Arabian king, the father-in-law of Herod Antipas. Herod afterward married the wife of his brother Philip, and in consequence of this the daughter of Aretas returned to her father. Enraged at the conduct of Herod, Aretas instituted hostilities against him, and destroyed his army.

40. Athens from Areopagus (foreground)

Complaint being made to the emperor, he sent Vitellius to punish Aretas, but while on the march news was received of the death of Tiberius, and the Roman army was withdrawn. It is probable that Caligula gave Damascus to Aretas as a free gift (A. D. 38), and he is mentioned as being king of that city by the apostle Paul (II Cor. 11:32).

Ar'gob (ăr'gŏb).

1. An accomplice of Pekah in the murder of Pekahiah, or, with Arieh, a prince of Pekahiah, whose influence Pekah feared, and whom he therefore slew with the king (II Kings 15:25), B. C. 759.

2. An elevated district or table-land, in Bashan, an island in form, some twenty by thirty miles in extent; elsewhere (Luke 3:1) called Trachonitis. It was allotted to the half tribe of Manasseh. The statement (Deut. 3:4) of there being sixty cities in this region is confirmed by recent discoveries. "The sixty walled cities are still traceable in a space of three hundred and eight square miles. The architecture is ponderous and massive: solid walls, four feet thick, and stones on one another without cement; the roofs, enormous slabs of basaltic rock like iron; the doors and gates are of stone eighteen inches thick, secured by ponderous bars. The land bears still the appearance of having been called 'the land of giants under the giant Og" (Porter, *Giant Cities of Bashan*).

Arid'ai (à-rīd'ā-ī), the ninth of the ten sons of Haman, slain by the Jews in Babylonia (Esth. 9:9).

Arid'atha (à-rīd'ā-thà), the sixth son of Haman, slain by the Jews (Esth. 9:8).

Ari'eh (ăr-yā'; *the lion*), either one of the accomplices of Pekah in his conspiracy against Pekahiah, king of Israel, or one of the princes of Pekahiah, who was put to death with him (II Kings 15:25), B. C. 737.

Ar'iel (ăr'Ĭ-ĕl; *lion of God*), one of the "chief men" sent by Ezra to Iddo at Casiphia to bring ministers for the house of God to go with the people to Jerusalem (Ezra 8:16), B. C. about 457.

In commenting upon Isa. 29:1, sq., Delitzsch understands Ariel to mean the "hearth of God," as a figurative name given to Jerusalem. He argues this from the fact of Ezekiel's giving (43:15, 16) this name to the altar of burnt offering in the new temple, and that Isaiah could not say anything more characteristic of Jerusalem than that Jehovah had a fire and a hearth there (Isa. 31:9, "furnace"). "By the fact that David fixed his headquarters in Jerusalem, and then brought the sacred ark thither, Jerusalem became a hearth of God."

Arimathae'a (ăr'Ĭ-mà-thē'à), the birthplace and sepulcher of Joseph in Judea. Here the body of Jesus was buried (Matt. 27:57; Mark 15:43; Luke 23:51; John 19:38). It is thought to be the same as Ramah, the birthplace of Samuel (I Sam. 1:1, 19), which by Keil and Delitzsch (*Com.*, in loc.) is identified with Ramah in Benjamin, about two hours N. W. of Jerusalem.

Ar'ioch (ăr'Ĭ-ŏk), perhaps Sumerian *êri-aku*, *servant of the moon-god*. 1. The king of Ellasar (Larsa, Senkereh, a city-state in S. Babylonia) who was in alliance with Chedorlaomer in his invasion of the Jordan Valley (Gen. 14:1, 9). Some connect this name with Warad-Sin (c. 1836-1824 B. C.) or Rim-Sin (c. 1824-1763 B. C.), sons of Kudur-Mabuk of Larsa. The chronology of this era, however, has not been definitely established. The events of Gen. 14 date c. 2080 B. C. in the Biblical chronological notices of Abraham's life. 2. Captain of the royal guard at Babylon under Nebuchadnezzar II (c. 605-562 B. C.). The name is perhaps the title of the official who, with other authority, had power to execute sentences of death (Dan. 2:14, 15, 24). *M. F. U.*

Aris′ai (å-rĭs′ī), the eighth of the ten sons of Haman, slain by the Jews in Babylonia (Esth. 9:9), B. C. about 480.

Aristar′chus (ă-rĭs-tär′kŭs; *the best ruler*), a native of Thessalonica, and a faithful adherent of the apostle Paul in his labors. He became the companion of Paul on his third missionary tour, accompanying him to Ephesus, where he was seized and nearly killed in the tumult raised by the silversmiths under Demetrius (Acts 19:29), A. D. 59. He left that city, accompanying Paul to Greece, thence to Asia (Acts 20:4), and subsequently to Rome (Acts 27:2), whither he was sent as a prisoner, or became such while there (Philem. 24), for Paul calls him his "fellow-prisoner" (Col. 4:10). Tradition makes him to have suffered martyrdom in the time of Nero.

Aristobu′lus (å-rĭs-tŏ-bū′lŭs; *best counselor*), a person to whose household Paul sends salutation (Rom. 16:10), A. D. 60. Tradition represents him as a brother of Barnabas, ordained a bishop by Barnabas or Paul, and as laboring and dying in Britain. Ramsay (*St. Paul the Traveller*, p. 353) identifies Aristobulus as a son of Herod the Great.

Ark, the name given to three vessels mentioned in the Bible.

1. **Noah's Ark** (Heb. *tēbä*, a *chest*), the vessel in which Noah and his family were saved during the Deluge. It was made of gopher (i. e., cypress) wood, which on account of its lightness and durability was employed by the Phoenicians for shipbuilding. A covering of pitch (bitumen) was laid on inside and outside, to make it watertight and, perhaps, as a protection against marine animals. The ark consisted of a number of "nests," or small compartments, arranged in three tiers, one above another—"with lower, second, and third (stories) shalt thou make it."

The ark was three hundred cubits long, fifty broad, and thirty high; and appears to have been built in the form of a chest, with flat bottom and flat (or slightly sloping) roof, being intended not for sailing, but merely to float upon the water. Light and air were furnished through a window, the construction of which we have not data sufficient to form an intelligent idea. It is uncertain whether the words, "in a cubit shalt thou finish it *above*," refers to the window or the ark. If to the window, then it would seem to imply that it was a cubit wide and ran the whole length of the ark. If to the ark, the passage can only signify that the window was placed within a cubit of the roof. The most probable conclusion is that the window was on the side. Some place the window on the roof, covering it with transparent (or translucent) material. The ark had a door in the side.

In addition to Noah and his family, eight persons in all (Gen. 7:7; II Pet. 2:5), one pair of all "unclean" animals, seven pairs of all that were "clean," and seven pairs of birds, with a contingent of "creeping things," were to be sheltered in the ark. As to the possibility of housing the animals, we must consider the extent of the flood, etc. *See* Flood.

2. **The Ark of Bulrushes** (Heb. same as above). In Exod. 2:3 it is recorded that when the mother of Moses could no longer hide him, she placed him among the reeds of the Nile in an ark (boat) of bulrushes, daubed with slime and pitch. This ark was made from the papyrus reed, which grows in the marshy places of Egypt. Pliny says that "from the plant itself they *weave* boats; and boats of this material were noted for their swiftness." They are alluded to in Isa. 18:2.

Sargon I, founder of a Semitic Empire in Babylonia c. 2400-2200 B. C., was similarly set afloat and rescued from death.

3. **Ark of the Covenant** (Heb. *'ärōn*, the common name for a *chest* or coffer).

(1) **Names.** It was called the "ark of the covenant" (Num. 10:33; Deut. 31:26; Heb. 9:4, etc.), because in it were deposited the two tables of stone, upon which were written the ten commandments, the terms of God's covenant with Israel; "the ark of the testimony" (Exod. 25:16, 22), the commandments being God's testimony respecting his own holiness and the people's sin; "the ark of God" (I Sam. 3:3; 4:11), as the throne of the divine presence. For full description, *see* Tabernacle.

(2) **History.** The history of the ark is in accordance with its intensely moral character. As the symbol of the Lord's presence, it was borne by the priests in advance of the host (Num. 10:33; Deut. 1:33; see also Psa. 132:8). At its presence the waters of Jordan separated, and only when it was carried to the farther shore did the waters resume their wonted course (Josh. 3:11-17; 4:7, 11, 18). The ark was carried about Jericho at the time of its downfall (Josh. 6:4-12). Very naturally, the neighboring nations, ignorant of spiritual worship, looked upon the ark as the god of Israel (I Sam. 4:6, 7), a delusion which may have been strengthened by the figures of the cherubim upon it.

The ark remained at Shiloh until the time of Eli, when it was carried along with the army, in the hope that it would secure victory for the Israelites against the Philistines. The latter were not only victorious, but also captured the ark (I Sam. 4:3-11); but they were glad to return it after seven months (5:7). It was taken to Kirjath-jearim (7:2), where it remained until the time of David. Its removal to Jerusalem was delayed three months by the death of Uzzah while carelessly handling it. Meanwhile it rested in the house of Obed-edom, from which it was taken with greatest rejoicing, to Mount Zion (II Sam. 6:1-19).

When the temple was completed the ark was deposited in the sanctuary (I Kings 8:6-9). In II Chron. 35:3 the Levites were directed to restore it to the holy place. It may have been moved to make room for the "carved image" that Manasseh placed "in the house of God" (II Chron. 33:7); or possibly on account of the purification and repairs of the temple by Josiah. When the temple was destroyed by the Babylonians the ark was probably removed or destroyed (II Esdr. 10:21,

22). Sacred chests were in use among other peoples of antiquity, and served as receptacles for the idol, or the symbol of the idol and for sacred relics.

Ark'ite, (ärk'īt), of Gen. 10:17; I Chron. 1:15, represents the inhabitants of present-day Tell Arka, some 80 miles N. of Sidon at the foot of Lebanon. Arkantu, mentioned by the great Egyptian conqueror Thutmose III (15th century B. C.) is evidently the same place. It was called Irkata in the Amarna Letters and was taken by Tiglath-pileser III of Assyria B. C. 738. *M. F. U.*

Arm, the common instrument of strength and agency, is often used in Scripture as the emblem of power. The "arm" of God is only another expression for his might (Psa. 89:13; Isa. 53:1). Hence *a stretched-out arm, making bare his arm,* ascribed to God, signifies his power and promptness to protect or punish (Exodus 6:6; Deut. 4:34; Isa. 52:10), a figure taken from the attitude of ancient warriors. *To break the arm* means to destroy one's power (I Sam. 2:31; Job. 22:9, etc.).

Armaged'don (är-má-gĕd'ŏn; Gr. *'Armageddon,* from Heb. *hăr Megiddo, hill or city of Megiddo,* Rev. 16:16). Megiddo occupied a very marked position on the southern rim of the plain of Esdraelon, the great battlefield of Palestine. It was famous for two great victories: of Barak over the Canaanites (Judg. 4:15), and of Gideon over the Midianites (Judg. 7); and for two great disasters: the deaths of Saul (I Sam. 31:8) and of Josiah (II Kings 23:29, 30; II Chron. 35:22). Armageddon becomes a poetical expression for terrible and final conflict.

41. Plain of Armageddon

To John the Revelator the ancient plain of Megiddo, the battle ground of the centuries, furnished a fit type of the great battle in which the Lord, at His advent of glory, will deliver the Jewish remnant besieged by the Gentile world powers under the Beast (Rev. 13:1-10) and the False Prophet (Rev. 13:11-18). Apparently the besieging hosts, whose advance upon Jerusalem is typically set forth in Isa. 10:28-32, and who are demon-energized (Rev. 16:13-16; Zech. 12:1-9) have retreated to Megiddo after the events of Zech. 14:2. There their decimation commences and is completed in Moab and Idumea (Isa. 63:1-3). This last grand battle of "the times of the Gentiles" and of this present age, finds fulfilment in the smiting-stone prophecy of Dan. 2:35, and ushers in "the day of the Lord," when God actively and visibly manifests His glorious power to the discomfiture and utter destruction of His enemies. Revised by *M. F. U.*

Arme'nia (är-mē'nĭ-á), Heb. ărărăt, for Akkadian *Urartu,* which occurs frequently in the Assyrian monuments. Sennacherib's sons escaped thither after murdering their father (II Kings 19:37). On one of the mountains of this region the ark of Noah rested (Gen. 9:4). The country extends from the Black to the Caspian Sea and from the Caucasus to the Taurus Mts. It was north of the Assyrian Empire. *M. F. U.*

Armlet. This word is not used in the A. V., being rendered in II Sam. 1:10 by "the bracelet on his arm." *See* Bracelet.

Armo'ni (är-mō'nĭ), the first named of the two sons of Saul, by Rizpah, who was given up by David to be hanged by the Gibeonites. He was slain with six of his brethren in the beginning of the barley harvest (II Sam. 21:8, sq.).

Armor, Arms. The weapons of the nations mentioned in the Bible were essentially the same, with modifications according to age and country. In giving a description of the several weapons, we adopt the ordinary division of Offensive Weapons (Arms) and Defensive Weapons (Armor).

    1. **Offensive Weapons.** (1) **Battle-ax** and **Mace.** The most primitive of weapons were the club and the throwing bat. The *club* at first consisted of a heavy piece of wood, of various shapes, used in hand-to-hand fighting. The *mace* (Heb. *bărzĕl*) was of wood, bound with bronze, about two and one-half feet long, with an angular piece of metal projecting from the handle, perhaps intended as a guard. At the striking end it was sometimes furnished with a ball. Maces were borne by the heavy infantry, and each charioteer was furnished with one. The Egyptian *battle-ax* was about two or two and one-half feet long, with a single blade secured by bronze pins, and the handle bound in that part to prevent splitting. The blade was shaped like the segment of a circle and made of bronze or iron. The *poleax* was about three feet in length, with a large metal ball, to which the blade was fixed. Allusions to these weapons are supposed to occur in Psa. 2:9; 35:3; Prov. 25:18. The *throwstick* is the same weapon seen figured on Egyptian and Assyrian monuments. "Axes" (Ezek. 26:9), literally *irons,* is used figuratively for weapons or instruments of war.

    (2) **Sword** (Heb. *hĕrĕb*). The Egyptian sword was short and straight, from two and one-half to three feet in length, usually double-edged and tapering to a point, and was used to cut and thrust. The king's sword was worn in his girdle, and was frequently surmounted by one or two heads of a hawk, the symbol of the sun, a title given to Egyptian kings. The sword thus worn was really a *dagger,* a common Egyptian weapon. It was from seven to ten inches in length, tapering gradually to a point, the blade, made of bronze, being thicker in the middle than at the edges. Assyrian swords were often richly decorated, the hilt embossed with lions' heads so arranged as to form both handle and crossbar. The sword of the Greeks and Romans generally had a straight two-edged blade, rather broad, and of nearly equal width from hilt to point. It was worn on the left side.

42. Shield, Sword and Girdle

The sword of the Hebrew resembled that of other oriental nations, and appears to have been short. That of Ehud was only a cubit (from eighteen to twenty-two inches) long. It was carried in a sheath held by the girdle (I Sam. 17:39; II Sam. 20:8); hence the expression "to gird one's self" with a sword means to commence war; and "to loose the sword," to finish it (I Kings 20:11).

Figurative. The sword itself is the symbol of war and slaughter (Lev. 26:25; Isa. 34:5, etc.), of divine judgment (Deut. 32:41; Psa. 17:13; Jer. 12:12; Rev. 1:16), and of power and authority (Rom. 13:4). The word of God is called "the sword" of the Spirit (Eph. 6:17). The sword is used in Scripture as illustrative of the word of God (Eph. 6:17; Heb. 4:12); Christ (Isa. 49:2; Rev. 1:16); the justice of God (Deut. 32:41; Zech. 13:7); the protection of God (Deut. 33:29); severe calamities (Ezek. 5:2, 17; 14:17; 21:9); deep mental affliction (Luke 2:35); the wicked (Psa. 17:13); their tongue (Psa. 57:4; 64:3; Prov. 12:18); their persecuting spirit (Psa. 37:14); their end (Prov. 5:4); false witnesses (Prov. 25:18); judicial authority (Rom. 13:4). *Drawing of sword* is figurative of war and destruction (Lev. 26:33; Ezek. 21:3-5); *sheathing it*, of peace and friendship (Jer. 47:6); *living by it*, of rapine (Gen. 27:40); *not departing*, of perpetual calamity (II Sam. 12:10).

(3) **The Spear, Javelin, Dart.** The *spear* is a weapon common to all nations of antiquity. That of the Egyptians was of wood, from five to six feet long, with the head of bronze or iron, usually with a double edge like that of the Greeks. The *javelin* was similar to the spear, but lighter and shorter, the upper extremity of the shaft terminating with a bronze knob surmounted by a ball. It was sometimes used as a spear for thrusting, and sometimes it was darted, the knob of the extremity keeping it from escaping the warrior's hand. The spear of the Assyrian infantry was short, scarcely exceeding the height of a man. That of the cavalry was longer. Several kinds of spears are mentioned in Scripture, but how the several terms used are to be understood is somewhat uncertain. (a) The *hănîth*, a "spear" of the largest kind, was the weapon of Goliath (I

Sam. 17:7, 45; II Sam. 21:19; I Chron. 20:5), and also of other giants (II Sam. 23:21; I Chron. 11:23) and mighty warriors (II Sam. 2:23; 23:18; I Chron. 11:11, 20). It was the habitual companion of King Saul, and it was this heavy weapon, and not the lighter "javelin," that he cast at David (I Sam. 18:10, 11; 19:9, 10) and at Jonathan (20:33). (b) Apparently lighter than the preceding was the *kîdōn (javelin)*. When not in action the *javelin* was carried on the back of the warrior (I Sam. 17:6, A. V. "target"). (c) Another kind of spear was *rōmăh*. In the historical books it occurs in Num. 25:7 and I Kings 18:28, and frequently in the later books, as in I Chron. 12:8 ("buckler"); II Chron. 11:12. (d) The *shĕlaḥ* was probably a lighter missile, or *dart* (see II Chron. 23:10; 32:5, "darts;" Neh. 4:17, 23, see marg.; Job 33:18; 36:12; Joel 2:8). (e) *shēbĕṭ*, a rod or staff, is used once only to denote a weapon (II Sam. 18:14).

Figurative. The spear is used figuratively of the bitterness of the wicked (Psa. 57:4); the instruments and effects of God's wrath (Hab. 3:11).

(4) **Bow and Arrow.** The bow was the principal weapon of offense among the Egyptians, Assyrians, and Hebrews. That of the Egyptians was a round piece of wood, from five to five and one-half feet long, either straight or bending in the middle when unstrung. The string was made of hide, catgut, or string. The Assyrian archer was equipped in all respects like the Egyptian, the bow being either long and slightly curved or short and almost angular. Among the Hebrews the bow, (Heb. *qĕshĕth*), and arrow

43. Assyrian Archers (part of engraved bronze band from gate at palace of Shalmaneser III)

(*hēṣ*) are met with very early in their history, both for the chase (Gen. 21:20; 27:3) and war (48:22). In later times archers accompanied the armies of the Philistines (I Sam. 31:3; I Chron. 10:3) and of the Syrians (I Kings 22:34). Among the Hebrews captains high in rank (II Kings 9:24), and even kings' sons (I Sam. 18:4), carried the bow, and were expert in its use (II Sam. 1:22). The tribe of Benjamin seems to have been especially addicted to archery (I Chron. 8:40; 12:2; II Chron. 14:8; 17:17); but there were also bowmen among Reuben, Gad, Manasseh (I Chron. 5:18), and Ephraim (Psa. 78:9). Of the form of the bow we can gather almost nothing. It seems to have been bent by the aid of the foot (I Chron. 5:18; 8:40; II Chron. 14:8; Isa. 5:28; Psa. 7:12, etc.). Bows of steel, or rather brass, are mentioned as if specially strong (II Sam. 22:35; Job 20:24). It is possible that in I Chron. 12:2 a kind of bow for shooting bullets or stones is alluded to (Wisd. 5:22, "stone-bow"). The arrows were carried in quivers (Heb. *t°lî*) hung on the shoulder or at the left side. They were probably of reed, and mostly tipped with flint points; others were of wood tipped with metal, about thirty inches long and winged with three rows of feathers. They were sometimes poisoned (Job 6:4), or tipped with combustible materials ("fiery darts," *those set on fire*, Eph. 6:16).

Figurative. This word is frequently used as the symbol of *calamity* or *disease* sent by God (Job 6:4; 34:6; Psa. 38:2; Deut. 32:34); the metaphor deriving propriety and force from the popular belief that all diseases were immediate and special inflictions from heaven. *Lightnings* are described as the arrows of God (Psa. 18:14; 144:6; Hab. 3:11). "The arrow that flieth by day" (Psa. 91:5) denotes some sudden danger. The *arrow* is also figurative of anything injurious, as a deceitful tongue (Jer. 9:8), a bitter word (Psa. 64:3), a false witness (Prov. 25:18). A good use of "arrow" is in Psa. 127:4, 5, where children are compared to "arrows in the hand of a mighty man"; i. e., instruments of power and action. The word is also used to denote the efficiency of God's word (Psa. 45:5). The *battle bow* is figurative for weapons of war and the military power (Zech. 9:10; 10:4).

(5) **The Sling** (Heb. *qĕlă‘*), may be justly reckoned as among the most ancient instruments of warfare (Job 41:28). This weapon was common among the Egyptians, Assyrians, and Hebrews. Later the Greek and Roman armies contained large numbers of slingers. The weapon was very simple, being made of a couple of strings of sinew, leather, or rope, with a leathern receptacle in the middle to receive the stone. After being swung once or twice around the head it was discharged by letting go one of the strings. Besides stones, plummets of lead shaped like an acorn were used, and could be thrown to the distance of six hundred feet. The stones were selected for their smoothness (I Sam. 17:40), and were considered as munitions of war. In action they were either carried in a bag (I Sam. 17:40) or lay in a heap at the feet of the slinger. Among the Hebrews the Benjamites were especially expert slingers (Judg. 20:16; comp. I Chron. 12:2).

Figurative. The rejection of one by Jehovah is represented by the expression, "The souls of thine enemies, them shall he sling out, as out of the middle of a sling" (I Sam. 25:29; while in Zechariah (9:15) sling stones represent the enemies of God, which "are trampled under feet like sling stones."

(6) **Engine, Battering-ram.** (a) (Heb. *ḥishābōn*, *contrivance*). The engines which went by this name (II Chron. 26:15) were the *balista*, used for throwing stones, and the *catapulta*, for arrows, an enormous stationary bow. Both of these engines were of various throwing power, stones being thrown of from fifty to three hundred pounds weight. Darts varied from small beams to large arrows, and their range exceeded one quarter mile. All these engines were constructed on the principle of the string, the bow, or spring. (b)

44. A Catapult

(Heb. *m°ḥî*, *stroke*, Ezek. 26:9), the *battering-ram*, so rendered (Ezek. 4:2; 21:22; Heb. *kăr*, *butting*). This instrument was well known both to the Egyptians and the Assyrians. The ram was a simple machine, consisting of a metal head affixed to a beam, which might be long enough to need one or two hundred men to lift and impel it. When it was still heavier it was hung in a movable tower and became a wonderful engine of war. Its object was to make a breach in the wall of a beleaguered town.

2. **Defensive Weapons.** (1) **The Shield.** The ancient soldier's chief defense, his shield, was various in form and material. The shield of the Egyptian was about one-half his height, and generally about twice as high as broad. It was probably formed of a wooden frame covered with rawhide, having the hair outward, with one or more rims of metal and metal studs. Its form resembled a funeral tablet, circular at the top and square at the base. A rare form of Egyptian shield was of extraordinary size and pointed at the top. The shields of the Assyrians in the more ancient bas-reliefs are both circular and oblong; sometimes of gold and silver, but more frequently of wicker work, covered with hides. The shield in a siege covered the soldier's whole person, and at the top had a curved point or a square projection like a roof, at right angles with the body of the shield. This was to defend the combatants against missiles thrown from the walls.

Shield is the rendering in the A. V. of the following words, of which the first two are the most frequent and important: (a) (Heb. *ṣĭnnä*, *protection*) was large enough to cover the whole body (Psa. 5:12; 91:4). When not engaged in conflict it was carried by the armor-bearer (I Sam. 17:7, 41). The word is used with "spear" as a formula for weapons generally (I Chron. 12:24; II Chron. 11:12). (b) (Heb. *mägēn*) was smaller, a buckler or target, probably for hand-to-hand fighting. The difference in size between this and the above-mentioned shield is evident from I Kings 10:16, 17; II Chron. 9:15, 16, where twice as much gold is named as being used for the latter as for the former. This shield is usually coupled with light weapons, as the bow (II Chron. 14:8) and darts (32:5). (c) *shĕlĕt*. The form of this shield is not well known. Although by some it is translated "quiver," and by others "weapons" generally, it is evident that *shields* is proper by comparing II Kings 11:10 with

II Chron. 23:9; II Sam. 8:7; I Chron. 18:7, 8. The *sōhērāh* "buckler" is found only in Psa. 91:4, and is used poetically. (d) Finally, we have the Gr. *thureos* (Eph. 6:16), a large oblong and square shield. The ordinary shield among the Hebrews consisted of a wooden frame covered with leather, and could be easily burned (Ezek. 39:9). Some shields were covered with brass, or copper, and when shone upon by the sun caused the redness mentioned in Nah. 2:3. Shields were rubbed with oil to render the leather smooth and slippery, and to prevent its being injured by the wet (II Sam. 1:21, 22; Isa. 21:5), as well as to keep the metal from rusting. Except in actual conflict, the shield was kept covered (Isa. 22:6). The golden shields mentioned in connection with the equipment of armies (I Macc. 6:30) were most probably only gilt; on the contrary, those of the generals of Hadadezer (II Sam. 8:7) and those Solomon made (I Kings 10:16, sq.; 14:26) are to be regarded as ornamental pieces of massive gold, such as were later sent to Rome as gifts (I Macc. 14:24; 15:18). Brazen shields also occur only in connection with leaders and royal guards (I Sam. 17:6; I Kings 14:27).

Figurative. The shield is illustrative of God's protection (Gen. 15:1; Deut. 33:29; II Sam. 22:3; Psa. 3:3; 5:12; 28:7; 33:20; 59:11; 84:9, 11; 115:9-11; 119:114; 144:2); truth of God (Psa. 91:4); salvation of God (II Sam. 22:36; Psa. 18:35); of faith (Eph. 6:16).

(2) **The Helmet.** The helmet of the Egyptians was usually of linen cloth quilted, which served as an effectual protection to the head, without the inconvenience of metal in a hot climate. The Assyrian helmet assumed different shapes in different ages, but its earliest form was a cap of iron, terminating in a point, and sometimes furnished with flaps, covered with metal scales, protecting the ears and neck and falling over the shoulders.

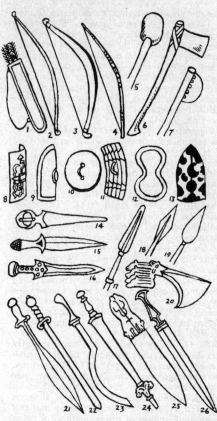

46. Ancient Weapons. Bows and Arrows (1-4); Maces and Axes (5-7); Shields (8-13); Daggers (14-16); Spears (17-19); Swords (20-26).

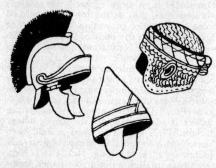

45. Helmets. Left, Roman (200 B. C.); center, Assyrian (750 B. C.); right, Sumerian (2500 B. C.).

We find several references to the *helmet* (Heb. *kōbă'*), as being in use among the Hebrews. They seem to have been commonly of brass (I Sam. 17:38).

Figurative. In Isa. 59:17 Jehovah is represented as arming himself for the defense of man, and among other articles he puts on is "a helmet of salvation," seeming to teach that salvation is the crowning act of God. The helmet as a part of the Christian's armor represents salvation (Eph. 6:17), "the hope" of salvation (I Thess. 5:8, Gr. an *obtaining*).

(3) **The Breastplate**, or **Cuirass.** The earliest material used to protect the body was probably the skins of beasts, which were soon abandoned for coats of mail. The cuirass of the Egyptians consisted of about eleven horizontal rows of metal plates, well secured by brass pins, with narrower rows forming a protection for the throat and neck. Each plate, or scale, was about an inch in width. In length the cuirass may have been little less than two and one-half feet, covering the thigh nearly to the knee; and in order to prevent its pressing too heavily on the shoulder it was bound with a girdle about the waist. Usually, however, that part of the body below the girdle was protected by a kind of kilt, detached from the girdle. Such was the covering of the heavy-armed troops. With the light-armed infantry, and, indeed, among the Asiatic nations in general, the quilted linen cuirass was in much demand.

The Assyrians used coats of scale armor and embroidered tunics, both of felt and leather. Among the Hebrews we have (a) the *breastplate* (Heb. *shiryōn, glittering*), enumerated in the description of the arms of Goliath, a "*coat* of mail," literally, a "*breastplate* of scales" (I Sam. 17:5), and further (v. 38), where *shiryon* alone is rendered "coat of mail." It may be noticed that this passage contains the most complete inventory of the furniture of a warrior to be found in the whole of the sacred history. *Shiryon* also occurs in I Kings 22:34 and II Chron. 18:33. The last passage is very obscure; the real meaning is probably "between the joints and the breastplate." (b) The *tăḥărā'* is mentioned but twice—in reference to the gown of the high priest (Exod. 28:32; 39:23). Like the English "habergeon," it was probably a quilted shirt or doublet put on over the head. Both of these terms are rendered "habergeon" (Exod. 28:30; 39:23; Job 41:26; II Chron. 26:14; Neh. 4:16).

Figurative. Being an efficient means of protection for the body, it is used metaphorically for *defense:* "the breastplate of righteousness" (Eph. 6:14), and "the breastplate of faith and love" (I Thess. 5:8).

(4) **Greaves** (Heb. *mĭṣhäh*, literally, a *facing*), for covering the leg, made of brass and widely known among the ancients, are mentioned in the A. V. only in the case of Goliath (I Sam. 17:6), and the *war boot* (Heb. *seʾōn*), a sort of half boot made of leather, studded with strong nails, only in Isa. 9:5 (literally, "every shoe"). We infer, therefore, that they did not belong to the common armor of the Hebrews.

(5) **Girdle** (Heb. *'ēzōr*), from which the sword was suspended, is frequently mentioned among the articles of military dress (Isa. 5:27; Eph. 6:14). It was of leather, studded with metal plates. When the armor was light the girdle was broad and girt about the hips; otherwise it supported the sword scarfwise from the shoulder. *See* Girdle.

Armor-bearer (Heb. *näsä' keli*, "one carrying weapons"), a person selected by prominent officers to bear their armor, to stand by them in danger, and to carry their orders, somewhat as adjutants in modern service (Judg. 9:54; I Sam. 14:6; 16:21; 31:4).

Armory, the place in which armor was deposited. In Neh. 3:19 mention is made of "the armory at the turning of the wall" in Jerusalem; probably the arsenal ("house of armor") which Hezekiah showed with so much pride to the Babylonian ambassadors (Isa. 39:2, Heb. *nĕshĕq*). A poetical allusion is made to armory in Cant. 4:4 (Heb. *tălpiyyäh*). In Jer. 50:25 God is said to have "opened his armory" (Heb. *'ōṣär*).

Army, represented in Scriptures by several Hebrew and Greek names.

1. **Jewish.** Although Israel was not to be a conquering people, yet it had to defend itself against hostile attacks, at first in the wilderness and afterward in the promised land. Hence Israel marched out of Egypt (Exod. 12:41; 13:18), as the host of Jehovah, armed. As such, the people were arranged according to their tribes and divisions of tribes (Num. 1-4), and every man above twenty years of age was enrolled for military service (Num. 1, sq.; 26:2) with the exception of the Levites (Num. 2:33). Up to what age military duty lasted is not given. Josephus states (*Ant.*, iii, 12, 4) that it was to the fiftieth year.

In time of war the number of fighting men needed was collected from the different tribes under the direction of inspectors (Heb. *shō-*

teʾrîm, Duet. 20:5; II Kings 25:19), by whom also the officers were appointed (Deut. 20:9). The principle on which these levies were made is not known to us. The law provided that anyone having built a new house, not yet consecrated; having planted a vineyard, and not having as yet enjoyed its fruit; or having betrothed but not yet married a wife, should not go to battle (Deut. 20:5-7). The fainthearted were also dismissed, in order that they should not discourage their brethren (Deut. 20:8). The army thus constituted was divided into companies of thousands, hundreds, and fifties under their respective officers (Num. 31:14), and still further into families (Num. 2:34; II Chron. 25:5; 26:12); each father's house probably forming a detachment, led by the most valiant among them. The provisioning of the army was laid on each tribe (Judg. 20:10; I Sam. 17:17, sq.). From the time of Moses to that of David the army of Israel consisted of footmen (I Sam. 15:4), and from the time Israel entered into Canaan until the establishment of the kingdom little progress was made in military affairs.

During the kingdom. Soon after the establishment of the kingdom a standing army was set up, the nucleus of which was the band of three thousand men selected by Saul (I Sam. 13:2; 24:2), and to which he constantly added men (I Sam. 14:52). Before David became king he had a band of six hundred men, gathered in his wars with Saul (I Sam. 23:13, 25:13), from whom his most noted captains were chosen (I Sam. 23:8, sq.). To these he added the Cherethites and Pelethites (II Sam. 8:18; 15:18; 20:7). Moreover, he organized a national militia in twelve divisions, each consisting of twenty-four thousand, and responsible for a month's service every year (I Chron. 27:1). At the head of the army when in active service was a commander-in-chief ("captain of the host," I Sam. 14:50).

The army hitherto had consisted entirely of infantry (I Sam. 4:10; 15:4), the use of horses having been prohibited (Deut. 17:16). David had reserved a hundred chariots from the spoil of the Syrians (II Sam. 8:4), which probably served as the foundation of the force which Solomon enlarged through his alliance with Egypt (I Kings 10:26, 28, 29).

The army, with the exception of a regularly maintained bodyguard (I Kings 14:28; II Kings 11:4, 11), was, strictly speaking, only a national militia, not in constant service, but in time of peace at home engaged in agriculture, and without pay. Even in war their pay probably consisted only of supplies, and a fixed portion of the spoil. These arrangements were kept up by his successors, and by some of them the military power was greatly strengthened by foot and horse (II Chron. 14:8; 17:14; 25:5, etc.). Sometimes foreign troops were hired as auxiliaries (II Chron. 25:6).

With regard to the arrangement and maneuvering of the army in the field, little is known. A division into three bodies is frequently mentioned (Judg. 7:16; 9:43; I Sam. 11:11). Jehoshaphat divided his army into five bodies, but retained the threefold principle of division, the heavy-armed troops of

Judah being considered as the proper army, and the two divisions of light-armed of the tribe of Benjamin as an appendage (II Chron. 17:14-18)." It is very difficult to ascertain the numerical strength of the Jewish army, the numbers given in the text being manifestly corrupted. The discipline and arrangement of the army, was gradually assimilated to that of the Romans, and the titles of officers borrowed from it.

2. **Roman Army.** The Roman army was divided into legions, the number of soldiers in a legion varying at different times. These legions were commanded by six tribuni ("chief captains," Acts 21:31), who commanded by turns. The tenth part of a legion, containing three hundred men, was called a *cohors*, cohort ("band," Acts 10:1); the cohort was divided into three maniples, and the maniple into two *centuries*, originally containing one hundred men, but later varying according to the strength of the legion. These centuries were under the command of centurions (Acts 10:1, 22; Matt. 8:5; 27:54). There were in addition to the legionary cohorts independent cohorts of volunteers. One of these was called the Italian (Acts 10:1), as consisting of volunteers, from Italy. There is a cohort named "Augustus" (Acts 27:1), which Meyer (*Com.*, in loc.) thinks to mean "the imperial cohort, one of the five cohorts stationed at Caesarea, and regarded as bodyguard of the emperor, employed here on special service affecting the emperor." *See* War.

Ar′nan (är′năn; Heb. from Arab., *"quick, lively*), probably the great-grandson of Zerubbabel, in the line of David's descendants (I Chron. 3:21), perhaps the same as Joanna (Luke 3:27), an ancestor of Jesus.

Ar′non (är′nŏn; *rushing torrent*), a river rising in the mountains of Gilead, E. of the Jordan, and reaching the Dead Sea through a stony and precipitous chasm of red and yellow sandstone. The name is also applied to the valley, or valleys, now known as "Wady Mojib," an enormous trench across the plateau of Moab. It is about seventeen hundred feet deep, and two miles broad from edge to edge of the cliffs which bound it, but the floor of the valley over which the stream winds is only forty yards wide. About thirteen miles from the Dead Sea the trench divides into two branches, one running N. E., the other S. S. E., and each of them again dividing into two. . . . Properly all the country from Jabbok to Arnon belonged northward to Ammon, southward to Moab. But shortly before Israel's arrival, *Sihon* (*q. v.*), an Amorite king from western Palestine, had crossed the Jordan, and driving Moab southward over Arnon, and Ammon eastward to the sources of the Jabbok, had founded a kingdom for himself between the two rivers" (Smith, *Hist. Geog.*, p. 558, sq.). It was afterward taken possession of by Israel on its way to Palestine, and Arnon became the boundary between Israel and Moab (Num. 21:13, 26; Josh. 12:1; Judg. 11:22; Isa. 16:2; Jer. 48:20).

A′rod (ā′rŏd; *humpbacked*), the sixth son of Gad (Num. 26:17), whose descendants were called Arodites, B. C. about 1700. He is called Arodi (Gen. 46:16).

Ar′odi, A′rodite. *See* Arod.

Ar′oer (ăr′ō-ēr; *nudity*).

1. A town on the N. bank of the Arnon (Deut. 2:36; 3:12; 4:48; Josh. 12:2; 13:9, 16; Judg. 11:26; I Chron. 5:8). As the southernmost town of Israel E. of Jordan, it has been called "the Beer-sheba of the East." It was fortified by Mesha as mentioned in the Moabite Stone (*q. v.*). Now called Arair, thirteen miles W. of the Dead Sea.

2. A town built by the Gadites (Num. 32: 34; Josh. 13:25; Judg. 11:33; II Sam. 24:5), connected with the history of Jephthah.

3. A city 12 miles S. E. of Beer-sheba, associated with David and his warriors (I Sam. 30:26-28; I Chron. 11:44), called now Ararah.

Ar′oerite (ăr′ō-ēr-īt), an inhabitant of Aroer (No. 3), probably that in the tribe of Judah (I Chron. 11:44).

Ar′pad (är′păd) rendered **Ar′phad** (är′făd) twice in A. V. is identified as Tell Erfad, thirteen miles north of Aleppo. It was a place of considerable importance in Assyrian times, being overrun by Adadnirari in 806 B. C., Ashurninari in 754, besieged and captured by Tiglath-pileser (742-740), and included in an uprising which was suppressed by Sargon in 720 B. C. It is commonly associated with the city-state of Hamath in Old Testament references, being not far distant (II Kings 18:34; 19:13, Isa. 10:9). *M. F. U.*

Arphax′ad (är-făx′ăd), the first antediluvian patriarch, son of Shem, and father of Salah, born two years after the deluge, and died aged four hundred and thirty-eight years (Gen. 11:10-13; I Chron. 1:17, 18). Arphaxad (R. V. and R. S. V. Arpachshad) has been frequently identified with the mountainous country on the Upper Zab River N. and N. E. of Nineveh, the Arrapachitis of the Greek geographers.

Arrow. *See* Armor, I, 4.

Artaxerx′es (är-tá-zērk′sēz).

1. The Persian king who, at the instigation of the enemies of the Jews, obstructed the rebuilding of the temple (Ezra 4:7-24), B. C. 522, which ceased until the second year of Darius, B. C. 520. He is doubtless the same as the Magian imposter Smerdis, who seized the throne B. C. 522, and was murdered after a usurpation of eight months.

2. Longimanus, who reigned over Persia forty years, B. C. 465-425. In the seventh year of his reign he commissioned Ezra to return to Jerusalem, granting large privileges to him and those accompanying him (Ezra 7:1, sq.), B. C. 457. About thirteen years later (B. C. 445) he granted permission to Nehemiah to assume control of the civil affairs at Jerusalem (Neh. 2:1-8).

Ar′temas (är′tĕ-màs, contraction of Gr. *Artemidoros; gift of Artemis*, i. e., Diana).

1. The name of a disciple mentioned in connection with Tychicus, one of whom Paul designed to send into Crete to supply the place of Titus, when he invited the latter to visit him at Nicopolis (Tit. 3:12), A. D. 65. According to tradition, he was bishop of Lystra.

2. *See* Diana (False gods).

Artificer (Heb. *hōrēsh*, or *hārāsh*), a fabricator of any material, as carpenter, smith, engraver, etc. (Gen. 4:22; I Chron. 29:5; II Chron. 34:11; Isa. 3:3). *See* Handicraft.

Artillery (Heb. *kelî, prepared*), use of the armor (quiver, bow and arrows) of Jonathan (I Sam. 20:40).

Arts. *See* Handicraft.

Ar'uboth (ăr'ŭ-bōth; *lattices*), a city or district, mentioned (I Kings 4:10) as the purveyorship of the son of Hesed. Probably to be identified with Arrabeh near Dothan.

Aru'mah (à-rū'mà; *height*), a place, in the neighborhood of Shechem, where dwelt Abimelech, the son of Gideon (Judg. 9:41).

Ar'vad (är'văd), an island off the coast of Phoenicia, rocky, two miles from the shore, and peopled by mariners and soldiers (Ezek. 27:8, 11). It is modern Ruwad, a little more than two miles from the shore to the S. of Tartus. On that small island are Phoenician remains; there "the family" of the Arvadites settled.

Ar'vadite (är'và-dīt; Gen. 10:18; I Chron. 1:16), an inhabitant of the island of Aradus, or *Arvad* (*q. v.*). The Arvadites were descended from the sons of Canaan (Gen. 10:18). They appear to have been in some dependence upon Tyre, as we find them furnishing a contingent of mariners to that city (Ezek. 27:8, 11). They took their full share in Phoenician maritime affairs, particularly after Tyre and Sidon fell under the dominion of the Greco-Syrian kings.

Ar'za (är'zà; *earthiness*), a steward over the house of Elah, king of Israel, in whose house, at Tirzah, Zimri, the captain of half of his chariots, conspired against *Elah* (*q. v.*), and killed him during a drunken debauch (I Kings 16:8-10).

A'sa(ā'sà; *healing*), cf. Arabic *'asa, to heal*; Aramic *'ăssâ, a physician*.

1. The son and successor of Abijah, king of Judah, who reigned forty-one years c. B. C. 916-873. (1) **Religious conduct.** On assuming the reins of government, Asa was conspicuous for his support of the worship of God, and opposition to idolatry. Even his grandmother, Maachah, was deposed from the rank of "queen mother" because she had set up an idol, which Asa overthrew and "burnt by the brook Kidron" (I Kings 15:13). Still, the old hill sanctuaries were retained as places of worship. He placed in the temple gifts dedicated by his father, and rich offerings of his own, and renewed the altar, which had apparently been desecrated (II Chron. 15:8). (2) **Wars.** The first ten years of his reign his kingdom enjoyed peace, which Asa utilized in fortifying his frontier cities and raising an army, which numbered at the beginning of hostilities five hundred and eighty thousand men (II Chron. 14:8), though this number has been thought an exaggeration of the copyist. In the eleventh year of his reign Zerah, the Ethiopian, invaded Judah with an army of a million men. Asa besought God for help, and, marching against Zerah, met and defeated him at Mareshah. He returned to Jerusalem with the spoil of the cities around Gerar, and with innumerable sheep and cattle (II Chron. 14:9-15). The prophet Azariah met Asa on his return, and encouraged him and the people to continue their trust in God. (3) **Re-**

forms. Asa carried on his reforms; a gathering of the people was held at Jerusalem, sacrifices were offered, and a covenant was made with Jehovah. To these ceremonies there came many from the kingdom of Israel, believing that God was with Asa (II Chron. 15). In the thirty-sixth year (according to some twenty-sixth) of his reign hostilities were begun by Baasha, king of Israel, who fortified Ramah, to prevent his subjects from going over to Asa. (4) **Alliance with Ben-hadad.** The good king then committed the great error of his life. He resorted to an alliance with Ben-hadad I, of Damascus, purchasing his assistance with treasures from the temple and the king's house. Ben-hadad made a diversion in Asa's favor by invading northern Israel, whereupon Baasha left Ramah. Asa took the material found there and built therewith Geba and Mizpah. His lack of faith was reproved by the seer Hanani, who told him that he had lost the honor of conquering the Syrians because of this alliance, and also prophesied war for the rest of his days. Asa, angered at Hanani, put him in prison, and oppressed some of the people at the same time (II Chron. 16:1, sq.). (5) **Sickness and death.** In the thirty-ninth year of his reign he was afflicted with a disease in his feet, and "sought not to the Lord," but depended upon the physicians. The disease proved fatal in the forty-first year of his reign. He died greatly beloved, and was honored with a magnificent burial (II Chron. 16:12-14).

2. A Levite, son of Elkanah and father of Berechiah, which latter resided in one of the villages of the Netophathites after the return from Babylon (I Chron. 9:16), B. C. after 536.

As'ahel (ās'à-hěl; *God's creature*).

1. The son of David's sister, Zeruiah, and brother of Joab and Abishai (II Sam. 2:18; I Chron. 2:16). He was an early adherent of David, being one of the famous thirty (II Sam. 23:24), and, with his son Zebadiah, was commander of the fourth division of the royal army (I Chron. 27:7). He was renowned for his swiftness of foot, and after the battle of Gibeon he pursued and overtook Abner, who reluctantly, and in order to save his own life, slew Asahel with a back thrust of his spear (II Sam. 2:18-23), B. C. about 1000. Joab, to revenge Asahel's death, slew Abner some years after at Hebron (II Sam. 3:26, 27).

2. One of the Levites sent by Jehoshaphat into Judah to teach the law of the Lord (II Chron. 17:8), B. C. after 875.

3. One of the Levites appointed by Hezekiah as overseer of the contributions to the house of the Lord (II Chron. 31:13), B. C. about 700.

4. The father of Jonathan, who was one of the elders that assisted Ezra in putting away the foreign wives of the Jews on the return from Babylon (Ezra 10:15), B. C. 457.

Asahi'ah (ā-sà-hī'à; *whom Jehovah made*), an officer of Josiah, who was sent with others to consult Huldah, the prophetess, concerning the book of the law found in the temple (II Kings 22:12-14), B. C. 624.

Asai'ah (ā-sà-ī'à; *whom Jehovah made*).

1. A prince of one of the families of the tribe of Simeon who, in the time of Hezekiah, drove

out the Hamite shepherds from the rich pastures near Gedor (I Chron. 4:36). B. C. about 700.

2. The son of Haggiah (I Chron. 6:30), and chief of the two hundred and twenty Levites of the family of Merari, appointed by David to remove the ark from the house of Obed-edom (I Chron. 15:6, 11), B. C. after 1000.

3. The "firstborn" of the Shilonites who returned to Jerusalem after the captivity (I Chron. 9:5), B. C. about 536.

4. The same (II Chron. 34:20) as *Asahiah* (*q. v.*).

A'saph (ā-săf; *collector*).

1. The father (or ancestor) of Joah, which latter person was "recorder" in the time of Hezekiah (II Kings 18:18, 37; Isa. 36:3, 22), B. C. about 710.

2. A Levite, son of Berachiah, of the family of Gershom (I Chron. 6:39; 15:17), eminent as a musician, and appointed by David to preside over the sacred choral services (I Chron. 16:5), B. C. after 1000. The "sons of Asaph" are afterward mentioned as choristers of the temple (I Chron. 25:1, 2; II Chron. 20:14, and elsewhere), and this office appears to have been made hereditary in the family (I Chron. 25:1, 2). Asaph was celebrated in after times as a prophet and poet (II Chron. 29:30; Neh. 12:46), and the titles of twelve of the Psalms (50, 73-83) bear his name, though in some of these (74, 79, 75) the "sons of Asaph" should be understood, as matters of late occurrence are referred to (Kitto, s. v.).

3. A "keeper of the king's forest," probably in Lebanon. Nehemiah requested Artaxerxes to give him an order on Asaph for timber to be used in the rebuilding of the temple (Neh. 2:8), B. C. about 445.

Asar'eel (ă-săr'ê-ĕl), the last named of the four sons of Jehaleleel, of the tribe of Judah (I Chron. 4:16).

Asare'lah (ăs-á-re'lá), one of the sons of the Levite Asaph, who was appointed by David in charge of the temple music (I Chron. 25:2). He is probably the same as Jesharelah (v. 14), and if so, was in the seventh of the (twenty-four) courses, B. C. after 1000.

Ascension of Christ, his glorious withdrawal, as to his bodily presence, from the earth, and entrance, as the God-man and mediatorial King, into heaven.

1. **The Fact.** The ascension was from the Mount of Olives forty days after the resurrection. (Predicted in Psa. 68:18; 110:11); then interpreted (Eph. 4:8-10; Heb. 1:13); also by Christ himself (John 6:62; 20:17). (2) Recorded (Mark 16:19; Luke 24:50, 51; Acts 1:9-11). (3) Recognized by St. John (passages above cited), and by other New Testament writers who based doctrines upon it (II Cor. 13:4; Eph. 2:6; 4:8-10; I Pet. 3:22; I Tim. 3:16; Heb. 1:13; 6:20). (4) Certified by the disciples who were eyewitnesses; by the words of the two angels; by Stephen and Paul and John, who saw Christ in his ascended state (Acts 1:9-11; 7:55, 56; 9:3-5; Rev. 1:9-18). (5) Demonstrated by the descent of the Holy Spirit on the day of Pentecost (Matt. 3:11; Luke 24:49; Acts 2:1-4, 33), and by the manifold gifts bestowed by the ascended Lord upon his Church (Eph. 4:11, 12).

47. Chapel of the Ascension (Mount of Olives)

2. **Doctrinal and Ethical Significance.** The visible ascension of Christ was the necessary sequel and seal of his resurrection (Rom. 6:9). It was the appropriate connecting link between his humiliation and glorification (Phil. 2:5-11). As consequences of the ascension the New Testament writers particularly note: (1) The removal of his bodily, but not his spiritual, presence from the earth; "Christ has passed into the heavens," but invisibly he is always near at hand (Heb. 4:14; Matt. 28:20; Acts 23:11; II Tim. 4:17). (2) The investure of Christ with power and dominion in heaven and earth. He is "at the right hand of God" (Matt. 28:18; Phil. 2:10; Heb. 12:2). (3) The perpetual intercession of Christ, as our great High Priest (Rom. 8:34; Heb. 5:20; 7:25). (4) The sending forth of the Holy Spirit, and the bestowment of other gifts upon the Church (Acts 2:33; Eph. 4:11, 12).

Of practical import, accordingly, the ascension of Christ is closely related to the peace and sanctification and hope of believers. (1) He is their heavenly advocate (I John 2:1). (2) He is still interceding for their perfection (John 17:20-24). (3) They are then encouraged to fidelity and to confident prayer (Heb. 4:14-16). (4) He powerfully attracts them to things above (Col. 3:1-4). (5) He has gone to prepare a place for them (John 14:2). (6) He awaits his perfect triumph over all his foes (Heb. 10:13). (7) He shall come again to judge the world (Acts 1:11; Matt. 25:31, 32).

As'enath (ăs'ê-năth; *who belongs to Neith*, i. e., the Egyptian Minerva), the daughter of Potipherah, priest of On, whom the king of Egypt gave in marriage to Joseph (Gen. 41:45), B. C. 1715. She became the mother of Ephraim and Manasseh (Gen. 46:20). Beyond this nothing is known concerning her.

A'ser, the Grecized form of Asher (Luke 2:36; Rev. 7:6).

Ash. See Vegetable Kingdom.

A'shan (ā'shăn; *smoke*), a Levitical city (I Chron. 6:59) in the low country of Judah, assigned first to Judah (Josh. 15:42), again to Simeon (Josh. 19:7; I Chron. 4:32) in which last passage it is given as a priests' city). Ain instead of Ashan is used in Josh. 21:16. Ashan is identified with Khirbet 'Ashan about five miles N. W. of Beer-sheba.

Ash'bea ('ăsh'bê-á), the head of a family mentioned as working in fine linen, a branch of the descendants of Shelah, the son of Judah (I Chron. 4:21).

Ash′bel (ăsh′bĕl), the second son of Benjamin (Gen. 46:21; I Chron. 8:1). His descendants were called Ashbelites (Num. 26:38).

Ash′belite. *See* Ashbel.

Ash′chenaz (ăsh′kĕn-ăz), a less correct form of Anglicizing *Ashkenaz* (*q. v.*), found in I Chron. 1:6 and Jer. 51:27.

Ash′dod (ăsh′dŏd), one of the five principal cities of the Philistines. Together with Gaza, Gath, Ekron and Ashkelon it formed what is known as the Philistine Pentapolis. These cities were at the zenith of their power at the time of Saul (c. 1020 B. C.) and continued to be important after the ascendancy of the Hebrew monarchy under the Davidic Dynasty (c. 1000-587 B. C.). Ashdod was situated between Ashkelon, a seaport, and Ekron, inland on the caravan route east to Lydda and west to Joppa. Sargon besieged and took the city (Isa. 20:1) despite its commanding position on a hill, which made it the envy of Israel. The Ark of God was carried by the Philistines to Ashdod after their victory at Ebenezer (c. 1050 B. C.) and carried into the temple of Dagon, an ancient Canaanite deity associated with agriculture, who was worshiped there (I Sam. 5). It was later carried to Gath and Ekron with similar disastrous results as at Ashdod. Mentioned some 21 times in the Old Testament, its palaces and temples (Amos 3:9) preserve its memory as a city of importance. Nehemiah in his day protested against Israelite men marrying wives from Ashdod and rearing children who could not speak "the Jews' language" (13:23-25). *M. F. U.*

Ash′dodites (ăsh′dŏ-dīts, Neh. 4:7), inhabitants of *Ashdod* (*q. v.*); less correctly rendered Ashdothites (Josh. 13:3).

Ash′dothites (ăsh′dŏ-thīts), a less correct mode (Josh. 13:3) of anglicizing the name *Ashdodites* (*q. v.*).

Ash′er (ăsh′ĕr; *happiness*), the eighth son of Jacob, and second of Zilpah, the maid of Leah (Gen. 30:13).

1. **Personal History.** Of this we have no record.

2. **The Tribe of Asher.** (1) **Number.** Asher had four sons and one daughter. Upon quitting Egypt the tribe numbered forty-one thousand five hundred, ranking *ninth*; and at the second census the number had increased to fifty-three thousand four hundred men of war, ranking *fifth* in population. (2) **Position.** During the march through the desert Asher's place was between Dan and Naphtali, on the N. side of the tabernacle (Num. 2:27). (3) **Territory.** The general position of the tribe was on the seashore from Carmel northward, with Manasseh on the S., Zebulun and Issachar on the S. E., and Naphtali on the N. E. The boundaries and towns are given in Josh. 19:24-31; 17:10, 11; Judg. 1:31, 32. (4) **Subsequent history.** The richness of the soil, and their proximity to the Phoenicians, may have contributed to the degeneracy of the tribe (Judg. 1:31; 5:17). In the reign of David the tribe had become so insignificant that its name is altogether omitted from the list of the chief rulers (I Chron. 27:16-22). With the exception of Simeon, Asher is the only tribe west of the Jordan which furnished no judge or hero to the nation. Anna, daughter of Phanuel, who was of the tribe of Asher, as a prophetess and a godly woman, recognized the infant Savior as the Messiah (Luke 2: 36-38).

Ashe′rah (á-shē′rá), a Canaanite goddess appearing as "Lady of the Sea" in the Shamra Literature of the 14th century B. C. *See* Gods, False.

Ash′erites (ăsh′ĕr-īts), descendants of *Asher* (*q. v.*) and members of his tribe (Judg. 1:32).

Ashes.

1. The ashes on the altar of burnt offering were removed each morning by a priest clad in linen (his official dress); and carried by him, attired in unofficial dress, to a clean place without the camp (Lev. 6:10, 11). According to the Mishna, the priest who was to remove the ashes was chosen by lot. The ashes of the red heifer (*see* Purification) had the ceremonial efficacy of purifying the unclean (Heb. 9:13), but of polluting the clean.

2. **Figurative.** It has been the custom in all ages to burn captured cities; and so, to *reduce a place to ashes* is a well-understood expression for effecting a complete destruction (Ezek. 28:18; II Pet. 2:6). A very frequent figurative employment of the word is derived from the practice of sitting among ashes, or scattering them upon one's person, as a symbol of grief and mourning (Job 2:8; 42:6; Isa. 58:5; Jer. 6:26; Matt. 11:21, etc.). In Ezek. 27:30 it is declared of the mourning Tyrians that "they shall wallow themselves in the ashes," expressive of great and bitter lamentation. *Eating* ashes is expressive of the deepest misery and degradation (Psa. 102:9; Isa. 44:20). Ashes are also used to represent things easily scattered, perishable, and, therefore, worthless. Thus Abraham speaks of himself as "dust and ashes" (Gen. 18:27), and the wicked are said to be "ashes under the soles of the feet" to the righteous (Mal. 4:3).

3. The early Christians naturally adopted a ceremony which had acquired so much significance. Tertullian speaks of the "substitution of sackcloth and ashes for a man's usual habit" as a regular ceremony of public confession and penance in the 2nd century. Penitents under excommunication used to sprinkle ashes upon their heads, and, standing at the doors of the churches, ask the prayers of those entering, that they might be readmitted to communion.

Ash′ima (ăsh′ĭ-má), the god of the people of Hamath. (II Kings 17:30). *See* Gods, False.

Ash′kelon (ăsh′kĕ-lŏn) (Askalon, Askelon, Ascalon in N. T. times), one of the five principal cities of Philistia, located on the fertile Maritime Plain some dozen miles north of Gaza. It probably derived its name from the *escallot* (scallion) which grew there. It has been excavated and shows stratigraphic layers of occupation from late Arabic at the summit, through the Crusader and N. T. periods down to an early Canaanite town which came to an end around 2000 B. C. In Samson's time Philistines occupied it (Judg. 14:19). Both Zephaniah (2:4) and Zechariah (9:5) foretold its destruction. Ashkelon was Herod the Great's birthplace and the residence of his sister Salome. Consequently he took an interest in

48. Roman Ruins, Askelon

the place, beautifying it with impressive colonnaded courts. The site was prominent in the period of the Crusades, but its chief interest is in the Biblical period. David mentions the city in his lament over Saul and Jonathan (II Sam. 1:20). *M. F. U.*

Ash′kenas (ăsh′kē-năz), the first-named of the sons of Gomer, son of Japhet (Gen. 10:3), and equivalent to Assyrian, *Ashkuz*, the Scythians (W. F. Albright, *O. T. Commentary*, 1948, p. 138). In the time of Jeremiah they dwelt in the neighborhood of Ararat and Minni (the Mannai of the Assyrian inscriptions) S. E. of Lake Van. They were rude and retarded in civilization and periodically overran extensive territory, so that their name came to be tantamount to barbarians. *M. F. U.*

Ash′nah (ăsh′nà), the name of two cities, both in the tribe of Judah (Josh. 15:33, 43). Neither of them has been positively identified.

Ash′penaz (ăsh′pē-năz), the master of the eunuchs, a chamberlain of Nebuchadnezzar, B. C. after 604, who was commanded to select certain Jewish captives to be instructed in "the learning and tongue of the Chaldeans" (Dan. 1:3). Among those whom he selected were Daniel and his three companions, Hananiah, Mishael, and Azariah, whose Hebrew names he changed to Babylonian (Dan. 1:7). The request of Daniel, that he might not be compelled to eat the provisions sent from the king's table, filled Ashpenaz with apprehension. But God had brought Daniel into favor with Ashpenaz, and he did not use constraint toward him, which kindness the prophet gratefully records (Dan. 1:16).

Ash′riel (ăsh′rĭ-ĕl), in I Chron. 7:14, more properly *Asriel (q. v.)*.

Ash′taroth (ăsh′tà-rŏth).

1. An ancient city of Bashan, E. of the Jordan (Deut. 1:4; Josh. 9:10; 12:4; 13:12,

31) in the half tribe of Manasseh. The inhabitants, including King Og, were giants. The town was the seat of the lewd worship of Astarte and capital of Og. By the time of Israel's entrance into the land, the iniquity of the inhabitants was full (Gen. 15:16) and God commanded the conquering Israelites utterly to exterminate them (Deut. 3:2-6). The site of the ancient city is identified with Tell Ashtarah 21 miles E. of the Sea of Galilee, the hill being surrounded by a well-watered plain.

2. Plural form of god Ashtoreth (Astarte). *See* Gods, False. *M. F. U.*

Ash′teroth Kar′naim (ăsh′tē-rŏth kär-nă′ĭm; *Ashteroth of the two horns*, Gen. 14:5). This was probably distinct from Ashtaroth. The Rephaim dwelt in Ashteroth Karnaim, a place probably at or near Tell 'Ashtarah. There was a temple here, dedicated to the principal female divinity of the Phoenicians; both the city, in later Hebrew times called Carnaim, and the temple are mentioned in Maccabees, and the reference seems to be the same place.

Ash′toreth, one of the names of a Sidonian goddess. *See* Gods, False.

Ash′ur (ăsh′ûr; *successful*), a posthumous son of Hezron (grandson of Judah, Gen. 46:12), by his wife Abiah (I Chron. 2:24). He had two wives, Helah and Naarah, by each of whom he had several sons (I Chron. 4:5), and through these he is called the "father" (founder) of Tekoa, which appears to have been the place of their eventual settlement.

Ashurban′ipal (ă-shûr-băn′ĭ-pàl; Assyrian "Ashur creates a son"), called also Asnapper (Osnapper) (*q. v.*), the grandson of Sennacherib (705-681 B. C.), and the last great Assyrian monarch (669-626 B. C.). His father was the famous Esarhaddon. He is renowned as a scholar and a protector of literature and art. His great library excavated at Nineveh has yielded a large quantity of cuneiform literature, numbering about 22,000 religious, literary and scientific texts. This vast corpus of material furnishes one of the main sources of information extant for the reconstruction of the history and civilization of ancient Assyria. Texts giving the ancient Babylonian versions of the creation and the flood found in the Nineveh beautified by this culture-loving king have shed much light on the Biblical account of these events recorded in Genesis. Ashurbanipal was on the throne of Assyria during a large part of Manasseh's long and wicked reign in Judah (c. 687-642 B. C.). The narrative of II Chron. 33 relates how Manasseh was deported to Babylon by the Assyrians (Esarhaddon or Ashurbanipal?). The authenticity of this event is supported by the fact Assyrian kings of this period did spend part of their time in Babylon. *M. F. U.*

Ashurna′sirpal II (à-shûr-nă′zĭr-pàl) (B. C. 883-859), a ruthless conqueror who brought the Assyrian empire to a place of dread power in all S. W. Asia. He built up a fighting machine that overran vast sections of the Neareastern world. He is notorious for his barbarous cruelty. His records are boasts of his inhuman brutality. The final edition of his annals was inscribed on the pavement slabs on the entrance of the Temple of Ninurta in

Calah, an ancient and ruined city (cf. Gen. 10:11) (now the Mound of Nimrod) where A. H. Lanyard began his Assyrian excavations in 1845. At the very beginning of the palace of Ashurnasirpal was uncovered. In a nearby small temple a half-life-size statue of the king was found. Inscribed thereon was the claim that he had conquered the whole region from the Tigris to the Great Sea (Mediterranean). *M. F. U.*

Ash'vath (ăsh'văth), the last named of the three sons of Japhlet, great-grandson of Asher (I Chron. 7:33).

A'sia (ā'shä), a name of doubtful origin, which, as a designation along with Europe and Africa, came into use in the 5th century B. C. The Scriptures do not mention Asia as a whole, the several references being to separate nations, or parts of the continent. In the New Testament the word is used in this narrower sense, sometimes for Asia Minor, and sometimes for Proconsular Asia, which latterly included Phrygia, Mysia, Caria, and Lydia. Proconsular Asia was governed by a proprator until the Emperor Augustus made it a proconsular province. Dr. J. Strong (*Cyc.*) thinks that "Asia" denotes the whole of Asia Minor in Acts 19:26, 27; 21:27; 24:18; 27:2; and that Proconsular Asia is referred to in Acts 2:9; 6:9; 16:6, 19:10, 22; 20:4, 16, 18; Rom. 16:5; I Cor. 16:19; II Cor. 1:8; II Tim. 1:15; I Pet. 1:1; and contained the seven churches of the Apocalypse (Rev. 1:4, 11). Luke appears to have used the term Asia in a still more restricted sense, as he counts Phrygia and Mysia as provinces distinct from Asia (Acts 2:9, 10; 16:6, 7).

A'sia, Churches of. See under their respective names.

Asiarchs (ā'shĭ-ärks; *rulers of Asia*, Acts 19:31), the ten superintendents of the public games and religious rites of proconsular Asia, who celebrated at their own expense the games in honor of the gods and emperor. Each city annually, about the time of the autumnal equinox, delegated one of its citizens with a view to this office; and out of the entire number ten were elected by the assembly of deputies. One of the ten, perhaps chosen by the proconsul, presided. It has been disputed whether only the president or the whole of the ten bore the title asiarch. From Acts 19:31 it would appear that all bore the title, and also that through courtesy it was extended to those who had held the office.

A'siel (ā'sĭ-ĕl; *created by God*), the father of Seraiah, and progenitor of one of the Simeonite chiefs that expelled the Hamites from the valley of Gedor, in the time of Hezekiah (I Chron. 4:35), B. C. before 715.

As'kelon (Judg. 1:18). *See* Ashkelon.

As'nah (ăs'nä), the head of one of the families of the Nethinim (temple servants) that returned from the Babylonian captivity with Zerubbabel (Ezra 2:50), B. C. about 536.

Asnap'per, (ăs'năp-ēr) or **Osnappar**, the name of a king mentioned only in Ezra 4:10, and called there the great and noble Asnapper (R. V. "Osnappar"). His name has been diligently sought in various Assyrian inscriptions, and he has been at times identified with Esar-haddon, and also with Sennacherib and

Shalmaneser. In 1875 it was first suggested by Gelzer that Asnapper is simply an Aramaean form of the Assyrian name Asshurbani-pal. This view, which seems so strange at first sight, is now almost universally accepted. The name Asshur-bani-pal seems greatly to have puzzled foreign writers and speakers, and the Greek form Sardanapallos, and the Latin Sardanapalus, both derived from Asshurbani-pal, are hardly less strange than the Aramaean form Asnapper.

Asshur-bani-pal (*q. v.*) followed his father Esar-haddon (*see* Esar-haddon) upon the throne of Assyria, by the express will of the latter. His long reign (669-626 B. C.) was one of the most brilliant in the annals of the Assyrian people. He was not a man of great native ability as was his father. He was not a great warrior, nor a great subduer of other lands. His reign was brilliant simply because he inherited a kingdom which his father had made strong without and within, and into which former kings had poured the wealth of plundered lands the whole world over. He had been carefully educated in the learning of the Babylonians, and no Assyrian king before ever had so little taste for war, and so great taste for knowledge, art, literature, and science. It was he who caused to be gathered into Nineveh the greatest library which had ever been assembled there. The books in it were written upon clay, it is true, but none the less were they real books, in that they contained records of the deeds, thoughts, and words of the men of the past. It is to this library that we owe much of what we know of the early history not only of Assyria, but also of Babylonia. While Asshur-bani-pal remained in Nineveh absorbed in his library, or in the worship of the gods, or in the pleasures of royalty, his armies, led by generals, were sent to carry on campaigns often in distant lands. His first campaign was in Egypt, where he carried on to a conclusion the efforts undertaken by his father, Esar-haddon. In two campaigns he drove Tirhaka from the country and set up Psammeticus as king in Memphis, to hold his throne as an Assyrian vassal. The other events of his reign are connected with stirring scenes. He besieged and took the city of Tyre; he defeated the Lydians under King Gyges, who had paid tribute to the Assyrians, and afterward played them false by giving aid to the Egyptians. He further drove back an Elamite invasion of his country, and later invaded Elam itself. By the will of his father Samash-shum-ukin, brother of Asshur-bani-pal, had been made king of Babylon, to rule in subjection to the great king in Nineveh. This arrangement worked poorly, and led to constant friction between the brothers. It was finally terminated by a war in which Asshur-bani-pal defeated the allied forces of the Babylonians, Elamites, and Arabians, and annexed Babylonia to Assyria. Many other campaigns into Arabia and in the West filled the years of his reign, most of them being almost certainly conducted by his generals. There is no Assyrian king whose career and whose name so well fit the narrative in Ezra 4:9, 10—*R. W. R.*

Asp. *See* Animal Kingdom.

As′patha (ăs′pȧ-thȧ), the third of the sons of Haman slain by the Jews of Babylonia (Esth. 9:7).

Asphalt. *See* Mineral Kingdom.

As′riel (ăs′rĭ-ĕl), a son of Gilead and great-grandson of Manasseh (Num. 26:31; Josh. 17:2). In I Chron. 7:14 the name is Anglicized Ashriel.

As′rielite (ăs′rĭ-ĕl-īt), a descendant of Asriel (Num. 26:31).

Add. *See* Animal Kingdom.

Assembly, the term used in the A. V. for several Hebrew words, elsewhere translated *"Congregation"* (*q. v.*). It is also the representative of the following: (1) *'äsäräh*, a *coming together*, especially for a *festal* occasion (Lev. 23:36; Num. 29:35; Deut. 16:8). (2) *mĭqrä'*, something *called*, a public meeting (Isa. 1:13; 4:5). (3) "General assembly" (Gr. *panēguris*, a festal gathering of all the people, Heb. 12:23), commonly believed to be the same as the Church. (4) *'ekklēsia*, a term in use among the Greeks from the time of Thucydides for an assemblage of the people for the purpose of deliberating (Acts 19:39).

As′shur (ăsh-ûr; a *step*), the second named of the sons of Shem (Gen. 10:22; I Chron. 1:17). His descendants peopled the land of Assyria. The word appears in Gen. 10:11, as if it were the name of a person, but the verse should be rendered as in the margin, "he went out into Assyria."

Asshu′rim (Gen. 25:3). *See* Ashurites.

As′sir (ăs′sĭr; *prisoner*).

1. A Levite, son of Korah (Exod. 6:24; I Chron. 6:22). His descendants constituted one of the Korhite families.

2. Son of Ebiasaph, great-grandson of the preceding, and father of Tahath (I Chron. 6:23, 37). There is some suspicion, however, that the name here has crept in by repetition from the preceding.

3. Son of Jeconiah, a descendant of David (I Chron. 3:17), unless the true rendering is "Jeconiah the captive," referring to the captivity of that prince in Babylon.

As′sos (ăs′ŏs), a seaport town in Mysia, on the N. shore of the Gulf of Adramyttium, and about thirty miles from Troas by sea, and opposite Lesbos. Paul came hither on foot from Troas to embark for Mitylene (Acts 20:13, 14). It is now a miserable village, bearing the name of Asso.

Assurance. 1. (Heb. *bĕtăh*, *security*, *trust*), mentioned (Isa. 32:17), together with "quietness," as the effect of righteousness (R. V. "confidence").

2. (Gr. *pistis*, *persuasion*, *credence*.) The resurrection of Jesus from the dead is given by Paul as the ground of assurance in believers (Acts 17:31).

3. (Gr. *plērophoria*, *entire confidence*.) In this sense it is used in Col. 2:2; I Thess. 1:5; Heb. 6:11; 10:22.

Assurance, a term brought into theology from the Scriptures, sometimes used broadly by theologians as referring to certitude respecting the validity of Christian revelation; most commonly employed to denote the firm persuasion of one's own salvation. The latter must of course include the former. In experi-ence the two are most closely connected. In both senses assurance is a product of the Holy Spirit (I Thess. 1:5; Col. 2:2; Heb. 6:11; 10:22; II Cor. 1:22; Rom. 8:16). See also other passages expressing "confidence," "boldness."

As to the assurance of personal salvation it must be emphasized that this must not be confused with the eternal security of a genuine believer. The latter is a fact due to God's faithfulness whether it is realized by the believer or not, while the former is that which one believes is true respecting himself at any given moment.

1. Assurance has been held, chiefly by Calvinists, to relate not only to present but also to final salvation. This is the logical outcome of the doctrine of unconditional election. It must stand or fall with that doctrine. Others, who regard mankind as in a state of probation, limit the assurance to present acceptance with God.

2. Is assurance the common privilege of believers? This the doctrine of the Roman Catholic Church answers in the negative "since no one can certainly and infallibly know that he has obtained the grace of God" (Council of Trent, sess. vi, ch. ix, "De Justificatione"). Luther and Melanchthon and many other of the reformers held strongly to the affirmative, and even made assurance the criterion of saving faith. Calvinistic doctrine has regarded assurance (implying not only present but also final salvation) as a special gift of grace possessed by relatively few believers, though, theoretically at least, within the privilege and duty of all. Methodist theology has given strong emphasis to assurance as the common privilege of all who truly believe in Christ; presenting, not the doubting and desponding type, but the confident and joyous type of religious experience as the one which is normal and scriptural.

3. As to whether assurance is of the essence of, or a necessary element in, saving faith the first Protestant Confession (Augsburg) held that it is involved therein in accordance with Luther's declaration that "he who hath not assurance spews faith out." Other and later utterances of the reformed doctrine discriminated between the act of justifying and saving faith and the assurance which comes as its result. The Westminster Assembly was the first Protestant synod, however, that formally declared assurance not to be of the essence of saving faith. Wesley, while seeming at times to teach the opposite view, nevertheless clearly held and taught that assurance is not involved in justifying faith or necessarily connected therewith. "The assertion, 'Justifying faith is a sense of pardon,'" he says, "is contrary to reason; it is flatly absurd. For, how can a sense of pardon be the condition of our receiving it?" For a most discriminating presentation of his views as to the relation of assurance to faith, see his works, vol. xii, pp. 109, 110.

4. As to the grounds of assurance, opinions have also varied, especially as to their order and relative importance. Calvinists are rather disposed to lay stress upon the external grounds of confidence instead of those that

are internal; i. e., the truths and promises of Scripture are dwelt upon more largely and strongly than the fruits of the Spirit and the "witness of the Spirit." *See* Spirit, Witness of. Wesley and other Methodist theologians emphasize chiefly the "witness of the Spirit," though they by no means undervalue the confidence that comes from the recognition of the validity of the truth and promises of God, and that which comes from finding in one's self the graces which surely proclaim the fact of personal salvation. The "witness of the Spirit" brings faith to its full development, so that, uplifted to a joyous experience of the new life, we become possessed more abundantly of the fruits of the Spirit, and the faith in God's word which was intellectual, rational, and dim or wavering becomes spiritual, living, and certain. Thus is realized "the full assurance of faith," and "of hope" and "understanding." *See* Westminster Con., art. xviii, "Of the Assurance of Grace and Salvation;" Hodge's *Systematic Theology;* Pope's *Compendium of Christian Theology;* Dorner's *System of Christian Doctrines,* introductory chapter, "The Doctrine of Faith;" Watson's *Theological Institutes;* Wesley's "Works," especially sermon on "The Witness of the Spirit;" Chamberlayne's *Saving Faith.* L. S. Chafer, *Systematic Theology,* vii: 21-24.

Assyr′ia (ă-sĭr′ĭ-à), the name of a country and the mighty empire that dominated the ancient Biblical world from 9th to the 7th century B. C.

1. **The Land of Assyria** was originally an exceedingly small tract, the triangular-shaped strip lying between the rivers Tigris and Zab, and bounded on the N. and E. by the Median and Armenian mountains. This territory was so small that it seems scarcely possible that a people confined within its borders could ever have reared an empire powerful enough to have dominated the civilized world. It is, however, to be remembered that it was not the people of this very narrow tract who made the world one vast tributary. That was done by a people of wider original possessions, for the land of Assyria was in close contact with Babylonia. The river Zab never formed a hard and fast boundary between the two lands. There was indeed no natural boundary at all. The political boundaries wavered back and forth in the great valley, just as political power went up and down. When Assyria was the stronger, then was the boundary pushed far below the Zab; when Babylonia became more powerful it retreated northward. So, also, westward the Tigris did not continue to confine the Assyrians on the W. At a very early period the borders were extended almost to the Euphrates. The populations of this wider country were absorbed into the kingdom of Assyria, and forgetting their origin became Assyrians to all intents and purposes. The world-wide dominion was achieved through the alliance with Babylonia, as well as by the absorption of the other peoples of the valley. During all their history the Assyrian people were of one family blood with the people of Babylonia, and their land was likewise of almost one piece. The land of Assyria is scarcely detachable from the Assyro-Babylonian land.

2. **The People.** The people who inhabited Assyria belonged to the great Semitic race. They had come originally, so it appears, from Babylonia to settle as colonists. They were not of pure race, for there had already been an intermixture of blood with the Sumerian people, who were the original inhabitants of the land. After this immigration the Babylonians continued the process of intermixture with successive invading peoples from Elam, Arabia, and elsewhere, but the Assyrians intermarried little with neighboring peoples, and held it a subject for much boasting that they were of purer blood than the Babylonians. In stature the Assyrians were of average modern European height, and were powerfully built. Their complexion was dark, the nose prominent, the hair, eyebrows, and beard thick and bushy. They were apparently of cheerful disposition, given to mirth and feasting, but of implacable cruelty. The pages of history are nowhere more bloody than in the records of their wars.

3. **Language and Literature.** The language of Assyria was closely akin to that of Babylonia, and may properly be regarded as practically the same language. It belongs to the Semitic family of languages, and is, therefore, akin to Arabic, Aramaean, and Hebrew. Unlike these three kindred languages, the Assyrian never developed an alphabet, though it did develop a few alphabetic characters. During its entire history the Assyrian language was prevailingly ideographic and syllabic. It expressed words by means of signs which represented the *idea;* thus there was a single sign for *sun,* another for *city,* another for *wood,* another for *hand.* These are called ideograms, and originated in considerable measure out of pictures, or hieroglyphs of the objects themselves. But besides these ideograms the language also possessed numerous syllabic signs such as *ab, ib, ub, ba, bi, bu.* By means of these words could be spelled out. Clumsy though this appears to be, the Assyrians were able to develop it far enough to make it a wonderfully accurate and sufficiently flexible tool. The materials on which they wrote were clay and stone, the use of which had come from Babylonia. In writing upon stone the characters were chiseled deeply into the surface, in regular lines, sometimes over raised figures of gods or kings. Writings thus executed were of monumental character, and could not be used for business or literary purposes. The great bulk of Assyrian literature has come down to us upon clay, and not upon stone. The clay tablets, as they are called, vary greatly in size. Some are shaped like pillows, two inches in length, by an inch and a quarter in width. Others are flat, and sometimes reach sixteen inches in length by nine or ten inches in width. The clay is also sometimes shaped like barrels, varying in height from five to nine inches, or like cylinders or prisms, which are found sometimes sixteen inches in height. When the soft clay had been formed into some one of these shapes the characters were formed by pressing into the surface a small metallic tool with a triangularly pointed end.

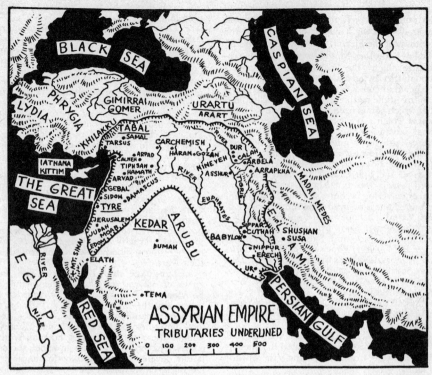

49. At its greatest extent the Assyrian Empire also included Egypt.

Each pressure formed a wedge-shaped, or cuneiform, depression, and by repeated indentations the characters were made. On these clay tablets the Assyrians wrote a varied literature. We have now in our possession vast stores of this literature, representing widely differing phases. There are found historical inscriptions, narrating in annalistic form the deeds of Assyrian monarchs; public documents, royal and private letters and dispatches; lists of taxes; innumerable business documents, such as receipts and bills of sale; religious documents, as hymns, prayers, incantations, and lists of omens; linguistic documents, as lists of signs and of words with explanations; astronomical lists of eclipses and the like; tables of square and cube roots; medical treatises and lists of recipes for the healing of disease. But a small part of this vast literature has been published in facsimile, or made accessible in translations in European languages. When they are made thus accessible they will give such an insight into the whole life of these people as we are able to obtain of very few peoples of antiquity.

4. **Religion.** The people of Assyria derived their religious ideas from Babylonia, and during all their history had constant contact with the mother country in this matter, as in others. The faith was polytheistic, and never shows in any text yet found any approach to monotheism. The god who stood at the head of the Assyrian pantheon was the great god Asshur, always honored as the divine founder of the nation. After him and below him are the gods

Anu, Bel, and Ea, the middle of whom, under slightly varying names and with changes of titles, was worshiped in Babylonia, and even far westward among other Semitic peoples. Besides this great triad, there was another consisting of the moon god Sin, the sun god Shamash, whose name appears in royal names so frequently, and Ishtar, the goddess of the crescent moon, and the queen of the stars; though her place in this triad is often taken by Ramman, the "thunderer," god of rain, of tempests, and of storms. These gods are invoked at times severally in phrases which seem to raise each in turn to a position of supremacy over the others. Early students of religious texts sometimes mistakenly supposed that these ascriptions of praise and honor were in reality tokens of monotheism. This is now well known to be a false inference. Monotheism is unknown, henotheism seems at times to be reached, but polytheism is the prevailing, as it was always the popular, belief. Besides these great triads of gods there were large numbers of minor deities, as well as countless spirits of heaven, earth, and sea. *See* Nergal.

The religious ceremonial of the Assyrians, with its sacrifices morning and evening, and its offerings of wine, milk, honey, and cakes was similar to that of Babylonia, but is not yet satisfactorily known, save in outline.

5. **Archaeology.** It is clear that the origin of the Assyrian commonwealth is to be found among Babylonian colonists (Gen. 10:11). Archaeology points also to this fact, and the

Assyrians themselves looked back to Babylonia as the motherland. Excavations made initially by Austin Layard, Hormuzd Rassam and Victor Place, early Assyriologists, and later diggings at Ashur (modern Qalat Sharqat) by a German Expedition under Walter Andrae (1903-1914) show that Assyrian beginnings are to be traced to c. 3000 to 1700 B. C. and that the site of the famous ancient city was occupied from the early part of the third millennium. Earliest literary references to the city occur in the texts recovered at Nuzu (Yorgan Tepe) east of Ashur, near Kirkuk in modern Iraq and dating from the 15th century B. C.

6. History. Under Shamshi-Adad I (c. 1748-c. 1716 B. C.) Assyria began to spread as a great city state, with strong fortifications and a splendid temple to house its national god, Ashur. From c. 1700-c. to 1100 B. C. the Old Assyrian Kingdom is to be dated, as the political power of Babylon declined. By the 14th century B. C. Assyria had arisen to a position of power comparable to Egypt on the Nile and the Hittite Empire in Asia Minor. Among the Amarna Tablets is a letter written by Ashur-uballit I, ("Ashur-has-given-life," c. 1362-c. 1327) to Amenhotep IV of Egypt in which the Assyrian monarch speaks as a royal equal. With Tiglath-pileser I (c. 1114-c. 1076) Assyria entered the period of empire, extending from c. 1100-633 B. C. This great conqueror was able to push Assyrian power westward to the Mediterranean Sea and northward to the region of Lake Van and the Mountains of Armenia. The next two centuries, however, marked a period of retrogression for Assyria until the rise of Ashurnasirpal II (883-859) who made his land a formidable fighting machine and who swept everything before his ruthless cruelty, as his annals tell. His son Shalmaneser III (858-824) inherited his father's gigantic fighting machine and conducted numerous campaigns against Syria-Palestine, in one of which he fought against Ahab of Israel at Karkar on the Orontes River in 853 B. C. and in another received tribute from "Jehu, son of Omri." Shalmaneser III styled himself "the mighty king, king of the universe, the king without a rival, the autocrat, the powerful one of the four regions of the world, who shatters the might of the princes of the whole world, who has smashed all of his foes as pots" (D. D. Luckenbill, Anc. Rec of Assyria and Babylonia, I, sect. 674). Despite his boasts Shalmaneser III died amid revolts which his son Shamsi-Adad V (823-811) also had to face. Adad-nirari III (810-783) kept Assyrian power aggressive, but under Shalmaneser IV (782-773), Ashur-dan III (772-755) and Ashur-nirari V (754-745) declension set in. Then the throne was seized by a great warrior and statesman, Tiglath-pileser III, who assumed the name of the illustrious conqueror Tiglath-pileser I of the eleventh century B. C. and brought back the empire to its glory, even conquering Babylon, where he was known as Pulu (cf. II Kings 15:19). This great warrior overran Israel, took tribute from Menahem, and transported his conquered peoples to distant sections of his empire. Soon after the death of Tiglath-

pileser, Hoshea of Israel attempted to revolt against Assyria. The new emperor, Shalmaneser V (726-722) thereupon laid siege to the Israelite capital of Samaria. Before the fall of the city had been fully consummated a new leader had seized the reins of power. He was Sharrukin II or Sargon II (721-705), whose new regime was inaugurated by the fall of the city. Sargon is mentioned but once in Scripture (Isa. 20:1), but as the result of the excavation of his splendid palace at Dur Sharrukin or Khorsabad, he is now one of the best known of Assyrian emperors. In 704 B. C. he was succeeded by his son Sennacherib, who held the throne of Assyria until 681 B. C., and was succeeded in turn by his son Esarhaddon

50. Winged-genius in Glazed Brick from the Palace of Sargon (Khorsabad)

(680-669), who ranks as one of the greatest Assyrian conquerors. Under Esarhaddon's son, Ashurbanipal, a scholar and a humanist instead of a great general, the Assyrian stranglehold on the Ancient world began to give way. In the intervening years till 612 B. C. when Nineveh fell and Assyrian civilization was snuffed out with startling suddenness, there were several undistinguished rulers. The Neo-Babylonian Empire arose on the ruins of Assyria, and a new historical epoch dawned. Revised by M. F. U.

As'taroth, As'tar'te, Asherah (q. v.). See Gods, False.

Astrology. See Magic.

Astronomy (Gr. 'astronomia, laws of the stars). This science probably owes its origin to the Chaldeans, there being evidence that they had conducted astronomical observations from remote antiquity. Callisthenes sent to his uncle, Aristotle, a number of these observations, of which the oldest must have dated back to the middle of B. C. 2300. "The Chaldean priests had been accustomed from an early date to record on their clay tablets the aspect of the heavens and the changes which took place in them night after night, the appearance of the constellations, their comparative brilliance, the precise moments of their rising and setting and culmination, together with the more or less rapid movements of the planets, and their motions toward or from one another." They discovered the revolution and eclipses of the moon, and frequently predicted with success eclipses of the sun (Maspero, *Dawn of Civilization*, p. 775, sq.).

The astronomy of China and India dates back to a very early period, for we read of two Chinese astronomers, Ho and Hi, being put to death for failing to announce a solar eclipse which took place B. C. 2169.

The Hebrews do not appear to have devoted much attention to astronomy, perhaps because *astrology*, highly esteemed among the neighboring nations (Isa. 47:9; Jer. 27:9; Dan. 2), was interdicted by the law (Deut. 18:10, 11). And yet we find as early as the Book of Job the constellations were distinguished and designated by peculiar and appropriate names (Job. 9:9; 38:31; also Isa. 13:10; Amos 5:8).

Asup'pim (á-sŭp'ĭm; *collections*), (I Chron. 26:15; *house of collections*, v. 17), a part of the temple assigned to the care of the family of Obed-edom. It appears to have been a building used for the storing of the temple goods, situated in the neighborhood of the southern door of the temple in the external court, and with probably two entrances (Keil, *Com.*, in loc.). The same word in Neh. 12:25 is incorrectly rendered (A. V.) "thresholds."

Asylum (Heb. *mĭqlät*), a place of safety where even a criminal might be free from violence from the avenger.

1. **Ancient.** From Exod. 21:14; I Kings 1:50, we see that the Hebrews, in common with many other nations, held that the altar, as God's abode, afforded protection to those whose lives were in danger. By the law, however, the place of expiation for sins of weakness (Lev. 4:2; 5:15-18; Num. 15:27-31) was prevented from being abused by being made a place of refuge for criminals deserving of death. The Mosaic law also provided "cities of refuge" (*q. v.*). Among the Greeks and Romans, the right of asylum pertained to altars, temples, and all holy shrines. These sanctuaries were exceptionally numerous in Asia. During the time of the Roman empire the statues of the emperors were used as refuges against momentary acts of violence. Armies in the field used the eagles of the legions for the same purpose.

2. **Christian.** In the Christian Church the right of asylum was retained, and extended from the altar to all ecclesiastical buildings. By act of Theodosius II (A. D. 431) not only the Church was to be considered sacred, but also the *atrium*, the garden, bath, and cells. Many abuses crept in, until the custom has either become extinct or greatly reformed.

Asyn'critus (á-sĭng'krĭ-tŭs; *incomparable*), the name of a Christian at Rome to whom St. Paul sends salutation (Rom. 16:14), A. D. 60.

A'tad (ā'tăd; *a thorn*). It is uncertain whether Atad is the name of a person or a descriptive appellation given to a "thorny" locality. At the threshing floor of Atad the sons of Jacob, and the Egyptians who accompanied them, "made a mourning" for Jacob seven days (Gen. 50:10, 11), B. C. c. 1871.

At'arah (ăt'á-rä; a *crown*), the second wife of Jerahmeel, of the tribe of Judah, and mother of Onam (I Chron. 2:26).

Atar'gatis (á-tär'gá-tĭs; from Gr. '*atargatis* from the Aramaic '*Atar* or '*Attar* (Astarte) plus '*Atah*. Probably the same form of the Phrygian *Atis*, a god of vegetation). A Syrian divinity, the great goddess of fertility among the Aramaeans. The worship of this goddess is not alluded to in the O. T., but II Macc. 12:26 mentions her temple at Carnion in Gilead. She was also worshipped at Ashkelon and the concomitants of her cult were those of the mother goddess of the Semites. *M. F. U.*

At'aroth (ăt'á-rŏth; *crowns*).

1. A city near Gilead, E. of Jordan, in a fertile grazing district (Num. 32:3). Rebuilt by the Gadites (v. 34).

2. A city on the border of Ephraim and Benjamin (Josh. 16:7). Called also Ataroth-adar (Josh. 18:13).

3. "Ataroth of the house of Joab," in the tribe of Judah, a city founded by the descendants of Salma (I Chron. 2:54).

A'ter (ā'tĕr; probably *shut up*).

1. A person "of" (probably descendant of) Hezekiah, whose family to the number of ninety-eight returned from the captivity (Ezra 2:16; Neh. 7:21), B. C. before 536.

2. The head of a family of Levitical "porters" to the temple, whose descendants went up to Jerusalem at the same time with the above (Ezra 2:42; Neh. 7:45), B. C. before 536.

3. One of the chief Israelites that subscribed the sacred covenant with Nehemiah (Neh. 10:17), B. C. about 445.

A'thach (ā'thăk), a city in Judah to which David sent a present of the spoils recovered from the Amalekites who had sacked Ziklag (I Sam. 30:30). Its site is Khirbet 'Attir near Enrimmon.

Atha'iah (ăth-á'yä; perhaps the same as Asaiah), a son of Uzziah, of the tribe of Judah, who dwelt in Jerusalem after the return from Babylon (Neh. 11:4), B. C. 445.

Athali'ah (á-thá-lī'áh).

1. The daughter of Ahab, king of Israel, doubtless by his wife Jezebel. She is called (II Chron. 22:2) the daughter of Omri, who was father of Ahab, but by a comparison of texts it would appear that she is so called only as being his granddaughter. (1) **Idolatry.** She was married to Jehoram, king of Judah, who "walked in the way of the house of Ahab," no doubt owing to her influence, "for he had the daughter of Ahab to wife" (II Chron. 21:6). After the death of Jehoram, Ahaziah came to the throne, and he also walked in the way of Ahab's house, following the wicked counsel of his mother (II Chron. 22:2, 3). (2) **Reign.** Ahaziah reigned one year, and was slain by Jehu, whereupon Athaliah resolved to seat herself upon the throne of David. She caused all the male members of the royal family to be put to death; only, Joash, the son of Ahaziah, escaping (II Kings 11:1), B. C. 842. Athaliah usurped the throne for six years,

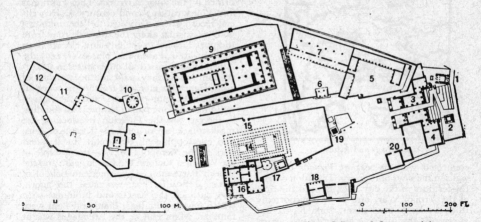

1. Nike Temple.   2. So called Monument of Agrippa.   3. Propylaea.   4. Picture Gallery.   5. Sanctuary of the Brauronia Artemis.   6. Propylon.   7. Chalkotheki.   8. Precinct of Zeus Polieus and Boukoleion.   9. Parthenon. 10. Temple of Roma.   11. Heroon of Pandion.   12. Service.   13. Great Altar of Athena.   14. Old Temple of Athena.   15. Propylon.   16. Erechtheum.   17. Pandroseum, Temple of Pandrosus, Sacred Olive Tree, Cecropium. 18. Dwelling of the Arrephori.   19. Promachos.   20. Service Building (?).

51. Plan of Acropolis by G. P. Stevens, American School of Classical Studies, Athens

842-836. Joash, in the meantime, had been concealed in the temple by his aunt. Jehosheba, the wife of Jehoiada, the high priest. In the seventh year, Jehoiada resolved to produce the young prince, and, arrangements having been made for defense in case of necessity, Joash was declared king. Athaliah, who was probably worhipping in the house of Baal, was aroused by the shouts of the people, and repaired to the temple, where her cry of "treason" only secured her own arrest. (3) **Death.** She was taken beyond the sacred precincts of the temple and put to death. The only other recorded victim of this revolution was Mattan, the priest of Baal (II Kings 11:1, sq.; II Chron. 23:1-17).

2. One of the sons of Jeroham, and a chieftain of the tribe of Benjamin, who dwelt at Jerusalem (I Chron. 8:26).

3. The father of Jeshaiah, which latter was one of the "sons" of Elam that returned with seventy dependents from Babylon under Ezra (Ezra 8:7), B. C. about 457.

Athanasian Creed. *See* Creeds.

Atheism (Gr. *'atheos, without God*), the denial of the existence of God. The term has always been applied according to the popular conception of God. Thus the Greeks considered a man *'atheos, atheist,* when he denied the existence of the gods recognized by the state. The Pagans called Christians atheists because they would not acknowledge the heathen gods and worship them. In the theological controversies of the early Church the opposite parties not infrequently called each other atheists.

When we speak of atheism proper, we speak of a phase of the controversy touching a great first cause of creation. The word, however, is not in favor, and is renounced even by those whose reasonings naturally lead up to it. The question may be fairly asked, Is blank atheism or antitheism possible to the human mind? And the answer must be finally given that it is not. If we appeal to Scripture, and such an

appeal should be allowed, we find that through the whole book there is no single allusion to men from whose mind the thought of God is erased. The book demonstrates everything about the Deity but his existence. It never descends to argue with an atheist. If it recognizes a man who is a disbeliever in God, it counts him a "fool" (Psa. 53:1). "In Eph. 2:12 the expression, *'atheoi en tō kosmō,* 'without God in the world,' the word *'atheoi, godless,* may be taken either with the active, neuter, or passive reference, i. e., either denying, ignorant of, or *forsaken* by God. The last meaning seems best to suit the passive tenor of the passage and to enhance the dreariness and gloom of the picture" (Ellicott, *Com.,* in loc.).

Atheism proper has mostly sprung from moral causes, and denotes a system of thought which the healthiest instinct of mankind has always abhorred. Even among the heathen the denial of the existence of the gods was proscribed and punished.

Athe'nian (Acts 17:21, rendered "of Athens" in v. 22), an inhabitant of *Athens* (*q. v.*).

Ath'ens (ăth'ĕnz), a city named after the patron goddess Athene and the capital of the important Greek state of Attica, which became the cultural center of the ancient pre-Christian world. It grew up around the 512-foot-high hill called the Acropolis and was

52. Agora (market place), Athens

105

53. Athens and Attica

connected with its seaport Piraeus by long walls in the days of its glory. Tradition carries the fortunes of the city back beyond the time of the Trojan War, and it was purportedly ruled by kings until about 1608 B. C., but afterwards the supreme authority was vested in archons. Two famous legislators appear in its history—Draco about 625 B. C., whose laws were pitilessly severe, and Solon about 595 B. C., whose enactments were more humane. After a great victory over the Persians at Marathon in 490 B. C. and at Salamis in 480 B. C., the Athenians were able to establish a small empire, with Athens as its capital and a substantial fleet as its protector. In the age of Pericles, an enlightened leader, art, literature and architecture flourished. But before the death of this great leader, the Peloponnesian War broke out (431 B. C.), eventuating in the surrender of Athens to Sparta in 404 B. C. Thereafter the city passed through many vicissitudes politically, but the culture and intellectual preeminence of its inhabitants gave them prestige despite varying political fortunes. Four great systems of philosophy flourished there—Platonic, Peripatetic, Epicurean and Stoic—attracting students from all over the ancient world. The city was captured by the Roman general Sulla in 86 B. C. and was under Roman rule when Paul came as a visitor (Acts 17:15). The remark of the sacred historian concerning the inquisitive nature of the Athenians (Acts 17: 12) is attested by the voice of antiquity. For

54. The Parthenon

instance, Demosthenes rebukes his countrymen for their love of constantly going about in the marketplace, asking one another, "What news?" The Apostle Paul's remark upon the "superstitious" (religious) character of the Athenians (Acts 17:22) is likewise con-

firmed by the ancient writers. Thus Pausanias and Philostratus, second century A. D. writers, record altars dedicated to "the unknown god" as existing along the two-mile road from the port Piraeus to the city and elsewhere in the city itself. Pausanias, moreover, says the Athenians surpassed all other states in the attention which they paid to the worship of gods. Hence the city was crowded in every direction with temples, altars, and other sacred buildings. Among pagan temples still standing in the city are the Theseion, overlooking the marketplace (agora q. v.), the Temple of Zeus, and overtopping all the architectural splendors of the Acropolis (q. v.)—the Temple of the Wingless Victory, the Erechtheum and the superb Parthenon. The American School of Classical Studies has excavated the agora, and outlined the streets and buildings with which Pericles, Phidias, Plato and Paul were familiar. Mars Hill or the Areopagus was at

55. Temple with Porch of Maidens, Acropolis

the west approach to the Acropolis. Here Paul preached the gospel of redemption through Christ to the devotees of three current philosophies—Platonism, Stoicism and Epicureanism. The Apostle argued against polytheism and offered salvation in the name of the one God manifested in Christ. Dionysius, an Areppagite, and a few others were converted (Acts 17:17). But Paul did not succeed in establishing a church at Athens, as at Corinth, Thessalonica, Philippi, Colossae and Ephesus. It was in Athens that Paul manifested evidence of his Hellenistic culture by familiarly quoting a verse (Acts 17:28) taken from an invocation to Zeus, written by a minor Cilician poet, Aratus (312-245 B. C.). Doubtless while in the city the great missionary saw the music hall or Odeion of Pericles (cf. I Cor. 13:1), the Stadium with its foot races (cf. I Cor. 9:24) and wrestling contests (cf. Eph. 6:12), and the great Tower and Waterclock of Andronicus (cf. Eph. 5:16). Likewise he may have visited the *keramikos* or potterymaking section of the city, which was famous (cf. Rom. 9:21). *M. F. U.*

Ath'lai (ăth'lī), a son of Bebai, who put away his strange wife on the return from Babylon (Ezra 10:28).

Atonement (Heb. *kāphăr*, to *cover, cancel;* Gr. *katallagē, exchange, reconciliation*).

1. **Definition.** In accordance with the force of these terms of Scripture the atonement is the covering over of sin, the reconciliation between God and man, accomplished by the

Lord Jesus Christ. It is that special result of Christ's sacrificial sufferings and death by virtue of which all who exercise proper penitence and faith receive forgiveness of their sins and obtain peace.

2. Scripture Doctrine. Terms and Methods. In addition to the terms above named there are other words used in the Scriptures which express the idea of atonement or throw special light upon its meaning. Of these may be here cited (a) *hilaskomai,* translated (Heb. 2:17) "to make reconciliation." Also Rom. 3:25; I John 2:2; 4:10, where the kindred noun is rendered "propitiation." (b) *lutron,* translated "ransom," "redemption" (Matt. 20:23; Mark 10:30; Luke 2:38; Heb. 9:12). By such words and in such passages as these the doctrine is taught that Christ died to effect reconciliation between God and man, to propitiate the divine favor in behalf of sinful men, and to redeem or ransom men from the penalties and the dominion of their sins.

There are also forms of expression in which the idea of substitution, or that Christ stands as our substitute in the economy of divine grace, appear with marked emphasis (Rom. 5:6-8; I Cor. 15:3; II Cor. 5:21; Gal. 3:13; Tit. 2:14; I Pet. 2:24; 3:18).

The divinely appointed sacrifices of the Old Testament dispensation are also full of significance, embracing as they did special offerings or sacrifices for sin. The uniform teaching of the New Testament is that these were typical of the sacrifice which Christ made of himself for the sins of the world.

3. Summary. While the Scriptures do not give a philosophical theory or explanation of the atonement, nor perhaps furnish us with data altogether sufficient for such a theory, still it is true that (a) The Scriptures reveal the atonement to us as an accomplished and completed fact (Heb. 9:13-26). (b) They represent this fact as necessary to human salvation (Luke 24:40-46, 47; Acts 4:12). (c) While the whole earthly life of Christ contained an atoning and even sacrificial element, the virtue of the atonement is to be found chiefly in his sacrificial death. His death was indispensable (John 3:14, 15). (d) In the atoning death of Christ was exhibited not only the holy wrath of God against sin, but quite as much the love of God toward sinful men (Rom. 3:25, 26; 5:6-8; John 3:16). (e) The gracious divine purpose realized in the atonement was inwrought with the creation of man. Redemption was in the thought and plan of the Creator so that man falling fell into the arms of divine mercy. The Lamb of God was "slain from the foundation of the world" (Rev. 13:8; I Pet. 1:19, 20). (f) The atonement is not limited, but universal in the extent of its gracious provisions (Heb. 2:9; I Tim. 2:5, 6; 4:10; Rom. 5:18; II Cor. 5:14, 15). (g) The universality of the atonement does not lead to universal salvation. The greater offer of salvation may be, and often is, rejected, and when the rejection is final the atonement avails nothing for the sinner (Mark 16:16; John 3:36; Heb. 10:26-29). (h) The atonement is the actual objective ground of forgiveness of sins and acceptance with God for all penitent believers (John 3:16; Acts 2:38; Eph. 1:7; Col. 1:14).

4. Theological Treatment. This branch of the subject calls for two classes of statements: (1) as to the history of the doctrine; (2) as to the theological views most generally held at the present time.

(1) **History.** During the early centuries of the history of the Church, and particularly prior to the Nicene Council (A. D. 325), Christian theology reflected, in the main, simply the teaching of the New Testament upon this subject. The attention of theologians was concentrated upon the person of Christ. There was but little speculation as to the method of the atonement or the exact ground of its necessity. That the sacrifice of Christ was vicarious, that he suffered in the stead of men, was, however, an idea constantly held; and that these sufferings were necessary to meet the requirement of divine righteousness was sometimes declared with emphasis. A fanciful notion, it is true, began to appear at that early period, a notion which afterward obtained some measure of prominence. Christ was regarded as a ransom paid to the devil to redeem men who by their sin had come under the dominion of the devil. This was taught by Origen (A. D. 230), and more emphatically by Gregory of Nyssa (A. D. 370). This view has also, but incorrectly, been attributed to Irenaeus (A. D. 180). Captious critics and infidels have often cited this incident in the history of theology in order to bring all theology into ridicule and contempt. But it is to be remembered that this phase of doctrine was always met with the strongest denial and opposition, as by Athanasius (A. D. 370) and Gregory of Nazianzum (A. D. 390). It was never the accepted doctrine of the Christian Church.

Anselm. Prominent in the history of the doctrine of the atonement must ever stand the name of Anselm, A. D. 1100. In his book, *Cur Deus Homo,* he brings out most clearly and emphatically the idea of the atonement as satisfaction to divine majesty. He viewed the necessity of atonement as entirely in the justice of God. He made this term "satisfaction," it has been said, "a watchword for all future time." Certain it is that what is known as the *satisfaction* theory of the atonement will ever stand associated with his name, although his satisfaction theory is not quite the same as that of the reformers.

Abelard. Chief among the opponents of Anselm was Abelard, A. D. 1141. He referred the atonement wholly to the love of God, and taught that there could be nothing in the divine essence that required satisfaction for sin. The death of Christ upon the cross was solely an exhibition of divine love. The effect is moral only. It is intended to subdue the hearts of sinful men, to lead them to repentance and devotion to Christ. Thus Abelard stands as the father of what is known as the *moral influence* theory.

Grotius. An epoch in the history of the doctrine was reached when Grotius, A. D. 1617, wrote his *Defensio fidei Cathol. de Satisfactione.* He wrote in refutation of the teaching of Socinus, who denied the vicarious character of Christ's death, and the need of any reconciliation of God with man. Grotius held fast to the vicariousness of Christ's sufferings, and used the term "satisfaction." But in his view it was a satisfaction to the requirements of moral government, and not to the justice which inheres in God himself. The necessity of the atonement, accordingly, he found not in the nature of God, but in the nature of the divine government. The purpose of the atonement is to make it possible to exercise mercy toward fallen and sinful men, and at the same time maintain the dignity of the law, the honor of the Lawgiver, and protect the moral interests of the universe. Grotius thus founded what is known as the *rectoral* or *governmental* theory.

The doctrines of Anselm, Abelard, and Grotius represent the principal tendencies of thought and discussion throughout the whole history of the doctrine. Under the treatment of various theologians these doctrines received modification more or less important; but in their leading principles these three forms of teaching have been the most prominent in the theology of the Christian Church.

(2) **Modern Views.** Aside from the opinion of rationalists and semirationalists, who wholly or in part reject the authority of Scripture, and accordingly attach but slight if any importance to Scripture teaching concerning the atonement, the three theories prominent in the past are still the prominent theories of the present. With various shadings and modifications, and attempts at interblending, they embody in the main the thinking of modern times upon this subject.

The moral influence theory, however, it should be said, has never obtained formal or general acceptance in any evangelical communion. It has been regarded justly as falling far short of adequately representing the teaching of Scripture. It contains some measure of truth, but leaves out the truth most essential, that of real, objective atonement. It reduces the atonement to an object lesson.

The thought of the Christian Church of to-day is divided in its adherence between the satisfaction and governmental theories; these theories appearing in various forms. But no one of these views most prominent is free from grave logical objections if held too rigidly and exclusively. Thus the satisfaction theory, if held in the sense that Christ actually bore the punishment for the sins of men, or that he literally, according to the figure of Anselm, paid the debt of human transgressors, after the manner of a commercial transaction, must lead logically to one or the other of two extremes—either that of a limited atonement or that of universalism. It tends also to antinomianism, to say nothing of other objections often raised. The governmental theory, held alone and too boldly, loses sight of the fact that the divine government must be a reflection of the divine nature, and that what is required by that government must be required also by some quality inherent in God. Further, this theory, if not guarded strongly, and by bringing in, in some form, the idea of satisfaction to divine justice, reduces the death of Christ to a great moral spectacle. It becomes, in fact, another moral influence theory.

A strong tendency, accordingly, of the present day is to seek some way of mediating between or of uniting the elements of truth found in these various theories. Certain it is that the Scriptures do represent the death of Christ as a most affecting manifestation of the love of God. Certain, also, it is that his death is represented as sacrificial, and required by the justice of God. And equally true it is that it is often viewed in its relations to divine law and the moral economy that God has established. And if the earnest attempts of devout thinkers do not succeed wholly in penetrating the mystery of the cross, and in bringing the exact meaning of Christ's death within the compass of their definitions, still it is held as beyond all question that the atonement wrought by Christ is a fundamental fact in human salvation, a real "covering" for sin, the divinely appointed measure for "reconciliation" between God and man.

5. **Extent of Atonement.** The extent of atonement is much less discussed than formerly. Many Calvinists have departed from the view they once strenuously held, that the atonement was for the elect only.

Literature—The literature of this subject is very extensive. Reference may here be made to *The Vicarious Sacrifice*, Bushnell—the moral influence theory; *Atonement in Christ*, Miley—the governmental theory; *Our Lord's Doctrine of the Atonement*, Smeaton—the satisfaction theory; also to the chapters treating this subject in such works of systematic theology as Pope's *Compendium of Christian Theology*, Van Oosterzee's *Christian Dogmatics*, Hodge's *Systematic Theology*, H. B. Smith's *System of Christian Theology.*—E. McC.

Atonement, Day of. *See* Festivals.

At'troth (Num. 32:35). *See* Ataroth.

At'tai (ă'tā-ī).

1. The son of a daughter of Sheshan, of the tribe of Judah, by his Egyptian servant, Jarha. He was the father of Nathan (I Chron. 2:35, 36).

2. One of David's mighty men, of the tribe of Gad, who joined David at Ziklag, whither he had fled from Saul (I Chron. 12:11).

3. The second of the four sons of King Rehoboam, by his second wife, Maachah, the daughter of Absalom (II Chron. 11:20).

Attali'a (ăt-à-lī'à), a seaport on the coast of Pamphylia, at the mouth of the river Cattarrhactes. The town was named after its founder, Attalus Philadelphus, king of Pergamos, 159-138 B. C. Paul and Barnabas on the way to Antioch stopped there (Acts 14:25). Its name in the 12th century appears to have been Satalia; it still exists under the name of Adalia.

Attire. *See* Dress.

Attitude. *See* Prayer, Salutation.

Augustus (à-gŭs'tŭs), the imperial title assumed by Octavius, successor of Julius Caesar. He was born A. U. C. 691 (B. C. 63), and was principally educated by his great-uncle, Julius Caesar, who made him his heir. After the death of Caesar, he acquired such influence that Antony and Lepidus took him into their triumvirate. He afterward shared the empire with Antony, and attained su-

56. Youthful Head of Augustus

preme power after the battle of Actium, B. C. 31, being saluted imperator by the Senate, who conferred on him the title Augustus in B. C. 27. He forgave Herod, who had espoused the cause of Antony, and even increased his power. After the death of Herod, A. D. 4, his dominions were divided among his sons by Augustus, almost in exact accordance with his will. Augustus was emperor at the birth and during half the lifetime of our Lord, but his name occurs only once (Luke 2:1) in the New Testament, as the emperor who ordered the enrollment in consequence of which Joseph and Mary went to Bethlehem, the place where the Messiah was to be born.

Aul. *See* Awl.

Aunt (Heb. *dōdäh, loving*), a father's sister (Exod. 6:20); also an uncle's wife (Lev. 18:14; 20:20).

Authorized Version (A. V.). *See* Bible.

A′va (āv′á, av′vah, II Kings 17:24), or **I′vah** (Iv′vah), II Kings 18:34; 19:13), identified with Tell Kafr 'Ayah on the Orontes S. W. of Homs.

Ave Maria (ä′vä mä-rē′ä) (*Hail Mary*).

1. The words of the angel Gabriel to the Virgin Mary, when announcing the incarnation (Luke 1:28), as rendered by the Vulgate.

2. The familiar prayer, or form of devotion, in the Roman Catholic Church, called also the "Angelical Salutation." It consists of three parts: (1) The Salutation of Gabriel, *Ave* (Maria) *gratia plena Dominus tecum; benedicta tu in mulieribus;* (2) the words of Elizabeth to Mary, *et benedictus fructus ventris tui;* (3) an addition made by the Church, *Sancta Maria, Mater Dei, ora pro nobis peccatoribus nunc et in hora mortis nostrae.* The whole Ave Maria, as it now stands, is ordered in the breviary of Pius V (1568) to be used daily before each canonical hour and after compline; i. e., the last of the seven canonical hours (*Cath. Dict.*, s. v.).

A′ven (ā′věn; *nothingness, vanity,* an *idol*).

1. The popular name of Heliopolis, in Lower Egypt, probably selected intentionally in the sense of an idol-city (Ezek. 30:17) because On-Heliopolis was from time immemorial one of the principal seats of the Egyptian worship of the sun, and possessed a celebrated temple of the sun and a numerous and learned priesthood.

2. The "high places of Aven" are the buildings connected with the image-worship at Beth-el, and which were to be utterly ruined (Hos. 10:8).

3. Mentioned as "the plain of Aven" (Amos 1:5), and thought by some to be the same as the plain of Baalbek, (*q. v.*), an early center of Baal worship. Others, however, connect the place with Awaniyek near Jerud on the road to Palmyra.

Avenger of Blood. *See* Blood, Avenger of.

A′vim (ăv′ĭm), **A′vims**, or **A′vites.**

1. A people among the early inhabitants of Palestine, whom we meet in the S. W. corner of the seacoast, whither they may have made their way northward from the Desert. The only notice of them which has come down to us is contained in a remarkable fragment of primeval history preserved in Deut. 2:23. Here we see them dwelling in the villages in the S. part of the Shefelah, or great western lowland, "as far as Gaza." In these rich possessions they were attacked by the invading Philistines, "the Caphtorim which came forth out of Caphtor," and who after "destroying" them and "dwelling in their stead," appear to have pushed them further N. Possibly a trace of their existence is to be found in the town "Avim" (or "the Avvim"), which occurs among the cities of Benjamin (Josh. 18:23). It is a curious fact that both the LXX. and Jerome identified the Avvim with the Hivites, and also that the town of ha-Avvim was in the actual district of the Hivites (Josh. 9:7, 17, comp. with 18:22-27).

2. The people of Avva, among the colonists who were sent by the king of Assyria to reinhabit the depopulated cities of Israel (II Kings 17:31). They were idolaters, worshipping gods called Bibhaz and Tartak. *See* Ava.

A′vith (ā′vĭth), a city of the Edomites, capital of King Hadad before there were kings in Israel (Gen. 36:35; I Chron. 1:46).

Awl (Heb. *mărşēă‘*, from verb signifying "to *bore*"), a boring instrument, probably of the simplest kind, and similar to those in familiar use at the present time. It occurs twice in the Scriptures (Exod. 21:6; Deut. 15:17).

Ax, the rendering in the A. V. of several original words:

1. *Garzen* (Heb., to *cut*). This appears to have consisted of a head of iron (Isa. 10:34), fastened with thongs or otherwise, upon a handle of wood, and so liable to slip off (Deut. 19:5; II Kings 6:5). It was used for felling trees (Deut. 20:19) and for shaping timber, perhaps like the modern adze.

2. *Hereb*, usually rendered "sword," is used of other cutting instruments; once rendered "ax" (Ezek. 26:9); probably a pickax, as it is said that "with his axes he shall break down thy towers."

3. *Kashil* occurs only in Psa. 74:6, and appears to have been a later word denoting a large ax.

4. *Magzerah*, "iron cutting tools" (K. and D., *Com.;* II Sam. 12:31).

5. *Ma'sad, hewing* instrument, rendered "tongs" (Isa. 44:12) and "ax" (Jer. 10:3. Some axes were shaped like chisels fastened to a handle, and such may have been the instrument named in Jeremiah; but as Isaiah (44:12) refers to the work of a blacksmith, this instrument was probably a chisel for cutting the iron upon the anvil.

6. *Qardom* is the commonest name for ax or hatchet. This is the instrument referred to in Judg. 9:48; I Sam. 13:20, 21; Psa. 74:5; Jer. 46:22, and was extensively used for felling trees.

7. The Greek word for ax is *'axine* (Matt. 3:10; Luke 3:9).

Figurative. The ax is used in Scripture as a symbol of divine judgment. John Baptist, referring probably to the excision of the Jewish people, says, "And now also the ax is laid unto the root of the trees." This denotes that it had already been stuck into the tree preparatory to felling it. The ax was also used as a symbol of human instrument, e. g., "Shall the ax boast itself against him that heweth therewith?" (Isa. 10:15), i. e., Shall the king of Assyria boast himself against God?

Axhead (*băr-zĕl*) (II Kings. 6:5) is literally "iron;" but as an ax is certainly intended, the passage shows that the axheads among the Hebrews were of iron. Those found in Egypt are of bronze, such as was anciently used; but they have been made them also of iron, the latter having been consumed by corroding. The Iron Age began 1200 B. C.

Axletree occurs only in I Kings 7:32, 33, as the translation of *yăd*, *hand*, the whole phrase being the *hands of the wheels*.

A'yin (ā'yĕn; in A. V. **A'in**, Heb. *'ayĭn*, an eye, a spring). The 16th letter of the Hebrew alphabet. It heads the sixteenth section of the 119th Psalm, in which passage (vs. 121-128) each verse begins with this letter in the original.

A place near Riblah in N. Palestine (Num. 34:11).

A place near Rimmon (Josh. 15:32).

A'zal (ā'zăl; *noble*), a place, evidently in the neighborhood of Jerusalem, and probably E. of the Mount of Olives (Zech. 14:5). Its site has not been identified, but the LXX. rendering *Iasol* suggests Wadi Yasūl, a tributary of the Kidron.

Azali'ah (ăz-à-lī'à; *reserved by Jehovah*), the son of Meshullam and father of Shaphan the scribe. The latter was sent with others by Josiah to repair the temple (II Kings 22:3; II Chron. 34:8), B. C. about 624.

Azani'ah (ăz-à-nī'à; *whom Jehovah hears*), the father of Jeshua, which latter was one of the Levites that subscribed the sacred covenant after the exile (Neh. 10:9), B. C. 445.

Azar'ael (Neh. 12:36). *See* Azareel (5).

Aza'reel (à-zā'rē-ĕl; *God has helped*).

1. One of the Korhites who joined David at Ziklag (I Chron. 12:6), B. C. before 1000.

2. The head of the eleventh division of the musicians of the temple (I Chron. 25:18), B. C. about 1000. Called Uzziel in v. 4.

3. The son of Jeroham, and prince of the tribe of Dan, when David numbered the people (I Chron. 27:22).

4. An Israelite, descendant of Bani, who renounced his Gentile wife after the return from Babylon (Ezra 10:41).

5. The son of Ahasai and father of Amashai, which last was one of the chiefs of one hundred and twenty-eight mighty men who served at the temple under the supervision of Zabdiel on the restoration from Babylon (Neh. 11:13, 14). He is probably the same as one of the first company of priests who were appointed with Ezra to make the circuit of the newly completed walls with trumpets in their hands (Neh. 12:36), where the name is rendered Azarael.

Azari'ah (ăz-à-rī'à; *helped* by *Jehovah*), a common name in Hebrew, and especially in the families of the priests of the line of Eleazar, whose name has precisely the same meaning as Azariah. It is nearly identical and is often confounded with Ezra, as well as with Zeraiah and Seraiah.

1. A son or descendant of Zadok, the high priest, in the time of David and one of Solomon's princes (I Kings 4:2), B. C. 960. He is probably the same as No. 6 below.

2. A son of Nathan, and captain of King Solomon's guards (I Kings 4:5).

3. Son and successor of Amziah, aking of Judah (II Kings 14:21; 15:1, sq.; I Chron. 3:12), more frequently called *Uzziah* (*q. v.*).

4. Son of Ethan and great-grandson of Judah (I Chron. 2:8).

5. The son of Jehu and father of Helez, of the tribe of Judah (I Chron. 2:38, 39).

6. A high priest, son of Ahimaaz and grandson of Zadok (I Chron. 6:9), whom he seems to have immediately succeeded (I Kings 4:2). He is probably the same as No. 1 above.

7. The son of Johanan and father of Amariah, a high priest (I Chron. 6:10, 11). He was probably high priest in the reigns of Abijah and Asa, as his son Amariah was in the days of Jehoshaphat.

8. The son of Hilkiah and father of Seraiah, which latter was the last high priest before the captivity (I Chron. 6:13, 14; 9:11; Ezra 7:1).

9. A Levite, son of Zephaniah and father of Joel (I Chron. 6:36). In v. 24 he is called Uzziah. It appears from II Chron. 29:12 that his son Joel lived under Hezekiah, and was engaged in the cleansing of the temple.

10. The prophet who met King Asa on his return from a victory over Zerah, the Ethiopian (II Chron. 15:1), where he is called the son of Oded, but Oded simply in v. 8. He exhorted Asa to put away idolatry and restore

the altar of God before the porch of the temple. A national reformation followed, participated in by representatives out of all Israel. Keil (*Com.*) thinks Obed in v. 8 is an interpolation.

11. Two sons of King Jehoshaphat (II Chron. 21:2), B. C. 875. M'Clintock and Strong (s. v.) conjecture that there is a repetition of name, and that there was but one son of that name.

12. A clerical error (II Chron. 22:6), for *Ahaziah* (*q. v.*), king of Judah.

13. A son of Jeroham, one of the "captains" who assisted Jehoiada in restoring the worship of the throne, opposing Athaliah and placing Joash on the throne (II Chron. 23:1).

14. The son of Obed, another of the "captains" who assisted in the same enterprise (II Chron. 23:1).

15. High priest in the reign of Uzziah. When the king, elated by his success, "went into the temple of the Lord to burn incense," Azariah went in after him, accompanied by eighty of his brethren, and withstood him (II Chron. 26:17, sq.).

16. Son of Johanan, and a chief of the tribe of Ephraim, one of those who protested against enslaving their captive brethren taken in the invasion of Judah by Pekah (II Chron. 28:12).

17. A Merarite, son of Jehalelel, who was one of those who cleansed the temple in the time of Hezekiah (II Chron. 29:12).

18. A high priest in the time of Hezekiah (II Chron. 31:10, 13), B. C. 719. He appears to have cooperated zealously with the king in that thorough purification of the temple and restoration of the temple services which was so conspicuous a feature in his reign.

19. The father of Amariah, and an ancestor of Ezra (Ezra 7:3).

20. Son of Maaseiah, who repaired part of the wall of Jerusalem (Neh. 3:23, 24), was one of the Levites who assisted Ezra in expounding the law (Neh. 8:7), sealed the covenant with Nehemiah (Neh. 10:2), and assisted at the dedication of the city wall (Neh. 12:33).

21. One of the nobles who returned from Babylon with Zerubbabel (Neh. 7:7). Called Seraiah in Ezra 2:2.

22. One of the "proud men" who rebuked Jeremiah for advising the people that remained in Palestine, after their brethren had been taken to Babylon, not to go down into Egypt; and who took the prophet himself and Baruch with them to that country (Jer. 43: 2-7).

23. The Hebrew name of *Abed-nego* (*q. v.*), one of Daniel's three friends who were cast into the fiery furnace (Dan. 1:7).

A′zaz (ā′zăz; *strong*), a Reubenite, the son of Shema and father of Bela (I Chron. v. 8).

Aza′zel (à-zā′zĕl; Heb. *'ăz'ăzĕl* likely for *'ăzălzĕl*, i. e., *an entire removal;* (Arab. *'azala, remove*), the Hebrew term translated in the A. V. (Lev. 16:8, 10, 26) "scapegoat." It is a word of doubtful interpretation, and has been variously understood.

1. By some it is thought to be the name of the *goat sent* into the desert. The objection to this is that in vers. 10, 26 the *Azazel* clearly seems to be that *for* or *to* which the goat is let loose.

2. Others have taken Azazel for the name of the place to which the goat was sent. Some of the Jewish writers consider that it denotes the height from which the goat was thrown; while others regard the word as meaning "desert places."

3. Many believe Azazel to be a personal being, either a spirit, a demon, or Satan himself. The cabalists teach that in order to satisfy this evil being and to save Israel from his snares, God sends him the goat burdened with all the "iniquities and transgressions" of his people once a year. But we think it entirely improbable that Moses under divine guidance would cause Israel to recognize a demon whose claims on the people were to be met by the bribe of a sin-laden goat.

4. The most probable rendering of Azazel is "complete sending away," i. e., solitude. The rendering then of the passage would be "the one for Jehovah, and the other for an utter removal." *See* Atonement, Day of; Scapegoat.

Azazi′ah (ā-zà-zī′ä; *strengthened by Jehovah*).

1. One of the Levites who were appointed to play the harp in the service of the tabernacle at the time when the ark was brought up from Obededom (I Chron. 15:21), B. C. about 991.

2. The father of Hoshea, who was prince of the tribe of Ephraim when David numbered the people (I Chron. 27:20), after 1000 B. C.

3. One of those who had charge of the temple offerings in the time of Hezekiah (II Chron. 31:13), B. C. 726.

Az′buk (ăz′bŭk), the father of Nehemiah, who was the ruler of the half of Beth-zur, and who repaired part of the wall after the return from Babylon (Neh. 3:16), B. C. before 445.

Aze′kah (à-zē′kä; *tilled*), a town in the plain of Judah (Josh. 15:35; I Sam. 17:1), with suburban villages (Neh. 11:30), and a place of considerable strength (Jer. 34:7). The confederated Amorite kings were defeated here by Joshua, and their army destroyed by an extraordinary shower of hailstones (Josh. 10: 10, 11). Joshua's pursuit of the Canaanites after the battle of Beth-horon extended to Azekah; and between it and Shochoh the Philistines encamped before the battle between David and Goliath (I Sam. 17:1). It was fortified by Rehoboam (II Chron. 11:9), was still standing at the time of the invasion of the kings of Babylon (Jer. 34:7), and was one of the places reoccupied by the Jews on their return from captivity (Neh. 11:30).

A′zel (ā′zĕl), the son of Eleasah, of the descendants of King Saul (I Chron. 8:37, 38; 9:43).

A′zem (ā′zĕm; a *bone*), a city in the tribe of Simeon, originally included within the southern territory of Judah, near Balah (or Bilhah) and Eltolad (Josh. 15:29; 19-3, I Chron. 4:29, A. V. "Eezem"). Probably Ummel 'Azam, 11 miles S. E. of Beer-sheba.

Az′gad (ăz′găd; *strong* in *fortune*), an Israelite whose descendants, to the number of 1,222 (2,322 according to Neh. 7:17), returned from Babylon with Zerubbabel (Ezra 2:12). A second detachment of one hundred and ten, with Johanan at their head, accompanied Ezra (Ezra 8:12). Probably the Azgad of Neh.

10:15 is the same person, some of whose descendants joined in the covenant with Nehemiah.

A'ziel (ā'zĭ-ĕl), a shortened form (I Chron. 35:20) for *Jaaziel* (*q. v.*), in v. 18.

Azi'za (à-zī'zà; *strong*), an Israelite, descendant of Zattu, who divorced the Gentile wife he had married after his return from Babylon (Ezra 10:27), B. C. 456.

Azma'veth (ăz-mā'vĕth; *strong as death*).

1. A Barhumite (or Baharumite), one of David's thirty warriors (II Sam. 23:31; I Chron. 11:33), and father of two of his famous slingers (I Chron. 12:3), B. C. about 1000.

2. The second of the three sons of Jehoadah (I Chron. 8:36), or Jarah (9:42), a descendant of Jonathan, B. C. after 1030.

3. Son of Adiel, and keeper of the royal treasury of David (I Chron. 27:25), B. C. about 1000.

4. A village of Judah or Benjamin (Neh. 12:29), called (7:28) Beth-azmaveth. It was occupied by Jews who returned with Ezra from Babylon. The notices of it seem to point to some locality in the northern environs of Jerusalem.

Az'mon (ăz'mŏn; *bonelike*), a place on the southern border of Palestine, between Hazaradar and "the river of Egypt)" (Num. 34:4, 5; Josh. 15:4).

Az'noth-Tabor (ăz'nŏth-tā'bŏr; *tops of Tabor*), a town in the W. of Naphtali, between the Jordan and Hukkok (Josh. 19:34). Perhaps Amm Jebeil near Mt. Tabor.

A'zor (ā'zōr), the son of Eliakim and father of Sadoc, in the paternal ancestry of Christ (Matt. 1:13).

Azo'tus (à-zō'tŭs), the Grecized form (Acts 8:40) of *Ashdod* (*q. v.*).

Az'riel ((ăz'rĭ-ĕl; *help of God*).

1. A mighty man of valor, and one of the heads of the half tribe of Manasseh beyond Jordan, who were taken into captivity by the king of Assyria as a punishment for their national idolatry (I Chron. 5:24), B. C. about 740.

2. The father of Jerimoth, which latter was

ruler of the tribe of Naphtali under David (I Chron. 27:19), B. C. about 1000.

3. The father of Seraiah, who with others was appointed by King Jehoiakim to apprehend Baruch, the scribe, and Jeremiah for sending him a threatening prophecy (Jer. 36:26), B. C. 606.

Az'rikam (ăz'rĭ-kăm; *help* against *the enemy*, or *my help arises*).

1. The last named of the three sons of Neariah, a descendant of Zerubbabel (I Chron. 3:23), B. C. about 404. He is perhaps the same as *Azor* (*q. v.*).

2. The first of the six sons of Azel, of the tribe of Benjamin (I Chron. 8:38; 9:44).

3. A Levite, son of Hashabiah and father of Hasshub (I Chron. 9:14; Neh. 11:15), B. C. before 536.

4. The governor of the king's house in the time of Ahaz, slain by Zichri, a mighty man of Ephraim (II Chron. 28:7), B. C. 741.

Azu'bah (à-zū'bàh; *forsaken*).

1. The daughter of Shilhi and mother of King Jehoshaphat (I Kings 22:42; II Chron. 20:31), B. C. before 875.

2. The wife of Caleb, the son of Hezron (I Chron. 2:18, 19), B. C. about 1471. *See* Jerioth.

A'zur (ā'zŭr; a less correct form of *Azzur*, *helper*).

1. The father of Hananiah of Gibeon, which latter was the prophet who falsely encouraged King Zedekiah against the Babylonians (Jer. 28:1), B. C. about 596.

2. The father of Jaazaniah, who was one of the men whom the prophet in vision saw devising false schemes of safety for Jerusalem (Ezek. 11:1), B. C. 594.

Az'zah (ăz'zàh; the *strong*), the more correct English form (Deut. 2:23; I Kings 4:24; Jer. 25:20) of *Gaza* (*q. v.*). The latter is the form given in the R. V.

Az'zan (ăz'zăn), the father of Paltiel, the prince of the tribe of Issachar, and commissioner from that tribe in the dividing of Canaan (Num. 34:26), B. C. c. 1370.

Az'zur (ăz'zŭr; *helper*), one of the chief Israelites who signed the covenant with Nehemiah on the return from Babylon (Neh. 10: 17), B. C. 445.

B

Ba'al (bā'àl; Heb. *bă'ăl, lord, possessor*).

1. A very common name for god among the Phoenicians. The word is also used of the master and owner of a house (Exod. 22:7; Judg. 19:22); of a landowner (Job. 31:39); of an owner of cattle (Exod. 21:28; Isa. 1:3), etc. The word is often used as a prefix to names of towns and men, e. g., Baal-gad, Baal-hanan, etc.

2. The name of the chief male god of the Phoenicians. *See* Gods, False.

3. A Reubenite, son of Reaia. His son Beerah was among the captives carried away by Tiglathpileser (I Chron. 5:5), B. C. before 740.

4. The fourth named of the sons of Jehiel, the founder of Gibeon, by his wife Maachah (I Chron. 8:30; 9:36).

5. The name of a place (I Chron. 4:33), elsewhere *Baalath-beer* (*q. v.*).

Ba'alah (bā'à-là; *mistress*).

1. A city on the northern border of the tribe of Judah (Josh. 15:10), one of the religious sanctuaries of the ancient Gibeonites, as it appears (Josh. 15:9) that Baalah and Kirjath-jearim were applicable to the same place. See I Chron. 13:6.

2. A city on the S. of Judah (Josh. 15:29). Called Balah (Josh. 19:3); also Bilhah (I Chron. 4:29).

57. Stele of the Canaanite Storm-God Baal Brandishing a Club and Wielding a Stylized Thunderbolt

3. A mountain on the N. W. boundary of Judah, between Shicron and Jabneel (Josh. 15:11), usually regarded as the same as Mount Jearim.

Ba'alath (bā'á-lăth; *mistress*), a town of the tribe of Dan (Josh. 19:44); supposed to be the place fortified by Solomon (I Kings 9:18; II Chron. 8:6).

Ba'alath-be'er (bā'á-lăth bē'ĕr; *mistress of the well*), a city of Simeon (Josh. 19:8), and probably the same as Baal (I Chron. 4:33). Doubtless identical with Ramoth-Negeb (Josh. 19:8). It is also the same as the *Bealoth* (*q. v.*) of Judah (Josh. 15:24).

Ba'albek (bā'ăl-bĕk), Gr. Heliopolis, "city of the sun," a popular ancient center of the worship of Baal in the region between Lebanon and Anti-Lebanon or "Hollow-Syria," later called Heliopolis when the Greeks associated Helios with Baal. The site may be identical with Baal-gad "in the valley of Lebanon under Mt. Hermon" (Josh. 11:17). Greek architectural skill and Rome's resources were lavished on Baalbek and its immense and beautiful temples. Although laid low by earthquakes and the ravishes of time, these imposing ruins including the Acropolis, Propylaea and the great court are still a magnificent mass of beauty. The Temple of Bacchus contains huge Corinthian columns 52 ft. high. The Temple of Jupiter-Hadad with its still-standing half-dozen Corinthian columns 60 ft. high are mute mementoes of the splendor of the place in Roman times. *M. F. U.*

Ba'al-Be'rith (bā'ăl-bĕ-rîth'), a god worshipped in Shechem. *See* Gods, False.

Ba'ale of Ju'dah (bā'á-lē of Jū'dá; *lords of Judah*), a city of Judah, from which David brought the ark into Jerusalem (II Sam. 6:2). Probably the same as *Baalah*, 1 (*q. v.*).

Ba'al-gad (bā'ăl găd; *lord of fortune*), a Canaanite city (Josh. 11:17; 12:7), at the foot of Hermon, hence called Baal-hermon (Judg. 3:3; I Chron. 5:23). Location uncertain.

Ba'al-ha'mon (bā'ăl hā'mŏn; *lord of the multitude*), the place where Solomon had a vineyard (Cant. 8:11) which he let out to "keepers." Location is unknown.

Ba'al-ha'nan (bā'ăl hā'nán; *lord of grace*).

1. An early king of Edom, son of Achbor, successor of Saul, and succeeded by Hadar (Gen. 36:38, 39; I Chron. 1:49, 50).

2. A Gederite, David's overseer of "the olive trees and sycamore trees in the low plains" (I Chron. 27:28), B. C. after 1000.

Ba'al-ha'zor (bā'ăl-hā'zōr; *having a village*), a place near Ephraim where Absalom had a sheep farm, and where he murdered Amnon (II Sam. 13:23). Probably the same as Hazor (Neh. 11:33), Now Tell'Asar.

Ba'al-her'mon (bā'ăl hĕr'mŏn; *lord of Hermon*).

1. A city of Ephraim near Mount Hermon (I Chron. 5:23). Probably identical with Baal-gad (Josh. 11:17).

2. A mountain E. of Lebanon (Judg. 3:3), from which the Israelites were unable to expel the Hivites. "*Baal-hermon* is only another name for *Baal-gad*, the present *Banjas*, under the Hermon (see Josh. 13:5)" (K. and D., *Com.*).

Ba'ali (bā'á-lī; *my master*). "Thou shalt call me Ishi; and shalt call me no more Baali" (Hos. 2:16). The meaning is that the Israel will enter into right relation with God, in which she will look toward him as her husband (Ishi), and not merely as *owner*, *master*. Calling or naming is a designation of the nature or the

58. Temple of Jupiter, Baalbek

true relation of a person or thing. Israel calls God her husband when she stands in the right relation to him; when she acknowledges, reveres, and loves him, as he has revealed himself, i. e., as the only true God. On the other hand, she calls him Baal when she places the true God on the level of the Baals, either worshipping other gods along with Jehovah, or by obliterating the essential distinction between Jehovah and the Baals.

Ba'alim (bā'ăl-ĭm), the plural of Baal. *See* Gods, False.

Ba'alis (bā'á-lĭs; *in exultation*), king of the Ammonites about the time of the Babylonian captivity, whom Jonathan reported to Gedaliah, the viceroy, as having sent Ishmael to slay him (Jer. 40:13, 14), B. C. 588.

Ba′al-me′on (bā′ăl-mĕ-ōn′; *lord of the dwelling*), one of the towns rebuilt by the Reubenites, and their names changed (Num. 32:38). Baal-Meon (*Beon*, v. 3; *Beth-Meon*, Jer. 48:23; and *Beth-Baal-Meon*, Josh. 13:17) is to be located at Ma′in 9 miles E. of the Dead Sea.

Ba′al-pe′or (bā′ăl-pē′ōr), a god of the Moabites. *See* Gods, False.

Ba′al-pera′zim (bā′ăl-pê-rā′zĭm; *possessor of breaches*), called Mount Perazim (Isa. 28:21), in central Palestine. Location unknown. Here David fought the Philistines (II Sam. 5:20; I Chron. 14:11). The place and the circumstances appear to be again alluded to in Isa. 28:21, where it is called Mount Perazim.

Ba′al-shal′isha (bā′ăl-shăl′ĭ-shá; *lord of Shalisha*), a place of Ephraim, not far W. of Gilgal (II Kings 4:38, 42). From this place a man brought provisions for Elisha.

Ba′al-ta′mar (bā′ăl-tā′mȧr; *lord of the palm trees*), one of the groves of Baal. Probably the palm tree of Deborah (Judg. 4:5). In the tribe of Benjamin near Gibeah of Saul (Judg. 20:33). The notices seem to correspond to the present ruined site Erhah, about three miles N. E. of Jerusalem.

Ba′al-zebub′ (bā′ăl-sĕ-bŭb′), the god of the Philistines at Ekron. *See* Gods, False.

Ba′al-ze′phon (bā′ăl-sĕ′fôn; *Baal of winter*, or *north*), a place belonging to Egypt on the border of the Red Sea (Exod. 14:2; Num. 33:7), mentioned in connection with Pi-hahiroth, on the journey of the Israelites. It must have been a well-known place, inasmuch as it is always mentioned to indicate the location of Pi-hahiroth, but its present location is unknown.

Ba′ana (bā′ȧ-ná).
1. The son of Ahilud, one of Solomon's twelve purveyors, whose district comprised Taanach, Megiddo, and all Beth-shean, with the adjacent region (I Kings 4:12), B. C. 960.
2. The father of Zadok, which latter person assisted in rebuilding the walls of Jerusalem under Nehemiah (Neh. 3:4), B. C. 445.

Ba′anah (bā′ȧ-ná), another form of *Baana*.
1. A son of Rimmon, the Beerothite. He, with his brother Rechab, slew Ishbosheth while he lay in his bed, and took the head to David in Hebron. For this David caused them to be put to death, their hands and feet to be cut off, and their bodies, thus mutilated, hung up over the pool at Hebron (II Sam. 4:2-12), B. C. about 992.
2. A Netophathite, father of Heleb, or Heled, which latter person was one of David's mighty men (II Sam. 23:29; I Chron. 11:30), B. C. about 1000.
3. The son of Hushai, and purveyor of King Solomon. His district was in Asher and Aloth (I Kings 4:16), B. C. 960. The name should be translated Baana.

Ba′ara (bā′ȧ-rȧ), one of the wives of Shaharaim, of the tribe of Benjamin (I Chron. 8:8). In v. 9, she is called Hodesh.

Baase′iah (bā′ȧ-sē′yȧ), a Gershonite Levite, son of Malchiah and father of Michael, in the lineage of Asaph the singer (I Chron. 6:40), B. C. before 1000.

Ba′asha (bā′ȧ-shá), the third sovereign of the separate kingdom of Israel, and the founder of its second dynasty. He reigned B. C. c. 900-877. Baasha was the son of Ahijah, of the tribe of Issachar, and conspired against King Nadab, the son of Jeroboam (when he was besieging the Philistine town of Gibbethon), and killed him and his whole family (I Kings 15:27, sq.). He was probably of humble origin, as the prophet Jehu speaks of him as being "exalted out of the dust" (I Kings 16:2). In matters of religion his reign was no improvement on that of Jeroboam, and he was chiefly remarkable for his hostility to Judah. He built Ramah "that he might not suffer any to go out or come in to Asa king of Judah" (I Kings 15:17). He was compelled to desist by the unexpected alliance of Asa with Ben-hadad I of Damascus. Baasha died in the twenty-fourth year of his reign, and was honorably buried in Tirzah, which he had made his capital (I Kings 15:33; 16:6). For his idolatries the prophet Jehu declared to him the determination of God to exterminate his family, which was accomplished in the days of his son Elah, by Zimri (I Kings 16:10-13).

Babbler, the rendering (Eccles. 10:11) of the Heb. *bă′ăl läshōn*, *master of the tongue*. The word is understood by some as *charmer*, by others as *slanderer*. Paul was called a "babbler" (Acts 17:18, Gr. *spermologos*, *seed picker*, as the crow), probably with a twofold meaning: (1) from the manner in which that bird feeds, a *parasite;* and (2) from its chattering voice.

59. Ziggurat of Babylon, Cast in Oriental Institute Museum

Ba′bel, Tower of. The building which the babel builders intended to construct and which became the symbol of their God-defying disobedience and pride (Gen. 11:1-6). This structure is brightly illuminated by a characteristic Mesopotamian building called the ziggurat. The Assyro-Babylonian word *ziqquratu* denotes a sacred temple tower and means a "pinnacle" or "mountain top." The Babylonian ziggurat was a gigantic artificial mound of sun-dried bricks. The oldest extant ziggurat is that at ancient Uruk, Biblical Erech (Gen. 10:10), modern Warka. This ancient temple tower dates from the latter part of the fourth millennium B. C. Nothing in the Biblical narrative indicates that the so-called Tower of Babel was a temple tower or ziggurat. It is simply called a tower (*migdal*). It seems clear that the Tower of Babel was the first structure of this sort ever attempted. And despite the fact of divine judgment on the first, the more than two dozen such later ziggurats are an imitation of the first to an extent and appear to constitute an attempt to avert any possibility of divine punishment by consecrating them to the guardian deity of the city. At Ur, the birthplace of Abraham, the god was Nannar and his holy shrine was set on the topmost stage. At Borsippa (Birs-Nimrûd) some 10 miles S. W. of Babylon, Nebo, the god of knowledge and literature, was the divinity. These ancient ziggurats were built in step-like stages. The highest one was seven stories, although the common height was three stories. The ziggurat at Uruk was a vast mass of clay stamped down hard and buttressed on the outside with layers of brick and bitumen. Similar structures at Ur, Babylon and Borsippa and other Mesopotamian cities illustrate the words of Gen. 11:3, 4: "Come, let us make brick, and burn them thoroughly. And they had brick for stone, and slime (bitumen) had they for mortar. And they said, Come, let us build us a city, and a tower, whose top may reach unto heaven; and let us make us a name, lest we be scattered abroad upon the face of the whole earth." Also illustrated is a salient difference between the building materials of the stoneless, alluvial plain of Babylonia and those of Palestine and Egypt. Sun-dried bricks were used for stone and slime (bitumen), which was abundant in the general regions of Babylon, was used for mortar.

The original Tower of Babel was probably constructed prior to B. C. 4000, when the arts and sciences had developed to such a degree as to contemplate building a city, and especially a tower "whose top may reach unto heaven" (Gen. 11:4). This phrase is not mere hyperbole, but an expression of pride and rebellion manifest by the Babel builders. Both Assyrian and Babylonian kings greatly prided themselves upon the height of their temples and boasted of having their tops as high as heaven.

Bab'ylon (băb'ĭ-lŏn). An ancient city-state in the plain of Shinar, derived from Accadian *babilu* ("gate of god").

1. **Name.** The name is derived by the Hebrews from the root *bālăl* ("to confound"), and has reference to the confusion of tongues at the Tower (Gen. 11:9). Thus the Biblical writer refutes any God-honoring connotation of the name. The Biblical account ascribes the founding of the ancient prehistoric city of Babylon to the descendants of Cush and the followers of Nimrod (Gen. 10:8-10). This statement distinguishes the people who founded the city (evidently the Sumerians) from the Semitic-Babylonians who afterward possessed it.

2. **Beginnings.** The beginnings of the city of Babylon are unknown to us except for the Biblical passage earlier mentioned (Gen. 10: 10). About B. C. 1830 the city began its rise to prominence. In the ensuing struggle with surrounding city-states, Babylon conquered Larsa and the first dynasty of Babylon was established. Such kings as Sumu-abu, Sumla-el, Sabum, Apel-Sin and Sin-mu-ballit ruled. Then the great Hammurabi (*q. v.*),

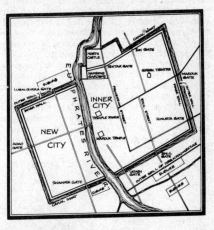

60. Babylon at the Time of Nebuchadnezzar as Reconstructed from Excavations and Clay-tablet Maps Recovered from the Ruins of the Great Metropolis. After E. Unger

about 1728-1686, ascended the throne and conquered not only all of S. Babylonia but extended his conquests as far north as Mari. At this famous city on the middle Euphrates, André Parrot, excavating for the Musée du Louvre (1933 ff.), unearthed thousands of cuneiform tablets, a vast royal palace, a Temple of Ishtar and a ziggurat. The city of Babylon did not reach the height of its glory, however, until the reign of Nebuchadnezzar II, (B. C. 605-562). Nebuchadnezzar made the city splendid and the king's own inscriptions are concerned largely with his vast building operations. Babylon was excavated thoroughly by the Deutsche Orientgesellschaft under the direction of Robert Koldewey, 1899 ff. (cf. *Das wieder erstehende Babylon*, 4th ed., 1925). Nebuchadnezzar's brilliant city included vast fortifications, famous streets like the Processional, canals, temples and palaces. The Ishtar Gate led through the double wall of fortifications and was adorned with rows of bulls and dragons in colored enameled brick. Nebuchadnezzar's throne room was likewise adorned with enameled bricks. The tall ziggurat was rebuilt. This Herodotus said rose to a height of eight stages. Near at hand was Esagila ("whose housetop is lofty"), the Temple of Marduk or Bel, which the king restored. Not far distant were the hanging gardens, which to the Greeks were one of the seven wonders of the world. How well the words of Dan. 4:30 fit this ambitions builder: "Is not this great Babylon, which I have built for the royal dwelling place by the might of my power and to the glory of my majesty?". The splendid Babylonian empire of Nebuchadnezzar was destined soon to fall. He was succeeded on the throne by Amel-Marduk (562-560), the Evil-Merodach of II Kings 25:27. This man was murdered by his brother-in-law, Nergal-shar-usur (560-556) whose son ruled only a few months and was succeeded by one of the conspirators, who made away with him. A noble named Nabunaid, or Nabonidus, then ruled, together with his son

Belshazzar (556-539; see Dan. 5); Nabonidus was the last king of the neo-Babylonian Empire. On October 13, 539 B. C., Babylon fell to Cyrus of Persia and from that time on the decay of the city began. Xerxes plundered it. Alexander the Great thought to restore its great temple, in ruins in his day, but was deterred by the prohibitive cost. During the period of Alexander's successors the area decayed rapidly and soon became a desert. From the days of Selucus Nicator (B. C. 312-280), who built the rival city of Seleucia on the Tigris, queenly Babylon never revived. The end of the greatest world city of antiquity had come.

61. Photo of Painting by Maurice Bardin of the Reconstruction according to Unger, Showing Procession Street Leading Through Famous Ishtar Gate; Hanging Gardens and Ziggurat, upper right

3. **Size and Appearance.** Herodotus says the city was in the form of a square, 120 stades (13 miles, 1,385 yards) on each side. It had two walls, inner and outer. The vast space within the walls was laid out in streets at right angles to each other, lined with houses three to four stories in height. He lists the following chief public buildings: (1) The Temple of Bel, consisting of a tower pyramidal in form, over eight stories, topped with a sanctuary. (2) The palace of the king. (3) The bridge across the Euphrates connecting the eastern and western sections of the city. Herodotus described the city as overwhelming in its size and magnitude. (Bk. I, 178-186). The next Greek writers whose records are important are Ctesias and Diodorus Siculus (II, 7f.). According to them the city was much smaller than Herodotus has represented, its circuit being 360 stades (41 miles, 6 yards). To the bridge of Herodotus, Diodorus has added a tunnel under the river and describes the hanging gardens of Nebuchadnezzar as rising in terraces, which supported full grown

trees. Hebrew accounts represent the city as great in size, beauty and strength; and in this they were amply sustained by the inscriptions and excavations.

4. **The Figurative Meaning.** In the prophetical writings, when the actual city is not meant, the illustration is to the "confusion" into which the whole social order of the world has fallen under Gentile world domination (Luke 21:24; Rev. 6:14). The divine order is given in Isaiah 11, that is, Israel in her own land the center of divine government of the world and the medium of the divine blessing, with Gentile nations blessed when associated with Israel. Anything else is politically mere "Babel." In the N. T. Babylon prefigures apostate Christendom, that is ecclesiastical Babylon, the great harlot (Rev. 17:15-18). It also prefigures political Babylon (Rev. 17:15-18), which destroys ecclesiastical Babylon. The power of political Babylon is destroyed by the glorious Second Advent of Christ (Rev. 16:14; 19:17). M. F. U.

Babylo'nia (Băb-ĭ-lō'nĭ-á), the eastern end of the so-called Fertile Crescent which had Babylon for its capital, called Shinar (Gen. 10:10; 11:2; Isa. 11:11), also land of the Chaldeans (Jer. 24:5; Ezek. 12:13).

1. **Principal Cities.** The region anciently comprised Sumer and Akkad. Akkad was the northern region of the lower alluvial plain of the Tigris-Euphrates, in which were Babylon, Borsippa, Kish, Kuthah, Sippar and Agade (Accad). Principal towns of Sumer were Nippur, Lagash, Umma, Larsa, Erech, (Uruk, Gen. 10:11), Ur, Abraham's city, and Eridu.

2. **Geography.** The two great rivers, Tigris and Euphrates, which have their source in the mountains of Armenia, have built up the alluvial plain of lower Babylonia. Heavily laden with silt, these mighty torrents gradually turned the upper reaches of the Persian Gulf into a marsh and finally into an absolutely flat and stoneless alluvial plain. The slow building of this plain has continued at the rate of 72 feet a year or a mile and one-half a century until today it stretches more than 300 miles southwestward to the present head of the Gulf. The present sites of Eridu, Ur and Lagash were probably on or very near the Persian Gulf about B. C. 3000. This fertile alluvial plain, irrigated by the Tigris and Euphrates Rivers, became the cradle of civilization. In this lower part of Mesopotamia, some 55 miles south of present Baghdad, there once stood on the shore of the Euphrates a city which bore the proud name of Bab-ilu, "gate of god," or Babylon. Although the history of the lower valley does not begin with this city, Babylon early became prominent and its name is attached primarily to this region which is now known familiarly as Babylonia.

3. **Early Inhabitants.** People called Sumerians preceded the Semites in lower Babylonia as far as the Biblical reports are concerned. They seem to have been "Hamitic" (Gen. 10:8-10) but scholars profess ignorance of their race and origin. They probably entered the plain of Shinar around B. C. 4500 and developed a high civilization. Their accomplishments included development of the

wedge-shaped cuneiform script. They were polytheistic. Originally each city-state had its own gods or goddesses, but eventually a triad pantheon developed: Anu (sky), Enlil (atmosphere and earth) and Ea (waters).

4. **Earliest History.** As the marshes dried up and areas of solid land appeared in lower Babylonia, civilization began. The earliest-known culture is dubbed Obeid, the name being derived from Tell el-Obeid, a small mound 4½ miles N. W. of the more famous site of Ur. The culture, characterized by a very definite style of pottery, is also known from the remains of other sites, including Ur. At Warka, the site of ancient Erech or Uruk, Some 35 miles up the Euphrates valley from Tell el-Obeid, appears the second culture of ancient Babylonia. It probably dates from the latter part of the 4th millennium B. C. At Warka was found another distinctive form of pottery, the oldest ziggurat (*see* Babel, Tower of), the first cylinder seals and the beginnings of writing. A further period in the early history of Mesopotamia is known from the findings at Jemdet Nasr, a site in the Mesopotamian Valley near Babylon. This culture with its characteristic pottery dates around B. C. 3200-3000. Its bronze tools indicate the beginning of the Bronze Age in Mesopotamia. During this period the important cities of Shuruppak (Fara), Eshnunna (Tell Asmar) and Kish were founded.

5. **Early Dynastic Period,** about B. C. 2800-2360. During this period dynasties of kings appear at Kish, Uruk, Ur, Awan, Hamazi, Adab and Mari. Among the rulers

in the First Dynasty of Kish was Etana "a shepherd, the one who to heaven ascended." The next dynasty is described as centering at the temple precinct of E-Anna, where the city of Uruk was subsequently built. Twelve kings were said to have reigned here for 2310 years including Gilgamesh, the epic hero. Excavations at Tell Asmar (ancient Eshnunna) reveal the art and religion of the middle phase of this early dynastic period. The First Dynasty of Ur indicates the last and culminating phase of the Dynastic Period. The Sumerian King List (Thorkild Jacobsen, *The Sumerian King List, Assyriological Studies,* Chicago 1939) states "Uruk was smitten with weapons; its kingship to Ur was carried. In Ur Mes-Anne-Pada became king and reigned 80 years." Four kings are mentioned as reigning 177 years. Then "Ur was smitten with weapons." The high degree of culture obtained under the First Dynasty of Ur is revealed in the famous royal cemetery uncovered there by C. Leonard Woolley. These tombs, dating around B. C. 2600, revealed a highly-developed culture. Another dynasty which flourished during the last phase of the Early Dynastic Period was that established by Ur-Nanshe at Lagash (Telloh) about 50 miles north of Ur. Reference is made in the inscriptions of Ur Nanshe to extensive building operations including construction of temples and digging canals. A later ruler named Eannatum claimed victories over Umma, Uruk, Ur, Kish and Mari. His battle against Umma is portrayed on the Stele of the Vultures. Subsequently Lagash fell again to Umma. The new conqueror was

62. Babylonian Empire.

Lugalzagesi, who was governor of Umma. This conqueror ultimately became king of Uruk and Ur and was one of the most powerful figures in Sumerian history. His quarter-century reign constituted the Third Dynasty of Uruk. His armies marched to the Mediterranean Sea.

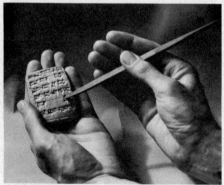

63. Babylonian Clay Tablet with Stylus in Correct Position for Writing Cuneiform

6. **The Old Akkadian Period**, about B. C. 2360-2180. Meanwhile the Semites were increasing in power in Babylonia under the leadership of the mighty Sargon, who had a humble origin and was placed in an ark of bullrushes like Moses. He built up a farflung empire and was succeeded by Rimush-manishtusu and Naram-Sin, Sargon's grandson, whose victory stele was discovered at Susa. But Naram-Sin's sprawling empire, extending from central Persia to the Mediterranean and N. E. Arabia to the Taurus Mountains, lasted only through the reign of his son Shargalisharri. Then Caucasian people, the Gutians, overran Babylonia.

7. **The Neo-Sumerian Period**, about B. C. 2070-1960. When Gutian power declined a Sumerian governor of Lagash, named Gudea, came into power. He is represented by numerous statues. Gudea built a famous temple, bringing cedar wood for it all the way from the Amanus Mountains of Northern Syria, part of the same general range as the Lebanon, from which Solomon over a millennium later was to cut cedar trees for the temple at Jerusalem (I Kings 5:6). With the downfall of the Gutians the powerful Third Dynasty of Ur arose in splendor under the leadership of Ur-Nammu, who took the new title of "king of Sumer at Akkad" and who erected a mighty ziggurat at Ur. He was succeeded by Dungi, Bur-Sin, Gimil-Sin and Ibi-Sin. It was apparently under this brilliant dynasty that Abraham was born and quitted the city.

8. **Elamite and Amorite Invasions**, about B. C. 1960-1830. Under Ibi-Sin Ur was sacked by the Elamites. Invading Amorites from Mari and elsewhere settled at Isin and Larsa. An Elamite ruler, Kirikiri, came into power at Eshnunna.

9. **Old Babylonia Period**, about B. C. 1830-1550. This was the period of the ascendancy of Babylon (q. v.), particularly under the great Hammurabi (q. v.). Excavations at the brilliant city of Mari on the middle Euphrates

have shed great light on this era. The Code of Hammurabi, discovered at Susa in 1901, was subsequently carried from Babylon and belongs to the period around B. C. 1700. It was during this time also that the famous epic of creation called *Enuma elish* assumed the form in which it was current for the next millennium. The discoveries at Nuzu, an ancient Hurrian center about 12 miles N. W. of modern Kirkuk, have shed a great deal of light on this period and especially the earlier patriarchal period.

10. **Kassite Invasion**, about B. C. 1550-1169. The Kassites who had been invading the land from the highlands to the east and N. E. for a number of centuries made themselves masters of the country. Finally Tukulti-Ninurta, king of Assyria (B. C. 1260-1232) invaded Babylonia and ruled for seven years, but was expelled.

11. **Dynasty II of Isin.** With the fall of the Kassites a new dynasty arose in Babylonia, Dynasty II of Isin. The kings were all native Babylonians, among them Nebuchadnezzar I (1146-23). He defeated the Elamites and the Hittites but was routed by the Assyrians. This dynasty came to an end in B. C. 1039.

12. **Later History.** About B. C. 1100-900 Aramaic tribes began invading Babylonia, and Assyria began to interfere in Babylonian affairs. Tiglath-pileser III (729 B. C.) (Pul; II Kings, 15:19) became king of Babylon. In 689 the city revolted against Sennacherib, who sacked and burned it to the ground. It was rebuilt by Esarhaddon and remained a part of Assyria until B. C. 625.

13. **Neo-Chaldean Empire.** B. C. 605-539. The new nation, the Chaldeans, under Merodach-baladan, who proclaimed himself king of Babylon (721), sent an embassy to Hezekiah, king of Judah, in 712, but was defeated by Sennacherib in 703. In B. C. 625 Nabopolassar became king of the Chaldeans and founded the Neo-Babylonian or Chaldean Empire. With Cyaxares, king of the Medes, he destroyed Nineveh in 612. His son Nebuchadnezzar defeated Necho of Egypt at Carcemish in 605. Now in control of all S. W. Asia, Nebuchadnezzar (605-562) entered his long and brilliant reign, destroying Jerusalem and making Babylon one of the most splendid of ancient cities. He was succeeded by his son Amel-Marduk (562-560). The latter was assassinated and Neriglissar (560-556) succeeded to the throne. Neriglissar's son reigned for nine months after Neriglissar's death and was also assassinated in 556. Then a Babylonian noble, Nabonidus, came to the throne; he appointed his son Belshazzar as co-regent (q. v.). In 539 B. C. Gobryas, one of Cyrus' generals, took Babylon, which remained under Persian rule B. C. 539-332. Alexander the Great controlled Babylon until 323. The Seleucidae ruled Babylon B. C. 312-171 and were succeeded by the Parthians who ruled from B. C. 171-A. D. 226. The Sassanian Dynasty ruled from A. D. 226-641 when Babylonia was conquered by the Moslem Arabs. After the fall of Jerusalem in A. D. 70 Babylonia became a seat of Jewish learning. M. F. U.

Babylo'nish Garment (Heb., *cloak of Shinar* or

Babylon), an ample robe with figures of men and animals either embroidered or interwoven in the fashion for which the Babylonians were noted. It came to mean a valuable piece of clothing in general (Josh. 7:21).

Ba'ca (bā'kȧ; "balsam tree" or "weeping"), an unidentified valley in Palestine (Psa. 84:6). It was possibly an imaginary poetical name, not intended to describe an actual location, but to stand for any experience of drought (cf. Arab. *baka'a,* "to be sparsely watered") in contrast to a well-watered experience ("who passing through the Valley of Baca, make it a *well*"); or it may be a reference to an experience of "weeping" with a play upon the Hebrew word *bäkäh* ("to weep"). If it actually refers to a place, it was likely so named from the balsam trees in it, which exude a tear-like gum (cf. the Valley of Rephaim, II Sam. 5:22, 23, R. V., where such trees were found). *M. F. U.*

Backbite, the rendering (Psa. 15:3) of Heb. *rägäl,* to *run about* tattling). In the New Testament the Gr. *katalaleō,* is to speak evil of, to traduce (Rom. 1:30; II Cor. 12:20). Everywhere this sin is warned against as being destructive and utterly unworthy of a believer.

Backsliding in the Heb. has the idea of "going back" (*sûg;* Prov. 14:14), "being stubborn or refractory like a heifer" (sōrēr; Hos. 4:16) and "turning back" (mĕshûbäh; Jer. 3:6 ff., 8:5; 31:22) to the old life of sin and idolatry. In the N. T. backsliding is set forth as involving a change of the believer's *standing* before God, but not of his *state.* The former is variable and depends upon daily contact with Christ, "walking in the light" (I John 1:7) and many other factors of the spiritual life. *Standing,* by contrast, refers to the believer's position "in Christ," which is grounded in the unchangeable and perfect work of Christ for the believer, while *state* describes the changing and imperfect condition of his soul from moment to moment and as affected by backsliding on the one hand, or spiritual progress on the other. Faith in Christ secures standing (John 1:12; Rom. 5:1, 2; 8:17; Eph. 1:3, 6; Col. 2:10; Heb. 10:19 etc.) but observance of all the laws of the spiritual life alone assures protection against backsliding. Compare I Cor. 1:2-9 (standing) with I Cor. 1:11; 3:1-4; 4:18; 5:2 (state). Backsliding not only results in a changed state or experience, but involves corrective chastening (Heb. 12:6; I Cor. 11:31), loss of rewards and fellowship (II Cor. 5:10, I John 1:7), curtailment of usefulness and in extreme cases physical death (I Cor. 5:5; I John 5:16) that the "spirit may be saved in the day of the Lord Jesus." Those who hold that one may fall from grace teach that backsliding may become complete, rather than partial, and that the individual must then be converted a second time. *M. F. U.*

Badger. *See* Animal Kingdom.

Bags made of leather or woven materials were in common use in Bible lands to hold money—lumps of gold or silver in most ancient times, (Isa. 42:6) and after the Persian period, minted coins. Water or wine bags were manufactured from skins of animals (Prov. 7:20). The shepherd's bag contained a heterogeneous assortment ranging from sling stones to food. Jesus referred to the common wallet for travelling in the scrip of Luke 12:33 (cf. Luke 10:4; 22:35, 36). Judas' bag was probably a small box or chest (John 12:6; 13:29). *M. F. U.*

Baha'rumite (bȧ-hä'rū-mīt), a native of *Bahurim* (*q. v.*); an epithet applied to Azmaveth, one of David's warriors (I Chron. 11:33). Called Barhumite in II Sam. 23:31.

Bahu'rim (bȧ-hū'rĭm; *young men*), a town of Judah on the road from Jerusalem to the Jordan, E. of Olivet (II Sam. 3:16). David had trouble here with Shimei, and was hidden by the spies (II Sam. 16:5; 17:18). Azmaveth is the only other native of this place except Shimei mentioned in Scripture (II Sam. 23: 31; I Chron. 11:33). It is identified with Râs et-Tmîm, just E. of Mt. Scopus, near Jerusalem.

Bail. *See* Surety.

Ba'jith (bā'jĭth; *house*), supposed to be a city in Moab, where there may have been a celebrated idol temple; by others it is rendered *temple house* (Isa. 15:2).

bakbak'kar (băk-băk'ẽr; *searcher*), one of the Levites inhabiting the villages of the Netophathites, after the return from Babylon (I Chron. 9:15), B. C. about 536.

Bak'buk (băk'bŭk; a *bottle*), the head of one of the families of the Nethinim that returned 'from Babylon with Zerubbabel (Ezra 2:51; Neh. 7:53), B. C. about 536.

Bakbuki'ah (băk-bū-kī'ȧ), a Levite, "second among his brethren," who dwelt at Jerusalem on the return from Babylon (Neh. 11:17). He was also employed on the watches, and was a porter of the gates (Neh. 12:9, 25), B. C. about 536.

Bake. *See* Bread.

Bakemeats (*food,* the *work of* the *baker*), baked provisions (Gen. 40:17).

Baking. *See* Bread.

Ba'laam (Bā-lȧm), a heathen diviner who lived at Pethor, which is said, in Deut. 23:4, to have been a city of Mesopotamia. Although doubtless belonging to the Midianites (Num. 31:8), he possessed some knowledge of the true God, and acknowledged that his superior powers as poet and prophet were derived from God, and were his gift. His fame was very great, and he became self-conceited and covetous. The Israelites having encamped in the plain of Moab (B. C. 1401), Balak, the king of Moab, entered into a league with the Midianites against them, and sent messengers to Balaam with "the rewards of divination in their hands" (Num. 22:5, sq.). Balaam seems to have had some misgivings as to the lawfulness of their request, for he invited them to remain over night, that he might know how God would regard it. These misgivings were confirmed by the express prohibition of God upon his journey. Balaam informed the messengers of God's answer, and they returned to Balak. A still more honorable embassy was sent to Balaam, with promises of reward and great honor. He replied that he could not be tempted by reward, but would speak what God should reveal. He requested them to tarry for the night, that he might know what the Lord would say unto him more. His importunity secured to him permission to accompany Balak's messengers with the divine injunction to speak as God should dictate. Balaam in the morning proceeded with the princes of Moab. But "God's anger was kindled against him, and the angel of the Lord stood in the way for an adversary against him." Though Balaam saw not the angel, the ass which he rode was aware of his presence. At first it turned into the field; again, in its terror, it pressed against the wall, squeezing Balaam's foot; upon the third appearance of the angel, there being no way of escape, it fell down. This greatly enraged Balaam, who smote her with a stick, whereupon the ass questioned Balaam as to the cause of the beating. He soon became aware of the presence of the angel, who accused him of perverseness. Balaam offered to return; the angel, however, told him to go on, but to speak only as God should tell him. Meeting Balak, he announced to him his purpose of saying only what the Lord should reveal. According to his direction seven altars were prepared, upon each of which Balak and Balaam offered a bullock and a ram. Thrice Balaam essayed to speak against Israel, but his utterances were overruled by God, so that, instead of cursings, there were blessings and magnificent prophecies, reaching forward until they told of "a star" rising "out of Jacob" (Num. 24:17). Balaam advised the expedient of seducing the Israelites to commit fornication (Num. 31:16). The effect of this is recorded in ch. 25. A battle was afterward fought with the Midianites, in which Balaam sided with them, and was slain (Num. 31:8).

Typical. The "error of Balaam" (Jude 1:11) was the diviner-prophet's mistake in concluding on the basis of natural morality, that God *must* righteously curse the nation Israel, seeing the evil in it. He was ignorant of the higher morality of the Cross, through which God enforces the awful sanctions of His law, at the same time manifesting His grace, so that He can be just and the justifier of a believing sinner. The "way of Balaam" (II Pet. 2:15) is the covetous conduct of the typical hireling prophet, solicitous only to commercialize His gift. The "doctrine of Balaam" (Rev. 2:14) was the teaching of the mercenary seer to abandon godly separation and a pilgrim character in favor of wordly conformity. Balaam taught Balak to corrupt the people who could not be cursed (Num. 31:15, 16; 22:5; 23:8) by seducing them to marry Moabite women and commit spiritual unchastity (James 4:4). Balaam as a prophet offers the strange spectacle of a prophet-diviner—a mixture of paganistic ritual with a true, though blurred knowledge of the true God. *M. F. U.*

Ba′lac, another form of *Balak* (Rev. 2:14).

Bal′adan (băl′à-dăn; Akkad. (He) *Marduk has given a son*).

1. The father of Merodach-baladan, king of Babylon in the time of Hezekiah, king of Judah (II Kings 20:12; Isa. 39:1), B. C. before 713.

2. A shortened form of Merodach-baladan (Isa. 39:1), or Berodach-baladan (II Kings 20:12).

Ba′lah (bā′là; to *decay*), a city in Simeon (Josh. 19:3), or Baalah (Josh. 15:29).

Ba′lak (bā′lăk; *destroyer, emptier*), the son of Zippor, and king of the Moabites (Num. 22:2, 4). He was so terrified at the approach of the victorious army of the Israelites, who, in their passage through the desert, had encamped near the confines of his territory, that he applied to Balaam to curse them, B. C. about 1400. His designs being frustrated in this direction, he acted upon Balaam's suggestion, and seduced the Israelites to commit fornication (Num. 25:1; Rev. 2:14).

Balances (Heb. *mō′znăyĭm*, i. e., *two scales*). That these were known to the early Hebrews and in common use is evident from the frequent reference to them in the Old Testament (Lev. 19:36; Job. 6:2; 31:6; Hos. 12:7, etc.). The probability is that the Hebrews used the common balances of Egypt. They were not essentially different from the balances now in use. Sometimes they were suspended by a ring, and in other cases the cross beams turned upon a pin at the summit of an upright pole, each end of the arm terminating in a hook, to which the precious metal to be weighed was attached in small bags.

Figurative. In a figurative sense the balance is employed in Scripture as an emblem of justice and fair dealing (Job 31:6; Psa. 62:9; Prov. 11:1). *Balances* used in connection with the sale of bread or fruit by weight is the symbol of scarcity (Rev. 6:5; see also Lev. 26:26; Ezek. 4:16, 17).

Bald Locust. See Animal Kingdom.

Baldness is mentioned in Scripture as a defect, interfering with personal beauty; and the more naturally so, as the hair was frequently allowed to grow with peculiar luxuriance as an ornament. Natural baldness appears to have been uncommon, and is alluded to as a mark of squalor and misery (Isa. 3:24; 15:2; Jer. 47:5). The address to Elisha, "Go up, thou baldhead" (II Kings 2:23), may mean that his scoffers referred to his age only. Baldness was expressly distinguished from leprosy, but had certain points of contact with it (Lev. 13:40-44). Artificial baldness was a mark of mourning (Jer. 16:6; Ezek. 7:18; Amos 8:10), and was forbidden to the Israelites on the ground of their being a holy people (Deut. 14:1, 2); it was a punishment inflicted upon captives (Deut. 21:12). The priests were forbidden to make baldness on their heads, as well as to shave off the corners of their beards (Lev. 21:5; Ezek. 44:20). The Jewish interpretation of this injunction excluded a bald priest from ministering at the altar, although baldness is not mentioned as a disqualification (Lev. 21:17-20). Baldness, by shaving, marked the conclusion of a Nazarite's vow (Num. 6:9, 18).

Balm. See Vegetable Kingdom.

Ba′mah (bā′mà; *height*), a high place where idols were worshiped. The word appears in its Hebrew form only in Ezek. 20:29, while in the first part of the verse it is translated "high place." By some the name is supposed to refer to some particular spot. Keil (*Com.*, in loc.) says that the word "is to be taken collectively, and that the use of the singular is to be explained from the antithesis to the one divinely appointed Holy Place in the temple, and not from any allusion to one particular *bamah* of peculiar distinction."

Ba'moth (bā'mŏth; *heights*), the forty-seventh station of the Israelites (Num. 21:19, 20) in the country of the Moabites, and probably the same as *Bamoth-baal* (q. v.).

Ba'moth-ba'al (bā'mŏth-bā'ăl; *heights of Baal*), a place E. of Jordan, and lying upon the river Arnon (Josh. 13:17). In the R. V. at Num. 21:28, called "the high places of Arnon." Bamoth-baal is called Beth-bamoth on the Moabite Stone (line 27, q. v.), and is located somewhere near Mt. Nebo.

Band, the representative of several Hebrew and Greek words, especially of *speira*, a cohort. *See* Army.

Ba'ni (bā'nī; *built*).

1. A Gadite, one of David's mighty men (II Sam. 23:36), B. C. about 1000.

2. A Levite, son of Shamer and father of Amzi, a descendant of Merari (I Chron. 6:46).

3. A descendant of Pharez and father of Imri, one of whose descendants returned from Babylon (I Chron. 9:4), B. C. long before 536.

4. One whose "children" (descendants or retainers), to the number of six hundred and forty-two, returned from Babylon with Zerubbabel (Ezra 2:10). He is elsewhere (Neh. 7:15) called Binnui. He is probably the one mentioned (Neh. 10:14) as having sealed the covenant.

5. The name of Bani is given (Ezra 10:29, 34, 38) three times as one who, either himself or his descendants, had taken strange wives after the captivity.

6. A Levite, whose son, Rehum, repaired a portion of the wall of Jerusalem (Neh. 3:17). Apparently the same Bani was among those who were conspicuous in all the reforms on the return from Babylon (Neh. 8:7; 9:4; 10:13). He had another son named Uzzi, who was appointed overseer of the Levites at Jerusalem; his own father's name was Hashabiah (Neh. 11:22).

Banish (Heb. *nādăḥ, to thrust out*, II Sam. 14:13, 14), **Banishment** (Heb. *mădŭăḥ, cause of banishment*, Lam. 2:14; Aram. *sharshah, rooting out*, Ezra 7:26). Banishment was not a punishment prescribed by the Mosaic law; but was adopted, together with the forfeiture of property, by the Jews after the captivity. It also existed among the Romans, together with another form of exile, called *disportatio*, which was a punishment of great severity. The person banished forfeited his estate, and was transported to some island named by the emperor, there to be kept in perpetual confinement (see Smith's *Dict. of Class. Antiq.*, s. v. "Banishment"). Thus the apostle John was banished to the island of Patmos (Rev. 1:9).

Bank in Scripture does not designate a financial institution for the custody of money but rather a *table* or *counter* (Gr. *trapeza*) at which a money-changer stood or sat, exchanging coins (Matt. 21:12; Mark 11:15; John 2:15). In Luke 19:23, however the word apparently approximates "bank" in the modern sense of the word. In the simple pastoral-agricultural economy of the Old Testament era loaning money among the Hebrews was not viewed favorably (Exod. 22:25; Lev. 25:37). In the New Testament period, however, not only was money lent between friends, but money-lending was a lucrative business. The banker presided at his table (Luke 19:23) and lent funds to others in pledge of mortgage (cf. Neh. 5:3, 4). Money-exchanging from one denomination to another, as shekels for the half-shekel for the Temple tax, or current coins for foreign money, such as the Hebrew shekel for the Roman denarius or Greek drachma, was a profitable branch of the ancient banking business. *M. F. U.*

Banner is the rendering of the Hebrew word *dĕgĕl*, denoting something "conspicuous," "easily seen" (cf. Akkad. *dagâlu. to see*, and *nēs*, cf. Heb. *nāsăs*, to be high, lofty?) Standards or symbols erected on poles, hilltops or other conspicuous places to rally tribes or armies, etc. are prominently referred to in Scripture (Num. 2:2; Num. 21:8f., Song 2:4; 6:4; Psa. 60:4; Isa. 11:10; 13:2; Jer. 4:21). The royal Sumerian tombs of Ur (c. 2900 B. C.) have yielded a famous standard inlaid with shell and lapis lazuli. The standards of the Twelve Tribes in the wilderness show the antiquity of such banners (Num. 2:2). *M.F.U.*

Banquet (generally Heb. *mĭshtĕh, drinking*).

Feasts are common in the Scripture narratives, and hospitality has always characterized life in Bible lands.

1. **Occasions.** Besides being a part of the religious observance of the great festivals, banquets or feasts were given on great family occasions, as a birthday (Gen. 40:20; Matt. 14:6), the weaning of a son and heir (Gen. 21:8), a marriage (Gen. 29:22; Judg. 14:10; Esth. 2:18; Matt. 22:2-4), the separation and reunion of friends (Gen. 31:27, 54), a burial (II Sam. 3:35; Jer. 16:7; Hos. 9:4), a sheep-shearing (I Sam. 25:2, 8, 36; II Sam. 13: 23-29).

2. **Time.** The usual time for holding the banquet was toward evening, corresponding to the dinners of modern times. To begin early was a mark of excess (Isa. 5:11; Eccles. 10:16). These festivals were often continued for seven days, especially wedding banquets (Judg. 14:12); but if the bride were a widow, three days formed the limit.

3. **Invitations, etc.** Invitations were sent out through servants (Prov. 9:3; Matt. 22:3, sq.) some time previous to the banquet; and a later announcement informed the expected guests that the arrangements were complete, and their presence was looked for (Matt. 22:8; Luke 14:7). This after-summons was sent only to those who had accepted the previous invitation, and to violate that acceptance for trivial reasons could only be viewed as a gross insult.

4. **Etiquette.** At a small entrance door a servant received the tablets or cards of the guests, who were then conducted into the receiving room. After the whole company had arrived the master of the house shut the door with his own hands, a signal that no others were to be admitted (Luke 13:25; Matt. 25:10). The guests were kissed upon their arrival (Tob. 7:6; Luke 7:45); their feet washed (Luke 7:44), a custom common in ancient Greece, and still found here and there in

Palestine; the hair and beard anointed (Psa. 23:5; Amos 6:6); and their places assigned them according to rank (I Sam. 9:22; Luke 14:8; Mark 12:39). In some cases each guest was furnished with a magnificent garment of a light and showy color, and richly embroidered, to be worn during the banquet (Eccles. 9:8; Rev. 3:4, 5). The refusal of such a mark of respect implied a contempt for the host and his entertainment that could not fail to provoke resentment (Matt. 22:11).

5. **Fare, etc.** In general the feasts of the Israelites were simple; but, no doubt, under the kings, with growing prosperity and luxury, riotous banquets were not unknown. Particularly choice dishes were set before the guest intended to be specially honored (I Sam. 9:24), sometimes double (I Sam. 1:5), and even fivefold portion (Gen. 43:34). In addition to a great variety of viands, wine was used, often drugged with spices (Prov. 9:2; Cant. 8:2); and the banquets frequently degenerated into drinking bouts (Isa. 5:12; Amos 6:5; Psa. 69:13).

The Jews of the Old Testament appear to have used a common table for all the guests, although persons of high official position were honored with a separate table. In some cases a ceremonial separation prevailed, as at Joseph's entertainment of his brethren (Gen. 43:32). In early times *sitting* was the usual posture (I Sam. 16:11; 20:5, 18); but later they adopted the luxurious practice of *reclining* upon couches (Luke 7:37, 38; John 12;2, 3).

In the houses of the common people the women and children also took part in the feast (I Sam. 1:4; John 12:3), the separation of the women not being a Jewish custom.

6. **Diversion.** At private banquets the master of the house presided, and did the honors of the occasion; but in large and mixed companies it was the ancient custom to choose a "governor of the feast" (John 2:8). This functionary performed the office of chairman, in preserving order, and also took upon himself the general management of the festivities. The guests were entertained with exhibitions of music, singers, and dancers, riddles, jesting, and merriment (Isa. 28:1; Wisd. 2:7; II Sam. 19:35; Isa. 5:12; 25:6; Judg. 14:12; Neh. 8:10; Amos 6:5, 6; Luke 15:25). *See* Festivals, Food.

Baptism, the application of water as a rite of purification or initiation; a Christian sacrament. *See* Sacraments.

The word "baptism" is the English form of the Gr. *baptismos*. The verb from which this noun is derived—*baptizo*—is held by some scholars to mean "to dip, immerse." But this meaning is held by others to be not the most exact or common, but rather a meaning that is secondary or derived. By the latter it is claimed that all that the term necessarily implies is that the element employed in baptism is in close contact with the person or object baptized. The Greek prepositions *en* and *eis* have played a very prominent part in discussions respecting the mode of baptism.

The scope of this article is limited mainly to Christian baptism, but as preliminary to this brief mention is made of:

1. **Jewish Baptism.** Baptisms, or ceremonial purifications, were common among the Jews. Not only priests and other persons, but also clothing, utensils, and articles of furniture, were thus ceremonially cleansed (Lev. 8:6; Exod. 19:10-14; Mark 7:3, 4; Heb. 9:10).

2. **John's Baptism.** The baptism of John was not Christian, but Jewish. It was, however, especially a baptism "unto repentance." The only faith that it expressed concerning Christ was that his coming was close at hand. They who confessed and repented of their sins and were baptized by John were thus obedient to his call to "prepare the way of the Lord."

Because the disciples whom Paul met at Ephesus (Acts 19:1-7) "knew no baptism but John's" (Acts 18:25, Weymouth), i. e. were ignorant of the Christian message and the baptism of the Holy Spirit, save as a prophesied event (Acts 19:4), they did not "receive the Holy Spirit, *when* they believed" (Acts 19:2). They had heard only John's message and received only John's baptism, which were introductory and merely preparatory. Faith in them could not bring the free gift of the Holy Spirit. The moment they heard and believed the new message of a crucified, risen and ascended Savior, they received the blessings of that message—the gift of the Holy Spirit, which included His baptizing ministry.

3. **Baptism of Jesus.** The baptism that Jesus received from John was unique in its significance and purpose. It could not be like that which John administered to others, for Jesus did not make confession. He had no occasion to repent. Neither was it Christian baptism, the significance of which we shall consider later. Jesus himself declared the main purpose and meaning of this event in his words, "Thus it becometh us to fulfill all righteousness." It was an act of ceremonial righteousness appropriate to his public entrance upon his mission as the Christ . . . which included His threefold office of prophet, priest and king, especially the second, for the essence of his redemptive work lies in His consecration as a Priest, the Great High Priest. In this office He offered not "the blood of bulls and goats," but Himself to put away sin (Heb. 9:24-26). It is this consecration to His redemptive priesthood that comes into clearest view in His baptism in Jordan. By "fulfilling all righteousness" our Lord meant the righteousness of obedience to the Mosaic Law. The Levitical law required all priests to be consecrated when they "began to be about 30 years of age" (Num. 4:3; Luke 3:23). The consecration was twofold—first the washing (baptism), then the anointing (Exod. 29:4-7; Lev. 8:6-36). When John on Jordan's bank "washed" (baptized) Jesus, the heavens were opened and the Holy Spirit came upon Him. This was the priestly anointing of Him Who was not only a priest by divine appointment, but an eternal priest (Psa. 110:4) and Who was thus divinely consecrated for the work of redemption (Matt. 3:16; Acts 4:27; 10:38).

4. **Baptism of Christ's Disciples.** That Christ himself baptized his disciples is a matter, to say the least, involved in doubt. While it is probable that at the beginning of his ministry our Lord baptized those who believed in him, he not long afterward delegated

this work to his disciples (John 4:1, 2). The office of Christ was and is to baptize with the Holy Spirit. His disciples administered the symbolical baptism, he that which is real (Matt. 3:11).

5. **Christian Baptism.** We consider the points of chief interest: (1) **Obligation.** The obligation of Christian baptism rests upon the command of Christ (Matt. 28:19). Though Christianity is a spiritual, and not in any large sense a ceremonial, religion, yet nevertheless Christ gave the command to baptize, which of course implies the further command to receive baptism. That this obligation is perpetual appears from the breadth of the command, and the far-reaching promise that was given in connection with it. The Quakers, among those who profess faith in Christ, are the chief opponents of this view. They rest their objection mainly upon the spiritual character of Christianity, and hold that the baptism of the Holy Spirit alone is requisite. They assert that water baptism was never intended to continue in the Church of Christ any longer than while Jewish prejudices made such an external ceremony necessary. (2) **Significance.** The nature and effect of baptism have been the subject of much controversy. The Roman Catholic, the Greek, and the Lutheran Churches, and many in the Church of England and Protestant Episcopal Church, hold that baptism is the direct instrument of regeneration. This is the so-called doctrine of baptismal regeneration. *See* Regeneration. Roman Catholics hold so strongly to this view that, accordingly, they also hold that all persons, adults or infants, who die unbaptized are excluded from heaven. Others have gone to the opposite extreme, taking the Socinian view, that baptism is merely a mode of professing faith in Christ, or a ceremony of initiation to the Christian Church. Others have reduced the rite to a symbol of purification, expressive of the purifying influence of the Christian religion. The doctrine of many evangelical Churches is that baptism is not only the rite of initiation into the Church of Christ, and not only a sign, but also a seal of divine grace. For example, the Westminster Confession, art. xxviii, says: "Baptism is a sacrament of the New Testament, ordained by Jesus Christ, not only for the solemn admission of the party baptized into the visible Church but also to be unto him a sign and seal of the covenant of grace of his ingrafting into Christ, of regeneration, of remission of sins, and of his giving up unto God through Jesus Christ, to walk in newness of life; which sacrament is, by Christ's own appointment, to be continued in his Church until the end of the world." As circumcision was the sign and seal of the Mosaic covenant, so baptism is construed as the sign and seal of the new covenant of the Gospel. On the one hand the person baptized becomes thus pledged to fidelity to Christ, and on the other hand baptism ratifies the divine pledge for the fulfillment of all his gracious promises to those who truly accept Christ. Baptism, in this view under the new dispensation, takes the place of circumcision under the old. This is taken as the fair implication of all those utterances of the apostle which represent Christians as numbered among the "faithful seed," "the chosen generation," "the circumcision," "the household of God." St. Paul distinctly declares this relation between the two rites (Col. 2:10-12). (3) **Proper subjects of baptism.** According to many groups, not only adults who repent of their sins and give evidence of faith in Christ, but also infants, the children of Christian parents, or under the care of those who will give them Christian nurture, are proper subjects for baptism. The following quotation admirably states the view of those who believe in infant baptism: "We hold that all children, by virtue of the unconditional benefits of the atonement, are members of the kingdom of God, and therefore graciously entitled to baptism; but as infant baptism contemplates a course of religious instruction and discipline, it is expected of all parents or guardians who present their children for baptism that they will use all diligence in bringing them up in conformity to the word of God; and they should be solemnly admonished of this obligation, and earnestly exhorted to faithfulness therein." Roman Catholics and others who teach that baptism is a saving rite, and absolutely essential to salvation, base their custom of infant baptism upon that ground. They who reject the baptism of infants do so because of their different view of the significance of the rite—a testimony of one's salvation. The Roman Catholic and Greek Churches, and most Protestant Churches, except Baptist, practice infant baptism. (4) **Mode.** The common doctrine of Christendom has been that all that is essential in the mode of baptism is the application of water "in the name of the Father, and of the Son, and of the Holy Ghost." It denies that immersion is the only valid baptism, and admits of sprinkling, pouring, and immersion. That immersion is a very ancient mode of baptism may be freely admitted. But the same may also be said of the other modes—sprinkling and pouring. Baptisms, or ceremonial purifications, among the Jews were performed undoubtedly in various ways. "Our Lord in his institution of baptism simply appropriated an ancient rite, and adapted it to the purposes of his kingdom. And he was silent as to the mode in which the water is to be applied. It is contrary to the whole spirit of Christ's teaching to attach great importance to details of ceremony. Also baptism, which is a universal rite, may properly, and sometimes must of necessity, be varied in mode according to climate and other circumstances." The Baptists hold "That Christian baptism is the immersion in water of a believer, into the name of the Father, and Son, and Holy Ghost; . . . that it is prerequisite to the privileges of a Church relation, and to the Lord's Supper." (5) **Administration.** The administration of baptism is commonly regarded as exclusively a prerogative of the ministerial office. But it is difficult, to say the least, to sustain this view by an appeal to the Scriptures. The wise and proper observance of Church order, however, has committed the performance of this rite to the ministers of the Church. The Roman Catholic Church teaches that baptism administered in extreme cases by a layman, or a woman, or

even a heretic is valid, though still ministers alone have the right to baptize. The same view obtains among Lutherans and others who hold strongly to the doctrine of baptismal regeneration.

Literature. The literature of this subject is abundant. Besides works upon systematic theology, see Bradbury, *Duty and Doctrine of Baptism*; Neander, *History of Doctrines;* Beecher, *Baptism, its Import and Modes;* Hibbard, *Christian Baptism, its Subjects, Mode, and Obligation.* For Baptist views, see Booth, *Apology for the Baptist;* Booth *Poedobaptism Examined;* Smith, *Arguments for Infant Baptism Examined;* Jewett, *On Baptism;* E. Fairfield, *Letters on Baptism;* J. Dale, *Classic Baptism, Johannic Baptism, Judaic Baptism.*

Baptism for the Dead, I Cor. 15:29). Of this difficult passage there are many expositions, a few of which we present:

1. The Cerinthians, the Marcionites, and other heretics had a custom, supposed to be referred to by the apostle. Persons who had been baptized had themselves baptized again for the benefit of people who had died *unbaptized* but *already believing,* in the persuasion that this would be counted to them as their own baptism. From this the apostle drew an argument to prove their belief in the resurrection. Meyer (*Com.,* in loc.) believes that this is the practice to which the apostle refers. "'For the benefit of the dead' remains the right interpretation."

2. Chrysostom believes the apostle to refer to the profession of faith in baptism, part of which was, "I believe in the resurrection of the dead." The meaning, then, would be, "If there is no resurrection of the dead, why, then, art thou baptized for the dead, i. e., the body?" Whedon (*Com.,* in loc.) holds to this interpretation, and says: "The apostolic Christians were baptized into the faith of the resurrection of the dead, and thereby they were sponsors *in behalf of* the dead, that the dead should rise."

3. Another interpretation, that of Spanheim, considers "the dead" to be martyrs and other believers who, by firmness and cheerful hope of resurrection, have given in death a worthy example, *by which* others were also animated to receive baptism. This interpretation, however, may perhaps also be improved if *Christ* be considered as prominently referred to among those deceased, by *virtue* of whose resurrection all his followers expect to be likewise raised.

4. Olshausen takes the meaning of the passage to be that "all who are converted to the Church are baptized *for the good* of the dead, as it requires a certain number (Rom. 11:12-25), a 'fullness' of believers, before the resurrection can take place."

5. "Over the graves of the martyrs." Vossius adopted this interpretation, but it is very unlikely that this custom should have prevailed in the days of St. Paul.

Baptism of Fire. It is clear from the immediate context of this reference (Matt. 3:9-12; Luke 3:16, 17) and from the general testimony of Scripture, that this baptism of fire is connected with judgment at the Second Advent of Christ as the baptism with the Holy Spirit

(Acts 1:5 with 11:16) is connected with grace flowing from the death, resurrection and ascension of Christ at His First Advent. As John F. Walvoord correctly observes, "While the Church Age is introduced with a baptism of the Spirit, the Kingdom Age is to be introduced with a baptism of fire" (*Doct. of the Holy Spirit,* Dallas, 1943, p. 165). At first glance it might seem singular that John the Baptist should speak of the First and Second Advents in such intimate connection, but he is merely expressing himself as many of the O. T. prophets did, who often envision the Lord's First and Second Comings in a blended view, and speak of both in the same clause (Cf. Isa. 61:1, 2 with Luke 4:16-21). Though some expositors, as Plumptre, have attempted to find a fulfillment of the baptism with fire in the "cloven-tongues like as of fire" (Acts 2:3), and others have construed it as a description of the baptizing work of the Holy Spirit as an experience to be sought in this age, a kind of "second Pentecost," these interpretations are manifestly erroneous. It is not Scriptural to pray for a baptism with fire, for there is no such baptism now, for the believer has been graciously delivered from wrath by the blood of Christ. M. F. U.

Baptism of Je'sus. *See* Baptism, 3.

Baptism of the Spirit. This momentous spiritual operation is set forth in the N. T. as the basis of all the believer's positions and possessions "in Christ" (Eph. 1:3; Col. 2:10; Col. 3:1-4, etc.). The operation is prophetic in the Gospels (Matt. 3:11; Mark 1:8; Luke 3:16, 17; John 1:33, 34); historic in the Acts (1:5 with 11:16), and doctrinal in the Epistles (I Cor. 12:13; Rom. 6:3, 4; Gal. 3:26, 27; Col. 2:9-12; Eph. 4:5). The Spirits' baptizing work, placing the believer "in Christ" occurred initially at Pentecost at the Advent of the Spirit, Who baptized believing Jews "into Christ." In Acts 8 Samaritans were so baptized for the first time. In Acts 10 Gentiles likewise were so baptized, at which point the normal order of the age was attained. Now, according to the clear teaching of the Epistles, every believer is baptized by the Spirit into Christ, the moment he is regenerated. He is also simultaneously indwelt by the Spirit and sealed eternally, with the privilege of being filled with the Spirit, as the conditions for filling are met. No subject in all the range of Biblical theology is so neglected, on one hand, or misunderstood and abused, on the other, as this. The baptism of the Spirit is widely confused with regeneration and with the indwelling, sealing and filling ministries of the Spirit, as well as with water baptism and a so-called "second blessing." For a comprehensive study of this important theme see *The Baptizing Work of the Holy Spirit* by Merrill F. Unger, Scripture Press, 1953, pp. 1-143. M. F. U.

Bar, a word of various meanings. (1) A bar, *crossbar* passing along the sides and rear of the *Tabernacle* (q. v.), through rings attached to each board, and thus holding the boards together (Exod. 26:26, sq.). (2) A bar or *bolt* for fastening a gate or door (Judg. 16:3; Neh. 3:3, sq.). The word is used figuratively of a rock in the sea (Jonah 2:6), the bank or shore of the sea (Job 38:10), of strong fortifications and impediments (Isa. 45:2; Amos 1:5).

Bar- (Aram., *son*), a patronymic sign, used like *Ben*, which had the same meaning. *Ben*, however, prevails in the pure Hebrew names of the Old Testament, and *Bar* in those of the New Testament, because much more used in the Aramaic and Syriac languages.

Barab'bas (bär-ăb'ȧs; Gr. *barabbas*, for Aram. *bar 'abba'*, *son of the father*, or *Abba*), a robber who had committed murder in an insurrection (Mark 15:7; Luke 23:19) in Jerusalem, and was lying in prison at the time of the trial of Jesus before Pilate, A. D. 29. The latter, in his anxiety to save Jesus, proposed to release him to the people, in accordance with their demand that he should release one prisoner to them at the Passover. Barabbas was guilty of the crimes of murder and sedition, making him liable to both Roman and Jewish law. But the Jews were so bent on the death of Jesus that of the two they preferred pardoning this double criminal (Matt. 27:20; Mark 15:11; Luke 23:18; John 18:40). "Pilate, willing to content the people, released Barabbas unto them, and delivered Jesus . . . to be crucified" (Mark 15:15).

Bar'achel (bär'ȧ-kĕl; *God has blessed*), the father of Elihu the Buzite, one of the three "friends" who visited Job in his affliction (Job 32:2, 6).

Barachi'ah. *See* Berechiah.

Barachi'as (bär-ȧ-kī'ȧs; *Barachiah*), the father of the Zechariah (Zacharias) mentioned in Matt. 23:35, as having been murdered by the Jews. *See* Zechariah.

Ba'rah. *See* Beth-barah.

Bar'ak (bär'ăk; *lightning*), the son of Abinoam of Kadesh, a city of refuge in the tribe of Naphtali (Judg. 4:6).

Personal History. He was summoned by the prophetess Deborah to take the field against the army of the Canaanitish king, Jabin, commanded by Sisera, with a force of

64. Probable Battleground of Barak and Sisera

ten thousand men from the tribes of Naphtali and Zebulun. He was further instructed to proceed to Mount Tabor, for Jehovah would draw Sisera and his host to meet him at the river Kishon, and deliver him into his hand. Barak consented only on the condition that Deborah would go with him, which she readily promised. Sisera, being informed of Barak's movements, proceeded against him with his whole army, including nine hundred chariots. At a signal given by the prophetess, the little army, seizing the opportunity of a providential storm, boldly rushed down the hill and utterly routed the host of the Canaanites. The victory was decisive: Harosheth was taken, Sisera murdered, and Jabin ruined (Judg. 4), between B. C. 1195-1155. The victory was celebrated by the beautiful hymn of praise composed by Barak in conjunction with Deborah (Judg. 5). Barak appears in the list of the faithful worthies of the Old Testament (Heb. 11:32).

Barbarian (Gr. *barbaros*, *rude*), was originally the Greek epithet for a people speaking any other than the Greek language. After the Persian wars it began to carry with it associations of hatred and to imply vulgarity and lack of culture. The Romans were originally included by the Greeks under the name *barbaroi*. But after the conquest of Greece, and the transference of Greek art and culture to Rome, the Romans took the same position as the Greeks before them, and designated as barbarians all who in language and manners differed from the Greco-Roman world. The word *barbarian* is applied in the New Testament, but not reproachfully, to the inhabitants of Malta (Acts 28:4), who were of Phoenician or Punic origin, and to those nations that had indeed some refinement of manners, but not the opportunity of becoming Christians, as the Scythians (Col. 3:11). The phrase "Greeks and Barbarians" (Rom. 1:14) means *all peoples*.

Barber (Heb. *gállāb*), occurs but once in the Scriptures (Ezek. 5:1); but, inasmuch as great attention was paid to the hair and beard among the ancients, the barber must have been a well-known tradesman. *See* Hair.

Barefoot (Heb. *yāḥēf*, *unshod*, Jer. 2:25). In the East great importance was attached to the clothing, and feelings respecting it were peculiarly sensitive, so that a person was looked upon as stripped and naked if he only removed an outer garment. To go *barefoot* was an indication of great distress (Isa. 20:2-4; II Sam. 15:30). Persons were also accustomed to remove their shoes when coming to places accounted holy (Exod. 3:5).

Barhu'mite (bär-hū'mīt), a transposed form (II Sam. 23:31) of the Gentile name *Baharumite* (*q. v.*).

Bari'ah (bȧ-rī'ȧ; *fugitive*), one of the five sons of Shemaiah, of the descendants of David, who are counted as six, including their father (I Chron. 3:22), B. C. before 410.

Bar-je'sus (bär-jē'sŭs; *son of Joshua*), otherwise called *Elymas* (*q. v.*), a demonized sorcerer-magician who withstood Barnabas and Paul (Acts 13:6).

Bar-jo'na (bär-jō'nȧ; *Son of Jonah*), the patronymic of the apostle Peter (Matt. 16:17; comp. John 1:42).

Bar'kos (bär'kŏs), the head of one of the families of Nethinim that returned from the captivity with Zerubbabel (Ezra 2:53; Neh. 7:55), B. C. 536.

Barley. *See* Vegetable Kingdom.

Bar'nabas (bär'nà-bàs; Gr. from Aram. *barnᵉbŭʾah*, *son of prophecy*, especially as it is manifested in exhortation and comfort), the name given by the apostles to Joses (Acts 4:36), probably on account of his eminence as a Christian teacher.

Personal History. Barnabas was a native of Cyprus, and a Levite by extraction. (1) **Charity.** Being possessed of land, he generously disposed of it for the benefit of the Christian community, and laid the money at the apostles' feet (Acts 4:36, 37). As this transaction occurred soon after the day of Pentecost he must have been an early convert to Christianity. (2) **Associated with Paul.** When Paul made his first appearance in Jerusalem Barnabas brought him to the apostles and attested his sincerity (Acts 9:27). Word being brought to Jerusalem of the revival at Antioch, Barnabas (who is described as "a good man, and full of the Holy Ghost and of faith") was sent to make inquiry. Finding the work to be genuine, he labored among them for a time, fresh converts being added to the Church through his personal efforts. He then went to Tarsus to obtain the assistance of Saul, who returned with him to Antioch, where they labored for a whole year (Acts 11:19-26). In anticipation of the famine predicted by Agabus the Christians at Antioch made a contribution for their poor brethren at Jerusalem, and sent it by the hands of Barnabas and Saul (Acts 11:27-30), A. D. 44. They, however, speedily returned, bringing with them John Mark, a nephew of the former (Acts 12:25). (3) **First Missionary journey.** By divine direction (Acts 13:2) they were separated to the office of missionaries, and as such visited Cyprus and some of the principal cities in Asia Minor (Acts 13:14). At Lystra, because of a miracle performed by Paul, they were taken for gods, the people calling Barnabas Jupiter (ch. 14:8-12). Returning to Antioch, they found the peace of the Church disturbed by certain from Judea, who insisted upon the Gentile converts being circumcised. Paul and Barnabas, with others, were sent to Jerusalem to consult with the apostles and elders. They returned to communicate the result of the conference, accompanied by Judas and Silas (ch. 15:1-32). (4) **Second missionary journey.** Preparing for a second missionary journey, a dispute arose between Paul and Barnabas on account of John Mark. "Barnabas determined to take Mark with them; Paul thought it not good to take him." The contention became so sharp that they separated, Barnabas with Mark going to Cyprus, while Paul and Silas went through Syria and Cilicia (ch. 15:36-41). At this point Barnabas disappears from the record of the Acts. Several times he is mentioned in the writings of St. Paul, but nothing special is noted save that Barnabas was at one time led away by Judaizing zealots. All else is matter of inference.

Barrel (Heb. *kǎd*, *jar*, *pitcher*), probably an earthen vessel used for the keeping of flour (I Kings 17:12, 14, 16; 18:33). In other places the word is rendered "pitcher" (*q. v.*).

Barren (Heb. *ʿäqär*, when spoken of persons). Barrenness, in the East, was looked upon as a ground of great reproach as well as a punishment from God (I Sam. 1:6, 7; Isa. 47:9; 49:21; Luke 1:25, etc.). Instances of childless wives are found (Gen. 11:30; 25:21; 29:31; Judg. 13:2, 3; Luke 1:7, 36). Certain marriages were forbidden by Moses, and were visited with barrenness (Lev. 20:20, 21). The reproach attached to barrenness, especially among the Hebrews, was doubtless due to the constant expectation of the Messiah, and the hope cherished by every woman that she might be the mother of the promised Seed. In order to avoid the disgrace of barrenness women gave their handmaidens to their husbands, regarding the children born under such circumstances as their own (Gen. 16:2; 30:3).

Bar'sabas (bär'sá-bǎs) in R. V. **Barsab'bas** (bär-sāb'ǎs; *son of Sabas*), a surname.

1. Of Joseph, a disciple who was nominated along with Matthias to succeed Judas Iscariot in the apostleship (Acts 1:23).

2. Of Judas, who, with Silas, was sent to Antioch in company of Paul and Barnabas (Acts 15:22).

Barthol'omew (bär-thŏl'ô-mū; *son of Tolmai*), one of the twelve apostles of Jesus, and generally supposed to have been the same person who, in John's gospel, is called Nathanael.

1. **Name and Family.** In the first three gospels (Matt. 10:3; Mark 3:18; Luke 6:14) Philip and Bartholomew are constantly named together, while Nathanael is nowhere mentioned. In the fourth gospel Philip and Nathanael are similarly combined, but nothing is said of Bartholomew. Nathanael must therefore be considered as his real name, while Bartholomew merely expresses his filial relation (Kitto).

2. **Personal History.** If this may be taken as true, he was born in Cana of Galilee (John 21:2). Philip, having accepted Jesus, told Bartholomew that he had "found him, of whom Moses in the law, and the prophets, did write, Jesus of Nazareth." To his question, "Can there any good thing come out of Nazareth?" Philip replied, "Come and see." His fastidious reluctance was soon dispelled. Jesus, as he saw him coming to him, uttered the eulogy, "Behold an Israelite indeed, in whom is no guile!" (John 1:45, sq.). He was anointed with the other apostles (Matt. 10:3; Mark 3:18; Luke 6:14), was one of the disciples to whom the Lord appeared after the resurrection (John 21:2), a witness of the ascension, and returned with the other apostles to Jerusalem (Acts 1:4, 12, 13). Tradition only speaks of his subsequent history. He is said to have preached the Gospel in India (probably Arabia Felix); others say in Armenia, and report him to have been there flayed alive and then crucified with his head downward.

3. **Character.** Nathanael "seems to have been one of those calm, retiring souls, whose whole sphere of existence lies not here, but 'Where, beyond these voices, there is peace.'

It was a life of which the world sees nothing, because it was '*hid* with Christ in God'" (Farrar).

Bartime'us (bär-tĭ-mē'ŭs; *son of Timoeus*), a blind beggar of Jericho, who sat by the wayside begging as our Lord went out of the city on his last journey to Jerusalem (Mark 10:46). Hearing that Jesus was passing, he cried for mercy, and in answer to his faith he was miraculously cured, and "followed Jesus in the way."

Ba'ruch (bä'rŭk; *blessed*).

1. The son of Zabbai. He repaired (B. C. 445) that part of the walls of Jerusalem between the north-east angle of Zion and the house of Eliashib the high priest (Neh. 3:20), and joined in Nehemiah's covenant (10:6).

2. Son of Col-hozeh, a descendant of Perez, a son of Judah. His son Maaseiah dwelt in Jerusalem after the captivity (Neh. 11:5).

3. Son of Neriah and brother of Seraiah, who held an honorable office in Zedekiah's court (Jer. 32:12; 36:4; 51:59). Baruch was the faithful friend and amanuensis of Jeremiah. In the fourth year of King Jehoiakim (B. C. about 604) Baruch was directed to write all the prophecies delivered by Jeremiah and read them to the people. This he did in the temple both that and the succeeding year. He afterward read them privately to the king's counselors, telling them that he had received them through the prophet's dictation. The king, when the roll was brought to him, cut it and threw it into the fire. He ordered the arrest of Jeremiah and Baruch, but they could not be found. Baruch wrote another roll, including all that was in the former and an additional prediction of the ruin of Jehoiakim and his house (Jer. 36). Terrified by the threats in the prophetic roll, he received the assurance that he should be spared from the calamities which would befall Judah (Jer. 45). During the siege of Jerusalem Jeremiah purchased the territory of Hanameel, and deposited the deed with Baruch (Jer. 32:12), B. C. 590. Baruch was accused of influencing Jeremiah in favor of the Chaldeans (Jer. 43:3; comp. 37:13), and he was thrown into prison with that prophet, where he remained until the capture of Jerusalem (Josephus, *Ant.*, x, 9, 1). By the permission of Nebuchadnezzar he abode with Jeremiah at Mizpah, but was afterward forced to go to Egypt (ch. 43:6). Nothing certain is known of the close of his life. According to one tradition, he went to Babylon upon the death of Jeremiah, where he died, the twelfth year after the destruction of Jerusalem. There are two apocryphal books which purport to be the productions of Baruch.

Barzil'lai (bär-zĭl'ā-i; *of iron*).

1. A wealthy and aged Gileadite of Rogelim, who showed great hospitality to David when he fled beyond Jordan from his son Absalom, B. C. c. 967. He sent in a liberal supply of provisions, beds, and other conveniences for the use of the king's followers (II Sam. 17:27). On the king's triumphant return Barzillai accompanied him over Jordan, but declined on the score of age (being eighty years old), and perhaps from a feeling of independence, to proceed to Jerusalem and

end his days at court. He, however, recommended his son Chimham to the royal favor (II Sam. 19:31-39). On his deathbed David recalled to mind this kindness, and commended Barzillai's children to the care of Solomon (I Kings 2:7).

2. A Meholathite, father of Adriel, which latter was the husband of Michal, Saul's daughter (II Sam. 21:8), B. C. before 1021.

3. A priest who married a descendant of Barzillai (1), and assumed the same name. His genealogy became so confused that his descendants, on the return from captivity, were set aside as unfit for the priesthood (Ezra 2:61; Neh. 7:63), B. C. before 536.

Ba'shan (bā'shăn), extended from Gilead in the S. to Hermon on the N., and from the Jordan to Salcah, the present Salkhat, on the E., and included Edrei (Deut. 3:10; Josh. 9:10), Ashtaroth (Deut. 1:4; Josh. 9:10, etc.), the present Tell-Ashtur, and Golan (Deut. 4:43; Josh. 20:8; 21:27). Golan, one of its cities, was a city of refuge. Its productiveness was remarked in the Old Testament (Psa. 22:12; Jer. 50:19). The western part is exceedingly fertile today. On the E. rise the Hauran Mountains to a height of six thousand feet. It was noted for its fine breed of cattle (Deut. 32:14; Ezek. 39:18). The cities are described by Moses as "fenced cities with high walls, gates, and bars." The inhabitants were giant-like men who were called Rephaim in the era of Abraham (Gen. 14:5).

Some of the deserted towns are as perfect as when inhabited. When Israel entered Canaan, Argob, a province of Bashan, contained "sixty fenced cities" (Deut. 3:4, 5; I Kings 4:13). After the exile Bashan was divided into four districts: Gaulonitis, or Jaulan, the western; Auranitis, or Hauran (Ezek. 47:16); Argob, or Trachonitis; and Batanaea, now Ard-el-Bathanyeh.

Ba'shan, Hill of. In Psa. 68:15 the poet says, "The hill of God is as the hill of Bashan; an high hill as the hill of Basham" (R. V. "A mountain of God is the mountain of Bashan; an high mountain is the mountain of Bashan"). "This epithet, not applicable to the long, level edge of the tableland, might refer either to the lofty triple summits of Hermon, or to the many broken cones that are scattered across Bashan, and so greatly differ in their volcanic form from the softer, less imposing heights of western Palestine" (Smith, *Hist. Geog.*, p. 550).

Ba'shan-ha'voth-ja'ir (bā-shăn-hā'vŏth-jā'ĭr; *the Bashan of the villages of Jair*), the name given by Jair to the places he had conquered in Bashan (Deut. 3:14). It contained sixty cities with walls and brazen gates (Josh. 13:30; I Kings 4:13). In Num. 32:41 called Havoth-jair, which is the correct name. The R. V. correctly translates Deut. 3:14. ". . . He called them, even Bashan, after his own name Havvoth-jair, unto this day."

Bash'emath (băsh'ē-măth; *fragrance*, elsewhere, I Kings 4:15, more correctly, "Basmath"), a daughter of Ishmael, the last married of the three wives of Esau (Gen. 36:3, 4, 13), from whose son, Reuel, four tribes of the Edomites were descended. When first mentioned she is called Mahalath (Gen. 28:9), while, on the other hand, the name Bashemath is in the narrative (Gen. 26:34) given to another of Esau's wives, the daughter of Elon the Hittite. It may have been the original name of one, and the name given to the other upon her marriage, for, "as a rule, the women received new names when they were married."

Basin (A. V. Bason). This word is employed for dishes, containers and bowls of various descriptions. 1. A large bowl, Heb. *mĭzräq*, was a part of the furnishing of the Tabernacle and the Temple, particularly in service at the altar of burnt offering (Num. 4:14) to hold the meal offering (Num. 7:13) and to receive sacrificial blood (Zech. 9:15; 14:20). It was commonly of gold or silver; sometimes of burnished brass (Exod. 27:3; Num. 7:84). In inordinate reveling wine is said to be drunk from such bowls (Amos 6:6). 2. A smaller vessel, Heb. *'ăggän*, was a vessel for washing, a laver, (Exod. 24:6). It was also a wine cup (Isa. 22:24, Cant. 7:23, translated "goblet"). 3. A shallow vessel, Heb. *săf*. A utensil for holding the blood of the victim (Exod. 12:22; Jer. 52:19), the oil for the sacred candlestick (I Kings 7:50), basins for domestic purposes (II Sam. 17:28) and for drinking (Zech. 12:2). The basin from which our Lord washed the disciples' feet (John 13:5), was called a *niptēr* signifying, evidently, a utensil for washing. *M. F. U. See* Bowl and Cup.

Basket. No less than five common Heb. words are employed to denote baskets or containers of different sizes, shapes and construction. Ancient art reliefs and sculptures and the etymological meaning of the words used show that the baskets were frequently woven or made of fibre from leaves of the palm tree or rushes, leaves and twigs. Some were used especially for holding bread (Gen. 40:16 f; Exod. 29:3, 23; Lev. 8:2, 26, 31; Num. 6:15, 17, 19). Egyptian bread baskets appear on ancient tombs. Baskets were used also in gathering grapes (Jer. 6:9) and carrying fruit (Amos 8:1, 2). In Egypt heavy burdens, as grain, were carried in large baskets swung from a pole hung on the shoulders. In the New Testament baskets are described as sometimes large enough to hold a man. Paul was lowered from the wall of Damascus in such a hamper (II Cor. 11:33). *M. F. U.*

Bas′math (băs′măth; *fragrance*), a daughter of Solomon, who became the wife of Ahimaaz, one of the king's purveyors (I Kings 4:15), B. C. about 965.

Bastard. The word occurs in Deut. 23:2 and Zech. 9:6. Its etymology is obscure, but it appears to denote anyone to whose birth a serious stain attaches. The Rabbins applied the term not to any illegitimate offspring, but to the issue of any connection within the degrees prohibited by the law (*see* Marriage). A very probable conjecture is that which applies the term to the offspring of heathen prostitutes in the neighborhood of Palestine, and who were a sort of priestesses to the Syrian goddess Astarte. In Zech. 9:6, the word is, doubtless, used in the sense of *foreigner*, expressing the deep degradation of Philistia in being conquered by other people.

1. Persons of illegitimate birth among the Jews had no claim to a share in the paternal inheritance, or to the proper filial treatment of children of the family. This is what is referred to in Heb. 12:8, where a contrast is drawn between the treatment which God's true children might expect, as compared with that given to such as are not so related to him.

2. Persons of illegitimate birth are forbidden, by the canon law, from receiving any of the minor orders without a dispensation from the bishop; nor can they, in the Latin Church, be admitted to holy orders, or to benefices with cure of souls, except by a dispensation from the pope. In the Church of England a bastard cannot be admitted to orders without a dispensation from the sovereign or archbishop.

Bat. *See* Animal Kingdom.

Bath. *See* Metrology.

Bathe, Bathing (Heb. *rähặs*). The hot climate of the East, with its abundant dust, made bathing a constant necessity for the preservation and invigoration of the health. This natural necessity was greatly furthered among the Israelites by the religious purifications enjoined by the law. For, although these precepts had a higher object, the teaching of personal purity, they could not fail to intensify the instinct of cleanliness, and to make frequent washing and bathing an indispensable arrangement of the life.

The Israelites, from early times, were accustomed not only to wash the hands and feet before eating, but also to bathe the body when about to visit a superior (Ruth 3:3), after mourning, which always implied defilement (II Sam. 12:20), but especially before any religious service (Gen. 35:2; Exod. 19:10; Josh. 3:5; I Sam. 16:5), that they might appear clean before God. The high priest at his inauguration (Lev. 13:6), and on the day of atonement before each act of propitiation (Lev. 16:4, 24), was also to bathe. To cleanse the body snow water was used, or lye put into the water (Job 9:30), also bran, according to Mishna. Bathing in running water was specially favored (Lev. 15:13), or in rivers (II Kings 5:10; Exod. 2:5). Baths were placed in the courts of private houses (II Sam. 11:2; Susanna 15). In the later temple there were bath rooms over the chambers for the use of the priests. The "pools," as those of Siloam and Hezekiah (Neh. 3:15, 16; II Kings 20:20; Isa. 22:11; John 9:7), were public baths, no doubt introduced in imitation of a Roman and Greek custom.

Bath′-sheba (băth-shē′bȧ; *daughter of the oath*), daughter of Eliam (II Sam. 11:3), or Ammiel (I Chron. 3:5), the granddaughter of Ahithophel (II Sam. 23:34), and wife of Uriah. She had illicit intercourse with David while her husband was absent at the siege of Rabbah, B. C. about 980. Uriah being slain by a contrivance of David, after a period of mourning for her husband Bath-sheba was legally married to the king (II Sam. 11:3-27). The child which was the fruit of her adulterous intercourse with David died, but she became the mother of four sons—Solomon, Shimea (Shammuah), Shobab, and Nathan (II Sam. 5:14; I Chron. 3:5). When Adonijah attempted to set aside in his own favor the succession promised to Solomon, Bath-sheba was employed by Nathan to inform the king of the conspiracy, and received from him an answer favorable to Solomon (I Kings 1:11-31). After the accession of Solomon she, as queen-mother, requested permission of her son for Adonijah to take in marriage Abishag the Shunammite (I Kings 2:21). The request was refused, and became the occasion of the execution of Adonijah (2:24, 25).

Bath'-shua (băth-shū'á), a variation of the name *Bath-sheba* (*q. v.*), the mother of Solomon (I Chron. 3:5).

Battering-ram. *See* Armor.

Battle. *See* Warfare.

Battle-ax. *See* Armor.

Battle-bow. *See* Armor.

Battlement, a breastwork, of wall or lattice, surrounding the flat roofs of Eastern houses, required as a protection against accidents (Deut. 22:8). "Battlements" is the rendering (Jer. 5:10) for the parapet of a city wall.

Bav'ai (băv'á-i), a son of Henadad, and ruler of the half part of Keilah. He repaired a portion of the wall of Jerusalem on the return from Babylon (Neh. 3:18), B. C. 445.

Bay (Heb. *läshōn, tongue*), the cove of the Dead Sea, at the mouth of the Jordan (Josh. 15:5; 18:19), and also of the southern extremity of the same sea (15:2). The same term is used (in the original) with reference to the forked mouths of the Nile ("the *tongue* of the Egyptian Sea," Isa. 11:15).

Bay, the color, according to the English version, of one of the spans of horses in the vision of Zechariah (6:3, 7). It is the rendering of *strong*. Keil and Delitzsch translate "speckled, powerful horses" (*Com.*, in loc.).

Bay Tree. *See* Vegetable Kingdom.

Baz'lith (băz'lĭth), the head of one of the families of Nethinim that returned to Jerusalem from the exile (Neh. 7:54). He is called Bazluth in Ezra 2:52.

Baz'luth (băz'lŭth), another form of *Bazlith*.

Bdellium. *See* Mineral Kingdom.

Beali'ah (bē-á-lī'á; *whose Lord is Jehovah*), one of the Benjamite heroes who went over to David at Ziklag (I Chron. 12:5), B. C. before 1000.

Be'aloth (bē'á-lōth).

1. A town in the southern part of Judah, i. e., in Simeon (Josh. 15:24), probably the same as Baalath-beer (19:8).

2. A district in Asher of which Baanah was commissary (I Kings 4:16, "in Aloth;" R. V. "Baloth").

Beam, timber used for building purposes (Matt. 7:3, sq.; Luke 6:41, 42). In the passages referred to reference is made to a common proverb among the Jews, respecting those who with greater sins reproved the lesser faults of others. *See* Mote.

Bean. *See* Animal Kingdom.

Bear. *See* Animal Kingdom.

Beard. *See* Hair.

Beast. *See* Animal Kingdom.

Beast, in a figurative or symbolical sense, is of frequent occurrence in Scripture, and generally refers to the sensual and groveling or ferocious and brutal natures properly belonging to the brute creation. The psalmist speaks of himself as being "like a beast before God," while giving way to merely sensuous consid-

erations (Psa. 73:22). The word is sometimes used figuratively of brutal men. Hence the phrase, "I fought with wild beasts at Ephesus" (I Cor. 15:32, comp. Acts 19:29), is a figurative description of a *fight with strong and exasperated enemies*. For a similar use of the word see Eccles. 3:18; II Pet. 2:12; Jude 10.

A wild beast is the symbol of selfish, tyrannical monarchies. The four beasts in Dan. 7:3, 17, 23, represent four kingdoms (Ezek. 34:28; Jer. 12:9).

In the Apocalypse the Beast obviously means a worldly power, whose rising out of the sea indicates that it owes its origin to the commotions of the people (Rev. 13:1; 15:2; 17:8).

The *four beasts* (Gr. *zōa, living creatures*, not *thērion* beast in the strict sense) should be rendered the *four living ones* (Rev. 4:6).

Beating, a punishment in universal use throughout the East. It appears to be designated by the Hebrew phrase "rod of correction" *shēbĕt mūsär*, Prov. 22:15). Beating with rods ("scourging," Lev. 19:20; "chastising," Deut. 22:18) was established by law, and was very common among the Jews (Prov. 10:13; 26:3). The person to be punished was extended upon the ground, and blows, not exceeding forty, were applied to his back in the presence of a judge (Deut. 25:2, 3). Among the Egyptians, ancient and modern, minor offenses were generally punished with the stick, and persons who refused to pay taxes were frequently brought to terms by a vigorous use of the stick. Superintendents were wont to stimulate laborers by the persuasive powers of the rod. The bastinado was inflicted on both sexes. *See* Punishments.

Beb'ai (bē'bā-ī).

1. The head of one of the families that returned with Zerubbabel from Babylon (B. C. about 536) to the number of six hundred and twenty-three (Ezra 2:11) or six hundred and twenty-eight (Neh. 7:16). At a later period twenty-eight more, under Zechariah, returned with Ezra (Ezra 8:11), B. C. about 457. Several of his sons were among those who had taken foreign wives (Ezra 10:28).

2. The name of one who sealed the covenant with Nehemiah (Neh. 10:15), B. C. 445.

Be'cher (bē'kĕr; *firstborn*, or *a young camel*, cf. Arab. *bakr*, young camel).

1. The second son of Benjamin, according to the list of both in Gen. 46:21 and I Chron. 7:6, but omitted in I Chron. 8:1. Some suppose that the word "firstborn" in the latter passage is a corruption of Becher; others, that Becher in the two passages above is a corruption of the word signifying "firstborn." Yet I Chron. 7:8 gives Becher as a person, and names his sons. He was one of the sons of Benjamin that came down to Egypt with Jacob, being one of the fourteen descendants of Rachel who settled there. At the numbering of the Israelites in the plain of Moab (Num. 26) there is no family named after him. But there is a Becher and a family of Bachrites among the sons of Ephraim. This has given rise to the supposition that the slaughter of the sons of Ephraim by the men of Gath had sadly thinned the house of Ephraim of its males, and that Becher, or his heir, married

an Ephraimitish heiress, a daughter of Shu-thelah (I Chron. 7:20, 21), and so his house was reckoned in the house of Ephraim.

2. Son of Ephraim; called Bered (I Chron. 7:20); his posterity were called Bachrites (Num. 26:35). He is probably the same as the preceding.

Becho′rath (bĕ-kō′răth; *firstborn*), the son of Aphiah, of the tribe of Benjamin, one of the ancestors of King Saul (I Sam. 9:1), B. C. long before 1030.

Bed, a common article of domestic furniture. In the ancient Near East, however, the poor and travelers often slept on the ground, using their outer garment as a covering (Gen. 28: 11; Exod. 22:26). Sometimes a bed might be no more than a mat of rough material easily carried about (Matt. 9:6), but regular beds raised above the ground to protect from dampness and drafts were early in existence (Deut. 3:11). The wealthy of Amos' day in the 8th century B. C. had beds of ivory (Amos 6:4) and expensive coverings and cushions (Amos 3:12). Beds of the wealthy often had a canopy. The Jewish bed may be described in five principal parts: a. *Mattress.* A mere matter of one or more garments. b. *Covering.* A finer garment than used for the mattress. In summer, a thin blanket or an outer garment worn by day (I Sam. 19:13) was sufficient. Hence the Mosaic law provided that this garment should not be kept in pledge after sunset, that the poor might not be without his covering (Deut. 24:13). c. *Pillow,* mentioned in I Sam. 19:13, apparently a material woven of goat's hair with which persons in the East covered the head and face while sleeping. d. *The Bedstead.* This was not always necessary. The divan or platform along the side or end of an Oriental room serving as a support for the bed with a frame seems implied in such references as II Sam. 3:31; II Kings 4:10; Esth. 1:6. e. *Ornamental Portions.* These consisted of pillows, a canopy, ivory carvings and probably mosaic work, purple and fine linen (Esth. 1:6, Cant. 3:9, 10; Amos 7:4). *M. F. U.*

Be′dad (bē′dăd; *separation*), the father of Hadad, a king in Edom (Gen. 36:35; I Chron. 1:46).

Be′dan (bē′dăn).

1. The name of a judge of Israel, not found in Judges, but only in I Sam. 12:11. It is difficult to identify him with any of the judges mentioned elsewhere, but it is probable that *Bedan* is a contracted form for the name of the Judge *Abdon* (*q. v.*).

2. The son of Ulam, the great-grandson of Manasseh (I Chron. 7:17).

Bedchamber (Heb. *ḥădăr ḥămmĭṭṭôth, room of beds,* II Kings 11:2; II Chron. 22:11; *ḥădăr mĭshkāb, sleeping room,* Exod. 8:3; II Sam. 4:7; II Kings 6:12). The "bedchamber" in the temple where Joash was hidden was probably a store chamber for keeping beds (II Kings 11:2; II Chron. 22:11). The position of the bedchamber in the most remote and secret parts of the palace seems marked in the passages, Exod. 8:3; II Kings 6:12.

Bede′iah (bĕ-dē′yȧ), one of the family of Bani, who divorced his Gentile wife on the return from Babylon (Ezra 10:35), B. C. 456.

Bedstead. *See* Bed.

Bee. *See* Animal Kingdom.

Beeli′ada (bē′ē-lī′ȧ-dȧ; *Baal has known*), one of David's sons, born in Jerusalem (I Chron. 14:7), B. C. after 1000. He is called Eliada (II Sam. 5:16; I Chron. 3:8).

Beel′zebub (bē-ĕl′zē-bŭb), a heathen deity, believed to be the prince of evil spirits (Matt. 10:25; 12:24, 27; Mark 3:22; Luke 11:15, sq.). By some Beelzebub is thought to mean *ba′al zebul,* the *dung-god,* an expression intended to designate with loathing the prince of all moral impurity. It is supposed, at the same time, that the name Beelzebub, the Philistine god of flies, was changed to Beelze*bul* ("god of dung"), and employed in an approbrious way as a name of the devil. Others prefer to derive the word from *ba′al zebul,* the *lord of the dwelling,* in which evil spirits dwell. The fact that Jesus designates himself as "master of the house" would seem to indicate that Beelzeboul had a similar meaning. *See* Gods, False.

Be′er (bē′ĕr; Heb. *b°′ēr,* an artificial *well,* distinguished from En, a *natural* spring). It is usually combined with other words as a prefix, but two places are known by this name simply:

1. A place in the desert on the confines of Moab, where the Hebrew princes dug a well with their staves and received a miraculous supply of water (Num. 21:16-18). It is probably the same as Beer-elim (Isa. 15:8).

2. A town in Judah to which Jotham fled for fear of Abimelech (Judg. 9:21), probably about eight Roman miles N. of Eleutheropolis, the present *el Bireh,* near the mouth of the Wady es Surâr.

Bee′ra (bē-ē′rȧ; a *well*), the last given of the sons of Zophah, a descendant of Asher (I Chron. 7:37).

Bee′rah (bē-ē′rȧ; a *well*), the son of Baal, a prince of the tribe of Reuben, and carried into captivity by the Assyrian Tiglath-pileser (I Chron. 5:6).

Be′er-e′lim (bē′ĕr-ē′lĭm; *well of heroes*), a spot named in Isa. 15:8 as on the "border of Moab," probably the S., Eglaim being on the N. end of the Dead Sea. It seems to be the same as Beer (Num. 21:16).

Bee′ri (bē-ē′rĭ; *of a fountain,* or *well*).

1. A Hittite, and father of Judith, a wife of Esau (Gen. 26:34), B. C. about 1950.

2. The father of the prophet Hosea (Hos. 1:1), B. C. before 748.

Be′er-lahai′-roi (bē′ĕr-lȧ-hī′roi; *the well of him that liveth and seeth me,* or *the well of the vision of life*), the fountain between Kadesh and Bered, near which the Lord found Hagar (Gen. 16:7, 14). In Gen. 24:62; 25:11, the A. V. has "the well of Lahai-roi."

Bee′roth (bē-ē′rŏth; *wells*).

1. One of the four cities of the Hivites who made a league with Joshua (Josh. 9:17). Beeroth was allotted to Benjamin (Josh. 18: 25), in whose possession it continued at the time of David, the murderers of Ish-bosheth belonging to it (II Sam. 4:2). Beeroth, with Chephirah and Kirjath-jearim, is in the list of those who returned from Babylon (Ezra 2:25; Neh. 7:29).

2. Beeroth of the children of Jaakan is named (Num. 33:31, 32; Deut. 10:6) as a place through which the Israelites twice

passed in the desert, being their twenty-seventh and thirty-third station on their way from Egypt to Canaan, probably in the valley of the Arabah.

Bee′rothite (bê-ê′rô-thīt), an inhabitant of *Beeroth* (*q. v.*) of Benjamin (II Sam. 4:2; 23:37).

Be′er-sheba (bē′ĕr-shē′bà; *well of the oath*, or *of seven*), a city in the southern part of Palestine, about midway between the Mediterranean Sea and the southern end of the Dead Sea. It received its name because of the digging of the well and making of a compact between Abraham and Abimelech (Gen. 21:31). It was a favorite residence of Abraham and Isaac (Gen. 26:33). The latter was living

65. Main Street, Beersheba

there when Esau sold his birthright to Jacob, and from the encampment round the wells Jacob started on this journey to Mesopotamia. He halted there to offer sacrifice to "the God of his father" on his way to Egypt. Beer-sheba was allotted to Simeon (I Chron. 4:28), and Samuel's sons were appointed deputy judges for the southernmost districts in Beer-sheba (I Sam. 8:2). Elijah fled to Beer-sheba, which was still a refuge in the 8th century, and frequented even by northern Israel (Amos 5:5; 8:14). The expression "from Dan to Beer-sheba" was a formula for the whole land. During the separation of the kingdoms the formula became *from Geba to Beer-sheba*, or *from Beer-sheba to Mount Ephraim*. After the exile Beer-sheba was again peopled by Jews, and the formula ran *from Beer-sheba to the valley of Hinnom* (Neh. 11:27, 30). There are still seven wells at Beer-sheba, and to the N., on the hills that bound the valley, are scattered ruins nearly three miles in circumference.

Beeshte′rah (bē′ĕsh-tē′rà), one of the two Levitical cities allotted to the Gershonites, out of the tribe of Manasseh beyond Jordan (Josh. 21:27). In the parallel list (I Chron. 6:71) Ashtaroth is given; and Beeshterah is only a contracted form of *Beth-Ashtaroth*, the "temple of Ashtoreth."

Beetle. See Animal Kingdom.

Beeves. See Animal Kingdom.

Beggar (Heb. *'ĕbyōn, destitute*, I Sam. 2:8; Gr. *ptōchos*, Luke 16:20, 22; Gal. 4:9; elsewhere *poor*). A beggar, whose regular business it was to solicit alms publicly, or to go promiscuously from door to door, as understood by us, was unknown to the Pentateuchal legislation. The poor were allowed privileges by the Mosaic

law, and indeed the Hebrew could not be an absolute pauper. His land was inalienable, except for a certain period, when it reverted to him or his posterity, and if this resource was insufficient he could pledge the services of himself and family for a valuable sum. In the song of Hannah (I Sam. 2:8), however, beggars are spoken of, and beggary is predicted of the posterity of the wicked, while it was promised not to be the portion of the seed of the righteous (Psa. 109:10; 37:25); so that then the practice was probable, though not uncommon. In the New Testament we read of beggars that were blind, diseased, and maimed seeking alms at the doors of the rich, by the waysides, and before the gate of the temple (Mark 10:46; Luke 16:20, 21; Acts 3:2).

Beginning (Heb. *rē′shîth, first*). "In the beginning" (Gen. 1:1) is used in an absolute sense. However, the "beginning" of John 1:1 used of Christ, the Logos, antedates that of Gen. 1:1, and refers to the eternal preëxistence of the Son. Gen. 1:1 merely gives the commencement of the physical universe and time. The "beginning" of I John 1:1 evidently refers to the commencement of Christ's public ministry.

　　Our Lord is styled the Beginning (Gr. *′Archē*) by both Paul and John (Col. 1:18; Rev. 1:8; 3:14), and it is worthy of remark that the Greek philosophers expressed the First Cause of all things by the same name.

Behead. See Punishment.

Behemoth (bĕ-hē′mŏth). See Animal Kingdom.

Be′kah (bē′kà), an early Jewish weight, being half a shekel. See Metrology, III.

Bel, the national god of Babylonia. See Gods, False.

Be′la (bē′là; *swallowed*).

　　1. A king of Edom, the son of Beor, and a native of the city of Dinhabah (Gen. 36:32, 33; I Chron. 1:43). From the name of his father, Beor, we may infer that he was a Chaldean by birth, and reigned in Edom by conquest. He may have been contemporary with Moses and Balaam.

　　2. The eldest son of Benjamin (Gen. 46:21; I Chron. 7:6, 7; 8:3), B. C. about 1640. From him came the family of the Belaites (Num. 26:38).

　　3. A son of Azaz, a Reubenite (I Chron. 5:8), "who dwelt in Aroer even unto Nebo and Baalmeon."

　　4. Another name (Gen. 14:2, 8) for the city of *Zoar* (*q. v.*).

Be′lah (bē′là), a less correct mode of Anglicizing (Gen. 46:21) the name *Bela* (*q. v.*), the son of Benjamin.

Be′laite (bē′là-īt), the patronymic (Num. 26:38) of the descendants of *Bela*, 2 (*q. v.*).

Be′lial (bē′lĭ-ăl), *worthlessness, wickedness*. Belial is often used in the A. V. as if it were a proper name, but beyond question it should not be regarded in the Old Testament as such; its meaning being *worthlessness*, and hence *recklessness, lawlessness*. The expression "son" or "man of Belial" must be understood as meaning simply a worthless, lawless fellow (Deut. 13:13; Judge. 19:22; 20:13, etc.).

　　In the New Testament the term appears (in the best manuscripts) in the form *Belias*, and not *Belial*, as given in A. V. The term, as used in II Cor. 6:15, is generally understood as applied to Satan, as the personification of all that is bad.

Believe. "To remain steadfast" (Heb. *'ămăn*, Gen. 15:6; Exod. 4:1; Num. 14:11, etc.). "To be persuaded" of God's revealed truth (Gr. *peithomai*, Acts 17:4; 27:11; 28:24). "To adhere to, rely on" God's promises (Gr. *pisteuō*, Matt. 8:13; Mark 5:36; John 3:16, etc.). Although belief as mere credence or confidence is exceedingly common and often the result of ignorance or deception, and not reposed in facts of knowledge or truth, yet in a Scriptural sense faith in its larger usage represents four principal ideas. The first is personal confidence in God; second, a creedal or doctrinal concept of the essential body of revealed truth (Luke 18:8; I Cor. 16:13; II Cor. 13:5, Col. 1:23; 2:7; Titus 1:13; Jude 1:3); third, faithfulness as an evidence or fruit of the believer's trust in God (Gal. 5:22, 23); fourth, a designation for Christ as the object of faith (Gal. 3:23, 25). As personal confidence in God, it is of immense importance clearly to distinguish three features of faith. (1) **Saving faith**, is inwrought confidence in God's promises and provisions in Christ for the salvation of sinners. It leads one to trust solely in the person and work of the Savior Jesus Christ (John 3:16; 5:24; Eph. 2:8-10). Such faith gives the believer an unchangeable and unforfeitable *position* described in innumerable passages as being "in Christ" (Rom. 8:1; Eph. 1:3, etc.). (2) **Sanctifying faith**, comprehends *knowledge* of and *trust* in our *position* "in Christ" (Rom. 6:1-10), so that one has experiential *possession* of Christ (Rom. 6:11). Compare Ephesians 1-3, setting forth the believer's position with Ephesians 4-6, his experience of that position. Sanctifying or sustaining faith appropriates the power of God for conforming one's position in Christ to one's enjoyment of the blessings of that position, but in no sense is it to be confused with saving faith, which results in that position. *All* believers have a *position* of sanctification (I Cor. 1:2 with 3:1-3; 5:5) and are "saints," and by faith are to realize that position in practice in living a saintly life (Eph. 4:1; Col. 3:1-4). All believers who have exercised "saving faith" in Christ *are* what they are "in Him," whether or not they ever realize it. The difference is that when they realize it and in faith act upon it, they begin to enjoy the benefits of it in daily living. (3) **Serving faith**, which acts upon the truth of divinely bestowed spiritual gifts and reposes confidence in all the details of divine enablement and appointments for service. "Hast thou faith? have it to thyself before God" (Rom. 14:22). This faith is accordingly a personal, individual matter. *M. F. U. See* also Faith.

Believers (Gr. *pistoi*), a term applied to Christian converts (Acts 5:14; I Tim. 4:12). It signifies those who have exercised saving faith in the person and work of Jesus Christ and who, as a result, have obtained a position which is denoted by the oft-recurring phrase in the New Testament "in Christ" (Eph. 1:3; I Cor. 1:2; Rom. 8:1, etc.). This "in-Christ" position wrought by the baptizing work of the Holy Spirit (I Cor. 12:13; Rom. 6:3, 4; Gal. 3:27; Col. 2:9-12) is the basis of all the believer's spiritual possessions. The New Testament presents Christian obligation as living in accordance with this position (Eph. 4:1; Rom. 6:11). The New Testament, therefore, presents the believer's position as unchangeable and unforfeitable as a result of the efficacy of Christ's atoning work and God's faithfulness. *M. F. U.*

Bell (Heb. *pă'ămōn*, something *struck*, Exod. 28:33, 34; 39:25, 26; *mĕşîllāh*, tinkling, Zech. 14:20). The bell is closely allied to the cymbal. The indentation of cymbals would be found to add to their vibrating power and sonority, and as this indentation became exaggerated nothing would be more probable than that they should eventually be formed into half-globes. This form is found in Roman and Greek sculpture. The most ancient bells yet discovered consist of a plate of metal, bent round and rudely riveted where the edges meet. Such were in use among the Assyrians and ancient Chinese.

1. Small golden bells were attached to the lower part of the blue robe (robe of the ephod) which formed part of the official dress of the high priest. These may have been partly for ornament, but partly also for use, to ring as often as the high priest moved, so as to announce his approach and retirement (Exod. 28:33-35).

2. In Isa. 3:16-18 reference is made to little tinkling bells, which are worn to this day by women upon their wrists and ankles to attract attention and gain admiration.

3. "Bells of the horses" (Zech. 14:20) were probably concave pieces or plates of brass, which were sometimes attached to horses for the sake of ornament. These by their tinkling served to enliven the animals, and in the caravans served the purpose of our modern sheep bells. In the passage referred to the motto "Holiness to the Lord," which the high priest wore upon his miter, being also inscribed upon the bells of horses, predicted the coming of a millennial age when all things, even to the lowest, should be sanctified to God.

Bellows (*blower*), Jer. 6:29 only, though other passages which speak of blowing the fire (Isa. 54:16; Ezek. 22:21), may refer to them; but as wood was the common fuel in ancient times, and kindles readily, a fan would generally be sufficient. Bellows seem to have been of great antiquity in Egypt, and were used at the forge or furnace. They were worked by the foot of the operator, pressing alternately upon two skins till they were exhausted, and pulling up each exhausted skin with a string held in his hand. The earliest specimens seem to have been simply of reed tipped with a metal point where it came in contact with the fire.

Belly (Heb. usually *bĕţĕn*, hollow; Gr. *koilia*; also Heb. *mē'îm*; Gr. *gaster*, especially the *bowels*). Among the Hebrews and most ancient nations the belly was regarded as the seat of the carnal affections, as being, according to their view, that which first partakes of sensual pleasures (Tit. 1:12; Phil. 3:19; Rom. 16:18).

Figurative. It is used figuratively for **the**

heart, the innermost recesses of the soul (Prov. 18:8; 20:27; 26:22). The "belly of hell," literally, "out of the womb of the nether world," is a strong phrase to express Jonah's dreadful condition in the deep (Jonah 2:2).

Belomancy, divination by arrows. *See* Magic.

Belshaz'zar (Bĕl-shăz'ĕr; Akkad. *Bel-shar-uṣur*, "may Bel protect the king") was the eldest son and co-regent of Nabonidus (B. C. 539), the last sovereign of the Neo-Babylonian Empire. The following passage explicitly states that before Nabonidus started on his expedition to Tema in Arabia he entrusted actual kingship to Belshazzar: "He entrusted a campaign to his eldest, firstborn son; the troops of the land he sent with him. He freed his hand, he entrusted the kingship to him. Then he himself undertook a distant campaign. The power of the land of Akkad advanced with him; towards Tema in the midst of the Westland he set his face. . . . He himself established his dwelling in Tema. . . . That city he made glorious. . . . They made it like a palace of Babylon . . ." The Babylonian records indicate that Belshazzar became co-regent in the third year of Nabonidus' reign (B. C. 553) and continued in that capacity until the fall of Babylon (B. C. 539). The Nabunaid Chronicle states that in the 7th, 9th, 10th and 11th year "the king was in the city of Tema. The son of the king, the princes and the troops were in the land of Akkad (Babylonia)." During Nabonidus' absence in Tema, the Nabunaid Chronicle explicitly indicates that the New Year's Festival was not celebrated but that it was observed in the 17th year upon the king's return home. Accordingly, it is evident that Belshazzar actually exercised the co-regency in Babylon and that the Babylonian records in a remarkable manner supplement the Biblical notices (Dan. 5; 7:1; 8:1). The Book of Daniel is thus not in error in representing Belshazzar as the last king of Babylon, as negative criticism was once so sure, nor can it be said to be wrong in calling Belshazzar "the son of Nebuchadnezzar" (Dan. 5:1). Even if Belshazzar were not lineally related to Nebuchadnezzar, which is doubtful since his mother, Nitocris, was evidently Nebuchadnezzar's daughter, the usage "son of," being equivalent in Semitic usage to "successor of," in the case of royalty would in this case still not be inaccurate. (cf. R. P. Dougherty, *Nabonidus and Belshazzar*, New Haven, 1929). In the Assyrian records Jehu is styled "the son of Omri;" actually Jehu was only a royal successor with no lineal relation at all. *M. F. U.*

Belteshaz'zar (bĕl-tē-shăz'ĕr; Akkad., *Balaṭsu-uṣur* (*Bel*), *protect his life*), the Babylonian name given to the prophet Daniel (Dan.1:7). *See* Daniel.

Ben (*son*), a Levite "of the second degree," one of the porters appointed by David to the service of the ark (I Chron. 15:18), B. C. 988.

Ben (Heb. *bĕn, son of*), often used as a prefix to proper names in Scripture, the following word being either a proper name, an appellative or geographical location, or even a number expressing age. Thus, a "son of 20 years" would mean 20 years old. Hadadezer Ben-rehob (II Sam. 8:3) would mean Hadadezer of

Beth-rehob, born or brought up in that place A "son of valor" (Heb. *bĕn ḥăyĭl*, Deut. 3:18) would mean a valorous one. *Son of* may, of course, mean a lineal father-son relationship, as with us (Gen. 4:25), or contrary to our usage to bear a more remote descendant as a grandchild (Gen. 46:24; II Kings 9:2, 20) or a great grandchild (Gen. 46:18). The Israelites were known as "the sons of Israel" (or Jacob) for centuries after the death of the patriarch (Mal. 3:6). The 70 souls that "came out of the loins of Jacob" (Exod. 1:5) included grandchildren. Usage extends to tribes or countries (Gen. 10:20-22), or even to a non-blood relation. Jehu, a usurper and founder of a new dynasty in Israel, and with no blood relationship whatever to the house of Omri is nevertheless styled "the son of Omri" in the Black Obelisk of Shalmanezer III of Assyria (D. D. Luckenbill, *Ancient Records of Assyria and Babylonia* I:590). *M. F. U.*

Bena'iah (bê-nā'yȧ; *built by Jehovah*).

1. The son of Jehoiada the chief priest (I Chron. 27:5), and a native of Kabzeel (II Sam. 23:20; I Chron. 11:22). He was placed by David (I Chron. 11:25) over his bodyguard of Cherethites and Pelethites (II Sam. 8:18; I Kings 1:38; I Chron. 18:17; II Sam. 20:23), and given a position above "the thirty" but not included among the "first three" of the mighty men (II Sam. 23:22, 23; I Chron. 11:24, 25; 27:6). He was a very valiant man and his exploits against man and beast which gave him rank are recorded in II Sam. 23:21; I Chron. 11:22. He was captain of the host for the third month (I Chron. 27:5). Benaiah remained faithful to Solomon during Adonijah's attempt on the crown (I Kings 1:8, sq.). Acting under Solomon's orders he slew Joab, and was appointed to fill his position as commander of the army (I Kings 2:35; 4:4), c. B. C. 938. Jehoiada the son of Benaiah, succeeded Ahithophel about the person of the king according to I Chron. 27:34. This is possibly a copyist's mistake for "Benaiah the son of Jehoiada."

2. A man of Pirathon, of the tribe of Ephraim, one of David's thirty mighty men (II Sam. 23:30; I Chron. 11:31), and the captain of the host for the eleventh month (I Chron. 27:14) B. C. 1000.

3. One of the princes of the families of Simeon, who dispossessed the Amalekites from the pasture grounds of Gedor (I Chron. 4:36), B. C. about 715.

4. A Levite in the time of David who "played with the psaltery on Alamoth" at the removal of the ark (I Chron. 15:18, 20; 16:5), B. C. about 990.

5. A priest appointed to blow the trumpet before the ark when David caused it to be removed to Jerusalem (I Chron. 15:24; 16:6), B. C. about 990.

6. A Levite of the sons of Asaph, the son of Jeiel and grandfather of Jahaziel, which latter was sent by God to encourage the army of Jehoshaphat against the Moabites (II Chron. 20:14), B. C. about 875.

7. A Levite in the time of Hezekiah who was one of the overseers of the offerings to the Temple (II Chron. 31:13), B. C. 726.

8-11. Four Jews who had taken Gentile

wives after the return from Babylon, B. C. 456. They were respectively of the "sons" of Parosh (Ezra 10:25), Pahath-moab (v. 30) Bani (v. 35), and Nebo (v. 43).

12. The father of Pelatiah, which latter was a "prince of the people" in the time of Ezekiel (Ezek. 11:1), B. C. before 592.

Ben-am′mi (bĕn-ăm′ĭ; *son of my kindred,*) son of Lot by his youngest daughter. He was the progenitor of the Ammonites (Gen. 19:38), B. C. 20th century.

Bench (Heb. *qĕrĕsh*, a *plank*, usually rendered *board*), once the rowing benches of a ship (Ezek. 27:6). The same Hebrew term is used (Exod. 26:15, sq.) for the boards of the *Tabernacle* (*q. v.*). *See* Chittim.

Ben′e-be′rak (bĕn′ĕ-bē′răk; *sons of lightning*), one of the cities of Dan (Josh. 19:45), the present Ibn Abrak, 4 mi. E. of Joppa. Sennacherib mentions it as one of the cities besieged and taken by him.

Benediction, an essential form of public worship was the priestly benediction, the form of which is prescribed in the law, "The Lord bless thee, and keep thee: the Lord make his face shine upon thee, and be gracious unto thee: the Lord lift up his countenance upon thee, and give thee peace" (Num. 6:24-26), the promise being added that God would fulfill the words of the blessing. This blessing was pronounced by the priest, after every morning and evening sacrifice, with uplifted hands, as recorded of Aaron (Lev. 9:22), the people responding by uttering an amen. This blessing was also regularly pronounced at the close of the service in the synagogues. The Levites appear also to have had the power of giving the blessing (II Chron. 30:27), and the same privilege was accorded the king, as the viceroy of the Most High (II Sam. 6:18; I Kings 8:55). Our Lord is spoken of as blessing little children (Mark 10:16; Luke 24:50), besides the blessing on the occasion of the institution of the Eucharist (Matt. 26:26).

Ben′e-ja′akan (bĕn′ē-jā′à-kăn; *children of Jaakan*), a tribe which gave their name to certain wells in the desert which formed one of the halting places of the Israelites on their journey to Canaan (Num. 33:31, 32). "*Bene-Jaakan* is simply an abbreviation of *Beeroth-bene-Jaakan*, wells of the children of *Jaakan*. Now if the children of Jaakan were the same as the Horite family of *Jakan* mentioned in Gen. 36:27, the wells of *Jaakan* would have to be sought for on the mountains that bound the *Arabah*" (K. and D., *Com.*, in loc.).

Ben′e-ke′dem (bĕn′ē-kē′dĕm; "sons of the East" i. e. "Easterners"), a people or peoples dwelling to the E. of Jordan, by which we are to understand not so much the Arabian desert, that reaches to the Euphrates, as Mesopotamia (Gen. 29:1; Job. 1:3; Judg. 6:3, 33; 7:12; 8:10, etc.).

Benevolence, Due (Gr. *hē opheilomenē eunoia* R. S. V. "conjugal rights"), a euphemism for marital duty (I Cor. 7:3).

Benha′dad (bĕn-hā′dăd), Heb. form of Aram. Bar-Hadad, *son of the god Hadad.*

1. **The Early Kings of Damascus.** The succession of Syrian kings who reigned at Damascus and elevated the city state to the height of its power. Under them it became the

inveterate foe of Israel for a full century and a half after B. C. 925. Biblical reference to the Ben-Hadads has been remarkably illuminated by archaeology as a result of the discovery of the inscribed stele of Ben-Hadad I, recovered in north Syria in 1940. This important royal inscription in general confirms the order of early Syrian rulers as given in I Kings 15:18, where Ben-Hadad is said to be the "son of Tabrimmon, the son of Hezion, king of Aram, who dwelled in Damascus." According to W. F. Albright's rendering of the Ben-Hadad monument, with the somewhat precarious restoration of the partly undecipherable portion, the sequence is identical: "Bir-Hadad, son of Tab-ramman, son of Hadyan, king of Aram." (cf. *Bulletin of Am. Schools of Oriental Research*, No. 87, Oct., 1942, pp. 23-29; No. 90, April, 1943, pp. 32-34). Bir Hadad is equivalent to Bar-Hadad (Heb. Ben-Hadad) and Tab-ramman and Hadyan are equatable with Heb. Tabrimmon and Hezion. The correct name of the first king of Damascus has been corroborated by archaeological evidence, but the identity of Rezon who seized Damascus during Solomon's reign and apparently ruled there (I Kings 11:23-25) is still unsolved. Is Hezion the same as Reson? If so, then the form Reson is secondary and may be regarded as a corruption of Hezion. If this is not the case, which apparently is unlikely, Rezon must be excluded from the dynastic list of I Kings 15:18, which is improbable since he was ostensibly the founder of the powerful Damascene state.

2. **Ben Hadad I.** By the time Ben Hadad entered into the succession of Syrian kings somewhere around B. C. 890, Syria had become the strongest state in this region of W. Asia and was ready to seize any opportunity to increase its territories. Such an occasion offered itself when the hard-pressed Asa, king of Judah (c. B. C. 917-876), sent an urgent appeal to Syria for help against Baasha, king of Israel (c. B. C. 900-877). Baasha pushing his frontier southward to within five miles of Jerusalem, proceeded to fortify Ramah as a border fortress commanding the capital of Judah (I Kings 15:17). Asa desperately sent what was left of the temple and royal treasury, despoiled so recently by the Egyptian pharoah Shishak, to Ben-Hadad as a bribe to entice Syria into an alliance with himself against Israel. This strategy was at least immediately successful for Ben-Hadad invaded northern Israel and forced Baasha to abandon Ramah (I Kings 15:20-22). But Asa committed a grievous mistake, for in courting the favor of Damascus against Israel, he granted Ben-Hadad an unparalleled opportunity for aggrandizement and gave a common enemy of both the Northern and the Southern Kingdoms a great advantage.

Formerly scholars almost universally distinguished between Ben-Hadad I, son of Tabrimmon, son of Hezion the contemporary of Asa and Baasha (I Kings 15:18) and Ben-Hadad the contemporary of Elijah and Elisha. Only occasionally did a Biblical scholar such as T. K. Cheyne recognize the possibility that the two might be identical (*Ency. Biblia*, Vol.

I, p. 531f). The majority, however, maintained that the so-called Ben-Hadad I died during the early years of the reign of Omri or Ahab (c. B. C. 865) and was succeeded by Ben-Hadad II. However, evidence furnished by the stele of Ben-Hadad I argues strongly for the identity of Ben-Hadad I and Ben-Hadad II (cf. *Bulletin of Am. Schools*, No. 83, pp. 14-22). In addition, careful research on the vexing problems of the chronology of the kings of Israel and Judah of this period has resulted in the reduction of regnal years, notably of Israel's kings, and obviated any serious objection to the equation on the grounds of an impossibly long reign for Ben-Hadad I.

A further argument commonly urged against the identification of Ben-Hadad I with Ben-Hadad II is the word of the vanquished Syrian monarch to King Ahab of Israel after the latter's notable victory at Aphek (modern Fiq) 3 miles E. of the Sea of Galilee, recorded in I Kings 20:34: "The towns which my father took from thy father I will restore. Thou shalt set up markets for thyself in Damascus as my father did in Samaria." This allusion can hardly be to Ahab's father Omri (c. B. C. 876-869) who founded the metropolis of Samaria as the capital of the Northern Kingdom, for available sources do not lend the least support to the hypothesis that the latter incurred a defeat in a coalition with Syria. The term "father," especially when used of royalty, must frequently be construed as "predecessor," as is commonly illustrated by the monuments. Doubtless towns taken from Israel by early Syrian kings such as Hezion or Tabrimmon are meant. Ben-Hadad's use of the term "Samaria" was evidently formulaic. The city had been so strategically situated and enjoyed such a prosperous growth that very soon after its establishment by Omri its name was used of the whole Northern Kingdom of which it was the capital. Ben-Hadad I warred against Ahab of Israel (I Kings 20:1). Ahab's brilliant strategy not only won this battle but also the one during the following year at Aphek (I Kings 20:26-43).

The next year, however, the appearance on the horizon of a powerful Assyrian army marching toward Syria-Palestine compelled Ahab and his hereditary foe Ben-Hadad to align themselves in a general coalition of neighboring kings to block the ambitious Assyrian invasion southward. The Monolith Inscription now in the British Museum records the military expeditions of Shalmaneser III (B. C. 859-824) and includes a description of his clash with the Assyrian coalition headed by "Hadadezer (Ben-Hadad), of Aram, (Damascus)" in B. C. 853. The battle took place at Karkar north of Hamath in the Orontes Valley, a strategic fortress city which guarded the approaches of lower Syria. Ahab "of Israel" is mentioned along with Ben-Hadad of Damascus. Ben-Hadad furnished 1200 chariots as over against Ahab's 2000, but Hadadezer (Ben-Hadad) furnished twice as many soldiers, 20,000 over against Ahab's 10,000. Shalmaneser's venture was evidently not very successful, despite his extravagant boasts. In B. C. 848 Shalmaneser III made another

thrust into Syria. He was again met by a coalition of "twelve kings of the seaboard" headed by Adadidri (Hadadezer of Damascus, i. e. Ben-Hadad I). Ben Hadad I's long energetic reign came to an end about B. C. 843 and by B. C. 841 Hazael, an influential official, had succeeded to the throne.

3. **Ben-Hadad II**, another Aramean king who ruled at Damascus. He was the son of Hazael. The latter sat on the throne at Damascus from c. B. C. 841-801. Ben-Hadad II was a weak ruler who signally failed to protect the far-reaching conquests of his father, Hazael, and Israel began to regain its fortunes. Although Aramaean power suffered in south Syria, Ben-Hadad II displayed remarkable vitality in the north, as shown by the important Stele of Zakir, king of Hamath, discovered in 1903 at modern Afis, S. W. of Aleppo in northern Syria. This significant monument, published by its discoverer H. Pognon in 1907, makes reference in lines 4 and 5 to Ben-Hadad II under the Aramaic form of his name "Bar Hadad, son of Hazael, king of Aram." He is presented as heading a coalition of kings against "Zakir, king of Hamath and Luash." The cause of the attack was the merger of two powerful independent states, Hamath and Luash. This political maneuver so upset the balance of power in Syria and was attended with such a serious threat to the autonomy of Damascus and other Syrian states that they were ready to go to war in order to break it up. Ben-Hadad II especially had reason to be made sensitive to any added threat to Syrian power since his losses to Israel in the south had seriously curtailed his sway in that direction. Zakir's victory over the coalition, in the celebration of which he set up his stele, furnished another indication of the essential weakness of Ben-Hadad II's might. In fact, his reign made possible Israel's power under Jeroboam II (c. B. C. 786-746). *M. F. U.*

Ben-ha′il (bĕn-hā′ĭl; *son of strength,* that is, *warrior*), one of the "princes" of the people sent by Jehoshaphat to teach the inhabitants of Judah (II Chron. 17:7), B. C. 875.

Ben-ha′nan (bĕn-hā′năn; *son of* one *gracious*), the third named of the four "sons" of Shimon, of the tribe of Judah (I Chron. 4:20).

Beni′nu (bē-nī′nū; *our son*), a Levite who sealed the covenant with Nehemiah (Neh. 10:13), B. C. 445.

Ben′jamin (bĕn′jà-mĭn; *son of my right hand,* or perhaps, "son of the South," Southerner).

1. The youngest of the sons of Jacob, and the second by Rachel (Gen. 35:18), born B. C. about 1900.

Personal History. Benjamin was probably the only son of Jacob born in Palestine. His birth took place on the road between Beth-el and Ephrath (Bethlehem), a short distance from the latter. His mother died immediately, and with her last breath named him Ben-oni (*son of my pain*), which name the father changed. We hear nothing more of Benjamin until the time when his brethren went into Egypt to buy food. Jacob kept him at home, for he said, "Lest peradventure mischief befall him" (Gen. 42:4). The story of his going to Joseph, the silver cup, his apprehension, etc., is familiar, and discloses nothing beyond a very strong affection manifested for him by his father and brethren.

The Tribe of Benjamin. In Gen. 46:21 the immediate descendants of Benjamin are given to the number of *ten*, whereas in Num. 26:38-40, only seven are enumerated, and some even under different names. This difference may probably be owing to the circumstance that some of the direct descendants of Benjamin died at an early period, or, at least, childless. (1) **Numbers.** At the first census the tribe numbered thirty-five thousand four hundred, ranking *eleventh*, but increased to forty-five thousand six hundred at the second census, ranking *seventh*. (2) **Position.** During the wilderness journey Benjamin's position was on the W. side of the tabernacle with his brother tribes of Ephraim and Manasseh (Num. 2:18-24). We have the names of the "captain" of the tribe when it set out on its long road (Num. 2:22); of the spy (13:9); of the families of which the tribe consisted when it was marshaled at the great halt in the plains of Moab, near Jericho (Num. 26:38-41, 63), and of the "prince" who was chosen to assist at the dividing of the land (Num. 34:21). (3) **Territory.** The proximity of Benjamin to Ephraim during the march to the promised land was maintained in the territories allotted to each. Benjamin lay immediately to the S. of Ephraim, and between him and Judah. (4) **Subsequent history.** We may mention, among the events of note, that they assisted Deborah. (Judg. 5:14); they were invaded by the Ammonites (10:9); that they were almost exterminated by the other tribes because they refused to give up the miscreants of Gibeah (chs. 19, 20); that the remaining six hundred were furnished with wives at Jabesh-gilead and Shiloh (ch. 21). To Benjamin belongs the distinction of giving the first king to the Jews, Saul being a Benjamite (I Sam. 9:1; 10:20, 21). After the death of Saul they declared themselves for Ish-bosheth (II Sam. 2:15, sq.; I Chron. 12:29). They returned to David (II Sam. 3:19; 19:16, 17). David having at last expelled the Jebusites from Zion, and made it his own residence, the close alliance between Benjamin and Judah (Judg. 1:8) was cemented by the circumstance that while Jerusalem actually belonged to the district of Benjamin, that of Judah was immediately contiguous to it. After the death of Solomon, Benjamin espoused the cause of Judah, and the two formed a kingdom by themselves. After the exile, also, these two tribes constituted the flower of the new Jewish colony (comp. Ezra 4:1; 10:9). The prediction of Jacob regarding Benjamin's future lot, or the development of his personal character in his tribe, is brief: "Benjamin shall raven as a wolf: in the morning he shall devour the prey, and at night he shall divide the spoil" (Gen. 49:27). The events of history cast light on that prediction, for the ravening of the wolf is seen in the exploits of Ehud the Benjamite (Judg. 3), and in Saul's career, and especially in the whole matter of Gibeah, so carefully recorded in Judg. 20. So, again, the fierce wolf is seen in fight in II Sam. 2:15, 16, at Gibeon, and

again in the character of Shimei. Some find much of the wolf of Benjamin in Saul of Tarsus, "making havoc of the Church."

Archaeology. The famous letters from the 18th century B. C. recovered from the site of the Middle-Euphrates city of Mari since 1933 mention the *Banu Yamina*, "sons of the right," i. e. "sons of the South" (Southerners), who were roving Bedouin in this vicinity at the time. Although some scholars (such as H. Parrot) are tempted to connect these wandering bands with the Biblical Benjamites or Benjaminites, and A. Alt allows the possibility, yet the Biblical tribe was born in Palestine and is never said to have been in Mesopotamia at all. The name Benjamin, meaning "Son of the Right," "Son of the South" or "Southerner" was a name likely to occur in various places, especially so at Mari, where the corresponding term "Sons of the Left," i. e. "Sons of the North" or "Northerners" is found. Directions N. and S. in the ancient Near East were determined by facing E. toward the sunrising—so left was North and right was South. Revised *M. F. U.*

2. A man of the tribe of Benjamin, second named of the seven sons of Bilhan, and the head of a family of warriors (I Chron. 7:10).

3. An Israelite, one of the "sons of Harim," who divorced his foreign wife after the exile (Ezra 10:32), B. C. 456. He seems to be the same person who had assisted in rebuilding (Neh. 3:23) and purifying (Neh. 12:34) the walls of Jerusalem.

Ben'jamite (běn'já-mīt; I Sam. 9:21; 22:7; II Sam. 16:11, etc.), the patronymic title of the descendants of the patriarch *Benjamin* (*q. v.*).

Be'no (bē'nō; *his son*), is given as the only son, or the first of the four sons, of Jaaziah the Levite, of the family of Merari, in I Chron. 24:26, 27.

Ben-o'ni (běn-ō'nĭ; *son of my pain*), the name given by the dying Rachel to her youngest son, but afterward changed (Gen. 35:18) by his father to *Benjamin* (*q. v.*).

Ben-Zo'heth (běn-zō'hěth; *son of Zoheth*), a person named (I Chron. 4:20) as the second son of Ishi, a descendant of Judah, or it may be that he was grandson of Ishi, being the son of Zoheth himself.

Be'on (bě-ōn'; perhaps an early scribal error for *Meon*, *q. v.*), one of the places fit for pasturage (Num. 32:3, "a place for cattle"). It is more properly called Beth-baal-meon (Josh. 13:17), more briefly Baal-meon (Num. 32:38), and Beth-meon (Jer. 48:23).

Be'or (bě'ōr; a *torch*).

1. The father of Bela, one of the kings of Edom (Gen. 36:32; I Chron. 1:43).

2. The father of Balaam, the prophet hired by Balak to curse the children of Israel (Num. 22:5), B. C. about 1400. In II Pet. 2:15 he is called Bosor.

Be'ra (bē'rá), king of Sodom at the time of the invasion of the five kings under Chedorlaomer, which was repelled by Abraham (Gen. 14:2, 17, 21), B. C. 21st century.

Ber'achah (běr'á-kä; a *blessing*).

1. One of the thirty Benjamite warriors who joined David at Ziklag (I Chron. 12:3).

2. A valley between Bethlehem and Hebron,

not far from En-gedi; noted as the place where Jehoshaphat overcame the Moabites and Ammonites (II Chron. 20:26).

Berachi'ah (bĕr-á-kī'á; I Chron. 6:39). *See* Berechiah, 2.

Berai'ah (bĕr-á-ī'á; *created by Jehovah*), next to the last named of the sons of Shimhi, and a chief Benjamite of Jerusalem (I Chron. 8:21).

66. Street Scene, Berea

Bere'a (bê-rē'á), a Macedonian city at the foot of Mount Bermius, once a large and populous city, the residence of many Jews, whose character for careful criticism in the study of the Scriptures was commended by St. Paul (Acts 17:10-13). Berea is now known as Verria, a place of some fifteen thousand people.

Berechi'ah (bĕr-á-kī'á; *blessed by Jehovah*).

1. One of the sons (according to most authorities), or a brother of Zerubbabel, of the royal line of Judah (I Chron. 3:20), B. C. 536.

2. The son of Shimea and father of Asaph, the celebrated singer (I Chron. 6:39, A. V., "Berachiah;" 15:17), B. C. 1000. He was one of the "doorkeepers for the ark" when it was removed from the house of Obed-edom (I Chron. 15:23).

3. The son of Asa, and one of the Levites that dwelt in the villages of the Netophathites after the return from Babylon (I Chron. 9:16), B. C. about 536.

4. The son of Meshillemoth, and one of the chiefs of Ephraim, who enforced the prophet Oded's prohibition of the enslavement of their Judaite captives by the warriors of the northern kingdom (II Chron. 28:12), B. C. 741.

5. The son of Meshezabeel and father of Meshullam, who repaired a part of the walls of Jerusalem (Neh. 3:4, 30). His granddaughter was married to Johanan, the son of Tobiah (Neh. 6:18).

6. The son of Iddo and father of Zechariah the prophet (Zech. 1:1, 7), B. C. before 520.

Be'red (bē'rĕd; *hail*).

1. A son of Shuthelah and grandson of Ephraim (I Chron. 7:20), supposed by some to be identical with Becher (Num. 26:35).

2. A town in the S. of Palestine (Gen. 16:14), between which and Kadesh lay the well Lahai-roi; supposed by some to be at El-Khulasah, twelve miles from Beer-sheba.

Be'ri (bē'rî; *well, fountain*), a son of Zophah, and a mighty warrior of the tribe of Asher (I Chron. 7:36).

Beri'ah (bê-rī'á; perhaps *prominent*, cf. Arab. *bara'a to excel*).

1. The last named of the four sons of Asher, and father of Heber and Malchiel (Gen. 46:17; I Chron. 7:30). His descendants were called Beriites (Num. 26:44, 45).

2. A son of Ephraim, so named on account of the state of his father's house when he was born. Some of Ephraim's sons had been slain by men of Gath "because they came down to take away their cattle" (I Chron. 7:23).

3. A Benjamite, and apparently son of Elpaal. He and his brother Shema were ancestors of the inhabitants of Aijalon, and expelled the people of Gath (I Chron. 8:13). His nine sons are enumerated in vers. 14-16.

4. The last named of the four sons of Shimei, a Levite of the family of Gershom (I Chron. 23:10, 11). His posterity was not numerous, and was reckoned with that of his brother Jeush.

Beri'ites (bê-rī'īts), only mentioned in Num. 26:44, and the descendants of *Beriah* (q. v.), son of Asher (Gen. 46:17; Num. 26:45).

Be'rites (bē'rīts), a people only mentioned in II Sam. 20:14, in the account of Joab's pursuit of Sheba, son of Bichri. Being mentioned in connection with Abel and Bethmaachah they seem to have lived in northern Palestine. Thomson (*Land and Book*) places them at Biria, N. of Safed. Biria he identifies with the Beroth, a city of the upper Galilee, not far from Cadesh, where, according to Josephus (*Ant.*, v, i, 18), the northern Canaanite confederacy pitched camp against Joshua. The story is told in Josh. 11, where, however, the camp is located at the waters of Merom.

Be'rith (bē'rīth), the god (Judg. 9:46). *See* Baal-berith, Gods, False.

Berni'ce (bĕr-nī'sē), the eldest daughter of Agrippa I, by his wife Cypros; she was espoused to Marcus, the son of Alexander, and upon his death was married to her uncle Herod, king of Chalcis, by whom she had two sons (Josephus, *Ant.*, xviii, 5, 4; xix, 5, 1). After the death of Herod she lived for some time with her own brother, Agrippa II, probably in incestuous intercourse. She was afterward married to Polemon, King of Cilicia, but soon deserted him and returned to her brother. With him she visited Festus on his appointment as procurator of Judea, when Paul defended himself before them all (Acts 25:13, 23; 26:30). She afterward became the mistress of Vespasian and his son Titus.

Bero'dach-bal'adan (bê-rō'dăk-băl'á-dăn), the king of Babylon who sent friendly letters and a gift to Hezekiah upon hearing of his sickness (II Kings 20:12). He is also called, in Isa. 39:1, *Merodach-baladan* (q. v.).

Beroe'a. *See* Berea.

Bero'thah (bê-rō'thá; Ezek. 47:16), or **Ber'-othai** (bê-rō'thī; *wells*, II Sam. 8:8). Ezekiel mentions Berothah in connection with Hamath and Damascus, as forming the northern boundary of the promised land as restored in his vision. Now identified with Bereitan in the Beqa about 35 miles N. of Damascus.

Be'rothite (bē'rō-thīt) an epithet of Naharai, Joab's armor-bearer (I Chron. 11:39), probably as a native of *Beeroth* (q. v.).

Beryl. *See* Mineral Kingdom.

Be'sai (bē'sī), one of the heads of the Nethinim,

whose descendants returned from Babylon (Ezra 2:49; Neh. 7:52), B. C. 536.

Besode'iah (bĕs-ô-dē'yà; *in the counsel of Jehovah*), the father of Meshullam, which latter repaired "the old gate" of Jerusalem (Neh. 3:6), B. C. 445.

Besom (bē'sŏm; a *broom*, Isa. 14:23, "besom of destruction"). To sweep away, as with a broom, is a metaphor still frequent in the East for utter ruin. Jehovah treats Babylon as rubbish, and sweeps it away, destruction serving him as a broom.

Besor (bē'sōr), a brook flowing into the Mediterranean, about five miles S. of Gaza. The place where two hundred of David's men remained while the other troops pursued the Amalekites (I Sam. 30:9, 10, 21). The present Wady es Sheriah, according to some; others claim its location in the wadi Ghazzeh.

Be'tah (bē'tà; *confidence*), called Tibhath (I Chron. 18:8), a city of Syria-Zobah, captured by David (II Sam. 8:8), and yielding much spoil of "brass." Probably a city on the eastern slope of Anti-Libanus.

Be'ten (bē'tĕn; *belly, hollow*), one of the cities on the border of the tribe of Asher (Josh. 19:25 only). Identified perhaps with *Abtun* E. of Mt. Carmel.

Beth (bĕth; *house*), the name of the second letter of the Hebrew alphabet (corresponding to Greek Beta, Latin B), so-named because originally the representation of a rude dwelling. As an appellative, Beth is the most general word for *house* (Gen. 24:32; 33:17; Judg. 18:31; I Sam. 1:7). From this general use the transition was natural to a house in the sense of a *family*. Beth is frequently employed in combination with other words to form the names of places.

Bethab'ara (bĕth-ăb'á-rà; *house of the ford*), the place on the E. bank of the Jordan where John was baptizing (John 1:28); placed by Conder at the ford 'Abarah, just N. of Beisan. The R. V. reads, "in Bethany beyond Jordan." Many of the best Greek manuscripts have "Bethany" instead of "Bethabara." This is not the Bethany near Jerusalem.

Beth-a'nath (bĕth-ā'năth; *house of (the goddess)*, Anath, modern el-Ba'neh, 12 miles E. of Acre), a fortified city of Naphtali, named with Beth-shemesh (Josh. 19:38; Judg. 1:33), from neither of which the Canaanites were expelled, although made tributaries (Judg. 1:33).

Beth-a'noth (bĕth-ā'nŏth; *house of (the goddess)* Anath), a town in the mountains of Judah (Josh. 15:59).

Beth'any (bĕth'á-nĭ; *house, place of unripe figs*).
1. A place on the E. of Jordan, the name of which is substituted in the R. V. for Bethabara (*see* John 1:28).
2. A village situated on the eastern slope of Mount Olivet, fifteen furlongs (about two miles) from Jerusalem. It is called also the *house of misery* on account of its lonely situation and the invalids who congregated there. It was the home of Lazarus, and associated with important events in Scripture history (Matt. 21:17; 26:6; Mark 11:11; 14:3; Luke 24:50; John 11:1; 12:1); called now Azariyeh, or Lazariyeh, "the place of Lazarus."

Beth-ar'abah (bĕth-ăr'à-bà; *house of the desert*), a town on the N. end of the Dead Sea, and one of six cities belonging to Judah on the N. border of the tribe (Josh. 15:6, 61). It was afterward included in the list of the towns of Benjamin (Josh. 18:22). It is called Arabah in Josh. 18:18.

Beth-a'ram (bĕth-ă'răm; Heb., *Bĕth-häräm*), a town of Gad, opposite Jericho, and 6 miles E. of Jordan (Josh. 13:27). Named Julias, or Livias, by Herod, after the wife of Augustus; and the present Tell er Rameh at the mouth of the Wadi Hesban, a source of celebrated hot springs where king Herod had a palace. Also called *Beth-haran (q. v.)*.

Beth-ar'bel (bĕth-ăr'bĕl; *house of Arbel*). In Hos. 10:14 we read of Ephraim, "All thy fortresses shall be spoiled, as *Shalman (q. v.)* spoiled Beth-arbel in the day of battle." "Beth-arbel is hardly the Arbela of Assyria—which became celebrated through the victory of Alexander—since the Israelites could scarcely have become so well acquainted with such a remote city, but in all probability the Arbela in *Galiloea Superior*, a place in the tribe of Naphtali between Sephoris and Tiberias" (K. and D., *Com.*). It is present-day Irbid, 4 miles N. W. of Tiberias.

Beth-a'ven (bĕth-ā'vĕn; *house of nothingness*, i. e., *idolatry*), a place in the mountains of Benjamin (Josh. 7:2; 18:12; I Sam. 13:5), E. of Beth-el (Josh. 7:2), and between it and Michmash (I Sam. 13:5).

The place mentioned in Hos. 4:15 is not the same, but, as Amos 4:4 and 5:5 clearly show, a name which Hosea adopted from Amos 5:5 for *Beth-el* (the present *Beitin*) to show that *Beth-el*, the house of God, had become Beth-aven, the house of idols, through the setting up of the golden calf there (I Kings 12:29).

Beth-azma'veth (bĕth-ăz-mā'vĕth), a village of Benjamin, the inhabitants of which, forty-two in number, returned with Zerubbabel from Babylon (Neh. 7:28; "Azmaveth," Neh. 12:29; Ezra 2:24). Its present site is Hizmeh, between Geba and Anathoth.

Beth-ba'al-me'on (bĕth-bā'ăl-mē'ŏn; *house of Baal-meon*), one of the places assigned to Reuben in the plains E. of Jordan (Josh. 13:17), known formerly as Baal-meon (Num. 32:38) or Beon (32:3), to which the Beth was possibly a Hebrew prefix. It is identified with the present ruins of Ma'in, in N. Moab, 4 miles S. W. of Medeba. It is mentioned in the Moabite Stone, 9, 30, as held by King Mesha.

67. Bethany

Beth-ba′rah (bĕth-bä′rȧ), a chief ford of Jordan. Possibly the place of Jacob's crossing (Gen. 32:22), S. of the scene of Gideon's victory (Judg. 7:24), and where Jephtha slew the Ephraimites (Judg. 12:4). Not identified.

Beth-bir′ei (bĕth-bĭr′ē-ī), a town of Simeon, inhabited by the descendants of Shimei (I Chron. 4:31); the Beth-lebaoth of Josh. 19:6, or simply Lebaoth (Josh. 15:32). Not identified with any present locality.

Beth′-car (bĕth-kär′; *sheep house*), the place to which the Israelites pursued the Philistines from Mizpah (I Sam. 7:6-12). From the unusual expression, "under Beth-car," it would seem that the place itself was on a height with a road at its foot. Its situation is not known.

Beth-da′gon (bĕth-dā′gŏn; *house of Dagon*, the fish god).

1. A city in the low country of Judah, about five miles from Lydda, near Philistia (Josh. 15:41). Present Khirbet Dajūn.

2. A town near the S. E. border of Asher (Josh. 19:27).

Beth-diblatha′im (bĕth-dĭb-lȧ-thä′yĭm; *house of two cakes of figs*), a city of Moab denounced by Jeremiah (Jer. 48:22); called Almon-diblathaim (Num. 33:46) and Diblath (Ezek. 6:14), a town once in possession of Israel (Moabite Stone, 30).

Beth′-el (bĕth′-ĕl; *house of God*).

1. A town about twelve miles N. of Jerusalem, originally Luz (Gen. 28:19). It was here that Abraham encamped (Gen. 12:8; 13:3), and the district is still pronounced as suitable for pasturage. It received the name of Beth-el, "house of God," because of its nearness to or being the very place where Jacob dreamed (28:10-22). Beth-el was assigned to the Benjamites, but they appear to have been either unable to take it or careless about doing so, as we find it taken by the children of Joseph (Judg. 1:22-26).

Being very close to the border of Ephraim, we are less surprised to find it in the kingdom of the Ten Tribes after the disruption of the kingdom. It seems to have been the place to which the ark was brought (Judg. 20:26-28). It was one of the three places which Samuel selected to hold court (I Sam. 7:16), and Jeroboam chose Beth-el as one of the two places in which he set up golden calves (I Kings 12:28-33). King Josiah removed all traces of idolatry, and restored the true worship of Jehovah (II Kings 23:15-20). Bethel was occupied by people returning from Babylon (comp. Ezra 2:28 with Neh. 11:31).

Beth-el being, as laid down by Eusebius and Jerome, twelve miles from Jerusalem and on the right hand of the road to Shechem, corresponds precisely to the ruins which bear the name Beitin. It stands upon the point of a low rocky ridge, between two shallow *wadies*, which unite and fall into the Wady Suweinit toward the S. E. According to excavated potsherds Beth-el began to be occupied as a city in the 21st century B. C. It suffered a severe destruction in the early 14th century B. C. (Albright). This is customarily referred to as a burning by the tribes of Israel during their conquest of Canaan. However, the destruction of Beth-el in the 13th century B. C. by a tremendous conflagration, shown by the

68. Representation of Astarte on a Seal Cylinder from Bethel, c. 1300 B. C.

excavations of the site in 1934 by a joint expedition of the Pittsburgh-Xenia Theological Seminary and the Am. Schools of Oriental Research under the leadership of Professor Albright, is to be connected with the later decimation by the tribe of Joseph, quite some time after Joshua's death (Judg. 1:22-26). It has nothing to do with the conquest which occurred shortly after B. C. 1400 (if the Biblical dates of the Exodus and conquest are followed). Burned brick, charred wreckage and ash-filled earth demonstrated the complete ruin of this stoutly constructed Canaanite predecessor of the city-shrine of later days. These same excavations have uncovered parts of a city wall dating about the 16th century B. C. The masonry of these ruined ramparts is the best Late Bronze Age (B. C. 1500-1200) domestic construction yet come to light in Palestine. Revised by *M. F. U.*

2. Knobel suggests that this is a corrupt reading for *Bethul* or *Bethuel* (Josh. 19:4; I Chron. 4:30), in the tribe of Simeon.

Beth′-el, Mount of, the southern range of mountains belonging to Beth-el (Josh. 16:1, 2). Beth-el is here distinguished from Luz because the reference is not to the town of Beth-el, but to the mountains, from which the boundary ran out to Luz.

Beth′-elite (bĕth′ē-līt), a name by which Hiel, who rebuilt Jericho (I Kings 16:34), was called, being a native of *Beth-el* (*q. v.*) in Benjamin.

Beth-e′mek (bĕth-ē′mĕk; *house of the valley*), a city of Asher, in the S. of the valley of Jiphthah-el (Josh. 19:27), not yet discovered, probably Tell Mimas, near 'Amqa, 6½ miles N. E. of Acre.

Be′ther (bē′thẽr; *dissection, separation*), a range of mountains named in Cant. 2:17, and perhaps the same as the "mountains of spices" (8:14).

Bethes′da (bē-thĕz′dȧ; Gr. from Aram. *Beth hesdä, house of grace*). A spring-fed pool with five porches where invalids waited their turn to step into the mysteriously troubled waters which were supposed to possess healing virtue. The fourth verse of the A. V., which mentions a periodic disturbance of the water affected by an angel, is not included in the R. V. because there is not sufficient attestation by early texts. Here Jesus healed the man who was lame for 38 years (John 5:2f.). It is now thought to be the pool found during the repairs in 1888 near St. Anne's Church in the Bezetha quarter of Jerusalem not far from the Sheep's Gate and Tower of Antonia. It is below the crypt of the ruined 4th century church and has a five-arch portico with faded frescoes of the miracle of Christ's healing. M. F. U.

Beth-e′zel (bĕth-ē′zĕl; *a place near*). A town mentioned in Mic. 1:11 in S. Judah, now identified with Deir el-'Asal about two miles E. of Tell Beit Mirsim.

Beth-ga′der (bĕth-gā′dĕr; *house of the wall*), a place in the tribe of Judah, of which Hareph is named as "father" or founder (I Chron. 2:51). Probably identical with *Gedor* (*q. v.*) of Josh. 15:58 or Geder.

Beth-ga′mul (bĕth-gā′mŭl; *house of recompense*), a city of Moab (Jer. 48:23). It is identified with Khirbet Jemeil, 6 miles E. of Dibon, between the Arnon and Ummer Raṣäs.

Beth-gil′gal (bĕth-gĭl′găl; *house of Gilgal*, Neh. 12:29), a place from which the sons of the singers gathered together for the celebration of the rebuilding of the walls of Jerusalem; doubtless the same as *Gilgal* (*q. v.*).

Beth-hacche′rem (Bĕth-hăk-ē′rĕm), in A. V. **Bethhaccerem** (bĕth-hăk′sē-rĭm; *house of the vineyard*). A Judean town (Neh. 3:14; Jer. 6:1) of such commanding height as to be a place for signaling upon occasions of invasion. It is commonly identified with 'Ain Karim, some 4½ miles W. of Jerusalem on the summit of Jebel 'Ali. Above this village are cairns which may have served as beacons. The Lachish Letters, discovered in 1935 by J. L. Starkey in the guard room adjoining the outer gate of the city of Lachish, an ancient fortress of Judah, tell of such a system of signaling. Letter No. 4 contains this passage: "We are watching for the signal stations of Lachish according to all the signals you are giving because we cannot see the signals of Azekah." Interestingly, the same term here employed for "fire signal" occurs in Jer. 6:1. "Flee for safety ye children of Benjamin, out of the midst of Jerusalem, and blow the trumpet at Tekoa, and raise up a signal on Beth-hacchE-rem; for evil looketh forth from the north and a great destruction."

Beth-hag′gan (bĕth-hăg′ăn; *house of the garden*), a place by way of which King Ahaziah fled from Jehu (II Kings 9:27, A. V., "garden house"). The "garden house" cannot have been in the royal gardens, but must have stood at some distance from the city of Jezreel, as Ahaziah went away by the road thither, and was not wounded till he reached the height of Gur, near Jibleam.

Beth-ha′ran (bĕth-hâ′răn), a fenced city E. of Jordan, "built," i. e., restored and fortified, by the Gadites (Num. 32:36). The same as *Beth-aram* (*q. v.*).

Beth-hog′la (Josh. 15:6), or **Beth-hog′lah** (18:19); (bĕth-hŏg′là; *house of a partridge*), a place on the border of Judah and of Benjamin, and belonging to the latter tribe (18:21). The name and location are to be found at 'Ain Hajlah, 4 miles S. E. of Jericho.

Beth-ho′ron (bĕth-hō′rŏn; *house* or *place of the hollow*), the name of two towns, an "upper"

and a "nether" (Josh. 16:3, 5; I Chron. 7:24; II Chron. 8:5), on the road from Gibeon to Azekah (Josh. 10:10, 11) and the Philistine plain (I Sam. 13:18). Beth-horon lay on the boundary line between Benjamin and Ephraim (Josh. 16:3, 5; 18:13, 14), was assigned to Ephraim, and given to the Kohathites (Josh. 21:22; I Chron. 6:68). It is said (I Chron. 7:24) that Sherah built Beth-horon the nether, and the upper, and Uzzen-sherah. The building referred to was merely an enlarging and fortifying of these towns. Sherah was probably an heiress, who had received these places as her inheritance, and caused them to be enlarged by her family.

"These places still exist, and are called by Arabic names meaning 'upper' and 'lower.' They are separated by about half an hour's journey. The upper village is about four miles from Gibeon, the road always on the *ascent*. The *descent* begins from the upper to the lower village, and that road is one of the roughest and steepest in Palestine; it is still used as the road from the coast, and is a key to the country; it was afterward fortified by Solomon. Old tanks and massive foundations exist" (Harper, *Bible and Mod. Dis.*, p. 159).

It was along this pass that Joshua drove the discomfited allies against whom he went out in defense of the Gibeonites (Josh. 10:10); and by the same route one of three companies of Philistine spoilers came against Israel (I Sam. 13:18).

The importance of the road upon which the two Beth-horons were situated, the main approach to the interior of the country from the hostile districts on both sides of Palestine, at once explains and justifies the frequent fortification of these towns at different periods of the history (I Kings 9:17; II Chron. 8:5; I Macc. 9:50; Judg. 4:4, 5).

Beth-jesh′imoth (bĕth-jĕsh′ĭ-mŏth; *house* or *place of deserts*), a town in Moab, not far E. of the mouth of the Jordan (Num. 33:49, "Beth-jesimoth;" Josh. 12:3; 13:20; Ezek. 25:9). Belonging to Sihon, king of the Amorites (Josh. 12:3).

Beth-jes′imoth, another form of *Beth-jeshimoth* (*q. v.*). In N. T. times Besimoth (Tell el-'Azeimeh).

Beth-le-aph′rah (bĕth-lē-ăph′räh; *house* or *place of dust;* so in R. V., Mic. 1:10; "house of Apharah" in the A. V.). Site unknown.

Beth-leba′oth (bĕth-lē-bā′ŏth; *house of lionesses*), a town in the lot of Simeon (Josh. 19:6), in the extreme S. of Judah (15:32), where it is given as *Lebaoth* (*q. v.*). The location of the site is near Sharuhen, but unknown.

Beth′-lehem (bĕth′-lē-hĕm; *house of bread*).

1. A town in Palestine, near which Jacob buried Rachel, then known as Ephrath (Gen. 35:19; 48:7). It is also called Beth-lehem Ephratah (Mic. 5:2), Beth-lehem-judah (I Sam. 17:12), Bethlehem of Judea (Matt. 2:1), and the city of David (Luke 2:4; John 7:42). The old name lingered long after Israel occupied Palestine (Ruth 1:2; 4:11; I Sam. 17:12; Psa. 132:6; Mic. 5:2, etc.). The city overlooks the main highway to Hebron and Egypt. The site of the city on a commanding limestone

ridge of the Judean highland has never been disputed.

After the conquest Beth-lehem fell to Judah (Judg. 17:7; I Sam. 17:12; Ruth 1:1, 2); Ibzan of Beth-lehem judged Israel after Jephthah (Judg. 12:8); Elimelech, the husband of Naomi and father-in-law of Ruth, was a Beth-lehemite (Ruth 1:1, 2), as was also Boaz (2:1, 4, 11).

David was born in Beth-lehem, and here he was anointed as future king by Samuel (I Sam. 16:1, sq.); here was the well from which David's three heroes brought him water (II Sam. 23:15, sq.), thought to be the same

69. Shepherds' Fields, Bethlehem

wells still existing in the N. side of the village, and three in number; it was the birthplace of the Messiah (Matt. 2:1), and its male children were slain by order of Herod (2:16, comp. Jer. 31:15; Mic. 5:2). This Beth-lehem is about five miles S. of Jerusalem, and elevated two thousand five hundred and fifty feet above the sea level, or one hundred feet higher than Jerusalem itself.

2. A town in the portion of Zebulun, named only in connection with Idala (Josh. 19:15). It is to be located at Beit Lahm, 7 miles N. E. of Nazareth.

Beth'-lehemite (bĕth'-lê-hĕm-īt), an inhabitant of *Bethlehem* (*q. v.*) in Judah (I Sam. 16:1, 18; 17:58; II Sam. 21:19).

Beth'-lehem-ju'dah (bĕth'-lê-hĕm-jū'dà), a more distinctive title (Judge. 17:7, 8, 9; 19:1, etc.; Ruth 1:1, 2; I Sam. 17:12) of *Bethlehem*, 1 (*q. v.*).

Beth-ma'achah (bĕth-mā'à-kà; *house of Maakah*), a place to which Joab went in pursuit of Sheba the son of Bichri (II Sam. 20:14). It was quite close to Abela, so that the names of the places are connected in v. 15, and afterward as Abel-beth-maachah (I Kings 15:20; II Kings 15:29); also called Abel-main (II Chron. 16:4). The modern site is Tell Abil, about 2½ miles W. N. W. of Laish (Dan) and 6 miles W. N. W. of Caesarea Philippi (Paneas) near the sources of the Jordan River.

Beth-mar'caboth (bĕth-mär'kà-bŏth; *place of chariots*), a town of Simeon, in the extreme S. of Judah, in which dwelt some of the descendants of Shimei (Josh. 19:5; I Chron. 4:31). Site uncertain.

Beth-me'on (bĕth-mē'ŏn; *house of habitation*), a place in the tribe of Reuben (Jer. 48:23); elsewhere (Josh. 13:17) in the full form *Beth-baal-meon* (*q. v.*).

Beth-nim'rah (bĕth-nĭm'rà; *house of the leopard*), one of the towns "built," i. e., fortified, by the tribe of Gad (Num. 32:36); called simply *Nimrah* (*q. v.*) in Num. 32:3.

Beth-pa'let (bĕth-pā'lĕt; *house of escape*), a town in the S. of Judah (Josh. 15:27), assigned to Simeon, and inhabited after the captivity (Neh. 11:26, A. V., "Beth-phelet"). Location uncertain.

Beth-paz'zez (bĕth-păz'ĕz; *house of dispersion*), a city of Issachar (Josh. 19:21). Probably modern Kerm el-Hadetheh.

Beth-pe'or (bĕth-pē'ôr; *house*, or *temple* of *Peor*), a place in Moab E. of Jordan, abominable for its idolatry. It belonged to Reuben (Josh. 13:20; Deut. 3:29; 4:46). It was the last halting place of the children of Israel, and in the valley near by was that in which Moses rehearsed the law to Israel and was buried (Deut. 4:44-46; 34:6).

Beth'phage (bĕth'fà-jē; Aram., *house of unripe figs*), on Mount Olives, and on the way from Jerusalem to Jericho, close to Bethany. A Sabbath day's journey from Jerusalem (Matt. 21:1; Mark 11:1; Luke 19:29). No trace of it now remains. It is not once mentioned in the Old Testament, though frequently in the Talmud.

Beth-phe'let (bĕth-fē'lĕt; Neh. 11:26). See Beth-palet.

Beth-ra'pha (bĕth-rä'fà; *house of Rapha*, or *giant*), a name occurring in the genealogy of Judas as a son of Eshton (I Chron. 4:12).

Beth-re'hob (beth-rē'hŏb; *house of the street*), a place near which was the valley where lay the town of Laish, or Dan (Judg. 18:28). This valley is the upper part of the Huleh lowland, through which the central source of the Jordan flows, and by which Laish-Dan, the present Tell el Qadi, stood. The Ammonites secured mercenary soldiers from Bethrehob to fight against David (II Sam. 10:6; Rehob, v. 8).

Bethsa'ida (bĕth-sā'ĭ-dà; Gr. from Aram., *bēth ṣaydä, house or place of fishing*).

1. A city in Galilee, on the W. coast of the Sea of Tiberias (John 1:44; 12:21). It was the native place of Peter, Andrew, and Philip, and a frequent resort of Jesus. Our Lord upbraided its inhabitants for not receiving his teachings (Luke 10:13). Robinson infers that Bethsaida was not far from Capernaum, as does also Edersheim. The latter says (*Life and Times of Jesus*, ii, 3, 4): "From the fact that Mark names Bethsaida, and John Capernaum, as the original destination of the boat, we would infer that Bethsaida was the fishing quarter of, or rather close to, Capernaum. . . . Further, it would explain how Peter and Andrew, who, according to John, were of Bethsaida, are described by Mark as having their home in Capernaum. . . . This also suggests that in a sense—as regarded the fishermen—the names were interchangeable, or, rather, that Bethsaida was the 'Fisherton' of Capernaum."

Robinson identifies as its probable site *'Ain et Tabighah*, a small village in a little wady, with a copious stream bursting from an immense fountain.

2. **Bethsaida of Gaulonitis**, afterward called Julias. There is every presumptive

evidence that the city in Gaulonitis, on the E. side of the sea, is that "in the desert place" where Christ fed the five thousand (Luke 9:10-17) and "healed them that had need of healing." Here he also restored the blind man to sight (Mark 8:22-26), as it would be on the road to Caesarea Philippi, next visited by our Lord (v. 27).

It was originally a small town; but Philip the tetrarch, having raised it to the rank of city, called it Julias, after Julia, the daughter of the Emperor Augustus (Josephus, *Ant.*, xviii, 2, 1). Philip died and was buried here. Some identify the locality with a spur of the mountains E. of the Jordan valley, called by the Arabs *El Tel*. It is without doubt to be placed at the east end of el 'Araj. Smith (*Hist. Geog.*, p. 458) thinks that it is not necessary to accept more than one Bethsaida.

70. Tell Husn, the Site of Bethshan

Beth'-shan (bĕth-shăn'; Heb. *house of security*, but more probably house of the Babylonian god Shahan, Phoenician Sha'an, the Sumerian serpent god). An ancient fortress city strategically commanding the Valley of Esdraelon (Tell el-Husn, "mound of the fortress") also known as Beth-shean (modern Beisan), New Testament Scythopolis. This great fortress site was founded before B. C. 3000 and has a long and interesting occupational history. After Thutmose III's brilliant victory at Megiddo (c. B. C. 1482) it passed into Egyptian hands and was garrisoned by Egyptian soldiers for almost 300 years. Two stelae of Seti I and one of Rameses II were uncovered here. At the time of the Conquest, around B. C. 1400, the inhabitants of the city and the plain had chariots of iron (Josh. 17:16) and the Israelites failed to drive out the Canaanites but developed strongly enough to make them pay tribute (Josh. 17:12-16). At the battle of Gilboa, around B. C. 1000, the town was either in Philistine hands or in alliance with them, for the Philistines fastened the bones of Saul and his sons to the wall of the city (I Sam. 31:10-13; II Sam. 21:12-14). The University of Pennsylvania Expedition at Bethshan, 1921-33, unearthed a temple which the excavators identified with the Temple of Ashtoreth in which Saul's armor was placed (I Sam. 31:10). I Chron. 10:10 refers to a second temple of Bethshan called the House of Dagon (*q. v.*) where Saul's head was hung. The excavations uncovered another temple to the south of the Temple of Ashtoroth which Alan Rowe identifies with the Temple of

Dagon. In the reign of Solomon the city gave its name to a district (I Kings 4:12). No mound in Palestine is more impressive than Bethshan, which yielded a number of Egyptian temples dating in the reigns of Amenhotep III (c. B. C. 1413-1377), Seti I (B. C. 1319-1301), Rameses II (B. C. 1301-1234). It has also revealed extensive fortress construction. In the level of City 7, from the reign of Amenhotep III, remains of the commandant's residence have been unearthed, showing spacious kitchen, lavatory and an immense silo for storing grain. A Canaanite migdol or fort tower was also found designed as a last place of refuge if the walls were breached. *M. F. U.*

Beth-she'mesh (bĕth-shē'mĕsh; *house of* the *sun*).

1. A sacerdotal city (Josh. 21:16; I Sam. 6:15; I Chron. 6:59) in the tribe of Dan, on the N. boundary of Judah (Josh. 15:10), toward Philistia (I Sam. 6:9, 12). The expression "went down" (Josh. 21:16; I Sam. 6:21) seems to indicate that the town was lower than Kirjath-jearim; and there was a valley of cornfields attached to the place (I Sam. 6:13). It was a "suburb city" (Josh. 21:16; I Chron. 6:59), and contributed to Solomon's expenses (I Kings 4:9). In an engagement between Jehoash, king of Israel, and Amaziah, king of Judah, the latter was defeated and made prisoner (II Kings 14:11, 13; II Chron. 25:21, 23). In the time of Ahaz the Philistines occupied it (II Chron. 28:18), and to this place the ark was returned (I Sam. 6:19). The number slain at Beth-shemesh for irreverently examining the holy shrine is recorded as fifty thousand and seventy. "In this statement of numbers we are not only struck by the fact that in the Hebrew the seventy stands before the fifty thousand, which is very unusual, but even more by the omission of the copula *waw*, which is altogether unparalleled. . . . We can come to no other conclusion than that the number fifty thousand is neither correct nor genuine, but a gloss which has crept into the text through some oversight" (K. and D., *Com.*, in loc.). It was identical with Irshemesh (Josh. 19:41), and is preserved in the modern *Ain-shems*, on the N. W. slopes of the mountains of Judah, a site known today as Tell er-Rumeileh.

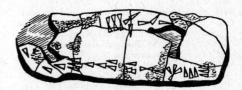

71. Tablet from Bethshemesh Inscribed in Ugaritic Alphabet

Pottery and scarabs demonstrate that the city was occupied from c. 2000 B. C.-c. 600 B. C. when the town was destroyed, probably by the armies of Nebuchadnezzar II.

2. A city near the southern border of Issachar, between Mount Tabor and the Jordan (Josh. 19:22). Unidentified.

3. One of the "fenced cities" of Naphtali (Josh. 19:38; Judg. 1:33), from which and

from Beth-anath the Canaanites were not driven out.

4. The name given by Jeremiah (43:13) to *On* (*q. v.*), the Egyptian city usually called Heliopolis.

Beth'-shemite (bĕth-shē'mīt), an inhabitant (I Sam. 6:14, 18) of the *Beth-shemesh* (*q. v.*) in Judea.

Beth-shit'tah (bĕth-shĭt'å; *house of the acacia*), a town not far from the Jordan to which the Midianites fled from Gideon (Judg. 7:22).

Beth-tap'puah (bĕth-tăp'ů-å; *house of apples*), a town about five miles W. of Hebron (Josh. 15:53), same as modern *Taffuh*. Another town in Judah was known by the simple name of *Tappuah* (*q. v.*).

Bethu'el (bē-thū'ĕl; perhaps *abode of God*).

1. A southern city of Judah, sometimes called Bethul or Beth-el (I Chron. 4:30; Josh. 19:4; 12:16; I Sam. 30:27). Named with Eltolad and Hormah.

2. The son of Nahor by Milcah; the nephew of Abraham, and father of Rebekah (Gen. 22:22, 23; 24:15, 24, 47). In ch. 25:20 and 28:5 he is called "Bethuel the Syrian." In the narrative of Rebekah's marriage he is mentioned as saying, "The thing proceedeth from the Lord" (ch. 24:50), while her brother Laban takes the leading part in the transaction.

Be'thul (bē'thŭl; contraction for *Bethuel*, a town in the S. of Simeon, named with Eltolad and Hormah (Josh. 19:4). Location uncertain.

Beth-zur' (bĕth-zûr'; *house of rock*), a strategic elevated fortress between Bethlehem and Hebron. The site has been excavated and yielded Middle Bronze Age ruins (c. 16th century B. C.) and a Maccabean fort, in which era it was called Bethsura. The site was fortified by Rehoboam (II Chron. 11:7), referred to in Nehemiah's time (Neh. 3:16), but was most prominent in Maccabean times. Here Judas Maccabeus defeated the Greeks under Lysias, B. C. 165. The name survives in the ruins of Beit Sur, 4 miles N. of Hebron, but the ancient location was at Khirbet et-Tubeiqah. *M. F. U.*

Bet'onim (bĕt'ô-nĭm; *hollows*), a town in the tribe of Gad (Josh. 13:26), located at Khirbet Batneh on Mount Gilead.

Betray (Gr. *paradidōmi*, *to give into the hands* of another), the term used of the act of Judas in delivering up our Lord to the Jews (Matt. 26:16; Mark 14:10; Luke 22:4, 6).

Betrothal. *See* Marriage.

Beu'lah (bū'lå; *married*), a prophetic figurative expression (Isa. 62:4), describing Palestine restored to God's blessing, not only after the Babylonian Exile but particularly after Israel's present world-wide dispersion and establishment in Palestine in the Millennial Kingdom. Israel in its relation to Jehovah is a weak but beloved woman who has Him for her Lord and Husband (Isa. 54:5) and who will yet be cleansed and restored to her Lord.

Beverage. *See* Drink.

Bewitch. To deceive or delude by Satanic and demonic power, as Simon Magus the sorcerer did to the people of Samaria (Acts 8:9), to thus "charm" or fascinate (Gal. 3:1).

Beyond, the region or country *beyond*. The phrase "beyond Jordan" frequently occurs in Scripture. To ascertain its meaning we must take into account the situation of the writer. With Moses, writing upon its eastern bank, it usually signified the country W. of the river (Gen. 50:10, 11; Deut. 1:1, 5; 3:8, 20; 4:46), but with Joshua after he crossed the river it meant the reverse (Josh. 5:1; 12:7; 22:7). In Matt. 4:15 "beyond Jordan" designates, after the two lands already mentioned, a new land as the theater of the working of Jesus, viz., Perea.

Be'zai (bē'zā-ī), the head of one of the families who returned from Babylon to the number of three hundred and twenty-four, including himself (Ezra 2:17; Neh. 7:23), B. C. 536. Either he or his family is probably referred to (Neh. 10:19) as sealing the covenant, B. C. 445.

Bezal'eel (bē-zăl'ê-ĕl; A. V. **Bez'alel**, bĕz'å-lĕl; *in the shadow* (protection) *of God*).

1. The artificer to whom was instrusted the design and construction of the tabernacle and its furniture in the wilderness. For this work he was specially chosen and inspired by Jehovah. With him was associated Aholiab, though Bezaleel appears to have been chief. He was the son of Uri, the son of Hur (Exod. 31:2-11; 35:30; 38:22), B. C. c. 1440.

2. One of the sons of Pahath-moab, who divorced his foreign wife after the captivity (Ezra 10:30), B. C. 456.

Be'zek (bē'zĕk; *lightning*).

1. The residence of *Adoni-bezek q. v.*), and inhabited by Canaanites and Perizzites (Judg. 1:4, 5). The location is uncertain but may well be Khirbet Bezqa near Gezer.

2. The place of gathering where Saul numbered the forces of Judah and Israel before going to the relief of Jabesh-gilead (I Sam. 11:8). Khirbet Ibziq, W. of Jordan and S. W. of Jabesh-gilead.

Be'zer (bē'zĕr).

1. The sixth named of the eleven sons of Zophah, of the descendants of Asher (I Chron. 7:37).

2. A Reubenite city of refuge E. of Jordan (Deut. 4:23; Josh. 20:8, etc.). Location uncertain.

Bible, the name commonly used to designate the 39 books of the O. T. and the 27 books of the N. T. These 66 books constitute a divine library which is nevertheless, in a vital sense, *one Book*.

1. **The Name Bible.** The development of the term "the Bible" to designate the "Book of books" is providential. It admirably expresses the unity of the Word of God. The English word "Bible" came originally from the name of the papyrus or byblos reed used extensively in antiquity for making scrolls and books. Byblos (O. T. Gebal) was so named because in that Phoenician seaport, trade and manufacture in papyrus writing-material was carried on. From about the 11th century B. C., or even earlier, papyrus rolls, grown in the Delta of Egypt, were shipped to Gebal. The word "Bible" comes from the Old French through the Latin *biblia*, from the Greek. Quite naturally the Greeks came to term a book *biblos* or a small book, *biblion*. By the 2nd century A. D. Greek Christians called their

sacred Scriptures *ta Biblia*, "the Books." When this title was subsequently transferred to the Latin, it was rendered in the singular and through Old French came into English as Bible.

2. **Other Designations.** In the O. T. and the Apocrypha the sacred writings are called "the books" (LXX *bibloi*, Dan. 9:2), "the holy books" (I Macc. 12:9), "the books of the law" (I Macc. 1:56), "book of the covenant" (I Macc. 1:57), etc. In the Prologue to Ecclesiasticus the Scriptures are referred to as "the law, the prophets, and the other books (*biblia*) of our fathers." In the N. T. the common designations for the O. T. books are "the Scriptures (writings; Matt. 21:42; Mk. 14:49; Luke 24:32; John 5:39; Rom. 15:4), the "holy Scriptures" (Rom. 1:2), "the sacred writings" (II Tim. 3:15). The Jewish technical division of "the law," "the prophets," and the "writings" is recognized in Luke 24:44. Another term for the whole is "the law and the prophets" (Matt. 5:17; 11:13; Acts 13:15). The term "law" is occasionally extended to include the other divisions (John 10:34; I Cor. 14:21). Paul employs also the expression "the oracles of God" (Rom. 3:2).

3. **Terms O. T. and N. T.** These terms have come into use since the close of the 2nd century to distinguish the Jewish and the Christian Scriptures. The word "testament" (literally, a will) denotes a covenant. In the R. V., accordingly, "testament" is generally corrected to covenant. However, these terms are not altogether accurate for the simple reason that the Mosaic covenant and the legal dispensation were still in operation throughout the lifetime and up to the death of Christ, when "the veil of the temple was rent in twain from the top to the bottom." This momentous event signified that a "new and living way" was open for all believers into the very presence of God with no other sacrifice or priesthood necessary save Christ (cf. Heb. 9:1-8; 10:19-22). It was only as a result of the death, burial and resurrection of Christ, the giving of the Holy Spirit at Pentecost (Acts 2), and the preaching of the gospel of grace that actually saw the outworking of the new covenant.

4. **Languages.** The O. T. is written mostly in Hebrew; the N. T. wholly in Greek. The parts of the O. T. not in Hebrew are Dan. 2:4-7:28; Ezra 4:8-6:18; 7:12-26; and Jer. 10:11. These sections are written in Aramaic, a related Semitic dialect which, after the exilic period, gradually took the place of Hebrew as the common language of the Jews. The ancient Hebrew was a Canaanite dialect closely akin to Phoenician and Ugaritic, a language spoken at Ugarit (modern Ras Shamra) in North Syria. At Ugarit, an important and extensive religious epic literature, shedding great light on Canaanite morality and religious practices, has been uncovered by Claude Schaeffer and the French Expedition (1929-37). N. T. Greek, so greatly illuminated by important papyri discoveries particularly from Egypt, has been shown to be not a special sacred dialect, as was formerly thought, but the common Hellenistic speech of the 1st century A. D. In no phase of its composition does the Bible show itself to be a book for the people more than in its use of everyday language of the Greek-speaking world of the period.

5. **The Divisions of the O. T. Books.** The 39 books of the O. T. were anciently divided by the Hebrews into three distinct classes: (1) *The Law*, (*Torah*) which comprised the five books of Moses—Genesis, Exodus, Leviticus, Numbers and Deuteronomy. These are the oldest of the Biblical books, Mosaic in origin, but incorporating much earlier material. (2) *The Prophets* (*Nebiim*) embraces the four earlier prophets, Joshua, Judges, Samuel and Kings and the four later prophets, Isaiah, Jeremiah, Ezekiel and the Twelve—Hosea, Joel, Amos, Obadiah, Jonah, Micah, Nahum, Habakkuk, Zephaniah, Haggai, Zechariah and Malachi. These were believed to have been written by those who had the prophetic office as well as the prophetic gift. (3) *The Writings* (*Kethubim*). These include poetical books (a) Psalms, Proverbs, Job (b) the Rolls —Canticles, Ruth, Lamentations, Ecclesiastes and Esther (c) prophetical historical books, Daniel, Ezra-Nehemiah and Chronicles. The Hebrew books number 24 and are identical in content with the 39 of the English order, the difference being made up by the division of Samuel, Kings and Chronicles into two books respectively instead of one, and by counting the twelve minor prophets individually instead of as one.

6. **Division of the N. T. Books.** By the middle of the 2nd century a Christian N. T. had come into existence. Early distinction had to be made (1) between the generally acknowledged and disputed books. As enumerated by Eusebius and substantiated by early lists such as the canon of Muratori (about 170 A. D.), quotations, versions and patristic use, the former included the four Gospels, Acts, 13 Epistles of Paul, I Peter and I John. With these may be placed Hebrews and Revelation. Disputed books included James, Jude, II and III John and II Peter. However, the complete acceptance of all of the books in our present N. T. canon may be dated from the Councils of Laodicea (about 363 A. D.) and Carthage (397 A. D.), which confirmed the catalogs of Cyril of Jerusalem, Jerome and Augustine.

7. **Origin and Growth.** Accepting the internal evidence, together with predictive prophecy and divine miracle, the following general conclusions have been accepted by conservative scholars: (1) The Pentateuch as it stands is historical and dates from the time of Moses. Moses was its real author, though it may have been revised and edited by later redactors, the additions being just as much inspired as the rest. (cf. Robert Dick Wilson, *A Scientific Investigation of the O. T.*, Philadelphia (1926), p. 11.) In other words, the Pentateuch is one continuous work, the product of a single writer, Moses. This Mosaic unity of the Pentateuch may, however, admit post-Mosaic additions or changes which do not abrogate the authenticity and integrity of the text. It is not inconsistent with Mosaic authorship of the Pentateuch to grant modification of archaic

expressions and place names, marginal glosses or explanatory scribal insertions which evidently crept into the text, and textual errors due to inadvertent mistakes of copyists. The latter constitute the legitimate domain of scholarly criticism. Examples of additions are Deut. 34:5-12, narrating Moses' death and burial. An evident gloss is furnished by Gen. 15:2, 3, which is untranslatable in the Hebrew unless one sees that a copyist's explanation eventually got into the text. (Gen. 14:14 and Deut. 34:1, where Leshem is called "Dan," although apparently this place did not receive its later name until after the Mosaic age (Judg. 18:29). Raamses (Exod. 1:11) seems clearly a modification of the earlier city Zoan or Avaris. (2) The book of Joshua is a literary unit distinct from the Pentateuch. It dates from the period of Joshua and in all likelihood was written in substance by Joshua himself (cf. 24:26). In any event, it was written early, as numerous internal evidences show. (3) The Song of Deborah (Judges 5) is an indubitably authentic monument of the age of the Judges, and the older parts of Judges, at least, are contemporaneous with the events they recount. (4) The age of Samuel, Saul and David and the monarchy was a period of literary activity, and saw the gradual rise of such books as I and II Sam., I and II Kings and many of the Psalms. (5) The Solomonic period saw the development of wisdom literature such as Proverbs, Canticles and Ecclesiastes. (6) To the period of the Divided Monarchy in the main belongs the extensive prophetic literature of the O. T. Obadiah and Joel are probably dated as early as the late ninth century B. C. To the eighth century B. C. belong Amos, Hosea and Jonah in the Northern Kingdom and Micah and Isaiah in the Southern Kingdom. Nahum, Zephaniah, Habakkuk and Jeremiah (including Lamentations) come in the late seventh century B. C. (7) Ezekiel and Daniel are exilic, and (8) Haggai, Zechariah and Malachi are postexilic, as well as such books as Esther, Ezra Nehemiah and Chronicles. Concerning unsound views, it is especially important to note that Isaiah 40-66 is assigned to a "second" or "third" Isaiah (q. v.) living about 540 B. C. or later, while a Maccabean date for the book of Daniel (c. 167 B. C.) is claimed by higher critics as one of the assured results of their research. But denials of the unity of Isaiah and the genuineness of Daniel (q. v.) are based upon false assumptions and unsound conclusions, and are challenged by believing scholars who refuse to abandon the fortress of a high and worthy doctrine of inspiration as set forth in the Word (II Tim. 3:15; II Pet. 1:20, 21). Conservative critics also refuse to surrender the historicity of Jonah (q. v.) or the authticity of Ezekiel's prophecies (q. v.) in the face of critical attack. *M. F. U.*

Biblia Pauperum (bĭb'lĭ-á paw'pĕr-ĭm; *Bible of the Poor*).

1. The name given to a Picture Bible, printed before the invention of movable types, on wood blocks. It had forty leaves printed on one side, on which forty scenes from the life of our Lord were depicted, with some Old Testament events, accompanied with an illustrative

text or sentence in Latin. It was not intended so much for the poor people as for the indigent friars, who were, doubtless, aided in their preaching by the pictures. The pictures in this book were copied in sculpture, paintings, and altar pieces. The stained-glass windows in Lambeth Chapel were copied from some of them.

2. A work of Bonaventura, in which Bible events are alphabetically arranged and accompanied with notes to aid preachers.

Bibliomancy (Gr. *biblion*, *Bible*, and *manteia*, *divination*), a kind of fortune-telling by means of the Bible, consisting of drawing texts of Scripture at random, from which inference was made of duty, future events, etc. It was introduced from paganism, which made a similar use of Homer, Virgil, and other writers. In the 12th century it was used for the detection of heretics and in the election of bishops. A sort of bibliomancy was in use among the Jews, which consisted in appealing to the very first words heard from anyone reading the Scriptures, and in regarding them as a voice from heaven.

Bich'ri (bĭk'rī; *first-born*), a Benjamite, whose son Sheba stirred up a rebellion against David after the death of Absalom (II Sam. 20:1, sq.), B. C. about 967.

Bid'kar (bĭd'kȧr), Jehu's captain and originally fellow-officer, who cast the body of Jehoram, the son of Ahab, into the field of Naboth after Jehu had slain him (II Kings 9:25), B. C. 842.

Bier (Heb. *miṭṭäh*, *bed*, II Sam. 3:31; Gr. *saros*, open *coffin*, funeral *couch*, Luke 7:14). The original form of the term is "beere," from the Anglo-Saxon "beran," *to bear*. The bier is in fact a hand-barrow on which to carry a corpse to burial. In Europe it was usually covered by a "hearse," or wagon-shaped framework, for the support of the "pall." A combination of the two placed on wheels makes the modern hearse.

Bigamy. *See* Marriage.

Big'tha (bĭg'thȧ; from Old Pers. *baga* + *da*, *gift of God*), one of the seven chamberlains who had charge of the harem of Xerxes (Ahasuerus) and were commanded by him to bring in Queen Vashti to the banquet (Esth. 1:10), B. C. 486-465.

Big'than, or **Bigtha'na** (bĭg'thăn or bĭg-thā'nȧ; Old Pers., cf. Bigtha). One of the chamberlains of Xerxes (Ahasuerus) who "kept the door." He conspired with Teresh against the life of the king, and being exposed by Mordecai was hanged with his fellow-conspirator (Esth. 2:21; 6:2), B. C. 486-465.

Big'vai (bĭg'vȧ-ī; Old Pers., *happy*, *fortunate*, from *baga*, *good luck*).

1. The head of one of the families of Israelites who returned from Babylon with Zerubbabel (Ezra 2:2; Neh. 7:7), with a large number of retainers—two thousand and fifty-six, Ezra 2:14; two thousand and sixty-seven, Neh. 7:19, B. C. 536. At a later period seventy-two males of his family returned with Ezra (ch. 8:14), B. C. about 457.

2. One of the chiefs of the people who subscribed to the covenant with Nehemiah (Neh. 10:16), B. C. 445. Perhaps the same as No. 1.

Bil'dad (bĭl'dăd), the Shuhite, (*q. v.*), and the second of the three friends of Job who disputed with him as to his affliction and character (Job. 2:11). In his first speech (ch. 8) he attributes the death of Job's children to their own transgression. In his second speech (ch. 18) he recapitulates his former assertions of the temporal calamities of the wicked, insinuating Job's wrongdoing. In his third speech (ch. 25), unable to answer Job's arguments, he takes refuge in a declaration of God's glory and man's nothingness. Finally, with Eliphaz and Zophar, he availed himself of the intercession of Job, in obedience to the divine command (ch. 42:9).

Bil'eam (bĭl'ê-ăm), a town in the western half of the tribe of Manasseh, and given with its "suburbs" to the Kohathites (I Chron. 6:70). Modern Bel'āmeh, 13 miles N. N. E. of Samaria.

Bil'gah (bĭl'gà; *cheerfulness*).

1. Head of the fifteenth course for the Temple service, as arranged by David (I Chron. 24:14), B. C. about 989.

2. A priest who returned from Babylon with Zerubbabel and Jeshua (Neh. 12:5, 18), B. C. 536. Perhaps the same as *Bilgal*, infra (Neh. 10:8).

Bil'gai (bĭl'gà-ĭ; *brightness, cheerfulness*), one of the priests whose descendants were sealed with Nehemiah after the restoration (Neh. 10:8), B. C. 445. Probably the same as *Bilgah*, supra.

Bil'hah (bĭl'hà), the handmaid of Rachel, given to her by Laban (Gen. 29:29), and bestowed by her upon her husband, Jacob, that through her she might have children, B. C. about 1930. Bilhah thus became the mother of Dan and Naphtali (Gen. 30:3-8; 35:35; 46:25). Her stepson Reuben afterward lay with her (Gen. 35:22), and thus incurred his father's dying reproof (Gen. 49:4).

Bil'han (bĭl'hăn).

1. A Horite chief, son of Ezer, son of Seir, dwelling in Mount Seir, in the land of Edom (Gen. 36:27; I Chron. 1:42).

2. A Benjamite, son of *Jediael* (*q. v.*) and father of seven sons (I Chron. 7:10).

Bill (Heb. *sēfer, writing*), is a word meaning anything that is written, e. g., a "bill of divorcement" (Deut. 24:1, 3; Isa. 50:1; Jer. 3:80 Matt. 19:7, Gr. *biblion*). The words in Job 31:35, "that mine adversary had written a book," would be better rendered, "that mine adversary had given me a *bill* of accusation" (i. e., of indictment). In Jer. 32:10-16, 44, "the evidence" (marg. "book") means a *bill* of purchase or sale. By "bill" (Gr. *gramma*, Luke 16:6, 7) a legal instrument is meant, which showed the amount of indebtedness, probably of tenants who paid rent in kind.

Bil'shan (bĭl-shăn; possibly from Akkad. *Bēlshun, their lord*), the name of one of the princes of the Jews who returned to Jerusalem with Zerubbabel after the captivity (Ezra 2:2; Neh. 7:7), B. C. 536.

Bim'hal (bĭm'hăl), a son of Japhlet and greatgreat-grandson of Asher (I Chron. 7:33).

Bind (*qāshăr'*). In the command, "Thou shalt bind them for a sign upon thine hand," etc., (Deut. 6:8) the "words are figurative, and denote an undeviating observance of the divine commands; and their literal fulfillment could only be a praiseworthy custom or well-pleasing to God when resorted to as the means of keeping the commands of God constantly before the eye" (K. and D., *Com.*, in loc.).

Binding and Loosing.

In Matthew 16:19 the power of binding and loosing is given to the Apostle Peter in connection with "the keys of the kingdom of heaven." A key in Scripture is a symbol of power and authority (Isa. 22:22; Rev. 1:18). Peter was thus given authority to open and close, not with reference to the church but in connection with "the kingdom of heaven." The history of the early church as recorded in the book of Acts makes clear the extent of this trust. It was Peter who opened the door to Christian opportunity on the day of Pentecost (Acts 2:14; 38-42), to the Samaritans (Acts 8:14-17) and to the Gentiles in Cornelius' household at Caesarea (Acts 10:34-46). Each of these pivotal passages marked the opening of religious opportunity in a dispensational sense to Jew, racially mongrel Samaritans and to Gentile. With the gospel of grace reaching out to the Gentiles in Acts 10, the normal course of the age was established. The Holy Spirit Who came at Pentecost to baptize the Jew into the body of Christ was now given to Samaritan and Gentile. This marked the extent of Peter's use of the keys of the kingdom of heaven and his power of binding and loosing. There was no other assumption of authority by the Apostle (Acts 15:7-11). In the Jewish council James, not Peter, presided (Acts 15:19; Gal. 2:11-15). The power of binding and loosing was shared by the other disciples. That it merely indicated special apostolic authority and power, and in no wise involved the determination of eternal destiny, is apparent from Rev. 1:18. Christ alone holds the keys of death and of Hades. To Peter alone was granted the special prerogative of opening gospel opportunity dispensationally at the beginning of the church age or present period, characterized preeminently by God's grace and extending from the formation of the church at Pentecost by the baptism of the Spirit (cf. Acts 1:5; 11:16 with I Cor. 12:13) to the outtaking of this body at the coming of Christ (I Cor. 15:53; I Thess. 4:13-27; II Thess. 2:1-8). *M. F. U.*

Bin'ea (bĭn'ê-à), a Benjamite, son of Moza and father of Rapha, of the descendants of King Saul (I Chron. 8:37; 9:43), B. C. about 850.

Bin'ui (bĭn'nū-î; *built*).

1. A Levite whose son, Noadiah, was one of those that assisted in weighing the gold and silver designed for the divine service on the restoration from Babylon (Ezra 8:33), B. C. about 457.

2. One of the "sons" of Pahath-moab, who put away his strange wife on the return from Babylon (Ezra 10:30), B. C. 456.

3. Another Israelite, of the "sons" of Bani, who did the same (Ezra 10:38), B. C. 456.

4. A Levite, son of Henadad, who returned with Zerubbabel from Babylon (Neh. 12:8), B. C. 536. He also (if the same) assisted in repairing the walls of Jerusalem (Neh. 3:24), B. C. 446, and joined in the covenant (Neh. 10:9), B. C. 410.

5. The head of one of the families of Israelites whose followers, to the number of six hundred and forty-eight, returned from Babylon (Neh. 7:15). In Ezra 2:10 he is called *Bani* (*q. v.*), and his retainers are numbered at six hundred and forty-two.

Bird. *See* Animal Kingdom, Food, Sacrifices.

Bir'sha (bĭr'shà; *with wickedness*), a king of Gomorrah, succored by Abraham in the invasion of Chedorlaomer (Gen. 14:2), B. C. about 2050.

Birth. *See* Child.

Birthday (Heb. *yōm hŭlĕdĕth,* Gen. 40:20; Gr. *ta genesia,* Matt. 14:6; Mark 6:21). The custom of observing birthdays was very ancient and widely extended. In Persia they were celebrated with peculiar honor and banquets, and in Egypt the king's birthday was observed with great pomp (Gen. 40:20). No reference is made in Scripture of the celebration of birthdays by the Jews themselves although the language of Jeremiah (20:14, 15) would seem to indicate that such occasions were joyfully remembered. By most commentators the feasts mentioned in Job. 1:13, 18, are thought to have been birthday festivals, but Delitzsch (*Com.,* in loc.) believes them to have been gatherings each day in the home of one of the brothers. The feast commemorative of "Herod's birthday" (Matt. 14:6) may have been in honor of his birth or of his accession to the throne (Hos. 7:5). The later Jews regarded the celebration of birthdays as a part of idolatrous worship. In the early Church the term "birthdays" was applied to the festivals of martyrs, the days on which they suffered death in this world and were born to the glory and life of heaven.

Birthright (Heb. *bĕkōräh'*; Gr. *prototokia, primogeniture*), the right of the firstborn; that to which one is entitled by virtue of his birth. *See* Firstborn.

Bir'zavith (bĭr'zà-vĭth). a name given in the genealogies of Asher (I Chron. 7:31) as the son of Malchiel and great-grandson of Asher.

Bish'lam (bĭsh'lâm; *in peace*) apparently an officer of Artaxerxes in Palestine at the time of the return of Zerubbabel from captivity. He wrote to the king against the Jews who were rebuilding the temple (Ezra 4:7) B. C. 529.

Bishop. *See* Elder.

Bishopric (Gr. *episcopē oversight*) the ministerial charge in the Church (Acts 1:20; I Tim. 3:1). In later times it is used to designate (1) the office and function of a bishop and (2) the district over which he has jurisdiction.

Bithi'ah (bĭ-thī'à; *daughter of Jehovah*) daughter of Pharaoh and wife of Mered, a descendant of Judah (I Chron. 4:18). It is thought that her sons are mentioned (v. 17) in the clause beginning "and she bare " etc. As the Pharaohs contracted marriages with royal families alone, Mered was probably a person of some distinction; or Bithiah may have been an adopted daughter of Pharaoh. It may be supposed that she became the wife of Mered through captivity.

Bith'ron (bĭth'rŏn; *cut, gorge, ravine*), a defile in the Arabah or Jordan valley (II Sam. 2:29) through which Abner and his men went after the death of Asahel.

72. Map of Bithynia

Bithyn'ia (bĭ-thĭn'ĭ-à), the N. W. province of Asia Minor. It is mountainous, thickly wooded, and fertile. It was conquered by the Romans 75 B. C. The letters of Pliny to the Emperor Trajan show that the presence of so many Christians in the province embarrassed him very much (I Pet. 1:1). Paul was not permitted to enter Bithynia (Acts 16:7), being detained by the Spirit.

Bitter (Heb. some form of *märrär'*; Gr. *pikros*). Bitterness in Scripture is symbolical of affliction, misery, servitude (Exod. 1:14; Ruth 1:20; Prov. 5:4), of wickedness (Jer. 4:18). A time of mourning and lamentation is called a "bitter day" (Amos 8:10). Habakkuk (1:6) calls the Chaldeans "that bitter and swift nation," i. e. having a *fierce* disposition. The "gall of bitterness" describes a state of extreme wickedness (Acts 8:23), while a "root of bitterness" (Heb. 12:15) expresses a wicked, scandalous person or any dangerous sin leading to apostasy. The "waters made bitter" (Rev. 8:11) is figurative of severe political or providential events.

Bitter Herbs. Because of the symbolical meaning of bitterness, bitter herbs were commanded to be used in the celebration of the *Passover* (*q. v.*) to recall the bondage of Egypt (Exod. 12:8; Num. 9:11). *See* Vegetable Kingdom.

Bittern. *See* Animal Kingdom.

Bitu'men (A. V. "slime"), a mineral pitch or asphalt of great utility in sealing objects against water and moisture. It was employed to calk the seams of boats, notably Noah's ark (Gen. 6:14), where it is significantly called *kōphĕr* (from *käphär,* "to cover"), so styled from its being overspread or overlaid. It is noteworthy that this is the same expression rendered "atonement" in Lev. 17:11, etc., for it is atonement that keeps out the waters of judgment and makes the believer's position "in Christ" safe. The ark is typical of the place of the believer "in Christ" (Eph. 1:1-14) and constitutes a type of our Lord as the refuge of His people from judgment (Heb. 11:7). Pitch was also used to bedaub the chest in which the baby Moses was concealed among the Nile flags (Exod. 2:3). Ancient deposits of bitumen existed at Hit on the Euphrates river above Babylon, and other places in Mesopotamia. It was widely used in ziggurat construction, as in the Tower of Babel (*q. v.*) (Gen. 11:3) in Babylonia and also in constructional decoration to hold tesserae of limestone or lapis lazuli, as such recovered architectural embellishments attest. *See also* Mineral Kingdom, asphalt. *M. F. U.*

Bizjoth'jah (bĭz-jŏth'já; *contempt of Jehovah*), one of the towns that fell to Judah (Josh. 15:28), probably the same as Baalath-beer 19:8). Site unknown.

Biz'tha (bĭz'thá; perhaps from Avestan *biz-da, double gift*), one of the seven eunuchs of the harem of Xerxes (Ahasuerus) who were ordered to bring Vashti forth for exhibition (Esth. 1:10), B. C. 486-465.

Black. *See* Colors.

Blains. *See* Diseases.

Blasphemy (Gr. *blasphēmia*, signifies the speaking of evil of God; Heb. *nāqǎb shēm 'Adōnai*, to curse the name of the Lord, Psa. 74:18; Isa. 52:5; Rom. 2:24). Sometimes perhaps, "blasphemy" has been retained by our translators when the general meaning, "evil-speaking," or "calumny," might have been better (Col. 3:8). There are two general forms of blasphemy: (1) Attributing some evil to God, or denying Him some good which we should attribute to Him (Lev. 24:11; Rom. 2:24). (2) Giving the attributes of God to a creature—which form of blasphemy the Jews charged upon Jesus (Luke 5:21; Matt. 26:65; John 10:36). The Jews, from ancient times, have interpreted the command, Lev. 24:16, as prohibiting the utterance of the name Jehovah, reading for it *Adonai* or *Elohim.*

Punishment. Blasphemy, when committed in ignorance, i. e., through thoughtlessness and weakness of the flesh, might be atoned for; but if committed "with a high hand," i. e., in impious rebellion against Jehovah, was punished by stoning (Lev. 24:11-16).

New Testament. Blasphemy against the Holy Spirit (Matt. 12:31; Mark 3:29; Luke 12:10), also called the *unpardonable sin*, has caused extended discussion. The sin mentioned in the gospels would appear to have consisted in attributing to the power of Satan those unquestionable miracles which Jesus performed by "the finger of God," and by the power of the Holy Ghost. It is questionable whether it may be extended beyond this one limited and special sin (*see* Sin, The Unpardonable).

Among the early Christians three kinds of blasphemy were recognized: (1) Of apostates and *lapsi* (lapsed), whom the heathen persecutors had compelled not only to deny, but to curse Christ. (2) Of heretics and other profane Christians. (3) Blasphemy against the Holy Ghost.

Blasting refers to two diseases which attack the grain: one to the withering or burning of the ears, caused by the East wind (Gen. 41:6, 23, 27); the other to the effect produced by a warm wind in Arabia, by which the green ears are turned yellow, so that they bear no grains (K. and D., *Com.*). *See* Mildew.

Blas'tus (blăs'tŭs; *sprout, shoot*), the chamberlain of King Herod Agrippa who acted as mediator between the people of Tyre and Sidon and the king (Acts 12:20), A. D. 44.

Blemish, a physical or mental defect. As the spiritual nature of a man is reflected in his bodily form, only a faultless condition of body could correspond to the holiness of a priest. Consequently all men were excluded from the priesthood, and all animals from being offered as sacrifices, who had any *blemish*. These blemishes are described in Lev. 21:17-23; 22:18-25; Deut. 15:21. "A flat nose" may mean any mutilation, while "anything superfluous" would seem to indicate "beyond what is normal, as an ill-formed member." The rule concerning animals extended to imperfections, so that if an animal free from outward blemish was found, after being slain, internally defective it was not offered in sacrifice.

Bless, Blessing. Acts of blessing may be considered: (1) When God is said to bless men (Gen. 1:28; 22:17). God's blessing is accompanied with that virtue which renders his blessing effectual, and which is expressed by it. Since God is eternal and omnipresent, his omniscience and omnipotence cause his blessings to avail in the present life in respect to all things, and also in the life to come. (2) When men bless God (Psa. 103:1, 2; 145:1-3, etc.). This is when they ascribe to him those characteristics which are his, acknowledge his sovereignty, express gratitude for his mercies, etc. (3) Men bless their fellow-men when, as in ancient times, under the spirit of prophecy, they predicted blessings to come upon them. Thus Jacob blessed his sons (Gen. 49:1-28; Heb. 11:21), and Moses the children of Israel (Deut. 33:1-29). It was the duty and privilege of the priests to bless the people in the name of the Lord (*see* Benediction). Further, men bless their fellow-men when they express good wishes and pray God in their behalf. (4) At meals. The psalmist says, "I will take the cup of salvation, and call upon the name of the Lord" (Psa. 116:13), an apparent reference to a custom among the Jews. A feast was made of a portion of their thank offerings when, among other rites, the master of the feast took a cup of wine, offering thanks to God for his mercies. The cup was then passed to all the guests, each drinking in his turn. At family feasts, and especially the Passover, both bread and wine were passed, and thanks offered to God for His mercies.

Blessing, The Cup of, a name applied to the wine in the Lord's Supper (I Cor. 10:16), probably because the same name was given to the cup of wine in the supper of the *Passover* (*q. v.*).

Blindness (*See* Diseases) was sometimes inflicted for political or other purposes in the East (I Sam. 11:2; Jer. 22:12). The eyes of captives taken in war were commonly put out. This practice was especially followed by the cruel Assyrians, as well as by Babylonians and others.

Figurative. In Scripture blindness is a term frequently used to denote ignorance or a want of spiritual discernment (Isa. 6:10; 42:18, 19; Matt. 15:14). Thus "blindness of heart" is a lack of understanding resulting from unbelief (Mark 3:5, marg.; Rom. 11:25).

Blood (Heb. *däm*; Gr. *haima*, the circulatory life-fluid of the body). A peculiar sacredness attached to blood, because of the idea that prevailed of its unity with the soul. We find this distinctively stated (Gen. 9:4): "But flesh with the life thereof, which is the blood thereof," etc. "This identification of the blood with the soul, which prevailed in antiquity, appears at first to have no further foundation than that a sudden diminution of the quantity of blood in the body causes death. But this phenomenon itself has the deeper reason that all activity of the body depends on the quantity of the blood. The blood is actually the basis of the physical life; and, so far, the soul, as the principle of bodily life, is preeminently in the blood. We are to understand this only of the sensuous soul, not of the intelligent and thinking soul" (Delitzsch).

Arising from this principle the Scriptures record different directions respecting blood:

1. **As Food.** When permission was given Noah to partake of animal food (Gen. 9:4) the use of blood was strictly forbidden. In the Mosaic law this prohibition was repeated with emphasis, though generally in connection with sacrifices (Lev. 3:8; 7:26). "The prohibition of the use of blood has a twofold ground: blood has the soul in itself, and in accordance with the gracious ordinance of God it is the means of expiation for human souls, because of the soul contained in it. The one ground is found in the nature of blood, and the other in its destination to a holy purpose, which, even apart from that other reason, withdraws it from a common use" (Delitzsch, *Bib. Psychology*, p. 283). Because of the blood the eating of bloody portions of flesh (Gen. 9:4), or of flesh with blood (Lev. 19:26; I Sam. 14:32), is also forbidden. The penalty was that the offender should be "cut off from the people," which seems to be death, but whether by the sword or by stoning is not known (Lev. 17:14). This prohibition was also made by the apostles and elders in the council at Jerusalem, and coupled with things offered to idols (Acts 15:29).

2. **Sacrificial.** A well-known rabbinical maxim, and recognized by the author of the Epistle to the Hebrews (9:22), was, "Without shedding of blood is no remission." The life is in the blood, as is often declared by Moses, and the life of the sacrifice was taken, and the blood offered to God, as a representative and substitute for the offerer (Lev. 17:11). *See* Sacrifice.

3. **Figurative.** "Blood" is often used for *life*: "Whoso sheddeth man's blood" Gen. 9:6); "His blood be upon us" (Matt. 27:25). "Blood" sometimes means *race* or *nature*; as, God "hath made of one blood all nations of men" (Acts 17:26). Sometimes it is used as a symbol of slaughter (Isa. 34:3; Ezek. 15:19). To "wash the feet in the blood of the wicked" (Psa. 58:10) is to gain a victory with great slaughter. To "build a town with blood" (Hab. 2:12) is by causing the death of the subjugated nations. Wine is called the *blood* of the grape (Gen. 49:11).

Blood and Water. *See* Crucifixion.

Blood, Avenger or **Revenger of** (Heb. *gō'ēl häddäm*, literally, *redeemer of blood*). At the root of the enactments of the Mosaic penal code there lies the principle of strict but righteous retribution, the purpose being to extirpate evil and produce reverence for the righteous God. This principle, however, was not first introduced by the law of Moses. It is much older, and is found especially in the form of *blood revenge* among many ancient peoples. It appears almost everywhere where the state has not yet been formed or is still in the first stages of development, and consequently satisfaction for personal injury falls to private revenge.

This custom of "blood calling for blood" exists among the Arabs of today. If a man is slain there can never be peace between the tribes again unless the man who killed him is slain by the avenger.

By this custom the life, first of all, but after it also the property of the family, as its means of subsistence, was to be protected by the nearest of kin, called a *redeemer*. The following directions were given by Moses: (1) The willful murderer was to be put to death, without permission of compensation, by the nearest of kin. (2) The law of retaliation was not to extend beyond the immediate offender (Deut. 24:16; II Kings 14:6; II Chron. 25:4, etc.). (3) If a man took the life of another without hatred, or without hostile intent, he was permitted to flee to a city of refuge (*q. v.*).

It is not known how long blood revenge was observed, although it would appear (II Sam. 14:7, 8) that David had influence in restraining the operation of the law. Jehoshaphat established a court at Jerusalem to decide such cases (II Chron. 19:10).

Blood, Issue of. *See* Diseases.

Bloody Sweat. In recording the scene in Gethsemane Luke says that our Lord's sweat "was as it were great drops of blood falling down to the ground" (22:44). These words are understood by many to express merely a comparison between the size and density of the drops of sweat and those of blood. But *blood* only receives its due in being referred to the *nature* of the sweat, and we infer that the words imply a *profusion of sweat* mingled with blood. "Phenomena of frequent occurrence demonstrate how immediately the blood, the seat of life, is under the influence of moral impressions. A feeling of shame causes the blood to rise to the face. Cases are known in which the blood, violently agitated by grief, ends by penetrating through the vessels which inclose it, and, driven outward, escapes with the sweat through the transpiratory glands" (Godet, *Com.*, in loc.). The phenomenon of "bloody sweat" under extreme emotional stress is recognized by medicine and is called *diapedesis*, or the seeping of the blood through the vessels without rupture.

Blot. This word is used in the sense of to obliterate; therefore *to blot out* is to destroy or abolish. To blot out sin is to fully and finally forgive it (Isa. 44:22). To blot men out of God's book is to withdraw his providential favors and to cut them off untimely (Exod. 32:32; comp. Deut. 29:20; Psa. 69:28). When Moses says, in the above passage, "Blot me, I pray thee, out of thy book," we understand the written book as a metaphorical expression, alluding to the custom of making a list of all citizens so that privileges of citizenship might be accorded them. "To blot out of Jehovah's book, therefore, is to cut off from living fellowship with the living God . . . and to deliver over to death. As a true mediator of his people, Moses was ready to stake his own life for the deliverance of the nation if Jehovah would forgive the people their sin. These words were the strongest expression of devoted, self-sacrificing love" (K. and D., *Com.*, in loc.).

The not blotting the name of the saints out of the book of life, etc. (Rev. 3:5), indicates their security and final vindication. A sinful act (Job 31:7) or reproach (Prov. 9:7) is termed a blot.

Blue. *See* Colors.

Boaner'ges (bō-à-nûr'jĕz; Gr. from Aram. "sons of thunder," "noise" *regōsha*. cf. Arab. *rejasa, to rumble*—thunder). An epithet used of James and John (Mark 3:17), denoting probably their fiery eloquence (so Jerome). It may, however, refer to their quick temper and disposition to violence (Luke 9:52-56). Compare Aram. *riggūshä* (Syriac *regshä*, tumult; *rugza*, "anger"). *M. F. U.*

Boar. *See* Animal Kingdom.

to Rome in Acts 27 is one of the best-known and vivid ancient adventures at sea. In O. T. times Egyptian ships not only plied the Nile but the Mediterranean coast. Traffic with Phoenician Byblos (O. T. Gebal) was especially well-known. These ships, called "Byblos Travelers," transported papyrus for papermaking and brought back various kinds of wood and expensive wines. From very early times flat-bottomed boats were capable of hauling heavy stones for Egyptian buildings hundreds of miles on the Nile. Similar flat-bottomed boats, caulked with bitumen, and timber rafts floated on inflated skins, were used on the Tigris and Euphrates Rivers. Traffic extended even to India via the Persian Gulf. Perhaps the most famous ships of antiquity were those of the Phoenicians that plied the Mediterranean and extended Phoenician art and culture as far west as Spain. These ships were propelled by sails and oars. *M. F. U.*

Bo'az (bō'ăz; possibly "fleetness" from Arab. *ba'aza* "to be nimble").

1. A wealthy Beth-lehemite, kinsman to Elimelech, the husband of Naomi. When Naomi and Ruth returned from the country of

73. An Egyptian Boat, ca. 1500 B. C.

Boats. As a farming people for the most part, inhabiting the central highland region of Palestine, the Hebrew people, unlike the Phoenicians, were not sea-minded. References to boats inside Palestine are not numerous. There were ferry boats across the Jordan River (II Sam. 19:18) and small fishing boats, which plied the Sea of Galilee (Mark 4:36; John 6:1, 23). David had to depend upon the Phoenician navy of Hiram. With Solomon the Hebrew navy was built. In this period Eziongeber was a copper refining center. The refining of copper was used as stock-in-trade for the commercial expeditions to Ophir in exchange for "ivory, apes and peacocks" (II Chron. 9:21). "Ships of Tarshish" that fetched gold from Ophir were evidently copper-smelting fleets. Although the Hebrews were a landloving people, there are a number of references to the boats of other nations (cf. Prov. 31:14; Psa. 107:23f; 104:26). Paul used coastal freighters for travel during his missionary journeys. His account of the voyage

Moab the latter received permission to glean in the fields of Boaz. He treated her generously, offering her much greater privileges than were usually accorded to gleaners. Finding that the kinsman of Ruth, who was more nearly related to her, would not marry her according to the "levirate law," Boaz voluntarily assumed its obligations. He married Ruth, and their union was blessed by the birth of Obed, the grandfather of David (Ruth 1-4), B. C. about 1070.

2. One of the pillars of Solomon's Temple. *See* Jachin.

Boch'eru (bō'kè-rōō; *firstborn*), one of the six sons of Azel, a descendant of King Saul (I Chron. 8:38).

Bo'chim (bō'kĭm; *weepers*), a place near Gilgal, called, as the name indicates, to remind of the tears shed by the unfaithful people of Israel upon God reproving them (Judg. 2:1, 5). It was W. of the Jordan, near the Dead Sea, and probably between Beth-el and Shiloh.

Body, the lowest part of man as a triune being,

in which his soul and spirit reside (I Thess. 5:23). In the body of a redeemed man the Holy Spirit dwells (I Cor. 6:19; II Pet. 1:13, 14) and his body is said to be peculiarly God's property (I Cor. 6:20). Its members are to be yielded unto God as instruments of righteousness rather than unto iniquity (Rom. 6:13, 19). **Figuratively.** The Apostle Paul uses the exquisite figure of the human body to portray the spiritual unity of believers in this age, from Pentecost to the out-taking of the church. This mystical body is formed by the baptizing work of the Spirit (I Cor. 12:13), which operation not only unites Christians to one another but to Christ (Rom. 6:3, 4; Gal. 3:27). "The body," Gr. (*sōma*) is differentiated from the *shadow* (*skia*), Col. 2:17. Thus the ceremonies of the law are figures and shadows realized in Christ. "The body of sin" (Rom. 6:6), called also "the body of this death" (Rom. 7:24) represents the physical body under the control of the old nature. Unless the Christian walks in the new nature under the power of the Holy Spirit, he will come under the contamination of the old nature, which is not eradicated or destroyed when he becomes a believer. The Apostle speaks of a *natural* body in opposition to a spiritual body (I Cor. 15:44). The spiritual body will be the body after glorification, no longer subject to sin or death. The body which is buried is natural, subject to dissolution. The resurrection body will be spiritual, no longer subject to natural law or to sin. *M. F. U.*

Bo'han (bō'hăn; a *thumb*), a Reubenite, in whose honor a stone was set up (or named), which afterward served as a boundary mark on the frontier of Judah and Benjamin (Josh. 15:6; 18:17).

Boil. *See* Diseases.

Bolster (Heb. *m⁽e⁾rǎ'äshäh'*, *at the head*, I Sam. 19:13, 16; 26:7, 11, 16), elsewhere rendered *Pillow q. v.*).

Bolt. *See* Lock.

Bond, the translation of several Hebrew and Greek words; an obligation of any kind (Num. 30:2, 4, 12). It is used to signify oppression, captivity, affliction (Psa. 116:16; Phil. 1:7). We read of the "bond of peace" (Eph. 4:3); and charity, because it completes the Christian character, is called the "bond of perfectness" (Col. 3:14). Bands or chains worn by prisoners were known as *bonds* (Acts 20:23; 25:14).

Bondage. *See* Service.

Bondmaid, Bondman, Bondservant. *See* Service.

Bone. This word is used figuratively, as, "bone of my bones, and flesh of my flesh" (Gen. 2:23), "of his flesh and of his bones" (Eph. 5:30), to mean the same nature, and the being united in the nearest relation. Iniquities are said to be in men's *bones* when their bodies are polluted thereby (Job. 20:11); and the state of the national death of Israel scattered among the Gentile nations is represented by the "valley of dry bones" (Ezek. 37:1-14).

Bonnet. *See* Dress.

Book (Heb. *sēfĕr;* Gr. *biblos*). The Hebrew word is much more comprehensive than our English *book*. It means anything *written*, as a *bill* of sale or purchase (Jer. 32, 12, sq.), a *bill*

of accusation (Job. 31:35), a *bill* of divorce (Deut. 24:1, 3), a letter (II Sam. 11:14), or a volume (Exod. 17:14; Deut. 28:58, etc.). Respecting the material, form, and making of books, *see* Writing.

There are some expressions in Scripture which may be suitably noticed here:

1. "To eat a book" (Ezek. 2:9; 3:2; Rev. 10:9) is a figurative expression, meaning to master the contents of the book; to receive into one's innermost being the word of God.

2. "A sealed book" is one closed up from view (Rev. 5:1-3), or one whose contents were not understood by those reading it (Isa. 29: 11). By a book "written within and on the back side" (Rev. 5:1) we understand a roll written on both sides.

3. "Book of the generation" means the genealogical records of a family or nation (Gen. 5:1; Matt. 1:1).

4. "Book of judgment" (Dan. 7:10), perhaps means books of accounts with servants; or, as among the Persians, records of official services rendered to the king, and the rewards given to those who performed them (Esth. 6:1-3). The "books" (Rev. 20:12) are referred to in justification of the sentence passed upon the wicked.

5. "The Book of Life" is a figurative expression originating from the ancient custom of keeping geneological records (Neh. 7:5, 64; 12:22, 23) and of registering citizens for numerous purposes (Jer. 22:30; Ezek. 13:9). God is accordingly represented as having a record of all His creation, particularly men under His special care. To be expunged from "the book of life" is to be severed from the divine favor and to incur an untimely death. Moses thus pleads that he might die, rather than that Israel should be destroyed (Exod. 32:32; Psa. 69:28). In the N. T. "the book of life" refers to the roster of righteous who are to inherit eternal life (Phil. 4:3; Rev. 3:5; 13:8; 17:8; 21:27), from which the saved are not to be blotted out (Rev. 3:5). In the Apocalypse "the book" (or "books") is presented as the divine record of the works of the unsaved at the Great White Throne Judgment (Rev. 20:12, 15), according to which the lost will suffer degrees of eternal punishment.

6. "Book of the Wars of the Lord" represents a memento of a larger literary efflorescence in early O. T. times than is represented in the canonical books. This early literary work, probably poetical, existed in Mosaic times (Num. 21:14). It was likely a collection of odes, celebrating God's glorious acts toward Israel, and recited over camp fires, just as the Bedouin do today. Similarly, "The Book of Jasher" (Josh. 10:13; II Sam. 1:18) seems to have been an early national chronicle of events in Israel, that stretched over several centuries of the early history of the Hebrews.

Booth (Heb. *sŭkkäh, hut,* or *lair;* often translated "tabernacle," or "pavilion"), a shelter made of branches of trees and shrubs (Gen. 33:17), and serving as a protection against rain, frost, and heat. Such were also the temporary green shelters in which the Israelites celebrated (Lev. 23:42, 43) the *Feast of Tabernacles (q. v.).*

Booty. *See* Spoil.

Bo'oz (bō'ŏz), the Grecized form (Matt. 1:5) of the Beth-lehemite *Boaz* (*q. v.*).

Border. 1. Generally (from Heb. *gĕbūl*), a boundary line. Boundary stones were commonly set up to mark off property lines (Deut. 19:14; 27:17; Prov. 22:28; 23:10). Many such markers have been excavated in Babylonia, where demarcation of fields in irrigation areas was especially important. One such "ancient landmark" survives from the reign of Nebuchadnezzar I (c. 1138 B. C.) and was unearthed at ancient Nippur.

Born Again. The new birth is a creative life-giving operation of the Holy Spirit upon a lost human soul, whereby in response to faith in Christ crucified (John 3:14, 15; Gal. 3:24), the believing one, "dead in trespasses and sins" (Eph. 2:1), is quickened into spiritual life, and made a partaker of the divine nature and of the life of Christ Himself (Gal. 2:20; Eph. 2:10; Col. 1:27; I Peter 1:23-25; II Peter 1:4). The complete necessity of this spiritual transaction is the result of fallen man's state of spiritual death, his alienation from God and his consequent utter inability to "see" (John 3:3) or "to enter" into "the kingdom of God" (John 3:5). No matter how moral, refined, talented or religious the natural or unregenerate man may be, he is blind to spiritual truth and unable to save himself (John 3:6; Psa. 51:5; I Cor. 2:14; Rom. 8:7, 8). It is patent, therefore, that the new birth is not the reformation of the old nature but the reception of a new nature. *M. F. U.* See Regeneration.

Borrow, Borrowing, as a matter of law, etc. *See* Loan.

We call attention to the much-debated act of the Israelites in "borrowing" from the Egyptians (Exod. 12:35). This was in pursuance of a divine command (Exod. 3:22; 11:2); and it suggests a difficulty, seeing that the Israelites did not intend to return to Egypt, or restore the borrowed articles. So considered the Israelites were guilty of an immoral act. The following are some of the attempts at explanation, briefly stated:

1. The Israelites borrowed, expecting to return in three days; but when Pharaoh refused to allow this Moses was instructed to demand the *entire* departure of Israel. After the smiting of the firstborn Israel was "thrust out," and had no opportunity of returning what they had borrowed.

2. After the borrowing the Egyptians made war upon the Israelites, and this breach of peace justified the latter in retaining the property as "contraband of war."

3. Ewald (*Hist. of Israel*, ii, 66) maintains that "since Israel could not return to Egypt, . . . and therefore was not bound to return the borrowed goods, the people kept them, and despoiled the Egyptians. It appears a piece of high retributive justice that those who had been oppressed in Egypt should now be forced to borrow from the Egyptians, and be obliged by Pharaoh's subsequent treachery to retain them, and thus be indemnified for their long oppression."

4. "The only meaning of *shä'ăl'* is *to ask* or *beg;* and the expression *yăsh'ûlûm'*, Exod.12:36), literally, 'they allowed them to ask,' i. e.,

the Egyptians received their petition with good will and granted their request. From the very first the Israelites asked without intending to restore, and the Egyptians granted their request without any hope of receiving back, because God had made their hearts favorably disposed toward the Israelites" (K. and D., *Com.*, 3:22). This view appears to be taken by Josephus (*Antiq.*, ii, 14, 6): "They also honored the Hebrews with gifts; some in order to secure their speedy departure; and others on account of neighborly intimacy with them." It evidently refers to the custom, which is fresh now as always in the unchangeable East, of soliciting a gift on the eve of departure, or on the closing of any term of service of any sort whatsoever. That this was the custom in that day, as it is now, is indicated in many Bible references to the giving of gifts (Gen. 12:16; 33:10, 11; Judg. 3:15-18, etc.); but more explicitly in the divine command to the Israelites themselves not to forget the backsheesh when they released a servant at the beginning of the sabbatical year (Deut. 15:13-15).

Bos'cath (bŏs'kăth; II Kings 22:1). *See* Bozkath.

Bosom.

1. The bunchy fold of the dress in front of the breast, into which idlers thrust the hand (Psa. 74:11), was used as a pocket or bag, in which bread, grain, and other kinds of food were carried (II Kings 4:39; Hag. 2:12; Luke 6:38; Gr. *kolpos*). Shepherds thus carried lambs (Isa. 40:11).

2. The front of the body between the arms; hence to "lean on one's bosom" is to so recline at table as that the head covers the bosom, as it were, of the one next him (John 13:23). The expression "into Abraham's bosom" (Luke 16:22) means to obtain the seat next to Abraham, i. e., to be partaker of the same blessedness as Abraham. Christ "is in the bosom of the Father" (John 1:18), i. e., "He who is most intimately connected with the Father, and dearest to him."

Bo'sor (bō'sŏr), the Grecized form (II Pet. 2:15) of *Beor* (*q. v.*), father of Balaam.

Botch. *See* Diseases.

Bottles. Two kinds of containers of liquids were common in ancient times—bottles of skin or earthenware. The latter were easily broken, and recovered pottery and shards constitute one of the most helpful ways the archaeologist has of describing and dating old cultures both in Palestine and Mesopotamia. Beautiful Halafian ware from Tell Halaf in N. Mesopotamie goes back to c. 4500 B. C. Obeidan ware from Tell Obeid, near Ur in Babylonia, dates around 3500 B. C.; Warkan ware from (Uruk, Erech, Gen. 10:11) 3200 B. C., Jemdet Nasr Ware around 3100 B. C. Jeremiah mentions the potter's earthen vessels (Jer. 19:1-10; 13:12-14). Bottles, frequently decorated with glass, held tears of mourners (Psa. 56:8) and were placed in tombs. They were popular in Egypt and Palestine. Bottles of skin were manufactured from whole animal hides by slowly drying them. Such leather containers are referred to in Gen. 21:14 and Josh. 9:4. Jesus referred to the wine bottle which bursts when new wine is put in the old skins (Matt.

9:17; Mark 2:22; Luke 5:37). Such skins were also used to churn butter. Skin bottles are common, even today, in Palestine. *M. F. U.*

Bottomless Pit (A. V. rendering of the Gr. *to phrear tēs 'abusson,* "the pit of the abyss," (Rev. 9:1, 2), the prison-house of the demons. In the end of the age myriads of these imprisoned evil spirits will be set free to indwell, torment and energize men (Rev. 9:1-21) to engage in a gigantic attempt to oppose Christ and God's kingdom-plans for the Jew in the millennial age to come (Rev. 16:13-16). At the Second Coming of Christ Satan and demons are remanded to the abyss (Rev. 20:1-3), which condition will make possible the kingdom-age on earth (Rev. 20:3). *M. F. U. See* Abyss, Hell, Tartarus, Lake of Fire.

Bow, as a weapon. *See* Armor.

    Figurative. The *bow* signifies *judgments* ready for offenders (Psa. 7:12); sometimes *lying* (Psa. 64:3; Jer. 9:3). "A deceitful bow" (Psa. 78:57; Hos. 7:16) represents *unreliableness.* "He bade them teach the use of the bow" (II Sam. 1:18). Bow here means "a song to which the title Kesheth (Heb. word for "bow") was given, not only because the bow is referred to (v. 22), but because it is a martial ode" (K. and D., *Com.,* in loc.).

Bow in the Clouds. *See* Rainbow.

Bowels, the translation of several Hebrew words and the Gr. *splanchna,* and often indicating the internal parts generally, the inner man, and also the *heart.* Thus the bowels are made the seat of tenderness and compassion (Gen. 43:30; Psa. 25:6, translated "tender mercies;" Phil. 1:8; Col. 3:12, etc.). "My bowels shall sound like an harp" (Isa. 16:11) is thus explained by K. and D. (*Com.*): "Just as the hand or plectrum touches the strings of the harp, so did the terrible things that he had heard Jehovah say concerning Moab touch the strings of his inward parts, and cause them to resound with notes of pain."

Bowing, an attitude of respect and reverence from the earliest times. Thus Abraham "bowed himself to the people of the land" (Gen. 23:7); Jacob, when he met Esau, "bowed himself to the ground seven times" (Gen. 33:3); and the brethren of Joseph "bowed down their heads, and made obeisance" (Gen. 43:28). The orientals in the presence of kings and princes often prostrate themselves upon the earth. Such customs prevailed among the Hebrews (Exod. 4:31; I Kings 1:53; 2:19; I Sam. 24:8).

    Bowing is frequently noticed in Scripture as an act of religious homage to idols (Josh. 23:7; II Kings 5:18; Judg. 2:19; Isa. 44:15, sq.), and also to God (Josh. 5:14; Psa. 22:29; 72:9; Mic. 6:6, etc.).

Bowl, the translation of several Hebrew words. We have no means of obtaining accurate information as to the material and precise form of these vessels. In the earliest times they were, doubtless, made of wood and shells of the larger kinds of nuts, and were used at meals for liquids, broth, or pottage (II Kings 4:40). Modern Arabs are now content with a few wooden bowls, although those of the emirs are not infrequently made of copper and neatly tinned. Bowls with Hebrew inscriptions have been found at Babylon. *See* Dish.

Bowman. *See* Armor.

Bowshot, the ordinary distance an archer could shoot an arrow (Gen. 21:16).

Box (Heb. *pak,* II Kings 9:1, 3; Gr. *alabastron,* Mark 14:3), a flask for holding oil or perfumery. The term "box" may have come into use because the flask was frequently inclosed in a box of wood or ivory.

Box Tree. *See* Vegetable Kingdom.

Boy (Heb. *yĕlĕd,* a young *boy* or *child,* Joel 3:3; Zech. 8:5; *nă"ăr,* Gen. 25:27), a term used of those who are from the age of infancy to adolescence.

Bo'zez (bō'ĕs). Between the passes through which Jonathan endeavored to cross over to go up to the post of the Philistines there was a sharp rock on this side, *Bozez;* and one upon the other, *Seneh* (I Sam. 14:4, 5). These rose up like pillars to a great height, and were probably the "hills" which Robinson saw to the left of the pass.

Boz'kath (bŏz'kăth), a town "in the plain" of Judea, near Lachish and Eglon (Josh. 15:39), and the birthplace of Adaiah, maternal grandfather of King Josiah (II Kings 22:1).

Boz'rah (bŏz'rà; *inclosure, fortress*).

    1. A city of Edom, and residence of Jobab (Gen. 36:33; I Chron. 1:44). This is the Bozrah of Isa. 34:6; 63:1; Jer. 49:13, 22; Amos 1:12; Mic. 2:12. It is present Buseirah. Bozrah was the metropolis of N. Edom (1200-700 B. C.) and was famous for its dyed garments (Isa. 63:1).

    2. A place in Moab (Jer. 48:24). Perhaps the same as Bezer.

Bracelet, an article of adornment very popular in ancient times, worn on the wrists or arms of both men and women (Ezek. 16:11; Cant. 5:14). Abraham's servant put such a piece of jewelry on Rebekah's wrist (Gen. 24:22). Israelites in the wilderness contributed gold or silver for the vessels of the Tabernacle from such a source (Num. 31:50). Saul wore such an armlet (II Sam. 1:10), and archaeology furnishes many examples of royal bracelets, such as those worn by Ashurnasirpal, Tiglath-pileser, Esarhaddon, and other emperors of Assyria. Bracelets were often gorgeously inlaid with precious stones and pearls and were popular in Egypt and Phoenicia, as well as Assyria and later in Rome. *M. F. U.*

Bramble. *See* Vegetable Kingdom.

Branch, the rendering of a number of Hebrew and Greek words. In the Scriptures, as well as elsewhere, the family is spoken of as a tree, and the members thereof as *branches.* From this has arisen a number of *figurative* expressions:

    1. A branch is used as a symbol of *prosperity* (Gen. 49:22; Job. 8:16; Prov. 11:28; Ezek. 17:6), and also of *adversity* (Job. 15:32; Psa. 80:11, 15; Isa. 25:5).

    2. "An *abominable* branch" (Isa. 14:19) may mean a branch withered, or a useless *sucker* starting from the root. The sentence might better be rendered, "But thou art cast out without a grave, like an *offensive* (i. e., useless) branch."

    3. "The *highest* branch" (Ezek. 17:3) is applied to Jehoiachin as king. "They put the branch to their nose" (Ezek. 8:17) is very obscure as to its meaning. By some the act

was thought to be expressive of contempt, similar to "they turn up the nose with scorn." Others understand a reference to the hypocrisy of the Jews who carried branches in honor of Jehovah but held them to the nose in scorn, outward worship but secret contempt. It may be that the branch was of a tree dedicated to Baal, and carried by them in his honor. The saying appears to be a proverbial one, but the origin and meaning have not yet been satisfactorily explained.

4. Christ the *Branch.* A branch is the symbol of kings descended from royal ancestors; and, in conformity with this way of speaking, Christ, in respect of his human nature, is called "a root out of the stem of Jesse, and a branch . . . out of his roots" (Isa. 11:1; Jer. 23:5; Zech. 3:8; 6:12). Christians are called branches of Christ, the Vine, with reference to their union with Him (John 15:5, 6).

Brand, in Zech. 3:2 (Heb. *'ûd*), means a wooden *poker* with which the fire is stirred; hence any burnt wood, a *firebrand* (also Amos 4:11; Isa. 7:4). In Judg. 15:5 (Heb. *lăppîd'*, in v. 4 "firebrand"); it is a *lamp* or *torch*, and so rendered elsewhere.

Brass. *See* Mineral Kingdom.

Bray. 1. The loud, harsh cry of an ass when hungry (Job. 6:5). It is used figuratively of the cry of persons when hungry (Job. 30:7).

2. To *pound* or *crush* as in a mortar (Prov. 27:22). Such a punishment is said to be still in use among the oriental nations.

Brazen. *See* Mineral Kingdom.

Brazen Sea. *See* Laver.

Brazen Serpent (Heb. *nähäsh' nĕhôshĕth', serpent of copper*). As the Israelites "journeyed from Mount Hor by the way of the Red Sea" they rebelled against God and against Moses. Punished by Jehovah with fiery serpents (*q. v.*), many of them died. At the command of God Moses made the figure of a serpent and set it upon a pole. Whoever of the bitten ones looked at it "lived," i. e., recovered from the serpent's bite (Num. 21:1-9). This brazen serpent afterward became an object of worship, under the name Nehushtan, and was destroyed by King Hezekiah (II Kings 18:4).

Figurative. From the words of our Lord (John 3:14) most commentators have rightly inferred that the "brazen serpent" was intended as a type of Christ as the Redeemer of the world, as "made sin for us" (II Cor. 5:21), and as bearing our judgment. Cf. the historical fulfillment in Matt. 27:46.

Bread. The word "bread" in the Bible is used in a very wide sense, often occurring as our "food," as in the petition, "Give us this day our daily bread." In strictness it denotes baked food, especially loaves. Its earliest reference is found in Gen. 18:5, 6.

1. **Material.** The best bread was made of wheat, called "flour" or "meal" (Judg. 6:19; II Sam. 1:24; I Kings 4:22, etc.); and when sifted the "fine flour" (Gen. 18:6; Lev. 2:1). A coarser bread was made of barley (Judg. 7:13; John 6:9-13). Millet, spelt, beans, and lentils were also used (Ezek. 4:9-12).

2. **Preparation.** To make "leavened bread" (Heb. *hämĕṣ', sour*) the flour was mixed with water, kneaded on a small kneading trough, with leaven added. These kneading troughs

may have been mere pieces of leather, such as are now used by the Arabs, although the expression "bound up in their clothes" (Exod. 12:34) favors the idea of a wooden bowl. The leavened mass was allowed time to rise (Matt. 13:33; Luke 13:21), sometimes a whole night (Hos. 7:6, "their baker sleepeth all the night"). When the time for making bread was short the leaven was omitted, and *unleavened* cakes were baked, as is customary among the Arabs (Gen. 18:6; 19:3; Exod. 12:39; I Sam. 28:24). Such cakes were called in Heb. *măṣṣäh', sweetness.*

Thin round cakes made of unleavened dough were baked on heated sand or flat stones (I Kings 19:6), by hot ashes or coals put on them—"ash-cakes" (Gen. 19:3; Exod. 12:39, etc.). Such cakes are still the common bread of the Bedouins and poorer Orientals. On the outside it is, of course, black as coal, but tastes well.

Old bread is described in Josh. 9:5, 12, as *crumbled* (Heb. *nĭqqūd', a crumb;* A. V. "moldy"), a term also applied to a sort of easily crumbling biscuit (A. V. "cracknels").

"From flour there were besides many kinds of confectionery made: (*a*) Oven-baked, sometimes perforated cakes kneaded with oil, sometimes thin, flat cakes only smeared with oil; (*b*) pancakes made of flour and oil, and sometimes baked in the pan, sometimes boiled in the skillet in oil, which were also presented as meat offerings; (*c*) honey cakes (Exod. 16:31), raisin or grape cakes (Hos. 3:1; Cant. 2:5; II Sam. 6:19; I Chron. 16:3), and heart cakes, kneaded from dough, sodden in the pan and turned out soft, a kind of pudding (II Sam. 13:6-9). . . . The various kinds of baked delicacies and cakes had, no doubt, become known to the Israelites in Egypt, where baking was carried to great perfection" (Keil, *Arch.,* ii, 126).

3. **Baking.** When the dough was ready for baking it was divided into round cakes (literally, *circles of bread;* A. V. "loaves," Exod. 29:23; Judg. 8:5; I Sam. 10:3, etc.), not unlike flat stones in shape and appearance (Matt. 7:9; comp. 4:3), about a span in diameter and a finger's breadth in thickness. The baking was generally done by the wife (Gen. 18:6), daughter (II Sam. 13:8), or a female servant (I Sam. 8:13). As a trade, baking was carried on by men (Hos. 7:4-6), often congregating, according to Eastern custom, in one quarter (Jer. 37:21, "bakers' street;" Neh. 3:11; 12:38, "tower of the ovens;" A. V. "furnaces").

4. **Egyptian Bread-making.** The following account of early bread-making is very interesting: "She spread some handfuls of grain upon an oblong slab of stone, slightly hollowed on its upper surface, and proceeded to crush them with a smaller stone like a painter's muller, which she moistened from time to time. For an hour and more she labored with her arms, shoulders, loins, in fact, all her body; but an indifferent result followed from such great exertion. The flour, made to undergo several grindings in this rustic mortar, was coarse, uneven, mixed with bran or whole grains, which had escaped the pestle, and contaminated with dust and abraded par-

ticles of the stone. She kneaded it with a little water, blended with it, as a sort of yeast, a piece of stale dough of the day before, and made from the mass round cakes, about half an inch thick and some four inches in diameter, which she placed upon a flat flint, covering them with hot ashes. The bread, imperfectly raised, often badly cooked, borrowed, from the organic fuel under which it was buried, a special odor, and a taste to which strangers did not sufficiently accustom themselves. The impurities which it contained were sufficient in the long run to ruin the strongest teeth. Eating it was an action of grinding rather than chewing, and old men were not infrequently met with whose teeth had gradually been worn away to the level of the gums, like those of an aged ass or ox" (Maspero, *Dawn of Civ.*, p. 320).

5. **Figurative**. The thin cakes already described were not cut but broken, hence the expression usual in Scripture of "breaking bread," to signify taking a meal (Lam. 4:4; Matt. 14:19; 15:36).

From our Lord's breaking bread at the institution of the Eucharist, the expression, *"breaking of,"* or *"to break bread,"* in the New Testament is used for the Lord's Supper (Matt. 26:26), and for the *agape*, or love feast (Acts 2:46).

"Bread of affliction" (literally *penury*) signifies to put one on the low rations of a siege or imprisonment (I Kings 22:27; Isa. 30:20).

"Bread of sorrows," (literally, "bread of labors," Psa. 127:2) means food obtained by toil.

"Bread of tears," (Psa. 80:5) probably signifies a condition of great sorrow.

"Bread of wickedness" (Prov. 4:17) and *"bread of deceit"* (Prov. 20:17) denote not only living or estate obtained by fraud, but that to do evil is as much the portion of the wicked as to eat his bread.

"Cast thy bread upon the waters" (Eccles. 11:1) is doubtless an allusion to the custom of sowing seed by casting it from boats into the overflowing waters of the Nile, or in any marshy ground. From v. 1 it is evident that charity is inculcated, and that, while seemingly hopeless, it shall prove at last not to have been thrown away (Isa. 32:20).

"Bread of Life" prefigures Christ as the Supplier of true spiritual nourishment (John 6:48-51). He is the bread of heaven and God's Word like bread is the spiritual "staff of life" (Matt. 4:4).

Bread, Show. *See* Showbread.

Breakfast. *See* Meals.

Breastplate. *See* Armor; High Priest, Dress of.

Breeches. *See* Priest, Dress of.

Brethren. *See* Brother.

Bribe, Bribery (Heb. *kōphĕr, redemption* money).

1. A payment made by a man to redeem himself from capital punishment. The expression "Of whose hand have I received any bribe to blind mine eyes therewith?" (I Sam. 12:3), means, "Of whom have I taken anything to exempt from punishment one worthy of death?"

2. (Heb. *shō'hăd, gift*). A present to avert punishment (II Kings 16:8; Prov. 6:35), or a bribe taken to pervert justice (I Sam. 8:3; Ezek. 22:12, A. V. "gifts").

Brick (Heb. *lᵉbēnäh'*, from *läbăn to be white*, from the whiteness of the clay out of which bricks were made; rendered "tile" in Ezek. 4:1). The earliest mention made of bricks in Scripture is in the account of the building of Babel (Gen. 11:3). In Exodus (ch. 5) we have the vivid description of the grievous hardship imposed upon the Israelites in making of bricks in Egypt.

1. **Babylonia**. The following account taken from Maspero (*Dawn of Civilization*, pp. 622, 623) will probably answer for all the countries of the East: "In the estimation of the Chaldean architects stone was a matter of secondary consideration. As it was necessary to bring it from a great distance and at considerable expense, they used it very sparingly, and then merely for lintels, thresholds, for hinges on which to hang their doors, for dressings in some of their state apartments, in cornices or sculptured friezes on the external walls of their buildings; and even then its employment suggested rather that of a band of embroidery carefully disposed on some garment to relieve the plainness of the material. Crude brick, burnt brick, enameled brick, but always and everywhere brick was the principal element in their construction. The soil of the marshes or of the plains, separated from the pebbles and foreign substances which it contained, mixed with grass or chopped straw, moistened with water, and assiduously trodden under foot, furnished the ancient builders with material of incredible tenacity. This was molded into thin, square brick, eight inches to a foot across and three or four inches thick, but rarely larger. They were stamped on the flat side, by means of an incised wooden block, with the name of the reigning sovereign, and were then dried in the sun. They were sometimes enameled with patterns of various colors." The Babylonian bricks were more commonly burned in kilns than those used at Nineveh, which are chiefly sun-dried like the Egyptian.

2. **Egyptian**. Egyptian bricks were not generally baked in kilns, but dried in the sun, although a brickkiln is mentioned by Jeremiah (43:9). Made of clay, they are, even without straw, as firm as when first put up in the reigns of the Thutmoids and others, whose names they bear. When made of the Nile mud they required straw to keep them from falling apart, and when laid up in walls were secured by layers of sticks and reeds. In size they varied from 20 or 17 inches to 14¼ inches long, 8¾ inches to 6½ inches wide, and 7 inches to 4½ inches thick.

Brickmaking was regarded as an unhealthy and laborious occupation by the Egyptians, and was, therefore, imposed upon slaves. Very naturally, the Hebrews, when enslaved by the Pharaohs, were put to this work. The use of brick as building material was, doubtless, quite general, although their friable nature often insured early decay. We have illustrations of walls, temples, storehouses, and temples having been built of bricks. The tomb of Rekhmire, grand vizier of Thutmose III (c. 1460 B. C.) depicts Semitic slaves busy with brickmaking. Raamses II (c. 1290 B. C.) rebuilt the older city Zoan-Avaris (Raamses of Exod 1:11) and the bricks are stamped with his name.

3. **Jewish.** The Jews learned the art of brickmaking in Egypt, using almost the identical method. Even now in Palestine bricks are made from moistened clay mixed with straw and dried in the sun.

Mention is made of the brickkiln in the time of David (II Sam. 12:31; comp. Nah. 3:14), and Isaiah complains (65:3) that the people built their altars of brick, instead of stone, as the law directed (Exod. 20:25).

Bridal Gift. See Marriage.

Bride, Bridegroom. See Marriage.

Figurative. The church is alluded to (Rev. 21:9) as "the *bride*, the Lamb's wife." The meaning is that as the bridegroom rejoices over the bride, so the Lord shall forever rejoice in his people and his people in him. Christ himself is also called "the bridegroom" in the same sense (John 3:29).

The figure of marriage is used also in the O. T. to denote the relationship between Jehovah and the Jewish nation, however, with this important contrast: Israel is portrayed as the *wife* of Jehovah (Hos. 2:2, 16:23), now because of unbelief and apostasy, disowned and dishonored, but yet to be restored (Hos. 2:14-23). The church, on the other hand, is a pure virgin, espoused to Christ (II Cor. 11:1, 2), which could never be true of an adulterous wife, although she is eventually to be restored in grace. In the mystery of the Divine-trinity it can be true that Israel is the adulterous wife of Jehovah (to be forgiven and reinstated), while the church is the virgin wife of the Lamb (John 3:29; Rev. 19:6-8). To break down this distinction between Israel, God's elect nation with a unique future when restored (Rom. 11:1-25), and the Church, the body (I Cor. 12:13) and bride of Christ (Eph. 5:25-27), formed by the baptizing work of the Holy Spirit during the period of Israel's national unbelief and setting aside, is to plunge Biblical prophecy into confusion. *M. F. U.*

Bridechamber. See Marriage.

Bridemaid, Brideman. See Marriage.

Bridge. Bridges were not in use in early Biblical times. Rivers were crossed either by ferries (II Sam. 19:18) or more commonly by fords (Judg. 3:28). Later, however, the Romans constructed masonry bridges, ruins of which survive to our day. A famous ruin of a bridge is the structure built across the Tyropoean Valley at Jerusalem by John Hycranus (134-104 B. C.), called "Robinson's Arch" from its modern discoverer. It was destroyed in 63 B. C. during Pompey's siege. Ruins of a famous Roman bridge are to be found near Beirut in Lebanon, north of the Dog River. *M. F. U.*

Bridle (Heb. *rĕ'sĕn, halter,* Job. 30:11; 41:13; Isa. 30:28; *mĕ'thĕg,* strictly the *bit,* as rendered in Psa. 32:9; *mǎhsōm',* a *muzzle,* only in Psa. 39:1; Gr. *chalinos, bit,* James 3:2; Rev. 14:20). The word bridle is used for that portion of the harness by which the driver controls the horse, and consists of the headstall, bit, and reins (Psa. 32:9). The Assyrians ornamented their bridles to a high degree.

It was customary to fix a muzzle of leather on refractory slaves (see Isa. 37:29). Prisoners of war were similarly treated. One of the Assyrian sculptures represents prisoners with a ring in the lower lip, to which is attached a thin cord held by the hand (II Kings 19:28).

Figurative. The providence of God in leading men and nations away from the completion of their plans is symbolized by the "bridle" and "hook" (II Kings 19:28; Isa. 30:28; 37:29; Ezek. 29:4). The restraints of law and humanity are called a bridle, and to "let loose the bridle" (Job 30:11) is to act without reference to these.

Brier. See Vegetable Kingdom.

Brimstone (Heb. *gŏphrĭth,* properly *resin;* Gr. *theion, flashing*). The Hebrew word is connected with *gopher* (Heb. *gŏphĕr*) and probably meant the *gum* of that tree. It was thence transferred to all inflammable substances, especially sulphur (*q. v.*). The cities of the plain were destroyed by a storm of fire and brimstone (Gen. 19:24).

Figurative. Apparently with reference to Sodom, brimstone is often used in Scripture to denote punishment and destruction (Deut. 29:23; Job 18:15; Psa. 11:6; Isa. 30:33; Ezek. 38:22; Luke 17:29; Rev. 9:17, etc.).

Bronze. An alloy of copper and tin, the ancient form in which copper was hardened for effective use in instruments and weapons. Copper was probably discovered about 5,000 B. C. by the Egyptians around Sinai. Deut. 8:9 and Job 28:2 tell of its being smelted from ore dug from the ground. In the Bible Heb. *nĕhōsĕth* and Gr. *chalkos* denote either copper or bronze, not brass, which is much more modern and is an alloy of copper and zinc. (See Minerals.) Palestine archaeology distinguishes several Bronze Ages—Early (3000 B. C.-2000 B. C.); Middle 2000-1500 B. C.); Late Bronze Age (1500-1200 B. C.), followed by the Iron Age (1200-300 B. C.). The Chalcolithic Age (before 3000 B. C.) was characterized by the transition from stone to copper. *M. F. U.*

Brook (Heb. generally *nǎhǎl;* Gr. *cheimarros,* a *torrent*).

1. A small stream, issuing from a subterranean spring and running through a deep valley, as the Arnon, Jabbok, Kidron, etc.

2. Winter streams arising from rains, but drying up in the summer (Job. 6:15).

3. The torrent bed, even though it be without water; so that it is sometimes doubtful whether the bed or stream is meant. The word is sometimes rendered "river," as in the case of the *brook* of Egypt, a small torrent in the southern border of Palestine (Num. 34:5; Josh. 15:4, 47).

Figurative. "My brethren have dealt deceitfully as a brook," etc. (Job. 6:15), is an expression of the failure of friends to comfort and help.

Brother (generally Heb. *'āh;* Gr. *adelphos*).

1. **Meanings.** Brother is a word extensively and variously used in Scripture. (1) A brother in the natural sense, whether the child of the same father and mother (Gen. 42:4; 44:20; Luke 6:14), or of the same father only (Gen. 42:15; 43:3; Judg. 9:21; Matt. 1:2; Luke 3:1, 19), or of the same mother only (Judg. 8:19). (2) A relative, kinsman, in any degree

of blood, e. g., a *nephew* (Gen. 14:16; 29:12, 15), or a *cousin* (Matt. 12:46; John 7:3; Acts 1:14, etc.). (3) One of the same tribe (Num. 8:26; 18:7; II Kings 10:13; Neh. 3:1). (4) A fellow-countryman (Judg. 14:3; Exod. 2:11; 4:18; Matt. 5:47; Acts 3:22, etc.), or one of a kindred nation, e. g., the Edomites and Hebrews (Gen. 9:25; 16:12; 25:18; Num. 20:14.) (5) An *ally, confederate,* spoken of allied nations as the Hebrews and Tyrians (Amos 1:9), or those of the same religion (Isa. 66:20; Acts 9:30; I Cor. 5:11; 11:2), probably the name by which the early converts were known until they were called "Christians" at Antioch (Acts 11:26). (6) A *friend, associate,* as of Job's friends (6:15; see also 19:13; Neh. 5:10, 14), of Solomon, whom Hiram calls his brother (I Kings 9:13). (7) One of equal rank and dignity (Matt. 23:8). (8) One of the same nature, a *fellow-man* (Gen. 13:8; Matt. 5:22, sq.; Heb. 2:17). (9) It is applied in the Hebrew to inanimate things, as of the cherubim it said, "their faces one to another" (Exod. 25:20; 37:9; literally, *a man his brother*) (10) Disciples, followers (Matt. 25:40; Heb. 2:11, 12).

2. **Figurative.** As *likeness* of disposition, habits, Job says (30:29), "I am a brother to dragons" (literally, *jackals*), i. e., I cry and howl like them. Among the Proverbs (18:9) is one which says, "He also that is slothful in his work is *brother* to him that is a great waster." The Jewish schools distinguish between a "brother" (i. e., an Israelite by blood) and "neighbor" (a proselyte). The Gospel extends both terms to all the world (I Cor. 5:11; Luke 10:29, 30).

Brotherly Kindness (Gr. *philadelphia,* II Pet. 1:7) is rendered "brotherly *love*" (Rom. 12-10; I Thess. 4:9; Heb. 13:1), "love of the brethren" (I Pet. 1:22). It is affection for our brethren, in the broad meaning of which word the Scriptures include our neighbors by all mankind, not excluding our enemies. We are not required to bestow equal love upon all, or recognize all as possessing an equal claim to it. It does not make men blind to the qualities of their fellows. While it requires obedience to the golden rule, a special and warmer love for our brethren in Christ is enjoined. Brotherly love requires the best construction of a neighbor's conduct, effort, and sacrifice for others, and forgiveness of injuries. *See* Charity.

Brotherly Love. *See* Brotherly Kindness.

Brothers of Our Lord. In Matt. 13:55 "James, and Joses, and Simon, and Judas" are named as the brothers of Jesus, while sisters are mentioned in v. 56. The sense in which the terms "brothers and sisters" is to be taken has been a matter of great discussion, some contending that they are to be regarded in their literal sense, others in the more general sense of relations. Several theories in support of the latter view have been advanced.

1. That they were our Lord's first cousins, the sons of Alphaeus (or Clopas) and Mary, the sister of the Virgin. Against this view it is urged that there is no mention anywhere of *cousins* or *kinsmen* of Jesus according to the flesh, although the term *cousin* (Gr. *'anepsios* is well known in New Testament vocabulary

(Col. 4:10); also the more exact term "sister's son" (Acts 23:16); also "kinsman" occurs eleven times (Mark 6:4; Luke 1:36, 58; John 18:26; Acts 10:24; Rom. 9:3, etc.). Thus it seems strange that if the *brothers of our Lord* were merely cousins they were never called such.

Again, if his cousins only were meant, it would not be true that "neither did his brethren believe on him" (John 7:5, sq.), for in all probability three of the four (viz., James the Less, Simon, and Jude) were apostles.

2. That they were sons of Joseph by a former marriage with a certain Escha, or Salome, of the tribe of Judah. The only ground for its possibility is the apparent difference of age between Joseph and the Virgin.

3. That they were the offspring of a levirate marriage between Joseph and the wife of his deceased brother, Clopas. This, however, is a mere hypothesis.

The arguments for their being the full brothers of Jesus are numerous, and, taken collectively, are very strong. (1) The words "firstborn son" (Luke 2:7) appear to have been used with reference to later born children. (2) The declaration that Joseph "knew her not till she had brought forth her firstborn son" (Matt. 1:25) does not necessarily establish the perpetual virginity of Mary. We must remember that "the evangelist employed the term 'firstborn' as an historian, from the time when his gospel was composed, and consequently could *not* have used it had Jesus been present to his historical consciousness as the *only* son of Mary. But Jesus, according to Matthew (12:46, sq.; 13:55, sq.), had also brothers and sisters, among whom he was the *firstborn*" (Meyer, *Com.,* on Matt. 1:25). (3) They are constantly spoken of *with* the Virgin Mary, and with no shadow of a hint that they were not her children. The *mother* is mentioned at the same time (Mark 3:31; Luke 8:19; John 2:12; Acts 1:14), just as in Matt. 13:55 the *father* and *sisters* are likewise mentioned along with him.

Brother's Wife (Heb. *y°bē'mĕth,* Deut. 25:7; "sister-in-law," Ruth 1:15). *See* Marriage, Levirate.

Brown (Heb. *ḥûm,* literally, *scorched*), the term applied to dark-colored (black) sheep (Gen. 30:32-40). *See* Colors.

Bruised, the rendering of at least eleven Hebrew and Greek words, is used in Scripture in a *figurative* sense. Thus Satan is said to bruise the heel of Christ (Gen. 3:15), i. e., to afflict the humanity of Christ, and to bring suffering and persecution on his people. The serpent's poison is in his head, and a wound in that part is fatal. So Christ is said to bruise the head of Satan when he crushes his designs, despoils him of his power, and enables his people to rise superior to temptation (Rom. 16:20). Our Lord was bruised when he had inflicted upon him the punishment due to our sins (Isa. 53:5, 10). The king of Egypt is called a "bruised reed" (II Kings 18:21), to mark his weakness and inability to help those trusting in him. Weak Christians are bruised reeds, which Christ will not break (Isa. 42:3; Luke 4:18).

Brutish (Heb. *bä'ăr*, "to be like an animal"), a term applied to one whose mental and moral perceptions are dulled by ignorance (Prov. 12:1), idolatry (Jer. 10:8, 14, 21, etc.). "The word must be explianed from Psa. 92:6, 'brutish,' foolish, always bearing in mind that the Hebrew associated the idea of godlessness with folly, and that cruelty naturally follows in its train" (Keil, *Com.*,on Ezek. 21:31).

Buck. *See* Animal Kingdom (art. Roebuck).

Bucket, a skin vessel with which to draw water (Isa. 40:15). In John 4:11 the Greek word *antlēma* is used.

Figurative. Bucket is used (Num. 24:7) for abundance, as water is the leading source of prosperity in the burning East. The nation is personified as a man carrying two buckets overflowing with water.

Buckler. *See* Armor.

Buffet (Gr. *kolaphizo*, to *strike with the fist*), rude maltreatment in general, whether in *derision* (Matt. 26:67; Mark 14:65), *affliction* (I Cor. 4:11), *opposition* (II Cor. 12:7), or *punishment* (I Pet. 2:20).

Building. *See* Architecture, House.

Figurative. "To build" is used with reference to children, and a numerous progeny (Ruth 4:11; II Sam. 7:27); and to the founding of a family. The Church is called a building (I Cor. 3:9, etc.); and the resurrection body of the Christian is denominated a building in contrast to a tent, symbolical of this mortal body (I Cor. 5:1).

Buk'ki (bŭk'ī).

1. The son of Jogli, and chief of the tribe of Dan, appointed by Moses as one of the commission to divide the inheritance among the tribes (Num. 34:22), B. C. c. 1400.

2. The son of Abishua and father of Uzzi, being great-great-grandson of Aaron (I Chron. 6:5, 51).

Bukki'ah (bŭ-kī'á), a Kohathite Levite, of the sons of Heman, the leader of the sixth band, or course, in the temple music service. The band consisted of himself and eleven of his kindred (I Chron. 25:4, 13), B. C. 1000.

Bul (bŭōl), the eighth ecclesiastical month of the Jewish year (I Kings 6:38). *See* Time.

Bull. *See* Animal Kingdom.

Figurative. In this sense *bull* represents powerful, fierce, and insolent enemies (Psa. 22:12; 68:30; Isa. 34:7).

Bullock. A young bull. *See* Animal Kingdom.

Bulrush. *See* Vegetable Kingdom.

Bulwark. Bulwarks in Scripture appear to have been rural towers, answering the purpose of the modern bastion. They were usually erected at certain distances along the walls, generally at the corners, and upon them were placed the military engines. *See* Fortifications.

Bu'nah (bŭō'ná; *discretion*), the second of the sons of Jerahmeel, the grandson of Pharez, the son of Judah (I Chron. 2:25).

Bunch, the rendering of several Hebrew words, as a bunch of hyssop (Exod. 12:22), a bunch of raisins (II Sam. 16:1), the bunch of a camel (Isa. 30:6).

Bundle, anything bound together, as a "bundle of myrrh" (Cant. 1:13), of "grain" (Matt. 13:30), of "sticks" (Acts 28:3). It is also used of money in a purse (Gen. 42:35).

Figurative. The speech of Abigail to David (I Sam. 25:29) may be rendered, as in R. V., "The soul of my lord shall be bound in the *bundle* of the living," and the words seem to refer to the safer preservation of the righteous on the earth. The metaphor is taken from the custom of binding up valuable things in a bundle to prevent injury.

Bun'ni (bŭn'ī; *built*). 1. One of the Levites who made public prayer and confession (Neh. 9:4), and joined Nehemiah in the solemn covenant after the return from Babylon (ch. 10:15), B. C. 445.

2. A Levite whose descendant, Shemaiah, was made an overseer of the temple after the captivity (Neh. 11:15), B. C. before 445.

Burden (Heb. *măssä*, a *lifting up*). This word is often used in the familiar meaning of a load. It has also frequently the meaning of an *oracle* from God; sometimes as a denunciation of evil (Isa. 13:1; Nah. 1:1), and also merely as a message, whether joyous or afflictive (Zech. 9:1; 12:1; Mal. 1:1).

Burial. *See* Dead, The.

Burial. 1. **Hebrew Custom.** Interment in Bible times followed soon after death, as is evident in the narratives of the burial of Sarah (Gen. 23:1-20), Rachel (Gen. 35:19, 20), and Rebekah's nurse (Gen. 35:8). The Hebrews did not normally cremate, except in most unusual cases of emergency, as in the case of Saul and his sons (I Sam. 31:11-13). Neither did they generally use coffins or embalm. Joseph's burial in a coffin (Gen. 50:26) and his being embalmed (as was his father Jacob, Gen. 50:2, 3) are to be explained as due to his eminent position and station in the land of the Nile. Ordinarily a body after being washed (Acts 9:37) and wrapped in a cloth or closely bound in bands (Matt. 27:59; John 11:44) was carried on a simple bier to the grave or vault (II Sam. 3:31; Luke 7:14), which was commonly a natural cave artificially cut out of the rock (Gen. 25:9, 10; Matt. 27:60). Unguents and perfumes were applied to the

74. Garden Tomb near "Gordon's Calvary"

body if they could be afforded (John 12:7; 19:39), or fragrant incense burned (Jer. 34:5). Mourners lamented with loud demonstrations of grief (Mark 5:38), and were often hired (Jer. 9:17).

2. **Egyptian Burials.** Egyptians took great pains to prepare their dead for the future life. Under the early dynasties trenches with flat stones (*mastaba*) laid over them were employed, and food and other essential commodities for the after-life were placed near the

body. The practice of placing one *mastaba* upon another resulted in a step pyramid, as the famous one at Saqqara from Dynasty III. From these developed the square-based perfect pyramids. These colossal structures, the most famous of which are located at Gizeh, from Dynasty IV, are architectural wonders that still amaze the world. In the complex interior of these great masses of stone the mummified bodies of royalty were interred. The intricate process of mummification, including embalming, required seventy days during which the viscera, except the heart, were removed and stored away in special animal-headed jars. The brains of the deceased were also removed and a resinous paste and linen used to stuff the body, while the body itself was carefully wrapped with linen bandages and cords. Jewels and scarabs were used to adorn the corpse, the latter enabling the mummy to be identified and dated. The mummy was set in a case, which was painted with the face of the deceased. The discovery of the lavish intact tomb of Tutankhamun (1922), a pharaoh of the 14th century B. C. (late Amarna Period) revealed incredible burial splendor. A whole series of fine metal coffins, including one of solid gold inlaid with lapis lazuli and carnelian were uncovered, as well as exquisite death masks of the ruler.

3. **Babylonian Burials.** Like the Egyptians, the Babylonians took great pains to prepare for the future life. The famous royal tombs from the First Dynasty of Ur, discovered by Sir Leonard Woolley and dating from about 2500 B. C., reveal rooms and vaults of brick and stone. The occupant of one of the tombs, identified by a lapis lazuli cylinder as Lady Shub-ad, lay upon a wooden bier, a golden cup near her hand. She wore an elaborate headdress, ornate earrings, and a golden comb with golden flowers set with lapis lazuli. Mass burials were discovered in several tombs. Twenty-five persons were interred with Lady Shubad. Other graves contained the remains of as many as six men and sixty-eighty women. Even chariots filled with treasures were driven into these tombs. Superb gold daggers, bowls, animals, helmets and other exquisitely wrought objects were interred with the deceased. But the graves of the common people were found to be simple rectangular pits. The body was wrapped in matting or put in coffins of wood, clay or wickerwork. Personal belongings as well as food and drink for the after-life were placed in the grave. Kindly provisions for the dead appear in the carefully folded hands in which there was a cup, once doubtless filled with water, for the need of the sleeper. Later Babylonians burned their dead and deposited their ashes in ornate funerary urns, as did Greeks and Romans. Hebrews in later times, indicated by the numerous ossuaries found in N. T. Palestine, also practiced cremation. *M. F. U.*

Burning. *See* Punishments.

Burning. "Burning instead of beauty" (Isa. 3:24, viz., *branding*). In Arabia the application of the *cey* with a red-hot iron plays a very important part in the medical treatment of both man and beast. You meet with many men who have been burned not only on their legs and arms, but in their faces as well. Burning thus appears to have been used as a symbol for disfigurement, as the contrary of beauty. The R. V. renders Isa. 3:24: "branding instead of beauty."

Burning Bush. *See* Bush.

Burnt Offering, Sacrifice. *See* Sacrifices.

Bury, Burying Place. *See* Dead, The; Tomb.

Bush (Heb. *s⁰nĕh, bramble;* Gr. *batos*), the burning bush, in which Jehovah manifested himself to Moses at Horeb (Exod. 3:2, etc.; Deut. 33:16; Mark 12:26; Acts 7:30, 35). This was probably the bramble.

Figurative. The thornbush, in contrast with the more noble and lofty trees (Judg. 9:15), represented the Israelites in their humiliation as a people despised by the world. The *burning* bush represents Israel as enduring the fire of affliction, the iron furnace of Egypt (Deut. 4:20), chastened but not consumed. *See* Vegetable Kingdom.

Bushel. *See* Metrology, II.

Busybody (Gr. *periergos, working around,* I Tim. 5:13; to *be overbusy,* II Thess. 3:11; *'allotriepiskopos,* "one who supervises others' affairs," I Pet. 4:15), a meddlesome person, emphatically condemned in the above passages.

Butler (Heb. *măshqĕh', one who gives drink*), a cup-bearer, as the word is rendered II Chron. 9:4, and an officer of honor in the royal household of Egypt (Gen. 40:1, 13). It was his duty to fill and bear the drinking vessel to the king. Nehemiah was cupbearer to King Artaxerxes (Neh. 1:11; 2:1).

Butter (Heb. *hĕm'äh, grown thick*). Although always rendered butter in the A. V., critics usually agree that the Hebrew word means *curdled milk* or curds. Indeed, it is doubtful whether butter is meant in any passage except Deut. 32:14, "butter of kine," and Prov. 30:33, "the churning of milk bringeth forth butter." The other passages will apply better to curdled milk than to butter. The ancient method of making butter was, probably, similar to that followed by the modern Bedouins. The milk is put into a skin, the tanned hide of a whole goat; this skin is hung up on a light frame or between two poles, and pushed steadily from side to side till the butter is ready. "When the butter has come, they take it out, boil or melt it, and then put it into *bottles* made of goats' skins. In winter it resembles candied honey; in summer it is mere oil" (Thomson, *Land and Book,* i, 393).

Buz (bōōz, *contempt*).

1. The second son of Nahor and Milcah (Gen. 22:21).

2. The father of Jahdo, of the tribe of Gad (I Chron. 5:14).

3. One of three tribes of northern Arabia. In Jer. 25:23 the following are mentioned: "Dedan, and Tema, and Buz, and all that are in the utmost corners."

Bu'zi (bōōz'î), a priest, father of Ezekiel the prophet (Ezek. 1:3), B. C. before 595.

Buz'ite (bōōz'īte), a term indicating the ancestry of Elihu, only found in Job 32:2, 6, "Elihu the son of Barachel the Buzite," indicating ancestry from the Arabian tribe of Buz.

Byways (Heb. *'ōrăḥ*, *way*, and *'ăqălqăl'*, *crooked*). It is recorded (Judg. 5:6) that "in the days of Shamgar, . . . the highways were unoccupied, and the travelers walked through by- ways." These byways were paths and circuitous routes which turned away from the high roads. They were resorted to in order to escape observation and for safety.

C

Cab. A Hebrew dry measure equal to about 2 quarts (II Kings 6:25). *See* Metrology, II.

Cab'bon (kăb'ŏn), a place in the "plain" of Judah (Josh. 15:40); possible the same as Machbenah (I Chron. 2:49).

Ca'bul (kā'bŭl, perhaps *sterile*, *worthless*), i. e., fettered land (Heb. *kĕbĕl*, *a fetter*).

1. A city on the E. border of Asher, at its N. side (Josh. 19:27), probably identical with the village of *Kabul*, 9 miles S. E. of Acre.

2. A district of Galilee, containing twenty "cities," which Solomon gave to Hiram, king of Tyre, in return for services rendered in building the temple. When Hiram saw them he was so displeased that he said, "What cities (i. e., What sort of) are these which thou hast given me, my brother? And he called them the land of *Cabul* unto this day" (I Kings 9:10-13). These cities were occupied chiefly by a heathen population, and were, probably, in a very bad condition. Or it may have been that, as the Phoenicians were a seafaring people, Hiram would prefer to have had coast cities than those inland.

Caesar (sē'zĕr), a name taken by—or given to —all the Roman emperors after Julius Caesar. It was a sort of title, like Pharaoh, and as such is usually applied to the emperors in the New Testament, as the sovereigns of Judea (John 19:15; Acts 17:7). It was to him that the Jews paid tribute (Matt. 22:17; Luke 23:2), and to him that such Jews as were *cives Romani* had the right of appeal (Acts 25:11); in which case, if their cause was a criminal one, they were sent to Rome (Acts 25:12, 21). The Caesars mentioned in the New Testament are Augustus (Luke 2:1), Tiberius (Luke 3:1; 20:22), Claudius (Acts 11:28), Nero (Acts 25:8). *See* each name.

75. Caesarea and Caesarea Philippi

Caesare'a (sĕs-à-rē'à; *pertaining to Caesar*).

1. **Caesarea Palaestinae** (i. e., "Caesarea of Palestine")—so called to distinguish it from Caesarea Philippi—or simply **Caesarea**, was situated on the coast of Palestine on the great road from Tyre to Egypt, and about half way between Joppa and Dora (Josephus, *War*, i, 21, 5). The distance from Jerusalem is given by Josephus (*Ant.*, xiii, 11, 2; *War*, i, 3, 5) as six hundred stadia; the actual distance in a direct line is forty-seven English miles. Philip stopped at Caesarea at the close of his preach-

76. Ruins at Caesarea and the Mediterranean

ing tour (Acts 8:40). Paul, to avoid Grecians who wished to kill him, was taken to Caesarea for embarkation to Tarsus (9:30). Here dwelt Cornelius the centurion, to whom Peter came and preached (10:1, sq.; 11:11), and to this city *Herod* (*q. v.*) resorted after the miraculous deliverance of Peter from prison (12:19). Paul visited Caesarea several times later (18:22; 21:8, 16), and was sent thither by the Roman commander at Jerusalem to be heard by Felix (23:23, 33; 25:1, sq.); and from Caesarea he started on his journey to Rome (27:1).

2. **Caesarea Philippi** (sĕs-à-rē'à fĭ-lĭp'ī; *Caesarea of Philip*), a town in the northern part of Palestine, about one hundred and twenty miles from Jerusalem, fifty from Damascus, and thirty from Tyre, near the foot of Mount Hermon. It was first a Canaanite sanctuary for the worship of Baal; perhaps Baal-hermon (Judg. 3:3; I Chron. 5:23). It was called by the Greeks *Paneas*, because of its cavern, which reminded them of similar places dedicated to the god Pan. In 20 B. C. Herod the Great received the whole district from Augustus, and dedicated a temple to the

emperor. Herod Philip enlarged it and called it Caesarea Philippi, to distinguish it from his father's on the seacoast. It was the northern limit of Christ's travels in the Holy Land (Matt. 16:13; Mark 8:27). The site of Caesarea is called Banias a paltry village.

Cage (*k^{e}lūb*), a "basket" or "cage" for keeping birds (Jer. 5:27) and fruit (Amos 8:1). On the Taylor Prism in the British Museum Sennacherib says of Hezekiah: "Himself like a caged bird, I shut up in Jerusalem . . ."

Ca'iaphas (kā'yȧ-făs), a *surname*, the original name being Joseph (Josephus, *Ant.*, xviii, 2, 2); but, the surname becoming his ordinary and official designation, it was used for the *name* itself. Caiaphas was the high priest of the Jews in the reign of Tiberius Caesar, at the beginning of our Lord's public ministry (Luke 3:2), and also at the time of his condemnation and crucifixion (Matt. 26:3, 57, etc.). He was appointed to this dignity through the curator, Valerius Gratus (probably A. U. C. 770-788 or 789, Meyer, *Com.*, on Luke), and held it during the whole procuratorship of Pontius Pilate, but was deposed by the proconsul Vitellus, A. D. about 38. He was the son-in-law of Annas, with whom he is coupled by Luke (*see* Note). His wife was the daughter of Annas, or Ananus, who had formerly been high priest, and who still possessed great influence and control in sacerdotal matters. After the miracle of raising Lazarus from the dead Caiaphas advocated putting Jesus to death. His language on this occasion was prophetic, though not so designed: "Ye know nothing at all, nor consider that it is expedient for us, that one man should die for the people, and that the whole nation perish not" (John 11: 49, 50). After Christ was arrested he was taken before Annas, who sent him to his son-in-law, Caiaphas, probably living in the same house. An effort was made to produce false testimony sufficient for his condemnation. This expedient failed; for, though two persons appeared to testify, they did not agree, and at last Caiaphas put our Saviour himself upon oath that he should say whether he was indeed the Christ, the Son of God, or not. The answer was, of course, in the affirmative, and was accompanied with a declaration of his divine power and majesty. The high priest pretended to be greatly grieved at what he considered the blasphemy of our Saviour's pretensions, and appealed to his enraged enemies to say if this was not enough. They answered at once that he deserved to die, but, as Caiaphas had no power to inflict the punishment of death, Christ was taken to Pilate, the Roman governor, that his execution might be duly ordered (Matt. 26:3, 57; John 18:13, 28). The bigoted fury of Caiaphas exhibited itself also against the first efforts of the apostles (Acts 4:6, sq.). What became of Caiaphas after his deposition is not known.

NOTE—"Annas and Caiaphas being the high priests" (Luke 3:2). Some maintain that Annas and Caiaphas then discharged the functions of the high priesthood by turns; but this is not reconcilable with the statement of Josephus. Others think that Caiaphas is *called* high priest because he then actually exercised the functions of the office, and that Annas is so called because he formerly filled the situation. But it does not thus appear why, of those who held the priesthood before Caiaphas, Annas in particular should be named, and not others who had served the office more recently than Annas. Meyer (*Com.*, in loc.) says: "Annas retained withal very weighty influence (John 18:12, sq.), so that not only did he continue to *be called by the name*, but, moreover, he also partially *discharged the functions* of high priest." Edersheim (*Life and Times of Jesus*, i, 264): "The conjunction of the two names of Annas and Caiaphas probably indicates that, although Annas was deprived of the pontificate, he still continued to preside over the Sanhedrin" (comp. Acts 4:6).

Cain (kān; a *smith*, *spear*).

1. The firstborn of the human race, and likewise the first murderer and fratricide. His history is narrated in Gen. 4, and the facts are briefly these: (1) **Sacrifice.** Cain was the eldest son of Adam and Eve, and by occupation a tiller of the ground. Upon a time he and his brother offered a sacrifice to God, Cain of the fruit of the ground and Abel of the firstlings of his flock. Cain's temper and offering (being bloodless) were not acceptable, while Abel's received the divine approval. (2) **Murder.** At this Cain was angered, and, though remonstrated with by the Almighty, he fostered his revenge until it resulted in the murder of his brother. When God inquired of him as to the whereabouts of Abel he declared, "I know not," and sullenly inquired, "Am I my brother's keeper?" The Lord then told him that his crime was known, and pronounced a curse upon him and the ground which he should cultivate. Cain was to endure, also, the torments of conscience, in that the voice of his brother's blood would cry unto God from the ground. Fearful lest others should slay him for his crime, he pleaded with God, who assured him that vengeance sevenfold would be taken on anyone who should kill him. He also gave him "a sign," probably an assurance that his life should be spared. Cain became a fugitive, and journeyed into the land of Nod, where he built a city which he named after his son, Enoch. His descendants are named to the sixth generation, and appear to have reached an advanced stage of civilization, being noted for proficiency in music and the arts.

The New Testament references to Cain are Heb. 11:4, where it is recorded, "By faith Abel offered unto God a more excellent sacrifice than Cain;" I John 3:12; Jude 11.

2. A city of the low country of Judah (Josh. 15:57), Khirbet Yaqin, 3 miles S. E. of Hebron.

Cai'nan (kā-ī'năn).

1. The son of Enos and great-grandson of Adam. He was born when his father was ninety years old. He lived seventy years, and begat Mahalaleel, after which he lived eight hundred and forty years (Gen. 5:9-14). His name is Anglicized *Kenan* in I Chron. 1:2.

2. The son of Arphaxad and father of Sala, according to Luke 3:35, 36, and usually called the second Cainan. He is nowhere found named in the Hebrew text, nor in any of the versions made from it, as the Samaritan, Aramaic, Syriac, Vulgate, etc. It is believed by many that the name was not originally in the text, even of Luke, but is an addition of careless transcribers from the Septuagint

Cake. *See* Bread.

Ca'lah (kā'lä), an ancient city of Assyria built by Nimrod or by people from his country

(Gen. 10:11). Shalmaneser I (c. 1280-1260 B. C.) made this place famous in his day. By the time of the great conqueror Ashurnasirpal II (883-859 B. C.) the site had fallen into decay. But this eminent warrior chose Calah as his capital. At this site, now represented by the mound of Nimrud, the young Assyriological pioneer Austen Henry Layard began his excavations in 1845. At the very outset of these diggings the splendid palace of Ashurnasirpal II was discovered with colossal winged man-headed lions guarding the palace entrance. In a small temple nearby a statue of Ashurnasirpal II was found in a perfect state of preservation. Numerous inscriptions of the emperor also came to light. Calah remained the favorite haunt of Assyrian kings for a century and a half. Here Layard recovered the famous Black Obelisk of Shalmaneser III in 1846, which, among other captives, portrays Jehu of Israel (c. 842-815 B. C.) bringing tribute to his Assyrian overlord. Valuable antiquities from Calah are housed in the Metropolitan Museum of Art in New York, the University Museum at Philadelphia and the Museum of Fine Arts in Boston. *M. F. U.*

Calamus. *See* Vegetable Kingdom.

Cal′col (kăl′kŏl), the fourth named of the five sons (or descendants) of Zerah (I Chron. 2:6). The same as *Chalcol* (*q. v.*).

Caldron, the rendering of several Hebrew words, all meaning a vessel for boiling flesh, either for domestic or ceremonial purposes (I Sam. 2:14; II Chron. 35:13; Job. 41:20; Jer. 52:18, 19; Ezek. 11:3, 7). Metallic vessels of this kind have been found in Egypt, Babylonia and Mesopotamia.

Ca′leb (kā′lĕb; a *dog*).

1. The son of *Jephunneh* (*q. v.*), the Kenezite, and chief of one of the families of Judah.

Personal History. (1) **A spy.** The first mention of Caleb was his appointment, at the age of forty years (Josh. 14:6, 7), as one of the twelve spies sent by Moses to explore Canaan (Num. 13:6, 17-25), B. C. c. 1440. (2) **A faithful report, and results.** On their return all the spies agreed respecting the preeminent goodness of the land, but differed in their advice to the people. While the ten others announced the inability of Israel to overcome the Canaanites, Caleb and Joshua spoke encouragingly. They admitted the strength and stature of the people, and the greatness of the walled cities, but were far from despairing. Caleb, stilling the people before Moses, exhorted them earnestly and boldly, "Let us go up at once and possess it; for we are well able to overcome it" (Num. 13:30). For this act of faithfulness, repeated the following day, Caleb and Joshua barely escaped being stoned by the people (Num. 14:10). Moses announced to the congregation, however, that they alone, of all the people over twenty years of age, should enter into the promised land, and in a plague that shortly followed the other spies died (Num. 14:26-38). A special promise was given to Caleb that he should enter the land which he had trodden upon, and that his seed should possess it (Num. 14:24). (3) **In Canaan.** We find no further mention of Caleb until about forty-five years after. The land was being divided, and he claimed the special

inheritance promised by Moses as a reward of his fidelity. His claim was admitted, and Joshua added his blessing. Caleb, who at the age of eighty-five years was still as strong for war as when he was forty, drove out the Anakim from Hebron (Josh. 14:6-15; 15:14). He then attacked Debir (Kirjath-sepher), to the S. W. of Hebron. This town must have been strong and very hard to conquer, for Caleb offered a prize to the conqueror, promising to give his daughter Achsah for a wife to anyone who should take it. Othniel, his younger brother took the city and secured Achsah and a tract of land (Josh. 15:13-19). We have no further information respecting Caleb's life or death.

NOTE—"There is no discrepancy between the accounts of the taking of Debir (Josh. 11:21, 22; 15:13-19), for the expulsion of its inhabitants by Joshua did not preclude the possibility of their returning when the Israelitish armies had withdrawn to the north" (Keil, *Com.*).

2. The last named of the three sons of Hezron (I Chron. 2:18), of the descendants of Judah, in I Chron. 2:9, where he is called *Chelubai*. His sons by his first wife, Azubah, or *Jerioth* (*q. v.*), were Jesher, Shobab, and Ardon (v. 18). After her death he married Ephrath, by whom he had Hur (v. 19), and perhaps others (v. 50). He had also several children by his concubines, Ephah and Maachah (vers. 46, 48).

3. The son of Hur and grandson of the preceding (I Chron. 2:50). No further information is given respecting him, save a mention of his numerous posterity.

Ca′leb-eph′ratah (kā′lĕb-ĕf′rȧ-thȧ), only in I Chron. 2:24: "And after that Hezron was dead in Caleb-ephratah," etc. "The town or village in which Caleb dwelt with his wife Ephrath may have been called Caleb of Ephrathah, if Ephrath had brought this place as a dower to Caleb (comp. Josh. 15:18). Ephrathah or Ephrath was the ancient name of Bethlehem, and with it the name Ephrath is connected, probably so called after her birthplace. If this supposition is well founded, then Caleb of Ephrathah would be the little town of Bethlehem" (Keil, *Com.*). Many scholars, however, adopt the LXX reading, "After the death of Hezron Caleb came unto Ephrath, the wife of Hezron, his father."

Calendar (Lat. *calendarium*, from *calere, to call*, because the priests *called* the people to notice that it was new moon), an ecclesiastical almanac, indicating the special days and seasons to be observed.

1. **Chaldean.** Their years were vague years of three hundred and sixty days. The twelve equal months of which they were composed bore names which were borrowed, on the one hand, from events in civil life, such as 'Simanu,' from the making of brick, and 'Addaru,' from the sowing of seed, and, on the other, from mythological occurrences whose origin is still obscure, such as 'Nisanu,' and 'Elul.' The adjustment of this year to astronomical demands was roughly carried out by the addition of a month every six years, which was called a second Adar, Elul, or Nisan, according to the place in which it was intercalated. The neglect of the hours and minutes in their calculations of the length of the year became

with them, as with the Egyptians, a source of serious embarrassment, and we are still ignorant as to the means employed to meet the difficulty.

2. **Egyptian.** Very early (4241 B. C., according to Breasted, *History of Egypt*, p. 32), the Egyptians divided the year into twelve months of thirty days each, with a sacred period of five feast days intercalated at the end of the year. The year began when Sirius first appeared on the eastern horizon at sunrise (the 19th of July on our calendar). Since this calendar year was a quarter of a day shorter than the solar year, it gained a full day every four years, and a full year in 1460 years. An astronomical event such as the heliacal rising of Sirius, when computed on the basis of the Egyptian calendar, may therefore be reckoned and dated within four years in terms of our reckoning, i. e. in years B. C. This is the calendar which Julius Caesar introduced into Rome and which was bequeathed to us by the Romans (see below). It has thus been in operation for over six millennia.

3. **Jewish.** The Israelites divided their year according to natural phenomena exclusively, combining, therefore, the solar and lunar year. The months began with the new moon, but the first month was fixed (after the Exodus and by the necessities of the Passover) by the ripening of the earliest grain, viz., barley. The lunar month averaging twenty-nine and one half days, a year of twelve months of thirty and twenty-nine days alternately resulted; but this involved a variation of eleven and twenty-two days alternately in eighteen out of nineteen years. To reconcile this lunar year with the year of the seasons, a thirteenth month was inserted about once in three years. That the Jews had anciently calendars wherein were noted all the feasts, fasts, and days on which they celebrated any great event of their history is evident from Zech. 8:19. Probably the oldest calendar is the *Megillath Taanith* ("volume of affliction"), said to have been drawn up in the time of John Hyrcanus, B. C. before 106. In the subjoined calendar it is assumed, as usual, that the first month of the Hebrew calendar, Abib or Nisan, answers nearly to half March and half April; the earliest possible commencement of the lunar year being on our fifth of March. *See* Chronology.

JEWISH CALENDAR

NAMES OF MONTHS		FESTIVALS	SEASON	WEATHER	CROPS, ETC.
HEBREW	ENGLISH				
A'BIB (Heb. *'ābib, green ears*), or NI'-SAN. Thirty days; first of *sacred*, seventh of *civil*, year.	March-April.	1. New moon (Num. 10: 10; 28:11-15). *Fast* for Nadab and Abihu (Lev. 10:1, 2). 10. Selection of paschal lamb (Exod. 12:3). *Fast* for Miriam (Num. 20:1), and in memory of the scarcity of water (20:2). 14. Paschal lamb killed in evening (Exod. 12:6). Passover begins (Num. 28:16). Search for leaven. 15. First day of unleavened bread (Num. 28: 17). After sunset sheaf of barley brought to temple. 16. "First fruits," sheaf offered (Lev. 23:10, sq.). Beginning of harvest, fifty days to Pentecost (Lev. 23:15). 21. Close of Passover, end of unleavened bread (Lev. 23:6). 15 and 21. Holy convocations (23:7). 26. *Fast* for death of Joshua.	Spring equinox.	*Wind* S.; sometimes sirocco. Fall of the "latter" or spring rains (Deut. 11:14). The melting snows of Lebanon and the rains fill the Jordan channel, and the river overflows in places its "lower plain" (Josh. 3:15; comp. Zech. 10:11).	*Barley* harvest begins in the plain of Jericho and in the Jordan valley; *wheat* coming into ear; uplands brilliant with shortlived verdure and flowers.
ZIF (Heb. *ziv, brightness*), or I'JAR. Twenty-nine days; second *sacred*, eighth of *civil*, year.	April-May.	1. New moon (Num. 1: 18). 6. *Fast* of three days for excesses during Passover. 10. *Fast* for death of Eli and capture of ark (I Sam. 4:11, sq.). 15. "Second" or "little" Passover, for those unable to celebrate in Abib; in memory of entering wilderness (Exod. 16:11).	Summer.	*Wind* S.; showers and thunder storms very rare (I Sam. 12:17, 18). Sky generally cloudless till end of summer.	Principal harvest month in lower districts. *Barley* harvest general (Ruth 1:22); *wheat* ripening on the uplands; *apricots* ripen. In Jordan valley hot winds destroy vegetation.

NAMES OF MONTHS		FESTIVALS	SEASON	WEATHER	CROPS, ETC.
HEBREW	ENGLISH				

SI'VAN (Heb. *sivän*). Thirty days; third third of *sacred*, ninth of *civil*, year.	May–June.	23. *Feast* for taking of Gaza by S. Maccabaeus; for taking and purification of temple by the Maccabees. 27. *Feast* for expulsion of Galileans from Jerusalem. 28. *Feast* for death of Samuel (I Sam. 25:1). 1. New moon. 2. "*Feast* of Pentecost," or "*Feast* of Weeks," because it came seven weeks after Passover (Lev. 23:15-21). 15, 16. Celebration of victory over Beth-san (I Macc. 5:52; 12:40, 41). 17. *Feast* for taking Caesarea by Asmonaeans. 22. *Fast* in memory of Jeroboam's forbidding subjects to carry first fruits to Jerusalem (I Kings 12:27). 25. *Fast* in memory of rabbins Simeon, Ishmael, and Chanina; *feast* in honor of judgment of Alexander the Great, in favor of Jews against Ishmaelites, who claimed Canaan. 27. *Fast*, Chanina being burned with books of law.		*Wind* N. W., also E.; and *khamseen*, or parching wind from southern deserts. Air still and brilliantly clear.	*Wheat* harvest begins on uplands; *almonds* ripen; *grapes* begin to ripen; *honey* of the Jordan valley collected May to July.
TAM'MUZ (Heb. *tämmüz*). Twenty-nine days; fourth of *sacred*, tenth of *civil*, year.	June–July.	1. New moon. 14. *Feast* for abolition of a book of Sadducees and Bethusians, intended to subvert oral law and traditions. 17. *Fast* in memory of tables of law broken by Moses (Exod. 32:19); and taking of Jerusalem by Titus.	Hot season.	*Wind* usually N. W., also E., and *khamseen* from S. Air still and very clear; heat intense; heavy dews.	*Wheat* harvest on highest districts; various *fruits* ripe. Springs and vegetation generally dried up. Bedouins leave steppes for mountain pastures. Elsewhere, country parched, dry and hard— "a dreary waste of withered stalks and burned-up grass" ("stubble," A. V.).
AB (Heb. *'äb*, *fruitful*). Thirty days; fifth of *sacred*, eleventh of *civil*, year.	July–August.	1. New moon; *fast* for death of Aaron, commemorated by children of Jethuel, who furnished wood to temple after the captivity. 9. *Fast* in memory of God's declaration against murmurers entering Canaan (Num. 14:29-31). 18. *Fast*, because in the time of Ahaz the evening lamp went out. 21. *Feast* when wood was stored in temple. 24. *Feast* in memory of law providing for sons and daughters alike inheriting estate of parents.		*Wind* E. Air still and very clear; heat intense; heavy dews.	Principal *fruit* month —grapes, figs, walnuts, olives, etc.; *vintage* begins (Lev. 26:5).
E'LUL (Heb. *'ēlül'*, good for *nothing*). Twenty-nine days; sixth of *sacred*, twelfth of *civil*, year.	August–September.	1. New moon. 7. *Feast* for dedication of Jerusalem's walls by Nehemiah. 17. *Fast*, death of spies bringing ill report (Num. 14:26). 21. *Feast*, wood offering. 22. *Feast* in memory of wicked Israelites, who were punished with death. (Throughout the month the cornet is sounded to warn of approaching new civil year.)		*Wind* N. E. Heat still intense (II Kings 4:18-20), much lightning, but rain rarely.	*Vintage* general; harvest of *dourra* and *maize*; *cotton* and *pomegranates* ripen.

NAMES OF MONTHS		FESTIVALS	SEASON	WEATHER	CROPS, ETC.
HEBREW	ENGLISH				
ETH'ANIM (Heb. *'ĕthănim, permanent*), or TIS'RI. Thirty days; seventh of *sacred*, first of *civil*, year.	September-October.	1. New moon; *New Year; Feast* of Trumpets (Lev. 23:24; Num. 29: 1, 2). 3. *Fast* for murder of Gedaliah (II Kings 25: 25; Jer. 41:2); high priest set apart for day of atonement. 7. *Fast* on account of worship of golden calf. 10. Day of atonement, *"the fast"* (Acts 27:9), i. e., the only one enjoined by the law; the first day of jubilee years. 15-21. *Feast* of Tabernacles. 22. Holy convocation, palms borne, prayer for rain. 23. *Feast* for law being finished; dedication of Solomon's temple.	Seed time, or earing.	*Wind* N. E. Dews very heavy. Former or early, i. e., autumnal, rains begin (Joel 2:23) to soften the ground (Deut. 11: 14); nights frosty (Gen. 31: 40).	Plowing and sowing begin as soon as ground is softened by the rain—in any weather as the time runs short (Prov. 20:4; Eccles. 11:4); *cotton* harvest.
BUL (Heb. *bûl*), or MARCHESH'-VAN. Twenty-nine days; eighth of *sacred*, second of of *civil*, year.	October-November.	1. New moon. 6, 7. *Fast* because Nebuchadnezzar blinded Hezekiah (II Kings 25: 7; Jer. 52:10). 17. Prayers for rain. 19. *Fast* for faults committed during Feast of Tabernacles. 23. Memorial of stones of altar profaned by Greeks (I Macc. 4:44). 26. *Feast* in memory of recovery after the captivity of places occupied by the Cuthites.		*Wind* N., N. W., N. E., S., S. W. Rainy month, partly fine; rains from S. and S. W.	*Wheat* and *barley* sown; *vintage* in northern Palestine; *rice* harvest; *fig* tree laden with fruit; *orange* and *citron* blossom; almost all vegetation has disappeared.
CHIS'LEU (Heb. *kĭslĕu*). Thirty days; ninth of *sacred*, third of *civil*, year.	November-December.	1. New moon. 2. *Fast* (three days) if no rain falls. 3. *Feast* in honor of Asmonaeans throwing out idols placed in temple court by Gentiles. 6. *Feast* in memory of roll burned by Jehoiakim (Jer. 36:23). 7. *Feast* in memory of Death of Herod the Great. 14. *Fast*, absolute if no rain. 21. *Feast* of Mount Gerizim; plowing and sowing of Mount Gerizim with tares, as Samaritans had intended to do with temple ground. 25. *Feast* of the dedication of the temple, or of Lights (eight days) in memory of restoration of temple by Judas Maccabaeus.	Winter begins. (John 10: 22).	Snow on mountains and stormy. Greatest amount of rainfall during year in December, January, and February.	Trees bare, but plains and deserts gradually become green pastures.
TE'BETH (Heb. *tĕ'bĕth*). Twenty-nine days; tenth of *sacred*, fourth of *civil*, year.	December-January.	1. New Moon. 8. *Fast* because the law was translated into Greek. 9. *Fast*, no reason assigned. 10. *Fast* on account of siege of Jerusalem by Nebuchadnezzar (II Kings 25:1). 28. *Feast* in memory of exclusion of Sadducees from the Sanhedrin.	Mid-winter.	*Wind* N., N. W., N. E. Coldest month; rain, hail, and snow (Josh. 10:11) on higher hills, and occasionally at Jerusalem.	Flocks leave highlands for the Jordan valley, and its cultivation begins; *oranges* ripening, and lower districts green with grain.

NAMES OF MONTHS		FESTIVALS	SEASON	WEATHER	CROPS, ETC.
HEBREW	ENGLISH				
SHE'BAT (Heb. *shebät'*), or SE'-BAT. Thirty days; eleventh of *sacred*, fifth of *civil*, year.	January-February.	1. New moon. 2. Rejoicing for death of King Alexander Jannaeus, enemy of the Pharisees. 4 or 5. *Fast* in memory of death of elders, successors to Joshua. 15. Beginning of the year of *Trees* (*q. v.*). 22. *Feast* in memory of death of Niscalenus, who ordered images placed in temple, and who died before execution of his orders. 23. *Fast* for war of the Ten Tribes against Benjamin (Judg. 20); also idol of Micah (18:11, sq.). 29. Memorial of death of Antiochus Epiphanes, enemy of Jews.	Winter.	*Wind* N., N. W., N. E. Gradually growing warmer. Toward end of month the most pleasant "cool season" begins.	*Almond* and *peach* blossom in warmer and sheltered localities; *oranges* ripe.
A'DAR (Heb. *'ädär*, *fire*). Twenty-nine days; twelfth of *sacred*, sixth of *civil*, year.	February-March.	1. New moon. 7. *Fast* because of Moses' death (Deut. 34:5). 8, 9. Trumpet sounded in thanksgiving for rain, and prayer for future rain. 12. *Feast* in memory of Hollianus and Pipus, two proselytes, who died rather than break the law. 13. *Fast* of Esther (Esth. 4:16). *Feast* in memory of Nicanor, enemy of the Jews (I Macc. 7: 44). 14. The first *Purim*, or lesser *Feast* of Lots (Esth. 9:21). 15. The great *Feast of Purim* (*q. v.*). 17. Deliverance of sages who fled from Alexander Jannaeus. 20. *Feast* for rain obtained in time of drought, in time of Alexander Jannaeus. 23. *Feast* for dedication of Zerubbabel's temple (Ezra 6:16). 28. *Feast* to commemorate the repeal of decree of Grecian kings forbidding Jews to circumcise their children.	Cold and rainy season, or spring.	*Wind* W. Thunder and hail frequent, sometimes snow. The latter rains begin, on which plenty or famine, the crops and pasture depend.	In valley of Jordan cultivation draws to an end, and *barley* ripens.

4. **Roman.** The ancient Roman year consisted of twelve lunar months, of twenty-nine and thirty days alternately, making three hundred and fifty-four days; but a day was added to make the number odd, which was considered more fortunate, so that the year consisted of three hundred and fifty-five days. This was less than the solar year by ten days and a fraction. Numa is credited with attempting to square this lunar year of three hundred and fifty-five days with the solar of three hundred and sixty-five; but how he did it is not certainly known. The Decemviri, B. C. 450, probably introduced the system of adjustment afterward in use, viz., by inserting biennially an intercalary month of twenty-three days between February 24 and 25, and in the fourth year a month of twenty-two days between February 23 and 24. But this gave the year an average of three hundred and sixty-six and a quarter days, or one too many; and it was the business of the pontiffs to keep the calendar in order by regular intercalation. Their neglect produced great disorder. The mischief was finally remedied by Julius Caesar, with the assistance of the mathematician Sosigenes. To bring the calendar into correspondence with the seasons the year 46 B. C. was lengthened so as to consist of fifteen months, or four hundred and forty-five days, and the calendar known as the Julian was introduced January 1, 45 B. C. The use of the

lunar year and the intercalary month was abolished, and the civil year was regulated entirely by the sun. Caesar fixed this year to three hundred and sixty-five and a quarter days, which is correct within a few minutes. After this the ordinary year consisted of three hundred and sixty-five days, divided into twelve months, with the names still in use.

5. **Gregorian.** The method adopted by Caesar answered a very good purpose for a short time, but after several centuries astronomers began to discover a discrepancy between the solar and the civil year. The addition of one day every fourth year would be correct if the solar year consisted of exactly three hundred and sixty-five and a quarter days, whereas it contains only three hundred and sixty-five days, five hours, forty-seven minutes, fifty-one and a half seconds. This makes the Julian year longer than the true solar year by about twelve minutes. In 1582 the Julian year was found to be about ten days behind the true time, the vernal equinox falling on the 11th instead of the 21st of March, its date at the Council of Nice, A. D. 325. Pope Gregory issued an edict causing the 5th of October to be called the 15th, thus suppressing ten days, and making the year 1582 to consist of only three hundred and fifty-five days; thus restoring the concurrence of the solar and civil year, and consequently the vernal equinox to the place it occupied in 325, viz., March 21. In order that this difference might not recur it was further ordained that every hundredth year (1800, 1900, etc.) should not be counted as a leap year, except every fourth hundredth, beginning with 2000. In this way the difference between the civil and solar years will not amount to a day in five thousand years. The pope was promptly obeyed in Spain, Portugal, and part of Italy. The change took place in France the same year by calling the 10th the 20th day of December. Gradually other countries adopted this style.

6. **Ecclesiastical.** Originally the ecclesiastical calendar was only an adaptation of Greek and Roman calendars, although Christian influence is seen in two calendars as early as the middle of the 4th century. This influence is shown in the setting of the Christian week side by side with the pagan, while the other, A. D. 448, contains Christian feast days and holidays, though as yet very few, viz., four festivals of Christ and six martyr days. The earliest known *pure Christian* calendar is of Gothic origin, from Thrace, in the 4th century. It is a fragment, merely thirty-eight days, but contains mention of seven saints.

Originally the martyrs were celebrated only where they suffered, and each Church had its own calendar, but in the Middle Ages the Roman calendar spread throughout the Western Church. From the 8th century combined calendars of saints and martyrs were made, and are found in great numbers. They are designed to suit all times, are supplied with means to ascertain the movable feasts, especially Easter.

The present Saints' Calendar of the Roman Catholic Church is very copious, and may be found more or less complete in its almanacs.

The German Lutheran Church retained the Roman calendar (with the saints' days of that age) at the Reformation. An Evangelical Calendar for the use of the Evangelical Church of Germany is issued annually.

The calendar of the Church of England may be found in the large edition of the Prayer Book, and consists of nine columns, containing, 1. The golden number or cycle of the moon; 2. Days of the month in numerical order; 3. Dominical or Sunday letter; 4. Calends, nones, and ides; 5. Holy days of the Church, as also some festivals of the Roman Church, for convenience rather than reverence; 6-9. Portions of Scripture and of the Apocrypha, appointed for the daily lessons.

Calf, the young of the ox species. The frequent mention in Scripture of calves is due to their common use in sacrifices. The "fatted calf" was considered by the Hebrews as the choicest of animal food. It was stall-fed, frequently with reference to a particular festival or extraordinary sacrifice (I Sam. 28:24; Amos 6:4; Luke 15:23). The allusion in Jer. 34:18, 19 is to an ancient custom of ratifying a *Covenant* (q v.). *See* Animal Kingdom.

Figurative. The expression "calves of our lips" (Hos. 14:2), and "fruit of our lips" (Heb. 13:15) signify *prayers* or *thanksgiving*, young oxen being considered as the best animals for thank offerings.

Calf, Golden. The idolatrous image of a young bull set up at Mount Sinai (Exod. 32:2 seq.) and later by Jeroboam at Bethel and Dan (I Kings 12:28). The young bull symbolized vitality and strength, and the Israelites sought to worship Jehovah under this representation. Doubtless the prevalence of bull worship in Egypt suggested this animal. Jeroboam also had likely seen the bull Apis worshipped in Egypt while he was a refugee at the court of Shishak (I Kings 11:40), but ancient tradition also influenced him, for he quotes Exod. 32:4 in advertising his new cult. Common among western Semites are gods represented as standing on an animal's back or as seated on an animal-borne throne. What Jeroboam likely did was to represent the invisible Jehovah bestride a young bull of gold. It is inconceivable that he would resort to the crass idea of actually expecting worship of a golden calf itself. *M. F. U.*

Calf, Worship of. *See* Gods, False.

Calker, a *repairer of* the *breach*, as in II Kings 12:8; 22:5, but elsewhere used as now for one who stops the seams in a vessel (Ezek. 27:9, 27), with pitch or bitumen.

Call, Calling (Heb. usually *qärä;* Gr. *kaleō*, to *call*).

1. **To Call for Help,** hence, to pray. We first meet this expression in Gen. 4:26: "Then began men to call upon the name of the Lord" (see also Psa. 79:6; 105:1; Isa. 64:7; Jer. 10:25; Zeph. 3:9). In this sense of invoking God in prayer, with an acknowledgment of his attributes, confession of sins, etc., "call" is used in the New Testament (Acts 2:21; 7:59; 9:14; Rom. 10:12; I Cor. 1:2).

2. **Divine Call.** The word "call" is used in Scripture with the following significations: (1) In the sense of "to name," "to designate" (Gen. 16:11; Deut. 25:8), and in the sense of

"to be," e. g., "His name shall be called Wonderful" (Isa. 9:6); i. e., he shall be wonderful, and so acknowledged. (2) In the designation of individuals to some special office or work, as the call of Bezaleel (Exod. 31:2), of judges, prophets, apostles, etc. (Isa. 22:20; Acts 13:2); of nations to certain functions, privileges, or punishments (Lam. 2:22; Isa. 5:26); particularly of Israel (Deut. 7:6-8; Isa. 41:9; 42:6; Hos. 11:1). (3) A condition of life, "Let every man abide in the same *calling* wherein he was called" (I Cor. 7:20). (4) **Call to salvation.** "To call" signifies to invite to the blessings of the Gospel, to offer salvation through Christ. This calling is, we believe, general, extending to all mankind. There is likewise a calling by the Spirit which is not resisted and clearly described as an efficacious calling. The efficacious calling of God is tantamount to His sovereign choice. There are now two elect companies in the world—Israel and the church. Both alike appear in Scripture as called by God. Israel's calling is national, while the calling of those who comprise the church is individual. It is wholly within the bounds of the efficacious calling that believers are termed *the called ones*. They are thus distinguished from the general mass who though subject to a general call are not efficaciously called. The efficacious call is the work of God in behalf of each elect person under grace. They are referred to as "the called according to His purpose" (Rom. 8:28). The Apostle goes on to declare that those whom God foreknew, He predestined; those whom He predestined, He called; those whom He called, He justified; and those whom He justified, He glorified (Rom. 8:29, 30). Calling, then, is that choice on the part of God of an individual through an efficacious working in his mind and heart by the Holy Spirit so that the will of the one who is called operates by its own determination in the exercise of saving faith. In this way two great necessities are provided; namely, only those are called whom God has predestined to be justified and glorified and those who are thus called, choose from their own hearts and minds to accept Christ as Savior. Revised by *M. F. U.*

Cal'neh (kăl'nĕ). 1. An ancient Babylonian city pertaining to Nimrod's kingdom (Gen. 10:10). Its location is uncertain. Some have identified Calneh with Nippur, an important excavated city in central Babylonia. Others see a connection with Kulunu, an ancient important city near Babylon. Another possibility is that Calneh may signify Hursagkalama, a twin city of Kish. 2. Calneh mentioned in Amos 6:2 together with Hamath may be Kullani, modern Kullanhu, about six miles distant from Arpad. *M. F. U.*

Cal'no (kăl'nō), a city referred to in Isaiah 10:9 as offering futile resistance to the overwhelming military power of Assyria. Doubtless the same as Calneh (2).

Cal'vary (Gr. *kranion*, a *skull*, but having its English form from the translators having literally adopted the Latin word *calvaria*, a bare *skull*; the Greek is the interpretation of the Hebrew *Golgotha*, *q. v.* Once, in Luke 23:33, the word occurs, the place where Christ was crucified, designated as the place of a skull

(Golgotha), either because of the shape of the mound or elevation or because a place of execution. Some claim that Moriah and Calvary are identical. The removal of the city wall from time to time renders it difficult to locate the spot. It would probably be a prominent place near to the public highway, for the Romans selected such places for public executions.

77. "Gordon's Calvary"

From the 4th century to the present day the sites of Calvary and of the Holy Sepulcher have been shown within the precincts of the Crusading Cathedral, standing where Constantine's Basilica was raised. Others identify the spot with "Gordon's Calvary." The site will remain uncertain till Jerusalem's N. wall at the time of Jesus is determined (cf. Heb. 13:12) and perhaps other evidence found.

Camel. For description of the camel, *see* Animal Kingdom.

Figurative. "It is easier for a camel to go through the eye of a needle, than for a rich man to enter into the kingdom of God" (Matt. 19:24) is a proverbial expression to show how difficult it is for a rich man who has the many temptations of wealth to leave them for the sake of Christ. The objection is made that the metaphor of an animal passing through a needle's eye is a bad one, and that the Gr. *kamēlos* ought to be read *kamilos*, a *cable*, "as for a *rope* to pass," etc. There appears, however, to be no such Greek word as *kamilos*, a *cable*. "To render the word by a *narrow gate*, a narrow *mountain pass*, or anything but a *needle* is inadmissible" (Meyer, *Com.*, in loc.).

"Ye blind guides, which strain at a gnat, and swallow a camel" (Matt. 23:24), is a

78. Camel (Dromedary)

proverb applied to those who superstitiously strive to avoid small faults and yet do not scruple to commit great sins. This is a reference to the custom of the Jews in "straining their wine," in order that there might be no possibility of swallowing with it any unclean animal, however minute (Lev. 11:42). This passage should be rendered, "Ye strain *out* the gnat," etc. Dr. Adam Clarke says that the "at" was substituted for "out" in the edition of 1611.

Camel's Hair. The long hair of the camel, which is somewhat woolly in texture, becomes, toward the close of spring, loose, and is easily pulled away in licks from the skin. The modern Arabs still weave it into a coarse sort of cloth for tent covers and coats for shepherds and camel drivers. Garments of this material were worn by John the Baptist in the wilderness (Matt. 3:4).

Figurative. It was an outward mark of that deadness to carnal enjoyment and mortification which marked John's mission as God's prophet in the apostasy of Israel. In this he imitated his great predecessor and type, Elijah (II Kings 1:8), in a time of similar degeneracy (see Zech. 13:4).

Ca′mon (kā′mŏn), the place of Jair's (the judge) burial (Judg. 10:5). Josephus (*Ant.*, v, 7, 6) states that Camon was a city of Gilead, while Eusebius and Jerome place it on the great road, six Roman miles N. of Legio, on the plain of Jezreel or Esdraelon. Polybius mentions it (doubtlessly correctly) among other cities of Gilead (*History* V, 70, 12).

Camp, Encampment (Heb. *măhănĕh, place of pitching a tent,* from *hănäh, to pitch a tent*), a term applied to any band or company presenting a regular and settled appearance; a nomad party at rest (Gen. 32:21); an army or caravan when on its march (Exod. 14:9; Josh. 10:5; 11:4; Gen. 32:7, 8), and the resting place of an army or company (Exod. 16: 13). Sometimes the verb refers to the casual arrangement of a siege (Psa. 27:3) or campaign (I Sam. 4:1). Among nomadic tribes war never attained the dignity of a science, and their encampments were consequently devoid of all the appliances of more systematic warfare. The art of laying out an encampment appears to have been well understood in Egypt long before the departure of the Israelites from that country, and it was there, doubtless, that Moses became acquainted with that mode of encampment which he introduced among the Israelites.

1. **Camp of Israel.** (1) **Arrangement.** During the sojourn in the wilderness, when the people for a long period had to be kept in a narrow space, it was necessary for the sake of order and safety to assign the several tribes and families to their respective positions, leaving as little as possible to personal rivalry or individual caprice. With the exception of some scattered hints, our information respecting the camp of Israel is found in Num., chaps. 2 and 3. The tabernacle occupied the center of the camp, following the common practice in the East of the prince or leader of a tribe having his tent in the center of the others. It should be borne in mind that Jehovah, whose tent was the tabernacle, was the leader of Israel. The tents nearest to the tabernacle were those of the Levites, whose business it was to watch it; the family of Gershon pitched to the west, that of Kohath to the south, and that of Merari to the north. The priests occupied a position to the east, opposite to the entrance of the tabernacle (Num. 3:38). The priests and Levites were under the immediate

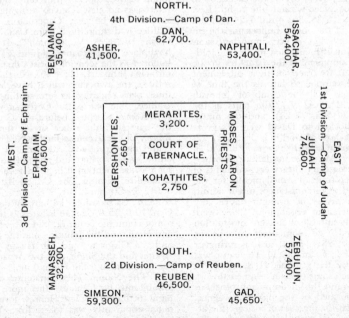

NORTH.
4th Division.—Camp of Dan.

DAN,
62,700.

ASHER,
41,500.

NAPHTALI,
53,400.

BENJAMIN,
35,400.

ISSACHAR,
54,400.

3d Division.—Camp of Ephraim.

WEST.

EPHRAIM,
40,500.

MERARITES,
3,200.

GERSHONITES,
2,650.

COURT OF
TABERNACLE.

MOSES, AARON,
PRIESTS.

KOHATHITES,
2,750.

1st Division.—Camp of Judah

EAST

JUDAH
74,600.

MANASSEH,
32,200.

ZEBULUN,
57,400.

SOUTH.
2d Division.—Camp of Reuben.

REUBEN
46,500.

SIMEON,
59,300.

GAD,
45,650.

79. Camp of Israel

supervision of Moses and Aaron (Num. 1:53; 3:21-38). The host of Israel was divided into four divisions and encamped in the following order: First, on the east, Judah, having associated with him Issachar and Zebulun; on the south, Reuben, Simeon, and Gad; on the west, Ephraim, Manasseh, and Benjamin; on the north, Dan, Asher, and Naphtali. Each division had its separate *Standard* (*q. v.*), and each family had a separate standard, around which it was to pitch its tents (Num. 1:52). The order of encampment was preserved on the march (Num. 2:17), the signal for which was given by a blast of the two silver trumpets (Num. 10:5). Sentinels were probably placed at the gates (Exod. 32:26, 27) in the four quarters of the camp. This was evidently the case in the camp of the Levites (comp. I Chron. 9:18, 24; II Chron. 31:2). (2) **Sanitary regulations.** The encampment of Israel, being that of the Lord's host, and with the Lord himself symbolically resident among them, was ordered to be kept in a state of great cleanliness. This was for the twofold purpose of preserving the health of so great a number of people and preserving the purity of the camp as the dwelling place of God (Num. 5:3, sq.; Deut. 23:14). The dead were buried without the camp (Lev. 10:4, 5); lepers were excluded till their leprosy departed (Lev. 13:46), and likewise all others with loathsome diseases (Lev. 15:2; Num. 5:2) or personal uncleanness (Deut. 23:10-12); those defiled by contact with the dead, whether slain in battle or not, were excluded from the camp for seven days; captives remained for a while outside (Num. 31:19; Josh. 6:23); the ashes from the sacrifices were carried to an appointed place without the camp, where the entrails, skin, horns, etc., and all that was not offered in sacrifice, were burnt (Lev. 4:11, 12; 6:11; 8:17); the execution of criminals took place without the camp (Lev. 24:24; Num. 15:35, 36; Josh. 7:24), as did the burning of the young bullock for the sin offering (Lev. 4:12). A very important sanitary regulation is mentioned in Deut. 23:12-14. The encampment of the Israelites in the wilderness left its traces in their subsequent history. The temple, so late as the time of Hezekiah, was still the camp of Jehovah (II Chron. 31:2, A. V., "the tents of the Lord;" comp. Psa. 78:28); and the multitudes who flocked to David were "a great host, like the host of God" (I Chron. 12:22, literally, "a great *camp*, like the *camp* of God").

2. **Military.** We have no definite information concerning the military encampments of Israel in later times. Formed merely for the occasion, and as circumstances might admit, they could scarcely be brought under very precise or stringent regulations. They were pitched in any suitable or convenient situation that presented itself—sometimes on a height (I Sam. 17:3; 28:4, etc.); near a spring or well (Judg. 7:1; I Sam. 29:1). The camp was surrounded by the rampart (I Sam. 17:20; 26:5, 7), which some explain as an earthwork thrown up round the encampment, others as the barrier formed by the baggage wagons. We know that, in the case of a siege, the attacking army, if possible, surrounded the

place attacked (I Macc. 13:43), and drew about it a line of circumvallation (II Kings 25:1), which was marked by a breastwork of earth (Isa. 62:10; Ezek. 21:22; comp. Job 19:12) for the double purpose of preventing the escape of the besieged and of protecting the besiegers from their sallies. To guard against attacks sentinels were posted (Judg. 7:20; I Macc. 12:27) round the camp, and the neglect of this precaution by Zebah and Zalmunna probably led to their capture by Gideon, and the ultimate defeat of their army (Judg. 7:19). The valley which separated the hostile camps was generally selected as the fighting ground (I Sam. 4:2; 14:15; II Sam. 18:6), upon which the contest was decided, and hence the valleys of Palestine have played so conspicuous a part in its history (Josh. 8:13; Judg. 6:33; II Sam. 5:22; 8:13, etc.). When the fighting men went forth to the place selected for marshaling the forces (I Sam. 17:20) a detachment was left to protect the camp and baggage (I Sam. 17:22; 30:24). The beasts of burden were probably tethered to the tent pegs (II Kings 7:10; Zech. 14:15).

Camphire. *See* Vegetable Kingdom.

80. Cana

Ca'na (kā'nà), "Cana of Galilee," a name found in the gospel of John only, but in such references no clew is given as to its locality; supposed to be near Capernaum. Cana of Galilee is distinguished from Cana of Asher (Josh. 19:28, A. V. "Kanah"). It was the birthplace of Nathanael (John 21:2), and honored as the scene of Christ's first recorded miracle (John 2:1, 11; 4:46). North of Nazareth lie the two sites which have at various times been regarded as representing Cana of Galilee. The one is the Christian village of *Kefr Kenna*, accepted before the Crusades as the true site; the other site is the ruin of *Kânah*, four or five miles farther N. The former is the more probable site, since it possesses ample water springs and abounds in fig trees such as are mentioned in John 1:48.

Ca'naanite, Si'mon The (Matt. 10:4; Mark 3:18). *See* Simon, 2.

Ca'naan, Ca'naanites (kā'nán, kā'ná-nīt). In Gen. 10:6, 15:8 Canaan is listed as the fourth son of Ham, the father of "Sidon his first born and Heth, and the Jebusite, and the Amorite, and the Girgasite, and the Hivite, and the Arkite, and the Sinite, and the Arvadite, and the Zemarite and the Hamathite."

1. **The Name.** The Canaanites were the inhabitants of Canaan, the more ancient name of Palestine. The Hebrew form of Canaan apparently was taken from Hurrian, signifying "belonging to the land of red-

81. Canaan

purple." From the 14th century B. C. on this designation came to be employed of the country in which the "Canaanite" or Phoenician traders exchanged for their commodities their most important commercial product, red-purple, which was obtained from the murex mollusks of Coastal Palestine and used for dyeing. In the Amarna Letters the "land of Canaan" is applied to the Phoenician coast, and the Egyptians called all western Syria by this name. By the time of the conquest the term Canaan signified the territory later called Palestine.

2. **Territory.** The name "land of Canaan" covers all Palestine west of the Jordan (Num. 34:3-12). This territory was situated between the great ancient empires of the Tigris-Euphrates and Halys Rivers on the one hand

and the great Egyptian empire of the Nile on the other. It was providential that the nation Israel with its testimony to the knowledge of the one true God and with its obligation to make known that fact, should inherit a country that formed a geographical bridge between the ancient centers of pagan civilization.

3. **Civilization.** The Canaanites were talented and early developed arts and sciences. Stout walled cities have been excavated and their construction was much superior to that of later Israelite buildings. They excelled in ceramic arts, music, musical instruments and architecture. The Solomonic temple was planned with the help of Phoenician artisans and architects. Craftsmen of Hiram of Tyre executed much of the work (I Kings 7:13-51). Decorations, architectural motifs and general styling were heavily indebted to Syro-Phoenician art. From all sections of Palestine, well-executed fortifications, ornate palaces and temples contrast strongly to the strata containing inferior Hebrew construction. The art treasures in ivory, gold and alabaster recovered from Canaanite Megiddo demonstrate Canaanite architectural elegance. Many of the treasures from Ras Shamra-Ugarit tell the same story. However, by the time of the Israelite conquest, Canaanite civilization had become decadent and was ripe for destruction. Among Canaanite cities excavated are Jericho, Bethel, Libnah, Lachish, Debir (Kiriath-sepher), Megiddo, Taanach, Beth-shan, Beth-shemesh, Byblos, Ras Shamra and Gezer.

4. **Canaanite Religion.** New vistas of knowledge of Canaanite cults and their degrading character and debilitating effect have been opened up by the discovery of the Ras Shamra religious epic literature from Ugarit in North Syria. Thousands of clay tablets stored in what seems to be a library between two great Canaanite temples dating from c. 15th-14th century B. C. give a full description of the Canaanite pantheon. Canaanite fertility cults are seen to be more base than elsewhere in the ancient world. The virile monotheistic faith of the Hebrews was continually in peril of contamination from the lewd nature worship with immoral gods, prostitute goddesses, serpents, cultic doves and bulls. El, the head of the pantheon, was the hero of sordid escapades and crimes. He was a bloody tyrant who dethroned his own father, murdered his favorite son and decapitated his own daughter. Despite these enormities, El was styled "father of years" (*abu shanima*), "the father of man," *abu adami*, ("father bull"), that is, the progenitor of the gods. Baal, the widely revered Canaanite deity, was the son of El and dominated the Canaanite pantheon. He was the god of thunder whose voice reverberated through the heavens in the storm. He is pictured on a Ras Shamra stele brandishing a mace in his right hand and holding in his left hand a stylized thunder bolt. The three goddesses were Anath, Astarte and Ashera, who were all three patronesses of sex and war. All were sacred courtesans. Other Canaanite deities were Mot (death), Reshep, the god of pestilence, Shulman, the god of health,

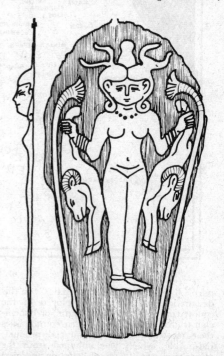

82. Left: Artist's drawing of gold pendant of the nude goddess of fertility from Ras Shamra. The sacred prostitute stands on a lion. The serpent symbolizes her fecundity. Her spiral locks and general posture identify her cult. **Right:** Another drawing of a gold pendant of the fertility goddess. The rams evidently portray sexual vigor.

Koshar, the god of arts and crafts, etc. These Canaanite cults were utterly immoral, effete and corrupt, dangerously contaminating and thoroughly justifying the divine command to destroy their devotees (Gen. 15:6).

83. A Phoenician Before the Sacred Candelabrum

5. The Conquest. After signal victories in Transjordan over Sihon, king of the Amorites and Og, king of Bashan, Israel under Joshua's leadership passed over the Jordan, and began the conquest. The story of the conquest is told in Joshua, chapters 1-12, and the allocation of the land to the various tribes is recounted in chapters 13-22. After the destruction of Jericho (around 1400 B. C., according to Garstang and in agreement with underlying O. T. chronology) and Ai (Josh. 6:1-8:29), the conquest of southern Canaan (chap. 10), and northern Canaan (chap. 11:1-5) is described. In Joshua 11:16-12:24 the conquest is summarized. The events recorded in the Bible are evidently highly selective. Summary statements embrace other conquests not specifically described in the book (cf. 21:43-45). Those that were included were considered sufficient to accomplish the author's purpose of proving God's faithfulness in giving them the land for their possession.

6. The Language. Languages of Canaan included Phoenician and Ugaritic. Hebrew seems to have been adapted from a Canaanite dialect. It originated from the old Phoenician alphabet. The origin of this proto-Semitic alphabet is still obscure. Examples of this rude

script discovered at Serabit el Khadem in the Sinaitic Peninsula in 1904-5 push alphabetic writing back to pre-Mosaic times. It is very interesting that this early (Sinai Hebrew) script was found in the general region where Moses was told to write (Exod. 17:8-14). But it is scarcely credible that the alphabet was invented in the desert wastes of the Sinaitic Peninsula. Since 1930 several very brief inscriptions dated between 1700-1550 have been found in Palestine and are more archaic than the letters from Serabit el Khadem. These apparently belong to the same alphabet. Proto-Sinaitic was demonstrably affected by Egyptian characters, in both the form of the letters and in the limitation of the alphabet to consonants. The alphabet itself was in all likelihood invented in Hyksos Egypt, or conceivably in Palestine at this or an earlier period. But old Hebrew goes back to the patriarchal age. Did Abraham find the Hebrew language in Palestine or did he bring it with him from Haran? The Hebrew patriarchs presumably spoke an Aramaic dialect while in Mesopotamia before their entrance into Palestine, but once in Palestine "they adopted a local Canaanite dialect which was not identical with the standard speech of the sedentary Canaanites, as may be linguistically demonstrated" (Albright, *From the Stone Age to Christianity*). This conclusion seems valid because old Hebrew is practically the same as Phoenician. Apparently it appears in the traditional name of Hebrew, "the language of Canaan" (Isa. 19:18). It is furthermore attested by early Canaanite and Hebrew inscriptions. These appear in Ugaritic about 1400 B. C., Canaanite inscriptions from Byblos and inscriptions from Cyprus, Sardinia and Carthage and other colonies in the western Mediterranean. Inscriptions made in Hebrew from Palestine including the Gezer Calendar (c. 925 B. C.), the Moabite Stone (c. 850 B. C.), the Samaritan Ostraca (c. 776 B. C.), the Siloam Inscription (c. 701 B. C.) and the Lachish Letters (589 B. C.) add further epigraphic evidence of the close association of Biblical Hebrew with Phoenician and other Canaanite dialects. *M. F. U.*

Can′dace (kăn′dá-sē), the title of that queen of the Ethiopians whose high treasurer was converted to Christianity under the preaching of Philip the evangelist (Acts 8:27), A. D. 34. Candace was probably a distinctive appellation borne by successive queens, as Pharaoh,

84. A sample of Ugaritic alphabet cuneiform writing: "He decides the suit of the widow. He judges the case of the orphan."—**The Legend of Danel,** II, V, 7b-8.

Ptolemy, etc. The country over which she ruled was that region in Upper Nubia which was called by the Greeks *Meroë*, where George Reisner identified pyramid tombs of reigning Candaces of Ethiopia constructed from c. 300 B. C.-300 A. D.

Candle, frequently used in Scripture, where *lamp* or *light* would be the more literal rendering. This is due to the general use of candles in England at the time of the translation of our present version of the Bible. *See* Lamp.

Candlestick, Golden. *See* Tabernacle.

Cane. *See* Vegetable Kingdom.

Canker. *See* Diseases.

Cankerworm. *See* Animal Kingdom.

Can′neh, mentioned only in Ezek. 27:23, and probably contracted form of the earlier Calneh (Gen. 10:10).

Canon of Scripture, The O. T.

1. **The Meaning of the Term.** If the testimony of Scripture is accepted, that God is the Author of the Bible and that the Holy Spirit worked upon men to receive and record His word for future generations, the important question was bound to arise (since many religious books were written during the O. T. period), *what particular books enjoy divine origin and hence are divinely authoritative*? This and similar problems concerning the origin of the 39 books of the O. T. and the 27 of the New constitute an historical inquiry concerning man's response to God's operation in giving the sacred oracles.

The Canon of Sacred Scripture is a phrase by which the catalog of the authoritative sacred writings is designated. The word for the expression, of Greek derivation, *kanōn*, and possibly a loan word from Semitic (Heb. *qānĕh*, Akkad. *qânu*) originally signified reed or measuring rod. Actually it indicated "that which measures;" that is, a standard, norm or rule; specifically, "that which is measured" by that standard, norm or rule. Those books which were measured by the standard or test of divine inspiration and authority and were adjudged to be "God-breathed" were included in "the canon." The term thus came to be applied to the catalog or list of sacred books thus designated and honored as normative, sacred and binding. Athanasius (c. A. D. 350) was the first person known with certainty to apply the term to sacred Scripture. Thereafter the concept became general both in the Greek and Latin churches. The Jewish idea was expressed technically in terms of a ritualistic formula known as "defiling the hands." The most likely explanation of this enigmatic phrase seems to be that of George Robinson Smith; namely, that the hands which had touched the sacred writings, that is, those that were really God-inspired, were rendered "taboo" with respect to handling anything secular. The high priest (Lev. 16:24) washed not only when he put on the sacred garments on the Day of Atonement but when he took them off. This seems to be the thought. When writings were holy they were said to "defile the hands."

2. **Contents of the Hebrew Canon.** The standard or Massoretic text of the O. T. contains 24 books, beginning with Genesis and concluding with II Chronicles. The arrangement is such that there are only 24 books instead of 39 as in the Protestant canon, but the subject matter is exactly the same. In other words, the O. T. canon of Protestantism is identical with that of the ancient Jews. The only difference is in the order and division of the books. In these matters the Protestant canon has been affected by the Septuagint, the version of the O. T. in Greek dated about B. C. 250-B. C. 160. The Greek version divides Samuel, Kings, Chronicles, Ezra-Nehemiah each into two books (making 8, instead of 4). The twelve minor prophets are divided into twelve instead of being counted as one, as in the Hebrew. This totals fifteen additional books, accounting for the 39. Modern Hebrew Bibles from the 16th century on also have the books divided into 39 but retain the ancient threefold division, Genesis opening and II Chronicles closing the canon. The 24-book division is as follows:

First: *The Law* (5 books)
    Genesis, Exodus, Leviticus, Numbers, Deuteronomy
Second: *The Prophets* (8 books)
    1. The Former Prophets (4 books)
        Joshua, Judges, Samuel, Kings
    2. The Latter Prophets (4 books)
        (1) Major (3 books)
            Isaiah, Jeremiah, Ezekial
        (2) Minor (1 book) The Twelve:
            Hosea, Joel, Amos, Obadiah, Jonah, Micah, Nahum, Habakkuk, Zephaniah, Haggai, Zechariah, Malachi
Third: *The Writings* ((11 books)
    1. Poetical (3 books)
        Psalms, Proverbs, Job
    2. Five Rolls (5 books)
        Song, Ruth, Lamentations, Ecclesiastes, Esther
    3. Historical (3 books)
        Daniel, Ezra-Nehemiah, Chronicles

3. **The Critical View of the Formation of the Canon of the O. T.** This hypothesis, which is a naturalistic attempt to account for the threefold division of the Hebrew Scriptures, maintains the gradual development of the Hebrew O. T. under three claims.

(1) **The First Claim.** The Hebrew canon first consisted of the Pentateuch and that alone.

(a) This is implied, the critics contend, in the expressed reverence paid to the Mosaic law in the post-exilic writings. The compiler of the Chronicles and Ezra-Nehemiah, it is stated, assumes the authority of the law in its finished form throughout the narration of post-exilic history. Malachi 4:4 appeals to the law of Moses as a sacred standard of doctrine for all Israel. **Reply.** But there is ample reason for an emphatic reference to the law of Moses after the exile. The catastrophe of the fall of the Northern Kingdom (II Kings 17:13-41) and the later captivity of Judah are time and again attributed to infraction of the law and the prophets. These are alike joined together as binding upon Judah and Israel. (Isa. 5:24; 30:9; Amos 2:4-6). It would be natural after the restoration to give special attention to that to which former disobedience had brought suffering and captivity. The question of whether or not the law of Moses was received as authoritative centuries before the exile is not in view. The reason Ezra stresses the law of Moses is that the specific evils current in the young restored community —foreign religions, Sabbath desecration and neglect of adequate temple worship, (Neh. 10:29 f.) were covered most comprehensively by the requirements of the law. The prophetic injunctions, although rooted in the Mosaic revelation, were not so direct and pointed.

(b) It is suggested, it is contended, in the special deference accorded the Pentateuch in later times. In this connection the critical theory stresses the Torah as the mainstay of Judaism and the object of Antiochus Ephiphanes' wrath (B. C. 168; II Macc. 1:57). The Pentateuch was not only the first installment of the translation of the Old testament into Greek, but the only portion carried out with the accuracy demanded by an authoritative edition. Philo attributes to Moses and the law the highest gift of inspiration. **Reply.** It is true that the law is exclusively spoken of in I Maccabees as adhered to by the faithful and forsaken by the godless (1:52; 2:21, 26 f.), but who would be so bold as to assert on that account that there were no other books in the canon at that late date? As far as the evidence from the LXX is concerned, the fact of an inferior translation for the prophets and the writings as compared with the law, even if it could be proved, might rest upon any number of other factors and not on a supposed non-canonization of the prophets and the writings. Philo's finespun theory of inspiration, like later rabbinical speculations, is mere fancy and offers no real weight.

(c) It is implied, say the critics, in the employment of the Torah in the synagogue service. From the Torah alone lessons were systematically read in public services of the synagogue. Not until later times (cf. Luke 4:17 f.) were lessons added from the prophets and then only to supplement and illustrate the Torah. **Reply.** Readings were confined to the law originally, not because it alone was canonical, but because the divine covenant relation with Israel rested upon it and hinged upon its faithful observation. This alone would give sufficient reason that from the very first institution of the synagogue the law should have a place in the worship. It would be only natural that soon selections from the prophets would be attempted to illustrate and emplify the law. The writings (Heb. *kethubim*) were more adaptable for reading on special occasions. The Psalms were sung in the temple and the five rolls were read on festal days. Selections from Job, Ezra-Nehemiah, Chronicles, Daniel and Proverbs were read throughout the entire night preceding the day of Atonement.

(d) It is implied by the subsequent use of "the law," signifying the whole Hebrew canon. This expression is assumed by critics to be a reminiscence of a much earlier usage as well as a recognition of the higher esteem in which the law was held (John 10:34; 15:25). Jesus refers to the Psalms as the law. In I Cor. 14:21 Isaiah is alluded to under the same designation. **Reply.** As the foundation of the whole Hebrew religious and liturgical sys-

tem, it was natural for the name of the Pentateuch to be figuratively applied to the whole, a part denoting the entirety. With perfect propriety all Scripture may be designated "the law" since it constitutes the revelation of God's purpose and will.

(e) The Samaritan Pentateuch points at least to the high probability that around B. C. 432 the Torah (the law) alone was canonical. Why did the Samaritans take only the Pentateuch? The critics see in this anomaly "presumptive evidence" that around B. C. 432 (cf. Neh. 13:28) the Torah alone was canonical among Jerusalem Jews. **Reply.** The mutilated canon of the Samaritans evidently originated like heretical sects in general. These groups accept what suits their own particular purposes, arbitrarily rejecting the rest. That the Samaritans did this is suggested by their deliberate alteration of Deut. 27:4 to read Mt. Gerizim instead of Mt. Ebal, in order to get divine sanction for the construction of their rival temple there. Since they deliberately did this, it is scarcely possible that they would have hesitated to reject any part of the sacred canon which spoke approvingly of worship at Shiloh or Jerusalem. Recognizing the force of this argument, Ryle, (*The Canon of the Old Testament*, p. 92 f.) suggests the inclusion of books like Joshua or Hosea which would have been inoffensive to the purposes of the Samaritans, had these writings at that time been canonical. But would a few isolated books outside the Pentateuch have offered any advantage? It would have in reality spoiled the unity and completeness which the Pentateuch afforded. The Samaritans were thus, as W. H. Green clearly remarks (*General Introduction to the Old Testament, The Canon*, New York, 1898, p. 100), "necessarily limited to the Pentateuch irrespective of the extent of the Jewish canon at the time."

(2) The Second Claim. The Prophets Were Not Added to the Hebrew Canon Until Between B. C. 300 and B. C. 200. The critical view acknowledges that the steps by which the prophets became canonical over a century and a half after the law "are, indeed, in a great measure hidden from our view" and that the evidence is "scanty." Ryle, *op. cit.*, p. 95 f.) However they insist upon the claim.

(a) It is implied, they claim, by the unpopularity of the prophets during the canonical period. As long as the prophets were not well received, it is maintained that it was very unlikely for their utterances and their writings to have been regarded as having canonical authority. Supposedly not until the power and prestige of the prophets were enhanced towards the end of the exilic period were the prophetic writings collected and canonized. This erroneous presupposition fails to see the real nature of Scriptural inspiration. The inspired Word of God possesses intrinsic binding authority and did not have to wait for intervals of time to give it this quality. Moreover, this quality is independent of the popularity or unpopularity of the prophet or the reception or rejection of his message. It is unwarrantedly assumed that "the incorporation of recent or almost contemporary work in the same collection with the older prophets would not have been approved" (Ryle, p. 106). But why should it not have been approved if inspired and thus possessing intrinsic authority? Why did many years have to slip away, for example, before Malachi's writings, written about B. C. 445, would be accepted, as Ryle contends?

(b) It is suggested by the date of the compilation of the book of Isaiah. Chapters 1-35 are in the main ascribed to Isaiah, while chapters 40-66, considered as non-Isaianic and late post-exilic, were added when the prophetical writings were being collected. The real author of this section being completely forgotten, they were simply appended to Isaiah's genuine prophecies. **Reply.** Only the critical hypothesis demands a long interval of time to attempt to offer some rational explanation for the unaccountable oblivion of the so-called second Isaiah. Not the internal evidence of the book itself, considered as a genuine work of Isaiah, but the assumptions of the critics, create the unanswerable question: How could so prominent a prophet with such unusual literary skill, who wrote near the end of the exile, be so completely forgotten that he was confused with another, who lived at an entirely different time and under completely different circumstances?

(c) It is implied in the date of the composition of the book of Daniel. Wildeboer concisely states the critical position: "At what time the division of the prophets was closed we are not informed. But on account of Daniel 9:2, whose author, living about B. C. 165, seems to know 'the books' as a collection with definite limits, and because the book of Daniel itself was unable to obtain a place in the second section, we fix the *terminus ad quem* about B. C. 200." (*Origin of the Canon of the Old Testament*, 1895, p. 116). **Reply.** The critical date of Daniel, about B. C. 167, is largely dictated by rationalistic presuppositions with regard to miracles and prophecies. There is no valid reason for rejecting the Danielic authorship which the book claims for itself. It is not true that the book was unable to obtain a place in the prophetic section of the canon. The rightful place, according to the Jewish criteria for arranging the threefold division, is in the third division. But if the book was not written until about B. C. 167, it may be asked, how did it gain credence in such a short time as to be quoted in I Macc. 2:59, 60? Or again it may be asked, why should it have been translated into Greek with other canonical books when, according to the uniform admission of the critics, this book would not have been in the canon at all if it were not considered to be the genuine work of the prophet Daniel?

(3) **The Third Claim.** The writings were not canonized until after the prophets, between B. C. 160-B. C. 105. The general position is that no steps were taken towards the formation of a third division until the second was closed. Reasons cited to support this presupposition are as follows:

(a) Considerable time had to elapse after Malachi for the general conviction to crystalize that prophecy had ceased and no more prophets were to be expected. Otherwise, it is

contended, Ezra-Nehemiah and Chronicles would have been placed with the other historical books, such as Samuel and Kings, and Daniel would have been inserted with other prophecies in the second section, if that division had not been previously closed when they were finally considered canonical. **Reply.** The order of the Hebrew canon is not the result of the character or contents of the various books. It is due to the official status or position of their authors. There is no need to assume that the second division was closed and could not be opened to admit these books.

(b) The general freedom and inaccuracy of the Greek rendering of the writings are proof against their canonization before B. C. 160. Dillmann, for example, maintains that the additions to Esther and Daniel in the Greek and the recasting of Chronicles and Ezra in the apocryphal Esdras furnish evidence that these books were not regarded as authoritative as the law and the prophets. **Reply.** It would be strange if stories so vivid and remarkable as Esther and Daniel would not arouse popular imagination. Later Targumic legends connected with the law are answer enough that canonicity is no bar to imaginative additions. The evidence from the Septuagint has been doubtless overdone and it is a subtle fallacy to assume that canonization always insures accurate translation or precludes imaginative fancy.

(c) The evidence of the prologue to Ecclesiasticus is opposed to the canonicity of the writings before B. C. 160. The supposed "vagueness" with which the author of the prologue about B. C. 132 refers to the third division is construed as a testimony to the late canonization of the writings. **Reply.** However this argument is invalid. So far from an imagined "vagueness," the language is remarkably definite. Actually the designation is very comprehensive. By referring to the third division as "the rest of the books" or "the other books of the fathers" the designation is just as unambiguous in the light of the miscellaneous contents of these writings as is the term "the law and the prophets." In fact, this statement in the prologue is in full agreement with the history of Josephus, who, flatly denying the critical hypothesis, asserts that the canon was completed and closed in the days of Artaxerxes, (B. C. 465-B. C. 425) and that since that time "not a soul has ventured to add or to remove or to alter a syllable" of the ancient records (*Contra Apionen* I:8). There is no proof whatever, despite the theorizing of the critics that, in the long interval between Malachi and the translator of Ecclesiasticus, the third division of the canon was still in the process of formation, much less that it was not formed until B. C. 160 or later.

4. **The Correct and Conservative View of the Development of the Hebrew Canon.** (1) **The Old Testament Books were written with the immediate idea of being held sacred and divinely authoritative.** Being divinely inspired, they possessed the stamp of canonicity from the first. The prophets were conscious that they were speaking the Word of God by inspiration. Often they prefix their spoken and written messages with an authori-

tative "thus saith the Lord," or some similar expression (cf. Exod. 4:15, 16; I Kings 16:1, II Kings 7:1; Jer. 13:1; Ezek. 1:3). Early in the history of Israel, God began the formation of the Book that was to constitute the revelation of Himself to man. The Decalogue was inscribed on stone (Deut. 10:4, 5), Moses' laws were written in a book (Deut. 31:24-26). Copies of this book were made (Deut. 17:18). Samuel also wrote in a book (I Sam. 10:25). The prophets wrote their inspired message (Jer. 36:32; Zech. 1:46). Ezra read the law publicly (Neh. 8:3). However, the precise way in which the entire group of Old Testament books was set apart and divinely inscribed as the Word of God is hidden from our eyes. Jewish tradition attributes these remarkable achievements to Ezra and the men of the Great Assembly, but these facts are also far from being clear. Since the writings of the prophets, as soon as they were issued, had tremendous authority as inspired Scripture, no formal declaration of their canonicity was needed to give them sanction. The divine Author Who inspired these writings, we may reasonably believe, acted providentially in behalf of their acceptance by the faithful. However their inspiration and consequent divine authority were inherent and not dependent on human reception or lapse of time to give them prestige or until there were no more living prophets, *or any other factor.* Canonical authority is not derived from the sanction of Jewish priests and leaders or from the Christian church. *That authority is in itself.* (2) *This view of the formation of the canon, however, is not the mere history of the production of the various books.* That Old Testament authors were fully conscious of their inspiration is clear from the internal evidence of the books themselves. There is no necessity, however, to think that they simply deposited their oracles in the temple, and they were immediately considered as a part of the sacred canon. Jeremiah 36:1-32 gives us an insight into how inspired Scripture had to face opposition and sometimes destruction. Canonization of books is not to be confused with their collection. Books were not made canonical by reason of their collection. They were collected because they were canonical, that is, possessed of divine authority by virtue of their inspired character. It is to be feared that modern scholars in making the collection and arrangement of Bible books a primary element in canonization have created an artificial idea which has led to serious misunderstanding and unsound views. The Jews had a canon of Scripture long before their holy writings were formally arranged in the threefold division and as a unified whole. (3) *The real basis of the threefold division of the Hebrew Scriptures is evidently the official position of the individual authors.* Moses was the writer of the books of the law in the first division. The writers in the second division were those who had the prophetic office, that is, the official status and calling of a prophet, as well as the prophetic gift (the enduement of inspiration). The authors in the third category had the prophetic gift but not the prophetic office. They were not *officially* prophets. David and Solomon were kings; Ezra was a scribe; Daniel, a government official; Nehemiah, a civil governor. This view seems to be the simplest and most satisfactory of all.

5. **The Christian Canon of the Old Testament.** In proportion as the fathers were more or less absolutely dependent on the Septuagint for their knowledge of Old Testament Scriptures, they gradually lost in common practice the sense of the difference between the books of the Hebrew canon and the Apocrypha. The history of the Christian canon is to be sought from definite catalogues, and not from isolated quotations. But even this evidence is incomplete and unsatisfactory, few of the catalogues being really independent. They evidently fall into two great classes, Hebrew and Latin; and the former, again, exhibits three distinct varieties, which are to be traced to the three original sources from which the catalogues were derived. The first may be called the pure Hebrew canon, which is that of the Church of England. The second differs from this by the *omission* of the book of Esther. The third differs by the *addition* of Baruch, or "the letter." During the first four centuries this Hebrew canon is the only one which is distinctly recognized, and it is supported by the combined authority of those fathers whose critical judgment is entitled to the greatest weight. The real divergence as to the contents of the Old Testament canon is to be traced to Augustine, whose wavering and uncertain language on the point furnishes abundant materials for controversy. In the famous passage (*De Doct. Christ.*, ii, 8 (13)) he enumerates the books which are contained in "the whole canon of Scripture," and includes among them the apocryphal books without any clear mark of distinction. The Council of Trent pronounced the enlarged canon, including the apocryphal books, to be deserving in all its parts of "equal veneration," and added a list of books to prevent the possibility of doubt. The Reformed Churches agreed in confirming the Hebrew canon of Jerome, and refused to allow any dogmatic authority to the apocryphal books; but the form in which this judgment was confirmed varied considerably in the different confessions. The English Church (Art. vi) appeals directly to the opinion of Jerome, and concedes to the apocryphal books, including 4 Esdras and the Prayer of Manasses, a use "for example of life and instruction of manners," but not for the establishment of doctrine. Revised by *M. F. U.*

Canon of Scripture (The N. T.). While the Churches of the West are divided as to the position of the Old Testament Apocrypha, they have joined in ratifying one canon of the New Testament. (1) **The apostles** claim for their writings a public use (I Thess. 5:27; Col. 4:16; Rev. 22:18) and an authoritative power (I Tim 4:1, etc; II Thess 2:6; Rev. 22:19), and Peter (II Pet. 3:15, 16) places the epistles of Paul in significant connection with "the other Scriptures." (2) **Apostolic fathers.** In the writings of the apostolic fathers, A. D. 70-120, with the exception of the epistles of Jude, II Peter, and II and III John, with which no coincidences occur, and I and II

Thessalonians, Colossians, Titus, and Philemon, with which the coincidences are very questionable, all the other epistles were clearly known, and used by them; but still they are not quoted with the formulas which preface citations from the Old Testament. (3) **Apologists.** The next period, 120-170 A. D.—the age of the apologists—carries the history of the formation of the canon one step further. The facts of the life of Christ acquired a fresh importance in controversy with Jew and Gentile. The oral tradition, which still remained in the former age, was dying away, and a variety of written documents claimed to occupy its place. Then it was that the canonical gospels were definitely separated from the mass of similar narratives in virtue of their outward claims, which had remained, as it were, in abeyance during the period of tradition. (4) **From A. D. 170-350.** The testimony of Iranaeus, Clement of Alexandria, and Tertullian extends to the four gospels, Acts, I Peter, I John, thirteen epistles of St. Paul, and the Apocalypse; and, with the exception of the Apocalypse, no one of these books was ever afterward rejected or questioned till modern times. (5) **From A. D. 303-397.** The persecution of Diocletian was directed in a great measure against the Christian writings, and some obtained protection by surrendering the sacred books. The Donatists may be regarded as maintaining in its strictest integrity the popular judgment in Africa on the contents of the canon of Scripture, and Augustine allows that they held in common with the Catholics the same "canonical Scriptures," and were alike "bound by the authority of both Testaments." The canon of the New Testament, as commonly received at present, was ratified by the third Council of Carthage (A. D. 397), and from that time was accepted throughout the Latin Church, though occasional doubts as to the Epistle to the Hebrews still remained. Meanwhile the Syrian churches still retained the canon of the Peshito. The churches of Asia Minor seem to have occupied a mean position as to the canon between the East and West. With the exception of the Apocalypse, they received generally all the books of the New Testament as contained in the African canon. (6) **The Reformation.** At the era of the Reformation the question of the New Testament canon became again a subject of great though partial interest. The hasty decree of the Council of Trent, which affirmed the authority of all the books commonly received, called out the opposition of controversialists, who quoted and enforced the early doubts. Erasmus denied the apostolic origin of the Epistle to the Hebrews, II Peter, and the Apocalypse, but left their canonical authority unquestioned. Luther set aside the Epistle to the Hebrews, St. Jude, St. James, and the Apocalypse, at the end of his version, and spoke of them and the remaining Antilegomena with varying degrees of disrespect, though he did not separate II Peter and II and III John from the other epistles (7) **Calvin.** Calvin, while he denied the Pauline authorship of the Epistle to the Hebrews, and at least questioned the authenticity of II Peter, did not set aside their canonicity, and

he notices the doubts as to St. James and St. Jude only to dismiss them. The language of the Articles of the Church of England with regard to the New Testament is remarkable. In the Articles of 1552 no list of the books of Scripture is given; but in the Elizabethan Articles (1562, 1571) a definition of Holy Scripture is given as "the canonical books of the Old and New Testament, *of whose authority was never any doubt in the Church*" (Art. vi). This definition is followed by an enumeration of the books of the Old Testament and of the Apocrypha; and then it is said summarily, without a detailed catalogue, "All the books of the New Testament, as they are commonly received, we do receive and account them for canonical." A distinction thus remains between the "canonical" books, and such "canonical books as have never been doubted in the Church;" and it seems impossible to avoid the conclusion that the framers of the Articles intended to leave a freedom of judgment on a point on which the greatest of the continental reformers, and even of Romish scholars, were divided.

Can'ticles. This delightful poem, also called the Song of Solomon, stands first in the list of the five Hebrew rolls or *megilloth*, which were short enough to be publically read on important anniversaries. Canticles comes first because it was read at the initial and greatest feast of the year, the Passover.

1. **The Name.** The term Song of Songs (1:1) is a Hebrew idiom denoting the superlative degree, that is, the best or most exquisite Song. The Greek *asma asmaton* and the Latin Canticum Canticorum, like the English "Song of Songs," slavishly transliterate the Hebrew idiom. The rendering "The Song of Solomon" is likewise deducted from the data of 1:1 ("a Song of Songs which is Solomon's") but is not a translation.

2. **The Form.** Interpretation of the Song depends to a large extent on the view taken of its form. Three distinct views are commonly held. The conservative (and we believe the correct view) construes it as a unified lyrical poem with a dramatic form of dialogue. The second view is that it is a drama or melodrama (Origen, Ewald, Koenig, Godet, etc.). Those subscribing to the third view hold it to be an anthology of loosely connected separate love lyrics (Lods, Haupt, Oesterly and Robinson, Pfeiffer, etc.) recited during wedding festivals (Budde, Cheyne, Goodspeed and Kassuto). That the Song is a homogeneous lyric, not an anthology of disconnected love poems without plan, is apparent from the following reasons: (a) Identical imagery and local color predominate in all parts of the Song, for example, the bridegroom (beloved) is compared to a young hart in 2:9, 17; 8:14. The bridegroom feeds his flock "among the lilies" in 2:16; 4:5; 6:2, 3. The bride is called "fairest among women" in 1:8; 5:9; 6:1. (b) The same persons appear in all parts of the poem: the bride (1:5; 2:16; 3:4; 6:90 7:10, 11; 8:2, 8), the bridegroom (1:7; 2:13; 4:8-5:1; 6:1; 7:11-13) and the daughters of Jerusalem (1:5; 2:7; 3:5, 10; 5:8, 16; 8:4). The view that the poem is a drama is scarcely tenable since it does not have sufficient action, plot or

dramatic sequence. The position that it is a collation of detached erotic lyrics is also unsatisfactory in the light of the unity of the poem. It is scarcely credible that the faithful of antiquity would have persisted in viewing as divinely inspired a poem of mere human love, especially when it was on such a plane often considered unedifying, and not allowed to be read by persons under thirty years of age among the Jews.

3. **The Interpretation.** Literal, allegorical and typical interpretations are commonly made. **The Literal Interpretation** construes the poem as a mere representation of human love without any higher or spiritual meaning. Edward J. Young sets forth a species of literal interpretation which is vaguely typical, viewing the poem as didactic and moral, and holding that it celebrates the dignity and purity of human love. (*Introduction to the O. T.* (1949), p. 327). Most modern interpreters resort to a shepherd hypothesis in which a third main character is introduced as the shepherd lover of the bride whom Solomon, villain-like, tries to seduce from her lover. The poem is thus made the triumph of pure love over lust, but under an obviously objectionable representation of Solomon. More serious, the shepherd has no tangible existence. **The Allegorical Interpretation** was common among ancient Jews and popularized among Christians by Origen. The Jewish interpretation represented the poem as setting forth Jehovah's love for Israel. To the Christian, it represented Christ's love for his church. Details were subject to extravagant interpretations. The view has much to be said in its favor. It accords the book a higher spiritual meaning and gives purpose to its canonical recognition. Furthermore, both the Old and New Testament set forth the Lord's relation to his people by the figure of marriage. In the O. T. however, Israel is presented as the wife of Jehovah (Hos. 2:19-23), in her sin and unbelief now divorced and yet to be restored (Isa. 54:5; Jer. 3:1; Hos. 1-3). On the other hand in the N. T. the church is portrayed as a virgin espoused to Christ (II Cor. 11:2; Eph. 5:23-32; Rom. 7:4; Rev. 19:6-8). The allegorical view fails in unnecessarily ruling out the actual historicity of the events and is subject to extravagant, far-fetched interpretation.

The Typical Interpretation has a mediating view between the two extremes, the literal and the allegorical. It neither denies the historical background nor encourages fantastic interpretations of details, since the typical foreshadows the anti-typical in only a few salient points. It avoids the secularity of the literal interpretation and finds an adequate purpose in the book in the typical relation between Solomon, elsewhere a type of Christ, and the Shulamite, type of the church, as the bride of Christ.

4. **The Author.** The natural indication of 1:1 "the Song of Songs, which is Solomon's" is that Solomon is the author, although the preposition may conceivably be translated "The Song of Songs which is *about* or *concerning* Solomon" (cf. 1:4; 3:7-11; 8:11). Numerous internal arguments also lend support to Solomonic authorship: the place names, evidences of royal luxury, the author's wide acquaintance with plants and animals (cf. I Kings 4:33). The presence of one or two Persian and Greek words need not dispose of the Solomonic authorship. It may simply indicate that the poem in the precise form in which we have it cannot be earlier than the third century B. C. (Eissfeldt). But one may at least inquire if even these features might be original in the light of the incredibly widespread extent of Solomonic commerce and an inevitable influx of foreign words. Likewise the Aramaisms may be the result of the inclusion of Aramaic countries in Solomon's realm. *M. F. U.*

Caper, the rendering in the R. V. of Heb. *'ăbîyyōnäh'*, provocative of *desire*, the *caper* berry (A. V. "desire," Eccles. 12:5). *See* Vegetable Kingdom.

86. Restored Synagogue at Capernaum

Caper'naum (kȧ-pẽr'nȧ-ŭm; "town of Nahum"), a city of Galilee, frequently mentioned by the evangelists in connection with the life of our Lord. It was on the western shore of the "Sea of Galilee" (Matt. 4:13; comp. John 6:24), lower than Nazareth and Cana, from which the road to it was one of descent (John 2:12; Luke 4:31). It was of sufficient size to be always called a "city" (Matt. 9:1; Mark 1:33); had its own synagogue, in which our Lord frequently taught (John 6:59; Mark 1:21; Luke 4:31-38)—a synagogue built by the centurion of the detachment of Roman soldiers which appears to have been quartered in the place (Luke 7:1; Matt. 8:8). But besides the garrison there was also a customs station, where the dues were gathered both by stationary (Matt. 9:9; Mark 2:14; Luke 5:27) and by itinerant (Matt. 17:24) officers.

85. Ruins of Ancient Synagogue, Capernaum

Capernaum was the residence of Jesus and his apostles, and the scene of many miracles and discourses. At Nazareth he was "brought up," but Capernaum was emphatically his "own city;" it was when he returned thither that he is said to have been "at home" (Mark 2:1). Here he chose the evangelist Matthew or Levi (Matt. 9:9). The brothers Simon Peter and Andrew belonged to Capernaum (Mark 1:29), and it is perhaps allowable to imagine that it was on the sea beach that they heard the quiet call which was to make them forsake all and follow Him (Mark 1:16, 17; comp. 28). It was here that Christ worked the miracle on the centurion's servant (Matt. 8:5; Luke 7:1), on Simon's wife's mother (Matt. 8:14; Mark 1:30; Luke 4:38), the paralytic (Matt. 9:1; Mark 2:1; Luke 5:18), and the man afflicted with an unclean demon (Mark 1:32; Luke 4:33). At Capernaum occurred the incident of the child (Mark 9:33; Matt. 18:1; comp. 17:24); and in the synagogue there was spoken the wonderful discourse of John 6 (see v. 59).

The doom pronounced against Capernaum and the other unbelieving cities (Matt. 11:23) has been remarkably fulfilled. Tell Hum, its now generally accepted site, is a mass of ruins adjacent to Bethsaida and Tabgha, and yielded a 3rd century A. D. synagogue when excavated.

87. Philistine Warriors in Time of Sennacherib

Caph'tor (kăf'tŏr), the place or country from which the Philistines originally came (Jer. 47:4; Amos 9:7; cf. Deut. 2:23). Caphtor is now identified with the recently discovered cuneiform *Kaptara* or Crete. For this reason the clause "whence came forth the Philistines?" is usually regarded as misplaced by a copyist and to belong after "Caphtorim" in Gen. 10:14. Such former identifications of

Caphtor as the Delta of Egypt or Cappadocia must now be abandoned. *M. F. U.*

Caphtorim (kăf-tŏr-îm'), the inhabitants of Caphtor or Crete (Deut. 2:23). In Gen. 10:14 "whence came forth the Philistines" should follow Caphtorim as the evidence of Amos 9:7 and Jer. 47:4 indicates. *See* Caphtor.

88. Cappadocia

Cappado'cia (kăp-à-dō'shĭ-à), a province in the eastern part of Asia Minor. Its boundaries were changed several times by the Roman emperors. In New Testament history it comprised Lesser Armenia. On the day of Pentecost it was represented at Jerusalem (Acts 2:9), and Peter refers to it (I Pet. 1:1); hence its interest for the Bible reader.

Captain, the rendering of numerous Hebrew and several Greek words, some of which require special consideration:

1. Prince or Leader (Heb. *sär;* Gr. *chiliarch*), a military title (I Sam. 22:2; II Sam. 23:19); also rendered "chief" (Gen. 40:2; 41:9), "prince" (Dan. 1:7,) "ruler" (Judg. 9:30), "governor" (I Kings 22:26). The "captain of the guard" (Acts 28:16) was the commander of the pretorian troops. The rank or power of an Israelitish captain was designated by the number of men under his command as "captain of fifty," or "captain of a thousand;" and the commander of the whole army was called the "captain of the host." *See* Army, Officer.

2. Ruler (Heb. *qäṣîn*), sometimes denotes a military (Josh. 10:24; Judg. 11:6 11; Isa. 22:3), sometimes a civil, command (Isa. 1:10; 3:6); in Isaiah rendered "ruler."

3. Adjutant (Heb. *shälîsh'*), properly a *third* man, or one of three. Some conclude from this that the term was applied to a higher order of soldiers, who fought from chariots, and so called because each chariot contained *three* soldiers, one of whom managed the horses while the others fought (Exod. 14:7; II Sam. 23:8, etc.). Others hold to the opinion that the *shälîsh* were third officrs in rank after the king, or commanded a third part of the army.

4. The "captain of the temple" (Luke 22:4; Acts 4:1; 5:24) was not a military officer, but a priest who had command of the Levitical temple police, known in Jewish writers a

"the man of the temple mount" (Edersheim, *The Temple*, p. 119). His duty was to visit the posts during the night and see that the sentries were doing their duty.

Figurative. Christ is called the "captain of our salvation" (Heb. 2:10; Gr. *'archēgos*), because he is the author of his people's salvation, and their leader. Jehovah announces himself to Joshua (5:14) as the "captain of the host," i. e., the head and protector of his people (Dan. 8:11, rendered "prince").

Captive, one taken in war. Such persons, as ancient inscriptions and reliefs show, were treated with great indignities and cruelty. Those who surrendered were led out with halters, as if for execution (I Kings 20:32); the victors set their feet upon the necks of captured kings and nobles (Josh. 10:24); cut off their thumbs, toes, or ears (Judg. 1:7; II Sam. 4:12; Ezek. 23:25); put out their eyes (II Kings 25:7). Captives were suspended by the hand (Lam. 5:12); made to lie down and be walked or driven over (Isa. 51:23); thrown among thorns, sawn asunder, beaten to pieces with thrashing machines, or had severe labor imposed upon them (Judg. 8:7; II Sam. 12:31; I Chron. 20:3). When a city was captured the men were usually put to death, the women and children sold as slaves (Isa. 47:3; II Chron. 28:8-15; Psa. 44:12; Mic. 1:11; Joel 3:3) or exposed to most cruel treatment (Nah. 3:5, 6; Zech. 14:2; Esth. 3:13; II Kings 8:12; Isa. 13:16, 18). Sometimes the people were transported (Jer. 20:5; 39:9, 10; II Kings 24:12-16) or made tributary (II Sam. 8:6; II Kings 14:14).

89. Blinding the Eyes of Captives

Captivity (properly some form of *shäbäh'*, to *take captive;* often expressed by other Hebrew words). This word may be taken in the strict sense of imprisonment, but in relation to the people of Israel it has come to mean expatriation. Captives and captivity are used in Scripture very much in the sense of exile, yet with the notion that this state of exile was compulsory, and that the persons thus exiled were in a dependent and oppressed condition. The violent removal of the entire population of a city or district is not an uncommon event in ancient history, and was much more humane than the selling of captives into slavery. Such deportation might arise from one of two motives—the desire of rapidly populating new cities, built for pride or policy, or to break up hostile organizations. In addition to the destruction of national existence such exile was made the more bitter from the sanctity attributed to special places and the local attachment to deity. Removal was thought to sever a people from the care and protection of

their God; indeed, it implied the defeat of such deity. Tiglath-pileser of Assyria (745-727 B. C.) inaugurated the practice of transporting whole conquered populations to distant parts of his empire (I Kings 15:29). In this policy he was followed by many of his royal successors including Sargon, Sennacherib and Esarhaddon and by Babylonian rulers, notably Nebuchadnezzar II (605-562 B. C.)

The bondage of Israel in Egypt, and their subjugation at different times by the Philistines and other nations, are sometimes spoken of as captivities; and the Jews themselves reckon their national captivities as four—the Babylonian, Persian, Grecian, and Roman. The general use of the term, however, is applied to the forcible deportation of the Jews under the Assyrian or Babylonian kings (Matt. 1:17).

1. **Captivity of Israel**. The removal of the ten tribes, though often spoken of as a single event, was a very complex process. The larger part of the people were carried away, not to Babylon, but to Assyria. The period during which their removal was gradually effected was not less than one hundred and fifty years. There were two of these captivities: (1) In the reign of Pekah, king of Israel, Tiglath-pileser III carried away, B. C. 740, the trans-Jordanic tribes (I Chron. 5:26) and the inhabitants of Galilee (II Kings 15:29; comp. Isa. 9:1) to Assyria. (2) In the reign of Hoshea, king of Israel, Shalmaneser, king of Assyria, twice invaded (II Kings 17:3, 5) the kingdom which remained, and his successor Sargon II took Samaria in 721 B. C., carrying away 27,290 of the population as he tells in his Khorsabad Annals. Later Assyrian kings, notably Esarhaddon (681-668 B. C.), completed the task.

2. **Captivity of Judah**. (1) **Date, etc.** The carrying away of the people of Judah was not accomplished at once. Sennacherib, B. C. after 705, is stated to have carried into Assyria two hundred thousand captives from the Jewish cities which he took (II Kings 18:13). Three distinct deportations are mentioned in II Kings 24:14 (including ten thousand persons) and 25:11, one in II Chron. 36:20, three in Jer. 52:28-30 (including four thousand six hundred persons), and one in Dan. 1:3. The two principal ones were: (1) When Jehoiachin with all his nobles, soldiers, and artificers were carried away; and (2) That which followed the destruction of Jerusalem and the capture of Zedekiah, B. C. 586. (Albright, 587 B. C.) The three mentioned by Jeremiah may have been contributions from the more distinguished portions of the captives, and the captivity of certain selected "children" (Dan. 1:3), B. C. 607, may have occurred when Nebuchadnezzar was colleague of his father, Nabopolassar. (2) **Condition of captives.** The condition of the captives must have had many an element of bitterness. They were humiliated with the memory of defeat and present bondage; if faithful to Jehovah they were subject to bitter scorn and derision (Psa. 137:3-5); they were required to pay for their existence in heavy services and tributes; those of high-priestly, noble, or royal

origin were treated with the utmost indignity (Isa. 43:28; 52:5). On the other hand, they were treated not as slaves, but as colonists. There was nothing to hinder a Jew from rising to the highest eminence in the state (Dan. 2:48), or holding the most confidential office near the person of the king (Neh. 1:11; Tob. 1:13, 22). The advice of Jeremiah (29: 5, etc.) was generally followed. The exiles increased in numbers and in wealth. They observed the Mosaic law (Esth. 2:8; Tob. 14:9). They kept up distinctions of rank among themselves (Ezek. 20:1). Their genealogical tables were preserved, and they were at no loss to tell who was the rightful heir to David's throne. They had neither place nor time of national gathering, no temple; and they offered no sacrifice. But the rite of circumcision and their laws respecting food, etc., were observed; their priests were with them (Jer. 29:1); and possibly the practice of erecting synagogues in every city (Acts 15:21) was begun by the Jews in the Babylonian captivity. (3) **Literature.** The captivity had also a contemporaneous literature. Tobit presents a picture of the inner life of a family of Naphtali among the captives of Nineveh. Baruch was written by one whose eyes, like those of Ezekiel, were familiar with the gigantic forms of Assyrian sculpture. Several of the Psalms appear to express the sentiments of Jews who were either partakers or witnesses of the Assyrian captivity. But it is from the three great prophets, Jeremiah, Ezekiel, and Daniel, that we learn most of the condition of the children of the captivity. (4) **Duration.** Jeremiah (25: 12; 29:10) predicted that the captivity should last for seventy years, and this prediction has aroused much discussion. The best explanation of the chronological problem involved is that there were two, if not more, coordinate modes of computing the period in question, used by the sacred writers, one *civil*, and extending from the first invasion by Nebuchadnezzar to the decree of Cyrus, B. C. 606-538; and the other *ecclesiastical*, from the burning of the temple to its reconstruction, B. C. 587(6)-517). The Babylonian captivity was brought to a close by the decree (Ezra 1:2) of Cyrus, B. C. 538, and the return of a portion of the nation under Sheshbazzar or Zerubbabel, B. C. 535; Ezra, B. C. 458, and Nehemiah, B. C. 445. The number who returned upon the decree of B. C. 538 was forty-two thousand three hundred and sixty, besides servants. Among them about thirty thousand are specified (comp. Ezra 2 and Neh. 7) as belonging to the tribes of Judah, Benjamin, and Levi. It has been inferred that the remaining twelve thousand belonged to the tribes of Israel (comp. Ezra 6:17). Those who were left in Assyria (Esth. 8:9, 11), and kept up their national distinctions, were known as *The Dispersion* (*q. v.*) (John 7:35; I Pet. 1:1; James 1:1). (5) **The ten tribes.** Of these little is known. (1) Some returned and mixed with the Jews (Luke 2:36; Phil. 3:5, etc.). (2) Some were left in Samaria, mingled with the Samaritans (Ezra 6:21; John 4:12), and became bitter enemies of the Jews. (3) Many remained in Assyria, and were recognized as an integral part of the dispersion (see Acts 2:9;

26:7). (4) Most, probably, apostatized in Assyria, adopted the usages and idolatry of the nations among whom they were planted, and became wholly swallowed up in them. (6) **Cause and effects of captivity.** The captivity in Babylon was the result that justly befell the covenant people from their becoming assimilated to heathen states. By accepting other gods they broke their covenant with Jehovah and placed themselves beyond his protection, which would be construed into indorsement of their conduct. "Repentance, and a return to the ancient, the everlasting, and the true God, from the delirium, the charms, and the seductions of the world, had indeed been for centuries the cry of the best prophets, ever growing in intensity" (Ewald, *Hist. of Israel*, v, 22, sq.). They now came to God in penitence and earnest prayer. The clearest proof of repentance is found in the establishment of four fast days, celebrated in four different months (Isa. 58:3, sq.; Zech. 7:5; 8:19). Thus the Jews who returned from captivity were remarkably free from the old sin of idolatry; and a great spiritual renovation, in accordance with the divine promise (Ezek. 36:24-28), was wrought in them. A new and deep reverence for at least the letter of the law and the institutions of Moses was probably the result of the religious services in the synagogue. The exile was also a period of change in the vernacular language of the Jews (see Neh. 8:8), and a new impulse of commercial enterprise and activity was developed.

3. **Captivity under the Romans.** (1) The fate of the Jews at the hands of the Romans far better deserves the name of captivity; for, after the massacre of many thousands, the captives were reduced to real bondage. Josephus tells us that one million one hundred thousand men fell in the siege of Jerusalem by Titus, and ninety-seven thousand were captured in the whole war. Those under seventeen were sold into private bondage; of the rest some were sent to the Egyptian mines, others into the provinces to be destroyed at the theaters by the sword and wild beasts (*Wars*, vi, 9, 3). (2) An equally dreadful destruction fell upon the remains of the nation, which had once more assembled in Judea, under the reign of Hadrian, and by these two wars the Jewish population must have been effectually extirpated from the Holy Land.

4. **Figurative.** "Children of the captivity" denotes those who were in captivity, or their posterity (Ezra 4:1). "The Lord turned the captivity of Job" (Job. 42:10) means that he released him from his sufferings and restored him to prosperity. "He led captivity captive" (Eph. 4:8) is a figurative allusion to the victory of Christ over the enemies of himself and his kingdom.

5. **Prophetic.** The O. T. speaks of a future restoration of Israel to God's favor in Palestine and as head of the nations in the Coming Age (the Millennium). Isaiah (11:11) calls it a "second" restoration. The Jews have never been restored but "once" and that was from Babylon. The Egyptian deliverance was not a restoration, because Palestine was never in

their possession until conquered by Joshua. The "second" and final restoration will be from their present world-wide dispersion (Jer. 16:14, 15; 24:6; Isa. 43:5-7) after the completion of "the times of the Gentiles" (Luke 21:24) at the Second Advent of Christ (Matt. 23:29). It will be a restoration in unbelief (Ezek. 36:24-27) to be followed by judgment and chastening in "the great tribulation" (Matt. 24:21-31; Jer. 30:4-7; Dan. 12:1) previous to their conversion (Zech. 12:10; I Cor. 15:8). It will be a national restoration (Ezek. 37:1-22; Rom. 11:25) and will usher in the mediatorial Davidic Messianic kingdom on earth. This millennial age with the Jew in his God-ordained position as a priestly nation at the head of the nations (Zech. 3:1-12) will constitute the last of God's ordered ages in time (Rev. 20:1-10) before the dawn of the eternal state (Rev. chaps. 21, 22). Revised by *M. F. U.*

Carbuncle. *See* Mineral Kingdom.

Car'cas (kär'kăs), the last named of the seven eunuchs who were commanded to bring Queen Vashti into the presence of King Ahasuerus at the royal feast (Esth. 1:10), B. C. about 478.

Carcase, the dead body of man or beast (Josh. 8:29; Isa. 14:19; Heb. 3:17, etc.). According to the Mosaic law: (1) The dead body of a human being rendered unclean the tent (or house) in which the man had died, with any open vessels therein, for seven days. It was no less defiling to touch the dead. (2) Contact with the carcase of any animal rendered unclean the one touching, carrying, or eating it unclean until evening (Lev. 11:39). For fuller particulars, *see* Uncleanness; Dead, The.

Car'chemish (kär'kē-mĭsh), a Hittite city on the right bank of the Euphrates commanding one of the best fords of that river (Jer. 46:24; Isa. 10:9). The site was excavated by Sir Leonard Woolley and T. E. Lawrence for the British Museum. An important Hittite culture was revealed, and the city formed the east capital of the Hittite empire. It lay just west of Haran and may have been visited by Abraham on his trek to Palestine. Sargon II of Assyria (c. 718 B. C.) took Carchemish. It was here that Nebuchadnezzar II defeated Nechoh of Egypt (605 B. C.), which event inaugurated the splendid Neo-Babylonian Empire and presaged the Babylonian captivity of the S. kingdom. *M. F. U.*

Care, Cares (Gr. *merimna*). The Greek word has the sense of being drawn in different directions, and answers to our *distraction*. It is used in the sense of anxiety in I Pet. 5:7, where it is contrasted with *melō*, to *be of interest* to, and may be read, "Casting all your anxiety upon him; for he is interested in you" (comp. Psa. 55:23; Luke 8:14; 21:34). In Matt. 13:22; Mark 4:19, the "care of this world" is anxiety about things pertaining to this earthly life. Paul uses the same word, "*care* of all the churches" (II Cor. 11:28).

Care'ah (kà-rē'à), the father of Johanan (II Kings 25:23); elswhere *Kareah* (*q. v.*).

Car'mel (kär'mĕl; a plant *field, park, garden*).
  1. As a common noun, rendered "fruitful field" (Isa. 10:18; 29:17; 32:15, 16), "plentiful field" (Isa. 16:10; Jer. 48:33), "plentiful

90. Mount Carmel with Haifa and the Mediterranean at Foot

country" (Jer. 2:7). In II Kings 19:23; II Chron. 26:10, it is incorrectly rendered as a proper name, "Carmel" (R. V. "fruitful field").
  2. A prominent headland of Palestine, bounding on the south the Bay of Acre, and running out almost into the Mediterranean, bearing about south-southeast for more than twelve miles, terminating suddenly by an eastern bluff. Its average height is one thousand five hundred feet. Carmel fell within the lot of the tribe of Asher (Josh. 19:26), which was extended as far south as Dor, probably to give the Asherites a share of the rich corn-growing plain of Sharon. The king of "Jokneam of Carmel" was one of the Canaanite chiefs who fell before the arms of Joshua. From earliest times the garden-like loveliness of Carmel was sacred to the Canaanite Baal and other oracles.
  That which has made Carmel most familiar is its connection with the history of Elijah and Elisha. Here Elijah brought back Israel to allegiance to Jehovah, and slew the prophets of the foreign and false god; here at his entreaty were consumed the successive "fifties" of the royal guard; but here, on the other hand, Elisha received the visit of the bereaved mother whose son he was soon to restore to her arms (II Kings 4:25, etc.). There is good reason to believe that a later incident in the life of the same great prophet took place on Carmel. This was when he "caused fire to come down from heaven" and consume the two "fifties" of the guard which Ahaziah had dispatched to take him prisoner, for having stopped his messengers to Baalzebub the god of Ekron (II Kings 1:9-15).
  Carmel is still clothed with the same excellency of wood which supplied the prophets of Israel and Judah alike with one of their most favorite illustrations (Isa. 33:9 Mic. 7:14).
  3. A town in the mountainous country of Judah (Josh. 15:55), familiar to us as the residence of Nabal (I Sam. 25:2, 5, 7, 40), and the native place of David's favorite wife, "Abigail the Carmelitess" (I Sam. 27:3; I Chron. 3:1). This was doubtless the Carmel at which Saul set up "a place," literally "a hand," after his victory over Amalek (I Sam. 15:12). And this Carmel, and not the northern mount, must have been the spot at which

King Uzziah had his vineyards (II Chron. 26:10). It is now called Kermel, about 9 miles S. E. of Hebron.

Car'melite (kär'měl-īt), the designation of Nabal (I Sam. 30:5; II Sam. 2:2; 3:3) and his wife Abigail (I Sam. 27:3; I Chron. 3:1, A. V. "Carmelitess"); also of *Hezrai* (*q. v.*), one of David's warriors (II Sam. 23:35), probably from being inhabitant of *Carmel q. v.*) in Judah.

Car'mi (kär'mī; *vine-dresser*).

1. The fourth son of Reuben (Gen. 46:9; Exod. 6:14), B. C. about 1870. His descendants were called Carmites (Num. 26:6).

2. The son of Hezron (Judah's grandson), and father of Hur (I Chron. 4:1). He is elsewhere called Caleb (ch. 2:18), or Chelubai (2:9).

3. The son of Zabdi (of the tribe of Judah), and father of Achan, the traitor (Josh. 7:1; I Chron. 2:7), B. C. before 1400.

Car'mites (kär'mīts), the patronymic of the descendants of *Carmi* (*q. v.*), the Reubenite (Num. 26:6).

Carnal (from Gr. *sarx, flesh*), having the nature of flesh, i. e., under the control of the animal appetites (Rom. 7:14); governed by mere human nature, not by the Spirit of God (I Cor. 3:1, 3, "fleshly"). It is mere human nature, the earthly nature of man apart from divine influence, and therefore prone to sin and opposed to God (Rom. 8:7; comp. Gal. 5:19, sq., where the works of "the flesh" are given)

Another sense is pertaining to the body, of things needed for the sustenance of the body (Rom. 15:27; I Cor. 9:11). The ceremonial parts of the Mosaic dispensation were carnal, relating to the bodies of men and beasts (Heb. 7:16; 9:10). The Christian's weapons are not carnal, i. e., not of human origin, not directed by human wisdom (II Cor. 10:4).

Carpenter (Heb. *ḥārûsh*, *artisan*, II Sam. 5:11; I Chron. 14:1; Isa. 44:13, etc.; Gr. *tekton*, Matt. 13:55; Mark 6:3). A general term, including an artificer in stone and metal, as well as wood. *See* Handicrafts.

Car'pus (kär'pŭs; *fruit*), a Christian of Troas, with whom the apostle Paul states that he left a cloak (II Tim. 4:13), probably when passing through Asia Minor for the last time before his martyrdom at Rome.

Carshe'na (kär-shē'nà), the first named of the seven "princes" or chief emirs of the court of Xerxes (Ahasuerus), with whom he consulted as to what course he should pursue toward Vashti, who had refused to appear at the royal banquet (Esth. 1:14). The name is evidently Old Persian, signifying "plowman."

Cart (Heb. *'ăgäläh*), something *revolving;* sometimes rendered "chariot," Psa. 46:9; "wagon," Gen. 45:19, sq.; Num. 7:8, sq.), a two-wheeled vehicle, used for transporting persons (Gen. 45:19) or freight (I Sam. 6:7, 8). They were drawn by cattle (II Sam. 6:3), and are to be distinguished from the war chariots drawn by horses. The wheels were sometimes made of solid blocks of wood, sometimes with spokes, as represented on the monuments of Egypt and Nineveh.

Figurative. The expression, "Woe unto them that draw . . . sin as it were with a *cart*

rope" (Isa. 5:18), is understood by some to refer to the binding of burdens upon carts, and so to the enslaving power of sin. Others use *cart rope* in the sense of a trace, and think that the metaphor is used to illustrate the heavy burdens which must be drawn by the sinner.

Carve, Carving. *See* Handicrafts.

Casement. *See* Lattice, House.

Casiph'ia (kà-sĭf'ĭ-à), a "place" of the Persian empire where Levites settled during the captivity, and whence Iddo and others joined Ezra (Ezra 8:17). Its location is unknown.

Cas'luhim (kăs'lū-hĭm), a Mizraite people or tribe (Gen. 10:14; I Chron. 1:12). The only clew we have as yet to the position of the Casluhim is their place in the list of the sons of Mizraim between the Pathrusim and the Caphtorim, whence it is probable that they were located in Upper Egypt.

Cassia. *See* Vegetable Kingdom.

Castaway (Gr. *'adokimos, not approved, disqualified*), a metaphor borrowed from the athletic games in which the contestant, being examined, is found to be rejected from receiving the prize because of the infraction of some rule of the game. In I Cor. 9:27 the Apostle is giving instruction concerning *rewards* and not *salvation*. These two lines of truth, so saliently differentiated in Scripture, are so commonly confused in theological thinking. Salvation, which is by "grace through faith" totally apart from "works" (Eph. 2:8-10) is not subject to loss or forfeiture, inasmuch as it is a divine gift and rests on the sure foundation of God's faithfulness (John 3:16; 4:10; Rom. 6:23). Rewards, on the other hand, are gained by works performed after one is saved (Matt. 10:42; Luke 19:17; II Tim. 4:7, 8; Rev. 2:10; 22:12). Furthermore, salvation is a present possession of the believer (John 3:36; 5:24; 6:47), while rewards are a future realization, to be dispensed at the Lord's Coming (Matt. 16:27; I Cor. 3:11-23; II Tim. 4:8). The R. S. V. of I Cor. 9:27 is accurate: "But I pommel my body and subdue it, lest after preaching to others I myself should be disqualified." *M. F. U.*

Casting. *See* Handicrafts.

Castle. In addition to its meaning of fortress (I Chron. 11:7), castles were, probably, towers used by the priests for observation, and for making known, through the sounding of trumpets, anything discovered at a distance (I Chron. 6:54). The "castles," Gen. 25:16, may have been inclosures for flocks or cattle, watchtowers from which shepherds watched their flocks. The "castle," Acts 21:34, refers to the quarters of the Roman soldiers in the fortress of Antonia, adjacent to the temple.

Cas'tor and Pol'lux (kăs'tōr and pŏl'ŭx). The Dioscuri, i. e., sons of Jupiter; Castor being a horse tamer, and Pollux (Gr. *Polydeucēs*), the master of the art of boxing. They were the ideal types of bravery and dexterity in fight, and thus became the tutelary gods of warlike youth. They were supposed to lend their aid to the mariner, who, in case of a storm, prays to them, and vows to sacrifice a lamb to them as soon as the storm ceases. The ship in which Paul sailed from Malta had for its sign Castor and Pollux (Acts 28:11).

Caterpillar. *See* Animal Kingdom.

Catholic Epistles. At the end of the Epistles stand seven—James, I and II Peter, I, II, III John, and Jude—which bear the name of *catholic*, or *general*. This title is inaccurate, for two of them, II and III John, are addressed to individuals; and two more to a designated circle of readers, James to "the twelve tribes which are in the dispersion," and I Peter to "the elect strangers of the dispersion," etc. The following explanations have been given of the term: (1) These epistles are "general letters of instruction, the name at first applied only to a part, but afterward including even those addressed to private persons;" (2) Because the different apostles were engaged in writing them; (3) Because of the *catholic* doctrine taught in them; (4) I Peter and I John, having from the beginning been received as authentic, obtained the distinction of being *catholic*, or universally accepted. As the others came to be thus received, they were called catholic.

Cattle. See Animal Kingdom.

Caul. 1. "The popular name for a membrane investing the viscera" (*Century Dict.*). "The liver-net, or stomach-net, which commences at the division between the right and the left lobes of the liver, and stretches on the one side across the stomach, and on the other to the regions of the kidneys" (K. and D., *Com.*, on Lev. 3:4). The *caul*, with the rest of the fat in the inside of the animal to be offered, and the two kidneys were burned upon the altar (Lev. 3:4, 5.)

2. "The *caul* of their heart" (Heb. $s^e g \delta r'$, *shut up*, Hos. 13:8) is either the *pericardium*, membrane about the heart, or the *breast*, as inclosing the heart.

3. Among the ornaments worn by the women in Isaiah's day (Isa. 3:18) were *cauls*, i. e., "hair-nets" (R. V. and A. V. "networks," R. S. V. "headbands"). *See* Dress.

Causeway (Heb. $m^e sill\ddot{a}h'$ from *sälăl, to throw up*), the raised way which led from the lower city up to the temple site (I Chron. 26:16, 18), which was afterward replaced by a bridge. In II Chron. 9:4 it is called an "ascent," and in 9:11 a "terrace."

Cavalry. *See* Army, War.

Cave. The chalky limestone of which the rocks of Syria and Palestine chiefly consist presents, as in the case in all limestone formations, a vast number of caverns and natural fissures, many of which have also been artificially enlarged and adapted to various purposes, both of shelter and defense. The most remarkable caves noticed in Scripture are: (1) That in which Lot dwelt after the destruction of Sodom (Gen. 19:30). (2) The cave of Machpelah (23:17). (3) Cave of Makkedah (Josh. 10:16). (4) Cave of Adullam (I Sam. 22:1). (5) Cave of Engedi (24:3). (6) The cave in which Obadiah concealed the prophets (I Kings 18:4), which was probably in the northern part of the country, where abundant caves fit for such a purpose might be pointed out. (7) Elijah's cave in Horeb (I Kings 19:9), the locality of which cannot be determined. (8, 9) The rock sepulchers of Lazarus and of our Lord (John 11:38; Matt. 20:60).

Caves were used as habitations (Num. 24:

21; Cant. 2:14; Jer. 49:16; Obad. 3), as places of refuge (Judg. 6:2; I Sam. 14:11), as prisons (Isa. 24:22; Zech. 9:11). *See* Dwelling.

Cedar. See Vegetable Kingdom.

Ce'dron (kē'drŏn; John 18:1). *See* Kidron.

Cellar, an underground vault for storage of wine and oil (I Chron. 27:27, 28). The word is also used to denote the *treasury* of the temple (I Kings 7:51) and of the king (14:26). *See* House.

Cen'chrea (sĕn'krĕ-à; *millet*), the eastern harbor of Corinth, the modern name of which is still Kenchreae, although the popular name is Kikries. It is about eignt miles from Corinth. Paul once sailed from this port (Acts 18:18). He also makes reference in Rom. 16:1 to the church established there.

Censer (Heb. *măhtäh*, a *firepan*; *mĭqtŏrĕth*, *vessel for burning incense*, from *qătăr*, *burn incense*), the vessel upon which the incense was burned in the sanctuary, and which was appointed to be set every morning on the altar of incense when the priest went in to trim the lamps, and again when he lighted them at even (Exod. 30:7, 8). Yearly, on the day of atonement, the high priest entered the holy of holies, bearing the censer, and threw upon the burning coals it contained the incense, holding the censer in his hand while the incense burned (Lev. 16: 12, 13).

No description is given of the censer, and therefore we are left in doubt as to its form and appearance. The probability is that, inasmuch as all fire upon which incense was burned was taken from the "brazen altar," every censer had a handle by which it could be carried. They are mentioned among the vessels of the tabernacle, which were to be wrapped up in proper coverings when the order was given to march (Num. 4:14); and from Lev. 10:1; Num. 16:6, 17, in which each ministering priest is spoken of as having his censer, it would seem that they existed in considerable numbers.

As to material, the censers were probably made of copper ("brazen"); and from the fact that the censers of the rebels were used as plates to cover the altar (Num. 16:38, 39) it would seem that they were simply square copper sheets, folded at the corners like the modern sheet-iron pan. Solomon prepared "censers of pure gold" for the temple (I Kings 7:50; II Chron. 4:22). In Rev. 5:8, 8:3, 5, the angel is represented with a golden censer.

The word *thumiastērion, place of fumigation,* rendered "censer" in Heb. 9:4, as a thing belonging to the tabernacle, probably means the "altar of incense."

Census. This term does not occur in the A. V., although found in the original (Matt. 17:25, *kēnsos,* A. V. "tribute"). The act is, however, referred to in the Heb. *mĭphqäd,* or *p^equdäh, numbering;* and the Gr. *'apographē, enrollment.*

1. **Old Testament.** According to the law of Moses (Exod. 30:12-14) every male Israelite of twenty years old and upward was enrolled in the army and was to pay half a shekel as atonement money. The following instances of a census being taken are given in the Old Testament: (1) Under the express direction of God (Exod. 38:26), in the third or fourth month after the Exodus during the encamp-

ment at Sinai, chiefly for the purpose of raising money for the tabernacle. The numbers then taken amounted to 603,550 men. (2) In the second month of the second year after the Exodus (Num. 1:2, 3). This census was taken for a double purpose: (*a*) To ascertain the number of fighting men from the age of twenty to fifty. (*b*) to ascertain the amount of the redemption offering due on account of all the firstborn, both of persons and cattle. The Levites, whose numbers amounted to 22,000, were taken in lieu of the firstborn males of the rest of Israel, whose numbers were 22,273, and for the surplus of 273, a money payment of thirteen hundred and sixty-five shekels, or five shekels each, was made to Aaron and his sons (Num. 3:39, 51). (3) Thirty-eight years afterward, previous to the entrance into Canaan, when the total number, excepting the Levites, amounted to 601,730 males showing a decrease of 1,870 (Num. 26:51). (4) In the reign of David the men of Israel above twenty years of age were 800,000, and of Judah 500,000, total 1,300,000. The book of Chronicles gives the numbers of Israel 1,100,000, and of Judah 470,000, total 1,570,000, but informs us that Levi and Benjamin were not numbered (I Chron. 21:6; 27:24). The time of this census belongs undoubtedly to the closing years of David's reign. The wrong of this census is thought by some to have consisted in the omission to collect the atonement money (see above) but the following explanation seems the correct one: "The true kernel of David's sin was to be found, no doubt, in self-exaltation, inasmuch as he sought for the strength and glory of his kingdom in the number of the people and their readiness for war" (K. and D., *Com.*, II Sam. 24:1-9). (5) The census of David was completed by Solomon by causing the foreigners and remnants of the conquered nations resident within Palestine to be numbered. Their number amounted to 153,600 (I Kings 5:15; II Chron. 2:17, 18), and they were employed in forced labor on his great architectural works (Josh. 9:27; I Kings 9:20, 21; I Chron. 22:2). The numbers in the armies under the several kings between Solomon and the captivity assist us in estimating the population at the various times referred to. The census taken of those who returned with Zerubbabel was to settle the inheritances in Palestine and to ascertain the family genealogies. The number was 42,360 (Ezra 2:64).

2. **New Testament.** St. Luke, in his account of the "taxing," says a decree went out from Augustus that all the world should be taxed, and in the Acts alludes to a disturbance raised by Judas of Galilee in the days of the "taxing" (Luke 2:1; Acts 5:37). The Roman census under the republic consisted, so far as the present purpose is concerned, in an enrollment of persons and property by tribes and households.

Centurion, the captains of the sixty *centuries* (companies of one hundred men) in the Roman legion. The centurion carried a staff of vinewood as his badge of office. There were various degrees of rank among the centurions according as they belonged to the three divisions of the *triarii, principes,* and *hastati,* and led

91. Roman Centurion

the first or second *centuria* of one of the thirty *manipuli.* The first centurion of whom mention is made in Scripture is the one who in our Lord's early ministry sent a request that he would recover his dying servant (Matt. 8:5-10). The other is Cornelius, an early convert to Christianity (Acts 10:1). Others are mentioned (Luke 7:2, 6; also in Acts). *See* Army.

Ce'phas (sē'fàs; Aram. *rock, stone*), a surname which Christ bestowed upon Simon Peter (John 1:42; I Cor. 1:12, sq.).

Ce'sar. *See* Caesar. **Cesare'a.** *See* Caesarea.

Chaff. Most generally "chaff" is the rendering of the Heb. *mōṣ,* the refuse of winnowed grain, consisting of husks and broken straw. In the East it was the custom to burn chaff, lest, with the changing wind, it might be blown again among the grain (Job 21:18; Psa. 1:4; 35:5; Isa. 17:13; 29:5; 41:15; Hos. 13:3; Zeph. 2:2).

In Isaiah (5:24; 33:11) the word rendered "chaff" is *hāshāsh',* and means *dry grass, hay.* It only occurs in the above passages.

Heb. *tĕ'bĕn,* rendered "chaff" in Jer. 23:28, is elsewhere (Exod. 5:7, 10, sq.) translated "straw." The "stubble" mentioned in Job 21:18) is *cut straw.*

In Daniel (2:35) the Aramaic word *'ūr* occurs.

Figurative. From its being the lighter and, comparatively speaking, worthless portion of the grain, *chaff* is used in Scripture as an emblem of that which is in doctrine or morals, of a similar nature; of false teaching (Jer. 23:28); evildoers, who must come to naught (Psa. 1:4; Isa. 33:11; Matt. 3:12).

Chain, the rendering of several Hebrew and Greek words. From very ancient times chains have been used, as at present, both for ornament, bondage, and badges of office.

1. **Badge of Office.** Instances of such are the golden chain on Joseph's neck (Gen. 41:42; Heb. *rābîd*, literally, *collar*) and the one promised to Daniel (Dan. 5:7; Heb. *hămûnēk*, *necklace*). In Egypt it was one of the insignia of a judge, who wore an image of truth attached to it; it was also worn by the prime minister. In Persia it was considered not only a mark of royal favor, but a token of investiture. In Ezek. 16:11 the chain is mentioned as the symbol of sovereignty.

2. **Ornamental.** Chains for ornamental purposes were worn by men, as well as women, in many countries, both of Europe and Asia, and probably this was the case among the Hebrews (Prov. 1:9; Heb. *'änäk, neck*). In addition to necklaces of pearls, corals, etc., other chains were worn (Judith 10:4), hanging down as far as the waist or even lower. Mention is made of "stepping chains" (Isa. 3:20; Heb. *se'ādōth, step-chains,* rendered "ornaments of the legs"), which were attached to ankle-rings to shorten the step and give it elegance. The "chains" (v. 19) were earrings.

3. **Chains** were used for the confinement of prisoners in a manner similar to our handcuffs (Judg. 16:21; II Sam. 3:34; Jer. 39:7; Heb. *nehōshĕth, bronze chains,* sometimes rendered "fetters"). The Romans frequently fastened the prisoner with a light chain to the soldier guarding him, as was the case with Paul (Acts 28:20); Eph. 6:20; II Tim. 1:16); and when the utmost security was desired two chains were used (Acts 12:6). The prophet Isaiah speaks (40:19) of silver chains in connection with idols, which may have been for ornament or to fasten them to their shrines.

4. **Figurative.** Chains are used as a symbol of oppression or punishment (Lam. 3:7; Psa. 149:8; Ezek. 7:23, etc.).
Pride is termed a chain which holds men in its power (Psa. 73:6).

Chalce′dony (kăl-sĕ′dô-nĭ). *See* Mineral Kingdom.

Chal′col (kăl′kŏl), one of the four sons of Mahol, who were famous for their wisdom before the time of Solomon (I Kings 4:31), B. C. before 960. In I Chron. 2:6, where the name is Anglicized Calcol, he and his brothers are given as the sons of Zerah, of the tribe of Judah.

Chalde′a (kăl-dē′á; from Accad. *kaldu*), originally a small territory in southern Babylonia at the head of the Persian Gulf but later, after the Neo-Babylonian empire of Nebuchadnezzar II (605-562 B. C.) the term came to include practically all of Babylonia extending north of Hit southward to the Gulf. *M. F. U.*

Chaldean (kăl-dē′ăn), a native of Chaldea. *See* Babylonia. The Chaldeans were a warlike, aggressive people from the mountains of Kurdistan. Apparently they were Haldians (or Khaldians), the inhabitants of Urartu, that is, Ararat or Armenia. The ancient Chaldeans are mentioned in the Babylonian inscriptions. They began to appear in Assyrian notices in the reign of Ashurnasirpal II (883-859 B. C.), though their existence as a people goes back well beyond 1000 B. C. When Tiglath-pileser

III (745-727 B. C.) became king of Assyria, he conquered Babylon. Here the Chaldeans and roving Aramean tribes were constantly disturbing the native king. In 731 B. C. Ukinzer, who came from one of the Chaldean cities, made himself king of Babylon. However, he was deposed by Tiglath-pileser III in 728 B C., who ascended the throne of Babylon and ruled under the name of Pul. Pul was followed on the Assyrian throne by Shalmaneser IV (726-722 B. C.). He was in turn succeeded on the throne of Babylon by Merodach-Baladan, a Chaldean. Merodach-Baladan was conquered by Sargon but continued as king until 709 B. C., when the latter became king of Babylon as well as of Assyria. At the time of Hezekiah (702 B. C.) Merodach-Baladan, son of Baladan, ruled in Babylon. It was not until about 625 B. C. that Chaldean power began to assert itself over Assyria. Nabopolasser at that time rebelled against Assyria and established the new Babylonian empire. He reconstructed the city of Babylon. In the fourteenth year of his reign (612 B. C.) with Cyaxerxes the Mede and the Scythian king he captured Nineveh and laid it waste (cf. Nahum 3:1-3). In 605 B. C. he was succeeded by his son Nebuchadnezzar II. Under Nebuchadnezzar II, Judah and Jerusalem were carried captive to Babylon, and the Chaldean armies over-ran the then-known world, with Nebuchadnezzar making the Babylon of his day the most splendid city of antiquity (cf. Dan. 4:30). Nebuchadnezzar was succeeded by his son Evil-Merodach (562-560 B. C.), who was murdered by his brother-in-law Neriglissar (560-558 B. C.). The next king, Labashi-Marduk, reigned only three months and was succeeded by the usurper Nabonidus, whose son Belshazzar (Dan. 5) was co-regent until the fall of the Chaldean empire in 538 B. C. That so small a land as Chaldea should produce a conquering race of sufficient power to overcome and rule the world of the time is one of the marvels of history. *M. F. U.*

Chaldean Astrologers.

Because of their proficiency in the science of astronomy and their skillful practice of astrology, the Chaldeans became a special caste of *astrologers.* In this sense the word is used in the book of Daniel (2:2, 10; 4:7, etc.). The explanation of this specialized name is easily understood. From 625 B. C. onward the Chaldeans held complete sway in Babylonia. The city of Babylon was their capital and was the very center of intellectual life in all western Asia. This intellectual activity was especially employed in the study of the stars, both scientific and as a means of divination. Astronomy and astrology were both sought after in the land. Hence Babylon became famous as the home of all sorts of magicians, sorcerers, diviners and other occultists. As scientists the Chaldeans founded the exact science of astronomy. For over a period of 360 years they kept meticulous astronomical records. One of their astounding contributions was to reckon a year of 365 days, six hours, fifteen minutes and forty-one seconds, a calculation that measures within thirty minutes of what modern instruments have worked out. As the Chaldeans held sway in Babylon, it was perfectly natural that they should give their name to the astrologists as well as astronomers who had made the city famous. *M. F. U.*

Chal'dee (kăl'dē). *See* Aramaic.

Chaldees (kăl-dēz'). This is a variant form of Chaldeans used in the expression "Ur of the Chaldees" (Gen. 11:31; Neh. 9:7). The qualifying phrase "of the Chaldees (Chaldeans)" is not an anachronism as many critics hold. (cf. Finegan, *Light From an Ancient Past*, 1946, p. 57). But as in the case of numerous archaic place names, it is a later scribal gloss to explain to a subsequent age when Abraham's native city Ur and its location had utterly perished, that the city was located in southern Babylonia, then known as Chaldea. After 1000 B. C. the race of the Chaldeans became dominant and it was, of course, quite natural for the Hebrew scribe to define the then incomprehensible foreign name by an appellation customary in his own day. Gen. 14 (vs. 2, 3, 7, 8, 17) offers a good example of such scribal glosses to explain archaic place-names. *M. F. U.*

Chalk. *See* Mineral Kingdom.

Chamber, as an apartment of a house (*q. v.*).

Figurative. The term "chamber" is used metaphorically in the Psalms (104:3, 13) for the heavens.

The expression, "Enter into my chambers," etc. (Isa. 26:20), is figurative of earnest prayer.

The "chambers of the south" (Job 9:9) are the constellations, or, perhaps, in a more general sense, the regions of the southern sky.

"Chambers of imagery" (Heb. "image apartments," Ezek. 8:12) is used by the prophet to denote the vision which he had of the idolatrous practices of the Jews in Jerusalem. "Image chambers" is the term applied to the rooms or closets in the houses of the people, in which idolatrous images were set up and secretly worshipped.

Chambering (Gr. *koitē, beds*), a word occurring only in Rom. 13:13, where it signifies lewd and licentious conduct, especially illicit intercourse.

Chamberlain (Heb. *sârîs, castrated,* sometimes translated "*Eunuch,*" *q. v.*), an officer confidentially employed about the person of the sovereign, as Potiphar (Gen. 39:1). This officer was introduced into the court by Solomon (I Kings 4:6; 16:9, "steward;" 18:3, "governor"). His duty seems at first to have been the superintendence of the palace and royal etiquette. Later this post became one of special and increasing influence, including the right of introduction to the king. He thus became the chief minister.

Erastus, the "chamberlain" of the city of Corinth, was one of those whose salutations to the Roman Christians are given (Rom. 16:23; Gr. *oikonomos*). The office was apparently that of public treasurer or *arcarius*. The *arcarii* were inferior magistrates having charge of the public chest, and were under the authority of the Senate.

Blastus, Herod's chamberlain (Acts 12:20; Gr. *koitōn*) was the chief *valet de chambre* of the king, and by reason of his office had great influence with Herod.

Chameleon. *See* Animal Kingdom.

Chamois. *See* Animal Kingdom.

Champion (Heb. *gǐbbōr,* I Sam. 17:51; elsewhere "mighty man"). The Hebrew phrase, rendered "champion" in I Sam. 17:4, 23, literally is a *man between the two,* a go-between, a challenger. So Goliath went between the armies of the Hebrews and Philistines, as the champion of the latter.

Cha'naan (kā'năn), another form (Acts 7:11; 13:19) of *Canaan* (*q. v.*).

Chance. The use of this word in Scripture has the sense of to *meet unexpectedly* (Deut. 22:6; II Sam. 1:6), an occurrence for which there seems to be no explanation (I Sam. 6:9), a *coincidence* (Luke 10:31), *opportunity* (Eccles. 9:11), *example* (I Cor. 15:37).

Chancellor (Aram. *bᵉēl tᵉēm, lord of judgment*), the title of the Persian governor of Samaria (Ezra 4:8, 9, 17).

Change of Raiment. *See* Dress.

Channel. 1. The rendering (Isa. 27:12) of *Shibboleth* (*q. v.*).

2. The bed of the sea, or of a river (Psa. 18:15; Isa. 8:7; Heb. *'ăpîq, valley*).

Chaos, a term not used in Scripture, but in frequent use to designate the unformed mass of primeval matter mentioned in Gen. 1:2. It comes from the Greek *chaos, immeasurable space*), and is used by Hesiod for the unfathomable gulf which was supposed to be the first of existing things. Some cosmogonies, as the Phoenician, retain the biblical terms descriptive of chaos, but changed into personal existences; e. g., the Hebrew term *bōhu, emptiness,* is transformed into Baau, the producing principle. According to Greek mythology, from Chaos arose the Earth, Tartarus, and Love, also Erebus and Night. Ovid describes chaos as a confused mass, containing the elements of all things which were formed out of it. The great majority of the cosmogonies, however, are atheistic, ascribing creation to inherent ability in matter, or to a blind necessity; while the Scriptures make it the act of God.

In Babylonian thought, however, matter and spirit are identified with each other and confused. Apsu (male) and Tiamat (female) are not only conceived as gods (spirit) but as cosmic forces (matter). Apsu is the primeval fresh water ocean and Tiamat, the primordial salt water ocean. Their union produces the gods and the universe. Tiamat (chaos) in her war with Marduk is slain and her corpse made into kosmos. Tiamat and *tehom* "the deep" of Gen. 1:2 are etymologically equivalent, but while the former is a mythical personality confused with matter, the latter is a common noun, without any mythological connotation whatever and simply describes the entire chaotic mass out of which the waters above the firmament were separated on the second day and out of which the dry land emerged on the third day. Tiamat and *tehom,* although cognate, are independent of each other and both go back to a common proto-Semitic form. Revised by *M. F. U.*

Chapel (Heb. *mǐqdäsh, holy place*), occurs only in Amos 7:13, where Beth-el is called "the king's chapel" by the high priest of the golden calf. The meaning appears to be that Beth-el was the royal capital, the principal seat of worship established by the king.

Chapiter, Capital, in modern architecture, the upper, ornamental part of a column. In Exod. 36:38; 38:17, 19, 28 (Heb. *rō'sh*, *head*), it refers to the capitals on the pillars of the tabernacle and its court. Once (II Chron. 3:15) the Heb. *ṣĕfĕth*, to *encircle*, is so rendered; elsewhere (I Kings, II Chron., and Jer. 52:22) the term is the rendering of the Heb. *kōthĕrĕth*, and refers to the capitals of the temple pillars.

Char′ashim (kär′à-shĭm; *craftsmen*). The "valley of Charashim" (I Chron. 4:14) was inhabited by craftsmen, and is called "valley of craftsmen" (Neh. 11:35); not far from Jerusalem.

Char′chemish (kär′kĕm-ish; II Chron. 35:20). See Carchemish.

Charger. 1. The rendering of the Heb. *q⁽ʿ⁾äräh*, literally, a *deep dish*; the silver dishes presented by the tribal chiefs (Num. 7) for the service of the tabernacle. The word is elsewhere translated "dish" (Exod. 25:29; 37:16; Num. 4:7). They weighed one hundred and thirty shekels each.

2. The "chargers" mentioned in Ezra 1:9 (Heb. *'ăgărṭāl*), thirty of gold and one thousand of silver, are supposed, by some, to have been *basins* for holding the blood of the sacrifices; by others, *baskets* for the first fruits.

3. The "charger" (Matt. 14:8, 11; Mark 6:25, 28; Gr. *pinax*) upon which Herodias bore the head of John the Baptist was probably a large *platter*, and the word is so rendered in Luke 11:39, sq.

In short, the word was properly a general term, indicating what bore or was loaded with any weight; hence, a saddle horse is still called a charger.

Chariot, the rendering of several Hebrew words and one Greek word, the indiscriminate use of which renders it difficult to know which kind of vehicle is meant. The same words are employed in speaking of chariots of war, state chariots, and even of wagons. The earliest mention of chariots in Scripture is where Joseph, as a mark of distinction, rode in Pharaoh's second chariot (Gen. 41:43); and later when he went in his own chariot to meet his father (46:29). Chariots also accompanied the funeral procession of Jacob, as a guard of honor (50:9). We next find them used for a *warlike* purpose (Exod. 14:7), when Pharaoh pursued the Israelites with six hundred chariots. Chariots date back to very early Sumerian times in Mesopotamia.

1. **Egyptian.** From the Egyptian monuments we are able to form a very correct idea of the chariots of that nation. They were all similar in form, having but two wheels, furnished on the right side with cases for bows and spears and arrows. The framework, wheels, pole, and yoke were of wood, with the wheels sometimes tipped with iron, and the axletrees ending with a scythe-like projection. The binding of the framework, as well as the harness, were of rawhide or tanned leather; while the floor was often made of rope network, to give a more springy footing to the occupants. The chariot was open behind, and here the charioteer entered. The sumptuous gold-stuccoed chariot of Tutankhamun was recovered from his lavish intact tomb.

From the Egyptian sculptures it would seem that an Egyptian army was composed exclusively of infantry and chariots. Chariots were manned sometimes with three men, the warrior, the shield-bearer, and the charioteer; sometimes with only one person. The presumption is that the horsemen and riders (Exod. 14:9; 15:1) were riders in the chariots; and the "captains" (14:7) were chariot-warriors, literally, "third" men, probably selected for their valor.

92. Egyptian (above) and Assyrian Chariots

2. **Assyrian.** From the sculptures we learn that the Assyrian chariot resembled the Egyptian in all material points. A very early chariot from Sumerian Ur is pictured with solid wooden wheels clamped around a copper core.

3. **Canaan.** The Canaanites had *iron* chariots (Josh. 17:18), "not *scythe* chariots, for these were introduced by Cyrus, but simply chariots tipped with iron" (K. and D., *Com.*, in loc.). Of these it is recorded that Jabin, king of Canaan, had nine hundred (Judg. 4:3). The number of chariots which the Philistines had in the time of Saul, viz., thirty thousand (I Sam. 13:5), appears excessive, the probability being that there is a mistake by the copyist, so that it would be more correct to read three thousand. David took from Hadadezer, king of Zobah, one thousand chariots (II Sam. 8:4), and later seven hundred from the Syrians (10:18), who, in order to recover their ground, collected from various countries thirty-two thousand (I Chron. 19:6, 7).

4. **Hebrew.** Hitherto the Israelites had few chariots, partly on account of the mountain-

ous nature of the country, partly owing to the prohibition against their multiplying horses. Solomon raised and maintained a force of one thousand four hundred chariots (I Kings 10:26) by taxation on certain cities. The chariots and the horses were imported chiefly from Egypt (I Kings 10:29). "Chariot cities" (II Chron. 1:14) were the depots and stables erected by Solomon on the frontiers of his kingdom, such as Beth-marcaboth, "the house of chariots" (Josh. 19:5), and Hazor-susah, "the village of horses" (I Kings 10:28). The famous stables excavated at Megiddo from Solomon's age strikingly confirm the Biblical notices, as do finds at his other "Chariot Cities," Hazor and Gezer.

5. **New Testament.** In the New Testament the only mention made of a chariot, except in Rev. 9:9, is in the case of the Ethiopian eunuch of Queen Candace (Acts 8:28, sq.).

6. **Figurative.** Chariots are frequently alluded to as symbols of power (Psa. 20:7; 104:3; Jer. 51:21; Zech. 6:1, 2); hosts or armies (II Kings 6:17; Psa. 68:17). Elijah, by his courage, faith, and power with God, was "the chariot of Israel, and the horsemen thereof" (II Kings 2:12). "Chariot" is likewise used poetically in Scripture to designate the rapid agencies of God in nature (Psa. 68:17; 104:3; Isa. 66:15; Hab. 3:8). "Chariot of the cherubim" (I Chron. 28:18) probable means the cherubim as the chariot upon which God enters or is throned (*see* cherubim, 3). "Chariot of fire, and horses of fire," (II Kings 2:11) signifies some bright effulgence which, in the eyes of the spectators, resembled those objects. "Chariot man" (II Chron. 18:33) is another name for "driver of chariot" (I Kings 22:34). "Chariots of the sun" are mentioned (II Kings 23:11) as being burned by Josiah. Horses and chariots were dedicated to the sun by its worshippers, under the supposition that that divinity was drawn in a chariot by horses. The rabbins inform us that the king and nobles rode in these chariots when they went forth to greet the morning sun. "The chariot of Israel" was an expression applied by Elisha to Elijah (II Kings 2:12). The meaning is thought to be that, as earthly kingdoms are dependent for their defense and glory upon warlike preparations, a single prophet has done more for the preservation and prosperity of Israel than all her chariots and horsemen.

Charity (Gr. *'agapē*; R. V. "love"). The only word in the Bible translated *charity* means *love*. It is affection, tender and passionate attachment, a sentiment of our nature excited by qualities in a person or thing which command our affection; a virtue of such efficacy that it is said to be the fulfilling of the law. Its absence invalidates all claim to the Christian name. It is the antithesis of selfishness. Luther calls it "the shortest and longest divinity." It is active, and dissatisfied if not blessing others. Christian love is piety, the greatest boon which God can give, for "God is love." "In it all human duty is summed up" (Matt. 22:37-40; Rom. 13:8; I Cor. 13:13). Love is the first-named element in the composite "fruit of the Spirit" (Gal. 5:22).

Charity, in modern speech, has other meanings: First, that sentiment which prompts us to think and speak well of others, judge their acts kindly, and make them happy; second, generosity to the poor; third, that which is thus given; and fourth, a benevolent foundation. *See* Brotherly Kindness, Love.

Charm, Charmer, Charming. *See* Magic.

Char'ran (kăr'ăn, Acts 7:2, 4). *See* Haran.

Chase. *See* Hunting.

Chaste, Chastity (Gr. *hagnos, dedicated*, hence, *holy, clean*), in scriptural sense: (1) Freedom from impure thoughts, imaginations, or desires (Phil. 4:8; I Tim. 5:22, "pure;" I Pet. 3:2); spoken of God (I John 3:3; James 3:17). (2) Pure from illicit sexual intercourse (II Cor. 11:2; Tit. 2:5).

Chasten. *See* Chastisement.

Chastisement, from the Greek *paideuo* (*to instruct, train, correct*) is the action of the Heavenly Father toward his wayward and disobedient child that he "should not be condemned with the world" (I Cor. 11:31, 32). This correction of the Father of His own offspring (Heb. 12:6) must in nowise be connected with condemnation. "There is no condemnation to them who are in Christ Jesus" (Rom. 8:1). "He that believeth on Him is not condemned" (John 3:18). A regenerated child of God has a position of a son and stands in the imputed merits of Christ and cannot come into condemnation. Chastening, therefore, is confined to sons in the family and it may be (1) *preventive*, as in the case of the Apostle Paul, who was given the thorn in the flesh to keep him humble (II Cor. 12:7-9). (2) *Corrective*, which is the disciplinary moving of the Father against His wayward son for the good of the son. (3) *Enlarging*, the object being "unto holiness," to bring forth the "fruit of righteousness" (Heb. 12:6; John 15:2). (4) *Vindictive*, as in the case of Job who vindicated God against the challenge and accusations of Satan that the patriarch did not really love God apart from his family, his possessions and himself. There is a difference between chastening and scourging. The latter represents the divine conquering of the human will that the redeemed life may be completely yielded to God (Rom. 12:1, 2). *M. F. U.*

Che'bar (kē'bär), a river or canal in the "land of the Chaldeans" (Ezek. 1:3), on the banks of which some of the Jews were located at the time of the captivity, and where Ezekiel saw his earlier visions (Ezek. 1:1; 3:15, 23, etc.).

Checker Work, *network*, supposed to be latticework, forming a balustrade upon the capitals of the columns in the temple (I Kings 7:17; "network" in v. 18.

Chedorlao'mer (kĕd-ŏr-lā-ō'mēr), a king mentioned in Gen. 14 as invading the Jordan Valley at the time of Abraham. He is called "king of Elam," a country east of Babylonia at the head of the Persian Gulf (Gen. 14:1, 4, 5). He was allied with three other Mesopotamian kings who fought against the five kings in the region of the Salt Sea. When the rulers of Sodom, Gomorrah, Admah, Zeboiim and Zoar threw off his hegemony, he attempted to crush all resistance. Abraham clashed with him and rescued Lot. Although all attempts to identify him have thus far failed, the episode is to be dated around the middle of the 21st century B. C. according to chronological notations in the Massoretic text of the Hebrew Bible. Former identification with Hammurabi (c. 1700 B. C.) is now completely untenable. *M. F. U.*

Cheek (*lěʾhî*). Smiting on the cheeck was considered in itself a great insult (Job 16:10; Lam. 3:30; Mic. 5:1; Luke 6:29). "Thou hast smitten all mine enemies upon the cheek bone" (Psa. 3:7) is figurative of utter destruction of those enemies. The cheek bone denotes the bone in which the teeth are placed, and to break that is to disarm the animal. "He hath the cheek teeth of a great lion" (Joel 1:6) refers to the hinder teeth, or grinders.

Cheese, the coagulated curd of milk pressed into a solid mass (Job 10:10; I Sam. 17:18; II Sam. 17:29). The Tyropoean Valley in Jerusalem is the Greek equivalent for "The Valley of the Cheese Makers." The making of cheese was an important industry in antiquity and this dairy product constituted a vital part of the diet of the Jews.

Among the regulations regarding food in the Mishna was that no cheese made by foreigners should be eaten, for fear that it might be derived from the milk of an animal which had been offered to idols.

Che'lal (kĕ'lăl; *completion*), one of the "sons" of Pahath-moab, who divorced his Gentile wife after the return from Babylon (Ezra 10:30), B. C. 456.

Chel'luh (kĕl'ā; *completed*), one of the "sons" of Bani, who divorced his Gentile wife after the return from captivity (Ezra 10:35), B. C. 456.

Che'lub (kē'lŭb; *basket, bird cage*).

1. The brother of Shuah and father of Mehir, of the tribe of Judah (I Chron. 4:11).

2. The father of Ezri, who was David's chief gardener (I Chron. 27:26), B. C. after 1000.

Chelu'bai (kĕ-lū'bī), one of the sons of Hezron (I Chron. 2:9); elsewhere in the same chapter (vers. 18, 42) called *Caleb* (*q. v.*).

Chem'arim (kĕm'á-rĭm; *ascetics*, Zeph. 1:4; elsewhere, II Kings 23:5, "idolatrous priests," and Hos. 10:5, "priests"), the priests appointed by the kings of Judah for the worship of the high places and the idolatrous worship of Jehovah.

Che'mosh (kē'mŏsh), the leading deity of the Moabites. *See* Gods, False.

Chena'anah (kĕ-nā'á-ná).

1. The fourth named of the seven "sons" of Bilhan, a Benjamite and mighty warrior, apparently, in the time of David (I Chron. 7:10), B. C. about 1000.

2. The father of the prophet Zedekiah, which latter opposed Micaiah and encouraged Ahab (I Kings 22:11, 24; II Chron. 18:10, 23), B. C. before 850.

Chen'ani (kĕn'á-nī; *established*), one of the Levites who conducted the devotions of the people after Ezra had read to them the book of the law (Neh. 9:4), B. C. 445.

Chenani'ah (kĕn-á-nī'á; *established by Jehovah*), chief of the Levites who, as master of song (I Chron. 15:22), conducted the grand musical services when the ark was removed from the house of Obed-edom to Jerusalem (15:27). He was of the family of Izharites, and was ap-

pointed over the inspectors of the building of the temple (26:29), B. C. about 1000.

Che'phar-haam'monai (kē'fàr-hă-ăm'ô-nĭ; *village of the Ammonites*), a place mentioned among the towns of Benjamin (Josh. 18:24). Site uncertain.

Chephi'rah (kē-fī'rá; *village, hamlet*), one of the Gibeonite towns of Benjamin (Josh. 18:26); now *Kefireh*, about eight miles from Jerusalem. Joshua made a league with its people (Josh. 9:17). It was occupied after the captivity by a remnant of Benjamin (Ezra 2:25; Neh. 7:29).

Che'ran (kē'răn), the last named of the four sons of Dishon, the Horite "duke" descended from Seir (Gen. 36:26; I Chron. 1:41).

Cher'ethim (kĕr'ĕ-thĭm; Ezek. 25:16), the regular plural of Cherethite. *See* Cherethites, No. 1.

Cher'ethites (kĕr'ĕ-thīts).

1. Those tribes of the Philistines who dwelt in the southwest of Canaan (I Sam. 30:14), and treated by Ezekiel (25:16, "Cherethim") and Zephaniah (2:5) as synonymous with Philistines. The LXX and Syriac rendered the words in these passages by *Cretans*, from which it is now known that the *Philistines* (*q. v.*) sprang from Crete, (cuneiform *Kaptara*).

2 "The Cherethites and the Pelethites," a collective term for David's life-guards (II Sam. 8:18; 15:18; 20:7, 23; I Kings 1:38, 44; I Chron. 18:17). The words are adjectives in form, but with a substantive meaning, and were used to indicate a certain rank, literally, the executioners and runners. At a later date they were called "the captains and the guard" (II Kings 11:4, 19; comp. I Kings 14:27).

93. Brook Cherith (at bottom of ravine) and St. George's Monastery

Che'rith (kĕ'rĭth), a brook in Transjordan where Elijah fled to hide (I Kings 17:3, 5). The traditional site of the brook is now the Wâdy Kelt, a wild glen which runs into the Jordan valley; but the Bible expression "facing" or "before" Jordan, would seem to imply that it was east of that river, and therefore in Elijah's own native country of Gilead. Wâdy Yabis, opposite Beth-shean, may be the place.

Che'rub (kē'rŭb), an Israelite of doubtful extraction, who accompanied Zerubbabel to Judea(Ezra 2:59; Neh. 7:61).

Cher'ub (chĕr'ŭb), **Cherubim** (Heb. *kʾrū-bîm*; Gr. *cheroubim*).

1. **Scripture Mention.** Cherubim are mentioned: (*a*) At the expulsion of our first par-

ents from Eden (Gen. 3:24), when their office was "to keep the way of the tree of life," i. e., to render it impossible for man to return to paradise and eat of the tree of life. In this account there is no mention of their nature or form. (*b*) We next read of them in connection with the furnishing of the tabernacle (Exod. 25:18, sq.), where directions are given to place two golden cherubim upon the top of the ark of the covenant. They were to be of "beaten work," i. e., beaten with the hammer and rounded, and not solid. They were fastened to the mercy seat (lid of the ark), and, facing each other, stretched out their wings so as to form a screen over the mercy seat. They were called the "cherubim of glory" (Heb. 9:5). Cherubim were also woven into or embroidered upon the inward curtain of the tabernacle (Exod. 26:1, sq.) and the veil (Exod. 26:31). (*c*) The two cherubim placed by Solomon in the holy of holies (I Kings 6:23, sq.; II Chron. 3:7-14) were made of olive wood, overlaid with gold. They had bodies ten cubits high, and stood upon their feet, like men. The length of their wings was five cubits. They stood with "their faces inward," i. e., toward the holy place, the outward wing of each cherub touching the wall and the tip of the other wings touching each other. (*d*) Other references are as follows: "He rode upon a cherub, and did fly" (II Sam. 22:11; Psa. 18:10); the vision of four cherubim (A. V. "living creatures") seen by Ezekiel (1:5, sq.; 10:1, sq.), and that of the "four beasts" in Rev. 4:6, sq. (*living creatures*):

94. Ivory Carving of Cherub from Megiddo, about 1180 B. C.

2. **Form.** From an excavated pair of cherubs supporting the throne of king Hiram of Byblos (c. 1200 B. C.) a creature with a lion's body, human face and conspicuous wings is indicated. The Assyrians and other Semitic peoples used symbolic winged creatures, notably winged lions and bulls to guard temples and palaces. Egyptians also had winged creatures in some of their temples. Griffins—winged sphinxes having lion's bodies and eagles heads, were familiar to the Hittites. The cherubim of Solomon are said to have "stood upon their feet" (II Chron. 3:13). Ezekiel says their appearance "had the likeness of a man" and that they had wings (10:8). The representations of the Bible stress the human likeness, but also indicate the animal charac-

teristics. Undoubtedly we are to think of the cherub as at Byblos; that is, as a winged lion with human face. In any case, they are celestial creatures belonging to the spiritual realm and not at all to be confounded with any natural identification.

3. **The Cherubim and the Throne.** As a winged lion with human head, that is, a winged sphinx, this hybrid animal appears hundreds of times in the iconography of western Asia between 1800 and 600 B. C. The fact that many representations picture the deity or king seated on a throne supported by two cherubs suggests that in the O. T. the Deity and His throne—both invisible—were similarly supported by symbolical cherubim. (Cf. W. F. Albright in *O. T. Commentary*, 1948, p. 148; Graham and May, *Culture and Conscience*, 1936, 195 f, 249 f.). Archaeology thus greatly illuminates the meaning of the cherubim both in Solomon's temple and the earlier tabernacle and enables I Sam. 4:4 (cf. Rev. 4:6) to be rendered thus ". . . the ark of the covenant of the Lord of Hosts Who is *enthroned* above the cherubim."

4. **The Meaning.** The cherubim from their position at the gate of Eden, upon the cover of the ark of the covenant and in Rev. 4 are evidently connected with vindicating the holiness of God against the presumptious pride of fallen man, who despite his sin, "did put forth his hand and take of the tree of life" (Gen. 3:22-24). Upon the ark of the covenant they looked down upon the sprinkled blood which symbolizes the perfect maintenance of God's righteousness by the sacrifice of Christ (Ex. 25:17-20; Rom. 3:24-26). The cherubim seem to be actual beings of the angelic order. They do not seem to be identical with the seraphim (Isa. 6:2). The cherubim apparently have to do with the holiness of God as violated by sin; the seraphim with uncleanness in the people of God. Revised by *M. F. U.*

Ches'alon (kĕs'á-lŏn), one of the landmarks on the west part of the north boundary of Judah (Josh. 15:10). Eusebius and Jerome differ as to its situation, but agree that it was a very large village near Jerusalem. Kesla, 10 miles W. of Jerusalem is its present site.

Che'sed (kĕ'sĕd), the fourth named of the sons of Nahor (Abraham's brother) by Milcah (Gen. 22:22).

Che'sil (kĕ'sĭl; *a fool*), a town in the south of Judah (Josh. 15:30), identical with Bethul and Bethuel (Josh. 19:4; I Chron. 4:30; "Beth-el," I Sam. 30:27).

Chest, the rendering of two distinct Hebrew terms: (1) '*ärōn*, invariably used for the ark of the covenant, and, with two exceptions, for that only. These exceptions are (*a*) the "coffin" in which the bones of Joseph were carried to Palestine (Gen. 50:26), and (*b*) the "chest" in which Jehoiada, the priest, collected the offerings for temple repairs (II Kings 12:9, 10; II Chron. 24:8-11). (2) *gᵉnäzîm*, used only in the plural, rendered "chests" (Ezek. 27:24) and "treasures" (Esth. 3:9, 4:7).

Chestnut. *See* Vegetable Kingdom.

Chesul'loth (kĕ-sŭl'ŏth), a town of Issachar (Josh. 19:18), probably identical with Chisloth-tabor (v. 12). Modern Iksal, near Nazareth, marks the ancient site.

Che′zib (kē′zĭb; *deceitful*), a town in which Judah was when Shelah, his third son, was born. (Gen. 38:5); probably the same as Achzib.

Chicken (Gr. *nossion*, Esdras 1:30; Matt. 23:37). *See* Animal Kingdom.

Chidon (kī′dŏn; a *spear*), thought by some to be an Israelite to whom belonged the thrashing floor where the accident to the ark, on its journey to Jerusalem, took place, as well as the death of Uzzah (I Chron. 13:9). It is more probable that it was the name of the *place*.

Chief, the rendering of a large number of Hebrew and Greek words, frequently in connection with official terms, as *"Chief Butler"* (*q. v.*), "Chief Captain" (*see* Army), "Chief of the Fathers" (*see* Father), "Chief of the Levites" (*see* Levites), "Chief Musician" *see* Music), *"Chief Porter"* (*q. v.*), "Chief Priests" (*see* Priest), "Chief Rulers" (*see* Synagogue).

Chief of Three, the official title of *Adino* (*q. v.*), the Ezrite (II Sam. 23:8, A. V. "chief among the captains;" marg. "head of the three").

Chiefs of Asia. *See* Asiarch.

Child, Children (Heb. properly *yĕlĕd*; Gr. *teknon*, something *born*). This term is often used in Scripture with considerable latitude; thus the descendants of a man, however remote, are called his sons or children. For other uses, see below.

1. **Desire for.** It is of children that the house, the family, is built (Gen. 16:2; 30:3, marg. "builded by her"). The conception and bearing of children was a matter of longing and joy among the Israelites, especially to the women (Gen. 24:60; 30:1; I Sam. 1:11). On the ground of the twofold blessing connected with creation and the covenant promise (Gen. 1:28; 12:2, 7; 13:16) a numerous group of children was considered as a special gift of God's grace (Deut. 28:4; Psa. 113:9; 128:3, sq.; Prov. 17:6; Eccles. 6:3), and sterility in marriage was thought to be a divine punishment (Gen. 16:2; 30:23; I Sam. 1:6, sq.; Isa. 47:9).

2. **Infants.** At childbirth women were helped by nurses, midwives, even in the time of the patriarchs (Gen. 35:17; 38:28; Exod. 1:15), although women in the East often give birth so easily as not to need this help. The newborn child, after having the navel cord cut, was bathed in water, rubbed with salt, and wrapped in swaddling clothes (Ezek. 16:4). As a rule, it was nursed and tended by the mother herself (Gen. 21:7; I Sam. 1:23; I Kings 3:21; Cant. 8:1), excepting in case of weakness or death or in princely families (II Kings 11:2; comp. Exod. 2:9). After eight days boys were circumcised (*see* Circumcision), and got their names from some remarkable circumstance connected with their birth (Gen. 25:25, sq.; 35:18; 38:29) or according to the mother's hopes or wishes (Gen. 4:25; 29:32, sq.; I Sam. 1:20), but in later times from some relative (Luke 1:61). Forty days after its birth, in the case of a boy, and eighty in the case of a girl, the mother had to offer a sacrifice of purification in the temple (Lev.

12:1-8), to present the male firstborn to Jehovah, and to redeem it with five shekels of silver (Num. 18:15, sq.; comp. with 4:47, and Lev. 27:5). The *weaning* of the child did not occur, in some cases, till it was two or three years of age (II Macc. 7:27), and was celebrated with festivities (Gen. 21:8), and on special occasions was accompanied with the offering of a sacrifice (I Sam. 1:23, 24).

3. **Training.** Both boys and girls, in their earlier years, were under the training of their mother (Prov. 31:1; II Tim. 1:5; 3:15), the daughters, no doubt, remaining so until their marriage. At the age of five years, probably, the boys were trained by their fathers, or in well-to-do families placed under the care of special tutors (Num. 11:12; Isa. 49:23; II Kings 10:1, 5; Gal. 3:24). This instruction was not only in reading and writing, but also in the Law, its commandments and doctrines, and the deeds and revelations of Jehovah to his people (Exod. 12:26; 13:8, 14; Deut. 4:10; 6:7, 20, sq.; 11:19; Prov. 6:20). Schools were not set up till a comparatively late time, and only in the larger cities. Gamaliel is said to have been the first who instituted schools for boys in cities.

4. **Children and the Law.** In the Decalogue reverence for parents is made a condition of children's prosperity (Exod. 20:12; Lev. 19:3; Deut. 5:16). If a child cursed his parents he was under the divine curse (Deut. 27:16), and was to be put to death equally with him who did violence to them (Exod. 21:15, 17; Lev. 20:9; Comp. Prov. 20:20; Matt. 15:4). Drunkenness, gluttony, and the like, persevered in against a father's warning, were punished by the elders of the city with stoning (Deut. 21:18-21).

Thus while the Law secured to the parents full authority over their children, it provided also against the abuse of full parental power. The father was not to deprive his firstborn of his rights of primogeniture in favor, for example, of a younger son by a second and more loved wife (Deut. 21:15-17). He could render nugatory a vow made by his daughter, but he must do so immediately upon hearing it; otherwise he could not prevent its fulfillment (Num. 30:4, 5). He had power to marry his daughters, and even to sell them into concubinage, but not to a foreign people (Exod. 21:7, sq.).

Children seem to have often been taken as bondsmen by creditors for debts contracted by the fathers (II Kings 4:1; Isa. 50:1; Neh. 5:5). Children who were slaves by birth are called in Scripture "those born in the house" (Gen. 14:14; 15:3; 17:23), "sons of handmaids" (Psa. 86:16; 116:16).

5. **Illegitimate.** Such children had no legal inheritance (Gen. 21:10; Gal. 4:30); they did not receive the training of legitimate sons (Heb. 12:8, "chastisement;" Gr. *paideia, education*); were excluded from the congregation (Deut. 23:2); and were despised by their brethren (Judg. 11:2).

6. **Figurative.** In the Scriptures, children, like sons or daughters, are used figuratively (*a*) to express a state of ignorance and of intellectual darkness (Matt. 11:16; I Cor. 13:11; 14:20; Eph. 4:14; Heb. 5:13); (*b*) of persons

who are distinguished, whether for good or evil, by some particular quality or power. Thus the expression "children of light" (Luke 16:8) is applied to those who have a knowledge of God through Christ; the "children of obedience" (I Pet. 1:14) are those submitting themselves readily to the will of God. The more immediate disciples of Jesus, who hailed him as the Bridegroom of his Church, are called "children of the bridechamber" (Matt. 9:15). On the other hand, we have such expressions as "child of hell" (Matt. 23:15), "children of the wicked one" (Matt. 13:38), "children of this world" (Luke 16:8).

Childbearing (Gr. *teknogonia*). As a part of the curse coming to our first parent, on account of sin, it was said to her, "In sorrow thou shalt bring forth children" (Gen. 3:16). Commenting on this, Delitzsch says: "That the woman should bear the children was the original will of God; but it was a punishment that henceforth she was to bear them in sorrow, i. e., with pains which threatened her own life as well as that of the child." The punishment consisted in an enfeebling of nature, in consequence of sin. The language of the apostle, "Notwithstanding she shall be saved in childbearing, if they continue in faith and charity," etc. (I Tim. 2:15), implies that a patient endurance of this penalty shall contribute to woman's spiritual benefit.

Childbirth. *See* Child, 2.

Children of God are only those who of the fallen race are regenerated as a result of faith in Christ. The believer's relationship to God as a child, accordingly, issues from the new birth (John 1:12, 13). But all regenerated people are not only children, that is born ones, but adult sons as well, children of God receive placing as sons (Eph. 4:5) by adoption (*q. v.*). The indwelling Spirit gives to the child of God the realization of his sonship or spiritual adulthood (Gal. 4:1-6). The popular doctrine of the fatherhood of God and the brotherhood of man is not taught in Scripture. Since man is fallen, a person only becomes a child by faith in Christ, and only members of the Father's family are brothers in any vital spiritual sense. Liberal theological thinking which seeks to break down this important Biblical distinction between the child of God "and the children of the devil" (John 8:44) is contrary to divinely revealed truth. It not only robs Christianity of its distinctive message but is provocative of great harm, confusion and empty Utopian dreaming. *M. F. U.*

Children of Israel. *See* Israel.

Chil'eab (kĭl'ê-ăb; *restraint* of the *father*), the second son of David, by Abigail, the widow of Nabal, the Carmelite (II Sam. 3:3), B. C. about 1000. He is called *Daniel* in the parallel passage (I Chron. 3:1).

Chil'ion (kĭl'ĭ-ŭn; *pining*), the younger son of Elimelech and Naomi, and husband of Orpah, Ruth's sister; he died childless in the land of Moab (Ruth 1:2, 5; 4:9), B. C. about 1100.

Chil'mad (kĭl'măd), a place or country mentioned in conjunction with Sheba and Asshur (Ezek. 27:23). The only name bearing any similarity to it is Charmande, a town near the Euphrates between the Mascas and the Babylonian frontier; but it is highly improbable

that this place was of sufficient importance to rank with Sheba and Asshur.

Chim'ham (kĭm'häm; *pining, longing*), a follower and, according to Josephus (*Ant.*, vii, 11, 4), a son of Barzillai, the Gileadite. Upon David's restoration after Absalom's rebellion, Chimham returned from beyond Jordan with him, and received marked favors at his hand, which were first offered to Barzillai, but declined on account of old age (II Sam. 19:37-40), B. C. 973. David probably bestowed upon him a possession at or near Bethlehem, on which, in later times, was an inn called after him (Jer. 41:17).

Chimney (Heb. *'ărŭbbäh'*, *lattice*). The expression "as the smoke out of the *chimney*" (Hos. 13:3) should be rendered "smoke out of the window," i. e., "window-lattice," as the houses were without chimneys. The same word is elsewhere translated "*Window*." *See* House.

Chin'nereth (kĭn'ê-rĕth; *harp-shaped*), or **Chin'neroth** (kĭn'ê-rŏth), (I Kings 15:20, "Cinneroth").

1. A fortified city in the tribe of Naphtali (Josh. 19:35 only), of which no trace is found in later writers, and no remains by travelers. By St. Jerome, Chinnereth was identified with the later Tiberias. On the temple walls of Karnak, at Thebes, Thutmose III (B. C. 1475) gives a list of Canaanitish towns submitting to him, among which Chinnereth is found.

2. **Sea of Chinnereth** (Num. 34:11; Josh. 13:27), the inland sea, which is most familiarly known to us as the "lake of Gennesaret." This is evident from the mode in which it is mentioned as being at the end of Jordan opposite to the "Sea of the Arabah," i. e., the Dead Sea; as having the Arabah or Ghor below it, etc. (Deut. 3:17; Josh. 11:2; 12:3). In the two latter of these passages it is in a plural form, Chinneroth. It seems likely that Cinnereth was an ancient Canaanite name existing long prior to the Israelite conquest.

Chi'os (kī'os), an island in the Grecian Archipelago, about five miles from the mainland; now Scio. It was once noted for wine. Paul anchored there (Acts 20:15).

Chis'lev (kĭs'lĕv) in A. V. **Chisleu** (kĭs'lū; Heb. *kĭslĕw* from Akkad. *kislimu*), the name of the third civil or ninth ecclesiastical month adopted from the Babylonians after the captivity (Neh. 1:1; Zech. 7:1). *See* Calendar, Time.

Chis'lon (kĭs'lŏn; *hopeful*), the father of Elidad, who, as one of the chiefs of Benjamin, was selected on the part of that tribe to divide Canaan (Num. 34:21).

Chis'loth-ta'bor (kĭs'lŏth-tā'bŏr; *flanks of Tabor*), a place near Tabor (Josh. 19:12), and probably the same as Chesulloth (v. 18).

Chit'tim, Kit'tim (kĭt'ĭm). A name of large signification (such as our Levant), applied to the islands and coasts of the Mediterranean in a loose way without fixing the particular part, though particular and different parts of the whole are probably in most cases to be understood. According to Josephus (*Ant.*, i 6, § 1) it is an ancestral name. "Chethimus possessed the island Chethima; it is now called Cyprus." By the Greeks the name was retained for the city Citium, a Phoenician colony of unknown antiquity on the southern coast, while "by the Hebrews all islands and most of the seacoasts are called Chethim." Modern scholars hold that the name was extended first from Citium to all Cyprus, and afterward to the coasts and islands, especially of Greece, though sometimes it was carried as far as Italy. In Maccabees, Chittim is Macedonia. The Vulgate in Numbers and the Vulgate and the Aramaic Targum in I Chron. 1:7 have "Italy," and in Ezek. 27:6 the Targum has "Apulia."

Among the Phoenicians *Kitti* meant Cyprians. Among the Hebrews we may perhaps say that the writers who showed most interest in and acquaintance with the maritime operations of Tyre, as Isaiah (see ch. 23), Jeremiah (25:22; 47:4), and Ezekiel (chs. 26, 27, 28), used almost entirely the longer and more accurate form *Kittiyim*, as Isa. 23:1, *kethibh* (but in 23:12 it is *Kittim*); Jer. 2:10; while authors more remote in space or time have the shorter form *Kittim* (Gen. 10:4; Num. 24:24; I Chron. 1:7; Dan. 12:30).

The name Chittim, being once given to these regions, might continue as a geographical term without regard to changes in population; but the association of Chittim in Gen. 10:4 with Javan and Elishah points to Greeks and Carians rather than to Phoenicians. If in Gen. 10:4 we read Rodanim, as in I Chron. 1:7, instead of Dodanim, we may with plausibility liken Javan, Elishah, Kittim, and Rodanim to Ionia, Elis, Citium, and Rhodes.

Cyprus was visited by Sargon I, about 2380 B. C. It paid tribute to Thutmose III in the 15th century B. C.; seven of its kings sent ambassadors to Sargon II, 709 B. C., who erected a monolith at Citium; ten of its kings sent envoys to Esar-haddon at the close of the war against Abdimiljuti and Sanduarri, 676 B. C.

Chi'un (ki'ŭn), a word occurring in the Bible only in Amos 5:26. It is generally revocalized *Kaiwan* or *Kewan*, i. e., Saturn (Ninib). Apparently the Masoretes gave the vocalization of *Shiqqus* ("a detestable thing," whence *Kiyyun*). R. S. V. translates "Kaiwan your star god." Stephen quotes "the star of the god Rephan" (Acts 7:43), the Chiun of Amos being read by the Septuagint translators Rephan, evidently the Egyptian name for Saturn. *M. F. U. See* Gods, False.

Chlo'e (Gr. klō'ē; *verdure*), a female Christian mentioned in I Cor. 1:11, some of whose household had informed the apostle Paul of divisions in the Corinthian Church. Whether she was a resident of Corinth or not we have no means of knowing.

Chor'ashan (kōr'à-shăn; *smoking furnace*). According to another reading it ought to be Bor-ashan. It was a place named (I Sam. 30:30) as the scene of David's hunting exploits; also probably identical with Ashan of Simeon (Josh. 15:42; 19:7).

Chora'zin (kô-rā'zĭn). This city, in the general vicinity of Bethsaida and Capernaum near the sea of Galilee, was upbraided by Jesus for its unbelief in the face of His mighty works and committed to destruction (Matt. 11:21; Luke 10:13). It is now identified with Kerazeh,

2½ miles north of Tell Hum (Capernaum). The ruins of a black basalt synagogue at this site have been known for many years. *M. F. U.*

Chosen (Heb. from *bāhǎr*; Gr. *'eklektos*), singled out from others for some special service or station. "Chosen" warriors are such as are picked out as being most skillful or best adapted to some service (Exod. 15:4; Judg. 20:16). The Israelites were a "chosen" people, God having set them apart to receive his word and maintain his worship (Psa. 105:43; Deut. 7:6, 7). Jerusalem was "chosen" as the seat of the temple (I Kings 11:13). Christ was *chosen* ("elect," Isa. 42:1) of God to be the Saviour of men. The apostles were "chosen before of God" to be witnesses of the resurrection (Acts 10:41). The declaration, "Many are called, but few chosen," means that the invitation is extended to many but that only few profit thereby so as to be finally accepted (Matt. 20:16; 22:14). *See* Election.

Choze'ba (kô-zē'bà; *deceitful*), a city in the lowlands of Judah, "the men" of which are named among the descendants of Shelah (I Chron. 4:22). the same as Chezib and Achzib (Gen. 38:5; Josh. 15:44).

Chrism. *See* Anointing.

Christ (Gr. *Christos*; *anointed*), the official title of our Saviour (occurring first in II Esdras 7:29, and constantly in the New Testament), as having been consecrated by his baptism and the descent of the Holy Spirit as our Prophet, Priest, and King. *See* Jesus.

Christ, Ascension of. *See* Ascension.

Christ, Crucifixion of. *See* Crucifixion.

Christ, Death of. *See* Atonement, Crucifixion.

Christ, Divinity of. *See* Incarnation.

Christ, Humanity of. *See* Incarnation.

Christ, Life of. *See* Jesus.

Christ, Offices of. *See* Jesus.

Christ, Person of. *See* Kenosis.

Christ, Resurrection of. *See* Resurrection.

Christian. A Christian is a believer in and a follower of Jesus Christ the Messiah. This name is more widely employed than any other designation of those who believe unto salvation. However, it occurs in the Sacred Text only three times: "And the disciples were called Christians first in Antioch" (Acts 11:26); "Then Agrippa said unto Paul, 'Almost thou persuadest me to be a Christian'" (Acts 26:28); "If any man suffer as a Christian, let him not be ashamed" (I Pet. 4:16). The term Christian is clearly a Gentile designation for believers since the word Christ upon which the term was constructed, suggests recognition of the Messiah, which no unbelieving Jew was prepared to do. Becoming a Christian, according to the N. T., is a very definite act with significant results. According to Lewis Sperry Chafer, no less than thirty-three simultaneous and instantaneous divine undertakings and transformations, which collectively constitute the salvation of a soul, take place the moment one exercises faith in Christ and is saved. Among these is that a believer in Christ has the guilt of his sins removed. Secondly he is taken out of Adam, the sphere of condemnation, and placed in Christ, the sphere of righteousness and justification. Thirdly, he is given a new standing by virtue of his being placed "in Christ" by the

Spirit's baptizing work (I Cor. 12:13; Rom. 6:3, 4) and "made . . . acceptable" (Eph. 1:6). A Christian then, as Chafer says, "Is not one who does certain things for God but . . . one for whom God has done certain things; he is not so much one who conforms to a certain manner of life as he is one who has received the gift of eternal life; he is not one who depends upon a hopelessly imperfect state but rather one who has reached a perfect standing before God as being in Christ." (*Systematic Theology* VII, p. 75.) *M. F. U.*

Christianity consists of the teachings and way of life made possible by the death, burial and resurrection of Christ and the giving of the Holy Spirit. These teachings were committed by Christ to his disciples and particularly by special divine revelation to the Apostle Paul, so that what was provided by Christ is given full-orbed doctrinal expression by the Apostle. Other N. T. writers give various aspects of Christian doctrine, but the most developed revelation concerning the person and work of Christ and of the Holy Spirit for the normal established course of the age was given to the great Apostle. His doctrinal epistles demonstrate that Christianity, although having its roots in Judaism, is not Judaism or a mixture of Judaism. It is a way of life, of salvation, the full expression of the gospel of the grace of God for this age in which God is visiting the Gentiles "to take out of them a people for his name" (Acts 15:14). After this period Christ will return and "build again the tabernacle of David which is fallen" (Acts 15:16), i. e., restore Israel for blessing in the coming millennial age.

To many Christianity is a general term descriptive of all that is not Jewish. To others it is synonymous with Christendom. In such cases, little attention is given to the distinctive features of Christian truth. *M. F. U.*

Christ'mas (*Christ's Mass*, or *Festival*), the annual festival held by the Christian Church in memory of the birth of Christ. It begins with the evening of December 24 (called *Christmas Eve*), and continues until Epiphany (January 6), the whole period being called *Christmastide*. It is more particularly observed on December 25, which is called *Christmas Day*, or simply *Christmas*.

As to whether our Lord's birth really occurred on December 25 ancient authorities are not agreed. Clement of Alexandria says that some place it on April 20, others on May 20, while Epiphanius states that in Egypt Jesus was believed to have been born on January 6. For a long time the Greeks had no special feast corresponding to Christmas Day. Chrysostom, in a Christmas sermon, A. D. 386, says: "It is not ten years since this day was clearly known to us, but it has been known from the beginning to those who dwell in the West." The whole Western Church unanimously agreed upon this date, and the Eastern Church adopted it without much contradiction.

Observance. As mentioned above, the whole period from Nativity to Epiphany was consecrated. The four Sundays preceding Christmas were incorporated with the cycle, under the title of the Advent, as a preparation for the festival. On Christmas Day, in the Roman Catholic Church, three masses were celebrated, viz., at midnight, dawn, and in the daytime, a custom still observed in collegiate and cathedral churches. "A mystical explanation of the three masses is given, and they are supposed to figure the three births of our Lord: of his Father before all ages, of the Blessed Virgin, and in the hearts of the faithful" (*Cath. Dict.*, s. v.).

Several non-Christian elements have crept into the observance of Christmas. The use of lighted tapers reminds us of the Jewish feast of purification. The giving of presents was a Roman custom; while the yule tree and the yule log are remnants of old Teutonic nature worship. Gradually the festival sank into mere revelry. In England an abbot of misrule was chosen in every large household; in Scotland an abbot of unreason, who was master of the house during the festival. The custom was forbidden by an act of Parliament in 1555; and the reformation brought in a refinement in the celebration of Christmas by emphasizing its Christian elements.

Christs, False (Gr. *pseudo christoi*), those who falsely claim to be the Messiah, and against whom our Lord warned his disciples (Matt. 24:24; Mark 13:22). About twenty-four such persons have had more or less prominence. *See* Antichrist.

Chronicles, Books of. In the Hebrew these two historical books were originally one work. The twofold Septuagint division did not become effective in modern Hebrew Bibles until the 16th century. The term Chronicle, from the Hebrew *divre hayyamim* ("events or annals of the days" i. e., "times" cf. I Chron. 27:24), was suggested by Jerome who said "the name might be better called a Chronicle of the entire divine history." The Septuagint styled the two books inaccurately *Paralipomena*, i. e., "things passed over or omitted" (from the books of Samuel and Kings), construing Chronicles as a mere supplement to these works. In the Hebrew canon the books of Chronicles come at the end of the third and last section.

1. **Purpose.** I and II Chronicles catalog the history of priestly worship from the death of Saul to the conclusion of the Babylonian captivity, when the book of Ezra takes up the account. Samuel and Kings present a prophetic standpoint over against the priestly approach of Chronicles. These books interpret the history of the Jerusalem priesthood in its growth and development from the time of David. It is not a mere supplement to the parallel books of Samuel and Kings, but emphasizes only those aspects of history that illustrate the observance of the priestly laws of Moses as a way to spiritual prosperity in Israel. Priestly genealogies and faithful Yahweh-worshipping kings are given prominence. The kings of the Northern Kingdom are, accordingly, passed over along with prophetic aspects, which are brought to the fore in Samuel and Kings:

2. **The Contents.**
Part I: Genealogies from Adam to Christ (1:1-9:44)
A. From Adam to Jacob, 1:1-2:2

A. Jacob's Posterity, 2:3-9:44

Part II: David's History, 10:1-29:30

A. Saul's Death, 10:1-14

B. Zion's Capture and David's Warriors, 11:1-12:40

C. David's Kingship, 13:1-22:1

D. David's Contribution to Tabernacle Worship, 22:1-29:30

Part III: Solomon's History, II Chron. 1:1-9:31

A. His Prosperity, 1:1-1:17

B. His Construction of the Temple, 2:1-7:22

C. His Work and Death, 8:1-9:31

Part IV: History of the Judahite Kings, 10:1-36:23

A. From Rehoboam to Zedekiah, 10:1-36:21

B. Cyrus' Edict (36:22-33)

3. **Author and Date.** Ezra is traditionally fixed as the author of Chronicles. W. F. Albright defends this thesis that the chronicler is Ezra and that he wrote between 400 and 350 B. C. Negative critics commonly assign the book considerably later. R. Pfeiffer sees nothing wrong with a date as late as 250 B. C. No conclusive argument can be advanced against authorship by Ezra around 400 B. C. or somewhat earlier. Arguments for a later date derived from the language and spirit of the work are not potent, since the diction of the chronicler is generally confessed to be similar to that of Ezra-Nehemiah and to come from the same period. Arguments based on the genealogies in I Chron. 3:17-24 are inconclusive, for the text as it stands does not permit determining whether five or eleven generations are listed after Zerubbabel and, accordingly, whether the last generation belongs to the period around 400 B. C. or around 270 B. C.

4. **Historical authenticity.** Critics have customarily depreciated the historical reliability of the chronicler's work. As W. F. Albright says "Chronicles contains a considerable amount of original material dealing with the history of Judah which is not found in Kings and . . . the historical value of this original material is being established by archaeological discoveries . . . (*Bulletin Am. Schools of Oriental Research* 100, 1945, p. 18). It is quite evident also that the writer's wide use of sources and his meticulous references to them disprove the critical notion that he was an inaccurate historian. The priestly slant of the book, as W. A. L. Elmslie correctly says, is "invaluable for the light it gives on the post-exilic priestly standpoint toward the past." (*How Come Our Faith*, 1949, p. 39), and must be evaluated on this score.

5. **Other "Chronicles."** It is manifest that the books of Chronicles and Ezra, though put into their present form by one hand, contain in fact extracts from the writings of many different writers, which *were extant at the time the compilation was made.* For the full account of the reign of David the compiler made copious extracts from the books of Samuel the seer, Nathan the prophet, and Gad the seer (I Chron. 29:29). For the reign of Solomon he copied from "the book of Nathan," from "the prophecy of Ahijah the Shilonite," and

from "the visions of Iddo the seer" (II Chron. 9:29). Another work of Iddo, "*the story* (or interpretation, *Midrash*) of the prophet Iddo," supplied an account of the acts and the ways and sayings of King Abijah (13:22); while yet another book of Iddo concerning genealogies, with the book of the prophet Shemaiah, contained the acts of King Rehoboam (12:15). For later times the "book of the kings of Israel and Judah" is repeatedly cited (II Chron. 25:26; 27:7; 32:32; 33:18, etc.), and "the sayings of the seers," or rather of Chozai (33:19, A. V. "seers"); and for the reigns of Uzziah and Hezekiah "the vision of the prophet Isaiah" (26:22; 32:32). Besides the above-named works there was also the public national record mentioned in Neh. 12:23. These "chronicles of David" are probably the same as those above referred to, written by Samuel, Nathan, and Gad. From this time the affairs of each king's reign were regularly recorded in a book (I Kings 14:29; 15:7, etc.); and it was doubtless from this common source that the passages in the books of Samuel and Kings identical with the books of Chronicles were derived (Smith, *Bib. Dict.*, s. v.). *M. F. U.*

Chronology, New Testament. Chronology is the scientific measurement of time according to the revolutions of the heavenly bodies, when it is said to be *astronomical*, or, according to particular events occurring among men on earth, when it is called *historical*.

1. **Difficulties of Chronology.** The Chronology of the New Testament relates alike to the dates when the several books of which it is composed were written, and to the historicity of the facts recorded in their contents. Thus the origin of the Christian era is involved. But the modern chronologist is confronted with no inconsiderable difficulty at the very outset to fix the *exact date* of the nativity of Jesus Christ, as the founder of Christianity, which synchronizes with the beginning of the Christian era. This is due to the fact that he is compelled to base his computation on dateless documents written in a remote antiquity. For neither sacred nor profane authors in those times were at all accustomed to record historical facts under distinct dates. All demands were satisfied when known occurrences were referred to definite periods, as within a certain generation, or under a specific dynasty, or within the reign of a given ruler already familiar to the contemporaries addressed; for our modern method of historical notation according to the calendar was something altogether unknown to the ancients. A fine illustration of the ancient method is furnished in the third gospel, wherein a chronological minute is made of the beginning of the Baptist's ministry, compacting away and synchronizing in a single sentence the names of the ruling Caesar at Rome, the several political rulers of Palestine under that emperor, the territories over which they presided, and even the high priests of the Jewish religion at Jerusalem (Luke 3:1, 2). Now it does not follow that because such documents were dateless they were unhistorical, or in any sense to be discredited. Rather, as such was the universal custom of the times with historians, a departure from that method would at once justify a

suspicion against an ancient document as unauthentic and incredible.

2. **Basis of Computation.** The argument relies upon three capital facts: (a) The star of the ancient wise men, a scientific conclusion; (b) the death of Herod the Great, with special reference to an eclipse of the moon; and (c) the enrollment of the Jewish population at the birth of Christ, by the Roman Quirinius. The scholarly Dr. Edward Robinson states: "The present Christian era, which was fixed by the abbot Dionysius Exiguus in the 6th century, assumes the year of the Christian era as coincident with the year 754 from the building of Rome. Our era begins in any case more than four years too late; i. e., from four to five years at least after the actual birth of Christ. This era was first used in historical works by the Venerable Bede early in the 8th century, and was not long after introduced in public transactions by the French kings Pepin and Charlemagne" (*Greek Harmony of the Gospels*).

Dionysius Exiguus did not give origin to the Christian era, he merely computed it. Considering the *data* then at his command, his work is as remarkable for its difficulty as for its measure of success. However, the *common consensus* of eminent biblicists is that he erred in his conclusion by at least four years: that the beginning of the Christian era should properly have been dated at A. U. C. 750 instead of 754, which would have been coincident with B. C. 4 of our present chronology. There are several scientific and historical *data* now to be considered as determinative of the time of the nativity of Jesus Christ, upon which the Christian era is based.

(1) **Star of the Wise Men.** *Matthew* alone notes the passage of the *Magi*, who had crossed the deserts of the East, guided by the presence of a strange star to the feet of the infant Jesus. They ask of Herod, "Where is he that is born King of the Jews? for we have seen his star in the east, and are come to worship him." The appearance of a star was the predicted sign of the Messiah's birth as made by Balaam, the Moses of the Midianites. It reads: "There shall come a Star out of Jacob, and a Scepter shall rise out of Israel. . . . Out of Jacob shall come he that shall have dominion" (Num. 24:17, 19).

In reference to the star of the Magi Dr. Schaff remarks: "The Saviour was not without a witness among the heathen. Wise men from the East—i. e., Persian Magi, of the Zend religion, in which the idea of a Zoziosh, or *redeemer*, was clearly known—guided miraculously by a star or meteor created for the purpose, came and sought out the Saviour to pay him homage" (Smith, *Bib. Dict.*, vol. ii, p. 1349, Hackett's ed.).

(1) *Jewish intimations*. (a) With reference to Balaam's prediction, the Jewish rabbis wrote in their Talmud: "When the Messiah shall be revealed there shall rise up in the east a star flaming with six colors" (R. Frey, *Messiah*, p. 137). "The star shall shine forth from the east, *and this is the star of the Messiah*. It shall shine forth from the east for fifteen days, and if it be prolonged it will be for the good of Israel" (Edersheim, *Jesus of Nazareth*, vol. i,

p. 212). (b) Those Jews who are still looking for their Messiah to come confidently expect a star to appear as the *sign of his advent*. So it was also in the early centuries of Christianity; and this explains why that celebrated messianic imposter succeeded so well in the reign of Hadrian, A. D. 132-135, who assumed the name *Bar-Kokheba*, i. e., "*the son of a star*," and issued coins bearing a star in allusion to Balaam's prediction. In his open rebellion against the Romans he found a large following of the Jews, but when made a prisoner he promised that if his captors killed him he would prove his Messiahship by rising from the dead. The Romans took him at his word and cut off his head. As he did not rise as he had promised, the Jews became disgusted and named him *Bar-Kozibar*, i. e., "*the son of a lie!*" (see Schaff's *Hist. Christ. Church*, vol. i, p. 402). (c) Dr. Schaff also mentions the learned rabbi named *Abarbanel*, or *Abrabanel*, as authority for the tradition of the Jews, "There was a conspicuous conjunction of planets . . . three years before the birth of Moses, in the sign Pisces," and that another "would occur before the Messiah's birth." This was fifty years before Kepler published his discovery of the conjunction of the planets Jupiter, Saturn, and Mars, in the sign Pisces, at the birth of Jesus. Kepler's discovery has since been verified by other eminent astronomers, "including Schubert, of Petersburg; Charles Pritchard, of London, honorable secretary of the Royal Astronomical Society; and Ideler and Encke, of Berlin." "Dean Alford accepts this view. . . . The mathematical calculation of Wieseler, placing the date of the appearance of the star at A. U. C. 750 is coincident with B. C. 4, the time of the corrected chronology of the nativity." "It is pronounced by Pritchard to be 'as certain as any celestial phenomenon of ancient date.'" "If we accept the results of these calculations of astronomers, we are brought to within two years of the nativity, viz., between A. U. C. 748 (B. C. 6) (Kepler), and 750 (B. C. 4) (Wieseler). The differences arise, of course, from the uncertainty of the time of the departure and length of the journey of the Magi" (*Hist.*, i, 115, 116, 119).

(2) *Chinese notations*. Dr. Edersheim mentions the astronomical tables of the Chinese as being honored by Humboldt, which contains an account of this star; and that "Pingre and others have designated it as a comet," whose appearance was coincident with the visit of the Magi, which would "seem to go before (them) in the direction of, and stand over, Bethlehem." "And here the subject must, in the present state of information, be left" (see *Jesus the Messiah*, i, 213).

(2) **Death of Herod the Great.** He was sometimes known as Herod I. The first gospel relates that "Jesus was born in Bethlehem of Judea, in the days of Herod the king" (Matt. 2:1; comp. Luke 1:5). Josephus, the celebrated Jewish priest and historian, born A. D. 37, affirms in both his historical works that Herod died in Jericho, in the valley of the Jordan, A. U. C. 750, or B. C. 4. It is known that his death occurred just before the Jewish Passover, on the 13th of March. This writer

further remarks that on "that very night there was an eclipse of the moon" (*Antiquities*, book xvii, ch. xvii, 6, § 4; *War*, i, ch. i, § 8). The fact of the eclipse is conspicuous for the reason that it is the only one mentioned by this writer, and that this circumstance furnishes a certain astronomical *datum* for determining the nativity, since Herod was then alive and "sought the young child's life."

When the Magi inquired of Herod respecting him "*born King of the Jews*," it filled him with consternation. "Herod the king . . . was troubled, and all Jerusalem with him." Fearing that the royal infant would be his supplanter, he "sent forth and slew all the *male infants* from two years old and under." Joseph meanwhile had fled with the holy family into Egypt, "until the death of Herod," when an angel directed him to return to the land of Israel, "for they were dead who sought the young child's life." Now, Josephus relates that Herod, just five days before he died, slew his own son Antipater, which reveals his horrible character. This fact seems to have been confused with the account of the massacre of the infant children at Bethlehem when the report reached the emperor at Rome. Thereupon Macrobius states that Augustus Caesar, recalling Herod's Jewish hatred of swine, said, "*It is better to be Herod's hog than to be his son*" ("*Melius est Herodis porcum esse quam filium*") (*Saturnalia Convivia*, ii, 4).

It is obvious that Jesus was born at least several months before the death of Herod; that the slaying of the innocents occurred between the birth of our Lord and the death of Herod; and withal, the moon's eclipse on that "very night" of his death renders it scientifically certain and ascertainable by mathematical calculation that Herod departed this life on March 13, A. U. C. 750, which is identical with the year B. C. 4, the year assumed as that of the nativity.

(3) **Enrollment of Cyrenius* (Quirinius).** Another chronological *datum* for determining the year of Christ's birth is furnished by the third gospel:

"Now it came to pass in those days, there went out a decree from Caesar Augustus, that all the world should be enrolled. *This was the first enrollment* made when Quirinius was governor of Syria. And all went to enroll themselves, every one to his own city. And Joseph also went up from Galilee, out of the city of Nazareth, into Judea, to the city of David, which is called Bethlehem, because he was of the house and family of David; to enroll himself with Mary. . . . And she brought forth her firstborn son" (Luke 2:1-7).

(1) *Method of registration.* This was a Roman registration conducted by the Jewish method. Every person was required to resort to his own tribal territory in order to be entered in the registry. By this simple but most significant circumstance Joseph and Mary left their residence in Galilee and came to their ances-

tral Bethlehem, in the territory of Judah, where Jesus was born; and Micah's prediction of the Messiah's birth was circumstantially realized: "Thou, Bethlehem Ephrathah . . . out of thee shall *one* come forth unto me who is to be ruler in Israel" (Mic. 5:2).

A headtax was imposed upon all men and women between the ages of fourteen and sixty-five (Schaff). Dr. Edersheim says: "In consequence of the decree of Caesar Agustus, Herod (the Great) directed a general registration to be made after the Jewish rather than the Roman manner. . . . All country people were to be registered in their own city; meaning thereby the town to which the village or place where they were born was attached. In so doing the house or lineage of each was marked. According to the Jewish mode of registration the people would have to be enrolled according to tribes, families, or clans, and the house of their fathers. . . . In the case of Joseph and Mary, whose descent from David was not only known, but where, for the sake of the unborn Messiah, it was most important that this should be distinctly noted, it is natural that in accordance with Jewish law they should go to Bethlehem" (*Jesus the Messiah*, i, 182, 183).

(2) *The two registrations.* There has been in the past an interesting question: How could Cyrenius conduct an enrollment of the Jews at the birth of Christ, B. C. 4, when it is a known fact that he was appointed governor of Syria and made a registry ten years later, viz., in A. D. 6? The answer is that Cyrenius was *twice* appointed to this service. In the first instance it was a census of the *population*, taken with a view of replacing their tribute to the empire in produce by a headtax in money; and in the second it was a registration of their *property*. The census occurred B. C. 4 to A. D. 1. It was begun by Sentius Saturninus, was then continued by Quintilius Varus until B. C. 4, and concluded by Cyrenius from the year B. C. 4 to A. D. 1, the time of the nativity. Luke expressly says, "*This was the first enrollment.*" The second enrollment by Cyrenius occurred A. D. 10-14, according to the correct chronology.

Now, Luke makes historical notation of *both* enrollments in a way that indicates a perfect understanding of them on the part of his contemporaries. He refers to the first as a principal fact connecting it with the birth of Jesus; he refers to the second enrollment incidentally, in narrating what Gamaliel said in defense of the apostles before the Sanhedrin. In recounting different rebellions against the Romans in that country, Gamaliel said, "After this man rose up Judas of Galilee *in the days of the enrollment*" (comp. Luke 2:1-3 and Acts 5:37). It is of this registration that Josephus says: "Under his administration (Cyrenius's as procurator of Judea) it was that a certain Galilaean whose name was Judas prevailed with his countrymen to revolt" (*War*, ii, 8, 1); "I mean that Judas who caused the people to revolt *when Cyrenius came to take an account of the estates of the Jews*" (*Ant.*, xx, 5, 2).

The latest word touching these enrollments is that given by the eminent Augustus W.

---

*Franciscus Junius is quoted as authority for the historical statement that "*the agent* through whom Saturninus carried out the census in Judea *was the* governor Cyrenius, according to Luke, ch. 2" (Schaff).

Zumpt, the classical scholar and archaeologist of Berlin, whose recent researches have secured us "full historical probability, and whose conclusions of the date of the birth of Christ at the time of the census taken B. C. 4 by Cyrenius is indorsed by the scholarly Mommsen, and accords with the view of Ideler, Bergmann, Browne, Ussher, and Sanclemente" (Schaff).

(3) *Patristic references.* These have their evidential value, coming from those who were so near in the succession of the apostles, and corroborating the historical character in the common understanding of their contemporaries respecting the census taken by Cyrenius at the time of the nativity. Manifold strength is added to these references in that they appeal directly to the registries of the Roman government for the truth of what they say. Justin Martyr (born A. D. 105) says: "Now there is a village in the land of the Jews, thirty-five stadia from Jerusalem, in which Christ was born, *as you can ascertain also from the registries of the taxing under Quirinius (Cyrenius) your first procurator in Judea*" (*First Apology*, ch. 34). Now, as Justin was defending the Christians from persecutions by the government, nothing could have been more unfortunate and fatal to his claim if the appeal to the public registries was false; but nothing could be stronger in evidence if the appeal was verified by the registration. This remark applies alike to Tertullian, of Carthage (born A. D. 160) who was a highly gifted lawyer, and who, writing with a different design from a different country, refers to the same enrollment, and the same *period*, when he says: "There is historical proof that at this very time *a census had been taken in Judea by Sentius Saturninus,* which might have satisfied their inquiry respecting the family and descent of Christ*" (*Marcion*, iv, ch. 19).

(4) *Accounts of Historians.* Dr. Schaff cites with approval several high authorities as historians on this subject. He says: "Cassiodorus and Suidas expressly assert the fact of a general census, and add several particulars which are not derived from Luke; e. g., Suidas says that Augustus elected twenty commissioners of high character and sent them to all parts of the empire to collect statistics of the population. . . . Hence Huschke, Wieseler, Zumpt, Plumptre, and McClellan accept their testimony as historically correct. . . . Wieseler quotes also John Malala, the historian of Antioch, as saying . . . that 'Augustus in the thirty-ninth year and tenth month of his reign (i. e., B. C. 5 or 6) issued a decree for a general registration throughout the empire.' Julius Caesar had begun a measurement of the whole empire, and Augustus completed it" (*Hist. Christ. Church*, vol. i, pp. 124, 125, note 4).

(5) *Affirmation of an enemy.* It is greatly to our advantage in the investigation of the truth of the gospels to cite the testimony of a conspicuous adversary of Christianity who lived in the early centuries of the era, touching this census taken by Cyrenius at the time of the nativity—Julian, born 331, a Roman emperor, known as "the Apostate," because, having been brought up a Christian, he repudiated this religion when he came to the

throne. When in possession of all the archives of the empire he wrote against the Christians as one so conscious of the certainty of his source of information that he adopts a defiant tone, especially in reference to the enrollment of Joseph and Mary at Bethlehem, as mentioned by Luke. There is absolutely no known record of evidence that Jesus was "enrolled as one of Caesar's subjects," unless it was at the time which Julian affirms. He says: "Jesus, whom you celebrate, was one of Caesar's subjects. If you dispute it, I will prove it. . . . For yourselves allow that he *was enrolled* with his father and mother *in the time of Cyrenius*." "But Jesus having persuaded a few among you, and those the worst of men, *has now been celebrated about three hundred years, having done nothing in his lifetime worthy of remembrance, unless anyone thinks it a mighty matter to heal lame and blind people, and exorcise demoniacs in the villages of Bethsaida and Bethany*" (Lardner's *Works*, vii, 626, 627).

(6) *Monumental inscription.* A monument has been unearthed at Rome between the Villa Hadriani and the Via Tiburtina. The name of him to whom the monument was dedicated is obliterated. Bergmann, Mommsen, and Merivale refer it to Cyrenius. Then it reads: "*Quirinius as proconsul obtained Asia as his province. As legate of the deified Augustus a second time, he governed Syria and Phoenicia*" (see Schaff's *Hist. Christ. Church*, i, 122, 123).

(7) *Christ's confirmation.* There is a direct implication of Christ's loyalty, as "one of Caesar's subjects," to "the powers that be," as on the notable occasion when he met the Jews with the answer, "*Render unto Caesar the things which are Caesar's*" (Matt. 22:15-22). This wonderfully wise reply which silenced his adversaries is a record which is exactly accordant with the witness of the emperor, who as the head of the imperial government had in his possession, for reference, all the registrations of the Jews. Julian said: "Jesus whom you celebrate was one of Caesar's subjects. If you dispute it I will prove it by and by; but it may as well be done now. For you yourselves allow that he was enrolled with his father and mother in the time of Cyrenius." This is an independent and complete confirmation of Matthew.

These, then, are the three principal arguments respecting the birth of Jesus, and therefore dating properly the Christian era at least four years earlier, viz.: (*a*) That based upon the science of astronomy relating to the Star of the Magi, as developed by Kepler and improved by other astronomers; (*b*) the death of Herod the Great, dated by the eclipse of the moon; and (*c*) the argument based on history due to the researches of Zumpt in regard to the date of Cyrenius's registration of the Jews. Respecting this census, in distinction from a later registration by the same person as indicated by Luke, the patristic appeals made by Justin and Tertullian to the documents in the possession of the government; the assumption of fact in the declaration by the Emperor Julian, who directly connects Christ with the census-taking of Cyrenius and his parents' registration; the confirmatory testimony of the secular historians Cassiodorus, Suidas, and

John Malala, of Antioch, to a universal registration throughout the world; the monumental reference at Rome to the same transaction of Cyrenius; and Christ's own conduct in holding himself to be "a subject of Caesar" by paying the usual imperial tribute to the receivers, are all so many facts corroborating the statement of Luke as historical, and fixing the beginning of the Christian era at least four years earlier than our present chronology does.

Literature. Dr. Philip Schaff's *History of the*

CHRONOLOGY OF THE BOOKS OF THE NEW TESTAMENT
THE HISTORICAL BOOKS

Book	Writer	Place	Addressed to	Date	Key Thought
1. *Synoptic gospels:*					
First gospel	Matthew	Judea	Jewish Christians	60-65	Jesus the true Messiah
Second gospel	Mark	Rome	Roman Christians	60-65	Jesus the Son of man
Third gospel	Luke	Caesarea	Greek Christians	58-65	Jesus Redeemer of mankind
2. *Fourth gospel*	John	Ephesus	Christian Church	90-100	Jesus incarnate Son of God
3. *Acts of Apostles*	Luke	Rome	Gentile world	58-65	Origin of apostolic churches

The foregoing represents what is regarded as approximately correct. The table following, however, represents the varied opinions of noted scholars respecting the several dates of the historical books of the New Testament. The first four persons named are known as eminent orthodox Christian writers; the others are recognized as holding more or less liberal views respecting the Scriptures.

BOOK	SCHAFF	ALFORD	HARMAN	MITCHELL	KEIM	HOLTZ-MANN	SCHEN-KEL	WEISS	HILGEN-FELD	RENAN	VOLKMAR	BAUR
Matthew	60-67	41-48	60-63	68-69	66	68	70	70	70	84	105-115	130
Mark	60-67	63	67-68	68-69	100	75	58	69	81	76	73	150
Luke	64-65	50-58	63	63-67	90	80	80	70-80	100	94	100-103	140
John	80-100	70-87	80	78-90	130	123	120	95	130	125	150	160
Acts	64	63		63-67								

THE PAULINE EPISTLES

Writings	Place	Addressed to	Date	Key Thought
1. *The earliest epistles written: two in number.*				
I Thessalonians	Corinth	Thessalonian Christians	52	Second advent of Jesus Christ.
II Thessalonians	Corinth	Thessalonian Christians	53	Misapprehension of advent corrected.
2. *Epistles universally accredited: four in number.*				
Galatians	Corinth or Ephesus	The church in Galatia	56	Salvation by faith.
I Corinthians	Macedonia	The church in Corinth	57	Resurrection of Jesus Christ.
II Corinthians	Macedonia	The church in Corinth	57	Defense of his apostleship.
Romans	Corinth	The Christians at Rome	58	Power of sin and grace.
3. *Epistles written in captivity: three in number.*				
Philippians	Caesarea or Rome	The church at Philippi	58-60	Spiritual encouragements given.
Ephesians	Rome	The church at Ephesus	62-63	Unity of Christian brethren.
Colossians	Rome	The church at Colosse	61-63	Correction of heretical views.
3. *The pastoral epistles: three in number.*				
I Timothy	Macedonia	Timothy	62-65	Church officers and their duties.
II Timothy	Rome	Timothy	65-66	Apprehension of his own death near.
Titus	Macedonia or Greece	Titus of Crete	65	Persons for churchly offices.
5. *A personal epistle: one in number.*				
Philemon	Rome	Master of Onesimus	65	Onesimus's slavery or freedom.
6. *A general epistle: one in number.*				
Hebrews	Palestine	Jewish Christians	63-64	High priesthood of Jesus Christ.

THE CATHOLIC EPISTLES

James	Jerusalem	Jerusalem	63-64	Duties: prayer, faith, works.
I Peter	Babylon	The dispersed Jews	64	Encouragement in Christian duties.
II Peter	Unknown	The Church at large	65	New heavens and new earth.
I John	Judea	The general Church	90-100	Love of Jesus and the brethren.
II John	Ephesus	Elect lady and children	90-100	Loyal obedience to Jesus Christ.
III John	Ephesus	Elder and beloved Gaius	90-100	The state of the Church.

BOOK OF THE APOCALYPSE

Revelation	Patmos* or Ephesus	Seven churches of Asia	68-69* or 96-98	The consummation of all things.

The foregoing represents what is regarded as approximately correct. The following table represents the varied opinions of Christian critics respecting the dates to be assigned to the several Pauline epistles:

	SCHAFF	ZAHN	ALFORD	BAGSTER	CONEYBEARE AND HOWSON	LEWIN	FARRAR	HARMAN	MITCHELL
Romans	58	58	58	59	58	58	58	58-59	58-60
I Corinthians	57	57	57	57-58	57	57	57	57-58	57-58
II Corinthians	57	57	58-59	57-58	57	57	58	57-58	57-58
Galatians	56	52	54-57	54-57	57	58	59	58-59	56-57
Ephesians	61	64	61-62	61-63	62	62	63	63	
Philippians		63	63	62-63	62	63	61-62	63	
Colossians		63	61-62	63	62	62	63	63	
I Thessalonians		53	52	52-53	52	52	52	52-54	
II Thessalonians		53	53	53	53	52	52	53-54	
I Timothy			67-68	65	67	64	66	65-66	
II Timothy		66	67-68	65	68	66	67	65-66	
Titus			67-68	65	67	64	66	65-66	
Philemon		63	61-62	63-64	62	62	63	63	

*If the apostle John was banished to Patmos under the reign of Nero, *as the internal evidence indicates*, he wrote the Apocalypse about A. D. 68 or 69, which was after the death of that emperor; but the gospel and epistles some years later. This view "is advocated or accepted by Neander, Lücke, Bleek, Ewald, DeWette, Baur, Hilgenfeld, Reuss, Düsterdieck, Weiss, Renan, Aubé, Stuart, Davidson, Cowles, Bishop Lightfoot, Westcott, and Schaff. The great majority of older commentators, and among the later ones Elliott, Alford, Hengstenberg, Ebrard, Lange, Hofmann, Godet, Lee, etc.," favor the traditional date, *as the external evidence indicates*, which is after Domitian's death in A. D. 96. John is said to have died a natural death in the reign of Trajan, about A. D. 98 (see Schaff, *Hist. Christ. Church*, i, pp. 429, 834).—*S. L. B.*

Christian Church, revised edition; Dr. Edward Robinson's *Greek Harmony;* McClintock and Strong's *Cyclopoedia;* Smith's *Bible Dictionary*, Hackett's edition; Edersheim's *Jesus the Messiah;* Josephus's *Antiquities; Ante-Nicene Fathers;* Lardner's *Works; Historical Evidences of the New Testament*, by the writer.—*S. L. B.*

Chronology, Old Testament. Of great importance is the location of events recorded in the O. T. in the frame of extra-Biblical history. Although many great problems still exist in this correlation, substantial strides in archaeological research have set the O. T. fairly accurately in the ancient Biblical world in general.

1. **Early Chronology of Genesis.** The initial chapters of the Bible do not indicate the date of the creation of the world or of man. Genesis 1:1 evidently puts the origin of the universe in the dateless past, allowing for all the ages outlined by the science of geology. According to Genesis, the appearance of man upon the earth is set forth as a result of a direct creative act of God and occurred at least over four millennia B. C. and perhaps as early as 7,000-10,000 years B. C. Byron Nelson, a conservative, argues for even greater antiquity of man (*Before Abraham, Prehistoric Man and Bible Life*, Minneapolis, 1948, p. 95). This, however, seems scarcely in focus with the indications of the Genesis account. On the other hand, the compressed chronology of Archbishop Ussher, who assumes unbroken succession of father-son relationship in the genealogical lists of Genesis 5 and 11, and who places the creation of man around 4,000 B. C., is untenable in the light of attested archaeological facts. For discussion of the problems involved see B. Ramm, "*The Christian View of Science And Scripture*." Grand Rapids, 1955.

2. **Pre-patriarchal Chronology.**

(1) **Neolithic Age c. 6000- c. 4500 B. C.** The first appearance of pottery c. 5000 B. C.

(2) **Chalcolithic Age c. 4500-3000 B. C.** Copper introduced along with stone implements, advance in pottery, early building activity, simple writing in Babylonia on clay c. 3500 B. C., irrigation cultures.

(3) **Early Bronze Age, 3000-2000 B. C.—** beginning of first great states. (*1*) *Babylonia*. (*a*) Early Dynastic Period c. 2800-2360 B. C. (*b*) Old Akkadian Period c. 2360-2180 B. C., Mesopotamian Period of great empire of Sargon I followed by Rimush, Manishtusu, Naram-Sin and Shargalisharri. (*c*) The Gutian Period c. 2180-2070 B. C. and Sumerian renaissance under the Third Dynasty of Ur, c. 2070-1960 B. C.

(2) *Egypt.* (*a*) Predynastic Period c. 5000-2900 B. C. (*b*) Protodynastic Period (Dynasties I-II c. 2900-2700 B. C.). (*c*) The Old Kingdom (Dynasties III-VI c. 2700-2200 B. C.), the great pyramids, vast imperial power. (*d*) First Intermediate Period c. 2200-2000 B. C. (Dynasties VII-XI).

3. **Patriarchal to Davidic Era c. 2000-1000 B. C.**

(1) **Middle Bronze Age c. 2000-1500 B. C.**

(*1*) *Mesopotamia*. Abraham's birth at Ur. c. 2160 B. C. (according to O. T. chronology preserved in Masoretic text), Abraham's entrance into Canaan c. 2086 B. C., Amorite invasion, establishment of Amorite dynasty from Mediterranean to Babylonia c. 2000-1700 B. C., the Mari Age revealed by excavations at the Middle Euphrates city c. 18th century B. C., First Dynasty of Babylon c. 1850-1550 B. C., the great Hammurabi c. 1700 B. C., Indo-Iranian-Hurrian invasion 18th and 17th centuries B. C., destruction of Babylon c. 1550 B. C. by Hittites.

(2) *Egypt.* The Great Middle Kingdom, Dynasty XII, c. 1990-1775 B. C. Egyptian control of Palestine-Syria, Egyptian sojourn of Israel c. 1817-1440 B. C. (chronology of Masoretic text), Joseph became prime minister and Jacob stood before one of the powerful pharoahs of this dynasty (Amenemes I-IV or Senwosret I-III); Israel continues in Egypt during the Hyksos period of foreign

domination c. 1775-1546 B. C., was oppressed by the great Thutmose III c. 1482-1450 B. C. of the New Kingdom (Dynasty XVIII) and quit the country under Amenhotep II c. 1450-1425 B. C.

(3) *Palestine.* Abraham enters Canaan c. 2086 B. C., Patriarchal Period 2086-1871 B. C. (chronology of the Massoretic text).

(2) **Late Bronze Age c. 1500-1200 B. C.**

(1) *Egypt—New Kingdom.* (a) Dynasty XVIII c. 1570-1319 B. C., Thutmose III c. 1482-1450 B. C., Amenhotep II c. 1450-1425 B. C., Israel quits Egypt c. 1440, enters Canaan around c. 1400 B. C. Important pharoahs of Amarna Period, Amenophis III c. 1413-1377, Amenophis IV (Akhnaton) 1377-1360 B. C.; solar monotheism. (b) Dynasty XIX c. 1319-1200 B. C., principal pharoahs Seti I c. 1319-1301 B. C., Rameses II The Great c. 1301-1234 B. C., wars with the Hittites at Kadesh c. 1298, treaty with them c. 1280, Merenptah c. 1235-1227, first mention of Israel in his stele c. 1230.

(2) *Mesopotamia.* Kassites in Babylonia c. 1500-1150 B. C., Mitannian state in northern Mesopotamia c. 1500-1370, war between Egypt and Mitanni, conquests of Hittites c. 1375.

(3) *Asia Minor.* Hittite Empire c. 1600-1200 B. C., clash with Egypt at Kadesh c. 1298 B. C., treaty with the Egyptians c. 1280.

(4) *Palestine.* (a) Amarna Period c. 1400-1360, destruction of Jericho c. 1400, entrance of Hebrews (Habiru?) into Palestine c. 1400, conquest of Palestine c. 1400-1360 (Massoretic Chronology). (b) Early Period of the Judges c. 1360-1200 B. C., oppression of Cushan-Rishathaim c. 1361-1353 B. C., deliverance by Othniel, period of peace c. 1353-1313 B. C. (Judg. 3:11), oppression by Eglon of Moab c. 1319-1295 B. C., period of peace after Ehud (Judg. 3:12-30) c. 1295-1215, oppression by Jabin (Judg. 4:1-24) c. 1215-1195 B. C.

(5) *The Greek World.* Acme of Minoan Civilization 15th century, downfall of Crete c. 1400 B. C., Mycenaean Civilization in Greece, trade with Asia c. 1400-1300 B. C.

(3) **Early Iron Age 1200-1000 B. C.**

(1) *Egypt.* Dynasty XX c. 1200-1085 B. C., Rameses III c. 1198-1167 B. C., stems invasion of sea peoples c. 1191 B. C., Philistines settle in large numbers in S. W. Palestine, Egypt loses hold on Palestine after c. 1150 B. C.

(2) *Mesopotamia.* General weakness of rulers with oppression of the great Tiglath-Pileser I who held northern Syria from c. 1105-1100 B. C.

(3) *Palestine.* Middle part of the period of the Judges, deliverance by Deborah (Judg. 4-5), an era of peace for 40 years c. 1195-1155 B. C., Midianite oppression seven years c. 1155-1148 B. C., era of peace under Gideon c. 1148-1108, Abimilech king at Shechem c. 1108-1105 B. C., Philistine ascendancy c. 1089-1059 B. C., Samson c. 1085-1065 B. C., judgeship of Eli c. 1065-1050 B. C., Saul and beginning of the monarchy c. 1020-1004 B. C., David king c. 1004.

4. **The Era of the Hebrew Kings c. 1000-587 B. C.**

(1) **Palestine.** (a) The United Monarchy: David c. 1004-965 B. C., Solomon c. 965-926 B. C. (according to J. Begrich). (b) The Dual Monarchy: c. 926-587 B. C.

JUDAH	ISRAEL
Rehoboam....c. 926-910 B.C.	Jeroboam I....c. 926-907 B.C.
Abijam......c. 910-908 B.C.	Nadab......c. 907-906 B.C.
Asa.........c. 908-872 B.C.	Baasha....c. 906-883 B.C.
Jehoshaphat..c. 872-852 B.C.	Elah.......c. 883-882 B.C.
Jehoram	Zimri......c. 882 B.C.
(or Joram)..c. 852-845 B.C.	Omri.......c. 882-871 B.C.
Ahaziah....c. 845-844 B.C.	Ahab......c. 871-852 B.C.
Athaliah....c. 845-839 B.C.	Ahaziah...c. 852-851 B.C.
Joash (or	Jehoram....c. 851-845 B.C.
Jehoash)...c. 839-800 B.C.	Jehu.......c. 845-818 B.C.
Amaziah....c. 800-785 B.C.	Jehoahaz....c. 818-802 B.C.
Uzziah (or	Joash......c. 802-787 B.C.
Azariah)..c. 785-747 B.C.	Jeroboam II..c. 787-747 B.C.
Jotham	Zechariah...c. 747-746 B.C.
(regent and	Shallum....c. 747-746 B.C.
king)......c. 758-743 B.C.	Manahem....c. 746-737 B.C.
Ahaz.......c. 742-725 B.C.	Pekahiah...c. 736-735 B.C.
Hezekiah....c. 725-697 B.C.	Pekah.....c. 734-733 B.C.
Manasseh....c. 696-642 B.C.	Hoshea....c. 732-724 B.C.
Amon.......c. 641-640 B.C.	Fall of Samaria....c. 721 B.C.
Josiah......c. 639-609 B.C.	
Jehoahaz.........c. 609 B.C.	
Jehoiakim....c. 608-598 B.C.	
Jehoiachin........c. 598 B.C.	
Zedekiah....c. 598-587 B.C.	
Fall of Jerusalem....587 B.C.	

(2) **Egypt.** (a) Libyan Dynasties XXII-XXIV c. 935-712 B. C., pharoah Shishak, who invaded Palestine. (b) Ethiopian Dynasty XXV c. 712-663 B. C., Assyria conquers Egypt c. 760 B. C. (c) Saite Dynasty XXVI c. 663-525 B. C., Pharoah Necho c. 609-597 B. C., Hophra c. 588-569 B. C., Necho defeated by Chaldeans at Haran in c. 609 B. C. and at Carchemish c. 605 B. C.

(3) **Mesopotamia.** (a) Assyrian Empire in a weakened form c. 1000-880 B. C., great conqueror Ashurnasirpal II 883-859 B. C., Shalmaneser III 858-824 B. C., Battle of Karkar 853 B. C. Assyrian push stopped by Ahab and Assyrian coalition. Tiglath-Pileser III 747-727 B. C. conquered coastal plain of Galilee, Gilead and Damascus 733-732 B. C., Samaria besieged by Shalmaneser V 727-722, captured by Sargon II 721 B. C., 27,290 leading citizens carried into exile, Sennacherib 705-681 invades Judea at the time of Hezekiah c. 701 B. C., Assyrian world power, Esarhaddon 681-669 B. C. conquers Egypt, Asshurbanipal 669-626 B. C., decline of Assyria, fall of Asshur to the Medes 614, Nineveh destroyed by the Medes and Babylonians 612 B. C. (b) The Chaldean Period c. 612-539, defeat of Assyria and Egypt under Necho at Haran c. 609 B. C., Nebuchadnezzar II c. 605-562 B. C., captivity of Judah, destruction of Jerusalem c. 587 B. C.

5. **The Era of the Exile and Return 587-400 B. C.**

(1) **Palestine.** Deportation of the leading citizens of Judah including Daniel 605 and Ezekiel 598, destruction of Jerusalem 587, Cyrus' proclamation 538, return under Zerubbabel 536 B. C., temple rebuilt 520-516 B. C., Ezra's return 458 B. C., Nehemiah's return 445 B. C., Malachi 400 B. C.

(2) **Persian Empire.** Conquers Babylon 539 B. C., death of Cyrus 530 B. C., Cambyses 530-522 B. C., conquers Egypt 525 B. C., Darius I the great, 522-486 B. C., Behistun Inscription; defeat at Marathon 490 B. C.,

Ahasuerus 486-465, campaign against Greece, defeat at Salamis 480 B. C., Artaxerxes I 465-424 B. C., Xerxes II 424-423 B. C., Darius I 423-404 B. C., Artaxerxes II 404-358 B. C., Artaxerxes III 358-338 B. C., Arses 338-336 B. C., Darius III 336-331 B. C.

(3) **Greece.** The Greeks defeat Persians Marathon 490 B. C., Salamis 480 B. C., golden age at Athens, Pericles 460-429 B. C., Herodotus 485-425 B. C., Socrates 469-400 B. C., Plato 430-350 B. C., Aristotle 384-322 B. C.

6. **The Greek Era 333-63 B. C.**

(1) **Macedonian Empire.** Philip 359-336, Alexander the Great, 336-323, conquest of Persia, reaches India 327 B. C., dies in Babylon 323 B. C.

(2) **Division of Alexander's Realm.** Gradually by 275 B. C. three leading kingdoms had emerged, which existed to the Roman Period.

(1) *Macedonia.* A line of kings ruled until made a Roman province in 146 B. C.

(2) *Egypt.* The Ptolemies:

Ptolemy I . . . . 323-285 B. C.
Ptolemy II . . . . . . 285-246 B. C.
Ptolemy III . . . . 246-221 B. C.
Ptolemy IV 221-203
Ptolemy V 203-180

This royal dynasty continued until Egypt was made a Roman province in 30 B. C.

(3) *Syria.* The Selucid Dynasty.

Seleucus I . . . . 312-280 B. C.
Antiochus I . . . . 280-261 B. C.
Antiochus II . . . . 261-247 B. C.
Seleucus II . . . . 247-226 B. C.
Seleucus III . . . . 226-223 B. C.
Antiochus III (The Great) 223-187 B. C.
Seleucus IV . . . . 187-175 B. C.
Antiochus-Epiphanes IV . 175-163 B. C.
Antiochus-Epiphanes V . . . 163-162 B. C.
Demetrius I . . . . 162-150 B. C.
Alexander Balas . . . . 150-145 B. C.
Demetrius II . . . . }145-138 B. C.
Antiochus VI . . . . }
Antiochus VII . . . . 139-129 B. C.

This dynasty continued in a weak form until Pompey's conquest of Syria, and it became a Roman province in 64 B. C.

(4) *Smaller Kingdoms From Alexander's Empire.* (a) *Pergamum*—under the Attalids until Attalus III 139-133, who bequeathed his kingdom to Rome. (b) *Bithynia*—under kings until Nicomedes III 94-74 B. C. bequeathed his kingdom to Rome.

(5) *Other Asia Minor Kingdoms.* (a) *Pontus*—under Mithridates I 337-301 and his successors until conquered by Rome in 50 B. C.

(b) *Galatia*—came under Roman rule on the death of Amyntas 37-25 B. C.

(6) *Parthian Kingdom* 248 B. C. extended sway to India. Defeated Crassus and threatened Syria and Asia Minor, repulsed by the Romans 39 B. C., the kingdom continued, but with declining power until A. D. 224.

(7) *Greek Cities*—allied with Rome against Macedonia, but Rome gradually absorbed Greece; destruction of Corinth 146 B. C. ends resistance, Greece organized as separate Roman province 27 B. C.

(8) *Palestine*—under strong Egyptian power until 198 B. C. when Syria gains ascendancy.

Maccabean revolt against Greek paganizing civilization 167 B. C. Judas Maccabeus 166-160 B. C., Jonathan 160-142 B. C., Simon 142-134 B. C., John Hyrcanus 134-104 B. C., Aristobulus II 66-63 B. C. Rome under Pompey assumes control over Palestine 63 B. C.

(9) *Nabataean Kingdom*—By 300 B. C. the Nabataeans were in possession of ancient Edom. From Petra, their capital, their power extended in all directions. Their control was limited by the Romans from 63 B. C. on but they did not become a Roman province until 106 A. D. *M. F. U.*

Chrysolite, Chrysoprase. *See* Mineral Kingdom.

Chub (kŭb; only Ezek. 30:5), a nation in alliance with Egypt, and probably near it. Some read *Lūb*, a singular form of *Lubim*, (Libyans), which elsewhere occurs only in the plural. Some propose *Nūb* (Nubia), as the Arabic version has Noobeh. But these emendations are only conjectures.

Chun (kŭn; I Chron. 18:8), a city of Hadarezer, king of Syria, in Aramzobah, on the highway to the Euphrates, and plundered by David for brass and copper wherewith to build the temple. Called Berothai (II Sam. 8:8). (*q. v.*). Probably the same as Berothah (Ezek. 47:16) (*q. v.*).

Church (Gr. *ekklēsia*, "called out," *ek* "out," *kaleo* "to call"). 1. **The Term, General Use.** The word church is employed to express various ideas, some of which are Scriptural, others not. It may be used to signify (1) The entire body of those who are savingly related to Christ. (2) A particular Christian denomination. (3) The aggregate of all the ecclesiastical communions professing faith in Christ. (4) A single organized Christian group. (5) A building designated for Christian worship.

2. **Simple New Testament Usage.** (1) **Definition.** In the N. T. the church fundamentally comprehends the whole number of regenerated persons specifically from Pentecost to the first resurrection (I Cor. 15:52; I Thess. 4:13-17) united organically to one another and to Christ by the baptizing work of the Holy Spirit (I Cor. 12:12, 13; Rom. 6:3, 4; Gal. 3:27; Eph. 4:5; Col. 2:10-12). According to the N. T. definition the church is the mystical body of Christ of which He is the head (Eph. 1:22, 23), being a holy temple for the habitation of God through the Spirit (Eph. 2:21, 22) is "one flesh" with Christ (Eph. 5:30, 31) and espoused to Him as a pure virgin to one husband (II Cor. 11:2-4). The word *ekklēsia*, however, is employed of any assembly, and the word in the Greek language implies no more; for example, the town meeting (*ekklēsia*) at Ephesus (Acts 19:39) and Israel called out of Egypt are spoken of as an assembly, *ekklēsia*, in the wilderness (Acts 7: 38), but in no sense was it a N. T. church except as a type of that which was to come. In addition to the church as the body of Christ, we find other meanings attached to the word in the N. T. It refers sometimes to the company of believers in a single province or city (cf. Rev. chaps. 2, 3), or those meeting in a particular place of worship. It is applied even to bodies of professed believers who have largely departed from the true faith and prac-

tice, though in such cases the title is no longer appropriate except as a reminder of what they once were or professed to be, or only as a convenient designation, the significance of which in such cases is wholly lost.

(2) **The Beginning of the Church.** That the true church as the body of Christ began on the day of Pentecost may be demonstrated in various ways. (1) Christ Himself declared it to be yet future. (2) It was founded upon the death, resurrection and ascension of Christ and such an accomplished fact was not possible until Pentecost (Gal. 3:23-25). (3) There could be no church until it was purchased with Christ's precious blood (Eph. 5:25-27), until He arose to give it resurrection life (Col. 3:1-3), until He ascended to be Head over all things to the church (Eph. 1:20-23) and until the Spirit came on Pentecost, through Whom the church would be formed into one body by the baptism of the Spirit. (4) The baptism of the Spirit prophesied by John (Matt. 3:11; Mark 1:8; Luke 3:16, 17; John 1:33) was still future at Acts 1:5. That it occurred between Acts 1:5 and Acts 11:16 is evident by a comparison of these two verses. It is obvious that the Holy Spirit, Who came at Pentecost, arrived to perform among His various ministries of regenerating, sealing, indwelling and filling, His distinctive ministry for this age, of baptizing into Christ, that is, into His body the church (I Cor. 12:13). It was just as impossible, considering the baptizing work of the Holy Spirit, that the church would have been formed before Pentecost as it was impossible that it should not have been formed after that date. Other views as to the time of the founding of the church include the period of Christ's earthly ministry, the days of Abraham, and the lifetime of Adam.

(3) **Purpose and Completion of the Church.** There is abundant Scripture that God's principal purpose in this particular age is the outcalling of the church, the body of Christ, from both Gentiles and Jews (Acts 15:14-18). This pivotal passage from Acts indicates God's divine purpose for this age in taking out from among the Gentiles a people for His name. The gospel during this present era has never anywhere saved all but in every place it has called out some. The church is thus still in the process of formation, principally from among Gentiles with comparatively few Jews, who constitute the remnant according to the election of grace (Rom. 11:5). When the body of Christ is complete, it will be removed or translated from the earthly scene (I Cor. 15:51-53; I Thess. 4:15-17; II Thess. 2:1; Rev. 3:10). After the out-taking of the church, the end-time apocalyptic judgments will fall upon Gentiles and unbelieving Jews. However, a remnant will be saved out of this "time of Jacob's trouble" (Jer. 30:5), and the Advent of Christ in glory will make the setting up of the millennial kingdom with the nation Israel reinstated in priestly communion and blessing (Zech. 3:1-10) as the light of the world (Zech. 4:1-14). Three views are held among premillennialists as to the time of Christ's return: before, in the middle of, and at the end of the tribulation.

(4) **Relation Between Christ and the Church.** Seven N. T. figures set forth this relation. (1) The Shepherd and the Sheep (John 10); (2) The Vine and the Branches (John 15); (3) The Cornerstone and the Stones of the Building (Eph. 2:19-22; I Cor. 3:9; I Pet. 2:5); (4) High Priest and the Kingdom of Priests (Heb. 5:1-10; 6:13-8:6; I Pet. 2:5-9; Rev. 1:6); (5) The Head and the Many-Membered Body (I Cor. 12:12-13; Eph. 4:4; I Cor. 12:27); (6) The Last Adam and the New Creation (I Cor. 15:22, 45; II Cor. 5:17); (7) The Bridegroom and the Bride (John 3:29; II Cor. 11:2; Eph. 5:25-33; Rev. 19:7, 8).

(5) **The Unity of the Church.** Our Lord's remarkable intercession for Christian unity in John 17:11, 20-23 was answered in the outpouring of the Holy Spirit at Pentecost and the Spirit's advent to baptize all who believe in Christ into one body. Christian unity is thus a reality—a position as a result of being "in Christ." It is not organizational unity but the unity of a living organism. The task of Christians is to realize this positional unity as an actuality by Christ-like conduct (Eph. 4:1-3) based on a sound doctrinal platform (Eph. 4:4-6). Only in this way can positional unity become experiential.

3. **Roman Catholic and Protestant Statements.** The authoritative utterances of Romanists and of Protestants illustrate this difference of view. For example, the *Catechism of Trent* (Roman Catholic) says: "The Church is one, because, as the apostle says, there is 'one Lord, one faith, one baptism;' but more especially because it has one invisible ruler, Christ, and one visible, viz., the occupant for the time being of the chair of St. Peter at Rome." Luther's *Larger Catechism* says: "I believe that there is upon earth a certain community of saints, composed solely of holy persons, under one Head, collected together by the Spirit; of one faith and one mind, endowed with manifold gifts, but united in love and without sects and divisions." The Church of England (Art. xix) says: "A congregation of faithful men, in which the pure word of God is preached, and the sacraments duly administered according to Christ's ordinance, in all those things that of necessity are requisite to the same." This is also the definition given by the Methodist Church. These quotations might be greatly multiplied; but enough is given to show the main line of divergence and the position and trend of Protestant doctrine upon this subject.

4. **The Ethics of the Church.** As visible institutions Churches must exercise government over their members. What rules of conduct they may properly impose and enforce is, however, a question of great importance. If the Church is, as Roman Catholics hold, infallible, because divinely inspired, then all that the Church may require is of divine obligation. If the Churches, as some seem to hold, are merely voluntary human societies formed for Christian purposes, then such rules as from a human standpoint may seem appropriate are binding upon those who enter and remain in their communion; though at the same time the obligation of entering or remaining becomes, to say the least, greatly

reduced. But if, according to the Protestant theory, the Churches are divine-human institutions, and not infallible, the rules of conduct must be in accordance with the teachings of the infallible word. The ethical standard of the visible Church must be simply that of the Holy Scriptures, otherwise the true idea of the Church is lost sight of and the Church assumes either too much or too little. Only by adhering to the word of God as the "rule of faith and practice" can the Churches save themselves from the two extremes: on the one hand, that of unduly magnifying the authority of the visible Church, or, on the other, that of laying aside its highest claim to recognition and obedience. Revised by *M. F. U.*

Churl (Heb. *kīlai, withholding,* Isa. 32:5, 7), a fraudulent person, a *deceiver.*

Churlish (the rendering of the Heb. *qāshěh, severe*), a word descriptive of a coarse, ill-natured fellow (I Sam. 25:3); probably the same in meaning as "hard" (Matt. 25:24).

Chu′shan-Rishatha′im. *See* Cushan-rishatha-im.

Chu′za (kōō′zà; Aram. *chuza', jug*), the "steward" of Herod (Antipas), whose wife, *Joanna* (*q. v.*), having been cured by our Lord either of possession by an evil spirit or of a disease, became attached to that body of women who accompanied him on his journeyings (Luke 8:3).

95. Cilicia

Cilic′ia (sĭ-lĭsh′ĭ-à), the southeasterly province of Asia Minor, and upon the Mediterranean Sea, with Tarsus, the birthplace of St. Paul, its capital. A Roman province, B. C. 67. The Jews of Cilicia had a synagogue at Jerusalem (Acts 6:9). It was famous for its goats' hair. Paul learned his trade of tentmaking here, and visited it soon after his conversion (Gal. 1:21; Acts 9:30). Cicero was once consul of it. Its climate was luxurious and attracted Greek residents (Acts 15:41; Acts 21:39).

Cinnamon. *See* Vegetable Kingdom.

Cin′nereth (sĭn′ē-rĕth), another form of *Chin-nereth* (*q. v.*).

Circle (Heb. *ḥūg*). "It is he that sitteth upon the circle of the earth" (Isa. 40:22). The same word is applied (Job. 22:14, rendered "circuit") to the *heavens,* which the ancients supposed to be a hollow sphere. The figure then is of Jehovah sitting or walking upon the heavens, which were thought to arch over the earth.

Circuit. (1) In I Sam. 7:16 (Heb. *sābǎb,* to *revolve*), a regular tour of inspection; in Eccles. 1:6, the periodical direction of the winds, which in the East are quite regular in their seasons. (2) In Job. 22:14 the Hebrew word is *ḥug, Circle* (*q. v.*). (3) The act of going round (Heb. *tᵉqūfāh, revolution*), the *apparent* diurnal revolution of the sun around the earth (Psa. 19:6), the completion of a year (Exod. 34:22; II Chron. 24:23, rendered "end of the year"), or of the term of pregnancy (I Sam. 1:20, rendered "the time was come about").

Circumcision (Heb. *mūlāh;* Gr. *peritomē,* a *cutting around*).

1. **The Ceremony** of circumcision consisted in cutting away the foreskin, i. e., the hood or fold of skin covering the head of the male organ. This is generally done by means of a sharp knife, but in more primitive times sharp stones were used (Exod. 4:25; Josh. 5:2, "knives of flint"). As a rule this act was performed by the father (Gen. 17:23), although it might be done by any Israelite, and, if necessary, women as well (Exod. 4:25), but never by a Gentile. In later times the operation was, in the case of adults, performed by a doctor. The Jews of the present day intrust it to a person called a *mohel* appointed especially for the purpose. In later times the naming of the child accompanied the act of circumcision (Luke 1:59).

2. **History.** After God had made a covenant with Abraham (Gen. 15) he commanded that, as a token of the covenant, every male should be circumcised; not merely the children and bodily descendants of Abraham, but also those born in his house and purchased slaves, and that in the case of children on the eighth day after birth. Every one not so circumcised was to be "cut off from his people" as having "broken the covenant" (Gen. 17:10-14).

Circumcision was formally enacted as a legal institute by Moses (Lev. 12:3; John 7:22, 23), and was made to apply, not only to one's own children, but to slaves, home-born or purchased; to foreigners before they could partake of the passover or become Jewish citizens (Exod. 12:48).

During the wilderness journey circumcision fell into disuse. This neglect is most satisfactorily explained as follows: The nation, while bearing the punishment of disobedience in its wanderings, was regarded as under temporary rejection by God, and was therefore prohibited from using the sign of the covenant.

As the Lord had only promised his assistance on condition that the law given by Moses was faithfully observed, it became the duty of Joshua, upon entering Canaan, to perform the rite of circumcision upon the generation that had been born in the wilderness. This was done, immediately upon crossing the Jordan, at or near Gilgal (Josh. 5:2, sq.).

From this time circumcision became the pride of Israel, they looking with contempt upon all those people not observing it (Judg. 14:3; 15:18; I Sam. 14:6; Isa. 52:1, etc). It became a rite so distinctive of them that their oppressors tried to prevent their observing it, an attempt to which they refused submission (I Macc. 1:48, 50, 60, 62).

The process of restoring a circumcised person to his natural condition by a surgical operation was sometimes undergone from a desire to assimilate themselves to the heathen around them, or that they might not be known as Jews when they appeared naked in the games. Against having recourse to this practice, from an excessive anti-Judaistic tendency, St. Paul cautions the Corinthians (I Cor. 7:18, 19). The attitude which Christianity, at its introduction, assumed toward circumcision was one of absolute hostility so far as the necessity of the rite to salvation or its possession of any religious or moral worth were concerned (Acts 15:5; Gal. 5:2).

3. **Pagan.** Circumcision was practiced by the Edomites, Moabites, Ammonites, and Egyptians, but among the last only by the priests and those who wanted to be initiated into the sacred mysteries. The practice has also been found to exist among the Ethiopians, Colchians, Congo Negroes, and many savage tribes in the heart of Africa; also among American Indian tribes, e. g., the Salivas, the Guamos, the Octamotos on the Orinoco, among the inhabitants of Yucatan and of Mexico, and, further, among the Fiji Islanders.

4. **Significance.** With respect to the symbolical significance of circumcision, it is said to have originated in phallus worship, but if so this would have no bearing on the Israelite view of the rite. It was practiced, say some, because of its medical advantages, as the warding off of disease through ease in cleanliness, or that it served to increase the generative powers, but these can hardly be received as proper explanations, for whole nations not practicing circumcision appear as healthy and fruitful. Nor can the rite be brought into connection with the idea of sacrifice, "the consecration of a part of the body for the whole," or even "as an act of emasculation in honor of the Deity, that has gradually dwindled down to the mere cutting away of the foreskin."

We must rather look for the significance of this rite in the fact that the corruption of sin usually manifests itself with peculiar energy in the sexual life, and that the sanctification of the life was symbolized by the purifying of the organ by which life is reproduced. But, as spiritual purity was demanded of the chosen people of God, circumcision became the external token of the covenant between God and his people. It secured to the one subjected to it all the rights of the covenant, participation in all its material and spiritual benefits; while, on the other hand, he was bound to fulfill all the covenant obligations. It had not, however, a sacramental nature; it was not a vehicle through which to convey the sanctifying influences of God to his people, but was simply a token of the recognition of the covenant relation existing between Israel and God.

The circumcision of the child on the eighth day seems to have been founded on the significance that attached to the number seven, so far as that number denotes a period of time. On the eighth day, when a new cycle of life began, the child entered into covenant with God. Again, it was not until the eighth day that the child was supposed to possess an independent existence.

5. **Figurative.** Circumcision was used as a symbol of purity of heart (Deut. 10:16; 30:6; comp. Lev. 26:41; Jer. 4:4; 9:25; Ezek. 44:7). "Who am of uncircumcised lips" (Exod. 6:12). By this figure Moses would seem to imply that he was unskilled in public address, as the Jews were wont to consider circumcision a perfecting of one's powers. Circumcision is also figurative of a readiness to hear and obey (Jer. 6:10).

6. **Christian Circumcision.** Christians are said to be circumcised in Christ (Col. 2:11). This circumcision is asserted to be "circumcision made without hands," that is, a spiritual reality and not a physical rite, the antitype and not the type. Physical circumcision was a putting off of a part of the flesh as a symbol of covenant relationship of God's people with a holy God. Christian circumcision is "putting off" not a part, but an entire "body of the flesh." "The body of the flesh" is the physical body controlled by the old fallen nature, which all possess, saved as well as unsaved. The "putting off" is positional truth, that is, truth which obtains as a result of the believer's being placed in Christ by the Spirit's baptizing work. Because the sin nature was judged by Christ in His death, so the believer by virtue of his organic union and identification with his Lord shares that "putting off" which Christ accomplished, just as he shares Christ's fulness and is declared "to be complete in Him." (Col. 2:10). The believer's circumcision is not only a spiritual reality consisting in the putting off of the body of the flesh; it is more precisely Christ's circumcision, effected by Him and imputed to the believer. "In whom," that is, in vital union with whom by Spirit baptism, "also ye are circumcised . . . by the *circumcision of Christ*" (Col. 2:11). Our Lord's circumcision mentioned in this passage has no reference to his physical circumcision when He was eight days old, but is a meaningful term the Apostle applies to Christ's death to the sin nature. It is the truth enunciated in Rom. 6:10, "For in that he died, he died *unto* sin once," and Romans 8:3 "For what the law could not do, in that it was weak through the flesh, God sending his own Son in the likeness of sinful flesh, and for sin, *condemned sin in the flesh*." It is thus apparent that the baptizing work of the Holy Spirit (I Cor. 12:13; Rom. 6:3, 4; Col. 2:12) effects spiritual circumcision. See *The Baptizing Work of the Holy Spirit* by Merrill F. Unger, 1953, pp. 91, 92.

Cis (sĭs), a Grecized form (Acts 13:21) of the name of *Kish* (q. v.), the father of King Saul.

Cistern (Heb. *b'ōr*, or *bōr*, a *dug place*), a receptacle for holding water (Prov. 5:15; Eccles. 12:6; Isa. 36:16; Jer. 2:13). Sometimes these were dug around a spring to retain the water coming therefrom. Those which generally bore the name of cisterns were covered reservoirs, dug out of the earth or rock, into which, in the rainy seasons, the rain or a flowing stream was conducted for storage. The absence of rain during the summer months (May to September) makes it necessary to collect and preserve the water, which falls in abundance during the remainder of the year. These cisterns were usually large pits, but sometimes extensive vaults, open only by a small mouth. The mouth was closed with a large flat stone, over which sand was spread to prevent easy discovery (Cant. 4:12, "sealed fountains"). Mud would naturally accumulate at the bottom of these cisterns, so that anyone falling therein would be likely to perish (Jer. 38:6; Psa. 40:2).

In cities, the chief dependence for water being upon cisterns, they were carefully made, either hewn out of the rock or constructed of masonry.

Empty cisterns were sometimes used as prisons; thus Joseph was cast into a pit (Gen. 37:22); and Jeremiah was also thrown into one (Jer. 38:6).

Figurative. (a) The breaking of the wheel at the cistern, used to draw up the bucket, is used (Eccles. 12:6) as an image of the dissolution of the bodily powers. (b) To "drink waters out of thine own cistern" (Prov. 5:15) means to confine one's self to pleasures legitimately his own. (c) "Broken cisterns" (Jer. 2:13) as tanks not only without feeding springs, but unable to even retain the water flowing into them, are symbols of all earthly, as compared with heavenly, means of satisfying man's highest needs.

Cities. *See* City.

Cities of Refuge. When the Israelites had come into the land of Canaan they were to choose conveniently situated as "cities of refuge," to which the manslayer who had killed a person by accident might flee. Three of these cities were located on each side of the Jordan (six in all). Those on the west of the Jordan were Kedesh in Galilee (I Chron. 6:76), Shechem in Mount Ephraim (Josh. 21:21; I Chron. 6:67), Hebron in Judah (Josh. 21:11; II Sam. 5:5; I Chron. 6:55); on the east of Jordan were Bezer, in the plain of Moab (Deut. 4:43; Josh. 20:8); Ramothgilead, in the tribe of Gad (Deut. 4:43; Josh. 21:38; I Kings 22:3); and Golan, in Bashan, in the half tribe of Manasseh (Deut. 4:43; Josh. 21:27; I Chron. 6:71). They were also Levitical cities. *See* Levite.

Regulations. The following were the regulations respecting the asylum offered by the cities of refuge. The *Avenger of Blood* (*q. v.*) was allowed to kill the manslayer if he overtook him before reaching the city (Num. 35:19). The fugitive before he could avail himself of the shelter must undergo a solemn trial, and prove to the congregation that the killing was accidental (Num. 35:12, 24); if acquitted of intentional killing he must remain within the city or its suburbs until the death of the high priest, and if found outside its limits might be put to death by the avenger of blood (Num. 35:25, sq.).

According to the rabbins, in order to aid the fugitive it was the business of the Sanhedrin to keep the roads leading to the cities of refuge in the best possible repair. No hills were left, every river was bridged, and the road itself was to be at least thirty-two cubits broad. At every turn were guide posts bearing the word *Refuge;* and two students of the law were appointed to accompany the fleeing man, to pacify, if possible, the avenger, should he overtake the fugitive.

Cities of the Plain. These cities were five in number, Sodom, Gomorrah, Admah, Zeboiim and Bela or Zoar (Gen. 13:12; 19:29). The Biblical notices that the district of Jordan where these cities were situated was extremely fertile and well peopled (c. 2065 B. C. according to the preserved chronology of the Massoretic text), but that not long afterwards was abandoned, are in agreement with archaeological facts (W. F. Albright, *The Archaeology of Palestine and the Bible*, pp. 133 sq.). It is now fairly certain that these cities were located in the Vale of Siddim (Gen. 14:3) and that this was the region in the southern portion of the Dead Sea now covered with water. The ruins of Bab ed-Dra' E. of the Dead Sea probably belong to the age of Sodom and Gomorrah. Its remains date from about the last third of the third millennium when occupation here came to an abrupt close. The Vale of Siddim with its towns was overtaken by a great catastrophe around the middle of the 21st century B. C. (Gen. 19:23-28). The Vale of Siddim was "Full of slime (i. e. asphalt) pits" (Gen. 14:10); petroleum deposits are still found in the area. Being on a great fault which forms the Jordan Valley, the Dead Sea of the Arabah, this region has been noted throughout history for its earthquakes. The cataclysm, although Scripture records only the miraculous elements, was doubtless due to violent earthquakes in which the salt and free sulphur of this area were mingled, which resulted in a gigantic explosion, hurling into the sky red hot the salt and sulphur, literally raining fire and brimstone over the whole plain (Gen. 19:24-28). The instance of Lot's wife being turned into a pillar of salt is reminiscent of the great salt mass in the valley, the Mount of Sodom, called by the Arabs *Jebel Usdum*. It is a spur some five miles long extending north and south at the S. W. end of the Dead Sea. Somewhere, inundated by the slowly rising water of the southern part of the Salt Lake the cities of the plain are evidently to be found. In N. T. times, their ruins were still visible, not yet being covered with water (Tacitus, *History* V:7; Josephus, *Wars of the Jews*, IV:4). M. F. U.

96. Mount of Sodom (*Jebel Usdum*)

Cities, Underground. *See* Edrei.

Citizenship (Gr. *politeia*, Acts 22:28, "freedom"), the rights and privileges of a native or adopted citizen as distinguished from a foreigner.

1. **Hebrew.** As the covenant people, and according to the Mosaic constitution (which was framed on a basis of religious rather than of political privileges and distinctions), the idea of the commonwealth (Eph. 2:12) was merged into that of the *Congregation* (*q. v.*).

2. **Roman** (Lat. *civitas*). In the fullest sense citizenship included the right of voting, of being elected to a magistracy, of appeal to the people, of contracting a legal marriage, of holding property in the Roman community. "As a rule, the Jewish communities in Roman cities are to be regarded in the light of *private associations of settlers*, which were recognized by the state and on which certain rights were conferred, but the members of which did not enjoy the rights of citizenship" (Schürer, *Jewish People*, ii, 270, sq.). Still there were quite a large number of towns in which the Jews enjoyed the *rights of citizenship*, as enumerated above. Individual Jews also had the rights of citizenship conferred upon them, as Paul (Acts 21:39), who, however, claimed it from being freeborn (22:28).

City (Heb. *'îr*, poetical *qîryâh*), in the most ancient times the only distinction between village and city was that an assemblage of houses and buildings surrounded by a wall was reckoned a city, and without such surroundings a village (Lev. 25:29-31; I Sam. 6:18; Ezek. 38:11).

Later, cities became distinguished by a large number of houses, as well as by the size, solidity, and magnificence of the buildings. "Cities and their villages" are commonly mentioned in the apportionment of the land to the tribes of Israel (Josh. 13:23, 28; 15:32, 36, 41, etc.), from which we infer that some villages belonged to and were dependent upon the cities. Naturally, with increased population and extension, villages and towns developed into cities, e. g., Hazar-addar (Num. 34:4), perhaps Hezron and Adar (Josh. 15:3); the two places being, probably, near together and growing into one. This may account for the fact that many places are designated now cities, now villages, as Bethlehem (John 7:42, "town;" Luke 2:4, "city").

The earliest notice in Scripture of city-building is of Enoch by Cain (Gen. 4:17). After the confusion of tongues the descendants of Nimrod founded Babel, Erech, etc., in the land of Shinar; and Asshur built Nineveh, Rehoboth, etc. (Gen. 10:10-12, 19). Such cities as Ur, Nippur, Kish, Eridu, Lagash, Nineveh, Ashur, etc. have been excavated and go back to 3,000 B. C. or earlier. The earliest Biblical description of a city, properly so called, is that of Sodom (Gen. 19:1-22), but cities existed in very early times on the sites of Jerusalem, Hebron, and Damascus; and it is plain that the Canaanite, who was "in the land" before the coming of Abraham, had already built cities. We read that the Israelites during their sojourn in Egypt were employed in building or fortifying the "treasure cities" of Pithom and Raamses (Exod. 1:11).

Hebrew Cities. The cities of Palestine were, judging from the large number mentioned in Joshua, relatively small, like most cities of very ancient times. They were like oriental cities of today, built with narrow, crooked streets (Eccles. 12:4; Cant. 3:2), with many squares near the gates, where markets and courts were held (Gen. 23:10; Ruth 4:1; Matt. 6:5, etc.). Few of the streets were paved, although, according to Josephus (*Ant.*, viii, 7), Solomon had the roads leading to Jerusalem laid with black stone. More certain are the statements that Herod the Great paved the main street in Antioch, and Herod Agrippa III Jerusalem with white stones. Many cities were surrounded with high walls, having strong gates and brazen or iron bars (Deut. 3:5; I Kings 4:13), and provided with watchtowers (II Sam. 18:24, sq.).

Later, especially under the kings, many places, particularly frontier towns and chief cities, and above all, Jerusalem, were strengthened by the erection of thick walls with battlements (II Chron. 26:6, sq.; Zeph. 1:16), and high towers raised partly over the gates (II Sam. 18:24; II Kings 9:17), partly at the corners of the walls (II Chron. 14:7; 32:5). Ditch and rampart were provided for the outside of the walls (II Sam. 20:15; Isa. 26:1; I Kings 21:23). Jerusalem's walls have been uncovered dating back to Jebusite times before 1,000 B. C.

Government. The government of Jewish cities was vested in a council of elders with judges (Deut. 16:18), who were required to be priests. Under the kings we find mention of a "governor" (I Kings 22:26; II Chron. 18:25). After the captivity Ezra made similar arrangements for the appointment of judges (Ezra 7:25). *See* Citizenship.

City, Fenced. A fortified city. *See* City, Fortress.

City, Holy, another name of Jerusalem (Neh. 11:1; Dan. 9:24), probably from the feeling that the sacredness of the temple extended in some measure over the city. It is so distinguished in the East to the present day.

City, Levitical. *See* Levitical Cities.

City of David, a portion of the S. W. hill of Jerusalem, including Mount Zion, where the fortress of the Jebusites stood. This fortress was reduced by David, who built a new palace and city, named after him (I Chron. 11:5).

Bethlehem, the native town of David, is also called, from that circumstance, the city of David (Luke 2:11).

City of God, a name given to Jerusalem (Psa. 46:4; comp. 48:1, 8), the appropriateness of which is evident from Deut. 12:5: "The place which the Lord your God shall choose out of all your tribes to put his name there, even unto his *habitation* shall ye seek, and thither thou shalt come."

City of Palm Trees. *See* Ir-Hattemarim.

City of Salt. *See* Ir-Hammelah.

City, Sacerdotal. *See* Priest.

City, Treasure (*city of provisions*, called "city of store," I Kings 9:19). Two such cities, *Pithom* and *Raamses* (*q. v.*), were built by the Israelites while in Egypt (Exod. 1:11), in which the produce of the land was housed. The Jewish kings had similar places of public deposit (II Chron. 8:4, 6; 16:4; 17:2).

Clau′da (klô′dá), a small island near the southwest shore of Crete. Pliny calls it Gaudos. Ptolemy calls it Klaudos. Now called Gozzo. It embraces about thirty families. Paul passed this island on his voyage to Rome (Acts 27:16).

Clau′dia (klô′dĭ-á; feminine of *Claudius*), a Christian female mentioned in II Tim. 4:21, as saluting Timotheus. By some she is thought to have been the daughter of the British king Cogidunus, and the wife of Pudens (mentioned in the same verse), and sent to Rome to be educated; that there she was the *protégée* of Pomponia (wife of the late commander in Britain, Aulus Plautius), and became a convert to Christianity. On the other hand, it may be said that this attempt at identification rests on no other foundation than the identity of the names of the parties, which, in the case of names so common as Pudens and Claudia, may be nothing more than a mere accidental coincidence (Conybeare and Howson's *St. Paul*, ii, 484, note).

Clau′dius (klô′dĭ-ŭs); (Gr. perhaps from *claudus, lame*).

1. The fourth Roman emperor (excluding Julius Caesar), who succeeded Caligula, January 25, A. D. 41. (1) **Early Life.** He was the son of Drusus and Antonia, and was born August 1, B. C. 10, at Lyons, in Gaul. Losing his father in infancy, he was left to the care and society of domestics, and despised by his imperial relatives. Notwithstanding the weakness of intellect resulting from this neglect, he devoted himself to literary pursuits, and was the author of several treatises. On the murder of Caligula he hid himself through fear of a similar fate, but was found by a soldier, who saluted him as emperor. (2) **As Emperor.** He was taken, almost by force, to the popular assembly, and constituted emperor chiefly by the pretorian guards, under the promise of a largess to each soldier. According to Josephus, the throne was, in a great measure, finally secured to him through the address and solicitation of Herod Agrippa. This obligation he returned by great favors to that personage, enlarging his territory, and appointing his brother Herod to the kingdom of Chalcis (Josephus, *Ant.*, xix, 5, 1), giving to this latter also, after his brother's death, the presidency over the temple at Jerusalem (Josephus, *Ant.*, xx, 1, 3). The Jews were generally treated by him with indulgence, especially those in Asia and Egypt (*Ant.*, xix, 5, 2, 3; xx, 1, 2), although those in Palestine seem to have, at times, suffered much oppression at the hands of his governors. About the middle of his reign those who abode at Rome were all banished (Acts 18:2), A. D. probably 49. The conduct of Claudius during his government, in so far as it was not under the influence of his wives and freedmen, was mild and popular, and he made several beneficial enactments. Having married his niece, Agrippina, she prevailed upon him to set aside his own son, Britannicus, in favor of her son, Nero, by a former marriage; but discovering that he regretted this step she poisoned him, A. D. 54.

2. Claudius Lysias (Acts 23:26). *See* Lysias.

Claw, the sharp, hooked end of the foot of a bird (Dan. 4:33) or animal (Deut. 14:6); the hoof solid or split.

Figurative. The expression "tear their claws in pieces" (Zech. 11:16) means to seize upon and eat the last morsel of flesh or fat.

Clay. *See* Mineral Kingdom.

Clean, Cleanness, the rendering of several Hebrew and Greek words, having the primary meaning of freedom from dirt or filth, and then of moral purity. Generally, however, they signify freedom from ceremonial defilement. *See* Purification, Purity, Uncleanness.

Cleft, the rendering of several Hebrew words.

1. A space or opening made by cleavage, as a fissure in a building (Amos 6:11; Isa. 22:9, "breaches"); crevice in a rock (Isa. 2:21; Cant. 2:14; Jer. 49:16).

2. The split in the hoof of an animal (Deut. 14:6).

Clem′ent (klĕm′ĕnt; *merciful*), a person (apparently a Christian of Philippi) mentioned by Paul (Phil. 4:3) as one whose name was in the book of life. This Clement was, by the ancient Church, identified with the bishop of Rome of the same name.

Cle′opas (klē′ō-pás; contraction of Gr. *kleopatros, of a renowned father*), one of the two disciples who were going to Emmaus on the day of the resurrection, when Jesus drew near and conversed with them (Luke 24:18). He questioned them as to the subject of their conversation, chided them for their ignorance and unbelief, and expounded to them the Scriptures which foretold his sufferings and glory. Arriving at Emmaus, they secured his presence at the evening meal, during which he was made known to them. They hastened back to Jerusalem and acquainted the disciples with what they had seen and heard. Cleopas must not be confounded with *Cleophas* (q. v.), or rather *Clopas*, of John 19:25.

Cle′ophas (klē′ō-fás), or rather **Clo′pas** (Gr. *klō′pás*), the husband of *Mary* (q. v.), the sister of Christ's mother (John 19:25); probably a Grecized form of *Alphaeus* (q. v.).

Clerk (Acts 19:35). *See* Town Clerk.

Cloak, an article of *Dress* (q. v.), as a covering or veil.

Figurative. That which conceals, and so, a pretext or excuse (John 15:22; I Pet. 2:16).

Closet (Heb. *ḥŭppāh, canopy*), a bridal couch with curtains (Joel 2:16; "chamber," Psa. 19:5). The same word is still employed by the Jews for the canopy under which the marriage ceremony is performed.

In the New Testament the word *tameion* is used in the sense of a place of privacy; any quiet room in one's home, as opposed to the synagogues and the streets (Matt. 6:6; Luke 12:3).

Cloth, Clothes, Clothing. *See* Dress.

Clothes, Rending of. *See* Rend.

Cloud. The allusions to clouds in Scripture, as well as their use in symbolical language, can only be understood when we remember the nature of the climate, where there is hardly a trace of cloud from the beginning of May to the close of September. During this season clouds so seldom appear and rains so seldom fall as to seem phenomenal, as was the case with the harvest rain invoked by Samuel

(I Sam. 12:17, 18) and the little cloud, not larger than a man's hand, which Elijah declared to be sure promise of rain (I Kings 18:44).

Clouds are referred to as showing forth the power and wisdom of God in their formation (Psa. 135:6, 7; 147:8; Prov. 8:28, etc.), and causing them to hold and dispense rain (Job 37:10, sq.; Prov. 3:20). They are called the "clouds of heaven" (Dan. 7:13; Matt. 24:30), "windows of heaven" (Gen. 7:11; Isa. 24:18), "bottles of heaven" (Job 38:37), "chambers" of God (Psa. 104:3, 13), "dust of God's feet" (Nah. 1:3).

Man's ignorance is illustrated by his inability to number the clouds (Job. 38:37), to account for their spreading (36:29), the disposing and balancing of them (37:15, 16), to cause them to rain (38:34), or stay them (38:37).

Figurative. Living much in the open air, and being of a poetical nature, the people of the East would naturally make clouds figurative of many things. Thus clouds are the symbol of armies and multitudes of people (Isa. 60:8; Jer. 4:13; Heb. 12:1). The sudden disappearance of threatening clouds from the sky is a figure for the blotting out of transgressions (Isa. 44:22). A day of clouds is taken for a season of calamity and of God's judgment (Lam. 2:1; Ezek. 30:3; 34:12; Joel 2:2). Naturally the cloud is a symbol of transitoriness (Job. 30:15; Hos. 6:4). The "cloud without rain" is the proverb for the man of promise without performance (Isa. 18:4; 25:5; Jude 12; comp. Prov. 25:14). False teachers are compared to "clouds that are carried with a tempest" (II Pet. 2:17). A wise ruler is said to be as the "light of . . . a morning without clouds" (II Sam. 23:4), while the favor of a king is compared to "a cloud of the latter rain, refreshing and fertilizing the earth" (Prov. 16:15). "Clouds returning after the rain" is figurative of the infirmities of old age; i. e., as after a rain one expects sunshine, so after pains one longs for comfort. As clouds in hot countries veil the oppressive glories of the sun, they are used to symbolize the divine presence, which they entirely or in part conceal (Exod. 16:10; 33:9; Num. 11:25; Job 22:14; Psa. 18:11, 12; Isa. 19:1). *See* Pillar of Cloud, Shekinah.

Cloud, Pillar of. *See* Pillar.

Clout. 1. The word used in Josh. 9:5, properly means to *cover*, i. e., to *patch*, and denotes that the sandals of the Gibeonites were mended, as if they had become old and worn during their journey. The primary sense of the word seems to have been a *blow*, as a "clout on the head." It was then applied to a bit of material clapped on, or hastily applied to mend a tear, a *patch*.

2. The "cast clouts" Jer. 38:11, 12; were old, torn clothes or rags put under the prophet's arms to prevent the cords cutting into the flesh while he was being drawn out of the dungeon.

Cni'dus (ni'dŭs), a town at the extreme southwest of Asia Minor, upon land jutting out between the islands of Rhodes and Coos (Acts 21:1). Venus was worshipped there. Paul sailed by this place (Acts 27:7).

Coal. Two Hebrew words are rendered "coal" or "coals:"

1. One (*pĕhĕm*) would seem to be applied to coals not yet lighted. It occurs three times—twice when the smith working with the coals is mentioned (Isa. 44:12; 54:16), and in Proverbs (26:21, "as coals are to burning coals"), where unlighted coals must be meant.

It has been disputed whether the Hebrews had mineral coal or merely charcoal. There is strong reason, however, that the former was used in ancient times. The mountains of Lebanon contain seams of coal which have been worked in recent times, and were, probably, not neglected by the Phoenicians. Charcoal was the "coal" in common use; thus coals of juniper or broom are mentioned (Psa. 120:4).

2. The other word (*gĕhĕlĕth, kindling*) signifies an ignited or *live* coal, and is of frequent occurrence (II Sam. 14:7; Job. 41:21; Psa. 18:8; Isa. 44:19; Ezek. 24:11, etc.); often with the addition of "burning" or of "fire" (Lev. 16:12; II Sam. 22:13, etc.).

The term "live coal" (Heb. *rĭspäh*, Isa. 6:6) appears to have been a hot stone used for baking upon (*see* I Kings 19:6, "a cake baken on the coals," Heb. *rĕsĕp*). In the expression "their visage is blacker than a coal" (Lam. 4:8) *coal* simply means *blackness* (R. V. "darker than blackness").

In the New Testament "fire of coals" (John 18:18) was probably of charcoal, on a chafing dish, used in the East for the sake of warmth. *See* Fuel.

Figurative. The expression, "They shall quench my coal which is left" (II Sam. 14:7), refers to the burning coal with which one kindles a fire, and is obviously a metaphor for extinguishing one's family.

"Coals of fire" (II Sam. 22:9, 13; Psa. 18:8, 12, etc.) is by some thought to be a figure for lightnings proceeding from God. The flame of red-hot coals pours out of him as out of a glowing furnace. This description is based entirely upon Exod. 19:18, where the Lord comes down upon Sinai in smoke and fire.

"Thou shalt heap coals of fire upon his head" (Prov. 25:22; Rom. 12:20) represents the shame and confusion which men feel when their evil is requited by good.

In Cant. 8:6 it is said, "Jealousy is cruel as the grave: the coals thereof are coals of fire, which hath a most vehement flame." In Hab. 3:5 "burning coals" seem to mean *fevers*.

Coast, an inaccurate rendering of several terms, meaning *border*, except in the expression "sea coast."

Coat. *See* Dress.

Coat of Mail. *See* Armor.

Cock, The, on tombs is a Christian symbol of the resurrection, the herald of life after the night of death. It is also a symbol of vigilance. *See* Animal Kingdom.

Cockatrice. *See* Animal Kingdom.

Cockcrowing. The habit of the cock in the East of crowing during the night at regular times gave rise to the expression "cockcrowing" to indicate a definite portion of time (Mark 13:35). The Romans called the last watch of the night, the break of day, about three o'clock, *gallicinium;* and the Hebrews designated the cockcrowing period by words signifying "the singing of the cock." Among the Hebrews we find no mention of the flight of the hours of the night except the crowing of the cock. *See* Time.

Cockle. *See* Vegetable Kingdom.

Coffer. The small chest which the Philistines placed upon the cart with the ark (I Sam. 6:8, 11, 15), and in which they deposited the golden mice and emerods that formed their trespass offering.

Coffin ('ärōn; Gen. 50:26, "and he was put in a coffin in Egypt"), undoubtedly a mummy chest made of sycamore wood, which was deposited in a room, according to Egyptian custom, and carried away with Israel at the Exodus. *See* Dead, Burial of, Burial.

The same Hebrew word is rendered "chest" (II Kings 12:10), and very frequently "*Ark*" (*q. v.*).

Coin. *See* Metrology, IV.

Col-Ho′zeh (kŏl-hō′zĕh; *all-seeing*), a descendant of Judah, being the son of Hazaiah, and father of one Baruch (Neh. 11:5), B. C. before 445. He had also a son named Shallum, who repaired part of the wall of Jerusalem after the captivity (Neh. 3:15).

Collar. 1. Any aperture. In Job 30:18 the opening by means of which the shirt was put on. The meaning of this passage seems to be that Job was so wasted by disease that his garments were not at all sustained by his person, but hung loosely from his neck.

2. A peculiar kind of pendant (Judg. 8:26; Heb. *nĕṭēfà'*, rendered "chains" in Isa. 3:19), probably pearl-shaped *Earrings* (*q. v.*).

Collection. 1. Joash ordered a collection for the repairing of the temple (II Chron. 24:6, 9). A chest was placed by the high priest at the entrance of the temple to receive the same. By making a distinction between this money and that given for the use of the priests a special appeal was made to the liberality of the people.

2. In the early age of the Christian Church the Christians of Palestine suffered greatly from poverty, probably due to ostracism. Paul made appeals to the Gentile Christians for aid (Acts 24:17; Rom. 15:25, 26; II Cor. 8 and 9; Gal. 2:10), recommending collections to be taken for this purpose on the "first day of the week" (I Cor. 16:1-3).

College (Heb. *mǐshnĕh, repetition,* II Kings 22:14), the residence of the prophetess *Huldah* (*q. v.*). The word *Mishneh* should be taken as a proper name, and as meaning a *district* or *suburb* of the city. The same term is used in Zeph. 1:10, and rendered "second," where the different quarters of Jerusalem are spoken of (see Neh. 11:9, in the original "upon the city second," i. e., over the second part of the city).

Collops. The thick flakes of fat flesh upon the haunches of a stall-fed ox, used as the symbol of irreligious prosperity (Job 15:27).

Colony. The city of Philippi was gifted by Caesar Augustus with the privileges of a *colony* (*colonia*). Antioch in Pisidia and Alexandria Troas both possessed the same character, but Philippi is the first case to which Scripture (Acts 16:12) calls our attention to this distinction. When the Romans conquered a town

they planted a body of their own citizens therein, as a kind of garrison, usually to the number of three hundred. These constituted a "colony of Roman citizens" (Lat. *colonia cibium Romanorum*), a sort of little Rome. Such a colony was free from taxes and military duty, its position as an outpost being regarded as an equivalent. It had its own constitution (a copy of the Roman), and elected its own senate and other offices of state. To this constitution the original inhabitants had to submit (Seiffert, *Dict. Class. Ant.*, s. v.).

Color (Acts 27:30), pretense.

Colors. The color sense, i. e., the distinction of color impressions in sensation, perception, and nomenclature, follows the same law as all human development—the law of progress from coarse to fine. The Jews had not reached such an advanced state of art that we should expect a wide acquaintance with colors. There are not, therefore, many colors mentioned in Scripture, and these may be arranged in two classes—those applied to natural objects, and artificial mixtures employed in *Dyeing* (*q. v.*) or *Painting* (*q. v.*).

1. **Natural.** (1) **White.** This term embraces the relatively as well as the absolutely white. In the full sense of the word the rays of the sun and those proceeding from a body raised to white heat are white, because all the colors of the spectrum are united in them. But even the daylight is not absolutely colorless, and the direct light of the sun seems yellowish, or, to speak poetically, golden. We are, therefore, prepared for a varied use of the term "white." Thus Matthew (17:2) writes, "His raiment was as white as the light;" and our Lord said, "The fields are already white to the harvest" (John 4:35); the ripening ears are white as distinguished from the green blade. The most common term is (Heb. *lābän*), which is applied to such objects as milk (Gen. 49:12), manna (Exod. 16:31), snow (Isa. 1:18), horses (Zech. 1:8), raiment (Eccles. 9:8); and a cognate word expresses the color of the moon (Isa. 24:23). Heb. *ṣǎḥ, sunny,* dazzling white, is applied to the complexion (Cant. 5:10); *hǐwwär,* a term of a later age, to snow (Dan. 7:9 only), and to the paleness of shame (Isa. 29:22); *sib,* to the hair alone. Another class of terms arises from the textures of a naturally white color. These were, without doubt, primarily applied to the material; but the idea of color is also prominent, particularly in the description of the curtains of the tabernacle (Exod. 26:1) and the priests' vestments (Exod. 28:6). (2) **Black.** Black and white are the extremest contrasts in Scripture, the former being where light and its colors have vanished. But then, as now, the term is used relatively, and includes the dark hues which approach black. The shades of this color are expressed in the terms (*shāḥōr, dusky*), applied to the hair (Lev. 13:31; Cant. 5:11); the complexion (Cant. 1:5), particularly when affected with disease (Job 30:30); horses (Zech. 6:2, 6); (*hûm,* literally, *scorched,* A. V. "brown," Gen. 30:32), applied to sheep; the word expresses the color produced by influence of the sun's rays; (*qādǎr,* literally, *to be dirty*), applied to a complexion blackened by sorrow or disease (Job 30:30), mourners'

robes (Jer. 8:21; 14:2), a clouded sky (I Kings 18:45), night (Mic. 3:6; Jer. 4:28; Joel 2:10; 3:15), a turbid brook (whence possibly *Kidron*), particularly when rendered so by melted snow (Job. 6:16). (3) **Red.** (Heb. *'ādōm*) is applied to blood (II Kings 3:22), a garment sprinkled with blood (Isa. 63:2), a heifer (Num. 19:2), pottage made of lentils (Gen. 25:30), a horse (Zech. 1:8; 6:2), wine (Prov. 23:31), the complexion (Gen. 25:25; Cant. 5:10; Lam. 4:7, A. V. "ruddy." *Reddish* is applied to a leprous spot (Lev. 13:19; 14:37). *Sārūq*, literally, *fox-colored*, *bay*, is applied to a horse (A. V. "speckled," Zech. 1:8), and to a species of vine bearing a purple grape (Isa. 5:2; 16:18). This color was symbolical of bloodshed (Zech. 6:2; Rev. 6:4; 12:3). (4) **Yellow** seems to have been regarded as a shade of green, for the same term *greenish* is applied to gold (Heb. *yerǎqrǎq*, Psa. 68:13, "yellow"), and to the leprous spot (Lev. 13:49). (5) **Green**, though frequently used, seldom refers to color. The Hebrew terms are *rǎ'ǎnān*, applied to what is *vigorous* and *flourishing* (Job. 15:32; Psa. 37:35; 52:8; Hos. 14:8); also used of that which is *fresh*, as oil (Psa. 92:10); and *yěrěk*, having the radical signification of *putting forth*, *sprouting*, and is used indiscriminately for all food products of the earth (Gen. 1:30; 9:3; Exod. 10:15; Isa. 15:6). Sometimes it is used for the sickly yellowish hue of mildewed grain (*see* Mildew), and also for the entire absence of color produced by fear (Jer. 30:6, "paleness"). "Green" is wrongly used in the A. V. for *white* (Gen. 30:37; Esth. 1:6), *young* (Lev. 2:14; 23:14), *moist* (Judg. 16:7, 8), *sappy* (Job 8:16), and *unripe* (Cant. 2:13).

2. **Artificial.** Dyeing, although known at an early period (Gen. 38:28; Exod. 26:1), is not noticed as a profession in the Bible; and the Jews were probably indebted to the Egyptians and Phoenicians for their dyes and the method of applying them. These dyes were purple (light and dark, the latter being the "blue" of the A. V.) and crimson; vermilion was introduced later. (1) **Purple** (Heb. *'ǎrgǎmän*). This color was obtained from a species of shellfish, the *murex trunculus*. "The dye taken from these shellfish is not their blood, but the slimy secretion of a gland which they have in common with all snails. This secretion is not at first red or violet, but whitish. When exposed, however, to the sunlight it begins to color like a photographic surface, and, passing through shades of yellow and green, settles into the purple color, which is a combination of red and violet light; and this mixed color, having sometimes more of a blue, sometimes more of a red hue, is ineffaceable. Purple was a monopoly of the Phoenicians. They, not only on their own but on other coasts, discovered shellfish yielding purple; but the oldest site of the purple trade was Tyre itself. At the present day, in the neighborhood of the miserable ruined village which bears the name of Tyre, there are found traces of these purple dyeworks, which were celebrated far into the Christian era. Purple was still costly in the time of the Roman supremacy. A mantle of the best purple of Tyre, such as the luxurious habits of the empire required, cost ten thou-

sand sesterces, i. e., over five hundred dollars" (Delitzsch, *Iris*, p. 65, sq.). Robes of a purple color were worn by kings (Judg. 8:26) and by the highest officers, civil and religious. They were also worn by the wealthy and luxurious (Jer. 10:9; Ezek. 27:7; Luke 16:19; Rev. 17:4; 18:16). (2) **Blue** (Heb. *tekēlěth*). This dye was procured from a species of shellfish found on the coast of Phoenicia, and called by modern naturalists *Helix Ianthina*. The tint is best explained by the statements of Josephus (*Ant.*, iii, 7, §7) and Philo that it was emblematic of the sky, in which case it represents, not the light blue of our northern climate, but the deep dark hue of the eastern sky. The A. V. has rightly described the tint in Esth. 1:6 (margin) as *violet*. This color was used in the same way as purple. Princes and nobles (Ezek. 23:6; Eccles. 40:4) and the idols of Babylon (Jer. 10:9) were clothed in robes of this color; the ribband and fringe of the Hebrew dress were to be of this color (Num. 15:38). (3) **Red** or **Crimson** (Isa. 1:18; Jer. 4:30, etc.). This color is expressed in Hebrew by several different terms: *Shäní* (Gen. 38:28-30), *tōlǎ'ǎth-shäní* (Exod. 25:4), or *tōlǎ'ǎth* simply (Isa. 1:18); *kǎrmíl*, (A. V. "crimson," II Chron. 2:7, 14; 3:14) was introduced at a late period, probably from Armenia, to express the same color. The first term expresses the brilliancy of the color, the second the worm or grub whence the dye was procured. This was a small insect of the size of a pea, which draws its nourishment from plants of the oak and other kinds by piercing them. The tint produced was *crimson* rather than scarlet. The only natural object to which it is applied in Scripture is the lips, which are compared to a scarlet thread (Cant. 4:3). Robes of this color were worn by the luxurious (II Sam. 1:24; Prov. 31:21; Jer. 4:30; Lam. 4:5; Rev. 17:4). This color was among the Greeks and Romans the proper color for the military cloak; and so it is a scarlet cloak which, according to Matthew, is put on the Saviour by the soldiers in Pilate's judgment hall. Mark and John say "purple," for the language of the people did not distinguish the two kinds of red. (4) **Vermilion** (Heb. *shä-shǎr*). This was a pigment used in fresco paintings, either for drawing figures of idols on the walls of temples (Ezek. 23:14), for coloring the idols themselves (Wisd. 13:14), or for decorating the walls and beams of houses (Jer. 22:14). Vermilion was a favorite color among the Assyrians, as is still attested by the sculptures of Nimroud and Khorsabad.

3. **Sacred**, or **Sacerdotal.** Purple, blue, scarlet, and white were the four colors prescribed by Moses. Of *four* colors were the ten curtains of the tabernacle, the veil, the curtain which hung at the entrance of the holy place, and the entrance into the court; the ephod, the girdle, and the breastplate of the high priest. Of *three* colors, viz., blue, purple, and scarlet, were the pomegranates which adorned the robe of the ephod. Of *one* color, white, were his under robe and miter; of *blue* were the fifty loops of the curtain, the cord by which the breastplate was fastened to the ephod, and that by which the diadem was attached to the miter. Of *one* color also, some-

times blue, sometimes purple, were the coverings of the sacred furniture of the tabernacle when it was carried from place to place; and of *one* color, white, were the clothes of the ordinary priests, with, probably, the exception of the particolored girdle.

4. **Figurative.** (1) *White* has a direct significance because light is white. White denotes purity, or, what is nearly the same, holiness. The priests were clothed in white as servants of the Holy One and as examples in holiness. White was also the ground color of the veil which divided the sanctuary, of the curtains, of the attire of the high priest. Garments of salvation are certainly garments of light (Psa. 27:1, "The Lord is my light and my salvation;" comp. Rev. 19:8). White was also the sign of *festivity* (Eccles. 9:8) and *triumph* (Zech. 6:3; Rev. 6:2). As the color of light (comp. Matt. 17:2) white was the symbol of *glory* and *majesty* (Dan. 7:9; Ezek. 9:3, sq.; Matt. 28:3; John 20:12; Acts 10:30). (2) *Black*, as the opposite of white or light, denotes *mourning*, *affliction*, *calamity*, and *death* (Jer. 14:2; Lam. 4:8; 5:10). It was also the sign of *humiliation* (Mal. 3:14, literally, "in black") and the omen of *evil* (Zech. 6:2; Rev. 6:5). (3) *Red* is the color of fire, and therefore of life: the blood is red because life is a fiery process. But *red*, as contrasted with white, is the color of selfish, covetous, passionate life. Sin is called red inasmuch as it is a burning heat which consumes man (Isa. 1:18). Red (crimson), as representing blood, designates the life principle of man and beast (Gen. 9:4-6) and the essential element of atonement (Isa. 63:2; Heb. 9:22). (4) *Green* was the emblem of *freshness*, *vigor*, and *prosperity* (Psa. 92:14, A. V. "flourishing;" 37:35, marg., "green"). (5) *Blue*. The purple blue, or hyacinth, points to heaven, and was the symbol of revelation. Among the Hebrews it was the Jehovah color, the symbol of the revealed God (comp. Exod. 24:10; Ezek. 1:26). Delitzsch says: "Blue denotes the softened divine majesty condescending to man in grace" (*Iris*, p. 48). It also represented reward. (6) *Purple*, as the dress of kings, was associated with *royalty* and *majesty* (Judg. 8:26; Esth. 8:15; Cant. 3:10; 7:5; Dan. 5:7, 16, 29, A. V. "scarlet").

Colos'sae, or **Colos'se** (kŏ-lŏs'ē), a city of mercantile importance on the Lycus, in Phrygia, about twelve miles above Laodicea. The most competent commentators think that the Christian church there was founded by Epaphras (Col. 1:2, 7; 4:12), and believe Col. 2:1 to prove that Paul had not been there previous to writing the epistle. The city was destroyed by earthquake in the ninth year of Nero and rebuilt. The modern town Chonas is at the ruins.

Colos'sians, Book of, an epistle of Paul written apparently from his Roman imprisonment (Acts 28:30, 31; Col. 4:3, 10, 18). Belonging also to this third group of Pauline Epistles are Philemon, Ephesians and Philippians.

1. **Occasion and Date.** The Epistle is a strong polemic against a Judaic-Gnostic heresy with its ceremonialism and doctrine of emanations. This unsound teaching sought to reduce Christianity to a legal system and

Christ to the position of a lesser god. Paul directed the impact of revealed truth against the Jewish element (circumcision, meats, drinks, fast days, new moons and Sabbaths, 2:11-16), an ascetic element (2:20-23), and a false philosophical and speculative element (2:8), with the worship of intermediary beings (2:18, 19). Apparently, Epaphras and his colleagues were unable to handle this situation and went to Rome to consult Paul about it (1:7, 8). The letter of reply was sent by Tychicus and Onesimus (4:7-9) toward the middle of Paul's two-year imprisonment at Rome, about A. D. 60.

2. **Plan.** Paul attacks the errors at Colossae by the clear presentation of counter truths. After first giving thanks for the Colossians' achievements and interceding for their progress (1:1-12), he expounds the supremacy of Christ over all principalities and powers (1: 13-19), the fullness of His redemption (1:20-23), and his own hardship in making known the gospel message (1:24-2:3). He warns the Colossian church against philosophic errors which set aside the provision of full deliverance from sin and freedom from legalism (2:4-15). He warns them accordingly to reject ritual prescriptions and the worship of inferior beings (2:16-19), emphasizing their complete position in Christ (2:20-3:4). He urges them to appropriate Christ's death and resurrection in practical Christian living (3:5-17) and in discharging the various special relations of life (3:18-4:6). He explains the mission of Tychicus and Onesimus (4:7-9), sends salutations (4:10-17), ending with a benediction (4:18).

3. **Outline.**

 Introduction (1:1-12)

 Part I. *Doctrinal Exposition*, 1:13-2:3
  1. Redemption, 1:13, 14
  2. Person of Christ, 1:15-19
  3. The Work of Christ, 1:20-23
  4. The Apostle's Participation in Christ's Program, 1:24-2:3

 Part II. *Doctrinal Polemicism*, 2:4-3:4
  1. Against false philosophy, 2:4-8
  2. In behalf of the Person and work of Christ, 2:9-15
  3. Resulting obligations, 2:16-3:4

 Part III. *Doctrinal Practice*, 3:5-4:6
  1. Practical appropriation of the death and resurrection of Christ, 3:5-17
  2. Appropriation of Christ's death and resurrection in domestic life, 3:18-4:1
  3. Appropriation of the death and resurrection in relation to the world, 4:2-6

 Part IV. *Personal Matters*, 4:7-17
  1. The mission of Tychicus and Onesimus, 4:7-9
  2. Salutations from Paul's associates, 4:10:14
  3. Paul's own greetings, 4:15
  4. The Laodicean message, 4:16, 17

 Conclusion, 4:18   M. F. U

Colt. *See* Animal Kingdom.

Comb. *See* Honeycomb; Bees, in Animal Kingdom.

Comfort (Heb. *nāḥăm, to comfort, give forth*

sighs; Gr. *parakaleō,* to *call alongside, help*). Our English word is from Lat. *confortare* (*con fortis*), *to strengthen much,* and means to ease, encourage, inspirit, enliven.

As pertaining to the life of believers it is the consolation and support which result from the gracious work of the indwelling Comforter, making clear to him his part in the great redemption, assuring him of the Saviour's love, and imparting peace and joy. The Greek noun is often translated *Consolation* (*q. v.*) in the New Testament.

Comforter, The. *See* Holy Spirit.

Coming of Christ, The. This great event, so prominent in both the Old and the New Testament, is a subject of much controversy, hostility and ignorance. It has been commonly set forth as one great cataclysmic event ending time and ushering in eternity with a concomitant so-called general resurrection and general judgment. This view, however, involves insuperable difficulties when the aggregate teaching of the Word is approached inductively. The various Scriptural statements can only be reconciled under the view that the coming of Christ will consist of two phases—a coming *for* His church, the body of Christ, (I Thess. 4:13-18, I Cor. 15:53, II Thess. 2:1, Rev. 3:10), and a coming *with* His church (Rev. 19:11-16). His coming for His church will result in its removal from the earthly scene to heaven. This climactic event will usher in a period of trouble at the end of the age, known as Daniel's seventieth week. At the conclusion of this period (at least seven years in length) in which human wickedness and rebellion will reach their acme, Christ will return with his glorified saints to conquer His enemies (Psa. 2; Zech. 14; Isa. 11) and to set up His millennial kingdom. This mediatorial Davidic kingdom will be the last of God's ordered ages in time. Only after it has run its course and Satan is loosed and all sinners judged (Rev. 20:11-15) will the eternal state be brought in. *M. F. U.*

Commandments, The Ten. *See* Decalogue.

Commerce. The exchange of products among men must have been coeval with the earliest history of mankind. The descendants of Cain in Genesis 4 initiated urban living, articles of art and craftsmanship (Gen. 4:21, 22), and engaged in commerce. The construction of the Noahic ark implied interchange of goods.

1. **Babylonia.** Among the early pre-Semitic Sumerians artistic craftsmanship and trade flourished as revealed by the exquisite jewelry and art objects recovered from the royal tombs at Ur dating no later than 2500 B. C. From the earliest levels of Mesopotamian

97. Drawing of a Painting, Syrian Ship Unloading in an Egyptian Harbor (ca. 1400 B. C.)

cities evidences of extended commerce are recovered. Babylonia was from most ancient times a great merchant nation dispensing wares by canal and river boat and by desert caravan. The city of Ur was a center of all kinds of manufacture, especially woolen goods. Babylonian merchants scattered widely, trafficking in not only their goods but peddling their arts and cuneiform system of writing. The Assyrian merchants invented the idea of checks—clay tablets denominating equivalent worth in silver. Ancient Sumerian and Akkadian kings imported cedar wood from Lebanon. The Fertile Crescent was a veritable beehive of camel caravans and river going ships. Early great syndicates of merchants controlled these trade routes stretching between Ur on the Lower Euphrates, Mari on the Middle Euphrates and Palmyra and Damascus westward, linking the lucrative trade marts of Egypt via Palestine-Syria.

2. **Phoenicia** was one of the greatest merchant nations of antiquity. Probably before 2400 B. C. they sailed boats between the coastal emporiums and Egypt. Through the centuries there was a continuous flow of commerce between Tyre, Sidon Gebal (Byblos) and Egypt. The latter city was especially known for the papyrus trade, lucrative commerce in Tyrian dyes and other commodities, as well as images of the goddess Astarte and the "Lady of Byblos." Tyre and Sidon as great commercial markets appear prominently in the Old Testament (Isa. 23:8, Ezek. 27).

98. Egyptian Bags of Money

3. **Egypt.** Egyptians early engaged in land and sea traffic. They imported cedar wood from Lebanon, pine from Cilicia, amber from the shores of the Baltic and tin to alloy copper for making bronze. Tiny Palestine was the bridge over which the ceaseless camel-caravan traffic flowed. Such a caravan laden with spices and perhaps nuts, balm and other commodities carried Joseph into Egypt (Gen. 39:1). Egyptian sailors plied the Red Sea. Caravan routes extended south carrying Egyptian grain in exchange for many exotic products.

4. **Israel.** Until Solomon's time the Hebrews were a simple agricultural and pastoral people. Solomon's diplomacy, foreign marriages, his control of the trade routes, his traffic in horses and chariots (I Kings 10:28, 29) between Kue (Cilicia) and Egypt, his construction of chariot cities and his voyages with Hiram of Tyre to Ophir (I Kings 9:26-28; 10:1-22), and his copper-mining in the Arabah and copper-refining at Ezion-Geber

99. Ancient Nile Boat

yielded the king an immense revenue and greatly extended Hebrew commerce. In 1938-40 Nelson Glueck excavated the remarkable copper furnace at modern Tell el-Kheleifeh (Ezion-Geber). It is now known that Solomon's smelting station had its counterparts in Phoenician metal refineries of Sardinia and Spain. Solomon's fleets putting out from Ezion-Geber laden with smelted ore brought back valuable goods obtainable in Arabian ports or from the adjacent coasts of Africa. Solomon's affluence was perhaps never equalled by his successors, but thereafter trade not only flourished through Palestine but the Jews enjoyed in their markets or *suks* exotic wares from Babylonia, Assyria, the Land of the Hittites, Egypt, Arabia and far-off Ophir. After the Babylonian captivity the commercial bent of the people was even more permanently fixed, and they never regained the simple pastoral nature or their economy of the earlier period.

5. **Greece.** c. 700 B. C. the Greeks became noted as great sea-going merchants in the Mediterranean world. As early as 650 B. C. they had trading posts in Egypt. Oil, wine, honey and exquisite Greek pottery were transported wherever ships could sail in the ancient civilized world. In this commercial activity they were preceded in the Aegean area by the highly developed culture and commerce of the Minoans and Mycenaeans—roughly contemporary with Moses and the period of the Judges.

6. **Aramaeans.** From the sixth century on Aramaean merchants became prominent all over the Fertile Crescent and they extended their commodities, culture and language so that the cumbersome cuneiform language was pushed out and later even Hebrew became a virtually dead language. As a result, by the first century A. D. Aramaic was the *lingua franca* of all S. W. Asia; it was therefore the native language of Jesus and His disciples.

M. F. U.

Communion. *See* Lord's Supper.

Communion of Saints, a part of Article iii of the Apostles' Creed: "I believe in the Holy Catholic Church, the communion of saints." The phrase is not found in the creeds of the Greek Church; and in the West we find it first in Faustus, Bishop of Reji, South Gaul, A. D. about 455. Among the views held are:

1. **Roman Catholic.** "The communion of saints consists in the union which binds together the members of the Church on earth, and connects the Church on earth with the Church suffering in purgatory and trium-

phant in heaven. The faithful on earth have communion with each other because they partake of the same sacraments, are under one head, and assist each other by their prayers and good works. . . . They communicate with the souls in purgatory by praying for them, . . . with the blessed in heaven by obtaining their prayers" (*Cath. Dict.*, s. v.).

2. **Protestant.** The Churches of the Reformation rejected these views, although Protestant definitions vary somewhat. (*a*) Luther declared the Church was the body of believers, who, by faith, were saints; hence the phrase was descriptive of the "Holy Church." So also the Reformed Church, at first in its symbols, the First Helvetic and the Scotch Confession of 1560. (*b*) Calvin understood it as a peculiarity of the Church. "It excellently expresses the character of the Church; as though it had been said that the saints are united in the fellowship of Christ on this condition, that whatever benefits God bestows upon them they should mutually communicate to each other." He is followed in the Geneva and Heidelberg Catechisms, and in the Westminster Catechism, which says: "All saints . . . being united to one another in love, they have communion in each other's gifts and graces, and are obliged to the performance of such duties, public and private, as do conduce to their mutual good, both in the inward and or ward man." (*c*) Christians have communion with the Father (I John 1:3; II Pet. 1:4), with Christ (I John 1:3; John 17:23), with the Holy Spirit (Phil. 2:1; II Cor. 13:14), with angels (Heb. 1:14; Luke 15:10; Matt. 17:10), with all saints on earth as the living members of Christ (John 1:7; Col. 2:19), and that they form one family with the saints who are in glory (Heb. 12:22, 23).

Community of Goods. The following picture of the early Church is given in Acts: "And all that believed were together, and had all things common," etc. (2:44, 45); "And the multitude of them that believed were of one heart and of one soul: neither said any of them that ought of the things which he possessed was his own; but they had all things common," etc. (4:32-34). From this we are not at liberty to assume in general "a distinguished beneficence, liberality, and mutual rendering of help," or "a prevailing willingness to place private property at the disposal of the Church;" but "a real community of goods" in the early Church at Jerusalem. In order the better to understand this community of goods the following characteristics must be noted: (1) It took place only in Jerusalem, and probably because of the poverty of the church in that city. There is no trace of it in any other church; on the contrary, the rich and poor continued to live side by side (I Cor. 16:2; II Cor. 9:5-7; I Tim. 6:17; James 5:1, sq.). (2) This community of goods was not ordained as a legal necessity, such as was practiced by the *Essenes* (*q. v.*). It was all left to the free will of the owners (Acts 5:3, 4), where the sin of Ananias was shown to be his *pretending* to give more than he really had done. (3) It was a continuation and extension of that community of goods which subsisted in the case of Jesus himself and his disciples, the wants of all being defrayed from a common purse; an earnest striving to carry out to the letter such commands as we find in Luke 12:33. Every age has witnessed an attempt to revive the Jerusalem dream of a life where should exist no distinctions of "order," and class, and where literally all things should be possessed in common; but every such attempt has failed as will present-day atheistic materialistic communism. The estimate of Paul and his brother apostles was the true one: they judged rightly when they declined to interfere with the established order of things among civilized peoples, or to recognize in any way a state of society which, however beautiful in theory, in practice would effectually bar all progress, and which would result only in confusion and misery.

Compassion. *See* Mercy.

Compel, the rendering in the A. V. (Matt. 5:41; 27:32; Mark 15:21) of the technical Greek term *'aggareuō*, literally, "to employ a courier." These couriers had authority to press into their service, in case of need, horses, vessels, even men they met. In Luke 14:23 the Greek word *'anakadzō* has the milder sense of *to urge*.

Conani'ah (kŏ-nȧ-nī'ȧ; *Jah has sustained*).

1. A Levite, ruler of the offerings and tithes in the time of Hezekiah (II Chron. 31:12, 13, A. V. "Cononiah").

2. One who made large offerings for the paschal sacrifices as renewed by Josiah (II Chron. 35:9).

Concision (Gr. *katatomē, cutting down, mutilation*), a contemptuous term used by Paul (Phil. 3:2) to denote the zealous advocates of circumcision; as though he would say, "Keep your eye on that boasted circumcision, or, to call it by its true name, 'concision,' or 'mutilation.'" In Gal. 5:12 he speaks more pointedly: "I would they (the same class of Judaizing teachers) were even *cut off*" i. e., done away with.

Concubine (Heb. *pīlĕgĕsh*, derivation uncertain), a secondary or inferior wife.

1. **Roman and Greek.** Among the Romans it was only at a comparatively late period that concubinage acquired any kind of legal sanction, and the *concubine* came to be substituted for the *mistress*. Among the Greeks, however, the distinction between wife and concubine was early established, the former being for the begetting of legitimate children and taking charge of the affairs of the house, the other for performing daily ministrations about the person.

2. **Hebrew.** Concubinage early came into general practice, for we read (Gen. 22:24) of Bethuel, the father of Rebekah, having not only his wife Milcah, but also a concubine, Reumah, who bore him four children. Indeed, concubinage substantially appeared when Abraham took Hagar as a sort of wife, by whom Sarah hoped he would have children—to be reckoned, in some sense, as her own, and to take rank as proper members of the family (Gen. 16:1, sq.). In the next generation of the chosen family we find no mention of a state of concubinage; Isaac seems to have had no partner to his bed but Rebekah,

and no children but Esau and Jacob. But the evil reappears in the next generation in an aggravated form; Esau multiplying wives at pleasure, and Jacob taking first two wives and then two concubines.

Nor was the practice ever wholly discontinued among the Israelites, for we see that the following men had concubines, viz., Eliphaz (Gen. 36:12), Gideon (Judg. 8:31), Saul (II Sam. 3:7), David (II Sam. 5:13), Solomon (I Kings 11:3), Rehoboam (II Chron. 11:21), Abijah (II Chron. 13:21). Indeed, in process of time concubinage appears to have degenerated into a regular custom among the Jews, and the institutions of Moses were directed to prevent excess and abuse by wholesome laws and regulations (Exod. 21:7-9; Deut. 21:10-14). The unfaithfulness of a concubine was considered as criminal (II Sam. 3:7, 8), and was punished with scourging (Lev. 19:20). In Judg. 19 the possessor of a concubine was called her "husband," her father is called the "father-in-law," and he the "son-in-law," showing how nearly the concubine approached to the wife.

Sometimes, to avoid debauchery, a female slave would be given to the son, and was then considered as one of the children of the house, and retained her rights as concubine even after the marriage of the son (Exod. 21:9, 10).

Christianity restores the sacred institution of marriage to its original character, and concubinage is ranked with fornication and adultery (Matt. 19:5; I Cor. 7:2). Still the practice of concubinage yielded only in the slowest and most gradual manner even to our Lord's explicit teachings. Long after the establishment of Christianity the state recognized concubinage as contradistinguished from marriage, though not in coexistence with it; and even as late as the Council of Toledo, A. D. 400, communion was allowed to persons living therein, while it excluded polygamists. For centuries concubinage was quite common among clergy and laity, being at first denied to the clergy, but only with general effect, about the period of the Reformation.

Concupiscence (Gr. *'epithumia*, a *longing*, Rom. 7:8; Col. 3:5), evil desire, generally in the sense of indwelling sin.

Condemnation. The Greek word; *krima*, is translated *judgment* and (often wrongly) *damnation*. Condemnation signifies the declaring an evildoer to be guilty; the punishment inflicted (I Cor. 11:32, 34); testimony by good example against malefactors (Matt. 12:41, 42). We use the word with the lighter meaning of censure, disapproval, blame, etc. As far as the justified believer is concerned, he faces no condemnation or judgment (Rom. 8:1). The guilt of his sin has been removed (Rom. chaps. 3-7) and he stands positionally "in Christ" and hence accepted "in the Beloved" (Eph. 1:6).

Conduit (Heb. *te'ālāh*, a *channel*, "watercourse," Job 38:25; "trench," I Kings 18:32-38). The aqueduct made by Hezekiah to convey the water from the upper pool of Gihon into the western part of Jerusalem (II Kings 18:17; 20:20; Isa. 7:3; 36:2). It seems to have been at first an open trench, but closed with masonry at the approach of the Assyrians. The aqueduct, though much injured, and not serviceable for water beyond Bethlehem, still exists; the water is conveyed from about two miles S. of Bethlehem, crossing the valley of Hinnom on a bridge of nine arches.

Coney. *See* Animal Kingdom.

Confection (Exod. 30:35), the perfume (v. 37) made by the temple apothecary.

Confectionary (I Sam. 8:13), a female perfumer.

Confession (Heb. from *yädäh*, literally, to *use*, i. e., extend the hand) is used in the Old Testament in the sense of acknowledging one's sin (Lev. 5:5; Job 40:14; Psa. 32:5). In the prayer of Solomon at the dedication of the temple he uses the expression "confess thy name" (I Kings 8:33, 35; II Chron. 6:24, 26), doubtless meaning the acknowledgment of Jehovah as the one against whom the Israelites might sin, and the justice of punishment meted out by him.

The Greek word rendered "confession" is *homologeō*, literally, to *say the same thing*, i. e., not to deny, and so to admit or declare one's self guilty of what he is accused. It is also used in the sense of a *profession*, implying the yielding or change of one's conviction (John 12:42; Acts 23:8; Rom. 10:9, 10; I Tim. 6:13, etc.).

Confusion of Tongues. *See* Babel; Tongues, Confusion of.

Congregation (Heb. *'ēdäh, assembly, mō'ĕd, festive gathering*).

1. **The Hebrew People** in its collective capacity under its peculiar aspects as a holy community, held together by religious rather than political bonds. Sometimes it is used in a broad sense as inclusive of foreign settlers (Exod. 12:19); but more properly, as exclusively appropriate to the Hebrew element of the population (Num. 15:15). Every circumcised Hebrew was a member of the congregation, and took part in its proceedings, probably from the time that he bore arms. It is important, however, to observe that he acquired no political rights in his individual capacity, but only as a member of a *house;* for the basis of the Hebrew polity was the house, whence was formed in an ascending scale the *family* or collection of houses, the *tribe* or collection of families, and the *congregation* or collection of tribes.

2. **The Comitia, or Legislative Assemblies.** (1) **Composition.** The persons composing the Comitia were judges, heads of families, genealogists (Heb. *shŏtĕrîm*), elders, and the princes of the tribes. These representatives formed the *congregation.* Comp. Exod. 12:3, "the congregation of Israel;" v. 21, "the elders of Israel;" further, Deut. 31:28, where we read, "the elders of your tribes and your officers;" and in v. 30, "the whole congregation of Israel." Thus both expressions are in every case identical, and *congregation* or *assembly* of Israel means the people of Israel present in their representatives.

(2) **Meetings.** The Comitia were convened by the judge or ruler, for the time being, and, in case of his absence, by the high priest (Josh. 23:1, 2; Num. 10:2-4; Judg. 20:27, 28). The place of assembling appears to have been at the door of the tabernacle (Num.

10:3; I Sam. 10:17); although some other place, commonly of some celebrity, was selected (Josh. 24:1; I Sam. 11:14, 15; I Kings 12:1). While in the wilderness the summons was given by blowing the holy trumpets; the blowing of *one* trumpet being the signal for a select convention, composed merely of the heads of the clans or associated families, and of the princes of the tribes; the blowing of two trumpets, the signal for convening the great assembly, composed not only of the above, but also of the elders, judges, and genealogists, and, in some instances, of the whole body of the people (Num. 10:2-4). When Israel was settled in Palestine notification of the assembly was sent by messengers.

(3) **Powers, etc.** In the congregation the rights of sovereignty were exercised, such as declaring war (Judg. 20:1, 11-14), making peace (Judg. 21:13-20), and concluding treaties (Josh. 9:15-21). Civil rulers and generals, and eventually kings, were chosen (I Sam. 10:17; II Sam. 5:1; I Kings 12:20). The congregation acted without instructions from the people, on their own authority, and according to their own views; still they were in the habit of proposing to the people their decisions for ratification (I Sam. 11:14; 15; comp. Josh. 8:33).

In the later periods of Jewish history the congregation was represented by the *Sanhedrin* (*q. v.*), and the term *Synagogue* (*q. v.*), applied in the Septuagint exclusively to the congregation, was transferred to the place of meeting. In Acts 13:43, however, it is used in a modern sense of an assemblage.

Congregation, Mount of (Heb. *hăr mō'ĕd*), supposed by some to refer to Mount Moriah as the site of the temple (Isa. 14:13), but Zion was neither a northern point of the earth, nor was it situated on the north of Jerusalem. "The prophet makes the king of Babylon speak after the general notion of his people, who placed the seat of the Deity on the summit of the northern mountains, which were lost in the clouds" (Delitzsch, *Com.*).

Congregation, Tabernacle of. *See* Tabernacle.

Coni'ah (cō-nī'à), another form of *Jehoiachin* (*q. v.*).

Cononi'ah (cŏn-ô-nī'à). *See* Conaniah.

Conscience (Lat. *conscientia, consciousness;* Gr. *suneidēsis*), the consciousness that a proposed act is or is not conformable to one's ideal of right, and manifesting itself in the feeling of *obligation* or *duty.* Conscience is not so much a distinct faculty of the mind, like perception, memory, etc., as an exercise of the judgment and the power of feeling, as employed with reference to moral truth. It implies moral sense "to discern both good and evil" (Heb. 5:14), and a feeling, more or less strong, of responsibility. Thus it will appear to be wrong to name conscience "the voice of God," although this is true, that the testimony of conscience certainly rests on a divine foundation, a divine law in man, the existence of which, its claims and judgments, are removed from his subjective control.

If a man knows his doing to be in harmony with this law his conscience is *good* (Acts 23:1; I Tim. 1:5, 19; Heb. 13:18; I Pet. 3:16, 21), *pure* (I Tim. 3:9; II Tim. 1:3), *void of offense.*

If his doing be *evil*, so also is his conscience, inasmuch as it is consciousness of such evil (Heb. 10:22); it is *defiled* (Tit. 1:15; I Cor. 8:7) when it is stained by evil deeds; or *seared with a hot iron* (I Tim. 4:2) when it is branded with its evil deeds, or cauterized, i. e., made insensible to all feeling.

Paul lays down the law that a man should follow his own conscience, even though it be weak; otherwise moral personality would be destroyed (I Cor. 8:10, sq.; 10:29, sq.).

Consecration, the rendering of several Hebrew and Greek words. It is the act of setting apart any thing or person to the worship or service of God.

1. **The Law of Moses** ordained that the firstborn, both of man and beast, should be consecrated to Jehovah; also that all the race of Abraham was in a peculiar manner consecrated to his worship, while the tribe of Levi and family of Aaron were more immediately consecrated to the service of God (Exod. 13:2; Num. 3:12; I Pet. 2:9). There were also consecrations, voluntary and of temporary or abiding nature (*see* Vow). Thus Hannah devoted her son Samuel to a lifetime service in the tabernacle (I Sam. 1:11); and David and Solomon appointed the Nethinim to a similar service in the temple (Ezra 8:20). The Hebrews sometimes devoted to the Lord their fields and cattle, spoils taken in war (Lev. 27:28, 29), vessels (Josh. 6:19), profits (Mic. 4:13), individuals (Num. 6:2-13; I Sam. 1:11; Luke 1:15), and nations (Exod. 19:6).

2. **In the New Testament** all Christians are consecrated persons. They are not only "a holy nation," but also "a royal priesthood" (I Pet. 2:9). The New Testament also recognizes special consecrations, as to the work of the Christian ministry, or to some particular service connected therewith (Acts 13:2, 3; I Cor. 12:28). *See* Ordination.

3. **Modern Use.** The uses of the term in modern times correspond in the main to the fundamental Scripture ideas. Thus in ecclesiastical phraseology it denotes the setting apart of a church for the purpose of worship, or the setting apart of a person to an office of the Christian ministry. The broadest and most important application is that which refers to the dedication of one's self to God, to be his possession and devoted to his service. Persons thus dedicating themselves are sanctified by the Spirit, and thus become in the true sense "consecrated." The Holy Spirit is both the seal and power of consecration. *See* Sanctification.

Consolation. *See* Comfort, Holy Ghost.

Constellations. *See* Astronomy, Star.

Consumption, end, consummation (Isa. 10:22, 23; 28:22). *See* Diseases.

Contention, immoderate strife or struggle in words to obtain an end, angry debate, discordant discussion, wrangling controversy, altercation, partisanship, putting one's self forward, factiousness (Prov. 13:10; 17:14; 18:6; Hab. 1:3; Acts 15:3, etc.; Rom. 2:18; see also Phil. 2:3; James 3:14, 16; in the plural, II Cor. 12:20; Gal. 5:20).

Contentment (Gr. *'autarkeia*). The word means "sufficiency," and is so rendered in II Cor. 9:8. It is that disposition of mind, through grace, in which one is independent of outward circumstances (Phil. 4:11; I Tim. 6:6, 8), so as not to be moved by envy (James 3:16), anxiety (Matt. 6:25, 34), and repining (I Cor. 10:10).

Contract. *See* Covenant.

Contrition (Heb. *däkä', bruised;* our English word is from Lat. *contritus*), penitence, humiliation, and grief for having sinned. The contrite soul is symbolized in the "bruised reed" (Matt. 12:20), which the Saviour "will not break." Contrition is the antecedent to pardon (Psa. 34:18; 51:17; Isa. 66:2). *Däkä'* is the word (Isa. 53:5, 10) rendered, "He was *bruised* for our iniquities;" "It pleased the Lord to *bruise* him." Roman Catholic theology names perfect repentance "contrition," and imperfect repentance "attrition."

Conversion (Gr. *'epistrophē*, Acts 15:3, rendered "conversion," literally, *turning toward*), a term denoting, in its theological use, the "turning" of a soul from sin unto God. The verb (*'epistrephō*) is sometimes rendered in the New Testament "to convert," sometimes simply "to turn." In its *active* sense it represents the action of one who is instrumental in "turning" or "converting" others (Luke 1:16; Acts 26:18; James 5:19, 21); *intransitively*, the action of men in their own conversion, i. e., the action of men empowered by divine grace to "turn" from sin "toward" God (Acts 3:19, R. V.).

The Hebrew terms of the Old Testament have a similar significance and use (Psa. 19:7; 51:13; Jer. 31:18; Ezek. 33:11). There is a measure of freedom in the Scripture use of these terms that should put us on our guard against attempts at too rigid definition. But in a general way it may be said that conversion in the Scriptures has a more exact and *restricted* meaning than is ascribed to it in common religious phraseology. Conversion is not justification, or regeneration, or assurance of reconciliation, however closely these blessings may be connected with true conversion. Like repentance and faith, both involved in conversion, conversion is an act of man which he is enabled to perform by divine grace.

Justification and regeneration are acts of God, which he invariably accomplishes for those who are converted, i. e., for those who, with repentance and faith, "turn" away from sin "toward" him (Acts 3:19). For a full and discriminating statement of the doctrine of conversion, see Pope, *Comp. Christian Doc.*, iii, 367-371. *See* Repentance.

Conviction (Gr. *'elegchō*, to convict, reprove, John 8:46, A. V. "convinceth." The R. V. changes the rendering to "convicteth." In I Cor. 14:24, A. V. "convinced" is in R. V. "reproved;" in Tit. 1:9 "convince" is changed to "convict," etc.). The meaning of conviction as a law term is *being found guilty*. In common language it means *being persuaded* or *convinced*. In *theology* it means *being condemned* at the bar of one's own conscience as a sinner in view of the law of God. It is the antecedent to repentance, and is often accompanied by a painful sense of exposure to God's wrath. It is the work of the Holy Spirit, showing the heinousness of sin and the soul's exposure to divine wrath. The means of conviction are ✸various: Gospel truth, the law read or heard, reflection, affliction, calamity, etc. It often comes suddenly, and may be stifled, as it surely is, if not heeded.

Convocation (Heb. *mǐqrä*, a *holy assembly*, i. e., a meeting of the people for the worship of Jehovah (Exod. 12:16, etc.). The following occasions were to be held as convocations: The *Sabbaths* (Lev. 23:2, 3); the *Passover*, the first and the last day (Exod. 12:16; Lev. 23:7, 8; Num. 28:18, 25); the *Pentecost, Feast of Weeks* (Lev. 23:21; Num. 28:26); the *Feast of Trumpets* (Lev. 28:24; Num. 29:1); the *Feast of Tabernacles*, first and last day (Lev. 23:35, 36; Num. 29:12); the one great *Fast*, the annual *Day of Atonement* (Lev. 23:27; Num. 29:7).

One great feature of the convocation was that no work was to be done upon these days, except what was necessary for the preparation of food; on the Sabbath even this was prohibited (Exod. 35:2, 3).

Cook, Cooking. *See* Food.

100. Coos

Co'os (kō'ŏs), a small island, formerly called Meropis, in the Aegean Sea (Acts 21:1), the birthplace of Hippocrates, celebrated for wines and beautiful stuffs. It is now called Stanchio, and has a population of about eight thousand. Paul spent the night on the island when on his voyage to Judea from Miletus.

Coping, the corbels, i. e., projecting stones on which the ends of timbers are laid (I Kings 7:9).

Copper. *See* Mineral Kingdom.

Coppersmith, a worker in any kind of metals; probably Alexander was so called (II Tim. 4:14) because copper was in such common use. *See* Handicrafts.

Cor. *See* Metrology, II, 1, (6).

Coral. *See* Mineral Kingdom.

Corban (kŏr'bán; Gr. *korban*, an *offering*), a name common to any sacred gift; the term in general use to denote sacrifice, its equivalent (Exod. 28:38) being *holy gifts*. All things or persons consecrated (or vowed) for religious purposes became *corban* and fell to the sanctuary. The Pharisees taught that as soon as a person had said to his father or mother, "Be it (or, It is) *corban* (i. e., devoted) whatever of mine shall profit thee" (Mark 7:11), he thereby consecrated all to God and was relieved from using it for his parents. This Jesus declared to be contradictory of the command which taught children to honor their parents. *See* Vows.

Cord, the rendering of several Hebrew words, the most comprehensive of which is *hĕbĕl*, from the root meaning to *twist*, hence the English *cable*. The term *cord* includes in its meaning rope, twine, thread, thongs, etc.

1. **The Material** of which cord was made varied according to the strength required. Flax was used for making ropes, string, and various kinds of twine; for large ropes, however, of ordinary quality and for common purposes, the fibers of the date tree were employed, as at the present day. The strongest rope was probably made of strips of camel hide, still used by the Bedouins for drawing water. Other materials are mentioned, as reeds, rushes, osier, etc.

2. **Uses.** The following uses of cord are mentioned: (1) For fastening a tent (Exod. 35:18; 39:40; Isa. 54:2). (2) For leading or binding animals, as a halter or rein (Psa. 118:27; Hos. 11:4). (3) For yoking them either to a cart (Isa. 5:18) or a plow (Job 39:10, A. V. "band"). (4) For binding prisoners (Judg. 15:13; Psa. 2:3; 129:4; Ezek. 3:25). (5) For bowstrings (Psa. 11:2) made of catgut; such are spoken of in Judg. 16:7 (A. V. "green withs," but more properly fresh or moist bowstrings). (6) For the ropes or "tacklings" of a vessel (Isa. 33:23). (7) For measuring ground (II Sam. 8:2; Psa. 78:55; Amos 7:17; Zech. 2:1); hence *cord* or *line* became an expression for an inheritance (Josh. 17:14; 19:9; Psa. 16:6; Ezek. 47:13), and even for any defined district (Deut. 3:4). (8) For fishing and snaring. (9) For attaching articles of dress, as the "wreathen chains," which were rather twisted cords, worn by the high priests (Exod. 28:14, 22, 24; 39:15, 17). (10) For fastening awnings (Esth. 1:6). (11) For attaching to a plummet. (12) For drawing water out of a well or raising heavy weights (Josh. 2:15; Jer. 38:6, 13).

3. **Figurative.** (1) To gird one's self with a cord was a token of sorrow and humiliation (I Kings 20:31-33; Job. 36:8). (2) To stretch out a cord over or about a city signifies to destroy it (Isa. 34:11; Lam. 2:8). Probably the meaning is that God brings about destruction with the same rigid exactness as that with which a builder carries out his well-considered plan. (3) Tent cords furnish several metaphors of stability (Isa. 33:20, "neither shall any of the cords thereof be broken," and Jer. 10:20, "all my cords are broken," signifying disaster). (4) "The cords of one's sins" (Prov. 5:22) are the consequences of wrongdoing. (5) As the tent supplied a favorite image of the human body, the cords which held it in its place represented the principle of life (Job 4:21; Eccles. 12:6). The "silver cord" (Eccles. 12:6) is supposed to be the spinal marrow, and is thought to refer to the silk and silver cord by which lamps were suspended, and the breaking of which allowed the lamp to be dashed to pieces. (6) A "threefold cord," i. e., one of three strands, is the symbol of union, the combination of many (Eccles. 4:12). (7) "I drew them with cords of a man" (Hos. 11:4) is an expression signify-

ing that God had employed *humane methods*, such as men employed when inducing others, as, for instance, a father guiding a child, who is learning to walk, with leading strings.

Core (kō'rê), a mode of Grecizing (Jude 11) the name *Korah* (*q. v.*).

Coriander. *See* Vegetable Kingdom.

Cor'inth (kŏr'ĭnth), a prominent Greek city.

1. **Physical Description.** Corinth was located upon an isthmus between the gulfs of Lepanto and Aegina connecting the Peloponnesus and the mainland, forty miles W. of Athens. It had two harbors, Cenchreae on the east and Lechaeum on the west. Its citadel, called Acrocorinthus, was built upon the rock two thousand feet above the level of the sea.

2. **History.** It had a mixed population of Romans, Greeks, and Jews. It was wealthy, luxurious, immoral, and vicious. In 146 B. C. the Romans destroyed it. Julius Caesar restored it, 46 B. C. Gallio, brother of Seneca, was proconsul when Paul first visited it. Upon the second visit Paul wrote his Epistle to the Romans, probably 58 A. D. The Gentile element prevailed in the Christian Church in Corinth. In 1462 the Turks gained possession of it and held it till the Greek revolution. Its former glory has entirely passed away. A miserable village called Gortho exists amid the ancient ruins. Paul's visit to Corinth is narrated in Acts 18. The American School of Classical Studies excavated there for thirty seasons, uncovering much of the city of Paul's day.

101. Modern Corinth

Corin'thian (kŏ-rĭn'thĭ-ản), an inhabitant of Corinth (*q. v.*).

Corinthians, First Epistle. This letter belongs to the second group of the Pauline Epistles, along with II Corinthians, Galatians and Romans. These are the greatest of the Pauline writings and deal with the most elevated themes that can engage the human mind.

1. **Authorship.** The Pauline authorship of I Corinthians is abundantly attested from the first century onward. Clement of Rome, the Didache, Ignatius, Polycarp, Hermas, Justin Martyr, Athenagoras, all lend their voice in support of the genuineness of the epistle. Irenaeus contains more than sixty quotations from I Corinthians; Clement of Alexandria quotes it more than 130 times; Tertullian quotes some 400 times. First Corinthians stands at the head of the Pauline Epistles in the Muratorian canon. Internal evidence is also abundant (cf. 1:1; 3:4; 6:22; 16:21). The way the book dovetails with the history in Acts also confirms it.

102. Bema or Judgment Seat at Corinth on Which Gallio Stood when Hearing Paul's Case

2. **Occasion and Date.** The occasion of the epistle was a letter of inquiry from Corinth concerning marriage and the eating of meats offered to idols (I Cor. 7:1; 8:1-13). This led the Apostle to write concerning the deepening divisions, increasing contentions and unjudged sin in the church (I Cor. 1:10-12; 5:1). The factions were due not to the open heresies, but to the carnality of the Corinthians, and to their being carried away by admiration for Greek wisdom and eloquence. The moral pollution of their city, which was notorious, was a continual temptation to them. Minor disorders took the form of abuse of spiritual gifts, particularly tongues and the sign gifts (I Cor. 14:1-28). False ideas concerning the resurrection were also corrected (chap. 15). The date of the Epistle varies with critical opinion. We know it was written from Ephesus (I Cor. 16:8, 9). It was seemingly written in the latter half of Paul's three-year ministry in that city (Acts 20:31; cf. 19:8-22). The spring of A. D. 54 or 55 is perhaps correct, although some would date it as late as A. D. 59.

3. **Purpose and Outline.** In correcting the current evils in the church, the Apostle presents the contents in the following plan:

Introduction, 1:1-9

Part I. *Rebuke of their Divisions*, 1:10-4:21

Part II. *The Problem of their Sensual Immorality*, chaps. 5-7

  1. Judgment of incest, 5:1-13

  2. Parenthetical—The law suits in heathen courts, 6:1-11

  3. Fornication and the sacredness of the body, 6:12-20

  4. Marriage and divorce, chap. 7

Part III. *The Problem of Food Offered to Idols*, 8:1-11:1

  1. General tenets, chap. 8

  2. The precept of forebearance, chap. 9

  3. Illustration from ancient Israel, 10:1:13

  4. Rebuke of idolatry, 10:14-22

  5. Christian liberty, 10:23-11:1

Part IV. *Problem of Public Worship*, 11:2-14:40

  1. Dress of women in public worship, 11:2-16

2. Regulations of the Lord's Supper, 11:17-34
3. Regulations concerning spiritual gifts, chaps. 12:14

Part V. *Doctrine of the Resurrection*, chap. 15

Part VI. *Practical Concerns of Paul*, 16:1-8 Conclusion, 16:19-24

103. Road from Corinth to Western Harbor of Lechaeum

Corin'thians, Second Epistle. This great epistle presents the vindication of Paul's apostleship and sets forth in a remarkable way the glory of the Christian ministry. The epistle discloses the heart of Paul and his conduct under physical weakness and persecution from the legalizers.

1. **Authenticity.** The internal evidence of II Corinthians vividly attests its genuineness. The distinctive elements of Pauline theology and eschatology are clearly seen throughout. However, the letter is not doctrinal or didactic, but intensely personal. Its absorbing interest is a recital of the events with which the apostle and the Corinthians were struggling at the time. A great deal is lacking concerning the circumstances calling forth the epistle, but the references to these events which do exist are so manifestly made in good faith that it is difficult for unbelief to reject Pauline authorship. External evidence, while not so clear as in the case of I Corinthians, yet is unambiguous in establishing the existence and the use of the letter, especially in the second century. Although Clement of Rome is silent, the epistle is quoted by Polycarp. It is referred to in the Epistle of Diognetus 5:12. It is sufficiently corroborated by Iraneus, Theophilus, Athenagoras, Tertullian and Clement of Alexandria.

2. **Date.** It was written from Macedonia, likely from Philippi, in the fall of 54 or 55 A. D., the same year in which I Corinthians was written or in the autumn of the succeeding year.

3. **Connection with I Corinthians.** After sending I Corinthians, it seems evident that news reached the apostle of growing opposition led by the Judaizing party. Paul was constrained to pay an immediate visit and found the reports only too true. Perhaps before the congregation at Corinth he was openly flouted. Returning to Ephesus he wrote a severe epistle which he sent on through the hand of Titus. Before Titus could return, events took a disastrous turn at Ephesus and Paul had to flee at the peril of his life. He went to Troas, but unable to await patiently there for tidings of the Corinthian issue, he crossed into Macedonia and met Titus there, possibly in Philippi. The news, happily, was reassuring. He then wrote again in the present epistle and sent it on by Titus and others.

3. **Value.** The letter is chiefly of value in showing us the concern of the apostle for his converts. In the circumstances of the epistle we find the intensity of his emotions and his great love for his converts. II Corinthians is also extremely valuable in setting forth the lofty character and the challenge of the Christian ministry. Paul sets forth his high calling as the most glorious work in which a man can engage. The Apostle himself received the ministry as divine and he accepted it with supreme devotion. Through all the sufferings, testings and buffetings which he suffered, we yet discern his triumphing in Christ.

4. **Outline.** The epistle may be divided into three parts:

Part I. Paul's guiding principle of conduct, 1:1-7:16

Part II. The collection for the poor saints at Jerusalem, 8:1-9:15

Part III. Paul's defense of his apostolic ministry, 10:1-13:14

Cormorant. *See* Animal Kingdom.

Cornelius (kôr-nē'lĭ-ŭs), a devout Roman proselyte, the first representative Gentile introduced to the gospel of grace (Acts 10:2).

1. **Personal History.** He was probably of the *Cornelii*, a noble and distinguished family at Rome (Acts 10:2).

2. **His Spiritual Status.** Was Cornelius saved before Peter's visit? A careful answer to this must be that he was *not* saved (Acts 11:14), his devotion, alms, prayers and visions (Acts 10:2) merely signifying that he was a Jewish proselyte. If he were regenerated, he most certainly was not baptized, indwelt and sealed by the Holy Spirit as every believer is in this age.

3. **Dispensational Importance.** The case of Cornelius marked the giving of the Holy Spirit to the Gentiles to undertake for them every ministry committed to Him in this present age, namely, the ministry of regeneration, baptism, indwelling, sealing and filling. The scene at Caesarea pictures the first representative Gentiles being baptized into the mystical body of Christ and becoming "fellow heirs" with the Jews, and partakers of His promise in Christ by the gospel (Eph. 3:6). In the book of Acts the gospel had now gone to Jew (Acts 2), to the racially mongrel Samaritan (Acts 8), and now to the Gentile (Acts 10). With the introduction to the latter the normal order of the age is established, when *every* believer, upon no other condition than simple faith in the finished redemptive work of Christ, is regenerated, baptized into the body of Christ, indwelt perpetually, sealed eternally, with the added privilege and duty of being filled continually as conditions for filling are complied with. Moreover, Cornelius' case marked the introduction of the gospel to the Gentiles. For the last time Peter used the "keys of the kingdom of heaven" (cf. Acts 2:14; 8:14, 15). He is the one who is sent to Cornelius, preaches the sermon and unlocks the message of grace (Acts 10:34 f.).

Without this simple dispensational distinction in the case of Cornelius as well as in the case of the pivotal passages, Acts 2 and Acts 8, the doctrine of the Holy Spirit in the Acts has become a grand jumble in modern cultism. For full discussion see Merrill F. Unger, *The Baptizing Work of the Holy Spirit* (1953), pp. 53-76.   —M. F. U

Corner Gate. This gate was at the northwest corner of Jerusalem (II Kings 14:13; II Chron. 25:23). See Jerusalem.

Corner Stone (Job 38:6; Isa. 28:16), the stone at the corner of two walls and uniting them; specifically, the stone built into one corner of the foundation of an edifice as the actual or nominal starting point of a building. From a comparison of passages we find mention of "a stone for foundations" (Isa. 28:16), "a stone for a corner" (Jer. 51:26, from which it would appear that corner stones were placed in different positions as regards elevation). The expressions "the head of the corner" (Psa. 118:22) and the "headstone" (Zech. 4:7) seem to warrant the conclusion that the "corner stone" is a term equally applicable to the chief stone at the top and that in the foundation.

 Figurative. The phrase "corner stone" is sometimes used to denote any principal person, as the princes of Egypt (Isa. 19:13, margin). Christ is called the "corner stone" in reference to his being the foundation of the Christian faith (Eph. 2:20) and the importance and conspicuousness of the place he occupies (Matt. 21:42; I Pet. 2:6).

Cornet. See Music, Instrumental.

Correction (Heb. *yāsăr*, to *instruct, chastise*; *yākăh*, to *manifest, reason with, reprove*). In "He that *chastiseth* the heathen, shall not he *correct*?" (Psa. 94:10) both Hebrew words are used in the above order. The man is styled happy whom God thus *correcteth* (Job 5:17). The Scriptures are for *correction* (II Tim. 3:16). In the Bible the word has the same double meaning as in other English literature, viz., *to reform, rectify*, free from errors, and to chastise or punish; the act of *correcting*. See Chastisement.

Corruption, the rendering of several Hebrew and Greek words, signifying (1) The decay of the body (Job 17:14; Psa. 16:10, etc.). (2) The blemishes which rendered an animal unfit for sacrifice (Lev. 22:25). (3) The demoralization of heart and life through sin (Gen. 6:12; Deut. 9:12), resulting in those sinful habits and practices which defile and ruin men (Rom. 8:21; II Pet. 2:12, 19). (4) Everlasting ruin (Gal. 6:8).

Corruption, Mount of, a hill near Jerusalem, where Solomon established high places for the worship of Ashtoreth, Chemosh, and Milcom, afterward overthrown by Josiah (II Kings 23:13). Tradition locates it at the eminence immediately south of the Mount of Olives.

Co'sam (kō'săm), the son of Elmodam and father of Addi, in the line of Joseph, the husband of Mary (Luke 3:28).

Cottage (1) A *hut* made of boughs (Isa. 1:8; Heb. *sŭkkăh*), for the purpose of temporary shelter. Being of slight structure, when the fruits were gathered they were either taken down or blown down by the winds of winter

(Job 27:18, "*booth*"). (2) Another Hebrew word (*mᵉlūnăh*), signifies a night lodge, or impermanent place of dwelling (from *lūn, to spend the night*). Usually merely the rough hut in which the vintager was sheltered (Isa. 1:8). In Isa. 24:20 it is a hanging bed. (3) The cottages mentioned in Zephaniah (2:6; Heb. *kᵉrōth*, literally, *diggings*) probably were excavations made by the shepherds as a protection against the sun.

Couch. See Bed.

Coulter (Heb. *'ēth*, I Sam. 13:20, 21), according to Isa. 2:4, Mic. 4:3, and Joel 3:10), is an iron instrument used in agriculture, the majority of the ancient versions rendering it *plow-share*.

Council. In the Old Testament *council* is the rendering of the Heb. *rĭgmäh'*, literally, a *heap* (Psa. 68:27), a throng or company of persons. Two Greek words are thus rendered in the New Testament:

 1. A consultation of persons (Matt. 12:14, *sumboulion*). In Acts 25:12 reference is made to a board of assessors or advisors, with whom the governors of the provinces took counsel before rendering judgment.

 2. Any assembly for the purpose of deliberating or adjudicating (*sunedrion*, a *sitting together*). Among the Jews these councils were: (1) The Sanhedrin. (2) The lesser courts (Matt. 10:17; Mark 13:9), of which there were two at Jerusalem and one in each town of Palestine. See Law, Administration of.

Counselor. In general, an adviser upon any matter (Prov. 11:14; 15:22; II Chron. 25:16, etc.), especially the king's state adviser (II Sam. 15:12; Ezra 7:28; I Chron. 27:33, etc.), and one of the chief men of the government (Job. 3:14; 12:17; Isa. 1:26; 3:3, etc.). In Mark 15:43 and Luke 23:50 the word probably designates a member of the Sanhedrin.

Coupling (Heb. *hăbăr*, to *join*), of curtains (Exod. 26:4, 5, 10; 28:27; 36:11, etc.), and wooden beams for fastening a building (II Chron. 34:11).

Course. This word is used in Scripture in the sense of *advance, progress* (II Thess. 3:1), *race*, a *career* (II Tim. 4:7), *path, direction* (Psa. 82:5), *running* as of a horse (Jer. 8:6; 23:10).

Course of Priests and Levites. The number of the priests and Levites had so increased that David divided them into twenty-four classes or orders, with a president at the head of each class. The order in which each of these classes was to take its turn was determined by lot, a new one being appointed every week, their duties beginning with one Sabbath and ending on the next (II Kings 11:9; II Chron. 23:8; see also I Chron. 24:1, where the twenty-four orders are enumerated; and 27: 1, sq.). See Levites, Priests.

Court (Heb. usually *hāṣēr*), an open inclosure; applied in Scripture mostly to the inclosures of the tabernacle and Temple (*q. v.*). It also means a yard of a prison (Neh. 3:25; Jer. 32:3), of a private house (II Sam. 17:18), and of a palace (II Kings 20:4; Esth. 1:5, etc.).

 "Court for owls" (Isa. 34:13) is rendered by Delitzsch (*Com.*, in loc.) "pasture for ostriches." He says that the Hebrew word corresponds to the Arabic for green, a green field, and takes it in the sense of a grassy place, such as is frequented by ostriches. In Amos (7:13) the Heb. word for "house" is rendered "court."

In the New Testament the Gr. *aulē* designates an open court (Rev. 11:2), while "kings' courts" is the rendering of the Greek word *basileion*, a *palace. See* House.

Courts, Judicial. *See* Law, Administration of.

Cousin, the rendering of the Gr. *sungenēs*, a blood relative or "kinsman," as elsewhere translated.

Covenant (Heb. *bᵉrith, cutting*), the term applied to various transactions between God and man, and man and his fellow-man. It is also rendered "league" (Josh. 9:6, 7, 11, etc.; Judg. 2:2; II Sam. 3:12, 13, 21; 5:3; I Kings 5:12, etc.), "confederacy" (Obad. 7). In the New Testament the word *diathēkē, disposition* or *will* respecting a person or thing, is used; sometimes it is translated "*Testament*" (*q. v.*), at other times "covenant."

1. **Application of the Term.** (1) Properly, of a compact between man and man; either between tribes or nations (I Sam. 11:1; Josh. 9:6, 15), or between individuals (Gen. 21:27), in which each party bound himself to fulfill certain conditions, and was promised certain advantages. In making covenants God was solemnly invoked as a witness (Gen. 31:50), whence the expression "a covenant of Jehovah" (I Sam. 20:8; comp. Jer. 34:18, 19; Ezek. 17:19), and an oath was sworn (Gen. 21:31). Accordingly, a breach of covenant was regarded as a heinous sin (Ezek. 17:12-20). The marriage compact is called "the covenant of God" (Prov. 2:17). As a witness to the covenant a gift was presented (Gen. 21:30), or a heap of stones set up (Gen. 31:52). (2) Improperly, of a covenant between God and man. As man is not in the position of an independent covenanting party, such a covenant is not strictly a mutual compact, but a promise on the part of God to arrange his providences for the welfare of those who should render him obedience.

2. **Covenants Mentioned.** The following covenants are mentioned in Scripture: (1) **The covenant with Noah,** in which God assured Noah that judgment would not again come to men in the form of a flood; and that the recurrence of the seasons and of day and night should not cease (Gen. 9; Jer. 33:20). (2) **The covenant with Abraham.** The condition of this covenant was that Abraham was to leave all his country, kindred, and father's house, and to follow the Lord into the land which he would show him. The promise was a fourfold blessing: (1) Increase into a numerous people; (2) Material and spiritual prosperity—"I will bless thee;" (3) The exaltation of Abraham's name—"make thy name great;" (4) Abraham was not only to be blessed by God, but to be a blessing to others, implicitly by the coming of the Messiah through his descendants (Gen. 12:1-3). Later this covenant was renewed, and Abraham was promised a son and numerous posterity (Gen. 15). About fourteen years after the making of the covenant it was renewed, with a change of his name and the establishment of circumcision, which was to be the sign of accepting and ratifying the covenant

Gen. 17). (3) **The covenant with Israel.** This took place at Sinai, when the people had intimated their acceptance of the words of the covenant as found in the Ten Commandments (Exod. 34:28; 24:3), and promised to keep the same. Their obedience to the commands of the law was to be rewarded by God's constant care of Israel, temporal prosperity, victory over enemies, and the pouring out of his Spirit (Exod. 23:20, sq.). The seal of this covenant was to be circumcision, and was called "Jehovah's covenant" (Deut. 4:13). It was renewed at different periods of Jewish history (Deut. 29; Josh. 24; II Chron. chaps. 15, 23, 29, 34; Ezra 10; Neh. chaps. 9, 10. (4) **Covenant with David.** This was in reality but another and more specific form of the covenant with Abraham, and had for its main object to mark with greater exactness the line through which the blessing promised in the Abrahamic covenant was to find accomplishment. The seed-royal thenceforth was to be in the house of David (II Sam. 7:12; 22:51), and, especially in connection with the One who was to be preeminently the child of promise in that house, all good, first to Israel, and then to all nations, should be realized (Psa. 2 and 22; Isa. 9:6, 7, etc.).

In adaptation to human thought such covenants were said to be confirmed by an oath (Deut. 4:31; Psa. 89:3).

3. **Ceremonies.** Covenants were not only concluded with an oath (Gen. 26:28; 31:53; Josh. 9:15; II Kings 11:4), but, after an ancient custom, confirmed by slaughtering and cutting a victim into two halves, between which the parties passed, to intimate that if either of them broke the covenant it would fare with him as with the slain and divided beast (Gen. 15:9, sq.; Jer. 34:18, sq.). Moreover, the covenanting parties were wont to have a common meal (Gen. 26:30, sq.; 31:54; comp. II Sam. 3:20 with v. 12), or at least to partake of salt (some grains of it). *See* Covenant of Salt.

Among the Medes, Lydians, Armenians, Arabs, Scythians, and other nations the parties to a treaty were wont to draw blood from their veins and to drink or lick it. This custom was unknown to the Israelites.

According to the Mosaic ritual, the blood of the victim was divided into halves; one half was sprinkled upon the altar, and the other upon the people (Exod. 24:6, sq.). The meaning of this seems to be that, in the sprinkling of the blood upon the altar, the people were introduced into gracious fellowship with God and atonement made for their sin. Through the sprinkling of the blood upon the people Israel was formally consecrated to the position of God's covenant people.

Covenant of Salt (Heb. *bᵉrith mĕläh*). Covenanting parties were accustomed to partake of salt, to make the covenant a *covenant of salt* (Num. 18:19; II Chron. 13:5), i. e., inviolably sure. The meaning appears to have been that the salt, with its power to strengthen food and keep it from decay, symbolized the unbending truthfulness of that self-surrender to the Lord embodied in the sacrifice, by which all impurity and hypocrisy were repelled.

Covenant, The New. In the New Testament we read of only two covenants—the *new* and the *old*, the former brought in and established by Christ, and the latter in consequence ceasing to exist. The *old*, i. e., the covenant of law, with all its outward institutions and ritualistic services, is regarded as *old* because its full and formal ratification took place before the other. In *germ* the *new* covenant (or that of *grace*) existed from the first; and partial exhibitions of it have been given all through the world's history. It was involved in the promise of recovery at the fall.

Covering the Head in prayer (I Cor. 11:4-6). "The Jewish men prayed with the head covered, nay, even with a veil before the face. Greek usage required that the head should be bare on sacred occasions; and this commended itself to Paul as so entirely in accordance with the divinely appointed position of man (v. 3) that for the man to cover his head seemed to him to cast dishonor on that position. His head ought to show to all (and its being uncovered is the sign of this) that no man, but, on the contrary, Christ, and through him God himself, is Head (Lord) of the man. . . . A woman, when praying, was to honor her head by having a sign upon it of the authority of her husband, which was done by having it covered; otherwise she dishonored her head by dressing, not like a married wife, from whose headdress one can see that her husband is her head, but like a loose woman, with whose *shorn* head the uncovered one is on a par" (Meyer, *Com.*, in loc.). The above command does not refer to private or family prayer.

Covert for the Sabbath. *See* Sabbath, Covert for.

Covetousness (Heb. *ḥâmăd*, to *desire; bĕṣă', dishonest gain;* Gr. *pleoneksia, the wish to have more*), an inordinate desire for what one has not, which has its basis in discontentment with what one has. It has an element of lawlessness, and is sinful because contrary to the command, "Be content with such things as ye have" (Heb. 13:5), because it leads to "trust in uncertain riches," to love of the world, to forgetfulness of God, and is idolatry (Col. 3:5), setting up wealth instead of God. It ranks with the worst sins (Mark 7:22; Rom. 1:29). Our Lord especially warns against it (Luke 12:15), as does St. Paul (Eph. 5:3, etc.). A man may be *covetous,* eager to obtain money, and not *avaricious* or *penurious,* i. e., unwilling to part with money, or *sordid* and *niggardly,* i. e., mean in his dealings. He may or may not be miserly.

The verb is also used in a good sense (I Cor. 12:31).

Cow. *See* Animal Kingdom.

Coz (kŏz; a *thorn*), the father of Anub and others of the posterity of Judah (I Chron. 4:8), where, however, his own parentage is not stated, unless he be a son or brother of Ashur (in v. 5).

Coz'bi (kŏz'bĭ; *false*), the daughter of Zur, a Midianitish prince. While in the act of committing lewdness with Zimri, an Israelitish chief, she was slain by Phinehas, who thrust a javelin through them both (Num. 25:15, 18), B. C. about 1401.

Crackling (Heb. *qōl, voice,* i. e., noise). "The crackling of thorns under a pot" (Eccles. 7:6) is a proverbial expression for a roaring but quickly extinguished fire.

Cracknel, a kind of biscuit baked hard and punctured with holes, such as the wife of Jeroboam sent to the prophet Ahijah (I Kings 14:3). The original word, in nearly the same form, is rendered "moldy" in Josh. 9:5, 12.

Craft, Craftsman. *See* Handicraft.

Craftiness, Crafty (Heb. *'ărăm,* to *be bare, cunning, subtilty;* Gr. *panourgia, adroitness, unscrupulousness*) are terms used in the Bible as applied to the sly, subtle, wily, deceitful, and fraudulent (Job. 5:12, 13; Psa. 83:3; Luke 20:23; I Cor. 3:19; II Cor. 4:2; 12:16, etc.).

Crane. *See* Animal Kingdom.

Creation, the work of God in bringing into existence the universe, including both the material and the spiritual worlds; in a more restricted sense, the bringing into existence and into its present condition the earth and the system to which it belongs.

1. **Christian View.** According to Christian doctrine, God alone is eternal. The system or systems of the material universe, as well as matter itself, also spiritual beings, except God, had a beginning. They were absolutely created, made "out of nothing," by the power of the almighty will. The first sentence of the Apostles' Creed is to be taken in its broadest and deepest sense, "I believe in God the Father Almighty, Maker of heaven and earth."

2. **Biblical.** The record of the creation in Genesis relates principally in its details to the creation of the earth, or the system to which the earth belongs, and to the creation of man. The first words of the record, however, at least suggest a still broader conception. Taking the account as a whole, we have revealed a succession of creative acts, constituting together one great process of creation. And whatever interpretations have been given as to the various stages of this process, or the "days" of creation, or of other particulars, the fact of chief import remains unclouded—that to God is ascribed the work of bringing into existence, by the free exercise of his creative power, the world and all orders of beings that are therein. This is the uniform teaching of the Old Testament Scriptures (Psa. 33:6; Isa. 45:18; Jer. 10:12, etc.). The doctrine of the New Testament upon this subject is not merely a repetition, but in some respects a development or further unfolding, of that contained in the Old. Thus, with greater explicitness the existence of superhuman intelligence is attributed in the New Testament Scriptures to divine creative power. As the heavenly and spiritual world comes more clearly into view in the New Testament, along with this comes more clearly the declaration that all spiritual beings, outside of God, owe their origin to him. Also, that creative "Word of the Lord," upon which such stress is laid in the Old Testament, in the New Testament is identified with Christ. The second person of the Trinity is revealed as the one most directly connected with the work of creation. In him creation has its explanation and its end (see John 1:3; I Cor. 8:6; Eph. 3:9-11; Heb. 1:2; 2:10; Col. 1:16).

3. **Antichristian Views.** It is requisite to distinguish clearly between Christian doctrine upon this subject and antichristian opposing theories. Particularly should be noted: (1) **Materialism**, which assumes the eternal existence of matter and regards matter as the fundamental principle of all things. This doctrine is atheistic. (2) **Pantheism**, which identifies the works of God, or the universe which God has created, with God himself—a form of speculation which often exercised a powerful charm over a certain class of minds, but which is, like materialism, essentially immoral. (3) **Emanationism**, which regards the things created, not as really creations produced by the free exercise of divine power, but as emanating or flowing forth from God as a stream issues from its fountain. This view regards God as merely passive. Logically, creation would be without beginning or end. No room is left for design in creation, to say nothing of other objections equally serious. (4) **Evolution**, a theory which, in its rigid materialistic form, has been taught so as to deny the Christian doctrine of creation. Abridged and modified forms of the theory, however, are held by many Christian scientists and theologians. Evolution becomes antichristian only when it seeks to explain the world and the existing order of things without recognizing the creative power and work of God. This it has often attempted, though in vain.

4. **Importance of Doctrine.** True doctrine upon this subject is both theoretically and practically of fundamental importance; (1) In relation to God, whose eternal greatness and majesty can be felt by us only when we conceive of him as "before all worlds" and the Creator of all. (2) Here, first of all, true religion establishes its claim upon us; for He who has created us and all things may rightfully require our worship and service. (3) In the creation we find also a true revelation, and he who recognizes this must admit the possibility and even the probability of more particular revelations. The objection to miracles in connection with revelation vanishes when one begins by accepting the miracle of creation. (4) This doctrine underlies all true repose of faith; for only when we apprehend the broad and wholesome teaching of the Scriptures upon this subject can we fully commit ourselves unto God "as unto a faithful Creator."

5. **Literature.** See works upon systematic theology, particularly Van Oosterzee's *Christian Dogmatics*, Pope's *Compendium of Christian Theology*, Hodge's *Systematic Theology*, Tayler Lewis's *Six Days of Creation*, Hugh Miller's *Testimony of the Rocks*, Janet's *Final Causes*. —E. McC.

Creature (Heb. *nĕphĕsh*, a *breathing* creature; Gr. *ktisis*, a making, *thing made*; *ktisma*, *formation*).

1. In Old Testament use "creature" is a general term for any animal (Gen. 1:21, 24, etc.).

2. In New Testament: (1) A term for the whole creation or for any created object, e. g., "Every creature of God is good" (I Tim. 4:4); "Nor height, nor depth, nor any other creature" (Rom. 8:39, etc.). (2) Humanity individually or collectively. "Preach the Gospel to every creature" (Mark 16:15); "The creature was made subject," etc. (Rom. 8:20, 21).

Creature, Living (Ezek. 1:5, sq.; 10:15, 17, 20). *See* Cherubim.

Creditor. *See* Debt, Loan.

Creed (*credere*, to believe), a statement of articles of belief which are fundamental and have been disputed. In the early Eastern Church a summary of this sort was called *the lesson* (Gr. *mathēma*), because the catechumens were required to learn it; also sumbalon (*symbolum*), a mark, token, or badge, as a seal ring—the proof of orthodoxy, whereby each Church may know its own members; also *canon*, the *rule*, viz., of faith.

The *first* object of creeds was to distinguish the Church from the world, from Jews and pagans. The earliest formularies contained simply the leading doctrines and facts of the Christian religion. The *second* object was to distinguish between persons professing the Christian faith, i. e., those who retained the apostolic doctrine, and those who had departed therefrom and fallen into errors on important points. The *Apostles' Creed* is of the first class, the *Nicene* and *Athanasian* of the second.

The Apostles' Creed is an early summary of the Christian faith, in which all Christian Churches, Greek, Roman, and Protestant, agree. By many writers of the Church of Rome it is held to have been written by the apostles themselves, but it is now generally admitted that, in its present form at least, it is not of earlier date than the fourth century.

The Athanasian Creed was supposed to have been drawn up by Athanasius, in the fourth century. But it so plainly rejects the errors of the Nestorians, Eutychians, and Monothelites, that it must have been written after the promulgation of these heresies.

The Nicene Creed was adopted at the Council of Nice, A. D. 325, and enlarged at the second Council of Constantinople, A. D. 381, by which the faith of the Church respecting the person of Christ was set forth in opposition to certain errors, especially Arianism. The Nicene Creed is held to be of authority in the Greek and Roman Churches, and is admitted by most Protestant Churches.

Creek (Gr. *kolpos, bosom*), an inlet from the sea, e. g., St. Paul's Bay, island of *Malta* (*q. v.*), where the apostle was wrecked (Acts 27:39).

Creeping Thing (Heb. *shĕrĕs*, an active mass of minute animals; or, Heb. *rĕmĕs, creeping*), a term used in Scripture (Gen. 1:24; 6:7, etc.) to designate reptiles, insects, aquatic creatures, and the smaller mammals.

Cres'cens (krĕs'ĕnz; *growing*), an assistant of the apostle Paul, who left Rome for Galatia (II Tim. 4:10). Of him nothing further is known; the accounts of his having been a preacher in Galatia, and having founded the Church in Vienne, are mere legendary glosses on this passage (Ellicott, *Com.*, in loco.).

Cre'tans (krē'táns). *See* Crete.

Crete, called now Candia, a large island in the Mediterranean, about one hundred and fifty miles in length and from six to thirty-five wide. It lies midway between Syria and

Malta. Anciently it possessed a great civilization. It is mountainous, and its famous peak is Mount Ida. The vessel, carrying *Paul* (*q. v.*) on his way to Rome, sailed along the southern coast of the island, where it was overtaken by a storm (Acts 27:7-21). The Cretes (Acts 2:11; "Cretians," Tit. 1:12, A. V.) are now called Cretans. It seems likely that a very early acquaintance existed between the Cretans and the Jews; and the special mention of the Cretans among those attending the great Pentecost (Acts 2:11) is just what we should expect. The Cretans had a name in ancient times for being good sailors; also for skill in archery and expertness in ambushing. Hence they were frequently engaged as light-armed troops by other nations.

104. Map of Crete and the Aegean Sea

The ancient notices of their character fully agree with the quotation which Paul produces from "one of their own poets" (Tit. 1:12): "The Cretans are always liars, evil beasts, slow bellies" (literally, *idle gluttons*). The classics abound with allusions to the untruthfulness of the Cretans; and it was so frequently applied to them that *krētizein*, "to act the Cretan," was a synonym to *play the liar*.

Crib (Heb. *'ēbūs, manger,* or *stall*), a stall (Prov. 14:4), or simply a manger to eat out of (Job 39:9; Isa. 1:3).

Crimson. *See* Colors, 2, (3).

Crisping Pin (Heb. *ḥārît, pocket,* Isa. 3:22), properly a pouch for holding money, generally carried by men in the girdle, or in a purse (*q. v.*); rendered "bag" in II Kings 5:23.

Cris'pus (krĭs'pŭs; *curled*), chief of the Jewish synagogue at Corinth (Acts 18:8), converted and baptized by the apostle Paul (I Cor. 1:14). According to tradition, he became afterward bishop of Aegina.

Crookbacked (Heb. *gĭbbēn,* to be *arched,* or *contracted*). A humpback (Lev. 21:20, 21) was one of the blemishes which unfitted a priest for the sacred service of the sanctuary.

Crop, that part of the bird which held the food, which, with its feathers, was cast among the ashes at the side of the altar, and not burned with the rest of the fowl (Lev. 1:16). *See* Sacrifice.

Cross (Gr. *stauros,* a *stake;* Lat. *crux*).

1. **Form.** The cross which was used as an instrument of death (*see* Crucifixion) was either a plain vertical stake to which the victim was fastened, with the hands tied or nailed above the head, or such a stake provided with a crossbar, to which the victim was fastened with the arms outstretched. Of this latter kind three varieties were known, so that there were four forms of the cross: (1) **Simple** (Lat. *simplex*), | ; (2) **St. Andrew's** (*decussata*), ✕; (3) **St. Anthony's** (*commissa*), ⊤; (4) **The Latin** (*immissa*), ✝

Other forms have been invented, and used as emblems, e. g., the Greek cross, consisting of four equally long arms, ✛; double cross, ✚ whose upper bar refers to the inscription by Pilate on the cross of Jesus; and the triple, ✚, ✚, of which the first is used by the pope, the second by the Raskolniks.

In addition to the transverse bar there was sometimes a peg, or other projection, upon which the body of the sufferer rested, to prevent its weight from tearing away the hands.

2. **Emblem.** That the cross was widely known in pre-Christian times as an emblem has been clearly shown by independent investigators. Indeed, it was a well-known heathen sign. The vestments of the priests of Horus, the Egyptian god of light, are marked ✛. At Thebes, in the tombs of the kings, royal cows are represented plowing, a calf playing in front. Each animal has a ✛ marked in several places on it. Rassam found buildings at Nineveh marked with the Maltese cross. Osiris, as well as Jupiter Ammon, had for a monogram a ✝ . The cross is found marked on Phoenician monuments at an early date.

In Christian times the cross, from being in itself the most vile and repulsive of objects, became in the minds of believers the symbol of all that is holy and precious. As Christ is the "wisdom of God and the power of God" unto salvation, it is but natural that those who experience the power of this salvation should glory in the cross. The exact time of its adoption as a Christian emblem is unknown. In the pre-Constantine period the sign of the cross seems to have been quite generally recognized by primitive Christians. They appear to have contemplated it only as a symbol, without any miraculous energy, and associated it with that which was hopeful and joyous. On the tombstones of the early Christians the cross was the emblem of victory and hope. It was only after superstition took the place of true spiritual devotion that the figure of the cross was used or borne about as a sacred charm.

In the latter part of the 3d century people signed the cross in token of safety, and laid stress on figures of it as a preservative against both spiritual and natural evil. This superstitious feeling was stimulated by the discovery of what was held to be the real cross upon which our Lord suffered. The empress Helena, mother of Constantine, about A. D. 326, visited Palestine, and was shown three crosses by a Jew. In order to know which was the genuine one, Macarius, bishop of Jerusalem, suggested that they be tested by their power of working miracles. One only being reported as possessing this quality, it was declared to be the real cross.

3. **As Signature.** As early as the 6th century it had become the custom to place three crosses (✝ ✝ ✝) near the signature of important documents, these having the value

of an oath on the part of the signer. Priests added it to their signatures, and bishops, as a sign of the dignity of their office, placed it before their signatures. Crosses were used in diplomatic documents as early as the 5th century. By tradition the cross is now used as a signature by those unable to write.

4. Figurative. The *cross* is used in Scripture, in a general way, for what is painful and mortifying to the flesh (Matt. 16:24). After the resurrection of our Lord the cross is spoken of as the representative of his whole sufferings from his birth to his death (Eph. 2:16; Heb. 12:2), and for the whole doctrines of the Gospel (I Cor. 1:18; Gal. 6:14); while the opposers of the Gospel were spoken of as enemies of the cross (Phil. 3:18). "The cross of Christ" (I Cor. 1:17) represents that Christ was crucified for man, and thereby procured his salvation.

Crow. *See* Animal Kingdom.

Crown. **1. Origin.** This ornament, which is both ancient and universal, probably originated from the fillets used to prevent the hair from being disheveled by the wind. Such fillets are still common, and they may be seen on the sculptures of Persepolis, Nineveh, and Egypt; they gradually developed into turbans, which by the addition of ornamental or precious materials assumed the dignity of miters or crowns. The use of them as ornaments probably was suggested by the natural custom of encircling the head with flowers in token of joy and triumph (Wisd. 2:8; Judith 15:13).

2. Bible Use. Several words in Scripture are rendered "crown:"

(1) *Nēzĕr*, (literally, something *set apart, consecration;* hence *consecrated* hair, as of a Nazarite) is supposed to mean a *diadem*. It was applied to the plate of gold in front of the high priest's miter (Exod. 29:6; 39:30); also to the diadem which Saul wore in battle, and which was brought to David (II Sam. 1:10), and that which was used at the coronation of Joash (II Kings 11:12). The crown was in universal use by priests, and in religious serv-

105. Royal Crowns: 1. Upper Egypt; 2. Upper and Lower Egypt; 3. Assyrian; 4. Laurel Crown; 5. Crown of Herod the Great; 6. Crown of Aretas

106. Helmet Crown of Upper Egypt Worn by King Narmer, Who Lifts a Mace to Slay a Kneeling Enemy

ices. Egyptian crowns such as that worn by Tutankhamun were elaborate and richly adorned with royal emblems. The crown worn by the kings of Assyria was a high miter frequently adorned with flowers, etc., and arranged in bands of linen or silk. Originally there was only one band, but afterward there were two, and the ornaments were richer.

(2) *'Atärāh, circlet;* Gr. *stephanos*), a more general word for crown, and used for crowns and head ornaments of various sorts. When applied to the crowns of kings it appears to denote the state crown as distinguished from the diadem, as, probably, the crown taken by David from the king of Ammon at Rabbah, and used as the state crown of Judah (II Sam. 12:30). As to the shape of the Hebrew state-crown we can form an idea only by reference to ancient crowns. The diadem of two or three fillets may have signified dominion over two or three countries. In Rev. 12:3; 13:1; 19:12, allusion is made to *many crowns* worn in token of extended dominion.

(3) *Kĕthĕr, chaplet*, the name given (Esth. 1:11; 2:17; 6:8) to the ancient Persian crown, which was, doubtless, the high cap or tiara so often mentioned by Greek historians.

(4) Other Hebrew terms rendered "crown" are *zēr*, a wreath or border of gold around the edge of the ark of the covenant (Exod. 25:11, etc.); and *qōdqōd*, the crown of the human head (Gen. 49:26, etc.). The Greek word *stemma*, is used only once in the New Testament (Acts 14:13) for the "garlands" used with victims.

3. Figurative. The crown was a symbol of victory and reward, victors being crowned in the Grecian games. These crowns were usually made of leaves, which soon began to wither. In opposition to these is the incorruptible crown (I Cor. 9:25; II Tim. 2:5), a crown of life (James 1:12; I Pet. 5:4; Rev. 2:10). The meaning of the crown of thorns placed on the head of Jesus (Matt. 27:29) was to insult him under the character of the king of the Jews. The crown is also used as an emblem of an exalted state (Prov. 12:4; 17:6; Isa. 28:5; Phil. 4:1, etc.).

Crown of Thorns. The Roman soldiers made a crown out of some thorny plant, and crowned our Lord in mockery (Matt. 27:29). "The object was not to cause suffering, but to excite ridicule; so that while we cannot altogether dissociate the idea of something painful from this crown of thorns we must not conceive of it as covered with prickles, which were intentionally thrust into the flesh. It is impossible to determine what *species* of thorn it was" (Meyer, *Com.*, in loc.). See Thorn.

Crucifixion. 1. **History.** This form of punishment was in use among the Egyptians (Gen. 40:19), the Carthaginians, the Persians (Esth. 7:10), the Assyrians, Scythians, Indians, Germans, and from the earliest times among the Greeks and Romans. After the conquest of Tyre, Alexander the Great ordered two thousand Tyrians to be crucified as punishment for the resistance which that city made. Crucifixion was abolished by Constantine, probably toward the end of his reign, owing, doubtless, to his increasing reverence for the cross. Punishment by the cross was confined to slaves or to malefactors of the worst class. Exemption from it was the privilege of Roman citizenship.

2. **Among the Jews.** Whether this mode of execution was known to the ancient Jews is a matter of dispute. The Hebrew words apparently alluding to crucifixion are *täläh* and *yäqä'*, generally rendered in the A. V. "to hang" (Num. 25:4; Deut. 21:22; II Sam. 18:10). The Jewish account of the matter is that the exposure of the body tied to a stake by the hands took place after death. The placing of the head on an upright pole has been called crucifixion. Crucifixion *after* death was not rare, the victim being first killed in mercy. The Jews probably borrowed this punishment from the Romans.

Among the Jews, as well as among the Romans, crucifixion was considered the most horrible form of death; and to a Jew it would seem the more horrible from the curse, "He that is hanged is accursed of God" (Deut. 21:23). Our Lord was condemned to it by the popular cry of the Jews (Matt. 27:23) on the charge of sedition against Caesar (Luke 23:21-23).

3. **Process.** Crucifixion was preceded by scourging with thongs, to which were sometimes added nails, pieces of bone, etc., to heighten the pain, often so intense as to cause death. In our Lord's case, however, this infliction seems neither to have been the legal scourging after sentence nor yet the examination by torture (Acts 22:24), but rather a scourging *before* the sentence to excite pity and procure immunity from further punishment (Luke 23:22; John 19:1). The criminal carried his own cross, or a part of it, in which

case another was compelled to share the burden (Luke 23:26). The place of execution was outside the city (I Kings 21:13; Acts 7:58; Heb. 13:12); arrived there, the condemned was stripped of his clothes, which became the perquisite of the soldiers (Matt. 27:35); and the cross having been previously erected he was drawn up and made fast to it with cords or nails, although sometimes he was fastened to the cross, which was afterward raised. The limbs of the victim were generally three or four feet from the earth. Before the nailing or binding took place a medicated cup was given out of kindness to confuse the senses and deaden the pangs of the sufferer (Prov. 31:6), usually of "wine mingled with myrrh," because myrrh was soporific. Our Lord refused it that his senses might be clear (Matt. 27:34; Mark 15:23).

If the nailing was the most painful mode in the first instance the other was more so in the end, for the sufferer was left to die of sheer exhaustion, and when simply bound with thongs, it might take days to accomplish the process; for usually a strong pin projected out of the central stem, on which the body of the sufferer rested. Instances are on record of persons surviving for nine days. Owing to the lingering character of this death our Lord was watched, according to custom, by a party of four soldiers (John 19:23), with their centurion (Matt. 27:66), to prevent the person being taken down and resuscitated. Fracture of the legs was resorted to by the Jews to hasten death (John 19:31). This was done to the two thieves crucified with Jesus, but not to him, for the soldiers found that he was dead already (John 19:32-34). The unusual rapidity of our Lord's death was due to the depth of his previous agonies, or may be sufficiently accounted for simply from peculiarities of constitution. Pilate expressly satisfied himself as to the actual death by questioning the centurion (Mark 15:44). In most cases the body was suffered to rot on the cross by the action of the sun and rain or to be devoured by birds and beasts. Sepulture was generally, therefore, forbidden, but in consequence of Deut. 21:22, 23 an express national exception was made in favor of the Jews (Matt. 27:58).

Cruse, the rendering of three Hebrew words:

1. *Săppăhăth*, literally, *spread out*, usually thought to be a *flask*, but more likely a shallow *cup* for holding water (I Sam. 26:11, 12, 16; I Kings 19:6) or oil (I Kings 17:12, 14, 16). "In a similar case in the present day this would be a globular vessel of blue porous clay, about nine inches diameter, with a neck of about three inches long, a small handle below the neck, and opposite the handle a straight spout, with an orifice about the size of a straw, through which the water is drunk or sucked" (Smith, *Bib. Dict.*, s. v.).

2. *Băqbŭq*, so called from the *gurgling* sound in emptying (I Kings 14:3), an "earthen bottle" (Jer. 19:1, 10).

3. *Ş'lohith*, probably a flat metal saucer of the form still common in the East. It occurs in II Chron. 35:13, "pans;" and other words from the same root are found in II

Kings 2:20, "cruse," and II Kings 21:13, "dish."

Crystal. *See* Mineral Kingdom.

Cubit. *See* Metrology, I.

Cuckow. *See* Animal Kingdom.

Cucumber. *See* Vegetable Kingdom.

Cumi (kū'mĭ; Gr. from Aramaic *qūmî*), "arise" (Mark 5:41).

Cummin. *See* Vegetable Kingdom.

Cup, the rendering mostly in the Old Testament of the Heb. *kôs;* in the New Testament, of the Gr. *protērion.*

1. **Egyptian.** These were very varied in form, the paintings upon the tombs representing many of elegant design, while others are deficient in both form and proportion. Many were of gold and silver (Gen. 44:2; comp. Num. 7:84), some being richly studded with precious stones, inlaid with vitrified substances in brilliant colors, and even enameled. They were also made of hard stones, pottery, glass, and porcelain.

107. An Egyptian Wishing Cup from Tutankhamun's Tomb

2. **Assyrian.** Cups and vases among the Assyrians were even more varied in form and design than among the Egyptians. The materials employed were about the same—precious metals, copper, bronze, glass, and pottery, both glazed and unglazed. Some of their drinking cups terminate in the head of a lion, with a handle. Other festal cups are more like bowls in form and fluted.

3. **Hebrew.** The cups of the Jews, whether of metal or earthenware, were probably borrowed from Egypt or from the Phoenicians, who were celebrated in that branch of workmanship. In Solomon's time all his drinking vessels were of gold (I Kings 10:21). The cups mentioned in the New Testament were often, no doubt, made after Greek and Roman models.

In Isaiah (22:24) the word translated "cup" signifies a *laver,* or basin (so rendered in Exod. 24:6, and "goblet," Cant. 7:2). The cups in I Chron. 28:17 were broad bowls for libation, improperly rendered "covers" (Exod. 25:29; 37:16; Num. 4:7).

4. **Cup of Divination.** The use of such cups was a practice common to Syria and Egypt as early as the time of the patriarch Jacob. Otherwise the question, "Is not this it in which my lord drinketh, and whereby indeed he divineth?" (Gen. 44:5) would have lost half

its force with the brethren of Joseph. Among the Egyptians this sort of divination consisted in pouring clean water into a goblet, and then looking into the water for representations of future events; or in pouring water into a goblet or dish, dropping in pieces of gold or silver, also precious stones, and the observing and interpreting the appearance of the water. Melted wax was also poured into the water, and the will of the gods interpreted by the variously shaped figures formed in this way. But we cannot infer from this that Joseph adopted this superstitious practice. The intention of the statement was simply to represent the goblet as a sacred vessel and Joseph as acquainted with the most sacred things.

5. **Figurative.** "Cup" is employed in both Testaments in some curious metaphorical phrases:

"The portion of the cup" is a general expression for the condition of life, prosperous or miserable (Psa. 11:6; 16:5; 23:5).

A "cup" is also the natural type of sensual allurement (Prov. 23:31; Jer. 51:7; Rev. 17:4; 18:6). Babylon is termed a "golden cup" to express its splendor and opulence.

"Cup of consolation" (Jer. 16:7). It was the oriental custom for friends to send viands and wine (the cup of consolation) to console relatives in mourning feasts (comp. II Sam. 3:35; Prov. 31:6).

"Cup of salvation" (Psa. 116:13) is probably the drink offering lifted in thanksgiving to God (Num. 15:5; 28:7).

"Cup of blessing" (I Cor. 10:16; called the "cup of the Lord," v. 21), i. e., the cup over which the blessing is spoken, when the wine contained in it is expressly consecrated by prayer to the sacred use of the Lord's Supper. It is called in Jewish writings, just as by Paul, "the cup of blessing," and is supposed to refer to the third cup of wine drunk at the passover feast, over which a special blessing was spoken. In I Cor. 10:21 it is contrasted with the "cup of demons," i. e., the cup drunk at heathen feasts.

The "cup of trembling," literally, "cup of reeling, intoxication" (Isa. 51:17, 22; Zech. 12:2), "cup of astonishment and desolation" (Ezek. 23:33), "cup of fury" (Isa. 51:17, 22; Jer. 25:15), "cup of indignation" (Rev. 14: 10) are figures representing the effects of Jehovah's wrath upon the wicked. God is represented as the master of a banquet, dealing madness and stupor of vengeance to guilty guests. There is in the prophets no more frequent or terrific image, and it is repeated with pathetic force in the language of our Lord's agony (Matt. 26:39, 42; John 18:11).

Cupbearer (Heb. *măshqĕh, one who gives drink to*), that officer of the household who tasted the wine and passed it to those at the table. He was often chosen for his personal beauty and attractions, and in ancient oriental courts was always a person of rank and importance. From the confidential nature of his duties and his frequent access to the royal presence, he possessed great influence. The chief cupbearer or butler to the king of Egypt was the means of raising Joseph to his high position (Gen. 41:9). Rabshakeh appears from his name to have filled a like office in the Assyrian court

(II Kings 18:17). Nehemiah was cupbearer to Artaxerxes Longimanus, king of Persia (Neh. 1:11; 2:1). Cupbearers are mentioned among the attendants of Solomon (I Kings 10:5; II Chron. 9:4).

Cure. *See* Diseases.

Curious Arts (Gr. *ta perierga, devious works*), magic, spoken of the black art as practiced by the Ephesian conjurors (Acts 19:19). The allusion is doubtless to the *Ephesian spells*, i. e., charms, consisting of letters or monograms, written on parchment and worn like amulets. *See* Magic.

Curse, the rendering of several Hebrew and Greek words. Many instances are recorded of cursing in the Scripture. Thus God cursed the serpent which had seduced Eve (Gen. 3:14); Cain, who slew his brother (4:11). He promised Abraham to curse those who should curse him. These divine maledictions are not merely imprecations, nor the expressions of impotent wishes; but they carry their effects with them, and are attended with all the miseries they denounce or foretell. Curses delivered against individuals by holy men (Gen. 9:25; 49:7; Deut. 27:15; Josh. 6:26) are not the expressions of revenge, passion, or impatience; they are *predictions*, and, therefore, not such as God condemns.

The Mosaic law forbade the cursing of father or mother (Exod. 21:17) on pain of death, of the prince of his people (22:28), of one that is deaf (Lev. 19:14) or perhaps absent so that he could not hear. Blasphemy, or cursing God, was a capital crime (Lev. 24:10, 11). *See* Anathema.

Curtains, the rendering in the A. V. of three Hebrew terms:

1. *Yᵉrî'äh,* the ten "curtains" of fine linen, and also the eleven of goats' hair which covered the tabernacle (Exod. 26:1-13; 36:8-17). The charge of these curtains and of the other textile fabrics of the tabernacle was laid on the Gershonites (Num. 4:25). Having this definite meaning, the word became a synonym for the tabernacle (II Sam. 7:2). Sometimes it means the sides of a tent (Isa. 54:2; Jer. 4:20; 10:20).

2. *Mäsäq,* the "hanging" for the doorway of the tabernacle (Exod. 26:36, etc.), and also for the gate of the court round the tabernacle (Exod. 27:16, etc.). *See* Tabernacle.

3. *Dōq, fineness,* occurs in the expression, "stretched out the heavens as a curtain" (Isa. 40:22), and appears to have been a fabric such as is used by rich orientals for a screen over their courts in summer.

Cush (Heb. *kûsh*).

1. A son (probably the eldest) of Ham. In the genealogy of Noah's children it is said, "Cush begat Nimrod" (Gen. 10:8; I Chron. 1:10). A number of his descendants are also mentioned.

2. A Benjamite, mentioned in the title of Psa. 7, respecting whom nothing more is known than that the psalm is there said to have been composed "concerning his words" (or affairs), B. C. 1000. He appears to have been an enemy of David and seeking an opportunity of injuring him, but to have been unsuccessful (v. 15).

3. **Land of.** The ancient designation of Ethiopia, that section of Africa contiguous to Egypt and the Red Sea, now known as Abyssinia (II Kings 11:9; Esther 1:1; Ezek. 29:10). In Genesis 2:13 and 10:8, the reference is to an earlier Asiatic (Mesopotamian) Cush, probably the Kassites (Cossaeans).

Cu'shan (kū'shăn), another form of Cush or perhaps an Arabian country occupied by Cushites (Hab. 3:7).

Chu'shan-Rishatha'im (kū'shăn-rĭsh-à-thā'-ĭm), evidently an obscure Hittite conqueror, who having annexed Mesopotamia (Mitanni) overran Palestine (Judg. 3:7-10). He left traces of his conquests at Bethshan, the stout Esdraelon fortress, and in other places (John Garstang, *Joshua-Judges*, p. 62, 364 seq.). The event is likely to be placed c. 1361-1353 B. C., in the latter part of the reign of Tutankhamun (c. 1366-1357 B. C.) and the first years of the regime of his general Harmhab, when Egyptian influence in Syria-Palestine had waned. *M. F. U.*

Cu'shi (kū'shĭ; *Cushite,* or *Ethiopian*).

1. The messenger sent by Joab to announce to David the success of the battle against Absalom, and the death of the young prince (II Sam. 18:21-23, 31, 32), B. C. about 970.

2. The father of Shelemiah, and greatgrandfather of Jehudi, which last was sent by the Jewish magnates to invite Baruch to read his roll to them (Jer. 36:14), B. C. before 604.

3. The son of Gedaliah and father of the prophet Zephaniah (Zeph. 1:1), B. C. before 620.

Cushion. *See* Bed.

Custom (Heb. *hălăq, way tax,* Ezra 4:13, 20; 7:24; Gr. *telos, tax,* I Macc. 11:35; Matt. 17:25; Rom. 13:7). *See* Tax.

Custom, Receipt of (Gr. *telōnion*), a term signifying *toll-house* (Matt. 9:9; Mark 2:14; Luke 5:27).

Cu'tha, or **Cuth** (kū'thà), name of a city of Babylonia mentioned twice only in the Old Testament. In one passage (II Kings 17:30) it is connected with the worship of the god Nergal; in the other (II Kings 17:24) it is mentioned along with Babylon and other cities as furnishing the people who were deported and settled in Samaria. The city of Cutha was located a short distance eastward of Babylon, where the village of Tell-Ibrahim now marks its former site. It was one of the most important cities of ancient Babylonia. In the opinion of some it was the capital city of an ancient kingdom which existed before the city of Babylon had risen to power in the country. However that may be, the city continued to be a center of power through the Assyrian period, and many Assyrian kings halted there to pay tribute of worship at the shrine of its great god Nergal, whose temple, known by the name of E-shid-lam, has been found in the ruins at Tell-Ibrahim. After the taking of Samaria by the Assyrians Sargon, king of Assyria, transported inhabitants from Avva, Babylon, Hamath, and Sepharvaim to Samaria, to take the place of those who had been removed into captivity. These people became known as Samaritans in later times, and a long enmity existed between them and the Jews. Among them the people of Cutha

108.

must have been prominent either because of numbers or of ability, for the new settlers were long called Cutheans. The history of Cutha shows periods of power and of decay. Sennacherib, king of Assyria, who destroyed Babylon, claims to have conquered Cutha in one of his great campaigns; and Nebuchadnezzar in a later day rebuilt and otherwise restored and beautified its temple. Cutha had two rivers or canals, and therefore probably possessed some commercial importance—R. W. R.

Cutting Off from the people. *See* Excommunication.

Cuttings (in the flesh), Lev. 19:28; 21:5; Jer. 48:37). Unnatural disfigurement of the body was prohibited by Moses, and seems to refer to the scratching of the arms, head, and face, common in times of mourning among the people of the East. The law gave the further prohibition, "Nor print any marks upon you" (Lev. 19:28); i. e., tattooing, a custom very common among the savage tribes, and still met with in Arabia. This prohibition had reference to idolatrous usages, but was intended to inculcate upon the Israelites a proper reverence for God's creation.

The priests of Baal cut themselves with knives to propitiate the god "after their manner" (I Kings 18:28). Herodotus says the Carians, who resided in Europe, cut their foreheads with knives at festivals of Isis; in this respect exceeding the Egyptians, who beat themselves on these occasions (Herod. ii, 61). Lucian, speaking of the Syrian priestly attendants of this mock deity, says that, using violent gestures, they cut their arms and tongues with swords. Tattooing indicated allegiance to a deity, in the same manner as soldiers and slaves bore tattooed marks to indicate allegiance or adscription. This is evidently alluded to in the Revelation (13:16; 17:5; 19:20), and, though in a contrary direction, by Ezekiel (9:4), by St. Paul (Gal. 6:17),

and perhaps by Isaiah (44:5) and Zechariah (13:6) (Smith, *Bib. Dict.*, s. v.). *See* Mark.

Cymbal. *See* Music.

Cypress. *See* Vegetable Kingdom.

Cy′prus (sī′prŭs), a large island in the Mediterranean off the coast of Syria. Its length is about one hundred and forty-eight miles, and its width from five to fifty miles. It was once inhabited by the Phoenicians. In 447 B. C. the Greeks controlled it. In 58 B. C. it fell to the Romans. On the death of Alexander the Great it had been incorporated with Egypt. It was an imperial province in 27 B. C. The first New Testament notice of Cyprus is in Acts 4:36, where it is mentioned as the native place of Barnabas. It appears prominently in connection with the early spread of Christianity (Acts 11:19, 20). Paul and Barnabas visited it A. D. 44. It was Paul's first missionary field (Acts 13:4-13). The Kittim of Gen. 10:4 and the Chittim of Isa. 23:1 were primarily the inhabitants of Citium, and then of the whole island.

Cyre′ne (sī-rē′nē), a city founded by the Greeks, upon a beautiful tableland one thousand eight hundred feet above the sea level. It was the capital of the district of Cyrenaica in Africa. It was a Greek city, but contained many Jews. Cyrene was represented in Jerusalem at the Pentecost (Acts 2:10). Simon, one of its people, helped Jesus bear his cross (Matt. 27:32). Cyrenian Jews had a synagogue at Jerusalem (Acts 6:9). It was destroyed in the 4th century by Saracens. It is waste and occupied now by wild beasts and Bedouins.

Cyre′nian (sī-rē′nĭ-ȧn; *of Cyrene*, Matt. 27:32; Acts 11:20), a native of Cyrene (A. V.), or Cyrenaica, in Africa (Mark 15:21, etc.).

Cyre′nius (sī-rē′nĭ-ŭs; whose full name was *Publius Silpicius Quirinus*) was the second of that name mentioned in Roman history, and was consul with M. Valerius Messala. Some years after, A. D. 6, he was made governor of

Syria, and made there and in Judea a census, or enrollment. He was a favorite with Tiberius, and on his death, A. D. 21, he was buried with public honors by the senate at the request of the emperor. The census above named seems, in Luke 2:2, to be identified with one which took place at the time of the birth of Christ, when Sentius Saturnius was governor of Syria. Hence has arisen considerable difficulty, which has been variously solved, either by supposing some corruption in the text of Luke, or by giving some unusual sense to his words. But A. W. Zumpt, of Berlin, has shown it to be probable that Quirinus was *twice* governor of Syria, and, by very striking and satisfactory arguments, fixes the time of his governorship at from B. C. 4 to A. D. 1; the second A. D. 6-10.

Cy′rus (sī′rŭs) II, the great, the conqueror of Babylon and ruler of that city from 539 B. C. until his death in 530 B. C., founded the vast Persian Empire. This great humane ruler holds an important position both in Biblical prophecy (Isa. 41:25; 44:28; 45:1-13) and history (Ezek. 1:1-8; 4:3-5; II Chron. 36: 22 ff.; Dan. 1:21; 10:1).

1. **Early History.** Cyrus II came to the throne of Anshan, an Elamite region, around 559 B. C. He clashed with a Median king, Astyages. When the Median army rebelled, Cyrus victoriously took Ecbatana and the Persians became ascendant.

2. **His Conquests.** Cyrus II extended his conquests with lightning-like rapidity, defeating Croesus, king of Lydia c. 546 B. C. Babylon fell to him in 539 B. C. Thus he laid the foundations of the vast Persian Empire under whose dominion Judea was to remain a province for the next two centuries. Cyrus established his capital at Pasargadae in the land of Parsa. On a ruined palace there the repeated inscription can still be read, "I, Cyrus, the king, the Achaemenid." From this palace comes the earliest extant Persian relief, a four-winged genius, perhaps representing the deified Cyrus.

3. **His Decree.** This edict recorded in II Chron. 36:22, 23 and Ezra 1:2, 3 gave permission to the Hebrew captives to go back to Palestine to rebuild their temple. "Thus saith Cyrus king of Persia, All the kingdoms of the earth hath Jehovah, the God of heaven, given me; and he hath charged me to build him a house in Jerusalem, which is in Judah. Whosoever there is among you of all his people, his god be with him, and let him go up to Jerusalem . . . and build the house of Jehovah . . ."

4. **His Inscriptions.** The famous cylinder of Cyrus found by Hormuzd Rassam in the 19th century is in remarkable agreement with the royal edict as set forth in the Bible. "From . . . Ashur and Susa, Agade, Ashnunnak, Zamban, Meturnu, Deri, with the territory of the land of Gutium, the cities on the other side of the Tigris, whose sites were of ancient found— the gods, who dwell in them, I brought back to their places and caused them to dwell in a habitation for all time. All their inhabitants

I collected and restored them to their dwelling places . . . may all the gods whom I brought into their cities pray daily before Bel and Nabu for long life for me . . ." (R. W. Rogers, *Cuneiform Parallels to the Old Testament* (N. Y., 1912), p. 383). This royal edict shows that Cyrus reversed the inhumane policy of displacing whole populations, as practiced by Assyrian and Babylonian conquerors. Thus his clemency and religious toleration with regard to the Jewish captives are readily understood. It is understandable how the Hebrew prophet sang of Cyrus as the deliverer whom Jehovah would raise up (Isa. 45:1-4). While the Hebrew prophet sang of the great conqueror anointed by the Lord for the particular task of restoring the Jewish captives, Cyrus claimed to be commissioned by the god Marduk. The famous inscription of the victor, preserved on a clay cylinder, contains the amazing story of triumphs of one who plainly saw himself as a man of destiny, and gives background to the prophetic message of the Hebrew seer. "Marduk . . . sought a righteous prince, after his own heart, whom he took by the hand. Cyrus, king of Anshan, he called by name, to lordship over the whole world he appointed him . . . to his city Babylon he caused him to go . . . his numerous troops in number unknown, like the water of a river, marched armed at his side. Without battle and conflict he permitted him to enter Babylon. He spared his city Babylon a calamity. Nabunaid, the king, who did not fear him, he delivered into his hand." (Rogers, *op. cit.*, p. 381).

109. Tomb of Cyrus, Pasargadae, Iran

5. **His End.** Cyrus was slain in battle 530 B. C. and buried in a still extant tomb at Pasargadae. In the small burial chamber a golden sarcophagus received Cyrus' body. Plutarch (c. 90 A. D.) says the tomb bore this inscription: "O man, whosoever thou art and whencesoever thou comest, for I know that thou wilt come, I am Cyrus and I won for the Persians their empire. Do not, therefore, begrudge me this little earth which covers my body." *M. F. U.*

D

Dab'areh (dăb'à-rě; Josh. 21:28). This name is incorrectly spelt in the A. V., and should be *Daberath* (*q. v.*).

Dab'basheth (dăb'ĕ-shĕth; *hump*), a town on the border of Zebulun (Josh. 19:11). Its location has not been positively identified.

Dab'erath (dăb'ĕ-răth; *pasture*), a Levitical town of Issachar (Josh. 19:12; I Chron. 6:72; *Dabareh*, Josh. 21:28). It lay at the western foot of Mount Tabor. The present insignificant village of Deburieh.

110. Dagger and Sheath

Dagger, any sharp instrument, especially a weapon of war (Judg. 3:16, 21, 22). *See* Armor.

Dagon. *See* Gods, False.

Daily occurs in the A. V. as the rendering of the Gr. *'epiousios*, *necessary* (Matt. 6:11; Luke 11:3), so that the phrase really means *the bread of our necessity*, i. e., *necessary for us*.

Daily Offering or **Sacrifice.** *See* Sacrifice.

Dalai'ah (dà-lī'à; I Chron. 3:24), the same name elsewhere more correctly Anglicized *Delaiah*, 1 (*q. v.*).

Dale, the King's, the name of a valley not far from Jerusalem and in the valley of Jehoshaphat, where Absalom built a family monument (Gen. 14:17; II Sam. 18:18). It is also called the "vale of Shaveh."

Da'leth (dä'lĕth), the fourth letter of the Hebrew alphabet. From Semitic "daleth" came Greek *delta*, whence Latin and English "d." See Psalm 119, section 4, where this letter begins each verse in the Hebrew.

Dalmanu'tha (dăl-mà-nū'thà), a place on the west coast of the Sea of Galilee, into parts of which Christ was said to have gone ("Magdala," Matt. 15:39). Dalmanutha itself is mentioned only in Mark 8:10. The place is identified with a village called Ain-el-Barideh —the "cold fountain." The village proper is called el-Mejdel, possibly the "Migdal-el" of Josh. 19:38.

Dalma'tia (dăl-mā'shĭ-à), a district east of the Adriatic, being a Roman province; a place visited by Titus (II Tim. 4:10). According to Rom. 15:19 Paul himself had once preached there, the place being referred to as Illyricum.

Dal'phon (dăl'fŏn), the second of the ten sons of Haman, killed by the Jews on the thirteenth of Adar (Esth. 9:7).

Dam (Heb. *'ēm, mother*). The Mosaic code had several regulations respecting treatment of parents, even among animals. Thus the young animal was to be with its mother seven days after birth before it could be sacrificed (Exod. 22:30; Lev. 22:27); a lamb was not to be seethed in its mother's milk (Exod. 23:19); a mother bird was not to be taken with her young (Deut. 22:6, 7).

Damages, remuneration or restitution prescribed in case of offense against the person, property, or name of another. *See* Law.

Dam'aris (dăm'à-rĭs; *gentle*), an Athenian woman converted to Christianity by Paul's preaching (Acts 17:34). Chrysostom and others believed her to have been the wife of Dionysius the Areopagite, but apparently for no other reason than that she is mentioned with him in this passage.

Dam'ascenes (dăm'à-sēns), inhabitants of Damascus (II Cor. 11:32).

Damas'cus (dà-măs'kŭs), said to be the oldest city in the East.

1. **Situation.** Damascus lies about seventy miles from the seaboard, upon the east of Anti-Lebanon, and close to the foot of the hills, in the valley of the Abana, a great plain about twenty-three hundred feet above the sea and thirty miles by ten in extent. This plain is called the Ghutah, and is shot all over by the cool, rapid waters of the Abana, which do equal service in bringing life and in carrying away corruption. It is very fertile, abounding in gardens, orchards, and meadows. It is to Abana that Damascus chiefly owes her importance and stability. Another important factor is that the city lies on the border of the desert, and that she is situated on the natural highway from the east to the west. Three

111. Panorama of Damascus

234

great roads go forth from her—west, south, and east. The western, or southwestern, road travels by Galilee to the Levant and the Nile. The southern, which leaves the city by the "Gates of God," takes the pilgrims to Mecca. The eastern is the road to Bagdad.

112. Damascus at Abana River (upper right)

2. **History.** Josephus (*Ant.*, i, 6) says that Damascus was founded by Uz, son of Aram. It is first mentioned in Scripture in connection with Abraham (Gen. 14:15), whose steward was a native of the place (15:2). We may gather from the name of this person, as well as from the statement of Josephus, which connects the city with the Aramaeans, that it was a Semitic settlement.

In the time of David "the Syrians of Damascus came to succor Hadadezer king of Zobah," with whom David was at war (II Sam. 8:5; I Chron. 18:5); but the Syrians were defeated, and David became master of the whole territory, garrisoning it with Israelites (II Sam. 8:6). In the reign of Solomon *Rezon* (*q. v.*) became master of Damascus (I Kings 11:23-25). The family of Hadad appears to have recovered the throne, as we find Ben-hadad in league with Baasha of Israel against Asa (I Kings 15:19; II Chron. 16:3), and after in league with Asa against Baasha (I Kings 15:20). The defeat and death of Ahab at Ramoth-gilead (I Kings 22:15-37) enabled the Syrians of Damascus to resume the offensive. Their bands ravaged Israel during Jehoram's reign and laid siege to Samaria.

Hazael, the servant of Ben-hadad, murdered the king (II Kings 8:15), and was soon after defeated by the Assyrians. He and his son waged successful war against Israel and Judah, but Joash defeated the Syrians thrice and recovered the cities of Israel (II Kings 13:3, 22-25). Jeroboam II (B. C. about 783) is said to have recovered Damascus (II Kings 14:28). Later (B. C. about 735) Rezin, king of Damascus, and Pekah, king of Israel, laid unsuccessful siege to Jerusalem (II Kings 16:5), but Elath—built by Azariah in Syrian territory—having been taken by Rezin, Ahaz sought the aid of Tiglath-pileser (II Kings 16:7, 8). Rezin was slain, the kingdom of Damascus brought to an end, the city destroyed, and its inhabitants carried captive into Assyria (v. 9; comp. Amos 1:5). It was long before Damascus recovered from this serious blow. We do not know at what time Damascus was rebuilt; but Strabo says that it was the most famous place in Syria during the Persian period. At the time of the Gospel history and of the apostle Paul it formed a part of the kingdom of Aretas (II Cor. 11:32), an Arabian prince, who held his kingdom under the Romans.

The mention of Damascus in the New Testament is in connection with the conversion and ministry of *Paul* (*q. v.*).

Dam'mim (dăm'im). *See* Ephes-dammim, Pas-dammim.

Damnation (rendering of several Greek terms, denoting *judgment, destruction,* etc.), a word used to denote the final loss of the soul, but not to be always so understood. Thus, in II Pet. 2:1, the expression "damnable heresies" means *destructive opinions;* "they that resist shall receive to themselves damnation" (Rom. 13:2), evidently *condemnation,* i. e., from the rulers. Again, in I Cor. 11:29, the *damnation* resulting from "eating and drinking unworthily" is *condemnation* (so rendered in v. 34). Just what it is to which the offender may be condemned lies with God. Some suppose temporal judgments from God and the censure of wise and good men. In Rom. 14:23, "He that doubteth is damned if he eat," i. e., is condemned by conscience and by God because he is not satisfied that he is right in so doing. *See* Punishment, Everlasting.

Dan, *judge,* the fifth son of Jacob and the first of Bilhah, Rachel's maid (Gen. 30:6).

1. **Personal History.** Of the patriarch himself no incident is preserved. By the blessing of Jacob on his deathbed it was settled that Dan and his other sons by handmaids should be legally entitled to a portion of the family inheritance.

2. **Tribe of Dan.** (1) **Numbers.** Only one son is attributed to Dan (Gen. 46:23), but it may be observed that "Hushim" is a plural form, as if the name, not of an individual, but of a family. At the exodus the tribe of Dan numbered sixty-two thousand seven hundred warriors (Num. 1:39), and at the second census sixty-four thousand four hundred, holding their rank as *second.* (2) **Position in camp.** Dan's position in the journey was on the north of the tabernacle, with Asher and Naphtali. The standard of the tribe was of white and red, and the crest upon it an eagle, the great foe to serpents, which had been chosen by the leader instead of a serpent, because Jacob had compared Dan to a serpent. Ahiezer substituted the eagle, the destroyer of

serpents, as he shrank from carrying an adder upon his flag. (3) **Prominent persons.** One who played a prominent part in the wanderings was "Aholiab, the son of Ahisamach, of the tribe of Dan" (Exod. 31:6, et. seq.). Samson was also a Danite (Judg. 13:2, sq.). (4) **Territory.** Dan was the last of the tribes to receive his portion, which was the smallest of the twelve. It had, however, great natural advantages, was very fertile, and had also a line of seacoast, which seems to have led them to engage in fishing and commerce, for in the war of Sisera and Barak Dan remained in ships (Judg. 5:17). It included the cities of Joppa, Lydda, and Ekron. (5) **Capture of Laish.** Crowded by the Amorites from the rich lowlands up into the mountains, the Danites turned their attention to territory in the north of Palestine. A force of six hundred men was sent, who captured and burned Laish, afterward rebuilding it and naming it Dan (Judg. 18:14-29). This city, with others, was laid waste by Ben-hadad (I Kings 15:20; II Chron. 16:4), and this is the last mention of the place. It is now called Tell el Kâdy ("mound of the judge").

Dan, Camp of (Judg. 13:25; 18:12, A. V. "Mahaneh-dan"), the name given to the district in which the Danites pitched before emigrating northward; or perhaps the location of some Danite families which remained.

Dan, City of. 1. Formerly Laish, but taken by the Danites and called *Dan* (q. v.).

2. There is a reference in Ezek. 27:29 in the A. V. to "Dan also" (Heb. *wᵉdăn*), but the R. V. has it correctly "Vedan," which has been thought to be Aden in Arabia, once the chief trading port of Arabia before the rise of Mochar.

"Dan even to Be'er-sheba." Dan being the northern boundary of Canaan, and Beersheba its most southerly town, this proverbial saying expressed the extreme length of the land (Judg. 20:1; I Sam. 3:20, etc.).

Dance.

1. **Among the Egyptians** the dance consisted mostly of a succession of figures, in which the performers endeavored to exhibit a great variety of gesture. Men and women danced at the same time or in separate parties, but the latter were generally preferred from their superior grace and elegance. Some danced to slow airs, adapted to the style of their movement—the attitudes they assumed frequently partook of a grace not unworthy of the Greeks—and others preferred a lively step, regulated by an appropriate tune. Graceful attitudes and gesticulation were the general style of their dance, but, as in other countries, the taste of the performance varied according to the rank of the person by whom they were employed, or their own skill; and the dance at the house of a priest differed from that among the uncouth peasantry or the lower classes of townsmen.

It was not customary for the upper orders of Egyptians to indulge in this amusement, either in public or private assemblies, and none appear to have practiced it but the lower ranks of society and those who gained their livelihood by attending festive meetings.

The dresses of the female dancers were light and of the finest texture, showing by their transparent quality the form and movement of the limbs. They generally consisted of a loose-flowing robe, reaching to the ankles, occasionally fastened tight at the waist, and round the hips was a small narrow girdle, adorned with beads or ornaments of various colors. Slaves were taught dancing as well as music, and in the houses of the rich, besides their other occupations, that of dancing to entertain the family or a party of friends was required of them; and free Egyptians also gained a livelihood by their performances. The dances of the lower orders generally had a tendency toward a species of pantomime; and the rude peasantry were more delighted with ludicrous and extravagant dexterity than with gestures which displayed elegance and grace. The Egyptians also danced at the temples in honor of the gods, and in some processions, as they approached the precincts of the sacred courts.

2. **The Greeks**, though they employed women who practiced music and dancing to entertain the guests, looked upon the dance as a recreation in which all classes might indulge, and an accomplishment becoming a gentleman; and it was also a Jewish custom for young ladies to dance at private entertainments (Matt. 14:6), as it is at Damascus and other Eastern towns.

3. **The Romans**, on the contrary, were far from considering it worthy of a man of rank or of a sensible person; and Cicero says: "No man who is sober dances, unless he is out of his mind, either when alone or in any decent society, for dancing is the companion of wanton conviviality, dissoluteness, and luxury." Nor did the Greeks indulge in it to excess; and effeminate dances or extraordinary gesticulation were deemed indecent in men of character and wisdom.

4. **Hebrew.** Among the Jews dancing was always a favorite social pastime among girls and women (Jer. 31:4), imitated by children playing on the street (Job 21:11; Matt. 11:17; Luke 7:32), and was engaged in by female companies in honor of national joys, especially of victories (I Sam. 18:6) and religious festivities (Exod. 15:20; Judg. 21:21). On such occasions, at least in more ancient times, men also testified the joy of their hearts by dancing (II Sam. 6:5, 14). A religious meaning belonged also to the torch dance, which arose later, by men in the temple on the first evening of the Feast of Tabernacles. The dances probably consisted only of circular movements, with artless rhythmical steps and lively gesticulations, the women beating cymbals and triangles (Judg. 11:34). When at national festivities other instruments were played (Psa. 68:25; 150:4). Of public female dancers, as are frequently found in the modern East, there is not a trace to be found in Old Testament times. Such dancing as that of Herodias's daughter before men at a voluptuous banquet (Matt. 14:6; Mark 6:22, sq.) was first introduced among the Jews through the influence of corrupt Greek customs.

The Jewish dance was performed by the sexes separately. There is no evidence from sacred history that the diversion was promiscuously enjoyed, except it might be at the erection of the deified calf, when, in imitation of the Egyptian festival of Apis, all classes of the Hebrews intermingled in the frantic revelry. In the sacred dances, although both sexes seem to have frequently borne a part in in the procession or chorus, they remained in distinct and separate companies (Psa. 68:25; Jer. 31:13). The dances of the virgins at Shiloh were certainly part of a religious festivity (Judg. 21:19-23).

A form of religious dancing sometimes made part of the public worship of the early Christians. The custom was borrowed from the Jews, in whose solemn processions choirs of young men and maidens, moving in time with solemn music, always bore a part. It must not be supposed that the "religious dances" had any similarity to modern amusements. They were rather processions, in which all who took part marched in time with the hymns which they sung. The custom was very early laid aside, probably because it might have led to the adoption of such objectionable dances as were employed in honor of the pagan deities. Prohibitions of dancing as an amusement abound in the Church fathers and in the decrees of the councils.

5. **Figurative.** Dancing in the Scriptures is symbolical of joy in contrast with mourning (Psa. 30:11, etc.).

Dan'iel (dăn'yĕl; *God is my judge*).

1. **The Son of David,** the second by Abigail, the Carmelitess (I Chron. 3:1). In the parallel passage, II Sam. 3:3, he is called Chileab.

2. **The celebrated prophet** and minister at the court of Babylon, whose life and prophecies are contained in the book bearing his name. Nothing is known of his parentage or family, but he appears to have been of royal or noble descent (Dan. 1:3) and to have possessed considerable personal endowments (Dan. 1:4). (1) **Early life.** He was taken to Babylon while yet a boy, together with three other Hebrew youths of rank—Hananiah, Mishael, and Azariah—at the first deportation of the people of Judah in the fourth year of Jehoiakim (B. C. 604). (2) **Enters the king's service.** He and his companions were obliged to enter the service of the royal court of Babylon, on which occasion he received the Chaldean name of Belteshazzar, according to the Eastern custom when a change takes place in one's condition of life, and more especially if his personal liberty is thereby affected (comp. II Kings 23:34; 24:17). Daniel, like Joseph, gained the favor of his guardian, and was allowed by him to carry out his wise intention of abstaining from unclean food and idolatrous ceremonies (1:8-16). His prudent conduct and absolute refusal to comply with such customs were crowned with the divine blessing and had the most important results. (3) **Interprets dreams.** After three years of discipline Daniel was presented to the king, and shortly after he had an opportunity of exercising his peculiar gift (1:17) of interpreting dreams—not only recalling the forgotten vision of the king, but also revealing its meaning (2:14, sq.). As a reward he was made "ruler over the whole province of Babylon" and "chief of the governors over all the wise men of Babylon" (2:48). Later he interpreted another of Nebuchadnezzar's dreams to the effect that he was to lose for a time his throne, but to be again restored to it after his humiliation had been completed (Dan. 4). (4) **In retirement.** Under the unworthy successors of Nebuchadnezzar Daniel appears to have occupied an inferior position (Dan. 8:27) and no longer to have been "master of the magicians" (4:8, 9), probably living at Susa (8:2). In the first year of King Belshazzar (7:1), B. C. about 555, he was both alarmed and comforted by a remarkable vision (ch. 7), followed by one two years later (ch. 8), which disclosed to him the future course of events and the ultimate fate of the most powerful empires of the world, but in particular their relations to the kingdom of God and its development to the great consummation. (5) **Restored to office.** He interpreted the handwriting on the wall which disturbed the feast of Belshazzar (5:10-28), and, notwithstanding his bold denunciation of the king, the latter appointed him the "third ruler of the kingdom" (5:29). After the fall of Babylon Darius ascended the throne and made Daniel the first of the "three presidents" of the empire (6:2). In deep humiliation and prostration of spirit he then prayed to the Almighty in the name of his people for forgiveness of their sins and for the divine mercy in their behalf; and the answering promises which he received far exceeded the tenor of his prayer, for the visions of the seer were extended to the end of Judaism (ch. 9). (6) **Persecution.** His elevation to the highest post of honor and the scrupulous discharge of his official duty aroused the envy and jealousy of his colleagues, who conspired against him. They persuaded the monarch to pass a decree forbidding anyone for thirty days to offer prayer to any person save the king. For his disobedience the prophet was thrown into a den of lions, but was miraculously saved and again raised to the highest posts of honor (ch. 6). (7) **Patriotism.** He lived to enjoy the happiness of seeing his people restored to their own land, and though his advanced age would not allow him to be among those who returned to Palestine, yet did he never for a moment cease to occupy his mind and heart with his people and their concerns (10:12). At the accession of Cyrus he still retained his prosperity (1:21; 6:28). (8) **Visions.** In the third year of Cyrus he had a series of visions, in which he was informed of the minutest details respecting the future history and sufferings of his nation to a period of their true redemption through Christ, as also a consolatory notice to himself to proceed calmly and peaceably to the end of his days, and then await patiently the resurrection of the dead (chaps. 10-12). It is not worthwhile to mention here the various fables respecting the later life and death of Daniel, as all accounts are vague and confused.

Character. In the prophecies of Ezekiel mention is made of Daniel as a pattern of righteousness (14:14, 20) and wisdom (28:3), and, since Daniel was still young at that time

(B. C. 594-588), some have thought that another prophet or the legendary Danel of the Ugaritic epic literature of the 14th century B. C. discovered at Ras Shamra, Syria, in 1929-1937, must be referred to. But Daniel was conspicuous for purity and knowledge at a very early age (Dan. 1:4, 17, 20), and he was probably over thirty years af age at the time of Ezekiel's prophecy. *See* Daniel, Book of.

3. **A priest** of the family of Ithamar who returned from the exile with Ezra (Ezra 8:2), B. C. about 457. He is probably the same as the priest Daniel who joined in the covenant drawn up by Nehemiah (Neh. 10:6), B. C. 445.

Daniel, Book of, one of the most important prophetical books of the O. T., indispensable as an introduction to N. T. prophecy dealing with the "times of the Gentiles" (Luke 21:24), the manifestation of the man of sin, the great tribulation, the second coming of Christ, the resurrection and the judgments. Daniel's visions encompass the whole period of Gentile world rule to its destruction and the setting up of the Messianic Kingdom.

1. **Contents.**

Part I. Daniel's visions under Nebuchadnezzar and his personal history to the reign of Cyrus, 1:1-6:28
   a. Reasons for Daniel's fame and prosperity, 1:1-21
   b. The image vision embracing Gentile world empire until its destruction by the "smiting stone," Christ and His second advent, 2:1-49
   c. Deliverance from the fiery furnace, 3:1-30
   d. Nebuchadnezzar's tree vision, 4:1-37
   e. Belshazzar's feast and the fall of Babylon, 5:1-31
   f. Deliverance from the lion's den, 6:1:28

Part II. Daniel's great prophetical visions, 7:1-12:13
   a. The four beasts and the second coming of Christ, 7:1-28
   b. Vision of the ram and the rough goat, 8:1-27
   c. Vision of the seventy weeks, 9:1-27 Embracing the first advent, 9:20-26 and Israel's final tribulation and the second advent, v. 27
   d. The vision of God's Glory, 10:1-21
   e. Prediction of the rule of the Ptolemies and Seleucidae and end-time events, 11:1-45
   f. The great tribulation, 12:1
      The resurrections, 12:2, 3
      Daniel's concluding message, 12:4-13

2. **The Danielic Authorship.** A Maccabean date (c. 167 B. C.) and the rejection of the traditional Danielic authorship are alleged assured achievements of modern criticism. These views, however, are built upon a number of highly plausible fallacies: a. *That Daniel's prophecy was placed among writings in the third section of the Hebrew canon and not among the prophets in the second division because it was not in existence when the canon of the prophets was closed, allegedly between 300-200 B. C.* This conclusion is based upon the unsound critical theory of canonization and also fails to take into account the official status of the prophet as a determining factor in the formation of the Hebrew canon. Although possessing the prophetic gift (Matt. 24:15), Daniel everywhere appears as a statesman and not as a prophet. b. It is assumed that because *Daniel is not mentioned in the list of writers in the book of Ecclesiasticus* (c. 180 B. C.) that the book, therefore, did not exist at that time. This argument from silence is dubious as neither Asa, Jehoshaphat or Ezra is mentioned. c. It is maintained that the *author of Daniel makes erroneous statements about history of the sixth century B. C.*, which would be incredible on the part of one who really lived during that period. The campaign of Nebuchadnezzar referred to in 1:1 is an example. But this again is an argument from silence for no extant source has proved this reference erroneous. Numbers of alleged discrepancies in chapter 5 have been obviated or cleared up by archaeological light, such as the existence of Belshazzar as king, who is called the son of (meaning nothing more than the royal successor of) Nebuchadnezzar. d. Alleged literary features of Daniel are adduced to prove its late date. There is no reason at all to conclude, for instance, that the three Greek words, names of musical instruments (Dan. 3:10), "demand a date" after the conquest of Palestine by Alexander the Great (332 B. C.), as S. R. Driver (*Introduction to the Literature of the O. T.*, p. 508) contends. It is becoming increasingly evident that Greek culture penetrated the Near East at a much earlier date than had formerly been supposed. Nebuchadnezzar's court was evidently highly cosmopolitan. If Jewish captives were required to furnish music (Psa. 137:3), why is it so incredible to believe that Greeks from Ionia, Lydia, Cilicia, and Cyprus were required to do the same? A slight Persian influence is certainly not astonishing since Daniel lived on into the Persian period. Neither is there anything decisive against Danielic authorship in the considerable Aramaic portions of the book. e. The critical claim that *the reference to Daniel in Ezekiel* (14:14 and 20; 28:23) *is to the ancient Semitic legendary figure of Danel*, who renders justice in the Ras Shamra poems of the fourteenth century B. C., is highly plausible, but certainly unsound. Why should Ezekiel classify a pagan figure with holy men such as Job and Noah? The fact is that the Ezekiel references furnish comparative historical evidence of the historicity of Daniel.

3. **Interpretation.** Considerable difference in interpretation of the great visions of Daniel is set forth by amillennial and premillennial commentators. Premillennialists contend that there will yet be established a future kingdom of Israel. Amillennialists generally view the first coming of Christ as an event initiating a spiritual Messianic kingdom. Premillennialists, on the other hand, see this as a vision of the destruction of Gentile world system, and "the Stone becoming a mountain and filling the whole earth" of the Monarchy Vision (2:31-45) is thought of as the establishment of the kingdom over Israel. Such a destruction of

Gentile world governments did not occur at the first advent of Christ. The Roman Empire was then at its height. Since the crucifixion, the Roman Empire has followed out the history marked in Daniel's great Monarchy Vision. Gentile world power still continues and it will only end by catastrophic judgment at Armageddon (Rev. 16:14; 19:21). Likewise in the great visions of chaps. 7 and 8, a difference of interpretation prevails. Premillennialists see the wild beasts portrayed in chap. 7 as picturing the outward voracious nature of the same world empires and Gentile world rule as exhibited in the monarchy vision of chap. 2. The "lion" of 7:4 is Babylon; the "bear" (7:5) is Media-Persia; the "leopard" (7:6) is Greece under Alexander; the nondescript beast of 7:7 is the Roman Empire; 7:8 gives a vision of the end of Gentile world dominion. Gentile world dominion in the end time will have "ten horns," (that is, ten kings Rev. 17:12), corresponding to the "ten toes" in the Monarchy Vision. "The little horn" of 7:8 prefigures Antiochus Epiphanes and through him the final Beast (II Thess. 2:4-8; Rev. 13:4-10). Chap. 7:9-12 presents the second coming of Christ in glory to set up His earthly kingdom. In chap. 8 the vision of the "ram" with the two horns and the "he-goat" with the one notable horn symbolizes the transfer of world power from Media-Persia in the East to Greece under Alexander in the West. The little horn prefigures Antiochus Epiphanes and through him the final Antichrist. The vision of the Seventy Weeks of chap. 9 constitutes one of the pivotal prophecies of the Bible, whether the amillennial interpretation of it as historical or the premillennial view as prophetic is adopted. Many prophetic Bible teachers hold that the Seventieth Week (q. v.) is yet future and corresponds to the Great Tribulation discoursed upon by our Lord in Matt. 24:21. Premillennialists, accordingly, see a gap or hiatus between vs. 26 and 27 in which they place the church period between the first and second advents. Amillennialists deny the "gap theory" and interpret the Seventy Weeks as fulfilled in connection with the first advent and the death of Christ 'and events closely connected with it. Dan. 11:1-12:13 gives a prophetic panorama from Darius to the man of sin (II Thess. 2: 3-4). The spirit of prophecy returns to Daniel's day. Daniel traces the remaining history of the Persian Empire to Greece, "the mighty king" of Greece (11:3). The division of Alexander's empire into four parts (11:4) as already predicted in 8:22, is here again foretold. Verses 4-20, in a most amazing fashion, minutely trace the wars between the Ptolemies and the Seleucidae of Syria. Antiochus Epiphanes occupies the vision down to vs. 36. From 11:36 the interpretation broadens out to the final little "horn." His prosperity continues until "the indignation" is accomplished (vs. 36). "The indignation" is the Great Tribulation (Dan. 12:1; Matt. 24:21). Verses 38-45 portray the little horn's career as an irresistible conqueror (40-44). He establishes the headquarters of his authority in Jerusalem. From this period begins the Great Tribulation which lasts for three and one-half

years (Dan. 7:25; 12:7, 11; Rev. 13:5). Thus the Book of Daniel, according to premillennialists, portrays the destruction of Gentile world power under the Beast or little horn. This is effected by the second coming of Christ and the establishment of the kingdom over Israel. M. F. U.

Dan'ite (Judg. 13:2; 18:1, 11; I Chron. 12: 35), one of the tribe of *Dan* (q. v.).

Dan-ja'an (dăn-jā'án; II Sam. 24:6). The LXX. and the Vulgate read "Dan in the woods." Opinions differ as to whether this is identical with Dan or Laish, or the ancient site called Danian in the mountains above Khan en-Nakura, south of Tyre, or a place near Gilead.

Dan'nah (dăn'ná; *murmuring*), a city in the mountains of Judah, about eight miles from Hebron (Josh. 15:49).

Da'ra (dä'rá), a contracted or corrupt form (I Chron. 2:6) of the name *Darda* (q. v.).

Dar'da (där'dá), a son of Mahal, one of the four men of great fame for their wisdom, but surpassed by Solomon (I Kings 4:31), B. C. before 960. In I Chron. 2:6, however, the same four names occur again as "sons of Zerah," of the tribe of Judah, with the slight difference that Darda appears as Dara. Although the identity of these persons with those in I Kings 4 has been much debated, they are doubtless the same.

Dari'us Hystas'pes (dá-rī'ús hĭs-tăs'pēz), king of Persia (521-486 B. C., Ezra 4:5, 24; 5:5-7; 6:1, 12, 15; Hag. 1:1; 2:10; Zech. 1:1, 7; 7:1), the restorer of the Persian empire founded by Cyrus the Great (*see* Cyrus). Cyrus was succeeded in 529 B. C. by his son Cambyses, who possessed his father's adventurous spirit without his commanding genius. He added first Phoenicia and Cyprus, and afterward Egypt, to the new empire, but failed in attempting to carry out impracticable schemes of conquest in North Africa and Ethiopia. Encouraged by these disasters to Cambyses a pretender seized the throne, claiming that he was Smerdis, the deceased younger son of Cyrus, who had not long survived his father's death. Cambyses, despairing of success against the usurper, put an end to his own life while on his homeward march. The impostor, after a reign of a few months, was dethroned by Darius, the son of Hystaspes, in 521 B. C., who headed an insurrection of the nobles against him. Darius was apparently the rightful heir

113. Darius (seated) Receives a Petitioner
(relief from Persepolis, Iran)

to the throne, being descended, collaterally with Cyrus, from the ancient royal line of Persia. The reign of Darius belongs more to general than to Bible history; but as he had great influence on the history of the world, as well as upon the fortunes of the Jews, we must notice the leading stages of his career. For our information we are indebted not only to the Greek historians, but to his own inscriptions, written in the Old Persian cuneiform alphabet, whose decipherment also gave the key to the more ancient and complex Assyrian and Babylonian system of ideograms and syllable signs. (1) **Period of revolt.** The genius for universal rule possessed by Cyrus, his power of conciliation, his generosity and tolerance, had kept his heterogeneous empire in peace and contentment for seventeen years after the submission of the Lydians and Greeks of Asia Minor and nine years after the capture of Babylon. But during the reign of Cambyses discontent and misrule prepared the way for open revolt, which at the accession of Darius was carried on in all parts of his dominions. To name the disaffected districts would simply be to enumerate the provinces of the empire, or, more summarily, the countries of which it was originally composed. Persia proper, Susiana (Elam), Media, Babylonia, Assyria, Armenia, Parthia, Hyrcania, with less known regions to the east, revolted successively or concurrently, while the governors of Asia Minor and Egypt quietly assumed their independence. But the energy and military skill of Darius everywhere prevailed, and the whole formidable uprising was quelled after six years' work of stern repression, so that by 515 B. C. the sole authority of Persia was recognized in all the lands that had been subdued by Cyrus and Cambyses. (2) **Period of reorganization.** Cyrus had made it his policy to interfere as little as possible with the modes of government followed by his several subject states. For example, in many countries the native kings were confirmed and encouraged in their autonomous administration upon the payment of a reasonable tribute, and in the smaller states native governors looked after the royal revenues and at the same time ruled their people in accordance with traditional methods. This whole system was changed by Darius, who abolished the local kingdoms and principalities, divided the whole empire into "satrapies," each satrap being a Persian official with supreme authority in civil affairs, and a division of the imperial army to support him and maintain the government against all outside attacks. Judges were also appointed with fixed circuits, and a system of posts was established, with royal roads extending everywhere for the transmission of dispatches and rescripts to and from the capital cities of Susa or Persepolis. Notice that this governmental system was an advance on the old Assyrian despotism, in that the sovereign ruled by delegated power, while still falling short of the representative systems that had their origin in the Greek republics. What is of particular importance to Bible readers is the application of the system to Palestine. There the returning exiles expected to found an autonomous princedom, but under Darius there was erected instead the Persian province of Judah, with imperial supervision over matters civil and religious. (3) **Period of foreign conquests.** Not content with the empire that fell to him by succession, Darius planned and carried out vast schemes of foreign conquest. The most important of these were the acquisition, about 512 B. C., of northwestern India, and the subjection, about 508 B. C., of the coast land between the Bosporus and the Grecian state of Thessaly. By the former the navigation of the lower Indus was controlled and the trade of India opened up by way of the Persian Gulf, with an enormous increase of the imperial revenue. The expedition which accomplished the latter result crossed the Bosporus, conquered maritime Thrace and Macedonia and the adjacent territory of the warlike Scythians to the north, whose inroads were a continual menace to the Asiatic provinces. Thus the Persian dominions now extended from the Caucasus to the borders of northern Greece and "from India even unto Ethiopia" (Esth. 1:1). (4) **Period of the Grecian wars.** These, as is well known, were precipitated by disturbances among the Greeks of the Asiatic coast. The revolt of the subject cities, in 501 B. C., was supported for a time by the European states of Athens and Eretria. It lasted till 494 B. C., and after its complete suppression steps were immediately taken by Darius for vengeance upon the foreigners. The first great expedition by land and sea, in 493, did not quite reach its destination, and the second by sea, in 490 was frustrated by the world-famous defeat at Marathon. These expeditions were led by generals of Darius, and he made plans for a third which he was to command in person. A revolt in Egypt, in 487, and his own death, in 486, put an end to the designs. He was succeeded by his son Xerxes, the Ahasuerus of the Book of Esther, whose mother was a daughter of Cyrus the Great. (5) **Darius and the Jews.** The exiles who returned under the protection of Cyrus (537 B. C.), having begun their political and religious life at Jerusalem, were thwarted in their efforts to rebuild the temple by the Samaritans and other adversaries, who accused them of intrigue and sedition against the Persian government. Cyrus, being occupied with his eastern wards, did not take upon himself to interfere for the prosecution of the work. His successor, Cambyses, had little sympathy with his struggling subjects. Thus the restoration of the sanctuary, so essential in all ways to the progress of the little nation, was delayed for seventeen years (Ezra 4:24). The accession of Darius gave new hope to the leaders of the Jews. In 520 B. C. the prophets Haggai and Zechariah stirred up the people to renewed efforts, and under their inspiration Zerubbabel, the civil leader of the colony, set earnestly to work (Ezra 5:1, 2). An appeal to Darius by Tattenai, the satrap of Syria (Ezra 5:3-17), embodying a memorial from the leaders of the Jews, resulted in the confirmation of their contention that their proceedings were not only lawful, but actually carried on under royal authority. Darius gave orders that search should be made, with the result that in Ecbatana the edict of Cyrus was found containing all that the Jews had claimed (Ezra 6: 1-5). Darius therefore made a new proclamation insisting that no obstacle should be put in the way of the people of Jerusalem; that the building of the temple should be forwarded; that interference with the work should be a capital offense, and that contributions should be made in money and goods from the king's local revenues toward the expenses of the restoration (Ezra 6:6-12). Accordingly the satrap and his officers with all diligence carried out the orders of Darius (6:13, sq.), with the result that the temple was finished and dedicated in the sixth year of Darius (516 B. C.).

114. Ruins of a Corner of Darius' Winter Palace, Persepolis, Iran

Darius the Mede (Dan. 5:31, 6:1, 6, 9, 25, 28; 9:1; 11:1) is to be identified with Gobryas (Gubaru), the governor of Babylon under Cyrus. Darius is most certainly another name for Gubaru. That he was styled "king" is to be regarded as not inaccurate in describing a man of Gubaru's authority since he was *amel pihate* of the city or province of Babylon, nor does this title usurp the absolute sovereignty of Cyrus (*q. v.*). Moreover, it is not necessary to discover cuneiform tablets dated according to the years of Darius' reign in order to substantiate the Biblical datings. These Biblical datings of Darius' reign (Dan. 9:1 and 11:1) are exactly paralleled by the datings of Belshazzar's reign (Dan. 7:1; 8:1). This conclusion is warranted since it is now known that the author of Daniel took into consideration Belshazzar's secondary position in the Babylonian Empire (cf. Dan. 5:7, 16, 29). Nor does the author of Daniel, while attributing far-reaching administrative powers to Darius detract from his subordination to Cyrus. Darius is said to have "received the kingdom" (Dan. 5:31) and to have been "made king over the realm of the Chaldeans" (Dan. 9:1). Behind these statements is the implication that Darius was not the supreme ruler of the Persian Empire. Daniel 6:28 portrays Daniel as prospering not in the consecutive reigns of two independent sovereigns, but during the reigns of two contemporary rulers, one being subordinate to the other. "So this Daniel prospered in the reign of Darius *and* in the reign of Cyrus the Persian." Gubaru (Gobryas), it is now known, appointed governors in Babylon after the fall of the city, and Cyrus departed for Ecbatana before the end of the year. The only possible ruler of Babylon was Darius, since Cambyses did not reign as subking until the following year, being removed from this honorary position after a few months, while Gubaru continued as governor of Babylon and the District Beyond the River for some years. Since the territory ruled by Gubaru was coextensive with the Fertile Crescent and included many different peoples and races, the description in Dan. 6:25-28 of Darius' decree is explainable. Neither does the decree of Darius in Dan. 6:7, 12 exclude the possibility of his being a subordinate ruler. Darius' second decree (Dan. 6:26), which was published to annul the first decree was addressed to "all the dominions of *my kingdom*," not the entire Persian Empire. "Unto all peoples, nations, and languages that dwell in all the earth" can be rendered "in all the land" (Dan. 6:25) and does not claim universal sovereignty for Darius. Moreover, Gubaru was doubtless "the son of Ahasuerus" and also a Mede. In the light of these various facts, it is maintained that Darius the Mede is to be identified with Gubaru the Governor of Babylon and that the book of Daniel is accurate in this historical reference. (The writer is indebted for this material to Prof. John C. Whitcomb, Jr. of Grace Theological Seminary, Winona Lake, Indiana, who wrote his master of divinity thesis (unpublished) on *The Historicity of Darius the Mede in the Book of Daniel*). M. F. U.

Darius the Persian (Neh. 12:22). This was Darius Codomannus, the last king of Persia (B. C. 336-330), whose empire was destroyed by Alexander the Great. He was a contemporary of the high priest Jaddua, who is referred to in the same verse. Thus the Bible brings before us nearly all the notable kings of Persia, from first to last.

Darkness (Heb. *hōshĕk, the dark;* Gr. *skotos*), in the physical sense, is specially noticed, on three occasions, in the Scriptures:

1. At the period of creation, when darkness, it is said, "was on the face of the deep," the dispelling of which, by the introduction of light, was the commencement of that generative process by which order and life were brought out of primeval chaos (Gen. 1:2-4).

2. The plague of darkness in Egypt (Exod. 10:21), "darkness that might be felt." *See* Plagues of Egypt.

3. The awful moment of our Lord's crucifixion, when "from the sixth hour there was darkness over all the land unto the ninth hour" (Matt. 27:45). Some, chiefly ancient writers, have insisted upon rendering "over all the *earth*," and account for it by an eclipse of the sun. But an eclipse of the sun could not be visible to the whole world, and, moreover, there could not have been an eclipse, for it was the time of full moon, when the moon could not come between the sun and the earth. The darkness would, therefore, seem to have been confined to Palestine, and may have been caused by an extraordinary and preternatural obstruction of the light of the sun by the sulphurous vapors accompanying the earthquake which then occurred.

The "thick darkness where God was" (Exod. 20:21) was doubtless the "thick darkness" in which "the Lord said he would dwell" (I Kings 8:12), and has reference to the cloud upon the mercy seat. "Cloud and darkness are round about him" (Psa. 97:2) refers to the inscrutability of the divine nature and working. The *darkness* connected with the coming of the Lord (Isa. 13:9, 10; Joel 2:31; Matt. 24:29, etc.) has reference to the judgments attendant on his advent.

Figurative. Darkness is used as symbolical of ignorance and spiritual blindness (Isa. 9:2; John 1:5; I John 2:8, etc.). With respect to the gloom associated with darkness it becomes significant of sorrow and distress; hence, "the day of darkness" is the time of calamity and trouble (Joel 2:2). Isa. 8:22; 9:2; 13:10, etc., refer to the unlighted streets of Eastern countries, and indicate the despair and wretchedness of the lost. Darkness affording a covering for the performance of evil, "the works of darkness" (Eph. 5:11) is employed to designate the more flagrant exhibitions of unrighteousness. Darkness is used to represent the state of the dead (Job. 10:21; 18:18).

Dar'kon (där'kŏn), one whose "children," or descendants, were among the "servants of Solomon" who returned from Babylon with Zerubbabel (Ezra 2:56; Neh. 7:58), B. C. about 458.

Darling (Heb. *yāḥîd; united, only*, hence *beloved;* Psa. 22:20; 35:17), one's *self.*

Dart, the rendering of several Hebrew and Greek words, meaning an arrow or light spear. The Hebrews are supposed to have discharged the arrow while on fire, to which allusion may be made in Deut. 32:23, 42; Psa. 7:13; 120:4; Zech. 9:14; Eph. 6:16. *See* Armor.

Da'than (dā'thăn; *of a spring,* or *well*), a Reubenite chieftain, son of Eliab, who joined the conspiracy of Korah, the Levite, and, with his accomplices, was swallowed up by an earthquake (Num. 16:1, sq.; 26:9; Deut. 11:6; Psa. 106:17), B. C. about 1435.

Daughter (Heb. *băth,* feminine of bēn, *son;* Gr. *thugatēr*) is used in Scripture, like son, with some latitude. In addition to its usual and proper sense of daughter, born or adopted, it is used to designate *a step-sister,* niece, or *any* female descendant (Gen. 20:12; 24:48; Num. 25:1; Deut. 23:17). More generally still it is used of the female branch of a family, or female portion of community, as "the daughters of Moab," of "the Philistines," "of Aaron" (Num. 25:1; II Sam. 1:20; Luke 1:5). Small towns were called daughters of neighboring large mother cities, as "Heshbon and all her daughters" (Num. 21:25, marg.); so Tyre is called the daughter of Zidon (Isa. 23:12).

Cities were commonly personified as women, and so, naturally, had the designation given to them of *daughters* of the country to which they belonged, as "daughter of Zion," "daughter of Jerusalem" (Isa. 37:22, etc.). The condition of daughters, that is, of young women, in the East, their employments, duties, etc., may be gathered from various parts of the Scriptures, and seems to have borne but little resemblance to that of young women of respectable parentage among ourselves. Rebekah drew and fetched water; Rachel kept

sheep, as did the daughters of Jethro, though he was a priest, or a prince, of Midian. They superintended and performed domestic services for the family. Tamar, though a king's daughter, baked bread.

Daughter-in-law (Heb. *kăläh;* Gr. *numphē*), means, literally, a *bride,* and is applied to a son's wife.

Da'vid.

1. **Name and Family.** His name in Hebrew means "beloved" or possibly "chieftain," as evidence from the Mari Letters indicates. Reference in these tablets to the plundering "Benjamites" is indicated by the word *dawîdum* ("leader"), which is apparently the original form of the name of Israel's most famous king. He was born in Bethlehem, the youngest son of a sheik of that town named Jesse (I Sam. 16:1; II Sam. 5:4). Apparently David had seven older brothers (I Sam. 16: 10).

2. **Early History.** His boyhood was spent as a shepherd. He was eminently gifted, being skilled in playing the lyre (I Sam. 16:18). David was conspicuous for valor, slaying a lion and a bear in defense of his father's flocks (I Sam. 17:34-36). As a humble shepherd lad he was anointed as Saul's successor by Samuel (I Sam. 16:1-13).

115. David Trying on Saul's Armor (Byzantine silver dish; c. 625 A. D.)

3. **His Relations with Saul.** As a result of Saul's disobedience to the divine command, he was rejected from the kingship and afflicted with melancholia, jealousy and hatred. David was summoned when the evil spirit, or demon, by God's permission came upon Saul. David played so well that Saul was refreshed and the evil spirit departed from him (I Sam. 16:14-23). When Saul's condition presumably improved, David returned to his pastoral pursuits at Bethlehem. On a visit to his brethren, who were fighting in Saul's army against the Philistines, the young shepherd lad whose valiant spirit was nurtured by communion with God was outraged by the cowardice of Saul's army, as it was defied by the Philistine

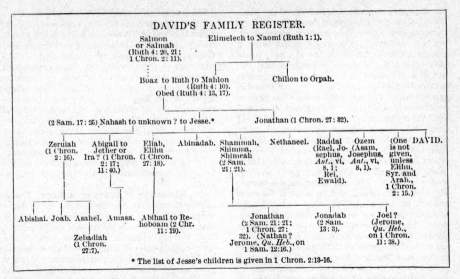

DAVID'S FAMILY REGISTER.

Salmon or Salmah (Ruth 4: 20, 21; 1 Chron. 2: 11).   Elimelech to Naomi (Ruth 1: 1).

Boaz to Ruth to Mahlon (Ruth 4: 10).   Chilion to Orpah.
Obed (Ruth 4: 13, 17).

(2 Sam. 17: 25) Nahash to unknown ? to Jesse.*   Jonathan (1 Chron. 27: 32).

Zeruiah (1 Chron. 2: 16). Abigail to Jether or Ira? (1 Chron. 2: 17; 11: 40.) Eliab, Elihu (1 Chron. 27: 18). Abinadab. Shammah, Shimma, Shimeah (2 Sam. 21: 21). Nethaneel. Raddai (Rael, Josephus, *Ant.*, vi, 8, 1; Rei, Ewald). Ozem (Asam, Josephus, *Ant.*, vi, 8, 1). (One DAVID, is not given, unless Elihu, Syr. and Arab., 1 Chron. 2: 15.)

Abishai. Joab. Asahel. Amasa. Abihail to Rehoboam (2 Chr. 11: 19). Jonathan (2 Sam. 21: 21; 1 Chron. 27: 32). (Nathan? Jerome, *Qu. Heb.*, on 1 Sam. 12:16.) Jonadab (2 Sam. 13: 3). Joel? (Jerome, *Qu. Heb.*, on 1 Chron. 11: 38.)
Zebadiah (1 Chron. 27:7).

* The list of Jesse's children is given in 1 Chron. 2:13-16.

giant-champion, Goliath. David's notable victory over the giant with a simple shepherd's sling and pebbles from the brook gained him national reputation. It was then that Saul made adequate inquiry concerning David's family connections. The result was that David was adopted in the court (I Sam. 17:55-18:2). As a warrior-courtier the young man won the loyal friendship of Saul's son Jonathan (I Sam. 18:1-4). Further clashes with the Philistines greatly enhanced David's reputation. Saul's insane jealousy and hatred against David were aroused when the women of Israel greeted the returning heroes with the song: "Saul hath slain his thousands, and David his ten thousands (18:5-9). From this point on David's life was in constant jeopardy. But he behaved himself so wisely that he attracted universal respect and love. Saul attempted to get rid of him by demanding that he slay 100 Philistines and provide proof of the fact. David performed the feat and received Michal, Saul's daughter. As a consequence, he was saved from death only by the loyalty of Jonathan and his wife, Michal.

4. **A Fugitive and an Outlaw.** The next several years of David's life were spent in fleeing from Saul's rage. Michal was given in marriage to another and was not restored to

David until after Saul's death. He saw Jonathan only by stealth. He fled to Samuel at Ramah, then fled to Nob where, on the pretext of a secret mission from Saul, he gained an answer from the oracle, food and the sword of Goliath. He then fled to Achish, king of Gath, where, as the slayer of Goliath, he feigned madness in order to avoid death at the hands of the Philistines (21:10-15). As an outlaw, David at the head of a band of supporters made the Cave of Adullum his headquarters (I Sam. 22:1, 2). In this general wild and mountainous region he was hunted like an animal. On several occasions Saul was at David's mercy, but he spared his life.

5. **Service under Achish.** Wearied with his wandering life, he at length crossed the Philistine frontier, not as before in the capacity of a fugitive but at the head of a sizeable force of 600 men (I Sam. 27:3, 4). Achish, king of Gath, gave him, after the manner of Eastern kings, the city of Ziklag on the Philistine frontier (27:6). From the Philistines David learned much military knowledge. While away from Ziklag the Amalekites burned the city and carried off the women and children. David was able to overtake the raiders and recover a vast amount of spoil. Two days after this victory an Amalekite arrived with the news of Saul's death at Gilboa.

6. **Early Activity as King.** Saul's death resulted in a crisis in the political history of Israel and a period of civil war followed. David took up his residence at Hebron in the hill country of Judah, some nineteen miles S. W. of Jerusalem. Here he was anointed king over the house of Judah and reigned seven and one-half years over that tribe (II Sam. 2:1-11). Meanwhile the long civil war between the house of Saul and the house of David eventuated in extermination of the house of Saul and David's being anointed king over all Israel (II Sam. 2:8-5:5). The most important event of his early reign was the capture of Jebusite Jerusalem and his making this the capital of the realm. Despite

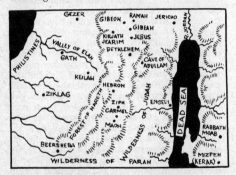

116. David's Wilderness Wanderings

the apparent impregnable defense of the place David took the stronghold, evidently not by climbing up the under-ground water-shaft, but by ascending the stout walls with a grappling hook. Although David's men probably scaled the walls of Jerusalem and did not gain entrance to the Jebusite fortress as previously thought, through the city's underground water system, archaeology has proved conclusively that the "stronghold of Zion" and subsequently "the city of David" (II Sam. 5:7) which the king constructed, were situated on the Eastern hill above the Gihon Fountain and not on the so-called Western hill of Zion. Having conquered the city David made it his capital, displaying great wisdom in this decision. The city stood on the border of Judah and Israel, and its neutral location tended to allay the jealousy between the northern and southern portions of his kingdom. Its liberation from the Canaanites opened the highway between Judah and the north which greatly facilitated both commerce and foreign intercourse and was a potent factor in the unity of the kingdom.

7. Subjugation of Neighboring States. A united Israel under a virile personality like David aroused the fear and jealousy of the Philistines, who were decisively defeated by David (II Sam. 5:17-25; I Chron. 18:1; II Sam. 21:15-22). So complete was David's subjugation of the inveterate enemy of Israel that their power was effectively nullified. David also conquered the Moabites, Arameans, Ammonites, Edomites and Amalekites (II Sam. 8:10; 12:26-31). He was enabled to build up a substantial empire for his son Solomon, which reached from Ezion-Geber on the Gulf of Aqabah in the south to the region of Hums bordering on the city-state of Hamath in the north (cf. W. F. Albright, *Archaeology and the Religion of Israel*, Baltimore, 1931, p. 131).

8. Organization of the Kingdom. David's administrative achievements, although overshadowed by his colorful personal skillful diplomacy and brilliant military strategy, were outstanding. This is clearly reflected in the extensive kingdom he left behind him and the preservation of accounts of efficient organization (Cf. I Chron. 22:17-27:34). His officialdom was organized in part at least on Egyptian models (Cf. Albright, *Op, cit.*, p. 120). Among official Egyptian institutions which he copied, probably through Phoenician or other channels, was the division of the functions between the "recorder," *mazkir*, and the "scribe," *sopher* (II Chron. 8:16, 17) and the Council of Thirty (Cf. I Chron. 27:6). He also efficiently organized his army (II Sam. 8:16) which included a special personal body guard of mercenaries, presumably of Philistine extraction, called Cherethites and Pelethites (II Sam. 8:18).

9. Establishment of Levitical Cities. Although these cities included the cities of refuge (Num. 35) which were provided for by Moses before entrance into the land and established by Joshua after the conquest (Josh. 21:2), it was very unlikely that before the time of Saul or David many of these places, such as Gezer, Ibleam, Taanach, Rehob in Asher,

Joknean and Naholal (Cf. Josh. 21) were actually apportioned to the Levitical priests, since these places were not in Israelite hands before that time. Towns such as Eltekeh and Gibbethon were under Philistine domination previous to the Davidic era. And such such places as Alemoth and Anathoth in the tribe of Benjamin could scarcely have been established as Levitical towns previous to the removal of the tabernacle to Nob in the time of Saul. It seems likely that they were apportioned to the Levites after David's conquest of Jebusite Jerusalem, making it his capital, since there is no doubt that he planned some kind of administrative reorganization of the Israelite confederation (Albright, *op. cit.*, p. 123).

10. Allocation of Cities of Refuge. A wise administrator like David would hardly have overlooked need for asylum for one unjustly accused of crime. Scholars are quite certain that the six cities of refuge as well as the forty-eight Levitical cities figured prominently in David's political reorganization. Such a provision would rule out clan and tribal vendettas which flourished during the period of the judges and were commonly very destructive (Judg. 8:1-4; Josh. 19:1-21:25). David's wise statesmanship was fully cognizant that a well-grounded kingdom would not tolerate blood feuds, and he was quick to take advantage of the Mosaic provision of six refuge cities, three on each side of the Jordan, for the purpose of consolidating the kingdom and contributing to its peace.

11. Jerusalem Made a Religious Center. His most important single act in this direction was the removal of the ark to Jerusalem from Keriath-jearim, where Israel's sacred chest had been, except for a very brief period at Beth-shemesh after the Philistines, in whose territory it had been kept since the battle of Ebenezer (c. 1050 B. C.), had brought it back to Israel. The first attempt to bring up the ark proved abortive (Cf. II Sam. 6:11-15; I Chron. 15:13), because it was not carried according to prescribed Mosaic regulations (Num. 4:5, 15, 19) and David's resort to the Philistine expedient of a new cart drawn by oxen (Cf. I. Sam. 6:7, 8) led to the death of Uzzah. Finally after four months and with great religious celebration the ark was brought up to the city of David (II Sam. 6:12-15) when David is said to have "danced before the Lord . . . girded with a linen ephod" (II Sam. 6:14). The ephod, now illustrated from the Assyrian and Ugaritic texts, was formerly an ordinary garment worn apparently especially by women. Not until later centuries did the ephod become restricted to religious and, subsequently, to priestly use. In Israel, however, it early became a distinctive part of the dress of the Levitical priesthood. Its use by David on this occasion was evidently in his capacity as Yahweh's anointed king and as His special representative. The Davidic tent was certainly copied after the specifications of the Mosaic prototype, as the one that had existed at Nob (I Sam. 21:1, 9).

12. Organization of Sacred Music. Despite modern criticism's denial that David organized Hebrew sacred music, archaeological

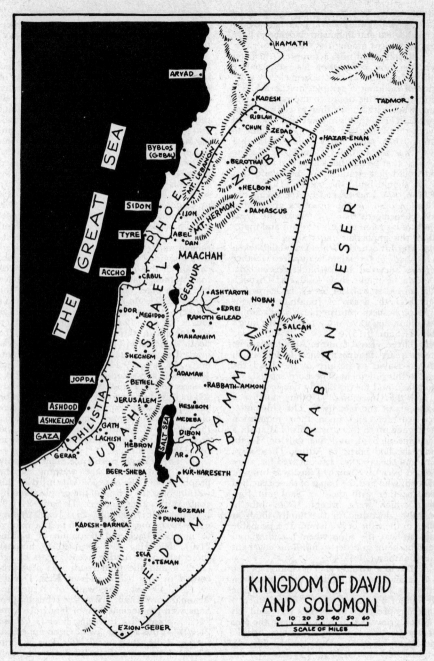

117.

KINGDOM OF DAVID
AND SOLOMON

0 10 20 30 40 50 60
SCALE OF MILES

findings tend to show there is nothing incongruous in the light of conditions existing in the ancient Near Eastern world around 1,000 B. C. with the Biblical representation of David as a patron saint of Jewish hymnology and the organizer of temple music. Palestinian musicians were well known in antiquity, as shown by the Egyptian and Mesopotamian monuments in the early nineteenth century B. C. Semitic craftsmen carried musical instruments with them when they went down into Egypt, as is shown by the famous relief from Beni-Hasan, 169 miles above Cairo. The epic religious literature discovered at Ras Shamra portrays the singers, "*sharim*," as forming a special class of personnel at Ugarit as early as 1400 B. C. The Old Testament narratives themselves give considerable prominence to David's musical and poetical gifts. Musical guilds have been shown by archaeological and linguistic evidence to have been prominent among the Canaanites.

13. **Resolve to build a temple.** After this event the king, contrasting his cedar palace with the curtains of the tabernacle, was desirous of building a temple for the ark. He communicated his desire to the prophet Nathan, who, without waiting to consult God, replied: "Do all that is in thine heart; for God is with thee." But the word of God came to Nathan that same night telling him that David was not to build a house for God to dwell in; that he had been a man of war; that God would first establish his house, and that his son should build the temple (II Sam. 7; I Chron. 17). Encouraged by the divine approbation, and by the promises given him, David henceforth made it one of the great objects of his reign to gather means and material for this important undertaking.

14. **Mephibosheth.** When David had taken up his abode in Jerusalem he inquired whether there yet survived any of Saul's descendants to whom he might show kindness. Through Ziba, an old steward of Saul's, he learned of Mephibosheth, a son of Jonathan. He sent for Mephibosheth, returned him Saul's family possessions, and gave him a place at the king's table (II Sam. 9:13).

15. **Three years' famine.** About this time a three years' famine terrified Israel, which induced David to inquire of the Lord the cause of this judgment. The Lord replied, "It is for Saul, and for his bloody house, because he slew the Gibeonites." Nothing further is known about the fact itself. The Gibeonites were sent for, and upon their requisition David gave up to them two sons of Rizpah, a concubine of Saul, and five sons of Merab, whom she had borne to Adriel. These were slain, and their bodies, left uncared for, were watched over by Rizpah. Word was brought to David, who had the bones of these crucified men, together with those of Saul and Jonathan, which were brought from Jabesh, honorably deposited in the family tomb at Zelah, in the tribe of Benjamin. It is probable that this was the time when David spared Mephibosheth, in order to fulfill his covenant with Jonathan (21:1-14).

16. **David's adultery.** The notion of the East, in ancient and modern times, has been that a well-filled harem is essential to the splendor of a princely court. This opened a dangerous precipice in David's way, and led to a most grievous fall. Walking upon the roof of his house, he saw a woman washing herself. The beauty of the woman excited David's lust, and he inquired of his servants who she was. "Bath-sheba, the daughter of Eliam, the wife of Uriah the Hittite," was the reply. Notwithstanding she was the wife of another, David sent for her, and she appears voluntarily to have acceded to his sinful purpose. In order to cover up his sin, and secure Bathsheba for his wife, David sent Uriah into battle under circumstances that caused his death, and thus added murder to his other crime. The clouds from this time gathered over David's fortunes, and henceforward "the

sword never departed from his house" (12:10). There followed the outrage of his daughter, Tamar, by his eldest son, Ammon, and the murder of the latter by the servants of Absalom (11:1-13:29).

17. **Absalom's rebellion.** Absalom fled and went to Talmai, the son of Ammihud, king of Geshur, where he remained three years, after which he was recalled to Jerusalem, but dwelt in his own house "two full years, and saw not the king's face." After this he sent for Joab, and through his mediation was admitted into his father's presence (ch. 14). Absalom soon began to aspire to the throne, and, under pretense of wanting to fulfill a vow, he gained permission to go to Hebron, where he strengthened his conspiracy. Hearing of Absalom's conduct, David fled from Jerusalem (15:13, sq.), and passed over Jordan, B. C. about 974. Mahanaim was the capital of David's exile, as it had been of the exiled house of Saul (17:24; comp. 2:8, 12). His forces were arranged under the three great military officers who remained faithful to his fortunes—Joab, captain of the host; Abishai, captain of "the mighty men;" and Ittai, who seems to have taken the place of Benaiah as captain of the guard (18:2). On Absalom's side was David's nephew, Amasa (17:25). The final battle was fought in the "forest of Ephraim," which terminated in the accident leading to the death of Absalom (18:1-33). The return was marked at every stage by rejoicing and amnesty (II Sam. 19:16-40; I Kings 2:7); and Judah was first reconciled. The embers of the insurrection still smoldering (II Sam. 19:41-43) in David's hereditary enemies of the tribe of Benjamin were trampled out by the mixture of boldness and sagacity in Joab, now, after the murder of Amasa, once more in his old position (ch. 20), and David again reigned in peace at Jerusalem.

18. **Three days' pestilence.** This calamity visited Jerusalem at the warning of the prophet Gad. The occasion which led to this warning was the census of the people taken by Joab at the king's orders (II Sam. 24:1-9; I Chron. 21:1-7; 27:23, 24). Joab's repugnance to the measure was such that he refused to number Levi and Benjamin (I Chron. 21:6). The king also scrupled to number those who were under twenty years of age (27:23), and the final result was never recorded in the "Chronicles of King David" (v. 24). Outside the walls of Jerusalem, Araunah, or Ornan, a wealthy Jebusite, perhaps even the ancient king of Jebuz (II Sam. 24:23), possessed a threshing floor (I Chron. 21:20). At this spot an awful vision appeared, such as is described in the later days of Jerusalem, of the angel of the Lord stretching out a drawn sword between earth and sky over the devoted city. The scene of such an apparition at such a moment was at once marked out for a sanctuary. David demanded, and Araunah willingly granted, the site; the altar was erected on the rock of the threshing floor; the place was called by the name of "Moriah" (II Chron. 3:1); and for the first time a holy place, sanctified by the vision of the divine Presence, was recognized in Jerusalem. It was this spot that afterward became

the altar of the temple, and therefore the center of the national worship.

19. **Adonijah's conspiracy.** Adonijah, one of David's elder sons, feared that the influence of Bath-sheba might gain the kingdom for her own son, Solomon, and declared himself to be the successor to his father.

20. **Solomon made king.** The plot was stifled, and Solomon's inauguration took place under his father's auspices (I Kings 1:1-53). By this time David's infirmities had

under the so-called "Coenaculum," but it cannot be identified with the tomb of David, which was emphatically within the walls (Smith).

Perhaps the best way to understand the family of David will be to study the accompanying table, in which are given his wives, children, and grandchildren, so far as known. The royal line was carried on through a union of the children of Solomon and Absalom (I Kings 15:2).

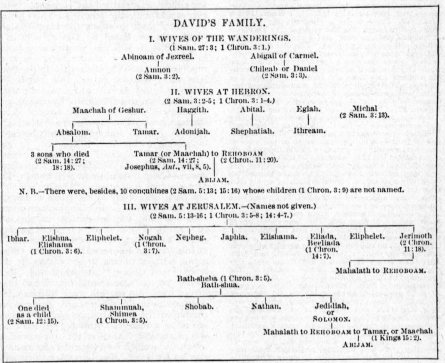

DAVID'S FAMILY.

I. WIVES OF THE WANDERINGS.
(1 Sam. 27:3; 1 Chron. 3:1.)

Abinoam of Jezreel.	Abigail of Carmel.
Amnon (2 Sam. 3:2).	Chileab or Daniel (2 Sam. 3:3).

II. WIVES AT HEBRON.
(2 Sam. 3:2-5; 1 Chron. 3:1-4.)

Maachah of Geshur.	Haggith.	Abital.	Eglah.	Michal (2 Sam. 3:13).
Absalom.	Tamar.	Adonijah.	Shephatiah.	Ithream.
3 sons who died (2 Sam. 14:27; 18:18).	Tamar (or Maachah) to REHOBOAM (2 Sam. 14:27; Josephus, *Ant.*, vii, 8, 5).	(2 Chron. 11:20).		
	ABIJAM.			

N. B.—There were, besides, 10 concubines (2 Sam. 5:13; 15:16) whose children (1 Chron. 3:9) are not named.

III. WIVES AT JERUSALEM.—(Names not given.)
(2 Sam. 5:13-16; 1 Chron. 3:5-8; 14:4-7.)

Ibhar.	Elishua, Elishama (1 Chron. 3:6).	Eliphelet.	Nogah (1 Chron. 3:7).	Nepheg.	Japhia.	Elishama.	Eliada, Beeliada (1 Chron. 14:7).	Eliphelet.	Jerimoth (2 Chron. 11:18).
							Mahalath to REHOBOAM.		

Bath-sheba (1 Chron. 3:5).
Bath-shua.

One died as a child (2 Sam. 12:15).	Shammuah, Shimea (1 Chron. 3:5).	Shobab.	Nathan.	Jedidiah, or SOLOMON.
				Mahalath to REHOBOAM to Tamar, or Maachah (1 Kings 15:2).
				ABIJAM.

grown upon him. An attempt was made to restore the warmth of his exhausted frame by the introduction of the young Shunammite, Abishag (1:1; 2:17). His last song is preserved—a striking union of the ideal of a just rule which he had placed before him, and of the difficulties which he had felt in realizing it (II Sam. 23:1-7). His last words, as recorded, to his successor, are general exhortations to his duty, combined with warnings against Joab and Shimei, and charges to remember the children of Barzillai (I Kings 2:1-9).

21. **Death.** He died at the age of seventy (II Sam. 5:4), and "was buried in the city of David" (I Kings 2:10, 11), B. C. about 960. After the return from the captivity "the sepulchers of David" were still pointed out "between Shiloh and the house of the mighty men," or "the guardhouse" (Neh. 3:16). His tomb, which became the general sepulcher of the kings of Judah, was pointed out in the latest times of the Jewish people. The edifice shown as such from the Crusades to the present day is on the southern hill of modern Jerusalem, commonly called Mount Zion,

22. **Character.** "If we proceed to put together, in its most general features, the whole picture of David which results from all these historical testimonies, we find the very foundations of his character to be laid in a peculiarly firm and unshaken trust in Jehovah, and the brightest and most spiritual views of the creation and government of the world, together with a constant, tender, and sensitive awe of the Holy One in Israel, a simple, pure striving never to be untrue to him, and the strongest efforts to return to him all the more loyally after errors and transgressions. . . . His mouth continually overflows with heartfelt praise of Jehovah, and his actions are ever redolent of the nobility inspired by a real and living fear of him (for the errors by which he is carried away stand out prominently just because of their rarity). . . . In the clear daylight of Israel's ancient history David furnishes the most brilliant example of the noble elevation of character produced by the old religion" (Ewald, *Hist. of Israel*, vol. iii, pp. 57, 58).

NOTE—**I Sam. 13:14.** "How," ask some, "could a man after God's own heart have murdered Uriah, and seduced Bath-sheba, and tortured the Ammonites?" An extract from one who is not a too-indulgent critic of sacred characters expresses at once the common sense and the religious lesson of the whole matter. "David, the Hebrew king, had fallen into sins enough—blackest crimes—there was no want of sin. And, thereupon, the unbelievers sneer, and ask, 'Is this your man according to God's heart?' The sneer, I must say, seems to me but a shallow one. What are faults, what are the outward details of a life, if the inner secret of it, the remorse, the temptations, the often-baffled, never-ended struggle of it, be forgotten? All earnest souls will ever discern in it (David's life) the faithful struggle of an earnest human soul toward what is good and best. Struggle often baffled —sore baffled—driven as into entire wreck, yet a struggle never ended, ever with tears, repentance, true unconquerable purpose, begun anew" (Carlyle, *Heroes and Hero-worship*, i, 277). **I Sam. 16:18; 17:42, 56.** There seems a contradiction between these two passages, the one describing David as a "mighty, valiant man, and a man of war," the others as "a youth, a stripling." The first description of David "does not presuppose he had already fought bravely in war, but may be perfectly explained from what David himself afterward affirmed respecting his conflicts with lions and bears (17:34, 35). The courage and strength which he then displayed furnished sufficient proofs of heroism for anyone to discern in him the future warrior" (Keil, *Com.*). **I Sam. 17:55, sq.** How can we reconcile Saul and Abner's ignorance of David, who had been musician and armorbearer to Saul? (16:14, sq.). Keil and Delitzsch (*Com.*) explain as follows: "The question put by Saul does not presuppose an actual want of acquaintance with the person of David and the name of his father, but only ignorance of the social condition of David's family, with which both Abner and Saul may hitherto have failed to make themselves more fully acquainted." Some explain by saying that after David played before Saul he returned to his home (which appears to be the fact, 18:2), and that his appearance had so changed as to make recognition impossible (Thomson, *Land and Book*, ii, 366, American ed.). **II Sam. 5:3.** The three anointings of David need give no trouble. The first (I Sam. 16:13) was a private, prophetic anointing; by the second (II Sam. 2:4) he was publicly recognized as king over Judah; by the third (II Sam. 5:3), as king over both Judah and Israel. **II Sam. 5:6-9.** Some see a discrepancy between the fact of the capture of "the stronghold of Zion" and the taking of Goliath's head to Jerusalem (I Sam. 17:54). Ewald (*Hist. of Israel*, iii, p. 72 answers, that clearly David did not carry the head to Jerusalem till afterward, when he was king. Keil (*Com.* on I Sam. 17:54) explains that the assertion made by some, that Jerusalem was not yet in possession of the Israelites, rests upon a confusion between the citadel of Jebus upon Zion, which was still in the hands of the Jebusites, and the city of Jerusalem, in which Israelites had dwelt for a long time (Josh. 16:63; Judg. 1:8). **II Sam. 6:20.** The proud daughter of Saul was offended at the fact that the king had on this occasion let himself down to the level of the people. She taunts him with having stripped himself, because while dancing and playing he wore somewhat lighter garments (such as the ordinary priestly garb) instead of the heavy royal mantle (Ewald, *Hist. of Israel*, iii, p. 127). **II Sam. 24:1** tells us that God moved David against Israel to say, "Go, number Israel and Judah." In I Chron. 21:1 it is alleged that Satan stood up against Israel, and provoked David to number the people. But the meaning is that God permitted Satan thus to move David in order that through his act an opportunity might arise for the punishment of Israel's sin. The command of David was not sinful in itself, but became so from the spirit of pride and vainglory out of which it originated, and which was shared with him by the people over whom he ruled (Taylor, *David*, p. 371). *M. F. U.*

David, City of.

1. Bethlehem of Judah was occasionally called "the city of David" (Luke 2:4, 11) because David grew up as a shepherd lad there.

2. The most ancient portion of the city of Jerusalem, that eastern hill inhabited by the Jebusites before it was conquered by David. David's account of the capture of "the stronghold of Zion . . . in the city of David" is recounted in II Sam. 5:6-8; I Chron. 11:4-8. Situated on a plateau of commanding height, 2500 feet above the Mediterranean and 3800

feet above the Dead Sea, the Jebusite fortress was scarped by natural rock for defense. Its stout walls, gates and towers were considered impregnable. So secure did the native Jebusite defenders consider themselves that they taunted David and the Israelite beseigers with the words: "You will not come in here but the blind and the lame will ward you off —thinking David cannot come in here" (II Sam. 5:6 R. S. V.). Despite its impregnability, David captured the fortress, and when the citadel was stormed the king said, "whoever would smite the Jebusites let him get up the water shaft to attack the lame and the blind who are hated by David's soul" (II Sam. 5:8 R. S. V.). This perplexing notation in the light of more recent evidence must be rendered "whoever getteth up with the hook (not water shaft or gutter) and smiteth the Jebusites . . ." As Albright says, "the word is now known to be typically Canaanite and the sense "hook" has been handed down through Aramaic to the modern Arabic. The hook in question was used to assist beseigers in scaling ramparts." ("The O. T. and Archaeology" in *O. T. Commentary*, Philadelphia, 1948, p. 149). However, Jerusalem's ancient water system is now well known. The fifty-foot-high water course ("Warren's Shaft") has been uncovered as the result of the excavations of the Palestine Exploration Fund, revealing that the inhabitants of the city (c. 2000 B. C.) had made a rock-cut passage, similar to that at Gezer and at Megiddo, to enable them to secure water from the Gihon spring without having to go outside the city walls. From the cave into which the Gihon spring entered a horizontal tunnel had been driven back into the hill some thirty-six feet west and twenty-five feet north. This conduit conducted the water into an old cave which served as a reservoir. Running up from this was a vertical tunnel at the upper end of which the women could stand to lower their jugs to get water. The Jebusite bastion with its twenty-foot thick wall has been verified by British archaeologists. Thus the City of David overlooks the Kedron and Hinnom valleys. David apparently did little to beautify the Jebusite city. Solomon, however, adorned it with magnificent buildings and made a worthy site of the Hebrew capital. *M. F. U.*

Dawn. See Time.

Day. See Time.

Day of Atonement. See Festivals.

Day of Christ is the period connected with reward and blessing of saints at the coming of Christ for His own. The expression occurs in I Cor. 1:8; 5:5; II Cor. 1:14; Phil. 1:6, 10; 2:16. In II Thess. 2:2 the A. V. has the Day of Christ incorrectly for the Day of the Lord. The Day of Christ is not the Day of the Lord. The latter is connected with earth judgments (Rev. 4:1-19:16), which come after the out-taking of the church, the body of Christ, and its glorification and judgment for works at the judgment seat of Christ. The Day of the Lord (Isa. 2:12; Rev. 19:11-21) cannot occur until after the church is completed (II Thess. 2:1 cf. II Thess. 2:2-12). *M. F. U.*

Day of Judgment. See Judgment.

Day of the Lord is the protracted period commencing with the Second Advent of Christ in glory and ending with the cleansing of the heavens and the earth by fire preparatory to the new heavens and the new earth of the eternal state (Isa. 65:17-19; 66:22; II Pet. 3:13; Rev. 21:1). The Day of the Lord as a visible manifestation of Christ upon the earth is to be distinguished from the Day of Christ. The latter is connected with the glorification of the saints and their reward in the heavenlies previous to their return with Christ to inaugurate the Day of the Lord. The Day of the Lord thus comprehends specifically the closing phase of the Tribulation and extends through the Millennial Kingdom. Apocalyptic judgments (Rev. 4:1-19:6) precede and introduce the Day of the Lord. *M. F. U.*

Day's Journey. See Metrology, I.

Daysman (Heb. *yākāḥ*, to *set right*), an *umpire* or *arbitrator* (Job 9:33), is an old English word derived from *day*, in the specific sense of a day *fixed for a trial*. The meaning seems to be that of some one to compose our differences, and the laying on of whose hand expresses power to adjudicate between the two persons. There might be one on a level with Job, the one party; but Job knew of none on a level with the Almighty, the other party (I Sam. 2:25). Such a mediator we have in Jesus Christ (I Tim. 2:5).

Dayspring (Heb. *shāḥăr*, Job 38:12; Gr. *'anatolē*, Luke 1:78), the first streak of daylight, the dawn; and so the early revelation of God in Christ to the soul.

Daystar (Gr. *phōsphoros, light-bearing*, Lat. *Lucifer*), the planet Venus, the morning star (II Pet. 1:19). The meaning of the passage is that the prophets were like a *lamp*, but Christ himself is the light of dawn, heralded by the "morning star" (Rev. 2:28; 22:16).

Deacon (Gr. *diakonos*, of uncertain origin), one who executes the commands of another, a servant.

1. **In a general sense** the term is applied to the "servant" of a king (Matt. 22:13); ministers (Rom. 13:4; literally, "deacons of God," i. e., those through whom God carries on his administration on earth); Paul and other apostles (I Cor. 3:5; II Cor. 6:3; I Thess. 3:2). As teachers of the Christian religion are called "deacons of Christ" in II Cor. 11:23; Col. 1:7; I Tim. 4:6, Christ is called the "minister (literally, *deacon*, Rom. 15:8) of the circumcision," as devoting himself to the salvation of the Jews. In addition to this general use of the word it was given a more specific meaning:

2. **Officer of the Church.** (1) **Origin.** In the New Testament deacons, or helpers, appear first in the church at Jerusalem. The Hellenistic Christians complained that their widows were neglected in favor of the Hebrew Christians "in the daily ministration" (Acts 6:1). This was a natural consequence of the rapid growth of the society, and of the apostles having more than they could properly attend to. Upon the recommendation of the apostles "seven men of honest report, full of the Holy Ghost and wisdom," were selected and set apart by prayer and laying on of hands. To deacons primarily was assigned the duty of ministering to the poor, and the oversight of temporal affairs of the Christian societies, yet retaining, as in the case of Stephen and Philip, the right to teach and baptize. *The qualifications* for this office, as enumerated by Paul (I Tim. 3:8, sq.), were of a nature to fit them for mingling with the Church in most familiar relations, to ascertain and relieve the wants of the poorer members with delicacy, and freedom from temptation to avaricious greed. On offering themselves for their work deacons were to be subject to a strict scrutiny (I Tim. 3:10). (2) **In the early Church.** A difference of opinion respecting the function of deacons prevailed in the early Church. Some contended that *no* spiritual function had been assigned them (Council Constantinople, Can. 18), whereas Ignatius styles them "ministers of the mysteries of Christ." Tertullian classes them with bishops and presbyters as guides and leaders to the laity. They evidently occupied the position of assistants to the higher clergy, exercising the spiritual functions or not, according to the sentiment of the age or wish of those whom they assisted. The deacons, also called *Levites*, received a different ordination from the presbyters, both as to form and the power it conferred; for in the ordination of a presbyter the presbyters who were present were required to join in the imposition of hands with the bishop, but the ordination of a deacon might be performed by the bishop alone. *Duties.* The duties of the deacon were: 1. To assist the bishop and presbyter in the service of the sanctuary; especially to care for utensils, etc., of the holy table. 2. In the administration of the Eucharist, to hand the elements to the people, but not to *consecrate* the elements. 3. To administer the baptism. 4. To receive the offerings of the people. 5. Sometimes, as the bishop's special delegates, to give to the penitents the solemn imposition of hands, the sign of reconciliation. 6. To teach and catechise the catechumens. 7. In the absence of bishop and presbyter to suspend the inferior clergy. In addition there were many minor duties. Deacons often stood in close relations with the bishop, and not infrequently looked upon ordination to the presbyterates as a degradation. The *number* of deacons varied with the wants of the individual church. The *qualifications* of a deacon were the same that were required in bishops and presbyters (I Tim. 3:1, sq.). (3) **In the modern Church** deacons are found as a distinct order of the clergy in the Roman Catholic, Church of England, Episcopal, Methodist Episcopal, German Protestant Churches. In the main their duties are the same, and consist in helping the clergy in higher orders. In the Presbyterian and Congregational Churches they are laymen, who care for the poor, attend to the temporal affairs of the Church, and act as spiritual helpers to the minister (see Schaff, *Hist. Christ. Ch.*, i, p. 135; Hurst, *Hist. Christ. Ch.*, p. 25; McC. and S., *Cyc.*).

Deaconesses, or female helpers, had the care of the poor and the sick among the women of the Church. This office was the most needful on account of the rigid separation of the sexes in that day. Paul mentions Phebe as a deaconess of the church of Cenchrea; and it seems probable that Tryphena, Tryphosa, and Persis, whom he commends for the labor in the Lord were deaconesses (Rom. 16:1, 12).

1. **In the Early Church** the apostolical constitution distinguished "deaconesses" from "widows" and "virgins," and prescribed their duties. The office of deaconess in the Eastern Church continued down to the 12th century. It was frequently occupied by the widows of clergymen or the wives of bishops, who were obliged to demit the married state before entering upon their sacred office.

2. **Qualifications.** Piety, discretion, and experience were in any case the indispensable prerequisites in candidates. During the first two centuries the Church more carefully heeded the advice of Paul that the deaconess should have been the wife of one husband, also that the Church should admit to this office only those who had been thoroughly tested by previous trusts, having used hospitality to strangers, washed the saints' feet, relieved the afflicted, diligently followed every good work, etc. (I Tim. 5:10); but at a later period there was more laxity, and younger and inexperienced women were admitted.

3. **Ordination.** The question of their ordination has been much debated. They were inducted into their office by the imposition of hands. Of this there is abundant proof. This would not necessarily imply the right to fulfill the sacred functions of the ministry.

4. **Duties.** The need of such helpers arose from the customs and usages of the ancient world, which forbade the intimate association of the sexes in public assemblies. They were to instruct the female catechumens, to assist in the baptism of women, to anoint with holy oil, to minister to the confessors who were languishing in prison, to care for the women who were in sickness or distress, and sometimes act as doorkeepers in the churches. It is plain that the deaconesses had other duties than those of keepers of the entrances of the church appointed for women, or even as assistants in baptism or instructors of candidates; they were employed in those works of charity and relief where heathen public opinion would not permit the presence of the deacons.

Dead, Baptism for the. See Baptism.

Dead, The. 1. **Egyptian.** The great care of the Egyptians was directed to their condition after death. They expected to be received into the company of that being who represented divine goodness if pronounced worthy at the great judgment day; and to be called by his name was the fulfillment of all their wishes. The dead were all equal in rank—king and peasant, the humblest and the hero. Virtue was the ground of admission into the land of the blessed, and reunion with the deity of which he was an emanation, receiving the holy name of Osiris. His body was so bound up as to resemble the mysterious ruler of Amenti (Hades); it bore some of the emblems peculiar to him; and bread, of a form which belonged exclusively to the gods, was given to the deceased in token of his having assumed the character of that deity. **Services.** These were performed by the priests (of the grade who wore the leopard skin) at the expense of the family. If the sons or relations were of the priestly order they could officiate, and the members of the family had permission to be present. The ceremonies consisted of a sacrifice (incense and libation being also presented) and a prayer. These continued at intervals as long as the family paid for them. The body after *Embalming* (*q. v.*) was frequently kept in the house, sometimes for months, in order to gratify the feeling of having those who were beloved in life as near as possible after death. The mummy was kept in a movable wooden closet, drawn on a sledge to and from the altar, before which frequent ceremonies were observed. It was during this interval the feasts were held in honor of the dead. Sometimes the mummy was kept in the house because the family were not possessed of a burial plot or they were denied the rites of burial on account of accusations brought against or debt contracted by the dead or his sons. This was considered a great disgrace, only to be removed by the payment of the debt, liberal donations in the service of religion, or the influential prayers of the priests. The form of the ritual read by the priest in pronouncing the acquittal of the dead is preserved in the tombs usually at the entrance passage. In this ritual the deceased is made to enumerate all the sins forbidden by the Egyptian law and to assert his innocence of each, persons of every rank being subjected to this ordeal. Every large city, as Thebes, Memphis, and some others, had its lake, at which the ceremonies were practiced. The Egyptians did not permit the extremes of degradation to be offered to the dead that the Jews sometimes allowed; and the body of a malefactor, though excluded from the precincts of the necropolis, was not refused to his friends for burial.

2. **Hebrew.** Immediately when life departed it was the office of a friend or son to close the eyes of the dead (Gen. 46:4) and to kiss the face (Gen. 50:1). The body was washed, wrapped in a linen cloth (Matt. 27:59, etc.), or the limbs separately wound with strips of linen (John 11:44), placed in a coffin (Luke 7:14), and if not buried immediately it was laid out in an upper room (II Kings 4:21; Acts 9:37). (1) **The embalmnig** of the dead took place after the Egyptian fashion in the case of Jacob and Joseph (Gen. 50:2, 26), but only imitated by the rich or distinguished so far that they anointed the dead with costly oil (John 12:7) and wound them in linen with spices, especially myrrh and aloes (John 19:39, 40). (2) **The burning** of bodies occurred to secure them from mutilation (I Sam. 31:12), in which case the bones were afterward buried (v. 13); or in times of war, where the multitude of deaths made burial impossible (Amos 6:10); finally, as a punishment inflicted on great criminals (Lev. 20:14; 21:9). The "making of a burning," usual when kings were buried (II Chron. 16:14; 21:19; Jer. 34:5), was a consuming of sweet-scented substances in honor of the dead. On high state occasions the vessels, bed, and furniture used by the deceased were burnt also. Such was probably the "great

burning" made for Asa. If a king was unpopular or died disgraced (II Chron. 21:19) this was not observed. (3) **Funeral and burial.** To remain unburied was considered the greatest indignity which could befall the dead (I Kings 13:22; 16:4; Jer. 7:33, etc.) because the corpse soon became the prey of wild beasts (II Kings 9:35). The law ordered that criminals should be buried on the day of execution (Deut. 21:23; comp. Josh. 8:29).

The speedy burial of the dead did not prevail in ancient times (Gen. 23:2), but arose when the law made dead bodies a cause of uncleanness (Num. 19:11, sq.; comp. Acts 5:6, 10).

To bury the dead was a special work of affection (Tobit 1:21; 2:8) and an imperative duty of sons toward their parents (Gen. 25:9; 35:29; Matt. 8:21), and next devolved upon relatives and friends (Tobit 14:16). The body was carried to the grave in a coffin, often uncovered, on a bier borne by men, with a retinue of relatives and friends (II Sam. 3:31; Luke 7:12-14; Acts 5:6, 10), while those prominent because of position, virtue, or good deeds were followed by a vast multitude (Gen. 50:7, 14; I Sam. 25:1; II Chron. 32:33).

The custom seems to have prevailed, as early as our Lord's life on earth, of having funeral orations at the grave. Even at the funeral of a pauper women chanted the lament, "Alas, the lion; alas, the hero!" or similar words, while great rabbis were wont to bespeak for themselves a warm funeral oration. After the funeral a meal was given (II Sam. 3:35; Hos. 9:4; Ezek. 24:17, 24), which later became scenes of luxurious display (Josephus, *War*, ii, 11). *See* Emblaming, Mourning, Tomb.

The word rendered "dead" (Job 26:5; Psa. 88:10; Prov. 2:18; 9:18; 21:16; Isa. 14:9; 26:14, 19) is (Heb. *ráphä'*), the *relaxed*, i. e., those who are bodiless in the state after death.

118. Dead Sea

Dead Sea, The. 1. **Name.** In Scripture it is called the *Salt Sea* (Gen. 14:3; Num. 34:12, etc.), the *Sea of the Plain* or *Arabah* (Deut. 3:17; 4:49, etc.), *East Sea* (Ezek. 47:18; Joel 2:20; Zech. 14:8, A. V. "former"). The name Dead Sea has been applied to it since the 2d century, and it was also called the Asphalt Sea by early writers.

2. **Location,** etc. The Dead Sea lies in the southern end of the Jordan valley, occupying the fifty-three deepest miles, with an average breadth of nine to ten miles. The surface is

twelve hundred and ninety feet below the level of the Mediterranean, but the bottom is as deep again, soundings having been taken of thirteen hundred feet in the northeast corner, under the hills of Moab; thence the bed shelves rapidly, till the whole southern end of the sea is only from eight to fourteen feet in depth. These figures vary from year to year, and after a very rainy season the sea will be as much as fifteen feet deeper, and at the southern end more than a mile longer. It is fed by the Jordan and four or five smaller streams, which pour into it six million tons of water a day. It has no outlet, but is relieved by evaporation, often so great as to form very heavy clouds. To this evaporation is due the bitterness of the sea. The streams which feed it are unusually saline, flowing through nitrous soil and fed by sulphurous springs. Chemicals, too, have been found in the waters of the sea, probably introduced by hot springs in the sea bottom. Along the shores are deposits of sulphur and petroleum springs, while the surrounding strata are rich in bituminous matter. At the southeast end a ridge of rock salt, three hundred feet high, runs for five miles, and the bed of the sea appears to be covered with salt crystals. "To all these solid ingredients, precipitated and concentrated by the constant evaporation, the Dead Sea owes its extreme bitterness and buoyancy. While the water of the ocean contains from four to six per cent of solids in solution, the Dead Sea holds from twenty-four to twenty-six per cent. The water is very nauseous to the taste and oily to the touch, leaving upon the skin, when it dries, a thick crust of salt. But it is very brilliant. Its buoyancy is so great that it is difficult to sink the limbs deep enough for swimming."

"Its shore is a low beach of gravel, varied by marl or salt marsh. Twice on the west side the mountain cliffs come down to the water's edge, and on the east coast there is a curious peninsula, El-Lisan (or the Tongue), though the shape is more that of a spurred boot. Ancient beaches of the sea are visible all round it, steep banks from five to fifty feet of stained and greasy marl, very friable, with heaps of rubbish at their feet, and crowned with nothing but their own bare, crumbling brows. Behind these terraces of marl the mountains rise precipitous and barren on either coast. To the east the long range of Moab, at a height of two thousand five hundred to three thousand feet above the shore, is broken only by the great valley of the Arnon. . . . On the west coast the hills touch the water at two points, but elsewhere leave between themselves and the sea the shore already described, sometimes one hundred yards in breadth, sometimes one and a half miles. From behind the highest terrace of marl the hills rise precipitously from two thousand to two thousand five hundred feet."

The prophet Ezekiel (47:1-12) gives a wonderful vision of a stream of water issuing from the temple, and with increasing volume sweeping down to the Dead Sea and healing its bitter waters, "teaching that there is nothing too sunken, too useless, too doomed, but by the grace of God it may be redeemed, lifted, and made rich with life" (Smith, *Hist. Geog.*, pp. 499-512).

The Dead Sea Scrolls. The last nine years (1947-1956) have witnessed phenomenal archaeological discoveries in Palestine, which are of tremendous importance to Biblical studies, and which are revolutionizing the approach to the text of the Old Testament as well as the background of the New Testament. In addition, the new manuscript material is shedding a flood of light on the intertestamental period from Malachi to John the Baptist. Since 1947 when a Bedouin shepherd stumbled upon a cave south of Jericho containing many scrolls of leather covered with Hebrew and Aramaic writing, besides some 600 fragmentary inscriptions, the archaeological world has been set agog as a result of the historical and philological importance of this new material. In 1952 new caves containing fragments of later scrolls inscribed in Hebrew, Greek and Aramaic were found. The announcement of these startling archaeological discoveries has been followed by the news of the recovery of additional manuscripts in still other caves in and around the Dead Sea area (James L. Kelso, "The Archeology of Qumran," *Jour. Bib. Lit.* LXXIV, Sept., 1955, p. 141-146).

1. **The Date of the Scrolls.** Despite the fact that a series of fantastic attacks was made against the antiquity and even the authenticity of the original group of these documents, three lines of evidence demonstrate that they have been correctly dated well before A. D. 70 by W. F. Albright and other competent paleographers (W. F. Albright, "The Bible After Twenty Years of Archeology," 1932-1952, in *Religion in Life* XXI, 4, 1952, p. 540). The first line of evidence is that of radiocarbon count, which dates the linen in which the scrolls were wrapped to a general era about 175 B. C. to 225 A. D. (Cf. O. R. Sellers, "Radiocarbon Dating of Cloth from the 'Ain Feshka Cave," *Bull. of the Am. Schs. of Or. Res.*, 123, Oct., 1951, p. 24 f.). More precise is the paleographic evidence. The forms of the letters employed by the various scribes in the recovered scrolls represent a period of more than a century. The letters themselves are intermediate between the known script of the third century B. C. and the middle of the first century A. D. Albright says, "All competent students of writing conversant with the available materials and with paleographic method" date the scrolls "in the 250 years before 70 A. D." (*Op. cit.*, p. 540). Frank M. Cross as a result of study of the evidence of the manuscripts from Qumran defines three periods: An archaic period, about 200-150 B. C., a Hasmonean period, about 150-130 B. C., and a Herodian period, about 30 B. C. to 70 A. D. ("The Oldest Manuscripts From Qumran" in the *Jour. Bib. Lit.* LXXIV, Sept., 1955, p. 164). Professor Cross shows that the preponderating majority of the manuscripts from Qumran stem from the second and third periods, especially the latter half of the second

119. **Climbing Up from Cave Four**

period and the latter part of the third period (*Ibid.* also "The Manuscripts of the Dead Sea Caves" in *Bib. Arch.* XVII, 1, Feb., 1954, p. 20). This coincides with the periods when activity at Khirbet Qumran was at its height, as the excavations at this most-important manuscript-yielding site (located about seven miles south of Jericho on the western shore of the Dead Sea) have shown (See Pére de Vaux, "Fouilles au Khirbet Qumran," *Revue Biblique* LXI, 1954, p. 231-236). The cave yielding the Dead Sea Scrolls was sealed sometime between 50 B. C. and 70 A. D. Later finds from the first cave date partly from the same period and partly from the second century A. D., when coming from later caves. The later fragments are inscribed in a script which is quite a bit later and is intermediate between the Dead Sea Scrolls and the earliest previously-known Hebrew fragments on parchment and on papyrus from the third and fourth centuries A. D. Greatly augmented numbers of recovered documents, some considerably earlier than the earliest of the finds at Cave One at Qumran, as well as later than the latest of them, make it possible for the paleographer to outline the history of the development of the script and "render incredible any attempt to date the Qumran scrolls after 70 A. D." (Frank M. Cross, *Bib. Arch.* XVII, 1, Feb., 1954, p. 20).

2. **The Contents of the Scrolls.** The contents of the new manuscripts from the Dead Sea caves are partly Biblical and partly intertestamental. The Biblical material includes two scrolls of Isaiah, one of which is complete, and most of the first two chapters of Habakkuk, beside fragments of all of the Old Testament books except Esther. Of the fragmentary manuscripts, the majority are from the Pentateuchal books, Isaiah or Psalms. However, fragments of Jeremiah and Daniel are numerous. To date some 100 Biblical manuscripts have been found. The Isaiah Scroll found in 1947, in the initial manuscript discovery, has remained the most famous of the finds. This complete document of Isaiah quite understandably created a sensation since it was the first major Biblical manuscript of great antiquity ever to be recovered. Interest in it was especially keen since it antedates by more than a thousand years the oldest Hebrew texts preserved in the Massoretic tradition, which is the basis of all recent Biblical translations and which does not go back earlier than 900 A. D. It is this fact that makes the Dead Sea Scrolls, containing the Hebrew text of the entire book of Isaiah and dating as early as 125-100 B. C. not only "the greatest manuscript discovery of modern times," (W. F. Albright, *Bib. Archeologist*, Vol. XI, 3, Sept., 1948, p. 55) but constitutes the documents themselves "the oldest existing manuscripts of the Bible in any language" (John C. Trever, *Bull. Am. Schs. Or. Res.* 113, Feb., 1949, p. 23). In the original batch of manuscripts of 1947 was also a Commentary on Habakkuk and the Manual of Discipline, of the pre-Christian Jewish sect of the Essenes. In the manuscripts purchased by the Hebrew University at Jerusalem was a later Isaiah scroll, more conformed to the

120. John Allegro with a Psalms Commentary from Cave Four

traditional Hebrew text, and a document called "War Between the Children of Light and Darkness," evidently growing out of the Maccabean struggles against Greek paganism (168-37 B. C.). There was also a collection of psalms. In February-March, 1949, the first cave was excavated by two well-known Palestinian archaeologists—Pere de Vaux and Lankester Harding. Numerous fragments of documents initially discovered in the cave were recovered, including fragments of Genesis, Deuteronomy and Judges, together with a fragment of Leviticus in old Hebrew script. Non-Biblical finds included a fragment of the Book of Jubilees, a work related to the Enoch literature, and some unknown material. From 1951-1954 the Essene community center at Khirbet Qumran was excavated, revealing remains of "a large rectangular structure which served . . . as the center of the communal life of the Sect whose members copied and preserved the MSS that were hidden in the caves nearby" (Charles T. Fritsch, *Jour. Bib. Lit.* LXXIV, Sept., 1955, p. 174). It is evident that the members of the Sect themselves inhabited the caves and were interred in the large cemetery between the main Community Building and the shores of the Dead Sea. Shortly after the excavations another cave was found at Qumran yielding fragments of Ruth, Isaiah, Psalms, Exodus, Jubilees and a liturgical document, which were bought by the Ecole Biblique and the Palestine Museum. Still another Qumran cave yielded inscribed copper strips, tightly rolled up, constituting a problem for modern science to unroll. When unrolled in 1956, they revealed a description of numerous sites where treasure was buried. In 1952 new caves at Murabba'at in another part of the "howling desert" yielded principally second century A. D. documents in Hebrew, Aramaic and Greek, including a few Biblical texts of Genesis, Exodus, Deuteronomy and Isaiah. Of special interest are several recovered Hebrew letters written by Simon ben Kaseba (bar Cocheba), leader of the Revolt of A. D. 132-1'35, to guerilla troops in the Murabba'at region. A notable exception to the second century A. D. date of this material is an archaic Hebrew papyrus piece, actually a palimpsest, giving a list of names and numbers and dating from the sixth century B. C. In the same general area other caves

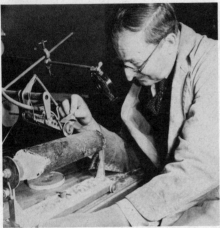

121. Prof. H. Wright Baker of Manchester's College of Technology Cutting the Copper Scroll from Cave Three

have been found. One group from Khirbet Mird, northeast of Mar Saba, contained Arabic papyri, Greek and Christo-Palestinian Syrian documents, with fragments of Biblical codices, all dating from late Byzantine and early Arabic periods. Another lot dates from the period of the bulk of the Murabba'at material. Among this group is a version of the Minor Prophets in Greek and a corpus of Nabataean papyri, both being of great Biblical and historical importance. The large and ever-increasing fund of manuscripts, Biblical and non-Biblical, particularly from the Qumran caves is challenging the energy and ingenuity of scholars to their full capacity. It is difficult as yet to predict the full import of this great body of Biblical material on textual criticism of the Old Testament, but the contribution to this most needy field will certainly be far-reaching. Vastly increased knowledge of the reliability of the Septuagint readings in textual criticism is bound to result. Historically the inter-Biblical period and the development of sectarian Judaism will be much better understood. The background of the New Testament will also be brightly illuminated and results which are bound to affect New Testament criticism are already assured. Radical late-date theories of the Gospel of John, which place the book after 150 A. D. on the ground that the conceptual imagery is Gnostic, are shown to be untenable. The Dead Sea Scrolls prove that the contents of John's

Gospel reflect the authentic Jewish background of John the Baptist and Jesus, not that of later times, and give evidence of ideas and influences illustrated in intertestamental literature. New discoveries in 1956 at cave 11, include two scrolls tentatively identified as Psalms and Leviticus. *See* Manuscripts, Dead Sea. *M. F. U.*

Deaf (Heb. *ḥĕrĕsh;* Gr. *kōphos,* blunted). Moses protected the deaf by a special statute. "Thou shalt not curse the deaf" (Lev. 19:14). This was because the deaf could not hear, and were therefore unable to defend themselves.

Figurative. Deafness is symbolical of inattentiveness or inability (Isa. 29:18; 35:5; Matt. 11:5, etc.).

Deal. *See* Metrology.

Dearth (Heb. *rä'äb, hunger;* Gr. *limos, scarcity*), a scarcity of provisions, resulting from failure of rain (I Kings 17:1), the plague of locusts (Psa. 78:46), or the lack of properly farming the land (Ruth 1:1). *See* Famine.

Death. A term which, in its application to the lower orders of living things, as animals and plants, denotes the extinction of vital functions, so that their renewal is impossible. With reference to human beings the term is variously defined according to the view held of human nature and life. The answer to the question, "What is death?" depends upon the answer given in the first place to the question, "What is man?" *See* Immortality.

Scripture Doctrine. The general teaching of the Scriptures is that man is not only a physical, but also a spiritual being; accordingly death is not the end of human existence, but a change of place or conditions in which conscious existence continues. (1) The doctrine of the future life is less emphatically taught in the Old Testament than in the New. The Old Testament Scriptures, however, frequently refer to death in terms harmonious with that doctrine (Eccles. 12:7; II Sam. 12:23; Psa. 73:24; Job. 14:14; Isa. 28:12). (2) In the New Testament this dark subject receives special illumination. In many cases essentially the same forms of representation are employed. Death is "a departure," a "being absent from the body," an "unclothing," a "sleep;" but with all is the clear and strong announcement of "life and immortality brought to light through the Gospel" (II Cor. 5:1-4; John 11:13; II Tim. 1:10; 4:6-7, etc.). (3) Death as a human experience, according to the Scriptures, is the result and punishment of sin. "The wages of sin is death." And though the word is often used in a spiritual sense, to denote the ruin wrought in man's spiritual nature by sin, yet in the ordinary physical sense of the word death is declared to have come upon the human race in consequence of sin. No such declaration is made as to the death of lower creatures (Gen. 2:17; 3:19; Rom. 5:12; 6:23; James 1:15). (4) A principal part of Christ's redemptive work is the abolishment of death. This is seen in part in man's present state, in the salvation which Christ effects from sin, which is "the sting of death," and in the taking away of the fear of death from true believers. The complete work of Christ in this respect will appear in the resurrection (II Tim. 1:10; I Cor.

15:22, 57; Heb. 2:24, 15). (5) **Man and lower creatures.** (1) The Scriptures make a deep distinction between the death of human beings and that of irrational creatures. For the latter it is the natural end of their existence; for the former it is an unnatural experience to which they are reduced because of sin, which is also unnatural. Man was not created to die. (2) The Scriptures nowhere affirm that death did not prevail over the lower creatures before the fall of man. Thus upon this point there is no conflict between the Scriptures and geology. (3) It does not follow, because man was created immortal, that his permanent abiding place was to be this world. The Old Testament Scriptures give two examples of men, Enoch and Elijah, who passed into the other world, but "did not see death." (See Martensen's *Christ. Dogm.*, Watson's *Institutes*, Pope's *Compend. Christ. Theol.*, Laidlaw's *Bible Doctrine Concerning Man*).—E. McC.

Debate. In addition to the usual meaning of friendly discussion, debate means quarrel, strife; thus, "Ye fast for strife and *debate*" (Isa. 58:4, R. V. "contention," Heb. *măṣṣäh*). Among evils of the Gentiles given in the Epistle to the Romans (1:29) Paul includes *debate;* the rendering of Gr. *eris*, wrangling, strife (A. V.).

De'bir (dē'bĭr) (Kiriath-sepher).

1. A frontier fortress of one of the five Amorite kings whom Joshua defeated and hanged (Josh. 10:3, 5, 16, 26).

2. A highland city of Judah about a dozen miles S. W. of Hebron, or about the same distance S. E. of Lachish. It was conquered by Joshua (Josh. 10:38 f). Later reoccupied, it was retaken by Othniel (Josh. 15:7, 15, 17). The Canaanites called it Kiriath-sepher ("book town") or Kirjath-sanna (Josh. 15:15, 49). W. F. Albright and Melvin Grove Kyle identify it as Tel Beit Mirsim, excavated from 1924 on. This site reveals clear occupational levels from c. 2200 B. C. The site offers a wealth of information about Hebrew pottery, masonry and industry. A jar handle inscribed "belonging to Eliakim, steward of Yaukin (Jehoikim) suggests that the site was occupied until the Babylonian captivity and the capture of king Jehoiachin in 598 B. C.

3. There was another Debir in Gad (Josh. 13:26) not far from Mahanaim, possibly the same as Lo-debar (II Sam. 17:27). *M. F. U.*

Deb'orah (dĕb'ō-ra; a *bee*).

1. The nurse of Rebekah (Gen. 35:8), whom she accompanied from the house of Bethuel (24:59). She is only mentioned by name on the occasion of her burial under the oak tree of Beth-el, named in her honor Allon-bachuth (*oak of weeping*, 35:8).

2. A prophetess, "the wife of Lapidoth," who judged Israel (Judg. 4:4) in connection with Barak, B. C. about 1120. (1) **Israel under Jabin.** After the death of Ehud the children of Israel fell away from the Lord, and were given into the hands of "Jabin, king of the Canaanites, who reigned in Hazor." He oppressed them severely for twenty years. (2) **Delivered by Deborah.** At this time Deborah, "the prophetess," dwelt under a palm tree (which bore her name) between Ramah and Beth-el, in Mount Ephraim, and hither the people came to her for judgment. She sent an inspired message to *Barak* (*q. v.*), bidding him assemble ten thousand men of Naphtali and Zebulun at Mount Tabor, for Jehovah would draw Sisera (Jabin's general) and his host to meet him at the river Kishon, and deliver them into his hand. Barak agreed, but only on the condition that Deborah would accompany him. Deborah consented, but assured him that the prize of victory, viz., the defeat of the hostile general, should be taken out of his hand, for Jehovah would sell Sisera into the hand of a woman (Jael). "And the Lord discomfited Sisera, and all his chariots, and all his host, with the edge of the sword before Barak." Sisera, taking refuge in the tent of Heber the Kenite, was slain by his wife, Jael. This success was followed up until Jabin was overthrown, and the land had rest forty years. (3) **Song.** This remarkable ode contained in Judges 5 is a poetic version of the same material contained in prose in Chapter 4. It is universally acclaimed a very early masterpiece of Hebrew poetry. Critics laud it as one of the first songs in Hebrew literature. Deborah has been widely acclaimed as its author. It is remarkable for its vividness of imagery, preserved archaisms and insight into the rude, barbaric life of the 12th century B. C.

Debt. 1. The rendering of several Hebrew and Greek words, with the general meaning of something *due*. In the Mosaic law the duty of aiding the poor was strongly emphasized (Deut. 15:7, sq.; comp. Psa. 37:26; Matt. 5:42), but all loans to fellow-Israelites were to be without interest (Deut. 15:2), and usury was looked upon with deepest contempt (Prov. 28:8; Ezek. 18:8, 13, 17, etc.). In any case of debt the creditor was expected to manifest the utmost consideration for the debtor, as a brother Israelite. Written notes of obligation (Deut. 15:2) were, at least after the period of exile, regularly in vogue (Jose-

122. Scene on a Megiddo Ivory Depicting Life in the Early 12th Century B. C. Palestine

phus, *Ant.*, xvi, 10, 8; *War*, ii, 17, 6). The "bonds" mentioned in the parable (Luke 16:6, sq.) may have been written on wax-covered tablets, or parchment, from which the numbers might easily be effaced. Of these "bonds" there were two kinds. The most formal, *shetar*, was not signed by the debtor, but only by the witnesses, who wrote their names (or marks) immediately below the lines of the document to prevent fraud. Generally it was further attested by the Sanhedrin of three, and contained the names of creditor and debtor, the amount owing, and the date, together with a clause attaching the property of the debtor. In fact, it was a kind of mortgage. When the debt was paid the legal obligation was simply returned to the debtor; if paid in part, either a new bond was written or a receipt given. The bond mentioned in the parable was different, being merely an acknowledgment of debt for purchases made, and was signed only by the debtor, witnesses being dispensed with.

2. **Regulations Respecting Debtors.** The creditor might secure what was due him by means of a mortgage, pledge, or bondsman. (1) If a pledge was to be taken for a debt the creditor was not allowed to enter the debtor's house and take what he pleased, but was to wait without (Deut. 24:10, 11; comp. Job 22:6; 24:7-9). (2) A mill or millstone, or an upper garment received as a pledge was not to be kept over night. These appear to be only examples of those things which the debtor could not, without great inconvenience, dispense with (Exod. 22:26, 27; Deut. 24:6, 12). (3) A debt could not be exacted during the Sabbatic year (Deut. 15:1-15), but at other times the creditor might seize, first, the hereditary land, to be held until the year of jubilee; or, secondly, the debtor's house, which could be sold in perpetuity, unless redeemed within a year (Lev. 25:25-33). Thirdly, the debtor might be sold, with wife and children, as hired servants (not slaves) until the jubilee (Lev. 25:39-41). (4) A person becoming bondsman or surety was liable in the same way as the original debtor (Prov. 11:15; 17:18).

Debtor. *See* Debt.

Decalogue (Gr. *deka*, "ten," *logos*, "word"). 1. **Name.** Decalogue is the name by which the Greek fathers designated "the Ten Commandments," which were written by God on tables of stone and given to Moses on Mount Sinai. In Hebrew the name is "ten words" *hǎddᵉbārîm 'ǎsěrěth*, Exod. 34:28; Deut. 4:13; 10:4). It is also called "the moral law," "the tables of testimony" (Exod. 34:29), "the tables of the covenant" (Deut. 9:9), and "the covenant" (Deut. 4:13). In the New Testament it is called "the commandments" *entolai*, Matt. 19:17, sq.; Rom. 13:9; I Tim. 1:9, 10, et al.).

2. **Versions.** There are two versions of the Decalogue given in the Pentateuch. The first is contained in Exod. 20, and the second in Deut. 5. These are substantially and almost verbally identical, excepting that the reasons given for the observance of the fourth commandment are not the same. In Exodus the reason is based on one's obligations to God as the Creator (Gen. 2:3). In Deuteronomy the reason assigned is one's duty to others and the memory of the bondage in Egypt. This variation has led many to the belief that the original law was simply "Remember the Sabbath day, to keep it holy." It may, however, be the fact that the form as it stands in Exodus is the divine original, but that Moses in reviewing the law just before his adieu to his people adds a fresh and fuller significance which the history of Israel suggested.

3. **Nature.** The Decalogue is a statement of the terms of the covenant which God made with his chosen people; and in this respect is to be distinguished from the elaborate system of law known as the Mosaic. The vast legal system of Israel, civil, criminal, judicial, and ecclesiastical, was framed after the covenant law, not with a view of expanding it, but to enforce it. As Fairbain suggests, its chief object was to secure through the instrumentality of the magistrate, that if the proper love should fail to influence the hearts and lives of the people, still the right should be maintained. The elaborate system was designed as an educator, to lead the people into the great principles of life embodied in the Decalogue and afterward exhibited in Christ. It was only a temporary expedient to achieve a given end, while the Decalogue is a statement of principles to continue for all time.

This unique place of the Decalogue is seen in the circumstance of its delivery. While all the rest of the law was given by God through the lips of Moses, this was spoken by God himself, and with an awful display of splendor and solemnity never before witnessed (Exod. 19). It appears also that angels were active in the promulgation of the law (Deut. 33:2, 3; Psa. 68:18; Acts 7:53; Gal. 3:19; Heb. 2:2). In addition to that these laws were written by God's own finger, and on durable tables of stone (Deut. 9:1). In the symbolism of the East the stone signified the perpetuity of the law written upon it. Written on both sides, it meant the completeness of the code.

Still another fact marks the unique place of the Decalogue. The tables of stone were put in the most sacred place in the world. In the tabernacle, in the "holy of holies," in the ark of the covenant. Thus they were plainly recognized as containing in themselves the sum and substance of what was held to be strictly required by the covenant.

4. **Contents.** That the Decalogue contains the essential principles of the moral law, and is therefore of permanent obligation, is affirmed in the New Testament. Jesus held it up as the perfect code. When the young man asked him the way of attaining eternal life, Jesus quoted from the Decalogue and told him to obey it and live (Mark 10:19; Luke 18:18-20). And again, after assenting to the two features of the Decalogue as the very essence of the law, he said, "This do, and thou shalt live" (Mark 12:28; Luke 10:28).

In his dispute with the Pharisees the chief point at issue was this: They exalted the minor law, the ceremonial observance, and threw the duties inculcated in the Ten Commandments in the background; he brought the Decalogue forward and gave it its true place. So did the apostles (Rom. 13:9). In the protracted discussion concerning the law, all Paul's examples are taken from these tables, or what they clearly forbade or required.

5. **Source.** The foundation and source of the moral law is God's character. "I am the Lord thy God, which brought thee out of the land of Egypt, out of the house of bondage," is the way the Decalogue is introduced. The Hebrew name here used (Everlasting Eternal Almighty) intimates that the principles of law have their standing in the character of God. "I am . . . thou shalt." That is the connection. And it is that that makes the moral law so awful in its unchangeable majesty. It is law because God is. It cannot be changed without changing the character of Jehovah himself. Right is what it is, because God is what he is, and therefore is as unchangeable as God.

The fact that God has placed the law of his own character on man is proof that man is capable of the divine. Expressing as it does man's true nature, to vary from its requirements is to fall below the dignity of true manhood. In this sense the Decalogue is, as the reformers taught, identical with the "eternal law of nature."

6. **Prohibitory.** The Decalogue is a series of prohibitions. The negative form is due to the shocking depravity of those to whom it was addressed. A prohibition means a disposition to do the thing prohibited. If men were not inclined to worship something other than God the first commandment would not be needed. If there was no murder in men's hearts the sixth commandment would not be required. And so of all the laws. Paul says, "The law was added because of transgressions." The law is put in the negative form for another reason, viz., the law can only restrain the act. It cannot implant the positive virtue. Statutory law may restrain and regulate actions. It cannot transform the sinful heart. It is of necessity negative.

7. **Divisions.** The Ten Commandments are not numbered in the sacred text, and the Church has been divided as to how the division should be made. There are three general modes of division attempted: (1) That which the reformed churches have adopted, and which is called the Philonic division. It makes Exod. 20:2, 3 the first commandment, vers. 4-6 the second, and v. 7 the third. This division is supported by the following reasons: (a) It is made on the principle that polytheism and idolatry are identical. (b) There are three ways of dishonoring God—in denying his unity, his spirituality, and his deity. (c) It divides the two tables into three and seven laws; three having a mystical reference to God, and seven to the Church. (d) It obviates the need of making the unnatural division of the commandment against covetousness into two. (2) The second division is called the Augustinian, and unites vers. 3-6 into one commandment; and divides the commandment concerning covetousness into two. By this method the Roman Church supported the legitimacy of sacred images which were **not** worshiped. (3) The third, or the Talmudic division, makes Exod. 20:2 the first commandment, and vers. 3-6 the second.

8. **Order.** The order in which these laws were written on the two tables of stone is not a matter of grave consideration. If the division were equal, as many think, then the law concerning honor to parents is exalted to a high rank, associated as it is with our duty to honor God. But even without a numerical equality of the two tables the division is philosophical. Our duties to God come first—his being, his worship, his name, and his day. Then come our duties to our fellow-men. They have their beginning in the home. Then they reach out beyond the home circle to all mankind, having regard, first, for our neighbor's life; second, to his wife; third, to his property; fourth, to his position. Finally, the tenth commandment touches the spring of all moral completeness, the desire of the heart. It is really the intent of the heart that determines the moral character of the act. It can not be reached by human legislation. It exposes to the conscience the utter failure of an act that might otherwise be blameless. It was this law that brought Paul with all his righteousness under sentence of condemnation (Rom. 7:7).

The two tables are summarized in the two great laws, "Thou shalt love the Lord thy God with all thy heart, and with all thy soul, and with all thy strength, and with all thy mind; and thy neighbor as thyself." *A. H. T.*

Decap′olis (Gr. dĕ-kăp′ô-lĭs; *ten cities*), a district containing ten cities in the northeastern part of Galilee, near the Sea of Galilee (Matt. 4:25; Mark 5:20; 7:31).

The cities were Scythopolis, Hippos, Gadara, Pella, Philadelphia, Gerasa, Dion, Canatha, Raphana, and Damascus. Damascus is the only one now entitled to the name of city. They were built originally by the followers of Alexander the Great, and rebuilt by the Romans in B. C. 65, by whom they had certain privileges conferred upon them.

Decision, Valley of, a figurative name (Joel 3:14) for the valley of *Jehoshaphat* (*q. v.*). The prophet gives in this passage a description of the nations streaming into the valley of judgment; following it with that of the appearance of Jehovah upon Zion in the terrible glory of the judge of the nations, and as a refuge of his people, Israel.

Decree, the rendering of a number of Hebrew and Greek words, sometimes translated "law," "edict." The enactments of kings in the East were proclaimed publicly by criers (Jer. 34:8, 9; Jonah 3:5-7) who are designated in Dan 3:4; 5:29, by the term *karozá*, the herald. Messengers, sent for that purpose, carried them to distant provinces, towns, and cities (I Sam. 11:7; Ezra 1:1; Amos 4:5), and they were publicly announced at the gate of the city, or other public place. In Jerusalem they were announced in the temple, where large numbers of people assembled, for which reason the prophets often uttered their prophecies there.

De′dan (dē′dăn).

1. A son of Raamah, son of Cush (Gen. 10:7; I Chron. 1:9).

2. A son of Jokshan, son of Abraham and

Keturah (Gen. 25:3; I Chron. 1:32). The usual opinion respecting these founders of tribes is that they first settled among the sons of Cush, wherever these latter may be placed; the second, on the Syrian borders, about the territory of Edom. But Gesenius and Winer have suggested that the name may apply to one tribe; and this may be adopted as probable on the supposition that the descendants of the Keturahite Dedan intermarried with those of the Cushite Dedan, whom the writer places, presumptively, on the borders of the Persian Gulf. The theory of this mixed descent gains weight from the fact that in each case the brother of Dedan is named Sheba. The passages in the Bible in which Dedan is mentioned (besides the genealogies above referred to) are contained in the prophecies of Isaiah (21:13), Jeremiah (25:23; 49:8), and Ezekiel (25:13; 27:15, 20; 38:13), and are in every case obscure. The probable inferences from these mentions of Dedan are: (1) That Dedan, son of Raamah, settled on the shores of the Persian Gulf, and his descendants became caravan merchants between that coast and Palestine. (2) That Jokshan, or a son of Jokshan, by intermarriage with the Cushite Dedan, formed a tribe of the same name, which appears to have had its chief settlement in the borders of Idumea, and perhaps to have led a pastoral life. A native indication of the name is presumed to exist in the island of *Dadan*, on the borders of the gulf (Smith).

Dedanim. *See* Dedan.

Dedicate (Heb. *ḥănăk*, to *initiate;* Gr. *qădăsh*, to *pronounce clean*), a religious service whereby anything is dedicated or consecrated to the service of God; as the dedication of the tabernacle by Moses (Exod. 40; Num. 7); the altar (Num. 7:84, 88); the temple, by Solomon (I Kings 8); the temple, by the returned exiles (Ezra 6:16, 17); the temple built by Herod (Josephus, *Ant.*, xv, 11, 6) (*see* Temple). Dedicatory solemnities were observed with respect to cities, walls, gates, and private houses (Deut. 20:5; Psa. 30, title; Neh. 12: 27). The custom still lingers in the dedication of churches, "opening" of roads, bridges, etc.

Dedication, Feast of. *See* Festivals.

Deed. *See* Land.

Deep, the rendering of several Hebrew and Greek words, used to denote: (1) The grave or abyss (Rom. 10:7; Luke 8:31); (2) The deepest part of the sea (Psa. 69:15; 107:24, 26); (3) Chaos, existing at creation (Gen. 1:2); (4) Hell, the place of punishment (Luke 8:31; Rev. 9:1, 11:7).

Defile, the rendering of several Hebrew and Greek words, generally meaning uncleanness, in a figurative or ceremonial sense. Many blemishes of person and conduct were, under the Mosaic law, esteemed as defilements. Under the Gospel moral defilement is specially emphasized (Matt. 15:18; Rom. 1:24). *See* Uncleanness.

Degree (Heb. *mă'ălăh*, a *step*). This term is used of a group of Levites "of the second *degree*" (I Chron. 15:18) in the sense of rank or order of enumeration. David, in the expression, "Thou hast regarded me according to the estate of a man of high degree" (I Chron. 17:17), seems to mean, "Thou hast visited .me in reference to my elevation." In Psa. 62:9 "degree" is evidently used in the sense of condition or rank, as also in Luke 1:52 and James 1:9 (Gr. *tapeinos, depressed, humiliated*). In I Tim. 3:13 (Gr. *bathmos*) the meaning is position (or "standing," R. V.). In reference to *degree* as applied to measurement, *see* Dial.

Degrees, Song of (*song of steps*), a title given to each of the fifteen psalms from 120 to 134 inclusive. Four of them are attributed to David, one is ascribed to the pen of Solomon, and the other ten give no indication of their author.

The opinion held by Rosenmüller, Herder, and others is that some of the psalms were written before the Babylonish captivity, some by exiles returning to Palestine, and a few at a later date; but that all were incorporated into one collection because they had one and the same character. With respect to the term rendered in the A. V. "degrees," a great diversity of opinion prevails among biblical critics. According to some it refers to the melody to which the psalm was to be chanted. Others, including Gesenius, derive the word from the poetical composition of the song and from the circumstance that the concluding words of the preceding sentence are often repeated at the commencement of the next verse (comp. 121:4, 5, and 124:1, 2 and 3, 4).

A good instance of the "step" style is found in Psa. 121: "I will lift mine eyes unto the hills, from whence cometh *my help. My help* cometh from the Lord, which made heaven and earth."

Aben-Ezra quotes an ancient authority, which maintains that the *degrees* allude to the fifteen steps which, in the temple of Jerusalem, led from the court of the women to that of the men, and on each of which steps one of the fifteen songs of degrees was chanted. The generally accredited opinion, however, is that they were pilgrim songs sung by the people as they went up to Jerusalem.

Deha'vites (dē-hā'vīts), Ezra 4:9 only; R. V. "Dehaites," one of the tribes transported by the king of Assyria to "the cities of Samaria" at the time of the captivity of Israel, B. C. 721. As they are named in connection with the Susanchites, or Susianans, and the Elamites they may be the widely diffused Aryan Daï, or Dahi, mentioned by Herodotus i, 125, among the nomadic tribes of Persia (Smith, *Bib. Dict.*, s. v.).

If Daï were transported by the Assyrians to Samaria it must have been a small detached section of the tribe analogous to the Hittites of southern Palestine. The *Daoi* of Herodotus, the Dahae of Pliny and Virgil, were a warlike and "numerous nomad tribe who wandered over the steppes to the east of the Caspian. Strabo has grouped them with the Sacae and Massagetae as the great Scythian tribes of inner Asia to the north of Bactriana." In the time of Alexander and later they were found about the rivers Oxus and Jaxartes. The name also appears in the vicinity of the Sea of Azof and of the river Danube. But all these places are far beyond the horizon of Assyria, nor can we find that the Assyrians ever mention such a race. On the whole, we incline to regard the identification as an interesting suggestion rather than an established fact. *W. H.*

De'kar (dē'kȧr; *stab*), the father of Solomon's purveyor in the second royal district, lying in the western part of the hill country of Judah and Benjamin, Shaalbim and Beth-shemesh (I Kings 4:9), B. C. before 960.

Delai'ah (dē-lī'ȧ; *freed by Jehovah*).

1. One of the sons of Elioenai, a descendant of the royal line from Zerubbabel (I Chron. 3:24), where the name is Anglicized *Dalaiah.* He probably belongs to the tenth generation before Christ (see Strong's *Harmony of the Gospels*, p. 17), B. C. about 300.

2. The head of the twenty-third division of the priestly order in the arrangement by David (I Chron. 24:18), B. C. about 980.

3. "Children of Delaiah" were among those that returned to Zerubbabel from certain parts of the Assyrian dominions, but who had lost the genealogical records (Ezra 2:60; Neh. 7:62), B. C. 536.

4. The son of Mehetabeel and father of the Shemaiah who advised Nehemiah to escape into the temple from the threats of Sanballat (Neh. 6:10), B. C. 445.

5. A son of Shemaiah and one of the princes to whom Jeremiah's first roll of prophecy was read (Jer. 36:12). He afterward vainly interceded with the king (Jehoiakim) to spare the roll from the flames (v. 25), B. C. 606.

Deli'lah (dē-lī'lȧ; *coquette*), a courtesan who dwelt in the valley of Sorek, beloved by Samson (Judg. 16:4-18), B. C. about 1060. Samson was inveigled by her into revealing the secret of his strength and the means by which he might be overcome. To this she was bribed by the lords of the Philistines, who gave her the large sum of eleven hundred pieces of silver for her services. She was probably a Philistine, and one who used her personal charms for political ends.

Deluge. *See* Flood.

De'mas (dē'mȧs), a companion of St. Paul (called by him his fellow-laborer in Philem. 24; see also Col. 4:14) during his first imprisonment at Rome. At a later period (II Tim. 4:10) we find him mentioned as having deserted the apostle through love of this present world, and gone to Thessalonica, A. D. 66.

Deme'trius (dē-mē'trĭ-ŭs).

1. A silversmith of Ephesus, who made "silver shrines for Diana" (Acts 19:24), i. e., probably, silver models of the temple or of its chapel, in which, perhaps, a little image of the goddess was placed. These, it seems, were purchased by foreigners, who either could not perform their devotions at the temple itself, or who, after having done so, carried them away as memorials or for purposes of worship. Demetrius, becoming alarmed at the progress of the Gospel under the preaching of Paul, assembled his fellow-craftsmen, and excited a tumult by haranguing them on the danger that threatened the worship of Diana, and, consequently, the profits of their craft. The tumult was quieted by the tact and boldness of the town-clerk, and Paul departed for Macedonia, A. D. (perhaps autumn) 55.

2. A Christian mentioned with commendation in III John 12, A. D. about 90. Further than this nothing is known of him.

Demon (Gr. *daimōn*, and its derivative *daimonion*). Once in the New Testament (Acts 17:

123. Bronze Figurine of the Demon God Pazuzu, 800-600 B. C.

124. Rear View of Pazuzu

18, A. V. "gods") used for deity, but usually inferior spiritual beings, angels who "kept not their first estate" (Matt. 25:41; Rev. 12:7, 9); the ministers of the devil (Luke 4:35; 9:1, 42; John 10:21, etc.). Satan is called the "prince of the devils" (Matt. 9:34; 12:24; Mark 3:22; Luke 11:15; Gr. 'archonti tōn daimoniōn). Demons are said to enter into (the body of) one to vex him with diseases (Luke 8:30, 32, sq.; Matt. 9:33; 17:18; Luke 4:35, 41, etc.). A person was thought to be possessed by a demon when he suffered from some exceptionally severe disease (Luke 4:33; 8:27); or acted and spoke as though mad (Matt. 11:18; Luke 7:33; John 7:20, etc.). According to a Jewish opinion which passed over to the Christians, demons are the gods of the Gentiles and the authors of idolatry. Paul, teaching that the gods of the Gentiles are a fiction (I Cor. 8:10, sq.), makes the real existences answering to the heathen conceptions of the gods to be *demons*, to whom he says they really sacrifice (I Cor. 10:20); according to I Tim. 4:1 pernicious errors are disseminated by demons. They are represented as "reserved in everlasting chains under darkness unto the judgment of the great day" (Jude 6; comp. II Pet. 2:4)

Demoniac (Gr. *daimonizomai, to be under the power of a demon,* rendered "possessed with a devil"), a term frequently used in New Testament of one under the influence of a demon. The verb "to be demonized" occurs, in one form or another, seven times in Matthew, four times in Mark, once in Luke, and once in John.

1. **Nature.** By some, demoniacs are thought to have been "persons afflicted with especially severe diseases, either bodily or mental (such as paralysis, blindness, deafness, loss of speech, epilepsy, melancholy, insanity, etc.), whose bodies, in the opinion of the Jews, demons had entered." But the evidence points to actual possession by spirits. "The demonized were incapable of separating their own consciousness and ideas from the influence of the demon, their own identity being merged, and to that extent lost, in that of their tormentors. In this respect the demonized state was also kindred to madness" (Edersheim, *Life of Jesus,* i, p. 608). (1) **The evangelists** constantly distinguish between demoniacal possession and all forms of mere disease, although sometimes occurring together. Thus, he "cast out the spirits . . . and healed all that were sick" (Matt. 8:16); they "brought unto him all sick people . . . and those which were possessed with devils, and those which were lunatic" (4:24); "they brought unto him all that were diseased, and them that were possessed with devils" (Mark 1:32; comp. verse 34). Here "lunatics" are specially distinguished from demoniacs. Matthew (9:32, 33) keeps the possession distinct from the dumbness with which he was also afflicted. Jesus called his disciples "together, and gave them power and authority over all devils, and to cure diseases" (Luke 9:1; comp. Matt. 10:1). In Mark 6:13 "they cast out many devils, and anointed with oil many that were sick, and healed them" (see Mark 3:15; Luke 6:17, 18). (2) **The evangelists** constantly assert that

the actions and utterances in demoniacal possessions were those of the evil spirits. The demons are the actual *agents* in the cases. Such statements are many: "The unclean spirits cried, saying," etc (Mark 3:11); "the devils besought him" (Matt. 8:31); "when the unclean spirit had torn him, and cried with a loud voice, he came out of him" (Mark 1:26; Luke 4:35). Similar in their tenor are Mark 9:20-26; Luke 9:42; 8:2; Acts 5:16. (3) **Not mere disease.** Some of the facts recorded are not compatible with any theory of mere disease, bodily or mental. One of these insuperable facts is found in the case recorded by three evangelists (Matt. 8; Mark 5; Luke 8), where the devils asked and received from Christ permission to pass from the demoniac into the herd of swine, and are declared to have done so, with the results there set forth. Again, there is the habitual assertion of Christ's divinity by these spirits and our Lord's recognition of the fact, while as yet not only the people, but the disciples did not know and characterize him, e. g., "I know thee who thou art, the Holy One of God" (Mark 1:24; Luke 4:34); "What have we to do with thee, Jesus, thou Son of God?" (Matt. 8:29; comp. Luke 4:41; Mark 3:11). That this was a genuine recognition, so understood by our Saviour, appears in this same passage; for "he straitly charged them that they should not make him known." Mark says (1:34) he "suffered not the devils to speak, because they knew him;" and Luke (4:41), "he rebuking them suffered them not to speak: for they knew that he was Christ." Epilepsy, lunacy, insanity, do not meet these several facts. Alford calls attention to a sort of double consciousness indicated in some of these cases, the utterance seeming to come now from the man and not from the evil spirit. In Acts 19:13-17 we find a distinction between "the evil spirit" who said, "Jesus I know, and Paul I know; but who are ye?" and "the man in whom the evil spirit was," who leaped on the sons of Sceva and overcame them. (4) **Jesus and demoniacs.** Jesus treated cases of demoniacal possession as realities. He is not only described as "charging," "rebuking," "commanding," and "casting out" the unclean spirits, but his direct addresses to them are recorded. Thus Mark 5:8-12; Matt. 8:29-32, "he [Jesus] said unto him, Come out of the man, thou unclean spirit. And he asked him, What is thy name? And he [the unclean spirit] answered, My name is Legion: for we are many. . . . And all the devils besought him, saying, If thou cast us out, suffer us to go away into the herd of swine. And he said unto them, Go." Again (Mark 1:25; Luke 4:34), he directly addressed the unclean spirit: "Hold thy peace, and come out of him." Was this all a show and a pretense on his part? He went further yet, for he deliberately argued with the Jews on the assumption of the reality of demoniacal possession, affirming that his casting out devils by the Spirit of God proved that the kingdom of God had come unto them (Matt. 12:23-27; Luke 11: 17-23). Questioned as to their inability to cast out an evil spirit Jesus replied, "This kind can come forth by nothing, but by prayer and fasting" (Mark 9:29). When the seventy returned and said to him with joy, "Lord, even the devils are subject to us through thy name," his answer was to the same effect: "I beheld Satan as lightning fall from heaven." We are further informed (Mark 3:14, 15) that in the solemn act of calling and appointing the apostles "he ordained twelve, that they should be with him, and that he might send them forth to preach, and to cast out devils." Clearly demonism was regarded by our Lord as a stern reality. See Merrill F. Unger, *Biblical Demonology*, Chicago, 1953, pp. 1-250.

2. **Cure.** "The New Testament furnishes the fullest details as to the manner in which demoniacs were set free. This was always the same. It consisted neither in magical means nor formulas of exorcism, but always in the word of power which Jesus spake or intrusted to his disciples, and which the demons always obeyed. In one respect those who were demonized exhibited the same phenomenon: they all owned the power of Jesus" (Edersheim, *Life of Jesus*, i, p. 480, sq.).

Den. The rendering of one Greek and several Hebrew words, meaning a *lair* of wild beasts (Job 37:8; Psa. 10:9; 104:22; Isa. 32:14); a *hole* of a venomous reptile (Isa. 11:8); a *fissure* in the rocks, caves used for hiding (Judg. 6:2; Heb. 11:38; Rev. 6:15), or resort for thieves (Matt. 21:13; Mark 11:17; Luke 19:46). For "Den of Lions" *see* Daniel.

Denarius. *See* Metrology, IV.

Denial. 1. Heb. *kāḥāsh*, to be *untrue*, *disown* (Josh. 24:28; Prov. 30:9).

2. Gr. *'aparneomai*, to affirm that one has no acquaintance or connection with another; of Peter denying Christ (Matt. 26:34, sq., 75); Mark 14:30, sq., 72; Luke 22:34, 61); to deny one's self, to lose sight of one's self and one's own interests (Matt. 16:24; Mark 8:34; Luke 9:23).

3. Gr. *'arneomai*, to *deny* an assertion (Mark 14:70) or event (Acts 4:16); to deny with accusative of the person is used of followers of Jesus who, for fear of death or persecution, deny that Jesus is their master and desert his cause (Matt. 10:33; Luke 12:9; II Tim. 2:12); and, on the other hand, of Jesus denying that one is his follower (Matt. 10:33; II Tim. 2:12). "Denying" God and Christ is used of those who, by cherishing and disseminating pernicious doctrines and immorality, are adjudged to have apostatized from God and Christ (II Pet. 2:1; I John 2:22, 23; Jude 4). "Denying ungodliness and worldly lusts" (Tit. 2:12) is to abjure, renounce.

Self-denial, in the scriptural sense, is the renouncing of all those pleasures, profits, views, connections, or practices that are prejudicial to the true interests of the soul. The understanding must be so far denied as to lean upon it in preference to divine instruction (Prov. 3:5, 6); the will must be denied so far as it opposes the will of God (Eph. 5:17); the affections when they become inordinate (Col. 3:5); the physical nature must be denied when opposed to righteousness (Rom. 6:12, 13); position (Heb. 11:24-26), pecuniary gain (Matt. 4:20-22), friends and relatives (Gen. 12:1) must be renounced if they stand in the way of religion and usefulness.

One's own righteousness must be relinquished, so as not to depend upon it (Phil. 3:8, 9); even life itself must be laid down if called for in the cause of Christ (Matt. 16:24, 25).

Denial of Christ. *See* Peter.

Deposit. *See* Property, Offenses Against.

Depravity. In theology the term depravity denotes the sinfulness of man's nature. *See* Sin, Original.

Depth. *See* Deep.

Deputy, the rendering of several words:

1. *Nĭṣṣāb* (*appointed*), a *prefect;* one set over others. This word is rendered "officer," or chief of the commissariat appointed by Solomon (I Kings 4:5, etc.).

2. *Pĕḥäh*, Esth. 8:9; 9:3; R. V. "governor," the Persian prefect "on this side" (i. e., west of) the Euphrates; modern form, *pasha.*

3. *Anthupatos, in lieu of anyone*, a *proconsul.* The emperor Augustus divided the Roman provinces into senatorial and imperial. The former were presided over by proconsuls appointed by the senate; the latter were administered by legates of the emperor, sometimes called propraetor (Acts 13:7, 8, 12; 18:12).

Der'be (dẽr'bē), a small town at the foot of Mount Taurus, about sixteen miles east of Lystra. Paul and Barnabas gained many converts here; possibly among them was Gaius (Acts 14:6, 20; 20:4). Paul passed through the place on his second missionary journey (16:1).

Desert is scarcely distinguished in ordinary language from *wilderness*, and in the English Bible the terms are used indiscriminately. In one place we find a Hebrew term treated as a proper name, and in another translated as a common name.

1. *Mĭdbar, pasture;* Exod. 3:1; 5:1, etc., usually rendered "wilderness" (Gen. 14:6, etc.), and applied to the country between Palestine and Egypt, including Sinai (Num. 9:5). When used with the article *mĭdbär* denotes the *wilderness of Arabia* (I Kings 9:18). Such pasture land in the East is very often an extensive plain or steppe, which during the drought and heat of summer becomes utterly parched and bare, so that the transition from pasture land to desert was quite easy and natural. That the word comprehends both meanings, see Psa. 65:13; Joel 2:22. But in many, and indeed the greater number of passages, the ideal of sterility is the prominent one (Gen. 14:6; 16:7; Deut. 11:24, etc.). In the poetical books "desert" is found as the translation of *mĭdbar* (Deut. 32:10; Job 24:5; Isa. 21:1; Jer. 25:24).

2. *'Arābāh* (*sterility;* rendered "desert" in Isaiah, Jeremiah, and Ezekiel; elsewhere usually "plain"). While this term primarily meant *plain,* it was not in the sense of pasture, but rather that of hollow or level ground, and especially the level of the Jordan valley, extending to the Red Sea (Deut. 1:1; 2:8; Josh. 12:1; hence also "sea of the *Arabah*" or "desert," Deut. 4:49; viz., the Dead Sea). In the East wide, extended plains are liable to drought and consequent barrenness; hence the Hebrew language describes a *plain,* a *desert,* and an *unfruitful waste* by the same word.

3. Yᵉshimōn (*desolation;* rendered "wilderness," Deut. 32:10; Psa. 68:7; "solitary," Psa. 107:4) is used with the definite article apparently to denote the waste tract on both sides of the Dead Sea. In such cases it is treated as a proper name in the A. V.; thus "the top of Pisgah, which looketh toward *Jeshimon*" (Num. 21:20). This term expresses a greater extent of uncultivated country than the others (I Sam. 23:19, 24; Isa. 43:19, 20).

4. Ḥorbäh (*desolation*), is generally applied to what has been made desolate by man or neglect (Ezra 9:9; Psa. 109:10; Dan. 9:12). The only passage where it expresses a natural waste or "wilderness" is Isa. 48:21, where it refers to Sinai. It is rendered "desert" only in Psa. 102:6; Isa. 48:21; Ezek. 13:4. The Greek word in the New Testament (*erēmos*) has the general meaning of *solitary, uninhabited*, and is sometimes rendered "wilderness."

Figurative. "Desert" or wilderness is used in Scripture as the symbol of temptation, solitude, and persecution (Isa. 27:10; 33:9); of nations ignorant or neglectful of God (32: 15; 35:1); of Israel when they had forsaken God (40:3). The desert was supposed to be inhabited by evil spirits, or at least occasionally visited by them (Matt. 12:43; Luke 11: 24).

Desire of All Nations (literally, the *delight* or *costly* of all the nations) is an expression (Hag. 2:7) understood by most of the earlier commentators as a title of the Messiah. Heb. *Ḥĕmdäh*, (*desire*), is the valuable possessions of the heathen, their gold and silver (v. 8), and the thought is that the shaking will be followed by this result, or produce this effect, that all that is valuable will come to fill the temple with glory.

Desolation, Abomination of. *See* Abomination.

Destroyer (Heb. *măshḥith*, an *exterminator*, Exod. 12:23), the agent employed in the slaying of the firstborn (Heb. 11:28; Gr. *hō holothrenōn*), the angel or messenger of God (II Sam. 24: 15, 16; II Kings 19:35; Psa. 78:49; Acts 12:23).

Destruction (Heb. *'ăbăddōn*, a *perishing*, Job 26:6; 31:12; Psa. 88:11; Prov. 15:11) means a place of destruction, abyss, and is nearly equivalent to *Sheol* (*q. v.*).

Destruction, City of. *See* On.

Deu'el (dū'ĕl; *known of God*), father of Eliasaph, the "captain" of the tribe of Gad at the time of the numbering of the people at Sinai (Num. 1:14; 7:42, 47; 10:20), B. C. about 1438. The same man is mentioned again (2:14), but here the name appears as *Reuel*, owing to an interchange of the two very similar Hebrew letters *D* and *R*.

Deuteronomy, Book of, the last book of the Pentateuch, completing the five books of Moses. The Jews called it "five-fifths of the law." It follows logically after Numbers. Numbers carries the history of the nation Israel to the events in the Plains of Moab to the E. of Jericho. Deuteronomy winds up the Mosaic age with three discourses from the great Lawgiver just before his death and the entrance of the people into the land of Canaan.

1. **The Name.** The name comes from the Septuagint through an inaccurate translation of Chapter 17:18 which is correctly rendered, "This is the copy (or repetition) of the law." It is apparent that the book is not a "second law" distinct from the law given at Sinai, as the name of the work might suggest. It is simply a partial restatement and exposition of former laws to the new generation which had been reared in the wilderness. The Jewish name of the book is *'Elleh haddevarim*, "These are the words" or simply *Devarim*, "Words." In Jewish tradition it is styled *Mishneh Torah*, meaning "repetition" or "copy of the law" (Deut. 17:18).

2. **The Author.** In most explicit terms the book itself asserts its authorship by Moses. "And Moses wrote this law, and delivered it unto the priests, the sons of Levi, who bore the ark of the covenant of the Lord, and unto all the elders of Israel" (Deut. 31:9). "And it came to pass, when Moses had made an end of writing the words of this law in a book, until they were finished, that Moses commanded the Levites, who bore the ark of the covenant of the Lord, saying, Take this book of the law and put it in the side of the ark of the covenant of the Lord your God, that it may be there for a witness against thee (Deut. 31:24, 26). No other book of the Pentateuch bears so emphatic a testimony of its Mosaic authorship. It is of unusual interest that critics most dogmatically reject the Mosaic authorship of this book in the face of these clear assertions. Over against these critical claims conservative scholars see ample evidence to maintain the Mosaic authenticity of this book. The general character of the writing, its code of conquest, its hortatory nature, its plan as a military law-book of a pilgrim people about to enter Canaan, together with the scope and spirit of the writing are peculiarly suited for the Mosaic era and completely unsuitable for a later age. Moses is mentioned more than forty times in the book, mostly as the authoritative author of the subject matter. The first person predominates. The language purports to come directly from Moses. If Moses is not the actual author, the book can hardly be excused from being a literary forgery, scarcely worthy of canonical Scripture.

3. **The Critical View of Authorship.** Deuteronomy has a central place in higher criticism of the Pentateuch. Rationalists maintain that it was written by an anonymous prophetic writer in the spirit of Moses between 715 and 640 B. C. It is claimed that it was first published in the eighteenth year of king Josiah, to bring about his great religious reformation (II Kings, Chaps. 22, 23). The principal reason assigned for the Josianic date is that the O. T. books do not give explicit witness to Deuteronomy especially in the matter of the law of the central sanctuary (Deut. 12:1-7). It is, accordingly, assumed not to have had an existence previously to Josiah's time. But an unbiased view of the Pentateuch reveals that the laws of Deuteronomy were both known and observed, existing in the form of written codified statutes, and made a marked impression on the Israelites from the period of their actual entrance into the land of Canaan. Examples are abundant. The "de-

votion" of Jericho (Josh. 6:17, 18) follows Deut. 13:15 ff. When Ai was captured, Israel took only "the cattle and the spoil" (Josh. 8:27) in keeping with Deut. 20:14. The body of the king of Ai was taken down from the gibbet before nightfall (Josh. 8:29 cf. Deut. 21:23). The altar on Ebal (Josh. 8:30, 31) recalls Deut. 27:4-6. Many other evidences occur. The law of the central sanctuary was also known in early Israel, as is proved by the fact that the east Jordanic tribes disavowed their memorial at the Jordan when accused by their fellow tribesmen of plurality of sanctuary (Josh. 22:29, 31 cf. Deut. 12:5). Elkanah went up annually to Shiloh, Israel's early sanctuary (I Sam. 1:3, 7). After the destruction of the central sanctuary Samuel sacrificed at Mizpah, Ramah and Bethlehem, evidently merely taking advantage of the law of Deut. 12:10, 11 because of the time of war. Hezekiah's revival (I Kings 18:4, 22) was inconceivably carried out without a knowledge of Deuteronomy and its unique law of the central sanctuary. Eighth-century prophets knew the law also. By their unsound views of Deuteronomy the partitionists have been led to discard Mosaic authenticity of the entire Pentateuch and have landed in the quagmire of doubt and uncertainty.

4. **Contents.**

Part I: First Mosaic Discourse, 1:1-4:43

Part II: Second Mosaic Discourse, 4:44-26:19

Part III: Third Mosaic Discourse, 27:1-30:20

Part IV: Historical Appendices, 31:1-34:12

 a. Moses' last words and Joshua's appointment, 31:1-30

 b. Moses' song and exhortation, 32:1-47

 c. Moses' sight of the Promised Land, 32:48-52

 d. Moses' parting blessing, 33:1-29

 e. Death and burial of Moses, 34:1-12

M. F. U.

Devil (Gr. *diabolos, accuser*).

1. One who slanders another for the purpose of injury, a calumniator, e. g., a gossip monger (I Tim. 3:11; II Tim. 3:3; Tit. 2:3).

2. "Devil" is the rendering of the Heb. *sā'îr, hairy* (Lev. 18:7), a "goat," or "satyr" (Isa. 13:21; 34:14). These were demon spirits that inhabited the desert, and whose pernicious influence was sought to be averted by sacrifice. The Israelites brought this superstition and the idolatry to which it gave rise from Egypt, where goats were worshiped as gods. These were the gods whom the Israelites worshiped in Egypt (Josh. 24:14; Ezek. 20:7; 23:3, 8, 9, etc.).

3 In Deut. 32:17; Psa. 106:37, the term rendered "devil" is *shade* (Heb. *shēd, demon*), and means an idol; since the Jews regarded idols as demons that caused themselves to be worshiped by men.

4. The greatest of all fallen spirits (Matt. 4:8-11; Rev. 12:9, etc.). This epithet refers to him as the "accuser of the brethren" (Rev. 20:10). In this role he is granted a certain power of sifting carnal believers (Job. 1:6-11; Luke 22:31, 32; I Cor. 5:5; I Tim. 1:20). Although this may even involve physical death, Satan's power over the believer is strictly permissive and limited, and believers are kept in faith through the advocacy of Christ (I John 2:1). At the commencement of the Great Tribulation, Satan's privilege of access to God as accuser will be terminated (Rev. 12:7-11). At Christ's glorious second advent Satan will be chained for the millennium (Rev. 20:2). Finally, he is loosed for a little season (Rev. 20:3, 7, 8) and will head a final attempt to overthrow God's kingdom. Defeated in this, he will be hurled to his eternal doom in the lake of fire. *See* Satan.

Devoted Thing. *See* Anathema.

Dew (Heb. *ṭăl*). "The dews of Syrian nights are excessive; on many mornings it looks as if there had been heavy rains, and this is the sole slackening of the drought which the land feels from May till October" (Smith, *Hist. Geog.*, p. 65) (Judg. 6:38; Cant. 5:2; Dan. 4:15, sq.). This partial refreshment of the ground is of great value, and would alone explain all the oriental references to the effect of dew. Thus it is coupled as a blessing with rain, or mentioned as a source of fertility (Gen. 27:28; Deut. 33:13; Zech. 8:12), and its withdrawal is considered a curse (II Sam. 1:21; I Kings 17:1; Hag. 1:10).

Figurative. Dew in the Scriptures is a symbol of the beneficent power of God, which quickens, revives, and invigorates the objects of nature when they have been parched by the burning heat of the sun (Prov. 19:12; Hos. 14:5). The silent, irresistible, and rapid descent of dew is used to symbolize the sudden onset of an enemy (II Sam. 17:12). "The dew of thy youth" (Psa. 110:3) is thought to be a figure of abiding youthful vigor. Dew is a token of exposure in the night (Cant. 5:2; Dan. 4:15, etc.)'; the symbol of something evanescent (Hos. 6:4; 13:3); and, from its noiseless descent and refreshing influence, the emblem of brotherly love and harmony (Psa. 133:3).

Diadem. The rendering in the A. V. of several Hebrew words:

1. *Ṣănîf*, something *wound about* the head, spoken of the turban of men (Job. 29:14), of women (Isa. 3:23, "hood"), of the high priest (Zech. 3:5), and the tiara of a king (Isa. 62:3).

2. *Ṣĕfîrăh*, circlet (Isa. 28:5), a royal tiara.

3. *Miṣnĕfĕth* (Ezek. 21:26) does not mean the royal diadem, like *Ṣănîf*, but the tiara of the high priest, as it does in every instance in the Pentateuch, from which Ezekiel has taken the word.

The difference in Greek between *diadem* (*diadēma*) and *crown* (*stephanos*) is carefully observed. The latter is a crown in the sense of a chaplet, wreath, or garland; the "badge of victory in the games, of civic worth, of military valor, of nuptial joy, of festal gladness." *Diadem* is a crown as the badge of royalty.

What the "diadem" of the Jews was we know not. That of other nations of antiquity was a fillet of silk, two inches broad, bound around the head and tied behind, the invention of which is attributed to Liber. Its color was generally white; sometimes, however, it was blue, like that of Darius, and it was sown with pearls or other gems (Zech. 9:16; comp. Mal. 3:17).

Dial (Heb. *mǎʿălāh*, *step*), for the measurement of time, erected by Ahaz (II Kings 20:11; Isa. 38:8), and called the "steps of Ahaz." As *mǎʿălāh* may signify either one of a flight of steps or degree, we might suppose the reference to be a dial plate with a gnomon indicator; but, in the first place, the expression points to an actual succession of steps, that is to say, to an obelisk upon a square or circular elevation ascended by steps, which threw the shadow of its highest point at noon upon the highest steps, and in the morning and evening upon the lowest, either on the one side or the other, so that the obelisk itself served as a gnomon. The step dial of Ahaz may have consisted of twenty steps or more, which measured the time of day by half hours, or even quarters. If the sign was given an hour before sunset the shadow, by going back ten steps of half an hour each, would return to the point at which it stood at twelve o'clock. When it is stated that "the sun returned," this does not mean the sun in the heaven, but the sun upon the sundial, upon which the illumined surface moved upward as the shadow retreated, for when the shadow moved back the sun moved back as well. The event is intended to be represented as a miracle, and a miracle it really was (Delitzsch, *Com.*, on Isa. 38:7, 8).

Diamond. *See* Mineral Kingdom.

Diana. *See* Gods, False.

Dib′laim (dĭb′lā-ĭm; *cakes* [of dried figs?]), the name of the father of Gomer, the wife of Hosea (Hos. 1:3), B. C. about 750.

Dib′lath (dĭb′lăth), properly **Dib′lah** (dĭb′lȧ), a place named only in Ezek. 6:14, as if situated at one of the extremities of the land of Israel. It is natural to infer that Diblah was in the north. The only name in the north at all like it is Riblah, and the letters *D* and *R* are so much alike in Hebrew and so frequently interchanged, owing to the carelessness of copyists, that there is a strong probability that Riblah is the right reading.

Di′bon (dī′bŏn, *pining*).

1. A town on the east side of Jordan, in the rich pastoral country, which was taken possession of and rebuilt by the children of Gad (Num. 32:3, 34). From this circumstance it possibly received the name of Dibon-gad. Its first mention is in the ancient fragment of poetry (Num. 21:30), and from this it appears to have belonged originally to the Moabites. We find Dibon counted to Reuben in the lists of Joshua (13:9, 17). In the time of Isaiah and Jeremiah, however, it was again in possession of Moab (Isa. 15:2; Jer. 48:18, 22; comp. 24). In the same denunciations of Isaiah it appears, probably, under the name of Dimon. In modern times the name Dhîbän still exists as a heap of ruins three miles north of the Arnon. It was among the ruins of Dibon that the Moabite Stone (*q. v.*) was discovered in 1868.

2. One of the towns which was reinhabited by the men of Judah after the return from captivity (Neh. 11:25). From its mention with Jekabzeel, Moladah, and other towns of the south there can be no doubt that it is identical with *Dimonah* (*q. v.*).

Di′bon-gad (dī′bŏn-găd), one of the halting places of the Israelites (Num. 33:45, 46). It was, no doubt, the same place which is generally called *Dibon*, 1.

Dib′ri (dĭb′rī; perhaps *eloquent*), a Danite, father of Shelomith, a woman whose son was stoned to death by command of Moses for blaspheming the name of the Lord (Lev. 24:11), B. C. c. 1420.

Didrachm. *See* Metrology, IV.

Did′ymus (dĭd′ĭ-mŭs; *twin*), a surname (John 11:16, etc.) of the apostle Thomas.

Diet (Heb. *ʾărūḥāh*), the term applied to the daily allowance apportioned by Evilmerodach, king of Babylon, to his royal captive, Jehoiachin, king of Judah (Jer. 52:34). Respecting the general use of the word. *See* Food.

Dignities (Gr. plural of *doxa*, *glory*), persons higher in honor (II Pet. 2:10; Jude 8), probably angels as being spiritual beings of preeminent dignity.

Dik′lah (dĭk′lȧ), the name of a son of Joktan (Gen. 10: 27; I Chron. 1:21). His descendants probably settled in Yemen and occupied a portion of it a little to the east of the Hejaz.

Dil′ean (dĭl′ē-ăn), a town in the low country of Judah (Josh. 15:38). Probably Tell en Negileh.

Dill, marginal and correct rendering (Matt. 23:23) of Gr. *anēthon*, translated in the text "anise." *See* Vegetable Kingdom.

Dim′nah (dĭm′nä; *dunghill*), a Levitical city in Zebulun (Josh. 21:35). In I Chron. 6:77 Rimmon is substituted for it.

Di′mon, the Waters of (dī′mŏn), some stream on the east of the Dead Sea, in the land of Moab, against which Isaiah is here uttering denunciations (Isa. 15:9). Gesenius conjectures that the two names Dimon and Dibon are the same.

Dimo′nah (dĭ-mō′nä), a city in the south of Judah (Josh. 15:22), perhaps the same as Dibon in Neh. 11:25.

Di′nah (dī′nä; *justice*), the daughter of Jacob by Leah (Gen. 30:21), and full sister of Simeon and Levi. While Jacob dwelt in Shechem Dinah was seduced by Shechem, the son of Hamor, the chief of the country. She was probably at this time about thirteen or fifteen years of age, the ordinary period of marriage in the East. Shechem proposed to make the usual reparation by paying a sum to the father and marrying her (Deut. 22:28, 29), but Jacob declined to negotiate until he had made known the facts to his sons and advised with them. Hamor proposed a fusion of the two peoples by the establishment of intermarriage and commerce. The sons, bent upon revenge, demanded, as a condition of the proposed union, the circumcision of the Shechemites. They assented, and on the third day, when the people were disabled, Simeon and Levi slew them all and took away their sister (Gen. 34). Dinah probably continued unmarried and went with her father into Egypt (46:15), B. C. about 1950.

Di′naite (dī′nȧ-īt), a name given to a part of the colonists placed in Samaria after it was taken by the Assyrians (Ezra 4:9). "They remained under the dominion of Persia, and took part with their fellow-colonists in opposition to the Jews under Artaxerxes, but nothing more is known of them" (Smith, *Bib. Dict.*, s. v.). They may have been the Armenian peoples known as Dayani to the Assyrians.

Dine, Dinner. *See* Eating, Food.

Din′habah (dĭn′hâbä), a city of Bela, king of Edom (Gen. 36:32; I Chron. 1:43). Location uncertain.

Diony′sius the Areopagite (dī-ô-nĭsh′ĭ-ŭs the ă-rē-ŏ′pà-gīt, Acts 17:19-34), an eminent Athenian converted to Christianity by the preaching of Paul on Mars' Hill. Nothing further is related of him in the New Testament, but Suidas recounts that he was an Athenian by birth and eminent for his literary attainments, that he studied first at Athens and afterward at Helipolis, in Egypt. The name of Dionysius has become important in Church history from certain writings formerly believed to be his, but now known to be spurious and designated as the Pseudo-Dionysian writings (McC. and S., *Cyc.*, s. v.).

Diot′rephes (dī-ŏt′rê-fēz; *Jove-nourished*), a person condemned by the apostle John in his third epistle. Desiring preeminence, he refused to see the letter sent by John, thereby declining to submit to his directions or acknowledge his authority. He circulated malicious slanders against the apostle and exercised an arbitrary and pernicious influence in the Church (III John 9, 10).

Discerning of Spirits, a spiritual gift enjoyed by certain in the apostolic age. This enabled its possessor to judge from what spirits the utterances they hear proceeded, whether the Holy Spirit, human or demoniac spirits; thus preserving the Church from misled influences (I Cor. 12:10; comp. I Cor. 14:29; I John 4:1).

Disciple. 1. This term occurs once in the Old Testament, as the rendering of Heb. *lĭmmûd*, one *instructed*, Isa. 8:16; rendered "learned" in 50:4; "taught" in 54:13.

2. **In the New Testament** it is the rendering of the Gr. *mathētēs, learner*, and occurs frequently. The meaning is one who professes to have learned certain principles from another and maintains them on that other's authority. It is applied principally to the followers of Jesus (Matt. 5:1; 8:21, etc.); sometimes to those of John the Baptist (Matt. 9:14) and of the Pharisees (Matt. 22:16). It is used in a special manner to indicate the twelve (Matt. 10:1; 11:1; 20:17).

DISEASES.

In treating this subject we call attention to the several diseases mentioned in Scripture, and to their treatment. Under the latter we introduce medicine, physician, remedies, etc.:

Ague (Heb. *qăddăḥăth*, Lev. 26:16, R. V. "fever"). This is doubtless generic for all the fevers of the land. They are intermittent, remittent, typhoid, typhus, besides the febrile states accompanying the various inflammations and the exanthemata. Malarial fevers are the most characteristic. They prevail especially in late summer and early autumn. In the swamps of the Hûleh and the irrigated gardens about the cities very malignant types of these fevers attack those who sleep in the foci of infection and those who work in the

poisonous atmosphere. Not infrequently patients die in the second or third paroxysm of such fevers. When they do not die from the violence of the poison they often drag on through weary months of constantly recurring attacks and suffer from congestion or abscess of the liver or spleen and other internal disorders.

Blains and **Boils** (Heb. *'ăbă'bû'äh; sh⁰ḥîn*, Exod. 9:9, 10). These are of several kinds: (1) Simple boils, which may be single or come out in large numbers and successive crops (Job 2:7), causing much suffering and some danger to the patient. They consist in a core, which is a gangrenous bit of skin and subcutaneous tissue, surrounded by an angry, inflamed and suppurating nodule, which finally bursts and lets out the core, after which the seat of the boil heals, leaving a permanent scar. (2) Carbuncles. These are very large boils, with a number of openings, leading to a considerable mass of dead cellular tissue and giving exit to the discharge of the same. Such was probably Hezekiah's boil (II Kings 20:7; Isa. 38:21). (3) Malignant pustules. These are due to infections from animals having splenic fever. The virus is carried by insects or in wool or hides or otherwise, and produces a black spot where it enters, surrounded by a dark livid purplish or dusky red zone, with vesicles and a hard area of skin infiltrated with anthrax bacilli. If the focus of the disease be not destroyed the blood is rapidly poisoned and the patient dies. (4) Probably all skin diseases in which there is suppuration in and beneath the cutis would have been included in the generic designation boils.

Blemish (Lev. 21:18-21, the rendering of several Hebrew words), any deformity or spot. Such disqualified their possessor from becoming a priest.

Blindness (Heb. *'iwwärōn*, Deut. 28:28, etc.). Eye affections are among the most common of all the diseases of Bible lands. Ophthalmia and other destructive diseases prevail to a frightful extent in Egypt. Among the lower classes it is, perhaps, the exception to see both eyes perfect. A very large proportion of the population has lost one eye, and the number of totally blind is excessive. While the ravages of eye diseases are not so frightful in Palestine and Syria they are sufficiently so to illustrate the very frequent (more than sixty times) references to blindness in the Bible. The causes are the heat, sunlight, dust, and, most of all, the uncleanly habits of the people, all of which favor the spread of diseases, which often in a single day destroy the eye.

Boils. *See* Blains.

Botch (Heb. *sh⁰ḥîn, burning*, Deut. 28:27, 35, R. V. "boil"), another rendering of the word elsewhere translated "boil."

Broken-Handed, Broken-Footed (Lev. 21: 19), a disqualification for the priesthood. Clubfoot and clubhand would also disqualify.

Bruises (Isa. 1:6; Jer. 30:12; Nah. 3:19, several Hebrew words), familiar accidents, often far more serious than would be supposed from their external marks.

Canker (II Tim. 2:17, A. V. marg., R. V. "gangrene"; Gr. *gaggraina*). The terrible disease, *cancer*, for which no remedy exists but the knife, is quite prevalent in the East, especially the form of it known as *epithelioma*. The sufferer from all forms of cancer has more or less acute pain, and ultimately ulceration, and, exhausted by bleeding or suppuration, at length dies worn out with its unspeakable agony. But this rendering, although it would suit the requisitions of the passage, is not the true one. *See* Gangrene.

Crookbacked (Heb. *gĭbbēn, arched*, Lev. 21:20). In the East it is quite common to see young girls carrying children on their shoulders, or perched on their hips. Many of these fall and experience irreparable injuries to their spines. Scrofulous disease of the spine is also very common and often results in angular curvature. The specimens of deformity of this class, which are to be seen by every wayside in Syria and Palestine, are lamentable. Those afflicted with such deformities were not allowed in the temple service.

Dropsy (Gr. *hudrōpikos, watery*, Luke 14:2). This is a symptom of a number of diseases, mostly of the heart, liver, kidneys, and brain, causing collections of water in the cavities o the body, or on its surface, or in the limbs. It is curable only if the disease causing it is amenable to treatment.

Dwarf. Dwarfs were not allowed in the priesthood (Lev. 21:20).

Emerods (Heb. *'ōphĕl, tumor*, Deut. 28:27, etc.), a painful disease, especially promoted by the sedentary habits of the orientals, and hence very common there. Although amenable to the advanced skill of the West, the popular medicine of the East has no cure for it. It was, therefore, a very terrible visitation (I Sam. 5:6, 9, 12; 6:4, 5, 11).

Flat Nose (Heb. *ḥărăm*, to be *blunt*, Lev. 21:18), a disqualification for the priesthood.

Flux (Gr. *dusenteria*). The "bloody flux" (Acts 28:8) was, no doubt, *dysentery*. This disease is very common in the East, and often fatal, not merely by its own violence, but by the abscess of the liver which it frequently causes. It is supposed that the disease of the bowels (II Chron. 21:15, 19) with which Jehoram was smitten was the advanced state of this disease, causing an invagination and procidentia.

Gangrene (R. V., II Tim. 2:17, for A. V. "canker"), mortification of any part of the body. The reference is probably to the variety known as senile gangrene. This disease begins at the end of a toe or finger, as a blackish spot, which gradually spreads over the rest of the toe, then to the other toes, and the foot, and leg, until at last the patient dies of blood poisoning. Even early and free amputation generally fails to save life, as the disease is in the constitution, and reappears in the stump. This course of the destructive process corresponds well with that of profane and vain babblings which (v. 16) "increase" (R. V. "proceed further") unto more ungodliness. *See* Canker.

Halt (Gr. *chōlos, limping*, Luke 14:21; John 5:3), lame, whether from rigidity, or amputation, or deformity.

Impotent (John 5:3), a general term for disabled.

Infirmity, a word used in the A. V. in three senses: (1) *Impurity* (Lev. 12:2, R. V. "impurity"). (2) *Deformity* (Luke 13:11). (3) A general term for *disability* (John 5:5; I Tim. 5:23). Besides these senses it is used figuratively for mental and spiritual weaknesses (Rom. 8:26, etc.).

Inflammation, a general and well-understood term (Lev. 13:28; Deut. 28:22).

Issue, a word used medically in three senses: (1) *Offspring* (Gen. 48:6). (2) *A flowing of blood* (Lev. 12:7; Matt. 9:20, etc.). (3) *Other discharges* (Lev. 15:2). These discharges rendered their victim unclean.

Itch (Heb. *ḥĕrĕs*, Deut. 28:27). It is probable that the word translated "itch" in this passage refers to some other tormenting skin disease, as eczema or prurigo, while that translated A. V. "scab," R. V. "scurvy" (Heb. *garabh*, Arab. *jarab*), is the true itch. *Jarab* is the classical name of this disease, and used for it also in common speech to this day (*see* Scurvy). Itch is a skin disease produced by the entrance of a parasitic insect into the substance of the skin. It causes intolerable itching, and the scratching produces deep furrows and excoriations. If left to itself it is interminable. Although curable by proper medical treatment, this was probably unknown to the Hebrews.

Lameness, impairment or loss of power in walking. It was a barrier to the priestly office (Lev. 21:18).

Leprosy (Heb. *ṣără'ăth*). Much confusion has arisen in the interpretation of the scriptural allusions to leprosy, from the fact that this word is used in English for a disease, *elephantiasis Graecorum*, wholly different in its symptoms, course, and termination from the Levitical and New Testament leprosy. The former is a constitutional, incurable, hereditary, more or less contagious disease, which sometimes begins with numbness of the extremities, with or without pain. There are dusky and livid swellings, and distortions of the hands and feet; nodules are formed in various parts of the body; ulcers open on the soles of the feet or at the ball of the heel. These extend to the bones, which become carious, and, as the ulceration spreads, the patient becomes more or less crippled. Tubercles are produced on the face, and folds of skin are raised on the forehead and cheeks, which give the so-called leonine expression to the countenance. Fever sets in, and ultimately the patient, often after a long and miserable life, succumbs. This disease may be the "botch" (A. V., Deut. 28:35, R. V. "boil") "in the knees and legs," and "from the sole of the foot to the crown of the head."

The biblical leprosy is a whiteness (Exod. 4:6) which disfigured its victim, but did not disable him. Naaman was able to exercise the functions of general of the Syrian army, although a leper. Both Old Testament and New Testament lepers went about everywhere. Leprosy is described in Leviticus as a white spot, spreading or disappearing, sometimes with a reddish base, or as raw spots. A victim of this superficial scaly disease (*lepra*, or *psoriasis*) was unclean only as long as the affection was partial. Once the whole body was covered he was clean, and could enter the temple (Lev. 13:12, 17).

The allusion to a boil (Lev. 13:18-28), with inflamed margins and whitened hairs, may refer to an Aleppo button, ending at its margin in a psoriasis, or a lupoid affection, which spreads for some distance around. This is quite common in the East. Levitical leprosy is self-terminable (Lev. 13:46). *Elephantiasis Graecorum* is neither curable, nor does it wear itself out.

The secret of the ceremonial uncleanness of persons with the various forms of tetter, eczema, lepra simplex, psoriasis, etc., is the piebald and mottled appearance, not the disease, for, as before said, a man wholly covered with the eruption was clean. When the lepers were cured by Christ the cure was called *cleansing* (Matt. 10:8; 11:15; Luke 7:22; 17:14). The victims were neither lame nor deformed. They were never brought on beds. The Mosaic law was full of prohibitions in regard to that which was not simple and uniform. A mottled or piebald animal could not be offered. A priest could not wear a patched or many-colored garment. Fungous growths on walls, mildew on clothes, were accounted leprosy, and made the tainted objects unclean. In this case surely it was the mottled blotched appearance that was objected to. The aim of the law was to inculcate by object lessons purity, simplicity, unity. When these objects were attained by uniformity in the eruption, even of leprosy, all over the body of the patient, he ceased to be ceremonially a leper. This disposes at once of the idea that scriptural lepers were isolated hygienically, as the victims of *elephantiasis Graecorum* are, lest they should infect others. For when perfectly leprous they were free to go where they would. (*See*, for a complete elaboration of this argument, *Sunday School Teacher*, London, May, 1880, pp. 183-188).

Lunacy (Matt. 4:24; 17:15). *See* Madness.

Madness (Heb. *shĭggä'ōn, raving*, Deut. 28:28). Madmen are twice mentioned (I Sam. 21:15; Prov. 26:18). Insanity is much more rare in the East than in the West. This is doubtless due to the freedom from the strain which so severely tests the endurance of the more active minds of the Japhetic stock. Little or no treatment is used. It is considered a merit to feed and clothe the insane if needy.

Maimed (Luke 14:21), a general term for severely injured.

Murrain (Heb. *dĕbĕr, pestilence*). We have no means of knowing what the epidemic was which constituted the fifth plague (Exod. 9:1-6). It may have been splenic fever, which sometimes prevails extensively.

Palsy (Gr. *paralutikos, loosened*). Paralysis comes from several causes: (1) Inflammation of the brain or spinal cord. This in the East is specially common in infancy, and in many cases leads to partial paralysis, as of the shoulder, arm, one or both legs, and sometimes the nerve of speech or hearing, or both. (2) Injuries of the spinal column. These are more apt to occur in adult life. (3) Pressure from curvature of the spine, or from tumors or other cause. (4) Apoplexy. The paralysis from the latter cause is sometimes cured. That from the others is incurable. The cases brought to our Saviour were undoubtedly of the incurable sort, and probably involved at least the lower limbs.

Pestilence (Heb. *dĕbĕr*; Gr. *loimos, plague*), a general term for diseases which attack large numbers of persons at the same time. They are not known to be due to organic germs. We have no means of knowing what particular pestilences from time to time scourged the Israelites.

Scab (Heb. for *săpăḥ*, Lev. 13:2, 6, 7; 14:56). The same root appears in the form of a verb (Isa. 3:17), *sippah*, to *afflict with a scab*. Both refer to the crust which forms on skin eruption. Such are common in many skin diseases and do not indicate any particular kind. Many diseases of the scalp produce them and cause the hair at the same time to fall out. This is regarded as a special calamity for women (Isa. 3:17). The term *yallepheth* (Lev. 21:20; 22:22), A. V. "scabbed," refers to some crustaceous disease of the skin of animals. The disease of horses, in which there is a scabby, eczematous state of the pastern, known in English as "scratches," is called *jatab* (itch) in Arabic.

Scall (Lev. 13:30, 35; 14:54), a somewhat general term for *eruptions*.

Scurvy (R. V., Deut. 28:27, for A. V. "scab"). We have given our reasons under *Itch* for preferring the rendering *itch* for the Heb. *garabh* here, instead of for *heres*, as in A. V., R. V. We do not see any reason to render it with R. V. "scurvy." Nor do we think the rendering of the same word (Lev. 21:20; 22:22), A. V., R. V., "scurvy" any better. *Itch* is its proper rendering. This would remove *scurvy* from the list of diseases mentioned in Scriptures.

Sores (Isa. 1:6; Luke 16:20; Rev. 16:11), a general term for ulcers.

Wen (Heb. *yăbbēl*), a cyst containing cebaceous and other matters, spoken of only in connection with animals intended for sacrifice (Lev. 22:22), but also common in men.

Withered (Heb. *yăbēsh*). The Nazarite's skin is spoken of as withered (Lam. 4:8), i. e., wrinkled and dry. A "withered hand" (Matt. 12:10, etc.; comp. I Kings 13:4-6) is one in which the muscles, and often the bones themselves, are shrunken, owing to loss of nerve power or stiffening of joints. Not infrequently the limb is much shorter, as well as more slender, than natural. When resulting from anything but recent disuse it is incurable.

Wounds are frequently alluded to. The binding up and pouring in oil and wine (Luke 10:34) was as good antiseptic treatment as was then known.

Worms. The worms which ate Herod (Acts 12:23) may have been maggots bred in some gangrenous sore.

Treatment of Diseases

The Hebrews were greatly inferior to their powerful neighbors of Egypt, Assyria, and Greece in scientific culture. We have no allusion in the Old Testament to scientific schools, and it is improbable that such existed. There were schools for the education of religious teachers, but we have no reason to believe that anything was taught in them except the Hebrew language itself and the various branches of canon law and interpretation. While their neighbors were evolving and cultivating mathematics, astronomy, history, logic, metaphysics, law, and medicine, and their learned men were committing to inscribed bricks, stone, papyrus rolls, and books full of treatises on all that they knew, the ancient Hebrews have not left us a single fragment of literature or science except the canonical Scriptures and the Apocrypha. Only by the most laborious search can we find in these Scriptures hints as to the scientific belief and practice which the Hebrews may have derived from their residence in Egypt and intercourse with their more enlightened and progressive rivals. The Talmud, the function of which was to gather up all that tradition had transmitted, and expound it by all that the ingenuity of its astute authors could furnish, does nothing to change our judgment that the Hebrews had little or no notion of the movement of the human mind which was taking place in other lands.

We have no reason to suppose that medicine affords any exception to the general state of the sciences among the Hebrews. It is exceedingly difficult to establish from the Bible the existence of such a science or of a proper order of medical practitioners in the earlier stages of Hebrew history. The allusions to the offices of the midwives (Gen. 35:17; 38:27-30; Exod. 1:15) give us no reason to suppose that they were an educated class, or had any knowledge of the art of accouchement greater than is possessed by their successors in Syria at the present day. There is nowhere in Scripture an intimation that a physician assisted at a confinement. The simple operation of circumcision was probably performed by heads of families or their dependents (Gen. 17:10-14; 34:24), or even women (Exod. 4: 25). The law provided that one who injured another should "pay for the loss of his time and cause him to be thoroughly healed" (Exod. 21:19). But this "causing to be healed" does not state nor necessarily imply a physician. Physicians embalmed Jacob (Gen. 50: 2), but they were Egyptians, not Hebrews. Job mentions physicians (13:4). Even so late as the time of Joram (850 B.C.), although he returned to Jezreel to be healed of wounds and sickness (II Kings 8:29), no mention is made of doctors. It is uncertain whether Asa's physicians (II Chron. 16:12, 915 B.C.) were natives or foreigners. The poetical allusion (Jer. 8:22, B.C. 626) is in the form of a question, "Is there no balm in Gilead? is there no physician there?" While it implies that physicians were then recognized as a guild, it does not make it certain that they were more than users of balsams and ointments for wounds. A few passages in Proverbs and one in Ecclesiastes have been quoted to prove that Solomon was versed in medicine (Prov. 3:8; 12:18; 17:22; 20:30; 29:1; Eccles. 3:3); but such an interpretation is quite fanciful. The allusions to diseases and remedies also tend to show that the conceptions of medicine were crude and popular. Of the diseases and deformities mentioned in the Pentateuch and Joshua we know ague, blains, boils, botch,

bruises, crookback, dwarf, emerods, flat nose, haltness, infirmity, inflammation, issue, itch, lameness, madness, wen, wound. Yet the most cursory glance at these terms shows that they are popular, not scientific. The "running issue" (Lev. 15:2, R.V. "issue out of his flesh"), "scab" (Deut. 28:27, R.V. "scurvy"), "scall" (Lev. 13:30), "leprosy" (Lev. 13:15), both of persons and things, "pestilence" (Exod. 5:3, etc.), "murrain" (Exod. 9:3), are uncertain. Of the treatment of these, except ceremonial and sacerdotal, we have not the faintest hint. The few remedies mentioned are evidently popular ones, as mandrakes, balm; or ingredients in unguents used for sacred purposes, not for healing, as calamus, cassia, cinnamon, myrrh, galbanum, onycha, stacte, frankincense; or condiments, as coriander.

Thus for the period of Hebrew history to the end of the Old Testament the Scripture reveals hardly a trace of medical science or art. This seems remarkable, considering the long residence of Israel in Egypt, where medicine was well established and cultivated to a high degree of excellence for those days. The Egyptians, owing to the practice of embalming, were well acquainted with human anatomy, as well as with that of the domestic animals. They also had a system of pathology and a considerable materia medica. They cultivated medicine to the point of dividing it into specialties as in modern times. But the Israelites in Egypt were apparently illiterate, and there is no reason to believe that any of them except Moses carried away any of the learning of Egypt. Although a considerable number of hygienic precepts exist in the Mosaic law, as circumcision, burying of excrements, etc. (Deut. 23:13), it is a strained interpretation to refer them to the medical knowledge or skill of the lawgiver. There was a tendency in all serious sickness to fall back on the religious ritual, and ultimately on the divine providence (Exod. 15:26; Psa. 103:3; 147:3; Isa. 30:26; Jer. 17:14; 30:17). When Asa "sought not to the Lord, but to the physicians" (II Chron. 16:12), the record speaks reproachfully. It is impossible to tell whether his diseased and swollen feet were dropsical or elephantiasical.

In the time of Christ the Jews had become enlightened by contact with Egypt, Babylon, Greece, and Rome. They certainly cultivated philosophy, law, and medicine. In the New Testament are mentioned dropsy, canker (cancer, or better, gangrene), bloody flux (dysentery), palsy, and lunacy. Physicians were a regular profession (Matt. 9:12; Mark 2:17; Luke 4:23; 5:31). Luke was the "beloved physician" (Col. 4:14). Physicians were numerous (Mark 5:26; Luke 8:43). They doubtless practiced according to the system then in vogue in the Greek and Roman world. But the vast number of the unrelieved stands out on every page of the gospels and gives to the ministry of Christ its peculiar hold on the people.

The following animal and vegetable substances used in medicine are alluded to under their several headings in the articles on *Animal*

Kingdom and *Vegetable Kingdom*: Anise, balm, calamus, cassia, cinnamon, cummin, dill, galbanum, gall, hyssop, leech, mandrake, mint, myrrh, stacte, wine.—*G. E. Post.*

Dish, the rendering in the A. V. of several Hebrew and Greek terms:

1. *Sēphĕl, low*, probably a shallow *pan* (a "dish" of *butter, curdled milk*, Judg. 5:25; "bowl" of water, Judg. 6:38).

2. *Şăllăhăth*, something to *pour* into, probably a *platter* (II Kings 21:13).

3. *Qĕʻărăh*, something *deep*, the gold "dishes" of the tabernacle (Exod. 25:29; 37:16; Num. 4:7; "charger" in Num. 7).

4. *Trublion*, Matt. 26:23; Mark 14:20, probably the same as No. 3.

In ancient Egypt and Judea each person broke off a small piece of bread, dipped it into the dish, and conveyed it to the mouth with a small portion of the contents of the dish. To partake of the same dish was to show special friendliness and intimacy.

Di'shan (dī'shăn; another form of *Dishon, antelope*), the name of the youngest son of Seir, the Horite, father of Uz and Aran, and head of one of the original tribes of Idumea (Gen. 36:21, 28, 30; I Chron. 1:38, 42).

Di'shon (dī'shŏn; *antelope*), the name of two descendants of Seir, the Horite.

1. Seir's fifth son, and head of one of the original Idumean tribes (Gen. 36:21, 30; I Chron. 1:38).

2. Seir's grandson, the only son of Anah, and brother of Aholibamah, Esau's second wife (Gen. 36:25; I Chron. 1:41).

Dispensations (Gr. *oikonomia, management of a household*, hence English *economy*).

A dispensation is an era of time during which man is tested in respect to obedience to some definite revelation of God's will. Seven such dispensations are recognized by many premillennialists. Other premillennialists speak of only three or four. Still others prefer not to be classed as dispensationalists at all. Those who hold to seven list them as follows:

1. **Innocence.** Man was created innocent, set in an ideal environment, placed under a simple test and warned of the result of disobedience. The woman fell through pride; the man, deliberately (I Tim. 2:14). Although God restored the sinning creatures, the dispensation came to an end at the judgment of the expulsion (Gen. 3:24).

2. **Conscience.** By an act of disobedience man comes to an experiential knowledge of good and evil. Driven out of Eden and placed under the Adamic Covenant, man was accountable to do all known good and to abstain from all known evil and to come before God by sacrifice. The result of this testing was complete degeneration ending in the judgment of the flood (Gen. 6-9).

3. **Human Government.** The declaration of the Noahic Covenant after the flood (Gen. 8:20-9:27) put man under a new test, featured by the inauguration of human government, the highest function of which was the judicial taking of life. Man is responsible to govern the world for God. That responsibility rests upon the whole race, Jew and Gentile. With the failure of Israel under the Palestinian Covenant (Deut. 28:30) and the consequent judg-

ment of the captivities "the times of the Gentiles" (Luke 21:24). began. The world is still Gentile-governed, and hence this dispensation overlaps other dispensations, and will not strictly come to an end until the second coming of Christ.

4. **Promise.** From the call of Abraham (Gen. 12:1) to the giving of the Mosaic law (Exod. 19:8). This disepnsation was under the Abrahamic Covenant and was exclusively Israelite.

5. **Law.** This era reaches from Sinai to Calvary. The period was a schoolmaster to bring Israel to Christ and was governed by the Mosaic Covenant (Exod. 20:1-31:18).

6. **Grace.** This period began with the death and resurrection of Christ (Rom. 3:24-26; 4:24, 25). The point of testing is no longer legal obedience to the law as a condition of salvation, but acceptance or rejection of Christ with good works as the fruit of salvation (John 1:12, 12; 3:36; I John 5:10-12). The predicted end of the testing of man under grace is the apostasy of the professing church (II Tim. 3:1-8) and the subsequent apocalyptic judgments.

7. **The Kingdom.** This is the last of the ordered ages regulating human life on the earth, previous to the eternal state. It involves the establishment of the Kingdom covenanted to David (II Sam. 7:8-17; Zech. 12:8; Luke 1:31-33; Luke 12:8). This will include Israel's restoration and conversion (Rom. 11: 25-27) and her rehabilitation as a high-priestly nation in fellowship with God and as head over the millennial nations (Zech. 3: 1-10; 6:9-15).

Dispersion of Israel (Gr. *diaspora*; rendered "dispersed," John 7:35; "scattered," James 1:1; I Pet. 1:1). Jewish communities settled in almost all the countries of the civilized world, remaining, on the one hand, in constant communication with the mother country, and, on the other, in active intercourse with the non-Jewish world.

1. **Causes** of the dispersion. These were of different kinds: The deportation by the Assyrian and Babylonian conquerors of large masses of the nation into their eastern provinces; the carrying to Rome by Pompey of hundreds of Jewish captives. Of greater importance, however, were the voluntary emigrations of Jewish settlers during the Graeco-Roman period to the countries bordering on Palestine, and to all the chief towns of the civilized world, for the sake chiefly of trade. The Diadochoi (successors of Alexander the Great), in order to build up their several kingdoms, offered to immigrants citizenship and many other privileges. Attracted by these circumstances, and perhaps influenced by adverse events at home, large numbers of Jews were induced to settle in Syria, Egypt, and Asia Minor, as well as in all the more important parts and commercial cities of the Mediterranean Sea.

2. **Extent.** That the dispersion became very widespread we have strong and varied evidence. The Roman Senate dispatched a circular 139-138 B. C.) in favor of the Jews to the kings of Egypt, Syria, Pergamos, Cappadocia, and Parthia, and to a great number of prov-

inces, towns, and islands of the Mediterranean Sea (I Macc. 15:16-24). It may hence be safely inferred that there was already a greater or less number of Jews in all these lands. See also the list of countries from which Jews had come to Jerusalem (Acts 2:9-11).

In Mesopotamia, Media, and Babylonia lived the descendants of the members of the ten tribes and of the kingdom of Judah carried thither by the Assyrians and Chaldeans. The "ten tribes" never returned at all from captivity, nor must the return of the tribes of Judah and Benjamin be conceived of as complete. These eastern Jewish settlements may also have been increased by voluntary additions, and the Jews in the provinces were numbered by millions (Josephus, *Ant.*, xi, 5, 2).

Josephus names Syria as the country in which was the largest percentage of Jewish inhabitants, and its capital, Antioch, was specially distinguished in this respect. In Damascus, according to Josephus, ten thousand (or according to another passage, eighteen thousand) Jews were said to have been assassinated during the war. Agrippa is authority for the statement that Jews had settled in Bithynia and in the uttermost corners of Pontus, which is confirmed by the Jewish inscriptions in the Greek language found in the Crimea. The entire history of the apostle Paul shows how widely the Jews had settled all over Asia Minor.

The most important with regard to the history of civilization was the Jewish colony in Egypt, and especially in Alexandria. Long before the time of Alexander the Great, Jewish immigrants were found there. In the time of Jeremiah many Jews went to Egypt for fear of the Chaldees (Jer. 41:17, 18), in opposition to the warning of the prophet (chaps. 42, 43), and settled in various parts of the country (44:1). Nebuchadnezzar appears, during his invasion of Egypt, to have carried to Babylon a considerable number of Jews from Alexandria.

The Jewish dispersion penetrated from Egypt to the westward, and was numerously represented in Cyrenaica. That it reached Greece is evident from the fact that Paul found synagogues in Thessalonica, Berea, Athens, and Corinth (Acts 17:1, 10, 17; 18:4, 7). Jews were also found in almost all the islands of the Grecian Archipelago and the Mediterranean Sea, and in some of these in large numbers.

In Rome there was a Jewish community numbering thousands, first appearing in that city during the time of the Maccabees. Judas Maccabeus sent an embassy to obtain assurances of its friendship and assistance (I Macc. 8:17-32); another was sent by Jonathan (12: 1-4), and a third by Simon (B. C. 140-139), which effected an actual offensive and defensive alliance with the Romans (I Macc. 14:24; 15:15-24).

But the settlement of Jews at Rome dates only from the time of Pompey, who after his conquest of Jerusalem (B. C. 63) took numerous Jewish prisoners of war with him to Rome. Sold as slaves, many of them were afterward given their liberty, and, granted Roman citizenship, formed a colony beyond the Tiber. They were expelled from Rome under Tiberius, and again by Claudius. But the Jews soon returned and, although looked down upon by the Romans, increased in wealth and numbers.

3. **Jewish Communities** in the dispersion. Of course there was only one way in which the scattered Israelites could maintain their native religion and usages, viz., by organizing themselves into *independent communities;* and that as a rule they were in the habit of doing, the nature of the organization varying according to time and place. Information respecting this feature of the dispersion in the East, Asia Minor, and Syria is very meager. In Alexandria and Cyrene they formed an independent municipal community within or coordinate with the rest of the city. A very important light is thrown upon the constitution of communities of the dispersion by a Jewish inscription found in Berenice, in Cyrenaica (probably B. C. 13), from which we find that the Jews of Berenice formed a distinct community, with *nine archons* at its head. With regard to the constitution of the Jewish communities of Rome and of Italy generally we are most thoroughly informed through the large number of Jewish epitaphs found in the cemeteries of Rome and Venosa. From these inscriptions we gather that the Jews living in Rome were divided into *a large number of separate and independently organized communities*, each having its own synagogue, *gerousia* (assembly of elders), and public officials. Two important privileges were allowed them: *the right of administering their own funds* and *jurisdiction over their own members*. Rome also granted them *exemption from military service*. In the older cities of Asia Minor, Syria, and Phoenicia there were instances in which individual Jews had the rights of citizenship conferred upon them, e. g., Paul (Acts 21:39). But as a rule the *Jewish communities* are to be considered as *private associations of settlers*. These had the right to claim the protection of the laws and enjoy the comforts and immunities of life.

4. **Religious Life.** Constant contact could not fail to have its effect upon the Jews in their development. The cultured Jews were not only Jews, but Greeks also, in respect to language, education, and habits; and yet in the depths of their hearts they were Jews, and felt themselves in all essentials to be in unison with their brethren in Palestine. One of the principal means employed for preserving and upholding the faith of their fathers was the *Synagogue* (*q. v.*).

There was also a *temple* at Leontopolis, with a regular Jewish temple service (B. C. 160- A. D. 73). *See* Temple. Collections were regularly received in every town, and at particular seasons forwarded to Jerusalem. The language employed in the religious services appears to have been usually Greek.

Dispersion of Mankind, the result of confusion of tongues at Babel (Gen. 11:6-9). In Gen. 10:5, 20, 31, we are told that the posterity of Noah were divided in their lands, every one according to his tongue, family, and nation; so that their distribution was undoubtedly conducted under the ordinary laws

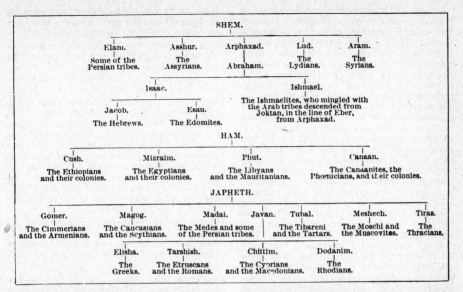

SHEM.				
Elam.	Asshur.	Arphaxad.	Lud.	Aram.
Some of the Persian tribes.	The Assyrians.	Abraham.	The Lydians.	The Syrians.

Isaac.	Ishmael.	
Jacob. The Hebrews.	Esau. The Edomites.	The Ishmaelites, who mingled with the Arab tribes descended from Joktan, in the line of Eber, from Arphaxad.

HAM.			
Cush.	Mizraim.	Phut.	Canaan.
The Ethiopians and their colonies.	The Egyptians and their colonies.	The Libyans and the Mauritanians.	The Canaanites, the Phoenicians, and their colonies.

JAPHETH.						
Gomer.	Magog.	Madai.	Javan.	Tubal.	Meshech.	Tiras.
The Cimmerians and the Armenians.	The Caucasians and the Scythians.	The Medes and some of the Persian tribes.		The Tibareni and the Tartars.	The Moschi and the Muscovites.	The Thracians.

Elisha.	Tarshish.	Chittim.	Dodanim.
The Greeks.	The Etruscans and the Romans.	The Cyprians and the Macedonians.	The Rhodians.

of colonization. The tenth chapter of Genesis presents an account of the principal descendants of Noah, followed by the description of that event which led to the division of race into many nations with different languages. The accompanying table shows the principal tribes that have been identified. For archaeological illumination of the Table of Nations (Gen. 10) *see* Merrill F. Unger, *Archaeology and the Old Testament* (Grand Rapids, 1954) pp. 73-104.

Divers, Diverse (Heb. *kĭl'ăyĭm, of two sorts*). The Jews were forbidden to bring together different kinds of materials, animals, or products, such as: (1) Weaving garments of two kinds of stuff, particularly of wool and linen; (2) sowing a field with mixed seed; (3) yoking an ox and an ass together; (4) breeding together animals of different species, e. g., to procure mules (Lev. 19:19; Deut. 22:9-11). The enactment concerning cloth would probably be better understood if we knew the exact meaning of Heb. *shă'ăṭnēz*, rendered "linen and woolen" (Lev. 19:19), and "garment of divers sorts" (Deut. 22:11). Perhaps the best explanation is "stuff of large meshes" (Koehler).

Divination (dĭv-ĭ-nā'shŭn). Divination as the art of obtaining secret knowledge, especially of the future, is a pagan counterpart of prophecy. Careful comparison of Scripture will reveal that inspirational divination is by demon power, whereas genuine prophecy is by the Spirit of God. The Biblical attitude toward divination is distinctly hostile (Deut. 18:10-12). The prophet of Jehovah is contrasted with diviners of all sorts and is set forth as the only authorized medium of supernatural revelation. Balaam (Num. 22-24) was a heathen diviner but rose to the status of a bona-fide prophet of the Lord, although he reverted to paganism. In Isa. 3:2; Judg. 27:9; Jer. 29:8; Ezek. 22:28 the diviner is classed with the prophet but this does not mean condonement of divination. It rather points to the apostasy

and pagan contamination of the era. Pure Yahwism is basically at variance with divination of every sort. Seeking knowledge of the future from any other source than the God of Israel was an insult to His holy Being and the revelation of Himself and His purpose for men. *See* M. F. Unger, *Biblical Demonology* (2nd ed. 1953), pp. 119-142. *M. F. U.*

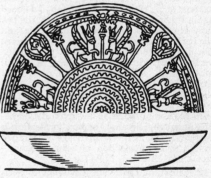

125. Divining Cup

Divorce, Divorcement (Heb. *kerîthŭth*; Gr. *'apostasion, cutting, separating*).

1. **Jewish Law.** A legal separation between man and wife, by means of a formal process of some sort. As the ordinances respecting marriage have in view the hallowing of that relation, so also was the Mosaic regulation in respect of divorce (Deut. 24:1-4). From this we learn that a man, finding in his wife something shameful or offensive, dismissed her from his house with a writ of divorcement. (1) **Temporary expedient.** Divorce, giving a writ, and causes of divorce seem to have been accepted by Moses by hereditary usage, and allowed because of the people's hardness of heart (Matt. 19:7, 8). The question of divorce was entirely at the will of the husband; the wife, not possessing equal privileges with the

271

husband, had no right of divorce. The action of Salome and others was done in defiance of law, and in imitation of Roman licentiousness. (2) **Ground of divorce.** There have been many interpretations of the expression "some uncleanness," given as the ground of divorce. It occurs also in Deut. 23:14 of things which profane the camp of Israel; and denotes something shameful or offensive. Adultery, to which some of the rabbins would restrict the expression, is not to be thought of, because this was to be punished with death. It is necessary, therefore, to understand by the phrase in question something besides adultery, something perhaps tending in that direction, something fitted to raise not unreasonable jealousy or distrust in the mind of the husband, and destroy the prospect of true conjugal affection and harmony between him and his wife. Still, a good deal was left to the discretion, and it might be the foolish caprice, of the husband; and so far from justifying it, on abstract principles of rectitude, our Lord rather admitted its imperfection, and threw upon the defective moral condition of the people the blame of a legislation so unsatisfactory in itself, and so evidently liable to abuse. (3) **Regulations.** But the giving "a bill (or rather 'book') of divorcement" (comp. Isa. 50:1; Jer. 3:8) would in ancient times require the intervention of a Levite, not only to secure the formal correctness of the instrument, but because the art of writing was then generally unknown. This would bring the matter under the cognizance of legal authority, and tend to check the rash exercise of the right by the husband. To guard against thoughtless and hasty divorce, the law provided that if a man dismissed his wife, and she became the wife of another man, he must not again take her to wife, not even if the second husband had divorced her, or even if he had died. "The remarrying of a divorced woman is to be regarded as a pollution, or on the same level with fornication, and the law condemns the reunion of such a divorced one with her first husband as 'an abomination before Jehovah,' because thereby fornication is carried still further, and marriage is degraded to the mere satisfaction of sexual passion" (Keil, *Bibl. Arch.*, ii, 173-175).

2. **Christian Law.** The teachings of Jesus upon the subject of divorce are found in Matt. 5:31, 32; 19:3-10; Mark 10:2-12; and Luke 16:18. Briefly they are: (1) The liberty given to a man by the Mosaic law to put away his wife (Deut. 24:1, sq.) was because of the hardness of the Jewish heart. (2) He who divorces his wife, except for fornication, and marries another, commits adultery (Matt. 19:9); and he who thus puts her away leads her to commit the same crime (Matt. 5:32). (3) He who marries a divorced woman commits adultery, and the woman who puts away her husband and marries another man (Mark 10:12) incurs the same kind of guilt. This last refers to the custom among the Greeks and Romans, viz., that the wife might also be the divorcing party. In Matt. 19:9 is given the one exception in favor of divorce, viz., *fornication*, i. e., *adultery;* because adultery destroys

what, according to its original institution by God, constitutes the very essence of marriage, the union of two in one flesh (vers. 5, 6).

Diz'ahab (dīz'á-hăb, *having gold*), a place in the wilderness of Sinai, not far from the Red Sea. It has been identified with *Mersa Dahab*, or *Mina Dahab*, i. e., "gold-harbor." Gold was most likely found there (Deut. 1:1).

Doctor (Gr. *didaskalos*, a *teacher*, Luke 2:46; 5:17; Acts 5:34). The Jewish teachers, at least some of them, had private lecture rooms, but also taught in public. Their method was the same as prevailed among the Greeks; any disciple being allowed to ask questions, to which the teacher gave reply. They did not have any official position, and received no salary other than voluntary gifts from their disciples, and were chiefly of the sect of the Pharisees. *See* Lawyer, Rabbi.

Do'dai (dō'dī; probably another form for *Dodo*), an Ahohite, who commanded the contingent for the second month under David (I Chron. 27:4); probably the same as *Dodo* (*q. v.*).

Dod'anim (dŏd'á-nĭm; Gen. 10:4; I Chron. 1:7, marg. of A. V. "Rodanim"), a family or race descended from Javan, the son of Japheth. The weight of authority is in favor of the former name. Dodanim is regarded as identical with Dardani. The Dardani were found in historical times in Illyricum and Troy; the former district was regarded as their original seat. They were probably a semi-Pelasgic race, and are grouped with the Chittim in the genealogical table, as more closely related to them than to the other branches of the Pelasgic race.

Dod'avah (dŏd'á-vá; *beloved of Jehovah*), a man of Mareshah, in Judah, and father of the Eliezer who predicted the wreck of Jehoshaphat's fleet auxiliary to Ahaziah (II Chron. 20:37), B. C. 874. R. V. has Dodavahu.

Do'do (dō'dō), perhaps a shortening of Dodavahu.

1. A descendant of Issachar, father of Puah, and grandfather of the judge Tola (Judg. 10:1), B. C. after 1300.

2. An Ahohite, father of Eleazar, one of David's three mighty men (II Sam. 23:9; I Chron. 11:12), B. C. before 1000. He seems to be the same as the *Dodai* mentioned in I Chron. 27:4 as commander of the second division of the royal troops under David.

3. A Beth-lehemite, and father of Elhanan, one of David's thirty heroes (II Sam. 23:24; I Chron. 11:26), B. C. before 1000.

Do'eg (dō'ĕg), an Edomite, and chief of Saul's herdsmen ("keeper of the king's mules," Josephus, *Ant.*, vi, 12, 1). He was at Nob when Ahimelech gave David assistance by furnishing him with the sword of Goliath and the showbread (I Sam. 21:7). Of this he informed the king, and, when others refused to obey his command, slew Ahimelech and his priests to the number of eighty-five persons (I Sam. 22:9-19), B. C. about 1000. This "act called forth one of David's most severe imprecative prayers (Psa. 52), of which divine and human justice seem alike to have required the fulfillment."

Dog. *See* Animal Kingdom.

Figurative. 1. In Bible times, as now, troops of hungry and half-wild dogs roamed about the fields and the streets feeding upon dead bodies and other offal (I Kings 14:11; 16:4; 21:19, 23; II Kings 9:10, 36; Jer. 15:3, etc.), and thus became objects of dislike. Thus fierce and cruel enemies were styled *dogs* (Psa. 22:16, 20; Jer. 15:3).

2. The dog being an *unclean* animal, the terms "dog," "dead dog," "dog's head," were used as terms of reproach, or of humiliation if speaking of one's self (I Sam. 24:14; II Sam. 3:8; 9:8; I Kings 8:13).

3. In the East "dog" is used for impure and profane persons, and was used by the Jews respecting the Gentiles (Matt. 15:26).

4. False apostles are called "dogs" on account of impurity and love of gain. (Phil. 3:2).

5. Those who are shut out of the kingdom of heaven are also called "dogs" (Rev. 22:15), on account of their vileness.

Doleful Creatures. *See* Animal Kingdom.

Door, the opening for ingress and egress, an essential part of a tent or house.

Figurative. "I will give the valley of Achor for a door of hope" (Hos. 2:15) refers, doubtless, to the defeat of Israel through the sin of *Achan* (*q. v.*), the encouragement given by Jehovah, and Joshua's uninterrupted success (Josh. 7:1, sq.).

An "open door" is used by Paul (I Cor. 16:9; II Cor. 2:12; Col. 4:3) as a symbol of the favorable opportunity for apostolic work. Our Lord speaks of himself as "the door" (John 10:9), and John of a "door opened in heaven" (Rev. 4:1).

Doorkeeper (Heb. *shō'ēr;* Gr. *thurōros*). "Doorkeepers for the ark are named (I Chron. 15:23, 24), whose duty was thought to be to guard the door of the tabernacle, so as to prevent anyone from coming carelessly to the ark." Persons were appointed to keep the street door of houses, and these were sometimes women (John 18:16; Acts 12:13).

"Doorkeeper" in Psa. 84:10 (marg. "to sit at the threshold") does not convey the right meaning of the original. It means one "at the threshold," either a beggar asking alms, or a passer-by merely looking in.

Doorpost, the rendering of Heb. *săph* (Ezek. 41:16), for *Threshold* (*q. v.*). Moses enjoined upon the Israelites that they should write the divine commands "upon the posts of thy house and thy gates" (Deut. 6:9; Heb. *mᵉzū-*

zäh). These words were figurative, and are expected to be understood spiritually. Placing inscriptions about the door of the house was an ancient Egyptian custom, and was evidently followed by the Israelites in very early times. Portions of the law were either carved or inscribed upon the doorposts, or else written upon parchment and inclosed in a cylinder or reed, and fixed on the right hand doorpost of every room in the house.

Doph'kah (dŏf'kà), one of the encampments of Israel in the desert, their eighth station (Num. 33:12, 13). It was located between Rephidim and the Red Sea; there is no satisfactory identification.

Dor (dōr; *dwelling*), an ancient city of the Canaanites (Josh. 11:2; 12:23). Its people were tributary to King Solomon (Judg. 1:27; I Kings 4:11). It was a Phoenician settlement on the coast of Syria, and is identified with Tantura, about eight miles N. of Caesarea.

Dor'cas (dôr'kăs; *gazelle*), a charitable and pious Christian woman of Joppa, whom Peter restored to life (Acts 9:36-41). The sacred writer mentions her as "a certain disciple named Tabitha, which by interpretation is called Dorcas," the reason of which probably is that she was a Hellenistic Jewess, and was called *Dorcas* by the Greeks, while to the Jews she was known by the name of *Tabitha* (*q. v.*).

127. Joseph P. Free (excavator) and Son Measure a Street at Dothan in a Level of Elisha's day (1956 season of excavation)

Do'than (dō'thán; probably, *two wells*), an upland plain on the caravan route from Syria to Egypt, about eleven miles N. of Samaria, and noted for its excellent pasturage; the scene of Joseph's forced slavery, and also of Elisha's vision of the mountain full of horses and chariots (Gen. 37:17; II Kings 6:13). One of the two wells found there now has the name of "the pit of Joseph" (*Jubb Yusuf*). It was the usual sort of pit or pond dug even now by Arabs and shepherds to get rain water, with sloping sides, perhaps ten feet

126. Mound of Dothan

128. Well at Dothan

deep. The excavation at the mound of Dothan, sixty miles by road north of Jerusalem, is being undertaken by the Wheaton Archaeological Expedition with Joseph P. Free as director. Beginning in the spring of 1953, Dr. Free has conducted annual excavations at the site. Iron Age Dothan has been uncovered with excavation of late bronze and earlier levels planned. See *Bulletin of the Am. Schools of Oriental Research*, No. 143, Oct. 1956; *Biblical Archaeologist*, May, 1956.

Double, the rendering of several Hebrew and Greek words, has many meanings. Thus the *Breastplate* (*q. v.*) was to be made of two thicknesses of cloth (Exod. 39:9). "Double money," the same value as before, with an equal value added thereto (Gen. 43:12, 15). "She hath received of the Lord's hand *double* for all of her sins" (Isa. 40:2) does not mean twice as much as she *deserved*, but *ample* punishment through her twofold captivity, the Assyrian and Roman. "For your shame ye shall have *double*" (Isa. 61:7) refers to the double possession of land, not only that which they had inherited, but extended far beyond their former borders. See Inheritance.

Double heart, *double* tongue, *double* mind are opposed to one that is simple, unequivocal, sincere (James 1:8; 4:8).

Doubt is that state of mind in which it hesitates between two contradictory conclusions. It may have some degree of belief, checked by a consciousness of ignorance. In this case it is provisional, waiting for more light. The New Testament gives several instances of this as worthy to be reasoned with.

Absolute *disbelief* is the belief of the opposite of that which faith holds.

Dough (Heb. *bāṣēq*, *swelling* from fermentation, Exod. 12:34, 39; Jer. 7:18, etc.; *'ărîsāh*, *meal*). Mention is made of Israel carrying their dough with them, before it was leavened, when they left Egypt (Exod. 12:34). Dough was sometimes baked with or without leaven. See Bread.

Dove Cote. "When traveling in the north of Syria many years ago I noticed in certain villages tall square buildings without roofs, whose walls were pierced inside by numberless pigeon-holes. In these nestled and bred thousands of these birds. Their foraging excursions extended many miles in every direction, and it is curious to notice them returning to their 'windows' like bees to their hives or like clouds pouring over a sharp ridge into the deep valley below (*see* Isa. 60:8). I have never seen them in Palestine" (Thomson, *Land and Book*).

Dove's Dung. *See* Animal Kingdom.

Doves and Turtledoves were the only birds that could be offered in sacrifice, being usually selected by the poor (Gen. 15:9; Lev. 5:7; 12:6; Luke 2:24); and to supply the demand for them dealers in these birds sat about the precincts of the temple (Matt. 21:12, etc.). *See* Animal Kingdom.

Figurative. The dove was the harbinger of reconciliation with God (Gen. 8:8, 10), and has since been the emblem of peace. It is also a noted symbol of tender and devoted affection (Cant. 1:15; 2:14, etc.), and likewise of mourning (Isa. 38:14; 59:11).

The dove symbolizes the Holy Spirit which descended upon our Saviour at his baptism, visibly with that peculiar *hovering motion* which distinguishes the descent of a dove (Matt. 3:16; Mark 1:10; Luke 3:22; John 1:32).

Dowry (Heb. *mōhăr*, *price* paid for a wife. Gen. 34:12; Exod. 22:17; I Sam. 18:25; *zĕbĕd*, a *gift*, Gen. 30:20). In arranging for marriage, as soon as paternal consent was obtained, the suitor gave the bride a betrothal or bridal gift, as well as presents to her parents and brothers. In more ancient times the bride received a portion only in exceptional cases (Josh. 15:18 sq.; I Kings 9:16). The opinion that the Israelites were required to buy their wives from the parents or relatives seems to be unfounded. The *mōhăr* in the Old Testament was not "purchase money," but the *bridal gift* which the bridegroom, after receiving the bride's assent, gave to *her*, not to the parents or kinsfolk. *See* Marriage.

Doxologies (Gr. *doxologia*, *giving glory*), ascriptions of glory or praise to God.

1. **Scriptural.** These abound in the Psalms (e. g., 96:6; 112:1; 113:1), and were used in the synagogue. The apostles very naturally used them (Rom. 11:36; Eph. 3:21; I Tim. 1:17). We have also examples of celestial doxologies (Rev. 5:13; 19:1). The song of the angels in Luke 2:14 is a doxology. As to the doxology in Matt. 6:13, *see* Lord's Prayer.

2. **Liturgical.** Three doxologies of special note have been used in church worship from a very early time: (1) The *Lesser Doxology*, or *Gloria Patri*, originally in the form, "Glory be to the Father, and to the Son, and to the Holy Ghost," to which was added later, "world without end," and still later brought to its present form: "Glory be to the Father, and to the Son, and to the Holy Ghost, as it was in the beginning, is now, and ever shall be, world without end. Amen." (2) The *Greater Doxology*, or *Gloria in Excelsis*, called also the *Angelic Hymn* (*q. v.*). (3) The *Trisagion*, as old as the 2d century, beginning, "Therefore, with angels and archangels, and with all the company of heaven, we laud and magnify thy glorious name."

Drag (Heb. *mĭkmĕrĕth*), is mentioned as being the object of worship by fishermen (Hab. 1:15, 16). It was a large fishing net, the lower part of which, when sunk, touches the bottom, while the upper part floats on the top of the water.

129. Akkadian Cylinder Seal: The Killing of the Hydra (from Tell Asmar, Iraq)

Dragon. *See* Animal Kingdom.

In the New Testament "dragon" (Gr. *drakōn*) is found only in Rev. 12:3, sq.; 13:2, 4, 11; 16:13; 20:2, and is used figuratively of Satan. The reason of this scriptural symbol is to be sought not only in the union of gigantic power with craft and malignity, of which the serpent is the natural emblem, but in the record of the serpent's agency in the temptation (Gen. 3).

In Christian art the dragon is the emblem of sin in general and idolatry in particular, having usually the form of a gigantic winged crocodile.

Dragon Well, probably the fountain of Gihon, on the west side of Jerusalem (Neh. 2:13).

Dram. *See* Metrology, IV.

Draught (Gr. *'aphedrōn*), a *privy, sink*; found only in Matt. 15:17; Mark 7:19. *See* Dung.

Draught House (Heb. *mǎḥǎrā'āh*, literally, *easing one's self*), a *privy* or *sink*. Jehu, in contempt of Baal, ordered his temple to be destroyed and the place turned into a receptacle for offal or ordure (II Kings 10:27).

Drawer of Water (Heb. *shō'ēb mǎyïm, drawer of water*). In the East water is often carried from the rivers or wells by persons who make it their trade, carrying water in goatskins slung on their backs, with the neck brought around under the arm to serve as a mouth. It was a hard and servile employment (Deut. 29:11), to which the Gibeonites were condemned (Josh. 9:21, 23).

Dream (Heb. *ḥǎlōm;* Gr. *'onar*). "The dream is a domain of experience, having an intellectual, ethical, and spiritual significance. Living in an earthly body, we have, as the background of our being, a dim region, out of which our thinking labors forth to the daylight, and in which much goes forward, especially in the condition of sleep, of which we can only come to a knowledge by looking back afterward. Experience confirms to us the assertion of Scripture (Psa. 127:2) that God giveth to his beloved in sleep. Not only many poetical and musical inventions, but, moreover, many scientific solutions and spiritual perceptions, have been conceived and born from the life of genius awakened in sleep.

"Another significant aspect of dreaming is the ethical. In the dream one's true nature manifests itself, breaking through the pressure of external relations and the simulation of the waking life. From the selfishness of the soul, its selfish impulses, its restlessness stimulated by selfishness, are formed in the heart all kinds of sinful images, of which the man is ashamed when he awakens, and on account of which remorse sometimes disturbs the dreamer. The Scriptures appear to hold the man responsible, if not for dreaming, at least for the character of the dream (Lev. 15:16; Deut. 23:10).

"A third significant aspect of dreams is the spiritual: they may become the means of a direct and special intercourse of God with man. The witness of conscience may make itself objective and expand within the dream-life into perceptible transactions between God and man. Thus God warned Abimelech (Gen. 20) and Laban (31:24) in a dream, and the wife of Pilate warned her husband against being concerned in the death of the Just One." The conviction of the sinfulness and nothingness of man is related by Eliphaz as realized in a dream (Job 4:12-21).

130. A Water Carrier

The special will of God is often revealed to men through dreams, of which the Scriptures mention many. Such are the dreams of Jacob in Beth-el (Gen. 28:12) and in Haran (Gen. 31:10-13), the dream of Solomon in Gibeon (I Kings 3:5), the dreams of Joseph the husband of Mary (Matt. 1:20), the night visions of Paul (Acts 16:9; 18:9; 23:11; 27:23). From I Sam. 28:6 we infer that God did at times answer sincere inquirers. Concerning the future the dreams of Nebuchadnezzar and Daniel are examples.

"Waking visions probably are to be distinguished from these prophetic dream visions, which the seer, whether by day (Ezek. 8:1; Dan. 10:7; Acts 7:55; 10:9-16) or by night (comp. Acts 16:9; 18:9), receives in a waking state."

The dreams of Joseph in his father's house (Gen. 37:5-11), which, as became plain to him subsequently (42:9), figuratively predicted to him his future eminence over the house of Jacob, the dreams of the chief butler and the chief baker of Pharaoh (Gen. 40), the dream of the soldier in the Midianitish camp in the time of Gideon (Judg. 7:13), are illustrations of dreams of presentiment.

According to Num. 12:6, dreams and visions (*q. v.*) are the two forms of the prophetic revelations of God. Too much reliance is not to be placed upon dreams (Eccles. 5:7).

"A good dream" was one of the three things —viz., a good king, a fruitful year, and a good dream—popularly regarded as marks of divine favor; and so general was the belief in the significance that it passed into this popular saying: "If anyone sleeps seven days without dreaming call him wicked" (as being unremembered by God) (*see* Delitzsch, *Biblical Psychology*, p. 324, sq.).

Interpretation of Dreams. Because the dream was looked upon as a communication from the gods there arose those who professed ability to interpret the same (*see* Magic). These were not to be listened to if they taught anything contrary to the law (Deut. 13:1, sq.; Jer. 27:9, etc.). Instances are given of God's aiding men to understand dreams and the divine lessons taught thereby, e. g., Joseph (Gen. 40:5, sq.; 41:7-32), Daniel (Dan. 2:19, sq.; 4:8).

Dregs. 1. The rendering of the Heb. *shĕmĕr*, Psa. 75:8, elsewhere *lees* of wine. As the wine was strained when about to be used, so the psalmist uses the figure of the strained wine being a portion of the righteous, while the wicked shall drink the dregs.

2. Heb. *qŭbbǎʻăth*, goblet, Isa. 51:17, 22, and rendered "dregs of the cup of my fury," but better, "the goblet of his fury."

Dress. In treating of this subject we call attention to: (1) Materials, color, and ornamentation; (2) Garments, forms, names, etc.; (3) Usages relating thereto.

1. **Materials, etc.** The first mention that occurs in Scripture of clothing is of the simple garments made by Adam and Eve from fig leaves (Gen. 3:7), which were followed by those made of the skin of animals (3:21). Skins were not wholly disused at later periods; the "mantle" worn by Elijah appears to have been the skin of a sheep or some other animal with the wool left on. It was characteristic of a prophet's office from its mean appearance (Zech. 13:4; comp. Matt. 7:15). Pelisses of sheepskin still form an ordinary article of dress in the East. The art of weaving hair was known to the Hebrews at an early period (Exod. 26:7; 35:6); the sackcloth used by mourners was of this material. John the Baptist's robe was of camel's hair (Matt. 3:4). Wool, we may presume, was introduced at a very early period, the flocks of the pastoral families being kept partly for their wool (Gen. 38:12); it was at all times largely employed, particularly for the outer garments (Lev. 13:47; Deut. 22:11, etc.). Flax was no doubt used in the earliest times to make linen garments. Of silk there is no mention at a very

early period, unless it be in Ezekiel (16:10, 13).

White was esteemed the most appropriate color for cotton cloth, and purple for others.

Ornamentation was secured by (1) weaving with previously dyed threads (Exod. 35:25); (2) gold thread; (3) introduction of figures, either woven into the stuff or applied by needlework. Robes decorated with gold (Psa. 45:13), and at a later period with silver thread (comp. Acts 12:21), were worn by royal personages; other kinds of embroidered robes were worn by the wealthy both of Tyre (Ezek. 16:13) and Palestine (Judg. 5:30; **Psa.**

131. Restoration Drawing of Ivory Plaque (Megiddo, Palestine) with a Female Figure, ca. 1350-1150 B. C.

45:14). The art does not appear to have been maintained among the Hebrews; the Babylonians and other Eastern nations (Josh. 7:21; Ezek. 27:24), as well as the Egyptians (v. 7), excelled in it. Nor does the art of dyeing appear to have been followed up in Palestine; dyed robes were imported from foreign countries (Zeph. 1:8), particularly from Phoenicia, and were not much used on account of their expensiveness; purple (Prov. 31:22; Luke 16:19) and scarlet (II Sam. 1:24) were occasionally worn by the wealthy. The surrounding nations were more lavish in their use of them; the wealthy Tyrians (Ezek. 27:7), the Midianitish kings (Judg. 8:26), the Assyrian nobles (Ezek. 23:6), and Persian officers (Esth. 8:15) are all represented in purple.

2. **Garments.** From the simple loin cloth, or apron, dress gradually developed in amount and character according to climate, and condition and taste of the wearer. Regarding the clothing of the patriarchs and ancient Israelites we have no exact information, but it was unquestionably very simple. It was not limited to what was indispensable to cover nakedness, for we read of various forms of clothing (Gen. 24:53; 37:3) and costly garments of byssus (Gen. 41:42; 45:22).

The making of clothes among the Israelites was always the business of the housewives, in which women of rank equally took part (I Sam. 2:19; Prov. 31:22, sq.; Acts 9:39).

While the costume of men and women was very similar, there was an easily recognizable distinction between the male and female attire of the Israelites, and accordingly the Mosaic law forbids men to wear women's clothes, and *vice versa* (Deut. 22:5).

(1) **The dress of men.** Among the Israelites these were (1) *Tunic* (Heb. *kᵉthōnĕth*, Exod. 28:4, 39; 29:5; II Sam. 15:32; Gr. *chitōn*, Matt. 5:40; Mark 6:9; Luke 3:11; 6:29, etc.; A. V. in each case "coat"). This was the most simple of all the garments worn, corresponding to an ordinary shirt or nightgown. It was probably made of two pieces sewn together at the sides, or else formed of one piece, with a place cut for the head to pass through. It afforded so slight a covering that persons who had on nothing else were called *naked* (I Sam. 19:24; II Sam. 6:20; John 21:7). Another kind reached to the wrists and ankles. It was in either case fastened around the loins with a girdle (*q. v.*), and the fold formed by the overlapping of the robe served as an inner pocket. Such a garment was worn by the priests (*q. v.*), and probably by Joseph (Gen. 37:3, 23) and Tamar (II Sam. 13:18). (2) The *Outer Tunic* (Heb. *mᵉʿîl*), a looser and a longer sort of a tunic, reaching to near the ankles; open at the top so as to be drawn over the head, and having holes for the insertion of the arms. As an article of ordinary dress it was worn by kings (I Sam. 24:4), prophets (I Sam. 28:14), nobles (Job 1:20), and youths (I Sam. 2:19). It may, however, be doubted whether the term is used in its specific sense in these passages, and not rather for any robe that chanced to be worn over the *kᵉthōnĕth* (1). Where two tunics are mentioned (Luke 3:11) as being worn at the same time, the second would be a *mᵉʿîl;* travelers generally wore two, but the practice was forbidden to the disciples (Matt. 10:10; Luke 9:3). (3) *Mantle* or *Cloak* (Heb. *sïmläh*, and other terms), a piece of cloth nearly square, a sort of blanket or plaid. In pleasant weather it was more conveniently worn over the shoulders than being wrapped around the body. While it answered the purpose of a cloak, it was so large that burdens, if necessary, might be carried in it (Exod. 12:34; II Kings 4:39). The poor wrapped themselves up wholly in this garment at night, spread their leathern girdle upon a rock, and rested their head upon it, as is customary to this day in Asia. Moses, therefore, enacted as a law what had been a

custom, that the upper garment, when given as a pledge, should not be retained overnight (Exod. 22:25, 26; Deut. 24:13; Job 22:6; 24:7). In the time of Christ the creditors did not take the upper garment or cloak, which it was not lawful for them to retain, but the coat or tunic, which agrees with the representation of Jesus (Matt. 5:40). There having occurred an instance of the violation of the Sabbath (Num. 15:32-41), Moses commanded that there should be a fringe upon the four corners of this garment, together with a blue cord or ribband, to remind the people of the heavenly origin of his statutes (Matt. 9:20; Luke 8:44). *See* Hem. The prophet's mantle was, probably, as a rule, a simple sheepskin with the wool turned outward. ·(4) *Breeches* or *Drawers* (Heb. *mïknäs, hiding*), a garment worn under the tunic for the fuller covering of the person. These trousers were worn by the priests, but do not appear to have been in general use among the Hebrews. *See* Priest, Dress of. (5) *Girdle* (the rendering of one Greek and several Hebrew words). The tunic when it was not girded impeded the person who wore it in walking. Those, consequently, who perhaps at home went ungirded went forth girded (II Kings 4:29; 9:1; Isa. 5:27; Jer. 1:17; John 21:7; Acts 12:8). There were formerly, and are to this day, two sorts of girdles in Asia: a common one of leather six inches broad and furnished with clasps, with which it is fastened around the body (II Kings 1:8; Matt. 3:4; Mark 1:6); the other a valuable one of flax or cotton, sometimes, indeed, of silk or of some embroidered fabric, a handbreadth broad, and supplied with clasps by which it was fastened over the forepart of the body (Jer. 13:1). The girdle was bound around the loins, whence the expressions, "The girdle of the loins" and "gird up your loins" (I Kings 18:46; Isa. 11:5; Jer. 1:17). The Arabians carry a knife or a poniard in the girdle. This was the custom among the Hebrews (I Sam. 25:13; II Sam. 20:8-10), a fact which admits of confirmation from the ruins of Persepolis. The girdle also answers the purpose of a pouch, to carry money and other necessary things (II Sam. 18:11; Matt. 10:9; Mark 6:8). (6) *Cap* or *Turban*. The words for headdress which occur in the Old Testament (Heb. *ṣänîf*, Job 29:14, "diadem;" *pᵉʾēr*, Isa. 61:3, A. V. "beauty;" 61:10, A. V. "ornaments") belong to the dress of men of rank. *Bonnet* (Heb. *mïgbäʿäh*), is used only of the priest's cap. Israelites, as a rule, seem not to have worn any cap, but to have confined their hair with a band or wrapped a cloth—generally known by us as a turban—around the head, as is still done in Arabia. *See* Diadem, Miter. (7) *Ephod*. The ephod (*q. v.*) and the *mᵉʿîl* (2), according to the Mosaic law, were appropriately garments of the high priest (*q. v.*), but were sometimes worn by other illustrious men (I Sam. 18:4; II Sam. 6:14; Job 29:14; Ezek. 26:16). (8) *Sandals, Shoes*. The covering for the feet were *sandals* (Heb. *näʿäläh;* Gr. *hupodēma, bound under* the feet), of leather and fastened with thongs. They were taken off upon entering a room or a holy place (Exod. 3:5; Josh. 5:15), while the poor and mourners went barefoot (II Sam. 15:30;

Isa. 20:2; Ezek. 24:17, 23). Men of rank had these sandals put on, taken off, and carried after them by slaves (Matt. 3:11; Mark 1:7; John 1:27).

(2) **The dress of women.** The difference between the dress of men and women was small, consisting chiefly in the fineness of the materials and the length of the garment. The dress of the hair in the two sexes was different, and another mark of distinction was that women wore a veil. (1) *Tunic.* Women wore the tunic as an *under dress* (Cant. 5:3), but it was probably wider, longer, and of finer material; the well-to-do wore also *shirts* (Heb. *sādin*, wrapper, Isa. 3:23, "fine linen"), and a kind of second tunic (male, 2), provided with sleeves and reaching to the ankles. (2) *Girdle.* This was frequently of fine woven stuff (Prov. 31:24) and studded with precious stones, and was worn lower down on the loins and more loosely than by men. (3) *Headdress.* (a) *Veil.* That of the lower class of Israelitish women is unknown, but the *veil* was regarded from ancient times by women of character as indispensable. Various kinds are mentioned: "The oldest kind seems to be (Heb. *ṣānif*, to *wrap*, Gen. 24:65; 38:14, 19), a cloak-like veil, a kind of mantilla which at a later time, perhaps made of finer stuff, was called *rādîd*, (*spreading*, Cant. 5:7; Isa. 3:23)." The *rāʻălāh*, (*fluttering*, Isa. 3:19) are veils flowing down from the head over the temples, hence waving with the action of walking, which were so adjusted to the eyes as to be seen through. Many understand *ṣămmāh*, (to *fasten* on; "locks," Cant. 4:1, 3; 6:7; Isa. 47:2; R. V. "veil") to be a veil; and that of one covering breast, throat, and chin, such as is still worn in Syria and Egypt. (b) The *mĭtpăḥăth*, Ruth 3:15; rendered "wimple" in Isa. 3:22), a sort of shawl or broad garment, and probably similar to the mantle (or cloak) worn by men. "As the cloaks worn by the ancients were so full that one part was thrown upon the shoulder and another gathered up under the arm, Ruth, by holding a certain part, could

receive into her bosom the corn which Boaz gave her" (Edersheim, *Sketches Jewish Life*). (c) The *kerchief* (Heb. *mĭspāḥăh, spread* out, Ezek. 13:18, 21) is understood by some as a close-fitting cap; but others think it to have been a long veil or headdress. "The Eastern women bind on their other ornaments with a rich embroidered handkerchief, which is described by some travelers as completing the headdress and falling without order upon the hair behind." In patriarchal times wives (Gen. 12:14) and young women (24:15, sq.) went about, especially when engaged in their household duties, without veils; and yet in so early times the betrothed veiled herself in the presence of the bridegroom (24:65), and lewd women veiled themselves (38:15). (4) *Sandal.* Sandals consisted merely of soles strapped to the feet, but ladies wore also costly slippers, often made of sealskin (Ezek. 16:10, A. V. "badgers' skin," R. V. "sealskin"), probably also of colored leather. Ladies of rank appear to have paid great attention to the beauty of their sandals (Cant. 7:1). They were embroidered or adorned with gems, and so arranged that the pressure of the foot emitted a delicate perfume. (5) *Stomacher* (Heb. *pᵉthîgîl*), a term of doubtful origin, but probably a gay holiday dress (Isa. 3:23). The garments of females were terminated by an ample border of fringe, which concealed the feet (Isa. 47:2; Jer. 13:22).

(3) **Luxurious articles of dress.** In addition to the essential and common articles of dress already mentioned a great many more of an ornamental kind were in use, especially among women of luxurious habits. In rebuking the women of Jerusalem Isaiah (3:16, sq.) mentions a number of these articles of luxurious dress. There is doubt as to the precise meaning of some of the words employed in the description, and little comparatively can now be known of the exact shape and form of several of the articles mentioned. They are (a) *Tinkling ornaments*, rings of gold, silver, or ivory, worn round the

132.   Man's   Babylonian   Egyptian   Hebrew   Women's
      Mantle   Dress c. 2000 B. C.   Dress c. 2000 B. C.   Royal Garb   Attire

ankles, which made a tinkling sound as the wearer walked. *See* Anklets. (*b*) *Cauls.* These were probably *headbands* or *frontlets*, i. e., plaited bands of gold or silver thread worn below the hair net and reaching from ear to ear. (*c*) *Round tires* (Heb. *săḥărōn*, a round *pendant;* "crescents," R. V.) the new moon being a symbol of increasing good fortune, and as such the most approved charm against the evil eye; fastened round the neck and hanging down upon the breast (Judg. 8:21). (*d*) *Chains*, "earrings" (R. V. "pendants"). (*e*) *Bracelets* (*q. v.*). According to the Targum, these were chains worn upon the arm, or spangles upon the wrist, answering to the spangles upon the ankles. (*f*) *Mufflers*, i. e., fluttering veils (*q. v.* above). (*g*) *Bonnets* (Heb. *peʾēr*, embellishment, R. V. "head tires") are only mentioned in other parts of Scripture as worn by men. (*h*) *Ornaments of the legs* (R. V. "ankle chains"), a chain worn to shorten and give elegance to the step. *See* Anklets. (*i*) *Headbands* (Heb. *qĭshshŭr*), *sashes*, and so rendered in R. V. (*k*) *Tablets* (Heb. *nĕphĕsh*, *breath*), smelling bottles (R. V. "perfume boxes"). (*l*) *Earrings* (Heb. *lăḥash*, *whisper*), an amulet (R. V.), i. e., gems or metal plates with an inscription upon them, worn as protection as well as ornament. *See* Earrings. (*m*) *Rings*, both ear and nose. *See* Rings. (*n*) *Changeable suits* (Heb. *măḥălāṣäh*), gala dresses, not usually worn, but taken off when at home. (*o*) *Mantles*, the second tunic. *See* above. (*p*) *Wimples*, the broad cloth wrapped round the body, such as Ruth wore (Ruth 3:15). *See* Veil (R. V. "shawl"). (*q*) *Crisping pins* (Heb. *härîṭ*, *cut out*, R. V. "satchel"), pockets for holding money (II Kings 5:23, "bags"), which was generally carried by men in the girdle or in a purse. (*r*) *Glasses* (R. V. "hand mirrors," *q. v.*). (*s*) *Fine Linen* (Heb. *sädin*, to *envelope*), veils or coverings of the finest linen, Sindu cloth. (*t*) *Hoods*, i. e., *headdress.* (*u*) *Veils* (*q. v.*), probably delicate, veil-like mantles thrown over the rest of the clothes.

Of course, garments varied greatly in material and ornamentation, according to ability and taste. Being often changed during marriage and other festive occasions, they were called *garments of change.* Kings and men of rank had always a large wardrobe of these, partly for their own use (Prov. 31:21; Job 27:16; Luke 15:22), partly to give away as presents (Gen. 45:22; I Sam. 18:4; II Kings 5:5; 10:22; Esth. 4:4; 6:8, 11).

(4) **Dress of foreign nations** mentioned in the Bible. That of the Persians is described in Dan. 3:21 in terms which have been variously understood, but which may be identified in the following manner: (1) The *sărbăl* (A. V. "coat"), *underclothing*, worn next the person; (2) *păṭîsh* (A. V. "hosen"), probably the outer tunic; (3) *kărbelä* (A. V. "hats"), mantle; while (4) the "other garments" *lᵉbūsh*, may mean coverings for the head and feet. In addition to these terms we have notice of a robe of state of fine linen (Heb. *tăkrîk*), so called from its ample dimensions (Esth. 8:15). References to Roman or Greek dress are few.

3. **Customs Relating to Dress.** "The length of the dress rendered it inconvenient for active exercise; hence the outer garments were

either left in the house by a person working close by (Matt. 24:18) or were thrown off when the occasion arose (Mark 10:50; John 13:4; Acts 7:58), or, if this was not possible, as in the case of a person traveling, they were girded up (I Kings 18:46; II Kings 4:29; 9:1; I Pet. 1:13). On entering a house the upper garment was probably laid aside and resumed on going out (Acts 12:8). In a sitting posture the garments concealed the feet; this was held to be an act of reverence (Isa. 6:2). The number of suits possessed by the Hebrews was considerable; a single suit consisted of an under and upper garment. The presentation of a robe in many instances amounted to installation or investiture (Gen. 41:42; Esth. 8:15; Isa. 22:21); on the other hand, taking it away amounted to dismissal from office (II Macc. 4:38). The production of the best robe was a mark of special honor in a household (Luke 15:22). The number of robes thus received or kept in store for presents was very large, and formed one of the main elements of wealth in the East (Job 27:16; Matt. 6:19; James 5:2); so that *to have clothing*=to be wealthy and powerful (Isa. 3:6, 7)" (Smith, *Bib. Dict.*, s. v.; Jahn, Keil).

Dress is used in Scripture in the following senses: (1) To *till* the soil (Heb. ʾăbăd, to *serve*, Gen. 2:15; Deut. 28:39; Gr. *geōrgeō*, Heb. 6:7). (2) *Preparation* of food (Heb. ʾäsäh, to *make*, Gen. 18:7, 8; I Sam. 25:18; II Sam. 12:4; 13:5, 7, etc.). (3) *Trimming* lamps (Heb. *yätäb*, *make right*, Exod. 30:7).

Drink. As a drink water took the first place, although milk was also extensively used, but considered as food (*q. v.*). For the better quenching of thirst the common people used a sour drink (Ruth 2:14), a sort of vinegar mixed with oil, perhaps also sour wine. The well-to-do drank wine, probably mixed with water, and often also spiced; also a stronger intoxicating drink, either date wine or Egyptian barley wine. *See* Wine.

Figurative. To "drink waters out of thine own cistern" (Prov. 5:15) is to enjoy the lawful pleasures of marriage. To "drink *blood*" (Ezek. 39:18) is to be satiated with slaughter. To "drink water by measure" (Ezek. 4:11) denotes scarcity and desolation.

Drink, Strong (Heb. *shēkär*, *intoxicant;* Gr. *sikera*), any *intoxicating* beverage. The Hebrews seem to have made wine (*q. v.*) of pomegranates (Cant. 8:2) and other fruits. In Num. 28:7 strong drink is clearly used as an equivalent to wine. "The following beverages were known to the Jews: (1) *Beer*, which was largely consumed in Egypt under the name of *zythus*, and was thence introduced into Palestine. It was made of barley; certain herbs, such as lupin and skirrett, were used as substitutes for hops. (2) *Cider*, which is noticed in the Mishna as *apple wine.* (3) *Honey wine*, of which there were two sorts—one consisting of a mixture of wine, honey, and pepper; the other a decoction of the juice of the grape, termed *debash* (honey) by the Hebrews, and *dibs* by the modern Syrians. (4) *Date wine*, which was also manufactured in Egypt. It was made by mashing the fruit in water in certain proportions. (5) Various other fruits and vegetables are enumerated by Pliny as supplying materials for *factitious* or home-made wine, such as figs, millet, the carob fruit, etc. It is not improbable that the Hebrews applied *raisins* to this purpose in the simple manner followed by the Arabians, viz., by putting them in jars of water and burying them in the ground until fermentation takes place" (Smith. *Bib. Dict.*, s. v.).

Drink Offering. *See* Sacrificial Offering.

Dromedary. *See* Animal Kingdom.

Dropsy. *See* Diseases.

Dross (Heb. *sig, refuse*), the impurities separated from silver, etc., by the process of melting (Prov. 25:4; 26:23); also the *base metal* itself prior to smelting (Isa. 1:22, 25; Ezek. 22:18, 19).

Figurative. Dross is used to represent the *wicked* (Psa. 119:119; Prov. 26:23), *sin* (Isa. 1:25), and *Israel* (Ezek. 22:18, 19).

Drought, the rendering of a number of Hebrew words. In Palestine from May till October there is little if any rain, and consequently this is the season of drought. The copious dews nourish only the more robust plants, and as the season advances the grass withers, unless watered by rivulets or the labor of man. It is the drought of summer (Gen. 31:40; Psa. 32:4); the parched ground cracks; the heaven seems like brass and the earth as iron (Deut. 28:23); prairie and forest fires are not uncommon (Isa. 5:24; 9:18, etc.).

Drown (Gr. *katapontizō*). Drowning was not a Jewish method of capital punishment, nor was it a *practice* in Galilee, but belonged to the Greeks, Romans, Syrians, and Phoenicians (Matt. 18:6).

Drum. *See* Music.

Drunk, Drunkard (Heb. some form of *shākăr*, to be *tipsy;* Gr. *metheuō*). Noah, who was probably ignorant of the fiery nature of wine, affords us the first instance of intoxication (Gen. 9:21). That the excessive use of strong drink was not uncommon among the Jews may be inferred from the striking figures furnished by its use and effect, and also from the various prohibitions and penalties (Psa. 107:27; Isa. 5:11; 24:20; 49:26; 51:17-22; Hab. 2:15, 16). The sin of drunkenness is strongly condemned in the Scriptures (Rom. 13:13; I Cor. 5:11; 6:10; Eph. 5:18; I Thess. 5:7, 8).

Figurative. Men are represented as *drunk* with sorrow, afflictions, and God's wrath (Isa. 63:6; Jer. 51:57; Ezek. 23:33); also those under the power of superstition, idolatry, and delusion, because they do not use their reason (Jer. 51:7; Rev. 17:2). *Drunkenness* sometimes denotes abundance, satiety (Deut. 32:42; Isa. 49:26). "To add drunkenness to thirst" (Deut. 29:19; R. V. "to destroy the moist with the dry") is a proverbial expression, meaning the destruction of one and all.

Drusil'la (drū-sĭl'à), youngest daughter of Herod Agrippa I, by his wife Cypros, and sister of Herod II, was only six years old when her father died in A. D. 44 (Josephus, *Ant.*, xix, 9, 1; xx, 7, 1, 2). She was early promised in marriage to Epiphanes, son of Antiochus, but the match was broken off in consequence of his refusing to perform his promise of conforming to the Jewish religion. She was married to Azizus, king of Edessa, but afterward

was induced by Felix procurator of Judea, to leave Azizus, and become his wife. In Acts 24:24 she is mentioned in such a manner that she may be naturally supposed to have been present when Paul preached before Felix in A. D. 57.

Duke (Lat. *dux*, a leader) is the translation of two Hebrew terms: (1) *Chief* (Heb. *'allūf, leader of a thousand*), the distinguishing title of Edomite and Horite phylarchs, i. e., head of a tribe or nation (Gen. 36:15-43; Exod. 15:15; I Chron. 1:51, 54). *'Allūf* is used rarely of Jews (Zech. 9:7; 12:5, 6, "governor"), and once of chiefs in general (Jer. 13:21, "captain"). (2) *Prince* (Heb. *nᵉsĭk, "anointed" one*), dukes of Sihon (Josh. 13:21), "properly *vassals* of Sihon, princes created by the communication or pouring in of power" (K. and D., *Com.*, in loc.). It is rendered "princes" (Psa. 83:11; Ezek. 32:30; Dan. 11:8) and "principal men" (Mic. 5:5).

Dulcimer. *See* Music.

Du'mah (dū'mà; *silence*).

1. A son of Ishmael, most probably the founder of an Ishmaelite tribe of Arabia, and so giving name to the principal place or district inhabited by that tribe (Gen. 25:14; I Chron. 1:30; Isa. 21:11).

2. A town in Judah (Josh. 15:52), the same as *Daumeh*, about ten miles S. W. of Hebron.

3. The region occupied by the Ishmaelites in Arabia (Gen. 25:14; I Chron. 1:30), retained in the modern *Dumat el Jeudel*.

4. **Figurative.** As used in Isa. 21:11, Dumah seems to be symbolical, meaning deep, utter "silence," and therefore the land of the dead (Psa. 94:17; 115:17).

Dumb (Heb. *'illēm, speechless;* Gr. *kōphos, blunted*, as to tongue, i. e., unable to speak, or as to ear, i. e., deaf). Dumbness has the following significations: (1) inability to speak by reason of natural infirmity (Exod. 4:11; Matt. 15:30; Luke 1:20, etc.). (2) By reason of want of knowing what to say or how to say it (Prov. 31:8); unwillingness to speak (Psa. 39:2, 9).

Dung, the rendering of several Hebrew and Greek words. In the case of sacrifices the dung was burned outside the camp (Exod. 29:14; Lev. 4:11; 8:17; Num. 19:5); hence the extreme opprobrium of the threat in Mal. 2:3. Particular directions were laid down in the law to enforce cleanliness with regard to human ordure (Deut. 23:12, sq.); it was the grossest insult to turn a man's house into a receptacle for it (II Kings 10:27, "draughthouse;" Ezra 6:11; Dan. 2:5; 3:29, "dunghill," A. V.); public establishments of that nature are still found in the large towns of the East. The use of this substance among the Jews was twofold: (1) as manure (*q. v.*), and (2) as fuel (*q. v.*).

Dung Gate (Neh. 2:13, "dung port;" 3:13, 14; 12:31), a gate of ancient Jerusalem, located at the southwest angle of Mount Zion. It was doubtless so called because of the piles of sweepings and garbage in the valley of Tophet below.

Dungeon. *See* Prison.

Dunghill, the rendering of three Hebrew words and one Greek, and meaning: (1) A heap of manure (Isa. 25:10; Luke 14:35).

(2) Privy (II Kings 10:27, "draughthouse;" Dan. 2:5).

Figurative. To sit upon a dung heap denoted the deepest degradation and ignominy (I Sam. 2:8; Psa. 112:7; Lam. 4:5).

Du'ra (dū'rā; Akkad. *dūru, circuit, wall*), a plain in the province of Babylon in which Nebuchadnezzar set up a golden image (Dan. 3:1). It is supposed that the site of the image is identified in one of the mounds discovered in the territory. Several localities in Babylon were called Duru. There is a river by this name, with Tulūl Dūra near by.

Dust. In the countries suffering from severe droughts the soil is often converted into dust, which, agitated by violent winds, brings terrific and desolating storms. Among the punishments against the Hebrews, in the event of forsaking Jehovah, was that, instead of rain, dust and ashes should fall from heaven (Deut. 28:24).

Figurative. To put dust on the head was the sign of the deepest grief (Josh. 7:6); sitting in the dust denotes degradation (Isa. 47:1); the "mouth in the dust" (Lam. 3:29) symbolizes suppliant and humble submission. Dust may mean the *grave* (Job. 7:21), *death* itself (Gen. 3:19; Psa. 22:15), a *numerous people* (Num. 23:10), or *low condition* (I Sam. 2:8; Nah. 3:18). The *shaking off the dust* is a sign of merited *contempt* with which the people rejecting the truth are reduced to the level of the Gentiles (Matt. 10:14; Acts 13:51). To "lick the dust" signifies the most abject submission (Psa. 72:9). To "cast dust" at anyone (II Sam. 16:13) may signify contempt, or, as some think, to demand justice (Acts 22:23). *See* Mourning.

Duty (Heb. *dāvär*, a *matter*, II Chron. 8:14; Ezra 3:4) means the task of each day. The other use of the word is that which a man owes to his wife or his deceased brother's widow (Deut. 25:5, 7; Heb. *'ōnäh, cohabitation*). In the New Testament the word is the rendering of the Greek *'opheideo*, to *be under obligation* (Luke 17:10; Rom. 15:27), and sigfies that which ought to be done.

Duty implies *obligation*. Such is the constitution of the human mind that no sooner do we perceive a given course to be *right* than we recognize also a certain *obligation* resting on us to pursue that course. Duties vary according to one's relations. Thus a man has duties to himself, the family, the state, and God. As his supremest relation is to God, and as God's commands are always right, therefore man's chief obligation is to God (I Cor. 10:31).

Dwarf (Heb. *däq, beaten* small, as in Lev. 16:12), an incorrect rendering for a *lean* or emaciated person (Lev. 21:20). Such a person was included among those who could not serve in the sanctuary. *See* Blemish.

Dwell. *See* House, Tent.

Figurative. God "dwelling in light" is said in respect to his independent possession of his own glorious attributes (I Tim. 6:16; I John 1:7); he *dwells in heaven* in respect to his more immediate presence there (Psa. 123:1); Christ *dwelt* (tabernacled) upon earth during his incarnation. To dwell has the sense of *permanent* residence. "God shall enlarge Japheth, and he shall *dwell* in the tents of Shem" (Gen. 9:27).

"To dwell under one's vine and fig tree" (I Kings 4:25) is to enjoy the possession of a home in one's own right. God dwells in the Church (Eph. 3:17-19) through the Holy Spirit (I Cor. 3:16; II Tim. 1:14); and believers are exhorted to "let the word of God dwell in them richly" (Col. 3:16; Psa. 119:11).

"Dwell deep," literally, "make deep for dwelling" (Jer. 49:8), seems to refer to a custom still common in Eastern countries of seeking refuge from danger in the recesses of rocks and caverns, etc.

Dwelling, the rendering of a number of Hebrew and Greek words. Human dwellings have varied from the earliest day to the present—caves, booths, tents, houses, and palaces —according to the character of the country, mode of living, and occupation, as well as the degree of culture.

Dyers. Nomadic society in Bible lands which not only wove its own textiles but dyed them. However, commercial guilds of specialists existed in this field. Fragments of wooden looms and dyeing vats were found at Lachish in South Judah. Clay loom weights were unearthed in some of the homes destroyed by Nebuchadnezzar. Long before Abraham's time Canaanites wove and dyed fine textiles. At Tell Beit Mirsim (Kirjath-Sepher) many loom-weights were recovered along with an elaborate setup for cloth production. In Syria, at Ugarit, remains of a dyeing establishment were recovered. The Canaanites were especially skillful in extracting purple dyes from murex shells. Byblus on the Mediterranean was not only noted for its papyrus production but for its cloth manufacture. Weavers and dyers in ancient Sumer went through a long period of apprenticeship. Egypt was noted very early for its superb linen. Fine awnings of blue, yellow and light green were exported. Weavers' beams (I Sam. 17:7) have been found in Biblical sites. Hebrews were more skillful at dyeing than almost any other artcraft. They used Tyrian murex shells yielding purple reds, and vegetable dyes. Vegetable matter and indigo were employed from very remote times. Pomegranate bark supplied black. Almond leaves yielded yellow. Potash, lime and grape treacle yielded indigo. *M.F.U.*

E

Eagle. *See* Animal Kingdom.

Figurative. Of great and powerful kings (Ezek. 17:3; Hos. 8:1); of the renovating and quickening influences of the Spirit in the godly, referring to the eagle's increase of vigor after the period of moulting (Psa. 103:5; Isa. 40:31); of God's strong and loving care of his people (Exod. 19:4; Deut. 32:11); the melting away of riches is symbolized by the swiftness of the eagle's flight (Prov. 23:5), also the rapidity of the movement of armies (Deut. 28:49; Jer. 4:13; 48:40), and the swiftness of man's days (Job 9:26); the height and security of its dwelling symbolizes the fancied but fatal security of the wicked (Jer. 49:16; Obad. 4). "Enlarge thy baldness as the eagle" (Mic. 1:16) is "a reference to the bearded vulture, or more probably the carrion vulture, which has the front of the head completely bald and only a few hairs at the back of the head. The words cannot possibly be understood as referring to the yearly moulting of the eagle itself" (K. and D., *Com.*, in loco).

Ear, the organ of hearing. We learn from Scripture that blood was put upon the right ear of the priests at their consecration (Exod. 29:20; Lev. 8:23), and of the healed leper in his cleansing (Lev. 14:14); that they were often adorned with rings (*see* Earring), and that servants who refused to leave their masters were fastened to the door by an awl bored through the ear as a mark of perpetual servitude (Exod. 21:6; Deut. 15:17).

Figurative. "To uncover the ear" (I Sam. 20:2, margin) is to reveal; to have the "ear heavy" (Isa. 6:10) or "uncircumcised" (Jer. 6:10) is to be inattentive and disobedient; the regard of Jehovah to the prayer of his people is expressed thus: "His ears are open to their cry" (Psa. 34:15).

Earnest (Gr. *'arrabōn, pledge*), money which in purchase is given as a pledge that the full amount will subsequently be paid. The Hebrew word *'ărābōn* was used generally for *pledge* (Gen. 38:17), *surety* (Prov. 17:18), and *hostage* (II Kings 14:14). The noun *earnest* occurs three times in the New Testament (II Cor. 1:22; 5:5; Eph. 1:14), and the meaning of the passages appears to be that the Holy Spirit is in the heart as an *earnest* money given for a guarantee of a future possession, the pledge of complete salvation. The gift of the Holy Spirit, comprising as it does "the power of the world to come" (Heb. 6:5), is both a foretaste and a pledge of future blessedness.

Earring. 1. **Egyptian, etc.** The earrings usually worn by Egyptian ladies were large, round, single hoops of gold, from one inch and a half to two inches and one third in diameter, and frequently of a still greater size, or made

of six rings soldered together; sometimes an asp, whose body was of gold set with precious stones, was worn by persons of rank as a fashionable caprice; but it is probable that this emblem of majesty was usually confined to members of the royal family. Earrings of other forms have been found at Thebes, but their date is uncertain, and it is difficult to say if they are of an ancient Egyptian age or of Greek introduction. Of these the most remarkable are a dragon and another of fancy shape, which is not inelegant. Some few were of silver, and plain hoops, like those made of gold already noted, but less massive, being of the thickness of an ordinary ring. At one end was a small opening, into which the curved extremity of the other caught after it had been passed through the ear. Others were in the form of simple studs. The ancient Assyrians, both men and women, wore earrings of exquisite shape and finish; and those on the later monuments are generally in the form of a cross.

133. Ancient Earrings

2. **Hebrew.** (1) *Ring* (Heb. *nĕzĕm*). Used both as a *nosering* and an *earring*, and differing little if any in form. It certainly means an earring in Gen. 35:4, but a nose jewel in Gen. 24:47; Prov. 11:22; Isa. 3:21; while its meaning is doubtful in Judg. 8:24, 25; Job. 42:11. (2) *Amulet* (Heb. *lăḥăsh, whispering*). This word, rendered in the A. V. "earrings" Isa. 3:20), is given "amulets" in the R. V. This latter more correctly represents the Hebrew word (meaning *incantations*), and these were gems or metal charms with an inscription upon them, which were worn for protection as well as ornament. On this account they were surrendered along with the idols by Jacob's household (Gen. 35:4). Chardin describes earrings, with talismanic figures and characters on them, as still existing in the East. Jewels were sometimes attached to the rings. The size of the earrings still worn in eastern countries far exceeds what is usual among ourselves; hence they formed a handsome present (Job. 42:11) or offering to the service of God (Num. 31:50). Earrings were worn by both sexes (Exod. 32:2).

Earth. The rendering of several Hebrew and Greek words. (*See* Mineral Kingdom.)

1. **Soil** (Heb. *'ădāmäh*), or ground, as in Gen. 9:20, where "husbandman" is literally *man of the ground.* The *earth* supplied the elementary substance of which man's body was formed (Gen. 2:7). According to the law, earth or rough stones were the material out of which altars were to be raised (Exod. 20:24); thought by some to symbolize the elevation of man to God. Others think it teaches that the earth, which has been involved in the curse of sin, is to be renewed and glorified by the gracious hand of God. Naaman's request for two mules' burden of earth (II Kings 5:17) was based on the belief that Jehovah, like heathen deities, was a local god, and could be worshiped acceptably only on his own soil.

2. **Land** (*'ĕrĕts*). K. and D. (*Com.*, on Gen. 2:5) thus distinguish between *field* (Heb. *sädĕh*), and *earth.* "*Sädĕh* is not the widespread plain of the earth, the broad expanse of land, but a field of arable land, which forms only a part of the earth or ground." The term is applied in a more or less extended sense: (1) To the whole world (Gen. 1:1); (2) to land as opposed to sea (Gen. 1:10); (3) to a country (Gen. 21:32); (4) to a plot of ground (Gen. 23:15); (5) to the ground on which a man stands (Gen. 33:3); (6) to "the inhabitants of the earth" (Gen. 6:11; 11:1); (7) to *heathen countries*, as distinguished from Israel especially during the theocracy (II Kings 18:25; II Chron. 13:9, etc.); (8) in a spiritual sense is employed in contrast with heaven, to denote things *carnal* (John 3:31; Col. 3:2, 5).

Earthen Vessel or **Earthenware.** See Pot, Potter.

Earthquake (Heb. *rằ'ăsh*, *vibration;* Gr. *seismos*), a tremulous motion or shaking of the earth caused by the violent action of subterraneous heat and vapors. That Palestine has been subject both to volcanic agency and to occasional earthquakes there can be no doubt. The recorded instances, however, are but few; the most remarkable occurred in the reign of Uzziah (Amos 1:1), which Josephus connected with the sacrilege and consequent punishment of that monarch (II Chron. 26: 16, sq.). Of the extent of that earthquake, of the precise localities affected by it, or of the desolations it may have produced—of anything, in short, but the general alarm and consternation occasioned by it, we know absolutely nothing. Earthquakes are mentioned in connection with the crucifixion (Matt. 27:51-54), the resurrection (Matt. 28:2), and the imprisonment of Paul and Silas (Acts 16:26). These, like that recorded in connection with the death of Korah (Num. 16:32), and with Elijah's visit to Mount Horeb (I Kings 19:11), would seem to have been miraculous rather than natural phenomena. Josephus (*Ant.*, xv, 52) gives an account of an earthquake which devastated Judea (B. C. 31). The Second Advent of Christ will be preceded and attended by gigantic earthquakes (Rev. 16:18, 19, and Zech. 14:4, 5).

Figurative. Earthquakes are symbolical of the judgments of God (Isa. 24:20; 29:6; Jer. 4:24; Rev. 8:5); of the overthrow of nations (Hag. 2:6, 22; Rev. 6:12, 13; 16:18, 19).

East, the direction toward the rising of the sun, denoted by the Hebrew word *mĭzrāh*, *rising* (Josh. 11:3; Psa. 50:1; 103:12; Zech. 8:7), used when the east is distinguished from the west or from some other quarter of the compass (Dan. 8:9; 11:44). Since the Hebrews faced the rising of the sun in telling direction, the east was "the front" (Heb. *qĕdĕm, what is the front;* Gen. 13:14; 28:14; Job 23:8, 9; Ezek. 47:18, sq.). This Hebrew word is also used in a geographical sense to describe a spot or country immediately *before* another in an easterly direction (Gen. 2:8; 3:24; 13:11). In Matt. 2:2, 9 the Greek expression for east means "rising," *anatolē:* "for we have seen his star in the east," that is, in its rising.

East, Children of the, Hebrew idiom for *Easterners* applied to peoples living east of Palestine (Judg. 6:3, 33; 7:12; 8:10; I Kings 4:30, etc.).

East Gate, the potter's gate, or the gate leading to the potter's field (Jer. 19:2). *See* Jerusalem.

East Sea. The Dead Sea was called the East Sea (Joel 2:20; Ezek. 47:18); while the Mediterranean Sea was called the West Sea (Num. 34:6). *See* Dead Sea.

East Wind (Heb. *qādīm, east*). *See* Winds.

Easter (Gr. *pascha*, from Heb. *pĕsăḥ*), the *Passover*, and so translated in every passage excepting "intending after Easter to bring him forth to the people" (Acts 12:4). In the earlier English versions Easter had been frequently used as the translation of *pascha*. At the last revision Passover was substituted in all passages but this. *See* Passover.

The word Easter is of Saxon origin, Eastra, the goddess of spring, in whose honor sacrifices were offered about Passover time each year. By the 8th century Anglo-Saxons had adopted the name to designate the celebration of Christ's resurrection.

Eating. *See* Food, Hospitality.

Figurative. "To eat" is spoken metaphorically of meditating upon and assimilating the word of God (Jer. 15:16; Ezek. 3:1; Rev. 10:9); familiar intercourse (Luke 13:26; comp. Tit. 1:16). "To eat the spoil of enemies" (Deut. 20:14) is to make use of it for one's own maintenance. "Eating and drinking" signifies enjoying one's self (Eccles. 5: 18), or to live in the ordinary way as distinguished from asceticism (Matt. 11:18; comp. Acts 10:41).

E'bal (*ē'băl;* to be *bare*, a *stone*).

1. A variant reading (I Chron. 1:22) for *Obal* (*q. v.*).

2. One of the sons of Shobal, son of Seir, the Horite, of Idumea (Gen. 36:23; I Chron. 1:40).

3. One of two mountains separated by the valley of Shechem. Ebal is two thousand seven hundred feet above the sea. The opposite mountain, Gerizim, is two thousand six hundred feet above the sea. The modern name of Ebal is Sitti Salamigah, so called after a Mohammedan female saint. Ebal is the mountain from the top of which were pronounced the blessings, and from Gerizim the cursings, of Israel (Deut. 11:29; Josh. 8:30-35). Conder considers that upon the top of this mount may be the site of Joshua's altar. The base of Mount Ebal has many sepulchral excavations.

E'bed (ē'bĕd; *servant*).

1. The father of *Gaal* (*q. v.*), who headed the insurrection at Shechem against Abimelech (Judg. 9:26-35), B. C. about 1100.

2. Son of Jonathan, and head of the descendants of Adin who returned (to the number of fifty males) from the captivity (Ezra 8:6), B. C. about 457.

E'bed-Me'lech (ē'bĕd-mē'lĕk; *servant of a king*), probably an official title equal to *king's slave*, i. e., *minister*, an Ethiopian at the court of Zedekiah, king of Judah, who was instrumental in saving the prophet Jeremiah from the dungeon and famine (Jer. 38:7-13). For his kindness he was promised deliverance when the city should fall into the enemy's hands (Jer. 39:15-18), B. C. 589. He is there styled a eunuch, and he probably had charge of the king's harem, an office which would give him free private access to the king.

Eb'en-e'zer (ĕb'ĕn-ē'zēr; *stone of the help*), a stone set up by Samuel after a signal defeat of the Philistines, as a memorial of the "help" received on the occasion from Jehovah (I Sam. 7:12). Its position is carefully defined as between Mizpeh and Shen. Neither of these points, however, has been identified with any certainty—the latter not at all.

E'ber (ē'bĕr).

1. The son of Salah and father of Peleg, being the third postdiluvian patriarch after Shem (Gen. 10:24; 11:14; I Chron. 1:18, 25). He is claimed as the founder of the Hebrew race (Gen. 10:21; Num. 24:24). In Luke 3:35 his name is Anglicized *Heber*.

2. The oldest of the three sons of Elpaal, the Benjamite, and one of those who rebuilt Ono and Lod, with their suburbs (I Chron. 8:12), B. C. 535.

3. The head of the priestly family of Amok, in the time of the return from exile under Zerubbabel (Neh. 12:20), B. C. 535.

Ebi'asaph (ē-bī'à-săf; *gatherer*), the son of Elkanah and father of Assir, in the genealogy of the Kohathite Levites (I Chron. 6:23). In v. 37 he is called a son of Korah, from a comparison of which circumstance with Exod. 6:24 most interpreters have identified him with *Abiasaph* (*q. v.*) of the latter passage; but (unless we there understand, not three sons of Korah to be meant, but only three in regular descent) the pedigrees of the two cannot be made to tally without violence. From I Chron. 9:19 it appears he had a son named Kore. In I Chron. 26:1 his name is abbreviated to *Asaph*.

Ebony. *See* Vegetable Kingdom.

Ebro'nah (ĕb-rō'nà; *passage*), the thirtieth station of the Israelites on their way from Egypt to Canaan (Num. 33:34, 35). Since it lay near Ezion-geber on the west, as they left Jotbathah, it was probably in the plain *Kâ'a en-Năkb*, immediately opposite the pass of the same name at the head of the Elamitic branch of the Red Sea.

Ecclesias'tes, Book of. (ĕ-klē'zĭ-ăs'tēz) The superscription 1:1 designates the book as "the words of the Preacher, the son of David, king in Jerusalem." "The Preacher," Hebrew *qōhĕlĕth*, apparently describes one who holds or addresses an assembly. Hebrew *qāhăl*. This

is the meaning evident in the Greek *ekklēsiastēs*, the Vulgate *concionator* and the English "preacher." Ecclesiastes was a roll which was read at the Feast of Tabernacles. The theme of the book is the vanity of mere earthly things contrasted to the knowledge and service of God.

1. **The Contents.**

Part I. The Subject Discussed: Vanity of everything, 1:1-3

Part II. Subject Proved, 1:4-3:22
 a. By the transitoriness of things, 1:4-11
 b. By the existence of evil, 1:12-18
 c. By the emptiness of pleasure, riches and work, 2:1-26
 d. By the certainty of death, 3:1-22

Part III. The Subject Developed, 4:1-12:8
 a. In Consideration of life's injustices, 4:1-16
 b. In Consideration of riches, 5:1-20
 c. In Consideration of man's end, 6:1-12
 d. In Consideration of man's sinfulness, 7:1-29
 e. In Consideration of inscrutable Divine Providence, 8:1-9:18
 f. In Consideration of life's disorders, 10:1-20
 g. In Consideration of the vanity of youth and age, 11:1-12:8

Part IV. The Conclusion, 12:9-14
 Reverence God and observe His commandments, 12:9-14

2. **Authorship.** Luther denied the Solomonic authorship, and it is at present very common to attribute the book to a much later writer or writers. Few, even among conservative scholars, today defend the Solomonic authorship. However, certain evidences point to the fact that Solomon wrote the book. 1:1 clearly attributes the book to Solomon. Definite texts in the book have reference to Solomon's widsom (1:16), his pleasures (2:3), his building exploits (2:4-6), his servants (2:7), and his wealth (2:8). If Solomon is not the writer, one must be prepared to defend the position that the author personates Solomon, as in the apocryphal Book of Wisdom (cf. Wisdom 6-9). Solomonic authorship, it may be said, need not be abandoned as incapable of scholarly defense despite critical unanimity. Romanist scholars Gietmann, Vigouroux and Cornely-Hagen, as well as some Protestant scholars, have defended the Solomonic authorship.

3. **Unity.** Numerous critics such as Winckler, Haupt, Kautzch and Barton deny unity of authorship and regard the book as composed of many later annotations to the original skeptical treatise in order to give the book an orthodox tone, but the language, style and theme of the entire book are against this view. Ernst Sellin and Otto Eissfeldt correctly defend the unity of the book, as do many of the church fathers such as Jerome, Gregory the Great and medieval scholastics such as Thomas Aquinas. (*See* E. W. Hengstenberg, Commentary on *Ecclesiastes*, Philadelphia, 1860; G. Gietmann "Ecclesiastes" in *Catholic Encyclopedia* V, 244-248; R. Gordis, *The Wisdom of Ecclesiastes*, New York, 1945.)

Eclipse of the Sun. No historical notice of an eclipse occurs in the Bible, but there are passages in the prophets which contain manifest allusion to this phenomenon (Joel 2:10, 31; 3:15; Amos 8:9; Mic. 3:6; Zech. 14:6). Some of these notices probably refer to eclipses that occurred about the time of the respective compositions; thus the date of Amos coincides with a total eclipse, which occurred February 9, B. C. 784, and was visible at Jerusalem shortly after noon; that of Micah with the eclipse of June 5, B. C. 716. A passing notice in Jer. 15:9 coincides in date with the eclipse of September 30, B. C. 610, so well known from Herodotus's account (i, 74, 103). The darkness that overspread the world at the crucifixion cannot with reason be attributed to an eclipse, as the moon was at the full at the time of the Passover.

Ed (Heb. 'ēd; a *witness*), a word inserted in the A. V. of Josh. 22:34, apparently on the authority of a few manuscripts, and also of the Syriac and Arabic versions, but not existing in the generally received Hebrew text.

E'dar (ē'dàr; a *flock*), the place where Jacob first halted after the burial of Rachel (Gen. 35:21).

E'den (ē'dĕn).

1. **Garden of.** Biblical notices locate the spot where the temptation and the fall occurred somewhere in the Tigris-Euphrates country, evidently in the easternmost third of the Fertile Crescent. "And a river went out of Eden to water the garden; and from thence it was parted, and became four heads. The name of the first is Pishon. . . . And the name of the second river is Gihon. . . . And the name of the third river is Hiddekel. . . . And the fourth river is the Euphrates (Gen. 2:10-14). Pishon and Gihon are presumably canals, called rivers in Babylonia, which connected the Tigris and Euphrates as ancient river beds. The Hiddekel (Babylonian *Idigla, Diglat*) is the ancient name of the Tigris. Friedrich Delitzsch located the site of Eden just north of Babylon where the Euphrates and Tigris closely approach each other. A. H. Sayce and others located it near Eridu, anciently on the Persian Gulf, but such identifications are now impossible. Both the Tigris and the Euphrates have shifted their river beds in the course of millennia and enormous deposits of silt have drastically changed the entire configuration of lower Babylonia. The slow building of the lower alluvial plain has continued seventy-two feet a year or a mile and one-half in a century, so that today the landed area stretches 300 miles southeastward from the approximate shore line of 3000 B. C. The two great rivers which were separated in antiquity, today flow across their own plain and swamps until they finally unite and flow together for at least 100 miles before reaching the Gulf. The important thing is that the Book of Genesis locates the beginning of human life in the very region which scientific archaeology has demonstrated to be the cradle of civilization. "No focus of civilization in the earth . . . can begin to compete in antiquity and activity with the basin of the eastern Mediterranean and the region immediately to the east of it—Breasted's Fertile Crescent." (W. F. Albright, *From the Stone Age to Christianity*, Baltimore, 1940, p. 6.)

2. One of the markets which supplied **Tyre** with richly embroidered stuffs (Isa. 37:12, 13; Ezek. 27:23). This city is the *Bit Adini* of the Assyrian monuments, a small kingdom situated on both sides of the Euphrates north of the Balikh River.

3. Son of Joab, and one of the Gershonite Levites who assisted in the reformation of public worship under Hezekiah (II Chron. 29:12), after c. 719 B. C. He is possibly the same Levite appointed by Hezekiah as one of those who were to superintend the distribution of the freewill offerings (II Chron. 31: 15). *M. F. U.*

E'der (ē'dẽr; *flock*).

1. A city of southern Judah, on the Idumaean border (Josh. 15:21), perhaps the same as *Edar* (*q. v.*).

2. The second of the three "sons" (descendants) of Mushi appointed to Levitical offices in the time of David (I Chron. 23:23; 24:30), B. C. after 1000.

Edification (Gr. *oikodomē, building*) means building up. A building is therefore called an edifice. Accordingly, the work of confirming believers in the faith of the Gospel and adding to their knowledge and graces is appropriately expressed by this term. Christians are said in the New Testament to be *edified* by understanding spiritual truth (I Cor. 14:3-5), by the work of "apostles, prophets, evangelists, pastors, and teachers" (Eph. 4:11, 12), and by good speech (4:29).

The means to be used for one's *upbuilding* are the study and hearing of God's word, prayer, use of the sacraments, meditation, self-examination, and Christian work of every kind. It is our duty to edify each other (I Thess. 5:11) by the exhibition of every grace of life and conversation.

The term is also applied to believers as "living stones" builded up into a habitation for the Lord, constituting the great spiritual temple of God (Eph. 2:20-22; I Pet. 2:5).

E'dom (ē'dŏm; *red*).

1. The name given to *Esau* (*q. v.*) after he bartered his birthright for a mess of *red* pottage (Gen. 25:30).

2. Edom stands also collectively for the *Edomites* (*q. v.*), as well as for their country, called also *Idumaea*.

E'domites (ē'dŏ-mīts), the descendants of Esau, who settled in the south of Palestine, and at a later period came into conflict with the Israelites (Deut. 23:7; Num. 20:14, sq.); frequently called merely *Edom* (Num. 24:18; Josh. 15:1; II Sam. 8:14, etc.).

1. **Country.** Edom, or Idumaea, was situated at the southeast border of Palestine (Judg. 11:17; Num. 34:3), and was properly called the land or mountain of *Seir* (Gen. 36:8; 32:3; Josh. 24:4; Ezek. 35:3, 7, 15). The country lay along the route pursued by the Israelites from Sinai to Kadesh-barnea, and thence back again to Elath (Deut. 1:2; 2:1-8), i. e., along the east side of the great valley of Arabah. On the north of Edom lay the territory of Moab, the boundary appearing to have been the "brook Zered" (2:13, 14, 18).

The physical geography of Edom is somewhat peculiar. Along the western base of the mountain range are low calcareous hills. These are succeeded by lofty masses of igneous rock, chiefly porphyry, over which lies red and variegated sandstone in irregular ridges and abrupt cliffs with deep ravines between. The latter strata give the mountains their most striking features and remarkable colors. The average elevation of the summit is about two thousand feet above the sea. Along the eastern side runs an almost unbroken limestone ridge, a thousand feet or more higher than the other. This ridge sinks down with an easy slope into the plateau of the Arabian desert. While Edom is thus wild, rugged, and almost inaccessible, the deep glens and flat terraces along the mountain sides are covered with rich soil, from which trees, shrubs, and flowers now spring up luxuriantly.

134. Edom

2. **The Edomites** were descendants of Esau, or Edom, who expelled the original inhabitants, the *Horites* (Deut. 2:12), whose rulers were sheikhs (Gen. 36:29, 30). A statement made in Gen. 36:31 serves to fix the period of the dynasty of the eight kings. They "reigned in the land of Edom before there reigned any king over the children of Israel;" i. e., before the time of Moses, who may be regarded as the first virtual king of Israel (comp. Deut. 33:5; Exod. 18:16-19). It would also appear that these kings were elected. The princes (A. V. "dukes") of the Edomites are named in Gen. 36:40-43, and were probably petty chiefs or sheikhs of their several clans.

3. **History.** Esau's bitter hatred to his brother Jacob for fraudulently obtaining his blessing appears to have been inherited by his latest posterity. The Edomites peremptorily refused to permit the Israelites to pass through their land (Num. 20:18-21). For a period of four hundred years we hear no more of the Edomites. They were then attacked and defeated by Saul (I Sam. 14:47). Some forty years later David overthrew their army in the "Valley of Salt," and his general, Joab, fol-

lowing up the victory, destroyed nearly the whole male population (I Kings 11:15, 16), and placed Jewish garrisons in all the strongholds of Edom (II Sam. 8:13, 14). Hadad, a member of the royal family of Edom, made his escape with a few followers to Egypt, where he was kindly received by Pharaoh. After the death of David he returned and tried to excite his countrymen to rebellion against Israel, but failing in the attempt he went on to Syria, where he became one of Solomon's greatest enemies (I Kings 11:14-23). In the reign of Jehoshaphat (B. C. 875) the Edomites attempted to invade Israel in conjunction with Ammon and Moab, but were miraculously destroyed in the valley of Berachah (II Chron. 20:22). A few years later they revolted against Jehoram, elected a king, and for half a century retained their independence (21:8). They were then attacked by Amaziah, and Sela their great stronghold was captured (II Kings 14:7; II Chron. 25:11, 12). Yet the Israelites were never able again completely to subdue them (28:17). When Nebuchadnezzar besieged Jerusalem the Edomites joined him, and took an active part in the plunder of the city and slaughter of the Jews. Their cruelty at that time seems to be specially referred to in the 137th Psalm. It was on account of these acts of cruelty committed upon the Jews in the day of their calamity that the Edomites were so fearfully denounced by the later prophets (Isa. 34:5-8; 63:1-4; Jer. 49:17; Lam. 4:21; Ezek. 25:13, 14; Amos 1:11, 12; Obad. 8, 10, sq.). On the conquest of Judah, the Edomites, probably in reward for their services during the war, were permitted to settle in southern Palestine, and the whole plateau between it and Egypt; but they were about the same time driven out of Edom proper by the Nabatheans. For more than four centuries they continued to prosper. But during the warlike rule of the Maccabees they were again completely subdued, and even forced to conform to Jewish laws and rites and submit to the government of Jewish prefects. The Edomites were now incorporated with the Jewish nation, and the whole province was often termed by Greek and Roman writers *Idumaea*. Immediately before the siege of Jerusalem by Titus, twenty thousand Idumaeans were admitted to the Holy City, which they filled with robbery and bloodshed. From this time the Edomites, as a separate people, disappear from the page of history. Scriptural indications that they were idolaters (II Chron. 25:14, 15, 20) are amply confirmed and illuminated by discoveries at Petra. For a discussion of the degrading practices of Edomite religion, see George L. Robinson, *The Saracophagus of an Ancient Civilization.*

Ed′rei (ĕd′rē-ī; *mighty*).

1. A fortified town of northern Palestine, situated near Kedesh and Hazor (Josh. 19: 37), site not known.

2. One of the metropolitan towns of Bashan beyond Jordan (Josh. 12:4, 5; 13:12; Deut. 3:19), and the place where King Og was defeated by the Israelites (Num. 21:33-35; Deut. 1:4; 3:1-3). It afterward fell to eastern Manasseh (Josh. 13:31; Num. 32:33).

"Its present name, *Ed-Dera'-ah;* first discovered by Consul Wetzstein in 1860, explored and mapped since by Schumacher in 1886. Accounts of this wonderful city have been given by others. I will condense the accounts. It is a *subterranean* city. There is a small court, twenty-six feet long, eight feet three inches wide, with steps leading down into it, which has been built as an approach to the actual entrance of the caves. Then come large basaltic slabs, then a passage twenty feet long, four feet wide, which slopes down to a large room, which is shut off by a stone door so this underground city could be guarded.

"Columns ten feet high support the roof of the chambers into which you now enter. These columns are of later period, but there are other supports built out of the basaltic rock. Then come dark and winding passages —a broad street, which had dwellings on both sides of it, whose height and width left nothing to be desired. The temperature was mild, no difficulty in breathing; several cross streets, with holes in the ceiling for air; a market-place, a broad street with numerous shops in the walls; then into a side street, and a great hall, with a ceiling of a single slab of jasper, perfectly smooth and of immense size. Airholes are frequent, going up to the surface of the ground about sixty feet. Cisterns are frequent in the floors. Tunnels partly blocked, too small for anyone now to creep through, are found. The two travelers from whom I have quoted believe that a far greater city exists than the portion they explored.

"This remarkable subterranean city was presumably hollowed out to receive the population of the upper town in times of danger, and the people were thus prepared to stand a siege on the part of the enemy for as long as their magazines were filled with food, their stables with cattle, and the cisterns with water.

"If, however, the enemy had found out how to cut off their supply of air by covering up the airholes the besieged would have had to surrender or perish. The average depth of the city from the surface of the ground is about seventy feet" (Harper, *Bib. and Mod. Dis.,* pp. 127-129).

Education. Although nothing is more carefully inculcated in the law than the duty of parents to teach their children its precepts and principles (Exod. 12:26; 13:8, 14; Deut. 4:5, 9, 10; 6:2, 7, 20, etc.), yet there is little trace among the Hebrews in earlier times of education in any other subject. Exceptions to this statement may perhaps be found in the instances of Moses himself, who was brought up in all Egyptian learning (Acts 7:22); of the writer of the book of Job, who was evidently well versed in natural history and in the astronomy of the day (Job. 38:31; chaps. 39, 40, 41); of Daniel and his companions in captivity (Dan. 1:4, 17); and, above all, in the intellectual gifts and acquirements of Solomon, which were even more renowned than his political greatness (I Kings 4:29, 34; 10:1-9; II Chron. 9:1-8). In later times the prophecies and comments on them, as well as on the earlier Scriptures, together with other sub-

jects, were studied. Parents were required to teach their children some trade. *See* Children, Father, Schools.

Effectual Calling. *See* Call.

Effectual Prayer. In James 5:16 the A. V. has "the *effectual fervent* (Gr. *'energoumenē*) prayer of a righteous man availeth much." The participle here has not the force of an adjective, but gives the reason why the prayer of a righteous man has outward success. The R. V. renders appropriately, "the supplication of a righteous man availeth much in its working."

Egg. Deut. 22:6 prohibits the taking of a sitting bird from its eggs or young. Eggs are mentioned as deserted (Isa. 10:14); of the cockatrice (59:5). Egg is contrasted with a scorpion (*q. v.*) as an article of food (Luke 11:12). Eggs were extensively used as food (*q. v.*).

Figurative. "The white of an egg" is used (Job. 6:6, "the juice of purslain," R. V. margin) as a symbol of something *insipid.*

Eg'lah (ĕg'lä; *heifer*), one of David's wives during his reign in Hebron and the mother of his son Ithream (II Sam. 3:5; I Chron. 3:3) B. C. about 1000. The clause appended to Eglah's name, viz., "David's wife," is not added to show that Eglah was David's principal wife, which would necessitate the conclusion drawn by the rabbins that Michal was the wife intended (Keil, *Com.*).

Eg'laim (ĕg'lā-ĭm) (Isa. 15:8). *See* En-eglaim.

Eg'lon (Heb. ĕg'lŏn; *calflike*), a Moabite king.

1. **Subdues the Israelites.** When Israel forsook the Lord again, the Lord strengthened Eglon against them. The king allied himself with the Ammonites and the Amalekites, invaded the land, and took "the city of palm trees," i. e., Jericho (B. C. c. 1300). Sixty years had passed since Jericho had been destroyed by Joshua. During that time the Israelites had rebuilt the ruined city, but they had not fortified it on account of the curse pronounced by Joshua upon anyone who should restore it as a fortress; so that the Moabites could easily conquer it, and, using it as a base, reduce the Israelites to servitude. Here Eglon built a palace (Josephus, *Ant.,* v, 4, 1, sq.), which he occupied at least in the summer months (Judg. 3:20).

2. **His death.** After the Israelites had served him eighteen years the Lord raised up a deliverer in the person of *Ehud* (*q. v.*), a Benjamite. He was deputed to carry a present to the king, and after he had done so retired with his attendants. Returning to the king, whom he found in his summer parlor, he informed him that he had a secret message from God. Eglon dismissed his attendants and rose to receive the divine message with reverence, when Ehud plunged a dagger into the body of the king, whose obesity was such that the weapon was buried to the handle, and Ehud could not draw it out again. Ehud locked the door of the room, went out through the porch, and escaped to Seirath, in Mount Ephraim. Through delicacy the servants waited for a long time before they opened the door, when they found Eglon dead upon the floor (Judg. 3:12-26).

E'gypt (ē'jĭpt).

1. The Country.

(1) **Name.** The ancient Egyptians knew their native country by the term *Kemet*, (the black land), from its dark-colored Nile mud in contrast with the red sands of the desert. The most common designation was Touï, the two countries, meaning Upper and Lower Egypt. The Canaanites called the land *Miṣri*. The Hebrew name employed in the O. T., *Miṣrayim*, is probably a dual, suggesting also the twofold ancient division of the country. Modern Arabs call it *Miṣr*. The Greeks called it *Aigyptos* as early as the Homeric period.

135. Egypt

(2) **Territory and Its Divisions.** In ancient times Egypt consisted mainly of (*a*) the narrow strip of land watered by the Nile, extending from Memphis or Cairo as far as the First Cataract and (*b*) the so-called Delta (from its resemblance to that letter of the Greek alphabet), the pie shaped area between the Mediterranean Sea and Cairo (measuring c. 125 miles N. and S. and 115, E. and W.). This geographic configuration of the country gave rise to the term Upper Egypt, denoting the long, narrow fertile valley and Lower Egypt, comprising the Delta. Egypt was accordingly about 550 miles long from the Mediterranean to the First Cataract and its average breadth about twelve miles. It was thus a very long and narrow country, its extremely fertile land comprising less than 13,000 square miles. Egypt in a very definite sense is the "gift of the Nile," as the ancient Greeks said. It de-

pends upon the exceedingly rich alluvial mud deposited by the annual inundation of the river from June to October. Irrigation was indispensable and agriculture was the foundation of its economy.

(3) **Its Protected Position.** Bounded on either side by untraversable deserts and mountains, the sea on the north, an exceedingly narrow valley and the river obstructed by cataracts on the south, Egypt was an isolated land. This geographic isolation was a prominent factor in its long and splendid history and brilliant civilization.

2. The Inhabitants.

(1) **The Original People and Language.** The ancient Egyptians were Hamitic peoples (Gen. 10:6). Later on an invasion from Babylonia, predominantly Semitic, came into the country and left its imprint upon the language and culture. Other elements such as the Nubian entered into the Egyptian mixture. At a late date the country was divided into 42 nomes, or provinces, 20 in Lower and 22 in Upper Egypt.

(2) **Their Language.** Egyptian is Hamitic, but may properly be called Hamito-Semitic. (*a*) The following linguistic areas may be noted: Old Egypt, Dynasties I-VIII, includes the language of the Pyramid Texts. (*b*) Middle Egyptian, the literary tongue of Dynasties IX-XVIII, and the vernacular language of the early part of the period, which became the classical norm imitated in later eras. (*c*) Late Egyptian, Dynasties XVIII-XXIV, which exists in business documents and to some extent in literary works. (*d*) Demotic, denoting the language in a popular script from Dynasties XXV to late Roman times, 700 B. C. until after 450 A. D. (*e*) Coptic, third century A. D. onward, the language of the Copts, the Christian descendants of the ancient Egyptians.

The earliest writing was heiroglyphic or picture language, including representations of common objects and geometric symbols. As early as the Old Kingdom scribes began to do away with cumbersome pictures in order to facilitate rapid writing. By the eighth century B. C. a demotic or popular writing came into vogue and was cursive in form. In 1799 Napoleon's expedition discovered the Rosetta Stone, a piece of black basalt bearing an inscription in heiroglyphics, demotic and Greek. This discovery, now in the British Museum, furnished the key to the decipherment of the Egyptian language. This feat was accomplished by the Frenchman François Champollion in 1822.

3. History of Egypt. Manetho, a priest of Sybennytos, c. 290 B. C., wrote a history of Egypt in Greek. He divided the history of united Egypt into thirty royal dynasties. The new minimal chronology begins the first of his dynasties around 2900 B. C. Our knowledge of the early and pre-dynastic periods comes from more recent archaeological discovery.

(1) **Early and Pre-Dynastic Periods.** c. 5000 B. C.-2900 B. C. Neolithic cultures appear from discoveries at Deir Tasa in Middle Egypt, in the Fayum and at Merimdeh Beni-Salameh. Calcolithic remains ap-

136. Granaries in Egypt

pear at Badari. Copper and fine pottery were used as well as green malachite for eye paint. Akin to the Badarians were the succeeding Amratians. The civilization of these people is to be dated around the middle of the fifth millennium B. C. and marks the beginning of the Pre-Dynastic Period. Cemeteries and village sites of Amratian culture exist from Badari to lower Nubia. They used copper and plied the Nile in boats made of bundles of papyrus. Their graves are distinctive, consisting of shallow oval pits accompanied by food, ornaments and weapons. The Amratian period was succeeded by the Gerzean. Pear-shaped maces, wavy-handled jars of clay, stone vessels of animal shapes and amulets representing the falcon, the cow, the bull, the toad and the fly were uncovered. In this period emerged the independent districts, each denoted by an ensign representing a plant or animal. Later the Greeks called them "nomes."

Eventually two powerful states came into existence, one in Upper Egypt and the other in the Delta. Ombos, near the modern town of Naqada, became the capital of Upper Egypt. The symbol of this kingdom was the so-called lotus. Behdet, near Alexandria, became the capital of Lower Egypt. The symbol of this kingdom was the papyrus which grows so luxuriously in the marshes of the Delta. Even after Egypt became a united country the two-kingdom tradition persisted. The rulers of all Egypt bore the title "king of Upper and Lower Egypt," and the symbol became a device in which the lotus and papyrus were combined. The Old Testament Hebrew name for Egypt remained literally "the two Egypts."

(2) **The Proto-Dynastic Period**, Dynasties I and II, c. 2900-2700 B. C. According to Manetho, Menes was the first king and reigned at This, not far from the great bend of the Nile below Thebes, near present-day Girga. The First and Second Dynasties are often called Thinite. The cemetery of the Thinite kings was in the desert near This, close by present-day Abydos. Sir W. M. Flinders Petrie excavated most of the tombs of this dynasty. See *The Royal Tombs of the I Dynasty*, 1900, and *The Royal Tombs of the Earliest Dynasty*, 1901, by Petrie. Like so many of the burial places of ancient Egyptians, the royal tombs at Abydos had already been plundered. Enough of the contents remained, however, to yield a profusion of jewelry, stone vases, copper vessels and other objects. Names

of a number of the kings were found, including Narmer, Aha, Zer and others, The slate palette of Narmer found at Hieronkonpolis has on the reverse the conspicuous figure of the king raising a mace to crush the skull of his enemy, whom he holds by the hair. On the king's head is a helmet-like crown of Upper Egypt. Behind the king is his servant bearing the king's sandals and a water vessel. Heads of Hathor the cow-goddess are around the king's belt and at the top of the palette. The falcon, as a royal symbol, holds a rope attached to a human head. Six papyrus stalks, symbolizing the marshes of Lower Egypt are depicted beneath the falcon. Below is a single barbed harpoon head and a rectangle representing a lake. The entire representation means that the falcon king has taken captive the people of the region of the Harpoon Lake in Lower Egypt.

(3) **The Old Kingdom, Dynasties III-IV**, c. 2700-2200, with capital at Memphis. King Zoser of the Third Dynasty built the famous Step Pyramid at Saqqara, the earliest large stone structure known in history, 190 feet high. Khufu, founder of the Fourth Dynasty, built the greatest of the pyramids at Gizeh. Originally 492 feet high, 755 feet square at the base, covering almost thirteen acres; 2,300,000 blocks of limestone, each weighing about 2½ tons, were required in its construction. Khafre, the successor of Khufu, constructed the second pyramid at Gizeh. Its present height is 447½ feet and is not considerably smaller than the Great Pyramid. The head of the great Sphinx, which stands to the east of the second pyramid, probably represents Khafre. Kings of the Fifth and Sixth Dynasties had inscriptions carved on the walls and inner passages of the pyramids. These are now known as the Pyramid Texts and deal with the glorious future life of the deceased kings in the presence of the sun god. The **Pyramid Texts** frequently have the form of

137. **Pyramids at Gizeh**

couplets with parallel thought arrangement, an early form of poetry which was to be used by the Hebrews two millennia later.

(4) **First Intermediate Period, Dynasties VII-XI**, c. 2200-1900. The pharaohs of this period were comparatively weak and ruled at Memphis and at Herakleopolis, some 77 miles south of Cairo. In the Eleventh Dynasty the Intefs and the Mentuhoteps ruled at Thebes, which was later destined to become Egypt's greatest capital.

(4) **Egypt's Strong Middle Kingdom, Dynasty XII**, c. 1900-1750. These kings were native Thebans, but ruled at Memphis and in the Fayum. This period was coeval with the patriarchal period in Palestine. Joseph became prime minister of and Jacob stood before one of the powerful pharoahs of this dynasty (Amenemes I-IV or Senwosret I-III). This period marked the classical efflorescence of Egyptian literature. Amenemes I composed a series of proverbs for his son. The Tale of Sinuhe portrays conditions in Syria and Palestine under the power of Egypt at this time. Senwosret III pushed the Egyptian Empire to the second cataract and extended his power into Syria. There was great commercial activity. A canal was constructed connecting the Red Sea to the nearest branch of the Nile in the eastern Delta. The mining industry in Sinai was developed into a permanent industry. Jewelry and art work from this period show remarkable design and accuracy of construction. The famous tomb of Khnumhotep II, a powerful noble under Senwosret II who

138. Painting on Wall of Khnumhotep's Tomb.
Depicting a Visit of Asiatics

lived at Beni Hasan 169 miles above Cairo, depicts the visit of 37 Asiatics to Egypt. These Semites bringing gifts remind us of Abraham's going down into Egypt. The picture gives an inscription reading thus: "The arrival, bringing eye paint, which 37 Asiatics bring to him." Their leader has the good Hebrew name "Sheik of the highlands Ibshe."

(6) **Second Intermediate Period, Dynasties XIII-XVII**, c. 1750-1570. The strong Middle Kingdom was succeeded by Dynasties XIII and XIV, characterized by weakness and futile struggles. This period of turmoil was followed by the invasion of the Hyksos, literally, "rulers of the foreign lands," commonly called the "Shepherd Kings." These foreign princes reigned almost a century and a half, comprising Dynasties XV-XVI. The Hyksos seem to have been mainly Semitic

with probable intermixture of Hittites and Hurrians. Avaris in the Delta was their capital. As the Hyksos period ran its course, Dynasty XVII came into power at Thebes. The last king of this dynasty, named Ahmose, completely expelled the Hyksos. The Hyksos introduced the horse and the chariot into the Nile Valley and transformed the peace-living Egyptians into a war-like nation.

139.

(6) **The New Empire**, c. 1570-1150 B. C., Dynasties XVIII-XX. This was the heyday of Egyptian splendor and building activity, as evidenced by the vast temple at Karnak. (See Steindorff and Keith Seele, *When Egypt Ruled the East*). Great pharoahs of this era include Amenhotep I, c. 1546-1525, Thutmose I, c. 1525-1508, Thutmose II, c. 1508-1504, Queen Hatshepsut, c. 1504-1482. She was succeeded by Thutmose III, the great conqueror and builder, c. 1482-1450. This warrior conducted seventeen campaigns and extended the empire to its widest limits in Palestine, Syria and the regions of the upper Euphrates and on the Nile up to the Fourth Cataract. At the battle of Megiddo, c. 1482 B. C., he defeated the Hittites. According to the chronology preserved in the Masoretic Text, he was probably the pharaoh of the oppression. Amenhotep II, c. 1450-1425, was apparently the pharoah under which the Children of Israel quit the country. The great empire began to decline after Thutmose III. Amenhotep III reigned from c. 1412-1375, "the Amarna Period," and was followed by his son Amenhotep IV, c. 1375-1366. This religious zealot is better known by the name of Akhnaton, and is famous for his solar monotheism. This cult was a reaction against the well-entrenched religion of Amun, the sun god of Thebes. Akhnaton established a new capital at Akhetaton (modern Tell el Amarna, where the famous Amarna letters were dis-

covered in 1886), nearly 300 miles below Thebes. Frantic calls for help against encroaching Habiru fill the Amarna correspondence. Under Tutankhamun the capital was re-established at Thebes. The lavish, intact tomb of this pharoah was discovered in 1922 by Howard Carter. Dynasty XIX was initiated by a general named Harmhab, c. 1353-1319, who restored traditional religion and organization. Ramesses I reigned for only a year, c. 1319, and was succeeded by Sethi I, c. 1318-1299. He showed imperial tendencies and began the conquest of Palestine-Syria, which his great son Ramesses II, c. 1299-1232, carried forward. This great pharoah, comparable to Thutmose III, clashed with the Hittites around c. 1293 at Kadesh on the Orontes. About a decade later he made a treaty with the Hittites. Merenptah (Merneptah) c. 1232-1222, succeeded the great conqueror. In his famous stele Israel is mentioned for the first time. Dynasty XX, c. 1200-1085, had about ten rulers by the name of Ramesses. Ramesses III, c. 1198-1167, was the greatest. He repulsed the invading sea peoples, including the Philistines. After him decline set in rapidly.

(8) **The Decline. Dynasties XXI-XXX**, c. 1085-332. Dynasty XXI, c. 1085-945. During this era the high priests of Amun at Thebes, Hrihor and his successors, and nobles of Tanis, Smendes and his successors, strove for supremacy. Meanwhile there was a Libyan penetration of the country and Sheshonk I (Biblical Shishak), a Libyan, seized the throne, inaugurating Dynasty XXIII, c. 945-745. Bubastis in the East Delta was now the capital. Dynasties XXIII-XXIV, c. 745-712, were likewise Libyan. Dynasty XXV, c. 712-663, was Nubian. By the middle of the eighth century B. C. a strong Nubian kingdom came into existence with a capital at Napata, just below the Fourth Cataract. By around 721 B. C. Piankhi, a Nubian king, advanced up the Nile and eventually captured Memphis. Shabaka, a brother of Piankhi, established the Nubian and Ethiopian Dynasty XXV, c. 712-663. Taharka, a son of Piankhi, was the last ruler. Around 680 B. C. Egypt became imperilled by the Assyrians. Esarhaddon conquered the Delta, and Taharka surrendered Lower Egypt. When the Assyrian army was withdrawn, Taharka once more became ruler of the whole country. Under Ashurbanipal the Assyrians made a new invasion c. 667 B. C. Ashurbanipal's second campaign eventuated in the sacking of Thebes, c. 663 (Nahum 3:8-10). Dynasty XXVI, c. 663-525, was founded by Psamtik (Psammetichus). It is sometimes called the Saite Dynasty, since the capital was at Sais in the Delta. He was a practical vassal of the Assyrians until c. 650 when the Assyrians had to withdraw their occupational forces because of a Babylonian revolt. Egyptian glory momentarily returned. Psamtik was succeeded by his son Necho II. c. 609-593. It was he who slew Josiah at Megiddo, c. 608, when the latter opposed his march toward Assyria. He was utterly routed by Nebuchadnezzar II and lost all Egypt's Asiatic possessions (II Kings 24:7). Henceforth Necho confined his energies chiefly to

Egypt, as did his son Psamtik II. The latter's son Apries (Hophra) unsuccessfully challenged Nebuchadnezzar's invasion of Palestine when Jerusalem fell (587 B. C.). Hophra lost his life in a civil war with Amasis II, c. 569-525, who succeeded him. In the days of Amasis, Nebuchadnezzar attempted to invade Egypt. At the end of his reign Amasis witnessed the rise of Cyrus the Great and the Persian Empire. His son Psamtik III reigned only a few months when he fell at Pelusium, 525 B. C. before the invading forces of Cyrus' son and successor, Cambyses II. From Dynasties XXVII-XXX Egypt was under Persian rule. In 332 B. C. the country was conquered by Alexander the Great. After his death in 323 B. C., the land came under the rule of the Ptolemies until the death of Cleopatra, 30 B. C., when it became a province of Rome.

140. Egyptian Gods, Osiris (left) and Re (right)

4. **Egyptian Religion.** The Egyptian religion was an utterly bewildering polytheistic conglomeration in which many deities of the earliest periods, when each town had its own deity, were retained. Re, the sun god, was worshipped at Heliopolis (On). Osiris, god of the Nile, became the god of fertility. With the ascendancy of Thebes, the local god Amun was elevated, and finally identified with Re under the compound Amun-Re. The moon also was worshipped as a god. Ptah, a god of Memphis, was known as the "great chief of artificers." It would be practically impossible to list all the gods sacred to Egyptians. Every object beheld, every phenomenon of nature, was thought to be indwelt by a spirit which could choose its own form, occupying the body of a crocodile, a fish, a cow, a cat, etc. Hence the Egyptians had numerous holy animals, principally the bull, the cow, the cat, the baboon, the jackal, and the crocodile. Some of the deities were composite, with human bodies and animal heads. Thoth, the scribe of the gods, had the head of an ibis; Horus, the sun god, that of a hawk. The idea of a universal god found expression under Akhnaton and for a brief period Aton was distinguished from the material sun. Despite crude nature worship among the Egyptians, there was a remarkable understanding of ethical conduct and, notably, mortality. Great pains were taken to insure the welfare of the deceased in the hereafter.

5. Relations with Israel. According to Biblical chronology preserved in the Massoretic Text of the Hebrew Bible, Jacob and his family went down into Egypt somewhere in the neighborhood of 1871 B. C., under the Twelfth Egyptian Dynasty of the Middle Kingdom. Abraham, early in the history of this powerful government, had gone down into Egypt in time of famine (Gen. 12:10-20) as the aged Jacob and his sons did in this later period under like circumstances (Gen. 46:6). Archaeology has yielded a number of evidences of Israel's sojourn in Egypt, among which are Egyptian personal names of Levites such as Moses, Assir, Pashhur, Hophni, Phineas, Merari and Putiel. These are all incontestably Egyptian. (Cf. Theophile Meek, "Moses and the Levites" in *The American Journal of Semitic Languages and Literatures* 56, pp. 117f. and *Hebrew Origins*, N. Y., 1950, p. 32.) Another indication are the Canaanite place names in the Delta before the New Empire, such as Succoth (Exod. 12:37), Baalzephon (Exod. 14:2), Migdal (Exod. 14:2), Zilu and very likely Goshen itself (Exod. 8:22; 9:26; W. F. Albright, *From the Stone Age to Christianity*, 1940, p. 184). The Egyptian plagues abound in authentic local coloring. About 1441 B. C. (Massoretic chronology), the Hebrews quitted Egypt after a 430-year sojourn (Exod. 12:40-41). This date is supported by the data in I Kings 6:1, which places the Exodus as 480 years before the fourth year of Solomon's reign, c. 961 B. C. Adding 480 to 961 gives 1441 B. C. Scholars, such as Albright, argue for a c. 1290 B. C. date. H. H. Rowley places it around 1225 B. C. Besides telescoping the period of the Judges, these later dates virtually rule out the possibility of fitting the Biblical chronology into the frame of contemporary history. John Garstang's excavations at Jericho favor the date c. 1441 and general conditions in Palestine, reflected in the Amarna Letters, do not make the equation impossible. Moreover, contemporary Egyptian history under the Eighteenth Dynasty permits the 1441 B. C. date. (For the early date and its arguments, see Merrill F. Unger's *Archeology and the Old Testament*, 1954, pp. 140-148, and objections to the early date, pp. 149-152.)

The son and successor of Ramasses II, Merenptah, set up a victory stele. This important monument found in the pharoah's mortuary temple at Thebes, in twenty-eight closely packed lines of inscription, celebrates his triumph over his enemies. The first extra-Biblical mention of Israel occurs on this inscription. The concluding portion of the stela reads as follows:

Askelon is carried captive, Gezer is conquered.
Yanoam is made as though it did not exist.
The people of Israel is desolate; it has no offspring;
Palestine has become a widow for Egypt.
All lands are united; they are pacified,
Everyone that is turbulent is bound by King Merenptah, giving life like Re every day.

Other notable contacts with Egypt occur in the days of Solomon, who married an Egyptian princess, and in the days of Rehoboam, when Judah and also Israel, as Archaeology has shown, was overrun and plundered by Shishak. In the days of Jeremiah, on the eve of the fall of Jerusalem, the prophet denounced the people for leaning upon Egypt. After the fall of the city and the murder of Gedaliah, Jeremiah and a number of those left in the land migrated to Egypt. In later periods, after Alexander's conquests and death, numerous Jews settled in Egypt, notably in Alexandria, under the favorable treatment of the Ptolemies. *M. F. U.*

Egypt, River of. Present-day Wadi el-Arish is a wide, shallow stream-bed forming the southern boundary of Judah. It drains surplus water of the wet season from the Wilderness of Paran into the Mediterranean. It forms a line of demarcation between Sinai and Palestine (Num. 34:5). It is some 96 miles N. E. of Kantara, the point of crossing the Suez Canal into Egypt proper.

E'hi (ē'hi; *brotherly*), one of the "sons" of Benjamin (Gen. 46:21). He is probably the grandson called *Ahiram* (*q. v.*) in Num. 26:38. In the parallel passage (I Chron. 8:6) he seems to be called *Ehud* (*q. v.*).

E'hud (ē'hŭd).

1. A descendant of Benjamin, progenitor of one of the clans of Geba that removed to Manahath (I Chron. 8:6). He seems to be the same as Ahiram (Num. 26:38), and if so, Ahiram is probably the right name, as the family were called Ahiramites. In I Chron. 8:1 the same person seems to be called Aharah, and perhaps also Ahoah in v. 4; Ahiah, v. 7; and Aher, I Chron. 7:12.

2. The third named of the seven sons o Bilhan, the son of Jediael and grandson of the patriarch Jacob (I Chron. 7:10).

3. A judge of Israel, the son (descendant) of Gera, a Benjamite. The name Gera was hereditary among the Benjamites (Gen. 46:21; II Sam. 16:5; I Chron. 8:3, 5).

Personal History. Ehud was the second judge of Israel, or rather of that part of Israel which he delivered from the Moabites. (1) **Israel under Moab.** Israel having lapsed into

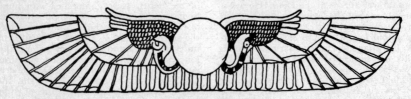

141. Winged Sun-Disk of Egypt, Symbol of the Sun-god, with Uraeus, the Sacred Snake on each side of Falconlike Wings

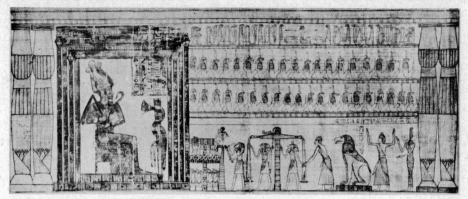

142. Judgment Scene, Weighing of the Heart

idolatry, the Lord strengthened Eglon, the king of Moab, against them. With the assistance of the Ammonites and the Amalekites he invaded the land and took Jericho (Judg. 3:12, 13) and held Israel under tribute eighteen years (B. C. c. 1314-1295.) (2) **Ehud slays Eglon.** Deputed by the children of Israel, Ehud brought a present (probably tribute) to Eglon. He departed with those who bore the gift, but, turning again at "the quarries (marg. *graven images*) that were by Gilgal," he presented himself before the king in his summer parlor. He secured the dismissal of the attendants by declaring that he had a "secret errand" unto Eglon. When they were alone, "Ehud said, I have a message from God unto thee," and the king rose to receive it with reverence. Immediately Ehud, who was left-handed, drew a dagger from his right thigh and plunged it so deeply into Eglon's abdomen that the fat closed upon the hilt and Ehud could not withdraw it. Leaving the room, he locked the door and fled by way of the quarries into Seirath. (3) **Overcomes Moab.** Ehud now summoned the Israelites to Seirath, in the mountains of Ephraim. First taking the fords of Jordan, he fell upon the Moabites, defeating them with a loss of ten thousand of their best men. And so the land had rest for eighty years (Judg. 3:15-30).

NOTE—"The conduct of Ehud must be judged according to the spirit of those times, when it was thought allowable to adopt any means of destroying the enemy of one's nation. The treacherous assassination of the hostile king is not to be regarded as an act of the Spirit of God, and therefore is not set before us as an example." Beyond his commission as deliverer of Israel we do not suppose that God gave Ehud any special commands, but left him to the choice of such measures and plans of conquest as his own judgment and skill might devise.

E'ker (ē'kẽr; Lev. 25:47), the youngest of the three sons of Ram, the grandson of Hezron (I Chron. 2:27).

Ek'ron (ĕk'rŏn; *extermination*), a city of the Philistines, about eleven miles from Gath. It belonged successively to Judah (Josh. 13:3) and Dan (Josh. 19:43) and to the Philistines (I Sam. 5:10). Here the ark was carried (I Sam. 5:10; 6:1-8). The fly god was worshipped here (II Kings 1:2). Robinson found its site at *Akir*, ten miles N. E. of Ashdod.

Ek'ronite (ĕk'rŏn-īt; Josh. 13:3; I Sam. 5:10),

an inhabitant of the Philistine city of *Ekron* (*q. v.*).

El (ĕl). This is a name by which God is called in the Old Testament—*El*, the God Elohim of Israel (Gen. 33:20). In prose it occurs more frequently with the modifier—*El Elyon* ("the Most High God" Gen. 14:18), *El Shaddai* ("God Almighty," Gen. 17:1), *El Hai* ("the Living God," Josh. 3:10), very commonly the plural of majesty *Elohim*. In poetry *el* is very common. The word often stands alone without any adjunct (Psa. 18:31; 33:48; 68:21; Job 8:3). *El* is a generic name for God in Northwest Semitic (Hebrew and Ugaritic), and as such it is also employed in the Old Testament for heathen deities (Exod. 34:14; Psa. 81:10; Isa. 44:10). The original generic term was *'ilum*, which dropping the mimation and the nominative case ending "*u*" became *el* in Hebrew. The word is derived from the root *'wl*, "to be strong, powerful," meaning "the strong one." In Canaanite paganism as reflected in the Phoenician historian Philo of Byblos, c. 100 A. D., and particularly in the epic religious literature unearthed at Ras Shamra, ancient Ugarit in North Syria, 1929-1937, *El* was the head of the Canaanite pantheon. According to Philo, *El* had three wives who were also his sisters. This fluidity of relationship is in accordance with the general irrationality and moral grossness of Canaanite cults. According to Philo, El was a bloody tyrant who dethroned his own father, Uranus, murdered his favorite son and decapitated his own daughter. The Ugaritic poems present him also as a lustful, morbid character. Despite these crimes, El was considered the exalted "father of years" (*abu shanima*), the "father of man" (*abu adami*) and "father bull," that is, the progenitor of the gods. Like Homer's Zeus, El was the father of men and gods. The utter moral abandon of El, as well as that of his son, Baal, and his three sister-wives, who were patronesses of sex and war, point to the degrading effects of Canaanite religion and offer adequate moral explanation for the inflexibly stern attitude of the Old Testament toward the religion of the Canaanites and to the Canaanites themselves. The Ras Shamra literature speaks of Canaan as the "land of el," where this deity was absolute in authority over lesser gods. El rapidly declined, however, and was largely supplanted by the worship of Baal, which was equally demoralizing. The Hebrew name of God, El, has, of course, no connection with paganism, but is a simple generic term. *M. F. U.*

El′adah (ĕl′a-dȧ; *God has decked*), one of the sons (rather than later descendants, as the text seems to state) of Ephraim (I Chron. 7:20); perhaps the same as Elead (*q. v.*) of v. 21, since several of the names (*see* Tahath) in the list appear to be repeated.

E′lah (ē′lȧ; *oak*, any large *evergreen*).

1. One of the Edomitish "dukes," or chieftains, in Mount Seir (Gen. 36:41; I Chron. 1:52).

2. The father of Shimei, one of Solomon's purveyors (I Kings 4:18), B. C. after 960.

3. The son and successor of Baasha, king of Israel (I Kings 16:8-10). He reigned for only parts of two years (B. C. c. 877-876), and was then killed while drunk by Zimri, in the house of his steward Arza (in Tirzah), who was probably a confederate in the plot. He was the last king of Baasha's line, and by this catastrophe the predictions of the prophet Jehu (I Kings 16:1-4) were accomplished.

4. The father of Hoshea, last king of Israel (II Kings 15:30; 17:1), B. C. c. 732-724.

5. One of the three sons of Caleb, the son of Jephunneh (I Chron. 4:15), B. C. c. 1380. This passage ends with the words "even (or *and*) Kenaz," showing that a name had been dropped out before it (Keil, *Com.*).

6. The son of Uzzi, and one of the Benjamite heads of families who were taken into captivity (I Chron. 9:8), or rather, perhaps, returned from it and dwelt in Jerusalem, B. C. 536.

7. *Vale of Elah.* Located eleven miles S. W. from Jerusalem, the scene of Goliath's death at the hands of David (I Sam. 17:2; 21:9). It is the modern Wady es-Sunt, or valley of the acacia tree. Its entrance from the Philistine plain is commanded by the famous Tell-es-Sâfiyeh.

E′lam (ē′lăm; *hidden*).

1. The first named of the sons of Shem (Gen. 10:22; I Chron. 1:17). His descendants probably settled in that part of Persia which was afterward frequently called by this name.

2. A chief man of the tribe of Benjamin, one of the sons of Shashak, resident at Jerusalem at the captivity or on the return (I Chron. 8:24), B. C. 536.

3. A Korhite Levite, fifth son of Meshelemiah who was one of the porters of the tabernacle in the time of David (I Chron. 26:3), B. C. 1000.

4. The progenitor of a family who returned with Zerubbabel (B. C. 536) to the number of twelve hundred and fifty-four (Ezra 2:7; Neh. 7:12). A further detachment of seventy-one men came with Ezra (Ezra 8:7). It was, probably, one of this family, Shechaniah, son of Jehiel, who encouraged Ezra in his efforts against the indiscriminate marriages of the people (Ezra 10:2), and six of the "sons of Elam" accordingly put away their foreign wives (Ezra 10:26).

5. In the same lists is a second Elam, whose sons, to the same number as in the former

case, returned with Zerubbabel (Ezra 2:31; Neh. 7:34), and which, for the sake of distinction, is called "the other Elam." "The coincidence of numbers is curious, and also suspicious, as arguing an accidental repetition of the foregoing name" (Smith, *Dict.*, s. v.).

6. One of the chiefs of the people who signed the covenant with Nehemiah (Neh. 10:14), B. C. 445.

7. One of the priests who accompanied Nehemiah and took part in the dedication of the new wall of Jerusalem (Neh. 12:42), B. C. 445.

E′lam (ē′lăm; Hebrew '*ēlām*, Akkadian *elamtu, highland*), the land beyond the Tigris and E. of Babylonia, bounded on the N. by Assyria and Media and on the S. by the Persian Gulf. Its capital was the very ancient city of Susa, O. T. Shushan. Elam was the center of a very ancient political power. Eannatum of Lagash was the first known person of history to mention Elam. He claims to have conquered it, but not much later under one of his successors, the Elamites plundered Lagash. The great Sargon of Agade styled himself "conqueror of Elam." His successor, Naram-Sin, mastered the entire land of Elam. As the result of the victories of this great Semitic dynasty of Agade, (c. 2400-2200 B. C.) the Elamites were kept in subjection for over 300 years. After the destruction of the Third Dynasty of Ur, c. 1960, Kudur Mabuk became master of Larsa and was succeeded by his sons, Warad-Sin and Rim-Sin. The great Hammurabi defeated Rim-Sin. Later on an Elamite conqueror carried the Code of Hammurabi to Susa, where it was recovered in 1901-2. In the Abrahamic era, Chedorlaomer, king of Elam, was powerful in Lower Babylonia and conquered even the country on the Jordan (Gen. 14:1-11). In the eighth and seventh centuries B. C. the mighty Assyrian empire intermittently had to struggle with the troublesome Elamites. About 645 B. C. Susa was taken. The Chaldeans conquered the Elamites (cf. Ezek. 32:24). Shushan became a capital of the Persian Empire. Some Elamites were forcibly settled in Samaria and joined in harrassing the Jews in their attempts to rebuild the temple (Ezra 4:9). Elamites were prominently present on the Day of Pentecost, when the Holy Spirit came (Acts 2:9). *M.F.U.*

E′lamites (ē′la-mīts; Ezra 4:9, Acts 2:9), the original inhabitants of the country called Elam; they were descendants of Shem, and perhaps received their name from an actual man, Elam (Gen. 10:22).

El′asah (ĕl′a-sȧ; *God has made*).

1. One of the sons of Pashur, a priest, who renounced his Gentile wife, whom he had married during the captivity or after (Ezra 10:22), B. C. 457.

2. The son of Shaphan, one of the two men who were sent on a mission by King Zedekiah to Nebuchadnezzar at Babylon. They at the same time took charge of the letter to Jeremiah the prophet to the captives in Babylon (Jer. 29:3), B. C. about 593.

E′lath (ē′lăth, ē′lŏth; *great trees*), a site located on the N. E. end of the Gulf of Aqabah. On their northward trek from Sinai Israelites passed Elath (Deut. 2:8) which was then a tiny village E. of the later Eloth and which was beside Ezion-geber. Ezion-geber, modern Tell el Keleifeh excavated by Nelson Glueck, lay E. of Elath, but from the tenth to the fifth century B. C. the place was known as Ezion-geber, later as Elath. Solomon gave Ezion-geber prominence by constructing a naval base and a copper smelting center there. Because of its strategic location it passed back and forth between Edomites and Jews in the two centuries between David and Uzziah (II Kings 14:33; 16:6). It was also a strategic stopping place for caravans coming from Arabia. *M. F. U.*

El-Beth′el (the *God of Bethel*), the name given by Jacob to the altar which he erected at Beth-el on his return from Laban (Gen. 35:7). It was built in memory of God's appearance to him in the vision of the "ladder" (Gen. 28:12, sq.; 35:7).

El′daah (ĕl′dä; *God of knowledge*), the last named of the five sons of Midian, Abraham's son by Keturah (Gen. 25:4; I Chron. 1:33), B. C. after 2,000.

El′dad (ĕl′dăd; *God has loved*), one of the seventy elders appointed to assist Moses in the administration of justice, B. C. c.1440. These elders were assembled before the door of the tabernacle and received the spirit of prophecy from God (Num. 11:24, 25). Eldad is mentioned along with Medad, another elder, as having received the same gift, although for some reason they were not with the other elders, but remained in the camp. A young man brought word to Moses that these two persons were prophesying in the camp, and Joshua entreated Moses to forbid them. But Moses replied: "Enviest thou for my sake? Would God that all the Lord's people were prophets, and that the Lord would put his Spirit upon them!" (Num. 11:26-29). The *mode* of prophesying, in the case of Eldad and Medad, was probably the extempore production of hymns chanted forth to the people. Compare the case of Saul (I Sam. 10:11).

Elder (Heb. *zäqēn, old*; Gr. *presbuteros, older;* Eng. *presbyter*). In early times books were scarce, and the aged of the tribes were the depositories of the traditions of bygone generations. The old men, moreover, had most experience and were the heads of large families, over whom they exercised supreme authority. Great reverence was paid to the aged among the Hebrews and other nations (Lev. 19:32; Deut. 32:7; Job 12:12; Prov. 16:31). Identifying old age with matured wisdom, knowledge, and experience, and as a reward for a virtuous and godly life, the aged were from time immemorial chosen to fill the official positions in the community. The name *elder* came to be used as the designation for the office itself.

1. **In the Old Testament** the term elder is applied to various offices; to Eliezer, who is described as the "eldest servant" (R. V. *elder,* i. e., *major-domo,* Gen. 24:2); the officers of Pharaoh's household (Gen. 50:7), and David's head servants (II Sam. 12:17). "The ancients of Gebal" (Ezek. 27:9) are understood to be the *master workmen.* The elders of Egypt (Gen. 50:7) were probably the state officers, and the term as denoting a political

office applied not only to the Hebrews and Egyptians, but also to the Moabites and Midianites (Num. 22:7). "According to patriarchal custom the fathers, standing by the right of birth (primogeniture) at the head of the several tribes and divisions of tribes, regulated the relations of the tribes and clans, punished offenses and crimes, and administered law and equity. Thus from the heads of tribes, clans, and families proceeded the *elders,* who, even before the time of Moses, formed the superiors of the people. For Moses and Aaron, on their arrival in Egypt, gathered the elders of Israel to announce to the people their divine commission to lead them out of the bondage of Egypt (Exod. 3:16, 18; 4:29)." They accompanied Moses in his first interview with Pharaoh (Exod. 3:18); through them Moses gave his communications and commands to the people (Exod. 19:7; Deut. 31:9); they were his immediate attendants in all the great transactions in the wilderness (Exod. 17:5); seventy of them accompanied Moses to Sinai (Exod. 24:1), when they were called *nobles.* Seventy of them were also appointed to bear the burden of government with Moses (Num. 11:16, 17). As in the legislation of Moses certain things were committed to the charge of the elders of each particular city (Deut. 19: 12; 21:3, etc.), it was clearly implied that the people, on their settlement in Canaan, were expected to appoint persons ("elders"), who would see that divine regulations were executed in the several districts (see Josh. 20:4; Judg. 8:16; Ruth 4:2, etc.). In the Psalms and the prophets elders are spoken of as a distinct class, with an official character, and occupying a somewhat separate position (Psa. 107: 32; Lam. 2:10; Ezek. 14:1, etc.). After the return from the Exile the office rose into higher significance and fuller organization. With every synagogue (*q. v.*) there was connected a government of elders, varying in numbers according to the population attached to it. The rulers of the synagogue and the elders of the people were substantially one, and a certain number of those elders belonged to the *Sanhedrin* (*q. v.*).

2. **In the New Testament** they were associated sometimes with the chief priests (Matt. 21:23), sometimes with the chief priests and scribes (Matt. 16:21), or the council (Matt. 26:59), always taking an active part in the management of public affairs. Luke speaks of the whole order by the collective term of eldership (Gr. *presbuterion,* Luke 22:26; Acts 22:5). There is no specific account given of the origin of the eldership in the apostolic Church. We find officers called interchangeably *elders* or presbyters and *bishops* (Gr. *episkopos, superintendent*). This office pertained to local congregations and was extended as the churches multiplied, and was distinguished from that of deacon. Elders first came into prominence on the scattering abroad of the disciples and the withdrawing of the apostles from Jerusalem, following the death of Stephen. They were associated with James to give direction to the affairs of the church, and appear to have been a well-known and established class of officials (Acts 11:30), and come

into greater prominence in association with the apostles (Acts 15:2). With the "brethren" they constituted the council at Jerusalem to which was referred the circumcision, and united with the apostles and the church in sending delegates to Antioch and other churches, who should convey the decision of the council (Acts 15:22, 23). When Paul visits Jerusalem for the last time he betakes himself to James, the president, where he finds all the elders assembled (Acts 21:18, sq.). The "elders" of the New Testament Church were the "pastors" (Eph. 4:11), "bishops or overseers" (Acts 20:28, etc.), "leaders" and "rulers" (Heb. 13:7; I Thess. 5:12, etc.) of the flock. They were also the regular teachers of the congregation, whose duty it was to expound the Scriptures and administer the sacraments (I Tim. 3:2; Tit. 1:9). The Jewish Christians, following the pattern of the synagogue as well as of political administration of cities, which was vested in a senate or college, readily adopted the *presbytery*. Consequently we meet it everywhere in the plural, and as a corporation at Jerusalem (Acts 11:30; 15:4, 6, 23; 21:18), at Ephesus (20:17, 28), at Philippi (Phil. 1:1), at the ordination of Timothy (I Tim. 4:14, etc.).

"The essential identity of presbyters and bishops in the apostolic age is a matter of well nigh absolute historic demonstration. The same officers of the church of Ephesus are alternately called presbyters and bishops. Paul sends greetings to the bishops and deacons of Philippi, but omits the presbyters because they were included in the first term, as also the plural indicates. In the pastoral epistles, when Paul intends to give the qualifications for all church officers he again mentions two, bishops and deacons, but the term presbyters afterward for bishops. Peter urges the presbyters to 'tend the flock of God, and to fulfill the office of bishops,' with disinterested devotion and without lording it over the charge allotted them. The interchange of terms continued in use to the close of the 1st century, as is evident from the epistle of Clement of Rome (about A. D. 95), and still lingered toward the close of the second" (Schaff, *Hist. Christ. Church*). The reason of the use of two terms for persons having the same essential functions has given rise to much discussion.

Two general suggestions have been made: (1) The term presbyter has been claimed to be of Jewish derivation, and to have been used at first only by Jewish-Christian congregations. In communities where a Christian church had sprung from the bosom of a local synagogue, and was therefore chiefly under the control of Jewish tradition and thought, the term presbyter, which was the name of the governing body of the synagogue, would be naturally transferred to officers of similar function in the Christian societies. It is likewise true that the term "bishop" is used to designate one of like official duty in the churches of almost exclusively Gentile origin. (2) A second theory is that the bishop of the Christian Church was analogous in office and function to that of the president of the heathen fraternities or clubs. To administer the funds of these organiza-

tions became a matter of primary importance, and the officer charged with this duty was termed an *episcopos*.

The peculiar environment of the first Christian believers compelled like provision for the exercise of systematic charities. Most of the early disciples were of the poorer class, and many more, upon profession of the Christian faith, became outcasts from their families and homes.

3. **In the Modern Church.** (1) In the Roman Catholic Church, the Church of England, and the Protestant Episcopal Church "priest" is generally used instead of "presbyter" or "elders," to designate the second order in the ministry (the three orders being bishops, priests, and deacons). (2) In the Methodist Church only two orders of ministers are recognized, elders and deacons, the bishop being chosen (*primus inter pares*) as superintendent. (3) Among Congregationalist and all Churches having the presbyterian form of government the two orders of elders and deacons are recognized. Among Presbyterians there are two classes of elders, viz., teaching elders (pastors) and ruling elders (laymen).

El'ead (ĕl'ē-ăd; *God has testified*), a descendant of Ephraim (I Chron. 7:21), but whether through *Shuthelah* (*q. v.*), or a son of the patriarch (the second Shuthelah being taken as a repetition of the first, and Ezer and Elead as his brothers), is not determined.

Elea'leh (ē-lē-ā'lĕ; *God has ascended*), a town of the Amorites, in the country east of the Jordan, in the tribe of Reuben (Num. 32:3-37). Prophetic threats were uttered against it (Isa. 15:4; 17:9; Jer. 48:34). The present El-Al, about a mile N. from Heshbon, marks the site.

Ele'asah (ĕl-ē-ē'á-sà), more properly *Elasah* (*q. v.*).

1. The son of Helez, one of the descendants of Judah, of the family of Hezron (I Chron. 2:39).

2. Son of Rapha, or Rephaiah, a descendant of Saul through Jonathan and Meribbaal, or Mephibosheth (I Chron. 8:37; 9:43), B. C. after 1030.

Elea'zer (ĕl-ē-ā'zẽr; *God is helper*), a common name among the Hebrews.

1. The high priest. The third son of Aaron by Elisheba, daughter of Amminadab (Exod. 6:23; 38:1). He married a daughter of Putiel, who bore him Phinehas (6:25), B. C. c. 1440. (1) **Succeeds to priesthood.** After the death of Nadab and Abihu without children (Lev. 10:1; Num. 3:4), Eleazar was appointed chief over the principal Levites, to have the oversight of those who had charge of the sanctuary (Num. 3:32). After the destruction of Korah and his company, Eleazar gathered up their censers out of the fire to make plates for a covering of the altar of burnt offering (16:37-39). With his brother Ithamar he ministered as a priest during their father's lifetime. (2) **As high priest.** Immediately before the death of Aaron Moses went with them both unto Mount Hor, where he invested Eleazar with the sacred garments, as the successor of Aaron in the office of high priest (Num. 20:25-29), B. C. about 1402. One of his first duties was, in conjunction with Moses, to

superintend the census of the people (26:1-4). He also assisted at the inauguration of Joshua (27:18-23) and at the division of the spoil taken from the Midianites (31:21). After the conquest of Canaan he took part in the division of the land (Josh. 14:1). The time of his death is not mentioned in Scripture. Josephus says that it took place about the same time as Joshua's, twenty-five years after the death of Moses. The high priesthood is said to have remained in the family of Eleazar until the time of Eli, into whose family, for some reason unknown, it passed until it was restored to the family of Eleazar in the person of Zadok (I Sam. 2:27; I Chron. 6:8; 24:3; I Kings 2:27) (Smith, s. v.).

2. An inhabitant of Kirjath-jearim, who was set apart by his fellow-townsmen to attend upon the ark while it remained in the house of his father, Abinadab, after it had been returned to the Hebrews by the Philistines (I Sam. 7:1, 2), B. C. before 1030. It is not stated that Eleazar was a Levite; but this is very probable, because otherwise they would hardly have consecrated him to be the keeper of the ark, but would have chosen a Levite for the purpose.

3. The son of Dodo the Ahohite, that is, possibly, a descendant of Ahoah, of the tribe of Benjamin (I Chron. 8:4), one of the three most eminent of David's thirty-seven heroes, who "fought till his hand was weary" in maintaining with David and the other two a daring stand after "the men of Israel had gone away." He was also one of the same three when they broke through the Philistine host to gratify David's longing for a drink of water from the well of his native Bethlehem (II Sam. 23:9, 17; I Chron. 11:12), B. C. about 998.

4. A Levite, son of Mahli, and grandson of Merari (B. C. after 1400). He is mentioned as having had only daughters, who were married by their "brethren," i. e., cousins (I Chron. 23:21, 22; 24:28).

5. The son of Phineas, and associated with the priests and Levites in taking charge of the sacred treasure and vessels restored to Jerusalem after the Exile (Ezra 8:33), B. C. about 457. It is not definitely stated, however, whether he was a priest or even a Levite.

6. One of the descendants of Parosh, an Israelite (i. e., layman) who, on returning from Babylon, renounced the Gentile wife whom he had married (Ezra 10:25), B. C. 456.

7. One of those who encompassed the walls of Jerusalem on their completion (Neh. 12:42), B. C. 445. He is probably the same as No. 5.

8. The son of Eliud, in the genealogy of Jesus Christ (Matt. 1:15).

Elect (Heb. *bāhîr, chosen*), and so rendered in II Sam. 21:6), used to denote those selected by God for special office, work, honor, etc. (Isa. 42:1; 45:4; 65:9, 22). The term was sometimes applied in the Early Church (1) to the whole body of baptized Christians; (2) to the highest class of catechumens *elected* to baptism; (3) and to the newly baptized, as especially admitted to the full privileges of the profession.

Election (Gr. *eklogē, choice,* a *picking out*).

1. **Bible Meaning.** This word in the Scriptures has three distinct applications. (1) To the divine choice of nations or communities for the possession of special privileges with reference to the performance of special services. Thus the Jews were "a chosen nation," "the elect." Thus also in the New Testament bodies of Christian people, or churches, are called "the elect." (2) The divine choice of individuals to a particular office or work. Thus Cyrus was elected of God to bring about the rebuilding of the temple. Thus the twelve were chosen to be apostles, and Paul to be the apostle to the Gentiles. (3) The divine choice of individuals to be the children of God, and therefore heirs of heaven.

It is with regard to election in this third sense that theological controversies have been frequent and at times most fierce. Calvinists hold that the election of individuals to salvation is absolute, unconditional, by virtue of an eternal divine decree. Arminians regard election as conditional upon repentance and faith; the decree of God is that all who truly repent of their sins and believe on the Lord Jesus Christ shall be saved. But every responsible person determines for himself whether or not he will repent and believe. Sufficient grace is bestowed upon everyone to enable him to make the right decision.

2. **The Calvinistic View.** The Westminster Confession, the standard of the Church of Scotland, and of the various Presbyterian Churches of Europe and America, contains the following statement: "God from all eternity did by the most wise and holy counsel of his own free will freely and unchangeably ordain whatsoever comes to pass; yet so as thereby neither is God the author of sin, nor is violence offered to the will of the creatures, nor is the liberty or contingency of second causes taken away, but rather established. Although God knows whatsoever may or can come to pass upon all supposed conditions, yet hath he not decreed anything because he foresaw its future, or as that which would come to pass upon such conditions. By the decree of God, for the manifestation of his glory some men and angels are predestinated unto everlasting life and others foreordained to everlasting death. These angels and men, thus predestinated and foreordained are particularly and unchangeably designed, and their number is so certain and definite that it cannot be either increased or diminished. Those of mankind that are predestinated unto life, God, before the foundation of the world was laid, according to his eternal and immutable purpose, and the secret counsel and good pleasure of his will, hath chosen in Christ unto everlasting glory, out of his mere free grace and love, without any foresight of faith, or good works, or perseverance in either of them, or any other thing in the creature, as conditions or causes moving him thereto; and all to the praise of his glorious grace. As God hath appointed the elect unto glory, so hath he, by the eternal and most free purpose of his will, foreordained all the means thereunto. Therefore, they who are elected, being fallen in Adam, are redeemed by Christ, are effectu-

ally called unto faith in Christ, by his Spirit working in due season; are justified, adopted, sanctified, and kept by his power through faith unto salvation. Neither are any other redeemed by Christ, effectually called, justified, adopted, sanctified, and saved, but the elect only. The rest of mankind God was pleased, according to the unsearchable counsel of his own will, whereby he extendeth or withholdeth mercy, as he pleaseth, for the glory of his sovereign power over his creatures, to pass by, and to ordain them to dishonor and wrath for their sin, to the praise of his glorious justice."

In support of this doctrine it is argued by Calvinistic theologians: (1) that according to the Scriptures election is not of works but of grace; and that it is not of works means that it is not what man does that determines whether he is to be one of the elect or not. For the descendants of Adam this life is not a probation. They stood their probation in Adam, and do not stand each one for himself. (2) That the sovereignty of God in electing men to salvation is shown by the fact that repentance and faith are gifts from God. These fruits of his Spirit are the consequences and signs of election and not its conditions. (3) The salvation which is of grace must be of grace throughout. The element of works or human merit must not be introduced at any point in the plan. And this would be the case if repentance and faith were the conditions of election. (4) That the system of doctrine called Calvinistic, Augustinian, Pauline, should not be thus designated. That though taught clearly by Paul, particularly in Rom. 8:9, it was taught also by others of the writers of sacred scripture, and by Christ himself. Reference is made to Matt. 11:25, 26; Luke 4:25-27; 8:10; John 6:37, 39, et al. (5) That the sovereignty of God is evidenced in dispensing saving grace is illustrated also in his establishing the temporal conditions of mankind. Some are born and reared in the surroundings of civilization, others of barbarism. And precisely so some are blessed with the light of the Gospel, while others, dwelling in pagan lands, are deprived of that light, and consequently are not saved.

This system of strict Calvinism above outlined has received various modifications by theologians of the Calvinistic school. The General Assembly of the Presbyterian Church in the United States of America, May, 1903, adopted the following: "We believe that all who die in infancy, and all others given by the Father to the Son who are beyond the reach of the outward means of grace, are regenerated and saved by Christ through the Spirit, who works when and where and how he pleases."

3. **The Arminian View.** The Arminian view of election has been in recent years more generally accepted than formerly, even among denominations whose teachings have been Calvinistic or indefinite upon this point. This view grounds itself, in opposition to Calvinism, upon the universality of the Atonement and the graciously restored freedom of the human will. Election, accordingly, is not absolute but conditional, contingent upon the proper acceptance of such gifts of grace as God by his Spirit and providence puts within the reach of men. Inasmuch as this subject involves the character and method of the divine government and the destiny of the entire race, it should be said: (1) That according to the Arminian doctrine the purpose of God to redeem mankind was bound up with his purpose to create. The Lamb of God was "slain from the foundation of the world." God would not have permitted a race of sinners to come into existence without provision to save sinners. Such provision must not be for only a part but for the whole of the fallen race. To suppose the contrary is opposed to the divine perfections. To doom to eternal death any number of mankind who were born in sin and without sufficient remedy would be injustice. (2) The benefits of the Atonement are universal and in part unconditional. They are unconditional with respect to those who, through no fault of their own, are in such a mental or moral condition as to make it impossible for them either to accept or reject Christ. A leading denomination emphasizes the doctrine that "All children, by virtue of the unconditional benefits of the Atonement, are members of the kingdom of God." This principle extends to others besides children, both in heathen and Christian lands. God alone is competent to judge of the extent to which, in varying degrees, human beings are responsible, and therefore of the extent to which the unconditional benefits of the Atonement may be applied. (3) The purpose or decree of God is to save all who do not, actually or implicitly, willfully reject the saving offices of the Lord Jesus Christ. Among those who have not heard the Gospel may exist "the spirit of faith and the purpose of righteousness." Thus virtually even those who have no knowledge of the historic Christ determine whether or not they will be saved through Christ. They to whom the Gospel is preached have higher advantages and more definite responsibilities. To them repentance toward God and faith in the Lord Jesus Christ are the conditions of salvation. (4) Upon all men God bestows some measure of his grace, restoring to the depraved will freedom sufficient to enable them to accept Christ and be saved. Thus, in opposition to Calvinists, Arminians assert that not only was Adam, but also his depraved descendants are in a stage of probation.

In behalf of this doctrine it is argued: (1) That the whole trend of the Scriptures is to declare the real responsibility of men, and their actual power to choose between life and death. (2) That the Scriptures explicitly teach that it is the will of God that all men should be saved. Only those perish who wickedly resist his will (I Tim. 2:4; 4:10; John 5:40; Acts 7:51, et al.). (3) The Scriptures declare the universality of Christ's Atonement, and in some degree the universality of its benefits (Heb. 2:9; John 1:29; 3:16, 17; I Cor. 15:22; Rom. 5:18, 19), and many other passages. (4) The doctrine of unconditional election necessarily implies that of unconditional reprobation; and that is to charge God with cruelty. (5) That unconditional election necessarily implies also the determinate number of the elect, a point which Calvinists hold, though they admit that they have for it no explicit teaching of Scripture. To the contrary, the Scriptures not only generally but particularly teach that the number of the elect can be increased or diminished. This is the purport of all those passages in which sinners are exhorted to repent, or believers warned against becoming apostate, or to "make" their "calling and election sure" (Matt. 24:4, 13; II Pet. 1:11, et al.). (6) That the Scriptures never speak of impenitent and unbelieving men as elect, as in some cases it would be proper to do if election were antecedent to repentance and faith, and not conditioned thereby. (7) That the whole theory of unconditional election is of the same tendency with fatalism. (8) That the logic of unconditional election is opposed to true evangelism. (9) That the essential features of the Arminian doctrine of election belong to the primitive and truly historic doctrine of the Church. Augustine was the first prominent teacher of unconditional election, and he, regardless of the logical inconsistency, granted that reprobation is not unconditional. This doctrine of Augustine was first formally accepted by the Church in A. D. 529, in the Canons of the Council of Orange, approved by Pope Boniface II. The prominency of unconditional election in the theology of Protestanism is due largely to the influence and work of John Calvin, who, at the age of twenty-five, wrote his *Institutes*, in which he not only set forth the Augustinian doctrine of unconditional election, but also taught unconditional reprobation. John Wesley, and his followers were responsible in a large degree for reviving and developing the doctrine of Arminius.

The limits of this article do not permit an examination of the contested passages of Scripture. For this, recourse must be had by the general reader to works of systematic theology and to the commentaries. For best presentation of the Calvinistic view of recent years, see Hodge, *Systematic Theology;* for Arminianism or Methodist view, see Watson, *Institutes;* Miley, *Systematic Theology;* Whedon, *On the Will;* Whedon, *Commentary on Romans;* Wesley. *Sermons*, particularly sermons 54, 62, 63. 64.—*E. McC.*

El'-elo'he-Is'rael (ĕl'ĕ-lō'hĕ-ĭz'rȧ-ĕl; the *mighty God of Israel*). Jacob called by this name an altar pitched before Shechem (Gen. 33:20) in accordance with his vow (28:21) to give glory to the "God of Israel."

Elements (Gr. *stoicheion, orderly*), the component parts of the physical universe. "The elements shall melt with fervent heat" (II Pet. 3:10, 12), i. e., reduced to as confused a chaos as that from which it was first created.

Figurative. The term is used figuratively of the elementary parts of religion (Heb. 5:12, "first principles"), the elements of religious training, or the ceremonial precepts common alike to the worship of the Jews and Gentiles (Gal. 4:3, 9); the ceremonial requirements, especially of Jewish tradition (Col. 2:8, 20). In Galatians and Colossians the word is rendered "rudiments." These types, "weak" and "beggarly," were suited to a condition of

comparative childhood, in which appeals must be made to the senses.

E'leph (ĕ'lĕf; *ox*), one of the towns allotted to Benjamin and mentioned in the second group of fourteen towns (Josh. 18:28). "Robinson (ii, p. 139) is, no doubt, correct in supposing it to be the present *Neby Samvil* (i. e., prophet, Samuel), two hours N. W. of Jerusalem" (K. and D., *Com.*).

Elephant. *See* Animal Kingdom.

Elha'nan (ĕl-hā'năn; *God is gracious*).

1. A distinguished warrior in the time of King David, who performed a memorable exploit against the Philistines, though in what that exploit exactly consisted and who the hero himself was it is not easy to determine (B. C. about 989). II Sam. 21:19 says that he was the "son of Jaare Oregim, the Bethlehemite," and that he "slew Goliath, the Gittite, the staff of whose spear was like a weaver's beam." In the A. V. the words "the brother of" are inserted to bring the passage into agreement with I Chron. 20:5, which states that "Elhanan, son of Jair [or Joar], slew Lahmi, the brother of Goliath, the Gittite, the staff of whose spear," etc. Of these two statements the latter is correct, the former containing a textual corruption, see E. Young, *Introduction to the O. T.* (1949), p. 182.

2. The name Elhanan also occurs as that of "the son of Dodo" (II Sam. 23:24; I Chron. 11:26), where he is given as one of "the thirty of David's guard." Perhaps his father had both names. "This Elhanan is not the same as the one mentioned above" (Keil, *Com.*).

E'li (ē'lī; *high*, i. e., God is high).

1. **Name and Family.** Eli was descended from Aaron through Ithamar (Lev. 10:1, 2, 12), as appears from the fact that Abiathar, who was certainly a lineal descendant of Eli (I Kings 2:27), had a son, Ahimelech, who is expressly stated to have been "of the sons of Ithamar" (I Chron. 24:3; comp. II Sam. 8:17).

2. **Personal History.** (1) **High Priest.** Eli is generally supposed to have been the first of the line of Ithamar who held the office of high priest (Josephus, *Ant.*, v, 11, 2). How the office ever came into the younger branch of the house of Aaron we are not informed, but it is very evident that it was no unauthorized usurpation on the part of Eli (I Sam. 2:27-30). (2) **Judge.** Eli also acted as judge of Israel, being the immediate predecessor of Samuel (I Sam. 7:6, 15-17), the last of the judges. He was also the first judge who was of priestly descent, and is said to have judged Israel forty years (4:18). (3) **His sons.** His sons, Hophni and Phineas, conducted themselves so outrageously that they excited deep disgust among the people and rendered the services of the temple odious in their eyes (I Sam. 2:12-17, 22). Of this misconduct Eli was aware, but contented himself with mild and ineffectual remonstrances (2:23, 24) where his station required severe and vigorous action (3:13). (4) **Prophetic warnings.** A prophet was sent to announce the destruction of the house of Eli, as a sign of which both his sons should be slain in one day; a faithful priest should be raised up in his place, and those who remained of Eli's house should come crouching

to him with the prayer to be put into one of the priest's offices to earn a morsel of bread (I Sam. 2-27-36). Another warning was sent to Eli by the mouth of the youthful Samuel (3:11-18). (5) **Death.** At last the Israelites rose against the Philistines, but were defeated near Eben-ezer. They then took the ark of the covenant into the camp, hoping thereby to secure the help of God; but in a succeeding engagement they suffered a still greater defeat, in which Eli's sons were slain. When tidings were brought to Eli that Israel was defeated—that his sons were slain, that the ark of God was taken—"he fell from off the seat backward by the side of the gate, and his neck brake, and he died: for he was an old man, ninety-eight years, and heavy" (I Sam. 4), B. C. about 1050. The final judgment upon Eli's house was accomplished when Solomon removed Abiathar from his office and restored the line of Eleazar in the person of Zadok (I Kings 2:27).

3. **Character.** The recorded history of Eli presents to us the character of Eli in three different aspects: (1) **The devoted high priest.** He takes particular interest in Hannah when he understands her sorrows and bestows upon her his priestly benediction (I Sam. 1:17; 2:20). He recognizes the divine message and bows in humble submission to the prophecy of his downfall (3:8, 18) and shows his profound devotion to God by his anxiety for the ark and his sudden fall and death at the tidings of its capture. We can find in him no indication of hypocrisy or lack of faith in God. (2) **As judge.** The fact that he judged Israel seems to prove that his administration was, on the whole, careful and just. But his partiality appears when his own sons are the offenders. (3) **As father.** Eli let his paternal love run away with his judgment; his fondness for his sons restrained him from the exercise of proper parental authority.

Eli'ab (ē-lī'ăb; *God is father*).

1. A son of Helon and the captain of the tribe of Zebulun who assisted Moses in numbering the people (Num. 1:9; 2:7; 10:16), B. C. about 1440. He is mentioned (7:24-29) as presenting the offering of his tribe at the dedication of the tabernacle.

2. A Reubenite, son of Pallu (or Phallu), whose family was one of the principal in the tribe, and father or progenitor of Dathan and Abiram, the leaders in the revolt against Moses (Num. 16:1, 12; 26:8, 9; Deut. 11:6), B. C. c. 1425. Eliab had another son, Nemuel (Num. 26:9).

3. The eldest brother of David (I Chron. 2:13) and first of the sons of Jesse who was presented to Samuel when he came to Bethlehem to anoint a king (I Sam. 16:6), B. C. about 1013. Eliab, with his two next younger brethren, was in the army of Saul when threatened by Goliath; and it was he who made the contemptuous inquiry, with which he sought to screen his own cowardice, when David proposed to fight the Philistine, "With whom hast thou left those few sheep in the wilderness?" (17:28). His daughter Abihail married her second cousin, Rehoboam, and bore him three children (II Chron. 11:18, 19). Eliab is supposed to be the same as Elihu.

"of the brethren of David" (I Chron. 27:18).

4. An ancestor of Samuel the prophet, being a Kohathite Levite, son of Nahath and father of Jeroham (I Chron. 6:27). In the other statements of the genealogy this name appears to be given as Elihu (I Sam. 1:1) and Eliel (I Chron. 6:34).

5. A valiant man of the Gadites, who joined David in the stronghold in the wilderness (I Chron. 12:9).

6. A Levite, who was one of the second rank of those appointed to conduct the music of the sanctuary in the time of David and whose part was to play on the psaltery. He also served as "porter," i. e., a doorkeeper (I Chron. 15:18, 20; 16:5), B. C. about 986.

Eli'ada (ē-lī'á-dá; *God is knowing*).

1. One of the youngest sons of David, born at Jerusalem, the child (as it would seem) of one of his wives, and not of a concubine (II Sam. 5:16; I Chron. 3:8, 9), B. C. after 1000. In I Chron. 14:7 the name appears in the form *Beeliada* (whom the *master has known*). As to the difficulty of David's using a name which contained *Baal* for one of its elements it is, at least, very doubtful whether that word, which literally means *master, husband*, had in David's time acquired the bad sense which *Baal* worship in Israel afterward imparted to it (Kitto, s. v.).

2. The father of Regon, who fled from the service of Hadadezer, king of Zobah, and became a captain of Syrian marauders who annoyed Solomon during his reign (I Kings 11:23), B. C. after 960. The name is Anglicized *Eliadah*.

3. A Benjamite and mighty man of war, who led two hundred thousand archers of his tribe to the army of Jehoshaphat (II Chron. 17:17), B. C. 875.

Eli'adah (ē-lī'á-dá; I Kings 11:23), a less correct mode of Anglicizing the name *Eliada* (No. 2, supra).

Eli'ah (ē-lī'á; whose *God is Jehovah*), a less correct mode of Anglicizing the name Elijah.

1. One of the "sons of Jeroham," and head of a Benjamite family resident at Jerusalem (I Chron. 8:27).

2. One of the "sons of Elam," who divorced his Gentile wife on returning from the exile (Ezra 10:26), B. C. 456.

Eli'ahba (ē-lī'á-bá; *God will hide*), a Shaalbonite, one of David's thirty chief warriors (II Sam. 23:32; I Chron. 11:33), B. C. about 1000.

Eli'akim (ē-lī'á-kĭm; *God will establish*).

1. Son of Hilkiah and prefect of the palace of King Hezekiah (II Kings 18:18; 19:2). (1) **History.** He succeeded Shebna in this office after the latter had been ejected from it as a punishment for his pride (Isa. 22:15-20), B. C. after 719. He was one of the three persons sent by Hezekiah to receive the message of the invading Assyrians (II Kings 18:18; Isa. 36:3, 11, 22) and afterward to report it to Isaiah. (2) **Character.** Eliakim was a good man, as appears by the title emphatically applied to him by God, "My servant Eliakim" (Isa. 22:20), and as was shown by his conduct on the occasion of Sennacherib's invasion (II Kings 18; 19:1-5), and also in the discharge of the duties of his high station, in which he acted as

a "father to the inhabitants of Jerusalem and to the house of Judah" (Isa. 22:21).

NOTE—The office that Eliakim held has long been a subject of perplexity to commentators. The ancients, including the LXX and Jerome, understood it of the priestly office. But it is certain, from the description of the office in Isa. 22, and especially from the expression in v. 22, "The key of the house of David will I lay upon his shoulder," that it was the king's house, and not the house of God, of which Eliakim was made prefect (Smith, *Dict.*, s. v.; Delitzsch, *Com.*). Most commentators agree that Isa. 22:25 does not apply to him, but to Shebna. Delitzsch, however, says: "Eliakim himself is also brought down at last by the greatness of his power on account of the nepotism to which he has given way."

2. The original name of *Jehoiakim* (*q. v.*), king of Judah (II Kings 23:34; II Chron. 36:4).

3. A priest in the days of Nehemiah, who assisted at the dedication of the new wall of Jerusalem (Neh. 12:41), B. C. 445.

4. Son of Abiud and father of Azor, of the posterity of Zerubbabel (Matt. 1:13). He is probably identical with Shechaniah (I Chron. 3:21).

5. The son of Melea and father of Jonan, in the genealogy of Christ (Luke 3:30), probably the grandson of Nathan, of the private line of David's descent, B. C. considerably after 1000.

E'liam (ē'lĭ-ăm; *God of the people*).

1. The father of Bath-sheba, the wife of Uriah and afterward of David (II Sam. 11:3). In the list of I Chron. 3:5 the names of both father and daughter are altered, the former to *Ammiel* and the latter to *Bath-shua*.

2. Son of Ahithophel, the Gilonite, one of David's "thirty" warriors (II Sam. 23:34), B. C. about 1000. The name is omitted in the list of I Chron. 11, but is now probably discernible as "Ahijah the Pelonite." The ancient Jewish tradition, preserved by Jerome, is that the two Eliams are one and the same person (Smith, *Dict.*).

Eli'as (ê-lī'ăs), the Grecized form in which the name of *Elijah* is given in the A. V. of the Apocrypha and New Testament.

Eli'asaph (ê-lī'ȧ-săf; *God has added*).

1. The son of Deuel (or Reuel), head of the tribe of Gad at the time of the census in the wilderness of Sinai (Num. 1:14; 2:14; 7:42, 47; 10:20), B. C. about 1438.

2. The son of Lael, and chief of the family of Gershonite Levites (Num. 3:24).

Eli'ashib (ê-lī'ȧ-shĭb; *God will restore*), a common name of Israelites, especially in the latter period of the Old Testament history.

1. A son of Elioenai, one of the latest descendants of the royal family of Judah (I Chron. 3:24).

2. A priest in the time of King David, head of the eleventh "course" in the order of the "governors" of the sanctuary (I Chron. 24:12), B. C. about 989.

3. A Levitical singer who repudiated his Gentile wife after the exile (Ezra 10:24), B. C. 556.

4. An Israelite of the lineage of Zattu, who did the same (Ezra 10:27), B. C. 456.

5. An Israelite of the lineage of Bani, who did the same (Ezra 10:36), B. C. 456.

6. The high priest of the Jews in the time of Nehemiah (B. C. 445). With the assistance of his fellow-priests he rebuilt the eastern city wall adjoining the temple (Neh. 3:1). His own mansion was, doubtless, situated in the same vicinity (3:20, 21). Eliashib was related in some way to Tobiah the Ammonite, for whom he prepared an anteroom in the temple, a desecration which excited the pious indignation of Nehemiah (13:4, 7). One of the grandsons of Eliashib had also married the daughter of Sanballat the Horonite (13:28). There seems to be no reason to doubt that the same Eliashib is referred to in Ezra 10:6, as the father of Johanan, with whom Ezra consulted concerning the transgression of the people in taking Gentile wives. He is evidently the same as the son of Joiakim mentioned in the succession of high priests (Neh. 12:10, 22).

Eli'athah (ê-lī'ȧ-thȧ; *God has come*), the eighth named of the fourteen sons of the Levite Heman, and musician in the time of David (I Chron. 25:4). With twelve of his sons and brethren he had the twentieth division of the temple service (25:27), B. C. about 970.

Eli'dad (ê-lī'dăd; *God of his love*), son of Chislon, and a chief of the tribe of Benjamin who represented his tribe among the commissioners appointed to divide the promised land (Num. 34:21), B. C. c. 1390.

E'liel (ē'lĭ-ĕl; *God is God*).

1. One of the heads of the tribe of Manasseh, on the east of Jordan, a mighty man (I Chron. 5:24).

2. The son of Toah and father of Jeroham, ancestors of Heman, the singer and Levite (I Chron. 6:34); probably identical with the *Eliab* of v. 27, and of the *Elihu* of I Sam. 1:1.

3. One of the descendants of Shimhi, and head of a Benjamite family in Jerusalem (I Chron. 8:20).

4. One of the descendants of Shashak, and also head of a Benjamite family in Jerusalem (I Chron. 8:22).

5. "The Mahavite," and one of David's distinguished warriors (I Chron. 11:46), B. C. 991.

6. Another of the same guard, but without any express designation (I Chron. 11:47).

7. One of the Gadite heroes who came across Jordan and joined David in his stronghold in the wilderness (I Chron. 12:11); possibly the same as No. 5 or 6, B. C. about 1000.

8. One of the eighty Hebronite Levites who assisted David in the removal of the ark to Jerusalem (I Chron. 15:9, 11), B. C. about 982.

9. One of the Levites appointed by Hezekiah to have charge of the offerings and tithes dedicated in the temple (II Chron. 31:13), B. C. about 719.

Elie'nai (ĕl-ĭ-ē'nī; *toward Jehovah are my eyes*), a descendant of Shimhi, and a chief of one of the Benjamite families resident at Jerusalem (I Chron. 8:20).

Elie'zer (ĕl-ĭ-ē'zēr; *God of help*).

1. "Eliezer of Damascus," mentioned in Gen. 15:2, 3, apparently as a house-born domestic and steward of Abraham, and hence likely, in the absence of direct issue, to become the patriarch's heir, B. C. about 2070. The common notion is that Eliezer was Abraham's house-born slave, adopted as his heir, and

meanwhile his chief servant, and the same who afterward sent into Mesopotamia to seek a wife for Isaac. "This last point we may dismiss with the remark that there is not the least evidence that 'the elder servant of his house' (Gen. 24:2) was the same with Eliezer" (Kitto).

NOTE—Much difficulty has arisen from the seeming contradiction in the two expressions "Eliezer of Damascus," and "one born in my house" (Gen. 15:2, 3). The question arises how could Eliezer have been a house-born slave, seeing that Abraham's household was never in Damascus. The answer is: the expression "the steward of my house," literally translated is, "the son of possession of my house," and is exactly the same as the phrase in v. 3, "the son of my house (A. V. 'one born in my house') is my heir." This removes every objection to Eliezer's being of Damascus, and leaves it more probable that he was not a servant at all, but a near relative, perhaps nearer than Lot. Some, indeed, identify Eliezer with Lot, which would afford an excellent explanation if Scripture afforded sufficient grounds for it (Keil, *Com.*; Kitto).

2. The second of the two sons of Moses and Zipporah, born during the exile in Midian, to whom his father gave this name, "because," said he, "the God of my fathers was my help, that delivered me from the sword of Pharaoh" (Exod. 18:4; I Chron. 23:15), B. C. before 1440. He remained with his mother and brother, Gershom, in the care of Jethro, his grandfather, when Moses returned to Egypt (Exod. 4:18), having been sent back by Moses (18:2). Jethro brought back Zipporah and her two sons to Moses in the wilderness after the exodus from Egypt (ch. 18). Eliezer had one son, Rehabiah, from whom sprang a numerous posterity (I Chron. 23:17; 26:25, 26). Shelomith, in the reigns of Saul and David (v. 28), who had the care of all the treasures of things dedicated to God, was descended from Eliezer in the sixth generation if the genealogy in I Chron. 26:25 is complete.

3. A son of Becher and grandson of Benjamin (I Chron. 7:8).

4. One of the priests who blew with trumpets before the ark when it was brought to Jerusalem (I Chron. 15:24), B. C. about 982.

5. Son of Zichri, and ruler of the Reubenites in the reign of David (I Chron. 27:16).

6. A prophet (son of Dodavah, of Mareshah) who foretold to *Jehoshaphat* (q. v.), that the fleet which he had fitted out in partnership with Ahaziah should be wrecked (II Chron. 20:37), B. C. after 875.

7. A chief of the Jews during the exile, sent by Ezra, with others from Ahava to Casiphia, to induce some Levites and Nethinim to join the party returning to Jerusalem (Ezra 8:16), B. C. 457.

8, 9, 10. A priest (descendant of Jeshua), a Levite, and an Israelite (of the lineage of Harim), who divorced their Gentile wives after the exile (Ezra 10:18, 23, 31), B. C. 456.

11. Son of Jorim and father of Jose, of the private lineage of David prior to Salathiel (Luke 3:29), B. C. before 588.

Elihoe'nai (ĕl-ĭ-hō-ē'nī; *toward Jehovah are my eyes*), son of Zerahiah, of the "sons of Pahath-moab," who returned with two hundred males from the exile (Ezra 8:4), B. C. 457.

Eliho'reph (ĕl-ĭ-hō'rĕf; *God of autumn*), son of Shisha, and appointed, with his brother Ahi-ah, royal scribe by Solomon (I Kings 4:3), B C. 959.

Eli'hu (ĕ-lī'hū; *my God is he*).

1. The son of Tohu and grandfather of Elkanah, Samuel's father (I Sam. 1:1). In the statements of the genealogy of Samuel in I Chron. 6, the name *Eliel* (q. v.) occurs in the same position—son of Toah and father of Jeroham (6:34); and also *Eliab* (6:27), father of Jeroham and grandson of Zophai. The general opinion is that Elihu is the original name, and the two latter forms but copyists' variations of it.

2. One of the captains of Manasseh (I Chron. 12:20) who followed David to Ziklag on the eve of the battle of Gilboa, and who assisted him against the Amalekites (I Sam. 30), B. C. about 1001.

3. One of the very able-bodied members of the family of Obed-edom (a grandson by Shemaiah), who were appointed porters of the temple under David (I Chron. 26:7), B. C. after 1000. Terms are applied to all these doorkeepers which appear to indicate that they were not only "strong men," as in the A. V., but also fighting men (*see* vers. 6, 7, 8, 12, in which the Hebrew words for army and warriors, or heroes, occur).

4. A chief of the tribe of Judah, said to be "of the brethren of David" (I Chron. 27:18), and hence supposed by some to have been his eldest brother, *Eliab* (I Sam. 16:6), B. C. 1000.

5. One of Job's friends. He is described as "the son of Barachel, a Buzite, of the kindred of Ram" (Job. 32:2). This is usually understood to imply that he was descended from Buz, the son of Abraham's brother Nahor. For his part in the remarkable discussion, *see* Job.

Eli'jah (ē-lī'jà; *my God is Jehovah*).

1. **The Prophet.** Elijah came from Tishbeh in Gilead, a district which shared deeply in the miseries of the kingdom of the Ten Tribes. Nothing is known concerning his family or birth.

Personal History. The better to understand his history let us briefly consider the condition of affairs when Elijah made his appearance. Ahab had taken for wife Jezebel, a Canaanite woman, daughter of Eth-baal. Of a weak and yielding character, he allowed Jezebel to establish the Phoenician worship on a grand scale—priests and prophets of Baal were appointed in crowds—the prophets of Jehovah were persecuted and slain, or only escaped by being hid in caves. It seemed as if the last remnants of true religion were about to perish. Jezebel had also induced Ahab to issue orders for the violent death of all the prophets of Jehovah who, since the expulsion of the Levites, had been the only firm support of the ancient religion (*see* I Kings 18:4, 13, 22; 19:10, 14; II Kings 9:7). (1) **Appears before Ahab.** Elijah suddenly appears before Ahab and proclaims the vengeance of Jehovah for the apostasy of the king. "As the Lord God of Israel liveth, before whom I stand," whose constant servant I am, "there shall not be dew nor rain these years, but according to my word." This was probably the conclusion of a warning, given to the king, of the consequences of his iniquitous course (B. C. about 875). Warned by God, he went and (2) **Hid by Cherith**, perhaps the present Wady Kelt. Here he remained, supported by ravens, until the brook dried up. Then another refuge was provided for him (3) **At Zarephath.** "The word of the Lord came unto him, saying, Arise, get thee to Zarephath . . . and dwell there." At the gate of the city he met the woman who was to sustain him, herself on the verge of starvation. Obedient to his request to prepare him food, she is rewarded by the miracle of the prolonging of the meal and oil, and the restoration of her son to life after his sudden death (I Kings

143. Elijah and the Widow's Son (stained glass, early 16th Century, Flemish)

17). (4) **Second appearance before Ahab.** For three years and six months there had been no rain (James 5:17). At last the full horrors of famine, caused by the failure of the crops, descended on Samaria. Elijah, returning to Israel, found Ahab yet alive and unreformed, Jezebel still mad upon her idols, and the prophets of Baal still deceiving the people. Elijah first presents himself (I Kings 18) to Obadiah, the principal servant of Ahab and a true servant of God. He requests him to announce his return to Ahab; and Obadiah, his fears having been removed by the prophet, consents. The conversation between Ahab and Elijah, when they met soon after, began with the question of the king, "Art thou he that troubleth Israel?" Elijah answers, unhesitatingly, "I have not troubled Israel; but thou and thy father's house, in that ye have forsaken the commandments of the Lord, and thou hast followed Baalim." He then challenges him to exercise his authority in summoning an assembly to Mount Carmel that the controversy between them might be decided. (5) **On Carmel.** Whatever were his secret purposes, Ahab accepted this proposal, and the people also consented. Fire was the element over which Baal was supposed to preside. Elijah proposes (wishing to give them every advantage) that, two bullocks being slain, and laid each upon a separate altar, the one for Baal, the other for Jehovah, whichever should be consumed by fire must proclaim whose the children of Israel were, and whom it was their duty to serve. There are few more sublime stories in history than this. On the one hand the servant of Jehovah, attended by his one servant, with his wild, shaggy hair, his scanty garb, and sheepskin cloak, but with calm dignity of demeanor and the minutest regularity of procedure. On the other hand the prophets of Baal and Ashtaroth—doubtless in all the splendor of their vestments (II Kings 10:22), with the wild din of their "vain repetitions" and the maddened fury of their disappointed hopes—and the silent people surrounding all; these form a picture which brightens into fresh distinctness every time we consider it. The Baalites are allowed to make trial first. All day long these false prophets cried to Baal, they leaped upon the altar, and mingled their blood with that of the sacrifice—but all is in vain, for at the time of the evening sacrifice the altar was still cold and the bullock lay stark thereon— "there was neither voice, nor any to answer, nor any that regarded." Then Elijah repaired the broken altar of Jehovah, and having laid thereon his bullock and drenched both altar and sacrifice with water until the trench about it was filled, he prayed, "Lord God of Abraham, Isaac, and of Israel, let it be known this day that thou art God in Israel, and that I am thy servant, and that I have done all these things at thy word." The answer was all that could be desired, for "the fire of the Lord fell, and consumed the burnt sacrifice, and the wood, and the stones, and the dust, and licked up the water that was in the trench." The people acknowledged the presence of God, exclaiming with one voice, "The Lord, he is God; the Lord, he is God." By his direction the juggling priests are slain, and Ahab informed that he might take refreshment, for God will send the desired rain. (6) **Prays for rain.** Elijah prays, God hears and answers; a little cloud arises, and, diffusing itself gradually over the entire face of the heavens, empties its refreshing waters upon the whole land of Israel. Ahab rides to Jezreel, a distance of at least sixteen miles, the prophet running before the chariot, but going no farther than "the entrance" of the city (I Kings 18). (7) **Flees from Jezebel.** The prophets of Baal were destroyed; Ahab was cowed; but Jezebel remained undaunted. She made a vow against the life of the prophet, who, attended by his servant—according to Jewish tradition the boy of Zarephath—took refuge in flight. The first stage in his journey was "Beer-sheba, which belongeth to Judah." Leaving his servant in the town he set out alone into the wilderness (I Kings 19:1-4). (8) **Under the juniper tree.** The labors, anxieties, and excitement of the last few days had proved too much even for that iron frame and that stern resolution. His spirit is quite broken, and, sitting beneath a juniper tree, he wishes for death. "It is enough; now, O Lord, take away my life; for I am not better than my fathers." But sleep and food, miraculously furnished, refreshed the weary prophet, and he went forward, in the strength of that food, a journey of forty days to Mount Horeb. (9) **At Horeb.**

Having rested in a cave one night the voice of the Lord came to him in the morning, asking, "What doest thou here, Elijah?" And then he again unburdens his soul and tells his grief: "I have been very jealous for Jehovah, but Israel has forsaken thy covenant; I stand alone, and my life is sought." He is directed to stand outside the cave, and "the Lord passed by" in all the terror of his most appalling manifestations. The fierce wind tore the solid

THE DIVIDED KINGDOM
IN ELIJAH'S TIME
JUDAH
ISRAEL
0 10 20 30 40 50 60

144.

mountains and shivered the granite cliffs of Sinai; the earthquake crash reverberated through the defiles of those naked valleys; the fire burnt in the incessant blaze of Eastern lightning. Like these, in their degree had been Elijah's own mode of procedure; but the conviction is now forced upon him that in none of these is Jehovah to be known. Then came the whisper of "the still small voice." Elijah knew the call, and, stepping forward, hid his face in his mantle and waited for the divine communication. Three commands were laid upon him—to anoint Hazael king over Syria; Jehu, the son of Nimshi, king over Israel; and Elisha, the son of Shaphat, to be his own successor. Of these three commands the first two were reserved for Elisha to accomplish; the last one was executed by Elijah himself (19:9-18). (10) **Finds Elisha.** The prophet soon found Elisha at his native place, Abel-meholah. Elisha was plowing at the time, and Elijah, without uttering a word, cast his mantle, the well-known sheepskin cloak, upon him, as if by that familiar action (which was also a symbol of official investiture) claiming him for his son. The call was accepted, and then began that long period of service and intercourse which continued until Elijah's removal (19:19-21). (11) **Reproves Ahab and Jezebel.** For about six years we find no notice in the sacred history of Elijah, till God sent him once again to pronounce sore judgment upon Ahab and Jezebel for the murder of the unoffending *Naboth* (*q. v.*). Just as Ahab was about to take possession of the vineyard he is met by Elijah, who utters the terrible curse (I Kings 21:19-25), B. C. 869. Ahab, assuming penitence, and afterward proving his sincerity, was rewarded by a temporary arrest of judgment; but it took effect upon his wicked consort and children to the very letter. (12) **Elijah and King Ahaziah.** Ahaziah had succeeded Ahab, his father, upon his death, and in the second year of his reign met with a serious accident. Fearing a fatal result, he sent to Ekron to learn at the shrine of Baal of the issue to his illness. But the angel of the Lord told Elijah to go forth and meet the messengers of the king. Questioned by Ahaziah as to the reason of their early return the messengers told him of their meeting the prophet and his prediction. From their description of him Ahaziah recognized Elijah, the man of God. Enraged he sent a captain with fifty men to take Elijah. He was sitting on top of "the mount," probably of Carmel. The officer addressed the prophet by the title most frequently applied to him, "Thou man of God, the king hath said, Come down. And Elijah answered and said, If I be a man of God, let fire come down from heaven, and consume thee and thy fifty. And there came down fire from heaven, and consumed him and his fifty." A second company shared the same fate. The altered tone of the leader of the third party, and the assurance of God that his servant need not fear, brought Elijah down. But the king gained nothing. The message before delivered was repeated to his face, and the king shortly after died. This was Elijah's last interview with the house of Ahab, and his last recorded appearance in person against the Baal worshipers (II Kings 1:2-17), B. C. c. 852. (13) **Warns Jehoram.** Jehoram, king of Judah, had married the daughter of Ahab, and walked "in the ways of the kings of Israel, as did the house of Ahab." Elijah sent him a letter denouncing his evil doings and predicting his death (II Chron. 21:12-15). This is the only communication with the southern kingdom of which any record remains. (14) **Closing scenes.** The faithful prophet's warfare is now accomplished, and God will translate him in a special manner to heaven. Conscious of this he determines to spend his last moments in imparting divine instruction to, and pronouncing his last benediction upon, the students in the colleges of Beth-el and Jericho. It was at Gilgal—probably not the ancient place of Joshua and Samuel, but another of the same name still surviving on the western edge of the hills of Ephraim—that the prophet received the divine intimation that his departure was at hand. Here he requested Elisha, his constant companion, to tarry while he goes on an errand of Jehovah. Perhaps the request was made because of the return of his old love for solitude, perhaps he desired to spare his friend the pain of too sudden a parting, or, it may be, he desired to test the affection of the latter. But Elisha would not give up his master, and they went together to Beth-el. The sons of the prophets, apparently acquainted with what was about to happen, inquired of Elisha if he knew of his impending loss. His answer shows how fully he was aware of it. "Yea, I know it; hold ye your peace." Again Elijah attempts to escape to Jericho, and again Elisha protests that he will not be separated from him. Under the plea of going to Jordan Elijah again requested Elisha to tarry, but still with no success, and two set off together toward the river. Fifty men of the sons of the prophets ascend the heights behind the town to watch what happens. Reaching the river, Elijah rolls up his mantle as a staff, strikes the waters, which divide, and they two go over on dry ground. What follows is best told in the simple words of the narrative: "And it came to pass, when they were gone over, that Elijah said unto Elisha, Ask what I shall do for thee, before I be taken away from thee. And Elisha said, I pray thee, let a double portion of thy spirit be upon me. And he said, Thou hast asked a hard thing: nevertheless, if thou see me when I am taken from thee, it shall be so unto thee; but if not, it shall not be so. And it came to pass, as they still went on, and talked, that, behold, there appeared a chariot of fire, and horses of fire, and parted them both asunder; and Elijah went up by a whirlwind into heaven." Elisha, at the wonderful sight, cried out, like a bereaved child, "My father, my father, the chariot of Israel, and the horsemen thereof!" The mantle of his master had, however, fallen upon Elisha, as a pledge that the office and spirit of the former were now his own (II Kings 2:1-13).

Character. Elijah's character is one of moral sublimity. His faith in God seemed to know no limit nor questioning. His zeal for Jehovah was an all-absorbing motive of his life, so that he justly said, "I have been very jealous for the Lord God of hosts." No danger nor duty was too severe to shake his confidence—no labor too great for his Lord. His courage was undaunted, even in the presence of royalty or famine. His obedience was simple and unquestioning as a child's. Tender of soul, he could sympathize with the widow when she lost her child, or weep over the sad condition of his deluded countrymen. Stern in principle, he was, in his opposition to sin, as fierce as the fire that more than once answered his command. He was by nature a recluse, only appearing before men to deliver his message from God, and enforce it by a miracle, and then disappearing from sight again.

NOTE—(1) *The Ravens.* Much ingenuity has been devoted to explaining away the obvious meaning of Elijah's ravens (I Kings 17:4, sq.). Michaelis supposes that the brook Cherith was a place where ravens were wont to congregate, and that Elijah took from their nests morning and evening the food which they brought to their young. Others have explained *'Orebim* to mean *Arabians;* others, the inhabitants of Orbo, or Oreb; and some have thought that the word might mean *merchants,* from *'arab, to traffic.* The text, however, plainly records a miracle (Whedon, *Com.,* in loco). (2) *Elijah's mocking.* Some have objected that Elijah's mockery of Baal's prophets was not in accordance with the spirit of Scripture—"not rendering railing for railing, but, contrarywise, blessing" (I Pet. 3:9). "In the case of Elijah ridicule was a fit weapon for exposing the folly and absurdity of idol worship. The prophet employed it with terrible effect" (Haley, *Dis.*). (3) *Letter to Jehoram.* This letter has been considered as a great difficulty, on the ground that Elijah's removal must have taken place before the death of Jehoshaphat, and, therefore, before the accession of Jehoram to the throne of Judah. That Jehoram began to reign during the lifetime of his father, Jehoshaphat, is stated in II Kings 8:16. He probably ascended the throne as viceroy or associate some years before the death of his father.

2. A priest of "the sons of Harim," who divorced his Gentile wife on returning from the exile (Ezra 10:21), B. C. 456.

Eli'ka (ē-lī'kà; perhaps *God has spued out, rejected*), a Harodite, and one of David's thirty-seven distinguished warriors (II Sam. 23:25), B. C. about 1000.

E'lim (ē'lĭm; *trees*), second station in the desert of Israel (Exod. 15:27; Num. 33:9), where they encamped for a month (Exod. 16:1). Here were "twelve wells (R. V. 'springs') of water and threescore and ten palm trees." The present Wady Gharandel.

Elim'elech (ē-lĭm'ĕ-lĕk; *God is king*), a man of the tribe of Judah who dwelt in Bethlehem-Ephratah in the days of the judges, B. C. probably before 1070. In consequence of a great dearth in the land he went with his wife, Naomi, and his two sons, Mahlon and Chilion, to dwell in Moab, where he and his two sons died (Ruth 1:2, 3; 2:1, 3; 4:3, 9).

Elioe'nai (ē-lĭ-ō-ē'nī; a contracted form of the name *Elihoenai*).

1. The eldest son of Neariah, son of Shemaiah, of the descendants of Zerubbabel (I Chron. 3:23, 24).

2. A prince of the Simeonites (I Chron. 4:36).

3. The fourth son of Becher, son of Benjamin (I Chron. 7:8).

4. Seventh son of Meshelemiah, one of the Korhite porters (doorkeepers) of the temple (I Chron. 26:3), B. C. about 960.

5. A priest of the sons of Pashur, who, at the instigation of Ezra, put away his Gentile wife

and offered a ram for a trespass offering (Ezra 10:22), B. C. 456. He is, perhaps, the same mentioned in Neh. 12:41 as one of the priests who accompanied Nehemiah with trumpets at the dedication of the wall of Jerusalem, B. C. 445.

6. An Israelite (*singer*) of the sons of Zattu, who likewise divorced his Gentile wife after the exile (Ezra 10:27), B. C. 456.

Eli'phal (ē-lī'fàl; *God his judge*), son of Hur, and one of David's mighty men (I Chron. 11:35), B. C. about 1000. *See* Eliphelet (3).

Eliph'alet (ē-lĭf'à-lĕt), a less correct mode of anglicizing (II Sam. 5:16; I Chron. 14:7) the name *Eliphelet* (q. v.).

El'iphaz (ĕl'ĭ-făz; *God of Gold*, or *God is fine gold*).

1. A son of Esau by Adah, his first wife, and father of several Edomitish tribes (Gen. 36:4, 10, 11, 16; I Chron. 1:35, 36).

2. One of the three friends who came to condole with Job in his affliction. They had agreed to meet together for this purpose, but, overpowered by feeling at the condition of their friend they sat down in silence for seven days (Job. 2:11). Eliphaz is called "the Temanite," and was probably of Teman, in Idumea. As Eliphaz, the son of Esau, had a son named Teman, from whom the place took its name, there is reason to conclude that this Eliphaz was a descendant of the former Eliphaz (Kitto). He is the first speaker among the friends and probably the eldest among them. He begins his orations with delicacy and conducts his part of the controversy with considerable address (chaps. 4, 5, 15, 22). On him falls the main burden of the argument that God's retribution in this world is perfect and certain, and that, consequently, suffering must be a proof of previous sin. The great truth brought out by him is the unapproachable majesty and purity of God (4:12-21; 15:12-16). But still, with the other two friends, he is condemned because they had "not spoken of God the thing that is right" (42:7). "In order that they may only maintain the justice of God they have condemned Job against their better knowledge and conscience" (Delitzsch). On sacrifice and intercession of Job all three are pardoned.

Eliph'eleh (ē-lĭf'ĕ-lĕ; *whom God makes distinguished*), a Merarite Levite, one of the gate-keepers appointed by David to play on the harp "on the Sheminith" on the occasion of bringing up the ark to the city of David (I Chron. 15:18, 21), B. C. about 982.

Eliph'elet (ē-lĭf'ĕ-lĕt; *God of deliverance*).

1. The third of the nine sons of David, born at Jerusalem, exclusive of those by Bath-sheba (I Chron. 3:6; 14:5), in which latter passage the name is written *Elpalet*, B. C. about 989.

2. The ninth of the same (I Chron. 3:8; 14:7; II Sam. 5:16), in which two latter passages the name is Anglicized *Eliphalet*. It is believed that there were not two sons of this name, but that one is merely a transcriber's repetition. The two are certainly omitted in Samuel, but, on the other hand, they are inserted in two separate lists in Chronicles, and in both cases the number of the sons is summed up at the close of the list.

3. One of David's distinguished warriors,

styled "the son of Ahasbai, the son of the Maachathite" (II Sam. 23:34), but, by some error and abbreviation, *Eliphal* (*q. v.*), son of Ur, in I Chron. 11:35.

4. The third of the three sons of Eshek, of the posterity of Benjamin, and a descendant of King Saul through Jonathan (I Chron. 8:39).

5. One of the three sons of Adonikam, who returned from Babylon with his brothers and sixty males (Ezra 8:13), B. C. 457.

6. A descendant of Hashum, who divorced his Gentile wife after the exile (Ezra 10:33), B. C. 456.

Elis′abeth (ê-lĭz′ȧ-bĕth; Gr. *Elisabeth*, from Heb. *'Elishĕbă', God her oath*), wife of Zacharias and mother of John the Baptist. She was a descendant of Aaron, and of her and her husband, this exalted character is given by the evangelist: "They were both righteous before God, walking in all the commandments and ordinances of the Lord blameless" (Luke 1:5, 6). They remained childless until well advanced in years, when an angel foretold to Zacharias the birth of John, and Zacharias, returning home, Elisabeth conceived (1:7-24). During five months she concealed the favor God had granted her; but the angel Gabriel discovered to the Virgin Mary this miraculous conception as an assurance of the birth of the Messiah by herself (1:24-38). Mary visited her cousin Elisabeth, and they exchanged congratulations and praised God together, Mary abiding with her for three months (1:39-56). When her child was circumcised she named him John. Upon her friends objecting that none of her kindred had that name an appeal was made to Zacharias. He wrote upon a tablet, "His name is John," and immediately speech was restored to him (1:58-64), B. C. 6.

Elise′us (ĕl-ĭ-sē′ŭs), the Grecized form of the name *Elisha* in the New Testament (Luke 4:27).

Eli′sha (ê-lī′shȧ). 1. **Name and Family.** (Heb. *'elisha', God his salvation*). The son of Shaphat, of Abel-meholah (in or near the valley of Jordan).

2. **Personal History.** (1) **Call.** Elisha, a husbandman, was plowing with a number of companions, himself with the twelfth plow. Elijah, on his way from Horeb to Damascus, found Elisha, and threw upon his shoulders his mantle—a token of investiture with the prophet's office and of adoption as a son. Elisha accepted the call, and delaying only long enough to kiss his father and mother and give a farewell feast to his people "arose and went after Elijah and ministered unto him" (I Kings 19:19-21), B. C. about 856. (2) **Elijah's ascension.** We hear no more of Elisha until he accompanied his master to the other side of Jordan, witnessed there his ascension, and with his fallen mantle parted the waters and was welcomed by the sons of the prophets as the successor of Elijah (II Kings 2:1-16), B. C. 846. (3) **At Jericho.** After this he dwelt at Jericho (II Kings 2:18). The town had lately been rebuilt by Hiel (I Kings 16:34), and was the residence of a body of the "sons of the prophets" (II Kings 2:5). While there he was waited upon by the citizens of the place, who complained to him of the foulness

145. Elijah's Spring, Across the Road from Old Jericho

of its waters. He remedied the evil by casting salt into the water at its source, in the name of Jehovah (2:19-22). (4) **Mocked.** Leaving Jericho he went to Beth-el, and upon nearing the latter place was met by a number of children who mockingly cried, "Go up, thou baldhead." This dishonor to God through his prophet was sternly rebuked by Elisha, and "two she-bears came out of the woods and tore forty-two of them. And he went from thence to Mount Carmel, and from thence he returned to Samaria" (II Kings 2:23-25). Objection has been made to the severity of the punishment visited upon the mocking children. "It is not said that they were actually slain (the expression is *bäqā', to rend*, which is peculiarly applicable to the claws of the bear). It is by no means certain that all of them were killed" (McClintock and Strong, s. v.). Kitto thinks that these children had been instigated by their idolatrous parents to mock Elisha, and that by this judgment the people of Beth-el were to know that to dishonor God's prophets was to dishonor him. (5) **Assists Jehoram.** Jehoram, king of Israel, and the kings of Judah and Edom were united in a campaign against Moab, endeavoring to suppress a revolt that occurred shortly after the death of Ahab. A difficulty arose from the lack of water. Elisha, being appealed to, requested a minstrel to be brought, and at the sound of the music the hand of Jehovah came upon him. He ordered pits to be dug to hold the abundant supply of water which he prophesied would be given them. The water which preserved their lives became the source of destruction to their enemies, for the next morning "the sun shone upon the water, and the Moabites saw the water on the other side as red as blood: and they said, This is blood: the kings are surely slain, and they have smitten one another: now therefore, Moab, to the spoil. And when they came to the camp of Israel, the Israelites rose up and smote the Moabites, so that they fled before them: but they went forward smiting the Moabites, even in their country" (II Kings 3:4-24). (6) **Widow's oil.** A widow of one of the sons of the prophets was in debt and her two sons about to be taken from her and sold by her creditors, as by law they had power to do (Lev. 25:39) and in her extremity she implored the prophet's assistance. Inquiring into her circumstances he learned that she had nothing but a pot of oil. This Elisha caused (in his absence, II Kings 4:5) to multiply until the widow had filled with it all the vessels she could borrow, and thus procured the means of payment (4:7). No place or date of the miracle is mentioned. (7) **Elisha and the Shunammite.** On his way between Carmel and the Jordan valley Elisha calls at Shunem. Here he is hospitably entertained by a rich and godly woman. Desiring to have him more than an occasional guest a chamber was prepared for his use. This room, called the *Aliyah* (the upper chamber), is the most desirable of the house, being retired and well fitted up. Elisha, grateful for the kindness shown him, asked of the woman if she would have him seek a favor for her of the king or captain of the host. She declined the prophet's offer, saying, "I dwell among mine own people." Gehazi, Elisha's servant, reminded him of the Shunammite's childless condition, and a son was promised her, which in due time was born (II Kings 4:8-17). When the child was large enough he went out to his father in the field. While there he was (probably) sunstruck, and soon died. The mother laid the dead child upon the prophet's bed, and hastening to the prophet in Carmel she made him acquainted with her loss, and Gehazi is sent before to lay Elisha's staff upon the face of the child. The child's life not returning Elisha shut himself up with the dead boy and, praying to God, "stretched himself upon the child; and the flesh of the child waxed warm" (4:18-37). (8) **Elisha at Gilgal.** It was a time of famine, and the food of the prophets must consist of any herbs that can be found. The great caldron is put on at the command of Elisha, and one of the company brought in his blanket full of such wild vegetables as he had collected and emptied it into the pottage. But no sooner have they begun their meal than the taste betrays the presence of some obnoxious herb, and they cry out, "O, thou man of God, there is death in the pot." In this case the cure was effected by meal which Elisha cast into the caldron (II Kings 4:38-41). Probably at the same time and place occurred the next miracle. A man from Baalshalisha brought to Elisha a present of the first fruits, which, under the law (Num. 18:8, 12; Deut. 18:3, 4), were the perquisites of the ministers of the sanctuary—twenty loaves of new barley and full ears of corn in the husk (perhaps new garden grain). This, by the word of Jehovah, was rendered more than sufficient for a hundred men (II Kings 4:42-44). (9) **Naaman cured.** Naaman, the chief captain of the army of Syria, was afflicted with leprosy, and that in its most malignant form, the white variety (II Kings 5:1, 27). Naaman, hearing of Elisha, informed the king, who sent him with a letter to the king of Israel. "And now," so ran Benhadad's letter, "when this letter is come unto thee, behold, I have therewith sent Naaman my servant to thee, that thou mayest recover him of his leprosy." Accompanying the letter were very rich presents of gold, silver, and raiment. The king of Israel saw only one thing in the transaction, viz., a desire on the part of Benhadad to pick a quarrel with him. The proph-

et, hearing of the matter, sent word to the king, "Let him come to me, and he shall know that there is a prophet in Israel." So Naaman stood with his retinue before Elisha's house. Elisha sent a messenger to the general with the simple instruction to bathe seven times in Jordan. Naaman is enraged at the independent bevahior of the prophet and the simplicity of the perscription, but, persuaded by his servants, obeyed Elisha, and was healed of his leprosy. Returning he appears in the presence of the prophet, acknowledges the power of God, and entreats Elisha to accept the present he had brought from Damascus. This Elisha firmly refuses and dismisses him in peace (5:1-27). (10) **Ax raised.** The home of the prophets becoming too small it was resolved to build nearer the Jordan. While one was felling a tree the ax head flew off and fell into the water. Appeal is made to Elisha: "And he cut down a stick, and cast it in thither: and the iron did swim," and was recovered (6:1-7). (11) **Thwarts the Syrians.** The Syrians warred against Israel, but their plans, however secret, were known to Elisha, who disclosed them to the king of Israel, and by his warnings saved the king, "not once nor twice" only. The king of Syria, learning that Elisha the prophet told of his plans, sent a detachment of men to take him. They came by night and surrounded Dothan, where Elisha resided. His servant was the first to discover the danger, and made it known to his master. At his request the eyes of the young man were opened to behold the spiritual guards which protected them. In answer to Elisha's prayer the Syrians were blinded, and Elisha offers to lead them to the place and person they sought. He conducted them to Samaria, where their blindness was removed and they found themselves in the presence of the king and his troops. The king, eager to destroy them, asked, "My father, shall I smite them? shall I smite them?" Elisha's object was gained when he showed the Syrians the futility of their attempts against him, and he, therefore, refused the king permission to slay them, and having fed them sent them away to their master (II Kings 6:8-23). "Was the deception (6:19) practiced toward the Syrians justifiable? Various answers have been given. Keil and Rawlinson apparently regard Elisha's statement simply in the light of a 'stratagem of war.' Thenius says: 'There is no untruth in the words of Elisha; for his home was not in Dothan, where he was only residing temporarily, but in Samaria; and the words "to the man" may well mean to his house.' Some regard the prophet's language as mere irony" (Haley's *Alleged Dis.*). (12) **Famine in Syria.** Ben-hadad, the king of Syria, now laid seige to Samaria, and its inhabitants were driven to great straits by reason of famine. Roused by an encounter with an incident more ghastly than all, Jehoram, the king (Josephus, *Ant.*, ix, 4, 4) vented, for some reason, his wrath upon Elisha, and, with an oath, he said, "God do so and more also to me if the head of Elisha, the son of Shaphat, shall stand on him this day." An emissary started to execute the sentence, but Elisha, warned of the danger, told those present not to admit him, assuring them that the king was hastening ("to stay the result of his rash exclamation," interprets Josephus, *Ant.*, ix, 4, 4). To the king Elisha promised that within twenty-four hours food should be plentiful. The next day the Syrian camp was found deserted. The night before God caused the Syrians to hear the noise of horses and chariots; and, believing that Jehoram had hired against them the kings of the Hittites and the king of Egypt, had fled in the utmost panic and confusion. Thus did God, according to the words of Elisha, deliver Samaria. Another prediction was accomplished; for the distrustful lord that doubted the word of Elisha was trampled to death by the famished people rushing through the gates of the city to the forsaken tents of the Syrians (II Kings 6:24-7-20). (13) **Shunammite's property restored.** Elisha, aware of the famine which God was about to bring upon the land, had advised his friend, the Shunammite, of it that she might provide for her safety. She left Shunem for the land of the Philistines, and there remained during the dearth. At the end of the seven years she returned and found her house and land appropriated by some other person. When she was come to the king to ask redress he was listening to a recital by Gehazi of the great things that Elisha had done, the crowning feat of all being that which he was then actually relating—the restoration to life of the boy of Shunem. The woman was instantly recognized by Gehazi. "My lord, O king, this is the woman, and this is her son, whom Elisha restored to life." The king immediately ordered her land to be restored, with the value of its produce during her absence (II Kings 8:1-6). (14) **Elisha at Damascus.** We next find Elisha at Damascus, whither he went to "anoint Hazael to be king over Syria." Ben-hadad was prostrate with his last illness, and sent Hazael, with a princely present to inquire of Elisha, "Shall I recover of this disease?" The answer of Elisha, though ambiguous, contained the unmistakable conclusion, "The Lord hath showed me that he shall surely die." The prophet fixed his earnest gaze upon Hazael and burst into tears. Inquired of as to the cause of his grief Elisha told him that he should be king and bring great evil upon the children of Israel. Hazael returned and told the king that the prophet had predicted his recovery. That was the last day of Ben-hadad's life, for on the morrow he was smothered, and Hazael reigned in his stead (II Kings 8:7-15). (15) **Jehu anointed.** While Hazael was warring against the combined force of the kings of Israel and Judah (II Kings 8:28) Elisha sent one of the "sons of the prophets" to anoint Jehu, the son of Jehoshaphat, king over Israel and prophesy concerning the fearful overthrow of the house of Ahab (9:1, sq.). (16) **Death.** We next find Elisha upon his deathbed. Here he is visited by Joash, the grandson of Jehu, who came to weep over the departure of the great and good prophet. The king is told that he will smite Syria but thrice, whereas if he had shown more energy in smiting the ground with the arrows he should have completely destroyed his foe (II Kings 13:14-19). (17) **In his tomb.** The power of the prophet does not end with

his death, for even in his tomb he restores the dead to life. A funeral was going on in the cemetery which contained the sepulcher of Elisha. Seeing a band of Moabites near by, the friends of the dead man hastily put him into the tomb of the prophet. The mere touch of his hallowed remains had power, for the man "revived, and stood up on his feet" (II Kings 13:20, 21).

3. **Character.** Elisha presents a very striking contrast to his master, Elijah, who was a true Bedouin child of the desert. Elisha, on the other hand, was a civilized man, preferring the companionship of men, dwelling in cities, and often in close connection with kings. Elijah was a man whose mission was to accuse of sin or bring judgment upon men because of it. Elisha, while defending the ancient religion, comes as the healer, and so his miracles were those of restoring to life, increasing the widow's oil, making pure the bitter waters. There is tender sympathy for friends, tears for his country's prospective woes. And yet there is firmness in maintaining the right, sternness of judgment, and seeming forgetfulness of self. "In spite of all the seductions to which he was abundantly exposed through the great consideration in which he was held he retained at every period of his life the true prophetic simplicity and purity and contempt for worldly wealth and advantages" (Ewald's *History of Israel*, iv, p. 83).

Eli'shah (ḗ-lī'shȧ), the oldest of the four sons of Javan (Gen. 10:4; I Chron. 1:7). He seems to have given name to "the isles of Elishah," which are described as exporting fabrics of purple and scarlet to the markets of Tyre (Ezek. 27:7). Elisha is Kittim or Cyprus (G. E. Wright and F. Filson (*Westminster Historical Atlas to the Bible* (1945, p. 109). It is the *Alashia* of the Amarna Letters. Cyprus with the Peloponnesus and the islands and coasts of the Aegean were rich in purple shells.

Elish'ama (ḗ-lĭsh'ȧ-mä; *God of hearing*).

1. The son of Ammihud, and "captain" of the tribe of Ephraim at the Exodus (Num. 1:10; 2:18; 7:48, 53; 10:22), B. C. c. 1440. From the genealogy in I Chron. 7:26 we find that he was the grandson of Joshua.

2. The second of the nine sons of David born at Jerusalem, exclusive of those by Bath-sheba (I Chron. 3:6), called in the parallel passages (II Sam. 5:15; I Chron. 14:5), by apparently the more proper name *Elishua* (*q. v.*).

3. The seventh of the same series of sons (I Chron. 3:8; 14:7). According to Samuel (II Sam. 5:14-16) there were only eleven sons born to David after his establishment in Jerusalem, and Elishama is eleventh of the series, B. C. after 1000.

4. An Israelite of the family of David, father of Nehemiah, and grandfather of Ishmael, who slew Gedaliah, the ruler appointed by Nebuchadnezzar over the people that were left in Judea (II Kings 25:25; Jer. 41:1), B. C. before 588.

5. An Israelite of the tribe of Judah and son of Jekamiah. In the Jewish tradition preserved by Jerome (*Qu. Hebr.* on I Chron. 2:41) he appears to be identified with No. 4.

6. One of the two priests sent with the Levites by Jehoshaphat to teach the law

through the cities of Judah (II Chron. 17:8), B. C. after 875.

7. A royal scribe, in whose chamber the roll of Jeremiah was read to him and other magnates and afterward deposited for a time (Jer. 36:12, 20, 21), B. C. about 604.

Elish'aphat (ē-lĭsh'a-făt; *God of judgment*), son of Zichri. One of the captains of hundreds by whose aid Jehoiada, the priest, placed Joash on the throne of Judah and overthrew Athaliah, the usurper (II Chron. 23:1, sq.), B. C. about 836.

Elish'eba (ē-lĭsh'ē-ba; *God of the oath*, i. e., worshiper of God), daughter of Amminadab and sister of Nahshon, the captain of the Hebrew host (Num. 2:3). She became the wife of Aaron, and hence the mother of the priestly family (Exod. 6:23), B. C. about 1440.

Elish'ua (ē-lĭsh'ū-a; *God of supplication*), one of the sons of David born at Jerusalem (II Sam. 5:15; I Chron. 14:5), called *Elishama* (*q. v.*) in the parallel passage (I Chron. 3:6), B. C. after 1000.

Eli'ud (ē-lī'ŭd; *God of majesty*), son of Achim and father of Eleazar, being the fifth in ascent in Christ's paternal genealogy (Matt. 1:14, 15), B. C. about 200 (McC. and S., *Cyc.*).

Eliz'aphan (ē-lĭz'a-făn; *God has concealed*).

1. The second son of Uzziel, and chief of the Kohathite Levites at the Exodus (Num. 3:30; Exod. 6:22), B. C. 1441. He, with his elder brother, Mishael, was directed by Moses to carry away the corpses of their sacrilegious cousins, Nadab and Abihu (Lev. 10:4). In Exodus and Leviticus the name is contracted into *Elzaphan*. His family took part in the ceremony of bringing the ark to Jerusalem in the time of David (I Chron. 15:8) and were represented in the revival under Hezekiah (II Chron. 29:13).

2. Son of Parnach and prince of the tribe of Zebulun, appointed to assist Moses in the division of the land of Canaan (Num. 34:25).

Eli'zur (ē-lī'zûr; *God his rock*), son of Shedeur and prince of the tribe of Reuben at the Exodus (Num. 1:5; 2:10; 7:30, 35; 10:18), B. C. 1440.

Elka'nah (ĕl-kā'na; *whom God has acquired*), the name of several men, all apparently Levites. There is much difficulty and uncertainty in the discrimination of the various individuals who bear this name.

1. The second son of Korah, according to Exod. 6:24, where his brothers are represented as being Assir and Abiasaph. But in I Chron. 6:22, 23, Assir, Elkanah, and Ebiasaph are mentioned in the same order, not as the three sons of Korah, but as son, grandson, and great-grandson, respectively; and this seems to be correct.

2. Son of Shaul, or Joel, being the father of Amasai, and ninth in descent from Kohath, the son of Levi (I Chron. 6:25, 36).

3. Son of Ahimoth, or Mahath, being father of Zuph, or Zophia, and great-grandson of the one immediately preceding (I Chron. 6:26, 35).

4. Another Kohathite Levite, in the line of Heman, the singer. He was the son of Jeroham and father of Samuel (I Chron. 6:27, 28, 33, 34), B. C. about 1106. He is described (I Sam. 1:1, sq.) as living at Ramathaim-zophim,

in Mount Ephraim, otherwise called Ramah; as having two wives, Hannah and Peninnah, with no children by the former till the birth of Samuel in answer to the prayer of Hannah. We learn also that he lived in the time of Eli, the high priest; that he was a pious man, going up yearly to Shiloh to worship and sacrifice (1:3). After the birth of Samuel Elkanah and Hannah continued to live at Ramah, and had three sons and two daughters (2:21). Elkanah, the Levite, is called an Ephraimite because, so far as his civil standing was concerned, he belonged to the tribe of Ephraim, the Levites being reckoned as belonging to those tribes in the midst of which they lived.

5. The father of one Asa, and head of a Levitical family resident in the "villages of the Netophathites" (I Chron. 9:16), B. C. long before 536.

6. A man of the family of Korhites, who joined David while he was at Ziklag (I Chron. 12:6), B. C. about 1002. He probably resided in the tribe of Benjamin, which included four Levitical cities. Perhaps he was the same person who was one of the two doorkeepers for the ark when it was brought to Jerusalem (15:23), B. C. about 982.

7. The chief officer in the household of Ahaz, king of Judah, slain by Zichri, the Ephraimite, when Pekah invaded Judah (II Chron. 28:7), B. C. about 735.

El'kosh (ĕl'kŏsh; *uncertain derivation*), the birthplace of the prophet Nahum; whence he is called "the Elkoshite" (Nah. 1:1). Two Jewish traditions assign widely different localities to Elkosh. In the time of Jerome it was believed to exist in a small village of Galilee, called to the present day Helcesaei (or Helcesei, Elcesi), which belief is more credible than the one which identifies Elkosh with a village on the eastern side of the Tigris, northwest of Khorsabad. This place, *Alkush*, is a Christian village, where the tomb of the prophet is shown in the form of a simple plaster box of modern style.

El'koshite (ĕl'kŏ-shīt). See Elkosh.

Ellas'ar (ĕl-lā'sär), a city of Babylonia, mentioned twice in Genesis (14:1, 9). Ellasar was located in Southern Babylonia, between Ur and Erech, on the left bank of the great canal Shat-en-Nil. The site of the city is now marked by the little mound called by the natives Senkereh. In an early period Ellasar played an important rôle in Babylonia. It was the center in southern Babylonia of the worship of the sun (called in Babylonian *Shamash*), as Sippar was in northern Babylonia the chief place of the same worship. The Babylonian form of the city's name was Larsa, and in later times it was known to the Greeks as Larissa. Its origin is entirely unknown to us, but its holy character and its religious leadership point to a high antiquity. About 2400 B. C. Ellasar was filling an influential place in Babylonia. It had then the leadership in southern Babylonia, and the kings of Larsa were at the same time kings of Sumer and Akkad. Of the dynasty which then ruled in Ellasar we know the names of only two kings, Nur-Ramman and Sin-iddina, the latter of whom built an important canal which connected the Shatt-en-Nil with the river Tigris.

Shortly after this time Ellasar was conquered by an invasion from Elam, and the Elamite king Kudur-Mabug, at that time a great conqueror even in the West, became possessed of the city. He did not, however, reside in the conquered city, but was there represented by his son, Eri-Aku, who is also known in the Babylonian inscriptions by the name of Rim-Sin. He was later conquered by Hammurabi, king of Babylon, who annexed the whole territory to the newly founded Babylonian empire.

Elm. *See* Vegetable Kingdom.

Elmo'dam (ĕl-mō'dăm), son of Er and father of Cosam, one of the ancestors of Christ in the private line of David (Luke 3:28). He is not mentioned in the Old Testament.

Elna'am (ĕl-nā'ăm; *God his delight*), father of Zeribai and Joshaviah, two of David's distinguished warriors (I Chron. 11:46), B. C. about 1000. "In the Septuagint the second warrior is said to be the son of the first, and Elnaam is given himself as a member of the guard."

Elna'than (ĕl-nā'thăn; *God the giver*).

1. An inhabitant of Jerusalem, whose daughter, Nehushta, was the mother of Jehoiachin, king of Judah (II Kings 24:8), B. C. before 597. He was, perhaps, the same as the son of Achbor sent by Jehoiakim to bring the prophet Urijah from Egypt (Jer. 26:22), and in whose presence the roll of Jeremiah was read, for the preservation of which he interceded with the king (Jer. 36:12, 25).

2, 3, 4. Three of the Israelites of position and understanding sent by Ezra to invite the priests and Levites to accompany him to Jerusalem (Ezra 8:16), B. C. 457.

Elo'him (ĕ-lō'hĭm; Heb. plural *'ĕlōhim;* singular *'ĕlōäh, mighty*), a term sometimes used in the ordinary sense of *gods*, whether true or false (Exod. 12:12; 35:2, 4, etc.), including Jehovah (Psa. 76:8; Exod. 18:11, etc.). Dr. W. Henry Green (in *Hom. Mag.*, Sept., 1898, p. 257, sq.) thus summarizes the principles regulating the use of Elohim and Jehovah in the Old Testament: "1. Jehovah represents God in his special relation to the chosen people, as revealing himself to them, their guardian and object of their worship; Elohim represents God in his relation to the world at large, as Creator, providential ruler in the affairs of men, and controlling the operations of nature. 2. Elohim is used when Gentiles speak or are spoken to or spoken about, unless there is a specific reference to Jehovah, the God of the chosen people. 3. Elohim is used when God is contrasted with men or things, or when the sense requires a common rather than a proper noun."

Elo'i (ĕ-lō'ī; Aram. *My God*), an exclamation quoted by our Saviour (Mark 15:34) on the cross from Psa. 22:1.

E'lon (ē'lŏn; *oak*).

1. A Hittite, father of Bashemath (Gen. 26:34), or Adah (Gen. 36:2), wife of Esau.

2. The second of the three sons of Zebulun (Gen. 46:14) and head of the family of Elonites (Num. 26:26).

3. An Israelite of the tribe of Zebulun, and judge for ten years (Judg. 12:11, 12).

4. One of the towns in the border of the tribe of Dan (Josh. 19:43), doubtless the same as Elon-beth-hanan (I Kings 4:9). Its site has not been identified.

E'lon-beth-ha'nan (ē'lŏn-bĕth-hā'năn). The same as *Elon*, 4.

E'lonite (ē'lŏn-īt), the patronymic applied to the descendants of *Elon* (*q. v.*), the son of Zebulun.

E'loth (ē'lŏth), another form (I Kings 9:26, etc.) of the city of *Elath* (*q. v.*).

Elpa'al (ĕl-pā'ăl; *God his ways*), the second of the two sons of Shaharaim by his wife Hushim, and progenitor of a numerous progeny. He was a Benjamite (I Chron. 8:11, 12, 18).

Elpa'let (ĕl-pā'lĕt), a contracted form (I Chron. 14:5) of the name *Eliphalet* (*q. v.*).

El-pa'ran (ĕl-pā'răn; *oak of Paran*), "the one oasis which is in mid-desert, on the great highway across the wilderness of Paran, known in later times as 'Qala' at Nukhl, . . . more commonly 'Castle Nakhl,' 'Castle of the Palm'" (Trumbull, *Kadesh-barnea*, p. 37). It was at "El-paran, which is by the wilderness," that Chedorlaomer halted before starting northward into Canaan (Gen. 14:5, 6). Ishmael dwelt in the wilderness of Paran, after he and his mother were expelled through the influence of Sarah (21:21).

El'tekeh (ĕl'tē-kĕh). R. V. has Elteke (ĕl-tē-kē), a Danite town assigned to the Levites (Josh. 19:40, 44:21:21, 23). The site was destroyed by Sennacherib c. 701 B. C. and in its vicinity a decisive battle was fought by the Assyrians and the Egyptians. It is located about seven miles N. N. W. of Timnah at the site of Khirbet el-Mukanna' some six miles S. S. E. of Ekron ('Akir). M. F. U.

El'tekon (ĕl'tē-kŏn; *God is straight*), one of the towns of the tribe of Judah, in the mountain district (Josh. 15:59); not identified.

Elto'lad (ĕl-tō'lăd; perhaps *God is generator*), one of the cities in the south of Judah (Josh. 15:30) allotted to Simeon (Josh. 19:4), and in possession of that tribe until the time of David (I Chron. 4:29); not identified.

E'lul (ē'lŭl; Heb. *'ĕlūl* from *Akkad. ulūlu*), the sixth month of the ecclesiastical, and twelfth of the civil year of the Jews. *See* Calendar, Time.

Elu'zai (ê-lū'zâ-ī; *God is my strength*), one of the Benjamite warriors who joined David at Ziklag (I Chron. 12:5), B. C. a little before 1000.

El'ymas (ĕl'ĭ-măs; probably from the Arabic *Aliman, a wise man*), a Jew named Bar-jesus, who had attached himself to the proconsul of Cyprus, Sergius Paulus, when Paul visited the island (Acts 13:6, sq.). Upon his endeavoring to dissuade the proconsul from embracing the Christian faith he was struck with miraculous blindness by the apostle (A. D. 44).

El'zabad (ĕl'zà-băd; *God has given*).

1. The ninth of the eleven Gadite heroes who joined David in the wilderness fastness of Judah (I Chron. 12:12), B. C. before 1000.

2. One of the sons of Shemaiah, the son of Obed-edom, the Levite. He served as a porter to the "house of Jehovah" under David (I Chron. 26:7), B. C. after 1000.

El'zaphan (ĕl'zà-făn), a contracted form (Exod. 6:22; Lev. 10:4) of the name *Elizaphan* (*q. v.*).

146. Egyptian Embalming

Embalm (Heb. *ḥănăt, to spice*), the process of preserving a corpse by means of spices (Gen. 50:2, 3, 26).

1. **Egyptians.** Egyptians preserved the body ostensibly to keep it in a fit state to receive the soul which once inhabited it. The soul was thought of as depending for its future fortunes upon those of the body. Physical decomposition robbed the soul of some part of itself and even was thought of as finishing altogether its existence when the corpse had entirely disappeared. Hence the Egyptians made every possible effort to preserve the body. There were various types of mummification, according to the financial ability of the deceased. During the Old Kingdom the viscera were removed to canopic jars of marble or alabaster. The lids of these jars were shaped like an animal deity who was supposed to watch over the body. During the seventy-day process of mummification the brains were removed and a resinous paste inserted in the cranial cavity. The body was then entwined elaborately in linen. After bandaging the body was put into a papyrus carton which was painted with elaborate religious symbols. Nobles were encased in three coffins. A mummy of a great pharoah, like Tutankhamun, was inserted in a series of precious containers. This monarch was interred in incredible splendor. The inner case of solid gold was inlaid with lapis lazuli, carnelian and enamel. Gorgeous jewels and scarabs bearing a royal seal of the ruler were placed in early Egyptian tombs. Occasionally a sceptre was placed in the hands of the deceased king. Herodotus tells of a type of embalming adopted by the poor. In this process they merely cleansed the body by an injection of *syrnoea* and salted it during seventy days, after which it was returned to the friends who brought it.

2. **Hebrew.** Joseph's and Jacob's embalming after the manner of the Egyptians was exceptional (Gen. 50:2, 26). However, wealthy people did anoint the bodies of their loved ones with costly oil (John 12:7) and wound them in linen with aromatic spices (John 19:39). *M. F. U. See* Burial.

Embroiderer. Weaving, plain sewing, and artistic needlework were practiced among the Hebrews as well as among their neighbors (Exod. 28:29; 35:25; 38:23; Judg. 5:30; Psa. 45:14). Long before Abraham's time the Canaanites wove fine textiles and had a flare for vivid colors. Remains of a dyeing establishment have been uncovered at Ugarit. Byblos and other Phoenician coastal cities were famous for their woven cloth and garments. From murex shells purple-red dye was extracted. Tell Beit Mirsim has yielded ample evidence of developed weaving, dyeing and artistic work on the loom. Mesopotamian mantles were proverbial for their beauty of color and adornment. Long before the time of Abraham a Babylonian ruler might have his own private factory for weaving materials. Egypt was famous not only for its fine linen, which Flinders Petrie said was as fine in the First Dynasty c. 2900 B. C. as our modern linen, but also for exquisitely embroidered garments and tapestries. It was in Egypt that the Israelites first learned the art of embroidery, and it would appear that certain families had arisen to distinction in the arts of weaving and embroidering, especially in the tribes of Judah and Dan (Exod. 35:30, 35; I Chron. 4:21). The O. T. especially refers to a high degree of artistic development in the priests' garments, the ephod and the gold, blue, scarlet and fine twined linen of the

147. Assyrian Embroidered Garment

Tabernacle vestments. Assyrian and Babylonian garments were mentioned as early as the time of Joshua (7:21) and as an article of commerce by Ezekiel (27:24). *M. F. U. See* Needlework and Weaving.

E'mek-Keziz. *See* Keziz.

Emerald. *See* Mineral Kingdom.

Emerods. *See* Diseases.

E'mim (ē'mĭm), the giant aborigines dispossessed By Moab. In Gen. 14:5-7, with which comp. Deut. 2:10-12, 20-23, we find all the region east of the Jordan once occupied by a series of races mostly described as giants—the Rephaim in Bashan, the Zamzummim dispossessed by the Ammonites (Deut. 2:20, 21); possibly the same as the Zuzim of Gen. 14:5, the Emim by the Moabites, and the Horim by the Edomites. The "Emims" of the A. V. is an incorrect double plural.

Emman'uel (ē-măn'ū-ĕl; *God with us;* i. e. *saviour*), a name given to Christ by Matthew (1:23) after Isa. 7:14. According to orthodox interpretation the name denotes the same as

God-man (*theanthrōpos*), and has reference to the personal union of the human nature and the divine in Christ.

Emma'us (ĕ-mā'ŭs; *hot baths*), a town seven and a half miles from Jerusalem (threescore furlongs), the scene of Christ's revelation of himself after his resurrection (Luke 24:13). Its real site is disputed, however. A number of places are held, by tradition and otherwise, to be the original site of Emmaus. Among them are Amwâs, or Emmaus-Nicopolis, Kubeibet, Khamesa, Beit Mizzeh, Kolonieh.

Em'mor (ĕm'môr), a Grecized form (Acts 7: 16) of the name *Hamor* (*q. v.*), the father of Shechem (Gen. 34:2).

En- (ĕn; *fountain*), a prefix to many names of places in Hebrew from there being a living spring in the vicinity.

E'nam (ē'năm; *double fountain*), one of the cities of Judah in the *Shefelah* or lowland (Josh. 15:34). From its mention with towns which are known to have been near Timnath this is very probably the place in the doorway (A. V. "an open place") of which Tamar sat before her interview with her father-in-law (Gen. 38:14).

E'nan (ē'năn; *having eyes*, i. e. "keen-eyed"), the father of Ahira, who was "prince" of the tribe of Naphtali at the time of the numbering of Israel in the desert of Sinai (Num. 1:15; 2:29; 7-78, 83; 10:27), B. C. c. 1440.

Encampment. See Camp.

Enchanter (Deut. 18:10), **Enchanters** (Jer. 27:9). See Magic.

Enchantment. The practice of magic or the speaking of certain words whereby evil supernatural forces are invoked in order to achieve supernatural effects over human beings, animals or natural phenomena. Under this category are included magic (Exod. 7:11), conjuration, exorcism (Acts 19:13-17), sorcery (Acts 8:9, 11; 13:8, 10). This traffic in quackery or in bone fide spiritism was forbidden by the law of Moses (Deut. 18:10). Sometimes magic is not easily distinguished from divination in the English versions (cf. Num. 23:23; 24:1; II Kings 17:17; Jer. 27:9. See Merrill F. Unger's *Biblical Demonology*, 1952, pp. 107-118, for a full discussion.)

End of the World. See Eschatology.

En'-dor (ĕn'dôr; *fountain of Dor*), a town about four miles from the foot of Mount Tabor. At present a "wretched hamlet" on the north shoulder of Little Hermon. The numerous caves in the hillsides suggest a fit dwelling place for such persons as the spiritistic medium to whom *Saul* (*q. v.*) resorted (I Sam. 28:7). See also Josh. 17:11; Psa. 83:10.

Ene'as (ē-nē'ăs). See Aeneas.

En-eg'laim (ĕn-ĕg'lā-ĭm; *fountain of two calves*), a place mentioned by Ezekiel (47:10) in the vision of holy waters. Identified with Ain Hajlah, N. of the Dead Sea, W. of Jordan.

En-gan'nim (ĕn-găn'ĭm; *fountain of gardens*).
1. A city of Issachar (Josh. 19:21; "Anem," I Chron. 6:73) allotted to the Levites (Josh. 21: 29), fifteen miles S. of Mount Tabor; the scene of Ahaziah's escape from Jehu (II Kings 9:27, "garden house"); identified with modern Jenin, a large town of four thousand inhabitants.

2. A town in Judah (Josh. 15:34); location unknown.

En-ge'di (ĕn-gē'dī; *fountain of the wild goat*).
1. A town, called also the city of palm trees (Gen. 14:7; II Chron. 20:2). It was situated about thirty miles S. E. from Jerusalem, on the edge of the wilderness and on the west shore of the Dead Sea. It is full of rocks and caves (I Sam. 23:29; Ezek. 47:10). The source of the fountain from which it derives its name is on the mountain side about six hundred feet above the sea.

It is called now 'Ain Jîdy (*spring of the kid*). Smith. (*Hist. Geog.*, p. 269, s. q.) describes it as a place of wonderful fertility, as most suitable for refuge, though with insignificant caves. None of them was large enough to have been the scene of such a story as I Sam. 24. The *strongholds* of David (23:29; 24:22) must have lain by the water, and the cave is described below them.

It was immediately after an assault upon the "Amorites, that dwelt in Hazezon-tamar," that the five Mesopotamian kings were attacked by the rulers of the plain of Sodom (Gen. 14:7; comp. II Chron. 20:2). Saul was told that David was in the "wilderness of En-gedi;" and he took "three thousand men and went to seek David and his men upon the rocks of the *wild goats*" (I Sam. 24:1-4). At a later period En-gedi was the gathering place of the Moabites and Ammonites who went up against Jerusalem and fell in the valley of Berachah (II Chron. 20:2). The vineyards of En-gedi were celebrated by Solomon (Cant. 1:14), its balsam by Josephus, and its palms by Pliny.

2. The "wilderness of En-gedi" (I Sam. 24:1) is doubtless the wild region west of the Dead Sea, which must be traveled to reach its shores.

Engine, a term applied in Scripture exclusively to military affairs. See Armor.

En-had'dah (ĕn-hăd'à), a city on the border of Issachar (Josh. 19:21); according to Knobel either the place by Gilboa called *Judeideh*, or else el-Hadethah, 6 miles E. of Mount Tabor.

En-hak'kore (ĕn-hăk'ō-rē; *fountain of the crier*), a spring which burst forth at the cry of Samson (Judg. 15:19). It has been identified with Ayun Kara, near Zoreah.

En-ha'zor (ĕn-hā'zôr; *fountain of the village*), one of the fenced cities in the inheritance of Naphtali, distinct from Hazor (Josh. 19:37). Probably Khirbet Hasireh near Hazzur.

En-mish'pat (ĕn-mĭsh'păt; *fountain of judgment*), the earlier name (Gen. 14:7) for *Kadesh* (*q. v.*).

Enmity (Heb. *'ēbäh*; Gr. *echthra*), deep-rooted hatred, irreconcilable hostility. God established perpetual enmity, not only between the serpent and the woman, but also between the human and the serpent race (Gen. 3:15). Friendship with the world (i. e., the corrupt part of it) is declared to be "enmity with God" (James 4:4), as being at variance with his plans for the promotion of righteousness (see I John 2:15, 16); so also the carnal mind is *enmity against* God (Rom. 8:7, 8), opposed to his nature and will. The ceremonial law is called "enmity" (Eph. 2:15, 16), referring to the hostility between Jew and Gentile, due to Judaical limitations and antagonisms, and more especially the alienation of both Jew and Gentile from God.

E'noch (ē'nŭk; *dedicated, initiated*), the name of two men, two others having their name given as *Hanoch* (*q. v.*).

1. The eldest son of Cain, who called the city which he built after his name (Gen. 4:17, 18).

2. The son of Jared (Gen. 5:18) and father of Methuselah (5:21, sq.; Luke 3:37). After the birth of Methuselah, in his sixty-fifth year, he lived three hundred years. After the birth of Methuselah it is said (Gen. 5:22-24) that Enoch "walked with God three hundred years, and was not; for God took him." As a reward of his sanctity he was transported into heaven without dying, and thus the doctrine of immortality was plainly taught under the old dispensation. In the Epistle to the Hebrews (11:5) the spring and issue of Enoch's life are clearly marked. Jude (vers. 14, 15) quotes from a prophecy of Enoch, but whether he derived his quotation from tradition or from writing is uncertain. The voice of early ecclesiastical tradition is almost unanimous in regarding Enoch and Elijah as "the two witnesses" (Rev. 11:3).

3. The first city mentioned in Scripture (Gen. 4:17), built by Cain, east of Eden and in the land of Nod.

E'nos (ē'nŏs; *a man*), the son of Seth and grandson of Adam (Gen. 5:6-11; Luke 3:38). He lived nine hundred and five years, and is remarkable on account of a singular expression used respecting him in Gen. 4:26, "Then began men to call upon the name of the Lord." Two explanations are given of this passage. One is the marginal reading, "Then began men to call themselves *by the name* of the Lord," in order, it would seem, to distinguish themselves from those who were already idolaters and were termed children of men; the other, "Then men *profanely* called on the name of the Lord," intimating that at that period idolatry began to be practiced among men. In I Chron. 1:1 the name is Anglicized *Enosh.*

E'nosh (ē'nŏsh, a more correct way of Anglicizing (I Chron. 1:1) the name *Enos* (*q. v.*).

"Enquire of the Lord" is a phrase often met with in early Scripture history. Rebekah is represented as going "to enquire of the Lord" (Gen. 25:22). During Jethro's visit to Moses we find the lawgiver vindicating his judicial office in these words, "Because the people come unto me to enquire of the Lord," etc. (Exod. 18:15, 16). In the tribal war against the Benjamites "the children of Israel enquired diligently of the Lord" (Judg. 20:27). We read also of this being done in the times of Saul, David, and Samuel (I Sam. 9:9; 10:22; II Sam. 2:1; 5:19, 23; I Chron. 14:10, 14). This longing of humanity for some material representation of divine direction and decision was responded to by Jehovah, who in different ways made known his counsel and guidance to those who "enquired" of him. This was done through the pillar of cloud, the shekinah, the urim and the thummim, and prophecy.

En-rim'mon (ĕn'rĭm'ŏn; *fountain of a pomegranate*), a place occupied by the descendants of Judah after the exile (Neh. 11:29), apparently the same as "Ain and Rimmon" (Josh. 15:32). It seems probable that they were so close together that in the course of time they grew into one. It is identified with Umm er-Rummāmin, 9 miles N. of Beersheba.

En-ro'gel (ĕn-rō'gĕl; *fountain of the treaders*), the "foot fountain," also called the "fullers' fountain." Here the fullers cleansed their garments by treading them in the water of the spring (Joel 15:7; 18:16; II Sam. 17:17; I Kings 1:9). This is the well of Job, "Bir Eyub," or the well of Jeremiah, and just below the junction of the valley of Hinnom and that of Jehoshaphat, about five hundred and fifty feet lower than the top of Mount Zion. Gihon Spring with which En-Rogel is sometimes confused, is farther north.

Ensample. *See* Example.

En-she'mesh (ĕn-shē'mĕsh; *fountain of the sun*), a landmark between Judah and Benjamin (Josh. 15:7; 18:17), east of the Mount of Olives; said to be the only spring on the way to Jericho, now called *Ain-Haud*, or "well of the apostles."

Ensign, the rendering of three Hebrew words, also translated *Banner* and *Standard.* The distinction between these three Hebrew terms is sufficiently marked by their respective uses. None of them, however, expresses the idea which "standard" conveys to our minds, viz., a *flag.* The standards in use among the Hebrews probably resembled those of the Egyptians and Assyrians—a figure or device of

148. Egyptian Standards

some kind elevated on a pole. (1) The Hebrew ensign (*nēs*) consisted of some well-understood signal which was exhibited on the top of a pole from a bare mountain top (Isa. 13:2; 18:3). What the nature of the signal was we have no means of stating. The important point to be observed is that the *nēs* was an occasional signal and not a military standard. (2) The Hebrew term for standard (*dĕgĕl*) is used to describe the standards which were given to each of the four divisions of the

Israelite army at the time of the Exodus (Num. 1:52; 2:2, sq.; 10:14, sq.). The character of the Hebrew military standards is quite a matter of conjecture; they probably resembled the Egyptian, which consisted of a sacred emblem, such as an animal, a boat, or the king's name. (3) The Hebrew "sign" (*'ōth*) denoted the standard of each tribe (Num. 2:2, sq.), and was different from the *děgěl*, the banner of three tribes together.

Figurative. It was customary to give a defeated party a banner as a token of protection, and it was regarded as the surest pledge of fidelity. God's lifting or setting up an ensign (Isa. 11:12) is a most expressive figure, and imports a peculiar presence, protection, and aid in leading and directing his people in the execution of his righteous will, and giving them comfort and peace in his service.

En-tap'puah (ĕn-tăp'ū-ä: *fountain of Tappuach*), a spring near the city of *Tappuah* (*q. v.*), put for that place in Josh. 17:7 (comp. v. 8).

Envy (Heb. *kĭn'äh;* Gr. *phthonos*), is (1) that discontented and mortified feeling which arises in the selfish heart in view of the superiority of another, nearly tantamount to jealosy (Psa. 37:1; 73:3; Prov. 24:1, 19; Phil. 1:15, etc.). (2) That malignant passion which sees in another qualities which it covets and hates their possessor (Prov. 27:4; Matt. 27:18; Rom. 1:29, etc.).

Envying is ill will, malice, spite (James 3:14). It is accompanied by every "evil work" (v. 16). It always desires and often strives to degrade others, not so much because it aspires after elevation as because it delights in obscuring those who are more deserving. It is one of the most odious and detestable of vices.

Epae'netus (ĕ-pē'nĕ-tŭs; *praised*), a Christian at Rome, greeted by St. Paul in Rom. 16:5 and designated as his beloved and the first fruit of Asia unto Christ.

Ep'aphras (ĕp'ȧ-frăs; probably a contraction of *Epaphroditus*), an eminent teacher in the Church at Colossae, denominated by Paul "his dear fellow-servant" and "a faithful minister of Christ" (Col. 1:7; 4:12), A. D. 62. It has been inferred from Col. 1:7 ("As ye also learned of Epaphras") that he was the founder of the Colossian Church. Lardner thinks that the expression respecting Epaphras in Col. 4:12, *ho ex humōn* (one of you), is quite inconsistent with the supposition of his being the founder of the Church since the same phrase is applied to Onesimus, a recent convert. The words are probably intended to identify these individuals as fellow-townsmen of the Colossians. He was at this time with Paul in Rome, and is afterward mentioned in the Epistle to Philemon (ver. 23), where Paul calls him *"my fellow-prisoner."* The martyrologies make Epaphras to have been the first bishop of Colossae and to have suffered martyrdom there.

Epaphrodi'tus (ĕ-păf-rō-dī'tŭs; belonging *to Aphrodite,* or Venus), a messenger of the church of Philippi to the apostle Paul during his imprisonment at Rome, intrusted with their contributions for his support (Phil. 2:25; 4:18). Paul seems to have held him in high appreciation, calling him his "brother," "companion in labor," and "fellow-soldier."

While in Rome, he contracted a dangerous illness, brought on by his ministering to the apostle (2:30). On his return to Philippi he was the bearer of the epistle to the Church there. Grotius and some other critics conjecture that Epaphroditus was the same as *Epaphras* mentioned in the Epistle to the Colossians. But though the latter name may be a contraction of the former the fact that Epaphras was most probably in prison at the time sufficiently marks the distinction of the persons.

E'phah (ē'fȧ; *gloom*).

1. The first named of the five sons of Midian (Gen. 25:4; I Chron. 1:33). His descendants formed one of the tribes of the desert connected with the Midianites, Shebaites, and Ishmaelites (Isa. 60:6, 7), and had its seat on the east coast of the Elanitic Gulf.

2. A concubine of Caleb, the son of Hezron, of the tribe of Judah (I Chron. 2:46).

3. One of the sons of Jahdai, probably a descendant of one of the sons of the foregoing (I Chron. 2:47).

Ephah (ē'fȧ), a measure for grain. *See* Metrology, II.

E'phai (ē'fī; *birdlike*), a Netophathite, whose sons were among the "captains of the forces" left in Judah after the deportation to Babylon, and who submitted themselves to Gedaliah, the Babylonian governor (Jer. 40:8). They warned Gedaliah of the plots against him, but were disbelieved by him (vers. 13-16), and probably were massacred with him by Ishmael (41:2, 3), B. C. 588.

E'pher (ē'fēr; *gazelle*).

1. The second named of the sons of Midian (Gen. 25:4; I Chron. 1:33), Abraham's son by Keturah.

2. An Israelite of the tribe of Judah, apparently of the family of Caleb, the son of Jephunneh (I Chron. 4:17).

3. The head of one of the families of Manasseh east, who were carried away by Tilgath-pileser (I Chron. 5:21-26), B. C. before 727.

E'phes-dam'mim (ē'fĕs-dăm'ĭm; *boundary of blood,* I Sam. 17:1), called Pas-dammim (I Chron. 11:13). The sanguinary contests between Israel and the Philistines gave it its name. It is modern Beit Fased ("house of bleeding").

Ephesians. *See* Ephesus.

Ephesians, Epistle to. Perhaps the sublimest of all the Pauline epistles. No part of N. T. revelation sets forth more clearly or more profoundly the believer's position "in Christ" and the results which should obtain in his practical experience. In contrast to Colossians and Galatians it is remarkably free of controversial elements. As Salmon notes, there have been students "who with an incredible lack of insight have construed it as an insipid production or a tedious and unskillful compilation." (*Exp. Gr. Testament* III, 208.)

1. **Authorship and Authenticity.** Ephesians has a strong claim to Pauline authenticity, both externally and internally. Clement of Rome, Ignatius, Polycarp, Hermas, Clement of Alexandria, Tertullian, Iranaeus, and Hippolytus give evidence of early and continued use of the Epistle. Internal evidence

likewise is decisive. The writer twice mentions his name (1:1 and 3:1). The organization of material is Pauline, beginning with doctrine (Chaps 1:3) and ending with experience based upon the doctrine (Chaps. 4-6). The language is definitely Pauline. According to Lewis "out of 155 verses in Ephesians, seventy-eight are found in Colossians in varying degrees of identity" (The Epistle to the Ephesians" in the *Int. Stand. Bible Ency.*, p. 956). I Peter, Hebrews and the Apocalypse apparently show acquaintance with Ephesians, indicating that Ephesians is earlier than I Peter, Hebrews and the Apocalypse. Ephesians was written from Rome in A. D. 64 (Acts 20-27). Tychichus was the bearer, together with the epistles of Colossians and Philemon. Since Ephesians is the most impersonal of Paul's letters and the words "to the Ephesians" are not in the best manuscripts, it seems that the letter was intended to be circularized, being sent to several churches, and may be referred to in Col. 4:16 as the Epistle to the Laodiceans. The letter would then be addressed "to the saints and faithful in Christ Jesus anywhere." The theme of the Epistle confirms this view.

Although the genuineness of the Epistle has been denied by Schleiermacher, de Wette, and others, there are strong arguments in its favor. Coleridge called it "the divinest composition of man."

2. **Position.** The Apostle's real object in writing this Epistle is to set forth the believer's union with Christ (1:3-14; 2:1-10), relating this to the union of Jew and Gentile in Christ (2:11-22). With the distinctive revelation of this truth to the Apostle (3:10-13), these sections give the believer's standing in Christ, and are doctrinal. Chapters 4-6 are practical and give our state. The Apostle in the doctrinal section offers two remarkable prayers that the power of the believer's position "in Christ" be understood and by faith be made an experience (1:15-23; 3:14-21). The practical exhortation based on the believer's position in Christ (4:1-6:9) pertains to his walk, which should be consonant with his position. Presented in 6:10-20 is the spiritual warfare of the Spirit-filled believer who through knowledge and faith translates his position into an everyday experience.

3. **Outline.**

Salutation: 1:1, 2.

Part I. The Believer's Position in Christ, 1:3-3:21
1. The elements of his position, 1:1-14
2. Prayer for knowledge and faith to appropriate the power of the position, 1:15-21
3. Christ the Head of the church, 1:22, 23
4. Method of Gentile salvation, 2:1-10
5. Union of Jew and Gentile in Christ, 2:11-18
6. The church as a temple inhabited by the Spirit, 2:19-22

Part II. The Church as a Special Divine Revelation, 3:1-12
1. Hidden in past ages, 3:1-6
2. Revealed especially to the Apostle Paul, 3:7-12
3. Second prayer for knowledge and faith to appropriate the power of the position, 3:13-21

Part III. The Walk of the Believer in Christ, 4:1-6:9
1. The walk worthy, 4:1-3
2. The walk as an expression of doctrinal unity, 2:4-6
3. The walk as a ministry of gifts, 3:7-16
4. The walk as a regenerated man, 4:17-29
5. The walk of the believer indwelt by the Spirit, 4:30-32
6. The walk as a child in God's family, 5:1-33
7. The walk of children and servants, 6:1-9

Part IV. The Warfare of the Spirit-filled Believer in Christ, 6:10-22
1. His power, 6:10
2. His armor, 6:11
3. His foes, 6:12-17
4. His resources, 6:18-22

Benediction, 6:23, 24   *M. F. U.*

Eph′esus (ĕf′ē-sŭs), the capital of proconsular Asia, and an opulent city on the western coast of Asia Minor, located on the banks of the Cayster and about forty miles S. E. of Smyrna. Its harbor was ample.

1. **History.** It was colonized as early as the 11th century B. C. by Androclus, the son of the Athenian king, Codrus. The Persians, Macedonians, and the Romans each put it under subjection. In 262 A. D. it was destroyed by the Goths, and afterward never rose to its former glory.

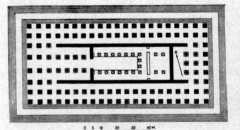

149. Plan of the Temple of Diana (Artemis), Ephesus

2. **Religion.** The Ephesians worshiped the Asiatic goddess Diana (*see* Gods, False), whose temple, one of the seven wonders of the world, made the city famous. The people, after the temple was destroyed by fire (B. C. 356), immediately rebuilt it. It is said that some of the magnificent columns are incorporated in the Church of St. Sophia.

There were many Jews in the city who were more or less influenced by Christianity (Acts 2:9; 6:9). Timothy was the bishop of the Church founded by St. Paul. To this Church Paul addressed one of his epistles. According to Eusebius St. John spent his last years in Ephesus. John opposed the doctrines of Nestorius, and Paul opposed the idolatry of those who made or worshiped shrines or practiced magic (19:13, sq.). His opposition resulted in a serious riot.

Several important councils were held in Ephesus, among which was the third ecumeni-

150. Remains of Amphitheatre, Ephesus, referred to in Acts 19:29

cal council (June 22-August 31, A. D. 431). A small Turkish town to-day represents the once noted city, which is called *Ayasaluk*.

Eph′lal (ĕf′lăl; *judge*), the son of Zabad, a descendant of Judah of the lineage of Sheshan (I Chron. 2:37).

E′phod (ē′fŏd), the father of Hanniel, the prince of the tribe of Manasseh, who was one of those appointed to divide the land among the tribes of Israel (Num. 34:23), B. C. c. 1390.

E′phod (ē-fŏd; *a covering*).

1. The Ephod and the Jewish Priesthood. A sacred garment of gold, blue, purple, scarlet and fine twined linen worn by the Jewish high priest (Exod. 28:40). The ephod fitted closely around the shoulders and was held by two straps. A hole in the top admitted the head. On top of each of the shoulder straps an onyx stone was encased in a filagree setting of gold and engraved with the names of six tribes of Israel (Exod. 28:9; 39:6, 7). The robe of the ephod was a garment different from the ephod. It was blue, sleeveless and fringed at the bottom with bells of gold and pomegranates of blue, gold, purple and scarlet (Exod. 28:31-35; 39:22-26). Ordinary priests wore a simpler linen ephod (I Sam. 22:18). Samuel wore such an ephod as a child (I Sam. 2:18), as did David when officiating before the ark as king (II Sam. 6:14).

2. The Ephod and Archaeology. Old Assyrian cuneiform tablets of the 19th century B. C. and the Ugaritic texts of the 15th show that an ephod (*epadu*), such as is mentioned in the O. T. as an important part of the holy attire of the Levitical priesthood was formerly an ordinary garment, worn especially, it would seem, by women. Only after many centuries did the *epadu* come to be restricted to religious and subsequently to priestly use. In Israel, however, it early came to be a distinctive part of the sacred dress of the Levitical priesthood. It was as Israel's anointed king and accordingly as a special representative of Jehovah that David wore a linen ephod on the occasion of the transfer of the ark of God to his capital city, Jerusalem. *M. F. U.*

Eph′phatha (ĕf′ā-thà; an Aramaic imperative meaning, "Be opened," i. e., receive power of hearing, the ears of the deaf and the eyes of the blind being considered as closed (Mark 7:34).

E′phraim (ē′frà-ĭm; *fruitful*), the second son of Joseph by Asenath, the daughter of Poti-

pherah (Gen. 46:20), born buring the seven years of plenty, B. C. about 1880.

1. Personal History. The first incident in Ephraim's history is the blessing of his grandfather, Jacob. Contrary to the intention of Joseph, Ephraim was preferred to Manasseh by Jacob, and upon him was conferred the birthright blessing (Gen. 48:17-19). Before Joseph's death Ephraim's family had reached the third generation (50:23), and it may have been about this time that the affray mentioned in I Chron. 7:21 occurred, when some of his sons were killed and when Ephraim named a son Beriah to perpetuate the memory of the disaster which had fallen on his house.

2. The Tribe of Ephraim. (1) **Numbers.** At the census in the wilderness of Sinai (Num. 1:32, 33; 2:19) its numbers were forty thousand five hundred, ranking *tenth*, and had decreased to thirty-two thousand five hundred at the second census, ranking *eleventh*. (2) **Position.** During the march through the wilderness the position of the sons of Joseph and Benjamin was on the west of the tabernacle (Num. 2:18-24), and the prince of Ephraim was Elishama, the son of Ammihud (1:10). According to rabbinical authority the standard of Ephraim was a golden flag, on which the head of a calf was depicted. The representative of Ephraim among the spies was the great hero, "Oshea, the son of Nun," whose name was changed by Moses to the more distinguished form (Joshua) in which it is familiar to us. (3) **Territory.** The boundaries of Ephraim are given in Josh. 16 (comp. I Chron. 7:28, 29). We are not able to trace this boundary line very exactly. But Ephraim occupied the very center of Palestine, embracing an area about forty miles in length from east to west and from six to twenty-five in breadth from north to south. It extended from the Mediterranean to the Jordan, having on the north the half tribe of Manasseh and on the south Benjamin and Dan (Josh. 16:5, etc.; 18:7, etc.; I Chron. 7:28, 29). The tribes of Ephraim and Manasseh were not at first contented with the size of their allotted portions, and were told by Joshua to go boldly and expel the inhabitants of the adjacent mountain and woodland country and occupy it (Josh. 17:14-18). (4) **Subsequent History.** "The tabernacle was set up in Ephraim at Shiloh" (Josh. 18:1). By this circumstance the influence of the tribe was increased, and we find it bearing itself haughtily. We have an example of this in their remonstrance to Gideon after his first victory, which that leader deemed prudent to pacify by a flattering answer (Judg. 7:24, 25; 8:1-3). With Jephthah they were still more incensed because, as they said, he had not solicited their aid. Jephthah boldly attacked and defeated them (12:1-6). At first the Ephraimites did not submit to the authority of David (II Sam. 2:8, 9), and though, after the death of Ishbosheth, a large body of them went to Hebron to join David and that monarch could speak of Ephraim as the strength of his head, yet the jealousy against Judah sometimes broke out (I Chron. 12:30; Psa. 60:7; II Sam. 19:40-43). David had his ruler in Ephraim (I Chron. 27:20) and Solomon his commissariat officer

(I Kings 4:8). Still the spirit and weight of the tribe were so great that Rehoboam found it necessary to repair to Shechem, a city within its borders, for his inauguration (I Kings 12:1). And then, on his foolish refusal of their demands, the ten tribes revolted, and established a different mode of worship (ch. 12). After this Ephraim was the main support of the northern kingdom, which came to be designated by its name, and the reunion of which with Judah was the hope of the prophets as the fulfillment of Israel's glory (Isa. 7:2; 11:13; Ezek. 37:15-22). After the captivity "children of Ephraim" dwelt in Jerusalem (I Chron. 9:3; comp. Neh. 11).

E′phraim, City of. In the wilderness was the town mentioned (John 11:54). It lay northeast of Jerusalem. Christ found refuge there when threatened with violence by the priests in consequence of raising Lazarus from the dead. Identified as *et Taiyibeh*.

E′phraim, Gate of. This was one of the gates of Jerusalem, on the north side of the city (II Kings 14:13; II Chron. 25:23).

E′phraim, Mount of, called also by other names, as "mountains of Israel" (Josh. 11:21) and "mountains of Samaria" (Jer. 31:5, 6; Amos 3:9). Joshua's burial place was among these mountains, at Timnath-heres, on the north side of the hill Gaash (Judg. 2:9). The earliest name given to the central range of mountains in Samaria was *Mount Ephraim*, just as the whole table land of Judah was called *Mount Judah*.

E′phraim, Wood of. When David's army had advanced into the field against Israel (those who followed Absalom) a battle was fought "in the wood of Ephraim" (II Sam. 18:6). All the circumstances connected with the battle indicate that it took place east of Jordan: Absalom had encamped in Gilead, and it is not stated that he had recrossed the Jordan; verse 3 ("that thou succor us out of the city") presupposes that the battle took place near Mahanaim; and after the victory the army returned to Mahanaim.

E′phraimite (ē′frā-ĭm-īt), a descendant of the patriarch Ephraim (Josh. 16:10; Judg. 12:4, 5, 6); also rendered *Ephrathite* (*q. v.*). The narrative in Judges seems to indicate that the Ephraimites had a peculiar accent, or *patois*, similar to that which in later times caused "the speech" of the Galileans to betray them at Jerusalem (Matt. 26:73).

E′phrain (ē′frā-ĭn), a city of Israel, which with its dependent hamlets Abijah and the army of Judah captured from Jeroboam (II Chron. 13:19). C. V. Raumer and others identify Ephron or Ephrain both with Ophrah of Benjamin, which, it is conjectured, was situated near or in Taiyibeh, to the east of Beth-el, and with the city of Ephraim (Keil, *Com.*, in loc.).

Eph′ratah (ĕf′rȧ-tȧ), or **Eph′rath** (ĕf′rȧth; *fruitfulness, fruitful*).

1. The second wife of Caleb, the son of Ezron, mother of Hur (I Chron 2:19) and grandmother of Caleb, the spy (ver. 50; 4:4), B. C. probably 1440.

2. The ancient name of Beth-lehem in Judah (Gen. 35:16, 19; 48:7), both of which passages distinctly prove that it was called

Ephrath or Ephratah in Jacob's time. The meaning of the passage, "Lo, we heard of it at Ephrath" (Psa. 132:6), is much disputed. The most obvious reference is to *Beth-lehem*, which is elsewhere known by that name.

Eph′rathite (ĕf′rȧ-thīt).

1. An inhabitant of Bethlehem (Ruth 1:2).

2. An Ephraimite (I Sam. 1:1; I Kings 11:26).

E′phron (ē′frŏn; perhaps *fawnlike*).

1. The son of Zohar, a Hittite; the owner of a field which lay facing Mamre, or Hebron, and of the cave contained therein, which Abraham bought from him for four hundred shekels of silver (Gen. 23:8-17; 25:9; 49:29, 30; 50:13), B. C. perhaps about 1950. By Josephus (*Ant.*, i, 14) the name is *Ephraim*, and the purchase money forty shekels.

2. A mountain the "cities" of which formed one of the landmarks on the north boundary of the tribe of Judah (Josh. 15:9). It was probably the steep and lofty mountain ridge on the west side of the Terebinth valley (Wady *Beit Hanina*).

Epicure′ans, The (ĕp-ĭ-kū-rē′ănz), derived their name from Epicurus (342-271 B. C.), a philosopher of Attic descent, whose "Garden" at Athens rivaled in popularity the "Porch" and the "Academy." The doctrines of Epicurus found wide acceptance in Asia Minor and Alexandria, and they gained a brilliant advocate at Rome in Lucretius (95-50 B. C.). The object of Epicurus was to find in philosophy a practical guide to happiness. True pleasure and not absolute truth was the end at which he aimed; experience and not reason the test on which he relied. It is obvious that a system thus framed would degenerate by a natural descent into mere materialism; and in this form Epicurism was the popular philosophy at the beginning of the Christian era (comp. Diog., L. x, 5, 9). When St. Paul addressed "Epicureans and Stoics" (Acts 17:18) at Athens the philosophy of life was practically reduced to the teaching of those two antagonistic schools (Smith).

Epistle (Gr. *epistolē, a written message*), the term employed to designate twenty-one out of twenty-seven of the writings of the New Testament, while Luke and the Acts are both prefaced by an epistle to Theophilus, a friend of the evangelist. They are known as *Paul's Epistles* and the *Catholic* or *General Epistles*.

1. **Paul's Epistles** number fourteen (if we include Hebrews), arranged in the New Testament not in the order of time as to their composition, but rather according to the rank of the places to which they were sent. It is not known by whom they were thus arranged. His letters were, as a rule, written by an amanuensis under his dictation, after which he added a few words in his own hand at the close. The epistles to Timothy and Titus are called pastoral epistles, from their being pastoral instructions from a pastor to a pastor.

Ephesians, Philippians, Colossians and Philemon are known as prison epistles because they were written during Paul's Roman imprisonment.

2. The **Catholic** or **General Epistles** were so called because they were not addressed to any particular church or individual, but to

Christians in general. Of these three were written by John, two by Peter, and one each by James and Jude. This division is strictly accurate, for I Peter and II and III John, although addressed to particular persons, have little in them that is properly local and personal.

Epistles, Spurious. Many of these are lost, but several are extant, of which the following are the principal:

1. The *Epistle of Paul to the Laodicaeans*. Marcion received as genuine an "Epistle of Paul to the Laodicaeans," early in the 2d century, but it is doubtful whether it is the one now extant in the Latin language. The original epistle was probably a forgery founded on Col. 4:16, "And when this epistle is read among you, cause that it be read also in the church of the Laodicaeans, and that *ye likewise read the epistle from Laodicaea*." Some have endeavored to identify it with a genuine epistle; Grotius thought it to be the Epistle to the Ephesians; Theophylact believed it to be I Timothy; others hold it to be I John, Philemon, etc.

2. *Third Epistle of Paul to the Corinthians*. Calvin, Louis Cappell, and others think that Paul wrote many other epistles besides those now known, basing their opinion on I Cor. 5:9. There is still extant, in the Armenian language, an epistle from the Corinthians to Paul, together with the apostle's reply. This epistle is quoted as Paul's by St. Gregory the Illuminator in the 3d century.

3. The *Epistle of Peter to James* is a very ancient forgery. Origen says that it was not to be reckoned among the ecclesiastical books, and that it was not written by Peter or any other inspired person. It is thought to be a forgery of some Ebionite in the beginning of the 2d century.

4. The *Epistles of Paul and Seneca* consist of eight long letters from the philosopher Seneca to the apostle Paul, with six from the latter to Seneca. Their antiquity is doubted. They are mentioned by St. Jerome and Augustine, and are generally rejected as spurious.

5. The *Epistle of Lentulus* to the Roman Senate, giving a description of the person of Christ, and some pretended epistles of the Virgin Mary, are generally rejected. *See* Bible.

Epoch, a point of time distinguished by some remarkable event, and from which succeeding years are numbered. *See* Era, Dispensation.

Er (ûr; *watchful*).

1. The eldest son of the patriarch Judah by Bath-shuah (daughter of Shuah), a Canaanitess (Gen. 38:2, 3). "Er was wicked in the sight of the Lord; and the Lord slew him" (ver. 7; Num. 26:19). It does not appear what the nature of his sin was; but, from his Canaanitish birth on his mother's side, it was probably connected with the abominable idolatries of Canaan (Smith).

2. The son of Shelah and grandson of Judah (I Chron. 4:21).

3. The son of Jose and father of Elmodam, in the ancestry of Joseph, the husband of Mary (Luke 3:28).

Era, a period during which years are numbered and dates are reckoned from some historical event.

1. **Jewish.** The ancient Jews used several eras in their computations: (1) From Gen. 7:11 and 8:13 it appears that they reckoned from the lives of the patriarchs or other illustrious persons; (2) From the Exodus from Egypt (Exod. 19:1; Num. 1:1; 33:38); (3) From the building of the temple (I Kings 9:10; II Chron. 8:1), and the reigns of the kings of Judah and Israel; (4) From the Babylonian captivity (Ezek. 1:1; 33:21; 40:1), and the dedication of the second temple; (5) Era of the Seleucidae, dating from the occupation of Babylon by Seleucus Nicator (312 B. C.); (6) From the time when their princes began to reign (I Kings 15:1; Isa. 36:1; Jer. 1:2, 3; also Matt. 2:1; Luke 1:5; 3:1); (7) Since the compilation of the Talmud the Jews have reckoned their years from the creation of the world, which they fix at B. C. 3761.

2. **Ancient Heathen.** (1) The First Olympiad placed in the year of the world 3228, and B. C. 776; (2) The taking of Troy by the Greeks, year of the world 2820 and B. C. 1184; (3) The voyage undertaken for the possession of the golden fleece, year of the world 2760; (4) Foundation of Rome (A. U. C.), B. C. 753; (5) Era of Nabonassar, B. C. 747; (6) Era of Alexander the Great, or his last victory over Darius, B. C. 330; (7) Julian Era, dating from the reform of the calendar by Julius Caesar, B. C. 45, Jan. 1; (8) Era of Diocletian, being the beginning of the first Egyptian year after the accession of that emperor, A. D. 284, August 29; (9) Among the Mohammedans, the Hegira, A. D. 622; (10) Among the modern Persians, the Era of Yezdegird III, A. D. 632, June 16.

3. **Christian.** For a long time the Christians had no era of their own, but followed those in common use in the different countries: In the western part of the Roman empire the *Consular* Era was used until the 6th century after Christ. The *Era of Diocletian*, called by the Christians the "Era of Martyrs" (*Aera Martyrum*) because of the persecutions in his reign, still used by the Abyssinians and Copts. The *Era of the Armenians*, when the Armenians, at the council of Tiben, separated from the main body of the Eastern Church by rejecting the council of Chalcedon, A. D. 552. The *Era of Constantinople*, or *Byzantine Era*, begins with the creation of the world, which it fixes at B. C. 5508. The *Vulgar* or *Christian Era*, beginning with the birth of Christ, is the ordinary count of years in the Christian countries. This era was invented in the 6th century by Dionysius Exiguus, who supposed that Christ was born December 25, A. D. 1, a date now universally considered to be at least three years too late. For several centuries the year was begun on March 25, the day of annunciation. In the 11th century the Dionysian Era was adopted by the popes, and has since been in universal use in the Western Church. *See* Chronology.

E′ran (ē′răn; *watchful*), son of Shuthelah (eldest son of Ephraim) and head of the family of the Eranites (Num. 26:36).

E′ranites (ē′răn-īts), descendants of Eran (Num. 26:36).

Eras′tus (ê-răs′tŭs; *beloved*), a Corinthian and one of Paul's disciples, whose salutations he sends from Corinth to the Church at Rome as those of "the chamberlain of the city"

(Rom. 16:23). The word so rendered (oikono-mos, Vulg. *arcarius*) denotes the city *treasurer* (or steward), an officer of great dignity in ancient times (Josephus, *Ant.*, vii, 8, 2); so that the conversion of such a man to the faith of the Gospel was a proof of the wonderful success of the apostle's labors in that city. We find Erastus with Paul at Ephesus as one of his attendants or deacons, whence he was sent along with Timothy into Macedonia, while the apostle himself remained in Asia (Acts 19:22). They were both with the apostle at Corinth when he wrote, as above, from that city to the Romans; at a subsequent period Erastus was still at Corinth (II Tim. 4:20), which would seem to have been the usual place of his abode.

E'rech (ē'rĕk; Akkadian Uruk), the city of Nimrod (Gen. 10-10), lying on the left bank of the Euphrates, is represented by modern Warka, situated about 100 miles S. E. of Babylon in a marshy region of the Euphrates. Here was discovered the first ziggurat, or sacred temple tower, and evidence of the first cylinder seals (Cf. Jack Finegan, *Light From the Ancient Past*, 1946, pp. 19-23). The Uruk ziggurat dates from the early part of the fourth millennium B. C. Erech, with Ur, Lagash and Eridu are among the oldest cities of southern Babylonia. *M. F. U.*

E'ri (ē'rī; *watching*), the fifth son of the patriarch Gad (Gen. 46:16) and ancestor of the Erites (Num. 26:16).

E'rite (ē'rīt), a patronymic designation (Num. 26:16) of the descendants of the Gadite *Eri* (*q. v.*).

Esa'ias (ē-zā'yăs), the Grecized form of Isaiah, constantly used in the New Testament.

Esar-had'don (ē-sär-hăd'ŏn; *Ashur* has given a brother), an eminent and powerful Assyrian emperor, successor of Sennacherib. He reigned 680-669 B. C.

1. **His Accession.** Sennacherib was assassinated in 681 B. C. by his two sons Adrammelech and Sharezer as a consequence of their jealousy of Esar-haddon, the emperor's favorite. Esar-haddon was away conducting a campaign and he immediately returned to Nineveh. The murderers escaped to Armenia.

151. Memorial Stone of Esar-haddon

2. **His Accomplishments.** The most important achievement of Esar-haddon was the restoration of the city of Babylon, destroyed by his father, Sennacherib. "... At the beginning of my rule, in the first year of my reign, when I took my seat upon the royal throne in might, there appeared favorable signs in the heavens and upon earth . . . through the soothsayers' rites encouraging oracles were disclosed, for the rebuilding of Babylon and the restoration of Esagila (temple of the gods). They caused the command (oracle) to be written down." (D. D. Luckenbill, *Ancient Records of Assyria and Babylonia II*, Sect. 646). Esar-haddon continues his description of the rebuilding of Babylon. "I summoned all my artisans and the people of Babylon in their totality . . . Babylon I built anew, I enlarged, I raised aloft, I made magnificent" (*Ibid*, Sect. 647). Esar-haddon also defeated Taharka, the pharoah of Egypt. The triumph over Taharka was commemorated by the victory stele set up at Senjirli in N. Syria, recovered in 1888 by the Germans. The king is depicted with a mace in his left hand, and in his right he pours out a libation to the gods, symbolized at the top of the stele. Ropes extending to the lips of two figures at his feet are shown in his left hand. Taharka is evidently one of the figures. The other seems to be Ba'alu of Tyre. Esar-haddon thus boasts of himself, "I am powerful, I am all powerful. I am a hero, I am gigantic, I am colossal," and for the first time an Assyrian monarch assumed the new title, "king of the kings of Egypt," boasting concerning Taharka, king of Egypt and Ethiopia . . . "daily without cessation I slew multitudes of his men and him I smote five times with the point of my javelin with wounds from which there was no recovery. Memphis, his royal city, in half a day, with mines, tunnels, assaults, I besieged, I captured, I destroyed, I defeated, I burned with fire" (Luckenbill II, Sects. 577-583). *M. F. U.*

E'sau (ē'sô; *hairy*, Gen. 25:25).

1. **Name and Family.** His surname, *Edom*, was given him from the *red* pottage (25:30). The eldest son of Isaac by Rebekah, and twin brother of Jacob.

2. **Personal History.** We have no account of the early life of Esau beyond an incident or two connected with his birth (Gen. 25:22-26), B. C. about 1980. As he grew up Esau became "a cunning hunter, a man of the field." He was, in fact, a thorough "son of the desert," who delighted to roam free as the wind of heaven, and who was impatient at the restraints of civilized or settled life. Still his father loved him, and none the less for the savory venison the son brought to him (25:28). (1) **Sells his birthright.** Coming in one day from the chase hungry and longing for food he saw Jacob enjoying a dish of pottage. He prayed Jacob to share his meal with him. Jacob set a price upon the food, even the birthright of his brother. This was, indeed, a large demand, for the birthright secured to its possessor immunities and privileges of high value—the headship of the tribe, both spiritual and temporal, and the possession of the great bulk of the family property, and carried with it the *covenant blessing* (Gen. 27:28, 29, 36;

Heb. 12:16, 17). Urged by hunger, however, Esau acceded to Jacob's demands, secured the food, and "despised his birthright" (Gen. 25: 29-34). (2) **Marries.** At the age of forty years Esau married two wives in close succession. These were both Canaanites, and, on account of their origin, were not acceptable to Isaac and Rebekah. The latter was especially grieved. "I am weary," she said (Gen. 27:46) "of my life because of the daughters of Heth." (1) His first wife was Adah, the daughter of Elon the Hittite (36:2), called Bashemath in 26:34. (2) His second wife was Aholibamah, the daughter of Anah, as all the accounts agree, except that in 26:34, where by some error or variation of names she is called Judith, the daughter of Beeri the Hittite. (3) Esau's third wife, taken from his own kindred, was Bashemath (otherwise called Mahalath, 28:9), sister of Nebajoth and daughter of Ishmael (36:3). (3) **Loses his father's blessing.** When Isaac was grown old and feeble he wished in the consciousness of approaching death, to give his blessing to his elder son. Without regard to the words which were spoken by God with reference to the children before their birth, and without taking any notice of Esau's frivolous barter of his birthright and his ungodly connection with Canaanites, Isaac maintained his preference for Esau. He commanded him to hunt game and prepare him a savory dish that he might eat and bless him. Rebekah sought to frustrate this plan, desiring to secure the inheritance for Jacob. Jacob successfully simulated Esau and secured the desired blessing, but had scarcely done so when Esau returned. When told that his brother had secured the prize he cried out, "Bless me, even me also, O my father!" Urging this entreaty again and again, even with tears, Isaac at length said to him: "Behold thy dwelling shall be the fatness of the earth, and of the dew of heaven from above; and by thy sword shalt thou live, and shalt serve thy brother: and it shall come to pass when thou shalt have the dominion, that thou shalt break his yoke from off thy neck." Thus deprived forever of his birthright by virtue of the irrevocable blessing, Esau hated his brother and vowed vengeance. But he said to himself, "The days of mourning for my father are at hand; then will I slay my brother Jacob." When Esau heard that his father had commanded Jacob to take a wife of the daughters of his kinsman Laban he also resolved to try whether by a new alliance he could propitiate his parents. He accordingly married his cousin Mahalath, the daughter of Ishmael (Gen. 28:6-9). (4) **Removes to Mount Seir.** Esau probably removed soon after this to Mount Seir, still retaining, however, some interest in his father's property in southern Palestine. It is probable that his own habits and the idolatrous practices of his wives and rising family continued to excite and even increase the anger of his parents; and that he, consequently, considered it more prudent to remove his household to a distance (Gen. 32:3). (5) **Reconciled to Jacob.** Esau was residing at Mount Seir when Jacob returned from Padan-aram, and Jacob, fearing lest Esau should desire to take revenge for

former injuries, sent messengers in order, if possible, to appease his wrath. In reply to his conciliatory message Esau came to meet him with four hundred armed men. "Jacob was greatly afraid and distressed. What must have been his surprise, when they neared each other, to see Esau running with extended arms to greet and embrace him! Esau "fell on his neck and kissed him, and they wept." Jacob had prepared a present for Esau, which the latter at first refused to take, but afterward accepted. Esau's offer to march with Jacob as a guard was declined, and Esau returned to Mount Seir (Gen. 32:3-33:16). (6) **Later history.** It does not appear that the two brothers met again until the death of their father. Mutual interest and fear constrained them to act honestly, and even generously, toward each other at this solemn interview. They united in laying the body of Isaac in the cave of Machpelah (Gen. 35:29). Then "Esau took all his cattle, and all his substance, which he had got in the land of Canaan"—such, doubtless, as his father, with Jacob's consent, had assigned to him—"and went into the country from the face of his brother Jacob" (36:6). Esau is once more presented to us (36:43) in a genealogical table, in which a long line of illustrious descendants is referred to "Esau, the father of the Edomites."

3. **Spiritual Message.** Esau serves as a good illustration of the natural man of the earth (Heb. 12:16, 17). In many respects a nobler man, in the natural, than Jacob, he was nevertheless destitute of faith. This was manifest in his despising the birthright because it was a spiritual thing, of value only as faith could see that value. The birthright involved the exercise of the priestly rights vested in the family head until the establishment of the Aaronic priesthood. The Edenic promise of the Satan-Bruiser was fixed in the family of Abraham (Gen. 3:15). The order of promise was Abel, Seth, Shem, Abraham, Isaac, *Esau.* As the first-born Esau was in the distinct line of the promise to Abraham of the Earth-Blesser (Gen. 12:3). For all that was revealed, these great Messianic promises might have been realized in Esau. For a fleeting, fleshly gratification Esau sold this birthright. Although Jacob's understanding of the birthright at the time was undoubtedly carnal and faulty, his desire for it, nevertheless, evidenced true faith. "And he that cometh unto God must believe that He is and is a Rewarder of them who diligently seek Him" (Heb. 11:6).

Eschatology (From Gr. *eschatos,* last and *logos, study*). A theological term employed to designate the doctrine of last things, particularly those dealing with the second coming of Christ and the events preceding and following this great event.

1. **Common Concept.** It is quite customary in treatises on systematic theology to find a very abbreviated eschatology and to discover a prevailing agnostic attitude that much cannot be known. This curtailment of such an important phase of Biblical theology is a very severe hindrance to the edification of the present-day church. Creedal systems and traditionalism have held the field in this realm

of theological thinking as in no other phase of theology. When one considers that approximately twenty-five per cent of divine revelation was prophetic when written, it is a tragedy to reduce this realm of theological thinking to the events immediately clustering around the second advent of Christ.

2. **Correct Concept.** Properly understood, eschatology is much broader than this. As Lewis Sperry Chafer says, "This, the last major division of systematic theology, is concerned with things to come and should not be limited to things which are future at some particular time in human history but should contemplate all that was future in character at the time its revelation was given. . . . A worthy eschatology must employ all prediction whether fulfilled or unfulfilled at a given time. In other words, a true eschatology attempts to account for all the prophecy set forth in the Bible." (Lewis Sperry Chafer, *Systematic Theology* IV, p. 255).

3. **General Scope.**

(1) Eschatology properly understood embraces the far-reaching prophecy concerning the Lord Jesus Christ as Prophet, Priest and King, as the Promised Seed, and with regard to the two Advents.

(2) It embraces prophecy concerning Israel's covenants. The four major covenants: that made with Abraham, that given through Moses, that made with David, and the New Covenant yet to be made in the Messianic Kingdom.

(3) It embraces prophecy concerning the Gentiles—their "times" (Luke 21:24), and their judgment.

(4) It embraces prophecies concerning Satan, evil, the "man of sin," etc.

(5) It embraces prophecy concerning the end of apostate Christendom.

(6) It embraces prophecy concerning the church, involving the translation of the living saints, the judgment seat of Christ, the marriage of the Lamb and the return of the glorified church to reign with Christ. A full-scale study of these great prophetic themes will comprehend the judgments, the resurrections, the mediatorial Messianic kingdom and the eternal state. *M. F. U.*

Esdrae′lon, Plain of (ĕs-drȧ-ē′lŏn). This name is the Greek modification of Jezreel (*God sows*). It is a large plain about twenty miles long and fourteen miles wide, famous for its fertility due to soil washed down from the neighboring mountains of Galilee and the highlands of Samaria. Esdraelon drains into the Mediterranean by the Wadi Kishon where Deborah's ancient battle was fought (Judg. 4:7; 5:21) and Elijah conducted his contest with the priests of Baal (I Kings 18:40). Important towns in ancient times, like Taanach, Megiddo and Bethshan, were built around the edge of the plain by Canaanite chariot kings. The valley has been a famous battleground through the centuries. Here the great Egyptian Thutmose III fought the confederate princes of Syria and Palestine. Here King Saul was slain by the Philistines (I Sam. 31:1-3). Here the conquering Israelites faced the Canaanite kings (Josh. 17:16). In the prophetic Scriptures the last great battle of

152. Plain of Esdraelon

the age will be fought at Armageddon, the ancient hill of the Valley of Megiddo west of Jordan in the Plain of Jezreel (Rev. 16:14-16; 19:17). This great conflict will be that in which Christ at His coming glory will deliver the Jewish remnant besieged by the Gentile world powers under the Beast and the False Prophet (Rev. 16:13-16; Zech. 12:1-9). Apparently the besieging hosts, alarmed by the signs preceding the Lord's Advent (Matt. 24:29, 30) fall back to Megiddo after the events of Zech. 14:2, where their destruction begins, with the decimation completed in Moab and the plains of Idumea (Isa. 63: 1-6). *M. F. U.*

E′sek (ē′sĕk; *contention*), one of the three wells dug by Isaac's herdsmen in the valley of Gerar, and so named because the herdsmen of Gerar disputed concerning its possession (Gen. 26:20).

Esh′baal (ĕsh′bā-ăl), or **Esh-ba′al** (ĕsh-bā′ăl; *man of Baal*), the fourth son of King Saul (I Chron. 8:33; 9:39). He is doubtless the same person as *Ish-bosheth* (I Sam. 31:2, comp. with II Sam. 2:8), since it was the practice to change the obnoxious name of *Baal* into *Bosheth* or *Besheth*, as in the case of Jerubbesheth for Jerubbaal and (in this very genealogy) of Mephibosheth for Meribbaal. The Hebrew term *bōshĕth*, meaning "shame," expressed the horror pious Yahwists felt toward the degenerate cults of Canaan.

Esh′ban (ĕsh′băn), the second named of the four sons of Dishon, the Horite (Gen. 36:26; I Chron. 1:41).

Esh′col (ĕsh′kŏl; *a bunch, cluster*).

1. A young Amoritish chieftain, who, with his brothers, Aner and Mamre, being in alliance with Abraham, joined him in the recovery of Lot from the hands of Chedorlaomer and his confederates (Gen. 14:13, 24), B. C. about 1955.

2. The valley in the neighborhood of Hebron, in which the spies found large grapes (Num. 13:23, 24). The valley probably took its name from the distinguished Amorite above mentioned.

Esh′ean (ĕsh′ē-ăn; *support*), the third named of a group of nine towns in the country round Hebron in Judah (Josh. 15:52). As the LXX reading is *Somah*, Knobel conjectures that Eshean is a corrupt reading for *Shema* (I Chron. 2:43) and connects it with the ruins of *Simia*, south of Daumeh (K. and D., *Com.*), A. V. and R. S. V. Eshan.

E′shek (ē′shĕk; *oppression*), a brother of Azel, a Benjamite, one of the late descendants of King Saul; the father of Ulam, the founder of a large and noted family of archers (I Chron. 8:39).

Esh′kalonite (ĕsh′kȧ-lŏn-īt), the designation (Josh. 13:3) of an inhabitant of *Ashkelon* (*q. v.*).

Esh′taol (ĕsh′tā-ŏl), a town in the northern part of the hilly region, at first assigned to Judah (Josh. 15:33), but afterward to Dan (19:41). Samson was born at or near Eshtaol (Judg. 13:24, 25; 16:31). From Eshtaol and the neighboring Zorah the Danites started on their expedition to secure more territory at Laish (18:2, sq.). Its location has been fixed at Eshwa‘ near Zorah, and 13 miles N. W. of Jerusalem.

Esh′taolite (ĕsh-tȧ-ō′līt), A. V. Esh-taulite, an inhabitant of Eshtaol.

Eshtemo′a (ĕsh-tĕ-mō′ȧ), or **Esh′temoh** (ĕsh′-tĕ-mō; *obedience*, Josh. 15:50), a mountain town of Judah, and afterward ceded to the priests (Josh. 21:14; I Chron. 4:17, 19). David, when at Ziklag, sent of his spoil to the elders of Eshtemoa (I Sam. 30:28), and Ishbah is mentioned (I Chron. 4:17) as its "father," i. e., lord. It is the present *Semua*, a village south of Hebron, with considerable ruins dating from ancient times.

Esh′ton (ĕsh′tŏn; *restful*), a son of Mehir and grandson of Chelub, of the tribe of Judah (I Chron. 4:11, 12).

Es′li (ĕs′lī), son of Nagge (Naggai) and father of Naum, of the maternal ancestry of Christ after the exile (Luke 3:25). He is probably the same as *Elioenai*, the son of Neariah and father of Johanan (I Chron. 3:23, 24).

Espousal, the mutual agreement between parties to marry. *See* Marriage.

   Figurative. This social institution is alluded to figuratively in the relationship of the Church as the bride of Christ (II Cor. 11:2; Eph. 5:25-32; John 3:29; Rev. 19:6-8). It is important to distinguish between Israel and the Church. Israel is the wife of Jehovah (Hos. 2:2; 2:16-23) now disowned but yet to be restored. This relationship is not to be confused with that of the Church of Christ. The Church is a virgin espoused to one Husband, which could never be said of an adulterous wife to be restored in grace. Israel is, accordingly, to be the forgiven and restored wife of Jehovah. Such relationships in dealing with deity, being figurative and expressing spiritual relationship, are not inconsonant or contradictory. I Cor. 10:32 clearly names three classes in this present age—Jews, Gentiles and the Church of God. All the unsaved are either Jews or Gentiles in this age. All saved people, whether Jews or Gentiles, are members of the Church, the Body of Christ, a distinct entity formed at Pentecost by the advent of the Spirit performing His baptizing work (Acts 1:5; 11:16; I Cor. 12:31) and to be completed at the coming of the Lord (I Cor. 15:53; I Thess. 4:13-17; II Thess. 2:1). *M. F. U.*

Es′rom (ĕz′rŏm), a Grecized form (Matt. 1:3; Luke 3:33) of the name of *Hezron* (*q. v.*), the grandson of Judah (I Chron. 2:5).

Essence, The Divine. Essence (from Latin verb *esse, to be*) signifies that which a person or thing is in himself or itself, apart from all that is accidental. Substance is a term of equivalent meaning. These terms are held by some to be more appropriate in philosophy than in theology. The Scriptures, it is truly said, contain no such abstract terms as essence and substance. At the same time it must be admitted that some of the names under which God has revealed himself, as Elohim and Jehovah, refer directly to the eternal divine essence. At all events theology has often made large use of these terms in its attempts to arrive at the proper and scriptural conception of God. The principal points in dispute have been, first, as to what extent, if any, the divine essence can be known to us; and, secondly, as to the relation existing between the attributes of God and his essence. The view best substantiated is that the attributes of God are not merely subjective conceptions, based upon certain only relatively true Scripture revelations, but that the attributes made known to us through the Scriptures are manifestations of what God is in himself. They are the living realization of his essence. Accordingly, while the divine essence is incomprehensible, we have nevertheless some measure of true knowledge of God, knowledge that relates to his very essence. (*See* God, Attributes of.) For full and discriminating discussion see Dorner, *System of Christian Doctrine*, vol. i, pp. 187-206; Pope, *Compendium of Christian Doctrine*, vol. i, pp. 246-252; Van Oosterzee, *Christian Dogmatics*, vol. i, pp. 234-238; Hodge, *Systematic Theology*, vol. i, pp. 366-370. *E. McC.*

Essenes′ (ĕs-sēnz′), a Jewish religious community, though differing in many respects from traditional Judaism.

   1. Identity. An ascetic community of men in Palestine and Syria forming the first cells of organized monasticism in the Mediterranean world. Their main colonies were near the northern end of the Dead Sea and around Engedi. The phenomenal discovery of non-Biblical literature among the famous Dead Sea Scrolls, including "The Manual of Discipline" and "The Commentary of Habakkuk," has shed a great deal of light on pre-Christian sects. The sect which owned and produced the Dead Sea Scrolls has striking affinities with the Covenanters of Damascus, the Essenes, the Therapeutae of Egypt and the John the Baptist movement. Millar Burrows has shown that the Judean Covenanters (his term for the Essenes) are the same Jewish sect as the Covenanters of Damascus. This new material corroborates Philo and Josephus, heretofore the primary sources for an understanding of the Essenes. For a comparison of this latest archaeological material with the older sources see W. H. Brownlee, "A Comparison of the Covenanters of the Dead Sea Scrolls with Pre-Christian Jewish Sects" in *The Biblical Archaeologist*, Vol. XIII, Sept. 1950, pp. 50-72 and pp. 56-66 dealing specifically with the Essenes.

   2. Origin. The origin of the Essenes is as obscure as their name. Josephus first mentions them (*Ant.*, xiii, 5, 9) in the time of Jonathan the Maccabee (about 150 B. C.), and speaks expressly of one Judas an Essene (105-104 B. C.). This would place the origin of the order in the 2d century before Christ. It is questionable whether they proceeded simply from Judaism or whether foreign and especially Hellenistic elements had not also an influence in their origin.

3. **Organization.** Their whole community was strictly organized as a single body, at the head of which were presidents (Gr. *epimelētai*), to whom the members were bound to unconditional obedience. One wishing to enter the order received three badges—a pickax, an apron, and a white garment. After a year's probation he was admitted to the lustrations. Another probation of two years followed, when he was allowed to participate in the common meals and to become a full member after first taking a fearful oath, in which he bound himself to absolute openness to his brethren and secrecy concerning the doctrines of the order to non-members. Only adults were admitted as members, but children were received for instruction in the principles of Essenism. Josephus says that the Essenes were divided into four classes according to the time of their entrance, the children being the first class, those in the two stages of the novitiate the second and third class, and the members proper the fourth class.

4. **Discipline.** Transgressions of members were tried by a court, and sentence was never pronounced by the votes of less than one hundred. What was once decided by that number was unalterable.

Excommunication was equivalent to a slow death, since an Essene could not take food prepared by strangers for fear of pollution. The strongest tie by which the members were united was the absolute *community* of goods. It is a law among them that those who come to them must let what they have be common to the whole order. They also have stewards appointed to take care of their common affairs. They choose fitting persons as receivers of revenues and of the produce of the earth, and priests for the preparation of the bread and food. There was *one* purse for all, and common expenses, common clothes, and common food at common meals. The needy of the order, as the sick and the aged, were cared for at the common expense, and special officers were appointed in every town to care for the wants of the traveling brethren. The *daily labor* of the members was strictly regulated. After prayer they were dismissed to their work by the presidents. They reassembled for purifying ablutions and the common meal, after which they went to work again, to reassemble for the evening meal. Although their chief employment was agriculture they carried on crafts of every kind; but trading was forbidden (as leading to covetousness), and also the making of weapons or any utensils that might injure men.

5. **Ethics, Manners, and Customs.** Philo competes with Josephus in sounding the praises of the Essenes. According to these authorities their life was abstemious, simple, and unpretending. They condemned sensual desires as sinful, abstained from wedlock, but chose other people's children while they were pliable and fit for learning; they only took food and drink till they had had enough, contenting themselves with the same dish day by day, and rejecting great expense as harmful to mind and body; they did not cast away clothes and shoes until they were utterly use-less, and only sought to acquire what was needed for the wants of life.

In addition to the general features of simplicity and moderation mentioned above we call attention to the following special points: (1) There was no *slave* among them, but all were *free*, mutually working for each other. (2) *Swearing* was forbidden as worse than perjury; "for that which does not deserve belief without an appeal to God is already condemned." (3) They *forbade anointing with oil*, regarding a rough exterior as praiseworthy. (4) *Bathing in cold water* was compulsory before each meal, after performing the functions of nature, or coming in contact with a member of a lower class of the order. (5) They considered *white* raiment as seemly for all occasions. (6) *Great modesty* was inculcated. In performing natural functions they dug with the pickax—which each member received—a hole one foot deep, covered themselves with a mantle (not to offend the brightness of God), relieved themselves into the hole, and threw in again the earth. In *bathing* they bound an apron about their loins; they avoided *spitting* forward or to the right hand. (7) They sent gifts of incense to the temple, but *offered no animal sacrifices* because they esteemed their own sacrifices more valuable. (8) The chief peculiarity of the Essenes was their common meals, which bore the character of *sacrificial feasts*. The food was prepared by priests, with the observance, probably, of certain rites of purification; for an Essene was not permitted to partake of any other food than this. The opinion that the Essenes abstained from *flesh* and *wine* is not supported by the older authorities.

6. **Theology, etc.** The Essenes held fundamentally the Jewish view of the world, entertaining an absolute belief in Providence, which they held in common with the Pharisees. Next to God the name of Moses the lawgiver was with them an object of the greatest reverence, and whoever blasphemes it is punished with death. In their worship the Holy Scriptures were read and explained. The Sabbath was so strictly observed that they did not on that day remove a vessel or even perform the functions of nature; and they seem to have kept to the priesthood of the house of Aaron.

They must have highly estimated their angelology as their novices had to swear carefully to preserve the names of the angels. Concerning their doctrine of the *soul* and of its *immortality* Josephus writes: "They taught that bodies are perishable, but souls immortal, and that the latter dwelt originally in the subtlest ether, but being debased by sensual pleasures united themselves with bodies as with prisons; but when they are freed from the fetters of sense they will joyfully soar on high as if delivered from long bondage. To the good (souls) is appointed a life beyond the ocean, where they are troubled by neither rain nor snow nor heat, but where the gentle zephyr is ever blowing. . . . But to the bad (souls) is appointed a dark, cold region full of unceasing torment."

A strange phenomenon presented on Jewish soil is the peculiar conduct of the Essenes with respect to the sun. To this they turned while praying, in opposition to the Jewish custom of looking toward the temple. From this and other customs it would appear that they were in real earnest in their religious estimation of the sun.

In conclusion we may observe that "Essenism is merely Pharisaism in the superlative degree." It was, however, influenced by foreign systems of theology and philosophy, of which four have been proposed, viz., Buddhism, Parseeism, Syrian heathenism, and Pythagoreanism.

The Essenes disappeared from history after the destruction of Jerusalem. Though not directly mentioned in Scripture they may be referred to in Matt. 19:11, 12; Col. 2:8, 18, 23. See Josephus, *Antiquities*, xviii, 1, 5; *Wars*, ii, 8, 2, sq.; Schürer, *Jewish People*, div. ii, vol. ii, 190, sq.; Edersheim, *Life and Times of the Messiah*, ii, 329, sq.

Es'ther (ĕs'tēr), the Jewish maiden chosen to be queen by Ahasuerus.

1. Name and Family. Esther was the new and probably Persian name given on her introduction to the royal harem. Her proper Hebrew name was *Hadassah* "Myrtle" (*q. v.*). As to the signification of Esther, it is "Ishtar," the name of the great Babylonian goddess. Gesenius quotes from the second Targum on Esther: "She was called Esther from the name of the star Venus, which in Greek is *Aster* (i. e., *astēr*, Eng. *star*)." Esther was the daughter of Abihail, a Benjamite and uncle of Mordecai (Esth. 2:15). Her ancestor, Kish, had been among the captives led away from Jerusalem by Nebuchadnezzar.

2. Personal History. Left an orphan, Esther was brought up by her cousin Mordecai, who held an office at Shushan in the palace (Esth. 2:5-7). (1) **Chosen queen.** Ahasuerus, Xerxes I (486-465 B. C.), having divorced his wife because she refused to comply with his drunken commands, search was made for the most beautiful maiden to be her successor. Those selected were placed in the custody of "Hegai, keeper of the women." The final choice among them remained with the king himself. That choice fell upon Esther, "for the king loved Esther above all the women, and she obtained grace and favor in his sight more than all the virgins; so that he set the royal crown upon her head, and made her queen instead of Vashti" (Esth. 2:8-17), B. C. about 478. (2) **Saves her people.** Esther, in obedience to Mordecai, had not made known her parentage and race (Esth. 2:10). But Haman, the Agagite, angry with Mordecai because he did not do him reverence, represented to the king that the Jews scattered through his empire were a pernicious nation. The king gave Haman full power to kill them all and seize their property (ch. 3). Upon being informed of this by Mordecai, Esther, who seemed herself to be included in the doom of extermination, resolved to plead for her people. She decided to present herself unbidden to the king, which was not according to law (4:16). She did so and, obtaining favor in his sight, made known her request. It was that the king and Haman would that day attend a banquet which she had prepared. At the banquet the king renewed his willingness to grant Esther

any request she might make. She extended an invitation to both for the morrow, and promised then to reveal her wishes (ch. 5). The next day Esther pleaded for her people and denounced Haman. The laws of the empire would not allow the king to recall a decree once uttered; but the Jews were authorized to stand upon their defense and this, with the known change in the intentions of the court, averted the worst consequences of the decree. The Jews established a yearly feast in memory of their deliverance called *Purim*, which is observed to this day (9:20, sq.).

3. Character. "The character of Esther, as she appears in the Bible, is that of a woman of deep piety, faith, courage, patriotism, and caution, combined with resolution; a dutiful daughter to her adopted father, docile and obedient to his counsels, and anxious to share the king's favor with him for the good of the Jewish people. That she was a virtuous woman, and, as far as her situation made it possible, a good wife to the king, her continued influence over him for so long a time warrants us to infer. There must have been a singular charm in her aspect and manners since she obtained favor in the sight of all that looked upon her (Esth. 2:15)." (McC. & S., *Cyc.*)

NOTE—The arguments against the genuineness of the story of Esther are: (1) The narrative implies that Vashti and Esther were the legitimate wives of "the great king" (Esth. 1:19; 2:4). The only wife of Xerxes, however, known to history was Amestris, married to him before the third year of his reign and who continued queen after his death. To this it is replied that the disgrace of Vashti may have been only temporary, and she was afterward restored to her queenship; or that Vashti and Esther were secondary wives, the latter certainly being selected from the king's harem. The title "queen" may have been used as a special honor in indicating the favor Esther had obtained with the king. (2) The king could not legally, and therefore it is supposed would not marry a wife not belonging to one of the seven great Persian families. "The marriage of Ahasuerus with a Jewess, even if we regard it as a marriage in the fullest sense, would not be more illegal or more abhorrent to Persian notions than Cambyses's marriage with his full sister. It is, therefore, just as likely to have taken place. If, on the other hand, it was a marriage of the secondary kind the law with respect to the king's wives would not apply to it" (Rawlinson, *Historical Illustrations of the Old Testament*).

Esther, Book of. The book is named from its principal character whose Hebrew name *Hadassah* (myrtle) was changed to the Persian name Esther. *See* Esther. The Jews call it Megilloth Esther, that is, the Esther Roll, and it is in the third section of the Hebrew Scriptures with the four other rolls, including the Song, Ruth, Lamentations and Ecclesiastes. These rolls were short and read on special feast days. The Esther Roll was read at the Feast of Purim.

1. Design. The purpose of the book is to demonstrate God's providential care of His people in their trials and persecutions and to furnish an explanation of the origin of the important Feast of Purim, first mentioned in II Maccabees 15:36.

2. Authenticity. It is common in critical circles to deny the historicity of the story except as history may be fictionized. A. Bentzen, accordingly, describes the book as an "historical novel" but is forced to confess "that the story teller knows something of the administration of the Persian kingdom and especially

153. Esther Before Ahasuerus (Menescardi)

the construction of the palace at Shushan." (Introduction II, 1948, p. 192.) The author's undeniable knowledge of Persian life and customs and his manifestly historical intent (Cf. 10:2) militate against the critics' contention of a fictional narrative. For example, it is alleged that Mordecai would have to be well over 100 years old to have gone in the first deportation in 597 B. C. The relative pronoun of this verse evidently refers to Kish, Mordecai's great grandfather; hence, this difficulty is obviated. It is also contended that Vashti, Esther and Mordecai are unknown to secular history in the reign of Xerxes I (c. 485-465 B. C.). But Esther evidently did not become queen until the seventh year of Xerxes' reign c. 478 B. C., after his return from his defeat in Greece, c. 480 B. C., when Herodotus specifically tells he paid attention to his harem. It is true that the queen is said to have been Amestris, but certainly Xerxes, from what we know of him personally and of his splendor and power, may well have had many other wives, if Solomon king over tiny Syria-Palestine had "700 wives, princesses, and 300 concubines" (I Kings 11:3). The contention that Esther (Ishtar), Mordecai (Marduk) and Vashti (the name of a Persian deity) were merely fictioned names is pure supposition carrying no weight with the devout student.

3. **Authenticity and date.** The book is anonymous. It is to be placed sometime during or near the reign of Artaxerxes Longimanus (c. 464-425 B. C.). This also accounts for its literary phenomena, since its diction is reminiscent of such late books as Ezra, Nehemiah and Chronicles. Critics who doubt the historicity of the book put it later in the Greek (third century B. C.) or Maccabean period (second century B. C.).

4. **Contents.**
Part I. The Jews in Danger, 1:1-3:15
  a. Esther made queen, 1:1-2:23
  b. Haman's plot against the Jews, 3:1-15
Part II. The Jews Delivered, 4:1-10:3
  a. Esther's courage brings deliverance, 4:1-7:10
  b. Vengeance over the Jews' enemies, 8:1-9:19
  c. The Feast of Purim, 9:20-32
  d. Mordecai's elevation at court, 10:1-3
                    M. F. U.

Esther, Fast of. *See* Festivals, III.

E'tam (ē'tăm; *hawk ground*).
1. "Rock Etam" was the place to which Samson retired after his slaughter of the Philistines (Judg. 15:8, 11). It is probably to be located near Zorah at 'Arak Isma'in.
2. A city of Judah fortified by Rehoboam (II Chron. 11:6), probably, from its position in the list, near Bethlehem and Tekoah. The Talmudists locate there the sources of the water from which Solomon's gardens and pleasure grounds were fed; from which it has been inferred that the site was identical with that of Solomon's Pools at el-Euruk, near Bethlehem. Probably it is the same Etam mentioned in I Chron. 4:3.

Eternal Life. This is a priceless treasure, the gift of God. It is not to be confused with mere endless existence, which all possess, saved as well as unsaved. Christ said, "I am come that they might have life and they might have it more abundantly" (John 10:10). This life is nothing less than "Christ in you, the hope of glory" (Col. 1:27). It is likened to a birth from above (John 3:3; John 1:13). It is dependent upon receiving Christ as Savior. "He that hath the son hath life, and he that hath not the son of God hath not life" (I John 5:12). Eternal life must not be confused with natural life. This form of life is subject to death and derived by human generation. Natural life has a beginning but no end. The difference is that one possessing mere natural life will be separated from God in the lake of fire eternally, whereas the one possessing eternal life will be united and in fellowship with God for all eternity. Thus, separation from God is eternal death; union with God is eternal life. *M. F. U.*

Eternity, an essential attribute of God. It is the infinitude of God in relation to duration, as his omnipresence is his infinitude in relation to space. His existence is without beginning and will never end. The thought of this divine attribute is necessarily included in that of God's absolutely independent existence. The eternity of God is declared in many places in the Scriptures. See Psa. 90:2; 102:26-28; Isa. 57:15; 44:6; I Tim. 6:16; II Pet. 3:8; Rev. 1:4, et al.

E'tham (ē'thăm), a place to the east of the present Suez Canal, on the border of the desert, where Israel made its second station after leaving Egypt (Exod. 13:20; Num.

33:6). At this point the Israelites were ordered to change their route (Exod. 14:2).

E'than (ē'thăn; *perennial, permanent*).

1. One of the four persons ("Ethan the Ezrahite, and Heman, and Chalcol, and Darda") who were so renowned for their sagacity that it is mentioned to the honor of Solomon that his wisdom excelled theirs (I Kings 4:31). Ethan is distinguished as "the Ezrahite" from the others who are called "sons of Mahol," unless the word *Mahol* be taken for "sons of music, dancing," etc., in which case it would apply to Ethan as well as to the others. In I Chron. 2:6 they are all given as "sons of Zerah." In the title to Psalm 89 an "Ethan the Ezrahite" is named as the author.

2. Son of Zimmah and father of Adaiah, in the ancestry of the Levite Asaph (I Chron. 6:42). In v. 21 he seems to be called *Joah*, the father of Iddo.

3. Son of Kishi, or Kushaiah, a Levite of the family of Merari. He was appointed one of the leaders of the temple music by David (as singer, I Chron. 6:44, or player on cymbals, chap. 15:17, 19), B. C. about 960. In the latter passages he is associated with Heman and Asaph, the heads of two other families of Levites; and, inasmuch as in other passages of these books (I Chron. 25:1, 6) the names are given as Asaph, Heman, and *Jeduthun*, it has been conjectured that this last and Ethan were identical. There is at least great probability that Ethan the singer was the same person as Ethan the Ezrahite (*see* No. 1), whose name stands at the head of Psalm 89, for it is a very unlikely coincidence that there should be two persons named Heman and Ethan so closely connected in two different tribes and walks of life.

Eth'anim (ĕth'ȧ-nĭm), another name for the month *Tisri* (q. v.). *See* Time.

Eth'baal (ĕth'bā-ăl; *with Baal*), a king of Sidon, father of Jezebel, the wife of Ahab (I Kings 16:31), B. C. before 875. According to Josephus (*Ant.*, viii, 13, 1 and 2), Ethbaal is called *Ithobalus* by Menander, who also says that he was a priest of Astarte, and, having put the king, Pheles, to death, assumed the scepter of Tyre and Sidon, lived sixty-eight years, and reigned thirty-two. We see here the reason why Jezebel, the daughter of a priest of Astarte, was so zealous a promoter of idolatry.

E'ther (ē'thĕr; *abundance*), one of a group of nine cities in the plain of Judah (Josh. 15:42), but eventually assigned to Simeon (19:7). Now identified with Khirbet el-'Ater, one mile N. W. of Beit Jibrin.

Ethio'pia (ē-thĭ-ō'pĭ-ȧ; Heb. *kūsh*), lying south of Egypt, corresponding to what is now called the Sudan, i. e., the country of the blacks. It was known to the Hebrews (Isa. 18:1; 45:14; Zeph. 3:10). The name Cush (A. V. "Ethiopia") is found in the Egyptian Keesh, evidently applied to the same territory. In the description of the garden of Eden, an Asiatic Cush is mentioned (Gen. 2:13). In all other passages the words Ethiopia and the Ethiopians—with one possible exception, "the Arabians that *were* near the Ethiopians" (II Chron. 21:16), which may refer to Arabians

opposite Ethiopia—may be safely considered to mean an African country and people or peoples (Kitto). The languages of Ethiopia are as various as the tribes. In Psa. 68:31, Isa. 45:14, and probably Zeph. 3:10, the calling of Ethiopia to the service of the true God is foretold. The case of the Ethiopian eunuch (Acts 8:27-39) indicates the spread of the old dispensation influence in that country and the introduction of the new.

Ethio'pian (ē-thĭ-ō'pĭ-ăn), (Num. 12:1; II Chron. 14:9; Jer. 13:23; 38:7, 10, 12), an inhabitant of *Ethiopia* (q. v.), or Cush; used of Zerah and Ebed-melech.

Ethio'pian Eunuch, chief officer of Candace, the Ethiopian queen, who was converted to Christianity through the instrumentality of Philip, the evangelist (Acts 8:27). He is described as *a power-wielding eunuch*, i. e., chief treasurer. In the East eunuchs were taken not only to be overseers of the harem, but also generally to fill the most important posts of the court and the closet. Tradition calls the Ethiopian *Indich* and *Fudich*, and makes him without historical proof, but not improbably, the first preacher of the Gospel among his countrymen. *See* Candace, Eunuch.

Ethio'pian Woman. Zipporah, the wife of Moses, is so described (Num. 12:1); elsewhere called the daughter of a Midianite (Exod. 2:21; comp. v. 16). Reference is probably made here to the Arabian Ethiopia. Ewald and Keil and Delitzsch think that allusion is made to another wife whom Moses married after the death of *Zipporah* (q. v.).

Eth'nan (ĕth'năn; *a gift*), a descendant of Judah, one of the sons of Helah, the wife of Ashur (I Chron. 4:7).

Eth'ni (ĕth'nī; *munificent*), the son of Zerah and father of Malchiah, a Levite of the family of Gershom (I Chron. 6:41).

Eubu'lus (û-bū'lŭs; *good in counsel*), a Christian at Rome whose greeting Paul sent to Timothy during his last imprisonment (II Tim. 4:21), A. D. 66.

Eucharist (û'kȧ-rĭst); (Gr. eucharistia, *giving of thanks*), one of the names of the *Lord's Supper* (q. v.).

Eu'nice (û-nī'sē; *good victory*), the mother of Timothy and the wife of a Greek (Acts 16:1; II Tim. 1:5), A. D. before 66. In both passages reference is made to her faith.

Eunuch (Gr. *eunouchos;* Heb. *sârîs*). The Greek word means literally "bed keeper," i. e., one who has charge of beds and bedchambers. The original Hebrew word clearly implies the incapacity which mutilation involves. Castration, according to Josephus (*Ant.*, lv, 8, 40), was not practiced by the Jews upon either man or animals; and the law (Deut. 23:1; comp. Lev. 22:24) is repugnant to this treatment of any Israelite. It was a barbarous custom of the East thus to treat captives (*Herod.*, iii, 49; vi, 32), not only of tender age, but, it should seem, when past puberty. The "officer" Potiphar (Gen. 37:36; 39:1, marg. "eunuch") was an Egyptian, married, and the "captain of the guard;" and in the Assyrian monuments a eunuch often appears, sometimes armed and in a warlike capacity, or as a scribe, noting the number of heads and amount of spoil, as receiving the prisoners, and even as officiating in religious ceremonies. The origination of the practice is ascribed to Semiramis, and is no doubt as early, or nearly so, as Eastern despotism itself. The complete assimilation of the kingdom of Israel, and latterly of Judah, to the neighboring models of despotism, is traceable in the rank and prominence of eunuchs (II Kings 8:6; 9:32; 23:11; 25:19; Isa. 56:3, 4; Jer. 29:2; 34:19; 38:7; 41:16; 52:25). They mostly appear in one of two relations, either military as "set over the men of war," greater trustworthiness possibly counterbalancing inferior courage and military vigor, or associated, as we mostly recognize them, with women and children. We find the Assyrian Rabsaris, or chief eunuch (II Kings 18:17) employed together with other high officials as ambassador. Some think that Daniel and his companions were thus treated (II Kings 20:17, 18; Isa. 39:7; comp. Dan. 1:3, 7) (Smith, *Bib. Dict.*). The court of Herod had its eunuchs (Josephus, *Ant.*, xvi, 8, 1; xv, 7, 4), as had also that of Queen Candace (Acts 8:27). We must remember that both the Hebrew and Greek terms were sometimes applied to those filling important posts, without regard to corporeal mutilation.

Figurative. The term is employed figuratively by our Lord (Matt. 19:12) with reference to the power, whether possessed as a natural disposition or acquired as a property of grace, of maintaining an attitude of indifference toward the solicitations of fleshly desires.

Euo′dias (û-ō′dĭ-ȧs; *a good journey*), a female member of the Church at Philippi, who seems to have been at variance with another female member named Syntyche (A. D. 58-60). Paul describes them as women who had "labored much with him in the Gospel," and implores them to be of one mind (Phil. 4:2, 3).

Euphra′tes (û-frā′tēz; Heb. *pᵉräth*, to *break* forth; Gr. *Euphratēs*). The river rises in the mountains of Armenia Major and flows through Assyria, Syria, Mesopotamia, and the city of Babylon, from seventeen hundred to eighteen hundred miles into the Persian Gulf. It receives the water of the Tigris and other small tributaries like the Chebar. It is navigable for small vessels for twelve hundred miles from its mouth. It floods like the Nile, becoming swollen, in the months of March, April, and May, by the melting of the snows. The Euphrates carries vast amounts of sediment into the gulf, so that it encroaches in its deposit upon that body at the rate of a mile and a half a century. Pliny and other writers tell marvelous stories of islands, a hundred miles and more out to sea, which have become part of the mainland in this way. It was the natural boundary of empire, so that to cross the Euphrates was to cross the Rubicon. It was the western boundary of Mesopotamia, dividing it from the "Land of Hatti," which included all land between the Euphrates and the Mediterranean: Babylon lay upon this, as Nineveh did upon the Tigris River. It flowed by other ancient cities, as Charchemish (II Chron. 35:20) and Sippar, Agade, Borsip-

154. Tigris-Euphrates Basin

pa, and Ur. It served like the Nile, to irrigate the country by means of artificial canals, making, according to Xenophon, the desert to become a garden of fertility. It is referred to under various names in Scripture (Gen. 2:14; 15:18; Deut. 1:7; 11:24; Josh. 1:4; II Sam. 8:3; II Kings 23:29; 24:7; I Chron. 5:9; 18:3; II Chron. 35:20; Jer. 13:4, sq.; 51:63). It is sometimes called the "flood."

Euroc′lydon (ū-rŏk′lĭ-dŏn) (Gr. *Euroklydōn; east* and *wave*, an *east waver*), the gale of wind in the Adriatic Gulf which off the south coast of Crete seized the ship in which Paul was finally wrecked on the coast of Malta (Acts 27:14). This gale is particularly described, and its circumstances admit of abundant illustration from experience of modern seamen in the Levant. As to the direction of the wind we quote: "The wind came *down from* the *island* and drove the vessel *off the island;* whence it is evident that it could not have been southerly. If we consider further that the wind struck the vessel when she was *not far* from Cape Matala (Acts 27:14), that it drove here *toward Claudia* (v. 16), which is an island twenty miles to the S. W. of that point, and that the sailors feared lest it should drive them into the Syrtis, on the African coast (ver. 17), an inspection of the chart will suffice to show us that the point from which the storm came must have been N. E., or rather to the E. of N. E., and thus we may safely speak of it as coming the E. N. E." (Conybeare and Howson, *Life and Epistles* of *St. Paul*, ii, 326).

Eu′tychus (û′tĭ-kŭs; *good fortune*), a young man of Troas who attended the preaching of Paul. The services were held in the third story of the house, the sermon long. lasting until midnight, and the air heated by the large company and the many lamps. Under these circumstances Eutychus was overcome with sleep and fell from the window near which he was sitting into the court below, "and was taken up dead." Paul went down, and extending himself upon the body embraced it, like the prophets of old (I Kings 17:21; II Kings 4:34). He then comforted his friends, "Trouble not yourselves; for his life is in him." Before Paul departed in the morning they brought the young man to him alive and well (Acts 20:5-12). Bloomfield (*New Testament*) proves that the narrative forbids us for a moment to entertain the view of those critics who suppose that animation was merely suspended.

Evangelist (Gr. *evangelistēs*, one *announcing good news*). In a general sense anyone who proclaims the mercy and grace of God, especially as unfolded in the Gospel; therefore pre-eminently to Christ, and the apostles whom he commissioned to preach the truth and establish his kingdom. It came, however, to be employed in the early Church as the designation of a special class, as in the following enumeration: "And he (Christ) gave some, apostles; and some, prophets; and some, evangelists; and some pastors and teachers" (Eph. 4:11). This passage, accordingly, would lead us to think of them as standing between the two other groups—sent forth as missionary preachers of the Gospel by the first, and as such preparing the way for the labors of the second. The same inference would seem to follow the occurrence of the word as applied to Philip (Acts 21:8). It follows from what has been said that the calling of the evangelist is the proclamation of the glad tidings to those who have not known them, rather than the instruction and pastoral care of those who have believed and been baptized. It follows also that the name denotes a *work* rather than an *order*. The evangelist might or might not be a bishop-elder or a deacon. The apostles, so far as they evangelized (Acts 8:25; 14:7; I Cor. 1:17), might claim the title, though there were many evangelists who were not apostles (Smith, *Bib. Dict.*, s. v.). In later liturgical language, the term applied to the reader of the Gospel for the day.

Eve (ēv; Heb. *hăwwäh*, *life giver*), the name given by Adam to the first woman, his wife (Gen. 3:20). It is supposed that she was created on the sixth day, after Adam had reviewed the animals. The naming of the animals led to this result, that there was not found a helpmeet for man. Then God caused a deep sleep to fall upon the man, and took one of his ribs and fashioned it into a woman, and brought her unto Adam (Gen. 2:18-22). Through the subtlety of the serpent Eve was beguiled into a violation of the one commandment imposed upon her and Adam. She took of the fruit of the forbidden tree and gave to her husband. Her punishment was an increase of sorrow and pregnancy (3:16). "That the woman should bear children was the original will of God; but it was a punishment that henceforth she was to bear them in sorrow, i. e., with pains which threatened her own life as well as that of the child" (*Delitzsch*). Three sons of Eve are named—Cain (4:1), Abel (v. 2), and Seth (5:3)—though the fact of other children is recorded (5:4).

Even, Evening, Eventide. *See* Time.

Evening Sacrifices. *See* Sacrifice.

Everlasting. *See* Eternity.

E'vi (ē'vī; *desirous*), one of the five kings of the Midianites slain by the Israelites in the war arising out of the idolatry of Baal-peor, induced by the suggestion of Balaam (Num. 31:8), and whose lands were afterward al-

lotted to Reuben (Josh. 13:21), B. C. 1441.

Evidence, the rendering in the A. V. of the Heb. *sēfĕr*, *book* (as usually rendered), or writing; hence a document of title, i. e., a *deed* (Jer. 32:10, 11, 12, etc.), and of the Gr. *elegchos*, *proof*, Heb. 11:1, R. V. "proving."

Evil is the comprehensive term under which are included all disturbances of the divinely appointed harmony of the universe. Christian doctrine, in accordance with the Scriptures, carefully distinguishes between physical and moral evil.

1. **Physical Evil**, or, as it is often called, natural evil, is disorder in the physical world. Such physical causes as militate against physical well-being are therefore called evils. That such evils are, to some extent at least, the effect or penalty of sin is a clear teaching of Scripture (Gen. 3:10-12, 8:16-19). To what extent physical sufferings are the necessary means to greater good is, however, a great question.

2. **Moral Evil**, or sin, is disorder in the moral world. It is the failure of rational and free beings to conform in character and conduct to the will of God. This is the greatest evil (*see* Rom. 1:18-32). How the existence of evil is compatible with the goodness of God is the question of *Theodicy* (*q. v.*). For discussion of moral evil *see* Sin.

Evildoer, one who is bad; from the Heb. *rā'ă'*, to *break*, and so to render worthless (Psa. 37:1; 119:115; Isa. 1:4, etc.). The Greek word (*kakopoios*), is identical with the English "Doer of evil" (I Pet. 2:12, 14; 3:16; 4:15).

Evil-favoredness, the general term for such blemish, scurvy, wound, etc., as rendered an animal unfit for sacrifice (Deut. 17:1; comp. Lev. 22:22-24).

E'vil-Mero'dach (ē'vĭl-mē-rō'dăk), name of a king of Babylon mentioned twice in the Old Testament (II Kings 25:27, and Jer. 52:31). The name, in the Babylonian language, is written Amel-Marduk; i. e., man (or servant) of the god Marduk, or Merodach. Evil-merodach was the son and successor of Nebuchadnezzar and reigned 562-560 B. C. Of his reign we have but meager details. According to Berosus and the canon of Ptolemy he was slain by his sister's husband, Neriglissar, who then made himself king in his stead. Josephus, in this probably following Berosus, makes him odious because of debauchery and cruelty. The Old Testament narrates a kindly and high-spirited act of his doing. In the first year of his reign he released from prison Jehoiachin, king of Judah, who had been thirty-seven years in confinement, "spake kindly unto him," and gave him a portion of his table for the rest of his life, honoring him above the other vassal kings who were at Babylon.

Ewes, the rendering in the A. V. of several Hebrew words for the female sheep. *See* Animal Kingdom.

Exactor (Heb. *nägăs*, to *drive, tax, tyrannize*, Isa. 60:17), a word used to signify a *driver* (taskmaster, Exod. 3:7; Job. 3:18; Isa. 9:3), or simply a driver of animals (Job 39:7); hence, exactor of debt (or tribute, Dan. 11:20; Zech. 9:8); hence, with oriental ideas of tyranny, a *ruler* (Isa. 3:12; 14:2; Zech. 10:4). In the passage, Isa. 60:17, it seems to mean *magistracy*, and we may read "righteousness shall be a substitute for the police force in every form" (Delitzsch, *Com.*).

Exchanger (Matt. 25:27, a *broker* or *banker*, i. e., one who exchanges money for a fee, and loans out to others for a rate of interest).

Excommunication, "a cutting off, deprivation of communion, or the privileges of intercourse; specifically, the formal exclusion of a person from religious communion and privileges" (*Cent. Dict.*, s. v.).

1. **Jewish.** The distinction between two kinds has been handed down: The *temporary* exclusion and the *permanent* ban, *hērĕm*, "*The Anathema*" (*q. v.*). The former of these, the *ban of the synagogue*, was among the later Jews, the excommunication or exclusion of a Jew, usually for heresy or alleged blasphemy, from the synagogue and the congregation, or from familiar intercourse with the Jews. This was a modification of the *anathema*, and owes its origin to Ezra 10:8, where we find that the *hērĕm* (anathema) excluded the man from the congregation and anathematized his goods and chattels, but did not consist in *putting him to death*. This ecclesiastical ban was pronounced for twenty-four different offenses, all of which Maimonides picked out from the Talmud. In the event of the offender showing signs of penitence it might be revoked. The excommunicated person was prohibited the use of bath, razor, and the convivial table, and no one was allowed to approach him within four cubits' distance. The term of punishment was thirty days, and it was extended to a second and third thirty days, if necessary. If still contumacious the offender was subjected to the second and severer excommunication, the *hērĕm*.

In the New Testament Jewish excommunication is brought before us in the case of the blind man (John 9:22), being exclusion from the synagogue, i. e., the *nĭdûî*. Some think that our Lord (in Luke 6:22) referred specially to three forms of Jewish excommunication.

2. **Christian.** Excommunication in the Christian Church is not merely founded on the natural rights possessed by all societies nor in imitation of the Jews. It was instituted by our Lord (Matt. 18:15-18), and consisted in the breaking off of all further Christian, brotherly fellowship with one who is hopelessly obdurate. We find the apostle Paul claiming the right to exercise discipline over his convert (II Cor. 1:23; 13:10), and that formal excommunication on the part of the Church was practiced and commanded by him (I Cor. 5:11; I Tim. 1:20; Tit. 3:10). The formula of *delivering* or *handing over to Satan* (I Cor. 5:5; I Tim. 1:20), admits of difference of interpretation. Some interpret it as being merely a symbol for excommunication, which involves "exclusion from all Christian fellowship, and consequently banishment to the society of those among whom Satan dwelt, and from which the offender had publicly severed himself" (Dr. David Brown in Schaff's *Popular Com.*, iii, p. 180). Dr. Alfred Plummer (*Pastoral Epistles*, p. 75, sq.) says

that "this handing over to Satan was an apostolic act—a supernatural infliction of bodily infirmity, or disease, or death, as a penalty for grievous sin. It is scarcely doubtful that St. Paul delivered Hymenaeus and Alexander to Satan, in order that Satan might have power to afflict their bodies, with a view to their spiritual amelioration."

3. **Nature of Excommunication.** We thus find excommunication consisted (1) in separation from the communion of the church; (2) having as its *object* the good of the sufferer (I Cor. 5:5) and protection of sound members (II Tim. 3:17); (3) that it was wielded by the highest ecclesiastical officer (I Cor. 5:3; Tit. 3:10), promulgated by the congregation to which the offender belonged (I Cor. 5:4), and in spite of any opposition on the part of a minority (II Cor. 2:6); (4) that it was for an indefinite duration or for a period; (5) that its duration might be abridged at the discretion and by the indulgence of the person imposing the penalty (v. 8); (6) that penitence was the condition of restoration (v. 7); (7) that the sentence was publicly reversed (v. 10) as it was publicly promulgated (v. 10).

Execution. *See* Punishments.

Executioner. The Hebrew word describes, in the first instance, the office of executioner, and, secondarily, the general duties of the bodyguard of a monarch. Thus Potiphar was "captain of the executioners" (Gen. 37:36; margin). That the "captain of the guard" himself occasionally performed the duty of an executioner appears from I Kings 2:25, **34.** Nevertheless the post was one of high dignity. The Gr. *spekoulătōr* (Mark 6:27), is borrowed from the Lat. *speculator;* originally a military spy or scout, but under the emperors transferred to the *bodyguard*.

Exercise, Bodily, exercise or training of the body, i. e., gymnastics (I Tim. 4:8). The apostle appears to disparage, not the athletic discipline, but rather that ascetic mortification of the fleshly appetites and even innocent affections (comp. I Tim. 4:3; Col. 2:23) characteristic of some Jewish fanatics, especially the *Essenes* (*q. v.*).

Exhortation (Gr. *paraklēsis*, literally a *calling near*, invitation) appears to have been recognized in the apostolic Church as a special supernatural or prophetic function (Rom. 12:8), probably a subordinate exercise of the general faculty of teaching (I Cor. 14:3). It has been defined as "the act of presenting such motives before a person as may excite him to the performance of duty." The Scriptures enjoin ministers to exhort men, i. e., to rouse them to duty by proposing suitable motives (Isa. 58:1; Rom. 12:8; I Tim. 6:2; Heb. 3:13); and it was also the constant practice of prophets (Isa. 1:17; Jer. 4:14; Ezek. 37), apostles (Acts 11:23), and of Christ himself (Luke 3:18) (McC. and S., *Cyc.*, s. v.).

Exodus, The. The great deliverance extended to the Israelites when "the Lord did bring the Children of Israel out of the land of Egypt" (Exod. 12:51), "with a mighty hand and with an outstretched arm" (Deut. 26:8), that is, "with full manifestation of divine power."

1. **Preparatory History.** The quiet life of

the patriarchs terminated in the circumstances subsequent to the selling of Joseph to the Ishmaelites and his later exaltation as viceroy in Egypt. According to the Biblical chronology preserved in the Massoretic text of the Hebrew Bible, the Israelites emigrated to Egypt around 1871 B. C. under the Twelfth Egyptian Dynasty of the Middle Kingdom c. 2000-1780 B. C. Multiplying rapidly in Egypt in the Land of Goshen (Gen. 46:26-34), identified with the area around the Wadi Tumilat in the eastern part of the Nile Delta, the Children of Israel soon became an important factor in Egyptian life. The Land of Goshen was one of the richest parts of Egypt, "the best of the land" (Gen. 47:11). Divine favor plus their happy location were factors in their increasing strength. Many scholars place Joseph's rise to power much later, during the Hyksos Period c. 1700 B. C. under the unnecessary supposition that it would be "an historical misrepresentation" to imagine that a young Semitic foreigner would have been elevated to such power under a native Egyptian dynasty like the Twelfth or the Eighteenth, but that such an event would be likely under the Semitic conquerors of Egypt, called the Hyksos. Unfortunately the period from 1780-1546 B. C. is one of great obscurity in Egypt, and the Hyksos conquest is as yet very imperfectly understood. Although the history of Joseph cannot yet be placed in the frame of known Egyptian history, Israel was in Egypt during this period of confusion and turmoil, and the notice of the accession of an oppressive pharoah called "a new king . . . who knew not Joseph" (Exod. 1:8) has reference to one of the pharoahs of the New Empire, after the expulsion of the despised Asiatics from Egypt. Consonant with this is the fact that the Israelites were settled about the Hyksos capital of Egypt in the "plain of Tanis" called "the field of Zoan" (Psa. 78:12).

2. **The Deliverance.** The ten plagues, like the story of Joseph are replete with authentic local coloring. Although the plagues are supernatural, they consist in the great increase of the normal intensity and introduction in unusual sequence of events and phenomena that were natural to Egypt. Israel's exit from Egypt, as outlined in the Bible narrative (Exod. 12:37; 13:17, 18, 20; 14:1, 2), has excited a vast amount of scepticism and debate among scholars. However, with increased archaeological knowledge, the Biblical itinerary is more and more credible.

3. **The Route of the Exodus.** In tracing this itinerary, it is important to observe that the translation of the Hebrew *Yam Suph* ("Red Sea") is plainly incorrect. The proper rendering is "Reed" or "Marsh" Sea. That this can scarcely denote the Red Sea or even its northeastern arm, the Gulf of Suez, is attested by the fact that no reeds exist in the Red Sea, and that the body of water they actually passed through formed a natural barrier between Egypt and the Sinai wilderness. On the other hand, to reach the Red Sea or its arm, the Gulf of Suez, the Israelites would have had to traverse a vast expanse of desert. The account most certainly implies the proximity of the Reed Sea to Succoth, modern

Tell el-Mashkutah, some thirty-two miles southeastward of their starting places from Raamses (Avaris-Zoan) (Exod. 12:37). The Reed or Papyrus Sea which the Israelites miraculously went through "may reasonably be supposed to be the Papyrus Lake or Papyrus Marsh known from an Egyptian document of the thirteenth century to be located near Tanis." (W. F. Albright, "The Old Testament Archaeology" in *O. T. Commentary*, Philadelphia 1948, p. 142). The crossing of the Reed Sea was doubtless in the area around Lake Timsah and just south of it. The topography of this region has been changed to some extent since the digging of the Suez Canal. At least one body of water, Lake Ballah, has disappeared. The vicinity of Lake Timsah between Lake Ballah and the Bitter Lakes may well have been more marshy than it is at present. The starting point for the tracing of the Biblical route of the Exodus was the identification of Raamses, earlier Avaris-Zoan, later Tanis. This city was the Hyksos capital, built c. 1720 B. C. It is located in the N. E. part of the Delta. Leaving Raamses (Tanis), the fleeing Israelite captives began their journey toward Canaan. The direct military route lay immediately parallel to the Mediterranean coast, past the Egyptian frontier fortress of Zilu (Thel) and thence by "the road of the land of the Philistines" (Exod. 13:17). This well guarded and carefully traveled highway giving access to the Egyptian Empire in Palestine and lower Syria would have brought the Israelites in immediate open conflict. Their morale and military organization were not equal to this. Quitting Succoth, located some ten miles east from Pithom (Exod. 1:11), now identified with Tell Retabeh, the Israelites set camp on the frontier of "the wilderness of the Red (Reed) Sea" (Exod. 13:18-20), that is, the region of Lake Timsah. Pi-hahiroth, said to be "between Migdol and the Reed Sea" and "in front of Baal-zephon" (Exod. 14:2), was most evidently Egyptian Pi-hathor in the general vicinity of Tanis. Migdol and Baal-zephon are Semitic names perfectly normal for this part of Egypt and attested by the inscriptions. However, their exact positions have not yet been determined, hence the Israelites in their circuitous journey (Exod. 13:18) may have gone farther northward than is commonly thought and crossed the water in the region of Lake Ballah. At any rate, the Biblical route as outlined in the Bible bears every evidence of reliability. *M. F. U.*

Exodus, The Date of. The date of Israel's departure from Egypt involves very difficult problems, and the subject is fraught with much confusion. Setting aside extreme views like those of Gardner, Hall, Wreszinski, etc., who regard the story of the Exodus as a garbled version of the Egyptian saga of Hyksos expulsion, or like those of Petrie, Eerdmans, Rowley, etc., who give it a very late date under Merneptah or even somewhat later, only two principal views exist. The first places the event around 1441 B. C. in the reign of Amenhotep II of the Eighteenth Dynasty; the second places it around 1290 B. C. in the reign of Rameses II in the Nineteenth Dynasty.

155. Thutmose III, thought by advocates of the early date of the Exodus to be the Pharoah of the great oppression

1. **The Biblical Date.** Despite the fact that any view of the date of the Exodus is plagued with problems so that many scholars contend that "the complete harmonization" of the Biblical account "and our extra-Biblical material is quite impossible" it is, nevertheless, true because of many considerations that the early date view (1441 B. C.) is the Biblical one. This is denied by many on the basis of Exodus 1:11 and other evidence. But if one carefully surveys all the Scriptural evidence, taking into consideration the whole time-scheme underlying the Pentateuch and the early history of Israel to the time of Solomon, it is clear that the O. T. places this great redemptive event around the middle of the 15th century B. C., rather than a full century and a half later. Evidence both within and without the Bible in support of this is not easily set aside. (1) **Explicit Scriptural Statement Places the Exodus about 1441 B. C.** In I Kings 6:1 it is explicitly stated that Solomon began to build "the house of Jehovah" "in the 480th year after the children of Israel were come up out of the land of Egypt." The fourth year of Solomon's reign, when he is said to have begun to build the temple, would be about 961 B. C. Since Solomon ruled forty years (I Kings 11:42), the fourth year of his reign would be variously computed by modern chronologists: 958 B. C. (Albright), 967 B. C. (Thiele), 962 B. C. (Begrich). Taking the year 961 B. C., which cannot be far wrong, the date 1441 B. C. as the date of the Exodus is computed, and 1871 B. C. as the time of the entrance of Israel into Egypt, since the sojourn there extended to 430 years (Exod. 12:20, 41). Albright's date of the Exodus (1290 B. C.) and H. H. Rowley's (1225 B. C.) must reject I Kings 6:1 as late and completely unreliable, despite the fact that the chronological notice it gives has every evidence of authenticity and obviously fits into the whole time scheme underlying the Pentateuch and the books of Joshua and Judges (cf. J. W. Jack, *The Date of the Exodus,*

Edinburgh, 1925, pp. 200-216). Scholars who thus drastically curtail the period of the Judges by a century and a half or two centuries, which the Biblical figures place about 1400 to 1050 B. C., practically reject the possibility of fitting the Biblical chronology into the framework of contemporary history. (2) **Contemporary Egyptian History Allows the 1441 B. C. Date of the Exodus.** This date falls very likely toward the opening years of the reign of Amenhotep II, (c. 1450-1425 B. C.), son of the famous conqueror and empire-builder, Thutmose III (c. 1482-1450 B. C.). The commanding person of Thutmose III, one of the greatest of the pharoahs, furnishes an ideal figure for the events of the Exodus. In the contemporary records of Amenhotep II, who would be the pharoah who hardened his heart and would not let the children of Israel go, of course no references occur to such national disasters as the ten plagues and the loss of the Egyptian army in the Red (Reed) Sea, much less to the escape of the Hebrews. But this circumstance is to be expected. The Egyptians were the last people to record their misfortunes. Nor is there any sign upon the mummy of Amenhotep II, discovered in 1898, to show that he was drowned at sea. Nor does the Bible state that he was, or that he personally accompanied his army into the water (Exod. 14:23-31). If Amenhotep II was the reigning pharoah of the Exodus, his eldest son was slain in the tenth plague (Exod. 12:29). It seems clear from the monuments that Thutmose IV (c. 1425-1412) was not the eldest son of Amenhotep II. The so-called

156. Amenhotep II, thought by advocates of the early date of the Exodus to be the Pharoah of the Exodus

Dream Inscription of Thutmose IV, recorded on an immense slab of red granite near the Sphinx at Gizeh, recounts the prophecy that the young Thutmose would one day be pharoah. Such a prophecy would have been pointless had the young man been the first-born son of Amenhotep, since the law of primogeniture was in force in Egypt at this time. Thutmose III was a great builder and employed Semitic captives in his wide-scale construction projects. His visier, named Rekhmire, left a tomb on which scenes of brick-making are depicted, recalling Exodus 5:6-19. Semitic foreigners are significantly found among the brick-layers on this tomb. The brick-layers are quoted as saying "He supplies us with bread, beer and every good thing," while the task-masters warn the laborers: "The rod is in my hand; be not idle." Finally Joseph died and "a new king arose over Egypt, who knew not Joseph" (Exod. 1:8). This ruler seems to have been the founder or an early king of the powerful Eighteenth Dynasty (1546-1319 B. C.). Since the Hyksos invasion of Egypt was led by

157. Captives Making Bricks, from Tomb of Rekhmire (official of Thutmose III), Bearded Semites Appear in Upper Register

Semites and not by Hurrians or Indo-Aryans, as recent studies have shown (W. F. Albright, *The O. T. and Modern Study*, Oxford, 1951, p. 44), it appears that the expulsion of the Hyksos around the middle of the 16th century B. C. was the important event that resulted in the oppression of the Israelites. Not until about 1570 B. C. were the Hyksos invaders driven out and the powerful Eighteenth Dynasty founded. Very likely under the kings of the Eighteenth Dynasty who preceded Tutmose III—Amenhotep I (1546-1525 B. C.), Thutmose I (1525-1508 B. C.) and Thutmose II (1508-1504 B. C.)—and under Queen Hatshepsut (1504-1482 B. C.), the Hebrew bondage became increasingly severe. About 1520 B. C. Moses was born, probably during the reign of Tutmose I, whose daughter, the well-known Hatshepsut, seems to have been the princess who found the baby Moses among the flags by the riverside (Exod. 2:5-10). After a struggle with Queen Hatshepsut, Thutmose III came into power about 1486 B. C. This event doubtless inaugurated the last and most severe phase of Israelite oppression. (3) **Contemporary Events in Palestine Substantiate the 1441 B. C. Date of the Exodus.** If the Exodus took place around 1441 B. C., the Israelites entered Canaan around 1401 B. C. Is there any evidence of such an invasion in extra-Biblical monuments? The Amarna Latters, which concern this very period (c. 1400-1366 B. C.), refer to such an invasion as has been known virtually from their discovery in 1886. These invaders, called Habiru, are etymologically actually equatable with the Hebrews. There are many serious problems involved, and the best scholars are divided on the matter, but the statement of J. W. Jack is still pertinent, especially in the light of plain statement and clear intimations of the O. T. concerning the date of the Exodus. "Who are these invaders of south

and central Palestine. . . . Who else could they be but the Hebrews of the Exodus, and have we not here the native version of their entry into the land?" (*Op. cit.* p. 128). For a full discussion see Jack, pp. 119-141.

In the Amarna Letters the correspondence of Abi-Hiba, governor of Jerusalem, with Pharoah Akhnaton (c. 1370 B. C.), Egyptian military aid is requested against the Habiru. The fall of Jericho favors the 1441 B. C. date of the Exodus as a result of the excavations of Ernest Sellin (1907-1909) and especially those of John Garstang (1930-1936). City D, which was taken by Joshua and the invading Israelites, was constructed about 1500 B. C. and fell around 1400 B. C.

2. **Objections to the Biblical Date.** Many scholars who set aside O. T. chronological notices as frequently of little historical value would strenuously object to calling the 1441 B. C. date of the Exodus the Biblical one. They would place it around 1290 B. C., urging the following objections:

(1) **It would be very improbable that Israel would have entered Egypt before the Hyksos period.** Abraham went to Egypt and moved freely in high circles under the Middle Kingdom (Gen. 13:10-12), and there is no reason why Joseph may not have done so at a later pre-Hyksos period, especially when his exaltation is presented in the O. T. narratives as entirely providential. Moreover, the details of the story have a strong Egyptian and not a Hyksos (Semitic) coloring. Had the reigning king been Hyksos, the Hebrew shepherds would not have been segregated in Goshen and a point made of the fact that "every shepherd is an abomination to the Egyptians" (Gen. 46:34).

(2) **Exodus 1:11 is supposed to place the Exodus definitely later.** But I Kings 6:1 is just as explicit for the earlier date. The question is, are these two notices at variance with one another? The explanation is that Raamses (Tanis, Avaris) is a modernization of its older name, and the fact that this site was called

158. Raamses II, often thought to be Pharoah of the Exodus, according to those who hold the late date

Raamses only from about 1300 to 1100 B. C. is not a decisive argument against the early date. The reference in Exodus 1:11 must be to the older city Zoan-Avaris where the oppressed Israelites labored centuries earlier. Since Zoan-Avaris was once a flourishing city before the Hyksos were driven out (c. 1570 B. C.), there was plenty of time for the Israelites in bondage to have constructed the earlier city as they went down into Egypt about 1870 B. C. Moreover, it is hardly conceivable that such renowned conquerors and builders like Thutmose III and Amenhotep II would have abandoned all interest in the Delta area, since this rich and vital territory was necessary to the security of their Asiatic domain.

(3) **Archaeological evidence fron Transjordan, Lachish and Debir, allegedly disprove the early date of the Exodus.** Nelson Glueck's surface explorations in Transjordan and in the Arabah are supposed to demonstrate that there was a gap in the sedentary population of this region from about 1900 to about 1300 B. C. so that had Israel come up out of Egypt about 1400 there would supposedly have been no Edomite, Ammonite and Moabite kingdoms to resist their progress. Only scattered nomads would have met them (cf. Num. 20:14, 17). But there is nothing in the narrative to demand anything more than a simple agricultural economy which would have left little or no material remains. Also archaeological evidence at Lachish and Debir is not sufficiently evident to set aside the whole testimony supporting the earlier date. *M. F. U.*

Ex′odus, Book of (ĕk′sô-dŭs; from the Gr. *ex*, "out," and *hodos*, "way" "a going out"). Whereas Genesis is the book of origins, Exodus is the book of redemption. Delivered out of Egyptian bondage the newly constituted nation is endowed with the law, priesthood and sacrificial system, providing for the worship and regulation of a redeemed people.

1. **The Name.** The book is named from the Latin, "exodus," through the LXX, *exodus*, signifying "out-going" or "departure" (cf. 19:1, Hebrews 11:22). The ancient Hebrews in accordance with their practice of designating the holy books from one or more of the opening words, called it *wᵉ ʾēllĕh shĕmōth* ("and these are the names"), or simply *shĕmōth*, ("names").

2. **The Aim.** The book of Exodus deals with the great event of the redemption from Egypt. It typifies our redemption and traces the constitution of Jacob's descendants as a theocratic nation at Mount Sinai. God, Who had hitherto been related to the Israelites only through the Abrahamic covenant, now brings Himself in relationship to them nationally through redemption. As a people selected to bring forth the promised Redeemer, they are put under the Mosaic covenant. The Divine Presence resides among them under the cloud of glory. The constitution, tabernacle, priesthood and sacrificial system are minutely typical of the Person and work of Christ (Note the message of the book of Hebrews). Exodus is preeminently the book of redemption.

3. **The Subject Matter.**

Part I. The Hebrews in Egypt, 1:1-12:36

Part II. The Hebrews in the Wilderness, 12:37-18:37

Part III. The Hebrews at Sinai, 19:1-40:38

4. **The Critical View.** Like Genesis and the rest of the Pentateuch, higher critics deny the Mosaic authorship and authenticity, claiming the book is a compilation of J, E and P sources. This partitionist theory, however, is constructed upon shaky presuppositions involving false literary criteria and philosophic hypotheses, notably the erroneous notion that the development of Israel and Israel's institutions were in nowise different from the progressive evolutionary development of other peoples. Sound views of inspiration must reject the essential claims of this so-called Graf-Keunen-Wellhausen theory of Pentateuchal criticism as being incompatible with the claims of the Pentateuch itself and its foundational place in the whole scheme of divine revelation and redemptive history.

5. **The Conservative View.** The book of Exodus is historical and from the time of Moses, who is its real author. As with the other books of the Pentateuch, the great Lawgiver may have used ancient sources, oral or written, but the Pentateuch bears the unmistakable hand of a one-author unity and bears the impress everywhere in miracle, prophecy, type and symbol of divine inspiration, historicity and authenticity. *M. F. U.*

Ex′orcism (ĕk′sôr-sĭzm). The practice of using magical words and ceremonies to expel evil spirits or demons. The phenomenon was characteristic of heathenism and incompatible with either the religion of Israel or Christianity. The Jews at Ephesus encountered by Paul (Acts 19:13-19) illustrate an attempt to mix pagan traffic in demonology with expulsion of evil spirits by the power of God. *See* Magic. *M. F. U.*

Expediency, Expedient (Gr. *sumpherō*, to *advantage*), "the principle of doing what is deemed most practicable or serviceable under the circumstances." A rule of expediency often referred to is that laid down by St. Paul: "Wherefore, if meat make my brother to offend, I will eat no flesh while the world standeth, lest I make my brother to offend" (I Cor. 8:13). The occasion of this declaration was his writing to the Corinthians respecting the Christian's attitude toward flesh offered up to idols (*q. v.*). This would give offense to some scrupulous consciences, while others, like St. Paul, might make light of the matter, so far as personal feeling was concerned. "It is impossible to state more strongly than does the apostle the obligation to refrain from indulging in things indifferent when the use of them is an occasion of sin to others. Yet it is never to be forgotten that this, by its very nature, is a principle the application of which must be left to every man's conscience in the sight of God. No rule of conduct founded on expediency can be enforced by church discipline. It was right in Paul to refuse to eat flesh for fear of causing others to offend, but he could not justly be subjected to censure had he seen fit to eat. The same principle is illustrated in reference to circumcision. The apostle utterly refused to circumcise Titus, and yet he circumcised Timothy, in both cases acting wisely and conscientiously. Whenever a thing is right or wrong, according to circumstances, every man must have the right to judge of those circumstances. Otherwise he is judge of another man's conscience, a new rule of duty is introduced, and the catalogue of *adiaphora* (i. e., things indifferent or nonessential), which has existed in every system of ethics from the beginning, is simply abolished" (T. W. Chambers, D.D., in Meyer's *Com. on I Cor. 8*).

Experience. We speak of our knowledge of sins forgiven and the favor of God enjoyed as our Christian *experience*. It means the practical trial of an acquaintance with the work of God in man which results in the consciousness of salvation. Thus experience is the personal trial of anything and the consequent knowledge of it.

Expiation, in the theological sense, denotes the end accomplished by certain divinely appointed sacrifices in respect to freeing the sinner from the punishment of his sins. The sacrifices recognized as expiatory are the sin offerings of the Old Testament dispensation (*see* Offerings; Sacrifice), and, preeminently, the offerings which Christ made of himself for the sins of the world (*see* Atonement).

The above definition is made somewhat general for the purpose of including both of the theories which accept expiation in any real sense.

1. The Calvinistic or Satisfaction view teaches that the sacrifice of Christ was expiatory in the sense that Christ suffered vicariously the punishment of the sins of the elect. The expiation thus is absolute in behalf of the limited number for whom it is made. For the non-elect, or reprobate, there is no expiation. *See* Election.

2. The Arminian theory of expiation holds that the sacrificial sufferings of Christ were not of the nature of punishment, but were a divinely appointed, though conditional, substitute for the punishment of the sins of all mankind. The sacrifice of Christ is expiatory in the sense that all who truly repent of their sins and believe on Christ have, on account of that sacrifice, their guilt canceled, the punishment of their sins remitted.

The two theories are alike in regarding Christ's sacrifice as the objective ground of forgiveness.

3. The third prominent theory of the atonement, the moral influence theory, admits of no necessity for sacrificial expiation and denies the expiatory character of sacrifices. According to this theory, Christ died to provide an example of devotion to truth and duty—the kind of devotion that might lead to a martyr's death.

As to the fact of expiation by sacrifice, it should be noted:

(1) The idea of expiation, or of seeking reconciliation with Deity, through sacrifices is a common feature of most if not all forms of religion. It is a fair supposition that, despite all the false conceptions held in connection with the idea, some measure of important truth lies at the bottom.

(2) Among the sacrifices appointed of God under the Old Testament dispensation there were sacrifices the purpose of which was clearly expiatory. Not only the simple and most natural understanding of such sacrifices, but also the divine teaching concerning them, was that they stood in important relation to the forgiveness of sins (*see* Lev. 17:11). Preeminent among these were the sacrifices on the great annual day of atonement. *See* Sacrifices; Offerings; Atonement, Day of.

It is not, however, to be understood that the blood of beasts of itself had expiatory value and effect, or that the offerings in a mechanical or commercial way wrought reconciliation (*see* Psa. 50; Isa. 1; Amos 5:22). It was only because of divine grace that these sacrifices availed for reconciliation. The sacrifices were not only appointed of God, but were also provided by him (Lev. 17:11; Psa. 50:10).

(3) In the New Testament dispensation, of which the Old was predictive and for which it was preparatory, the sacrifice which Christ offered of himself is conspicuously set before us as the ground of the forgiveness of sins. Christ is "the Lamb of God which taketh away the sin of the world." He is the "Lamb slain from the foundation of the world." It was Christ's own declaration that his blood was shed "for the remission of sins." *See* also John 3:14; Col. 1:14, 20; Heb. 9:13, 14; Heb. 10:1-12, and many other passages.

As to the necessity of expiation, whence it arises, *see* Atonement. E. McC.

Eye is used as the symbol of a large number of objects and ideas, as: (1) A *fountain* frequently; (2) *Color* (Num. 11:7, in the Hebrew; *see* margin); (3) The *face* or *surface* (Exod. 10:5, 15; Num. 22:5, 11, as "the face, i. e., eye of the land"); the expression "between the eyes" means the *forehead* (Exod. 13:9, 16); (4) In Cant. 4:9 "eye" seems to be used poetically for look; (5) "Eye" (Prov. 23:31, A. V. "color") is applied to the beads or bubbles of wine when poured out; (6) "Before the eyes" (Gen. 23:11, 18; Exod. 4:30) means in one's presence; "in the eyes" (Gen. 19:8) of any one means according to his judgment or opinion; "to set the eyes" (Gen. 44:21; Job 24:23; Jer. 39:12) upon anyone is to regard with favor, but may also be used in a bad sense (Amos 9:8); (7) Many of the passions, such as envy, pride, pity, etc., being expressed by the eye, such phrases as the following occur: "Evil eye" (Matt. 20:15, i. e., *envious*); "bountiful eye" (Prov. 22:9); "wanton eyes" (Isa. 3:16); "eyes full of adultery" (II Pet. 2:14); "the lust of the eyes" (I John 2:16); "the desire of the eyes" (Ezek. 24:16) denotes whatever is a great delight. (8) "To keep as the apple (pupil) of the eye" (Deut. 32:10; Zech. 2:8) is to preserve with special care; "as the eyes of servants look unto the hand of their master" (Psa. 123:2) is an expression which seems to indicate that masters, especially in the presence of strangers, communicated with their servants by certain motions of their hands.

Eyes, Blinding of. *See* Punishments.

Eyes, Covering of the (Gen. 20:16), a phrase of much disputed significance, understood by some to mean that Abimelech advised Sarah and her women, while in or near towns to conform to the general custom of wearing veils (*q. v.*). Another view is the following: "By the 'covering of the eyes' we are not to understand a veil, which Sarah was to procure for a thousand shekels, but it is a figurative expression for an atoning gift, . . . so that he may forget a wrong done, and explained by the analogy of the phrase he covereth the faces of the judges, i. e., he bribes them (Job 9:24)" (K. and D., *Com.*, in loc.).

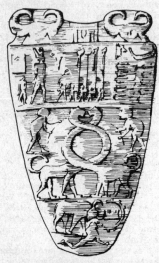

159. Palette on Which Eye Paint Was Ground in Very Early Egypt. The necks of the monsters formed a cavity to hold the paint.

Eyes, Painting the, or rather the eyelids, is a very ancient practice known to the Hebrews and to the Egyptians millennia before them. About 4000 B. C. the Bedarians of Egypt were accustomed to grind green malachite on slate palettes to use for eye-paint. This was not only a beauty aid but an excellent germicide. It is still used by Africans, and is particularly effective when spread around the eyes as a protection against flies. One of the finest monuments of Narmer, one of the kings of the First Dynasty of Egypt, c. 2900 B. C., is a palette found at Hierakonpolis. The palette, similar to those on which the Egyptians had long ground eye paint, is of a very large size befitting a great king. The painting of the eyelids was doubtless copied by the Hebrews from their Egyptian, Phoenician and Mesopotamian neighbors. Jezebel is spoken of as having "painted her eyes" (II Kings 9:30 R. S. V.). This practice was also very common in Phoenicia. Painting of the eyes is mentioned among other things by which women thought to win admiration. Compare Jer. 4:30: "enlarge your eyes with paint" (R. S. V.) and Ezek. 23:40: "For them you painted yourself, painted your eyes and decked yourself with ornaments" (R. S. V.). Eye paint was also prepared from antimony ore which, when pulverized, produced a black powder with

160. Styles of Eye-Painting

metallic brilliancy. It was generally made into an ointment and applied to the eyebrows and eye-lashes with an eye-pencil.
                                              M. F. U.

Eyesalve (Gr. *kollourion*, diminutive of *kollura*, coarse bread of cylindrical shape), a preparation shaped like a *kollura*, composed of various materials and used as a remedy for tender eyelids (Rev. 3:18).

E′zar (ē′zar), a less correct mode of Anglicizing (I Chron. 1:38) the name *Ezer* (*q. v.*).

Ez′bai (ĕz′bå-ī), the father of Naarai, one of David's mighty men (I Chron. 11:37), B. C. after 1000.

Ez′bon (ĕz′bŏn).
   1. The fourth son of the patriarch Gad (Gen. 46:16), called also (Num. 26:16) *Ozni*.
   2. The first named of the sons of Bela, the son of Benjamin (I Chron. 7:7).

Ezeki′as (ĕz-ē-kī′ăs), a Grecized form (Matt. 1:9, 10) of the name of King *Hezekiah* (*q. v.*).

Eze′kiel (ē-zēk′yĕl), one of the four greater prophets.
   1. **Name and Family.** (Heb. *yᵉhĕzqē′l*, *God will strengthen*). The son of a priest named Buzi.
   2. **Personal History.** Ezekiel was taken captive in the captivity of Jehoiachin, eleven years before the destruction of Jerusalem (II Kings 24:12-15). He was a member of a community of Jewish exiles who settled on the banks of the Chebar, a "river" or canal of Babylonia. It was by this river, "in the land of the Chaldeans," that God's message first reached him (Ezek. 1:3). His call took place "in the fifth year of King Jehoiachin's captivity (1:2, B. C. 592), in the thirtieth year, in the fourth month." It now seems generally agreed that it was the thirtieth year from the new era of Nabopolassar, father of *Nebuchadnezzar* (*q. v.*). We learn from an incidental allusion (24:18)—the only reference which he makes to his personal history—that he was married and had a house (8:1) in his place of exile, and lost his wife by a sudden and unforeseen stroke. He lived in the highest consideration among his companions in exile, and their elders consulted him on all occasions (8:1; 11:25; 14:1; 20:1, etc.). The last date he mentions is the twenty-seventh year of the captivity (29:17), so that his mission extended over twenty-two years.
   3. **Character.** He is distinguished by his firm and inflexible energy of will and character, and we also observe a devoted adherence to the rites and ceremonies of his national religion. Ezekiel is no cosmopolite, but displays everywhere the peculiar tendencies of a Hebrew educated under Levitical training. We may also note in Ezekiel the absorbed

recognition of his high calling, which enabled him cheerfully to endure any privation or misery, if thereby he could give any warning or lesson to his people (ch. 4; 24:15, 16, etc.), whom he so ardently loved (9:8; 11-13).

Ezekiel, Book of. This major prophecy takes the name of the prophet whose writing it records. Ezekiel was the son of a priest named Buzi and without doubt a priest himself (1:3). Together with king Jehoiachin he was taken captive to Babylon in 597 B. C. He settled in Babylonia in a place called Tel-abib (1:1; 3:15) by the River Chebar, a great canal S. E. of Babylon. He began his ministry in the fifth year of the captivity of Jehoiachin when he was about thirty years old (Cf. 1:1). His ministry lasted about twenty-two years, until 571 B. C. (Ezek. 29:17), his last dated prophecy. It is not certain whether he survived to see king Jehoiachin liberated by Evil-Merodach in 560 B. C.

1. **Authorship and Date.** The unity and authenticity of the book of Ezekiel were not seriously attacked until comparatively recent times. As late as 1924 Gustav Hoelscher observed that the critical knife had been laid on practically all the O. T. prophetic books except Ezekiel's prophecy. Accordingly, following the methods of Duhm, he dissected the book, leaving not much more than one-tenth of it as authentic—the comparatively few rhythmical sections. The rest, the prosaic parts, he assumed were written by fifth-century authors.

V. Herntrich, *Ezekielprobleme*, 1932, although largely rejecting Hoelscher's theses, approached the book in essentially the same way. W. A. Irwin rejects chapters 40-48 entirely and accepts only 250 verses of the rest. (*The Problem of Ezekiel*, Chicago, 1943). In 1930 C. C. Torrey rejected the book as a pseudo-epigraph of Palestinian origin and dated it c. 230 B. C. (*Pseudo-Ezekiel and the Original Prophecy*, New Haven, 1930, p. 150). N. Messel, 1945, and A. Bentzen, 1949, advocate similar if not such drastic views. Criticism of Ezekiel illustrates the wearisome story of negative criticism. It is conceived in doubt and born in complete confusion and uncertainty. The critics' subtle attempts to solve the so-called "problem of Ezekiel" need not trouble the reverent Christian student who firmly believes in and has a vital knowledge of the supernatural in his own experience. Negative critical views are largely dictated by disbelief in the supernatural. Containing so many supernatural visions and apocalyptic imagery which, like the book of Daniel, is reflected in the book of the Revelation, it was inevitable that negative criticism would dismember the book despite manifold evidences of its genuineness which the older critics like Cornill freely admitted (*Einleitung*, p. 76). The arrangement and plan, the accurate dating, the use of the first person and the clear-cut prophetic purpose all point to genuine authorship by Ezekiel.

2. **Purpose.** Ezekiel's mission was one of comfort to the captives in Babylon, comprising "all the house of Israel" (Cf. 37:11, 15-24). Ezekiel directed his prophecies toward demonstrating that Jehovah was justified in permitting the captivity of his people. This is the dominant theme in chapters 8-33. Proof is presented that instead of wiping them out, as God had done with other nations who had committed similar abominations, His dealing with his own covenant people was preventive and corrective. The purpose was to instruct them to know that He was God and that the neighboring nations exulting over their fall would be judged (25:1-32:32) and that the nation would finally be restored in the mediatorial Davidic kingdom (33:1; 48:35). The phrase "they shall know that I am God" occurs above thirty times in 6:7-39:28.

3. **The Contents.**

Introduction: Ezekiel's call and commission, 1:1-3:27

Part I. Prophecies against Judah and Jerusalem, 4:1-24:27

Part II. Prophecies against surrounding nations, 25:1-32:32

1. Against Amon, 25:1-7
2. Against Moab, 25:8-11
3. Against Edom, 25:12-14
4. Against Philistia, 25:15-17
5. Against Tyre, 26:1-28:19
6. Against Sidon, 28:20-26
7. Against Egypt, 29:1-32:32

Part III. Prophecies of Israel's final restoration, 33:1-48:35

1. Events preceding the restoration, 33:1-39:29
   a. Wicked purged out, 33:1-33
   b. False shepherds give way to True Shepherd, 34:1-31
   c. Restoration of the land, 36:1-15
   d. Restoration of the people, 36:16-37:28
   e. Judgment of enemies, 38:1-39:24
   f. Vision of the restored nation, 39:25-29

2. Worship in the Kingdom, 41-48:35
   a. Millennial temple, 40:1-43:27
   b. Millennial worship, 44:1-46:24
   c. Millennial land, 47:1-48:35

M. F. U.

E'zel (ē'zĕl; *separation*, see I Sam. 20:19), the memorial stones, or place of the meeting and parting of David and Jonathan. The margin of the A. V. has "that showeth the way;" the margin of the R. V. has "this mound."

E'zem (ē'zĕm; I Chron. 4:29). See Azem.

E'zer (ē'zĕr; *help*).

1. The father of Hushah, one of the posterity of Hur, of the tribe of Judah (I Chron. 4:4).

2. A son (or descendant) of Ephraim, who, with Elead, was slain by the aboriginal inhabitants of Gath "because they came down to take away their cattle" (I Chron. 7:21).

3. The first named of the Gadite champions who went to David at Ziklag (I Chron. 12:9), B. C. after 1000.

4. The son of Jeshua, the ruler of Mizpah, who repaired part of the city walls near the armory (Neh. 3:19), B. C. 445.

5. One of the priests who assisted in the dedication of the walls of Jerusalem under Nehemiah (Neh. 12:42), B. C. 445.

6. One of the sons of Seir, and native princes of Mount Hor (Gen. 36:21, 27, 30; I Chron. 1:42, 38), in which last verse the name is Anglicized "Ezar."

Ezion-geber (ē′zĭ-ŏn-gē′bẽr; Elath, modern Tell el Kheleifeh), Solomon's naval base and copper-refining port at the head of the Gulf of Aqabah (I Kings 9:26). Under Nelson Glueck's direction the American Schools of Oriental Research and the Smithsonian Institute have excavated this important site of the Hebrew monarchy. Archaeological finds show remains of complex masonry in which five strata of occupation covering five centuries were unearthed. Most important of these finds was a copper-smelting refinery. This refinery is the largest and most complex to be recovered from ancient times and shows how King Solomon developed copper mining and refining in the Arabah and made this venture one of the most lucrative sources of his proverbial lavish income. Phoenician technicians who built the seaport of Ezion-geber for Solomon were widely experienced in the art of setting up copper furnaces and refineries at the smelting settlements in Sardinia in Spain (the later Tartessus) which were called *Tarshish.* After these, the ships specially equipped for transporting such ore and metal cargoes were called Tarshish ships (Cf. Frederic Thieberger, *King Solomon*, London, 1947, p. 206). The construction of the copper refinery at Ezion-geber was uncommonly good, as Glueck has noted (*The Other Side of the Jordan*, New Haven, 1940, pp. 50-113). Copper thus became Solomon's principal export and his merchants' main stock-in-trade (*Ibid.*, p. 85). Solomon's navy setting sail from Ezion-geber laden with smelted ore brought back in exchange valuable cargoes obtainable in Arabian ports or from nearby coasts of Africa. Solomon's Phoenician engineers and advisers selected Ezion-geber in order to give their smelting furnaces the benefit of the fierce winds which blow perpetually down the deep Arabah rift. Solomon as a "copper king" thus had his ancient Pittsburgh located on the Red Sea.

Ez′nite (ĕz′nīt), apparently the patronymic of *Adino* (*q. v.*) given (II Sam. 23:8) as chief among David's captains. Concerning this doubtful rendering Luther expresses the following opinion: "We believe the text to have been corrupted by a writer, probably from some book in an unknown character and bad writing, so that *orer* should be substituted for *adino*, and *ha-eznib* for *eth hanitho*;" that is to say, the reading in the Chronicles (I Chron. 11:11), "he swung his spear," should be adopted (K. and D., *Com.*).

Ez′ra (ĕz′rá; *help*).

1. The priest who led the second expedition of Jews back from Babylonian exile in Palestine, and the author of the book bearing his name (*see* the last four chapters, in which he speaks in the first person).

Family. Ezra was a lineal descendant of Phineas, the grandson of Aaron (Ezra 7:1-5), being a son of Seraiah, who was the grandson of Hilkiah, high priest in the reign of Josiah. He is described as "a ready scribe in the law of Moses" (v. 6); "a scribe of the words of the commandments of the Lord, and of the statutes of Israel" (v. 11); "Ezra the priest, a scribe of the law of the God of heaven" (v. 12).

History. (1) **Appointed leader.** Ezra's priestly extraction acted as a powerful lever for directing his vigorous efforts specifically to the promotion of religion and learning among his people. It is recorded (Ezra 7:10) that Ezra "had prepared his heart to seek the law of the Lord, and to do it, and to teach in Israel statutes and judgments." Living in Babylon he gained the favor of King Artaxerxes, and obtained from him a commission to go up to Jerusalem (B. C. about 459). The king's commission invited all the Israelites, priests, and Levites in the whole empire, who so wished, to accompany Ezra. Of these a list amounting to one thousand seven hundred and fifty-four is given (ch. 8); and these, doubtless, form part of the full list of the returned captives contained in Nehemiah (ch. 7), and in duplicate (Ezra 2). Ezra was allowed to take with him a large freewill offering of gold and silver, and silver vessels, contributed by the Jews, by the king himself, and by his counselors. He was also empowered to draw upon the king's treasures beyond the river for any further supplies required; and all priests, Levites, and other ministers of the temple were exempted from taxation. Ezra received authority to appoint magistrates and judges in Judea, with power of life and death over all offenders (7:11-28). His credentials were indorsed by the seven principal members of the royal council (v. 14). (2) **Preparations.** Ezra assembled the Jews who accompanied him on the banks of the river Ahava, where they halted three days in tents. As mentioned above, the number was about one thousand five hundred, and included several of highpriestly and Davidic descent. Upon inspection he found that they had not a single Levite among them, and sent a deputation to Casiphia, where many of them lived, and succeeded in inducing thirty-eight Levites and two hundred and twenty servants of the temple to join their expedition (8:15-20). The valuable offerings to the temple he placed in the custody of twelve of the most distinguished priests and Levites; but such was his trust in God and his lofty courage, that he refrained from asking a royal escort (v. 22). After fasting and other pious exercises (vers. 21-23), the company started on their journey on the twelfth day of the first month (in the spring) of the seventh year of Artaxerxes I. (3) **At Jerusalem.** They reached Jerusalem without accident at the beginning of the fifth month (7:8). Three days after their arrival the treasures were weighed and delivered to the proper custodians, burnt sacrifices were offered by the returned exiles, and the king's commissions were delivered to viceroys and governors (8:32-36). In accordance with the royal decree, Ezra was now to be firmly established in Jerusalem as chief judge; empowered to settle everything relating to the religion of the Jews, and the life which was regulated by it. Ezra soon found, to his great distress, that the people of Jerusalem had paid no regard to the law forbidding the marriage of Israelites with heathen. Overwhelmed by his emotion, he sank to the ground, utterly unstrung and weeping bitterly. Men of tender conscience gathered around him, and all remained in mourning until the hour of the evening sacrifice, when Ezra poured out his soul in prayer (9:1-15). By this time a great congregation had gathered about Ezra, and "wept very sore." At length Shechaniah declared the guilt of the people and their wish to comply fully with the law. A general assembly was called to meet in Jerusalem within three days to decide what course should be pursued. They assembled on the twentieth day of the ninth month amid a great storm of rain, and having confessed their sin, they proceeded to the remedy with order and deliberation. All the strange wives were put away, including even those who had borne children, by the beginning of the new year (ch. 10). (4) **Later history.** Whether Ezra remained after the events recorded above, occupying about eight months, or returned to Babylon, is not known. It is conjectured by some that Ezra remained governor until superseded by Nehemiah; others think that he continued his labors in conjunction with Nehemiah. Our next mention of him is in connection with Nehemiah, after the completion of the walls of Jerusalem. The functions he executed under Nehemiah's government were purely of a priestly and ecclesiastical character; such as reading and interpreting the law of Moses to the people, praying for the congregation, assisting in the dedication of the walls, and proclaiming the religious reformation effected by Nehemiah (Neh. 8:9; 12:26). In the sealing of the covenant (10:1, sq.), Ezra perhaps sealed under the patronymic Seraiah or Azariah (v. 2). As Ezra is not .mentioned after Nehemiah's departure for Babylon, and as everything fell into confusion in Nehemiah's absence, it is not unlikely that Ezra had again returned to Babylon before Nehemiah. (5) **Character.** Ezra had a profound love for the word of God, and "prepared his heart to seek the law of the Lord, and to do it, and to teach in Israel statutes and judgments" (Ezra 7:10); he was a man of excellent judgment (7:25), of large conscientiousness (9:3, sq.), which led him deeply to deplore sin and strenuously to oppose it. So great was his sense of dependence upon God that every step he took was marked by some devout acknowledgment of the divine help, "according to the good hand of God upon him" (7:6, 9, 27, 28; 8:22, 31).

2. A descendant of Judah, the father of several sons. His own parentage is not given (I Chron. 4:17).

3. The head of one of the twenty-two courses of priests which returned from captivity with Zerubbabel and Jeshua (Neh. 12:1), B. C. 536. The same name appears in v. 13, where it is stated that his son, Meshullam, was chief of his family in the time of the high priest Joiakim (*see* v. 12); also in v. 33, as one of the chief Israelites who formed the first division that made the circuit of the walls of Jerusalem when rebuilt, B. C. 445.

Ezra, Book of. In the Ancient Hebrew Scriptures Ezra and Nehemiah were classified as one book, called "the Book of Ezra." Since 1448 Hebrew Bibles have the twofold arrangement Ezra and Nehemiah, as in our English renderings. In the Septuagint Ezra and Nehemiah follow Chronicles. This seems a more logical and primitive idea since Ezra and Nehemiah carry on the history at the point where Chronicles leaves off, and since the Massoretic notes on the Writings stand at the conclusion of Nehemiah and not Chronicles. Critics commonly consider Chronicles, Ezra and Nehemiah as originally a single work, but the reasons deducted are not completely satisfying.

1. **Authorship and Date.** There is no solid reason why the authorship of the book by Ezra should be given up, despite the theorizing of modern critics. It is possible that a later inspired compiler consulted Ezra's memoirs written in the first person (Ezek. 7:27-9:15). However, it is very likely that Ezra himself compiled this material as a framework for the book and filled out the remaining parts written in the third person from other sources to make it a unified whole. Assuming that Ezra is also the author of Chronicles, according to tradition, then the book of Ezra must have followed Chronicles somewhere during the period of 430-400 B. C., or a little later. Ezra's activity is evidently to be placed during the reign of Artaxerxes (465-424 B. C.) but Chronicles and the book of Ezra may have been written considerably later. Modern negative criticism construes the book as a compilation dating at least a century or more subsequent to Ezra's time. It is therefore accorded little historical authenticity. Such invalid criticisms as the claim of the non-historicity of the title "king of Persia" (1:1, 2, etc.) are often made. The terms, as common sense would suggest, are used interchangeably and occur in the same passages (Ezra 1:1, 2, 7, 8; 7:1, 7) as one would now refer to "the president" or "the President of the United States" without implying by the latter term that a new nation had superseded the United States. A heathen king, moreover, although a "king of kings" might naturally be styled simply "king of Persia" even if such usage is rare on the monuments. Critics make the charge of chronological confusion in Ezra 4:6-23. Events in the reign of Xerxes (485-465 B. C.) and Artaxerxes (465-425 B. C.) come before events in the reign of Darius (521-485 B. C.) in chapter 5, but Ezra simply finishes one subject before proceeding to the next, even at the expense of chronological sequence, which any other writer would be inclined to do. The Decree of Cyrus recorded in Hebrew (Ezra 1:1-4) and Aramaic (6:3-5) is supposed to involve contradiction, but the one in Hebrew was evidently made by Cyrus when he first conquered Babylon and naturally has a Jewish coloring. The second, in Aramaic, was evidently a formal record drawn up for the official archives at Ecbatana and consequently has a Babylonian coloring. There is no reason to suppose that both are not historical and authentic.

3. **Outline.**

Part I. Return under Zerubbabel, 1:1-6:22
  1. First return of the captives, 1:1-2:70
    a. Cyrus' decree, 1:1-11
    b. Register of exiles, 2:1-7

2. The restoration of popular worship,
   3:1-6:22
   a. Temple rebuilt, 3:1-6:15
   b. Temple dedicated, 6:16-22
Part II. Reforms under Ezra, 7:1-10:44
1. Second return of exiles, 7:1-8:36
2. Abolishment of heathen marriages,
   9:1-10:44

M. F. U.

Ez′rahite (ĕz′rȧ-hīt), the patronymic of the Levites Heman and Ethan (I Kings 4:31; titles of Psa. 88, 89). Their Levitical descent is

not at variance with the epithet Ezrahite (or Ezrachite), for they were incorporated into the Judean family of Zerach. Thus the Levite (Judg. 17:7) is spoken of as belonging to the family of Judah because he dwelt in Bethlehem of Judah.

Ez′ri (ĕz′rī; *helpful*), son of Chelub, superintendent for King David of those "who did the work of the field for tillage of the ground" (I Chron. 27:26), B. C. after 1000.

Ez′rite. *See* Abi-ezrite.

F

Fable (Gr. *muthos, myth*), a fictitious story employed for the purpose of enforcing some truth or precept. Neander, *Life of Christ*, thus distinguishes between the parable and fable: "The parable is distinguished from the fable by this, that, in the latter qualities or acts of a higher class of beings may be attributed to a lower, e. g., those of men to brutes; while in the former the lower sphere is kept perfectly distinct from that which it seems to illustrate. The beings and powers thus introduced always follow the law of their nature, but their acts, according to this law, are used to figure those of a higher race." Of the fable, we have but two examples in the Bible, (1) That of the trees choosing their king, addressed by Jotham to the men of Shechem (Judg. 9:8-15); (2) that of the cedar of Lebanon and the thistle, as the answer of Jehoash to the challenge of Amaziah (II Kings 14:9).

In the New Testament fable is used for *invention, falsehood* (II Pet. 1:16). "The fictions of the Jewish theosophists and Gnostics, especially concerning the emanations and orders of the aeons, i. e., spirits of the air, are called myths" (A. V. Fables; I Tim. 1:4; 4:7; II Tim. 4:4; Tit. 1:14).

Face. There is nothing peculiar in the use of this word in Scripture, except with reference to God. Applied to God, it denotes his *presence.* In such phrases as "Seeing the face of the Lord," "The face of the Lord is set against them that do evil," "The cry came before the face of the Lord," it is evidently all one with God's manifested presence. The declaration made by Jehovah to Moses, "there shall no man see me, and live" (Exod. 33:20), seems to contradict the joyful assertion of Jacob, "I have seen God face to face, and my life is preserved" (Gen. 32:30). The apparent discrepancy is to be explained by the different respects in which the expression is used in the two cases. The face of God, as involving the full blaze of his manifested glory, no mortal can see and live; but when veiled and appearing with the softened radiance of the human countenance, revived and quickened life is the natural result. The word is also used in the sense of *favor* (Psa. 44:3; 67:1; Dan. 9:17), and signifies also *anger*, justice, severity (Gen. 16:6, 8; Exod. 2:15; Rev. 6:16), it being natural for men to express these feelings in their countenances. "To set one's face" denotes to

determine fully and resolve, and "to fall on the face" is an attitude of *fear* and *reverence*. To see one "face to face" is to enjoy a direct, clear sight of him, and not a reflection in a mirror.

Faces, Bread of, is the showbread (*q. v.*), which was always in the presence of God.

Fair, the rendering of several Hebrew and Greek words. In the East exposure to the sun makes a great difference in the complexion of women. Those of high condition carefully avoid such exposure, and retain their fairness, which becomes a distinguishing mark of quality as well as an enhancement of beauty (Gen. 12:11-13; Cant. 1:15, 16).

Fair Ha′vens (Gr. *kaloi limenes, good harbors*), a harbor in the island of Crete (Acts 27:8), "near the city of Lasea, which, as Smith has shown conclusively, is the small bay, two leagues E. of Cape Matala, still bearing the same name in the modern Greek dialect, (*Limeōnas kalois*)" (Ramsey, *St. Paul*, p. 321).

Fairs (Ezek. 27:12-27). This word is only found in Ezekiel, and does not mean *fairs*, but *wares*, as the R. V. renders it, and as the A. V. has it in v. 33. The essential meaning of the Hebrew seems to be an *exchange*, or *equivalent*, alluding to the frequency of *barter* in ancient trade.

Faith (Gr. *pistis*), belief, trust—especially in a higher power. The fundamental idea in Scripture is steadfastness, faithfulness.

1. **Scripture Use of Word.** The word is used in Scriptures, (1) Most frequently in a subjective sense, denoting a moral and spiritual quality of individuals, by virtue of which men are held in relations of confidence in God and fidelity to him. (2) In an objective sense, meaning the body of truth, moral and religious, which God has revealed—that which men believe. Examples of this use of the word are not numerous, though they occur occasionally, as in Phil. 1:27; I Tim. 1:19; 6:20, 21; Jude 3, 20.

The word occurs but twice in our English version of the Old Testament, the idea being expressed by other terms, as "trust," etc.

This article is confined in the further discussion to faith in the sense first named. The following points are of chief importance:

2. **Philosophical.** Faith, viewed philosophically, must be regarded as lying at the basis of all knowledge. Anselm's famous utterance, "Crede ut intelligas," "Believe that you may

know," expresses the truth in contrast with the words of Abelard, "Intellige ut credas," "Know that you may believe." Truths perceived intuitively imply faith in the intuitions. Truths or facts arrived at by logical processes, or processes of reasoning, are held to be known because, first of all, we have confidence in the laws of the human mind. Our knowledge obtained through the senses has underneath it faith in the senses. To this extent Goethe spoke wisely when he said, "I believe in the five senses." A large part of knowledge rests upon human testimony, and of course this involves faith in the testimony.

The distinction between matters of faith and matters of knowledge must not be drawn too rigidly, inasmuch as all matters of knowledge are in some measure matters also of faith. The distinction, when properly made, recognizes chiefly the different objects to which our convictions relate, and the different methods by which we arrive at these convictions. The convictions themselves may be as strong in the one case as in the other.

3. **Theological.** Faith in the theological sense contains two elements recognized in the Scriptures. There is an element that is intellectual; also an element, of even deeper importance, that is moral. Faith is not simply the assent of the intellect to revealed truth; it is the practical submission of the entire man to the guidance and control of such truth. "The devils believe and tremble."

Indispensable as is the assent of the intellect, that alone does not constitute the faith upon which the Scriptures lay such emphasis. The essential idea is rather that of fidelity, faithfulness, steadfastness. Or, as has been well said, "Faith, in its essential temper, is that elevation of soul by which it aspires to the good, the true, and the divine." In illustration may be cited particularly John 3:18-21; Rom. 2:7; 4:5; Heb. ch. 11; James 2:14-26.

4. **Intellectual.** Viewed more particularly with reference to its intellectual aspect, faith is properly defined as the conviction of the reality of the truths and facts which God has revealed, such conviction resting solely upon the testimony of God.

These truths and facts are to a large extent beyond the reach of the ordinary human processes of acquiring knowledge. Still they are of the utmost importance in relation to human life and salvation. God has therefore revealed them. And they who accept them must do so upon the trustworthiness of the divine testimony. This testimony is contained in the Holy Scriptures. It is impressed moreover by the special sanction of the Holy Spirit. (*See* John 3:11, 31:33; 16:8-11; I John 5:10, 11, and many other places.)

5. **Results of Faith.** They who receive the divine testimony and yield to it cordial and full assent become partakers of heavenly knowledge. Their knowledge comes by faith, yet none the less is it knowledge. The Scriptures, it is true, recognize the difference between walking by faith and walking by sight, and thus the difference between the objects and methods of sense-perception and those of faith. Also the difference is noted between the acquisition of human learning and philosophy

and the contents of the divine revelation. But still the Scriptures represent true believers as persons who "know the things that are freely given . . . of God." Christ said to his disciples, "Unto you it is given to know the mysteries of the kingdom of God" (Luke 8:10; *see* also John 8:31, 32; I Cor. 1:5, 6, 21-30; 2:9-16; Eph. 1:17; I Tim. 2:4).

6. **Reason and Faith.** The relation of reason to faith is that of subordination, and yet not that of opposition. The truths of revelation are in many cases above reason, though not against it. Such truths were revealed because reason could not discover them. They are therefore to be accepted, though the reason cannot demonstrate them. But this inability of reason to discover or to demonstrate is one thing; irrationality, as involving absurdity, or contradiction of the intuitions of the intellect or conscience, or contradiction of well-established truth, is another.

Reason has its justly recognized and appropriate function in examining and weighing the evidences of revelation, also in interpreting or determining the force of the terms in which the revelation is given. But when the reality and meaning of revelation are thus reached reason has done its work, and it remains for faith to accept the contents of the revelation, whatever they may be.

It should be said, however, that the evidence of the saving truth of revelation, most convincing for many, is not that which appeals directly to reason. Many lack ability or opportunity to investigate the rational evidences of Christianity. But to them with all others the announcement of the truth comes attended by the ministration or direct testimony of the Holy Spirit. They are thus made to feel that they ought to repent and believe the Gospel. If they yield to this conviction they obtain forgiveness of their sins and become new creatures in Christ Jesus. The Spirit bears witness to their acceptance with God. And thus in the experience of salvation they have indubitable proof of the reality of revelation. In all this reason is subordinate to faith, but by no means opposed to it (I Cor. 1:21-31; John 16:8-11; Rom. 8:14-17; I John 5:9-11).

7. **Condition of Salvation.** As has been assumed in the foregoing, faith is the condition of salvation. It is not the procuring cause, but the condition, or instrumental cause. It is frequently associated in the Scriptures with repentance; and thus the conditions of salvation, as commonly stated in Protestant doctrine, are repentance and faith. But in reality true faith and true repentance are not separate or to be distinguished too rigidly from each other. Faith is fundamental. Repentance implies faith. Faith is not real saving faith unless it includes repentance. (*See* Repentance.) Saving faith may therefore be properly defined, for those who have the light of the Gospel, as such belief in the Lord Jesus Christ as leads one to submit completely to the authority of Christ, and to put complete and exclusive trust in him for salvation. (*See* John 3:14-16, and many other places.)

Faith, which is the condition of salvation, is also, in an important measure, one of the results of salvation. In the justified and regenerated soul, faith is deepened and developed by the influence of the Holy Spirit. In its essential quality faith is unchanged, but it acquires greater steadiness; and as the word of God is studied and its contents spiritually apprehended faith becomes broader and richer in the truths and facts which it grasps.

Thus in its beginning and completion faith is one of the fruits of the Spirit (Gal. 5:22).

For fuller discussion see works of Systematic Theology, particularly Lewis Sperry Chafer's *Systematic Theology* III: 372-378; VI: 293-294.
E. McC.

Faith, Rule of. In the early Church the summary of doctrines taught to catechumens, and to which they were obliged to subscribe before baptism. It was afterward applied to the Apostles' Creed. In modern theology it denotes the true source of our knowledge of Christian truth.

1. **Protestant Doctrine.** One of the chief doctrinal elements of the Reformation was the sufficiency of the Scriptures for faith and salvation. Thus the Methodist Church teaches: "The Holy Scriptures contain all things necessary to salvation; so that whatsoever is not read therein, nor may be proved thereby, is not to be believed as an article of faith, or be thought requisite or necessary to salvation" (*Meth. Dis.*, v, 5).

2. **Roman Catholic** teaching is: "The Church is the ordinary and the infallible means by which we know what the truths are which God has revealed. The testimony of the Church is the *rule* by which we can distinguish between true and false doctrine. . . . A person must believe that the Church cannot err, and that whatever it teaches is infallibly true" (*Cath. Dict.*, s. v.).

Faith, The Christian. "To those who receive the light, in the sense of not refusing it, revelation is one whole, and all its glorious system of truth is received and surely believed. To them it is both objectively and subjectively *the Faith*; and, inasmuch as Christianity has brought it in all fullness into the world, it is to them the *Christian Faith*. This phrase has therefore a larger meaning. It signifies that it is not their philosophy simply, the glory of their reason, the tradition they have derived from their fathers, but the rich inheritance which the Holy Spirit has given to that one supreme faculty of their souls, the faith which is the *evidence of things not seen*. It is a body of truth which, as reason did not give it, so reason cannot take it away. It is a region in which they walk by faith, which their faith habitually visits, in which their faith lives, and moves, and has its being" (Pope, *Compend. Christian Theol.*, p. 45).

Faithfulness (Heb. *'ĕmūnāh, faithfulness, stability*), an attribute ascribed to God in many places, especially in the Psalms (36:5; 89:2 sq.; Isa. 11:15, etc.), which exhibits his character as worthy of the love and confidence of man, and assures us that he will certainly fulfill his promises, as well as execute his threats against sin. It covers "temporal blessings (I Tim. 4:8; Psa. 84:11; Isa. 33:16); spiritual blessings (I Cor. 1:9); support in

temptation (I Cor. 10:13) and persecution (I Pet. 4:12, 13; Isa. 41:10); sanctifying afflictions (Heb. 12:4-12); directing in difficulties (II Chron. 32:22; Psa. 32:8); enabling to persevere (Jer. 32:40), and bringing to glory (I John 2:25)."

Faithfulness is also predicated of men: "He was a *faithful* man" (Hebrew *trustworthy*, Neh. 7:2); "who then is that faithful (trusty) and wise steward?" (Luke 12:42, etc.) "*The Faithful*" was the general and favorite name in the early Church to denote baptized persons.
Falcon. *See* Animal Kingdom.
Fall of Man, a term of theology which is not found in Scriptures, though the essential fact is a matter of Scripture record and of clear though not frequent reference. The particular account is in Gen. 3. The most explicit New Testament references are Rom. 5:12-21; I Cor. 15:21, 22, 45-47; II Cor. 11:3.

The character of the primitive record in Genesis has been the subject of much discussion. Some have contended that the account is purely literal; others, that it is figurative, poetic, or allegorical; still others, rationalistic or semirationalistic, relegate the whole matter to the realm of the mythical. This last view, of course, cannot be consistently held by anyone who accepts the Scriptures as of divine authority.

It must be admitted that the account leaves room for many questions both as to its form and its meaning in relation to incidental details. But still the great, underlying, essential facts are sufficiently clear, especially when the account is taken in connection with other Scriptures. They are as follows:

1. **Bible Doctrine.** (1) The fall of our first parents was an epoch or turning point in the moral history of the race. It was in itself an epoch of great and sad significance and of far-reaching results.

(2) Man at his creation was in a state of moral purity. In connection with his freedom there was of necessity the possibility of sin. But still there was no evil tendency in his nature. God pronounced him, with other objects of his creation, "good." He was made in the image and likeness of God.

(3) As a moral being man was placed by God in a state of probation. His freedom was to be exercised and tested by his being under divine law. Of every tree in the garden he might freely eat, except the tree of knowledge of good and evil. At one point there must be restraint, self-denial for the sake of obedience. "He could not have the whole world and save his own soul."

(4) The temptation to disobedience came from an evil source outside himself. In Genesis only the serpent is mentioned. In the New Testament the tempter is identified as Satan, who employed the serpent as his instrument (II Cor. 11:3, 14; Rom. 16:20; Rev. 12:9).

(5) The temptation came in the form of an appeal to both man's intellect and to the senses. The forbidden fruit was presented as "good for food" and "to be desired to make one wise." Thus the allurement was in the direction of sensual gratification and intellectual pride.

(6) At the beginning of the sin lay unbelief.

The tempted ones doubted or disbelieved God and believed the tempter. And thus, under the strong desire awakened by the temptation, they disobeyed the divine command.

(7) By this act of disobedience "sin entered into the world and death by sin." Shame and alienation from God were the first visible consequences. The image of God, which contained among its features "righteousness and true holiness," was marred and broken, though not completely lost. (*See* Image of God.) Expulsion from Eden followed. The ground was cursed on account of sin. Sorrow and toil and struggle with the evil in human nature became the lot of mankind.

2. **Theological Views.** As to the theological treatment of this topic it should be particularly noted:

(1) **Rationalistic.** A favorite view of rationalistic or evolutionist theologians is that the fall was a necessary incident in man's moral development. The fall is sometimes, therefore, spoken of as "a fall upward." It was a step forward from the savage or animal state to the practical knowledge of good and evil, and thus, through the experience of sin, toward the goal of developed moral purity. But this view ignores the essential evil of sin. It makes sin only an imperfect or disguised good, and is, for that reason and others, opposed to the plain teaching of Scripture.

(2) **Calvinistic view.** The Calvinistic types of theology regard the fall in two ways: (*1*) The supralapsarian, or most rigid view, includes the fall under the divine decree. (*2*) The sublapsarian, the less rigid but less logically consistent view, represents the divine decree as relating to the condition produced by the fall. Out from the race fallen in Adam God elected a certain number to salvation. The human race is not in a state of probation. The sin of our first parents closed the probationary period of human history.

(3) **Arminian view.** The Arminian theology regards the fall not as predetermined by a divine decree, but as foreseen and provided against by divine grace. It asserts that but for the redemptive purpose of God in Christ the race of fallen descendants of Adam would not have been permitted to come into existence. When man fell he did not "fall upward," but he fell into the arms of redeeming mercy. Probation is still the condition of mankind. For though man is fallen and therefore under the bondage of sin, through Christ, the second Adam, man has his moral freedom restored to such an extent that he can avail himself of the provisions that God has made for his salvation.

3. **The Fall and Archaeology.** The so-called Myth of Adapa has often been adduced as offering a parallel to the Bible account of the fall of man. This claim, however, is ill-founded. There is not the slightest reason to look for the fall in the literature of the Babylonians as such a concept is contrary to their whole system of polytheistic speculation. In Genesis man is created in the image of a holy God. But the Babylonians, like other ancient heathen peoples, notably the Greeks and the Romans, fashioned their gods good and bad

in the image of man. Such deities schemed, hated, fought and killed one another. Of such dubious moral character, it was impossible that they be thought of as creating anything morally perfect, neither could man formed out of the blood of such deities (the foolish Babylonian notion) possess anything but an evil nature. No fall was possible because man was created evil and in heathenistic thought had no state of innocence from which to fall. Nevertheless further features of the legend of Adapa are interesting by way of similarity or contrast. The "food of life" corresponds to "fruit" of the "tree of life" (Gen. 3:3, 22). The two accounts are in agreement that eternal life could be obtained by eating a certain kind of food. Adam, however, forfeited immortality for himself because of the sinful desire to be "like God" (Gen. 3:5). Consequently he was exiled from the garden lest he should eat "of the tree of life . . . and live forever" (Gen. 3:22). Adapa was already endued with wisdom by the gods. He failed to become immortal not because of disobedience or presumption, like Adam, but because he was obedient to his creator, Ea, who deceived him. The Babylonian tale, like the Biblical narrative, deals with the perplexing question why man must suffer and die. In contrast, the answer is not that man fell from his moral integrity and that sin into which he fell involved death, but that man forfeited his opportunity to get eternal life in consequence o being deceived by one of the gods. The origin of human sin is not at all in view in the Adapa story. This is basic in the theologically pivotal third chapter of Genesis. The two narratives, the Biblical and the Babylonian, are poles apart despite superficial resemblances.

E. McC. revised by *M. F. U.*

For full discussion see works of systematic theology, as Pope, *Compend. Christian Theology;* Watson, *Theological Institutes;* Van Oosterzee, *Christian Dogmatics;* Delitzsch, *Biblical Psychology;* Fletcher, *Appeal;* C. Hodge, *Systematic Theology,* L. S. Chafer, *Systematic Theology;* A. Strong, *Systematic Theology;* Gustav Oehler, *Theology of the O. T.*

Fallow Deer. *See* Animal Kingdom.

Fallow Ground, a field plowed up and left for seeding; as summer fallow, properly conducted, is a sure method of destroying weeds (Jer. 4:3; Hos. 10:12).

Fallow Year. *See* Sabbath.

False Christs, those who falsely claim to be Messiah foretold by Jesus (Matt. 24:24; Mark 13:22). Nothing is known of the historical fulfillment of this prophecy, but Josephus (*Wars,* vii, 11, 1) mentions *Jonathan* as a pretender.

False Prophet, the, is the Second Beast of Rev 13:11-18 (Cf. Rev. 16:13; 19:20; 20:10). Twice he is associated with the First Beast (Anti-Christ) and once with the Dragon (Satan). As the Dragon and the First Beast are persons, so must he be a person. Jesus had a prophetic foreview of him when He said, "There shall arise false Christs and false prophets and shall show great signs and wonders insomuch that if it were possible they should deceive the very elect" (Matt. 24:24). Here our Lord distinguishes between false Christs and false prophets. It seems clear, therefore, that the Anti-Christ and the False Prophet cannot be the same. The False Prophet will be a miracle worker. By evil supernatural power he will bring fire down from heaven and will command the people of the Tribulation Period to make "an image of the Beast" in order to worship it, having power to give life to the image to cause it to speak and to demand that all who will not worship it shall be put to death (Rev. 11:15). And he causes all "both small and great, both rich and poor, both free and slave to be marked on the right hand or the forehead so that no one can buy or sell unless he has the mark that is the name of the Beast or the number of its name" (Rev. 13:16, 17). He will thus be a consummation of deception and wickedness, this being signified by his mystical number, 666. As an aid to the Anti-Christ, he is one of the principal characters revolting against God at the end time, immediately prior to Christ's Second Advent. *M. F. U.*

Familiar Spirit (Heb. *'ob*), is a divining demon present in the physical body of the conjurer. "A man, or also a woman, that hath a familiar spirit (literally, 'in whom there is a divining demon'), or a wizard, shall surely be put to death: they shall stone them with stones; their blood shall be upon them" (Lev. 20:27). The term "familiar" is used to describe the foreboding demon because it was regarded by the English translators as a servant ("famulus"), belonging to the family ("familiaris"), who was on intimate terms with and might be readily summoned by the one possessing it. Thus a familiar spirit is a divining demon and the ancient world, as well as the modern, had traffic in spiritism, not as mere chicanery, but as a spiritual reality of evil nature. The significance of the Hebrew term *'ob* is disputed. It may be related to the Arabic root *'awaba* ("to return"), with reference to the divining spirit who periodically returns to the medium. The commonest view, however, associates the fundamental etymological significance with "something hollow" as a "leathern bottle" or "wine skin" (Job. 32:19). Assuming the fundamental notion of "hollowness," various explanations are suggested as accounting for it, such as calling the divining spirit an *'ob* because of the hollow tone of its voice as issuing from a cave or opening in the ground. Greek and Roman oracles were commonly situated among the deep caverns, which were considered to communicate with the spirit world. This was notably true of Apollo's famous oracle at Delphi. (*See* T. K. Oesterreich, *Possession, Demoniacal and Other*, pp. 312 s. q., E. Langton, *Essentials of Demonology*, pp. 96-98.) Gesenius has the idea that the connection between "bottle" and "necromancer" probably arose "from regarding the conjurer, while possessed by the demon, as a bottle, i. e., vessel, case, in which the demon was contained." (Hebrew and English Lexicon, *in loc.*). *M. F. U.*

Family. The family relation is the institution of God lying at the foundation of all human society. Christian ethics leave nothing wanting of the main elements of that institution. It confirms monogamy: "From the beginning of the creation God made them, male and fe-

male. For this cause shall a man leave his father and mother, and cleave to his wife" (Matt. 19:5; Mark 10:6, 7). So Christian legislation is clear and positive respecting the relation of marriage, of parents and children, of masters and servants, and the regulation of all the household. Parental obligations include the maintenance of children (I Tim. 5:8) and their education in its fullest sense (Exod. 12:26, 27; Deut. 6:6, 7; Eph. 6:4).

The filial obligations are obedience (Luke 2:51; Eph. 6:1; Col. 3:20), reverence (Exod. 20:12; comp. Eph. 6:1, 2), and grateful requital (I Tim. 5:4; comp. John 19:26). The moral teaching of Christianity has a very marked bearing on the relation between master and servants. Although the mutual rights, duties, and responsibilities are not in their widest range matter of direct statute in the Scriptures, the principles laid down by Paul are of permanent application. On the employer's side there is the obligation of justice (Col. 4:1); on the side of the servants there is enjoined the duty of obedience, fidelity, and honesty (Tit. 2:9, 10; Col. 3:22, 23; Eph. 6:5, 6). Thus the family occupies a prominent place throughout Scripture, is the first form of society, and has continued to be the germ and representative of every fellowship (Pope, *Christ. Theol.*, iii; Westcott, *Social Aspects of Christianity*, p. 19, sq.).

Family, or **Father's House,** one of the divisions of the people of Israel. *See* Israel, Classification of.

Famine occupies a conspicuous place in Scripture among the troubles with which God's people had to contend. It is mentioned as one of the scourges which God sent to chastise men for their wickedness (Lev. 26:21, 26; Psa. 105:16; Lam. 4:4-6; Ezek. 14:21).

1. **Causes.** Several causes of famine are given: (1) God's blessing withheld (Hos. 2:8, 9; Hag. 1:6); (2) Want of seasonable rain (I Kings 17:1; Jer. 14:1-4; Amos 4:7, sq.). "In Egypt a deficiency in the rise of the Nile, with drying winds, produces the same results. The famines recorded in the Bible are traceable to both these phenomena; and we generally find that Egypt was resorted to when scarcity afflicted Palestine. In the whole of Syria and Arabia the fruits of the earth must ever be dependent on rain, the watersheds having few large springs and the small rivers not being sufficient for the irrigation of even the level lands. If, therefore, the heavy rains of November and December fail the sustenance of the people is cut off in the parching drought of harvest time, when the country is almost devoid of moisture" (Smith, *Dict.*, s. v.). (3) Rotting of seed in the ground (Joel 1:17); (4) Blasting and mildew (Amos 4:9; Hag. 2:17; (5) Devastation by enemies (Deut. 28:33, 51). In addition to the above causes may be given the imperfect knowledge of agriculture which prevailed, in consequence of which men had few resources to stimulate, or in unfavorable seasons and localities, to aid the productive powers of nature. Means of transit were defective, rendering it often impossible to relieve the wants of one region even when there was plenty in another. Despotic governments and frequent wars and

desolation greatly interrupted agricultural industry.

2. **Characteristics.** These famines were often long continued (Gen. 41:27) and of great severity (Gen. 12:10; II Kings 8:1; Jer. 52:6), accompanied with wars (Jer. 14:15; 29:18), and followed by pestilence (Jer. 42: 17; Ezek. 7:15; Matt. 24:7). During the time of famine people fed upon wild herbs (II Kings 4:39, 40), asses' flesh and ordure (II Kings 6:25; Lam. 4:5) and human flesh (Lev. 26:29; II Kings 6:28, 29), while provisions were sold by weight and water by measure (Ezek. 4:16).

3. **Instances.** Famines are mentioned as occurring in the days of Abraham (Gen. 12:10), of Isaac (26:1), of Joseph (41:53-56), of the Judges (Ruth 1:1), of David (II Sam. 21:1), of Ahab (I Kings 17:1; 18:2), of Elisha (II Kings 4:38), during the siege of Samaria (II Kings 6:25), in the time of Jeremiah (Jer. 14:1, sq.), during the siege of Jerusalem (II Kings 25:3), after the captivity (Neh. 5:3), in the reign of Claudius Caesar (Acts 11:28), before the destruction of Jerusalem (Matt. 24:7).

Figurative. Famine is symbolic of the withdrawal of God's word (Amos 8:11, 12) and the destruction of idols (Zeph. 2:11).

Fan (Heb. *zäräh*, to *toss* about; *mizrěh;* Gr. *ptuon*), a sort of long-handled, wooden shovel, with which grain was thrown up against the wind in order to separate the chaff therefrom (Isa. 30:24; Matt. 3:12; Luke 3:17). At the present day in Syria a large wooden fork is used.

Figurative. To *fan* is used in the sense of to *scatter*, as enemies (Isa. 41:16); to "fan at the gates" (Jer. 15:7) is to cause defeat and dispersion on the border of the land; "whose fan is in his hand" (Matt. 3:12) refers to Christ as judge, separating evil from good.

Fanners, rendering in the A. V. (Jer. 51:2), but properly "strangers," and so translated in the R. V.

Farm. *See* Agriculture.

Farthing. *See* Metrology, IV.

Fast, Fasting (Heb. *şûm*, to *cover* the mouth; Gr. *nēsteuō*, to *abstain*). In the early ages men subsisted largely upon the spontaneous productions of the earth and the spoils of the chase; and owing to the uncertainty of obtaining food fasting was often compulsory. Superstitious ignorance could easily interpret this compulsion into an expression of the divine will, and so consider fasting as a religious duty. It was thought that the gods were jealous of the pleasures of men, and that abstinence would propitiate their favor. As a result we find that fasting as a religious duty is almost universal.

1. **Jewish.** The word fasting (Heb. *şûm*) is not found in the Pentateuch, but often occurs in the historical books (II Sam. 12:16; I Kings 21:9-12; Ezra 8:21) and the prophets (Isa. 58:3-5; Joel 1:14; 2:15; Zech. 8:19, etc.). The expression used in the law is "afflicting the soul" (Lev. 16:29-31; 23:27; Num. 30:13), implying the sacrifice of the personal will, which gives to fasting all its value. (1) **Observance.** The Jewish fasts were observed with various degrees of strictness. When the

fast lasted only a single day it was the practice to abstain from food of every kind from evening to evening, whereas in the case of private fasts of a more prolonged character it was merely the ordinary food that was abstained from. To manifest a still profounder humbling of the soul before God in repentance and mortification on account of one's sin and the punishment with which it had been visited, it was not unusual to put on sackcloth, rend the garments, and scatter ashes over the head (II Sam. 13:19; I Kings 21:27; I Macc. 3:47; Lam. 2:10; Jonah 3:5, sq.). In I Sam. 7:6 it is said that Israel "drew water, and poured it out before the Lord, and fasted on that day." To "pour out thine heart like water" (Lam. 2:19) seems to denote inward dissolution through pain and misery. In connection with the fast it would be a practical confession of misery and an act of deepest humiliation before the Lord. (2) **Different fasts.** (1) The Mosaic law prescribed only one public occasion of strict fasting, viz., once a year on the great Day of Atonement (*q. v.*). This observance seems always to have retained some prominence as "the fast" (Acts 27:9). But as to the nature of the observance we are nowhere expressly informed, excepting that food was interdicted from evening to evening (Lev. 23:27-29). (2) The Hebrews, in the earlier period of their history, were in the habit of *fasting* whenever they were in hard and trying circumstances (I Sam. 1:7), misfortune, and bereavement (I Sam. 20:34; 31:13; II Sam. 1:12), in the prospect of threatened judgments of God (II Sam. 12:16; I Kings 21:27), on occasions of falling into grievous sin (Ezra 10:6), or to avert heavy calamity (Esth. 4:1, sq.). (3) Extraordinary fasts were appointed by the theocratic authorities on occasions of great national calamity in order that the people might humble themselves before the Lord on account of their sins, thus avert his wrath, and get him to look upon them again with his favor (Judg. 20:26; I Sam. 7:6; II Chron. 20:3; Joel 1:14; 2:12; Jer. 36:9; Ezra 8:21; Neh. 1:4; II Macc. 13:12).

2. **Post-Exilic.** There is no mention of any other periodical fast than that on the Day of Atonement in the Old Testament, except in Zech. 7:1-7; 8:19. These anniversary fast days were observed from about the time of the captivity, and were as follows: (1) The seventeenth day of the fourth month, viz., Tammuz, or July. This fast was instituted in memory of the capture of Jerusalem (Jer. 52:6, 7; Zech. 8:19). (2) The ninth day of the fifth month, Ab, or August, in memory of the burning of the temple (II Kings 25:8; Zech. 7:3; 8:19). (3) The third of the seventh month, Tishri, or October, in memory of the death of Gedaliah (Jer. 40:4; Zech. 7:5; 8:19). (4) The tenth day of the tenth month, Tebeth, or January, in memory of the commencement of the attack on Jerusalem (Zech. 8:19; II Kings 25:1; Jer. 52:4). (5) The fast of *Esther* (*q. v.*), kept on the thirteenth of Adar (Esth. 4:16). "Subsequent to the captivity, and with the growth of the Pharisaic spirit, the fasts became much more frequent generally, till ere long they assumed the form

of ordinary pious exercises, so that the Pharisees fasted regularly on the second and fifth day of every week (Matt. 9:14; Luke 18:12), while other Jewish sects, such as the Essenes and Therapeutae, made their whole worship to consist principally of fasting. For new archaeological light in the practices of these pre-Christian Jewish sects *see* W. H. Brownlee, "A Comparison of the Covenanters of the Dead Sea Scrolls with Pre-Christian Jewish Sects," in the *Biblical Archaeologist* XIII, Sept., 1950 pp. 50-72. There was, however, no fasting on the Sabbath, on festival and gala days in Israel, and on the day immediately preceding the Sabbath or a festival" (Judith 8:6). That in the lapse of time the practice of fasting was lamentably abused is shown by the testimony of the prophets (Isa. 58:4, sq.; Jer. 14:12; Zech. 7:5).

3. **New Testament**. In the New Testament the only references to the Jewish fasts are the mention of "the fasts" in Acts 27:9 (generally understood to denote the Day of Atonement) and the allusions to the weekly fasts (Matt. 9:14; Mark 2:18; Luke 5:33; 18:12; Acts 10:30). These fasts originated some time after the captivity. They were observed on the second and fifth days of the week, which being appointed as the days for public fasts (because Moses was supposed to have ascended the Mount for the second tables of the law on a Thursday and to have returned on a Monday) seem to have been selected for these private voluntary fasts.

Our Lord sternly rebuked the Pharisees for their hypocritical pretenses in the fasts which they observed (Matt. 6:16, sq.) and abstained from appointing any fast as part of his own religion (Matt. 9:14; 11:18, 19). Prayer and *fasting* are mentioned (Matt. 17:21; Mark 9:29) as means for promoting faith and as good works. Mention is made of fasting in the Apostolic Church (Acts 13:3; 14:23; II Cor. 6:5). In the last passage the apostle probably refers to *voluntary fasting*, as in chap. 11:27 he makes a distinction between fasting and "hunger and thirst."

4. **Christian Church**. After the Jewish custom fasting was frequently joined with prayer that the mind, unincumbered with earthly matter, might devote itself with less distraction to the contemplation of divine things. As the Pharisees were accustomed to fast twice a week, on Monday and Thursday, the Christians appointed Wednesday and especially Friday as days of half fasting or abstinence from flesh in commemoration of the passion and crucifixion of Jesus. They did this with reference to the Lord's words, "When the bridegroom shall be taken from them, then shall they fast" (Matt. 9:15).

In the 2d century arose also the custom of quadragesimal fasts before Easter, which, however, differed in length in different countries, being sometimes reduced to forty hours, sometimes extended to forty days, or at least to several weeks. Perhaps equally ancient are the nocturnal fasts or vigils before the high festivals, suggested by the example of the Lord and the apostles. On special occasions the bishops appointed extraordinary fasts and applied the money saved to charitable purposes, a usage which became often a blessing to the poor.

By the 6th century fasting was made obligatory by the Second Council of Orleans (A. D. 541), which decreed that anyone neglecting to observe the stated time of abstinence should be treated as an offender. In the 8th century it was regarded as meritorious, and failure to observe subjected the offender to excommunication. In the Roman Catholic and Greek Churches fasting remains obligatory, while in most Protestant Churches it is merely recommended.

Fat (Heb. *hēlĕb*). "The Hebrews distinguished between the suet or pure fat of an animal and the fat which was intermixed with the lean (Neh. 8:10). Certain restrictions were imposed upon them in reference to the former: some parts of the suet, viz., about the stomach, the entrails, the kidneys, and the tail of a sheep, which grows to an excessive size in many Eastern countries and produces a large quantity of rich fat, were forbidden to be eaten in the case of animals offered to Jehovah in sacrifice (Lev. 3:3, 9, 17; 7:3, 23). The ground of the prohibition was that the fat was the richest part of the animal, and therefore belonged to God (3:16). The presentation of the fat as the richest part of the animal was agreeable to the dictates of natural feeling, and was the ordinary practice even of heathen nations. The burning of the fat of sacrifices was particularly specified in each kind of offering" (Smith, *Dict.*, s. v.).

Figurative. Next to blood, the bearer of life (Lev. 17:14), stood the fat as the sign of healthfulness and vigor. "The fat of the earth," "the fat of the wheat, of the oil, and the wine," even "the fat of the mighty," though to our view somewhat peculiar expressions were familiar to the Hebrews, as indicating the choicest specimens or examples of the several objects in question (Gen. 45:18; Deut. 32:14; Num. 18:12, marg. "Fat;" II Sam. 1:22).

Father (Heb. *'āb;* Gr. *patēr*, literally *nourisher*, protector).

1. **Meanings**. This word, besides its natural sense of progenitor (Gen. 19:31; 44:19, etc.), has a number of other meanings, as: (1) **Any ancestor**, near or remote (I Kings 15:11; II Kings 14:3), e. g., a *grandfather* (Gen. 28:13; 31:42; 32:9, etc.); a *great* grandfather (Num. 18:2; I Kings 15:11, 24, etc.); frequently in the plural *fathers*, i. e., *forefathers* (Gen. 15:15; Psa. 45:16). (2) **Founder**, i. e., the first ancestor of a tribe or nation (Gen. 10:21; 17:4, 5; 19:37, etc.). Here we may refer to Gen. 4:21 ("the father of all such as handle the harp and organ," i. e., the founder of a family of musicians, the inventor of the art of music. Jabal was "the father of those who dwell in tents" (Gen. 4:20). The author of a family or society of persons animated by the same spirit as himself; thus Abraham was "the father of all them that believe" (Rom. 4:11). The *author* or maker of anything, especially a *creator* ("hath the rain a *father*?" Job 38:28). In this sense God is called the *father of men* and *angels* (Isa. 63:16; 64:8; Eph. 3:14, 15, etc.). He is also called the Father of lights, i. e., stars (James 1:17). The above topical

senses come from the notion of *source, origin;*
others are drawn from the idea of paternal
love and care, the honor due a father, etc.
(3) **Benefactor**, as doing good and providing
for others as a father (Job. 29:16, "I was a
father to the poor"). Eliakim, the prefect of
the palace, was called "a father to the inhabitants of Jerusalem" (Isa. 22:21). The
Messiah is the "everlasting father" (Isa. 9:6);
God, the *father* of the righteous and of kings
(II Sam. 7:14; I Chron. 17:13, 22; Psa.
89:26). (4) **Teacher**, from the idea of paternal
instruction (I Sam. 10:12); priests and prophets were called *father*, as teachers (II Kings
2:12; 5:13, etc.). In a similar sense the prime
minister, as chief adviser, is called the king's
father (Gen. 45:8). (5) **Intimate relationship,**
as, "I have said to corruption, Thou art my
father" (Job 17:14).

2. **Place and Authority.** The position and
authority of the father as the head of the
family is expressly assumed and sanctioned in
Scripture as a likeness of that of the Almighty
over his creatures. It lies, of course, at the root
of that so-called patriarchal government
(Gen. 3:16; I Cor. 11:3), which was introductory to the more definite system that followed,
but did not wholly supersede it. "While the
father lived he continued to represent the
whole family, the property was held in his
name, and all was under his superintendence
and control. His power, however, was by no
means unlimited or arbitrary, and if any occasion arose for severe discipline or capital punishment in his family he was not himself to
inflict it, but to bring the matter before the
constituted authorities" (Deut. 21:18-21). The
children, and even the grandchildren, continued under the roof of the father and grandfather; they labored on his account and were
the most submissive of his servants. The property of the soil, the power of judgment, the
civil rights belonged to him only, and his sons
were merely his instruments and assistants.
The father's blessing was regarded as con-
ferring special benefit, but his malediction
special injury, to those on whom it fell (Gen.
9:25, 27; 27:27-40; 48:15, 20; ch. 49); and
so also the sin of a parent was held to affect,
in certain cases the welfare of his descendants
(II Kings 5:27). The father, as the head of the
household, had the obligation imposed upon
him of bringing up his children in the fear of
God, making them well acquainted with the
precepts of the law, and generally acting as
their instructor and guide (Exod. 12:26;
Deut. 6:20, etc.). Filial duty and obedience
to both parents were strictly enforced by
Moses (Exod. 20:12); and any outrage against
either parent, as a blow (Exod. 21:15), a
curse (v. 17; Lev. 20:9), or incorrigible rebellion against their authority (Deut. 21:18,
sq.), was made a capital offense.

Father, God the, is a term which represents
several scriptural conceptions.

1. The term designates the first person of the
Holy Trinity. God has revealed himself as
Father, Son, and Holy Spirit. To the Eternal
Son the Father stands related as to no other
being, and finds in the Son the perfect and
infinite object of his love. With this highest
meaning in view the apostles speak of God as
"the Father of the Lord Jesus Christ" (*see*
Eph. 1:17; I Cor. 8:6; I Pet. 1:3). Thus also,
while Christ taught his disciples to address
God in prayer as "our Father," he did not
use that form himself. He spoke of God as
"my Father" and "your Father," but at the
same time he made it plain that he distinguished between the relation in which they
stood to God and that in which he himself
stood. The first words of the Apostolic Creed,
"I believe in God the Father Almighty," are
first of all a recognition of this deep truth of
holy Scriptures. *See* Trinity.

2. In the Old Testament Scriptures God is
in quite a number of conspicuous instances
called the Father of the Jewish nation. The
chosen nation owed its origin and continued
existence to his miraculous power and special
care. As their father he loved, pitied, rebuked,
and required the obedience of his people (*see*
Deut. 32:6; Hos. 11:1; Psa. 103:13; 68:5;
Mal. 1:6).

3. In the New Testament, which brings the
fact of the fatherhood of God into greater
prominence and distinctness, God is represented as the Father of various objects and
orders of beings which he has created. The
term thus used refers to the natural relationship between God and his creatures, and has
a significance more or less profound according
to the different natures and capacities of these
objects or orders of beings. Thus God is "the
Father of lights," the heavenly bodies (James
1:17). Also he is "the Father of spirits" (Heb.
12:9). He is particularly the Father of man,
created after his image (Acts 17:26; Luke
3:8).

4. God is in a special sense the Father of his
redeemed and saved people. While all the
hope of the Gospel rests upon the fact of the
fatherly love of God for mankind even in its
sinfulness (*see* John 3:16; Luke 15:11-32), still
only they who are actually saved through
Jesus Christ are admitted to the privileges of
children in the divine household. Christ taught
only his disciples to pray "our Father." He
said to the unbelieving Jews, "Ye are of your
father, the devil" (John 8:44). The spiritual
and moral relationship destroyed by sin must
be restored by gracious, divine renewal (John
1:12; Rom. 8:14-16, et al.). *See* Adoption.
E. McC.

Father-in-Law. One giving a daughter in
marriage (Exod. 3:1; 4:18); one related by
affinity (Gen. 38:25; I Sam. 4:19, 21). A
wife's father (John 18:13).

Father's Brother (Heb. *dōd*), strictly *one beloved* (Isa. 5:1; an *uncle* (Num. 36:11; II Kings
24:17); in Exod. 6:20 used in the feminine,
Father's Sister, an Aunt.

Father's House, the name given to *families*
among the Israelites (Josh. 22:14; comp.
7:14, 16-18). *See* Israel, Classification of.

Fathom. *See* Metrology, I.

Fatling. 1. An animal put up to be fatted for
slaughter (Heb. *mᵉrî'*, II Sam. 6:13; I Kings
4:23; Isa. 11:6; Ezek. 39:18; Matt. 22:4).

2. A *marrowy* sheep (*q. v.*), especially of the
fat-tailed variety (Heb. *mēăḥ*, Psa. 66:15).

Fatted Fowl (Heb. *bărbŭrîm 'ăbŭsîm*), are mentioned among the daily provisions for Solomon's table (I Kings 4:23). The R. S. V.

renders the Hebrew "fatted fowl." Evidently the "lark-heeled cuckoo," is meant. The cuckoo is a delicacy, in Greece and Italy, even today. L. Koehler, Lexicon, in loco. *See* Animal Kingdom.

Fear (Heb. *yĭr'äh, reverence,* and other Hebrew words meaning *terror,* Exod. 15:16, etc.; *carefulness,* Josh. 22:24, R. V.; *trembling,* Prov. 29:25; *fright,* Job 41:33; Gr. *phobos, dread, terror,* Matt. 14:26, etc.). Fear is that affection of the mind which arises on the conception of approaching danger. The fear of God is of several kinds: Superstitious, which is the fruit of ignorance; servile, which leads to abstinence from many sins through apprehension of punishment; and filial, which has its spring in love, and prompts to care not to offend God and to endeavor in all things to please him. It is another term for practical piety and comprehends the virtues of the godly character (Psa. 111:10; Prov. 14:2), while its absence is characteristic of a wicked and depraved person (Rom. 3:18). It is produced in the soul by the Holy Spirit, and great blessing is pronounced upon those who possess this Christian trait: His angels protect them (Psa. 34:7); they are "under the shadow of the Almighty" (Psa. 91:5, 6). This fear would subsist in a pious soul were there no punishment of sin. It dreads God's displeasure, desires his favor, reveres his holiness, submits cheerfully to his will, is grateful for his benefits, sincerely worships him, and conscientiously obeys his commandments. Fear and love must coexist in us in order that either passion may be healthy, and that we may please and rightly serve God. "The fear of the Lord" is used for the worship of God, e. g., "I will teach you the fear of the Lord" (Psa. 34:11), and for the law of God (19:9). The "fear of Isaac" (Gen. 31:42, 53) is God, whom Isaac worshiped with reverent awe. The "fear of man" is that dread of the opinions of our neighbors which makes us cowards in the performance of those duties which we fancy they do not practice (Prov. 29:25).

Feast. *See* Banquet, Festivals.

Feast of Charity. *See* Agape.

Feeble Knees, a term used to express the results of overexertion, as in an athletic contest, and, figuratively, of *weariness of mind, low spirits* (Heb. 12:12).

Feeble-Minded (Gr. *oligopsuchos, little spirited*), often occurs in the Septuagint, and signifies one who is laboring under such trouble that his heart sinks within him; and may mean here one despairing of working out his salvation (I Thess. 5:14, R. V. "fainthearted")

Feeling. In Eph. 4:19 we find this, "who being past feeling have given themselves over to lasciviousness," etc. The Greek word *apalegeō,* means "to become insensible to pain, callous, and so indifferent to truth, honor, or shame." The writer of the epistle to the Hebrews (4:15) tells us that "we have not a high priest which cannot be touched with the *feeling* of our infirmities." Here we have the Greek *sumpatheō, to feel for, to have compassion on.* Dorner thus speaks of feeling as an element of man's nature: "In *feeling* he has existence within himself, in *will* he exists in a state of movement from self outward, in *knowledge* in movement

from without inward. . . . Like the other spiritual faculties, so called, *feeling* is receptive of infinite as of finite truth. Feeling is a third element alongside of knowledge and will. The strength of feeling depending very much on individual mental temperament, this forms no security for the purity or healthiness of religious feeling. With respect to the contents of feeling, in religious feeling the reference to a definite idea of God will likewise exert an influence, and upon its accurate or confused character—in short, upon its completeness— will the nature of religion depend. A religion, for example, acquainted merely with God's physical attributes will stand lower than one that has heard of his holiness, or, still more, of his love. Feeling alone, occupied merely with self and brooding upon self, may easily become one-sided and selfish. Knowledge, as the product of revelation, we call *illumination.* Revelation must possess power by its contents to inspire and intensify the *will,* and under this aspect it is *quickening,* while the *feeling* (the spiritual consciousness of self or life) is enhanced in freedom and blessedness" (Dorner, *Christ. Doct.,* ii, 109, 119, etc.).

Feet. *See* Foot.

Fe'lix (fē'lĭx; *happy*), the Roman procurator before whom Paul was arraigned (Acts 24).

1. **Elevation and Crimes.** He was originally a slave, and for some unknown service was manumitted by Claudius Caesar. He was appointed by this emperor procurator of Judea on the banishment of Ventidius Cumanus, probably A. D. 53. Suetonius speaks of the military honors which the emperor conferred upon him, and specifies his appointment as governor of the province of Judea, adding an innuendo which loses nothing by its brevity, viz., that he was the husband of three queens or royal ladies ("*trium reginarum maritum*"). Tacitus, in his *History,* declares that during his governorship in Judea he indulged in all kinds of cruelty and lust, exercising regal power with the disposition of a slave; and in his *Annals* (xi, 54) he represents Felix as considering himself licensed to commit any crime, relying on the influence which he possessed at court. Having a grudge against Jonathan, the high priest, who had expostulated with him on his misrule, he made use of Doras, an intimate friend of Jonathan, in order to get him assassinated by a gang of villains, who joined the crowds that were going up to the temple worship, a crime which led subsequently to countless evils by the encouragement which it gave to the Sicarii, or leagued assassins of the day, to whose excesses Josephus ascribes, under Providence, the overthrow of the Jewish state. While in office he became enamored of Drusilla, a daughter of King Herod Agrippa, who was married to Azizus, king of Emesa, and through the influence of Simon, a magician, prevailed upon her to consent to a union with him. With this adulteress Felix was seated when Paul reasoned before him (Acts 24:25). Another Drusilla is mentioned by Tacitus as being the (*first*) wife of Felix.

2. **Hears Paul.** Paul, having been arrested at Jerusalem, was sent by Claudius Lysias to Felix at Caesarea (Acts 23:23, sq.), where he was confined in Herod's judgment hall till his

accusers came. After five days they arrived, headed by Ananias, the high priest. Their case was managed by Tertullus, who, to conciliate Felix, expressed gratitude on the part of the Jews, "Seeing that by thee we enjoy great quietness, and that very worthy deeds are done unto this nation by thy providence" (24:1, 2). He then proceeded to accuse Paul, charging him, first, with sedition; secondly, with being "a ringleader of the sect of the Nazarenes;" and, thirdly, with an attempt to profane the temple at Jerusalem (vers. 5, 6). The evident purpose was to persuade Felix to give up the apostle to the Jewish courts, in which case his assassination would have been easily accomplished. Felix now gave the prisoner permission to speak, and the apostle, after briefly expressing his satisfaction that he had to plead his cause before one so well acquainted with Jewish customs, refuted Tertullus step by step. Felix deferred inquiry into the case for the present. "When Lysias comes down," he said, "I will know the uttermost of this matter." Meanwhile he placed him under the charge of the centurion who had brought him to Caesarea (24:10-23). Some days after Felix came into the audience chamber with his wife Drusilla, and the prisoner was brought before them. As a faithful preacher he spoke to the Roman libertine and the profligate Jewish princess. As he reasoned of righteousness, temperance, and judgment to come, "Felix trembled." But still nothing is decided, Felix saying, "Go thy way for this time; when I have a convenient season I will call for thee." We are informed why the governor shut his ears to conviction, and even neglected his official duty and kept his prisoner in cruel suspense: "He hoped also that money should have been given him of Paul, that he might loose him" (vers. 24-26). Hence he frequently sent for Paul and had many conversations with him. But his hopes were unfulfilled, and he retained the apostle a prisoner for two years (v. 27).

3. **Summoned to Rome.** Meantime the political state of Judea grew more embarrassing. It was during the two years of Paul's imprisonment that disturbances took place in the streets of Caesarea. In the end Felix was summoned to Rome, and the Jews followed him with their accusations. Thus it was that he was anxious "to show the Jews a pleasure," and "left Paul bound" (v. 27). At Rome he was saved from suffering the penalty due to his atrocities by the influence of his brother Pallas.

Felloes (Heb. *ḥishshŭk, conjoined*), the curved pieces which joined together form the rim of a wheel (I Kings 7:33).

Fellow. 1. A contemptuous use of Hebrew (*'îsh*, I Sam. 29:4); Greek (*anēr*), words for *man*.

2. The rendering (Heb. *rĕă'*), *friend, associate*, etc. (Exod. 2:13; Judg. 7:13, etc.), (*hābēr*, Eccles. 4:10).

3. The rendering of Heb. *'āmîth, neighbor*, in that remarkable passage, "Awake, O sword, against my shepherd, and against the man that is my *fellow*" (Zech. 13:7). The expression "man, who is my nearest one," implies much more than unity or community of vocation, or that he had to feed the flock like Jehovah. The idea of nearest one (or fellow) involves not only similarity in vocation, but community of physical or spiritual descent, according to which he whom God calls his neighbor cannot be a mere man, but can only be one who participates in the divine nature or is essentially divine. This passage is quoted and applied to himself by our Lord (Matt. 26:31).

Fellowship.

Fellowship means companionship, a relation in which parties hold something in common, familiar intercourse. Christians have *fellowship* with the Father and the Son (I John 1:3) and the Holy Spirit (II Cor. 13:14), and with one another (I John 1:7). As is the case between men, no one can be in fellowship with God unless he possess like purposes and feelings (I John 2:3-6), with love (Rom. 8:38, 39). The *fellowship* of believers embraces confession of faults one to another with prayer (James 5:16); assembly, with exhortation and provoking to love and good works (Mal. 3:16; Heb. 10:24, 25); partaking the Lord's supper (I Cor. 11:24, 25); "ministering to the saints" (Acts 11:29; Rom. 12:13; 15:25; I Cor. 16:1, 2; II Cor. 8:4; Heb. 13:16); bearing the infirmities of the weak and edification (Rom. 15:1). Love for and fellowship with one another are necessary to, and an evidence of fellowship with God (I John 4:12). Christ prayed that his people might have fellowship with each other (John 17:21). Fellowship with God is essential to fruitfulness (John 15:4).

Fence (Heb. *gāder*, an *inclosure;* Num. 22:24; Psa. 62:3; 80:12). Fences were built of unmortared stones, to protect cultivated lands, sheepfolds, etc. In the crevices of such fences serpents delighted to hide (Eccles. 10:8; comp. Amos 5:19).

Figurative. In Psa. 62:3 the wicked are compared to a tottering *fence* and bowing wall, i. e., their destruction comes suddenly See Hedge.

Fenced City, the rendering of several Hebrew words; sometimes translated "stronghold" (II Chron. 11:11), "fort" (Isa. 29:3). The broad distinction between a city and a village in biblical language consisted in the possession of walls. The city had walls, the village was unwalled or had only a watchman's tower, to which the villagers resorted in times of danger. A threefold distinction is thus obtained: (1) Cities; (2) unwalled villages; (3) villages with castles or towers (I Chron. 27:25). The district east of the Jordan, forming the kingdoms of Moab and Bashan, is said to have abounded from very early times in castles and fortresses, such as were built by Uzziah to protect the cattle and to repel the inroads of the neighboring tribes, besides unwalled towns (Deut. 3:5; II Chron. 26:10). When the Israelites entered Canaan they found many fenced cities (Num. 13:28; 32:17; Josh. 11:12, 13; Judg. 1:27-33), some of which held out for a long period, e. g., Jerusalem was held by the Jebusites till the time of David (II Sam. 5:6, 7; I Chron. 11:5). *See* Cities, Fortifications.

Fens. *See* Vegetable Kingdom.

Ferret (R. V. "gecko"). *See* Animal Kingdom.

Ferryboat (Heb. *'ăbārāh, crossing*), a vessel for crossing a stream (II Sam. 19:18). Floats or rafts for this purpose were used from remote times (I Kings 5:9, and paintings on Egyptian monuments). A ferryboat still crosses the Jordan ford near Jericho.

Festivals. Besides the daily worship, the law prescribed special festivals be from time to time observed by the congregation. One Hebrew name for festival was *hăg* (from the verb signifying to *dance*), which, when applied to religious services, indicated that they were occasions of joy and gladness. The term most fitly designating, and which alone actually comprehended all the feasts, was *mō'ēd*, (a *set time* or *assembly, place of assembly*). What is meant by this name, therefore, was the stated assemblies of the people—the occasions fixed by the divine appointment for their being called and meeting together in holy fellowship, i. e., for acts and purposes of worship. There is also the Greek *heortē* (*festival, holy day*).

The date of every Mosaic festival without distinction, no matter what its special object may have been, gave evidence of being connected in some way or other with the number *seven*. So every seventh day, every seventh month, every seventh year, and lastly, the year that came after the lapse of seven times seven years, was marked by a festival. Again, the Passover and the Feast of Tabernacles extended over seven days; the number of special convocations (*q. v.*) during the year was seven—two at the Passover, one at the Pentecost, one at the Feast of Trumpets (or New Moon), one on the Day of Atonement, and two at the Feast of Tabernacles. All the festivals instituted by the law of Moses may be arranged in two series, Septenary and Yearly. In addition are the Post-Exilic and Doubtful Festivals. *See* table below:

TABLE OF FEASTS.

Septenary Festivals, or Cycles of Sabbaths, including:

Weekly Sabbath (Exod. 20:8-11; 31:12, sq.; Lev. 23:1-3).

Seventh New Moon, or Feast of Trumpets (Num. 28:11-15; 29:1-6).

Sabbatic Year, i. e., every seventh year (Exod. 23:10, 11; Lev. 25:2-7).

Year of Jubilee (Lev. 25:8-16; 27:16-25). New Moon (Num. 10:10; 28:11).

Yearly Festivals:

Feast of Passover and Unleavened Bread (Exod. 12:1-28; 23:5, sq.; Lev. 23:4-8; Num. 28:16-25; Deut. 18:1-8).

Pentecost, or Feast of Weeks (Exod. 34:22; Lev. 23:15; Num. 28:26; Deut. 16:10).

Day of Atonement (Lev. 16:1-34; Exod. 30:10-30; Num. 29:7-11).

Feast of Tabernacles (Lev. 23:34-42; Num. 29:12, sq.; Neh. 8:18; John 7:2, 37).

Post-Exilic Festivals, some of which were kept as regularly as those prescribed by Moses: Feast of Purim (Esth. 9:24-32).

Feast of Dedication (I Macc. 4:52, sq.; II Macc. 10:6, sq.; John 10:22).

These festivals are treated in this article in the above order.

I. *Serpentary Festivals.*

1. The Weekly Sabbath. In addition to entire cessation from all work the Sabbath was observed by a holy assembly, the doubling of the morning and evening sacrifices (Num. 28:9, sq.). and the presentation of new showbread in the Holy Place (Lev. 24:8). *See* Sabbath.

2. The Seventh New Moon, or **Feast of Trumpets** (Heb. *yōm tᵉrū'āh, day of blowing,* Num. 29:1), the Feast of the New Moon (*q. v.*), which fell on the seventh month, or Tishri. This differed from the ordinary festivals of the new moon on account of the symbolical meaning of the seventh or sabbatical month, and partly, perhaps, because it marked the beginning of the *civil* year. This month was distinguished above all the other months of the year for the multitude of ordinances connected with it, the first day being consecrated to sacred rest and spiritual employment, the tenth being the day of Atonement, while the fifteenth began the Feast of Tabernacles. (1) **Sacrifices.** (*a*) The usual morning and evening sacrifices, with their meat and drink offerings. (*b*) The ordinary sacrifice for the New Moon, except the sin offering, viz., two young bullocks, one ram, seven yearling lambs, with their meat and drink offerings (Num. 28:11, sq.). (*c*) Another festive offering of one young bullock, one ram, seven lambs, with their meat and drink offerings, together with "one kid of the goats for a sin offering, to make an atonement for you" (Num. 29:1-6). (2) **Observance.** This day was observed as a feast day, in the strict sense, by resting from all work, and as a memorial of blowing of horns, by a holy convocation. In later times, while the drink offering of the sacrifice was being poured out, the priests and Levites chanted Psalm 81, while at the evening sacrifice they sang Psalm 29. Throughout the day trumpets were blown at Jerusalem from morning to evening. In the temple it was done even on a Sabbath, but not outside its walls. "The Day of Atonement, which falls on this month, provides full expiation of all sins and the removal of all uncleanness; and the Feast of Tabernacles, beginning five days thereafter, provides a foretaste of the blessedness of life in fellowship with the Lord. This significance of the seventh month is indicated by the sounding of trumpets, whereby the congregation present a memorial of themselves loudly and strongly before Jehovah, calling on him to vouchsafe the promised blessings of grace in fulfillment of his covenant" (Keil, *Arch.*, ii, p. 10). The fact that Tisri was the great month for sowing might easily have suggested the thought of commemorating on this day the finished work of creation; and thus the Feast of Trumpets came to be regarded as the anniversary of the beginning of the world. The rabbins believed that on this day God judges all men, and that they pass before him as a flock of sheep pass before a shepherd.

3. Sabbatic Year, the septennial rest for the land from all tillage and cultivation as enjoined by Moses (Exod. 23:10, 11; Lev. 25:2-7; Deut. 15:1-11; 31:10-13). (1) **Names**, etc. The four names given to this festival by

Moses express some feature connected with its observance. These names are (1) *Rest of Entire Rest* (Heb. *sh̬e̬băth shăbbăthōn, Sabbath of Sabbatism*, Lev. 25:4, A. V. "Sabbath of rest"), because the land was to have a complete rest from cultivation; (2) *Year of Rest* (Heb. *sh̬e̬năth shăbbăthōn, Year of Sabbatism*, Lev. 25:5), because the rest was to extend through the year; (3) *Release* (Heb. *sh̬e̬mĭttäh*, Deut. 15:1, 2), or more fully *the Year of Release* (Heb. *sh̬e̬năth hăshsh̬e̬mĭttäh*, Deut. 15:9), because in it all debts were remitted; (4) *the Seventh Year* (Heb. *sh̬e̬năth hăshshēbă'*, Deut. 15:9), because it was to be celebrated every seventh year. (2) **Design.** The spirit of the Sabbatic year is that of the weekly Sabbath. The rest which the land was to keep in the seventh year was not to increase its fruitfulness by lying fallow, nor merely to be a time of recreation for laboring men and beasts, needful and useful as this may be. It was rather to afford true spiritual rest and quickening, with their attendant life and blessing. "Thus Israel, as the people of God, was to learn two things: First, that the earth, though created for man, was not merely that he might turn its powers to his own profit, but that he might be holy to the Lord and participate also in his blessed rest; next, that the goal of life for the congregation of the Lord did not lie in that incessant laboring of the earth which is associated with sore toil in the sweat of the brow (Gen. 3:17, 19), but in the enjoyment of the fruits of the earth, free from care, which the Lord their God gave and ever would give them if they strove to keep his covenant and to take quickening from his law" (Keil, *Arch.*, ii, p. 12). Such an institution as the Sabbatic year might seem, at first sight, to be impracticable. But we are to remember that in no year was the owner of land allowed to reap the whole harvest (Lev. 19:9; 23:22). Unless the remainder was entirely gleaned there might easily have been enough to insure quite a spontaneous crop the ensuing year, while the vines and olives would yield fruit of themselves. Then, too, the unavoidable inference from Lev. 25:20-22 is that the owners of land were to lay by grain in previous years for their own and their families' need. (3) **Time, observance**, etc. The Sabbatic year, like the year of Jubilee, began on the first day of the civil year, viz., the first of the month Tisri. Though this was the time fixed for the celebration of the Sabbatic year during the time of the second temple, yet the tillage and cultivation of certain fields and gardens had already to be left off in the sixth year. Thus it was ordained that fields upon which trees were planted were not to be cultivated after the feast of Pentecost of the sixth year, while the cultivation of grain fields was to cease from the feast of the Passover (Mishna, *Shebith*, i, 1-8). The keeping of the Sabbatic year is very distinctly attested by I Macc. 6:49, 53, and Josephus, *Antiq.*, xiii, 8, 1; xiv, 10, 6; xv, 1, 2, etc., and also that it was observed by the Samaritans (Josephus, *Antiq.*, xi, 8, 6).

The laws respecting this year were (1) That the soil, the vineyards, and the olive yards were to have perfect rest (Exod. 23:10, 11;

Lev. 25:2-5). Rabbinical regulations carried the law to such an extent that anything planted wittingly or unwittingly had to be plucked up by its roots (Mishna, *Terum*, ii, 3). (2) That the spontaneous growth of the fields or of trees (comp. Isa. 37:30) was for the free use of the poor, the hireling, stranger, servants, and cattle (Exod. 23:10, 11; Lev. 25:2-5). An especially fruitful harvest was promised for the sixth year (Lev. 25:20, 21). (3) The third enactment enjoins the remission of debts, with the exception of foreigners (Deut. 15:1-4). This does not seem to denote the entire renunciation of what was owed, but the not pressing it during the Sabbatic year. This enactment does not forbid the voluntary payment of debts, but their enforced liquidation. Also that no poor man should be oppressed by his brother. (4) Finally, at the feast of Tabernacles in this year, the law was to be read to the people—men, women, children, and strangers—in solemn assembly before the sanctuary (Deut. 31:10-13).

The Sabbatic year seems to have been systematically neglected. Hence Jewish tradition explains (see II Chron. 36:21) that the seventy years' captivity was intended to make up for the neglect of Sabbatical years. After the return from captivity this year was most strictly observed.

4. **Jubilee** (Heb. *yōbēl*, a *blast* of a trumpet), usually in connection with the year of Jubilee (Lev. 25:28); also called the *"Year of liberty"* (Ezek. 46:17). Its relation to the Sabbatic year and the general directions for its observance are found in Lev. 25:8-16, 23-55. Its bearing on lands dedicated to Jehovah is given in Lev. 27:16-25. It is not mentioned in Deuteronomy, and the only other reference to it in the Pentateuch is in Num. 36:4. (1) **Time.** After the lapse of seven Sabbaths of years, or seven times seven years, i. e., forty-nine years, the trumpet was to sound throughout the whole land, and the fiftieth year was to be announced and hallowed as Jubilee year. This was not the forty-ninth year, as held by some chronologists. Decisive against this view is the fact "that in Lev. 25:10, sq., not only is the fiftieth year expressly named as the year of Jubilee, but the forty-nine years which make seven Sabbatic years are expressly distinguished from it" (Winer, *R. W. Buch*, art. *Jubeljahr*). (2) **Observance**. It should be noticed that the observance of Jubilee was to become obligatory upon the Israelites after they had taken possession of the promised land and had cultivated the soil for forty-nine years. The ancient Talmudic tradition, which appears to be correct, is that the first Sabbatic year was the twenty-first, and the first Jubilee the sixty-fourth after the Jews came into Canaan, for it took them seven years to conquer it and seven more to distribute it. The only enactment as to the *manner* of its observance is that it should be announced with the blowing of trumpets, the Jubilee which proclaimed to the covenant nation the gracious presence of its God. Because the Scriptures do not record any particular instance of the public celebration some have denied or questioned whether the law of Jubilee ever came into actual opera-

tion. In favor of its actual observance are: (1) The probability arising from the observance of all the other festivals. (2) The law of the inalienability of landed property really obtained among the Hebrews (Num. 36:4, 6, 7; Ezek. 46:17). (3) The unanimous voice of Hebrew tradition. (3) **Laws.** The law states three respects in which the Jubilee was to be hallowed, i. e., separated from other years: (1) *Rest for soil.* No sowing, reaping, nor gathering from the unpruned vine (Lev. 25:11). Thus the soil enjoyed a holy rest, and man was freed from the sore labor of sowing and reaping, and in blessed rest was to live and enjoy the bounty provided by Jehovah in the sixth year (v. 21). (2) *Reversion of landed property* (Lev. 25:10-34; 27:16-24). The law of Moses provided that all the promised land was to be divided by lot among the Israelites, and that it was to remain absolutely inalienable. Therefore, at Jubilee all property in fields and houses situated in villages or unwalled towns, which the owner had been obliged to sell through poverty and which had not been redeemed (*see* Redemption), was to revert without payment to its original owner or his lawful heirs. The only exceptions were houses in walled cities, which remained with the buyer unless redeemed within one year (25:29, 30), and the fields which, unless redeemed by the owner, had been sold and thereby rendered unredeemable (27:17-21) and reverted to the priests. (3) *Manumission of Israelites.* Every Israelite, who through poverty had sold himself to one of his countrymen or to a foreigner settled in the land, if he had been unable to redeem himself or had not been redeemed by a kinsman, was to go out free with his children (Lev. 25:29-35, 39, sq.). Thus ownership of a person was changed into a matter of hire (vers. 40, 53). It would seem that there must have been a perfect remission of all debts in the year of Jubilee from the fact that all persons who were in bondage for debt, as well as all landed property of debtors, were freely returned. Thus the Jubilee year became one of freedom and grace for all suffering, bringing not only redemption to the captive and deliverance from want to the poor, but also release to the whole congregation of the Lord from the sore labor of the earth, and representing the time of refreshing (Acts 3: 19) which the Lord provides for his people. For in this year every kind of oppression was to cease and every member of the covenant people find his Redeemer in the Lord, who brought him back to his possession and family.

5. **New Moon** (Heb. *rō'sh ḥōdĕsh, beginning of month,* Num. 10:10; 28:11). The ordinary New Moons, i. e., all except the seventh, were raised out of the rank of ordinary days, but not to that of festivals. They may be called demi-feast days, and will therefore be inserted here. (1) **Origin.** Many nations of antiquity celebrated the returning light of the moon with festivities, sacrifices, and prayers. Some think that the object of Moses in providing for this occasion was to suppress heathen celebrations of the day. There was, however, a deeper meaning in this observance. The new moon stood as the representative of the month. "For a single day a burnt offering sufficed, in

which the idea of atonement was subordinate to the idea of consecration to the Lord. But for the month, in view of sins committed and remaining unexpiated during the course of the past month, a special sin offering must be brought for their atonement; and thus, on the ground of the forgiveness and reconciliation with God thereby obtained, the people might be able in the burnt offering to consecrate their life anew to the Lord. (2) **Mode of Ascertaining the New Moon.** As the festivals, according to the Mosaic law, were always to be celebrated on the same day of the month, it was necessary to fix the commencement of the month, which was determined by the appearance of the new moon, for the new moon was reckoned not by astronomical calculation, but by actual personal observation. On the thirtieth day of the month watchmen were placed on commanding heights round Jerusalem to watch the sky. As soon as each of them detected the moon he hastened to a house in the city which was kept for the purpose, and was there examined by the president of the Sanhedrin. When the evidence of the appearance was deemed satisfactory the president rose up and formally announced it, uttering the words, "It is consecrated." The information was immediately sent throughout the land from the Mount of Olives by beacon fires on the tops of the hills. The religious observance of the day of the new moon may plainly be regarded as the consecration of a natural division of time. (3) **Sacrifices.** (*a*) The usual morning and evening sacrifices, with their meat and drink offerings. (*b*) Special sacrifices, consisting of two young bullocks, one ram, and seven lambs of the first year, as a burnt offering, with their meat and drink offerings. A goat was also presented as a sin offering, at which time the priests blew the silver trumpets (Num. 28:11-15; 10:10). (4) It is evident from the writings of the prophets and from post-Exilian documents that the New Moon was an important national festival. It was often called a feast along with the Sabbath (Psa. 81:3; Isa. 1:13; Ezek. 46:1; Hos. 2:11), on which all business ceased (Amos 8:5), the pious Israelites waited on the prophets for edification (II Kings 4:23), many families and clans presented their annual thank offerings (I Sam. 20:6, 29), social gatherings and feasting were indulged in (vers. 5, 24), and the most devout persons omitted fasting (Judith 8:6).

II *Yearly Festivals.* These were:

1. **The Passover** and **Feast of Unleavened Bread,** the most important of the three great annual festivals of Israel. (1) **Name and Signification.** It was indifferently called the Feast of the Passover and the Feast of Unleavened Bread, but where the object was to mark the distinction between the Passover as a sacrifice and as a feast following the sacrifice the latter was designated the Feast of Unleavened Bread (Lev. 23:5, sq.). The Hebrew word *pĕsăḥ* (from *päsäḥ,* to *leap over,* figuratively, to *spare, show mercy*) denotes: (1) *An overstepping;* (2) The *paschal sacrifice* by virtue of which the *passing over* was effected (Exod. 12:21, 27, 48; II Chron. 30:15). The *paschal meal* was on the evening of the 14th Nisan,

while the seven days following are called the *feast of unleavened bread* (Lev. 23:5, 6), hence the expression *the morrow of the Passover* for the 15th Nisan (Num. 33:3; Josh. 5:11). The whole feast, including the paschal eve, is called *the festival of Unleavened Bread* (Exod. 23:15; Lev. 23:6; Ezra 6:22; Luke 22:1, 7; Acts 12:3; 20:6); but the simple name *Passover* (Heb. *pĕsăḥ*) is the one commonly used by the Jews to the present day for the festival of unleavened bread (II Chron. 30:15; 35:1, 11; Mark 14:1; Gr. *pascha*. (2) **Institution.** The Passover was instituted in memory of Israel's preservation from the last plague visited upon Egypt (the death of the firstborn) and their deliverance from bondage (Exod. 12:1-28). "The deliverance of Israel from Egypt was accompanied by their adoption as the nation of Jehovah. For this a divine consecration was necessary that their outward severance from Egypt might be accompanied by an inward severance from everything of an Egyptian or heathen nature. This consecration was imparted by the Passover, a festival which was to lay the foundation of Israel's birth (Hos. 2:15; Exod. 6:6, 7) into the new life of grace and fellowship with God and to perpetuate it in time to come" (K. and D., *Com.*, on Exod. ch. 12). (3) **Observance. (1)** *At the Exodus.* At its first institution, just before the Exodus, the keeping of the Passover was as follows: Every head of a family chose a male of the first year without blemish from the small cattle, i. e., from the sheep or goats, on the 10th Nisan (Exod. 12:3). Later it became the fixed practice to take a *lamb*. On the 14th Nisan the victim was slain "between the two evenings" (Exod. 12:6); according to the Karaite Jews between actual sunset and complete darkness, but understood by the Pharisees and Rabbins as the time when the sun begins to descend to his real setting (from 3 to 6 P. M.). A bunch of hyssop was dipped in the blood of the animal and applied to the two posts and the lintel of the house where the meal was to be eaten. Then the whole animal, without breaking a bone, was roasted and eaten by each family, including slaves and strangers, if circumcised. If the number of the family was too small the neighboring family might unite in the eating. It was eaten that same night with unleavened bread and bitter herbs, probably endives, wild lettuce, which are eaten by Jews of the present day in Egypt and Arabia with the paschal lamb. The meal was eaten the same evening, all who partook having their loins girded, shoes on their feet, and a staff in hand, ready to march out of Egypt. What of the lamb could not be eaten was to be burned on the morrow, and nothing of it was to be carried out of the house (12:1-13, 21-23, 28, 43-51). According to Jewish authorities this was called the "Egyptian" passover in distinction from the "Permanent" passover. The paschal lamb was a sacrifice, combining in itself the significance of the sin offerings and holy offerings, i. e., it shadowed reconciliation as well as glad fellowship with God; the lamb suffered instead of the partakers. There being no fixed sanctuary the houses were converted into such places of grace or altars, and the blood put on the posts and lintel of the door

was the sign that the house was to be spared. With this sparing and reconciliation accomplished through forgiveness of sins there was immediately associated the meal, and thus the *sacrificium* becomes the *sacramentum*, the sacrificial flesh becomes a means of grace. The unleavened bread symbolized the spiritual purity, after which Israel in covenent with the Lord is to strive; and the bitter herbs were intended to call to mind the bitter experiences which the Israelites had suffered in Egypt. (2) *After the Exodus.* The following supplementary enactments were introduced after the Exodus: All male members of the congregation were to appear before the Lord with "the first of the first fruits" (Exod. 23:14-19), the first sheaf of the harvest to be offered on "the morrow after the Sabbath" (Lev. 23:4-14); those prevented from keeping the Passover on the 14th Nisan were to observe it on the fourteenth of the following month (Num. 9:6-14); special sacrifices were to be offered each day of the festival (Num. 28:16-25); the paschal animals were to be slain in the national sanctuary, and the blood sprinkled on the altar instead of the door-posts and lintels of the several dwellings (Deut. 19:1-8).

The Feast of Unleavened Bread followed immediately on the Passover, and lasted seven days, from the 15th to the 21st Nisan (or Abib). On each of these days, after the morning sacrifice, a sacrifice in connection with the feast was presented; unleavened bread alone was eaten (Exod. 12:15-20; 13:6-8; Deut. 16:3-8. (1) **Sacrifices.** (*a*) The usual morning and evening sacrifices, with their meat and drink offerings. (*b*) Two young bullocks, one ram, seven lambs of the first year, with their meat and drink offerings. These were presented after the morning sacrifice (Num. 28:19-24). (2) **Convocations.** The first and seventh days of the feast were celebrated by a holy convocation and resting from work, with the exception of preparing food. On the intervening days work might be carried on unless the weekly Sabbath fell on one of them, in which case the full strictness of Sabbath keeping was observed, and the special feast sacrifice was not presented until after the Sabbath offering. (3) **Barley sheaf.** On the second feast day (16th Nisan) the first sheaf of the new harvest (barley) was symbolically offered to the Lord by waving—not burned on the altar—accompanied with a lamb of the first year for burnt offering, with its meat and drink offerings. Previous to this offering neither bread nor roasted grain of the new harvest was allowed to be eaten (Lev. 23:9-14). Those attending presented freewill, burnt, and holy offerings of sheep and oxen (Exod. 23-15, sq.; Deut. 16:2, sq.), and sacrificial meals were eaten. The feast closed on the 21st, with rest from work and a holy convocation. (4) **History.** Scripture records that the Passover was kept on the evening before the Israelites left Egypt (Exod. 12:28), the second year after the Exodus (Num. 9:1-5), and then not again until they entered Canaan (Exod. 13:5; Josh. 5:10). Only three instances are recorded in which the Passover was celebrated between the entrance into the promised land and the Babylonian captivity, viz., under

Solomon (II Chron. 8:13), under Hezekiah when he restored the national worship (II Chron. 30:15), and under Josiah (II Kings 23:21; II Chron. 35:1-19). But the inference that the Passover was only celebrated on these occasions seems the less warranted, that in later times it was so punctually and universally observed. (5) **Post-Exilic observance.** After the return of the Jews from captivity the celebration of the Passover, like that of other institutions, became more regular and systematic; and its laws, rites, manners, and customs faithfully transmitted to us. These were the same as those in the time of Christ and his apostles, and are, therefore, of the utmost importance and interest to us in understanding the New Testament. We give the various practices in connection with the days of the festival on which they were respectively observed.

(a) *The Great Sabbath* (10th Nisan) is the Sabbath immediately preceding the Passover, and is so called (in the Calendar) because, according to tradition, the 10th of Nisan, when the paschal lamb was to be selected, originally fell on the Sabbath. In later legislation the animal was not required to be set aside four days beforehand, yet the Sabbath was used for the instruction of the people in the duties of this great festival. In addition to the regular ritual, special prayers bearing on the redemption from Egypt, the love of God to Israel, and Israel's obligation to keep the Passover, were prescribed for that Sabbath. Mal. 3:1-4:6 was read as the lesson of the day, and discourses were delivered explanatory of the laws and domestic duties connected with the festival. This is likely the Sabbath referred to in John 19:31.

(b) *The 13th Nisan.* On the evening of the 13th Nisan, which, until that of the 14th, was called the *"preparation for the Passover"* (John 19:14), every head of a family searched for and collected by the light of a candle all the leaven. Before beginning the search he pronounced the following benediction: "Blessed art thou, O Lord our God, King of the universe, who hast sanctified us with thy commandments, and hast enjoined us to remove the leaven." After the search he said, "Whatever leaven remains in my possession which I cannot see, behold, it is null, and accounted as the dust of the earth."

(c) *The 14th Nisan.* This day, called until the evening *the preparation for the Passover*, was also known as the "first day of Passover" (Lev. 23:5-7). Handicraftsmen, with the exception of tailors, barbers, and laundresses, were obliged to cease from work, either from morning or from noon, according to the custom of the different places in Palestine. No leaven was allowed to be eaten after noon, when all that had been found on the preceding or this day must be burned. On the 14th Nisan every Israelite who was physically able, not in a state of Levitical uncleanness, nor further distant from Jerusalem than fifteen miles, was to appear before the Lord with an offering in proportion to his means (Exod. 23:15; Deut. 16:16, 17). Women, though not legally bound to appear in the sanctuary, were not excluded from it (I Sam. 1:7; Luke 2:41, 42).

(d) *Offering of the Paschal Lamb.* This lamb must, of course, be free from all blemish, and neither less than eight days nor more than exactly one year old. Each paschal lamb was to serve a "company" of not less than ten nor more than twenty, the representatives of each company going to the Temple. The daily evening sacrifice (Exod. 29:38, 39), usually killed at the eighth hour and a half (i. e., 2:30 P. M.), and offered up at the ninth and a half hour (i. e., 3:30 P. M.), was on this day killed at 1:30 and offered at 2:30 P. M., an hour earlier; and if the 14th of Nisan happened on a Friday it was killed at 12:30 and offered at 1:30 P. M., two hours earlier than usual, so as to avoid any needless breach of the Sabbath.

Before the incense was burned or the lamps were trimmed the paschal sacrifice had to be offered. It was done on this wise: The first of the three festive divisions, with their paschal lambs, was admitted within the court of the priests. Each division must consist of not less than thirty persons. Immediately the massive gates were closed behind them. The priests blew a threefold blast from their silver trumpets when the Passover was slain. Altogether the scene was most impressive. All along the court up to the altar of burnt offering priests stood in two rows, the one holding golden, the other silver bowls. In these the blood of the paschal lambs, which each Israelite slew for himself (as representative of his company at the paschal supper), was caught up by a priest, who handed it to his colleague, receiving back an empty bowl, and so the bowls with the blood were passed up to the priest at the altar, who jerked it in one jet at the base of the altar. While this was going on a most solemn "hymn" of praise was raised, the Levites leading in the song and the officers either repeating after them or merely responding. "The HALLEL (*q. v.*) was recited the whole time, and if it was finished before all the paschal animals were slain it might be repeated a second and even a third time. Next the sacrifices were hung up on hooks along the court, or laid on staves which rested on the shoulders of two men (on Sabbaths they were not laid on staves), then flayed, the entrails taken out and cleansed, and the inside fat separated, put in a dish, salted, and placed on the fire of the altar of burnt offering. This completed the sacrifice.

"The first division of officers being dismissed, the second entered, and finally the third, the service in each case being conducted in precisely the same manner. Then the whole service concluded by burning the incense and trimming the lamps for the night." If it was the Sabbath the first division waited in the court of the Gentiles, the second between the ramparts, i. e., the open space between the walls of the court of the women and the trellis work in the temple, while the third remained in its place. . . . At dark all went out to roast their paschal sacrifices. According to Jewish ordinance the paschal lamb was roasted on a spit of pomegranate wood, the spit passing through from mouth to vent. If it touched the oven the part so touched must be cut away, thus carrying out the idea that the lamb must not be defiled by any contact with foreign matter. It was not to be "sodden," because the flesh must remain pure, without the admixture even of water, and no bone of it was to be broken.

(e) *The Paschal Supper.* As the guests gathered around the paschal table they were arrayed in their best festive garments, joyous and at rest, as became the children of a king. To express this idea the Rabbins insisted that at least a part of the feast should be partaken of in a recumbent position. The left elbow was placed on the table, the head resting on the hand, with sufficient room between each guest for the free movement of the right hand. This explains in what sense John "was leaning on Jesus' bosom," and afterward "lying on Jesus' breast," when he leaned back to speak to him (Luke 22:14, sq.; John 13:23, 25). The father, or other person presiding, took the place of honor at the table, probably somewhat raised above the rest.

The paschal supper commenced by the head of the "company" pronouncing a benediction over the first cup of wine, which had been filled for each person. It was then drunk, and a basin of water and a towel were handed round, or the guests got up to wash their hands (John 13:4, 5, 12), after which the blessing belonging thereto was pronounced.

These preliminaries ended, a table was brought in, upon which was the paschal meal. The president of the feast first took some of the herbs, dipped it in the sauce (Heb. *charoseth*), ate of it, and gave to the others (Matt. 26:23; John 13:26). Immediately after this all the dishes were removed from the table (to excite the more curiosity), and the second cup of wine was filled. Then the son asked his father as follows: "Wherefore is this night distinguished from all other nights? For on all other nights we eat leavened or unleavened bread, but on this night only unleavened bread? On all other nights we eat any kind of herbs, but on this night only bitter herbs? On all other nights we eat meat roasted, stewed, or boiled, but on this night only roasted? On all other nights we dip (the herbs) only once, but on this night twice?" In reply the head of the house related the whole national history, commencing with Terah, Abraham's father, Israel's deliverance from Egypt, the giving of the law; and the more fully he explained it all the better.

The paschal dishes were now placed back upon the table. The president took up in succession the dish with the Passover lamb, that with the bitter herbs, and that with the unleavened bread, briefly explaining the import of each; the first part of the Hallel was sung (Psa. 113 and 114), with this brief thanksgiving at the close: "Blessed art thou, Jehovah our God, King of the universe, who hast redeemed us and redeemed our fathers from Egypt." The second cup of wine was then drunk, and hands were washed a second time, with the same prayer as before, and one of the two unleavened cakes broken and "thanks given."

Pieces of the broken cake, with "bitter herbs" between them, and "dipped" in the charoseth, were next handed to each of the company. This, in all probability, was "the sop" which, in answer to John's inquiry about the betrayer, the Lord "gave" to Judas (John 13:25, sq.; Mark 14:22; Luke 22:21).

The paschal supper itself consisted of the unleavened bread, with bitter herbs, of the so-called Chagigah (i. e., a voluntary peace offering made by private individuals), and the paschal lamb itself. After that nothing more was to be eaten, so that the flesh of the paschal sacrifice might be the last meat partaken of. But since the cessation of the paschal sacrifice the Jews conclude the supper with a piece of unleavened cake, called the *Aphikomen*, or after dish. Hands were again washed, the third cup was filled, and grace after meat said. The service concluded with the fourth cups over which the second portion of the Hallel was sung (Psa. 115, 116, 117, 118), the whole ending with the so-called "blessing of the song."

(*f*) *The 15th Nisan, Unleavened Bread.* On this day there was a holy convocation, and it was one of the six days on which, as on the Sabbath, no manner of work was allowed, with this exception, that while on the Sabbath the preparation of necessary food was not allowed (Exod. 16:5, 23, 29; 35:2, 3), on holy convocation it was permitted (Exod. 12:16; Lev. 23:7; Num. 28:18). The other five days on which the Bible prohibits servile work are the seventh of this festival, the day of Pentecost, New Year's Day, and the first and last of the Feast of Tabernacles.

In addition to the ordinary sacrifices there were offered on this and the following six days two bullocks, a ram, and seven lambs of the first year (with meat offerings) for a burnt offering, and a goat for a sin offering (Num. 28:19-23). Besides these public sacrifices voluntary offerings were made by each individual appearing before the Lord in Jerusalem (Exod. 23:15; Deut. 16:16). The Jewish canons prescribed that this freewill offering should be, 1. A burnt offering, worth not less than sixteen grains of corn; 2. A festive offering of not less value than thirty-two grains; 3. A peace, or joyful offering (Deut. 27:7), the value to be determined by the offerer (Deut. 16:16, 17).

(*g*) *The 16th Nisan, Cutting Barley Sheaf.* This day was also called "*the morrow after the Sabbath;*" and on it the omer of the first produce of the harvest (i. e., barley) was waved before the Lord (Lev. 23:10-14). Though for obvious reasons it was customary to choose barley grown in the sheltered Ashes valley across the Kedron, there were no restrictions, save that the barley was to be grown in Palestine, and without being forced by manuring and artificial watering. On the 14th Nisan delegates from the Sanhedrin had marked out the spot whence the first sheaf was to be cut, by tying together in bundles, while still standing, the barley to be reaped. When the time came for cutting the sheaf (i. e., the evening of the 15th Nisan, even though it was a Sabbath), just as the sun went down, three men, each with a sickle and basket, set formally to work. In order to bring out all that was distinctive in the ceremony, they first asked of the bystanders three times each of the following questions: "Has the sun gone down?" "With this sickle?" "Into this basket?" "On this Sabbath?" and, lastly, "Shall I cut?" Having each time been answered in the affirmative, they cut down the barley to the amount of one ephah (nearly three and a half pecks). The ears were brought into the court of the temple and threshed out with canes or stalks, so that the grains might not be crushed. The grain was then "parched" on a pan perforated with holes, so that each grain might be touched by the fire, and finally exposed to the wind. It was then ground and sifted to the requisite fineness, which was ascertained by one of the "Gizbarim" (treasurers) plunging his hand into it, the sifting process being continued as long as any of the flour adhered to the hand. In this manner the prescribed omer of flour was secured and offered in the temple on the 16th Nisan. Whatever was in excess of an omer was redeemed, and could be used for any purpose. The omer of flour was mixed with a "log" of oil, and a handful of frankincense put upon it, then waved before the Lord, and a handful taken out and burned on the altar (Lev. 2:15, 16). This was what is popularly, though not very correctly, called "the presentation of the first, or wave sheaf."

(*h*) *The 17th to the 20th Nisan.* These days constituted a half holy day, and were "*the lesser festival.*" As regards work during this period all that was necessary for the public interest or to prevent private loss was allowed, but no new work of any kind for public or private purposes might be begun. The following work was allowed: Irrigating dry land; digging watercourses; repairing conduits, reservoirs, roads, market places, baths; whitewashing tombs, etc. Dealers in fruit, garments, or utensils were allowed to sell privately what was required for immediate use. In the temple the additional sacrifices appointed for the festival were offered up, and the lesser Hallel was sung instead of the greater.

(*i*) *The 21st Nisan*, or the last day of the Passover, was observed by a holy convocation, and was celebrated in all respects like the first day, except that it did not commence with the paschal meal.

(*j*) *The Second, or Little Passover*. Anyone prevented by Levitical defilement, disability, or distance from keeping the regular Passover might observe the "second," or the "little Passover," exactly a month later (Num. 9:9-12). In this "second" Passover both leavened and unleavened bread might be kept in the house; the Hallel was not to be sung at the paschal supper; no Chagigah was offered. The supper could not be eaten by any defiled person.

(*k*) *Release of Prisoners*. It is not certain whether the release of a prisoner at the Passover (Matt. 27:15; Mark 15:6; Luke 23:17; John 18:39) was a custom of Roman origin, or whether it was an old Jewish usage, which Pilate allowed them to retain.

(*l*) *Preparations for the Passover*. A month previous (the 15th Adar) bridges and roads had been repaired for the use of pilgrims. This was also the time for administering the testing draught to women suspected of adultery (*q. v.*), for burning the red heifer (Num. 19: 1, sq.), and for boring the ears of those wishing to remain in bondage. One of these preliminary arrangements is specially interesting as recalling the words of the Saviour. Any dead body found in the field was buried where found; and, as the pilgrims coming to the feast might have contracted "uncleanness" by unwittingly touching such graves, it was ordered that all "sepulchers" should be "whitened" a month before the Passover. Evidently, it was in reference to what our Lord saw going on around him at the time he spoke, that he compared the Pharisees to "whited sepulchers, which indeed appear beautiful outward, but are within full of dead men's bones, and of all uncleanness" (Matt. 23:27). Two weeks before the Passover, and at the corresponding time before the other two great festivals, the flocks and herds were to be tithed and the treasure chests publicly opened and emptied. Lastly, "many went out of the country up to Jerusalem before the Passover, to purify themselves" (John 11:55; comp. I Cor. 11:27, 28).

(6) **Present observance.** The Jews of today continue to celebrate the Passover largely as in the days of the second temple. Several days before the festival all utensils are cleansed; on the eve of the 13th Nisan the master of the house, with a candle or lamp, searches most diligently into every hole and crevice of the house to discover any leaven which may remain about the premises. Before doing so he pronounces the benediction, following with the formal renunciation of all leaven. On the 14th Nisan (the Preparation Day) all the firstborn males above thirteen years of age fast, in commemoration of the sparing of the Jewish firstborn in Egypt. On this evening the Jews arrayed in festive garments, offer up the appointed prayers in the synagogue. Returning to their homes they find them illuminated and the tables spread with the following food: Three unleavened cakes are put on a plate; a shank bone of a shoulder of lamb, having a small bit of meat thereon, and an egg roasted hard in hot ashes, are in another dish; the bitter herbs are in a third dish, while the sauce (Heb. *charoseth*) and salt water, or vinegar, are put into two cups. The whole family, including the servants, are gathered around the table, and the food, with four cups of wine, are partaken of with blessings and benedictions. The same service is gone through the following evening, as the Jews have doubled the days of holy convocation.

2. **Pentecost** (Gr. *Petēkostē, fiftieth*, i. e., *day*), the second of the three great annual festivals, the others being the Passover and Tabernacles. The most important Bible passages relating to it are Exod. 23:16; Lev. 23: 15-22; Num. 28:26-31; Deut. 16:9-12. (1) **Names and signification.** This festival is called: 1. *The Feast of Weeks* (Exod. 34:22; Deut. 16:10, 16; II Chron. 8:13), because it was celebrated seven complete weeks, or fifty days, after the Passover (Lev. 23:15, 16). 2. *The Feast of Harvest* (Exod. 23:16), because it concluded the harvest of the later grains. 3. *The day of first fruits* (Num. 28:26), because the first loaves made from the new grain was then offered on the altar (Lev. 23:17). (2) **Origin and import.** The Scriptures do not clearly attach any historical significance to this festival, but seem to teach that Pentecost owes its origin to the harvest which terminated at this time. It is to be expected that, in common with other nations of antiquity who celebrated the ingathering of grain by offering to the Deity, among other firstling offerings, the fine flour of wheat, the Jews would recognize Jehovah's bounty with the first fruits of their harvest. The Jews, at least as early as the days of Christ, connected with the Passover, and commemorated on the 6th Sivan, the giving of the Decalogue. It was made out from Exod. ch. 19 that the law was delivered on the fiftieth day after the Exodus. It has been conjectured that a connection between the event and the festival may possibly be hinted at in the reference to the observance of the law in Deut. 16:12. The Pentecost was essentially linked to the Passover—that festival which, above all others, expressed the fact of a race chosen and separated from other nations—and was the solemn termination of the consecrated period. (3) **The time of the festival.** The time fixed for celebrating the Pentecost is the fiftieth day from "*the morrow after the Sabbath*" of the Passover (Lev. 23:11, 15, 16; or, as given in Deut. 16:9, seven full weeks after the sickle was put to the corn. The precise meaning of the word Sabbath in this connection, which determines the date for celebrating this festival, has been from time immemorial a matter of dispute. The Boethusians and the Sadducees in the time of the second temple, and the Karaites since the 8th century of the Christian era, have taken "Sabbath" in the sense of the *seventh day of the week*, and have maintained that the omer was offered on the day following that weekly Sab-

bath which might happen to fall within the seven days of the Passover. This would make Pentecost always come on the first day of the week. Against this many arguments are presented, showing that such an opinion involves many arbitrary and improbable arrangements. Commenting on Lev. 23:15-22, K. and D. (*Com.*, in loco) say that "*Sabbaths* (v. 15) signifies weeks. Consequently, 'the morrow after the seventh Sabbath' (v. 16) is the day after the seventh week, not after the seventh Sabbath." It is therefore evident that the Jews, who during the second temple kept Pentecost fifty days after the 16th Nisan, rightly interpreted the injunction in Lev. 23: 15-22. The fiftieth day, according to the Jewish canons, may fall on the 5th, 6th, or 7th of Sivan. (4) **Observance, Pentateuchal.** The Mosaic ordinances provided that on the day of Pentecost there was to be a holy convocation, on which no manner of work was to be done; all the able-bodied men of the congregation to be present (unless legally precluded) at the sanctuary, and a special sacrifice offered (Lev. 23:15-22; Num. 28:26-31). The sacrifices offered were (*a*) The morning and evening sacrifices, with their meat and drink offerings. (*b*) A burnt offering, consisting of seven lambs, one young bullock, two rams, with their meat and drink offering (Lev. 23:18; Num. 28:26, sq.). (*c*) Then was presented the two wave loaves, the new meat offering, of two tenths of an ephah of new flour (Lev. 23:17). (*d*) With the loaves were presented: A kid of the goats for a sin offering and two lambs for a peace offering. The firstling loaves, with the two lambs (peace offering), were devoted to the Lord, by waving, as a thank offering for the harvest which had been gathered in during the seven previous weeks. The words, "Ye shall bring out of your habitations wave loaves" (Lev. 23:17), are not to be understood as if every head of a house was to bring two such loaves, but that the two loaves were presented for the whole people. "Out of your habitations" appears to mean that they were to be loaves prepared for the daily nourishment of the house, and not specially for a holy purpose, or paid for out of the treasury. Freewill offerings, presented by each person in proportion to the blessings received from God. These might be burnt, meat, drink, or other offerings (Deut. 16:10). This festival was to be a season of rejoicing, in which were to share the children, men and maid servants, the Levites, the stranger, the fatherless, and the widow (Deut. 16:11). Israel was also to recall their bondage in Egypt and admonished to keep the divine law (Deut. 16:12). (5) **Observance, Post-Exilian.** From Acts (2:9-11) we infer that, perhaps more than to any other great festival, the Jews came from distant countries to Jerusalem. On the day before Pentecost the pilgrims entered Jerusalem, and the approach of the holy convocation was proclaimed in the evening by blasts of the trumpets. The great altar was cleansed in the first watch, and immediately after midnight the temple gates were thrown open. Before the morning sacrifice all burnt and peace offerings brought by the people were examined by the priests. The following

order was observed for the various sacrifices: (*a*) The regular morning sacrifice. (*b*) The festive offerings, as prescribed (Num. 28:26-30); the Levites chanting the Hallel, in which the people joined. (*c*) The firstling loaves, with their accompanying offerings. These loaves were prepared as follows: "Three *seahs* of new wheat were brought to the temple, threshed like other meat offerings, ground and passed through twelve sieves, and the remainder was redeemed and eaten by anyone. Care was taken that the flour for each loaf should be taken separately from one and a half *seah;* that it should be separately kneaded with luke-warm water (like all thank offerings), and separately baked in the temple itself. The loaves were made the evening preceding the festival; or, if that fell on the Sabbath, two evenings before. These loaves, with the two lambs, formed part of the same wave offering." (*d*) The freewill offerings of the people, which formed the cheerful and hospitable meal of the family, and to which the Levite, the widow, the orphan, the poor, and the stranger were invited. (6) **Present day observance.** This festival is annually and sacredly kept by the Jews on the 6th and 7th Sivan—i. e., between the second half of May and the first half of June, thus prolonging it to two days. In accordance with the injunction in Lev. 23:15, 16, the Jews regularly count every evening the fifty days from the second day of passover until Pentecost, and recite a prayer over it. The three days preceding the festival, on which the Jews commemorate the giving of the law, are called *the three days of separation and sanctification*, because the Lord commanded Moses to set bounds about the mount, and that the people should sanctify themselves three days prior to the giving of the law (Exod. 19:12, 14, 23).

On the preparation day the synagogues and private houses are adorned with flowers and odoriferous herbs; the males purify themselves by immersion and confession of sins, put on festive garments, and resort to the synagogue, where, after evening prayer, the hallowed nature of the festival is proclaimed by the cantor in the blessing pronounced over a cup of wine. The same is also done by every head of a family before the evening meal. After supper, either in the synagogue or in private houses, the reading of Scripture continues all night, the reason given being that, when God was about to reveal his law to Israel, he had to waken them from sleep, and to remove that sin they now keep awake during the night. In the general festival service of the morning special prayers are inserted for the day, which set forth the glory of the Lawgiver and of Israel; the great Hallel is recited; the lesson from the law (Exod. 19:1, 20, 26), the *Maphtir* (Num. 18:26-31), and the lesson from the prophets (Ezek. 1:1-28; 3:12), are read; the evening prayer (*Musaph*) is offered, and the benediction is received by the congregation, their heads covered by the fringed wrapper. On the second evening they again resort to the synagogue, use the ritual for the festivals, in which are again inserted special prayers for this occasion, chiefly on the greatness of God and the giving of the law and the decalogue. The sanctification of the festival is again pronounced, both by the prelector in the synagogue and the heads of the families at home. Prayers different from those of the first day, also celebrating the giving of the law, are mingled with the ordinary prayers; the Hallel is recited, as well as the book of Ruth; the lesson read from the law is Deut. 15:19-16:17, and the lesson from the prophets is Hab. 2:20-3:19, or 3:1-19; prayer is offered for departed relatives; the *Musaph Ritual* is recited; the priests pronounce the benediction, and the festival concludes after the afternoon service, as soon as the stars appear or darkness sets in.

3. **Atonement, Day of** (Heb. *yōm hăkkĭp-pūrîm*), the day appointed for a yearly, general, and perfect expiation for all the sins and uncleanness which might remain, despite the regular sacrifices. (1) **Signification.** The Levitical ritual was a constant reminder that "The law . . . can never, with those sacrifices which they offer year by year continually, make the comers thereunto perfect" (Heb. 10:1). Even with the most scrupulous observance of the prescribed ordinances many sins and defilements would still remain unacknowledged, and therefore without expiation. This want was met by the appointment of a yearly, general, and perfect expiation of all the sins and uncleanness which had remained unatoned for and uncleansed in the course of the year (Lev. 16:33). Thus on the Day of Atonement Israel was reconciled unto Jehovah, which was necessary before the Feast of Tabernacles, which feast prefigured the ingathering of all nations. In connection with this point it may also be well to remember that the Jubilee year was always proclaimed on the Day of Atonement (Lev. 25:9). (2) **Time.** The tenth day of the seventh month, or *Tishri* (October), and the fifth of Atonement (Lev. 16:1-34; Num. 29:7-11). The day was a high Sabbath, on which no work was done; and all the people were to afflict their souls, i. e., to fast (from the evening of the 9th to the evening of the 10th), under penalty of being cut off from Israel (Lev. 23:27-32). The chronological link connecting the Day of Atonement with the death of Aaron's sons (Lev. 10:1-5) was intended to point out that event as leading thereto, and also to show the importance and holiness attached to an entrance into the inmost sanctuary of God (Lev. 16:1, 2). (3) **Sacrifices.** From Lev. 16:5-28; Num. 29:7-11, it would appear that the sacrifices for the day were as follows: (*a*) The ordinary morning sacrifice. (*b*) The expiatory sacrifices for the priesthood, viz., a young bullock. (*c*) The sin offering for the people, a kid of the goats for Jehovah and another for Azazel. (*d*) The festive burnt offerings of the priests and people. and, with them, another sin offering. (*e*) The ordinary evening sacrifice. Of course, if the Day of Atonement fell on a Sabbath, besides all these, the ordinary Sabbath sacrifices were offered. (4) **Ceremonies. 1.** *Preparation.* The center point of this feast was the expiation offered by the high priest after the morning sacrifice. In later times, at least, the high priest underwent a special preparation for this service. Seven days before he had left his own home and taken up his residence in the temple chambers. A substitute was provided, lest the high priest should die or become Levitically unclean. During this week he practices the various priestly duties, such as sprinkling the blood, burning incense, lighting the lamps, offering the daily sacrifices, etc.; for every part of the service on Atonement Day devolved upon the high priest, and he must make no mistake. Further, he was to abstain from all that could render him unclean or disturb his devotions. On the morning of the Day of Atonement the high priest bathed his entire person; not in the place ordinarily used

by the priests, but one specially set apart for him. He then put on the holy garments—the coat, drawers, girdle, and head dress of white cloth—thus signifying that he was entirely cleansed from the defilement of sin and arrayed in holiness. **2.** *Expiatory rites.* Everything being in readiness, the high priest slew the bullock (the sin offering for himself and his house), then filled a censer (coal pan, Exod. 25:38) with burning coals from the altar of burnt offerings, and, putting two handfuls of incense into a vase, bore them into the holy of holies. He poured the incense upon the coals, "that the cloud of the incense may cover the mercy seat." As the burning incense was a symbol of *prayer*, this covering of the mercy seat with the cloud of incense was a symbolical covering of the glory of the Most Holy One with prayer to God, and thus served as protection to the worshiper. The high priest now returned to the altar of burnt offering to fetch some of the blood of the bullock, which he sprinkled upon the mercy seat ("eastward," Lev. 16:14) and seven times upon the ground before it. After this he slew the goat selected for a sin offering, and did with its blood as with the blood of the bullock, viz., sprinkled it upon and before the mercy seat. He thus made atonement for the holy of holies, because of the uncleanness of both priests and people (v. 16). He was now required to atone for the "tabernacle of the congregation" ("tent of meeting," R. V.), which he did by sprinkling the blood of both the bullock and the goat, first on the horns of the golden altar once, and then seven times toward the altar, on the ground (see Exod. 30:10). Atonement having been made for the building, the high priest was to expiate the altar of burnt offering, which he did by first putting some of the blood of the bullock and the he-goat upon the horns of the altar, and sprinkling it seven times. Thus the dwelling, the court, and all the holy things were expiated and cleansed. The question how often the high priest on this day went into the holy of holies is not of great importance. The biblical account seems to indicate that he entered four times: 1. With the incense, while a priest continued to agitate the blood of the bullock lest it should coagulate; 2. With the blood of the bullock; 3. With the blood of the goat; 4. To bring the censer, which, according to the Talmud, was done after the evening sacrifice. The high priest then, going out into the court of the tabernacle, laid his hands on the head of the scapegoat, confessing over it all the sins and transgressions of the people. It was led away, by a man standing ready, into the wilderness, and there let go free, to signify the carrying away of Israel's sins which God had forgiven. *See* Azazel. **3.** *Festive offerings.* He then went into the tabernacle, took off his white garments, laid them down there (because they were only to be worn in the expiatory ritual of this day), washed himself "in the holy place" (in the laver of the court), put on his usual official robes, and completed his own and the people's burnt offering in the court, at the same time burning the fat of the sin offerings on the altar. But both of the sin offerings were carried without the camp and burned, with skin, flesh, and dung. The persons who had taken the live goat into the wilderness and burned the sin offerings outside the camp were, before they returned into it, to wash their clothes and bathe their bodies (Lev. 16:2-29). "This act of expiation for the people and the holy places being finished, there was presented immediately before the evening sacrifice, according to Jewish tradition, the offering prescribed for the feast of the day, a goat as sin offering, a bullock, a ram, and several lambs as burnt offerings, with the corresponding meat and drink offerings (Num. 29:7, 11), and therewith the feast of the day was closed." According to the Rabbins the high priest on this day (1) Performed all the duties of the regular daily service; (2) Sprinkled the blood eight times, once toward the ceiling and seven times on the floor; (3) After returning the third time from the holy of holies to the holy place he sprinkled the blood of bullock and goat toward the veil, mixed the blood of the two victims together, sprinkled the altar of incense with the mixture, pouring out what remained at the foot of the altar of burnt offering; (4) The two goats were similar in appearance (size and value). The lots with which they were chosen were originally of boxwood, later of gold; (5) The high priest, as soon as he received the signal that the goat had reached the wilderness, read some lessons from the law, and offered prayer; (6) Very strict rules are given by the Mishna for the fasting of the people. (5) **Modern observance.** The strict Jews, on the day previous to the Day of Atonement, provide a cock which is slain by an inferior rabbi; the person whose property it is then takes the fowl by the legs, swings it over the heads of himself and company, and at the same time prays to God that the sins committed by them during the year may enter the fowl. This fowl seems to be a substitute for the scapegoat of old. In the evening, after a sumptuous repast, they go to the synagogue dressed in their best. After a blessing by the clerk each contributes toward the free gift offering, after which begins the evening prayer, the reader, the chief rabbi, and many of the congregation clad with the shroud in which they are to be buried, continuing in prayer and supplication for upward of three hours. Some remain all night, and those who go to their homes come again in the morning at five o'clock and remain until dark. The following is the order for the day: Morning prayers; the usual prayers and supplications peculiar to the day; reading the portion from Lev. 16, the *maphter* (Num. 19: 7-11), the portion from the prophets (Isa. 57:14 to end of ch. 58); the prayer of the *musaph*, i. e., *addition*, which makes mention of the additional sacrifices (Num. 29:7), and supplicates Jehovah to be propitious; the offering of the day from Num. 29:7-27. They abstain from food altogether during the day. *See* Expiation.

4. **Tabernacles, Feast of,** the third of the great annual feasts, the other two being the Passover and Pentecost. (1) **Names.** *1. The Festival of Tents* (Heb. *hăg hăssŭccōth,* A. V.

"Feast of Tabernacles," II Chron. 8:13; Ezra 3:4; Zech. 14:16, 18, 19); Gr. *skēnopēgia,* John 7:2), because the Israelites were commanded to live in booths during its continuance (comp. Lev. 23:43). *2. The Feast of Ingathering* (Heb. *hăg hā'ōsîf,* Exod. 23:16; 34:22), because it was held after the ingathering of the harvest and fruits. *3. The Festival of Jehovah* (Heb. *hăg Yhwh,* Lev. 23:39, or simply *the festival* (I Kings 8:2; II Chron. 5:3), because it was the most important or well known. The principal passages referring to this feast are: Exod. 23:16; Lev. 23:34-36, 39-43; Deut. 16:13-15; 31:10-13; Neh. ch. 8. (2) **Origin and import.** The origin of this feast is by some connected with Succoth, the first halting place of the Israelites on their march out of Egypt, and the booths are taken to commemorate those in which they lodged for the last time before they entered the desert. It was ordered by Moses in the regulations he gave to the Israelites respecting their festivals, and unites two elements: The *ingathering* of the labor of the field (Exod. 23:16), the fruit of the earth (Lev. 23:39), or the ingathering of the threshing floor and the wine press (Deut. 16:13), and the dwelling in booths, which were to be matters of joy to Israel (Lev. 23:41; Deut. 16:14). The dwelling in booths was to be a reminder to them of the fatherly care and protection of Jehovah while Israel was journeying from Egypt to Canaan (Deut. 8:9, sq.). "In comparison with the 'house of bondage' the dwelling in booths on the march through the wilderness was in itself an image of freedom and happiness" (K. and D., *Com.,* in loco). Such a reminder of God's loving care and Israel's dependence would, naturally, keep the Israelites from pride and self-conceit. (3) **Time of Festival.** It began on the 15th of Tisri (the seventh month), five days before the Day of Atonement, and although, strictly speaking, it lasted only seven days (Deut. 16:13; Lev. 23:36; Ezek. 45:25), another day was added (Neh. 8:18). This day was observed with a Sabbatic rest. (4) **Observance.** To distinguish between the Pentateuchal enactments and the rites, ceremonies, etc., which gradually obtained, we divide the description of its observance into three sections: *1. Mosaic.* On the first day of the feast, booths were constructed of fresh branches of fruit and palm trees, "boughs of thick trees," i. e., thick with leaves and willows. These were located in courts, streets, public squares, and on house roofs. In these every home-born Israelite was to dwell during the festival, in memory of their fathers dwelling in booths after their exodus from Egypt (Lev. 23:40; Neh. 8:15). The day was also to be observed as a Sabbath and a holy convocation, in which no secular work was to be done, and all able-bodied male members of the congregation not legally precluded were to appear before the Lord. The booth in Scripture is not an image of privation and misery, but of protection, preservation, and shelter from heat, storm, and tempest (Psa. 27:5; 31:20; Isa. 4:6). The following is a table of the sacrifices offered during this festival:

Day.	Bull-ocks.	Rams.	Lambs.	Goats, sin offer-ing.
1st....	13	2	14	1
2d....	12	2	14	1
3d....	11	2	14	1
4th....	10	2	14	1
5th....	9	2	14	1
6th....	8	2	14	1
7th....	7	2	14	1
Total	70	14	98	7
8th....	1	1	7	1

Each bullock, ram, and lamb was accompanied with its prescribed meat and drink offering. The above sacrifices were offered after the regular morning sacrifice (Num. 29:12-34). Every Sabbatical year the law was to be read publicly in the sanctuary on the first day of the festival (Deut. 31:10-13). The six following days were half festivals, probably devoted to social enjoyments and friendly gatherings, when every head of a family was to extend hospitality, especially to the poor and the stranger (Deut. 16:14). To these seven days there was added an eighth, the twenty-second of the month, as the close of the feast. This day was observed with a Sabbatic rest and holy convocation, but had only a simple sacrifice, similar to the first and tenth days of the seventh month (Num. 29:35-38). See table of sacrifices above. There is only one instance recorded of this festival being celebrated between the entrance into the Promised Land and the Babylonian captivity (I Kings 8:2; II Chron. 7:8-10; Neh. 8:17). 2. *Post-Exilic.* After the Babylonian captivity the Feast of Tabernacles began to be strictly and generally kept, and more minute definitions and more expanded applications of the concise Pentateuchal injunction were imperatively demanded, in order to secure uniformity of practice, as well as to infuse devotion and joy into the celebration.

It was ordained that the booth must be a detached and temporary habitation, constructed for the festival and not for permanent residence; the interior must neither be higher than twenty cubits nor lower than ten palms; it must have not less than three walls, and so thatched as to admit the view of the sky and the stars, and the part open to the rays of the sun was not to exceed the part shaded by the cover; it must not be under a tree, covered with a cloth, or with anything which contracts defilement or does not derive its growth from the ground. The furniture of the booths must be of the plainest, and only such as was fairly necessary. Every Israelite was to dwell in the booth during the whole of the seven days of the festival, while his house was to be only his occasional abode; and he was only to quit the booth when it rained heavily. Even a child, as soon as it ceases to be dependent upon its mother, must dwell in the booth. The only persons exempt were those deputed on pious missions, invalids, nurses, women, and infants.

There was a controversy between the Pharisees and Sadducees respecting the use of the branches of trees mentioned in Lev. 23:40; the latter, from Neh. 8:15, 16, understanding them to be for the erection of the booths, while the Pharisees applied them to what the worshipers were to carry in their hands. The Rabbins ruled that the *aethrog*, or citron, was "the fruit of the goodly trees," and "the boughs of thick trees" meant the myrtle, provided it had "not more berries than leaves." Every worshiper carried the *aethrog* in his left hand, and in his right the *lulab*, or palm, with myrtle and willow branch on either side of it, tied together on the outside with its own

kind, though on the inside it might be fastened even with a gold thread. The *lulab* was used in the temple on each of the seven festive days; even children, if able to shake it, being bound to carry one.

14th Tisri. This was the day before the feast and was the *Preparation Day.* On this day the pilgrims came to Jerusalem and prepared all that was necessary for the solemn observance of the festival. When the evening set in the blasts of the priest's trumpets on the temple mount announced the advent of the feast. As at the Passover and at Pentecost the altar of burnt offering was cleansed during the first night watch, and the temple gates were thrown open immediately after midnight. The time till the beginning of the ordinary morning sacrifice was occupied in examining the various sacrifices and offerings that were to be brought during the day. If this day was the Sabbath all *lulabs* had to be deposited somewhere in the temple, as it was contrary to law to carry the palms on the Sabbath from the booths of the pilgrims to the temple.

15th Tisri. While the morning sacrifice was being prepared a priest, accompanied with music, went down to the Pool of Siloam, whence he drew water into a golden pitcher capable of holding three *logs.* On the Sabbaths the water was brought from a golden vessel in the temple itself, to which it had been carried from Siloam the preceding day. At the same time that the procession started for Siloam another went to a place in Kedron valley (i. e., Motza), whence they brought willow branches. These they stuck on either side of the great altar, bending them over so as to form a canopy. The priest who had gone to Siloam so timed his return as to join his brother priests as they carried the sacrifice to the altar. On reaching the water gate he was welcomed by three blasts of the trumpet. He ascended the steps of the altar with another priest, who carried a pitcher of wine for a drink offering. They turned to the left, where there were two silver basins with holes in the bottom; the basin for the water at the west with a narrower hole, that for the wine at the east with wider hole, so that both might get empty at the same time. Into these respective basins the water and wine were poured; the people shouting to the priest, "Raise thy hand," to show that he really poured the water into the basin. The reason for this was that Alexander Jannaeus, a Sadducee (about 95 B. C.), had shown his contempt for the Pharisees by pouring the water upon the ground. He was pelted by the people with their *aethrogs*, and the soldiers being called in nearly six thousand Jews were killed in the temple.

As soon as the altar was decorated with the willow branches the morning sacrifice was offered. While these sacrifices were being offered the Levites chanted the *Great Hallel*, as at the Passover and Pentecost. When the choir came to the words, "O give thanks unto the Lord" (Psa. 118:1), and again when they sang, "O work then now salvation, Jehovah" (Psa. 118:25), and once more at the close, "O give thanks unto the Lord" (Psa. 118:29), all the worshipers shook their *lulabs* toward the altar. The chant finished, the priests marched around the altar, exclaiming, "Hosanna, O Jehovah; give us help, O Jehovah, give prosperity" (Psa. 118:25). The benediction was then pronounced and the people dispersed, amid the repeated exclamation, "How beautiful art thou, O altar!" or, "To Jehovah and thee, O altar, we give thanks!" This prayer for succor was applied to Christ, when the multitude greeted Jesus on his entry into Jerusalem (Matt. 21:8, 9; John 12:12, 13).

Each pilgrim betook himself to his booth, there to enjoy his social repast with the Levite, the stranger, etc. On the first day of the festival every Israelite carried about his *lulab*, or palm, all day—to the synagogue, on his visits to the sick and mourners.

16th to 20th Tisri, called also *the middle days of the feast* (John 7:14), or *the lesser festival.* These days were half holy days, on which necessary food or raiment might be privately purchased, and work required for the observance of the festival might be performed. During these days the sacrifices were offered, the palm and the citron were used, and the priests marched round the altar as on the first day of the festival, with this exception, that the number of animals offered diminished daily.

21st Tisri, or *the last day of the feast* (but according to some authorities this title was given to the 22d Tisri). This seventh day of the festival was distinguished from the other days as follows: After the *Musaph*, or special festival sacrifices of the day, the priests marched seven times around the altar, instead of once, as on other days; the willows which surrounded the altar were then so thoroughly shaken by the people that the leaves lay thickly on the ground; the people also brought palm branches and beat them to pieces at the side of the altar, from which the day was called *the day of willows*, and *the branch-threshing* day. This over, the children who were present threw away their palms and ate up their *aethrogs*, or citrons; on the afternoon of this day the pilgrims began to move the furniture from the booths, the obligation to dwell in them ceasing at that time. This, the great Hosanna day, was regarded as one of the four days whereon God judges the world. It seems altogether probable that it was on this day that Jesus uttered those memorable words, "If any man thirst, let him come unto me, and drink" (John 7:37).

22d Tisri. This eighth day was added as the close of the festival, and was observed with Sabbatic rest and holy convocation. It had only a simple sacrifice (similar to the first and tenth day of the seventh month; *see* table of sacrifices above). The people dwelt no longer in booths, the joyful procession for the drawing of water was discontinued, the illumination of the court of the women ceased, and the palms and willows were not used.

The ceremony of drawing the water was repeated every morning during the seven days of the festival, but was discontinued on the eighth.

When the Feast of Tabernacles fell on a Sabbatic year the reading of portions of the law (Deut. 31:10-13) was afterward confined to one book of the Pentateuch, the number of synagogues in which the law was read every week rendering it less needful to read extensive portions in the temple. A peculiarity of this festival was that on the first seven days all the twenty-four orders of the priests officiated, while at all the other festivals only those served upon whom the lot fell (comp. I Chron. 24:7-19). On the eighth day the twenty-four orders were not all present; only those upon whom the lot fell. As the close of the first day of the feast was celebrated, the "joy of the pouring out of water," the worshipers descended to the court of the women, where great preparations had been made. Four golden candelabras were there, each with four golden bowls, against each candelabra a ladder resting, upon them standing four lads from the rising youth of the priests, with pitchers of oil, wherewith they fed the lamps, while the cast-off breeches and girdles of the priests served for wicks. The light from these lamps illuminated the whole city, and around them danced distinguished men, with lighted torches in their hands, singing hymns and songs of praise. The Levites, stationed on the fifteen steps which led into the court, and corresponding to the fifteen psalms of degrees, i. e., *steps* (Psa. 120-134), accompanied the songs with harps, psalteries, cymbals, and other musical instruments. The dancing, as well as the music, continued until daybreak. It is probable that Jesus referred to this custom when he spoke those well-known words, "I am the light of the world" (John 8:12).

3. Since the dispersion. Save the adaptation of the rites to the altered condition of the nation, the Jews of the present day continue to celebrate the Feast of Tabernacles as in the days of the second temple.

As soon as the Day of Atonement is over every Orthodox Jew begins to erect his booth in which he and his family are to take up their abode during the festival, and he also provides himself with a *lulab* (palm) and *aethrog* (citron). The festival commences on the eve of 14th Tisri (Preparation Day), all the Jews, attired in festive garments, resorting to the synagogues, where, after the evening prayer, the hallowed nature of the festival is proclaimed by the cantor in the blessing pronounced over the wine. After the evening service every family resorts to its booth, which is illuminated and adorned with leaves and fruit, and in which the first festive meal is taken. Before this is eaten the head of the family pronounces the sanctity of the festival over a cup of wine. Each member of the family washes his hands, pronouncing the prescribed benediction while drying them, and all begin to eat. Orthodox Jews sleep in the booths all night.

The following morning, the first day of the feast, they resort to the synagogue, holding the palms and citrons in their hands, laying them down during the former part of the prayer, but taking them up after the eighteen benedictions, when about to recite the Hallel. Holding the palm in the right hand and the citron in the left, they recite the following prayer: "Blessed art thou, O Lord our God, King of the universe, who hast sanctified us with thy commandments, and hast enjoined us to take the palm branch." Then each turns his citron upside down and waves his palm branch three times toward each point of the compass, and the legate of the congregation pronounces the benediction; the Hallel is chanted; the lessons are read from the law (Lev. 22:26, 23:44; Num. 29:12-16), and from the Prophets (Zech. 14:1-21). After this the *Musaph* prayer is recited; and when the reader comes to the passage where the expression *priests* occurs the Aaronites and the Levites rise, and, after the latter have washed the hands of the former, the priests, with uplifted hands, pronounce the sacerdotal benediction (Num. 6:24-27) upon the congregation, whose faces are veiled with the *Talith*. The elders then march round the Ark, in the center of the synagogue, the legate carrying the scroll and the rest palm branches, repeating the *Hosanna* and waving the palms in memory of the procession round the altar. The morning service concluded, the people betake themselves to their booths to partake of the festive repast with the poor and the stranger. About five or six o'clock they recite, in the synagogue, the *Minchah* prayer, answering to the daily evening sacrifice in the temple.

The ritual and rites of the second evening and morning are similar to those of the first; the lesson from the prophets, however, is from I Kings 8:2-21. After the afternoon service of this day the middle days of the festival begin, which last four days, when the ritual is like that of ordinary days, a few prayers being inserted in the regular formula; lessons are read on each day, and the procession goes round the ark.

The seventh day, i. e., *the Great Hosanna*, is celebrated with peculiar solemnity, inasmuch as it is believed that on this day God decrees the weather, or, rather, the rain, for the future harvest. On the evening previous every Israelite supplies himself with a small bunch of willows tied with palm bark. Some pious Jews read all night from Deuteronomy, the Psalms, the Mishna, etc., and are immersed before the morning prayer. Candles are lighted at the time of morning service, and after the morning prayer (similar to those of the preceding days) seven scrolls are taken from the ark, from one of which the lesson is read. After prayer the procession, headed by the rabbi and the legate, with those carrying the scrolls, goes seven times round the ark, or the reading desk, reciting the Hosannas and waving their palms. The palms are then laid down and the willows beaten.

On the evening of the seventh day the festival commences which concludes the whole cycle of the feast. Being a day of holy convocation, the *Kiddush* (i. e., proclamation) of its sanctity is offered. On the following morning, in the synagogue, the prayers of the first two days are offered; the special lesson of the day is read; the *Musaph*, or additional prayer, is offered, and the priests pronounce the benediction. The people no longer take their meals in the booths on this day. On the evening of this day begins the festival called *the Rejoicing of the Law*. The eighteen benedictions are recited, all the scrolls taken from the ark, into which a lighted candle is placed. A procession of distinguished members is headed by the legate; they hold the scrolls in their hands and go around the reading desk; the scrolls are then put back into the ark, except the one placed upon the desk, from which is read the last chapter of Deuteronomy, all persons in the synagogue being called to the reading, including children. The evening service over, the children leave the synagogue in procession, carrying banners with sundry Hebrew inscriptions.

On the following morning the Jews resort again to the synagogue, recite the *Hallel* after the eighteen benedictions, empty the ark of all its scrolls, put a lighted candle into it, and, with the scrolls go round the reading desk, amid jubilant songs. The scrolls are returned to the ark, with the exception of two, from one of which is read Deut. ch. 33, whereunto four persons are at first called; then all the little children, and then again several adults. The first of these is known as *the Bridegroom of the Law*, and after the cantor has addressed him in a lengthy Hebrew formula the last verses of the Pentateuch are read, the reading being followed by all the people exclaiming, *be strong!* Gen. 1:1-2:3 is read, to which another is called who is known as *the Bridegroom of Genesis*, to whom is delivered a Hebrew formula; the *Maphtir* (i. e., Num. 29:35-30:1) is read from another scroll; the *Mustaph*, or additional special prayer for the festival, and the service is concluded. The rest of the day is spent in rejoicing and feasting.

The design of this festival is to celebrate the annual completion of the perusal of the Pentateuch, inasmuch as on this day the last section of the law is read. Hence the name of the festival, *The Rejoicing of Finishing the Law*.

III. *Post-Exilic Festivals*. To the yearly festivals instituted by the Mosiac law several were added after the Exile, of which some were as regularly kept as the Mosaic yearly feasts. They were the following:

1. **Purim** (Heb. *pūrim, lots*, Esth. 9:26, 31), was instituted by Mordecai, at the suggestion of Esther, in memory of the extraordinary deliverance of the Jews of Persia from the murderous plot of Haman. It was generally adopted, though not at first without opposition. (1) **Name and signification.** The name *Purim, lots*, was given to this festival because of the casting of lots by Haman to decide when he should carry into effect the decree issued by the king for the extermination of the Jews (Esth. 9:24). The name was probably given to the festival in irony. (2) **Observance.** The only directions given respecting the observance of the festival is (Esth. 9:17-24), that Mordecai ordered the 14th and 15th of Adar to be kept annually by the Jews; that these two days should be days of feasting and joy, of the interchange of presents, and of sending gifts to the poor; and that the Jews agreed to continue the observance of the festival as it was begun. No mention is made of any special sacrifice. At the present day the festival is kept as follows: The day preceding (13th Adar) is kept as a fast day (called "the Fast of Esther"), in accordance with the command of the queen (Esth. 4:15, 16), sundry prayers, expressive of repentance, etc., being introduced into the ritual for the day. As on all fast days, Exod. 32:11-14; 34:1-11 are read as the lesson for the law, and Isa. 55:6-56:8 as the Haphtarah. If 13th Adar falls on a Sabbath the fast is kept on the Thursday previous. As soon as the stars appear the festival commences, candles are lighted, all the Jews resort to the synagogue, where, after the evening service, the benediction is pronounced, and the book of Esther is read by the prelector. As often as the name of Haman is mentioned in the reading the congregation stamp on the floor, saying, "Let his name be blotted out. The name of the wicked shall rot!" while the children spring rattles. After the reading the congregation exclaims, "Cursed be Haman; blessed be Mordecai!" etc.; the benediction is said, and all go home and partake of milk and eggs. On the 14th, in the morning, the people go to the synagogue; several prayers are inserted into the regular ritual; Exod. 17:8-16 is read as the lesson from the law, and Esther, as on the pre-

vious evening. The rest of the festival is given up to rejoicing, exchange of presents, games, etc. Rejoicings continue on the 15th, and the festival terminates on the evening of this day.

2. **Dedication, Feast of** (Heb. *ḥănŭkkăh*), called in I Macc. 4:52-59 "the dedication of the altar," and by Josephus (*Ant.*, xii, 7, 7) "the feast of lights." It was a popular and joyous festival, and commemorated the purifying of the temple, the removal of the old polluted altar, and the restoration of the worship of Jehovah by Judas Maccabeus, B. C. 164.

This feast began on the 25th Chisleu (December), and lasted eight days, but did not require attendance at Jerusalem. Assembled in the temple, or in the synagogues of the places where they resided, the Jews sang "Hallel," carrying palm and other branches; and there was a grand illumination of the temple and private houses. The real origin of the illumination of the temple is unknown, although tradition says that when the sacred "candlesticks" of the restored temple were to be lighted only one flagon of oil, sealed with the signet of the high priest, was found to feed the lamps. This was *pure* oil, but only sufficient for one day—when, lo, by a miracle, the oil increased, and the flagon remained filled for eight days, in memory of which the temple and private houses were ordered to be illuminated for the same period. No public mourning or fast was allowed on account of calamity or bereavement. The similarity between this festival and the "Feast of Tabernacles" would seem to indicate some intended connection between the two. Our Lord, without doubt, attended this festival at Jerusalem (John 10: 22). It is still observed by the Jews.

IV. *Festivals as types*. According to many Bible teachers, the seven feasts of the Lord of Lev. 23 constitute a prophecy and foreshadowing of future events, part of which have been fulfilled and part yet to be fulfilled. They are "the shadow of things to come," of which Christ is the body or substance (Col. 2:16, 17). The seven annual feasts may be divided into two sections of four and three. The first section includes the Passover, the Feast of Unleavened Bread, the Feast of First Fruits and Penetecost. The second group, separated by a four-month period, includes the Feast of Trumpets, the Day of Atonement and the Feast of Tabernacles. The three great festivals were the Passover, Pentecost and Tabernacles. The first four feasts foreshadowed truths concerning this present gospel age; the last three foreshadow blessing in store for Israel. The first four are historic; the last three, prophetic. Those who hold the typical view of the Hebrew feasts, teach the significance of each as follows:

1. **Passover.** The Passover (Lev. 23:4, 5) speaks of Calvary and of redemption by blood from Egypt, the type of the world; and from pharaoh, a type of Satan; and from Egyptian servitude, a type of sin. The festival speaks of our redemption from sin by the Lamb of God (I Pet. 1:19), Christ being our Passover (I Cor. 5:7).

2. **Unleavened Bread** (Lev. 23:6-8) typifies the holy walk of a believer consequent

upon redemption (I Cor. 5:8; 11:23-33; II Cor. 7:1; Gal. 5:7-9). The divine order is eloquent. First, redemption followed by a holy walk. The eating of unleavened bread and the putting away of all leaven from the household portrays holiness, as leaven is a figure of "malice and wickedness" (I Cor. 5:8) and is not befitting a believer's walk.

3. **First Fruits.** (Lev. 23:9-14). This feast is typical of resurrection, first of Christ, then of "them that are Christ's at His coming" (I Cor. 15:23, I Thess. 4:13-18). When the priest on the day of Christ's resurrection waved the sheaf of first fruits in the temple, it was before a rent veil and was but an antiquated form, for the substance had come and the shadow had passed away. Joseph's empty tomb proclaimed that the great first fruit sheaf had been reaped and waved in the heavenly temple. This feast has been completely fulfilled in Christ.

4. **Pentecost.** (Lev. 23:15-22). The antitype is the coming of the Holy Spirit at Pentecost to form the Church, the body of Christ. Because the church is not yet glorified and contains evil, leaven is present (Matt. 13:33; Acts 5:1). The two loaves, are not a sheaf of separate stalks loosely tied together, but a real union of particles making loaves or a homogeneous body. At Pentecost the Holy Spirit by His baptizing work formed the separate disciples into one organism, the body of Christ (Acts 1:5 with Acts 11:16 and I Cor. 12:13). The Church had to begin on Pentecost because it was the first historical instance of the Spirit's baptizing work (Cf. Merrill F. Unger, *The Baptizing Work of the Holy Spirit*, 1953, pp. 53-65). Although leaven was in the two loaves offered at Pentecost, typifying Jew and Gentile made one in Christ (Cf. Eph. 3:1-10), yet the leaven has been baked, that is, sin in the redeemed has been judged in Christ. The four-month period between Pentecost and Trumpets was occupied in gathering in the harvest, typical of the present Church period before Christ takes up again with Israel.

5. **Trumpets** (Lev. 23:23-25) speaks of the regathering of Israel to its home land after the out-gathering of the Church. Matt. 24:31 speaks of the Son of Man at His Second Advent sending His angels with a great sound of a trumpet to gather together His elect (of Israel) from the four winds, from one end of heaven to the other.

6. **Day of Atonement** (Lev. 23:26-32) envisions Israel's national cleansing from sin (Rom. 11:25) and refers to the time when a "fountain will be open to the house of David and to the inhabitants of Jerusalem for sin and for uncleanness" (Zech. 13:1). It portrays their future conversion as a nation at the Second Advent of Christ (Zech. 12:9-14).

7. **Tabernacles** (Lev. 23:33-44). The antitype of this feast has not yet appeared. Peter anticipated it, however, on the Mount of Transfiguration when he said, "Lord, it is good for us to be here. If Thou wilt, let us make here three tabernacles, one for Thee and one for Moses and one for Elijah" (Matt. 17:4). What Peter desired, the dwelling of heavenly and earthly people on the earth, was not possible in that age but will be possible in the conditions of the mediatorial Davidic kingdom. Then the kingdom of the heavens will bring heaven and earth in closer union. The Feast of Tabernacles is thus prophetic of Israel's millennial rest. The Feast of Tabernacles will be a memorial to Israel, going back to Egypt and forward to millennial rest, as the Lord's supper now points back to a finished redemption until Christ appears. The eighth day following the Sabbath (Lev. 23:39) points to the new heaven and the new earth following the millennium and to the dispensation of the fullness of times before the eternal state.

Revised by *M. F. U.*

Fes′tus, Por′cius (fĕs′tŭs, pôr′shĭ-ŭs); the successor of Felix as the Roman governor of Judea, appointed by the emperor Nero probably in the autumn of A. D. 60 (C. and H., *Life and Epistles of St. Paul*). Three days after his arrival at Caesarea (the political metropolis) he went up to Jerusalem. Here he was met by the "high priest and the chief of the Jews, who informed him against Paul." They requested, as a favor, that he would allow Paul to be brought up to Jerusalem, the plea, doubtless, being that he should be tried before the Sanhedrin. The real purpose, however, was to kill him while on the way. Festus refused to comply, and told them that they must meet the accused face to face at Caesarea. After eight or ten days Paul was summoned before Festus and asked whether he was willing to go to Jerusalem; but the apostle, knowing full well the danger that lurked in this proposal and conscious of the rights he possessed as a Roman citizen, refused to accede and replied boldly to Festus, concluding with, "I appeal unto Caesar." About this time Herod Agrippa, with his sister, Berenice, came on a complimentary visit to Festus, and was consulted by the governor. The result was an interview between the three and Paul, in which the latter delivered a famous discourse and was pronounced innocent. But having appealed to Caesar Festus sent him to Rome (Acts chaps. 25, 26). A few other facts are mentioned concerning Festus. Judea was in the same disturbed state that it had been in under the procuratorship of Felix. He took part with Agrippa against the priests, who built a wall to obstruct Agrippa's view of the temple, but allowed an appeal to Nero, who decided in favor of the Jews. He probably died in summer of A. D. 62. *See* Paul.

Fetters, shackles or chains for binding prisoners either by the wrists or ankles. The Philistines bound Samson with fetters of copper, or bronze (Judg. 16:21). Manasseh and Zedekiah, kings of Judah, were bound with fetters by the Chaldeans and carried to Babylon (II Chron. 33:11; II Kings 25:7). The "man with an unclean spirit" was bound with fetters and chains (Mark 5:4). In the original several words are used.

The Egyptians inclosed the hands of their prisoners in an elongated fetter of wood, made of two opposite segments, nailed together at each end, such as are used in securing prisoners in Egypt at the present day.

Fever. *See* Diseases.

Fidelity (Gr. *pistis*), "is that grace in the servant which shows him to be worthy of his

Master's trust. Thus our Lord says, 'Who then is that faithful and wise steward,' etc. (Luke 12:42). Paul gives the description of the faithful servant as 'showing all good fidelity' (Tit. 2: 10). The same word which expresses our trust in God's fidelity expresses his trust in ours. It is a grace which stands alone as having the epithet *good*, and it must pervade the whole of life. Here then are all the elements of our ethics: The Master commits a trust, and the trustworthy servant shows fidelity in all things. It may be that the very faith which trusts God is the strength of the faithfulness which God may trust. Fidelity extends to the whole of life, with special reference to our individual vocation. Nothing is excluded from the sphere of this duty. Fidelity, as the test applied to service, is guarded by threatenings and stimulated by the hope of reward" (Matt. 25:23, 26, 30) (Pope, *Christ. Theol.*, iii, 220-223).

Field (Heb. *sädĕh, smoothness*). This word does not exactly correspond to our "field." The two words agree in describing *cultivated* land, but differ in point of extent, the *sädĕh* being specifically applied to what is *uninclosed*, while *field* conveys the notion of inclosure. On the one hand *sädĕh* is applied to any cultivated ground, whether *pasture* (Gen. 29:2; 31:4; 34:7; Exod. 9:3), *tillage* (Gen. 37:7; 47:24; Ruth 2:2, 3; Job. 24:6; Jer. 26:18; Mic. 3:12), *woodland* (I Sam. 14:25, A. V. "ground;" Psa. 132:6), or *mountain top* (Judg. 9:32, 36; II Sam. 1:21), and in some instances in marked opposition to the neighboring wilderness, as the field of Shechem (Gen. 33:19), the field of Moab (Gen. 36:35; Num. 21:20, A. V. "country;" Ruth 1:1), and the vale of Siddim (Gen. 14:3, 8).

On the other hand the *sädĕh* is contrasted with what is inclosed, whether a *vineyard* (Exod. 22:5; Lev. 25:3, 4; Num. 22:4, etc.), a garden, or a city (Deut. 28:3, 16), unwalled villages ranking in the eyes of the law as fields (Lev. 25:31). The term often implies a place remote from a house (Gen. 4:8; 24:63), a sense more fully expressed by "the open field" (Lev. 14:7, 53; 17:5; Num. 19:16) and naturally coupled with the idea of exposure and desertion (Jer. 9:22; Ezek. 16:5; 32:4; 33:27; 39:5).

Fields were marked off by stones, which could be easily removed (Deut. 19:14; 27:17; comp. Job 24:2; Prov. 22:28; 23:10). Being unfenced, fields were liable to damage from straying cattle (Exod. 22:5), hence the necessity of constantly watching flocks and herds. From the absence of inclosures cultivated land of any size might be termed a *field*, whether of limited area (Gen. 23:13, 17; Isa. 5:8), one's entire inheritance (Lev. 27:16, sq.; Ruth 4:5; Jer. 32:9), public land about a town, *ager publicus* (Gen. 41:48; Neh. 12:29), not applied, however, to the "suburbs" of Levitical cities immediately adjacent to the walls and considered as part of the town (Josh. 21:11, 12), and lastly the territory of a people (Gen. 14:7; Num. 21:20, A. V. "country," etc.).

Fields were occasionally called after remarkable events, as "Helkath-hazzurim," *the field of strong men* (II Sam. 2:16), or the use to which it may have been put, as "the fuller's

field" (II Kings 18:17), "potter's field" (Matt. 27:7).

The expression "fruitful field" (Isa. 10:18; 29:17; 32:15, 16), and "plentiful field" (16: 10, etc.) are not connected with *sädĕh*, but with *kărmĕl*, (a *park*, or well-kept wood), as distinct from a wilderness or forest (II Kings 19:23; Isa. 37:24, A. V. "Carmel," etc.).

Fifties. *See* Israel, Classification of.

Fig. *See* Vegetable Kingdom.

Fig Leaves. *See* Dress.

Fight. *See* Warfare.

Fillet, an erroneous rendering in the A. V. of *hăshŭqîm* (*joinings*, Exod. 38:17, 28; 27:17), the rods which joined together the tops of the pillars round the court of the Tabernacle (*q. v.*) and from which the curtain was suspended (Exod. 27:10, 11, etc.); *hut*, thread (as elsewhere rendered), i. e., a *measuring line* (Jer. 52:21).

Filth, Filthy, the rendering of several Hebrew and Greek words and meaning "foul matter," "anything that soils or defiles." In II Chron. 29:5 and Ezra 6:21 the filth from which the Jews were to cleanse the temple and themselves was the abomination of idolatry. Filth is used as the equivalent of *moral impurity* (Ezek. 36:25; II Cor. 7:1; James 1:21, etc.). In I Cor. 4:13 it is used to denote *outsweepings*, that which is worthless. The expression "that the filthiness of it may be molten in it" (Ezek. 24:11) seems to mean that the pot was to be placed empty upon the fire that the rust may be burned away by the heat. The *filthiness* of the pot was the rust upon it.

Fine, Fines. *See* Punishments.

Finering. *See* Metal, Workers in, art. "Handicrafts."

Finger. Besides its usual meaning it is used:

Figuratively, to denote the special and immediate agency of anyone. The Egyptian magicians said of the plagues, "This is the finger of God," i. e., done by God himself (Exod. 8:19). The tables of stone were said to have been "written with the finger of God" (Exod. 31:18) under his personal direction. The heavens are said to be the work of God's fingers, i. e., his power (Psa. 8:3); and Christ said, "If I by the finger of God cast out devils" (Luke 11:20).

"The putting forth of the finger" (Isa. 58:9) signifies a scornful pointing with the fingers at humbler men, and especially at such as are godly. "Four fingers" is the measure of thickness used by Jeremiah (52:21).

Fining Pot. *See* Metals, Workers in, art. "Handicrafts."

Finisher (Gr. *teleiōtēs, completer*), spoken of Jesus (Heb. 12:2) as one who in his own person raised faith to its perfection and so set before us the highest example of faith.

Fins were a distinctive mark of such fish as might be eaten under the Mosaic law (Lev. 11:9, 10, 12; Deut. 14:9, 10). *See* Food.

Fir. *See* Vegetable Kingdom.

Fire. The invention of fire antedates history and seems to be assumed in the first sacrifice of Cain and Abel (Gen. 4:3). No nation has yet been discovered which did not know the use of fire; but the way in which it was first procured is unknown. Entering so largely into the life of men it has naturally been the subject of many legends. The ancient Chaldeans looked upon Gibir (or Gibil), the lord of fire, as their most powerful auxiliary against the Annunaki, an order of inferior but malignant beings. Gibir is addressed as the one who lightens up the darkness, who melts the copper and tin, the gold and silver. According to Greek mythology Prometheus, when Zeus denied fire to mortals, stole it from Olympus and brought it to men in a hollow reed. For this he was punished by being chained on a rock in the wilds of Scythia.

The various uses of fire are given in the following sections:

1. **Domestic.** The preparation of food presupposes the use of fire, which the Israelites seem, at least in later times, to have produced by striking steel against flint (II Macc. 10:3), although the oldest method known was that of rubbing two pieces of wood together. Besides for cooking purposes fire is often needed in Palestine for warmth (Jer. 36:22; Mark 14:54; John 18:18). Sometimes a hearth, with chimney, was constructed, on which lighted wood, or pans of charcoal, was placed. In Persia a hole made in the floor is sometimes filled with charcoal, on which a sort of table is set covered with a carpet, the company drawing the carpet over their feet. Rooms are warmed in Egypt with pans of charcoal. The use of charcoal in reducing and fashioning metals was well known among the Hebrews. *See* Metals, Workers in, art. "Handicrafts."

2. **Laws Regulating Fire.** The law forbade any fire to be kindled on the Sabbath, even for culinary purposes (Exod. 35:3; Num. 15:32, sq.). This did not, probably, forbid the use of fire for warmth. The dryness of the land in the hot season made fires the more likely to occur (Judg. 9:15), and the law ordered that anyone kindling a fire which caused damage to grain should make restitution (Exod. 22:6; comp. Judg. 15:4, 5; II Sam. 14:30).

3. **Religious.** Fire was used to consume the burnt offerings and the incense offering, beginning with the sacrifice of Noah (Gen. 8:20) and continued in the ever-burning fire on the altar. "In the sacrificial flame the essence of the animal was resolved into vapor; so that when a man presented a sacrifice in his own stead, his inmost being, his spirit, and his heart ascended to God in the vapor, and the sacrifice brought the feeling of his heart before God" (K. and D., *Com.*). This altar-fire was miraculously sent from God (Lev. 6:9, 13; 9:24), like the fire of Jehovah which consumed the sacrifices of David and Solomon (I Chron. 21:26; II Chron. 7:1). Keil and Delitzsch (*Com.*, Lev. 9:24) say: "The miracle recorded in this verse did not consist in the fact that the sacrificial offerings placed upon the altar were burned by fire which proceeded from Jehovah, but in the fact that the sacrifices, which were already on fire, were suddenly consumed by it." Fire was to be constantly burning upon the altar without going out, in order "that the burnt offering might never go out, because this was the divinely appointed symbol and visible sign of the uninterrupted worship of Jehovah, which

the covenant nation could never suspend either day or night without being unfaithful to its calling" (K. and D., *Com.*, Lev. 6:12). If by any calamity the sacred fire was extinguished, according to the Talmud, it was only to be rekindled by friction. Fire for sacred purposes obtained elsewhere than from the altar was called "*strange fire*," for the use of which Nadab and Abihu were punished with death by fire from God (Lev. 10:1, 2; Num. 3:4; 26:61). When the Israelites returned with booty taken from the Midianites, Eleazer, whose duty it was to see that the laws of purification were properly observed, told them that "the ordinance of the law" was that all articles which could bear it were to be drawn through the fire, and then sprinkled with the water of purification (Num. 31:21-23). The victims slain for sin offerings were afterward consumed by fire without the camp (Lev. 4:12, 21; 6:30; 16:27; Heb. 13:11). The Nazarite, on the day when the time of his consecration expired, shaved his head and put the hair into the altar fire, under the peace offering that was burning, and thus handed over and sacrificed to the Lord the hair which had been worn in honor of him (Num. 6:18).

4. **Penal.** Capital punishment was sometimes aggravated by burning the body of the criminal after death (Lev. 20:14; 21:9; Josh. 7:25; II Kings 23:16). *See* Punishments, Warfare.

5. **Figurative.** Fire was a symbol of the Lord's presence and the instrument of his power, either in the way of approval or of destruction (Exod. 14:19, 24; Num. 11:1, 3, etc.). Thus Jehovah appeared in the burning bush and on Mount Sinai (Exod. 3:2; 19:18). In the midst of fire he showed himself to Isaiah, Ezekiel, and John (Isa. 6:4; Ezek. 1:4; Rev. 1:14), and will so appear at his second coming (II Thess. 1:8). Jehovah guided the Israelites through the wilderness with the pillar of fire (Exod. 13:21). God is compared to fire, not only because of his glorious brightness, but on account of his anger against sin, which consumes sinners as fire does stubble (Deut. 32:22; Isa. 10:17; Ezek. 21:31; Heb. 12:29). Fire is illustrative of: The Church overcoming her enemies (Obad. 18); the word of God (Jer. 5:14; 23:29); The Holy Spirit (Isa. 4:4; Acts 2:3); the zeal of saints (Psa. 39:3; 119:139), and of angels (Psa. 104:4; Heb. 1:7); of lust (Prov. 6:27, 28), and of wickedness (Isa. 9:18); of the tongue (Prov. 16:27; James 3:6); the hope of hypocrites (Isa. 50:11; persecution (Luke 12:49-53), and of judgments (Jer. 48:45; Lam. 1:13; Ezek. 39:6). Fire, in its symbolical use, is also spoken of as purifying—the emblem of a healing process effected upon the spiritual natures of persons in covenant with God (Isa. 4:4; Mal. 3:2).

Fire Baptism. *See* Moloch, Worship of; Baptism.

Fire, Strange. *See* Fire, III.

Fire Worship, or *pyrolatry.* As a symbol of purity, or of the divine presence and power, or as one of the constituent elements, or as typifying the destructive element in nature, fire has been from early times the object o worship by many peoples, e. g., the ancient

Persians and Medes. The faith of the Magi made the elements of nature the direct objects of worship. These were fire, water, earth, and air, of which the first was considered the most energetic and sublime. So the priest built an altar, and the sacred fire caught from heaven was kindled and kept burning always. The priest was the Holy Magus. No other might attend the altars or conduct the mystic rites. No breath of mortal might be blown upon the sacred flame without pollution; the burning of dead bodies was a horrid profanation, and of the sacrificial offerings only a fragment of fat was given to the flame. This worship among the Canaanites is frequently referred to in the Scriptures, and the people warned against joining in its abominations (Lev. 18:21; Deut. 12:31; I Kings 11:7; II Chron. 28:3; Ezek. 16:20, 21, etc.). In spite, however, of these warnings, the people caused their children to pass through the fire to Molech. *See* Gods, False.

Fire worship was practiced also among the Carthaginians, Scythians, the ancient Germans, the ancient inhabitants of Great Britain; and traces of it are found in Mexican and Peruvian worship. The Mexican god of fire, *Xiuhtecutli* (the Lord of Fire), was a very ancient deity. He is represented naked, with his chin blackened, with a headdress of green feathers, carrying on his back a kind of serpent, with yellow feathers, thus combining the fire colors. . . . Sacrifices was offered to him daily. In every house the first libation and the first morsel of bread were consecrated to him. And as an instance of the astounding resemblance between the religious development of the Old World and that of the New, the fire in Mexico, as in ancient Iran and other countries of Asia and Europe, in every house must be extinguished on a certain day in every year; and the priest of *Xiuhtecutli* kindled fire anew by friction before the statue of the god. . . . "At set of sun" of this day "all who had prisoners of war or slaves to offer to the deity brought forward their victims, painted with the colors of the god, danced along by their side, and shut them up in a building attached to the teocalli of fire. At midnight each owner severed a lock of the hair of his slave or slaves, to be carefully preserved as a talisman. At daybreak they brought out the victims, the priests took them upon their shoulders, and flung their human burden upon the fire" (Reville, *Religions of Mexico and Peru*, p. 62, sq., 83). Among the Peruvians "Fire, considered as derived from the sun, was the object of profound veneration. Strange as it may seem at first sight, the symbol of fire was stones. But . . . stones were thought to be animated by the fire that was supposed to be shut up within them, since it could be made to issue forth by a sharp blow. A perpetual fire burned in the Temple of the Sun and in the abode of the Virgins of the Sun. It was supposed that fire became polluted and lost its divine nature by too long contact with men. The fire must be renewed from time to time, and this act was performed yearly by the chief priest of Peru, who kindled wood by means of a concave golden mirror" (ibid., p. 162, 163).

Firebrand. 1. A torch. The firebrand used by Samson (Judg. 15:4), was probably a torch made of resinous wood or other material tenacious of flame. His tying the foxes tail to tail was to prevent them from running to their holes, and by impeding their progress to more effectual execution. Similar conflagrations produced by animals, particularly by foxes, were well known to Greeks and Romans.

2. Arrows fitted with combustibles (Prov. 26:18; comp. Eph. 6:16).

3. The fag ends of wooden pokers (literally, fire stirrers), which would not blaze any more, but only continue smoking (Isa. 7:4; Amos 4:11).

Firepan.

1. Snuff dishes, i. e., dishes to receive the snuff when taken from the lamps of the holy place (Exod. 25:38).

2. An ashpan or vessel used for taking away the coal from the fire on the altar (Exod. 27:3; Lev. 16:12, etc.).

Fires (Heb. *'ûr*). In Isa. 24:15 we read, "Glorify ye the Lord in the fires," but which is better rendered in the R. V. "East." The lands of the Asiatic East were called *'ûrîm*, the lands of light, i. e., the sun-rising, as opposed to the West, i. e., "from the sea" (v. 14).

Firkin. *See* Metrology, II.

Firmament (Heb. *räqîă'*, *expanse*, Gen. 1:6, 14, 15, 17), the pure and transparent expanse of ether which envelops the globe. This was made by God on the second day of creation, for the purpose of separating the sea from the clouds. As used in the record of creation, firmament, includes not merely the lower heavens, or atmospheric sky, with its clouds and vapors, but the whole visible expanse up to the region of the fixed stars. For it is said that on the fourth day God made in the firmament sun, moon, and stars. A controversy has arisen respecting the sense attached by the Hebrew writers to "firmament," chiefly on account of the ancient translations given of it, and the poetical representations found of the upper regions of the visible heavens in some parts of Scripture. The Septuagint renders *stereōma*, meaning generally "some compact mass," while the Vulgate has *firmamentum*, a *prop* or *support*. Hence it has been argued that the Hebrews understood by the word something solid, capable of bearing up the waters which accumulate in masses above, and even of having the heavenly bodies affixed to it as a crystalline pavement. As proof of this view such passages are quoted as speak of the foundations of heaven shaking (II Sam. 22:8), of its pillars trembling (Job 26:11), of the windows or doors of heaven (Gen. 7:11; Psa. 78:23; Mal. 3:10), or of the sky being "strong as a molten looking-glass" (Job 37:18). But these expressions are manifestly of a figurative nature.

First-Begotten. *See* Firstborn.

Firstborn (Heb. several words from *bäkăr*, to *burst forth*; Gr. *prōtotokos*), applied equally to animals and human beings. By the firstborn, in a religious point of view, we are to understand the first of a mother's offspring (Exod. 12:12). *See* Inheritance.

Figurative. The expression "firstborn" stands for that which is most excellent. Thus Jesus Christ is "the firstborn of every creature" (Heb. 12:23). "The firstborn of the poor" (Isa. 14:30) means the *poorest of the poor.* "The firstborn of death" (Job 18:13) is that disease which Bildad has in his mind as the one more terrible and dangerous than all others. Diseases are conceived of as the children of death.

Firstborn, Destruction of. *See* Plagues of Egypt.

Firstborn in Israel. In memory of the death of Egypt's firstborn and the preservation of the firstborn of Israel, all the firstborn of Israel, both of man and beast, belonged to Jehovah (Exod. 13:2, 15; comp. 12:11-15).

1. **Sanctification of the Firstborn of Man.** This was closely connected with Israel's deliverance from Egypt, and the object of that deliverance was their sanctification. Because Jehovah had delivered the firstborn of Israel they were to be sanctified to him. The fundamental element upon which this sanctification rests is evidently the representative character of the firstborn, standing for the entire offspring. Moreover, the firstborn of newly married people were believed to represent the prime of human vigor (Gen. 49:3; Psa. 78:51). Then, too, all Israel were in outward standing and covenant relationship the Lord's firstborn, being the national representatives of a redeemed Church, to be brought out of every kindred, tongue, and people, and as such they were a nation of priests (Exod. 4:22, 23; 19:6).

2. **Redemption.** The firstborn was the priest of the whole family. The honor of exercising the priesthood was transferred, by the command of God through Moses, from the tribe of Reuben, to whom it belonged by right of primogeniture, to that of Levi (Num. 3:12-18; 8:18). In consequence of this fact, that God had taken the Levites to serve him as priests, the firstborn of the other tribes were redeemed. They were presented to the Lord when a month old, and, according to the priest's estimation, were redeemed by a sum not exceeding five shekels (Num. 18:16). When the Levites were set apart Moses numbered the firstborn of Israel, to exchange them for the Levites. The number of the firstborn of the twelve tribes amounted to 22,273 of a month old and upward. Of this number 22,000 were exchanged for the 22,000 Levites. This left 273 to be redeemed, whose redemption money (1,365 shekels) was to be paid to Aaron and his sons as compensation for the persons who properly belonged to Jehovah (Num. 3:40, sq.). The Jewish doctors held that if the child died before the expiration of thirty days the father was excused from payment; if the child was sickly, or appeared otherwise to be inferior to children generally, the priest could estimate it at less than five shekels; or, if he found the parents were poor, he might return the money after the ceremony. When the mother's days of purification were accomplished, and she could appear in the temple, she brought the child to the priest to be publicly presented to the Lord (Luke 2:22). The Jews still observe this law of redemption when the firstborn male is thirty days old, inviting to their house friends and a priest to a meal on the following day. The priest, having invoked the divine blessing

upon the meal and offered some introductory prayers, etc., looks at the child and the redemption money placed before him, and asks the father to choose between the money and the child. Upon the father's reply that he would rather pay the redemption money, the priest takes it, swings it round the head of the child, in token of his vicarious authority, saying, "This is for the firstborn; this is in lieu of it; this redeems it," etc. When the firstborn is thirteen years old he fasts the day before the feast of Passover, in commemoration of the sparing of the firstborn in Egypt.

3. **Redemption of the Firstborn of Animals.** (1) **Of clean animals.** The firstborn male of animals was devoted to the Lord, and, if a clean animal, was sacrificed to him. It was to be brought to the sanctuary within a year, dating from the eighth day after birth, and there offered in sacrifice; the blood sprinkled upon the altar, the fat burned upon it, while all the remaining flesh (as the breast and the right shoulder, in the case of peace offerings) belonged to the priest (Num. 18:17, sq.; comp. Exod. 13:13; 22:30; 34:20; Neh. 10:36). If the animal had some severe blemish—happened to be blind or lame—it was eaten at home by the owner. Before the sacrifice the animal was not to be used for any work, as it belonged to the Lord (Deut. 15:19). (2) **Of unclean animals.** The firstborn of unclean animals were to be redeemed according to the valuation of the priest, with the addition of a fifth; and if this was not done it was to be sold at the estimated value. By this regulation the earlier law, which commanded that an ass should either be redeemed with a sheep or put to death (Exod. 13:13; 34:20), was modified in favor of the revenues of the sanctuary and its servants. Nothing, however, that a man had devoted (banned) to the Lord of his property (man, beast, or field) was to be sold or redeemed, because it was most holy (Lev. 27:28, 29). The same is true with regard to the produce of the soil—i. e., the products of agriculture—the first of which (i. e., the best of the *firstlings* of which) were sacred to the Lord (Exod. 23:19; Deut. 18:4). *See* First Fruit.

4. **Birthright** (Heb. *bᵉkōrāh*), the term applied to the peculiar advantages, privileges, and responsibilities of the firstborn among the Israelites. The firstborn was the object of special affection to his parents and inherited peculiar rights and privileges. Before these are given it will be proper to call attention to the fact that, in case a man married a widow with children by a former husband, the firstborn, as respected the second husband, was the eldest child by the second marriage. Attention is also called to the additional fact that, before the time of Moses, the father might transfer the right of primogeniture to a younger child; but the practice occasioned much contention (Gen. 25:31, 32), and a law was enacted overruling it (Deut. 21:15-17). The rights and privileges of the firstborn were: *1.* The *firstborn* received a double portion of the estate, the other sons single and equal portions. Thus, for example, if there were five sons the property would be divided into six portions, of which the eldest son received two sixths, each

of the others one sixth. Where there were two wives, one loved, the other hated, the father is not to prefer the later-born son of the favorite wife to the older firstborn of the hated one, but is to give the right of primogeniture (with two portions of the estate) to the beginning of his strength (Deut. 21:15-17). Jacob took away the right of primogeniture from Reuben because of his incestuous conduct (Gen. 49:4; comp. 35:22), and transferred it to Joseph by adopting his two sons (Gen. 48:20-22; I Chron. 5:1). 2. The *firstborn* was the head of the whole family. Originally the priesthood belonged to the tribe of Reuben, as the firstborn, but was transferred to the tribe of Levi (Num. 3:12-18; 8:18). The firstborn enjoyed an authority over those who were younger similar to that possessed by a father (Gen. 35:23, sq.; II Chron. 21:3). As head of the family he had also, according to patriarchal custom, to provide food, clothing, and other necessaries in his house for his mother till death, and his unmarried sisters till their marriage.

First Day of the Week. *See* Lord's Day, Sunday.

First Fruit (Heb. *rē'shîth, first; bǐkkūr, first ripe;* Gr. *'aparchē, beginning*). Like the firstborn of man and beast, the first fruits were sacred to Jehovah, as Lord of the soil (Exod. 23:19; Deut. 18:4, etc.).

1. **Character of, etc.** (1) *In general, first fruits* included those in the raw state (as grain and fruit); those prepared for use as food (wine, oil, flour, and dough), including even wool (Exod. 22:29; 23:29; 34:26; Deut. 18:4, etc.). (2) The firstling sheaf at the Passover (*q. v.*) presented by the congregation before the commencement of the grain harvest (Lev. 23:10, 11). Josephus says that the sheaf was of barley, and that, until this ceremony had been performed, no harvest work was to be done (*Ant.*, iii, 10, 5). (3) The firstling loaf at Pentecost (*q. v.*), when the harvest was completed. Two of these loaves, made of the new flour (wheat) and leavened, like the sheaf above mentioned, were waved before the Lord (Lev. 23:15; Exod. 34:22; Num. 28:26).

2. **Offering of First Fruits, etc.** Regarding the *firstling* (*see* Passover and Pentecost, art. "Festivals"), no private offerings of first fruits were allowed before the public oblation of the two loaves (Lev. 23:15, 20). The law nowhere specifies the amount that was to be given in the shape of offerings of this kind, but leaves it to each individual's discretion; only it provided that the choicest portions were always to be offered (Num. 18:12). Neither is it stated in the law what were to be the different products of the soil from which firstlings were to be offered, but that the whole produce of husbandry was meant is implied in the spirit of the law itself. Accordingly, in the time of Hezekiah, firstlings of grain, wine, oil, honey, and of the whole produce of the soil, were offered (II Chron. 31:5). This may further be inferred from the regulation to the effect that, of every tree bearing edible fruit which any Israelite might plant, the fruits of the fourth year, the earliest period at which they could be eaten, were to be sacred to the Lord; and,

consequently, they must have been presented to him as an offering (Lev. 19:23, sq.).

3. **Manner of Offering.** The first fruits were brought in a basket to the sanctuary and presented to the priest, who was to set the basket down before the altar of the Lord. Then the offerer recited the story of Jacob's going to Egypt, and the deliverance of his posterity therefrom, and acknowledged the blessings with which God had visited him (Deut. 26:2-11). It being found almost impracticable for every Israelite to go on this mission to Jerusalem, the following custom arose. The inhabitants of a district prepared a basket with seven kinds of ripe fruit, arranged in the following order: Barley in the bottom, then wheat, olives, dates, pomegranates, figs, and grapes. This basket was watched all night by a company of at least twenty-four persons, who stayed in the open market place, being afraid to go into a house lest the death of an inmate should cause pollution. In the morning the company set out for Jerusalem. An ox (to be the peace offering) went before them with gilded horns and an olive crown upon its head, the people singing, "I was glad when they said unto me, Let us go into the house of the Lord" (Psa. 122:1). On approaching Jerusalem a messenger was sent to announce their arrival, and the first fruits were tastefully arranged. The officiating priest, the Levites, and the treasurers went out to meet them (the number of officials depending upon the size of the party), and accompanied them into the city, singing, as they entered, "Our feet stand within thy gates, O Jerusalem" (Psa. 122:2). The piper, who led the music of the party, continued to play until the procession came to the mount of the temple. Here everyone, even the king, took his own basket upon his shoulders and went forward till they came to the court of the temple, singing, "Praise ye the Lord; praise God in his sanctuary," etc. (Psa. 150). The Levites responded with "I will extol thee, O Lord!" etc. Then the pigeons which were hung about the baskets were taken for burnt offerings. With the baskets still upon their shoulders everyone began the story of Jacob till he came to the words, "A wandering Syrian was my father" (see Deut. 26:3-5), when he let down his basket, holding it by the brim. The priest then put his hands under it and waved it, the offerer continuing to recite the story. When he reached Deut. 26:10, "And now, behold, I have brought the first fruits," etc., he put the basket beside the altar and, having prostrated himself, departed. After passing the night in Jerusalem the pilgrims returned the following day to their homes.

4. **Exemptions.** Exemptions were made in the case of: Those who simply possessed the trees, without owning the land, for they could not say, "The land which thou has *given me.*" Those living beyond the Jordan could not bring first fruits in the proper sense of the libation, not being able to say the words of the service, from "the land that floweth with milk and honey" (Deut. 26:10-15). A proselyte, though bringing the offering, was not to recite the service, being unable to say, "I am come to the country which the Lord sware

unto *our fathers to give us.*" Stewards, servants, slaves, women, sexless persons, and hermaphrodites were not allowed to recite the service, because they could not use the words, "I have brought the first fruits of *the land, which thou, O Lord, hast given me*" (Deut. 26:10), they having originally had no share in the land.

5. **Historical.** After the time of Solomon the corruption of the nation led to neglect of these as well as of other legal enactments, and their restoration was among the reforms brought about by Hezekiah (II Chron. 31:5, 11). Nehemiah also, after the captivity, reorganized the offerings of first fruits of both kinds and appointed places to receive them (Neh. 10: 35, 37; 12:44). An offering of first fruits, brought to Elisha, was miraculously increased so as to feed one hundred persons (II Kings 4:42). First fruits were sent to Jerusalem by Jews living in foreign countries (Josephus, *Ant.*, xvi, 6, 7).

6. **Figurative.** Of the Jewish nation it was said, "Israel was holiness unto the Lord, and the *first fruits* of his increase" (Jer. 2:3). In the New Testament first fruits are emblematical of abundance, excellence, and sample of full harvest. Paul says that Christians "have the first fruits of the Spirit" (Rom. 8:23), i. e., the first manifestations of the Spirit in the Gospel dispensation. Christ was "the first fruits of them that slept," i. e., the first who rose from the dead (I Cor. 15:20, 23; 16:15; Rom. 11: 16, etc.). Converts are called first-fruits, as Epenetus (Rom. 16:5).

Fish. *See* Animal Kingdom.

    Figurative. This term is used to signify the inhabitants of Egypt (Ezek. 29:4, 5); the visible Church (Matt. 13:48); defenseless people taken by the Chaldeans (Hab. 1:14). In Christian symbolism the fish is of great significance. "It is among the earliest art forms, and pertains to a period of Church history which causes it to be among the most interesting and important objects in the whole range of Christian symbolism. It is generally thought to be the symbol of Christ. The word in Greek was made up of the initial letters of the words in the article of faith so dear to the early Church: I, Ιησοῦς, Jesus; X, Χριστός, Christ; Θ, Θεοὐ, of God; Υ, Υἱός, Son; Σ, Σωτήρ, Saviour—Jesus Christ, Son of God, Saviour. The fish is also used to represent Christ's disciples. Probably, as suggested by Tertullian, the water and the rite of baptism were prominently in their thought, while secondary reference may have been had to the parable of the net or to the command of Christ to Peter and Andrew, 'Follow me, and I will make you fishers of men' " (Matt. 4:18, 19).

Fish Gate (Heb. *shā‘ăr hǎddǎgîm, gate of the fishes*), the name (II Chron. 33:14; Neh. 3:3; 12:39) of one of the gates of *Jerusalem* (*q. v.*). It probably took its name from the fact of fish being brought through it on the way to the city, or from the fish market being located near it.

Fish Pool, in general a pond or reservoir; thought by our translators at Cant. 7:4 to be intended for fish (*q. v.*), such as were anciently constructed for pleasure angling.

Fisher. In addition to the usual meaning, the

Lord called his disciples "fishers of men" (Matt. 4:19; Mark 1:17). *See* Fishing.

Fishhook.

1. The prophet Amos (4:2), in denouncing the voluptuous grandees of Samaria, predicts as follows: "God will take you away with hooks, and your posterity with fishhooks." The reference is undoubtedly to the practice of Egyptians, Assyrians and other ancient conquerors of putting fishhooks in the lips of captives (see II Chron. 33:11, R. V. margin).

2. A ring placed in the mouth of fish and attached to a cord to keep them alive in the water (Job 41:1, 2). *See* Fishing.

161. Fishing (Egyptian Inscription)

Fishing has always been an industry pursued by a large number of people in Palestine. The natives are exceedingly fond of fish, and pay double to triple the price for it that they do for meat. The methods of taking fish mentioned in the Bible are: 1. *Angling* with a hook (Isa. 19:8; Hab. 1:15; Job 41:1; Amos 4:2). 2. *Spearing* (Job 41:7). In this passage the reference is to the crocodile, but he is included under the generic idea of fish as conceived by the Hebrew mind, i. e., a creature living more or less in the water. 3. *Netting*. They used the cast net (Ezek. 26:5, 14; 32:3; 47:10; Hab. 1:15, 17; Mic. 7:2; Eccles. 7:26; Matt. 4: 18, sq.; Mark 1:16, etc.). This consists of a net with fine meshes and of a circular form, about fifteen feet in diameter. The margin is loaded with leaden sinkers. To the center of the net is attached a long piece of fish line. This is held in the left hand, while the net, which has been previously gathered up in the right, is cast by a broad sweep of the arm over an area of the shallow water close to the shore, where the fisherman has previously observed a shoal of fish. The center of the net is now drawn up by means of the cord, and the fisherman wades into the water and secures the catch. The *seine* is also very much used. Half of it is loaded into one boat and the other half in another, and the boats then separate, paying out the net as they go and inclosing a vast area of the water. When all the net has been paid out the boats draw it toward the shore and land the ends of the net. The two crews now commence to draw in their respective ends of the net, thus inclosing the draught of fishes and gradually landing them (Matt. 13:

48). At other times the two boats inclose a circle in the water and draw the fishes into the boats (Luke 5:4-9). The seine is also mentioned in the Old Testament (Isa. 19:8; Hab. 1:15). The writer has seen a fisherman in Egypt bore a hole through the tails of fishes caught by a hook and string them on a cord, and fasten one end of the cord to a stake in the water to keep them fresh. Four of Christ's twelve disciples were fishermen. Christ promises them that they shall become fishers of men (Mark 1:17, etc.).—G. E. P.

Fitches. *See* Vegetable Kingdom.

Flag. *See* Vegetable Kingdom.

Flag. *See* Standard.

Flagon (Heb. *nēbĕl, a skin,* Isa. 22:24), A bottle or pitcher made either of skin or earthenware (Isa. 30:14). The word sometimes occurs with the force of a musical instrument, generally rendered "psaltery," but sometimes "viol."

Flake, the dewlaps or flabby parts on the belly of the crocodile (Job. 41:23), which are firmly attached to the body and do not hang loosely as on the ox.

Flame. *See* Fire.

Flank, the internal muscles of the loins near the kidneys, to which the fat adheres (Lev. 3:4, 10, 15; 7:4); hence the viscera in general, figuratively for the inmost feelings (Psa. 38:7, "loins"). The expression "he maketh collops of fat on his flanks" (Job 15:27) is used to denote the results of self-pampering.

Flax. *See* Vegetable Kingdom.

Flea. *See* Animal Kingdom.

Fleece (Heb. *gēz, sheared,* Deut. 18:4; Job. 31: 20), the wool of a sheep, whether on the living animal, shorn off, or attached to the flayed skin. The miracle of Gideon's fleece (Judg. 6:37, 39, 40) consists of the dew having fallen one time upon the fleece, without any on the floor, and that at another time the fleece remained dry while the ground was wet with dew.

Flesh. This word has various meanings, as follows: 1. In a general sense of the whole animal creation, man or beast (Gen. 6:13, 17, 19; 7:15, 16, 21; 8:17; Matt. 24:22; I Pet. 1:24). 2. Of the flesh of the living body, both of men and beasts (Gen. 41:2, 19; Job 33:21; I Cor. 15:39); and as distinguished from other parts of the body, e. g., from bones (Luke 24:39). 3. In the sense of our word *meat,* i. e., the flesh of cattle used for food (Exod. 16:12; Lev. 7:19; Num. 11:4, 13); *see* Food. 4. The body as distinguished from the *spirit* (Job. 14:22; 19:26; Prov. 14:30; Isa. 10:18, margin; John 6:52; I Cor. 5:5; II Cor. 4:11; 7:1; Col. 2:5; I Pet. 4:6); so also "flesh and blood" as a periphrasis for the whole animal nature or man (Heb. 2:14). 5. Human nature, man (Gen. 2:23; Matt. 19:5, 6; I Cor. 6:16; Eph. 5:25-31); also of the incarnation of Christ (John 1:14; 6:51; Rom. 1:3; Eph. 2:15; Col. 1:22; Heb. 5:7; 10:20, etc.). 6. Natural or physical origin, generation, relationship (Gen. 29:14; 37:27; Judg. 9:2; II Sam. 5:1; 19:13; John 1:13; Rom. 9:8; Heb. 2:11-14; 12:9); of one's countryman (Rom. 9:3; 11:14; Acts 2:30; Gal. 4:23); a fellow-mortal (Isa. 58:7). 7. The sensuous nature of man, "the animal nature," without any suggestion of depravity, sexual desire (John 1:13); with cravings which excite to sin (Matt. 26:41; Mark 14:38). 8. Mere human nature, the earthly nature of man apart from divine influence, and therefore prone to sin and opposed to God; accordingly it includes in the soul whatever is weak, low, debased, tending to ungodliness and vice (see Rom. 8:3, 5, 6; II Cor. 7:5; Gal. 5:16; Eph. 2:3). 9. As a modest, general term for the secret parts (Gen. 17:11; Exod. 28:42, margin; Lev. 15:2, 3, 7, 16, 19; II Pet. 2:10; Jude 7). *See* Food.

Flesh and Blood, an expression denoting man as fallible, liable to err (Matt. 16:17; comp. Gal. 1:16; Eph. 6:12).

Flesh Hook, an instrument used in sacrificial services (Exod. 27:3; 38:3; Num. 4:14; I Chron. 28:17; II Chron. 4:16); probably a *fork,* with its many tines bent back to draw away the flesh. The implement in I Sam. 2:13, 14, is stated to be three-tined, and was apparently the ordinary fork with prongs for culinary purposes, of course, of large size.

Flesh "Offered to Idols" (I Cor. 8:1, sq.; comp. Acts 15:20). This consisted of those parts of the animals offered in heathen sacrifices which remained over after the priests had received their share, and which were either eaten in the temple, or at home in connection with sacrificial feasts, or else (by poor or miserly persons) sold in the flesh markets. This was a very practical matter, as the Christian might easily come to eat such meat, either through being invited to a feast by heathen acquaintances (10:27), or by buying it in the market (10:25), and thereby offense would be given to scrupulous consciences. On the other hand, those of freer spirit, and with more of Paul's own mode of thinking, might be apt to make light of the matter, and withal forget how a Christian out to spare the weak. *See* Expediency.

Flesh Pot. This was probably a bronze vessel with three legs used for culinary purposes by the Egyptians, such as is represented in the paintings of the tombs (Exod. 16:3).

Flies. *See* Animal Kingdom.

Flint. *See* Mineral Kingdom.

Float. A raft for conveying bulky substances by water. Thus Solomon contracted with Hiram, king of Tyre, to have cedars cut on the western side of Mount Lebanon and floated to Jaffa (I Kings 5:9). Sometimes spelled "flote" (II Chron. 2:16).

Flock. Figurative. In addition to the usual sense of sheep (*see* Animal Kingdom), taken collectively the term is applied both to Israel as a nation in covenant relation to Jehovah as well as to the N. T. Church (Isa. 40:11; Matt. 26:31; Luke 12:32; I Pet. 5:2, 3). "Flock of the slaughter" (Zech. 11:4) is an expression that may be applied either to a flock that is being slaughtered or to one that is destined to be slaughtered in the future. From verse 11 Israel is the flock referred to, and not the human race. "Israel was given up by Jehovah into the hands of the nations or imperial powers to punish it for its sin. But as these nations abused the power intrusted to them and sought utterly to destroy the nation of God, which they ought only to have chastised, the Lord takes charge of his people as their shepherd" (K. and D., *Com.,* in loco).

Flood or **Deluge.** The account of this phenomenal world-engulfing event is recounted in Genesis 6-9. It comprehends the bulk of space given by divine revelation to the events in the early redemptive history of man, eclipsing even the space given to the Creation and the Fall.

1. **The Bible Account.** The historical recital in Genesis pointedly sets forth the wickedness of man as the cause of the flood (6:5-7, 11-13), Noah's building of an ark in which he and his family were to be saved during the coming flood, the entrance of Noah, his family and the animals into the ark and God's deliverance from the catastrophe because of Noah's righteousness. Isa. 54:9 refers to the flood as "the waters of Noah." Jesus puts His sanction upon the historicity of the event (Matt. 24:37, sq.; Luke 17:26). Peter speaks of "the longsuffering of God which waited in the days of Noah while the ark was preparing wherein few, that is eight souls, were saved by water" (I Pet. 3:20) and cites it as an example of God's righteous judgment (II Pet. 2:5).

Table of Events	Genesis
Noah, in his six hundredth year, enters the ark with his family...	7:1-9
The rain begins on seventeenth of second month, and lasts forty days......................	7:10-17
The rain ceases; the waters prevail.	7:18-24
The ark rests on Ararat, seventeenth day of seventh month....	8:1-4
Tops of mountains visible, first day of tenth month..............	8:5
Raven and dove sent out.........	8:6-9
Dove again sent out seven days after, and returns with olive branch......................	8:10, 11
Dove sent out the third time, after seven days, and returns no more.	8:12
Ground becomes dry, six hundred and first year, first month and first day; covering of ark removed....................	8:13
Noah leaves the ark, second month, twenty-seventh day...........	8:14-19

2. **Primitive Tradition of a Flood.** The tradition of the flood was persistent among ancient Oriental peoples. In lower Mesopotamia, the ancestral home of Abraham, the flood was well remembered as a great catastrophe in human history and was preserved through oral tradition and upon cuneiform tablets. The Sumerian King List (See Thorkild Jacobsen, *The Sumerian King List, Assyriological Studies* XI, Chicago, 1939) after recording eight antediluvian kings interrupts the sequence with the following significant statement before proceeding to the postdiluvian rulers: "(Then) the Flood swept over (the earth). After the flood had swept over (the earth) (and) when kingship was lowered (again) from heaven kingship was (first) in Kish." (See A. Leo Oppenheim in *Ancient Near Eastern Texts*, Princeton, 1950, p. 265). In ancient times the Tigris-Euphrates Valley was subject to frequent floods when these great rivers overflowed their banks. Evidence

of a flood at Ur and at Kish has been construed as pointing to the Biblical deluge but, as H. Frankfort has shown, these deposits do not even belong in the same century. According to the Scriptural representations the flood was a world-wide catastrophe.

3. **The Sumerian Account of the Flood.** The oldest version of the flood is the Sumerian record on a cuneiform tablet from ancient Nippur in north central Babylonia dating before the second millennium B. C. The third column on the tablet introduces the flood. The flood hero is named Ziusudra, a king-priest. The next column portrays Ziusudra receiving a communication from the gods. In column five the deluge has broken upon the world and the hero is riding in a huge boat:

"When for seven days and seven nights
The flood had raged over the land
And the huge boat had been tossed on the great waters by the storms,
The sun god arose shedding light in heaven and on earth.
Ziusudra made an opening in the side of the great ship.
Before the sun god he bowed his face to the ground.
The king slaughtered an ox, sheep he sacrificed in great numbers."

(J. Finegan, *Light From the Ancient Past*, Princeton, 1946, p. 27). In the last column Ziusudra is immortalized and conducted to a paradise called "the Mountain of Dilmun."

4. **The Babylonian Account of the Flood.** This constitutes the eleventh book of the Assyro-Babylonian epic of Gilgamesh. These tablets were unearthed at ancient Nineveh in 1853 by H. Rassam. Not until 1872 were they deciphered and recognized as a startling extra-Biblical account of the flood. The flood account as contained in the Gilgamesh epic offers the most striking and detailed similarity to Gen. 6-8. Ziusudra, the Sumerian Noah, appears as Utnapishtim, "day of life." Gilgamesh, a demi-god and king of Uruk, Biblical Erech (Gen. 10:10), in search of the secret of immortality finds the immortalized flood hero Utnapishtim. In explaining the secret of his immortality, he recounts the cause of it as his passing through the experience of the flood and being given eternal life as a result. In Utnapishtim's account the gods determine to destroy the earth by a deluge. According to divine directions the Babylonian hero constructs an enormous boat in the form of a cube, pitching it within and without with bitumen, and taking aboard gold, silver, his family, craftsmen, beasts of the field and a boatman. The fierce storm is pictured as "gathering with the first glow of dawn." Adad, the god of tempest and rain, roared. The Annunaki gods lifted up their torches, emblazoning the land with lightning flashes:

"The gods were frightened by the deluge,
And shrinking back they ascended to the heavens of Anu.
The gods crouched like dogs."

(11, lines 113-115)

At the terrible decimation of human life the gods weep. Six days and six nights the storm raged. On the seventh day the flood ceased.

The Babylonian hero looks out from the boat and surveys the catastrophic scene:

"I looked at the weather: stillness had set in,
And all mankind had turned to clay.
The landscape was as level as a flat roof.
I opened a hatch, and light fell upon my face.
Bowing low, I sat and wept,
Tears running down on my face.
(lines 132-137)

The poem tells how the ship landed on Mt. Nisir, commonly identified with Pir Omar Gudrun in the mountain country east of ancient Assyria, a peak of about 9,000 feet. As Mt. Nisir held the ship captive, the Babylonian hero sent out birds:

"When the seventh day arrived,
I sent forth and set free a dove
The dove went forth, but came back;
There was no resting place and she turned round.
Then I sent forth and set free a swallow,
The swallow went forth, but came back;
There was no resting place for it and she turned round.
Then I sent forth and set free a raven.
The raven went forth and, seeing that the waters had diminished,
He eats, circles, caws, and turns not round.
Then I let out (all) to the four winds and offered a sacrifice."   (lines 145-155)

When sacrifices were offered to the gods,

"The gods smelled the savor,
The gods smelled the sweet savor,
The gods crowded like flies about the sacrificer."   (lines 156-161)

The account ends with the gods engaged in altercation concerning the responsibility of the flood and with Utnapishtim and his wife being immortalized.

"Hitherto Utnapishtim has been but human.
Henceforth Utnapishtim and his wife shall be like unto us gods.
Utnapishtim shall reside far away, at the mouth of the rivers!"

5. **A Comparison of Biblical and the Babylonian Accounts. The Resemblances:** (1) Both accounts represent the flood as definitely planned, by the one true God in Genesis; by numerous quarreling deities in the Babylonian version who childishly disclaim responsibility when they see the terriffic havoc wrought. (2) In each case the judgment is revealed to the flood hero. (3) Both accounts set forth defection in the human race as the cause. In the Genesis account it is the outrageous sin of the antediluvians with no blurred moral element. In the Babylonian account the moral element is completely blurred as a consequence of a complete lack of sin or sins or distinction between the righteous and unrighteous. (4) In each case the hero is delivered with his family and with animals, although the number surviving in the Babylonian account is larger than the Biblical account. (5) A huge boat appears in both cases, the Babylonian vessel having a displacement about five times that of Noah's ark. Both are pitched to make them water tight. (6) Both stories indicate physical causes of the catastrophe. Violent wind, rain and electrical storm constitute the causes in the pagan account. In the Genesis account nothing short of a globe-encircling catastrophe is indicated. "All the fountains of the great deep were broken up and the windows of heaven were opened (Gen. 7:11). This can only mean lowering the mountainous regions and raising of ocean beds in violent shiftings of the earth's crust. "The openings of the windows of heaven" seems to indicate the complete atmospheric change, signified by the rainbow (Gen. 9:3). Previous to the flood atmospheric rain did not occur (Cf. Gen. 2:5, 6). The huge sources of water seemingly came from large subterranean springs and from the condensation of a huge vapory mist that covered the earth unstead of clouds. II Pet. 3:7 disputes any contention that the Bible presents the flood as merely local, no matter what geological or astronomical or other difficulties such a representation may offer. (7) The account of the duration of the flood is given in both stories—a total of 371 days in the Biblical account; only six days in the Babylonian account. Both give similar striking details which are almost sensational. The sending out of the birds and the landing of the ship on a mountain are examples. The Bible account specifies "the Mountains of Ararat" (Gen. 8:4). The name is identical with the Assyrian name Urartu, denoting the general mountainous territory of Armenia, north of Assyria (Cf. II Kings 19:37; Jer. 51:27; Isa. 37:38). The landing of the Babylonian boat was on Mt. Nisir, west of Assyria. The Biblical account of sending out of birds with a raven sent out first and a dove released on three occasions is much more reasonable than the sending out of a dove first, a swallow second and finally a raven. The raven normally would be sent out first since it is a carrion-loving bird and can withstand inclement weather. (8) In both cases the hero worships after his deliverance. Utnapishtim offered sacrifice and poured out a libation, burning "sweet cane, cedar and myrtle." Noah similarly offered burnt offerings. In both cases the deity "smelled" the soothing fragrance (Gen. 8:21). (9) Both heroes are recipients of special blessings after the catastrophe. Divinity and immortality are granted Utnapishtim and his wife. Noah is blessed with the power of multiplying and replenishing the earth, to exercise dominion over the animals, originally given at creation, and he is given reassurance that there would not be another flood of such proportions.

6. **The Differences.** (1) Despite the startling similarity between the Biblical and Babylonian accounts of the flood, the underlying differences are much more significant and fundamental. The two accounts are completely different in their theological concepts. The chaste monotheism of Genesis elevates every aspect of the flood story. In contrast the crass polytheism of the cuneiform accounts vitiates the Babylonian story at every turn. Whereas the Genesis account attributes the flood to the one infinitely powerful and holy God, the Babylonian tradition comprehends a crowd of quarreling, disagreeing, self-accusing deities who either crouch in fear "like dogs" or "swarm like flies" around the

sacrifice offered by the flood hero. (2) The two accounts are poles apart in their moral concepts. The ethical element in the cuneiform story is completely blurred with hazy views of sin. The cause of the flood is entirely confused, and the justice of it compromised. The whole episode is more the result of the caprice of the gods than a necessary punishment for sin. As a result, the ethical and didactic value of these stories is greatly depreciated. In contrast the solid morality of the Biblical account gives the Genesis story the highest didactic and spiritual value. (3) The two accounts differ in their philosophic conconcepts. The Babylonian account hopelessly confuses spirit and matter and makes both eternal. The causation is attributed to a multitude of deities. Thunder is Adad, the god of storm and rain, in action. It is Ninurta, the god of winds and irrigation, that causes the dikes to give way. Lightning is the activity of the Annunaki, judges of the underworld, who "raise their torches," illuminating the land. The picture of the one supreme God as Creator and Sustainer of all, Who controls all the phenomena of His creation, is in striking contrast.

7. **Explanation of the Similarities.** The most widely accepted explanation is that the Hebrew borrowed from the Babylonian account. To the conservative student, this is incredible. The superlative loftiness of the monotheistic account in the light of the utter crudity of the Babylonian tradition renders this view not only extremely unlikely but practically impossible, especially as the theory cannot be proved. It is also extremely unlikely that the Babylonians borrowed from the Hebrew, inasmuch as the earliest known tablets are considerably older than the book of Genesis, upon any consideration of the date of the latter. It is possible, however, that the Hebrew account may have been current in some form or other centuries before it assumed its present form. The likely explanation is that both the Hebrew and Babylonian accounts go back to a common source of fact, which originated in an actual occurrence. The flood occurred sometime long before 4000 B. C. The memory of this great event persisted in tradition. The Babylonians received it in a completely corrupted and distorted form. Genesis portrays it as it actually occurred, and as the Spirit of God gave it to meet special needs in the history of redemption. *M. F. U.*

Floor, a level, or open area, as the "place" or square near the gates of oriental cities (I Kings 22:10; II Chron. 18:9, A. V. "void place" in both passages). *See* House, Pavement, Thrashing Floor.

Flotes. *See* Float.

Flour, ground grain for making bread, the support of life in the ancient world. At first barley alone was ground, but afterward wheat, as only the poor used barley. As to the method of making flour, both mortars and mills were employed. *See* Bread; Mills. Fine flour was presented in connection with sacrifices in general, and by the poor as a sin offering (Lev. 5:11-13).

Flower (Heb. *pĕrăḥ*, a *calyx*), the term applied to the floral ornaments of the golden candle-stick (Exod. 25:31, sq.; 37:17; I Kings 7:26), and also the artificial lily ornaments round the edge of the great laver (I Kings 7:26; II Chron. 4:5).

Flowers. Figurative. Flowers, from their speedy decay, are representative of the shortness of human life (Job 14:2; Psa. 103:15; I Pet. 1:24); the speedy downfall of the kingdom of Israel (Isa. 28:1), and the sudden departure of the rich (James 1:10, 11). *See* Vegetable Kingdom.

Flute. *See* Musical Instruments.

Flux, Bloody. *See* Diseases.

Fly. *See* Animal Kingdom.

Foal, an ass's colt (Gen. 49:11; Zech. 9:9; Matt. 21:5). *See* Animal Kingdom.

Foam (Heb. *qĕṣĕp*, a *splinter*). The original word is rendered "foam" in Hos. 10:7, "As for Samaria, her king is cut off as the *foam* upon the water. It means a broken branch, a fagot, or splinter. Cf. the R. S. V. rendering: "Samaria's king shall perish like a chip on the face of the waters."

Fodder. The original word properly signifies a mixture, and is rendered "corn" in Job 24:6, and "provender" in Isa. 30:24.

Follower (Gr. *mimētēs*, an *imitator*). Paul urges Christians to be "followers of me," etc., meaning that they were to imitate him in all good things (I Cor. 4:16; 11:1, etc.); also to take God as an example (Eph. 5:1). In Phil. 3:17 the "followers" were to be co-imitators.

Folly, *Silliness* (Prov. 5:23, etc.); *emptiness* (Gen. 34:7), and many others. Other terms in the original may be rendered "thickheadedness" (Eccles. 2:3), "senselessness" (II Tim. 3:9), "heedlessness" (II Cor. 11:1), "self-confidence" (Psa. 85:8), "insipidity" (Job 24:12; Jer. 23:13). As a word in common use, *folly* is a weak or absurd act, and *foolishness* is a want of wisdom or judgment.

Food. Represented in the original by several Hebrew and Greek words.

1. **In Early Times.** The articles of food used by men are determined largely by the products of the country which they inhabit, and change with the growth of culture. At first men lived upon roots, vegetables, and the fruit of trees, all of which articles were known by the general name of *food* (Heb. *lĕḥĕm*, Gen. 1:29). It was not till after the Flood that God allowed men the use of the flesh of animals (Gen. 9:3), but it is very probable that the Cainite Jubal, "the father of such as dwell in tents and have cattle" (Gen. 4:20), used not only the milk and wool obtained from the flock, but also ate of the flesh of the cattle. That before the Flood the flesh of animals was converted into food may be inferred from the division of animals into clean and unclean (Gen. 7:8), and after the Flood it is expressly mentioned that animals were slain for food (Gen. 9:3, 4).

2. **In the Patriarchal Age** the flesh of animals, both tame and wild, was eaten. Leguminous food (i. e., beans, peas, etc.) was used, and a preparation of lentils (*q. v.*) seems to have been a common and favorite dish (Gen. 25:34). Use was also made of honey, spices, and nuts (Gen. 43:11). As early as the time of Abraham the art of preparing bread was carried to some degree of perfection.

3. **Among the Egyptians.** Egyptians had a great variety of foods. Egyptian wall paintings reveal much concerning the manner of eating. Genesis 40 reminds us of an occasion when the king elevated his chief butler and baker. The plentiful foods served at a typical palace banquet included fowls, fish of all sorts, barley-beer and elaborate condiments. Huge jars of wine were brought in and guests were given bent glass tubes which they dipped directly into the jars. Both men and women attended feasts. Men guests were clean shaven. They wore white banquet garments. Around their necks were elaborate jewels. Women guests wore long white gowns of transparent fineness with exquisite jewelry. Paintings of the city of Akhetaton, built c. 1387-1366 B. C. show us the king and his wife Nofretete and his three young daughters feasting in their wide banqueting hall. Fragrant garlands hanging from pillars add to the festal scene. Slaves wave ivory handled ostrich fans to cool the heated atmosphere of the Egyptian evening. The banqueting table was gayly bedecked with bright cushioned chairs.

4. **Among the Mesopotamians.** The lower Mesopotamian region offered many species of legumes to choose from. Beans, lentils, peas, fitches, kidney beans, onions, cucumbers, egg plants, pumpkins and wheat and barley were considered indigenous. The date palm and other fruit-trees abounded. A very early Babylonian domestic scene portrays a mother from Ur feeding a bunch of the famous Euphrates dates to her baby on her knee. One of the earliest banquet scenes which exists is recorded on a tiny lapis lazuli cylinder seal in the Museum of the University of Pennsylvania. This interesting art object, executed c. 3000 B. C., depicts a banquet of the now famous Queen Shub-ad. Fleece-skirted domestics dispense goblets of wine to guests seated on small stools. Other palace servants wave fans. A musician stands on one side performing on a harp. (M. S. and J. Lane Miller, *Ency. of Bible Life*, N. Y., 1944, pp. 229-319).

5. **Among the Israelites.** While in Egypt the Israelites shared in the abundance of that land, where they "sat by the fleshpots and did eat bread to the full" (Exod. 16:3); and they recalled in the wilderness with regret and murmuring "the fish, the cucumbers, the melons, the leeks, the onions, and the garlic" (Num. 11:5). The subject of food among the Israelites will be considered as follows: Articles prohibited; articles allowed; food, its preparation; meals, etc.

(1) **Articles prohibited.** Animal food was limited by the Mosaic law: (*a*) By the primeval distinction between clean and unclean, under which distinction were forbidden to be used as food: Quadrupeds which do not ruminate (i. e., chew the cud) or have cloven feet (Lev. 11:4-8; Deut. 14:7, 8). Fishes without scales and fins, e. g., eels and all shell fish (Lev. 11:9-12). Birds of prey and such as feed upon worms and carrion (Lev. 11:13-19). Serpents and creeping insects; insects which sometimes fly and sometimes go upon their feet, with the exception of some of the locust kind (Lev. 11:20-24, 42). (*b*) By the sacrificial ordinances was forbidden the eating of all

blood of cattle and birds and bloody flesh (Lev. 3:17; 7:26; 17:10-14; Deut. 12:16, 23; comp. Gen. 9:4; I Sam. 14:32, sq.). The fatty portions which, in the sacrifice of oxen, sheep, and goats, were burned upon the altar (Lev. 3:17; 7:23, 25); also everything consecrated to idols (Exod. 34:15). (*c*) For sanitary reasons, doubtless, the following was forbidden as food: the flesh of cattle that had fallen down dead or had been torn by wild beasts (Exod. 22:31; Lev. 11:39, sq.; Deut. 14:21), as well as food prepared with water on which the dead body of an unclean insect had fallen (Lev. 11:33, 34). All food and liquids remaining in an uncovered vessel in the tent or chamber of a dying or dead man (Num. 19:14, 15). In addition, it was forbidden to "seethe a kid in his mother's milk" (Exod. 23:19; 34:26; Deut. 14:21). The reason for this, according to light from the Ras Shamra tablets, is that the Canaanites employed such a practice in one of their sacred rituals. Besides these, according to ancient tradition, the Israelites, perhaps from a feeling of reverence, denied themselves the use of the sinew of the hip (Gen. 32:32).

(2) **Articles allowed.** These were partly vegetable and partly animal, with salt for seasoning. Grain formed the chief nourishment, roasted in the fire, especially wheat kernels—still a favorite food in Palestine, Syria, and Egypt. But it was frequently baked into bread. Milk was an article of daily food; not only the milk of cows, but also of sheep and goats (Deut. 32:14; Prov. 27:27); sometimes sweet, sometimes sour, thick, or curdled. The latter still forms, after bread, the chief food of the poorer classes in Arabia and Syria, nor is it wanting on the tables of well-to-do persons. The Israelites, no doubt, prepared *cheese* of different kinds, and very likely *butter* also (Prov. 30:33). "Much liked also were honey of bees; perhaps, also, grape honey (must of sweet grapes boiled to a syrup), and wood honey of wild bees (I Sam. 14:25; Matt. 3:4), in which Palestine was and still is rich; raisins, dried figs (I Sam. 25:18), date cakes (II Sam. 16:1), and various fresh fruits." *Vegetables.*—Of these those chiefly used were pulse, lentils, and beans, with onions, garlic, and cucumbers; also green herbs—sometimes raised in gardens (I Kings 21:2), sometimes growing in the fields (Prov. 15:17). *Animal food.*—The flesh of oxen, sheep, and goats ranks first, while the flesh of calves, lambs, and kids was greatly prized; perhaps, also, that of pigeons and turtle doves. The rich had upon their tables stag, antelope, buck, and various kinds of winged game (I Kings 4:23; Neh. 5:18). *Fish* were supplied in great abundance from the lake of Gennesaret (John 21:11; comp. Matt. 14:17; 15:34), while in after times the Phoenicians brought fish to Jerusalem from the sea (Neh. 13:16). *Locusts* were eaten by the poorer people (Lev. 11:22; Matt. 3:4; Mark 1:6); sometimes salted and roasted (or fried), sometimes boiled in water and buttered.

(3) **Preparation of Food.** Grain was eaten at first without any preparation, and the custom of thus eating it had not entirely disappeared in the time of Christ (Matt. 12:1).

After the uses of fire were known grain was parched. Later the introduction of the mortar and mill furnished flour, which was made into bread (*q. v.*). As to the preparation of vegetables and flesh, we learn that so early as the time of Isaac it was customary to prepare soup of lentils (Gen. 25:29, 34) and flesh (27:14). Vegetables, pulse, and herbs were cooked in pots (II Kings 4:38; Num. 11:8; Judg. 6:19; I Sam. 2:14) and seasoned with oil. Roasting on a spit was perhaps the oldest way of cooking flesh, but less common among the Israelites than boiling, roast flesh being used only by the rich and better classes (I Sam. 2:15), as is still the case in the East. When cooked in pots (I Sam. 2:14; II Chron. 35:13), it was lifted out with a three-pronged fork and brought to the table with the broth (Judg. 6:19). All the flesh of the slain animal, owing to the difficulty of keeping it in warm climates, was commonly cooked at once. The Israelites seem to have boiled the flesh of young animals in milk. Locusts were frequently roasted, as they still are in the East. "Their wings and feet are taken off and their intestines extracted; they are salted, fixed upon a sharp piece of wood, placed over the fire, and at length eaten. They are likewise prepared by boiling them. Sometimes they are salted and preserved in bottles and, as occasion requires, are cut in pieces and eaten" (Lev. 11:22; Matt. 3:4). Salt (*q. v.*) was very anciently used (Num. 18:19; comp. II Chron. 13:5). In most ancient times the animal was slain by the master of the house, although he were a prince, and the cooking also was done by his wife (Gen. 18:2-6; Judg. 6:19), with the help of female slaves. In the houses of the upper classes there were also special cooks (II Sam. 9:23, sq.), and in the larger cities bakers (Hos. 7:4).

(4) **Meals, etc.** Besides a simple breakfast the Israelites had two daily meals; at midday (Gen. 18:1; 43:16, 25; Ruth 2:14; I Kings 20:16), and their principal meal at about six or seven in the evening (Gen. 19:1, sq.; Ruth 3:7). They were accustomed to wash their hands both before and after eating (Matt. 15:2; Mark 7:2; Luke 11:38), because food was lifted to the mouth with the fingers (*see* Washing). Prayers were also offered (I Sam. 9:13). In the older times it was the custom to sit at the table (Gen. 27:19; Judg. 19:6; I Sam. 20:5, 24; I Kings 13:19), but later it was usual to recline upon cushions or divans. The food was taken to the mouth with the right hand, a custom still prevalent in the East (Ruth 2:14; Prov. 26:15; John 13:26). *See* Banquet; Drink.

Fool. Represented by a large number of Hebrew and Greek words. The word is used in Scripture with respect to *moral* more than to intellectual deficiencies. The "fool" is not so much one lacking in mental powers, as one who misuses them; not one who does not reason, but reasons wrongly. In Scripture the "fool," by way of eminence, is the person who casts off the fear of God, and thinks and acts as if he could safely disregard the eternal principles of God's righteousness (Psa. 14:1; 92:6; Jer. 17:11; Prov. 14:9, etc.). Yet in many passages, especially in Proverbs, the term has

its ordinary use, and denotes one who is rash, senseless, or unreasonable. The expression "thou fool" (Matt. 5:22) is used in the *moral* sense, means "wicked," and seems to be equivalent to judging one as worthy of everlasting punishment. *See* Folly.

Foolishness. *See* Folly; Fool.

Foot. The word "feet" is used in Scripture for the sake of delicacy, to express the parts and the acts which it is not allowed to name. Hence, "the hair of the feet," "to open the feet," etc. "To cover the feet" (I Sam. 24:3; Judg. 3:24) is a euphemism for performing the necessities of nature, as it is the custom in the East to cover the feet. The Jews neglected the feet, and bared them in affliction (II Sam. 15:30; 19:24; Ezek. 24:17); stamped them on the ground in extreme joy or grief (Ezek. 6:11; 25:6); showed respect by falling at the feet (I Sam. 25:24; I Kings 4:37; Esth. 8:3; Mark 5:22), reverence by kissing another's feet (Luke 7:38), subjection by licking the dust from the foot (Isa. 49:23); while the subjugation of enemies was expressed by placing the foot on their necks (Josh. 10:24; Psa. 110:1). The feet of enemies were sometimes cut off or maimed (Judg. 1:6, 7; II Sam. 4:12). Uncovering the feet was a mark of adoration (Exod. 3:5).

Figurative. "To be at any one's feet" is used for being at the service of another, following him, or receiving his instruction (Judg. 4:10; Acts 22:3). The last passage, in which Paul is described as being brought up "at the feet of Gamaliel," will appear still clearer if we understand that, as the Jewish writers allege, pupils actually did sit on the floor before, and, therefore, at the feet of, the doctors of the law, who themselves occupied an elevated seat. "He set my feet upon a rock" (Psa. 40:2) expresses the idea of stability. "Thou has set my feet in a large place" (Psa. 31:8) denotes liberty. "Sliding of the feet" is figurative for yielding to temptation (Job 12:5; Psa. 17:5; 38:16; 94:18). "Treading under foot" (Isa. 18:7; Lam. 1:15) implies complete destruction. To "wash" or "dip" one's feet in oil or butter (Deut. 33:24; Job 29:6) is to possess abundance; "dipped in blood" (Psa. 68:23), of victory. "To keep the feet of the saints" (I Sam. 2:9) is to preserve them from stumbling. "Lameness of feet" (Psa. 35:15, A. V. "adversity;" marg. "halting;" Jer. 20:10, etc.) denotes affliction. "To set one's foot" in a place signifies to take possession (Deut. 1:36; 11:24). "To water with the foot" (Deut 11:10) refers to irrigation, which was effected by foot pumps, and by turning the small streams of the garden with the foot. A striking phrase, borrowed from the feet, is used by Paul (Gal. 2:14): "When I saw that they walked not uprightly;" literally, "with a straight foot."

Foot Washing. *See* Washing.

Footman. Employed in the A. V. in two senses: 1. The military use of the word is the infantry in the army (*q. v.*). 2. In the special sense of a runner (*q. v.*).

Footsteps. Footprints are held to be indicative of one's character, their direction a proof of his tendencies. Therefore to watch one's footsteps is to seek a cause for accusation (Psa. 17:5, 11).

Footstool (Heb. *kĕbĕš*, something *trodden* upon), an article of furniture, used to support the feet when sitting in state, as upon a throne (II Chron. 9:18. The divine glory which resided symbolically between the cherubim above the ark of the covenant is supposed to use the ark as a footstool (I Chron. 28:2; Psa. 99:5; 132:7). The earth is called God's footstool by the same expressive figure which represents heaven as his throne (Psa. 110:1; Isa. 66:1; Matt. 5:35).

Forbearance (Gr. *'anochē*, a *holding back*, *delaying*, Rom. 2:4; 3:25). "The forbearance of God and his long suffering—the two terms exhausting the one idea—denote the disposition of God, in accordance with which he indulgently tolerates sins and delays their punishment (Meyer, *Com.*, in loco).

Forces (Hebrew, specially *hăyĭl*, *strength*). In a military point of view it is applied to army, fortifications, etc. In Isa. 60:5, 11 the phrase "forces of the Gentiles" seems to be used in its widest sense to denote not only the subjugation of the heathen, but also the consecration of their *wealth* (the rendering in the R. V.), "their resources."

Ford, a shallow place in a river or other body of water which may be crossed on foot or by wading (Gen. 32:22; Josh. 2:7; Judg. 3:28; 12:5, 6, A. V. "passages;" Isa. 16:2). The fords of the Jordan are frequently mentioned. A little above the Dead Sea two fords cross the Jordan near Jericho, passable for the most of the year, connecting roads from the Judean hills with highways from Gilead and Moab. The passage from Samaria into Gilead was made easy by an extraordinary number of fords through the Jordan. The depth of the Jordan fords varies from three feet to as much as ten or twelve (Smith, *Hist. Geog. of Holy Land*, pp. 266, 337, 486). Mention is also made of the ford of the Jabbok (Gen. 32:22) and of Arnon (Isa. 16:2). The "passages" of the Euphrates (Jer. 51:32) "are not merely those over the main river, but also those over the canals cut from it to add strength, whether fords, ferries, or light wooden birdges, which must have existed alongside the one stone bridge over the river for purposes of intercourse" (Orelli, *Com.*, in loco).

Forefront is used in its present sense, as the foremost part or place, e. g., the *forefront* of a building or of a battle (Ex. 26:9; II Sam. 11:15, etc.

Forehead (Heb. *mēṣăḥ*, to *shine*). The practice of veiling the face in public for women of the higher classes—especially married women —in the East, sufficiently stigmatizes with reproach the unveiled face of women of bad character (Gen. 24:65; Jer. 3:3). Reference is made to this when Israel is called "impudent" (literally, "of an hard forehead," R. V.), while courage is promised to the prophet when Jehovah says, "I have made the forehead strong (R. V. 'hard') against their foreheads" (Ezek. 3:7, 8). The custom among many oriental nations both of coloring the face and of impressing on the body marks indicative of devotion to some special deity or religious sect

is mentioned by various writers. In Ezekiel (9:4-6) we read that the Hebrew letter "t" (in early times made in the form of a cross) should be placed upon the foreheads of those who mourned the abominations of Israel, that they might be spared (see Rev. 7:3; 9:4; 14:1; 22:4); in the opposite sense as servants of Satan (Rev. 13:16, 17; 14:9, etc.). The "jewels for the forehead," mentioned by Ezekiel (16:12), and in margin of A. V. (Gen. 24:22), were in all probability nose-rings (Isa. 3:21).

Foreigner (Heb. *năkrî*, *stranger*, Deut. 15:3; Obad. 11; *tōshàb*, Exod. 12:45, *dweller*, as distinguished from a native; Gr. *paroikos*, *dwelling near*, Eph. 2:19), one living in a country of which he is not a native, i. e., in the Jewish sense, a Gentile. The Kingdom of God, temporarily limited to the one people of Israel, yet bore within it the germ of universality, of diffusion among all people. The covenent made with Abraham was from the beginning not exclusively confined to the natural posterity of Israel's twelve sons. As a practical proof that the redemption which was to be prepared through him and his seed was intended to all races of the earth, Abraham was commanded to circumcise every male belonging to his house. Hereby his servants, who amounted to hundreds, are included in his house, made partakers of the covenant promises, and incorporated with the promised seed.

Privileges. When the Israelites went up out of Egypt a large, mixed multitude of foreigners accompanied them (Exod. 12:38; Num. 11:4; Josh. 8:35), and were not rejected by them. Among the Israelites there were at all times individuals of other (heathen) peoples. To such were granted toleration and several privileges, in return for which compliance with the following regulations was insisted upon. They were required, for example, not to blaspheme the name of Jehovah (Lev. 24:16); not to indulge in idolatrous worship (Lev. 20:2); not to commit acts of indecency (Lev. 18:26); not to do any work on the Sabbath (Exod. 20:10); not to eat leavened bread during the Passover (Exod. 12:19); not to eat any manner of blood or flesh of animals that had died a natural death or had been torn by wild beasts (Lev. 17:10, 15). Under such circumstances the law accorded to foreigners not only protection and toleration, but equal civil rights with the Israelites. They could even acquire fixed property, lands (Lev. 25:47, sq.), and offer sacrifices to the Lord (Num. 15:15, sq., 26, 29).

Citizenship. Should he desire to enjoy the full rights of citizenship a stranger submitted to circumcision, thus binding himself to observe the whole law, in return for which he was permitted to enjoy to the full the privileges and blessings of the people of the covenant (Rom. 9:4), with whom, in virtue of this right, he was now incorporated (Exod. 12:48). The parties excluded from this fellowship were the Edomites and Egyptians resident in Israel —only, however, till the third generation (Deut. 23:7, 8); the seven Canaanitish nations, doomed to destruction and excluded forever (Exod. 34:15; Deut. 7:1-4); the Ammonites and Moabites, "even to the tenth generation" —i. e., forever—because of their opposition to the Israelites entering Canaan (Deut. 23:3).

Figurative. "Foreigners" in Eph. 2:19 denotes those who, being in a state of nature, are without citizenship in God's kingdom, as opposed to "fellow-citizens." In I Pet. 2:11 "foreigners" (A. V. "strangers") are those who live as strangers on the earth, i. e., with their citizenship in heaven (Phil. 3:20, R. V.).

Foreknowledge. *See* God, Attributes of.

Foreordination. *See* Election.

Forerunner (Gr. *prodromos*, one who is sent before to take observations or act as a spy, a scout, a light-armed soldier. In Heb. 6:20 it is used in the sense of one who comes in advance to a place whither the rest are to follow, viz., Jesus Christ (comp. John 14:2).

Foreship, ("forepart"), the prow of a ship (*q. v.*) (Acts 27:30, 41).

Foreskin, the loose fold of skin on the distinctive member of the male sex, which was removed in circumcision (*q. v.*), the *glans penis* artificially uncovered. Circumcision being a symbol of purification, the foreskin was a type of corruption; hence the phrase, "foreskin of the heart" (Deut. 10:16; Jer. 4:4) to designate a carnal or heathenish state (Rom. 2:29). It was sometimes brought as a trophy of slain Gentiles (I Sam. 18:25; II Sam. 3:14).

Foreskins, Hill of. A place at or near Gilgal, so called from the fact that the foreskins of the Israelites were buried there when the nation was circumcised (Josh. 5:3).

Forest. *See* Vegetable Kingdom.

Figurative. Forest is used symbolically to denote a city, kingdom, and the like (Ezek. 20:46, where the "forest of the south" denotes the kingdom of Judah). Kingdoms which God has threatened to destroy are represented under the figure of a forest, destined to be burned (Isa. 10:17, 18, 19, 34, where the briars and thorns denote the common people, while "the glory of the forest" are the nobles and others of high rank. See also Isa. 32:19; 37:24; Jer. 21:14; 22:7, etc.). The forest is the image of unfruitfulness as contrasted with a cultivated field or vineyard (Isa. 29:17; 32:15; Jer. 26:18; Hos. 2:12).

Forgiveness is one of the most widely misunderstood doctrines of Scripture. It is not to be confused with human forgiveness which merely remits a penalty or charge. Divine forgiveness, on the other hand, is one of the most complicated and costly undertakings, demanding complete satisfaction to meet the demands of God's outraged holiness.

1. **In the Old Testament.** "The priest shall make atonement for them and it shall be forgiven them" (Lev. 4:20). However, O. T. sacrifices only had a typical significance and served as a covering (Heb. *kāphăr*, to cover, to aid, Deut. 21:8; Gen. 50:17, etc.) from sin until the appointed time when God should deal finally with sin through the death of Christ. It is thus obvious that the transaction was to some extent incomplete on the Divine side. Of necessity sin was pretermitted. However, the offender received full forgiveness (Cf. Rom. 3:25, Acts 17:30).

2. **For the Unsaved.** Forgiveness under this consideration is never an isolated oper-

ation but always connected as an integral part of the whole divine undertaking for man called "salvation." Forgiveness is only one of the many transformations wrought of God in the unsaved in response to simple faith in Christ. Thus forgiveness of sin is not equivalent to salvation. It is merely negative. All else in the comprehensive term "salvation" is gloriously added (John 10:28; Rom. 5:17).

3. **For the Believer Who Sins.** The great foundational truth respecting the believer in relationship to his sins is the fact that his salvation comprehends the forgiveness of all his trespasses past, present and future so far as condemnation is concerned (Rom. 8:1; Col. 2:13; John 3:18; John 5:24). Since Christ has vicariously borne all sin and since the believer's standing in Christ is complete, he is perfected forever in Christ. When a believer sins, he is subject to chastisement from the Father, but never to condemnation with the world (I Cor. 11:31, 32). By confession the Christian is forgiven and restored to fellowship (I John 1:9). It needs to be remembered that were it not for Christ's finished work on the cross and His present intercession in heaven, the least sin would result in his banishment from God's presence and eternal ruin.

4. **Sin Unto Death.** Persistent or scandalous sin in the believer in face of Divine grace and his perfect standing in Christ may eventuate in a sin resulting in physical death. "If any man see his brother sin a sin which is not unto death, he shall ask, and He shall give him life for them that sin not unto death. There is a sin unto death: I do not say that he shall pray for it (I John 5:16; cf. I Cor. 5:1-5). Both John 15:2 and I Cor. 11:30 point out that God reserves the right to cut off the physical life of a believer who has ceased to be a worthy witness in the world. Such a cutting off does not mean that the one who has died is lost. It merely signifies more drastic chastisement to the end that a believer might not be condemned with the world (I Cor. 11:31, 32).

5. **The Unpardonable Sin.** This was a specific sin possible only during the earthly life of our Lord when he was ministering in the power of the Holy Spirit. Under those unique conditions a person who attributed to Satan the power of the Holy Spirit, so visibly and openly manifested, was guilty of this peculiar sin. For this reason there could be no forgiveness in the age then present or in the age immediately following (Matt. 12:22-32; Mark 3:22-30). Since no such conditions exist in this age, the unpardonable sin is now impossible. An unpardonable sin and the gospel of "whosoever will" cannot coexist. Were such a sin possible today, every gospel invitation would specifically shut out those who had committed such a trespass.

6. **As an Obligation Among Men.** The believer who belongs to this age is exhorted to be kind unto other believers, and unbelievers as well, tenderhearted and forgiving to one another as God "for Christ's sake hath forgiven you" (Eph. 4:32). The basis of the plea for such forgiveness is that one has been himself so graciously forgiven.

Fork (Heb. *sheʿlish kilshōn, three of prongs*, only in I Sam. 13:21), a three-pronged fork, i. e., pitchfork, with which to handle hay, straw, etc.

Fornication Gr. *porneia*, is used of illicit sexual intercourse in general (Acts 15:20, 29; 21:25; Rom. 1:29; I Cor. 5:1; 6:13, 18; 7:2, etc.). It is distinguished from "adultery" (Gr. *moicheia*, in Matt. 15:19; Mark 7:21; Gal. 5:19). Jahn (*Bibl. Arch.*, § 158) thus distinguishes between adultery and fornication among nations where polygamy exists: "If a married man has criminal intercourse with a married woman, or with one promised in marriage, or with a widow expecting to be married with a brother-in-law, it is accounted *adultery*. If he is guilty of such intercourse with a woman who is unmarried it is considered *fornication*." At the present time adultery is the term used of such an act when the person is married, fornication when unmarried; and *fornication* may be defined as lewdness of an unmarried person of either sex. Its prohibition rests on the ground that it discourages marriage, leaves the education and care of children insecure, depraves and defiles the mind more than any other vice, and thus unfits for the kingdom of God (I Cor. 6:9, etc.). Our Lord forbids the thoughts that lead to it (Matt. 5:28).

Figurative. The close relationship between Jehovah and Israel is spoken of under the figure of marriage, Israel being the unfaithful wife of the Lord, now rejected but yet to be restored.

The Church of the N. T. is a pure virgin espoused to Christ (II Cor. 11:2), and thus differentiated from the Nation Israel (I Cor. 10:32). The worship of idols is naturally mentioned as *fornication* (Rev. 14:8; 17:2, 4; 18:3; 19:2); as also the defilement of idolatry, as incurred by eating the sacrifices offered to idols (Rev. 2:21). *See* Idolatry.

Fort, Fortification, Fortress. The Hebrew people, never very well equipped with arms or possessing military knowledge, and surrounded by powerful neighbors, early learned it was "better to take refuge in the Lord than to put confidence in princes." (Psa. 118:9). In the Theocracy the Divine ideal was that real protection was in faith in the God of Israel. Such burning faith in God's power protected Moses, Joshua, Deborah, Samson, Jonathan, David and other national heros; yet early in her history Israel had to fight to survive.

1. **Pre-Israelite Fortification.** When Joshua and Israel invaded Palestine, they faced formidable Canaanite defenses. Stoutly walled cities erected on mounds which seemed to reach to heaven dotted "the land of milk and honey." Canaanites were famous for their masonry and by 2000 B. C. had erected massive defenses. Such excavated sites as Jericho, Shechem, Taanach, Lachish, Gezer and Beth-shan have yielded plentiful information concerning the formidableness of Canaanite fortifications. The reports of the Mosaic spies were literally true. They did find great fortified strongholds. Even before the Phoenicians, their Amorite predecessors, from c. 2500 B. C. had massive fortifications. At Megiddo,

the old Amorite fort overlooking Esdraelon had an area of twenty acres. The recital of the Israelite struggle to attain the strongholds of the Amorites, Hittites, Perrizites and Jebusites is true to archaeological excavations. The impregnable walls of Jebusite Jerusalem, which David finally took, have been fully verified. At Ugarit in North Syria a cuneiform tablet was found which listed the military equipment kept in the royal Ugaritic arsenal. At Ras Shamra there was a lively trade in horses. Jericho's famous walls are featured in the Biblical narrative as well as in their archaeological excavations. The taking of

162. Stout Walls of Jericho (reconstructed)

Jericho has been to a large extent verified by the archaeologist's spade. At Jericho, John Garstang located a series of walled cities, one above another: City A, 3000 B. C., City B, c. 2500 B. C., City C was larger than its predecessors and was surrounded by stout walls with stone glacis and outer moat. This city belonged to the Hyksos era and suffered destruction c. 1500 B. C. City D, taken by Joshua, was constructed c. 1500 B. C. It had a double wall of brick. A massive six-foot-thick wall was erected on the edge of the mound. An inner wall (twelve feet thick) was separated from it by a space of twelve to fifteen feet. The wall originally reached perhaps thirty feet. Like Jericho, Bethel, occupied almost constantly from 2000 B. C. or earlier, had well constructed city walls. The stout fortifications of Bethel were consumed by a terrific conflagration.

2. **Fortifications Under Monarchy.** A good example of an early citadel of Israel is Saul's fortress in Gibeah (present Tell el-Ful), located in the hill country about four miles north of Jerusalem. It was excavated in 1922–23 by W. F. Albright. At the bottom of the mound, fortress No. 1 showed traces of destruction by fire and is probably the one mentioned in Judg. 20:40. (Cf. W. F. Albright, *Young's Analytical Concordance*, 20th Edition, 1946, p. 32). Fortress No. 2, just above the first, is identified with Saul's stronghold. The structure, 170 ft. x 155 ft., had casemated walls and separately bonded corner towers. The outer wall was about six feet thick and was defended by a glacis or sloping base. The castle comprised two stories and contained a massive stone staircase. Above Saul's structure is a third fortress characterized by a series of stone piers. This citadel suffered destruction by fire, perhaps in the Syro-Ephraimite wars. Egyptian art records two of the towers of the military architects at Gibeah. Together these

"fenced" cities constituted a strong system of defense. The most notable link in the chain was Beth-shan, guarding the eastern approaches to the famous battlefield of Esdraelon. In fact, Tell el-Husn, modern name of Beth-shan, means "Mount of the Fortress." Clarence Fisher, Alan Rowe and other excavators have unearthed fortress constructions at this important site. Megiddo was another great fortified location (Josh. 12:21; Judg. 5:19; II Kings 23:29). It not only had a strong wall, gates and towers but, during Solomon's era, was one of his chariot cities. Lachish in S. E. Palestine was another famous fort, excavated by J. L. Starkey and others.

3. **Other Fortresses of Bible Times.** Samaria, founded by Omri and made glorious by the Omri dynasty of the ninth century B. C. had a great bastion. Jeroboam II of the eighth century made it an almost impregnable location with high walls and formidable fortifications. Damascus was another ancient city whose N. T. walls are familiar from the experiences of Paul. From a house built on the city wall he escaped in a basket (Acts 9:25). The Greek city of Athens was also fortified and the city walls connected the capital with her twin harbors at Phaleron and Piraeus. Corinth was another famous fortified site. The ancient Greek walls were constructed on the Acro-Corinthus above the commercial city on the Isthmus. The commercial city, now well known, reveals traces of the city walls including the Isthmian Gate and the ruins of the extensive wall joining Corinth with its harbor at Lechaeum. Syracuse on the island of Sicily also had mighty fortifications in Bible times. This famous fortress stemmed the invasion of the armed savage Carthaginians for thirty-eight years, thus defending Hellenic culture in the mid-Mediterranean. Ancient Babylon, Nineveh and Ashur, Ur and other Mesopotamian cities were mighty fortresses from ancient times. The Babylon of Nebuchadnezzar II, as revealed by the records of Herodotus and the accounts of Robert Koldewey, tell of mammoth walls which stretched across the Tigris-Euphrates plain about the city. The incredible splendors of the city, including its hanging gardens, its famous Ishtar Gate, ziggurat and temples, were thus defended by a vast system of fortifications. The Ishtar Gate bore reliefs of bulls and dragons, symbolic of Chaldean prowess. This ornate, square-towered portal guarded the city's entrance to the north wall. Assyrian kings such as Sargon II adorned and defended their palaces with massive gates. The Roman walls of Paul's time, which had already existed for centuries, were formidable but never as famous as those at Jerusalem. The remains of many ancient gates are to be found at Rome. *M. F. U.*

Figurative. As illustrative of divine protection to those who trust him, the Lord is compared to a fortress (II Sam. 22:2; Psa. 18:2; 31:3; 71:3, etc.). "The fortress also shall cease from Ephraim" (Isa. 17:3), is an expression signifying that she loses her fortified cities, which were once her defense. To overthrow one's fortress is to rob it of defense, to humiliate (Isa. 25:12). Of the righteous man it is said, "his place of defense shall be the munitions of rocks" (Isa. 33:16,), i. e., God's protection shall be to him as the impregnable walls of a fortress upon a rock. "I have set thee for a tower and a *fortress* among my people," etc. (Jer. 6:27), is rendered by Orelli, *Com.*, in loco, "an assayer to my people, a piece of ore" (Heb. from *bĕṣĕr, broken off*), "that thou mayest test their walk."

Fortuna′tus (fôr-tū-nä′tŭs; *fortunate*), a disciple of Corinth, of Roman birth or origin, as his name indicates, who visited Paul at Ephesus, and returned, along with Stephanas and Achaicus, in charge of that apostle's First Epistle to the Corinthian Church (I Cor. 16: 17). "The household of Stephanas" is mentioned in 1:16 as having been baptized .by Paul himself; perhaps Fortunatus and Achaicus may have been members of that household. There is a Fortunatus mentioned at the end of Clement's First Epistle to the Corinthians, who was possibly the same person.

Forum Appii. See Appii Forum.

Foundation, the lowest part of a building, and on which it rests.

Figurative. By foundation is sometimes understood the *origin* (Job 4:19), where men are represented as dwelling in clay houses, whose foundation, i. e., *origin*, was in the dust (comp. Gen. 2:7; 3:19). It is also used in the sense of *beginning*, as "the foundation of the world" (Matt. 13:35; 25:34, etc.). The expression is illustrative of Christ: "Behold, I lay in Zion for a foundation stone," etc. (Isa. 28:16; I Cor. 3:11); of the doctrines of the apostles (Eph. 2:20); the first principles of the Gospel (Heb. 6:1, 2); the Christian religion (II Tim. 2:19); of the righteous (Prov. 10:25); the wise man is one who lays his foundation upon a rock (Luke 6:48); the good minister, who builds on the true foundation—Jesus Christ (I Cor. 3:10).

Fountain is a natural source of living water. the same word as "eye" in Hebrew, *ʿȧyin* (Gen, 16:7; Deut. 8:7; 33:28; I Sam. 29:1; Prov. 8:28). Often the Hebrew word used denotes a place of a fountain or running water (Lev. 11:36; Josh. 15:9; Psa. 74:15; 114:8; Prov. 25:26), a well-watered place (Psa. 84:6). It is also spoken of an inflow of the sea (Gen. 7:11; 8:2). In Ecc. 12:16 and Isa. 35:7; 49:10 the original word *mȧbbūʿȧ* has the idea of a gushing source of water. An artificial source of flowing water, such as a cistern or a reservoir may be denoted by the Hebrew word *mȧqōr* (Lev. 20: 18; Psa. 36:9; 68:26; Prov. 5:18; 13:14; 14: 27; Jer. 2:13). The Greek *pēgē* occurs in Jas. 3:11, 12; Rev. 7:17; 8:10; 14:7; 21:6).

M. F. U.

Figurative. Of God (Psa. 36:9; Jer. 17:13); as the source of grace (Psa. 87:7); of Christ (Zech. 13:1); of the manifestations of divine grace (Isa. 41:18; Joel 3:18); of Israel, as the father of a numerous posterity (Deut. 33:28); of a good wife (Prov. 5:18); of spiritual wisdom (Prov. 16:22; 18:4, in both passages rendered "wellspring"); of the Church (Cant. 4:12; Isa. 58:11, "spring of water"). See Spring, Well.

Fowl. See Animal Kingdom; Food; Sacrifice.

In the New Testament "fowls" is the rendering most frequently of the Gr. *ta peteina,* which comprehends all kinds of birds (Matt. 13:4; Mark 4:4, etc.).

Fowler (from Heb. *yāqōsh*, to *lay snares;* Psa. 91:3; 124:7; Prov. 6:5; Jer. 5:26; Hos. 9:8), one who took birds by means of nets, snares, decoys, etc. Among the Egyptians "fowling was one of the great amusements of all classes. Those who followed this sport for their livelihood used nets and traps, but the amateur sportsman pursued his game in the thickets, and felled them with the throw-stick. . . . The throwstick was made of heavy wood, and flat, so as to offer little resistance to the air in its flight, and the distance to which an expert could throw it was considerable. It was about one foot and a quarter to two feet in length, and about one and a half inches in breadth, slightly curved at the upper end. They frequently took with them a decoy bird, and in order to keep it to its post, a female was selected, whose nest, containing eggs, was deposited in the boat" (Wilkinson, *Ancient Egyptians*, i, 234, sq.). By the Mosaic law any one finding a bird's nest was forbidden to take the mother with the eggs or young (Deut. 22:6, 7), lest the species be extinguished; or, perhaps, to impress upon men the sacredness of the relation between parent and young.

Fox. *See* Animal Kingdom.

Figurative. The proverbially cunning character of the fox is alluded to in Scriptures, as in Ezek. 13:4, where the prophets of Israel are said to be like foxes in the desert; and in Luke 13:32, where our Lord calls Herod "that fox." The fox's fondness for grapes is alluded to in Cant. 2:15.

Frankincense. *See* Incense, Vegetable Kingdom.

Fraud. *See* Law.

Fray (Heb. *hārăd*, to *frighten*, Deut. 28:26; Jer. 7:33; Zech. 1:21), an old word, signifying to frighten, to scare away.

Freedom (Heb. *hŭpshäh*, *liberty;* Gr. *politeia, citizenship*, Acts 22:28).

1. **Hebrew.** Every Israelite (man or maid) who had become a slave might not only be redeemed at any time by his relatives, but, if this did not take place, he was bound to receive his freedom without payment in the seventh year, with a present of cattle and fruits (Exod. 21:2, sq.; Deut. 15:12-15). Indeed all slaves of Hebrew descent, with their children, obtained freedom without ransom in the jubilee year (Lev. 25:41). If the man was single when he went into slavery, he was liberated alone; whereas the wife brought into slavery with her husband received her freedom at the same time with him (Exod. 21:2, sq.; Jer. 34:8, sq.). The emancipation of slaves among Greeks and Romans was tolerably common. The Greeks had no special legal form for the process, and consequently no legal differences in the legal *status* of freedom. At Athens they took the position of resident aliens, and were under certain obligations to their liberators as patrons.

2. **Roman.** Among the Romans emancipation was either formal or informal. (1) Of formal emancipation there were three kinds: (*a*) the *manumissio vindictā*, in which the owner appeared before the magistrate with the slave. A Roman citizen laid a staff upon the slave's head and declared him free, whereupon the master, who was holding the slave with his hand, let him go as a symbol of liberation. (*b*) The *manumissio censu*, in which the master enrolled the slave's name in the list of citizens. (*c*) The *manumissio testāmentō*, or manumission by will, in which the master declared his slave free, or bound his heir to emancipate him. (2) Informal emancipation took place in virtue of an oral declaration on the part of the master, in the presence of friends, or by letter, or by inviting the slave to the master's table. After formal emancipation they at once became Roman citizens, but, not being free-born, were not eligible to office and were excluded from military service. Informal emancipation conferred only practical freedom without civil rights (Seyffert, *Dic. Class. Antiq.* (s. v.). Freedom is used (Acts 22:28; comp. 21:39) for citizenship (*q. v.*).

Freedom. 1. **Theological.** *An attribute of God.* This is declared by the apostle Paul, in harmony with the unanimous testimony of the Scriptures, in the words, "Who worketh all things after the counsel of his own will" (Eph. 1:11). By this term theology expresses the fact that God is a self-determining agent, a free personal being acting purely in accordance with his own perfections. The reason of the divine purpose and act is to be found only in God himself. Inasmuch as God is eternally and unchangeably what he is, we must recognize in God, in a proper sense, an absolute necessity. But it is a necessity which not only does not conflict, but is identical, with his perfect freedom. The creation—the existence of all things that are not God—must be referred to the divine freedom. God could be under no necessity to create. But if he creates, his creation, the order, the laws he establishes among them, must reflect his wisdom and goodness and holiness—in a word, Himself. At this point the doctrine of the divine freedom reveals sharply its opposition to Pantheism, which asserts that all things, even sin (the sinfulness of which it denies), are but necessary manifestations or unfoldings of the Divine Being. *See* Pantheism.

The freedom of God is exercised and illustrated in his government of his moral creatures. It has pleased God to create intelligences possessed of moral freedom, and to make their ultimate destiny contingent upon the right use of their freedom. This is a necessary feature of the government which God has established over the world of moral beings he has seen fit to create. God has manifested his perfect freedom in creating such a world and adapting his methods to the exigencies that arise in its history. This view of the divine freedom is to be maintained in opposition to the exaggerated and unscriptural view of the divine sovereignty which, despite all merely verbal qualifications, actually reduces the freedom of moral creatures to a nullity, and regards their destinies as unalterably fixed by an eternal, divine decree. *See* Sovereignty of God.

2. **Human.** In what has been said above the freedom of man, as that of other moral intelligences, has been assumed. The doctrine of human freedom, or of freewill, the subject

of so much controversy, requires, however, particular discussion.

(1) **Definition.** By freedom of the will, in the proper sense, is meant the power of contrary choice, i. e., the power of the mind to choose in some other direction than that in which the choice is actually made. Theologically freedom refers especially to the power to choose between good and evil, righteousness and unrighteousness. On the one hand, by those who uphold this doctrine, it is asserted that man freely determines his own volitions; on the other, by necessitarians, it is held that these volitions are determined by conditions, influences, and circumstances with which they are connected as rigidly and powerfully as effects are connected with causes in the material world.

(2) **Parties to controversy.** Prominent among those who deny human freedom are materialists. This position is also the natural result of Dualism and Pantheism. Also that form of Theism which fails to recognize the divine freedom finds no freedom in man. The attitude of Calvinistic theology upon this subject has been the occasion of much dispute and probably of some misunderstanding. The extreme doctrines of foreordination, of unconditional election and reprobation, held by Calvinists, as well as some of the terms by which they describe man's actual condition have been claimed by Arminians to be logically equivalent to a denial of man's freedom. And yet it may truly be said that Calvinism, generally speaking, has steadfastly proclaimed the responsibility of man as a free moral agent. On the whole, belief in the freedom of the will, properly interpreted, may be regarded as the unanimous, if not always coherently spoken, belief of the Christian Church.

(3) **Theological interpretation.** The doctrine of human freedom relates not only to man's original condition before the fall, but also to his present fallen condition, as that of bondage to sin; and still further to the condition to which he is brought through redemption by Christ. (a) Man was created in the image of God, and accordingly was endowed with perfect moral freedom. Sin resulted from the abuse of freedom. (See Fall of Man; Sin.) (b) In consequence of the sin of the first human pair mankind has inherited a depraved nature. So that while the natural freedom of man is not lost in respect to many things, yet with respect to meeting the requirements of the divine law, man is of himself in a state of complete moral inability (see Rom. 7:19-24, et al). This is to be held in opposition to Pelagianism (See Pelagianism). (c) The actual condition of mankind, as morally fallen, is, however, greatly modified by the grace of God that has come to the race through redemption. Through regeneration and sanctification the bondage of sin is completely destroyed, and thus believers become "free indeed."

(4) **Arguments for freedom.** (a) Appeal is made to universal consciousness. The common experience of men is that while choosing one way they feel that they might choose another. (b) Freedom is essential to all moral responsibility. And moral responsibility is one of the intuitions of the human mind. (c) The

denial of freedom must logically lead to the denial of moral distinctions in human affairs. (d) In addition to the above, which are purely rational arguments, is the general force of Scripture teaching, which uniformly represents man as invested with the power of choosing between right and wrong, and between sin and salvation.

Literature.—(Arminian) Watson, *Theological Institutes;* Pope, *Compendium of Christian Theology;* Whedon, *Freedom of the Will;* (Calvinstic) Edwards, *Inquiry on the Freedom of the Will;* Hodge, *Systematic Theology.* E. McC—revised by *M. F. U.*

Freedom, Year of, or Jubilee. *See* Festivals.

Freeman (Gr. *apeleutheros,* one *set free*), a person who had been freed (I Cor. 7:22). In Gal. 4:22, 23, 30, a strong distinction is drawn between the freewoman and the bondmaid. *See* Freedom.

Freewill Offering. *See* Sacrificial Offering.

Friend, a person with whom one has friendly intercourse (Gen. 38:12, 20; II Sam. 13:3; Job 2:11; 19:21, etc.); also a *lover, one beloved* of a woman (Cant. 5:16; Jer. 3:1, A. V. "lovers," 20; Hos. 3:1); and in Judg. 14:20 it is used in the sense of "the friend of the bridegroom" (John 3:29), who asked the hand of the bride and rendered service at the marriage (*q. v.*).

Comrade, Matt. 11:16, A. V. "fellow"), used in kindly address (Matt. 20:13; 22:12; 26:50)—Gr. *hetairos.*

One attached by affection (Gr. *philos*) frequently used in the New Testament, as Jas. 2:23; 4:4.

Fringe (Heb. *gᵉdîl, twisted* thread, i. e., a *tassel,* Deut. 22:12; *ṣîṣîth, flowery, bloomlike,* and so *tassel,* Num. 15:38, 39). Fringes were ordered to be sewn upon the hem of the outside garment, to remind the Israelites of the commandments of God, that they might have them constantly before their eyes and follow them. These fringes (tassels) were made of twisted blue thread and fastened upon each corner of the garment. The color (blue) was used to remind the Jews of the heavenly origin of the law. Fringed garments, elaborately wrought, were very common among the ancient Egyptians and Babylonians.

Frog. *See* Animal Kingdom.

Frontlet (Heb. *ṭôphāphāh,* to *bind,* only in Exod. 13:16; Deut. 6:8; 11:18). "The expression in Deut. 6:8, 'Thou shalt bind them for a sign upon thine hand, and they shall be as frontlets between thine eyes,' does not point at all to the symbolizing of the divine commands by an outward sign to be worn upon the hand, or to bands with passages of the law inscribed upon them, to be worn on the forehead between the eyes. . . . The line of thought referred to merely expresses the idea that the Israelites were not only to retain the commands of God in their hearts, and to confess them with the mouth, but to fulfill them with the hand, or in act and deed" (K. and D., *Com.* in loco). But the Jews, after their return from captivity, construed the injunction literally, and had portions of the law written out and worn as badges upon their persons. They are still worn by modern Jews, and consist of strips of parchment, on which are written four passages of Scripture (Exod. 13:2-10, 11-17; Deut. 6:4-9; 13-22). These are rolled up in a case of black calfskin, attached to a stiffer piece of leather having a thong one finger broad and one and a half cubits long. *See* Phylactery.

Frost (Heb. *kᵉphōr*, so called from *covering* the ground, "hoar frost," Exod. 16:14; Job 38:29; Psa. 147:16; also *qᵉrăḥ*, *smooth*, as ice, so rendered Job 6:16; 38:29), frozen dew. It appears in a still night, when there is no storm or tempest, and descends upon the earth as silently as if it were produced by mere breathing (Job 37:10).

Frowardness, perverseness (Deut. 32:20); deceit, falsehood (Prov. 2:12; 6:14, etc.).

Fruit. *See* Garden; Vegetable Kingdom.

Figurative. The word fruit is often used figuratively in Scripture: Of offspring, children (Exod. 21:22; Psa. 21:10; Hos. 9:16); also in such phrases as "fruit of the womb" (Gen. 30:2; Deut. 7:13, etc.); "fruit of the loins" (Acts 2:30); "fruit of the body" (Psa. 132:11; Mic. 6:7). Also in a variety of forms, as: "They shall eat the fruit of their doings," i. e., experience the consequences (Prov. 1:31; Isa. 3:10; Jer. 6:19; 17:10); the "fruit of the hands" is used for gain, profit; boasting is the "fruit of the stout heart" (Isa. 10:12); a man's words are called the "fruit of the mouth" (Prov. 12:14; 18:20; Heb. 13:15; Hos. 10:13); "fruit of lies;" "the fruit of the righteous" (Prov. 11:30) is his counsel, example, etc.; the "fruit of the spirit," enumerated in Gal. 5:22, 23, are those gracious habits which the Holy Spirit produces in the Christian, given more briefly as "goodness, righteousness, and truth" (Eph. 5:9); the "fruits of righteousness" (Phil. 1:11) are such good works as spring from a gracious frame of heart. Fruit is also the name given to a charitable contribution (Rom. 15:28).

Frying Pan, a pot for boiling meat, etc. (Lev. 2:7; 7:9). It was, probably, deeper than the "baking pan" (Lev. 2:5) which was used for baking bread.

Fuel. In most Eastern countries there is a scarcity of wood and other materials used by us for fuel. Consequently almost every kind of combustible matter is eagerly sought for, such as the withered stalks of herbs and flowers (Matt. 6:28, 30), thorns (Psa. 58:9; Eccles. 7:6), and animal excrements (Isa. 9:5, 19; Ezek. 4:12-15; 15:4, 6; 21:32). At the present time wood or charcoal is employed in the towns of Syria and Egypt, although the people of Palestine use anthracite coal to some extent. *See* Coal.

Fugitive, the rendering of several Hebrew words, meaning to *wander*, a *refugee, deserter,* etc.

Fuller. *See* Handicrafts.

Fuller's Field, a spot near Jerusalem (II Kings 18:17; Isa. 36:2; 7:3) so near the walls that one speaking there could be heard on them (II Kings 18:17, 26). The pool mentioned is probably the one now known as Birket-el-Mamilla, at the head of the Valley of Hinnom, a little west of the Yafa gate. The position of the fuller's field is thus indicated.

Fuller's Soap. Figurative. The powerful cleansing properties of *borith*, or soap, are employed by the prophet Malachi (3:2) to represent the prospective results of the Messiah's coming (comp. Mark 9:3). *See* Fuller under Handicrafts.

Fullness. 1. That portion of the corn and wine which was to be offered to Jehovah as a tithe or first fruits (Exod. 22:29, margin; Num. 18:27).

2. (Gr. *plērōma, that which has been filled*). This term has been variously used in Scripture. (*a*) The "fullness of time" is the time when Christ appeared—"When the fullness of the time was come God sent his Son" (Gal. 4:4). (*b*) The fullness of Christ is the superabundance with which he is filled (John 1:16; Col. 1:19; 2:9). In the last passage, "In him dwelleth all the fullness of the Godhead bodily," means that the whole nature and attributes of God are in Christ. (*c*) The Church, i. e., the body of believers, is called the fullness of Christ (Eph. 1:23), as it is the Church which makes him a complete and perfect head.

Funeral. 1. **Egyptian.** When the body was buried, either in the hills, there to be preserved by the conservative influence of the sand, or, having been embalmed, was placed in a sarcophagus of hard stone, whose lid and trough, hermetically fastened with cement, prevented the penetration of any moisture, the soul was supposed to follow the body to the tomb, and there to dwell, as in its eternal house, upon the confines of the visible and invisible world. Funeral sacrifices and the regular cultus of the dead originated in the need experienced for making provision for the sustenance of the manes after having secured their lasting existence by the mummification of their bodies. Unless supplied with food the soul (or double) was supposed to wander abroad at night in search thereof. Therefore food and vessels of wine and beer were brought to the tomb, that they might enjoy that which was thought to be necessary for the maintenance of their bodies.

2. **Among the Ancient Israelites.** What

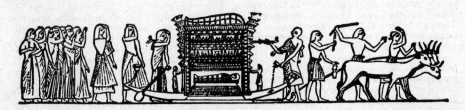

163. Egyptian Funeral

form or ceremonies of obsequies were observed is to us almost unknown, except that the act of interment was performed by the relations (sons, brothers) with their own hands (Gen. 25:9; 35:29; Judg. 16:31; comp. Matt. 8:21, 22). In later times the Jews left this office to others, and in Amos 5:16 it is spoken of as something shocking that kinsmen should be obliged to carry the corpse to the grave. As soon as possible after death the body was washed (Acts 9:37), then wrapped in a large cloth (Matt. 27:59; Mark 15:46; Luke 23:53), or all its limbs wound with bands (John 11:44), between the folds of which, in cases of persons of distinction, aromatics were laid or sprinkled (John 19:39, sq.). At public funerals of princes sumptuous shrouds were used, and there was a prodigious expense of odors. The body was removed to the grave in a coffin (probably open), or on a bier (II Sam. 3:31), borne by men (Luke 7:14; Acts 5:6, 10), with a retinue of relatives and friends (II Sam. 3:31; Luke 7:12). The Talmud speaks of funeral processions with horns, in a long train (Job 21:33), with loud weeping and wailing (II Sam. 3:32). Female mourners were hired for the purpose, who prolonged the lamentation several days. The burial was followed by the funeral meal (II Sam. 3:35; Jer. 16:5, 7; Hos. 9:4; Ezek. 24:17, 22).

Furlong. *See* Metrology, I.

Furnace.

1. A smelting oven of livestone, kiln (Gen. 19:28; Amos 2:1) or oven for making bricks (Exod. 9:8, 10; 19:18).

2. A large crucible apparently with an opening at the top for casting in materials (Dan. 3:22, 23), and a door at the ground from which to take the metal (v. 26). The Persians used this device for inflicting capital punishment (Cf. Jer. 29:22; Hos. 7:7; II Macc. 7:5).

3. A cylindrical fire pot such as is commonly used in dwelling houses in the East (Gen.

15:17). They are still in use among the Arabs. N. T. references to a furnace either for smelting, burning earthenware or baking bread are found in Matt. 13:42, 50; Rev. 1:15; 9:2.

Figurative. A refining furnace is used figuratively to describe a state of trial (Deut. 4:20; Isa. 48:10). *M. F. U.*

Furnaces, the Tower of (Neh. 3:11; 12:38). This was one of the towers of the middle or second wall of Jerusalem, at its northwest angle, adjoining the "corner gate," and near the intersection of the present line of the Via Dolorosa with the street of St. Stephen. It may be the same as the "Baker's Street" (Jer. 37:21).

Furniture. 1. The rendering in the A. V. of the Heb. *kăr, pad,* a camel's litter or canopied saddle, in which females are accustomed to travel in the East at the present day (Gen. 31:34).

2. The name given to the sacred things in the tabernacle and their utensils (Exod. 31:7, sq.; 35:14; 39:33). In Nah. 2:9 it is used for "ornamental vessels."—Heb. *kᵉlî,* something *prepared.*

For furniture in its usual sense, *see* House, III.

Furrow, a trench in the earth made by a plow (Psa. 65:10; Hos. 10:4). In Hos. 10:10 "furrows" had better be rendered "transgressions," referring, according to some, to the golden calves at Dan and Beth-el, but according to others to their apostasy from Jehovah and the royal house of David. (comp. ch. 3:5).

Future Life. *See* Life; Immortality.

Fury (Heb. *hēmäh, heat;* or *ḥārōn, burning*), intense anger, attributed to God metaphorically, or speaking after the manner of men (Lev. 26:28; Job. 20:23; Isa. 63:3, etc.). It is the spontaneous reaction of the divine holiness against sin treasured-up and ripe for judgment. *See* Anger.

G

Ga'al (gā'ăl; *loathing*), the son of Ebed (Judg. 9:26, sq.). He was probably a freebooter, and was welcomed to Shechem because the Shechemites hoped that he would be able to render them good service in their revolt from Abimelech. At the festival at which the Shechemites offered the first fruits of their vintage in the temple of Baal, Gaal strove to kindle their wrath against the absent Abimelech. His rebellious speech was reported to Abimelech by the town prefect, Zebul. On receiving this intelligence Abimelech rose up during the night with the people that were with him, and placed four companies in ambush against Shechem. When Gaal went out in the morning upon some enterprise, and stood before the city gate, Abimelech rose up with his army out of the ambush. Gaal fled into the city, but was thrust out by Zebul, and we hear of him no more, B. C. c. 1008-1105.

Ga'ash (gā'ăsh; *quaking*), more accurately Mount Gaash, in the district of Mount Ephraim. On the north side of the hill was Timnath-serach, the city given to Joshua (Josh. 24:30). Here Joshua was buried. The "brooks," that is, *valleys* of Gaash are mentioned in II Sam. 23:30; I Chron. 11:32.

Ga'ba (gā'bá; Josh. 18:24; Ezra 2:26; Neh. 7:30), a less correct rendering of *Geba* (*q. v.*).

Gab'bai (găb'å-ī; *tax gatherer*), a chief of the tribe of Benjamin, who settled in Jerusalem after the captivity (Neh. 11:8), B. C. before 445.

Gab'batha (găb'å-thá; Aram. *gabbᵉthä, ridge, knoll, hill*), the place mentioned in John 19:13, where it is stated that Pilate, alarmed by the insinuation of the Jews, "If thou let this man go thou art not Caesar's friend," went into the pretorium again, and brought Jesus out to them. He then pronounced formal sentence against Jesus, having taken his seat upon the tribunal in a place called the Pavement (Gr. *lithostrōton, stone strewn*), but in the Hebrew Gabbatha. It is probable that the Greek name was given to the spot from the nature of its pavement, and the Hebrew from its shape.

Ga'briel (gā'brĭ-ĕl; *man* or *hero of God*), the word used to designate the heavenly messenger, sent to explain to Daniel the visions which he saw (Dan. 8:16; 9:21), and who announced the birth of John the Baptist to his father, Zechariah (Luke 1:11), and chat of the Messiah to the Virgin Mary (Luke 1:26). From Daniel 12:1, it is apparent that Michael is the special champion of the nation Israel and will be Israel's special defender during the Great Tribulation. As to his relation to other angels and archangels, the Scriptures give no information; but in the book of Enoch "the four great archangels, Michael, Raphael, Gabriel, and Uriel," are described as reporting the corrupt state of mankind to the Creator, and receiving their several commissions. In the Rabbinical writings Gabriel is represented as standing in front of the divine throne, near the standard of Judah. The Mohammedans regard Gabriel with profound reverence, affirming that to him was committed a complete copy of the Koran, which he imparted in successive portions to Mohammed. He is styled in the Koran the Spirit of Truth and the Holy Spirit, and it is alleged that he will hold the scales in which the actions of men will be weighed in the last day.

Gad (găd; *fortune*). 1. **Son of Jacob.**

(1) **Name and Family.** Jacob's seventh son, the firstborn of Zilpah, Leah's maid, and whole brother to Asher (Gen. 30:11-13; 46:16, 18), B. C. perhaps about 1850.

(2) **Personal History.** Of the life of the individual Gad nothing is preserved, and therefore we must proceed immediately to speak of:

(3) **The Tribe of Gad.** *1. Numbers.* At the time of the descent into Egypt seven sons are ascribed to him (Gen. 46:16), remarkable from the fact that a majority of their names have plural terminations, as if those of families rather than persons (Smith). At the first census Gad had forty-five thousand six hundred and fifty adult males, ranking *eighth;* and at the second census forty thousand five hundred, ranking *tenth. 2. Position.* They were attached to the second division of the Israelitish host, following the standard of Reuben, and camping on the south of the tabernacle, their chief being Eliasaph, the son of Deuel, or Reuel (Num. 1:14; 2:10-16). *3. Territory.* In common with Reuben, Gad requested Moses to give them their portion on the east of Jordan, because they had "a great multitude of cattle." Upon being assured that they would assist their brethren in the conquest of Canaan, Moses granted them their request. The country allotted to Gad appears, speaking roughly, to have lain chiefly about the center of the land east of Jordan. To Reuben and Gad was given the territory of Sihon, between the Arnon and the Jabbok, and as far east as Jazer, the border of the Ammonites, but the division is hard to define (see Num. 32:34, sq.; Josh. 13:15, sq.). "The land is high, well suitable for flocks. . . . there is water in abundance, and therefore the vegetation is rich" (Harper, *Bible and Mod. Dis.*, p. 262). *4. Subsequent History.* The Gadites were a warlike race, and they bravely aided their brethren in the

conquest of Canaan (Josh. 4:12; 22:1-4). Surrounded by the Ammonites, Midianites, and many other hostile tribes, they yet nobly defended their country. One of their greatest victories was that gained over the descendants of Ishmael, the tribes of Jetur, Nephish, and Nodab, from whom they took enormous booty (I Chron. 5:18-22). The seat of Ishbosheth's sovereignty was established in this territory, for Abner brought him to Mahanaim, and there he reigned (II Sam. 2:8), and there he was assassinated. Many, however, of the Gadite chiefs had joined David while in the hold (I Chron. 12:8); and when, years later, he was obliged to flee across the Jordan, he found a welcome and help (II Sam. 17:24, 27-29). In the division of the kingdom, Gad, of course, fell to the northern state, and many of the wars between Syria and Israel must have ravaged its territory (II Kings 10:33). At last, for the sins of the people, Tiglath-pileser carried the Gadites and the neighboring tribes away captive into Assyria (II Kings 15:29; I Chron. 5:26).

2. The "Seer," or "the king's seer," i. e., David's (II Sam. 24:11; I Chron. 21:9; 29: 29; II Chron. 29:25), was a prophet who appears to have joined David when in "the hold," and at whose advice he quitted it for the forest of Hareth (I Sam. 22:5), B. C. before 1000. We do not hear of him again until he reappears in connection with the punishment inflicted for the numbering of the people (II Sam. 24:11ª19; I Chron. 21:9-19). But he was evidently attached to the royal establishment at Jerusalem, for he wrote a book of the Acts of David (I Chron. 29:29), and also assisted in settling the arrangements for the musical service of the "house of the Lord" (II Chron. 29:25).

Gad (găd; "good fortune"), a Canaanite god of fortune often appearing in Hebrew compounds cf. Baal-gad (Josh. 11:17; Migdal-gad Josh. 15:37). *See* Gods, False.

Gad'ara (găd'à-rà), the capital of the Roman province of Perara, east of the Jordan, about six miles from the Sea of Galilee, opposite Tiberias. The scene of the healing, by the Saviour, of the demoniac was Gadara. The modern village, Um-Keis, is in the midst of ruins intimating the grandeur of the ancient Gadara. *See* Gadarenes.

Gadarenes (găd-à-rēnz'), the inhabitants of *Gadara* (*q. v.*), mentioned in the account of the healing of the demoniacs (Mark 5:1; Luke 8:26, 37). It is also the correct reading in Matt. 8:28 (and is so rendered in the R. V. and R. S. V.), where "Gergesenes" must be supposed to owe its origin to a confusion in the matter of geography by an ancient copyist.

Gad'di (găd'ī; *fortunate*), son of Susi, of the tribe of Manasseh, sent by Moses to represent that tribe among the twelve "spies" on their exploring tour through Canaan (Num. 13: 11), B. C. c. 1441.

Gad'diel (găd-ĭ-ĕl; *fortune of Gad*), son of Sodi, of the tribe of Zebulun. One of the twelve "spies" sent by Moses to explore Canaan (Num. 13:10), B. C. c. 1441.

Ga'di (gā'dī, a *Gadite*), the father of the usurper Menahem, who went up from Tirzah, and came to Samaria and slew Shallum, king

of Israel (II Kings 15:14), and reigned ten years over Israel (v. 17), B. C. about 741.

Gad'ites (găd'īts; the descendants of *Gad* (*q. v.*), the son of Jacob (Num. 34:14; Deut. 3:12, 16; 4:43; 29:8, etc.).

Ga'ham (gā'hăm; *to burn*), one of the sons of Nahor (Abraham's brother) by his concubine Reumah (Gen. 22:24), B. C. about 2100.

Ga'har (gā'här), one of the chief Nethinim whose descendants returned with Zerubbabel from the captivity to Jerusalem (Ezra 2:47; Neh. 7:49), B. C. before 536.

Ga'ius (gā'yŭs; Latin *Caius*).

1. A Macedonian who accompanied Paul in some of his journeys, and was seized by the populace at Ephesus (Acts 19:29), A. D. about 54.

2. A man of Derbe, who accompanied Paul on his return from Macedonia into Asia, probably to Jerusalem (Acts 20:4).

3. An inhabitant of Corinth, the host of Paul, and in whose house the Christians were accustomed to assemble (Rom. 16:23). He was baptized by Paul (I Cor. 1:14).

4. The person to whom John's third epistle is addressed. "He was probably a convert of St. John (v. 4), and a layman of wealth and distinction in some city near Ephesus, A. D. after 90. The epistle was written for the purpose of commending to the kindness and hospitality of Gaius some Christians who were strangers in the place where he lived."—*Smith*.

Ga'lal (gā'lăl; *rolling*), the name of two Levites after the exile.

1. One of those who dwelt in the villages of the Netophathites and served at Jerusalem (I Chron. 9:15), B. C. about 536.

2. A descendant of Jeduthun, and father of Shemaiah, or Shammua (I Chron. 9:16; Neh. 11:17), B. C. before 445.

Gala'tia (gà-lā'shĭ-à). The Roman Galatia was the central region of the peninsula of Asia Minor, with the provinces of Asia on the west, Cappadocia on the east, Pamphylia and Cilicia on the south, and Bithynia and Pontus on the north (Acts 16:6; 18:23; I Cor. 16:1; Gal. 1:2, etc.). It would be difficult to define the exact limits. In fact they were frequently changing. At one time there is no doubt that

164. Map of Galatia

this province contained Pisidia and Lycaonia, and therefore those towns of Antioch, Iconium, Lystra, and Derbe, which are conspicuous in the narrative of St. Paul's travels. **Gala'tians** (gȧ-lā'shĭ-ȧns). They were called by the Romans *Galli*, and were a stream from that torrent of barbarians which poured into Greece in the 3d century B. C., and which recoiled in confusion from the cliffs of Delphi. Crossing over into Asia Minor they lost no time in spreading over the whole peninsula with their arms and devastation, dividing nearly the whole of it among their three tribes. They levied tribute on cities and kings, and hired themselves out as mercenary soldiers. It became a Roman province under Augustus, reaching from the borders of Asia and Bythnia to the neighborhood of Iconium, Lystra, and Derbe, "cities of Lycaonia." Henceforth this territory was a part of the Roman empire.

"The Galatians are frequently called Gallo-Grecians, and many of the inhabitants of the province must have been of pure Grecian origin. Another section of the population, the early Phrygians, were probably numerous, but in a lower and more degraded position. The presence of a great number of Jews in the province implies that it was, in some respects, favorable for traffic. . . . The Roman itineraries inform us of the lines of communication between the great towns near the Halys and the other parts of Asia Minor. These circumstances are closely connected with the spread of the Gospel" (C. and H., *Life and Epist. of St. Paul*, i, 247).

Religious Matters. The Galatians had little religion of their own, and easily adopted the superstitions and mythology of the Greeks. Paul introduced the Gospel among them (Acts 16:6; 18:23; Gal. 1:6; 4:3), visiting them in person. When detained by sickness he sent Crescens to them (II Tim. 4:10). Soon after Paul left Galatia, missionaries of the Judaizing party came, and taught the necessity of circumcision for the higher grade of Christian service; declared that the apostle did, in effect, preach circumcision (Gal. 5:11), thus casting doubt upon Paul's sincerity. Such teaching caused defection among the converts to Christianity, and he wrote his epistle vindicating himself against the charges of the Judaizing party.

Galatians, Epistle to, the letter of the Apostle Paul containing his great defense of the gospel of grace against legalistic perversion or contamination.

1. **Early Testimony.** The early church gives unambiguous testimony to this document. Marcion put it at the head of his *Apostolikon* (140 A. D.). Athenagoras, Justin Martyr and Melito quote it. Evidences of it appear in Ignatius and Polycarp. With the other Pauline epistles it appears in the oldest Latin, Syriac and Egyptian translations and in the Muratorian Canon of the second century. No trace of doubt as to the authority, integrity or apostolic genuineness of the epistle comes from ancient times.

2. **Destination and Date.** Although the Pauline authorship of Galatians is well established, its destination, occasion and date are surrounded by critical difficulties. It was addressed to "the churches of Galatia" (Gal. 1:2). The Roman province of Galatia included not only Galatia proper, peopled largely by Celts from Gaul, but also portions of Lycaonia, Pisidia and Phrygia, all situated on the south. That Paul addressed the churches in the south part of Galatia is supported by the following facts. (1) He and Barnabas had visited the cities of Iconium, Lystra, Derbe and Pisidian Antioch, all in south Galatia, and had established churches in the vicinity during the first missionary journey (Acts 13:4; 14:18). (2) Familiar reference to Barnabas (Gal. 2:1, 9, 13) would be unexplainable in a letter sent to northern Galatia, where Barnabas seems to have been unknown. (3) In the south Galatian cities there were Jews who might have caused the events mentioned in the letter (Acts 13:14-51; 14:1; 16:1-3). If the "South Galatian theory" is subscribed to, Galatians may have been written either at Antioch in Syria at the consummation of the first missionary journey (Acts 14:26-28) or at Ephesus in the course of the third missionary journey (Acts 19:10). The Apostle's visit to Jerusalem (Gal. 2:1-10) is thought to be identical to that alluded to in Acts 11:30. If this is so, Galatians may have been sent from Antioch around 48 A. D. prior to Paul's third visit to Jerusalem to attend the apostolic gathering of Acts 15. According to this theory, Galatians would be the earliest of the Apostle's letters. There are strong reasons, however, to support the hypothesis that Galatians was written at Ephesus (c. 52 A. D.) during the same time as the other great epistles.

3. **The Occasion.** Galatians has been called the "Magna Charta of Christian liberty" and the "Christian's Declaration of Independence." The difficulty that produced this important epistle was caused by Jewish believers who proclaimed a mixture of Judaism and Christianity. The Apostle had proclaimed the free grace of God for all men through the death of Christ. The legalizers contended that Christianity could only work within the sphere of the Mosaic law. Faith in Christ, involving the free gifts of the Holy Spirit, was not sufficient. Obedience to the Mosaic law (Gal. 2:16, 21; 3:2; 5:4, etc.), which requires observance of festal days, (Gal. 5:3; 6:12) and the Sabbath (Gal. 4:10), was stressed. Had the Judaizers won, Christianity merely would have been a sect within Judaism. The situation called for all the skill and wisdom the great Apostle could muster. With invincible logic he vindicated Christianity on the sole basis of man's acceptance of Christ. Men are justified by the finished work of the Redeemer and in no manner by forms and ceremonies. Galatians was an echo of the great truth of justification so masterfully set forth in Romans.

4. **Outline.**

Introduction: 1:1-5

Part I. The Apostolic Vindication, 1:6-2:21
1. The occasion, 1:6, 7
2. The authenticity of his gospel, 1:8-10
3. Divine origin of it, 1:11-24
4. The official endorsement of it, 2:1-10
5. The explanation of his conduct, 2:11-21

Part II. Doctrinal Justification, Chaps. 3 and 4

1. The faulty conduct of the Galatians, 3:1-5
2. Abraham's example, 3:6-9
3. Legal deliverance by Christ, 3:10-14
4. The purpose of the law, 3:15-18
5. Law related to the promise, 3:19-22
6. Superiority of the condition under faith compared with that under law, 3: 23-4:11
7. Paul and the Galatians, 4:12-20
8. The two covenants, 4:21-31

Part III. The Practical Application, 5:1-6:10

1. Warning of the right use of freedom, 5:1-15
2. The way to spiritual growth, 5:16-26
3. Exhortation to patience and brotherly love, 6:1-5
4. Exhortation to liberality, 6:6-10
5. Warning against Judaizers, 6:11-16

Conclusion: 6:17, 18   M. F. U.

Galbanum. *See* Vegetable Kingdom.

Gal'eed (găl'ē-ĕd); *heap of witness*, the name given by Jacob to a pile of stones erected by Jacob and Laban as a memorial of their covenant (Gen. 31-47, 48). It is Hebrew, but the name given by Laban, Jegar-sahadutha, is Aramaic, known probably to Nahor's family, while Abraham and his descendants learned the kindred dialect of Hebrew.

Galilae'an (găl-ĭ-lē'ăn), a native, or inhabitant of Galilee (Matt. 26:69; Acts 1:11; 5:37; John 4:45, "of Galilee"). The Galilaeans were generous and impulsive, of simple manners, earnest piety, and intense nationalsim. They were also excitable, passionate, and violent. The Talmud accuses them of being quarrelsome, but admits that they cared more for honor than for money. Their religious observances were simple, differing in several points from those of Judea. The people of Galilee were specially blamed for neglecting the study of their language, charged with errors in grammar, and especially with absurd malpronunciation, sometimes leading to ridiculous mistakes. Thus there was a general contempt in Rabbinic circles for all that was Galilaean. The Galilaeans were easily recognized by their dialect and tone, as is seen by the detection of Peter as one of Christ's disciples (Mark 14:70). The name was applied by way of reproach to the early Christians. Julian generally used this term when speaking of Christ or Christians, and called Christ "the Galilaean God." He also made a law requiring that Christians should be called by no other name, hoping thereby to abolish the name of Christian. It is said that he died fighting against the Christians, and as he caught the blood from a wound in his side, threw it toward heaven, saying, "Thou hast conquered, O Galilaean!"

Gal'ilee (găl'ĭ-lē; Heb. *gălîlăh, circle or circuit*). Palestine (*q. v.*) was divided into three provinces—Judea, Samaria, and Galilee. Galilee occupied the upper part of the land, being the northwest province. In the time of Christ it included more than one third of western Palestine, extending from the base of Mount Hermon, on the north, to the ridges of Carmel and Gilboa, on the south, and from the Jordan to the Mediterranean Sea, about fifty by twenty-five miles in extent. Solomon once offered the tract to Hiram, who declined it, after which Solomon colonized it. It embraced a large northern portion of the tribe of Naphtali, and was called Galilee of the Gentiles. There are very many Scripture references to it. The first three gospels are occupied largely with Christ's ministry in Galilee. Of his thirty-two parables nineteen were spoken in Galilee, and twenty-five of his thirty-three great miracles were performed in Galilee. In this province the Sermon on the Mount was spoken. Here our Lord was transfigured.

165. Galilean Terrain at Edge of Nazareth

Gal'ilee, Sea of. This is called by four different names in Scripture: The "Sea of Chinnereth" (Heb. *kĭnnĕrĕth, harpshaped*), the shape of the sea (Num. 34:11; Josh. 12:3; 13:27); the "Lake of Gennesareth" (Luke 5:1, Gr. *Gennēsaret*, the name of the extended plain adjoining the lake; the "Sea of Tiberias" (John 6:1; 21:1). This is the name used by the natives at this time—*Bahr Tarbariyeh*. The name "Galilee" is used (Matt. 4:18; 15:29). The lake is distant from Jerusalem about sixty miles; is from eighty to one hundred and sixty feet deep, with abundance of fish. The river Jordan, which makes a steep descent, falling on the scale of sixty feet to a mile, for the distance of more than twenty-five miles, enters the lake, The waters of the lake are blue and sweet. The lake, about which so much of the life of Jesus was passed, though six hundred and eighty feet below the Mediterranean Sea, was the center of busy life. Nine cities, each with a population of not less than fifteen thousand, bordered it. It was the very highway of rich traffic between Damascus and the sea. The customhouse duties, from which Christ took Matthew, were of no little import. The hot springs brought multitudes to be cured. George Adam Smith, says concerning the industries of Galilee: "They were agricultural, fruit growing, dyeing, and tanning, with every varying department of a large carrying trade, but chiefly boatbuilding, fishing, and fish curing. Of the last, which spread the lake's fame over the Roman world before its fishermen and their habits became familiar through the Gospel, there is no trace in the Evangelists. The fisheries themselves were pursued by thousands of families. They were no monopoly; but the fishing grounds, best at the north end of the lake, where the streams entered, were

166. Sea of Galilee

free to all. And the trade was very profitable."
It was on and about this lake that Jesus did
many of his most wonderful miracles. Eighteen
of the thirty-three recorded miracles of Christ
were probably done in the immediate neighborhood of the Sea of Galilee. In the city of
Capernaum alone he performed ten of these.

Gall.

1. **Bitter substance** (Heb. *m^erērāh*), denotes
etymologically "that which is bitter;" see Job
13:26, "thou writest bitter things against me."
Hence the term is applied to the "bile" or
"gall" from its intense bitterness (Job 16:13;
20:25); it is also used of the "poison" of
serpents (Job 20:14), which the ancients erroneously believed was their gall. *See* Vegetable
Kingdom.

2. **Poisonous herb** (Heb. *rō'sh*), generally
translated "gall" by the A. V., is in Hos. 10:4
rendered "hemlock;" in Deut. 32:33 and Job
20:16 *rō'sh* denotes the "poison" or "venom"
of serpents. From Deut. 29:18 and Lam. 3:19,
comp. with Hos. 10:4, it is evident that the
Hebrew term denotes some bitter, and perhaps poisonous plant. Other writers have supposed, and with some reason (from Deut. 32:
32), that some berry-bearing plant must be
intended. Gesenius understands "poppies."
The capsules of the *Papaveraceae* may well give
the name of the *rō'sh* ("head") to the plant in
question, just as we speak of poppy *heads*. The
various species of this family spring up quickly
in cornfields, and the juice is extremely bitter.
A steeped solution of poppy heads may be
"the water of gall" of Jer. 8:14.

3. **Bitter secretion** (Gr. *cholē*, greenish?) It
is recorded that the Roman soldiers offered
our Lord, just before his crucifixion, "vinegar
(R. V. and R. S. V. 'wine') mingled with
gall" (Matt. 27:34), and "wine mingled with
myrrh" (Mark 15:23). The Jews were in the
habit of giving the criminal a stupefying drink
before nailing him to the cross, probably with
the purpose of deadening pain. Much discussion has arisen both as to the nature of the
potion presented to Jesus and its purpose.
Perhaps the following is about correct: "Gall"
is to be understood as expressing the bitter
nature of the draught, and its purpose was to
strengthen the Lord for the trial of suffering
before him.

Gallery, a term in architecture, signifying *projection* of a story or portico, an *offset, terrace*
(Ezek. 41:15; 42:3, 5). Their exact form is a
matter of conjecture.

Galley. *See* Ship.

Gal'lim (găl'ĭm); *heaps* a city of Benjamin,
north of Jerusalem. It was the native place of

Phalti, to whom David's wife Michal had
been given (I Sam. 25:44; Isa. 10:30). Site
uncertain.

Gal'lio (găl'ĭ-ō) proconsul of Achaia (Acts 8:
12, etc.). *See* Paul.

Gallows. *See* Punishments.

Gama'liel (gȧ-mā'lĭ-ĕl; *reward of God*).

1. **Son of Pedahzur**, and the captain of the
tribe of Manasseh (Num. 7:54; 10:23), who
was appointed to assist Moses in numbering
the people at Sinai (1:10; 2:20). He made an
offering, as tribe prince, at the dedication of
the altar (7:54), and was chief of his tribe at
starting on the march through the wilderness
(10:23), B. C. c. 1440.

2. **Doctor.** The grandson of the great Hillel,
and himself a Pharisee and celebrated doctor
of the law. His learning was so eminent and
his character so revered that he is one of the
seven who, among Jewish doctors only, have
been honored with the title of "Rabban." He
was called the "Beauty of the Law," and it is
a saying of the Talmud that "since Rabban
Gamaliel died the glory of the law has ceased."
He was a Pharisee, but anecdotes are told of
him which show that he was not trammeled by
the narrow bigotry of the sect. He rose above
the prejudices of his party. Candor and wisdom seem to have been the features of his
character, and this agrees with what we read
of him in the Acts of the Apostles, that he
was "had in reputation of all the people" (C.
and H., *Life and Epistles of St. Paul*). When
the apostles were brought before the Sanhedrin, and enraged the council by their courage
and steadfastness, the latter sought to slay
them. But this rash proposal was checked by
Gamaliel, who, having directed the apostles
to withdraw, thus addressed the council: "Ye
men of Israel, take heed to yourselves what
ye intend to do as touching these men. . . .
Refrain from these men, and let them alone;
for if this counsel or this work be of men, it
will come to nought; but if it be of God, ye
cannot overthrow it" (Acts 5:34-39). His counsel prevailed, and the apostles were dismissed
with a beating. We learn from Acts 22:3 that
he was the preceptor of the apostle Paul.
Ecclesiastical tradition makes him become a
Christian and be baptized by Peter and Paul,
together with his son Gamaliel and with Nicodemus. The Clementine Recognitions (1:65)
state that he was secretly a Christian at this
time. But these notices are altogether irreconcilable with the esteem and respect in which
he was held even in after times by the Jewish
Rabbins. The interference of Gamaliel in behalf of the apostles does not prove that he
secretly approved of their doctrine. He was a
dispassionate judge, and reasoned in that affair
with the tact of wordly wisdom and experience,
urging that religious opinions usually gain
strength by opposition and persecution (5:35,
37), while, if not noticed, they are sure not to
leave any lasting impression on the minds of
the people if devoid of truth (v. 38), and that
it is vain to contend against them if true (v.
39). M'C. and S., *Cyc.*

Games. This word does not occur in Scripture,
though frequent reference is made to the things
signified by it.

1. **In Bible Lands.** A taste for social games

in Oriental lands goes back to very ancient times. Sir Leonard Woolley recovered a fine Sumerian game board from Ur in lower Mesopotamia dating from before 3000 B. C. Dice from nearly every locality of the ancient east have been recovered in ivory, pottery and numerous other substances. Gaming boards from the Eighteenth Egyptian Dynasty from c. 1560-1350 B. C. have been recovered in large numbers. A gaming board with men of clay going back to almost 5000 B. C. has been brought to light in Egypt. In the University Museum at Philadelphia there is a pink alabaster draught board from Abydos dated c. 2900 B. C. Ivory strips with one side painted black were used in the place of dice. Marbles go back to early times and were popular in the Eighteenth Dynasty. At Tell Beit Mirsim (Kirjath-sepher) in Palestine a complete set of gaming pieces has been recovered from a royal palace. The Hyksos horsemen who invaded Egypt played at draughts for diversion. They had a square ivory board and used

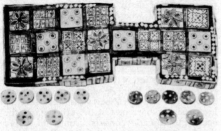

167. Gaming Board from Ur (about 2500 B. C.)

pyramid-like dice. On the pavement of Herod's Praetorium in Jerusalem a most elaborate gaming board has been recovered. The kind of plays used on this gaming board can be figured out. A gaming board from Crete from a royal recreation room is indescribably magnificent in silver, gold, ivory and crystal. The board is more than one yard long. Its ivory framework is set with gold plate trimmed with mosaic of rock crystal and blue enamel. Around its rim it is clustered with marguerites with crystal centers set in blue enamel. The top of the board is incised with nautilus shells, descriptive of the Minoan islanders. Toys abound from ancient Bible times. Miniature houses, animals and every-day scenes are depicted. Children of the well-to-do were well supplied with diversion. There are dolls with moveable joints and life-like hair. Toys from Tell Beit Mirsim include whistles, rattles and dolls. In Egypt elite social groups had hunting parties in the marshes. Carved sticks and wooden boomerangs were used. Harpoons, fishing spears and bronze fishhooks have turned up. (See M. S. and J. Lane Miller, *Ency. of Bible Life*, New York, 1944, pp. 391-392.) *M. F. U.*

2. **Hebrew.** With regard to juvenile games, the notices are very few. The only recorded sports, however, are keeping tame birds (Job 41:5) and imitating the proceedings of marriages or funerals (Matt. 11:16). With regard to manly games, they were not much followed by the Hebrews; the natural earnestness of their character and the influence of the climate alike

indisposed them to active exertion. The chief amusement of the men appears to have consisted in conversation and joking (Jer. 15:17; Prov. 26:19). A military exercise (probably a war dance) seems to be noticed in II Sam. 2:14. Indeed the public games of the Hebrews seem to have been exclusively connected with military sports and exercises; and it is probable that in this way the Jewish youth were instructed in the use of the bow and sling (I Sam. 20:20, 35-40; Judg. 20:16; I Chron. 12:2). In Jerome's day the usual sport consisted in lifting weights as a trial of strength, as also practiced in Egypt. Dice are mentioned by the Talmudists, probably introduced from Egypt. Public games were altogether foreign to the spirit of Hebrew institutions; the great religious festivals supplied the pleasurable excitement and the feelings of national union which rendered the games of Greece so popular, and at the same time inspired the persuasion that such gatherings should be exclusively connected with religious duties. Accordingly the erection of a *gymnasium* by Jason was looked upon as a heathenish proceeding (I Macc. 1:14; II Macc. 4:12-14). The entire absence of verbal or historical reference to this subject in the gospels shows how little it entered into the life of the Jews.

3. **Grecian.** The more celebrated of the Grecian games were four in number: The Isthmian, held on the Isthmus of Corinth, in a grove sacred to Poseidon, from B. C. 589, held in the first month of spring, in the second and fourth years of each Olympiad; the Nemean, celebrated in the valley of Nemea, in honor of Zeus; the Olympian, celebrated in honor of Zeus at Olympia; and the Pythian, held from B. C. 586 on the Crissaean plain, below Delphi, once in four years, in the third year of each Olympiad. The Olympic games were by much the most celebrated, and in describing these we describe the others, with certain differences of no account. They were celebrated once every four years, and hence a period of four years was termed an Olympiad, by which period the Greeks reckoned their time. "The festival consisted of two parts: *1.* **The presentation of offerings**, chiefly to Zeus, but also to the other gods and heroes, on the part of the Eleans, the sacred embassies, and other visitors to the feast; and *2.* **The contests.** These consisted at first of a simple match in the *stadium* (I Cor. 9:24-27), the race being run in heats of four, the winners in each heat competing together, the first in the final heat being proclaimed victor; later the runners had to make a circuit of the goal and return to the starting point; then came the long race, where the distance of the *stadium* had to be covered six, seven, eight, twelve, twenty, or twenty-nine times; the fivefold contest, consisting of leaping, running, quoit, spear throwing, and wrestling; boxing; chariot racing in the hippodrome; *pancration* (a combination of wrestling and boxing); racing in armor, and competitions between heralds and trumpeters. Originally only men took part in the contests, but after B. C. 632 boys also shared in them. At first the contests were only open to freemen of pure Hellenic descent, but they were afterward opened to Romans. Permission to view

the games was given to barbarians and slaves, while it was refused to women. All competitors were obliged to take an oath that they had spent at least ten months in preparation for the games, and that they would not resort to any unfair tricks in the contests. Judges, varying in number from one to twelve, but after B. C. 348 always ten, kept guard over the strict observance of all regulations and maintained order. Transgressions of the laws of the games and unfairness on the part of competitors were punished by forfeiture of the prize or by fines of money, which went to the revenue of the temple. The name of the victor, as well as his home, were proclaimed aloud by the herald and a palm branch presented him by the judges. The actual prize he only received on the last day of the festival. This was originally some article of value, but at the command of the Delphic oracle this custom was dropped, and the victors were graced by a wreath of the leaves of the sacred wild olive, said to have been originally planted by Neracles. Brilliant distinctions awaited the victor on his return home, for his victory was deemed to have reflected honor on his native land at large. He was accorded a triumph, and at Athens received 500 *drachmae*, the right to a place of honor at all public games, and board in the *prytaneum* for the rest of his life" (Seyffert, *Dict. Class. Antiq.*). These games were often held in the Hellenic towns of Palestine, being introduced by Herod into Caesarea and Jerusalem. In the former town he built a stone theater and a large amphitheater. St. Paul's epistles abound with allusions to the Greek contests (see I Cor. 4:9; 9:24-27; 15:32; Phil. 3:14; Col. 3:15; II Tim. 2:5; 4:7, 8; Heb. 10:33; Heb. 12:1). A direct reference to the Roman beast-fights (Gr. *ethēriomachēsa*) is made by St. Paul when he says, "If after the manner of men I fought with beasts at Ephesus," (I Cor. 15:32). Paul takes for granted that his readers were acquainted with what he describes in such strong language, and that they would take it figuratively, since they knew that his citizenship would exclude him from condemnation to such punishment. It is here a significant *figurative* description of the fight with stong and exasperated enemies.

Gam'madim (găm'ă-dĭm), mentioned as defenders of the towers of Tyre (Ezek. 27:11). Various explanations have been given of the meaning of the term, but the most probable is "warriors," "brave men," used as an epithet applied to the native troops of Tyre. R. S. V. renders "Men of Gamad." Perhaps Kumidi in N. Syria is meant, mentioned in the Amara letters.

Ga'mul (gā'mŭl; *rewarded*), the chief of the twenty-second course of priests, among whom the services of the sanctuary were distributed by lot in the time of David (I Chron. 24:17), B. C. after 1000.

Gaoler. *See* Jailer.

Gap (Heb. *pĕrĕṣ breach*), an opening in a wall (Ezek. 13:5); "breaches" (Amos 4:3). Such a break was exceedingly dangerous in time of siege.

Figurative. The corruption was so great in Israel that Ezekiel (22:30) declares "that not a man could be found who should enter into the gap as a righteous man, or avert the judgment of destruction by his intercession."

Garden, an enclosed plot of ground carefully cultivated. The term (Heb. *găn*, Gr. *kēpos*). applies to flower gardens (Cant. 6:2), spice plantations (4:16), orchards (6:11), kitchen gardens (Deut. 11:10), and probably parks (II Kings 9:27; 21:18, 26). Bible lands have been for the most part denuded of their forests. Even groves of nonfruit-bearing trees are rare, except in the neighborhood of cities and villages. The mountain tops are generally bare. The same is true of the table lands of the interior. The grain fields and pastures are usually at a distance from the villages, not surrounded by fences or hedges, but extending unbroken for miles in every direction, often without a single tree to diversify their surface. On the other hand the vegetable gardens, fruit orchards, mulberry groves, and such trees as are cultivated for timber, like the poplar, are grouped in and around the villages and towns, where they are accessible to the people, can be easily guarded from poachers, and above all where they can be irrigated from the water supply which is the life of the place.

The western landscape exhibits fields and pastures, divided by fences, walls, and hedge rows, interspersed with groves or scattered trees, and dotted with picturesque cottages, with here and there a village or town, the outskirts of the town being usually more or less waste or barren. On the other hand the eastern landscape consists usually of broad areas sown with uniform crops of cotton or cereals, or terraced hillsides planted with vines, mulberries, or figs, or bleak mountain tops, often with scarcely a shrub to clothe the gray rocks, and not infrequently one may take in at a glance these varied features of the scenery without seeing a single human habitation. Suddenly, on rising above a knoll in the plains, or turning an angle in the valleys, he comes upon a scene of ravishing beauty. A village, perched on the top of a rounded hill or clinging to the mountain side, or a city in a broad plain, surrounded and interspersed with luxuriant gardens, orchards, and groves of shade and timber trees, among which wind silvery streams, and over which is a haze which transforms all into a dream. As he enters this paradise the voice of the nightingale, the goldfinch, and the thrush, and the odors and bright colors of innumerable flowers and fruits, charm his senses. Such a scene greeted Mohammed as he looked from the barren chalk hills of Anti-Lebanon over the oasis of Damascus, and he feared to enter lest he should no longer care for Paradise.

An Eastern garden is wholly unlike a Western. It is generally surrounded by a high wall of mud or stone (Prov. 24:31), or hedges or fences (Isa. 5:5), usually composed of a tangle of brambles, thorns, or canes to prevent intrusion. The door has a wooden boltlock, by the side of which is a hole for the hand to be put through from the outside to reach the lock, which is fastened on the inner face (Cant. 5:4, 5). Over the gate or inside the garden is a booth or lodge of boughs (Isa. 1:8), or a room, often in the shape of a tower (Mark

12:1), for the watchman. On the trees are scarecrows (Gr. *probaskanion*, Ep. Jer. 69). These consist of the figure of a man perched on the limb of a tree, or of rags tied to the branches, or of the body of a bird. These gardens are not laid out with the precision of the West, with paths and beds. The vegetables, however, are planted in rows by the shallow ditches or furrows through which the water is conveyed to them (Psa. 1:3; Eccles. 2:6). This water is turned from one furrow to another either by a hoe or by moving the earthen bank which separates them by a shove of the foot (Deut. 11:10). Sometimes the vegetables are planted in a sunken parallelogram, surrounded by a low, earthen wall, in which an opening is made by the foot until the space is filled with water, and then the earth is shoved back in the same way and retains the water. This process is repeated over the whole plantation. Many gardens have fountains or wells (Cant. 4:15). To this allusion is made in the name En-Gannim, "Fountain of Gardens," the modern Jennîn. In the orchards and gardens were planted vines, olives (Exod. 33:11), figs, pomegranates, walnuts (Cant. 6:11), flowers (Cant. 6:23), henna, spikenard, saffron, calamus, cinnamon, frankincense, myrrh, aloes, and various spices (R. V., Cant. 4:13, 14), and a great variety of vegetables and fruits. The gardens and parks of Solomon (Eccles. 2:5, 6) are supposed to have been in Wadi 'Urtâs, and the "pools" (v. 6) are still in good preservation. The "King's garden" (II Kings 25:4, etc.) was near the pool of Siloam, at Bîr Ayyûb, which is probably En-rogel.

The delight which the ancients derived from their gardens is the subject of many allusions in Canticles. It is exactly reproduced in oriental gardens today. Seated on a mat or rug by the bank of a rushing stream, under the shade of the orange or apricot, which tempers the brightness while not obscuring the glory of the sunshine, in an atmosphere laden with the odors of flowers, and musical with the songs of the nightingales and plaintive with the cooings of the turtle-doves, he whiles away hours, eating the luscious fruits which droop over his head, drinking of the pure, cold water, conversing with his friends, or, soothed by these influences, he sinks into a tranquil slumber, in which he dreams of the paradise of God.—*G. E. P.*

Figurative. A "watered garden" (Isa. 58:11; Jer. 31:12) was an emblem of fertility. A "tree planted by the waters" (Jer. 17:8; comp. Psa. 1:3) was the emblem of the righteous. A waterless garden (Isa. 1:30) was a desert.

Garden House, the rendering (II Kings 9:27) of Heb. *bêth hăggän,* "Ahaziah fled by the way of the garden house." "The 'garden house' cannot have formed a portion of the royal gardens, but must have stood at some distance from the city of Jezreel, as Ahaziah went by the road thither, and was not wounded till he reached the height of *Gur,* near Jibleam" (Keil, *Com.*). Some think that a place is denoted. In Canticles (1:16) the bride looks with delight upon the summer house shaded with verdure, and containing the divan, inviting to luxurious repose.

Gardener, a class of workmen alluded to in Job 27:18, and mentioned in John 20:15. *See* Garden.

Ga′reb (gä′rĕb; *scabby*). 1. An Ithrite, i. e., a descendant of Jethro, or Jether, and one of David's mighty men (II Sam. 23:38; I Chron. 11:40), B. C. about 1000.

2. A hill near Jerusalem, apparently N. W. (Jer. 31:39).

Garland (Gr. *stemma*). In heathen sacrifices it was customary to adorn the victims with fillets and garlands, and also to put garlands on the head of their idol before sacrifice. These garlands were generally composed of such trees or plants as were esteemed most agreeable to the god who was to be worshiped. It is recorded (Acts 14:13) that the priest at Lystra came out to meet Paul and Barnabas with "oxen and garlands," but whether to adorn the oxen or the apostles is uncertain.

Garlic, Garlick. *See* Vegetable Kingdom.

Garments. When the people proclaimed Jehu king they took their garments and put them under him on the stairs (II Kings 9:13), probably thus making an improvised throne for him. The spreading of garments in the streets before persons to whom it was intended to show particular honor was a very ancient and general custom. Thus the people spread their garments in the way before Jesus (Matt. 21:8), while some strewed branches. The simple and uniform shape of garments encouraged the practice of gathering a large number together (Job. 27:16; Matt. 22:11, 12; James 5:1, 2), and of keeping them on hand to present to those whom it was desired to honor (Gen. 35:2; II Kings 5:5; II Chron. 9:24). *See* Dress.

Gar′mite (gär′mĭt), an epithet of Keilah (*q. v.*) in the obscure genealogy (I Chron. 4:19) of Mered (*q. v.*).

Garner. *A depository* (usually rendered a *treasure*) but really the place where goods are laid up (Joel 1:17).

A place for storing away anything, especially a granary (Psa. 144:13); Matt. 3:12; Luke 3:17); elsewhere "barn." *See* Granary.

Garnet. *See* Mineral Kingdom.

Garrison (from Heb. näsăb to *stand* firm), a military or fortified post (I Sam. 13:23; 14:1, 6, etc.; II Sam. 23:14). In Ezek. 26:11 an improper rendering is given of the Heb. *măṣ-ṣ^ebōth* which always means a standing object or monumental *column;* here pillars dedicated to Baal, two of which are mentioned by Herodotus (ii, 44) as standing in the temple of Hercules at Tyre, one of gold, the other of emerald; not images of gods, but pillars, as symbols of Baal.

Gash′mu (găsh′mŭ), a prolonged form (Neh. 6:6) of the name Geshem (*q. v.*).

Ga′tam (gā′tăm; *puny*), the fourth named of the sons of Eliphaz, the son of Esau, and founder of an Edomitish tribe (Gen. 36:11, 16; I Chron. 1:36), B. C. about 1800.

Gate (generally the rendering of Heb. *shă‘ăr, opening,* and Gr. *pulē,* from *pělō, to turn),* the entrance to inclosed grounds, buildings, cities, etc.

1. **Various Names.** In the Scriptures we find mentioned: (1) *Gates of cities,* as the "fish," "sheep gate," etc., of Jerusalem (Neh. 1:3; 8:3; Jer. 37:13); the gates of Sodom (Gen.

19:1), of Gaza (Judg. 16:3). (2) *Gates of palaces* (Neh. 2:8). (3) *Gates of the temple* (*q. v.*). (4) *Gates of tombs* (Matt. 27:60, A. V. "door"). (5) *Gates of prisons* (Acts 12:10). (6) *Gates of camps* (Exod. 32:26, 27; see Heb. 13:12).

2. **Material, etc.** We are not informed as to what materials the Israelites used for the inclosures and gates of their temporary camps. In Egyptian monuments such inclosures are indicated by lines of upright shields, with gates apparently of wicker, defended by a strong guard. Gates of *brass* (Psa. 107:16; Isa. 45:2, "bronze") and of *iron* (Acts 12:10) were, probably, only sheeted with plates of these metals. Gates of *stone* and of pearls are mentioned in Isa. 54:12; Rev. 21:21, and are supposed to refer to such doors, cut out of a single slab, as are occasionally found in ancient countries. Gates of wood were probably used in Gaza (Judg. 16:3). The doors themselves of the larger gates mentioned in Scripture were two-leaved, plated with metal, closed with locks, and fastened with metal bars (Deut. 3:5; Psa. 107:16; Isa. 45:1, 2). Gates not defended by iron were of course liable to be set on fire by an enemy (Judg. 9:52). The gateways of royal palaces and even of private houses were often richly ornamented. Sentences from the law were inscribed on and above the gates (Deut. 6:9; Isa. 54:12; Rev. 21:21). In later Egyptian times the gates of the temples seem to have been intended as places of defense, if not the principal fortifications. The gateways of Assyrian cities were arched or squareheaded, sometimes flanked by towers. The entrance to their own royal mansions was a simple passage between two colossal human-headed bulls or lions.

3. **Purposes.** The gate was the place for great assemblies of the people (Prov. 1:21), as they passed into and out of the city. This naturally led to the custom of using gates as places for public deliberation; reading the law and proclamations (II Chron. 32:6; Neh. 8:1, 3); holding court (Deut. 16:18; 17:8; Ruth 4:11; II Sam. 15:2, etc.); gathering news (Gen. 19:1), and gossip (Psa. 69:12); attracting the attention of the sovereign or dignitary at his going out or coming in (Esth. 2:19, 21; 3:2). The priests and prophets seem to have delivered their discourses, admonitions, and prophecies at the gates (Isa. 29:21; Amos 5:10; Jer. 17:19, 20; 26:10). Criminals were punished outside the gates (I Kings 21:10, 13; Acts 7:58; Heb. 13:12). Pashur smote Jeremiah and put him in the stocks at the high gate of Benjamin (Jer. 20:2). In heathen cities the open spaces near the gates appear to have been sometimes used as places for sacrifice (Acts 14:13; comp. II Kings 23:8). Being positions of great importance the gates of cities were carefully guarded and closed at nightfall (Deut. 3:5; Josh. 2:5, 7; Judg. 9:40, 44).

4. **Figurative.** Gates are thus sometimes taken as representing the city itself (Gen. 22:17; 24:60; Deut. 12:12; Judg. 5:8; Ruth 4:10; Psa. 87:2; 122:2). "The gates of *righteousness*" (Psa. 118:19) are thought to mean the temple gates. The gates of *death* and *hell* occur (Job 38:17; Psa. 9:13; Mic. 2:13) as symbols of power and empire. In Matt. 16:18 by the "gates of hell" must be understood all

aggressions by the infernal empire upon the Christian Church.

Gath (găth; *wine press*), one of the cities of the Philistine pentapolis. The site is uncertain, for the city disappeared mysteriously by some unexplained disaster hinted at in Amos 6:2. Tell es-Safiyeh; ten miles E. of Ashdod and ten miles S. E. of Ekron is favored as its site. This was a famous Crusader location, from which Richard the Lionhearted made his raids on caravans near Beersheba. Araq-'el-Menshiyeh, six miles W. of Beit Jibrin has also been defended as the location of Gath. Wherever the ancient city was, it was the nearest of the large Philistine towns to Hebrew territory. It had a reputation for huge men like Goliath (I Sam. 17). Achish was king at the time of David and befriended him during Saul's persecution, giving him the town of Ziklag. Subsequently David captured Gath (I Chron. 18:1). Rehoboam, Solomon's son and successor, fortified it (II Chron. 11:8). The Aramaean king, Hazael of Damascus, captured Gath in his advance on Jerusalem (II Kings 12:7). *M. F. U.*

Gath'-he'pher (găth-hē'fĕr; *winepress of digging*) a town of Zebulun, in lower Galilee, 3 miles from Nazareth. It was Jonah's birthplace (II Kings 14:25), whose reputed tomb is shown at the village of El-Meshad, at the top of the hill, as *Neby-Yûnas*. In Josh. 19:13 the town is called Gittah-hepher.

Gath-rim'mon (găth-rĭm'ŏn; *winepress of Rimmon or pomegranate*).

1. A Levitical city in the tribe of Dan. It was situated near Joppa, in the plain of Philistia (Josh. 19:45; 21:24; I Chron. 6:69). The Gath-rimmon of Josh. 21:25 is evidently a copyist's error, occasioned by the wandering of the eye to the previous verse.

2. Also a city of the same name in the half tribe of Manasseh, called in I Chron. 6:70 Bileam.

Gaulani'tis (gô-lă-nī'tĭs), a province ruled by Herod Antipas, east of the Lake of Galilee. The name is derived from "Golan," one of the cities of refuge in the territory of Manasseh (Josh. 20:8; 21:27; Deut. 4:43). *See* Golan.

Gay (Gr. *lampros*, bright), a term equivalent to *magnificent*, *sumptuous*, as applied to clothing (James 2:3; "goodly" in v. 2).

Ga'za (gā'zȧ, *stronghold*), like Damascus, one of the most ancient cities of the world, being a border Canaanite city before Abraham. Its Hebrew name is Azzah (Deut. 2:23; I Kings 4:24; Jer. 25:20). It was the capital of the Philistines. Its earliest inhabitants were the Avims, who were conquered by a Philistine tribe called the Caphtorims (Josh. 13:2, 3). It was the scene of Samson's prowess and humiliation (Judg. 16:1-3); also of Philip's Christian service (Acts 8:26). Modern Gaza (Ghuzzeh) serves as the administrative center of the Gaza Strip, which is crowded with Arab refugees.

Ga'zathites (gā'zȧ-thīts), a designation (Josh. 13:3) of the inhabitants of the city of Gaza; rendered Gazites (Judg. 16:2).

Gazelle. See Animal Kingdom.

Ga'zer (gā'zĕr; II Sam. 5:25; I Chron. 14:16). *See* Gezer.

Ga′zez (gā′zĕz; *shearer*).

1. A "son" of Caleb (son of Hezron, son of Judah) by his concubine Ephah (I Chron. 2:46).

2. A grandson of the same Caleb, through his son Haran (I Chron. 2:46).

Ga′zites (gā′zīts) the designation (Judg. 16:2) of the inhabitants of Gaza; rendered "Gazathites" (Josh. 13:3).

Gaz′zam (găz′ăm) the progenitor of one of the families of Nethinim that returned from the captivity with Zerubbabel (Ezra 2:48; Neh. 7:51), B. C. before 536.

Ge′ba (gē′bà; *hill*), a Levitical city of Benjamin (Josh. 21:17; comp. I Kings 15:22; I Sam. 13:3, 16, etc.), situated north of Jerusalem. The Philistines were smitten from Geba unto Gaza by David (II Sam. 5:25), and Gaza was rebuilt by Asa (I Kings 15:22; II Chron. 16:6). "From Geba to Beer-sheba" expressed the whole extent of the kingdom of Judah (II Kings 23:8). It is identified with Jeba, near Michmash.

Gebal (gē′băl). 1. A very ancient Phoenician trading city on the Mediterranean, present-day Gebeil on the Mediterranean twenty-five miles N. of Beirut (Josh. 13:5; I Kings 5:18 R. S. V.). The Greeks called the city Byblos, meaning "book," because here "paper" was

168. Gebal Harbor

made from imported Egyptian papyrus reeds. On this ancient writing material, expense accounts, state correspondence, religious texts and important documents were inscribed. The Phoenicians of Gebal (Gebalites or Geblites, Josh. 13:5) were expert masons, especially in stone-cutting (Cf. I Kings 5:18 R. S. V.). Gebalites were also famous for their boat building and caulking (Ezek. 27:9). These famous ships of antiquity were known as "Byblos travelers" and ran between Phoenica and Egypt. Their cargo consisted of cedar for mummy cases, oils for mummification, fancy woods, etc., returning with gold, metal wares, perfumes and papyrus reeds. Ships of Byblos plied the Mediterranean as did those of Tyre and Sidon. One of the features of the Amarna Letters is the correspondence of Rib-addi with the Egyptian pharoah. Wenamon tells of his visit to Byblos around 1100 B. C. Near Byblos the voluptuous Adonis rites in honor of Ashtarte were notorious. Excavations at Gebal, going back to c. 3000 B. C. or earlier, have revealed a long and interesting occupational history. The sarcophagus of Ahiram, king of Byblos in the eleventh century B. C., is important especially because of the alphabetic inscription it contains, which is a link in the development of the Phoenician alphabet.

169. Sarcophagus of Ahiram, found at Gebal

2. N. E. Edom, known also as Teman (Psa. 83:7), allied itself with Moabites and Arabians against Israel. *M. F. U.*

Ge′ber (gē′bẽr; *warrior*), the son of Uri, and one of Solomon's purveyors, having jurisdiction over Gilead (I Kings 4:19). His son (probably) had charge of Ramoth-gilead (v. 13), B. C. after 1000.

Ge′bim (gē′bĭm; *cisterns;* in Isa. 33:4, "*locusts;*" in Jer. 14:3, "*pits*"), a city of Benjamin, between Anathoth and Nob, mentioned only in Isa. 10:31, identified by various scholars with Khirbet ed-Duweir. Others suggest Bath el-Battash.

Geck′o. *See* Animals.

Gedali′ah (gĕd-à-lī′à; *made great by Jehovah*).

1. **The Son of Juduthun** and his second assistant in the Levitical choir selected by David for the temple service (I Chron. 25:3, 9), B. C. before 960.

2. **A Descendant of Jeshua**, and one of the priests who divorced their Gentile wives after the Babylonish captivity (Ezra 10:18), B. C. 456.

3. **The Son of Pashur**, and one of the Jewish princes who, hearing a prophecy of Jeremiah, conspired to accuse and imprison the prophet (Jer. 38:1, sq.), B. C. 589.

4. **The Son of Ahikam** (Jeremiah's protector, Jer. 26:24), and grandson of Shaphan. After the destruction of the temple (B. C. 587) Nebuchadnezzar departed from Judea, leaving Gedaliah as governor. He was stationed, with a Chaldean guard, at Mizpah. Gedaliah had inherited his father's respect for Jeremiah (Jer. 40:5, sq.), and was, moreover, enjoined by Nebuzar-adan to look after his safety and welfare (39:11-14). Having established his government at Mizpah, the inhabitants, who had fled at the advance of the Chaldean armies, or when the troops of Zedekiah were dispersed in the plains of Jericho, quitting their retreats, began to gather around him. Gedaliah advised submission and quietness, promising them, on this condition, the undisturbed enjoyment of their possessions. The labors of the field were ·resumed, and they "gathered wine and summer fruits very much" (40:12). Jeremiah joined Gedaliah; and Mizpah became the resort of Jews from various quarters (40:6, 11), many of whom, as might be expected at the end of a long war, were in a demoralized state, unrestrained by religion, patriotism, or prudence. The wise, gentle, and prosperous reign of Gedaliah did not secure

him from the foreign jealousy of Baalis, king of Ammon, and the domestic ambition of Ishmael, a member of the royal family of Judah (Josephus, *Ant.* x, 9, 3). The latter came to Mizpah with a secret purpose of destroying Gedaliah. Gedaliah, generously refusing to believe a friendly warning which he received of the intended treachery, was murdered, with his Jewish and Chaldean followers, two months after his appointment. After his death the Jews, anticipating the resentment of the king of Babylon, gave way to despair. Many, forcing Jeremiah to accompany them, fled to Egypt, under Johanan (II Kings 25:22-26; Jer. 40:13; 41:18).

Ged′eon (gĕd′ē-ŏn), the Grecized form of Gideon). The judge Gideon (*q. v.*), thus Anglicized in Heb. 11:32.

Ge′der (gē′dẽr; *walled*), a city of the Canaanites taken by Joshua (Josh. 12:13); identical probably with Gedor (*q. v.*).

Gede′rah (gĕ-dē′rä; *sheepcote*), a city of Judah with a Phoenician title. It is the feminine form of Geder (Josh. 12:13), and its plural is Gederoth (15:41). Identified with Jedireh 4 miles N. W. of Zorah and Eshtaol.

Ged′erathite (gĕd′ē-rȧ-thīt). an epithet of Josabad, one of David's famous warriors at Ziklag (I Chron. 12:4), so called from being a native of Gedor or Gederah.

Ged′erite (gĕd′ē-rīt), an epithet of Baal-hanan, David's overseer of olive and sycamore groves in the low plains of Judah (I Chron. 27:28), probably so called from being a native of Geder or Gederah.

Ged′eroth (gĕd′ē-rŏth; *fortresses*), a town in the "valley" of Judah (Josh. 15:41), and captured by the Philistines from Ahaz (II Chron. 28:18).

Gederotha′im (gĕd′ē-rô-thā′ĭm; *double wall*), named (Josh. 15:36) among the valley towns of Judah.

Ge′dor (gē′dŏr; *a wall*).

1. A chief of the Benjamites resident at Jerusalem (I Chron. 8:31; 9:37), B. C. before 536.

2. An ancient city in the mountains of Judah (Josh. 15:58), some of whose inhabitants joined David at Ziklag (I Chron. 12:7). It was probably to this town that Josabad the Gederathite belonged (I Chron. 12:4). Some identify it with Geder. The village is now called Jedûr.

3. It is said in I Chron. 4:39, "They went to the entrance of Gedor, even unto the east side of the valley," etc. It is impossible to determine exactly the location of this Gedor, but it is not to be identified with No. 2.

Geha′zi (gĕ-hā′zĭ, *valley of vision*), the servant of Elisha. The first mention of him is his reminding his master of the best mode of rewarding the kindness of the Shunammitess (II Kings 4:12 sq.). He was present when she told the prophet of her son's death, and was sent to Elisha to lay his staff upon the face of the child, which he did without effect (4:25-36). The most remarkable incident in his career is that which caused his ruin. When Elisha declined the rich gifts of Naaman, Gehazi coveted at least a portion of them, He therefore ran after the retiring chariots, and requested, in his master's name, a portion of the gifts, on the pretense that visitors had ar-

rived for whom he was unable to provide. He asked a talent of silver and two garments; and the grateful Syrian made him take two talents instead of one. Having hid the spoil, he appeared before Elisha, who asked him where he had been, and on his answering, "Thy servant went no whither," the prophet denounced his crime, and told him that the leprosy of Naaman should cleave to him and to his seed forever. "And he went out from his presence, a leper as white as snow" (II Kings 5:20-27). We afterward find Gehazi recounting to King Joram the great deeds of Elisha, and, in the providence of God, it happened that while he was speaking of the restoration of the child of the Shunammite woman she, with her son, appeared before the king to claim her house and lands, of which she had been despoiled during the recent famine. Struck by the coincidence, the king immediately granted her request (II Kings 8:1-6).

NOTE— *Gehazi made a leper.* The punishment inflicted on Gehazi, though severe, cannot justly be reckoned too hard for the occasion. "There was a great complication of wickedness in his conduct. He first arrogated to himself a superior discernment to that of the Lord's prophet; then he falsely employed the name of that prophet for the purpose which the prophet himself had expressly and most emphatically repudiated; further, as an excuse for aiming at such a purpose, he invented a plea of charity, which had no existence but in his own imagination; and, finally, on being interrogated by Elisha after his return, he endeavored to disguise his procedure by a lie. Such accumulated guilt obviously deserved some palpable token of the divine displeasure" (M'C. and S., *Cyc.*). See Elisha.

Gehen′na (gĕ-hĕn′ȧ; Gr. *Geenna*, for the Heb. *hĭnnōm*, the *Valley of Hinnom*), a deep, narrow glen to the south of Jerusalem, where the Jews offered their children to Moloch (II Kings 23:10; Jer. 7:31; 19:2-6). In later times it served as a receptacle of all sorts of putrefying matter, and all that defiled the holy city, and so became the representative or image of the place of everlasting punishment, especially on account of its ever-burning fires; and to this fact the words of Christ refer when he says "the fire is not quenched." "The passages of the New Testament show plainly that the word 'gehenna' was a popular expression for 'hell' of which Jesus and his apostles made use, but it would be erroneous to infer that Jesus and his apostles merely accommodated themselves to the popular expression, without believing in the actual state of the lost." In the N. T. the word gehenna falls many times from the lips of Christ in most awesome warning of the consequences of sin (Matt. 5:22, 29, 30; 10:28; 18:9; 23:15, 33; Mark 9:43, 45, 47; Luke 12:5). He describes it as a place where "their" worm never dies and their "fire" is never to be quenched. Gehenna is identical in meaning with the "lake of fire" (Rev. 19:20; 20:10, 14, 15). Moreover the "second death" and "the lake of fire" are identical terms (Rev. 20:14). These latter Scriptural expressions describe the eternal state of the wicked as forever separated from God and consigned to the special abode of unrepentant angels and men in the eternal state. The term "second" is employed relating to the preceding physical death of the wicked in unbelief and rejection of God (John 8:21-24). That the "second death" ("lake of fire" or gehenna) is not annihilation is shown clearly by Rev. 19:20 and 20:10. After 1000 years in the lake of fire the Beast and False Prophet still exist there undestroyed. The words "forever and ever" ("to the ages of the ages") describing the destiny of the lost in Heb. 1:8, also apply to the duration of the throne of God as eternal in the sense of being unending. Thus is represented the punishment of the wicked. Gehenna, moreover, is not to be confused with Hades or Sheol (*q. v.*), which describe the intermediate state of the wicked previous to the judgment and the eternal state. *See* Hades, Lake of Fire, Tartarus, Hell, Hinnom. *M. F. U.*

Gel′iloth (gĕl′ĭ-lŏth, *circles*), a place on the boundary of Judah and Benjamin (Josh. 18:17), and probably another form of Gilgal (Josh. 15:7).

Gemal′li (gē-măl′ĭ; *camel driver*), the father of Ammiel, which latter was the Danite representative among those who explored the land of Canaan (Num. 13:12), B. C. c. 1440.

Gemari′ah (gĕm-à-rī′à; *Jehovah has perfected*).

1. The son of Hilkiah, who, with Elasah, son of Shaphan, were sent to Babylon as ambassadors by King Zedekiah. They also took charge of a letter from Jeremiah to the Jewish captives at Babylon, advising them to settle peaceably in the land of captivity, promising deliverance after seventy years, and warning them against false prophets (Jer. 29:3, sq.), B. C. about 597.

2. The son of Shaphan, one of the nobles of Judah, and a scribe of the temple in the time of Jehoiakim. Baruch read aloud the prophecies of Jeremiah to the people at the official chamber of Gemariah (or from a window in it), which was attached to the new gate of the temple built by King Jotham (Jer. 36:10; comp. II Kings 15:35). Gemariah's son, Michaiah, having reported this to his father, Baruch was invited to repeat the reading, at the scribe's chamber in the palace, before Gemariah and others, who gave an account of the matter to the king (Jer. 36:11-20). He, with the others, heard the divine message with fear, though Gemariah and two others besought the king not to destroy the roll (36:21-25), B. C. about 608.

Genealogy (Gr. *genealogia;* Heb. *sēphĕr tōlᵉdōth.* "the book of the generations"), race accounts or family registers tracing the descent and ancestral relationships of tribes and families. The older histories being usually drawn up on a genealogical basis, "genealogy" is often extended to the whole history, as "the book of the generation of Jesus Christ" includes the whole history contained in that gospel (comp. Gen. 2:4, etc.). This genealogical form of history was not peculiar to the Hebrew or the Semitic races, for the earliest Greek histories were also genealogies.

1. **The Redemptive Purpose of God** in respect to the higher interests of mankind took from the first a specific family direction, and it was of importance that at least the more prominent links in the successive generations of those more nearly connected with the development of that purpose should be preserved to future times. It is the genealogy of mankind in its bearing on this higher interest —reaching through the line of Seth to Noah,

then from Noah through the line of Shem to Abraham, then again through the lines of Isaac, Jacob, Judah, and David to Christ— over which the providence of God has most carefully watched, and which it has most fully exhibited in the historical records of Scripture. The promise of the land of Canaan to the seed of Abraham, Isaac, and Jacob successively, and the separation of the Israelites from the Gentile world; the expectation of Messiah as to spring from the tribe of Judah; the exclusively hereditary priesthood of Aaron with its dignity and emoluments; the long succession of kings in the line of David; and the whole division and occupation of the land upon genealogical principles by the tribes, families, and houses of fathers, gave a deeper importance to the science of genealogy among the Jews than perhaps any other nation.

2. **Different Genealogies.** "In Gen. 35:22-26 we have a formal account of the sons of Jacob, the patriarchs of the nation, repeated in Exod. 1:1-5. In Gen. 46 we have an exact genealogical census of the house of Israel at the time of Jacob's going down to Egypt. When the Israelites were in the wilderness of Sinai their number was taken by divine command 'after their families, by the house of their fathers.' According to these genealogical divisions they pitched their tents, and marched, and offered their gifts and offerings, chose the spies, and the whole land of Canaan was parceled out among them."

David, in establishing the temple services, divided the priests and Levites into courses and companies, each under the family chief. When Hezekiah reopened the temple and restored the temple services, he reckoned the the whole nation by genealogies. Zerubbabel's first care seems to have been to take a census of those who had returned from Babylon and to settle them according to their genealogies (see I Chron. 9:2, sq.). In like manner Nehemiah gathered "together the nobles, and the rulers, and the people, that they might be reckoned by genealogy" (Neh. 7:5; 12:26). That this system was continued in after times, at least as far as the priests and Levites were concerned, we learn from Neh. 12:22; and we have incidental evidence from the apocryphal books (I Macc. 2:1-5; 8:17; 14:29) of the continued care of the Jews still later to preserve their genealogies. Another proof is the existence of our Lord's genealogy in two forms, as given by Matthew and Luke. The mention of Zacharias as "of the course of Abia," of Elizabeth as "of the daughters of Aaron," and of Anna, the daughter of Phanuel, as "of the tribe of Aser," are further indications of the same thing (Luke 1:5; 2:36). From all this it is abundantly manifest that the Jewish genealogical records continued to be kept till near the destruction of Jerusalem. But there can be little doubt that the registers of the Jewish tribes and families perished at the destruction of Jerusalem, and not before.

"The Jewish genealogies have two forms, one giving the generations in a descending, the other in an ascending scale. Examples of the descending form may be seen in Ruth 4:18-22, or I Chron. 3; of the ascending I Chron. 6:33-43, A. V.; Ezra 7:1-5. Females are named in genealogies when there is anything remarkable about them, or when any right or property is transmitted through them (see Gen. 11:29; 22:23; 25:1-4; 35:22-26; Exod. 6:23; Num. 26:33; I Chron. 2:4, 19, 35, 50, etc.)" (Smith. *Bib. Dict.*, s. v.).

3. **Abbreviated Genealogies.** B. B. Warfield showed more than a generation ago that the Bible genealogies contained gaps ("The Antiquity and Unity of the Human Race," *Studies in Theology*, New York, 1932, pp. 235-258). The genealogies in Exod. 6:16-24, Ezra 7:1-5 and Matt. 1:1-17 contain omissions. This is most certainly the case also in the genealogies of Gen. 5 and 11. To use these genealogical lists in Genesis to calculate the creation of man (c. 4004 B. C.), as Archbishop Ussher has done, is not only unwarranted from a comparative study of Scriptural genealogies, but incontestably disproved by the well-attested facts of modern archaeology. The total length of the period from the creation of man to the flood and from the flood to Abraham is not specified in Scripture. That the genealogies of Gen. 5 and 11 are most assuredly drastically abbreviated and have names that are highly selective is suggested by the fact that each list contains only ten names, ten from Adam to Moses and ten from Shem to Abraham. It is quite evident that symmetry was the goal in constructing these genealogical lists rather than a setting forth of unbroken descent from father to son, in contrast to modern registers of pedigree. Such symmetry with the omission of certain names is obvious from the genealogy of Matt. 1:1-17. This fact is further corroborated by the evident latitude used in ancient Semetic languages in the expressions "begat," "bare," "father" and "son." This usage is completely contrary to English idiom. Thus to "beget" a "son" may mean to beget an actual child or a grandchild or a great grandchild, or even distant descendants. Usage extends to tribes or countries (Gen. 10:2-22), and even to non-blood relationship. Jehu, the usurper and founder of a new dynasty in Israel and with no blood connection whatever to the House of Omri, is nevertheless called "son of Omri" by Shalmaneser III of Assyria. (Daniel David Luckenbill, *Ancient Records of Assyria and Babylonia* I, Sect. 590.) Nebuchadnezzar is called the "father of" Belshazzar who was actually the son of Nabonidus, a usurper (Dan. 5:2). Accordingly, as J. H. Raven says in the regular recurring formula, "A lived . . . years and begat B, and A lived after he begat B . . . years and begat sons and daughters, and B lived . . . years and begat C." B may not be the literal son of A but a distant descendant. If so, the age of A is his age at the birth of the child from whom B is descended. Between A and B, accordingly, many centuries may intervene. The Genesis genealogical lists are not intended to divulge the antiquity of man upon the earth, but to set forth the line of the promised Redeemer (Gen. 3:15) from Adam to Abraham and to show the effects of sin and the altered conditions brought about by the flood and upon human vitality and longevity. Added evidence that the genealogies of Gen. 5

and 11 contain extensive breaks is demonstrated by the fact that they allow only about 4000 years from the creation of Adam to Christ. On the other hand, modern archaeology clearly traces sedentary pottery cultures such as that from Tell Halaf well before 4000 B. C. To place the flood so late as 2348 B. C., as is the case if the genealogies are employed for chronological purposes, is archaeologically fantastic. This great cataclysm certainly took place long before 4000 B. C. Revised by *M. F. U.*

Genealogy of Jesus Christ. *See* Chronology, New Testament; Jesus.

Generation. The word generation is used in at least three shades of meaning in the Scriptures, which are closely related and growing out of each other. (1) The radical meaning is that of the production of offspring, in which sense it is applied to the offspring of an individual, or successions of offspring noted in a genealogical table, and called a "book for generations" (Gen. 5:1; 37:2; Matt. 1:17, etc.), i. e., lists of successive lines of descent from father to son. (2) A period of time. Differing as the intervals do in this respect, *generation* could never be intended to mark a very definite period, and must be understood with considerable latitude. The term is used in the sense of time or successive divisions of time. For *generation* in the sense of a *definite* period of time, see Gen. 15:16; Deut. 23:2, 3, 8, etc. As an indefinite period of time: for time *past*, see Deut. 32:7; Isa. 58:12; for time *future*, see Psa. 45:17; 72:5, etc. (3) The word is also taken to denote the persons actually constituting a specific generation, as exponents of its state or character, as: "this generation" (Matt. 11:16), "an evil and adulterous generation" (Matt. 12:39), "faithless and perverse generation" (Matt. 17:17), "crooked and perverse generation" (Phil. 2:15). Delitzsch (*Com.*, on Isa. 53:8) thus defines generation: "We must adhere to the ordinary usage, according to which *dôr* signifies an age, or the men living in a particular age; also, in an ethical sense, the entire body of those who are connected together by similarity of disposition" (Psa. 14:5).

Gen′esis (jĕn′ĕ-sĭs; the book of origins, Gr. *genesis*, origin), stands traditionally as the introductory book of the entire body of Hebrew sacred literature and of revealed truth in general.

1. **The Name.** The book takes its name from the title given to it in the LXX version which is derived from the heading of its ten parts *hē biblos geneseos* (2:4; 5:1; 6:9; 10:1; 11:10; 11:27; 25:12; 25:19; 36:1; 37:2). The Hebrews style the book *bᵉrēshîth*, meaning "in the beginning."

2. **The Design.** As the book of beginnings Genesis recounts the beginning of the physical creation of all plant, animal and human life as well as human institutions and social relationships. The book illustrates (as does the entire Bible) the principle of selection. Those events necessary to introduce the drama of human redemption are narrated: The creation, the fall, the flood, the call of Abraham and foregleams of the promised redeemer (3:15, 16; 12:1-3; 49:10).

3. **The Outline.**

Part I. The Primeval History of Mankind, 1:1-11:26
1. The creation, 1:1-2:25
2. From the fall to the flood, 3:1-5:32
3. The flood, 6:1-9:29
4. From the flood to Abraham, 10:1-11:26

Part II. The Patriarchal History of Israel, 11:27-50:26
1. Abraham, 11:27-25:10
2. Isaac, 25:11-28:9
3. Jacob, 28:10-36:43
4. Jacob's sons, particularly Joseph, 37:1-50:26

4. **The Literary Scheme.** The narrative of Genesis is hung upon a geneological skeleton marked by the phrase which occurs ten times, "These are the generations of." Under this arrangement the book of Genesis is outlined as follows:

(1) The generations of the heavens and the earth (1:1-4:26); (2) The generations of Adam (5:1-6:8); (3) The generations of Noah (6:9-9:29); (4) The generations of Noah's sons (10:1-11:9); (5) The generations of Shem (11:10-26); (6) The generations of Terah (11:27-25:11); (7) The generations of Ishmael (25:12-18); (8) The generations of Isaac (25:19-35:29); (9) The generations of Esau (36:1-37:1); (10) The generations of Jacob (37:2-50:26).

5. **The Critical View.** Critics partition the book of Genesis and view it as comprised of composite sources pieced together by a late exilic or post-exilic redactor. J, the Jehovist, possibly wrote about 850 B. C., in the south (Judah), employing the name Jehovah. E, the Elohist, is said to have used the name Elohim, writing about 750 B. C., in the north (Ephraim). The narrative sections J and E were allegedly fitted into the Scriptural history of the origin of the Jewish nation, called the Priestly Code (P) about 500 B. C. This documentary theory, which was subtly developed, highly plausible and universally popular, is a highly traditional product of modern rationalistic skepticism and is based on late literary criteria, unsound philosophic presuppositions and a manifest enmity against the miraculous and the prophetic elements which constitute the warp and woof of the Pentateuch. (See Edward J. Young, *Introduction to the O. T.*, 1949, pp. 183-276.

6. **The Chronology.** Genesis leaves both the date of the creation of the world and of man an unsettled question. According to Genesis 1:1 the earth was created in the dateless past. The appearance of man upon the earth is described as accomplished by a direct act of God which occurred at least over 4,000 years B. C. and perhaps as early as 7,000-10,000 B. C. However, any considerably earlier date for the creation of man such as the evolutionists' greatly expanded ages is out of focus with the Genesis narratives. Moreover, the geneologies of Chapters 5 and 11 cannot be validly used to calculate the creation of man about 4004 B. C., as Archbishop Ussher has done; first, because these geneologies are evidently symmetrical rather than unabridged, and the date 4004 B. C. for man's creation is uncon-

trovertably disproved by the well attested findings of archaeology. The total length from the period of the creation of man to the flood and from the flood to Abraham is not specified in Genesis. That these geneological lists are drastically shortened and contain highly selective names is suggested by the fact that each list contains only ten names, ten from Adam to Noah and ten from Shem to Abraham. Symmetry is clearly aimed at with the omission of certain names, as is also true of the geneology of Matt. 1:1-17. Another reason that these geneologies cannot be used for dating purposes is that the Hebrew expressions "beget," "bare," "father" and "son" are used with great latitude of meaning in ancient Semitic languages in idiom quite alien to English. To beget a son may, of course, mean to bear an immediate male descendant (Gen. 4:25), or contrary to our usage, to bear a more remote descendant as a grandchild (cf. Gen. 46:25; II Kings 9:2, 20) or a great grandchild (Gen. 46:18). Usage extends even to tribes or countries (Gen. 10: 21, 22) or even to a non-blood relationship. Jehu, a usurper and the founder of a new dynasty, and with no blood relationship whatever to the house of Omri is, notwithstanding, called the "son of Omri" on the Black Obelisk of Shalmaneser III of Assyria. Likewise, Nebuchadnezzar is called "father of Belshazzar," who was actually the son of Nabonidus, the usurper (Dan. 5:2). Accordingly it appears how precarious it is to calculate dates on the basis of the genealogies of Genesis. The purpose of these lists is not to show the age of men upon the earth but to trace outstanding respective names in the line of the Messianic Redeemer (Gen. 3:15) from Adam to Abraham, and to show the effects of sin and the altered conditions caused by the flood upon human longevity. Modern archaeology has discovered highly developed sedentary pottery cultures, such as that at Tell Halaf, well before 4,000 B. C. This shows how untenable it is to place man's creation about 4,000 B. C. It also proves how archaeologically fantastic it is to date the deluge so late as 2348 B. C., as would be the case if the Genesis geneologies are employed for chronological ends. The deluge, as a world-wide catastrophe that it certainly was, took place long before 4,000 B. C.

Gennes'aret (gĕ-nĕs'á-rĕt; *garden of riches*). The earliest use of the name is in I Macc. 11:67, Genesar. The Targums identify the name with Chinnereth (Deut. 3:17; Josh. 19:35), which is applied both to the lake and the town.

1. **The Town.** This stood on the west shore of the lake, called in Old Testament *Chinnereth* (*q. v.*).

2. **The District.** A small region of Galilee, on the west shore of the lake, visited by Jesus on his way south to Capernaum (Matt. 14:34).

3. **Lake** (Luke 5:1). The name given to the *Sea of Galilee* (*q. v.*).

Gentile. 1. **Old Testament.** The Heb. *gōyîm* signified the nations, the surrounding nations, *foreigners* as opposed to Israel (Neh. 5:8).

2. **New Testament.** (1) The Greek *ethnos*

in the singular means a people or nation (Matt. 24:7; Acts 2:5, etc.), and even the Jewish people (Luke 7:5; 23:2, etc.). It is only in the plural that it is used for heathen (gentiles). (2) *Hellēn*, literally Greek, John 7:35; Rom. 3:9). The A. V. is not consistent in its treatment of this word, sometimes rendering it by "Greek" (Acts 14:1; 17:4; Rom. 1:16; 10:12), sometimes by "Gentile" (Rom. 2:9, 10; 3:9; I Cor. 10:32). The latter use of the word seems to have arisen from the almost universal adoption of the Greek language.

3. **Relation to Israel.** What rendered the Jews a distinct and honored class was simply their election of God to the place of his peculiar people, by which they became the recognized depositories of his truth and the consecrated channels of his working among men. The distinction between Israel and other nations, as was shown in the covenant with Abraham, was to be only for a time; and believing Gentiles in no age were excluded from sharing in the benefits conferred upon the Jews, when they showed themselves willing to enter into the bond of the covenant.

Hedged in by a multitude of special institutions and taught to consider a nonobservance of these customs as uncleanness, and blinded by an intense national pride, the Jews seemed often to regard the heathen as only existing for the purpose of punishing the apostasy of Judea (Deut. 28:49; I Kings 8:33, etc.), or of undergoing vengeance for their enmity toward her (Isa. 63:6).

"Considering the wall of strict separation which, as regards matters of religion the Jews had erected between themselves and the Gentiles, it would not readily occur to one that these latter were also permitted to take part in the worship at Jerusalem. It may be accounted for, however, by reflecting how formal and superficial the connection often is between *faith* and *worship*. To present a sacrifice in some famous sanctuary was often no more than an expression, on the part of the offerer, of a cosmopolitan piety, and not intended to be an expression of the man's creed. This might take place at Jerusalem, for there was no reason why the Jewish people and their priests should discountenance an act intended to do honor to their God, even though it were purely an act of politeness. Accordingly we find the Old Testament itself proceeding on the assumption that a sacrifice might be legitimately offered even by a Gentile" (Lev. 22:25) (Schürer, *Jewish People*, Div. II, vol. i, 299, sq.; also ii, p. 311).

The form which the adhesion of Gentiles to Judaism assumed, and the extent to which they observed the ceremonial laws of the Jews, was of a very varied character. Tertullian speaks of Gentiles who, while observing several Jewish ordinances, continued notwithstanding to worship their own deities. On the other hand, those who submitted to circumcision thereby bound themselves to observe the whole law to its fullest extent. Between these two extremes there would be a manifold series of gradations. The "God-fearing" Gentiles mentioned (Acts 10:2, 22; 13:16, 26, 43; 16:14; 17:17; 18:7) were, probably, those who adopted the Jewish mode of worship, attended the synagogues, but restricted themselves to certain leading points of the ceremonial law, and so were regarded as outside the fellowship of Jewish communities (Schürer, ii, 311, sq.). *See* Heathen.

4. **In Prophecy.** In the prophetic Word there is a clear distinction between "Jews, Gentiles and the Church of God" (I Cor. 10:32). In this present age all the saved are members of "the Church of God." Unsaved people are either Jews, who are nationally set aside in the present age, or Gentiles. The Word of God clearly outlines the future of the Gentiles. Having their origin in Adam they consequently also have their natural headship in him as do unsaved Jews. Having partaken of the fall, they are nevertheless the subjects of prophecy which foretells that some of them will yet share as a subordinate people with Israel in her coming Kingdom glory (Isa. 2:4; 60:3, 5, 12; 62:2; Acts 15:17). Their condition from Adam to Christ rests upon a fivefold indictment "without Christ, being aliens from the commonwealth of Israel, and strangers from the covenants of promise, having no hope, and without God in the world" (Eph. 2:12). Consequent upon the death, resurrection and ascension of Christ and the advent of the Spirit, admission to gospel privilege was accorded to Gentiles (Acts 10:45; 11:17-18). In the present age of the Church from Pentecost to the outtaking of the body of Christ, God is calling out an elect company from among the Gentiles (Acts 15:14) to form the Church. The salvation of this age is not a question of sharing Israel's earthly covenants, which even Israel is not now enjoying, but rather the grace brought by Jesus Christ in being privileged to partake of a heavenly citizenship. Prophecy reveals, too, that the mass of Gentiles will not in the present age enter by faith into these blessings. Consequently Gentiles move on as "the nations" to the end of their stewardship as earth rulers. The termination of this period will be the end of the "times of the Gentiles" (Luke 21:24; Dan. 2:36-44). The nations will thus pass through the tribulation judgments (Rev. 4:19) and will be judged as nations at the Second Coming of Christ (Matt. 25:31-46). The basis of the judgment will be the treatment of the Jew—"my brethren." The sheep will enter into the Millennial Kingdom; the goats, into everlasting fire prepared for the devil and his angels (Matt. 25:41). "And these shall go away into everlasting punishment: but the righteous into life eternal" (25:6). The Gentile is also distinctly revealed in the eternal state. After the creation of the new heavens and the new earth, when the New Jerusalem comes down from God out of heaven (Rev. 3:12; 21:2, 10) "the nations of them which are saved shall walk in the light of it: and the kings of the earth do bring their glory and honor into it . . . and they shall bring the glory and honor of the nations into it" (Rev. 21:24-26). Gentiles thus always remain distinct from the nation Israel, therefore, there is no defensible reason for misapplying this great body of Scripture bearing on the Gentiles either to the Jew or to the Church God. *See* Jews, Heathen.

Gentiles, Court of the. *See* Temple.

Gentleness (Heb. *'ănăwäh, condescension,* Psa. 18:35; Gr. *Epieikeia, clemency,* II Cor. 10:1). "All God's going back from the strictness of his rights as against men, all his allowing of their imperfect righteousness and giving a value to that which, rigidly estimated, would have none; all his refusal to exact extreme penalties; all his remembering whereof we are made and measuring his dealings with us thereby" (Trench, *Syn. of N. T.*), God demands the same of us toward our fellows (Matt. 18:23). The helping grace of God, that practical hearkening on the part of God, when called upon for help, which was manifested in the bettered condition of the Psalmist (II Sam. 22:36; Psa. 18:35). Four Greek words are rendered "gentle" or "gentleness," all of them with the underlying meaning of affable, kindly.

Genu'bath (gē-nū'băth; *theft*), the son of Hadad, of the Edomitish royal family, by the sister of Tahpenes, the queen of Egypt, and reared in Pharaoh's household (I Kings 11:20). He was born in the palace of Pharaoh and weaned by the queen herself, and was on the same footing as the sons of the king.

Ge'ra (gē'rà) the name of at last three Benjamites, perhaps from *gēr* (Heb. *Sojourner*).

1. The son of Bela and grandson of Benjamin (I Chron. 8:3); probably the same as the one mentioned (with some confusion) in verses 5, 7, unless one of these be identical with No. 2. In Gen. 46:21 he is given as the son of Benjamin, and there appears among the descendants of Jacob at the time of his removal to Egypt, B. C. about 1871. In I Chron. 7:7, Uzzi occupies the same position as Gera elsewhere in the genealogy.

2. The father (or ancestor) of Ehud the judge (Judg. 3:15), B. C. before 1295.

3. The father of Shimei, which latter cursed David when he fled from Absalom (II Sam. 16:5; 19:16, 18; I Kings 2:8), B. C. before 966.

Gerah, the smallest weight and coin among the Hebrews. *See* Metrology, III, IV.

Ge'rar (gē'rär), a Philistine city figuring prominently in the patriarchal narratives of Abraham (Gen. 20) and of Isaac (Gen. 26). Both of these patriarchs had somewhat similar experiences with their wives and King Abimelech (*q. v.* of Gerar). Tell el-Jemmeh, partly excavated by the great Egyptian archaeologist, Sir Flinders Petrie, is undoubtedly the important mound representing the ancient city. Excavation at the site revealed occupational levels from the Late Bronze Age through Byzantine times. In antiquity it likely controlled the lucrative caravan route. The multiplicity of objects found indicate sustained wealth. Incense altars from the sixth to the fourth centuries B. C., decorated with men and camels, point to the fact that Gerar was on the important spice and incense route from Arabia. It was situated on the border between Palestine and Egypt, but was located on an inland route more protected than the coastal military and commercial route.—*M. F. U.*

Ger'asene, an inhabitant of Gerasa (*q.v.*). Several manuscripts read *Gerasēnōn,* instead of *Gergesēnōn,* in Matt. 8:28.

Ger'gesa (gûr'gĕ-sà) or Ger'asa (gĕr'à-sà). There is diversity of opinion concerning the location of the place where Jesus healed the demoniac. Kersa, apparently formerly Gergesa, on the eastern shore of the Galilean Sea across from Magdala seems to be the most likely location. It has a topography fitting the details of the narrative (Luke 8:33). There was a Gadara (Muqeis) some half-dozen miles S. E. of the south end of the Sea of Galilee, but this does not suit Mark 5:13. Christ's miracle of healing is sometimes still identified with Gerasa, the splendid Nabataean city of Jerash, some forty miles S. E. of the Sea of Galilee in Transjordan, but this seems extremely unlikely in view of the great distance from the scene of Christ's Perean ministry. However, our Lord may have been in this magnificent city. Certainly some to whom He ministered lived there. The result of His ministry certainly extended there (Mark 5:20). Jerash was called the "Pompeii of the East." It is the best preserved Palestinian city from the Roman era. The British School of Archaeology in Jerusalem, The American Schools of Oriental Research and Yale University have done extensive work at this ruin. See Carl H. Kraeling, *Gerasa, City of the Decapolis,* The Am. Schools of Oriental Research, New Haven, Conn. The Temple of Artemis at Gerasa and the Temple of Dionysius, the wine god, and other famous buildings reveal the elegance of this metropolis. What is more interesting to the Bible student is that at Jerash the decline of paganism can be traced in masonry, as the form and fabric of pagan temples were incorporated into Christian churches, such as St. Theodore's and the Cathedral. Jerash was rivaled in size by Palmyra and in cultic importance by Syrian Baalbek. *M. F. U.*

Gergesene' (gûr'gĕ-sēnz), the reading in the A. V. and R. S. V. in the account of the expulsion of the swine by our Lord (Matt. 8:28), instead of Gadarene (Mark 5:1; Luke 8:26).

Ger'izim (gĕr'ĭ-zīm), the mountain of the Gerizzites, situated opposite Mount Ebal, over the valley of Shechem, which was about three miles in length and not wider than will allow the hearing of a voice across. Gerizim is 2,849 ft. above the Mediterranean and is called today Jebel el-Tor. From its summit most of Palestine can be seen. It was the scene of the parable of the trees and brambles (Judg. 9:7, sq.). Tradition attempts to locate here Abra-

170. **Mount Gerizim**

ham's altar built for the sacrifice of Isaac, also his interview with Melchizedek. After the captivity Manasseh, by permission of Alexander the Great, built a temple on Gerizim, and the Samaritans joined together the worship of idols and the true God (II Kings 17: 33). This temple was destroyed by John Hyrcanus c. 128 B. C. To this day the sect offers annual paschal sacrifice on the top of the mount according to the prescriptions of Exod. 12. Moses commanded (Deut. 11:29; 27:12) that from Mount Gerizim the blessings of the law should be proclaimed, while its curses should proceed from Mount Ebal (comp. Josh. 8:33).

Ger'shom (gûr-shŏm; *sojourner* Exod. 2:22, cf. Arab *jarash*, "bell").

1. The elder of the two sons of Moses, born to him in the land of Midian by Zipporah (Exod. 2:22; 18:3), B. C. before 1441. He, with his brother Eliezer, held no other rank than that of simple Levites, while the sons of their uncle Aaron held all the privileges of the priesthood (I Chron. 23:15, 16; 26:24), a proof of the rare disinterestedness of Moses. Shebuel, one of his descendants, was appointed ruler of the treasury under David (I Chron. 26:24-28).

2. The oldest son of Levi (I Chron. 6:16, 17, 20, 43, 62, 71; 15:7), elsewhere written Gershon (*q. v.*).

3. The son of one Manasseh (according to the text), and father of Jonathan, which last acted as priest to the Danites who captured Laish (Judg. 18:30); but, according to a more correct reading, he is not different from the son of Moses. The Talmud explains the substitution of "Manasseh" for "Moses" in the text by asserting that Jonathan did the works of Manasseh, and was therefore reckoned in his family.

4. A descendant of Phinehas, who went up with Ezra from Babylon (Ezra 8:2), B. C. 457.

Ger'shon (gûr'shŭn; *expulsion*), the eldest of the three sons of Levi, apparently born before the migration of Jacob's family into Egypt (Gen. 46:11; Exod. 6:16), B. C. c. 1871. But, though the eldest born, the families of Gershon were outstripped in fame by their younger brethren of Kohath, from whom sprang Moses and the priestly line of Aaron (I Chron. 6:2-15). At the census in the wilderness the Gershonites numbered seven thousand five hundred males (Num. 3:22), the number of efficient men being two thousand six hundred and thirty (4:40). The sons of Gershon had charge of the fabrics of the tabernacle—the coverings, curtains, hangings, and cords (3:25, 26; 4:25, 26). In the encampment their station was behind the tabernacle, on the west side (3:23). When on the march, they went with the Merarites, in the rear of the first body of three tribes—Judah, Issachar, Zebulun—with Reuben behind them. In the apportionment of the Levitical cities thirteen fell to the lot of the Gershonites—two in Manasseh beyond Jordan, four in Issachar, four in Asher, and three in Naphtali. In the time of David the family was represented by Asaph "the seer" (I Chron. 6:39-43). It is not easy to see what special duties fell to the lot of the Gershonites in the service of the tabernacle

after its erection at Jerusalem, or in the temple. They were appointed to "prophesy"—i. e., probably, to utter or sing inspired words, perhaps after the special prompting of David himself (25:2). Others of the Gershonites, sons of Laadan, had charge of the "treasures of the house of God, and over the treasures of the holy things" (26:20-22), among which precious stones are specially named (29:8). In Chronicles the name is, with two exceptions (6:1; 23:6), given in the slightly different form of "Gershom."

Ger'shonites (gûr-'shŏn-īts), the descendants of Gershon, one of the sons of Levi (Num. 3: 21; 4:24, 27; Josh. 21:33, etc.). As to the office and duties of the Gershonites, *see* Levites.

Ge'sham (gē'shăm), or rather **Ge'shan**(gē'-shăn), the third son of Jahdai, among the descendants of Caleb (I Chron. 2:47), B. C. after 1440.

Ge'shem (gē'shĕm; *shower*), an Arabian (Neh. 2:19; 6:1), and one of the enemies of the Jews on the return from the exile, especially in the plots against the life of Nehemiah (6:2), B. C. 445. Geshem, we may conclude, was an inhabitant of Arabia Petraea, or of the Arabian Desert, and probably the chief of a tribe which, like most of the tribes on the eastern frontier of Palestine, was, in the time of the captivity and the subsequent period, allied with the Persians, or with any peoples threatening the Jewish nation; for the wandering inhabitants of the frontier, doubtless, availed themselves largely, in their predatory excursions, of the distracted state of Palestine, and dreaded the reestablishment of the kingdom. The Arabians, Ammonites, and Ashdodites are recorded as having "conspired to fight against Jerusalem and to hinder" its repairing. The name is identical with Gashmu (*q. v.*), being the Hebraized form with the dropping of the nominative ending "u" and *gashm* resolving into *geshem*.

Ge'shur (gē'shŭr; *bridge*), a principality in Syria on the east of Jordan, adjoining the north border of the Hebrew territory, and lying between Mount Hermon, Maachah, and Bashan (Deut. 3:13, 14; Josh. 12:5). This Aramaean principality was ruled over by Talmai, whose daughter David married (II Sam. 3:3). It was the possession of Manasseh, although its original inhabitants were not expelled (Josh. 13:13). Thither Absalom fled after killing Amnon (II Sam. 13:37, 38), from which Joab returned him to Jerusalem (14: 23). It is stated (I Chron. 2:23) that "Jair took Geshur, and Aram. . . . even threescore cities." While these places were taken, they were held only as subject territories.

Gesh'uri, (gĕsh'ū-rī) Deut. 3:14; Josh 13:2), or **Gesh'urites** (gĕsh'ū-rīts Heb.), (Josh. 12: 5; 13:11, 13; I Sam. 27:8), the inhabitants of Geshur (*q. v.*), bordering on Aram, to the east of Jordan.

Ge'ther (gē-'thĕr; derivation uncertain), the name of the third son of Aram (Gen. 10:23). He is mentioned in I Chron. 1:17 as one of the sons of Shem, probably meaning "grandson of." It is uncertain where his posterity settled.

Gethsem'ane (gĕth-sĕm'à-nē; Gr. from Aram. *oil press*), the olive yard at the foot of the

Mount of Olives, to which Jesus was accustomed to retire (Luke 22:39) with his disciples, and which was the scene of his agony (Mark 14:32; Luke 22:44; John 18:1). There are two traditional places called Gethsemane. One is in the possession of the Latin Church.

171. Garden of Gethsemane

It consists of a triangular spot, some seventy paces in circumference. It is inclosed by a fence and contains some very large and old olive trees, besides a flower garden. The Greeks have set up another traditional Gethsemane, located farther up Mount Olivet. Dr. Thomson (*Land and Book*, ii, p. 483, sq.) says that he is inclined to think both are wrong, and he would place the garden in a very secluded spot several hundred yards northeast of the other traditional sites.

Geu'el (gê-ū'ĕl; *majesty of God*), the son of Machi, of the tribe of Gad, and one of the men sent by Moses to search the land of Canaan (Num. 13:15), B. C. 1440.

Gez'er (gĕz'ĕr), a very ancient city on the Shephalah above the Maritime Plain, eighteen miles N. W. of Jerusalem and seventeen miles S. E. of Jaffa. The site was strategic since it guarded one of the few roads of access from Jaffa to Jerusalem. Tell Jezer is the modern town of Khirbet Yerdeh. It is called Gezer (II Sam. 5:25; I Chron. 14:16 A. V.). The site has been excavated by R. A. S. Macalister. The occupation of the site goes back to prehistoric times. Semitic Canaanites arrived about the second half of the third millennium B. C. Their decendants occupied the city when the Israelites came into the land under Joshua. Joshua evidently smote the king of Gezer (Josh. 12:12), yet the Canaanites somehow regained control of the city and remained safe behind their fourteen-foot thick walls (Judg. 1:29). The Hebrews are said to have compelled the Gezerites to do manual work (Josh. 16:10), but the city remained under Canaanite control until Solomon's time, when the Egyptian pharaoh, whose daughter married Solomon, destroyed the city and gave its ruins to the Jewish monarch as a wedding gift (I Kings 9:16). Solomon remodeled the town into one of his chariot cities (I Kings 9:15-19; 10:26). Macalister excavated the site from 1902-1908 under the Palestine Exploration Fund (British). His famous discoveries included a Middle or Bronze Age tunnel which ran back under the city ninety-four feet below the rock surface to a spring. A reservoir capable of holding 2,000,000 gallons

of water was also uncovered. The stout walls of Gezer explain why the Israelites were not able to take it. The well-known Gezer Calendar containing the program of the Palestinian farmer in the Saul-Davidic age and translated by W. F. Albright from Hebrew characters dating around 925 B. C. runs thus:

"His (or, a man's) two months are (olive) harvest;
His two months are grain planting;
His two months are planting;
His month is hoeing up of flax;
His month is barley harvest;
His month is harvest and festival;
His two months are vine tending;
His month is summer fruit."

The Egyptian conquest of Gezer is recounted in the Merenptah Stele which significantly contains the only allusion to Israel yet found in a Nile valley inscription, dated c. 1224 B. C.

172. Hebrew Calendar from Gezer

Gez'rites, (gĕz'rīts) the name given in the A. V. of I Sam. 27:8 to a tribe associated with the Amalekites and Geshurites, "of old the inhabitants of the land, as thou goest to Shur, even unto the land of Egypt." The three were attacked, plundered, and exterminated by David during his stay in the land of the Philistines. This is all that is known of the tribe, and even the name is in doubt. Gezrites (Heb. *hăgizrî*, strictly "the Gizrite") is the rendering of the *geri* of I Sam. 27:8, where the kethîbh has *hăgizrî*, which may be Girzite, Gerizite, or Gerizzite. The Alexandrian manuscript of the LXX has *ton Gezraion*; Vulgate Gerzi and Gezri. The R. V. has Girzites in the text and Gizrites in the margin. Gesenius himself, and after him Stanley, reading, as we suppose, Gerizite, supposed an old-time connection between this tribe and Mount Gerizim. If we read Gezrites, it would naturally mean inhabitants of Gezer; but Gezer being fifty miles distant in the territory of Ephraim, seems too far off to have been reached by David on this raid.—W. H.

173. Hebrew-Phoenician Scripts Showing the Comparative Date of the Gezer Calendar

Ghost, the archaic English form of the German *Geist*, or spirit, and the translation of several Hebrew and Greek words signifying *breath, life, spirit* (Job 11:20; Jer. 15:9; Matt. 27:50; John 19:30). In the New Testament it frequently occurs as the designation of the third person in the Trinity—the *Holy Ghost* (*q. v.*). other phrases in which it occurs are those rendered "to give up the ghost," etc., all simply signifying to *die* (Gen. 25:17; Lam. 1:19, etc.). *See* Holy Ghost.

Gi'ah (gī'à; *bursting forth as a fountain*), opposite the hill Ammah, on the way to the desert of Gibeon, mentioned in the account of the pursuit of Abner by Joab and Abishai (II Sam. 2:24).

Giant, an abnormally tall and powerful human being of ancient Bible lands; the rendering of several Hebrew words.

1. **Nephilim** (nĕf'ĭ-lĭm; Hebrew *nᵉphilîm*). The form of the Hebrew word denotes a plural verbal adjective or noun of passive signification, certainly from *naphal*, "to fall," so that the connotation is "the fallen ones," clearly meaning the unnatural offspring which were in the earth in the years before the flood, "and also after that" (Num. 13:33), "when the sons of God came in unto the daughters of men" (Gen. 6:4). The mention of the great stature of the Nephilim, the sons of Anak, in the evil report which the ten spies brought of the land of Canaan (Num. 13:33) together with the Septuagint rendering, *gigantes*, suggested the translation giants. The real idea of the word must have been "fallen ones" or monsters of mixed human and angelic birth, like the rebellious Titans. They were exceedingly wicked and violent so that "every imagination" of the thoughts of men's hearts "was only evil continually" (Gen. 6:5). *See* Merrill F. Unger, *Biblical Demonology*, pp. 45-52.

2. **Rephaim** (rĕf'ā-ĭm; Hebrew *rᵉphā'îm*, *shades, ghosts*). The aboriginal giants who inhabited Canaan, Edom, Moab and Ammon. In Abraham's time, c. 1950 B. C., Chedorlaomer defeated them. At the period of the Conquest, c. 1440 B. C., Og, king of Bashan, is said to have alone remained of this race (Deut. 3:11; Josh. 12:4; 13:12). His huge bedstead of iron is particularly mentioned.

3. **Anakim** (ăn'à-kĭm; Hebrew *'ănāqîm, sons of Anak*). In Num. 13:33 the Anakim are classed with the Emim and the Rephaim on account of their gigantic size.

4. **Emim** (ĕm'ĭm), a race which inhabited the country of the Moabites (Gen. 14:5), and which is pictured as "great and many and tall as the Anakim" (Deut. 2:11).

5. **Zamzumim** (zăm'zŭm-ĭm), a giant race inhabiting the land of Ammon (Deut. 2:20).

6. **Other references.** From a remnant of the Anakim in Philistine Gath came the famous Goliath (I Sam. 17:4). Two of the Philistine giants are mentioned in II Sam. 21:16-22. The tradition of a giant race persisted in the ancient Near East and goes back in the Genesis account to intercourse between fallen angels and mortal women. Although this so-called angel hypothesis of Gen. 6:1-4 is disclaimed by many Bible students, it is a clear implication of the original. Says W. F. Albright, "Yahweh was believed to have created astral as well as terrestrial beings and the former were popularly called, 'the host of heaven' or 'the sons of God'. In Gen. 6:1 ff., for example, . . . the (astral) gods who had intercourse with mortal women who gave birth to heroes (literally, meteors, *nephilim*), an idea that may often be illustrated from Babylonian and Greek mythology. But the Israelite who had this section recited, unquestionably thought of intercourse between angels and women (like later Jews and Christians)." *From the Stone Age to Christianity*, (1940), p. 226.

Gib'bar (gĭb'är; *mighty man, a hero*), an Israelite whose descendants, to the number of ninety-five, returned with Zerubbabel from Babylon (Ezra 2:20), B. C. before 536. This is probably an error for the remnants of the natives of Gibeon (Neh. 7:25).

Gib'bethon (gĭb'ĕ-thŏn; *mound, a height*), a Philistine city (Josh. 19:44; 21:23), within the bounds of the tribe of Dan, and assigned to the Kohathites (21:23). Nadab, king of Israel, was slain under its walls (I Kings 15:27; 16:15).

Gib'ea (gĭb'ē-à; *hill*), a place built or occupied, in connection with Machbenah, by Sheva (I Chron. 2:49), perhaps the same as Gibeah (Josh. 15:57).

Gib'eah (gĭb'ē-à; Hebrew same as above), a *hill*, as the word is sometimes rendered.

1. **Gibeah-haaraloth**, "the hill of the foreskins" (Josh. 5:3, margin).

2. **Gibeah of Judah**, situated in the mountains of that tribe (Josh. 15:57), where the prophet Habakkuk is said to have been buried. It lay from seven to ten miles S. W. of Jerusalem, and is identified by Robinson with Jebah.

3. **Gibeah of Benjamin** (Judg. 19:14; I Sam. 13:16; II Sam. 23:29), known also as "Gibeah of Saul" (I Sam. 11:4; Isa. 10:29), the scene of the inhuman crime recorded in Judg. 19:12, sq., and for which the Benjamites were nearly exterminated. It was Saul's birthplace, and continued to be his residence after he became king (I Sam. 10:26; 11:4; 15:33, etc.), and here the Gibeonites hung his descendants (II Sam. 21:6). Saul's Gibeah has been excavated by W. F. Albright. The modern site is Tell el-Fûl, meaning "hill of beans." The site revealed twelve levels of history. An Israelite town, apparently referred to in Judg. 19 and 20, was destroyed by fire. Saul's rustic stronghold with its sturdy polygonal masonry was erected c. 1015 B. C. The outer citadel walls, 170 x 155 feet, were eight to ten feet thick. The castle comprised two stories with a stone staircase. The casemented walls and separately bonded towers are peculiar to this period. In the audience chamber David played his harp to soothe the demon-possessed Saul (I Sam. 16:23). Among the interesting objects found were grinding stones, spinning whorls, cooking pots, burnished ware and a gaming board. Storage bins for oil, wine and grain, still holding their contents when excavated, were also found in the royal palace. *M. F. U.*

4. **Gibeah at Kirjath-jearim**, where the ark remained from the time the Philistines returned it until it was taken to Jerusalem (II Sam. 6:3, 4; comp. I Sam. 7:1, 2).

5. Gibeah is rendered "hill" in the following passages: "the *hill* that pertained to Phineas," in Mount Ephraim, where Eleazar was buried (Josh. 24:33), identified with Khirbet Jibia, five miles N. of Guphna, toward Shechem; "hill of Moreh" (Judg. 7:1); "hill of God" (I Sam. 10:5); "hill of Hachilah" (I Sam. 23:19; 26:1); "hill of Ammah" (II Sam. 2:24); "hill of Gareb" (Jer. 31:39).

Gib'eath (gĭb'ē-ăth; Josh. 18:28), same as Gibeah, III.

Gib'eathite (gĭb'ē-à-thīt), a native of Gibeah (I Chron. 12:3), Shemah by name, who was the father of two Benjamites who joined David.

Gib'eon (gĭb'ē-ŏn; *hill city*), one of the Hivite cities which, through deception, effected a league with Joshua (Josh. 9:3-17), thus escaping the fate of Ai and Jericho. It was afterward allotted to Benjamin, and made a Levitical town (18:25; 21:17). After the destruction of Nob by Saul the tabernacle was set up here, and remained until the building of the temple (I Chron. 16:39; I Kings 3:4, 5; II Chron. 1:3, sq.). When the Amoritish kings besieged Gibeon, Joshua hastened to its relief and a great battle followed, to the great discomfiture of the Amorites (*See* Joshua). From Jer. 41:16 it would seem that after the destruction of Jerusalem by Nebuchadnezzar, Gibeon again

became the seat of government. It produced prophets in the days of Jeremiah (28:1). "Men of Gibeon" returned with Zerubbabel (Neh. 7:25). Gibeon is located about eight miles N. W. of Jerusalem on the route to Joppa. Other events in the history of Gibeon include the battle between Ishbosheth and David (II Sam. 2:8-17; 3:30) and the execution of the seven sons of Saul (II Sam. 21:1-9). Gibeon was an important place of worship in Solomon's time (I Kings 3:4; II Sam. 20:8). There he had his famous dream. On the Karnak Relief of Pharoah Shishak, Gibeon is mentioned as one of the trophies of his invasion of Palestine (I Kings 14:25 f. "in the fifth year of Rehoboam"). Shishak's carved reliefs also show captives taken in his Palestinian invasion. (*See* Leon Legrain, *Les Temples de Karnak*). Gibeon (El-Jib) was excavated in 1956 by a team representing the University of Pennsylvania Museum and the Church Divinity School of the Pacific. The walls and parts of the city water system were uncovered.—*M. F. U.*

174. Steps Leading down to Pool of Gibeon
(see II Sam. 2:8-17)

Gib'eonites (gĭb'ē-ŏn-īts), the people of Gibeon and perhaps also of the three cities associated with Gibeon (Josh. 9:17). Upon the victorious advance of the Israelites the inhabitants of Gibeon attempted to anticipate the danger which threatened them by means of a stratagem, and to enter into a friendly alliance with Israel. A delegation waited upon Joshua at Gilgal, representing themselves as ambassadors from a far country, desirous of making a league with him. They made this appear probable by taking "old sacks upon their asses, and wine bottles, old, and rent, and bound up; and old shoes and clouted (i. e., mended) upon their feet, and old garments upon them; and all the bread of their provision was dry and moldy." They declared that all these tokens of age and wear had come to them upon their journey. Upon these representations they were received as friends and an alliance made with them. Upon the discovery of the stratagem by which they had obtained the protection of the Israelites, they were condemned to be perpetual bondmen, hewers of wood and drawers of water for the congregation, and for the house of God and altar of Jehovah (Josh. 9:23, 27). Saul appears to have broken this covenant, and in a fit of enthusiasm or patriotism to have killed some and devised a general massacre of the rest (II Sam. 21:1, 2, 5). This was expiated many years after by giving up seven men of Saul's descendants to the Gibeonites, who hung them or crucified them "before Jehovah"—as a kind of sacrifice—in Gibeah, Saul's own town (vers. 4, 6, 9). From this time there is no mention of the Gibeonites as a distinct people, but many writers include them among the *Nethinim* (*q. v.*), who were appointed for the service of the temple (I Chron. 9:2).

Gib′lites (correctly A. V., R. S. V. Gebalites; gē′băl-īts), inhabitants of Gebal or Byblus a maritime town of Phoenicia. *See* Gebalities.

Giddal′ti (gĭ-dăl′tĭ; *I have made great*), the ninth son of Heman, and head of the twenty-second course of Levitical musicians in the tabernacle under David (I Chron. 25:4, 29), B. C. after 1000. The office of these brothers was to sound the horn in the Levitical orchestra (v. 5).

Gid′del (gĭd′ĕl), the name of two men whose descendants returned from the captivity with Zerubbabel.

1. One of the Nethinim (Ezra 2:47; Neh. 7:49), B. C. before 536.

2. One of "Solomon's servants," i. e., perhaps of the Canaanitish tribes enslaved by Solomon (Ezra 2:56; Neh. 7:58; comp. I Kings 9:21), B. C. before 536.

Gid′eon.—1. **Name and Family.** (Heb. (gĭd′ē-ŏn; *tree feller*, i. e., *warrior*). He was son of Joash the Abi-ezrite, of the tribe of Manasseh, and resided at Ophrah in Gilead, beyond Jordan.

2. **Personal History.** (1) **Condition of Israel.** Another relapse into evil brought Israel under the oppression of the Midianites for seven years. With Midian were allied Amalek and "the children of the east" (of Jordan). Their power pressed so severely upon the Israelites that the latter "made them the dens which are in the mountains, and caves, and strongholds." The allies encamped in their territory, destroyed the crops, "till thou come unto Gaza, and left no sustenance for Israel, neither sheep, nor ox, nor ass," so that "Israel was greatly impoverished" (Judg. 6:1-6). But before helping them the Lord sent a prophet (name not given) to reprove them for their disobedience and bring them to repentance. (2) **Call of Gideon.** In such a time of distress Gideon was threshing wheat in the winepress to conceal it from the Midianites. While thus engaged the angel of the Lord appeared to him and addressed him in these words: "The Lord is with thee, thou mighty man of valor." To this Gideon made the despondent reply, "If the Lord be with us, why then is all this befallen us?" Then Jehovah (revealing himself) said, "Go in this thy might, and thou

shalt save Israel from the hand of the Midianites: have not I sent thee?" Doubtful of the means by which he might accomplish so great a work, he requested a sign from heaven. This was granted to him; for when he presented his offering of a kid and unleavened cakes, the angel touched it, and it was consumed by fire. Recognizing Jehovah, he was filled with fear; but being comforted he built an altar (*Jehovah-shalom, the Lord send peace*, Judg. 6:11-24). (3) **Destroys an altar of Baal.** The first thing for Gideon to do was to purify his father's house from idolatry, and sanctify himself by sacrificing a burnt offering. That night God commanded him to throw down the altar of Baal, belonging to his father, and cut down the grove by it. Then he was to build an altar unto the Lord, and offer thereon a seven-year-old bullock of his father's. Assisted by ten servants, Gideon obeyed the vision during (probably) the following night, through fear of those around. Gideon, being identified as the perpetrator of the act, was in danger of being stoned. But his father took the part of his son, and told the people to allow Baal to plead for himself. From this circumstance Gideon received the name of *Jerubbaal*, i. e., "Let Baal plead" (Judg. 6:25-32). (*See* Baal). (4) **The sign of the fleece.** When the Midianites and their allies once more invaded the land of Israel the Spirit of the Lord came upon Gideon, and he gathered together an army from the tribes of Manasseh, Asher, Zebulun, and Naphtali. Before going into battle he asked for a sign from God of the success of his undertaking. He asked that the dew should fall on a fleece spread upon the threshing floor, while the ground all around should be dry. In the morning the fleece was so wet that Gideon wrung out of it a bowl of water. The next night the wonder was reversed, the soil being wet and the fleece perfectly dry (6:36-40). "The sign itself was to manifest the strength of divine assistance to his weakness of faith. Dew, in the Scriptures, is a symbol of the beneficent power of God, which quickens, revives, and invigorates the objects of nature when they have been parched by the burning heat of the sun's rays" (K. and D., *Com.*). (5) **Midianites defeated.** Assured by this double sign, Gideon advanced against the enemy, and encamped near the brook Harod, in the valley of Jezreel. *See* Esdraelon, Valley of. The army of the Midianites and their allies numbered about one hundred and thirty-five thousand (Judg. 8:10), while the Israelites mustered only thirty-two thousand. Nevertheless, "the Lord said unto Gideon, The people that are with thee are too many for me to give the Midianites into their hands, lest Israel vaunt themselves against me, saying, Mine own hand hath saved me." Gideon, therefore, made the usual proclamation (Deut. 20:8), that all the faint-hearted might withdraw; and twenty-two thousand availed themselves of this opportunity. Even this number the Lord regarded as too great, and so Gideon was commanded to test them in the matter of drinking. Those who knelt to drink were rejected, and only those were chosen who "lapped of the water with his tongue, as a dog lappeth," i. e., to take the water from the brook with the hollow of their hand, and lap it into the mouth with their tongue as a dog does. This test reduced the number to three hundred men. These took the provision from the people, and the war trumpets; so that every one of the three hundred had a trumpet and (as the provisions were probably kept in vessels) a pitcher as well. That night Gideon overheard a man telling to his fellow a dream which he had had, viz., that of a cake of barley bread overthrowing a tent. Regarding this dream as significant of divine cooperation, Gideon began the attack without delay. He divided his three hundred men into three companies, gave them all trumpets and empty pitchers, with torches in their hands. The pitchers were to hide the burning torches during the advance, and to increase the noise at the time of the attack by dashing them to pieces. The noise and sudden lighting up of the burning torches would naturally deceive the enemy as to the numbers of Gideon's army. His stratagem was eminently successful, and the enemy, thrown into a complete rout, "fled to Beth-shittah in Zererath, and to the border of Abel-meholah, unto Tibbath" (7:1-23). (6) **The Ephraimites.** In order to cut off the enemy's retreat at the Jordan, Gideon sent notice to the Ephraimites to "take before them the waters unto Beth-barah and Jordan" (3:28). The Ephraimites responded, took possession of the waters mentioned, captured the two princes, Oreb and Zeeb, put them to death, and brought their heads to Gideon. This latter act amounted to an acknowledgment of Gideon's leadership, but they were greatly annoyed because he had made war upon and defeated the enemy without first summoning them to the field. Serious consequences were avoided by the tact of Gideon in speaking in a lowly spirit of his doings in comparison with theirs (7:24-8:3). The gleaning of Ephraim is the victory over the Midianites and the capture of the two princes. The vintage of Abiezer, Gideon's victory with his three hundred men. (7) **Destroys Succoth.** Passing over Jordan in his pursuit of the Midianites, he was refused assistance by the people of Succoth and Penuel. Upon his return he destroyed both places (8:4-17). (8) **Avenges his brethren.** Gideon inquired of the two captive kings of Midian (Zebah and Zalmunna), "What manner of men were they whom ye slew at Tabor?" And they answered, "As thou art, so were they; each one resembled the children of a king." He then told them that these persons were his brethren, and commanded Jether, his firstborn, to slay them. But Jether fearing to do so, Gideon slew them, "and took away the ornaments that were on their camels' necks" (8:18-21). (9) **Refuses the crown.** Gideon, having so gloriously delivered Israel from the severe and long oppression of the Midianites, was offered by the Israelites an hereditary crown. "*The men of Israel*" were probably only the northern tribes already mentioned in chap. 6:35, who had suffered most severely from the Midianite oppression and had rallied about Gideon. The temptation to accept the government of Israel was resisted by Gideon, probably, because he thought the government of Jehovah

in Israel amply sufficient, and did not consider himself or his sons called to found an earthly monarchy. (10) **Remaining acts and death.** Gideon made the request that the people should give him the golden earrings taken with the spoil, which they willingly consented to do, and brought them to the amount of seventeen hundred shekels (about fifty pounds). He made thereof a golden ephod, and put it in his own city, Ophrah. This was probably a magnificent coat, made of the gold and purple, and not an image (*see* Ephod). It proved a snare to Israel, to himself, and house: to Israel, because they made it an object of worship; to Gideon and his house, because he invaded the prerogative of the Aaronic priesthood, and gave an impetus to the worship of Baal after his death. The evil consequences of this false step in religion was realized in the miserable sequel of Gideon's family. The history of Gideon is concluded in Judg. 8:28-32. The Midianites had been so humiliated that "they lifted up their heads no more. And the country was in quietness forty years in the days of Gideon." A few other notices are given respecting his family, to prepare the way for the history of his sons after his death. "And Jerubaal, the son of Joash, went and dwelt in his own house;" retiring into private life. In addition to the seventy sons born of his many wives, he had a son by his concubine who lived in Shechem, and to this son he gave the name of Abimelech. Gideon died at a good old age, and was buried in his father's sepulcher at Ophrah, B. C. about 1215-1190.

Gideo'ni (gĭd-ē-ō'nĭ; *warlike*), a Benjamite whose son, Abidan, was a prominent man of his tribe, and was employed in numbering the people (Num. 1:11; 2:22; 7:60, 65; 10:24), B. C. about 1400.

Gi'dom (gī'dŏm; *cutting*, i. e., *desolation*), a place east of Gibeah, toward the wilderness (of Beth-el), where the routed Benjamites turned to escape to the rock Rimmon (Judg. 20:45).

Gier Eagle. *See* Animal Kingdom.

Gift. The giving and receiving of presents has in all ages been not only a more frequent, but also a more formal and significant proceeding in the East than among ourselves. We cannot adduce a more remarkable proof of the important part which presents play in the social life of the East than the fact that the Hebrew language possesses no less than fifteen different expressions for the one idea. Several of these have a distinct and specific meaning, indicative of the relation of giver and receiver, or of the motive and object of the presentation.

1. From the Hebrew root *näthăn*, "to give," we have several words, meaning a *gratuity* (Prov. 19:6); to secure favor (Prov. 18:16; 21:14), in religious thankfulness (Num. 18:11), or in dowry (Gen. 34:12), in inheritance (Gen. 25:6; II Chron. 21:3; Ezek. 46:16, 17), or as a bribe (Prov. 15:27; Eccles. 7:7, etc.).

2. From the Heb. (*näsä'*, to *raise*) we have words signifying *pecuniary assistance* (Esth. 2:18) and a *present* in token of respect (II Sam. 19:42). Perhaps the inherent idea of these terms is that of *oblation* to a superior, a *dish of honor* for special guests (II Sam. 11:8), the

"collection" for the sanctuary (II Chron. 24: 6, 9).

3. More distinctly in the sense of a votive offering is Heb. *minḥäh*, an *oblation* or propitiatory gift (II Sam. 8:2, 6; I Chron. 18:2, 6, etc.), and in several other passages where the word has the accessory idea of *tribute*.

4. Other words are mercenary in character. Thus Heb. *shôḥăd* is a gift for the purpose of escaping punishment, presented either to a judge (Exod. 23:8; Deut. 10:17) or to a conqueror (II Kings 16:8).

5. In Greek the usual terms are generally derived from *didōmi*, (to *give*), and have a very wide meaning, as did the Hebrew.

"It is clear that the term 'gift' is frequently used where we should substitute 'tribute' or 'fee.' The tribute of subject states was paid not in a fixed sum of money, but in kind, each nation presenting its particular product; and hence the expression 'to bring presents'—to own submission (Psa. 68:29; 76:11; Isa. 18: 7). Friends brought presents to friends on any joyful occasion (Esth. 9:19, 22), those who asked for information or advice to those who gave it (II Kings 8:8), the needy to the wealthy from whom any assistance was expected (Gen. 43:11; II Kings 15:19; 16:8); on the occasion of a marriage, the bridegroom not only paid the parents for his bride (A. V. 'dowry'), but also gave the bride certain presents (Gen. 34:12; comp. Gen. 24:22). The nature of the presents was as various as were the occasions. The mode of presentation was with as much parade as possible. The refusal of a present was regarded as a high indignity. No less an insult was it not to bring a present when the position of the parties demanded it (I Sam. 10:27)" (Smith, *Bib. Dict.*, s. v.).

Gift of Tongues. *See* Tongues, Gift of.

Gifts, Spiritual (Gr. *charismata*, *gifts of grace*). This term outside of the Pauline epistles is only used once in the New Testament, viz., I Pet. 4:10, in the sense of the *gift of divine grace*. The expression, "But every man hath his proper gift of God" (I Cor. 7:7), seems to imply continence or some other gracious endowment in its place. In II Cor. 1:11 the "gift" was deliverance from great peril to life. Paul calls that which he intends to communicate to the Romans through his personal presence among them a *spiritual gift of grace* (Rom. 1:11), "because in his apprehension all such instruction, comfort, joy, strengthening, etc., as are produced by his labors, are regarded not as procured by his own human individuality, but as a result which the Holy Spirit works by means of him—the gracious working of the Spirit, whose organ he is" (Meyer, *Com.*, in loco).

The "free gift," "gift by grace" (Rom. 5: 15, 16) is the economy of divine grace, by which the pardon of sin and eternal salvation are appointed to sinners in consideration of the merits of Christ laid hold of by faith (comp. Rom. 6:23); plural of the several blessings of the Christian salvation (Rom. 11: 29).

In the technical Pauline sense "gifts" denote *extraordinary powers*, distinguishing certain Christians and enabling them to serve the Church of Christ, the reception of which

is due to the power of divine grace operating in their souls by the Holy Spirit (Rom. 12:6; I Cor. 1:7; 12:4, 31; I Pet. 4:10); specially the sum of those powers requisite for the discharge of the office of an evangelist (I Tim. 4:14; II Tim. 1:6). The fullest list of these charismata, or spiritual gifts, is given in I Cor. 12.

Concerning spiritual gifts Cremer says: "Their number is as various as the needs of the Church, and neither the enumeration of I Cor. 12, nor of Eph. 4, nor Rom. 12 can be regarded as exhaustive. But those are permanent which are necessary for the government of the Church, and those temporary which had a miraculous element, as the miraculous gifts of the apostles. But among the latter is not to be included the 'gift of proclaiming the Gospel so as to produce faith' (Weiss). The apostolic charismata bear the same relation to those of the ministry that the apostolic office does to the pastoral office, and consist in the power to lay the foundations of the Church. They are therefore not repeated, as the Irvingites hold, for there are no circumstances calling for their repetition" (article in Schaff-Herzog).

Gi'hon (gī'hŏn; *a gushing fountain*. 1. One of the four rivers of Eden (Gen. 2:13). The Gihon and also the Pishon are presumably canals (called rivers in Babylonia), which connected the Tigris and Euphrates as ancient river beds. Biblical notices place the Garden of Eden, where the Temptation and Fall occurred, somewhere in the Tigris-Euphrates Valley, evidently at the easternmost third of the Fertile Crescent. Shifting river beds and accumulation of enormous deposits of river silt make the task of locating the site of the Pishon or the Gihon virtually impossible. But the other two rivers, Euphrates and Tigris, are well known.

2. The intermittent spring which constituted Jerusalem's most ancient water supply, situated in the Kedron Valley just below the eastern hill (Ophel). This abundant source of water was entirely covered over and concealed from without the walls, and was conducted by a specially built conduit to a pool within the walls where a besieged citizenry could get all the water it needed. "Why should the kings of Assyria come and find much water?" The people queried in the time of Hezekiah (II Chron. 32:2-4). Hezekiah's Tunnel, 1777 feet long and hewn out of the solid rock, and comparable to tunnels at Megiddo and Gezer, conducted the water to a reservoir within the city. From the top of Ophel the ancient Jebusites (c. 2000 B. C.) had cut a passage through the rock where water pots could be let down a 40-foot shaft to receive the water in the pool fifty feet back from the Gihon. Early excavations at Jerusalem by the Palestine Exploration Fund under the direction of Sir Charles Warren (1867) resulted in finding the forty-foot rock-cut shaft. It is now known as Warren's Shaft. Conrad Shick in 1891 discovered an ancient surface canal which conveyed water from the Gihon Spring to the old pool of Siloam, located just within the S. E. extremity of the ancient city. Isaiah seems to have made an illusion to the softly flowing

waters of this gentle brook when he spoke poetically of "the waters of Shiloah that go softly" (Isa. 8:6). *M. F. U.*

Gil'alai (gĭl'á-lī; perhaps (*The Lord*) *has rolled away*), one of the priests appointed by Nehemiah to aid Zechariah in the musical services under Ezra at the dedication of the walls of Jerusalem (Neh. 12:36), B. C. 445.

Gilbo'a (gĭl-bō'á). Its name was probably suggested by the spring or fountain about half a mile E. of the city of Jezreel, which stood on the western extremity of the mount. Parallel and six miles N. of this range is another, called the "hill of Moreh," but called by travelers "Little Hermon." The beautiful valley of Jezreel lies between the two. It was at Gilboa that Saul and his three sons were slain in the battle with the Philistines (I Sam. 28: 4; 31:1, 8; I Chron. 10:1). When David heard of the disaster he incorporated in his beautiful ode all the conditions, geographical, military, and social (II Sam. 1:19-25).

Gil'ead (gĭl'ê-ăd; cf. Arab. *jala'ad, to be rough*).

1. **The mountain region** east of the Jordan, called "the mount of Gilead" (Gen. 31: 25), extending from the Sea of Galilee to the upper end of the Dead Sea, about sixty miles long and twenty wide, bounded on the north by Bashan, and on the south by Moab and Ammon (Gen. 31:21; Deut. 3:12-17), called now Jebel Jelâd or Jelûd. Upon it is the site of the ancient city of Ramoth-gilead, now identified by Nelson Glueck with Tell Ramith in the N. part of the country. Its scenery is beautiful. The hills are fertile and crowned with forests. Scripture names oak trees and herds of cattle as found there (Gen. 37:25; Num. 32:1). Reuben and Gad desired to possess this territory because in need of pasture for their herds (Deut. 3:12-17). The occupants now are, as in early times, hardy, fighting men. The name Gilead is seldom used in the Bible beyond Old Testament history.

2. **A city** "of them that work iniquity," etc. (Hos. 6:8). "Hosea calls Gilead (district) a city of evil-doers, as being a rendezvous for wicked men, to express the thought that the whole land was as full of evil-doers as a city is of men" (K. and D., *Com.*).

3. **The son of Machir** and grandson of Manasseh; his descendants bore his name as a patronymic (Num. 26:29, 30).

4. **Father of Jephthah** the judge, and descendant of the above (Judg. 11:1, 2).

5. **Son of Michael** and father of Jaroah, of the tribe of Gad (I Chron. 5:14).

Gil'eadites, the (Judg. 12:4, 5; Num. 26:29; Judg. 10:3), a branch of the tribe of Manasseh, descended from Gilead. There appears to have been an old-standing feud between them and the Ephraimites, who taunted them with being deserters. See Judg. 12:4, which may be rendered: "And the men of Gilead smote Ephraim, because they said, Ye Gileadites are fugitives of Ephraim among the Manassites." "The meaning of these obscure words is probably the following: 'Ye are an obscure set of men, men of no name, dwelling in the midst of two most noble and illustrious tribes.' "

Gil'gal (gĭl'găl; *rolling*).

1. A place in the Jordan valley not far from Jericho, called Geliloth (Josh. 18:17). Here the Israelites first encamped after they crossed Jordan, and here were the twelve stones set up as a memorial (Josh. 4:19, 20). Samuel judged here (I Sam. 7:16); Agag was slain here (I Sam. 15:33).

2. Gilgal of Elijah and Elisha (II Kings 2:1, 2; 4:38), a locality probably four miles distant from Beth-el and Shiloh.

3. In Josh. 12:23 occurs the name of a regal Gilgal. In the R. V. the term "king of the nations of Gilgal" is exchanged for "the king of Goiim in Gilgal," and Parker says the word Goiim probably means the nomad people who had been driven away by Joshua.

Gi'loh (gī'lō), in the mountains of Judah (Josh. 15:51), the birthplace and the scene of the miserable suicide of the traitor Ahithophel (II Sam. 15:12; 17:23). Probably the present Khirbet Gala, 5 miles N. N. W. of Hebron. Giloh stands probably for the original Gilon (cf. II Sam. 15:12; 23:34). *See* Gilonite.

Gi'lonite (gī'lŏn-īt), an epithet of the traitor Ahithophel (*q. v.*), doubtless from his city, Giloh (II Sam. 15:12; 23:34).

Gim'el (gĭm'ĕl; *camel*). Gimel is the third letter of the Hebrew alphabet, pronounced like English "g" and corresponding to Greek *gamma*. It stands at the head of the 3rd section of Psalm 119, in which each verse commences with this letter in the Hebrew.

Gim'zo (gĭm'zō; a *place abounding in sycamores*), a town in the low country of Judah. Now Jimzu, three miles from Ludd or Lydda.

Gin, an old English word for *trap*, and the rendering of two words:

1. (Heb. *mōqēsh*). A *noose* or "snare," as elsewhere rendered (Psa. 140:5; 141:9; Amos 3:5).

2. (Heb. *pǎh*). A *plate* of metal, hence a *trap* (Job 18:9; Isa. 8:14); elsewhere "snare."

Gi'nath (gī'năth), the father of *Tibni* (*q. v.*), king of the northern tribes of Israel (I Kings 16:21, 22).

Gin'netho (gĭn'ê-thô), a corrupt reading (Neh. 12:4) for the name *Ginnethon*.

Gin'nethon (gĭn'ê-thŏn; *gardener*), one of the "chiefs" of the priests that returned from the captivity with Zerubbabel (Neh. 12:4, where the reading is "Gennetho") and subscribed the covenant with Nehemiah (10:6). His son, Meshullam, is mentioned as contemporary with the high priest Joiakim (12:16), B. C. 536-410.

Girdle, as an article of clothing, *see* Dress; Priests, Clothing of.

Figurative. To "gird (or girdle) up the loins" was a common expression for putting one's self in readiness for any service that might be required (Luke 12:35; I Pet. 1:13). Girdles of sackcloth were worn as marks of humiliation and sorrow (Isa. 3:24; 22:12). The girdle was a symbol of strength, activity, and power (Job 12:17; 30:11; Isa. 23:10 margin; 45:5; 22:21; I Kings 20:11). "Righteousness and faithfulness" are called the girdle of the Messiah (Isa. 11:5), and the perfect adherence of the people of God to his service is spoken of as the "cleaving of the girdle to a man's loins" (Jer. 13:11).

Gir'gashites (gûr'gá-shīt) or **Gir'gasite** (gûr'-gá-sīt), one of the seven Canaanite nations whose land was given to Israel. Josh. 24:11

seems to place them west of the Jordan. In Gen. 10:16 and I Chron. 1:14 the Girgashite is descended from Canaan. The Girgashites are enumerated among the devoted Canaanite nations only in Gen. 15:21; Deut. 7:1; Josh. 3:10; 24:11; Neh. 9:8.

Girl (Heb. *yăldäh*, literally, *one born*), in the ordinary sense (Joel 3:3; Zech. 8:5), but of a marriageable "damsel" (Gen. 34:4).

Gis'pa (gĭs'pà), one of the two overseers of the Nethinim in Ophel, at Jerusalem, after the captivity (Neh. 11:21); but whether he was himself also of that class is not stated, although this is probable from the fact that his associate, Ziha, was (Ezra 2:43), B. C. 445.

Git'tah-he'pher (gĭt-à-hē'fẽr; Josh. 19:13). *See* Gath-hepher.

Git'taim (gĭt'à-ĭm; *two winepresses*), the place to which the Beerothites fled (II Sam. 4:3), perhaps through fear of vengeance for the murder of Ishbosheth. It is mentioned (Neh. 11:33) in the list of cities inhabited by the Benjamites after the captivity, identified with Gamteti of the Amarna Letters and located at or near Ramleh.

Git'tite (gĭt'īt), an inhabitant, or properly native, of the Philistine city, Gath (Josh. 13:3), six hundred of whom attached themselves to David and became part of his bodyguard (II Sam. 15:18, 19). *Obed-edom* (*q. v.*), in whose house the ark was placed for a time (6:10), is called a Gittite, probably from his birthplace, the Levitical city of Gath-rimmon in the tribe of Dan (Josh. 21:24; 19:45).

Git'tith (gĭt'ĭth), a musical term in title of Psa. 8, 81, 84. It may refer to a musical instrument characteristic of Gath or to "The March of the Gittite Guard."

Gi'zonite (gī'zō-nīt), an inhabitant of Gizoh, Hashem by name, who was the ancestor of two of David's warriors (I Chron. 11:34). Gizonite seems to be a corruption of Gunite (see Rahlf's LXX); cf. Num. 26:48.

Glass.

1. **Egyptian.** The discovery of glass was made very early by the Egyptians and the Phoenicians. The opaque variety was known by the Nile-dwellers as far back as the end of the third millennium B. C. Perfume bottles, bracelets, tear bottles and beads were manufactured of Egyptian glass from the time of the New Empire (c. 1500 B. C.) on. Exquisite shades of blue, yellow and red, seen today in tomb jewelry, were common among the wealthy. Animals were made of glass as well as strings of beads at the time of Thutmose III (c. 1450 B. C.). King Tutankhamun's tomb (14th century B. C.) yielded colorful glass vases and cups.

2. **Phoenician.** Phoenicians at an early period produced glass and exquisite jewelry. Pliny recounts how that one day a vessel put into the Byblos harbor near the Belus River and landed with blocks of niter, the sailors using this substance to support cooking utensils on the sand shore. They were amazed, so the account goes, to find the fires melted salt and sand in a flow of glass. However true this story is, the sand of the Belus River was long famous as an ingredient of fine glass, and some would give Phoenician craftsmen in

glass priority over the Egyptian. Sidon was famous for glassware at an early age. In the Byblos district of Lebanon a new find of Phoenician glassware was made in 1942 in the course of the construction of the Haifa to Tripoli railroad.

3. **Roman.** Transparent glass came in later as a luxury in the Roman Age. It was a distinct artistic improvement over the opaque variety of ancient Egyptians and Phoenicians. In the N. T. period after the discovery of transparent Roman glass, Alexandria in Egypt became world-famous as a center of the production of beautiful glassware. This reputation was maintained for a long period. Fine beakers, bowls, flasks and goblets, bottles both for perfume and wine, were costly wares exported throughout the entire Mediterranean world and even as far as Britain. Corinth, after the Pauline Period, also developed a reputation for the production of fine Roman glass of varied colors.

4. **Biblical.** In the light of transparent Roman glass, the Patmos seer's references become much more comprehensible when he speaks of "a sea of glass mingled with fire" (Rev. 15:2) and when he refers to the New Jerusalem with its streetway of "pure gold as it were transparent glass." We also find in the Apocalypse the expression "like unto clear glass" (21:18), "as it were transparent glass" (21:21). In both passages "glass" is the rendering of the Greek *hualos*. In the reference of Rev. 4:6 and 15:2 the adjective form of this Greek word is used, meaning *of glass*, *transparent*. Caution must be exercised, however, in translation references to glass. The familiar passages, "and now we see through a glass darkly" (I Cor. 13:12), and "like a man beholding his natural face in a glass" (Jas. 1:23) allude to a *mirror* (Gr. *esoptron*). Probably one

175. Metal Mirror

of the highly polished metal mirrors such as were in vogue in Egypt, Pompeii and throughout the Roman world is meant. Among the numerous articles used by fashionable Jewish women in Isaiah's time were "hand mirrors" used for "well set hair" (Isa. 3:23, 24). Evidently these worldly daughters of Zion, that is, "Zion women," carried vanity cases as women do today, and a polished bronze mirror is apparently implied (Heb., *gĭllāyōn*, polished metal plates). When Job said, Hast thou with Him spread out the sky, which is strong, and as a molten looking glass?" (Job. 37:18), he had in mind the metal type of "looking glass." *M. F. U.*

Glean. Moses provided a liberal treatment of the poor at the harvest season. In reaping the field the owner was not to "wholly reap the corners," etc. (Lev. 19:9, sq.); i. e., he was not to reap the field to the extreme edge, nor gather together the ears left upon the field in the reaping. In the vineyard and olive plantation the fallen fruit was to be left for the distressed and the foreigner (comp. Deut. 24: 20-22), hence the proverb of Gideon (Judg. 8:2). *See* Agriculture.

Glede. *See* Animal Kingdom.

Glorify. 1. To make glorious or honorable, or to cause to appear so (John 12:28; 13:31, 32; Acts 3:13, etc.); especially of the resurrection of Christ and his ascension (John 7:39; 12: 16).

2. The bringing of Christians to a heavenly condition and dignity (Rom. 8:30).

3. To *glorify* (I Cor. 6:20) is to "show forth his praise" by obedience to his law. Thus the "heavens declare the glory of God" in obedience to the law of creation, and much more do men glorify him by willing obedience to the moral law (I Cor. 10:31; John 17:5).

Glory in the A. V. usually represents the Heb. *kābōd, weight,* and Gr. *doxa,* although a number of other words in the original are thus rendered.

In the applications of the word "glory" in Scripture it is easy to trace the fundamental idea involved in it. Properly it is the exercise and display of what constitutes the distinctive excellence of the subject of which it is spoken; thus, in *respect to God,* his glory is the manifestation of his divine attributes and perfections, or such a visible effulgence as indicates the possession and presence of these (Exod. 33:18, 19; 16:7, 10; John 1:14; 2:11; II Pet. 1:17, etc.). God's "glory is the correlative of his holiness . . . is that in which holiness comes to expression. Glory is the expression of holiness, as beauty is the expression of health." In *respect to man,* his glory is found in the things which discover his honorable state and character, such as wisdom, righteousness, superiority to passion, or that outward magnificence which is expressive of what, in the lower sphere, bespeaks the high position of its possessor.

"By a very natural extension, the term *glory* is used for the property or possession itself, which tends to throw around its subject a halo of glory, or in some respect to crown it with honor; as when the glory of man is identified with his soul; the glory of Lebanon with its trees (Isa. 60:13); the glory of herbs with the beauty of their flower (40:6); the glory of God with his infinite perfections, and especially with his pure and unchanging righteousness (3:8; 42:8). In this last sense God is the

glory of his people (Jer. 2:11; Zech. 2:5), because he is the living root and spring of all that distinguishes them for good; and they are his glory in the other sense (Jer. 13:11; 33:9), inasmuch as it is through their holy and blessed state, through the wonderful things done for them and by them, that his own glorious perfections are manifested before the eyes of men. There are no applications of the word in Scripture but what may without difficulty be reduced to the one or the other of those now indicated" (*Imp. Dict.,* s. v.).

Glutton (Hebrew from *zälăl,* to *shake,* hence to *be loose,* morally), a voluptuary, debauchee (Deut. 21:20; Prov. 23:21); "riotous" in Prov. 23:20; 28:7. "Gluttonous" (Matt. 11: 19; Luke 7:34) is a free liver.

Gnash (Heb. *härăq*), to *grate* the teeth; "to gnash with the teeth," and "gnashing of teeth," are expressions denoting rage or sorrow (Job 16:9; Lam. 2:16).

Gnat. *See* Animal Kingdom.

Goad. An instrument for guiding oxen, the long handle of which might be used as a formidable weapon (Judg. 3:31). The instrument, as still used in the countries of southern Europe and western Asia, consists of a rod about eight feet long, brought to a sharp point and sometimes cased with iron at the bigger end, to clear the plow of clay.

Figurative. "To kick against the goads," A. V. "the pricks" (Acts 9:5), was proverbially used by the Greeks for unavailing resistance to superior power.

Goat. *See* Animal Kingdom; Food; Scapegoat.

Goat's Hair; Skin. *See* Dress, Tabernacle.

Go'ath (gō′ăth), a place near Jerusalem, mentioned by Jeremiah (Jer. 31:39) in his prophecy of the city's restoration. The site is unknown, but probably west of the city.

Gob (gŏb; *a pit*), II Sam. 21:18, 19; called Gezer (I chron. 20:4), the place where the brother of Goliath of Gath defied Israel, but was slain by Jonathan, the son of Shimei or Shammah. In the Syriac version Gob is "Gath," and the Heb. text is uncertain.

Goblet (Heb. *'ăggän*), a trough for washing garments; thus any laver, basin, bowl (Cant. 7:2; comp. Exod. 24:6, "basin;" Isa. 22:24, "cup"). In form and material the goblet was probably like those found in the Egyptian ruins, of silver, gold, bronze, porcelain, and even of wood.

God. 1. **Names of God.** The two essential and personal names of God in the Hebrew Scriptures are Elohim and Jehovah (more correctly Yahweh); the former calling attention to the fullness of divine power, the latter meaning "He who is," and thus declaring the divine Self-existence. These terms are varied or combined with others to bring out or emphasize certain attributes of the Godhead, such variations or combinations being rendered in our English version, "God Almighty," "The Living God," "The Most High," "The Lord," or "The God of Hosts." The English word God is identical with the Anglo-Saxon word for "good," and therefore it is believed that the name God refers to the divine goodness. (See Oehler's *Theol. of Old Test.,* Strong's and Young's *Concordances.*)

2. **Doctrine Defined.** The scriptural or

Christian doctrine of God must be distinguished not only from anti-theistic theories, but also from other theories more or less approximating that doctrine. God as revealed through the Scriptures is the one Infinite and Eternal Being. He is purely spiritual, the Supreme Personal Intelligence, the Creator and Preserver of all things, the perfect Moral Ruler of the universe; he is the only proper object of worship; he is the tri-personal—the Father, Son, and Holy Spirit constituting one Godhead (Gen. 1:1; Exod. 34:14; Psa. 90:1, 2; 139:7-12; Job 26; Jer. 23:2-4; Matt. 3:16, 17; 28:19; John 4:24; I John 4:16, etc.). The above does not present fully, as we shall see later, the contents of revelation concerning God. But it is sufficient for the purpose of making the distinctions named.

(1) **Theism.** Theism, as the term is most commonly used, is equivalent to monotheism, and particularly in the sense of recognizing the one God as distinct from the world, the personal Creator and Governor of all things. Accordingly the following are specified as (*a*) *Atheism*, avowed opposition to a belief in one supreme God; (*b*) *Polytheism*, holding a multiplicity of gods; (*c*) *Pantheism*, identifying God with the universe; (*d*) *Materialism*, recognizing no existence save that of matter; (*e*) *Agnosticism*, denying all knowledge of God and all possibility of knowing him, thus being in practical effect equivalent to Atheism.

(2) **Deism.** Deism and Theism are etymologically equivalent terms, yet a distinction is found in their application. Deism has appeared in various forms, but in general it has been distinct from Theism in that, though holding to the existence of a personal God who has created the world, it has regarded God as holding himself aloof from the world and leaving it to the government of natural laws.

(3) **Theism and Christian doctrine.** Theism lies at the basis of all Christian doctrine, and yet is not to be regarded as comprehending that doctrine in all its fullness. This must appear most plainly in the consideration of the attributes of God and the mode of the divine existence.

(4) **The knowledge of God.** As to man's knowledge of God two questions have been the subjects of much controversy: the first relating to the possibility of true knowledge of the divine Being, the second the source or method of such knowledge.

First. Can God be known? The Scriptures declare that God is incomprehensible (see Job 11:7; 21:14; 36:26; Psa. 77:19; Rom. 11:33). Perfect or complete knowledge of God is not attainable by man upon the earth. But equally true it is that the Scriptures represent God as revealing himself to man, and that a sufficient though limited measure of true knowledge of God is put within the reach of human beings. The important distinction to be maintained at this point is that between partial and perfect knowledge. We cannot comprehend God, and yet we can truly know him. Our blessedness, our eternal life even, is in such knowledge (see Matt. 11:27; John 17:3; Rom. 1:19, 20; Eph. 1:17; Col. 1:10; I John 5:20).

The prevailing faith of the Christian Church in all ages has been in accord with these teachings of Scripture.

Both theological and philosophical speculation, however, have often diverged from this view, and in both directions. For example, defenders of the Arian heresy in the fourth century held that God could be fully known. They thus sought to meet the appeals of their opponents to the unsearchableness of God. The Mystics of the Middle Ages also claimed the possibility of perfect knowledge of God. Through the life of love in God they held that the soul could contemplate him immediately and clearly, and thus arrive at complete knowledge. In modern times the tendency of error, in the main, is in the opposite direction. The incomprehensibility of God and his unknowableness are conceived in such a one-sided or exaggerated form as to shut out the possibility of any measure of real knowledge. Agnosticism is an extreme illustration. The doctrine of Mansel in his *Limits of Religious Thought* betrays the same tendency.

Second. As to the source or method of the knowledge of God, it is held by many theologians that the idea, and consequently some knowledge of God, is innate. By this is meant, however, only that all men have naturally a conviction that there is a Being upon whom they are dependent and to whom they are responsible. The arguments for and against this view are too minute and extended to be here presented. Van Oosterzee's statement is weighty: "Belief in God is by no means the necessary product of abstract reasoning, but has its firm basis in the whole nature and being of man." It is also said with much force that the Scriptures do not seek to prove the existence of God, but simply assume or assert the fact as one that men ought to be prepared to recognize. The rational proofs of the existence of the divine Being are not, however, to be regarded otherwise than of great value. They are mainly drawn from nature, from history, and from humanity. It is sometimes rashly asserted that arguments built upon these foundations are antiquated or useless. Nevertheless they remain, whatever may be their changes of form, in all essential respects, valid and of great use in confirming and explaining the belief in God which is in some sense natural to every human heart. It is to be observed also that nature and man and history bring to us a general revelation from God—a fact not seldom recognized in the Scriptures (see Psa. 19:1-3; Acts 14:17; 17:26, 27; Rom. 1:19, 20; 2:15).

Accordingly study in these directions yields not only evidences of the existence of the divine Being, but also some knowledge of his character.

Special revelation, for which the Holy Scriptures are the appointed vehicle, affords us the necessary and sufficient knowledge of God. The Scriptures throughout are harmonious in their teachings. The God of the Old Testament is also the God of the New. And yet the Scriptures exhibit a progress in the revelation.

The New Testament doctrine of God is distinguished from that of the Old, first, in that it presents with peculiar distinctness and fullness the divine fatherhood. Second, it declares likewise the divine sonship of Jesus Christ, "God manifest in the flesh." The God-man is the fullest disclosure of the divine nature, and the Redeemer and Saviour of mankind. Third, the distinct divine personality and peculiar office of the Holy Spirit is brought most clearly into view. And thus comes what at most was but intimated in the Old Testament, the doctrine of the Trinity. *See* Trinity.

3. **The Attributes of God.** From the Scriptures is derived in the largest measure our knowledge of the attributes of God. By the word attributes in this connection is meant the properties or qualities of the divine Being, and particularly those which are made known to us through the revelation which he has given of himself. They are not to be regarded as mere human conceptions, but as true representations of the divine nature. Nor are they to be thought of as otherwise than absolutely inseparable from that nature. They blend harmoniously with each other in the unity of the one Being, God.

Theologians differ to some extent in their statements of the essential truth of Scripture at this point, varying in their use of terms, also in classification and arrangement. But they generally agree in recognizing the following as the revealed attributes of God, viz.: Spirituality, Infinity, Eternity, Immutability, Self-sufficiency, Perfection, Freedom, Omnipotence, Omnipresence, Omniscience, Justice, Truth, Love, Mercy, and Grace.

For discussion of attributes see separate heads.

Literature—Works of systematic theology: Van Oosterzee, Pope, Hodge, Watson; Bowne, *Studies in Theism;* Foster, *Theism;* article in *Encyc. Brit.*, "Theism," by Professor Flint.   E. McC.

God, the Unknown. Paul, in his address on Mars' Hill, said that he had seen in Athens "an altar with this inscription, 'To the unknown God'" (Acts 17:22, 23). That there actually stood at Athens such an altar appears historically certain, since Paul appeals to his own observation, and that, too, in the presence of the Athenians themselves. But there are corroborating external proofs, since Lucian, Pausanias, and Philostratus mention altars at Athens consecrated "to the unknown gods." The question naturally arises, What definite god is meant? Different answers have been given, but the following is probably correct: On important occasions, when the reference to a god known by name was wanting, as in public calamities, of which no definite god could be assigned as the author, in order to honor or propitiate the god concerned by sacrifice, without lighting upon the wrong one, altars were erected which were destined and designated *agnōstō theō* (to the unknown god).

Goddess. *See* Gods, False.

Godhead. As used in theology the term means: 1. The Divine Nature; deity. 2. The Supreme Being, especially as comprehending all His attributes. 3. Divinity, a heathen god or goddess. The Scriptural term Godhead is used of divinity or deity (Gr. *theiotēs*; Rom. 1:20):

"Ever since the creation of the world His invisible nature, namely, his eternal power and deity, has been clearly perceived in the things that have been made" (R. S. V.). In Col. 2:9 "Godhead" (Gr. *theotēs*) is also used in the sense of deity (divinity): "for in Him the whole fullness of deity dwells bodily" (R. S. V.). In Acts 17:29 the adjective (Gr. *theios*) "God-like," is used: "Being then God's offspring we ought not to think that the Deity is like gold or silver or stone, a representation by the art and imagination of man." *M. F. U.*

Godliness, the rendering of Gr. *eusebeia, reverence,* in Scripture everywhere *piety toward God* (Acts 3:12, A. V., "holiness;" I Tim. 2:2; 4:7, 8; 6:3, 5, 6, 11). It is the sum of religious virtues and duties, bringing to its possessor blessedness here and hereafter (I Tim. 4:8). "The mystery of godliness" (I Tim. 3:16) is the mystery which is held by godliness and nourishes it. Once (I Tim. 2:10) godliness is the rendering of *theosebeia, reverence toward God.*

Gods (Heb. *'ĕlōhim*). This term for deity is used in a threefold connotation in the O. T. 1. In a singular sense of the One True God in a plural of majesty or excellence. It is construed with a singular verb or adjective (Gen. 1:1; II Kings 19:4, 16; Psa. 7:10; 57:3; 78:56); but with a plural verb only in certain phrases. 2. All gods or deities in general, "the gods of the Egyptians" (Exod. 12:12), "strange gods" (Gen. 35:2, 4; Deut. 29:18); "new gods" (Deut. 32:17). 3. Of judges or prophets as those, "unto whom the Word of God came" (John 10:35; Psa. 82:6), and whom God consequently dignified with authority to bear His Own Name (Exod. 21:6; 22:8). The medium of Endor said to Saul concerning the spirit she brought up at the seance: "I see a god ('elohim) coming up out of the earth" (I Sam. 28:13). The expression is difficult and unusual in that it is the same word for "God" or "gods;" but that the particular reference is not to Yahweh or to heathen deities or demons is evident from Saul's immediate query, "What form is *he* of?" (vs. 14). It is apparent that this is another case where *'elohim* is employed of a judge or prophet. The designation was plainly apropos of Samuel, the last and greatest of the judges and the first of the prophets. This usage of *'elohim* as referring to God's earthly representatives is denied by some critics, and the R. S. V. renders "God" in Exod. 21:6; 22:8; such a rendering is manifestly unsustained by the context and by a general comparison of Scripture. *M. F. U.*

GODS, FALSE

Under the head of idolatry (*q. v.*) will be discussed the general subject of the evil, which proved so attractive and fatal to the Israelites, viz., the worship of false gods. In this article we only present the gods specially named in Scripture, whether worshiped by Israel or other nations. They are given in alphabetical order.

Adram′melech (a-drăm′ĕ-lĕk; Adar is king). This deity was worshiped in N. W. Mesopotamia under the name of Adad-Milki, which is a form of the Syrian god Hadad. In honor of Adrammelech the colonists of Samaria, who had been brought from Sephar-vaim, burned their children in the fire (II Kings 17:31). The deity is associated with Anammelech. Some have identified the two as being a double god but this is hypothetical. *M. F. U.*

Anam'melech (á-năm'ĕ-lĕk; Anu is king). Anu was the Babylonian god of the sky and one of the gods revered by the people of the Babylonian city of Sepharvaim (II Kings 17:36). When these Sepharvites were transported to Samaria they honored this repugnant deity by burning their children in the fire, worshipping him in the fashion of Molech, the god worshipped particularly by the children of Ammon (I Kings 11:7). *See* Adrammelech. *M. F. U.*

176. Fight Between Gods and a Monster (from Palace of Ashurnasirpal II, Assyria)

Ash'ima (ăsh'imá), the god of Hamath introduced by the colonists settled in Samaria by Shalmaneser (II Kings 17:30).

Asherah (á-shē'rá), plural, Asherim, a pagan goddess, who is found in the Ras Shamra epic religious texts discovered at Ugarit in North Syria (1929-1937), as Asherat, "Lady of the Sea" and consort of El. She was the chief goddess of Tyre in the 15th century B. C. with the appelation *Qudshu*, "holiness." In the Old Testament Asherah appears as a goddess by the side of Baal, whose consort she evidently came to be, at least among the Canaanites of the South. However, most Biblical references to the name point clearly to some cult object of wood, which might be worshipped or cut down and burned, and which was certainly the goddess' image (I Kings 15:13, II Kings 21:7). Her prophets are mentioned (I Kings 18:19) and the vessels used in her service referred to (II Kings 23:4). Her cult object, whatever it was, was utterly detestable to faithful worshippers of Yahweh (I Kings 15:13) and was set up on the high places beside the "altars of incense" (*hammanim*) and the "stone pillars" (*masseboth*). Indeed, the "stone Pillars" seem to have represented the male god Baal (cf. Judg. 6:28), while the cult object of Ashera, probably a tree or pole, constituted a symbol of this goddess (See W. L. Reed's *The Asherah in the Old Testament*, Texas Christian University Press). But Asherah was only one manifestation of a chief goddess of Western Asia, regarded now as the wife, now as the sister of the principal Canaanite god El. Other names of this deity were Ashtoreth (Astarte) and Anath. Frequently represented as a nude woman bestride a lion with a lily in one hand and a serpent in the other, and

styled *Qudshu* "the Holiness," that is, "the Holy One" in a perverted moral sense, she was a divine courtesan. In the same sense the male prostitutes consecrated to the cult of the *Qudshu* and prostituting themselves to her honor were styled *qedishim*, "sodomites" (Deut. 23:18; I Kings 14:24; 15:12; 22:46). Characteristically Canaanite the lily symbolizes grace and sex appeal and the serpent fecundity (W. F. Albright, *Archeology and the Religion of Israel*, Baltimore, Johns Hopkins Press, 1942, pp. 68-94). At Byblos (Biblical Gebal) on the Mediterranean, north of Sidon, a center dedicated to this goddess has been excavated. She and her colleagues specialized in sex and war and her shrines were temples of legalized vice. Her degraded cult offered a perpetual danger of pollution to Israel and must have sunk to sordid depths as lust and murder were glamorized in Canaanite religion. On a fragment of the Baal Epic, Anath appears in an incredibly bloody orgy of destruction. For some unknown reason she fiendishly butchers mankind, young as well as old, in a most horrible and wholesale fashion, wading ecstatically in human gore up to her knees—yea, up to her throat, all the while exulting sadistically. In Canaan there was a tendency to employ the plural forms of deities Ashtoreth (Ashtoroth), Asherah (Asherim), Anath (Anathoth) to summarize all the various manifestations of this deity. In like fashion the Canaanite plural *Elohim* ("gods") was adopted by the Hebrews to express all the excellencies and attributes of the one true God. *M. F. U.*

177. Astarte Plaque from Tell Beit Mirsim, (about 1450 B. C.)

Ash'toreth (ăsh'tô-rĕth), Astarte, a Canaanite goddess. In south Arabic the name is found as 'Athtar (apparently from '*athara, to be fertile, to irrigate*), a god identified with the planet Venus. The name is cognate with Babylonian Ishtar, the goddess of sensual love, maternity and fertility. Licentious worship was conducted in honor of her. As Asherah and Anat of Ras Shamra she was the patroness of war as well as sex and is sometimes identified with these goddesses. The Amarna Letters present Ashtoreth as Ashtartu. In the Ras Shamra Tablets are found both the masculine form 'Athtar and the feminine 'Athtart. Ashtoreth worship was early entrenched at Sidon (I

Kings 11:5, 33; II Kings 23:13). Her polluting cult even presented a danger to early Israel (Judg. 2:13; 10:6). Solomon succumbed to her voluptuous worship (I Kings 11:5; II Kings 23:13). The peculiar vocalization Ashtoreth instead of the more primitive Ashtaroth is evidently a deliberate alteration by the Hebrews to express their abhorrence for her cult by giving her the vowels of their word for "shame" (*bosheth*). *M. F. U.*

Astar′te, the Greek name for *Ashtoreth* (q. v.).

Baal (bā′ăl), common Canaanite word for "master, lord," was one of the chief male deities of the Canaanite pantheon, now well-known from the religious epic literature dis-

178. Ras Shamra Stele, with the Great Canaanite. God El Receiving Homage from the King of Ugarit (14th Century B. C.)

covered at Ras Shamra (ancient Ugarit of the Amarna Letters) from 1921-1937. Baal was the son of El, the father of the gods and the head of the Canaanite pantheon, according to the tablets from Ugarit. He is also designated as "the son of Dagon" (Heb. *dagan*, "grain"), an ancient Canaanite and Mesopotamian deity associated with agriculture. Baal was thus the farm god who gave increase to family and field, flocks and herds. He was likewise identified with the storm-god Hadad whose voice could be heard in the reverberating thunder that accompanied rain, which was so necessary for the success of the crops. *Canaanite Worship*. The inhabitants of Canaan were addicted to Baal worship, which was conducted by priests in temples and in good weather outdoors in fields and particularly on hilltops called "high places." The cult included animal sacrifice, ritualistic meals, and licentious dances. Near the rock altar was a sacred pillar or *maṣṣebah*, and close by the symbol of the *asherah*, both of which apparently symbolized human fertility. High places had chambers for sacred prostitution by male-prostitutes (*kedishim*) and sacred harlots (*kedeshoth*) (I Kings 14:23, 24; II Kings 23:7). The gaiety and licentious character of Baal worship always had a subtle attraction for the austere Hebrews bound to serve a holy God under a rigorous moral code. *Baal Names*. In times of lapse Hebrews compounded the names of their children with Baal—for example, Jerubbaal (Judg. 7:1); Ishbaal (I Chron. 8:33; 9:39), Meribbaal (I Chron. 8:34; 9:40) which in times of revival and return to Yahwism were altered, the *baal* element being replaced by "bosheth," meaning "shame." Thus pious Israelites express their horror of Baal worship; examples are Jerubbosheth (for Jerubbaal) (II Sam. 11:21), Ishbosheth (for Ishbaal) (II Sam. 2:8), Mephiboseth (for Merribaal) (II Sam. 4:4; 9:6, 10). Numerous place names also occur, such as Baal-gad ("Lord of good fortune," Josh. 11:17), Baal-hamon ("Lord of wealth," Song 8:11), Baal-hazor ("Baal's village," II Sam. 13:23), Baal-meon ("Lord of the dwelling," Num. 32:38), Baal-peor ("Lord of the opening," Deut. 4:3), Baal-Tamar ("Lord of the palm tree," Judg. 20:33) and others.

Ba′al-berith′ (bā′ăl-bē-rîth′; *lord of the covenant*). Under this title the great N. W. Semitic weather god Baal was worshipped at Shechem after the death of Gideon (Judg. 8:33; 9:4). Occasionally he was spoken of as El-berith, "the god of covenant" (Judg. 9:46). The Canaanites were brought into the Israelite fold by treaty, conquest or gradual absorption. The Bene Hamor ("Sons of the Ass") of Shechem were incorporated in such a way. This is indicated from various early references to them and to their god Baal-Berith (lord of covenant). The sacrifice of an ass was an essential feature of a treaty among the Amorites of the Mari Period (c. 1700 B. C.) (Cf. W. F. Albright, *From the Stone Age to Christianity*, 1940, p. 231). *M. F. U.*

Ba′alim (bā′ăl-ĭm; Heb. pl. of *Ba′al*). This is a general term including not images of Baal but various concepts of the god. There were numerous Baalim as Baal-shamem (lord of heaven) of the Phoenicians and Palmyraeans; Baal-Melkart of the Tyrians; Baal-Saphon of the Canaanites of Ugarit. There is a distinction, too, between the Baalim, as Baal-berith, Baal-Peor and Baal-zebub. *M. F. U.*

Ba′al-pe′or (bā′ăl-pē′ôr; Baal of Peor), a Moabite deity worshipped on the summit of Mt. Peor with immoral rites. The name is probably another form of Chemosh (q. v.). The Israelites were seduced into the immorality of this licentious worship in the Plains of Moab (Num. 25:1-9; Psa. 106:28; Hos. 9:10). *M. F. U.*

Ba′al-ze′bub (bā′ăl-zē′bŭb), the form of the name of Baal as worshipped at the Philistine city of Ekron. Baal, under this aspect of worship, was viewed as the producer of flies and hence able to control this pest, so common in the East. He was consulted by Ahaziah of Israel, c. B. C. 849 (II Kings 1:2-16). A N. T. rendering of the name is Beelzebul (R. S. V.) Beelzebub (A. V.) meaning, "lord of the (heavenly) habitation." Pharisees called Beelzebub (Beelzebul) the "prince of the demons" (Matt. 12:24). Our Lord denied that He expelled demons by the power of Beelzebub (Luke 11:19-23). It is a matter of divine revelation that demonism is the dynamic of idolatry. (I Cor. 10:20; "No, I imply that what pagans sacrifice they offer to demons and not to God. I do not want you to be partners with demons," R. S. V.). Many of the Jews from the period of the restoration and down through N. T. times believed that heathen deities were demons. The heathen deities were, of course, nothing, but behind them were evil spirits or demons energizing their worship. (Cf. Merrill F. Unger, *Biblical Demonology*, pp. 58-61).

M. F. U.

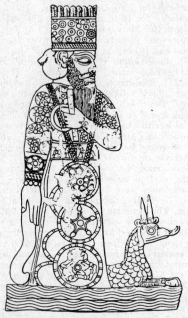

179. Marduk

Bel (bāl) (Akkad. Bēlū, cognate of Heb. *bāʻăl*, *lord*), the patron god of Babylon (Jer. 51:44) identified with Marduk, head of the Babylonian pantheon. The Hebrews called him Merodach. As a sun god his festival was celebrated in the spring at the beginning of the year, since the sun's rays were then most potent in reviving nature. The Babylonians paid him supreme tribute and exalted him to the headship of their pantheon shortly after B. C. 2000. According to *Enuma elish*, the Babylonian account of creation, Marduk was elevated to this superior position because of his slaying Tiamat, the goddess of chaos. He was worshiped in Esagila, the lofty temple at Babylon. *M. F. U.*

Be'rith. *See* Baal-berith.

Calf Worship.

1. An image was made of gold earrings and other ornaments by the Hebrews and worshipped under the direction of Aaron (Exod. 32:1-6; Deut. 9:16). This was evidently a representation of Yahweh as the God of their deliverance from Egypt. It seems scarcely possible that this incident represents bull worship as witnessed in Egypt, for there the bull was a living animal (Apis). Among many eastern nations there is evidence of the worship of the bull as the emblem of strength and the symbol of generative power. The winged

bull was common among the Assyrians. In Egypt the term bull was a favorite term applied to a king or a god.

2. Jeroboam I, after the division of the monarchy, set up two golden calves at Bethel in the south of his country and Dan in the north, to offset interest in the temple at Jerusalem (I Kings 12:29). This was evidently an accommodation to Canaanite bull cults and certainly cannot mean that the people worshipped the image itself, but rather they thought of Yahweh enthroned invisibly above the calf. Among Israel's immediate neighbors —Canaanites, Arameans and Hittites—"deities were nearly always represented as standing on the back of an animal or as on a throne borne by animals, but never as themselves in animal form" (W. F. Albright, *From the Stone Age to Christianity*, Baltimore, 1940, p. 229). The storm god of Mesopotamia, for example, is depicted on 2nd millennium B. C. seal cylinders in the form of a lightning bolt set upright on a bull's back (*Ibid.*). Although conceptionally there is little difference between representing the invisible Deity as enthroned above the cherubim (I Sam. 4:4; II Kings 19:15), or as standing on a bull, except that the former represent beings of the realm of the supernatural which defend the holiness (Gen. 3:24) and throne of God (Ezek. 1:5; Rev. 4:6-9), nevertheless Jeroboam's innovation was extremely dangerous. The bull affiliations of Baal, "lord of heaven," were too closely connected with the more degrading aspects of pagan cults to be safe. The Northern Kingdom, consequently, fell to the peril of idolatrous pollution as a result. *M. F. U.*

Cas'tor (kăs'tôr) and **Pol'lux** (pŏl'ŭx) Gr. *dioskouroi*, *sons of Jupiter*). Castor was a horse tamer and Pollux master of the art of boxing. Castor became mortal, having fallen in a contest with Idas and Lynceus, the sons of their paternal uncle Aphareus. Pollux, the immortal son of Zeus, prayed his father to let him die too. Zeus permitted him to spend one day among the gods, his peers, the other in the lower world with his beloved brother. According to another story Zeus, in reward for their brotherly love, set them in the sky as the constellation of the Twins, or the morning and evening star. They are the ideal types of bravery and dexterity in fight.

The ancient symbol of the twin gods at Lacedaemon was two parallel beams, joined by cross-pieces, which the Spartans took with them into war. They were worshipped at Sparta and Olympia with Hercules and other heroes. As gods of the sea they were worshiped especially in Ostia, the harbor town of Rome. The only mention of them in Scripture is that the ship in which Paul sailed from Malta bore the sign of "Castor and Pollux" (Acts 28:11).

Che'mosh (kē'mŏsh) was the national deity of the Moabites, honored with horribly cruel rites like those of Molech, to whom children were sacrificed in the fire. It is very interesting archaeologically to note that the anger of Chemosh is said in the famous Moabite Stone to be the reason for Israel's subjugation of Moab (Cf. Judg. 11:24). Solomon made a fatal mistake, whatever his reason might have been, of rearing an altar to Chemosh in Jerusalem (I Kings 11:7). This abomination was not destroyed until Josiah's purge almost three centuries later (II Kings 23:13). So infatuated were the Moabites with Chemosh that they were known as "the children of Chemosh" (Num. 21:29); that is, "worshippers par excellence of Chemosh." *M. F. U.*

Chi'un (kī'ŭn; Heb. *Kiyyŭn*). The name of this deity should in all likelihood be vocalized *Kaiwan* or *Kewan* as representing Akkad. *Kaiwānu*, the name of Ninib or Saturn. The unusual spelling in the Massoretic text is evidently the result of the intentional pointing for the vowels of *shikkuṣ*, meaning "a detestable thing." Accordingly, the A. R. V. renders it "shrine." The R. S. V. renders the passage (Amos 5:26), where the word occurs only once in the Hebrew Bible, "Kaiwan your star-god." *See* Rephan. *M. F. U.*

180. Dagon

Da'gon (dā'gŏn; Heb. *dāgōn*, corn, evidently a diminutive of *dag*, "fish"). An ancient Mesopotamian deity, early transported to the west. Dagon is generally represented as having the body or trunk of a fish, with human head and hands, as being the symbol of water and all the vivifying natural powers which take effect in warm countries through water. The Babylonian-Assyrian, and later Canaanite Dagon, is described by Philo of Byblos as the god of grain. This has been abundantly verified by the North Syrian religious texts from Ras Shamra. There Dagon is associated with agriculture and is described as the father of the great god Baal. Dagon was revered among the early Phoenicians. He had importance as the national god of the Philistines, who set up temples in his honor at Ashdod, Gaza and elsewhere. Numerous towns were named after him, such as Beth-Dagon (Josh. 15:41). His temple has been found at Ugarit near to that of Baal with features found in later Hebrew architecture. Instances connected with the temple of Dagon are the scene of Samson's death (Judg. 16:23-30), the experiences connected with the Hebrew ark at Ashdod (I Sam. 5:1-7) and the fastening of Saul's head in the temple of Dagon at Beth-shan, which has been excavated at this famous fortress site guarding the eastern approaches of Jezreel.
M. F. U.

Dia'na (dī-ă'nà), a goddess known among the Greeks as Artemis and among the Romans as Diana. Like Apollo she was armed with bow and arrow, which she used against monsters and giants, but she was also a beneficent and helpful deity. As Apollo was the luminous god of day, she with her torch was a goddess of light by night, and in course of time became identified with all possible goddesses of moon and night. Her proper domain is that of nature, being a mighty huntress, sometimes chasing wild animals, sometimes dancing, playing, or bathing with her companions. To her all beasts of the field were sacred, but her favorite animal all over Greece was held to be the hind. As goddess of the chase she had also influence in war, and the Spartans before battle sought her favor by the gift of a goat.

Diana (Artemis) was also a protectress of youth, especially those of her own sex. Young girls revered the virgin goddess as the guardian of their maiden years, and before marriage offered her a lock of their hair, their girdle, and their maiden garment. She was supposed to assist at childbirth. In early times human sacrifices had been offered to Artemis. A relic of this was the yearly custom observed at Sparta, of flogging the boys till they bled, at the altar of a deity known as *Artemis Orthia*.

"Diana of the Ephesians" was not a Greek divinity, but Asiatic. This is shown by the fact that eunuchs were employed in her worship—a practice quite foreign to Greek ideas. She was not regarded as a virgin, but as mother and foster-mother, as is clearly shown by the multitude of breasts in the rude effigy. She was undoubtedly a representative of the same power presiding over conception and birth which was adored in Palestine under the name of Ashtoreth. Her worship, frantic and fanatical after the manner of Asia, was traced back to the Amazons. Her temple at Ephesus was one of the wonders of the world, but its great glory was the "image which fell down from Jupiter" (Acts 19:35). Images claiming so lofty an origin were to be found in other cities than Ephesus. Once in the year there was a public festival in honor of the goddess at Ephesus, to which all the Ionians who could do so repaired with their wives and children, bringing costly offerings to Diana and rich presents for the priests. Great gain came to the silversmiths in making and selling small images of the goddess (*see* Acts 19:23, sq.).

Gad, a Canaanite deity improperly rendered "troop" (Isa. 65:11), was the god of good fortune, supposed to be the deified planet Jupiter. This star is called by the Arabs "the greater luck" as the star of good fortune.

Ju'piter (jū'pĭ-tēr), the Latin form of Greek, Zeus. In the Italian mythology Jupiter was the highest god in heaven, and identical with the Greek Zeus, not only in nature but also in name, for Jupiter is compounded of *Iŏuvis* and *pater*. As in the course of time the Italian god became identified with the Greek, he was regarded as a son of Saturn and of Ops, corresponding with the Greek Uranus and Rhea respectively. From Jupiter comes all that appears in the heavens. As Lucetius he is the bringer of light, the cause of the dawn, as well as of the full moon. Just as the calends (1st) of each month are sacred to Juno, so the ides (13th or 15th), which are full-moon days, are sacred to Jupiter. He controls all weather, sends the lightning and rain, was the giver of wine, the decider of battles and giver of vic-

181. The Temple of Jupiter in Athens with the Acropolis as a Background

tory, watches over justice and truth, and is therefore the most ancient and most important god of oaths.

Jupiter is mentioned in Acts 14:12, 13, where it is recorded that the people of Lycaonia cried: "The gods are come down to us in the likeness of men. And they called Barnabas, Jupiter, and Paul, Mercurius, because he was the chief speaker." Barnabas was probably identified with Jupiter because of his majestic appearance. Paul was identified with Mercury because he was the god of eloquence. The temple of Jupiter at Lystra appears to have been outside the gates, as was frequently the custom.

In Acts 19:35 it is stated that the Ephesians believed that their statue of Diana fell down from Jupiter.

Mal′cham (măl′kăm; *their king*). The national god of the Ammonites equated sometimes with Molech or Moloch (*q. v.*). Malcham (R. S. V. "Milcom") was an "abomination" worshiped by Solomon (I Kings 11:5, 33 and extirpated by Josiah (II Kings 23:13). *See* Milcom.
M. F. U.

Me′ni (mē′nĭ; Heb. *mĕnî, destiny* or *fate*). Name of the god of destiny or fortune worshiped by the ancient Hebrews in time of apostasy (Isa. 65:11): "But you who forsook the Lord, who forget my holy mountain, who set a table for Fortune and fill cups of mixed wine for Destiny" R. S. V. Fortune is "Gad" (*q. v.*) and Destiny is "Meni." M. F. U.

Mer′cury (mûr′kû-rĭ), the Roman god of commerce and protector of the grain trade, and identical with Hermes, who was the son of Zeus and the Naiad, daughter of Atlas. He was the inventor of the lyre, the herald of the gods, and guide of the dead into Hades; the god of mining, of crops, and of roads. He was also the patron of trade and even of theft, of games, and of oratory. He is mentioned in Acts 14:12, where it is stated that the people of Lystra took Paul to be Mercurius, probably because of his eloquence.

Mero′dach (mê-rō′dăk, the Hebrew name for the Akkad. *Marduk*). *See* Bel, Baal. Merodach (Marduk) was the head-god of the Babylonian pantheon and the patron god of the city. Merodach's exaltation as head of the Babylonian pantheon is featured in the Babylonian story of creation, *Enuma elish.* He was worshipped by Nebuchadnezzar, the Assyrians, and notably by Cyrus the Great. Cyrus lauds Merodach as a "righteous prince." Jer. 51:

44 and Isa. 46:1 mention this deity. Merodach's name appears compounded with many prominent personages outside Scripture and in Scripture and in Bible history in such names as Merodach-baladan and Evil-merodach.
M. F. U.

Mil′com (mĭl′cŭm), another form of *Malcham* (*q. v.*), the national god of the Ammonites, called (I Kings 11:5; II Kings 23:13), "the abomination of the Ammonites."

Mo′lech (mō′lĕk; Heb. *melek, king*), a destable Semitic deity honored by the sacrifice of children, in which they were caused to pass through or into the fire. Palestinian excavations have uncovered evidences of infant skeletons in burial places around heathen shrines. Ammonites revered Molech as a protecting father. Worship of Molech was stringently prohibited by Hebrew law (Lev. 18:21; 20:1-5). Solomon built an altar to Molech at Tophet in the Valley of Hinnon. Manasseh (c. B. C. 686-642) in his idolatrous orgy also honored this deity. Josiah desecrated the Hinnom Valley altar but Jehoiakim revived the cult. The prophets sternly denounced this form of heathen worship (Jer. 7:29-34; Ezek. 16:20-22; 23:37-39; Amos 5:26). No form of ancient Semitic idolatry was more abhorrent than Molech worship. M. F. U.

Mo′loch (mō′lŏk), another form in English Amos 5:26; Acts 7:43) of *Molech* (*q. v.*).

Ne′bo (nē′bō; Akkad., *Nābū*), a Babylonian deity (Isa. 46:1), the god of wisdom and literature. Borsippa near Babylon was the special center of his worship. The last great Assyrian emperor, Ashurbanipal (B. C. 669-633), the "Osnapper" of the O. T. (Ezra 4:10), acted in the interests of Nebo and was a patron of learning and education. An inscription of Ashurbanipal reads thus: "I, Ashurbanipal, learn the wisdom of Nabu, the entire art of writing on clay tablets." In the Nabunaid Chronicle, at the time of the rule of Nabunaid's son Belshazzar, Nabu together with Bel was very prominent. Speaking of Nabonidus (Akkadian Nabunaid) the Chronicle says: "The king for the month Nisan did not come to Babylon; Nabu did not come to

182. Reconstruction of Baalbek Temple Complex (Baalbek, Syria)

Babylon; Bel did not go forth (from Esagila); the New Year's festival was not celebrated." (Jack Finegan, *Light from the Ancient Past*, 1946, p. 190). M. F. U.

Nehush′tan (nê-hŭsh′tăn; a *brazen* or copper *thing*), a contemptuous epithet applied to the brazen serpent (*q. v.*), which the Israelites had turned into an object of worship (II Kings

18:4). Among the first acts of Hezekiah was the destruction of all traces of the idolatrous rites which had gained a fast hold upon the people. Among other objects of superstitious reverence and worship was this serpent, which, in the course of a thousand years, had become invested with a mysterious sanctity, which easily degenerated into idolatry.

Ner'gal (nŭr'găl), the Babylonian sun god (II Kings 17:30). The center of his cult was Cuthah from which Babylonian city, among others, colonists were brought to Samaria after the deportation of the ten tribes (II Kings 17:24-30). Its site is at Tell Ibrahim, N. E. of Babylon. Nergal was also the god of pestilence and war and had charge of the nether world. The name occurs as a formative element in the name of one of Nebuchadnezzar's princes, Nergalsharezer, who held the office of Rab-mag (Jer. 39:3, 13). *M. F. U.*

Nib'haz (nĭb'hăz), an idol worshipped by the Avvites, displaced persons from the Assyrian empire brought to colonize Samaria after the captivity of the Northern Kingdom (II Kings 17:31). This deity is identified by Hommel with *Ibna-haza*, an Elamite god. *M. F. U.*

183. Sumerian Deity

Nis'roch (nĭs'rŏk), a god with a temple at Nineveh and worshipped by Sennacherib (B. C. 705-681). It was in the house of this god while at worship that Sennacherib was assassinated (II Kings 19:37; 37:38). This divinity has not as yet been clearly identified. Some construe it as an intentional perversion of the name of Marduk or as a composite containing Ashur; others equate him with Assyrian Nusku. *M. F. U.*

Pol'lux. *See* Castor.

Rephan (rē'făn), A. V. Rem'phan, à stellar deity said to have been worshipped by the Israelites in the desert (Acts 7:43). The R. S. V. renders "the star of the god Rephan." The quotation in Acts is from a corrupted translation of Kaiwan (Akkad. Kaimanu), the

name of Saturn, and was understood to be the god Chiun (Amos 5:26 A. V.). *See* Chiun, Siccuth. *M. F. U.*

Rim'mon (rĭm'ŭn; *pomegranate*), a Syrian deity, worshipped at Damascus, where there was a temple or "house of Rimmon" (II Kings 5: 18). It is probably a contracted form for *Hadad-Rimmon*, since *Hadad* was the supreme deity or sun-god of the Syrians. Hadad, with the modification expressed by Rimmon, would be the sun-god of the late summer, who ripens the pomegranate and other fruits. In this sense he has been thought to be the personification of the power of generation, since the pomegranate, with its abundance of seeds, is used in the symbolism of both oriental and Greek mythology along with the Phallus as a symbol of the generative power, and is also found upon Assyrian monuments.

Satyr (săt'ĕr). In the A. V. Heb. *sä'îr*, (*shaggy, hairy*) is rendered "satyr." The reference is clearly to demonic creatures which would dance among the ruins of Babylon (Isa. 13: 21) and among the remains of Edomite cities (Isa. 34:14). "He goat" is the common signification of the name, but in Lev. 17:7 and II Chron. 11:15 R. V. the reference is clearly to some object of idolatrous reverence. It either refers to idols having the appearance of goats or, more likely, to the demon-agencies energizing the idol in question. The demonic reference is clearly indicated by Rev. 18:2 where the language is quoted from the Septuagint and the word "demons" is used. Thus the prophet has in mind evil spirits or demons. In Greek and Roman mythology a satyr was a sylvan god, Bacchus' companion. As a goat-like creature he had a brutal and lustful nature. The connection between Greek gods and the Hebrew representations is that of the idol and the demon power behind it. *M. F. U.*

Sic'cuth (sĭ'kooth), apparently the proper name of a stellar deity (Amos 5:26), rendered by E. R. V., R. S. V. "Sakkuth," but in the A. V. and A. R. V. translated "tabernacle"; that is, Hebrew "Succoth." Interpreted as a proper name, it corresponds to Sakkut, the Babylonian designation of the planet Saturn. The Babylonians also called the planet Saturn *Kaimanu*, that is, in modernized form Kaiwanu or Chiun (*q. v.*), (Amos 5:26). As in the case of Hebrew *Kiyyun*, the vocalization of the Hebrew word for "a detestable thing" (*shĭqqūs*) was given to it, resulting in Siccuth. *See* Rephan. *M. F. U.*

Suc'coth-Be'noth (sŭc'ŏth-bē'nŏth), an idol set up in Samaria (II Kings 17:30) by displaced Babylonians. This deity has been identified with Zarpanitum, the consort of Marduk, the patron god of Babylon (Rawlinson and Schrader). Others have connected him with the Akkadian expression *sakkut binuti*, the supreme arbiter of the world. This is construed as a title of Marduk and the form Succoth-benoth represents a Hebraization of it (Friedrich Delitzsch). *M. F. U.*

Tam'muz (tăm'ŭz). Ezekiel refers to the worship of this Babylonian deity in a vision of his apostate brethren who were enamored of this cult. The prophet saw the women weeping for this god at the North Gate of Jerusalem temple (Ezek. 8:14). Tammuz was known by the

Babylonians as Dumuzi, god of pasture and flocks, of subterranean water and of vegetation. He was the husband-brother of Ishtar (Asherah, fertility goddess). Tammuz supposedly died every autumn when he departed to the underworld. Thence he was recovered by the disconsolate Ishtar. His reappearance marked the bursting forth of life in the springtime. The fourth Babylonian month, July, was named in honor of Tammuz, which name was applied in later post-Biblical times by Jews to their fourth month, June-July. Tammuz is equated with the Greek Adonis and the Egyptian Osiris. Allusions to the worship of Tammuz cults seem to be referred to in Jer. 22:18, Amos 8:10, and Zech. 12:10. The worship of this god was widespread throughout the Fertile Crescent from Babylonia-Assyria to Palestine-Syria. The rites of Tammuz included a divine marriage of the king annually to the fertility goddess in the person of a temple priestess. Tammuz worship was especially notorious at Byblus (Biblical Gebal q. v.) on the Mediterranean. M. F. U.

Tar′tak (tär′tăk), a heathen deity mentioned with Nibhaz (q. v.) as introduced into Samaria by the Avvite settlers (II Kings 17:31).

Gog (gŏg).

1. Son of Shemaiah and father of Shimei, and one of the descendants of Reuben (I Chron. 5:4).

2. The prince of Rosh, Meshech, and Tubal (A. V. "the chief prince of Meshech and Tubal"), whom Ezekiel said would invade the restored land of Israel from the far distant northern land by the appointment of God in the last times, and with a powerful army of numerous nations (38:1-9), with the intention of plundering Israel, now dwelling in security, that the Lord may sanctify himself upon him before all the world (v. 10-16). When Gog shall fall upon Israel, he is to be destroyed by a wrathful judgment from the Lord, that the nations may know that God is the Lord (vers. 17-23). On the mountains of Israel will Gog with all his hosts and nations succumb to the judgment of God (39:1-8).

Ezekiel 38, 39, which deal with Gog, the prince, and Magog, his land, describe the actual invasion of Palestine by a great northern confederacy, ostensibly headed up by Russia. The scene depicts a gigantic outburst of anti-Semitism and a colossal attempt to overrun Palestine and annihilate the Jew. Russia and the northern powers have been persecutors of dispersed Israel, and it is consonant with the covenants and promises of Israel, which are yet to be fulfilled (Cf. Gen. 15:18 sq.; Deut. 33 sq.), that divine destruction should be precipitated at the climax of the last mad attempt to destroy the remnant of Israel in Jerusalem and Palestine. The entire prophecy belongs to the "Day of the Lord" (Isa. 2:10-22; Rev. 19:11-21) and evidently precedes the actual battle of Armageddon by a number of years. The prophetic perspective concerning Gog, however, includes the final revolt of the nations at the close of the mediatorial Messianic Kingdom (Rev. 20:6-9). M. F. U.

Go′lan (gō′lăn), one of the three cities of refuge on the east of Jordan, the others being Bezer and Ramoth (Deut. 4:43; comp. Josh. 20:8; 21:27; I Chron. 6:71). It became the head of the province of Gaulanitis, one of the four provinces in which Bashan was divided after the Babylonian captivity, and probably identical with the modern *Jaulân*, in Western Hauran.

Gold. See Mineral Kingdom.

Golden City (Heb. *mădhēbäh*), a term applied to Babylon (Isa. 14:4) and occurring nowhere else. "Not one of the early translators ever thought of deriving this word from the Aramaean *dehab* (gold), but translated the word as if it were *marhebah* (haughty, violent treatment). We understand it, according to *madmenah* (dunghill) in chap. 25:10, as denoting the place where they were reduced to pining away, i. e., as applied to Babylon as the house of servitude where Israel had been wearied to death" (Delitzsch, *Com.*, in loco). The R. S. V. renders "insolent fury."

Goldsmith. See Handicrafts.

Gol′gotha (gŏl′gŏ-thä; *place of a skull*). The gospels and tradition disagree as to the locality. John (19:41, 42) locates the place by saying, that "in the garden near" the place where Jesus was crucified there was a new sepulcher, and that he was here laid, for it was nigh at hand, and it was the Jew's preparation day. The Scripture references place the spot outside of the city, and from Matt. 27:33, and Mark 15:29, it is to be concluded that the place of crucifixion was on the public highway or road. On the contrary, the place of tradition is quite a distance within the city limits. The fact that the city wall may have been changed in the rebuilding of the city by Hadrian, etc., etc., is met with the fact of the general uncertainty of localities located by tradition, being matters of hearsay without the records. See Calvary.

Goli′ath (gō-lī′ăth).

1. **Name and Family.** Goliath, although repeatedly called a Philistine, was probably descended from the old Rephaim, of whom a scattered remnant took refuge with the Philistines after their dispersion by the Ammonites (Deut. 2:20, 21; II Sam. 21:22).

2. **Personal History.** The only mention made of Goliath is his appearance as the champion of the Philistines, and his death at the hands of David (I Sam. 17), B. C. c. 1010. The Philistines had ventured upon another inroad into the country, and had taken up a firm position on the slope of a mountain, Ephes-dammim, between Shochoh and Azekah, in western Judah. Israel encamps over against them on the slope of a second mountain, at a place called the Valley of the Terebinth, and between the two camps lies a deep, narrow valley, which seems destined as a field on which the warriors of either side may exercise their valor. And now from the Philistine camp there advances a champion, Goliath of Gath, six cubits and a span high (which, taking the cubit at twenty-one inches, would make him ten and a half feet high), with a bronze helmet, and clothed in a coat of mail the weight of which was five thousand shekels, and a spear like the shaft of a weaver's beam.

Forty days he terrifies the people by challenging, morning and evening, to single combat any of Israel's warriors. David had been sent to his brethren with provisions, and, hearing the challenge of Goliath, inquired its meaning. Upon being told, he offered to become Israel's champion, and sallied forth armed with a sling and five smooth stones. He answered the scornful taunt of the giant with, "This day will the Lord deliver thee into mine hand." He smote Goliath in the forehead, and, slaying the fallen champion, cut off his head. "When the Philistines saw their champion was dead, they fled," and were pursued by the Israelites with great slaughter.

The giant was over nine feet. The "four cubits and a span" under ordinary calculation would make him at least this height. Skeletons recovered in Palestine attest the fact that men as tall as Goliath once lived in that general region. Critics commonly reject the historical reliability of the David-Goliath narrative, adducing contradictions in the account. An alleged contradiction is II Sam. 21:19, which reports that "Elhanan . . . slew Goliath the Gittite . . ." while I Sam. 17:50, 51 (Cf. 19:5; 21:9; 22:10, 13) asserts that David did so. Moreover, I Chron. 20:5 reports that "Elhanan the son of Jairi slew Lahmi, the brother of Goliath the Gittite . . ." If this glaring error was in the original the final redactors of Samuel were guilty of a most obvious and stupid blunder and must be considered as incredibly incompetent. The explanation of the apparent discrepancy is that the passage in Samuel has suffered corruption in the course of transmission. A careful study of the original suggests that the reading both in Samuel and Chronicles originally was either "And Elhanan the son of Jairi slew Lahmi and the brother of Goliath" or "Elhahanan the son of Jairi the Bethlehemite slew the brother of Goliath." The obvious original is that both passages substantiate that David slew Goliath and Elhanan slew "the brother of Goliath." (For suggested emendation see Edward Young, *Introduction to the O. T.*, 1949, p. 181f.; S. R. Driver, *Notes on the Hebrew Text of the Books of Samuel*, Oxford, 1913; *International Critical Commentary in. loc.*, p. 354 f.)

                                      M. F. U.

Go′mer (gō′mĕr).

1. The eldest son of Japheth, and father of Ashkenaz, Riphath, and Togarmah (Gen. 10:2, 3). The name afterward occurs as that of a tribe (*See* Ezek. 38:6), probably the Cimmerians, who dwelt, according to Herodotus, on the Maeotis, in the Taurian Chersonesus (K. and D., *Com.*).

2. The name of the daughter of Diblaim, a harlot who became the wife or concubine (according to some, in vision only) of the prophet Hosea (Hos. 1:3), B. C. about 785.

Gomor′rah (gō-môr′rȧ); apparently meaning, "submersion;" cf. Arab. *ghamara*, to over-flow, to inundate). The city in the Plain of Jordan (Gen. 10:19; 13:10) which, with Sodom, became the type of intolerable wickedness and was destroyed by fire (Gen. 19:24, 28). Like Sodom, its ruler was vanquished by a Mesopotamian confederacy which invaded the Jordan Valley in the time of Abraham (Gen.

14:8-11). The Biblical notices point out that the district of the Jordan where Sodom, Gomorrah, Admah, Zeboiim and Zoar were located was exceedingly productive and well peopled around 2054 B. C., but that not long afterward was abandoned. This circumstance is in full agreement with archaeological findings. (*See* W. F. Albright, *The Archeology of Palestine and the Bible*, p. 133 ff.). These cities were located in the Vale of Siddim (Gen. 14:3). Probably this was the area at the southern end of the Dead Sea, now covered with water.

184. Map of the Lower Dead Sea Area Showing the Cities of "the Plain of Jordan" (Gen. 13:10)

Somewhere in the vicinity of 2050 B. C. this region was overwhelmed by a great conflagration. The country was said to have been "full of slime (asphalt) pits" (Gen. 14:10). Bitumen deposits are still to be found in that area. Being on the fault-line forming the Jordan Valley, the Dead Sea and the Arabah, this region has been the scene of earthquakes throughout history. The Biblical account sets forth the miraculous elements, but geological activity was doubtless a factor. The salt and free sulphur of this area, now a burned-out region of oil and asphalt, were mingled by an earthquake to form a violent explosion. Evidently salt and sulphur were blasted into the sky red hot so that literally it rained fire and brimstone over the whole plain (Gen. 19:24, 28). Lot's wife being turned into a pillar of salt is reminiscent of "the Mount of Sodom" known to the Arabs as *Jebel Usdum*, a five-mile-long salt mass stretching N. and S. at the southeastern end of the Dead Sea. Somewhere under the slowly rising water of the southern part of the lake the five cities of the plain are to be found. According to Tacitus' *History* V:7, and Josephus' *Wars of the Jews*, IV:4, their ruins were still visible in classical and N. T. times, not yet being covered with water. M. F. U.

Goodly Trees (Heb. *'ēṣ hädär, trees of ornament*). The Israelites were directed to take "boughs of goodly trees" (i. e., carry about in festive procession) on the first day of the *Feast of Tabernacles* (*q. v.*), in memory of their having dwelt in booths (Lev. 23:40). The expression, "goodly trees," probably included not only the orange and citron, which were placed in gardens for ornament rather than for use, but also myrtles, olive trees, palms, and others which had beauty or pleasant odor.

Goodman (Gr. *oikodespotēs*, Matt. 20:11; 24: 43; Mark 14:14; Luke 22:11), rendered "master of the house" (Matt. 10:25; Luke 13:25; 14:21); "householder" (Matt. 13:27; 20:1, etc.). "Goodman" (Prov. 7:19) is the rendering of the Hebrew *'ish, man*, i. e., husband.

Goodness. In some places *kindness* seems more especially meant; e. g., "The earth is full of the goodness—loving-kindness, R. V.—of the Lord" (Psa. 33:5). In others it expresses the supreme benevolence, holiness, and excellence of the divine character, the sum of all God's attributes. "I will make all my goodness pass before thee" (Exod. 33:19). In common use *goodness* is the opposite of *badness*, the quality of character which makes its possessor lovable; excellence more particularly of a religious kind, virtue, righteousness.

Gopher. *See* Animal Kingdom.

Gopher Wood. *See* Vegetable Kingdom.

Go'shen (gō'shĕn). This northeastern section of the Egyptian Delta region is usually called "the land of Goshen," "country of Goshen" (Gen. 47:27), or simply "Goshen" and "the land of Rameses" (Gen. 47:11; cf. Ex. 12:37). In this region the Israelites under Jacob settled during the prime-ministership of Joseph (Gen. 46: 28f.). This was a very fertile section of Egypt, excellent for grazing and certain types of agriculture, but apparently not particularly inviting to the pharoahs because of its distance from the Nile irrigation canals. It extends thirty or forty miles in length centering in Wadi Lumilat and reaches from Lake Timsa to the Nile. It was connected with the name of Rameses because Rameses II (c. 1290-1224 B. C.) built extensively in this location at Pithom (Tell er Retabeh) and Rameses (Zoan-Avaris-Tanis). Tanis was called the House of Rameses (c. 1300-1100 B. C.). The references to the city of Rameses in Exod. 1:11 must be to the older City Zoan-Avaris where the oppressed Israelites labored centuries earlier. It seems clearly evident, therefore, that the reference to the name Rameses in Exod. 1:11 must be construed as a modernization of an archaic place name and have reference to the earlier city Zoan-Avaris.
M. F. U.

2. A district of southern Palestine, lying between Gaza and Gibeon, its name probably being given in remembrance of Egypt (Josh. 10:41); 11:16). In the latter passage the maritime plain of Judah, the *Shefelah*, is expressly mentioned, and if Goshen was any part of that rich plain, its fertility may have suggested its name.

3. A town mentioned in company with Debir, Socoh, and others as in the mountains of Judah (Josh. 15:51), in the group on the southwest part of the hills.

Gospel (Anglo Saxon, *godspell*, "good story"), good news, and employed as the equivalent of the Greek *'euaggelion*. This word in the earlier Greek language signified "a present given to one who brought good tidings," or "a sacrifice offered in thanksgiving for such good tidings having come." In later Greek it was employed for the good tidings themselves. It is used to signify:

1. The good news of the death, burial and resurrection of Christ as provided by our Lord and preached by His disciples (I Cor. 15:1-4). The gospel then is full and free deliverance from sin on the basis of simple faith in Jesus Christ, the Vicarious Sinbearer (Eph. 2:8-10). In this aspect the gospel has two phases: one, to the unsaved: "Christ died for me" (John 3:16; 3:34; Acts 16:30, 31); secondly, the gospel to the saved: "I died in Christ" (Rom. 6:2-10) with a key to the experiential realization of this fact in the life furnished by Rom. 6:11.

2. Forms of the Gospel to be Differentiated. Many Bible teachers make a distinction in the following:—(1) *The Gospel of the Kingdom*. The good news that God's purpose is to establish an earthly mediatorial kingdom in fulfillment of the Davidic Covenant (II Sam. 7:16). Two proclamations of the gospel of the kingdom are mentioned, one, past, beginning with the ministry of John the Baptist, carried on by our Lord and His disciples and ending with the Jewish rejection of the Messiah. The other preaching is yet future (Matt. 24:14), during the Great Tribulation, and heralding the Second Advent of the King. Closely connected, although perhaps not identical in its emphasis with the gospel of the kingdom, is the everlasting gospel (Rev. 14:6) preached to earth dwellers during the latter part of the Tribulation. (2) *The Gospel of God's Grace* (see No. 1 above). Paul calls this gospel of the grace of God "my gospel" (Rom. 2:16) because the full doctrinal content based upon the gospel of the grace of God embraces the revelation of the result in the outcalling of the Church, her relationship, position, privileges and responsibility. This distinctive Pauline truth honeycombing Ephesians and Colossians is interwoven in all of the Pauline writings.

3. "Another gospel" (Gal. 1:6; II Cor. 11: 4) "which is not another." This consists of any denial or perversion of the gospel of the grace of God. Its essential stamp is that it denies the full efficacy of God's grace alone to save, keep and perfect, and introduces some sort of human merit. In Galatia it was legalism. Its teachers are under God's terrible anathema. The relation of the gospel to the law of Moses has been a source of much confusion. Under grace the Ten Commandments are all presented, except that involving the observance of the seventh day. However, they are to be operative not to find favor with God but because the redeemed one has already found favor and eternal life and possesses the indwelling Spirit to work them out in daily conduct.

4. The four stories of our Lord's life published by Matthew, Mark, Luke and John. The writers are called Evangelists. These accounts are "gospels" because they recite the events in the life, death, resurrection, ascension of our Lord and predicted bestowment of the Spirit, making possible "the gospel."
M. F. U.

Gospels. *See* Bible, Books of.

Gospels, the Four. The term *Gospel* is an old English word (used A. D. 1250-1350) derived from the Saxon God-spel, i. e., God, and spel, *story;* from spellian, *to tell,* meaning "*literally a narrative of God*" (Skeat) as realized in the life of Jesus Christ. It is so used in both the Authorized and the Revised Version (Webster). Gospel is not *a translation* of the Greek word *euaggelion*; as is constantly supposed, but "it is the nearest idiomatic equivalent" known to the sacred writers (Schaff). The word gospels is applied in a specific sense to the first four books of the New Testament, because each one gives a distinct memoir of Jesus Christ; and so exclusively and completely are the contents of these four gospels occupied with the Lord's life that had there never been *the historical Christ,* who lived and died, who rose from the dead and ascended into heaven, those four gospels would have no right to exist.

Different in authorship, different in the standpoint of the.writer, different in the parts and period of our Lord's life traversed, different also in the omissions and additions of each, the four gospels constitute one harmonious whole: one in subject, one in source, one in history, one in purpose and in power; and each biographer relates independently his own story of Jesus with that inimitable simplicity and truth which commends itself "to every man's conscience in the sight of God."

1. **Writers of the Gospels.** The authors of the four gospels were severally Matthew, Mark, Luke, and John (see under several names). They were not all fishermen as is often supposed. They were from different secular occupations, and from various parts of the country.

Patristic testimony regarding both the authors and the order of the several gospels is very conclusive. Irenaeus (born about A. D. 115), the pupil of Polycarp, who was the disciple of the apostle John, says: "It is not possible that the gospels can be either more or fewer than they are now" (*Against Heresies,* iii, 8). Origen (b. 185) "attests that he knows only four gospels . . . which are the only undisputed ones in the whole Church of God throughout the world;" and he names them in the exact order as they have come down to us (Eusebius, *Eccl. Hist.,* B. vi, ch. 25, p. 231, Cruse's translation). The famous Fragment known as the. *Muratorian Canon* (dating A. D. 170) is torn off in the first part, leaving a few words in the last of Mark's gospel, but gives Luke and John in that order. As the part due to Matthew has disappeared, and is found nowhere else, it is easy to understand that it was the part which was lost. Eusebius (b. 260), the first historian of the Church whose work has come down to us, while discussing the books of the New Testament, says: "Among the first must be placed *The Holy Quaternion of the Gospels*" (Euseb., *E. H.,* iii, 25, p. 99).

(1) **Matthew** wrote at Jerusalem, before starting out to evangelize the nations; *Mark* wrote at Rome, before starting out to establish the faith in Egypt; *Luke* wrote in Greece, or while sharing Paul's imprisonment at Caesarea; *John* wrote at Ephesus after his exile at Patmos. Clement of Alexandria (b. 150)

affirms that Matthew continued his stay at Jerusalem with the other apostles, busy with his own countrymen for a period of twelve years after the crucifixion (Strom., vi, 5, 53). Eusebius says: "The Holy Apostles and disciples of our Saviour, being scattered over the whole world, Thomas, according to tradition, received Parthia as his allotted region; Andrew received Scythia, and John Asia, where, after continuing for some time, he died at Ephesus. Peter appears to have preached through Pontus, Galatia, Bithynia, Cappadocia, and Asia, to the Jews that were scattered abroad; who also finally coming to Rome, was crucified with his head downward, having requested of himself to suffer in this way" (*E. H.,* iii. c. 1, p. 70).

Theodore of Mopsuestia says: "For a good while the apostles preached chiefly to Jews in Judea. Afterward Providence made way for conducting them to remote countries. Peter went to Rome; the rest elsewhere; John, in particular, took up his abode in Ephesus. About this time the other evangelists, Matthew, Mark, and Luke, published their gospels, which were soon spread abroad all over the world" (cited by Lardner, v, 299). The author of the *Imperfect Work* (about A. D. 560) wrote: "The occasion of Matthew's writing is said to be this: There was a great persecution in Palestine, so that there was danger lest all the faithful should be dispersed. That they might not be without teaching, though they should have no teachers, they requested Matthew to write for them a history of all Christ's words and works, that wherever they should be, they should have with them the ground of their faith" (Lard., v, p. 300). Exactly when Matthew's gospel was written is at present indeterminate. Ancient writers differ in dates. Theophylact, of the 11th Christian century, and Euthymius, of the 12th century, state that it was produced "eight years after the ascension," which would be about A. D. 41 or 42 of our current chronology. But the more ancient writers give a later date. The Paschal Chronicle of the 7th century says, "about fifteen years after our Lord's ascension." with which Nicephorus Callisti, of the 14th century, agrees. This would be about A. D. 48. But Irenaeus, Bishop of Lyons, in the 2nd century, and at only one remove from the apostle John, says: "Matthew indeed produced a gospel written among the Hebrews in their own dialect, while Peter and Paul proclaimed the gospel and founded the Church at Rome. After the departure (death) of these, Mark, the disciple and interpreter of Peter, also transmitted to us in writing that which had been preached by Peter. And Luke, the companion of Paul, committed to writing the gospel preached by him (Paul). Afterward John, the disciple of our Lord, the same that lay in his bosom, also published the gospel while he was yet in Ephesus, in Asia" (Euseb., *E. H.,* v, c, 8). In no case could this have been earlier, but probably later than A. D. 61, the year Paul arrived at Rome a prisoner. Epiphanius, Bishop of Cyprus in A. D. 367, who is accounted high authority in these matters, says that Matthew wrote first (of the four evangelists) and Mark soon after, being a companion of Peter at Rome; that Mark and Luke were both of the seventy disciples sent out to the Gentiles; that both were offended at Christ's words recorded in John 6:44; that Peter recovered Mark, and Paul recovered Luke to the Christian faith afterward; that Mark wrote the second gospel and Luke the third, and John wrote the fourth and last gospel (see Lard., iv, pp. 187, 188).

By whom the gospel of Matthew was given in our present Greek form is unknown, but probably by himself. The concensus of critical scholars is that it is not a mere translation, but an original composition. Socrates, the historian, states that Matthew went to Ethiopia, where he is said to have died a a natural death. Eusebius says that Pantaenus, the philosopher, who afterward became a Christian, and was placed at the celebrated school at Alexandria, penetrated as far as the Indies, and "there found his own arrival anticipated by some who there were acquainted with the gospel of Matthew, to whom Bartholomew, one of the apostles, had preached, and left them the gospel of Matthew in Hebrew, which was also preserved until this time" (see *E. H.*, v, 10, p. 178).

(2) **Mark** is the evangelist who wrote the second gospel. Papias, Bishop of Hierapolis in the first half of the 2d century, furnished the earliest notice of this gospel. He says: "Mark, having been the interpreter of Peter, wrote down accurately whatever he remembered, without however recording in order what was either said or done by Christ. *For neither did he hear the Lord, nor did he follow him* (as did the Twelve) . . . So then Mark committed no error in thus writing down such details as he remembered; for he made it his own forethought not to omit or misrepresent any details that he heard (from Peter)" (Euseb., *E. H.*, iii, 39). Jerome observes of Mark, that "taking his gospel which himself had composed, he went to Egypt and at Alexandria founded a church of great note;" and in his *Book of Illustrious Men*, says: "Mark, the disciple and interpreter of Peter, at the desire of the brethren at Rome, wrote a short gospel according to what he had heard related by Peter, which, when Peter knew it, he approved it and authorized it to be read in the churches" (see Lard., v, 334). Universal testimony is to the effect that Mark wrote down in his gospel as best he could the substance of Peter's preaching; and the gospel itself confirms by internal evidence the testimony of the fathers in many respects. For while it details in a graphic manner important facts, it is at once the briefest and least complete of the four gospels. Nevertheless, it represents fairly the impulsive and energetic Peter, and the very omissions and additions indicate the style of the apostle. Justin Martyr, who wrote about A. D. 140-150, and was born before the death of the apostle John, cites from the *Memoirs of Peter* the names given to James and John by Jesus, who called them "Boanerges," or sons of thunder; a circumstance mentioned only in Mark's gospel (3:17). Jerome, after mentioning Mark as having composed his gospel, and gone to Egypt, and founding a notable church at Alexandria, states that this

evangelist "died in the eighth year of the reign of Nero." As Nero ruled the empire A. D. 54-68, this would place the death of Mark in the year 62 (Lard., v, 331).

Three things are made evident as related to Mark's gospel by these patristic citations: *1.* That Mark composed his gospel of the substance preached by Peter; *2.* that Peter "knew" of the fact, and both approved and authorized his gospel to be read in the several churches; *3.* that all this was accomplished before the death of Peter at Rome.

(3) **Luke,** by common consent, was the writer of the third gospel and of Acts. Even such writers as the Frenchman Renan, known as hostile to Christianity, fully concede this fact as incontestable. The third gospel is derived from different sources, but all legitimate authorities, as it is confessedly due to those apostles who "from the beginning were eyewitness and ministers of the word" (Prologue of chap. 1). Nevertheless, it is the most complete gospel of them all, and the only one which observes a strictly historical method, the first three gospels being biographical sketches, or as designated by Justin Martyr, *"Memoirs of the Apostles"*. It is to be remarked that both Luke's gospel and Acts are dedicated to one Theophilus (friend of God), which was a custom in those days, obligating those thus receiving a copy as a gift to exert themselves to give the work circulation (Lee).

(4) **John** is the author of the fourth gospel. After extraordinary research and testing, the criticism of the best scholarship of the age ascribes this work to that apostle "whom Jesus loved." No classic writing of equal antiquity is so well attested by both external and internal evidence as John's gospel. It has been said, so peculiar and marked is this writing, that if we did not know who its author was, we should have to imagine a personage of such character for its authorship.

2. **Designations of the Writers.** (1) **Evangelists.** In organizing the workers for the kingdom of Christ "He gave some, apostles; some, prophets; and some, evangelists . . . for the perfecting of the saints" (Eph. 4:11, 12). Evangelists appear to have been appointed to a certain *work*, rather than to be a specific order in the apostolic Church. They were afterward known as *euangelistai, evangelists,* whose function was that of missionary preachers, who are described by Eusebius as "leaving their country they performed the office of evangelists to those who proclaim Christ; they also delivered to them the books of the holy gospels. The Holy Ghost also wrought many wonders through them, so that as soon as the gospel was heard men voluntarily gathered in crowds and eagerly embraced the true faith with their whole minds." The evangelists were "bringers of good tidings given to the heralds of salvation through Christ, who are not apostles" (Thayer). In the time of Chrysostom the term was applied to *the writers of the gospels"* (Cremer). The four gospels were composed within a short period, if measured by the lapse of time, but at long intervals, if measured by the course of events.

A just distinction is to be noted as between the first and fourth gospel written by two of

Christ's disciples, who were eyewitnesses of facts stated, and the second and third gospels, which were written by evangelists *who did not* witness the facts they record. Mark and Luke were not of the Twelve at least. The distinction relates to the kind of testimony which each class furnishes. Matthew and John were identified with the original "Twelve" disciples who were chosen by our Lord to accompany him throughout his ministry, "beginning from the baptism of John unto the same day that he was taken up" to heaven (Matt. 10:2-5; Acts 1:22). They were so chosen, as Mark and Luke were not, to be "witnesses of all things which he did both in the land of the Jews and in Jerusalem," whose perfectly familiar knowledge of Jesus was such that they even "did eat and drink with him after he rose from the the dead." These were they whom he "commanded" "to preach unto the people and to testify" (Acts 10:39, 41, 42). As seen, Papias, who was almost within touch of the apostles, says that Mark neither heard the Lord, nor did he follow him. Even if Epiphanius be correct in identifying Mark and Luke with the seventy disciples, it does not follow from the evidence that they were with Jesus "from the beginning," and certainly not at the end, if they became offended at Christ's words, "and walked no more with him." Neither of these writers professes to have been eyewitnesses of the scenes which he records; but quite to the contrary, Luke makes declaration of other sources of information. However, this is no detriment at all to the claim of these two gospels as being equally historical and credible with the others. Mark reports the substance of Peter's sermons which he had often heard repeated in public or in private conversations; and Peter was an eyewitness, and Luke acknowledges his obligation to those who were "eyewitnesses and ministers of the word."

Nor do these facts reduce the contents of the second and third gospels to the character of mere "traditions," as some have assumed. Traditions may be, and often are, thoroughly historical, since the mere act of writing does not render anything historical. But these two gospels were *not* handed down from one generation to another, or from father to son, as must be the case with "*tradition;*" they were written deliverances to contemporaries of Christ and his apostles, who were themselves cognizant of many facts recorded in these gospels. These writings of Mark and Luke were never questioned by those who lived in their time, and were in a position to know or deny the historicity and credibility of their statements. Their gospels were not of the character of traditions any more than the records taken in the courts, of the testimony of witnesses, are to be called mere "traditions," which would obviously be a vicious misuse of language.

(2) **Synoptists.** The writers of the first three gospels are known as Synoptists in distinction from the fourth gospel; and the first three gospels are called the synoptic gospels; from *sun, together,* and *opsis, view.* The reference is to the parallel narratives in the facts recorded and the statements made by Matthew, Mark, and Luke. John's gospel is very different in character, being intentionally supplementary to the accounts given by the synoptists. Clement of Alexandria says: "The three gospels previously written, having been distributed among all, and also handed down to him [i. e., John], they say that he admitted them, giving his testimony to their truth; but that there was wanting in the narrative the account of the things done by Christ among the first of his deeds, and at the commencement of the gospel. . . . For it is evident that the other three evangelists only wrote the deeds of our Lord for one year after the imprisonment of John the Baptist, and intimated this in the very beginning of their history. . . . The Apostle John, it is said, being entreated to undertake it, wrote the account of the time not recorded by the former evangelists, and the deeds done by our Saviour which they have passed by (for these were the events that occurred before the imprisonment of John), and this very fact is intimated by him when he says (2:11): "This beginning of miracles did," etc. (Euseb., iii, c. 24). Clement elsewhere says: "But John, last of all, perceiving that what had reference to the body in the gospel of our Saviour was sufficiently detailed, and being encouraged by his familiar friends and urged by the Spirit, wrote a spiritual gospel" (Ib., vi, 14).

The synoptists in traversing the same ground with each other exhibit certain agreements and disagreements in statement which are really remarkable. These divergencies relate alike to matter and method, yet without invalidating the account. For the last century it has been a problem for the ripest scholarship and keenest criticism to solve. The careful analysis and consideration have been carried on nearly to exhaustion, and no satisfactory solution has been reached from sheer insufficiency of *data*, now after the lapse of nearly two thousand years. These several writers indicate their individuality of character and independence of each other in a manner that excludes the thought of either collision or collusion in their testimony. For they evince not the slightest consciousness of any error as possible, and evidence not the slightest concern that anything that they record could be disputed by contemporaries who might be supposed to be at times as familiar with certain public events as themselves. Unquestionably they neglect the strict chronological order of events, in that they aim at the higher end of spiritual sequence, which is always kept in sight. Mere deviations of statement are certainly not to be taken as contradictions. The variations of the first three gospels furnish a clear case of what in the courts is known as "Substantial truth under circumstantial variety of testimony in manner and detail," as in any other case of testimonies from different witnesses who are honest. For, as Dr. Schaff admirably remarks, "It is a generally acknowledged principle in legal evidence that circumstantial variation in the testimony of witnesses confirms their substantial agreement."

3. **Origin of the Gospels.** Very evidently the several gospels had their origin in a common source. There is not the slightest proof, however, that they were derived from some

prior and unknown writing of some unknown and imaginary author. Their character precludes the assumption. The four gospels owe their existence solely to one source, as they are exclusively occupied with one subject, viz., the *historical Person of Jesus Christ*. His life is no ideal creation, and the contents of the gospels are the not the outgrowth of exuberant fancy. The evangelists themselves were utterly incapable of even conceiving ideally, much less developing, such a unique character as that of the perfect Man delineated on their pages. There must first have been the *real God-Man* made manifest to their gaze, present to the apprehension through the senses, realized and known to their mind, by long and familiar contemplation, to have furnished to the race such an imperishable portraiture of the living Christ of God.

The origin of the four gospels was clearly historical, although somewhat progressive in character. First, there was the Christly Presence whose very personality and spirituality spoke so directly to men's consciousness that at his word they turned from their occupation instantly, and with a loving cheer, "left all . . . and followed him" (Matt. 4:21, 22; Luke 5: 27). Then the gospel which he himself *orally* declared, the miracles which he wrought to confirm the word, the truths which he taught in conversation, as one who gazed upon the invisible world; and the passion which he endured at the end, in maintenance of his teachings—are the things which made a powerful and imperishable impression upon mankind. After that the apostles took up the story of his life, and began to preach with strange power that Jesus was the realization of Jewish prediction, was the true Messiah of the Jews, the incarnate Son of God, the wonderful Redeemer of mankind. For about thirty years after the crucifixion, while whole communities were religiously reformed or revolutionized by Christian doctrine, no pen had yet traced a single line about Jesus Christ in the gospels. At last, all these *oral teachings* both by Christ and his apostles crystallized in written and permanent form known to us as the four gospels, to be the heritage of the generations to come, down to the end of time. *The oral and the written teachings were equally authoritative and the product of inspired minds* (Comp. II Pet. 1:21; II Tim. 3:16, 17; I Thess. 2:13; II Thess. 2:15; Acts 15:22-28). Jesus directed his disciples to go "teach all nations" (Matt. 28:20); but he did not restrict them to any one *mode* of teaching, and speech and writing are but different methods of instruction for those who are present or absent.

(1) **Matthew.** In point of time, the best biblical scholars give priority to Matthew's gospel (Schaff). Origen mentions "the four gospels as the only undisputed ones in the whole Church of God throughout the world," and that "*the first is written by Matthew, the same who was a publican, but afterward an apostle of Jesus Christ, who having published it for the Jewish converts, wrote it in Hebrew.*" That Matthew wrote his gospel in the Hebrew language is amply attested by Papias, Irenaeus, Pantaenus, Origen, Eusebius, Cyril of Jerusalem, Epiphanius, and Jerome. Traces of this

fact may be found in his use of certain Hebrew words found nowhere else than in a Jewish vocabulary. Such are *Immanuel* (Heb. '*immänü'ēl;* Gr. *Emmanouēl,* "*God with us,*" 1: 23); *Golgotha* (Heb. *gŭlgōlĕth,* Chald. *gŭlăltä';* Gr. *Golgotha, a skull,* 27:33); *Raca* (Gr. *hraka, a simpleton,* 5:22); *Eli* (Heb. '*ēli;* Gr. *ēli,* "*My God,*" 27:46). Pantaenus, the Christian philosopher, avers that in his evangelism he had penetrated so far as the Indies, where he found those who are acquainted with Matthew's Hebrew gospel, which Bartholomew, one of the apostles, had preached to the natives (see Euseb., *E. H.,* v, 10, p. 178).

That Matthew wrote as early as the period assigned is evident from citations made therefrom by one who was a disciple of the apostles. Barnabas, whose epistle is now dated A. D. 70-79, mentions many incidents recorded in the several gospels as well as in Paul's earlier epistles, such as Christ's choosing the twelveapostles, the mockery of Jesus by Herod Antipas and his soldiery, the casting lots for his garments, etc., and then cites the very words of Matthew (9:13, also in Mark 2:17): "*I came not to call the righteous, but sinners" to repentance.* Not only is this passage cited *as being Scripture,* but as determinative that he was not quoting from an *oral gospel,* he says, "*As it is written, Many are called, but few chosen;*" —*sicum scriptum est* (Epis. of Barnabas, ch. 4, close) (see Matt. 22:14, and 20:16 of Authorized Version; the latter reference is omitted in the English Revised Version). This is the first distinct reference made by an apostolic father to a *written* gospel. The document known as the *Didaché of the Apostles,* which was written in the last decade of the 1st century, makes much use of this Gospel of Matthew, particularly of the Sermon on the Mount, which Matthew is by far the most copious in quoting. The *Didaché* was in existence while the apostle John was still living, and proves that Matthew's written gospel was well known in the 1st century. So Justin writes of the "Memoirs," or "Memorabilia of the Apostles which are called Gospels" in both his *Apologies* and *Dialogue.* Papias says that "Matthew composed his history [*ta logia,* i. e., *the divine oracles*] in the Hebrew dialect, and everyone translated them as he was able" (Euseb., iii, c. 38, p. 116). Clement of Alexandria says, referring to the first and third gospel: "Those which contain the genealogies were written first" (Euseb., *E. H.,* vi, c. 14, p. 220).

(2) **Mark.** Respecting the difficulties which confronted Peter at Rome, and his success, Eusebius says: "The declaration of the truth prevailed and overpowered all, and the divine word itself, now shining from heaven upon men and flourishing upon earth and dwelling with his apostles, prevailed and overpowered every opposition" (ii, c. 14). Clement of Alexandria says: "The gospel of Mark was occasioned in the following manner: When Peter had proclaimed the word publicly at Rome, and declared the gospel under the influence of the Spirit, as there was a great number present, they requested Mark, who had followed him from afar, and remembered well what he had said, to reduce these things to writing, and that after composing the gospel,

he gave it to those who requested it of him" (Euseb., *E. H.*, vi, 14).

Clement, in another place, says: "So greatly did the splendor of piety enlighten the minds of Peter's hearers, that it was not sufficient to hear but once, nor to receive *the unwritten* doctrine of the Gospel of God, but they persevered in every variety of entreaties to solicit Mark as the companion of Peter, and whose gospel we have, that he should leave them a monument of the doctrine thus orally communicated in writing. Nor did they cease their solicitations until they had prevailed with the man, and thus became the means of that history which is called *the gospel of Mark*." Peter "having ascertained what was done, by the revelation of Spirit, was delighted," and . . . "the history obtained his authority for the purpose of being read in the churches" (Euseb., *E. H.*, ii, c. 15, pp. 52, 53).

(3) **Luke.** This evangelist, in the prologue of his gospel, professes to have received information from those who "from the beginning were eye-witnesses and ministers of the word," and that he himself "had a perfect understanding of all things from the very first," respecting which he now proposed to write (1:2, 3). Clement remarks that "Luke also in the commencement of his narrative premises the cause which led him to write, showing that many others having rashly undertaken to compose a narration of matters that he had already completely ascertained, in order to free us from the uncertain suppositions of others, in his own gospel he delivered *the certain account* of those things that he himself had fully received from his intimacy with Paul, and also his intercourse with the other apostles" (Euseb., *E. H.*, iii, 24). In the sense that he possessed several sources of information, his gospel is the most composite of the four, in its contents. It is safe to believe that it was composed in the period between A. D. 58 and 63, but probably not *published* until after the death of Paul. "Mark and Luke wrote at a time when their writings might be approved, not only by the Church, but also by the apostles still living" (Augustine).

(4) **John.** In respect to this evangelist Clement again observes: "After Mark and Luke had already published their gospels, they say that John, who, during all this time, was preaching the gospel without writing, at length proceeded to write it on the following occasion: The three gospels previously written, having been distributed among all, and also handed to him, they say that he admitted them, giving his testimony to their truth; and that there was only wanting in the narrative the account of the things done by Christ, among the first of his deeds and at the commencement of the gospel. . . . The apostle, therefore, in his gospel gives the deeds of Jesus before the Baptist was cast into prison, but the other evangelists mention the circumstances after that event. One who attends to these circumstances can no longer entertain the opinion that the gospels are at variance with each other, as the gospel of John comprehends the first events of Christ's life, but the others, the history that took place in the latter part of the time. It is probable, there-

fore, that for these reasons John has passed by in silence the genealogy of our Lord, because it was written by Matthew and Luke; but he commenced with the doctrine of the divinity as the part reserved for him by the divine Spirit, as if for a superior" (Euseb., *E. H.*, iii, c. 24, pp. 98, 99).

The celebrated Fragment of the New Testament known as *the Muratorium Canon*, which dates about A. D. 170, thus accounts for the origin of John's gospel: that at Ephesus the apostles and elders showed John the first three gospels, which he read and approved, and then urged him to write the fourth gospel; that thereupon John desired to seek the Lord's will, and proposed to make it the subject for fasting and prayer for three days; that meantime anyone receiving a revelation respecting it should immediately communicate it to the others; that on the first night Andrew the disciple reported a vision that John should narrate all matters in his own name, and the others should assist him. Thereupon, John proceeded to write his gospel, with the special view of supplementing any details omitted by the other evangelists, and generally omitting particulars which they had inserted in the first three gospels. This account serves to explain the special indorsement given by these assistants, which now is included in the text, at the close of the fourth gospel, in these words: "*This is the disciple which testifieth of these things and wrote these things; and* we know that his testimony is true" (John 21:24) (see Westcott's *Canon*, p. 214).

4. **Objects of the Gospels.** Each evangelist naturally had some special object in view in composing his gospel, and that gave it prominence. *Matthew*, being himself a Jew, wrote in the Jewish language for the special benefit of all Jewish converts and people. Accordingly he records the evidence that Jesus Christ was truly the realization of the Jews' Messiah, and hence traces Christ's *royal descent* from Abraham as the progenitor of the Jewish race, down through the line of Davidic *kings*, and thereby proves that Jesus was the *true King of* "*the kingdom of heaven*," in distinction from an earthly monarchy of common expectation. The accentuation of the phrase is made obvious by the fact that the "kingdom of heaven" does not occur in any other evangelist, but occurs in the first gospel, no less than thirty-two times (Westcott). *Luke*, on the other hand, was a Greek, and wrote his gospel in the Greek language—the language of common intercourse among the nations—for the special advantage of all the Greek-speaking Gentiles. He therefore naturally neglects the proof of the Jewish Messiah as secondary in the interest of the Gentiles, and traces Christ's *natural descent* down from Adam, as the progenitor of the whole human race, acknowledging Jesus Christ as *the Redeemer*, not of the Jews only, but of universal mankind. *Mark's* surname being Roman, and he being Peter's interpreter in preaching to the Romans at Rome, at their urgency wrote his gospel in the interests of the Roman converts and people, concerning "*the kingdom of God*" which now had come to them. *John* wrote his gospel long after the other evangelists, with the purpose of

supplementing the first three gospels, writing for the special edification and evangelization of the Christian Churches. Thus the four gospels had each a specialty, but not an exclusive purpose in writing; for these specialties are but the variations of the one great Gospel adapted to all men, in the interests of every age, until the end of the world.

5. **Contents of the Gospels.** (1) **Titles.** These are prefixed to the several gospels, introducing them as "According to Matthew," "According to Mark," *etc.*, which do not appear on the earliest manuscripts which have come down to us. This, however, is not to be understood as saying that these indications of authorship are not entirely correct and authentic. For while it is not absolutely known, it is very highly probable that this formula was placed there by the direction of the Church first receiving them, with a view to properly designating them for permanent future use.

(2) **Contents.** Matthew and Luke *open* their gospels with the genealogies and birth of Jesus; Mark, with the baptismal ministrations of the Baptist; and John, with the mystery of the incarnation. Matthew *closes* his gospel with Christ's great commission to go "disciple all nations;" Mark, with the successes which should crown the ministry of the apostles; Luke, with the indescribable joy experienced by the disciples returning from Christ's ascension; and John, with the assurance that a world of books could not describe the words and deeds of Christ to men. As to those contents of the gospels which relate to our Lord's ministry, the characteristic differences may properly be remarked. Matthew gives special prominence to our Lord's *discourses* on the mountains, as related to the ancient prophecies (5-7); Mark gives in simplest but graphic narrative, a vivid picture of Christ's *miracles*, of which he records nearly as many as the other two evangelists (5-8); Luke gives prominence to the *parables* of Jesus elsewhere unrecorded (13-17); while the evangelist John discourses profoundly respecting the *preexistence* of Christ, and his *wonderful prayers* (chaps. 1, 10, 12:27-30; 17). "Matthew groups together doctrinal teachings in the form of great discourses; he is a *preacher*. Mark narrates events as they occur to his mind; he is a *chronicler*. Luke reproduces the external and internal development of events; he is a *historian*" (Godet). John declares the profound doctrine of the incarnation; he is a *theologian*.

Matthew's *narration* occupies about one-fourth of his gospel; Mark's about one-half, and Luke's about one-third" (Norton). "If the total contents of the gospels be represented by one hundred, there are seven peculiarities in Mark, forty-two in Matthew, fifty-nine in Luke, and ninety-two in John" (Westcott). "One half of Mark is found in Matthew, one fourth of Luke is found in Matthew, one third of Mark is found in Luke. . . . If the extent of all the coincidences be represented by one hundred, their proportion is: Matthew, Mark, and Luke have fifty-three coincidences; Matthew and Luke have twenty-one; Matthew and Mark have twenty; and Mark and Luke have six coincidences" (Schaff).

Matthew's gospel serves as the connecting link between the Old Testament and the New. His Sermons of Christ are larger in extent than all the others together. He makes constant reference to the civil law of Moses, correcting wrong impressions and tendencies of the Jewish people. His familiarity with the land of the Jews, its geography and topography, is indicated in his assumption of such knowledge on the part of the Jews. That the contents of Mark's gospel, as already indicated, was the substance of Peter's preaching which Mark reported, is accordant with the affirmations of Papias, Irenaeus, Clement of Alexandria, Tertullian, Origen, Eusebius, and Jerome. Tertullian (b. 150), referring to the second and third gospel, says: "That which Mark published may be affirmed to be Peter's, whose interpreter Mark was. For even Luke's form of the gospel men usually ascribe to Paul. And it may well seem that the works which the disciples publish belong to their masters" (Adv. Marcion, iv, c. 5).

In the incorporation and also in the omission of certain significant facts, Mark indicates that Peter's statements were the basis of his gospel, especially those related to the apostle. In his *opening chapter* the evangelist mentions that Peter's home was "the house of Simon and Andrew" (1:16, 29); and in the *closing* chapter he records the message of the angel of the resurrection: "Go your way, tell his disciples *and Peter* that he goeth before you into Galilee; there shall ye see him" (16:17). There is a parallel statement amounting almost to identity of words in one of the last sentences of Mark (16:19), and in Peter's First Epistle: "So the Lord Jesus . . . was received up into heaven, and sat down at the right hand of God," and "Jesus Christ, who is on the right hand of God, having gone into heaven" (I Pet. 3:22, Eng. R. V.; comp Acts 2:25, 33-36).

Among the contents of Mark's gospel are two miracles of unusual character to be noted; one wrought upon the deaf and dumb man in Decapolis, at which the people "were above measure astonished, saying he hath done all things well. He maketh even the deaf to hear, and the dumb to speak" (7:37). Another miracle was that wrought upon a blind man of Bethsaida, whose cure was not instantaneous, but gradual, in that at first he only "saw men, as trees, walking;" but who at Jesus's touch, "saw all things clearly" (8:22-26).

Mark's gospel is the least literary and least complete of the four. His style is crude, his vocabulary limited, his narrative abrupt and often broken off suddenly, suggestive of *the speaker* whom he is reporting, rather than the graceful writer. Despite all this, it is the peculiarity of the contents of his gospel that they are always interesting, because the thoughts are sharply presented in a series of pictures, rapid, vivid, and often dramatic. All this is the marked characteristic of all Peter's public addresses. Mark's remarkable impressibility and memory are distinctively illustrated herein. Sometimes the evangelist gives delicate touches of shade and coloring to persons and scenes which he describes. He notes particularly the manly emotions and passions of Jesus in the stir of events; such as his positions (1:12), his gestures (9:35; 10:23), his expression of countenance (8:12), his movements (3:34; 5:32; 9:35; 11:11), his repose (4:38), his wonder (6:6), his indignation (3:5), his tenderness (6:31; 6:34; 8:23; 10:21). The same particularity is observable in mentioning persons, parties, places, and in noting times: of persons (1:29, 36; 3:6; 11:11; 13:3; 15:21; 16:7); of places (2:1, 13; 3:7; 4:1; 5:20; 7:31); of times (1:35; 4:35; 6:2; 11:11; 14:68; 15:25).

Luke's gospel in contents is the most particular in details, the most historical in order, and the most complete in character of them all. His is preeminently the gospel of Christ's humanity; the gospel of "the Son of Man;" and the gospel of salvation for the universal human race. He alone narrates Christ's prayer on the cross for his enemies, and his promise of paradise to the penitent thief, closing with a brief description of our Saviour's benediction with uplifted hands upon the world which he had just redeemed, as he ascended into the heavens. His style indicates culture. He possessed a wealth of vocabulary. He is remarkable for his carefulness in historical details. He uses about one hundred and eighty terms in his gospel alone, not found elsewhere in the writings of the New Testament, many of which are rare and even technical. An illustration is furnished in his remarkable description of Paul's shipwreck in Acts, in which he gives no less than seventeen nautical terms with entire correctness. He notices with the observance of a trained physician the subjects of diseases, of sufferings, and the miracles of healing. He mentions Peter's mother-in-law, who was distressed with *a great fever*" (4:38); the *fever and dysentery* which had seized upon Publius of Melita (Acts 28:8), and Christ's deadly sufferings in the garden, so that "his sweat was as it were great drops of blood falling down to the ground" (Luke 22:44).

John, the loving disciple whom Jesus loved, survived all the other disciples, and unto him it was reserved to close the apostolic age. He was the preeminent personage whose part it was to close also the story of our Lord's life. "His gospel is the golden sunset of the age of inspiration" (Schaff). It was written at Ephesus, a city of prominence in "Asia," the name of the most western province of Asia Minor, long after the Jerusalem of John's early manhood was made a heap of ruins in A. D. 70. Writing at such a remote point both in distance and time, and especially under the circumstances which gave rise to his gospel, it would not be expected that he would need to parallel the lines and traverse the territory traced by the synoptists. Accordingly he neglects the genealogical ancestry of our Lord, the birth of the Baptist, the story of Christ's temptation, his baptism in the Jordan, his transfiguration, the choosing of the twelve disciples, and the account of the demons cast out. He records nothing of the Sermon on the Mount, the Lord's Prayer, the destruction of Jerusalem, or of the end of the world. On the other hand, John begins his gospel with "the beginning" of time, discourses of Christ's preexistent state, and identifies Jesus as the Word with the uncreated God by his incarnation.

The witness of the Baptist that Jesus was the Son of God, is incorporated in his writings. He thence passes into the spiritual birth of men, the bread and water of life, and enlarges upon the mission and comfort of the Holy Spirit. John includes the accounts of Nicodemus, the woman of Samaria, and six miracles not mentioned by the synoptists: the first, which occurred at the marriage of Cana of Galilee; and the last, the most wonderful of miracles, the raising of Lazarus from death to life. At the close he confesses that he omits "many other things" "which are not written in this book;" but then carefully states that "These things are written that ye might believe that Jesus is the Christ, the Son of God; and that believing, ye might have life through his name" (20:30, 31; 21:25).

It is evident that the writer of the fourth gospel is a Jew, and is familiar with Jewish facts, personages, and places in history. A delegation of Jewish "priests and Levites from Jerusalem" asked the Baptist, "Who art thou?" (1:19); Philip saith, "We have found him of whom Moses in the law and the prophets did write, Jesus of Nazareth" (1:45). "How is it that thou, being a Jew, askest drink of me, which am a woman of Samaria?" (4:9, 10). "Salvation is of the Jews" (4:22). "Now Jacob's well was there" (4:6). "This is that prophet which should come into the world" (6:14). There is also evident a familiarity with the geography: "These things were done in Bethabara, beyond Jordan, where John was baptizing" (1:28); "Go wash in the pool of Siloam" [at Jerusalem] (9:7). "Philip was from Bethsaida, the city of Andrew and Peter" (1:44); "There was a marriage in Cana of Galilee" (2:1); "John also was baptizing in Aenon near Salim" (3:23). "Then cometh he to a city of Samaria, which is called Sychar, near a parcel of ground that Jacob gave to his son Joseph" (4:5). So also of the topography about the Holy City: "Now there is at Jerusalem by the sheep-market a pool which is called in the Hebrew tongue Bethesda, having five porches" (5:2); and we read of "in the temple in Solomon's porch" (10:23); "over the brook Kedron where was a garden" (18:1), "the judgment-seat in a place called The Pavement, but in the Hebrew Gabbatha" (19:13), and "the place called the place of the skull, which is called in the Hebrew, Golgotha" (19:17).

6. Characteristics of the Gospels. If Matthew's gospel is the most majestic and powerful in citations from the Old Testament, Mark's is clearly the briefest and most incomplete in the historical sense, while Luke's is the most composite with reference to his various sources, and John the most profound and impressive for its advance doctrine. Matthew conducts the essential Jewish argument in the Jewish tongue, for the Jewish people. He traces Christ's ancestral kings, he records the Sermon on the Mount; he disregards the chronological order of events, following similarity of matter, looking constantly to spiritual sequence.

Lange remarks of Mark's gospel, as a prominent characteristic, the alternation of *rest and labor constantly noted* by that evangelist in

Christ's public life. After his baptism, Jesus retired to the wilderness of Judea, before engaging in preaching in Galilee (1:12). He withdrew himself with his disciples to the sea, and to "a small ship," before he began the work of miracles upon "plagues" and the casting out "unclean spirits" who cried out, "Thou art the Son of God" (3:7-12).

Luke's characteristic is his completeness and his exactness in all matters of detail. It has been called the gospel of womanhood. Throughout from the very first chapter to the last, the noble and womanly deeds of devoted women are remarked. Elizabeth the wife of the saintly priest, and mother of the Baptist; Mary "the wedded Maid and Virgin Mother;" "Anna a prophetess, the daughter of Phanuel, of the tribe of Aser;" the sorrowing but gladdened widow of Nain, whose dead son was lifted into life; the woman with the issue of twelve years' standing; the nameless woman who anointed Christ's feet in the house of Simon the Pharisee; the guiltless, but much abused Mary Magdalene, who was the first to visit the sepulcher; the Mary and Martha who with Lazarus composed the first Christian family at Bethany; the poor widow who cast into the treasury her two mites, which was all the living she had; the weeping "daughters of Jerusalem" whom Jesus addressed so thoughtfully from the cross; the women of Galilee who brought with them spices to the sepulcher of our Lord; the woman in the beautiful parable of the lost piece of silver—these all attest what prominence Luke "the beloved physician" gave to womanhood in his gospel.

Another characteristic of Luke's authorship is that he brings so much sunshine and cheer in his gospel. From the first to last there are "words of joy and gladness." To Zacharias it was said, "Thou shalt have joy and gladness" (1:14). To the shepherds with their flocks on the hills of Bethlehem, it was said, "Behold I bring you good tidings of great joy which shall be to all people" (2:10). The seventy disciples return with joy, because even demons are subject to them through Christ's name (10:17). So the shepherd recovers his sheep and returns with joy; the lost piece of silver is found and neighbors and friends are asked to join in the joy and cheer it brought to them all; the angels in heaven rejoice over one sinner that repenteth (ch. 15). In that surprise in the presence of the risen Lord, the disciples "believed not for joy" and wonder (24:4); and at last, when Jesus "was parted from" his disciples, and was taken up into heaven, the apostles worshiped him, and returned to Jerusalem with great joy (24:51, 52). Is it any wonder that the skeptical Renan should declare that the third gospel is the most beautiful book ever written, when viewed from a purely literary and humanitarian standpoint?

Four characteristics mark the gospel of John. These are (1) the inimitable simplicity of its style, which engages the thoughtful interest of the child quite as much as that of the man; (2) the profound doctrine of the incarnation of Jesus Christ, which of course transcends human understanding, but so is one's own life incomprehensible; (3) the preeminent spirituality of its character, and this is attributable to the devout personality of its author; and (4) finally, John's gospel is to be recognized in a supreme sense as the gospel of love. His sentences are brief and sententious; sometimes antithetical, but oftener running in parallelisms after the style of Hebrew poetry. His vocabulary is not large, but is sufficient. "The light shineth in darkness, and the darkness comprehendeth it not." "A servant is not greater than his lord; neither one that is sent greater than he that sent him." The author of the fourth gospel and the three synoptists traverse the territory of our Lord's life from opposite starting points. That is, the synoptists begin with our Saviour's *manhood*, and develop progressively along the lines of his Messiahship and miracles until the doctrine of his deity is to be clearly apprehended. On the contrary, John begins with his preexistence and Godhead and descends gradually through his Messiahship to the plane of his manhood among men. The synoptists trace his claims as the God-Man through his external history; but John lays claim at once to Christ's dignity by opening up to our apprehension his internal nature as the Son of God through the incarnation. Hence the author of the fourth gospel supplements but does not repeat the thrice-told story of the first three evangelists, filling their omissions with most interesting matter, seldom overlapping their narratives, and then only to give added details, and so supplement the whole. Added years, and matured experience, and deep reflections with increased spirituality, and a constant faith and abounding love, gave to this apostle the highest qualifications for the production of his gospel. He uses the verb *to believe* (*pisteuein*) about two hundred times; twice as often as the synoptists. This writer especially speaks as an eyewitness: "We beheld his glory; glory of the only begotten of the Father, full of grace and truth" (1:14), and near the close of the gospel, he records his affirmation that there were "many other signs which Jesus did *in the presence of his disciples* which are not written in this book; but these are written that ye might believe that Jesus Christ is the Son of God, and that believing ye might have life through his name" (20:30, 31).

7. **Credibility of the Gospels.** It seems strange that this point should be discussed in view of such documents. "The credibility of the gospels would never have been denied if it were not for the philosophical and dogmatic skepticism which desires to get rid of the supernatural and miraculous at any price" (Schaff).

(1) **Signatures.** An objection to the credibility of the gospels is based upon the fact that they bear no signatures to authenticate sacred authorship. The case is different with the epistles of the New Testament. Paul's thirteen epistles *invariably* open with a declaration of his authorship as an apostle of Jesus Christ (see Rom. 1:1); and sometimes it appears again embodied in the text near the close of the epistle (I Cor. 16:21; Col. 4:18; II Thess. 3:17, comp. Phil. 5:9). For this marked difference in documents of equal antiquity, there is

required a justifying explanation. Fortunately we have not far to go for the sufficient reason. Chrysostom (b. 347) states the case fully thus: "Moses did not put his name to the first five books [of the Bible], nor did the historian who wrote after him . . . nor did Matthew, or Mark, or Luke, or John, put their names to their writings. . . . What is the reason for this? [Because] they delivered their writings [directly] *to those who were present*, when it was needless to put their name down; [but the apostle Paul] sent his writings *to those who were at a distance*, in the form of an epistle, where the addition of the name is necessary" (Homily 4, on Matt.). There was besides great critical care exercised by Paul in this regard in order to prevent imposture, especially as he employed amanuenses in writing, but left his autograph deposited with the several churches addressed, accompanied with certain marks or signs which should indicate by comparison the real authentication of any given document purporting to be apostolical. This special precaution against fiction and forgery is clearly set forth in II Thess. 3:17: "*The salutation of Paul in mine own hand, which is the token in every epistle; so I write.*" No other writings of equal antiquity can furnish such evidence of their authenticity as these sacred writings.

(2) **Simplicity.** Another evidence of credibility is *internal*, manifested in the absolute simplicity and sincerity of purpose on the part of the evangelists. These apostolic men unhesitatingly record their own ignorance and stupidity which had subjected them to repeated reproof from Christ; their carnal ambitions for place and power; their utter failure to work a miracle after they had been duly authorized by the Master (Matt. 17:14-21; Mark 9:14-29); how they forbade another to work miracles because he did not follow the disciples (Luke 9:38, 39). Further, they make it a matter of circumstantial record against themselves that Peter openly denied his Master; that Judas was guilty of treachery and was bribed by a small price; that out of sheer fear, all the disciples forsook Jesus when he was arrested in the garden. After the crucifixion they confess the deep despondency and despair of all the apostles; their absolute disbelief in the fact of Christ's resurrection; their consequent return to former secular pursuit at the sea of Galilee. Without strictures on the horrid cruelties of the crucifixion, without concealments or exaggeration, without explanation or extenuation, they confess their own faults and foibles. Facts just as they occurred, have to speak for themselves, and the record unexplained and unjustified, goes down to all future generations, to be read and known of all men. In their profound sincerity they evidence no reservations, and no concern respecting their own, or each others' fame; they do not even seem to inquire what will be the effect of all this touching the Christian cause thereafter. Their whole trend is to tell the story of Jesus which had taken full possession of their souls; and the account receives an added charm from the very simplicity and sincerity for the absolute truth of the narrative.

(3) **Confirmation.** The credibility as well as the authenticity of the gospels is confirmed by an ancient disbeliever, Celsus (b. about 135-140) who was an eclectic philosopher who championed the literary assault upon Christianity and the Christians, in a work entitled *A True Word* (*Logos Alēthēs*). It was published about a century after the gospels. Having evidently a copy of these Scriptures in his possession, he makes adverse criticisms upon about one hundred and twenty facts which are mentioned in their contents. Among these particulars he refers to Jesus as having descended from the Jewish kings, that at first Joseph was suspicious of Mary's chastity, that Jesus was born in a small village in Judea, that Mary was married to an unnamed carpenter, that a strange star appeared at Christ's birth, that Herod slew the children of Bethlehem, that an angel directed Joseph and family to flee into Egypt, that they were recalled to their home in Nazareth, and that Jesus was called a Nazarene. Then to clinch his charges he emphasizes the fact that these gospels were written by Christ's disciples. His words are: "The disciples of Christ wrote such statements regarding him" (Origen, *Contra Celsum*, B. ii, ch. 16). "As you yourselves have recorded" (Ib. ii, 49; 53). "*All these statements are taken from your own books*," in addition to which we need no other witness; for you fall by your own swords" (Ib. ii, 74). Celsus never cites an apocryphal gospel as authority, for he knew that only these four had ever been acknowledged as genuine by the Christian world, upon which they relied with an implicit and absolute faith. At this early date this enemy of Christianity corroborated and authenticated the authenticity and historicity of the four gospels.

8. **Canonicity of the Gospels.** The canon of the New Testament was formed and established directly between the apostolic writers and the several churches addressed. No council whatever of the church had any part in its formation. About the middle of the 2d century certain false writings known as *Apocryphal Gospels* first appeared, purporting to give a sketch of the childhood and early life of Jesus. They were mere romances, strangely puerile writings, unhistorical in character as a whole, yet with shreds of truth borrowed from the genuine history. These apocryphal books were put in circulation about a century after the genuine gospels had been published. About A. D. 363 the small Council of Laodicaea, as the first instance of the kind, took formal action in recording a list of the genuine books of the New Testament, to preserve the just distinction between those which had always been accepted and those which were known to be apocryphal. To prevent imposition, expecially in remoter churches, this council made a public declaration of the Canon just as it had been maintained and known to be, from the time of the apostles themselves. Now obviously this action was not *original*, but simply *confirmatory of that which the church had held from the beginning as settled* respecting canonical books. It was, in intention and in fact, a standing *protest against* those other books which were known as *spurious*. Having done this *as a public, and formal declaration and confirmation of the faith of*

the church respecting the sacred books, its work was done. The council originated nothing, inaugurated nothing, and except in the *ratifying sense*, "settled" nothing.

The epistles being sent to distant churches were always received with critical caution and care. To find acceptance at all, they had to come under due apostolic sanctions and bear significant *tokens* from the writers thereof that they were genuine, and not spurious (II Thess. 3:17).

Literature—Eusebius, *Ecclesiastical History*, Cruse's translation, London; Schaff, *History of the Christian Church*, vol. i; Harman, *Introduction to the Study of the Scriptures*; Westcott, *Introduction to the Study of the New Testament*; Westcott, *Canon of the New Testament*, 1881; Van Oosterzee, *Person of Christ*, 1876; Schaff, *Person of Christ*, N. Y.; Gladstone, *Impregnable Rock of Holy Scripture*; Prof. Given, *Truth of Scripture Revelation*, etc.; Sayce, *Higher Criticism and the Verdict of the Monuments*, 1894; Rawlinson, *Historical Evidences of the Truth of the Scripture Records*, N. Y.; Faussett, *Summary of Gospel Incidents*, etc.; Renan, *Life of Jesus*; Chrysostom, *Homilies on the New Testament*; Ante-Nicene Fathers (in English); Conybeare, *Monuments of Early Christianity*; Chadwick, *Christ Bearing Witness to Himself*, N. Y.; Lardner's Works, 10 vols.; Bowman, *Historical Evidences of the New Testament. S. L. B.*

Gourd. *See* Vegetable Kingdom.

Government of God. *See* Theocracy, Israel.

Government of Israel. *See* Israel.

Governor, one who rules by authority delegated from a supreme ruler to whom he is responsible. In such a role, Joseph as Prime Minister of Egypt was called its governor (Gen. 42:6; 45:26). Gedaliah was governor for Nebuchadnezzar II in Palestine after the Fall of Jerusalem (587 B. C.; Jer. 40:5; 41:2). Persian governors had administration over the Jews after the captivity. Zerubbabel and Nehemiah, though Jews by birth, were Persian administrators (Neh. 5:14, 18; Hag. 1:14). At the time of our Lord, although Pontius Pilate's actual Roman title was procurator, he was actually the governor of Judea at the time of the crucifixion, and is so named (Matt. 28:14). *M. F. U.*

Go'zan (gō'zăn), a northeastern Mesopotamian city located on the Habor River, a tributary of the Euphrates. It lay east of the important patriarchal city of Haran and N. W. of the great Assyrian metropolis of Nineveh. The Assyrians deported the Israelites to Gozan after the capture of the capital of Samaria (II Kings 17:6; 18:11; 19:12; I Chron. 5:26). The Assyrians called Gozan, *Guzanu*. It is the Gauzanitis of Ptolomey. Baron von Oppenheim discovered a new culture at Tell Halaf, ancient Gozan, in 1911 and 1913. Halafian pottery, now proverbial for its beauty, dates from c. 4000 B. C. *M. F. U.*

Grace. "Grace is what God may be free to do, and indeed what he does, accordingly, for the lost after Christ has died on behalf of them." (Lewis Sperry Chafer, *Systematic Theology* VII, p. 178). It is thus apparent that God's grace is to be distinguished from his mercy and love (Eph. 2:4, 5) "But God Who is rich in mercy for His great love wherewith He loved us, even when we were dead in sins, hath quickened us together with Christ, by grace ye are saved." Mercy is therefore the compassion of God which moved him to provide a Saviour for the unsaved. Had God been able to save even one soul on the ground of His sovereign mercy alone, He could have saved every person on that basis, as Lewis Sperry Chafer points out, and the death of Christ would not have been a necessity. Divine love on the other hand is the motivating plan behind all that God does in saving a soul. But since God is holy and righteous and sin is a complete offense unto Him, His love or His mercy cannot operate in grace until there was provided a sufficient satisfaction for sin. This satisfaction makes possible the exercise of God's grace. Grace thus rules out all human merit. It requires only faith in the Saviour. Any intermixture of human merit violates grace. God's grace thus provides not only salvation but safety and preservation for the saved one, despite his imperfections. Grace perfects forever the saved one in the sight of God because of the saved one's position "in Christ." Grace bestows Christ's merit and Christ's standing forever (Rom. 5:1; Rom. 8:1; Col. 2:9, 10) "For in Him dwelleth all the fullness of the Godhead bodily and *ye are complete in Him* . . . " Grace thus obviates any obligation to gain merit, and the law system as a merit-system is no longer applicable to a believer, since he is no longer "under the law" but "under grace" (Rom. 6:14). The problem of a holy life is met in the gospel of grace by the fact that the saved one has entirely a new position "in grace" instead of "in Adam" (Rom. 5:12-20). And being baptized "into Christ" (Rom. 6:1-10) he is "dead indeed unto sin and alive unto God." Knowledge of and faith in this glorious "in-Christ" position (Rom. 6:11) is the key that makes it actual in the believer's everyday experience. Rewards for faithfulness and practical holiness of life are to be dispensed, but this is a truth not to be confused with an unforfeitable and unmerited salvation. *M. F. U.*

Grace at Meals, a short prayer at table, returning thanks to God for food provided and asking the divine blessing thereon. The propriety of such an act is evident from the injunction (Rom. 14:6; I Cor. 10:31; I Tim. 4:4), and from the example of our Lord (Mark 8:6, 7; Luke 24:30). Among the Jews "grace" was said both before and after meals, and also by women, slaves, and children. Regulations were made down to the pettiest detail, viz.: what form was to be used for the fruits of the trees; what for wine; what for the fruits of the ground; for bread; for vegetables; for vinegar; for unripe fallen fruit; for locusts, milk, cheese, eggs; and scholars contended as to when this and that form was suitable. . . . When such restriction was laid upon prayer by the legal formula, it could not but be chilled into an external performance (Schürer, *Jewish People*, Div. ii, vol. ii, 117 sq.).

Graft, Graff (Gr. *egkentrizō*, to *prick in*). Grafting is the process in horticulture by which a portion of a plant is made to unite with another plant, whether of the same kind or of another variety or species. The plant upon which the operation is performed is called the stock; the portion inserted or joined with it, the scion or graft. The usual process was to take shoots or buds from approved trees, and to insert them on others, where, with proper care, they continued to grow. Thus fruit was kept from degenerating, for the grafts received nourishment from the stocks, but always produced fruit of the same sort as the tree from which they were taken.

The apostle Paul makes use (Rom. 11:17-24) of a figure which has something striking. He compares the Jewish theocracy to a good olive tree, the Gentiles to a wild one, of which a branch is engrafted upon the former, and which by that means acquires fruitfulness.

Grain (Heb. *ṣᵉrōr, packed,* i. e., *kernel;* Gr. *kokkos, kernel*), used (Amos 9:9; Matt. 13:31, etc.) in the singular and not as we do in a collective sense. *See* also Corn in Vegetable Kingdom.

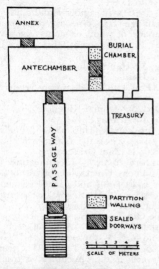

185. Plan of King Tutankhamun's Tomb

Granary. *See* Storehouse.
Grape. *See* Vegetable Kingdom.
Grass. *See* Vegetable Kingdom.
Grasshopper. *See* Animal Kingdom.
Grate, a copper network, movable by a copper ring at each corner, and placed below the top of the great altar (Exod. 27:4; 35:16; 38:4, 5, 30; 39:39). *See* Altar.
Grave.
1. **Egyptian.** The Egyptians were distinguished above other peoples of the ancient Biblical world for their attention to burial and the after-life. Believing in a future existence that was a higher form of their earthly life, all sorts of physical comforts were interred with the deceased. Besides food and drink, household pets were embalmed and placed in the tomb and often happy scenes from the earth-life of the deceased were painted on the sarcophagi or on the tomb walls. (See John Garstang, *Burial Customs of Ancient Egypt* and Steindorff and Seele, *When Egypt Ruled the East*). The very poor, it is true, were simply interred clotheless and uncoffined beneath the

sand, but even in this extremity food and water were placed alongside the deceased. People of wealth were buried in a mastaba during the early dynasties. This was a development from the simple trench into which the body had been lowered and a pile of dirt heaped upon it. The mastaba consisted of a rectangular structure of brick or stone placed over the grave. In the vicinity of the great pyramids at Gizeh and at Saqqarah numberless mastabas of the nobility have been uncovered. In the case of royalty the pyramid was used, as the Great Step Pyramid at Saqqarah, belonging to the Third Dynasty. This and other pyramids developed from the mastaba when several of these structures were placed one on top of another. Still further developments were the colossal pyramids at Gizeh. King Zoser of the Third Dynasty was interred in the step pyramid at Saqqarah. Khufu, Khafre and Menkaure were honored by the great Gizeh pyramids. The Fifth Dynasty pyramids at Abusir, south of Gizeh, were much smaller. In the splendid New Kingdom, when Egypt ruled the East, the mastaba and pyramid had become outmoded. The style for rock-cut tombs was in vogue. Examples of these are the tombs of Thutmose III at Thebes and Queen Hatshepsut's exquisite mortuary temple. The story of the sumptuous tomb of Tutankhamun reads like a fairy tale. Akhnaton's tomb consisted of a passage cut into the rocky hill leading to a column-supported hall where the sarcophagus of the pharoah lay. Whether temples or rock-cut sepulchres, reliefs were carved on the walls; and paintings made in bright colors depicted happy scenes from the earthly life of the deceased.

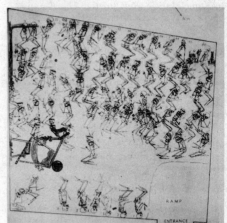

186. Sumerian Royal Death Pit

2. **Mesopotamian and Persian.** Much is now known of graves from the Royal Tombs at Ur. Sumerian royalty, like the Egyptians, desired creature comforts to follow them in death. So courtiers and horses and servants were buried alive. This is indicated by the tomb of Queen Shub-ad and her husband at Ur. She was buried in great splendor. Babylonians at a considerably later date practiced cremation like the Romans, placing the

ashes of the deceased in artistic glazed crematory urns. The great kings of Persia—Darius, Xerxes, and Artaxerxes—cut their tombs out of solid rock near Persepolis. Those of Darius I and Artaxerxes I have a column-adorned facade. Darius is pictured worshipping Ahura Mazda in front of a fire altar. The tomb of Cyrus the Great was built near Parsargadae, N. E. of Persepolis. Alexander the Great, two centuries later, found Cyrus' tomb looted, with the remains of the founder of the Persian Empire lying upon the floor.

3. **Greek.** Early pre-Hellenic Greek tombs were shaped like bee-hives. Later, lavish tombs such as King Mausolus' of Caria (c. 350 B. C.) became the prototype of succeeding mausoleums. Greek sarcophagi were also very handsomely executed. Tomb reliefs are in the highest tradition of Hellenic art. At Marathon, the so-called Soros is an artificial mound thrown up little by little to mark the spot where almost 200 Athenians fell in 490 B. C., heroically defending their democratic land against the invasion of Persia. This constitutes the unique "community tomb."

4. **Roman.** Early Romans practiced cremation, placing the ashes of the deceased in columbaria ("pigeon lodgings"). Such columbaria were found near Virgil's tomb at Naples, at Rome's seaport of Ostia, at Pompeii and in many Roman cities of the Middle East. Many of these were artistically carved. Well-known cities of first century Rome had a "Street of the Sepulchres." When Paul came into Rome over the Appian Way, he passed hundreds of tombs of wealthy Romans of the Imperial Period, some consisting of flat slabs, others standing pillars, mausoleums and some towers. Burial in the catacombs was common in Rome of the early Christian era. Compartments in the rock received the bodies and were shut with panels inscribed with the name of the deceased along with an emblem of the sacred monogram, the fish, the shepherd or a praying man (orans).

5. **Hebrew.** Among the Jews graves were sometimes mere cavities, dug out of the earth (Gen. 35:8; I Sam. 31:13); natural caves or grottoes (Gen. 23:17); artificial tombs hewn out in the rock, provided with galleries and chambers, preference being given to places outside cities (Luke 7:12; John 11:30). Only kings and prophets (I Kings 2:10; 16:6; I Sam. 25:1; 28:) were buried in cities. The rich had, no doubt, family burying places (Gen. 23:20; Judg. 8:32; II Sam. 2:32; I Kings 13:22), while the poorer classes would doubtless have their public ones (Jer. 26:23; II Kings 23:6; comp. Matt. 27:7). Graves hewn in the rock, or laid out in natural caves, were closed with large flat stones (Matt. 27:60; 28:2; John 11:38). Monuments were set up in the very early times on or over graves (Gen. 35:20; comp. Job 21:32; II Sam. 18:18), which afterward took the form of magnificent mausoleums with pyramids and many kinds of emblems (I Macc. 13:27, sq.).

Probably there were burying places attached to each village in ancient times, as we find in the case of Nain, where the graveyard remains to this day.

In post-exilic times it was sought to restore and adorn the graves of the prophets and other holy persons, and this was particularly affected by the Pharisees, to testify their reverence for the prophets (comp. Matt. 23:30, sq.).

Flat stones laid upon graves had upon them a marking to warn passers-by lest they should contract uncleanliness by touching the grave. For this end also the tombs were whitewashed every year on the 15th of Adar.

There are scriptural traces of the popular idea that graves were the residence of demons (comp. Matt. 8:28), who were, perhaps, connected with soothsaying (Acts 16:16); while others refer such allusions to the supernatural notions respecting offering to the manes of the departed. *M. F. U.* See Tomb.

Grave Clothes (Gr. *keiria, winding sheet*). From early times the body was washed (Acts 9:37), then wrapped in a linen cloth (Matt. 27:59), or the limbs separately wound with strips of linen (John 11:44).

Graved. See Graving under Handicrafts.

Graven Image (Heb. *pěsěl,* or *pᵉsîl, a carving*), a figure made of wood or stone (Exod. 20:4; Deut. 27:15), to represent Jehovah. See Image Worship.

Graving. See Handicrafts.

Gray. See Hair.

Grease (Psa. 119:70), elsewhere rendered fat (*q. v.*).

Great Owl. See Animal Kingdom.

Greaves. See Armor, 2, (4).

Gre′cia (grē′shĭ-à), (Heb. *yāwän,* usually rendered *Javan* (*q. v.*), the Latin form (Dan. 8:21; 10:20; 11:2) of Greece (*q. v.*).

Grecians (grē′shĭ-àns).—**Identification.** In the Old Testament, Greeks, inhabitants of Greece and the coast lands and islands belonging to the Greek race; in the New Testament, Hellenists, or Greek-speaking Jews.

In the Old Testament Javan (Heb. *yāwän*), is translated "Greece" (A. V. of Zech. 9:13, R. V. and R. S. V. throughout) and "Grecia" (A. V. of Dan. 8:21; 10:20; 11:2); in Joel 3:6, *yᵉwänîm,* q. d., "Javanites" is translated "Grecians." In the New Testament the versions distinguish between *Hellēnes,* "Greeks" by birth, as opposed to *Ioudaioi,* "Jews," whence *Hellēnes* is sometimes applied to Gentiles in general; and *Hellēnistai,* "Grecians," i, e., Greek-speaking Jews, as opposed to *Hebraioi,* home Jews dwelling in Palestine. The difference between the two versions in Acts 11:20 and 18:17 results from a difference between the Greek texts which they followed.

In the New Testament, then, Grecians or Hellenists were foreign Jews who spoke Greek, which the conquests of Alexander had made the language of the educated throughout the civilized world, and "also the language of the masses in the great centers of commerce." Some would also include under the name "Hellenists" proselytes of Greek birth.

There are legends of early Jewish settlements in Arabia, Ethiopia, and Abyssinia. Indeed, the natural overflow of a vigorous people inheriting the business energy of their father Jacob would have united with the varying fortunes of war to carry numbers of Jews far beyond the limits of Palestine at a remote period. Of the influence of the Jews who were scattered abroad in these early ages it is impossible to form an estimate. Theirs was not professedly a missionary religion; but wherever the faithful Jew went he carried the knowledge of the true God, as did Naomi (Ruth 1: 15, 16; 2:12), or, indirectly, Naaman's maid (II Kings 5:3, 11); and, as far as his influence extended, he carried that combination of religion and lawful commerce which the great missionary explorer, Livingstone, thought so desirable.

But the Dispersion, as a distinct element influencing the entire character of the Jews, dates from the Babylonian exile. Its limits had been extended by the Greek conquests in Asia, by the colonizing policy of some of the successors of Alexander the Great, and by the persecutions of Antiochus, so that at the beginning of the Christian era the Dispersion was divided into three great sections—the Babylonian, the Syrian, the Egyptian.

From Babylon the Jews spread throughout Persia, Media, and Parthia; but the settlements in China belong to a modern date. Nisibis, in northeast Mesopotamia, became a colonizing center. In Armenia the Jews arrived at the greatest dignities.

We find them throughout Asia Minor even to its western coast. They were numerous in Cyprus, and were important enough in Delos and in Cos to receive religious recognition from the Romans. The Jews of the Syrian provinces gradually formed a closer connection with their new homes, and together with the Greek language adopted in many respects Greek ideas. Hence arose Hellenism.

This Hellenizing tendency, however, found its most free development at Alexandria. The Jewish settlements established there by Alexander and Ptolemy I became the source of the African dispersion, which spread over the north coast of Africa, and perhaps inland to Abyssinia. At Cyrene and Berenice (Tripoli) they formed a considerable portion of the population. It was Jason of Cyrene who wrote " 'in five books' a history of the Jewish war of liberation, which supplied the chief materials for the second book of the Maccabees."

The Jewish settlements in Rome either resulted from "the occupation of Jerusalem by Pompey, B. C. 63, or were largely increased by that event. Under the favor of the early emperors they increased, till in the time of Claudius they had become formidable on account of their numbers and dissensions, and were banished from the city" (Acts 18:2; comp. Suet., *Claud.*, 25, "*Judoeos impulsore Chresto assidue tumultuantes Roma expulit*"). But they soon flowed back and were quite numerous (Acts 28:17, ff.) and conspicuous (Mart., *Ep.*, xi, 94; Juv., *Sat.*, iii, 14).

Thus at the day of Pentecost there were at Jerusalem devout Jews out of every nation under heaven (Acts 2:5). For, though scattered through so many remote lands, the Dispersion was still bound together in itself and to its mother country by religious ties. The temple was the acknowledged center of Judaism, and the faithful Jew everywhere contributed the half shekel toward its maintenance. But, while the fires of patriotism burned

unquenched and unquenchable throughout the Jewish world, it was impossible to maintain pharisaic strictness and rigor in these remote lands. Egypt, for example, was beyond the reach of the beacon fires which signaled the time of appearance of the new moon, and beyond the Sabbath reading of the Hebrew Scriptures. The influence of the Dispersion on the rapid promulgation of Christianity can scarcely be overrated. The course of the apostolic teaching followed in a regular progress the line of Jewish settlements. This we can see by following the travels of St. Paul in the Acts. Throughout the apostolic journeys the Jews were the class to whom "it was necessary that the word of God should be first spoken" (Acts 13:46); and they in turn were united with the mass of the population by the intermediate body of "the devout," which had recognized in various degrees the faith of the God of Israel.

The Hellenistic system was so widely diffused as to form an excellent preparation for a world religion. It was strong enough to give the new faith a good start, yet too weak to restrain its growth or to smother its free spirit in a mass of Judaic details and reduce it to the position of an advanced Judaism. The steadfast adhesion of the Hellenistic system to the historic faith, with its comparative freedom from Pharisaic narrowness, well qualified it to be the nurse of a new religion which was to be an expanded but not enfeebled development of the old. The purely outward elements of the national life were laid aside with a facility of which history offers few examples, while the inner character of the people remained unchanged.

The Septuagint version of the Old Testament had given the Hellenists a Bible in the universal language of the New Testament world. In the fullness of time, when the great message came, a language was prepared to receive it; and thus the very dialect of the New Testament forms a great lesson in the true philosophy of history, and becomes in itself a monument of the providential government of mankind. W. H.

Greece was properly that country in Europe inhabited by the Greeks (I Macc. 1:1), but in Acts 20:2, apparently designating only that part of it included in the Roman province of Macedonia (*q. v.*). Greece is sometimes described as a country containing the four provinces of Macedonia, Epirus, Achaia (or Hellas), and Peloponnesus, but more commonly only the two latter are to be understood as comprised in it. There seems to have been little intercourse between Greece and the Hebrews, until the Macedonian conquest of the East; hence the few references in the Old Testament. Greece is mentioned in Gen. 10:2, 4, under the name Javan (*q. v.*); the Jews and Greeks are said to have met in the slave market (Joel 3:6); and Greece is spoken of as "the rough goat," by Daniel (8:21).

At the beginning of the Christian era those territories which now form the kingdom of Greece formed the Roman province of Achaia, with the proconsul residing at Corinth. As a place of learning, however, Athens held the first rank, and study there was held indispens-

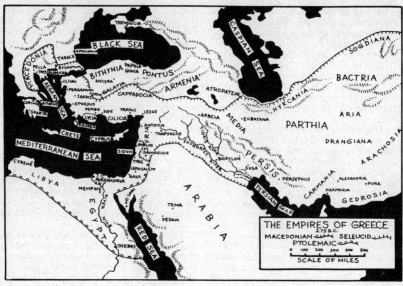

THE EMPIRES OF GREECE
275 B.C.
MACEDONIAN ∿∿∿∿ SELEUCID ⊔⊔⊔⊔
PTOLEMAIC ∿∿∿∿
0   100   200   300   400   500
SCALE OF MILES

187

able to a Roman youth wishing to distinguish himself. Her schools of grammar, rhetoric, dialectics, and philosophy, were crowded.

Christianity was first planted in Greece by Paul, who visited Philippi (Acts 16:12), then Thessalonica, Berea, Athens, and Corinth (chaps. 17, 18). Dionysius the Areopagite, who was converted through the apostle's address on Mar's Hill, is said to have become the Bishop of Athens. *See* Grecians, Paul.

Greek, an inhabitant of Greece.

Green. *See* Color.

Greeting. *See* Salutations.

Greyhound. *See* Animal Kingdom.

Grind. *See* Mill.

Figurative. To oppress the poor by exaction (Isa. 3:15, "to grind the faces of the poor").

The expression, "Let my wife grind unto another" (Job 31:10) means, let her become another's menial (comp. Exod. 11:5; Isa. 47: 2).

Grisled, or Grizzled (Heb. *bārōd*, *spotted*), partly colored or variegated, as goats (Gen. 31:10, 12), or horses (Zech. 6:3, 6).

Grove, the rendering of two Hebrew words.

1. *Asherah*, (Heb. *'ăshērāh*, *fortunate*). It is generally admitted that this word cannot mean either a green tree or a *grove*, for the simple reason that the words *to make* (I Kings 14:15; 16:33; II Kings 17:16, etc.), *to set up* (II Kings 17:10), *to stand up* (II Chron. 33:19), and *to build* (I Kings 14:23), used to denote the erection of an Asherah, are not one of them suitable to a tree or grove. On the other hand the Asherah is spoken of as being set up under, or by the side of, the green tree. Asherah (*q. v.* under Gods, False) was a Canaanite goddess, now well-known from the Ugaritic Literature, and the idol (or wooden column) of her was generally set up beside the altars of Baal.

2. **Grove** (Heb. *'ēshĕl*, Gen. 21:33), really means the *tamarisk* tree, which with its long life, hard wood, and evergreen leaves, is a type of the ever-enduring grace of the faithful covenant-keeping God. In the religions of the ancient heathen world groves play a prominent part. In the old times altars only were erected to the gods. It was thought wrong to shut up the gods within walls, and hence, as Pliny expressly tells us, trees were the first temples; and from the earliest times groves are mentioned in connection with religious worship (Gen. 12:6, 7; 13:18; Deut. 11:30; A. V. "plain"). The groves were generally found connected with temples, and often had the right of affording an asylum. Some have supposed that even the Jewish Temple had an inclosure planted with palm and cedar (Ps. 92:12, 13) and olive (Ps. 52:8), as the mosque which stands on its site now has. This is more than doubtful; but we know that a celebrated oak stood by the sanctuary at Shechem (Josh. 24:26; Judg. 9:6).

Guard.

1. Hebrew word for a "cook" (*ṭabbāh*), as butchering fell to the lot of the cook in Eastern countries it gained the secondary sense of "executioner," and is applied to the bodyguard of the kings of Egypt (Gen. 37:36) and Babylon (II Kings 25:8; Jer. 39:9; 41:10; Dan. 2:14).

2. Hebrew word for a "runner" (*rāṣ*), the ordinary term employed for the attendants of the Jewish kings, whose office it was to run before the chariot (II Sam. 15:1; I Kings 1: 5), and to form a military guard (I Sam. 22: 17; II Kings 10:25; 11:6; II Chron. 12:10).

3. The Hebrew words for "watch" (*mĭsh-mĕrĭth*, *mĭshmăr*), express properly the *act of watching*, but are occasionally transferred to the persons who kept watch (Neh. 4:9, 22; 7:3; 12:9; Job 7:12).

Guardian Angels. *See* Angels.

Gudgo′dah (gŭd-gō′dà), *cutting*, *cleft*), the fortieth station of the Israelites, between Mt. Hor and Jotbath (Deut. 10:7). The name appears to be preserved in the present wady *Ghudhagidh*. Same as Horhaggidgad (Num. 33:32).

434

Guest. *See* Hospitality.

Guest Chamber (Gr. *kataluma*, to *break up*, i. e., a *journey*), any room for the entertainment of guests (Mark 14:14; Luke 22:11); rendered *Inn* in Luke 2:7. *See* House.

Guilt. *See* Sin.

Gulf (Gr. *chasma*, *chasm*), an impassable space, such as is represented to exist between the abode of Abraham and the lost rich man (Luke 16:26).

Gu'ni (gū'nī; *colored, dyed*).

1. One of the sons of Naphtali (B. C. perhaps about 1870, but not necessarily born before the migration to Egypt (Gen. 46:24; Num. 26:48; I Chron. 7:13). His descendants are called *Gunites* (Num. 26:48).

2. Father of Abdiel and grandfather of Ahi, which last was chieftain of the Gileadite Gadites (I Chron. 5:15).

Gu'nite (gū'nīt), a general name of the descendants of Guni (*q. v.*), of the tribe of Naphtali (Num. 26:48).

Gur (gûr; a *whelp* as *abiding* in the lair), an ascent near Ibleam, on the road from Jezreel to Beth-haggan, where the servants of Jehu overtook and slew Ahaziah the king (II Kings 9:27). It has not been identified.

Gurba'al (gûr-bā'ăl; *sojourn of Baal*), a place in Arabia captured by Uzziah (II Chron. 26:7); not identified.

Gutter (Heb. *ṣǐnnûr*).

1. This term occurs in the proposal of David that some one should "get up to the gutter and smite the Jebusites" (II Sam. 5:8, a: v.) R. S. V. has "the water shaft," but more recent evidence points to "a grappling hook" used by besiegers in scaling ramparts. The word is now known to be typically Canaanite and the sense "hook" has been handed down through Aramaic to modern Arabic. *See* W. F. Albright in *O. T. Commentary*, 1948, p. 149

2. Drinking troughs (Exod. 2:16), into which Jacob placed peeled rods when the sheep came to drink (Gen. 30:38, 40).

H

Haahash'tari (hā-à-hăsh'tà-rī), the last mentioned of the four sons of Naarah, the second wife of Ashur, of the tribe of Judah (I Chron. 4:6).

Haba'iah (hà-bā'yà; *Jehovah has hidden*), a priest whose descendants returned with the captivity with Zerubbabel, but were degraded from the priesthood, not being able to trace their genealogy (Ezra 2:61); Neh. 7:63), B. C. about 536.

Habak'kuk (hà-băk'ŭk; *embrace*, or perhaps the name of a plant, cf. Akkad. *hambakuku*), the eighth in order of the twelve minor prophets. Nothing certain is known as to the circumstances of Habakkuk's life, as we have only apocryphal and conflicting accounts. In the headings to his book (chaps. 1:1, and 3:1) Habakkuk is simply described as a man who held the office of prophet. From the conclusion to the psalm in ch. 3, "To the chief singer on my stringed instruments" (v. 19), we learn that he was officially qualified to take part in the liturgical singing of the temple, and therefore belonged to one of the Levitical families who were charged with the maintenance of the temple music, and, like the prophets Jeremiah and Ezekiel, who sprang from priestly households, belonged to the tribe of Levi. This is supported by the superscription of the apocryphon of Bel and the Dragon, "Habakkuk the son of Joshua of the tribe of Levi" (K. and D., *Com.*).

Habak'kuk, Book of. The prophecy is named from its evident author (1:1). Practically nothing is known of Habakkuk. From the reference "to the Chief Musician on my stringed instruments" (3:19) combined with the reference to Habakkuk as "the son of Jesus of the tribe of Levi" in the apocryphal legend of Bel and the Dragon, some scholars such as S. Mowinckel have come to the conclusion that the prophet was a Levitical member of the temple choir.

1. **Time of Composition.** The book is evidently to be placed in the general period of the rise of the Neo-Babylonian Empire around 620 B. C. since allusion is made to the Chaldean invasion (1:5, 6). The preferred date of many critics is in the latter portion of Josiah's reign (c. 625-608 B. C.) or in the reign of Jehoiakim (608-597 B. C.). B. Duhm, E. Sellin and C. C. Torrey unwarrantedly emend *Kasdim*, that is, Chaldeans, in 1:6 to *Kittim* (Cypriotes), declaring that the prophecy was aimed at Alexander the Great, and date the book that late.

2. **Criticism.** Literary critics have handled the book of Habakkuk roughly. Karl Marti leaves only seven verses of the entire book intact. B. Duhm, who is scarcely to be called conservative, says that Marti treats the book as cruelly as Yahweh is said to treat the house of the ungodly (3:13) "Thou didst crush the head of the wicked, laying him bare from thigh to neck" (R. S. V.). Critics differ considerably with regard to the unity of chapters one and two. Chapter three is more commonly derived from chapters one and two and dated in the fourth or third century B. C. (Pfeiffer). However, the theme of both is the same. Both contain linguistic likenesses. Chapter three is specifically called the Prayer of Habakkuk (3:1). The technical musical terms contained in it need not be relegated to a post-exilic period for they were evidently in use in preexilic times in the psalter.

3. **Content.**

Part I. Prophet's Twofold Complaint, 1:1-2:20

 A. The First Complaint, 1:1-11

  1. Israel's sin and God's silence, 1:2-4

188. Dead Sea Scroll of Habakkuk, "pesher" interpretation

2. God's reply: the Chaldean invasion, 1:5-11
B. The Second Complaint, 1:12-2:20
   1. Chaldean cruelty and God's silence, 1:12-2:1
   2. God's response: Israel's salvation; woes upon the Chaldeans, 2:2-20
Part II. Prayer of the Prophet, 3:1-19
A. Title, 3:1
B. Initial request, 3:2
C. A Theophany, 3:3-15
D. An unperturable faith, 3:16-19

4. Canonicity. The book is quoted prominently in the N. T. and the references there give Habakkuk significance theologically (cf. Acts 13:41 with Hab. 1:5; Rom. 1:17, Gal. 3:11, Heb. 10:38 with Hab. 2:4). Both Jewish and Christian thought have accorded the book canonical authority. M. F. U.

Habazini'ah (hăb-à-zĭ-nī'à), the father of one Jeremiah, and grandfather of the chief Rechabite, Jaazaniah, which last the prophet Jeremiah tested with the offer of wine in the temple (Jer. 35:3), B. C. about 607.

Hab'ergeon, an old English word for *breastplate*. See Armor, II, (3).

Habitation, the rendering of several Hebrew and Greek words, and used in the general sense of a place to dwell in (Psa. 69:25); 104: 12; Acts 1:20, etc.).

Figurative. God is called the "habitation of his people" (Psa. 71:3; 91:9). Justice and judgment are the habitations of God's throne (89:14), since all his acts are founded on them (117:2). Palestine, Jerusalem, the tabernacle, and the temple are called the habitation of God, for in them he signally showed his presence (Psa. 132:5, 13; Eph. 2:22). God is said to "inhabit the praises of Israel" (Psa. 22:3), i. e., Jehovah is the object of and graciously receives the praises of his people. Eternity is represented as Jehovah's habitation (Isa. 57: 15), i. e., the eternally dwelling One, whose

life lasts forever and is always the same. See House, Tent.

Ha'bor (hā'bôr; *joining together*), a river of Mesopotamia, identified with the modern Khabur. It flows south through Gozan and after a course of 190 miles meets the east branch of the Euphrates. Deported Israelites from Samaria were settled on its banks by Tigth-lapileser III, of Assyria (745-727 B. C.; I Chron. 5:26) and by Sargon II (721-705 B. C.; II Kings 17:6; 18:11).

Hachali'ah (hăk-à-lī'à; R. V. and R. S. V. correctly Hacaliah, the father of Nehemiah, the governor after the captivity (Neh. 1:1; 10:1), B. C. before 446.

Hachi'lah (hà-kī'là; *dark*), a hiding place of David at the time the Ziphites proposed betraying him to Saul (I Sam. 23:19; 26:1, 3). Hachilah appears to have been the long ridge now called El Kôlah, where there is a high hill with a ruin, called Yŭkîn.

Hach'moni (hăk'mô-nī; *wise, skillful*), a man only known as the father (or ancestor, comp. I Chron. 27:2) of Jashobeam, the chief of David's warriors (I Chron. 11:11, where *son of Hachmoni* is rendered "Hachmonite," for which the parallel passage (II Sam. 23:8) has "Tachmonite"), and also of Jehiel, the companion of the princes in the royal household (I Chron. 27:32), B. C. considerably before 1000. Hachmon or Hachmoni was, no doubt, the founder of a family to which these belonged. The actual father of Jashobeam was Zabdiel (27:2), and he is also said to have belonged to the Korhites (12:6); possibly the Levites descended from Korah (McC. and S., *Cyc.*).

Hachmonite (hăk'mô-nīt). See Hachmoni.

Ha'dad (hā'dăd; *sharp, fierce*), probably an official title, like Pharaoh, and the names of several men. It is found occasionally in the altered form, Hadar.

1. One of the sons of Ishmael (Gen. 25:15, "Hadar;" I Chron. 1:30), after B. C. c. 1900.

2. The son of Bedad, and king of Edom. He gained an important victory over the Midianites on the field of Moab. He was the successor of Husham, and established his court at Avith (Gen. 36:35; I Chron. 1:46).

3. Another king of Edom, successor of Baalhanan. The name of his city was Pai (Pau), and his wife's name Mehetabel (I Chron. 1: 50). He is called Hadar in Gen. 36:39, where his death is not mentioned.

4. An Aramaean deity identified with their own weather god Rammon (Heb. Rimmon). Adad (Hadad) was an ancient Mesopotamian deity, god of the storm and thunder. The name Hadad occurs in many compound names of Aramaeans, such as Hadadezer, Ben-Hadad ("son of Hadad").

5. A prince of the royal house of Edom. In his childhood he escaped the massacre under Joab, and fled with some followers into Egypt. Pharaoh treated him very kindly, and gave him his sister-in-law in marriage. By her he had a son, Genubath, who was brought up in the palace with the sons of Pharaoh. After David's death Hadad resolved to recover his dominion, but Pharaoh opposing him, he left Egypt and returned to his own country (I Kings 11:14, sq.). It does not appear from the text, as it now stands, what was the result of this attempt, further than he was one of the troublers of Solomon's reign (v. 14). Our version makes v. 25 refer to Rezon, but the Septuagint has, "*This is the evil which Adar did*." The meaning then will be, This same kind of mischief (incursions in the land of Israel like those of Rezon) wrought also Hadad.

Hadade′zer (hă-dăd-ē′zĕr; *Adad* his *help*), son of Rehob, and king of the Aramaean state of Zobah. While on his way to establish his dominion (B. C. about 984) he was defeated in the neighborhood of the Euphrates (II Sam. 8:3). From ch. 10 (v. 7, sq.) we learn that Joab commanded the forces of Israel. Hadadezer made preparations for the campaign of the following year on a far larger scale. When David heard that Hadadezer was gathering great armies on the Euphrates, he determined to anticipate his attack. He marched in person with his troops over Jordan to the northeast, and, at Helam, a place unknown to us, a decisive battle was fought. The Aramaeans from both sides of the Euphrates were completely routed (II Sam. 8:4; 10:18), and the power of Hadadezer was so thoroughly broken that all the small tributary princes seized the opportunity of throwing off his yoke.

Hadadrim′mon (hă-dăd-rĭm′ŏn), (two Syrian deities), a place in the valley of Megiddo (Zech. 12:11). The lamentation on account of the death of the good king Josiah, who lost his life in battle here, was so great as to pass into a proverb (II Chron. 35:22-25).

Ha′dar (hā′dăr; perhaps *chamber*). 1. One of the "sons of Ishmael" (Gen. 25:15), given in I Chron. 1:30 as Hadad (*q. v.*).

2. An Edomite king who succeeded Baalhanan (Gen. 36:39). The name of his city, and the name and genealogy of his wife, are given. In the parallel list in I Chron. 1 he appears as Hadad. We know from another source (I Kings 11:14, sq.) that Hadad was

one of the names of the royal family of Edom. *See* Hadad, 3.

Hadare′zer (hă-dà-rē′zĕr; *Adad* his *help*), the form (II Sam. 10:16, 19; I Chron. 18:3, sq.; 19:16, 19) of Hadadezer (*q. v.*).

Had′ashah (hăd′-à-shä; *new*), a city in the valley of Judah (Josh. 15:37), between the hilly region and the Philistine border.

Hadas′sah (hà-dăs′sà; *myrtle*), the earlier Jewish name of Esther (Esth. 2:7). *See* Esther.

Hadat′tah (hà-dăt′à; *new*), one of the extreme southern towns of Judah (Josh. 15:25). The Massoretic accents of the Hebrew connect Hadattah with Hazor preceding, making it read "new Hazor." Apparently el-Hudeira S. E. of Tuwāni towards the Dead Sea.

Ha′des (Gr. *hadēs, unseen*). This word does not occur in the English Bible, either as a general or proper name, but is found several times in the original (Matt. 11:23; 16:18; Luke 10:15; 16:23; Acts 2:27, 31; Rev. 1:18; 6:8; 20:13, 14; I Cor. 15:55, but in the last passage the true reading is *thanatos, death*).

The following views of Hades may be well noted:

1. The ancient Greek view of Hades, and the Roman view of *Orcus*, or *Inferna*, is that of a place for all the dead in the depth of the earth; dark, dreary, cheerless, shut up, inaccessible to prayers and sacrifices, ruled over by Pluto. This presiding god was the enemy of all life, heartless, inexorable, and hated accordingly by gods and men.

2. The Hebrew Sheol (*q. v.*) is the equivalent for Hades, and is likewise the subterranean abode of all the dead until the judgment. It was divided into two departments, paradise or Abraham's bosom for the good, and Gehenna or hell for the bad.

3. In the New Testament, as will be seen above, the term Hades is of comparatively rare occurrence; in our Lord's own discourses it is found only three times, and on two of the occasions by way of contrast to the region of life and blessing. From a consideration of the various passages the following may be a just conclusion: "It seems as if in the progress of God's dispensations a separation had come to be made between elements that orginally were mingled together, so that Hades was henceforth appropriated, both in the name and in the reality, to those who were reserved in darkness and misery to the great day; and other names, with other and brighter ideas, were employed to designate the intermediate resting place of the redeemed. These latter pass immediately upon death into the presence of their Lord (John 14:2, 3; Phil. 1:23). Such being the nature of the scriptural representation on the subject, one must condemn the fables that sprung up amid the Dark Ages about the limbus, or antechamber of hell, and the purgatorial fires, in which it was supposed even redeemed souls had to complete their ripening for glory" (*Imp. Dict.*, s. v.).

4. Luke 16:19-31, which sets forth the account of the Rich Man and Lazarus (and which strictly speaking is not a parable), indicates a difference in Hades after the ascension of Christ. Before this far-reaching event it seems clear that Hades was in two compart-

ments, the domicile respectively of saved and unsaved spirits. "Paradise" and "Abraham's bosom," both common Jewish terms of the day, were adopted by Christ in Luke 16:22; 23:43, to designate the condition of the righteous in the intermediate state. The blessed dead being with Abraham were conscious and "comforted" (Luke 16:25). The dying thief was on that very day to be with Christ in "Paradise." The unsaved were separated from the saved by a "great gulf fixed" (Luke 16:26). The rich man, who is evidently still in Hades, is a representative case and describes the unjudged condition in the intermediate state of the wicked. As to his spirit, he was alive, fully conscious and in exercise of his mental faculties and also tormented. It is thus apparent that insofar as the unsaved dead are concerned, no change in their abode or state is revealed in connection with the ascension of Christ. At the sinners' judgment of the Great White Throne, Hades will surrender the wicked. They will be judged and be cast into the Lake of Fire (Rev. 20:13, 14; See Lake of Fire). However, with regard to the state of the righteous and the location of Paradise, Christ's ascension has evidently worked a drastic change. The Apostle Paul was "caught up to the third heaven . . . into Paradise" (II Cor. 12:1-4). Paradise, therefore, now denotes the immediate presence of God. When Christ "ascended up on high" he "led a multitude of captives" (Eph. 4:8-10). When it is immediately added that He "descended first into the lower parts of the earth", evidently the Paradise division of Hades, he set free the saved spirit denizens of the underworld. Thus during the present Church age, the redeemed who die, that is, fall asleep, are "absent from the body"; at home with the Lord." The wicked by contrast are in Hades, both awaiting resurrection, one the resurrection to life and the other the resurrection to condemnation. *See* Intermediate State, Gehenna, Lake of Fire, Eternal Punishment.

M. F. U.

Ha'did (hā'dĭd; *sharp pointed*), a place in Benjamin, seven hundred and twenty of whose inhabitants returned from captivity (Ezra 2: 33, where some copies read Harid; Neh. 7:37; 11:34). Located at Haditheh, 3 miles E. N. E. of Lydda.

Had'lai (hăd'lī; *ceasing, resting*), the father of Amasa, which latter was one of the Ephraimites who opposed the captives of Judah in the civil war between Pekah and Ahaz (II Chron. 28:12), B. C. about 735.

Hado'ram (há-dō'răm).

1. The fifth of the thirteen sons of Joktan (Gen. 10:27; I Chron. 1:21), and supposed to be progenitor of a tribe in Arabia Felix. It is impossible to identify the tribe in question.

2. The son of Toi (Tou), king of Hamath, sent by his father (with valuable presents of gold, silver, and brass vessels) to congratulate David on his victory over their common enemy, Hadadezer, king of Syria (I Chron. 18:10), B. C. about 984. In the parallel narrative of II Sam. 8, the name is given as Joram. This, being a contraction of Jehoram, which contains the name of Jehovah, is peculiarly an Israelitish appellation (Smith, s. v.).

3. Chief officer of the tribute in the time of Rehoboam, son of Solomon. He was stoned to death by the people of the northern tribes when sent by the king to collect the usual taxes (II Chron. 10:18), B. C. about 934. Probably the same person as Adoniram in I Kings 4:6; 5:14.

Ha'drach (hā'drăk), the name of a country mentioned by Zechariah (9:1). It occurs in the late Assyrian monuments as *Hatarrika* and is located on the Orontes S. of Hamath and N. of Damascus.

Haemorrhoids. *See* Diseases, Emerods."

Haft, an old form of handle, e. g., of a dagger (Judg. 3:22).

Ha'gab (hā'găb; *a locust*), one of the Nethinim whose descendants returned from Babylon under Zerubbabel (Ezra 2:46), B. C. before 536.

Hag'aba (hăg'á-bä; also *a locust*, Ezra 2:45), one of the Nethinim whose descendants returned from the captivity with Zerubbabel (Neh. 7:48), B. C. before 536.

Hag'abah (hăg'á-bä; Ezra 2:45), another form of the preceding.

Ha'gar (hā'gär; derivation uncertain), a native of Egypt, servant of Abraham (Gen. 21:9, 10), and handmaid of Sarah (16:1).

1. **Abraham's Wife.** Sarah, continuing for so long a time childless, determined to become a mother by proxy (not uncommon in the East) through her handmaid, whom she gave to Abraham as a secondary wife (Gen. 16), B. C. c. 2050. This honor was too great for the weak and ill-regulated mind of Hagar; and no sooner did she find herself likely to become the mother of her master's heir than she openly triumphed over her less favored mistress. Sarah, deeply wounded, complained to Abraham, who gave her power to act as she thought best toward Hagar.

2. **Flight.** As soon as Sarah made her feel her power, Hagar fled, doubtless intending to return to Egypt by a road used from time immemorial, that ran from Hebron past Beersheba "by the way of Shur." There the angel of the Lord found her by a well, and directed her to return to her mistress and submit to her, promising her the birth of a son and numerous descendants.

3. **Return.** Obedient to the heavenly visitor, and having distinguished the place by the name of Beer-lahai-roi, Hagar returned again to the tent of Abraham, where in due time she had a son. Abraham called him, as directed by the angel (v. 11), Ishmael, "God shall hear." About fourteen years after Isaac was born, and when he was weaned, two or three years later, Ishmael greatly offended Sarah by mocking her son. Sarah insisted upon his expulsion from the family, together with Hagar.

4. **Expelled.** Abraham, though displeased, consented, being divinely instructed to follow Sarah's advice. Hagar and her son were sent away. In the desert, the strength of Ishmael gave way, and she laid him down under one of the stunted shrubs of that region. She withdrew about a bowshot's distance, unwilling to see his dying sufferings, and wept. The angel of the Lord appeared with a comforting promise of her son's increasing greatness, and directed her to a fountain, from which she

189. Hagar in the Wilderness (Carat)

filled the bottle and gave her son to drink. We have no account of Hagar's subsequent history beyond what is involved in that of Ishmael, who established himself in the wilderness of Paran, in the neighborhood of Sinai, and was married to an Egyptian woman (Gen. 21:1-21). In Gal. 4:24, the apostle Paul, in an allegory, makes Hagar represent the Jewish Dispensation, which was in bondage to the ceremonial law, as Sarah represents the true Church of Christ, which was free from this bondage.

Hagarenes', (hăg-à-rēnz'), **Ha'garites** (hā'-gà-rīts), (Psa. 83:6, A. V. Hagarenes, R. V. Hagarenes, marg. Hagrites; I Chron. 5:10, A. V. Hagarites, R. V. Hagrites; 19, 20, A. V. Hagarites, R. V. Hagrites; comp. 27:31, A. V. Hagerite, R. V. Hagrite), a nation living east of Palestine who were dispossessed by Reuben, Gad. and east Manasseh, in the days of Saul. To this time I Chron. 5:10 refers. Vers. 18-22 seem at first sight to refer to the days of Jotham and Jeroboam II. But we incline to think that v. 18 is a resumption of the narrative of v. 10, which is interrupted by the genealogy of Gad (vers. 11, 17), the more because Pekah, in whose reign the first captivity took place (II Kings 15:29), was contemporary with Jotham (II Kings 15:32), so that little time would be left for the occupation by Israel (I Chron. 5:21).

The power of the Hagarenes is shown by the force sent against them (I Chron. 5:18), and their wealth in flocks and herds by the spoil (v. 21). Their subsequent hostility appears from Psa. 83:6, where they are mentioned next to Moab. In I Chron. 27:31 Jaziz, the Hagrite, keeps the flocks of David, very likely in his ancestral regions. Mibhar, "the son of Haggeri" may equally well mean "son of a Hagrite." We need find no discrepancy between this and II Sam. 23:35, "Bani the Gadite," since the two accounts are connected with different periods of David's life, about thirty years apart, and it is not likely that the persons about him were exactly the same.

It is generally supposed that the Hagarenes were the descendants of Hagar. This is favored by the fact that of the three names, Jetur, Nephish, and Nodab, which are mentioned in I Chron. 5:19, apparently as names of Hagrite tribes or chiefs, two, Jetur and Nephish, appear in Gen. 2:5, 15 as names of sons of Ishmael. In Psa. 83:6 Ishmaelites are distinguished from Hagarenes; but it may be as a general and special term, as the Parisians might be distinguished from the French in one passage, and in another all might be called French, or, as among the seven nations of Canaan, one was called especially Canaanites.

Smith (*Bib. Dict.*) thinks the name and location of the Hagarenes may be represented by *Hejer*, the Agrae of Ptol., v, 19, 2, and Strabo, xvi, 767. Gesenius (12th ed.) thinks that the *agraioi* of Strabo were probably another section of the same race. We only know them by the land taken from them east of Gilead; but as a pastoral tribe they no doubt traversed at different times a good deal of territory. Jetur is thought to be represented by Iturea.—W. H.

Ha'gerite, (hā'gĕ-rīt), a designation of Jaziz (*q. v.*), who was overseer of David's flocks (I Chron. 27:31). *See* Hagarite.

Hag'gai (hăg'gā-ī; *festal*), the tenth in order of the twelve minor prophets, and the first of the three who, after the return of the Jews from the Babylonian exile, prophesied in Palestine. Of the place and year of his birth, and his descent, nothing is known. He commenced to prophesy in the second year of Darius Hystaspes (Hag. 1:1). Together with Zechariah, he urged the renewal of the building of the temple, which had been suspended after the reign of Cyrus, and obtained the permission and assistance of the king (Ezra 5:1; 6:14). Animated by the high courage of these devoted men, the people prosecuted the work with vigor, and the temple was completed and dedicated in the sixth year of Darius, B. C. 516.

Haggai, Book of. Haggai lived at the same time as Zechariah and, as an older man, labored with the younger man to encourage the returned Babylonian exiles to finish rebuilding the temple. Work on this structure had been started in the second year of Cyrus, late in B. C. 536 but had been abandoned because of difficulties and opposition.

1. **Occasion.** In the second year of the Persian monarch Darius (520 B. C.) Haggai (Heb. "festal") preached his four prophetic messages. Excerpts of these sermons compose the canonical book. The first prophetic utterance (1:1-15) was preached in August-September 520 B. C., the second (2:1-9), September-October, 520 B. C., the third (2:10-19) November-December 520 B. C., and the fourth (2:20-23), November-December.

2. **Outline.**

Part I. Plea to finish the temple, 1:1-15
Part II. Prophecies of the millennial temple, 2:1-9
Part III. Promise of present blessing upon finishing the temple, 2:10-19
Part IV. Prophecy of the future destruction of Gentile world power, 2:20-23

3. **Authorship.** Since the addresses of the prophet, as we now possess them, are severely curtailed resumés and since the prophet is always spoken of in the third person, critics such as Oesterly and Robinson deny that the book as it now stands is from Haggai's hand. They claim it is to be attributed, in all prob-

ability, to a contemporary who wrote down the salient points of the prophet's sermons. The arguments of brevity, however, and use of the third person are not convincing reasons why the entire book may not have been written by Haggai himself. If Haggai wrote under inspiration, there is no reason why he might not have used short excerpts from his larger discourses or have employed the third person. *M. F. U.*

Hag′geri (hăg′gê-rĭ; a *Hagerite*). "Mibhar, son of Haggeri," was one of the mighty men of David's guard, according to the catalogue of I Chron. 11:38. The parallel passage (II Sam. 23:36) has "Bani the Gadite."

Hag′gi (hăg′ĭ; *festive*), the second of the seven sons of the patriarch Gad (Gen. 46:16), and progenitor of the family of Haggites (Num. 26:15).

Haggi′ah (hăg-gī′à; *festival of Jehovah*), a Levite of the family of Merari, apparently the son of Shimea and the father of Asaiah, which last seems to have been contemporary with David (I Chron. 6:30).

Hag′gites (hăg′ĭts), the family title of the descendants of Haggi (*q. v.*), the son of Gad (Num. 26:15).

Hag′gith (hăg′gĭth; *festive*), a wife of David, known only as the mother of Adonijah (II Sam. 3:4; I Kings 1:5, 11; 2:13; I Chron. 3: 2). She was probably married to David after his accession to the throne, B. C. 1000.

Hagiog′rapha (hăg-ĭ-ŏg′ra-phà; *holy writings*), a name sometimes applied to the third division of the Scriptures, called by the Jews "The Writings," and consisting of the Psalms, Proverbs, Job, Daniel, Ezra, Nehemiah, Ruth, Esther, Chronicles, Canticles, Lamentations, and Ecclesiastes. This division was so manifestly arbitrary that it was never accepted as a proper one by the Church.

Ha′i (hā′ĭ), another form (Gen. 12:8; 13:3) of Ai (*q. v.*).

Hail. 1. (Gr. *chaire, be cheerful, rejoice*). A salutation conveying a wish for the welfare of the person addressed (Luke 1:28); continued among our Saxon forefathers in "Joy to you," and "Health to you."

2. Congealed rain (Heb. *bärad*, Gr. *chalaza*, with which God defeated an army of Canaanites (Josh. 10:11, "the Lord cast down great stones from heaven upon them unto Azekah, and they died"). This phenomenon, which resembled the terrible hail in Egypt (Exod. 9: 24), was manifestly a miraculous occurrence produced by the omnipotent power of God, for the hailstones did not injure the Israelites who were pursuing the enemy. That hail, though uncommon, was not absolutely unknown in Egypt, we learn from the testimony of travelers from ancient times to the present. In Palestine, "hail is common, and is often mingled with rain and with thunder storms (comp. Psa. 18:12, 13, etc.), which happen at intervals through the winter, and are frequent in the spring" (Smith, *Hist. Geog.*, p. 64).

As a hailstorm is generally accompanied by lightning, we find in Scripture hail and fire (i. e., lightning) mentioned together (Exod. 9:23; Psa. 78:48; 105:32, etc.).

Figurative. Hail is the symbol of divine vengeance upon kingdoms and nations, as the enemies of God and his people (Isa. 28:2, 17; 32:19; Hag. 2:17).

Hailstone (Heb. *'ĕbĕn bäräd*), a stone of hail (Josh. 10:11). See above.

Hair (properly Heb. *sē'är;* Gr. *thrix, threeks*). The customs of ancient nations regarding the hair varied considerably.

1. Of the Head. (1) **The Egyptians.** According to Herodotus, the Egyptians "only left the hair of their head and beard grow in mourning, being at all other times shaved." This agrees perfectly with the authority of the sculptures and of Scripture, where Joseph is said to have "shaved himself," when sent for from prison by Pharaoh (Gen. 41:14). Love of cleanliness seems to have been the motive for this custom, and the priests carried this so far that they shaved the whole body every three days. Even the heads of young children were shaved, certain locks being left at the front, sides, and back. Women always wore their own hair, and they were not shaved even in mourning, or after death. Wigs were also worn, though rather by women than by men.

(2) **Assyrian.** In the Assyrian sculptures the hair always appears long, combed closely down upon the head, and shedding itself in a mass of curls upon the shoulders. Herodotus testifies that the Babylonians wore their hair long. The very long hair, however, that appears in the figures on the monuments is supposed to have been partly false, a sort of headdress to add to the effect of the natural hair.

(3) **Greeks.** The Greeks of the oldest times regarded long hair in man as an ornament, and only cut it as a sign of mourning. At Athens, down to the Persian wars, the hair was worn long, and fastened up into a knot by a needle in the form of a grasshopper. A free Athenian citizen did not wear his hair very short, or he would have been mistaken for a slave, who would be obliged to do so. The Greek women, to judge from existing monuments, followed an extraordinary variety of fashions, but all of them sought to cover the forehead as much as possible. Hairpins (made of ivory, bronze, silver, and gold), fillets, and nets were used in dressing the hair. Both Greek and Roman ladies tried by artificial means to give their dark hair a fair or ruddy complexion.

(4) **Hebrews.** The Hebrews bestowed special care on the hair and beard (see below); regarding thick, abundant hair as an ornament, while the bald head was regarded even to insults (II Kings 2:23). Long flowing hair was worn only by youths in more ancient times (II Sam. 14:26; Cant. 5:11), and by Nazarites during the term of their vow (Num. 6:5). Women always wore their hair long (Cant. 4:1; Luke 7:38; John 11:2; I Cor. 11:15), and put up in plaits (II Kings 9:30); so the Nazarite (Judg. 16:13, 19). Fashionable ladies were in the habit of curling artificial locks (Isa. 3:24). The fashionable braided hair, in which the Jewesses of a later time probably imitated the style of Roman ladies, is censured by the apostles as unsuitable for Christians (I Tim. 2:9; I Pet. 3:3). Even men began at that time to curl their hair, a practice which was generally condemned (Josephus, *Ant.*, xiv, 9, 4),

the usual custom for men being to cut the hair from time to time with a razor (Ezek. 44:20), but without shaving it bare. Female hairdressers, who are first mentioned in the Rabbinical writers, may have existed in more ancient times, for barbers are mentioned in Ezek. 5:1.

2. The Beard. (1) Customs. Western Asiatics have always cherished the beard as the badge of the dignity of manhood, and attached to it the importance of a feature, e. g., the eye or nose. The Egyptians, on the contrary, sedulously, for the most part, shaved the hair of the face and head, and compelled their slaves to do the like. The enemies of the Egyptians, including probably many of the nations of Canaan, Syria, and Armenia, etc., are represented nearly always bearded. In the Ninevite monuments is a series of battle views from the capture of Lachish, by Sennacherib, in which the captives have beards very like some of those in the Egyptian monument. There is, however, an appearance of conventionalism both in Egyptian and Assyrian treatment of the hair and beard on monuments, which prevents our accepting it as characteristic.

(2) **Hebrew regulations, etc.** Among the Hebrews the beard was considered as an ornament, and was not shaven, but only trimmed (II Sam. 19:25). The dressing, trimming, anointing, etc., of the beard was performed with much ceremony by persons of wealth and rank (Psa. 133:2). The removal of the beard was a part of the ceremonial treatment proper to a leper (Lev. 14:9). Size and fullness of beard are said to be regarded, at the present day, as a mark of respectability and trustworthiness. The beard is the object of an oath, and that on which blessings or shame are spoken of as resting. The custom was and is to shave or pluck it and the hair out in mourning (Isa. 15:2; 50:6; Jer. 41:5; 48:37; Ezra 9:3; Bar. 6:31); to neglect it in seasons of permanent affliction (II Sam. 19:24), and to regard any insult to it as the last outrage which enmity can inflict (II Sam. 10:4). The beard was an object of salutation (II Sam. 20:9), and it was a custom to swear by it (Matt. 5:36). The law forbade the deforming of the head by cutting away the hair round it, and of the beard by cutting the corners (Lev. 19:27). This is understood to mean that the hair was not to be cut in a circle from one temple to another, as among the Arabs; nor that portion of the face where the beard and hair met be shaved. By some these regulations are thought to have reference to the fact that among some nations these customs are part of idolatrous worship.

Figurative. Hair was a symbol of that which was of the *least value* in man's person (I Sam. 14:45; II Sam. 14:11; I Kings 1:52; Matt. 10:30; Luke 12:7; 21:18); of *great number* (Psa. 40:12; 69:4); a *minute distance* (Judg. 20:16). White or gray hair is the symbol of honor or authority, and is thus entitled to respect (Lev. 19:32; Prov. 16:31; Dan. 7:9; Rev. 1:14); sometimes of approaching decay, as of Israel (Hos. 7:9). To cover the beard (A. V. "upper lip"), i. e., to cover the face up to the nose, is a sign of mourning (Lev. 13:45), of trouble

and shame (Ezek. 24:17); Mic. 3:7), and is really equivalent to covering the head (Jer. 14:4; Esth. 6:12).

Hak'katan (hăk'á-tăn, or rather **Ka'tan** (kā'-tăn; *little*, or *junior*), a descendant (or native) of Azgad, and father of Johanan, which last returned with one hundred and ten male retainers from Babylon with Ezra (Ezra 8:12), B. C. before 457.

Hak'koz (hăk'ŏz; I Chron. 24:10). See Koz.

Haku'pha (há-kū'fà; *crooked, bent,* cf Arab. *hakafa, to be curved*), one of the Nethinim who returned from Babylon with Zerubbabel (Ezra 2:51; Neh. 7:53), B. C. about 538.

Ha'lah (hā'là), the district in the Assyrian Empire into which the captive Israelites were taken by the Assyrian kings (II Kings 17:6; 18:11; I Chron. 5:26), and situated on the banks of the Khabour, evidently near Gozan.

Ha'lak (hā'lăk; *bare*), the Smooth or Bald Mountain, mentioned in the description of Joshua's conquests in Canaan (Josh. 11:17; 12:7). Doubtless this ridge is referred to in Num. 34:3, 4; Josh. 15:2, 3, under the name Ascent of Akrabbim. It is now located N. N. E. of Abdeh, which is on the Wadi el-Marra.

Hal'hul (hăl'hŭl), a town in the highlands of Judah, in which tradition says Gad, the seer of David, was buried (Josh. 15:58); preserved in the ruins of Halhûl, about 4 miles north of Hebron.

Ha'li (hā'lī; *jewel*), one of the towns assigned to Asher (Josh. 19:25), not definitely located.

Hall. See House.

Hal'lel (hăl'ĕl; Heb. *hālēl*, Gr. *humnos, praise*), the name of a particular part of the hymnal service chanted at certain festivals. This service received the designation "hallel" because it consists of Psalms 113-118, which are psalms of praise and begin with Hallelujah. It is also called the "Egyptian Hallel," because it was chanted in the temple while the Passover lambs, first enjoined in Egypt, were slain. This Hallel was also chanted after the morning sacrifice on the Feast of Pentecost, the eight days of the Feast of Tabernacles, and the eight days of the Feast of Dedication. It was chanted too in private families on the first evening of Passover. The Great Hallel was so called because of the reiterated response after every verse, "For thy mercy endureth forever" (Psa. 136). It was recited on the first evening of the Passover, at the supper, by those wishing to have a fifth cup, i. e., one above the enjoined number. The hymn sung by Jesus and his disciples after the Last Supper (Matt. 26:30) is supposed to have been part of this Hallel.

Hallelu'jah (hăl-ê-lū'yà; (Heb. *hăl⁰lū-yäh, praise ye Jah*, i. e., Jehovah; Gr. *'allēlovia*, evidently a common form of adoration and thanksgiving in Jewish worship, as appears from its frequent employment at the beginning and close of many of the Psalms (see Psa. 106, 111, 113, 117, 135). In the great hymn of triumph in heaven over the destruction of Babylon the large multitude in chorus, like the voice of mighty thunderings, burst forth, "Allelujah, for the Lord God omnipotent reigneth," in response to the voice from the throne saying, "Praise our God, all ye his servants" (Rev. 19:1-6).

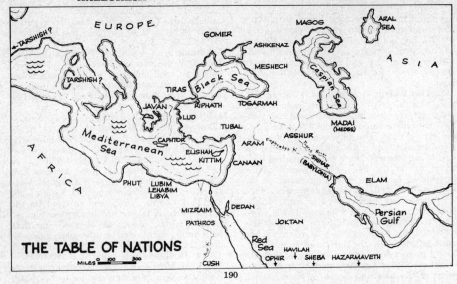

THE TABLE OF NATIONS

MILES 0   100   300

190

Hallo′hesh (hă-lō′hĕsh; *the whisperer, enchanter*), the father of Shallum, which latter assisted Nehemiah in repairing the walls of Jerusalem (Neh. 3:12), where the name is Anglicized "Halohesh." He was one of the popular chiefs who covenanted with Nehemiah (Neh. 10:24), B. C. 445.

Hallow, Hallowed (Heb. *qādăsh*, to *set apart, consecrate;* Gr. *hagiazo,* to *make sacred*). Spoken of a *person* who consecrates himself to God (Isa. 65:5); of Christ undergoing death to consecrate himself to God (John 17:19; comp. 10:36; Gal. 1:15); of *things.* e. g., the altar, the temple (Exod. 29:36; Lev. 8:15; Num. 7:1; I Kings 8:64); the *Sabbath* in keeping it holy (Exod. 20:8, etc.). In general, Christians are the hallowed (Acts 20:32; 26:18, A. V. "sanctified"), as those who, freed from impurity, have been brought near to God through their faith and sanctity. *See* Sanctification.

Halo′hesh (hălō′hĕsh; Neh. 3:12). *See* Hallohesh.

Ham (hăm; *hot*), the youngest of the three sons of Noah (Gen. 5:32). Like his brothers he was married at the time of the Deluge, and with his wife was saved from destruction in the ark (7:13). After the Deluge he provoked the wrath of his father by an act of indecency toward him which occasioned a far-reaching prophecy (9:21, sq.). A list of his descendants is given in chap. 10:6-18, as follows:

The Hamitic peoples are presented in Genesis 10:8-10 as developing earthly imperial power in their first appearance in human history. This power, moreover, is implied to be evil. Nimrod is said to have been "a mighty hunter before the Lord" (Gen. 10:9). The simple construction of this passage, so commonly misinterpreted, is that Yahweh took note of his royal character as that of a "hunter," which was the exact opposite of the divine ideal of a king—that of a shepherd (Cf. II Sam. 5:2; 7:7; Rev. 2:27). A hunter gratifies himself at the expense of his victim. On the other hand, a shepherd spends himself for the good of the subjects of his care. Hamitic imperial power is said to have begun in Babel, Erech, Akkad and Calneh (Gen. 10: 10). The cities of Babylon, Erech and Akkad are now well known. They were among the earliest great capitals of the civilized world and were located "in the land of Shinar." This term denotes the entire alluvial plain of Babylon between the Tigris and the Euphrates, in approximately the last 200 miles of these great rivers as they flowed in ancient times. This region was divided according to the cuneiform accounts into the northern portion called Akkad in which Babel (Akkad. *Babilu,* signifying gate of god) and the city of Akkad (Agade) were situated. The southern portion was called Sumer, in which Erech,

HAM.

I. CUSH	II. MIZRAIM	III. PHUT	IV. CANAAN.
1. Seba; 2. Havilah; 3. Sabtah; 4. Raamah; 5. Sabtecha; 6. Nimrod.	1. Ludim; 2. Anamim; 3. Lehabim; 4. Naphtuhim; 5. Pathrusim; 6. Casluhim; Caphtorim.		1. Sidon; 2. Heth; 3. Jebusite; 4. Amorite; 5. Girgasite; 6. Hivite; 7. Arkite; 8. Sinite; 9. Arvadite; 10. Zemarite; 11. Hamathite.
Sheba; Dedan.	Philistim.		

Cush, Mizraim, and Phut were the progenitors of the tribes that peopled Africa, and Canaan became the father of those that principally occupied Phoenicia and Palestine.

ancient Uruk, modern Warka, was located. This, the cradle of ancient civilization, was the first center of imperialism under the Hamitic peoples.

442

The name of Ham alone, of the three sons of Noah, if our identification be correct, is known to have been given to a country (Psa. 78:51; 105:23; 106:22).

NOTE: Gen. 9:24: "His younger son." It is questionable whether the adjective "younger" literally, "little" is to be taken as comparative, in the sense of "the younger," or as superlative, meaning "the youngest." Keil and Delitzsch (Com., in loco.) prefer the former, and take the order in which the three names stand as an indication of their relative ages. Others accept the superlative and consider Ham to be the youngest son (McC. and S., Cyc.). Gen. 9:25: "Cursed be Canaan!" "To understand the words of Noah with reference to his sons we must bear in mind, on the one hand, that as the moral nature of the patriarch was transmitted by generation to his descendants, so the diversities of character in the sons of Noah foreshadowed diversities in the moral inclinations of the tribes of which they were the heads; and, on the other hand, that Noah, through the Spirit and power of that God with whom he walked, discerned in the moral nature of his sons, and the different tendencies which they already displayed, the germinal commencement of the future course of their posterity, and uttered words of blessing and of curse, which were prophetic of the history of the tribes that descended from them" (K. and D., Com.).

"**Ham, they of**" (I Chron. 4:40). The Simeonites, wishing to extend their territory "went to the entrance of *Gedor*" (q. v.), and there found these Hamites who "dwelt there of old." They may have been Egyptian Cushites, or even Canaanites (I Chron. 1:8). This only is certain, that they were a peaceful shepherd people, dwelling in tents, and therefore nomads.

Ha'man (hā'măn), the son of Hammedatha the Agagite, prime minister of Ahasuerus, the Persian king (Esth. 3:1), B. C. after 486. As Agag was a title of the kings of the Amalekites, it is supposed that Haman was descended from the royal family of that nation. He, or his father, probably found their way to Persia as captives or hostages. His intrigues against Mordecai and the Jews, the discovery of his plot, and his own execution, are graphically delineated in the Book of Esther. Prideaux (*Connexion*, anno 453) computes the sum which he offered to pay into the royal treasury at more than two million sterling pounds (ten million dollars).

Ha'math (hā'măth; *fortress*), a very ancient city-state, capital of the upper Syria, in the valley of the Orontes, and most important town, as Shalmanezer claims to have captured eighty-nine towns belonging to it. Originally a Canaanite colony (Gen. 10:18). In the time of Hezekiah it was taken by the Assyrians (II Kings 18:34) and was annexed to the Assyrian empire, B. C. 720. It was located in a fertile and well watered valley at the foot of Lebanon. Its modern name is "Hamah," and it is here that those inscribed stones, called "Hamath" stones, were first noticed by Burckhardt in 1810, afterward rediscovered by Sir Richard Burton and Tyrwhitt Drake, and of which squeezes were shown in London in 1872 which are now known to be "Hittite."

Hamath. The city kingdom of Hamath was prominent in O. T. history from the time of David onward and is well known from the Assyrian monuments. Its site has been extensively excavated, revealing a distinctive Hittite occupation. In the famous Battle of Karkar in 853 B. C., Hamath was prominently joined with Ben Hadad of Damascus and Ahab, king of Israel, against the encroachments of Shalmaneser III of Assyria. Despite this valiant stand, Hamath later succumbed to the Assyrians. Citizens of Hamath were transplanted into the Northern Kingdom when Israel fell (II Kings 17:24, 30). Some Israelites were also transplanted to Hamath. In later Assyrian history Hamath became a province of Syria and subsequently of Persia in the time of Nehemiah. M. F. U.

Ham'athite (hăm'ȧ-thīt; the inhabitants Gen. 10:18; I Chron. 1:16), or rather founders of *Hamath* (q. v.).

Ha'math-Zo'bah (hā'mŏth-zō'bȧ; II Chron. 8:3), supposed to be the same as *Hamath* (q. v.). Some think it different, and distinguished therefrom by the suffix "Zobah." It is, however, most likely to be identical with the well-known city Hamath on the Orontes, Hadadezer's Empire was large in extent and in all likelihood comprehended the region of Hamath, captured by Solomon (II Chron. 8:3).

Ham'math (hăm'ăth; *warm springs*), one of the fortified cities in the territory allotted to Naphtali (Josh. 19:35). It is not possible from this list to determine its position, but the notices of the Talmudists leave no doubt that it was near Tiberias, one mile distant—in fact, that it had its name, Chammath, "hot baths," because it contained those of Tiberias. Josephus mentions it under the name of Emmaus as a village not far from Tiberias. The *Hummâm*, at present three in number, still send up their hot and sulphureous water at a spot rather more than a mile south of the modern town. In the list of Levitical cities given out of Naphtali (Josh. 21:32), the name of this place seems to be given as Hammoth-dor, and in I Chron. 6:76 it is further altered to Hammon.

Hammeda'tha (hăm-ê-dā'thȧ), father of the infamous Haman, and commonly designated as "the Agagite" (Esth. 3:1, 10; 8:5; 9:24), though also without the title (9:10).

191. Code of Hammurabi, c. B. C. 1700

Ham'melech (hăm'ê-lĕk; *the king*), father of Jerahmeel, which latter was one of those commanded by Jehoiakim to arrest Jeremiah and Baruch (Jer. 36:26), B. C. before 605. It is uncertain whether this was the same as Hammelech, the father of Malchiah, into whose dungeon Jeremiah was afterward cast (Jer. 38:6), B. C. before 589. Others, however, regard the word in both cases as an appellative, referring in the first passage to Jehoiakim and in the latter to Zedekiah. *Compare* Hammoleketh.

Hammer, an implement described by four Hebrew words in the O. T. A heavy wooden mallet used for driving in tent pins was called a *hălmūth* (Judg. 5:26). Another type of heavy maul was called a *kēlăf* (Psa. 74:6). A smaller tool suitable for the gold beater (Isa. 41:7) and the quarrymen (Jer. 23:29) was called a *păṭish*. A tool evidently very similar to the *păṭish*, and doubtless a pointed hammer of the stone cutter and smith (I Kings 6:7; Isa. 44:12) and in general a workman's hammer (Judg. 4:21) was called a *măqqäbäh*. M. F. U.

Hammol'eketh (hă-mŏl'ê-kĕth; *the queen*), a woman introduced in the genealogies of Manasseh as daughter of Machir and sister of Gilead (I Chron. 7:17, 18), and as having among her three children Abiezer, from whose family sprang the great judge Gideon. The Jewish tradition is that "she used to reign over a portion of the land that belonged to Gilead," and that for that reason her lineage has been preserved. *See* Hammelech.

Ham'mon (hăm'ŏn; *glowing, warm*).

1. A town in the territory of Asher (Josh. 19:28), apparently midway between Naphtali and Sidon. Present site not certain.

2. A Levitical city of Naphtali assigned to the Gershonites (I Chron. 6:76), and answering to the similar names of *Hammath* and *Hammoth-dor* (q. v.).

Ham'moth-dor (hăm'mŏth-dōr; *hot springs of Dor*), a city of Naphtali (Josh. 21:32); probably the same as *Hammath* (q. v.).

Hammura'bi (hăm-ōō-rä'bê), the sixth king of the famous First Dynasty of Babylon, formerly identified with Amraphel of Gen. 14:1. This identification is now no longer possible as a result of the thousands of clay tablets recovered from the middle Euphrates city of Mari in 1937, and information based upon the Khorsabad List. New sources of information enable us to place Hammurabi's reign c. 1728-1686 (Albright). This is at least three centuries subsequent to the age of Abraham. Hammurabi exalted Babylon as his capital. His city had a ziggurat. He adorned the cities of Asshur and Nineveh. His reign was one of great prosperity, advance in astronomy, architecture, mathematics and literature. The Creation and Flood Epics were edited in his day and have descended to us in the form

193. Lamgi-Mari, Early King of Mari in the Time of Hammurabi

which they took under his reign. Copies of these epics dating about B. C. 640, were found in the library of Ashurbanipal at Nineveh. Hammurabi's Black Stele from the city of Ur was inscribed in both the Semitic and Sumerian languages. Hammurabi is famous in large part for his code of laws discovered in 1901-2 by Jacques de Morgan at Susa, where it had been carried by Elamite raiders. This famous code offers interesting parallels to Pentateuchal laws, preceding them by at least three centuries, and adapted to an urban irrigation culture in contrast to the simple agrarian culture of Palestine. M. F. U.

Ham'onah (hăm'ō-nà; *multitude*), the figurative name of the place in the valley in which the burial of Gog and his forces are prophetically announced to take place (Ezek. 39:16).

Ha'mon-gog (hā'mŏn-gŏg; *multitude of Gog*), the name given by the prophet Ezekiel (39:11) to the valley in which the slaughtered army of Gog are described as being buried. *See* Gog.

Ha'mor (hā'môr; *a he-ass*), a Hivite, from whom (or his sons) Jacob purchased the plot of ground in which Joseph was afterward buried (Gen. 33:19; Josh. 24:32; Acts 7:16, in which last passage the name is Anglicized *Emmor*), and whose son, Shechem, seduced Dinah (Gen. 34:2). As the latter appears to have founded the city of Shechem, Hamor is also named as the representative of its inhabitants (Judg. 9:28), in the time of Abimelech. Neither his character and influence (indicated by his title "prince"), nor his judicious behavior in the case of his son, saved him from the indiscriminate massacre by Dinah's brothers.

Hamu'el (hà-mū'ĕl; *heat*, or *anger of God*), the son of Mishma and (apparently) father of

DET.   HA – AM – MU – RA – BI

192. Hammurabi's name in cuneiform writing. The first sign is a determinative denoting a man's name.

Zacchur, of the tribe of Simeon (I Chron 4:26).

Ha'mul (hā'mŭl; *pitied*, *spared*), the second of the two sons of Pharez, son of Judah (I Chron. 2:5). He could not have been born, however, before the migration of Jacob into Egypt (as appears to be stated in Gen. 46:12), since Pharez was not at that time grown up (38:29).

Ha'mulites (hā'mū-līts); the descendants (Num. 26:21) of Hamul.

Hamu'tal (hă-mū'tăl; *kinsman of the dew*), daughter of Jeremiah of Libnah, wife of King Josiah and mother of King Jehoahaz (II Kings 23:31; 24:18; Jer. 52:1), B. C. 639.

Hanam'eel (hȧ-năm'ē-ĕl); R. V. Han'amel (*God has compassion*), the son of Shallum and cousin of Jeremiah, to whom, while Jerusalem was besieged, he sold a field in Anathoth (Jer. 32:6-12), B. C. about 590. The prohibition to sell Levitical estates applied merely to their alienating them from the tribe. "The transaction was intended to evince the certainty of restoration from the impending exile by showing that possessions, which could be established by documents, would be of future value to the possessor" (vers. 13-15).

Ha'nan (hā'năn; *merciful*).

1. One of the sons (or descendants) of Shashak, one of the chief men of Benjamin, residing at Jerusalem (I Chron. 8:23).

2. The last named of the six sons of Azel the Benjamite (I Chron. 8:38; 9:44).

3. Son of Maachah, and one of David's mighty men (I Chron. 11:43), B. C. 1000.

4. One of the Nethinim whose posterity were among those that returned from the captivity with Zerubbabel (Ezra 2:46; Neh. 7:49), B. C. 536.

5. One of the Levites who assisted Ezra in expounding the law to the people (Neh. 8:7), B. C. 445. He also sealed the covenant made by Nehemiah (10:10). He is probably the same as the one mentioned in chap. 13:13, as the son of Zaccur, who, on account of his integrity, was appointed to distribute the Levitical revenues among his brethren.

6. A chief of the people who subscribed the covenant drawn up by Nehemiah (Neh. 10:22). The same name occurs in ver. 26.

7. The son of Igdaliah, and an officer about the Lord's house. Into the chamber of his sons Jeremiah brought the Rechabites in order to test their temperance (Jer. 35:4), B. C. about 607.

Hanan'eel, Tower of (hȧ-năn'ē-ĕl; *God has favored*), a tower which formed part of the wall of Jerusalem (Neh. 3:1; 12:39). From these two passages, particularly from the former, it might almost be inferred that Hananeel was but another name for the Tower of Meah; at any rate they were close together, and stood between the sheep gate and the fish gate. This tower is further mentioned in Jer. 31:38. The remaining passage in which it is named (Zech. 14:10) also connects this tower with the "corner gate," which lay on the other side of the sheep-gate. The R. V. and R. S. V. read "tower of Hananel (hăn'ȧ-nĕl).

Hana'ni (hȧ-nā'nī; *gracious*).

1. One of the sons of Heman, appointed by lot, in the time of David, for the service of song in the sanctuary. Hanani had charge of the eighteenth division (I Chron. 25:4, 25), B. C. after 1000.

2. A prophet who rebuked Asa, king of Judah, for seeking help from the king of Syria against Baasha, king of Israel. In punishment for his defection from the true God, Hanani threatened him with wars during the remainder of his reign. Enraged at the prophet's boldness, the king put him in prison (II Chron. 16:7-10), B. C. 879. This Hanani is probably the same as the father of the prophet Jehu, who denounced Baasha (I Kings 16:1, 7) and King Jehoshaphat (II Chron. 19:2; 20:34).

3. One of the sons (or descendants) of Immer, who had taken a strange wife during the captivity (Ezra 10:20).

4. One of the "brethren" of Nehemiah, who, with others, went from Jerusalem to Shushan, sent probably by Ezra, and brought information concerning the condition of the returned Jews. Their information probably led to the mission of Nehemiah (Neh. 1:2). Hanani returned to Judea, and, together with one Hananiah, was placed in charge of the gates of Jerusalem, to see that they were opened and shut at the proper hours, morning and evening (7:2), B. C. 445.

5. A priest, one of the musicians who officiated in the ceremonial of purifying the walls of Jerusalem when they had been rebuilt (Neh. 12:36), B. C. 445.

Hanani'ah (hăn-ȧ-nī'ȧ; *Jehovah was favored*).

1. One of the sons of Zerubbabel, who was of the family of David (I Chron. 3:19). His sons are given as Pelatiah and Jesaiah (ver. 21).

2. One of the sons of Shishak, and a chief of the tribe of Benjamin (I Chron. 8:24).

3. A son of Heman, appointed by David to take charge of the sixteenth division of Levitical muscians (I Chron. 25:4, 23), B. C. about 1000.

4. "One of the king's captains" in the army of Uzziah, king of Judah (II Chron. 26:11), B. C. after 783.

5. An Israelite, of the family of Bebai, who renounced his Gentile wife after the captivity (Ezra 10:28), B. C. 456.

6. "The son of one of the apothecaries" (or makers of the sacred ointments and incense, Exod. 30:22-38), who repaired part of the wall of Jerusalem (Neh. 3:8), B. C. 445. Possibly the same as No. 5.

7. The son of Shelemiah, and one of the priests who repaired the wall of Jerusalem opposite their houses, "from above the horse gate" (Neh. 3:30), B. C. 445.

8. The "ruler of the palace," and the person who was associated with Nehemiah's brother, Hanani, in charge of the gates of Jerusalem. He is described as "a faithful man," and one that "feared God above many" (Neh. 7:2), B. C. 445. His office seems to have been one of authority and trust, and perhaps the same as that of Eliakim, who was "over the house" in the reign of Hezekiah.

9. The name of one of the "chief of the people" who sealed the covenant made by Nehemiah and the people to serve the Lord (Neh. 10:23), B. C. 445.

10. A priest, apparently son of Jeremiah, after the captivity (Neh. 12:12); probably the

same as one of those who celebrated the completion of the walls of Jerusalem (ver. 41), B. C. 445.

11. Son of Azur, a prophet of Gibeon, who uttered false prophecies in the fourth year of Zedekiah, king of Judah. He publicly prophesied in the temple that within two years Jeconiah and his fellow-captives, with the vessels of the Lord's house, which Nebuchadnezzar had taken away to Babylon, should be brought back to Jerusalem. He sought to uphold his prophecy by taking off from the neck of Jeremiah the yoke which he wore by divine command (Jer. 27:2), in token of the subjection of Judea and the neighboring countries to the Babylonian empire. Jeremiah was bidden to go and tell Hananiah that for the wooden yokes which he had broken he should make yokes of iron, "that they may serve Nebuchadnezzar." Jeremiah also added this rebuke and denunciation: "Hear, now, Hananiah: The Lord hath not sent thee; but thou makest this people to trust in a lie. Therefore, thus saith the Lord: Behold, I will cast thee from off the face of the earth: this year thou shalt die, because thou hast taught rebellion against the Lord. So Hananiah the prophet died the same year in the seventh month" (Jer. 28:1-17), B. C. about 593. "The history of Hananiah is of great interest, as throwing much light upon the Jewish politics of that eventful time, divided as parties were into the partisans of Babylon on one hand, and Egypt on the other. It also exhibits the machinery of false prophecies, by which the irreligious party sought to promote their own policy in a very distinct form" (McC. and S., *Cyc.*).

12. The father of Zedekiah, who was one of the princes to whom Michaiah reported Baruch's reading of Jeremiah's prophecies (Jer. 36:12), B. C. about 604.

13. The grandfather of Irijah, the captain of the guard at the gate of Benjamin, who arrested the prophet Jeremiah upon the supposition that he intended to desert to the Chaldeans (Jer. 37:13), B. C. 597.

14. The original name of Shadrach, one of the three Hebrew children, by which latter name he is better known (Dan. 1:6, 7, 11, 19; 2:17).

Hand (Heb. *yäd*), the *open* palm; *kăph*, the *hollow* of the hand; Gr. *cheir.*

Figurative. Being the member of the body which is chiefly employed in active service, the *hand* is used in Scripture with a great variety of applications founded upon and suggested by this natural employment, thus: (1) Hands are the symbols of human action; *pure* hands represent pure actions, *unjust* hands injustice; while "hands full of blood" denote actions stained with cruelty, etc. (Psa. 90:17; Job 9:30; I Tim. 2:8; Isa. 1:15). (2) *Washing* the hands was a symbol of innocence (Deut. 21:6, 7; Psa. 26:6; Matt. 27:24). (3) The hand, in general, was the symbol of *power* and *strength*, especially the *right* hand (Exod. 15:6; Psa. 17:7). "*Holding by the right hand*" was expressive of support (Psa. 73:23; Isa. 41:13); *standing at the right hand* indicated *protection* (Psa. 16:8; 109:31; 110:5); *to lean upon* the hand of another was a mark of *familiarity*, as well as of *superiority* (II Kings 5:18; 7:17);

to give the hand, as to a master, was a sign of *submission* (II Chron. 30:8, margin), and to kiss the hand denoted *homage*, (I Kings 19:18; Job 31:27); pouring water on another's hands signified to serve him (II Kings 3:11); to "seal up the hand" is to prevent one from working, e. g., by reason of the cold (Job 37:7); to withdraw the hand is to withhold support (Psa. 74:11), while to cut it off was to practice extreme self-denial (Matt. 5:30). The open hand is figurative of liberality (Deut. 15:8; Psa. 104:28), the closed hand of illiberality (Deut. 15:7). The right hand was used to indicate the South, and the left the North (Job 23:9; I Sam. 23:19; II Sam. 24:5). The right hand was the place of honor (I Kings 2:19) and power (Mark 14:62). "I will turn my hand upon thee" (Isa. 1:25) signifies a movement of the hand, hitherto at rest, either for the purpose of inflicting punishment upon the person named (Amos 1:8; Jer. 6:9; Ezek. 38:12; Psa. 81:14), or though this is seldom the case, for the purpose of saving one (Zech. 13:7).

Customs. Men lifted up their hands in prayer (Job 11:13; I Tim. 2:8), also in taking an oath (Gen. 14:22, etc.); smote the hands together over the head as a gesture of extreme grief (II Sam. 13:19); Jer. 2:37); the accuser stood at the right hand of the accused in a trial (Psa. 109:6; Zech. 3:1); the right hand of the priest was touched with blood of the consecration ram (Exod. 29:20; Lev. 8:23, 24). The Jews washed their hands before eating (Matt. 15:2; Mark 7:3), or after touching an unclean person (Lev. 15:11); servants were directed by movements of the hand of master or mistress (Psa. 123:2); the hand was kissed in idolatrous worship (Job 31:27); treaties were made and sureties entered into by joining hands (II Kings 10:15; Job 17:3; Prov. 6:1; 17:18); the hand was placed under the thigh of a person to whom an oath was made (Gen. 24:2, 3; 47:29, 31); joy was shown by clapping the hands (II Kings 11:12; Psa. 47:1); while smiting them together expressed extreme anger (Num. 24:10; Ezek. 21:14, 17).

Handbreadth. *See* Metrology, I.

HANDICRAFTS.

The word handicraft is not found in Scripture, and yet it is very appropriate, inasmuch as most of the mechanical work of olden times was performed by hand.

1. **Earliest Examples.** Archaeological discoveries have revealed remarkable evidences left by the non-Semitic Sumerians who arrived in the Plain of Shinar in lower Babylonia sometime before 4000 B. C. The excavations of Abram's city of Ur have uncovered exquisite jewels, many of which may be seen in the University Museum of Philadelphia. The horde of jewels recovered from the Royal Tombs is especially valuable. Queen Shubad's tomb was fabulously adorned. Apparently demonstrating complete loyalty to the beautiful queen, sixty-eight of her court ladies had walked alive into the tomb. In full regalia, the royal sepulchre remained untouched until 1927 when retrieved by Sir Leonard Woolley. The artistic skill of the workmen of that day is revealed in the Queen's diadem of minute

beads, palmettes, flowerettes, rosettes and exquisitely thin rolled gold. This splendor furnished the background for carved stags, antelopes and bearded bulls. The Queen wore a jeweled cap of gold, its silver fillets adorned with beech leaves. Heavy gold earrings were in her ears. She was also bedecked with a necklace, gold pins, and fish-shaped amulets. Another remarkable example of Sumerian art was a solid gold helmet of a warrior. Also found were finely wrought golden tumblers, dainty cosmetic boxes, a paint cup, and a silver toilet box with a lid carved from sea shells showing a lion attacking a goat. At Tepe Gawra, an ancient city mound in north Mesopotamia, objects of gold, silver and electrum were dug up. Also found were ivory combs banded with gold and studded with precious stones. Jewels go back to very early times in Egypt and seem only to have been preceded by the Sumerians. Stone necklaces and bracelets from the Badarian civilization (c. B. C. 3500) have been found. Predynastic Egyptian artists developed fine styles. By the Twelfth Dynasty, from c. B. C. 2000-1750, Egyptian craftsmanship in jewelry reached a high mark in beauty, color and design. Egyptian jewelry is noted for its good taste and its fine execution. Sumerian and early Egyptian artists are also known for their skill in wood, leather, stone and various other materials.

2. **Biblical Notices.** The first craftsman we read of in Scripture, Tubal-Cain (Gen. 4:22) was a worker in metals, indicating that metalworking was one of the earliest crafts among the Hebrews. This circumstance becomes so much the more significant as the general Hebrew term for an artisan, *hädäsh*, primitively denotes a worker in metals, or at least in some hard material. The Hebrews, when they left Egypt, had among them skilled workmen in gold, silver, brass, wood, leather, as is evident from the building of the tabernacle. But, when these artists died, the development of the mechanical arts seemed to have come to a standstill (Judg. 5:8; I Sam. 13:19). Even in the time of Solomon the Hebrews needed the teaching of the Phoenicians (II Sam. 5:11; I Kings 5:1, sq.; 7:13, sq.).

Manual labor was generally held in low esteem by the Greeks, in later times many free citizens declining to engage in it at all. The Romans also seem to have thought that there was something objectionable in mechanical labor, and in many wealthy homes this was mostly done by slaves. To pursue a trade was, at least in later times, not considered degrading among the Jews. Indeed, at this time all the rabbinical authorities were working at some trade, and it became the fashion to affect hard labor: the great Hillel being a woodcutter; his rival Shammai a carpenter; and among the celebrated rabbis of after times we find shoemakers, tailors, carpenters, sandal makers, smiths, potters, builders, etc. Nor were they ashamed of their manual labor. It was a rabbinical principle, that "Whoever does not teach his son a trade, is as if he brought him up to be a robber."

Apothecary (Exod. 30:25, 35; 37:29; Eccles. 10:1), rendered "confectionaries" (I Sam. 8: 13). *See* Perfumer, below; article *Perfume*.

Armorer. In I Sam. 8:12, it is recorded that Samuel told the Israelites that if they chose a king he would take their sons and set them to make his instruments of war; i. e., to be engaged in the arts of warfare rather than in those of peace. As to the work of the armorer, it can be better understood by consulting article *Armor*.

Baker (Heb. *'äphäh*, to *cook*), makers of bread and pastry, a department then more varied than that of cook (Gen. 40:1, sq.; 41:10; Hos. 7:4, 6). In Jer. 37:21 it is stated that bread was brought daily "out of the baker's street," a baker's bazaar, which would indicate that bakers formed a guild by themselves.

In Egypt the bakery profession was one of great importance. A Biblical reminiscence of this was the unfortunate baker who was placed in prison in the Joseph story. The baker's dream recounts all sorts of fancy baked food (Gen. 40). Egyptian bakers were required to give strict account of their stocks of materials to the overseer of granaries. Miniature models of such scenes have come down to us from excavated tombs. Closely associated with the baker was the miller. Mother and daughter had this task among the common people. The job consisted in turning with wooden handles the heavy grinding stones, sometimes a foot-and-a-half in diameter. In more primitive times the grain was simply crushed in a curvature of the rock with a small hand stone. Public millers had a humming trade, asses turning the stones. At Ostia, the port of Rome, and at Pompeii, recovered mills indicate a booming business requiring large storehouses. The Bible refers frequently to the miller (Exod. 11:15; Judg. 16:21; Matt. 24: 41; Luke 17:2). *M. F. U.*

194. An Egyptian Tomb Model, Showing a Brickmaker at Work

Brickmaker. Brickmaking, a mere manual occupation with nothing to stimulate the clever workmen to creative craftsmanship, was only followed by the meanest of the community who had not even the satisfaction of working for themselves. Thus, the Israelites were forced to this mean occupation in Egypt. Bricks were a government monopoly. The pay for a tale of them was a small remuneration for this laborious drudgery in mud. Egypt and Babylonia with mighty rivers and alluvial silt excelled in brick construction. (*See* Brick). However, these lowly workmen were essential to building trades in Biblical lands. Guilds or unions of brickmakers travelled in groups through the country ready to perform service where needed. An example of large-scale brick making and brick laying comes to us from the splendid reign of Thutmose III (c. 1483-1450 B. C.). The tomb of Thutmose's grand visier, named Rekhmire, near Thebes, is adorned with scenes and inscriptions describing his

195. Modern Egyptian Mud Bricks Drying in the Sun

career. In one of these pictures Rehkmire leans on a staff and inspects stone-cutters, brickmakers, sculptors and builders who toil before him. Brick making in ancient Egypt was a process involving the breaking up of the Nile mud with mattocks, moistening it with water and then mixing it with sand and chopped straw (Exod. 5:6-19). Then placed in molds, it was put in the sun to bake. Semitic foreigners appear on the tomb making and laying bricks, working on the Temple of Amun. The brick-layers say: "He supplies us with bread, beer and every good sort" while the taskmaster says to the builders: "The rod is in my hand; be not idle." (Cf. P. E. Newberry, *The Life of Rekhmara;* James Breasted, *Ancient Records of Egypt*, 1906-7, II, Section 758 ff.). This reference to brick making is all the more significant inasmuch as Thutmose III (according to the Massoretic chronology), was the pharoah of the oppression. *M. F. U.*

Builders. Besides brickmaking and bricklaying, carpentry and stone-masonry were important trades in the ancient world.

1. **Carpenters.** The Egyptian carpenter was more important than the Palestinian. There were palaces and wealthy houses to beam and trim, wooden mummy cases to cut out, furniture to make, irrigation pumps (*shadufs*) to erect, large rivergoing vessels and smaller boats to make, and implements of various sorts to fashion. Especially noteworthy are the large barges which transported huge blocks of limestone and sandstone and giant obelisks; also, such large works as pillars, gates, temple and palace doors. Carpenter's tools such as adzes, axe heads and chisels have been re-

covered. Palestinian carpenters in early Israel did not develop a high degree of skill. Palestinian dwellings, even of the peasantry, were of mud brick or stone so that woodwork for construction purposes was at a minimum. Solomon, therefore, had to import Phoenician craftsmen to build his royal palaces and the temple. After the Solomonic era, however, carpentry was cultivated. Nebuchadnezzar II carried away carpenters (Jer. 24:1). The Palestinian carpenter must have had tools very similar to those used in Egypt. Sandstone served as a plane, saws with flint teeth were mounted on a frame, and a heavy stone served as a hammer. The adze was an all-around tool. At the time of Isaiah carpenters developed great skill, not only in common construction work, but in idol making (Cf. Is. 44:12-17).

2. **Stone Masons.** The worker in stone was indispensable in Palestine as in the land of the Nile. The vast palaces, tombs, pyramids, temples and obelisks required consummate skill on the part of a multitude of stone workers. The mighty pyramids with their minute constructional accuracy testify to the high development of the art of construction in early

196. Egyptian Stone Artisans

Dynastic Egypt. In early Israel before the prosperity of the Davidic-Solomonic era, stone houses among the Israelites were not common; Hiram of Tyre's craftsmen, however, gave impetus to stone masonry. There were building trades in Jerusalem during the Hebrew monarchy. When public buildings or the temple fell into disrepair, money was raised by public subscription. And it was paid out "to the carpenters and the builders who worked upon the House of the Lord and to the masons and the stone cutters, as well as to buy timber and quarried stone for making repairs on the House of the Lord. (II Kings 12:11, 12). Timber was cut by woodmen specially qualified for this work. Solomon boasted that the Sidonians were expert timber-cutters. Solomon's temple was built out of fine quarry-chiseled marble (I Kings 7:9-12). Jesus laid stress upon the importance of a solid foundation in building in a country where heavy rains might occur (Matt. 7:24-27). *M. F. U.*

Calker, a repairer of leaks in a vessel (Ezek. 27:9, 27), where Tyre is represented as a ship.

Carpenter. *See* Wood, Workers in, below, Builders.

Carver, the rendering of six Hebrew words, meaning to engrave. sculpture, and carve. Carving was carried on to a great extent by the Egyptians both upon buildings and furniture. The arts of carving and engraving were much in demand in the building of the tabernacle and the temple (Exod. 31:5; 35:33; I Kings 6:18, 35; Psa. 74:6), as well as in the ornamentation of the priestly dresses. Carving of timber is mentioned (Exod. 31:5), and a minute description of the process of idol making is given in Isa. 44:13, sq.

Confectioner. *See* Perfumer, below; article Perfume.

Dyer. This word does not occur in Scripture, but we have mention of skin dyed, and of various colored curtains in the tabernacle (Exod. 25:4, 5; 26:14, etc.), and of Lydia, as a seller of purple (Acts 16:14). The dyeing of purple was actively carried on, especially in Thyatira, and an inscription found there particularly mentions the guild of dyers of that place.

Embalming, a distinct craft. *See* article Embalm.

Embroiderer. *See* articles Embroiderer; Needlework.

Founder (Judg. 17:4; Jer. 6:29; 10:9, 14; 51:17). *See* Metal, Workers in, below.

Fuller (Heb. *kābăs*, to *wash;* Gr. *gnapheus*, a clothes *dresser*). The art of the fuller is of great antiquity, and seems to have, at a very early period, reached a comparative degree of perfection. Many persons, both men and women, were engaged in cleaning cloths and stuffs of various kinds, and the occupations of the fuller form some of the subjects of Egyptian sculptures. It is probable that they were only a subdivision of the dyers. The trade of the fullers, so far as it is mentioned in Scripture, appears to have consisted chiefly in cleansing garments and whitening them (Mark 9:3). The process of fulling and cleansing cloth, so far as it may be gathered from the practice of other nations, consisted in treading or stamping on the garments with the feet or with bats in tubs of water, in which some alkaline substance answering the purpose of soap had been dissolved. In early times, before and even after the invention of soap, potash, niter, and several earths were employed for cleaning cloths, as well as various herbs, many of which are still in use among the Arabs. The "fuller's field" (II Kings 18:17; Isa. 7:3; 36:2) was near Jerusalem, and its mention would seem to indicate that it was a well-known resort of this craft. *See* Fuller's Field, Soap.

Gardener. *See* Garden, Agriculture.

Glass Worker. The Egyptians and Phoenicians very early made opaque glass, and developed the art of making vases, jewelry, bottles, etc. *See* article on Glass.

Goldsmith. The Hebrews called this technician "a refiner" (*sōrēph*), melter of gold (Neh. 3:8, 32; Isa. 40:19; 41:7; 46:6; Mal. 3:2, 3). From very early antiquity gold has been used in jewels.

1. **Egyptian.** Gold was known long before silver in Egypt. Silver much later came from Asia Minor and was known as "white gold" by Egyptian jewelers. Gold was dug from the eastern desert and the Egyptian wadis. Its shining splendor attracted men before they knew how to write. Gold was very commonly used in Egypt, even being covered with inlay of stones or enamel. King Tutankhamun's solid coffin and his death mask inlaid with precious stones and enamel are well-known

examples of Egyptian prodigality in the use of this metal. The pectoral pendant of King Senwosret (c. B. C. 1887-1849), found in the tomb of his daughter Princess Sit Hat Hor Yunet, near her father's pyramid at el Lahun, is of gold lavishly inlaid with precious stones. The cartouche of the king is at the center. This was very likely the pharaoh who occupied the throne when Israel entered Egypt.

2. **Babylonian.** The head tire of Queen Shub-ad of Sumerian Ur (c. B. C. 2700-2500), recovered from the Royal Tombs by Woolley, is a superb illustration of the work of Sumerian-Semitic artists who were executing their finest work in gold c. 3200-2600 B. C. The gold flowers springing from the "Spanish comb," the fillet of golden leaves, the heavy golden earrings and the various necklaces done in semi-precious stones give us a good idea of the wonderful skill of the Sumerian goldsmiths. Also glyptic artists produced solid gold cylinder seals with fine intaglio designs. These show exquisite artistic beauty, as well as a vast variety of golden cups, helmets, and other objets d'art. Gold and electrum objects from Mesopotamia and Tepe Gawra would grace any artistic display of the present day. In ancient Oriental kingdoms special quarters were given over to the goldsmiths, who created fashionable articles for the court and sacred vessels for the temples.

3. **Biblical.** In the Old Testament anklets, bracelets, diadems, necklaces, nose rings, earrings, finger rings, crowns, coronets, camel crescents, gold hair nets, pendants, perfume boxes, jewel caskets and amulets are mentioned. Solar discs and lunar crescents (Cf. Isa. 3:18) have been excavated at Ras Shamra, ancient Ugarit. Amulets or magical pendants to ward off evil spirits were very common. The Jewish priest's ephod (Exod. 39) had four rows of three stones each, one gem representing each of the twelve Israelite tribes. Mentioned are "sardius, topaz and carbuncle" in the first row; and the second row, "an emerald, a sapphire, and a diamond;" and the third row, "a jacinth, an agate, and an amethyst;" and the fourth row, "a beryl, an onyx and a jasper;" they were enclosed in settings of gold filigree. Gems of gold fastened the resplendent breast plate to the high priest's ephod at the shoulders (Exod. 39:22-24). The lavish jewel finds at Ur, the home of Abraham, and other Mesopotamian cities make the account in Exodus thoroughly credible. The golden calf (Exod. 32) wrought out of the people's "jewels of silver and jewels of gold" is another example of the art of the goldsmith among the Hebrews. Rebecca's jewelry consisted of a "gold ring weighing half a shekel, two bracelets for her arms weighing ten gold shekels" (Gen. 24:22, 30). Saul and Jonathan had jewels of beauty. In II Sam. 1:10 the Amalekite says concerning the slaying of Saul: "And I took the crown that was on his head and the armlet which was on his arm and I have brought them here unto my lord." David's royal jewels included not only a crown but buckles, shields and spears. His vast bounty as a result of his conquests enabled him to amass a horde of jewels that constituted a royal fortune and gave his son Solomon a start on his splendid reign (Cf.

I Chron. 28, 29). To the vast wealth in gold and precious stones inherited from his father David, Solomon added great quantities of metal and precious stones acquired by tribute, exploitation, marriage doweries and his own business enterprises in spice trade, horses, copper-mining in the Arabah and trade at Ezion-geber. Especially did a vast influx of gold characterize his reign. *M. F. U.*

Figurative. The prevalent idea of No. 2 is the *subtle* work of the fine arts, and with this well agrees the use of the word in Prov. 6:18, "the heart that *deviseth* wicked imaginations" (comp. I Sam. 23:9; literally, to *forge*). In the passage, "Behold, I have graven thee upon the palms of my hands" (Isa. 49:16), there is an allusion to the ancient custom of puncturing ornamental figures and mementoes upon the hand, arm, and forehead, and coloring the punctures with indigo, cypress, etc. This gives us the figure of Zion being as close to God as he is to himself, and facing him amid all the emotions of his divine life.

Leather, Workers in (Heb. *'ōr;* Gr. *dermatinos,* Matt. 3:4). The probability is that the Israelites obtained much of their knowledge of the making of leather from the Egyptians. Part of the process of curing skins is introduced in the sculptures, and that of dyeing them is mentioned in the Bible (Exod. 25:5). In one instance a man is represented dipping the hide into a vase, probably containing water, in which it was suffered to soak, preparatory to the lime being applied to remove the hair, a process very similar to that adopted at the present day in the East. The tanning and preparation of leather was also a branch of art in which the Egyptians evinced considerable skill; the leather cutters constituted one of the principal subdivisions of the fourth class, and a district of the city was exclusively appropriated to them in the Libyan part of Thebes. Of leather they made thongs, shoes, sandals, the coverings and seats of chairs or sofas, bow cases, and most of the ornamental furniture of the chariot; harps were also adorned with colored leather, and shields and numerous other things were covered with skin prepared in various ways. Reference is made (II Kings 1:8; Matt. 3:4) to girdles of leather.

Mason. *See* article House; Stone, Workers in, below.

Metal, Workers in.

1. **Egyptian.** Metal working and mining developed early in Egypt. In the Pyramid Age (c. 2900 B. C.-c. 2450 B. C.) skilled metal workers were producing ingenious bronze rip saws, often six feet in length for heavy woodwork. The huge pyramid stone blocks were cut by special-type saws. Vast quantities of gold for Egypt's skillful goldsmiths were imported from east African Punt. Egyptian craftsmen made wide use of copper, perhaps unintentionally alloyed at the earlier periods. As early as the First Dynasty, Egyptians pioneered in the copper-rich Sinai Peninsula. They developed skill in copper smelting and compounding metals, evidently knowing the value of alloys. Egyptians had slave labor imported from Midian and Edom, who worked first in the Sinai copper mines and later in the turquoise mines, well known from the First

Dynasty on. The famous Queen Hatshepsut, who lived c. 1500 B. C. and was evidently the contemporary of Moses, cultivated the turquoise mines of Sinai. In this Sinai region occurs a very early alphabetic script. What is most interesting is that Moses himself is said to have written in this very region.

2. **Mesopotamian.** Like the Egyptians, the early non-Semitic Sumerians before 3000 B. C. and later the Semitic Babylonians developed very high skill in various types of metal work. Their work in gold is now well known. They also used copper, later bronze, and finally iron. Sacred and non-sacred utensils, tools of every description, weapons, idols, and ornaments have been produced in profusion by the archaeologist's spade.

3. **Israelite.** References to metals in the O. T. are numerous. Gold, silver, iron and copper-bronze appear frequently on its pages. Gold, silver and copper were used in the tabernacle. David took vast quantities of copper in war, and his successor, Solomon, developed the lucrative copper-mining and copper-smelting industries in the Arabah. Solomon lavishly used gold, silver and copper in the construction of the temple. His seaport-copper refinery at Ezion-geber has been unearthed at Tell el-Kheleifeh by Nelson Glueck in 1938-39. Blast furnaces there were constructed as to take advantage of the fierce winds sweeping down the Arabah. Ingots of raw copper not only supplied the vast quantities needed for the temple and palaces at Jerusalem, but also furnished Solomon's stock-in-trade for his *tarshish* fleets which brought back exotic woods, precious stones, gold, ivory and apes (I Kings 9:26-28). Solomon's "tarshish" ships were really refinery-fleets, as Albright has shown. They were similar to the Phoenician fleets in the Mediterranean which transported the same ore from the refineries of Sardinia and Spain. Iron was introduced into Israel in the period of Saul who, as a result of his victories over the Philistines, broke their tight monopoly on this important metal (I Sam. 13:19, 20). When Saul and David broke the power of the Philistines, the iron-smelting formula became public property and metal was popularized in Israel. This worked an economic revolution in Palestine, making possible a higher standard of living. It is not surprising, therefore, to read that in amassing materials supplied to Solomon for the building of the temple "David prepared iron in abundance for the nails, for the doors of the gates and for the couplings" (I Chron. 23:2). Also, mention is made of saws, arrows and axes of iron (I Chron. 20:3). For the working of metals, three different trades were early developed in Israel: that of the *smith* in iron (Isa. 44:12; II Chron. 24:12), including the *locksmith* (II Kings 24:16); the *coppersmith* (I Kings 7:14) and the *gold* and *silversmith* (Judg. 17:4, A. V. "founder"). We read of axes and other iron instruments (Num. 35:16; Deut. 19:5; 27:5), while vessels and cooking utensils were of brass (or copper). The working (hammering) of iron was probably known to the patriarchs. In later times arms and other things, formerly made of copper, such as chains, bolts and

armor, were made of iron (Cf. Judge 16:21 with Job 20:24; Psa. 107:16, 149:8; Isa. 45:2). Copper-working apparently was not older than that of iron, both originating with Tubal Cain (Gen. 4:22), only copper ore, being found more frequently solid in large masses, and more easy to work than iron ore, was more widely spread in earlier ages. The iron of very early antiquity was meteorite, and not smelted from ore. Smelted iron did not come into common use until the Iron Age, 1200-300 B. C. Copper was used for all sorts of vessels, weapons, armor, mirror (Exod. 38:8), and statues (Dan. 5:4, 23). Casting was certainly known and practiced among the Hebrews (Judg. 17:4; I Kings 7:46; II Chron. 4:17). In the last two passages we are told that the workmen employed by Solomon cast the metal vessels, etc., of the temple in the clay soil of Jordan. *M. F. U.*

Perfumer. The perfumes used in the religious services, and in later times in the funeral rites of monarchs, imply knowledge and practice in the art of the "apothecaries" (i. e., perfumers), who appear to have formed a guild or association (Exod. 30:25, 35; Neh. 3:8; II Chron. 16:14; Eccles 7:1; 10:1; Eccles. 38:8). *See* Ointment, Perfume.

Orientals delighted in perfumes and cosmetics. Especially in Egypt a knowledge of fragrant spices and oils was cultivated. The carved back of the chair of King Tutankhamun in the Cairo Muesum shows the queen placing the finest perfume of the realm on the shoulder of the young king. From the ornate tomb of Queen Shub-ad of Ur, before the third millennium B. C. on down to noble ladies of many lands, examples survive of the perfumer's art. And toilet-sets from the boudoirs of many ancient queens have survived to illustrate the development of the beautician's art. The spice and frankincense trade of the ancient world built up enormous wealth. Moses and the Israelites learned much from the perfume industry of Egypt.

1. **Sacred Incense.** Moses in giving the formula for incense to be used exclusively in the tabernacle specified as follows: "take . . . sweet spices, stacte and onycha, and galbanum: sweet spices with pure frankincense: of each there shall be a like weight; and thou shalt make of it an incense of perfume after the art of the perfumer, seasoned with salt . . . and thou shalt beat some of it very small" (Exod. 30:34-36). Stacte was a gum resin exuded from the storax tree. Onycha was probably related to benzoin. Galbanum was a brown yellowish resin exuded from a carrot-like plant found in the ancient East. Frankincense was a white aromatic gum secreted from trees related to the terebinth, found in S. W. Arabia, Abyssinia and India.

2. **Sacred Anointing Oil.** In the holy anointing oil (used in the tabernacle) the "finest spices" were enumerated in Exod. 30: 22-25 as "liquid myrrh," "sweet smelling cinnamon," "aromatic cane," "cassia," . . . "and of olive oil a hin: and he shall make of these a sacred anointing oil blended as by the perfumer: a holy anointing oil it shall be." Myrrh was made from an aromatic resin exuded from a balsam-like shrub which grows in parts of the Arabian desert or from Syrian-Palestinian rock roses. Punt, in east Africa, had groves of myrrh trees. Queen Hatshepsut's sailors from Egypt in the fifteenth century B. C. were amazed to see native huts built among these groves. Sweet cinnamon was made from the bark of a tree known in the Solomonic era in Palestine and in Babylonia. Cassia was a type of cinnamon. Calamus, or sweet cane, came from a far country (Jer. 6:20). It is mentioned as a sweet smelling plant in the Song of Solomon 4:14. It is evidently of the flag-family and thrives in damp places, as does the iris.

3. **Other Perfumes.** Spikenard (Syrian nard) was a highly valuable ingredient of ointments. It may have come from the pasture lands of the Himalayas. At any rate, it was extremely expensive. Judas criticized the extravagance of Mary when she anointed Christ's feet with it (John 12:3-9). Henna, or camphire, a yellow-flowered shrub furnishing ancient dyeing matter for finger and toe nails was often mixed with spikenard. Aloes may be Indian sandalwood or, as thought by some, the gum of the eagle tree of India. Mixed with myrrh and cinnamon it was a highly valued perfume (Psa. 45:8; Prov. 7:17).

Plasterer. *See* articles House; Plaster.

Potter. Pottery making is one of the oldest crafts of civilized man. The art of ceramics was invented at the close of the Late Stone Age in the Near East, perhaps as early as 5000 B. C. The simple pottery sherds which have survived the millennia tell a story of the tastes and destinies of nations. Recovered pottery fragments are one of the best allies of the archaeologist in dating ancient civilizations and identifying strata of culture from varied mounds. Archaeologists identify ancient cultures by the type of pottery unearthed. For example, in Mesopotamia, the exquisite Halafian ware (c. B. C. 4500-4000) from Tell Halaf, marks a specific culture. Samarran ware, found at Samarra on the Tigris, dates c. B. C. 3800. Characteristic Obeidan pottery from Tell Obeid near Ur marks civilization c. B. C. 3500. Warkan ware from Erech (Uruk), dates around B. C. 3200. Jemdet Nasr ware dates c. B. C. 3200-3000. The invention of the pottery wheel marked a revolution in ancient cultures and paralleled the beginning of the historical period in Egypt (c. B. C. 3000). At Lachish in south Judah a potter's workshop with a simple pottery wheel dating from c. B. C. 1500 was unearthed. Pottery found at Jericho, at Ugarit, at Megiddo and practically all other Palestinian sites illustrates the Biblical notices of this ancient craft. The Israelites, of course, had pottery in the wilderness. Biblical references of this craft occur in Isa. 45:9 and Jer. 18:3. At Jerusalem there was a royal establishment of potters (I Chron. 4:23) from whose employment, and from the fragments cast away in the process, the Potter's Field perhaps received its name (Isa. 30:14).

Figurative. There are several allusions to both the potter and his fabrics. The breaking of pottery is used, from its fragile nature, to illustrate the ease with which God punishes the wicked (Psa. 2:9; Isa. 30:14; Jer. 19:11);

from its cheapness, the depreciation of good men (Lam. 4:2). The thorough acquaintance of the potter with both the clay and the vessel that he made therefrom is used to illustrate God's knowledge of humanity. The power of the potter in molding the clay is used to illutrate the absolute power of God in molding the destinies of men (Rom. 9:21). To place one's self as clay in the hands of God, as the potter, is a striking figure of complete trust and surrender (Isa. 64:8). The phrase "throw to the potter" (Zech. 11:13) is apparently a proverbial expression for contemptuous treatment, although we have no means of tracing its origin satisfactorily. "As the words read, they can only be understood as signifying that the potter was in the house of Jehovah when the money was thrown to him: that he had either some work to do there, or that he had come there to bring some earthenware for the temple kitchens" (see 14:20; Keil and Delitzsch, *Commentary*, in loco.). M. F. U.

Refiner. *See* Metals, Workers in.

Rope. Ropes, strings, and various kinds of twine were made by the ancients of flax and other materials. For large ropes of ordinary quality, and for common purposes, the fibers of the date tree were employed by the Egyptians as at the present day, and many specimens of these durable materials have been found in the excavations of Upper and Lower Egypt. In a tomb at Thebes, of the time of Thutmose III, is represented the process of twisting thongs of leather, which is probably the same as that adopted in ropemaking.

The Scripture references to rope are but few: The binding of Samson with them by Delilah (Judg. 16:11, 12); in Ahithopel's counsel to drag down with ropes the supposed place of David's retreat (II Sam. 17:13); the servants of the defeated Syrian king, Benhadad, coming to Ahab with ropes round their necks (I Kings 20:31, 32), as a sign of absolute surrender; and in the account of Paul's shipwreck (Acts 27:32).

Figurative. Isaiah directs a woe against those guilty of impiety thus: "Woe unto them that draw iniquity with cords of vanity, and sin as it were with a cart rope" (5:18). "There is a bitter sarcasm involved in the bold figure employed. They were proud of their unbelief, but this unbelief was like a halter with which, like beasts of burden, they were harnessed to sin, and therefore to the punishment of sin, which they went on drawing farther and farther, in ignorance of the wagon behind them" (Delitzsch, *Com.*, in loco).

Shipbuilder. The Hebrews were not a seafaring or ship-building people but sea-faring occupations were very prominent in the great empires on the Nile, Tigris-Euphrates and the Phoenician coastal cities.

1. **Egyptian.** The Egyptians were the earliest Mediterranean boat-builders, with the Phoenicians of Byblos running a close second. Small flat-bottomed boats were useful for fishing and fowling in the Delta marshes. Very large barges transported stone from Upper Egypt. Trading boats plied the river as well as funereal barges which carried mummies and tomb-adornments along the river. Some of the barges were sacred to the sun god.

2. **Phoenician.** The Phoenicians early developed a reputation for their boats and skill in manning them. Although these were often no larger than a coastal New England fishing boat, they carried on extensive trade over all the Mediterranean. With the masts of cedar, flooring of fir, oars of oak and rowing benches of ivory inlaid with box wood and sail cloth made in the looms of Egypt, these vessels put out from Sidon, Arvad, and Tyre. In the Solomonic era (c. 960 B. C.) Phoenician boatbuilders and mariners were employed by the Hebrew monarch to develop a *tarshish* ("ore smelting") fleet at Ezion-geber, modern Tell el Kheleifeh, to carry smelted copper ore from the Arabah to southern Arabian and north African ports. There it was exchanged for gold, silver, ivory and two kinds of monkeys.

3. **Mesopotamian.** At a very early period the Sumerians and later the Babylonians built boats of reed basket work caulked with bitumen. The Assyrians constructed skin boats and rafts of timber by the eighth century B. C. These were precursors to the *guffahs* which still ply the Euphrates. The sea-borne traffic for Babylon, which arrived through the Persian Gulf, from India and Africa, bringing exotic spices and luxury articles, consisted of wooden boats not drastically different from the Phoenician and Egyptian craft.

4. **Greek.** By 600 B. C. the Greeks were developing distinctive boats, making improvements on Egyptian and Phoenician models. Bow and stern were turned up. Corinthian war ships were double-decked, one deck for rowers and the other for fighters. Their ships were large, requiring anchors and employing slave labor.

5. **Biblical.** The tribe of Dan apparently had ships (Judg. 5:17). Solomon's *tarshish* fleet (I Kings 9:26-28) takes a prominent place but it was an unusual feature of Solomon's prosperity and splendor. Ferry boats crossing the humble Jordan are mentioned (II Sam. 19: 15, 18). Small ferries still cross the Jordan. The Galilean fishing boats in which Jesus went back and forth across the Sea of Galilee are prominent in the Gospels. The ships in which the Apostle Paul sailed in his Mediterranean missionary journeys are mentioned conspicuously in the Books of Acts. M. F. U.

Shoemaker. *See* Leather, Workers in, above.

Silversmith. *See* Metals, Workers in, above.

Stonecutter. *See* Stone, Workers in.

Stone, Workers in.—1. **Egyptians.** The Egyptians, at a remote period, used stone implements; and we find that stone-tipped arrows continued to be occasionally used for hunting long after the metal head had been commonly adopted. The same prejudice in favor of an ancient custom retained the use of stone knives for certain religious purposes, examples of which have been found in excavations and tombs.

"The most ancient buildings in Egypt were constructed of limestone, hewn from the mountains bordering the valley of the Nile; but so soon as the durability of sandstone was ascertained the quarries of Silsilis were opened, and these materials were universally adopted. Immense blocks of stone were quarried here and transported to their destined localities.

197. A Cosmetic Jar from Tutankhamun's Tomb

The obelisks transported from the quarries of Syene, at the first cataracts, to Thebes and Heliopolis, vary in size from seventy to ninety-three feet in length. Small blocks of stone were sent from the quarries by water to their places of destination in boats or on rafts, and if any land carriage was required, they were placed on sledges and rollers; but those of very large dimensions were dragged the whole way by men, overland. . . . The immense weight of stone shows that the Egyptians were well acquainted with mechanical powers and the mode of applying a locomotive force with the most wonderful success. . . . The hieroglyphics on obelisks and other granite monuments are sculptured with a minuteness and finish which is surprising, even if they had used steel as highly tempered as our own" (Wilkinson, *Ancient Egyptians*, II, 156, 300 sq.).

2. Hebrews. Stone work among the Hebrews consisted of the hewing and smoothing of stones and marble for great buildings. They were also skillful in cutting and engraving precious stones for ornaments (Exod. 35:33). From the fact that David secured masons from Hiram (II Sam. 5:11; I Chron. 14:1) we infer that the Hebrews were not as skillful as the Tyrians.

As will be seen from the above, the ancients employed substantially the same appliances as are used in working stone today, and the great pyramids, temples, aqueducts, etc., of the East testify to their skill.

Tailor. *See* article Dress.

Tanner. *See* Leather, Workers in, above.

Tools. Metal workers used the anvil, hammer (Isa. 41:7), tongs, chisel, or graving tool (Exod. 32:4), bellows (Jer. 6:29), melting pot (Prov. 17:3), and for large castings the furnace (Ezek. 22:18).

Weaver. The weaving of the common, coarser, and finer woolen, linen, cotton, and hair cloths into garments, covers, tent curtains, etc., was the business of the housewives, as well as the spinning of flax, wool, cotton, goat's and camel's hair (Exod. 35:25, sq.; II Kings 23:7; Prov. 31:13, 19). But the art of weaving, strictly so called (Exod. 27:16), with inwrought flowers and figures, was done by men, as well as the weaving of fine bysus, in which the sons of Selah were engaged even in Egypt (I Chron. 4:21). Hence the particular manipulations of this business were so generally known that in figurative language we often read of the weavers' beam (I Sam. 17:7; II Sam. 21: 19), the shuttle (Job 7:6), warp and woof (Lev. 13:48, sq.; Judg. 16:13), etc. *See* article on Embroiderer.

Wood, Workers in.—1. **Egyptian.** Carpenters and cabinetmakers were a very numerous class of workmen, and their occupations form one of the most important subjects in the paintings which represent the Egyptian trades. From these we learn that the Egyptians made the various wooden parts of houses (doors, etc.), boxes, tables, sofas, chairs, etc. With the carpenters may be mentioned the wheelwrights, makers of coffins, and the coopers; and this subdivision of one class of artisans shows that they had systematically adopted the partition of labor. The makers of chariots and traveling carriages were of the same class. Palanquins, canopies, and wooden chests for traveling and religious purposes were the work of cabinetmakers or carpenters; but the makers of coffins were distinct from both of these. The boat builders and basket makers were subdivisions of workers in wood. The occupation of the cooper was comparatively limited in Egypt, where water and other liquids were carried or kept in skins and earthenware jars; and the skill of the cooper was only required to make wooden measures for grain, which were bound with hoops of either wood or metal. Among the many occupations of the carpenter, that of veneering is noticed in the sculptures of Thebes as early as the time of the New Kingdom, about B. C. 1450.

2. Israelites. As among the Egyptians the carpenter, joiner, carver, sculptor, wagon maker and basket maker all worked in wood. These trades or occupations were probably never strictly separated from one another. Mention of the first three is made in connection with the building of the tabernacle (Exod. 25:10, sq.; 35:30, sq.; 37:1, 10, 15, 25). The Israelitish princes had wagons—covered ones too—in the desert, which they probably brought from Egypt (Num. 7:3), and baskets are mentioned (Num. 6:15, sq.; Deut. 26:2, 4); but of coopering there is not a trace.

3. Tools. The usual tools, among the Egyptians, of the carpenter were the ax, adz, handsaw, chisels of various kinds, the drill, and two sorts of planes (one resembling a chisel, the other apparently of stone, acting as a rasp on the surface of the wood, which was afterward polished by a smooth body, probably of stone); and these, with the ruler, plummet, right angle (square), a leather bag containing nails, the hone, and the horn of oil, constituted the principal, and perhaps the only implements he used.

Among the Israelites the following tools for carpenters and joiners are incidentally mentioned: the ax, hatchet, saw, plane, level, compass (Isa. 44:13), hammer, and pencil (or red lead).

Handkerchief (Gr. *soudarion; sweat cloth*). The *soudarion* is noticed in the New Testament as a wrapper to fold up money (Luke 19:20); as a cloth bound about the head of a corpse (John 11:44; 20:7), being probably brought from the crown of the head under the chin, and, lastly, as an article of dress that could be easily removed (Acts 19:12), probably a handkerchief worn on the head like the *keffieh* of the Bedouins. *See* Dress.

Handle (Hebrew, plural *kǎppŏth*, literally *hands*), the thumb pieces or knobs of the bolt or latch to a door (Cant. 5:5). *See* Lock.

Handmaid or **Handmaiden** (Heb. *shǐphḥāh*, or *'āmäh*, Gen. 16:1; Ruth 3:9, etc.; Gr. *doulē*, Luke 1:38, etc.). A maidservant, as both Hebrew terms are often translated, the latter being rendered "handmaid" in a deprecatory sense. *See* Service.

Hands, Imposition of. This occurs in Scripture as a patriarchal usage, as Jacob's laying his hands upon the heads of Joseph's children (Gen. 48:14); as well as in later times, when Jesus placed his hands upon children presented to him for *his* blessing (Matt. 19:15). The imposition of hands formed part of the ceremonial observed on the appointment and consecration of persons, as of Joshua by Moses (Num. 27:18-20; Deut. 34:9); and also sometimes attended the healing of persons by a prophet (II Kings 4:34), though in this instance Elisha placed his hands upon the hands of the child. In the Gospel age the action was, undoubtedly, used in connection with the bestowal of supernatural gifts, or the miraculous effects of the Holy Spirit (Mark 5:23, 41; 7: 32), although our Lord extended his hands *over* the apostles in blessing them at the Mount of Olives (Luke 24:50). The apostles laid their hands upon sick folk and healed them (Matt. 9:18; Mark 6:5, etc.); and at times also laid their hands upon the baptized, that they might receive the special gifts of the Spirit (Acts 8:15-18; 19:6). A quite natural extension of this practice was to apply it to those who were set apart to the sacred office in the Church—the men already possessed of delegated power and authority proceeding, like Moses in respect to Joshua, to put some of their own honor upon those chosen to the same responsible and dignified position (Acts 14:3; I Tim. 4:14). "Not that the mere act could confer any special spiritual power, but it was employed as a fit and appropriate symbol to denote their full and formal consent to the bestowal of the divine gift; and, being accompanied by prayer to Him who alone can really bestow it, might ordinarily be regarded as a sign that the communication had actually taken place."

Ecclesiastical Uses. In the rites of the early Church the imposition of hands was used in confirmation, which generally was an accompaniment of baptism, and symbolized the reception of the Holy Ghost. It was also prac-

ticed in ordination (*q. v.*). In the modern Church the Roman Catholics use the imposition of hands in the ceremonies which precede extreme unction, in ordination and confirmation (in both of which services it has received a sacramental efficacy). In the mass, previous to the consecration of the elements, the priest extends his hands over the people in blessing. The Church of England and the Protestant Episcopal churches employ it as a symbolical act in baptism and confirmation. The Methodist, the Presbyterian, and Congregational Churches employ it only in ordination.

Handstaff (Heb. *mǎqqēl*, a *rod* or *staff*), a javelin (Ezek. 39:9). *See* Armor, I, (3).

Handwriting (Gr. *cheirographon, what one has written with his own hand*), specially a note of hand, or writing in which one acknowledges that money has either been deposited with him or lent to him by another, to be returned at an appointed time.

Figurative. It is applied in Col. 2:14 (R. V. "bond") to the Mosaic law, which shows men to be chargeable with offenses for which they must pay the penalty.

Ha'nes (hä'nēz), a place in Egypt only mentioned in Isa. 30:4: "For his princes were at Zoan, and his messengers came to Hanes." Hanes has been supposed by Vitringa, Michaelis, Rosenmüller, and Gesenius to be the same as Heracleopolis Magna in the Heptanomis. This identification depends upon the similarity of the two names. Other scholars, however, are disposed to identify Hanes with Tahpanhes, a fortified town on the E. frontier. This is the identification of the Aramaic paraphrase on the passage.

Hanging. *See* Punishment.

Han'iel (hǎn'ǐ-ěl), the less correct form (I Chron. 7:39) of *Hanniel* (*q. v.*).

Han'nah (hǎn'à; *grace, favor*), wife of Elkanah (a Levite of Ephratah) and mother of Samuel. Although childless, she was much beloved by her husband, but was greatly distressed by the insults of Elkanah's other wife, Peninnah, who had children. On one of her visits to Shiloh she vowed before the Lord, if he would give her a son, to devote him to his service. Her manner, speaking in an inaudible tone, attracted the attention of the high priest, Eli, who suspected her of drunkenness. From this suspicion she easily vindicated herself, and, receiving a blessing from Eli, returned to her home with a lightened heart. Before the end of the year Hannah became the mother of a son, whom she named Samuel, B. C. about 1106. When Samuel was old enough to dispense with her maternal services Hannah took him to Shiloh and presented him, with due form, to the high priest (I Sam. 1:1-25). The joy of Hannah found expression in an exulting song of thanksgiving. It is specially remarkable that in this song (2:10) is the first mention in Scripture of the word "anointed" or Messiah, and, as there was no king in Israel at the time, it seems the best interpretation to refer it to Christ. There is also a remarkable resemblance between this song and that of Mary (Luke 1:46, sq.). Hannah came up to Shiloh every year to visit Samuel and to bring him a coat. She received the kindly notice of Eli, and, blessed of God, bare after Samuel three sons and two daughters (2:21).

Han'nathon (hăn'ȧ-thŏn; probably *favored*), a place on the northern boundary of Zebulun (Josh. 19:14), apparently about midway between the Sea of Galilee and the valley of Jiphthah-el.

Han'niel (hăn'ĭ-ĕl; *grace of God*).

1. The son of Ephod, prince of the tribe of Manasseh, and one of those appointed by Moses to divide the land among the several tribes (Num. 34:23).

2. One of the sons of Ulla, and a chief of the tribe of Asher (I Chron. 7:39, where the name is less correctly Anglicized *Haniel*).

Ha'noch (hā'nŏk; dedicated, *initiated*).

1. The third son of Midian, and grandson of Abraham and Keṭurah (Gen. 25:4; I Chron. 1:33, A. V. "Henock"), B. C. after 1950.

2. The oldest son of Reuben (Gen. 46:9; Exod. 6:14; I Chron. 5:3), from whom came "the family of the Hanochites" (Num. 26:5), B. C. perhaps about 1850.

Ha'nochites. (hă'nō-kīts). *See* Hanoch, II.

Ha'nun (hā'nŭn; *favored*).

1. The son and successor of Nahash, king of the Ammonites (II Sam. 10:1, sq.; I Chron. 19:2-6). David, who had received kindness from Nahash, sent an embassy to condole with Hanun on the death of his father, B. C. about 984. The young king, led by his courtiers, misapprehended the object of the mission and shamefully treated the ambassadors. Their beards were *half* shaven and their garments cut off at the middle, and in this plight they were sent back to David. News being brought to the king of the affront, he commanded the ambassadors to tarry in Jericho until their beards grew. He vowed vengeance, and Hanun, anticipating war, called to his aid the Syrians. The power of the Syrians, however, was broken in two campaigns, and the Ammonites were left to their fate.

2. A Jew who was associated with the inhabitants of Zanoah in repairing the valley gate of Jerusalem after the captivity (Neh. 3:13), B. C. 445.

3. The sixth son of Zalaph, who repaired part of the walls of Jerusalem (Neh. 3:30), B. C. 445.

Haphra'im (hăf-rä'yĭm; *double pit*), a place near the borders of Issachar, mentioned as between Shunem and Shihon (Josh. 19:19). Probably et-Taiyibeh N. W. of Bethshan.

Ha'ra (hä'rȧ), a province of Assyria, mentioned (I Chron. 5:26) as one of the localities to which Tiglath-pileser deported the two and a half trans-Jordanic tribes. Being joined with Hala, Habor, and the River Gozan, all situated in western Assyria, between the Tigris and Euphrates, we may safely conclude that Hara was in their neighborhood.

Har'adah (hăr'ȧ-dȧ; *place of terror*), the twenty-fifth station of the Israelites in the desert (Num. 33:24); perhaps at the head of the valley northeast of Jebel Araif en Nakah.

Ha'ran (hā'răn; cf. Akkad. *ḥarränü, road caravan route*).

1. One of the three sons of Terah, brother of Abraham, and the father of Lot, Milcah, and Iscah. He died in his native place (Ur) before his father, Terah (Gen. 11:26, sq.), B. C. probably before 2250.

2. The son of Ephah, a concubine of Caleb, and father of Gazez (I Chron. 2:46), B. C. after 1440.

3. (Hebrew same as No. 1). One of the three sons of Shimei, a Gershonite, who was appointed by David to superintend the offices at the tabernacle (I Chron. 23:9), B. C. about 960.

4. **Ha'ran, City of.** In A. V. of N. T. "Charran." An ancient and still-existing North Mesopotamian commercial city on the Belikh River, sixty miles from its entrance into the Euphrates. It was located in Padan-aram ("field of Aram"). The city was on the busy caravan road connecting with Nineveh, Asshur and Babylon in Mesopotamia, and with Damascus, Tyre and Egyptian cities in the west and south. It was a natural stopping-off-place for Terah and Abraham in their trek to Palestine. Interestingly Haran, like Ur, was a center of the moon god cult. Whether Terah was a worshiper of the moon god Sin and refused to break with his idolatry is an open question (Gen. 11:31, 32). At any rate, when Terah died at Haran, Abraham and his nephew Lot and their families continued their migration S. W. into Canaan, passing through the hill country of Shechem and on to Bethel. Abraham and his clan kept in touch with Haran. Isaac's wife Rebecca was fetched thence from Nahor, a neighboring city of Haran (Gen. 24). Jacob's wife Rachel also came from this region (Gen. 28, 29), where Jacob himself spent twenty years. The Mari Tablets unearthed in excavations at Mari by the Museé du Louvre under the leadership of André Parrot mention Nahor. These tablets belong to the eighteenth century B. C. Haran too was a flourishing city in the nineteenth and eighteenth centuries B. C., as is known from frequent references to it in cuneiform sources. Cuneiform tablets from Nuzu, a small Assyrian town S. W. of Kirkuk, greatly illuminate the partriarchal age. Such social usages as family teraphim (Gen. 31:19), death-bed blessing (Gen. 27) and employment of concubines to insure heirs (Gen. 16:3) are referred to in the Nuzu Letters. The city of Haran remained important throughout the centuries. Here the Assyrians made their last stand (609 B. C.) and three years later it fell to the Medes. who destroyed it and drove the Assyrians back across the Euphrates. *M. F. U.*

Ha'rarite (hă'rȧ-rīt), the designation of three of David's guard.

1. **Agee**, a Hararite (II Sam. 23:33).

2. **Shammah**, the Hararite (II Sam. 23:33).

3. **Sharar** (II Sam. 23:33) or **Sacar** (I Chron. 11:35), the Hararite, was the father of Ahiam, another member of the guard.

Harbo'na (här-bō'nȧ; Avestan, *the bald man*), one of the seven chamberlains of King Ahasuerus, or Xerxes, commanded by him to exhibit the beauty of Queen Vashti to his courtiers (Esth. 1:10). He also suggested to the king the hanging of Haman (7:9, A. V. "Harbonah"), B. C. about 478.

Harbo'nah (här-bō'nȧ; Esth. 7:9). *See* Harbona.

Harden. "To harden one's face" (Prov. 21:29) is to put on an impudent, shameless face. "To harden the neck" (II Kings 17:14; Neh. 9:29; Prov. 29:1, etc.) is to be stubborn, self-willed.

Hardness of Heart, (Matt. 19:8; Mark 3:5), destitution of feeling; obtuseness to spiritual things; obduracy, wickedness. In common use —stinginess, solidity, firmness. In Ezek. 3:7 "hardhearted" evidently means morally hardened.

Hare. *See* Animal Kingdom.

Ha′reph (hä′rĕf; *reproachful*), the "father" of Bethgader and "son" of Caleb of Judah by one of his legitimate wives (I Chron. 2:51), B. C. about 1190.

Ha′reth (hä′rĕth; thicket, also **Hereth** (hē′-rĕth), as in R. S. V. This is the place in the wooded mountain to which David fled from Saul (I Sam. 22:5). Possibly the scene of the incident narrated in II Sam. 23:14-17; I Chron. 11:16-19.

Harha′iah (Heb. hȧr-hā′yȧ), the father of Uzziel, "of the goldsmiths," which latter repaired part of the walls of Jerusalem after the captivity (Neh. 3:8), B. C. 445.

Har′has (här′hăs; II Kings 22:14), given in II Chron. 34:22 as *Hasrah* (*q. v.*).

Har′hur (här′hŭr), one of the Nethinim whose posterity returned from Babylon with Zerubbabel (Ezra 2:51; Neh. 7:53), B. C. before 536.

Ha′rim (hä′rĭm; perhaps *consecrated, devoted* or *flat-nosed*).

1. The head of the third course of priests as arranged by David (I Chron. 24:8), B. C. after 1000.

2. An Israelite, whose descendants, to the number of three hundred and twenty males, or one thousand and seventeen in all, returned from Babylon with Zerubbabel (Ezra 2:32, 39; Neh. 7:35, 42), B. C. before 536. But among these some are enumerated (Ezra 10:21) as priests in the corresponding lists of those who renounced their Gentile wives, and others (10:31) as ordinary Israelites. Others consider Harim to be a place, and identify it with the village *Charim*, situated eight English miles N. E. of Jaffa (McC. and S., *Cyc.*).

3. The father of Malchijah, who repaired part of the wall of Jerusalem (Neh. 3:11), B. C. before 445.

4. One of the priests who signed the sacred covenant of Nehemiah (Neh. 10:5), B. C. 445.

5. A chief of the people who signed the covenant (Neh. 10:27), B. C. 445.

6. One of the priests who returned from Babylon (Neh. 12:15). In the former list the name is changed to Rehum (v. 3), B. C. about 536.

Ha′riph (hä′rĭf; *autumnal*).

1. An Israelite, whose descendants (or possibly a place whose inhabitants), to the number of one hundred and twelve, returned from Babylon with Zerubbabel (Neh. 7:24), probably the same as Jorah (Ezra 2:18), B. C. before 536.

2. A chief of the people who gave his hand to the covenant made by Nehemiah (Neh. 10:19), B. C. 445.

Harlot, Whore, etc., are terms promiscuously used in the A. V. for several Hebrew words of widely different meaning.

1. *A Lewd Woman.* (Heb. *zōnäh*), is the word which occurs most generally in the Old Testament, and expresses licentious action on the part of either men or women, married or unmarried; also used to describe the misconduct of a concubine or secondary wife (Judg. 19:2). This word is often rendered in the A. V. by the first of the above English words (Gen. 34:31, etc.), and without apparent reason by the second (Prov. 23:27, etc.). From Gen. 38:15 it would appear that such women were marked either by a veil or some peculiarity in its size or mode of wearing it, although Jahn (*Bib. Arch.*, p. 141) thinks that all lewd women went without the veil, and that Tamar assumed a veil for the purpose of concealing herself from her father-in-law. The effort to identify the term harlot with innkeeper (Josh. 2:1; Judg. 16:1) seems hardly justifiable.

2. *Temple Prostitute,* (Heb. *qᵉdēshäh*, to *consecrate;* in the three passages, Gen. 38:21, 22; Deut. 23:17; Hos. 4:14), one "set apart to a sacred purpose," according to the infamous rites in use among the votaries of certain deities in Canaan and neighboring countries. Herodotus refers to the infamous custom of the Babylonians, who compelled every native female to attend the temple of Venus once in her life, and to prostitute herself in honor of the goddess. Such prostitution was forbidden by the law of Moses (Lev. 19:29; 21:9), yet it seems to have been assumed that the harlot class would exist, and the prohibition of Deut. 23:18, forbidding offerings from the wages of such sin, is perhaps due to the contagion of heathen example.

3. *"The Strange Woman"* (Heb. *näkrîyäh*, I Kings 11:1; Prov. 5:20; 6:24; 7:5; 23:27). There is a difference of opinion as to the circumstances in which such a name was given to harlots. The simplest account seems to be that it refers to a man leaving his own rightful wife for another, who ought to be strange to him (Prov. 5:17, 18, 20). Another explanation is that the earliest and most frequent offenders against purity were "strange women," in the sense of foreigners, like the Midianite women in the days of Moses (Num. 25:1, sq.), Canaanites, and other Gentiles (Josh. 23:13).

4. *An Unchaste Female.* (Gr. *pornē* Matt. 21:31, 32; Luke 15:30; I Cor. 6:15, 16; Heb. 11:31; James 2:25), any woman, married or single, who practices unlawful sexual indulgence, whether for gain or for lust. The representation given by Solomon is no doubt *founded* upon facts, and therefore shows that in his time prostitutes plied their trade upon the "streets" (Prov. 7:12; 9:14, etc.; Jer. 3:2; Ezek. 16:24, 25, 31).

Figurative. The term "harlot" is used figuratively for *idolatress* (Isa. 1:21; Jer. 2:20; Rev. 17:1, 5, 15; 19:2). *See* Fornication; Illegitimacy.

Harne′pher (hȧr-nē′fĕr), one of the sons of Zophah, a chief of the tribe of Asher (I Chron. 7:36).

Harness, Harnessed, the act of fastening animals to a cart or vehicle, e. g., *yoking* cattle (I Sam. 6:7, 10; A. V. "tie") or horses (Jer. 46:4). From the monuments we see that the harness of the Egyptian war chariots was of leather, richly decorated, many colored, and studded with gold and silver.

Ha'rod (hā'rŏd; *trembling or terror*), the spring at which the test of drinking was applied before the battle of Israel with the Midianites (Judg. 7). The well bursts out of the source "some fifteen feet broad and two feet deep, from the very foot of Gilboa." It is identical with the present fountain '*Ain Jalud*, a mile E. from Jezreel, and opposite Shunem.

Ha'rodite (hā'rô-dīt). Shammah and Elika, two of David's heroes (II Sam. 23:25) were so called, probably from their being natives of *Harod* (*q. v.*). In I Chron. 11:27 an error in writing gives us Harorite.

Har'oeh (hăr'ô-ĕ; I Chron. 2:52). *See* Reaiah.

Ha'rorite (hā'rô-rīt; I Chron. 11:27), another form for *Harodite* (*q. v.*), an epithet of Shammoth, one of David's heroes.

Haro'sheth (hà-rō'shĕth) **of the Gentiles**, a city in the north of Palestine, the home of Sisera (Judg. 4:2, 13, 16). Harper thinks the name signifies "forests," and says "there still are the densely wooded slopes." Easton says "the name in the Hebrew is *Harosheth ha Gojim*, i. e., 'the smithy of the nations,' probably so called because here Jabin's iron war chariots, armed with scythes, were made." Jabin's great army gathered here preparatory to battle and defeat (Judg. 4). It is identified as Tell 'Amar on the northern bank of the Kishon, 16 miles N. N. W. of Megiddo.

Harp. *See* Music, p. 766.

Harrow (Heb. *hărîts*, II Sam. 12:31; I Chron. 20:3). The word so rendered in the above passages is probably a threshing machine, the verb rendered "to harrow" (Job 39:10), expresses apparently the "breaking of the clods" (Isa. 28:24; Hos. 10:11), and is so far analogous to our harrowing, but whether done by any such machine as we call "a harrow" is very doubtful.

Har'sha (här'shà; possibly *silent, dumb*), one of the Nethinim whose descendants returned from Babylon with Zerubbabel (Ezra 2:52; Neh. 7:54), B. C. before 536.

Hart. *See* Animal Kingdom.

Ha'rum (hā'rŭm; *exalted*), the father of Aharhel, the "families" of which latter are enumerated among the posterity of Coz, of the tribe of Judah (I Chron. 4:8).

Haru'maph (hà-rū'măf; *snub-nosed*), "father" of Jedaiah, which latter was one of the priests who repaired part of the walls of Jerusalem (Neh. 3:10), B. C. 445.

Har'uphite (här'ŭ-fīt), a patronymic applied to Shephatiah (I Chron. 12:5), which denotes either one descended from *Haruph* (*q. v.*), or a native of *Hariph* (*q. v.*).

Ha'ruz (hā'rŭz; *gold*, or cf. S. *Arab*; *be covetous* or *eager*), a citizen of Jotbah, and father of Meshullemeth, who became the wife of King Manasseh and mother of King Amon (II Kings 21:19), B. C. before 641.

Harvest (Heb. qāṣîr, *a cutting*. The crops in the southern parts of Palestine and in the plains come to maturity about the middle of April, but in the northern and mountainous sections they do not become ripe till three weeks, or more, later. The harvest began with the barley and the festival of the Passover (Lev. 23:9-14; II Sam. 21:9, 10; Ruth 2:23) and ended with the wheat (Gen. 30:14; Exod. 34:22) and the festival of Pentecost (Exod. 23:16). *See* Agriculture.

Figurative. Harvest is a figurative term for *judgment* (Jer. 51:33; Hos. 6:11; Joel 3:13; comp. Rev. 14:15); of a season of *grace* (Jer. 8:20); a time when many are ready to receive the Gospel (Matt. 9:37, 38; John 4:35); and, as the harvest is considered as the *end* of the season, so our Lord says, "The harvest is the *end* of the world" (Matt. 13:39). *Dew* in harvest, causing the plants to ripen with rapidity and luxuriance, is a symbol of God's fostering care (Isa. 18:4); *cold* in harvest is refreshing, like a faithful messenger (Prov. 25:13); while *rain* in harvest, being untimely, is a symbol of honor given to a fool (26:1).

Hasadi'ah (hăs-àdî'à; *favored by Jehovah*), one of the five sons of Zerubbabel mentioned in I Chron. 3:20.

Hasenu'ah (hăs-ê-nū'à), an Israelite of the tribe of Benjamin, whose descendants dwelt in Jerusalem after the captivity (I Chron. 9:7), B. C. before 536.

Hashabi'ah (hăsh-à-bī'à; *Jehovah reckons, imputes*).

1. The son of Amaziah and father of Malluch, of the family of Merari (I Chron. 6:45).

2. The son of Bunni and father of Azrikam, of the family of Merari (I Chron. 9:14; Neh. 11:15), B. C. before 445.

3. The fourth of the six sons of Jeduthun (I Chron. 25:3), who had charge of the twelfth course of singers (v. 19), B. C. after 1000.

4. A Hebronite, appointed by David on the west side of Jordan "in all the business of the Lord, and in the service of the king" (I Chron. 26:30), B. C. after 1000.

5. Son of Kemuel, and ruler of the Levites in David's time (I Chron. 27:17), perhaps the same as No. 4.

6. One of the chief Levites who made voluntary offerings of victims for the Passover kept by King Josiah (II Chron. 35:9), B. C. about 639.

7. One of the Levites who responded to the invitation of Ezra to act as a minister in the house of the Lord (Ezra 8:19), B. C. about 457.

8. One of the chief priests into whose care Ezra intrusted the bullion and other valuables for the sacred vessels at Jerusalem (Ezra 8:24). He is probably the same whose father, Hilkiah, is mentioned in Neh. 12:21, B. C. 457.

9. The son of Mattaniah and father of Bani (Neh. 11:22), B. C. before 445.

10. A chief of the Levites (Neh. 12:24), who repaired part of the walls of Jerusalem (3:17), and subscribed the covenant of fidelity to Jehovah (10:11), B. C. 445.

Hashab'nah (hà-shăb'nà; probably for Hashabiah), one of the chiefs of the people who subscribed Nehemiah's covenant (Neh. 10:25), B. C. 445.

Hashabni'ah (hà-shăb-nī'à; *Jehovah has taken account*).

1. Father of Hattush, which latter repaired part of the walls of Jerusalem (Neh. 3:10), B. C. before 445.

2. A Levite who was among those who officiated at the solemn fast under Ezra and

457

Nehemiah when the covenant was sealed (Neh. 9:5), B. C. 445.

Hashbad'ana (hăsh-băd'á-nà), one of those who stood at Ezra's left hand while he read the law to the people (Neh. 8:4), B. C. 445.

Ha'shem (hā'shĕm). The sons of Hashem, the Gizonite, are named among the members of David's guard (I Chron. 11:34; the *Jashen* of II Sam. 23:32), B. C. before 1047.

Hashmo'nah (hăsh-mō'-nà), the thirtieth station of the Israelites in the wilderness (Num. 33:29, 30), near Mount Hor. It was located, apparently, near the intersection of *Wady el-Jerafeh* with *Wady el-Jeib*, in the Arabah.

Ha'shub (hā'shŭb).

1. The son of Pahath-moab, and one of those who repaired part of the walls of Jerusalem (Neh. 3:11), B. C. 445. Perhaps he is the same person mentioned (10:33) as one of the chief Israelites who joined in the sacred covenant of Nehemiah.

2. Another who assisted in the building of the wall of Jerusalem (Neh. 3:23), B. C. 445.

3. A Levite, son of Azrikam and father of Shemaiah, which last was one of those resident in the "villages of the Netophathites," and having general oversight of the temple (Neh. 11:15; I Chron. 9:14, in which latter passage the name is more correctly Anglicized "Hasshub"), B. C. before 445.

Hashu'bah (há-shū'bà; *esteemed*), one of the five sons of Zerubbabel (Keil, *Com.*)꜕ but according to some authorities the son of Pedaiah, the descendant of David (I Chron. 3:20).

Ha'shum (hā'shŭm).

1. An Israelite whose posterity (or perhaps a place whose inhabitants), to the number of two hundred and twenty-three, came back from Babylon with Zerubbabel (Ezra 2:19), or three hundred and twenty-eight in all (Neh. 7:22). Seven men of them married foreign wives, from whom they separated (Ezra 10:33), B. C. before 536.

2. One of those who stood up with Ezra while he read the book of the law to the people (Neh. 8:4), B. C. about 445.

3. The head of a family who sealed the covenant made by Nehemiah and the people (Neh. 10:18), B. C. 445.

Hashu'pha (há-shoō'fà; Neh. 7:46). See Hasupha.

Has'rah (hăs'rà), the father (or mother) of Tikvath and grandfather of Shallum, which last was husband of Huldah the prophetess (II Chron. 34:22). The parallel passage (II Kings 22:14) gives the name, probably by transposition, in the form *Harhas*. Hasrah is said to have been "keeper of the wardrobe," perhaps the sacerdotal vestments, B. C. before 639.

Hassena'ah (hăs-ĕn-ā'á), a Jew whose sons rebuilt the fish gate in the repair of the walls of Jerusalem (Neh. 3:3), B. C. before 445. In Ezra 2:35; Neh. 7:38; the name is given without the article. *Senaah* (*q. v.*).

Has'shub (hăs'shŭb; I Chron. 9:14). See Hashub, 3.

Hasu'pha (há-soō'fà), one of the Nethinim whose descendants returned from Babylon with Zerubbabel (Ezra 2:43; Neh. 7:46, in which latter passage the name is less correctly Anglicized *Hashupha*, *q. v.*), B. C. before 536.

Hat (Dan. 3:21), "a mantle," in the R. V., but evidently "a cap" or type of head wear. *See* Dress.

Ha'tach (hā'tăk); R. V. and R. S. V. **Hathach** (hā'thăk), a eunuch in the palace of Xerxes, appointed to wait on Esther, and who acted for her in her communications with Mordecai (Esth. 4:5, 6, 9, 10), B. C. about 478.

Hate (Heb. *sānē'*; Gr. *miseō*), in the root of the Hebrew word is the idea of ugliness, deformity; hence to regard with feelings contrary to love; to abhor, to loathe, to cherish dislike to. In both the Hebrew and Greek words we find the above meaning in some places (e. g., II Chron. 18:7; Psa. 45:7; Matt. 24:10, etc.); while in others the meaning is "to regard with less love" (e. g., Deut. 21:15, 16; Prov. 13:24; Mal. 1:3; Rom. 9:13).

The requirement to hate father and mother, wife and children, etc., and one's own life (Luke 14:26), means that all earthly ties and love must be subordinate to love for Christ.

God's hatred is toward all sinful thoughts and ways. It is a feeling of which all holy beings are conscious in view of sin, and is wholly unlike the hatred which is mentioned in the Scriptures among the works of the flesh (Gal. 5:20).

Ha'thath (hā'thăth; *terror*, as in Job 6:21), son of Othniel and grandson of Kenaz, of the tribe of Judah (I Chron. 4:13), consequently also grandnephew and grandson of Caleb (v. 15; comp. Judg. 1:13), B. C. probably after 1170.

Hati'pha (há-tī'fà; Aram., *captive*), one of the Nethinim whose posterity returned from Babylon with Zerubbabel (Ezra 2:54; Neh. 7: 56), B. C. before 536.

Hat'ita (hăt'ĭ-tà; Aram., *dug up, furrowed*), some **Hati'ta** (há-tī'tà) one of the "porters" (i. e., Levitical temple *janitors*) whose descendants returned from Babylon (Ezra 2:42; Neh. 7: 45), B. C. before 536.

Hat'si Ham Men'uchoth (hăt'sī hăm mĕn'ŭkŏth); I Chron. 2:52, margin). *See* Manahethites.

Hat'til (hăt'ĭl), one of the descendants of "Solomon's servants" whose posterity returned from Babylon with Zerubbabel (Ezra 2:57; Neh. 7:59), B. C. before 536.

Hat'tush (hăt'ŭsh; derivation uncertain).

1. One of the sons of Shemaiah, among the posterity of Zerubbabel (I Chron. 3:22), B. C. after 536.

2. A descendant of David who accompanied Ezra to Jerusalem (Ezra 8:2), B. C. 457.

3. Son of Hashabniah, and one of those who rebuilt the walls of Jerusalem (Neh. 3:10), B. C. 445. Perhaps identical with No. 2.

4. One of the priests who united in the sacred covenant with Nehemiah (Neh. 10:4), B. C. about 445.

5. A priest who returned from Babylon with Zerubbabel (Neh. 12:2), B. C. 536.

Hauran' (há-ōō-rán'; "hollow" or "black land of basaltic rock"), a mound-dotted extinct volcanic plateau E. of the Lake of Galilee and S. of Damascus and Mt. Hermon. This region is roughly co-terminus with O. T. Bashan. The region is extremely fertile and forms a natural granary. Numerous ghost-towns exist in its area, some of them constructed of basalt and called in the O. T. "the giant cities of Bashan." In later Graeco-Roman times the area, smaller than formerly, was known as Auranitis. This was one of the four provinces which Augustus gave to Herod the Great (c. 23 B. C.). Subsequently it formed a part of Philip's tetrarchy. Ezra. 47:16, 18 envisions Hauran as a boundary for restored Israel.

Haven, the rendering of two Hebrew and one Greek word, and having the meaning of our words, "port," or "harbor."

Hav'ilah (hăv'ĭ-là; perhaps *sandy*, Cf. Heb. *ḥôl, sand*).

1. A region encompassed by the Pison branch of Eden's river. It is represented as richly producing gold, onyx and bdellium—an aromatic gum (Gen. 2:11, 12). This region is not to be confused with the Havilah of the Joktanites (Gen. 10:29; 25:18; I Sam. 15:7) or of the Kushites (Gen. 10:7; I Chron. 1:9). This region evidently skirted Babylonia and was on the boundary "as thou goest to Assyria."

2. A district evidently N. of Sheba in Arabia, between Ophir and Hazarmaveth. Its people were nomads (Ishmaelites, Gen. 25:18). Apparently its boundaries were very fluid and reached into North Arabia, as is indicated by the narrative of Saul's warfare with the Amalekites (I Sam. 15:7).

3. The second son of Cush (Gen. 10:17; I Chron. 1:9).

4. The twelfth-named of the thirteen sons of Joktan (Gen. 10:29; I Chron. 1:23). *M. F. U.*

Ha'voth-Ja'ir (hā'vŏth-jā-ĭr; *huts or hamlets of Jair*), a district of villages in Bashan, east of the Jordan, which the son of Manasseh took and called by his name (Num. 32:41).

Deut. 3:14 says that "Jair took all the country of Argob and Maachathi, and called them Bashanhavoth-jair." In Judges (10:4) it is recorded that Jair the Gileadite and judge had thirty cities called Havoth-jair.

Hawk. *See* Animal Kingdom.

Hay. *See* Vegetable Kingdom.

Haz'ael (hăz'â-ĕl; *God beholds*, i. e., *cares for*), an officer of Benhadad, king of Syria, whom Elijah was commanded to anoint to be king in his stead (I Kings 19:15).

1. **Consults Elisha.** When Elisha was at Damascus, Hazael was sent by his master, then ill, to consult the prophet respecting his recovery (II Kings 8:7-13), B. C. about 843. The answer was that he *might* certainly recover. "Howbeit," added the prophet, "the Lord hath showed me that he shall surely die." He then looked steadily upon Hazael till he became confused, on which the man of God wept. Upon Hazael asking, "Why weepeth my lord?" Elisha replied, "Because I know the evil that thou wilt do unto the children of Israel," etc. Hazael exclaimed, "But what is thy servant, the (not *a*) dog, that he should do this great thing?" The prophet responded, "The Lord hath showed me that thou shalt be king over Syria."

2. **Kills Benhadad.** Hazael returned and told Benhadad the prophet's answer. The next day he took a cloth, dipped it in water, and spread it over the face of the king, who, in his feebleness, and probably in his sleep, was smothered, and died what seemed a natural death (II Kings 8:15).

3. **King.** He ascended the throne and was soon engaged in hostilities with Ahaziah, king of Judah, and Jehoram, king of Israel, for the possession of Ramothgilead (II Kings 8:28). A text from Asshur mentions the significant dynastic change at Damascus and strikingly confirms the Biblical account of Hazael's accession (II Kings 8:7-15): "Adadidri forsook his land" (i. e. died violently or was murdered). Hazael, son of nobody, seized the throne." Evidence from the stela of Ben-hadad from the region of Aleppo in North Syria, discovered in 1940, indicates that the Adadidri of this account is none other than Benhadad I and that the Ben-hadad in the Biblical account is neither an error nor a gloss for Adadidri as E. J. Kraeling surmises (*Aram and Israel*, p. 77 and 79, Note 1), but is the same person (Albright, *Bulletin of the Am. Schools* 87, p. 26).

4. **Wars.** Hazael was soon confronted by Jehu of Israel (c. 842-815 B. C.), a dangerous usurper like himself. Jehu incurred the implacable hatred of Hazael by submitting to Shalmaneser III in the Assyrian invasion of 841 B. C. rather than joining the Syrian coalition to resist the enemy's advance. Shalmanezer's Black Obelisk actually shows Jehu kneeling before the Assyrian emperor presenting "tribute of Iaua (Jehu), son of Omri." Hazael, single-handed, stemmed the Assyrian invasion of 841 B. C. and was able at least to ward off a crushing blow. Until 837 B. C., which marked Shalmanezer's final effort to subdue central and southern Syria, Hazael was free to satisfy his lust for territorial expansion. He began relentlessly to thresh Gilead and Bashan "with threshing instruments of iron" (II Kings 10:32, 33; Amos 1:3, 4).

5. **Hazael and Joahaz.** Hazael renewed his relentless attacks on Israel at Jehu's death (815 B. C.) and reduced his son Joahaz (815-801 B. C.) to an extreme stage of abasement (II Kings 13:1-9, 22, 25). So powerful did Hazael become that he took possession of the Philistine plain, destroyed Gath and besieged Jerusalem. He was bought off by the payment of a large sum raised by stripping the temple (II Kings 12:17, 18).

6. **As a Conqueror.** In extending his sway to the south, Hazael became the most powerful of the Aramaean conquerors who ruled at Damascus. In fact, he became the chief power in all Syria. However, the reappearance of Assyria in the west under Adadnirari III (807-782 B. C.) demonstrated that Hazael's empire built on brute force lacked intrinsic solidarity. Whereas a unified Syria had met and checked Shalmaneser's advance under Ben-hadad I at Karkar in 853 B. C., Adadnirari's westward push gave no proof at all of such solidarity. Damascus did escape actual destruction, but was put under an oppressive tribute. According to the Saba'a Stele, discovered in 1905, Adadnirari says "To march against Aram I gave command. Mari' (Hazael) I shut up in Damascus, his royal city. One hundred talents of gold, 1000 talents of silver . . . I received" (D. D. Luckenbill, II, Sect. 735). Even such countries as *Bit Humri*

(Israel) and *Palastu* (Philistia) revolted in the crisis and sent tribute to Assyria. From the upper portion of a slab found at Nimrud (Calah), the cuneiform inscription of Adadnirari lists among other countries "Tyre, Sidon, Humri (Omriland, Israel), Edom, Palastu (Philistia)" as lands which he says "I brought into submission to my feet. Tribute and tax I imposed upon them." (Luckenbill, *op. cit.*, Sect. 739).

7. After an extended rule of at least forty years, Hazael died in 801 B. C. or slightly later. Adadnirari III for the year 802 B. C. and likely several years earlier, names *Mari'* as a king at Damascus. This circumstance must be accounted for under the supposition that the term is a second name of Hazael and is merely a popular title of the kings of Damascus. According to Albright, it is an abbreviation of a name like *Mari-hadad*—"Hadad is my lord" (*Bulletin of Am. Schools* 87, p. 28, Note 16). An inscription from an ivory recovered from the site of Arslan Tash in North Syria carries the name "Our lord Hazael" and dates from the time of Adadnirari III (F. Thureau-Dangin, A. Barrois, G. Dossin and M. Dunand, *Arslan Tash*, Paris, 1931, p. 135-138). It is significant in computing the date of Hazael's death. Other similar ivories found at Nimrud are dated somewhat later since an Assyrian tablet of inventory lists them as booty from Damascus at the time of Hazael's successor (*See* C. C. McCown, *The Ladder of Progress in Palestine*, N. Y., 1943, p. 198).
M. F. U.

Haza′iah (hȧ-zā′yȧ; *Jehovah beholds*), son of Adaiah and father of Col-hozeh, a descendant of Pharez (Neh. 11:5), B. C. before 536.

Ha′zar (hā′zȧr; an *inclosure*), a term frequently prefixed to geographical names in order to indicate their dependence as *villages* upon some town or noted spot. Gesenius (*Heb. Lex.*, s. v.) says that Hazar is "spoken also of the movable villages or encampments of nomadic tribes, who usually pitch their tents in a circle, or so as to form an inclosure." The African Arabs, who originally emigrated from Arabia, have retained many of their ancestral customs. When these Arabs are in a region where they are liable to attacks from enemies, they pitch their tents in a circle, with their cattle and goods in the center. The whole is then fenced in with a low wall of stones, in which are inserted thick bundles of thorny acacia, the tangled branches and long needlelike spikes forming a perfectly impenetrable hedge around the encampment. *See* Hazar-Addar, etc.

Ha′zar-ad′dar (hā′zȧr-ăd′ȧr; *village of Addar*), a place in the southern desert part of Palestine, between Kadeshbarnea and Amon (Num. 34:4; simply *Adar* in Josh. 15:3).

Ha′zar-E′nan (hā′zȧr-ē′năn; *village of fountains*), a village named as a boundary place (Num. 34:9, 10; Ezek. 47:17; 48:1), probably located east-northeast of Damascus and identified as Kiryatein on the road to Palmyra. "And the border from the sea shall be Hazarenan, the border of Damascus," cannot have any other meaning than that the northern boundary, which started from the Mediterranean Sea, stretched as far as *Hazar*-Enan,

the frontier city of Damascus (Kiel, *Com.*, Ezek. 47:17).

Ha′zar-Gad′dah (hā′zȧr-găd′ȧ; *village of fortune;* Josh. 15:27), a town in the extreme south of Judah. Perhaps identified with Khirbet Ghazza.

Ha′zar-Hat′ticon (hā′zȧr-hăt′ĭ-kŏn; *middle village*), named in the prophecy of Ezekiel (47:16) as the ultimate boundaries of the land. Its location has not been ascertained.

Ha′zarma′veth (hā′zȧr-mā′vĕth; *village of death*), one of the sons of Joktan (Gen. 10:26; I Chron. 1:20), or a district of Arabia Felix settled by him.

Ha′zar-Shu′al (hā′zȧr-shū′ȧl; *village of jackals*), a town the identifications of which are all conjectural. It was upon the south border of Judah (Josh. 15:28; Neh. 11:27), but afterward included in the territory of Simeon (Josh. 19:3; I Chron. 4:28).

Ha′zar-Su′sah (hā′zȧr-sū′sȧ; *village of horses*), a city that fell to the tribe of Simeon (Josh. 19:5), identified by some with Sansannah (15:31), one of Solomon's "chariot cities" (II Chron. 1:14). Probably Sūsīyeh, near Eshtemoa.

Haz′azon-ta′mar (hăz′ȧ-zŏn-tā′mȧr; (II Chron. 20:2). *See* Hazezon-tamar.

Hazel. *See* Vegetable Kingdom.

Hazelelpo′ni (hăz-ė-lĕl-pō′nī, or rather **Zelelpo′ni** (zė-lĕl-pō′nī), the sister of Jezreel and others of the sons of Etam, a descendant of Judah (I Chron. 4:3).

Haze′rim (hȧ-zē′rĭm; *villages*), the name of a place (Deut. 2:23); or, perhaps, a general designation of many towns by the name of Hazor, or Hagar, found among the *Avites* (*q. v.*), in northwest Arabia Petraea.

Haze′roth (hȧ-zē′rŏth; *villages*), the sixteenth station of the Israelites, and their second after leaving Sinai (Num. 11:35; 12:16; 33:17, 18; Deut. 1:1). At Hazeroth the people tarried (Num. 11:35; here occurred the sedition of Miriam and Aaron (chap. 12), after which Israel removed to "the wilderness of Paran."

Haz′ezon-ta′mar (hāz′ė-zŏn-tā′mȧr; the ancient name of Engedi (Gen. 14:7); in II Chron. 20:2) called Hazazon-tamar.

Ha′ziel (hā′zĭ-ĕl; *vision of God*), a "son" of the Gershonite Shimei, and chief of the family of Laadan (I Chron. 23:9), B. C. about 960.

Ha′zo (hā′zō), one of the sons of Nahor by Milcah (Gen. 22:22), B. C. after 2100. He must, in all likelihood, be placed in Ur of the Chaldees, or the adjacent countries.

Ha′zor (hā′zŏr; *enclosure, village*).

1. A chief city of north Palestine (Josh. 11:10), near Lake Huleh, and the seat of Jabin, a powerful Canaanitish king, who sent out a summons to the neighboring kings to assist him against Joshua (11:1, sq.). Like other strong places in that part, it stood on a mount or "tell" (Josh. 11:13, A. V. "strength"), but the surrounding country was doubtless flat and suitable for chariot manoeuvers (see vers. 4, 6, 9; Judg. 4:3). Another, Jabin, king of Canaan, oppressed Israel, from whose yoke deliverance was obtained by Deborah and Barak, after which Hazor remained in possession of the Israelites, and belonged to the tribe of Naphtali (Josh. 19:36; Judg. 4:2, sq.; I Sam. 12:9). It

was one of the places which Solomon fortified and for which he made a tax levy (I Kings 9:15). Its inhabitants were carried off to Assyria by Tiglath-pileser (II Kings 15:29; Josephus, *Ant.*, ix, 11, 1). Hazor is mentioned in the Amarna Letters (227:3 and letter 228:23 f.). It is identified with Tell el-Wakkas (Qedeh) 3¾ miles W. of the Bridge of the Daughters of Zion, near the headwaters of

198. Scene at 1955 Hebrew University Excavations at Hazor. Yigael Yadin, standing in left foreground, was director.

the Jordan. A team of archaeologists from the Hebrew University, Jerusalem, began excavation at Hazor in 1955.

2. A city in the south of Judah (Josh. 15: 23), perhaps Hezron, near to Kadesh-barnea (v. 3). This is thought to have been the central town of that name, the other Hazors, Hazor-hadattah, etc., being probably so called for distinction's sake.

3. "The kingdoms of Hazor" (Jer. 49:28-33); probably a district of Arabia; "it may be a collective name, and refer to settled, not wandering Arabs, dwelling in strong farmsteads. The tents of these nomads, and the insignificant Bedouin villages, without doors and bars, present a strange contrast to the great cities of Syria, with their magnificent palaces (vers. 23-27); and yet even the former contain precious goods, tempting the foreigner's greed" (Orelli, *Com.*, in loc.).

4. A city inhabited by the Benjamites after the captivity (Neh. 11:33); possibly the modern Khirbet Hazzur, 4 miles N. N. W. of Jerusalem. From the places mentioned with it, as Anathoth, Nob, etc., it would seem to have been a little north of Jerusalem.

Ha'zor-Hadat'tah (hā'zŏr-há-dăt'á; "New Hazor," Josh. 15:25). *See* Hadattah.

He (hā), the fifth letter of the Hebrew alphabet, pronounced like English "h." In the Hebrew of Psalm 119:33-40 each verse begins with this letter.

Head. This part of the body has generally been thought to be the seat of intelligence, while the heart, or the parts near it, were the place of the affections (Gen. 3:15; Psa. 3:3; Eccles. 2:14). In Scripture the *head* is sometimes put for the whole person (Gen. 49:26; Prov. 10:6), or for the life itself (Dan. 1:10; I Sam. 28:2).

Customs. The head was bowed: in worshipping God (Gen. 24:26; Exod. 4:31), and as a token of respect (Gen. 43:28). In *grief* the head was covered up (II Sam. 15:30; Esth. 6:12), shorn (Job. 1:20), sprinkled with dust (Josh. 7:6; Job 2:12), or the hands placed

thereon (II Sam. 13:19; Jer. 2:37). *Shaving* the head was forbidden to the priests and Nazarites (Lev. 21:5, 10; Num. 6:5). Lepers always went with the head uncovered (Lev. 13:45), while women generally covered the head in public (Gen. 24:65; I Cor. 11:5). The heads of criminals and enemies slain in war were often cut off (Matt. 14:10; Judg. 5:26; I Sam. 17:51, 57; 31:9).

Diseases. The head was liable to leprosy (Lev. 13:42-44), scab (Isa. 3:17), internal disease (II Kings 4:19; Isa. 1:5). *See* Diseases.

Figurative. The head is illustrative of God (I Cor. 11:3), of Christ (I Cor. 11:3; Eph. 1:22; Col. 2:19), of *rulers* (I Sam. 15:17; Dan. 2:38), of *chief men* (Isa. 9:14, 15); of the *chief city* of a kingdom (Isa. 7:8). The *covered* head is a symbol of defense and protection (Psa. 140:7), or of subjection (I Cor. 11:5, 10); *made bald* signifies heavy judgments (Isa. 3:24; 15:2; 22:12; Mic. 1:16); *lifted up*, of joy and confidence (Psa. 3:3; Luke 21:28); of *pride*, etc. (Psa. 83:2); of *exaltation* (Gen. 40:13; Psa. 27:6); *anointed*, of joy and prosperity (Psa. 23:5); *shaking the head* is a gesture of mockery at another's fall (Isa. 37:22) or misfortune (Psa. 22:7; Jer. 18:16; Matt. 27:39). The head is, according to Scripture, evidently the noblest part of man. Because in the head the human organism culminates Christ is called the "Head of the Church;" and for the same reason the head is the general metaphorical appellation of him who is most exalted, the most excellent, the chief. He who blesses lays his hand upon the head of the person to be blessed, and he who consecrates on the head of the person to be consecrated. Precisely for the same reason tongues of fire are distributed on the heads of the apostles: it was a heavenly laying on of hands.

Head of the Church. On account of the very intimate union that exists between Christ and the Church he is called the head (Eph. 4:15; 5:23), and the Church his body (4:12; Col. 1:24), inseparably united. Not only does the Church, as a body, stand in need of Christ (Col. 2:19; Eph. 4:15, 16), but the apostle ventures the bold expression that Christ also needs the Church, as that which belongs to his completeness. Believers are baptized by the Holy Spirit into Christ (Rom. 6:3, 4; Gal. 3:27) and into His Body. The figure of body and head is used more than any other to represent the service and manifestation of Christ through his redeemed people of this age. Christ is not only Head of His mystic Body, the Church, He is also Head of the Bride (Eph. 5:23-33). This last figure again presents the Church in the unique relationship it sustains to Christ, which will be realized after its glorification and the Marriage of the Lamb.

Headband (Hebrew plural, *kĭshshûrîm*), probably a *girdle* (Isa. 3:20; "attire," Jer. 2:32). *See* Dress.

Headdress. *See* Dress.

Headstone. In Zech. 4:7 Christ, under the symbolism of a Stone, is presented as the Head of the corner (Acts 4:11; I Pet. 2:7). The whole company of believers is viewed as a building of God, composed of living stones, Christ being the Headstone of the corner

(Eph. 2:19-22). In the millennial age, toward which the golden candlestick of Zech. 4:1-7 points, Christ will be manifested also as the Headstone of the temple of His restored covenant people Israel, the golden candlestick of Zech. 4:2 more specifically speaking of converted Israel as the light of the world in the Kingdom Age. *See* Corner Stone.

Heady (Gr. *propetēs, falling forward*), a term applied to one form of wickedness, viz., those who are rash, reckless (II Tim. 3:4).

Heal. *See* Diseases.

Heap, the rendering of several Hebrew words, with the general meaning of a collection of things so as to form an elevation. The term was applied to a pile of earth or stones covering over or marking the place of a grave (Josh. 7:26; 8:29; II Sam. 18:17); to the ruins of walls and cities (Job. 8:17; Isa. 25:2; Jer. 9:11); a pile (e. g., of rubbish, Neh. 4:2; of grain, Cant. 7:2; of sheaves, Ruth 3:7; Hag. 2:16, etc.).

Heart (Heb. mostly *lēb;* Gr. *kardia*). According to thorough investigation and evidence of Scripture in all its parts, the heart is the innermost center of the natural condition of man. The heart is: (1) The center of the bodily life, the reservoir of the entire life-power (Psa. 40:8, 10, 12), and indeed in the lowest physical sense; for eating and drinking, as strengthening of the heart (Gen. 18:5; Judg. 19:5; I Kings 21:7; Acts 14:17, etc.), becomes the strengthening of the whole man. (2) The center of the rational-spiritual nature of man; thus when a man determines upon anything, it is called to "presume in his heart to do so" (Esth. 7:5); when he is strongly determined, he is said to "stand steadfast in his heart" (I Cor. 7:37); what is done gladly, willingly, and of set purpose, is done "from the heart" (Rom. 6:17). The heart is the seat of love (I Tim. 1:5) and of hatred (Lev. 19:17). Again, the heart is the center of thought and conception; the heart knows (Deut. 29:4, Prov. 14:10), it understands (Prov. 8:5; Isa. 44:18; Acts 16:14), it deliberates (Neh. 5:7, marg.), it reflects (Luke 2:19), and estimates (Prov. 16:9). The heart is also the center of the feelings and affections: Of joy (Isa. 65:14); of pain (Prov. 25:20; John 16:6); all degrees of ill will (Prov. 23:17; Acts 7:54; James 3:14); of dissatisfaction, from anxiety (Prov. 12:25) to despair (Eccles. 2:20); all degrees of fear, from reverential trembling (Jer. 22:40) to blank terror (Deut. 28:28; Psa. 143:4). (3) The center of the moral life; so that all moral conditions, from the highest love of God (Psa. 73:26), even down to the self-deifying pride (Ezek. 28:2, 5), darkening (Rom. 1:21) and hardening (Isa. 6:10; 63:17; Jer. 16:12; II Cor. 3:15), are concentrated in the heart as the innermost life circle of humanity (I Pet. 3:4). The heart is the laboratory and place of issue of all that is good and evil in thoughts, words, and deeds (Mark 7:21; Matt. 12:34); the rendezvous of evil lusts and passions (Mark 4:19, comp. 15; Rom. 1:24); a good or evil treasure (Luke 6:45); the place where God's natural law is written in us (Rom. 2:15), as well as the law of grace (Isa. 51:7; Jer. 31:33); the seat of conscience (Heb. 10:22; comp. I John 3:19-

21); the field for the seed of the divine word (Matt. 13:19; Luke 8:15). It is the dwelling place of Christ in us (Eph. 3:17); of the Holy Spirit (II Cor. 1:22); of God's peace (Col. 3:15); the receptacle of the love of God (Rom. 5:5); the closet of secret communion with God (Eph. 5:19). It is the center of the entire man, the very hearth of life's impulse.

Hearth, the rendering of several Hebrew words:

1. A *brazier,* or portable *furnace,* in which fire was made in the king's winter apartment (Jer. 36:22, 23), Heb. *'āh.*

2. A fire pan or basin for holding fire (Zech. 12:6), for roasting in (I Sam. 2:14), or for washing, "laver" (Exod. 30:18, etc.), Heb. *kīyyōr.*

3. A *burning,* so rendered in Isa. 33:14), a fagot for fuel (Psa. 102:3), and from the same root, *yākăd,* a burning mass upon a hearth (Isa. 30:14), Heb. *mōqēd.*

Heat, the rendering of several Hebrew and Greek words, having besides its ordinary meaning several peculiar uses in Scripture.

Figurative. The heat of the sun is symbolical of tribulation, temptation, or persecution (Matt. 13:6, 21; Luke 8:6-13). A gentle heat of the sun signifies the favor and bounty of the prince, while a fierce heat denotes punishment (see Psa. 121:6). "Heat of the day" (Matt. 20:12) is united with burden to denote severe toil.

Heath. *See* Vegetable Kingdom.

Heathen (Heb. *gōyîm, troop*). At first the word *gōyîm* denoted generally all the nations of the world (Gen. 18:18; comp. Gal. 3:16), but afterward the Jews became a people distinguished from the other nations. They were a separate people (Lev. 20:23; 26:14-38), and the other nations were heathen. With these nations the Israelites were forbidden to associate (Josh. 23:7), to intermarry (Josh. 23:12; I Kings 11:2), or to worship their gods. Owing to its position these nations penetrated into Palestine, and the advance of heathen culture could not be prevented. For that very reason the lines of defense against all illegality were only the more strictly and carefully drawn by the vigilance of the scribes. "Two points especially were not to be lost sight of in guarding against heathen practices—heathen idolatry and heathen non-observance of the Levitical law of uncleanness. With respect to both the pharisaism of the scribes proceeded with extreme minuteness. For the sake of avoiding even an only apparent approximation of idolatry, the Mosaic prohibition of images (Exod. 20:4, sq.; Deut. 4:16, sq.; 27:15) was applied with the most relentless consistency." Not only did they declare themselves ready to die rather than to allow a statue of Caligula in the temple (Josephus, *Ant.,* xviii, 3, 8), but the Jews also repudiated pictorial representations in general, such as the trophies in the theater or the eagle at the gate of the temple. Very minute and exact regulations were made to prevent any encouragement of idolatry or contact therewith: e. g., an Israelite was not to have any business transaction with a Gentile during the three days preceding or the three days following a heathen festival, while on the festival itself an

Israelite was to hold no kind of intercourse with the town; all objects possibly connected with idolatrous worship were forbidden, wood taken from an idol grove was prohibited, and bread baked by it could not be eaten, or if a weaver's shuttle was made of such wood its use was forbidden, as well as cloth woven therewith. A Gentile—as a nonobserver of the laws of purification—was unclean, and all intercourse with him was defiling, including his house and all objects touched by him (John 18:28). Provisions coming from the heathen were not to be eaten by Jews, although they were allowed to trade in them. A strictly legal Israelite could not at any time sit at meat at a Gentile table (Acts 11:3; Gal. 2:12) (Schurer, Div. II, vol. i, 51, sq.). *See* Gentile.

Heave Offering. *See* Sacrificial Offerings.

Heave Shoulder. *See* Sacrificial Offerings.

Heaven, the rendering of several Hebrew and Greek words:

1. **Material.** (1) **The Sky** (Heb. *shämăyĭm, lofty*), by far the most frequent designation of *heaven* in the Hebrew Scriptures, and meaning the firmament, which appears like an arch spread out above the earth, and represented as supported on foundations and pillars (II Sam. 22:8; Job. 26:11), with the rain descending through its gates or windows (Psa. 78:23; comp. Gen. 28:17). We find such expressions as *toward heaven, heavenward* (Gen. 15:5; 28:12); "under the *heavens*," i. e., on earth (Eccles. 1:13; 2:3); "under the whole heaven," i. e., the *whole* earth (Gen. 7:19; Deut. 2:25; Job. 28:24, etc.); "the heavens and the earth," i. e., the universe (Gen. 1:1; 2:1). Akin to this word is *height* (Heb. *märōm, elevation*), which, though not rendered "heaven," has doubtless a celestial signification (Psa. 68:18; 93:4; 102:19), rendered "on high," "the height." (2) *A wind* (Heb. *gălgăl, a wheel*), rendered "heaven" in Psa. 77:18, but meaning a *whirlwind*. (3) *Clouds* (Heb. *shăhăq, cloudy dust, vapor*), the sky or heavens; serene (Job 37:18) or as covered with clouds (37:21); from which descend the rain and dew (36:28; Prov. 3:20), and manna (Psa. 78:23; comp. Isa. 45:9), and whence the thunder is heard (Psa. 77:18). Also put for the clouds themselves (Job. 38:37). (4) Closely connected with (3) is (4) *Celestial Expanse* (Heb. *räqĭă', that which is spread out*), rendered in the A. V. "firmament" (*q. v.*). (5) Of the Greek terms, *ouranos*, like (1), signifies the *heights*, and thence the vaulted expanse of the sky; the region where clouds and tempests gather (Matt. 16:2; Luke 4:25); the region above the sky, the seat of things eternal and perfect, where God and the other heavenly beings dwell (Matt. 5:34; 23:22, etc.). This heaven Paul (II Cor. 12:2) seems to designate the third heaven. *Mid-heaven* (Gr. *mesouranēma*). Thus the sun is said to be in mid-heaven at noon.

2. **Spiritual.** Scriptures evidently specify three heavens, since "the third heaven" is revealed to exist (II Cor. 12:2). It is logical that a third heaven cannot exist without a first and second. Scripture does not describe specifically the first and second heaven. The first, however, apparently refers to the at-

mospheric heavens of the fowl (Isa. 2:18) and clouds (Dan. 7:13). The second heaven may be the stellar spaces (Cf. Gen. 1:14-18). It is the abode of all supernatural angelic beings. The third heaven is the abode of the Triune God. Its location is unrevealed. Until this present age, it has not been entered by any created being, angelic or human. It is the divine plan at present to populate the third heaven. It is a place (John 14:1-3). It is called "glory" (Heb. 2:10). Those who enter it will be perfected forever (Heb. 10:14) and made partakers of Christ's fullness, (John 1:16) which is all fullness (Col. 1:19) and which comprehends the very nature of the Godhead bodily (Col. 2:9). The Apostle John was called into heaven (Rev. 4:1). The Apostle Paul was caught up to the third heaven (II Cor. 12:1-9). He was prohibited, however, from revealing what he saw and heard. Heaven is a place of beauty (Rev. 21:1-22:7), of life (I Tim. 4:8), service (Rev. 22:3), worship (Rev. 19:1-3) and glory (II Cor. 4:17).

Heaving and Weaving. *See* Sacrificial Offerings.

He'ber (hē'bĕr; Nos. 1, 2, 3, Heb. *'ēbĕr,* of the *other side,* i. e., of the river, *immigrant*).

1. The last named of the seven chiefs of the Gadites in Bashan (I Chron. 5:13).

2. One of the sons of Elpaal, and a chief of the tribe of Benjamin (I Chron. 8:17).

3. A Benjamite and son of Shashak (I Chron. 8:22), B. C. before 598.

(Nos. 4, 5, 6, Heb. *hĕbĕr, fellowship*).

4. Son of Beriah and grandson of Asher (Gen. 46:17; I Chron. 7:31, 32). His descendants are called *Heberites* (Num. 26:45).

5. "A descendant of *Hobab* (*q. v.*), whose wife, Jael, slew Sisera (Judg. 4:17, sq.). He is called Heber the Kenite (Judg. 4:11, 17; 5:24), which seems to have been a name for the whole family (Judg. 1:16). Heber appears to have lived separate from the rest of the Kenites, leading a patriarchal life. He must have been a person of some consequence from its being stated that there was peace between the house of Heber and the powerful King Jabin. At the time the history brings him under our notice his camp was in the plain of Zaanaim, near Kedesh, in Naphtali" (Kitto).

6. Probably a son of Mered (of Judah) by Jehudijah, and "father" of Socho (I Chron. 4:18).

He'berite (hē'bĕr-īt), a descendant of *Heber q. v.* No. 4), of the tribe of Asher (Num. 26:45).

He'brew Language. The language of the Hebrews and of the Old Testament Scriptures, with the exception of a few chapters written in Aramaic. It is called Hebrew nowhere in Scripture, but this is not surprising when we remember how rarely that name is employed to designate the Israelites. It is called "the language of Canaan" (Isa. 19:18), as distinguished from that of Egypt; and the "Jewish language" (II Kings 18:26, 28), as distinguished from the Aramaean. The Hebrew belongs to the Semitic or Shemitic group of languages.

1. **Characteristics.** (1) **Sound.** The Hebrew has a predominance of guttural sounds—at least four, if not five; the use of very strong

letters, which may be represented by *tt*, *ts*, *kk* (or *kh*); the vowels are kept in strict subordination to the consonants, it being a rare and exceptional case when a word or syllable begins with a vowel. (2) **Roots, etc.** Like other Semitic languages, the Hebrew is characterized by the three-letter root. This is expanded into a variety of conjunctional forms, expressing intensity, reflexiveness, causation, etc., modifications of the root idea being indicated, not by additions to the root, but by changes within the root. (3) A peculiar use of the *plural*, not only denoting plurality, but likewise extension, in space or time. (4) In composition the Hebrew is simple, pictorial, and poetical.

2. **History.** Hebrew was already in spoken and written use when Moses and the Israelites came up out of Egypt (c. 1440 B. C.). The evidence of the Pentateuch and the witness of archaeology support this fact. The Proto-Semitic script, discovered by Petrie early in the twentieth century, and the discovery of a simple alphabetic Semitic script closely akin to Hebrew at Ras Shamra-Ugarit on the North Syrian coast, 1929-1937, add new evidence that Hebrew was available as a literary vehicle for Moses, the first inspired penman of Scripture "Ugaritic," belonging to the Amarna Age, late fifteenth and fourteenth centuries B. C. (Cf. Cyrus Gordon, *The Living Past*, New York, 1941, p. 103-135), was coeval with the Mosaic age. Although there is not the slightest need to suppose that Moses wrote in any other script than the primitive prongshaped alphabet of early Hebrew, yet, as one brought up in the Egyptian court (Exod. 2:10) and well versed in Egyptian sciences and heiroglyphics (Acts 7:22), he could have written in Egyptian. Besides, he was likely familiar with Akkadian, the *lingua franca* of all south western Asia at the time, a fact proved by the Amarna Letters.

3. **Origin.** Hebrew originated from the old Phoenician alphabet from which all alphabets in current use, Semitic and non-Semitic, were ultimately derived. The origin of this proto-Semitic alphabet is still unclear, although an early example of the rude script was discovered at Serabit el Khadem in the Sinaitic Peninsula in 1904-05. Albright dates this script in the early fifteenth century (*Bulletin of the Am. Schools of Oriental Research* 110 April, 1948, p. 22). It is of more passing interest that this proto-"Sinai-Hebrew Script" was discovered in the very area in which Moses was commanded to write (Exod. 17:8-14), but early Hebrew goes back to the time of Abraham. The question is, Did the patriarch import it from Haran or find it in Palestine? The patriarchs evidently used an Aramaic dialect in Mesopotamia, but when they came into Canaan they adopted a local Canaanite dialect, which was not identical with the standard speech of the sedentary Canaanites, as may be linguistically demonstrated (W. F. Albright, *From the Stone Age to Christianity*, p. 182). Since old Hebrew is practically identical with Phoenician, this conclusion seems inescapable. The Canaanite origin of Hebrew is attested by Ugaritic and Phoenician. Numbers of important Canaanite inscriptions have been re-

covered, notably the Sarcophagus of Ahiram of Byblos, 11th century B. C. Later Phoenician inscriptions from Cyprus, Sardinia and Carthage and other colonies of the Mediterranean show the Canaanite affinities of Hebrew. The Gezer Calendar (c. 925 B. C.) written in perfect classical Hebrew, followed by the Moabite Stone (c. 850 B. C.) written in the language of Moab, which was very closely akin to Hebrew, as well as later inscriptions from Samaria from the time of Jeroboam II, help to trace the development of Hebrew as a closely aligned Canaanite dialect. Particularly enlightening is the Siloam Inscription (c. 701 B. C.) cut in Hezekiah's rock conduit and notably the Lachish Letters, which give us the Hebrew spoken and written at the time of Jeremiah.

4. **Written Hebrew.** The round-bosomed letters of present-day Hebrew Bibles are evidently a modification of Aramaic characters. The famous Dead Sea Scrolls from the second century B. C. are written in this type of letter as well as the Nash Papyrus, dated c. 125 B. C. The vowel points in modern Hebrew Bibles were not added until 600-800 A. D. and were the work of Massoretic scholars, notably at Tiberias in Palestine. *M. F. U.*

He′brew of the Hebrews. A Hebrew of Hebrew parentage *and* ancestry; a Hebrew of pure blood (Phil. 3:5). Owing to the loss of private records in earlier times there might have been many a Benjamite left in Palestine who could not prove a pure Hebrew descent. On another occasion Paul seems to appeal in similar case, "Are they Hebrews? So am I" (II Cor. 11:22). That the expression did not refer to being born in Palestine is shown by Paul himself saying, "I am a man which am a Jew of Tarsus" (Acts 21:39). The expression "Hebrew of the Hebrews" reflects a Semitic idiom denoting the superlative degree, and meaning "a Hebrew in every sense of the word." cf. "Song of Songs" (Cant. 1:1) "the superlative Song" or "holy of holies," i. e., "the *most holy* place."

Hebrews. The first person in the Bible called a Hebrew is Abram (Gen. 14:13). Thereafter his descendants through Isaac and Jacob were known as "Hebrews" (Gen. 40:15); 43:32; Exod. 2:11). The origin of the name Hebrew offers a difficult problem. The term may be derived from the prominent Semitic progenitor, Eber, the ancestor of Abraham (Gen. 10: 21, 22). Again "Abram the Hebrew" (Gen. 14:13), may be "Abram who crossed the river," that is, the Euphrates (Josh 24:2, 3). Accordingly, the Septuagint translates "Abram, the Hebrew" *hä ′Ibhrî*, from *′ābhär* "to cross over." Gen. 14:13 has *ho peratēs*, "the one who crossed over." Another archaeological and linguistically appealing possibility is the widely discussed question whether or not the Habiru, featured in the Nuzian-Hittite and Amarna documents of the fifteenth and fourteenth centuries B. C. are not to be identified, in part at least, with the Hebrews. For the scholar who follows the underlying chronology of the Massoretic Text and places the Exodus c. B. C. 1440, the identification Hebrew (Habiru) fits extremely well. The Habiru in central Palestine, reflected in the

Amarna Letters, were in this case in part at least Biblical Hebrews. *M. F. U.*

Hebrews, Epistles to. *See* Bible.

This magnificent epistle, from the standpoint of doctrinal contribution and literary excellency is in many ways without peer among N. T. books. This book is of unparalleled importance in expounding the transition from the old Levitical economy to Christianity. It eloquently sets forth the foundation Judaism furnished Christianity in Messianic type, symbolized in prophecy.

1. **Attestation and Authorship.** External evidence unmistakably attests the early existence of the epistle. Clement of Rome, Polycarp, Justin Martyr, Dionysius of Alexandria, and Theophilus of Antioch quote from it. However, Marcion and the Muratorian Fragment do not recognize it. Eusebius, Origen, Athanasius and others held that it was written by Paul, but the authorship has remained uncertain. The writer of the epistle does not mention his name, which is contrary to the custom of the Apostle. Moreover, the writer to the Hebrews uses the Septuagint throughout except possibly at 10:30, whereas Paul employs both the Hebrew and the Septuagint. The style and vocabulary are not particularly Pauline.

2. **Occasion and Date.** It seems clear that the temple was still in existence and the ritual still continued. The present tense is repeatedly used in this connection (8:4, 13; 9:4, 5, 9; 10:1, 8, 11; 13:10, 11). The readers had evidently been Christians for a long time and had suffered severely. A date c. 67-69 A. D. would seem to fit the internal evidence.

3. **Purpose.** The writer aims to establish the supremacy of Christ and Christianity (1:1-10:18), and to warn those who accepted Christ of the dangers of apostasy (6:4-8; 10:26-31; 13:14-19). In view of the antiquated nature of Judaism the writer also exorts his readers to make a complete break with it (12:18-13:17). To accomplish this purpose the writer in closely knit argument establishes the superiority of Christ over angels, over Moses and Joshua and over O. T. priesthood and ritual.

4. **Outline.**
Introduction: 1:1-4.
Part I. The Son superior to the angels, 1:5-2:18
  1. O. T. proof, 1:5-14
  2. Resulting obligation, 2:1-4
  3. Reasonableness of the Son's humiliation, 2:5-18
Part II. The Son superior to Moses and Joshua, Chaps. 3:1-4:16
  1. To Moses, 3:1-6
  2. Failure under Moses and Joshua, 3:7-4:2
  3. Provided rest, 4:3-10
  4. Necessity of attaining this rest, 4:11-13
  5. Christ's triumph as High Priest our incentive to draw near, 4:14-16
Part III. The superiority of Christ's High Priesthood, Chaps. 5:1-7:28
  1. His high priestly qualifications, 5:1-10
  2. Necessity of comprehending spiritual truth, 5:11-6:20

  3. Melchisedec aspect of Christ's High Priesthood, 7:1-25
  4. Christ's High Priesthood contrasted with the Levitical, 7:26-28
Part IV. The superiority of Christ's High Priestly ministry, 8:1-10:18
  1. The circumstances (Chaps. 8), 8:1-13
  2. Contrast of sanctuary and service under the two covenants, 9:1-28
  3. Contrast of Levitical sacrifices and Christ's sacrifice, 10:1-18
Part V. Practical application, 10:19-12:29
  1. Plea for faithfulness, 10:19-39
  2. Call to achieve by others' example, 11:1-12:4
  3. Consolation by fact of sonship, 12:5-13
  4. Warning against apostasy, 12:14-17
  5. Argument from the higher position of the Christian, 12:18-29
Conclusion: Social and religious obligations, personal instructions, 13:1-25. *M. F. U.*

199. Hebron

He′bron (hē′brŭn; *a community; alliance*).

1. A town in the mountains of Judah, about two thousand eight hundred feet above the Mediterranean Sea, and between Beersheba and Jerusalem, being about twenty miles from each. It was named Kirjath-arba (Gen. 23:2; Josh. 14:15; 15:13), also *Mamre* (*q. v.*), after Mamre the Amorite (Gen. 13:18; 35:27). It is now called el-Khulil. Among those who lived there were the Canaanites and the Anakim (Gen. 23:2; Josh. 14:15; 15:13), Abraham (Gen. 13:18), Isaac and Jacob (Gen. 35:27). David made it his royal residence (II Sam. 2:1-4; 5:5; I Kings 2:11); also Absalom (II Sam. 15:10). Sarah was buried here (Gen. 23:17-20); Joshua took Hebron (Josh. 10:36, 37; 12:10) and Caleb retook it (Josh. 14:12). The Romans also captured and destroyed it. The mosque of Hebron covers the remains of some of the patriarchs, and it is with difficulty that any Christian gains admission to the sacred building.

2. The third son of Kohath, and a grandson of Levi; a younger brother of Amram, father of Moses and Aaron (Exod. 6:18; Num. 3:19; I Chron. 6:2, 18; 23:12), B. C. before 1440. His descendants are called *Hebronites* (Num. 3:27, etc.).

3. The son of Mareshah, and, apparently, grandson of Caleb, of the posterity of Judah (I Chron. 2:42, 43), B. C. after 1400.

He′bronite (hē′brŭn-īt), a descendant of Hebron, the third son of Kohath (Exod. 6:18; Num. 3:19, comp. v. 27; I Chron. 26:23, 30, 31). We find them settled in Jazer, in Gilead, "mighty men of valor," seventeen hundred in number, who were superintendents for King David (I Chron. 26:31, 32), while twenty-seven hundred others held the same position over the two and a half tribes (v. 30).

Hedge, the rendering of several Hebrew and Greek words, most of them used to denote that which surrounds or incloses, whether it is a stone wall (Prov. 24:31; Ezek. 42:10), or a fence of other materials. A vineyard hedge (Psa. 89:40; I Chron. 4:23; Jer. 49:3) was common in Palestine (Heb. *gādēr* or *g⁰dērāh*), and the second Hebrew word is employed to describe the wide walls of stone, or fences of thorn (Eccles. 10:8), which served as a shelter for sheep in winter and summer (Num. 32:16). The word *m⁰sūkāh* means a thorn hedge (Mic. 7:4). See Wall.

Figurative. A hedge is used figuratively of God's protection (Job 1:10); of the sluggard's way (Prov. 15:19); afflictions (Job 3:23; 19:8); judgments (Lam. 3:7; Hos. 2:6); holy ordinances (Isa. 5:2; Matt. 21:33); broken hedge, figurative of the removal of protection (Psa. 80:12; Isa. 5:5).

Heg'ai (hĕg'ā-ī), or **He'ge** (hē'gē). Esth. 2:3, the eunuch having charge of the harem of Xerxes, and the preparation of the females sought as concubines for him (Esth. 2:8, 15), B. C. about 478.

He'ge (hē'gē), the same as *Hegai* (Esth. 2:3, q. v.).

Heifer. See Animal Kingdom; Sacrifices.

Figurative. As the heifer, or young cow, was not used for plowing, but only for treading out the grain, when it ran without any headstall, the expression an "unbroken heifer" (Hos. 4:16; A. V. "backsliding") is used for refractoriness. A similar sense is attached to the expression, "calf of three years old" (Isa. 15:5; Jer. 48:34). "To plow with another man's heifer" (Judg. 14:18), is to take an unfair advantage of another. An heifer that "loveth to tread out the corn" (Hos. 10:11), is figurative of one choosing pleasant, productive, and profitable labor; because in threshing the animal was allowed to eat at pleasure (Deut. 25:4). "An heifer of three years old" (Isa. 15:5) is one still in freshness and fullness of its strength, and is used figuratively of a nation still strong. "Fair," of the beauty and wealth of Egypt (Jer. 46:20). "At grass," of the luxurious Chaldeans (50:11).

Heifer, Red. See Sacrificial Offerings.

Heir. See Inheritance.

He'lah (hē'lä; *ornament, necklace*), one of the two wives of Ashur, the father of Tekoah, by whom she had three sons (I Chron. 4:5, 7).

He'lam (hē'lăm; II Sam 10:16, 17). Memorable as the place located betwen the Euphrates and the Jordan, where David routed the Syrians under Hadadezer. The town named Alema (I Macc. 5:26) modern 'Alma in the Hauran is the probable location.

Hel'bah (hĕl'bà; *fatness*), a town of Asher not far from Sidon, and one of the places from which the Canaanites were not expelled (Judg. 1:31). Identified with Mahalliba of the Assyrian monuments, N. E. of Tyre.

Hel'bon (hĕl'bŏn; *fat*, i. e., fertile), a place named only in Ezek. 27:18, where "the wine of Helboa" is mentioned among the commodities furnished by Damascus to the great market of Tyre. "It still exists in the village of *Helbon*, a place with many ruins three and a half miles N. of Damascus in the midst of a valley of the same name" (Keil, *Com.*, in loc.).

Hel'dai (hĕl'dā-ī).
1. A Netophathite, and descendant of Othniel, chief of the twelfth division (twenty-four thousand), of David's forces (I Chron. 27:15), B. C. about 960. In I Chron. 11:30 (where he is called *Heled*) his father's name is said to be Baanah; and in the parallel passage (II Sam. 23:29) he is called *Heleb*.
2. One returned from the captivity, whom the prophet Zechariah was directed to take with him when he went to crown the high priest Joshua as a symbol of the future Messiah's advent (Zech. 6:10), B. C. 519. The name is written *Helem* in v. 14.

He'leb (hē'lĕb; *fat, fatness*), son of Baanah the Netophathite, and one of David's warriors (II Sam. 23:29); elsewhere more correctly called *Heled* (I Chron. 11:30), or, still better, *Heldai* (I Chron. 27:15).

He'led (hē'lĕd), son of Baanah, a Netophaphathite, and one of David's warriors (I Chron. 11:30), called in the parallel passage (II Sam. 23:29) *Heleb*, but more accurately *Heldai* (I Chron. 27:15).

He'lek (hē'lĕk; *a portion*), the second son of Gilead, of the tribe of Manasseh, whose descendants were called *Helekites* (Num. 26:30; Josh. 17:2).

He'lekites (hē'lĕk-īts), the descendants of Helek (Num. 26:30). "Children of Helek" (Josh. 17:2).

He'lem (hē'lĕm). 1. The brother of Shamer and great-grandson of Asher (I Chron. 7:35), B. C. probably before 1440. Perhaps the same as *Hotham* (v. 32).
2. One assisting Zechariah in typical crowning of the high priest (Zech. 6:14), probably by erroneous transcription for *Heldai* (v. 10).

He'leph (hē'lĕf), a city mentioned as the starting point of the northern border of Naphtali, beginning at the west (Josh. 19:33).

He'lez (hē'lĕz; perhaps, *strength*).
1. One of David's mighty men (II Sam. 23:26), an Ephraimite of Pelon (I Chron. 11:27), and captain of the seventh monthly course (I Chron. 27:10), B, C. about 970.
2. Son of Azariah and father of Eleasah, of the tribe of Judah (I Chron. 2:39).

He'li (hē'lī), the father-in-law of Joseph, and maternal grandfather of Christ (Luke 3:23).

Hel'kai (hĕl'kā-ī; probably a shortened form of Hilkiah), son of Meraioth, and one of the chief priests in the time of the high priest Joiakim (Neh. 12:15), B. C. after 536.

Hel'kath (hĕl'kăth; *portion, field*), a town assigned to the tribe of Asher, on the eastern border (Josh. 19:25), and one of the Levitical cities (21:31). In I Chron. 6:75 *Hukok* is an old copyist's error.

Hel'kath-Haz'zurim (hĕl'kăth-hăz'û-rĭm, *smoothness of the rocks*, others *field of the sharp edges*), the name given to the plain near the pool of Gibeon, because of the deadly combat of twelve of the adherents of Ishbosheth with as many of David's, which appears to have brought on a general engagement, resulting in the defeat of the men of Israel (II Sam. 2:12-17).

Hell, a term which in common usage designates the place of future punishment for the wicked. Other meanings in many instances are expressed by this term, which must be recognized to prevent mistakes and confusion. In some cases it refers to the grave, in others to the place of disembodied spirits without any necessary implication as to their happines or unhappiness. This fact, however, does not militate against the correctness of the belief indicated by the common use of the term, a belief which rests upon many passages of Scripture for its support.

1. **Scripture Terms.** The words of the original Scriptures rendered "hell" in the English A. V. are three in number. With a solitary exception (II Pet. 2:4 *tartaroō*, to *incarcerate*) they are the only words thus translated. These, however, are not the only terms, as we shall see, in which the idea of a place of future penal suffering for the wicked is clearly and strongly expressed. The three words are as follows:

(1) **Sheol.** Without entering into the discussion as to the derivation or root meaning of this term of the Old Testament Scriptures, it may be sufficient to say, that this word occurs sixty-five times. In our A. V. it is translated thirty-one times "grave," thirty-one times "hell," and three times "pit." The general idea is "the place of the dead;" and by this is meant, not the grave, but place of those who have departed from this life. The term is thus used with reference to both the righteous and the wicked: of the righteous (Psa. 16:10; 30:3; Isa. 38:10, etc.), of the wicked (Num. 16:33; Job 24:19; Psa. 9:17, et al.). This is in accordance with the general character of the Old Testament revelation, which presents much less clearly and strongly than the New the doctrine of the future life with its distinct allotments of doom. But there are many hints, and more than hints, of the difference in the conditions of the departed. The Psalmist prays: "Draw me not away with the wicked, and with the workers of iniquity" (Psa. 28:3; see also Isa. 33:14; 66:24; Dan. 12:2).

(2) **Hades.** One of the New Testament terms rendered "hell" like the Old Testament "sheol" is comprehensive, and has a quite similar significance. It refers to the underworld, or region of the departed, the intermediate state between death and the resurrection. It occurs eleven times in the New Testament, viz.: Matt. 11:23; 16:18; Luke 10:15; 16:23; Acts 11:27, 31; I Cor. 15:55; Rev. 1:18; 6:8; 20:13, 14. The A. V. renders the word "hell" in every case with one exception, viz.: I Cor. 15:55, where it gives "grave." The R. V., however, substitutes "hades" for "hell," leaving the word untranslated, thus representing, as it is held, more correctly the original idea. It is not to be denied that the distinction thus recognized between "hades," and "hell," as a place of misery is a valid one. Nevertheless it is equally plain that our Lord, in certain of his words, associated judgment and suffering with the

condition of some of the inhabitants of "hades" (e. g., Matt. 11:23; Luke 16:23). *See* Hades.

(3) **Gehenna** (*q. v.*), the valley of Hinnom. A place where the Jewish apostasy, the rites of Moloch, were celebrated (I Kings 11:7). It was converted by King Josiah into a place of abomination, where dead bodies were thrown and burnt (II Kings 23:13, 14). Hence the place served as a symbol, and the name was appropriated to designate the abode of lost spirits. In this way the term was used by our Lord.

The word occurs twelve times in the New Testament, and in every case it is properly translated "hell," denoting the eternal state of the lost after resurrection. That is, the meaning of the English word which overbears all others is particularly the meaning of Gehenna (see Matt. 5:22, 29, 30; 10:28; 18:9; 23:15, 33; Mark 9:43, 45, 47; Luke 12:5; James 3:6).

The distinction between hades (the intermediate state) and Gehenna ("eternal hell") is of importance, because not only is it necessary to the understanding of quite a large number of passages in the New Testament, but also it may prevent misconstruction and remove uncertainty as to Christ's teaching with regard to the future state of the wicked. It also has important bearing upon the doctrine of "Christ's descent into hell" (hades) and that of the "Intermediate State."

2. **Scripture Synonyms.** The Bible doctrine of hell is by no means confined to the terms above mentioned, and to the passages in which they appear. There are many phrases in which the overshadowing idea is presented with great distinctness, such as "unquenchable fire," "the blackness of darkness," "furnace of fire," "torment in fire and brimstone," "the smoke of their torment," "the lake which burneth with fire and brimstone," "where their worm dieth not," "the place prepared for the devil and his angels." Van Oosterzee well remarks: "There is no doubt that Holy Scripture requires us to believe in a properly so-called *place* of punishment, in whatever part of God's boundless creation it is to be sought. That the different images under which it is represented cannot possibly be taken literally will certainly need no demonstration; but it is perhaps not unnecessary to warn against the opinion that we have to do here with mere imagery. Who shall say that the reality will not infinitely surpass in awfulness the boldest pictures of it?"

For theological treatment of doctrine, *See* Punishment, Future, Gehenna.

Hel′lenist (hĕl′ĕn-ĭst), a term employed of a person who spoke Greek but was not racially of the Greek nation. The expression is especially used of Jews who adopted the Greek language and, to some extent, Greek customs and culture. In both Acts 6:1 and 9:29 the R. S. V. correctly renders the original text as Hellenists. The A. V. translates simply Grecians.

Helmet. *See* Armor, 2 (2).

He′lon (hē′lŏn; *valorous, strong*), the father of Eliab, which latter was prince of the tribe of Zebulun at the Exodus (Num. 1:9; 2:7; 7:24, 10:16), B. C. 1440.

Help. Besides its usual meaning of *assistance*, a technical application is given the term in two passages.

1. "Helps," *boētheia*, an apparatus for securing a leaking vessel, by means of ropes, chains, etc., forming a process of undergirding (Acts 27:17).

2. "Helps" (Gr. *antilēpsis*; a *laying hold of*), the ministrations of the deacons, who have care of the sick (I Cor. 12:28), where it is used in the senses of *helpers*.

Helpmeet (Heb. *'ēzĕr kⁿnĕgdō*; a *help as his counterpart*), i. e., an aid suitable to him, such as the man stood in need of (Gen. 2:18, generally now punctuated so as to read a "helpmeet for him").

Helve (Heb. *'ēs, wood*), the handle or wooden part (Deut. 19:9) of an ax (*q. v.*).

Hem of a Garment, the extremity, border of the outer garment (Exod. 28:33; 39:24-26; Matt. 9:20; 14:36). The importance which the later Jews, especially the Pharisees, attached to this portion of the dress (Matt. 23:5, A. V. "borders") was founded upon the regulation Num. 15:38, 39. The fringe did not owe its origin to this regulation, but was originally the ordinary mode of finishing the robe; the ends of the threads composing the woof being left in order to prevent the cloth from unraveling.

He'mam (hē'măm), the son of Lotan, the eldest son of Seir (Gen. 36:22). The same as Homam (*q. v.*).

He'man (hē'măn; *faithful*).

1. One of the four persons celebrated for their wisdom, to which that of Solomon is compared (I Kings 4:31). He is probably the same as the son of Zerah and grandson of Judah (I Chron. 2:6). The mention of these men together as famous for their wisdom does not at all require that we should think them contemporaries.

2. Son of Joel and grandson of Samuel (*Shemuel*) the prophet, the Kohathite, and one of the leaders of the temple music as organized by David (I Chron. 6:33 where singer should rather be rendered *musician;* 15:17; 16:41, 42), B. C. about 970. This, probably, is the Heman to whom the eighty-eighth Psalm is ascribed. He had fourteen sons and three daughters. "Asaph, Heman, and Jeduthun are termed 'seers' (II Chron. 35:15), which refers rather to their genius as sacred musicians than to their possessing the spirit of prophecy (I Chron. 15:19; 25:1; II Chron. 5:12, although there is not wanting evidence of their occasional inspiration" (McC. and S., *Cyc.*).

He'math (hē'măth).

1. A Kenite, ancestor of the Rechabites (I Chron. 2:55).

2. An incorrect Anglicized form (I Chron. 13:5; Amos 6:14) of *Hamath* (*q. v.*).

Hem'dan (hĕm'dăn; *pleasant*), the first named of the four "children" of Dishon, which latter was a son of Seir, and one of the Horite "dukes" in Mount Seir (Gen. 36:26). In I Chron. 1:41 the name is, by an error of transcribers, written *Amram.*

Hemlock. *See* Vegetable Kingdom.

Hen. *See* Animal Kingdom.

Hen (hĕn; favor, *grace*), the son of Zephaniah, to whom the prophet was sent with a sym-

bolical crown (Zech. 6:14); probably a figurative name for *Josiah* (v. 10). "By the LXX and others the words are taken to mean 'for the favor of the son of Zephaniah' " (Smith, *Dict.*).

He'na (hē'nȧ; signification unknown), a city probably in Mesopotamia, mentioned in connection with Hamath, Arpad, etc., as having been overthrown by Sennacherib before his invasion of Judea (II Kings 18:34; 19:13; Isa. 37:13). It is probably the city of *Ana* on the Euphrates.

Hen'adad (hĕn'ȧ-dăd; *favor of Hadad*), a Levite, whose sons were active in the restoration after the captivity (Ezra 3:9). Two of the latter, Bavai and Binnui, are named (Neh. 3:18, 24; 10:9), B. C. before 536.

He'noch (hē'nŭk; I Chron. 1:3, 33). *See* Enoch.

He'pher (hē'fēr; a *pit, well*).

1. The youngest son of Gilead and great-grandson of Manasseh (Num. 27:1). He was the father of Zelophehad (Num. 26:33; 27:1; Josh. 17:2, 3), and his descendants were called *Hepherites* (Num. 26:32), B. C. before 1400.

2. The second son of Ashur (a descendant of Judah) by one of his wives, Naarah (I Chron. 4:6), B. C. after 1440.

3. A Mecherathite, one of David's heroes, according to I Chron. 11:36. The name does not appear in the list given in Samuel, and is supposed to be an interpolation, or identical with *Eliphelet* of II Sam. 23:34.

4. A royal city of the Canaanites, taken by Joshua (12:17), and used by Solomon for commissary purposes (I Kings 4:10). It is to be sought for in the neighborhood of Socoh, in the plain of Judah.

He'pherite (hē'fēr-īt), a descendant of Hepher 2 (Num. 26:32).

Heph'zi-bah (hĕf'zĭ-bȧ; *my delight* is *in her*).

1. The queen of Hezekiah and mother of King Manasseh (II Kings 21:1), B. C. before 690.

2. A symbolical name given to Zion by Isaiah (62:4). Zion had been called "Forsaken," but now is called Hephzi-bah, as the object of God's affection. This prophetic appellation will find fulfilment in the future conversion and millennial blessing of the nation Israel.

Herald (Heb. *kärōz*, only in Dan. 3:4), a crier, a herald, from an old Persian word *khresii* (Keil, *Com.*, in loc.). The several Greek words usually rendered "preach" in the New Testament have the meaning of to proclaim as a herald, while the word "preacher" (I Tim. 2:7; II Tim. 1:11; II Pet. 2:5) would be more correctly rendered *herald.*

Herb. *See* Vegetable Kingdom.

Herbs, Bitter (Heb. *mⁿrōrîm*). The Israelites were commanded to eat "bitter herbs" with the Passover bread (Exod. 12:8; Num. 9:11) in remembrance of the bitterness of their bondage in Egypt (Exod. 1:14). "The *Mishnah* mentions these five as falling within the designation of 'bitter herbs,' viz., lettuce, endive, succory, what is called 'Charchavina (urtica, beets?) and horehound' "(Edersheim, *The Temple*, p. 204).

Herd (Heb. *bäqär;* Gr. *agelē*). "The herd was greatly regarded both in the patriarchal and Mosaic period. The ox was the most precious stock next to horse and mule. The herd yielded the most esteemed sacrifice (Num. 7:3; Psa. 69:31; Isa. 66:3); also flesh meat and milk, chiefly converted, probably, into butter and cheese (Deut. 32:14; II Sam. 17:29), which such milk yields more copiously than that of small cattle. The full-grown ox was hardly ever slaughtered in Syria; but, both for sacrificial and convivial purposes, the young animal was preferred (Exod. 29:1). The agricultural and general usefulness of the ox, in plowing, threshing, and as a beast of burden (I Chron. 12:40; Isa. 46:1), made such a slaughtering seem wasteful. The animal was broken to service probably in his third year (Isa. 15:5; Jer. 48:34). In the moist season, when grass abounded in the waste lands, especially in the 'south' region, herds grazed there. Especially was the eastern table land (Ezek. 39:18; Num. 32:4) 'a place for cattle.' Herdsmen, etc., in Egypt were a low, perhaps the lowest caste; but of the abundance of cattle in Egypt, and of the care there bestowed on them, there is no doubt (Gen. 47:6, 17; Exod. 9:4, 20). So the plague of hail was sent to smite especially the cattle (Psa. 78:48), the firstborn of which also were smitten (Exod. 12:29). The Israelites departing stipulated for (Exod. 10:26), and took 'much cattle' with them (12:38). Cattle formed thus one of the traditions of the Israelitish nation in its greatest period, and became almost a part of that greatness. When pasture failed, a mixture of various grains (Job 6:5) was used, as also 'chopped straw' (Gen. 24:25; Isa. 11:7; 65:25), which was torn in pieces by the threshing machine and used probably for feeding in stalls. These last formed an important adjunct to cattle keeping, being indispensable for shelter at certain seasons (Exod. 9:6, 19)" (Smith, *Bib. Dict.*).

Herdman (Heb. *bōqēr,* a tender of oxen; in distinction from *rōʿî,* a feeder of sheep). The rich owners of herds placed them in charge of herdsmen, who watched the cattle to keep them from straying, to protect them from wild beasts, and lead them to suitable pasture. Usually they carried a staff furnished with a point of iron (*see* Goad) and had also a wallet or small bag for provisions, etc. (I Sam. 17:40, 43; Psa. 23:4; Mic. 7:14; Matt. 10:10; Luke 9:3, 4). They wore a cloak, with which they could envelop the entire body (Jer. 43:12); and their food was always simple, sometimes only the chance fruit they might find (Amos 7:14; Luke 15:15). Their wages consisted of the products of the herd, especially of the milk (Gen. 30:32, sq.; I Cor. 9:7). The occupation of herdsman was honorable in early times (Gen. 47:6; I Sam. 11:5; I Chron. 27:29; 28:1). Saul himself resumed it in the interval of his cares as king; also Doeg was certainly high in his confidence (I Sam. 21:7). Pharaoh made some of Joseph's brethren "rulers over his cattle." David's herdmasters were among his chief officers of state. The prophet Amos at first followed this occupation (Amos 1:1; 7:14). *See* Shepherd.

Heʹres (hēʹrĕz; *mountain of the sun*), a city of Dan, near Aijalon, which the Ammonites continued to hold (Judg. 1:35), but as tributaries.

Keil (*Com.,* in loc.) thinks it only another name for *Ir-shemesh,* i. e. Beth-shemesh.

Heʹresh (hēʹrĕsh; *silent, dumb*), one of the Levites that dwelt in the "villages of the Netophathites," near Jerusalem, on the return from captivity (I Chron. 9:15), B. C. 536.

Heresy (Gr. *hairesis,* a *choice*), means, in the New Testament: 1. A chosen course of thought and action; hence one's chosen opinion, tenet, and so a sect or party, as the Sadducees (Acts 5:17); the Pharisees (15:5; 26:5); the Christians (24:5, 14; 28:22). 2. Dissensions arising from diversity of opinions and aims (Gal. 5:20; I Cor. 11:19). 3. Doctrinal departures from revealed truth, or erroneous views (Tit. 3:10; II Pet. 2:1). Against such departures the apostles vigorously warned the Church (Acts 20:29; Phil. 3:2).

In the Early Church. In the apostolic age we find three fundamental forms of heresy, which reappear with various modifications in almost every subsequent period.

(1) **Judaistic.** "The Judaizing tendency, the heretical counterpart of Jewish Christianity, so insists on the unity of Christianity with Judaism, as to sink the former to the level of the latter, and make the Gospel merely a perfected law. It regards Christ also as a mere prophet, a second Moses, and denies, or at least wholly overlooks, his priestly and kingly offices, and his divine nature in general. The Judaizers were Jews in reality, and Christians only in appearance and name. They held circumcision and the whole moral and ceremonial law of Moses to be still binding, and the observance of them necessary to salvation. Of Christianity as a new, free, and universal religion, they had no conception. The same heresy, more fully developed, appears in the 2d century under the name of *Ebionism.*"

(2) **The Paganizing or Gnostic Heresy.** "This exaggerates the Pauline view of the distinction of Christianity from Judaism, sunders Christianity from its historical basis, resolves the real humanity of the Saviour into a Docetistic illusion (i. e., the heavenly Being, whose nature is pure light, suddenly appearin as a sensuous apparition). The author of this baptized heathenism, according to the uniform testimony of Christian antiquity, is Simon Magus, who unquestionably adulterated Christianity with pagan ideas and practices, and gave himself out, in pantheistic style, for an emanation of God. This heresy, in the 2d century, spread over the whole Church, east and west, in various schools of *gnosticism.*"

(3) **Syncretistic Heresy.** As attempts had already been made, before Christ, by Philo and others to blend the Jewish religion with heathen philosophy, especially that of Pythagoras and Plato, so now, under the Christian name, there appeared confused combinations of these opposing systems, forming either a paganizing Judaism or a Judaizing paganism, according as the Jewish or the heathen element prevailed.

"Whatever their differences, however, all these three fundamental heresies amount at last to a more or less distinct denial of the central mystery of the Gospel—the incarnation of the Son of God for the salvation of the world. They make Christ either a mere man or a mere superhuman phantom; they allow, at all events, no real and abiding union of the divine and human natures in the person of the Redeemer."

Heresy disturbed the unity of doctrine and of fellowship in the early Church, which was therefore forced to exclude those holding false doctrine from its communion. Once excluded, they formed societies of their own. This was the case with the Novations, Gnostics, Donatists, etc. *See* Schaff (*Hist. Christ. Church*, p. 88, sq.).

Heretic. *See* Heresy.

Heritage. *See* Inheritance.

Her′mas (hûr′măs; Gr. *Hermas, Mercury*), a Christian resident at Rome to whom St. Paul sends greeting (Rom. 16:14). Irenaeus, Tertullian, and Origen agree in attributing to him the work called *The Shepherd*, but this is greatly disputed. He is celebrated as a saint, in the Roman calendar, on May 9.

Her′mes (hûr′mēz; the Greek name of Mercury), a man mentioned (Rom. 16:14) as a disciple in Rome. "According to the Greeks he was one of the seventy disciples and afterward Bishop of Dalmatia" (Calmet, *Dict.*, s. v.).

Hermog′enes (hûr-mŏj′ê-nēz; *Mercury-born*), a disciple in Asia Minor mentioned by the apostle Paul, along with Phygellus, as having deserted him, doubtless from fear of the perils of the connection (II Tim. 1:15). Nothing more of him is known.

200. Mount Hermon

Her′mon (hûr′mŏn; *sacred mountain*), a mountain which formed the northermost boundary (Josh. 12:1) of the country beyond the Jordan (11:17), which Israel conquered from the Amorites (Deut. 3:8). It must, therefore, have belonged to Anti-Libanus (I Chron. 5:23; comp. Deut. 4:48; Josh. 11:3, 17, etc.). It is identified with the present Jebel *es-Sheik*, i e., Sheik's Mountain, situated thirty miles S. W. of Damascus and forty miles N. E. of the sea of Galilee. Its height is 9,101 feet above the Mediterranean sea. In Deut. 4:48 it is called Mount *Sion*, i. e., a high mountain, being by far the highest of all mountains in or near Palestine. The ancient inhabitants of Canaan had sacred places on the high mountains and the hills. We need not wonder, then, that Hermon should have been selected for the altar and the sacred fire. Hermon was the

religious center of primeval Syria. Its Baal sanctuaries not only existed, but gave it a name, before the Exodus (Josh. 11:17). The view from perpetually snow-clad Hermon is magnificent. From the torrid Dead Sea region its cooling snows can be seen 120 miles distant, Its melting glaciers form the main source of the turbulent Jordan. The Psalmist speaks (Psa. 133:3) of the "dew of Hermon." The snow on the mountain condenses the vapors during the summer so that abundant dews descend upon it while the surrounding country is parched. One of its tops is actually *Abu-Nedy*, i e., "father of dew."

It has been widely held that the Hermon region was the scene of our Lord's transfiguration. If so, Christ traveled from Bethsaida, on the northwest shore of the Sea of Galilee, to the coasts of Caesarea Philippi; thence he led his disciples "into a high mountain apart, and was transfigured before them." Afterward he returned, going toward Jerusalem through Galilee (comp. Mark 8:22-28; Matt. 16:13; Mark 9:2-13, 30-33).

Her′monites (hûr′mŏn-īts), properly "the Hermons," with reference to the three summits of Mount Hermon (Psa. 42:6).

Her′od (hĕr′ŭd). This was not a personal name, but the family or surname. It belonged alike to all the generations of the Herodian house as known to the Scriptures. Much confusion has arisen from not having recognized this simple fact. Hence some have even questioned the inerrancy of Luke in that he called Herod Antipas "Herod," when Josephus uniformly calls him "Antipas." But the point assumed is itself a mistake. For Luke mentions him as "Herod," and "Herod the tetrarch," and as "Herod the tetrarch of Galilee" in the same chapter (3:1, 19); and Josephus repeatedly calls him "Herod the tetrarch," and "Herod the tetrarch of Galilee," and "that Herod who was called Antipas" (*Ant.*, xviii. ch. 2, § 3; ch. 7, § 1; ch. 9, §§ 5 and 6; *War*, ii, ch. 9, § 1). The identification therefore is perfect as regards the person, the official title, the political geography; and Luke's mention is strictly historical. All the descendants of Herod the Great down to the fourth generation, who were identified with the government of Palestine and are mentioned in the New Testament, are known in history by the surname Herod; Herod Archaelaus, Herod Antipas, Herod Philip II, Herod Agrippa I, and Herod Agrippa II.

I. Her′od the Great, B. C. 37-4.

1. *History.* The father of Herod the Great was named Antipater. He was of Idumaean blood. The Idumaeans were of the Edomite stock, the descendants from Esau. (Josephus, *Ant.*, xiv, ch. 8, § 5; *Wars*, i, ch. 10, § 3). They occupied a southern district of Palestine known as the *Negeb*, located between the Mediterranean and the Dead Sea and southward. By conquest John Hyrcanus brought the Idumaeans into Palestine about B. C. 130, and as they conformed to the Jewish rite of circumcision they embraced the Jewish religion. However, the Jews regarded the Idumaeans with considerable suspicion and prejudice, calling them but "half Jews" (*Ant.*, xiv, ch. 15, § 2; xx, ch. 8, § 7). Josephus

records that Herod was appointed procurator of Galilee when only fifteen years of age (*Ant.*, xiv, ch. 9, § 2); but probably the age of twenty-five was intended (see Whiston's note in loco). Mark Antony gave Herod a tetrarchy (*Ant.*, xiv, ch. 13, §§ 1 and 2; *War*, i, ch. 12, § 5), and afterward he persuaded the Roman Senate to make Herod a king (*Ant.*, xiv, ch. 14, § 4). The great Roman historian Tacitus affirms that Herod was placed on the throne by Mark Antony, and that Augustus (Caesar) enlarged his privileges (*Hist.*, v, 9). But Herod did not succeed in asserting his royal rights over Palestine until he had captured Jerusalem, B. C. 37. Nevertheless, his coronation by Caesar was made an occasion of great magnificence (*Wars*, i ch. 20, § 3).

2. **Architecture.** Herod had a passion for ostentatious display in the direction of magnificent architecture and monuments, as had also all his ruling descendants after him. Jerusalem, as the metropolis of the land, was the recipient from him of much munificence in the way of architectural monuments. To conciliate the Jews, who had been alienated by his cruelties, he with much address proposed to reconstruct their ancient temple which Solomon had originally built, though it has been shrewdly suspected that he entertained the sinister motive to possess himself of the public genealogies collected there, especially those relating to the priestly families, unto whom they were of paramount importance and interest. It is said that he thereby hoped to destroy the genealogy of the expected Messiah, lest he should come and usurp his kingdom. However that may be, he endeavored to make the Jewish nation understand that he was doing them a great kindness without cost to them, and he promised that he would not attempt to build them a new temple, but merely restore to its ancient magnificence the one originally built by David's son. For the restoration made by Zerubbabel upon the return of Israel from the captivity of Babylon seems to have fallen short in architectural measurement, in height some sixty cubits (*Ant.*, xv, ch. 11, § 1), and the whole was becoming marked with decay. To this end Herod took down the old temple to its very foundations, and engaged one thousand wagons to draw stones and ten thousand skilled workmen to teach the priests the art of stonecutting and carpentering.

The temple proper which he erected was one hundred cubits in length and twenty cubits in height. It was constructed of white stone, each one being twenty-five cubits long and eight in height. Surmounting this structure was a great white dome adorned with a pinnacle of gold, suggestive of a mountain of snow as seen from afar (*Ant.*, xv, ch. 11, §§ 2 and 3). The Jewish tradition holds that "the temple itself was built by the priests in one year and six months, when they celebrated its completion with Jewish feast and sacrifices; but that the cloisters and outer inclosures were eight years in building." However that may be, additions were made continuously from year to year; so that though Herod began the rebuilding B. C. 20, as a whole it was literally true that the temple was "built

in forty and six years," when the Jews so asserted to Jesus (John 2:20). But the end was not yet, for the work was really continued until A. D. 64, just six years before the final destruction of the temple by the Roman soldiers of Titus. Even then, when the Romans under Vespasian made incursion into Palestine in 64, Herod's great grandson, Herod Agrippa II was making expensive preparations to "raise the holy house twenty cubits higher" (*War*, v, ch. 1, § 5).

The destruction of the temple occurred on the Jewish Sabbath, August 10, in the year 70. When Jerusalem was captured, the temple was burned, the Jewish people were expatriated; and never since has sacrifice been offered up to God on Jewish altars.

About the same time Herod rebuilt the temple at Samaria, "out of a desire to make the city more eminent than it had been before, but principally because he contrived that it might at once be for his own security and a monument of his magnificence" (*Ant.*, xv, ch. 8, § 5). He is also credited with having erected a monument over the royal tombs at Jerusalem, after having attempted to rob the dead of their sacred treasures, "such as furniture of gold and precious goods that were laid up there" (*Ant.*, xvi, ch. 7, § 1).

3. **Character.** Herod was not only an Idumaean in race and a Jew in religion, but he was a heathen in practice and a monster in character. During his administration as king he evidenced himself to be exceedingly crafty, jealous, cruel, and revengeful. He exercised his kingly power with the disposition of a very despot. This characteristic was illustrated in its worst form toward the several members of his own family. He had nine or ten wives (*War*, ii, ch. 28, § 4), and on the merest suspicion put to death his favorite wife, Mariamne, and also her brothers, Aristobulus and Alexander (*War*, i, ch. 11, § 6, close), and at last, when on his own deathbed, just five days before he died himself, he ordered his son, Antipater, to be slain (*Ant.*, xv, ch. 7, §§ 5-7; *War*, i, ch. 22, § 5; *Ant.*, xv, ch. 6, § 2, close; ch. 3, § 3; xvi, ch. 11, § 7; xvii, ch. 7, § 1; *War*, i, ch. 33, § 7). It is no wonder that Augustus should have ridiculed this Jewish king, saying that "It is better to be Herod's hog than to be his son!" It is easy to understand how it is accordant with his character that the inquiry made by the Magi, "Where is he that is born King of the Jews?" should so arouse his jealous spirit that he should "seek the young child to destroy him," and "sent forth and slew all the male children that were at Bethlehem" (Matt. 2:13, 16). One of Herod's most infamous crimes in the purpose was, when he was on his deathbed, to command that "the principal men of the entire Jewish nation" should come to his presence, whom he then shut up in the hippodrome and surrounded them by soldiers, and ordered that immediately after his own death, which he

expected soon, they should all be killed, *that it might seemingly, at least, afford "an honorable mourning at his funeral!"* The royal wretch died, but the order was never executed (*Ant.*, xvii, 6, 5; *War*, i, ch. 33, § 8).

II. Her′od Archaela′us (B. C. 4-A. D. 6). He was the eldest of the three sons who succeeded the father in the government of Palestine—the son of Malthace, the Samaritan wife (*War*, i, ch. 33, § 7).

1. **Accession.** His father provided in his will that Archaelaus should become *a king* at his own death; but a deputation of fifty Jews of distinction, by the consent of Quintilius Varus, Prefect of Syria, sailed to Rome and protested against such measure, urging that instead there might be a theocracy under the civil authority of a Roman procurator. It is said that eight thousand Jews met and hailed these deputies with shouts of joy in sympathy with this movement.

2. **Ethnarchy.** When the Emperor Augustus had read the will and heard the protestations against Archaelaus, he refused his royalty, and instead appointed him ethnarch over one half of his father's kingdoms, including therein Samaria, Judea, and Idumaea, promising, however, that if his ruling his people should justify the measure he would thereafter make him a king over the same territory.

3. **Government.** But Archaelaus began at once to usurp kingly prerogatives without and against imperial authority. Soon his course produced tumults and revolts, which he sought to reduce to peace by cruelties and terrorism. On the occasion of a certain Passover he slew three thousand Jewish subjects, "till the temple was full of dead bodies; and all this was done . . . by one who pretended to the lawful title of king" (*Ant.* B., xvii, ch. 9, §§ 3-6; *War*, B. ii, ch. 6, §§ 1, 2; ch. 7, §3).

4. **Deposition.** In consequence of the complaints made against the ethnarch Archaelaus was deposed in the year 6 of corrected chronology, which was early in the tenth year of his government, and he was banished to Vienna in Gaul (France), where at length he died. His territory was then reduced to a Roman province and placed under the authority of Coponius as procurator.

5. **Scripture Reference.** A single incidental allusion is made in the gospels to Archaelaus, but it is in exact accordance with his character. It was probably near the close of the first year of Christ's infancy that Joseph and Mary returned from Egypt, intending to go to Galilee by way of Jerusalem. "But when he heard that Archaelaus was reigning over Judea in the room of his father, Herod (the Great), he was afraid to go thither, and he turned aside into the parts of Galilee" (Matt. 2:22). (For criticism on the expression "Archaelaus was reigning," *see* Herod Antipas, 8).

III. Her′od An′tipas (ăn′tĭ-pás; B. C. 4-A. D. 39). This prince was the full but younger brother of Archaelaus (*Ant.*, xvii, ch. 1, § 3).

1. **Character.** As a ruler he was regarded as "sly, ambitious, luxurious, but not so able as his father" (Schürer). Hausrath does him the scant courtesy of calling him "a wily sneak!" Of him Jesus said, "Go ye and tell *that fox*, behold, I cast out devils" (Luke 13:32). His administration was characterized throughout with cunning and crime, intensely selfish and utterly destitute of principle.

2. **Tetrarchy.** His father had contemplated making him a king, to reign over the territory ruled by Archaelaus, which constituted one half of his own kingdom, but subsequently concluded to alter his will, making him a mere "tetrarch" of Galilee and Perea, which embraced but one fourth of the original territory (*Ant.*, xvii, ch. 8, § 1), and Caesar afterward confirmed the will and "made Antipas tetrarch" (*War*, i, ch. 33, § 7). Besides this testimony a coin exists which distinctly proves the historicity of this tetrarchy. It was struck in the year 33, and reads on the obverse side, "Of Herod the Tetrarch;" and on the reverse side, "Tiberias," as the capital of the tetrarchy.

3. **Marriages.** Herod Antipas was first married to the daughter of Aretas, an Arabian king of Petraea. Nevertheless he intrigued with Herodias, the wife of his half-brother, Philip I, who was a tetrarch of noble standing, in whose house Antipas was a guest. The two eloped together, although both were married at the time (*Ant.*, xviii, ch. 5, § 1). Now Herodias was granddaughter of Herod the Great, and sister of Herod Agrippa I, and the wife and niece of Herod Philip I.

4. **John and Antipas.** The scandalous conduct of Herod Antipas and Herodias is cited in the first three gospels in connection with the reproof administered by John the Baptist to Herod Antipas, and is treated quite at large by Josephus (Matt. 14; Mark 6; Luke 9; *Ant.*, xviii, ch. 7, § 1). For John said, "It is not lawful for thee to have thy brother's wife" (Mark 6:18); and Luke adds, "Herod the tetrarch being reproved by him for Herodias, Philip's wife, and for all the evils which he had done, added yet this above all, that he shut up John in prison" (3:19, 20).

The first two gospels mention "the daughter of Herodias," but neither gives her name. Josephus says that ner name was Salome (*Ant.*, xviii, ch. 5, § 4). The occasion referred to by both evangelists and historian, in which so much interest centers, was a festive party of the nobles of the land who assembled at the tetrarch's palace to celebrate the anniversary of Herod's birthday. Salome here first appears in this scene in sacred history. On the mothers' side she was granddaughter of Simeon, the high priest. Now the fact that a child was born to Philip and Herodias by the first marriage of the mother was a bar to her second marriage under Jewish law. Her marriage to Antipas, while her proper husband and his proper wife were still living, was the more aggravating to the Jews because she was a Jewess and belonged to the royal family; and their infamy was the more conspicuous in that Herod Antipas was the ruler of the Jews and had shamelessly put the Jewish laws at defiance (Lev. 18:18; 20:21).

This anniversary was the occasion, and this daughter, Salome, was made the guilty person by whom this infamous Herodias secured the revenge of a bad woman for the reproof given her husband for living with her unlawfully. Salome having danced before the nobles to the great fascination and gratification of Herod, he promised her anything she might ask of him, to the half of his kingdom. Herodias saw her opprotunity and induced her daughter to request the head of John the Baptist, who was then in prison near at hand. The executioner was sent to the prison at once and the ghastly gift was given. John the Baptist was beheaded, the man who of all men born of women was greatest (Matt. 11:11; Luke 7:28). The voice of one crying in the wilderness was at last silenced. The rough and rugged prophet of righteousness ceased to live. "His disciples came and took up the body and buried it, and went and told Jesus" (Matt. 14:12).

The place of the Baptist's prison was anciently known as Machaerus, but the modern name is Mkaur. It is located in the mountain fastnesses with a deep ravine below, on the eastern shore of the Dead Sea, between Abarim and Pisgah, not far from the northern extreme of the sea. It is said that the rock-hewn dungeon is beneath the splendid banquet hall in which the nobility were entertained when the swordsman was sent to bring in the prisoner's head. It was here in the same mountains in which Israel sought for the grave of her first prophet (Moses), was the last prophet (John) entombed.

5. **Treacheries.** It was now the thirty-ninth year of our chronology when Caius Caligula had been for two years upon the imperial throne at Rome. He soon discovered the real character of Herod Antipas. Ascertaining that as tetrarch he was intriguing with a Roman officer of the army named Sejanus, and had been confederating with the king of Parthia against the Roman empire, and had laid in store armors for seventy thousand men of war, Antipas was soon to be called to judgment. Meantime Herodias was most urgent that the tetrarch should go to Rome and make request that he might receive a crown as king. Moreover, he was extremely jealous of his nephew Herod Agrippa I, who had already received a kingdom. Antipas had deeply offended Agrippa by insulting reflections on his condition of poverty before he had had royalty bestowed on him. Agrippa was in relations of intimacy with the emperor, and kept him posted as to these movements of his uncle Antipas. At length Antipas unwillingly was constrained to go to Rome and request that the first will of his father might be granted him by the emperor. Herod Agrippa I immediately sent his freedman named Fortunatus to Rome with the necessary documents to prove these accusations, and Agrippa himself followed in a few days to confront Antipas with the facts and proofs in person. Antipas was just having his first interview when Fortunatus entered and handed the letters at once to the emperor. When Agrippa had also arrived, and all the accusations against Antipas were understood by the emperor, he challenged Antipas to deny the charges preferred of his treachery toward the imperial government, in confederating with Sejanus, and with Artabanus, king of Parthia, and the secret storing of arms against himself. The tetrarch could not deny these accusations, and so confessed his guilt.

6. **Antipas Deposed.** Thereupon Caligula deprived Herod Antipas of his tetrarchy "and gave it by way of addition to Agrippa's kingdom," confiscated his money, and sent him and his wife into perpetual banishment in Lyons, Gaul (France), and eventually in Spain, where he died (*Ant.*, xviii, ch. 7, §§ 1, 2; *War*, ii, ch. 9, § 6). Dion Cassius also relates that "Herod the Palestinian, having given a certain occasion by reason of his brothers (nephew) was banished beyond the Alps, and his estates of the government confiscated to the state" (Book lv, Caesar Augustus, 27).

7. **Jesus and Antipas.** It is now in place to consider the relations of our Saviour and this tetrarch during the week of the great crucifixion. It was about six years before Herod Antipas was deposed and exiled. From the time that this Herod had slain the Baptist, this crime had haunted his conscience. When then he heard of the deeds done by Jesus, "he was perplexed, because it was said of some that John had risen from the dead." "And Herod said, John have I beheaded, but who is this of whom I hear such things?" And he said, "This is John the Baptist; he is risen from the dead; and therefore mighty works do show forth themselves in him" (Luke 9:7; Matt. 14:2).

201. Coin of Herod Antipas

We find Herod Antipas at Jerusalem when Jesus was before Pilate on trial for his life. When Pilate understood that Jesus was from Galilee, the territory of Antipas, "he sent him to Herod as belonging to his jurisdiction." "And when Herod saw him, he was exceedingly glad; for he was desirous to see him of a long season, because he had heard many things of him, and he hoped to see some miracle done by him." Nevertheless, as Christ did not reply to his questions of curiosity, he was offended, and "Herod with his men of war set him at nought, and mocked him, and arrayed him in gorgeous robe, and sent him again to Pilate. And the same day Pilate and Herod were made friends together; for before they were at enmity between themselves" (Luke 23:5-12; comp. Acts 4:27).

8. **Kingship of Antipas.** Criticism has found difficulty in understanding how the evangelists mention that "*Archaelaus was reigning* over Judea in the room of his father Herod (the Great)" as if he were *a king*, whereas Archaelaus was but an ethnarch, and his father ruled a *kingdom* (Matt. 2:22). So also Herod Antipas is repeatedly called "*a king*" in the first two gospels when his principality was merely a tetrarchy (Matt. 14:1, 9; Mark 6:14, 22-27). Alford says, "Herod was not king properly, but only a tetrarch." Wescott states

that "he was called king by courtesy."
Whedon says that he was so called "in compliance with custom;" and Farrar, "It is only popularly that he is called king." The determining argument, however, is fatal to all these conjectural opinions, and is based upon the *usus* of the word king, at the time the evangelists employed it, and not in its *modern* restricted sense. We now apply the term absolutely and exclusively to *royalty*, but in the time of Augustus and afterward, it was applicable not only to a soverign ruler, but "in a general and lower sense applied equally to *a prince, ruler, viceroy, and the like*" (Robinson's *Greek Dictionary of the New Testament*, on Basileus, and also Basilenō). The appellation was applied "to a chief, a captain, a judge . . . *to a king's son, a prince, or anyone sharing in the government;* generally a lord, a master, a householder, *and after Augustus, to any great man*" (Liddell and Scott's *Greek Dictionary*, 1883, on Basileus). Josephus (born A. D. 37), who lived in the time of the apostles, confirms this usage when he relates that Herod the Great altered his will, "*and therein made Antipas king*," when in fact he was merely made tetrarch (*War*, i, ch. 32, § 7).

IV. Her′od Phil′ip II (B. C. 4-34 A. D.).

1. **Philip the Tetrarch.** This Herod was also the son of Herod the Great and Cleopatra. He should not be confounded with a half brother of the same name, who was the son of Mariamne, and known as Philip I. By his father's will Philip I was excluded from all government rights on account of the supposed treachery on the part of his mother toward her husband (*War*, i, ch. 30, § 7). He married his niece Herodias, who afterward eloped with her husband's half brother Herod Antipas. Philip I and Herodias had a daughter named Salome, who figured in the death of John the Baptist. Philip II, the tetrarch, married this Salome.

2. **Tetrarchy.** With characteristic accuracy Luke refers to this "Philip," and is confirmed in all particulars by Josephus and contradicted in none. This Jewish historian gives us definitely the countries included in his tetrarchy. He mentions how Herod the Great by will provided that his own kingdom should be divided between his three sons; Archaelaus taking half the territory, as already described, to be ruled as an ethnarchy, and the remaining half to be divided into two parts, to be called tetrarchies, meaning each a fourth part, to be given to the "two sons, Philip (II) and Antipas;" and that "Batanaea and Trachonitis and Auronitis (i. e., Gaulonitis) and parts of Jamnia . . . were to be made subject to Philip;" under the name of tetrarchy (*Ant.*, xvii, ch. 11, § 4; ch. 8, § 1). These regions were located in northeastern Palestine. There is in existence a coin struck by the authority of Philip II, in the reign of the Emperor Tiberius, which bears the following superscription:

Obverse, "Tiberius Augustus Caesar"—Tiberios Sebastos Kaiser.

Reverse, "Of Philip Tetrarch"—Philippou tet [rarches].

Philip's subjects were mostly Syrians and Greeks. He had a peaceful rule for thirty-seven years.

3. **Conduct.** This tetrarch was altogether the best of all the Herods. He is described as "a person of moderation and quietness in the conduct of his life and government," whose consideration for his subjects was remarkable; that when he traveled among them he was careful to have his tribunal on which he sat in judgment to follow him in his progress, and when anyone met him who wanted assistance, he made no delay but had his tribunal set immediately wheresoever he happened to be, and sat down upon it and heard his complaint. Moreover, he left monuments of himself worthy of his name in improvements for his people. At Paneas, at the base of Mount Hermon, in the north, at the principal source of the Jordan, he built a new city with much magnificence, called Caesarea Philippi (Matt. 16:13). It is now but a mere ruin. This city must be distinguished from Caesarea on the Mediterranean Sea. He also erected Bethsaida to the rank of a city, whose site was a little north of the Sea of Galilee on the upper Jordan, and he gave it the name Julias, after Julia, "the profligate daughter of Augustus" (*Ant.*, xviii, ch. 2, § 1; *War*, ii, ch. 9, § 1).

4. **Death.** After a long rule, distinguished for its moderation and equity, this worthy tetrarch died A. D. 34, which was "in the thirtieth year of the reign of Tiberius." He was greatly beloved by his people. He had married Salome, the daughter of Herodias, but they left no children. Upon his death his territory was annexed to the Roman province of Syria. "When he was carried to his monument, which he had already erected for himself beforehand, he was buried with great pomp" (*Ant.*, xviii, ch. 4, § 6).

5. **Philip and the Gospels.** He is mentioned by Luke as "Philip, tetrarch of the Iturea," which is the Greek name for the country lying at the base of the Lebanon mountains (Luke 3:1). "When Jesus came into the coasts (Mark, Gr. *tas kōmas, the villages*) of Caesarea Philippi, he asked his disciples, saying, Whom do men say that I, the Son of man, am. . . . But whom say ye that I am? Simon Peter said, Thou art the Christ, the Son of the living God. Jesus said, Blessed art thou, Simon Bar-jona: for flesh and blood hath not revealed it unto thee, but my Father which is in heaven" (Matt. 16:13-17; Mark 8:27-30). It was in this region that Jesus began to teach them that "the Son of man must suffer many things, and be rejected of the elders and chief priests and scribes, and be slain, and be raised the third day" (Luke 9: 22). "But they understood not that saying, and were afraid to ask him" (Mark 9:32).

Thus the second generation of the Herodians known to the gospels pass out of history.

We come now to the third generation of the Herods, the first of whom is

V. HER′OD AGRIP′PA I (A. D. 37-44).

1. **Princely Life.** This Agrippa was the son of Bernice and Aristobulus, a son of Herod the Great, who slew him. He was born B. C. 10, and died A. D. 44. He was the child of two first cousins, and was himself married to another cousin, who was the daughter of his

aunt, who again was married to an uncle! Josephus mentions him as "Agrippa," and "Agrippa the Great" (*War*, i, ch. 28, § 1; *Ant.*, xvii, ch. 2, § 2; xviii, ch. 5, § 4). In the New Testament he is called either by his surname "Herod," or "Herod the king" (Acts 21:1, 6, 7, 11, 19-21). He was brought up and educated at Rome, as were most of the Herodian princes. Agrippa appears to have been a man of gracious manners, of kindly spirit in the main, gifted with extraordinary powers of eloquence, and quite vain. In religion he was a zealous rather than a devout Jew, attentive to "tithe of mint and anise and cummin," but neglectful of "the weightier matters of the law, judgment, mercy, and faith." He was keenly fond of popularity, and possessed much personal magnetism (*Ant.*, xix, ch. 6, §§ 1, 2; xix, ch. 7, § 3).

2. **Reverses.** Agrippa and Caius (Gaius) Caligula, the heir apparent to the imperial throne, in early life became warm personal friends, a fact which afterward was greatly to the advantage of this prince. For out of this intimacy came some remarkable surprises and reverses of fortune to Agrippa. One day these friends were riding out together in a chariot, and Eutychus, a freedman, was their charioteer. In the course of conversation, Agrippa enthusiastically stretched out his hands and said confidingly to Caligula that he wished that old Tiberius would die, that Caius Caligula might assume the purple and the throne. The freedman, overhearing the remark, reported it to the emperor Tiberius, who at once peremptorily ordered Agrippa to be put in chains and then imprisoned. Wearing his robe of distinction, the order was executed, and Agrippa was placed among the criminals of the State. This humiliation was endured, however, but six months, when Tiberius died, and Caligula at once became emperor (*Ant.*, xviii, ch. 6, § 6; *War*, ii, ch. 9, § 5).

3. **Kingship.** A few days after the imperial funeral Agrippa was summoned to appear at the new emperor's palace—the palace of Caligula. Having shaved and changed raiment, he presented himself hopefully in the presence of the new emperor, his friend, who immediately proceeded to "put a diadem upon Agrippa's head and appointed him to be king of the tetrarchy of (his uncle) Philip (and Lysanius); also . . . changed his iron chain for a gold one of equal weight," which he hung about his neck. Afterward this golden chain was "hung up within the limits of the temple at the treasury (at Jerusalem), that it might be a memorial of the severe fate he had lain under; . . . a demonstration how the greatest prosperity may have a fall, and that God sometimes raises what is fallen down. . . . For this chain thus dedicated afforded a document to all men that King Agrippa had once been bound in a chain for a small cause, but recovered his former dignity and was advanced to be a more illustrious king" (*Ant.*, xviii, ch. 6, §§ 10, 11; xix, ch. 6, § 1). The Senate at Rome also gave him the honorary position of pretor.

4. **Assumes Government.** In the second year of Caligula's reign Agrippa requested leave of the emperor to return home to Pales-

tine and take possession of his kingdom (*Ant.*, xviii, ch. 5, § 11). Accordingly he sailed on the Mediterranean, in the usual course, to Alexandria in Egypt. At this time the Jews and Greeks of the city were in very unpleasant relations with each other. When the Greeks saw this Jewish King, accompanied by his bodyguard, exploiting much gold and silver, they spitefully took occasion to mock him with the meanest insults. They even engaged a poor, naked, idiot boy, named Carabas, who was the butt of the street boys, placed on him a crown of paper, clothed him in mat cloth, and with a stick in his hand to represent a scepter and a bodyguard composed of *the gamin* of the city, they derided the new king on the stage (see Philo's *Flaccum*, §§ 5 and 8). But when Agrippa reached his subjects in Palestine the Jews were astonished to see him returning as a king, and he was received with apparent satisfaction.

5. **Memorable Services.** In accordance with his promise on leaving the emperor at Rome, having organized and established his kingdom, King Agrippa I returned to the imperial capital. It was about this time that Caligula developed unmistakable indications of insanity, and, among other things, demanded that he should be universally deified and adored as a god, and that all men should swear by his name. He filled his Jewish subjects with the utmost horror when he ordered Petronius, president of Syria, to place a gilded statue of the emperor in the holy of holies of the temple at Jerusalem to be worshiped. For when they submitted to become subjects of the empire they were guaranteed all their own national and religious rights. A similar attempt at Alexandria had occasioned both tumults and massacres. An embassy composed of Jews, who were the principal men among them, was organized, with the eminent Philo at their head, to persuade Caligula to desist from this inexpressible wrong. But when they went to the emperor he refused them his presence, and bade Philo "Begone!" Petronius meantime, with an army, marched to Jerusalem. At Ptolemais the Jews flocked by the ten thousand to petition the Syrian prefect not to compel them to "violate the laws of their forefathers;" but that, if he persisted in carrying out the imperial order, to first kill them, and then do what he was resolved upon (*Ant.*, xviii, ch. 8, §§ 1-6). Petronius was touched with this loyalty of their faith, and, dismissing the Jews, promised to send to Rome in their interests in this matter. Meantime Agrippa, who was at this time at Rome, furnished in honor of Caligula a magnificent banquet; and when the emperor was full of wine, and Agrippa had drank to his health, Caligula generously proposed in return everything that might contribute to Agrippa's happiness, and, so far as was in the emperor's power, he should be at his service. With admirable tact and address Agrippa declined to receive anything in his own behalf, as he had already received so much; but, in behalf of his brethren at home, he said, "This is my petition, that thou wilt no longer think of the dedication of that statue which thou hast ordered to be set up in the Jewish temple by Petronius." Caligula thereupon, "as

a favor to Agrippa," rescinded the order (*Ant.*, xviii, ch. 8, §§ 1-8). Nevertheless, because Petronius so far disobeyed Caligula's orders as to make representations, and so delay executing his orders, the emperor ordered the prefect to commit suicide; but the order was delayed at Rome, and very soon Caligula died by the dagger of the assassin, named Chaerea, whom the emperor had outrageously insulted. This was in A. D. 41.

6. **Enlarged Kingdom.** Claudius, a weak-minded man, who had been the laughing-stock of the court, now came to the front. Through the friendly offices of Herod Agrippa I, who with great diplomacy used his influence adroitly with the Senate favorably for this man, he was made emperor. As a return for being elevated to the imperial succession in the house of the Caesars and the empire of the world, Claudius published edicts in favor of the Jews, and greatly enlarged the dominions of Agrippa by adding Judea, Samaria, and Abylene, so that his realm was now almost as extensive as was his grandfather's, King Herod the Great, lacking only Idumaea (*Ant.*, xix, ch. 5, § 1; *War*, ii, ch. 11, § 5). Evidence of the historicity of this account is furnished in a coin struck by Herod Agrippa I, at Caesarea. It reads:

Obverse: Basileus megas Agrippa Philo-kaiser.

Reverse: Kaisar ē Sebastō Aimeni.

Obverse: "Agrippa the Great, Lover of Caesar."

Reverse: "Caesar on Port Sebastus."

Sebaste is the standing Greek word for Augustus, the title assumed by several emperors. "Cumanus took one troop of horsemen, called the troop of Sebaste, out of Caesarea" (*War*, ii, ch. 12, § 5).

7. **Humiliations Imposed.** Though having received royalty, with the added heritage of his grandfather's kingdom, Herod Agrippa was at one time made to feel that, after all, his dominion was a mere dependency upon the Roman power which dominated the nations included in the empire. Being of Idumaean origin, it is related that on one occasion, before his kingdom had been enlarged by Claudius, when the Feast of Tabernacles was observed, the lesson from the law for the day was read: "Thou shalt in any wise set him king over thee whom the Lord thy God shalt choose. . . . Thou mayest not set a stranger over thee which is not thy brother" (Deut. 17: 15). He, remembering that he was of foreign stock, and was so recognized by his brethren, Agrippa, from bitter anticipations, burst into tears before them all; but the people, sympathizing with him, exclaimed, "Fear not, Agrippa, thou art our brother!" For the law required also, "Thou shalt not abhor an Edomite, for he is thy brother. . . . The children that are begotten of them shall enter into the congregation of the Lord in their third generation" (Deut. 23; ch. 7, § 8). Agrippa thus was clearly entitled to this consideration; he was at a remove of the third generation at least from the Idumaeans or Edomites.

Now Agrippa resided mostly at Jerusalem. He commenced the building of impregnable walls to fortify the city. But Marsus Vibius, prefect of Syria, ordered the constructions discontinued on the mere grounds of suspicion. The king, like his ancestors, was fond of ostentatious display. He had once invited a number of petty kings contiguous to his own realm to be his guests and accept his hospitality at the city Tiberias, where royal spectacles were to be witnessed. Marsus Vibius came also from Syria. Agrippa and the five kings thinking to do him honor, went forth in a chariot about seven furlongs to meet the prefect. But Marsus, being suspicious of the real meaning of hospitable popularity and display of the public games, offered a great affront to all concerned when he ordered the five kings to proceed at once and quietly to their respective homes (*Ant.*, xix, ch. 7, § 2; Ibid., ch. 8, § 1).

8. **Christian Persecutions.** Herod Agrippa I is known in the New Testament simply as "Herod." He was the only Herod who had royalty bestowed upon him and governed all Palestine since the death of his grandfather, Herod the Great, who died soon after the birth of Jesus. He is mentioned only in the Book of Acts, where he is named twice in the same chapter in connection with two different events (ch. 12). Although usually an affable man, he was exceedingly ambitious to please his Jewish subjects, and this passion led him to become a persecutor of the Christians in the little community at Jerusalem. The record reads: "Now about this time Herod the king stretched forth his hands to vex (*kakaō*, to maltreat, exasperate) certain of the Church. And he killed James, the brother of John (sons of Zebedee), with the sword; and because he saw it pleased the Jews he proceeded further to take Peter also," with a view of slaying him after the Passover was ended (Acts 12:1-3). But Peter was delivered by night by the interposition of an angel. Now this procedure was exactly accordant with the Jewish Talmud in the Mishna, which reads thus: "The ordinance of putting to death by the sword is this, the man's head is cut off with a sword, as is accustomed to be done *by royal command*" (Professor Lomby, *Com.*, in loco; comp. *Ant.*, xix, ch. 9, § 3).

9. **Death.** Agrippa and his deputies and other dignitaries of the land assembled at Caesarea, at the seaside, to celebrate the games at a festival and to offer vows for the safety and prosperity of the Emperor Claudius. Early in the morning of the second day of the celebration the king presented himself to the people clad in "a garment made wholly of silver and of a texture truly wonderful." When the sun's rays touched his dress the reflections shone out in a surprising splendor. Josephus says that the people exclaimed that "he was a god," and that "the king did neither rebuke them nor reject their impious flattery" (comp. Acts 12:19-23). After five days the king "departed this life, being in the fifty-fourth year of his age and in the seventh of his reign." "For he reigned four years under Caius (Caligula) Caesar, three of them were over Philip's tetrarchy only, and on the fourth he had that of Herod (Antipas) added to it; and he reigned besides those three years under the

reign of Claudius Caesar" (*Ant.*, xix, ch. 8, § 2).

VI. HER'OD AGRIP'PA II (A. D. 53-70).

1. **Identification.** Much confusion and difficulty have been experienced to identify these two historical personages—father and son—as they bear exactly the same name. Nevertheless, they are known in both profane and sacred history by different appellations. Outside of Scripture the elder is called Herod Agrippa I and the younger as Herod Agrippa II. But in the New Testament the father is named either "Herod," as he is repeatedly called in the same chapter (Acts 12:6, 11, 19-21), or "Herod the king" (12:1); whereas the son, in contradistinction from the father, is called either "Agrippa" (25:22, 23; 26:32), or "King Agrippa" (25:26; 26:27, 28). True, both were kings and bore the same name, but they were not both rulers at the same time and their kingdoms were different. So far as appears in Scripture, Herod Agrippa I was king of all Palestine proper during the period A. D. 41-44; while Herod Agrippa II was king of perhaps one third of that country, lying to the north and northeast, during the period A. D. 52-70, when his government was utterly destroyed by the Roman-Jewish war and the Jewish nation ceased to be. As to scriptural incidents associated with each, it was Herod Agrippa I who beheaded James, the brother of John, and also imprisoned Peter at Jerusalem (12:13); but it was Herod Agrippa II who went to Caesarea, whom Paul called "king" or "King Agrippa" in his memorable defense at Caesarea (26:2, 7, 13, 19, 26, 27), and whom Luke calls either "Agrippa" or "King Agrippa" in narrating the same occasion (25:13, 22-24, 26; 26:28, 32).

2. **Youth.** When Herod Agrippa I died, in A. D. 44, he left this son and three daughters, named Bernice, Mariamne, and Drusilla (*Ant.* xviii, ch. 5, § 4; xix, ch. 9, § 1). Agrippa was born A. D. 27, and was but a stripling of seventeen years of age at his father's death, resident at the imperial capital, receiving his education under the patronage of the emperor. "Now Agrippa, the son of the deceased was, at Rome and brought up with Claudius Caesar" (*Ant.*, xix, ch. 9, § 2). This emperor at first contemplated placing young Agrippa immediately upon his father's throne to rule all Palestine; but better counsels prevailing, he concluded that it would be "a dangerous experiment" for "so young a man," who was without any experience, to undertake to govern so large a kingdom (*Ant.*, xix, ch. 9, § 2). "So Claudius made the country a Roman province, and sent Cuspius Fadus to be procurator of Judea and the whole of the kingdom" (*Ant.*, xix, ch. 9, § 2; *War*, ii, ch. 11, § 6).

3. **Royalty.** When his uncle, Herod, king of Chalcis, died, in A. D. 48, Agrippa junior had attained the twenty-first year of his age. Claudius now appointed him to be governor of that vacant kingdom. At the same time he was made superintendent of the Jewish temple at Jerusalem and manager of its treasury, with full power to remove the high priests from office at will, an authority which he frequently exercised, as did his uncle before him (*Ant.*, xx, ch. 8, § 11; xx, ch. 9, §§ 1, 4, 6; xx, ch. 1,

§ 3). These frequent changes of the high priesthood for political reasons rendered Herod Agrippa II quite unpopular with the Jews.

It is not quite clear whether royalty was conferred upon this Agrippa when he was appointed at Chalcis over his uncle's vacant kingdom, but it is quite certain he had this distinction at least when he was transferred to another and greater kingdom. His royal residence was finally established at Caesarea Philippi, at the southwestern base of Mt. Hermon, which is at the principal source of the River Jordan.

4. **Kingdom.** Josephus remarks: "Now, after the death of Herod, king of Chalcis, Claudius set Agrippa, the son of Agrippa, over his uncle's kingdom, while Cumanus took upon him the office of procurator of the rest (of the territory), which was a Roman province" (*War*, ii, ch. 12, § 1). He also mentions that about the year 53, "when Claudius had completed the twelfth year of his reign, he bestowed upon Agrippa (II) the two former tetrarchies of Philip and Lysanius, but took from him Chalcis when he had been governor thereof four years (*Ant.*, xx, ch. 7, § 1; *War*, ii, ch. 12, § 1), and removed him to a greater kingdom" (*War*, ii, ch. 12, § 8). His realm was now situated in the north and northeast of Palestine, but the regions known as Peraea, and Judea, Samaria, and Galilee, which belonged to the kingdom of his father, were never included in the kingdom of King Herod Agrippa II. A coin exists, struck by the authority of the second Herod, at Caesarea Philippi, the capital of his new kingdom, in the imperial reign of Nero, which reads thus:

Obverse: "Nero Caesar."

Reverse: "By King Agrippa, Neronias."

That is, the city Caesarea Philippi is renamed "Neronias" in honor of Nero, the reigning emperor at that time.

5. **End.** Herod Agrippa II, unlike his father was never popular with his subjects. It appears to have been the purpose of the procurator, Florus, to goad the Jews into revolt and war with the whole Roman empire by his own official and infamous conduct toward those people. "Multitudes of Jews addressed themselves to the king (Agrippa II) and to the high priests, and desired that they might have leave to send ambassadors to Nero against Florus" (*War*, ii, ch. 17, § 4). But Agrippa, seeing the evils to arise, in a public address endeavored to dissuade the Jews from their warlike purpose, an appeal which ended in tears, and greatly moved the impassioned people addressed. But when Agrippa saw that the inevitable had come, he joined his forces with those of the Romans and made war upon his abused and aggrieved subjects (*War*, ii, ch. 17, § 4). In a battle before Gamala Herod was wounded in the elbow by a stone, but continued in the command of his own troops until the Romans had destroyed both Agrippa's kingdom and the Jewish commonwealth. The war closed in the capture of Jerusalem in the year 70. Agrippa then retired to Rome, where at length he died, in the seventy-third year of his age, A. D. 100, and in the third year of the reign of the emperor Trajan.

Josephus makes special note of the fact that

Titus, the Roman general, affixed his signature to the history of the Roman-Jewish war, as written by himself, and authenticated its statements as being historical, and, moreover, when he was emperor, ordered the publication of his books; and that Josephus then had in his possession sundry letters from Herod Agrippa II attesting the truth of his historical narrative as one who was an eye-witness of the facts therein stated (*Life*, § 65).

Princesses of the House of the Herods.— *Herodias, Bernice, Drusilla.* The Herodian princesses were not themselves Jewish rulers, but were married to those who were. They belonged to the royal family by birth. There were others, but these are the only ones mentioned in the historical New Testament.

I. **Hero′dias.** *See* under Herod Antipas, 3 and 4.

II. **Bernice.** 1. **Personality.** This princess was the eldest daughter of King Herod Agrippa I and Cypros, and she was therefore the sister of King Herod Agrippa II and Drusilla; and she was the wife of Herod, king of Chalcis, "who was both her husband and uncle." She was sometimes called "a queen," but in reality never wore a crown. Bernice was a woman of rarest beauty and charms of person. Tacitus mentions her as "Queen Bernice (who) at that time (was) in the bloom of youth and beauty" (*Hist.* ii, 81).

2. **Character.** Her husband dying in A. D. 48, Bernice was but twenty years of age. However, after that event her character was held much in question on the score of chastity. She had retired to the home of her brother Agrippa II, and even their relations with each other were regarded with grave suspicion (*Ant.*, xx, ch. 7, § 3). In order to cast off evil surmises respecting them, she accepted marriage with Polemo, king of Pontus, who was induced to take the step "on account of her riches;" but their married life together was of but short duration, as not long afterward Bernice forsook her husband and returned to her brother Agrippa (*Ant.*, xx, ch. 7, § 3, comp. Tacitus, *Hist.*, ii, 81; Suetonius, Titus, vii; *Juvenal's Satires*, 155-157). No intimation of Bernice's reputation is given in the references in the New Testament.

3. **Publicity.** She figures conspicuously besides her unmarried brother, Herod Agrippa II, in places of public interest and assemblies, on several occasions. In one instance they went together to Jerusalem to quiet the warlike spirit aroused among the Jews by the exasperating cruelties perpetrated by, and the conduct of, the notorious Gessius Florus, the procurator. Bernice appeared in the gallery of the auditorium overlooking the excited and surging multitude, to whom Agrippa made a powerful appeal that they should not revolt against the Roman power. "When Agrippa had thus spoken, both he and his sister, wept, and by their tears repressed a great deal of the violence of the people" (*War*, ii, ch. 16, §§ 1-5). They went together again when "King Agrippa (II) was going to Alexandria, to congratulate Alexander (the procurator) upon his having obtained the government" of Judea (*War*, ii, ch. 15, § 1). And now once again they are found together at Caesarea on the

sea, to extend courtesy of greetings and congratulations to Portius Festus upon the occasion of his entering upon office as procurator of that country, while Paul was in custody there as a prisoner (Acts 25). From the lips of Festus, King Agrippa learned the particulars respecting the eloquent prisoner whom his predecessor Felix had left "bound," because "he was willing to show the Jews a pleasure." Already had Paul been imprisoned two years, and the official Jews of Jerusalem had been clamoring for his life. Agrippa having expressed a desire to hear Paul speak in defense of the Christian faith, Festus promised him opportunity "on the morrow." Accordingly, "when Agrippa was come and Bernice with great pomp, and was entered into the place of hearing, with the chief captains and principal men of the city, at Festus's command Paul was brought forth" (Acts 25:22, 23). Bernice was now conspicuously seated beside her brother, King Agrippa. At this time the princess was thirty-two years of age, and "sat blazing with all her jewels" before the gazing public, listening to the apostle's immortal defense (Acts 26).

III. **Drusil′la.** Herod Agrippa I left three daughters, named Bernice, Mariamne, and Drusilla, in that order of their age (*Ant.*, xviii, ch. 5, § 4). When the father died in A. D. 44, Drusilla was but a prattling child of six summers. As she grew into womanhood she became a celebrated beauty, and was the envy of even her sister Bernice.

1. **Marriages.** Being a Jewess of a family of distinction, she accepted in marriage Azizus, king of Edessa (Emesa), on the express condition that he would conform to the required ceremony of becoming a Jew. At one time "while Felix the procurator of Judea saw this Drusilla, he fell in love with her; for she did indeed excel all other women in beauty." Felix sent a Jew "to persuade her to forsake her husband and marry him; and he promised that if she would not refuse him, he would make her a happy woman." She accepted this proffer, and was "prevailed upon to transgress the laws of her forefathers and marry Felix. And when he had a son by her, he named him Agrippa" (*Ant.*, xx, ch. 7, §§ 1, 2). This son and mother perished in the eruption of Mount Vesuvius in the Christian year 79.

2. **Husband.** Claudius Felix was a man of low origin, and obviously of the lowest instincts. He "had been a slave (in Rome), in the vilest of all positions, at the vilest of all epochs, in the vilest of all cities" (Farrar). Tacitus says that as a procurator "Antonius Felix exercised the prerogatives of a king, with the spirit of a slave, rioting in cruelty and licentiousness;" a man who "supposed he might perpetrate with impunity every kind of villiany" (*Annals*, xii, 54). Suetonius remarks that "in consequence of his elevation (to be procurator of Judea), he became the husband of three queens" (Claudius, c. 28).

3. **At Caesarea.** During the procuratorship, when "Felix came (to Caesarea) with his wife Drusilla, which was a Jewess, he sent for Paul and heard him concerning the faith in Christ Jesus. And as he reasoned of righteousness, and temperance (i. e., self-control), and the

TABLE OF THE HERODIAN FAMILY

GIVING THE NAMES ONLY OF THOSE MENTIONED IN THE FOREGOING DISCUSSION AND THOSE NAMED IN THE NEW TESTAMENT.

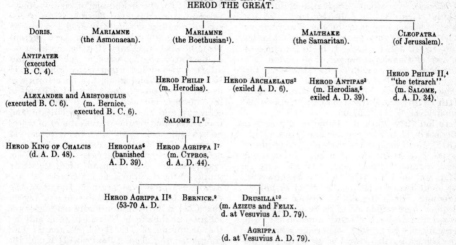

HEROD I[1], or
HEROD THE KING, or
HEROD THE GREAT.

[1]"Herod the King," Matt. 2; Luke 1:5. [2]Herod "Archaelaus," Luke 19:12-27; Matt. 2:22. [3]"Herod" Antipas "the tetrarch," Matt. 14:1; Luke 3:1, 19; Mark 6:14. [4]Herod "Philip" "the tetrarch," Matt. 14:1, 6; Luke 3:1, 19; 9:7; Mark 6:34. [5]"Herodias," Matt. 14:3, 6; Mark 6:17. [6]Salome, Matt. 14:6; Mark 6:22, 28; Luke 3:19. [7]"Herod" Agrippa [I] "the king," Acts 12:1, 2. [8]Herod "Agrippa" II, Acts 25:13-27; 26. [9]"Bernice," Acts 25:13, 23; 26:30. [10]"Drusilla," Acts 24:24.

judgment to come, Felix was terrified, and answered, Go thy way for this time; and when I have a convenient season, I will call thee unto me." He hoped that bribe money would be given him to release Paul, and accordingly sent for him the oftener; but, when he was to be succeeded by the honorable Porcius Festus, "Felix left Paul bound" to please the Jews (Acts 24:24-27). Thus closed the scene and the procuratorship of Felix at Caesarea.

Literature.—Conybeare and Howson, *Life and Epistles of St. Paul;* Thomas Lewin, *Life and Letters of St. Paul;* Prideaux, *The Old and New Testaments Connected;* Milman, *History of the Jews;* Thomas Lewin, *Fasti Sacri;* Stanley, *Jewish Church;* Ewald, *History of Israel,* 1867; Schürer, *Jewish People in the Time of Jesus Christ;* 1885; Wellhausen, *History of Israel and Judah,* 1891; Farrar, "The Herods;" Yahn, *Hebrew Commonwealth,* 1828; Hausrath, *History of the New Testament Times,* 1878; Keim, *Jesu of Nazara,* 1878; Edersheim, *Life and Times of Jesus the Messiah,* 1885; Rénan, *History of the People of Israel;* Smith's *Bible Dictionary,* Hackett's edition; Kitto, *Biblical Cyclopoedia;* McClintock and Strong, *Cyclopoedia;* Reuss, *History of the New Testament;* Bowman, S. L., *Historical Evidences of the New Testament.*—S. L. B.

Hero′dians (hĕ-rō′dĭ-ănz), a party among the Jews of the apostolic age, and keenly opposed to Jesus (Matt. 22:16; Mark 3:6; 12:13); but of which no explicit information is given by any of the evangelists. The party was, probably, formed under Herod the Great, and appears to have had for its principle that it was right to pay homage to a sovereign who might be able to bring the friendship of Rome and other advantages, but who had personally no title to reign by law and by religion. On this question they differed from the Pharisees (Matt. 22:16, 17), although they coalesced with them in disguised opposition, or in open union against Jesus, in whom they saw a common enemy. The Herodians were obviously something more than a political party, something less than a religious sect.

Hero′dias (hĕ-rō′dĭ-ăs; feminine of Herod), the daughter of Aristobulus—one of the sons of Mariamne and Herod the Great—and sister of Herod Agrippa I. See Herod, III, 4.

Hero′dion (hĕ-rō′dĭ-ŏn; derived from *Herod*), a Christian at Rome to whom Paul sent a salutation as his kinsman (Rom. 16:11).

Heron. See Animal Kingdom.

He′sed (hē′sĕd; *grace, kindness*), the name of a man whose son (Ben-hesed) was Solomon's purveyor in the districts of Aruboth, Sochoh, and Hepher (I Kings 4:10), B. C. after 960.

Hesh′bon (hĕsh′bŏn; *reckoning*), originally a Moabitish town, but when the Israelites arrived from Egypt it was ruled over by Sihon, styled both "king of the Amorites" and "king of Heshbon." It was taken by Moses (Josh. 21:23-26), and became a Levitical city (Josh. 21:39; I Chron. 6:81), in the tribe of Reuben (Num. 32:37; Josh. 13:17); but, being on the border of Gad, is sometimes assigned to the latter (Josh. 21:39; I Chron. 6:81). Heshbon, now Hesbân, is twenty miles E. of Jordan, and 4,000 ft. above the turbulent stream as it enters the Dead Sea. It is the site of an excellent spring which made it an extremely desirable location. Its extensive ruins, particularly from the Roman Period are still visible.

Figurative. In Cant. 7:4 the eyes of the Shulamite are likened to the "fishpools of Heshbon," by the gate of Bath-rabbim. The bright pools in the stream which runs beneath Hesbân on the west are probably intended (Harper).

Hesh'mon (hĕsh'mŏn), a town in the south of Judah (Josh. 15:27), perhaps the same as Azmon (v. 4).

Heth (hĕth), the forefather of the nation of the *Hittites* (*q. v.*) called "sons and children of Heth" (Gen. 23:3, 5, 7, 10, 16, 18, 20; 25:10; 49:32). Once we hear of the daughters of Heth (Gen. 27:46). In the genealogical tables of Gen. 10 and I Chron. 1, Heth is named as a son of Canaan, younger than Zidon, the firstborn, but preceding the Jebusite, the Amorite, and the other Canaanitish familes. The Hittites were, therefore, a Hamitic race.

Heth (hāth), the 8th letter of the Hebrew alphabet. Cf. Ps. 119:57-64.

Heth'lon (hĕth'lŏn), the name of a place on the northern border of Palestine (Ezra 47:15; 48:1). In all probability the "way of Hethlon" is the pass at the northern end of Lebanon, and is thus identical with "the entrance of Hamath" in Num. 34:8, etc. It may, however, be identified with Heitela, N. E. of Tripoli.

Hewing. The Gibeonites, having deceived Joshua, were sentenced to serve as "hewers of wood and drawers of water unto all the congregation" (Josh. 9:21), a service which was performed by the lowest class of the people (Deut. 29:11). In I Kings 5:15 it is recorded that Solomon "had fourscore thousand hewers in the mountains."

Hez'eki (hĕz'ĕ-kī; *my strength*, or perhaps an abbreviation for Hezekiah), one of the "sons" of Elpael, a chief resident of Jerusalem (I Chron. 8:17, 18). Hizki (R. V. and R. S. V.).

Hezeki'ah, King (hĕz-ê-kī'à; in the A. V. of the N. T. Ezeki'as, the Greek form of the Hebrew *Jehovah is strength*).

1. **The Twelfth Sovereign** (excluding Athaliah), of the separate kingdom of Judah, ruling from c. B. C. 715-687. He was a son of Ahaz, born c. B. C. 736 (II Kings 18:1, 2; II Chron. 29:1).

2. **As a Reformer.** As a godly king his first act was to purge, repair and reopen the temple which had been neglected and polluted during the idolatrous reign of his weak father, Ahaz. His task consisted of rooting out Canaanite fertility cults and other pagan contaminations. Hezekiah's reformation was so thorough that he did not even spare "the high places." These centers of contaminated worship on hill tops "he removed, and broke down the images, cut down the groves." A still more decisive act was the destruction of the brazen serpent of Moses (Num. 21:9) which had become an idolatrous object. His great reformation (Cf. II Chron. 29:1-36; II Kings 18:3-7) was followed by the great celebration of the Passover (II Chron. 30), to which not only all Judah was summoned, but also the remnant of the ten tribes.

3. **As a Warrior.** (1) War with Philistines. Early in his reign (c. B. C. 714) Hezekiah assumed an aggressive war against the Philistines. He not only retook the cities which his father had forfeited (II Chron. 28:18) but even dispossessed the Philistines of their own cities except Gaza (II Kings 18:8) and Gath, (Josephus, *Ant.*, ix, 13:3). Accordingly, he came to exercise a sort of suzerainty over the Philistine cities, and Ashdod under its Greek prince was induced to lead them in the revolt against Assyria. (2) Early Relations with Assyria. Hezekiah inherited the Assyrian menace from his father who mortgaged the Judean kingdom to "the giant of the Semites." From c. B. C. 715, the beginning of his own independent rule, Hezekiah faced a series of Assyrian invasions which featured his reign. As a wise and godly ruler, he made every attempt to build up his country that he might eventually throw off the Assyrian yoke which his father had saddled upon it by alliance (II Kings 16:7-9). The purport of his reform was to fortify the moral and spiritual defenses of his country. He also built up the national economy and the military. Agriculture and trade expanded by the establishment of warehouses and stock yards at strategic places (II Chron. 32:28, 29), a national system of defenses was inaugurated (II Chron. 32:5-7), and Jerusalem was given an adequate water supply in the event of siege (II Chron. 32:30). Ample warning was granted Judah of the Assyrian peril. In Hezekiah's fourth regnal year (724 B. C.)—undoubtedly his regency is meant—Shalmaneser V had begun, and by the beginning of 721 B. C. Sargon II had completed, the siege of Samaria (II Kings 18:9-11). In the ensuing interval the Assyrian menace moved ever nearer. In 711 B. C. Sargon claimed the credit of a campaign against Ashdod. The Assyrian record (Isa. 20:1) clearly outlines that it was the Assyrian commander-in-chief "tartan" (Assyrian *turtannu*, "second in rank") who actually conducted the campaign. See W. F. Albright, *O. T. Commentary*, Philadelphia, 1948, p. 161. (3) Sennacherib and Hezekiah. Early in the reign of Sennacherib, Hezekiah revolted against Assyria. The Assyrian preoccupation in lower Mesopotamia with the irrepressible Chaldeans of the sea lands under Merodach-baladan, king of Babylon, coupled with Hezekiah's consciousness of his own prosperity were prime factors in the revolt. It was the same Merodach-baladan who, pretending to congratulate Hezekiah upon his recovery from a serious illness, tried with lavish gifts to win over Judah into a coalition which was being secretly formed against Assyria (Isa. 39:108). This Merodach-baladan was twice ruler of Babylon (722-710 B. C., 703-702 B. C.), and his embassy to Judah was apparently dispatched in the latter part of the earlier period of his reign. Hezekiah manifested egotistical folly in showing Merodach-baladan's emissaries all his treasures. Isaiah, foreseeing the future strengthening of the Chaldeans, severely rebuked Hezekiah's foolishness. In B. C. 701 the Assyrian emperor launched his great western campaign as a punitive measure against Hezekiah and other Palestinian-Syrian rebels. This important campaign is not only vividly described in the Biblical record but is also contained in the annals of Sennacherib which were recorded on clay cylinders, or prisms. The edition of these annals is found on the so-called Taylor Prism of the British Museum, with a copy on a prism of the Oriental Institute of the University of Chicago. In detail Sennacherib depicts his third campaign, which included the siege of Jerusalem. After the subjugation of Philistine coastal towns and

Philistine strongholds, together with Moabite, Edomite and other cities, he refers to a victorious battle near Altaku (Eltekeh), where Palestinian forces were reinforced by Egyptian bowmen and chariotry. Then Sennacherib makes a lengthy reference to his attack on Hezekiah's realm. "As for Hezekiah, the Jew, who did not submit to me, all 46 of his strong walled cities as well as the small cities in their neighborhood . . . I besieged and took. 200,150 people, great and small, male and female, horses, mules, asses, camels, cattle and sheep without number I brought away from them and counted as spoil. Himself, like a caged bird, I shut up in Jerusalem, his royal city. Earth works I threw up against him—the one coming out of his city gate I turned back to his misery. The cities of his which I had despoiled I cut off from his land and to Mitinti, king of Ashdod, Padi, king of Ekron, and Sili-bel, king of Gaza, I gave them." Sennacherib goes on to tell how the "terrifying splendor" of his majesty overcame Hezekiah. This Assyrian monarch boasts placing Hezekiah under a large tribute, carrying away gems, antimony, jewels, couches of ivory, elephant hides, maple, boxwood and all kinds of valuable treasures as well as his daughters, his harem and his musicians. The account of Sennacherib's western campaign recorded in the Taylor Prism is evidently the same as that

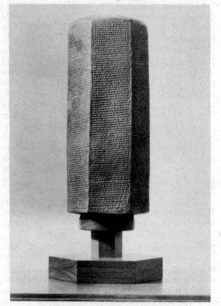

202. Clay Prism of King Sennacherib, Describing His Siege of Jerusalem

described in II Kings 18:13-19:37; II Chron. 32:1-12 and Isa. 36:1-37:28. There are numerous striking points of agreement, as well as some difficulties. For example, when Sennacherib invaded Palestine he is said to have captured many of the fortified Judean cities (II Kings 18:13) and to have threatened Jerusalem with a great army dispatched from Lachish under "Tartan and Rabsaris and Rabshakeh" (II Kings 18:17). A sculpture

recovered at Nineveh shows Sennacherib sitting upon his chair throne at Lachish and receiving rich spoils while unfortunate prisoners are tortured. These details fit well into the Biblical account. Moreover, it is now known from the monuments that Tartan (Assyrian *turtannu*, "second in rank"), Rabshakeh (Assyrian *rab-shaqu*, "chief officer") and Rabsaris (Assyrian *rabu-sha-reshi*, originally "chief eunuch") were titles of high Assyrian officials and not personal names at all (Millar Burrows, *What Mean These Stones*, New Haven, 1941, p. 43f.). Hezekiah's tribute is placed at thirty talents of gold in both sources but at only 300 talents of silver in II Kings 8:14 as compared with 800 which the Assyrian king mentions. E. Schrader reconciles the two differences on the basis of the Babylonian light and Palestinian heavy talent, while George Barton suggests a textual corruption (*Archaeology and the Bible*, 7th Ed., 1937, p. 473). (4) Sickness and Death. The Assyrians, despite their boasts, were not able to take Jerusalem. Toward the end of his reign Hezekiah became dangerously ill (II Kings 20:1; II Chron. 32: 24; Isa. 38:1). His kingdom was still in a perilous state from the Assyrian menace. Having no heir at the time, Hezekiah prayed that his life might be spared. He was granted a fifteen-year extension of life and died a natural death peacefully (c. B. C. 687).

4. **Siloam Tunnel.** Hezekiah is famous archaeologically for the steps he took to supply fresh water within the city walls of Jerusalem. "He made a pool, and the conduit, and brought water into the city" (II Kings 20:20). In Chronicles it is appended that "the same Hezekiah also stopped the upper spring of the waters of Gihon and brought them down on the west side of the City of David (II Chron. 22:30). The intermittent spring of Gihon, Jerusalem's most ancient water supply, was located below the steep eastern hill (Ophel) in the deep Kidron Valley. It was thus exposed to enemy attack. Hezekiah completely covered over this ancient spring and diverted it through a conduit 1777 feet long and hewn out of solid rock into a reservoir within the city walls. Tunnels at Megiddo and Gezer are similar to this amazing engineering feat of Hezekiah's workmen.

5. **Siloam Reservoir.** In addition to the tunnel, Hezekiah built a larger reservoir, called the Pool of Siloam. The pool measures about 20 x 30 feet. In Jesus' day the blind man who was healed was directed to go and wash in this pool (John 9:7-11).

6. **The Siloam Inscription.** Hezekiah's tunnel was made famous by a remarkable inscription upon it accidently discovered in 1880 by a boy wading in the pool. This six-line memorial, beautifully cut on the wall of the conduit in classical Hebrew characters about nineteen feet from the Siloam end of the acqueduct, has great paleographic value on a par with the Moabite Stone. The inscription translated runs thus: "The boring through is completed. Now this is the story of the boring through. While the workmen were still lifting pick to pick each toward his neighbor and while three cubits remained to be cut through, each heard the voice of the other who called his neighbor,

since there was a crevice in the rock on the right side. And on the day of the boring through the stone cutters struck, each to meet his fellow pick to pick; and there flowed the waters to the pool for 1200 cubits and 100 cubits was the height of the rock above the heads of the stone cutters."

He'zion (hē'zĭ-ŏn; *vision*), the father of Tabrimon and grandfather of Ben-hadad I, to whom Asa sent silver and gold from the sacred treasury to secure his aid against Baasha (I Kings 15:18), B. C. before 915. In the absence of all information, the natural suggestion is that he is the same person as Rezon, the contemporary of Solomon (I Kings 11:23), the two names being very similar in Hebrew, and still more so in the versions (Smith).

He'zir (hē'zĭr; *swine, boar*).

1. The head of the seventeenth course of priests as established by David (I Chron. 24:15), B. C. after 1000.

2. One of the heads of the people who sealed the solemn covenant with Nehemiah (Neh. 10:20), B. C. 445.

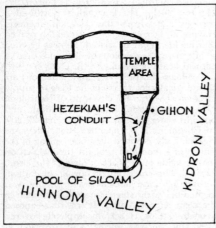

203. Jerusalem at the Time of Hezekiah ca. 700 B. C.), Showing Hezekiah's Conduit (Siloam Tunnel)

Hez'rai (hĕz'rā-ī; II Sam. 23:35), the same as *Hezro* (*q. v.*).

Hez'ro (hĕz'rô), a Carmelite; one of David's mighty men (I Chron. 11:37). He is called in the margin and in II Sam. 23:35 *Hezrai* (*q. v.*).

Hez'ron (hĕz'rŏn).

1. The third son of Reuben (Gen. 46:9; Exod. 6:14; I Chron. 4:1; 5:3). His descendants were called *Hezronites* (Num. 26:6).

2. The elder of the two sons of Pharez and grandson of Judah (Gen. 46:12; Ruth 4:18, 19; I Chron. 2:5, 9, 18, 21, 24, 25). He is called *Esrom* in Matt. 1:3.

3. A place on the southern boundary of Judah, west of Kadesh-barnea (Josh. 15:3, 25). In the latter passage it is identified with *Hazor* (*q. v.*).

Hez'ronites (hĕz'rŏn-īts), the descendants of *Hezron*, No. 1 (*q. v.*).

Hid'dai (hĭd'ā-ī), one of the "thirty" heroes of David, "of the brooks of Gaash" (II Sam. 23:30). In I Chron. 11:32 he is given as *Hurai* (*q. v.*).

Hid'dekel (hĭd'ê-kĕl; Heb. *Hiddekel;* Sumerian, *Igna;* Babylonian, *Idigla, Diglat;* Old Persian, *Tigra;* Greek, Tigris). The Hiddekel is thus the ancient name of the Tigris (Gen. 2:14; Dan 10:4). Modern Arabs still call it Diglah. The Pishon and the Gihon mentioned in connection with the rivers of Eden (Gen. 2:10-14) are presumably canals, called rivers in Babylonia, which connected the Tigris and Euphrates as ancient river beds. Biblical notices thus place the Garden of Eden somewhere in the Tigris-Euphrates country, evidently in the easternmost third of Breasted's "Fertile Crescent." The Tigris has its chief source in central Armenia, originating on the southern slope of the Anti-Taurus. Two eastern sources rise out of Lake Van. As the river flows E. S. E. through the Kurdistan Mountains, it is gradually augmented by various tributaries such as the Upper and Lower Zab and the Dyalah. In ancient times the Tigris entered separately into the Persian Gulf; now it joins the Euphrates and mingles with its waters for more than 100 miles in the Shatt-al-Arab before entering the Persian Gulf. The entire length of the Tigris to the junction of the Euphrates is 1146 miles and is only slightly more than half the length of the latter stream. On the banks of the Tigris were located Nineveh and the ancient Assyrian city of Ashur.

Hi'el (hī'ĕl; perhaps, *God liveth*), a native of Beth-el, who rebuilt Jericho in the reign of Ahab (I Kings 16:34), and in whom was fulfilled the curse pronounced by Joshua (Josh. 6:26), B. C. after 875.

Hierap'olis (hē-êr-ăp'ô-lĭs; city of the mythical Amazon queen, Hiera). This important center of Christian influence was situated near Colossae and Laodicea in the Lycus River valley of Phrygia. It is referred to only in Col. 4:13 (Cf. Acts 19:10). Paul evidently did not preach there. Other of the early Christians did, possibly Philip the Evangelist and John, as is commonly believed. The hot baths of Hierapolis, noted for their medicinal benefits, drew patrons of the Plutonium ("Entrance to Hades"). The city was a wealthy dyeing center. Extensive ruins, including two theatres, a gymnasium and baths have been excavated. If was a cosmopolitan city with a considerable Jewish population. Four early Christian churches have been found in this city.

Hi'eroglyph'ics (hī'ĕr-ô-glĭf'ĭks; from Gr. *hieros, sacred*, and *gluphen*, to *carve*). Pictures of objects, as of an animal, tree, bird, etc., representing a word, syllable, or single sound, and intended to convey a meaning. The name was first applied to the engraved marks and symbols found on the monuments and other records of ancient Egypt. The key to these inscriptions was the *Rosetta Stone* (*q. v.*). The Egyptian hieroglyphics were generally engraved, but in old temples are found in high relief, generally from right to left, but read either vertically or horizontally. They ceased to be written about 300 A. D. *See* Writing.

Higgai'on (hĭ-gī'yŏn), possibly a musical note. It is transliterated in Psa. 9:16; translated "solemn sound" in Psa. 92:3, and "meditation" in Psa. 19:14.

High Place (from Canaanite *bamah*, pl. *bamoth, ridge,* Heb. *elevation of land*), localities chosen as places of worship of God or idols. The high places were features of Canaanite religion and the conquering Israelites were commanded to destroy them when they entered Canaan (Num. 33:52; Deut. 33:29). Israel came in contact with the high places of the Moabites before they entered the land (Num. 21:28; 22:41). Being defiled by Canaanite fertility cults and other paganistic pollutions, the high places were often connected with licentiousness (Hos. 4:11-14) and immorality (Jer. 3:2). One of the best known high places is the "Conway High Place" at Petra (*See* W. F. Albright, *The Archaeology of Palestine,* p. 161-165). The Ugaritic tablets of the late fifteenth century B. C. from Ras Shamra show that animals were sacrificed in the high places of Baal in North Syria. Always contiguous to the rock altar was a sacred pillar, *maṣṣebah,* being a sacred pole having phallic associations, capped with a symbol of the *ashera,* evidently denoting female fertility. Male prostitutes, *kedeshim* and sacred courtesans, *kedeshoth* (I Kings 14:23, 24; II Kings 23:7) maintained chambers for cultic prostitution in honor of the heathen deity. At Gezer first-born babies were slain and their bodies placed in jars near the high place (Cf. Isa. 57:5). The idea of a high place, indicated by early shrines, was that elevation of the cultic center gave impressiveness. Babylonians devised artificial hills called ziggurats. The Greeks loved their lofty Mt. Olympus and their Acropolis. The worship of Jehovah, contrary to the law of Moses which specified one altar for all Israel, was often conducted on high places. The Mosaic prescription was a safeguard to protect the people from idolatrous associations and corruption. The worship of the God of Israel at other altars was allowable only in times of great stringency, as after the fall of Shiloh when the temple had not yet been erected (I Kings 3:2, 4; II Chron. 1:3). High places were legitimate also in the Northern Kingdom when access to the Jerusalem temple was no longer possible. After Solomon, who grievously sinned in erecting high places to his heathen wives (I Kings 11:1-8), this heathenistic institution prevailed among many kings of the Davidic line. Jehoram, Jehoshaphat's son, made high places in the mountains of Judah (II Chron. 21:11), as did Ahaz. Hezekiah broke them down (II Kings 18:4, 22). Manasseh in his idolatrous orgy re-erected them (II Kings 21:3). They were again destroyed by Josiah (II Kings 23:5, 8, 13). The prophets denounced the high places (Ezek. 6:3). Emphasis was placed on the fact that Zion was the place to worship (Isa. 2:2; 8:18; Joel 2:1; 3:17; Amos 1:2; Micah 4:1, 2.). *M. F. U.*

High Priest. *See* Priest, High.

Highest (Heb. *'elyōn, elevated*), a title ascribed to Jehovah (Psa. 18:13; 87:5), and in the New Testament (Gr. *hupsistos*) of the highest region, i. e., *heaven* (Matt. 21:9; Mark 11:10; Luke 2:14, etc.); also of rank, the most high God (Mark 5:7; Luke 8:28, etc.).

Highway (usually Heb. *mᵉsillāh*), an embanked road or raised causeway. *See* Roads.

Hi'len (hī'lĕn; I Chron. 6:58). *See* Holon.

Hilki'ah (hĭl-kī'á; *portion of Jehovah*)

1. The father of Eliakim, who was overseer of the household in the time of Hezekiah (II Kings 18:18, 26, 37; Isa. 22:20; 36:3, 22; 37:2), B. C. c. 715.

2. High priest in the reign of Josiah. According to the genealogy in I Chron. 6:13 (*see* Neh. 11:11) he was son of Shallum, and, from Ezra 7:1, apparently the ancestor of Ezra, the scribe. His high priesthood was rendered particularly illustrious by the great reformation effected under it by King Josiah (II Kings 23:4, sq.; II Chron. 34:9, sq.) by the solemn Passover kept at Jerusalem in the eighteenth year of the king's reign (II Chron. 35:1, sq.), and, above all, by the discovery which he made in the house of the Lord of a book which is called "the Book of the Laws" (II Kings 22:8) and "the Book of the Covenant" (23:2), B. C. 639.

NOTE—A difficult and interesting question arises: What was the book found by Hilkiah? Kennicott is of opinion that it was the original autograph copy of the Pentateuch written by Moses which Hilkiah found, but his argument is far from conclusive. Our means of answering this question seem to be limited: (1) To an examination of the terms in which the depositing the book of the law by the ark was originally enjoined; (2) To an examination of the contents of the books discovered by Hilkiah, as far as they transpire; (3) To any indications which may be gathered from the contemporary writings of Jeremiah, or from any other portions of Scripture. A consideration of all these points raises a strong probability that the book in question was the book of Deuteronomy (Smith). The probability is that the book found by Hilkiah was the same which was intrusted to the care of the priests and was to be put in the side of the ark (Deut. 31:9-26), and that this was the entire body of the Mosaic writing and not any part of it, seems the only tenable conclusion (Kitto).

3. A Merarite Levite, the son of Amzi and father of Amaziah (I Chron. 6:45).

4. The second son of Hosah, a Merarite, appointed by David as doorkeeper of the tabernacle (I Chron. 26:11), B. C. about 995.

5. One of those who stood at the right hand of Ezra while he read the law to the people (Neh. 8:4), B. C. about 445.

6. One of the chief priests who returned from Babylon with Zerubbabel and Jeshua (Neh. 12:7). His son Hashabiah is mentioned in v. 21, B. C. 536.

7. A priest of Anathoth and father of the prophet Jeremiah (Jer. 1:1), B. C. before 626.

8. Father of Gemariah, who, with Elasah, was sent by Zedekiah with a message to the captives at Babylon (Jer. 29:3), B. C. before 599.

Hill, the rendering of several words in the original.

1. **Hill.** (Heb. *gĭbᵉ'äh; high*), from a root which seems to have the force of curvature or humpishness. A word involving this idea is peculiarly applicable to the rounded hills of Palestine. (Exod. 17:9; I Sam. 7:1, etc.).

2. **Mountain** (Heb. *hăr*). Our translators have also employed the English word *hill* for the very different term *hăr,* which has a much more extended sense than *gĭbᵉ'äh,* meaning a whole district rather than an individual eminence, and to which our word "mountain" answers with tolerable accuracy. This exchange is always undesirable, but it sometimes occurs so as to confuse the meaning

of a passage where it is desirable that the topography should be unmistakable. For instance, in Exod. 24:4, the "hill" is the same which is elsewhere in the same chapter (12, 13, 18, etc.), consistently and accurately rendered "mount" and "mountain." The country of the "hills," in Deut. 1:7; Josh. 9:1; 10:40; 11:16, is the elevated district of Judah, Benjamin, and Ephraim, which is correctly called "the mountain" in the earliest descriptions of Palestine (Num. 13:29), and in many subsequent passages. In II Kings 1:9 and 4:27, the use of the word "hill" obscures the allusion to Carmel, which in other passages of the life of the prophet (e. g., I Kings 18:19; II Kings 4:25) has the term "mount" correctly attached to it.

3. "A going up" (Heb. *mä'ălĕh, elevation*). On one occasion the word is rendered "hill" (I Sam. 9:11), better "ascent."

4. In the New Testament the word "hill" is employed to render the Greek word (*bounos, hillock*), but on one occasion it is used for *oros*, elsewhere "mountain," so as to obscure the connection between the two parts of the same narrative (Luke 9:37).

Hill Country, the rendering in the Old Testament (Josh. 21:11) of *Har* (*see* Hill, 2); and in the New Testament of the Gr. *oreinos, mountainous* (Luke 1:39, 65); and meaning Mount Ephraim. The rendering "hill country" is misleading. "With their usual exactness the Hebrews saw that these regions (i, e., the mountains of Judah, Ephraim, and Naphtali) formed part of one range, the whole of which they called not by a collective name, but singularly—the mountain" (Smith, *Hist., Geog.*, p. 53).

Hil'lel (hĭl'lĕl; *praising*), a Pirathonite, and father of the judge Abdon (Judg. 12:13, 15), B. C. before 1070.

Hin. *See* Metrology, II, 2 (2).

Hind. *See* Animal Kingdom.

Hinge, the rendering of two Hebrew words, viz., *şîr*, to *open*, Prov. 26:14, and *pôth* literally an *interstice*, I Kings 7:50. Doors in the East turn rather on pivots than what we call hinges. They were sometimes made of metal (e. g., Solomon had hinges made of gold in the temple, I Kings 7:50, or, at least, plated with gold), but generally of the same material as the door itself. These pivots worked in sockets —above and below—in the door frame. The weight of the door resting on the lower pivot, it would open with much less ease than one working on our hinges, especially when the lower socket became worn (Prov. 26:14).

Hin'nom (hĭn'ŏm).

1. **An unknown person** whose name is given to the "Valley of Hinnom" (Josh. 18:16; Neh. 11:30); elsewhere (Josh. 15:8; II Kings 23:10; II Chron. 33:6, etc.) called "the valley of the son," or "children of Hinnom."

2. **Valley of Hinnom**, otherwise called "the valley of the son," or "children of Hinnom," a deep and narrow ravine, with steep, rocky sides to the south and west of Jerusalem, separating Mount Zion to the north from the "Hill of Evil Counsel," and the sloping rocky plateau of the "plain of Rephaim" to the south. The earliest Bible mention of the Valley of Hinnom is in Josh. 15:8; 18:16, where the boundary line between the tribes of Judah and Benjamin is described as passing along the bed of the ravine. On the southern brow, overlooking the valley at its eastern extremity, Solomon erected high places for Molech (I Kings 11:7), whose horrid rites were revived from time to time in the same vicinity by the later idolatrous kings. Ahaz and Manasseh made their children "pass through the fire" in this valley (II Kings 16:3; II Chron. 28:3; 33:6), and the fiendish custom of infant sacrifice to the fire-gods seems to have been kept up in Tophet, at its southeast extremity for a considerable period (Jer. 7:31; II Kings 23:10). To put an end to these abominations the place was polluted by Josiah, who rendered it ceremonially unclean by spreading over it human bones, and other corruptions (II Kings 23:10, 13, 14; II Chron. 34:4, 5), from which time it appears to have become the common cesspool of the city, into which its sewage was conducted, to be carried off by the waters of the Kidron, as well as a lay-stall, where all its solid filth was collected. From its ceremonial defilement, and from the detested and abominable fire of Molech, if not from the supposed overburning funeral piles, the later Jews applied the name of this valley *Ge Hinnom, Gehenna*, to denote the place of eternal torment. The name by which it is now known is *Wâdy Jehennam*, or *Wâdy er Rubêb*. *See* Gehenna, Hell, Lake of Fire, Punishment, Future.

Hip and Thigh, a proverbial expression for a *great slaughter* (Judg. 15:8), like the Arabic "war in thigh fashion," or the German "cutting arm and leg in two."

Hi'rah (hī'rà), an Adullamite, and friend of Judah (Gen. 38:1, 12; comp. v. 20).

Hi'ram (hī'răm; probably shortened from *'aḥiram, exalted brother*, Heb. and Phoenician), generally in the Chronicles "Huram;" and "Hirom" in I Kings 5:10, 18; 7:40). Hiram (Ahiram) was a common Phoenician royal name, as is attested by the inscriptions, notably that discovered on the sarcophagus of Ahiram at Byblus (Biblical Gebal, *q. v.*, Psa. 83:7; Ezek. 27:9) discovered in 1923-1924 by a French expedition under M. Montet and dating probably from B. C. 11th century. See W. F. Albright, *Archaeology and the Religion of Israel*, p. 40. However, it is impossible under present sources of knowledge to identify Hiram of Tyre with Ahiram of Byblus.

1. **King of Tyre**, who sent an embassy to David after the latter had conquered the stronghold of Zion and taken up his residence in Jerusalem. It seems that the dominion of this prince extended over the western slopes of Lebanon; and when David built himself a palace, Hiram materially assisted the work by sending cedar wood from Lebanon, and skillful workmen to Jerusalem (II Sam. 5:11; I Chron. 14:1). He reigned c. B. C. 970-936. It was the same prince who sent an embassy of condolence and congratulation when David died and Solomon ascended the throne. In consideration of large quantities of corn, wine, and oil sent him by Solomon, the king of Tyre furnished from Lebanon the timber required for the temple, delivering it at Joppa, the port of Jerusalem (I Kings 5:1, sq.; 9:11,

sq.; II Chron. 2:3, sq.). He also supplied large quantities of gold, and received from Solomon in return twenty towns in Galilee (I Kings 9:11-14), which, when he came to inspect them, pleased him so little that he applied to them a name of contempt (*Cabul*), and restored them to Solomon (I Kings 9:12, 13; II Chron. 8:2). It does not, however, appear that the good understanding between the two kings was broken by this unpleasant circumstance, for it was after this that he admitted Solomon's ships to a share in the profitable trade of the Mediterranean (I Kings 10:22); and Jewish sailors, under the guidance of Tyrians, were taught to bring the gold of Ophir (I Kings 9:26-28) to Solomon's two harbors on the Red Sea. Dius, the Phoenician historian, and Menander of Ephesus, assign to Hiram a prosperous reign of thirty-four years, and relate that his father was Abibal, his son and successor Baleazar. Others (later writers, as Eusebius, after Tatian, *Proep. Ev.*, x, 11) relate that Hiram, besides supplying timber for the temple, gave his daughter in marriage to Solomon. Some have regarded this Hiram as a different person from the friend of David, arguing from the long reign necessary, if he was the same who assisted David to build his house. Hiram I was a powerful ruler since at this era southern Phoenicia was consolidated under one king who ruled at Tyre, but who was officially styled "King of the Sidonians."

Another Hiram, king of Tyre, is mentioned in the royal records of the great Assyrian conqueror Tiglath-pileser III (744-727 B. C.).

2. The son of a widow of the tribe of Naphtali, and of a Tyrian father. He was sent by King Hiram to execute the principal works of the interior of the temple, and the various utensils required for the sacred services (I Kings 7:13, 14, 40). It is probable that he was selected for this purpose by the king, in the notion that his half-Hebrew blood would render him the more acceptable at Jerusalem, B. C. about 960.

Hire. *See* Wages.

Hireling (Heb. *säkîr;* Gr. *misthōtos*), a laborer employed on hire for a limited time (Job 7:1; 14:6; Mark 1:20), as distinguished from one belonging to his master. Naturally, as a temporary laborer, he would feel much less interest as compared with the shepherd or permanent keeper of the flock (John 10:12, 13). *See* Service.

Hiss (Heb. *shärăq,* to *whistle*). (1) This term usually expresses insult and contempt (Job 27:23); and mingled astonishment and contempt, as by beholders of the ruined temple (I Kings 9:8; II Chron. 7:21). (2) It is also used in the sense of to *allure,* to *entice;* as a bee keeper, who by hissing (whistling) induced the bees to come out of their hives and settle on the ground (Isa. 5:26; 7:18).

History, New Testament and Early Christianity. From the birth of Christ until the accession of the last of the house of the Herods, Herod Agrippa II, embracing fifty years, is a period without a parrallel in history for changes and complications in the several governments and political geography of Palestine.

The conspectus following synchronizes the reign of the Roman emperors of the first Christian century, the numerous high priests of the Jews, and the different political governments of that country, with the Christian history of the same period.

A CONSPECTUS OF THE NEW TESTAMENT AND CHRISTIANITY OF THE FIRST CENTURY.

DATE.	EMPERORS.	CHRISTIAN HISTORY.	HIGH PRIEST.	PALESTINIAN RULERS.
B. C. 4.	Augustus (Octavius).	PROBABLE BIRTH OF JESUS CHRIST.	Eleazar appointed by Archaelaus. Jesus ben Sie. Joazar (second time.)	DEATH of Herod the Great, March 13. Three sons succeed him, viz.: (*a*) Herod Archaelaus, ethnarch of one half of the territory: Samaria, Judea, and Idumaea. (*b*) Herod Antipas, tetrarch of one fourth, viz.: Galilee and Peraea. (*c*) Herod Philip, tetrarch of Panias, Auranitis, Batania, and Trachonitis. Quirinius (Cyrenius) *registers the Jewish population.*
A. D. 6.	Augustus.		Annas (Hanan).	Archaelaus deposed and banished; his territory becomes a Roman province. Coponius, procurator of Judea, A. D. 6-9, under the governor of Syria. Quirinius registers *Jewish Property.*
A. D. 9.	Augustus.	JESUS VISITS JERUSALEM (Luke 2).		Marcus Ambivius, procurator of Judea, A. D. 9-12.
A. D. 12.	Augustus.			Annius Rufus, procurator of Judea, A. D. 12-15.
A. D. 14.	Augustus. dies Aug. 19. Tiberius succeeds A. D. 14-37.			
A. D. 15.	Tiberius.		Ishmael ben Phabi.	Valerius Gratus, procurator, A. D. 15-26.
A. D. 16.	Tiberius.		Eleazar ben Hanan.	

DATE.	EMPERORS.	CHRISTIAN HISTORY.	HIGH PRIEST.	PALESTINIAN RULERS.
A. D. 17.	Tiberius.		Simon ben Kamhith.	
A. D. 18.	Tiberius.		Joseph Kaiaphas ("Caiaphas"), A. D. 18-36.	
A. D. 26.	Tiberius.	*Ministry of John the Baptist.*		Pontius Pilate, procurator, A. D. 26-36.
A. D. 27.	Tiberius.	Baptism of Jesus; his ministry begins. First Passover, March 22. First Galilean circuit (Matt. 4; Mark 1; Luke 4).	Caiaphas.	Pontius Pilate, procurator.
A. D. 28.	Tiberius.	March 29, Christ's Second Passover. Second Galilean circuit (John 5; Matt. 13).	Caiaphas.	Pontius Pilate, procurator.
A. D. 29.		April 16, Third Passover. Third Galilean circuit (Matt. 9:10; Mark 6; Luke 9). Oct., Feast of Tabernacles (John 7). Dec., Feast of Dedication (John 10).	Caiaphas.	Pontius Pilate, procurator.
A. D. 30.	Tiberius.	March 30, Christ at Bethany. Fourth Passover week. Christ betrayed Thursday night, Apr. 4. The crucifixion, April 6. The resurrection, April 9. The ascension, May 17. The pentecost, May 27. First miracle by the apostles (Acts 3); Sanhedrin imprison Peter and John (Acts 4).	Caiaphas.	Pontius Pilate, procurator.
A. D. 31.	Tiberius.	Ananias and Sapphira die. Apostles imprisoned, but delivered by an angel; summoned before Sanhedrin. Gamaliel interposes. Apostles beaten (Acts 5).	Caiaphas.	Pontius Pilate, procurator.
A. D. 34.	Tiberius.		Caiaphas.	Pontius Pilate, procurator; Philip, the tetrarch, dies. Vitellius, legate of Syria.
A. D. 36.	Tiberius.	Saul leads in persecutions. Ethiopian converted by Philip (Acts 8).	Jonathan ben Hanan by Vitellius.	Pontius Pilate deposed. Marcellus succeeds, A. D. 36.
A. D. 37.	Tiberius. dies March 16; Caligula succeeds A. D. 37-41.	Stephen martyred; Saul converted and spends three years in Arabia (Acts 9; Gal. 1:18).	Theophilus by Vitellius.	Caligula gives Herod Agrippa I tetrarchies of Philip and Lysanius. Maryllus sent to Judea as hipparch.
A. D. 39.	Caligula.			Herod Antipas deposed; Publius Petronius, governor of Syria. March 16, Caligula attempts to put his statue in the temple at Jerusalem.
A. D. 40.	Caligula.	Paul visits Jerusalem; plots made against his life; he goes to Tarsus (Acts 9). Christianity passes to the Gentiles; Cornelius converted and baptized (Acts 10, 11).		
A. D. 41.	Caligula dies Jan. 24. Claudius succeeds	Gentile Christians multiply at Antioch, Syria, and are *first called Christians at Antioch* (Acts 11).	Simon Kantheras by Agrippa I.	Herod Agrippa I made king over Samaria, Abylene, and Judea by Caligula and Claudius, A. D. 41-44.
A. D. 42.	Claudius.	Barnabas brings Paul from Tarsus to Antioch. Agabus predicts a great famine (Acts 11).	Matthias ben Hanan by Agrippa I.	Herod Agrippa I, king of Palestine, A. D. 41-44.
A. D. 43.	Claudius.		Elionaeus ben Kantherus by Agrippa I.	
A. D. 44.	Claudius.	James beheaded by Agrippa I; Peter released from prison by an angel (Acts 12).	Joseph ben Kamhith by Herod of Chalcis.	Herod Agrippa I exploits at Caesarea in the theater, and dies five days after, aged fifty-four years (Acts 12). Claudius makes Cuspius Fadus procurator of Judea.
A. D. 45.	Claudius.	Paul and Barnabas sent on first missionary journey to the Gentiles (Acts 13, 14).		Theudas executed.
A. D. 46.	Claudius.			Tiberius Alexander, procurator, A. D. 46-48.

DATE.	EMPERORS.	CHRISTIAN HISTORY.	HIGH PRIEST.	PALESTINIAN RULERS.
A. D. 47.	Claudius.		Ananias by Herod of Chalcis.	
A. D. 48.	Claudius.	Judaizers visit Antioch; Paul and Barnabas sent to Jerusalem; Council decrees liberty to Gentiles (Acts 15).		Ventidius Cumanus, procurator of Judea. Herod of Chalcis dies, and Claudius gives his principality to Herod Agrippa II, son of Herod Agrippa I.
A. D. 50.	Claudius.	Paul and Silas's second missionary journey to Gentiles (Acts 15-17).	Ishmael ben Phabi (younger) by Agrippa II.	
A. D. 51.	Claudius.	Paul and Silas visit cities in Asia Minor and Europe. The Macedonian vision. Paul and Silas at Philippi are whipped and imprisoned. Paul goes to Athens; preaches his memorable discourse on Mars' Hill.		
A. D. 52.	Claudius.	Paul meets Aquila and Priscilla. Writes First Epistle to the Thessalonians.		Antonius Claudius Felix, procurator of Judea, A. D. 52-60. King Agrippa II pleads for Jews at Rome.
A. D. 53.	Claudius.	Paul before Gallio at Achaia; leaves Corinth and visits Ephesus (Acts 18). Writes Second Epistle to the Thessalonians.		
A. D. 54.	Claudius. dies. Accession of Nero, A. D. 54-68.	Paul visits Jerusalem again. Makes third missionary journey.		
A. D. 55.	Nero.	Paul is two years at Ephesus; meets Apollos (Acts 18). A tumult arises. Town clerk quiets the people (19). Paul goes to Macedonia and Greece (20).		
A. D. 57.	Nero.	Paul writes both epistles to the Corinthians, also to the Galatians. Goes to Corinth, staying three months.		
A. D. 58.	Nero.	Writes the epistles to the Romans. With Luke leaves Corinth for Macedonia, Troas, and Miletus, returning to Jerusalem via Tyre and Caesarea. Agabus illustrates prediction with Paul's girdle; Philip's four daughters prophesy. A tumult at Jerusalem; Paul is assaulted, but rescued by the Roman captain; addresses the mob; is sent to Caesarea by night. Paul's defense before Felix (19-24).		
A. D. 59.	Nero.	Paul imprisoned at Caesarea for two years (24).		
A. D. 60.	Nero.	Paul defends himself before Festus and King Herod Agrippa II at Caesarea (25, 26). His voyage to Rome; shipwrecked at Melita (Malta); spends winter there (27, 28).		Portius Festus, procurator of Judea, A. D. 60-62.
A. D. 61.	Nero.	Voyage resumed, lands at Puteoli; thence to Rome afoot; is delivered to Burrus, the pretorian prefect of Nero. Lives for two years in his own hired house (27, 28).	Joseph Kabi, by Agrippa II.	
A. D. 62.	Nero.	Paul writes to Philemon, Colossians, Philippians, Ephesians. Acts of the Apostles closes. Conybeare and Howson conjecturally	Hanan ben Hanan, and Jesus ben Damnai, by Agrippa II. trace Paul's life	further as follows:
A. D. 63.	Nero.		Jesus ben Gamaliel, by Agrippa II.	
A. D. 64.	Nero.	Nero burns Rome, and persecutes Christians for his own crime.		Gessius Florus, procurator.

DATE.	EMPERORS.	CHRISTIAN HISTORY.	HIGH PRIEST.	PALESTINIAN RULERS.
A. D. 65.	Nero.	Paul travels to Spain.	Matthias ben Theophilus, by Agrippa II.	
A. D. 66.	Nero.	Paul visits churches in Asia Minor.		
A. D. 67.	Ñero.	Writes First Epistle to Timothy, also to Titus.	Phannias appointed by the people.	
A. D. 68.	Nero commits suicide. Galba succeeds.	Paul is martyred at Rome.		Marcus Antonius Julianus, procurator. (Josephus, *War*, vi, 4, 3).
A. D. 69.	Successively Galba, Otho, and Vitellius.	Apostles go abroad to evangelize the nations.		
A. D. 70.	Vespasian.			Titus captures Jerusalem.
A. D. 79.	Vespasian dies, and Titus succeeds, 79-81.			
A. D. 81.	Titus dies, Domitian succeeds.	Domitian persecutes Christians.		
A. D. 96.	Domitian dies, and Nerva succeeds.			
A. D. 98	Trajan.	The apostle John dies.		
A. D. 100.	Trajan.			Herod Agrippa II, dies at Rome in Trajan's reign, aged seventy-three years, having ruled twenty-two years and survived the war thirty years.

NOTE—The dates for the high priests given above are the conclusions of Ewald and Schurer, but are not claimed to be exact, yet closely approximate.

TABULATION OF THE HIGH PRIESTS AND PROCURATORS OF JUDEA.

HIGH PRIESTS.		PROCURATORS OF JUDEA.	SCHURER.	LEWIN.	WHITE-HOUSE.	McCLINTOCK STRONG'S CYCLO.
	B. C.		B. C.	B. C.	B. C.	B. C.
Joazar ben Boethus.	4	Archaelaus as ethnarch.	4	4	3	4
Eleazar.		Herod Antipas as tetrarch.	4	4	3	4
Jesus ben Sie.	4	Philip II as tetrarch.	4	4	3	4
Joazar (second time).						
	A. D.		A. D.	A. D.	A. D.	A. D.
*ANNAS (Hanan).	6	Archaelaus is deposed.	6	6	7	6
		Coponius, procurator.	6	6-9	7-9	6-9
		Marcus Ambivius.	9	9-12	9-12	9-12
		Annius Rufus.	12	12-15	12-15	12-15
Ishmael ben Phabi.	15	Valerius Gratus.	14	15-26	15-26	15-26
Eleazar ben Hanan.						
Simon ben Kamithus.	17					
*JOSEPH KAIAPHAS.	18					
	34	Herod Philip II dies.				
Jonathan ben Hanan.	36	Marcellus.	36		36-38	36-38
Theophilus ben Hanan.	37	Maryllus (hipparch).	37	37	39	37-40
	39	Herod Antipas deposed.				
Simon Kantheras.	41	Herod Agrippa I king.	39	41-44		41-44
Matthias ben Hanan.						
Elionaeus ben Kantheras.						
Joseph ben Kamydus.	44	Cuspius Fadus.	44	44-46	44-46	45-46
		Tiberius Alexander.	46	46-48	46-48	47-49
Ananias ben Nebeaeus.	47	Ventidius Cumanus.	48	48-50	48-51	49-53
Jonathan.						
Ishmael ben Phabi (Junior)	50	Antonius Claudius Felix.	52	50-58	51-60	53-55
		Portius Festus.	60	58-60	60-62	55-62
Joseph Kabi ben Simon.	61					
Hanan ben Hanan (Ananus).	62	Florus Albinus.	62	60-64	62-64	
Jesus ben Damni.	62					

High Priests.	A. D.	Procurators of Judea.	Schurer. A. D.	Lewin. A. D.	White-house. A. D.	McClintock Strong's Cyclo. A. D.
Jesus ben Gamaliel.	63	Gessius Florus.	64	64		65
Matthias ben Theophilus.	65					
Phannias ben Samuel.	67					
		Marcus Antonius Julianus (Josephus, *War*, b. vi, cn. 4, §3.) *See Luke 18:13, 24; John 18:13, 14.				69-70

Literature.—Tacitus, *History* and *Annals;* Josephus, *Antiquities* and *Roman-Jewish War;* William Smith, *Bible Dictionary;* Conybeare and Howson, *Life and Epistles of St. Paul;* Thomas Lewin's *Life and Letters of St. Paul;* Thomas Lewin, *Fasti Sacri;* Schürer, *Jewish People in the Times of Jesus Christ;* Milman, *History of the Jews;* Ewald, *History of Israel;* Farrar, on The Herods; S. L. Bowman, *Historical Evidences of the New Testament.*— S. L. B.

History, Old Testament. To write an Old Testament history, even in the briefest possible compass, would be to deal critically with the greater portions of the Bible narrative and to relate it to the contemporary scene. Since this contemporary scene has been marvelously extended as a result of archaeological research, such a task is here impossible. Therefore, the following conspectus of Old Testament history is substituted. In locating such pivotal events as Abraham's entrance into Canaan, the Exodus, and the Conquest in the frame of contemporary history, the author adheres to the numbers preserved in the Massoretic text of the Hebrew Old Testament, thus placing Abraham's birth c. B. C. 2161, his entrance into Palestine c. B. C. 2086, the Egyptian Sojourn c. B. C. 1871-1441, the Exodus c. 1441 and the Conquest c. B. C. 1400. Scholars who do not hold to the Old Testament chronological scheme place Abraham anywhere from B. C. 2000 to B. C. 1600, the Egyptian sojourn not until c. B. C. 1720 or later, and the Exodus c. B. C. 1290 in the reign of Raamses II or in the reign of Merneptah (c. 1230) or even later toward the close of the thirteenth century B. C. These views, however, cannot be reconciled with the general chronological scheme underlying Genesis through Kings, despite alleged archaeological evidence adduced in their support. Therefore, the following table is presented (*see* also Chronology):

A CONSPECTUS OF OLD TESTAMENT EVENTS CORRELATED WITH CONTEMPORARY HISTORY

DATE	EVENTS IN BIBLICAL HISTORY	EVENTS IN CONTEMPORARY HISTORY
Dateless Past	Creation of the World.	Various Geologic Ages. Prehistoric Stone Ages.
Probably B. C. 10,000 or Earlier	Creation of Man. Development of Cainite Civilization.	Farming, Domestication of Animals, crude arts, first villages founded.
Probably Before B. C. 5000	The Flood.	
c. B. C. 5000	Development into nations of descendants of Noah—Shem, Ham and Japheth.	Early Chalcolithic Age, pottery developed, copper introduced. Badarian, Amratian cultures in Egypt.
c. B. C. 4700	Tower of Babel erected. Confusion of tongues.	First great buildings erected in Babylonia. Earliest levels of Nineveh, Tepe Gawra, Tell ed-Judeideh, etc.
c. B. C. 4500-3000	Development of urban cultures in Babylonia.	Halafian Culture (c. 4500), Obeidan Culture (c. 3600) at Tell Obeid near Ur. Warkan (Uruk, Erech) (c. 3200); writing invented, earliest cylinder seals; Jemdet Nasr Culture (c. 3000).
c. B. C. 3000-2700 c. B. C. 2700-2200	Noah to Abraham } { Continuous spiritual declension and lapse of Noah's descendants into idolatry.	Union of Egypt Dynasties I, II (c. 2900-2700). Early Dynastic or Sumerian Period in Babylonia (c. 2800-2360). EGYPTIAN OLD KINGDOM (Pyramids), Dynasties III-VI (c. 2700-2200). First Semitic Dynasty (Sargon I) (c. 2360-2180).
c. B. C. 2250-2200	Terah born	First Intermediate Period or Dark Age in Egypt (c. 2200-1989).
c. B. C. 2161	Birth of Abraham.	Gutian Rule in Babylonia (c. 2180-2070). Sumerian revival under Third Dynasty of Ur (c. 2070-1960).
c. B. C. 2086	Abraham's entrance into Canaan.	Ur-Nammu, Dungi, Bur-Sin, Gimil-Sin and Ibi-Sin rule in power at Ur, Abraham's birthplace.
c. B. C. 2075	Invasion of Mesopotamian kings (Gen. 14).	
c. B. C. 2050	Destruction of Sodom and Gomorrah.	
c. B. C. 1950	Isaac.	Fall of Ur (c. 1960). Elamite princes in Isin and Larsa in lower Babylonia. Small Amorite and Elamite states in Babylonia.
c. B. C. 1871	Israel's entrance into Egypt.	Strong Middle Kingdom in Egypt (Dynasty XII).
	Joseph's Viceroyship.	Amenemes I-IV, Senwosret I-III (c. 1989-1776 B. C.).

DATE	EVENTS IN BIBLICAL HISTORY			EVENTS IN CONTEMPORARY HISTORY
c. B. C. 1780	Israel in Egypt.			First Dynasty of Babylon (c. 1850-1550). Hammurabi, (c. 1728-1689). Mari Age. Hyksos Period of foreign domination in Egypt (c. 1720-1570).
c. B. C. 1520	Moses born.			New Empire, Dynasty XVIII (c. 1570-1150), Kamose, Thutmose I, II, Queen Hatshepsut (c. 1570-1482).
c. B. C. 1485	Final phase of Israelite oppression.			Thutmose III (c. 1482-1450).
c. B. C. 1441	Exodus from Egypt.			Amenhotep II (c. 1450-1425).
c. B. C. 1441	Israel in the Wilderness.			Thutmose IV (c. 1425-1412).
c. B. C. 1401	Fall of Jericho.			Amenhotep III (c. 1412-1387). Amarna Period.
c. B. C. 1400 to 1361	Conquest of Canaan. Period of Joshua and Elders.			Invasion of Palestine by Habiru. Amenhotep III (Ikhnaton) (c. 1387-1366). Advance of Hittites.
c. B. C. 1361	Oppression of Cushan-Rishathaim.			Tutankamun in Egypt (c. 1366-1357).
c. B. C. 1353	Othniel's Deliverance—forty years peace.			Harmhab—decline of Egyptian influence in Palestine.
c. B. C. 1313	Oppression by Eglon of Moab.			Seti I, pharaoh (c. 1314-1290).
c. B. C. 1295	Ehud's Deliverance.			Raamses II (c. 1290-1224)— brilliant reign.
c. B. C. 1295	Peace for 80 years.			Hittite advance into Syria. Merneptah's Stele mentions Israel in Palestine.
c. B. C. 1215	Jabin's Oppression.			Weak kinglets on throne of Egypt—Amenmose, Siptah, Seti II.
c. B. C. 1195-1155	Deborah's Exploit. Forty-year peace.			Raamses III (c. 1198-1167). Invasion of Sea Peoples repulsed. Greek History: The Trojan War (c. 1200).
c. B. C. 1155	Midianite Oppression.			Decline of Egyptian power—weak reign of Raamses IV and V.
c. B. C. 1148	Gideon's Victory and Judgeship.			Egypt power in Palestine practically nil.
c. B. C. 1148	40-year peace after Gideon.			
c. B. C. 1108	Abimelech king at Shechem.			Peleset (Philistines) increase in power.
c. B. C. 1105	Ammonite Oppression, Jephthah judge.			
c. B. C. 1099	Philistine Ascendancy.			
c. B. C. 1085	Samson is Judge.			
c. B. C. 1065	Eli is Judge.			
c. B. C. 1050	Battle of Ebenezer, Philistines take ark.			Great Empires on Tigris-Euphrates, Halys and Nile decline leaving Syria-Palestine open for conquests of David (c. 1004-965) and the splendor of Solomon's reign (c. 965-926).
c. B. C. 1020	Saul and beginnings of Monarchy.			
c. B. C. 1004	David king of Judah.			
c. B. C. 998	David king of all Israel.			
c. B. C. 965	Solomon			
c. B. C. 926	Division of the Monarchy.			Rezon seizes power in Damascus (c. 930).
	Kingdom of Judah	*Kingdom of Israel*		
c. B. C. 926	Rohoboam	Jeroboam I		Shishak's Invasion (c. 921).
c. B. C. 910		Abijam		
c. B. C. 908		Asa		Aramaean Kingdom of Damascus expands under Hezion and Tabrimmon.
c. B. C. 907	Nadab			
c. B. C. 906	Baasha			
c. B. C. 900				Aramaeans of Damascus ascendant under Hezion.
c. B. C. 883		Elah		
c. B. C. 882		Zimri Omri		Benhadad I of Damascus.
c. B. C. 871		Ahab	Elijah	Rise of Assyria: Ashurnasirpal II (883-859). Conquests of Shalmaneser III (859-824). Battle of Karkar: Syrian coalition vs. Assyria (853).
	Jehoshaphat Jehoram			
c. B. C. 852		Ahaziah		
c. B. C. 851		Jehoram		
	Ahaziah			

DATE	EVENTS IN BIBLICAL HISTORY	EVENTS IN CONTEMPORARY HISTORY
c. B. C. 845	Athaliah Jehu Jehoash Jehoahaz } Elisha Joash	Jehu surrenders to Assyrians. Shamshi-Adad V (823-811). Adad-nirari III (810-783).
c. B. C. 802	Amaziah	Decline of Assyria.
c. B. C. 787	Jeroboam II } Amos	
c. B. C. 785	Uzziah	
c. B. C. 747	Jotham Zechariah	Tiglath-pileser III (745-727) overruns Syria-Palestine.
c. B. C. 742	Ahaz Isaiah Shallum	
c. B. C. 746	Micah Menahem Hosea	
c. B. C. 736	Pekahiah	
c. B. C. 734	Pekah	
c. B. C. 732	Hoshea	Damascus falls to Assyria (732).
c. B. C. 725	Hezekiah	Shalmaneser V (727-722) besieges Samaria.
c. B. C. 721	Samaria Falls	Sargon II (722-705) takes Samaria.
	Kingdom of Judah.	
c. B. C. 701		Sennacherib (705-681) invades Judah.
c. B. C. 696	Manasseh's idolatrous reign.	
c. B. C. 641	Amon	Sennacherib's death (681). Esarhaddon's reign (681-669) conquers Egypt. Ashurbanipal (669-626).
c. B. C. 639	Josiah.	
c. B. C. 609	Josiah slain by Necho.	Asshur falls to Medes (614). Nineveh falls to Medes and Babylonians (612). Defeat of Assyrians and Egyptians by Necho (609).
c. B. C. 608	Jehoahaz. Jehoiakim.	
c. B. C. 605	Daniel carried to Babylon. Jeremiah.	Nebuchadnezzar defeats Necho (609). Nabopolassar's death (605). Nebuchadnezzar II (605-562).
c. B. C. 598	Jehoiachin. Zedekiah.	Jehoiachin and Ezekiel, etc. carried to Babylon (598).
c. B. C. 587	Fall of Jerusalem. Daniel's career in Babylon. Ezekiel's prophesies to Exiles.	Lachish Letters (c. 589). Jerusalem destroyed (587). Nebuchadnezzar's conquests (Egypt). Evil-Merodach, liberation of Jehoiachin (c. 561). Neriglassar (560-556). Nabunaid (Nabonidus) (556-539).
c. B. C. 539	Fall of Babylon.	Belshazzar (coregent with Nabunaid).
c. B. C. 538	Edict of Cyrus.	
c. B. C. 536	Return of remnant. Rebuilding of temple begun.	Rule of Cyrus, founder of Persian Empire till death (530). Cambyses king of Persia (530-522);
c. B. C. 522		Darius I (522-486).
c. B. C. 520	Ministry of Haggai and Zechariah. Building of Temple resumed.	
c. B. C. 516	Temple completed by Zerubbabel.	Defeat of Persians at Marathon (490). Xerxes I (Ahasuerus) (486-465). Persian defeat at Salamis (480).
c. B. C. 476	Esther Queen.	
c. B. C. 458	Ezra's return. Revival of the law.	Artaxerxes I (465-424).
c. B. C. 445	Nehemiah's return to rebuild walls.	Periclean Age in Greece (460-429). Herodotus, Socrates, Plato.
c. B. C. 432	Malachi prophesies.	See CHRONOLOGY, O. T.—*M. F. U.*

Hitt′ites (hĭt′ĭts; Heb. *Ḥitti, Ḥittim, Ḥeth*).

1. **Old Testament References.** A people mentioned frequently in the O. T., forty-seven times under their own name and fourteen times as descendants of Heth (Gen. 10:15). In the days of Abraham a group of them were located in the neighborhood of Hebron (Gen. 23:1-20), from whom the patriarch bought a burial place. Esau married Hittite wives (Gen.

204.

26:34, 35; 36:2). The spies sent out by Moses found Hittites located in the hill country (Num. 13:29). The Hittites were among the dwellers of Canaan at the time of the conquest and offered opposition to Israel (Josh. 9:1, 2; 11:3). They were located near a territory held by Israel, for the inhabitants of Luz built a new city in Hittite territory (Judg. 1:26). As the land was gradually conquered, the Hittites were not driven out by Israel, but remained, and in some cases intermarried. They appear in various ways at later times. Hittites were among David's followers (I Sam. 26:6). Uriah, whom David put to death, was a Hittite (II Sam. 11:3). Solomon had Hittite women in his harem (I Kings 11:1), while many of this people were impressed to forced labor (I Kings 9:20, 21). These various Biblical allusions used to be treated with great skepticism, but the Hittites offer an example of archaeology's resurrection of an ancient people, so that today the Hittites and Hittite culture are well known.

2. **Archaeological Discovery.** It is now known that the center of Hittite power was in Asia Minor. There an empire that once vied with Egypt and Assyria, but had been long forgotten, has been discovered by modern archaeologists. A missionary at Damascus named William Wright and the Orientalist A. H. Sayce were among the first scholars to piece together the picture of this ancient imperial people from scattered monuments (Wright, *The Empire of the Hittites*, 1884; Sayce, *The Hittites, the Story of a Forgotten Empire*, Rev. Ed. 1925). Knowledge was vastly increased by the discovery of a German professor named Hugo

Winckler of thousands of cuneiform tablets at Boghaz-keui, a Hittite capital located on the great bend of the Halys River, ninety miles east of Angora. This phenomenal discovery was made in 1906-07 and 1911-12. A Czech scholar, Friedrich Hrozny, and other linguists have deciphered Hittite cuneiform used between B. C. 1900 and 1100. This accomplishment has opened up a vast Hittite literature consisting of their annals, religious texts and myths in Sumero-Akkadian characters received from the Hurrians (Horites). Portions of Hittite legal codes have also been discovered.

3. **Periods of Hittite Power.** Two chief periods of Hittite power are to be distinguished. The first refers back to the time of the First Dynasty of Babylon (c. B. C. 1600-1450). The second comprises the new Hittite kingdom which was powerful in the years c. B. C. 1400-1200. This latter kingdom was consolidated by a powerful ruler at Boghaz-keui named Subbiluliuma. This mighty conqueror incorporated into his empire the Mesopotamian kingdoms of Mitanni and of the Hurri and pushed his army southward into Syria to the very confines of Palestine. The king of Mitanni, whom he conquered, was named Tushratta, well-known from his

205. Hittite Soldier Armed with Axe

correspondence with Amenhotep III and IV of Egypt (J. A. Knudtzon, *Die el Amarna Tafel*) (Num. 17:25; 27:29). Tushratta gave his daughter to be the wife of Amenhotep III. Subbiluliuma was followed by Arandash and then Arandash's brother, Mershilish was followed by his son, Mutwatallish. The latter clashed with Raamses II in the famous Battle of Kadesh and almost defeated the proud pharoah. The brother and second king after Mutwatallish was Hattushilish, who signed a non-agression pact with Raamses II. This agreement was sealed by the marriage of the Hittite king's daughter to Raamses II. Around 1200 B. C. Egyptian power went into temporary eclipse and the Hittite empire came to its end. The capital at Boghaz-keui fell. However, Hittite kingdoms continued to exist at Senjirli, Carchemish, Sakjegeuzi, Hamath and other places.

4. **Language and Culture.** The Hittites were non-Semitic, probably Aryan, the first Indo-Europeans to cross the Caucasus into Armenia and Cappadocia. They brought with them pre-Indo-European language, the harbinger of Sanskrit, Greek, Latin, Slavonic and Teutonic tongues. They formed a cultural tie between Europe and Mesopotamia.

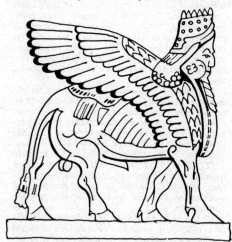

206. Man-headed Winged Bull; Part Man, Part Lion or Bull, Part Eagle. This creature was set up by Assyrian and Hittite kings to protect entrances.

5. **Agressiveness.** Many scholars consider the Hittites as the third most influential of ancient peoples of the Middle East, rivaling the Egyptians and the Mesopotamians. Hebrews dreaded them as well as the empires on the Tigris and Euphrates. About 1550 they destroyed the Babylonian capital of the great Hammurabi. Their agressiveness is demonstrated also in their commercial activities, carrying on extensive trade in horses with Solomon. Like the Hyksos and the Mitanni and other peoples of Western Asia, the Hittites were noted for fine horses, the clay tablets revealing much information about this matter. The Hittites also kept secret the iron-smelting formula when iron was regarded almost as valuable as silver and gold. Not until two centuries later did the Philistines come into this knowledge and not until the Saul-Davidic era did Israel learn it.

6. **Religion.** Hittite religion is a grand medley of Egyptian and Babylonian deities. They transported Ishtar of Nineveh as far west as Asia Minor. Marduk, the patron god of Babylon, is said on one tablet to have gone to the land of the Hittites where he sat upon his throne for twenty-four years. With Egyptian deities they also assimilated the gods of Syria and Asia Minor. Hittites early dwelt in what later became prominent centers of early Christianity: Tarsus, Iconium, Lystra, etc. The famous Ephesian Diana may have been a Hittite Artemis. Hittite gods are frequently depicted astride the backs of animals or enthroned between them. However, they are not actually presented as animals. This was evidently the arrangement in Jeroboam's cultic calves at Dan and Bethel, with Jehovah invisibly enthroned. *M. F. U.*

Hi′vites (hī′vīts; Cf. Heb. *ḥăwwäh, tent village, Arab ḥiwaʻ, collection of tents,* Heb. *the Hivite.* One of the seven nations of Canaan, who were to be destroyed by the Israelites (Deut. 7:1, and elsewhere; comp. Gen. 10:17). The focus of the Hivites seems to have been in the north. In Josh. 11:3 the Hivites dwelt "under Hermon, in the land of Mizpeh"; in Judg. 3:3, they "dwelt in Mount Lebanon, from Mount Baal-hermon unto the entering in of Hamath"; in II Sam. 24:7, "all the cities of the Hivites" are numbered apparently near Tyre. And all these seem to be in some sense official locations of the Hivite race, rather than mere chance settlements. But the name Hivite may be a descriptive term like *Amorites* (*q. v.*), and not a local name, for we find Hivites in other localities. Hamor, the father of Shechem, was a Hivite. The whole story (Gen. 34:2-31) shows them to have been warmhearted, impulsive, and overconfident (v. 23), yet overtrustful (v. 21), and given to trade and to the multiplication of flocks and herds rather than to war. It is hinted that the absence of any attempt at revenge confirms this impression of unwarlike character, as does the ease with which Abimelech took the city, though indeed at last not without hard fighting (Judg. 9:22-49) and by the "unmilitary character" of his slayer and her weapon (v. 53). Perhaps the name of their god, Baal-berith, *Baal of the league,* may confirm this impression of their unwarlike character. In Josh. 9:7, 17 we find Hivites occupying four confederate cities (Gibeon, Chephirah, Beeroth, and Kirjath-jearim) in the western half of the territory assigned. Here we find the same foresighted keenness and the same disposition to gain their ends by diplomacy rather than by arms; but their craft this time is less self-confident and more successful.

The Hivite form of government is not described, but the mention of "our elders and all the inhabitants of our country" (Josh. 9:11) certainly indicates one in which the people had considerable voice, since the sending of an embassy of unconditional peace is one of the highest acts of sovereignty. So Hamor and Shechem "communed with the men of their city" (Gen. 34:20-24), and reasoned, but did not attempt to command.

There is confusion between Hivite and Horite (Hurrian) in the original text of Gen. 36:2, 20, 29; Josh. 9:7 and Josh. 9:13, lxx. It is possible the Hivites were an ethnic subdivision of the Horites (Hurrians).

Hizki′ah (hĭz-kī′à; *strengthened of Jah*), an ancestor of Zephaniah the prophet (Zeph. 1:1), B. C. before 630.

Hizki'jah (hĭz-kī'à; Hebrew same as above). According to the punctuation of the A. V. a man who sealed the covenant of reformation with Ezra and Nehemiah (Neh. 10:17). But there is no doubt that the name should be taken with that preceding it, as "Ater-Hizki-jah," a name given in the lists of those who returned from Babylon with Zerubbabel (Smith, s. v.). *See* Hezekiah.

Hoarfrost (Heb. *kᵉphōr*, Exod. 16:14; Psa. 147:16; Job 38:29, "hoary"). *See* Frost.

Ho'bab (hō'băb; *beloved*), the son of Raguel the Midianite (Num. 10:29; Judg. 4:11), B. C. 1440. He has usually been identified with Jethro (*see* Exod. 18:5, 27, compared with Num. 10:29, 30); but it is rather his father, Reuel, to whom the title "Moses's father-in-law" is intended to apply in Num. 10:29. That Jethro and Reuel (Raguel) were names of the same person seems evident from Exod. 2:18, 21; 3:1. Hobab would, therefore, be the brother-in-law of Moses. When Jethro returned to his home (Exod. 18:27) Moses prevailed upon Hobab to remain (as seems implied by the absence of any refusal to his second importunity in Num. 10:32) and act as guide through the desert. We find his descendants among the Israelites (Judg. 4:11).

Ho'bah (hō'bà), a place, north of Damascus, to which Abraham pursued the kings who had pillaged Sodom (Gen. 14:15). Location uncertain.

Hod (hŏd; *majesty*), one of the sons of Zophah, of the tribe of Asher (I Chron. 7:37).

Hoda'iah (hō-dā'yä; *majesty of Jah*), the first named of the seven sons of Elioenai, of the descendants of Zerubbabel (I Chron. 3:24); probably a brother of the Naum of Luke 3:25.

Hodavi'ah (hō-dà-vī'à; *praise of Jehovah*).

1. One of the chief men of the tribe of Manasseh, east of Jordan at the time of the Assyrian captivity (I Chron. 5:24).

2. Son of Hasennah and father of Meshullam, of the tribe of Benjamin (I Chron. 9:7), B. C. before 536.

3. A Levite, whose descendants (to the number of seventy-four) returned from Babylon with Zerubbabel (Ezra 2:40), B. C. before 536. In the parallel passage (Neh. 7:43) his name is written *Hodevah*. He is probably the same as *Judah* (Ezra 3:9).

Ho'desh (hō'dĕsh; *a month*), one of the wives of Shaharaim, of the tribe of Judah, several of whose children are enumerated (I Chron. 8:9), in v. 8 more correctly *Baara* (q. v.).

Hode'vah (hō-dē'và; *majesty of Jah*, Neh. 7:43). *See* Hodaviah, 3.

Hodi'ah (hô-dī'à; Hebrew same as Hodijah), one of the two wives of Mered (I Chron. 4:19), and the mother of Jered and Heber and Jekuthiel; she is called (v. 18) Jehudijah (*the Jewess*, i. e., his Jewish wife, as distinguished from Bithiah, who was an Egyptian).

Hodi'jah (hô-dī'jà; *majesty of Jehovah*).

1. One of the Levites who assisted Nehemiah in expounding the law (Neh. 8:7; 9:5). From the association of his name in Neh. 10:10, with some of those mentioned in connection with his in chap. 8:7, we conclude that he is the same person, B. C. 445.

2. Another Levite mentioned in Neh. 10:13,

as one of those who signed the covenant with Nehemiah.

3. One of the Israelites who became parties with Nehemiah in the sacred covenant (Neh. 10:18).

Hog'lah (hŏg'là; perhaps *partridge*, Cf. Arab. *hajal, partridge*), the third of the five daughters of Zelophehad the Gileadite, to whom, in the absence of male heirs, portions were assigned by Moses (Num. 26:33; 27:1; 36:11; Josh. 17:3).

Ho'ham (hō'hàm; derivation uncertain), the king of Hebron, who joined the league against Gibeon, but was overthrown in battle by Joshua and slain after being captured in the Cave of Makkedah (Josh. 10:3), B. C. after 1400.

Hold (*fortress*, as often rendered), the term especially applied to the lurking places of David (I Sam. 22:4, 5; 24:22, etc.).

Holiness (Heb. *qōdĕsh; hagiōsunē;* in both cases "separation," or "setting apart," holy, from Sax. "halig," "whole," "sound"). Holiness is therefore a general term to indicate sanctity, or separation from all that is sinful, or impure, or morally imperfect; moral wholeness. The term is used with reference to persons, places, and things.

1. **Holiness of God.** Holiness is one of the essential attributes of the divine nature. It is, on the one hand, entire freedom from moral evil, and upon the other, absolute moral perfection. The Scriptures lay great stress upon this attribute of God (*see* Exod. 15:11; I Sam. 2:2; Psa. 71:22; 99:9; 111:9; Isa. 6:3; Hab. 1:12; Rev. 15:4, etc.). Of greatest consequence, also, in this connection, is the revelation of God's holiness in the character and work of Jesus Christ. *See* Christ, Sinlessness of; Atonement.

By the holiness of God, it is not implied that he is subject to some law or standard of moral excellence external to himself, but that all moral law and perfection have their eternal and unchangeable basis in his own nature. He is the One in whom these eternal sanctities reside, who is himself the root and ground of them all. In this sense it is said without qualification, "There is none holy as the Lord" (I Sam. 2:2); "Thou only art holy" (Rev. 15:4).

Religious and Moral Bearings. The holiness of God is set before us in the Scriptures as of great practical consequence.

(*a*) It is the special ground of reverence, awe, and adoration (*see* Psa. 71:22; 111:9; Isa. 6:3, et al.). (*b*) It is the standard of all holiness (*see* Matt. 5:48; I Pet. 1:16, et al.). (*c*) It implies necessarily the divine opposition to, and condemnation of all sin (Hab. 1:13; I Sam. 6:20; Isa. 6:5, et al.). (*d*) The contemplation of this attribute is accordingly peculiarly adapted to awaken or deepen the human consciousness of sin. *See* Scriptures above referred to. (*e*) It is revealed to men, nevertheless, as setting before them the highest end of their aspiration, and hope, and endeavor (*see* Exod. 19:6; Lev. 20:7; Heb. 12; I Pet. 1:16).

2. **Holiness in Moral Creatures Generally.** The Scriptures represent the unfallen angels as "holy" (Matt. 25:31; Mark 8:38); men

also in many instances are thus represented (II Kings 4:9; II Chron. 35:3; Ezra 8:28; Mark 6:20; I Pet. 2:5).

But in all such cases the following distinctions are to be borne in mind: (*a*) Holiness of the most exalted type in the creature, as in the holy angels, is less than the holiness of God. Their holiness is perfect conformity to the will of God, one infinitely superior to themselves. The holiness of God is absolute; its law is in the perfection of his own Being. (*b*) God is in the most complete sense separate from evil. In him is no possiblity of sin. With infinite comprehension he perfectly measures the enormity of sin and hates it with a perfect hatred. The angels are finite in their capacities, and however holy, there exists for them at least the abstract possibility of sinning. For such reasons, probably, it is written, "There is none holy as the Lord" (I Sam. 2:2); "He charged his angels with folly" (Job 4:18), and "Behold, he putteth no trust in his saints (angels); yea, the heavens are not clean in his sight" (Job 15:15). In connection with the last passage, says Dillmann, "In comparison with the all-transcending holiness and purity of God, the creatures which ethically and physically are the purest are impure."

Holiness in man, with respect to which the foregoing, is certainly suggestive, requires further consideration.

3. **Holiness in Man.** Of this it is to be noted, (1) That in many cases the holiness ascribed to men in the Scriptures is simply ceremonial, formal. They are persons "separated," "set apart," or dedicated to holy services. They were expected or required, however, along with this outward dedication, to lead holy lives, and to be inwardly dedicated, a requirement frequently lost sight of. Thus the priests and the Levites are spoken of in the Old Testament as "holy." (2) The holiness predicated or required of men, upon which the Scriptures everywhere lay almost exclusive stress, is that of character and conduct. (3) Man appears before us in the Scriptures as a fallen being, and, as he appears to our observation, by nature unholy and sinful. Created in the image of God, he has lost one of the most essential features of that image—holiness. (4) Holiness, so far as it appears in man anywhere, is an outcome of God's gracious work in salvation, and yet not without the proper exertion of one's own free will, and the putting forth of strenuous effort (Eph. 4:22, 24). (5) Exalted attainments in holiness are possible for men, and often realized in this life (Luke 1:75; II Cor. 7:1; I Thess. 3:13). (6) The whole tone of Scripture accords with the weighty exhortation, "Follow peace with all men and holiness, without which no man shall see the Lord" (Heb. 12:14). (6) The N. T. teaches that the believer was sanctified positionally when he was saved by virtue of his being presented "in Christ" (I Cor. 1:2, 30), that he is being sanctified experientially as he reckons upon his position in Christ (Rom. 6:11) and that he will be ultimately sanctified in the sense of full conformity to Christ in glorification (Rom. 8:30, 31). *See* Sanctification.

4. **Holy Place, Things, etc.** The Scriptures also ascribe holiness to places (e. g., the Temple, and the "most holy place" therein), and to things, as the altars and other accessories of worship. By holiness in such instances is meant "separation" or dedication to holy uses, and of course there is implied no moral quality or inherent sanctity in the objects themselves. They were to be treated with reverence, as should churches and accessories of worship in these days, because of the holiness of God to whose service they are dedicated. *See* Holiness, Ceremonial.—E. McC. revised by *M. F. U.*

Holiness, Ceremonial. Jehovah had called Israel to be "a kingdom of priests, and an holy nation" (Exod. 19:6), having placed them in covenant fellowship with himself. In this covenant relationship he established an institution of salvation, which furnished the covenant people with the means of obtaining the expiation of their sins and securing righteousness before God and holiness of life with God (*see* also Lev., chaps. 11-15, 17, 18; Deut. 14:1-21). This holiness was shown in certain ceremonies and laws:

1. The dedication of the firstborn (Exod. 13:2, 12, 13; 22:29, 30, etc.), and the offering of all firstlings and first fruits (Deut. 26:1, sq.).

2. The distinction between clean and unclean food (Lev., ch. 11; Deut., ch. 14).

3. Provision for purification (Lev., chaps. 12-15; Deut. 23:1-14). *See* Purification.

4. Laws against disfigurement (Lev. 19:27; Deut. 14:1) and against excessive scourging (Deut. 25:3).

5. Laws against unnatural marriages and lusts (Lev., chaps. 18, 20).

6. Holiness of priests (*q. v.*), Levites (*q. v.*), and holiness of sacred places. *See* Tabernacle; Temple, etc.

7. Of times. *See* Festivals.

Ho'lon (hō'lŏn; *sandy*).

1. A town in the mountains of Judah (Josh. 15:51), given to the priests (21:15). Location is unknown.

2. A city in the plain of Moab upon which judgment was pronounced by Jeremiah (48: 21). Not identified, although named in connection with Jahazah, Dibon, and other known places.

Holy Ghost. *See* Holy Spirit.

Holy Ghost, Sin Against. *See* Sin, the Unpardonable.

Holy of Holies. *See* Tabernacle.

Holy Place. *See* Tabernacle, Temple.

Holy Spirit, the third Person in the Trinity.

1. **Scriptural Designations** (Heb. *rūăḥ, 'ĕlōhim, Spirit of God;* or *rūăḥ, YHWH, Spirit of Jehovah;* Gr. *to pneuma to hagion,* the "Holy Ghost," or "the Holy Spirit"). Frequently the term is simply "the Spirit," or "the Spirit of the Lord," or "the Spirit of God," or "the Spirit of Jesus Christ" (Matt. 3:16; Luke 3:22; 4:18; Acts 5:9; Phil. 1:19).

2. **Theological Statements.** The doctrine of the Holy Spirit has about it the difficulty that belongs to that of the Trinity, or the existence of God as a purely spiritual being; the difficulty that arises from the narrow limits of the human understanding. Nevertheless the Scriptures bring to us their definite representations of truth. And with these Christian

thought must concern itself. The chief topics of theology respecting the Holy Spirit are: (1) His personality; (2) His deity; (3) His relation to the Father and to the Son; (4) His office or work.

(1) **Personality.** The historic and prevailing doctrine of the Christian Church, in accordance with the Scriptures, has been that the Holy Spirit is a person distinct from the Father and the Son, though united to both in the mysterious oneness of the Godhead. He is not simply a personification or figurative expression for the divine energy or operation, as some have held at various periods of the history of the Church (Anti-Trinitarians), but an intelligent agent, possessed of self-consciousness and freedom. In proof of this it is justly said: *1.* That the Scriptures which ascribe distinct personality to the Father and the Son, with equal explicitness ascribe distinct personality to the Holy Ghost. Prominent illustrations of this are found in Matt. 3:16, 17; 28:19; John 14:16, 17; 15:26. *2.* The pronouns used with reference to the Holy Spirit are invariably personal pronouns, e. g., John 16:13 14; Acts 13:2. *3.* The attributes of personality, self-consciousness, and freedom are ascribed to the Holy Spirit (I Cor. 2:10; 12:11). *4.* The relations described as existing between the Holy Spirit and mankind are such as to emphaisze his personality. The Spirit strives with man (Gen. 6:3). He instructs, regenerates, sanctifies, and comforts believers (John 16:13, 14; 3:5; 14:16; I Pet. 1:2). We are warned not to "sin against," "not to resist " not "to grieve," nor to quench the Holy Spirit (Matt. 12:31, 32; Acts 7:51; 4:30; I Thess. 5:19).

(2) **Deity.** The deity of the Holy Spirit has been but little disputed in the Church by those who have admitted his personality. The Arian heresy of the 4th century, which represented the Holy Spirit as the earliest of all the creatures of the created Son, is the chief exception to the general rule. The Scriptures which establish the personality of the Holy Spirit, in many cases, as must have been noted, also establish his deity. Beyond this, attention is commonly called to the following sure indications of Holy Scripture: *1.* The Holy Spirit is distinctly called God, and names are given to him that properly belong to God (Acts 5:3, 4; Isa. 6:9; comp. Acts 28:25; Jer. 31:31-34; Heb. 10:15; II Cor. 3:17, 19). *2.* Divine attributes, as knowledge, sovereignty, eternity, are ascribed to the Holy Spirit (I Cor. 2:11; 12:11; Heb. 9:14). *3.* Divine works, as creation and the new birth, are attributed to him (Gen. 1:2; Job 26:13; John 3:3, 8). *4.* Worship and homage such as belong only to God are paid to the Holy Spirit (Isa. 6:3-10; comp. Acts 28:25-27; II Cor. 13:14). And harmonious with this is the fact that the sin against the Holy Spirit is the unpardonable sin (Matt. 12:31, 32). *See* Sin, Unpardonable.

(3) **Relation to Trinity.** The relation of the Holy Spirit to the Father and to the Son is a subject with respect to which the faith of the Church developed slowly. The controversies of the first four centuries related principally to the Son. The Council at Nicaea, A. D. 325, gave forth simply this clause respecting the

third Person in the Trinity: "And we believe in the Holy Spirit." The second Council at Constantinople, A. D. 381, added the words "the Lord and Giver of life who proceeds from the Father, who is to be worshiped and glorified with the Father and the Son, and who spake through the prophets." At the third Synod of Toledo, A. D. 589, the words *"filio que"* (and the Son) were added, so as to assert the procession of the Holy Ghost from the Son as well as the Father. This was a principal cause of the division between the Western and Eastern Churches, the former maintaining, the latter denying, that the Holy Spirit proceeds from both the Father and the Son (*see* Shedd, *Hist. of Doctrine*, vol. i, pp. 355-362). The prevailing doctrine may be thus summed up: *1.* The Holy Ghost is the same in substance and equal in power and glory with the Father and the Son. *2.* He is, nevertheless, as to his mode of subsistence and operation, subordinate to both the Father and the Son, as he proceeds from them and is sent by them, and they operate through him (John 15:26; 16:15; 14:26; Phil. 1:19; Acts 11:17).

(4) **Office.** Well says Van Oosterzee: "Happily, not the sounding the depths of the Holy Spirit's nature, but the receiving and possessing of the Holy Spirit himself, is for us, even as Christian theologians, the main point." Hence, without detracting from the value of what has preceded, of paramount importance is the office and work of the Holy Spirit. This is indicated as follows: *1.* The Spirit is the immediate source of all life, physical and intellectual (Psa. 104:29; Isa. 32:14, 15; Job 32:8; 33:4; Gen. 2:7; Exod. 31:2, sq.; Num. 11:17, et al.). *2.* He bore an important part in the coming of Christ in the flesh and the qualifying of his human nature for his work (Luke 1:35; John 3:34; 1:32). *3.* He is the revealer of all divine truth. The Holy Scriptures are especially the product of the Holy Spirit (Mic. 3:8; John 14:26; 16:13; I Cor. 2:10-13; II Tim. 3:16). *4.* He moves upon the hearts and consciences of all men, attending revealed truth with his power wherever it is known, and even where it is not known, affording some measure of divine light and gracious influence (Acts 2:17; John 16:8-11; I Cor. 2:4). *5.* He convicts men of sin, graciously aids them in repentance and faith; regenerates, comforts, and sanctifies believers; bears witness to their acceptance with God and adoption as God's children; dwells in them as the principle of a new and divine life. In addition to Scripture before quoted, *see* Rom. 8:14-16; I Cor. 6:19; II Cor. 3:18 (*see* Spirit, Witness of). *6.* He also exercises guidance in the ministrations of the Church, calling men to various offices and endowing them with qualifications for their work (Acts 13:2; I Cor. 12:4-11).

5. **Special Work in the Believer.** The Holy Spirit in this particular age from Pentecost to the outtaking and glorification of the Church, the Body of Christ, performs a special work in every believer the moment he exercises saving faith in Christ. Simultaneously with regenerating him the Spirit baptizes the believer into union with other believers in the Body (I Cor. 12:13) and into union with Christ, Himself

(Rom. 6:3, 4). This is an unique and distinctive ministry of the Spirit during this age. The Holy Spirit also indwells every believer perpetually (John 14:17; Rom. 8:9; I Cor. 6:19, 20) and seals every believer unto the day of redemption (Eph. 4:30). In addition, the Holy Spirit fills every believer when special conditions of filling are met (Eph. 5:18).

6. **Dispensational Ministry.** According to the prophetic announcement of John the Baptist of the Spirit's baptizing work (Matt. 3:11; Mark 1:8; Luke 3:16, 17; John 1:32, 33), the death, resurrection and ascension of Christ were to inaugurate the new age of the Holy Spirit's ministry. Our Lord prophetically announced a drastic change in the Holy Spirit's operation in the age which was to begin. At Pentecost (Acts 2) the Holy Spirit came as the ascension gift. He came, moreover, in a sense in which he was not here before and to perform all the ministries delegated to Him in this age, namely, regenerating, baptizing, sealing and indwelling every believer with the added privilege of each believer being filled with the Spirit, if he meets the conditions of filling. The distinctive ministry of the Spirit for this age is His baptizing work. This occurred for the first time in Acts 2 (Cf. Acts 1:5, Acts 11: 14-16). The first occurrence of the baptizing work of the Spirit in Acts 2 marked the birthday of the Christian Church. In Acts 8 the racially mongrel Samaritans were admitted to gospel privilege and granted the gift of the Holy Spirit, which included the Spirit's baptizing work, placing them in the Church, the Body of Christ. In Acts 10 the Gentiles were likewise admitted. This latter instance marks the normal course of the age. Every believer upon the simple condition of faith in Christ is regenerated, baptized into the Body, the Church, indwelt perpetually, sealed eternally and given the privilege of being continuously filled. Old Testament saints and all pre-Pentecost experience came short of these tremendous blessings which are the heritage of every genuine believer in this age. E. McC. revised by *M. F. U.*

Holyday. 1. The rendering of the Heb. *ḥāgăg,* to *dance,* a festival celebrated by sacred dances (Exod. 5:1), and so a public solemnity (Psa. 42:4).

2. In Col. 2:16 "holyday" is the rendering of the Gr. *heortē,* a feast, and often so translated.

Ho′man (hō′măn; Cf. Heb. *hāmăm, confuse, make a noise*), one of the sons of Lotan, and grandson of Seir the Horite (I Chron. 1:39). In the parallel passage (Gen. 36:22) his name is written Hemam.

Home. *See* Family; Household.

Homeborn. *See* Service.

Homer. *See* Metrology, II.

Honesty. "Honest" is generally rendered in the R. V. "honorable" and "seemly." Gr. *semnotēs* has the meaning of *gravity, probity, purity* (I Tim. 2:2). "Honestly" (Rom. 13:13; I Thess. 4:12) is the rendering of the Gr. *euschēmonōs,* and means *seemly, properly, with propriety.* In general, honesty stands for upright disposition, rectitude in dealing with others, probity, purity.

Hon′ey, a sweet thick fluid manufactured by bees from flowers and fruits and placed in the cells of the comb (Judg. 14:8; Psa. 19:10). Sweets have always been craved by Orientals, and honey was much esteemed as an article of food (Gen. 43:11; II Sam. 17:20). It was very often eaten directly from the honey comb, or prepared in other ways (Exod. 16:31; I Sam. 14:26). Canaan is often described in the O. T. as a land "flowing with milk and honey" (Exod. 3:8, 17 etc.). This graphic figure portrays the fertile land supplying rich pasturage for cattle, which give such abundant milk the land is said to flow with it, and producing many kinds of flowers, giving food to honey-producing bees. Wild honey was frequently deposited in rocks (Deut. 32:13), in trees (I Sam. 14:25) and, upon occasion, in the carcases of animals (Judg. 14:8). It was sought after for making many kinds of pastries and condiments. Honey was not only produced from bees but also artificially from dates and grapes (Arab. *dibs;* Josephus, *Wars,* IV. 8, 3). Honey was excluded from the offerings made by fire unto the Lord (Lev. 2:11), apparently because, like leaven, it produces fermentation. Honey was often presented as a gift (Gen. 43: 11; I Kings 14:3). John the Baptist had "wild honey" as an important part of his diet (Matt. 3:4). Honey in general supplied the place of sugar. For example, 300 pounds of grapes produced 100 pounds of *dibs,* and when diluted with a little water, furnished a kind of sugar (Exod. 16:31).

Figurative. Honey and milk are used to denote sweet discourse (Cant. 4:11). The Word of God is compared with honey as spiritually delectable (Psa. 19:10; 119:103) and honey taken in due quantities is illustrative of moderation in pleasure (Prov. 25:16, 27). *See* Bees, Animal Kingdom. *M. F. U.*

Honor, the rendering of several Hebrew and Greek words, meaning: (1) Respect paid to superiors: to God (I Chron. 16:27; Psa. 66:2; 96:6; Dan. 11:38; John 5:23; Rev. 5:12); to parents and kings, including submission and service (Exod. 20:12; Matt. 15:4; I Pet. 2:17); the esteem due to virtue, wisdom, glory, reputation, and probity (Prov. 15:33; 22:4; 29: 23). (2) The reward, emolument, position, given to subjects (Num. 22:17, 37; II Chron. 1:11, 12; Esth. 6:3, 6, 9), and the final reward of righteousness (John 5:44; Rom. 2:7; Heb. 2:7; II Pet. 1:17).

Hood (Heb. *ṣānîf, to wind around,* Isa. 3:23), a headdress composed of twisted cloths of various colors; a turban. *See* Dress.

Hoof (Heb. *pärsäh,* to *split, divide*), the cleft foot of neat cattle (Exod. 10:26; Lev. 11:3, etc.), and also of the horse, though not cloven (Isa. 5:28; Jer. 47:3). The parting of the hoof is one of the main distinctions between clean and unclean animals. *See* Animal.

Hook. 1. A ring, such as we place in the nose of a bull to lead him about (II Kings 19:28; Isa. 37:29; Ezek. 29:4, etc.); an allusion in the first two passages to the absolute control of Jehovah over Sennacherib. A similar method was adopted for leading captives, as Manasseh (II Chron. 33:11).

2. A peg, or pin, upon which the curtains were hung in the tabernacle (*q. v.*).

3. A vine dresser's pruning hook (Isa. 2:4; 18:5; Mic. 4:3; Joel 3:10).

4. Double or forked pegs, upon which the carcases of beasts were hung for flaying (Ezek. 40:43).

5. A fleshhook for taking joints of meat out of the boiling pot (Exod. 27:3; I Sam. 2:13, 14). *See* Fishhooks.

Hope is in the N. T. sense the *expectation of good* (Gr. *elpis*). This original word denotes a joyful and contented expectation of eternal salvation (Acts 23:6; 26:7; Rom. 5:4f; I Cor. 13: 13). Because of God's manifested salvation in Christ, and because He is the Source of all the believer's expectations, He is styled the "God of hope" (Rom. 15:13). Paul calls his converts his *hope*, not as the cause but as objects of his hope. In the O. T. hope is expressed by several different words such as *safety, security* and *trust* (Heb. *bĕṭaḥ,* Psa. 16:9; 22:9, etc.). Another Heb. word denoting *refuge,* in the sense of firm and certain expectation, is *mibṭāḥ* (Prov. 22: 19; Job 8:14; Psa. 42:5; 71:5). The word "refuge" in the sense of a *shelter* was also used to denote hope (Heb. *maḥăsĕḥ,* Psa. 62:8; Jer. 17:7, 17; Joel 3:16). Another expression denotes something *waited for* (Heb. *mĭqwĕh,* Ezra 10:2). In Zech. 9:12 still another term is employed (Heb. *tĭqwäh;* "the prisoners of hope"); here described are those cherishing expectation of deliverance. The fountain-head of hope is the death, burial and resurrection of Christ (I Pet. 1:3). "Christ in you" is the "hope of glory" (Col. 1:27). In the N. T. hope is also marked by an eschatological significance. For example, Titus 2:13; where the coming of the Lord is called "the Blessed Hope," that is, the expectation giving joy to the Christian in promise of future glorification. *M. F. U.*

Hoph′ni (hŏf′nī), the first named of the two sons of the high priest Eli (I Sam. 1:3; 2:34), who fulfilled their hereditary sacerdotal duties at Shiloh. Their brutal rapacity and lust, which increased with their father's age (2:12-17, 22), filled the people with indignation, and provoked the curse which was denounced against their father's house, first by an unknown prophet (vers. 27-36), and then by the youthful Samuel (3:11-14). They were both slain on the same day, and the ark was captured by the Philistines (4:10, 11), B. C. about 1050 at the battle of Ebenezer. The Scriptures call them "sons of Belial" (2:12).

Hoph′ra (hŏf′rà). *See* Pharaoh-Hophra.

Hor, Mount (hōr; *the mountain*), the name of two mountains.

1. The mountain on which Aaron died (Num. 20:25, 27). The word Hor is regarded by the lexicographers as an archaic form of Har, the usual Hebrew term for "mountain." The few facts given us in the Bible regarding Mount Hor are soon told. It was "on the boundary line" (Num. 20:23) or "at the edge" (33:37) of the land of Edom. It was the halting place of the people next after Kadesh (20:22; 33:37), and they quitted it for Zalmonah (33:41) in the road to the Red Sea (21:4). It was during the encampment at Kadesh that Aaron was gathered to his fathers. The most commonly accepted site of Mount Hor is at the east of the 'Arabah, the highest and most conspicuous of the whole range of the sandstone mountains of Edom, having close beneath it on its eastern side the mysterious city

of Petra. The tradition has existed from the earliest date. It is now the Jebel Nebi-Harûn, "the mountain of the Prophet Aaron." This identification, does not however, meet the full requirements of the narrative. "There is a mountain which fully meets the requirements of the Bible text, and the natural demands of the narrative, as to the Mount Hor where Aaron died and was buried. That mountain is Jebel Madurah, near the western extremity of Wady Feqreh, a little to the southwest of the passes es-Sufâh and el-Yemen. Its formation, its location, its name, go to identify it with the place of Aaron's burial, and there is even a smack of tradition in its favor. . . . In its location, Jebel Madurah stands at a triangular site, where the boundaries of Edom, of Canaan, and the Wilderness of Zin meet. It is at the extremest northwest boundary of Edom, yet it is not within that boundary line. It is on the very verge of the land of promise, yet it is not within the outer limits of that land" (Trumbull, *Kadesh-Barnea,* p. 129 sq.).

2. A mountain named only in Num. 34:7, 8, as one of the marks in the northern boundary of the land of promise. Its identification is difficult. The Mediterranean was the western boundary; the first point was Mount Hor, and the second "the entrance of Hamath." R. A. S. Macalister equates it with Mt. Hermon, The reference is evidently to the whole Lebanon range or a prominent peak of the range.

Ho′ram (hō′ràm), the king of Gezer, who, coming to the relief of Lachish, was overthrown by Joshua (Josh. 10:33), B. C. after 1400.

Ho′reb (hō′rĕb; *dryness, desert,* Exod. 3:1; 17: 6; 33:6; Deut. 1:2, 6, 19, etc.; I Kings 8:9; 19:8; II Chron. 5:10; Psa. 106:19; Mal. 4:4), in the opinion of some a lower part or peak of Sinai from which one ascends towards the south the summit of Sinai (Jebel Musa); but according to others a general name of the whole mountain of which Sinai was a particular summit. *See* Sinai.

Ho′rem (hō′rĕm), one of the "fenced cities" of Naphtali (Josh. 19:38), between Migdal-el and Beth-Anath. Exact location not known.

Hor-Hagid′gad (hōr′-hă-gĭd′găd), the name of the thirty-third station of Israel in the desert (Num. 33:32, 33), probably the same as their forty-first station, *Gudgodah* (*q. v.*) (Deut. 10:6, 7).

Ho′ri (hō′rī). *See* Horite.

1. A son of Lotan, and grandson of Seir (Gen. 36:22; I Chron. 1:39).

2. In Gen. 36:30, "Hori" has in the original the article prefixed, i, e, the *Horite;* and is the same word as that which in vers. 21, 29, is rendered in the A. V. "the Horites."

3. A Simeonite, whose son Shaphat was the commissioner of his tribe, sent by Moses to explore the land of Canaan (Num. 13:5), B. C. c. 1401.

Ho′rim (hō′rĭm; Deut. 2:12, 22). *See* Horite.

Ho′rite (hō′rīt; Heb. *Ḥori,* pl. *Ḥorim*).

1. **Biblical references.** In the Pentateuchal books there are a number of references to an enigmatic people called Horites; translated Horims in the A. V. of Deut. 2:2, 22. These people were defeated by Chedorlaomer and

the invading Mesopotamian army (Gen. 14:6). They were governed by chieftains (Gen. 36:29, 30). They are described as having been exterminated or destroyed by Esau's descendants (Deut. 2:2, 22). This unknown people used to be thought of as a very local and restricted group of cave-dwellers named "Horites," being thought of as derived from Heb. *hor*, cave. Other than this alleged etymological description, the Horites remained completely obscure, not appearing in the Bible outside the Pentateuch or in extra-Biblical literature.

2. **Archaeological Discovery.** Within the past forty years, however, archaeology has brought to light evidences of the Hurrians (the Biblical Horites), who now occupy a prominent place on the stage of ancient history. This ethnic group is now known not only to have existed but to have played a far-reaching role in ancient Near Eastern cultural history. As a result of the recovery of the Hurrian civilization, the popular etymology which connects them with troglodytes have generally been abandoned. Excavations at Mari on the middle Euphrates, about seven miles N. of Abou Kemal, conducted since 1933 by the Musée du Louvre, have unearthed numerous Hurrian tablets. To this early phase of Hurrian literature (c. B. C. 2400-1800) belong some of the Hurrian religious texts found at the ancient Hittite capital of Hattushash (Boghaz-keui) in Asia Minor. But the most important discovery regarding the Hurrians comes from Nuzu, present-day Yorgan Tepe, a dozen miles S. W. of modern Kirkuk. In the old Akkadian period (c. B. C. 2360-2180) this city was known as Gasur, with a predominently Semitic population, but before the eighteenth century B. C. the city had become an important center of the Hurrians. It was known as Nuzu. At this period the Hurrians were a dominant ethnic element through the Middle East. Thousands of clay tablets were uncovered at Nuzu. These were inscribed by Hurrians in the Babylonian language, but contained many native Hurrian words. A large number of these tablets are to be dated in the fifteenth century B. C., and they give much information concerning the life of the Hurrian people. Remarkable parallels from Nuzu tablets concerning marriage, adoption and social customs, such as those that prevailed in the patriarchal period of Genesis, occur. Scholars are still busy translating thousands of clay tablets shedding light on the Hurrians and other peoples of western Asia. As this material becomes accessible, the puzzle of the Biblical Horites is becoming solved.

3. **National affiliations.** The Hurrians were non-Semitic, who before the second millennium B. C. migrated into northern Mesopotamia. Their homeland was evidently the region south of the Caucasus. They appear first upon the pages of history c. B. C. 2400 in the Zagros Mountain region east of the Tigris. After the Gutian victory over the last kings of Akkad, the Hurrians seem to have inundated northern Mesopotamia, especially the east Tigris country. Hurrian names were common even in south Mesopotamia during the Third Dynasty of Ur (c. B. C. 1960), and they continued to be numerous under the First Dynasty of Bablyon (c. B. C. 1830-1550). *M. F. U.*

Hor'mah (hôr'må; *a devoted place, destruction*), the chief town of a Canaanitish king in the south of Palestine (Josh. 12:14), near which the Israelites were discomfited by the Amalekites when against the advice of Moses they attempted to enter Canaan by that route (Num. 14:45; comp. 21:1-3; Deut. 1:44). It was afterward taken by Joshua and assigned to Judah (Josh. 15:30), but finally fell to Simeon (19:4; I Chron. 4:30). Hormah has not been positively identified, though Tell es-Seba' about 3 miles E. of Beersheba is a likely location.

Horn (Heb. *qĕrĕn, projecting;* Gr. *keras*). Horns are mentioned in Scripture as being used for:

1. **Trumpets.** These were at first merely horns perforated at the tip; such as are still used for calling laborers to meals. Later they were made of metal, as the silver trumpets of the priests (Num. 10:1, sq.). Those used at the overthrow of Jericho (Josh. 6:4, 6, 13) were, probably, large horns or instruments in the shape of a horn, which gave a loud, far-sending note (see Lev. 23:24; 25:9).

2. **Vessels.** Horns being hollow and easily polished, have been used in ancient and modern times for drinking and kindred purposes, such as a *flask* or vessel made of horn to hold oil (I Sam. 16:1, 13; I Kings 1:39), or toilet bottle containing antimony for blacking the eyelashes. *See* Inkhorn.

3. The projections of the altar of burnt offering (Exod. 27:2) and of the altar of incense (30:2) at their four corners, were called "horns." By laying hold of these horns of the altar of burnt offering, a criminal found safety (I Kings 1:50; 2:28), if his offense was accidental (Exod. 21:14).

4. The peak or *summit* of a hill was called a *horn* (Isa. 5:1, margin) (see illustration below).

5. In Hab. 3:4, "he had horns coming out of his hand;" the context implies *rays of light* (comp. Deut. 33:2).

Figurative. Two principal applications of this metaphor will be found—*strength* and *honor*. Horns being the chief source of attack and defense with the animals to which God has given them, they are employed in Scripture as emblems of power; of God (Psa. 18:2; Hab. 3:4), of Christ (Luke 1:69; Rev. 5:6), of Ephraim (Deut. 33:17), of the wicked (Psa. 22:21; 75:10), of kingdoms (Dan. 7:7, 8, 24; 8:3, 5, 6, 20), of antichristian powers (Rev. 13:1; 17:3, 7).

The *budding*, or *spouting* of horns, is figurative of the commencement or revival of a nation or power (Psa. 132:17; Ezek. 29:21); *raising up*, of arrogance (Psa. 75:4, 5); *exalting*, of increase of power and glory (I Sam. 2:1, 10; Psa. 89:17, 24; 92:10; 112:9); *pushing with*, of conquests (Deut. 33:17; I Kings 22:11; Mic. 4:13); *bringing down*, or degradation (Job 16:15, "I have defiled," i. e., laid low, "my horn in the dust," as a wounded animal); *cutting off*, of destruction of power (Psa. 75:10; Jer. 48:25; Lam. 2:3).

Hornet. *See* Animal Kingdom.

Horona'im (hôr'ō-nā'ĭm; *double cave*), a city of Moab, on the mountain slope of Luhith, along the route of the invading Assyrians (Isa.

15:5; Jer. 48:3, 5, 34). Cf. The Moabite Stone, 31. It is probably el-'Arak.

Hor'onite, the (hôr'ô-nīt), an epithet of Sanballat (only in Neh. 2:10, 19; 13:2). Fürst and the latest (12th) German edition of Gesenius derive it from Beth-Horon, while Dr. Strong's *Exhaustive Concordance* and Robinson's Gesenius take it from Horonaim. On the latter supposition Sanballat was a Moabite; and this would accord well with his connection with Tobiah, the Ammonite. But if the term is from Beth-Horon, he was probably a Samaritan, or related to the Samaritans. This would agree with Josephus, who says: "He was a Cuthean by birth, of which stock were the Samaritans also" (*Ant.*, xi, 7, § 2).—W. H.

Horse. *See* Animal Kingdom.

Figurative. On account of the strength of the horse, it has become the symbol of war (Deut. 32:13; Psa. 66:12; Isa. 58:14; Zech. 9:10; 10:3); of *conquest*, as in Cant. 1:9; the bride advances with her charms to conquest, "as a company of horses in Pharaoh's chariots." The war horse rushing into battle is figurative of impetuosity of the wicked in sin (Jer. 8:6). In Zechariah (6:2-7) the prophet mentions horses that were red, black, white, and speckled. The red horses symbolize war, the black pestilence, the speckled famine, while the white points to the glorious victories of the ministers of the divine judgment.

Horse Gate, a gate in the old wall of Jerusalem (*q. v.*), at the west end of the bridge leading from Zion to the temple (Neh. 3:28; Jer. 31:40), perhaps so called because the "horses of the sun" (II Kings 23:11) were led through it for idolatrous worship (II Chron. 23:15).

Horse-Leech. *See* Animal Kingdom.

Horses, Horsemen. In antiquity the Hittites cultivated horses. This animal seems to have been introduced from inner Asia. Horses were bred by the fierce Mitanni, who wrote about horses in Hittite cuneiform. The horse was introduced into Egypt apparently by the Hyksos invaders c. 1750 B. C. The horse, even as a dray animal, was apparently unknown, even in the great Pyramid Age (2800-2400 B. C.). Egyptian wall reliefs depict simply asses and donkeys but no horses at the earlier periods. From the Hyksos the Egyptians acquired a taste for horse-drawn chariots. Horse-drawn chariotry pursued the fleeing Israelites (Exod. 14:8, 26-29). The introduction of the horse into lower Mesopotamia is still obscure. When Israel entered Palestine, they found people of the plains equipped with horses and chariots of iron (Judg. 1:19). Not until the period of the monarchy, after 1020 B. C., did the hill-dwelling Israelites possess horse-drawn chariots such as their neighbors owned. David hamstrung the horses he captured from his enemies, doubtless in obedience to Deut. 17:16: "Only he (the future king) must not multiply horses for himself or cause the people to return to Egypt in order to multiply horses . . ." Solomon, disregarding the Deuteronomic injunctions, equipped his army with thousands of horses and chariots (II Chron. 9:25). Excavations at Megiddo and Gezer have uncovered his well-built stables and quarters for their horsemen. The stone mangers and hitching posts can be plainly seen. Solomon also had

as one of his pet commercial projects horse and chariot-trade between Egypt and Asia Minor, bringing hand-made chariots (and evidently horses too) from Egypt and transshipping fine horses from Cilicia. In early Israel mules were traditionally royal mounts (II Sam. 18:9; Zech. 9:9; Matt. 21:5). Kings of Judah and Israel had numerous horses, and Ahab of Israel is mentioned on the Assyrian monuments as furnishing a very sizable contingent of horses and chariotry in the Syrian coalition against Shalmaneser II at Karkar (853 B. C.). The Assyrians were great horse-lovers, Assyrian monarchs often using them for lion-hunting. Persian kings made large use of horses as couriers (Cf. Zech. 1:8-11; 6:1-8). Romans employed cavalry escorts for important prisoners, such as for Paul enroute to Antipatris (Acts 23:23, 32). Chariot-racing was a favorite diversion in their ampitheatres. In Bible times horses were unshod and driven with bit and bridle. They were often sumptuously adorned (Mark 11:8), frequently with bells (Zech. 12:14). *M. F. U.*

Ho'sah (hō'sà; *hopeful*).

1. A city of Asher, at a point on the boundary line where it turned from the direction of Tyre toward Achzib (Josh. 19:29); location unknown.

2. A Levite of the family of Merari, who, with thirteen of his relatives, was appointed doorkeeper to the ark after its arrival in Jerusalem (I Chron. 16:38). In the latter distribution (26:10, 11, 16) the gate Shallecheth, on the west side of the temple, fell to him, B. C. about 988.

Hosanna (Gr. *hosannah*, from Heb. *hōshî'āh-nā'*, *save now*), the cry of the multitude as they thronged in our Lord's triumphal procession into Jerusalem (Matt. 21:9, 15; Mark 11:9, 10; John 12:13). The psalm from which it was taken (the 118th) was one with which they were familiar from being accustomed to recite the 25th and 26th verses at the Feast of Tabernacles. On that occasion the *Hallel*, consisting of Psalms 113-118, was chanted by one of the priests, and at certain intervals the multitudes joined in the responses, waving their branches of willow and palm, and shouting as they waved them hallelujah, or hosanna, or "O Lord, I beseech thee, send now prosperity" (Psa. 118:25). On each of the seven days during which the feast lasted, the people thronged in the court of the temple, and went in procession about the altar, setting their boughs bending toward it, the trumpets sounding as they shouted hosanna. It was not uncommon for the Jews in later times to employ the observances of this feast, which was preeminently a feast of gladness, to express their feelings on other occasions of rejoicing (I Macc. 13:51; II Macc. 10:6,7). *See* Hallel.

The early Christian Church adopted this word into its worship. It is found in the apostolical constitutions connected with the great doxology, "Glory be to God on high," and was frequently used in the communion service, during which the great doxology was sung.

Hose, Hosen (Aram. *paṭîsh*, Dan. 3:21). The

better rendering of this term appears to be *tunic*, an undergarment. *See* Dress.

Hose′a (Heb. *hōshē′ă, deliverer*), the son of Beeri, and the first of the minor prophets as they appear in the A. V.

1. **Time.** In the first verse of his prophecy it is stated that "the word of the Lord came unto Hosea, in the days of Uzziah, Jotham, Ahaz, and Hezekiah, kings of Judah, and . . . of Jeroboam, king of Israel." Dr. J. F. McCurdy dates the beginning of Hosea's public life at B. C. 748, and Hezekiah's death at B. C. 690, which would make the prophet's ministry extend over a period of about fifty-eight years. The book furnishes strong presumptive evidence in support of this chronology.

2. **Place.** There seems to be a general consent among commentators that the prophecies of Hosea were delivered in the kingdom of Israel, and that he was a subject of that kingdom. This is favored not only by the fact that his prophetic addresses are occupied throughout with the kingdom of the ten tribes, but also by the peculiar style and language of his prophecies, which have here and there an Aramaean coloring, and still more by the intimate acquaintance with the circumstances and localities of the northern kingdom (5:1; 6:8, 9; 12:12; 14:6), which even goes so far that he calls the Israelitish kingdom "the land" (1:2), and the king of Israel "our king" (7:5). It has been conjectured that Hosea, having long appealed in vain to his countrymen, retired to Judah, and that there his prophecy was committed to writing in its present form.

3. **The Prophet's Family Relations.** It is recorded in 1:2-9 that Hosea, at the command of God, took an impure woman (Gomer, the daughter of Giblaim) to wife, and had by her two sons (Jezreel and Loammi) and one daughter (Lo-ruhamah), and in 3:1, 2, that by the divine command he purchased an adulteress. These statements have given rise to much discussion as to their literal or allegorical interpretation. Dr. Strong (Mc. and S., *Cyc.*, s. v.) expresses the opinion that "There were two marriages by the prophet: first in chaps. 1, 2, of a woman (probably of lewd inclinations already) who became the mother of three children, and was afterward repudiated for her adultery; and the second, in ch. 3, of a woman at least attached formerly to another, but evidently reformed to a virtuous wife. Both these women represented the Israelitish nation, especially the northern kingdom, which, although unfaithful to Jehovah, should first be punished and then reclaimed by him." Dr. Keil (*Com.*, in loc.) says, "No other course is left to us than to picture to ourselves Hosea's marriages as internal events, i. e., as merely carried out in that inward and spiritual intuition in which the word of God was addressed to him; and this removes all the difficulties that beset the assumption of marriages contracted in outward reality."

Hosea, Book of.

Hose′a (hô-zē′á; Heb. *Hoshea, salvation*). In the A. V. of N. T. his name occurs as Osee (ō′zē), from the Gr. form. The prophet bore the name used once of Joshua and the same borne by Hoshea, the last ruler of the Northern Kingdom.

1. **Span of His Ministry.** This is indicated in the superscription to the book: "In the days of Uzziah (c. B. C. 767-739), Jotham (c. B. C. 739-735), Ahaz (c. B. C. 735-715) and Hezekiah (c. B. C. 715-686), kings of Judah, and the days of Jerobam II (c. B. C. 781-753) . . ., king of Israel" (Hos. 1:1). The prophetic ministry of Hosea extended well beyond Jeroboam II's death into the period of civil war in which Zachariah (c. 753), Shallum (c. 752), Menahem (c. 752-741), Pekahiah (c. 741-739), Pekah (c. 739-731) and Hoshea (c. 731-722) reigned, until the fall of Samaria. For this reason some scholars, such as R. Pfeiffer (*Introduction*, 1940, p. 566) view the reference to Hezekiah and other Judean kings in 1:1 as an interpolation. This is not necessitated since the recorded prophecies of Hosea are obviously only a compendium of his activity which extended into the early years of Hezekiah's reign. Whether the prophet was carried into Assyrian captivity is not known. Like Jeremiah of Judah, later he was the prophet of doom to the Northern Kingdom.

2. **Purpose.** Hosea is the prophecy of God's unchanging love for Israel. Despite their contamination with Canaanite paganism and fertility cults, the prophet bent every effort to warn the people to repent in the face of God's perpetual love for them. His theme is fourfold: Israel's idolatry, wickedness, captivity and restoration. Throughout the entire book, however, he weaves the theme of the love of God for Israel. Israel is depicted prophetically as Jehovah's adulterous wife, shortly to be put away, but eventually to be purified and restored. These momentous events are set forth in the divine comment that the prophet marry an harlot. The offspring of this union are given names symbolic of Hosea's chief prophecies: Jezreel, the dynasty of Jehu is to be extirpated; Lo-ruhamah, "not shown mercy," a prophecy of the Assyrian captivity; Lo-ammi, "not my people," temporary rejection of Israel (Cf. Rom. 11:1-24); Ammi, "my people," final restoration of the nation (Cf. Rom. 11:25, 26) in the end time (Hos. 1:2-2:23).

3. **Contents.**

Part I. Israel, Jehovah's Faithless Wife, Repudiated and Restored, 1:1-3:5
   A. The first symbolic marriage, 1:1-2:23
      1. Rejected Israel, birth of Jezreel, Lo-ruhamah, Lo-ammi, 1:1-9
      2. Comforted Israel, 1:10, 11
      3. Chastised Israel, 2:1-13
      4. Restored Israel, 2:14-23
   B. The second symbolic marriage, 3:1-5
      1. The marriage itself, 3:1-3
      2. The symbolic meaning, 3:4, 5
Part II. Israel, the Object of God's Love, Reestablished as a repentant and restored nation, 4:1-14:9
   A. Israel's guilt, 4:1-19
   B. The Divine displeasure, 5:1-15
   C. The repentant remnant's cry, 6:1-3
   D. Jehovah's response, 6:4-13:8
   E. Final restoration, 13:9-14:9

4. **Authorship and Genuineness.** The book is unquestionably authored by "Hosea, the

son of Beeri ..." (1:1). Even the critical school commonly admits this unity. Two types of passages were sometimes denied to Hosea by late nineteenth century criticism, namely those dealing with Judah and those promising restoration and blessing. Actually, there is no compelling reason for denying to Hosea any of the prophecy. More recent criticism tends to deny fewer passages as later interpolations. (A. Bentzen, *Introduction* II, 1949, p. 33 and Oesterley and Robinson, *Introduction to the O. T.*, p. 349). While granting the "possibility, even the probability" that certain passages in which Judah is mentioned may be later interpolations, critics by no means insist upon it and, regarding the passages on restoration, assert that the evidence "does not justify us in dogmatically asserting that they are not the work of Hosea himself." Divine authority and authenticity of the book are indicated quotations from the prophet are found in the N. T. (Cf. Hos. 11:1, Matt. 2:15; Hos. 6:6, Matt. 9:13 and 12:7; Hos. 10:8, Luke 23:20; Hos. 2:23, Rom. 9:25; Hos. 13:14, I Cor. 15:55; Hos. 1:9, 10 and 2:23, I Pet. 2:10).
M. F. U.

Hosha′iah (hŏ-shā′yà; *Jah has saved*).

1. A man who assisted in the dedication of the wall of Jerusalem after it had been rebuilt by Nehemiah (Neh. 12:32), B. C. 445.

2. The father of a certain Jezaniah, or Azariah, who was a man of note after the destruction of Jerusalem by Nebuchadnezzar, and besought Jeremiah to favor the flight of the remnant of the Jews into Egypt (Jer. 42:1; 43:2), B. C. 586.

Hosha′ma (hŏ-shā′mà), or **Hosh′ama** (hŏsh′à-mà; *Jah has heard*), one of the sons of King Jehoiachin, born during his captivity (I Chron. 3:18), B. C. after 597.

Hoshe′a (hŏ-shē′à; Hebrew same as Hosea).

1. The original name of Joshua, the son of Nun (Deut. 32:44); sometimes written Oshea, as Num. 13:8, 16.

2. The son of Elah, and last king of Israel. He conspired against and slew his predecessor, Pekah (II Kings 15:30), "in the twentieth year of Jotham." Tiglath-pileser set up Hoshea as the nominal king of Samaria, but as his personal representative (B. C. about 733). He did not become established on the throne till after an interregnum of at least eight years, viz., in the twelfth year of Ahaz (II Kings 17:1). It is declared of him that "he did that which was evil in the sight of the Lord, but not as the kings of Israel that were before him" (v. 2). Shortly after his accession he submitted to the supremacy of Shalmaneser, who appears to have entered his territory with the intention of subduing it by force if resisted (II Kings 17:3); and indeed seems to have stormed the strong caves of Beth-arbel (Hos. 10:14), but who retired pacified with a present. Intelligence that Hoshea had entered into negotiations with So, king of Egypt, prompted Shalmaneser to return and punish the rebellious king with imprisonment for withholding the tribute (II Kings 17:4). He was probably released by the payment of a large ransom, but a second revolt soon after provoked the king of Assyria to march an army into the land of Israel; and after a three

years' siege Samaria was taken and destroyed, and the ten tribes were carried away beyond the Euphrates, B. C. 721 (II Kings 17:5, 6; 18:9-12). Of the future fortune of Hoshea we know nothing.

3. Son of Azaziah and prince of the tribe of Ephraim in the time of David (I Chron. 27: 20), B. C. about 1000.

4. One of the chiefs of Israel who joined in the sacred covenant with Nehemiah after the captivity (Neh. 10:23), B. C. 445.

Hospitality. In oriental lands, and still in some countries of belated civilization, it was and is felt to be a sacred duty to receive, feed, lodge, and protect any traveler who might stop at the door. The stranger was treated as a guest, and men who had thus eaten together were bound to each other by the strongest ties of friendship, which descended to their heirs, confirmed by mutual presents. With the Greeks hospitality was a religious duty, as was the case with Hebrews, enjoined by the law of Moses (Lev. 19:34). The present practice of the Arabs is the nearest approach to the ancient Hebrew hospitality. A traveler may sit at the door of a perfect stranger and smoke his pipe until the master welcomes him with an evening meal, and may tarry a limited number of days without inquiry as to his purposes, and depart with simple "God be with you" as his only compensation. As the Hebrews became more numerous inns were provided, but these did not entirely supersede *home hospitality*. The Old Testament gives illustrations of it in Gen. 18:1-8; 19:1-3; 24:25, 31-33, etc. Job says (31:32), "The stranger did not lodge in the street, but I opened my doors to the traveler." The neglect of the law of hospitality is illustrated in the case of the Rich Man and Lazarus (Luke 16:19-25).

The spirit of *Christian* hospitality is taught in the New Testament (Luke 14:12-14). The Gr. *philoxenos* (a *lover of strangers*) is the word for hospitality in Tit. 1:8; I Pet. 4:9; and *philoxenia* (*love of strangers*) in Rom. 12:13; Heb. 13:2.

Host. 1. In a social sense.

(1) Literally a *stranger* (Gr. *xenos*), i. e., one who receives and entertains hospitably (Rom. 16:23), where "and of the whole Church" is added; meaning that Gaius received all the members of the Church who crossed his threshold, or kindly permitted the Church to worship in his house.

(2) "One who receives all comers", an innkeeper, host (Luke 10:35; Gr. *pandocheus*).

2. In a military sense. *See* Army.

Host of Heaven, (*army of the skies*, Gen. 2:1). The sun, moon, and stars, under the symbol of an army; in which the sun is considered as king, the moon as his vicegerent, the stars and planets as their attendants (comp. Judg. 5:20). The worship of the host of heaven was one of the earliest forms of idolatry (*q. v.*), and was common among the Israelites in the times of their declension from the pure service of God (Deut. 4:19; II Kings 17:16; 21:3, 5; Jer. 19:13; Zeph. 1:5; Acts 7:42).

The "host of heaven," referred to in Dan. 8:10, 11, appears to be figurative for "the holy people," i. e., Israel (see 8:24). The comparison of Israel to the "hosts of heaven" has its root in this, that God, the King of Israel, is called the God of Hosts ("the Prince of the Host," v. 11), and by the *hosts* are generally to be understood the stars or angels; but the tribes of Israel also, who were led by God out of Egypt, are called "the hosts of Jehovah" (Exod. 7:4; 12:41). As in heaven the angels and stars, so on earth the sons of Israel form the host of God. This comparison serves, then, to characterize the insolence of Antiochus (the "horn," Dan. 8:9) as a wickedness against heaven and the heavenly order of things (Keil, *Com.*, in loc.).

Jehovah is frequently mentioned as "Jehovah, God of hosts," i, e., of the celestial armies (Jer. 5:14; 38:17; 44:7; Hos. 12:5, etc.). The Heb. *Sabaoth, hosts,* is ·used by the apostles Paul and James (Rom. 9:29; James 5:4).

Hostage (Heb. *tǎʻǎrūbäh; suretyship*), one delivered into the hand of another as security for the performance of a pledge or engagement. In ancient times it was very usual for conquered kings or nations to give hostages for the payment of tribute, of continuance in subjection; thus Joash, king of Israel, exacted hostages from Amaziah, king of Judah (II Kings 14:14; II Chron. 25:24).

Ho'tham (hō'thăm; a *seal ring*), one of the sons of Heber, the grandson of Asher (I Chron. 7:32). He is probably the same as *Helem*, whose sons are enumerated in v. 35, and grandsons in vers. 36, 37.

Ho'than (hō'thăn; Hebrew same as *Hotham*), an Aroerite, father of Shama and Jehiel, two of David's "valiant men" (I Chron. 11:44), B. C. about 1000.

Ho'thir (hō'thĭr), the thirteenth son of *Heman* (*q. v.*), who, with eleven of his kinsmen, had charge of the twenty-first division of Levitical singers (I Chron. 25:4, 28), B. C. after 1000.

Hough (hŏk; Heb. *ʻäqǎr, to extirpate*), the method employed to render useless the captured horses of an enemy (Josh. 11:6; comp. Gen. 49:6, margin), since the Israelites were forbidden to use that animal (II Sam. 8:4; I Chron. 18:4). It consisted in *hamstringing*, i. e., severing "the tendon Achilles" of the hinder legs.

Hour. *See* Time.

House (Heb. *bayity;* Gr. *oikia*). The beginning of house building is lost in the darkness of primeval times and reaches back in the sacred record to the days of Cain (Gen. 4:17). While the Israelites did not become dwellers in cities till the sojourn in Egypt and after the conquest of Canaan (Gen. 47:3; Exod. 12:7; Heb. 11:9), the Canaanites, the Assyrians, and the Egyptians were from an early period builders of houses and cities. Of course houses would vary much, according to the climate, tastes, and condition of the people. And yet we find some leading characteristics in the oriental house, distinguishing it from that of northern latitudes.

1. **Material.** The material for house building is determined partly by what is to be had in the locality, partly by the object of the buildings and the means of the builders. The houses of the rural poor in Egypt, as well as in most parts of Syria, Arabia, and Persia are for the most part mere huts of mud or sunburnt bricks. Those of the Israelites were probably mostly made of brick burned or merely dried in the sun, or of lime and sandstone. Only houses of the rich, and palaces, were built of hewn stone (I Kings 7:9; Isa. 9:10) or white marble (I Chron. 29:2). For mortar there was used clay or lime, or gypsum (Isa. 33:13; comp. Deut. 27:4) and asphalate (Gen. 11:3). The beams, doorposts, doors, windows, and stairs were commonly of sycamore (Isa. 9:10); in more ornamental buildings, of olive, cypress, cedar, and sandal (I Kings 7:2; Jer. 22:14).

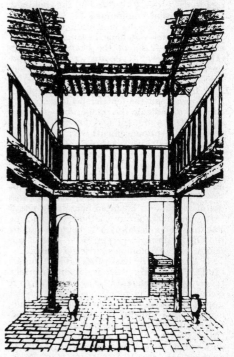

207. Reconstruction of a Middle or Upper Class House at Ur During the Time of Abraham

2. **Exterior.** Only large palaces, it would appear, were built of more than one story, at least in earlier times; so the palace of Solomon, the house of Lebanon (I Kings 7:2, sq.), the three story side chambers of Solomon's Temple (6:5, sq.). There is no other mention in Scripture of any house in Palestine with more than one story, for Acts 20:9 refers to Troas.

(1) **The walls** were whitewashed outside and inside with lime or gypsum, palaces with bright-colored vermilion (Jer. 22:14). The exterior of a dwelling house of the better kind in Palestine is for the most part plain and unattractive, having but few openings or projections, such as to give relief and variety. These openings are not more than the doorway and two or three latticed windows.

(2) **The roof** is commonly flat, has never any chimneys, and does not overhang the external walls. In the poorer class of houses the roofs were made of earth, stamped and rolled upon a foundation of boughs or rafters. The nature of these roofs readily explains the transaction referred to in Mark (2:4) and Luke

(5:19). Probably the bearers of the paralytic in their anxiety broke up the simple materials of the roof, and through the aperture let him down into the presence of Jesus. The better class of houses had their roofs laid with tiles and stone. The outer edge was provided with a breastwork or latticelike railing to prevent falling (Deut. 22:8). The roof is one of the most important parts of an Eastern house, every kind of business and amusement at times proceeding upon it. We have Rahab hiding the spies beneath the stalks of flax laid on the roof to dry (Josh. 2:6). We find the roof used for confidential communing (I Sam. 9:25), for sleeping (v. 26), for lamentation (Isa. 15:3; Jer. 48:38), for watching the approach of an enemy (Isa. 22:1), or the bearer of tidings (II Sam. 18:24, 33). Booths were built upon the roof (Neh. 8:16), and altars for idolatrous worship (II Kings 23:12; Jer. 19:13; Zeph. 1:5). Upon the roof, as in a most public place, Absalom spread the tent for his father's con- cubines, to indicate the unalterable estrange- ment between himself and David (II Sam. 16:21, 22). Announcements were made from the roof (Matt. 10:27; Luke 12:3). It was usual to have two flights of steps to ascend to the roof, one within the house and one in the street, which latter would afford a more ready escape than through the house (Matt. 24:17).

(3) **The porch** (Heb. *'ūlām, vestibule*) was not uncommon in Egyptian houses, but was a very unusual feature in the houses of ancient Palestine, no reference to it being found in the Old Testament, except in the case of the temple and of Solomon's palace (I Kings 7:6, 7; II Chron. 15:8; Ezek. 40:7). The "porch" (Judg. 3:23, Heb. *mǐsděrōn*) is an incorrect rendering, the reference being probably to a colonnade running along the outside of the upper room of Eglon's palace and communi- cating with a staircase. In the A. V. we read of a porch attached to the high priest's palace (Matt. 26:71, Gr. *pulōn*), which was likely the gate or entrance to the house from the street, as elsewhere (Acts 10:17; 12:14; 14:13; Rev. 21:12). The *stoa* (John 5:2), bore no resem- blance to the porch of a dwelling house, but was rather a colonnade, or cloisters, or a dis- tant building, used as a place of resort in the heat of the day. The porch of the palace was a place of judgment for the king (I Kings 7:7, 8).

(4) **Door.** Doors were commonly made of wood, the more expensive being of cedar (Cant. 8:9); but doors made of single slabs of stone, some inches thick, occasionally ten feet high, and turning on stone pivots, are found in the old houses and sepulchers in Syria. The doorways of Eastern houses are sometimes richly ornamented, though they are generally mean in appearance even when belonging to sumptuous dwellings. The doorway from the street into the court is usually guarded within from sight by a wall or some arrangement of the passages, and had a stone seat for the porter and other servants. Over the door the Israelites were directed to write sentences from the Law.

(5) **Court** (Heb. *hāṣēr, inclosed*). The court was one of the great characteristics of the Eastern house, the latter being built to in-

208. Villa of Wealthy Egyptian in Old Kingdom

close one, two, and even three courts. Some of the finest houses in Damascus have as many as seven. The court nearest the entrance is variously arranged, according as it is the only one, or the house has two or more. If there is only one court, it is an open space or quad- rangle, round which the apartments for the inmates, and in country places also the sheds for the cattle, are arranged. A house of a somewhat better description usually consisted of the court, three or four storerooms on the ground floor, with a single chamber above, from which a flight of stairs leads to the court. The houses of men of rank, and palaces, were usually built with a roomy court, surrounded with porticoes and galleries, paved, provided with well (II Sam. 17:18) and baths (11:2), probably planted with trees, and forming the reception room of the house. If there were three or more courts, all except the outer one were alike in size and appearance; but the outer one, being devoted to the more public life and intercourse with society, was mate- rially different from all the others. Into this court the principal apartments look, and are either open to it in front or are entered from it by doors. Over the doorway leading from the street is a projecting window with a lattice more or less elaborately wrought, which, ex- cept in times of public celebrations, is usually closed (II Kings 9:30). An awning is some- times drawn over the court and the floor strewed with carpets on festive occasions. The stairs to the upper apartments are in Syria usually in a corner of the court. Around part, if not the whole, of the court is a veranda, often nine or ten feet deep, over which, when there is more than one floor, runs a second gallery of like depth with a balustrade. If there are more than three courts the second is for the use of the master of the house, where he is attended by his eunuchs, children, and females, and sees only those whom he may call from the third court, where they dwell.

It was into this court that Esther came to invite the king to visit her part of the palace, but she would not on any account have gone into the outer court.

(6) **Windows.** The window of an Eastern house had no glass, consisted generally of an aperture inclosed with latticework, and was small so as to exclude the heat. The windows usually look into the court, but in every house one or more look into the street, making it possible for a person to observe the approach of another without himself being visible (Judg. 5:28; II Sam. 6:16; Prov. 7:6; Cant. 2:9). Where houses were built against the city wall it was not unusual for them to have projecting windows surmounting the wall and looking into the country. From such a window the spies escaped from Jericho (Josh. 2:15) and Paul from Damascus (II Cor. 11:33). Daniel's room had several windows, and his lattices were open when his enemies found him at prayer (Dan. 6:10). The projecting nature of the window, and the fact that a divan or raised seat encircles the interior, so that persons sitting at the window are near the aperture, easily explains the fall of Ahaziah and Eutychus (II Kings 1:2; Acts 20:9).

209. Palestinian House

(7) **The pillar** formed a very important feature in oriental building, partly, perhaps, as a reminiscence of the tent, with its supporting poles, and partly from the use of flat roofs. Pillars were used to support flat roofs or awnings; also to support curtains (Exod. 26:32). The circumstance of Samson's pulling down the house by means of the pillars may be explained by the fact of the company being assembled on tiers of balconies above each other, supported by central pillars on the basement; when these were pulled down the whole of the upper floors would fall also (Judg. 16:26).

(8) **Chimney.** The ancient house did not have chimneys; the word so rendered (Hos. 13:3) means a hole through which the smoke escaped, and in use only in the poorer houses, where wood was used for fuel. In the better class of houses the rooms were warmed by charcoal in braziers (Jer. 36:22; Mark 14:54; John 18:18), or a fire at night might be kindled in the open court (Luke 22:55).

3. **Interior.** (1) **The upper room** (Heb. *ʿălīyyäh*, Gr. *huperōon*), was on the roof, and, being the most desirable place in the house, was often given up to favored guests; but it must not be confounded with the guest chamber (*q. v.*, below). Usually the Scriptures mention one upper room, as if there were only one (Judg. 3:23; I Kings 17:19; II Kings 4:11; Acts 9:39; 20:8), but in the larger houses there were several (II Chron. 3:19; Jer. 32:13, 14). Frequent mention is made of them in connection with kings, who seem to have used them as summer houses because of their coolness (Judg. 3:20; II Kings 1:2; 23:12). The summer house spoken of in Scripture was very seldom a separate building, the lower part of the house being the winter house and the upper the summer house. This room was used for meditation and prayer (Mark 14:15; Luke 22:12), set apart for the prophets (I Kings 17:19; II Kings 4:10), and, on account of their size and coolness, as places of meeting (Acts 1:13; 20:8), and for similar reasons the dead were laid out in it (9:39). An upper room appears to have been built over the gateways of towns (II Sam. 18:33).

(2) **Guest chamber** (Heb. *lĭshkäh*, Gr. *kataluma*). This room was placed opposite the entrance into the court, and was used by the master of the house for the reception of all visitors. It is often open in front and supported in the center by a pillar. It is generally on the ground floor, but raised above the level of the court. This would seem to have been the guest chamber where our Lord ate his last passover (Mark 14:15; Luke 22:11), being not the "upper room," but a ground room elevated. Before entering the guests take off their shoes; so our Lord is thought to have had his feet bare when the woman washed them (Luke 7:38).

(3) **Other rooms.** There are seldom any special bedrooms in Eastern houses, except in those of the wealthy (II Kings 11:2; Eccles. 10:20; II Sam. 4:5). In Egypt there were such (Gen. 43:30; Exod. 8:3), as also in Syria (II Kings 6:12). In houses generally a low divan, raised round the sides of the room, serves for seats by day, and on it are placed the beds for sleeping during the nights. The *ceilings* (*q. v.*) of the principal apartments were adorned with much care, and often at great expense. The *kitchen*, where there is an inner court, is always attached to it, as the cooking is performed by the women. The furniture of this apartment consists of a sort of raised platform of brick, with receptacles on it for fire, answering the "boiling places" of Ezekiel (46:23). The fuel used was usually charcoal, and the food cooked in pots and chafing dishes.

(4) **Furniture.** The *furniture* in ancient Eastern houses was generally simple, owing probably to the people living so much out of doors. And though we have no exact information respecting the furniture of houses in Palestine, it is probable that they indulged, as did surrounding nations, as wealth permitted, in many luxuries. For the furnishing of an apartment the Israelites appear to have held the following articles indispensable: A bed, table, seat, and candlestick, i. e., lamp (II Kings 4:10). To these were added, for the complete

furnishing of a house, the necessary cooking, eating, and drinking vessels. In the houses of the wealthy these articles were not only provided in great abundance, but were also costly and luxurious. The rooms were furnished with cushions and couches (sofa or divan), which served also as beds, and were covered with costly carpets (Prov. 7:16) and soft pillows (Ezek. 13:18, 20). The bedsteads were inlaid with ivory (Amos 6:4), and the tables and stools, which were much more in use among the Israelites than at present in the East (II Kings 4:10; Prov. 9:14), were artistically wrought. The eating and drinking vessels were of gold and silver, and the needful wardrobes and chests were not wanting.

Figurative. The word "house" is often used in Scripture in the sense of lineage, or family; thus Joseph was of the house of David (Luke 1:27; 2:4); offspring (II Sam. 7:11; Psa. 113:9); household (Gen. 43:16; Isa. 36:3). Heaven is the house of God (John 14:2); the grave is the house appointed for all living (Job 30:23; Isa. 14:18); the body is called a house (II Cor. 5:1).

Household, the rendering generally of the same Hebrew and Greek words as are rendered "house," and meaning the members of a family living in the same dwelling, including servants and dependents. In Job 1:3 the word *'ăbūdāh,* (literally "service") appears to mean a retinue of servants. The expression "they of Caesar's household" (Phil 4:22) seems to refer to some of the servants of the emperor.

One of the divisions of the Hebrews, as tribes, families, households, etc. *See* Israel, Constitution of.

Housetop, the flat roof of an Eastern house (*q. v.*).

Figurative. Some of these roofs were covered with earth rolled hard, which, softened by rain, would afford nourishment for grass seeds. When the returning drought and heat came the grass speedily withered, a proper illustration of momentary prosperity followed by ruin (II Kings 19:26; Psa. 129:6; Isa. 37:27).

Huk'kok (hŭk'ŏk), a city on the southern border of Naphtali, near to Aznoth-tabor (Josh. 19:34). Robinson and Van de Velde identify it with Yakuk, five miles W. of the site of Capernaum and this is now generally accepted. There is another Hukkok (I Chron. 6:75, A. V. "Hukok") in Asher. In Josh. 21:31 it is Helkath instead of Hukkok, a case in which the two names are applied to one place.

Hu'kok (hū'kŏk; I Chron. 6:75). *See* Hukkok.

Hul (hŭl; *circle*), the second son of Aram, and grandson of Shem (Gen. 10:23; I Chron. 1:17). The geographical location of the people whom he represents is not positively known. Quite probable seems the identification either with Huleh around Lake Merom or with Hūli'a in the Mount Massius regions mentioned by Ashurnasirpal.

Hul'dah (hŭl'dà; *mole, weasel*), a prophetess, the wife of *Shallum* (*q. v.*), who was keeper of the wardrobe. She dwelt, in the reign of Josiah, in that part of Jerusalem called the Mishneh (*second* or *double,* perhaps "*suburb,*" or "*lower city*"). To her the king sent Hilkiah the priest,

Shaphan the scribe, and others, to consult respecting the denunciations in the lately found book of the law. She then delivered an oracular response of mingled judgment and mercy, declaring the not remote destruction of Jerusalem, but promising Josiah that he should be taken from the world before these evil days came (II Kings 22:14-20; II Chron. 34:22-28), B. C. about 639. Huldah is only known from this circumstance.

Human Sacrifice. *See* Sacrifice.

Human Soul. *See* Soul.

Humanity of Christ. *See* Christ, Incarnation of.

Humbleness (Col. 3:12), elsewhere rendered Humility (*q. v.*).

Humiliation of Christ, an expression which refers to the earthly life of the Lord Jesus Christ, and contrasts his condition during that period, on the one hand, with the glory of his preexistent state, and, on the other, with his subsequent exaltation.

Scripture Teaching. The fact, the constituent features, the end, and the ethical significance of Christ's humiliation, are all matters of explicit Scripture teaching.

(1) **The fact** was more than suggested in certain utterances of the Lord himself (see John 3:13; 6:62; 16:28; 17:5). In deepest harmony with such utterances, as well as with the declared facts of our Lord's earthly history, was apostolic teaching; e. g., Paul said, "he humbled himself" (Phil. 2:8; see also II Cor. 8:9; Heb. 2:9, 10, 16; Rev. 1:18). According to the import of these and other passages the humiliation of Christ began with his incarnation and culminated in his death upon the cross, and came to its end in his exaltation to the right hand of God.

(2) **Nature.** An examination of the Scripture bearing upon this subject shows that the humiliation consisted; (*a*) in his voluntary incarnation; (*b*) in not only entering into union with human nature, but also in assuming a manhood which, though sinless, was still subject to the infirmities of man's moral condition (*see* Rom. 8:3); (*c*) in that "he was made under the law" (Gal. 4:4, 5), i. e., subjected to legal measures and obligations appropriate only for human beings; (*d*) in standing as the representative of sinners (II Cor. 5:21); (*e*) in his sacrificial death; (*f*) his humiliation was made more conspicuous by poverty, persecutions, and the scorn and cruelties which he suffered at the hands of blind and sinful men.

(3) **The end** of his humiliation was, (*a*) in a subordinate sense, the fulfillment of certain types and predictions of the Old Testament dispensation (*see* Matt. 2:23; 27:35; John 12:38, et al.); (*b*) chiefly, that Christ might come in the most complete sense into oneness with mankind, and thus accomplish human redemption (II Cor. 5:21; 8:9, et al.).

(4) **Its ethical import** appears in that (*a*) thus Christ sets before the world the most perfect example of unselfishness (*see* Matt. 20:28; II Cor. 8:9); (*b*) likewise of patience and humility (Matt. 10:24, 25; 11:29; Heb. 12:2, 3).

For theological treatment we refer to Van Oosterzee's *Dogmatics,* vol. ii, pp. 540-550; Pope's *Compendium of Christian Doctrine,* vol.

ii, pp. 152-166, and other works of systematic theology.—E. McC.

Humility (Heb. *'ănăwăh, gentleness, affliction;* Gr. *tapeinophrosunē, lowliness of mind;* Prov. 15:33, et al.; Acts 20:19 in R. V. is *"lowliness of mind"*). The heathen moralists had not the idea; their *humility* (from *humus, earth*) meant meanness of spirit. Christian humility is that grace which makes one think of himself no more highly than he ought to think (Rom. 12:3). It requires us to feel that in God's sight we have no merit, and in honor to prefer our brethren to ourselves (Rom. 12:10), but does not demand undue self-depreciation or depressing views of one's self, but lowliness of self-estimation, freedom from vanity. It is enjoined of God (Col. 3:12; James 4:6). The word is about equivalent to *meekness* (Psa. 25:9), and is essential to discipleship to Christ (Matt. 18:3, 4).

Hundreds. One of the groups (Exod. 18:21) into which Moses divided the people of Israel. *See* Israel, Classification of.

Hunger (Heb. *ră'ēb*), the rendering of the same Hebrew and Greek words that are sometimes rendered "famine" (*q. v.*).

    Figurative. Our Lord, in his Sermon on the Mount (Matt. 5:6), uses hunger as symbolic of deep and earnest longing after righteousness.

Hunt, Hunter, Hunting (Heb. *ṣăyĭd,* to *lie in wait;* *rădăph,* to *run after*). Naturally, the pursuit and capture of wild animals became very early a means of sustenance and of pleasure.

210. Hunter and Hounds (Egyptian)

1. **Egyptians.** In Egypt the desert had its perils and resources; the lion, leopard, panther, and other dangerous beasts being found there. The nobles, like the Pharaohs of later times, regarded as their privilege or duty the stalking and destroying of these animals. The common people hunted the gazelle, oryx, mouflon sheep, ibex, wild ox, and the ostrich, and such humbler game as the porcupine and the long-eared hare. To scent and retrieve the game, the hyena ran side by side with the wolf-dog and the lithe Abyssinian grayhound.

When the Egyptian wished to procure animals without seriously hurting them, he used the net for birds, and the lassoo and the *bola* for quadrupeds, these being less injurious than the spear and arrow. The *bola* was made of a single rounded stone, attached to a strap about five yards long. When the stone was thrown the cord twisted round the legs, muzzle, or neck of the animal pursued, and the hunter was able to bring down his half-strangled prey.

2. **Chaldeans.** Among this people the chase was a favorite pastime, and afforded substantial additions to the larder. It was, however, essentially the pastime of the great noble, who hunted the lion and bear in the wooded covers or the marshy thickets of the river bank; the gazelle, ostrich, and bustard on the elevated plains or rocky table lands of the desert. Recovered reliefs show that Assyrian kings especially delighted in lion-hunting. Ashurbanipal is presented most vividly in his chariot spearing a leaping lion.

3. **Biblical.** The chase is mentioned as being pursued as early as the time of Nimrod, who was "a mighty hunter before the Lord" (Gen. 10:9); but it does not appear to have formed a special occupation among the Israelites. It was practiced by farmers and shepherds (*q. v.*), partly for the sake of food (Gen. 27:3, sq.; Prov. 12:17), partly in defending their flocks against beasts of prey (I Sam. 17:34).

Hunters used the bow and arrow (Gen. 27:31), slings (I Sam. 17:40), nets, snares, and pits, especially for larger animals, such as gazelles (Isa. 51:20) and lions (II Sam. 23:20; Ezek. 19:4).

The following regulations are given in the Mosaic law: 1. The products of the land in the Sabbatic year were to be left in part to serve the wants of the beasts of the field (Exod. 23:11; Lev. 25:7). 2. If eggs or young birds were taken from a nest, the mother was allowed to escape (Deut. 22:6, sq.). 3. Israelites and strangers among them were required to let the blood flow from edible wild beasts and birds taken in the hunt, and to cover it with earth (Lev. 17:13), because containing the life it was considered holy.

Hu'pham (hū'făm), apparently one of the sons of Benjamin (Num. 26:39), and founder of the family of the Huphamites. He is supposed to be the same as *Huppim*. From I Chron. 7:12, 15, it would appear that Huppim was a grandson of Benjamin.

Hu'phamites (hū'fȧ-mīts), the descendants (Num. 26:39) of *Hupham* (*q. v.*).

Hup'pah (hŭp'ȧ; *covering, protection*), a priest in David's time, having charge of the thirteenth of the twenty-four classes into which the king divided the priests (I Chron. 24:13), B. C. 1000.

Hup'pim (Gen. 46:21; I Chron. 7:12). *See* Hupham.

Hur (hûr; a *hole, prison*), the name of five men.

1. A man who is mentioned in connection with Moses and Aaron on the occasion of the battle with Amalek at Rephidim, when with Aaron he stayed up the hands of Moses (Exod. 17:10, 12). He is mentioned again in 24:14 as being, with Aaron, left in charge of the people by Moses during his ascent of Sinai, B. C. c.

1440. He was, according to Josephus (*Ant.*, iii, 2, 4), the husband of Miriam, the sister of Moses.

2. The grandfather of Bezaleel, the chief artificer of the tabernacle—"son of Uri, son of Hur—of the tribe of Judah" (Exod. 31:2; 35:30; 38:22). In the lists of the descendants of Judah in I Chron. the pedigree is more fully preserved. Hur there appears as one of the great family of Pharez. He was the son of Caleb ben-Hezron by a second wife, Ephrath (2:19, 20; comp. v. 5, also 4:1), the first fruit of the marriage (2:50; 4:4), and the father, besides Uri (2:20), of three sons, who founded the towns of Kirjath-jearim, Bethlehem, and Beth-gader (v. 51), B. C. before 1440 (Smith, *Dict.*).

3. The fourth named of the five kings of Midian who were slain (with Balaam) by the Israelites, under the leadership of Phineas (Num. 31:8), B. C. about 1401. In a later mention of them (Josh. 13:21) these five Midianites are termed "*dukes of Sihon*," properly, "*vassals*."

4. A person whose son (Ben-Hur) was the first named of Solomon's twelve purveyors. His district was in Mount Ephraim (I Kings 4:8), B. C. about 960.

5. Father of Rephaiah, which latter is called "ruler of the half part of Jerusalem" after the captivity, and who assisted in repairing its walls (Neh. 3:9), B. C. before 445.

Hu'rai (hū'rā-ī), a native of the valleys ("brooks") of Mount Gaash, and one of David's valiant men (I Chron. 11:32); called less correctly (II Sam. 23:30) *Hiddai*, B. C. 953.

Hu'ram (hū'rȧm), another form of *Hiram* (*q. v.*).

1. A Benjamite, son of Bela, the firstborn of the patriarch (I Chron. 8:5).

2. The form in which the name of the king of Tyre in alliance with David and Solomon—and elsewhere given as *Hiram*—appears in Chronicles (II Chron. 2:3, 11, 12; 8:2, 18; 9:10, 21).

3. The same change occurs in Chronicles in the name of Hiram the artificer, which is given as Huram (II Chron. 2:13; 4:11, 16).

Hu'ri (hū'rī), the son of Jaroah, and father of Abihail, of the descendants of Gad in Bashan (I Chron. 5:14).

Husband. *See* Marriage.

Husbandman (properly Heb. *'ish 'ăclämäch, man of the ground;* Gr. *geōrgos, land worker*), a farmer or other worker of the soil. Husbandry is among the most ancient and honorable occupations (Gen. 9:20; 26:12, 14; 37:7; Job 1:3; Isa. 28:24-28; John 15:1).

Figurative. God is compared to a husbandman (John 15:1; I Cor. 3:9). The various operations of husbandry (*see* Agriculture), such as sowing of seed, harvesting, etc., furnish many apt illustrations in Scripture.

Husbandry. *See* Agriculture.

Hu'shah (hū'shȧ; *hurry; haste*), son of Ezer, and descendant of Hur, of the family of Judah (I Chron. 4:4), whence probably the patronymic *Hushathite* (II Sam. 21:18; I Chron. 11:29; 20:4). He seems to be the same person that is called *Shuah* in I Chron. 4:11. Comp. *Husham*.

Hu'shai (hū'shä-ī; *hasty*), an Archite, and a prominent actor in the history of Absalom's rebellion. When David fled from Jerusalem, Hushai joined him, but, at David's suggestion, returned to the city for the purpose of serving his master, as occasion might offer (II Sam. 15:32, sq.). He offered his allegiance to Absalom (16:16, sq.), and was invited by him to a conference, which should decide the prince's action. Hushai advised delay in the pursuit of the king until ampler preparation had been made, thus defeating the counsel of Ahithophel (17:5-22). The immediate result was the suicide of the defeated Ahithophel (v. 23), and the ultimate consequence was the crushing out of the rebellion, B. C. about 977. He is called the "friend" of David (II Sam. 15:37), and "the king's companion," i. e., *vizier*, or intimate adviser (I Chron. 27:33). Baanah, Solomon's vicegerent in Asher (I Kings 4:16), was doubtless his son.

Hu'sham (hū'shâm; *hastily*), a Temanite, successor of Jobab and predecessor of Bedad, among the native princes of Mount Seir before the usurpation of the Edomites (Gen. 36: 34, 35; I Chron. 1:45, 46).

Hu'shathite, the (hū'shȧ-thīt), the designation of one of the heroes of David's guard, Sibbechai (II Sam. 21:18; I Chron. 11:29; 20:4; 27:11). Josephus, however, calls him a Hittite. In II Sam. 23:27 he is named Mebunnai, a mere corruption of Sibbechai. *See* Hushah.

Hu'shim (hū'shĭm; *hasters*).

1. The son of Dan (Gen. 46:23); given *Shuham* in Num. 26:42.

2. A name given as that of "the *sons* of Aher," or Aharah, the third son of Benjamin (I Chron. 7:12; comp. 8:1), and therefore only a plural form for *Shuham*, as a representative of his brethren.

3. One of the wives of Shaharaim, a Benjamite, in the country of Moab, by whom he had Abitub and Elpaal (I Chron. 8:8, 11).

Husk. *See* Vegetable Kingdom.

Huz, (hŭz), eldest son of Nahor and Milcah (Gen. 22:21). *See* Uz.

Huz'zab (hŭz'ȧb; Heb. *näṣȧb, to establish*). This word is erroneously rendered (Nah. 2:7) as a proper name. The meaning appears to be as follows: The prophet has been declaring that "The gates of the rivers shall be opened, and the palace shall be dissolved," and he cries out, as if against objectors, "It is established," i. e., is determined (by God).

Hyacinth. *See* Jacinth, Mineral Kingdom.

Hyena. *See* Animal Kingdom.

Hyk'sos (hĭk'sŏs; Egyptian for "rulers of foreign lands"), a mixed race, predominantly N. W. Semitic, which invaded Egypt (c. B. C. 1720-1550). They reigned during Dynasties XV and XVI. Their capital was at Avaris-Tanis in the Delta. Archaeological excavations have uncovered many Hyksos remains. They introduced the horse and chariot into Egypt as well as the composite bow. These implements of war made possible the New Empire of Egypt after B. C. 1550 and the expulsion of the Hyksos. The Hyksos Dynasties of Egypt were brought to an end when Khamose and Ahmose expelled them from the Delta (c. B. C. 1600-1550). Amenhotep I inaugurated the splendid strong Eighteenth Dynasty (c. B. C.

1546-1319). While many scholars maintain the Exodus took place under the Nineteenth Dynasty, the chronological data preserved in the Massoretic text undeniably places this event in the Eighteenth Dynasty. The Hyksos erected large earthen enclosures for their horses. This type of construction can be seen at Jericho, Shechem, Lachish, and Tell el-Ajjul. They also erected many temples to Baal. There are evidences of the worship of the mother goddess. Common in Hyksos levels are cultic objects such as nude figurines, serpents and doves, showing their complete devotion to this type of degrading worship. Hyksos burial customs are distinctive as is their chariotry. *M. F. U.*

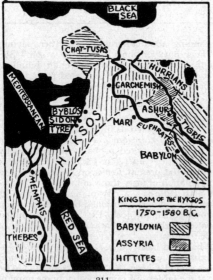

211.

Hymenae′us (hĭ-mĕn-ē′ŭs; *pertaining to Hymen, god of marriage*), a person in Ephesus twice named in the Epistles of Timothy, who, with Alexander (I Tim. 1:20) and Philetus (II Tim. 2:17) had departed from the truth in faith and practice.

1. **Error.** The chief doctrinal error of these persons consisted in maintaining that "the resurrection was past already" (II Tim. 2:18). The precise meaning of this expression is by no means clearly ascertained; the most general and perhaps best founded opinion is, that they understood the resurrection in a figurative sense of the great change produced by the gospel dispensation. Thus he stands as one of the earliest of the Gnostics.

2. **Sentence.** "Whom I have delivered unto Satan" (I Tim. 1:20). The exact meaning of this formula has been much discussed. Some think it means simply excommunication; others, supernatural infliction of corporeal punishment; others, both combined. Elliott (*Com.*, in loc.) says: "We conclude, then, with Waterland, that 'delivery over to Satan' was a form of Christian excommunication, declaring the person reduced to the state of a heathen, *accompanied with* the authoritative infliction of bodily disease or death." Satan was

212. Examples of Hyksos Pottery from Jericho

held to be the instrument or executioner of all these visitations (cf. I Cor. 5:5; I John 5:16).

Hymn. *See* Music.

Hypocrisy (Heb. from *hănēf*, to *defile*, and so rendered in Jer. 3:9; Gr. *hupokrisis*, an *answer, to play a part*), dissimulation of one's real character or belief; a false assumption of character or belief. In Isa. 32:6 we have the expression "to practice hypocrisy" with the meaning of dealing craftily. The Greek word signifies the part taken by an actor; hence outward show. Hypocrisy is professing to be what one is not, and is generally applied to religious character.

Hypocrite. The hypocrite is a double person, natural and artificial; the first he keeps to himself, the other he puts on, as he does his clothes, to make his appearance before men. Hypocrites have been divided into four classes: 1. The *wordly* hypocrite, who makes a profession of religion and pretends to be religious, merely from worldly considerations (Matt. 23:5). 2. The *legal* hypocrite, who relinquishes his vicious practices, in order thereby to merit heaven, while at the same time he has no real love to God (Rom. 10:3). 3. The *evangelical* hypocrite, whose religion is nothing more than a bare conviction of sin; who rejoices under the idea that Christ died for him, and yet has no desire to live a holy life (Matt. 13:20). 4. The *enthusiastic* hypocrite, who has an imaginary sight of his sins and of Christ; talks of remarkable impulses and high feelings, etc., while he lives in the most scandalous practices (II Cor. 11:14).

Hyssop. In some of the sacrifices the relation between the shed blood and the transgressor was made manifest by the sprinkling on him of part of the blood. This was done with a bunch of hyssop. The first record of this use of hyssop is in connection with the Exodus, when the Israelites employed it to sprinkle the doorposts with the blood of the paschal lamb (Exod. 12:22). It was also used in connection with the ceremony of purifying lepers (Lev. 14:4-7), and in sprinkling blood on the leprous house (vers. 48-53). Hyssop was also used in the peculiar ordinance appointed for the purification of ceremonial uncleanness contracted by touching a dead body (Num. 19:1, sq.). *See* Sacrificial Offerings, 7.

The simplest form of the hyssop sprinkler is the "bunch" which each father in Israel hastily prepared before leaving Egypt. In the Mosaic ritual the bunch of hyssop was tied with a scarlet thread (Num. 19:6). In the account of the crucifixion (John 19:28, 29) it is recorded, "they filled a sponge with vinegar, and put it upon hyssop, and put it to his mouth." In the parallel passages of Matthew and Mark no reference is made to the hyssop, but it is said that the sponge was put upon a reed. Some explain the difference of statement by the supposition that the hyssop was fastened to a reed; others that the Greek term rendered "reed" was a long stalk of hyssop; others, as Haley (*Alleged Discrepancies*, p. 235), think that drink was twice offered to our Lord.

Figurative. The Psalmist, having in view the frequent use of hyssop in the ceremonial law, as a means by which the virtue of the sacrifice was transferred to the transgressor, applies it figuratively to the purification of the soul from guilt when he prays, "Purge me with hyssop, and I shall be clean" (Psa. 51:7). In alluding to Solomon's botanical knowledge it is said "He spake of trees, from the cedar tree that is in Lebanon even unto the hyssop that springeth out of the wall" (I Kings 4:33). The tall cedar and the *humble hyssop* at once suggests the most extensive range in the vegetable world. *See* Vegetable Kingdom.

I

I Am ('*ĕhyĕh 'ăshĕr 'ĕhyĕh, I am Who I am*), a name of God (Exod. 3:14, lit. God *is he who is*), the absolute *I*, the self-existent *One*.

Ib'har (ĭb'hàr; *choice*), one of the sons of David, born to him in Jerusalem (II Sam. 5:15; I Chron. 3:6; 14:5), B. C. after 1000.

Ib'leam (ĭb'lē-ăm), a city—with suburban towns—within the natural boundaries of Asher, but assigned to Manasseh (Josh. 17:11); one of the towns from which Manasseh failed to expel the Canaanites (v. 12). It is called *Bileam* (I Chron. 6:70), a Levitical city (comp. Josh. 21:25, where it is called Gathrimmon). Probably preserved in the ruins of *Khirbet-belameh*, 1¼ miles S. of Jenin.

Ibene'iah (ĭb-nē'yà; *built by Jah*), a son of Jeroham, who, with other Benjamites, returned to Jerusalem after the captivity (I Chron. 9:8), B. C. after 536.

Ibni'jah (ĭb-nī'jà; *building of Jah*), the ancestor of Meshullam, a Benjamite, who settled in Jerusalem after the return from Babylon (Josh. 9:8), B. C. after 536.

Ib'ri (ĭb'rī; an *Eberite*, or "Hebrew"), the last of "the sons of Merari by Jaaziah," apparently a descendant of Levi in the time of David (I Chron. 24:27).

Ib'zan (ĭb'zăn), the tenth "judge of Israel" (Judg. 12:8-10). He was of Bethlehem, probably the Bethlehem of Zebulun (so Michaelis and Hezel), and not of Judah (as Josephus says). He governed seven years, B. C. probably after 1080. The prosperity of Ibzan is marked by the great number of his children (thirty sons and thirty daughters), and his wealth by their marriages, for they were all married.

Ice (Heb. *qĕrăḥ, smooth*, Job. 6:16; 38:29; Psa. 147:17). "On the Central Range (in Palestine) snow has been known to reach a depth of nearly two feet, and the pools at Jerusalem have sometimes been covered with ice. But this is rare" (Smith, *Hist. Geog.*, p. 65).

Ich'abod (ĭk'à-bŏd; *where is the glory? inglorious*), the son of Phinehas, and grandson of Eli. The wife of Phinehas was about to become a mother when she heard that her husband was slain in battle, that Eli was dead, and that the ark of God had been taken by the Philistines. Under such circumstances her labor was fatal. When lying at the point of death the women standing about sought to cheer her, saying, "Fear not; for thou hast borne a son." She only replied by naming the child Ichabod, adding, "The glory is departed from Israel: for the ark of God is taken" (I Sam. 4:19-22), B. C. about 1050. The only other mention of Ichabod is in I Sam. 14:3, where it is stated that his brother, Ahitub, was father of *Ahiah* (*q. v.*), who acted as high priest for Saul.

Ico'nium (ī-kō'nĭ-ŭm), a celebrated city of Asia Minor, visited probably three times by the apostle Paul (Acts 13:51; 14:1, 19, 21; 16:2), the present *Konia*, or *Konieh*, having a population of forty thousand.

Id'alah (ĭd'à-là), a city of Zebulun, near its western border, mentioned between Shimron and Bethlehem (Josh. 19:15). It is identified with Khirbet el Huwara about ½ mile S. of Beit Lahm.

Id'bash (ĭd'băsh; *honeyed*), a descendant of Judah who, with his two brothers and a sister, are said (I Chron. 4:3, R. V. "sons of") to be "of the father of Etam," probably meaning of the lineage of the founder of that place, or perhaps they were themselves its settlers.

Id'do (ĭd'ō). 1. The father of Ahinadab, Solomon's purveyor in the district of Mahanaim (I Kings 4:14), B. C. before 960.

2. A Gershomite Levite, son of Joah, and father of Zerah (I Chron. 6:21); perhaps more correctly called *Adaiah* in v. 41.

3. Son of Zechariah, and ruler of the half tribe of Manasseh east (I Chron. 27:21), B. C. 960.

4. Hebrew same as No. 2, a seer whose "visions" against Jeroboam incidentally contained some of the acts of Solomon (II Chron. 9:29). He appears to have written a chronicle or story relating to the life and reign of Abijah (13:22), which he seems to have called *Midrash*, or "exposition," and also a book "concerning genealogies," in which the acts of Rehoboam were recorded (12:15), B. C. after 934. These books are lost, but they may have formed part of the foundation of the existing books of Chronicles.

5. The father of Berechiah and grandfather of the prophet Zechariah (Zech. 1:1, 7), although in other places Zechariah is called "the son of Iddo" (Ezra 5:1; 6:14; Neh. 12:16). Iddo returned from Babylon with Zerubbabel (Neh. 12:4), B. C. 536.

6. The chief of the Jews established at Casiphia. It was to him that Ezra sent for Levites and Nethinim to join his company. Thirty-eight Levites and two hundred and twenty Nethinim responded to his call (Ezra 8:17-20), B. C. 457. It would seem from this that Iddo was a chief person of the Nethinim, and also that this is one of the circumstances which indicate that the Jews, in their several colonies under the exile, were still ruled by the heads of their nation and allowed the free exercise of their worship (Kitto).

Idle (Gr. *argos*). A peculiar use of this word is, "I say unto you, that *every idle word* that men shall speak, they shall give an account thereof" (Matt. 12:36). Here the term *idle* means *unprofitable, pernicious*. The Greek word *ēros*, may be rendered *nonsensical, absurd* (Luke 24:11).

Idol, Image. These are the rendering of a large number of Hebrew and Greek words, and may be divided as follows: (1) Abstract terms, which, with a deep moral significance, express the degradation associated with, and stand out as a protest of the language against, the enormities of idolatry; (2) Those which apply to the idols or images, as the outward symbols of the deity who was worshipped through them; (3) Terms relating to material and workmanship.

1. **Abstract Terms.** (1) **An empty thing** (Heb. *'āwĕn*), rendered elsewhere "nought," "vanity," "iniquity," "wickedness," "sorrow," etc., and only once "idol" (Isa. 66:3). The primary idea of the root seems to be emptiness, nothingness, as of breath or vapor; and, by a natural transition, in a moral sense, wickedness in its active form of mischief, and then, as the result, sorrow and trouble. Hence *'āwĕn* denotes a vain, false, wicked thing, and expresses at once the essential nature of idols and the consequences of their worship.

(2) **A nonentity** (Heb. *'ĕlîl*, good for *nothing*) is thought by some to have a sense akin to that of "falsehood," and would therefore much resemble (1), as applied to an idol. It is used of the idols of Noph or Memphis (Ezek. 30:13). In strong contrast with Jehovah it appears in Psa. 96:5; 97:7.

(3) **Terrifying thing** (Heb. *'ēmîm*), so-called from the terror they inspire in their devotees. (Jer. 50:38). In this respect it is closely connected with number 4.

(4) **A horrible thing** (Heb. *mĭflĕṣĕth*), a "fright," "horror," applied to the idol of Maachah, probably of wood, which Asa cut down and burned (I Kings 15:13; II Chron. 15:16), and which was unquestionably the phallus, the symbol of the productive power of nature and the nature-goddess Ashera.

(5) **A shameful thing** (Heb. *bōshĕth*, "shame," Jer. 11:13; Hos. 9:10), applied to Baal or Baal-peor, as characterizing the obscenity of his worship.

(6) **Logs, blocks** (Heb. *gĭllūlîm*, such as are rolled (*gālăl*) like helpless logs. (Ezek. 30:13). The expression is applied, principally in Ezekiel, to false gods and their symbols (Deut. 29:17; Ezek. 8:10, etc.). It stands side by side with other contemptuous terms in Ezek. 16:36; 20:8; as, e. g. *shĕkĕṣ*, "filth," "abomination" (Ezek. 8:10), and

(7) **An abomination** (Heb. *shĭqqūṣ*, *filth, impurity*, especially applies to that which produced ceremonial uncleanness Ezek. 37:23; Nah. 3:6). As referring to the idols themselves, it primarily denotes the obscene rites with which their worship was associated, and hence, by metonymy, is applied both to the objects of worship and also to their worshippers.

2. **Names of Idols.** Terms applied more directly to the images or idols, as the outward symbols of the deity who was worshipped through them.

(1) **A likeness** (Heb. *sĕmĕl* or *sēmĕl*, *semblance*), rendered "idol" (II Chron. 33:7, 15); "figure" (Deut. 4:16); "image" (Ezek. 8:3, 5). It corresponds to the Latin *simulacrum*.

(2) **A representation** (Heb. *ṣĕlĕm*, a *shadow*). It is the "image" of God in which man was created (Gen. 1:27; comp. Wisd. 2:23), distinguished from "likeness," as the "image" from the "idea" which it represents, though it would be rash to insist upon this distinction. But whatever abstract term may best define the meaning *ṣĕlĕm*, it is unquestionably used to denote the visible forms of external objects, and is applied to figures of gold and silver (I Sam. 6:5; Num. 33:53; Dan. 3:1), such as the golden image of Nebuchadnezzar, as well as to those painted upon walls (Ezek. 23:14). "Image" perhaps most nearly represents it in all passages. Applied to the human countenance (Dan. 3:19, "form"), it signifies the "expression."

(3) **An appearance** (Heb. *tĕmūnäh*, rendered "image" in Job 4:16; elsewhere "similitude" (Deut. 4:12); "likeness" (Deut. 5:8). "Form," or "shape" would be better.

(4) **Something formed or fashioned** (Heb. *'äsäb*, *'ĕṣĕb*) (Jer. 22:28) or *'ōṣĕb* (Isa. 48:5), "a figure," all derived from a root *'äṣäb*, "to work," or "fashion," are terms applied to idols as expressing that their origin was due to the labor of man.

(5) **A form** (Heb. *ṣîr*), once only applied to an idol (Isa. 45:16). The word signifies "a form," or "mold," and hence an "idol."

(6) **Stone monument** (Heb. *măṣṣēbäh*), anything *set up*, a "pillar" (Gen. 28:18; 31:45; 35:14, 15). Such were the stones set up by Joshua (Josh. 4:9) after the passage of the Jordan, and at Shechem (24:26), and by Samuel, when victorious over the Philistines (I Sam. 7:12). When solemnly dedicated they were anointed with oil, and libations were poured upon them. The word is applied to denote the obelisks which stood at the entrance to the Temple of the Sun at Heliopolis (Jer. 43:13). The Palladium of Troy, the black stone in the Kaaba at Mecca, said to have been brought from heaven by the angel Gabriel, and the stone at Ephesus "which fell down from Jupiter" (Acts 19:35), are examples of the belief, anciently so common, that the gods sent down their images upon earth.

(7) **Incense-altar** (Heb. *hămmänîm* from *hmm, be hot, stand for heating, brazier*), the mention of which is joined with statues of Astarte (Lev. 26:30; Isa. 17:8; 27:9; Ezek. 6:4, 6; II Chron. 14:5; 34:7) several times; while from II Chron. 34:4 it appears that they stood upon the altars of Baal.

(8) **Something to look at** (Heb. *măskîth*, Lev. 26:1; Num. 33:52 Ezek. 8:12, with the root apparently from *săkăh, to look at, behold*, Lev. 26:1; Num. 33:52; Ezek. 8:12). The general opinion appears to be that *ĕbĕn măskîth* signifies a stone with figures graven upon it.

(9) **Teraphim.** Household deities. *See* Teraphim.

3. **Material, etc.** Terms relating to the material and workmanship of the idol.

(1) **An artistically executed likeness** (Heb. *pĕsĕl*), usually rendered in the A. V. "graven or carved image," but "quarries" in Judg. 3:19, 26). The verb is employed to denote the fine work of the stone worker, after receiving it from the quarries (Exod. 34:4; I Kings 5:18). The term *pĕsĕl* was applied, however, to images of metal and wood, as well as those of stone (Deut. 7:25; Isa. 30:22; 40:19; Hab. 2:19).

(2) **A metal-cast idol** (Heb. *nĕsĕk, nēsĕk*, and *măssēkăh*), are evidently synonymous (Isa. 41: 29; 48:5; Jer. 10:14) in later Hebrew, and denote a "molten" image, the last term being often used in distinction from *pĕsĕl* (Deut. 27:15; Judg. 17:3, etc.).

4. **Forms of Idols.** Among the earliest objects of worship, regarded as symbols of deity, were meteoric stones; then rough, unhewn blocks, and later stone columns or pillars of wood, in which the divinity worshiped was supposed to dwell. The Bible does not give us many traces of the forms of idolatrous images. *Dagon* (*q. v.*), god of the Philistines, had a figure partly human, terminating in a fish. *See* Idolatry.

Idolatry. 1. Definition and Classification. In a general sense idolatry is the paying of divine honors to any created thing; the ascription of divine power to natural agencies. Idolatry may be classified as follows: (*a*) The worship of inanimate objects, as stones, trees, rivers, etc.; (*b*) of animals; (*c*) of the higher powers of nature, as the sun, moon, stars; and the forces of nature, as air, fire, etc.; (*d*) hero-worship, or of deceased ancestors; (*e*) *idealism*, or the worship of abstractions or mental qualities, as justice. Another classification is very suggestive: (*a*) the worship of Jehovah under image or symbol; (*b*) the worship of other gods under image or symbol; (*c*) the worship of the image or symbol itself. Each of these forms of idolatry had its peculiar immoral tendency. *See* Gods, False; Idol.

2. **Idolatry of Israel's Neighbors.** Israel adopted in the course of her history many idolatrous practices from her heathen neighbors. (1) **Egyptian.** The Egyptians had a bewildering conglomeration of deities. It is impossible to list all the gods sacred to this people. Every aspect of nature, every object looked at, animate as well as inanimate, was viewed as indwelt by a spirit which could select its own form, occupying the body of a cow, a crocodile, a fish, a human being, a tree, a hawk, etc. In their hieroglyphic inscriptions and their tomb paintings ancient Egyptian artists have left impressions of literally thousands of deities. The Pyramid Texts mention some 200. The Book of the Dead catalogs 1200. The great deity, the sun god,

Amun-re, was one of the principle deities. Many of the Pharoahs were believed to incarnate Amun-Re. Akhenaton, around 1380 B. C., switched from the worship of Amun as the state religion to the solar disc, Aton (and approached monotheism). An entire shake-up in the religious constitution of the nation followed. When Tutankhamun went back to Amun worship there was a similar political upheaval. Egypt venerated her fertility gods and her Isis; a counterpart of Astarte was adopted as far west as Italy. In Pompeii the ruins of a little temple of Isis is extant. Egyptians venerated Osiris, an agricultural deity, consort of Isis and the father of young Horus,

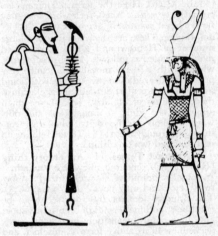

213. Egyptian Gods
Left: Ptah; Right: Horus

who became successor of Osiris when the latter became the underworld god. Osiris was immensely influential. He was associated with the life-giving waters of the Nile River. At Heliopolis, Biblical On, gods worshipped included Nut, Seb, Isis, Set, Osiris, Temu, Tefnut, Shu and others, besides a lesser group of deities. The sight of animal- and bird-headed Egyptian deities such as Ptah, Knum, Hathor, Set, Sobek, etc., must have been thoroughly repulsive to the Hebrews, and yet the splendor and attraction of Egyptian cults must have been dazzling to the less spiritually minded.

(2) **Canaan.** Fertility cults nowhere controlled people more completely than in Canaan. When Israel entered Palestine, the Canaanites were in the last stages of degradation as the result of centuries of worshipping degrading deities. The only safe recourse for the virile Bedouin from the wilderness was complete separation and annihilation of the Canaanites and their religion. Orgiastic nature worship, fertility cults in the form of serpent symbols, unbounded license and moral abandon could only be met with a severe code of ethics. El, a heartless, unbridled tyrant had three wives or consorts who were patrons of sex and war. Baal was the great N. W. Semitic god of the storm. At Tyre Melcarth was honored. Koshar was the Vulcan of the Canaanite; Hauron, the shepherd god. Mot was the

214. Canaanite Shrine with Cult Stones, from
the Jericho Level Destroyed by Joshua

god of death. The Ras Shamra Texts speak of
a sun goddess Shapash. In the worship of these
various deities prostitution was glorified. Veneration of Astarte continued for many centuries until the Christian emperor Constantine,
in the fourth century A. D., destroyed the
Venus and the Adonis cult centers. There
were also various pillar cults which had a
degrading cultic significance, as at Gezer and
Ader in Moab.

(3) **Babylonia and Assyria.** Very early inhabitants of Mesopotamia paid homage to
fertility gods. There the famous goddess of
propagation, Ishtar, was thought of as descending to the underworld to seek her young
husband, Tammuz. Other gods of production
were Dagon, who in the West became father
of Baal and brother of the virgin goddess of
fertility, Anath. Babylonians also worshipped
the sky god, An; En-lil, the wind god; Enki,
earth and water god; Ningal, the mother
goddess, Namuzi (and Tammuz of the Bible);
Utu, the sun god; Nannar, the moon god;
Marduk, another form of the sun god who
later became the chief god of Babylon; and
Ashur, the principal god of the Assyrians.
Along with Ishtar, their immoral goddess of
love, they worshipped Nabu, patron of learning, Nergal, god of war and the underworld,
and Nusqu, the god of fire. The later Chaldeans especially revered the gods of fire and
of the heavens, as a result of their interest in
astrology. Perhaps Babylonia exerted a greater
influence upon Israelite religion than either
Canaan or Egypt. However, Abraham, by his
divine call, was brought out of paganism,
and although he knew the many gods at Ur,
particularly the moon god, Sin, who was also
worshipped at Haran, nevertheless his vision
of the "God of Glory" (Acts 7:2) purged out
the intermixture of idolatry. Along with the
moon god Sin, Shamash, the sun god, was
greatly venerated among the Babylonians and
Assyrians. Numerous cuneiform tablets depict

scenes of Shamash worship. The cuneiform
and monumental finds of the Sumerian-Akka-
dian peoples in Mesopotamia give us richer
archaeological information of Mesopotamian
religion than the records of Egypt. Stone and
clay inscriptions, literary tablets unearthed in
such temple libraries as that at ancient
Nippur, S. E. of Babylon, the Tell Farah
tablets from central Babylonia, and the thousands of clay tablets from Lagash (B. C. 26th
century) yield a great fund of religious information. Tablets from the royal library of King
Sargon II of Assyria (B. C. 721-705), augmented by Sennacherib and Esarhaddon, give
further information. The phenomenal finds
from the great library of Ashurbanipal (B. C.
668-633) have shown how potent a factor
Sumero-Akkadian religion was in the ancient
Biblical world. M. F. U.

3. **Idolatrous Usages.** Mountains and high
places were chosen spots for offering sacrifice
and incense to idols (I Kings 11:7; 14:23),
and the retirement of gardens and the thick
shade of woods offered great attractions to
their worshippers (II Kings 16:4; Isa. 1:29;
Hos. 4:13). The host of heaven was worshipped
on the housetop (II Kings 23:12; Jer. 19:13;
32:29; Zeph. 1:5). The priests of the false
worship are sometimes designated Chemarim,
a word of Syriac origin, to which different
meanings have been assigned. It is applied to
the non-Levitical priests who burnt incense on
the high places (II Kings 23:5) as well as to
the priests of the calves (Hos. 10:5). In addition to the priests there were other persons intimately connected with idolatrous rites, and
the impurities from which they were inseparable. Both men and women consecrated
themselves to the service of idols: the former
as *kedêshim*, for which there is reason to believe
the A. V. (Deut. 23:17, etc.) has not given
too harsh an equivalent; the latter as *kedês-
hôth*, who wove shrines for Astarte (II Kings
23:7). The same class of women existed among
the Phoenicians, Armenians, Lydians, and Babylonians (Epist. of Jer., v. 43). They are
distinguished from the public prostitutes (Hos.
4:14), and associated with the performances
of sacred rites. Besides these accessories there
were the ordinary rites of worship which idolatrous systems had in common with the religion of the Hebrews. Offering burnt sacrifices
to the idol gods (II Kings 5:17), burning incense in their honor (I Kings 11:8), and
bowing down in worship before their images
(I Kings 19:18), were the chief parts of their
ritual; and from their very analogy with the
ceremonies of true worship were more seduc-
tive than the grosser forms.

4. **Idolatry Among the Israelites.** Although
of a family which worshiped strange gods
(Josh. 24:2), yet Abraham still worshipped
one true God when He revealed himself to
him, and called him to leave his native land
for Canaan (Gen. 12:1). The teraphim which
Rachel took with her (Gen. 31:19) were household gods of an inferior kind, which might be
combined with the worship of the one supreme
God. Hence we find no idolatry in the strict
sense either among the patriarchs or Israelites
in Egypt and under Moses, but only solitary
traces of idolatry and image worship, whereby

the knowledge and worship of God was so far polluted, but not supplanted (Gen. 30:27; 31:53). The traces of idolatry which have been sought in Exod. 17:7; Num. 25:2; Josh. 24:14; Ezek. 20:7; and Amos 5:25, 26 prove nothing more than disturbances of pure Jehovah worship by image worship, heathen superstition, and proneness to fleshly sins. The golden calf (Exod. 32) was intended to be a representation of Jehovah after an Egyptian pattern. Amos (5:25) in his rebuke seems to have in view image worship, but not the service of the Assyrian idols Sakkuth and Kewan. The worship of Baal-peor was a temporary apostasy, brought about by the temptations to licentious indulgence offered by the rites of that deity.

215. High Place, Petra

The people of Israel were first seduced into apostasy from Jehovah, into heathen idolatry by the Canaanites, who had not been rooted out. This apostasy took place during the time of the judges. The various gods to whose service the Israelites gave themselves were *Canaanitish;* and after the invasion of Palestine by the Assyrians, *Assyrian* idols were added. After the death of Joshua and the elders who outlived him, Israel forsook Jehovah "and served Baal and Ashtaroth" (Judg. 2:13); and from this time its history becomes little more than a chronicle of the inevitable sequence of offense and punishment (Judg. 2:12-14). Idolatry becomes the national sin, even Gideon, the judge and a Levite (Judg. 17:7) giving occasion to, or assisting in idolatrous worship. In later times the practice of secret idolatry was carried to greater lengths. Images were set up on the corn floors, in the wine vats, and behind the doors of private houses (Isa. 57:8; Hos. 9:1, 2); and to check this tendency the statute in Deut. 27:15 was originally promulgated. Under Samuel's administration a fast was held and purificatory rites performed, to mark the public renunciation of idolatry (I Sam. 7:3-6). But in the reign of Solomon all this was forgotten. Each of his many foreign wives brought with her the gods of her own nation; and the gods of Ammon, Moab, and Zidon were openly worshiped.

(1) **Among the ten tribes.** Jeroboam, fresh from his recollections of the Apis worship of Egypt, erected golden calves at Beth-el and at Dan, and by this crafty state policy severed effectively the kingdoms of Judah and Israel (I Kings 12:26-33). But Jeroboam's calves

were doubtless intended to fasten the worshipper's attention upon Yahweh, thought of as invisibly represented above the animals, astride their backs. The deity astride a bull was a very common conception illustrated by ancient Near-Eastern iconography. The successors of Jeroboam followed in his steps, till Ahab, who married a Zidonian princess, at her instigation (21:25), built a temple and altar to Baal, and revived all the abominations of the Amorites (21:26). Henceforth Baal worship became so completely identified with the northern kingdom that it is described as walking in the way or statutes of the kings of Israel (II Kings 16:3; 17:8), as distinguished from the sin of Jeroboam. The conquest of the ten tribes by Shalmaneser was for them the last scene of the drama of abominations which had been enacted uninterruptedly for upward of two hundred and fifty years. In the northern kingdom no reformer arose to vary the long line of royal apostates; whatever was effected in the way of reformation was done by the hands of the people (II Chron. 31:1).

(2) **Idolatry in Judah.** Rehoboam, the son of an Ammonite mother, perpetuated the worst features of Solomon's idolatry (I Kings 14:22-24); and in his reign was made the great schism in the national religion. The first act of Hezekiah on ascending the throne was the restoration and purification of the temple which had been dismantled and closed during the latter part of his father's life (II Chron. 28:24; 29:3). The iconoclastic spirit was not confined to Judah and Benjamin, but spread throughout Ephraim and Manasseh (II Chron. 31:1), and to all external appearance idolatry was extirpated. But the reform extended little below the surface (Isa. 29:13). With the death of Josiah ended the last effort to revive among the people a purer ritual, if not a purer faith. Idolatry spread fearfully in the last times of the kingdom of Judah, until it brought down on the people the punishment of captivity in Babylon. This exile bore wholesome fruit, for in captivity the Jews wholly gave up gross idolatry; with the exception of certain of those who had returned to Palestine, marrying heathen wives and sharing their worship, which departure was corrected by Ezra (Ezra 9:1, sq.). Later a new danger presented itself in Greek influence brought into Asia by Alexander; and some place-hunting Jews were base enough to adopt Greek idolatry. So far was the nation from showing any inclination to idolatry that the attempt of Antiochus Epiphanes was utterly baffled by the Jews (I Macc. 2:23-26). The erection of synagogues has been assigned as a reason for the comparative purity of the Jewish worship after the hatred for images acquired by the Jews in their intercourse with the Persians.

5. **Idolatry and the Law.** Israel had entered into a solemn compact with Jehovah, accepting him as the only God, and pledging themselves faithfully to serve him (Exod. 19:3-8; 20:2, sq.). Idolatry, therefore, to an Israelite was a state of offense (I Sam. 15:23), a political crime of the gravest nature, high treason against his king. It was a transgression of the covenant (Deut. 17:2, 3), *"the evil"* preeminently in the eyes of Jehovah (I Kings

21:25). Idolatry was a great wrong because of the licentious rites associated with it (Rom. 1:26-32), thus debauching the morals of its adherents. Regarded in a moral aspect, false gods are called "stumbling blocks" (Ezek. 14: 3), "lies" (Amos 2:4; Rom. 1:25), "abominations" (Deut. 29:17; 32:16; I Kings 11:5; II Kings 23:13), "sin" (Amos 8:14, comp. II Chron. 29:18); and with a profound sense of the degradation consequent upon their worship, they were characterized by the prophets as "shame" (Jer. 11:13; Hos. 9:10), "strange gods" (Deut. 32:16), "new gods" (Judg. 5:8), "devils—not God" (Deut. 32:17; I Cor. 10: 20, 21), and as denoting their foreign origin, "gods of the foreigner" (Josh. 24:14, 15). Their powerlessness is indicated by describing them as "gods that cannot save" (Isa. 45:20), "that made not the heavens" (Jer. 10:11), "nothing" (Isa. 41:24; I Cor. 8:4), "wind and confusion" (Isa. 41:29), "vanities of the Gentiles" (Jer. 14:22; Acts 14:15).

Many customs associated with idolatry were forbidden by the law. Maimonides tells us that the prohibition against sowing a field with mingled seeds, and wearing garments of mixed material was because some idolaters attributed a kind of magical influence to the mixture (Lev. 19:19). It was also forbidden to interchange the garments of the sexes (Deut. 22:5); to cut the flesh for the dead (Lev. 19: 28; I Kings 18:28), and make a baldness between the eyes (Deut. 14:1), as being associated with idolatrous rites. Eating of things offered was a necessary appendage to sacrifice (comp. Exod. 18:12; 32:6; 34:15; Num. 25: 2). The printing upon one's person was forbidden to the Israelites (Lev. 19:28), because idolaters branded upon their flesh some symbol of deity they worshipped, as the ivy leaf of Bacchus (3 Macc. 2:29).

216. Roman Road, Petra

6. **Penalties.** The first and second commandments are directed against idolatry of every form. Individuals and communities were equally amenable to the rigorous code. The individual offender was devoted to destruction (Exod. 22:20); his nearest relatives were not only bound to denounce him and deliver him up to punishment (Deut. 13:2-10), but their hands were to strike the first blow when, on the evidence of two witnesses at least, he was stoned (Deut. 17:2-5). To attempt to seduce others to false worship was a crime of equal enormity (Deut. 13:6-10). An idolatrous nation shared a similar fate.

Figurative. The term idolatry is used to designate *covetousness*, which takes mammon for its god (Matt. 6:24; Luke 16:13; Eph. 5:5; Col. 3:5). *Appetite* or gluttony is also included under idolatry (Phil 3:19; comp. Rom. 16: 18; II Tim. 3:4). *See* Gods, False.

Idumae'a (ĭd-û-mē'á). In the A. V. of O. T. and Apocrypha, Idume'a (Gr. *pertaining to Edom*). This is a term employed by Greeks and Romans in a slightly different spelling for the country of Edom (Mark 3:8 and in A. V. only Isa. 34:5, 6; Ezek. 35:15; 36:5). After the Fall of Jerusalem (B. C. 587) the Edomites began to advance northward (Ezek. 36:5). By B. C. 312 the Nabataeans, who established themselves in Edom, drove them from Petra.

217. Amphitheater, Petra

The Edomites were gradually pushed into the southern half of Judea, including the region around Hebron, an area which the Greeks later called Idumaea. Judas Maccabaeus warred against them and a half-century later John Hyrcanus completely subdued them and imposed the rite of circumcision, and invoked the old Jewish law of assembly (Deut. 23:7f). Julius Caesar in 47 B. C. appointed an Idumaean, Antipater, procurator of Judea, Samaria and Galilee. Herod, son of Antipater, was crowned king of the Jews in 37 B. C. When Titus besieged Jerusalem in 70 A. D. the Idumaeans joined the Jews in rebellion against Rome. Josephus says that 20,000 Idumaeans were admitted as defenders of the Holy City. Once within, they proceeded to rob and kill, but these traitors received the same fate as the few surviving Jews when Rome took over Jerusalem. Idumaea, or Edom, ceased to be. Gen. 27:40 was fulfilled in the words of Jesus (Matt. 26:52). M. F. U.

I'gal (ī'gàl; He (God) redeems).

1. The son of Joseph, and agent from Issachar to spy the land of Canaan (Num. 13:7), B. C. 1441.

2. The son of Nathan of Zobah, and one of David's mighty warriors (II Sam. 23:36), B. C. about 962. In the parallel list (II Chron. 11:38) the name is given as "*Joel* the brother of Nathan."

3. *See* Igeal (I Chron. 3:22).

Igdali'ah (ĭg-dà-lī'à; *great is the Lord*), the father of Hanan, into the chamber of which latter Jeremiah brought the Rechabites to propose the test of their temperance (Jer. 35:4), B. C. about 600.

I'geal (ĭ'gê-àl; *He (God) redeems*), one of the

sons of Shemaiah, of the descendants of Zerubbabel (I Chron. 3:22), B. C. after 536.

Ignorance. The term implies *error, going astray* (Lev. 4:2, "If a soul sin through ignorance"). In the New Testament the Greek means *want of knowledge;* sometimes simple, excusable want of information (Acts 17:30); sometimes inexcusable (Eph. 4:18); sometimes moral blindness or *sinful* ignorance (Acts 3:17).

I'im (ī'ĭm; *heaps, ruins*).

1. A city in the extreme south of Judah (Josh. 15:29), and doubtless included within the territory of Simeon, as the associated places were (19:3). It is probably to be identified with the ruins of Deir el-Ghawi, near Umm Deimneh.

2. A contracted form (Num. 33:45) of *Ije-abarim* (q. v.).

I'je-ab'arim (ī'jĕ-ăb'á-rĭm; *ruins of Abarim*), the forty-seventh station of the Israelites in the wilderness, "in the borders of Moab" (Num. 33:44), or "before Moab, toward the sun-rising" (21:11).

I'jon (ī'jŏn; a *ruin*), a frontier town in the north of Palestine, in the hills of Naphtali—a store city. It was captured in the days of Asa by Benhadad (I Kings 15:20; II Chron. 16: 4), and later by Tiglath-pileser (II Kings 15:29). It is thought to be *el-Khîam*, in the fertile valley of Merj 'Ayûn (" the meadow of springs"), northwest of Dan.

Ik'kesh (ĭk'kĕsh; *crooked, perverse*), the father of Ira the Tekoite, which latter was one of David's famous warriors (II Sam. 23:26; I Chron. 11:28), and captain of the sixth regiment of his troops (I Chron. 27:9), B. C. 1000.

I'lai (ī'lâ-ī), an Ahohite, and one of David's heroes (I Chron. 11:29), called *Zalmon* in the parallel list (II Sam. 23:28), B. C. 1000.

Illuminated (from Gr. *phōtizō*, to *give light*), a term meaning imbued with a saving knowledge of the gospel, and so applied to Christians (Heb. 6:4, A. V. "enlightened"; 10:32). In the early Christian Church it was used to denote the baptized.

Illyr'icum (ĭ-lĭr'ĭ-kŭm), a region lying between Italy, Germany, Macedonia, and Thrace, having on one side the Adriatic Sea, and on the other the Danube. It answers to the present Dalmatia; by which name, indeed, the southern part of Illyricum itself was known, and whither Paul informs Timothy that Titus had gone (II Tim. 4:10). It is of uncertain dimensions, being understood differently by Greek and Roman writers. It is only once mentioned in the New Testament, and that simply as the extreme limit to which, in the direction of Rome, Paul carried the gospel message (Rom. 15:19). It is difficult to ascertain the exact meaning of this passage. The expression "round about" may be joined with Jerusalem, and signify its *neighborhood* (as Alford); or it may be joined with "unto Illyricum" and denote the *circuit* of the apostle's journey "as far as Illyricum," an expression warranted by the indefinite phrase of Luke, "those parts" (Acts 20:2).

Image, also rendered "graven image," "molten image," etc. *See* Idol.

Image, Nebuchadnez'zar's (Heb. *ṣĕlĕm*, a *resemblance*), Nebuchadnezzar saw in his dream a great metallic image which was terrible to look upon. It was not an idol image, but a *statue*, and from the description given was evidently in human form. The image appears divided as to its material into five parts—the head of fine gold, breast and arms of silver, the "belly (the abdomen) and thighs" (loins) of brass (i. e., copper), the legs with upper part of thighs of iron, and the feet of clay (Dan. 2:32, 33). Thus it will be seen the material becomes inferior from the head downward, finally terminating in clay. While Nebuchadnezzar was contemplating this image a "stone was cut out without hands," broke loose from the mountain, struck against the lowest part of the image, broke the whole of it into pieces, and ground all of its material to powder. The expression "without hands" signifies without human help.

Nebuchadnezzar's dream, as unravelled by Daniel, describes the course and end of "the times of the Gentiles" (Luke 21:24; Rev. 16: 19); that is, of the Gentile world power to be destroyed at the Second Coming of Christ. "The stone . . . cut out of the mountain without hands" symbolizes Christ returning as "King of Kings and Lord of Lords" to set up His millennial kingdom. The four empires represent Babylon, Media-Persia, Greece under Alexander, and Rome. The latter power is seen divided first into two legs, fulfilled in the eastern and western Roman Empires and then into ten toes (cf. Dan. 7:26). The ten-toed form will be the condition of Gentile world domination at the time of the returning Smiting Stone (Dan. 2:34, 35). The Gentile world system is destroyed by a sudden crushing blow, not by a gradual process. At the first advent of Christ neither the sudden crushing blow took place nor did the ten-toed condition occur. M. F. U.

In Dan. (ch. 3) is an account of a golden image set up by Nebuchadnezzar in the plain of Dura. It probably represented his patron god, Bel-Merodach, and adoration to it was a test of loyalty. As its height was out of proportion to its breadth (six cubits) ten to one, it is probable that a tall pedestal is included in its measurement.

Image of God. 1. **As Borne by Man** (Heb. *ṣĕlĕm, resemblance;* accompanied in Gen. 1:26; 5:1 by *dᵉmûth,* "likeness"). Attempts have been made by modern as well as ancient writers to base important distinctions upon the use of the two words. But such attempts are regarded generally as instances of overrefined or fantastic exegesis. The double expression is for the purpose of giving strength and emphasis to the idea of godlikeness in man as set forth in these passages. Likeness added to image tells us that the divine image which man bears is one corresponding to the original pattern.

The conception of man as created after the image of God is justly held to be of great importance, and fundamental in theology. It is foremost among the Bible representations of man; it is bound up in the account of his creation; it appears in striking relation elsewhere, sometimes with the same, at others with different expressions (Gen. 9:6; Psa. 8; James 3:9; Eph. 4:24; Col. 3:10; comp. Matt. 5:48; Luke 6:36; Acts 17:28, 29; I Pet. 1:15,

16; II Pet. 1:4, where the exalted capacity and nature of man are assumed).

Significance of the idea. This has been a favorite battleground of theologians, partly due to the brevity of the Scripture statements, and more largely to the different theological presuppositions with which the subject has been considered. An outline of the history of speculation, or of doctrine, upon this point cannot be given here. Evidently the Scriptures proclaim resemblance of some most important character between the constitution of man and the divine nature. The creature man is exalted above all the other creatures of the earth, as the account shows, in that he is a copy of the Creator. And, what is also of great moment, according to the representations of Scripture, this image survived the fall, and, though blurred, still exists. The sacredness of human life is based upon this fact (Gen. 9:6). The cursing tongue as well as the violent hand for the same reason must be restrained (James 3:9). As to the effect of the fall and man's sinful history upon God's image in man the Scriptures are almost wholly silent. Paul (Rom. 3:23) declares that "all have sinned and *come short* of the glory of God," a statement equivalent to saying that the glorious image is, because of sin, less than it once was, There are also recognitions of loss in this respect, through sin, where, in the famous passages Eph. 4:24; Col. 3:10, the apostle speaks of the "new man," or man's renewal. But, as the best theologians commonly agree, the representations of Scripture are such as to create the impression that in some lofty sense "the divine image is inalienable from man." As to what constituted this image originally, and as to what it still constitutes, it should be said that a too frequent mistake has been to concentrate attention upon some single feature instead of comprehending all those excellent characteristics, which, according to the Scriptures, belonged, or belong, to man, and which constitute his likeness to his Maker. Also the effort has been made to distinguish too sharply between that in the likeness which has been lost through sin and that which is permanent. Man's nature has generally suffered loss from sin, but even in those respects in which the loss has been greatest, "in righteousness and true holiness," the loss is not such but that, through grace, he is capable of divine renewal. With these preliminaries in view, the chief significance of the idea, or the contents of the divine image, may be summarized as follows: (1) *Spirituality.* Man's likeness to God is not, as some of the early Latin fathers fancied, a bodily likeness. "God is a Spirit." And the first great point of resemblance between man and his Creator is found in man's spiritual nature. His life is inbreathed from God—a distinguishing fact in his creation (see Gen. 1:7; Job 32:8). With this stands connected the fact of man's immortal nature and destiny, for God is "the Eternal Spirit." The general teaching of Scripture is that this feature survives. (2) *Personality.* God is a person; he is conscious of his own existence. He is the Supreme Intelligence. He is free. Man is also self-conscious; is endowed with intelligence, **rationality,** and freedom. And at this point,

despite sin, still may be discerned in man wonderful vestiges of his inherent greatness and likeness to the divine. (3) *Holiness.* God is the Holy One. Man was created pure, with no inherent tendency to sin; not with such righteousness as must be developed and confirmed by habitual practice of good, but still with such positive qualities in his nature that he was "after the image and likeness" of the righteous and holy God. (4) *Love.* "God is love." The cardinal virtue, or moral excellence, proclaimed for man in the Scriptures is love. Man originally bore and again may bear the divine likeness in this respect. But here, as elsewhere, we see the necessity for restoration. (5) *Dominion.* God is sovereign. He created man to rule (see Gen. 1:26; Psa. 8:6; et al.). Whether the place assigned to man in the creation is to be considered a feature of his likeness to the divine, or, in the consequence of that likeness, is a question that has been much discussed. The latter is the more exact view, as reference is here to his position rather than to his nature. And yet man's royalty in the natural world is still so great that it must suggest his original complete fitness for it. For related topics, *see* Righteousness, Original; Sin, Original; Grace; Immortality.

2. **Christ the Image of God.** In two passages of the New Testament Christ is thus designated. In Col. 1:15 he is "the image of the invisible God;" in Heb. 1:3 he is "the brightness of God's glory," "the express image of his person" (comp. John 1:1; 17:25, 26).

Ellicott well remarks, "The Son is the Father's image in all things, save only in being the Father." Christ has appeared in the world as the perfect manifestation of God. And that he called himself "the Son of man" is not opposed to this fact. For if man in his original state bore the divine image, certainly he must bear it who is not only perfect in his human nature, but is also the "only begotten Son" of God. What this designation of Christ may convey to us as to the eternal relations between the Father and the Son is a deep matter which cannot here be considered. But it should be noted that this "second man," this "Lord from heaven," this eternal "Word," this "image of the invisible God," appears in the New Testament as the Author of salvation. And, besides, the end of this salvation is conformity to his image. In the Old Testament man appears created after the image of God; in the New "the Son is the prototype of redeemed or renewed humanity" (see Rom. 8:29; Col. 3:10, 11; comp. Rom. 8:19 with I John 3:2; Phil. 3:21; II Cor. 3:18; I Cor. 15:47, 49).

Literature.—See Van Oosterzee, *Dogmatics,* vol. 1, p. 359, sq; Especially valuable. Laidlaw, *Bible Doctrine of Man.* See also Martensen, *Christian Dogmatics,* 136-141; Wuttke, *Christian Ethics,* vol. i, 37, sq.; Oehler, *Theologie des Alten Testaments,* 219, sq.—E. McC.

Image Worship. *See* Idol; Idolatry.

Imagery (Heb. *măskîth,* an *image* Lev. 26:1; *picture,* Num. 33:52). "The chambers of his imagery" is an expression found in Ezek. 8:12, in the description given by the prophet of the vision shown him of the Temple. The prophet appears to have been conducted out of the inner court through its northern gate into the outer court and placed in front of the northern gate, which led into the open air. There was a hole in the wall, and on breaking through the wall, by the command of God, he came to a door. Entering it, he saw all kinds of figures of animals portrayed on the wall of the rooms; in front of these seventy of the elders of Israel were standing and praying reverence to the images of the beasts with burning incense. The vision was a revelation of what was going on through the whole of Israel. The secret chamber is figurative of the idolatry secretly practiced by the people; the number, seventy, represents the whole nation. The picture on the walls, representing animal worship, showed the great degradation of the nation's religion, which was justified by the elders under the delusion that "The Lord seeth not; the Lord hath forsaken the earth;" that is to say, not that "He does not trouble himself about us, but that he does not know what we do; and has withdrawn his presence and help." Thus they denied God's omniscience and omnipresence. "Chambers of imagery" is a term applied to the rooms or closets in the homes of the people in which idolatrous images were set up and worshiped.

Imagination is the image-making, pictorial faculty of the mind, reproducing and recombining former thoughts and experiences. It illustrates, adorns, and illuminates our speech and writing by presenting new views and applications of things, truths, and conceptions. It is the artist's great qualification, and the supreme talent of the inventor, finding expression in painting and sculpture, new machinery, architecture, landscape gardening, etc.

Imagination is the rendering of the Heb. *sh⁽e⁾rîrûth, firmness*, generally in a bad sense, i. e., *hardness of heart* (Deut. 29:19; frequently in Jeremiah); *yēṣĕr, form, conception* (Gen. 6:5; 8:21; Deut. 31:21, etc.); Gr. *dialogismos, deliberating with one's self* (Rom. 1:21); *dianoia, way of thinking* (Luke 1:51).

Im'la (ĭm'lä; *full*), the father of Micaiah, which latter was the prophet who ironically foretold the defeat of the allied kings of Judah and Israel against Ramoth-gilead (II Chron. 18: 7, 8). In the parallel passage (I Kings 22:8, 9) his name is written *Imlah*.

Im'lah (ĭm'lä; I Kings 22:8, 9). See Imla.

Imman'uel (ĭm-măn'ū-ĕl). See Emmanuel.

Immateriality, not consisting of matter. This quality is predicated of God and the human soul. "Finite and passive matter, with its divisibility, is not in his essence. The absolute Being is thoroughly one with itself, and is not composite; the composite is divisible, the divisible is finite and material; thus all this cannot be applied to God" (Dorner, *Christ. Doctrine*, i, 238). God is also free from the limitations to which matter is subject, i. e., from the limits of space and time. The immateriality of God is therefore the basis of the qualities of eternity, omnipresence, and unchangeableness.

The immateriality of the soul includes simplicity as another of its qualities, but it is not superior to the limitations of space and time, since the soul needs the body as a necessary organ of its life.

Im'mer (ĭm'ẽr; *sheep, lamb*), the name of several priests.

1. The father of Meshillemith (I Chron. 9: 12), or Meshillemoth (Neh. 11:13), some of whose descendants took a conspicuous part in the sacred duties at Jerusalem after the exile. His descendants, to the number of one thousand and fifty-two, returned from Babylon with Zerubbabel (Ezra 2:37; Neh. 7:40). He is probably the one some of whose descendants divorced their Gentile wives (Ezra 10:20), B. C. long before 536. By some he is identified with Nos. 4 and 5.

2. A priest in the time of David, and head of the sixteenth sacerdotal division (I Chron. 24:14).

3. One who accompanied Zerubbabel from Babylon, but was unable to prove his Israelitish descent (Ezra 2:59; Neh. 7:61), B. C. 536. "It does not clearly appear, however, that he claimed to belong to the priestly order, and it is possible that the name is only given as that of a place in the Babylonish dominions from which some of those named in the following verses came" (McC. and S., s. v.).

4. The father of Zadok, which latter repaired part of the walls of Jerusalem (Neh. 3:29), B. C. before 445.

5. The father of Pashur, which latter "smote Jeremiah the prophet, and put him in the stocks" (Jer. 20:1, 2), B. C. before 605.

Immortality, "Exemption from death and annihilation;" with reference to man, unending personal existence beyond the grave.

Viewed strictly, the idea of man's future life is not altogether identical with that of his immortality. And yet practically the question, "If a man die shall he live again?" covers the whole matter.

1. Scripture Doctrine. (1) **The Old Testament.** The idea of individual immortality is not as prominently and emphatically set forth in the Old Testament as in the New, it being the purpose and method of the Old Testament writers to present, not so much the contrast between the present and the future, as that between the chosen people and the heathen nations. It is national life, and not that of individuals, which occupies the foremost place. Nevertheless, the assertion, made even by certain Christian writers, that the doctrine of the future life is not taught in the Old Testament Scriptures, is unwarranted. And the supposition, which has sometimes been entertained, that the patriarchs and prophets and the Jewish people generally held no such doctrine is unreasonable and opposed to fact. It is to ascribe to them lower views of man's nature and future destiny than prevailed among the nations with which they came in contact. It is to regard the recipients and custodians of special revelation as less enlightened than others to whom such privileges had not been afforded. That the Jews, with the exception of the Sadduces, universally believed in man's immortal nature when Christ came is beyond dispute. And there is sufficient evidence to show that such had been their belief during the preceding centuries of their history. For example, such common expressions as "Was gathered unto his people," and the prohibition of necromancy, or invocation of the dead, clearly testify to the popular Hebrew belief in continued conscious existence beyond the grave. If the number of passages in the Old Testament explicitly affirming this doctrine is not large it should not, therefore, be a matter of cavil. The fact of life after death is taken for granted. Its recognition pervades the general drift or spirit of these ancient Scriptures. Thus man is represented as created in the image of God, and therefore a creature whose chief existence is spiritual, and not to be obliterated by the death of the body. His highest good is constantly set before us, as found in the divine favor and fellowship. All temporal good is insignificant in comparison with this. "The prosperity of the wicked" is not to be envied, because of the "end" which is understood in "the sanctuary." In the same place of clear and holy light is seen the contrasted condition and prospect of the righteous. "I am continually with thee; thou hast holden me by my right hand. Thou shalt guide me by thy counsel and afterward receive me to glory" (Psa. 73). Thus the whole drift or tendency is to turn the thoughts of the people from the present toward the future. And besides there are several places in the Old Testament where the doctrine of a future life is plainly asserted. The sixteenth psalm, especially as connected with the apostolic comments (Acts 2:27; 13:35) is a case in point (see also Psa. 17:15; Isa. 26:19; Dan. 12:2, 3).

(2) **The New Testament.** In II Tim. 1:10 Paul speaks of Christ "who hath abolished death, and brought life and immortality to light through the Gospel." Literally the phrase "brought to light" means "has illuminated," or "shed light upon." It is certainly not implied here that the doctrine of immortality was unknown to the world before Christ came. For some sort of belief in that doctrine had been common, if not universal, among the Gentile nations, as well as among the Jews. It means that "the Gospel pours light upon and discloses the author, origin, and true nature of life and immortality to our view" (see Whedon, *Com.*, on above passage). It should be added that, not only among the Jews, some, particularly the Sadducees, had cast away the belief and hope of a future life, but also false philosophy and prevailing corruption had weakened or destroyed the faith of many among the Gentiles. The mission of Christ, therefore, was not only to "shed light upon immortality" by means of definite and authoritative instruction, but also by his life and death and resurrection to make it possible for men to attain to an immortality that should be blessed. Accordingly, we find explicit utterances from Christ in large number with respect to this subject. He argued with the Sadducees against their unbelief. And his argument is significant as showing, not only Christ's own affirmation of a future deathless life, but also his affirmation of that doctrine as taught in the Old Testament (*see* Luke 20:27-38). He taught the doctrine plainly; he illustrated it by parables; it ran as a solemn undertone through all his teachings (*see* Matt. 5:12; 8:11, 12; 12:32; 13:36, 43; 18:8, 9; 22:11-13; 25:1-13, 31-46; Mark 8:35-37;

Luke 12:4, 5; 13:24-29; 16:19-31; 18:29, 30; John 3:16; 5:39, 40; 6:47-58; 10:28; 11:25; 14:1-6, et al.). It should be noted that in the passages referred to Christ speaks of the future, not only of the righteous, but also of the wicked; also, that he speaks of a blessed immortality as attainable only through himself. The teachings of the apostles, as found in other parts of the New Testament, are as we might expect, equally explicit with those of Christ. It is unnecessary to cite illustrations. As it has well been said, "The obligation which even in this respect the world owes to the Gospel of the Cross is one which cannot be overrated" (Van Oosterzee).

2. **Theological.** The prevalent and almost unvarying faith of the Christian Church has been in harmony with the teachings of the Holy Scriptures in holding to endless future life, not only for the righteous, but also for the wicked. In early Church history, however, there are a few traces, or isolated examples, of what has come to be known as the doctrine of conditional immortality. By this is meant not only the immortal blessedness, but also immortality itself is to be won by the saving union with Christ. Man is not by nature immortal; he becomes immortal upon the condition that he receives a new and spiritual life. The fate of the wicked accordingly will be annihilation (see Hagenbach, *Hist. of Doctrine*, vol. 2, p. 16). This view has been promulgated in some measure in recent times in England and in this country. The chief objections to it, and which must make it untenable, are that it loses sight of the inherent dignity of human nature, and is opposed also by those teachings of the Scripture which represent the punishment of the wicked as of equal duration with the reward of the righteous. See Annihilation; Punishment, Future.

From the standpoint of theology immortality is not a doctrine that requires scientific proof. It belongs to the realm of faith; and here, as elsewhere, faith may rest upon the revelation of God. Doubts have often been expressed by theologians as to whether reason alone can furnish satisfactory proof of that doctrine. And it is generally admitted that in an exact or scientific way it cannot be demonstrated. Nevertheless, while not conclusive, some of the arguments commonly adduced are of recognized force, as, e. g., the *teleological*, viz., That the mental capacities are fitted for a larger development than is afforded by the imperfect conditions of the present life, and therefore we may reasonably expect a future field for their exercise and expansion; also the *historical*, the general and enduring belief in a future state of rewards and punishments, as manifesting a correspondence between such belief and the essential features of human nature. The words of Plato may be regarded as applicable to this whole class of arguments, where, in a passage of the *Phoedo*, he makes one of the speakers to say that if a man can do no better on a matter of such practical importance as faith in the future world "he ought to choose out the best and most irrefragable human opinion about it, and upon that, like a mariner on a raft, risk his way through the storms of life, unless he can proceed more easily and safely on the more sure vehicle of some divine word."

Belief in immortality is most secure when united with a living faith in God; and that must mean God as revealed in the Holy Scriptures. With the right conception of God as a starting point theologians bring forward considerations of the utmost importance. We present at this point, in somewhat condensed form, the argument of Van Oosterzee: "The recognition of God's *supremacy* excludes the representation that man might by a voluntary deed entirely annihilate himself, and thus after the greatest misdeeds withdraw himself from the hands of the Supreme Judge. God's *justice* demands that the balance between virtue and happiness should not only be preserved and restored in secret, but should be revealed and maintained in the sight of all; this certainly is not done, or is only imperfectly effected, on this side of the grave. . . . The *holiness* of God requires that we should choose the good unconditionally, even before life itself; this requirement would be unreasonable, and self-denial would be alike a crime and folly if it led to self-annihilation. The *wisdom* of God would not have provided man with a preeminent moral disposition if the term of his existence had been limited to this life. It is the most highly developed minds which find themselves here least satisfied, and who at their highest attainment would desire to be able to begin, not only once again, but even in an infinitely better way. . . . The *goodness* of God, finally, would not have implanted so deeply in our hearts this desire for continuance if that desire must continue unsatisfied forever. The fear of death makes man much more unhappy than the beast if there be no immortality. . . . The satiety of life, which is observable in some people, does not prove the contrary, since it is just the opposite of real satisfaction. Men are satiated with this form of life because they have not found *life* in it; they are satiated with the *esse*, not with the *vivere*, which is the highest aspiration of the soul. Here, if anywhere, the aspiration proves the reality of the object of desire" (see Van Oosterzee's *Dogmatics*, vol. i, pp. 371, 372). Van Oosterzee adds: "Still this only becomes infallibly *certain* when the believer is conscious of his life in personal communion with God."

The philosophic treatment of the doctrine, also the history of the belief in immortality, do not come within the scope of this article, and accordingly are only dealt with incidentally. E. McC.

Literature.—The literature of this subject is most abundant. In addition to works referred to we cite a few others of special importance: Laidlaw, *Bible Doctrine Concerning Man;* Channing, *Works*, iv, p. 169; Chalmer, *Works*, x, 415; Alger, *Critical History of the Doctrine of a Future Life;* L. S. Chafer, *Systematic Theology*, II, 152-53, 155; VII, 190-191. Hodge, *Systematic Theology*, iii, 716, sq.; A. H. Strong, *Systematic Theology*, 984-997; Seeberg, *History of Doctrines* cf. index; Addison, *Life Beyond Death in the Beliefs of Mankind.*

Immutability, the divine attribute of unchangeableness. The Scripture declarations of this attribute are most clear and emphatic. It is indicated in the title under which God made himself known to Moses, "I Am," "I Am That I Am" (*see* Exod. 3:14; Num. 23:19; 32:11; 102:25-27; Mal. 3:6; James 1:17).

From this it is to be understood that God is eternally the same in his essence, in the mode of his existence, in his perfections, in the principles of his administration.

This attribute is essential to deity. To think of God otherwise than unchangeable is to think of him otherwise than perfect.

Immutability is not, however, to be confounded with immobility. God acts, and his actions vary with reference to different ends. His affections toward the same persons change according to the changed attitude of those persons toward him. Thus, according to the representations of Scripture, the God who "is not man that he should repent" nevertheless does "repent," an accommodation of language to express the truth above stated. In reality such changes in the divine operations and affections are illustrations of the fact and character of divine immutability (*see* Num. 23:19; Psa. 90:13; Jonah 3:9, 10; Ezek. 33:7-19).

The proper conception of God's unchangeableness is to be derived only from the Scriptures, and the sublimity of the conception therein given is one of the indications of divine revelations (see Van Oosterzee's *Christ. Dogmatics*, vol. i, p. 257, sq.; Watson's *Institutes*, vol. i, 398, sq.; and other works of systematic theology).—E. McC.

Im'na (Ĭm'nà; *he will restrain*), one of the sons, apparently, of Helem, the brother of Shamer, a descendant of Asher (I Chron. 7:35; comp. v. 40).

Im'nah (Ĭm'nà; cf. Arab. *yumnah, good luck, fortune*).

1. The first named of the sons of Asher (I Chron. 7:30), called *Jimnah* in Gen. 46:17; B. C. about 2000.

2. The father of Kore, which latter, a Levite, had charge of the east gate of the temple, and was appointed by Hezekiah over the freewill offerings (II Chron. 31:14), B. C. c. 715.

Importunity (Gr. *anaideia*, from Homer down, *shamelessness, impudence*), spoken of an importunate man, persisting in his entreaties (Luke 11:8; comp. Luke 18:1; I Thess. 5:17).

Imposition of Hands. See Hands, Imposition of.

Impotent. *See* Diseases.

Imprecation. *See* Curse.

Imprecatory Psalms. *See* Psalms.

Impurity. *See* Uncleanness.

Imputation is one of the major doctrines of Christianity. It has produced a great deal of theological controversy (see Hagenbach and Shedd, *History of Doctrine*). The actual word *impute* means to "reckon over unto one's account." The case of the Apostle's writing to Philemon concerning whatever his runaway slave Onesimus might owe him gives a perfect Scriptural illustration of the meaning of the word: "Put that on mine account" (Phil. 1:18). Three major imputations are expounded in Scripture:

1. **Of Adam's sin to the race.** This is the clear teaching of Rom. 5:12-21. Verse 12 clearly indicates that death has come upon

all men "because all men sinned." The tense of *sinned* is the aorist and does not therefore concern the sin of men in their daily experience. But the passage clearly indicates that all men sinned when Adam sinned and thereby incurred the penalty of physical death upon themselves as a consequence. In demonstrating that this passage does not have reference to personal sins, we call attention to the Apostle's observation that between the time of Adam and Moses, before the Mosaic law was instituted, all died. Likewise all irresponsible persons such as infants and imbeciles died, although they were never guilty of willful sin as in the case of Adam. Many theologians object to this teaching of real imputation; that is, of reckoning to each person that which is antecedently his own. But Scripture furnishes a close parallel in the record of Levi, who was supported by tithes and is specifically said to have paid tithes while being in the loins of his great-grandfather, Abraham (Heb. 7:9, 10), that is, when Abraham paid tithes to Melchizedek.

2. Of the sin of the human race to Christ. This involves a judicial imputation inasmuch as the sin was never antecedently Christ's, and when laid upon Him became His in a fearful sense. In this grand fact the truth of the gospel lies. Although the theological term *impute* is not employed with regard to the laying of the sin of Adam's race upon the Sinbearer, the idea is obviously contained in such expressions as "laid on Him the iniquity of us all," "Who bore our sins," "made Him to be sin" (Isa. 53:5, 6; I Pet. 2:24; II Cor. 5:21).

3. Of the righteousness of God to the believer. The great theme of the Book of Romans has to do with the doctrinal expression of imputation of the righteousness of God to the believer as it pertains to his salvation. It is quite obvious, therefore, that this truth is of great consequence to the Christian's salvation. The Pauline epistles in general clearly show that this phase of imputation is the groundwork of the Christian's acceptance and standing before an infinitely holy God. Only this righteousness can find acceptance for salvation and through it alone one may enter heaven. The pregnant phrase "*the righteousness of God*" (Rom. 1:17; 3:22; 10:3) signifies not merely that God Himself is righteous but that there is a righteousness which proceeds from God. Since no human being in God's eyes is righteous (Rom. 3:10), it is clear that an imputed righteousness, the very righteousness of God Himself, is sinful man's only hope of acceptance with the Holy One. Possessing this righteousness is the only thing that fits one for the Presence of God (Col. 1:12; Phil. 3:9). When this righteousness is imputed by God to the believer, it becomes his forever by a judicial act, since it was not antecedently the believer's. It is thus patent that this demands a righteousness which is made over to the believer, just as Christ was made to be sin for all men (II Cor. 5:21). By the believer's baptism by the Spirit "into Christ" this righteousness is made a legal endowment by virtue of the death of Christ. Indeed, imputed righteousness becomes a reality on the basis of the fact

that the believer is "in Christ." As hitherto one was "in Adam" (Rom. 5:12-21), so by the Spirit's baptism (Rom. 6:3, 4) he is now placed in the resurrected Christ and is a recipient of all that Christ is, even of the "righteousness of God" which Christ is. It is a transcendent truth that Christ is made to the believer the "righteousness of God" (I Cor. 1:30), and being "in Christ" the believer is "made" the righteousness of God (II Cor. 5:21). The glory of this "in Christ" position is beyond description or human comprehension "for by one offering He hath perfected forever them that are sanctified" (Heb. 10:14). The "fulness of Christ" (John 1:16; Col. 1:19; 2:9, 10) becomes the believer's portion in Christ, "for in Him dwells all the fullness of the Godhead bodily, and ye are complete in Him . . ." The basis of the legality of such imputation, resulting in such a position for the believer, resides in the fact that Christ offered Himself without spot to God (Heb. 9:14). This means that Christ not only was made a sin offering, but His death (by which remission of sin is made legally possible on the basis that He substituted for those who believe, and presented Himself as an offering well-pleasing to God) also made possible a release of all that He is in infinite merit, bestowing this merit on the meritless. When others did not possess and could not gain a standing and merit before God, He released His own Self in infinite perfection for them. As the cross furnishes the legal basis for the remission of sin, so it furnishes likewise the legal basis for the imputation of righteousness. Both aspects of a sweet savor and a non-sweet savor in the estimation of the Father are typically expounded in the five offerings of Lev. 1-5. There was that in the death of Christ which was a non-sweet savor to God manifested in the terrible words, "My God, My God, why hast Thou forsaken Me?" (Psa. 22:1; Matt. 27:46). The character of the perfect, sinless Lamb of God (Heb. 9:14) suggests the sweet-savor aspect. Thus the sweet savor aspect of Christ's offering and its accomplishment in the believer by his union with Christ through the work of the Holy Spirit is the legal ground for the imputation of God's righteousness to the believer. Foundational to essential Christian teaching and the essence of the gospel are these three imputations. They are typical in the Mosaic system; antitypical in the Christian era. *M. F. U.* (*See* Atonement, Faith, Justification, Grace, Gospel, Righteousness, Sanctification). (Lit., A. A. Hodge, *Outlines of Theology*, 348-366; 407-08; 501, 502; L. S. Chafer, *Systematic Theology* II, 296-315; III, 243-244; V, 143-144; VII, 191-194; A. H. Strong, *Systematic Theology*, 593-637).

Im'rah (ĭm'rá; *he*, i. e., God, *resists*), one of the sons of Zophah, of the tribe of Asher (I Chron. 7:36). *See* Hotham.

Im'ri (ĭm'rī).

1. The son of Bani and father of Omri of Judah (I Chron. 9:4), B. C. before 536.

2. The father of Zaccur, which latter repaired part of the wall of Jerusalem (Neh. 3:2), B. C. before 445.

Inability. Scripture represents fallen man as utterly lost and unable to please God or to save himself. The divine revelation is that God hath concluded both Jew and Gentile under sin (Rom. 3:9). God's final verdict is the whole world is guilty before Him (Rom. 3:9-20). Justification by faith in Christ crucified is the one and only remedy for sinners (Rom. 3:21-5:11). God enables men to believe; and when they believe they receive a new life and a new nature, in addition to the indwelling Spirit which imparts the dynamic for holy living and serving well pleasing to God. *M. F. U.*

Incantation. *See* Magic.

Incarnation (Lat. *in* and *caro,* "flesh"), the act of assuming flesh; in theology, the gracious voluntary act of the Son of God in assuming a human body and human nature.

1. **The Christian Doctrine** of the incarnation, briefly stated, is that the Lord Jesus Christ is one person with two natures indissolubly united, the one nature being that of the eternal Son of God, the other that of man, in all respects human, "yet without sin." It includes the miraculous conception and birth of Christ. The incarnation is absolutely without parallel in history. The fabled incarnations of pagan religions are at most only indications of the vague longing of humanity for union with the divine, and are thus in some sense imaginative anticipations of the Christian reality. The incarnation is also to be distinguished from theophanies, or those appearances of a divine person in human form (often bearing the title "the Angel of Jehovah"), of which the Old Testament gives instances (see Gen. 33:24-30; Exod. 3:2-7; 14:19; Josh. 5:13-15; 6:1; Judg. 6:11-22; Dan. 3:25). These are to be regarded as preintimations, or occasional prophetic manifestations of that which was to be permanently realized in Christ (*see* Theophanies).

2. **Scripture Teachings.** In addition to the gospel record of the miraculous conception and birth of Christ (see Luke 1:26-35; 2:1-14, comp. with Matt. 2:1-15), the Scriptures disclose this doctrine in several ways.

(1) **Old Testament.** In the Old Testament prophecies, which represent Christ as a person both human and divine, he is set forth in "the seed of the woman," a descendant of Abraham, of Judah, and of David, "a man of sorrows." But he is also called "the mighty God," "the everlasting Father," "the Son of God," "the Lord (Jehovah) our righteousness." While these familiar Scriptures do not formally state the doctrine of the incarnation, they logically suggest, or lead up to it.

(2) **New Testament.** Also in the New Testament there are many passages which present the elements of this doctrine separately—Christ is represented as a man, with a human body and a rational human soul; physically and mentally he is truly human. The designation "the Son of man" occurs more than eighty times in the gospels. But elsewhere this same person claims for himself, and has ascribed to him, the attribute of Deity. For Scripture reference *see* Humanity and Divinity of Christ.

(3) There are numerous instances in which these two elements of Christ's personality are combined in the statement, or in which they are brought without hesitation or reserve close together (e. g., Matt. 11:8; 16:27; 22:42-45; 25:31-46; Mark 14:60-64; Luke 9:43, 44; John 3:31; Rom. 5:15, 21; I Cor. 15:47).

(4) While the doctrine does not rest for its authority upon isolated proof-texts, but rather upon the Scripture revelation as a whole, still there are certain utterances of great weight in which the truth is distinctly, and we may say even formally, stated (*see* John 1:1-14, comp. I John 1:1-3; 4:2, 3; Rom. 1:2-5; Phil. 2:6-11; I Tim. 3:16; Heb. 2:14). The only way in which the force of these teachings can be set aside or lessened is by proving lack of authority on the part of the Scriptures. It should be added that the only way in which the Scriptures can be understood or intelligently interpreted is in the light of the essential facts of the incarnation.

3. **Theological Development of the Doctrine.** The early centuries of the history of the Church were marked in an unusual degree by speculations concerning the person of Christ. The representation of Scripture raised many questions among thinkers, and led to numerous attempts to give scientific form and elaborateness to the doctrine of the incarnation. These speculations were affected in some instances by Jewish opinions and prejudices held by members of the Christian communion, but more frequently by one form or another of pagan philosophy. It is not surprising, therefore, that various styles of error, heresies which became historic, appeared, and were overthrown, during those centuries. Among the prominent heresies were the following, viz.:

(1) **Ebionism,** or the doctrine of the Ebionites, a Jewish sect which existed even in the time of the apostles. This error arose from mistaken Jewish preconceptions concerning the Messiah, and consisted in the denial of the divine nature of Christ.

(2) **Gnosticism,** a name indicating the assumption of superior capacity for knowledge (Gr. *gnōsis,* "knowledge"). Gnosticism in its diverse forms received its impulse, and in the main its guidance, from pagan philosophy. In different ways it denied the humanity of Christ, even to the extent of denying the reality of his human body.

(3) **Sabellianism,** which at bottom was a denial of the tri-personality of God, denied, accordingly, the existence of the Son of God, as a distinct person, before the incarnation. The union between the divine and human natures in Christ was held to be but temporary.

(4) **Arianism** denied that the Son was of the same essence with the Father, but held that the essence in both was similar. Hence the conclusion reached that Christ was created, though the greatest of all creatures. In connection with this heresy was the fierce contention over *homoousios,* "same substance," and *homoiousios,* "similar substance," a discussion to which uninformed persons, who do not realize the importance of the issue involved, sometimes sneeringly refer.

(5) **Apollinarianism,** resting upon the Platonic distinction between body, soul, and spirit, as three distinct elements in man, viewed Christ as having a human body and soul, or animal life, but not a human spirit,

the seat of rationality and intelligence. Instead of the latter was the divine nature of Christ. Thus Christ was not completely human.

The study of the heresies of early Church history is especially valuable because the errors of modern times, as Socinianism, Unitarianism, and Rationalism, are simply these ancient and oft-refuted heresies revived. It would be a mistake to suppose that during those centuries the faith of the Christian Church was reduced to confusion. It has been said with much force, "The faith of the common people is determined by the word of God, by the worship of the sanctuary, and by the teachings of the Spirit. They remain in a great measure ignorant of, or indifferent to, the speculations of theologians. It cannot be doubted that the great body of the people from the beginning believed that Christ was truly a man, was truly God, and in one person" (Hodge, vol. ii, p. 398). Nevertheless, it is to be remembered that systematic treatment of this great subject was indispensable, not only to meet the demands of the most thoughtful minds, but also to afford guidance to the popular teachings of the Church; especially to prevent such teachings departing from the truth revealed in the Holy Scriptures. The discussions of the early period of the Church practically determined in its general form the faith of Christendom as to the person of Christ for all the centuries that have followed. At present the question is more frequently asked by theologians than formerly "whether the Son of God would still have become incarnate had not sin entered the world." By some it is held that the Son held such an original relation to man that incarnation would have taken place even then as an event essential to man's attainment of his high destiny, though not of course under circumstances of humiliation. For judicious treatment of this not simply curious question the reader is referred to Van Oosterzee's *Christian Dogmatics*, vol. i, p. 298, sq. Also, the significance of the phrase used by Paul (Phil. 2:7, *heauton ekenōse*, properly rendered in the R. V. "emptied himself") is at present receiving unusual attention, though much discussed as "a most profound question" centuries ago. In considering this *kenosis*, or self-abnegation on the part of the Son of God, the correct distinction appears to be that between the *possession* and the *use* of the divine attributes. The laying aside of the possession conflicts with the idea of the divine immutability. That Christ did not use or exercise his divine properties in their fullness during his humiliation is evident from the Scriptures. His power to work miracles was never exerted for himself, but often for others. He bore "the form of a servant." He admitted, asserted, a limitation to his knowledge in one respect (see Mark 13:32), though manifesting and declaring himself possessed of divine knowledge in others (see Matt. 11:27; John 3:12, 13). But truly says Van Oosterzee, "The subject remains a divine mystery of which we cannot sound the depths, and can only approximately indicate the peculiar nature and meaning" (see Van Oosterzee's *Christian Dogmatics*, vol. ii, p. 543, sq.). *See* art. Kenosis.

4. **Theoretical and Practical Value of the Doctrine.** The doctrine of the incarnation is fundamental in Christian theology. In its light we find in Christ a new and the highest revelation of God; also a revelation of man in his original pure and perfect nature, most exalted and capable of union with God. The sinlessness of Christ, also his miraculous works, are here explained. Only thus can be reconciled the contrasting and seemingly contradictory facts of his earthly life; his human limitations on the one hand and the manifestation of divine attributes and the exercise of divine prerogatives (as in the forgiveness of sins) on the other. The atonement depends for its efficacy upon the fact that Christ was "God manifest in the flesh;" likewise the value of his intercession, his sympathetic relation to his people, and his power to impart to them a new and holy life, and bring them to everlasting exaltation and glory (see Heb. 2:9-18; 4:14-16; John 1:12; I John 1:4; 3:1-3). E. McC.

Literature.—In addition to works already cited, Dorner, *System of Christian Doctrine;* Watson, *Theological Institutes;* Shedd, *History of Doctrine;* Dorner, *History of the Doctrine of the Person of Christ;* Neander, *History of the Development of Christian Dogmas;* Gore, *The Incarnation of the Son of God;* Godet, *Commentary on St. Luke,* vol. 1, p. 151, sq.; Liddon, *The Divinity of our Lord,* § vii; C. A. Briggs, *The Incarnation of the Lord;* B. B. Warfield, *The Lord of Glory;* James Stalker, *The Christology of Jesus;* Chafer, *Systematic Theology* I, 348-64; V, 39-176.

Incense (Hebrew usually *qᵉṭōrĕth*, once applied to the *fat* of rams, the part always burned in sacrifice; once *qittēr*, Jer. 44:21, both from the Hebrew, to *smoke;* sometimes *lᵉbōnāh,* Isa. 43:23; 60:6; 66:3; Jer. 6:20; 17:26; 41:5, *frankincense*), an aromatic compound which gives forth its perfume in burning. Its most general use in Scripture is that perfume which was burned upon the Jewish altar of incense (*see* Tabernacle). Both among the Hebrews and Egyptians we find no other trace of incense than in its sacerdotal use, but in Persian sculptures we see it burned before the king.

1. **Material.** The incense employed in the service of the tabernacle was called *incense of the aromas* (Heb. *qᵉṭōrĕth sămmîm*), the ingredients of which are given in Exod. 30:34, 35. These consisted of: (1) *Stacte* (Heb. *nāṭāf*), i. e., "not the juice squeezed from the highly fragrant myrrh tree, but probably a species of *gum storax* resembling myrrh;" (2) *Onycha* (Heb. *shᵉḥĕlĕth,* literally, a *scale*), the shell of the perfumed mollusk, *blatta byzantina,* found in the Mediterranean and Red Seas, and yielding a musky odor when burned; (3) *Galbanum* (Heb. *ḥĕlbᵉnäh,* literally, *fat*), a gum that is obtained by making incisions in the bark of a shrub growing in Syria, Arabia, and Abyssinia; and (4) *Pure frankincense* (Heb. *lᵉbōnāh,* literally, *white*), a pale yellow, semitransparent, pungent resin, which, when burnt, is very fragrant, grown in Arabia and Judea.

2. **Preparation.** The A. V. says "of each there shall be a like *weight,*" i. e., equal parts of the various ingredients, but Abarbanel, Aben Ezra, and others think that the meaning is, each ingredient was, in the first place, to be

pounded by itself, and then mixed with the rest, for it is possible that the ingredients did not all admit of being pounded to the same extent. Besides, it was to be *salted* (A. V. "tempered"), was to be "pure and holy," i. e., unadulterated with any foreign substance, and was to be reserved exclusively for sacred use, any other application of it being forbidden on pain of being "cut off from his people."

3. **Sacred Use.** The person selected to burn incense upon the altar of incense was Aaron, but in the daily service of the second temple the office devolved upon the inferior priests, from among whom one was chosen by lot (Luke 1:9). Uzziah was punished for presuming to infringe upon this prerogative of the priests (II Chron. 26:16, 21). The times of offering incense were, in the morning, at the time of trimming the lamps, and in the evening, when the lamps were lighted (Exod. 30:7, 8). On the day of atonement (*see* Festivals) the high priest offered the incense.

4. **Figurative.** Incense in Scripture is the symbol of prayer. "Let my prayer be set before thee as incense" (Psa. 141:2; see Isa. 60:6). In Rev. 5:8; 8:3, 4 we meet with the same idea. But "it is not prayer alone that is expressed by incense. . . . A good or evil savor was to Israel the symbol of a good or godless life; and when, therefore, the sanctuary of God was kept continually filled with fragrance, they beheld in this the sweet savor, not of prayer alone, but of that life to which, as a priestly nation, they were called" (Dr. Wm. Milligan, *Bib. Ed.*, iii, 226, sq.). *See* Tabernacle; Temple.

Incest, the crime of cohabitation with a person within the degrees forbidden by the Levitical law (Lev. 18:1-18). The prohibition of incest and similar sensual abominations is introduced with a general warning as to the licentious customs of the Egyptians and Canaanites, and an exhortation to walk in the judgments and ordinances of Jehovah. Intercourse is forbidden (1) with a mother; (2) with a stepmother; (3) with a sister or half-sister; (4) with a granddaughter, the daughter of either son or daughter; (5) with the daughter of a stepmother; (6) with an aunt, sister of either father or mother: (7) with the wife of an uncle on the father's side; (8) with a daughter-in-law; (9) with a sister-in-law, or brother's wife; (10) with a woman and her daughter, or a woman and her granddaughter; (11) with the sister of a living wife. No special reference is made to sexual intercourse with a daughter, being a crime regarded as not likely to occur; with a full sister, i. e., the daughter of one's father and mother, being included in No. 3; or with a mother-in-law, included in No. 10. Those mentioned in Nos. 1, 2, 3, 8, and 10 were to be followed by the death of the criminals (Lev. 20:11, 12, 14, 17), on account of their being accursed crimes (Deut. 23:1; 27:20, 22, 23); while the punishment of those guilty of Nos. 6, 7, 9 was to bear their iniquity and die childless (Lev. 20:19-21). *See* Marriage.

Incontinency (Gr. *akrasia*, *want of self-control*, I Cor. 7:5; II Tim. 3:3), absence of that virtue which consists in restraining concupiscence.

Incorruption (Gr. *aphtharsia*, is applied to the body of a man as exempt from decay after the resurrection (I Cor. 15:42, 50, 53, 54).

In Rom. 2:7 and II Tim. 1:10 the Greek word is rendered *immortality*, and in Eph. 6:24, *sincerity*, R. V. *uncorruptness*. The crown of the saints is *incorruptible* (I Cor. 9:25), also their "inheritance" (I Pet. 1:4). The meaning is ever-enduring, unchanging.

Independence of God. God is absolute and not dependent upon any thing or person outside of himself for his existence. "His being and perfections are underived, and not communicated to him, as all finite perfections are by him to the creature." (1) He is independent as to his knowledge (Isa. 40:13, 14); (2) in power (Job 36:23); (3) as to his holiness, his bounty and goodness (Rom. 9:18).

India (Heb. *hōdū*), the limit of the territories of Ahasuerus in the east (Esth. 1:1; 8:9). The country so designated is not the peninsula of Hindustan, but the region through which the Indus River flowed—the Punjab.

Infant Baptism. *See* Baptism.

Infant Salvation. *See* Salvation.

Infinity, unlimited extent of space or duration or quantity. As designating an essential attribute of God the term refers to his unlimited existence, capacity, energy, and perfections.

The word infinity does not occur in the Scriptures, and yet, properly understood, it is an appropriate term, and necessary to express certain Scripture revelations concerning God. God is not subject to the limitations of time or space. Thus infinity expresses both his eternity and his immensity. Also his power and knowledge and other perfections exist in unlimited fullness.

This idea of God, necessary to our conception of him, can be held by us only in a negative form, this being due to the finite nature of our understanding. It is nevertheless a positive idea and represents the actual fact that God in his being and attributes transcends, not only our comprehension, but also all limits that must everywhere else be recognized. God is the only infinite existence.

Care must, however, be exercised not to conceive of the infinity of God in a material manner. God is the infinite Spirit. His presence pervades and fills all space, but not necessarily to the exclusion of other and finite existences. The mistake of Spinoza, and Pantheists generally, has been that of applying to God the material conception of infinity. And upon the principle of the impenetrability of matter, or that two bodies cannot occupy the same space at the same time, the conclusion has been reached that the being of God includes all things, or that all things are parts or manifestations of God. The idea of infinity brought forward by Mr. Mansel in *The Limits of Religious Thought* is also essentially of the same character, though he avoids the Pantheistic conclusion by appealing from philosophy to faith for the right conception of God. It must be borne in mind that the infinity of God is that of Spirit, and to spirit the ideas of extension and impenetrability do not apply, as they do to matter. And further, the infinite Spirit is necessarily one capable of creating finite existences. And withal there must ever be the proper acknowledgment of the incapacity of the human mind to argue adequately upon this and certain other subjects. E. McC.

For discriminating discussion see Pope's *Compend. of Christ. Theol.*, vol. i, p. 293, sq.; also Hodge's *System. Theol.*, vol. i, p. 380, sq.; L. S. Chafer, *System Theol.*, I, 215-16; VII, 199-200; A. H. Strong, *System. Theol.*, 275-295; A. A. Hodge, *Outlines of Theol.* 140f.

Infirmity (Heb. *măḥălāh*, Prov. 18:14; Gr. *astheneia, weakness or frailty* of body, A. V. *sicknesses*, Matt. 8:17; translated *weakness* in I Cor. 15:43; II Cor. 13:4). In Rom. 6:19, "*infirmity* of your flesh" means the weakness of human nature as respects understanding. Paul says in I Cor. 2:3; "I was with you in *weakness*," meaning inability to do great things, want of skill in speaking, or of human wisdom. In Heb. 5:2 and 7:28, the high priest is spoken of as "compassed with *infirmity*," which means tendency to sin, unlike our great High Priest. In Heb. 4:15; "We have not a high priest which cannot be touched with the feeling of our *infirmities*," it denotes all human disabilities. Also in Rom. 8:26 and II Cor. 12:5, 9. The Gr. *nosos*, is rendered *sickness, disease* (Luke 7:21, etc.). Matt. 8:17 contains both words. In Rom. 15:1 sins of *infirmity* are referred to, which are such as are attributable to excusable ignorance, unavoidable surprise, or constitutional weakness. *See* Diseases.

Inflammation. *See* Diseases.

Ingathering, Feast of. *See* Festivals. (Feast of Tabernacles).

Inheritance. The following laws prevailed among several nations:

1. **Greek.** If a person died intestate, leaving sons, all of equal birthright, and none of them disinherited, the sons inherited the property in equal parts, the eldest probably receiving the same as the rest. Daughters were provided with dowries, which went back to the remaining heirs in case the daughter was divorced or childless after marriage. If a man had no son, he usually adopted one to continue the family and its religious worship; and if he had daughters he would marry one of them to the adopted son, in which case the chief share of the inheritance fell to his daughter and her husband, the rest receiving dowries. If only daughters survived, the succession passed to them, and the next of kin had a legal right to one of the heiresses and could claim to marry her, even though she had married another before receiving the inheritance. A man marrying an heiress was bound by custom and tradition, if he had sons, to name one as heir to the property coming with his wife, and thus restore the house of his maternal grandfather. Children born out of wedlock were illegitimate, and had no claim to the estate of the father. If a man died intestate, leaving no heirs either of his body or adopted, his nearest relations in the male line inherited, and in default of these, those in the female line as far as children of first cousins.

2. **Roman.** If a man died intestate leaving a wife and children of his own body or adopted, they were his heirs; this did not apply, however, to daughters who had passed into the hands of their husbands, or of children who had been freed by emancipation from the power (*potestas*) of their father. If a man left no wife or children, the *agnati*, or relations of the male line, inherited, according to the de-

gree of their kinship. If there were no *agnati*, and the man was a patrician, the property went to his *gens*. The relations in the female line (*cognati*) were generally not entitled to inherit by the civil law.

3. **Hebrew.** The Hebrew institutions relative to inheritance were of a very simple character. Under the patriarchal system the property was divided among the sons of the legitimate wives (Gen. 2:10; 24:36; 25:5), a larger portion being assigned to one, generally the eldest, on whom devolved the duty of maintaining the females of the family. The sons of concubines were portioned off with presents (Gen. 25:6). At a later period the exclusion of the sons of unlawful wives was rigidly enforced (Judg. 11:1, sq.).

The possession of land, which Israel received by lot from God, was to remain the inalienable property of the several families. According to an old-standing custom, the father's property went to his sons, the firstborn receiving a double portion, the other sons single and equal portions—i. e., of five sons the firstborn got two sixths, and each of the others a sixth of the father's entire property. In consideration of this division, the firstborn, as head of the family, had to provide food, clothing, and other necessaries in his house, not only for his mother, but also for his sisters until their marriage. This custom was more precisely defined by Moses: the father could not deprive his firstborn of his birthright by mere caprice (Deut. 21:15-17), but it might be taken away because of a trespass against the father as, in the case of Reuben (Gen. 49:4; I Chron. 5:1). *See* Firstborn.

If there were no sons, it went to the daughters (Num. 27:8), on the condition that they did not marry out of their own tribe (Num. 36:6, sq.; Tob. 6:12; 7:13), otherwise the patrimony was forfeited. If there were no daughters, it went to the brother of the deceased; if no brother, to the paternal uncle; and, failing these, to the next of kin (Num. 27:9-11). In the case of a widow being left without children, the nearest of kin on her husband's side had the right of marrying her, and in the event of his refusal the next of kin (Ruth 3:12, 13); with him rested the obligation of redeeming the property of the widow (Ruth 4:1, sq.) if it had been either sold or mortgaged. If none stepped forward to marry the widow, the inheritance remained with her until her death, and then reverted to the next of kin. The land being thus so strictly tied up, the notion of *heirship*, as we understand it, was hardly known to the Jews.

TABLE SHOWING ORDER OF SUCCESSION AS HEIRS.

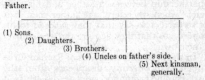

Father.
(1) Sons.
(2) Daughters.
(3) Brothers.
(4) Uncles on father's side.
(5) Next kinsman, generally.

If the testators were possessed of what we call *personal* property—i. e., flocks and herds, stores of change of raiment, precious metals, or jewels, which last, in oriental countries, is still the favorite mode of investment—the portions of the younger children, as well as gifts or dowers for the daughters, were usually provided from this source. The strict law of entail with regard to land did not at all fetter the testator in the disposition of his personal property. It was to this latter that the request of the younger son referred. He asked that the third part of the movable property, which would naturally come to him at his father's death, should be granted him now (Luke 15:12). Testamentary dispositions were of course superfluous. The references to wills (*q. v.*) in St. Paul's writings are borrowed from the usages of Greece and Rome, whence the custom was introduced into Judea.

Inheritance, Spiritual. "The metaphor of the spiritual 'inheritance' is peculiarly, though not exclusively, Pauline. St. Peter employs it twice (I Pet. 1:4; 3:9), St. James once (2:5), but St. Paul in a multitude of instances. It is closely interwoven with the substance of the longest and most intricate arguments in his epistles; it appears in the reports of his sermons in the Acts; he alone of all the sacred writers employs it in what may be described as the most daring of all theological conceptions—that which is embodied in the celebrated definition of believers as 'heirs of God and joint heirs with Christ.' To our minds heirship involves no more than the idea of the acquisition of property by succession, and the idea of succession is manifestly inapplicable with reference to the eternal God. That the heirship to which St. Paul alludes is Roman and not Hebrew, is evident not only from the accompanying reference to adoption, but also from the fact that it is a joint and equal heirship."

Sir Henry Maine writes (*Ancient Law*): "The notion (among the Romans) was that though the physical person of the deceased had perished, his legal personality had survived and descended unimpaired to his heirs or co-heirs, in whom his identity (so far as the law was concerned) was continued" (p. 181). "The testator lived on in his heir or in the group of his co-heirs. He was in law the same person with them" (Ibid., p. 188). "In pure Roman jurisprudence the principle that a man lives on in his heir—*the elimination, so to speak, of the fact of death*—is too obviously for mistake the center round which the whole law of testamentary and intestate succession is circling" (Ibid., p. 190). Contrary to the well-known maxim of English law, *Nemo est heres viventis* ("No one is heir of the living"), according to Roman law, the moment a child was born he was his father's heir. Paul the Jurist (3d century, A. D.) observes that there is a species of copartnership between a father and his children; "when, therefore, the father dies, it is not so correct to say that they succeed to his property, as that they acquire the free control of their own."

"In the light of the theories of Roman jurisprudence incongruity disappears from the great Pauline metaphor, and we discern in it a new sublimity. Instead of the death of the ancestor being essentially connected with the idea of inheritance, we find this circumstance 'eliminated.' The heir has not to wait for the

moment of his father's decease. In and through his father he is already a participator in the family possessions. The father does not die, but lives on forever in his family. Physically absent, he is spiritually present, not *with* so much as *in* his children. In this phrase, 'the heirs of God,' there is presented a most vivid view of the intimate and eternal union between the believer and God, and of the faithful soul's possession in present reality, and not merely in anticipation of the kingdom of God on earth and in heaven" (W. E. Ball, LL.D., *Mag. of Christ. Literat.*, p. 344, sq.).

Iniquity. 1. Heb. *'āwōn*, perversity, depravity, sin (Gen. 4:13, A. V. "punishment," etc.); guilt contracted by sinning (Exod. 20:5, etc.); anything unjustly acquired (Hos. 12:8); penalty of sin (Isa. 5:18); calamity, misery (Psa. 31:10). The Heb. is:

2. Heb. *'ĕwĕl* (Job 34:10) and Heb. *'āwălāh* (II Chron. 19:7), mean perverseness.

3. In the New Testament the Greek words are very expressive. Thus *adikia*, rendered "unrighteousness," "wrong," means "that which is not just" (Matt. 7:23, et al.), *anomia* and *paranomia*, "without law" and "transgression of law" (Matt. 23:28; II Thess. 2:7; II Pet. 2:16); while *ponēria* (Matt. 22:18; Luke 11:39; Rom. 1:29; I Cor. 5:8, etc.) signifies depravity, wickedness, malice.

In ordinary usage the term means absence of equity, wickedness, sin, etc.

Injuries. *See* Law, Offenses.

Ink (Heb. *d^eyō*, Jer. 36:18; Gr. *melan*, black, II Cor. 3:3; II John 12; III John 13). The ink of the ancients was composed of powdered charcoal, lampblack or soot, mixed with gum and water. It was intensely black and would retain its color for ages, but was easily erased from the parchments with sponge and water (see Num. 5:23, sq.). When needed for use some of the dry preparation was mixed with water until about the consistency of modern printer's ink. It was thus less adapted for rapid work than modern ink. Both the Egyptians and the Hebrews made use of different colors for writing, some of the books of the latter having been written, according to Josephus, in red, blue, purple, gold, and silver tints.

Ink-Horn (Heb. *qĕsĕth*, a round *vessel*). This consists of a long tube for holding pens, sometimes made of hard wood, but generally of metal—brass, copper, or silver. It is about nine or ten inches long, one and a half or two inches wide, and half an inch deep. To the upper end of this case the inkstand is attached. This is square or cylindrical, with a lid moving on hinges and fastening with a clasp. The inkhorn was carried in the girdle.

Inn (Heb. *mālōn*, Gen. 42:27; 43:21; Exod. 4:24, a "resting place for the night;" while the Gr. *kataluma*, is used for an "inn," Luke 2:7; an "eating room," A. V. *guest chamber*, Mark Mark 14:14; Luke 22:11). In the East hospitality was religiously observed, and therefore, in our sense of the term, inns were not known. Khans, or caravansaries, are the representatives of European inns, and were only gradually established. It is doubtful whether there is any allusion to them in the Old Testament, the meaning in Gen. 42:27; Exod. 4:

24; Jer. 9:2, being only the *station*, the place of rest for the night, either under a tent or in a cave. The first trace of an inn may be found in Jer. 41:17, "the habitation of Chimham" (Heb. *gērūth*), although this may simply be a proper name as the R. S. V. renders; "Geruth Chimham." The *pandocheion* (Luke 10:34) probably differed from the *kataluma* (Luke 2: 7) in having a "host" or "innkeeper" (Luke 10:35), who supplied some few of the necessary provisions and attended to the needs of travelers left to his charge. In these hostelries bazaars and markets were held, animals killed and meat sold, also wine and cider; so that they were a much more public place of resort than might at first be imagined.

The origin of caravansaries is unknown. Perhaps they were established at first by traders who regularly passed the same road. Now they are spread over the whole of the East, being found in cities, villages, and even the open highway. They consist of large buildings of stone arranged in a square, which inclose a spacious court. They are frequently of two stories, the lower containing stores and vaults for goods and stalls for cattle, the upper for travelers. They have a well or a large reservoir.

It appears that houses of entertainment were sometimes, as in Egypt (Herod. ii, 35), kept by women, whose character was suspicious. But the inference that the women mentioned in Josh. 2:1; Judg. 16:1; I Kings 3:16 were innkeepers seems rather forced.

Innocency (Heb. *nĭqqāyōn*, literally *clearness*, Gen. 20:5; Psa. 26:6; 73:13; Hos. 8:5; *zāqū*, *purity*, Dan. 6:22). The Hebrews considered innocence as consisting chiefly in an exemption from external faults, but this is a very different standard of morality from that of the Gospel (Matt. 5:28; John 3:25) or even of the Old Testament (Psa. 51:6). Innocence is sometimes used as an exemption from punishment (Jer. 46:28, Heb. "I will not treat you as one innocent;" also Nah. 1:3; Psa. 18:26).

Innocents, Slaughter of (Matt. 2:16), the slaying of the young children of Bethlehem, by order of Herod, in the hope of killing Jesus. *See* Herod I.

Inscription. *See* Writing.

Inspiration. The doctrine of the inspiration of Scripture is of immense importance. This is at once apparent when one considers that all evangelical Christian doctrines are developed from the Bible and rest upon it for authority. L. Boettner is correct when he calls the Biblical teaching of inspiration "the mother and guardian of all the others" (*Studies in Theology*, 1947, p. 48). An unsound view of inspiration of Scripture is bound to countenance unsound views, produce distorted teachings or serious gaps in essential doctrinal systematization, or offer a temptation to too easy subscription to plausible but unsound scientific or philosophic theorizings.

1. **The Scriptural Definition of Inspiration.** In defining divine inspiration in the distinctive sense in which it is employed in the Holy Scriptures, the difference in meaning of this expression from revelation and illumination must be carefully comprehended. (1) **Revelation.** Revelation, which may be oral or written,

may be defined as an operation of God communicating to man truth which otherwise man could not know. Since man was created in God's image and endowed with capacity to know God, it is rational to expect that God would communicate Himself and His mind to man. If unfallen man, being a finite creature, needed divine revelation and instruction (Gen. 2:16, 17; 3:8), how much more fallen man completely incapacitated by sin. (2) **Inspiration** is "a supernatural influence exerted on the sacred writers by the Spirit of God, by virtue of which their writings are given Divine trustworthiness" (B. B. Warfield, "Inspiration," *Int. Stand. Bible Ency.*, p. 1473). In defining Scriptural inspiration three factors must be kept in mind: first, the primary efficient *Cause*, the Holy Spirit, Who acts upon man; second, the subject of inspiration, man, the *agent* upon whom the Holy Spirit acts directly; third, the *result* of inspiration, *a written revelation, once for all given, thoroughly accredited and tested by miracle and fulfilled prophecy* (cf. J. E. Steinmueller, *Companion to Scripture Studies*, N. Y., 1941, Vol. I, p. 5, 14). (3) **Illumination.** Illumination is a ministry of the Holy Spirit which enables all who are in right relation with God to understand the objective written revelation. Thus, revelation involves *origin*, inspiration, *reception* and *recording* and illumination, *understanding* or *comprehending* the written objective revelation. In other words, revelation comprehends God *giving* truth. Inspiration embraces man under divine control accurately *receiving* the truth thus given. Illumination deals with man's *understanding* the God-given, inspired revelation (I Cor. 2:14). Revelation as it concerns Holy Scripture had a specific time period involving the inspiration of certain sovereignly-chosen individuals as the recipients of the revelation. It is plain that both of these divine operations have ceased. In contrast, illumination is continuously operative in all those who qualify for this ministry of the Holy Spirit.

2. **The Scriptural Doctrine of Inspiration.** (1) **The Fact of Inspiration** is stated in II Tim. 3:16, 17, which the A. V. correctly renders "All Scripture is given by inspiration of God, and is profitable for doctrine, for reproof, for correction, for instruction in righteousness: That the man of God may be perfect, throughly furnished unto all good works." Five great truths of inspiration are herein taught: first, the plenary inspiration of the Bible, "all"; secondly, the plenary inspiration specifically of the O. T., plainly implying the entire N. T. also, that is "all Scripture"; thirdly, the Divine authorship of Scripture—"given by inspiration of God" ("God-breathed"); fourthly, the supreme value of all Scripture to the spiritual life, "profitable for doctrine, for reproof, for correction and instruction in righteousness"; fifthly, the holy purpose of Scripture, "that the man of God may be perfect (complete), throughly furnished unto all good works." (2) **The Fact of Inspiration Implied.** The sacred authors were prophets and apostles of God's Word in the highest sense of the term. Scripture is filled with such expressions as "the Word of the Lord came, saying" (I Kings 16: 1); "thus saith the Lord unto me. . . ." (Jer.

13:1). "The Word of the Lord came expressly unto Ezekiel" (Ezek. 1:3). The Apostle Paul and others claimed to speak by direct revelation (Eph. 3:1-10), etc. Prophets spoke of future events (such as Moses' foretelling the coming of the great Prophet, Christ) and have had their predictions verified during succeeding centuries. David (Psa. 22) and Isaiah (Chap. 53) minutely prophesied the sufferings, death and resurrection of Christ. Daniel previewed the rise of Persia, Greece and Rome (Dan. 2:37-40; 7:4-7). Some prophets, such as Moses, Elijah and Elisha, had their messages authenticated by miracle. Others had irresistible compulsion to speak, such as Jeremiah (chap. 20:9). These were often commanded to write their utterances, or wrote under Divine leading (Exod. 24:4; Deut. 27:8; Isa. 30:8; Jer. 30:2; Luke 1:1-3, etc.). (3) **Nature of Inspiration.** "Knowing this first, that no prophecy of the Scripture is of any private interpretation. For the prophecy came not in old time by the will of man: but holy men of God spake as they were moved by the Holy Ghost" (II Pet. 1:20, 21). This pivotal passage deals with the question *how* Scripture was inspired. First, it declares how it did not originate—it is not of "private interpretation," that is, it is not the result of human research nor the product of the writer's own thought. It did not come into being "by the will of man." Man did not propose to write it, decide its subject matter or outline its arrangement. Secondly, this passage tells how the Scriptures did originate. "Men," that is, certain divinely selected men, "spake from God," the Source. These inspired men were borne or carried along by the Holy Spirit, the message being *His, not theirs.* Accordingly, if it can be demonstrated that we have the words they spoke and wrote transmitted substantially in identical form with the original documents, and the science of textual criticism enables this to be done, then a charge of error is a charge against God, not against men except, of course, where the supposed "error" may be due to textual corruption in the long course of transmission. Where the text has unquestionably suffered in transmission, the labors of devoted scholars are directed to its restoration. This is done through ancient versions, textual variants and other linguistic and historical evidence continuously being made available by archaeology and various other phases of sound Biblical research.

3. **Other Scriptural Proofs of the Inspiration of the Scriptures.** God spoke through O. T. prophets (Heb. 1:1, 2). The O. T. Scriptures are inviolable (John 10:34-36). The indefectability and certainty of promise and prophecy are clearly seen in the oft-recurring expression "that it might be fulfilled" (Matt. 1:22; 2:15, 23; 8:17; 12:17, etc.) and in such Scriptures as Matt. 24:35, "Heaven and earth shall pass away but my Word shall not pass away." Jesus quoted the O. T. as authoritative (Matt. 4:4, 7, 10). The Holy Spirit in the prophets equipped them for their ministry (I Pet. 1:10, 11). The Spirit of God spoke through David (II Sam. 23:1, 2), and other prophets. Besides the Scriptural proofs, unbroken Jewish and Christian tradition attest the inspiration of Holy Scripture.

4. **The True Biblical Doctrine of Inspiration.** Scripture nowhere fully explains the precise *modus operandi* of inspiration, yet it is possible to formulate a doctrine which is in agreement with all the plain and sufficient Scriptural revelation vouchsafed to us. This doctrine almost universally rejected today on the basis of alleged philosophic, scientific, historical, archaeological and linguistic difficulties involved, is called *verbal, plenary inspiration.* It is sometimes called the *dynamic view.* This view holds that the superintendency of the Holy Spirit rendered the writers of Scripture infallible in their communications of truth and inerrant in their literary productions. Yet it leaves room for the fullest play of the personality, style and background of the individual authors. By verbal inspiration is signified that in the *original writings* the Holy Spirit led in the choice of each word used (cf. I Cor. 2:13; John 10:34-36). Compare Gal. 3:16, where the problem turns upon the singular or plural of a word. By plenary inspiration is meant that the accuracy which verbal inspiration insures is extended to every portion of the sacred revelation, so that it is as a whole and in all its constituent parts, infallible as to truth and final as to divine authority. This is the traditional teaching of the Church, and is that doctrine set forth by Christ and the apostles. This teaching preserves the dual authorship of Scripture (the divine and the human) in perfect balance, ascribing to each that consideration which is accorded in the Bible.

5. **Results of Inspiration.** The Bible having been brought into existence by the supernatural action of the Holy Spirit upon the sacred writers, the question is what is the result of this divine process in the product itself. (1) **The Absolute Inerrancy of the Autographa.** Absolute freedom from error must be attributed to the original copies cf the inspired writings. It is unthinkable that inaccuracy and mistake can co-exist with inspiration. Can God Who is Supreme Truth speak that which is untrue? The claim of verbal, plenary inspiration for the original writings, however, does not extend to the multitudinous transcriptions and various translations, both ancient and modern. Inerrancy applies to transcriptions as the Massoretic-Hebrew Text and the Greek N. T. Text and the translations such as the Septuagint, Vulgate, Syriac, Luther's Bible, and various English versions only insofar as they reproduce exactly the original autographic manuscripts. Since none of the original manuscripts, of course, are in existence, critics commonly reject the inerrancy of the autographa as "an assumption for which there is no warrant in sound reason" (G. Maines, *Divine Inspiration*, p. 109). But the fact and the truth rest not upon "reason" but upon the clear revelation of the Scriptures themselves (II Tim. 3:16; II Pet. 1:20, 21). (2) **Providential Preservation of Scripture with Regard to its Substance.** The Holy Spirit, it is reasonable to conclude, also had a definite ministry in preserving the inspired Scriptures through millennia of transmission.

Possible errors which have crept in as a result of copyists' slips, glosses, etc. are the domain of lower criticism and here the Christian scholar may find a worthy task for his labors. The high development of N. T. textural citicism as the result of many manuscript finds has given us the transmitted text in a very high degree of purity. Lack of manuscript evidence in the O. T. field has seriously curtailed textual criticism and hence there are many more unresolvable textual difficulties in the O. T. than in the New. Recent phenomenal manuscript finds such as the Dead Sea Scrolls (notably the Isaiah Manuscript) are tending to alleviate this condition regarding the O. T. text. (3) **Scriptural Inerrancy Embraces Scientific Features.** In this realm, although serious problems exist, there are no proved facts of science that necessitate abandonment of the Scriptural doctrine of inspiration. Many scientific theorizings would seem to suggest this, but when the Bible is correctly placed in the prescientific era in which it had its birth, its alleged scientific inaccuracies are much less formidable than the liberal or neo-orthodox interpreter would have us believe. (4) **Scriptural Inerrancy Embraces Historical and Literary Features.** In no field has the Bible been more seriously challenged than in the historical. While it is true many serious historical problems still remain, such as the existence of the Philistines in patriarchal times, the date of the Exodus, the identity of Darius the Mede in the Book of Daniel, archaeology has made colossal contributions toward resolving many of these problems. The existence of Sargon II, the Hittites and the Horites (the Hurrians), the religion of the Canaanites, the historicity of the patriarchs and many other serious problems have been cleared up. Although there is almost universal rejection of a thoroughly sound teaching of Biblical inspiration in our day, the conservative scholar with an abundance of this new apologetic material at his disposal may well hesitate before abandoning this solid foundation of true Biblical exposition and theological systematization.

M. F. U.

Instant, Instantly. In addition to the usual use of the word (i. e., a particular point of time), several Greek words are used in the New Testament. These words imply *to be urgent*, urgently, or fervently, as will be seen from the following passages (Luke 7:4; 23:23; Acts 26:7; Rom. 12:12). In II Tim. 4:2 we find "be instant in season and out of season." The literal sense is "stand ready"—"be alert" for whatever may happen.

Instruction. See Education; Children; Schools.

Instrument (Heb. *k^eli*, something *prepared*), a general term for any *apparatus*, as implement, utensil, weapon, vessel, furniture, etc. The expression "instruments of unrighteousness," etc. (Rom. 6:13; Gr. *hopla adikias*) is a part of a figure in which sin as a ruling power would employ the members of the body as *weapons* against holiness.

Insult. Such treatment of another, in word or deed, as expresses contempt. It is not definitely noticed in the Mosaic law; only the reviling of a ruler was forbidden (Exod. 22:28), but without any special penalty attached. The severity with which disrespect toward sacred persons was regarded appears from II Kings 2:23, sq. See Mockery.

Integrity (Heb. *tōm, completeness*) has various shades of meaning: *simplicity* or *sincerity* (Gen. 20:5; Psa. 25:21; 78:72); *entirety* as Job when under grievous trial (Job 2:3, 9; 27:5; 31:6; comp. Psa. 26:1; 41:12, etc.).

Intention, purpose, design, the deliberate exercise of the will with reference to the consequences of an act attempted or performed.

It is one of the fundamental principles of ethics that the moral quality of an action is in the intention. This is a general principle, however, to be guarded by the fact that no one is at liberty to do evil that good may come. See Ethics.

In the doctrine of the Roman Catholic Church the idea of intention plays a peculiarly important part in connection with the efficacy of the sacraments. Thus the efficacy of baptism depends upon the intention of the priest. "He must have the intention to baptize indeed, i, e., to do what the Church does, or what Christ has ordained" (Deharbe, *Catechism*, p. 251). Also, more generally, in the decrees of the Council of Trent (11th canon, section 7) it is stated: "If anyone shall say that in ministers, while they effect and confer the sacraments, there is not required the intention at least of doing what the Church does, let him be anathema." In opposition to this is the 26th Article of Religion of the Church of England, which declares that the unworthiness or wickedness of ministers "hinders not the effect of the sacraments . . . which be effectual because of Christ's institution and promise, although they be ministered by evil men." See Sacraments.

Intercession (Heb. *pägă*, to *come upon;* Gr. *entunchanō*, to *meet with, to come between*).

1. **Intercession of Christ.** This belongs to the office of Christ as priest (*q. v.*) and refers generally to the aid which he extends as mediator between God and mankind (*see* Mediation). In a particular sense Christ is represented as drawing near to God and pleading in behalf of men. Thus, in harmony with the idea of intercession, he is called our Advocate. The prayers and praises of believers are acceptable to God through Christ's intercession (see I John 2:1; Rom. 8:27; Heb. 4:14-16; 7:25; 13:15; I Pet. 2:5; Rev. 8:3).

The objects of Christ's intercession are (1) The world, the whole of humanity, which he represents. On no other ground can we understand how a guilty race could be permitted to extend its existence upon the earth under the moral government of God. In the broadest meaning of the term Isaiah says, "He made intercession for the transgressors" (Isa. 53:12). (2) The great body of his people. In a special and peculiarly appropriate and emphatic sense Christ pleads the cause of those who are savingly united to him. He prays for them as "not for the world" (see John 17). (3) Individuals, and particularly those who penitently put their trust in him. "The Head of every man is Christ" (I Cor. 11:3). "If any man sin we have an Advocate with the Father" (I John 2:1).

2. **Intercession of the Holy Spirit.** In one

important passage (Rom. 8:26) this is particularly mentioned, and refers to the aid of the Holy Spirit afforded to believers that they may offer truly appropriate prayers.

3. **Intercession of Christians.** Roman Catholics believe in the intercession of the saints, i. e., of canonized departed spirits. This is rejected by Protestants as unscriptural because it derogates from the character of Christ, who is the only and sufficient mediator between God and man, also because of the supposition involved that there exists a class of glorified human beings who have personal merits of their own on account of which they may plead effectually for others. A great truth, however, is to be recognized in that it is the privilege and duty of all Chrisitans to pray effectively, as well as put forth efforts, for their fellowmen. This is intercession in a subordinate though still important sense. The propriety and validity of such human intercession is illustrated in the Scriptures of both Testaments (see I Sam. 12:23; I Kings 18:36, 37; Luke 12; Matt. 5:44; I Tim. 2:1, et al.).

Interest. *See* Usury.

Intermarriage. *See* Marriage.

Intermediate State, a phrase employed in theology in two ways: First, it is sometimes used to designate the interval between the death and resurrection of Christ. This is Van Oosterzee's exclusive use of the term. Second, the use which is by far more general refers the term to the condition of mankind after death and before the resurrection and final judgment. The following discussion, therefore, embraces these two distinct though importantly related subjects.

1. **Of Christ.** The condition or situation of the God-man during the period in which his body lay in the grave may be a matter for reverent inquiry, but not one for much of dogmatic statement. For the latter there is not sufficient Scripture basis.

(1) We may look upon our Lord at this point as affording another illustration of his acceptance of human conditions in that he existed for a time as a disembodied spirit, and for a time awaited his resurrection and glorification. The words spoken to Mary, "I am not yet ascended to my Father" (John 20:17), would seem to indicate that his spirit, which had been disembodied, had not attained to the final blessedness. On the other hand, his promise to the penitent thief certainly had a glorious meaning (comp. with II Cor. 12:2-4; Rev. 2:7).

(2) At the same time the intermediate state may be regarded as the transition between our Lord's humiliation and exaltation. In one sense, at all events, it was the beginning of his exaltation. For though he was "dead and buried," even in death he triumphed over death, in that his body "saw no corruption" (Acts 2:27; 13:37). Also, it is held that in entering the world of spirits our Lord did so triumphantly, and took possession of the kingdom of the dead. Reference is made in this connection to Rom. 14:9; 10:7; Eph. 4:8, 9; Col. 2:15; I Pet. 3:18, 19; but the precise character of Christ's activity during this interval is one of those obscure matters upon which speculation has been abundant, and

has often gone beyond the proper warrant of Holy Scripture.

(3) Christ's descent into hell is a phrase the proper meaning of which has been a subject of endless controversy. That the phrase should continue to be used is, in view of its ambiguity and liability to abuse, at least open to question.

The Apostles' Creed contains in its fifth article the words "He descended into hell." But it is universally conceded that they did not appear in that creed or any other before the 4th century. The purpose for which the clause was introduced is in dispute. It remains in the Apostles' Creed as used by the Roman and Greek and Lutheran Churches and the Church of England. The Protestant Episcopal Church prefaces the Creed with a note permitting the substitution of the words "He went into the place of departed spirits," as meaning the same as the words of the Creed. The Methodist Church omits the words altogether. *See* Creeds; also *Westminister Catechism* answer to question 50.

The phrase "descent into hell," or any proper equivalent does not appear in the New Testament. The words quoted by St. Peter (Acts 2:30, 31), much relied upon, are quoted also by St. Paul (Acts 13:34, 53), but in such a way as to show that both apostles had in mind solely the resurrection of our Lord as preceded by his actual death and burial. But for the exposition of these and other passages (as Eph. 4:8-10; I Tim. 3:16, and especially I Pet. 3:19-21; 4:6), the meaning of which is disputed, reference must be made to the works of Scripture exegetes.

It would be vain to attempt here to outline the history of speculation in connection with this subject. It should be said, however, that the view that Christ's activity during his intermediate state embraced the preaching of his Gospel was held by quite a considerable number of the early Church fathers. The advantages of this preaching were regarded as offered to both Jews and Gentiles in Hades. This view, as is well known, has been revived and brought into considerable prominence within recent years. But that this Gospel proclamation by our Lord in the world of spirits has ever been repeated (if it ever existed), or that others have been commissioned to similar work, must certainly remain a matter of pure and perilous conjecture. Upon the inference taken from this view of probation and the offer of salvation beyond the grave, further remark will be made in the second part of this article.

The Roman Catholic view of the descent is interwoven with the peculiar ideas of the Roman Church as to the various divisions of the world of spirits. The purpose of Christ in the descent was to deliver the saints of Israel and others from the *limbus patrum*, and conduct them to heaven (see *Cat. Council Trid.*, art. v.).

The doctrine of the Greek Church represents Christ as descending into Hades for the purpose of offering redemption "to those who were subject to Satan on account of original sin, releasing believers, and all who died in piety under the Old Testament dispensation."

The Lutheran doctrine has presented considerable variations. But prominent amid the conflict of opinions is the view of the later

Lutheran theologians, which regards the "descent into hell" as taking place not before, but immediately after the resurrection. The period of the intermediate state was passed in Paradise. Early on Easter morning before the risen Lord manifested himself to men, he went soul and body to hell, the abode of the lost, and there proclaimed his power over the devil and his angels. The "descent," according to this view, belonged emphatically to Christ's exaltation. The greatest extravagance of opinion upon this subject was that taught by Johannes Hoch in the 16th century, viz., that the soul of Christ descended into hell to suffer punishment while his body lay in the grave. That such a thought could find any measure of acceptance is, as has been said, "the opprobrium of one of the darkest chapters of historical theology."

Without going further, sufficient has been presented to illustrate the sentence quoted by Van Oosterzee: "On this subject also it is wiser, after David's fashion (Psa. 139:18) to meditate on one's couch than to write thereupon." *See* Hell.

Literature for this part of the subject, in addition to works of systematic theology referred to below: Pearson *On the Creed;* J. S. Semler, *De Vario Impari Veterum Christi ad Inferos;* A. Dietmaler, *History Dogma de Descensu Christi ad Inferos;* Dorner, *Person of Christ;* Hacker, *Dissert de descensu Christi ad Inferos.* For views of various commentators, ancient and modern, as well as Alford's own view on I Pet. 3:18-20, see Alford's *Commentary on New Testament*, vol. iv, part i, p. 368. Whedon's *Commentary* on I Peter is worthy of special attention with respect to the passage in question.

2. **Of Mankind.** This likewise is a subject upon which the light of the Scripture is not abundant. There is, however, a progress to be noted when we compare the revelations of the New with those of the Old Testament. That the human spirit continues to exist consciously after the death of the body is a fact most clearly established upon a biblical basis, to say nothing of the strength of philosophical arguments upon the matter (*see* Immortality). That a most powerful contrast is declared between the state of the righteous and that of the wicked, not only after the final judgment, but also during the interval between that event and the death of the body should also be regarded as beyond question. But still the precise condition or situation in which the departed spirit finds itself immediately after death is another matter, upon which even the teachings of the New Testament are not full, or always most explicit. Accordingly speculation has been rife, and has frequently illustrated the peril of attempting to be "wise above that which is written." It is not practicable here to do more than to indicate by the most general outline the various theories that have found their advocates, and, besides this, to suggest the conclusions that may be derived fairly from the Scriptures.

(1) The belief has been held by many at different times in the history of the Church that during the intermediate state the soul is unconscious. Strictly speaking, the theory has sometimes gone beyond this, and denied the existence of any spiritual principle in man that may survive the disorganization of the body. A modification of the theory of the unconscious state, or sleep of the soul, has appeared in the speculation that the soul while disembodied can take no note of the succession of events, and thus no note of time, and therefore, so far as consciousness is concerned, the moment of death is practically identical with that of resurrection. Without delaying, in order to criticize these speculations upon philosophic grounds, it may be sufficient to say that in all its forms the theory in question is opposed to the picture of conscious life given by our Lord in the account of The Rich Man and Lazarus; also to the general representations of the Apocalypse. The fact upon which stress is often laid, that in the New Testament the dead are sometimes spoken of as sleeping, and the saints "sleep in Jesus" (I Thess. 4:14), proves nothing in favor of the theory. For this is simply a figurative expression with reference to the resemblance which death bears to sleep; and, besides this, sleep is one thing and utter unconsciousness is another.

(2) In contrast with the preceding is the theory which obliterates the intermediate state by representing human beings as entering at the moment of their death upon their final condition. Redemption according to this condition (that of Gnosticism) accomplishes its final triumph in the deliverance of the spirit from the body, while St. Paul represents the final triumph as the resurrection, the "redemption of the body" (see Rom. 8:19-23; I Cor., ch. 15). This theory also ignores the final judgment as represented in the Scriptures.

(3) The theory of a purgatory, or intermediate state of suffering between heaven and hell, for the discipline and purification of those who finally are to enter heaven, belongs to the Roman Church. It is part of an elaborate system of doctrine concerning the souls of the departed developed by mediaeval theology. It has no foundation in Scripture. It is opposed by such Scriptures as pronounce those "who die in the Lord" as "blessed," or "with Christ." It dishonors the perfect atonement of our Lord. It has led to the great abuse of the sale of masses for the dead. *See* Purgatory.

(4) Within recent years has been presented, sometimes with great apparent force, the theory which regards the intermediate state as one of probation and opportunity to choose the way of life, particularly for those who, from no fault of their own, have not in the present world known the Gospel. This theory rests for its Scripture support mainly upon I Pet. 3:19-21; 4:6, much controverted passages to which reference has already been made. Interwoven with this theory are what may be regarded as overstrained conceptions of the necessity of probation in every case for the development of moral life, and of the necessity of an intellectual apprehension of the historic Christ in order to secure salvation (*see* Probation; also Faith; also Arminian view of the application of the benefits of the atonement in article on *Election*). It should be said that many, if not most, of the advocates of this view guard it, or attempt to guard it, in such

a way as not to encourage men in the rejection of the Gospel, for they admit, as all must, that the whole tone of Scripture, at least for those who hear the Gospel, is to the effect: "Behold now is the accepted time; behold now is the day of salvation" (see also Luke 16:25-31).

(5) From what is revealed in the Scriptures it may reasonably be concluded (*a*) that the intermediate state is not for the wicked that of their final misery, nor for the righteous that of their completed and final blessedness. They await the resurrection and the judgment of the great day (see Matt. 25:31-46; John 5:28, 29) (*see* Resurrection; Judgment). (*b*) The state of those "who die in the Lord" is, even for this period, pronounced "blessed." It is so, for the reason that though they wait for the final consummation, they are "with Christ" (see Rev. 14:4, 13; Phil. 1:23; John 14:1, 3; Luke 23:43, et al.). (*c*) For those who have willfully rejected the offer of salvation through Christ there is no ground of hope based upon Scripture that after death that offer will be renewed. It is proper to emphasize this statement in view of the spirit of presumption fostered by conjectural dealing with this most awful of all themes. E. McC. *See* Hell, Hades, Gehenna, Lake of Fire, Eternal Punishment.

Literature.—Works of systematic theology of special value: L. S. Chafer, *System. Theol.*, IV, 413-15; VII, 202-3; See also A. A. Hodge, Charles Hodge, A. H. Strong.

Interpretation of Scripture. *See* Inspiration.

Iphedei′ah (ĭf-ê-dē′yȧ; *Jehovah redeems*), one of the "sons" of Shashak, and a chief of the tribe of Benjamin, resident at Jerusalem (I Chron. 8:25), B. C. before 588.

Also **Iph-de′iah** (ĭf-dē′yȧ) R. V. and R. S. V.

Iph′tahel. *See* Jiphthael.

Ir (ĭr; a *city*), the father of Shuppim (Shupham) and Huppim (Hupham), of the tribe of Benjamin (I Chron. 7:12); probably identical with one of the sons of Benjamin (Gen. 46:21), and, therefore, not, as often supposed, the same as **Iri** (I Chron. 7:7).

I′ra (ī′rȧ), the name of three of David's favorite officers.

1. A Jairite, and "chief ruler about David" (II Sam. 20:26), B. C. after 1000.

2. A Tekoite, son of Ikkesh, and one of David's thirty warriors (II Sam. 23:26; I Chron. 11:28). He was afterward placed in charge of the sixth division of troops (I Chron. 27:9), B. C. 993.

3. An Ithrite, one of David's "valiant men" (II Sam. 23:38; I Chron. 11:40), B. C. about 993.

I′rad (ī′răd), one of the antediluvian patriarchs of the Cainite line, son of Enoch, and father of Mehujael (Gen. 4:18).

I′ram (ī′răm), the last named of the Edomite phylarchs in Mount Seir, apparently contemporary with Horite kings (Gen. 36:43; I Chron. 1:54).

Ir-hahe′res (ĭr-hȧ-hē′rĕz; A. V. "the city of destruction"), the name or an appellation of a city in Egypt, mentioned only in Isa. 19:18. There are various explanations. 1. "The city of the sun," a translation of the Egyptian sacred name of Heliopolis. This is the rendering of the R. S. V. 2. "The city of Heres," a transcription in the second word of the Egyptian sacred name of Heliopolis, Ha-ra, "the abode (literally, 'house') of the sun." 3. "A city destroyed," literally, "a city of destruction," meaning that one of the five cities mentioned should be destroyed, according to Isaiah's idiom. 4. "A city preserved," meaning that one of the five cities mentioned should be preserved. A very careful examination of the 19th chapter of Isaiah, and of the 18th and 20th, which are connected with it, makes the third explanation most likely.

I′ri (ī′rī), the last named of the five sons of Bela, son of Benjamin (I Chron. 7:7).

Iri′jah (ī-rī′jȧ; *Jehovah sees* or *provides*), son of Shelemiah, and a captain of the ward at the gate of Benjamin, who arrested the prophet Jeremiah on the pretense that he was deserting to the Chaldeans (Jer. 37:13, 14), B. C. about 597.

Ir-na′hash (ĭr-nā′hăsh; *city of a serpent*, marg. "city of Nahash"), thought by some to be a city founded (rebuilt) by Tehinnah (I Chron. 4:12). It is apparently to be rendered rather "city of copper" (cf. I Chron. 4:14) and to be connected with Nahas (Copper Ruin) located near the N. end of the 'Arabah.

I′ron (ī′rŏn), one of the "fenced" cities of Naphtali (Josh. 19:38), probably the present village of *Jarûn*, southeast of Bint-Jebeil.

Iron. *See* Mineral Kingdom.

Figurative. Iron is used in Scripture as the symbol of *strength* (Dan. 2:33, etc.), of *stubbornness* (Isa. 48:4); of severe *affliction* (Deut. 4:20; Psa. 107:10); of a *hard, barren soil* (Deut. 28:23); of harsh exercise of *power* (Psa. 2:9; Rev. 2:27).

Ir′peel (ĭr′pê-ĕl; *God will heal*), a city of the tribe of Benjamin (Josh. 18:27). From the associated names it would seem to have been located in the district west of Jerusalem.

218. A Herd in the Old Kingdom, Fording an Irrigation Canal

Irrigation. There is a reference to artificial irrigation by conduits in the "water partings, canals" (Job 38:25; Prov. 21:1). Besides, they were well known to the Israelites from Egypt (Deut. 11:10), for there water is brought from the Nile, its canals and reservoirs, to the higher-lying regions in various ways: sometimes by *draw wells* with a long lever (now called *Shaduf*); sometimes by large *dredge wheels* moved by the foot, over which passes a long endless rope with earthen jars fixed to it such as are still in use (Deut. 11:10), though the phrase "wateredst it with thy foot" may refer to pushing aside the soil between one furrow and another, so as to allow the flow of water; sometimes by more complex machines moved by oxen; sometimes by carrying it on the shoulder in buckets.

Ir-she′mesh (ĭr-shē′mĕsh; *city of the sun*), a city of Dan, on the border between Eshtaol and Shaalabbin (Josh. 19:41), the same as Bethshemesh (I Kings 4:9).

I′ru (ĭ′rū), the first named of the sons of Caleb, the son of Jephunneh (I Chron. 4:15), B. C. after 1440.

I′saac (ī′zăk).—1. **Name and Family.** (Heb. *yĭṣḥäq*, *laughter*, i. e., *mockery*). The only son of Abraham by Sarah. The name Isaac was fitly chosen by Jehovah for the child in commemoration of supernatural birth (Gen. 17:19), and of the *laughing* joy it occasioned.

2. **Personal History.** (1) **Early Life.** The birth of Isaac occurred (B. C. about 2061) when Abraham was a hundred years old and his mother ninety (Gen. 21:5; comp. 17:17). He was circumcised when he was eight days old, and his mother's skeptical laughter was turned into exultation and joy. The next event recorded of Isaac is his weaning, probably (according to Eastern custom) when he was two years old (21:8, sq.). In honor of the occasion Abraham made a great feast, as an expression, no doubt, of his joy. This happiness was naturally shared by the mother and the friends of the parents. But *Ishmael* (*q. v.*) saw no occasion for gladness to him—being supplanted in the more peculiar honor of the house by this younger brother. He mocked (*see* Note) and so angered Sarah that she insisted upon his being sent away. (2) **Offering.** We are next informed of the event connected with the command of God to offer Isaac up as a sacrifice on a mountain in the land of Moriah (ch. 22), B. C. perhaps 2045. He was probably about sixteen years of age; according to Josephus (*Ant.*, i, 13, 2) twenty-five. It appears from the narrative that Isaac was not aware that he was to be offered until the act was in process of being accomplished (Gen. 22:7, 8), and then there was no resistance; nor, so far as we are informed, did Isaac raise any objection. His conduct proved him to be a fitting type of Him who came to do not his own will, but the the will of Him that sent him. (3) **Marriage.** A long gap occurs in the narrative of Isaac's life, and we hear nothing of him till his marriage to Rebekah. We may reasonably infer that a period of twenty years or more elapsed since the last event recorded concerning him; for his marriage took place after his mother's death, which occurred when Isaac was thirty-

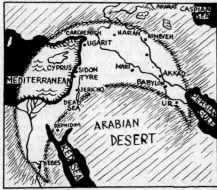

219. Breasted's Fertile Crescent in Patriarchal Times

seven years old. In obedience to the command of Abraham, his trusty servant went to Mesopotamia to take, under divine direction, a partner from among his own kin for his son. Rebekah was chosen, and became the wife of Isaac when he was forty years of age (ch. 24), B. C. about 2021. (4) **Death of Abraham.** Previous to his death Abraham made a final distribution of his property, leaving to Isaac his possessions, while the sons of Hagar and Keturah were sent away with presents into the east country (Arabia). Isaac and Ishmael buried their father in the cave of Machpelah, and Isaac took up his residence "by the well Lahai-roi" (25:5-11). (5) **Children.** After about twenty years (B. C. about 2001), and in answer to prayer, Rebekah gave birth to two sons Jacob and Esau (25:21, sq.). As the boys grew Isaac gave a preference to Esau, perhaps from his robust character, while Jacob, "a plain man, dwelling in tents," was the favorite of his mother. (6) **Denies his wife.** A famine in the land compelled Isaac to seek food in some foreign land, but he was admonished by God not to go down to Egypt, but to continue in the promised land. The Lord renewed the promise to him and to his seed, and confirmed the promise made to his father. Isaac did not so fully trust the divine protection, but that he was led by his fears into an error. While dwelling in the neighborhood of Gerar he had the weakness to call Rebekah his sister, lest the people might kill him if they knew her to be his wife. Upon learning the truth Abimelech, the Philistine king, rebuked Isaac for his prevarication, but allowed him to remain in the land (26:1-11). (7) **Later life.** Isaac remained in the land of the Philistines, cultivated a portion of ground, and in the same year reaped a hundredfold. His flocks and herds multiplied greatly. This so excited the envy of the Philistines that they drove him from their territory. He reopened the wells which his father had digged, and which the Philistines had filled up; digging also several new ones, which they claimed as theirs. Withdrawing from one after another, he dug one which he was allowed to keep unmolested; and, in token of his satisfaction at the peace he enjoyed, he called it Rehoboth (*Room*, Gen. 26:12-22). Thence he returned to Beersheba, where the Lord appeared to him and repeated the covenant blessing. Abimelech also sought and obtained from Isaac a covenant of peace (26:24-33). When Esau was forty years of age, and Isaac a hundred, the former married Judith and Bashemath, daughters of Canaan, "which were a grief of mind to Isaac and Rebekah" (vers. 34, 35). (8) **Isaac's blessing.** The last prominent event in the life of Isaac is the blessing of his sons (27:1, sq.). Being old and dim of sight, and supposing that his death was near at hand, Isaac called Esau and requested him to take venison and to make him "savory meat," that he might eat and bless him before he died. Rebekah, hearing his request, sought to frustrate his intention, and to secure the blessing for Jacob. While Esau was absent, Rebekah prepared the "savory meat," and Jacob, disguised so as to resemble his hairy brother, deceived his father and obtained the blessing.

Upon the discovery of the deception Isaac, remembering, no doubt, the prediction that "the elder should serve the younger," declined to revoke the words he had uttered, but bestowed an inferior blessing upon Esau. This so angered Esau that he seems to have looked forward to Isaac's death as affording an opportunity for taking vengeance upon his brother. The aged patriarch was therefore induced, at his wife's entreaty, to send Jacob into Mesopotamia, that he might take a wife "of the daughters of Laban" (27:41-28:6). (9) **Death.** After some time Jacob returned and found his father at Mamre, in "the city of Arba, which is Hebron, where Abraham and Isaac so-

220. Hebron, City of the Patriarchs (see Gen. 35:27)

journed." Here Isaac died at the age of one hundred and eighty years, and was gathered unto his people, and his sons, Esau and Jacob, buried him (35:27-29), B. C. about 1881.

(3) **As a Type.** Many Bible students teach that Isaac in his various relations presents a type of Christ. Those who hold such a view see Isaac in his surrender and submission to the sacrifice on Moriah (Gen. 22) as a type of Christ "obedient unto death" (Phil. 2:5-8). Abraham is set forth as a type of the Father Who "spared not His Own Son but delivered Him up for us all" (John 3:16; Rom. 8:32). The ram miraculously caught in the thicket and sacrificed instead of Isaac is a type of substitutionary atonement—Christ offered as a burnt offering in the place of sinners (Heb. 10:5-10). Abraham saying, "I and the lad will go yonder and worship and will come again to you" (Gen. 22:5) comprehends resurrection (Heb. 11:17-19). In Gen. 24 Isaac again appears as a type of Christ as the Bridegroom. "Whom not having seen" the bride, Rebekah, (a type of the Church, the *ecclesia,* the virgin bride of Christ) loves (Gen. 24:16; II Cor. 11:2; Eph. 5:25-32). Isaac going out into the field to meet and receive his bride (Gen. 24:63; I Thess. 4:14-16) is a picture of the Bridegroom. Again, Abraham appears as a type of the Father and the unnamed servant, a type of the Holy Spirit Who does not "speak of Himself," but takes the gifts of the Bridegroom to woo the bride (John 16:13, 14). Thus the servant enriches the bride (Gal. 5:22; I Cor. 12:7-11) and conducts her to the bridegroom.

(4) **Isaac and Archaeology.** The name Isaac, like that of Jacob, is an abbreviated

theophorous name whose full form would be Yitshaq-'el (cf. Ya'qub'el). These names belong to types now well known in the environment from which the early Hebrews sprang. The name Abraham also has been found in Mesopotamia, showing that it was actually a name in use at the time. The name Jacob occurs in tablets of the eighteenth century B. C. from Chagar Bazar in northern Mesopotamia and also as a place name in Palestine in the fifteenth century B. C. in Thutmose III's list. The Nuzu Letters, excavated between 1925 and 1941 not far from modern Kirkuk, not only illustrate patriarchal customs and life in general but give an example of the circumstances of the birth of Ishmael (Gen. 16:1-6). Nuzu marriage regulations stipulate that if a wife is barren she must furnish her husband with a slave wife. Later when Sarah had herself given birth to Isaac and determined that Hagar and her child be disinherited, the patriarch's reluctance to comply with her demand was readily comprehensible in the light of the common practice at Nuzu. There the law stipulated that in case the slave wife should bear a son, that son must not be expelled. It is clear in the light of Nuzian parallels why Abraham was loath to agree with Sarah's illegal demand, and doubtless he would have refused to do so, despite his concern for Isaac, had not a Divine dispensation over-ridden the law. Revised by *M. F. U.*

Isa'iah (ī-zā'yà; *Jehovah saves*).

Personal History. Very little information has come to us respecting the history of Isaiah. His father's name was Amoz (Isa. 1:1), but of what tribe we do not know. Isaiah is thought to have lived in Jerusalem, near the temple (ch. 6), and married a prophetess, by whom he had a son named Maher-shalal-hash-baz (8:3); another son, Shear-jashub, being mentioned in 7:3. His dress was suitable to his vocation (20:2), viz., a coarse linen or hairy overcoat of a dark color, such as was worn by mourners. (1) **Time of the prophet.** Isaiah prophesied under the reigns of Uzziah, Jotham, Ahaz, and Hezekiah, kings of Judah. The first period of his ministry was in the reigns of Uzziah (B. C. 783-738) and Jotham (750-738 as regent, 738-735 as sole ruler), in which he preached repentance without success, and, consequently, had to announce judgment and banishment. The second period extended from the commencement of the reign of Ahaz (735-719) to that of the reign of Hezekiah; the third from the accession of Hezekiah (719-705) to the fifteenth year of his reign. After this he took no further part in public affairs, but he lived till the commencement of Manasseh's reign, when, according to a credible tradition, he suffered martyrdom by being sawn asunder. To this Heb. 11:37 is supposed to be an allusion. (2) **Writings.** Isaiah was the author of a biography of King Uzziah (II Chron. 26:22), and of Hezekiah (32:32), as well as of the sublime prophecies that bear his name. Both biographies have been lost, together with the annals of Judah and Israel into which they had been inserted. He is by general consent the greatest of all Hebrew writers, and so fully does he describe the person and offices of the Messiah, that

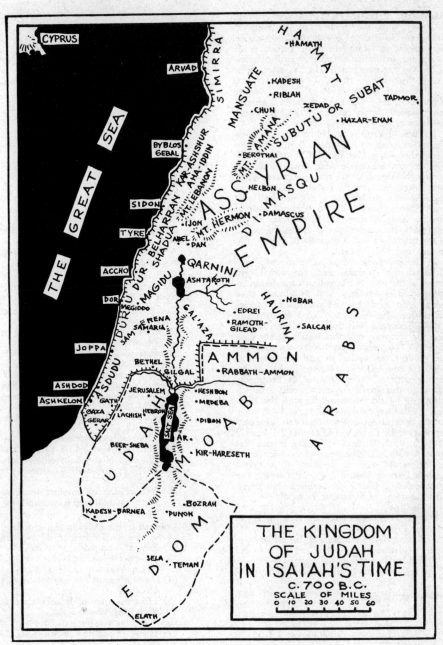

THE KINGDOM
OF JUDAH
IN ISAIAH'S TIME
C. 700 B.C.
SCALE OF MILES
0 10 20 30 40 50 60

221.

from the time of Jerome he has been known as the evangelical prophet. (3) **Position.** Isaiah appears to have held a high rank in Jerusalem, for Hezekiah, when sending a deputation to him, chose his highest officers and the elders of the priests (II Kings 19:2). It is exceedingly probable that he was the head and chief of the prophetic order, holding in Jerusalem the same rank which Elisha had held in the prophetic schools in Israel. His authority greatly increased after the fulfilment of his prophecies by the Babylonian exile, the victories of Cyrus, and the deliverance of the covenant people. Even Cyrus was induced (Josephus, *Ant.*, xl, 1, 1 and 2) to set the Jews at liberty by the prophecies of Isaiah concerning himself.

Concerning the opinion of a "second Isaiah," see Isaiah, Book of. *See* Jesaiah.

Isaiah, Book of. Isaiah (Heb. *Yᵉshāʿyāhû, Jehovah is salvation*), is the greatest of the Hebrew prophets. His general prophecies are without peer as far as beauty of style, versatility of treatment, brilliance of imagery and splendor of diction are concerned. He has often been called "the Prince of O. T. Prophets" (cf. B. A. Copass, *Isaiah, Prince of O. T. Prophets,* Nashville, 1944). His book is the first among the so-called "latter prophets," and his name has been given to his prophetic collection.

1. **Time of Prophecy.** He resided and ministered in Jerusalem from c. B. C. 740, the "year that King Uzziah died" until c. B. C. 700, or somewhat later. He thus prophesied during the kingship of Uzziah, Jotham, Ahaz and Hezekiah, kings of Judah (1:1). He was married to a prophetess (8:3) and had two sons: Shearjashub (7:3), "a remnant will return," and Maher-shalal-hash-baz (8:3), "hurry booty, hasten prey." Thus the name of the first child had a promise of mercy; the second, one of judgment.

2. **The purpose.** Isaiah in his ministry emphasized the spiritual and the social. He struck at the root of the nation's trouble in its apostasy and idolatry and sought to save Judah from its moral and political and social corruption. However, he failed to turn the nation Godward. His divine commission carried the warning that this would be the case (6:9-12). Thereupon he boldly declares the inevitable crash of Judah and the preservation of a small Godly remnant (6:13). However gleams of hope radiate his prophecy. Through this small remnant world-wide redemption would eventuate through the Messiah at His First Advent (9:2, 6; 53:1-12, etc.). At the Second Advent national salvation and restoration for Israel would result (2:1-5; 9:7; 11:1-16; 35:1-10; 54:11-17). The theme that Israel would one day be a Messianic nation to the world and a medium of universal blessing (yet to be fulfilled), with which the prophecies of Isaiah are imbued, has given him the name of Messianic Prophet.

3. **Outline.**

Part I. Prophecies from the Standpoint of the Prophet's Own Time, 1:1-35:10
  a. Prophecies concerning Judah and Jerusalem, 1:1-13:6
    (1) General introduction, 1:1-31
    (2) Millennial blessing through cleansing, 2:1-4:6
    (3) Israel's castigation for her sins, 5:1-30
    (4) The prophet's call and commission, 6:1-13
    (5) Immanuel's prophecy, 7:1-25
    (6) Prophecy of Assyrian invasion, 8:1-22
    (7) Messianic prediction, 9:1-21
    (8) Assyrian punishment, 10:1-34
    (9) Millennial restoration, 11:1-16
    (10) Millennial worship, 12:1-6
  b. Prophecies against foreign nations, 13:1-23:18
    (1) Babylon, 13:1-14:23
    (2) Assyria, 14:24-27
    (3) Philistia, 14:28-32
    (4) Moab, 15:1-16:14
    (5) Damascus, 17:1-14

    (6) Land beyond the rivers of Ethiopia, 18:1-7
    (7) Egypt, 19:1-25
    (8) Assyria's conquest, 20:1-6
    (9) Desert areas, 21:1-22:25
    (10) Tyre, 23:1-18
  c. Prophecy of kingdom establishment, 24:1-27:13
    (1) The Great Tribulation, 24:1-23
    (2) Character of the Kingdom, 25:1-12
    (3) Restored Israel, 26:1-27:13
  d. Prophecies concerning Judah and Assyria, 28:1-35:10
    (1) Danger and deliverance, 28:1-33:24
    (2) The Day of the Lord, 34:1-17
    (3) Full millennial blessing, 35:1-10
Part II. Historical Interlude, 36:1-39:8
  a. Sennacherib's invasion, 36:1-37:38
  b. Hezekiah's sickness and recovery, 38:1-22
  c. Arrival of Babylonian envoys; prophecy and captivity, 39:1-8
Part III. Prophecies of Redemption and Restoration from the Idealistic Standpoint of the Babylonian Exile, 40:1-66:24
  a. Comfort to the exiles, the promise of restoration, 40:1-28:22
    (1) Message of comfort—promise of Messianic restoration, 40:1-11
    (2) Basis of comfort—God's character, 40:12-31
    (3) The reason for comfort—Jehovah's vindication against idolators by raising up Cyrus the Deliverer, 41:1-29
    (4) The Comforter—Jehovah's Servant, 42:1-25
    (5) The result of the comfort—a nation restored, 43:1-45:25; the downfall of the Babylonian idols, 46:1-12; and Babylon itself, 47:1:15
    (6) Exhortation of comfort to those yet to be delivered from captivity, 48:1-22
  b. Comfort to the exiles in the prophecy of the Messiah-Redeemer, 49:1-57:21
    (1) His call and work, 39:1-26
    (2) His obedience, 50:1-11
    (3) His redemption, 51:1-52:12
    (4) His atonement and exaltation, 53:13-53:12
    (5) His guarantee of Israel's restoration, 54:1-17
    (6) Worldwide salvation, 55:1-13
    (7) His warnings and promises, 56:1-57:21
  c. Comfort in the prophecy of Israel's future glory, 58:1-66:24
    (1) Obstacles to Israel's restoration removed, 58:1-59:21
    (2) Jerusalem's exaltation in the Messianic Age, 60:1-22
    (3) Messiah's ministry for Israel and the world, 61:1-11
    (4) God's concern for Jerusalem, 61:1-12
    (5) Messiah's conquest of Israel's enemies, 63:1-14

(6) The remnant's prayer, 63:15-64:
12
(7) Jehovah's response, 65:1-25
(8) Kingdom blessing, 66:1-24

4. **Date and Authorship.** Until about the middle of the eighteenth century the traditional view that Isaiah wrote the entire prophecy was almost universally held. However, since 1775, when J. C. Doederlein denied Isaiah's authorship of chapters 40-66, it has been common for critics to speak of a "second Isaiah." This unknown writer allegedly wrote in the period immediately before the end of the Babylonian captivity (c. 550-539 B. C.). B. Duhm went a step farther and denied the unity of chapters 40-66. He invented a "third Isaiah" for chapters 55-66. Duhm is followed notably by K. Elliger and E. Sellin. Other critics divide the third Isaiah into a school of writers, rather than attribute it to an individual. In 1928 C. C. Torrey in his book entitled, *The Second Isaiah*, advanced the hypothesis that chapters 34-66 (36-39 excluded) were by one author living in Palestine. He thus presented strong evidence for the unity of this section.

5. **Rejection of the Critical View.** (1) **First Critical Claim:** *The standpoint of the writer of chapters 40-66 is exilic and precludes Isaiah's authorship on the basis of the historic function of prophecy.* The argument is not that the standpoint of the writer is exilic. This is freely admitted. The question is whether under the influence of the Spirit of Prophecy, a prophet might not be naturally transported into the future to describe coming events to a future generation. Critics who rule out the supernatural and admit at most a premonition or "brilliant intuition" (cf. Robert Pfeiffer, *Introduction*, p. 423) are compelled to deny the possibility of such an occurrence as supernatural projection into the future and, accordingly, must refuse Isaiah's authorship of the second part of the book. But the critical arguments are inconclusive and thus to reject the unity of the book on the basis of the *analogy of prophecy* (see S. R. Driver, Introduction, 9th ed., p. 236-243), maintaining that a prophet never projects himself into an ideal standpoint in the future except when the transference to that state is transient (for example Isa. 5:13-15; 9:1-6; 23:1, 14) is not correct. Actually examples occur in Ezekiel (Ezek. 40:2), who was transported from Babylon during the captivity "into the land of Israel . . ." to behold from the idealistic future standpoint of the millennium the extended vision of the millennial temple and Israel in the Land during the future Kingdom Age (Ezek. 40-48). Similarly, Ezekiel is brought out "in the Spirit of the Lord" and set down in the midst of a valley "full of bones" (37:1). In this case the prophet is projected into the ideal standpoint of Israel's final world-wide dispersion and regathering. John was evidently similarly projected into the future Day of the Lord (Rev. 1:10) to behold the protracted events of that future period (Rev. 4:1-19:21). Paul was caught up to the third heaven (II Cor. 12:2-4). Accordingly, to reject the unity of chapters 40-66 on the basis that Isaianic authorship

violates the "historic function of prophecy" is unsustained. The prophet, says Driver (*op. cit.*, p. 237), "speaks always, in the first instance, to his own contemporaries; the message which he brings is intimately related to the circumstances of his time; his promises and predictions, however far they reach into the future, nevertheless rest upon the basis of the history of his own age, and correspond to the needs which are then felt." However, it is open to serious doubt whether the words of consolation of the so-called "second Isaiah" were not appropriate for the faithful, persecuted believers in the early reign of Manasseh. The Fall of Jerusalem and Sennacherib's invasion were events that brought the possibility of exile very close and for all that was revealed, such an exile may have taken place almost immediately. Critics fail to see that the essential notion of prophecy involving the direct operation of the Holy Spirit upon the faculties of man, cannot be circumscribed by time or space or comprehended to any extent apart from the supernatural. If critics admit a transient projection into the future, why may there not be an extended projection? (2) **The Second Claim.** *The differences in style between the two sections of the book preclude Isaiah's authorship of chapters 40-66.* This argument is extremely precarious and highly subjective, failing to take into consideration that an author of Isaiah's versatility may change his style in the course of a long literary career of possibly over forty years. Then too, critics are impressed by similarities of style between the two. Some even assert that the similarities led later redactors to append this second section to Isaiah's genuine prophecy. (3) **Third Critical Claim.** *Differences in theological concepts of the two sections indicate separate authorship.* This is the weakest of all. In the first Isaiah God's majesty is supposedly emphasized; God's infinity by the second Isaiah. Also the prominent idea of a remnant in the first part is supposedly unemphasized in the second part. But such arguments reveal the essential unsoundness of the entire critical view.

6. **Unity of the Book.** To the weakness of the critical arguments must be added other reasons supporting the unity of the Book of Isaiah which commend themselves to conservative scholars. (1) **The N. T. Witness.** The weight of this argument cannot be dismissed by contending that Biblical writers do not concern themselves with points of technical introduction. This may be true, but the manner of quotation, as in John 12:38-41, is so direct and personal that the actual author is indicated. (See also John 3:3; Luke 3:4; John 1:23, also cf. Matt. 8:17; 12:18-21; John 12:38-41; and Paul's quotation, Rom. 9:27-33; 10:16-21). (2) **Implicit Illustrations** *to the second part of Isaiah in exilic prophets point to Isaiah's authorship.* (Cf. Nahum 1:15 with Isa. 52:7; Jer. 31:35 with Isa. 51:15; Jer. 10:1-16 with Isa. 41:7 and 44:12-15; Zeph. 2:15 with Isa. 47:8, 10). (3) **The Voice of Tradition.** The Isaiah Manuscript, the Dead Sea Scrolls, the Septuagint evidence, Jewish tradition, Josephus, the Apocrypha, the Church fathers and the general witness of Christians down to the middle of the eighteenth

century are against the idea of a second and third Isaiah. The general testimony of the greatness of the second Isaiah from a literary and prophetic point of view, involves the critical contention in difficulty. If this writer was so great, the greatest of the prophets, why did his reputation dwindle so rapidly that by the second century B. C. he was almost an anonymity and his great prediction confused with a much lesser light, Isaiah the son of Amoz, whose stature had so phenomenally increased that Ecclesiasticus gives him such high praise? (4) **Evidence that the author of Is.** *40-66 was a native Palestinian favors Isaianic unity of the entire prophecy.* C. C. Torrey's second Isaiah, although arguing for a different author for the second section, presents a favorable defense of the unity of chapters 40-66 and its Palestinian authorship. *M. F. U.*

Is′cah (ĭs′kà), the daughter of Haran, and sister of Milcah and Lot (Gen. 11:29; comp. v. 31). Jewish tradition, as in Josephus (*Ant.,* i, 6, 5), Jerome and the Targum Pseudo-Jonathan identifies her with *Sarah* (*q. v.*).

Iscar′iot (ĭs-kăr′ĭ-ŏt; probably from Heb. *'ish qᵉrîôth, man of Kerioth*), a surname of *Judas* (*q. v.*) the traitor, to distinguish him from others of the same name (Matt. 10:4, etc.).

Ish′bah (ĭsh′bà; *he will praise*), a descendant of Judah, and founder ("father") of Eshtemoa; he was probably a son of Mered by his wife Hodiah (I Chron. 4:17). (*See* Mered). He is perhaps the same as *Ishi* (*q. v.*) in v. 20 and apparently identical with the *Naham* (*q. v.*) of v. 19.

Ish′bak (ĭsh′băk; *leaving*), a son of Abraham and Keturah (Gen. 25:2; I Chron. 1:32); B. C. after 2030, and the progenitor of a tribe of northern Arabia.

Ish′bi-be′nob (ĭsh′bī-bē′nŏb), one of the Rephaim, a gigantic warrior, "whose spear weighed three hundred shekels of brass," who attacked David, but was slain by Abishai (II Sam. 21:16), B. C. about 970.

Ish-bo′sheth (ĭsh-bō′shĕth; *man of shame*), the youngest of Saul's four sons (II Sam. 2:8; I Chron. 8:33; 9:39; in the two later passages his name is given as *Esh-Baal,* "the man of Baal"). The name evidently offers an example of rendering the "Baal" element by "*bōshĕth,*" Hebrew for "shame," showing the abhorrence with which heathens gods were held.

Personal History. (1) **Succeeds Saul.** Ish-bosheth was the only son who survived his father, his three brothers being slain with Saul in the battle of Gilboa, B. C. about 1000. Being the oldest of the royal family, he was, according to the law of oriental succession, the heir to the throne. His uncle, Abner, loyally espoused his cause, but the whole kingdom was in ruins; while hardly a single city west of the Jordan either could or would acknowledge the rule of the house of Saul. Abner, therefore, took Ish-bosheth beyond the Jordan, to the city Mahanaim, and announced him as Saul's successor (II Sam. 2:8, 9). Abner appears to have first undertaken to reunite under his protection the country of the east, and then reconquer the territory subdued by the Philistines. The order in which these districts were retaken seem to be indicated in v. 9. While Abner was making these

efforts some five years probably elapsed, leaving the length of Ish-bosheth's reign two years (v. 10). He was forty years old when he began to reign. Even the semblance of authority which he possessed he owed to the will and influence of Abner, who kept the real control of affairs in his own hands, carrying on all wars and negotiations with David (II Sam. 2:12, sq.; 3:6-12). (2) **Breaks with Abner.** At length Ish-bosheth accused Abner (whether justly or not is not stated) of cohabiting with Rizpah, his father's concubine, which, according to oriental custom, was considered treason. When Ish-bosheth accused him of this, he fell into a great rage, and announced his intention of handing over the kingdom to David. Ish-bosheth made no reply, "because he feared him." Soon after Abner made proposals to David, and the latter demanding Michal, his former wife, Ish-bosheth forced Phaltiel to give her up (3:12-16). While carrying on negotiations with David, Abner fell a victim to the resentment of Joab for the death of Asahel (v. 17, sq.). (3) **Death.** When Ish-bosheth heard that Abner was dead, "his hands were feeble," and he was soon after murdered, while taking his midday rest, by Rechab and Baana, probably to revenge a crime of his father, or in the hope of obtaining a reward from David. They met with a stern reception from that king, who rebuked them for the cold-blooded murder, and ordered them to be executed. The head of Ish-bosheth was buried in the sepulcher of Abner in Hebron (4:2-12), B. C. about 996.

Ish′i (ĭsh′ī; *salutary*).

1. The son of Appaim and father of Sheshan, and descendant of Judah (I Chron. 2:31).

2. Another descendant of Judah, but through what line does not appear (I Chron. 4:20); his sons were Zoheth and Ben-zoheth.

3. A Simeonite, four of whose sons led their brethren in the invasion of Mt. Seir, and the dispossession of the Amalekites (I Chron. 4: 42), B. C. before 715.

4. One of the chiefs of Manasseh east, who were "mighty men of valor, famous men" (I Chron. 5:24), B. C. about 720.

Ishi′ah (ī-shī′à), the fifth son of Izrahiah, great-grandson of Issachar (I Chron. 7:3).

Ishi′jah (ĭsh-ī′jà; Heb. same as above), one of the "sons" of Harim, who renounced his Gentile wife after the captivity (Ezra 10:31), B. C. 456.

Ish′ma (ĭsh′mà), a descendant of Judah, given as one of the sons "of the father (founder) of Etam" (I Chron. 4:3).

Ish′mael (ĭsh′mà-ĕl; *God will hear*), the name of several men.

1. **Son of Abraham** (Gen. 16:15, 16).

Personal History. Ishmael was the eldest son of Abraham by Hagar, his Egyptian concubine, when the patriarch was eighty-six years old, fourteen years before the birth of Isaac (Gen. 21:5), B. C. c. 2085. The place of his birth was Mamre. (1) **Circumcision.** The next recorded event of his life is his circumcision, he then being thirteen years of age (Gen. 17:25), at which time the Lord renewed to Abraham in more definite terms the promises made to Abraham respecting Ishmael (v. 20). Up to this time Abraham appears to have considered Ishmael as the heir of promise, and to have entertained great affection for him. (vers. 17, 18). (2) **Expulsion.** Ishmael is not mentioned again until the weaning of Isaac, when Ishmael was probably between fifteen and sixteen years of age. During the festivities of the occasion, Ishmael, angered doubtless by his blighted hopes, gave way to some insulting expressions of mockery. Sarah speedily detected him, and said to Abraham, "Cast out this bondwoman and her son: for the son of this bondwoman shall not be heir with my son, even with Isaac." Grieved at the demand of Sarah, he only yielded when influenced by a divine admonition. The beautiful and touching picture of Hagar's departure and journey is thus recorded: "And Abraham rose up early in the morning, and took bread, and a bottle of water, and gave it unto Hagar, putting it on her shoulder, and the child, and sent her away; and she departed, and wandered in the wilderness of Beer-sheba. And the water was spent in the bottle, and she cast the child under one of the shrubs. And she went, and sat her down over against him a good way off, as it were a bowshot; for she said, Let me not see the death of the child. And she sat over against him, and lifted up her voice and wept" (Gen. 21:6-16). The Lord appeared to Hagar, opened her eyes, and she saw a well of water, and thus saved the life of the lad. Again the cheering promise is renewed to her of her son, "I will make him a great nation" (v. 18). (3) **Marries.** Thus miraculously preserved, the lad "grew and dwelt in the wilderness (Paran), and became an archer." It would seem to have been his mother's wish to return to Egypt, but this being prevented, she took him an Egyptian wife (Gen. 2:121). We have no account of Ishmael having any other wife, and if this be the case, she was the mother of twelve sons (Gen. 25:13-15) and one daughter. This daughter, being called the "sister of Nebajoth" (Gen. 28:9), the limitation of the parentage of the brother and sister seems to point to a different mother for Ishmael's other sons. (4) **After life.** Of this we know but little. Ishmael was present, with Isaac, at the burial of Abraham (Gen. 25:9). The sacred historian gives us a list of his twelve sons, tells us that Esau married his daughter Mahaloth (28:9), and closes up the brief sketch in these words: "And these are the years of the life of Ishmael, a hundred and thirty and seven years: and he gave up the ghost and died, and was gathered unto his people. And they dwelt from Havilah unto Shur, that is before Egypt, as thou goest toward Assyria: and he died in the presence of all his brethren" (25:17, 18).

Character. Ishmael appears to have been a wild and wayward child, and doubtless the perfect freedom of desert life, and intercourse with those who looked upon him as heir-apparent of their great chief, tended to make him impatient of restraint, and overbearing in his temper. His harsh treatment by Sarah, his disappointment in not becoming the heir of Abraham, and the necessity of earning a scanty living by his sword and bow, would naturally wound his proud spirit and make him what the angel had predicted, "A wild man; his hand will be against every man, and every man's hand against him" (16:12).

NOTE—Gen. 16:12. Keil (*Com.*) considers the expression, "He shall dwell in the presence of all his brethren," to mean that "Ishmael would maintain an independent standing before all the descendants of Abraham," and adds: "The Ishmaelites have continued to this day in free and undiminished possession of the extensive peninsula between the Euphrates, the Straits of Suez, and the Red Sea, from which they have overspread both Northern Africa and Southern Asia." Smith (*Cycl.*) says that the passage "seems only to signify that he dwelt near them;" which view, Dr. Strong (McC. and S., *Cycl.*) says, "is confirmed by the circumstance that the Israelites did, in fact, occupy the country bordering that in which the various tribes descended from Abraham or Terah had settled—the Ishmaelites, Edomites, Midianites, Ammonites, etc." **Gen. 21:14.** The age of Ishmael at the time of his expulsion has given occasion to considerable discussion. He was doubtless thirteen years of age (Gen. 17:25) at the time of his circumcision, and the time of his expulsion about two or three years later (Gen. 21:5-8). The translation of Gen. 21:14, which seems to speak of Ishmael as an infant is infelicitous. It is unnecessary to assume that the child was put on Hagar's shoulder, the construction of the Hebrew not requiring it; and the sense of the passage rendering it highly improbable. Hagar carried "it," the *bottle*, on her shoulder. The fact of the lad being overcome by thirst and fatigue before his hardy Egyptian mother, is not remarkable, especially when we remember God's miraculous interposition in her behalf.

2. Son of Azel, a descendant of Saul through Meribbaal, or Mephibosheth (I Chron. 8:38; 9:44), B. C. before 588.

3. A man of Judah, whose son (or descendant), Zebadiah, was "ruler of the house of Judah," under Jehoshaphat (II Chron. 19:11), B. C. about 875. The office of "ruler," etc., was that of lay president of the supreme court in Jerusalem.

4. Son of Jehohanan, of Judah, and captain of a "hundred," who assisted Jehoiada in restoring Joash to the throne (II Chron. 23:1), B. C. c. 836.

5. One of the "sons" of Pashur, who relinquished his Gentile wife after the exile (Ezra 10:22), B. C. 456.

6. Murderer of Gedaliah, who was the superintendent, under the king of Babylon, of the province of Judea. His full description is "Ishmael, the son of Nathaniah, the son of Elishama, of the seed royal" of Judah (Jer. 41:1; II Kings 25:25). "Whether he was actually a son of Zedekiah or a king, or more generally, that he had royal blood in his veins—we cannot tell." (2) **Crime.** During the siege of Jerusalem he, like many others of his countrymen (Jer. 40:11), had fled across the Jordan, where he found a refuge at the court of Baalis, then king of Bene-Ammom (Josephus, *Ant.*, x, 9, 2). Gedaliah had taken up his residence at Mizpah, a few miles N. of Jerusalem, where the prophet Jeremiah resided with him (Jer. 40:6). Ishmael had been instigated by Baalis to slay Gedaliah (v. 14), and his intention was made known by Johanan who offered to put Ishmael to death. To this Gedaliah would not consent, and a short time after, Ishmael and ten companions, "princes of the king," came to him and were by him entertained at a feast (vers. 15, 16). He returned the kindness shown him by murdering Gedaliah and all his attendants, including some Chaldean soldiers who were there. So secretly was the deed executed that for two days it remained undiscov-

ered. On the second day he saw a party of eighty devotees, bringing incense and offerings to the temple, who, at his invitation, turned aside to the residence of Gedaliah. As they passed into the city he closed the gates and slew all but ten, who escaped by the offer of heavy ransoms. He then carried off the daughters of King Zedekiah, and the people of the town, and started for the country of the Ammonites. The massacre was soon made known, and Ishmael was quickly followed by Johanan and his companions, who "found him by the great waters that are in Gibeon" (41:1-12), B. C. 588. Ishmael, with eight of his men, escaped, and went to the Ammonites. Nothing more is recorded of this marvel of craft and villainy.

Ish'maelite (ĭsh'mȧ-ĕl-īt), a descendant of Ishmael. The term is probably sometimes used as a general name for all the Abrahamic peoples from Egypt to the Euphrates, and perhaps to the Persian Gulf, their headquarters being in western Arabia. In Gen. 37:25, 27, 28 the name "Ishmaelites" may have been applied in general to the caravan, which included a body of Midianite merchantmen. The same relation may exist in Judg. 8:22, 24; in v. 24 that kind of traders may have been called "Ishmaelites" as the name *Canaanites* (*q. v.*) was used for merchants, since the Ishmaelites were caravan traders from the remotest times.

Mohammed claimed descent from Ishmael. Though, in the confusion of the Arab genealogies, the names are lost beyond the twenty-first generation before the prophet, the claim is probable enough, since the pre-Mohammedan law of blood revenge, which required every one to know his ancestors for four generations back, would prevent all confusion in regard to race. And, after making due allowance of mixture with Joktanites and Keturahites, we may fairly regard the Arabs as essentially an Ishmaelite race.

In II Sam. 17:25 Amasa, Absalom's commander-in-chief, was the son of "Ithra an Israelite," but in I Chron. 2:17 "the father of Amasa was Jether the Ishmaelite." If one reading is wrong, "Ishmaelite" is more likely to be correct, inasmuch as the fact of Amasa's father being an Israelite would be too common to demand special mention. But, "according to Jardri, Jether was an Israelite, dwelling in the land of Ishmael, and thence acquired his surname, like the house of Obed-edom the Gittite." Or, as there were Israelites who bore the name of Ishmael (see especially I Chron. 8:38; 9:44; also II Chron. 19:11; 23:1; Ezra 10:22; II Kings 25:23-25; Jer. 40:8-41:15), it might well be that Jether or Ithra was descended from some Israelite named Ishmael. —W. H.

Ishma'iah (ĭsh-mā'yȧ; *Jehovah will hear*), son of Obadiah, and ruler of the tribe of Zebulun in the time of David (I Chron. 27:19), B. C. 1000.

Ish'meelite (ĭsh'mê-ĕl-īt; Gen. 37:25, 27, 28; 39:1; I Chron. 2:17). *See* Ishmaelite.

Ish'merai (ĭsh'mê-rī), one of the family of Elpaal, a chief Benjamite resident at Jerusalem (I Chron. 8:18), B. C. before 588.

I'shod (ī'shŏd; *man of renown*), a son of Hammoleketh, and, from his near connection with

Gilead, probably an important person (I Chron. 7:18).

Ish'pan (ĭsh'păn), one of the "sons" of Shashak, a chief Benjamite residing at Jerusalem (I Chron. 8:22), B. C. before 588.

Ish'tob (ĭsh'tŏb; *man of Tob*), one of the small kingdoms or states which formed part of the general country of Aram (II Sam. 10:6, 8). *Ish-tob* is not to be taken as one word and rendered as a proper noun, . . . but 'the men of Tob.' *Tob* was the district between Syria and Ammonitis, where Jephthah had formerly taken refuge. *See* Tob.

Ish'uah (ĭsh'û-ȧ), the second named of the sons of Asher (Gen. 46:17; I Chron. 7:30, A. V. "Isuah"). He appears to have left no issue (comp. Num. 26:44).

Ish'uai (ĭsh'û-ī; (I Chron. 7:30). *See* Ishui, 1.

Ish'ui (ĭsh'û-ī), the name of two men.

1. The name is given as Isui (Gen. 46:17), Jesui (Num. 26:44), and Ishuai (I Chron. 7: 30), the third son of Asher, and founder of the family of "Jesuites."

2. The second named of Saul's sons by Ahinoam (I Sam. 14:49; comp. v. 50). In the list of Saul's genealogy, in I Chron., chaps. 8, 9, his name is omitted. Some, therefore, claim that he died young. In I Sam. 31:2 his place is occupied by Abinadab, with whom others identify him.

Island, Isle (Heb. *'î*).

1. The radical sense of the Hebrew word seems to be "habitable places," as opposed to water, and in this sense it occurs in Isa. 42:15, "I will make the rivers islands."

2. Any maritime district, whether belonging to a continent or to an island; thus it is used of the shore of the Mediterranean (Isa. 20:6; 23:2, 6), and of the coasts of Elishah (Ezek. 27:7), i. e., of Greece and Asia Minor. In this sense it is more particularly restricted to the shores of the Mediterranean, sometimes in the fuller expression, "islands of the sea" (Isa. 11: 11). Occasionally the word is specifically used of an island, as of Caphtor or Crete (Jer. 47: 4). But more generally it is applied to any region separated from Palestine by water, as fully described in Jer. 25:22.

The "many isles" (Ezek. 27:3) may have been the islands and coasts of Arabia, on the Persian Gulf and Erythraen Sea.

Ismachi'ah (ĭs-mȧ-kī'ȧ; *Jah will sustain*), one of the Levites charged by Hezekiah with the superintendence of the sacred offerings under the general direction of the high priest and others (II Chron. 31:13), B. C. about 719.

Isma'iah (ĭs-mā'yȧ; *Jehovah hears*), a Gibeonite, one of the chiefs of the warriors who joined themselves to David when he was at Ziklag (I Chron. 12:4), B. C. before 1000. He is described as "a hero (Gibbor) among the thirty and over the thirty," i. e., David's bodyguard, but his name does not appear in the lists of the guard in II Sam., ch. 23, and I Chron., ch. 11. Possibly he was killed in some encounter before David reached the throne (Smith).

Is'pah (ĭs'pȧ), one of the "sons" of Beriah, a chief Benjamite (originally from the neighborhood of Aijalon) resident at Jerusalem (I Chron. 8:16), B. C. before 588.

Is'rael (ĭz'râ-ĕl; *having power with God, or God's fighter*).

1. **Jacob,** the name conferred by the angel Jehovah upon *Jacob* (*q. v.*) at Peniel (Gen. 32:28).

2. **Israelites,** i. e., the whole people of Israel, the twelve tribes; called the *children of Israel* (Josh. 3:17; 7:25; Judg. 8:27; Jer. 3:21); the *house of Israel* (Exod. 16:31; 40:38); *in Israel* (I Sam. 9:9); and *land of Israel* (I Sam. 13:19; II Kings 6:23). Sometimes the whole nation is represented as one person: "Israel is my son" (Exod. 4:22; Num. 20:14; Isa. 41:8; 42:24; 43:1, 15: 44;1, 5). Israel is sometimes put emphatically for the *true Israelites*, the faithful, those distinguished for piety and virtue (Psa. 73:1; Isa. 45:17; John 1:47; Rom. 9:6; 11:26; Gal. 6:16). In the expression (Isa. 49:3), "Thou art my servant, O Israel," Christ is undoubtedly referred to.

Israelites was the usual name of the twelve tribes, from their leaving Egypt until after the death of Saul, but after the defection of the ten tribes, they arrogated to themselves the name of the whole nation (II Sam. 2:9; 10, 17, 28; 3:10, 17; 10:40-43; I Kings 12:1). The kings of the ten tribes were called *kings of Israel*, and the descendants of David, who ruled over Judah and Benjamin, were known as *kings of Judah;* and in the prophets of that period *Judah* and *Israel* are put in opposition (Hos. 4:15; 5:3, 5; 6:10; 7:1; 8:2, 3, 6, 8; 9:1, 7; Amos 1:1; 2:6; 3:14; Mic. 1:5; Isa. 5:7). Yet in Isa. 8:14 the two kingdoms are called the "houses of Israel."

After the Babylonian captivity the returned exiles, though mainly of Judah, resumed the name of Israel as the designation of their nation, but as individuals they are called Jews in the Apocrypha and New Testament. The expression "to all Israel in Judah and Benjamin" (II Chron. 11:3) characterizes all who had remained true to the house of David as Israel, i, e., those who walked in the footsteps of their progenitor Israel (Jacob) (Keil, *Com.*, in loc.).

Israel seems to have been used to distinguish laymen from priests, Levites, and other ministers (Ezra 6:16; 9:1; Neh. 11:3).

Is'rael, Classification. *See* Israel, Constitution of.

Is'rael, Constitution of. Properly to understand this subject it must be remembered that the Israelites are sometimes spoken of as one of the nations, and with a *civil* constitution. At other times they are mentioned as the people adopted into covenant with Jehovah, when reference is made to the *theocratic* constitution.

1. **The Civil Constitution.** This had respect to the classification of the people, succession and right of inheritance (*q. v.*), land (*q. v.*), and property.

Classification. The nation, in virtue of its descent from the twelve sons of Israel, formed a great family called "the house of Israel." Genealogically it was divided (Josh. 7:14, 16-18) into:

(1) **Tribes** (Heb. *măṭṭĕh*, or *shēbĕṭ*, both meaning *branch*, the former term being applied to the tribe in its genealogical branches, the latter as being under one scepter). Tribal divisions are found among many ancient peo-

ples, as the Edomites, Ishmaelites, Arabs, etc. The Hebrew tribes were founded by the twelve sons of *Jacob* (*q. v.*) as the tribal fathers of the people. An exception to this rule was made in the case of Joseph's sons, Ephraim and Manasseh, they being raised to the position of heads of tribes, having been adopted by Israel as his sons (Gen. 48:5). This would make, strictly speaking, thirteen tribes, but only twelve are uniformly reckoned (see Exod. 24:4; Josh. 4:2, sq., etc.), because Levi, as intrusted with the service of worship, occupied a mediatorial position between Jehovah and Israel; consequently no special tribal territory was allotted to them (Josh. 13:14, 33), but they dwelt in towns scattered through all the other twelve tribes. When the Levites were so reckoned Ephraim and Manasseh are included together as the tribe of Joseph (Num. 26:28; comp. v. 57; Josh. 17:14, 17). This tribal organization was still further established and completed by the giving of the land of Canaan to the Israelites according to their tribes, clans, and fathers' houses. Such a firm root did this organization take that it survived the troublous times of the judges, and was not dissolved by the introduction of the monarchy. We find the heads of tribes exercising great influence on the election of kings (I Sam. 8:4, sq.; 10:20, sq.; II Sam. 3:17, sq.; 5:1, sq.), consulted by them on all important state affairs (I Kings 8:1; 20:7; II Kings 23:1), and sometimes asserting their influence with great energy (I Kings, ch. 12). Though the tribal organization lost its firm basis with the carrying away of the people into exile, the elders maintained the internal administration and guidance of the people both in and after the exile (Jer. 20:1; Ezek. 14:1-5; 20:1). In the prophetic vision which Israel had of the future condition of his sons (Gen. 49:3, sq.), he thus enumerates them: *1*. Reuben, the firstborn; *2*. Simeon, and, *3*. Levi, instruments of cruelty; *4*. Judah, whom his brethren shall praise; *5*. Zebulun, dwelling at the haven of the sea; *6*. Issachar, a strong ass; *7*. Dan, the judge; *8*. Gad, overcome and overcoming; *9*. Asher, whose bread shall be fat; *10*. Naphtali, a hind let loose, giving goodly words; *11*. Joseph, a fruitful bough; *12*. Benjamin, a wolf. In this enumeration it is remarkable that the subsequent division of the tribe of Joseph into the two branches of Ephraim and Manasseh is not yet alluded to. Respecting the vexed question of the territory occupied by the several tribes, *see* Land; Palestine.

(2) **Families or clans** (Heb. *mĭshpähōth; circle of relatives*), the first subdivision under tribes, founded from the beginning by Jacob's grandchildren (the sons of his own or adopted sons), and also by grandchildren and great-grandchildren of the twelve heads of the tribes. Of the fifty-seven of the families into which the twelve tribes were divided in the last year of their wilderness travels (Num. 26) two belonging to Judah were formed by his grandchildren (v. 21); to Manasseh one family founded by his grandson Gilead, and six by Gilead's sons or Manasseh's great-grandsons (vers. 29-38); to Ephraim, a family founded by his grandson Eran (v. 36); to Benjamin, two families by his grandchildren, the sons of Bela

(v. 40); and to Asher, two families by his grandchildren, the sons of Beriah (v. 45). The principle according to which not only sons but grandsons and great-grandsons were raised to be founders of families is unknown.

(3) **Households** (Heb. *băyĭth, house; bēth 'āb, house of father*), a technical expression denoting the larger subdivisions or family groups into which the "families" (clans) fell. "Father's house" also denotes that family which had the primacy in every tribe or family, or that house which belonged to the father of a tribe or his representative in each division of the people.

(4) **Men** (Heb. *gĕbĕr*, a *person*), fathers with wife and children.

Government. "According to patriarchal custom, the fathers, standing by right of birth (primogeniture) at the head of the several tribes and divisions of tribes, regulated the relations of the tribes and clans, directed their common affairs, settled disputes as they arose, punished offenses and crimes, and administered law and equity. By founding clans grandchildren were often put on an equality with sons; the heads of clans and fathers' houses gradually attained to almost equal authority and standing with the heads of tribes, for each governed within his own circle, as far as was possible in that state of servitude to which the Israelites were gradually reduced in Egypt. Thus from the heads of tribes, clans, and families proceeded *elders* (*q. v.*), who, even before the time of Moses, formed the superiors of the people" (Keil, *Arch.*, ii, 312, sq.).

2. **Theocratic Constitution.** As we have already seen, the Israelites possessed in their tribal constitution the elements of a state, and it was not until their adoption into covenant with Jehovah, the Lord of the whole earth (Exod. 19:5), that they received through Moses the laws and ordinances for the kingdom which they were to establish in Canaan. This constitution is called a *theocracy* (Gr. *theokratia, rule of God*), and has its root in the peculiar relation into which Jehovah entered with the people of Israel, whom he chose to carry out his purposes of redemption (Psa. 44:4; 58:24; 74:12; Isa. 43:14, 15). According to Keil (*Arch.*, pp. 320, 321), the theocracy "consists essentially in these three things: (*a*) God himself, as Lawgiver, orders or modifies the relations of the religious and common life of the people by immediate revelation given to Moses. (*b*) He takes into his own hand the control and government of the Israelitish state or kingdom, in that he is ever really present to his people, makes known his will in important state affairs by the Urim and Thummim, by prophets, and, when necessary, interposes in a miraculous way, judging, punishing, blessing. (*c*) Finally he raises up for the people the needed leaders and rulers, and furnishes them with the power required for their office. Thus all the human superiors of the Israelites were, in the strictest sense of the word, servants and representatives of God, who had only to carry out his law, to execute his will. The one Lord and sovereign was Jehovah, the covenant God, who, as Lawgiver, supreme Judge and Ruler of his people, united in himself all the powers constituting the state, and directed them by his servants."

Under the theocracy we find that Jehovah called Moses to be the organ of his will in the *giving of the law;* that the *judicial power* was intrusted to the princes of the tribes and elders of the congregation (*see* Classification, above; Elders); the *executive* was held sometimes by the princes of the tribes, sometimes by men called of Jehovah in extraordinary cases to lead and govern the people, and invested with sovereign power; the *priesthood*, with the high priest at its head, stood between the congregation or its individual members and Jehovah in religious matters; and, lastly, as a check to the overstraining of priestly power, and to all hierarchal ambition, were the *prophets*, who, with divine authority and power, and without respect of persons, admonished all ranks to keep within the limits of the law.

Is′rael, Kingdom of. An earthly kingdom was not incompatible with the theocracy (*q. v.*), if the kings submitted unconditionally to the will of Jehovah, and, as earthly representatives of his sovereignty, wished only to execute his laws and judgments. It was not the original intention of Jehovah to leave his people as sheep without a shepherd, but to set over them a man who should lead them (Num. 27:16, sq.), as he gave them Moses and Joshua, and afterward judges from Othniel to Samuel. Knowing that Israel would long for a king, God gave a promise to the patriarchs that kings should go forth from their loins (Gen. 17:6, 16; 35:11); this promise was renewed by Moses (Deut. 28:36), and a law given relating to the king (17:14-20), whereby the earthly kingdom was incorporated in the theocracy.

1. **Law of Kingdom.** This law (Deut. 17:14, sq.) does not prescribe an earthly kingdom, but only arranges for such if desired by Israel. It provides that (1) one of their own people, and not a stranger, shall be chosen; (2) That he shall not multiply horses, i. e., strengthen his power by a standing army; (3) "Neither shall he multiply wives," that would serve to gratify lust and give oriental splendor to his court (comp. I Kings 11:3); (4) He shall carefully study the law, a copy of which was to be given him, and guide his rule thereby. This "law of the kingdom" was proclaimed by Samuel, written "in a book, and laid up before the Lord" (I Sam. 10:25).

Still further, the king set by Jehovah over his people was not a constitutional prince elected by the people, but was independent. He owed his selection to God, and was dependent upon him alone, and was bound to carry out the Mosaic law, and follow out the will of Jehovah as made known by his prophets (I Sam. 10:24; 16:1, 13; 13:13; 15:26, sq.). Thus Saul and afterward David were chosen by Jehovah to be princes over Israel, and anointed by Samuel to their office.

The kingdom was not firmly established under truly theocratic meaning by Saul. He unduly exalted himself, and was rejected because of his opposition to the will of Jehovah (*see* Saul). *David* (*q. v.*), on the contrary, was always faithful to the theocratic idea, and carefully watched over its institutions. Thus the earthly kingdom became the visible representation of Jehovah's sovereignty over Israel.

The kingdom, although intended to be

hereditary as among other peoples (Deut. 17: 20; comp. I Sam. 13:13), first became so under David in virtue of the divine promise (II Sam. 7:12, sq.). The law of succession was that the eldest or firstborn son followed his father on the throne (II Chron. 21:3), though not without exceptions (II Chron. 11:22; II Kings 23:34). If the successor was a minor a regency intervened, or the queen mother acted as sovereign (I Kings 15:13), or the high priest became guardian (II Kings 12:2).

2. **Administration.** Kings, as the "anointed of the Lord," were considered by the people as holy persons (I Sam. 24:7, 11; 26:11, 16, 23; II Sam. 1:16) without being deified, or becoming inaccessible to their subjects. In the highest cases of appeal they pronounced sentence personally (II Sam. 15:2; I Kings 3:9, 16, sq.), usually led their army in war (I Sam. 12:2, sq.; II Sam. 5:6, etc.), and publicly arranged for and conducted festivals (I Sam., ch. 6; I Kings, ch. 8).

3. **Officials.** As a bodyguard the kings had the *Cherethites* (*q. v.*) and *Pelethites* (*q. v.*), who also executed the sentences pronounced by them (II Sam. 15:18; 20:7, etc.). They were supported in their administration by many officials who served as *princes* (I Kings 4:2), or counselors. In II Sam. 8:16-18; 20:23-26; I Chron. 27:32-34 and I Kings 4:1-6 the following officials are named: (*a*) The head of the army, or commander-in-chief; (*b*) The commander of the Cherethites and Pelethites; (*c*) The recorder, probably the keeper of the state archives; (*d*) The scribe, or secretary of state; (*e*) The high priest; (*f*) Privy counselors (*Cohanim*, or friends of the king), called also "chief about the king" (I Chron. 18:17), "old men that stood before Solomon" (I Kings 12:6), "them that were in the king's presence" (II Kings 25:19; Jer. 52:25); (*g*) The overseer of public works (I Kings 5:16); (*h*) The royal treasurer, i. e., having charge of the treasures in Jerusalem, with assistant treasurers having charge of the royal fields, vineyards, flocks, etc. (I Chron. 27:25-31) besides "officers" who acted as chief tax collectors (I Kings 4:7-19); (*i*) The court marshal, or prefect of the palace (v. 5). There were also the cupbearer (10:5), keeper of the wardrobe (II Kings 10:22), and inferior servants.

In addition, after the fashion of oriental courts, but at variance with the law (Deut. 17:17), there were a large number of wives and concubines (II Sam. 5:13; I Kings 11:3; II Chron. 11:21), who, on the death of the king, became the property of his successor (II Sam. 12:8).

4. **Revenue.** This was derived from the following sources: (*a*) Voluntary gifts from subjects (I Sam. 10:27; 16:20), and from foreign visitors (I Kings 10:10, 25: II Chron. 32:23); (*b*) Regular contributions made by subjects (I Kings 4:7; comp. I Sam. 17:25); (*c*) Tribute paid by subject peoples (II Sam. 8:2; II Kings 3:4; Isa. 16:1); (*d*) The share of spoil taken in war (II Sam. 8:11; 12:30); (*e*) The produce of the royal domains, i, e., of the fields, vineyards, flocks, etc. (I Chron. 27:25, sq.; II Chron. 26:10), and the gain by commerce, etc. (I Kings 10:11, 14, 22).

5. **Continuance.** Israel, as the legitimate

kingdom, lasted until the destruction of the state by the Chaldeans, but the apostate ten tribes, revolting under the lead of Jeroboam, perished much earlier (*see* Chronology). Respecting Israel as a separate kingdom, *see* History, Old Testament.

Is'sachar (ĭs'á-kär; *he will bring reward*).

1. **The Ninth Son of Jacob** and the fifth of Leah (Gen. 30:18), B. C. about 1925. He was born at Padan-aram, and but little is recorded of him.

2. **The Tribe of Issachar.** (1) **Numbers.** At the descent into Egypt four sons are ascribed to him, who founded the four chief families of the tribe (Gen. 46:13; Num. 26:23, 25; I Chron. 7:1). The number of fighting men, when the census was taken at Sinai, was fifty-four thousand four hundred, ranking *fifth* (Num. 1:28, 29); at the second census the number had increased to sixty-four thousand three hundred, ranking *third* (26:25). (2) **Position.** Issachar's place during the journey to Canaan was on the east of the tabernacle, with his brothers Judah and Zebulun (2:3-8). At this time the captain of the tribe was Nethaneel, the son of Zuar (1:8). He was succeeded by Igal, the son of Joseph, who went as one of the spies (13:7), and he again by Paltiel, the son of Azzan, who assisted Joshua in apportioning the land of Canaan (34:26). (3) **Territory.** The allotment of Issachar lay above that of Manasseh. The specification of its boundaries and contents is contained in Josh. 19:17-23. (4) **Subsequent history.** Jacob's prophecy, "Issachar is a strong ass crouching down between two burdens; and he saw that rest was good, . . . and became a servant unto tribute" (Gen. 49:14, 15), was fulfilled by Issachar paying tribute to the various marauding tribes attracted to its territory by the richness of the crops.

3. **One of the Korhite Levites**, seventh son of Obed-edom, and one of the doorkeepers of the house of the Lord (I Chron. 26:5).

Isshi'ah (ĭs-shī'á; *lent by Jehovah*), the name of two men.

1. The first of the sons of Rehabiah, and great-grandson of Moses (I Chron. 24:21; comp. 26:25, where he is called *Jeshiah*).

2. The second son of Uzziel (grandson of Levi), and father of Zechariah (1 Chron. 24:25; comp. 23:20 where, he is called *Jesiah*).

Issue. This term has the meaning of off-spring (Gen. 48:6; Matt. 22:25); of anything ignoble, worthless, and is applied to the large and hitherto ignoble family of Eliakim, who would fasten upon him and climb through him to honor (Isa. 22:24); and of the emission of a stallion, to whom the idolatrous paramours of Judah are compared (Ezek. 23:20). *See* Diseases.

Is'uah (ĭs'ū-á; I Chron. 7:30). *See* Ishuah.

Is'ui (ĭs'ū-ī; Gen. 46:17). *See* Ishui, 1.

Ital'ian (ĭtăl'ĭ-ăn; *of* or *from Italy*, Acts 10:1). This only mention of the name in Scripture is in connection with the "band" to which Cornelius belonged. It was probably a cohort of Italians separate from the legionary soldiers, and not of the Italian Legion.

It'aly (ĭt'á-lĭ), occurs five times in Scripture (Acts 18:2; 27:1; 6, Heb. 13:24, and *subscription*). From these passages we have testimony respecting the Jewish colony in Italy, the commerce between it and Asia, and the spread of Christianity. The Italy of the New Testament denotes the whole natural peninsula between the Alps and the Straits of Messina.

Itch. *See* Diseases.

Ith'ai (ĭth'á-ī; I Chron. 11:31). *See* Ittai.

Ith'amar (ĭth'á-mär; *palm-coast*, Gesenius), the fourth and youngest son of Aaron (Exod. 6:23; Num. 3:2; I Chron. 6:3), B. C. before 1440. He was consecrated to the priesthood along with his brothers (Num. 3:3), and after the death of Nadab and Abihu, they leaving no children (Num. 3:4), he and Eleazar were appointed to their places in the priestly office (Lev. 10:6, 12; Num. 3:4; I Chron. 24:2). We learn nothing more of Ithamar, save that the property of the tabernacle (the curtains, hangings, pillars, cords, and boards) was placed under his charge (Exod. 38:21), and that he superintended its removal by the Gershonites and Merarites (Num. 4:28, 33). Ithamar with his descendants occupied the position of common priests till the high priesthood passed into his family in the person of Eli, under circumstances of which we are ignorant. Abiathar, whom Solomon deposed, was the last high priest of that line, and the pontificate reverted to the elder line of Eleazar in the person of Zadok (I Kings 2:27). A priest by the name of Daniel, of Ithamar's posterity, returned from Babylon (Ezra 8:2).

Ith'iel (ĭth'ĭ-ĕl; perhaps, *God with me*).

1. The son of Jesaiah and father of Maaseiah, a Benjamite, one of whose posterity returned with a party from Babylon (Neh. 11:7), B. C. long before 536.

2. A person mentioned along with Ucal in Prov. 30:1, to whom the words of Agur's prophecy was addressed.

Ith'mah (ĭth'má; bereavement, *orphan-hood*), a Moabite, and one of David's supplementary bodyguard (I Chron. 11:46), B. C. 950.

Ith'nan (ĭth'năn), one of the cities of south Judah (Josh. 15:23), not identified.

Ith'ra (ĭth'rá), an Israelite (but more correctly an *Ishmaelite*, according to I Chron. 2:17, where he is called *Jether*), and father of Amasa (David's general) by Abigail, David's sister (II Sam. 17:25; I Kings 2:5), B. C. before 1000.

Ith'ran (ĭth'răn; *abundance, excellence*).

1. One of the sons of Dishon, grandson of Seir the Horite (Gen. 36:26; comp. v. 30; I Chron. 1:41).

2. One of the sons of Zophah, the great-grandson of Asher (I Chron. 7:37). Perhaps the same as *Jether*, in v. 38.

Ith'ream (ĭth'rē-ăm; *residue of the people*), David's sixth son, born of Eglah in Hebron (II Sam. 3:5; I Chron. 3:3), B. C. about 1000.

Ith'rite (ĭth'rīt), the descendants of a Jether resident in Kirjath-jearim (I Chron. 2:53). David's heroes, Ira and Gareb (11:40; II Sam. 23:28) belonged to the family of *Jether* (*q. v.*).

It'tah-ka'zin (ĭt'á-kā'zĭn; *time of a judge*), a city, near the eastern boundary of Zebulun (Josh. 19:13), not identified. (R. S. V., Eth-kazin).

It'tai (ĭt'á-ī).

1. "Ittai the Gittite," i. e., a native of Gath, a Philistine in the army of David, who first appeared on the morning of David's flight from Absalom and Jerusalem. The king saw him coming with those who remained faithful, and besought him as "a stranger, and also as an exile, and as one who had but recently joined his service, to return and not ally himself to a doubtful cause. But Ittai declared himself to be the king's slave (A. V. 'servant'), and determined to share his master's fortunes. He was allowed to proceed, and passed over the Kedron with the king and his company (II Sam. 15:19, sq.), B. C. 970. When the army was numbered and organized by David at Mahanaim, Ittai appeared in command of a third part of the force, and seems to have enjoyed equal rank with Joab and Abishai (II Sam. 18:2, 5, 12). We learn nothing more of Ittai, excepting traditions and speculations which seem very improbable" (Smith, *Dict.*).

2. The son of Ribai, a Benjamite of Gibeah, one of David's thirty heroes (II Sam. 23:29). In the parallel list of I Chron. 11:31 the name is given as *Ithai*.

Iturae'a (ĭt-û-rē'á), a small province on the northwestern border of Palestine, lying along the base of Mount Hermon, and a portion of the tetrarchy of Philip (Luke 3:1). It lies N. E. of the Sea of Galilee, E. of the sources of the Jordan River.

Jetur, the son of Ishmael, gave his name, like the rest of his brethren, to the little province he colonized (Gen. 25:15, 16). Ituraea, with the adjoining provinces, fell into the hands of a chief called Zenodorus; but about B. C. 20 they were taken from him by the Roman emperor, and given to Herod the Great, who bequeathed them to his son Philip (Luke 3:1). Caligula gave Ituraea to Herod Agrippa I. When Herod Agrippa died Ituraea was incorporated into the province of Syria under procurators.

I'vah (ī'vá) A. V. and R. S. V. Ivvah, II Kings 17:24, one of the cities of the Assyrians, from which they brought colonists to repeople Samaria (II Kings 18:34; 19:13; comp. Isa. 37:13); called *Ava* (*q. v.*) in II Kings 17:24.

222. Megiddo Ivory Box with Cherubs and Lions
(c. 1250 B. C.)

Ivory was imported into Tyre by "men of Dedan" (Ezek. 27:15) and "ships of Tarshish" (I Kings 10:22), and used in ornamenting houses, constructing furniture, etc., as in the present day in the East. The tusks are called "horns" (Ezek. 27:15).

Iz'ehar (īz'ê-här; Num. 3:19), the same as Iz-har.

Iz'eharites (īz'ê-här-īts). *See* Izharites.

Iz'har (īz'här; *anointing*), the second son of Kohath, the son of Levi and father of Korah (Exod. 6:18, 21; Num. 16:1; I Chron. 6:2, 18, 38; 23:12, 18). In Num. 3:19, the name is given "Izehar." His descendants are called *Izharites*, B. C. about 1440.

Iz'harites (īz'här-īts), a family of Kohathite Levites, descended from Izhar, the son of Kohath (I Chron. 24:22; 26:23, 29), and rendered Izeharites in Num. 3:27.

Izli'ah. *See* Jezliah.

Izrahi'ah (ĭz-rà-hī'à; *Jehovah will bring forth*).
1. The son of Uzzi and great-grandson of Issachar (I Chron. 7:3).
2. A Levite (Neh. 12:42), A. V. *Jezraiah q. v.*).

Iz'rahite (ĭz'rà-hīt), a patronymic epithet of Shamhuth, one of David's generals (I Chron. 27:8); probably so called as being descended from Zerah, Judah's son.

Iz'ri (ĭz'rī; the *Jezerite*), the leader of the fourth division of Levitical singers under David (I Chron. 25:11); probably the same as *Zeri*, of the sons of Jeduthun, mentioned in v. 3, B. C. 1000.

J

Ja'akan (jā'á-kăn), the ancestor of the Bene-jaakan, round whose well the children of Israel encamped, once after they left Mosera (Num. 33:30-32), and again in a reverse direction after they left Kadesh-barnea, before they reached Mount Hor or Mosera (Deut. 10:6), B. C. before 1440. He was the son of Ezer and grandson of Seir (I Chron. 1:42), where the name is given as *Jakan*. In Gen. 36:27, the name appears in the simple form *Akan*.

Jaako'bah (jà-à-kō'bà; another form of Jacob), one of the prosperous descendants (*n°sî'îm*, princes) of Simeon that emigrated to the valley of Gedor in the time of Hezekiah (I Chron. 4:36), B. C. about 710.

Ja'ala (jā'á-là; *wild goat*), one of the Nethinim ("servants of Solomon"), whose descendants (or perhaps a place whose former inhabitants) returned from the captivity with Zerubbabel (Neh. 7:58); called in the parallel passage (Ezra 2:56) by the equivalent name *Jaalah*, B. C. before 536.

Ja'alah (jā'á-là; Ezra 2:56). *See* Jaala.

Ja'alam (jā'á-lăm), the second named of Esau's three sons by Aholibamah in Canaan (Gen. 36:5, 14: I Chron. 1;35).

Ja'anai (jā'á-nī), one of the chief Gadites resident in Bashan (I Chron. 5:12).

Ja'are-or'egim (jā'á-rê-ôr'ê-jĭm), the father of *Elhanan* (*q. v.*), a Bethlehemite, who smote Goliath the Gittite (II Sam. 21:19), but in I Chron. (20:5) it is stated that "Elhanan the son of Jair slew Lahmi the brother of Goliath," etc. The reading in Chronicles is probably the correct one, the word Oregim having crept in from the next line through oversight of the copyist.

Ja'asau (jā'á-sô; *they will do*), an Israelite of the "sons" of Bani, who renounced his Gentile wife after the return from Babylon (Ezra 10: 37), B. C. 456. R. S. V. Ja'asu.

Jaa'siel (jà-ā'sĭ-ĕl; *God makes*), the son of Abner, and ruler of the tribe of Benjamin in the time of David (I Chron. 27:21). By some he is identified with Jasiel, the Mesobaite, and one of David's bodyguard (I Chron. 11:47), B. C. about 1000.

Jaazani'ah (jà-ăz-à-nī'à; *Jehovah hears*).
1. The son of Jeremiah (not the prophet), and a chief man of the Rechabites, whom the prophet tested as to their obedience to Jona-

dab, their founder, by the offer of wine (Jer. 35:3, sq.), B. C. 606.
2. A Maachathite, son of Hoshaiah, and one of the "captains" who accompanied Johanan to pay his respects to Gedaliah at Mizpah (II Kings 25:23; Jer. 40:8), and after his assassination asked Jeremiah's advice (Jer. 42:1). He appears to have assisted Johanan in recovering the prey from Ishmael (41:11, sq.), and to have gone to Egypt with the rest (43:4, 5). In Jer. 40:8; 42:1, the name is changed to *Jezaniah*. He is doubtless the person called *Azariah* in Jer. 43:2, B. C. 588.
3. The son of Shaphan, leader of the seventy elders of Israel, seen by Ezekiel, in his vision, offering idolatrous worship at Jerusalem (Ezek. 8:11), B. C. 592.
4. The son of Azur, one of the "princes" among the twenty-five men seen (in a vision) by Ezekiel at the east gate of the temple, "devising mischief and giving wicked counsel" (Ezek. 11:1, sq.), B. C. 592.

Ja'azer (jā'á-zēr; *helpful*) or **Ja'zer** (jā'zēr), a town east of Jordan, in or near to Gilead (Num. 32:1, 3). It was taken by Israel from the Amorites (21:32), was assigned to the tribe of Gad (Num. 32:1, 3, 35), and was constituted a Levitical city (Josh. 21:39; I Chron. 26:31). It must have been a place of importance, as it gave its name to a district and dependent towns (Num. 21:32). From its being mentioned between Dibon and Nimrah, it would seem to have been located on the high plain north of Heshbon. Jaazer is mentioned in connection with the census under David (II Sam. 24:5; I Chron. 26:31), and also in the prophecies of Isaiah (16:8, 9) and Jeremiah (48:32). Père Abel identifies the site with Khirbet Jazzir, S. of Salt near Ain Hazir.

Jaazi'ah (jà-à-zī'à; *comforted* by *Jehovah*), apparently the third son or descendant of Merari the Levite, and founder of an independent house in that family (I Chron. 24:26, 27). Neither he nor his descendants are mentioned elsewhere (see 23:21-23; Exod. 6:19). The word Beno, which follows Jaaziah, should probably be translated "his son," i, e., the son of Merari (McC. and S.).

Jaa'ziel (jà-ā'zi-ĕl; *comforted* by *God*), a Levitical musician among those of the subordinate part

(I Chron. 15:18); the same as the Aziel who was one of those that performed the *soprano* (v. 20), B. C. after 1000.

Ja′bal (jā′bȧl), the son of Lamech and Adah, the brother of Jubal (Gen. 4:20), where he is described as "the father of such as dwell in tents, and have cattle." This obviously means that Jabal was the first who adopted that nomadic life still followed by many Arabian and Tartar tribes in Asia.

223. Plains of Jabbok

Jab′bok (jăb′ŏk), a stream east of the Jordan, which empties into that river nearly midway between the Dead Sea and the Sea of Galilee, or about forty-five miles S. of the latter. Its headwaters rise on the edge of Moab, only about eighteen miles E. of the Jordan. The river flows at first toward the desert under the name of Ammân, past Rabbath-Ammon; there turns N., fetches a wide compass N. W., cuts the Gilead range in two, and flows in a very winding channel W. S. W. to the Jordan. Its whole course, counting its windings, is over sixty miles. It is shallow and always fordable, except where it breaks between steep rocks. Its valley is fertile, has always been a frontier and a line of traffic. It was anciently the border of the Ammonites (Num. 21:24; Deut. 2:37; 3:16), and afterward became the boundary between the kingdoms of Sihon and Og (Josh. 12:2, 5). The earliest notice of it is the account of the mysterious struggle of Jacob with Jehovah, and the interview with his brother Esau (Gen. 32:22, sq.), both of which took place on Jabbok's southern bank. The Jabbok is now called Zerka, "the blue river."

Ja′besh (jā′bĕsh; *dry, parched*).

1. The father of *Shallum* (q. v.), which latter slew Zachariah, king of Israel, and reigned only a month (II Kings 15:10, 13, 14), B. C. before 742.

2. The short form (I Chron. 10:12 only) of *Jabesh-gilead* (q. v.).

Ja′besh-Gil′ead (jā′bĕsh-gĭl′ē-ăd; *Jabesh of Gilead*), a town of Gilead beyond Jordan, distant a night's journey from Beth-shan (I Sam. 31:11; II Sam. 2:4), and lying within the territory assigned to the eastern half-tribe of Manasseh (Num. 32:29, 40). Its inhabitants were severely punished because they did not respond to the call against Benjamin (Judg. 21:8-14), every man being put to the sword and

four hundred maidens being given to the Benjamites.

The city survived the loss of its males, and is next heard from as being besieged by Nahash the Ammonite. He offered to spare its inhabitants if they would agree to have their right eyes put out (to render them unfit for military service). Being allowed seven days to ratify the treaty, they appealed to Saul, who raised a large army and defeated the Ammonites (I Sam. 11:1, sq.).

This service was gratefully remembered, and when Saul and his sons were slain in Mount Gilboa (I Sam. 31:8) the men of Jabesh, after a night march, took down their corpses, burned them, and buried their ashes "under a tree at Jabesh." For this kindly act David sent his blessing (II Sam. 2:5).

Its site is not defined in Scripture. Josephus (*Ant.*, vi, 5, 1) calls Jabesh the metropolis of Gilead. Robinson (*Bib. Res.*, p. 320) supposes it to be the ruins of *ed-Deir* in the Wady *Yabis*.

Nelson Glueck however, locates it about 10 miles S. E. of Bethshan on twin mounds, Tell el-Meqbereh and Tell Abu Kharaz on the Wadi Yabis (Jabesh) flowing into the Jordan S. of the Lake of Galilee.

Ja′bez (jā′bĕz; *he makes sorrowful*).

1. A descendant of Judah, but of what family is not apparent. The only mention made of him is this remarkable account: "And Jabez was more honorable than his brethren: and his mother called his name Jabez, saying, Because I bare him with sorrow. And Jabez called on the God of Israel, saying, O that thou wouldest bless me indeed, and enlarge

224. Baptismal in the Jabbok

my coast, and that thine hand might be with me, and that thou wouldest keep me from evil, that it may not grieve me! And God granted him that which he requested" (I Chron. 4:9, 10). Keil (*Com.*, in loc.) supposes that this is a record of a vow made by Jabez, the conditions only being given. "The reason of this is, probably, that the vow had acquired importance sufficient to make it worthy of being handed down only from God's having so fulfilled his wish that his life became a contradiction of his name, the son of pain having been free from pain in life, and having attained to greater happiness and reputation than his brothers."

2. A place inhabited by "the families of the Scribes" (I Chron. 2:55), apparently in Judah. It is nowhere else mentioned.

Ja′bin (jā′bĭn; *he (God) understands*) probably a royal title at Hazor, like Agag among the Amalekites.

1. A king of Hazor, who organized a confederacy of the northern princes against the Israelites. These assembled with their hosts near the waters of Merom, where Joshua surprised this vast army and overthrew it. He then took Hazor and slew Jabin (Josh. 11:1-14), B. C. about 1370.

2. Another king of Hazor, and probably a descendant of the former. He is called "king of Canaan" (Judg. 4:2) in distinction from the kings of other nations, such as Moab, Mesopotamia, etc. (Keil, *Com.*). He seems to have had unusual power, as he is credited with nine hundred chariots of iron. The idolatry of the Israelites having lost them the divine protection, they became subject to Jabin, who "mightily oppressed" them for twenty years. From this they were delivered by the great victory won by Barak over the forces of Jabin. commanded by Sisera (4:3-16), B. C. about 1215-1195. The war still continued until it ended in the overthrow of Jabin. His name is mentioned in Psa. 83:9.

Jab′neel (jăb′nē-ĕl; *God builds, causes to build*).

1. A town on the northern boundary of Judah (Josh. 15:11), probably the same as *Jabneh* (*q. v.*).

2. A city on the border of Naphtali (Josh. 19:33). Little or no clew can be obtained relative to its situation.

Jab′neh (jăb′nĕ; *he (God) causes to be built*), probably the same as Jabneel (1), a point on the northern boundary of Judah, between Mount Baalah and the Mediterranean Sea. There was a constant struggle between the Danites and the Philistines, and it is not surprising that we find Jabneh in the hands of the latter. Uzziah captured this place along with Gath and Ashdod (II Chron. 26:6). Josephus calls it *Jamnia*. It still exists as a good-sized village, under the name of *Jebuah*, about two miles from the sea, seven miles S. of Joppa.

Ja′chan (jā′kăn), one of seven chief Gadite "brothers" resident in Bashan (I Chron. 5:13).

Ja′chin (jā′kĭn; *he (God) establishes*).

1. The fourth son of Simeon (Gen. 46:10; Exod. 6:15), called *Jarib* in I Chron. 4:24, founder of the Jachinites (Num. 26:12).

2. One of the priests residing in Jerusalem after the captivity (I Chron. 9:10; Neh. 11:10).

3. Head of the twenty-first course of priests in the time of David (I Chron. 24:17).

4. Jachin and Boaz were the names of two columns in the porch of Solomon's temple (I Kings 7:15-22; II Chron. 3:17). *See* Temple.

It has been convincingly shown that the names of these two columns stood for the initial words of dynastic oracles which were inscribed upon them (R. B. Y. Scott, *Jour. of Bib. Lit.*, 58, 1939, p. 143 f.; cf. Paul Garber, *Bib. Archaeologist* Feb, 1951, p. 8 f.). The Jachin formula may have been, "Yahweh will establish (*yakin*) thy throne forever," or something similar, and the "Boaz" oracle may have run, "In Yahweh is the king's strength," or something of that sort. Frequently Jachin and

225. Artist's Conception of the Chapiters or Capitals of Jachin and Boaz

Boaz have been interpreted as sacred obelisks similar to those erected beside great Egyptian temples at Thebes and Heliopolis, or beside the Temple of Melcarth at Tyre. This view is possible, since Solomon did, apparently, make concessions to the architectural fads of his day. Sometimes they have been viewed as stylized trees or again as cosmic pillars, like the Pillars of Hercules. The best interpretation seems to be that put forth by Robertson Smith years ago, who viewed them as "gigantic cressets or fire altars." W. F. Albright adopts Robertson Smith's essential view that Jachin and Boaz were immense fire altars, adducing proof from the painted tombs of Marisa in southern Palestine, where similar incense burners appear. Albright presents added evidence from the Egyptian Djed Pillar, a sacred emblem of Osiris which bears certain affinities to these structures. Most important is the fact that each of the shafts of the two pillars is represented as being crowned with an oil basin or a lamp stand, Heb. *gülläh* (I Kings 7:41); cf. Zech. 4:3 (W. F. Albright, *Archaeology and the Religion of Israel*, p. 144-148, *Bull. of Am. Schs. of Or. Res.* 85, 1942, pp. 18-27). Thus imitating Phoenician models, these immense incense stands illuminated the facade of the Moriah temple. They doubtless caught the first glint of the Jerusalem sunrise, or were wrapped in mists of the Kidron Valley. With their blazing, smoking wicks, they recalled to worshippers the fiery, cloudy pillar that led Israel of old through the wilderness. The north Syrian shrine uncovered at Tell Tainat, like Solomon's edifice, had two columns situated at its portico. Such pillars flanking the main entrance of temples were common in Syria, Phoenicia and Cyprus in the first millennium

B. C. Spreading eastward, they came into vogue in Assyria. They are to be found in Sargon's Temple at Khorsabad, late eighth century B. C., and westward to the Phoenician colonies in the western Mediterranean. (*See* Boaz). *M. F. U.*

Jacinth. *See* Mineral Kingdom.

Jackal. *See* Animal Kingdom.

Ja′cob (jā′kŏb; *heel-catcher, supplanter*) by popular etymology; but perhaps "he whom God protects" from S. Arab. and Ethiopic *'akaba, guard, keep.*

1. **The Patriarch.** The second born of the two sons of Isaac and Rebekah, his conception being supernatural, in answer to Isaac's prayer. He was born when his father was sixty years old, probably at the well Lahai-roi (Gen. 25:21-26; comp. v. 11), B. C. about 2001.

Personal History. It is recorded that Jacob grew up to be "a plain man, dwelling in tents," preferring the quiet of a home life to the active, dangerous career of a hunter. He was the favorite of his mother, while Isaac's partiality was shown toward Esau. (1) **Buys Esau's birthright.** The first incident mentioned is his purchase of Esau's birthright at the paltry price of a mess of pottage, thus making use of his brother's hunger to advance his own interests. "The birthright consisted afterward in a double portion of the father's inheritance (Deut. 21:17); but with the patriarchs it embraced the chieftainship, rule over the brethren and the entire family (Gen. 27:29), and the title to the blessing of promise (27:4, 27-29), which included the future possession of Canaan and of covenant fellowship with Jehovah (28:4)" (Keil and Delitzsch, *Com.*). (2) **Obtains Isaac's blessing.** Isaac, now aged, was about to pronounce his blessing upon Esau, his elder son, which blessing acted with all the force of a modern testamentary bequest. This was thwarted by the deception practiced upon him by Rebekah and Jacob, the latter personating Esau and helping out his mother's fraud by direct falsehood. Thus Jacob received his father's blessing (27:1-29). (3) **Jacob's flight.** Esau hated his brother because of his deception and its success, and resolved to slay him, only delaying until a sufficient time after the probably near death of his father. Rebekah, informed of Esau's purpose, advised Jacob to flee to her brother Laban, in Haran, obtaining Isaac's consent by the plea that she wished Jacob to marry one of his kinswomen and not a daughter of Canaan. Isaac blessed Jacob again and sent him away (27:41-28:5). Jacob's age is arrived at thus: Joseph was thirty years old when introduced to Pharaoh; and, allowing for seven years of plenty and two of famine (45:6), Joseph was thirty-nine years old when Jacob went to Egypt, at which time Jacob was one hundred and thirty years of age; therefore Joseph was born before Jacob was ninety-one. His birth occurred in the fourteenth year of Jacob's sojourn in Mesopotamia (30:25; 29:18, 21, 27), which would make Jacob's flight to have taken place in his seventy-seventh year. (4) **Dream at Beth-el.** On his journey he stopped at Luz for the night, and was there favored with the vision of the ladder and the ascending and descending angels. God

there confirmed to him the promises given to his fathers, and promised him protection on his journey and a safe return to his home. In recognition of the divine presence Jacob called the place Beth-el, and made a vow, and dedicated a tenth of all God gave him to Jehovah (28:10-22) (*see* Ladder). (5) **Serves Laban.** Arrived at Haran, Jacob met Rachel, Laban's daughter, by whom Jacob's coming was made known to her father. After a month Laban inquired what wages Jacob desired for his services, and he asked for Rachel on the condition of a seven years' service. At the expiration of the time, which seemed to Jacob "but a few days for the love he had to her," Laban availed himself of the customs of the country to substitute his elder daughter, Leah. Upon the discovery of the deception, Laban excused himself, saying: "It must not be so done in our country, to give the younger before the first-born"—a perfectly worthless excuse, for if it had been the custom in Haran, Laban should have told Jacob of it before. Another seven years' service gained for Jacob his beloved Rachel. Leah became the mother of Jacob's firstborn, Reuben, three other sons successively following, viz., Simeon, Levi, and Judah. Rachel, bearing no children, gave to Jacob her maid Bilhah, who bore Dan and Naphtali. Two other sons, Gad and Asher, were born of Leah's maid, Zilpah. Leah bare two more sons, Issachar and Zebulun, and a daughter, Dinah. At length Rachel became the mother of a son, whom she called Joseph (29:1-30:24). A number of years later Benjamin was born. After Jacob's fourteen years had expired he was induced by Laban to remain six years longer, and, by a hardly honorable artifice, increased greatly in wealth. This displeased Laban, so that a separation was deemed advisable (30:25-31:16). (6) **Flees from Laban.** Gathering together his family and property, he set out for Canaan, B. C. about 1960. On the third day Laban learned of Jacob's departure and followed after him, but was warned by God not to hinder his return. After much reproach and recrimination peace was restored, and Laban returned to his home (31:17, sq.). Shortly after the departure of Laban, Jacob met a company of angels, and called the place, in honor of them, Mahanaim (*two hosts*). (7) **News from Esau.** Jacob sent messengers to Esau with a friendly greeting, who brought word that his brother was on the way to meet him with four hundred men. Greatly alarmed and distressed, he divided his people, with the flocks and herds, into two companies, so that if one was attacked the other might escape. Jacob also prepared a present from his substance for Esau, hoping thus to pacify his brother. (8) **Wrestling.** Then came a night of prayer, during which the angel of the Lord wrestled with him (see Note). In attestation of his power with God, through faith, his name was changed from Jacob to *Israel* ("wrestler with God"). His request, viz., to know the name of the person with whom he wrestled, was denied him, but Jacob named the place, near Jabbok, the remarkable transaction, Peniel, "*the face of God*" (32:24, sq.). (9) **Reconciled to Esau.** In the morning Jacob saw Esau, with his army, approaching, and sent forward, first his hand-maids, then Leah and her children, and lastly Rachel and Joseph. Esau's bitter feelings gave way at the sight of his brother, his liberal gifts, and earnest entreaties. They embraced as brothers, and, for aught we know, maintained friendly relations for the rest of their lives. Jacob remained for a while on the other side of Jordan, at Succoth. He then came to She-chem, and pitched before the city of Shalem, and purchasing a plot of ground, "erected there an altar, and called it El-Elohe-Israel," i. e., *Mighty one, God of Israel* (33:1-20). Here

226. Jacob's Well

is located the well called after Jacob (John 4: 6). (10) **Goes to Beth-el.** Having been brought into collision with the people of Shechem, be-cause of the violation of Dinah and the re-venge taken by her brothers, Jacob was com-manded to go and dwell in Beth-el. He took the strange gods found in his family and buried them "under the oak which is by Shechem." There God appeared to Jacob again and blessed him, renewing the Abrahamic cove-nant. (11) **Bereavement.** While journeying from Bethel to Ephrath his beloved wife, Ra-chel, died in giving birth to her second son, Benjamin (35:20). Not long after this Jacob was sorely afflicted in the loss of his beloved son, Joseph, who was sold by his brethren (ch. 37), and by the death of Isaac. (12) **Egypt.** The great famine, predicted by Joseph, becoming very sore in Canaan, Jacob sent his sons down into Egypt to purchase grain. He retained Ben-jamin, his youngest son, "lest mischief should befall him." His sons returned with a good supply of food, and told him that they had been taken for spies, and could only disprove the charge by carrying Benjamin to the "lord of the land." His credulity was greatly tested when his sons came home with the tidings that "Joseph is yet alive." Convinced, however, of the truth of their story, he decided to go and see him before he died. On his way he was encouraged by a vision at Beer-sheba. He came to Egypt, and was affectionately re-ceived by Joseph (chap. 42:46), B. C. about

1871. By him he was presented to Pharaoh, and he and his family located in Goshen (47:1-12). This pharaoh was doubtless one of the powerful rulers of the splendid Twelfth Dynasty (2000-1780 B. C.). (13) **Death.** After a residence of seventeen years in Egypt "the time drew near that Israel must die," and, calling Joseph to him, acquainted him with the divine promise of the land of Canaan, and took from him a pledge that he would bury him with his fathers. He then adopted Joseph's sons, Ephraim andManasseh, as his own, and pronounced his benediction upon his sons. And when Jacob had made an end of com-manding his sons, he gathered up his feet in the bed and "yielded up the ghost" (49:33), at the ripe age of one hundred and forty-seven years (47:28), B. C. about 1854. His body was embalmed, carried with great care and pomp into the land of Canaan, and de-posited with his fathers and his wife Leah in the Cave of Machpelah (50:1-13). His de-scendants were led out from Egypt by Moses, and entered Canaan under the leadership of Joshua. The twelve tribes of which the nation was composed were named after his sons, with the exception that Joseph was represented by his sons Ephraim and Manasseh. The list of Jacob's descendants (46:8-27) was probably made up at the time of his decease, as we find mentioned sons of Benjamin, himself a mere youth when he went to Egypt. (14) **Scripture references.** "Hosea, in the latter days of the kingdom, seeks (12:3, 4, 12) to convert the descendants of Jacob from their state of alien-ation from God, by recalling to their memory the repeated acts of God's favor shown to their ancestor. And Malachi (1:2) strengthens the desponding hearts of the returned exiles by assuring them that the love which God be-stowed upon Jacob was not withheld from them. Besides the frequent mention of his name in conjunction with those of the other two patriarchs, there are distinct references to events in the life of Jacob in four books of the history of Jacob's birth to prove that the favor of God is independent of the order of natural descent. In Heb. 12:16, and 11:21, the trans-fer of the birthright and Jacob's dying bene-diction are referred to. His vision at Beth-el and his possession of land at Shechem are cited in John 1:51, and 4:5, 12. And Stephen in his speech (Acts 7:12, 16) mentions the famine which was the means of restoring Ja-cob to his lost son in Egypt, and the burial of the patriarch in Shechem" (Smith, *Bib. Dict.*).

Character. Jacob appears to have inherited the gentle, quiet, and retiring character of his father; also a selfishness and a prudence which approached to cunning. These showed them-selves in his reprehensible deception of his father, his dealings with Esau, and the means which he employed to make his bargain with

CHILDREN OF JACOB

By Leah.	By Rachel.	By Bilhah.	By Zilpah.
(1) Reuben	(12) Joseph	(5) Dan	(7) Gad
(2) Simeon	(13) Benjamin	(6) Naphtali	(8) Asher
(3) Levi			
(4) Judah			
(9) Issachar			
(10) Zebulun			
(11) Dinah			

his uncle (Laban) work to his own enrichment. We must remember, however, that he was inured to caution and restraint in the presence of a more vigorous brother; that he was secretly stimulated by a belief that God designed for him some superior blessing; that he was compelled to leave home to preserve his life, and obliged to cope with an avaricious and crafty uncle. But "God revived the promise over which he had brooded for sixty years, since he learned it in childhood from his mother. Angels conversed with him. Gradually he felt more and more the watchful care of an ever-present spiritual Father. Face to face he wrestled with the representative of the Almighty. And so, even though the moral consequences of his early transgressions hung about him, and saddened him with a deep knowledge of all the evil of treachery, and domestic envy, and partial judgment, and filial disobedience, yet the increasing revelations of God enlightened the old age of the patriarch; and at last the timid 'supplanter,' the man of subtle devices, waiting for the salvation of Jehovah dies, the 'soldier of God,' uttering the messages of God to his remote posterity" (Smith *Bib. Dict.*).

Figurative. The "*God of Jacob*" (Exod. 3:6; 4:5; II Sam. 23:1; Psa. 20:1; Isa. 2:3); simply "*Jacob*" (Psa. 24:6) where the term '*ĕlōhî*, God, appears to have been dropped from the text; and "*mighty One of Jacob*" (Psa. 132:2), are titles of *Jehovah* as the national deity. For the house or family of Jacob, i. e., the Israelites, we have the "house of Jacob" (Exod. 19:3; Isa. 2:5, 6; 8:17, etc.), "Seed of Jacob" (Isa. 45:19; Jer. 33:26), "the sons of Jacob" (I Kings 18:31; Mal. 3:6); "congregation of Jacob" (Deut. 33:4), and simply "Jacob" (Num. 23:7, 10, 23; 24:5, 17, 19, etc.); and the expression "in Jacob" (Gen. 49:7; Lam. 2:3), i. e., among the Jewish people.

Archaeological Light. The Nuzu Letters, excavated 1925-1941 on the ancient site of Nuzu, S. E. of Nineveh, shed great light on the patriarchs, particularly Jacob. One of the tablets parallels to some extent the relationship between Jacob and Laban (Gen. 29-31). Although the element of adoption, which is present in the Nuzu document is absent in the Biblical story, in the case from Nuzu a man adopts another as his son, giving him his daughter to wife and making him and his children heirs, unless the adopter should later beget a son of his own. In the Nuzu account, the adopted son was to receive an equal share of the estate with the actual son. However, the son's children would in this instance forfeit any right (C. H. Gordon, *Biblical Archaeologist* 3, Feb. 1940, p. 2 f.). It is also specified that the adopted son would not be entitled to take another wife in addition to the daughter of his adopted father.

Esau's selling of his birthright to Jacob (Gen. 25:27-34) is also illustrated by the rites of primogeniture at Nuzu. There a legal arrangement existed whereby the privileges of the first-born could be transferred to another. In one case they were transferred to one who was not actually a brother but was adopted as a brother. In another case, actual brothers were involved, as Esau and Jacob, and the

one who surrendered his rights received three sheep in return, to some extent at least comparable to the meal which Esau got.

The teraphim which Rachel stole from Laban (Gen. 31:34) are also illustrated from the Nuzu information. These were plainly household gods, implying leadership of the family and, in the case of a married daughter, insured her husband the right of the property of her father (Gordon, *Review Biblique*, 44, 1935, pp. 35 f.). Since Laban evidently had sons of his own when Jacob quitted him, they alone had the right to their father's gods, and the theft of these household idols by Rachel was a serious offense (Gen. 31:91, 30, 35) aimed at preserving for her husband, Jacob, the chief title to Laban's estate (cf. Jack Finegan, *Life from the Ancient Past*, Princeton, 1946, p. 55). It is interesting also to note that the name Jacob, which stands evidently for *Ya'qub-'el*, "May El protect," occurs in tablets of the eighteenth century B. C. from Chagar Bazar in north Mesopotamia (C. J. Gadd, *Iraq*, 1949, p. 38, Note 5). The name Jacob likewise occurs as a Palestinian place-name in Thutmose III's list of the fifteenth century B. C. *M. F. U.*

2. **The Father of Joseph**, the husband of the Virgin Mary (Matt. 1:15, 16), B. C. before 40.

Jacob's Well. *See* Jacob.

Ja'da (jā'dä; *knowing*), the last named of the two sons of Onam, a descendant of Judah through Jerahmeel; his two sons are likewise mentioned (I Chron. 2:28, 32).

Ja'dau (jā'dô; *knowing*), one of the sons of Nebo who divorced his Gentile wife after the exile (Ezra 10:43).

Jaddu'a, (jă-dū'á; *knowing*).

1. One of the chiefs of the people who subscribed the covenant made by Nehemiah (Neh. 10:21), B. C. 445.

2. The son of Jonathan (Neh. 12:11), and the last high priest mentioned in the Old Testament (v. 22). This is all that we learn of him from Scripture, but we gather pretty certainly that he was a priest in the reign of the last Persian king, Darius Codommanus, and that he was still priest after the Persian dynasty was overthrown, i. e., in the reign of Alexander the Great. Josephus (*Ant.*, xi, 8, 3-6) makes Jaddua high priest when Alexander invaded Judea, but the balance of his story does not deserve credit.

Ja'don (jā'dŏn; *judge*), a Meronothite who assisted in reconstructing the walls of Jerusalem after the return from Babylon (Neh. 3:7), B. C. 445.

Ja'el (jā'ĕl; *ibex, wild goat*), the wife of Heber the Kenite, and slayer of Sisera. Sisera took refuge, after the defeat of the Canaanites by Barak, in the tent of Jael, there being peace between the house of Heber and Jabin, king of Hazor. He would not, probably, have so openly violated all ideas of oriental propriety, by entering a woman's apartments, but for Jael's earnest invitation. She covered him with a quilt (A. V. "mantle"), and gave him milk to drink. Fearing discovery by his pursuers, he exacted a promise from her to preserve the secret of his concealment, and fell into a heavy sleep. Jael took one of the great wooden pins (A. V. "nail") which fastened down the cords of the tent and drove it into the temples of Sisera, until it penetrated the ground, or floor. "So he died." Barak, coming up in his pursuit of Sisera, was met by Jael, who showed him the deed she had performed (Judg. 4:17-22), B. C. about 1195.

NOTE.—Many have sought to justify the conduct of Jael; others see in it a scriptural indorsement of murder. It is not necessary to accept either alternative. The Scripture narrative simply gives the incident as a fact. Jael violated her offered hospitality, so universally sacred to the oriental mind, committing the sins of lying, treachery, and assassination. These are nowhere justified by God's word. Nor can we accept the assumption of Calovius, Buddeus, and others, that Jael offered Sisera her hospitality in perfect sincerity, and that after he was asleep was instigated by the Spirit of God to do the deed. She probably acted from prudential motives, and seeing that the Hebrews were victorious, and her people were at peace with Jabin, and fearing vengeance from them for sheltering Sisera, she conceived the purpose of slaying the sleeping and helpless man. Much more difficult is it to explain the eulogistic notice which Jael receives in the triumphal ode of Deborah and Barak, "Blessed above women shall Jael the wife of Heber the Kenite be; blessed shall she be above women in the tent," etc. (Judg. 5:24-27). We "question whether any moral commendation is *directly* intended. What Deborah stated was a *fact*, viz., that the wives of the nomad Arabs would undoubtedly regard Jael as a public benefactress, and praise her as a popular heroine. She certainly was not 'blessed' as a pious and upright person is blessed when performing a deed which embodies the noblest principles, and which goes up as a memorial before God, but merely as one who acted a part that accomplished an important purpose of heaven" (McC. and S., *Cyc.*, s. v.). "*In the days of Jael*" (Judg. 5:6). The Jael here mentioned has been supposed by some (e. g. Gesenius, Robinson, Furst, and others) to have been a local judge of the Israelites in the interval between Shamgar and Jabin. The reasons for this supposition are: 1. That the state of things described in Judg. 5:6, as existing in the days of Jael the wife of Heber, whose time was famous for the restoration of the nation to a better. 2. That the wife of a stranger would hardly have been named as marking an epoch in the history of Israel. But there is no evidence of such an interval or of such a judgeship; and it is, therefore, more natural to refer the name to the wife of Heber as the most prominent character in the period referred to. The circumstance that the name Jael is *masculine* in the Hebrew is of no force, as it is freely used (literally) of the female deer (Prov. 5:19) (McC. and S.).

Ja'gur (jā'gẽr), a town of southern Judea, on the border of Edom, mentioned (Josh. 15:21) as part of the portion of Judah. Probably Tell Ghurr, N. of Bir el-Meshash.

Jah, a contraction (Psa. 68:4) for *Jehovah* (*q. v.*). Jah also enters into the composition of many Hebrew words, as Adonijah, Isaiah, etc.

Ja'hath (jā'hăth).

1. Son of Reaiah (or Haroeh), of the posterity of Hezron, and father of two sons, Ahumai and Lahad (I Chron. 4:2).

2. A son of Shimei, grandson of Gershom and great-grandson of Levi (I Chron. 23:10). Considerable confusion occurs respecting *Shimei* (*q. v.*) and his sons. In v. 9 the three sons of Shimei are, by some error (probably the transposition of the latter clause), attributed to his brother Laadan, while in v. 11 Jahath is stated to have been "chief" (i. e., most numerous in posterity) of the *four* sons of Shimei. A similar disagreement appears in the parallel passage (I Chron., ch. 6) where Jahath (v. 43) occurs as the son of Gershom, and again (v. 20) as a son of Libnah (i. e., Laadan), instead of Shimei.

3. One of the sons of Shelomoth an Izharite of the family of Kohath, appointed by David

to a prominent place in the sacred services (I Chron. 24:22), B. C. about 960.

4. A Merarite Levite, and one of the overseers of the temple repairs carried on by King Josiah (II Chron. 34:12), B. C. 639.

Ja'haz (jā'hăz), a town in the tribe of Reuben, mentioned in connection with Moab (Isa. 15:4). It was called *Jahaza* (Josh. 13:18), *Jahazah* (21:36), and *Jahzah* (I Chron. 6:78). Sihon the Amorite was defeated here (Num. 21:33; Deut. 2:32). On the Moabite stone, lines 19, 20, the name is spelled like the shorter Hebrew form, and the place is given as a fortress, and seemingly near Dibon, but its exact location is not known.

Ja'haza (jā'hȧ-zȧ; Josh. 13:18), and **Jaha'zah** (jȧ-hā'zȧ; Josh. 21:36; Jer. 48:21), other renderings of the Hebrew *Jahaz* (*q. v.*).

Jahazi'ah (jā-hȧ-zī'ȧ; *Jehovah sees*), son of Tikvah, apparently a priest, one of those assisting Ezra in ascertaining which of the Jews had married Gentile wives after the return from Babylon (Ezra 10:15), B. C. 457.

Jaha'ziel (jȧ-hā'zĭ-ĕl; *God sees*).

1. One of the Benjamite warriors who deserted Saul and came to David when he was at Ziklag (I Chron. 12:4), B.C. shortly before 1000.

2. One of the priests, in the reign of David, appointed with Benaiah to blow the trumpet before the ark when it was brought to Jerusalem (I Chron. 16:6), B. C. about 986.

3. The third "son" of Hebron, the grandson of Levi, through Kohath (I Chron. 23:19; 24:23).

4. Son of Zechariah, a Levite of the family of Asaph, who was inspired by Jehovah to prophesy to Jehoshaphat his victory over the Moabites and others who were invading the country (II Chron. 20:14, sq.), about 875.

5. A son of Jahaziel, was chief of "the sons of Shechaniah," and returned with Ezra from Babylon with three hundred males (Ezra 8:5), B. C. 457.

Jah'dai (jä'dâ-ī), a descendant, apparently, of Caleb, of the family of Hezron; his sons' names are given, but as his own parentage is not stated (I Chron. 2:47) it can only be conjectured.

Jah'diel (jä'dĭ-ĕl), one of the heroes of the tribe of Manasseh east of Jordan (I Chron. 5:24).

Jah'do (jä'dō), a Gadite, son of Buz and father of Jeshishai, of the descendants of Abihail, resident in Gilead (I Chron. 5:14), B. C. before 771.

Jah'leel (jä'lê-ĕl), the last named of the three sons of Zebulun (Gen. 46:14; Num. 26:26). His descendants are called *Jahleelites* (Num. 26:26), B. C. before 1640.

Jah'leelites (jä'lê-ĕl-īts), the descendants of *Jahleel* (*q. v.*).

Jah'mai (jä'mâ-ī), one of the "sons" of Tola, grandson of Issachar (I Chron. 7:2).

Jah'zah (I Chron. 6:78). *See* Jahaz.

Jah'zeel (jä'zê-ĕl; *allotted by God*), the first named of the sons of Naphtali (Gen. 46:24). His descendants are called *Jahzeelites* (Num. 26:48). In I Chron. 7:13 the name is written *Jahziel* (*q. v.*).

Jah'zeelites (jä'zê-ĕl-īts; Num. 26:48), the descendants of *Jahzeel* (*q. v.*).

Jah'zerah (jä'zĕ-rȧ), the son of Meshullum

and father of Adiel, a priest (I Chron. 9:12), B. C. long before 536. He is probably the same as Azareel (Neh. 11:13).

Jah′ziel (jä′zē-ĕl; I Chron. 7:13). *See* Jahzeel.

Jailor (Gr. *desmophulax*, Acts 16:23), a keeper of a prison (*q. v.*).

Ja′ir (jā′ĭr; *he enlightens*).

1. The son of Segub, which latter was descended from Judah on his father's side (I Chron. 2:22), and from Manasseh on his mother's side. Moses reckons Jair as belonging to Manasseh (Num. 32:41; Deut. 3:14; see also I Kings 4:13), probably on account of his exploits and possessions in Gilead (I Chron. 2:23). He settled in the part of Argob bordering on Gilead, where we find the small towns taken (retaken) by him named collectively Havoth-jair, or "Jair's villages" (Num. 32:41; Deut. 3:14; I Kings 4:13; I Chron. 2:22). They are said to have numbered *twenty-three* (I Chron. 2:22), *thirty* (Judg. 10:4), and *sixty* (I Chron. 2:23; Josh. 13:30; I Kings 4:13). Perhaps the whole sixty were captured by him and his relatives, and twenty-three of them were assigned to him, others being added afterward (Mc. and S., *Cyc.*).

2. The eighth judge of Israel, a Gileadite in Manasseh (Josephus, *Ant.*, v. 7, 6), and probably a descendant of the preceding. He ruled twenty-two years, and his opulence is thus recorded: "And he had thirty sons that rode on thirty ass colts, and they had thirty cities, which were called Havoth-jair unto this day, which are in the land of Gilead." The twenty-three villages of the more ancient Jair were probably among the thirty which this Jair possessed. He was buried in Camon, probably in the same region (Judg. 10:3-5).

3. The father of Elhanan, who slew Lahmi, the brother of Goliath (I Chron. 20:5), B. C. before 1018. In the parallel passage (II Sam. 21:19) we find "*Jaare*."

4. A Benjamite, son of Shimei and father of Mordecai, Esther's uncle (Esth. 2:5), B. C. before 518.

Ja′irite, the (jā′ĭr-īts; II Sam. 20:26). *See* Ira.

Ja′irus (jā′ĭ-rŭs), a ruler of a synagogue, probably at Capernaum, whose only daughter Jesus restored to life (Mark 5:22; Luke 8:41; comp. Matt. 9:18), A. D. 27. Some have wrongfully inferred, from our Saviour's words, "The maid is not dead, but sleepeth," that the girl was only in a swoon (Olshausen, *Com.*, i, 321; Neander, *Leben Jesu*, p. 347; McC. and S., *Cyc.*).

Ja′kan (jā′kăn; I Chron. 1:42). *See* Jaakan.

Ja′keh (jā′kĕ; *pious*, cf. Arab. *waka, preserve, be pious*), the father of Agur, whose sayings are given in Prov. 30:1, sq. Beyond this mention we have no clew to the existence of either person. There is great difference of opinion as to the person intended. The traditional view is that which gives the word a figurative import (*yĭqqähäh, obedience*), and applies it to David. Others understand a real name of some unknown Israelite, which seems very likely. The R. S. V. renders: "The words of Agur Son of Jakeh of Massa."

Ja′kim (jā′kĭm; *God sets up*).

1. One of the "sons" of Shimhi, a Benjamite resident at Jerusalem (I Chron. 8:19).

2. Head of the twelfth course of priests as arranged by David (I Chron. 24:12), B. C. about 970.

Ja′lon (jā′lŏn), the last named of the four sons of Ezra, of the tribe of Judah, and, apparently, of a family kindred with that of Caleb (I Chron. 4:17).

Jam′bres (jăm′brēz), a person named as opposing Moses (II Tim. 3:8). *See* Jannes.

James (jāmz), more correctly **Jaco′bus** (jà-kō′-bŭs; Gr. *Iakōbos*—Jacob).

1. **The Son of Zebedee** (Matt. 4:21; Mark 1:19; Luke 5:10) and Salome (comp. Matt. 20:20; Mark 15:40; 16:1), and the elder brother of John the Evangelist (Mark 5:37).

Personal History. James appears first in the sacred narrative as following his occupation of fisherman, he and his brothers being partners with Simon Peter (Luke 5:10). When called by our Lord to be his followers in the spring or summer (A. D. 27), James and his brother responded with an alacrity that renders them models of obedience (Matt. 4:21; Mark 1:19). We find him named among the twelve who received (A. D. 28) a call to apostleship (Matt. 10:2; Mark 3:14; Luke 6:13; Acts 1:13). These brothers and Peter seemed for some reason to be especially fitted to live in close intimacy with the Master, and were associated on several interesting occasions. They alone were present at the transfiguration (Matt. 17:1; Mark 9:2; Luke 9:28), at the raising of Jairus's daughter (Mark 5:37; Luke 8:51), and at the garden of Gethsemane during our Lord's agony (Mark 14:33; Matt. 26:37); and with Andrew they listened to the Lord's private discourse on the fall of Jerusalem (Mark 13:3). Through mistaken views of the Messiah's kingdom, and an ambition to share in its glory, they joined in the request made to Jesus by their mother (Matt. 20:20-23; Mark 10:35). James was the first of the apostles to suffer martyrdom, being slain with the sword by command of Herod (Acts 12:2), A. D. 44. Many legends are recorded of James, but as they have no good foundation they had better be omitted.

227. Traditional Tombs
Left to right: Absalom, St. James, the Prophet Zechariah

Character. From the desire to punish the inhabitants of a certain village in Samaria, because they declined to receive Jesus (Luke 9:52-54), we infer that James and John were warm and impetuous in temperament. They were called by our Lord (Mark 3:17) Boanerges—*sons of thunder*—probably on account of their boldness and energy in discharging their apostleship.

2. **James the Less**, another of the twelve apostles. He was the son of Alphaeus (Matt.

10:3; Mark 3:18; Luke 6:15; Acts 1:13) and Mary, the sister of our Lord's mother (Matt. 27:56; Mark 15:40; Luke 24:10; John 19:25), and was called James the Less (*hō mikros, the little*) because he was younger than James the son of Zebedee, or on account of his low stature (Mark 16:1). His mother is supposed by some to have been called sister, i. e., sister-in-law, of Mary the mother of Jesus, because of their marriage to two brothers, Cleophas and Joseph. It has also been conjectured that Alphaeus died without issue, and that his wife was espoused by Joseph, on which account James is styled the (legal) son of Alphaeus and the (reputed half) brother of our Lord. James had two brothers, Judas (or Jude) the apostle and Joses (Matt. 27:56; Luke 6:16).

3. **The Brother of the Lord.** The natural interpretation of the passages Matt. 13:55; Mark 6:3 indicates that James and his brothers and sisters were sons and daughters of Joseph and Mary, the mother of Jesus. He was not one of the twelve apostles (Matt. 10:2-4), nor at first a believer in Jesus (John 7:5). From Acts 1:13, 14 we conclude that his former skepticism had passed away, as it is stated there that "his brethren" continued with the apostles and others in the "upper room" after the ascension. Although he was not one of the twelve, yet he was vouchsafed a vision of the risen Lord (I Cor. 15:5, 7). Like Paul and Barnabas, he received the title of apostle (Gal. 1:19), and was recognized by the zealots for the law as their leader (2:12). He occupied a prominent, if not the chief, place in the Church at Jerusalem (v. 9), was president of the first council (Acts 15:13), and, with the elders, received Paul upon his return from his third missionary tour (21:18), A. D. 57. He was the author of the epistle that bears his name. Eusebius tells us that James was surnamed "the Just" by the ancients on account of his eminent virtue.

NOTE.—By many James *the son of Alphaeus* and James *the brother of our Lord* are considered as identical; but this view is insisted upon principally by those who hold to the perpetual virginity of Mary, for which there is not the slightest evidence in Scripture any more than there is for "Immaculate Conception." They therefore insist that the words *brethren* and *sisters* are not to be taken in their literal sense, but in the more general one of relations, and argue that they were either (1) stepbrothers and sisters or (2) cousins. Without introducing the argument for either theory they have been dropped as untenable. That James was literally the Lord's brother is the view held by Stier, Fitch, Andrews, Farrar, Neander, Alford, Demarest, Whedon, and others. For discussion of this subject, see Whedon, *Com.*, Matt. 13:35; Andrews, *Life of our Lord;* Eadie, *Com.*, Gal. 1:19; Alford, *Introd. to James;* Woodsworth, *Introd. to James;* Johnstone, *Lectures on the Epist. of James.*

James, Epistle of. The chief of the five epistles called "catholic" or "general," in their titles in the A. V. (James, I and II Peter, I John and Jude); these epistles were addressed not to individual churches, as were most of the Pauline Epistles, but to Christians in general.

1. **Nature and Purpose.** The book is a homily written to the twelve tribes which are scattered abroad; that is, to Jewish Christians of the Dispersion. The author's aim was to rally Christians from their worldliness to the practical privileges of their profession. The

epistle has been called the most Jewish book in the N. T. Some even would go so far as to ascribe it to a non-Christian Jew and maintain that it was later adapted to Christian use by two or three phrases containing the name of Christ (1:1; 2:1). However the Christianity of the epistle is seen not so much in its subject matter as in its spirit. It is an interpretation of the O. T. law and the Sermon on the Mount in the light of the Christian gospel. The author shows acquaintanceship with the apocrypha, and was evidently influenced especially by two, Ecclesiasticus and the Wisdom of Solomon.

2. **Attestation.** Not until toward the end of the fourth century (the Third Council of Carthage, 397 A. D.) did the Epistle of James become generally recognized as canonical. Eusebius classed it among the antilegomena, yet quotes James 4:11 as scripture. It is omitted in the Muratorian canon, yet the epistle was more widely known in the first three centuries than has been supposed. The Old Syriac Version included it. Hermas evidently used it. James is frequently referred to in the Testaments of the Twelve Patriarchs. Ignatius evidently knew it as well as Polycarp, but none of these shows certain dependence upon James. However, Origin, Cyril of Jerusalem, Athanasius, Jerome and Augustine recognized the epistle as Scripture. The internal evidence is stronger than the external. The epistle thoroughly harmonizes with what we know of this James from Josephus (*Antiquities* XX:9) and the Book of Acts (15:13-21; 21:17-25) and from Galatians (1:19; 2:9, 10), as well as with the well-known circumstances of Jewish Christians in the Dispersion. The supposed opposition to Paul is purely imaginary. Properly interepreted, the opposition disappears. In the absence of doctrinal content, if there had been a forger, he would most assuredly have chosen the name of some well-known apostle and not the more or less obscure name of James, the Lord's brother.

3. **Authorship.** *See* James 3.

4. **Destination.** James evidently intended his epistle for the large number of Christian Jews scattered throughout the Roman Empire. He may have slanted it with particular reference to the eastern dispersion, since Peter addresses the Diaspora in Asia Minor where the Epistle of James, it is conjectured, would be less likely known. The Book of Acts records that there were Jews in almost every city where Christianity was planted, as at Jerusalem on the Day of Pentecost (Acts 2:9-11). Many of these were converted to Christianity and carried the message back home with them. It was to these Jewish believers that James addressed his letter.

5. **The Date.** The Epistle of James may be presumed to be very early, possibly the first epistle to Christians. This is indicated by the early martyrdom of James, according to tradition in the year 62 A. D. Much more substantial reasons, however, are adduced from the internal evidence. The epistle shows no trace of the distinctive references concerning the new age, the outcalling of the Church, the features of grace or of the relationship of Gentile converts to the law of Moses, which

resulted in the Jerusalem Council of Acts 15, over which James presided. The general absence of doctrine in the epistle, its Palestinian atmosphere, and its O. T. flavor combine to substantiate this view. The epistle shows no evidence of the Fall of Jerusalem.

6. **The Plan.** The apostle undertakes to deal with the needs of his fellow Christian believers in the Dispersion. After a brief greeting (1:1) (1) he exhorts his readers to take the proper attitude toward testings and trials (1:2-18); (2) and warns them to react properly toward the Word of God (1:19-27). (3) He rebukes a demonstration of carnal partiality (2:1-13). (4) He expounds the uselessness of faith apart from works (2:14-26). (5) He inveighs against the sin of an uncontrolled tongue (3:1-12). (6) He expounds true and false wisdom (3:13-18). (7) He advises them against quarrelsomeness, worldiness and pride (4:1-10). (8) He inculcates brotherly consideration (4:11, 12). (9) He criticizes the spirit of their business activity (4:13-5:6). (10) He calls them to patient endurance of life's misfortunes (5:7-12). (11) He shows them what to do when afflicted (5:13-18) and (12) He stresses the need for restoring a person who has gone astray (5:19, 20).

7. **Outline.** James deals with the mature believer (3:2).

Salutation—(1:1).
1. The mature believer's reaction toward trials, 1:2-18
2. His reception of the Word, 1:19-27
3. His treatment of others, 2:1-13
4. His genuine faith, 2:14-26
5. His control of the tongue, 3:1-12
6. His attitude toward true wisdom, 3:13-18
7. His amiableness, spirituality, humility, 4:1-10
8. His concern for his fellows, 4:11, 12
9. His discretion in business, 4:13-5:6
10. His patient endurance, 5:7-12
11. His conduct when afflicted, 5:13-18
12. His concern for a straying brother, 5:19, 20   *M. F. U.*

Ja'min (jā'mĭn; *right hand*).
1. The second son of Simeon (Gen. 46:10; Exod. 6:15; I Chron. 4:24), B. C. about 1871. He was founder of the family of the Jaminites (Num. 26:12).
2. The second son of Ram, the fourth in descent from Judah (I Chron. 2:27).
3. One of the priests who expounded the law to the people when read by Ezra (Neh. 8:7), B. C. about 445.

Ja'minites, the (jā'mĭn-īts), the descendants of Jamin the son of Simeon (Num. 26:12).

Jam'lech (jăm'lĕk; *whom (God) makes king*), a chief of the tribe of Simeon, apparently one of those whose family invaded the valley of Gedor in the time of Hezekiah (I Chron. 4:34), B. C. about 715.

Jangling (Gr. *mataiologia*, I Tim. 1:6), vain talking and, in Tit. 1:10 the noun, "vain talkers," i. e., those who utter empty, senseless things.

Jan'na (jăn'à), the son of Joseph and father of Melchi, the sixth in ascent from Christ on his mother's side (Luke 3:24), B. C. about 200. R. S. V. renders Jannai.

Jan'nes (jăn'ĕz). Jannes and Jambres are two of the Egyptian magicians who attempted by their enchantments to counteract the influence on Pharaoh's mind of the miracles wrought by Moses (II Tim. 3:8; comp. Exod. chaps. 7, 8).

Jano'ah (jà-nō'à; *quiet*), a place apparently in the north of Galilee, or the "land of Naphtali," one of those taken by Tiglath-pileser in his first incursion into Palestine (II Kings 15:29). No trace of it appears elsewhere.

Jano'hah (jà-nō'hà; Heb. same as Janoah), a place on the boundary of Ephraim (Josh. 16:6, 7). Eusebius gives it as twelve miles E. of Neapolis. A little less than that distance from Nablus, and about southeast in direction, two miles from Akrabeh, is the village of Yanûn, doubtless the ancient Janohah, but now a miserable village with extensive ruins of antiquity.

Ja'num (jā'nŭm; *asleep*), a town of Judah in the mountain district, apparently not far from Hebron (Josh. 15:53), not identified.

Ja'pheth (jā'fĕth; *widespreading*), one of the three sons of Noah (Gen. 5:32; 6:10; 7:13; 9:18; 10:1; I Chron. 1:4, 5). Although he is mentioned last in these passages, yet we learn from Gen. 10:21 (comp. 9:24) that he was the eldest of the three. He and his wife were preserved in the ark (Gen. 7:7; I Pet. 3:20). He had seven sons (Gen. 10:2; I Chron. 1:5), and his descendants occupied the "isles of the Gentiles" (Gen. 10:5), i. e., the coast lands of the Mediterranean Sea in Europe and Asia Minor. His act of filial piety when, with Shem, he covered his father's nakedness, is recorded in Gen. 9:20-27.

Japhi'a (jà-fī'à; *may he* i. e., God, *cause to be bright*).
1. The king of Lachish who, with three other kings, joined Adoni-zedek, king of Jerusalem, against Joshua, but was defeated and slain after confinement in the cave of Makkedah (Josh. 10:3, sq.), B. C. about 1395.
2. One of the sons of David, born to him by one of his wives, whose name is not given, at Jersualem (II Sam. 5:15; I Chron. 3:7; 14:6), B. C. after 1000.
3. A town on the eastern part of the southern boundary of Zebulun, situated on the high ground between Daberath and Gittah-hepher (Josh. 19:12). Dr. Robinson (*Researches*, iii, 194) identifies it with modern Yafa, about one and a half miles S. W. of Nazareth. This undoubtedly is the correct site.

Japh'let (jăf'lĕt; *he*, i. e., God, *will rescue*), a son of Heber and great-grandson of Asher, and father of three sons and a daughter (I Chron. 7:32, 33). Some think it to have been a branch of his descendants (Japhleti) that are mentioned in Josh. 16:3 as having settled along the border between Ephraim and Dan, but this is improbable.

Japh'leti (jăf'lĕ-tī). The boundary of "the Japhleti" is one of the landmarks on the south boundary line of Ephraim (Josh. 16:3). Perhaps the name preserves the memory of some ancient tribe who at a remote age dwelt on these hills (Smith, *Bib. Dict.*).

Ja'pho (jā'fō), the Hebrew form (Josh. 19:46) of *Joppa* (*q. v.*).

Ja'rah (jā'rà; *honey*, I Chron. 9:42). *See* Jehoadah.

Ja'reb (jā'rĕb; *he will contend; contentious*), occurs as a proper name in Hos. 5:13; 10:6, where a "King Jareb" is spoken of as the false refuge and final subjugator of the kingdom of Israel. It is a figurative title of the king of Assyria.

Ja'red (jā'rĕd; perhaps *descent*), an antediluvian patriarch, the fifth from Adam. He was the son of Mahaleel and father of Enoch (Gen. 5:15-20; I Chron. 1:2; "Jered," Luke 3:37).

Jaresi'ah (jăr-ê-sī'ȧ; origin uncertain), one of the "sons" of Jehoram, a chief man of Benjamin resident at Jerusalem (I Chron. 8:27).

Jar'ha (jär'hȧ), the Egyptian slave of Sheshan, a descendant of Jerahmeel. He was married to the daughter of his master, and, in consequence, obtained his freedom. Sheshan having no sons, his posterity were traced through this connection (I Chron. 2:34-41). Some suppose that the name of Jarha's wife as Ahlai (v. 31; comp. 34), but the masculine form of the word, and the use of Ahlai (11:41) for a man, is adverse to this conclusion. Others suppose Ahlai to be a clerical error for Attai (v. 35); others again that Ahlai was a name given to Jarha on his incorporation into the family of Sheshan, while still others conjecture that Ahlai was a son of Sheshan, born after the marriage of his daughter.

Ja'rib (jā'rĭb), *he will contend, contender*.

1. A son of Simeon (I Chron. 4:24), given in Gen. 46:10 as *Jachin* (*q. v.*).

2. One of the "chief men" sent by Ezra to procure a priest "for the house of God" on the return from Jerusalem (Ezra 8:16), B. C. about 457.

3. A priest of the "sons" of Jeshua, who divorced his Gentile wife after the captivity (Ezra 10:18), B. C. 456.

Jar'muth (jär'mŭth; *elevation, height*).

1. A town in the low country of Judah (Josh. 15:35), and the seat of the Canaanitish king Pirim. He was one of the five who conspired to punish Gibeon for having made alliance with Israel (10:3, 5), and who were routed at Beth-horon and put to death by Joshua at Makkedah (v. 23). It is identified with the modern Yarmuk, a village with the remains of walls and cisterns of early date.

2. A Levitical (Gershonite) city in the tribe of Asher (Josh. 21:29), called Remeth (19:21) and Ramoth (I Chron. 6:73).

Jaro'ah (jȧ-rō'ȧ; cf. Arab. *wariha, to be soft*), a chief man of the tribe of Gad resident in Bashan (I Chron. 5:14), B. C. before 740.

Ja'shen (jā'shĕn; *sleeping*), a person several of whose "sons" are named as among David's famous bodyguard (II Sam. 23:32), called (I Chron. 11:34) Hashem the Gizonite. The discrepancies between the two passages may, perhaps, best be reconciled by understanding the two brave men referred to as being Jonathan Ben-shammah (or Ben-shageth) and Ahiam Ben-sharar (or Ben-sacar), grandsons of Jashen (or Hashem) of Gizon, in the mountains of Judah—hence called Hararites, B. C. before 1000.

Ja'sher, Book of (jā'shēr), R. V. and R. S. V. Ja'shar, the *book of the righteous*, A. V. "Book of Jasher," (Josh. 10:13; II Sam. 1:17, 18), the book of the upright or righteous man, that is to say, of the true members of the theocracy, or godly men. From the two references given it has been justly inferred that the book was a collection of odes in praise of certain heroes of the theocracy, with historical notices of their achievements interwoven. That the passage in Joshua quoted from this work is extracted from a song is evident enough, both from the poetical form of the composition and also from the parallelism of the sentences. The reference in II Sam. 1:18 is to an elegy upon Saul and Jonathan in the Book of Jasher. By some the Book of Jasher is supposed to have perished in the captivity.

Jasho'beam (jȧ-shō'bê-ăm; *let the people return*).

1. A Hachmonite, one of David's warriors, and the first named of the two lists given of them (II Sam. 23:8, "the Tachmonite," marg. "Joshebbassebet;" I Chron. 11:11). The former passage attributes to him the defeat of eight hundred, the latter of three hundred Philistines. This is accounted for by Kennicott (*Diss.*, i, 95, 96) as follows: " . . . , the initial letter of the Hebrew words for *three* and *eight*, being used as an abbreviation, a mistake arose." Dr. Strong (McC. and S., *Cyc.*, s. v.) inclines to the supposition that "Jashobeam, or Josheb-bash-shebeth (II Sam. 23:8; margin) was the name or title of the chief, Adino and Eznite being descriptive epithets, and Hachmonite the patronymic of the same person." The exploit of breaking through the host of the Philistines to procure a draught of water from the well of Bethlehem is ascribed to the three chief heroes, and therefore to Jashobeam, the first of the three (23:13-17), B. C. before 1000. See Josheb-bash-shebeth.

2. One of the Korhites who joined David at Ziklag (I Chron. 12:6), B. C. before 1000.

3. One who commanded twenty-four thousand, and did duty in David's court in the month Nisan (I Chron. 27:2). He was the son of Zabdiel, and, if the same as No. 1, his patronymic of "the Hachmonite" must refer to his race or office.

Ja'shub (jā'shŭb; *he returns*).

1. The third son of Issachar, and founder of the family of the Jashubites (Num. 26:24; I Chron. 7:1). He is called Job (Gen. 46:13), perhaps by contraction, or corruption, or substitution, B. C. before 1871.

2. One of the sons of Bani, a layman in the time of Ezra who had to put away his foreign wife (Ezra 10:29) B. C. 456.

Jashu'bi-Le'hem (jȧ-shū'bĭ-lē'hĕm; *returner of bread*), a person or a place named among the descendants of Shelah, the son of Judah by Bath-shua the Canaanitess (I Chron. 4:22). It is probably a place, and we should infer that it lay on the western side of the tribe, in or near the Shefelah.

Ja'shubites, the (jā'shŭ-bīts), the family founded by Jashub the son of Issachar (Num. 26:24).

Ja'siel (jā'sĭ-ĕl; I Chron. 11:47). See Jaasiel.

Ja'son (jā'sŭn; *healing*), of Thessalonica, was the man who entertained Paul and Silas in that city. The mob, in consequence, assaulted his house, and, not finding his guests, dragged Jason before the ruler, who released him on security (Acts 17:5-9). He is probably the same as the Jason mentioned in Rom. 16:21, as a kinsman of Paul, and probably accompanied him to Corinth (A. D. 54).

Jasper. *See* Mineral Kingdom.

Jath'niel (jăth'nĭ-ĕl; *God bestows*), the fourth son of Meshelemiah, a Korhite Levite, one of the doorkeepers of the temple (I Chron. 26: 2), B. C. about 960.

Jat'tir (jăt'ĭr), a city in the mountains of Judah (Josh. 15:48), and with its suburbs assigned to the priests (Josh. 24:14; I Chron. 6:57). David was accustomed to visit Jattir in his freebooting days, and sent to his friends there gifts taken from his enemies (I Sam. 30:27). According to Eusebius and Jerome it was in their time a large place inhabited by Christians, twenty miles from Eleutheropolis, probably on the site occupied by the ruins of 'Attir.

Ja'van (jā'văn; Heb. *yāwän*, Arab. *yunan, Greece, Greeks*), the fourth named of the sons of Japheth, and father of Elishah, Tarshish, Kittim, and Dodanim (Gen. 10:2, 4; I Chron. 1:5, 7). The name appears in Isa. 66:19, where it is coupled with Tarshish, Pul, and Sud, and more particularly with Tubal and the "isles afar off," as representatives of the Gentile world; in Ezek. 27:13, among the places where the Syrians obtained articles of traffic; in Dan. 8:21; 10:20 (comp. 11:2; Zech. 9:13 A. V. "Graecia"), where Alexander the Great is styled king of Javan. A comparison of these passages leave no doubt that Javan was the name given to Greece by the Hebrews, and believed to be the country settled by his posterity. Javan refers more precisely to the Ionians who inhabited the coasts of Lydia and Caria, and whose cities were important commercial emporia two centuries before those on the Peloponnesus. Sargon II (721-705) first mentions them in Assyrian records as the result of an encounter with them in a naval battle.

Javelin. *See* Armor, 1 (3).

Jaw (Hebrew usually *lᵉḥî*, rendered *jawbone; jaws*, Psa. 22:15; *jaw teeth*, Prov. 30:14; *cheek teeth*, Joel 1:6). The jawbone of an ass was the weapon with which Samson once did great slaughter (Judg. 15:15). *See* Cheek.

Ja'zer (jā'zẽr; Num. 32:1, 3; Josh. 21:39; II Sam. 24:5; I Chron. 6:81; 26:31; Isa. 16:8, 9; Jer. 48:32). *See* Jaazer.

Ja'ziz (jā'zĭz), a Hagarite, and overseer of David's flocks (I Chron. 27:31), which were probably pastured east of Jordan, where the forefathers of Jaziz had lived for ages (comp. vers. 19-22).

Jealousy (Heb. *qĭn'äh*, Gr. *zēlos*), properly suspicion of a wife's purity (Num. 5:14); often used of Jehovah's sensitive regard for the true faith of his people (Exod. 20:5, etc.; II Cor. 11:2); used for anger or indignation, or intense interest for the welfare of another (Psa. 79:5; I Cor. 10:22; Zech. 1:14; 8:2). "'I, Jehovah thy God, am a jealous God,' who will not transfer to another the honor that is due to himself (Isa. 42:8; 48:11), nor tolerate the worship of any other god (Exod. 34:14), but who directs the warmth of his anger against those who hate him (Deut. 6:15) with the same energy with which the warmth of his love (Cant. 8:6) embraces those who love him, except that love in the form of grace reaches much farther than wrath" (K. and D., *Com.*, in loc.). When speaking of the jealousy

of God, we are to understand this language to be employed to illustrate, rather than represent the emotions of the divine mind. The same causes operating upon the human mind would produce what we call anger, jealousy, repentance, grief, etc.; and therefore, when these emotions are ascribed to the mind of God, this language is used because such emotions can be represented to us by no other.

Jealousy, Image of (Heb. *sēmĕl hăqqĭn'äh*), the image seen by Ezekiel in the vision of the abominations of Jewish idolatry (Ezek. 8:3, 5). The idolatrous object was such as to excite the jealousy (*q. v.*) of Jehovah; probably Baal or Asherah, whose image had already been placed in the temple by Manasseh (II Kings 21:7). "As the God of Israel, Jehovah cannot tolerate the image and worship of another god in *his* temple. To set up such an image in the temple of Jehovah was a practical renunciation of the covenant, a rejection of Jehovah on the part of Israel as its covenant God" (Keil, *Com.*, in loc.).

Jealousy Offering (Heb. *mĭnḥăth qᵉnä'ōth*, literally *offering of jealousies*, an intensive plural). If a man suspected his wife of adultery without her having been caught in the act, or without his having witnesses to prove her supposed guilt, then he was required to bring her to the priest, along with an offering (Num. 5:12, sq.). It consisted of a tenth of an ephah of barley flour, without oil or incense, called "an offering of jealousy, an offering of memorial." The priest set her before Jehovah, poured holy water (Exod. 30:18) into an earthen basin, and put dust into it from the floor of the sanctuary. Uncovering her head, he put the offering into her hand; and holding the water in his hand, he pronounced a solemn oath of purification before her, to which she responded, Amen, amen.

The dust was strewn upon the water . . . as an allusion to the fact that dust was eaten by the serpent (Gen. 3:14) as a curse of sin, and therefore as a symbol of a state deserving a curse, a state of the deepest humiliation and disgrace (Psa. 72:9; Isa. 49:23; Mic. 7:17). On the very same ground an earthen vessel was chosen, that is to say, one quite worthless in comparison with a copper one. The loosening of the hair of the head is to be regarded here as a removal or loosening of the female headdress, and a symbol of the loss of the proper ornament of female morality and conjugal fidelity. . . . The priest, as a representative of God, held the vessel in his hand, with the water in it, which was called the "*water of bitterness, the curse-bringing*," inasmuch as, if the crime imputed to her was well-founded, it would bring upon the woman bitter suffering as the curse of God.

The priest wrote these curses, those contained in the oath, in a roll, and washed them with the bitter water, i. e., washed the writing in the vessel, so that the words of the curse should pass into the water, and be imparted to it; a symbolical act, to set forth the truth that God imparted to the water the power to act injuriously upon a guilty body, though it would do no harm to an innocent one.

After all this was done he gave her the water to drink (Num. 5:11-31); although, according to v. 26, not till after the presentation of the sacrifice and the burning of the memorial upon the altar.

It cannot be determined with any certainty what was the nature of the disease threatened in the curse; but the idea of the curse seems to have been properly enunciated by Theodoret, "the punishment shall come from the same source as the sin." The punishment was to answer exactly to the crime, and to fall upon those bodily organs which had been the instruments of the woman's sin, viz., the organs of child-bearing.

Jealousy, Waters of. *See* Jealousy Offering.

Je'arim (jē'a-rĭm; *forests*), a mountain named in specifying the northern boundary of Judah (Josh. 15:10), having *Chesalon* (*q. v.*) upon it as a landmark.

Jeat'erai (jē-ăt'ē-rī), a Levite of the family of Gershom (I Chron. 6:21), generally thought to be the same called Ethni in v. 41. R. V. and R. S. V. Jeath'erai.

Jeberechi'ah (jē-bĕr-ē-kī'á; *Jehovah blesses*), the father of Zechariah (not the prophet), which latter Isaiah took as one of the witnesses of his marriage with "the prophetess" (Isa. 8:2), or, as Delitzsch thinks (*Com.*, in loc.), as witnesses of the writing upon the tablet, B. C. about 742.

Je'bus (jē'bŭs), the name of Jerusalem under Jebusite control (Josh. 15:8; Judg. 19:10); it was also called Jebusi (Josh. 18:16, 28). Jebusite Jerusalem, which David captured (II Sam. 5:8), has been shown by archaeological excavation to have been the S. W. hill, and to have been fortified by stout walls, which have been uncovered. The Jebusite city was south of the Temple area on Moriah. *See* Jerusalem.

Jeb'usite, Jeb'usites (jĕb'ū-sīt; Hebrew always singular *hăyᵉbûsî*, II Sam. 5:6; 24:16, 18; I Chron. 21:18, and *yᵉbûsî* in II Sam. 5:8; I Chron. 11:6; Zech. 9:7), one of the Canaanitish nations who were to be dispossessed by Israel. In the list of the doomed nations the Jebusites always come last, except in Ezra 9:1; Neh. 9:8. But this was not because they were of no account. They were mountaineers (Num. 13:29; Josh. 11:3). Their city was Jerusalem (Josh. 15:63), "which is Jebus" (I Chron. 11:4). Their warlike character is shown by their whole history. It was Adonizedek, king of Jerusalem, who raised the confederacy against Gibeon (Josh. 10:1-4). The Jebusites were summoned to take part in the confederacy headed by Jabin, king of Hazor (11:3). The king of Jerusalem was among those smitten by Joshua (12:10), and from Josh. 12:7 we might infer that Israel had taken their territory. But they still retained at least their royal city (Judg. 1:21) till the time of David (II Sam. 5:6-8; I Chron. 11:4-6). Living on the border between Judah and Benjamin, the Jebusites dwelt with Judah (Josh. 15:63) and with Benjamin (Judg. 1:21), to which tribe Jerusalem belonged (Josh. 18:28). It is presumably implied that neither tribe was able to dislodge them.

The only real appearance of Jebusites after this is in the story of Araunah (II Sam. 24:16-24), or Ornan (I Chron. 21:14-27), the Jebusite. Neh. 9:8 is a historical reminiscence, and probably Zech. 9:7; but Ezra 9:1 certainly seems to imply the existence of the Jebusites as a distinct heathen tribe.

Jebusites and Archaeology. Archaeology has shown that Jebusite Jerusalem lay on the eastern hill south of the higher ground which in the tenth century B. C. became Solomon's temple area. The Jebusites did not select the better location because this high place above the Kidron was already occupied by a Canaanite temple which the Jebusites did not care to displace. The site they developed as an impregnable bastion was a tiny triangle bounded by the Kidron, Tyropoeon and Zedek Valleys. Its bold rock escarpments made an ideal fortification site and its water supply from the Gihon Spring made it secure. When David took the city of the Jebusites, it was named Davidsburg, or City of David. As a result of the labors of such men as Sir Charles Warren, Clermont-Ganneau, Hermann Guthe, F. Bliss, Capt. R. Weill, John Garstang and J. W. Crowfoot, the modern limits of the City of David have been determined. Portions of the Jebusite city wall and fortifications were uncovered, including the great western gate. In part these probably go back to B. C. 2000. Evidence brought to light shows that the city which David captured was shaped like a huge human footprint about 1250 feet long and 450 feet wide, a total of not more than eight acres, comparable to the same area within the walls of Tell en-Nebeh, and the six acres of Canaanite Jericho (cf. the thirty acres of contemporary Megiddo). However, its stout walls and elevated position and perennial water supply made it virtually impregnable. David's prowess, however, took it by storm. *M. F. U.*

Jecami'ah (jĕk-a-mī'á; I Chron. 3:18), elsewhere *Jekamiah* (*q. v.*).

Jecholi'ah (jĕk-ō-lī'á; *able through Jehovah*), wife of Amaziah, king of Judah, and mother of Azariah, or Uzziah (II Kings 15:2), B. C. about 797. In II Chron. 26:3 her name is given as *Jecoliah*.

Jechoni'as (jĕk-ō-nī'ás), the Greek form (Matt. 1:11, 12) of the name of King *Jechoniah* (*q. v.*).

Jecoli'ah (jĕk-ō-lī'á; II Chron. 26:3). *See Jecholiah*.

Jeconi'ah (jĕk-ō-nī'á), an altered form of the name of King *Jehoiachin* (*q. v.*), found in I Chron. 3:16, 17; Esth. 2:6; Jer. 24:1; 27:20; 28:4; 29:2.

Jeda'iah (jē-dā'yá; *Jehovah has been kind*, cf. Arab. *yadā, to do good*).

1. (Heb. *yᵉdāyāh*). The son of Shimri and father of Allon, of the ancestors of Ziza, a chief Simeonite, who migrated to the valley of Gedor (I Chron. 4:37), B. C. before 715.

2. (Hebrew same as No. 1). Son of Harumaph, and one of those who repaired the walls of Jerusalem (Neh. 3:10), B. C. 445.

3. (Heb. *yᵉdă'yāh*; *Jehovah knows*). The chief of the second division of priests as arranged by David (I Chron. 24:7), B. C. about 960.

4. (Hebrew same as No. 3). A priest officiating in Jerusalem after the captivity (I Chron. 9:10; Neh. 11:10); in the latter passage called the son of Joiarib (probably a corrupt reading). He seems to have belonged to the family of Jeshua, nine hundred and seventy-three of his relatives accompanying him from Babylon

(Ezra 2:36; Neh. 7:39). A Jedaiah is mentioned in Neh. 12:6, 7, 19, 21, but whether the same person or not is difficult to decide, some (Smith, *Bib. Dict.*) holding that there were two priestly families of this name. He is probably identical with the Jedaiah whom the prophet was directed to crown with the symbolical wreath (Zech. 6:10-14), B. C. 536-517.

Jedi'ael (jĕ-dī'å-ĕl; *known of God*).

1. One of the "sons" of Benjamin, ancestor of many Benjamite families, numbering, according to David's census, seventeen thousand two hundred warriors (I Chron. 7:6, 10, 11). He is usually identified with Ashbel (I Chron. 8:1), but may have been a later descendant of Benjamin, who reached the first rank by reason of the fruitfulness of his house and the decadence of elder branches.

2. The son of Shimri, and one of David's heroes (I Chron. 11:45), and, perhaps, the chief of Manasseh who joined David at Ziklag (12:20), B. C. before 1000.

3. The second son of Meshelemiah, and a Korhite of the Levitical family of "the sons of Asaph." He was appointed a doorkeeper of the tabernacle by David (I Chron. 26:2), B. C. about 960.

Jedi'dah (jĕ-dī'då; *beloved*), the daughter of Adaiah of Boscath, wife of King Amon and mother of Josiah (II Kings 22:1), B. C. 640.

Jedidi'ah (jĕ-dĭ-dī'å; *beloved by Jehovah*), the name given by God through Nathan to Solomon (II Sam. 12:25).

Jedi'thun (jĕ-dī'thŭn), the form given in I Chron. 16:38; Neh. 11:17; Psa. 39, title; and 77, title, of *Jeduthun* (q. v.).

Jedu'thun (jĕ-dū'thŭn; *praise, praising*), a Merarite, and one of the masters of the sacred music appointed by David (I Chron. 16:38, sq.; 25:1, 3, etc.), B. C. about 960. From a comparison of I Chron. 15:17, 19 with 16:41, 42; 25:1, 3, 6; II Chron. 35:15, some identify him with Ethan. In II Chron. 35:15 he is called the "king's seer." His sons appear sometimes as exercising the same office (I Chron. 25:1, 3), at others as doorkeepers (16:42). His descendants are mentioned (II Chron. 29:14) as taking part in purifying the temple in the reign of Hezekiah, and later still (Neh. 11:17; I Chron. 9:16) employed about the singing. His name is used (II Chron. 35:15) instead of Jeduthunites (sons of Jeduthun).

Jee'zer (jĕ-ē'zĕr; *helpless*, abridged for *Abiezer*), a son of Gilead of Manasseh (Num. 26:30), elsewhere (Josh. 17:2, etc.) called *Abiezer* (q. v.).

Jee'zerites (jĕ-ē'zĕr-īts), the descendants (Num. 26:30) of Jeezer.

Je'gar-Sahadu'tha (jĕ'går-så-hăd-ū'thå; Aramaic, *heap of testimony*), the Aramaean name given by Laban the Syrian to the heap of stones which he erected as a memorial of the compact between Jacob and himself, while Jacob commemorated the same by setting up a pillar (Gen. 31:47), as was his custom on several other occasions. Galeed, a "witness heap," is given as the Hebrew equivalent.

Jehale'leel (jĕ-hăl-ē'lê-ĕl; *praiser of God*), a descendant of Judah whose own immediate parentage is not known. Four of his sons are enumerated (I Chron. 4:16).

Jehal'elel (jĕ-hăl'ê-lĕl; Hebrew same as above),

a Merarite Levite whose son, Azariah, took part in the restoration of the temple in the time of Hezekiah (II Chron. 29:12), B. C. 719.

Jehde'iah (jĕ-dē'yå).

1. A descendant of Shubael, or Shebuel, of the family of Gershom, and head of a division of the Levitical temple as attendants arranged by David (I Chron. 24:20; comp. 23:16), B. C. about 960.

2. A Meronothite who had charge of the royal asses under David (I Chron. 27:30), B. C. 1000.

Jehez'ekel (jĕ-hĕz'ĕ-kĕl; *God will strengthen*), the head of the twentieth "course" of priests under David (I Chron. 24:16). *See* Ezekiel.

Jehi'ah (jĕ-hī'å; *Jehovah liveth*), a Levite associated with Obed-edom as "doorkeeper of the ark" when brought by David to Jerusalem (I Chron. 15:24), B. C. 982. Called Jehiel, or Jeiel, in v. 18.

Jehi'el (jĕ-hī'ĕl).

1. A Benjamite, apparently the founder ("father") of, and resident at, Gibeon, and the husband of Maachah. A number of his sons are named (I Chron. 9:35, sq.; comp. 8:29).

2. The son of Hothan, an Aroerite, one of David's heroes (I Chron. 11:44), B. C. 993.

3. A Levite "of the second degree," appointed by David to play upon a psaltery on the occasion of the removal of the ark to Jerusalem (I Chron. 15:18, 20), in which former passage he and those named with him are called "porters." He is apparently the *Jehiah* of v. 24. By some he is identified with the Gershonite head of the Bene-Laadan in the time of David (23:8), who had charge of the treasures (29:8). If so, his descendants were called *Jehieli* (Jehielites, 26:21), B. C. 982.

4. Son of Hachmoni (or a Hachmonite), who was "with the king's sons," probably as tutor (I Chron. 27:32). The mention of Ahithophel (v. 33) seems to fix the date before the revolt, B. C. perhaps about 976.

5. The second named of the six brothers of Jehoram, and son of King Jehoshaphat (II Chron. 21:2). These brothers were all murdered by Jehoram upon his accession (v. 4), B. C. 850.

6. One of the descendants ("sons") of Heman the singer, who assisted King Hezekiah in his reformations (II Chron. 29:14), and probably the same person who was appointed one of the superintendents of the sacred offerings (31:13), B. C. 719.

7. One of the "rulers of the house of God," who contributed liberally toward the temple sacrifices in the time of King Josiah (II Chron. 35:8), B. C. 639.

8. The father of Obadiah, which latter returned with two hundred and eighteen males of the sons of Joab from Babylon, with Ezra (Ezra 8:9), B. C. before 457.

9. A priest, one of the "sons" of Harim, who divorced his Gentile wife after the exile (Ezra 10:21), B. C. 457.

10. One of the "sons" of Elam, who put away his Gentile wife after the captivity (Ezra 10:26), and probably the father of Shechaniah, who proposed that measure (v. 2), B. C. 457.

Jehi'eli (jĕ-hī'ĕ-lī; *Jehielite*), a Gershonite Levite of the family of Laadan. His sons had charge of the treasures of the Lord's house (I Chron. 26:21, 22), B. C. before 960.

Jehizki'ah (jĕ-hĭz-kī'á; same as *Hezekiah, Jehovah strengthens*), the son of Shallum, one of the leaders of Ephraim, who, at the instance of Obed the prophet, insisted upon the liberation of the captives brought into Samaria by the army under Pekah in the campaign against Judah (II Chron. 28:12; comp. vers. 8, 13, 15), B. C. about 741.

Jeho'adah (jĕ-hō'á-dá; *whom Jehovah adorns*), son of Ahaz, the great-grandson of Jonathan, the son of Saul (I Chron. 8:36), called *Jarah* (*q. v.*) in I Chron. 9:42, R. V. and R. S. V. Jehoaddah.

Jehoad'dan (jĕ-hô-ăd'ăn; perhaps, *Jehovah delights*), a woman of Jerusalem, queen of Joash and mother of Amaziah (II Kings 14:2; II Chron. 25:1), B. C. 825.

Jeho'ahaz (jĕ-hō'á-hăz; *Jehovah has laid hold of*, abbreviated, Jo'ahaz).

1. The son and successor of Jehu, the twelfth king of Israel after the division of the kingdom (II Kings 10:35). He reigned seventeen years B. C. 815-799. Following the sins of Jeroboam, his forces were defeated by the Syrians until they were reduced to fifty horsemen, ten chariots, and ten thousand footmen. In his humiliation he besought Jehovah, and a deliverer was granted to Israel, probably in the person of *Jehoash* (*q. v.*), his son, who expelled the Syrians and reestablished the affairs of the kingdom (II Kings 13:1-9, 25).

2. The third son of Josiah by Hamutal, called *Shallum* in I Chron. 3:15, where he is given as the fourth son, but by a comparison of II Kings 23:31, and II Chron. 36:11, we find that Zedekiah was the younger. After his father had been slain in resisting the progress of Pharaoh-necho, Jehoahaz was raised to the throne, at the age of twenty-three years, in preference to his elder brother, Jehoiakim (II Kings 23:31, 36). He was anointed at Jerusalem (v. 30), and found the land full of trouble, but free from idolatry (v. 24). He is described as an evil-doer (v. 32) and an oppressor (Ezek. 19:3), but seems to have been lamented by the people (Jer. 22:10; Ezek. 19:1). Pharaohnecho, upon his return from the Euphrates, removed him from the throne, and put Jehoiakim in his place. Jehoahaz was taken first to Riblah in Syria, and then to Egypt, where he died. His reign lasted only three months, B. C. 608.

3. The name given (II Chron. 21:17; 25:23) to the youngest son of Jehoram, king of Judah; usually called *Ahaziah* (*q. v.*).

Jeho'ash (jĕ-hō'ăsh; *Jehovah has given*, cf. Arab. *'asa, 'awasa*, to bestow).

1. The eighth king of Judah, and son of King Ahaziah (II Kings 11:2), by Zibiah (II Kings 12:1; II Chron. 24:1). He was born B. C. about 843. His aunt, Jehosheba, saved him from the massacre by *Athaliah* (*q, v.*). At the age of seven years he seems to have been the only living descendant of Solomon, and was then brought into the temple and anointed king. *Jehoida* (*q. v.*), the high priest, thought the time ripe for overthrowing the power of Athaliah, the usurper, and secured the cooperation of the royal bodyguard. The noisy greeting that was accorded Jehoash brought

Athaliah to the temple, where she was seized and slain, B. C. about 836. Jehoash behaved well as long as Jehoida, his uncle, lived. Excepting that the high places were still resorted to for incense and sacrifice, pure religion was restored, and the temple was repaired. But after the death of his aged counselor, evil advisers led him into sin; the law was neglected, idolatry prevailed, and God's anger kindled against him. Prophets were sent to warn him, but the ungrateful king responded by putting to death Zechariah, the son and successor of his benefactor Jehoiada. In about a year Hazael, king of Syria, came against him, overcame his forces, and, appearing before Jerusalem, was bought off with the treasures of the temple. Jehoash also suffered from a painful malady, and was at length slain by his own servants, B. C. about 797. He was buried in the city of David, but not in the sepulcher of the kings (II Kings chaps. 11, 12; II Chron. 24). He is one of the three kings omitted in the genealogy of Christ (Matt. 1:8).

2. The son and successor of Jehoahaz, king of Israel. (1) **Reign.** He became viceroy to his father (II Kings 13:10), reigning thirteenth over the separate kingdom sixteen years, including his viceroyship, B. C. 799-783. According to the scriptural account, Jehoash "did that which was evil in the sight of the Lord; he departed not from all the sins of Jeroboam, the son of Nebat, who made Israel sin: but he walked therein" (II Kings 13:11). Josephus says (*Ant.*, ix, 8, 6) that "He was a good man, and in disposition was not at all like his father." The statement in Kings is supposed by some to refer to the first part of his reign, while that of Josephus relates to the latter part, after a reclamation. (2) **Interview with Elisha.** Jehoash held Elisha in great veneration, and when he heard of the prophet's last illness he went to his bedside, wept over him, and said, "O, my father, my father, the chariot of Israel, and the horsemen thereof." The prophet promised him deliverance from the Syrian yoke in Aphek, and bid him smite upon the ground. The king smote thrice and then stayed, whereupon the prophet rebuked him for staying, and limited to three his victories over Syria. These promises were accomplished after the prophet's death, Jehoash in three successive victories overcoming the Syrians and retaking from them the towns which Hazael had rent from Israel (II Kings 13:10, sq.). (3) **War.** The success of Jehoash appears to have made Amaziah, king of Judah, jealous, and he sought a quarrel with him. Jehoash replied with the parable of the "Thistle and the Cedar." But Amaziah was determined in his purpose, and a war ensued in which Jehoash was victorious. Having defeated Amaziah in Beth-shemesh, in Judah, he advanced against Jerusalem, broke down the walls to the extent of four hundred cubits, and carried away the treasures both of the temple and the palace, together with hostages for the future good behavior of Amaziah (II Chron. 25:17-24). Jehoash, soon after his victory, died in peace, and was buried in Samaria (II Kings 14:8-16).

Jehoha'nan (jĕ-hô-hā'năn; *Jehovah is favorable*).

1. A Korhite, and head of the sixth division

of the Levitical temple porters (I Chron. 26: 3), B. C. about 960.

2. The second named of the "captains" of Jehoshaphat, king of Judah. He commanded two hundred and eighty thousand men (II Chron. 17:15), and is, probably, the same whose son Ishmael supported Jehoiada in the restoration of prince Jehoash (23:1), B. C. about 875.

3. An Israelite of the family of Bebai, who divorced his Gentile wife after the exile (Ezra 10:28), B. C. 456.

4. A leading priest, descendant of Amariah, which latter returned with Zerubbabel. He was contemporary with Joiakim (Neh. 12:13; comp. vers. 2 and 12), B. C. considerably after 536.

5. A priest who took part in the musical services at the dedication of the walls of Jerusalem by Nehemiah (Neh. 12:42), B. C. 445.

Jehoi'achin (jĕ-hoi'á-kĭn; *Jehovah will establish*), son of Jehoiakim, king of Judah, and Nehushta, daughter of Elnathan of Jerusalem; called also Coniah (1) **Reign.** He succeeded his father as the nineteenth king over the separate kingdom, and reigned three months and ten days, B. C. 597. His age at his accession was eighteen years, according to II Kings 24:8, but eight years according to II Chron. 36:9 (see *Note*). Jehoiachin "did that which was evil in the sight of the Lord," and probably opposed the interests of the Chaldean empire, for in three months after his accession we find Nebuchadnezzar laying siege to Jerusalem, as Jeremiah had predicted (Jer. 22:18-30). Immediately after Jehoiachin's succession the Egyptians were completely driven out of Asia, the fortresses south of Jerusalem were invested, and numbers of the inhabitants of the lowlands carried away as prisoners. Jerusalem was at the time quite defenseless, and in a short time Jehoiachin surrendered at discretion (with the queen-mother, and all his servants, captains, and officers) to Nebuchadnezzar, who carried them, with the eunuchs and harem, to Babylon (Jer. 24:1, 29; comp. Ezek. 17:2). The number of captives is given in II Kings 24:14 as ten thousand, including warriors, craftsmen, and others. Nebuchadnezzar also took the treasures found in palace and temple (v. 13), and placed Mattaniah, the only surviving son of Josiah, on the throne, changing his name to Zedekiah (II Kings 24:14-17). (2) **Captivity.** Jehoiachin was placed in prison in Babylon, where he remained for thirty-six years, until the death of Nebuchadnezzar, when Evil-merodach not only released him, but gave him a seat at his own table and an allowance for his support (II Kings 25:27-30; Jer. 52:31-34), B. C. 561. We learn from Jer. 28:4, that four years after he had gone to Babylon there was an expectation at Jerusalem of Jehoiachin's return, but Jeremiah accuses Hananiah, who thus prophesied, of falsehood (v. 15). The tenor of Jeremiah's letter of the elders of the captivity (ch. 29) would seem to indicate that there was a party among the captivity who were looking for the overthrow of Nebuchadnezzar and the return of Jehoiachin. Neither Daniel nor Ezekiel makes any further allusion to him, except that Ezekiel dates his prophesies by the year

"of King Johoiachin's captivity" (1:2; 8:1; 24:1, etc.), the latest date being the twenty-seventh year (29:17; 40:1). (3) **Jehoiachin and Archaeology.** The archaeologist's spade has given remarkable minute corroboration of the Biblical notices of Jehoiachin's captivity. In excavations near the Ishtar Gate of Babylon almost 300 clay tablets dating from 595-570 B. C. were recovered from some fourteen rooms. These important documents contain receipts of barley, oil and other supplies which had been rationed to captive artisans and workmen exiled from many lands. King Jehoiachin appears as "Yaukin, king of the land of Yahud (Judah)" as the recipient of these rations. Moreover, the cuneiform tablets carry the names of Jehoiachin's five sons and their Jewish attendant, named Kenaiah. These tablets, discovered by E. F. Weidner, point to the fact that several of the sons were born before 592 B. C., with the eldest, Shealtiel, father of Zerubbabel, born c. 598 B. C. at the latest, which makes Zerubbabel at the time of the reconstruction of the second temple (c. 520-516 B. C.) older than had been commonly supposed. In addition, three clay jar handles dug up at Beth Shemesh and Kiriath-sepher (see Debir) were impressed with a seal in old Phoenician script "belonging to Eliakim, steward of Yaukin." This indicates that the crown property was in charge of Eliakim during Jehoiachin's exile and that Zedekiah, expecting a possible return of his royal nephew, did not seize the property of the rightful ruler. (See Biblical Archaeologist V, 4, Dec. 1942).

NOTE.—(1) *Jehoiachin's Age.* He was at his accession eighteen years of age, according to II Kings 24:8, but only eight according to II Chron. 36:9. The usual explanation of this difference is that he reigned ten years in conjunction with his father. This would make him eight at the beginning of his joint reign, and eighteen when he began to reign alone. "The probability is that 'eight' in the latter text is a corruption (the *yodh*, 10, being dropped out)" (Haley, *Discrepancies*). (2) *Time of Capture.* His capture was in Nebuchadnezzar's eighth year, according to II Kings 24:12; but in the seventh according to Jer. 52:28. This discrepancy may have arisen either from a slight mistake in numeral letters or else from a different method of counting regnal years (Haley, *Discrepancies*). (3) *Childless.* The expression (Jer. 22:30) "Write ye this man childless" refers to his having no legally reckoned successor on the throne, for he had children (Orelli, *Com.*, in loc.).

Jehoi'ada (jĕ-hoi'á-dà; *Jehovah knows*).

1. The father of Benaiah, one of David's chief warriors (II Sam. 8:18; 20:23; 23:20, 22; I Kings 1:8, sq.; 2:25, sq.; 4:4; I Chron. 11:22, 24; 18:17; 27:5), B. C. before 1000. He is probably the same person mentioned as leader of three thousand seven hundred Aaronites who assisted David at Hebron (I Chron. 12:27). In I Chron. 27:34 his name seems to have been transposed with that of his son, although Keil (*Com.*, in loc.) suggests that the Jehoiada mentioned there was a grandson of this Jehoiada.

2. The high priest at the time of Athaliah's usurpation, about B. C. 842, and during most of the reign of Jehoash. He married Jehosheba, daughter of King Jehoram and sister of King Ahaziah. When *Athaliah* (*q. v.*) slew the royal family, Jehoiada with his wife stole and secreted Jehoash, and after six years placed him on the throne. In this revolution Jehoiada showed great tact and ability. He waited until

public sentiment seemed ripe for a change, and then entered into secret alliance with the chief partisans of the house of David and of the true religion. He gathered at Jerusalem the Levites from the different cities, and concentrated a large concealed force in the temple by the expedient of not dismissing the old courses of priests and Levites when their successors came to relieve them. These were armed by means of the shields and armor deposited in the temple treasury by David, divided into three bands, and posted at the principal entrances. The courts were filled with people favorable to the cause, and then Jehoiada produced the young king, and crowned and anointed him, and presented him with a copy of the Law, according to Deut. 17:18-20. Nor did Jehoiada forget the sanctity of the temple, none but the priests and ministering Levites being allowed to enter; and strict orders having been given that Athaliah should not be slain within its precincts. The new reign was inaugurated by a solemn covenant between himself, as high priest, and the people and king to renounce the worship of Baal, which was followed by the destruction of the altar and temple of Baal and the death of his priest, Mattan. His influence over the young king was very beneficial, who ruled well and prosperously during Jehoiada's lifetime. The restoration of the temple in the twenty-third year of his reign was carried on under Jehoiada's supervision. For account of this work see II Kings, ch. 12, and II Chron., ch. 24. At length he died at the age of one hundred and thirty years (II Chron. 24:15), and, as a signal honor, was buried "in the city of David among the kings," B. C. perhaps 798. He is, doubtless, the same as Berechiah (Barachias, Matt. 23:25), whose son Zechariah was slain by command of the king (II Chron. 24:20-22).

3. The son of Paseah, apparently one of the chief priests who with Meshullam repaired the "old gate" of Jerusalem (Neh. 3:6), B. C. 446.

4. A priest who was in Jerusalem when the Jews were led into captivity, but who was displaced, Zephaniah being put in his stead (Jer. 29:26).

Jehoi′akim (je̅-hoi′å-kĭm; *Jehovah raises up*), the eighteenth king of the separate kingdom of Judah.

1. **Name and Family.** His original name was Eliakim, but its equivalent, Jehoiakim, was given him by Pharaoh-necho, the Egyptian king. He was the second son of Josiah by Zebudah, the daughter of Pedaiah of Rumah (II Kings 23:36), born B. C. about 633.

2. **Personal History.** (1) **Made king.** Jehoiakim's younger brother, Jehoahaz, or Shallum (Jer. 22:11), was made a king at the death of his father, Josiah. The intention, probably, was for him to follow up his father's policy in siding with Nebuchadnezzar against Egypt. Pharaoh-necho, having overcome all resistance with his victorious army, deposed Jehoahaz, made him a prisoner in Riblah, and afterward took him to Egypt. He set Eliakim upon the throne, B. C. 608, changing his name to Jehoiakim, and charged him with collecting a tribute of one hundred talents of silver and a talent of gold, nearly two hundred

thousand dollars (II Kings 23:33-35; II Chron. 36:3, 4). (2) **Made a vassal.** After the battle of Carchemish Nebuchadnezzar captured Jerusalem, and, taking the king prisoner, "bound him in fetters to carry him to Babylon." He also took "of the vessels of the house of the Lord," and carried them to the temple of Bel (his god) in Babylon (II Chron. 36:6, 7). Nebuchadnezzar, for some reason, seems to have abandoned his intention of conveying Jehoiakim to Babylon, and restored him to his throne as a vassal (II Kings 24:1; Jer. 25:1). (3) **Destroys the roll.** In the fourth year of Jehoiakim's reign the prophet Jeremiah caused a collection of his prophecies to be written out by Baruch and publicly read in the temple. This coming to the knowledge of the king, he sent for it and had it read before him. He listened to only a small portion of it, and then took the roll, and, cutting it in pieces, burned it in the fire. But Jeremiah was bidden to take another roll and write upon it the same words, with the addition of another and an awful denunciation (Jer., ch. 36). (4) **Rebellion and death.** After three years of subjection Jehoiakim, deluded by the Egyptian party in his court (comp. Jeosephus, *Ant.*, x, 6, 2), withheld his tribute and rebelled against Nebuchadnezzar (II Kings 24:1). This step was taken against the earnest protestation of Jeremiah, and in violation of his oath. We are not informed as to what moved Jehoiakim to this rebellion, but it may be that seeing Egypt entirely severed from the affairs of Syria since the battle of Carchemish, and Nebuchadnezzar wholly occupied with distant wars, he hoped to make himself entirely independent. His reign was now turbulent and unhappy. Bands of Chaldeans, Syrians, Moabites, and Ammonites came against him and cruelly harassed the country. It was perhaps at this time that the great drought occurred described in Jer., ch. 14 (comp. Jer., ch. 15, with II Kings 24:2, 3). In the closing years of his reign the Ammonites appear to have overrun the land of Gad (Jer. 49:1), and other nations ravaged Israel (Ezek., ch. 25). Jehoiakim came to his end, as was predicted, in a violent manner, and his body was thrown over the wall, perhaps to convince the enemy of his death. It was afterward taken away and given an unhonored burial (Jer. 22:18, 19; 36:30; II Kings 23:36; 24:1-7; II Chron. 36:4-8), B. C. 597.

3. **Character.** Jehoiakim was a vicious and irreligious man, and one who encouraged the abominations of idolatry (Jer. 19, which chapter is supposed to refer to his reign). The vindictive pursuit of *Urijah* (*q. v.*), and the indignities offered to his corpse by the king's command, are samples of his irreligion and cruelty (26:20-23). His daring impiety is shown by his treatment of the roll containing Jeremiah's prophecy; and his selfishness is shown by his spending large sums in building magnificent palaces for himself when the land was impoverished by the tributes laid upon it by Egypt and Babylon (22:14, 15).

NOTE.—(1) *No Successor.* In Jer. 36:30 it is predicted of Jehoiakim that "He shall have none to sit upon the throne of David," While II Kings 24:6 states that "Jehoiachin his son reigned in his stead." In answer, we state that Jehoiachin's reign lasted but three months, and the Hebrew term rendered "sit" in Jeremiah implies some degree of permanance; and hence there is no collision between the passages (Haley, *Discrepancies*, p. 346). (2) *Carried to Babylon*, etc. It is stated in II Chron. 36:6 that Nebuchadnezzar bound Jehoiakim in fetters to carry him to Babylon; but in II Kings 24:6 it is said that he "slept with his fathers," and in Jer. 22:19 that his body should be "cast forth beyond the gates of Jerusalem." The probability is that he was bound with the intention of carrying him to Babylon, but instead was slain and his corpse ignominiously treated (Rawlinson).

Jehoi′arib (jê-hoi′à-rĭb; *Jehovah will contend*), head of the first of the twenty-four courses of priests, as arranged by David (I Chron. 24: 7), B. C. about 961. Some of his descendants returned from the Babylonian captivity (I Chron. 9:10; Neh. 11:10, A. V. "Joiarib"). Jewish tradition asserts that only four of the courses returned from Babylon, viz., Jedaiah, Immer, Pashur, and Harim, and that they were subdivided into six each, to keep up the old number of twenty-four. But we find that other of the priestly courses are mentioned as returning (Neh. 10:2-8), and in the list (12:1-7) that Jehoiarib is expressly mentioned. In the other passages the name is abbreviated, both in Hebrew and A. V., to *Joiarib* (*q. v.*).

Jehon′adab (jê-hŏn′à-dăb) also Jonadab (jŏn′à-dăb; *Jehovah is magnanimous*).

1. The son of Shimeah, and nephew of David, and a friend of Amnon. He gave the latter the wicked advice that resulted in the ensnaring of Amnon's sister, Tamar (II Sam. 13:), B. C. about 974. When Amnon was murdered by Absalom, and the exaggerated report reached David that all the princes were slaughtered, Jonadab was aware of the real fact, and, being with the king, assured him that Amnon alone was slain (vers. 32, 33; A. V. shorter form "Jonadab").

2. A son (or descendant) of Rechab, the founder of a peculiar tribe, who bound themselves to abstain from wine, and never to relinquish the nomadic life. This mode of life, partly monastic, partly Bedoiun, was adhered to from generation to generation, and when, many years after the death of Jehonadab, the Rechabites were forced to take refuge from the Chaldean invasion within the walls of Jerusalem, nothing would induce them to transgress the rule of their ancestor (Jer. 35:19, A. V. "Jonadab"). The single occasion in which Jehonadab appears before us in the historical narrative is in II Kings 10:15, sq., B. C. about 842. Jehu was advancing, after the slaughter of Betheked, on the city of Samaria, and met Jehonadab. Upon being assured that he was in sympathy with the king, he was taken up into the chariot and intrusted with the king's secret, viz., the destruction of the Baalites. He then proceeded to Samaria in the royal chariot. It may be that Jehonadab had been commissioned by the people of Samaria to meet the king on the road and appease him. If so, his venerable character, his rank as head of a tribe, and his neutral position, well qualified him for the task. No doubt he acted with Jehu throughout, but the only occasion in which he is expressly mentioned is when he went with Jehu through the temple of Baal to turn out any who might happen to be in the mass of pagan worshipers (II Kings 10: 23).

Jehon′athan (jê-hŏn′à-thăn; *Jehovah has given*).

1. The full Hebrew form of the name *Jonathan* (*q. v.*), the eldest son of King Saul. The name is given in the A. V. in the shorter form.

2. The son of Uzziah, and superintendent of certain of King David's storehouses (I Chron. 27:25), B. C. after 1000.

3. The name of one of the Levites sent by Jehoshaphat through the cities of Judah to teach the law to the people (II Chron. 17:8), 17:8), B. C. 875.

4. The name of a priest (Neh. 12:18), and a representative of the family of Shemaiah (v. 6) in the days of Joiakim, B. C. after 536.

Jeho′ram (jê-hō′răm; *Jehovah is high*). contracted form *Joram*.

1. The son of Ahab and Jezebel, and successor of his brother Ahaziah, who died childless. He was the tenth king on the separate throne of Israel, and reigned twelve years. (II Kings 1:17; 3:1), B. C. about 853-842.

Personal History. (1) **War against Moabites.** After the death of Ahab the Moabites, who had been tributary to Israel, asserted their independence; and their king, *Mesha* (*q. v.*), withheld his tribute of one hundred thousand lambs and one hundred thousand rams, with the wool. Thereupon Jehoram asked and obtained the help of Jehoshaphat (king of Judah) in a war against the revolting Moabites. While marching through the wilderness of Edom the armies were in great danger through lack of water. Jehoshaphat suggested an inquiry of some prophet of Jehovah, and Elisha was found with the host. He severely rebuked Jehoram, and bid him inquire of the prophets of Baal; but afterward predicted a great victory over the Moabites. The king was directed to have many ditches dug in the valley, and was assured that they would be filled immediately with water. The Moabites, advancing, saw the water reddened like blood with the rays of the morning sun, and concluding that the allies had fallen out and slain each other, advanced incautiously. They were put to rout, and their land utterly ravaged (II Kings 3:1-25). (2) **Invasion of Samaria.** A little later war again broke out between Syria and Israel, and we find Elisha befriending Jehoram. The king was made acquainted with the secret counsels of the Syrian king, and was thus enabled to defeat them; and the blinding of the Syrian soldiers by God procured a cessation of the invasion (II Kings 6:8-23). (3) **Further disasters.** But it seems probable that when the Syrian inroads ceased, and he felt less dependent upon the aid of the prophet, he relapsed into idolatry, and was rebuked by Elisha, and threatened with a return of the calamities from which he had escaped. Refusing to repent, a fresh invasion by the Syrians and a close siege of Samaria actually came to pass, according, probably, to the word of the prophet. Hence, when the terrible incident arose, in consequence of the famine, of a woman boiling and eating her own child, the king immediately attributed the evil to Elisha, the son of Shaphat, and determined to take away his life. The providential interposition by which both Elisha's life was saved and the city delivered is narrated in II Kings, ch. 7, and Jehoram appears to have returned to a friendly feeling toward Elisha (II Kings 8:4, sq.). (4) **Alliance with Ahaziah.** It was very soon after the above events that Elisha went to Damascus and predicted the revolt of Hazael and his accession to the throne of Syria in the room of Ben-hadad. Jehoram seems to have thought the revolution in Syria, which immediately followed Elisha's prediction, a good opportunity to pursue his father's favorite project of recovering Ramoth-gilead from the Syrians. He accordingly made an alliance with his nephew Ahaziah, who had just succeeded Joram on the throne of Judah, and the two kings proceeded to occupy Ramoth-gilead by force. The expedition was an unfortunate one. Jehoram was wounded in battle, and obliged to return to Jezreel to be healed of his wounds (II Kings 8:29; 9:14, 15), leaving his army under Jehu to hold Ramoth-gilead against Hazael. Jehu, however, and the army under his command, revolted from their allegiance to Jehoram (II Kings, ch. 9), and, hastily marching to Jezreel, surprised Jehoram, wounded and defenseless as he was. Jehoram, going out to meet him, fell pierced by an arrow from Jehu's bow on the very plat of ground which Ahab had wrested from Naboth the Jezreelite; thus fulfilling to the letter the prophecy of Elijah (I Kings 21:21-29). With the life of Jehoram ended the dynasty of Omri. Jehoram, like his father, was an idolater, laying aside his worship of Baal, probably after his rebuke by Elisha, but still clinging to the abominations of Jeroboam (I Kings 12:26, 31, 32).

2. Eldest son and successor of Jehoshaphat, and fifth king on the separate throne of Judah. He was crowned at the age of thirty-two, and reigned eight years, about B. C. 850-843 (II Kings 8:16; II Chron. 21:1-6). Jehosheba, his daughter, was wife to the high priest Jehoiada. As soon as he was fixed on the throne he put his six brothers to death, with many of the chief nobles of the land. He then, probably at the instance of his wife, Athaliah, the daughter of Ahab, proceeded to establish the worship of Baal (II Kings 8:18, 19). A prophetic writing from the aged prophet Elijah (II Chron. 21: 12-15) failed to produce any good effect upon him. This was in the first, or second year of his reign. The remainder of it was a series of calamities. First the Edomites, who had been tributary to Jehoshaphat, revolted from his dominion, and, according to old prophecies (Gen. 27:40), established their permanent independence. Next Libnah, one of the strongest fortified cities in Judah (II Kings 19:8), rebelled against him. Then followed invasions of armed bands of Philistines and of Arabians, who stormed the king's palace, put his wives and all his children, except his youngest son, Ahaziah, to death (II Chron. 22:1), or carried them into captivity, and plundered all his treasures. He died of a terrible disease (II Chron. 21:19, 20) early in the twelfth year of his brother-in-law Jehoram's reign over Israel.

Character. Jehoram was an impious and cruel tyrant, manifesting his impiety by the setting up of Baal worship in the high places, and prostituting the daughters of Judah to the infamous rites of Ashteroth; and showing his cruelty by the murder of all his brothers—the

first example of that abominable mode of avoiding a disputed succession.

Note.—(1) *Jehoram's accession.* It is stated in II Kings 1:17 that Jehoram, the son of Ahab, began to reign in the second year of Jehoram, the son of Jehoshaphat; while in II Kings 8:16 it says that the latter began to reign in the fifth year of the former. To reconcile these statements let us remember that Jehoram, the son of Jehoshaphat, was for some time joint ruler with his father. Now, suppose that in the second year of this joint reign Jehoram (son of Ahab) began his reign; then that in the fifth year of the latter the former began to reign alone. This will make the joint reign about five years long. (2) *Jehoram's sons.* In II Chron. 21:16, 17 it is stated that the sons of Jehoram were taken captive; but in II Chron. 22:1 that they were slain. The presumption is that they were first taken captive and afterward slain.

3. One of the priests sent by Jehoshaphat to instruct the people in the law (II Chron. 17: 8), B. C. after 875.

Jehoshab′eath (jê-hŏ-shăb′ê-ăth; *Jehovah is an oath*), the form in which the name of *Jehosheba* (*q. v.*) is given in II Chron. 22:11. It is stated here, but not in Kings, that she was the wife of Jehoiada, the high priest.

Jehosh′aphat (jê-hŏsh′á-făt; *Jehovah judged*).

1. Son of Ahilud, who filled the office of recorder or annalist in the courts of David (II Sam. 8:16; 20:24; I Chron. 18:15) and Solomon (I Kings 4:3), B. C. 984-965.

2. Son of Paruah, one of the twelve purveyors of King Solomon (I Kings 4:17). His district was Issachar, B. C. about 960.

3. The fourth king of the separate kingdom of Judah was the son of Asa (by Azubah), whom he succeeded on the throne when he was thirty-five years old, and reigned twenty-five years (about 875-850). His history is to be found among the events recorded in I Kings 15:24; II Kings 8:16, or in a continuous narrative in II Chron. 17:1-21:3. He was contemporary with Ahab, Ahaziah, and Jehoram. (1) **Strengthens himself.** At first he strengthened himself against Israel by fortifying and garrisoning the cities of Judah and the Ephraimite conquests of Asa (II Chron. 17: 1, 2). But soon afterward the two Hebrew kings, perhaps appreciating their common danger from Damascus and the tribes on their eastern frontier, formed an alliance. Jeshoshaphat's eldest son, Jehoram, married Athaliah, the daughter of Ahab and Jezebel. (2) **Resists idolatry.** In his own kingdom Jehoshaphat ever showed himself a zealous follower of the commandments of God; he tried, it would seem not quite successfully, to put down the high places and groves in which the people of Judah burnt incense (I Kings 22:43; II Chron. 17:6; 20:33). In his third year he sent out certain princes, priests, and Levites, to go through all the cities of Judah, teaching the people out of the Book of the Law (II Chron. 17:7-9). Riches and honors increased around him. He received tribute from the Philistines and Arabians, and kept up a large standing army in Jerusalem (II Chron. 17:10, sq.). (3) **Alliance with Ahab.** He went to Samaria to visit Ahab and become his ally against the Syrians. Desirous of consulting the Lord, Micah was sent for; but he did not make the impression upon Jehoshaphat which might have been expected, or else the king felt bound in honor not to recede. He came very

near falling a victim to the plan that Ahab had laid for his own safety, but escaped and returned to Jerusalem in peace (I Kings 22:1, sq.; II Chron., ch. 18-19:1). There he met the just reproaches of the prophet Jehu, and went himself through the people, "from Beersheba to Mount Ephraim," reclaiming them to the law of God (II Chron. 19:1-3). (4) **Further reforms.** He tried to remedy the many defects in the local administration of justice and applied himself to their remedy. He appointed magistrates in every city, and a supreme council at Jerusalem, composed of priests, Levites, and "the chief of the fathers," to which difficult cases were referred, and appeals brought from the provincial tribunals (II Chron. 19:4-11). (5) **Commerce.** Turning his attention to foreign commerce, he built at Ezion-geber, with the help of Ahaziah, a navy designed to go to Ophir; but it was wrecked at Ezion-geber. He afterward, through the advice of Eliezer, the prophet, declined the cooperation of the king of Israel, and the voyage prospered. The trade was, however, soon abandoned (II Chron. 20:35-37; I Kings 22:49). (6) **Wars.** After the death of Ahaziah, king of Israel, Jehoram, his successor, persuaded Jehoshaphat to join him in an expedition against Moab. The allied armies were saved by a miraculous supply of water, and were afterward victorious over the enemy (II Kings 3:4-27). Another war, and to Jehoshaphat much more dangerous, was kindled by this. The Moabites turned their wrath against him, and induced the Ammonites, the Syrians, and the Edomites to unite with them. Jehoshaphat, believing that his help was to come from God, proclaimed a fast, and the people assembled in Jerusalem, to implore divine assistance. "And Jehoshaphat stood in the congregation of Judah and Jerusalem, in the house of the Lord, before the new court. . . . O our God, wilt thou not judge them? for we have no might against this great company that cometh against us; neither know we what to do; but our eyes are upon thee." After he ceased praying Jehaziel, a Levite, pronounced deliverance in the name of the Lord, assuring Judah of the overthrow of the enemy without a blow from them. And so it happened; for the allies quarreled among themselves and destroyed each other. This great event was recognized by the surrounding nations as the act of God, and they allowed Jehoshaphat to close his life in quiet (II Chron. ch., 20). During the last years of his reign his son *Jehoram* (*q. v.*) was associated with him in the government. His name (Josaphat) occurs in the ancestral list of our Lord (Matt. 1:8).

Character. The character of Jehoshaphat is thus summed up: "Jehoshaphat sought the Lord with all his heart" (II Chron. 22:9). His good talents, the benevolence of his disposition, and his generally sound judgment, are shown not only in the great measures of domestic policy which distinguished his reign, but by the manner in which they were executed. No trace can be found in him of that pride which dishonored some and ruined others of the kings who preceded and followed him.

4. Son of Nimshi and father of King Jehu (II Kings 9:2, 14), B. C. before 842.

5. One of the priests who (I Chron. 15:24) were appointed to blow trumpets before the ark when it was carried from the house of Obed-edom to Jerusalem, B. C. about 982.

Jehosh'aphat (jḗ-hŏsh'à-făt), **Valley of,** the name given to the valley situated between Jerusalem and the Mount of Olives, which in modern times had been used by the Jews as a burying-ground. There is a typical use of the word, in a sense of divine judgments upon the enemies of God and his people (Joel 3:2, 12). In this valley Jehoshaphat overthrew the united enemies of Israel (II Chron. 20:26, A. V. "valley of Berachah").

228. Kidron Valley, Wall of Jerusalem on Right

From about the fourth century A. D. the Valley of Jehoshaphat has been identified with the Kidron. This identification is based on Joel 3:2, 12 and particularly Zechariah, chapter 14, but since no actual valley bore this name in pre-Christian antiquity, Joel's prophetic employment of it is figurative of the place where the judgment of the nations will take place prior to Christ's Second Advent and the setting-up of the millennial kingdom.

Jehosh'eba (jḗ-hŏsh'-ē-bà; *Jehovah her oath*, that is, worshiper of Jehovah), the daughter of Joram, sister of Ahaziah, aunt of Joash, all kings of Judah, and wife of Jehoiada, the high priest (II Kings 11:2). Her name in the Chronicles (II Chron. 22) is given *Jehoshabeath*. As she is called (II Kings 11:2), "the daughter of *Joram*, sister of Ahaziah," it has been conjectured that she was the daughter, not of Athaliah, but of Joram by another wife. By her the infant Joash was rescued from the massacre of the seed royal by Athaliah, and he and his nurse secreted in the palace and afterward in the temple (II Kings 11:2, 3; II Chron. 22:11, 12). He was brought up, probably, with her sons (II Chron. 23:11), who assisted at his coronation (B. C. 842).

Jehosh'ua (jḗ-hŏsh'ū-à; Num. 13:16), or **Jehosh'uah** (I Chron. 7:27), fuller forms in the A. V. of the name *Joshua* (*q. v.*).

Jeho'vah (jḗ-hō'và; Heb. YHWH, LXX. usually *ho Kurios*, the name of God most frequently used in the Hebrew Scriptures; but commonly represented—we cannot say rendered—in the A. V. by "Lord."

1. **Pronunciation.** The true pronunciation of this name, by which God was known to the Hebrews, has been entirely lost, the Jews themselves scrupulously avoiding every mention of it, and substituting in its stead one or other of the words with whose proper vowel

points it may happen to be written, usually the name Adonai. They continued to write *Yhwh*, but read Adonai. Where God is called "*My Lord Jehovah*" (Heb. Adonai *Yhwh*), to avoid the double Adonai, Elohim was substituted. When the vowel points were added to the Hebrew text the rule, in the case of words written but not read, was to attach to these words the vowels belonging to the words read in place of them. Thus they attached to *Yhwh* the points of *'ădōnāy*; hence the form *Yᵉhōwäh* and the name Yᵉh′v′h. The strong probability is that the name Jehovah was anciently pronounced *Yähwĕh*, like the *Iabe* of the Samaritans. This custom, which had its origin in reverence, and has almost degenerated into a superstition, was founded upon an erroneous rendering of Lev. 24:16, from which it was inferred that the mere utterance of the name constituted a capital offense. According to Jewish tradition, it was pronounced but once a year by the high priest on the Day of Atonement when he entered the Holy of Holies; but on this point there is some doubt. On the authority of Maimonides we learn that it ceased with Simeon the Just. But even after the destruction of the second temple instances are met with of individuals who were in possession of the mysterious secret.

2. **Import.** The passage in Exod. 3:14 seems to furnish designedly a clew to the meaning of the word. When Moses received his commission to be the deliverer of Israel, the Almighty, who appeared in the burning bush, communicated to him the name which he should give as the credentials of his mission: "And God said unto Moses, *I am that I am* (Heb. *'ĕhyĕh 'ăshĕr 'ĕhyĕh*), and he said, Thus shalt thou say unto the children of Israel, *I am* hath sent me unto you."

In both names *'ĕhyĕh* and *Yhwh*, the root idea is that of *underived existence*. When it is said that God's name is *He Is*, simple being is not all that is affirmed. *He is* in a sense in which no other being *is*. He is; and the cause of his being is in himself. *He is because he is.* . . . From the idea of *underived and independent existence*, which seems to be the root idea in this divine name, follows that of *independent and uncontrolled will and action*.

3. **When Made Known.** "The words 'By my name *Jehovah* was I not known to them' (Exod. 6:3) do not mean, however, that the patriarchs were altogether ignorant of the name Jehovah. When Jehovah established his covenant with Abram he said, 'I am *El Shaddai*, God Almighty,' and from that time forward manifested himself to Abram and his wife as the Almighty, in the birth of Isaac, which took place apart altogether from the powers of nature, and also in the preservation, guidance, and multiplication of his seed; now he was about to reveal himself to Israel as *Jehovah*, as the absolute Being working with unbounded freedom in the performance of his promises" (K. and D., *Com.*, on Exod. 6:3). Respecting the difference between Jehovah and Elohim, *see* Elohim.

Jeho′vah-Ji′reh (jė-hō′vȧ-jī′rĕ; *Jehovah will see*, i. e., *provide*), the name given by Abraham to the mount on which the angel of the Lord appeared to him and not only arrested

the sacrifice of Isaac, but provided a ram in his place (Gen. 22:14). *See* Moriah.

Jeho′vah-Nis′si (jė-hō′-vȧ-nĭs′ī; *Jehovah my banner*), the name given by Moses to an altar which he erected upon the hill where he sat with uplifted hands during the successful battle against the Amalekites (Exod. 17:15). Nothing is said about sacrifices being offered upon the altar, and it has been suggested that the altar with its expressive name was merely to serve as a memorial to posterity of the gracious help of Jehovah.

Jeho′vah-Sha′lom (jė-hō′vȧ-shä′lŏm; *Jehovah-peace*), the name given to an altar erected by Gideon in Ophrah after Jehovah had given him the commission to deliver Israel from the Midianites, confirming it by miracles and a message of peace (Judg. 6:24). As it was a time of backsliding, Gideon gave expression to his surprise and gratitude by erecting this altar a monument to Jehovah as the God of peace.

Jeho′vah-Sham′mah (jė-hō′vȧ-shăm′ȧ; *Jehovah is there*), the figurative name given by Ezekiel (48:35, A. V. "The Lord is there") to millennial Jerusalem seen by him in his vision. The expression signifies that Jehovah has turned his favor once more to Jerusalem which will enjoy great prosperity as the capital of the earth in the Kingdom Age.

Jehoz′abad (jė-hŏz′ȧ-băd; *Jehovah endowed*).

1. The son of Shomer (or Shimrith), a Moabitess, and one of the two servants who assassinated King Jehoash of Judah in that part of Jerusalem called Millo (II Kings 12:21; II Chron. 24:26), B. C. about 797.

2. A Korahite Levite, second son of Obed-edom, and one of the porters of the south gate of the temple, and of the storehouse appointed by David (I Chron. 26:4, 15), B. C. about 967.

3. The last named of Jehoshaphat's generals, who had the command of one hundred and eighty thousand troops (II Chron. 17:18), B. C. about 875.

Jehoz′adak (jė-hŏz′ȧ-dăk; *Jehovah has justified*), A. V. "Josedech" in Haggai and Zechariah; also contracted Jozadak in Ezra and Nehemiah), son of the high priest Seraiah at the time of the Babylonian captivity (I Chron. 6:14, 15), B. C. 588. Whether he succeeded to the high priesthood after the slaughter of his father (II Kings 25:18-21) is not known. But if he did he had no opportunity of performing the functions of his office, as he was carried to Babylon by Nebuchadnezzar (I Chron. 6:15). He probably died in exile, as his son Joshua (Jeshua) was the first high priest who officiated after the return from captivity (Hag. 1:1, 12, 14; 2:2, 4; Zech. 6:11; Ezra 3:2, 8; 5:2; 10:18; Neh. 12:26).

Je′hu (jē′hū; Gesenius, *Jehovah is He*).

1. The son of Hanani; a prophet of Judah, but whose ministrations were chiefly directed to Israel. His father was probably the seer who rebuked Asa (II Chron. 16:7). He must have begun his career as a prophet when very young. He first denounced Baasha (I Kings 16:1, 7), and then, after an interval of thirty years, reappears to reprove Jehoshaphat for his alliance with Ahab (II Chron. 19:2, 3). He survived Jehoshaphat and wrote his life (20:34), B. C. about 879-850.

2. The eleventh king of the separate kingdom of Israel.

Family. Jehu was the son of Jehoshaphat (II Kings 9:2), and the grandson of Nimshi, although sometimes called the latter's son (I Kings 19:16).

Personal History. The first appearance of Jehu is when, with a comrade in arms, Bidkar, he rode behind Ahab on the journey from Samaria to Jezreel (II Kings 9:25). Elijah was commanded at Horeb to anoint him king, but, for unknown reasons, did not do so (I Kings 19:16, 17). (1) **Anointed king.** Jehu meantime, in the reigns of Ahaziah and Jehoram, had risen to importance. He was, under the last-named king, captain of the host in the seige of Ramoth-gilead. While in the midst of the officers of the besieging army a youth suddenly entered, of wild appearance, and insisted on a private interview with Jehu. They retired into a secret chamber. The youth uncovered a vial of sacred oil, poured it over Jehu's head, and after announcing to him the message from Elisha, that he was appointed to be king of Israel and destroyer of the house of Ahab, rushed out of the house and disappeared. Jehu's countenance, as he reentered the assembly of officers, showed that some strange tidings had reached him. He tried at

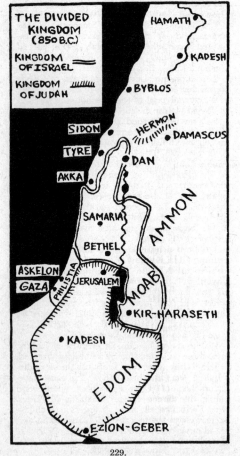

THE DIVIDED KINGDOM (850 B.C.)

KINGDOM OF ISRAEL

KINGDOM OF JUDAH

HAMATH

KADESH

BYBLOS

SIDON

HERMON

DAMASCUS

TYRE

DAN

AKKA

SAMARIA

AMMON

BETHEL

ASKELON

PHILISTIA

JERUSALEM

GAZA

MOAB

KIR-HARASETH

KADESH

EDOM

EZION-GEBER

229.

first to evade their questions, but then revealed the situation in which he found himself placed by the prophetic call. In a moment the enthusiasm of the army took fire. They threw their garments under his feet, so as to form a rough carpet of state; then blew the royal salute on their trumpets, and thus ordained him king (II Kings 9:1-13), c. B. C. 842 (2) **Slays the kings.** Jehu accepted the kingdom, and immediately began to make it secure. He cut off all communication between Ramoth-gilead and Jezreel, and set off at full speed with Bidkar, whom he had made captain of his host. Jehoram was there (suffering from wounds received at the hands of the Syrians), as well as Ahaziah, king of Judah, who had come to see him. The watchman told of the coming of a company, and as it neared the city he announced to the kings that "the driving is like the driving of Jehu" (9:20). When near the city the alarm was taken, and the two kings hastened out and met Jehu in the field of Naboth. In answer to the question of Jehoram, "Is it peace, Jehu?" the latter replied, "What peace, so long as the whoredoms of thy mother Jezebel and her witchcrafts are so many?" Then he drew his bow and smote Jehoram, while his followers pursued and mortally wounded Ahaziah. Jehu advanced to Jezreel and fulfilled the divine warning on Jezebel. The queen appeared at the palace window as if to welcome Jehu, but he shouted, "Who is on my side?" Two eunuchs appeared, and at his command they threw her from the window (9:14-37). (3) **Destroys house of Ahab.** Jehu then sent a letter to the rulers, challenging them to set up one of the young princes as king, and fight out the matter. They replied that they were ready to submit to him; whereupon he ordered them to appear the next day with the heads of all the royal princes of Samaria, which they did. He explained that he must be regarded as the appointed minister of the divine decrees against the house of Ahab, and proceeded to slay all the officers of the late government who would most likely disturb his own reign (10:1-11). Proceeding to Samaria he met forty-two sons (or nephews) of Ahaziah, king of Judah, and put them to the sword (II Kings 10:12-14; II Chron. 22:8). (4) **Destroys Baalites.** On his way to Samaria he met Jehonadab, the Rechabite, to whom he confided his purpose of exterminating the Baalites. Arriving at Samaria, he announced that he was to be even more enthusiastic in the service of Baal than Ahab had been, and summoned them to come and sacrifice to that god. When they were assembled in the temple, clad in their sacerdotal garments, Jehu offered the chief sacrifice, Jehonadab joining in the deception. At a concerted signal the eighty trusted guards fell upon and massacred the worshippers, and thus at one blow exterminated the heathen population of Israel. The temple and image of Baal were demolished and the sanctuary became a resort for the basest uses (II Kings 10:15-28). (5) **Sin and punishment.** Jehu sinned against God in not overturning the golden calves worshipped in Beth-el and Dan, and thus continued in the sin of Jeroboam. For this it was foretold that his dynasty should only extend to four generations. (6) **His wars.** After his violent political and religious purge in Israel, Jehu incurred the implacable hatred of Hazael (*q. v.*) of Damascus by submitting to Shalmaneser III, king of Assyria, in the Assyrian invasion of 841 B. C., rather than joining Syria in a coalition against the encroachments of "the

230. One of the Panels of the Obelisk of Shalmaneser III, Showing Jehu Paying Tribute to the Assyrian, 841 B. C.

giant of the Semites." The Black Obelisk of Shalmaneser III, which Austen Layard found in the imperial palace at Nimrud, displays Jehu actually prostrating himself before the Assyrian emperor. The accompanying inscription reads: "Tribute of Iaua (Jehu), son of Omri. Silver, gold, a golden bowl, a golden beaker, golden goblets, pitchers of gold, lead, staves for the hand of the king, javelins I received from him" (D. D. Luckenbill, *Ancient Records of Assyria and Babylonia*, Chicago, 1927, Vol. I, section 590). But Assyrian withdrawal for the time from the West and Hazael's growing power, must have made Jehu lament his Assyrian appeasement policy. The Aramaeans began to "thresh" Gilead and Bashan "with threshing instruments of iron" (II Kings 10:32, 33; Amos 1:3, 4) before Jehu passed off the scene around 815 B. C. M. F. U.

Character. Jehu was a very positive and ambitious character; quick to decide upon a plan of action, and equally ready in execution. He was prudent, calculating, and passionless. The narrative justifies us, we think, in judging that his zeal for God was regulated very much by his zeal for Jehu. "He must be regarded, like many others in history, as an instrument for accomplishing great purposes rather than as great or good in himself. In the long period during which his destiny, though known to others and perhaps to himself, lay dormant; in the ruthlessness with which he carried out his purposes; in the union of profound silence and dissimulation with a stern, fanatic, wayward zeal, he has not been without his likenesses in modern times" (Smith, *Dict.*, s. v.).

3. The son of Obed and father of Azariah, of the tribe of Judah (I Chron. 2:38).

4. A Simeonite, son of Josibiah, and one of the chief Simeonites who moved into the valley of Gedor in search of pasturage during the reign of Hezekiah. They smote and dispossessed the original inhabitants (I Chron. 4:35-41), B. C. about 713.

5. An Antothite, one of the chief of the slingers of Benjamin, who joined David at Ziklag (I Chron. 12:3), B. C. before 1000.

Jehub′bah (jĕ-hŭb′à; *hidden*), a man of Asher, son of Shamer, or Shomer, of the house of Beriah (I Chron. 7:34).

Jehu′cal (jĕ-hū′kăl; *Jehovah is able*), the son of Shelemiah, and the person who was sent with Zephaniah by King Hezekiah to Jeremiah to request that he would pray to Jehovah in behalf of the kingdom (Jer. 37:3). He afterward joined with his associates in requesting the death of the prophet because of his unfavorable response (38:4), in which verse he is styled one of "the princes." In 38:1 his name is given in the abbreviated form Jucal.

Je′hud (jĕ′hŭd; *praise*), a town on the border of Dan, named between Baalath and Bene-berak (Josh. 19:45). The modern site is Ya-zūr, 5 miles S. E. of Joppa.

Jehu′di (jĕ-hū′dī; *a man of Judah, a Jew*), the son of Nethaniah, employed by the princes of Jehoiakim's court to bring Baruch to read Jeremiah's denunciation (Jer. 36:14), and then by the king to fetch the volume itself and read it to him (vers. 21, 23), B. C. 608.

Jehudi′jah (jĕ-hû-dī′jà; *Jewess*), not a proper name, as in the A. V.), the wife, probably, of Mered (I Chron. 4:18). The following readjustment of the text is proposed to clear away its obscurity: "These are the sons of Bithiah the daughter of Pharaoh, which Mered took, and she bare Miriam, etc., and his wife Jehudijah bare Jered," etc. (Jamieson, Fausset, and Brown, *Com.*, in loc.). She is probably the same as *Hodiah* (v. 19).

Je′hush (jĕ′hŭsh), son of Eshek, a remote descendant of Saul (I Chron. 8:39).

Jei′el (jĕ-î′-ĕl).

1. A Reubenite of the house of Joel at the time of the taking of some census, apparently on the deportation of the trans-Jordanic tribes by Tilgath-pilezer (I Chron. 5:7), B. C. about 740.

2. A Merarite Levite appointed by David to assist in the removal of the ark to Jerusalem (I Chron. 16:5). He is probably the same as the one mentioned in the same verse as performer on "psalteries and harps," and identical with the "porter" (15:18) and musician (v. 21), B. C. about 982.

3. A Levite, and great-grandfather of Jehaziel, who predicted success to Jehoshaphat against the Ammonites and Moabites (II Chron. 20:14), B. C. considerably before 875.

4. The scribe who, with others, kept the account of the numbers of King Uzziah's troops (II Chron. 26:11), B. C. about 769.

5. A Levite of the sons of Elizaphan, who assisted in the restoration of the temple under King Hezekiah (II Chron. 29:13), B. C. 719.

6. One of the chief Levites in the time of Josiah, who assisted in the rites of the great Passover (II Chron. 35:9), B. C. about 639.

7. One of the "last sons" of Adonikam, who, with sixty males, formed part of the caravan of Ezra from Babylon to Jerusalem (Ezra 8:13), B. C. about 457.

8. An Israelite of the "sons" of Nebo, who had taken a foreign wife and had to relinquish her (Ezra 10:43), B. C. 457.

Jekab′zeel (jĕ-kăb′zĕ-ĕl; *God will gather*), a

town in Judah (Neh. 11:25), probably identical with *Kabzeel* (*q. v.*).

Jekame′am (jĕk-à-mē′ăm; *the people will rise*), a Levite, the fourth in rank of the "sons" of Hebron in the Levitical arrangement established by David (I Chron. 23:19; 24:23), B. C. about 960.

Jekami′ah (jĕk-à-mī′à; *Jehovah will rise*).

1. The son of Shallum and father of Elishama, of the descendants of Sheshan of Judah (I Chron. 2:41), B. C. probably about 588.

2. In A. V. "Jecamiah." The fifth named of the sons of King Jeconiah (I Chron. 3:18), born to him during the captivity, B. C. after 597.

Jeku′thiel (jê-kū′thĭ-ĕl; *God will support*, cf. Arab. *qata*, to *sustain, nourish*), a man recorded in the genealogies of Judah (I Chron. 4:18) as the son of Mered by his Jewish wife (A. V. Jehudijah), and in his turn the father, or founder, of the town of Zanoah.

Jemi′ma (jê-mī′mà, R. V. and R. S. V. Jemimah; *a pigeon, dove*), the name of the first of the three daughters born to Job after his restoration to prosperity (Job. 42:14).

Jem′uel (jĕm′-û-ĕl; *day of God*), the eldest son of Simeon (Gen. 46:10; Exod. 6:15); elsewhere (Num. 26:12) called *Nemuel*.

Jeph′thae (jĕf′thē), the Greek form (Heb. 11: 32) of *Jephthah* (*q. v.*).

Jeph′thah (jĕf′thà; *he will open*), the ninth judge of Israel, the illegitimate son of Gilead.

1. **Personal History.** (1) **A Freebooter.** In consequence of his illegitimacy, he was banished from his father's house, and took up his residence at Tob, a district of Syria, not far from Gilead (Judg. 11:1-3). Here it was that he became head of a marauding party, and when a war broke out between the Israelites and the Ammonites, he probably signalized himself. (2) **Leader of Israel.** This induced the Israelites to seek his aid as commander; and though at first he refused, in consequence of their ill-treatment of him, yet, on their solemn covenant to regard him as their leader, he consented. In this capacity he was successful, and, in a war which soon followed, the Ammonites were defeated with great loss (11:3-33). On the eve of the battle he made a vow (vers. 30, 31) that whatever should come forth from his house first to meet him on his return home he would devote to God. This turned out to be his daughter, an only child, who welcomed his return with music and dancing. (See below). (3) **Quarrel with Ephraimites.** His victory over the Ammonites was followed by a quarrel with the Ephraimites, who challenged his right to go to war without their consent, and used threatening language toward him. Jephthah remonstrated with them, and then, gathering his forces, gave the Ephraimites battle, defeating them with great loss. The Gileadites then seized the fords of Jordan, and made those attempting to cross pronounce the word "Shibboleth;" but if anyone pronounced it "Sibboleth," they knew him to be an Ephraimite, and slew him on the spot (12:1-6). (4) **Rule and death.** The remainder of Jephthah's rule seems to have been peaceful, lasting about six years (B. C. 1105-1099). He was buried in his native region, in one of the cities of Gilead (12:7).

2. **Character.** Jephthah appears to have been a daring, intrepid man, skilled in war, quick to avenge injuries, and ready to defend the helpless as well as to forgive wrong. He does not seem to have been rash and impetuous, notwithstanding his vow, for he did not take the sword at once, but waited until negotiations with the king of Ammonites had been without effect.

3. **Jephthah's Vow.** Volumes have been written on what is generally termed "Jephthah's rash vow;" the question is whether, in doing to his daughter according to his vow, he actually offered her in sacrifice or not. That he really did so is a horrible conclusion, but one that it seems impossible to avoid. The following may be taken as a summary of the arguments on both sides:

(1) **In favor of actual sacrifice**, the following arguments are urged: *1.* The express terms of the narrative, "I will offer it up for a burnt offering," and "he did according to his vow." *2.* The fact that Jephthah was a half heathen, and that the circumstances took place where the heathen dwelt in great numbers, and where human sacrifices were not unknown. *3.* That Jephthah's excessive grief on seeing his daughter come forth to meet him can only be accounted for on the supposition that he considered her devoted to death. *4.* That the mourning for Jephthah's daughter for four days in the year can be reconciled only with the supposition that she was an actual sacrifice. *5.* That there is nothing in the history to show that his conduct was sanctioned by God.

(2) **In opposition it is urged:** *1.* By translating the Hebrew prefix (which is rendered *and* in our version), *or*, all difficulty will be removed. His words would then read, "shall surely be the Lord's, *or* I will offer a burnt offering;" and not unfrequently the sense requires that the Hebrew should be thus rendered (Lev. 27:28) where there is a similar meaning of the conjunctive *waw*. *2.* He cannot be understood as declaring an intention to offer as a burnt offering whatever might come forth to meet him, since he might have been met by what no law or custom permitted to be so offered. *3.* The sacrifice of children to Moloch is expressly forbidden, and declared an abomination to the Lord (Lev. 20:2, 3); and it would be a yet higher insult to offer them to the Lord. *4.* There is no precedent for such an offering. *5.* No father by his own authority could put even an offending child to death, much less one that was innocent (Deut. 21:18-21; I Sam. 14:24-45). *6.* It is said he did to her "according to his vow," and "she knew no man," which conveys the idea that she was devoted to a life of celibacy; and that what the daughters of Israel bewailed was not her death, but her celibacy (Judg. 11:38-40). There appears to have been a class of women devoted exclusively to the temple service who were Nazarites (Exod. 38: 8); the word rendered *assembled* means *engaged in service*. To this company of females reference is made (I Sam. 2:22; see also Luke 2:37). To such a company of devoted women Jephthah's daughter might be set apart. One of the strongest points on this side of the argument is, that the Hebrew word *lethanoth*,

rendered *to bewail*, rather meant *to celebrate;* these daughters of Israel went yearly, not to lament, but with songs of praise to celebrate, the daughter of Jephthah. The prominence given to the daughter's virginity, as an argument against Jephthah's sacrifice, we think is hardly warranted. It is probably mentioned to give greater force to the sacrifice, as it would leave him without issue, which in the East was considered a special misfortune (Ewald, *Hist. Israel;* K. and D., *Com.;* Robertson, *Early Religion of Israel;* Mc. and S., *Cyc.;* Smith, *Bib. Dict.*, and others).

Jephun'neh (jḗ-fŭn'ĕ; *he is ready*).

1. The father of Caleb, which latter was a faithful explorer of Canaan with Joshua (Num. 13:6; 14:6, sq.; 26:65; 32:12; 34:19; Deut. 1:36; Josh. 14:6, sq.; 15:13; 21:12; I Chron. 4:15; 6:56), B. C. before 1414. He was a descendant of Caleb, the son of Hezron (I Chron. 4:4, 15).

2. One of the sons of Jether, of the descendants of Asher (I Chron. 7:38), B. C. probably before 1017.

Je'rah (jē'rȧ; *moon, month*), the fourth son of Joktan (Gen. 10:26; I Chron. 1:20).

Jerah'meel (jḗ-rä'mē-ĕl; *God will compassionate*).

1. The firstborn son of Hezron, son of Pharez, son of Judah (I Chron. 2:9, sq.). His descendants were called Jerahmeelites.

2. A Merarite Levite, the representative of the family of Kish, probably the son of Mahli (I Chron. 24:29; comp. 23:21), B. C. about 960.

3. Son of Hammelech, who was employed by Jehoiakim to make Jeremiah and Baruch prisoners, after he had burnt the roll of Jeremiah's prophecy (Jer. 36:26), B. C. about 608.

Jerah'meelite (jḗ-rä'mē-ĕl-īt; I Sam. 27:10; 30:29), descendants of Jerahmeel, 1.

Je'red (jē'rĕd; *descent*).

1. One of the patriarchs before the flood (I Chron. 1:2), the name, in Gen. 5;15-20, is given as *Jared* (*q. v.*).

2. A son, apparently, of Ezra, of the tribe of Judah, by his wife *Jehudijah* (*q. v.*). He is named as the father (founder) of Gedor (I Chron. 4:18), B. C. perhaps about 1640.

Jer'emai (jĕr'ḗ-mī; *high*), one of the "sons" of Hashum, who divorced his wife after the return from Babylon (Ezra 10:33), B. C. 457.

Jeremi'ah (jĕr-ḗ-mī'ȧ; *Jehovah will lift up, exalt* or *will rise*). In A. V. of N. T. Jeremy (jĕr'ḗ-mĭ) and Jeremias (jĕr-ḗ-mī'ȧs).

1. An inhabitant of Libnah, the father of Hamutal, wife of Josiah and mother of Jehoaahaz and Zedekiah (II Kings 23:31; 24:18; Jer. 52:1), B. C. before 608.

2. One of the chief men of the tribe of Manasseh east, apparently about the time of their deportation by the Assyrians (I Chron. 5:24), B. C. about 727.

3. One of the Benjamite warriors who joined David at Ziklag (I Chron. 12:4), B. C. before 1000.

4, 5. The fifth and tenth in rank of the Gadite adventurers who joined David's troops in the wilderness (I Chron. 12:10, 13), B. C. before 1000.

6. One of the priests who subscribed the sacred covenant along with Nehemiah (Neh. 10:2); probably the same as one of those who followed the princes in the circuit of the newly repaired walls with the sound of trumpets (12:34), B. C. 445.

7. A priest who accompanied Zerubbabel from Babylon to Jerusalem (Neh. 12:1). It is probably himself or his course that is mentioned in v. 12, B. C. 536.

8. The son of Habazaniah and father of Jaazaniah, which last was one of the Rechabites whom the prophets tested with the offer of wine (Jer. 35:3), B. C. before 626.

9. The second of the greater prophets of the Old Testament.

Family. Jeremiah was the son of Hilkiah, a priest of Anathoth, in the land of Benjamin (Jer. 1:1). Many writers, both ancient and modern, have supposed that his father was the Hilkiah mentioned in II Kings 22:8. Against this hypothesis, however, there have been urged (Keil, Ewald, Orelli, and others) the facts, (1) That the name is too common to be a ground of identification. (2) That the manner in which Hilkiah is mentioned is inconsistent with the notion of his having been the high priest of Israel. (3) That neither Jeremiah himself nor his opponents allude to himself. (4) That the priests who lived at Anathoth were of the house of Ithamar (I Kings 2:26), while the high priests, from Zadok down, were of the line of Eleazar.

History. (1) **Early life.** The word of the Lord came to Jeremiah while he was still very young (Jer. 1:6), and happened in the thirteenth year of the reign of King Josiah (B. C. 626), while the prophet still lived in Anathoth. He appears to have remained in his native city until he was obliged to leave in order to escape the persecution of his fellow-townsmen (Jer. 11:21), and even of his own family (12:6). He then took up his residence at Jerusalem. (2) **Under Josiah.** He probably assisted King Josiah in the reformation effected during his reign (II Kings 23:1, sq.). The movement in behalf of true religion ceased as soon as the influence of the court was withdrawn; and the prophet bewailed the death of this prince as the precursor of the divine judgments for the national sins (II Chron. 35:25). (3) **Under Jehoahaz.** The short reign—three months—of this king gave little scope for prophetic action, and we hear nothing of Jeremiah during this period. (4) **Under Jehoiakim**, B. C. 608-597. The king had come to the throne as the vassal of Egypt, and for a time the Egyptian party was dominant in Jerusalem. Jeremiah appeared as the chief representative of the party that favored the supremacy of the Chaldeans as the only way of safety. In so doing he had to expose himself to the suspicion of treachery, and was interrupted in his ministry by "the priests and prophets," who, with the populace, brought him before the civil authorities, urging that capital punishment should be inflicted on him for his threatenings (Jer. 26). The princes of Judah endeavored to protect him, and appealed to the precedent of Micah the Morasthite, who had uttered a like prophecy in the reign of Hezekiah; and so for a time he escaped. Ahikam, the son of Shaphan, seems to have had influence to secure the prophet's safety. In the fourth year of Jehoiakim he was commanded to write the predictions which had been given him. Probably as a measure of safety he was, as he says, "shut up," and could not himself go to the house of the Lord. He therefore deputed Baruch to write the predictions and to read them publicly on the fast day. Baruch was summoned before the princes, who advised that both he and Jeremiah should conceal themselves, while they endeavored to influence the mind of the king by reading the roll to them. Jehoiakim read three or four leaves and then destroyed the roll. He gave orders for the immediate arrest of Baruch and Jeremiah, who, however, were preserved from the angry king. The prophet, at the command of God, rewrote the roll, adding "besides unto them many like words" (Jer. 36:22). To this period is assigned the prophecy in the valley of Benhinnom (Jer. 19), and his ill treatment at the hand of *Pashur* (*q. v.*). (5) **Under Jehoiachin,** B. C. 597. We still find Jeremiah uttering his voice of warning during the closing days of the reign of Jehoiakim and the short reign of his successor, Jehoiachin (Jer. 13:18; comp. II Kings 24:12; Jer. 22:24-30). He sent a letter of counsel and condolence to those who shared the captivity of the royal family (chaps. 29-31). (6) **Under Zedekiah.** In the fourth year (B. C. 593) of this monarch's reign Hananiah prophesied that the power of the Chaldeans would be destroyed and the captives restored from Babylon (28:3); and corroborated his prophecy by taking off from the neck of Jeremiah the yoke which he wore by divine command (27:2). Jeremiah was told to "Go and tell Hananiah, saying, Thus saith the Lord; thou hast broken the yokes of wood; but thou shalt make for them yokes of iron. For thus saith the Lord of hosts, the God of Israel; I have put the yoke of iron upon the neck of all these nations, that they may serve Nebuchadnezzar, king of Babylon" (28:13, 14). It was probably not until the latter part of the reign of Zedekiah that the prophet was put in confinement, as we find that "they had not put him into prison" when the army of Nebuchadnezzar commenced the siege of Jerusalem (37:4, 5). Jeremiah had declared what would be the fatal issue (ch. 24), and was incarcerated in the court of the prison adjoining the palace, where he predicted the certain return from the impending captivity (32:37). Jeremiah's suffering reached its climax under this king, especially during the siege of Jerusalem. The approach of the Egyptian army, and the consequent withdrawal for a time of the Chaldeans, brightened the prospects of the Jews, and the king entreated Jeremiah to pray to the Lord for them. The answer received from God was that the Egyptians would go to their own land, and that the Chaldeans would return and destroy the city (37:7, 8). This irritated the princes, who made the departure of Jeremiah from the city the pretext for accusing him of deserting to the Chaldeans. He was cast into prison in spite of his denial, where he would doubtless have perished but for the interposition of Ebedmelech, one of the royal eunuchs (37:12-38: 13). The king seems to have been favorably inclined toward the prophet, but, for fear of the princes, consulted with him secretly (38:

14-28). In one of these secret interviews Jeremiah obtained a milder imprisonment in the "guard-court" belonging to the royal citadel (37:17, sq.). While in prison he bought, with all requisite formalities, the field at Anathoth, which his kinsman Hanameel wished to get rid of (32:6-9), thus showing his faith in his country's future. (7) **Under Nebuchadnezzar.** Nebuchadnezzar took the city (B. C. 586 Albright's date, 587), and gave a special charge to his captain, Nebuzaradan, to free Jeremiah and to follow his advice (39:11, 12). He was, accordingly, delivered from the prison, and the choice given him either to go to Babylon or remain with his own people. He chose the latter, and went to Mizpah with Gedaliah, who had been appointed governor of Judea. After the murder of Gedaliah he advised Johanan, the recognized leader of the people, to remain in the land (42:7, sq.). The people refused to heed his advice, under the plea that he was acting in the interest of the Chaldeans, removed to Egypt, and took Jeremiah and Baruch with them (43:6, 7). While there he still sought to turn the people who had so long rebelled against the Lord to him (ch. 44). His writings give us no further information respecting his life, but it is probable that he died in Egypt soon after. (8) **Traditions.** There is a Christian tradition that Jeremiah was stoned to death by the Jews at Tahpanhes. An Alexandrian tradition reported that his bones had been brought to that city by Alexander the Great. On the other hand, there is the Jewish statement that, on the conquest of Egypt by Nebuchadnezzar, he, with Baruch, made his escape to Babylon, and died there in peace. (9) **Archaeology.** In 1935 J. L. Starkey discovered 18 ostraca with Hebrew writing in the ancient Phoenician script in a guard room adjoining the outer gate of the city of Lachish (cf. Harry Torczyner, *Lachish I: The Lachish Letters*, 1938; W. F. Albright, Bulletin 70, *Am. Schls. Orient. Res.*, April, 1938, p. 11-17). Still additional ostraca were found in the last campaign in 1938. These letters were written by a certain Hoshaiah, who was at some military outpost, to a man named Jaosh, evidently the high commanding officer at Lachish. Nebuchadnezzar had attacked and partly burned Lachish about a decade previously in Jehoiachin's reign. These letters, however, belong to the layer of ashes representing the final destruction of the city and are to be dated early in 588 B. C. when Nebuchadnezzar was beginning his final siege of Jerusalem together with that of Lachish and Azekah. These so-called Lachish Letters have immense paleographic value and shed much historical light on the time of Jeremiah. The good Hebrew names and expressions used, such as "weakening the hands of the people," remind us of Jer. 38:4. *M. F. U.*

Character. "In every page of Jeremiah's prophecies we recognize the temperament which, while it does not lead the man who has it to shrink from doing God's work, however painful, makes the pain of doing it infinitely more acute, and gives to the whole character the impress of a deeper and more lasting melancholy. He is preeminently 'the man that hath seen afflictions'" (Lam. 3:1). He reveals himself in his writings "as a soul of gentle nature, yielding, tenderhearted, affectionate, with almost a woman's thirst for love, with which certainly the iron, unbending firmness, and immovable power of resistance belonging to him in his prophetic sphere are in strange contrast" (Orelli, *Com.*, p. 11).

Jeremiah, Book of.

Jeremiah's prophecies are named after the prophet himself, *Yirmeyahu* or *Yirmeyah*. His ministry extended over the last tragic forty years of the kingdom of Judah to the destruction of Jerusalem and the deportation of its inhabitants to Babylon.

1. The Purpose. The prophetic oracles of Jeremiah constitute a stern warning to Judah and its capital city, Jerusalem, to abandon idolatry and apostasy to escape the inevitable consequence of the seventy-year Babylonian captivity (25:1-14). The prophet's sermons met with intense opposition from a society fanatically addicted to idolatry. The brave prophet, however, discharged his ministry despite continual persecution and danger of death. The tense threesided contest for world dominion between Assyria, Egypt and Babylon form the background of his prophetic career. Because he predicted the triumph of Babylon and the consequent captivity of Judah and repeated warning against useless alliance with Egypt, he incurred almost universal disfavor. A note of doom dominates his message. Against this dark background, passages setting forth Messianic hope flash through his prophecies. These great foregleams of a better day (cf. 23:5 f.; 30:4-11; 31:31-34; 33:15-18) point to the final restoration of Israel. This is not to be confused however with the restoration from Babylon, but points to a period of unparalleled tragedy (30:3-10) through the manifestation of David's righteous Branch, Jehovah-Tsidkenu (23:6; 30:9). These great Messianic prophecies are yet to be fulfilled (Acts 1:7; 15:14-17) in the future millennial kingdom (Rom. 11:15-29).

2. The Outline.

Introduction: The prophet's call, 1:1-19

Part I. Prophetic Oracles Against Jerusalem and Judah, 2:1-45:5

  a. In the reign of Josiah and Jehoiakim, 1:1-20:18

    (1) First Oracle—National Sin and Ingratitude, 2:1-3:5

    (2) Second Oracle—Destruction from the North, 3:6-6:30

    (3) Third Oracle—Threat of Exile, 7:1-10:25

    (4) Fourth Oracle—The Broken Covenant and the Sign of the Girdle, 11:1-13:27

    (5) Fifth Oracle—The Drought, 14:1-15:21; the Sign of the Unmarried Prophet, 16:1-17:18; Warning regarding the Sabbath, 17:19-27

    (6) Sixth Oracle—Sign of the Potter's House, 18:1-20:18

  b. During Various Periods until Jerusalem's Destruction, 21:1-39:18

    (1) Zedekiah and the people's punishment, 21:1-29:32

    (2) Future Messianic Kingdom, 30:1-32:26

    (3) Sin of Zedekiah; the loyalty of the Rechabites, 34:1-35:19

    (4) Jehoiachin's opposition, 36:1-32

    (5) Jerusalem's experiences during the seige, 37:1-39:18

  c. After the Fall of Jerusalem, 40:1-45:5

    (1) Jeremiah's ministry to the remnant in the land, 40:1-42:22

    (2) Jeremiah's ministry in Egypt, 43:1-44:30

    (3) Jeremiah's message to Baruch, 45:1-5

Part II. Prophecies Against the Nations, 46:1-51:64

  a. Against Egypt, 46:1-28

  b. Against Philistia, 47:1-7

  c. Against Moab, 48:1-47

  d. Against Ammon, 49:1-6

  e. Against Edom, 49:7-22

  f. Against Damascus, 49:23-27

  g. Against Arabia, 49:28-33

  h. Against Elam, 49:34-39

  i. Against Babylon, 50:1-51:64

Part III. Historical Appendix:

Judah's Fall and Captivity, 52:1-30

Jehoiachin's liberation, 52:31-34

3. Authorship and Authenticity. Numerous arguments support the fact that Jeremiah "the son of Hilkiah, of the priests that were in Anathoth in the land of Benajmin" (1:1), is the author of the book. (1) **Internal Evidence.** The prophet dictated all his prophecies in the beginning of his ministry to the fourth year of Jehoiakim to his secretary, Baruch. This material consists of well over half the prophet's ministry. When this roll was destroyed by king Jehoiakim (36:23), the prophet dictated another edition, which included much new material (36:32). This is not the present book since many portions of the book of Jeremiah bear a later date in his prophetic career (for example, 21:1; 24:1, etc.), still others show evidence of being composed in the later portion of his ministry. Internal evidence demonstrate that the prophet authored the entire book. Chapter 52 is a possible exception. This was possibly appended to his prophecies from II Kings 24:18-25:30, with which it is practically identical. (2) **External proof.** O. T. references to the prophecies are explicit (cf. Daniel's allusion to the prediction of the seventy year's captivity, Dan. 9:2; Jer. 25:11-14; 29:10). II Chron. 36:21 and Ezek. 1:1 confirm this prophecy and the general period of Jeremiah. Extracanonical evidence adds its voice. Ecclesiasticus 49:6, 7 traces the destruction of Jerusalem to the rejection of Jeremiah's warning and prophecies. Josephus (*Ant.*, x, 5:1) and the Talmud confirm the same fact. In the N. T., Matt. 2:17, 18 quotes Jer. 31:15. Matt. 21:13, Mark 11:17 and Luke 19:46 quote from Jeremiah 7:11. Rom. 11:27 has reference to Jer. 31:33f. Heb. 8:8-13 also quotes from this passage. Christian tradition also adds its testimony to the Jeremian authenticity of the prophecy. (3) **Apparent composite character of the book.** This is explained by the fact that the book was written in stages. The earlier edition was destroyed. It was reissued later with additions. Subsequent prophecies were collated and doubtless edited by Baruch. For this reason the contents are not always in systematic order or chronological sequence. The wide divergence between the Septuagint and the Massoretic Hebrew is difficult to account for and seems to comprehend two different forms of the book. (4) **Modern criticism fails to disprove Jeremian authenticity.** Critical theories are to a large extent subjective. Robert Pfeiffer conjectures that Baruch combined the prophet's book with his own, redoing many of the prophetic speeches in his own "deuteronomistic style" (*Intr.*, 1940, p. 55). It is contended that even Baruch's book was later extensively revised with both prose and poetic editions. But such a procedure on the part of a pious disciple like Baruch is unreasonable. A. Bentzen rejects the idea that Baruch authored the "deuteronomistic sections." Bentzen thinks that Jeremiah was used by "deuteronomistic zealots" (*Intr.*, 1949, p. 119). H. Birkeland assumes that the book contains several complexes of traditions (*Zum hebraeischen Traditionswesen*, 1938, p. 42), but the old idea of a nucleus of traditions subsequently expanded is without factual foundation. Critical theories are bereft of any valid substitute for Jeremian authorship of the prophecy. *M. F. U.*

Jeremi′as (jĕr-ē-mī′ās), a Grecized form of the name Jeremiah the prophet (Matt. 16:14).

Jer′emoth (jĕr′ē-mŏth; *tall* cf. Arab. *warima, to be thick, tall, swollen*).

1. A Benjamite chief, a son of the house of Beriah and Elpaal (I Chron. 8:14; comp. 12 and 18). His family dwelt at Jerusalem, B. C. apparently about 588.

2. A Merarite Levite, son of Mushi (I Chron. 23:23), called *Jerimoth* in I Chron. 24: 30, B. C. about 960.

3. Son of Heman, head of the thirteenth course of musicians in the divine service (I Chron. 25:22); probably the same called *Jerimoth* in v. 4, B. C. about 960.

4. One of the "sons of Elam" who put away his strange wife after the captivity (Ezra 10: 26), B. C. 456.

5. One of the "sons of Zattu" who had taken strange wives, and put them away after the return from Babylon (Ezra 10:27), B. C. 456.

6. The name which appears in the same list as "and *Ramoth*" (v. 29). *See* Ramoth.

Jer′emy (jĕr′ē-mī), a familiar form of the name Jeremiah (Matt. 2:17; 27:9).

Jeri′ah (jē-rī′à), a Kohathite Levite, chief of the great house of Hebron when David organized the Levitical service (I Chron. 23:19; 24:23), B. C. about 960. His name is given as *Jerijah* in I Chron. 26:31.

Jer′ibai (jĕr′ĭ-bī; *Jehovah contends*), the second named of the sons of Elnaam, and one of David's bodyguard (I Chron. 11:46), B. C. after 1000.

Jer′icho (jĕr′ĭ-kō; possibly *place of fragrance* or *moon-city*), an ancient city in the wide plain where the Jordan valley broadens between the Moab mountains and the western precipices, and situated on the route of Israel after it crossed the Jordan under Joshua (Josh. 3: 16). The first mention of Jericho in Scripture is in connection with the advance of Israel to Canaan; they "pitched in the plains of Moab, on this side Jordan by Jericho" (Num. 22:1). From the manner and frequency in which it is referred to it would seem to have been the most important city of the Jordan valley at that time (Num. 31:12; 34:15; 35:1, etc.). The spies sent by Joshua were entertained in Jericho by *Rahab* (*q. v.*), for which they promised her protection when the city should be destroyed; which promise was religiously observed (Josh. 2:1-21; 6:25). The miraculous capture of Jericho, and the sin and punishment of Achan, and the curse pronounced upon anyone who should attempt to rebuild it, are graphically recorded (Josh. 6:1-7:26). Jericho was given to the tribe of Benjamin (Josh. 18:21), "and from this time a long interval elapses before Jericho appears again upon the scene. It is only incidentally mentioned in the life of David in connection with his embassy to the Ammonite king (II Sam. 10:5). And the solemn manner in which its second foundation under Hiel, the Beth-el-ite, is recorded (I Kings 16:34) would certainly seem to imply that up to that time its site had been uninhabited. It is true that mention is made of 'a city of palm trees' (Judg. 1:16; 3:13) in existence apparently at the time when spoken of. However, once actually rebuilt, Jericho rose again slowly into consequence. In its immediate vicinity the sons of the prophets sought retirement from the world: Elisha 'healed the spring of the waters;' and over against it, beyond Jordan, Elijah 'went up by a whirlwind into heaven' (II Kings 2:1-22). In its plains Zedekiah fell into the hands of the Chaldeans (II Kings 25:5; Jer. 39:5). In the return under Zerubbabel the 'children of Jericho,' three hundred and forty-five in number, are comprised (Ezra 2:34; Neh. 7: 36); and it is even implied that they removed thither again, for the 'men of Jericho' assisted Nehemiah in rebuilding that part of the wall of Jerusalem that was next to the sheep-gate (Neh. 3:2). The Jericho of the days of Josephus was distant one hundred and fifty stadia from Jerusalem and fifty from the Jordan."

231. Air View of Tell es-Sultan
(Old Testament Jericho)

In the New Testament Jericho is mentioned in connection with Jesus restoring sight to the blind (Matt. 20:30; Mark 10:46; Luke 18: 35), and his being entertained by Zaccheus (Luke 19:1, sq.); and, finally, it was introduced in the parable of the good Samaritan,

232. Area C, Jericho, the Canaanite City
Destroyed by Joshua, 1955 Excavation

which, if not a real occurrence, derives interest from the fact that robbers have ever been the terror of the road from Jerusalem to Jericho.

Archaeological Excavations. Excavations at the site of the ancient town point to the fall of the city to Joshua and the Israelites around 1400 B. C. The ancient strategic fortress commanding the entrance to Canaan from the east is represented by the modern mound known as Tell es-Sultan. The springs at this site yield a plentiful supply of water. Through the excavations of Ernst Sellin and the Deutsche Orientgesellschaft (1907-1909), and particularly those of John Garstang (1930-1936), the occupational history of the ancient city has been determined. The site was occupied in Neolithic times before B. C. 4500. In the Chalcolithic era, B. C. 4500-3000, a series of successive cities stood there. Professor Garstang assigned alphabetic names to later cities which occupied the site. City A was dated c. B. C. 3000, City B was founded c. B. C. 2500, and was destroyed c. B. C. 1700. City C was larger than its predecessors. It was adorned with a splendid palace and was surrounded with stout walls, stone glacis and outer mote. This city belonged to the Hyksos period and suffered destruction around B. C

233. Jericho, Area B, a General Air View of the Citadels (Assyrian and Persian periods, 8th, 4th centuries, B. C.)

1500. City D, captured by Joshua, was constructed c. B. C. 1500. At this time the old palace of the preceding city was rebuilt and the new city protected by a double wall of brick. A redoubtable 6-foot thick wall was built on the edge of the mound. The inner wall was separated from it by a space of from

twelve to fifteen feet and was itself twelve feet thick. The wall was originally about thirty feet high. The city was crowded, comprising only about a half-dozen acres. This explains the erection of houses over the space between the inner and outer wall. Accordingly, Rahab is represented as having let the spies down "by a cord through the window, for her house was upon the side of the wall, and she dwelt upon the wall" (Josh. 2:15). The walls of City D display evidence of violent destruction. The outer wall had tumbled forward down the slope of the mound and the inner wall with the houses built upon it had covered the intervening space. Ashes, charred timbers, reddened masses of stone and brick show that a fire accompanied the fall of the city. The natural conclusion is that this destruction of Jericho's walls is that depicted so graphically in Josh. 6. This conclusion is strengthened by the fact that after this complete destruction Jericho lay in ruins and was not reconstructed until the time of City E, which belongs to the time of Ahab, (c. B. C. 860) when Hiel the Bethelite rebuilt the town (I Kings 16:34). Garstang dates the destruction of Jericho City D, c. 1400 B. C., which agrees admirably with the Biblical notices. Advocates of the late date theory of the Exodus, such as G. E. Wright and W. F. Albright, claim to have disproved Garstang's date. But much confusion remains among those who, like Albright, would place the destruction of Jericho c. B. C. 1300, in which case it can neither be connected historically with the destruction of City D as recounted in Joshua 6, nor fits into their date of the Exodus (c. 1280 B. C.). *See* Exodus, Date of.

234. Excavating New Testament Jericho

Excavations at O. T. Jericho were resumed in 1952 by the British School of Archaeology in Jerusalem, Kathleen Kenyon, director, and the American Schools of Oriental Research. Work continues to the present. Miss Kenyon's discoveries date mostly to the pre-literary period at Jericho.

Dr. James Kelso of Pittsburgh-Xenia Theological Seminary and Dimitri Baramki of the Palestine Department of Antiquities excavated at N. T. Jericho in 1950. Among other discoveries, they unearthed a large palace attributed to Herod the Great and Archelaus.

M. F. U.

235. The Mound of New Testament Jericho

Jer'iel (jĕr'ĭ-ĕl; *God sees*), a man of Issachar, one of the six heads of the house of Tola mentioned in the census in the time of David (I Chron. 7:2), B. C. perhaps after 1000.

Jeri'jah (jĕr-ī'já), a different form (I Chron. 26:31) of the name *Jeriah* (*q. v.*).

Jer'imoth (jĕr'ĭ-mŏth; cf. Jeremoth).

1. The fourth named of the four sons of Bela, son of Benjamin and founder of a Benjamite house which existed in the time of David (I Chron. 7:7; comp. v. 2), B. C. after 1689.

2. One of the "sons" of Becher (I Chron. 7:8), and head of another Benjamite house, B. C. about 1017.

3. One of the Benjamite archers and slingers that joined David at Ziklag (I Chron. 12:5), B. C. before 1000.

4. The last named of the sons of Mushi, the son of Merari (I Chron. 24:30); elsewhere called *Jeremoth.*

5. One of the sons of Heman, head of the fifteenth ward of musicians (I Chron. 25:4, 22); called in the latter verse *Jeremoth* (B. C. about 960).

6. Son of Azriel, ruler of the tribe of Naphtali in the reign of David (I Chron. 27:19), B. C. about 1000.

7. Son of King David, whose daughter Mahalath was the first wife of Rehoboam, her cousin Abihail being the other (II Chron. 11:18), B. C. before 974. He is not named in the list of David's children (I Chron. ch. 3, or 14:4-7), and it is probable that he was the son of a concubine, and such is the Jewish tradition. The passage II Chron. 11:18 is not quite clear, since the ward "daughter" is a correction of the *qeri;* the original text had *bēn* i. e., "son".

236. Royal Egyptian Scarab Signets of the Last Kings of Jericho

8. A Levite, and one of the overseers of the temple offerings in the reign of Hezekiah (II Chron. 31:13), B. C. 729.

Je'rioth (jĕ'rĭ-ŏth; *tent curtains*), apparently the second wife of Caleb, the son of Hezron (I Chron. 2:18), B. C. about 1440. The Vulgate renders this as the son of Caleb by his first-mentioned wife, and father of the sons named; but this is contrary to the Hebrew text, which is closely followed by the LXX. Perhaps the connective *waw* should be rendered by *even,* thus making Jerioth but another name for Azubah.

Jerobo'am (jĕr-ō-bō'ăm; *the people multiplied*).

1. **The First King of Israel,** the son of Nebat, an Ephraimite, by a woman named Zeruah (I Kings 11:26).

Personal History. (1) **Noticed by Solomon.** At the time when Solomon was constructing the fortifications of Millo underneath the citadel of Zion, his sagacious eye discovered the strength and activity of the young Ephraimite who was employed on the works, and he raised him to the rank of superintendent over the taxes and labors exacted from the tribe of Ephraim (I Kings 11:28), B. C. after 960. (2) **Future foretold.** On one occasion, when leaving Jerusalem, he encountered Ahijah, "the prophet" of the ancient sanctuary of Shiloh. Ahijah stripped off his new outer garment and tore it into twelve shreds, ten of which he gave to Jeroboam, with the assurance that, on obedience to his laws, God would establish for him a kingdom and dynasty equal to that of David (vers. 29-40). (3) **Flight into Egypt.** Jeroboam, probably, began to form plots and conspiracies, for Solomon sought to take his life, whereupon he fled to Egypt. He received the protection of pharaoh Shishak, and remained there until the death of Solomon (v. 40), B. C. about 926. (4) **Revolt of Israel.** Upon the accession of Rehoboam Jeroboam appears to have headed a deputation who asked for a redress of grievances. The harsh answer of Rehoboam rendered a revolution inevitable, and Jeroboam was called to be "king of Israel" (12:1-20). (5) **As king.** He selected Shechem as his capital, but for some cause not known removed the seat of government to Penuel, west of Jordan. He later returned to the east of Jordan and took up his permanent residence at Tirzah (I Kings 12:25; comp. 15:21, 33; 16:6, sq.; Josh. 12:24). The policy of Jeroboam was to bring about a religious as well as political disruption of the kingdom. He therefore sought to discourage the yearly pilgrimages to the temple at Jerusalem. To this end he established shrines at Dan and Beth-el, sanctuaries of venerable antiquity, and at the extremities of the kingdom. He set up "golden calves," doubtless thought of, according to a widespread Semitic custom of viewing deities enthroned on the backs of animals, as representing Jehovah's invisible Presence, and united the pontificate to his crown (I Kings 12:26-33). While officiating at the altar a man of God appeared and announced the coming of King Josiah, who should burn upon that altar the bones of its ministers. Jeroboam attempted to arrest him, when the arm that he stretched forth was smitten with palsy, but in answer to his prayer was healed (13:1-10). Jeroboam continued his idolatrous practices, making "the lowest of the people priests of the high places" (v. 31), and his contumacy soon brought about the extinction of his dynasty. His son Abijah fell sick, and Jeroboam sent his wife in disguise to the prophet Ahijah, who, however, recognized her and predicted her son's death. She returned to Tirzah, "and when she came to the threshold of the door the child died." Jeroboam seems never to have recovered from the blow, and died soon after, having reigned twenty-two years (14:1-20), B. C. c. 926-c. 904. Jeroboam waged constant war with the house of Judah, but the only act distinctly recorded is a battle with Abijah, the son of Rehoboam, in which he was defeated, and for the time lost the important cities of Beth-el, Jeshanah, and Ephraim (II Chron. 13:1-19).

Character. Jeroboam was perhaps a less remarkable man than the circumstances of his being the founder of a new kingdom might lead us to expect. His government exhibits but one idea—that of raising a barrier against the reunion of the tribes. Of that idea he was the slave and victim; and, although the barrier which he raised was effectual for his purpose, it only served to show the weakness of the man who could deem needful the protection for his separate interests which such a barrier offered.

2. **Jeroboam II** was the son of the successor of Jehoash, and the fourteenth king of Israel B. C. c. 787-747). Notwithstanding he followed the example of the first Jeroboam in keeping up the idolatry of the golden calves, the Lord had pity upon Israel. Jeroboam brought to a successful issue the wars which his father had undertaken, and delivered Israel from the Syrian yoke (comp. II Kings 13:4; 14:26, 27). He took the chief cities of Damascus (II Kings 14:28; Amos 1:3-5) and Hamath, and restored to Israel the ancient eastern limits from Lebanon to the Dead Sea (II Kings 14:25; Amos 6:14). He reconquered Ammon and Moab (Amos 1:13; 2:1-3), restored to the trans-Jordanic tribes their territory (II Kings 13:5; I Chron. 5:17-22). But it was merely an outward restoration. The sanctuary at Beth-el was kept up in royal state (Amos 7:13), but drunkeness, licentiousness, and oppression prevailed in the country (Amos 2:6-8; 4:1, 6:6; Hos. 4:12-14; 1:2), and idolatry was united with the worship of Jehovah (Hos. 4:13; 13:6). Amos prophecied the destruction of Jeroboam and his house by the sword (Amos 7:9, 17), and Hosea (1:1) also denounced the crimes of the nation.

Excavations at Samaria, the capital of the Northern Kingdom, have confirmed its popularity and splendor in the eighth century B. C. (See J. W. Crowfoot, Kathleen M. Kenyon and E. L. Sukenik, *The Buildings at Samaria*, 1942). Jeroboam II refortified the city with a great double wall. In exposed sections, this reached as much as 33 feet in width, constituting fortifications so substantial that the mighty Assyrian army took three years to capture the city (II Kings 17:5). The splendid palace of limestone with strong rectangular tower and extensive outer court, hitherto assigned to the Ahab era, almost certainly belongs to Jeroboam II (J. Finegan, *Life From the Ancient Past*, Princeton, 1946, p. 155). The jasper seal discovered by Schumacher at Megiddo and inscribed "Shema, servant of Jeroboam," is to be connected with Jeroboam II rather than Jeroboam I, as is now epigraphically certain. The efflorescence of art in this prosperous era is proved by the lifelike and magnificently executed lion which appears upon the seal.

Amos' prophecies shed light on the augmentation of commerce and wealth in Jeroboam's realm and its consequent luxury and moral declension. Increased tribute poured in, creating a wealthy class which was utterly selfish and unscrupulous (Amos 2:6; 8:6). Simple dwellings of unburned brick gave way to "houses of hewn stone." Ahab's ivory palace, evidently decorations only are meant, was imitated by many of the wealthy land owners (Amos 3:15; 5:11; I Kings 22:39). Loose feasting was the order of the day (Amos 6:4-6). Religion degenerated into mere ritualism devoid of righteousness and morality (Amos 4:4; 5:5; 8:14). The evils of the time called for divine retribution. Jeroboam's house was to be visited with the sword (Amos 7:9). Somewhere around 746 B. C. Jeroboam died a natural death, but his son and successor, Zachariah, after a six-month reign, was assassinated by a usurper, inaugurating a period of sheer decline and civil strife. M. F. U.

NOTE.—Some regard the prophecy of Amos, that Jeroboam should die by the sword, a failure, as there is no evidence that his death was other than natural, for he was buried with his ancestors in state (II Kings 14:29). The interregnum of eleven years which intervened before the accession of his son Zachariah (14:29; comp. with 15:8) argues some political disorder at the time of his death. But the probability rather is that the high priest, who displayed the true spirit of a persecutor, gave an unduly specific and offensive turn to the words of Amos, in order to inflame Jeroboam the more against him.

Jero'ham (jê-rō'hăm; *compassionate*).

1. The son of Elihu and father of Elkanah, the father of Samuel (I Sam. 1:1; I Chron. 6:27, 34), B. C. before 1171.

2. The father of several Benjamite chiefs residing at Jerusalem (I Chron. 8:27), B. C. before 536.

3. The father of Ibneiah, a Benjamite chief who was a resident of Jerusalem (I Chron. 9:8), B. C. probably before 536. Perhaps the same as No. 2.

4. A priest whose son Adaiah was one of the priests residing at Jerusalem (I Chron. 9:12). The same names are given as father and son in Neh. 11:12, and are probably identical. B. C. before 536.

5. An inhabitant of Gedor, and father of

Joelah and Zebadiah, who joined David at Ziklag (I Chron. 12:7), B. C. before 1000.

6. A Danite whose son (or descendant) Azareel was ruler over his tribe in the time of David (I Chron. 27:22), B. C. before 1000.

7. Father of Azariah, which latter was one of the "captains of hundreds" by whose assistance Jehoiada placed Joash on the throne of Judah (II Chron. 23:1), B. C. before 836.

Jerubba'al (jĕr-ŭb-bā'ăl; *Baal will contend*), a surname given by his father to Gideon, the judge of Israel, because he destroyed the altar of Baal (Judg. 6:32; 7:1; 8:29, 35; 9:1, 2, 5, 16, 19, 24, 28, 57; I Sam. 12:11).

Jerubbe'sheth (jĕr-ŭb-bē'shĕth; *contender* with *shame*, i. e., *idol*), a name for Jerubbaal in which Baal is branded *bosheth* (*besheth*), the Hebrew word for "shame." This epithet of Gideon (II Sam. 11:21) was given to avoid pronouncing the name (Exod. 33:13) of a false god (viz., Baal).

Jeru'el (jĕ-rū'ĕl; *founded by God*). "The wilderness of Jeruel" is mentioned (II Chron. 20:16) by Jahaziel as the place where Jehoshaphat would meet the Moabites and Ammonites and overcome them. This "wilderness" was, doubtless, a part of the great stretch of flat country, bounded on the south by Wady el Ghâr, and extending from the Dead Sea to the neighborhood of Tekoa, and now called *el Hasasah*.

Jeru'salem (jĕ-rū'sá-lĕm), the first city of Palestine. "The Holy City" for three great world religions: Christianity, Judaism and Islam.

1. **Name.** The etymology of the name is not certain. It is apparently of Semitic origin connected with the Heb. *shālōm* (*shalem*), meaning "peace," or identified with *salem* (Gen. 14:18; Psa. 76:2). An Egyptian notice from the third quarter of the 19th century B. C. mentions *Urusalimum*. The Tell el Amarna correspondence of the 14th century B. C. refers to the town as *Urusalim* meaning, evidently, "City of Peace." The Assyrians called it *Ursalimmu*. Romans and Greeks called it *Hierosolyma*. To the Arabs it is *El Kuds*, meaning "Holy Town."

2. **Location.** "The Holy City" is located 14

miles W. of the Dead Sea, 33 miles E. of the Mediterranean. Bethlehem lies about five miles to the S. E. The city is situated on a rocky plateau at an elevation of 2,550 feet. It is 3800 feet above the level of the Dead Sea. It is accurately poetized as "beautiful in elevation, the joy of the whole earth" (A. S. V. Psa. 48:2). Its location has helped to give it prestige. It was exclusive, with no river frontage like Babylon, Thebes, Rome or Memphis; no harbor like Tyre, Sidon nor Alexandria. It was off the main highways between Asia Minor and Egypt. It possessed a good water supply from the ancient Gihon Spring (*q. v.*) (The Virgin's Fountain) in the Kidron and En Rogel (*q. v.*) or Job's Well at the junction of the Kidron and the Hinnon Valleys. It was centrally located and ideal for the capital of the united kingdom of Israel in the Davidic-Solomonic era (c. 1000-930 B. C.) and of Judah (c. 930 B. C. -587 B. C.).

238. Church of the Holy Sepulcher, Jerusalem

3. **The Climate.** Being high in elevation and fanned by the afternoon breeze from the Mediterranean, Jerusalem has a mean annual temperature of 63 degrees. However, the temperature can mount to 100 degrees in summer and drops to 25 degrees in the winter. Snow occasionally falls, sometimes to a depth of one foot, but does not last long.

4. **General Boundary of David's City.** Jebusite Jerusalem of David's day was located on the S. E. hill and as C. C. McCown describes it, was "shaped somewhat like a gigantic human foot-print about 1250 feet long and 400 wide. . . ." The enclosed area was about eight acres, a small strip of land compared to Megiddo's thirty (cf. C. C. McCown, *The Ladder of Progress in Palestine*, p. 239). Manasseh (c. B. C. 687-642) is said by the chronicler to have built "an outer wall to the city of David on the west side of Gihon in the valley even to the entrance of the Fish Gate" (II Chron. 33:41). Nehemiah's wall apparently followed the wall that had existed in the early monarchy from the west, south and east sides of the city, but at the Hippicus Tower near the present Jaffa Gate, edged north west and comprised evidently the Corner Gate. Then it took a northeasterly course, pierced by the Gate of Ephraim, the Old Gate, and the Fish Gate. It touched the northwest angle of the Temple area. The line of Nehemiah's wall and of the later North walls vitally concerns the disputed site of Calvary and the Garden

237. Hills and Valleys of Jerusalem

Tomb. The walls and gates of Jerusalem of Nehemiah's time are minutely described. The gates at Jerusalem include the following: Sheep Gate, Fish Gate, Old Gate, Valley Gate, Dung Gate, Fountain Gate, Water Gate, Horse Gate and East Gate. Towers include that of Hammeah, of Hananel and of Furnaces. The walls include Broad Wall, Wall of Pool Shelah, and Wall of Ophel. Herod surrounded the sanctuary area of his day with beautifully fashioned masonry walls. At least four of these walls were constructed in ancient times. The walls and gates as seen in Jerusalem today are due in large part to Suleiman the Magnificent, 16th century A. D. The present walls of Jerusalem have 35 towers and eight gates, the Damascus, Herod's, Stephen's, the Dung Gate, the Zion Gate, the Jaffa Gate, the New Gate and the Golden Gate.

5. **History.** The history of Jerusalem from the time of Joshua to its destruction by Titus, a period of fifteen centuries, is a succession of changes, revolutions, sieges, surrenders, famines, each followed by restorations and rebuilding. The city's greatest glory was reached under the reign of King Solomon, who built the temple and a royal palace, besides very greatly enlarging and strengthening the walls of the city. Jerusalem's greatest humiliation possibly was reached under the reign of An-

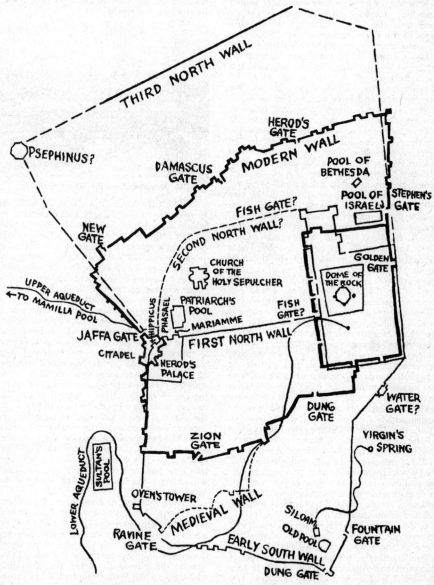

239. Jerusalem's Walls and Gates

tiochus Ephiphanes, B. C. 175-163, when the most violent and cruel efforts were made to destroy the Jews and their religion. For the earliest record of Jerusalem we must go to the description of the boundaries of Judah and Benjamin (Josh. chaps. 15 and 18). Until David captured the entire city from the Jebusites (II Sam. 5:7; I Chron. 11:6) these ancient inhabitants had always been in possession of a part of it. From the time when David brought the Ark of God into the city (II Sam. 6:2-16) until the rebuilding of the walls under Nehemiah, the metropolis was almost continuously added to and embellished. Notable improvements included Hezekiah's vast structures for aqueduct and water supply and the enclosing with an outside wall of Zion and the City of David. During fifty years of the Exile, and immediately succeeding the capture of the city of Nebuchadnezzar, it lay in ruins. Cyrus the Great decreed the return of the captive Jews to their city and the rebuilding of the city walls, which by Nehemiah's time had been broken down for one hundred and forty years. (Neh. 4:7-22). Under Nehemiah the city regained much of its former glory. Alexander the Great, in 332 B. C., showed much favor to the Jews, exempting them in some degree from tribute. In 320 B. C., because the Jews refused to fight and defend themselves on the Sabbath day when Ptolemy Soter attacked the city, it was captured, and many of its inhabitants were removed to Africa. The prosperity of the city under Antiochus the Great, 200 B. C., was undone by the infamy of Antiochus Epiphanes, against whom the oppressed Jews revolted in 165 B. C. when a great victory was gained over Antiochus by an army led by Judas Maccabaeus. The period from the death of Judas Maccabaeus, B. C. 161, until the city was captured by Pompey in B C. 63, was marked by the occurrence of strife and disorder in Jerusalem. In the dissensions between the political rulers and the religious sects of Pharisees and Sadducees probably not less than fifty thousand people fell victims. Crassus plundered the temple of treasure, which, together with that taken from the city, amounted to ten million dollars. About six years afterwards a Roman army under Herod the Great captured the city. The city soon again became restored to much of its former grandeur. Under Herod the temple was enlarged and beautified. It was in this state of things that Christ found the city. Under Herod the city was given a better water supply. Under Herod's grandson, Herod Agrippa, in 41 B. C., the area of the city wall was doubled. Bad government by Roman procurators, appointed over Judea as a Roman province, led to disaster and discontent, until finally Titus laid siege to the city and captured it with the sacrifice of one million lives.

6. **The Early Church.** After the death and resurrection of Christ, Jerusalem became the scene of the most stirring events connected with Christianity, beginning with the day of Pentecost and including much of the history contained in the Acts of the Apostles. The Gospel was first proclaimed here in strict obedience to the command of Christ (Acts 1:4).

The church here increased rapidly (ch. 5). Here the first martyr was sacrificed (ch. 7); here Paul sat at the feet of Gamaliel, and here he preached, and it was from here that he was taken to Caesarea and Rome. In Jerusalem the great council was held, at which the question of the rite of circumcision was discussed, and during which addresses were made by Peter, Barnabas, Paul and James. James was the president of the council, occupying a very prominent place, if, indeed, not the first place in the church. Herod here put an end to the career of James by beheading him (Acts 12). The extreme severity of the persecutions tended to scatter abroad the Christians, which resulted in the dissemination of the gospel throughout the world.

240. Jerusalem from the Mount of Olives

7. **The City After 70 A. D.** In 70 A. D. the Romans destroyed the city and massacred its inhabitants. Under Hadrian the Romans began to refortify Jerusalem as a Gentile city and hold it against its former inhabitants. The Jewish revolt (132-135 A. D.) under Bar Cocheba was evidently due to this circumstance. It was suppressed, the rebuilding of the city resumed and completed. The new city was called Colonia Aelia Capitolina. This name described it as a Roman colony. Aelia was in honor of Hadrian, whose prenomen was Aelius, and Capitolina because it was dedicated to Jupiter Capitolinus. A temple was dedicated to this heathen god where the former Jewish temples had stood on Mt. Moriah. The name of Aelia continued for several centuries. Constantine removed the ban against Jews entering the Holy City. Both Constantine and his mother built churches in the city. In 614 A. D. the Persians under Chosroes II captured Jerusalem and massacred the inhabitants. From 637-1517 the city alternated between the possession of Moslems and Christians, the Crusaders capturing it in 1099. Three times since that time has the city been in Christian hands and as many times fallen into the hands of the Moslems.

8. **Archaeology.** As a result of excavations, Sir Charles Warren discovered that the inhabitants of Jerusalem c. 2000 B. C. had made a rock-cut passage similar to the one at Gezer and Megiddo to enable them to secure water from the Gihon Spring without having to go outside the city walls. From the cave into which the Gihon Spring emptied, a horizontal tunnel had been driven back into the hill some 36 feet west and 25 feet north. This con-

duit brought the water back into an old cave which thus served as a reservoir. Running up from this was a 40-foot vertical tunnel, since known as "Warren's Shaft." At the top of this in ancient times there was a platform where women could stand to lower their jars and draw up the water. From this a sloping passage ran up with its entrance within the city walls. It is possible David's men gained access to the Jebusite fortress though this underground water system (II Sam. 5:7), but this is now disputed. It seems they rather scaled the walls. The so-called "Robinson's Arch" and "Wilson's Arch" are especially interesting discoveries. Both are large stone remains of two ancient bridges which connected the Hasmonaean palaces at the N. E. brow of the western hill in the Temple area. "Robinson's Arch," some 39 feet from the S. W. angle of W. wall of the Temple area, consists of three courses of huge stones jutting from the wall and forming a part of the spring of a mighty arch. The entire span of this arch is calculated to have been over 41 feet. This ancient viaduct crossed the Tyropoeon Valley with about eight arches. While Sir Charles Warren was exploring the south end of Wilson's Arch, he discovered a room which he called "Masonic Hall." Some of the masonry still visible in Jerusalem today in the lower courses of the Citadel and Herod's enlarged Temple area, as well as the tomb of Absalom from the Herodian period, were seen by Jesus. See excellent discussion in Harper's Bible Dictionary (New York, 1955).

9. **The Modern City.** The modern city occupies the site of the ancient ruin. The modern wall, built in 1542, varies from 20 to 60 feet in height. The site of the former magnificent temples, that of Solomon, Zerubbabel and Herod, is occupied by a Moslem mosque,

241. Moslem Dome of the Rock on Site of the Temple

the Dome of the Rock, and called also the Mosque of Omar, built by Abd el-Melik in 686 A. D. In World War I Palestine was conquered by the British under General Allenby, and Jerusalem surrendered Dec. 9, 1917. Since that time Palestine has undergone remarkable growth. Zionism has flourished, the State of Israel has emerged (1948), and Jerusalem is a flourishing capital divided at present by the Jew and Arab, with the State of Israel growing economically and culturally.

10. **Prophecy.** Prophetic Scripture outlines a brilliant future for Jerusalem. During the millennium it is to be the capital of the earth, (Isa. 60:1-22; Zech. 14:1-20; Ezek. chaps. 40-

48). The Second Coming of Christ will eventuate in the destruction of Israel's enemies, the judgment of the nations, the deliverance of the Israelite remnant and the establishment of the Kingdom. But before that great event Israel will go through the time of the Great Tribulation (Jer. 30:7) under the terrible rule of the Anti-Christ. Only as the remnant looks upon Him Whom they have pierced will they be converted (Zech. 12:10 through 13:1) and at last recite the penetential strains of Isaiah 53. *M. F. U.*

Jeru′salem, New. This is the City of God which comes down out of heaven described in Rev. 21:2; 21:10. This city is the one "which hath foundations" and which Abraham saw by faith (cf. Heb. 11:8-10). It is described in Heb. 12: 22-24. Christ makes mention of it in his message to the church in Philadelphia (Rev. 3:12). In full correspondence with the description as given in Heb. 12:22-24, the Church is present; the angels are present; a company of "just men made perfect," to which Israel would belong, is present; and Christ the Mediator and God the Father are present. Taking the measurements of the city literally, the breadth and height are equal, being 12,000 furlongs, which which would be 1500 miles each way. The glory of the eternal city is described in terms of being pure gold. The city descends from heaven and is to be doubtless considered as something distinct from heaven. It is named for the bride of Christ, the Church, evidently because she has some superior right to it or forms the chief body of redeemed humanity to occupy it. However other peoples and beings enter her gates, making it clearly a cosmopolitan center. It must be clearly remembered that when the last two chapters of the Bible describe the future eternal state of all things, they differentiate at least four different abodes: a. the new heaven; b. the new earth; c. the bridal city; d. "and without," which is evidently identical with the lake of fire or the second death (Rev. 20:14, 15; 21:8; 22:15). But in this changed situation with its different dwelling-places the place of residence is no longer subject to change. This is the consummation of revelation in which time merges into eternity. *M. F. U.*

Jeru′sha (jē-rū′shà; *taken in marriage, possessed*), the daughter of Zadok and queen of Uzziah. She was the mother of Jotham, king of Judah (II Kings 15:33), B. C. 738. Called also *Jerushah.*

Jeru′shah (jē-rū′shà), another form (II Chron. 27:1) of the name *Jerusha* (q. v.).

Jesa′iah (jē-sā′yà; I Chron. 3:21; Neh. 11:7), another form of *Jeshaiah* (q. v.).

Jesha′iah (jē-shā′yà; *Jehovah saves*).

1. The second-named of the sons of Hananiah, the son of Zerubbabel (I Chron. 3:21), another form of *Jesaiah*, B. C. after 536.

2. One of the sons of Jeduthun, appointed as a sacred harper (I Chron. 25:3) at the head of the eighth division of Levitical musicians (v. 15), B. C. after 1000.

3. The son of Rehabiah, of the Levitical family of Eliezer. His descendant, Shelomith, was over the sacred treasury in the time of David (I Chron. 26:25; comp. 24:21, where he is called Isshiah), B. C. after 1000.

4. Son of Athaliah, and chief of the family of Elam. He returned from Babylon with seventy males (Ezra 8:7), B. C. about 457.

5. A Levite of the family of Merari, who, in company with Hashabiah, met Ezra at Ahava, on the way from Babylon to Palestine (Ezra 8:19), B. C. about 457.

6. Father of Ithiel, a Benjamite, whose descendant, Sallu, resided in Jerusalem after the exile (Neh. 11:7, A. V. "Jesaiah"), B. C. before 445.

Jesh'anah (jĕsh'à-nà; *old*), one of the cities of Israel, which was taken with its suburbs from Jeroboam by Abijah, king of Judah (II Chron. 13:19). It is only mentioned in this connection, and its site has not been ascertained.

Jeshare'lah (jĕsh-à-rē'là; perhaps, *upright toward God*), head of the seventh division of the Levitical musicians (I Chron. 25:14). He was a son of Asaph, and his name is given (ver. 2) as *Asarelah*.

Jesheb'eab (jĕ-shĕb'ē-ăb; perhaps, *father's seat*), the head of the fourteenth course of priests as arranged by David (I Chron. 24:13), B. C. before 960.

Je'sher (jĕ'shẽr; *uprightness*), one of the sons of Caleb, the son of Hezron, by his wife Azubah (I Chron. 2:18), B. C. about 1440.

Jesh'imon (jĕsh'ĭ-mŏn; *a waste, a desolation*). The title simply designates the place, which lies north of the Dead Sea (Num. 21:20; 23:28; I Sam. 23:19, etc.). "In the Old Testament the wilderness of Judea is called the Jeshimon, a word meaning devastation, and no term can better suit its haggard and crumbling appearance. It covers some thirty-five miles by fifteen . . . short bushes, thorns, and succulent creepers were all that relieved the brown and yellow bareness of the sand, the crumbling limestone, and scattered shingle. Such is Jeshimon, the wilderness of Judea. It carries the violence and desolation of the Dead Sea Valley right up to the heart of the country, to the roots of the Mount of Olives, to within two hours of the gates of Hebron, Bethlehem, and Jerusalem" (Smith, *Hist. Geog.*).

Jeshi'shai (jĕ-shī'shâ-ī; *aged*), the son of Jahdo and father of Michael, one of the ancestors of the Gadites who dwelt in Gilead (I Chron. 5:14), B. C. long before 740.

Jeshoha'iah (jĕ-shô-hā'yà), a chief of the Simeonites, and one of those who emigrated to Gedor (I Chron. 4:36). B. C. about 715.

Jesh'ua (jĕsh'ū-à; a later form of Joshua, *Jehovah is salvation*).

1. A priest in the reign of David, to whom the ninth course fell by lot (I Chron. 24:11, in which passage it is Anglicized *Jeshuah*), B. C. about 960. Perhaps the same as the one mentioned in Ezra 2:36; Neh. 7:39, whose descendants returned from Babylon.

2. A Levite appointed by Hezekiah, with others, to distribute the sacred offerings among their brethren (II Chron. 31:15), B. C. 719.

3. Son of Jehozadak, first high priest of the third series, viz., of those after the Babylonian captivity, and ancestor of the fourteen high priests his successors down to Joshua or Jason, and Onias or Menelaus, inclusive. Jeshua,

like his contemporary Zerubbabel, was probably born in Babylon, whither his father, Jehozadak, had been taken captive while young (I Chron. 6:15). He came up from Babylon in the first year of Cyrus with Zerubbabel (Ezra 2:2; Neh. 7:7; 12:1, 7, 10), and took a leading part with him in the rebuilding of the temple and the restoration of the Jewish commonwealth (Ezra 3:2, 8, 9; 4:3; 5:2), B. C. 536-446. Besides the great importance of Jeshua as a historical character, from the critical times in which he lived, and the great work which he accomplished, his name Jesus, his restoration of the temple, his office as high priest, and especially the two prophecies concerning him in Zech. 3 and 6:9-15, point him out as an eminent type of Christ. He is called *Joshua* (Hag. 1:1, 12; 2:2, 4; Zech. 3:1, 3, 6, 8, 9).

4. A descendant (or native) of Pahath-moab, mentioned with Joab as one whose posterity, numbering two thousand eight hundred and twelve (Ezra 2:6), or two thousand eight hundred and eighteen (Neh. 7:11), returned from Babylon, B. C. before 536.

5. A Levite named along with Kadmiel as one whose descendants ("children of Hoderah"), to the number of seventy-four, returned from Babylon (Ezra 2:40; Neh. 7:43), B. C. before 436.

6. The father of Jozabad, which latter was appointed by Ezra one of the receivers of the offering for the sacred service (Ezra 8:33), B. C. about 457.

7. A Jew whose son Ezer repaired the part of the wall ("over against the going up to the armory") under Nehemiah (Neh. 3:19), B. C. 445.

8. A Levite, probably son of Azaniah (Neh. 10:9), who assisted in explaining the law to the people under Ezra (Neh. 8:7; 9:4, 5; 12:8), B. C. about 445.

9. Joshua, the son of Nun, is called Jeshua in Neh. 8:17.

10. Son of Kadmiel, one of the Levites who served in the temple, "to praise and to give thanks" after the restoration in the time of Eliashib (Neh. 12:24), B. C. about 406. Perhaps, however, "son" is here a transcriber's error for "and," in which case this Jeshua will be the same as No. 5 (McC. and S., *Cyc.*).

11. A city of Judah inhabited after the captivity (Neh. 11:16); perhaps Tell es-Sa-'weh.

Jesh'uah (jĕsh'ū-à; I Chron. 24:11). See Jeshua, 1.

Jesh'urun (jĕsh'ū-rŭn; *upright*), an honorable surname given to Israel (Deut. 32:15; 33:5, 26; Isa. 44:2, A. V. ''Jersurun''), and representing Israel as a nation of just or upright men. The epithet *righteous nation*, as we may render *Jeshurun*, was intended to remind Israel of its calling, and involved the severest reproof of its apostasy.

Jesi'ah (jĕ-sī'à; I Chron. 12:6; 23:20). See Isshiah.

Jesim'iel (jĕ-sĭm'ĭ-ĕl; *God will place*), one of the thirteen Simeonite princes who, in the time of Hezekiah, migrated to the valley of Gedor for purposes of conquest (I Chron. 4:36).

Jes'se (jĕs'ē), a son (or descendant) of Obed, the son of Boaz and Ruth (Ruth 4:17, 22;

Matt. 1:5, 6; Luke 3:32; I Chron. 2:12). He had eight sons (I Sam. 17:12), the youngest of whom was David. Jesse's wealth consisted chiefly of sheep, for whom David acted as shepherd (I Sam. 16:11; 17:34, 35). The last historical mention of Jesse is in relation to the asylum which David procured for him from the king of Moab (I Sam. 22:3), B. C. before 1000.

Although Jesse was a prominent lineage, yet he himself was unknown and of modest station in life. In such great Messianic passages as Isa. 11:1 and 10, allusion is made to this fact. After Saul had become estranged from David, he approbriously called him "the son of Jesse," thereby displaying his scorn toward him (I Sam. 20:31; 22:7; 25:10). *M. F. U.*

Jesting (Gr. *eutrapelia*,; *pleasantry, humor, facetiousness*) is used in a bad sense (Eph. 5:4), as scurrility, ribaldry, low jesting.

Jes'ui (jĕs'ū-ī; Num. 26:44). *See* Ishui, No. 1.

Jes'uites (jĕs'ū-īts; Num. 26:44), descendants of *Ishui,* No. 1.

Jes'urun (jĕs'ōō-rŭn; Isa. 44:2). *See* Jeshurun.

Je'sus Christ (jē'zŭs krīst). In order to study understandingly the life of our Lord, recourse should first be had in brief to the broad teachings of the New Testament respecting the character, relations, and claims of the Lord Jesus Christ. He is the one subject whose history fills the four gospels. We should properly *apprehend,* though we cannot *comprehend,* the divine personality set forth in these Scriptures; that personality whose words, deeds, and sufferings, and whose *revealing names and titles* are recorded therein for our learning.

1. **Names Assigned to our Lord.** Matthew opens his gospel as "the book of the generations of Jesus Christ the Son of David." Both designations are here used as a personal name, although usually "Christ" is a term employed rather as an appellative or common name.

(1) **The personal name** of our Lord was *Jesus,* which signifies *Saviour.* It is carefully accented by repetitions in the record as being highly important. (*a*) He was so called prospectively by Gabriel unto Mary: "Thou hast found favor with God: and behold thou shalt conceive in thy womb and bring forth a Son, *and thou shalt call his name Jesus*" (Luke 1:31). (*b*) He was so named by the angel to Joseph in his supernatural dream respecting Mary and the child: "She shall bring forth a Son, and thou shalt call his name *Jesus, for he shall save his people from their sins*" (Matt. 1:21). (*c*) He was so called on the day of his birth: "She brought forth her firstborn son, and he called his name Jesus" (Matt. 1:25). (*d*) He was so called when his name was officially bestowed at circumcision: "*His name shall be called Jesus who was so named of an angel before he was conceived in the womb*" (Luke 2:21).

(2) **His official appellative** was *Christ,* which means *the Anointed One.* Here *the Messiah and the Christ of the Scriptures* meet and identify themselves in the personality of Jesus, who was the Anointed of God as the Prophet, Priest, and King *Christos* = Christ = *the Anointed;* (Heb. *Mäshîäḥ, Messiah = the Anointed*). "*God anointed Jesus of Nazareth with the Holy Ghost, and with power,* who went about doing good, and healing all that were oppressed of

the devil; for God was with him" (Acts 10:38). Andrew, who had been one of the Baptist's disciples, when he turned to follow Jesus "first findeth his own brother Simon, and saith unto him, *We have found the Messiah,* which is, being interpreted, *the Christ*" (John 1:35, 40, 41). "It was revealed" unto the just and devout Simeon "by the Holy Ghost, that he should not see death before he had seen *the Lord's Christ*" (Luke 2:25, 26). Peter, answering the Lord's question, said: "*Thou art the Christ,* the *Son of the living God*" (Matt. 16:16).

(3) **Other titles** ascribed to our Lord. The Jehovah of the Old Testament is the Jesus of the New. (*a*) Jesus is called "*the son of Man*" (*ho huios tou anthrōpou*). With this formula Jesus usually addressed himself to the apprehension of his disciples. The reasons are quite obvious: Jesus was in his condition of humility; he was, as yet, thus best known to his followers in his humanity. He was to be cognized as the promised "seed of the woman," and withal, he was that Perfect Man whose unique mission into this world was to be the Redeemer of lost mankind. (*b*) Jesus is called distinctively "*the Son of God*" (*ho huios tou theou*). This title expresses the deity of the Lord Jesus as distinguished from his humanity. In Scripture this designation is never applied to his miraculous birth, or exclusively to his Messiahship, which, however, is included, but invariably to his original relation to the Father as he was in his preexistence before he assumed humanity. Our Lord declares himself to be the Son of God, and includes his Messiahship as based upon his proper oneness and equality with God, either by direct expression or indirectly by implication (for full discussion, see Cremer, *Biblio-Theol.*, Lex. of New Testament, 1880, p. 562). That relation made the Messiahship possible, as expressed in "God sending his own Son in the likeness of sinful flesh" (Rom. 8:3). The reference is not to the incarnation or miraculous conception of Christ, but to his oneness with God in the glory which he had with the Father before the world was (John 17:5). Jesus said to the Jews: "Say ye of him whom the Father hath sent into the world, Thou blasphemest, *because I said I am the Son of God?*" (John 10:36; comp. 9:35-37; Matt. 26:33, 64). The Jews understood that Jesus made this high claim, and would stone him, because that he, being a man, had made himself God (John 10:33); and Paul reaffirms the claim when he represents Jesus Christ as "being in the form of God, thought it not robbery to be equal with God," "that at the name of Jesus every knee shall bow, of things in heaven, and things in earth, and things under the earth, and every tongue shall confess that Jesus Christ is Lord, to the glory of God the Father" (Phil. 2:5-8). (*c*) Jesus is called "*God our Saviour*" (*ho Sōtēros hēmōn Theos*). These passages express Christ's unity and identity with God, illustrating the character of the preexistence of Jesus. Hence, the apostle Paul speaks of "the commandment of God our Saviour" (I Tim. 1:1; Tit. 1:3); of "the kindness and love of God our Saviour" (Tit. 3:4); of that which "is good and acceptable in the sight of God our Saviour" (I Tim. 2:4); and that men should "adorn the doctrine of God

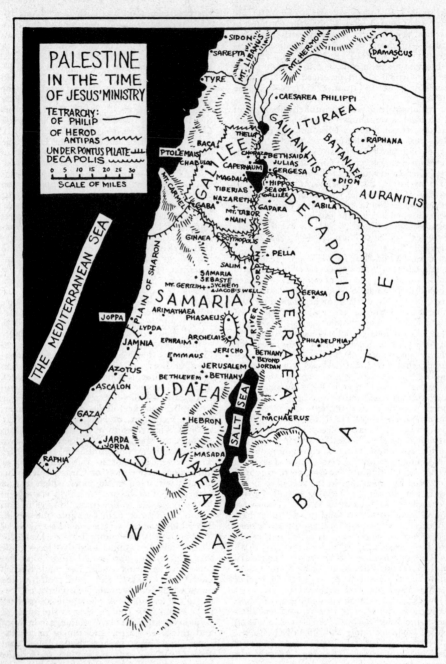

PALESTINE
IN THE TIME
OF JESUS' MINISTRY

TETRARCHY:
OF PHILIP ————
OF HEROD
ANTIPAS ∿∿∿∿
UNDER PONTUS PILATE ⊥⊥⊥
DECAPOLIS ∿∿∿∿

0 5 10 15 20 25 30
SCALE OF MILES

242.

our Saviour in all things" (Tit. 2:10), "looking for that blessed hope and the glorious
appearing of the great God and our Saviour
Jesus Christ" (Tit. 2:13).

2. **Ground of Christian Belief.** The four
gospels are occupied in furnishing facts illustrative of Jesus Christ and his work as related
to mankind; also in teaching his relation to
God. As these Scriptures derive all their char-

acter and significance from his personality and
life—without which they would have no
occasion to exist—our faith in their teaching
reposes on the following propositions: (1) The
absolutely unique and perfect manhood of
Jesus Christ among men; (2) The realization
in him of all the Messianic predictions of
Scripture; (3) All his miracles being restora-
tive, were part of his redemptive plan; (4)

The resurrection of Jesus from the dead, an absolute historical fact; (5) The transformation secured in the character of the individual believer; (6) The Spirit's witness to personal adoption in Christian consciousness; (7) Pre-eminence of the Christian nations as seen on the atlas of the world.

The details of our Lord's life may now be studied with advantage.

TIME	NO.	OUR LORD'S LIFE	MATT Ch. Ver.	MARK Ch. Ver.	LUKE Ch. Ver.	JOHN Ch. Ver.
B.C.		*Preliminary Facts.*				
	1	Luke's preface to his gospel			1:1-4	
6	2	Prediction to Zacharias of the Baptist's birth			1:5-25	
5	3	Gabriel's annunciation to Mary of Messiah's birth			1-26:28	
5	4	Mary visits Elizabeth and her prophetic hymn			1:39-56	
5	5	Birth of John and Zacharias's prophetic hymn			1:57-70	
5	6	Joseph's dream respecting Mary's chastity	1:18-25			
		Birth and boyhood of Jesus.				
	7	Genealogy of Christ's royal and natural ancestry	1:1-17		3:23-38	
4	8	Our Lord's nativity at Bethlehem	1:18,25		2:1-7	1:1-14
4	9	The angel's revelation in song to the shepherds			2:8-20	
4	10	The infant Jesus receives his name by circumcision			2:21	
4	11	Child presented at the temple for legal redemption			2:22-39	
4	12	Visit of the Magi to Herod at Jerusalem	2:1-12			
4	13	Herod's consternation and inquiries	2:3-7			
4	14	The Magi visit the village of Bethlehem	2:10-12			
3	15	Herod's jealousy and resentment aroused	2:7,8,16			
3	16	Flight of Joseph and family into Egypt	2:13-15			
3	17	Herod massacres the male infants of Bethlehem	2:16-18			
2	18	Recall of the holy family from Egypt	2:19-21			
1	19	Returning, they fear Herod Archaelaus the ethnarch	2:22			
		[Here follow about ten years of silent history.]				
A.D.						
9	20	Jesus at twelve, with the Sanhedrists in the Temple			2:40-52	
		[Here follow about eighteen years of silent history.]				
26	21	John the Baptist inaugurates his ministry	3:1-12	1:3-8	3:1-18	
27	22	Inauguration of Jesus Christ to his ministry	3:13-17	1:9-11	3:21-23	
27	23	Jesus made subject to the temptations of Satan	4:1-11	1:12,13	4:1-11	
27	24	Baptist witnesses that Jesus is the Son of God				1:19-36
27	25	Two of John's disciples leave him and follow Christ				1:35-42
27	26	Philip and Nathaniel also now become his disciples				1:43-51
27	27	The first miracle wrought by Jesus Christ in Cana				2:1-12
		From the first to the second Passover.				
27	28	Traders' animals expelled from the temple with scourge				2:13-22
27	29	Interview of Nicodemus with Jesus by night				3:1-21
27	30	Baptist witnesses the second time for Christ				1:15-34
27	31	Christ's disciples baptize other followers				3:22
27	32	The imprisonment of John the Baptist by Antipas	14:3-5	6:17-20	3:19,20	
27	33	Jesus thereupon leaves Judea for Galilee	4:12	1:14,15	4:14,15	4:1-3
27	34	Jesus converses with Samaritan woman at the well	4:12			4:4-42
27	35	Jesus opens his public ministry in Galilee	4:14	1:14,15	4:14,15	4:43-45
27	36	The nobleman seeks Jesus at Cana to heal his son				4:46-54
		From the second to the third Passover.				
28	37	Jesus visits Jerusalem during the Passover				5:1
28	38	Healed an infirmity of thirty-eight years				5:2-9
28	39	Jews dispute Christ's right to heal on Sabbath				5:10-17
28	40	Jews affirm that Christ claimed equality with God				5:18-47
28	41	Returns to Nazareth and proves his Messiahship			4:15-22	
28	42	Rejected at Nazareth, he dwells at Capernaum	4:13-16		4:23-31	
28	43	Resumes public teaching here and works miracles	4:17-25	1:21,22	4:31,32	
28	44	Miracle of fishes: calls Peter, Andrew, James and John	4:18-22	1:16-22	5:1-11	
28	45	Jesus casts out an unclean spirit in synagogue		1:22-28	4:33-37	
28	46	Peter's wife's mother miraculously cured of fever	8:14-17	1:29-34	4:38-41	
28	47	Christ's first circuit in Galilee with disciples	4:23-25	1:35-39	4:42-44	
28	48	He cures a leper who gives him great fame	8:2-4	1:40-45	5:12-16	
28	49	Returning to Capernaum, heals the paralytic	9:2-8	2:1-12	5:17-26	
28	50	Call of Matthew and the feast at his house	9:9-13	2:13-17	5:27-32	
28	51	Discussion with Jews about the disciples' fasting	9:14-17	2:18-22	5:33-39	
28	52	Disciples pluck ears of grain on the Sabbath	12:1-8	2:23-28	6:1-5	
28	53	Jesus healed the man's withered hand on Sabbath	12:9-14	3:1-6	6:6-11	
28	54	Our Lord heals multitudes at the seaside		3:7-12		
28	55	After a night of prayer, Jesus chooses the twelve	10:1-42	3:13 19	6:12-19	
28	56	Jesus preaches on the mountains of Galilee	5,6,7	{4:21-25} {9:43-48}	6:20-49	
28	57	Centurion's servant healed miraculously by Christ	8:5-13		7:1-10	
28	58	The widow's son of Nain restored to life			7:11-17	
28	59	Baptist's inquiry from his prison at Machaerus	11:2-6		7:18-23	
28	60	Christ's eulogy upon his cousin, the Baptist	11:7-19		7:24-35	
28	61	He upbraids cities where he had wrought miracles	11:20-30			
28	62	Woman anoints his feet in Pharisee's house			7:36-50	
28	63	Second circuit of two days' preaching in Galilee			8:1-3	
28	64	Returning to Capernaum, he heals the demoniac	12:22-37	3:22-30	11:14-26	

TIME	NO.	OUR LORD'S LIFE	MATT Ch. Ver.	MARK Ch. Ver.	LUKE Ch. Ver.	JOHN Ch. Ver.
28	65	His mother and kinsfolk think Jesus to be insane	12:46-50	3:19-21	8:19-21	
28	66	From a vessel he preaches seven parables	13:1-3	4:1-34	8:4-18	
28	67	Asleep at sea, he awoke and stayed the storm	8:23-27	4:35-41	8:22-25	
28	68	Jesus cures two demoniacs among the Gadarenes	8:28-34	5:1-20	8:26-40	
28	69	Return to west shore, he raises Jarius's daughter	9:18-25	5:21-24	8:40,41	
28	70	Heals woman of issue of blood twelve years	9:20-22	5:25-34	8:43-48	
28	71	Christ rejected the second time at Nazareth	13:54-58	6:1-6		
28	72	Third circuit of Jesus's preaching in Galilee	9:35-38	6:6		
28	73	The twelve are sent forth to work miracles	10:1-42	6:7-13	9:1-6	
28	74	Herod Antipas beheads John at Machaerus	14:1-12	6:14-29	9:7-9	
28	75	The twelve returning report their successes		6:30	9:10	
28	76	Crosses Galilean Sea and feeds five thousand	14:13-21	6:31-44	9:10-17	
28	77	Returning he walks the sea in storm and night	14:22-46	6:45-56		6:15-24
28	78	The five thousand fed, find Jesus at Capernaum				6:22-71

29 April. *From the third unto the fourth Passover.*

TIME	NO.	OUR LORD'S LIFE	MATT Ch. Ver.	MARK Ch. Ver.	LUKE Ch. Ver.	JOHN Ch. Ver.
29	79	Jesus delays going to the third Passover				7:1-10
29	80	Many cures by Christ on Gennesaret plain	14:34-36	6:53-56		
29	81	Pharisees refuted about washing hands	15:1-20	7:1-23	6:39	
29	82	Visits Tyre and Sidon; cures Syro-Phoenician	15:21-28	7:24-30		
29	83	Returns by Decapolis making many cures	15:29-31	8:31-37		
29	84	Jesus feeds four thousand on the mountain	15:29-38	8:1-9		
29	85	He recrosses Galilean Sea to Magdala (west)	15:39	8:10		
29	86	Thence sails to Bethsaida-Julias (east of Jordan)	16:1-4	8:13,22		
29	87	Cures blind man who saw men as trees walking		8:22-26		
29	88	Passes into regions of Caesarea Philippi	16:13	8:27-30		
29	89	Jesus asks the disciples their opinion of him	16:13-20	8:27-30		
29	90	Jesus begins now to predict his own death	16:21	8:31	9:21,22	
29	91	Christ's transfiguration on Mount Hermon	17:1-13	9:2-13	9:28-36	
29	92	Descending he casts out a demon	17:14-21	9:14-29	9:37-43	
29	93	Jesus again predicts his own death and rising	17:22,23	9:30-32	9:44,45	
29	94	Half shekel provided in the fish's mouth	17:24-27			
29	95	Disciples contend who shall be greatest	18:1-35	9:33-50	9:45-50	

Oct. *Feast of Tabernacles six months after Passover.*

TIME	NO.	OUR LORD'S LIFE	MATT Ch. Ver.	MARK Ch. Ver.	LUKE Ch. Ver.	JOHN Ch. Ver.
29	96	Jesus goes to Jerusalem and teaches in temple				7:1-10
29	97	Puts severest test to human consciousness				7:17
29	98	The people are divided as to Christ's doctrine				7:11-44
29	99	Nicodemus defends Jesus before the Sanhedrin				7:45-53
29	100	Christ, the Jews, and the adulteress				8:1-11
29	101	Jesus now claims to be the Light of the World				8:12-20
29	102	His preexistence before Abraham was				8:42,56-58
29	103	Jesus escapes from the stoning of the Jews				8:59
29	104	He gives sight to the beggar born blind				9:1-41
29	105	He announces himself the Good Shepherd				10:1-16
29	106	He again calls himself the Son of God	26:63,64			{ 9:35-37 / 10:36
29	107	Christ finally leaves Galilee			9:51-56	
29	108	Requisites for discipleship to Christ			9:51-56	
29	109	Seventy disciples sent forth to work			10:1-16	
29	110	They return rejoicing in their success			10:17-20	
29	111	Tempting lawyer and the Good Samaritan			10:25-24	
29	112	Jesus visits Martha and Mary (Bethany)			10:38-42	
29	113	Teaches disciples the Lord's Prayer	6:5-12		11:1-4	
29	114	Miracles on demoniacs ascribed to Beelzebub			11:14-26	
29	115	Disciples admonished as to Pharisees			12:1-3	
29	116	Dangers and duties of discipleship			12:3-53	
29	117	He declines arbitrating an inheritance			12:13-21	
29	118	Counsels, parables, and predictions			12:21-59	
29	119	A woman's spirit of infirmity cured			13:10-17	
30	120	Christ at the feast of dedication				10:22-29
30	121	Test question before stoning Jesus				10:31-38
30	122	Jesus escapes and goes to Peraea				10:39-42
30	123	Lazarus sick, he returns to Bethany				11:1-16
30	124	Christ describes Antipas as a fox			13:31,32	
30	125	He miraculously cures the man afflicted with dropsy			14:1:6	
30	126	The parable of the great supper			14:7-24	
30	127	The perils of discipleship			14:25-35	
30	128	The lost sheep; lost silver; the lost son			15:3-32	
30	129	The unjust steward: rich man and Lazarus			16:1-30	
30	130	Miracle of the resurrection of Lazarus				11:17-46
30	131	Sanhedrin conspire against Christ's life				11:47-53
30	132	Leaving Jerusalem he goes to Ephraim				11:54

Christ's last journey to Jerusalem through Samaria.

TIME	NO.	OUR LORD'S LIFE	MATT Ch. Ver.	MARK Ch. Ver.	LUKE Ch. Ver.	JOHN Ch. Ver.
30	133	Cures ten lepers on borders of Samaria			17:11-19	
30	134	The judge and the importunate widow			18:1-8	
30	135	Self-righteous Pharisee and publican			18:9-14	
30	136	Jesus goes to Jerusalem by Peraea	19:1,2	10:1		
30	137	Pharisees question Jesus about divorce	19:3-12	10:2-12		
30	138	Christ's love and blessing for little children	19:13-15	10:13-16	18:15-17	
30	139	Rich young ruler and the discipleship	19:16-30	10:17-31	18:18-31	
30	140	Compensation of laborers in vineyard	20:1-16			
30	141	Jesus foretells his death third time	20:17-19	10:32-34	18:31-34	
30	142	Request of special favor for James and John	20:20-38	10:35-45		
30	143	Bartimaeus and another blind man cured	20:29-34	10:46-52	18:25,19	

TIME	NO.	OUR LORD'S LIFE	MATT. Ch. Ver.	MARK Ch. Ver.	LUKE Ch. Ver.	JOHN Ch. Ver.
30	144	Zacchaeus called down from a sycamore tree......................			19:2-10	
30	145	Men thought the kingdom of God was now near...................			19:11	
30	146	Jesus counsels by the nobleman and his money...................			19:12-28	
		Last Jewish Sabbath beginning at sunset Friday.				
30	147	A woman anoints Christ's head and feet (Bethany).............	26:6-13	14:3-9	....	12:1-8
30	148	At Jerusalem Jews seek for our Lord's life....................				11:55-57
30	149	Crowds visit Bethany to see Lazarus and Jesus.................				12:9-11
		Last week of Passover ending with the crucifixion.				
		First Day, Sunday, April 2.				
30	150	Christ's triumphal entrance into Jerusalem....................	21:1-11	11:1-11	19:29-40	12:12-19
30	151	Approaching nigh the city, he wept over Jerusalem.............			19:41-44	
30	152	Jesus entered the temple inspecting its affairs................		11:11		
30	153	He retired to Bethany to spend the night.....................	21:17	11:11		
		Second Day, Monday, April 3.				
30	154	Returning next day hungry he cursed the fig tree..............	21:18-22	11:12-14	....	
30	155	He cleansed the temple again at end of his ministry............	12:12,18	11:15-17	19:45,46	
30	156	Jesus healed the blind and lame in the temple.................	21:14			
30	157	At evening Jesus left the city for Bethany...................		11:19		
		Third day, Tuesday, April 4.				
30	158	Returning he explains the lesson of the fig tree..............	21:20-22	11:20-26		
30	159	Duty to forgive in order to be forgiven......................		11:25,26		
30	160	The duty and power of faith in God urged....................	21:21,22	11:22-24		
30	161	Jesus teaches daily the people in the temple..................			19:47	
30	162	The Sanhedrists challenge his authority to teach..............	21:23-27	11:27-33	20:1-18	
30	163	Responds: Parable of two sons and a vineyard.................	21:28-32	12:1-16		
30						
30	164	The Sanhedrists sought to lay hands on Jesus.................	21:43,44	12:12	{19:47,48} {12:19,20}	8:37
30	165	Parable of a king, his son, and his vineyard.................	22:1-14			
30	166	Herodians and Pharisees try to catch his words..............	22:15-22	12:13-17	20:19-26	
30	167	Sadducees cavil about the resurrection same day..............	22:23-33	12:18-27	20:27-40	
30	168	Jesus with the lawyer and the great commandment............	22:35-40	12:28-34		
30	169	If David's son, how does David call him Lord.................	22:41-46	12:35-37	20:41-44	
30	170	Warnings and woes for scribes and Pharisees.................	23:1-36	12:38-40	20:45-47	
30	171	Christ's tearful prediction respecting Jerusalem...............	23:37-39	....	13:34,35	
30	172	A poor widow's two mites appreciated by Jesus...............		12:41-44	21:1-4	
30	173	Some Greeks desire to see Jesus Christ......................				12:20-22
30	174	Jesus prays and the Father answers from heaven..............				12:27-30
30	175	From Mount Olivet Jesus predicts downfall of Jerusalem........	24:1-42	13:..	21:5-37	
30	176	Christ's answer concerning the judgment day.................	{24:36-51} {25:1-51}			
		Fourth Day, Wednesday, April 5.				
30	177	Judas Iscariot conspires against Christ's life.................	26:1-16	14:1-11	22:1-6	
30	178	But many of the Sanhedrin believed on Christ................				12:42
		Fifth Day, Thursday, April 6.				
30	179	Jesus sends forth two disciples for Passover..................	26:17-29	14:12-16	22:7-13	
		Sixth Day, Friday, April 7.				
30	180	Jesus observes Passover at sunset on Friday..................	26:20-35	14:17-31	22:14-23	
30	181	Strife of the disciples who should be greatest................			22:24-30	
30	182	Thereupon Jesus himself washes disciples' feet...............			13:1-20	
30	183	Jesus institutes and administers Lord's Supper...............	26:26-29	14:22-25	22:15-20	
30	184	Jesus foretells and designates his betrayer..................	26:20-25	14:17-21	22:21-23	13:21-29
30	185	Judas after the supper withdraws to betray him..............				13:27-30
30	186	Jesus predicts the scattering of the twelve...................	26:31-35	14:27-31	22:31-38	13:36-38
30	187	Farewell words of Christ with his disciples.................				{14:4,25-31} {16:1-33}
30	188	He enters into prayer and agony in Gethsemane..............	26:30-46	14:26-42	22:39-46	18:1
30	189	Judas now identifies and betrays Jesus.....................	26:47-56	14:42-46	22:47-51	18:2-9
30	190	Peter cuts off Malchus's ear, which Jesus healed.............	26:51-56	14:47-50	22:49-53	18:10,11
30	191	Jesus before Annas at night, and Caiaphas at dawn............	26:59-68	14:53,54	{3:2} 22:54	18:13,24
30	192	Peter thrice denies that he knew the Lord...................	26:69-75	14:66-72	22:54-62	18:25-28
30	193	Jesus avows that he is the Christ of God...................	26:59-68	14:55-65	22:63-71	18:19-24
30	194	Christ before Pilate for sentence to death..................	27:1-14	15:1-5	23:1-5	18:28-38
30	195	Pilate sends Jesus to Herod Antipas of Galilee...............			23:6-12	
30	196	Herod and soldiers mock Jesus with robe, crown, and reed........	27:27-37	15:16-20		{18:39,40} {19:1-16}
30	197	Pilate exonerates Jesus, but people require Barabbas...........	27:15-26	15:6-15	23:13-25	
30	198	Judas remorsefully returns his reward......................	27:3-10	....	{Acts} {1:16-20}	
30	199	Jesus bears his cross, relieved by Simon....................	27:31-33	15:21	23:26	19:16,17

TIME	NO.	OUR LORD'S LIFE	MATT. Ch. Ver.	MARK Ch. Ver.	LUKE Ch. Ver.	JOHN Ch. Ver.
		Particulars related to Christ's crucifixion and resurrection.				
30	200	The place of crucifixion was called Golgotha*.....................	27:33	15:22	23:33	19:17,18
30	201	He was crucified in companionship of malefactors................	27:38	15:27	23:32,33	19:18
30	202	The three hours of preternatural darkness.......................	17:45	15:33	23:44,45	....
30	203	His garments divided among the Roman soldiers..................	27:35	15:24	23:34	19:23,24
30	204	The jeers and gibes of enemies unto Christ......................	27:39-44	15:29-32	23:35-43	....
30	205	Tenderness and sympathy manifested by friends.................	27:36-56	15:40,41	23:47-49	19:25-27
30	206	The rending of the veil of the temple..........................	27:51	15:38	23:45	....
30	207	The rending of the rocks by an earthquake......................	27:51			
30	208	The resurrection of the bodies of the saints....................	27:52,53			
		The seven sayings of Jesus on the Cross.				
30	209	Prayer for his murderers: "Father forgive them"..............			23:34	
30	210	Promise to the penitent thief: "This day shalt"...............			23:42,43	
30	211	Jesus commits his mother to John: "Behold thy son"..........				19:26,27
30	212	The premonitory thirst of Jesus: "I thirst"..................	27:48	15:36		19:28-30
30	213	His loud outcry of agony: "Eloi, Eloi, lama," etc............	27:46	15:34-37	23:46	
30	214	Christ's final word touching his mission: "It is finished"......				19:30
30	215	He commends his spirit unto God: "Father, into thy hands".....	27:50	15:37	23:46	
30	216	Having completed his sufferings, Jesus expired.................	27:50	15:37	23:46	19:30
30	217	Treatment by soldiers of Christ's dead body....................				19:31-37
30	218	Officer of the day testifies Jesus "was the Son of God".........	27:54			
30	219	Treatment by friends of Christ's dead body....................	27:57-61	{15:42-47 16:1	23:50-56	19:38-42
		Seventh Day, Saturday, April 8.				
30	220	Custody of Christ's body after its burial......................	27:62-66	....		
		FROM CHRIST'S RESURRECTION TO HIS ASCENSION.				
		First day's appearance, Easter, April 9.				
30	221	Women at dawn, with spices, find an empty tomb..............	28:1,2	16:1-6	24:1-8	20:1
30	222	Mary Magdalene runs to tell Peter and John..................				20:2
30	223	The others stay at the sepulcher and talk with the angels........	28:2-7	16:5-7	24:4-8	
30	224	Peter and John run to the empty sepulcher....................			24:12	20:3-10
30	225	Christ's first appearance is to Mary Magdalene.................		16:9		20:11-17
30	226	His second appearance is to Mary, Salome, and Joanna..........	28:8-10	16:8	24:9-10	
30	227	Watch report to chief priests the facts known.................	28:11			
30	228	The watch take a bribe to falsify the facts....................	28:12-15			
30	229	His third appearance was to Peter, first Sabbath..............			24:34	1 Cor. 15:5
30	230	Fourth appearance was to two going to Emmaus................		16:12,13	24:13-35	
30	231	Fifth appearance that day to disciples, Thomas being absent.....		16:14	24:36-49	20:19-23
		Appearance of Christ after the first day.				
30	232	Sixth appearance to the ten, Thomas present..................				20:24-29
30	233	Seventh appearance to eleven on mountain in Galilee............	28:16-20	16:15-18		
30	234	Eighth appearance to seven fishing in Galilee..................				21:1-24
30	235	Ninth appearance to five hundred in mountain of Galilee........	28:16			1 Cor. 15:6
30	236	Tenth appearance to James, place not noted...................				Ib. 15:7
30	237	He was seen, not now and then, but literally, *"through forty days"* viz., in every one of the forty days (Acts 1:3-9). He was also seen by Paul when he was converted near Damascus (I Cor. 15:8), and by Stephen when he "saw Jesus standing at the right hand of God" (Acts 7:56), and by the Apostle John again in the apocalyptic vision (Rev. 1:5-18)				

*"*Golgatha*" was written in Aramaic, *gulgalta'*, and in Hebrew *gulgoleth;* but in Greek, *to Kranion*, and in Latin *Calvaria*, rendered "Calvary" in Luke 23:33—all meaning *"the place of a skull."* The three Hebrew evangelists give the Hebrew designation, but Luke being himself a Greek, designates the place by the Greek term. S. L. B.

Literature.—See a standard *Harmony of the Gospels* such as Faussett, Withrow, Strong, Robinson, A. T. Robertson; or a *Life of Christ* such as Weiss, Neander, Farrar, Andrews, and the works of Lange, Ellicott, Edersheim, D. Smith and Sanday.

Je'sus, Offices of. "Jesus is, in virtue of his incarnation, anointed mediator between God and man. His work was the fulfillment and consummation of the ancient prophetical, priestly, and regal functions to which the typical servants of God under the old economy were anointed. These offices he began to discharge on earth, and continues to discharge in heaven. While considering them as distinct, it is important to remember that they are one in the mediatorial work" (Pope, *Christ. Theol.*, p. 196).

1. The Prophetic Office. We call Christ our highest prophet because he is the perfect revealer of the counsel and will of God for the salvation of sinners. As such he comes with supreme credentials, the Truth and the Light of men. The Lord not only speaks of himself as a prophet (Matt. 13:57; John 13:33), but also receives this name from others without contradiction (Matt. 21:11; John 3:2: 4:19; 6:14; 9:17), and declares that he is come into the world in order to bear witness of the truth (John 18:37). His disciples call him Prophet and Apostle (Luke 24:19; Acts 3:22-24; Heb. 1:1; 3:1; II Pet. 1:18, sq.; Rev. 1:5).

Christ came as the greatest Prophet, Priest and King. As "the revealed of God" *par excellence* He fulfilled Deut. 18:15: "The Lord thy God will raise up unto thee a Prophet from the midst of thee, of thy brethren, like unto Me; unto Him ye shall hearken."

2. **Priestly Office.** Here on earth our Lord was a Priest in a preeminent sense, both in His sacrifice of Himself for the sins of the world and in His intercession. He is also our present High Priest interceding for us in heaven. Jesus' baptism in Jordan was evidently a Divine setting-apart of the Messiah for His threefold office of Prophet, Priest and King, especially as a priest for therein was the essence of His work manifested in human redemption. *See* Intercession, Mediation, Propitation.

243. Church of the Nativity, Bethlehem

3. **Kingly Office.** All the O. T. prophecies concerning the kingdom have in view Christ's Kingly office. (1) Christ will in the future occupy David's throne as David's heir (II Sam. 7:16; Psa. 89:20-27; Isa. 11:1-16; Jer. 33:19-21). (2) He was born as a King (Matt. 2:2. (3) He came into the world as a King (Luke 1:32, 33). (4) He was rejected as a King (Mark 15:12, 13; Luke 19:14). (5) He died as a King (Matt. 27:37). (6) He is coming again as a King (Rev. 19:16). Christ is never called "King of the Church" although the term is used, in the worship of the Church (I Tim. 1:17). He is "King of the Jews" (Matt. 2:2) and "Head of the Church" (Eph. 1:22, 23). At His Second Coming Christ will set up the Davidic mediatorial kingdom and reign as a King-Priest (Zech. 6:11-13). His millennial reign will be mediatorial in the sense that God will reign through Christ. The mediatorial kingdom will continue until all enemies, angelic and human, will be put down (I Cor. 15:25-28). However, Christ's Kingly reign is eternal (II Sam. 7:15; Psa. 89:36, 37; Isa. 9:6, 7) inasmuch as Christ goes on reigning by the same authority of the Father (I Cor. 15:28). *See* Kingdom of God.

Je'ther (jē'thĕr; *eminence, abundance, surplus*).

1. Jethro, the father-in-law of Moses (Exod. 4:18, marg.).

2. The firstborn of Gideon's sons, who, when called upon to execute the captured Midianitish kings, Zebah and Zalmunna, timidly declined on account of his youth (Judg. 8:20). According to Judg. 9:18, he was slain, with sixty-nine of his brothers, by the hands of Abimelech.

3. The father of Amasa, captain general of Absalom's army (I Kings 2:5, 32). Jether is merely another form of Ithra (II Sam. 17:25), the latter being probably a corruption. He is

described in I Chron. 2:17, as an Ishmaelite, which again is more likely to be correct than the "Israelite" of the Hebrew in II Sam. 17, or the "Israelite" of the Hebrew in II Sam. 17, or the "Jezreelite" of the LXX and Vulgate in the same passage (K. and D., *Com.*, in loc.). Kimchi suggests "that in the land of Ishmael Jether was called the Israelite from his nationality, and in that of Israel they called him the Ishmaelite on account of his living in the land of Ishmael."

4. The son of Jada, a descendant of Hezron, of the tribe of Judah (I Chron. 2:32).

5. The son of Ezra, whose name occurs in a dislocated passage in the genealogy of Judah (I Chron. 4:17).

6. The chief of a family of warriors of the line of Asher, and father of Jephunneh (I Chron. 7:38). He is probably the same as Ithran (v. 37).

Je'theth (jē'thĕth), (derivation uncertain), one of the phylarchs (A. V. "dukes") who came of Esau (Gen. 36:40; I Chron. 1:51).

Jeth'lah (jĕth'lä), R. V. and R. S. V. Ithla, (*a hanging or lofty place*), a city on the borders of the tribe of Dan, mentioned only in Josh. 19:42, probably Beithul, 3 miles E. of Yalo (Aijalon).

Jeth'ro (jĕth'rō; *excellence, superiority*), a priest or prince of Midian, both offices probably being combined in one person. Moses spent the forty years of his exile from Egypt with him, and married his daughter Zipporah (Exod. 3:1; 4:18), B. C. c. 1475. By the advice of Jethro, Moses appointed deputies to judge the congregation and share the burden of government with himself (Exod. 18); and on account of his local knowledge he was entreated to remain with the Israelites throughout their journey to Canaan (Num. 10:31, 33). It is said in Exod. 2:18, that the priest of Midian whose daughter Moses married was Reuel; afterward, at ch. 3:1, he is called Jethro, as also in ch. 18; but in Num. 10:29, "Hobab the son of Raguel the Midianite" is apparently called Moses' father-in-law (comp. Judg. 4: 11). The probability is that Jethro and Raguel were but different names of Moses' father-in-law (the former being either a title, or a surname showing the rank of Raguel in his tribe), and that the son, Hobab, was his brother-in-law.

Je'tur (jē'tûr), one of the twelve sons of Ishmael (Gen. 25:15; I Chron. 1:31). His name stands also for his descendants, the Ituraeans (I Chron. 5:19), living east of the northern Jordan (Luke 3:1).

Jeu'el (jē-ū'ĕl), a descendant of Zerah, who, with six hundred and ninety of his kindred, dwelt in Jerusalem after the captivity (I Chron. 9:6), B. C. 536.

Je'ush (jē'ŭsh).

1. The first of the three sons of Esau by Aholibamah, born in Canaan, but afterward a sheik of the Edomites (Gen. 36:5, 14, 18; I Chron. 1:35), B. C. after 1950.

2. The first-named son of Bilhan, the grandson of Benjamin (I Chron. 7:10), B. C. considerably after 1900.

3. A Levite, one of the four sons of Shimei, of the Gershonites. He, with his brother Beriah, not having many sons, were reckoned as the

third branch of the family (I Chron. 23:10, 10, 11), B. C. about 960.

4. The first named of the three sons of Rehoboam, apparently by Abihail, his second wife (II Chron. 11:19), B. C. after 926.

Je′uz (jē′ŭz; *counselor*), the head of a Benjamite house, one of the sons of Shaharaim, born of his wife Hodesh in Moab (I Chron. 8:10).

Jew (jōō; Heb. *yᵉhûdî*, a Jehudite, i. e., descendant of Judah; Gr. *Ioudaios*, a name formed from that of the patriarch Judah, and applied first to the tribe or country of Judah, or to a subject of the kingdom of Judah (II Kings 16:6; 25:25; Jer. 32:12; 38:19; 40:11; 41:3; 52:28) in distinction from the seceding ten tribes, the Israelites. From the time of the Babylonian captivity, as the members of the tribe of Judah formed by far the larger portion of the remnant of the covenant people, Jews became the appellation of the whole nation (II Macc. 9:17; John 4:9; Acts 18:2, 24). The original designation of the Israelitish people was the *Hebrews*, as the descendants of Abraham. Thus Paul was appropriately called a Hebrew, and still later the terms Hebrew and Jew were applied with little distinction. *See* Israel, Hebrew.

Jewel, Jewelry. In all ages and among all peoples the love of ornament has expressed itself in the making and wearing of objects of beauty such forms as were attainable. Very early, as soon indeed as the use of metals was known, the making of jewelry, in our sense of the word, began. In the prehistoric bronze age we find multitudes of objects for personal adornment made of that material; and articles of silver and gold, set with stones, are preserved to us from the very dawn of history. The almost universal practice of burying such treasures with the remains of their owners has been a priceless boon both to history and archaeology in revealing to us the arts, the commerce, the culture, and the migrations of perished races and civilizations.

(Exod. chaps. 28 and 39). The royal jewels and the insignia of orders of nobility in Europe and the ecclesiastical jewelry of the Greek and Roman Catholic churches are modern examples of 3 and 4. In addition to these uses it may be noted that in ancient times, and still in the East, where money could not be invested as it is with us, the precious stones and elaborate jewelry formed one of the safest and most convenient ways of preserving great wealth in small bulk, easy to transport and to secrete.

2. **Scripture Terms.** Four Hebrew words are rendered in the A. V. "jewels:"

(1) *Sᵉgŭläh*, *shut up*, *treasure*, is connected with the idea and habit referred to in No. 4 (see Mal. 3:17), and often used figuratively (Exod. 19:5; Psa. 135:4, A. V. "treasure").

(2) *Kᵉli*, is something *wrought* or *prepared*, an article of silver or gold (Gen. 24:53; Exod. 3:22; 11:2; 12:35; Num. 31:50, 51), and more generally (Isa. 61:10; Ezek. 16:39). This is also an indefinite term, often, perhaps, meaning vessels or implements, at other times decorations or trappings, as in last passage cited.

(3) *Ḥĕlyäh*, an ornament or trinket (Hos. 2:13), again very general in character.

(4) *Nĕzĕm*, a *ring*, the only term that is at all specific, generally rendered *earring*, and clearly so in Gen. 35:4; Exod. 32:2, 3; Ezek. 16:12; but a *nosering* (Prov. 11:22; Isa. 3:21), while in many other cases (Gen. 24:22, 20, 47; Num. 31:50, 51; Judg. 8:24-26; Prov. 25:12, etc.), although the former is the rendering, agreeably to modern and Western ideas, the latter may very probably be the original sense.

The nosering in some form is an oriental custom of great persistency. It is sometimes two or two and a half inches in diameter (as in Arabia, especially in the Nejed), or less (as with the women of Anatolia); and sometimes, as in the region of Damascus, is reduced to a mere jeweled stud, like our earrings within the last generation.

244. Metal Workers in Old Kingdom Egypt
Upper left: weighing the metal; middle: furnace with men at blow pipes; right: casting and hammering; lower: making costly ornaments and jewelry

1. **The Uses** of jewelry have been various: (1) Mere personal adornment (Exod. 11:2; Isa. 3:19, 20); (2) Gifts and tokens of friendship or affection of our most familiar associations (Gen. 24:22, 53; Ezek. 16:11); (3) In sacred and religious ceremonials (Gen. 41:42; Dan. 5:7, 16, 29); and (4) The priestly jewels

Other forms of jewelry need but brief reference. Bracelets and necklaces are familiar in all ages and nations; but in ancient times they were largely worn, especially the former, by men, as is conspicuously shown in the Assyrian sculptures, and implied in Scripture passages, as Num. 31:50. The large, massive golden bracelets of both men and women were sometimes made hollow, as is now done, and filled with sulphur, partly to lighten their weight and partly to save material. This has been proved by Phoenician examples, and was, probably, frequent. Some of the ancient necklaces were very beautiful; much use was not made of precious stones, but of glass and glazed earthenware, especially in Phoenician jewelry, as beads and pendants mingled with gold.

The passage (Cant. 1:10), "Thy cheeks are comely with rows *of jewels*," probably refers to a style of ornament seen in many Cypriote figures, a series of coins, hung by small chains or links from behind the ears and coming down by the sides of the face in pendant "rows."

3. **Egyptian.** The art of manufacturing jewelry had reached great perfection in Egypt at a very early date. Nothing in ancient gilt or gem-work, and scarcely anything now, can surpass in elegance the jewelry found with mummies of the royal family of the 12th dynasty. The jewelled treasuries of Tutankhamun

245. Earrings from King Tutankhamun's Tomb

of the resplendent 18th dynasty were incredibly magnificent. His tomb when opened in 1922 was intact. The tombs were systematically violated and robbed in ancient times, probably, it is thought, during the period of the Hyksos; but a few had escaped intact, and in them were found the mummies of several princesses, with their jewels. Among these were necklaces, bracelets, etc., exquisitely wrought and set with pearls, carnelian, emerald, and lapis lazuli; other articles inlaid with these same stones somewhat in the manner of *cloisonne* enamel, and two very remarkable crowns, like delicate wreaths, the one incrusted with flowers of gems and bearing a fanlike spray of similar flowers, with stems and leaves of gold; the other a lacelike garland of gold with forget-me-nots of gems and beads of lapis lazuli (comp. Ezek. 16:12). The most familiar form of Egyptian jewelry is that of the so-called scaraboid seals. Many of them, doubtless, were used more as ornaments than as actual seals, though frequently employed for the latter purpose.

4. **Assyrian.** The jewelry of Assyria and Babylonia may be characterized generally as large, heavy, and showy, but not graceful or delicate. The form best known to us, however, is that of the peculiar "Chaldean cylinders," or rolling seals, which, like the Egyptian scarabs, were largely worn as ornaments and charms. Herodotus mentions a cylinder seal, a staff and some other articles, as forming part of the regular outfit of a Babylonian gentleman for all dress occasions; and with this may be compared the much more ancient account of Judah (Gen. 38:18). Sumerian jewelled wealth is lavishly illustrated by the royal tomb of Queen Shubad, discovered by Woolley at ancient Ur.

5. **Phoenician.** With regard to the Phoenician artisans in Judea, it is not necessary to suppose that they resided there, save, perhaps in the principal cities; but they very probably traveled through the country doing a little business from place to place. Some writers observe that this custom may still be seen in the East; the itinerant goldsmith and jeweler comes with his small portable furnace, crucible, and stock in trade, and sets up business for a day or two in a Syrian or Roumanian hamlet. The women bring their treasured coins to be fashioned into bracelets, bangles, or rings, and the artificer deducts a little percentage for his work. This method is probably very ancient and widespread. Excavations in the Royal Tombs of Byblos have yielded abundant evidences of Phoenician jewel-craft. In the National Museum of Lebanon gleaming objets d'art displaying Phoenician skill can be seen today.

6. **Hebrew.** Of course, the most interesting and important articles of Hebrew jewelry are those connected with the worship of the tabernacle, especially the high priest's breastplate, of which such particular descriptions are given. The style of workmanship must have been Egyptian in character; the Israelites had been living there for generations, and must have been familiar with the art of that country, while long cut off from association with Mesopotamia. At a later period of their history they came under Assyrian and Babylonian influence, and largely in art matter of their Phoenician neighbors. We have seen how the latter borrowed and mingled the art styles of Egypt and Mesopotamia, developing no originality, though much of skill and delicacy in treatment. It would seem, therefore, that the influences dominating Hebrew art in jewelry must have been first Egyptian, then Phoenician, and finally Chaldean.

At this point a few words should be said as to the differences between ancient and modern jewelry. The whole method of cutting stones in facets is modern and European; all Eastern and all ancient jewelry is quite different; the stones are dressed *en cabochon*, as modern jewelers call it, i. e., in rounded forms with smooth or polished convex surfaces. This mode we still employ for opaque and translucent gems, such as turquoises, opals, moonstones, and "carbuncle" garnets; but anciently it was universal. This method gives none of the brilliant flashing effect now so highly esteemed, which results from the internal reflection and refraction of the rays of light from the numerous facets; hence the ancients seem to have cared less for transparency than we do; and to make up for the loss of beauty in this regard they paid more attention to engraving gems than the moderns. Any collection of ancient jewelry will show a large proportion of opaque and semitransparent stones, all *en cabochon*, rounded, and many beautifully sculptured with cameos, intaglios, or inscriptions. In this work the ancients excelled; and the fineness, sharpness, and boldness of their gem engraving cannot be surpassed, indeed, can scarcely be equaled by steam workmen with the best of tools and magnifiers (*see* Anklets, Bracelets, Precious Stones, Ring).—*D. S. M.*, revised by *M. F. U.*

Jew'ess, (jōō'ĕs), a woman of Hebrew extraction, without distinction of tribe (Acts 16:1; 24:24). It is applied in the former passage to Eunice, the mother of Timothy, who was unquestionably of Hebrew origin (comp. II Tim. 3:15), and in the latter to Drusilla, the wife of Felix, and daughter of Herod Agrippa I.

Jewish (Gr. *Ioudaïkos*), of or belonging to Jews. The apostle Paul warns his young brother against Jewish legends, i. e., the Rabbinical legends (Tit. 1:14).

Jew'ry (jōō'rĭ), Luke 23:5; John 7:1), the Jewish nation, i. e., the kingdom of Judah, later Judea (Dan. 5:13).

Jezani'ah (jĕz-à-nī'à; Jer. 40:8; 42:1). *See* Jaazaniah, 1.

Jez'ebel (jĕz'ĕ-bĕl; perhaps, *non-cohabited, unhusbanded*), the daughter of Ethbaal, king of Tyre and Sidon, and queen of Ahab. Her father had formerly been a priest of Astarte, but had violently dispossessed his brother Phelles of the throne.

1. **Personal History.** The first mention of Jezebel in the sacred narrative is her marriage with Ahab (I Kings 16:31), B. C. about 871. (1) **Introduces idolatry.** The first effect of her influence was the immediate establishment of the Phoenician worship on a grand scale at the court of Ahab. At her table were supported no less than four hundred and fifty prophets of Baal and four hundred of Astarte (I Kings 16:31, 32; 18:19), while the prophets of Jehovah were slain by her orders (I Kings 18:13; II Kings 9:7). (2) **Opposes Elijah.** When at last the people, at the instigation of *Elijah* (*q. v.*), rose against her ministers and slaughtered them at the foot of Carmel, and when Ahab was terrified into submission, she alone retained her presence of mind; and when she received, in the palace of Jezreel, the tidings that her religion was all but destroyed (I Kings 19:1), she vowed to take the life of the prophet. (3) **Secures the death of Naboth.** When she found her husband cast down by his disappointment at being thwarted by Naboth, she took the matter into her own hands (I Kings 21:7). She wrote a warrant in Ahab's name, which was to secure the death of *Naboth* (*q. v.*). To her, and not Ahab, was sent the announcement that the royal wishes were accomplished (21:14), and she bade her husband go and take the vacant property. On her, accordingly, fell the prophet's curse as well as on her husband (21:23). (4) **Influence.** Her policy was so triumphant that there were

at last but seven thousand people who had not bowed the knee to Baal, nor kissed the hand of his image. Through her daughter Athaliah, queen of Judah, the same policy prevailed for a time in that kingdom. She survived Ahab fourteen years, and maintained considerable ascendency over her son Jehoram. (5) **Death.** When Jehu entered Jezreel Jezebel was in the palace, which stood by the gate of the city, overlooking the approach from the east. She determined to face the destroyer of her family, whom she saw rapidly advancing in his chariot. She painted her eyelids in the Eastern fashion with antimony, so as to give a darker border to the eyes and make them look larger and brighter, possibly in order to induce Jehu, after the manner of Eastern usurpers, to take her, the widow of his predecessor, for his wife, but more probably as the last act of regal splendor. She tired her head (i. e., adorned her head and hair with a queenly headdress), and, looking down upon him from the high latticed window in the tower, she met him by an allusion to a former act of treason in the history of her adopted country. Jehu looked up from his chariot. Two or three eunuchs of the royal harem showed their faces at the windows, and, at his command, dashed the ancient princess down from the chamber. She fell immediately in front of the conqueror's chariot. When, afterward, he wished to show respect to her corpse as that of "a king's daughter," nothing was found of her but the skull, the palms of her hands, and the soles of her feet (II Kings 9:7, 30, sq.), B. C. about 841.

2. **Character.** Jezebel was a woman in whom, with the reckless and licentious habits of an oriental queen, were united the sternest and fiercest qualities inherent in the Phoenician people. The wild license of her life, the magical fascination of her arts or of her character, became a proverb in the nation (II Kings 9:22). Long afterward her name lived as the byword for all that was execrable. In the Revelation (2:20) she is used as a type of false teachers who, as the Church of Rome, developed, wedded Christian doctrine to pagan ceremonies, as Jezebel engulfed Israel in idolatry.

Je'zer (jē'zēr; *form, purpose*), the third named of the sons of Naphtali (Gen. 46:24; Num. 26:49; I Chron. 7:13), and progenitor of the Jezerites (Num. 26:49), B. C. before 1870.

Je'zerites (jē'zēr-īts; Num. 26:49). *See* Jezer.

Jezi'ah (jĕ-zī'à; *whom Jehovah sprinkles*), an Israelite of the "sons" of Parosh, who put away his heathen wife after the exile (Ezra 10:25), B. C. 456.

Je'ziel (jē'zĭ-ĕl), a "son" of Azmaveth, and one of the skilled Benjamite archers, who joined David at Ziklag (I Chron. 12:3), B. C. before 1000.

Jezli'ah (jĕz-lī'à; cf. Arab. *yazaliy, eternal, unceasing*), one of the "sons" (or descendants) of Elpaal, and apparently a chief Benjamite resident at Jerusalem (I Chron. 8:18), B. C. probably about 588. R. V. and R. S. V. Izliah.

Jezo'ar (jē-zō'ēr), the son of Helah, a wife of Ashur, the father (founder) of Tekoa (1 Chron. 4:7).

Jezrahi'ah (jĕz-rà-hī'à; *Jehovah will shine*), the superintendent of the singers at the dedication of the walls of Jerusalem after the exile (Neh. 12:42), B. C. 445.

Jez'reel (jĕz'rĕ-ĕl; *God sows*).

1. A descendant of the father (or founder) of Etam, of the line of Judah (I Chron. 4:3).

2. The oldest son of the prophet Hosea, so called because of the great slaughter predicted by his father (Hos. 1:4, 5), B. C. about 748.

246. Valley of Jezreel and Road to Nazareth

3. The name of a city in Issachar (Josh. 19: 18), and the plain in which it was located (I Sam. 29:1; Hos. 1:5). It was situated about fifty-five miles N. of Jerusalem, and is identified with the present *Zerin*. Here the kings of Israel had a palace (II Sam. 2:8, sq.), and here the court often resided (I Kings 18:45; II Kings 10:11). In or near the town was a temple of Baal, and an asherah (A. V. "grove," I Kings 16:32, 33); and the palace of Ahab (I Kings 21:1; 18:46) was on the eastern side of the city forming part of the city wall (comp. I Kings 21:1; II Kings 9:25, 30, 33). The seraglio in which Jezebel lived was on the city wall, with window facing to the east (II Kings 9:30). Nearby was the vineyard of Naboth, coveted by King Ahab, and secured by Jezebel through the cruel death of Naboth (I Kings 21:1, sq.).

(1) **Jezreel, blood of** ("I will avenge the blood of Jezreel upon the house of Jehu," Hos. 1:4), is generally understood to be put for the murders perpetrated by Ahab and Jehu at this place. But the divine venegeance is to be visited upon the house of Judah, and would seem, therefore, to be because of his acts. This may be, not because of his extermination of the house of Ahab, in which he fulfilled the divine command, but by reason of the motives which actuated Jehu. That he was moved by evil and selfish motives is evident (see II Kings 10:29, 31).

(2) **Jezreel, ditch of.** The fortification, or intrenchment, surrounding the city, outside of which Naboth was executed (I Kings 21:23, marg.).

(3) **Jezreel, fountain of.** "The fountain which is Jezreel" (I Sam. 29:1) is mentioned as the spot near which the Isrealites pitched their camp in one of their campaigns against the Philistines. At present it is called *Ain Jalûd* (or *Ain Jalût*), i. e., Goliath's fountain, probably because it was regarded as the scene of Goliath's defeat. It is a very large fountain issuing from the foot of the mountain on the northeast border of Gilboa.

(4) **Jezreel, portion of.** The field or country adjacent to the city, where the crime of Ahab had been perpetrated, and its retribution was to be exacted (II Kings 9:10, 21, 36, etc.).

(5) **Jezreel, tower of.** One of the turrets or bastions guarding the entrance of the city, and where the watchman was stationed (II Kings 9:17).

(6) **Jezreel, valley of,** lying on the northern side of the city, between the ridges of Gilboa and Moreh. Its name was afterward extended to the whole plain of Esdraelon (Josh. 17:16; Judg. 6:33; Hos. 1:5). Smith suggests that the "word for 'vale,' *emeq*, literally *deepening*, is a highlander's word for a valley as he looks *down* into it, and is never applied to any extensive plain away from hills."

4. A town in the mountains of Judah, mentioned between Juttah and Jokdeam (Josh. 15:56), and probably the native place of Ahinoam, one of David's wives (I Sam. 25:43; 27:3); not yet discovered.

Jez'reelite (jĕz'rĕ-ĕl-īt), an inhabitant of *Jezreel* (*q. v.*), in Issachar (I Kings 21:1, 4, 6, 7, 15, 16; II Kings 9:21, 25).

Jez'reelitess (jĕz'rĕ-ĕl-ĭ-tĕs; I Sam. 27:3; 30:5; II Sam. 2:2; 3:2; I Chron. 3:1), a woman of Jezreel in Judah.

Jib'sam (jĭb'săm; *fragrant, pleasant*), one of the "sons" (descendants) of Tola, the son of Issachar, in David's army (I Chron. 7:2), B. C. about 1000. Or he may have been a son of Tola, with descendants in the army of David. A. V. and R. S. V. render Ibsam.

Jid'laph (jĭd'lăf; *he weeps*), the seventh named of the eight sons of Nahor (Abraham's brother) by Milcah (Gen. 22:22), B. C. perhaps about 2100.

Jim'na (jĭm'nà), (Num. 26:44), **Jim'nah** (Gen. 46:17). *See* Imnah.

Jim'nite (jĭm'nīt) (Num. 26:44), descendants of Jimna.

Jiph'tah (jĭf'tà; *he will open*), a city in the lowland district of Judah (Josh. 15:43), not positively identified, but located by some at the ruined village *Jimrin*.

Jiph'thah-el (jĭf'thà-ĕl; *God will open*), a valley at the intersection of the line between Asher and Naphtali, with the northern boundary of Zebulun (Josh. 19:14, 27). It is probably "no other than the large Wady *Abilin*, which takes its rise in the hills in the neighborhood of Jefât" (Robinson, *Bib. Res.*, p. 107). R. V. and R. S. V. Iphtahel.

Jo'ab. 1. (jō'ăb; *Jehovah is father*). A "captain of the host" of David.

Family. Joab was one of the three sons of Zeruiah, the sister of David. His father is not named in the Scriptures, but Josephus (*Ant.*, vii, 1, 3) gives his name as Suri. He seems to have resided at Bethlehem, and to have died before his sons, as we find mention of his sepulcher at that place (II Sam. 2:32).

Personal History. (1) **First appearance.** Joab's first appearance was in connection with his brothers, Abishai and Asahel, in command of David's army, when they went against Abner, who was championing the claims of Ishbosheth to the throne. The armies met at the pool of Gibeon, a general action was brought on, and Abner worsted. In his flight he killed Asahel, who was pursuing him (II Sam. 2:13-32), B. C. about 1000. (2) **Avenges Asahel.** Joab was greatly angered at the death of his brother, but postponed his revenge. Abner, quarreling with Ishbosheth, came to David in Hebron, in order to enlist in his service. When Joab returned from some warlike excursion, and was informed of Abner's visit, he chided the king, and accused Abner of treachery. He then sent messengers after Abner, who returned at once and was slain by Joab. David reprobated the act, but seems to have been in fear of his able and intrepid nephew (II Sam. 3:8-39). (3) **In chief command.** At the siege of Jerusalem Joab succeeded in scaling the height upon which the fortress stood, and was made "chief and captain" of the army of all Israel, of which David was now king (II Sam. 5:6-10; I Chron. 11:5-8). He immediately undertook, in conjunction with David, the fortification of the city (II Sam. 5:9; I Chron. 11:8). He had a chief armorbearer of his own, Naharai, a Beerothite (II Sam. 23:37; I Chron. 11:39), and ten attendants to carry his equipment and baggage (II Sam. 18:15). He had the charge of giving the signal by trumpet for advance or retreat (18:16). He was called by the almost regal title of "Lord" (11:11), "the prince of the king's army" (I Chron. 27:34). His usual residence was in Jerusalem, but he had a house and property, with barley fields adjoining, in the country (II Sam. 14:30), in the "wilderness" (I Kings 2:34), probably on the northeast of Jerusalem (comp. I Sam. 13:18; Josh. 8:15, 20), near an ancient sanctuary, called from its nomadic village "Baal-hazor" (II Sam. 13:23; comp. with 14:30), where there were extensive sheepwalks. (4) **Military achievements.** These were conducted by him in person, and may be divided into three campaigns: (*a*) That against the allied forces of Syria and Ammon. Joab attacked and defeated the Syrians, while his brother did the same to the Ammonites. The Syrians rallied with their kindred beyond the Euphrates, and were finally routed by David himself (II Sam. 10:1, sq.). (*b*) The second was against Edom. The decisive victory was gained by David himself in the "valley of salt," and celebrated by a triumphal monument (8:13). But Joab had the charge of carrying out the victory, and remained for six months, extirpating the male population, whom he then buried in the tombs of Petra (I Kings 11:15, 16). (*c*) The third was against the Ammonites. They were again left to Joab (II Sam. 10:7-19). At the siege of Rabbah the ark was sent with him, and the whole army was encamped in booths or huts round the beleaguered city (11:1, 11). After a sortie of the inhabitants, which caused some loss to the Jewish army, Joab took the lower city on the river, and then sent to urge David to come and take the citadel, that the glory of the capture might pertain to the king (12:26-28). (5) **Services to David.** Joab served David faithfully, both in political and private relations, and showed himself to be truly devoted to his interests. (*a*) *Joab and Uriah.* During the Ammonite war Joab lent himself to the king's passion, and secured the death of Uriah the Hittite (II Sam. 11:1-25). (*b*)

Joab and Absalom. When Absalom accomplished the death of Amnon, Joab effected his return by means of the widow of Tekoah; and when he revolted, Joab's former intimacy with the prince did not impair his fidelity to the king. He followed him beyond the Jordan, and in the final battle of Ephraim, slew Absalom in spite of David's injunction to spare him, and when no one else had courage to act so decisive a part (II Sam. 18:2, 11-15). (*c*) When David resolved to number the people Joab endeavored to dissuade him from his purpose, and, unsuccessful in this, performed the task so tardily as to afford the king an opportunity of reconsidering the matter (24:1-4). (6) **Murder of Amasa.** David, to conciliate the powerful party which had supported Absalom, offered the command of the army to Amasa. Joab was grievously offended by this act of the king, and when Amasa tarried longer than the time allowed him to assemble his forces, Joab had an opportunity of displaying his superior resources. Abishai was ordered to pursue the revolting Sheba (perhaps with Joab in command, K and D.), and when Amasa came up to meet them at Gibeon he was treacherously slain by Joab (II Sam. 20:4-13). (7) **Joins Adonijah.** Shortly before the death of David a demonstration was made in favor of his eldest surviving son, Adonijah, and Joab joined his party. The prompt measures taken rendered Adonijah's demonstration abortive (I Kings 1:7, 15, sq.). (8) **Death.** Hearing of the death of Adonijah, Joab fled for refuge to the altar. Solomon, hearing of this, sent Benaiah to put him to death; and as he refused to come forth, Benaiah slew him. His body was buried in the wilderness of Judah (I Kings 2:5, 28-34), B. C. about 962.

Character. Joab was a man of great military prowess, valiant, and capable. He was revengeful, and not above treachery in order to gratify his vengeance. While treating his king with but little ceremony he was, nevertheless, truly devoted to his interests. His principles did not prevent him from serving his master's vices as well as his master's virtues. Altogether he appears in history as one of the most accomplished and unscrupulous warriors that Israel ever produced.

2. In I Chron. 2:54 there is mention of "Ataroth, the house of Joab." What Joab is meant is uncertain, but it is supposed to refer to No. 1.

3. The son of Seraiah (son of Kenaz), a Judaite and progenitor of the inhabitants of Charashim, or craftsmen (I Chron. 4:14).

4. The head of a family whose descendants, with those of Jeshua, to the number of two thousand eight hundred and twelve (Ezra 2:6), or two thousand eight hundred and eighteen (Neh. 7:11), returned from Babylon with Ezra. It is not certain whether Jeshua and Joab were sons of Pahath-Moab, or whether, in the registration of those returned, the descendants of Jeshua and Joab were represented by the sons of Pahath-Moab. The Joab mentioned in Ezra 8:9 is probably the same person, B. C. 445.

Jo′ah (jō′à; *Jehovah is brother*).

1. Son of Asaph and "recorder" of King

Hezekiah, and one of the messengers sent to receive the insulting message of Rabshakeh (II Kings 18:18, 26, 37; Isa. 36:3, 22), B. C. about 719.

2. A Levite of the family of Gershom, son of Zimnah and father of Iddo (I Chron. 6:21). He is probably the same person who, with his son Eden, assisted Hezekiah in the reformation of the temple worship (II Chron. 29:12), B. C. about 719. He is identified with Ethan, mentioned in I Chron. 6:42.

3. The third son of Obed-edom, one of the porters for the tabernacle in the time of David (I Chron. 26:4), B. C. after 1000.

4. Son of Joahaz, and recorder for King Josiah. He was appointed one of the superintendents of the temple repairs (II Chron. 34:8), B. C. 639.

Jo'ahaz (jō'á-hăz; *Jehovah holds*), the father of Joah, which latter was recorder in the reign of Josiah (II Chron. 34:8), B. C. 639.

Joan'na (jō-ăn'á; *Joannas*).

1. The son of Rhesa and grandson of Zerubbabel, in the lineage of Christ (Luke 3:27).

2. (Gr. *Jōanna*, probably feminine of *Jōannēs, John*). The wife of Chuza, the steward of Herod Agrippa (Luke 8:3). She, with other women, had been cured of grievous diseases by the Saviour, or received material benefits from him, and ministered to him and his disciples. She was also one of the women to whom Christ appeared after the resurrection (Luke 24:10).

Jo'ash (jō'ăsh; Heb. *Yō'äsh, Jehovah has given*, Arab. *'asa, to give*).

1. The father of Gideon, who, although himself an idolater, ingeniously screened his son from those desiring to avenge his overthrow of the altar of Baal (Judg. 6:11, 29-31; 7:14; 8:13, 29). He was buried in Ophrah, where he lived (8:29-32).

2. A person who was ordered by King Ahab to imprison Micaiah the prophet for denouncing the allied expedition against Ramoth-gilead (I Kings 22:26; II Chron. 18:25), B. C. about 853. In both passages he is styled "the king's son," which is usually taken literally. Some, however, suggest that the title may merely indicate a youth of princely stock; others, that Melek, translated *king*, is a proper name.

3. King of Judah (II Kings 11:2; 12:19, 20; 13:1, 10; 14:1, 3, 17, 23; I Chron. 3:11; II Chron. 22:11; 24:1, 2, 4, 22, 24; 25:23, 25). *See* Jehoash, 1.

4. King of Israel (II Kings 13:9, 12, 13, 14, 25; 14:1, 23, 27; II Chron. 25:17, 18, 21, 23, 25; Hos. 1:1; Amos 1:1). *See* Jehoash, 2.

5. A descendant of Shelah, son of Judah, mentioned among those "who had the dominion in Moab" (I Chron. 4:22). The Hebrew tradition, quoted by Jerome and Jarchi, applies it to Mahlon, the son of Elimelech, who married a Moabitess.

6. A son of Shemah (or Hasmath), the Gibeathite, who, with his brother Ahiezer and other "mighty men," joined David at Ziklag (I Chron. 12:3).

Jo'ash (Heb. *Yō'äsh, Jehovah has come, hastened*).

1. One of the "sons" (descendants) of Becher, son of Benjamin, and a chieftain of his family (I Chron. 7:8).

2. The person having charge of the "cellars of oil" under David and Solomon (I Chron. 27:28), B. C. after 1000.

Jo'atham (jō'á-thăm), Jotham the son of Uzziah (Matt. 1:9).

Job (jōb), the third named of the sons of Issachar (Gen. 46:13), called Jashub (Num. 26:24; I Chron. 7:1). *See* Jashubi.

Job, Book of.

This splendid dramatic poem belongs to the Wisdom Literature of the O. T. It is universally recognized as superb literature. The poem takes its name from its chief character, Job, *'iyyōb*. Interestingly enough, the name occurs in the Berlin Execration Texts as the name of a certain prince in the region of Damascus in the nineteenth century B. C. (*Bull. of Am. Schls.* 82, 1941, p. 36). The name also is found in the Amarna correspondence dating c. 1400 B. C. as a prince of Pella. Job of the Biblical story was a dweller in the land of Uz (1:1), which evidently lay somewhere between Damascus on the north and Edom on the south; that is, in the steppes E. of Palestine-Syria.

1. **The Subject of the Book.** The Book of Job centers around the perplexing question why the righteous suffer and how their suffering can be reconciled with the infinite goodness and holiness of God. Job's three friends offer practically the same answer (chap. 3-31). They imply that suffering is always the outcome of sin. Job desperately asserts his innocence and at times appears almost delirious under the unjust insinuations. He almost borders upon accusing God of injustice but he recoups his confidence in the Divine Goodness and protests he will be finally vindicated. At this juncture Elihu comes on the scene and appears with the divine message elaborated in the N. T., that sufferings are very often the medium of refining the righteous, the chastisements of a Father Who loves His children, and by no means the action of a vindictive or implacable God (chaps. 32-37). God speaks to Job out of the whirlwind, humbling him and bringing him to a realization that he, himself, is to be abhorred before the Divine Presence (42:1-6). His self-abnegation and spiritual refining are a prelude to his restoration (42:7-17).

2. **The Argument.**

Prologue: Testing of Job, 1, 2

Part. I. Job Falsely Comforted by his Friends, 3-31

   a. First cycle of speeches, 3-14: Job's speech followed by those of his three friends, each in turn answered by Job

   b. Second cycle of speeches, 15-21: Each friend speaks to Job and is answered by him

   c. Third cycle of speeches, 22-31: Eliphaz and Bildad speak until answered by Job

Part II. Speeches of Elihu, 32-37

   a. First speech—purpose of affliction, 32-33

   b. Second speech—God vindicated, 34

   c. Third speech—The advantages of piety, 35

d. Fourth speech—God's greatness and
Job's ignorance, 36-37
Part III. Speeches of God, 38-42:6
a. First speech—Creation declares God's
all-power. Job's conversion, 38:1-
40:5
b. Second speech—Power of God and
human weakness. Job's humility,
40:6-42:6
Epilogue: Job's friends rebuked, Job restored, 42:7-17

3. **Time and Composition.** Great disagreement prevails as to the composition. Critics
date the composition of the book anywhere
from patriarchal times (Ebrard) to as late as
400 B. C. (Eissfeldt, Volz) or even the third
century B. C. (Cornhill). Probably the most
likely date is the Solomonic era, (Franz, Delitzsch, Keil) because it bears evidence of the
creative beginning period of wisdom literature.
It comprehends ideas similar to parts of Proverbs (cf. Job. 15:8 and chap. 28 with Prov. 8).

4. **Authenticity.** It is customary among
critics to deny the authenticity of (1) Prologue
and Epilogue; (2) Chapter 28, the poem of
Divine Wisdom; (3) Description of leviathan
and behemoth (40:10-41:25); (4) The discourses of Elihu (32:1-37:24). No valid reason
can be adduced for ascribing the prologue and
epilogue to a later author. "The dialogue cannot have had any independent existence," as
A. Bentzen correctly observes. "In 8:4-29:5
it presupposes the description of Job's illness
as given in the narrative" (*Intr.* II, p. 175).
Chapter 28 cannot be proved to be extraneous
although the passage is admittedly loosely
connected with the context, but so are other
choice literary pieces of the book. If, as is
certainly true, "the finest literary masterpieces
are to be found among these incidental pieces
and in digressions rather than in the argu-
mentative scaffolding of the book," as Pfeiffer
admits, why reject this passage and retain
others when "to remove even some of them
would greatly reduce the value of the original
poem and imply that the poetic genius of the
supplementers was equal, if not superior, to
that of the original poet?" (*Intr.*, p. 686). The
same answer may be given to the critical
contention that the descriptions of leviathan
(crocodile) and behemoth (hippopotamus) in
40:15-41:34 are a subsequent insertion. The
language and ideas of this passage are similar
to the remainder of the book (cf. 40:15
and 39:15 with 5:23; 41:9 with 3:9, etc.).
Elihu's speeches are rejected because he does
not appear in the prologue or epilogue. He is
not merely a loquacious interrupter. He adds
a momentous truth that affliction of the righteous is disciplinary (33:16-18; 27-30; 36:10-
12). Elihu's speeches answer Job's problem
and get him ready for Jehovah's appearance
and words from the whirlwind. There would
be a genuine lack in the book if the Elihu
sections were omitted. He does not appear in
the epilogue because, unlike Job's friends, he
did not merit rebuke. His contribution to the
solution of the problem of the book invalidates
the rejection of this portion. *M. F. U.*

Jo'bab (jō'băb; *howler, one who calls shrilly*).
1. The last in the order of the sons of Joktan
(Gen. 10:29; I Chron. 1:23).

2. Son of Zerah of Bozrah, and one of the
"kings" of Edom (Gen. 36:33, 34; I Chron.
1:44, 45), B. C. probably before 1440.
3. The king of Madon, a royal city of the
Canaanites. Assisting Jabin, king of Hazor,
against Joshua, they were both by him overcome (Josh. 11:1), B. C. after 1370.
4. A Benjamite, and the first named of the
sons of Shaharaim by his wife Hodesh (I
Chron. 8:9).
5. One of the "sons" (probably descendants)
of Elpaal, a chief of Benjamin at Jerusalem
(I Chron. 8:18), B. C. probably about 588.

Joch'ebed (jŏk'ĕ-bĕd; *Jehovah her glory*), the
wife of Amram, and mother of Miriam, Aaron,
and Moses (Num. 26:59), B. C. c. 1520. In
Exod. 6:20 it is expressly declared that she
was the sister of Amram's father, and, consequently, her husband's aunt. It was contrary
to the law for persons thus related to marry,
and several attempts have been made to prove
a more distant relationship. Kitto says:
"The fact seems to be that where this marriage
was contracted there was no law forbidding
such alliances, but they must in any case have
been unusual, although not forbidden; and
this, with the writer's knowledge that they
were subsequently interdicted, sufficiently accounts for this one being so pointedly mentioned." So Kiel and Delitzsch (*Com.*, in loc.).

Jo'ed (jō'ĕd; *Jehovah his witness*), the son of
Pedaiah, and grandfather of Sallu, which last
was one of the Benjamites chosen to dwell in
Jerusalem after the captivity (Neh. 11:7), B.
C. before 536.

Jo'el (jō'ĕl; *Jehovah is God*).
1. The eldest of the two sons of Samuel, appointed by him as judges in Beer-sheba. By the
taking of bribes and perversion of judgment
they led to the popular desire for a monarchy
(I Sam. 8:2), B. C. before 1030. In I Chron.
6:28 by a clerical error he is called Vashni.
He is named as the father of Heman, the
Levitical singer (I Chron. 6:33; 15:17).
2. A descendant of Simeon, one of those
whose families emigrated to the valley of
Gedor (I Chron. 4:35), B. C. about 715.
3. A descendant of Reuben, but by what
line or in what degree of proximity is uncertain (I Chron. 5:4, 8).
4. A chief of the Gadites resident in Bashan
(I Chron. 5:12), B. C. perhaps about 782.
5. A Kohathite Levite, son of Azariah, and
father of Elkanah (I Chron. 6:36). He is
probably the Joel who assisted Hezekiah in
his restoration of the temple services (II Chron.
29:12), B. C. 719.
6. The third named of the four sons of
Izrahiah, a chieftain of the tribe of Issachar
in the time of David (I Chron. 7:3), B. C.
about 1000.
7. Brother of Nathan, and one of David's
mighty men (I Chron. 11:38), B. C. about
1000. He is called "Igal the son of Nathan" in
II Sam. 23:36. Kennicott decides in favor of
the former as most likely to be the genuine
text (*Dissertations*, pp. 212-214).
8. A Levite, chief of the family of Gershom,
who, at the head of one hundred and thirty,
was appointed by David to assist in removing
the ark (I Chron. 15:7, 11), B. C. after 1000.
He is probably the same as the third of the

"sons" of Laadan (23:8), and also with the son of Jehiel, who was one of the keepers of the "treasures of the dedicated things" (26: 22) (Keil).

9. Son of Pediah, and chief, in the time of David, of the half tribe of Manasseh west (I Chron. 27:20), B. C. about 1000.

10. One of the "sons" of Nebo, who put away his Gentile wife after the return from Babylon (Ezra 10:43), B. C. 456.

11. Son of Zichri, and "overseer" of the Benjamites resident at Jerusalem after the captivity (Neh. 11:9), B. C. about 536.

12. Son of Pethuel, and second of the twelve minor prophets (Joel 1:1; Acts 2:16). Nothing is known of his life, and all that can be inferred with any certainty from his writings is that he lived in Judah, and probably prophesied in Jerusalem. The date of his ministry is also a disputed point, some making him contemporary with Amos and Isaiah, during the reign of Uzziah, B. C. about 770; others (Keil, *Com.*) assign him to the first thirty years of Jehoash.

Joel, Book of.

Joel was a prophet of the Southern Kingdom. His name means "Jehovah is God." His frequent addresses to the priesthood would seem to indicate that he, himself, was a member of the priesthood.

1. **Purpose.** The prophet has in mind to warn the nation to repent in the light of approaching judgment. He also stirs up the faithful among the people to believe the promises of God involving coming salvation and destruction of the enemies of God's kingdom. In the prophecy a terrible plague of insects is made the occasion of great prophetic significance (Joel 1:13, 14) adumbrating the Day of the Lord. Chapter 2 demonstrates this fact when the scourge of locusts fades out of the picture and the future Day of Jehovah comes into full view. The prophetic imagery foreshadows the end time of the present age; that is, the period of the "times of the Gentiles" (Luke 21:24; Rev. 16:14). The Battle of Armageddon is also prefigured as well as the regathering of Israel and Kingdom blessing. Joel presents the following order of events: (1) The invasion of Palestine by Gentile nations under the leadership of the Beast and the False Prophet (Joel 2:1-10; cf. Armageddon, Rev. 16:14). (2) Decimation of the invading hordes by the Lord's host (Joel 2:11 cf. Rev. 19:11, 21). (3) Judah's conversion in the land (Joel 2:12-17). (4) The Lord's promise of deliverance (Joel 2:18-27). (5) The pouring out of the Holy Spirit preceding the Kingdom Age (Joel 2:28, 29). (6) The Second Advent of Christ with the establishment of the mediatorial kingdom (Joel 2:30-32; cf. Acts 15:15-17). (7) The judgment of the nations (Joel 3:1-16). (8) Realization of full millennial conditions (Joel 3:17-21; cf. Zech. 14:1-21).

2. **Analysis.**

Part I. The Day of the Lord in Prophetic Type, 1:1-20

    a. The prophet, 1:1

    b. The locust plague, 1:2-7

    c. Repentance and prayer of the afflicted people, 1:8-20

Part II. The Day of the Lord Itself in Prophecy, 2:1-32

    a. The invaders, 2:1-10

    b. The Lord's host at Armageddon, 2:11

    c. Repentant remnant in Palestine, 2:12-27

    d. The Lord's response to the remnant, 2:18-29

    e. Signs of the Day of the Lord, 2:30-32

Part III. The Judgment of the Nations in Prophecy, 3:1-16

    a. Israel reinstated, 3:1

    b. The nations judged, 3:2, 3

    c. Pheonicia and Philistia condemned, 3:4-8

    d. The call to arms and the judgment, 3:9-16

Part IV. Millennial blessing in prophecy, 3:17-21

    a. Jerusalem's ascendancy, 3:17

    b. Judah's prosperity, 3:18

    c. Egypt and Edom's desolation, 3:19

    d. Explanation of Jerusalem's exaltation, 3:20, 21

3. **Authorship.** As early as 1872, M. Vernes denied the Joel authorship (cf. 1:1). Vernes maintained that chapters 3 and 4 were not authored by the same person as 1 and 2. Such cirtics as J. W. Rothstein, Sievers, B. Duhm and Paul Haupt also deny the unity of the book. These views have not met with wide acceptance, however (cf. L. Dennefelt, *Les Problemes du Livre de Joel*, Paris, 1926 and J. Smith, W. H. Ward and J. Bewer, *Joel* in Int. Crit. Com., N. Y., 1911; A. S. Capelrud, *Joel Studies*, Uppsala, 1948).

4. **The Date.** Critics commonly date Joel's prophecy anywhere from the division of the kingdom (c. 932 B. C.) to the time of Malachi (c. 400 B. C.) or even later. The safest date seems to be pre-exilic. The reign of Joash (835-796 B. C.) is most appropriate for the prophecy. Several lines of argument would seem to indicate that Joel's prophecy is early. Its style and general spirit are dissimilar to that of Haggai, Zechariah and Malachi, post-exilic prophets. Its language and style rather belong to the period of Hebrew classical literature. Joel's diction seems reminiscent of Amos, who seems to have made use of Joel (cf. Joel 3:16 with Amos 1:2; Joel 3:18 with Amos 9:13). Perhaps significant is the lack of the mention of a king in the book. Joash was a minor and for a long time under the guardianship of Jehoida, the high priest. Then too, Israel's enemies are the Phoenicians and Philistines (3:4) and the Egyptians and Edomites (3:19), not the Assyrians and the Babylonians who harrassed Israel from Amos' period to the Exile. Cornhill, Oesterley and Robinson, Merx and S. R. Driver agree for a post-exilic date but their evidence is inconclusive. Joel 3:2 is supposed to allude to the exile but this is clearly a predictive passage of the nation's present-day scattering and by no means needs to refer to the Babylonian captivity. The mention of the *Jevanim* or "Ionians" does not necessitate a date after the Exile. These people are alluded to in the Assyrian records of the 8th century B. C. Arguments based on the silence with regard to a king or idolatrous places of worship in the Northern Kingdom

are pointless. Such mention is also lacking in Nahum, Jonah, Zephaniah and Obadiah.

M. F. U.

Joe'lah (jô-ē'là, *furthermore*), one of the two sons of Jeroham of Gedor who joined David at Ziklag (I Chron. 12:7), B. C. before 1000.

Joe'zer (jô-ē'zẽr; *Jehovah his help*), one of the Korhites who united themselves to David at Ziklag (I Chron. 12:6), B. C. before 1000.

Jog'behah (jŏg'bê-hà; *hillock*), one of the "fenced cities" rebuilt by the Gadites (Num. 32:35). It is mentioned (Judg. 8:11) as in the route of Gideon while pursuing the Midianites. Its name still exists in Jubeihah 6 miles N. W. of Rabbath Amman.

Jog'li (jŏg'lī; *exiled*), the father of Bukki, which latter was appointed from the tribe of Dan on the commission for dividing the land of Canaan (Num. 34:22), B. C. about 1380.

Jo'ha (jō'hà; probably *Jehovah revives*).

1. One of the sons of Beriah the Benjamite, and a chief of his tribe resident at Jerusalem (I Chron. 8:16). B. C. perhaps about 588.

2. A Tizite who, with his brother Jediael, was one of David's mighty men (I Chron. 11 : 45), B. C. 1000.

Joha'nan (jō-hā'năn; contracted form of Jehohanan, *God is gracious*).

1. The son of Careah (Kareah), one of the Jewish chiefs who rallied around Gedaliah on his appointment as governor (II Kings 25: 23; Jer. 40:8). He also warned the governor of the purpose of Ishmael to assassinate him, and offered to slay Ishmael, but Gedaliah refused to listen to his advice (Jer. 40:13-16). After the murder of Gedaliah, Johanan led in the pursuit of the assassin and rescued the people he had taken captive (41:11-16). He then consulted with Jeremiah as to what course the remnant of the people should pursue, but when told by the prophet to remain in the land he and his associates refused, and retired (taking Jeremiah with them) to Tahpanhes, in Egypt (43:1-7). From this time we lose sight of him and his fellow-captains, and they, doubtless, shared the threatened punishment (v. 11, sq.), B. C. 586.

2. The eldest son of Josiah, king of Judah (I Chron. 3:15). He probably died early, as Scripture makes no further mention of him, B. C. after 639.

3. The fifth son of Elioenai, one of the descendants of Zerubbabel (I Chron. 3:24), B. C. probably after 400. He is identified by some with Nahum, mentioned (Luke 3:25, A. V. "Naum") among the ancestry of Christ.

4. Son of Azariah, and father of Azariah, high priests (I Chron. 6:9, 10), and by some thought to have been the same as Jehoiada (II Chron. 24:15).

5. One of the mighty men who joined David at Ziklag (I Chron. 12:4), B. C. before 1000. He was probably a Benjamite.

6. The eighth named of the Gadite warriors who rallied to the support of David in the hold in the wilderness (I Chron. 12:12), B. C. before 1000.

7. The father of Azariah, which latter insisted upon sending home the captives taken from Judah (II Chron. 28:12), B. C. about 735.

8. The son of Hakkatan, of the "sons" of Azgad, who returned, with one hundred and ten males, from Babylon with Ezra (Ezra 8: 12), B. C. about 457.

9. A priest, the "son" of Eliashib, into whose chamber Ezra retired to mourn over the marrying of Gentiles wives by the Jews (Ezra 10: 6). He is identified with the Johanan mentioned in Neh. 12:22, 23.

10. The son of Tobiah the Ammonite, who married the daughter of Meshullum, the priest (Neh. 6:18), B. C. 445.

John. 1. **The Apostle** (jŏn; Gr. *'Iōannēs* from Heb. *Yōhänän*, *Jehovah is gracious*), the son of Zebedee, a fisherman on the Sea of Galilee, probably not of the poorer class (Mark 1:20; Luke 5:10), and Salome (Mark 15:40; comp. Matt. 27:56). We have no information respecting the religious character or personal participation of Zebedee in the events of the Gospel history, but his mother was one of the women who followed Jesus even to his crucifixion (Matt. 27:56; Mark 15:40).

Personal History. (1) **Early life.** John was probably the son of Zebedee and Salome and younger brother of James (Matt. 4:21), and lived in Bethsaida (Luke 5:10; John 1:44). The mention of the "hired servants" (Mark 1:20), of his mother's "substance" (Luke 8:3), of "his own home" (John 19:27), as also his acquaintance with Caiaphas the high priest (John 18:15), implies a position of at least considerable influence and means. His mother, who manifested an earnest desire for the welfare of her sons (Matt. 20:20), probably early instructed him in religious things; and his trade of fisherman was adapted to holy meditation, since it would lead him frequently to pass whole nights in stillness upon the water. (2) **Introduction to Jesus.** The incident recorded in John 1:35-39, would seem to indicate that John had become a disciple of John the Baptist. His mention of Andrew only by name is consistent with his usual manner of naming himself as "that other disciple," "the disciple whom Jesus loved." One day, about the hour of evening sacrifice, John Baptist pointed to Jesus walking by, and said, "Behold the Lamb of God!" His two disciples immediately followed Jesus, and inquired where he dwelt. To this question the Master replied, "Come and see;" and they "abode with him that day, for it was about the tenth hour." John was probably among the disciples who followed their new teacher to Galilee (John 1:43), who were with him at the marriage feast of Cana (2:2), journeyed with him to Capernaum, and thence to Jerusalem (2: 12, 23), and came back through Samaria (4: 5). He then returned to his former occupation. (3) **As apostle.** At last the time came when the disciples were to enter into closer relation to Jesus, and become his apostles. John, with his brother James, Simon, and Andrew, were called at the same time, after the incident of the miraculous draught of fishes (Mark 1:19, 20; Luke 5:10). John, with Peter and James, was distinguished above the other apostles, entering more fully into the Master's feelings and plans, and receiving in return his confidence and love. Mention is made of John at the restoration of Peter's mother-in-law

(Mark 1:29-31); at the ordination of the twelve apostles (3:17), where he and his brother received from Jesus the surname *Boanerges;* at the raising of Jairus's daughter (Mark 5:35-37; Luke 8:51); at the transfiguration (Matt. 17:1; Mark 9:2; Luke 9:28); rebuking one who cast out devils in the Lord's name, because he was not one of their company (Luke 9:49); seeking to call down fire from heaven upon a village of the Samaritans (9:54); joining with his mother and James in asking for the highest places in the kingdom of the Master (Matt. 20:20-28; Mark 10:35-45); with Jesus upon the Mount of Olives when he foretold the destruction of Jerusalem (Mark 13:3); sent by the Master to prepare, with Peter, the passover (Luke 22:8); asking Jesus, at the supper, who would betray him (John 13:23-26); with Peter and James in Gethsemane (Mark 14:32, 33). When the betrayal is accomplished Peter and John follow afar off, and, through the personal acquaintance between the latter and Caiaphas, gain admittance into the palace (John 18:15, 16); he was the only disciple present at the crucifixion, and was appointed by Jesus to care for Mary as a son (19:26, 27). (4) **Friendship for Peter.** Notwithstanding the denial of Peter he and John continued friends, and are afterward often mentioned together. To them Mary Magdalene first runs with the tidings of the emptied sepulcher (20:2); they are the first to hasten thither (20:4-8). For at least eight days they remain in Jerusalem (20:26), after which we find them on the Sea of Galilee pursuing their old calling (21:1). John is the first to recognize his risen Lord; Peter the first to plunge into the water and swim toward the shore where he stood (21:7). The affection and anxiety of Peter for John is shown in his question put to the Master, "Lord, and what shall this man do?" (21:21). (5) **History of the Acts.** The same union continues between Peter and John. Together they witness the ascension, share in the election of Matthias and the pentecostal baptism. Together they enter the temple as worshippers (Acts 3:1), are imprisoned and protest against the threats of the Sanhedrin (4:3 sq.). They were also sent together to preach to the Samaritans (8:14). John and the rest of the apostles remained at their post despite the persecution of Saul (8:1). He did not meet Paul when the latter came back to Jerusalem as a convert (Gal. 1:19); but this, of course, does not make the inference necessary that he had left Jerusalem. During the persecution under Herod Agrippa he lost his brother by martyrdom (Acts 12:2), while his friend Peter sought safety in flight (12:18, 19). Fifteen years after Paul's first visit he was still at Jerusalem (Conybeare and Howson, *Life and Epistles*), one of the "pillars" of the Church, and took part in settling the controversy between the Jewish and Gentile Christians (Acts 15:6, 13; Gal. 2:9). Of the work of the apostle during this period we have hardly the slightest trace. (6) **After his departure from Jerusalem.** John probably remained in Judea till the death of Mary released him from his trust. When this took place we can only conjecture. There are no signs of his being at Jerusalem at the time of St. Paul's last visit (Acts 21). "Assuming the authorship of the epistles and Revelation to be his, the facts which the New Testament writings assert or imply are: *1.* That, having come to Ephesus, some persecution drove him to Patmos (Rev. 1:9). *2.* That the seven churches in Asia Minor were the special objects of his affectionate solicitude (1:11); that in his work he had to encounter men who denied the truth on which his faith rested (I John 4:1; II John 7), and others who disputed his authority (III John 9, 10)." If to this we add that he must have outlived all, or nearly all, of those who had been the friends and companions even of his maturer years; that this lingering age gave strength to an old impression that his Lord had promised him immortality (John 21:23); that, as if remembering the actual words which had been thus perverted, the longing of his soul gathered itself up in the cry, "Even so, come, Lord Jesus" (Rev. 22:20), we have stated all that has any claim to the character of historical truth. Tradition tells us that he was shipwrecked off Ephesus, and arrived there in time to check the progress of the heresies which sprang up after Paul's departure; that in the persecution under Domitian he was taken to Rome, and that the boiling oil into which he was thrown had no power to hurt him; returned to Ephesus, attested the truth of the first three gospels, writing the fourth to supply what was wanting; introduced the Jewish mode of celebrating the Easter feast; and that, when all capacity to work and teach was gone—when there was no strength even to stand—he directed himself to be carried to the assemblage of believers, and simply said, with a feeble voice, "Little children, love one another." (7) **Writings.** The following books of the New Testament are generally accepted as having been written by the apostle John: the gospel and the three epistles bearing his name and the Revelation.

2. One of the family of the high priest, who, with Annas and Caiaphas, sat in the council before whom the apostles Peter and John were summoned for their cure of the lame man and preaching in the temple (Acts 4:6). "Lightfoot identifies him with Rabbi Johanan ben Zaccai, who lived forty years before the destruction of the temple, and was president of the great synagogue after its removal to Jabne, or Jamnia. Grotius merely says he was known to rabbinical writers as 'John the priest'" (Smith, *Dict.*, s. v.).

3. The Hebrew name of the evangelist Mark, who throughout the narrative of the Acts is thus designated (Acts 12:12, 25; 13:5; 15:37).

John, The Gospel of, the fourth gospel of the N. T., regarded by many as the deepest and most wonderful book in the N. T. Although in one sense of the word it is simple, direct, penetrating and to be understood by common folk, yet in another respect it is a sublimely profound revelation fathomed only by the deeply spiritual scholar. Some have called it "the greatest book in the world."

1. **Purpose.** The real aim of the Gospel of John is spiritual. Although many different opinions have been advanced, the purpose is

stated clearly and unequivocally in chapter 20:30, 31: "Many other signs truly did Jesus in the presence of the disciples, which are not written in this book: But these are written, that ye may believe that Jesus is the Christ, the Son of God; and that believing you may have life in His Name." It is quite evident from this statement that the author's intent is to conduct men to saving faith in Christ as the Son of God and so enable them to obtain eternal life. The deity of Christ is thus proved by miraculous signs, consisting of a selective group of miracles which he enumerates as demonstrating Christ's Messiahship. A careful reading of the gospel will also disclose that the author seeks to accomplish this in various other ways by presenting the true Person and and work of the Savior and by a variety of telling figures describing Christ, such as the Bread of Life, the Light of the World, the Good Shepherd, the Truth, the Way, the Life and the Vine. To accomplish his spiritual aim, John records eight miracles and all but two, the feeding of the 5000 (6:4-14) and the walking on the sea (6:15-21) are peculiar to John. This wondrous book has a literary unity; the miracles, the discourses, the imagery and the figures are all selected in order to attain its purpose. In the synoptic gospels the miraculous works of Jesus are very frequently performed out of mercy, but in the Gospel of John they are presented as attestations of His Messiahship that men may believe on him as Christ the Savior.

2. The Literary Plan.

Part I. Prologue: The Deity and Glory of the Son of God, 1:1-5

Part II. The Incarnation and Reception of the Son of God, 1:6-18

Part III. The Son of God revealed to Israel, 1:19-12:50

Part IV. The Son of God Instructs His Disciples, chaps. 13-17

Part V. The Son of God Glorified in His Passion, chaps. 18, 19

Part VI. The Son of God Revealed in Resurrection Power and Glory, chaps. 20, 21

3. **The Author.** Internal evidence that the author is "the disciple whom Jesus loved, who also leaned on his breast at supper" (21:20 cf. 21:4) and that this is the Apostle John is supported by numerous lines of evidence. (1) *He was a contemporary of the events described.* The writer was known to the high priest and entered the high priest's residence in company with Jesus (18:15). He alone narrates the fact that it was the high priest's servant whose ear Peter cut off (18:10). He deals with questions of the period before the destruction of Jerusalem and not with controversies of the second century when Gnostic and Ebionite defections were active (cf. 6:15; 11:47-50). Numerous other details point to the contemporary scene. (2) *He was a Jew of Palestine.* He shows acquaintance with the Hebrew as is shown by its opening words (cf. Gen. 1:1). Three times he quotes from the Hebrew (12:40; 13:18; 19:37). He knows intimately the Hebrew festivals, that of Passover (2:13 and 23; 6:4; 13:1; 18:28), the feast of Tabernacles (7:27), and the Feast of Dedication (10:22). Jewish customs and habits of thought are

familiar to him, such as questions of purification (3:25; 11:55), marriage customs, especially the way of arranging water pots (2:1-10), Jewish burial customs (11:38, 44; 19:31; 19:40). He shows first-hand knowledge of Palestine, that there is a descent from Cana to the Sea of Galilee (2:12) and that Jacob's well is deep (4:11). Such places are familiar to him as Ephraim (11:54), Aenon (3:23), Mt. Gerizim (4:20), Jerusalem and the Kidron (18:1), Bethesda and Siloam (5:2; 9:7) and Golgotha (19:17, etc.). (3) *He was John, the beloved apostle.* This is a general deduction sustained from the above facts. He indicates the hours of events recounted (1:39; 4:6, 52; 19:14). He reports quotations of Philip (6:7; 14:8), Thomas (11:16; 14:5), Judas (14:22) and Andrew (6:9). He leaned on Jesus' breast at the Last Supper (13:23-25) and accordingly numbered among the three, Peter, James and John. Moreover Peter is distinguished from the author by name, as in 1:41, 42; 13:6 and 8, and James had suffered martyrdom long before the writing of the gospel (Acts 12:2). He characteristically introduces himself (13:23; 19:26; 20:2; 21:7, 20). These general facts make it difficult to escape the conclusion that John the Apostle wrote the fourth gospel.

4. **Authenticity.** External evidence for the early date and apostolic authorship of the Gospel of John is as substantial as that for any N. T. book. Early evidence is found in the Epistle of Barnabas. Tatian quotes the fourth gospel in his Diatessaron, as well as Theophilus of Antioch. The Muratorian Canon says "John, one of the disciples, wrote the fourth book of the gospels." From the time of Irenaeus the evidence becomes incontrovertible. He frequently quotes the gospel and in such a way as to show it had been for a long time used in the churches. This testimony is perhaps most important considering he was a pupil of Polycarp, and Polycarp was a friend of the Apostle John. Clement of Alexandria and Tertullian of Carthage often quote from the Gospel of John.

5. **The Date.** The date of the fourth gospel is to be assigned between 85 and 95 A. D. A papyrus bit containing two verses of the Gospel of John has been discovered and belongs to the Papyrus Rylands and is dated c. 140 A. D. This bit of evidence suggests that the fourth gospel was in existence as early as the first half of the second century and at that time was already in wide use. *M. F. U.*

John, First Epistle of.

The First Epistle of John is in the nature of a family letter from the Heavenly Father to His "little children" who are in the world. The great theme of the epistle is fellowship in the family of the Father. The intimacy of the epistle has always had great attraction for the people of God.

1. **Occasion and Date.** The epistle was apparently written to compete with various forms of error, particularly Cerinthian Gnosticism. False teachers of this cult had denied the essential truth of the incarnation, that Christ had come in the flesh, maintaining that matter was evil. The writer also combatted false mysticism that denied the reality of the sin-nature in the Christian. He also

inveighed against those who violated Christian fellowship and rejected Christian morality and love. The First Epistle of John is in a sense a moral and practical application of the Gospel. The time between the two could not have been very long. It was probably written a little later than the Gospel, around 90 A. D. or 95.

2. **The Purpose.** The Apostle plainly refutes the false ideas of the errorists. He does this positively, giving fresh interpretation and application of the Gospel to the exigencies of his time. He shows the reality of the fellowship with the Father and that believers possess eternal life now in this world. He stresses the close connection of the possession of eternal life with the manifestation of love, right conduct and sound morality.

3. **The Outline.** The Apostle apparently does not develop his thought in progressive fashion but in what has been called a "spiral" manner. The author rather treats a number of related topics and interweaves them. For this reason outlining the epistle is difficult and to some extent arbitrary. The book is commonly divided into two principal parts.

Part I. Family Fellowship, 1:1-3:24
1. The basis of this fellowship, the Incarnation, 1:1-3
2. Family fellowship with the Father and the Son, 1:3, 4
3. Conditions of family fellowship, 1:5-3:24
   a. Walking in the light, 1:5-7
   b. Realization of the indwelling sin nature, 1:8
   c. Forgiveness by confession, 1:9, 10
   d. Christ's advocacy maintains fellowship, 2:1, 2
   e. The tests of fellowship, obedience and love, 2:3-3:24

Part II. Family Fellowship in the World, 4:1-5:21
1. Warning against false teachers, 4:1-6
2. Description of God's true child, 4:7-10
3. Manifestations of life of love, 4:11-21
4. Faith as a conquering principle in the world conflict, 5:1-21 *M. F. U.*

John, Second and Third Epistles.
These two letters are extremely short. Each was sent by the elder or presbyter (II John:1; III John:1). They were authored in the province of Asia probably between 95 and 100 A. D. Second John is addressed evidently to a Christian mother and her family, styled "elect lady and her children." The Second Epistle, as in the First, gives prominence to the commandment of love. It warns against false teachers (v. 7). These heretics were to be treated with sternness and shown no hospitality. The key phrase of the Second Epistle is "the truth," by which John means the body of revealed truth, the Scriptures. The Epistle is in three divisions.
Part I. "The truth" and love are joined together in true Christian life, vs. 1-6
Part II. The danger of unscriptural ways, vs. 7-11
Part III. A superscription, vs. 12-13

The Third Epistle of John, like the Second, was written by the Apostle probably around 95 A. D. The aged Apostle arraigned the church for permitting one Diotrephes to exercise dominating authority in the church. In the primitive church such a thing was incredible. This domineering individual had rejected the apostolic authority. Historically this small Epistle outlines the commencement of clericalism and priestly arrogation of authority which in later centuries was to develop in such evil proportions. The believer's resource in such a day of declension is also given. John does not write as an apostle but as an elder, and the letter is addressed not to a church but to a faithful man in the church, to comfort and sustain those who were adhering to the primitive simplicity. The third letter of John stresses personal responsibility in a day of declension.

The outline is as follows:
Part I. Personal greetings to "the well beloved" Gaius, vs. 1-4
Part II. Instructions concerning ministers, vs. 5-8
Part III. Warning against the power-loving Diotrephes, vs. 9-11
Part IV. The praiseworthy Demetrius, vs. 12-14 *M. F. U.*

John The Baptist. (*John the baptizer*), the forerunner of Jesus Christ. He and his mission were foretold by Isaiah (40:3; comp. Matt. 3:3), and by Malachi (3:1).

1. **Family.** John was of the priestly race by both of his parents, his father, Zacharias, being a priest of the course of Abia, or Abijah (I Chron. 24:10), and his mother, Elizabeth, was "of the daughters of Aaron" (Luke 1:5). His birth—through the miraculous interposition of almighty power, by reason of his parents' extreme age—was foretold by an angel sent from God, who at the same time assigned to him the name of *John*. He was born in the hill country (whither his mother had gone, probably for the sake of privacy) six months before the birth of our Lord (perhaps B. C. 5).

2. **Personal History.** (1) **Early life.** On the eighth day he was brought to be circumcised, and friends of his parents proposed to call him Zacharias, after his father. But his mother required that he should be called John, a decision which his father, still speechless, confirmed by writing on a tablet. He was set apart as a Nazarite, according to the angelic injunction (Luke 1:15; comp. Num. 6:1-21). All that we know of the period between this time and the beginning of his ministry is contained in a single verse: "The child grew and waxed strong in spirit, and was in the deserts till the day of his showing unto Israel" (Luke 1:80). (2) **Beginning of ministry.** At length, in the fifteenth year of the reign of Tiberius Caesar (A. D. 25), John began to preach, and attracted to himself a great multitude from "Jerusalem, and all Judea, and all the region round about Jordan" (Matt. 3:5). To them he proclaimed the near approach of "the kingdom of heaven," and administered the rite of baptism "unto repentance." His birth, his hard, ascetic life, the general expectation that some great one was about to appear, served to attract this great multitude, for "John did no miracle" (John 10:41). (3) **Meeting with Jesus.** Before long Jesus presented himself to John, to re-

ceive baptism at his hand, which John declined to administer, until our Lord's declaration that "Thus it becometh us to fulfill all righteousness" (Matt. 3:15). (4) **Subsequent ministry.** With the baptism of Jesus John's more especial office ceased. The king had come, and there was little further need of the herald. We learn that John and his disciples continued to baptize some time after our Lord entered upon his ministry (John 3:23; 4:1). He also instructed his disciples in certain moral and religious duties, as fasting (Matt. 9:14; Luke 5:33) and prayer (Luke 11:1). We learn also that he still continued to be a witness to Jesus, so confidently pointing him out as the Lamb of God that two of his own disciples were led to accept Jesus as the true Messiah, and became his followers (John 1:29, sq.; v. 35-37). (5) **Imprisonment and death.** Shortly after this his public ministry was brought violently to a close. Herod Antipas had taken Herodias, his brother Philip's wife, and when John reproved him for this and other sins (Luke 3:19), Herod cast him in prison, the castle of Machaerus, on the eastern shore of the Dead Sea. While confined there he sent two of his disciples with the inquiry, "Art thou he that should come?" This was doubtless done in order to assist his disciples in transferring their allegiance to Jesus, as Jesus himself bore testimony to the steadfastness of John (7:19-28). Herodias, embittered against John, determined upon his death, but was prevented by Herod's conviction that John was a just man (Mark 6:20) and his fear of the people (Matt. 14:5). But at last her opportunity arrived, and taking advantage of a promise given by Herod to her daughter, Herodias bade her order the head of John the Baptist. The king reluctantly complied, and sent an executioner, who beheaded him in the prison. His disciples, when they heard of his death, buried his body and went and told the Lord (Matt. 14:3-12; Mark 6:17-29).

3. **Character.** The nature of John the Baptist was full of impetuosity and fire—a very Elijah. His life, however, was characterized by the graces of self-denial, humility, and holy courage. His abstinence was so great that some thought him possessed, and said, "He hath a devil." In his humility he declined the honors which an admiring multitude almost forced upon him, and declared himself to be *no one*— a voice merely—calling upon the people to prepare for the reception of the one whose shoe-latchet he was not worthy to unloose. And when that one came, he recommended his own disciples to attach themselves to him, furnishing the world an example of gracefully accepting the fact, "He must increase, but I must decrease." For his courage in speaking the truth he went a willing victim to prison and to death.

NOTE—*John's acquaintance with Jesus.* Much discussion has arisen concerning the apparent contradiction in Matt. 3:13, 14, and John 1:31, 33. In the former John evidently recognized Jesus, while in the latter he says, "I knew him not." The truth seems to be that John knew Jesus, but was not certain of his Messiahship. It was necessary for him, before asserting positively that Jesus was the Christ, to have undoubted testimony of the fact. This was given him in the descent of the Holy Ghost in the form of a dove, as John himself declares (John 1:33).

Joi′ada (joi′à-dà; *Jehovah knows*), a contraction of *Jehoiada* (q. v.), the son and successor of Eliashib in the high priesthood, and succeeded by his son Jonathan (Neh. 12:10, 11, 22). Another of his sons married a daughter of Sanballat, on which account he was banished by Nehemiah (Neh. 13:28), B. C. before 445.

Joi′akim (joi′à-kĭm; *Jehovah establishes*), a contraction of *Jehoiakim* (q. v.), a high priest, son of Jeshua, and father of Eliashib (Neh. 12:10, 12, 26), B. C. before 445.

Joi′arib (joi′à-rĭb; *Jehovah will contend*).

1. A man "of understanding," and one of those with whom Ezra consulted upon the subject of obtaining a company of Levites to return with him to Jerusalem (Ezra 8:16). This conference took place at the river Ahava (v. 15), and resulted in sending a delegation to "Iddo the chief at the place Casiphia," who responded with a large number of the desired ministers (vers. 17-20), B. C. about 457.

2. A descendant of Judah, son of Zechariah, and father of Adaiah, probably through Shelah (Neh. 11:5), B. C. before 445.

3. The founder of one of the courses of priests, and father of Jedaiah (Neh. 11:10). It is thought that there is some error in the list by which he is given as the father of Jedaiah, for in I Chron. 9:10 (where his name is given in full, Jehoiarib), he ranks with Jedaiah and Jachin as heads of courses of priests (see Kiel, in loc.).

4. A priest who returned with Zerubbabel from Babylon (Neh. 12:6). His son, Mattenai, was a contemporary with the high priest Joiakim (v. 19), B. C. 536.

Joining, cramps or binders in the wall of a building (I Chron. 22:3).

Jok′deam (jŏk′dē-ăm), a city of Judah, in the mountains (Josh. 15:56), apparently south of Hebron.

Jo′kim (jō′kĭm; contraction of *Joiakim*), a descendant of Shelah, the son of Judah (I Chron. 4:22). *See* Joiakim.

Jok′meam (jŏk′mē-ăm), one of the places given to the Levites with its suburbs (I Chron. 6: 68). It is in the Jordan Valley. The A. V. gives it as Kibzaim (Josh. 21:22), and "Jokneam" (I Kings 4:12).

Jok′neam (jŏk′nē-ăm), a city in Palestine on the border of Zebulun's allotted portion (Josh. 12:22; 19:11; 21:34; I Kings 4:12). Called also Jokmeam (I Chron. 6:68). The modern Tell Kaimon, twelve miles S. W. of Nazareth.

Jok′shan (jŏk′shăn), the second son of Abraham and Keturah (Gen. 25:2, 3; I Chron. 1:32). His sons Sheba and Dedan are the ancestors of the Sabaeans and Dedanites that peopled a part of Arabia Felix.

Jok′tan (jŏk′tăn), second named of the two sons of Eber, a descendant of Shem. His brother was Peleg (Gen. 10:25, 26, 29; I Chron. 1:19, 20, 23).

Jok′theel (jŏk′thē-ĕl).

1. A city in the low country of Judah, mentioned between Mizpeh and Lachish (Josh. 15:38).

2. The name given by King Amaziah to Selah—the stronghold of the Edomites—after he captured it from them (II Kings 14:7; comp. II Chron. 25:11-13).

Jo′na (jō′nȧ; John 1:42), same as *Jonas* (*q. v.*).

Jon′adab (jŏn′ȧ-dăb; *Jehovah gives*), a shortened form of the name *Jehonadab* (*q. v.*).

1. The son of Shimeah, and nephew of David (II Sam. 13:3, 32, 35).

2. The Rechabite (Jer. 35:6, 8, 10, 14, 16, 18, 19).

Jo′nah (jō′nȧ; *dove*), the fifth in order of the minor prophets, was the son of Amittai, and was born in Gath-hepher, in the tribe of Zebulun (II Kings 14:25).

Personal History. Jonah flourished probably in or before the reign of Jeroboam II. (B. C. c. 782-753, Thiele's dates), and predicted the successful conquests, enlarged territory, and brief prosperity of the Israelitish kingdom under that monarch's sway (II Kings 14:25). What else we know of Jonah's history is to be gathered from the book that bears his name. He was commissioned by Jehovah to go and prophesy to the Ninevites, but for some reason was reluctant to obey, and attempted to flee to Tarshish. He went to Joppa, and there embarked upon a ship bound for that port. A violent storm arose, and the captain of the vessel called upon Jonah to pray to his God to save them. As the storm did not abate, the sailors proceeded to cast lots, believing that some person on board the ship had caused the anger of God, as manifested in the tempest. Jonah was singled out as the culprit, and at his suggestion they unwillingly cast him into the sea. By the appointment of God he was swallowed by a great fish, which upon the third day cast him out upon dry land. Jonah was again commanded to go to Nineveh, and immediately obeyed. The people repented, a fast was appointed, and the city was not destroyed. Provoked at the sparing of Nineveh, Jonah in his displeasure prayed to Jehovah to take his life, as his proclamation had not been fulfilled. God taught him, by means of the rapidly growing and speedily decaying gourd, that it was proper for him to exercise mercy toward the repentant city (Jonah 1:1-4:11).

NOTE.—(1) Much objection has been urged against the truth of the story of Jonah and the fish. It is simply said, "The Lord had prepared a great fish to swallow up Jonah." The species of marine animal is not defined, and the Greek *ketos* is often used to specify, not the genus whale, but any large fish or sea monster. All objection to its being a whale which lodged Jonah in its stomach, from the straitness of throat or rareness of haunt in the Mediterranean, are thus removed. Since the days of Bochart it has been a common opinion that the fish was of the shark species, *Lamia canis carcharias*, or "sea dog." Entire human bodies have been found in some fishes of this kind. Still, granting all these facts, the narrative is miraculous, and nothing is impossible with God. (2) Various interpretations are given of "the sign of the prophet Jonas" (Matt. 12:39). Keil (*Com.*, in loc.) says: "The mission of Jonah was a fact of symbolical and typical importance, which was intended not only to enlighten Israel as to the position of the Gentile world in relation to the kingdom of God, but also to typify the future adoption of such of the heathen as should observe the word of God, into the fellowship of the salvation prepared in Israel for all nations." Whedon (*Com.*, in loc.) says: "The mission of Jonah was a fact of symbolical and typical importance, which was intended not only to enlighten Israel as to the position of the Gentile world in relation to the kingdom of God, but also to typify the future adoption of such of the heathen as should observe the word of God, into the fellowship of the salvation prepared in Israel for all nations." Whedon (*Com.*, in loc.) explains: "Our Lord, even in refusing a *sign*, gives a

sign. His prophecy of his burial, after the manner of the swallowing of Jonah, was in itself a miracle of foreknowledge, and so a proof of his Messiahship."

Jonah, Book of.

This literary production is listed among the Minor Prophets, and is unique in that it is not a collection of Jonah's prophecies, but a biographical account of Jonah's ministry in Nineveh. It teaches the lesson that God's grace went beyond the boundaries of Israel to embrace the nations. It is placed among the Minor Prophets because the experience and the career of Jonah are prophetic of the death, burial and resurrection of Christ and the consequent blessing upon the Gentiles.

1. **Literary Character.** Critics commonly view the book as legend, myth, or parable. The book is correctly evaluated as history. There is not the slightest reason to stumble over the miraculous and to brand it as legend or myth. The miracles of the book of Jonah are a piece with those that honeycomb all Scripture, particularly the Pentateuch. The storm, Jonah being swallowed by the sea monster, the conversion of the Ninevites and the racinus, or gourd, are no more incredible than the dividing of the Red Sea, the cloudy and fiery pillar, manna from heaven, water out of the flint, or the resurrection of Christ. The latter is directly connected with Jonah's experience in the great fish (Matt. 12:39-41; Luke 11:29-32). The book is certainly designed to be viewed as historical. There is nothing in it to suggest otherwise. To assert that our Lord's words regarding Jonah did not imply His belief in the historicity of events is highly artificial and arbitrary. Ancient Jewish opinion looked upon the account as historical (Josephus, *Ant.*, ix, 10, 2). The general Jewish and Christian tradition has followed the same view. Although the book is historical, it is more than history. Its right to the position in the twelve Minor Prophets is due to the fact that it is *predictive* or *typical* history. In its prophetic aspects the Book of Jonah has very important ramifications. In one sense of the word, Jonah in his ministry prefigures Christ in His specific character as The Sent One, being buried, raised from the dead and carrying salvation to the nations. In another aspect of his ministry, Jonah portrays Israel nationally, outside of its own land, as since 70 A. D., a serious trouble to the Gentiles, yet meanwhile witnessing to them. Finally they are cast out by the Gentiles, but preserved through their future tribulation at the end of this age (Dan. 12:1). At the time of the Second Advent of Christ they find salvation and deliverance (Rom. 11:25, 26) becoming world-wide witnesses to the Gentiles in the future earthly Davidic millennial kingdom (Zech. 8:7-23).

2. **Author and Date.** It is by no means impossible that Jonah himself was the author of this book in the eighth century B. C. This is the predominating tradition. It is true there are Aramaisms in the book. This is made mention of by the critics. But such forms occur in early as well as in late O. T. books and are to be found in the Ras Shamra epics from Ugarit, dating c. 1400 B. C. Robert Pfeiffer imagines that an historical blunder occurs in

the designation of the Assyrian emperor as the "king of Nineveh" (3:6) and the description of Nineveh as "an exceeding great city of three days' journey" (3:3). Pfeiffer, moreover, asserts that it is "physiologically improbable" for a man to survive three days within a fish. But the expression "Nineveh *was* a great city" does not imply a date after 600 B. C., but merely points to the dimensions of the city as Jonah found them. Luke 24:13 constitutes a parallel. This verse states that Emmaus "*was* from Jerusalem about three-score furlongs." In answer to Pfeiffer's rationalistic position, it should be noted that Christ believed in the historicity of the miracle narrated in Jonah (Matt. 12:39, 40; Luke 11:29, 30). To deny the miraculous here is to limit God, who is certainly able to preserve a man alive for three days in a fish. The term "king of Nineveh" can scarcely be carped at. The Israelites normally spoke of the ruler of Assyria as king, cf. similar references to surrounding kings (I Kings 21:1; 20:43; II Kings 3:9, 12; II Chron. 24:23). The universalistic ideas of the book are not a late and strange development, but appear early (cf. Gen. 9:29). To assert that such teaching was confined to the post-exilic era is arbitrary. The period of Jonah can be fitted into historical conditions at Nineveh under Semiramis, the queen regent, and her son Adad-Nirari III (810-782 B. C.). The God Nebo was worshipped, and constituted an approach to monotheism reminiscent of Amenophis IV of Egypt in the fourteenth century B. C. Jonah preached in Nineveh in the closing years of this reign, or earlier in the reign of Assurdan III (771-754 B. C.). This period was favorable for Jonah's ministry. Whether the plagues recorded in Assyrian history in 765 and 759 B. C. and the total eclipse of 753 B. C., regarded as portents of divine wrath, prepared the Ninevites for his message, is not known.

3. **The Contents.**
Part I. The Prophet's First Call and Disobedience, 1:1-2:10
   a. The Divine commission and his flight, 1:1-3
   b. The storm, 1:4-7
   c. The confession, 1:8-12
   d. The prophet's being thrown in the sea, 1:13-17
   e. His intercession and salvation, 2:1-10
Part II. The Prophet's Second Call and His Obedience, 3:1-4:11
   a. He goes to Nineveh, 3:1-4:11
   b. The Ninevites repent, 3:5-9
   c. The city is saved, 3:10
   d. Jonah is angered, 4:1-4
   e. Jonah is reproved, 4:5-11

4. **The Unity of the Book.** Critics commonly reject the psalm in chapter 2, but if this psalm is removed, the symmetry of the book is undeniably destroyed. The book obviously falls into two halves, the first half, Chapters 1 and 2; the second half, Chapters 3 and 4. Moreover, 1:1-3a is practically identical with 3:1-3a. Also, it is to be noted that 2:2 and 4:2 both mention Jonah's praying. In one case there is a complaint and in the other, a song of thanksgiving. The rejection of 2:2-9, accordingly, destroys the basic symmetry of the book. Critics assert that in 2:1 it is said that Jonah prayed, but what follows is not a prayer but a song of praise for deliverance. But such a critical censure is pointless, displaying ignorance of the fact that thanksgiving is the very heart of prayer. In addition, critics maintain that the song of thanksgiving for deliverance occurs prior to the deliverance, but not until verse 10 is it said that Jonah was cast upon the dry land. Julius Wellhausen even went so far as to say that the mention of weeds in 2:5 exploded the idea that Jonah was in the fish's belly. His remark that "weeds do not grow in a whale's belly" (*Die Kleinen Propheten*, 1898, p. 221) has become proverbial, but Edwin J. Young, (*Introduction to the O. T.*, 1949, p. 257) shows clearly that Wellhausen and other objectors to the genuineness of 2:2-9 miscomprehend the meaning of the psalm completely. Says Young, "Of course weeds do not grow in whales' bellies. But this is not a psalm of thanksgiving *for deliverance from a whale's belly.* It is rather a song of thanksgiving for *deliverance from drowning.* The figures of speech employed in this psalm have reference to drowning, not to a whale's belly. Furthermore, there is not one scintilla of evidence which makes this psalm purport to have reference to deliverance from the belly of a fish. The school of negative criticism has unjustly imputed to this psalm a meaning which it was never intended to bear." (For conservative discussion see Robert Dick Wilson, "The Authenticity of Jonah" in *Princeton Theological Review*, Vol. 16, p. 280-298; 430-456; H. C. Trumbull, "The Reasonableness of the Miracle of Jonah" in the *Lutheran Church Review*, 1911). *M. F. U.*

Jo'nan (jō'năn), the son of Eliakim, and father of Joseph, among the maternal ancestors of Christ (Luke 3:30). He is not mentioned in the Old Testament.

Jo'nas (jō'năs; Gr. *'Iōnas*, for the Hebrew Jonah).
   1. The prophet Jonah (Matt. 12:39, 40, 41; 16:4; Luke 11:29, 30, 32).
   2. The father of the apostle Peter (John 21:15-17). In John 1:42 the name is given as Jona.

Jon'athan (jŏn'à-thăn; a contracted form of *Jehonathan, Jehovah has given*).
   1. **The Son** (or descendant) **of Gershom,** the son of Moses (Judg. 18:30). Jonathan, who was a Levite, resided at Bethlehem, and, leaving that place to seek his fortune, came to Mount Ephraim, to the home of Micah. This person made Jonathan an offer to receive him into his house as priest, which offer he accepted (17:7-13). Not long after five Danite spies, looking for a suitable place for settlement, came to the house of Micah, and inquired of Jonathan respecting the success of their journey. He replied, "Go in peace: before the Lord is your way wherein ye go." Afterward, when a company of six hundred Danites were on their way to occupy Laish, they went to Micah's house, appropriated the carved image, the ephod, the teraphim, and the molten image. Jonathan accepted their invitation to accompany them, and became their priest. This office remained in his family

until "the day of captivity of the land" (18:1-30).

NOTE.—There is little doubt but that Jonathan was a descendant of Moses, and we have, therefore, to explain the expression "son of Manasseh." It is supposed that in the name Moses *Mosheh*, the single letter *n* (*nun*) has been interpolated, changing it into Manasseh, in order to save the character of the great lawgiver from the stain of having an idolator among his immediate descendants.

2. **The eldest son of Saul**, king of Israel. (1) **Personal history.** Jonathan first appears in history some time after his father's accession, being at that time at least thirty years of age. In the war with the Philistines, commonly called, from its locality, "the war of Michmash," he commanded one thousand men of the three thousand which composed Saul's standing army. He was encamped at Gibeah, and "smote the garrison of the Philistines" in Geba (I Sam. 13:2, 3), B. C. c. 1020. Saul and the whole population rose, but unsuccessfully, and the tyranny of the Philistines because harsher than ever. From this oppression Jonathan resolved to deliver his people, and, unknown to any but his armorbearer, he attacked the garrison at Michmash (14:1, 4-14). A panic seized the garrison, spread to the camp, and thence to the surrounding bands. This was increased by an earthquake and by the combined assault of various bodies of Israelites hidden in the mountains. Saul and his band joined in the pursuit of the Philistines, having forbidden any man to taste of food until the evening. Ignorant of this command and accompanying curse, Jonathan partook of some honey while passing through the forest. This coming to the knowledge of Saul, he would doubtless have fulfilled his vow and have sacrificed Jonathan, but the people interfered in his behalf (14:16-45). Jonathan is next introduced to us as the bosom friend of David. Their friendship began on the day of David's return from the victory over Goliath, and was confirmed by a solemn covenant, which was ratified by Jonathan giving his friend his mantle, sword, girdle, and bow (18:1-4). Shortly after this he pleaded with his father in behalf of David, and secured a reversal of the royal decree against the latter's life (19:1-7). The king's madness soon returned, and David fled. The friends met, however, by the stone of Ezel, and entered into a second covenant, pledging themselves to strive for each other's safety, and David swearing to show kindness to the family of Jonathan when he should be delivered of his enemies. He again pleaded with his father to spare David, which so enraged the king that he "cast a javelin at him," with the evident intention of taking his life. The next day he communicated the failure of his mission to David, and they parted to meet only once more (20:1-42). This last meeting was in the forest of Ziph, during Saul's pursuit of David. Jonathan gave expression to his confidence in his friend's elevation to the throne. "They two made a covenant before the Lord," and parted to meet no more (23:15-18). We hear no more of Jonathan until the battle of Gilboa, when, with his father and his two brothers, he was slain by the Philistines (31:2, 8). His remains were carried to Jabesh-gilead and

buried there (v. 13), but were afterward removed, with those of his father, to Zelah in Benjamin (II Sam. 21:12-14). Jonathan left one son, Mephibosheth, who was five years old at the time of his death (4:4), B. C. about 1000. (2) **Character.** Jonathan was a man of lofty daring, who did not shrink to place himself in the greatest danger for the sake of his country. But his most noticeable characteristic was his ardent and unselfish devotion to his friends, which led him to give up his hopes of the throne, and even expose himself to death, for the sake of those he loved. Notwithstanding that his affection for his father was repelled by the latter, owing to the king's insanity, he cast his lot with his father's decline, and "in death they were not divided."

3. **Son of Abiathar**, the high priest, who adhered to David during the rebellion of Absalom (II Sam. 15:27, 36). He remained at En-rogel to report to his master the proceedings in the camp of the insurgents, but, being discovered, fled to Bahurim, and escaped by hiding in a well (17:17-21), B. C. about 970. Later his loyalty to the house of David is shown by announcing to the ambitious Adonijah the forestallment of his measures by the succession to the throne of Solomon (I Kings 1:42, 43). B. C. c. 966.

4. **The son of Shimeah** (Shammah), and nephew of David, who slew a gigantic relative of Goliath, and became one of David's chief warriors (II Sam. 21:21; I Chron. 20:7). He is probably the same who is mentioned as secretary of the royal cabinet (I Chron. 27:32, where *dôd* is translated "uncle").

5. **The son of Shage** the Hararite, and one of David's famous warriors (II Sam. 23:32; I Chron. 11:34).

6. **The second son of Jada**, the grandson of Jarahmeel, of the family of Judah. Jether dying without issue, this branch of the line was continued through Jonathan's two sons, Peleth and Zaza (I Chron. 2:32, 33).

7. **Father of Ebed**, which latter was an Israelite of the "sons" of Adin, who returned with Ezra from Babylon with fifty males (Ezra 8:6), B. C. before 457.

8. **Son of Asahel**, employed with Jahaziah in separating the people from their Gentile wives (Ezra 10:15), B. C. 457.

9. **Son of Joiada**, and father of Jaddua, Jewish high priests (Neh. 12:11); elsewhere (12:22) called *Johanan* (*q. v.*). Josephus relates (*Ant.*, xi, 7, 1, 2) that he murdered his own brother, Jesus, in the temple, because Jesus was endeavoring to get a high priesthood from him through the influence of Bagoses, the Persian general.

10. **A priest**, the descendant of Melicu, in the time of Joiakim (Neh. 12:14), B. C. between 536 and 549.

11. **Son of Shemaiah**, and father of Zechariah, a priest who blew the trumpet at the dedication of the wall (Neh. 12:35), B. C. after 536. He is probably the same as Jehonathan (v. 18).

12. **A scribe** in the time of King Zedekiah, in whose house Jeremiah was imprisoned by the princes of Judah (Jer. 37:15, 20; 38:26), B. C. 589.

13. **One of the sons of Kareah**, who, with

others, held a conference with Gedaliah, the Babylonian governor of Jerusalem (Jer. 40:8, B. C. 588.

Jo'nath-E'lem-Recho'kim (jō'năth-ē'lĕm-rê-kō'kĭm), a term in title of Psalm 56. *See* Musical Terms.

Jop'pa (jŏp'pà; Heb. *yāphō, beauty*); a very old city on the Mediterranean, about thirty miles N. W. of Jerusalem. It is supposed to have got its name from the mass of sunshine which its houses reflected. It is a very ancient city, being enumerated in the lists of the great conqueror Thutmose III (15th cent. B. C.), and occurring in the Amarna Letters of the early 14th century. It was included in the portion assigned to Dan (Josh. 19:46, A. V. "Japho"). Its harbor naturally made it the port of Jerusalem. Thither Hiram floated down from Tyre the fir trees of Lebanon (II Chron. 2:16), and, later, Zerubbabel, acting on the edict of Cyrus, caused to be brought here the cedar trees from the same mountains (Ezra 3:7). Here Jonah embarked for Tarshish (Jonah 1:3). In Joppa Peter wrought the miracle on Tabitha (Acts 9:36), resided for quite a time with Simon the tanner (v. 43), and saw the vision of the great sheet let

247. Traditional House of Simon the Tanner, Joppa

down from heaven (10:5, 16), and here received the summons from Cornelius (v. 17, sq.). Jonathan Maccabeus captured Joppa in B. C. 148 (I Macc. 10:76). Simon, suspecting its inhabitants, set a garrison there (I Macc. 12:34), and upon the restoration of peace, established it again as a haven (14:5). The city was twice destroyed by the Romans, and changed hands several times during the crusades. It was made in the 4th century the seat of a bishopric. The city is now called Jaffa, or Yâfa, and is a thriving metropolis in the state of Israel.

Jo'rah (jō'rà), a man whose descendants (or place whose former inhabitants), to the number of one hundred and twelve, returned from

248. Modern Jaffa and Ancient Ruins

the Babylonian captivity (Ezra 2:18; Hariph in Neh. 7:24), B. C. about 536.

Jo'rai (jō'rà-ī; same as *Jorah*), the fourth named of seven Gadite chieftains (I Chron. 5:13), the place of whose residence is not given, unless, as Keil conjectures (*Com.*, in loc.), v. 16 mentions it. In that case they dwelt in Gilead, in Bashan, B. C. perhaps about 782.

Jo'ram (jō'răm; *Jehovah is high*, a shortened form of *Jehoram, q. v.*).

1. Son of Toi, king of Hamath, who was sent by his father to congratulate David upon his victory over Hadadezer (II Sam. 8:9, 10), B. C. about 986. He is called Hadoram in I Chron. 18:10.

2. One of the descendants of Eliezer (I Chron. 26:25). In Matt. 1:8, *Jehoram (q. v.)*.

Jor'dan, river of (Hebrew generally with article *hǎyyǎrdēn, the descender*, probably from the rapid descent of the stream). It is now called El Urdan, or Esh Sheryah, or the watering-place, and is the chief river of Palestine.

Jor'dan, Valley of (Heb. *'Arăbǎh;* rendered "the plain," Josh. 18:18, marg., "the champaign," Deut. 11:30, "the desert," Ezek. 47:8). Its modern name is El Ghor. For convenience we treat both the river and valley in the same article.

The valley of the Jordan is a rift more than one hundred and sixty miles long, counting from just below Lake Huleh, where the dip below sea level begins, to the point on the Arabah S. of the Dead Sea where the valley rises again to sea level. It is from two to fifteen miles broad, and falls as deep as one thousand two hundred and ninety-two feet below sea level, while the bottom of the Dead Sea is one thousand three hundred feet deeper still. In this valley is the Jordan river; two great lakes—Huleh and Galilee—respectively twelve and fifty-three miles long; large tracts of arable land, especially about Gennesaret, Bethlehem, and Jericho.

249. River Jordan

Geologists claim this valley is due to volcanic action, forcing up two long folds of limestone, running north and south, with a diagonal ridge shutting off the Dead Sea from the Red Sea, and inclosing a part of the old ocean bed. "There then followed a period of great rains, with perpetual snow and glaciers

Galilee. Six miles above the lake it is crossed by the Bridge of the Daughters of Jacob on the high road between Damascus and Galilee.

2. **The Lower Jordan.** The Jordan Valley between the Lake of Galilee and the Dead Sea is sixty-five miles long. On the west are the mountains of Galilee and Samaria, with the

250. The Rift of the Jordan Valley

on Lebanon, during which the valley was filled with fresh water to an extent of two hundred miles, or one long lake from the Sea of Galilee to some fifty miles S. of the present end of the Dead Sea. How the valley passed from that condition to its present state is not clear" (Smith, *Hist. Geog.*, p. 470).

"In this valley are six distinct sections: the Beka'a, or valley between the Lebanons; the Upper Jordan, from its sources at the foot of Hermon through Lake Huleh to the Lake of Galilee; this lake itself; the lower Jordan to its mouth at Jericho; the Dead Sea; and thence to the Gulf of 'Akaba, the Wady 'Arabah" (p. 471).

1. **The Upper Jordan.** "The great valley of Palestine, as it runs out from between the Lebanons, makes a slight turn eastward round the foot of Hermon, so that Hermon not only looks right down the rest of its course, but is able to discharge into this three fourths of the waters which gather on its high and ample bulk." Four streams which unite before entering Lake Huleh contest the honor of being considered as the source of Jordan: (1) The Nahr Bareighit, which comes down the Merj 'Arun; (2) the Nahr Hasbany, which springs half a mile to the N. of Hasbeya, from a buttress of Hermon, and flows down between Hermon and the Jebel Dahar, the longest of the four, but having much less water than the two following; (3) the Nahr Leddân, the shortest but heaviest, springing from Tell-el-Kadi, in the bosom of the valley itself; and (4) Nahr Banias, rising in the very roots of Hermon, and having the largest number of tributarites. These last two have generally been considered as the sources of Jordan.

This whole district was given (B. C. 20) to Herod the Great by Augustus, and the town he built was known as Caesarea Philippi. To this region Jesus repaired to avoid Jewish hostility, and it is this district that is referred to in Psa. 42. It was, in a military point of view, the northern gate of Palestine; and here in Dan lay the limit of the land of Israel. At the lower end of this district lay Lake Huleh, without doubt the Lake Semechonitis of Josephus (*Ant.*, v, 5, 1; *Wars*, iii, 10, 7), and probably also the waters of Merom of the book of Joshua (11:5, 6). From the lower end of the lake the river Jordan enters the Great Rift below the level of the sea, falling six hundred and eighty feet in less than nine miles, and then glides quietly into the Lake of

break between them of the Vale of Jezreel. On the east are the flat hills of Gilead, some two thousand feet above the Jordan, broken by the valleys of the Yarmuk and Jabbok. Between these ranges of hills the valley is from three to fourteen miles wide. Much of this valley is very fertile, vegetation being extremely abundant, especially in the spring. There is, however, much sour land, jungle, obtrusive marl, and parched hillsides, all justifying the name of desert. "Down this broad valley there curves and twists a deeper, narrower bed, perhaps one hundred and fifty feet deeper and from two hundred yards to a mile broad." This is the breadth to which the Jordan rises when in flood, once a year (Josh. 3:4; Eccles. 24:26). Further we come to the Jordan itself, from ninety to one hundred feet broad, rapid and muddy. The depth varies from three feet at some fords to ten or twelve. In the sixty-five miles the descent is six hundred and ten feet, an average of fourteen feet a mile. But few towns have been built in the Jordan valley, for the following reasons: From early spring to late autumn the heat is intolerable, the temperature rising as high as one hundred and thirty degrees in August; in ancient times the valley was infested with wild beasts; the frequent incursions of Arabs. The importance of the Jordan in Scripture would seem to arise from its being a frontier and boundary (Gen. 32:10; Deut. 3:20; 27:4; Josh. 1:2; Num. 34:10-12), and a military frontier (Judg. 7:24; 12:5). To pass the Jordan was figurative of decision; like crossing the Rubicon. Many of the most remarkable

251. Parade in Amman, Jordan;
Wedding of King Hussein

names and events of Scripture are associated with the Jordan: Joshua leading Israel into the promised land, the parting of Elijah and Elisha, Naaman being healed in its waters, David crossing it to escape from the rebellious Absalom, and the baptism of Jesus by John.

With the partition of Palestine in 1948, much of the Jordan valley came under the control of the Hashemite Kingdom of the Jordan, with its capital at Amman. *See* Palestine.

252. Amman, Jordan, Street Scene

Jo'rim (jō'rĭm), the son of Matthat and father of Eliezer, maternal ancestors of Jesus (Luke 3:29).

Jor'keam (jôr'kē-ăm; A. V. Jor'ko-am), the son of Raham, descendant of Caleb; or the name of a place in the tribe of Judah (I Chron. 2:44).

Jos'abad (jŏs'á-băd), another form of Jozabad (No. 1).

Jos'aphat (jŏs'á-făt), a Grecized form (Matt. 1:8) of the name Jehoshaphat, king of Judah.

Jo'se (jō'sē), one of the maternal ancestors of Jesus (Luke 3:29), not mentioned in the Old Testament.

Jos'edech (jŏs'ē-dĕk), another form of Jehozadak, or Jozadak, the son of Seraiah (Hag. 1:1, 12, 14, 2:2, 4; Zech. 6:11).

Jo'seph (jō'zĕf; *may he;* i. e., Jehovah *add*), the name of the following men:

1. **Son of Jacob.** Joseph was the elder son of Jacob and Rachel, born while his father was still serving Laban (Gen. 30:22-25), B. C. about 1910. *See* Note.

Personal History. After his birth Joseph is mentioned in connection with his father's flight (Gen. 33:2, 7), and then no more until he was seventeen years of age. (1) **Position in family.** As the child of Rachel, and "son of his old age" (37:3), and doubtless also for his excellence of character, he was beloved by his father above all his brethren. This, together with the fact that he reported to his father the evil conduct of the sons of Bilhah and Zilpah, caused his brethren to hate him. Their jealousy was aggravated by Jacob's showing his preference in presenting Joseph with a dress, probably a long tunic with sleeves, worn by youths of the richer class (37:2-4). A still greater provocation was the telling of his dreams, that seemed to foreshow his preeminence in the family (v. 5-11). (2) **Sold into slavery.** Such was Joseph's relation to his brethren when his father sent him from the vale of Hebron to Shechem to inquire concerning their welfare. They were not at Shechem, but were found by Joseph in Dothan. His appearance aroused their hatred, and, with the exception of Reuben, they resolved to kill him. He interfered in Joseph's behalf, and persuaded them to cast him into a pit, intending "to deliver him to his father again." This they accordingly did, after stripping him of his tunic. While they were eating bread a company of Arabian merchants (Ishmaelites) appeared, and, at the suggestion of Judah and in the absence of

253. Joseph Sold by His Brethren

Reuben, Joseph was sold to them for twenty shekels of silver. Dipping Joseph's tunic in the blood of a kid, they sent it to Jacob, that he might believe that his favorite had been torn in pieces by some wild beast. Their trick succeeded, and Joseph was mourned as dead. The merchants sold Joseph to Potiphar, an officer of Pharaoh, and he became an Egyptian slave (37:12-36), B. C. about 1897. (3) **Slave life.** In the service of Potiphar Joseph behaved himself so discreetly, and was so led of God, that he found great favor with his master, who gave him the direction of all his affairs. Refusing, however, to gratify the improper request of his master's wife, he was accused by her of unchastity and thrust into prison. Here, also, God was with Joseph, procuring him favor in the eyes of the governor of the prison, so that he intrusted all the prisoners to his care, leaving everything to his supervision (39:1-23). While here he interpreted correctly the dreams of two of his fellow-prisoners—Pharaoh's chief butler and baker—disclaiming any human skill, and acknowledging that the interpretations were of God. These interpretations were fulfilled three days afterward, on the king's birthday (ch. 40). (4) **Exaltation.** After two years Pharaoh had two prophetic dreams which the magicians and wise men of Egypt were unable to interpret. The butler, calling to mind the service rendered him by Joseph, advised his royal master to put his skill to the test. Joseph was sent for and interpreted the dreams as foretelling seven years of plenty to be followed by seven years of famine. He followed up this interpretation by advising Pharaoh to "look out a man discreet and wise, and set him over the land of Egypt." This counsel pleased Pharaoh and his ministers, who believed that Joseph possessed the spirit of supernatural insight and wisdom. Joseph was appointed ruler over Pharaoh's house, and over all the land; in other words, became grand vizier of Egypt. Pharaoh called him Zaphnath-paaneah (*saviour of the world*), and married him to Asenath, daughter of Poti-pherah, the priest of On. This promotion took place when Joseph was thirty years of age (41:1-46), B. C. about

1883. During the seven years of plenty Joseph prepared for the years of famine to follow by carefully husbanding the grain, which was so abundant as to be beyond measurement. During these years his two sons, Manasseh and Ephraim, were born (41:47-52). When scarcity began Joseph was in a condition to supply the wants of Egypt, and also of surrounding nations. He put all Egypt under Pharaoh—first the money, then the cattle, the land (excepting the priests'), and eventually the Egyptians themselves becoming the property of the crown. The people were distributed according to the cities in which the grain was stored, and were instructed to pay a tax to the crown of one fifth of the product of the soil (41:53-57; 47:14-26). (5) **Joseph and his brethren.** Early in the time of famine the brethren of Joseph, excepting Benjamin, went to Egypt to buy food. Applying to Joseph, who had supreme control over the stores of Egypt, he was not recognized, but knew his brethren, and seems to have resolved to make them feel and acknowledge the wrong they had done him. He acted as a foreigner toward them, speaking harshly to them, inquired whence they had come, and accused them of being spies. This charge they denied, and told him particularly about their family. After putting them in ward for three days he sent them home to bring back their youngest brother as proof of their veracity, keeping Simeon as

254. Egyptians Selling Corn to Semites

hostage. Having with great difficulty secured Jacob's permission, they took Benjamin, a present, double money to repay the sum placed by order of Joseph in each man's sack, and returned to Egypt. The presence of his younger brother assured Joseph of the truth of his father's welfare, and, yielding to his natural impulses, he made himself known to his brethren. He inquired again concerning his father; told them not to grieve because of the sin they had committed in selling him, as God had overruled it for their welfare; charged them to return to Canaan and bring Jacob and their families to Egypt, and that he would provide for them during the five remaining years of famine. These events reached the ear of Pharaoh; he approved all that Joseph had done, and gave commandment that Jacob and his family should forthwith come into Egypt (42:1-45:24). (6) **Welcomes Israel.** Israel, convinced that Joseph still lived, went to Egypt, where he was tenderly welcomed and provided for, and placed in the land of Goshen. When he died he was embalmed by order of Joseph, and carried by him to Canaan and laid in the cave of Machpelah (45:25-50:13). (7) **Remaining history.** Upon his return from Canaan Joseph found his brethren in fear lest, his father being dead, he would punish them. He assured them that this was not his purpose,

and promised still to nourish them and their little ones. Joseph lived to be one hundred and ten years of age, and, dying, took an oath of his brethren that they would carry up his bones to the land of promise. After his death he was embalmed and "put in a coffin in Egypt" (50:14-26), B. C. about 1800. This promise was religiously kept, as "Moses took the bones of Joseph with him" (Exod. 13:19), and they were at length put in their final resting place at Shechem (Josh. 24:32).

Character. In Joseph we recognize the elements of a noble character—piety, pure and high morality, simplicity, gentleness, fidelity, patience, perseverance, an iron will, and an indomitable energy.

Chronology. The Joseph story, according to the Biblical chronology preserved in the Massoretic Hebrew text, is to be placed c. 1871 B. C. i. e., during the splendid Twelfth Dynasty. However, many scholars have concluded that it would be an "historical misinterpretation" (Alexis Mallon, *Les Hebreux en Egypte, Orientalia* III, 1921, p. 67), to imagine that a young Semitic foreigner would have been lifted up to such power under native Egyptian dynasties. This would be more likely, it is claimed, under the Hyksos-Semitic conquerors of Egypt. It is unfortunate that this period of the Hyksos invasion is to a large extent unknown. Everybody agrees, however, that Israel was in Egypt during this period of confusion and turmoil (c. 1750-1550) and that the notice that an oppressor called "a new king . . . who knew not Joseph" (Exod. 1:8) refers to one of the pharoahs of the New Empire, after the hated Asiatic Hyksos were expelled from Egypt. With this tallies the fact that the Israelites were in residence in the "Plain of Tanis," called "the field of Zoan" (Psa. 78:12). This was the Hyksos capital of Egypt. *M. F. U.*

Archaeology. That Jacob and his sons went down into Egypt under Joseph's viziership has been denied by some of the more radical critics (cf. Leroy Waterman, *Jour. Am. Or. Soc.*, lvii, p. 375-380; *Am. Jour. Sem. Lang.*, lv, p. 25-43). But this historical tradition is so inextricably woven into the fabric of Jewish history that it "cannot be eliminated without leaving an inexplicable gap" (W. F. Albright, *From the Stone Age to Christianity*, Baltimore, 1904, p. 183 f.). In addition to this general conclusion, numerous evidences of Israel's sojourn in Egypt appear in the Genesis-Exodus part of the Pentateuch. Most astonishing are the surprising number of Egyptian personal names showing up in the Levitical genealogies. (Theophile Meek, "Moses and the Levites," *Am. Journ. Sem. Lang. and Lit.* lvi, p. 117 f.). Unquestionably Egyptian are such names as Moses, Hophni, Phineas, Merari, Putiel (first element) and Assir. I Sam. 2:27 further corroborates this fact. Critics unwarrantably, however, deny that the other tribes sojourned in Egypt on the basis that the Egyptian names are apparently confined to the Levitical tribe. Another evidence of the Egyptian sojourn is the authentic local coloring which appears in numerous aspects of the Pentateuchal account. Many bits of Egyptian coloring exist "which are beautifully illustrated by Egyptological discoveries" (W. F. Albright in *Young's Analytical Concordance*, 20th Ed., 1936, p. 27). When the writer, for instance, mentions the title of Egyptian officials such as the "chief of the butlers" and "chief of the bakers" (Gen. 40:2) they are those of *bona fide* palace officials mentioned in Egyptian documents. (See G. E. Wright and F. Filson, Westminster *Hist. Atlas to the Bible*, 1945, p. 28b). Other examples occur in Gen. 39:4; Gen. 41:40; Gen. 41:42, 43. Such striking examples as the famines of Egypt (cf. Gen. 41) are illustrated by at least two Egyptian officials who give a resume of their charities on the walls of their tombs, listing dispensing food to the needy "in each year of want." One inscription from c. 100 B. C. actually mentions the famine of seven years' duration in the days of Pharaoh Zoser of Dynasty III about 2700 B. C. Such items as dreams, the presence of magicians (cf. Gen. 41:8), mummification (Gen. 50:2, 26) and Joseph's life span of 110 years (Gen. 50:22), the traditional length of a happy, prosperous life in Egypt, are all well illustrated by the monuments. The family of Jacob, some seventy persons (Gen. 46:26, 27) were settled down in Goshen (Gen. 46:26-34). This area has been identified with the eastern part of the Delta around the Wadi Tumilat. The region around this Wadi, especially north of it, was one of the most fertile parts of Egypt, "the best of the land" (Gen. 47:11). A fine archaeological parallel is the representation of a group of W. Semitic immigrants going down to Middle Egypt around the year 1900 B. C. The scene is sculptured on the tomb of one of Senwosret II's officials named Khnumhotep at Beni Hasan. A party bringing barter products from S. W. Asia appear under the leadership of "Sheik of the highlands, Ibshe." The name and the faces are clearly Semitic. Thick black hair falls to the neck, and their beards are pointed. They are dressed in long cloaks and are armed with spears, bows and throw sticks. The accompanying inscription reads "the arrival, bringing eye paint, which thirty-seven Asiatics bring to him" (Jack Finegan, *Light From the Ancient Past*, 1946, p. 83). Another bit of evidence are the Canaanite place names in the Delta. These include Succoth (Exod. 12:37), Baal-zephon (Exod. 14:2), Migdol (Exod. 14: 2), Zilu (Tell Abu Zeifah) and very likely Goshen itself (Exod. 8:22; 9:26) (See W. F. Albright, *From the Stone Age to Christianity*, 1940, p. 184). M. F. U.

2. The father of Igal, the spy delegated from Issachar to explore Canaan (Num. 13: 7), B. C. 1209.

3. One of the sons of Asaph who were appointed chiefs of the first division of sacred musicians by David (I Chron. 25:2, 9), B. C. about 960.

4. A Jew of the family of Bani who divorced his Gentile wife after the captivity (Ezra 10: 42), B. C. 456.

5. Son of Shebaniah, and one of the chief priests after the captivity (Neh. 12:14), B. C. after 536.

6. The husband of Mary and foster-father of our Lord. By Matthew (who gives the line of royal descent) he is said to have been the son (i. e., son-in-law) of Jacob, whose lineage is traced through David up to Abraham. Luke (giving the line of natural descent) represents him as the son of Heli, and traces his origin up to Adam. Only a few statements respecting Joseph appear in Holy Writ. While living at Nazareth (Luke 2:4) he espoused Mary (1: 27), but before he took her home as his wife she proved to be with child. Grieved at this, and yet not wishing to make a public example of Mary, Joseph purposed quietly to separate from her "by simply a note of dismissal, or bill of divorcement." He was dissuaded from taking this step by the assurance of the angel that Mary had conceived under a divine influence (Matt. 1:18, sq.). Joseph obeyed the divine command and took Mary as his wife (1:24). Shortly after he was obliged, by the decree of enrollment from Augustus Caesar, to leave Nazareth with his wife and go to Bethlehem. When the shepherds came he was there with Mary and her babe; he went with them to the temple to present the infant according to the law, and, warned by an angel, took them down to Egypt, where he remained until, directed by a heavenly messenger, he returned to the land of Israel. His intention to reside in Bethlehem was changed through fear of Archaelaus, and he took up his abode in Nazareth (2:1-23), where he carried on his trade of carpenter. When Jesus was twelve years old Joseph took him and Mary to Jerusalem to keep the Passover, and upon their return to Nazareth continued to act as his father (Luke 2:41-51). The sacred writings furnish no additional information respecting Joseph, and the origin of all the earliest stories and assertions of the fathers concerning him is to be found in the apocryphal gospels.

7. The son of Mattathias and father of Janna, maternal ancestors of Jesus (Luke 3: 24).

8. The son of Judah and father of Semei, maternal ancestors of Jesus (Luke 3:26).

9. The son of Jonan and father of Judah, among Christ's maternal ancestors (Luke 3: 30).

10. Of Arimathaea, "an honorable counselor, who waited for the kingdom of God," and was a secret disciple of Jesus. The crucifixion seems to have wrought in him positive convictions, for, upon learning of the death of our Lord, he "went in boldly unto Pilate and craved the body of Jesus." Pilate, having learned from the centurion who had charge of the execution that Jesus was actually dead, gave the body to Joseph, who took it down from the cross. After it had been embalmed at the cost of Nicodemus, another secret disciple (John 19:38, 39), Joseph had the body wrapped in linen, and deposited it in a new tomb belonging to himself and located in a garden "in the place where Jesus was crucified" (Matt. 27:58-60; Mark 15:43-46; Luke 23:50, sq.). Luke describes Joseph as "a good man and a just," and adds that "he had not consented to the counsel and deed of them," i. e., of the Jewish authorities. From this remark it seems to be evident that he was a member of the Sanhedrin.

11. Surnamed Barsabas, was one of the two persons whom the primitive Church nomi-

nated, immediately after the resurrection of
Christ, praying that the Holy Spirit would
show which one should be apostle in place of
Judas. When the lots were cast Matthias was
chosen (Acts 1:23-25). Joseph also bore the
name of *Justus*, and was one of those who had
"companied with the apostles all the time that
the Lord Jesus went in and out among them,
beginning from the baptism of John" until
the ascension (vers. 21, 22).

Jo'ses (jō'sĕz; Greek form of Joseph).

1. The son of Mary and Cleopas, and
brother of James the Less, Simon, and Jude.
He was, consequently, one of those who are
called "the brethren" of our Lord (Matt.
13:55; 27:56; Mark 6:3; 15:40, 47). He alone
of his brethren was not an apostle.

2. A Levite of Cyprus (Acts 4:36), surnamed
by the apostle *Barnabas* (*q. v.*).

Jo'shah (jō'shà), son of Amaziah, and one of
the princes of Simeon, the increase of whose
family led them to remove to the valley of
Gedor, from which they expelled the Hamites
(I Chron. 4:34), B. C. about 711.

Josh'aphat (jŏsh'à-făt; *Jehovah judges*), a Mith-
nite, and one of David's mighty men (I
Chron. 11:43), B. C. about 1000.

Joshavi'ah (jŏsh-à-vī'à), a son of Elnaam, and,
with his brother Jeribai, associated with the
bodyguard of David (I Chron. 11:46), B. C.
1000.

Joshbeka'shah (jŏsh-bē-kā'shà; perhaps *he*, i.
e., God, *returns a hard fate*), a son of Heman,
and leader of the seventeenth division of the
temple musicians (I Chron. 25:4, 24), B. C.
about 960.

Jo'sheb-Basse'bet (jō'shĕb-băs-sē'bĕt; *sitting
in the council*), the Tachmonite, the chief of
David's three heroes (II Sam. 23:8, marg.;
R. V. Josheb-basshebeth); called in I Chron.
11:11, *Jashobeam* (*q. v.*).

Josh'ua (jŏsh'û-à).

1. The assistant and successor of Moses.—
Name (Heb. *Yᵉhōshū'ă*, *Jehovah is salvation*),
changed by Moses (Num. 13:16) from *Hoshea*,
salvation (Num. 13:8).

Family. The son of Nun, the son of Elishama, prince of the tribe of Ephraim (Exod.
33:11; Num. 1:10).

Personal History. (1) **In battle.** In the
Bible the first mention of Joshua is as the
victorious commander of the Israelites in their
battle against the Amalekites at Rephidim
(Exod. 17:8-16), B. C. c. 1440. (2) **On Mount
Sinai.** When Moses ascended Sinai to receive
for the first time (Exod. 24:13) the two tables,
Joshua, who is called his minister or servant,
accompanied him part of the way, and was
the first to accost him on his return (32:17).
(3) **In charge of tabernacle.** After the defection of Israel and their worship of the golden
calf, Moses moved the tabernacle outside of
the camp, and, returning to the congregation, left it in charge of Joshua (33:11). (4)
An unwise request. When it was told Moses
that Eldad and Medad prophesied in the
camp, Joshua requested him to forbid them,
which request elicited that famed reply of
Moses, "Enviest thou for my sake? would
God that all the Lord's people were prophets,
and that the Lord would put his Spirit upon
them" (Num. 11:27-29). (5) **A spy.** Soon

after Joshua was appointed as one of the
twelve chiefs sent (13:8, 16, 17) to explore
the land of Canaan. He and *Caleb* (*q. v.*) were
the only ones that gave an encouraging report of their journey, and exhorted the people
to go up and possess the land (14:6-9). (6)
Appointed ruler. The forty years of wandering were almost passed, and Joshua, because
of his faithfulness, was one of the few survivors (26:65). Moses, by direction of God
(Num. 27:18-23; Deut. 1:38), invested him
solemnly and publicly with authority, in connection with Eleazar, over the people (Deut.
3:28). (7) **With Moses in the tabernacle.** It
was revealed to Moses that he was soon to die,
and that he should appear with Joshua in
the tabernacle. And while in the presence of
God Moses gave his faithful minister a
"charge," and said, "Be strong and of good
courage: for thou shalt bring the children of
Israel into the land which I sware unto them;
and I will be with thee" (Deut. 31:14, 23).
(8) **Assumes charge of Israel.** Under the
direction of God, again renewed (Josh. 1:1),
Joshua, now in his eighty-fifth year, and "full
of the spirit of wisdom" (Deut. 34:9), assumed
the command of the people (B. C. c. 1400.
From Shittim he sent spies into Jericho, who
were lodged and secreted by *Rahab* (*q. v.*),
and returned to Joshua with an account of
the fear of the people because of the Israelites

255. Excavations at Jericho

(Josh., ch. 2). (9) **Entrance into Canaan.**
The next morning after their return Joshua
broke camp at Shittim and moved down to
the edge of Jordan, which at this season, the
harvest (April), overflowed the banks (Josh.
3:15). On the third day the officers instructed
the people in the order of the march, and
Joshua bade them sanctify themselves for the
morrow. In the morning the priests advanced
in front of the people bearing the ark, and
when their feet touched the water the river
was divided. They took their position in the
midst of the river bed, and there remained
until the people had all passed over. Meanwhile twelve chosen men, one from each tribe,
took twelve stones from the spot where the
priests stood, leaving in their place twelve
other stones taken from the dry land. When
all this was done Joshua commanded the
priests to come up out of Jordan; and as soon
as they reached dry ground the waters of
Jordan returned and overflowed its banks as
before (4:1-18). (10) **In Canaan.** The host
encamped that night at Gilgal, in the plains

609

of Jericho, and there Joshua set up the twelve stones taken from Jordan as a perpetual memorial of the dividing of its waters (4:19-24). At the command of God, Joshua caused the people to be circumcised; which rite seems to have been neglected in the case of those born after the Exodus (5:5). Four days after the crossing of Jordan the Passover was celebrated; and the Israelites eating the next day of bread made from the corn of the land, the manna ceased (5:10-12). (11) **Capture of Jericho.** As Joshua was meditating how to attack Jericho, he saw a warrior with a drawn sword in his hand, who, in reply to Joshua's challenge, announced himself as the "captain of the host of Jehovah," and gave the divine plan for the capture of the city (vers. 13, 14). The men of war, and priests carrying trumpets and the ark, were to compass the city once each day for six days, and seven times on the seventh day, when the walls of the city

256. Types of Late Bronze Age Pottery in Use at the Time of the Israelite Conquest of Jericho

would fall. Following the directions given, Joshua beheld the fall of the city, put the inhabitants to death, and destroyed the property found therein. The only exception was Rahab and her household, and the silver and gold and vessels of brass and iron, which were placed in the sacred treasury (ch. 6). (12) **The first defeat.** The next undertaking was the capture of Ai, (*q. v.*), which the spies informed Joshua would be easily accomplished. But three thousand men were sent to take it—so sure seemed victory. They were repulsed and chased to Shebarim, with a loss of thirty-six men. Joshua made inquiry of the Lord as to the reason of the defeat of Israel, and was told of the taking of spoil from Jericho by one of the Israelites. A lot was ordered, which resulted in fixing the crime upon *Achan* (*q. v.*), and the destruction of himself, family, and property (ch. 7). (13) **Taking of Ai.** Joshua then formed a plan for taking Ai by stratagem, which met with complete success. The city was destroyed with all its inhabitants, its king hanged on a tree, and buried under a great heap of stones, the only memorial of the city (Josh. 8:1-29). After this Joshua caused the law to be engraven upon stones on Mount Ebal, and read to the people stationed upon that mountain and Mount Gerizim (8:30-35). (14) **Craft of the Gibeonites.** When the kings of the Hittites and other nations west of Jordan heard of the fall of Ai, they armed themselves against Joshua. But the Gibeonites, a confederacy of several cities not far from the encampment of

the Israelites, sent ambassadors in torn clothes, with old sacks and musty bread, pretending that they had come from a distant country and wished to make a covenant with Israel. They obtained a treaty which was respected by Joshua, he merely making them "hewers of wood and drawers of water for the congregation of and for the altar of the Lord" (ch. 9). (15) **Battle of Gibeon.** Alarmed by the defection of the Gibeonites, Adonizedek, king of Jerusalem, made a league with the kings of Hebron, Jarmuth, Lachish, and Eglon, and laid siege to Gibeon. Joshua hastened to their help, marching by night from Gilgal, and, taking the Amorites by surprise, utterly routed them near Bethhoron. Joshua was aided in this battle by an unprecedented hailstorm, which slew more than fell by the sword; and by a miraculous lengthening of the day, which enabled him to pursue the fugitives even to Makkedah (Josh. 10:1-14). (16) **Subsequent conquests.** This great battle was followed by the conquest of Makkedah, Libnah, Lachish, Gezer, Eglon, Hebron, and Debir. In this one campaign Joshua subdued the southern half of Palestine, from Kadeshbarnea to Gaza, the eastern and western limit of the southern frontier; and he led the people back to Gilgal (Josh. 10:15-43). In another campaign he marched to Lake Merom, where he met and overthrew a confederacy of the Canaanitish chiefs of the north, under Jabin, king of Hazor; and in the course of the war led his victorious soldiers to the gates of Zidon and into the valley of Lebanon, under Mount Hermon, but left the cities standing, with the exception of Hazor. In six years Joshua was master of the whole land from Mount Halak, at the ascent of Mount Seir on the south, to Baalgad, under Mount Hermon, on the north. His conquests were six nations, with thirty-one kings, including the Anakim, the old terror of Israel (11:1-12:24). (17) **Dividing the inheritance.** Joshua now, in conjunction with Eleazar and the heads of the tribes, proceeded to apportion the promised land, including the part as yet unconquered, asking for his portion Timnath-serah, a city of Mount Ephraim (Josh., chaps. 13-19). After the inheritance of five of the tribes had been determined Joshua removed to Shiloh, where he set up the tabernacle and assembled the people (18:1). Seven tribes had not received their inheritance, and Joshua reproved them for not taking possession of the land. Three men were appointed from each tribe to survey the rest of the land and to divide it into seven portions, which, with their several cities, they described in a book. The survey being finished, Joshua cast lots for the seven portions before the tabernacle in Shiloh (18:2-10). Six cities of refuge were appointed by the people themselves, three on the west of Jordan and three on the east of Jordan (ch. 20). The Levites having claimed the right given to them by Moses, received forty-eight cities and their suburbs, which were given up by the several tribes in proportion to the cities they severally possessed (Josh. ch. 21; comp. Num. 35:1-8). The warriors of the trans-Jordanic tribes were then dismissed in peace to their homes (Josh. 22:1-30). (18) **Old age and death.** After an interval of rest Joshua convoked an assembly from all Israel, and delivered to them two solemn addresses concerning the marvelous fulfillment of God's promises to their fathers. He warned them of the conditions upon which their property depended, and caused them to renew their covenant with God at Shechem. He died at the age of one hundred and ten years, and was buried in his own city, Timnath-serah (Josh. 24:29), B. C. about 1365.

Character. It is difficult to form an estimate of Joshua's character, because the man is overshadowed by the very greatness of the events in which he is placed. And yet this is not a dishonor to him, but a glory; a *lesser* man would have been seen and heard more. His life, though recorded with fullness of detail, shows no stain. By the faithful serving of his youth he was taught to command as a man; as a citizen he was patriotic in the highest degree; as a warrior, fearless and blameless; as a judge, calm and impartial. He was quite equal to every emergency under which he was to act—valiant without temerity, active without precipitation. No care, no advantage, no duty, is neglected by him. He ever looked up for and obeyed divine direction with the simplicity of a child, and wielded the great power given him with calmness, unostentation, and without swerving, to the accomplishment of a high, unselfish purpose. He earned, by manly vigor, a quiet, honored old age, and retained his faith and loyalty, exclaiming, in almost his dying breath, "As for me and my house, we will serve the Lord!"

NOTE—1. The severe treatment of the Canaanites has provoked considerable comment. That Joshua was right because he acted under the command of Jehovah has been justified by two facts: (a) The excessive wickedness of the Canaanites (Lev. 18:21-24). (b) The contamination of their example (Deut. 7:1-5). Archaeology has corroborated the abandoned wickedness and utter debilitating effect of Canaanite cults. Religious literature excavated at Ras Shamra (1929-1937) presents the Canaanite pantheon as utterly immoral. The chief god, El, is a monster of wickedness. His son, Baal, great N. W. Semitic god of the thunder, is no better. The three famous goddesses, Ashera, Anath and Ashtoreth are patronesses of sex and war and their bloodiness and lustfulness must have reduced Canaanite civilization to extremely sordid depths. This archaeological picture of Canaanite religion fully supports Philo o Byblus' estimate of the utter corruption of Canaanite cults, and removes critical doubt of the authenticity of Philo's material.

NOTE—2. The lengthening of the day of the battle of Gibeon has elicited much skepticism and called forth many theories. The miraculous event may have consisted in the expansion of the rotary motion of the earth, or an extraordinary refraction of the light so as to be visible over the whole globe. Kiel suggests that the day merely seemed lengthened because the work accomplished by the Israelites was so great. *M. F. U.*

2. A native of Beth-shemesh, an Israelite, the owner of the field into which the cart came which bore the ark on its return from the land of the Philistines (I Sam. 6:14, 18), B. C. about 1076.

3. The governor of Jerusalem at the time of the reformation by Josiah (II Kings 23:8), B. C. 621.

4. The son of Josedech (Hag. 1:1, 12, 14), a high priest in the time of Haggai and Zechariah, better known under the name of *Jeshua* (see *Jeshua*, No. 2). In Zechariah (3:1-10) Joshua, as pontiff, represents the people in the garb of slaves, and afterward clothed with the new and glorious garments of deliverance. This symbolic action prefigures the future national cleansing of Israel at the Second Advent of Christ and her reconstitution as a nation in the millennial kingdom. When messengers came to Jerusalem, from the remnant of the captivity in Babylon, to offer presents of gold and silver to the temple, the prophet was directed to have some of their offerings made into crowns for Joshua, as a symbol of the sacerdotal and regal crowns of Israel which were to be united on the head of the Messiah (Zech. 6:10, 11).

Joshua, Book of. The name, meaning "Jehovah saves," well describes the character of Joshua's military career.

1. **The Purpose.** The book of Joshua demonstrates God's faithfulness to his promise by leading Israel into the land of Canaan as he had previously led them out of Egypt (Gen. 15:18; Josh. 1:2-6). The account of the conquest is highly selective and abbreviated. Those events which are enumerated are deemed sufficient for the purposes the author had in mind.

2. **The Typical Meaning.** According to I Cor. 10:11 events of the Exodus, the wilderness wandering and the conquest of Canaan are highly typical. "Now all these things happened unto them for examples," literally, "as types." Accordingly, Joshua is a type of Christ as our conquering commander. The redemption out of Egypt and the passage of the Red Sea typify our being baptized by the Holy Spirit into union with Christ (cf. I Cor. 10:2): "And they were all baptised unto (into) Moses in the cloud and in the sea." This redemptive experience prefigures the position the Christian has by virtue of being in Christ by the Spirit's baptising work (I Cor. 12:13; Eph. 1:3; Rom. 6:2, 3; Col. 2:9-12). The crossing of Jordan is a type of our death with Christ *experientially*, as the crossing of the Red Sea is a type of our *positional* death in Christ. Claiming by faith our experience based upon our position is set forth by crossing the Jordan and entering the land of conflict and victory (Eph. 6:10-20). Canaan is not a type of heaven, but a type of meeting our spiritual enemies in victorious Christian living. It is "reckoning ourselves to be dead indeed unto sin and alive unto God" in union with Christ (Rom. 6:11). Every believer is positionally "dead to sin" and "alive to God." The difference is when he reckons it true, it becomes experientially actual. The Canaanites, Perizzites, Hivites, etc. may speak of our spiritual enemies (Eph. 6:12).

3. **The Outline.**
Part I. The Conquest of the Land, 1:1-12:24
    a. Commission of Joshua, 1:1-9
    b. Preparation to cross Jordan, 1:10-2:24
    c. Jordan crossed, 3:1-4:24
    d. Israel circumcised, etc. at Gilgal, 5:1-15
    e. Capture of Jericho and Ai, 6:1-8:29
    f. Altar on Mt. Ebal erected, 8:30-35
    g. Deception of Gibeonites, 9:1-27
    h. Conquest of southern Canaan, 10:1-43

i. Conquest of northern Canaan, 11:1-15
j. Summary of the conquest, 11:16-12:24
Part II. Division of the Land, 13:1-22:34
  a. Instruction of Joshua, 13:1-7
  b. Eastern tribes assigned, 13:8-33
  c. Western tribes assigned, 14:1-19:51
  d. Cities of refuge provided, 20:1-9
  e. Levitical towns chosen, 21:1-45
  f. Eastern tribes sent away, 22:1-34
Part III. Joshua's Farewell Address and
    Death, 23:1-24:33

4. Authorship and Date. The book is anonymous. That the book however, was composed in substance by Joshua himself or by an inspired writer soon after his death is supported by the following facts: (1) The account has the vividness of an eye witness (Josh. 5:1, 6). Such events as the sending out of the spies (chap. 2). the crossing of Jordan (chap. 3), the capture of Jericho and Ai (chaps. 6-8), etc. are described with great vividness of detail. (2) Parts of the book, at least, are written by Joshua (cf. 24:26; 18:9). (3) The narrative was written very early. Rahab, the harlot, was still alive (6:25). That the Jebusites were "dwelling with the children of Judah in Jerusalem unto this day" (15:63) points to a pre-Davidic date (cf. II Sam. 5:5-9). Such references as the Canaanites dwelling at Gezer (16:10) are pre-Solomonic, because the pharaoh of Egypt slew the Canaanite inhabitants and gave the cities as a present to his daughter, Solomon's wife. Jerusalem was not yet an Israelite capital (18:16, 28). Archaic names of cities appear, such as Baalah, later Kirjath-jearim (15:9). The Gibeonites were still "hewers of wood and drawers of water" (9:27), whereas in Saul's day they suffered massacre and their status had been changed (II Sam. 21:1-9). (4) Although the book is early and doubtless authored by Joshua himself, yet minor details in the present form of the work cannot be assigned to Joshua's original work (cf. the account of his death (24:29-31; 13:20) and the strange use of the term "mountains of Judah and of Israel" (11:21). The reference to the book of Jasher (Josh. 10:13) does not constitute a legitimate argument that the book of Joshua was written during David's reign or later, since reference is made to the book of Jasher then. Almost nothing is known of the book of Jasher, which may have been an anthology of national heroes, expanded from century to century to include contemporary celebrities.

5. Relation to the Pentateuch. Denying that the book of Joshua is a literary unit, the critics weave it into their theory of the Pentateuch and have coined the unsound critical term "Hexateuch" to fit their hypothesis. The sources J (Jehovistic) and E (Elohistic) are claimed to be the two primary sources of chapters 1-12, revised later by Deuteronomic writers. Chapters 13-22 are said to be from a priestly source (P) and were added to JED around 400 B. C. That the "Hexateuch" is purely a critical invention is proved from the following reasons: (1) It is of a piece with the documentary hypothesis of the Pentateuch and is founded upon the same false literary, historical and religious philosophical presuppositions. (2) Certain pronounced linguistic

peculiarities which appear in the Pentateuch are absent from the book of Joshua. (3) There is no historical evidence that Joshua was ever thought of as forming a unit with the Pentateuch. The Samaritans took only the Pentateuch, which would have been inconceivable had Joshua at that time formed a "Hexateuch," and especially so when the book apparently favors the Samaritans by its references to Shechem (Josh. 24:1, 32).

6. Authenticity and Credibility of the Book. To the believing student the book of Joshua by its own internal evidence and the implicit and explicit references to it in the N. T. (Heb. 11:30, 31) and the intimate fashion in which its typology is interwoven in the N. T. revelation of God's redemption in Christ (Heb. 3:7-4:11, cf. 4:8) stamp it as genuine. *M. F. U.*

Josi′ah (jō-sī′á; perhaps, *Jehovah heads*, cf. Arab. *'asa, cure, nurse*).

1. The sixteenth king of the separate kingdom of Judah; the son of King Amon and his wife Jedidah. Josiah, at the early age of eight years, succeeded his father on the throne of Judah (II Kings 21:26; 22:1; II Chron. 34:1), B. C. 639. (1) **Idolatry overthrown.** In the eighth year of his reign "he began to seek after the God of David his father" (II Chron. 34:3), and manifested that enmity to idolatry in all its forms which distinguished his character and reign. In the twelfth year of his reign "he began to purge Judah and Jerusalem from the high places, and the groves, and the carved images, and the molten images." So strong was his detestation of idolatry that he ransacked the sepulchers of the idolatrous priests of former days and burned their bones upon the idol altars, before they were overthrown. He did not confine his operations to Judah, but went over a considerable part of Israel, with the same object in view; and at Beth-el, in particular, executed all that the prophet (I Kings 13:2) had foretold (II Kings 23:1-19; II Chron. 34:3-7), (2) **Temple repaired.** In the eighteenth year of his reign Josiah proceeded to cleanse and repair the temple. The task was committed to Shaphan, the state secretary; to Maaseiah, the governor of the city; and to the chancellor, Joah. All parties engaged in the work displayed such fidelity that the money could be given to them without reckoning (II Kings 22:3-7; II Chron. 34:8-13). (3) **Finding of the law.** In the course of this pious labor the high priest, Hilkiah, discovered in the sanctuary "a book of the law" by Moses. He reported his discovery to Shaphan, who conveyed the volume to the king, and read it in the royal presence. Alarmed by the penalties threatened in the law, Josiah sent several of his chief counselors to consult with the prophetess Huldah, who replied that although these dread penalties would be inflicted, he should be gathered to his fathers in peace before the days of punishment came. Perhaps with a view of averting the threatened doom, Josiah convened the people at Jerusalem; and, after the reading of the law, made a solemn covenant with Jehovah (II Kings 22:8-23:3; II Chron. 34:14-32). To ratify the renewal of the covenant Josiah appointed the Passover to be held at

the legal time, which was accordingly celebrated on a scale of unexampled magnificence. But it was too late; the hour of mercy had passed; for "the Lord turned not from the fierceness of his great wrath" (II Kings 23:21-23, 26; II Chron. 35:1-19). (4) **Death**. Not long after this Pharaoh-Necho, king of Egypt, sought a passage through Josiah's territory, on his way to fight against Carchemish, on the Euphrates. Josiah, disguising himself, went out to battle, and was mortally wounded by a random arrow and taken to Jerusalem, where he died (B. C. 608). "Jeremiah lamented for Josiah; and all the singing men and the singing women spake of Josiah in their lamentations to this day;" i. e., in the lamentation which they were wont to sing on certain fixed days, they sung also the lamentation for Josiah (II Kings 23:29, 30; II Chron. 35: 20-25). Both Jeremiah and Zephaniah mention Josiah in their prophecies.

2. The son of Zephaniah, residing in Jerusalem after the captivity, in whose house Zechariah was to crown the high priest Joshua (Zech. 6:10), B. C. 519.

Josi′as (jō-sī′ás), the Grecized form of *Josiah* (Matt. 1:10, 11).

Josibi′ah (jō-sĭ-bī′à; *dweller with Jehovah*), the son of Seriah, of the tribe of Simeon. His son Jehu was one of those who migrated to Gedor (I Chron. 4:35), B. C. before 711.

Josiphi′ah (jŏs-ĭ-fī′à; *Jehovah will increase, add*), one of the family of Shelomith, whose son led up one hundred and sixty males under Ezra to Jerusalem from Babylon (Ezra 8:10), B. C. about 457.

Jot, rather Iota, the smallest letter of the Greek alphabet (*i*), from the Heb. *yod*, and answering to the *i* or *y* of the European languages. It is used figuratively to express the minutest trifles (Matt. 5:18), as *alpha* and *omega* are used to express the beginning and the end.

Jot′bah (jŏt′bà; *goodness, pleasantness*), the city of Haruz, whose daughter Meshullemeth was the mother of King Amon (II Kings 21:19). It is possibly to be identified with Jotapata (Khirbet Jefāt), 7 miles N. of Sepphoris.

Jot′bath (jŏt′bă̄th; Deut. 10:7). See Jotbathah.

Jot′bathah (jŏt′bá-thà; *goodness, pleasantness*), one of the Israelitish encampments (Num. 33: 33, 34); "Jotbath" in Deut. 10:7.

Jo′tham (jō′thăm; *Jehovah is upright*).

1. The youngest of Gideon's legitimate seventy sons, and the only one of them who escaped the massacre ordered by Abimelech (Judg. 9:5), B. C. perhaps about 1108. After Abimelech had been made king by the Shechemites, Jotham appeared on Mount Gerizim and protested against their act in a beautiful parable, in which the trees are represented as bestowing upon the bramble the kingly honor which had been refused by the cedar, the olive, and the vine (vers. 7-21). We hear no more of him, but are informed that three years later the curse that he uttered was accomplished (v. 57).

2. The eleventh king of Judah, and son of King Uzziah by Jerusha, daughter of Zadok. After his father was smitten with leprosy Jotham conducted the government for him until his death (about thirteen years), when he ascended the throne, being then twenty-five

years of age (II Kings 15:5, 32, 33; II Chron. 27:1), B. C. about 738. Jotham reigned in the spirit and power of his father, and avoided any assumption of the priestly functions which proved so disastrous to his father. He was unable, however, to correct all of the corrupt practices of the people. He built the upper gate of the temple—i. e., the northern gate of the inner court— and continued the fortifying of Jerusalem, which his father had begun. He also built "cities in the mountains of Judah, and in the forests he built castles and towers." He waged war successfully against the Ammonites, who seem to have refused to pay to Jotham the tribute which they paid to Uzziah (II Chron. 26:8). For three years after their defeat he compelled them to pay one hundred talents of silver and ten thousand measures each of wheat and barley (27: 2-5). After a reign of sixteen years, including his joint reign with Uzziah, Jotham died, and was buried in the sepulcher of the kings (II Kings 15:38; II Chron. 27:8, 9), B. C. about 735.

3. A descendant, apparently, of Caleb, and one of the six sons of Jahdai (I Chron. 2:47).

Journey, Day's; Sabbath Day's. See Metrology.

Joy (usually some form of Heb. *gîl*, to *leap*, or *spin round* with pleasure); a stronger term than *sĭmḥāh*, (Psa. 30:5, etc.); *māsōs*, Job 8:19, etc.), rejoicing; (Gr. *chara*, Matt. 2:10), gladness; the cause or occasion of joy (Luke 2:10; I Thess. 2:20).

1. Joy is a delight of the mind arising from the consideration of a present, or assured possession of a future good. When moderate it is called *gladness;* raised suddenly to the highest degree it is *exultation* or *transport;* when the desires are limited by our possessions it is *contentment;* high desires accomplished bring *satisfaction;* vanquished opposition we call *triumph;* when joy has so long possessed the mind that it has settled into a temper, we call it *cheerfulness.* This is natural joy.

2. There is a *moral joy,* which is a self-approbation, or that which arises from the performance of any good actions; this kind of joy is called peace, or serenity of conscience; if the action be honorable, and the joy rise high, it may be called *glory.*

3. *Spiritual.* This is called a "fruit of the Spirit" (Gal. 5:22); "the joy of faith" (Phil. 1:25); "the rejoicing of hope" (Heb. 3:6). Its objects are: God himself (Psa. 43:4; Isa. 61: 10); the promises (Phil. 3:3; I Pet. 1:8); the Gospel (Psa. 89:15); the prosperity of Christ's kingdom (Acts 15:3; Rev. 11:15, 17); the happiness of a future state (Psa. 16:9-11; Rom. 5:2; 15:13; Heb. 3:6). This spiritual joy is permanent (John 16:22; Phil. 4:4); unspeakable (I Pet. 1:8).

Joz′abad (jŏz′à-băd; contraction of *Jehozabad, Jehovah endowed*).

1. An inhabitant of Gederah, and one of the famous Benjaminte archers who came to David at Ziklag (I Chron. 12:4, A. V. "Josabad"), B. C. before 1000.

2, 3. Two of the "captains" of Manasseh having this name, joined David when retreating to Ziklag (I Chron. 12:20), B. C. before 1000.

4. One of the subordinate overseers, under

Conaniah and Shimei, who had charge of the first fruits, tithes, and consecrated gifts in the time of Hezekiah. He was probably a Levite (II Chron. 31:13), B. C. about 719.

5. One of the Levite princes who made offerings at the solemnization of the Passover by Josiah (II Chron. 35:9), B. C. about 621.

6. A Levite employed with others by Ezra to weigh the silver and gold and vessels brought from Babylon for the sanctuary (Ezra 8:33), B. C. about 457. He is probably the same as the chief Levite who afterward had "the oversight of the outward business of the house of God" (Neh. 11:16), B. C. 445.

7. One of the priests, of the "sons" of Pashur, who put away his Gentile wife after the captivity (Ezra 10:22), B. C. 456.

8. A Levite who also divorced his Gentile wife (Ezra 10:23), B. C. 456. Perhaps identical with No. 9.

9. One of the Levites who assisted Ezra in expounding the law to the people (Neh. 8:7), B. C. about 445.

Joz′achar (jŏz′a-kȧr; *Jehovah has remembered*), the son of Shimeath, an Amonitess, and one of the two servants of Joash, king of Judah, who formed a conspiracy against him and slew him in Millo (II Kings 12:21; II Chron. 24:25, 26; in the latter passage the name is given as Zabad), B. C. 839. R. V. and R. S. V. Joz′acar.

Joz′adak (jŏz′a-dăk) (Ezra 3:2, 8; 5:2; 10:18; Neh. 12:26). *See* Jehozadak.

Ju′bal (joo′băl), the second son of Lamech by Adah, a descendant of Cain. He is described as the inventor of the "harp and organ," perhaps the *lyre* and *mouthorgan*, or pipe (Gen. 4: 21). According to Josephus (*Ant.*, i, 2, 2), "he cultivated music, and invented the psaltery and cithara."

Jubilee. *See* Festivals, I, 4.

Ju′cal (joo′kăl), an abbreviated form (Jer. 38: :1) of *Jehucal* (*q. v.*).

Ju′da (joo′dȧ), an incorrect English form of the name Judas or Judah.

1. The patriarch *Judah*, son of Jacob (Luke 3:33; Heb. 7:14; Rev. 5:5; 7:5).

2. One of the brethren of our Lord (Mark 6:3). His name is given more correctly in Matt. 13:55, as *Judas*.

3, 4. Maternal ancestors of our Lord (Luke 3:26, 30).

Judae′a. *See* Judea.

Ju′dah (joo′dȧ). 1. **The Patriarch—Name and Family.** (Heb. *Yᵉhūdäh, may he*, i. e., *God, be praised*), was the fourth son of Jacob and Leah, and whole brother to Reuben, Simeon, and Levi, older than himself, and Issachar and Zebulun younger (Gen. 29:35), B. C. about c. 1950.

Personal History. (1) **Treatment of Joseph.** It was by Judah's advice that his brethren sold Joseph to the Ishmaelites instead of taking his life. By the light of his subsequent conduct we see that his action on this occasion arose from a generous impulse, although the form of the question he put to them has been sometimes held to suggest an interested motive: "What profit is it if we slay our brother and conceal his blood? Come and let us sell him" (Gen. 37:26, 27). (2) **Removes to Adullam.** After the sale of Joseph, Judah removed

to Adullam, and married a woman of Canaan named Shuah, by whom he had three sons, Er, Onan, and Shelah. Er married a woman whose name was Tamar, and, dying childless, Judah bestowed his wife upon his second son, Onan, who also died without children. Judah was reluctant to bestow his only surviving son upon this woman, and put her off on the plea that he was not of sufficient age (38:1-11). (3) **Judah's sin.** Tamar, actuated by the usual passion of Eastern women for children, conceived the plan of associating herself with Judah himself, under the guise of a loose woman. Having waylaid him on the road to Timnath, she accomplished her object. The result of the painful affair was the birth of two sons, Zara and Pharez (38: 12, sq.). (4) **Becomes leader.** Though not the firstborn, Judah "prevailed above his brethren" (I Chron. 5:2) and we find him subsequently taking a decided lead in all the affairs in the family. When it became necessary to go a second time into Egypt for food, he remonstrated with Jacob against his detention of Benjamin, and undertook to be responsible for the safety of the lad (Gen. 43:3-10). When the cup was found in Benjamin's sack, and punishment from Joseph seemed imminent, Judah's earnest prayer for his father and brethren and his offer of himself as slave so moved upon his princely brother that he could no longer retain his secret (44:16-34). Soon, too, it is Judah who is sent by Jacob to smooth the way for him in the land of Goshen (46:28). We hear nothing more of him till he received, along with his brethren, the final blessing of his father (49:8-12).

The Tribe of Judah. (1) **Numbers.** When Judah went into Egypt he had three sons, but so greatly did this family increase that it numbered, at the first census, seventy-four thousand six hundred, being first in population of all the tribes. At the second census it numbered seventy-six thousand five hundred, still retaining its rank. Its representative among the spies, and also among those appointed to partition the land, was the great Caleb, the son of Jephunneh (Num. 13:6). (2) **Position.** During the march through the desert Judah's place was in the van of the host, on the east side of the tabernacle, with his kinsmen Issachar and Zebulun (2:3-9; 10:14). According to rabbinical authority, Judah's standard was green, with the symbol of a lion (Keil). (3) **Portion in Canaan.** Judah was the first tribe which received its allotted possessions west of the Jordan, and this territory included fully one third of the whole land. When the land was again distributed, by actual survey, a portion was given to Simeon. The boundaries and contents of the territory allotted to Judah are given at great length (Josh. 15:20-63; *see* Fig. 258). (4) **Relation to other tribes.** During the rule of the judges, Judah maintained an independent spirit toward the other tribes; and while they acquiesced in the Benjamite (Saul's) appointment as king, it could hardly have been with a very good grace, as may be inferred from the very small contingent they supplied to that monarch's army against Amalek (I Sam. 15:4). (5) **As a kingdom.** When Judah established David as king, and removed the sanctuary to Jerusalem, the Ephraimites were dissatisfied, and seized the first opportunity of setting up an independent kingdom. Then the history of Judah as a tribe lapsed into that of *Judah as a kingdom*. Then followed a varied history of wars, vassalage, and occasional prosperity. Against Judah were arrayed Israel, Egypt, Syria, and finally the country was ravaged by the king of Babylon; Jerusalem was burnt with fire, the holy temple laid in ashes, the people taken away into captivity, and then Judah was no more (II Kings chaps. 24, 25; Jer. chaps. 39-41).

2. A Levite who returned to Jerusalem with Zerubbabel (Neh. 12:8), B. C. about 536. He is perhaps the same person whose son aided in rebuilding the temple (Ezra 3:9, A. V. "Jeshua"), although the latter may be the same as Hodaviah (2:40).

3. The son of Senuah, a Benjamite, and "second over the city" of Jerusalem. Dr. Strong (see *Cyc.*, s. v.) maintains that the true translation is "over the second city," and that Judah was prefect over Acra, or the Lower City (Neh. 11:9), B. C. 445.

4. One of those (priest or Levite is not stated) who followed the Jewish princes around the southern portion of the rebuilt wall of Jerusalem (Neh. 12:34), B. C. 445. He is perhaps identical with the musician named in v. 36.

Ju′dah, Kingdom of. *See* History, Old Testament; Judah.

Ju′das (jōō′dás; Greek form, 'Ioudas, of Heb. *Judah*).

1. The Patriarch Judah, son of Joseph (Matt. 1:2, 3). *See* Judah.

2. Iscariot (Gr. *'Iskariōtēs, inhabitant of Kerioth*), the son of Simon, and one of our Lord's twelve apostles.

Personal History. (1) **His call.** We learn nothing of Judas previous to his call (Matt. 10:4; Mark 3:19; Luke 6:16), and yet the appearance of his name in the lists of the apostles would seem to indicate that he had previously declared himself a disciple. It does not seem necessary to speculate upon the motives that influenced Judas to become a disciple, or to attempt a solution of the question why such a man was chosen for the office of an apostle. (2) **As treasurer.** When the twelve became an organized body, traveling hither and thither, receiving money and other offerings, and distributing to the poor, it became necessary that some one should act as steward, and we learn (John 12:4-6; 13:29) that this duty fell to Judas. And then, probably finding himself in possession of larger sums than before, there came covetousness, unfaithfulness, and embezzlement (12:4-6). (3) **Treachery foretold.** Some time previous to the betrayal of Jesus "many of his disciples went back, and walked no more with him" (6:66), probably influenced by the disappointment of their earthly expectations, or fearful of coming evil. In deep sadness of heart he asked his disciples the question, "Will ye also go away?" Receiving assurance of faithfulness from the disciples through Peter, "Jesus answered them, Have not I chosen you twelve, and one of you is a devil? He spake of Judas Iscariot the son of Simon: for he it was that should betray him, being one of the twelve" (6:70, 71),

indicating that even then the greed of immediate or the hope of larger gain kept him from "going back;" that hatred was taking the place of love, and leading him on to a fiendish malignity. The scene at Bethany (Matt. 26:6-13; Mark 14:3-9; John 12:3-9) showed how deeply the canker had eaten into his soul. The warm outpouring of love calls forth no sympathy. He utters himself, and suggests to others, the complaint that it is a waste. Under the plea of care for the poor he covers his own miserable theft. (4) **Betrayal of Jesus.** Previous to the feast of the Passover Judas had gone to "the chief priests and captains," and covenanted with them for money to betray Jesus to them (Matt. 26:14, sq.; Mark 14:10, sq.; Luke 22:3, sq.). He seems to have concealed his treachery, however, for we find him still with the disciples. At the beginning of the last supper he is present, his feet are washed, he hears the fearful words, "Ye are clean, but not all," and the Master's teaching the meaning of the act (John 13:2, sq.). Reclining near Jesus, he hears him tell the disciples that "One of you shall betray me," and asks with the others, "Is it I?" And then, fully given over to the evil one, and beyond reclaim, Satan enters into him, and Jesus said unto him, "That thou doest, do quickly." Judas rose from the feast, and was a disciple no more (Matt. 26:20, sq.: John 13:26-30), and shortly after he completed the betrayal. He knew the garden whither Jesus and the disciples often resorted, and he came accompanied by a band of officers and servants, to whom he made known his Master by a kiss (Matt. 26:47-49; Mark 14: 43-45; Luke 22:47, 48; John 18:1-5). Jesus replied to that kiss with the words of stern, sad reproach, "Judas, betrayest thou the Son of man with a kiss?" (Luke 22:48). (5) **Remorse and death.** When Judas had time for reflection, and saw that Jesus was condemned, he was conscience stricken. Returning to the priests, he confessed his crime and hurled down the money, which they refused to take (Matt. 27:3-5). Feeling, perhaps, that there was for him no restoration; that he was, indeed, "the son of perdition" (John 17:12), "he departed, and went and hanged himself" (Matt. 27:5). He went "to his own place" (Acts 1:18-25).

NOTE.—Between these two passages (Matt. 27:5; Acts 1:16-25) there appears at first sight a discrepancy. In Matthew it is stated "He cast down the pieces of silver in the temple and departed, and went and hanged himself." In Acts (ch. 1) another account is given. There it is stated: (1) That instead of throwing the money into the temple he bought a field with it. (2) That instead of hanging himself, "falling headlong, he burst asunder in the midst, and all his bowels gushed out." (3) That for this reason, and not because the priests had bought it with the price of blood, the field was called "Aceldama." The fact would seem to be that Judas hanged himself, probably with his girdle, which either broke or became untied, and threw him heavily forward upon the jagged rocks below, thus inflicting the wound mentioned by Peter in the Acts. The apparent discrepancy in the two accounts as to the disposition of the money may be thus explained: "It was not lawful to take into the temple treasury, for the purchase of sacred things, money that had been unlawfully gained. In such case the Jewish law provided that the money was to be restored to the donor, and, if he insisted on giving it that he should be induced to spend it for something for the public weal. By a fiction of law the money was still considered to be Judas's, and to have been applied by him in the purchase of the well-known 'potter's field'" (Edersheim, *Life of Jesus*, ii, 575).

Character. The strongest element in the character of Judas was doubtless avarice, and there is no vice at once so absorbing, so unreasonable, and so degrading as the vice of avarice. The dissappointment of every expectation which had first drawn him to Jesus, the intolerable rebuke of that sinless life, and, lastly, the sight of Mary's lavish sacrifice, which brought no gain to himself, increased his alienation to repugnance and hate, so that Judas became capable of the deed that has given his name an everlasting stain.

3. Mentioned, with James and Simon, as a son of Mary (Matt. 13:55; Mark 6:3, A. V. "Juda").

4. Judas Lebbaeus, surnamed Thaddeus (Matt. 10:3; Mark 3:18). Luke (6:16) simply designates him "Judas of James," which probably means that he was the brother of *James the Less* (*q. v.*). We find mention of Judas among the twelve apostles (Matt. 10:3; Mark 3:18; Luke 6:16), besides which the only circumstance recorded of him in the gospels consists in the question put by him to our Lord (John 14:22): "Judas saith unto him (not Iscariot), Lord, how is it that thou wilt manifest thyself unto us, and not unto the world?" Nor have we any account of his proceedings after the resurrection, for the traditions respecting him are lacking in authority, associating him with the foundation of the Church at Edessa. The author of the Epistle of Jude has usually been identified with Judas.

5. Of Galilee, who stirred up a sedition among the Jews soon after the birth of Jesus (Acts 5:37). According to Josephus, he was born in Gamala, and the sedition occurred in A. D. 6. He was destroyed, and his followers scattered by Cyrenius, proconsul of Syria and Judea.

6. A Jew who lived in Damascus, in the street called Straight, probably the "Street of Bazaars." Paul went thither to lodge, and Ananias went there by direction of God, and recovered Saul from his blindness (Acts 9:11). The so-called "House of Judas" is still shown in an open space called "the Sheyk's Place," a few steps out of the Street of Bazaars.

7. Surnamed Barsabas, a disciple, and one of the deputation sent to confirm the Syrian Christians. The epistle having been read to the Church assembled at Antioch, Judas and Silas exercised their prophetical gifts for the confirmation of the believers, after which Judas returned to Jerusalem (Acts 15:22, 27, 32).

Jude (Jude, ch. 1), the brother of James, and author of the last of the general epistles, usually identified with Judas. 4.

Jude, Epistle of, one of the general letters dealing primarily with false teachers (Jude 1:4-6) and in this respect resembling II Pet. Jude expresses affectionate solicitude for the Christians (vs. 1-3, 17-25) and urges them to contend "for the faith once for all delivered to the saints." His language is extremely stern toward heretics. He denounces and threatens them rather than refuting them. Although the Epistle deals with conditions that were incipient in the writer's time, nevertheless the scope of the book comprehends conditions at the end of the age and so has a suitable place before the Book of Revelation.

1. **Authorship.** According to the testimony of the book itself, it was written by "Jude, a servant of Jesus Christ and brother of James" (vs. 1). Since James was one of the brothers of Jesus, Jude was likewise one of His brethren. Matt. 13:55 and Mark 6:33 indicate that Jesus had a brother by that name. Six other Judes or Judases are referred to in the N. T., but the writer of this epistle is not to be confused with any of them. He differentiates himself from others of the same name by mention of his brother, rather than his father. The reason for this is that his brother was much better known among his readers. Jude was not an apostle, as indicated by the omission of the apostolic title. Almost nothing is known about the life of Jude, except that he was evidently one of the younger brothers of Jesus. He was apparently convinced of the deity of Christ after the resurrection and is numbered with the disciples in the upper room after the ascension (Acts 14).

2. **Authenticity.** Hermas, Polycarp, Athenagoras, Theophilus of Antioch, Tertullian, Clement of Alexandria and Eusebius give early attestation to the authority of the book. Jude is more strongly attested than II Pet. This is somewhat astonishing when one considers its lack of apostolic authorship, its shortness, its polemic character and its alleged reference to apocryphal literature. Clement of Alexandria, Tertullian, Augustine, Jerome and other church fathers maintained that Jude actually makes reference to the apocrypha. For this reason many early fathers rejected it as authentic. Verse 9 was thought to have been a quotation from the Assumption of Moses and verse 14f. was supposed to be taken from the Book of Enoch. It is possible that Jude quotes a passage from a known uncanonical book, not by way of endorsement, but because he used this particular statement as divinely given.

3. **The Background.** The general character of the Epistle does not permit a certain determination of the locality of its composition or its destination. It may be that the letter was intended for the same people as those to whom his brother James addressed his letter.

4. **Occasion and Date.** The inroads of apostasy and heretical doctrine stirred up the author to write and to warn the faithful Christians against the danger. The author cites important examples of defection in the O. T. and the result, notably the defection of the Israelites when they came up out of Egypt; defection among angelic beings, evidently in connection with the flood (vs. 6) and the apostasy of Sodom and Gomorrah. Jude gives an eloquent and impassioned polemic against the apostate teachers (vs. 8-19). He concludes his Epistle with comfort to Christians by reminding them of their first duty. The date is undeterminable; any time from 66 A. D. to 75-80 A. D. could be possible. It is commonly dated around 75 A. D. by Zahn, and others.

5. The Outline.

Introduction, vs. 1, 2

Part I. The Occasion of the Letter: The Apostasy, vs. 3, 4

Part II. Historical Examples of Apostasy vs. 5-7

1. Of Israel, vs. 5
2. Of angelic beings, vs. 6
3. Of Sodom and Gomorrah, vs. 7

Part III. Description of False Teachers, vs. 8-13

Part IV. Authoritative Declarations of God's Judgment of the Wicked, vs. 14-19

Part V. Encouragement of True Believers and Their Full Duty to Christ, vs. 20-23

1. Edification and prayer in the Holy Spirit, vs. 20
2. Preservation in the love of God and expectation of Divine mercy, vs. 21
3. Exhortation to soul winning, vs. 22, 23

Conclusion: Benediction, vs. 24, 25

M. F. U.

257. Mount of Temptation, Judean Wilderness

Jude'a (jōō-dē'å), the name of the southernmost Roman division of Palestine. Judea is very small, for if you include the whole maritime plain and the desert, it does not amount to more than two thousand square miles. But it never included the whole of the plain. Apart from the Shephelah and the plain, Judea was fifty-five miles long, from Bethlehem to Beersheba, and from twenty-five to thirty miles broad, about one thousand three hundred and fifty square miles, of which nearly one half was desert. On the east was the Jordan and its valley, and, coming west, the desert, then the "hill country," then the Shephelah (or low hills), and, finally, the maritime plain. On the north Judea was bounded by Samaria, and on the south by the desert.

The wilderness of Judea extends from the beach of the Dead Sea to the very edge of the central plateau (or hill country), thus obliging travelers from the east to journey for from five to eight hours through a waterless desert. Three well-watered spots are on its eastern edge, Jericho, 'Ain Feshkah (ten miles to the south), and 'Ain Jidi (or Engedi, eighteen miles farther). From Jericho there start into Judea three roads, from 'Ain Feshkah one, and from Engedi one. The roads from Jericho run northwest to Ai and Beth-el, southwest to Jerusalem, and south southwest to the lower Kedron and Bethlehem. Just after this last crosses the Kedron it is joined by the road

from 'Ain Feshkah. The road from Engedi breaks into two branches, one running northwest to Bethlehem and Jerusalem, a wild and difficult road, never used by caravans, the other branch turns southwest to Yuttah and Hebron.

Smith (*Hist. Geog.*, p. 310) says that the three features of Judea's geography which are most significant in her history are, "her pastoral character, her neighborhood to the desert, her singular unsuitableness for the growth of a great city." Two, at least, of the prophets were born in face of the wilderness of Judea—Amos at Tekoah, and Jeremiah at Anathoth. The wilderness was the scene of David's refuge from Saul; here John the Baptist prepared for his mission, and here our Lord suffered his temptation.

Although physically the most barren and awkward, Judea was morally the most famous and powerful of the provinces of Syria. Her character and history are thus summed up: "At all times in which the powers of spiritual initiative or expansion were needed, she was lacking, and so in the end came her shame. But when the times required concentration, indifference to the world, loyalty to the past, and passionate patriotism, then Judea took the lead, or stood alone in Israel, and these virtues even rendered brilliant the hopeless, insane struggles of her end. Judea was the seat of the one enduring dynasty of Israel, the site of their temple, the platform of their chief prophets. After their great exile they rallied round her capital, and centuries later they expended upon her fortresses the last efforts of their freedom. It is, therefore, not wonderful that they should have won from it the name which is now more frequent than either their ancestral designation of Hebrews or their sacred title of Israel" (Smith, *Hist. Geog.*, pp. 259, 260).

Judge. For judge in the general sense of magistrate, *see* Law, Administration of.

Judges, the. There is a restricted sense of the word *judge*, in which it means that officer who presided over the affairs of the Hebrews in the period between Joshua and the accession of Saul.

1. Age of the Judges. "In those days there was no king in Israel, but every man did that which was right in his own eyes" (Judg. 17:6; 18:1; 19:25). This sentence, frequently and earnestly repeated, gives us the keynote of the whole Book of Judges. Each tribe took thought for itself how best to secure and maintain an adequate territory, so that separate interests of all sorts soon became prevalent, and regard for the general welfare was more and more forgotten. This separation of the parts of the nation was aided by the early disunion and jealousies of the several tribes, no one of which held the preeminence. The consequences of this internal discord were so threatening that it became a very grave question whether the nation would be able to hold even the soil on which its peculiar religion and culture were to attain their full development. Then, too, the ancient inhabitants still retained their hold on large tracts, or on important positions throughout the country. The neighboring powers still looked upon the newcomers as an easy prey to incursion and devastation, if not to actual subjugation. Nor did Israel escape the pernicious influence of idolatry, both of Canaan and the surrounding countries. The following is the review of the period of the judges: The children of Israel did evil against Jehovah, though he had manifested special favor to them; he sold them into the hand of this enemy or that; they cried to him in their trouble; he raised up a deliverer who saved them; the land had rest; again they

sinned; and again the same cycle was repeated.

2. **The Judges.** Under the circumstances mentioned above the people were left an easy prey to idolatrous influences; they seemed incapable of grasping the idea of a divine and invisible King; therefore God allowed them judges in the persons of faithful men, who acted, for the most part, as agents of the divine will, regents of the invisible King, holding their commission directly from him or with his sanction. They would thus be more

258.

inclined to act as dependent vassals of Jehovah than kings, who would naturally have notions of independent rights and royal privileges. In this greater dependence of the judges upon the divine King we see the secret of their institution. As to the nature of the office it appears to have resembled that of the Roman dictator, to which it has been compared, with this exception, that the dictator laid down his power as soon as the crisis which had called for its exercise had passed away; but the Hebrew judge remained invested with his high authority during life (I Sam. 4:18; 7:15). Sometimes these judges commenced their career with military exploits, but this was not always the case. Eli and Samuel were not military men; Deborah judged Israel before she planned the war against Jabin; and of Jair, Ibzan, Elon, and Abdon, it is at least uncertain whether they ever held any military command. The origin of their authority must in all cases be traced ultimately to Jehovah, owing to the very nature of the theocracy (II Sam. 7:7), yet this did not prevent differences of detail in the manner of their appointment. In Judg. 2:16 it is distinctly stated that "the Lord *raised up* judges" (comp. 3:10; 6:34; 11:29; 13:25). One, Barak, was named by a prophetess, who was herself acknowledged as a judge of Israel (4:5, 6). Of others it is simply said that they *arose* (10:1, 3), while Jephthah furnishes a clear instance of *popular election* (10:18; 11:5, 6).

3. **Name and Function.** The name in Hebrew is the participle of *shäphät, to judge, pronounce* judgment. The judges were men (excepting Deborah) who procured justice or right for the people of Israel, not only by delivering them from the power of their enemies but also by administering the laws and rites of the Lord (Judg. 2:16-19). *Judging* in this sense was different from the administration of civil jurisprudence, and included the idea of government such as would be expected from a king (see I Sam. 8:5, 6; II Kings 15:5). Alongside with the extraordinary rule of the judges, the ordinary administration of justice and government of the commonwealth still remained in the hands of the heads of the tribes and the elders of the people.

4. **Chronology of the Period.** The following is the data of this period as we find it in the Book of Judges:

	YEARS
1. Oppression by Cushan-rishathaim (3:8)....	8
Deliverance by Othniel and rest (3:9-12)...	40
2. Oppression by the Moabites (3:14).........	18
Deliverance by Ehud and rest (3:15-13)....	80
Shamgar as judge (3:31).....................	
3. Oppression by King Jabin (4:2, 3).........	20
Deliverance by Deborah and Barak and rest (4:4-5:31)...............................	40
4. Oppression by the Midianites (6:1)........	7
Deliverance by Gideon and rest (6:2-8:28)..	40
Abimelech's reign (9:22)...................	3
Tola, judge (10:1, 2)......................	23
Jair, judge (10:3)........................	22
5. Oppression by the Ammonites (10:8)......	18
Deliverance by Jephthah, judge (11:1-12:7).	6
Ibzan, judge (12:8-10)....................	7
Elon, judge (12:11, 12)...................	10
Abdon, judge (12:13-15)..................	8
6. Oppression by the Philistines (13:1)........	40
Samson judged Israel during this period (15:20; 16:31) twenty years................	
Total............................	390

If we add to this:

(a) The time of Joshua, not distinctly mentioned................................	20
(b) The time of Eli, judge (I Sam. 4:18)......	40
	450

And adding still further:

(c) The times of Samuel and Saul combined..	40
(d) The reign of David (II Sam. 5:4; I Kings 2:11)..................................	40
(e) The reign of Solomon to the building of the temple (I Kings 6:1)..................	3

The whole time from the entrance of Israel into Canaan to the building of the temple.....	533
Add forty years for wandering in the desert, and we have..................................	573

But according to I Kings 6:1, the temple was built in the four hundred and eightieth year after the Israelites left Egypt. The apostle Paul says: "And after that he gave unto them judges about the space of four hundred and fifty years, until Samuel the prophet" (Acts 13:20). There can be but little doubt that some of the rulers were contemporaneous, which would greatly reduce the length of the period. *See* Chronology, History, Old Testament.

Judges, Book of. The book of the O. T. which carries on the history of God's chosen people through the era intervening from the death of Joshua (c. B. C. 1375) to the era of Samuel (c. B. C. 1075), a period of roughly three centuries.

1. **Purpose.** The Book of Judges aims to demonstrate that defection from Jehovah incurs severe punishment and servitude. Only by turning back to God can restoration be enjoyed. Thus the judges were charismatic leaders, raised up by God to deliver His theocratic people. Only by heeding their Spirit-directed message and following them in deliverance against their enemies could restoration be accomplished. The O. T. judges performed two functions. By divine power and Spirit-anointed leadership they delivered the people from enemy oppression. Having accomplished this, they ruled over them and administered government in the name of Israel's God. In their governmental capacity they correspond roughly to the *shufetim* of Phoenicia and the *sufetes* of Carthage who, were akin to the Roman consuls. (See Zellig Harris, *A Grammar of Phoenician Language*, New Haven, 1936). The events illustrating the spiritual principle of restoration upon repentance are selective. Often they are coeval rather than chronological in sequence. Evidently long periods are passed over without comment. Quite a few of the judges are mentioned by name only, without any word of their particular deliverance. Since the book reports seven apostasies, seven servitudes to seven heathen nations, and seven deliverances, it is evidently put in a symmetrical form. A parallel in church history is found in the professing church since the apostolic age, in which the rise of numerous sects and the forfeited sense of the unity of the Spirit and of one body appear.

2. **Critical View of Literary Composition and Date.** The prevailing literary view of Judges, while not intimately connected with Pentateuchal criticism, is built on many of the same fallacies. It construes the book of Judges as a collection of old hero tales which were taken from two chief sources denominated J

and E. These two documentary strata were supposed to have been fused in the latter half of the seventh century B. C. into one with a few small additions, such as the minor judges, to form substantially the present book (10:1-5; 12:8-15). A Deuteronomist somewhat later supposedly gave a pragmatic religious interpretation to the whole which, according to Julius Bewer, (*The Literature of the O. T.*, N. Y., 1933, p. 230) was "distorted and wrong" from "an historical point of view." It is also maintained that the book did not attain its precise present form until around 200 B. C.

3. **Conservative View of Literary Composition and Date.** The evidence of the book itself coupled with tradition on the other hand, indicates that it was written sometime during the early years of the Hebrew monarchy, probably in the era of Saul around 1020 B. C. Samuel, as a member of the prophetic school, may well have been the author-compiler. This is supported by the following evidence: (1) The author was undoubtedly a compiler to a large extent. This is necessitated by the simple consideration that the events extended over several centuries. The compiler, for example, selected the prose account of the deliverance of Deborah (chap. 4) and the early poem, The Song of Deborah, in chap. 5. More prominence was accorded the stories of Gideon and Samson. This is evidently explained by their high didactic value. (2) The book displays a unity of one author-editor. Its symmetrical development and unified plan are the result of the early influence of the book of Deuteronomy as a genuine Mosaic composition. In this important book blessing in Canaan is promised on the terms of obedience to the divine law and punishment is threatened upon the breaking of it (Deut. 28:1-68). Critics who reject the Mosaic authenticity of Deuteronomy explain this intense pragmatic interpretation as the work of a so-called Deuteronomistic Work of History (cf. Aage Bentzen, *O. T. Intr.*, ii, p. 87), but this is the result of an unsound assumption and a false view of the date and genuineness of the book of Deuteronomy. (3) The book evidently belongs to the period of Saul (cf. the statement in Judges 1:21 that "the Jebusites dwell with the children of Benjamin in Jerusalem until this day." This notice could not have been penned after David's conquest of Zion in the seventh year of his reign (c. 996 B. C.; II Sam. 5:6-8). The statement "in those days there was no king in Israel (Judg. 17:6; 18:1; 19:1; 21:25) points to the early period of the monarchy. (4) Hebrew tradition names Samuel as the author. The internal evidence and Hebrew tradition lend their voice to a position which is defended by many Christian conservative scholars. For critical views see G. F. Moore, *Int'l. Crit. Commentary*, 1895; and C. F. Burney, *The Book of Judges with introduction and notes*, 2nd ed., London, 1920; Otto Eissfelt, *Die Quellen des Richterbuches*, Leipzig, 1925; J. Garstang, *Joshua: Judges*, London, 1937.

4. **Outline.**

Part I. Introduction to the Period, 1:1-2:5

  1. Political conditions, 1:1-36

  2. Religious conditions, 2:1-5

Part II. The Period of the Judges, 2:6-16:31

  1. Religious condition of the entire period, 2:6-3:6

  2. The Judges:

    a. Othniel, 3:7-11

    b. Ehud, 3:12-30

    c. Shamgar, 3:31

    d. Deborah and Barak, 4:1-5:31

    e. Gideon and Abimelech, 6:1-9:57

    f. Tola, 10:1, 2

    g. Jair, 10:3-5

    h. Jephthah, 10:6-12:7

    i. Ibzan, 12:8-10

    j. Elon, 12:11, 12

    k. Abdon, 12:13-15

    l. Samson, 13:1-16:31

Part III. The Double Appendix, 17:1-21:25

  1. The idolatry of Micah and the Danites, 17:1-18:31

  2. The crime at Gibeah and its punishment, 19:1-21:25

M. F. U.

Judgment. In this article we treat of judgment: 1. Right of private; 2. Judgments of men; 3. Judgments of God; and 4. Judgment, the final.

1. **Judgment, Right of Private.** The matters in question at this point relate:

(1) To the right of individuals to interpret the Scriptures for themselves, or to form their own judgments as to the meaning of the Scriptures. This is an issue principally between Roman Catholics and Protestants. It is asserted by the Roman Church that the Church is the divinely authorized and infallible interpreter of Scripture revelation. It is admitted that many questions of details in connection with the study of the Bible should be left to scientific research. But still it is held that in all controversies with respect to the meaning of particular passages, also that, as to the general doctrine of the Scriptures the decision of the Church is final. The only course that is safe or right for the people is to submit unreservedly to the judgment of the Church. In opposition to this Protestants generally hold that the Bible is a book for the people. It is God's message to be received and read, and, in its great general meaning, to be apprehended directly by the people themselves. The prophets of the Old Testament spoke to the people. The gospels and the epistles were for popular use and instruction. And while parts of Holy Scripture are difficult or impossible to understand without skilled interpretation, still the truth essential to salvation is within the reach of all. Christ has not appointed any class or body of men in the Church as interpreters of the Scriptures in any such sense as to make their interpretation final or supreme before the conscience and intelligence of the people. The responsibility for religious faith and conduct belongs to the individual. He has not the right to submit himself blindly in these respects to the guidance of others. It is to be maintained, however, that everyone is bound to exercise diligence and to use all proper means for the right understanding of moral truth, to pay respect to the judgment of those wiser than himself, and especially to pay heed to those interpretations of the Scriptures which have generally prevailed, or have been uni-

versal, in the history of the Christian Church.

(2) The place of private judgment in Churches not professing infallibility. The claim of the Church of Rome to infallibility covers not only the interpretation of Scripture, but other matters resting professedly upon tradition, with respect to which the Church has rendered formal decision. Protestants meet this twofold assumption with their historic watchword, "The Bible the only and sufficient rule of faith and practice." And yet the extent to which private judgment may be rightfully exercised in Protestant Churches is a question by no means settled. At the one extreme are those who hold that the Church should present very few, if any, doctrinal tests of membership; that reliance should be placed upon vigorous Christian institutions as most likely to lead to a real and general Christian belief. This is the view of the Broad Church party in the Church of England and others of so-called liberal tendencies. At the other extreme are those who would impose upon the membership of Protestant Churches not only a detailed system of doctrine, but also ethical regulations which are not supported by the Scriptures. With this is asserted strictly the obligation of membership in these Churches. The more moderate position is that Churches for their very existence must have a basis of general doctrine which rests unmistakably upon the Scriptures, and must prescribe a line of conduct resting upon the same authority. The difficulties, both theoretical and practical, grow out of a lack of proper conception of the Church and of the Churches. For discussion of this we refer to the article in this work, *Church.*

(3) The liberty of private judgment in relation to the state. Civil government is clearly recognized by the Scriptures as resting upon divine authority. Obedience to the state may therefore be said, in general terms, to be a divine requirement (see Rom. 12:1-5; I Pet. 2:13-15). But it is equally clear that in order to exact justly obedience from citizens or subjects the state must confine its action within its proper sphere. The function of the state is to protect life and property, and to preserve social order. When civil government attempts to enforce assent to religious doctrines, or to enact laws which require disobedience to the commandments of God, then the right of private judgment must be asserted. "We ought to obey God rather than men." There are other cases, into which we cannot here enter, in which a perversion or abuse of civil power must be met by the exercise of individual conscience. This is a principle, nevertheless, which in a free and popular government needs to be carefully guarded. For discussion of this point, see Hodge, *Systematic Theology,* vol. iii, p. 356-360; Lieber, *Political Ethics.*

2. **Judgments of Men.** The Scriptures recognize it to be necessary that, under proper limitations, men should form and express judgments relative to their fellow-men.

(1) There is the necessity of private, unofficial judgment. We must constantly form estimates of the conduct and character of others for our own guidance and safety and usefulness. "By their fruits ye shall know them."

The prohibition of judging, in Matt. 7:1, is not opposed to this, as must be seen in vers. 6, 7 of the same chapter. We are forbidden to usurp God's place as judge; also to pass rash and unjust and uncharitable and needless judgments.

(2) It is also necessary that men should judge officially. Human government is divinely authorized. And the exercise of judicial functions is essential to all government. All judges, however, are to remember that they are subject to the judgment of God, and to exercise their office equitably and with due moderation. (see Rom. 13:1-5; I Pet. 2:13, 14).

Judgments, the. Theologians have often maintained that there is one general judgment. This is a tenet strongly intrenched in Christian theology. But a careful inductive study of all the Scriptures involved demonstrates that there are at least eight distinct judgments described in the Bible.

1. **The Judgment of the Cross.** This is the judgment upon sin effected by Christ when He said "It is finished" (John 19:30). It is the basis of the believer's salvation when he believes. Christ has borne the sinner's guilt and as a substitute for all on behalf of whom He died, sin has been judged. In the Person of the Divine Substitute, the one who believes on Christ has been hailed to court, sentenced to condemnation and executed in the Person of his Substitute (John 5:24; Rom. 8:1; Gal. 3:13; Heb. 9:26-28; I Pet. 2:24).

2. **The Judgment of Believers.** This takes the form of divine correction and chastisement (I Cor. 11:30-32; Heb. 12:3-15; John 15:1-9). The Apostle says: "If we would judge ourselves, we should not be judged, but when we are judged, we are chastened of the Lord that we might not be condemned with the world" (I Cor. 11:31, 32). This, then, involves God's disciplinary action against a sinning saint. "The sin unto death" (I John 5:16 cf. I Cor. 5:1-5; Acts 5:1-11) occurs when the believer, through deliberate continued sin brings reproach upon the name of Christ and upon his salvation by free grace, forfeits his physical life "that his spirit might be saved in the Day of the Lord Jesus."

3. **The Believer's Works.** This judgment concerns only Christians and it is not a matter of judgment for sins which have been judged at the cross and with which the believer will not be faced again (John 5:24; Rom. 8:1), but involves the Divine appraisal of the Christian's works and service. This will entail reward or loss of reward (II Cor. 5:10; Rom. 14:10; Eph. 6:8; II Tim. 4:8). *See* Judgment seat of Christ.

4. **The Judgment of Self.** This is referred to in I Cor. 11:31, 32. It has reference to stern criticism of a Christian of his own ways with accommodation to the divine will and immediate confession of and turning away from all sin (I John 1:7-9). True confession is equivalent to self-judgment and involves immediate cleansing and restoration to fellowship and "walking in the light."

5. **Judgment of the Nations.** This judgment is referred to in Matt. 25:31-46. It involves the Divine dealing with the nations on the basis of their treatment of Israel. The

"goat" nations on the left hand involve those peoples who are sent to the lake of fire. The "sheep" nations on the right hand enter the millennial kingdom. The peculiar basis of this judgment is the way all nations have dealt with Israel during the tribulation period preceding the Second Advent of Christ. O. T. prophecy is clear in its prediction that some Gentile nations will enter the coming kingdom of Israel (cf. Isa. 60:3; 61:6; 62:2). These nations will be subordinate to Israel. As the millennial state merges into the eternal state, Gentile nations are still asserted to be on the earth when the heavenly Jerusalem descends from heaven (Rev. 21:24, 26).

6. **The Judgment of Israel.** Ezek. 20:33-44 gives clear teaching that Israel must come into judgment before being restored in the millennial kingdom. This O. T. teaching has confirmation in the N. T. from the Parable of the Ten Virgins (Matt. 25:1-13) (See Joel 3:11-15). Prophecy seems to teach that there will be a general resurrection of all truly regenerated Israelites of the past dispensation to be judged. Those who had a kingdom hope are to arise and enter the earthly glory (cf. Ezek. 37:1-14; Dan. 12:1-3).

7. **The Judgment of Angels.** These are fallen angels and are evidently judged in connection with the Great White Throne (I Cor. 6:3; II Pet. 2:4; Jude 1:6; Rev. 20:10).

8. **The White Throne Judgment.** This last great assize comprehends the judgment of all unsaved of all ages (Rev. 20:11-15). The basis will be works, which evidently suggests differences and degrees of punishment. All who are not found in "the book of life" are cast into "the lake of fire." This is called "the second death," which means final and complete cutting off from God's presence and a sin-cleansed universe.

For theologians who object to these various judgments, a simple choice must be made of following traditional theology or the plain teachings of the Scripture inductively formulated. The present author considers that the doctrine of a general judgment is incompatible with inductive logic in handling the Scriptures.
M. F. U.

259. Interior, Pilate's Judgment Hall

Judgment Hall (Gr. *praitōrion*, "headquarters" in a Roman camp; the palace of a governor). The Greek word pretorium is so rendered in Mark 15:16; in Matt. 27:27 it is given in the A. V. as *common hall;* in Phil. 1:13, *palace;* in John 18:28, *hall of judgment;* and in the same

verse; John 18:33; 19:9; Acts 23:35, *judgment hall.*

1. In John 18:28, 33; 29:9, it is the residence which Pilate occupied when he visited Jerusalem. The site of Pilate's pretorium in Jerusalem has given rise to much dispute, some supposing it to be the palace of King Herod, others the tower of Antonia; but it has been shown elsewhere that the latter was probably the pretorium, which was then and long afterward the citadel of Jerusalem.

2. In Acts 23:35 Herod's judgment hall, or pretorium, in Caesarea, was doubtless a part of that magnificent range of buildings the erection of which by King Herod is described in Josephus.

3. The word "palace," or "Caesar's court," in the A. V. of Phil. 1:13, is a translation of the same word, pretorium. It may here have denoted the quarter of that detachment of the pretorian guards which was in immediate attendance upon the emperor, and had barracks in Mount Palatine.

Judgment Seat (Gr. *bēma,* a *step*), a raised place mounted by steps; used of the official seat of a judge (Matt. 27:19; John 19:13; Acts 18:12, 16, sq.; 25:6); of the judgment seat of Christ (Rom. 14:10; II Cor. 5:10); of the structure, resembling a throne, which Herod built in the theater at Caesarea, and from which he used to view the games and make speeches to the people (Acts 12:21).

Judgment Seat of Christ. This assize is spoken of in II Cor. 5:10: "For we must all appear before the judgment seat of Christ; that everyone may receive the things done in his body, according to that he hath done, whether it be good or bad." The manifestation of the believer's works is in question in this judgment. It is most emphatically not a judgment of the believer's sins. These have been fully atoned for in the vicarious and substitutionary death of Christ, and "remembered no more forever" (Heb. 10:17). It is quite necessary, however, that the service of every child of God must be definitely scrutinized and evaluated (Matt. 12:36; Rom. 14:10; Gal. 6:7; Eph. 6:8; Col. 3:24, 25). As a result of this judgment of the believer's works, there will be "reward" or "loss" of reward. In any eventuality, the truly-born-again believer will be saved (I Cor. 3:11-15). The judgment seat, literally *bema,* is evidently set up in heaven previous to Christ's glorious Second Advent to establish His earth-rule in the millennial kingdom (Matt. 16:27; I Cor. 4:15; II Tim. 4:8; Rev. 22:12). The out-taking of the church, according to I Thess. 4:13-18; I Cor. 15:51-58, must first be fulfilled. The judgment seat of Christ is necessary for the appointment of places of rulership and authority with Christ in His role of "King of Kings and Lord of Lords" at His revelation in power and glory.
M. F. U.

Judgments of God. *See* Judgments, the.

Judicial Blindness.

1. The Bible speaks of three types of blindness: physical, spiritual and judicial. Instances of physical blindness appear in Scripture (John 9:25). Jesus often healed physical blindness in His earthly ministry. In John 9:29-41

physical blindness and its cure portrays judicial blindness and its cure.

2. Spiritual Blindness. Spiritual blindness is that state affecting truth. "But if our gospel be hid it is hid to them that are lost: in whom the god of this world hath blinded the eyes of them that believe not, lest the light of the glorious gospel of Christ, Who is the image of God, should shine unto them (II Cor. 4:3, 4). Numerous scriptures portray the unsaved as blinded and held under the power of Satan (John 8:44; Col. 1:13; Eph. 2:1, 2). Salvation involves the taking away of this Satanic veil. Spiritual blindness also extends to carnal Christians. Yielding to sin on the part of a believer, or failing to walk by the Spirit, involves diminution of spiritual perception: "And I, brethren, could not speak unto you as spiritual but unto carnal, even as unto babes in Christ" (I Cor. 3:1). The correction of blindness in the carnal believer can only be brought about by a separation from carnality and his yielding to the Holy Spirit (I Cor. 2:6-16).

3. Judicial Blindness. This phase of blindness or hardness of heart is characteristic of the nation Israel as a result of its rejection of Messiah. It extends throughout the entire Christian age since the crucifixion of Christ. In Rom. 11:1-5 the Apostle describes Israelites as under a double election, the national election and their individual election. He points out that nationally they have been temporarily set aside but that through individual election of grace when the present age of the outcalling of the Church is completed, Israel will be brought into judgment, refined and restored to its national election. For this reason Israel's blindness is described by the Apostle to be "in part" (Rom. 11:25), thus indicating the remnant of Israel who will be saved in this present age and who become members of the Church, the body of Christ. Judicial blindness of Israel is implied in such great scriptures as Jer. 31:35-37; Isa. 6:9, 10; Mark 4:12; Luke 8:10; Acts 28:26, 27; John 12:37-41. We are told in II Cor. 3:14-16 that a covering is upon the heart of the understanding of Jews "when Moses is read." However, when the nation shall turn to the Lord "the veil shall be taken away." The difficult problem is, that although Scripture declares that for their own national sins they are nationally blinded, yet not all of them are blinded, and only partially so for the period of the outcalling of the Church. The Apostle says: "For I would not, brethren, that you should be ignorant of this mystery, lest you should be wise in your own conceits; that blindness in part is happened to Israel, until the fullness of the Gentiles be come in. And so shall all Israel be saved; as it is written, there shall come out of Sion the Deliverer, and shall turn away ungodliness from Jacob: for this is my covenant unto them, when I shall take away their sins" (Rom. 11:25-27).

M. F. U.

Ju′dith (jōō′dĭth; *Jewess*), the daughter of Beeri, the Hittite, and one of Esau's two wives (Gen. 26:34). She is elsewhere called *Aholibamah* (q. v.).

Ju′lia (jōō′lĭ-á; feminine of *Julius*), a female disciple at Rome to whom Paul sent salutations (Rom. 16:15).

Ju′lius (jōō′lĭ-ŭs), the centurion who conducted Paul to Rome. At Sidon he allowed Paul to visit his friends, and treated him courteously throughout the voyage (Acts 27: 1, 3, 43), A. D. 62.

Ju′nia (jōō′nĭ-á) or rather **Ju′nias** (jōō′nĭ-ás), a Christian at Rome to whom Paul sent a salutation in connection with Andronicus as "kinsmen and fellow-prisoners, who are of note among the apostles, who also were in Christ before" himself (Rom. 16:7), A. D. 60. From his calling them kinsmen it is supposed that they were of Jewish extraction.

Juniper. *See* Vegetable Kingdom.

Ju′piter (jōō′pĭ-tĕr), the supreme god of the Romans, Greek Zeus. *See* Gods, False.

Ju′shab-He′sed (jōō′shăb-hē′sĕd; *returner of kindness*), according to some, the son of Pedaiah (I Chron. 3:20); but according to Keil (*Com.*, in loc.) the last named of the sons of Zerubbabel. Keil thinks that the two groups of sons (vers. 19, 20) are mentioned separately because they had different mothers.

Justice, in Ethics, is a term of comprehensive meaning. It refers to both disposition and conduct. For various Hebrew and Greek words rendered justice or righteousness in the Scriptures, we refer to Young's or Strong's *Concordance*. The Latin word "*justitia*" is defined by Cicero as "*animi affectio suum cuique tribuens*" (*De Finibus*, v, 23, 65). This definition he expands elsewhere so as to have justice include religion, filial affection, fidelity, lenity in moderating punishment, and kindly benevolence (*Partitiones Orat.*, 22, 78). Thus the term is used in a general sense for "what is right, or as it should be." The New Testament conception of justice thoroughly accords with this. Justice is not only respect for the rights of one's fellow-men, as of life, property, and reputation. In the broadest sense it includes the proper recognition of man's duty toward God. It begins with that (see Matt. 22:21, 37, 38, and many other places). With respect to man's relation to man, it includes several details often forgotten as items of justice. Thus charity or love is an obligation of righteousness (Rom. 13:8). Thus respect for human nature is enjoined in the precept "Honor all men" (I Pet. 2:17). Thus also courtesy and hospitality (I Pet. 3:8; 4:9). In short, man in his relation to man is to reflect the justice or righteousness of God; with the exception, considered below, that man, as an individual, is not to administer retributive justice. The public administration is a most important part of social ethics, and, as just noted, entirely distinct from the ethics of individual life. Here it is to be borne in mind that in human courts where just laws are properly administered, are reflections, at least, of the distributive justice, that is divine (*see* Judgments of Men). The judicial function of the state, must however, be confined within its proper limits, taking cognizance of only external conduct, and this so far as it relates to the protection of life, property, reputation, and social order. And yet justice is not to be administered merely upon grounds of social expediency but because it is justice (*see* Punishment). *E. McC.*

Justice of God (Heb. *ṣĕdĕk, right, rightness*). In theology, as in the Scriptures, the terms justice and righteousness are used synonymously. The justice of God is both an essential and a relative attribute of the divine existence. It is a necessary outflow from the holiness of God. It is that in positive form which is negatively described as holiness, or separateness from evil. And, further, it is the holiness of God as manifested and applied in moral government. *See* Holiness of God.

The justice or righteousness of God is proclaimed emphatically in the Scriptures of the Old and New Testaments (e. g., Gen. 18:25; Psa. 11:7; John 17:25; Heb. 6:10). In accordance with the Scripture, divine justice, i. e., perfect justice, is everywhere in the divine administration. God is the righteous Governor of the wold. His laws are equitable and practicable. This is legislative or rectoral justice. God is also the righteous Judge. The sentences he pronounces, the rewards he bestows, the penalties he inflicts, are all righteous. This is the judicial or distributive justice (see Deut. 32:3, 4; Psa. 36:6; 19:7-10; 119:142; 97:2; Isa. 33:22; Acts 10:34; Rom. 2:11; Rev. 15:3; 16:7, et al.).

The relation of the justice to the grace of God cannot be considered here fully. It should be remarked, however, that the revelation of his highest grace in Christ was "to declare his righteousness" (Rom. 3:25, 26; *see* Grace; Atonement). Also the rewards graciously apportioned to the eternally saved vary in measure, and have respect to the individual character and deeds of those who receive them (*see* Judgment, the Final). The righteousness or justice of God, also like his holiness, is communicable to men. It is the work of divine grace to impart to men rightness by renewal "in righteousness and true holiness" (Eph. 4: 23, 24; Isa. 46:13; 51:5; 56:1; Rom. 10:3). *See* Image of God.

There is no warrant for the statement that the Old Testament magnifies the justice of God more than does the New. The New Testament brings to light most distinctly the economy of grace, by no means lost sight of in the Old. But, at the same time, it reveals most fully the triumph of the righteous kingdom of God, culminating in the final judgment.—*E. McC.*

Justification. Justification is a divine act whereby an infinitely Holy God judicially declares a believing sinner to be righteous and acceptable before Him because Christ has borne the sinner's sin on the cross, and "has been made unto him righteousness" (I Cor. 1:30; Rom. 3:24). Justification springs from the fountain of God's grace (Titus 3:4-5). It is operative as the result of the redemptive and propitiatory sacrifice of Christ, Who has settled all the claims of the law (Rom. 3:24, 25; 5:9). Justification is on the basis of faith and not by human merit or works (Rom. 3:28-30; 4:5; 5:1; Gal. 2:16). In this marvelous operation of God the infinitely Holy Judge judicially declares righteous the one who believes in Jesus (Rom. 8:31-34). A justified believer emerges from God's great court room with a consciousness that Another, his Substitute, has borne his guilt, and that he stands without accusation before the bar of God (Rom. 8:1, 33, 34). Justification makes no one righteous, neither is it the bestowment of righteousness as such but rather declares one to be justified whom God sees as perfected once and forever in His Beloved Son. As Lewis Sperry Chafer says; "Therefore, this may be stated as the correct formula of justification: The sinner becomes righteous in God's sight when he is in Christ: he is justified by God freely, all without a cause, because thereby he is righteous in His sight" (*Systematic Theology*, vii, p. 222). *M. F. U.*

2. Historical. Throughout the whole history of this doctrine the principal point of difference and dispute has been as to whether faith is the only condition of justification, or whether good works in connection with faith are also to be regarded as an instrumental cause. Upon this question opinion has run to opposite extremes—those of Antinomianism and the doctrine of penances and works of supererogation. A chief cause of error has been an undue magnifying of the intellectual element in faith at the expense of the element that is moral and practical. Even in the earliest days of Christianity the tendency was manifest to regard faith as merely a mental assent to Christian doctrine. The possessor of such faith deemed himself as having fully met the Gospel requirement, though regardless of the claims of Christian service, and even of ordinary morality. Passages in the epistles of St. Paul and St. James were written to correct this Antinomian error (e. g., Rom. 6:1; Gal. 5:16-25; James 2:14-26). Partly as a recoil from this error the demand arose that, in addition to good works as evidences of true faith in believers, the sins of believers should be expiated by penances. And still further came in a false idea of the character of good works. Instead of the clear recognition of the only relative and imperfect character of the righteousness of even the best Christians, the distinction was made between the divine commands and the divine counsels, and the belief obtained footing that by keeping both men might do more than meet the divine requirements. Thus the scriptural doctrine of justification by faith became, to a considerable extent, beclouded in the early period of the history of the Church. The abuses which later became prevalent in the Roman Catholic Church through the failure to maintain the Scripture conception of faith and through the false conception of good works, are well known. Without entering in detail into the views of this, or of the Greek Church, it must suffice us to emphasize the fact that the rescuing of the Scripture doctrine upon this subject, largely, though not wholly, lost sight of for a long time, was the work of the reformation of the 16th century. Justification by faith is a fundamental doctrine of Protestant and evangelical Christianity. It stands opposed to those rationalistic conceptions of sin, and the attitude of God toward it, which reduce justification to a nullity, and to those views of Christian merit, cherished by Romanism, which derogate from the efficacy of Christ's atonement, and at the same time it holds before men the great hope of the Gospel, and lays deep the foundation of Christian morality. *E. McC.* revised by *M. F. U.*

Jus'tus (jŭs'tŭs; *just*).

1. The surname of Joseph, called also Barsabas, who, with Matthias, was selected by the apostles as candidates for the place made vacant by the apostasy of Judas Iscariot (Acts 1:23).

2. A disciple living at Corinth, in whose house, near the synagogue, Paul preached to the Gentiles (Acts 18:7), B. C. 54.

3. Called also Jesus, a Jewish Christian, named in connection with Mark by Paul, as being his "only fellow-workers" at Rome when he wrote to the Colossians (Col. 4:11), B. C. 64.

Jut'tah (jŭt'á; *inclined*), a Levitical city in the mountains of Judah (Josh. 15:55; 21:16). It was allotted to the priests, but in the catalogue (I Chron. 6:57-59) the name has escaped. It is supposed to have been the residence of Zacharias and Elizabeth, and the birthplace of John the Baptist (Luke 1:39). It is doubtless, the present *Jutta*, or *Jitta*, about five miles S. of Hebron.

K

Kab'zeel (kăb'zê-ĕl; *God has gathered*), a city in the south of Judah, the birthplace of Benaiah (Josh. 15:21; II Sam. 23:20; I Chron. 11:22). In Neh. 11:25 it is called *Jekabzeel* (*q. v.*).

Ka'desh (kā'dĕsh; *consecrated*), more fully **Ka'-desh-Bar'nea** (kā'dĕsh-bär'nê-å), a spot where the Israelites twice encamped while journeying from Egypt to Palestine, being their nineteenth and thirty-seventh station. Its original name would seem to have been *Rithmah* (*q. v.*), becoming Kadesh when the tabernacle rested there; *En-Mishpat* (*q. v.*), "Fountain of Judgment," when judgment was passed upon the Israelites; and *Meribah* (*q. v.*) when it was the place of murmuring and strife.

From Kadesh-barnea Moses sent messengers to explore the promised land, and, returning, they made their report. The people rebelled, and even went so far as to choose a captain to lead them back to Egypt (Num. 14:4). In consequence Kadesh, the *sanctuary*, became En-Mishpat, a "Fountain of Judgment," when the rebellious people were sentenced to complete forty years of wandering. Israel determined to obtain possession of Canaan (14:39, 40), and pushed into the "south country" (the Negeb), i. e., the high land between the desert and Canaan proper. They were, however, defeated by the Amorites (Deut. 1:44) and the Amalekites (Num. 14:45).

1. **Scripture References.** The first mention of Kadesh-barnea is in connection with the devastating march of *Chedorlaomer* (*q. v.*), king of Elam, in the days of Abraham (Gen. 14:1-16). Kadesh is mentioned in connection with the flight of Hagar (16:7), where it is recorded that she rested by "the fountain in the way of Shur," between Kadesh and Bered (v. 14). Again it is recorded that Abraham moved from Hebron, and sojourned at a point "between Kadesh and Shur" (20:1). Some think that the rebellion of Korah and his company occurred at Kadesh, and that it was there "the earth opened her mouth and swallowed them up" (Num. 16:1-31). It was certainly at Kadesh that Miriam died and was buried (20:1), and that Moses struck the rock when he had been told only to speak to it (vers. 2-11). This was the third time that it was the "Fountain of Judgment" by Jehovah passing judgment upon Moses for his impatience, presumption, and lack of reverent obedience (vers. 12-24). Then Kadesh, *consecrated* (place), *sanctuary*, became Meribah, or *strife* (v. 13).

A long halt at Kadesh followed (Deut. 1:46), and it would appear that the Israelites scattered about in the valleys of the desert, leading a nomad life, having all this time Kadesh as the northernmost limit of their roving, and as, in a peculiar sense, the center of their occupancy, or the pivot of their wanderings. Thus passed thirty-seven years, during which Israel did not advance one single step toward the occupancy of the promised land. Then they came together in Kadesh, "even the whole congregation" (Num. 20:1; Deut. 2:1), as if it was the rendezvous and rallying point of the scattered nation.

It was from Kadesh that Moses sent messengers to the king of Edom with the request that Israel might pass through his country on the way to Canaan (Num. 20:14-21), and also with like request to the king of Moab (Judg. 11:16, 17).

2. **Location.** This has been successfully identified with 'Ain Kadeis, some seventy miles south of Hebron. Water was the determining factor of the location (Num. 20:2f). With the region some five or six miles to the north, which was also well watered, Israel acquired the most livable part of the Sinai Peninsula. This circumstance offers the reason for their extended stay at this place.

Kad'miel (kăd'mĭ-ĕl; *God is in the van*).

1. One of the Levites who, with his family, returned from Babylon with Zerubbabel, and apparently a representative of the descendants of Hodaviah, or, as he is elsewhere called, Hodaveh or Judah (Ezra 2:40; Neh. 7:43; 12:8, 12, 24). He assisted in the various reforms of that period (Ezra 3:9), B. C. 536.

2. A Levite who assisted in leading the devotions of the people after they were taught the law by Ezra (Neh. 9:4, 5), signed the covenant (10:9), B. C. 445. He is thought to have been a son of No. 1.

Kad'monites (kăd'mŏn-īts), a tribe mentioned only in Gen. 15:19 as one of the nations to be dispossessed by Israel. As an adjective the name means "eastern," or "ancient." Quite probably, therefore, the Kadmonites were "Bene-Kedem" (Judg. 6:33, A. V. "children of the East"), i. e., "tribes who roved in the great waste tracts on the east and southeast of Palestine." *W. H.* revised by *M. F. U.*

Kal′lai (kăl′á-ī; *swift, light*), son of Sallai, and a chief priest in the time of the high priest Joiakim (Neh. 12:20), B. C. after 635.

Ka′nah (kā′ná; *place of reeds*).

1. A stream which empties into the Mediterranean between Caesarea and Joppa, after serving as a boundary between Ephraim and Manasseh (Josh. 16:8; 17:19). It is identified by some as the river Aujeh.

2. A town in the north of Asher (Josh. 19:28). It possesses colossal ruins and figures of persons, which cuttings are supposed to be of Phoenician origin.

Kaph (kăf; Heb. *kăph, palm of hand*), 11th letter of the Hebrew alphabet, cf. Psa. 119:81-88 where this letter begins each verse in the Hebrew.

Kare′ah (ká-rē′á; *bald*), the father of Johanan and Jonathan, Jewish princes in the time of Gedaliah, the Babylonian governor of Jerusalem (Jer. 40:8, sq.; 41:11, sq.; 42:1, 8; 43:2, 4, 5). Elsewhere called *Careah* (*q. v.*).

Kar′ka (kär′ká; *ground, floor*), a place named in the description of Judah's lot, and between the Mediterranean and the Dead Seas (Josh. 15:3). It has not been identified.

Kar′kor (kär′kôr; cf. Arab. *karkar, soft level ground*), a place east of the Jordan where Gideon's three hundred men, "faint yet pursuing," captured Zebah and Zalmunna (Judg. 8:10). Its location cannot be determined with accuracy.

Kar′tah (kär′tá; *city*), a town in the tribe of Zebulun, assigned (Josh. 21:34) to the Levites of the family of Merari.

Kar′tan (kär′tăn; *town, city*), present-day Khirbet el-Kureiyeh, one of the cities of refuge in Naphtali, belonging to the Gershonite Levites, not far from the Sea of Galilee (Josh. 21:32; Kirjathaim, I Chron. 6:76).

Kat′tath (kăt′ăth), one of the towns of Zebulun (Josh. 19:15), probably the same as Kitron (Judg. 1:30).

Ke′dar (kē′dẽr; Heb. *qădăr, to be dark*, but cf. Arab. *qadara, to be able, mighty*).

1. The second son of Ishmael, and father of the tribe bearing his name (Gen. 25:13; I Chron. 1:29). Of Kedar little is known, but his posterity are frequently mentioned (see 2).

2. Kedar, in the stricter sense, was a nomadic tribe of Ishmaelites, which wandered as far as the Elanitic gulf; but it is usually used in Scripture as the collective name of the Arabic tribes (Bedouins) generally (Cant. 1:5; Isa. 21:16, 17; 42:11; 60:7; Jer. 2:10; 49:28; Ezek. 27:21). In Psa. 120:5 Kedar and Mesech are put for barbarous tribes.

Ked′emah (kĕd′ĕ-má; *eastward*), the last named son of Ishmael, and probably head of an Arab tribe of the same name (Gen. 25:25; 1 Chron. 1:31).

Ked′emoth (kĕd′ĕ-mŏth; *eastern places*), a city of Reuben, assigned with its suburbs ("villages") to the Levites of the Merari family (Josh. 13:18; 21:37; I Chron. 6:79). "Out

of the wilderness of Kedemoth" Moses sent a deputation to Sihon, king of the Amorites, with a request to pass through his land (Deut. 2:26).

Ke′desh (kē′dĕsh; *sacred place, sanctuary*).

1. A city in the extreme south of Judah (Josh. 15:23), and probably the same as *Kadesh-barnea* (*q. v.*).

2. A city in the tribe of Issachar, given to the Levites of the family of Gershom (I Chron. 6:72; called "Kishion," Josh. 19:20; "Kishon," 21:28).

3. A "fenced city" of Naphtali (Josh. 19:37), and one of the cities of refuge (Josh. 20:7). Its king was slain by Joshua (12:22). It was the residence of Barak (Judg. 4:6); was captured by Tiglath-pileser (II Kings 15:29), and was a well-known place after the captivity (I Macc. 11:61, sq.). It is now an insignificant village, still bearing the ancient name, to the northwest of the lake of Huleh.

Ke′desh Naph′tali (kē′dĕsh-năf′tá-lī), (Judg. 4:6). See Kedesh 3.,

Kehela′thah (kĕ-hē-lā′thá; *assembly convocation*), one of the stations (twenty-third) of the children of Israel in the desert (Num. 33:22, 23).

Kei′lah (kē-ī′lá), a city in the plains of Judah, which David once relieved from a siege by the Philistines, but its inhabitants were false and sought to deliver him up to Saul (I Sam. 23:1-13; Neh. 3:17). The site is satisfactorily identified with Khirbet Kila, about 8½ miles N. W. of Hebron. In the time of Nehemiah Keilah was so considerable a city as to have two prefects, who assisted in repairing the walls of Jerusalem (Neh. 3:17, 18).

Kela′iah (kē-lā′yá), one of the Levites who divorced his Gentile wife after the captivity (Ezra 10:23, A. V. "the same is Kelita"). See Kelita.

Kel′ita (kĕl′ĭ-tá; perhaps *dwarf;* cf. Arab. *qulāt*), one of the Levites who put away his Gentile wife after the captivity (Ezra 10:23; assisted Ezra to expound the law (Neh. 8:7); and signed the covenant made by Nehemiah (10:10), B. C. 456.

Kem′uel (kĕm′û-ĕl; *assembly of God*).

1. One of the sons of Abraham's brother Nahor (Gen. 22:21), and father of Bethuel (Gen. 24:15), B. C. about 2150.

2. The son of Shiphtan, and commissioner to represent Ephraim in the partition of the land of Canaan (Num. 34:24), B. C. about 1375.

3. The father of Hasabiah, who was ruler of the Levites in the time of David (I Chron. 27:27), B. C. about 1000.

Ke′nan (kē′năn; I Chron. 1:2). See Cainan.

Ke′nath (kē′năth; *possession*), a city in Gilead which, with its "villages," was taken from the Canaanites by Nobah, and afterward called by his name (Num. 34:42). It is mentioned (I Chron. 2:22, 23), apparently as taken by Jair. Kenath is now Kanawat, a ruined town east of Bashan, on the west side of the Hauran Mountains. It overlooks a vast region, and is surrounded by a cluster of cities, all within a distance of from half an hour to two hours from it. . . . The number of ruined buildings of all kinds is very considerable.

Ke′naz (kē′năz).

1. One of the sons of Eliphaz, the first-born

of Esau. He became chief of one of the Edomitish tribes of Arabia Petraea (Gen. 36:11, 15; I Chron. 1:36). In Gen. 36:42; I Chron. 1:53, we have according to Keil and Delitzsch (*Com.*, in loc.), a list, not of persons, but of capital cities of the several kingdoms.

2. A brother of Caleb, and father of Othniel, who took Kirjath-sepher and received Caleb's daughter Achsah as a prize (Josh. 15:17; Judg. 1:13; 3:9, 11; I Chron. 4:13), B. C. about 1400-1370.

3. The son of Elah, and grandson of Caleb (I Chron. 4:15).

Ke′nezite (kē′něz-īt), **Ken′izzite** (kěn′ĭ-zīt), alike in the Hebrew *hăqqᵉnĭzzî*. The Kenizzites are mentioned only in Gen. 15:19, where they are named between the Kenites and the Kadmonites among the nations to be dispossessed by Israel. They probably dwelt somewhere in the southern part of Canaan. They were related to the Kenites and like them were skilled metal-workers of the copper-rich Jordan Vallay and the Arabah (*see* Kenite). In Gen. 36:11, 15 Kenaz is a son of Eliphaz, the son of Osan; and in Gen. 36:42 Kenaz appears among the dukes of Edom. This might lead us to think that the Kenizzites were an Edomite tribe, if they had not been mentioned so long before. The case is similar to that of *Amalek* (*q. v.*); but the occurrence of the name Kenaz in vers. 15, 42 makes it appear that Kenaz may have been a more common name than Amalek. In Num. 32:12; Jos. 14:6, 14, the same Hebrew (A. V. "Kenezite," R. V. "Kenizzite") is an epithet of Caleb or of Jephunneh in the phrase, "Caleb the son of Jephunneh the Kenezite" (Kenizzite). It is quite probable that Caleb was descended from the Edomite Kenaz. This is argued from Josh. 15:13; "Unto Caleb, the son of Jephunneh, he gave a part *among the children of Judah*," and 14:14, "Hebron became the inheritance of Caleb, the son of Jephunneh, the *Kenezite* unto this day, because that he wholly followed the *Lord God of Israel*." The same is indicated by Edomite and Horite names in the genealogy of Caleb. Thus, besides Kenaz (Gen. 36:11, 15), we find Shobal (comp. I Chron. 2:52 with Gen. 36:20); Manahethites (I Chron. 2:52; comp. Manahath, Gen. 36:23); Korah (Gen. 36:14, 16, 18, with I Chron. 2:43); the Ithrites (I Chron. 2:53, comp. Ithran, Gen. 36:26); Elah (II Chron. 4:15, comp. Gen. 36:41); and Jephunneh has been compared with Pinon (Gen. 36:41).—*W. H.* revised by *M. F. U.*

Ke′nites (kē′nīts; *pertaining to copper smiths*), a group of metal smiths who traveled throughout the mineral-bearing region in the Wadi Arabah. They were descended from the Midianites, and developed extraordinary skill in metal work. They early settled down along the S. W. shore of the Dead Sea, S. E. of Hebron (Judg. 1:16). Hobab, the son of Reuel, was a Kenite and acted as a guide to Israel in the wilderness (Judg. 1:16; 4:11). Their nomadism is suggested in the O. T. by numerous individual Kenites described as living in various places. Besides their residence S. E. of Hebron, they were found in the Wadi Arabah (Num. 24:20-22), in Naphtali (Judg. 4:11) and in the Davidic-Solomonic era are mentioned in southern Judah (I Sam. 15:6; 27:10). Heber, mentioned in Judg. 4:11; 5:24 was a Kenite and the ascetic Rechabites mentioned in I Chron. 2:55 were also of Kenite extraction. *M. F. U.*

Ken′izzites (kěn′ĭ-zīts) (Gen. 15:19). See Kenezite.

Keno′sis (kē-nō′sĭs; Gr. *kenōsis, an emptying*), a Greek word used in theology with reference to the self-abnegation of the Son of God in becoming incarnate, and entering upon his state of humiliation. This use of the term is based upon Phil. 2:7, where the phrase *heauton ′ekenōse* occurs (rendered in the A. V. "made himself of no reputation," translated literally in the R. V. "emptied himself"). The same idea of self-deprivation, or the laying aside of something that Christ possessed as a divine person in his preexistent state, finds expression in other places in the Scriptures (e. g., John 17:5), where our Lord speaks of "the glory" which he had with the Father "before the world was," also (II Cor. 8:9) where St. Paul says of Christ, "though he was rich, yet for your sakes he became poor."

The profound and difficult question naturally raised, is, in what sense did the Son of God lay aside his divine riches in becoming the God-man: of what "glory" did he divest himself; what are we to understand by the kenosis, or "emptying of himself?" The question is inwoven with the mystery of the incarnation. It is a part of the mystery. And the inquiry soon leads to depths that are unfathomable, because of the incomprehensibility of God, and the inability of the human mind to conceive adequately the divine mode of existence. And yet, fidelity to the Scriptures, and the proper demands of the intellect, foster the attempt to penetrate the mystery as far as possible, even though the result may fall far short of the full solution.

A brief survey of the fluctuations of doctrine and conjecture upon this subject will be helpful. Historically, the question has presented many phases, among them these: Was the Son of God during his earthly sojourn in the flesh self-deprived in any measure of his divine attributes? If he still retained them fully in his possession, was their exercise or use for the time surrendered; and if so, to what extent, and under what regulating principles? Was the consciousness of our Lord simply human, the divine consciousness for the time non-existent, or awakening in him only gradually; or was his consciousness throughout that of the God-man?

The ancient Church, with but few exceptions, taught that the Son did not retain the divine glory for himself, for his own advantage, while yet he did not cease even in the flesh to be what he eternally was. "That emptying," said Hilary, "is by no means the annihilating of the heavenly nature." The theology of the Middle Ages so honored the divine nature of Christ as to overlook all limitations assumed in the union of that nature with the human. Thomas Aquinas admitted only an outward development in age and wisdom as in the sight of men.

The kenosis became the subject of much controversy between the theologians of Giessen and Tübingen early in the 17th century, the former (Menzer and Feurborn) maintaining that if Christ did not during his humiliation actually divest himself of his attributes, as omnipotence and omniscience, etc., he did lay aside their use; the latter (Haffenreffer, Thummius, Nicolai, Oriander) contending that the kenosis was only a concealment or veiling of their use. Later Thomasius (*Person and Work of Christ*) took the ground positively of self-abdication of the divine attributes on the part of Christ, assuming a sleeplike unconsciousness of the divine nature of the Son during our Lord's earthly life, and the exclusion of the Son from the Trinity during that period. Gess (*Die Lehre von der Person Christi*) Georg Ludw. Hahn (*Theologie der N. T.*) take substantially the same ground. This scanty outline is sufficient to show the perilous paths that are followed when the attempt is made to push speculation too far in this direction. Likewise it must be apparent that the conclusion reached should be such as not to deny the absolute unchangeableness of God, nor the constant completeness of the divine nature in the Son even in the days of his humiliation; while, on the other hand, the reality of his loving self-abasement in his entrance into fellowship with humanity should be duly recognized. And all reflection upon this subject, as upon many others, must be under the guidance, and within the limits, of Scripture teaching.

That the "Word made flesh" was truly God, as well as man, with divine nature and attributes undiminished, cannot be doubted by anyone who believes the first chapter of St. John's gospel, to say nothing of the force of other Scriptures.

Whether the consciousness of his divine nature was from the very outset possessed by our Lord is a matter upon which the Scriptures are silent. St. Luke, however, furnishes a glimpse that is suggestive when the child Christ says, "Wist ye not that I must be about my Father's business?" (Luke 2:49, 50). And certain it is that he clearly expresses this consciousness during the years of his ministry (e. g., John 14:9-11; 8:58; 10:30; 17:25).

As to the divine attributes in Christ, the distinction seems valid between their full possession and their constant exercise. That he constantly possessed the attributes of deity is inseparable from faith in his divine, and, therefore, unchangeable nature. And yet the use of these same properties appears to have been in some way limited. This must be manifest to anyone who attentively reads the gospels. And the law of this limitation is found in the love and self-sacrifice which led our Lord to the complete acceptance of his human and earthly lot. He who "emptied himself" "took upon him the form of a servant." The two expressions are mutually explanatory. Thus He who was "in the form of God" and "thought it not robbery to be equal with God," placed himself in relation to the Father in the lowly position of a servant (John 5:30; 4:34; 17:4, 18; 14:28; Matt. 26:39); he was also the servant of mankind (Matt. 20:28; Luke 22:26, 27); he never wrought miracles for himself, but often did so for others (comp.

Matt. 4:3, 4; 14:15-21; 15:32-39); he admitted and asserted a limitation to his knowledge with respect to one matter, but manifested and declared himself to be possessed of divine knowledge with respect to other matters, and even the highest. And here the fullness of his knowledge was always at the service of his love (comp. Mark 13:32; Matt. 11:27; John 3:12, 13; 17:25, 26). He neither exercises his omnipotence nor exhibits his omniscience for his own advantage and glory, but for the performance of his saving work among men.

Two other expressions in the same passage (Phil. 2:5-8) throw light upon the kenosis. Before the kenosis Christ was "in the form of God;" afterward he was "made in the likeness of men," "formed in fashion as a man." Here the contrast is between the *manifestations of being* and *character* which naturally belonged to the Son of God, and the veiling of the divine glory which came to pass when he became incarnate. What the "form of God" was which the Son laid aside, the apostle does not tell us; but evidently it was such manifestation of the divine being as was befitting to him who "deemed it not a prize to be on an equality with God." St. Paul elsewhere writes that God "dwelleth in light which no man can approach unto" (I Tim. 6:16). In strongest contrast with this was all the outward appearance of the earthly life of our Lord. He left the companionship of angels for that of men. The angels are the servants of God. Though on special occasions they were sent to minister to him (Matt. 3:11; Luke 22:43), Christ never called for them (see Matt. 27:53).

Two features of the incarnate life of the Son of God are emphasized by St. Paul for ethical purposes in connection with the kenosis: first, self-sacrificing love (Phil. 2:3-5); second, obedience (Phil. 2:8, 12, 13). The sequence, the exaltation of Christ (vers. 9-11), has the gloriously hopeful suggestion and promise for all his followers. *See* Incarnation; Humiliation of Christ.

Literature.—For compact history of views, see Lange on Phil., p. 38. For doctrine, see Van Oosterzee, *Christ. Dogm.*, vol. ii, §§ xcv and ci; Doner, *Hist. of Doct. of Person of Christ*, i-ii, 29; Gore, *Incarnation of the Son of God*, pp. 176-179; 284, 285.—E. McC.

Kere' (kĕ-rā', kĕ-rē') (Aram. passive part. *qᵉrē*, signifying "what is to be read"). This is a marginal reading in the traditional Hebrew Massoretic text. In the opinion of the Jewish scholars (Massoretes) this was the superior reading and was to be substituted or read for what was written in the text, called the *kethib* *q. v.* Actually the vowel pointings of the *kethib* were to be read with the *kere*.

Ker'en-Hap'puch (kĕr'ĕn-hăp'ŭk; *paint-horn*, i. e., *cosmetic box*), the name given to the youngest daughter of Job after his restoration to prosperity (Job 42:14).

Ke'rioth (kē'rĭ-ŏth; *cities*).

1. A city of southern Judah, and probably included within Simeon (Josh. 15:25). It seems to be the place alluded to in the name of Judas Iscariot, a native of Kerioth. It has been identified with Khirbet el-Karyathein, about 4½ miles S. of Tell Mā'in.

2. A city of Moab mentioned by Jeremiah

(Jer. 48:24, 41) and Amos (2:2, A. V. "Kirioth") in their prophecies of its overthrow by the Babylonians. It occurs on the Moabite Stone, (line 13).

Ke'ros (kē'rŏs), one of the Nethinim whose descendants returned with Zerubbabel to Jerusalem after the captivity (Ezra 2:44; Neh. 7:47), B. C. before 536.

Kethib (kĕ-thēv', also written *kethiv*, kĕ-thēve', an Aram. passive part. (kĕ-thîb), *written*. The *kethib* was the reading actually occurring in the Hebrew text and represented, even though an inferior reading in the opinion of the Massoretic scholars, an ancient traditional reading deserving of some credence. The vowels on the *kethib* were meant to be superimposed upon the marginal or *kere* reading (*See* Kere). The *Kethib Kere* device proves the high veneration of Massoretic scholars for the traditional readings and for sacred regard for the text together with their extreme unwillingness to change it, even in the case of an inferior traditional reading. *M. F. U.*

Kettle (Heb. *dūd, boiling*), a large pot for cooking (I Sam. 2:14; elsewhere rendered "pot," Psa. 81:6; Job 41:20; "caldron," II Chron. 35:13). From I Sam. 2:14, it is evident that this vessel was used in preparing the peace offerings, as it is said: "All that the flesh hook brought up the priest took for himself."

Ketu'rah (kĕ-tū'rá; *incense*), the second wife (or concubine, I Chron. 1:32) of Abraham (Gen. 25:1, 4). By Abraham she had six sons, who, after they grew to manhood, were established "in the east country," that they might not interfere with Isaac. It is generally supposed that she was married to Abraham after the death of Sarah; but against this it is urged that it is very improbable that six sons should have been born to Abraham by one woman, and that, too, after he was one hundred and forty years old, and that he should have lived to see them arrive at adult age. It has therefore been suggested that Keturah had been Abraham's secondary or concubine wife before the death of Sarah, and that she was raised to the dignity of a full wife after that event. Through the offspring of Keturah Abraham became the "father of many nations."

Key. As an instrument for fastening, *see* Lock.

Figurative. Because of its power to open to, or exclude from, all treasures of a city or house, the key is often used in Scripture as a symbol of *power* and *authority*, whether in Church or State. Thus Isaiah speaks (22:22) of the key of David being given to Eliakim, as the most influential adviser of the king. The power of the keys consisted not only in the supervision of the royal chambers, but also in deciding who was and who was not to be received into the king's service.

With reference to the administration of the house of David in the higher sense, our Lord is represented as having the key of David (Rev. 3:7), receiving and excluding whom he pleases, and committing to his apostles—to Peter first as the most prominent member of the apostolic body—the keys of the kingdom (Matt. 16:19; 18:18). *See* Peter.

"The key of knowledge" (Luke 11:52) of spiritual things is the Scriptures, which the Scribes reserved exclusively to themselves. The

260. Ancient Prison Keys

figure used by our Lord is that of *knowledge* being a temple, into which the Scribes should have led the people, but whose gate they closed and held the key with jealous care, even their commentaries hiding rather than revealing knowledge.

Kezi'ah (kĕ-zī'á; *cassia*), Job's second daughter, born to him after his adversity (Job 42:14).

Ke'ziz (kē'zĭz), a city of Benjamin (Josh. 18: 21, A. V. "Valley of Keziz"), the name of which is still preserved in the Wady el Kaziz, on the road from Jerusalem to Jericho, southeast of the Apostles' Well.

Khan (kän), the more common Arabic name for the establishments which correspond to our inn (*q. v.*).

Kib'roth-Hatta'avah (kĭb'rŏth-há-tä'-á-vá; *the graves of lust*), one of the stations of the Israelites, probably in Wady Murrah, about thirty miles N. E. of Sinai. It was the scene of murmuring and discontent, followed by most severe punishment (Num. 11:34, 35; 33:16, 17; Deut. 9:22; Psa. 78:30, 31).

Kib'zaim (kĭb'zā'ĭm; a *double heap*), a city of Ephraim, assigned to the Kohathite Levites (Josh. 21:22), called *Jockmeam* in I Chron. 6:68. Its site is not ascertained. (*See* Jokmeam).

Kid, the young of the goat. See Animal Kingdom; Sacrificial Offerings.

Kidney (Heb. *kĭlyäh;* Gr. *nephros*). The kidneys, two in number, are situated in the back part of the abdomen, one on each side of the vertebral column, and surrounded by a mass of fat and areolar tissue. They are for the purpose of separating from the blood certain materials which, when dissolved in a quantity of water, also separated from the blood, constitute the urine.

1. The kidney with its surrounding fat was part of the burnt offering (Exod. 29:13, 22; Lev. 3:4, 10, 15; 4:9; 8:16, 25, etc.). See Sacrificial Offerings.

2. The Hebrew word is sometimes applied to *kernels* of grain, from their kidneylike shape (Deut. 32:4).

3. **Figurative.** When the kidney is used figuratively, it is rendered in the A. V. "reins."

In the ancient system of physiology the kidneys, from their sensitiveness, were believed to be the seat of desire; and the Scripture brings the tenderest and most inward experience of a manifold kind into association with them.

"When man is suffering most deeply within he is pricked in his kidneys (reins, Psa. 73:21). When fretting affliction overcomes him, his kidneys are cloven asunder (Job 16:13; comp. Lam. 3:13); when he rejoices profoundly, they exult (Prov. 23:16); when he feels himself very penetratingly warned, they chasten him (Psa. 16:7); when he very earnestly longs, they are consumed away within his body (Job 19:27); when he rages inwardly, they shake (I Macc. 2:24). . . . God is frequently called the Trier of the heart and reins; and of the ungodly it is said that God is far from their reins (Jer. 12:2), i. e., that he, being withdrawn back into himself, allows not himself to be perceived by them" (Delitzsch, *Psychology*, p. 317).

Kid′ron (kĭd′rŏn; *turbid, dusky, gloomy;* Gr. *Kedrōn*, John 18:1, A. V. "Cedron"), the brook or wintry torrent which flows through the Valley of Jehoshaphat. The name was also applied to its bed, the *valley* of Kidron. It is thus described by Smith (*Hist. Geog.*, p. 511):

261. The Valley of the Kidron and Jerusalem from the Mount of Olives

"To the north of Jerusalem begins the torrent-bed of the Kidron. It sweeps past the Temple Mount, past what were afterward Calvary and Gethsemane. It leaves the Mount of Olives and Bethany to the left, Bethlehem far to the right. It plunges down among the bare terraces, precipices, and crags of the wilderness of Judea—the wilderness of the scapegoat. So barren and blistered, so furnace-like does it (the valley) become as it drops below the level of the sea, that it takes the name of Wady-en-Nar or the Fire Wady. At last its dreary course brings it to the precipices above the Dead Sea, into which it shoots its scanty winter waters; but all summer it is dry." The valley is only twenty miles long, but with a descent of three thousand nine hundred and twelve feet. The place where it enters the Jordan is a narrow gorge about twelve hundred feet deep.

Kidron is the brook crossed by David when fleeing from Absalom (II Sam. 15:23, 30); Solomon fixed upon it as the limit of Shimei's walks (I Kings 2:37); beside it Asa destroyed and burned his mother's idol of Asherah (I Kings 15:13); here Athaliah was executed

(Josephus, *Ant.*, ix, 7, 3; II Kings 11:16). It then became the regular receptacle for the impurities and abominations of the idol worship, when removed from the temple and destroyed by the adherents of Jehovah (II Kings 23:4, 6, 12; II Chron. 29:16; 30:14); and in the time of Josiah this valley was the common cemetery of Jerusalem (II Kings 23:6; Jer. 26:23; 31:40).

Kin. *See* Kindred.

Ki′nah (kī′nà; *lamentation dirge*), a city in the extreme south of Judah toward Edom (Josh. 15:22). Kinah is located at the head of Wadi el Keini.

Kindness and **Loving-Kindness** (Heb. *ḥĕsĕd, desire, zeal*), zeal toward another in a good sense: (1) Of men, as shown in doing mutual favors, benefits (Gen. 21:23; II Sam. 10:2); compassion for the afflicted (Job 6:14, A. V. "pity"). The formula "to do" or "show kindness" is very frequent in Scripture (II Sam. 3:8; 9:1, 7), and in II Sam. 9:3, there is the expression "that I may show the kindness of God unto him," i. e., "like that of God," or "for the sake of God." (2) Of God toward men, as shown in *mercies, benefits,* etc. (Psa. 31:21; 107:43; 117:2, etc.). Kindness is also the rendering of the Gr. *chrēstotēs, moral goodness,* and so *benignity* (Rom. 2:4; Gal. 5:22, A. V. "goodness"; II Cor. 6:6; Eph. 2:7; Col. 3:12).

Kindred is the rendering in the A. V. of the following Hebrew and Greek terms:

1. *Family* (Heb. *mĭshpāḥāh*, usually so rendered). This word corresponds to our word *clan*, and is used of the different tribes of Canaanites (Gen. 10:18); a subdivision of the Israelites (Exod. 6:14; Num. 1:20, etc.), and figuratively for a nation (Jer. 5:9; 8:3; 25:9; 20:32; Mic. 2:3), and is rendered *kindred* (Gen. 24:41; Josh. 6:23; Ruth 2:3; Job 32:2), in all of which it refers to relationship, to *consanguinity*, more or less remote.

2. *Lineage* (Heb. *mōlĕdĕth*), hence a *person* born, a *child* (Gen. 28:9; Lev. 18:9, 11); persons of the *same family* or *lineage* (Gen. 12:1; 24:4; 31:3; 43:7; Num. 10:30; Esth. 2:10; 8:6). In some of these instances the relation is only that of common nationality.

3. *Acquaintance* (Heb. *mōdăʿăth, acquaintance,* Ruth 3:2), is used to express blood relationship.

4. *Near relative* (Heb. *gōʾēl, near of kin*). This term is applied to one who is so related as to possess the rights and obligations of a kinsman, avenger (*q. v.*). It is generally used to denote the nearest kinsman, able to redeem (Ruth 4:1, 3:12).

5. *Brother* (Heb. *ʾāḥ*). This term occurs as *kindred* in the A. V. only in I Chron. 12:29, but occurs frequently elsewhere in a wide sense, including all collateral relationships, whether by consanguinity, affinity, or simple relationship. From this term comes *brotherhood*. The Hebrews also expressed consanguinity by such words and phrases as *flesh* (Gen. 37:27; Isa. 58:7); *bone and flesh* (Gen. 29:14; Judg. 9:2; II Sam. 5:1, etc.); *flesh of his flesh* (A. V. "near of kin," Lev. 18:6; "nigh of kin," 25:49).

6. In the New Testament the following Greek words are rendered *kindred: genos,* the

most general and frequent term, our *kin*, i. e., blood relationship; its derivative, *suggeneia*, *co-relationship; patria*, (Acts 3:25), descent in a direct line (Luke 2:4, "lineage;" Eph. 3:15, "family"); *phulē, offshoot*, a *tribe* (Rev. 5:9; 7:9; 11:9; 13:7, etc.), a *tribe*. Of the special names denoting relation by consanguinity, the principal will be found explained under their proper heads, *Father, Brother*, etc. It will be there seen that the words which denote near relation in the direct line are used also for the superior or inferior degrees in that line, as grandfather, grandson, etc. The words which express collateral consanguinity are: (1) Uncle; (2) Aunt; (3) Nephew; (4) Niece (not in A. V.); (5) Cousin. The terms of affinity are: *1.* (*a*) Father-in-law, (*b*) Mother-in-law; *2.* (*a*) Son-in-law, (*b*) Daughter-in-law; *3.* (*a*) Brother-in-law, (*b*) Sister-in-law. The domestic and economic questions arising out of kindred may be classed under the heads of *Family, Marriage, Inheritance,* and *Blood Revenge.*

Kine (Cows). *See* Animal Kingdom.

Figurative. Kine is used figuratively: Of proud and wealthy rulers (Amos 4:1); well favored, of years of plenty (Gen. 41:2, 26, 29); lean, of years of scarcity (41:3, 27, 30).

King (Heb. and Aram. *mĕlĕk ruler;* Gr. *basileus*).

1. **General Use of Term.** This term is used with considerable latitude in Scripture, and is often applied where some inferior epithet would correspond better with modern ideas. Thus, when we read of the king of Sodom, of Gomorrah, of Admah, of Zeboim (Gen. 14:2) all towns lying within a very limited distance—it is manifest that we must understand the term *king* in the sense of a local ruler. This, and many similar notices, shows a prevailing tendency in early times toward monarchical government. Whenever the people of a district settled down and formed themselves into a regular community it was under the presidency of a regal head. Not in Egypt alone, but in Salem, in Gerar, in all the little towns to which the patriarchs came, a king invariably appears on the scene. Thus, in so small a country as Canaan *thirty-one* kings were conquered by Joshua (Josh. 12:9, 24); while Adonibezek speaks of having subdued *seventy* (Judg. 1:7).

2. **Hebrew Use of Term.** Among the Israelites king was the title applied to the supreme head of the nation from about B. C. 1020-587. (1) **Occasion.** The immediate occasion for the substitution of a regal form of government for that of the judges (*q. v.*) seems to have been the siege of Jabesh-gilead by Nahash, king of the Ammonites (I Sam. ch. 11; 12:12), and the refusal to allow the inhabitants of that town to capitulate, except on humiliating and cruel conditions (11:2, 4-6). The Israelites seem to have been convinced that they could not succeed against their formidable enemies unless, like other nations, they placed themselves under the rule of a king. Probably another influencing cause was the disgust excited by the corrupt administration of affairs by the sons of Samuel and the desire for a radical change (8:3-5). Accordingly, the original idea of a Hebrew king was twofold: First, that he should lead the people to battle in time of war; and, secondly, that he should execute judgment and

justice to them in war and peace (8:20). (2) **Powers.** Besides being commander in chief of the army, supreme judge and absolute master of the lives of his subjects, the king exercised the power of imposing taxes upon them, and of exacting from them personal service and labor. The degree to which the exaction of personal labor might be carried on a special occasion is illustrated by King Solomon's requirements for building the temple. The king of Israel had also another claim to respect and obedience, as the vicegerent of Jehovah (I Sam. 10:1; 16:13), and, as it were, his son, if just and holy (II Sam. 7:14; Psa. 89:26, 27; 2:6, 7). Set apart as a consecrated ruler, and anointed with the holy oil (Exod. 30:33; I Kings 1:39), he became "the Lord's Anointed." (3) **Court.** A ruler who had so much authority, human and divine, was naturally distinguished by outward honors and luxuries. Thus, gradually, he came to have a court of oriental magnificence. When the kingdom was at its height he sat on a throne of ivory, covered with pure gold, at the feet of which were two figures of lions; and was dressed in royal robes (I Kings 22:10; II Chron. 18:9); his insignia were a golden crown, perhaps radiant with gems (II Sam. 1:10; 12:30; II Kings 11:12; Psa. 21:3), and a royal scepter. He was treated with the utmost consideration, those who approached him bowing to the ground (I Sam. 24:8; II Sam. 19:24). He had a more or less extensive harem, guarded by eunuchs (I Sam. 8:15; II Kings 24:12, 15, etc.). (4) **Succession.** The law of succession to the throne is somewhat obscure, but it seems most probable that the king during his lifetime named his successor. This was certainly the case with David (I Kings 1:30; 2:22) and with Rehoboam (II Chron. 11:21, 22). At the same time, if no partiality for a favorite wife or son intervened, there would always be a natural bias of affection in favor of the eldest son. (5) **Officers.** The recorder, or chronicler, whose duty it was to write the annals of the king's reign; the scribe, or secretary (II Sam. 8:17; 20:25; II Kings 12:10, etc.); chief steward, or officer "over the house" (Isa. 22:15; 36:3); the king's friend (I Kings 4:5) or companion; the keeper of the wardrobe (II Kings 10:22); the captain of the bodyguard (II Sam. 20:23); officers over the king's treasure, his storehouses, laborers, vineyards, olive trees, sycamore trees, camels, and flocks (I Chron. 27:25-31); the commander in chief of the army (II Sam. 11:1; 20:23; I Chron. 27:34); the royal counselors (I Chron. 27:32; Isa. 3:3; 19:11, 13). (6) **Revenues:** the following sources are mentioned. The royal demesnes, cornfields, vineyards, and olive gardens; the produce of the royal flocks (I Sam. 21:7; II Sam. 13:23; II Chron. 26:10; I Chron. 27:25); a nominal tenth of the produce of corn lands and vineyards and of sheep (I Sam. 8:15, 17); a tribute from merchants who passed through the Hebrew territory (I Kings 10:14); presents made by his subjects (I Sam. 10:27; 16:20; I Kings 10:25; Psa. 72:10); in the time of Solomon the king had trading vessels of his own at sea (I Kings 10:22). It is probable that Solomon and some other kings may have derived some revenues from commercial ventures (I Kings 9:28); the spoils of war taken from conquered nations and the tribute paid by them (II Sam. 8:2, 7, 8, 10; I Kings 4:21; II Chron. 27:5); lastly, an undefined power of exacting compulsory labor, to which reference has been already made (I Sam. 8:12, 13, 16).

3. **New Testament Use of Term.** Owing to the peculiar political relations of the Jews the title "king" has very different significations: The Roman *emperor* (I Pet. 2:13, 17); and so the "seven kings" (Rev. 17:10) are thought to be the first seven Caesars; Herod Antipas (Matt. 14:9; Mark 6:22), although he was only *tetrarch* (comp. Luke 3:19); the ten provincial representatives of the Roman government (Rev. 17:12), as being supreme each in his own jurisdiction.

4. **Figurative.** "King" is used symbolically to signify the possessor of supreme power (Prov. 8:15, 16); it is applied to God, as the sole proper sovereign and ruler of the universe (I Tim. 1:17); to Christ as the sole head and governor of his Church (I Tim. 6:15, 16; Matt. 27:11; Luke 19:38; John 1:49; 18:33, 37); to men, as invested with regal authority by their fellows (Luke 22:25; I Tim. 2:1, 2, etc.). The people of God are called *kings* and *priests* (Rev. 1:6; comp. Psa. 49:14; Dan. 7: 22, 27; Matt. 19:28; Luke 22:29, 30; I Cor. 6:2, 3, etc.); Death, the "king of terrors" (Job 18:14); the "leviathan" (*q. v.*), "a king over all the children of pride" (Job 41:34). *See* History, Old Testament; Israel, Kingdom of.

Kingdom of God; Kingdom of Heaven. The "kingdom of God" is evidently a more comprehensive term than the "kingdom of heaven" and embraces all created intelligences both in heaven and on earth who are willingly subject to God and thus in fellowship with him. The "kingdom of heaven," more precisely the "kingdom of the heavens," is a term descriptive of any type of rulership God may assert on the earth at a given period. As a predicted kingdom it has reference to the establishment of the kingdom of Israel on the earth (Acts 1:6) and is the subject of extended glowing prophecies in the O. T. (Psa. 2:6; 16:9; 72:1; Isa. 11:1; 32:1; 65:17; Jer. 33:15; Dan. 7:13, 14; Micah 4:1; Zech. 9:10; 12:1; 14:9). As a covenanted kingdom, the kingdom of heaven becomes the national hope of Israel (II Sam. 7:4-17). John the Baptist, Christ and the Apostles announced the kingdom unto national Israel as "at hand." That offer was rejected. As a result the "kingdom of heaven" in its earthly manifested form was postponed until Christ's Second Advent. Widespread attempts to "bring in the kingdom" on the basis of Christ's First Advent are misplaced. According to the clear teaching of the Bible it will be realized only in connection with the Second Advent. The testimony of Scripture agrees completely with this fact. According to Matt. 13 the present gospel age represents the mystery form of the kingdom. "Since the kingdom of heaven is no other than the rule of God on the earth, He must now be ruling to the extent of full realization of those things which are termed 'the mysteries' in the N. T. and which really constitute the new message

of the N. T." (Lewis Sperry Chafer, *Systematic Theology* vii, p. 224). The "kingdom of the heavens," that is, the manifested rule of God on the earth in the mediatorial Davidic kingdom, of course, will not be realized until the future millennial period. The kingdom of God and the kingdom of heaven, as Lewis Sperry Chafer points out, are not identical despite the fact that "Matthew employs the terminology of the kingdom of heaven" and Mark and Luke, when presenting practically the same teaching, employ the term "kingdom of God." According to Scripture the "children of the kingdom" may be taken out (Matt. 8:12; 24:50, 51; 25:28-30). This fate cannot be applied to the kingdom of God and its members (John 3:18). The parable of the wheat and the tares (Matt. 13:24-30, 36-43) and that of the good and bad fish (Matt. 13:47-50), are spoken only of the kingdom of heaven. The parable of the leaven, however, (Matt. 13:33; Luke 13:21) is applied to both kingdoms. "Leaven represents evil doctrine rather than evil persons, and evil doctrine may and does corrupt both kingdoms" (*Op. cit.*, p. 224-25). M. F. U.

Kingdom of Israel. *See* Israel, Kingdom of; Constitution of.

Kingdom of Judah. *See* Judah, Kingdom of.

Kingly Office of Christ. *See* Jesus, Offices of.

Kings, I and II, Books of. These books are named from the opening word of first Kings in the Hebrew text, *weˈhammelek,* meaning *and the king,* and from the fact that this section of Scripture deals with the kings of Israel and Judah in their historical setting, in one case to the fall of Samaria (722-721 B. C.) and in the other case to the Babylonian captivity. In the Greek and the Vulgate it is recorded as 3rd and 4th Kings. In modern Hebrew Bibles it appears as I and II Kings after I and II Samuel. The book was originally single-volumed like Samuel.

1. **The Scope.** As an historical narrative the Books of Kings carry on the recital of the history of Israel where I and II Sam. leave off, just prior to the death of David. The historical narrative is carried forward to the Fall of Samaria in the case of the Northern Kingdom and until the thirty-seventh year of King Jehoiachin's captivity in Babylon. The time span is from c. 972-560 B. C.

2. **Chronology.** The task of harmonizing the synchronous reigns of the kings of Judah and Israel has been a very difficult problem, exercising the ingenuity of scholars for many years. More recent chronologists include F. X. Kugler, *Von Moses bis Paulus,* Muenster, 1922; J. Begrich, *Die Chronologie der Koenige von Israel und Judah,* Tuebingen, 1929; S. Mowinckel, *Die Chronologie der israelitischen und jeudeschen Koenige,* Leyden, 1932; M. Vogelstein, *Biblical Chronology,* Part I, Cincinnati, 1944. Numerous factors complicate the chronology of the monarchic period such as co-regencies, ancient calendar reckonings, synchronisms, etc. Very enlightening is Edwin R. Thiele's *The Mysterious Number of the Hebrew Kings,* Chicago, 1951. W. F. Albright has also made valuable contributions to the chronological study of this period in his article "The Chronology of the Divided Monarchy" in

Bulletin of the American Schools 100, p. 16-22. Albright observes co-regencies and synchronisms but reduces the reigns of Judahite kings as well as the number of Israelite kings, especially in the case of the Omrides. These and other studies have somewhat reduced vexing problems, yet few of the dates of this period are absolutely fixed, but in most cases are perhaps not more than five years wrong.

3. **Authorship.** The Talmud (*Baba Bathra*, 14b) names Jeremiah as the author. J. E. Steinmueller (*A Companion to Scripture Studies*, Vol. ii, p. 98f) espouses this view. He maintains that the Jeremian authorship does not rule out the composition of the book at Babylon, since tradition holds that Nebuchadnezzar carried Jeremiah to Babylon, after the latter had conquered Egypt in his thirty-seventh year (568 B. C.). In Babylon Jeremiah died as an aged man past ninety. Under this view Jeremiah wrote II Kings 25:27-30 in Babylon, although the remainder of the book may have been compiled long before that time.

4. **Sources.** The writer, whether he was Jeremiah or not, was in all probability a contemporary of Jeremiah and also a prophet who was deeply distressed at the spiritual declension of Judah. The author makes free mention of sources which he evidently used extensively. He refers to the Book of the Acts of Solomon (I Kings 11:41). The Book of the Chronicles of the Kings of Israel is mentioned seventeen times. The Books of the Chronicles of the Kings of Judah are referred to fifteen times.

5. **Critical View.** Higher critics commonly place the original edition of the Book of Kings shortly after the death of Josiah, somewhere between 609 and 600 B. C. The claim is made that the writer was the first to use historical materials derived from the recently discovered Book of Deuteronomy, which initially is alleged to have appeared in 621 B. C. The book is supposed to be a religious and not an historical work. Critics call it a Deuteronomistic history (cf. Pfeiffer, *Introduction*, p. 380). The unique law of the central sanctuary appearing in Deuteronomy 12 is supposed to be the guiding principle for evaluating each king. Thus, authentic history is supposedly ruled out. It is also maintained that c. 550 B. C., during the exilic period, a second Deuteronomist added the history to the liberation of King Jehoiachin (II Kings 25:27-30) and made various additions to the book. Wellhausen critics assume that this Deuteronomist also redid the Pentateuchal books, except Leviticus, together with Joshua, Judges and Samuel. Supposedly a few additions were finally made by a priestly writer until the time it was canonized (c. 200 B. C.).

6. **Repudiation of the Critical Position.** This critical view must be rejected because it is unsound and of one piece with the partitioning of the Pentateuch. The same erroneous philosophical, historical and literary suppositions underlie the notion of a Deuteronomistic work of history as underlie the unsound partitioning of the Pentateuch. The objectionable theory is that the book discovered in the 18th year of Josiah's reign (II Kings 22:3-8) was Deuteronomy and that alone, and that this book was composed shortly before its discovery and passed off as a pious fraud, alleged to be the law of Moses. It is a far sounder view to accept early Pentateuchal evidences of the existence of Deuteronomy rather than to invent this artificial theory and to reject all such inferences as later glosses or redactorial additions. Moreover, the critical theory must be rejected because the Deuteronomic stamp is no less original with other O. T. books than it is with the Book of Kings. It is pure supposition to view Joshua, Judges and Samuel as originally written without the background of the Deuteronomic laws. It must not be denied, however, that the author of Kings had a pragmatic and religious motive. He was not supplanting existing histories, but writing a religious history. This history is not to be accounted as distorted or arbitrary simply because it deals with the rulers of the theocratic kingdoms on the basis of the loyalty to the Word of God.

7. **Outline.**

Part I. Solomon's Rule, I Kings 1:1-11:43
  a. His accession, 1:1-53
  b. David's charge, 2:1-46
  c. Solomon's marriage and wisdom, 3:1-28
  d. His administration, 4:1-34
  e. His building activities, 5:1-8:66
  f. His prosperity and splendor, 9:1-10:29
  g. His apostasy, 11:1-43

Part II. The Contemporaneous reigns of the Judahite and Israelite Kings, I Kings 12:1-II Kings 17:41

Part III. The Reigns of the Judahite Kings to the Fall of Judah, II Kings 18:1-25:30
  a. Hezekiah, 18:1-20:21
  b. Manasseh, 21:1-18
  c. Amon, 21:19-26
  d. Josiah, 22:1-23:30
  e. Jehoahaz, 23:31-35
  f. Jehoiakim, 23:36-24:7
  g. Jehoiachin, 24:8-17-25:27-30
  h. Zedekiah, 24:18-25:26

M. F. U.

King's Garden. *See* Garden.
King's House. *See* Palace.
King's Mother. *See* Queen.
King's Sepulcher. *See* Tomb.
Kinsman (Heb. *gō'ēl, redeemer*). This Hebrew term for kinsman is used to imply certain obligations arising out of that relationship, and has for its primary meaning *coming to the help* or *rescue* of one. The *gō'ēl* among the Hebrews was the nearest living male blood relation, and on him devolved certain duties to his next of kin.

1. **Blood Avenger.** The most striking office of the kinsman *gō'ēl* was that of blood avenger (*q. v.*). Although the word is peculiar to the Hebrew language, the institution which it represents is common to several branches of the Semites. The unit of Semitic society is the clan, a body of persons united to one another by blood, a family on a somewhat enlarged scale. The members of the clan, closely bound by blood ties to one another, feel a mutual responsibility for one another. A wrong done to a single member is a crime against the entire clan. The obligation, therefore, rests

upon the clan to punish the wrongdoer; and in the case of a murder committed it is a positive obligation to seek, not, indeed, vengeance, but avengeance. The blood of the murdered man cries up from the ground, and the cry is heard loudest by that member of the clan who stands nearest to the dead. The crime consists in the spilling of the blood—its waste, rather than in the extinction of life. The son is enjoined to avenge the blood of his father, the brother is obliged to punish a crime committed against his sister. "Lynch law" is the most primitive form of justice; and *gōʼēl* is the "avenger," legitimately constituted as such, and recognized by the verdict of ancient Semitic society. If the killing was accidental the *gōʼēl* had no claim, unless the slayer left the city of refuge before the death of the high priest in whose reign the crime was committed.

2. **Redeemer.** It was the duty of a kinsman (i. e., "redeemer") to redeem the paternal estate which his nearest relative might have sold through poverty (Lev. 25:25; Ruth 4:4), to ransom his kinsman who may have sold himself (Lev. 25:47, sq.), to act as go-between in case a person wished to make restitution to a relative. If there was no kinsman, then the compensation went to the priest, as representing Jehovah, the king of Israel (Num. 5:6, sq.). From Ruth (chaps 3, 4) it has been inferred that among the duties of kinsman *gōʼēl* was that of marrying the widow of a deceased kinsman's widow. But the Levirate law expressly limits the obligation to a brother. The nearest kinsman had the right to redeem the land, which, perhaps, involved the marrying the widow of the deceased owner, according to usage. *See* Marriage, Levirate; Redeemer

Kir (kĭr; *wall*), the place to which Tiglath-pileser led captive the people of Damascus (II Kings 16:9), according to the prophecy of Amos (1:3-5), and from which at some time the Aramaeans emigrated to Syria (Amos 9:7). Delitzsch (*Com.*, on Isa. 22:6) identifies the Kir in this passage with that mentioned in Kings and Amos. It seems to have been situated on the river Kur (*Kuros*), which takes its rise in Armenia.

Kir of Moab (kĭr of Mōʼăb), one of the two strongly fortified cities of Moab (Isa. 15:1), the other being Ar. It is probably the same as *Kir-haraseth* (*q. v.*).

Kir-Harʼaseth (kĭr-härʼȧ-sĕth; *city of pottery*, some read "new city"), II Kings 3:25; "Kir-hareseth," Isa. 16:7; "Kir-haresh," 16:11; "Kir-heres," Jer. 48:31, 36; and Kir of Moab, Isa. 15:1), a strongly fortified city of Moab, which is now known as Kerak, and is distant from Jerusalem about fifty miles. Joram, king of Israel, took the city, and destroyed all but its walls (II Kings 3:25). Mesha, its king, endeavored with seven hundred men to fight his way through the besiegers; but when this attempt failed, in his desperation, he took his firstborn son, who was to succeed him as king, and offered him as a sacrifice upon the wall. From the other passage cited it would appear to have been restored before Isaiah's time, and ravaged by the Babylonians.

Kirʼioth (kĭrʼĭ-ŏth) (Amos 2:2). *See* Kerioth.

Kirʼjath (kĭrʼjăth; *city*), a city belonging to Benjamin (Josh. 18:28). By some it is identified with Kirjath-jearim, but this is disputed.

Kirjathaʼim (kĭr-jăth-thāʼĭm; *double city*), or "Kiriathaim."

1. A city of refuge in Naphtali (I Chron. 6:76); elsewhere (Josh. 21:32) called *Kartan* (*q. v.*).

2. A very ancient town east of Jordan, from which the gigantic *Emim* (*q. v.*) were expelled by the Moabites (Gen. 14:5, A. V. "Kiriathaim;" comp. Deut. 2:9, 10). It was next held by the Amorites, from whom it was taken by the Israelites, and assigned to Reuben (Num. 32:37; Josh. 13:19). During the Assyrian exile the Moabites again took possession of this and other towns (Jer. 48:1; Ezek. 25:9, A. V. both "Kiriathaim"). *See* Moabite Stone, line 10. Harper and others identified it with the ruins of El Kŭreiyât, between Madeba and Dibon.

Kirʼjath-Arʼba (kĭrʼjăth-ärʼbȧ; *city of Arbah*), a city in the mountains of Judah, and named after Arba the Anakite (Gen. 23:2; Josh. 14:15; 15:54; 20:7; Judg. 1:10; Neh. 11:25), but better known as *Hebron* (*q. v.*).

Kirʼjath-Aʼrim (Ezra 2:25). *See* Kirjath-jearim.

Kirʼjath-Baʼal (kĭrʼjăth-bāʼăl; *city of Baal*), another name (Josh. 15:60; 18:14) for *Kirjath-jearim* (*q. v.*).

Kirʼjath-Huʼzoth (kĭrʼjăth-hūʼzŏth; *city of streets*), a city of Moab, to which Balak took Balaam to offer up sacrifice (Num. 22:39). Balak undoubtedly expected through these offerings to propitiate Jehovah and secure his favor to the Moabites. It was near Bamoth-baal (v. 41).

Kirʼjath-Jeʼarim (kĭrʼjăth-jēʼȧ-rĭm; *city of forests;* **Kirʼjath-Aʼrim** kĭrʼjăth-āʼrĭm; contracted form), a Gibeonite town (Josh. 9:17), first assigned to Judah (Josh. 15:60; Judg. 18:2), but afterward to Benjamin (Josh. 18:28). It was called Baalah (15:9) and Kirjath-baal (v. 60). "This must have lain somewhere about Mount Jearim, the rugged, wooded highlands which look down on the basin of Sorek from the north of the great defile. But the exact site is not known with certainty. Some think that it was the present Kuriet 'Enab to the north of Mount Jearim, and others Khurbet 'Erma to the south, near the mouth of the great defile. Each of these, it is claimed, echoes the ancient name; each suits the descriptions of Kirjath-jearim in the Old Testament. For the story of the ark, Khurbet 'Erma has the advantage, lying close to Beth-shemesh, and yet in the hill country. Leaving the question of the exact site open, we must be satisfied with the knowledge that Kirjath-jearim lay on the western border of Benjamin; once the ark was set there; it was off the debatable ground of the Shephelah and within Israel's proper territory. Here in the field of the woods it rested till David brought it up to Jerusalem (II Sam. 6:2, 3, 12; I Chron. 15:1-29; comp. Psa. 132).

Kirʼjath-Sanʼnah (kĭrʼjăth-săʼnȧ), called also Kirjath-sepher (kĭrʼjăth-sēfʼĕr) or "city of books." This S. Judah city of the hill country has been identified with Tell Beit Mirsim, some 13 miles W. S. W. of Hebron. Melvin Grove Kyle and W. F. Albright excavated the site from 1924 on. The results were most happy, revealing clear strata with occupation from c. 2200 B. C. At this place masonry of the Canaanites, Egyptians, Hyksos and Hebrews can be seen. This site has greatly increased knowledge of Hebrew craftsmanship, particularly pottery making, building and dyeing. Here a jar handle was recovered marked "Belonging to Eliakim, steward of Yaukin" (Jehoachin). Othniel took Debir and received Caleb's daughter Achsah as a reward (Josh. 15:7, 15). The city was given over to the descendants of the priesthood (Josh. 21:15).

M. F. U.

Kish (kĭsh).

1. The father of King Saul (I Sam. 9:3; 10:11, 21; 14:51; I Chron. 9:39; 12:1; 26: 28). He was a wealthy Benjamite, the son of Ner (I Chron. 8:33; 9:39), and grandson of Abiel, the "son" of (I Sam. 9:1), being used in the general sense of male descendant. No incident respecting him is mentioned with the exception of his sending Saul after the lost asses (9:3), and that he was buried in Zelah (II Sam. 21:14), B. C. about B. C. c. 1025. He is called *Cis* in Acts 13:21.

2. The third son of Jehiel (of Gibeon) and Maachah, a Benjamite of Jerusalem (I Chron. 8:30; 9:36).

3. The second son of Mahli (grandson of Levi). His sons married their cousins, the daughters of his brother Eleazar (I Chron. 23:21, 22; 24:29), B. C. probably before 1440.

4. Another Levite, also of the family of Merari. He was the son of Abdi, and assisted Hezekiah in cleansing the temple (II Chron. 29:12), B. C. 719.

5. A Benjamite, and great-grandfather of Mordecai (Esth. 2:5), B. C. considerably before 478.

6. An ancient lower Mesopotamian city 8 miles E. of Babylon. Excavated palaces, temples, canals and *ziggurat* (temple tower) give much information on Babylonian life before Abram's residence at Ur. Sargon I (c. 2380 B. C.) was a native of Kish. Hammurabi (c. 1700 B. C.) adorned the city.

Kish′i (kĭsh′ĭ; I Chron. 6:44). *See* Kushaiah.

Kish′ion (kĭsh′ĭ-ŏn; *hard ground*), a city of Issachar (Josh. 19:20), assigned to the Levites of the family of Gershon and for a city of refuge (21:28, A. V. "Kishon"). It is erroneously transcribed Kedesh (I Chron. 6:72).

Ki′shon (kī′shŏn; *bending, winding,*) and "Kison," Psa. 83:9; also known as the "waters of Megiddo" (Judg. 5:19), a torrent or winter stream in Central Palestine. It rises in the hills about Tabor and Gilboa, and running in a northeast direction through the plains of Esdraelon and Acre, empties into the Mediterranean Sea at the foot of Mount Carmel. The two channels of the stream unite a few miles N. of Magiddo. The channel of the united stream is here deep and miry, the ground for some distance on each side is low and marshy, and the fords during winter are always difficult, and often, after heavy rain, impassable; yet in summer, even here, the whole plain and river bed are dry and hard. Indeed, during the greater part of the year the stream is confined to a few miles next the sea. The modern name is *Nahr el Mukatta‘*, i. e., "the river of

slaughter" (comp. I Kings 18:40). In the song of Deborah (Judg. 5:21) it is spoken of as "that ancient river."

It was a little to the south of Kishon, viz., at Megiddo, that *Sisera* (*q. v.*) was defeated. While the battle raged a violent storm of wind and rain came (5:20, 21), and the plain became a marsh and the dry river bed a foaming torrent. This, of course, greatly interfered with the fighting of Sisera's cavalry and charioteers. Kishon was also the scene of the destruction of the prophets of Baal. Their slaughter doubtless took place near the foot of Carmel.

Ki′son (kī′sŏn; Psa. 83:9), another form of *Kishon* (*q. v.*).

Kiss. Kissing the lips by way of affectionate salutation was customary among near relatives of both sexes, both in patriarchal and in later times (Gen. 29:11; Cant. 8:1). Between individuals of the same sex, and in a limited degree between those of different sexes, the kiss on the cheek as a mark of respect or an act of salutation has at all times been customary in the East. In the Christian Church the kiss of charity was practiced not only as a friendly salutation, but as an act symbolical of love and Christian brotherhood (Rom. 16:16; I Cor. 16:20; II Cor. 13:21; I Thess. 5:26; I Pet. 5:14). It was embodied in the earlier Christian offices, and has been continued in some of those now in use. Among the Arabs the women and children kiss the beards of their husbands or fathers. The superior returns the salute by a kiss on the forehead. In Egypt an inferior kisses the hand of a superior, generally on the back, but sometimes, as a special favor, on the palm also. To testify abject submission, and in asking favors, the feet are often kissed instead of the hand. The written decrees of a sovereign are kissed in token of respect; even the ground is sometimes kissed by orientals in the fullness of their submission (Gen. 41:40; I Sam. 24:8; Psa. 72:9, etc.). Kissing is spoken of in Scripture as a mark of respect or adoration to idols (I Kings 19:18; Hos. 13:2), (Smith, *Bib. Dict.*, s. v.).

Kite. *See* Animal Kingdom.

Kith′lish (kĭth′lĭsh), a town in the valley of Judah (Josh. 15:40). It is identified by some with *Jelameh;* by others it is thought to be found in Tell *Chilchis*, to the S. S. E. of Beit-jibrin.

Kit′ron (kĭt′rŏn; *figurative, knotty*), a city in Zebulun, from which the Israelites did not expel the Canaanites (Judg. 1:30), probably the same as *Kattath* (*q. v.*). A. Alt locates it at Tell el-Far about 7½ miles S. E. of Haifa.

Kittim. *See* Chittim.

Knead, the preparation of dough by working it into a mass with the hands; a task usually performed by women (Gen. 18:6; I Sam. 28: 24; II Sam. 13:8, etc.), but sometimes by men (Hos. 7:4).

Kneading Trough, the vessel in which the dough was mixed and leavened and then left to rise (Exod. 8:3; 12:34; "store" in Deut. 28:5, 17). The Arabs use for this purpose a leather which can be drawn up into a bag by running a cord along the border, in which they often prepare and carry their dough. It is not probable that the troughs of the Hebrews, in the references above, were like these, as they were not a nomadic people. *See* Bread.

Knee. The expression "to bend the knee" has for its primary notion that of *breaking down*, and then to *invoke God, to bless* (II Chron. 6:13; Psa. 95:6; Dan. 6:10; Matt. 17:14). To bend the knee signifies also to give or receive a blessing, because the person blessed kneels. In this sense it refers to: (1) The benediction of dying parents (Gen. 27:4, 7, 10, 19); (2) of the priest to the people (Lev. 9:22, 23); (3) of a prophet (Num. 24:1; Deut. 33:1). It also signifies "to salute," which is connected with blessing (II Kings 4:29).

The expression, "And he made his camels to kneel down" (Gen. 24:11), means that they were to rest.

"To bow the knee" is to perform an act of worship (I Kings 19:18; Isa. 66:3, where the rendering is "he blessed an idol").

Kneeling in prayer was a practice of great antiquity; and references are made to it in both the Old Testament and New Testament (II Chron. 6:13; Psa. 95:6; Dan. 6:10; Luke 22:41; Acts 7:60; 9:40; 21:5; Eph. 3:14).

Figurative. Knees are used symbolically for *persons* (Job 4:4; Heb. 12:12).

Knife, the rendering of several Hebrew terms, but not important enough to be given.

1. **Material.** The knives of the Egyptians, and of other nations in early times, were probably only of hard stone, and the use of the flint or stone knife was sometimes retained for sacred purposes after the introduction of iron and steel. Herodotus (ii, 86) mentions knives both of iron and of stone in different stages of the same process of embalming. The same may perhaps be said to some extent of the Hebrews.

Lachish yielded an inscribed Hyksos knife. Hittite daggers have been recovered at Bethshan from about 1470 B. C. Till the time of Saul and David iron and "steel" knives with ivory handles were rare being monopolized by the iron-smelting Philistines.

2. **Uses**, etc. In their meals the Jews, like other orientals, made little use of knives, but they were required both for slaughtering animals either for food or sacrifice, as well as cutting up the carcasses (Lev. 7:33, 34; 8:15, 20, 25; 9:13; Num. 18:18; I Sam. 9:24, etc.). Smaller knives were in use for paring fruit (Joseph) and for sharpening pens (Jer. 36:23). The razor was often used for Nazaritic purposes, for which a special chamber was reserved in the temple (Num. 6:5, 9, 19; Ezek. 5:1, etc.). The pruning hooks of Isa. 18:5 were probably curved knives. The lancets of the priests of Baal were pointed knives (I Kings 18:28) and the suffering caused by cutting themselves with these knives was supposed to secure from Baal a favorable hearing. The knives which with other articles of temple furniture were brought back from Babylon were doubtless used for killing and dissecting the sacred victims (Ezra 1:9).

Knock (Heb. *dāphăq;* Gr. *krouō,* Cant. 5:2; Judg. 19:22, "beat;" Matt. 7:7; Rev. 3:20, etc.). "Though orientals are very jealous of their privacy, yet they never knock when about to enter your room, but walk in without warning or ceremony. It is nearly impossible to teach Arab servants to knock at your door. They give warning at the outer gate, or entrance, either by calling or knocking. To stand and *call* is a very common and respectful mode; and thus it was in Bible times, and to it there are many very interesting allusions. Moses commanded the holder of a pledge to stand without, and call to the owner thereof to come forth (Deut. 24:10). This was to avoid the insolent intrusion of cruel creditors. Peter stood knocking at the outer gate door (Acts 12:13, 16), and so did the three men sent to Joppa by Cornelius (Acts 10:17, 18). The idea is that the guard over your privacy is to be placed at the entrance to your premises" (Thomson, *Land and Book,* i, 191, sq.). The expression, "ask, seek, knock" (Matt. 7:7; Luke 11:9), is the climax depicting the rising of prayer into intense fervor.

Knop, an archaic translation of original words denoting the spheroidal decorations of the seven-branched candlestick (Exod. 25:31-36; 37:17-22). The meaning is "knob" or "bud" of a flower. The same is true of the ornamentation of the temple (I Kings 6:18) and the Molten Sea (I Kings 7:24). *See* Tabernacle.

Knowledge.

The expression "to know" sometimes means *to approve* of and take delight in (Psa. 1:6; Rom. 8:29); to cherish (John 10:27); to experience (Eph. 3:19). In Job 7:10 it is used of an inanimate object, "He shall return no more to his house, neither shall his place know him any more." By a euphemism "to know" frequently denotes sexual intercourse (Gen. 44:1).

Knowledge may be partial (I Cor. 13:9). It implies discovery, detection; as through the law comes the knowledge of sin (Rom. 3:20). Knowledge is spoken of as an emblematical person, and as the gift of God (Prov. 1:29; 8:10, etc.). Knowledge may be perverted, and thus become the medium of evil (Isa. 47:10; Rom. 1:28; I Cor. 8:1). Respecting divine knowledge, *see* Omniscience.

Ko'a (kō'á). This word occurs only in Ezek. 23:23, in the prophetic denunciations of punishment to the Jewish people from the various nations whose idolatries they had adopted: "The Babylonians, and all the Chaldeans, Pekod and Shoa, and Koa, and all the Assyrians with them." The Koa are evidently to be equated with *Kutu (Ku)* located E. of the Tigris and S. of the lower Zab.

Ko'hath (kō'hăth), the second son of Levi (Gen. 46:11), and the father of Amram, Izehar, Hebron, and Uzziel (Num. 3:19). Of his personal history we only know that he went down to Egypt with Levi and Jacob (Gen. 46:11); that his sister was Jochebed (Exod. 6:20); and that he lived to the age of one hundred and thirty-three years (6:18), B. C. about 1871. His descendants, the *Kohathites* (*q. v.*), formed one of the three great divisions of the Levites, and contained the priestly family descended from Aaron (6:18-20). In the service of the tabernacle their duty was to bear the ark and the sacred vessels (Num. 4:15; 7:9). The inheritance of the Kohathites who were not priests lay in the half tribe of Manasseh in Ephraim (I Chron. 6:61-70) and in Dan. (Josh. 21:5, 20-26).

Ko'hathites (kō'há-thīts), the descendants of Kohath, the second of the three sons of Levi (Gershon, Kohath, Merari), from whom the three principal divisions of the Levites derived their name (Gen. 46:11; Num. 3:17; II Chron. 34:12, etc.). *See* Levites, 5 (1).

Kola'iah (kō-lā'yá; *voice of Jehovah*).

1. A Benjamite, and remote ancestor of Sallu, which latter dwelt in Jerusalem after the captivity (Neh. 11:7), B. C. long before 445.

2. The father of Ahab, which latter was a false prophet denounced by Jeremiah (Jer. 29:21), B. C. about 626.

Ko'rah (kō'rá).

1. **The third son of Esau** by his Canaanite concubine Aholibamah (Gen. 36:5, 14, 18; I Chron. 1:35), B. C. about 1950. He was born in Canaan before Esau migrated to Mount Seir (Gen. 36:5-9), and became the head of a petty Edomitish tribe (36:18), where "duke" means "tribe head." "Korah, in Gen. 36:16, has probably been copied by mistake from v. 18" (K. and D., *Com.*, in loc.).

2. **The Levite** who conspired with Dathan and Abiram against Moses. Korah was the son of Izhar, the brother of Amram, the father of Moses and Aaron, making him cousin to these leaders of Israel (Exod. 6:21; Num. 16:1). About all that we know of Korah is in connection with the conspiracy of which he was one of the leaders (Num. 16:1-49). (1) **Reasons for conspiracy.** Korah was probably influenced by jealousy because the high honors and privileges of the priesthood had been exclusively appropriated by the family of Aaron. Moses having supreme authority in civil affairs, the whole power over the nation would seem to have been engrossed by him and Aaron. The particular grievance which rankled in the minds of Korah and his company was their exclusion from the office of priesthood—and their being confined—those among them who were Levites—to the inferior service of the tabernacle. (2) **Complaint.** Having joined to himself Dathan and Abiram and two hundred and fifty "princes of the assembly," Korah appeared with them before Moses and Aaron, and charged them with usurpation of privileges and offices rightfully belonging to others. Moses no sooner heard this charge than he fell upon his face, as if to refer the matter to the Lord (comp. Num. 14:5), and declared that the decision should be left to Jehovah. He told them to appear the next day with censers and incense. (3) **Destruction.** The next day the rebels presented themselves before the tabernacle, along with Moses and Aaron; and the whole congregation were gathered at the instigation of Korah. The Shekinah appeared, and a voice commanded Moses and Aaron to separate themselves from the congregation, that they might not share in its destruction for making common cause with the conspirators. The two leaders prayed that the people might be spared, and that Jehovah would confine his wrath to the leaders of the rebellion. The congregation, instructed by Moses, withdrew, and, after Moses had appealed to what was about to happen as a proof of the authority by which

he had acted, the earth opened and then closed over the fallen tents of Korah, Dathan, and Abiram. The other two hundred and fifty rebels, who were probably in front of the tabernacle, were then consumed by "fire from the Lord," B. C. about 1430. The censers of the rebels were made into plates to form an outer covering to the altar, a warning of the just judgment of God (v. 38, sq.). The next morning the whole congregation murmured against Moses and Aaron, and charged them with having slain the people of Jehovah. Notwithstanding the prayers of Moses and his brother, they could not avert the bursting forth of wrathful judgment. A plague destroyed fourteen thousand seven hundred (vers. 41-50), and the high priesthood of Aaron was confirmed (ch. 17). As the descendants of Korah afterward became eminent in the Levitical service, it is clear that his sons were spared. They were probably living in separate tents, or separated themselves from the conspirators at the command of Moses. He is referred to in Num. 26:9-11; I Chron. 6:22, 37. In Jude (v. 11; A. V. "Core") Korah is coupled with Cain and Balaam, and is held up as a warning to presumptuous and self-seeking teachers.

3. **Son of Hebron.** The eldest of the four sons of Hebron, of the family of Caleb and tribe of Judah (I Chron. 2:43), B. C. considerably after 1380.

Ko'rahite (kō'rá-hīt; I Chron. 9:19, 31), *Korhite*, or *Korathite*, that portion of the Kohathite Levites who were descended from *Korah* (*q. v.*). *See* Levites, 5 (1).

Ko'rathites, the (kō'rá-thīts; Num. 26:58). *See* Korahite.

Ko're (kō'rê; *crier*, or a *partridge*).

1. A Levite, the son of Ebiasaph, and father of Shallum, who was doorkeeper of the tabernacle (I Chron. 9:19). in I Chron. 26:1, Kore is named as the father of Meshelemiah (or Shelemiah), a temple warden, B. C. about 960.

2. (I Chron. 26:19). Erroneous translation for *Korahites*.

3. Son of Imnah, a Levitical keeper of the East Gate, appointed by Hezekiah to receive the thank offerings and distribute them to the priests (II Chron. 31:14), B. C. 719.

Kor'hites, the (kōr'hīts; Exod. 6:24; I Chron. 12:6; 26:1; II Chron. 20:19). *See* Korahite.

Koz (kŏz; a *thorn*), the head of the seventh division of priests according to the arrangement of David (I Chron. 24:10), where the name is translated *Hakkoz*, B. C. about 975. He is probably the same whose descendants were excluded by Nehemiah from the priesthood because of their defective pedigree (Ezra 2:61; Neh. 7:63). To the same family seems to have belonged Meremoth, who repaired two portions of the walls of Jerusalem, one portion of which extended from the door of the high priest's house to the end of it. (Neh. 3:4, 21). *See* Coz.

Kusha'iah (kû-shā'yà), a Merarite Levite, whose son Ethan was appointed a chief assistant of Heman in the temple music by David (I Chron. 15:17), B. C. 975. In I Chron. 6:44, he is called *Kishi*.

L

La'adah (lā'á-dá; uncertain meaning), the second son of Shelah (son of Judah), and "father" (founder) of Mareshah (I Chron. 4:21).

La'adan (lā'á-dăn; as above).

1. An Ephraimite, the son of Tahan, and grandfather of Elishama, which latter was prince of his tribe at the Exodus (I Chron. 7:26), B. C. before 1440.

2. The first named of the two sons of Gershom, the son of Levi (I Chron. 23:7-9; 26: 21). He is called *Libni* (6:17). Keil (*Com.*, in loc.) thinks that Laadan was a later descendant of Gershom than Libni, and that the Shimei of v. 9 was a descendant of Libni, not elsewhere mentioned.

La'ban (lā'bǎn; *white*).

1. The son of Bethuel (Gen. 28:5), grandson of Nahor, Abraham's kinsman, and brother of Rebekah (Gen. 24:15, 29); an Aramaean herd owner of Mesopotamia. He united with his father, according to the usual custom, in consenting to the marriage of Rebekah to Isaac (24:50, sq.), B. C. about 1920. When their son Jacob became of marriageable age his parents directed him to take a wife from the daughters of Laban, and Jacob complied (28:2, 5). Laban arranged with his nephew to give him Rachel to wife on condition of seven years' service, but on the wedding night led Leah, his eldest daughter, into the bridechamber. When complained to by Jacob he made the weak excuse, "It must not be so done in our country, to give the younger before the firstborn." But, to satisfy Jacob, he promised to give him Rachel in a week if he would serve him seven years longer. To this Jacob consented, and eight days later was wedded to the woman he loved (29:15-30). At the end of the second period of seven years Jacob desired to return to Canaan, but Laban persuaded him to remain, and made a contract with him to keep his flocks. By a cunning artifice Jacob made this bargain result greatly to his own advantage (30:25-43), and at the end of six years left stealthily for his former home (31:1-21). Three days after, Laban, hearing of Jacob's flight, started in pursuit, and overtook him on the seventh day at Mount Gilead. The night before he was warned by God in a dream "not to speak to Jacob either good or bad," i. e., not to threaten or persuade him to return. He confined himself to bitter reproaches; told Jacob that he had power to do him harm if God had not forbidden him, and accused him of stealing his gods (the teraphim). Rachel concealed the theft by resorting to a trick well calculated to deceive. Thereupon Jacob grew angry and remonstrated with Laban, who at once proposed a covenant of peace. This was celebrated with a feast, and the next morning Laban departed to his own place (31:22, sq.).

2. A place in the desert, on the route of the Israelites (Deut. 1:1), probably identical with *Libnah* (Num. 33:20).

Labor, the rendering of a large number of Hebrew and Greek terms. The teaching of Scripture (Gen. 2:15) is that man, even in his state of innocency, was to lead a life of activity, which was very different, however, from the trouble and restlessness of the weary toil into which he was plunged by sin. Exercise of some kind was essential to his wellbeing (Eccl. 5:12). In consequence of the fall, the earth no longer yielded spontaneously the fruits requisite for man's maintenance, but he was obliged to secure the necessaries of life by labor and strenuous exertion (Gen. 3:19).

"*Work*, as distinguished from *labor*, is not so much a term denoting a lighter kind of labor as a general and comprehensive term applied to the performance of any task, whether easy or severe. '*Avōdāh* is the execution of a definite daily task, whether in field labor (Psa. 104: 23) and mechanical employment (Exod. 39: 32) on the one hand, or priestly service and the duties connected with the worship on the other (Exod. 12:25, 26; Lev. 23:7, sq.), i. e., such occupations as came under the denomination of labor, business, or industrial employment" (K. and D., *Com.*, on Exod. 20:8).

That labor was held in high respect we gather from such expressions as, "Seest thou a man diligent in business (skilled in his work), he shall stand before kings" (Prov. 22:29; comp. 10:4; 12:24, 27). When Nebuchadnezzar carried the Jews away into captivity he found among them a thousand craftsmen and smiths (II Kings 24:14-16; Jer. 29:2).

The ancient rabbins regarded manual labor as honorable, and urged it upon all as a duty. In the Talmud we find such sayings as the following: "He who does not teach his son a craft is, as it were, bringing him up to robbery;" "Labor is greatly to be prized, for it elevates the laborer, and maintains him."

Value of Labor. The following values of labor are given by F. R. Conder (*Bib. Ed.*, iii, 223, sq.): "The *denarius*, which was the Roman equivalent for a quarter shekel, was a day's pay of a Roman soldier. This was in exact accordance with the price, mentioned in the parable of the laborers in the vineyard, of a penny a day. The limit between the proper subject for alms for the purpose of support and the independent man was fixed by the oral law at the receipt of two hundred *zuzae*, that is to say, to one shekel per week, . . . This was considered by the law of Moses to be the lowest rate at which life was to be supported." *See* Handicrafts, Service.

Lace (Heb. *päthîl*, *twined*), the blue *cord* with which the high priest's breastplate was tied to the ephod (Exod. 28:28, 37; 39:21, 31). The Hebrew term is rendered "ribband" (Num. 15:38); "thread" (Judg. 16:9, etc.).

262. Fortress of Lachish in Judah with Double Wall and Triple Gate (reconstructed)

La'chish (lā'kĭsh), a royal Canaanite city and one of the chief fortresses of Judah, identified with the large 22-acre mound now known as Tell ed-Duweir. It is situated 30 miles S. W. of Jerusalem, 15 miles W. of Hebron. It is of immense strategic importance, dominating the old road from the Palestinian highland to the Nile valley. The site was excavated by the Wellcome-Marston Archaeological Expedition in 1933. The work was supervised by J. L. Starkey until his murder by bandits early in 1938. The excavation of this site, ranking in importance with Beth-shan and Megiddo, was thereafter carried on by Charles H. Inge and Lankester Harding. The city was occupied several millennia before Abraham and was an important city still standing when the Israelites invaded Palestine. Its king, Japhia, joined a confederacy against Joshua (Josh. 10:3, 5) but was captured by the Israelites (Josh. 10:31-35; 12:11). It was rebuilt or fortified by Rehoboam (II Chron. 11:9). It had a reputation for strength. Amaziah fled hither and was slain (II Kings 14:19; II Chron. 25:27). Lachish was strong enough to resist the seige of Sennacherib when on his way to Egypt (II Kings 18:13-17; II Chron. 32:9; Isa. 36:2; 37:8). The city experienced two destructions by Nebuchadnezzar, one in 598 B. C. when Jehoiachin and the Jerusalem citizens were carried into captivity (II Kings 24) and another in 587 B. C. when the city was reduced to ashes. After the exile it was reoccupied (Neh. 11:30). Micah (1:13) denounced Lachish because it was the first to

grant admission to the iniquities of Israel into Judah i. e., the idolatry of the image worship of the ten tribes. (See Micah 1:5; Amos 3:14). The powerful Sennacherib in his advance upon Palestine (c. 701 B. C.) besieged Lachish (II Chron. 32:9; II Kings 18:17-19:37). The cuneiform inscriptions relate the story of the attack on Lachish. Among Sennacherib's records is an account of his capture of 46 Judaean cities. The Assyrian emperor boasts of shutting up Hezekiah "like a bird" in Jerusalem, his royal city. Archaeological evidences of the Assyrian siege are numerous. The Hyksos period from c. 1730-1560 B. C. has been traced in corresponding strata with Lachish. Especially important is the deep defense ditch or fosse characteristic of the period, used evidently as an enclosure for animals, perhaps horses. The Tell el Armana Letters (c. 1380 B. C.) mention the city. Numbers of inscrip-

264. Decoration on Bichrome Ware from Lachish, c. 1500 B. C.

tions have been found at the site, notably a broken bowl written in Egyptian apparently by an Egyptian tax collector enumerating certain wheat deliveries. This is dated in the "year 4" of a certain pharaoh. Many scholars connect this notation with Merenptah (c. 1230 B. C.). This is one bit of evidence which leads some scholars to place the date of the Exodus in the 13th century under the XIX Dynasty. Also found in a Late Bronze Age temple at Lachish were a bowl and a jar inscribed in an early Canaanite script. This script is identical with that of the proto-Semitic inscriptions found at Serabit el-Khadem on the Sinai Peninsula and in similar levels at Shechem, Gezer and Beth Shemesh. Most important of all of the Lachish discoveries are the so-called Lachish Letters. These priceless documents, of vast epigraphic importance, illustrate the Hebrew current in the time of Jeremiah. They are to be dated between the two Babylonian sieges of Lachish (598-587 B. C.). Eighteen of these pieces of ancient inscribed pottery were found in 1935, to which three more were added in 1938. (See Harry Torczyner, *La-*

263. A Lachish Letter

265. Ivory Inlay from Lachish (13th Century B. C.)

chish I, The Lachish Letters, 1938; W. F. Albright, *Bull. Am. Schs.* 70, 1938, p. 11-17
also *Bull.* 80, 1940, p. 11-13; *Bull.* 82, p. 24.
Practically all of these ostraca were written
by a certain Hoshaiah, who was stationed at
a military outpost, to a man named Jaosh,
evidently the high commanding officer at Lachish. (See Jack Finegan, *Life From the Ancient
Past,* p. 162). M. F. U.

Lad (Heb. *nă'ăr*). This term is applied to the
young from the time of infancy to that of
adolescence—of an infant just born (Exod.
2:6; Judg. 13:5, 7; I Sam. 4:21); of a boy
not yet full grown (Gen. 21:16, sq.; 21:12;
22:12; Isa. 7:16; 8:4); and a of youth nearly
twenty years of age (Gen. 34:19; 41:12; I
Kings 3:7; II Sam. 18:5, 29); and occasionally of a *girl,* or maiden (Gen. 24:14, 16; 34:3,
12; Deut. 22:15, sq.). In some of the above
passages the A. V. renders "child." *See*
Children.

Ladder (Heb. *sŭllăm, staircase*). This word occurs only in the account of Jacob's dream at
Beth-el (Gen. 28:12, "and behold a ladder
set up on the earth, and the top of it reached
to heaven," etc.). By many the rendering
"staircase" is preferred, and is supposed to
apply to the rocky mountain side. The vision
that Jacob saw of angels ascending and descending teaches the fact of communication
between heaven and earth, and the ministry
of angels. To us there is a deeper meaning
since the incarnation. The true staircase by
which heavenly messengers ascend and descend is the Son of man. It is he who really
bridges the interval between heaven and earth,
God and man. However, the true fulfillment
of Jacob's vision will not take place till the
Millennial Age when the covenant with
Abraham confirmed in Isaac and Jacob will
be realized (John 1:49-51).

La'el (lā'ĕl; *to, belonging to God* i. e., devoted
to him), the father of Eliasaph, who was chief
of the Gershonites at the time of the Exodus
(Num. 3:24), B. C. 1210.

La'had (lā'hăd; *oppression,* cf. Arab. *lahada, to
press down, overburden*), the second of the two
sons of Jahath, a descendant of Judah (I
Chron. 4:2), B. C. after 1210.

Lahai'-roi (là-hī'roi; Gen. 24:62; 25:11), elsewhere *Beer-Lahai-roi* (*q. v.*).

Lah'mam (lā'măm), a city in the plain of
Judah (Josh. 15:40), perhaps among the Phil-

istines west of the highlands of Judea. It is
thought to be represented by the ruins of
el-Lahm, near Beit-Jibrin.

Lah'mi (lä'mī), named as the brother of Goliath, and slain by Elhanan (I Chron. 20:5).
Dr. Strong (McC. and S., *Cyc.,* s. v.) considers
this an incorrect reading for Bethlehemite, as
in the parallel passage (II Sam. 21:19). Winer,
Keil, Deutsch, Grove, and others maintain
that Chronicles gives the true reading. *See*
Goliath.

La'ish (lā'ĭsh; a *lion*).
 1. A native of Gallim, a Benjamite, to whose
son Phalti Saul gave David's wife Michal (I
Sam. 25:44; II Sam. 3:15), B. C. about 1015.
 2. A place in the north of Palestine (Judg.
18:7, 14), about four miles from Paneas, at the
head of the Jordan. It was taken by the restless Danites and included within their territory. It is called also Leshem and Dan (Josh.
19:47; Judg. 18:7, 29; Jer. 8:16), now identified with *Tell-el-Kady,* "the mound of the
judge," to the north of the waters of Merom
(Josh. 11:5).
 3. A place mentioned in Isa. 10:30, and
thought by some to be the modern *el-Isawiyeh,*
about a mile N. E. from Jerusalem. R. V. and
R. S. V. Laishah.

Lake (Gr. *limnē,* a *pool*), a term used in the
New Testament only of the Lake of Gennesaret (Luke 5:1, 2; 8:22, 23, 33), and the
"lake of fire" (Rev. 19:20; 20:10, 14, 15;
21:8). *See* Gehenna.

Lak'kam (lăk'ăm), A. V. **La'kam** (lā'kăm; *an
obstruction,* cf. Arab. *lakama, to obstruct a road-
way*), a place in the northeast of Naphtali
(Josh. 19:33).

La'ma (lä'mä), a term signifying *why,* quoted
from Psa. 22:1 by our Saviour on the cross
(Matt. 27:46; Mark 15:34).

Lamb. Lambs and young rams form an important part of almost every sacrifice in the O. T.
(Num. 6:14; Lev. 4:32 (*See* Sacrifice). The
term is used typically of Christ as the Sin
Bearer of the world (John 1:29, 36). It was
evidently used early to describe the redemption to be brought by the long-awaited Messiah (Isa. 53:7). The sheep speaks eloquently
of the coming Redeemer and Sin-Bearer. Especially significant is the use of the figure of
the lamb as a symbol of Christ in the Apocalypse. There the lamb-lion figure portrays
Christ in His future victory as crowned be-

LAMB

cause of His redemptive work (Rev. 5:12-13; 7:9; 22:1, 3). The term "marriage supper of the Lamb" (Rev. 19:7-9) symbolizes the union of Christ and His Church in glory previous to His Second Coming to the earth to destroy His enemies, oust earthly Satanic power and to set up the long awaited mediatorial kingdom of Israel (Rev. 19:11-17). *M. F. U.*

Lamb, as the symbol of Christ (John 1:36; I Pet. 1:19; Rev. 13:8), was typified by the paschal lamb (*q. v.*), and travestied by the Antichrist, who sets himself up as the true Christ, professing to imitate the Redeemer, and whose False Prophet is described as "another beast coming up out of the earth; and he had two horns like a lamb" (Rev. 13:11).

Lamb of God, a title given to our Lord (John 1:29, 36; comp. Acts 8:32; I Pet. 1:19). In these passages Christ is likened to a sacrificial lamb on account of his death, innocently and patiently endured, to expiate sin. In the Revelation John beheld "a lamb as it had been slain, having seven horns and seven eyes, which are the seven spirits of God sent forth into all the earth" (Rev. 5:6); i. e., invested with the attributes of God, omnipotence and omniscience, and sharing the universal empire and homage of the universe.

Lame, a general term signifying imperfect, either by birth or injury. Lameness is mentioned among the bodily imperfections which would exclude a son (descendant) of Aaron from entering the holy place or offering sacrifices (*q. v.*). A person thus afflicted might, however, eat of the sacrifices, like other priests (Lev. 21:17-23).

La'mech (lā'mĕk).

1. The fifth in descent from Cain, being the son of Methusael and the father of Jabal, Jubal, Tubalcain, and the latter's sister, Naamah (Gen. 4:18-22). Lamech took two wives, Adah and Zillah, and was thus the first to practice polygamy. To the narrative of Lamech we are indebted for the only example of antediluvian poetry (vers. 23, 24):

> "Adah and Zillah, hear my voice;
> Wives of Lamech, hearken unto my speech:
> For a man I slew for my wound,
> And a young man for my stripes.
> For sevenfold is Cain avenged,
> And Lamech seven-and-seventyfold."

Many views have been entertained as to the meaning of these words. Keil (*Com.*, in loc.) says that "in the form of pride and arrogance Lamech celebrates the inventions of Tubalcain;" and the idea of the song is, "Whoever inflicts a wound or stripe on me, whether man or youth, I will put to death; and for every injury done to my person I will take ten times more vengeance than that with which God promised to avenge the murder of my ancestor Cain." Turner (*Companion to Genesis*, p. 209) says "that he had slain a young man, not in cold blood, but in consequence of a wound or bruise he had himself received; and on the ground, apparently, of a difference between his case and that of Cain's—viz., that he had done *under* provocation what Cain had done *without* it—he assures himself of an interest in the divine guardianship greater than that granted to Cain."

2. The son of Methuselah and father of

LAMENTATIONS, BOOK OF

Noah. He lived to be seven hundred and seventy-seven years of age (Gen. 5:25-31; I Chron. 1:3; Luke 3:36).

La'med (lä'mĕd; *oxgoad*). Letter 12 of the Hebrew alphabet corresponding to Greek *lambda*, English "l." It stands before the twelfth section of Psa. 119 in which each verse of the Hebrew begins with this letter.

Lament. *See* Mourning.

Lamentations, Book of, one of the so-called Megilloth, or Rolls, found in the third part of the Hebrew canon. The work consists of five elegiac poems lamenting the destruction of Jerusalem at the time of the Babylonian captivity. It is termed *Ekah* (How!) in the Hebrew from its initial word. The Gr. rendering in the Septuagint is *Threnoi*, rendered as Lamentations in the Latin. The name of Jeremiah is usually appended as the traditional author.

1. **Purpose.** Lamentations portrays the reaction of a devout Israelite toward the destruction of the theocracy. The tragic scene presents God's people so corrupt that Jehovah has forsaken His sanctuary and abandoned it to enemies. The poet celebrates the Lord's righteousness but bewails the iniquity of the nation. The inhabitants are called upon to repent. The whole note is one of deep tragedy. The Lord's people from whom salvation would eventually come have become so vile as to be fit only to be destroyed.

2. **The Form.** The first four elegiac poems are alphabetic. In the first two (chaps. 1 and 2) a new letter of the Hebrew alphabet opens each verse, which has three parts. In the third lamentation (chap. 3) three verses are allotted to each of the 22 letters of the alphabet, and every verse in each group of three begins with the same letter. In the fourth dirge, one verse composed of two members is distributed to each letter. The last dirge is not alphabetic but consists of 22 verses. The meter is what is known as *qinah*, a special elegiac arrangement. The first member of the verse is longer than the second; sometimes it is called the "limping verse." Instead of being balanced and reinforced by the second, it is faintly echoed, giving the effect of the whole dying away in a plaintive cadence.

3. **Authorship.** Many scholars such as Chaney, Ewald, Eissfeldt, Pfeiffer and others dismiss authorship by Jeremiah. The main reason given in support of this is that the tradition is unreliable, being removed by three centuries from the age of the prophet. Internal evidence in comparison with Jeremiah's other writings, and several historical allusions are used as alleged evidence. In reply it may be said that if Jeremiah is not the author, no other contemporaneous writer fits the category with any show of probability. Denying Jeremiah's authorship, critics are cast into complete confusion concerning the question of who the author was. The long-sustained tradition of Jeremiah's authorship could hardly have arisen without solid basis. Argument from differences in vocabulary are extremely precarious. Supporting Jeremiah's authorship is a strong and persistent tradition dating from the time of the Greek version. The Vulgate and the Targum of Jonathan,

641

as well as many of the church fathers and numerous later commentators follow this tradition. Internal evidence is also suggestive. The scenes are life like in their portrayal and suggest an eye witness. A comparison of the Lamentations with Jeremiah's other writings also show points of similarity, and the sensitive temperament of the great prophet is reflected in the elegiac poems. (See S. R. Driver, *Intro.*, 1913, p. 462 for similarities). *M. F. U.*

Lamp (Heb. *nēr lăppîd*, torch, Gr. *lampas*). The terms *candle* and *candlestick* are frequent in the A. V., where *lamp* and *lampstand* would have been more literal renderings. Although lamps are frequently mentioned in Scripture, no indication is given of their form and structure. The natural supposition is that they were similar to those employed in surrounding countries, especially Egypt, to which in matters of art and comfort the Israelites stood nearly related. The following are the references to lamps:

1. That part of the golden candlestick (*q. v.*) which bore the light; also of the ten golden candlesticks in the Temple of Solomon (Exod. 25:37; I Kings 7:49; II Chron. 4:20; 13:11; Zech. 4:2).

2. A torch, such as were carried by the soldiers of Gideon (Judg. 7:16, 20), and, perhaps, similar to those which Samson tied to the foxes' tails (15:4). *See* Torch.

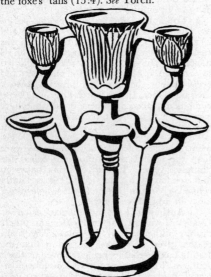

266. Egyptian Lamp from
King Tutankhamun's Tomb

3. Lamps for domestic use. The form of these may probably be inferred from the prevailing shape of ancient specimens from neighboring nations that have come down to us. In the British Museum there are various forms of ancient Egyptian lamps, of terra cotta and bronze, with ornaments in bas-relief. It seems that the Hebrews, like other ancient and modern orientals, were accustomed to burn lamps overnight in their chambers, which custom gave rise to several symbols. Modern Egyptian lamps consist of small glass vessels with a tube at the bottom

containing a cotton wick twisted around a piece of straw.

4. The use of lamps fed with oil in marriage processions is alluded to in the parable of the ten virgins (Matt. 25:1). These probably were similar to the modern Egyptian lantern, called *fanoos*, a sort of folding lantern.

267. Roman Lamp (upper); Ancient Lamp
from the Catacombs (lower)

5. **Figurative.** Lamp is used as symbolical of: The word of God (Psa. 119:105; Prov. 6: 23); the omniscience of Christ (Dan. 10:6; Rev. 1:14); salvation of God (Gen. 15:17; Isa. 62:1); God's guidance (II Sam. 22:29; Psa. 18:28, "candle"); spirit of man (Prov. 20:27, "candle"); ministers and wise rulers (John 5:35, "light;" II Sam. 21:17, marg.); completely put out, the destruction of him who curses his parents (Prov. 20:20).

Lance (Heb. *kîdōn*; Jer. 50:42, usually called "spear"), a javelin in distinction from the long-handled spear. *See* Armor I (3).

Lancet (Heb. *rōmăḥ*, to *hurl*, I Kings 18:28). This word is elsewhere rendered and appears to mean a javelin, or light spear. It may mean the iron point or head of a lance. *See* Armor I (3).

Land. Respecting the cultivation of land by the Hebrews, *see* Agriculture.

Land and Property. 1. **Distribution.** The patriarchs were promised for their posterity the possession of Canaan on the west of Jordan. Owing to the opposition of the Amorites, who had formed two large kingdoms on the east of Jordan, the Israelites were compelled to wage war with Sihon of Heshbon and Og of Bashan. Defeated by Israel, their territory was taken and divided by Moses, who gave it to the tribes of Reuben and Gad, and the half tribe of Manasseh. They were allowed to enter upon their possession, however, only after having fulfilled their promise of sending all their men of war in aid of their brethren over the Jordan (Num., ch. 32; Deut. 2:26-3:20; Josh. 13:15-32).

Joshua had charge of the taking and dividing of Canaan, and, having defeated thirty-one kings and taken their cities, he proceeded, by divine command, to divide the whole land among the remaining tribes, according to the boundaries fixed by Moses (Num. 34:1-35:8). The portion of each tribe was fixed by lot, i. e., by lot it was decided where each tribe was to be located (26:52-56; 33:54). Then the compass, size, and boundaries of the several territories were settled and regulated by the commission appointed for the purpose, consisting of Eleazar the priest, Joshua, and twelve princes of the tribes mentioned by name (Num. 34:16-29; Josh. 14:1). Naturally the extent of territory assigned to each tribe depended upon its number (Num. 33:54). A committee was formed of three men out of each tribe to survey the land (Josh. 18:4-9), i. e., not to measure it geometrically, but to have it described according to the number of its cities and villages, its soil, etc. The land was subdivided, so that every clan and father's house received an inheritance for itself. All the land was not immediately taken possession of, for the Canaanites were not extirpated. In the course of time the Canaanites left in the land were subjugated, and their land became the property of the Israelites. As to the division of the cities, towns, and villages, the Old Testament does not give any clear account.

Israel was taught that they had conquered Canaan only by the help of Jehovah (Psa. 44:3), and that the land was and remained the property of Jehovah, the covenant God (Lev. 25:23). Though the land was promised to the children of Israel for an everlasting possession (Gen. 13:15, sq.), yet their retaining it was conditional on their faithful fulfillment of its covenant obligations (Lev. 26:32, sq.; Deut. 4:26, sq.; 11:19, sq.), and even the ground did not become Israel's property in such a way that the possessor could dispose of it as he willed.

2. **Laws.** (1) **Rest.** (*a*) That Israel might be constantly reminded of the condition upon which it held the land, a year of rest for the ground was to be observed every seventh year, "a Sabbath for the Lord" (Lev. 25:4); and every fiftieth year was to be a jubilee, in which everyone returned to his property (25:10, 13). (*b*) *Sale.* The land was not to be sold in perpetuity, but there was a provision for redeeming the land by the seller or next of kin (25:23, 24); and if not redeemed before, the land reverted without payment in the jubilee year to its original possessor or his heir (v. 28). Thus every sale of land became a lease, since only its produce was sold, till the jubilee (25:15, 16). (2) **Redemption.** In case the owner or his next of kin wished to redeem the land, then the years that had elapsed since the sale were reckoned, and the buyer received only as much purchase money as would be due for the time remaining till the next jubilee (Lev. 25:25-27). This right of redemption in the jubilee held *absolutely* for (1) property in lands and houses in villages and unwalled places; (2) for the houses of the Levites in the cities allotted for them, and the attached fields (25:31-34). In a *limited* way it held: (1) the dwelling house in walled cities; for them the right of redemption lasted only a full year from the day of sale (vers.

29, 30); (2) for the fields vowed unto the Lord, with the limitation, that if they were not recovered for the prescribed valuation, but were sold to another, they did not revert in the jubilee to their original possessor or his heir, but as being holy to Jehovah like a devoted field, became the property of the priests (27:14-21). Houses in walled cities were not so closely connected with the land, which the Lord gave to his people for an inheritance, that they could be regarded as inalienable. (3) **Consecration.** A bought field could be consecrated to the Lord by the buyer only so far as it had become his property. Strictly speaking, he had only bought its produce until the jubilee, and could, therefore, vow only this to Jehovah. If he ransomed it he ransomed it for himself till the jubilee; if he did not ransom it, the sanctuary had the use of it for this interval, after which the field reverted in either case without payment to the original owner (Lev. 27:22-24). An hereditary owner could vow a portion to Jehovah, who had given him all. In such a case ransom was allowed till the jubilee by the payment of the value of the harvests till this date with an added fifth. Then the field remained his property, and from the jubilee onward its produce again belonged to him cost free. If not redeemed it was understood that he had given it wholly to Jehovah, and it became the property of the priests (27:16-21).

Landmark (Heb. *g⁽e⁾būl*), a mark to designate the boundary of land; a stone, stake, or other monument. The removal of such landmark was prohibited by the Mosaic law (Deut. 19:14; 27:27; Prov. 22:28; comp. Job 24:2), on account of the close connection in which a man's possession as the means of his support stood to the life of the man himself. Landmarks were held sacred by other nations; by the Romans, for example, who held them so sacred that removal was punished with death.

Lane (Gr. *hrumē*, Luke 14:21) a narrow way or passage in a town, shut in by buildings on both sides (Matt. 6:2; Acts 9:11; 12:10, A. V. "street").

Languages. The ancient Biblical world was thoroughly polyglot. Important was Sumerian, a non-Semitic pictograph and sign language current in southern Babylonia previous to 3000 B. C. The Semitic Babylonians brought in Akkadian, written in cuneiform characters. The great family of Semitic languages included its Eastern branch, Assyrian-Babylonian (Akkad.); N. W. Semitic, Aramaic, Ugaritic, Hebrew and Phoenician; S. Semitic, Arabic, Ethiopic and Amharic. The language of the Philistines still remains obscure. The Moabites spoke a dialect very similar to Hebrew, as shown by the Moabite Stone discovered in 1868. The Gezer Calendar (c. 925 B. C.), the Siloam Inscription (c. 702 B. C.) and the Lachish Letters (c. 589 B. C) give us epigraphic evidence of the development of Hebrew. (See HEBREW LANGUAGE). The Ugaritic Tablets from Ras Shamra (1929-1937) have greatly illuminated Canaanite dialects, and being closely associated with Hebrew, have shed much light on the language of the O. T. As a cultural bridge between the great Nile Empire and the empires on the

Halys in Asia Minor and on the Tigris-Euphrates in Mesopotamia, the ancient Hebrews came constantly in contact with various languages. Now well known are Hittite, Hurrian and Semitic dialects spoken in antiquity. Excavations at Boghaz-Keui, Mari on the Middle Euphrates, . . . and at Nuzu in the Tigris country have yielded a whole vast cuneiform literature in Hittite and Hurrian. At the end of the O. T. period (c. 400 B. C.) Hebrew began to fade out and Aramaic became the *lingua franca* of S. W. Asia as Akkadian had been in the Armana Period (c. 1400 B. C.). By the time of Jesus, Aramaic was the common vernacular in Palestine with *koine* Greek a universal language since Alexander's conquests in the fourth century B. C. The Latin of the Roman Empire also became a kind of *lingua franca*. The superscription on the cross was hence written in Greek, Latin and Hebrew (Aramaic) (Luke 23:38).

M. F. U.

Lantern (Gr. *phanos, shining*). This word occurs only in John 18:3, where it is recorded that the party which went to Gethsemane were provided "with lanterns, and torches, and weapons." A lantern is simply a lamp with a covering of some sort to protect it from the wind and other violence. Therefore too sharp a distinction between it and lamp is not to be drawn, and not infrequently either term might be indifferently used. The lamps, e. g., of Gideon's band were lanterns rather than lamps in the ordinary sense; and when the psalmist speaks of "a lamp to his path" (Psa. 119:105), we naturally conclude that he refers to some kind of lantern. As the streets of Eastern towns are not lighted at night, and never were so, lanterns are used to an extent unknown to dwellers in modern towns. *See* Lamp.

268. Ruins of Theatre at Laodicea

Laodice′a (lå-ŏd-ĭ-sē′à). Of the several cities named Laodicea in Syria and Asia Minor, only one is mentioned in the Scriptures, viz., the one situated on the confines of Phrygia and Lydia, on the banks of the Lycus, and about forty miles from Ephesus—not far from Colossae. After having been successively called Diosopolis and Rhoas, it was named Laodicea, in honor of Laodice, the wife of Antiochus II (B. C. 261-246), who rebuilt it. It was destroyed by an earthquake (A. D. 66, or earlier) and rebuilt by Marcus Aurelius. It was the seat of a Christian Church (Col. 2:1; 4:13, 15, 16; Rev. 1:11). It is now a heap of ruins, called by the Turks *Eski-hissar*, or "old castle."

Laodice′a, Church at. Among the residents of this city at the time of the apostles were many Jews; and it is probably owing to this fact that a Christian Church was planted here at so early a date. It appears from the epistle to the Colossians (4:15, 16) that Paul never visited Laodicea, but hearing, most probably, from Epaphras of the false doctrines spread in that city, he wrote to the Colossians desiring that his epistle to that Church should also be read in Laodicea. The message of the Spirit (Rev. 3:14-22) to the Church of Laodicea was an awful warning. *See* Laodiceans, Epistle to.

The Laodicean condition describes the spiritual lukewarmness and worldliness which will pervail in the professing church of Christ at the end of the age. Rich, cultured, religious ritualistic—this church will have become so self-satisfied and wordly as to have ostracised Christ completely. He is represented prophetically as standing on the outside knocking for admission (Rev. 3:20). No longer is He admitted by the corporate body, but stands outside extending an invitation to individuals. The awful spiritual condition, so utterly nauseating to God, calls forth one of the boldest figures used in the N. T. "So then, because thou art lukewarm and neither cold or hot, I will vomit thee out of my mouth" (cf. II Tim. 3:1-8 for the spiritual and moral conditions at the end of the Church Age). *M. F. U.*

Laodice′ans, Epistle to. In Col. 4:16 Paul desires that the epistle from Laodicea "be read at Colossae." From this it has been supposed that Paul wrote an epistle to the Laodiceans, which is no longer extant. Jerome and Theodoret mention such an epistle, and it was also referred to at the second council of Niceaea. The epistle assuming to be that in question, and which is generally condemned as spurious, is found in some copies of the New Testament printed in Germany; and Calmet in his dictionary gives a full translation of it. Some (Conybeare and Howson) have thought that the epistle to the Ephesians is the one alluded to by the apostle. Another explanation of the passage is that St. Paul intended the letter of the Laodiceans *to him*, conveyed by Epaphras, to be read in the church of Colossae, together with the apostolic epistle to the Colossians themselves; and that as the epistle to the Colossians was in some sense an answer to the Loadiceans, it would be necessary that both should be read in the church of Laodicea also (*Imp. Dict.*, s. v.).

Lap (Heb. *bĕgĕd*, II Kings 4:39, a *garment; ḥēq*, Prov. 16:33, the *bosom; ḥōṣĕn, bosom*, Neh. 5:13). The fold of the garment in which orientals are accustomed to carry articles in lieu of pockets; thus one of the sons of the prophets gathered "wild gourds (*q. v.*) his lap full" (II Kings 4:39). *See* Dress.

The psalmist prayed, "render unto our neighbors sevenfold into their bosom their reproach" (Psa. 79:12). The same allusion occurs in Luke 6:38, "Give, and it shall be given unto you; good measure, pressed down, and shaken together, and running over, shall men give into your bosom."

Lap′idoth (lăp′ĭ-dŏth; *torches*), the husband of

the prophetess Deborah (Judg. 4:4), B. C. about 1195.

Lapped, Lappeth (Heb. *läqăq*, to *lick* up as a dog, I Kings 21:19, etc.). Lapping was the test of Gideon's men (Judg. 7:5, 6), and is still in the East supposed to be an evidence of that readiness which fits men for active service. The meaning is that these men, instead of kneeling down to drink, employed the hand to carry the water to their mouths. Practice gives a peculiar tact in this mode of drinking; and the passage of the hand between the water and the mouth is so rapidly managed as to be comparable to that of the dog's tongue in similar circumstances. Again, the water is dexterously jerked into the mouth before the hand is brought close to it, so that the hand is reaching for a new supply before the preceding has been swallowed.

Lapwing. *See* Animal Kingdom.

Lasciviousness (Gr. *'aselgeia*, that which *excites disgust*), unbridled lust, licentiousness, wantonness. In the list of the evil products of the heart given by our Lord (Mark 7:22) it is uncertain what particular vice is spoken of; gluttony and venery (Jude, ch. 4; I Pet. 4:3); carnality (II Cor. 12:21; Gal. 5:19; Eph. 4:19).

Lase'a (là-sē'à), a city of Crete, near Fair Havens (Acts 27:8). If the vessel in which Paul was sailing stopped any length of time it is probable that Paul visited Lasea. Its ruins are located near Cape Leonda, about five miles from Lasea.

La'sha (lā'shà), one of the places named in defining the border of the Canaanites (Gen. 10:19). Jerome, Jonathan, and the Jerusalem Targum identify it with Calirrhoe, a place with sulphur baths, east of the Dead Sea, in Wady Zerka Ma'in.

Lasha'ron (là-shā'rŏn; *of* or *to Sharon*), signification unknown), one of the thirty-one Canaanitish towns, west of Jordan, smitten by Joshua (Josh. 12:18). Perhaps, the LXX preserves the original reading "the king of Aphek (which belongs) to Sharon."

Last Day. *See* Judgments, the.

Last Time. *See* Eschatology.

Latchet (Heb. *serōk*, *thong*; Gr. *himas*, *strap*, i. e., *tie*), the strap or cord used by the orientals to fasten the shoe upon the foot (Isa. 5:27; Mark 1:7; Luke 3:16; John 1:27).

Figurative. In Isa. 5:27, the prophet uses the poetical figure, "neither shall the girdle of their loins be loosed, nor the latchet of their shoes be broken;" to illustrate the tightness and durability of their equipment. The expression, "the latchet of whose shoes I am not worthy to unloose" (Mark 1:7; Luke 3:16; John 1:27), and that in Matt. 3:11, "whose shoes I am not worthy to bear," refer to the fact that in the East to bear the sandals of their masters, as well as to fasten them on or take them off, was the business of slaves of the lowest rank. "That I will not take from a thread even to a shoe latchet" (Gen. 14:23) is figurative for the smallest or most worthless thing belonging to the king of Sodom.

Lat'in (lăt'ĭn; *Roman*, Luke 23:38), the vernacular language of the Romans, although most of them in the time of Christ likewise spoke Greek.

Lattice, the rendering of the following words:
1. *A lathed aperture* (Heb. *'ĕshnäb*), a lattice window, through which the cool breezes pass (Judg. 5:28; "window," Prov. 7:6).
2. *A net* (Heb. *sebäkäh*, II Kings 1:2), probably a screen before a window.
3. *A window lattice* (Heb. *ḥĕrĕk*, Cant. 2:9).

The object of the lattice is to keep the apartments cool by intercepting the direct rays of the sun, and at the same time permit a free circulation of the air through the trellis openings. Perhaps the network through which Ahaziah fell and received his mortal injury was on the parapet of his palace (II Kings 1:2).

Laughter. "In Scripture it usually expresses joy (Gen. 21:6; Psa. 126:2; Eccles. 3:4; Luke 6:21); sometimes mockery (Gen. 18:13; Eccles. 2:2; James 4:9); also security (Job 5:22). When predicated of God (Psa. 2:4; 59:8; Prov. 1:26) it signifies that he despises or pays no regard to the person or subject" (McC. and S., *Cyc.*, s. v.).

Laver (Heb. *kiyyōr*, something *round*, a *basin*), the basin at which the priests washed their hands and feet while engaged in their public ministrations. The laver of the tabernacle differed from that of the temple.

1. **Tabernacle Laver.** This was made by divine direction (Exod. 30:18) of "brass" (i. e., copper or bronze) out of the metal mirrors of the Hebrew women (38:8). It was placed between the tabernacle and the great altar, so as to be convenient for the priests' use when going from the altar to the tabernacle (30:20, 21; 40:32). It consisted of two parts, viz., the laver proper and foot or pedestal. Neither the form nor size is given. Regarding its shape, something may be deduced from the etymology of the Hebrew term and its use in other passages. *Kiyyōr* "is derived from a root that seems primarily to mean *excavation by hammering*, and this would naturally yield a semiglobular hollow, which form is confirmed by the convenience for a lavatory, like a washbowl or basin, and by the similar shape of the molten sea and the smaller lavers, which took its place in the temple (I Kings 7:38, 40, 43, etc.), and which are denoted by the same word. The laver proper was probably used as the receptacle for the water, which was allowed to run down upon the hands and feet of those washing."

The "foot" (Heb. kēn, *support*), was, doubtless, circular in shape, and formed another basin. It was evidently an expansion of the shaft, probably with a turned-up rim. As no mention is made of a vessel in which was washed the parts of the victims offered in sacrifice, the laver probably served this purpose. No direction is given as to the kind of water to be used; but the Jewish commentators state that any kind might be employed, provided that it be renewed daily. "In the account of the offering by the woman suspected of adultery there is mention made of 'holy water' mixed with dust from the floor of the tabernacle, which the woman was to drink according to certain rites (Num. 5:17). Most probably this water was taken from the laver. Perhaps the same should be said of the 'water of purifying' (Num. 8:7), which was sprinkled on the Levites on the occasion of their consecration to the service of the Lord in the tabernacle" (Fairbairn). Like other sacred vessels, the laver was consecrated with oil (Lev. 8:10, 11). No mention is made in the Hebrew text of the mode of transporting the laver, but in Num. 4:14, a passage is added in the LXX agreeing with the Samaritan version, which prescribes the method of packing it, viz., in a purple cloth, protected by a skin covering.

2. **Temple Lavers.** Owing to the increased number of priests and victims in Solomon's temple, greater facilities were needed for washing; *ten* lavers were used for the sacrifices and the "molten sea" for the ablutions of the priests (II Cor. 4:6). Of these we have minuter descriptions than of the tabernacle laver. (1) **The "molten sea"** (Heb. *yäm, sea*). This was a huge round basin, five cubits high and ten cubits in diameter at the brim, "and a line of thirty cubits did compass it about" (I Kings 7:23-26). Perhaps the circumference measurement was of the bowl at the water line, and not including the projected rim. It was made of strong bronze, a hand breadth in thickness. "Its brim was bent outward in a cuplike form, and made to resemble the flower of the lily, while underneath two rows of 'knops' (coloquintidas, i. e., wild cucumbers or apples), ten to every cubit, ran around the sea for ornament." In II Chron. 4:3, we have "the similitude of oxen" instead of "knops." It is possible that *bakarim*, oxen, may be a corruption of *pekaîm* (Clark, *Com.*, in loc.). The capacity of this huge basin was two thousand baths (comp. *bath*). The number three thousand baths (II Chron. 4:5) is thought to be an error of a transcriber. The water was doubtless drawn from this basin by means of faucets. This laver was supported by twelve brazen oxen, three looking toward each point of the compass, while it is probable that they all stood upon one and the same basement of metal. (2) **The ten lesser lavers.** For full description of these see I Kings 7:27-39. In order to convey water to any part of the courts where it might be needed for washing such things as they offered for the burnt offering (II Chron. 4:6), ten beautifully ornamented bronze trucks (A. V. "*bases* of brass") were prepared, five of them being placed on the south and five on the north side of the altar. These trucks were all alike in form, size, and casting; and were square chests, four cubits long, the same wide, and three cubits high. They were constructed with flat panels, (A. V. "borders"), supported by stiles (A. V. "ledges"); the panels being ornamented with figures of lions, oxen, and cherubim. Each truck had four bronze wheels and bronze axles, and the four feet thereof had shoulderpieces (I Kings 7:30). The meaning seems to be that the chests had feet at each corner, and that these rested upon the axles in such a manner as to raise the chest above the rim of the wheels (v. 32), and under the borders were four wheels. Keil supposes that the shoulderpieces ran up each corner from the foot and reached to the lower side of the laver, thus helping to support it (A. V. "under the laver were undersetters, molten at the side of every addition," v. 30). The wheels were one and one half cubits high, in construction resembling that of chariot wheels, and their hubs, felloes, spokes, and axletrees were cast in bronze. The top of the trucks were constructed for the purpose of holding the lavers. They were made with stiles and panels, like the sides, but appear to have been arched so as to rise in the center, terminating in a circular receptacle (A. V. "chapiter"), one half cubit high by one and one half diameter, for the laver. These stiles and panels were ornamented with graved cherubim, lions, and palm trees. The lavers were four cubits in diameter, corresponding with the trucks, narrowing down at the base to one and one half cubits, and held forty baths (about four hundred and forty gallons), just one fiftieth of the capacity of the great laver. Some have thought that these trucks were made of so great height in order to bring the laver near the height of the altar. It may be that these chests (trucks) opened at the sides, and were really tanks for washing the sacrifices in, the water coming into them from the lavers by means of a pipe. After use they could be wheeled away and cleansed.

3. In the second temple there appears to have been only one laver of brass, with twelve instead of two stopcocks, and a machine for raising water and filling it.

4. **Typical Meaning.** The laver is a type of Christ cleansing the believer-priest from the defilement of sin (John 13:2-10; Eph. 5:25-27). The priests, after serving at the brazen altar (type of Christ's cross on which our Whole Burnt Offering purchased our redemption) could not enter the holy place of God's manifested presence, till hands and feet were cleansed.

Law (Heb. *töräh, teaching, instruction;* Gr. *nomos*), a term employed almost 200 times in the Bible and signifying the revealed will of God with respect to human conduct. It includes all the Divine commands and precepts for regulating man's moral life without and within. It is used in six different senses in Scripture. (1) *That which is enacted by man* (Gen. 9:6; Matt. 10:15; Luke 20:22; I Tim. 1:8-10; II Tim. 2:5). Law in this aspect embraces that which established human government requires of those under its jurisdiction. (2) *The Law of Moses.* This was a divinely instituted rule of life mediated through Moses to govern God's covenant people, Israel, in Canaan. It regulated their common, everyday conduct and was a covenant of works (Exod. 19:5, 6). They were never able to keep this covenant and it will be superseded by the New Covenant (Jer. 31:31-34; Heb. 8:8-13). The Mosaic code of laws included *The Commandments* (Exod. 20:1-17), the *Judgments* stipulating their social life (Exod. 21:1-23:33) and *Ordinances*, directing Israel's worship (Exod. 25:1-31:18). This Mosaic system, including the Ten Commandments as a way of life, came to an end with the death of Christ (John 1:17; Rom. 10:4). The Mosaic age was preceded (Exod. 19:4) and followed (John 1:17) by grace. In the gracious dispensation inaugurated as the result of the atonement of Christ, all the Ten Commandments appear in the epistles except that regarding the seventh day and are operative not as stern "thou shalt nots" but as gracious duties and privileges of a redeemed people, possessing the dynamic of the Holy Spirit, willingly and effectively to carry out their injunctions. The Mosaic law was thus a temporary divine administration in effect only until Christ should come. It had the definite ministry of imparting to sin the character of transgression (Rom. 5:13; Gal. 3:19). (3) *The Law of Grace*. This category includes the doctrines and precepts of grace addressed to the redeemed child of God in this age. It must be carefully noted that the Christian is not under law. Grace has imparted to him all the merit that he could ever need (John 1:16; Rom. 5:1; 8:1; Col. 2:9, 10). Being "in-lawed" to Christ (I Cor. 9:20, 21) does not mean that the Christian is without law, but it does mean, as one redeemed by grace, he has the duty, or rather gracious privilege, of not doing that which is displeasing to God and fully discharging that which is well pleasing to him on the basis of a manifestation of spontaneous gratitude for his salvation in grace. (4) *God's Will*. The revealed will of God in any situation becomes a law to the Christian, although it embraces all God's revealed pleasure for any people at any time. Thus the word *law* in the Book of Romans is sometimes used in referring to something other than the Law of Moses (Rom. 7:15-25; Rom. 8:4). (5) *Natural Law Written on the Heart*. This aspect of law is closely connected with the revealed will of God, but it is to be distinguished in that it is what God requires of all of his creatures. "For when the Gentiles, which have not the law, do by nature the things contained in the law, these, having not the law, are a law unto themselves: Which show the work of the law written in their hearts, their conscience also bearing witness, and their thoughts the meanwhile accusing or else excusing one another (Rom. 2:14, 15). (6) *The Kingdom Rule of Life*. This is the aspect of law which will be in force in the future millennium. Matt. 5:1-7:29 gives a resume of it. It seems unthinkable to many theologians that there will be a reinstatement of law after the age of grace. But that such is the case is clearly taught in Ezekiel's great prophecy of millennial conditions described in chapters 40-48, and also appears under the text of that which is legal by its aim to secure merit (Matt. 6:14, 15). But the legal administration of the millennium will be an exalted and spiritualized economy and will operate under ideal conditions with Satan bound, a large ministry and operation of the Holy Spirit and the personal Presence of Christ.

M. F. U.

Law of Mo'ses (Heb. *tōräh, Mōshĕh*), signifies the whole body of Mosaic legislation (I Kings 2:3; II Kings 3:25; Ezra 3:2); called with reference to its divine origin *the law of Jehovah* (Psa. 19:8; 37:31; Isa. 5:24; 30:9). In the latter sense it is called by way of eminence, *The Law* (Heb. *hăttōräh*, Deut. 1:5; 4:8, 44; 17:18, 19; 27:3, 8). The law is especially embodied in the last four books of the Pentateuch. Respecting the question of the *origin*

of the Mosaic law, we quote from Dr. J. Robertson, *Early Religion of Israel*, p. 335, sq.: "It occurs at once as a striking thing that the uniform tradition is, that Moses gave laws and ordinances to Israel; and that it is not a blind ascription of everything to some great ancestor may be gathered from the fact that there are ordinances and customs which are not traced to him. The Sabbath is made as old as the creation; circumcision is a mark of the covenant with Abraham; sacrifices are pre-Mosaic; and the abstaining from the sinew that shrank is traced to the time of Jacob. The body of laws, however, that formed the constitution of Israel as a people is invariably referred to Moses. The persistence with which it is represented that law, moral and ceremonial, came from Moses, and the acceptance of the laws by the whole people as of Mosaic origin, proves at least that it was a deeply-seated belief in the nation that the great leader had given some formal legal constitution to his people. . . . The testimony of a nation is not so lightly to be set aside; it is the work of criticism to explain and account for tradition, not to give it the lie."

For a recent study see George E. Mendenhall, "Law and Covenant in Israel and the Ancient Near East" in *The Bib. Archaeologist* Vol. XVII, 2 (May, 1954, pp. 26-46); 3, (Sept., 1954) pp. 49-76.

Principles. At the root of the Mosaic code lies (1) the principle of strict but righteous retribution, and its intention is to extirpate evil and produce reverence for the righteousness of the holy God in the heart of the people; (2) Punishment should correspond to the heinousness of the offense, that there shall fall upon the culprit what he has done to his neighbor; the punishment is to be limited to the guilty party, and not be extended to his children (Deut. 24:16); (3) It commands with unsparing severity the punishment of all presumptuous disobedience to God and to his holy ordinances; and, (4) finally, "it threatens a curse and severe punishments from God, the avenger of all evil, for offenses which either escape the eye of civil justice, or which, like apostasy from the Lord to idolatry, may prevail to such a degree that the arm of the earthly magistrate is overpowered and paralyzed by the spirit of the time." In analyzing the Mosaic code we adopt the division, usual in systems of law—the civil, criminal, judicial, constitutional, ecclesiastical, and ceremonial.

1. Civil. (1) **Of persons.** (*a*) *Of Father and children*. The authority of the father to be sacred; cursing, smiting (Exod. 21:15, 17; Lev. 20:9); stubborn and wilful disobedience to be considered as capital crimes; but punishment of death was vested only in the congregation (Deut. 21:18-21); vow of daughter conditional upon consent of father (Num. 30:3-5). *Inheritance*. Right of the *firstborn* to a double portion not to be set aside by partiality (Deut. 21:15-17); inheritance allowed to daughters in default of sons, if the heiress married within her own tribe (Num. 27:6-8; comp. ch. 36); *unmarried daughters* entirely dependent upon their fathers (30:3-5). (*b*) *Husband and Wife*. The power of husband over wife such as to make the wife dependent even to the fulfilling of an engagement before God, as in the case of a vow (30:6-15); but a widow or divorced wife became independent, and was bound by any vow she may have made (v. 9); upon marriage the husband was excused from war or public duties for one year (Deut. 24:5); *marriages* within certain degrees were forbidden (Lev. 18:1, sq.); *divorce* for "uncleanness" allowed, but the divorced wife could not be taken back after marriage to another (Deut. 24:1-4); *slander* against a wife's virginity punishable by fine and by deprival of power of divorce, but if wife was proven guilty she was put to death (Deut. 22:13-21); *a slave wife*, bought or captive, not to be actual property, nor to be sold; if ill-treated, freed (Exod. 21:7-9; Deut. 21:1, sq.); *raising up of seed* (Levirate law) a right to be claimed by widow with a view of preserving the family (Deut. 25:5-10). (c) *Master and slave. Power of master limited*, so that death under chastisement was punishable (Exod. 21:20), and maiming gave liberty (vers. 26, 27); *Hebrew slave* freed at the Sabbatical year (his wife and children, if they entered bondage with him, to go out with him), unless he formally consented to remain in perpetual servitude (Exod. 21:1-6; Deut. 15:12-18); but in any case he seems to have received his freedom and that of his children at the jubilee (Lev. 25: 10); if sold to a resident alien ("stranger"), he was always redeemable, at a price proportional to the distance from the jubilee (25:47-54). *Foreign slaves* were held and inherited as property forever (25:45, 46), and fugitive slaves from other nations were not to be given up (Deut. 23:15). (d) *Strangers* seem never to have been *sui juris*, or able to protect themselves; and kindness toward them was enjoined as a duty (Exod. 22:21; Lev. 19:33, 34). (2) **Law of things.** (a) *Land and property.* All land was considered as belonging to Jehovah, with its holders as his tenants (Lev. 25: 23); *sold land*, therefore, was to return to its original owners at the jubilee, the price of sale to be calculated accordingly, and redemption on equitable terms to be allowed at all times (25:25-28); a *house sold* to be redeemed within one year, and if not, to pass away altogether (25:29, 30); land to rest in Sabbatic and jubilee years, and spontaneous growth of these years to be for poor, stranger, etc. (Lev. 23:22; Deut. 24:19-21). *Houses of Levites*, or those in unwalled villages, to be redeemed at any time, in the same way as land, and Levitical suburbs inalienable (Lev. 25:31-34); *sanctified* land or houses, tithes, or unclean firstlings might be redeemed at the addition of one fifth their value (reckoned by priest according to distance from the jubilee), if devoted and unredeemed by owner, to be hallowed at the jubilee forever, and given to the priests (25:14-39); Inheritance (q. v.). The following were the regulations respecting *losses:* If two men strove together, and as a result one should be disabled from work, the other must pay for the lost time (Exod. 21: 19); claims for losses from trespass, or for any lost thing, were to be brought before the judges, and adverse judgment was followed by the payment of double to the other (22:9);

a man finding any lost thing, and denying it, was obliged, when he wished to present a trespass offering, to restore the lost thing with an added fifth to the one to whom it belonged (Lev. 6:4, 5). The general principle upon which these enactments were based was that an Israelite's fellow-countrymen were his brothers; and he was always to act the brotherly part. Therefore, whenever he found anything that was lost he was commanded to care for it, and to make diligent search for its owner with a view of restoration (Deut. 22:3). (b) *Laws of debt. All debts* to an Israelite to be released at the Sabbatical year, but they might be exacted of strangers (Deut. 15:1-11); *interest*, from an Israelite, not to be taken (Exod. 22:25-27; Deut. 23:19, 20). Pledges not to be insolently or ruinously exacted (Deut. 24:6, 10-13, 17, 18). (c) *Taxation. Census money*, a poll-tax (of a half shekel) to be paid for the service of the tabernacle (Exod. 30:12-16); *spoil* in war, divided equally between combatants and the congregation, of the combatant's half one five hundredth, and of the people's one fiftieth, given as a heave offering unto the Lord (Num. 31:26, sq.); *Tithes* (q. v.); *poor laws* providing for the legal right of the poor to *glean* fields and vineyards (Lev. 19:9, 10; Deut. 24:19-22); for the hungry to eat of grain, etc., on the spot (Deut. 23:24, 25); for payment of wages daily (24:15); *maintenance of priests, see* Priest.

2. **Criminal.** (1) **Offenses against God,** which were considered as treason. These offenses were all forbidden, in principle, by the Ten Commandments. *First Command.* Acnowledgment of false gods (Exod. 22:20), and all idolatry (Deut., ch. 13; 17:2-5). *Second Command.* Witchcraft and false prophecy (Exod. 22:18; Deut. 18:9-22; Lev. 19:31). *Third Command.* Blasphemy (Lev. 24:15, 16). *Fourth Command.* Sabbath breaking (Num. 15: 32-36). Punishment in all cases, death by stoning. Idolatrous cities to be utterly destroyed. (2) **Offenses against man.** *Fifth Command.* Parents, disobedience to, cursing, or smiting of (Exod. 21:15; 17; Lev. 20:9; Deut. 21:18-21); also disobedience to priest or supreme judge. Punishment, death by stoning (comp. I Kings 21:10-14; II Chron. 24:21). *Sixth Command.* (1) *Murder*, punished without sanctuary, reprieve, or satisfaction (Exod. 21: 12, 14; Deut. 19:11-13). If in a quarrel a *pregnant* woman is struck, and she lose her child, fine was exacted; but if she suffered other injury, full retribution (Exod. 21:22, sq.). Death of a slave actually under the rod to be punished (21:20, 21). (2) *Death* by an ox known to gore, punishable by death of ox and owner, but as this was not an intentional crime the owner was allowed to redeem his forfeited life by expiation money (21:28-30). (3) *Accidental homicide*, escaped the avenger by flight to city of refuge till death of high priest (Num. 35:9-28; Deut. 4:41-43; 19:4-10). (4) *Death at hands of unknown person*, to be expiated by formal disavowal and sacrifice by elders of the nearest city (Deut. 21:1-9). *Seventh Command.* (1) *Adultery*, punished by death of both offenders; *rape* of married or betrothed woman, by death of offender (22:22-27). (2) *Rape* or *seduction* of unbetrothed virgin, to be

compensated by marriage, with dowry (fifty shekels), and without power of divorce; or, if she be refused, by payment of full dowry (Exod. 22:16, 17; Deut. 22:28, 29). (3) *Unlawful marriages* (incestuous, etc.), to be punished, some by death, some by childlessness (Lev., ch. 20). *Eighth Command.* (1) *Theft.* Stolen property found on thief, if an ox, ass, or sheep, punished by twofold restoration; if killed or sold, then restoration to be made, fivefold for an ox and fourfold for a sheep (Exod. 22:1-4). If unable to make restitution, thief might be sold (v. 3); if he was killed while breaking in the thief might be slain as an outlaw (v. 2). (2) *Trespass*, injury to things or money lent, to be compensated (22:5-15). (3) *Perversion of justice*, by bribes, threats, etc., strictly forbidden (23:6-9). (4) *Kidnapping*, to be punished by death (Deut. 24:7). *Ninth Command. False witness*, punished with that which he wished done to the one against whom he testified (Exod. 23:1-3; Deut. 19: 16-21). *Slander* of a wife's chastity punished by fine and loss of power of divorce (Deut. 22:18, 19). *Tenth Command.* For the tenth commandment, *see* Decalogue, 8. In addition to the above, it was forbidden to remove boundary lines, under penalty of a curse (Deut. 27: 17); neighbor's straying beast to be returned (Exod. 23:4, sq.), or helped if in trouble (Deut. 22:1-4); injury done to the field or vineyard of another by beast or fire, to be compensated by best of one's own (Exod. 22: 5); the killing of a beast to be made good, beast for beast (Lev. 24:18); a blemish caused to another punished by *lex talionis*, or damages (Exod. 21:18; 19, 22-25; Lev. 24:19, 20).

3. **Mosaic and Near Eastern Laws.** As a result of archaeological excavations, especially of the past three decades, the Law of Moses appears in a much clearer context. The Code of Hammurabi, dating from c. 1700 B. C., and discovered at ancient Susa (Biblical Shushan) in 1901-2, has been classic in illuminating and illustrating Mosaic law. Now, however, Sumerian, Babylonian, Assyrian, Hittite and Canaanite codes are shedding their light on the Mosaic legislation. Especially must be mentioned the laws of Lipit-Ishtar, king of Isin, in central Babylonia, dating c. 1875 B. C., and even the earlier laws of Eshnunna, an ancient city N. E. of modern Baghdad. (See Francis R. Steele, *Am. Jr. Arch.* III, 1948, pp. 445-450; Albrecht Goetze, *Sumer* IV, 1948, pp. 63-102; P. A. Pohl, *Orientalia* XVIII, 1949, pp. 126-129). In this new context the famous Code of Hammurabi appears as a comparative late-comer in Babylonia. The Code of Eshnunna, antedating Hammurabi's Code by almost two centuries, contains the first exact parallel to any Biblical law, namely that concerning the division of oxen after a fatal combat between the animals (Exod. 21:35). In addition to these codes must be mentioned the old Babylonian and Assyrian tablets from Kanish in Cappadocia (19th cent. B. C.). A wealth of legal material (belonging to the 15th century B. C.) has also been recovered at Nuzu, near modern Kirkuk, since 1925. Assyrian laws have been recovered by the Germans in the city of Asshur on the Tigris, much of it coming from

the period of Tiglathpileser I (c. 1110 B. C.). Hittite laws have also come to light and date a century or two earlier than the laws of Tiglathpileser. In comparison with these various laws "the Book of the Covenant exhibits a combination of simplicity in economic life and ethical humanitarianism in human relations which could have arisen only in early Israel" (W. F. Albright in *The O. T. in Modern Study*, 1951, p. 39f.).

4. **Mosaic Law and the Code of Hammurabi.** This famous seven-foot tall piece of black diorite which regulated the commercial, domestic, social and moral life of the Hammurabi period (c. 1728-1676 B. C.) constitutes one of the most astonishing legal finds in history. It antedates the Mosaic legislation by three centuries. This famous legal code illuminates the Mosaic laws. As a result of the careful study of the two bodies of material, it will be found that the Mosaic code is neither borrowed nor dependent upon the Babylonian, but is unique in those specific features that suited Israel's need as an elect, theocratic nation. In comparing the two it might be said: (1) *The Mosaic and Hammurabi codes are different in content.* Moses' laws contain numerous ritual regulations and religious stipulations. The Code of Hammurabi is almost purely civil. (2) *The Two Codes Regulate Different Societies.* Hammurabi's laws govern an urban, commercial, thickly-settled irrigation culture. Mosaic laws govern a simple agricultural, pastoral people not urbanized or commercially developed but conscious of their divine calling. The two codes vary in their morality. Alfred Jeremias succinctly states the essential contrast of the two bodies of laws. He points out in the Babylonian code "(1) There is no control of lust. (2) There is no limitation of selfishness through altruism. (3) There is nowhere to be found a postulate of charity. (4) There is nowhere to be found the religious motif which recognizes sin as the destruction of the people because it is in opposition to the fear of God. In the Hammurabi Code every trace of religious thought is absent; behind the Israelite law stands ever the ruling will of the Holy God; it bears throughout a religious character" (*The O. T. in the Light of the Ancient East*, 1911, Vol. II, p. 112). It may be fairly said that the resemblances or the likenesses between the two codes are traceable to similarity of antecedents and general intellectual and cultural heritage. Revised by *M. F. U.*

5. **Judicial.** See Law, Administration of.

6. **Constitutional.** See Israel, Constitution of.

7. **Ecclesiastical and Ceremonial**, including: (1) **The law of sacrifice** and offerings (*see* Sacrifice, Offerings). (2) **The law of holiness** (*see* Holiness, Ceremonial).

Law, Administration of.

1. **Judges and Courts.** (1) **Early courts.** In patriarchal times the head of the house had the judicial power over his household, even over life and death (Gen. 38:24). With the increase of families this power naturally passed over to the heads of tribes and clans; but after the exodus those who sought justice naturally turned to Moses (Exod. 18:13, sq.). Moses, unable to keep up with the demands

made upon him, acting on Jethro's advice, chose from among the elders "able men, such as feared God, men of truth, hating covetousness." These he appointed as rulers over thousands, hundreds, fifties, and tens, who should act as judges in all small matters, while the more difficult matters should be brought to Moses for decision (Exod. 18:19-26; Deut. 1:13-18). The relation of these judges to one another is not exactly defined in Scripture; but it may have consisted in this, that the judges over thousands were appointed to settle the disputes between the tribes and chief clans of the people; the judges over hundreds, etc., the quarrels and the different contentions between the larger and smaller divisions of the clans and families. (2) **Local courts.** After the entrance into Canaan the same general rules remained in force. For this period there is only the quite general command: "Judges and officers (*shoterim*) shalt thou make thee in all thy gates (cities), that they may judge the people with just judgment" (Deut. 16:18). These officials were the *local justices*, who, in the several cities, pronounced finally on all minor controversies, i. e., such as were easy to decide by law, and to punish the guilty. For more difficult cases, viz., such as had been referred to Moses, a *higher court* is appointed, having its seat at the place of the sanctuary, and to consist of priests and judges; with the high priest and a (secular) supreme judge (Deut. 17:8; 19:16, sq.). In this court the lay judge conducted the investigation (19:18), while the priest gave guidance from the law (Lev. 10:11); finally the judge pronounced sentence. (3) **Senate.** Besides these local courts, the elders of every city formed a *senate* or *magistracy*, whose duty it was, as representatives of the congregation, to remove the evil from the midst of them. This senate decided various simple family matters which required no deeper judicial investigation, punished the guilty even with death, and delivered up the deliberate manslayer to the avenger of blood (Deut. 19:12). Among the cases which came under the jurisdiction of this senate were a rebellious son (21:18, sq.), a husband's charge against the virgin chastity of his wife (22:13, sq.), and the refusal in the matter of levirate marriage (*q. v.*). These matters belonged rather to the department of government than to the administration of justice in the strict sense; and the elders took up these cases as the upholders of good order. *In David's time.* David, after his wars, arranged the affairs of his kingdom; and among the other appointments set apart six thousand Levites to be *shoterim* and judges (I Chron. 23:4; comp. 26:29). It is doubtful if these Levites were associated with the local courts, the probability being that they were appointed to administer the payments of the people for the sanctuary, to watch over them, and in disputed cases to give judicial decisions. Jehoshaphat, desirous of spreading the knowledge of the law (II Chron. 17:7-9), put judges in all the fortified cities (19:5-7), and provided a supreme tribunal in Jerusalem, consisting of Levites, priests, and heads of tribes, presided over by the high priest (for the interest of Jehovah) and the prince of the house of Judah

(for the king's interest), with functions of an exclusively judicial character. *Post-exilic times.* Josephus (*Wars*, ii, 14, 1) mentions *local courts* that discharged judicial functions; and local sanhedrins are referred to as those to which the believers would be delivered (Matt. 10:17; Mark 13:9). These lesser courts were empowered to deal with criminal cases of a serious nature, even to the sentencing of murderers. We may also regard as belonging to the same category those courts that in Matt. 5:22, are assumed to be inferior to the high court of the sanhedrin; and similarly with regard to the "elders" of Capernaum (Luke 7:3). The most subordinate of these courts consisted of seven persons; although three judges were considered sufficient to decide certain cases. There is a statement in the Mishna to the effect that an inferior sanhedrin consisted of twenty-three persons, and that one of this sort was assigned to every town with a population of at least one hundred and twenty, or, according to R. Nehemiah's view, of at least two hundred and thirty, in order that there might be a judge for every ten inhabitants. (4) **The Sanhedrin**, the great council in latter times (*see* Sanhedrin).

2. **Judicial Procedure.** The course of justice was very simple. The judges appointed by Moses were to judge the people "at all seasons" (Exod. 18:22); while the lawgiver himself sat with Aaron and the princes of the congregation before the tabernacle (Num. 27:2; comp. Exod. 18:19, sq.). Judges in the cities, after the custom of the ancient East, had their seat at the gate (Deut. 21:19; 22:15; Prov. 22:22; Amos 5:11, 15) and on the open squares. Before them the litigants appeared, and presented their case orally (Deut. 1:16; 21:19; 25:1); and the accused who did not appear was summoned (25:8); counsel are unknown in the Old Testament. The supreme judges of the people administered justice in public; e. g., Deborah under a palm (Judg. 4:5), the kings in the gate or court of the palace (II Sam. 15:2, 6; comp. 14:4, sq.; I Kings 3:16); Solomon made a porch of judgment in his palace (I Kings 7:7). Later the princes sat for judgment at the entrance of the new gate of the temple (Jer. 26:10, sq.). The judge was bound to hear and examine closely (Deut. 1:16, sq.; 13:14). The *proof* varied according to circumstances. It might be a simple oath (Exod. 22:11), the word of accuser if a parent (21:18), a token (Deut. 22:15, 17). Generally the declarations of witnesses were taken, and those of two or three were required to make testimony valid (19:15), especially in criminal cases (Num. 35:30; Deut. 17:6). Witnesses were to be rigidly questioned, and if a witness was found to be false he was to be punished with the punishment which would have fallen upon the accused (Deut. 19:18, 19). From Prov. 18:18; 16:33, it would appear that other evidence lacking the lot was applied, though it is not mentioned in the Pentateuch, but only in Josh. 7:14, and I Sam. 14:40, sq., as an immediate divine decision. *Sentence.* Sentence was pronounced orally, although under the kings the judges seem to have written their sentences (Isa. 10:1). *Punishment.* This was executed without de-

lay (Num. 15:36; Deut. 22:18); was administered before the judge (Deut. 25:2, sq.), probably by the officers of the court; if capital it was stoning by the whole congregation (Num. 15:36) or the people of the city (Deut. 22:21), the witnesses being the first to cast a stone (13:9; 17:9), which could hardly be expected of a witness who was not fully satisfied of the truth of his testimony; or by the avenger of blood (Num. 35:19, sq.). After the introduction of the kingdom punishment was administered by the servants of the king (II Sam. 1:15), or by the royal guard in case of state or treasonable offenses (I Kings 2:25, 34, 46; II Kings 10:25).

Lawgiver (Heb. *mᵉhōqēq;* Gr. *nomothetēs*), used in the usual sense of lawgiver (Deut. 33:21; Isa. 33:22); of God as the supreme lawgiver and judge (James 4:12); but elsewhere a *scepter*, as a badge of power (Num. 21:18; Psa. 60:7; Gen. 49:10).

Lawyer (Gr. *nomikos*, according to *law*), a term used to signify one who is *conversant with the law*, "jurist" (Matt. 22:35; Luke 7:30; 10:25; 11:45; 14:3; Tit. 3:13), and probably applied to a scribe (*q. v.*) in his practical administration of the law in the pronounciation of legal decisions. It is not accidentally that the expression is so frequently used by St. Luke. He purposes by the repetition to make clear to his Roman readers the character of the Jewish scribes.

Laz'arus (lăz'á-rŭs; abridged form of Heb. *Eleazar*).

1. A beggar named in the story of the rich man (Luke 16:20-25), whose patient piety in this world was rewarded with bliss in the other. This is the only instance of a proper name being in a parable.

2. A man of Bethany, and the brother of Mary and Martha. He was a personal friend of Jesus, by whom he was raised from the dead four days after his burial (John 11:1-44). Later, when a supper was given to our Lord, Lazarus was present, and many people gathered through a desire to see the resurrected man. So convincing an evidence of Jesus's power was very distasteful to the chief priests, and they "consulted that they might put Lazarus also to death" (12:1-10). This they probably did not do, but satisfied themselves with the death of Jesus. According to an old tradition in Epiphanius (*Hoer.*, lxvi, 34, p. 652), Lazarus was thirty years old when restored to life, and lived thirty years after.

269. Tomb of Lazarus, Bethany

Lead. *See* Mineral Kingdom.

Leaf. Fig leaves are mentioned as forming the first covering of Adam and Eve (Gen. 3:7).

Figurative. Leaves, as the outward manifestation of life in the tree, are used symbolically, as: a bright, fresh-colored leaf, showing that it is richly nourished, is figurative of *prosperity* (Psa. 1:3; Jer. 17:8); a faded leaf, on the contrary, showing a lack of moisture and nourishment, becomes an emblem of adversity and decay (Job. 13:25; Isa. 64:6). In Ezekiel's vision of the holy waters the blessings of Messiah's kingdom are spoken of under the image of trees growing on a river's bank and with fadeless leaves (Ezek. 47:12), which should be good as medicine (comp. Rev. 22:1, 2). **Leaf of a door** (Heb. *ṣēlä'*, a *side*). Keil (*Com.* in loc.) thinks that this refers to doors made in two sections, like the "Dutch doors," that could be open either above or below. Their height in this case would be sufficient to allow the priests to pass through with the lower half only open. In Isa. 45:1, a "two-leaved gate" refers to a double gate. **Leaf of a book** (Heb. *dĕlĕth*). In Jer. 36:23; it is said that "when Jehudi had read three or four leaves he cut it (the roll) with the penknife." "Leaves" here denotes the columns, the four-cornered squares into which the rolls were divided.

League. *See* Covenant.

Le'ah (lē'á), the eldest daughter of Laban, who by a deceit of her father became the wife of Jacob (Gen. 29:16-23). She was not so good-looking as her sister Rachel, having weak eyes, which is probably the reason of Jacob's preference for the younger sister. Leah had six sons, Reuben, Simeon, Levi, Judah (29:32-35), Issachar, and Zebulun (30:17-20), and a daughter, Dinah (v. 21). She probably died in Canaan, as she is not mentioned in the migration to Egypt (46:6), and was buried in Hebron (49:31).

Leasing, an old English word equivalent to lying. Lies, as elsewhere rendered.

Leather. *See* Handicraft, Writing.

Leaven, a substance added to dough to cause it to rise, from Latin *levamen*, that is, *that which raises*, from *lavere, to raise*.

1. **Terms.** The Hebrew term *sᵉ'ōr* occurs only five times in Scripture, in four of which (Exod. 12:15, 19; 13:7; Lev. 2:1) it is translated "leaven" and in the fifth (Deut. 16:14) "leavened bread." This probably denotes the small portion of dough left from the preceding baking which had fermented and turned acid. Its distinctive meaning is *fermented* or *leavened mass*. The Hebrew expression *măṣṣäh, sweet*, means without leaven (Lev. 10:12); thus the Hebrew terms for the meaning of fermented or sour. The Gr. term is *zumē* and has the same latitude of meaning as the general Hebrew words for leaven.

2. **Preparation.** In early times leaven was made from fine white bran kneaded with must or with the meal of certain plants such as fitch or vetch, or from barley mixed with water and then allowed to stand until it turned sour. In later times it was made from bread flour kneaded without salt and kept until it passed into a state of fermentation.

3. **Levitical Regulations.** The Mosaic Law

strictly forbade the use of leaven in the priestly
ritual (Lev. 2:11). Typically this signified that
the offering was to be a type of purity, and
leaven, which causes disintegration and corruption, symbolized evil and the energy of
sin. To the Hebrew mind, whatever was in a
decayed state suggested the idea of uncleanness and corruption. Amos (4:5) in the light
of the prohibitions of the law, ironically commands the Jews of his day to "offer a sacrifice
of thanksgiving *with leaven*." In two instances,
however, the law permits its use with the
offering of the new loaves presented at Pentecost (Lev. 23:17) and in connection with the
praise offering (Lev. 7:13). The reason for the
exception at Pentecost is that the two wave
loaves of fine flour typify the N. T. Church
brought into being by the baptism of the
Holy Spirit (Acts 2:1-4; I Cor. 12:12, 13).
The two wave loaves typifying the Church
contain leaven because there is evil in the
Church; but it is to be carefully noted that
the loaves with leaven were baked; that is,
the manifested evil in the body of Christ, the
Church, was judged in the death of Christ.
Leaven, then, is symbolic or typical of evil,
always having this implication in the O. T.
(cf. Gen. 19:3; Exod. 12:8, 15-20, 34, 39).
In the N. T. its symbolic meaning is also
clear. It is "malice and wickedness" as contrasted with "sincerity and truth" (I Cor. 5:
6-8). It represents evil doctrine (Matt. 16:12)
in its threefold manifestation of Phariseeism,
Sadduceeism and Herodianism (Matt. 16:6;
Mark 8:15). Religious externalism constituted
the leaven of the Pharisees (Matt. 23:14, 16,
23:28). A skeptical attitude toward the supernatural was the leaven of the Sadducees
(Matt. 22:23, 29). The spirit of wordly compromise was the leaven of the Herodians
(Matt. 22:16-21; Mark 3:6). The parable of
the leaven "which a woman took and hid in
three measures of meal until the whole was
leavened" is in agreement with the unvarying
Scriptural meaning of leaven. *M. F. U.*

Leba′na (lĕ-bä′nä; Neh. 7:48). *See* Lebanah.
Leb′anah (lĕb′à-nà), **Leba′nah** (lĕ-bä′nä;
white, poetically the *moon*), one of the Nethinim
whose descendants returned from Babylon
with Zerubbabel (Ezra 2:45; Neh. 7:48),
B. C. about 536.

Leb′anon (lĕb′á-nŏn; *white*, from the snow on
its peaks), the loftiest and best known mountain range of Syria, forming the northern
boundary of Palestine. It is really a branch
running southward from the Caucasus, and

at its lower end forking into two parallel
ranges—the *eastern*, or Anti-Lebanon, and the
western, or Lebanon proper. The mountain
chain of Lebanon begins at the great valley
connecting the Mediterranean with the plain
of Hamath ("the entrance of Hamath," Num.
34:8), and runs southwest till it sinks into the
plain of Acre and the low hills of Galilee. Its
extreme length is one hundred and ten miles,
and the average breadth at its base about
twenty miles. Its average height is from six
thousand to eight thousand feet; the highest
peak—*Jebel Mukhmel*—is about ten thousand
two hundred feet, and the *Sannin* about nine
thousand feet. The highest peaks are covered
with perpetual ice and snow, and the line of

271. The Lebanon Region

cultivation reaches to the height of about six
thousand feet. In the mountain recesses wild
beasts range, as of old (II Kings 14:9; Cant.
4:8). Lebanon is remarkable for the grandeur
and beauty of its scenery, and supplied the
sacred writers with many expressive similes
(Psa. 72:16; 104:16-18; Cant. 4:15; Isa. 2:13;
35:2; 60:13; Hos. 14:5). It was noted for its
cedars (Psa. 29:5; Cant. 5:15), its wines (Hos.
14:7), and its cool waters (Jer. 18:14).

The *eastern* range, or Anti-Lebanon, has its
center at Mount Hermon, from which a number of ranges radiate like the ribs of a half-
opened fan. The first runs northeast, parallel
to Lebanon, from which it is separated by the
valley of Coele-Syria, or the *Beqa‛* whose average breadth is about six miles. Its elevation is
not more than four thousand five hundred
feet. As it advances northward its features
become wilder and grander, and the elevation increases until, above the plain of Zebe-
dâny, it attains an elevation of about seven
thousand feet. There is little change until it
reaches the parallel of Ba'albek, when it be-

270. The Mountains of Lebanon

gins to fall, and declines gradually until at length it sinks down into the plain of Hamath. The lowest and last of the Anti-Lebanon ranges runs nearly due east along the plain of Damascus, continuing onward to Palmyra. Its average elevation is not more than three thousand feet, and, with the exception of a few peaks, it does not rise more than seven hundred feet above the plain.

272. Cedars of Lebanon

The Climate of Lebanon varies greatly. In the plain of Dan, at the source of the Jordan, the heat and vegetation are almost tropical. The coast along the western base of Lebanon, though very sultry during the summer months, is not unhealthy. The sea breeze setting in in the evening keeps the night comparatively cool, and the air is dry and free from malaria. In the plains of Coele-Syria and Damascus snow falls, sometimes eight inches deep. The main ridges of both ranges are generally covered with snow from December to March. During the summer the higher parts of the mountain are cool and pleasant, rain seldom falling between June 1 and September 20.

History. Lebanon is first mentioned (Deut. 1:7; 11:24) as a boundary of the country promised to Israel; and to those who had lived in Egypt or the desert Lebanon must have seemed a paradise. It was originally inhabited by a number of independent, warlike tribes, some of whom Joshua conquered near Lake Merom (Josh. 11:2-18). They are said to have been of Phoenician stock (Pliny, v, 17; Eusebius, Onom., s. v.; comp. I Kings 5). Farther norther were the Hivites (Judg. 3:3), the Giblites and Arkites. The Israelites never completely subdued them, but the Phoenicians appear to have had them under their power, as they supplied themselves and Solomon with timber from their forests (I Kings 5:9-11; Ezek. 27:9, sq.). Still later the king of Assyria felled its timber for his military engines (Isa. 14:8; 37:24; Ezek. 31:16). In the fourth century B. C. the whole country was incorporated with the country or kingdom of the Seleucidae. Today the Republic of Lebanon, embracing much of what was ancient Phoenicia, exists as an independent state.

Figurative. Lebanon is used to symbolize that which is great, strong, beautiful, as: (1) The army of Asshur (Isa. 10:34); (2) A proud people (Isa. 29:17); (3) The Jews (Jer. 22:6, 23; Hab. 2:17); (4) Perhaps of the temple, in

which was timber from Lebanon; (5) mourning of Lebanon, of deep affliction (Ezek. 31: 15).

Leba'oth (lĕ-bā'ŏth; Josh. 15:32), see Beth-Lebaoth.

Lebbae'us (lĕ-bē'ŭs; courageous), a surname of Judas or Jude (Matt. 10:3), one of the twelve apostles. He was called also Thaddaeus, which Meyers (Com., in loco.) thinks was his regular apostolic name.

Lebo'nah (lĕ-bō'nà; frankincense), a town near Shiloh, north of the spot where the young men of Benjamin were directed to capture the Shilonite maidens at the yearly festival (Judg. 21:19). It is, doubtless, the same as Lubban, 3 miles N. W. of Shiloah.

Le'cah (lē'kà), a place in the tribe of Judah founded by Er (I Chron. 4:21), not elsewhere mentioned.

Leech. See Animal Kingdom (Horseleech).

Leeks. See Vegetable Kingdom.

Lees (Heb. shĕmĕr, something preserved). "Wines on the lees" are wines which have been left to stand upon their lees after the first fermentation is over, which have thus thoroughly fermented, and have been kept a long time, and which are then filtered before drinking; hence wine both strong and clear; in which case it was used figuratively for the full enjoyment of blessedness in the perfected kingdom of God (Isa. 25:6). Allowed to remain upon the lees, the wine became thick and syrupy, and symbolized the sloth, indifference, and gross stupidity of the ungodly (Jer. 48:11; Zeph. 1:12). To drink the lees ("dregs," A. V., Psa. 75:8) was an expression for the endurance of extreme punishment.

Left. The left hand was esteemed of ill omen, hence the term sinister as equivalent to unfortunate. This was especially the case among the Greeks and Romans. The Greek term was used in taking auguries; but these omens were euphemistically called euōnuma, which in fact were regarded as unlucky, i. e., which came from the left, sinister omens (for which a good name was desired). Among the Hebrews the left hand indicated the north (Gen. 14:15; Job 23:9), the person's face being supposed to be turned toward the East.

Left-handed (Heb. 'ittēr yăd yᵉmînō, shut as to his right hand), a term applied to one who is unable to use skillfully his right hand (Judg. 3:15; 20:16). It can hardly mean an ambidexter, since the expression "shut as to his right hand" would preclude the fact of ability to use both hands alike. An instance of using both hands dexterously is given in I Chron. 12:2. Perhaps this power of using the left hand may have come through cultivation.

Leg. The bones of the legs of crucified persons were broken to hasten death (John 19:31). See Crucifixion.

Legerdemain. See Magic.

Legion, a main division of the Roman army, nearly equivalent to our regiment. It comprised a much larger number of men, running from three thousand men to about six thousand at the time of Christ. See Army.

Figurative. The word legion came to mean a great number or multitude, e. g., of angels (Matt. 26:53) and of evil spirits (Mark 5:9; comp. v. 15).

Leha′bim (lē-hā′bĭm), a people reckoned among the Midianitish stock (Gen. 10:13; I Chron. 1:11). The Lehabim are undoubtedly the fair-haired, blue-eyed Libyans, who as far back as the nineteenth and twentieth dynasties had been incorporated into the Egyptian army. At one time they occupied much the same place in Egyptian history as was subsequently occupied by the Lydians, and the twenty-second dynasty, that of Shishak was, of Libyan extraction, and owed its rise to power to the influence of the Libyan troops.

Le′hi (lē′hī; a *cheek*, or *jawbone*), the place in Judah where Samson slew the Philistines with a jawbone (Judg. 15:9, 14, 16). The R. V. has in Judg. 15:19, "the hollow place that is in Lehi." The spring in the hollow place he called En-hakkore, "the fountain of him that prayed."

Lem′uel (lĕm′ů-ĕl, belonging *to God*), a person of whom nothing is known, except that to him the admonitory apothegms of Prov. 31: 2-9, were addressed by his mother. The rabbinical commentators identify Lemuel with Solomon, which seems the most likely conjecture. Others (as Grotius) refer the epithet to Hezekiah, while others (as Gesenius) think that it refers to some neighboring petty Arabian prince.

Lend. *See* Loan.

Lentile. *See* Vegetable Kingdom.

Leopard. *See* Animal Kingdom.

Figurative. The leopard is illustrative of God in his judgments (Hos. 13:7); of the Macedonian kingdom (Dan. 7:6); of Antichrist (Rev. 13:2); *tamed*, of the wicked subdued by truth and grace (Isa. 11:6).

Leper (Heb. *Şärä‘, smite*). **Leprosy** (Heb. *şärä‘äth, a smiting, a scourge*). Concerning the nature of leprosy, *see* Diseases. Here will be considered the Mosaic regulations respecting the existence of leprosy and the purification therefrom. The law for leprosy treats of:

1. **Leprosy in Man.** (1) **Symptoms,** etc. The priest was to decide whether the leprosy was: (*a*) In its dangerous forms when appearing on the skin (Lev. 13:2-28), on the head and beard (vers. 29-37); (*b*) in harmless forms (vers. 38, 39); and (*c*) when appearing on a bald head (vers. 40-44); (*d*) instructions were given for removal of the leper from the society of men (vers. 45, 46). While thus excluded the leper was to wear mourning costume, rend his clothes, leave the hair of his head disordered, keep the beard covered (Ezek. 27:17, 22), and cry "Unclean! unclean!" that everyone might avoid him for fear of being defiled (Lam. 4:15), and as long as the disease lasted he was to dwell apart without the camp (Lev. 13:45, 46; Num. 5:2, sq.; 12:15, etc.). Respecting the symptoms the priest was to decide as to whether they indicated leprosy or some other disease. (2) **Purification.** The ceremonial prescribed for the purification of persons cured of leprosy is based upon the idea that this malady is the bodily symbol, not so much of sin merely as of death. Accordingly the rite of purification resolved itself into two parts: (1) The readmission of the sufferer (Lev. 14:1-9), who had been looked upon as dead, into the society of the living, and preparation for his return to fellowship with the covenant people. This ceremony, therefore, took place without the camp. The officiating priest caused two clean and living birds, along with some cedar wood, scarlet wool, and hyssop to be brought. One of the birds was killed over running water, i. e., water from a spring or stream, in such a way that the blood would flow into the water. He then dipped into this the living bird, the cedar, the scarlet wool, and the hyssop—the symbol of duration of life, vigor of life, and purity. He then sprinkled it seven times upon the leper, after which the living bird was set free, thus symbolizing that the leper was at liberty to return to society. The slain bird, though not having a sacrificial character, seems intended to show that the leper was saved from death by intervention of divine mercy. The sprinkling was repeated *seven* times. The symbolical cleansing was followed by the shaving off of the hair, which was peculiarly liable to be affected by the leprosy; bathing the body in water, and washing the clothes. (2) admission to camp (Lev. 14:10-32), i. e., to resume living in his tent, was obtained after a *second* cleansing, on the eighth day. On this day the priest presented the candidate, with the necessary offerings, before the Lord. These offerings were: two he-lambs, one ewe lamb, three tenth deals flour mingled with oil, and one log of oil. The priests waved one of the he-lambs and the log of oil for a trespass offering. The lamb was then slain, and some of the blood was put upon the tip of the ear, the hand, and the foot of the person. These same organs were afterward anointed with oil, and after the priest had sprinkled some of the oil seven times before the Lord the remainder was poured upon the head of the person to be dedicated. The she-lamb was then offered for a sin offering, for the purpose of making atonement (v. 19), after which the burnt and meat offerings were presented. In case the person was poor he offered one lamb, two turtledoves, or two young pigeons (vers. 21:32). Thus the restored leper was admitted again to communion with the altar and Israel.

2. **Leprosy in a House.** The law concerning this was made known to Moses, as intended for the time when Israel should possess Canaan and dwell in houses. This leprosy manifested its presence by depressions of a greenish or reddish color on the walls, and was of vegetable formation. When these indications were observed the owner of the house reported to the priest, who directed that the whole contents of the house should be taken out, in order to prevent everything within it from becoming unclean. He then examined the walls of the house, and if he saw symptoms of the plague ordered the house closed for seven days. If on the seventh day the leprosy gave evidence of spreading he ordered the affected stones to be removed, the inside of the house to be scraped, the affected parts removed replaced by others, and the walls plastered with fresh mortar. If, after these precautions, the evil should reappear, the leprosy was pronounced of a malignant type, the house was pulled down, while stones, timber, and rubbish were removed to an unclean

place without the city. Any person entering the house, who ate or slept in it, was accounted unclean and was required to wash his clothes. If it was found that the plague had not spread after the house was plastered, the priest declared it free from the disease, and after sprinkling it seven times with the same kind of sprinkling water as was used in the case of human leprosy, he purified it, and made atonement for it that it might be clean (Lev. 14:33-53).

3. **Leprosy in Fabrics.** The leprosy in woolen or linen fabrics and leather is probably the result of damp or ill ventilation, causing the material to rot. Leprosy in woolen or linen *clothes* or *fabrics*, or in *leather*, was also indicated by greenish or reddish spots upon them. The presence of these were reported to the priest, who ordered the affected article to be shut up for seven days. If the spots had spread by the eighth day, the article was burned; if not, it was ordered washed and shut up another seven days. If then similar spots appeared, the article or material was burned; but if the leprous spot had yielded to the washing but left a stain, the stained portion was cut out and the remainder pronounced clean. In case no further indication of the disease appeared, the material was washed the second time and pronounced clean (Lev. 13:47-59). The Jewish laws exempted dyed material from liability to leprosy.

Le'shem (lē'shĕm), a city in North Palestine (Josh. 19:47), elsewhere called Laish (*q. v.*).

Le'thech (lē'thĕk), a Hebrew word in margin of Hos. 3:2, and meaning a measure for grain. In the A. V. it is rendered "a half homer." The R. S. V. renders "a letheck of barley." *See* Metrology, II.

Letter is used both as an alphabetical character and correspondence (*see* Writing and Epistle). The words of the apostle (Gal. 6:11), "Ye see how large a letter I have written unto you with mine own hand," is thus explained by Meyer (*Com.*, in loc.): "In accordance with his well-known manner in other passages, *Paul adds to the letter, which up to this point he had dictated, the conclusion from verse 11 onward in his own handwriting* . . . But this close of our epistle was intended to catch the eyes of the readers as *something so especially important, that from verse 12 to the the end the apostle wrote with very large letters,* just as we, in writing and printing, distinguish by letters of a larger size anything that we wish to be considered as peculiarly significant."

Figurative. "The letter" is used by the apostle Paul in opposition to the spirit (Rom. 2:27, 29; 7:6; II Cor. 3:6, 7). In general *letter* is used to denote the Mosaic law, and mere external obedience thereto.

Letu'shim (lĕ-tū'shĭm; *hammered, oppressed*), the second son of Dedan, grandson of Abraham by Keturah (Gen. 25:3), B. C. considerably after 1950. The plural form of the three sons of Dedan would seem to indicate *tribes* descended from him. *See* Dedan.

Leum'mim (lĕ-ŭm'ĭm; *nations, peoples*), the last of the three sons of Dedan, grandson of Abraham by Keturah (Gen. 25:3), or more probably a tribe descended from Dedan, among

whose descendants they appear as third. Some have identified them with the *Alumeōtai* of Ptolemy (vi, 7, § 24); but the Alumeotae of Central Arabia have been quite as probably thought to correspond to Almodad. In the Sabaean inscriptions, however, the forms *l'mm* and *l'mym* occur.

Le'vi (lē'vī; a *joining*), the third son of Jacob and Leah (Gen. 29:34), B. C. probably 1950.

1. **Personal History.** (1) **Avenges Dinah.** One fact alone is recorded in which Levi appears prominent. His sister *Dinah* (*q. v.*) was seduced by Shechem, and, according to the rough usage of the times, the stain could only be washed out by blood. Simeon and Levi took this task upon themselves. Covering their scheme with fair words and professions of friendship, they committed a cowardly and repulsive crime (Gen. 34). (2) **Levi and Joseph.** Levi shared in the hatred which his brothers bore to Joseph, and joined in the plots against him (37:4). (3) **Migrates to Egypt.** With his three sons, Gershon, Kohath, and Merari, Levi went down into Egypt (46:11), and as one of the four eldest sons we may think of him as among the five (47:2) specially presented to Pharaoh. Then comes the last scene, when Jacob, on his deathbed, recalls Levi's old crime and expresses his abhorrence of it (49:5-7). *See* Levites.

2. Father of Matthat and son of Melchi, third preceding Mary among the ancestors of Jesus (Luke 3:24) B. C. considerably before 22.

3. The father of another Matthat, and son of Simeon, in the maternal line between David and Zerubbabel (Luke 3:29), B. C. after 876.

4. An apostle. *See* Matthew.

Leviathan. *See* Animal Kingdom.

Levirate Marriage (from Lat. *Levir*, a *husband's brother*), the name applied to the custom among the Hebrews that when an Israelite died without leaving male issue, his nearest relative should marry the widow, and continue the family of his deceased brother through the first-born son of such union, he becoming the heir of the former husband. If the brother did not choose to marry the widow she subjected him to gross insult. *See* Marriage, Levirate.

Le'vites (lē'vīts; Heb. *benē lēwî, sons of Levi*, or simply *lēwî, "Levites"*), a patronymic title which, besides denoting all the descendants of Levi (Exod. 6:25; Lev. 25:32; Josh. 21:3, 41), is also the distinctive title of that portion of the tribe which was set apart for the service of the sanctuary, subordinate to the priests (Num. 8:6; Ezra 2:70; John 1:19, etc.). It is sometimes added as an epithet, and we read of "the priests of the Levites" (Josh. 3:3; Ezek. 44:15).

1. **Their Appointment.** No reference is made to the consecrated character of the Levites in Genesis. Tracing its descent from Leah, the tribe would naturally take its place among the six chief tribes sprung from the wives of Jacob, and share with them a superiority over those who bore the names of the sons of Bilhah and Zilpah. The work of Aaron, and his greater brother Moses, would give prominence to the family and tribe to which they belonged. And again the tribe stood separate

and apart as the champions of Jehovah, after the sin of making the golden calf. If the Levites had been sharers in the sin of the golden calf, they were, at any rate, the foremost to rally round their leader when he called on them to help him in stemming the progress of the evil. But we are told that the tribe of Levi was specially chosen by God for the purpose of intrusting to it the care and administration of holy things (Num. 3:5, sq.; 8: 14-19). They were consecrated to Jehovah as his peculiar property, instead of the firstborn (*q. v.*) of the whole nation, these latter being replaced by the Levites, while all over and above the number required were ransomed at the rate of five shekels a head (18:16).

2. **Division** of the tribe of Levi. Different functions having been assigned to the separate houses of the Levitical branch of the tribe, we insert the following table, formulated from Exod. 6:16-25 and Num. 3:17-20, italicising the priestly branch.

LEVI
- GERSHON { Libni. Shimei.
- KOHATH
  - Amram { Aaron { Eleazar. Ithamar } ; Moses.
  - Izhar { Korah. Nepheg. Zichri.
  - Hebron.
  - Uzziel { Mishael. Elzaphan. Zithri.
- MERARI { Mahli. Mushi.

In Num. 3:21 Libni and Shimei are mentioned as fathers of families, as is Hebron also (3:27). The design of the genealogy appears to be to give the pedigrees of Moses and Aaron, and some other principal heads of the family of Aaron (*see* Exod. 6:25).

3. **Age and Qualifications.** A Levite's period of service was from twenty-five to fifty years of age (Num. 8:24, 25); after the latter age he ceased from "work," and acted as overseer. The age of thirty years (Num. 4:3-49) has been variously explained, some thinking it to have arisen from an error of the copyist, others that it referred to the time of transporting the tabernacle, others that the first selection of Levites was those from twenty-five to fifty, but that *all future* Levites had to commence service at twenty-five. The Septuagint solves the difficulty by uniformly reading twenty-five instead of thirty. No other qualification than that of age is mentioned, although the regulations in force among the priests respecting deformity and cleanness doubtless applies also to the Levites.

4. **Duties.** The functions of the whole tribe of Levi were to preserve the law of Jehovah in all its integrity and purity, to see that its requirements were duly complied with, to dispense justice in accordance with its enactments, and to transmit it to posterity (Lev. 10:11; Deut. 17:18; 31:9-13; 33:10; comp. II Chron. 17:8-10; Neh. 8:9; Ezek. 44:23; Mal. 2:7, sq.). The Levites, apart from their priestly portion, were to act as assistants to the sons of Aaron "in all the service of the tabernacle" (Num. 18:4), but they were forbidden to touch any sacred furniture or the altar until it had been covered by the priests

(4:5-15). As the tabernacle was the sign of the presence among the people of their unseen King, so the Levites may be compared to a royal guard; indeed the terms "host" (4:3) and "service" (v. 30) are rendered "warfare" in the margin. When the people settled in Canaan it was the duty of the Levites, acting as police, to guard the sanctuary, to open and close it, to look after the cleaning of it and the furniture, to prepare the showbread, and to do whatever other baking was needed in connection with the sacrifices, to lead the music (*q. v.*) during worship, to assist the priests in slaughtering and skinning the animals for sacrifice, to examine the lepers according to law, to look after the temple stores, and such like. For the heavier and more menial duties of their office, the Levites were assisted by *temple slaves.* Thus the Gibeonites had been appointed to act as hewers of wood and drawers of water (Josh. 9:21). David and other kings presented to the sanctuary persons to perform services of such a nature (Ezra 8:20), probably prisoners of war who had become proselytes, called after the captivity *Nethinim* (*q. v.*).

5. **Classification.** The better to systematize their service, Moses divided the Levites into three sections by their respective descent from the sons of Levi, viz., Gershon, Kohath, and Merari. They were under the general supervision of Eleazar, the son of Aaron, with aids having charge of a section (Num. 3:32).

(1) **The Kohathites**, with Elizaphan as leader (Num. 3:30). *Number*, at the building of the tabernacle, eight thousand six hundred men (3:28), with two thousand seven hundred and fifty qualified for active service (4:36). *Place of encampment*, south side of the tabernacle (3:29). *Duty*, charge of the ark, table of showbread, candlestick, altars of burnt offering and of incense, the sacred vessels used in the service, and the veil (3:27, sq.; 4:4, sq.).

(2) **Gershonites**, with Eliasaph as leader (Num. 3:24). *Number*, seven thousand five hundred men, with two thousand six hundred and thirty for active service (3:22; 4:40). *Place of encampment*, west side of tabernacle (3: 23). *Duty*, charge of curtains, the tent (i. e., above the planks), the coverings and the hanging for the door of the tabernacle, the hangings of the court and the court entrance, their cords and instruments of service, also the work of taking down and setting these up (3:25, 26; 4:22-28).

(3) **Merarites**, with Zuriel as leader (Num. 3:35). *Number*, six thousand two hundred men, with three thousand two hundred qualified for active service (3:34; 4:44). *Encampment*, north side of tabernacle (3:35). *Duty*, charge of planks, bars, pillars, and sockets of the tabernacle; also the pillars of the court, their sockets, pins, cords, and tools pertaining thereto (3:36, sq.; 4:29, sq.). Owing to the heavy nature of the materials which they had to carry, four wagons and eight oxen were assigned to them; and in the march both they and the Gershonites followed immediately after the standard of Judah, and before that of Reuben, that they might set up the tabernacle against the arrival of the Kohathites (7:8).

6. **Consecration.** The consecration of the Levites began with sprinkling them with the "water of purifying" (marg. "sin-water"), followed by shaving off the hair of the entire body, washing of clothes, accompanied by the sacrifice of two bullocks, fine flour and oil (Num. 8:6-15). The water of purifying (or sin-water) is thought by some to be the same as that used in the purification for leprosy (Lev. 13:6, 9, 13), while others understand it to be the water in the laver, provided for the purpose of cleansing the priests for the performance of their duties. After this purification they were brought before the door of the tabernacle, and set apart for service by the laying on of the hands of the elders.

7. **Revenues and Residence.** Chosen from among the whole people to be Jehovah's peculiar possession, the Levites did not obtain, like the rest of the tribes, any inheritance in the land of Canaan. Their portion was to be Jehovah himself (Num. 18:20; Deut. 10:9, etc.), who ordained that they should have set apart for them four cities out of every tribe, along with the necessary pasture for their cattle (Num. 35:1-8). Besides this they received the tithes due to Jehovah from the fruits of the fields, from the flocks and herds (Lev. 27:30-33; comp. Num. 18:21-24), of the first fruits (Exod. 23:19; Lev. 2:14; 23:17, etc.), of the firstborn (Exod. 13:12, sq.; Lev. 27:26; Num. 18:15, sq.; Deut. 15:19), as well as certain portions of the sacrificial offerings of the people (Num. 18:8-11, 19). Of the tithes the Levites had to turn over a tithe to the priests (18:26, sq.). The Levites lived for the greater part of the year in their own cities, and came up at fixed periods to take their turn of work (I Chron. chaps. 25, 26). How long that term lasted we have no sufficient data for determining.

8. **History, etc.** (1) **Till death of Solomon.** It may be well to add a few additional facts to those already given. We have seen that the Levites were to take the place of the earlier priesthood of the firstborn as representatives of the holiness of the people; that they acted as the royal guard, waiting upon Jehovah; and that they alone bore the tabernacle and its sacred furniture. Failing to appreciate their holy calling, that section of the Levites whose position brought them into contact with the tribe of Reuben conspired with it to reassert the old partriarchal system of a household priesthood, but were severely punished by divine interposition (Num. 16:1, sq.). Joshua, the successor of Moses, faithfully planned to continue the Mosaic ideal of the Levites as the priestly caste, providing them with cities to dwell in and servants from the conquered Hivites. During the period of the Judges we have only scanty material respecting the Levites, but the conduct of the people would seem to indicate that either the Levites failed to bear witness to the truth or had no power to enforce it. The shameless license of the sons of Eli may be looked upon as the result of a long period of decay affecting the whole order. Samuel, himself a Levite (I Chron. 6:28, 33), infused new life into the organization. His rule and that of his sons, and the prophetical

character now connected with the tribe, tended to give them the position of a ruling caste; and perhaps the desire of the people for a king was a protest against the assumption of the Levites of a higher position than that originally assigned them.

David definitely recognized their relation to the priesthood, and publicly admitted their claim to be the bearers of the ark (I Chron. 15:2). In the procession which entered Jerusalem bringing the ark to its final resting place, the Levites were conspicuous, wearing their linen ephods and appearing in their new character as minstrels (15:27, 28). The education which the Levites received for their peculiar duties, no less than their connection, more or less intimate, with the schools of the prophets, would tend to make them, so far as there was any education at all, the teachers of the others, the transcribers and interpreters of the law, the chroniclers of the times in which they lived.

(2) **During the divided kingdom.** "The revolt of the ten tribes, and the policy pursued by Jeroboam, led to a great change in the position of the Levites. They were the witnesses of an appointed order and a central worship. He wished to make the priests the creatures and instruments of the king, and to establish a provincial and divided worship. The natural result was that they left the cities assigned to them in the territory of Israel, and gathered round the metropolis of Judah (II Chron. 11:13, 14). In the kingdom of Judah they were, from this time forward, a powerful body, politically as well as ecclesiastically. We find them prominent in the war of Abijah against Jeroboam (13:10-12). They are sent out by Jehoshaphat to instruct and judge the people (19:8-10). The apostasy that followed on the marriage of Jehoram and Athaliah exposed them for a time to the dominance of a hostile system; but the services of the temple appear to have gone on, and the Levites were again conspicuous in the counter revolution effected by Jehoiada (ch. 23), and in restoring the temple to its former stateliness under Joash (24:5). The closing of the temple under Ahaz involved the cessation at once of their work and of their privileges (28:24). Under Hezekiah they again became prominent, as consecrating themselves to the special work of cleansing and repairing the temple (29:12-15); and the hymns of David and of Asaph were again renewed. Their old privileges were restored, they were put forward as teachers (30:22), and the payment of tithes, which had probably been discontinued under Ahaz, was renewed (3:14). The genealogies of the tribe were revised (v. 17), and the old classification kept its ground. The reign of Manasseh was for them, during the greater part of it, a period of depression. That of Josiah witnessed a fresh revival and reorganization (34:8-13). In the great passover of his eighteenth year they took their places as teachers of the people, as well as leaders of their worship (35:3, 15). Then came the Egyptian and Chaldean invasions, and the rule of cowardly and apostate kings. Then the sacred tribe showed itself unfaithful. They had, as the penalty of their sin, to witness the destruction of the temple and to taste the bitterness of exile."

(3) **After the captivity.** "The position taken by the Levites in the first movements of the return from Babylon indicates that they had cherished the traditions and maintained the practices of their tribe. It is noticeable that, in the first body of returning exiles, they were present in a disproportionately small number (Ezra 2:36-42). Those who do come take their old parts at the foundation and dedication of the second temple (3:10; 6:18). In the next movement under Ezra their reluctance was even more strongly marked. None of them presented themselves at the first great gathering (8:15). The special efforts of Ezra did not succeed in bringing together more than thirty-eight, and their places had to be filled by two hundred and twenty of the Nethinim (v. 20). Those who returned with him resumed their functions at the feast of tabernacles as teachers and interpreters (Neh. 8:7), and those who were most active in that work were foremost also in chanting the hymnlike prayer which appears in ch. 9 as the last great effort of Jewish psalmody. They are recognized in the great national covenant, and the offerings and tithes which were their due are once more solemnly secured to them (10:37-39). They take their old places in the temple and in the villages near Jerusalem (12:29), and are present in full array at the great feast of the dedication of the wall. The two prophets who were active at the time of the return, Haggai and Zechariah, if they did not belong to the tribe, helped it forward in the work of restoration. The strongest measures were adopted by Nehemiah, as before by Ezra, to guard the purity of their blood from the contamination of mixed marriages (Ezra 10:23); and they are made the special guardians of the holiness of the Sabbath (Neh. 13:22). The last prophet of the Old Testament sees, as part of his vision of the latter days, the time when the Lord 'shall purify the sons of Levi' (Mal. 3:3). The guidance of the Old Testament fails us at this point, and the history of the Levites in relation to the national life becomes consequently a matter of inference and conjecture" (Smith, *Dict. of Bible*).

(4) **In New Testament.** The Levites appear but seldom in the history of the New Testament. Where we meet with their names it is as the type of a formal heartless worship, without sympathy and without love (Luke 10:32). The mention of a Levite at Cyprus in Acts 4:36 shows that the changes of the previous century had carried that tribe also into "the dispersed among the Gentiles."

Levitical Cities. As the Levites were to "have no inheritance in their land" (Num. 18:20), Moses commanded the children of Israel, i. e., the rest of the tribes, to give towns to the Levites to dwell in of the inheritance that fell to them for a possession, with pasturage round about the cities for their cattle (Num. 35:2, sq.). The pasturage (A. V. "suburbs") were to "reach from the wall of the city and outward 1,000 cubits round about. And ye shall measure without the city on the east side 2,000 cubits." These dimensions have occasioned great difficulty because of the apparent contradiction in the two verses, as specifying first 1,000 cubits and then 2,000.

Of the many explanations given of these measurements the following two seem most probable: According to the Talmud (*Erubin*, 51a), the space "measured from the wall 1,000 cubits round about" was used as a common or suburbs, and the space measured "from without the city on the east side," etc., was a further tract of land of 2,000 cubits, used for

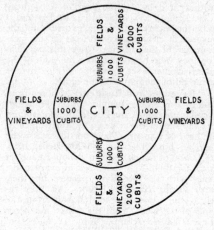

273.

fields and vineyards, the former being "the suburbs," properly so called, and the latter "the fields of the suburbs," as represented in Figure 273. The above explanation takes for granted, which seems probable, that the cities were circular in form. Keil and Delitzsch indorse the explanation given by J. D. Michaelis: "We must picture the towns and the surrounding fields as squares, the pasturage as stretching 1,000 cubits from the city wall in every direction, and the length of each outer side as 2,000 cubits, apart from the length of the city wall; so that if the town itself occupied a square of 1,000 cubits (Fig. 274), the outer side of the town fields would measure 2,000+1,000 cubits in every direction; but if each side of the city was only 500 cubits long (Fig. 275), the outer side of the town fields would measure 2,000+500 cubits in every

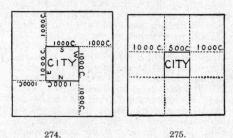

274.   275.

direction." Of these cities six were to be cities of refuge (*q. v.*), and thirteen allotted to the priests' portion of the tribe. Which cities belonged to the priests, which to the nonpriestly portion of the tribe, and how they were distributed among the other tribes (Josh. 21:3, sq.), is shown in the following table:

(1) *Kohathites:*

(a) Priests....	Judah and Simeon....	9
	Benjamin............	4
(b) Not priests	Ephraim............	4
	Dan.................	4
	Half Manasseh (west)..	2
	Half Manasseh (east)..	2
(2) *Gershonites*...	Issachar.............	4
	Asher..............	4
	Naphtali............	3
	Zebulun............	4
(3) *Merarites*....	Reuben..............	4
	Gad.................	4
	Total............	48

These cities were not given entirely to the Levites as their own property, but as many houses in the towns as sufficed for their necessities. These could be redeemed if sold at any time, and reverted to them without compensation in the year of jubilee, even if not redeemed before (Lev. 25:32, 33); but such portion of the city as was not taken possession of by them, together with the fields and villages, continued the property of those tribes to which they had been assigned by lot.

Leviticus. As Exodus is the book of redemption, Leviticus is the book of cleansing, worship and service of the redeemed people.

1. **The Name.** The name describes its contents, for it deals with the law of the priests, the sons of Levi, Leviticus being taken from the Vulgate, *Leviticus* (through the Septuagint *Leueitikon*). The designation sets forth the book admirably as a manual of the O. T. priesthood (Heb. 7:11). The Jews, however, commonly designate the book from its opening phrase *wayiqra*, "and he called." Leviticus is a priestly book which sets forth the way of the priestly approach to God. Its inspired N. T. commentary, the Epistle to the Hebrews, describes the same approach in the dispensation of grace. Being a hand-book of Levitical directions, it has very little narrative, and such brief passages as the episode of the strange fire offered by Nadab and Abihu (10:1, 2), are most intimately connected with the illustrations of the law given.

2. **The Literary Character.** The book incontrovertibly claims Mosaic authorship. Some 56 times in 27 chapters the claim is made that these laws were divinely given through Moses. This is the traditional view. However, higher Pentateuchal criticism denies the Mosaic authenticity of Leviticus. Critics commonly assign it to the so-called Priest Code, abbreviated P, which is frequently dated about 500 B. C., or a little later. Some critics think that Leviticus 17-27 is distinct enough from P to be designated H ("Holiness Code"), which is assumed to be combined with P to form our present book. Thus the critics can hardly escape making the book of Leviticus a pious forgery.

3. **Weakness of the Critical Theory.** The hypothesis of an exilic date (S. R. Driver) or post-exilic date (Julius Bewer) for the so-called Priestly Code is filled with serious objections for the conservative. Morally it involves the dishonesty of passing off as Mosaic what was not Mosaic at all. This procedure is manifestly inconsistent with the moral standards of a prophet or any adequate view of

inspiration. There is also the historical absurdity of getting so late a concoction of laws accepted at all or, what is even more incredible, approved as directly mediated by God to Moses. In addition there is the legal inanity which is manifested in foisting the code in its Mosaic dress and wilderness framework on a post-exilic economy. Critics describe the purpose of Leviticus as arousing the post-exilic community to organize "a theocracy which was to be symbolized and realized in a hierocracy" (Julius Bewer, *The Literature of the O. T.*, N. Y., 7th Ed. (1947), p. 259) but this is highly artificial, arbitrary and against internal evidence of the book itself. Moreover, archaeological discoveries have shown that codification of law in the Near East came early, rather than late, as critics used to assert. There is therefore no objective reason for dating Old Testament legislation late. *See* under Law of Moses, #3. Mosaic and Near Eastern Laws.

4. **The Contents.**

Part I. *Directions for Coming to God*, 1:1-16:34

  a. Directions for Priestly Sacrifices, 1:1-17:38

  b. Directions for Priestly Consecration, 8:1-9:24

  c. Directions for Priestly Violation, 10:1-20

  d. Directions for Priestly Purification, 11:1-15:33

  e. Directions for the Day of Atonement, 16:1-34

Part II. *Directions for Fellowship with God*, 17:1-27:34

  a. Directions Preserving Holiness, 17:1-22:33

  b. Directions Governing Religious Feasts, 23:1-44

  c. Directions for Lamps, Shew Bread, etc., 24:1-23

  d. Directions for Sabbatic Year and Jubilee, 25:1-26:2

  e. Promises and Warnings, 26:3-46

  f. Directions Concerning Vows and Tithes, 27:1-34   *M. F. U.*

Levy (Heb. *măs, tribute*), the term applied to a company of thirty thousand Israelites raised by Solomon (I Kings 5:13). They were free Israelites, who to pay tribute (or tax) worked four months in the year, felling trees under the direction of subjects of Hiram. Another *levy* was of Canaanites, who were assigned to tributary labor (9:15), in this case for the erection of buildings.

Lewd (Gr. *ponēros*), in a moral sense *evil, wicked* (Acts 17:5).

Lewdness (Gr. *hradiourgēma*, literally *doing things easily*, or *boldly*), a piece of knavery, rascality (Acts 18:14). Elsewhere these terms are used in their proper sense of *licentiousness* (Heb. *zĭmmäh*, etc., *badness*, Judg. 20:6; Jer. 11:15; Ezekiel frequently; Hos. 6:9), once (Hos. 2:10) the *parts of shame* (Heb. *năblūth*).

Libation, the act of pouring wine on the ground in divine worship. Sometimes other liquids have been used, as oil, milk, water, honey, but mostly wine. Among the Greeks and Romans it was an essential part of solemn sacrifices. Libations were also in use among the Hebrews, who poured a hin of wine on the victim after it was killed, and the several pieces of the sacrifice were laid on the altar ready to be consumed in the flames. *See* Offerings.

Liberality, a generous disposition of mind, resulting in large giving, i. e., according to one's ability; largeness of mind; catholicity. In I Cor. 16:3 "a gracious, act" or "benevolence" (Gr. *charis*) is indicated.

Lib′ertines (lĭb′ẽr-tēns; Latin, *"freedmen"*). This occurs but once in the New Testament: "Certain of the synagogue, which is called of the Libertines" (Acts 6:9). The interpretation of this word has been various. Some think these Libertines were manumitted Roman slaves, who having embraced Judaism had their synagogue at Jerusalem. Others, owing to the geographical names given to other synagogues in the same verse, infer that this must have the same meaning, and suppose that Jews dwelling in Liberatum, a city or region in proconsular Africa, are meant. Others, with far greater probability, appeal to Philo, and understand the word as denoting Jews who had been made captive by the Romans under Pompey, but were afterward set free, and who, although they had fixed their abode at Rome, had built at their own expense a synagogue at Jerusalem, which they frequented when in that city.

Liberty, Christian, or evangelical liberty, a phrase which covers several New Testament representations of the Christian life.

1. Believers are emancipated from the bondage of Satan, the domination of sin, from guilt, and the fear of death (*see* John 8:31-36; Acts 26:17, 18; Rom. 7:24, 25; 8:15; Heb. 2:14, 15). Spiritual union with Christ, involving the service of Christ, is compatible with perfect freedom; inasmuch as we are thus restored to the right relationship to God and brought into harmony with his will (*see* Matt. 11:28-30; James 1:25).

2. Christians are not under obligation to observe the distinctly Jewish regulations, Circumcision, the sign of the old covenant, with the whole body of ceremonial and economic requirements essential to the chosen nation during the period that was preparatory to the Gospel, under the Gospel is set aside. These features of religion, once imposed by special revelation, were annulled by the incoming of the new dispensation. They were not in keeping with the proper magnifying of the grace of Christ, the dignity and inward liberty of redeemed souls, their moral elevation and illumination, their relationship as children of God. Nor were they adapted to Christianity as designed to be the universal religion of the world (*see* John 4:20-24; Acts 15:1-29; Gal. 2:1-21; 5:1-6; Heb. 8:10, 13).

3. The phrase also refers to the privilege of Christians to regulate their lives as individuals with respect to matters which are morally indifferent. The New Testament instructions upon this point were developed for the most part on account of the attempt to impose Jewish regulations upon converts of Christianity, but the principles set forth are of much broader application, and are still of great importance (*see* Rom. 13:1-23; 14:14; I Cor. 7:8; also Scriptures referred to above).

With respect to such things are as not commanded or forbidden in the word of God Christian liberty may be exercised and should be allowed. Actions are not to be pronounced sinful which are not sinful. Nonessentials are not to be elevated to the place of essential virtues. Proper room must be left for the exercise of individual judgment or of enlightened Christian conscience. But this liberty with respect to things indifferent is not absolute. Its exercise is under the limitations of the laws of self-preservation, of expediency, of duty, or of love. Concession should be made for the sake of "the weak," though care should be taken not to make them in such a way, or to such an extent, as to perpetuate their weakness or to promote superstition. If the former be not done "the weak" are needlessly injured. If the latter is omitted the principle of evangelical liberty is violated, Christians are reduced to unchristian thraldom, and the progress of Christ's kingdom is obstructed.

E. McC.

Lib′nah (lĭb′nà; *whiteness*).

1. The twenty-first station of the Israelites in the wilderness (Num. 33:20, 21); not identified.

2. A city of the Canaanites, near Lachish, captured by Joshua (Josh. 10:29-32; 12:15); the birthplace of Josiah's queen, Hamutal (II Kings 23:31). It was strongly fortified when Sennacherib laid siege to it, and the Assyrian army was cut off (II Kings 19:8, 9, 35). It was a Levitical city in the tribe of Judah (Josh. 21:13), and has been identified with the modern Tell es Safi.

Lib′ni (lĭb′nī; *white*).

1. The first son of Gershon, the son of Levi (Exod. 6:17; Num. 3:18, 21; I Chron. 6:17, 20), B. C. after 1900. His descendants are called Libnites (Num. 3:21; 26:58).

2. The son of Mahli, son of Merari (I Chron. 6:29). It is probable that he is the same as the preceding, and that something has been omitted from the text (Smith, *Dict.*, s. v.).

Lib′nite (lĭb′nīt; *white*), a descendant of Libni, the Levite (Num. 3:21; 26:58).

Lib′ya (lĭb′yà), the country of the Lubim (Gen. 10:13), the tract lying on the Mediterranean between Egypt and Carthage (Ezek. 30:5; 38:5; Acts 2:10). Cyrene was one of its cities. *See* Lubim.

Lice. *See* Animal Kingdom.

Lie. A lie is the utterance by speech or act of that which is false, with intent to mislead or delude. In Scripture the word is used to designate all the ways in which men deny or alter the truth in word or deed, as also evil in general. Good is designated as the truth, and evil as its opposite. Hence the Scriptures most expressly condemn lies (John 8:44; I Tim. 1:9, 10; Rev. 21:27; 22:15). The Bible mentions instances of good men telling lies, but without approving them, as that of Abraham (Gen. 12:13; 20:2), Isaac (ch. 26), Jacob (ch. 27), the Hebrew midwives (Exod. 1:15-19), Michal (I Sam. 19:14, sq.), David (I Sam. ch. 20).

Lieutenants, (Aram. *'ăhăshdărpᵉnîm*), the official title of the satraps or viceroys who governed the provinces of the Persian empire; it is rendered "lieutenant" in Esth. 3:12, 8:9;

9:3; Ezra 8:36; and "prince" in Dan. 3:2; 6:1, etc.

Life as used in the Bible life denotes:

1. **That which is physical** or natural; that is, mere animal life (Gen. 6:17; 7:15). It thus often has reference to man's bodily life upon the earth, its relative value and transient duration (e. g. Exod. 1:14; Psa. 17:14; 63:3; James 4:14). This form of life propagated by human generation is subject to physical death. Nevertheless, as it involves the whole man, this life is endless in every human being, saved or unsaved. Natural life has a beginning but no end. For the saved it involves eternal life or endless union and fellowship with God. For the unsaved it involves eternal existence in separation from God.

2. **Eternal.** This is the gift of God as a result of faith in Jesus Christ (Eph. 2:8-10). It must not be confused with mere endless existence, which is true of the unsaved. It involves the endless continuance and perfection of blessedness and communion with God entered upon by the saved on the earth. For example: Matt. 18:8-9; Luke 18:30; John 3:15, 16; 6:40; 17:3; Rom. 2:7 (*See* Immortality). Thus John writes "He that hath the Son hath life and he that hath not the Son of God hath not life" (I John 5:12; cf. John 10:10 with Col. 10:27).

3. **Absolute Life.** God in Christ, as self-existent or absolute life is the Source of all life (John 4:26; 14:6; Col. 3:4; I John 1:1, 2; 5:20).

4. **Manner of Life**, as in Luke 8:14; Eph. 4:18; I Tim. 2:2; I John 2:16). *M. F. U.*

Lift (Heb. *näsä'*; Gr. *airō*). Besides the general meaning of raising, this word has figurative meanings:

1. To *lift up the hands* is, among the orientals, a common part of taking an oath (Gen. 14:22; Exod. 6:8, marg.). To lift up one's hand *against* another is to attack, to fight him (II Sam. 18:28; I Kings 11:26).

2. To lift up one's *face* in the presence of another is to appear boldly in his presence (II Sam. 2:22; Ezra 9:6).

3. *To lift up one's hands, eyes, soul,* or *heart unto the Lord*, are expressions describing the sentiments and emotion of one who prays earnestly or ardently desires anything.

Light (mostly Heb. *'ōr;* Gr. *phōs*). Light is declared by the Scriptures to have come into existence by the express fiat of the Almighty, and to have been in existence long before man or the present races of animals or vegetables had their being (Gen. 1:3).

Of all the benefits which we have, as inhabitants of this lower world, received from God, there are few more remarkable than the possession of light, with an organization enabling us to make use of it. By means thereof, we come into possession of much of our knowledge, many of our comforts and necessities, to say nothing of its wonderful purity, delicacy, and variety of colors which it reveals to the eye of man. It is not at all surprising, therefore, that it should exercise a vast influence over the imagination of man and lead to its worship. Such being the case, we find many instances in the Word where such tendency is discouraged. *See* Sun, Worship of.

Figurative. The Almighty himself is frequently spoken of as connected with the idea of light. Thus "God is light" (I John 1:5); the "Father of lights" (James 1:17). God is addressed as one "Who coverest thyself with light, like as with a garment" (Psa. 104:2), and as "dwelling in the light which no man can approach unto" (I Tim. 6:16). Great sublimity is introduced by the combination of figures of darkness and light, and by making them mutually enhance each other (Psa. 18:11; Exod. 24:15-17). Jesus, as the one who brings the true knowledge of God, is called "the light of men" (John 1:4; see also Matt. 4:16; John 1:9; 8:12; 12:35, 36). Light is continually used as figurative of holiness and purity (Prov. 6:23; Isa. 5:20; Rom. 13:12). Light also, as might naturally be expected, is frequently used for spiritual illumination, especially that illumination which is effected in the soul by the indwelling Spirit of God (II Cor. 4:6; Eph. 5:14; I Peter 2:9). Again, light is used as the figure in general for that which cheers or renders prosperous, and is applied with much force to spiritual joy arising from the happy influences of the Spirit of peace. Hence the frequent use of the expression, "The light of thy countenance." "The Lord is my light and my salvation" (Psa. 27:1); and "Light is sown for the righteous and gladness for the upright in heart" (Psa. 97:11). A striking variety is given in Job 37:21, "Men see not the bright light in the cloud," their trouble so oppressing them that all seems dark, and they observe not the happier times in store for them. The Word of God is compared to a light (Psa. 119:105). The figure is also applied to the heavenly state (Isa. 60:19, 20; Col. 1:12; Rev. 21:23; 22:5). Finally, the figure is applied to Christians in general (Matt. 5:14; Eph. 5:8), and to holy men, as John the Baptist (John 5:35). *See* Lamp.

Lightning (Heb. *bäräq, gleam;* Gr. *'astrapē*). In Syria lightnings are frequent in the autumnal months, seldom a night passing without a great deal of lightning, sometimes accompanied with thunder. A squall of wind and clouds of dust usually precede the first rains.

Figurative. Lightning is used as a symbol of God's glorious and awful majesty (Rev. 4:5); as his edicts, enforced with destruction to those that oppose him (Psa. 18:14; 144:6; Zech. 9:14); and, accompanied with thunder and hail, of great plagues, so that men blasphemed on account thereof.

Lign-Aloes. *See* Vegetable Kingdom.

Ligure. *See* Mineral Kingdom.

Lik'hi (lĭk'hī), the third named of the four sons of Shemidah, son of Manasseh (I Chron. 7:19), B. C. after 1876.

Lily. *See* Vegetable Kingdom.

Lily Work, part of the ornamentation of the two pillars which were erected (II Chron. 3:15) before the (temple) house. The pillars were surmounted by capitals ("chapiters"), and these were covered to a depth of four cubits with sculpture in the form of flowering lilies, below which was a cubit of network and pomegranates (I Kings 7:19, 22).

Lime. *See* Mineral Kingdom.

Line, the rendering of several Hebrew words

and one Greek word, with various meanings. Thus we have a line as our measuring line (II Sam. 8:2; I Kings 7:15, 23; Amos 7:17; Isa. 34:17; Ezek. 40:3; 47:3), a cord (Josh. 2:18, 21, etc.). There can be little doubt that the Hebrews acquired the art of measuring land from the ancient Egyptians, who were early acquainted with it. The language of Josh. 18:9, "And the men went and passed through the land, and described it by cities into seven parts in a book," evidently indicates that a survey of the whole country had been made.

Figurative. The word "line," as a string of a musical instrument, is put for *sound* (Psa. 19:4); while in the expression "not to boast in another man's line of things" (II Cor. 10: 16) the meaning probably is, not within the boundary line of another to boast of what is already done. In Isa. 28:10, 13, the expression "line upon line, line upon line," etc., is a sneer intended to throw ridicule upon the smallness and vexatious character of the prophet's interminable and uninterrupted chidings. The word also means a *portion* as described by measurement (Psa. 16:6).

Lineage (Gr. *patria*, paternal *descent*, "kindred," Acts 3:25; "family," Eph. 3:15; family or race, Luke 2:4). See Genealogy.

Linen. Linen was well known in the ancient Biblical world. The Egyptians were especially famous for their fine linen. The flax was planted in Egypt in November and gathered

⅔ SIZE

276. Flax

almost four months later. It had to be separated from its seeds, bunched, retted, laid in the sun and immersed in water to bleach and soften for crushing. The flax fibres were beaten out of the woody portions and it was drawn by a comb-like implement into thread for weaving on looms. Palestine as well as Egypt developed dexterity in weaving fine linens. Flax prospered in the tropical climate around Jericho. Rahab is said to have had dried flax on the top of her roof. Blooming flax is a common sight in Biblical lands. The Hebrew word *pishtĕh* is rendered "linen" in Lev. 13:47; Deut. 22:11; Jer. 13:1, etc. and "flax" in Josh. 2:6; Judg. 15:14; Prov. 31: 13; Isa. 19:9; Ezek. 40:3; Hosea 2:5, 9. This expression refers not only to flax (Judg. 15: 4) but also to the plant itself (Josh. 2:6) and the manufacture from it. It was used for nets (Isa. 19:9), girdles (Jer. 13:1), measuring

lines (Ezek. 40:3) as well as priestly dress (Ezek. 44:17, 18). (*See* Flax). The Hebrew expression *būṣ* from a root signifying *to be white* (Akkad., *buṣu*) is apparently a late word for fine linen and appears to be identical with Greek *bussos*. It was employed for the attire of the Levitical choir (II Chron. 2:12), for the loose upper garment worn by kings over the close-fitting tunic (I Chron. 15:27) and for the veil of the temple, embroidered by the skill of Tyrian craftsmen (II Chron. 3:14). Mordecai was arrayed in robes of *fine linen* and purple (Esther 8:15) when honored by the Persian monarch, and the dress of the rich man in Luke 6:19 was purple and *fine linen* (*bussos*). The merchandise of mystical Babylon contained as one of its commodities fine linen (with purple and scarlet) (Rev. 18: 12). The Hebrew word *shēsh*, an Egyptian word denoting linen or *byssus*, was brought to Tyre (Ezek. 27:7) and was one of the offerings brought out of Egypt by the Israelites (Exod. 25:4; 35:6). It seems apparent that *shēsh* is identical with Hebrew *buṣ*. It is used to describe the garments of Joseph (Gen. 41: 42), of priests (28:5; 39:2f), also the curtains and veil of the tabernacle (Exod. 26:1, 31, 36; 27:9, 16, 18 etc.). Linen was extensively used in wrapping the dead, as in the burial of our Lord. This practice was evidently of Egyptian influence. In the Land of the Nile mummy wrappings were of incredible proportions and were exclusively of linen. Laodicea in Asia Minor was an important center of linen weaving. Such cities as Byblos, Tyre and Bethshan were famous as linen-manufacturing cities as late as the fourth century A. D. *M. F. U.*

Figurative. Linen is used as an emblem of moral purity (Rev. 15:6), and of luxury (Luke 16:19).

Lintel, (Heb. *măshqōph, overhanging*), the beam which forms the upper part of the framework of a door (Exod. 12:22, 23; rendered "upper door post" in v. 7). This the Israelites were commanded to mark with the blood of the paschal lamb on the memorable occasion when the passover was instituted.

Li'nus, (lī'nŭs), one of the Christians at Rome whose salutations Paul sent to Timothy (II Tim. 4:21), A. D. 64.

Lion. See Animal Kingdom.

Figurative. The strength (Judg. 14:18; II Sam. 1:23), courage (II Sam. 17:10; Prov. 28:1, etc.), and ferocity (Gen. 49:9; Num. 24: 9) of the lion was proverbial. Hence the lion was symbolical of Israel (Num. 24:9), of the tribe of Judah (Gen. 49:9), of Gad (Deut. 33: 20), Dan (Deut. 33:22, "a lion's whelp"), of Christ (Rev. 5:5), of God in protecting his Church (Isa. 31:4), of God in executing judgments (Isa. 38:13; Lam. 3:10; Hos. 5:14; 13: 8), of the boldness of saints (Prov. 28:1), of brave men (II Sam. 1:23; 23:20), of cruel and powerful enemies (Isa. 5:29; Jer. 49:19), of persecutors (Psa. 22:13; II Tim. 4:17), of Satan (I Pet. 5:8), of imaginary fears of the slothful (Prov. 22:13; 26:13). The *tamed* lion is symbolical of the natural man subdued by grace (Isa. 11:7; 65:25), while the roaring of a lion is used to characterize a king's wrath.

Lip (Heb. *sáphäh* with the idea of *termination*).

In addition to its literal meaning the word is often used in the original for an edge or border, as of a cup, a garment, the sea, etc. It is often put as the organ of speech, thus: "To open the lips," is to begin to speak (Job 11:5; 32:20); to "refrain the lips" is to keep silence (Psa. 40:10; Prov. 10:19). "Uncircumcised of lips" (Exod. 6:12), i. e., not of ready speech, is the same as "slow of speech" (4:10). The "fruit of the lip" (Heb. 13:15) is a metaphor for *praise*, and by a bolder figure we have "the calves of the lips" (Hos. 14:2) for a thank offering. "Lip" stands in Scripture for language or dialect (I Cor. 14:21). The moral quality of speech is represented by "lying lips," i. e., *falsehood* (Prov. 10:18; comp. 17:4, 7) or *wickedness* (Psa. 120:2) or *truth* (Prov. 12:19). Ardent professions are represented by "burning lips" (Prov. 26:23); a pleasant discourse by "sweetness of lips" (Prov. 16:21). To "shoot out the lip" (Psa. 22:7) has always been an expression of the utmost scorn and defiance; so "unclean lips" are used to express an unfitness to impart or receive divine communications (Isa. 6:5, 7), and the touching of the lip with a "live coal" is figurative for cleansing it. To "cover the lip," i. e., the beard, was a sign of mourning, as in the case of a leper (Lev. 13:45), of trouble and shame (Ezek. 24:17; Mic. 3:7).

Liquor, the juice of olives and grapes (Exod. 22:29; Num. 6:3; Cant. 7:2). *See* Wine.

277. Egyptian Litter

Litter (Heb. *ṣāb*, Isa. 66:20), a sedan, or palanquin, borne by men or animals, which was in general use throughout the East.

Little Owl. *See* Owl in *Animal Kingdom*.

Liver (Heb. *kābēd, heavy, weighty,* as the *heaviest* of the viscera). The word often occurs in the natural sense, as indicative of a vital organ in the animal system, and especially with reference to the part of animals slain in sacrifice (Exod. 29:13, 22; Lev. 3:4, 10, 15; 4:9, etc.). *See* Sacrificial Offerings. The liver was used by the ancients for the purpose of divination (*q. v.*), and such use was not unknown to the Jews, though it is only once referred to in the Scriptures, and then with reference to the conduct of a heathen prince (Ezek. 21:21). In common with other ancient peoples, the Israelites were wont to identify the liver more with the source and center of life than we do, and sometimes put *liver* where we would put *heart* (*see* Prov. 7:23; Lam. 2:11).

Living Creatures (Ezek., chaps. 1, 3, 10; Rev. 4:6-9, A. V. "beasts;" R. V. "living creatures"), are identical with *Cherubim* (*q. v.*).

Lizard. *See* Animal Kingdom.

Loaf (Heb. *kikkär, circle;* Gr. *'artos;* sometimes only *lěḥěm, bread*), a round cake, or biscuit, the usual form of bread among the Orientals (Exod. 29:23; Judg. 8:5; I Sam. 10:3; I Chron. 16:3; Matt. 14:17; Mark 6:38, etc.). *See* Bread, Offering.

Lo-am'mi (lō-ăm'ī; *not my people*), the figurative name given by the prophet Hosea to his second son by Gomer, the daughter of Diblaim (Hos. 1:9), to denote the rejection of the kingdom of Israel by Jehovah. Its significance is explained in vers. 9, 10.

Loan. The law of Moses did not contemplate any raising of money by loans to obtain capital; and such persons as bankers and sureties, in the commercial sense (Prov. 22:26; Neh. 5:3), were unknown in the early ages of the Hebrews. The law made the following provisions respecting loans:

1. **Interest.** It strictly forbade any interest to be taken for a loan to any poor person, and at first, as it seems, even in the case of a foreigner; but this prohibition was afterward limited to the Hebrews only, from whom, of whatever rank, not only was no usury on any pretense to be exacted, but relief to the poor by way of loan was enjoined, and excuses for evading this duty were forbidden (Exod. 22:25; Lev. 25:35-37; Deut. 15:3, 7-10; 23:19, 20).

As commerce increased, the practice of usury, and so also of suretyship, grew up; but the exaction of it from a Hebrew appears to have been regarded to a late period as discreditable (Prov. 6:1, 4; 11:15; 17:18; 20:16; Psa. 15:5; Jer. 15:10; Ezek. 18:13; 22:12). Systematic breach of the law in this respect was corrected by Nehemiah after the return from captivity (Neh. 5:1-13). The money changers, who had seats and tables in the temple, were traders whose profits arose chiefly from the exchange of money with those who came to pay their annual half shekel.

2. **Pledges.** In making loans no prohibition is pronounced in the law against taking a *pledge* of the borrower, but certain limitations are prescribed in favor of the poor. (1) The outer garment, if taken in pledge, was to be returned before sunset. (2) The prohibition was absolute in the case of (*a*) the widow's garment (Deut. 24:17), and (*b*) a millstone of either kind (24:6). (3) A creditor was forbidden to enter a house to reclaim a pledge, but was to stand outside till the borrower should come forth to return it (24:10, 11). (4) The original Roman law of debt permitted the debtor to be enslaved by his creditor until the debt was discharged; and he might even be put to death by him. The Jewish law, as it did not forbid temporary bondage in the case of debtors, so it forbade a Hebrew debtor to be detained as a bondsman longer than the seventh year, or, at farthest, the year of jubilee (Exod. 21:2; Lev. 25:39-42; Deut. 15:9).

Lock (Hebrew verb *nā'al,* to *fasten;* noun *măn'ăl*). The doors of the ancient Hebrews were secured by bars of wood or iron, the latter generally used in the entrances of fortresses, prisons, and towns (see Isa. 45:2). The locks are usually of wood, and consist of a partly hollow bolt from fourteen inches to two feet long for external doors or gates, or from seven to nine inches for interior doors. The bolt passes through a groove in a piece attached to the door into a socket in the doorpost. In the groove-piece are from four to nine small iron or wooden slidingpins or wires, which drop into corresponding holes in the bolt, and fix it in its place (Neh. 3:3, 6, 13-15). The key has a certain number of iron pegs at one end, which correspond to the holes in the bolt of the lock, into which they are introduced to open the lock; the former pins being thus pushed up, the bolt may be drawn back. These keys were from seven inches to two feet in length, and so heavy as sometimes to be as much as a man could conveniently carry. It is to a key of this description that the prophet probably alludes: "And the key of the house of David will I lay upon his shoulder" (Isa. 22:22). But it is not difficult to open a lock of this kind even without a key, viz., with the finger dipped in paste or other adhesive substance. The passage, Cant. 5:4, 5, is thus probably explained.

Locust. See Animal Kingdom.

Figurative. The locust is used in Scripture as a symbol of *destructive enemies*. See the highly poetical description in Joel (1:6, 7; 2:2-9); of armed men (Nah. 3:17).

Lod (lŏd), I Chron. 8:12; Ezra 2:33; Neh. 7:37; 11:35) is, without doubt, the city of Lydda (Acts 9:32, etc.). See Lydda.

Lo-de'bar (lô-dē'bàr; *no pasture*), probably identical with Debir (Heb. Lidebir, Josh. 13: 26 R. S. V. margin), in Gilead, north of the brook Jabbok, not far from Mahanaim, the residence of Ammiel, whose son Machir entertained Mephibosheth (II Sam. 9:4, 5), and afterward sent supplies to David (17:27). The place is identified with Ummed-Dabar, S. of the Wadi el-'Arab, E. of the Jordan.

Lodge (Heb. *lin* or *lūn*, to *stop over night*, and several Greek words); (1) In the general sense of stopping for rest, or the place of lodging (Gen. 24:23; Josh. 4:3; Ruth 1:16, etc.). (2) A shed or lodge for the watchman of a garden (Isa. 1:8, "The daughter of Zion is left as a cottage in a vineyard, as a *lodge* in a garden of cucumbers," etc.). The "lodge" here referred to was a little temporary hut for a shelter from heat by day and the cold dews by night. It is usually built on an elevation of ground, with room for only one person, who in this solitude watches the ripening crop. "The point of comparison, therefore, is that in the vineyard and cucumber field not a human being is to be seen in any direction; and that there is nothing but the cottage and the lodge to show that there is any human being there at all. So did Jerusalem stand in the midst of desolation reaching far and wide—a sign, however, that the land was not entirely depopulated" (Delitzsch, *Com.*, in loc.). The Hebrew word sometimes means a hanging bed, or hammock, which was often used in hot climates (Isa. 24:20, "cottage").

Loft (Heb. *'ălĭyyäh*, *lofty*), the upper chamber of a private house (I Kings 17:19).

Log. See Metrology, II.

Logos. See Word.

Loin (the rendering of several Hebrew words and one Greek word), the part of the back and sides between the hip and the ribs, which, being, as it were, the pivot of the body, is most sensibly affected by pain or terror (Deut. 33:11; Job 40:16; Psa. 38:7, etc.). It is used by euphemism for the generative power (Gen. 35:11; I Kings 8:19; II Chron. 6:9). This part of the body was especially girt with sackcloth in token of mourning (Gen. 37:34; I Kings 20:31, 32; Psa. 66:11; Isa. 20:2, etc.).

Figurative. "If his loins have not blessed me" (Job 31:20) is an expression in which the blessing of the thankful (29:13) is transferred from the person to the parts of the body benefited by the warmth imparted. The loose and flowing garments of the Orientals required to be gathered at the waist before engaging in any exertion or enterprise; hence, "to gird up the loins" (I Kings 18:46; Job 38:3; 40:7; Prov. 31:17, etc.) is used as a figure for vigorous effort.

Lo'is (lō'ĭs; perhaps *agreeable*), the maternal grandmother of Timothy, his father being a Greek (Acts 16:1). She was commended by the apostle Paul for her faith (II Tim. 1:5).

Long-Suffering (Heb. *'ĕrĕk 'ăppăyĭm*, *slow to anger*; Gr. *makrothumia*), that disposition of God in accordance with which he delays the punishments of men (Exod. 34:6; Num. 14: 18; Psa. 86:15; Jer. 15:15; Rom. 2:4; 9:22; I Tim. 1:16; I Pet. 3:20; II Pet. 3:9, 15). It is also mentioned as one of the Christian graces, and is shown in bearing troubles and ills, in a slowness in avenging wrongs (II Cor. 6:6; Eph. 4:2; II Tim. 4:2).

Looking-Glass. See Mirror.

Loop. By loops the curtains of the tabernacle were fastened to their corresponding knobs. They were probably made of goat's hair cord, and were dyed blue (Exod. 26:4, sq.; 36:11, sq.). See Tabernacle.

Lord, the rendering of several Hebrew and Greek words, which have a very different meaning from each other:

1. *Jehovah* (*yahweh*) (Heb. *YHWH*, *self-existent*), Jehovah. This is used as a proper name of God only, and should have been retained in that form by the translators. See Jehovah.

2. *Lord* (Heb. *'Adōn*), an early word denoting ownership; hence, absolute control. It is not properly a divine title, being used of the owner of slaves (Gen. 24:14, 27; 39:2, 7; A. V. "master"); of kings as the lords of their subjects (Isa. 26:13); of a husband as lord of the wife (Gen. 18:12). It is applied to God as the owner and governor of the whole earth (Exod. 23:13; Psa. 114:7). It is sometimes used as a term of respect, like our *sir;* but with a pronoun attached ("my lord"), and often occurs in the plural.

3. *Adonai* (Heb. *'ădōnai*), emphatic, *the Lord;* and by many regarded as the plural of No. 2. It is used chiefly in the Pentateuch; always where God is submissively and reverently addressed (Exod. 4:10, 13; Josh. 7:8); also when God is spoken of (I Kings 13:9; 22:6, etc.). The Jews, out of a superstitious reverence for the name Jehovah, always, in reading, pronounce *Adonai* where *Jehovah* is written. The

similar form, *with the suffix*, is also used of men, as of Potiphar (Gen. 39:2, sq.; A. V. "master"), and of Joseph (42:30, 33).

4. *Lord, Master* (Gr. *kupios, supreme*), he to whom a person or thing belongs, the master, the one having disposition of men or property, as the "Lord of the vineyard" (Matt. 20: 8; 21:40; Mark 12:9; Luke 20:15); the "Lord of the harvest" (Matt. 9:38; Luke 10:2); the "master of the house" (Mark 13:35); "Lord of the Sabbath" (Matt. 12:8; Mark 2:28; Luke 6:5), as having the power to determine what is suitable to the Sabbath, and of releasing himself and others from its obligation. The term is also a title of honor, expressive of the respect and reverence with which servants salute their master (Matt. 13:27, A. V. "sir;" Luke 13:8; 14:22, etc.); employed by a son in addressing his father (Matt. 21:30, A. V. "sir"); by citizens toward magistrates (27: 63, A. V. "sir"); by anyone wishing to honor a man of distinction (Matt. 8:2, 6, 8; 15:27; Mark 7:28; Luke 5:12, etc.); by the disciples in saluting Jesus their teacher and master (Matt. 8:25; 16:22; Luke 9:54; John 11:12, etc.). This title is given to *God*, the ruler of the universe, both with the article *ho kurios* (Matt. 1:22; 5:33; Mark 5:19; Luke 1:6, sq.; Acts 7:33; II Tim. 1:16, 18, etc.), and without the article (Matt. 21:9; 27:10; Mark 13:20; Luke 2:9, 23, 26; Heb. 7:21, etc.). The title is also applied to Jesus as the Messiah, since by his death he acquired a special ownership of mankind, and after his resurrection was exalted by a partnership in the divine administration (Acts 10:36; Rom. 14:8; I Cor. 7:22; 8:6; Phil. 2:9-11).

5. *Baal* (Heb. *bă'ăl, master*), applied only to heathen deities, or to man as husband, etc., or to one specially skilled in a trade or profession. *See* Baal.

6. Several other and less important words in the original are rendered "Lord" in the A. V. They are: *Shălîsh*, (II Kings 7:2, 17), an officer of the third rank; *răb*, (Dan. 2:10), a chief, or captain; *mărē', master*, (2:10), an official title; *sĕrĕn*, a Philistine term found in Joshua, Judges, and I Samuel, where "the *lords* of the Philistines" are mentioned; (*răbrĕbăn, magnate*), used in reference to certain Babylonian nobles (Dan. 4:36; 5:1, 9, 10, 23; 6:17), and its Greek equivalent, *Rabboni* (*q. v.*); *săr*, a head person, title of nobility (Ezra 8:25).

The Lord's Day. This, the first day of the week in the Christian order, commemorates the new creation with Christ Himself as its resurrected Head. It is not a mere changeover from the Sabbath, but a new day marking a new dispensation. The Sabbath related to the old creation (Exod. 20:8-11; 31:12-17; Heb. 4:4). There are prophetic adumbrations of the Lord's Day in the O. T. (Psa. 1:18, 22-24; cf. Acts 4:11, 12; Matt. 28:1; cf. Lev. 23:11). The term "Christian Sabbath" is scarcely Biblically defensible. This day of grace marks the beginning of the week with a day of privilege, whereas the Sabbath came at the end of a week of labor, an order expected under the law. It must carefully be remembered that the Lord's Day, the term "Sunday" (*q. v.*) being of pagan origin, is strictly a Christian

institution. It is not for all men, and it is scarcely Biblically justified to attempt to legislate its observance upon unsaved people. As Lewis Sperry Chafer points out, "Men are not justified in returning to the rules provided for the Sabbath in order to secure directions for the observance of the Lord's Day. When Christ came from the grave, He said to His friends 'Rejoice' (cf. Psa. 118:24) and 'go tell . . .' (Matt. 28:9, 10, literal rendering). These words may well be taken as a wise direction respecting observance of the day. The Lord's Day, moreover, can be extended to all days whereas the Sabbath could not be (cf. Rom. 14:5, 6)" (*Systematic Theology* vii, p. 229). *M. F. U.*

The Lord's Prayer. This prayer is in reality a prayer for the kingdom and in the kingdom (Matt. 6:8-15; 7:7-11). "Thy kingdom come. Thy will be done in earth as it is in heaven" can only be realized in its contextual meaning in the coming millennial kingdom. There is no doubt that this prayer, so universally recited and often sentimentally entrenched in human affections because of childhood training, was nevertheless evidently not intended as a ritual prayer for this age. Its petitions, however, are remarkably comprehensive and it has served as a vehicle of blessing for countless millions. The prayer is not given as a set form which is to be slavishly followed, but rather as setting forth the general sentiments and desires which are acceptable to Him whom we address in prayer. *M. F. U.*

Lord's Supper (Gr. *kuriakon deiphon*, a *meal belonging to the Lord*).

1. **Name.** The meal established by our Lord (I Cor. 11:20), and called "supper" because it was instituted at supper time. Synonymous with this is the phrase "the Lord's table" (10:21), where we also find the name "the cup of the Lord." Other terms were introduced in the Church, such as *communion* (Gr. *koinōnia, participation,* i. e., a festival in *common,* I Cor. 10:16), and *eucharist* ("a giving of thanks"), because of the hymns and psalms which accompanied it.

2. **Its Origin.** Of this we have the accounts recorded by Matthew (26:26-29), Mark (14: 22-25), Luke (22:19, sq.), and by the apostle Paul (I Cor. 11:24-26), whose words differ very little from those of Luke. The only difference between Matthew and Mark is that the latter omits the words "for the remission of sins." Paul declares (I Cor. 11:23) that the account which he wrote to the Corinthians he "received of the Lord," which would seem to imply a communication made to himself personally by the Lord, contrasting it with the abuse among them.

Jesus instituted the supper while he was observing the Passover with his disciples; so that some references to that feast should be given. The following order of observing the Passover prevailed at the time of Christ: (1) Meeting of celebrants, the head of the household, or celebrant, blessing a cup of wine, of which all partook. (2) Washing the hands, accompanied with a benediction. (3) Table set with paschal lamb, unleavened bread, bitter herbs, and sauce. (4) The celebrant first, and then others, dipped a portion of bitter herbs into the sauce and ate them. (5) Dishes removed and cup of wine brought, followed by an interval for asking questions as to this strange procedure, and then wine passed. (6) Table set again, the celebrant repeating the commemorative words which opened what was strictly the paschal supper, a solemn thanksgiving and Pslams 103 and 104. (7) Second washing of hands with a short blessing, breaking of one of the two cakes of unleavened bread, with thanks. Bread partaken of after dipping it, with the bitter herbs, into the sauce. (8) Flesh eaten with bread, another blessing, a third cup of wine, known as the "cup of blessing." (9) Fourth cup, with recital of Psa. 115-118, from which this cup was known as the cup of the Hallel, or of the Song. (10) There might be, in conclusion, a fifth cup, provided that the great Hallel was sung over it (possibly Psa. 120-138).

"Comparing the ritual thus gathered from rabbinic writers with the New Testament, and assuming (1) that it represents substantially the common practice of our Lord's time; and (2) that the meal of which he and his disciples partook was either the Passover itself or an anticipation of it, conducted according to the same rules, we are able to point, though not with absolute certainty, to the points of departure which the old practice presented for the institution of the new. To 1 or 3, or even to 8, we may refer the first words and the first distribution of the cup (Luke 22:17, 18); to 2 or 7, the dipping of the sop (John 13:26); to 7, or to an interval during or after 8, the distribution of the bread (Matt. 26:26; Mark 14:22; Luke 22:19; I Cor. 11:23, 24); to 9 or 10 ('after supper,' Luke 22:20), the thanksgiving and distribution of the cup, and the hymn with which the whole was ended."

"The original eucharistic meal was symbolic. The broken bread and the consecrated cup were also prophetic of the work which Christ was to accomplish for his disciples and the world. The real sacrifice, of which this sacrament was to be a remembrance, was yet to be accomplished; hence the supper was so far prophetic. The bread was to symbolize the broken body and the cup the blood, which was the pledge of the covenant between God and man" (Bennett, *Christ. Arch.*, p. 416).

3. **Observance.** The Passover was an annual festival, but no rule was given as to the time and frequency of the new feast, although the command, "Do this as oft as ye drink it" (I Cor. 11:25) suggested a more frequent observance. It would appear that the celebration of the Lord's Supper by the first disciples occurred daily in private houses (Acts 2:46), in connection with the agape or love feast, to indicate that its purpose was the expression of brotherly love. The offering of thanks and praise (I Cor. 11:24; 10:16) was probably followed with the holy kiss (Rom. 16:16; I Cor. 16:20). It was of a somewhat festive character, judging from the excesses which Paul reproved (I Cor. 11:20), and was associated with an ordinary meal, at the close of which the bread and wine were distributed as a memorial of Christ's similar distribution to the disciples. From the accounts in the Acts (2:42, 46) and from Paul's letter to the Corin-

thians (11:20, 21) it is safely inferred that the disciples contributed each a share of the food necessary for the meal, thus showing a community of love and fellowship. To this unifying power of the eucharist Paul evidently refers (I Cor. 10:16, 17). From the account given in I Cor. 11:17-34, it is evident that each person ate of that which he brought, and held therein his own private meal in place of the Lord's Supper. There was not a proper waiting for the distribution of the elements by a church officer, and there seems to be no evidence that a priestly consecration and distribution of the bread and wine were regarded as necessary to the validity of the sacrament. 'Tis true a blessing was spoken over the cup (I Cor. 10:16), but every Christian man, probably, might offer this blessing at that time, when the arrangements of church life as regards public worship were as yet so little reduced to fixed order.

4. **Early Church.** Under Trajan the strict edicts against secret societies compelled the separation of the agape from the Lord's Supper; the former, being adjudged by the emperor to pertain to the secret clubs, was discontinued, and the Lord's Supper was connected with the public worship. From the circumstance that unbaptized persons, and such as were under church discipline, as well as others not in full communion with the church, were excluded from the assembly before the celebration of the Lord's Supper, the idea of mystery soon attached to this rite.

In the earliest notices of the Lord's Supper a simple and almost literal imitation of the meal as instituted by Christ is prevalent. In the "Teaching of the Twelve" the instructions for celebrating the eucharist are as simple and archaic as those respecting baptism. In Justin Martyr's account of the Lord's Supper is noticed an almost like simplicity as in the "Teaching." A change is in the fact that special celebrants or officers are now recognized: "There is brought to the president of the brethren bread and a cup of wine mixed with water." The deacons distribute the consecrated elements and carry away a portion to those who are absent. In Tertullian's account there is scarcely more formality.

In ante-Nicene times the following order was observed: The prayers, the kiss of peace between man and man, and woman and woman; the oblation or offerings for the feast, the poor, and the clergy; and the communion of the partaking of the consecrated elements. The wine was mingled with water, and the communicants, standing, received both elements in the hands of the officiating deacons. Portions of the sanctified bread were sometimes borne to their homes by the members, where the family communion was repeated in one kind. The custom of the apostolic Church for all communicants to make offerings of bread and wine and other things to supply the elements of the holy eucharist, and gifts to the poor, was continued through all the early history of Christianity and in a modified form until the 12th century.

As Church government and discipline developed, the ceremonies connected with the eucharist became more formal and involved.

Extended and carefully prepared liturgical forms appear, the work of great Churchmen or councils. Based upon the earlier and simpler order of consecration and communion, they were often of great length and accompanied with many impressive ceremonies, especially frequent musical recitations by the choirs and responses by the people.

At the institution of the Lord's Supper Christ used *unleavened bread*. The primitive Christians carried with them the bread and wine for the eucharist, and took the bread in common use, viz., leavened. When this custom ceased the Greeks retained the leavened bread, while in the Latin Church the unleavened bread became common since the 8th century. The custom of breaking the bread (I Cor. 11:24) was discontinued by the Roman Catholic Church when, in the 12th and 13th centuries, the host or holy water was cut in a peculiar way, so as to represent upon it a crucified Saviour. The Reformed Churches reintroduced the use of common bread and the breaking of it.

We have no evidence as to whether the wine used by Christ was pure, mixed with water, fermented, or unfermented; although general practice, as well as other facts, would lead to the conclusion that it was fermented.

5. **Controversies.** (1) **Transubstantiation.** The Council of Trent teaches that, after the consecration, the body and blood, together with the soul and divinity of our Lord Jesus Christ, are contained "truly, really, and substantially in the sacrament of the most holy eucharist," and it anathematizes those who say that Christ's body and blood are there in sign and figure only. Furthermore, the Roman Catholic Church teaches "that the worship of sacrifice was not to cease in the Church, and the Council of Trent defines that in the eucharist or mass a true and proper sacrifice is offered to God" (*Cath. Dict.*, s. v.). (2) **Lutheran.** The Lutheran Church rejects transubstantiation, while insisting that the body and blood of Christ are mysteriously and supernaturally united with the bread and wine, so that they are received when the latter are. This is called *consubstantiation*. (3) **Spiritual Presence view.** According to this view, "this hallowed food (the bread and wine), through concurrence of divine power, is in verity and truth, unto faithful receivers, *instrumentally* a cause of that mystical participation whereby I make myself wholly theirs, so I give them in hand an actual possession of all such saving grace as my sacrificial body can yield, and as their souls do presently need, this is to them, and in them, my body" (Hooker, *Eccles. Polity*, book v, 167). "The body of Christ is given, taken, and eaten in the supper only after a heavenly and spiritual manner. And the means whereby the body of Christ is received and eaten in the supper is faith" (*Discipline, Methodist Church*, Art. 18). (4) **Symbolic or Zwinglian view.** According to this view, partaking of the Supper merely commemorates the sacrificial work of Christ, and its value to the participant consists only in the bestowal of a blessing.

Lo-Ruha′mah (lō-rōō-hä′má; *not pitied, not favored*), the name divinely given to the second child (a daughter) of the prophet Hosea (1:6) to indicate that the Lord will not continue to show compassion toward the rebellious nation, as he hitherto has done under Jeroboam II (II Kings 13:23). In Hos. 2:23 the expression is translated "her that had not obtained mercy." A *daughter* is named to represent the effeminate period which followed the overthrow of the first dynasty, when Israel was at once abject and impious. When God restored his favor to the people her name was changed to *Ruhamah* (*q. v.*).

Loss. *See* Law of Moses, Civil, 2, *a*.

Lot. 1. (Heb. *gōräl*, a *pebble*; *ḥēbēl, measuring line, portion*; Gr. *lanchanō*, to *cast lots*, Luke 1:9; *klēros, pebble, bit of wood* to cast lots with (Acts 1:26). The custom of deciding doubtful questions by lot is one of great extent and high antiquity, recommending itself as a sort of appeal to the Almighty, secure from all influence of passion or bias, and is a sort of divination employed even by the gods themselves (Hom., *Il.*, xxii, 209; Cic., *De Div.*, i, 34; ii, 41). Among the Jews also the use of lots, with a religious intention, direct or indirect, prevailed extensively. The religious estimate of them may be gathered from Prov. 16:33. The following historical or ritual instances are: (1) Choice of men for an invading force (Judg. 1:1-3; 20:9); (2) Partition of the soil of Palestine among the tribes (Num. 26:55; Josh. 18:10; Acts 13:19), of Jerusalem, i. e., probably its spoil or captives among captors (Obad. 11), of the land itself in a similar way (I Macc. 3:36); apportionment of possessions, or spoil, or of prisoners, to foreigners or captors (Joel 3:3; Nah. 3:10; Matt. 27:35); (3) Settlement of doubtful questions (Prov. 16:33; 18:18), a mode of divination among heathen by means of arrows, two inscribed and one without mark (Hos. 4:12; Ezek. 21:21), detection of a criminal (Josh. 7:14, 18), appointment of persons to offices or duties, as the priests (Luke 1:9); also successor to Judas (Acts 1:26); selection of the scapegoat on the Day of Atonement (Lev. 16:8, 10). *See* Urim and Thummim.

2. That which falls to one by lot, as a *portion* or *inheritance* (Deut. 32:9; Josh. 15:1; I Chron. 16:18; Psa. 105:11; 125:3; Isa. 17:14; 57:6; Acts 8:21; comp. Acts 13:19).

Lot (lŏt), the son of Haran and nephew of Abraham.

1. **Family.** The following genealogy exhibits the family relations (Gen. 11:27, sq.).

2. **Personal History.** Lot's father dying (Gen. 11:28), he was left in the charge of his grandfather, Terah, with whom he migrated to Haran (11:31), B. C. c. 2120. After the death of Terah, Lot accompanied Abraham to Canaan (12:4, 5) B. C. c. 2086, and thence to Egypt, and back again to Canaan (12:10; 13:1). (1) **Separation.** The flocks and herds of both increased so greatly that the land did not furnish pasture enough, and, consequently disputes arose between their herdsmen. To put an end to strife Abraham proposed a separation, and magnanimously left the choice of territory to his nephew, who selected the plain of Jordan and fixed his abode at Sodom (13:5-12). (2) **A prisoner.** A few years after, Lot was carried away by Chedorlaomer, along

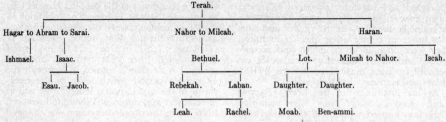

Terah.

| Hagar to Abram to Sarai. | Nahor to Milcah. | Haran. |

Ishmael.   Isaac.   Bethuel.   Lot.   Milcah to Nahor.   Iscah.

Esau. Jacob.   Rebekah.   Laban.   Daughter.   Daughter.

Leah.   Rachel.   Moab.   Ben-ammi.

with other captives from Sodom, but was rescued and brought back by Abraham (14:12:16), B. C. c. 2060. (3) **Escape from Sodom.** When Jehovah had determined to destroy Sodom, Lot was still residing there, and, sitting at the city gate, met the messengers (angels) of the Lord. He pressed them to pass the night at his house, and they yielded to his entreaty. While they were at supper the house was beset by a number of the inhabitants, who demanded, with the basest violation of hospitality, that the strangers should be delivered up to them for a most shameful purpose. Lot went out to them, shut the door behind him to protect his guests, and resisted the base demands of the crowd. This enraged them still more, and they were about to break in the door when the angels pulled Lot into the house, shut the door, and smote the people with blindness. Lot was then informed of the coming destruction of the city, and exhorted to remove his family, and in the morning was hastened away by the angels. Instead of cheerfully obeying the commandment to flee to the mountain, Lot entreated that he might be allowed to take refuge in Zoar, the smallest of the cities of the plain. While on their way Lot's wife, disobedient to the divine command, "Look not behind thee," lingered behind, probably from a longing for her home and earthly possessions, and "became a pillar of salt" (*see* Note). Lot, actuated by fear, soon left Zoar and removed to a cave in the neighboring mountains (19:1-30). (4) **Daughters' crime.** While there his daughters, dreading the extinction of their family, resolved to procure children through their father. This they succeeded in doing by making him drunk with wine, and in that state seducing him into an act of which he would not in soberness have been guilty. The son of the elder daughter was Moab, progenitor of the Moabites and of the younger Ben-ammi, "the father," i. e., ancestor of the Ammonites (19:31-38). Lot is not mentioned again in the O. T., and the time and place of his death are unknown. He is alluded to in II Pet. 2:7, 8 and being described as a "righteous man" is clearly revealed as the type of a carnal wordly believer in contrast to Abraham, the man of faith.

NOTE—*Lot's wife.* The turning of Lot's wife into a pillar of salt has often been regarded as one of the difficulties of the Bible, but is not so necessarily. "We are not to suppose that she was actually turned into one, but having been killed by the fiery and sulphureous vapor with which the air was filled and afterward incrusted with salt, she resembled an actual statue of salt" (K. and D., *Com.*, in loco). *Lot's daughters.* The narrative of the conduct of these women is related without comment by the sacred writer. There is no concealment, no extenuation. The very fact of their securing Lot's intoxication is evi-

dence that he was too good a man to accede to their wishes while in his right mind. See Sodom, Gomorrah.

Lo'tan (lō'tăn), the first-named son of Seir, the Horite, and a prince of Idumaea prior to the ascendency of the Esauites (Gen. 36:20, 29; I Chron. 1:38). His sons were Hori and Heman (or Homan) (36:22; I Chron. 1:39), and through his sister, Timna, he was related to Eliphaz, Esau's son (Gen. 36:12).

Love (Heb. *'ăhăbāh;* Gr. *'agapē*), chiefly represented in the Scriptures as an attribute of God, and as a Christian virtue. Its consideration, therefore, belongs to both theology and ethics.

1. An attribute of God. According to the Scriptures, God has feeling, affection, though rationalistic theologians (e. g., Schleiermacher, Bruch) have asserted the contrary. We must derive our conceptions of God from the special revelation which he has given of himself; and this declares his love as strongly as his existence. It is held by some to be inadequate to speak of love as a divine attribute, "God is love" (I John 4:8, 16). The Scriptures contain no equivalent statements with respect to other qualities of the divine nature. Love is the highest characteristic of God, the one attribute in which all others harmoniously blend. The love of God is more than kindness or benevolence. The latter may be exercised toward irrational creatures, but love is directed toward rational, personal beings. The eternal love of God has never been without its object; a fact upon which we receive some light from the Scripture revelation of the threefold personality of God (*see* Trinity; *see* also Matt. 3:17; John 15:9; 17:23-26). The gracious love of God to men, even to sinful men, is most strongly declared in both the Old and the New Testaments (e. g., Exod. 34:6; Isa. 63:9; Jer. 31:3; John 3:16; I John 4:10). The love of God underlies all that he has done and is doing, although many facts exist which we cannot reconcile with his love on account of our limited understanding. The highest disclosure and most complete proof of divine love is in redemption (*see* Rom. 5:8; 8:32-39; I John 4:9, 10). The reality and power of this love are properly apprehended only under the influence of the Holy Spirit. "The love of God is shed abroad in our hearts by the Holy Ghost which is given unto us" (Rom. 5:5).

2. A Christian virtue. Love is the preeminent virtue inculcated and produced by Christianity. The whole law is summed up in love, not in the sense of rendering all other requirements nugatory, but in the sense that love is fundamental, and expresses the spirit of all others, and with enlightenment will lead

to the observance of all others (*see* Matt. 22: 37-39; 5:43-48; John 14:15, 21; 15:12-14; Rom. 13:8; I Cor., ch. 13; Gal. 5:14). Accordingly love is declared to be the chief test of Christian discipleship (*see* John 13:35; Matt. 5:44; I John 3:14). Also, love is the highest motive 'r ground of moral actions. Without this all other motives fall short of furnishing the true stimulus of Christian living. As all sin roots itself in selfishness, so all virtue springs out of love; and yet the love which is presented in the New Testament as the mainspring of holy living is grateful love 'as distinct from the love that is wholly disinterested. "We love him because he first loved us," are words which rightly express the whole matter (*see* I John 4:19, also II Cor. 5:14; Rom. 12:1, 2). The contention of Fenelon that true Christian love should be disinterested, that we must love God exclusively on account of his perfection, so that if he did not bless us, but were to cast us off, we would love him still, finds no support in the Scriptures. It contains a measure of truth inasmuch as it emphasizes the warning that we are certainly not to love the gifts of God more than the giver, and that we are not to love God wholly on account of his gifts. In reality, grateful love includes adoring love, or that which loves God for his own sake. Christian love, it is also important to note, is made possible only by divine grace. It is one of the fruits of the Spirit (Gal. 5:22; see also I John 3:14). *E. McC.*

Love Feast (Gr. *'agapē*).

1. **Meaning.** Feasts expressing and fostering mutual love, which used to be held by Christians in connection with the Lord's Supper (whether before or after is uncertain), and at which the poorer Christians mingled with the wealthier and partook in common of the food provided by the wealthy (Jude, ch. 12). The expression, "sporting themselves with their own deceivings" (II Pet. 2:13), is rendered in some texts "living luxuriously in their agapae."

2. **Mode of Celebrating.** The bishop or presbyter presided. Before eating the guests washed their hands, and prayer was offered; then followed the reading of Scripture, and questions by the person presiding, reading or reciting accounts from other churches, which aroused sympathy and sometimes called for assistance; partaking of the feast and collection for orphans and widows, the poor, and prisoners; the kiss of charity, and conclusion by prayer (Rom. 16:16; I Cor. 16:20; I Thess. 5:26; I Pet. 5:14).

3. **Decline.** It appears from the passages already referred to, and from I Cor., ch. 11, that at an early period the agapae were perverted from their original design, and the heathen began to tax them with impurity. The Roman authorities suspected the agapae of belonging to the class of *Hetoerioe* (secret societies), which were often employed for political purposes, and as such denounced by imperial edict. On account of these and similar irregularities, and probably in part to elude the notice of their persecutors, the eucharist came to be celebrated by itself and before daybreak. The council of Laodicea, 28th canon, forbade holding the agapae in the

churches, and this was confirmed by the Council of Carthage (can. 29, A. D. 397).

4. **Modern Observance.** The Moravians observe the love feast on various occasions, "generally in connection with a solemn festival or preparatory to the holy communion. Printed odes are often used, prepared expressly for the occasion. In the course of the service a simple meal of biscuit and coffee or tea is served, of which the congregation partake together. In some churches the love feast concludes with an address by the minister" (*Moravian Manual*, 1859, p. 161). Wesley borrowed the practice from the Moravians, "in order to increase in them (persons in class) a grateful sense of all God's mercies." The only food is a little bread and water, and the exercises generally consist of singing, prayer, and the relation of Christian experience. These love feasts are observed by the Wesleyans and Methodists of America.

Loving-Kindness (Heb. *ḥěsěd, desire, ardor*). In a good sense *ḥěsěd* is zeal toward anyone, *kindness, love*. Of God toward men, *goodness, mercy, grace* (Psa. 17:7; 26:3; 36:7, 10, etc.). Figuratively, it is used of God as a merciful benefactor (144:2, "My goodness"). In the plural, *mercies, benefits* from God (89:2, "mercy;" v. 49; 25-6; Isa. 63:7).

Low, Lower, Lowest. The expression, "low parts of the earth," means properly *valleys;* hence, by extension, *sheol*, or the under world, as the place of the dead (Ezek. 26:20; Psa. 63:9, rendered "lower"). The "lower parts of the earth" (Isa. 44:23) is not hades, but the interior of the earth, with its caves, its pits, and its deep abysses. The "lowest parts of the earth" (Psa. 139:15) is used figuratively for any hidden place, as the womb.

Lu'bim (lū'bĭm; Nah. 3:9; II Chron. 12:3; II Chron. 16:8; Dan. 11:43), an African race, the primitive Libyans. They are always mentioned in connection with Egyptians and Ethiopians. They formed part of the armies of Shishak (II Chron. 12:3) and of Zerah (16:8), and they helped No-amon, or Thebes (Nah. 3:9). In Dan. 11:43 they pay court to a northern conqueror. The Lubim were probably the Rebu, or Lebu, of the Egyptian monuments,. a fair race of Semitic type, warlike, but not able to stand against Merneptah and Rameses II. Their home appears to have been on the north coast of Africa, west of Egypt. They doubtless belonged to the oldest stream of colonization which flowed westward along the northern coast of Africa. The territory of the Lubim and their kindred tribes may be likened to that of the great Arab tribe of the Benee 'Alee, which extends "from Egypt to Morocco." "Reduced by the Egyptians about 1250 B. C., and afterward driven inland by the Phoenician and Greek colonists, they still remain on the northern confines of the great desert, and even within it and in the mountains, while their later Semitic rivals pasture their flocks in the rich plains." Probably the Mizraite Lehabim (Gen. 10:13; I Chron. 1: 11) are the same as the Lubim.—*W. H.* revised by *M. F. U. See* Libya.

Lu'cas (lū'kās), a "fellow-laborer" of Paul during his imprisonment at Rome (Phil., v. 24), A. D. 64. He is doubtless the same as *Luke* (*q. v.*).

Lu'cifer (lōō'sĭ-fēr; Heb. *hēlēl, brightness*). This designation, referred to Satan, is coupled with the epithet "son of the morning" and clearly signifies "bright star" (Isa. 14:12-14), probably what we call the "morning star." As a symbolical representation of the king of Babylon in his pride, splendor and fall, the passage goes beyond the Babylonian prince and invests Satan who, at the head of this present world-system, is the real though invisible power behind the successive world rulers of Tyre, Babylon, Persia, Greece and Rome. This far-reaching passage goes beyond human history and marks the beginning of sin in the universe and the fall of Satan and the pristine, sinless spheres before the creation of man. Similarly Ezekiel (28:12-14), under the figure of the king of Tyre, likewise traces the fall of Satan and the corruption of his power and glory. In the Ezekiel passage Satan's glorious and splendid unfallen state is described. In Isa. 14:12-14 his fall is depicted. In both passages representation is not of Satan as confined to his own person, but as working in and consummating his plans through earthly kings and potentates who take to themselves divine honors and who, whether they actually know this or not, rule in the spirit and under the aims of Satan. Dan. 10:13 and Eph. 6:12 show that there are human as well as superhuman agencies in world governments in the Satanic world system. (For the Satanic World System and Its Character see Merrill F. Unger's *Biblical Demonology*, 2nd. ed., 1953, p. 181-192, and "Demonism and World Governments," pp. 192-200). *M. F. U.*

Lu'cius (lū'shĭ-ŭs) (for Lat. *Lucius*, surnamed the "Cyrenian"), one of the "prophets and teachers" at Antioch who, at the command of the Holy Spirit, ordained Barnabas and Saul (Acts 13:1; Rom. 16:21), A. D. 45.

Lud, Lu'dim (lŭd, lū'dĭm; Gen. 10:22; I Chron. 1:17; Isa. 66:19; Ezek. 27:10; *Ludim*, Gen. 10:13; I Chron. 1:11; see also Ezek. 30:5; Jer. 46:9).

The Lud of Gen. 10:22, I Chron. 1:17, was the fourth son of Shem; the Ludim of Gen. 10:13, I Chron. 1:11, were the first mentioned among the descendants of Mizraim, the second son of Ham. In Jer. 46:9 and Ezek. 30:5, Lūd and Lūdĭm are associated with African nations, and partly so in Isa. 66:19 and Ezek. 27:10. Our first impulse would be to refer all these prophetic passages, especially Jer. 46:9 and Ezek. 30:5 to the Mizraite tribe. It is hinted, however, that the Lud and Ludim of the prophets may have been the Ionian and Carian mercenaries which were employed in the Egyptian army from the time of Psammethichus I to the final subjugation of the country. This might explain the ambiguous manner in which they are associated with both Asiatic and African nations. In the time of the prophets Lydia might well be taken to represent the western part of Asia Minor. *See* Lydians.—*W. H.* revised by *M. F. U.*

Lu'hith (lū'hĭth; Jer. 48:5; Isa. 15:5), a Moabite town situated upon an eminence, whither the people fled from the invading Babylonians.

Luke (lūk; Gr. *Loukas;* Lat. *Lucanus*), the evangelist and author of the gospel bearing his name and the Acts of the Apostles. *See* Gospels; Bible, Books of.

Personal History. The materials found in Scripture for a life of Luke are very scanty, and seem to yield the following results: (1) That Luke was of Gentile origin. This is inferred from the fact that he is not reckoned among those "who are of the circumcision" (Col. 4:11; comp. 5:14). When and how he became a physician is not known. (2) That he was not "an eyewitness and minister of the word from the beginning" (Luke 1:2). (3) On the supposition of Luke's being the author of the Acts we gather from those passages in which the first person *we* is employed the following information: That he joined Paul's company at Troas and sailed with them to Macedonia (Acts 16:10, 11); he accompanied Paul as far as Philippi (16:25-17:1), but did not share his persecution nor leave the city, for here the third person *they* is used. The first person *we* does not reappear until Paul comes to Philippi at the end of his third journey (20:6), from which it is inferred that Luke spent the intervening time—a period of seven or eight years—in the city or neighborhood; and as the *we* continues to the end of the book, that Luke remained with Paul during his journey to Jerusalem (20:6-21:18), was that apostle's companion to Rome (27:1), sharing his shipwreck (28:2), and reaching the imperial city by way of Syracuse and Puteoli (28:12-26). According to the epistles he continued to be Paul's "fellow-laborer" till the end of his first imprisonment (Philem. v. 24; Col. 4:14). The last glimpse of the "beloved physician" (II Tim. 4:11) discovers him to be faithful amid general defection. Tradition, since the time of Gregory of Nazianzus, makes Luke a martyr; yet not unanimously, since accounts of a natural death slip in. *Where* he died remains a question; certainly not in Rome with Paul, for his writings are far later (Meyer, *Com.*, on Luke, introduction).

Luke, Gospel of, the third synoptic gospel, a work of high literary quality ascribed by almost universal Christian tradition to Luke, the beloved physician, and traveling companion of Paul.

1. **Charactistics.** Renan viewed Luke's gospel as "the most beautiful book that has ever been written." The subject matter as well as the author's literary talent combine to give the book an interesting appeal and polish conspicuous in the N. T. The elevated subject matter was a challenge to the author's literary endeavor. Whereas Matthew presents Christ as King, Mark presents Him as a Servant, John presents him as the Son of God, and Luke presents him as the Son of Man, the Human-Divine One in contrast to John's the Divine-Human One. The term "Son of Man" acts as a key phrase, and 19:10 is commonly taken as the key verse: "For the Son of Man is come to seek and to save that which was lost." Consonant with his purpose, Luke narrates those events which demonstrate the humanity of Christ. The divine genealogy is traced to Adam. A detailed account of Christ's mother and of His infancy and childhood is presented. The parables included by Luke have a human touch. Although Luke beautifully sets forth

the humanity of the Divine One, he carefully shields His deity and kingship (Luke 1:32-35). It has truly been said that Luke is the gospel of "the Man Whose Name is The Branch" (Zech. 6:12). Luke is distinctive in that it catalogs much material which is not included in the other evangels. This new material amounts to more than 50 per cent of its content. For example, Luke has a joyous note and records five great outbursts of song—Elizabeth's *Beatitude*, Mary's *Magnificat*, Zachariah's *Benedictus*, the angels' *Gloria in Excelsis*, and Simeon's *Nunc Dimittis*. His gospel is emphatically "good tidings of great joy."

2. **Purpose.** The evangelist avers to write in order that Theophilus "might know the certainty" of the things wherein he had been instructed (1:4). Theophilus seems to have been a Gentile, and the epithet *kratistos*, often given to persons of rank (Acts 23:26; 24:3; 26:5) suggests that he was an individual of eminence, most likely a recent convert. Some think that he was a *patronos libri* and acted as a patron for the production of the book. Everyone is of the opinion that the gospel was intended for people at large, especially the Greek-speaking world.

3. **The Date.** Since the book was written before the Acts, which is to be dated c. 61 A. D., it was likely written while Paul was at Caesarea. Since internal evidence that Luke wrote both the gospel and the Book of Acts (and he divulges the fact that the gospel was written first, Acts 1:1), it must be concluded that the gospel was penned prior to 61 A. D. Luke was in Cesaraea where Paul was in prison (Acts 27:1). This circumstance would furnish him opportunity for the research he mentions with such fine literary style and classical flourish in 1:1-4.

3. **Attestation.** External evidence is very strong concerning the early existence and use of Luke. Justin Martyr quotes 22:44; 23:46. The Muratorian Fragment calls the third gospel "Luke." Heggesippus, Tatian, the unbeliever Celsus, Marcion, Clement of Alexandria and Tertullian all refer to "Luke." Robertson's statement in the *International Standard Bible Encyclopedia* on Luke sums up the evidence, "Surely the general use and acceptance of the third gospel in the early second century is beyond reasonable doubt. It is not easy to decide when the actual use began, because we have so little data from the first century."

4. **The Outline.**

Introduction, 1:1-4

Part I. The Son of Man in His human relationships, 1:5-2:52

Part II. The Son of Man in His baptism, ancestry and testing, 3:1-4:13

Part III. The Son of Man in His ministry as Prophet-King in Galilee, 4:14-9:50

Part IV. The Son of Man's journey from Galilee to Jerusalem, 9:51-14:44

Part V. The Son of Man offered as Israel's King, His rejection and sacrifice, 19:45-23:46

Part VI. The Son of Man in resurrection ministry and ascension, 24:1-53

          M. F. U.

Lunatic. *See* Diseases, Demoniac.

Lust, the rendering of several Hebrew and Greek words with various meanings:

1. Intense longing desire, "my *lust* shall be satisfied upon them" (Exod. 15:9; Num. 11:34; Deut. 12:15, etc.).

2. In the ethical sense *lust* is used to express sinful desire—sinful either in being directed toward forbidden objects, or in being so violent as to overcome self-control, and to engross the mind with earthly, carnal, and perishable things.

"By lusts Paul, like Peter and James, understands, not the natural appetites of the body, but the sinful, godless inclinations (Rom. 1:24), whether these be of a sensuous or of a spiritual nature. He purposely quotes the Old Testament commandment against sinful lust (Exod. 20:17; Deut. 5:21) in such a manner that it is not any definite objects of lust, but the longing for them as such that he calls forbidden (Rom. 7:7). In his sense every lust is a product of sin (v. 8), which compels us to obey the lusts of the body (6:12); every natural appetite may be perverted by sin into lust (13:14). Such passages as I Thess, 2:17; Phil. 1:23 have naturally nothing to do with this technical use of the word *lust* (Gr. *epithumia*)" (Weiss, *Theology of New Testament*, i, p. 328).

Luz (lŭz; *almond tree*).

1. The ancient (Canaanite name of Beth-el (Gen. 28:19; 35:6; 48:3), or a town which formerly stood upon or near the latter city (*see* Beth-el). In Josh 16:2 "Luz is distinguished from Beth-el because the reference is not to the town of Beth-el, but to the southern range of mountains belonging to Beth-el, from which the boundary ran out to the town of Luz, so that this town, which stood upon the border, was allotted to Benjamin (18:13)" (K. and D., *Com.*).

2. A town in the land of the Hittites, built by an inhabitant of the former Luz. He was spared when the latter was destroyed by the Benjamites (Judg. 1:23-26). Luweiziyeh, a ruin 4½ miles N. W. of Banias is suggested as the site by Conder.

Lycao'nia (lĭk-ȧ-ō'nĭ-ȧ), a small Roman province of Asia Minor, bounded north by Galatia,

278. Lycaonia

east by Cappadocia, south by Isauria, and west by Phrygia. It is not very fertile, though level, and therefore adapted to pasturage. Its cities are Derbe, Iconium, and Lystra. The "speech of Lycaonia" (Acts 14:11) was a corrupt Greek mingled with Assyrian. Paul preached in this region (14:1-6), and revisited it (16:1, 2).

Ly'cia (lĭ'shĭ-à), a mountainous province in the southwest of Asia Minor belonging to Rome. Patara and Myra are its towns, which were visited by Paul (Acts 21:2; 27:5). It is a part of the region now known as *Tekeh*.

Lyd'da (lĭd'à), a town about 11 miles S. E. of Joppa, called in the Old Testament Lod (I Chron. 8:12), while its modern name is Ludd. It is located in the midst of a rich and fertile plain. It was one of the most westerly of the Jewish settlements after the exile, the site of which is described as Ge-haharashim, the valley of the smiths or craftsmen. It was here that Peter healed the paralytic, and secured many converts (Acts 9:32-35). It was not Jewish, but pagan, under the name of Diospolis. *See* Lod.

Lyd'ia (lĭd'ĭ-à), a seller of purple of the city of *Thyatira* (*q. v.*) who dwelt in Philippi. She sold the purple-dyed garments from Thyatira in Philippi, and traded in both the cheap and expensive merchandise. As her husband is not mentioned, and she was a householder, she was probably a widow. She was not by birth a Jewess, but a proselyte, as the phrase "who worshipped God" imports. Converted by the preaching of Paul, and baptized by him, she pressed upon him the use of her house so earnestly that he was constrained to accept (Acts 16:14, 40). Whether she was one of "those women who labored with Paul in the gospel at Philippi" (Phil. 4:3) it is impossible to say.

Lyd'ia, Lyd'ians (lĭd'ĭ-à, lĭd'ĭ-ănz), the words used in the A. V. for lūd, (Ezek. 30:5); and lūdim, (Jer. 46:9); *see* under *Ludim*. In Homer's time the country was occupied by Pelasgic Meonians, kindred of the Trojans. The Lydians came in with Lydus, son of Atys, from which Lydus, with his brothers Mysus and Car, descended Lydians, Mysians, and Carians respectively. To what race the Lydians belonged it is impossible to tell. To the Greeks they and their language was barbarous, but they were highly civilized, and with the Carians "were in many respects little inferior to the Greeks." Their commercial enterprise was an "industrial power" in its day, and was to them a source of great and lasting prosperity. Before their subjugation by Persia they were warlike, and their cavalry was the best of its time. To them is ascribed the invention of the games (*paignia*) which they had in common with the Greeks, of retail trade, and of the coining of gold and silver.

After the dynasty of Lydus followed that of the Herakleids, beginning with Agron, son of Ninus, son of Belus, son of Alcaeus, son of Hercules (Herod. i, 7). This connects at least the reigning family with Assyria. After reign-

ing for twenty-two generations (five hundred and five years) this line ended with Candaules (Myrsilus), and was followed by Gyges, the first of the Mermnadae, at a time variously estimated before and after 708 B. C. These Mermnadae, who are thought to have been really Lydians, reigned till the fall of their last king, Croesus, 546 B. C. Under the Romans Lydia was part of the Roman province of Asia.

Josephus (*Ant.*, i, 6, § 4) makes Lud the ancestor of the Lydians; but as the *Ruten* or *Luden* of the Egyptian monuments for the 13th-15th century B. C. seem to have come from a place north of Palestine and near Mesopotamia, it has been conjectured that the Lydians may have gone from this place to Asia Minor, being displaced by the Assyrians.—*W. H.*

Lysa'nias (lĭ-sā'nĭ-ŭs), a tetrarch or governor of the region known as Abilene. This country was drained by the Abana River and located between Baalbek on the north side of Mt. Hermon and Damascus. This Lysanias ruled in the time of John the Baptist (Luke 3:1) in the fifteenth year of Tiberias. Some critics insist that Lysanias, the son of Ptolemy, who reigned in Chalcis in Coelesyria (40-34 B. C.) gave the name to this tetrarchy and that Luke has made an historical blunder. Lysanias, however, who ruled Chalcis is never styled tetrarch nor does Abila appear in his kingdom. In 37 A. D. the emperor Caligula appointed Herod Agrippa king of the tetrarchy of Philip and added Lysanias to the tetrarchy. The tetrarchy of Lysanias with capital at Abila some 18 miles N. W. of Damascus was distinct from the kingdom of Chalcis. (Josephus, *Ant.*, xix, 5, 1; xx, 7, 1). In the time in which Luke writes, the region about Abila was ruled by the tetrarch Lysanias, and Luke is correct. *M. F. U.*

Lys'ias (lĭs'ĭ-ăs), *Claudius*, the "chief captain" in command of the Roman troops in Jerusalem, who rescued Paul from the fury of the Jews (Acts 12:31-38; 22:24-30), and sent him under guard to the procurator Felix at Caesarea (23:17-30; 24:7, 22), A. D. 55.

2. A general under Antiochus Epiphanes and Antiochus Eupator (I Macc. 3:32-37). *See* Maccabees, the.

Lys'tra (lĭs'trà), a town of *Lycaonia* (*q. v.*), where Paul preached after being driven from Iconium (Acts 14:2-7). Here he healed a lame man, and because of this was taken by the inhabitants to be the god Mercury (v. 8, sq.). Through the influence of Jews from Antioch and Iconium the tide was turned, and Paul was stoned nearly to death (v. 19; II Tim. 3:11). Paul left for Derbe, but soon returned (Acts 14:21). It is not definitely stated that he ever visited Lystra again, but the route of his third missionary journey (18:23) makes it probable. Lystra was a Roman colony located on a hill about 1 mile N. W. of Khatyn Serai, which is situated 18 miles S. S. W. of Iconium.

M

Ma'acah, or **Ma'achah** (mā'à-kà; *oppression*).

1. The last named of the four children of Nahor by his concubine Reumah (Gen. 22: 24). Whether this child was son or daughter is not stated.

2. One of David's wives, and the mother of Absalom. She was the daughter of Talmai, king of the Geshur, lying to the north of Judah (II Sam. 3:3), between Hermon and Bashan.

3. A city and small Syrian kingdom at the foot of Mount Hermon, near Geshur (Josh. 13:13; II Sam. 10:6, 8; I Chron. 19:7). The kingdom embraced the southern and eastern declivities of Hermon, and a portion of the rocky plateau of Iturea. The Israelites included this territory in their grant, but never took possession of it (Josh. 13:13). Its king contributed one thousand men to the Syrian alliance against David (II Sam. 10:6-8), which was defeated (v. 19).

4. The father of Achish, king of Gath, to whom Shimei went in pursuit of two runaway servants, and by so doing forfeited his life by going beyond the limits prescribed by Solomon (I Kings 2:39).

5. The mother of King Abijam. She was the daughter of Abishalom, and wife of Rehoboam (I Kings 15:2), B. C. about 926. In v. 10 she is called the "mother" of Asa, but there "mother" is used in a loose sense, and means "grandmother." The following seem to be the facts: Maachah was the granddaughter of Absalom (Abishalom), and the daughter of Tamar (Absalom's only daughter), and her husband was Uriel of Gibeah (II Chron. 11: 20-22; 13:2). Because of the abuse of her power as "queen mother" in encouraging idolatry, Asa "removed her from being queen" (I Kings 15:10-13; II Chron. 15:16).

6. The second named of the concubines of Caleb (son of Hezron), and the mother by him of several children (I Chron. 2:48).

7. The sister of Huppim and Shuppim, and wife of Machir, by whom he had two sons (I Chron. 7:15, 16).

8. The wife of Jehiel, and mother of Gibeon (I Chron. 8:29; 9:35).

9. The father of Hanan, one of David's valiant men (I Chron. 11:43).

10. The father of Shephatiah, military chief of the Simeonites in the time of David (I Chron. 27:16), c. 1000 B. C.

Maach'athi (mâ-ăk'à-thī) (Deut. 3:14), **Maach'athites** (mā-ăk'à-thīts), inhabitants of Maac(h)ah, a small kingdom near Palestine, probably in the stony desert of *el-Kra*, "which is to this day thickly studded with villages." It lies east of Argob (*Lejah*), between that and the *Sufâ*. There were Maachathite warriors among the mighty men of Israel. One is apparently the father of Ahasbai in II Sam. 23: 34, one was the father of Jezaniah, or Jaazaniah (II Kings 25:33; Jer. 40:8); another, Eshtemoa (I Chron. 4:19), may have taken the title from Maachah, Caleb's concubine (I Chron. 2:48). Indeed, so common was Maachah as a personal name that other Ma-

achathites may have received the epithet in the same way. It is possible that the kingdom Maac(h)ah may have taken its name from the Maachah of Gen. 22:24. The Maachathites are mentioned in Joshua in connection with the Geshurites as bordering the terriotry of Og, king of Bashan (12:5; comp. 13:11), but not dispossessed by Israel.

Maada'i (mā-à-dā'ī), a Jew of the family of Bani, who divorced his Gentile wife after the captivity (Ezra 10:34), B. C. 456.

Maadi'ah (mā-à-dī'à; *ornament of Jehovah*), one of the priests who returned from Babylon with Zerubbabel (Neh. 12:5), B. C. about 536. He is thought to be the same as *Moadiah* (v. 17).

Maa'i (mâ-ā'ī), one of the priests appointed to perform the music at the celebration of the completion of the walls of Jerusalem after the exile (Neh. 12:36), B. C. 445.

Maal'eh-Acrab'bim (mâ-ăl'ê-à-krăb'ĭm; *steep of scorpions*, i. e., "scorpion-hill"), a pass in the southeast border of Palestine (Josh. 15:3), called "the ascent of Akrabbim" (Num. 34:4). It is identified with the steep pass of *es Sufah*.

Ma'arath (mā'à-răth; *desolation*), a place in the mountains of Judah (Josh. 15:59), not positively identified, perhaps Beit Ummar, about 7 miles N. of Hebron.

Maase'iah (mâ-à-sē'yà; *work of Jehovah*).

1. One of the Levites of the second class of appointed musicians "with psalteries upon Alamoth," at the bringing up of the ark from the house of Obed-edom (I Chron. 15:18, 20), B. C. about 982.

2. One of the "captains of hundreds" who assisted the high priest Jehoiada in raising Joash to the throne of Judah (II Chron. 23: 1), B. C. 836.

3. A "ruler" (steward) who assisted Jeiel the scribe in arranging the army of King Uzziah (II Chron. 26:11), B. C. about 783.

4. A person slain by Zichri, an Ephraimite hero, in the invasion of Judah by Pekah, king of Israel (II Chron. 28:7), B. C. about 735. Maaseiah is called the "king's son;" but this should not, probably, be interpreted literally, "for in the first years of his reign, in which this war arose, Ahaz could not have had an adult son capable of bearing arms, but" Maaseiah was likely "a royal prince, a cousin or uncle of Ahaz" (Keil, *Com.*, in loc.).

5. The "governor of the city," appointed by King Josiah to cooperate with Shaphan and Joah in repairing the temple (II Chron. 34: 8), B. C. 621. He is probably the same as Maaseiah, the father of Neriah, and grandfather of Baruch and Seraiah (Jer. 32:12; 51:59).

6. One of the priests of the descendants of Jeshua, who divorced his Gentile wife after the captivity (Ezra 10:18), B. C. 456.

7. Another priest of the "sons" of Harim who put away his Gentile wife after the exile (Ezra 10:21), B. C. 456. He is probably the one who belonged to the chorus that celebrated the completion of the walls (Neh. 12: 42), B. C. 445.

8. A priest of the "sons" of Pashur, who

divorced his Gentile wife after the return from Babylon (Ezra 10:22), B. C. 456. Perhaps the same as one of the trumpeters who joined in celebrating the building of the walls of Jerusalem (Neh. 12:41), B. C. 445.

9. An Israelite, descendant of Pahath-moab, who put away his Gentile wife after the exile (Ezra 10:30), B. C. 456.

10. A Jew, whose son Azariah repaired a portion of the walls of Jerusalem after the return from Babylon (Neh. 3:23), B. C. 445.

11. One of those who stood at the right hand of Ezra while he read the book of the law to the people (Neh. 8:4), B. C. about 445.

12. One of the priests who, with the Levites, expounded the law as it was read by Ezra (Neh. 8:7), B. C. about 445.

13. One of the "chief of the people" who joined in the covenant with Nehemiah (Neh. 10:25), B. C. 445.

14. The son of Baruch, and one of the descendants of Judah who dwelt in Jerusalem after the captivity (Neh. 11:5), B. C. about 536. In I Chron. 9:5, the same person is, probably, given as *Asaiah*.

15. The son of Ithiel, a Benjamite, and one whose descendants resided in Jerusalem after the return from Babylon (Neh. 11:7), B. C. before 536.

16. A priest, whose son Zephaniah was sent by Zedekiah, king of Judah, to inquire of the prophet Jeremiah during the invasion by Nebuchadnezzar (Jer. 21:1; 29:21, 25; 37:3), B. C. before 589.

17. The son of Shallum, and a "keeper of the door" of the temple, with a chamber in the sacred edifice (Jer. 35:4), B. C. about 607.

Maas'iai (mâ-ăs'ī-ī; *work of Jehovah*, A. V. and R. S. V. Ma'asai), the son of Adiel, descendant of Immer, and one of the priests resident at Jerusalem after the captivity (I Chron. 9:12), B. C. probably after 536.

Ma'ath (mā'áth), a person named as the son of Mattathias, and father of Nagge in the maternal ancestry of Jesus (Luke 3:26). As no such name appears in the Old Testament pedigrees, it is thought that this name has been accidently interpolated from the Matthat (v. 24).

Ma'az (mā'ăz; *anger*), the first named of the three sons of Ram, the firstborn of Jerahmeel, of the descendants of Judah (I Chron. 2:27), B. C. after 1440.

Maazi'ah (mâ-à-zī'á; *Jehovah is a refuge*).

1. The head of the last (twenty-fourth) course of priests as arranged by David (I Chron. 24:18), B. C. before 960.

2. One of the priests who sealed the covenant made by Nehemiah (Neh. 10:8), B. C. about 445.

Mac'cabees, The, (măk'à-bēz). The Asmonaean family, distinguished in Jewish history, from B. C. 167 till the time when Judea became a province of Rome, were called Maccabees from Judas, a distinguished member of the house, whose surname was Maccabaeus.

1. **Name.** The etymology of the word is uncertain. Some have maintained that it was formed from the combination of the initial letters of the Hebrew sentence, "Who among the gods is like unto thee, Jehovah?" (Exod. 15:11), which is supposed to have been inscribed upon the banner of the patriots. Another derivation has been proposed, which, although direct evidence is lacking, seems satisfactory. According to this, the word is formed from *Makkâbâh*, "a hammer," giving a sense not altogether unlike that in which Charles Martel derived a surname from his favorite weapon. Although the name *Maccabees* has gained the widest currency, that of *Asmonaeans*, or *Hasmonaeans*, is the proper name of the family. This name probably came from Chasmon, the great-grandfather of Mattathias.

2. **Pedigree.** The relation of the several members of the family will be seen in the accompanying table.

THE ASMONAEAN FAMILY.

Chasmon ("of the sons of Joarib;" comp. 1 Chron. 24:7).

Johanan (Gr. Ἰωαννης).

Simeon (Gr. Συμεων, Simon; comp. II Pet. 1:1).

Mattathias (Matthias, Joseph., *War*, i, 1, 3). B. C. 167.

Johanan (Johannes) (Gaddis) ("Joseph," II Macc. 8:22), B. C. 161.	Simon (Thassi), B. C. 135.	Judas (Maccabeus), B. C. 161.	Eleazar (Avaran), B. C. 163.	Jonathan (Apphus), B. C. 143.
Judas B. C. 135.	Johannes Hyrcanus I, B. C. 106.	Mattathias, B. C. 135.	Daughter *to* Ptolemaeus (I Macc. 16:11, 12).	
Salome (Alexandra) *to* Aristobulus I, B. C. 105.	Antigonus, B. C. 105.	Jannaeus Alexander B. C. 78. to Alexandra,	son	son
Hyrcanus II, B. C. 30.		Aristobulus II, B. C. 49.		
Alexander *to* Alexander, B. C. 28. | B. C. 49.		Antigonus, B. C. 37.		
Mariamne to Herod the Great, B. C. 29.	Aristobulus, B. C. 35.			

3. **History.** The Maccabees first came into
notice through the terrible persecution of the
Jews under Antiochus Epiphanes. His accession was immediately followed by desperate
efforts of the Hellenizing party at Jerusalem
to assert their ascendency. Jason, brother of
Onias III, the high priest, secured the high
priesthood, and bought permission (2 Macc.
4:9) to carry out his design of habituating the
Jews to Greek customs (4:7, 20). Three years
later Menelaus supplanted Jason by a larger
bribe, and the latter fled to the Ammonites (4:
23-26). During the absence of Antiochus on his

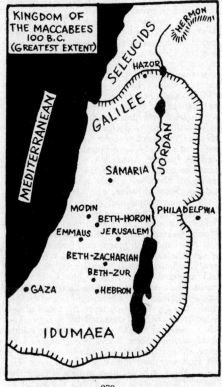

KINGDOM OF
THE MACCABEES
100 B.C.
(GREATEST EXTENT)

SELEUCIDS
HERMON
HAZOR
GALILEE
MEDITERRANEAN
JORDAN
SAMARIA
MODIN
BETH-HORON
PHILADELPHIA
EMMAUS JERUSALEM
BETH-ZACHARIAH
BETH-ZUR
GAZA
HEBRON
IDUMAEA

279.

second invasion of Egypt, he was reported as
dead, and Jason seized the opportunity of recovering his office, took the city, and inflicted
all manner of cruelties on the inhabitants. Antiochus, on hearing of this, and supposing that
there was a general revolt of the Jews, hastily
returned to Jerusalem, laid siege to the city,
put forty thousand of its inhabitants to death,
and sold as many more into slavery. He despoiled the temple of its precious vessels and
furniture, and returned to Antioch laden with
the treasure. On occasion of his fourth and
last invasion of Egypt, he was arrested by the
Roman ambassadors and ordered to leave the
country on pain of the wrath of the Roman
Senate (Dan. 11:30). On his way homeward
he passed through Palestine, and vented his
wrath upon the Jews, commissioning his lieutenant Apollonius, with an army of twenty-
two thousand men, to destroy Jerusalem.
Taking advantage of the Sabbath, he came

upon the people assembled in their synagogues, massacred the men, and made the
women and children captives. He burned the
city, erected a fort on an eminence commanding the temple, so that the worshippers approaching it were slain; while the place itself
was defiled with every abomination; and the
daily sacrifice was made to cease, according
to the prediction of Daniel (8:9-12; 11:31).
Matters were brought to a height by the
famous decree of Antiochus, commanding that
all the people should conform to the religion
of the sovereign on pain of death. This brought
about the Maccabean war.

(1) **Mattathias.** At the time of the great
persecution he was already advanced in years,
and the father of grown-up sons. He was a
priest of the course of Joarib, the first of the
twenty-four courses (I Chron. 24:7), and, consequently, of the noblest blood. He retired to
Modin, a little town west of Jerusalem. He
was required to sacrifice on the heathen altar,
but refused. A Judean coming forward to
sacrifice, Mattathias, carried away by his zeal,
smote him, overthrew the altar, summoned
all the faithful to follow him, and fled with
his sons into the wilderness. He was joined by
many from various parts of the country; in
many places the idolatrous altars were overthrown, and the old Israelite usages and customs reintroduced. Mattathias did not long
survive the fatigues of active service. He died
B. C. 166, and "was buried in the sepulcher
of his father at Modin."

(2) **Judas.** Mattathias himself named Judas
—apparently his third son—as his successor in
directing the war of independence (I Macc.
2:66). The energy and skill of "the Maccabee,"
as Judas is often called in II Maccabees, fully
justified his father's preference. It appears that
he had already taken a prominent part in the
first secession to the mountains (II Macc. 5:
27), where Mattathias is not mentioned. His
first enterprises were night attacks and sudden
surprises (8:6, 7); and when his men were
encouraged by these means he ventured on
more important operations and defeated Apollonius (I Macc. 3:10-12) and Seron (13-24) at
Beth-horon. Shortly afterward Antiochus Epiphanes, whose resources had been impoverished by the war (27-31), left the government
of the Palestinian provinces to Lysias. Lysias
organized an expedition against Judas; but
his army, a part of which had been separated
from the main body to effect a surprise, was
defeated by Judas at Emmaus with great
loss, B. C. 166 (46-53); and in the next year
Lysias himself was routed at Bethsura. After
this success Judas was able to occupy Jerusalem, except the "tower" (6:18, 19), and he
purified the temple (4:36, 41-53) on the 25th
of Chisleu, exactly three years after its profanation (1:59). The next year was spent in
wars with frontier nations (ch. 5); but in spite
of continued triumphs the position of Judas
was still precarious. In B. C. 163 Lysias laid
siege to Jerusalem. The accession of Demetrius
brought with it fresh troubles to the patriot
Jews. A large party of their countrymen, with
Alcimus at their head, gained the ear of the
king, and he sent Nicanor against Judas.
Nicanor was defeated, first at Capharaslama,

and again in a decisive battle at Adasa, near to the glorious field of Bethhoron (B. C. 161) on the 13th Adar (I Macc. 7:49; II Macc. 15:36), where he was slain. This victory was the greatest of Judas' successes, and practically decided the question of Jewish independence; but it was followed by an unexpected reverse. A new invasion under Bacchides took place. Judas was able only to gather a small force to meet the sudden danger. Of this a large part deserted him on the eve of the battle; but the courage of Judas was unshaken, and he fell at Eleasa, the Jewish Thermopylae, fighting at desperate odds against the invaders. His body was recovered by his brothers and buried at Modin "in the sepulcher of his fathers," B. C. 161.

(3) **Jonathan.** After the death of Judas the patriotic party seems to have been for a short time wholly disorganized, and it was only by the pressure of unparalleled sufferings that they were driven to renew the conflict. For this purpose they offered the command to *Jonathan*, surnamed Apphus (*the wary*), the youngest son of Mattathias. He retired to the lowlands of the Jordan (I Macc. 9:42), where he gained some advantage over Bacchides (B. C. 161), who made an attempt to hem in and destroy his whole force. After two years Bacchides again took the field against Jonathan, B. C. 158. This time he seems to have been but feebly supported, and after an unsuccessful campaign he accepted terms which Jonathan proposed; and after his departure Jonathan "judged the people at Michmash" (v. 73), and gradually extended his power. The claim of Alexander Balas to the Syrian crown gave a new importance to Jonathan and his adherents. The success of Alexander led to the elevation of Jonathan, who assumed the high-priestly office (10:21); and not long after he placed the king under fresh obligations by the defeat of Apollonius, a general of the younger Demetrius (ch. 10). After the death of Alexander Jonathan attached himself to Antiochus VI. He at last fell a victim to the treachery of Tryphon, B. C. 144 (I Macc. 11:8-12:4).

(4) **Simon.** As soon as Simon, the last remaining brother of the Maccabaean family, heard of the detention of Jonathan in Ptolemais by Tryphon, he placed himself at the head of the patriot party. His skill in war had been proved in the lifetime of Judas (I Macc. 5:17-23), and he had taken an active share in the campaigns of Jonathan (11:59). Tryphon, after carrying Jonathan about as a prisoner for some little time, put him to death; and then, having murdered Antiochus, seized the throne. On this Simon made overtures to Demetrius II, B. C. 143, which were favorably received, and the independence of the Jews was at length formally recognized. The long struggle was now triumphantly ended, and it remained only to reap the fruits of victory. This Simon hastened to do. The prudence and wisdom for which he was already distinguished at the time of his father's death (2:65), gained for the Jews the active support of Rome (15:16-21), in addition to the confirmation of earlier treaties. After settling the external relations of the new state upon a sure basis,

Simon regulated its internal administration. With two of his sons he was murdered at Dok by Ptolemaeus, B. C. 135 (I Macc. 16:11-16).

(5) **John Hyrcanus** was the next leader of the family. Having been unanimously proclaimed high priest and ruler at Jerusalem, he marched against Jericho to avenge the death of his father and brothers. The threats of Ptolemy against the mother of Hyrcanus caused him to protract the siege, until the sabbatical year obliged him to raise it. But Ptolemy, after killing her and her sons, fled to Philadelphia. Antiochus soon after invaded Judea, and , besieging Jerusalem, reduced Hyrcanus to great extremity. At the feast of Passover, however, he granted a truce for a week, supplied the besieged with sacrifices, and ended with conceding a peace on condition that the Jews surrendered their arms, paid tribute for Joppa and other towns, and gave him five hundred talents of silver and hostages. Ewald (*History*, v, p. 344) says that "John sought relief in his financial difficulties by opening the tomb of David. The treasures which he found there enabled him not only to pay the required redemption money, but also to enlist foreign mercenaries." John himself immediately accompanied the king to Parthia, where Antiochus was killed. Hyrcanus availed himself of the opportunity to shake off the Syrian yoke and establish the independence of Judea, which was maintained until it was subjugated by the Romans. He also captured several towns beyond the Jordan; destroyed the Samaritan temple on Mount Gerizim; captured the towns of Dora and Marissa in Idumaea, and forced the rite of circumcision upon the people; renewed a treaty, offensive and defensive, with Rome, and amassed great wealth. His sons, Antigonus and Aristobulus, conducted a campaign against the Samaritans; and when Antiochus Cyzicenus came to the relief of the Samaritans, he was defeated by Aristobulus. After a year or so Samaria fell into the hands of Hyrcanus. Soon after, being exposed to some indignity from a Pharisee, he openly left that sect and joined the Sadducees. He passed the rest of his days in peace, built the castle of Baris on a rock within the fortifications of the temple, called by Herod "Antonia." His reign lasted about thirty years.

(6) **Aristobulus** succeeded his father, John Hyrcanus, as high priest and governor. He was the first since the captivity to assume the title of king. He starved his mother to death and imprisoned three of his brothers. He only reigned one year.

(7) **Alexander Jannaeus** succeeded to his brother Aristobulus, slaying one brother who displayed ambition, but leaving the other alone. After varying fortunes, he found himself at the head of sixty thousand men, and he marched in triumph to Jerusalem. After a reign of twenty-seven years he died, B. C. 78.

Alexander was succeeded by Hyrcanus II, and he was induced to enter private life by his brother Aristobulus II. Aristobulus, offering to surrender Jerusalem, was thrown into chains by Pompey. Hyrcanus was restored by Pompey to the high priesthood. He carried Aristobulus and family to Rome; but Alexander, the son of Aristobulus, escaped, and, raising a considerable force, garrisoned Machaerus, Hyrcania, and the stronghold of Alexandrion. He was subdued by Gabinius. No sooner had he done so than Aristobulus escaped from Rome and established himself in Alexandrion. He was taken prisoner and sent in chains to Rome, but his son Antigonus was released. Alexander, with eighty thousand men, opposed the Romans, but was put to flight. He was subsequently executed by Metellus Scipio, B. C. 49. Thus Hyrcanus retained the sovereignty, but Antipater enjoyed the real power. He found, however, a troublesome enemy in Antigonus, son of Aristobulus, who allied himself with the Parthians, and for a time held Jerusalem and kept Herod in check. At Masada, a city on the west coast of the Dead Sea, Antigonus was nearly successful, until Herod obliged him to raise the siege. He afterward suffered defeat by Herod, and was vanquished by the Roman general Sosius, sent to Anthony, by whom, at the request of Herod, he was put to death, B. C. 37.

Thus perished the last of the Maccabees, who seemed to inherit something of their ancient spirit. Hyrcanus, who previous to this had been incapacitated for the priesthood by having his ears cut off, was put to death in his eightieth year, B. C. 30. Herod married Mariamne, in whom the race of the Asmonaeans came to an end, and by her marriage passed into the Idumaean line of the Herodians.

Two of the first generation of Maccabees, though they did not, like their brothers, attain to leadership, shared their fate—Eleazar, by a noble act of self-devotion; John, apparently the eldest brother, by treachery. Probably history affords no parallel to the courage with which this band of men dared to face death, one by one, in a holy cause. "The Maccabees inspired a subject-people with independence; they found a few personal followers, and they left a nation" (*McC.* and *S., Cyc.*; Smith, *Bib. Dict.*; Ewald, *History of Israel*). *See* Maccabees; Books of, under Apocrypha.

280. Macedonia

Macedo′nia (măs-ē-dō′nĭ-à), a country lying north of Greece, whose rivers were the Strymon and the Axius, and whose mountains were Olympus and Athos. Some of its chief cities were Amphipolis, Apollonia, Berea, Neapolis, Philippi, and Thessalonica. It was conquered by the Romans, 168 B. C. Under the

famous Philip and his son, Alexander the Great, it attained the summit of its power (B. C. 359-323) Paul was summoned to preach in Macedonia by a vision (Acts 16:9; 20:1). The history of his journey through Macedonia is given in detail in Acts (16:10-17:15). He again passed through this province (20:1-6), and, after many years, probably visited it for a third time (Phil. 2:24; I Tim. 1:3). *See* Paul.

Machae′rus (mà-kē′rŭs; *the Black Fortress*) a strong fortress of Petraea, and the place, according to Josephus (*Ant.*, xviii, 5, 2), of John the Baptist's beheading. It was built by Alexander Jannaeus as a check against Arab marauders (Josephus, *Wars*, vii, 6, 2), demolished by Gabinius when he made war against Aristobulus, and rebuilt by Herod. It was situated in the gorge of Callirhoe, one of the valleys east of the Dead Sea, three thousand eight hundred and sixty feet above this sea and two thousand five hundred and forty-six feet above the Mediterranean. "Its ruins, now called *M'khaur*, are still visible on the northern end of Jebel Attarûs." *See* John the Baptist.

Mach′banai (măk′bà-nī), the eleventh of the Gadite warriors who joined themselves to David in the wilderness (I Chron. 12:13), about 1002 B. C. R. V. and R. S. V. Mach′-bannai.

Machbe′nah (măk-bē′nà), if a man, was the son of Sheva, and the one after whom the place of the same name was called (I Chron. 2:49).

Ma′chi (mā′kī), the father of Geuel, who represented the tribe of Gad among the explorers of Canaan (Num. 13:15), B. C. c. 1440.

Ma′chir (mā′kĭr; *sold*).

1. The eldest son of Manasseh (Josh. 17:1), who had children during the lifetime of Joseph (Gen. 50:23), B. C. after 1876. He was was the founder of the family of the Machirites (Num. 26:29), who settled in the land taken from the Amorites (Num. 32:39, 40; Deut. 3:15; Josh. 13:31; I Chron. 2:23). Owing to the fact of Machir's grandson, Zelophehad having only daughters, a special enactment was made as to their inheritance (Num. 27:1; 36:1; Josh. 17:3). His daughter became the wife of Hezron and mother of Segub (I Chron. 2:21). Machir's mother was an Aramitess, and by his wife, Maachah, he had several sons (7:14-16).

2. A descendant of the former, a son of Ammiel, residing at Lo-debar, who took care of the lame son of Jonathan until he was provided for by David (II Sam. 9:4, 5), and afterward hospitably entertained the king himself at Mahanaim (17:27-29), B. C. about 984-967.

Ma′chirites (mā′kĭr-īts; "the Machirite;" only in Num. 26:29), descendants of Machir (1), who was son of Manasseh by an Aramite concubine. The wife and children are named in I Chron. 7:16, 17; but the statement in v. 17, "These are the sons of Gilead, the son of Machir, the son of Manasseh," with the declaration that "Machir begat Gilead" would add Gilead to the list of Machir's sons. At the same time the enumeration of the Gileadites by families in Num. 26:29-32, together with the account of the peopling of Gilead in Num.

36:39, 40, gives some color to the opinion that if "Machir begat Gilead" Gilead is used collectively for the inhabitants of Gilead, like Moab for the Moabite nation, and the like, and that what is meant is that Machir was the ancestor of the Gileadites. The wife of Machir, who seems to have been a Benjamitess, was Maachah, the sister of Huppim and Shuppim (I Chron. 7:12, 15). And Abiah (2:24) was the last wife of Hezron (v. 21), son of Pharez (v. 5), son of Judah (v. 4). Thus did the Machirites connect Manasseh with both Judah and Benjamin. The daughters of Zelophehad, whose story is told in Num. 26:33; 27:1-11; 36:1-12; Josh. 17:3-6, were Machirites. The law which prevented confusion of inheritances by tribal intermarriages was first made in regard to this case (Num. 36:1-12), and was not in existence at the time of the before-mentioned intermarriages. See more under *Manassites.—W. H.*

Machnade′bai (măch-nă-dē′bī; *what is like the liberal*?), an Israelite of the "sons" of Bani who put away his Gentile wife after the captivity (Ezra 10:40), B. C. 456.

281. Entrance to Mosque over Cave of Machpelah

Machpe′lah (măk-pē′là; perhaps *double*), a field containing a cave, bought by Abraham for a burying place (Gen. 23:9, 17) and where he buried Sarah (v. 19). Abraham was buried there (25:9), Isaac and Rebekah, his wife, and Leah, the wife of Jacob (49:30), and later Jacob also (50:13). This is the last biblical mention of the cave of Machpelah; and there is no reason to think that any building was erected on the spot before the captivity. The cave was in *Hebron* (*q. v.*), and is now marked by a Mohammedan mosque, in which are shown the so-called tombs. Each is inclosed in a chapel, or shrine, closed with gates, and below the floor. Moslem and Christian have together held this sanctuary for six hundred years. The building, from the immense size of some of its stones and the manner in which they are fitted together, is supposed by some to have been erected in the time of David or Solomon, while others ascribe it to the time of Herod or later.

Mad. *See* Madness.

Mada′i (mà-dā′ī; a *Mede*), the third son of Japheth (Gen. 10:2; I Chron. 1:5), from whom the Medes descended. We hear of Madai upon the Assyrian monuments, about B. C. 840, where they are called Amadâ, and found by the Assyrian army in Media Atropatênê.

Ma′dian (mā′dĭ-ăn; Acts 7:29). *See* Midian.

Madman′nah (măd-măn′à, *dunghill*), a town in the extreme south of Judah (Josh. 15:31), afterward assigned to Simeon. From I Chron. 2:49 it appears to have been founded or occupied by Shaaph, the son of Maachah, Caleb's concubine. It is, perhaps, identical with Miniay, or Minieh, south of Gaza.

Mad′men (măd′měn; *dunghill*), a town in Moab, threatened with the sword from the Babylonian invasion (Jer. 48:2), identified as Khirbet Dimneh 2½ miles N. of Rabba.

Madme′nah (măd-mē′nà; *dunghill*), a town (Isa. 10:31) named on the route of the Assyrian invaders, north of Jerusalem, between Nob and Gibeah. The same word in Isa. 25:10 is rendered "dunghill," but the verse may mean "that Moab will be trodden down by Jehovah as straw is trodden to fragments on the threshing floors of Madmenah."

Madness. Besides its proper meaning of mania (*see* Diseases), the term "mad" is used in Scripture of a violent disturbance of the mental faculties: (1) From overstudy (Acts 26:24, 25); (2) from sudden and startling intelligence (12:15); (3) of false prophets (Isa. 44:25; Hos. 9:7); (4) the result of inebriety (Jer. 25:16; 51:7); (5) in derision, with reference to the ecstatic utterances of the prophets when in a state of holy exaltation (II Kings 9:11; Jer. 29:26); (6) furious passion, as a persecutor (Acts 26:11; Psa. 102-8); (7) idolatrous hallucination (Jer. 50:38), or wicked and extravagant jollity (Eccles. 2:2); (8) a reckless state of mind (10:13), bordering on delirium (Zech. 12:4), whether induced by overstrained mental effort (Eccles. 1:17; 2:12), blind rage (Luke 6:11), or depraved tempers (Eccles. 7:25; 9:3; II Pet. 2:16).

Ma′don (mā′dŏn; *strife*), a Canaanitish city, in the north of Palestine, ruled by a king named Jobab (Josh. 11:1), and captured by Joshua (12:19). It is probably to be identified with the village of Madîn, near Hattin, west of the Sea of Galilee.

Mag′bish (măg′bĭsh; probably *sturdy, strong*, cf. Akkad. *gabshu, massive, powerful*), the name of a man (or place) whose descendants, to the number of one hundred and fifty-six, returned to Palestine with Zerubbabel (Ezra 2:30).

Mag′dala (măg′dà-là; Aram. *migdᵉla, tower*), a small town of Galilee, on the west shore of the Lake of Gennesaret, between Capernaum and Tiberias, mentioned only in Matt. 15:39 (Dalmanutha in the parallel passage, Mark 8:10), and may be the same as Migdal-el (Josh. 19:38). It was the birthplace of Mary Magdalene, i. e., the Magdalene. It is now probably the small village of *el-Mejdel*, three miles N. W. of Tiberias.

Mag′dalen (măg′dà-lĕn), or **Magdale′ne** (măg-dà-lē′nĕ), the surname of *Mary*, 2.

Mag′diel (măg′dĭ-ĕl), one of the chiefs of Edom, descended from Esau (Gen. 36:43; I Chron. 1:54).

Ma′gi (mā′jī), Gr. *magoi* singular, *magos* from Old Persian *magav*); A. V. "wise men" in Matt. 2:1, 7, 16; "sorcerer" in Acts 13:6, 8.

1. **In the Old Testament.** In the Hebrew text of the Old Testament the word occurs but twice, and then only incidentally. Among the Chaldean officers sent by Nebuchadnez-

zar to Jerusalem one had the name or title of Rab-mag (Jer. 39:3, 13). This word has been interpreted as equivalent to *chief of the magi*. However, it seems here simply to mean "great prince" Akkad. *rab* ("great") and *mugi*, ("prince"). The term magi was used as the name for priests and wise men among the Medes, Persians, and Babylonians. These persons were supposed to be adepts in that secret learning which in remote antiquity had its seat in Egypt, and later in Chaldea, from which latter fact they were often called "Chaldeans" (Dan. 2:2, sq.; 4:7; 5:7, 11, 30). They formed five classes: the *Hartummim*, expounders of sacred writings and interpreters of signs (Dan. 1:20; 2:2; 5:4); the *Ashaphim*, conjurers (2:10; 5:7, 11); the *Mekashephim*, exorcists, soothsayers, magicians, diviners (Dan. 2:2; comp. Isa. 47:9, 13; Jer. 27:9); the *Gozerim*, casters of nativities, astrologists (Dan. 2:27; 5:7, 11); and the *Kasdim*, Chaldeans in the narrower sense (2:5, 10; 4:4; 5:7). The magi took their places among "the astrologers and stargazers and monthly prognosticators." It is with such men that we have to think of Daniel and his fellow-exiles as associated. They are described as "ten times wiser than all the magicians and astrologers" (1:20). The office which Daniel accepted (5:11) was probably identical with that of the Rab-mag who first came before us.

2. **Later Meaning.** We find that the word *magi* presented itself to the Greeks as connected with a foreign system of divination and the religion of a foe whom they had conquered; and soon became a byword for the worst form of imposture. The swarms of impostors that were to be met with in every part of the Roman empire, known as "Chaldei," "Mathematici," and the like, bore this name also. We need not wonder, accordingly, to find that this is the predominant meaning of the word as it appears in the New Testament. The noun and the verb derived from it are used by St. Luke in describing the impostor, who is therefore known distinctively as Simon Magus (Acts 8:9). Another of the same class (Bar-jesus) is described (13:8) as having, in his cognomen Elymas, a title which was equivalent to Magus. In one memorable instance, however, the word retains its better meaning. In the gospel of Matthew, written according to the general belief of early Christian writers for the Hebrew Christians of Palestine, we find it, not as embodying the contempt which the fraud of impostors had brought upon it, but in the sense which it had of old, as associated with a religion which they respected, and of an order of which one of their own prophets had been the head. Thus, the evangelist would probably see in them men at once astronomers and astrologers, but not mingling any conscious fraud with their efforts after a higher knowledge (Matt. 2:1). The indefinite expression, "from the east" (see Matt. 8:11; 24:27; Luke 13:29; Rev. 21:13), leads us to assume that the writer himself had no more precise information at his command. "It is entirely baseless to determine their *number* from the *threefold* gifts, and to regard them as *kings* on account of Psa. 68:30, 32; 72:10; Isa. 49:7; 60:3, 10." From a very early period the Church has believed

the magi to be the first Gentile worshippers of the Christ. "The expectations of the Jews, that their Messiah was to rule over the *world*, might at that period have been sufficiently disseminated throughout the foreign countries of the East to lead heathen astrologers, for the object in question, to the Jewish capital" (Meyer, *Com.*, in loc.; Smith, *Bib. Dict.*, s. v.). *See* Star.

Magic, Magicians (from Heb. *ḥĕrĕṭ*, to *engrave*, and so to *draw magical lines* or *circles*), the art or science of working wonders beyond the ordinary powers of man. "Magic may be divided into two classes—natural or scientific, and supernatural or spiritual—the one attributed its wonders to a deep, practical acquaintance with the powers of nature; the other to celestial or infernal agency. But both systems seem to have taken their origin in traditional accounts of early miracles—in attempts to investigate how such miracles were performed, and whether it were possible or not to imitate them. The theory of atoms held by the Epicureans appears to have been the basis of most magical speculations. It may be expressed somewhat after this manner: All changes in nature take place by the operation of atoms, and must *ultimately*, therefore, be effected by mechanical action. Wherever man can substitute artificial action of the same kind, he can produce the same effects as those of nature. It required, in the first place, a knowledge of the mode in which nature acted; and, secondly, the power of applying the same agencies. On the other hand, the spiritual or geotic (literally "terrestrial," and so *superstitious*) magic relied entirely on the powers of spiritual beings; it demanded no knowledge of nature, and rarely required any moral or intellectual preparation. Its works were understood to be purely miraculous; and those who practiced it claimed the wonder-working power only by means of mighty and unseen intelligences in obtaining communion with and authority over whom their science consisted" (*Imp. Bib. Dict.*, s. v.). As will be seen in the article *Magi*, there were among the Egyptians, Babylonians, etc., classes who were expert in magical arts. We will refer to these before calling attention to the Scripture accounts.

1. **Egypt.** The god Thot, having pointed out the evil to men, gave to them at the same time the remedy. The magical arts, of which he was the repository, made him virtual master of the other gods. Their mystic names, their secret weaknesses, the perils they most feared, ceremonies by which they could be subdued, prayers which they must grant under penalty of misfortune or death, were all known to him. This wisdom, transmitted to his worshippers, gave them the same authority in heaven, earth, or the nether world. Thus, they could bind or loose Osiris, Sit, Anubis, or even Thot himself; send them forth, recall them, constrain them to work or fight for them.

Very naturally, this great power exposed the magicians to temptations, being often led to use it to the detriment of others, to satisfy spite, or gratify their grosser appetites. Many made a gain of their knowledge, putting it at the service of the ignorant who would pay for it. They pretended to be able to bring on sicknesses, deceptive or terrifying dreams, specters, constrain the wills of men, cause women to be victims of infatuation, etc. Magic was not supposed to be all powerful against destiny; thus, fate decreed that the man born on the twenty-seventh of Paophi would die of a snake bite, but magic might decide as to the year in which his death would occur. Still more efficacious were the arts of magic in combating the influences of secondary deities, the evil eye, and the spells of man. After expelling the hurtful deity it was necessary to restore the health of the victim, and thus the magician was naturally led to the study of medicine. Magic was also invoked against magic, and thus rivalry arose among magicians.

Among the officers of distinction in the royal household were the "masters of the secrets of heaven," those who see what is in the firmament, on the earth, and in hades; those who know all the charms of the soothsayers, prophets, or magicians. The laws of the seasons and the stars, propitious months, days, or hours, presented no mysteries to them, drawing, as they did, their inspiration from the magical books of the god Thot. They understood the art of curing the sick, interpreting dreams, invoking or obliging the gods to aid them, etc. The great lords themselves deigned to become initiated into the occult sciences, and were invested with these formidable powers; sorcery was not considered incompatible with royalty, and the magicians of Pharaoh often took Pharaoh himself as a pupil. The Egyptians thought "that everything that happened was owing to the action of some divinity. They believed, therefore, in the incessant intervention of the gods; and their magical literature is based on the notion of frightening one god by the terrors of a more powerful divinity, either by prayer placing a person under the protection of his divinity, or by the person actually assuming its name and authority. Sometimes threats are uttered against a god; or rather, as an Egyptian priest (Abammom by name) said, the daimones, i. e., subordinate ministers of the gods" (Maspero, *Dawn of Civilization*, pp. 212, 281, 282; Renouf, *Religion of Ancient Egypt*, p. 219, sq.).

2. **Chaldea.** The Chaldeans believed that the operations of nature were not carried on under impersonal and unswerving laws, but by voluntary and rational agents, swayed by an inexorable fate against which they dared not rebel, but still free enough and powerful enough to avert by magic the decrees of destiny, or at least to retard their execution. "From this conception of things each subordinate science was obliged to make its investigations in two perfectly distinct regions; it had first to determine the material facts within its competence—such as the position of the stars, for instance, or the symptoms of a malady; it had then to discover the beings which revealed themselves through these material manifestations, their names and characters. When once it had obtained this information, and could lay its hand upon them, it could compel them to work on its behalf; science was thus nothing else than the application of magic to a particular class of phenom-

ena. . . . Chaldea abounded with soothsayers (*q. v.*) no less than with astrologers (*q. v.*), to whom the sick were confided, as expert in casting out demons and spirits. Consultations and medical treatment were, therefore, religious offices, in which were involved purifications, offerings, and a whole ritual of mysterious words and gestures. The use of magical words was often accompanied by remedies, which were for the most part grotesque and disgusting in their composition; (these) filled the possessing spirits with disgust, and became the means of relief owing to the invincible horror with which they inspired the persecuting demons. . . . The neighboring barbaric peoples were imbued with the same ideas as the Chaldeans regarding the constitution of the world and the nature of the laws which governed it. They lived likewise in perpetual fear of those invisible beings whose changeable and arbitrary will actuated all visible phenomena. . . . In the eyes of these barbarians, the Chaldeans seemed to be possessed of the very powers which they themselves lacked" (Maspero, *Dawn of Civ.*, p. 780, sq.).

3. **Scripture Accounts.** The earliest account of any magical proceedings recorded in Scripture is to be found in the history of Rachel (Gen. 31:19, 30, 32-35). This would seem to indicate the practice of magic in Padan-aram at that early time. The teraphim were consulted by the Israelites for oracular answers (Judg. 18:5, 6; Zech. 10:2). The only account of divining by teraphim is in the record of Nebuchadnezzar's advance against Jerusalem (Ezek. 21:19-22).

In Gen. 44:5, referring to the cup found in Benjamin's sack, we read: "Is not this it in which my lord drinketh, and whereby indeed he divineth?" (*see* Cup, 4). It is certainly not to be inferred that Joseph actually adopted this superstitious practice. The intention of the statement may simply have been to represent the goblet as a sacred vessel, and Joseph as acquainted with its common divinatory use.

In the histories of Joseph and Moses the magicians are spoken of as a class. When Pharaoh's officers were troubled by their dreams, being in prison, they were at a loss for an interpreter. Before Joseph explained the dreams he disclaimed the power of interpreting save by the divine aid, saying, "(Do) not interpretations (belong) to God? Tell me (them), I pray you" (Gen. 40:8). In like manner, when Pharaoh had his two dreams, we find that he had recourse to those who professed to interpret dreams. Joseph, being sent for on the report of the chief of the cupbearers, was told by Pharaoh that he had heard that he could interpret a dream. From the expectations of the Egyptians and Joseph's disavowals, we see that the interpretation of dreams was a branch of the knowledge to which the ancient Egyptian magicians pretended.

The Bible narrative of the events immediately preceding the Exodus introduces the magicians. When the rod of Aaron was changed into a serpent, it is said that Pharaoh called his magicians, and "they also did in like manner with their enchantments" (Exod. 7:11). The same is said of their imitation of the first and second plague (7:22; 8:7). But when they attempted to imitate Moses in the plague of the lice, they were unsuccessful, for it is recorded that "the magicians did so with their enchantments to bring forth lice, but they could not" (8:18). Whether the magicians really did what they appeared to do, or only performed a clever trick, has been a question of much dispute. Some contend that they did produce the same sort of miracle as that wrought through Moses, and that this was through demoniacal influence. It would seem the writer's intention to intimate that the Egyptian magicians considered Moses to be one of their own profession—what he did, that they claimed to be able to do also—he worked by the same means, and only exceeded them in degree. And this was unquestionably the opinion of the king himself. That they could not produce lice is not conclusive proof against their having acted through supernatural agency. It is quite evident from Scripture that Satanic and demonic power, although great, is definitely limited and can only go so far. They admitted that this plague was from Jehovah, and the next plague, that of boils, attacked them to their discomfiture.

Balaam (see Num. 22:6, sq.; Josh. 13:22) furnishes us another case of a man accustomed to use incantations; and it is evident that Balak believed, in common with the whole ancient world, in the real power and operation of the curses, anathemas, and incantations pronounced by priests, soothsayers, etc.

Saul attempted to obtain a knowledge of the future in ungodly ways, and commanded his servants to seek for a woman that had a familiar spirit; the mistress of a conjuring spirit with which the dead were conjured up for the purpose of making inquiry concerning the future (see Necromancy, below). The supernatural terror with which the account is full cannot however be proved to be due to this art; for it has always been held by sober critics that the appearing of Samuel was permitted for the purpose of declaring the doom of Saul, and not that it was caused by the witch's incantations. The witch is no more than a bystander after the first; she sees Samuel, and that is all.

The prophets, through their condemnation of them, tell us that magical practices prevailed among the Hebrews in the later days of the two kingdoms. Isaiah (2:6) says that the people were "soothsayers like the Philistines," understood by Delitzsch (Com., in loc.) to mean "cloud-gathers," or "storm-raisers." In another place (8:19) he reproves the people for seeking those "that have familiar spirits, and wizards that peep" (R. V. "chirp") and mutter; while in 47:12, 13, the magic of Babylon is characterized by the prominence given to astrology. Micah (3:5-7) refers to the prevalence of divination among those who were such pretended prophets as the opponents of Jeremiah, not avowed prophets of idols as Ahab's seem to have been.

Jeremiah was constantly opposed by false prophets, who pretended to speak in the name of the Lord, saying that they had dreamt, when they told false visions, and who practiced various magical arts (Jer. 14:14; 23:25, sq.; 27:9, 10).

From Ezekiel (8:7-12) we learn that fetishism was among the idolatries which the Hebrews, in the latest days of the kingdom of Judah, had adopted from their neighbors. The passage (13:18) is thought by some to refer to the making of amulets; while others believe that it is figurative of hiding the truth. See Kerchief.

Daniel, when taken captive, was instructed in the learning of the Chaldeans, and placed among the wise men of Babylon (2:18), by whom we are to understand the magi, for the term is used as including magicians, sorcerers, enchanters, astrologers, and Chaldeans, the last being apparently the most important class (2:2, 4, sq.; comp. 1:20). As in other cases the true prophet was put to the test with the magicians, and he succeeded where they utterly failed.

After the captivity it is probable that the Jews gradually abandoned the practice of magic. Zechariah speaks indeed of the deceit of teraphim and diviners (10:2), and foretells a time when the very names of idols should be forgotten and false prophets have virtually ceased (13:1-4), yet in neither case does it seem certain that he is alluding to the usages of his own day. In the Apocrypha we find indications that in the later centuries preceding the Christian era magic was no longer practiced by educated Jews.

In the New Testament we read very little of magic. Philip the deacon found in Samaria Simon, a famous magician, known as Simon Magus (q. v.), who, while having great power with the people, is not said to have been able to work wonders. At Paphos, Elymas, a Jewish sorcerer and false prophet, was struck blind for a time at the word of Paul (Acts 13:6-12); while at Ephesus, certain Jewish exorcists, signally failing in their endeavor to cast out demons, abandoned their practice of the magical arts. We have also the remarkable case of Paul casting out the "spirit of divination" from a damsel who "brought her masters much gain by foretelling" (Acts 16:16-18). "Our examination of the various notices of magic in the Bible gives us this general result: They do not, as far as we can understand, once state positively that any but illusive results were produced by magical rites. They therefore afford no evidence that man can gain supernatural powers to use at his will."

4. **Magic Forbidden.** The law contains very distinct prohibitions of all magical arts. Besides several passages condemning them, in one place there is a specification which is so full that it seems evident that its object is to include every kind of magical art. The Israelites are commanded in the place referred to not to learn the abominations of the peoples of the promised land. Then follows this prohibition: "There shall not be found among you anyone that maketh his son or his daughter to pass through the fire, or that uses divination, or an observer of times, or an enchanter, or a witch, or a charmer, or a consulter with familiar spirits, or a wizard, or a necromancer" (Deut. 18:10, 11). It is added that these phenomena of demon-inspired paganism are

abominations, and that because of them the Canaanites were driven out from before the Israelites.

5. **Various Forms.** As stated in article *Divination* (*q. v.*), there were forms of ascertaining the divine will, and future events which were taken in good sense, and, therefore, not forbidden. Two other classes of divination are mentioned in Scripture—those forbidden and those without special sanction or reprobation. We group these together for greater convenience in the study of the subject:

(1) **Astrologers**, called by the Hebrews "dividers of the heavens." They are mentioned with "stargazers" (Isa. 47:13). They apparently "cut up the heavens" into certain sections in order to trace the course of them, making an effort to foretell the future. They were a part of the court of Nebuchadnezzar II (Dan. 1:20) and were characteristic of ancient courts such as that of Babylon and Chaldea. Astrology was widely practiced among heathen nations, but was accounted illegitimate among the Hebrews, being considered inconsistent with the worship of Jehovah and classified, (as in Isa. 47:12, 13), with occultism and demon-inspired paganism. The Hebrew and Aramaic words translated "astrologers" (Dan. 1:20; 2:27; 4:7, 5:7) are all translated in the R. V. "enchanters."

(2) **Belomancy**, or divination by arrows. It is said of the king of Babylon, "he made his arrows bright" (Ezek. 21:21), (R. S. V.—"he shakes the arrows") more strictly, the quiver with the arrows. On this practice itself Jerome writes: "He consults the oracle according to the custom of his nation, putting his arrows into a quiver, and mixing them together, with the names of individuals inscribed or stamped upon them, to see whose arrow will come out, and which state shall be first attacked." In this case Jerusalem was the ill-fated object of this divination, as we learn from the next verse, "At his right hand was the divination for Jerusalem." The arrow lot of the ancient Greeks was similar to this; also that of the ancient Arabs. Another kind of arrow lot was by shooting. Three suitors of an Eastern princess decided their claims by shooting each an arrow inscribed with his own name. The arrow taking the longest flight indicated the name of the successful competitor. This sort of divination is not to be confounded with the arrow shot by Jonathan, which was an understood sign; nor the shooting of the arrows by Joash, king of Israel, at the command of the prophet, in which we have a symbolical prophecy.

(3) **The Chaldeans.** Among others consulted by the king of Babylon respecting his dream were the Chaldeans. Among an Aramaic people the priests in a stricter sense were called Chaldeans, from the fact of the ancient supremacy of the Chaldean people in Babylonia. These Chaldeans sought their greatest glory in the study of astrology, and also possessed the knowledge of divination from omens, of expounding of dreams and prodigies, and of skilfully casting horoscopes (Keil, *Com.*, on Dan. 2:2).

(4) **Charm** (Heb. *lāḥăsh*, to *whisper*), a word used to express *serpent charming* (Psa. 58:5; Jer.

8:17; Eccles. 10:11). In the first of these passages *lāḥăsh* occurs in connection with the Hebrew word *ḥĕbĕr* meaning, a *confederacy*, (i. e., with the spirits of the other world), which is rendered in the same manner and has a similar meaning. It is certain that from time immemorial certain people of the East have exercised remarkable power over even the most poisonous of serpents (*see* Serpent Charmer). The "charmer" mentioned in Deut. 18:11 is one who pronounced a ban, probably referring to the custom of binding or banning by magical knots. Another reference to charmer is found in Isa. 19:3 (Heb. *hā'iṭṭîm, mutterers*), and is thought to refer to ventriloquists.

(5) **Divination, diviners.** Generally speaking, "divination differs from prophecy in that the one is a human device while the other is a divine gift—the one an unwarranted prying into the future by means of magical arts, superstitious incantations, or natural signs, arbitrarily interpreted; the other a partially disclosed insight into the future by the supernatural aid of Him who sees the end from the beginning" (*Imp. Dict.*, s. v.). In Scripture the diviners were *false* prophets, and divination was allied to witchcraft and idolatry (Deut. 18:10, 18; Josh. 13:22; Jer. 27:9, etc.), and energized by demon power (cf. I Cor. 10:20, 21).

(6) **Dreams, divination by.** The Hebrews, along with other Orientals, greatly regarded dreams, and applied for their interpretation to those who undertook to explain them. Such diviners were called *oneirocritics* and the art itself *oneiromancy*. Dreams were looked upon from the earliest antiquity as premonitions from their idol gods to future events. Opposed to this was the command of Jehovah forbidding his people from observing dreams and from consulting explainers of them. Those who pretended to have prophetic dreams and to foretell future events, even though what they foretold came to pass, if they had any tendency to promote idolatry, were put to death (Deut. 13:1-4). In opposition to the word of God no prophets were to be received, although they rained signs and wonders—not even an angel from heaven (Gal. 1:8).

(7) **Enchantment.** The practice of conjurors and exorcists in employing incantations or magic rigmaroles in enlisting the aid of evil spirits to effect some design or in purportedly setting free the demonized from their torments. Cf. Daniel 2:2, 10, R. V. It appears as the heathen counterpart of prayer. *See* Divination, Enchantment, Sorcery.

(8) **Exorcist** (Gr. *'exorkistēs, one who exacts an oath*), one who employs a formula of conjuration for expelling demons (Acts 19:13). The use of the term exorcists in this passage, as the designation of a well-known class of persons to which the individuals mentioned belonged, confirms what we know from other sources as to the common practice of exorcism among the Jews. Among all the references to exorcism, as practiced by the Jews, in the New Testament (Matt. 12:27; Mark 9:38; Luke 9:49, 50), we find only one instance which affords any clew to the means employed (Acts 19:13). In this passage it is said that "certain

of the vagabond Jews, exorcists, took upon them to call over" a demoniac "the name of the Lord Jesus, saying, We adjure you by Jesus whom Paul preacheth." *See* Demon, Exorcism.

(9) **Familiar spirits, consulter with.** *See* Necromancer, below, Familiar Spirit, Witch.

(10) **Idolomancy**, i. e., consulting with images, literally *teraphim*. These household gods of the Semitic nations are often mentioned in the Old Testament from the time of Laban (Gen. 31:19). They were wooden images (I Sam. 19:13) consulted as "idols," from which the excited worshippers fancied that they received oracular responses (Ezek. 21:21; Zech. 10:2).

(11) **Magician**, a general term including all those who worked wonders beyond the ordinary powers of man. See head of this article.

(12) **Necromancer** (Heb. *dōrēsh 'ēl hăm-mēthîm, one who inquires of the dead*), one who pretends to be able by incantations to call up the dead to consult them respecting things unknown to the living. A few, such as Cicero (*Tusc.*, i, 16, 37), scouted the idea, but the practice held its ground in pagan and even Christian lands until the present. The Eastern magi were especially famed for necromantic skill. The necromancer was supposed to be the possessor of a conjuring spirit, i. e., of a spirit with which the dead were conjured up, for the purpose of making inquiry concerning the future (*see* Lev. 19:31). Such a person was the so-called "witch" (really "spiritistic medium") of Endor, to whose incantations the shade of Samuel responded (*see* Saul). It is evident from her exclamation that she was surprised at this appearance, and that she was not really able to conjure up departed spirits or persons who had died. The familiar spirit (Heb. *'ōb*, a leather *bottle*), was supposed to be granted to the necromancer as a servant or attendant, and bound to him by the ties or obligations of witchcraft. To the spirits of the departed thus evoked the necromancer lent a low, soft, almost whispering voice (Isa. 8:19; comp. 19:3), as seemed natural for such shades. It is not certain that these mutterings and whisperings were produced by ventriloquism, although this may be the case, as ventriloquism was one of the arts of ancient jugglers. "In most parts of Greece necromancy was practiced by priests or consecrated persons in the temples: in Thessaly it was the profession of a distinct class of persons called Psychagogoi (evokers of spirits)." Necromancy was forbidden to the Israelites as a heathen superstition (Lev. 19:31), and they who disobeyed were threatened with death (Lev. 20:6; Deut. 8 11). Still it found its way among them, especially when idolaters occupied the throne (II Kings 21:6; II Chron. 33:6; Isa. 8:19, 29:4; comp. 19:3, where the Egyptian enchantments are mentioned).

(13) **Prognosticators** (Heb. *mōdī'îm lēhŏdä-shîm, making known as to the months*) are mentioned in Isa. 47:13, where the prophet is enumerating the astrological superstitions of the Chaldeans, who foretold the future by observing the phases of the moon. *See* Astrology.

(14) **Rabdomancy** (Gr. *hrabdos*, a *staff*, and *manteia, divination*), divination by rods. Cyril of Alexandria calls this an invention of the Chaldeans, and describes it as consisting in this, that two rods were held upright, and then allowed to fall while forms of incantation were being uttered; and the oracle was inferred by the way in which they fell, whether forward or backward, to the right or to the left. This custom is referred to in the passage, "And their staff declareth unto them" (Hos. 4:12), as an evidence of the tendency of Israel to idolatry.

(15) **Soothsayer, soothsaying.** The soothsayer (diviner) was the pagan counterpart of the prophet, prognosticating future events, or professing to do so (Josh. 13:22) by various arts. Actually diviners were energized by evil powers, as the prophet of the Lord was under the control of the Holy Spirit.

(16) **Sorcery** (Heb. from *kāshăf*, to *whisper*; Gr. *mageia*, Acts 8:11; *pharmakeia, medication*). A sorcerer was one who professed to tell the lot of others, to have power with evil spirits (Isa. 47:9, 12; Dan. 2:2), and was severely denounced (Mal. 3:5; Rev. 21:8; 22:15). This art was also practiced in connection with pharmacy, the mixing of drugs and medical compounds (Rev. 9:21; 18:23). *See* Sorcery.

(17) **Splanchnomancy**, divination by inspection of entrails, was practiced in Rome by the Etrurian soothsayers, and frequently referred to by Greek and Latin writers. Cicero (*De Divin.*, ii, 15) mentions the importance of the *liver* in divination of this kind. One example of this is contained in Scripture (Ezek. 21:21), where it is said that the king of Babylon "looked in the liver," when he came to the "parting of the way," to decide as to his future course. Liver-divination was especially widespread in Assyria-Babylonia and thousands of clay tablets dealing with omens and incantations have been dug up.

(18) **Stargazer** (Heb. *hōzēh, beholder*, and *kōkäb, star*), one who pretends to foretell what will happen by observing the stars (Isa. 47:13). *See* Astrology, above.

(19) **Witch, witchcraft**, generally the rendering of the same original words translated "sorcery," "sorcerer" (see above). In I Sam. 15:23 it is the rendering of the Heb. *qěsěm, lot*, and is the pretended divination in connection with the worship of idolatrous and demoniacal powers. *See* Witch.

(20) **Wizard** (Heb. *yĭdde'ōnî, a knowing* one), a term denoting a person pretending to be wise; but the term is usually employed as the masculine of witch. A wizard might employ any of the magical arts (Lev. 19:31; 20:27; I Sam. 28:3, 9), and the Israelites were forbidden to consult any such (Deut. 18:11). For further discussion see M. F. Unger, *Biblical Demonology* (1952), with full bibliography pp. 228-238.

Magistrate, the rendering in the A. V. of several Hebrew and Greek words, and referring to a public civil officer. Among the Hebrews, Greeks, and Romans the corresponding term had a much wider signification than the term magistrate with us.

1. "There was no magistrate in the land" (Judg. 18:7) would be better rendered "no

one who seized the government to himself," etc.

2. "Magistrates and judges" (Ezra 7:25) ought to be rendered "judges and rulers."

3. *Archōn, first,* rendered *magistrate* (Luke 12:58), signifies *one first in power.* Similar in derivation and meaning is Gr. *Archē* (Luke 12:11) *"magistrates";* Tit. 3:1, "principalities"). *Archōn* is used of the Messiah as "the prince of the kings of the earth" (Rev. 1:5), and of Moses as the judge and leader of the Israelites. It is spoken of magistrates of any kind, e. g., the high priest (Acts 23:5); of civil judges (Acts 16:19); a ruler of the synagogue (Matt. 9:18, 23; Mark 5:22; Luke 8:41); persons of influence among the sects at Jerusalem, who were also members of the Sanhedrin (Luke 14:1; 18:18; 23:13, 35; 24:20, etc.); of Satan, the *prince* of the fallen angels (Matt. 9:34; Mark 3:22; Luke 11:15; John 12:31; Eph. 2:2, etc.).

4. General (Gr. *stratēgos*), properly signifies the *leader of an army, commander;* but in the New Testament a *civic commander* (Acts 16:20, 22, 35, 36, 38; Tit. 3:1). In Roman colonies and municipal towns the chief magistrates were usually two in number (called *duumviri*). These had the power of administering justice in the less important cases. *See* Israel, Constitution of.

Ma′gog (mā′gŏg; *region of Gog*) is mentioned in Gen. 10:2; I Chron. 1:5, as the second son of Japhet, but understood by some to be the name of a people. Magog is associated with Gomer in Genesis, with Gog also in Ezekiel (38:2; 39:6). Gog is described by the prophet as belonging to "the land of Magog," the situation of which is defined by its proximity to "the isles" of the Aegean. It is clear that Lydia is meant, and that by Magog we must understand "the land of Gog." Scholars have sought to identify Gog with Gugu (Gyges), king of Lydia and with *Gagaia* of the Amarna Letters. *See* Gog.

Ma′gor-Mis′sabib (mā′gŏr-mĭs′á-bĭb; *terror round about*), the name given by Jeremiah to Pashur (*q. v.*), emblematical of his fate (Jer. 20:3-6).

Mag′piash (măg′pĭ-ăsh), one of the chief Israelites who joined the covenant made by Nehemiah (Neh. 10:20), B. C. 445.

Maha′lah (má-hā′lá; I Chron. 7:18). *See* Mahlah, No. 2.

Maha′laleel (má-hā′lá-lē′ĕl; *praise of God*). A. V. and R. S. V. Mahal′alel (má-hăl′á-lĕl).

1. The son of the patriarch Cainan, the grandson of Seth. Born when his father was seventy years of age, he himself became the father of Jared at the age of sixty-five, and died when he was eight hundred and ninety-five years old (Gen. 5:12-17; I Chron. 1:2; Luke 3:37), in which passage the name is Anglicized Maleleel.

2. An Israelite of the tribe of Judah and family of Perez (Pharez), and ancestor of Athaiah, who resided in Jerusalem after the captivity (Neh. 11:4), B. C. before 536.

Ma′halath (mā′há-lăth; *sickness*).

1. The daughter of Ishmael and third wife of Esau (Gen. 28:9; 36:3; in the latter passage called *Bashemath*).

2. The granddaughter of David, daughter

of Jerimoth, and wife of Rehoboam (II Chron. 11:18), B. C. 926.

3. Part of title of Psalms 53 and 88. *See* Musical Terms.

Ma′hali (mā′há-lī; Exod. 6:19). *See* Mahli.

Mahana′im (mâ-há-nā′ĭm; *double camp,* or *double host,* was so called because the host of God joined that of Jacob as a safeguard), a place beyond the Jordan, north of the brook Jabbok, where the angels of God appeared to Jacob (Gen. 32:1, 2). The name was afterward given to the town then existing, or afterward founded, in the neighborhood. It was on the boundary of Gad and Manasseh, as well as of Bashan (Josh. 13:26, 30), and was a city of the Levites (Josh. 21:38; I Chron. 6:80). Here Ishbosheth reigned and was assassinated (II Sam. 2:8, 12; 4:5-8). Many years after David repaired to Mahanaim, and was entertained by Barzillai (II Sam. 17:24, 27; I Kings 2:8). Near this appears to have been fought the battle between the forces of David and Absalom (II Sam., ch. 18). It was named as the station of one of the twelve officers who had charge, in monthly rotation, of the provisions for Solomon's establishment (I Kings 4:14). It has not been positively identified, but it may be that it is represented by a ruined site under the name of *Maneh,* 2½ miles N. of Ajlun.

Ma′haneh-Dan (mā′há-nĕ-dăn; *camp of Dan;* R. V. "Mahaneh-dan"), a place at which six hundred Danites once encamped before the capture of Laish (Judg. 18:11-13). It was "behind," i. e., west of Kirjathjearim; and was called "Dan after the name of their father" (18:29).

Mahar′ai (má-hăr′â-ī; *swift, hasty*), the Netophathite who was one of David's mighty men (II Sam. 23:28; I Chron. 11:30), and was appointed captain, for the tenth month, of a contingent of twenty-four thousand men (I Chron. 27:13), B. C. about 975.

Ma′hath (mā′hăth).

1. A Kohathite, son of Amasai and father of Elkanah, in the ancestry of Heman (I Chron. 6:35), B. C. before 1000.

2. Another Kohathite, who, with his brother Levites, took part in the restoration of the temple under Hezekiah (II Chron. 29:12), and was afterward appointed one of the overseers of the sacred offerings (31:13), B. C. c. 715.

Ma′havite (mā′há-vīt), apparently a patrial designation of Eliel, one of David's guard (I Chron. 11:46). As no place or person *Mahavah,* or *Mahavai,* is anywhere else alluded to from which the title could have been derived, a corruption in the text is supposed. Bertheau suggests that it should read, "he of Mahanaim."

Maha′zioth (má-hā′zĭ-ŏth; *visions*), one of the fourteen sons of Heman the Levite (I Chron. 25:4), and appointed by lot leader of the twenty-third division of temple musicians (v. 30), B. C. before 960.

Ma′her-Shal′al-Hash′-Baz (mā′hĕr-shăl′ăl-hăsh′băz; *spoil hastens, prey speeds*), are words which Isaiah was commanded to write upon a tablet, and afterward to give as a symbolical name to a son to be born to him (Isa. 8:1, 3).

Mah′lah (mä′là; *disease*).

1. The eldest of the five daughters of Zelophehad, of the tribe of Manasseh, who married among their kindred, and so kept their inheritance (Num. 26:33; 27:1; 36:11; Josh. 17:3).

2. Given in the A. V. Mahalah, as the name of a child, whether son or daughter is uncertain, of Hamoleketh, the sister of Gilead, a Manassite (I Chron. 7:18).

Mah′li (mä′lī; *weak, sickly*).

1. The eldest son of Merari and grandson of Levi (Exod. 6:19, A. V. *Mahali;* Num. 3:20; I Chron. 6:19; 23:21; 24:26; Ezra 8:18). He had three sons, named Libni (I Chron. 6:29), Eleazar, and Kish (23:21; 24:28), and his descendants were called *Mahlites* (Num. 3:33; 26:58).

2. A son of Mushi, a son of Merari, and therefore nephew of the preceding (I Chron. 23:23; 24:30). He had a son, Shamar (6:47), B. C. before 1440.

Mah′lite (mä′līt), a descendant of *Mahli* (*q. v.*), the son of Merari (Num. 3:33; 26:58).

Mah′lon (mä′lŏn; *sickly*), the elder of the two sons of Elimelech the Bethlehemite and Naomi. Having removed to Moab with their parents, Mahlon married Ruth the Moabitess, and died without issue (Ruth 1:2, 5; 4:9, 10), B. C. before 1070.

Ma′hol (mä′hŏl; a *dance*), a person who seems to have been the father of Heman, Chalcol, and Darda, men renowned for their wisdom before the time of Solomon (I Kings 4:31). If these are the same as those given (I Chron. 2:6) as the sons of Zerah, the word must be taken, as elsewhere, to denote simply their pursuit as musical composers, an art ever connected with dancing.

Maid, Maiden, the rendering of several Hebrew and Greek words, differing in meaning beyond the mere matter of sex:

1. *N*e*qēbäh* (Lev. 12:5 only, a *maid child*), a female from the sexual form. Similar in meaning is *nă′ărăh′* (II Kings 5:2, 4; Ezra 2:4, 9, 13; Prov. 9:23), corresponding to Gr. *paidiskē*, Mark 14:66; Luke 22:56), a *girl* from infancy to adolescence.

2. *Bēthūlāh′*, (Exod. 22:16; Judg. 19:24; Job 31:1; Psa. 78:63; Jer. 2:32; 51:22), a *virgin*, from the idea of *separation*. Similarly '*ăl*e*māh′ veiled, kept* out of *sight*, Exod. 2:8).

3. *'Amāh′* (Gen. 30:3; Exod. 21:20; Lev. 25:6, etc.); *shiphe*hāh′* (Gen. 30:7, sq.; Psa. 123:2; Isa. 24:2), a *maidservant*.

Mail, Coat of. *See* Armor.

Maimed (from Heb. *hărăs*, to *wound*, Lev. 22:22; Gr. *kullos*, rocking about, Matt. 15:30, 31; 18:8; Mark 9:43; *anapēros, crippled*, Luke 14:13, 21), deprived by violence of some necessary member. Such sacrifices were not allowed to be offered (*see* Lame, Sacrifices).

Mainsail. *See* Ship.

Ma′kaz (mä′kăz; *end, boundary*), one of the places in the district under the supervision of "the son of Dekar" (I Kings 4:9), one of Solomon's purveyors. Its situation is unknown.

Maker, a term usually applied to God as creator (Job 4:17; 36:3; Psa. 95:6; Prov. 22:2; Isa. 17:7, etc.; Hos. 8:14). It is used of *man* in Isa. 22:11 and Hab. 2:18. The expression "And the strong shall be as tow, and the *maker* of it as a spark" (Isa. 1:31), has a better reading in the margin and the R. V., "and his *work* as a spark." The meaning seems to be "that the fire of judgment need not come from without. Sin carries the fire of indignation within itself, and an idol is, as it were, an idolater's sin embodied and exposed to the light of day" (Delitzsch, *Com.*, in loc.).

Makhe′loth (măk-ē′lŏth; *assemblies*), the twenty-sixth station of Israel in the wilderness, between Haradah and Tahath (Num. 33:25, 26); present location unknown.

Makke′dah (măk-ē′dà; *herdsman's place*), a royal Canaanite city in the low country of Judah (Josh. 12:16), located near the place at which Joshua put to death five kings who had fought against Israel (Josh. 10:10-29). It was afterward assigned to Judah (15:41). George Smith identifies this place with *el-Mughâr*, "the caves," to the southwest of Ekron, yet admits it as doubtful.

Mak′tesh (măk′tĕsh; *mortar*), a peculiar mortar-shaped valley, generally supposed to have been the Tyropean Valley. Ewald thinks it to have been that part of the city of Jerusalem known as the Phoenician quarter (Zeph. 1:11).

Mal′achi (măl′à-kī; *messenger*), the last both of the minor prophets and Old Testament writers (Mal. 1:1). The circumstances of Malachi's life are unknown, only as they may be inferred by his prophecies. He seems to have been contemporary with Nehemiah, if we may judge from the agreement found between them in the reproof administered for the marriage of Gentile wives (comp. 2:11, sq., with Neh. 13:23, sq.) and negligent payment of tithes (Mal. 3:8-10 with Neh. 13:10-14), B. C. 432.

Malachi, Book of, the last of the O. T. books and the last of Minor Prophets.

1. **The Name.** Malachi (1:1) means *my messenger* in Hebrew. It is common in critical circles to deny that Malachi was an historical person, and to make the prophecy anonymous. It is claimed that Malachi is merely an appellative or symbolical expression suggesting the mission of the real author. The reference to "my messenger" in 3:1 is supposed later to have suggested the name. The Greek version renders 1:1 "by the hand of his messenger" but uses the title, Malachias. The Targum of Jonathan ben Uzziel assumes that by Malachi Ezra the scribe is referred to. It is better to take the name Malachi as an abbreviated form of *Malakiyah*, "the messenger of Jehovah." It is highly unreasonable to assume the anonymity of the book. None of the other major or minor prophets is anonymous. Nor is it necessary to suppose that 1:1 is connected with 3:1.

2. **Author and Date.** The book is obviously a unit, the work of one man. Practically nothing is known of the life of Malachi except what suggestions may be gleaned from the book itself. Certain evidence, however, enables one to fix upon the approximate date of the prophecy. A Persian governor was in authority in Jerusalem, and is called a *pehah* (1:8). The temple had been completed for some time and the religious ritual was for a long time practiced (1:7-10; 3:8). It is patent from these elements of internal evidence that the proph-

ecy is to be dated after Haggai and Zechariah. Religious zeal had waned and enough time had elapsed for abuses to become evident. Personal piety, especially of the priests, had degenerated (1:6-8), foreign marriages flourished (2:10-12) and paying tithes for temple support had fallen into neglect. The book is reminiscent of the era of Ezra-Nehemiah. A date around 455 B. C. or later would be probable.

3. **Unity and Authenticity.** Critics have been in general agreement as to the unity of the book. Editorial additions are taken to be inconsequential. Chapter 2:11, 12 is looked upon as being a later interpolation by Cornill and Marti. Chapter 4:4-6 (Heb. text 3:22-24) is sometimes construed to be an interpretation of 3:1 and, according to A. Bentzen, "probably a later commentary." But all of these critical contentions are pure conjecture. The N. T. fully attests the canonical and doctrinal authority of Malachi (cf. Mal. 4:5, 6 with Matt. 11:10, 14; 17:11, 12; Mark 9:10, 11; Luke 1:17; cf. Mal. 3:1 with Matt. 11:10 and Mark 1:2; Mal. 1:2, 3 with Rom. 9:13). (For a critical discussion see C. C. Torrey, "The Prophecy of Malachi," *Jour. Bibl. Lit.*, 1898, pp. 1-15; J. M. P. Smith, "The Book of Malachi" in *Int'l. Crit. Commentary*, 1912).

3. **Outline.**
Introductory Appeal—God's Love for Israel, 1:1-5
Part. I. Warning Against Priests' Sins, 1:6-2:9
   a. Their carelessness and their ritual functions, 1:6-2:4
   b. Their slovenly teaching, 2:5-9
Part II. Forewarning Against the People, 2:10-4:3
   a. 1st Warning: Against Treachery, 2-10:16
   b. 2nd Warning: Of Judgment, 2:17-3:6
   c. 3rd Warning: To Repent, 3:7-12
   d. 4th Warning: God's Condemnation, 3:13-4:3
Part III. Concluding Solemn Warning, 4:4-6
   a. To observe the Mosaic law, 4:4
   b. To have in mind the (Second) Coming of Christ, 4:5, 6
　　　　　　　　　　　　　　　　M. F. U.

Mal'cham (măl'kăm; *their king*).
1. A Benjamite, and fourth named of the seven sons of Shaharaim by his wife Hodesh (I Chron. 8:9).
2. A false god (Zeph. 1:5). *See* Gods, False.

Malchi'ah (măl-kī'á), or **Malchi'jah** (măl-kī'-jä; *Jehovah is King*).
1. A Gershonite Levite in the ancestry of Asaph (I Chron. 6:40).
2. A priest, the father of *Pashur* (I Chron. 9:13; Jer. 21:1; in other passages "Malchijah," Neh. 11:12; Jer. 38:1), B. C. before 589.
3. The head of the fifth division of the sons of Aaron as arranged by David (I Chron. 24:9, Malchijah), B. C. before 967.
4. An Israelite, formerly resident (or descendant) of Parosh, who put away his Gentile wife after the captivity (Ezra 10:25), B. C. 456.

5. Another Israelite of the same place (or parentage) who did the same (Ezra 10:25, "Malchijah"), B. C. 456.
6. A Jew of the family (or town) of Harim who divorced his Gentile wife (Ezra 10:31), B. C. 456. He also assisted in repairing the walls of Jerusalem (Neh. 3:11, A. V. "Malchijah"), B. C. 445.
7. The son of Rechab, the ruler of part of Bethhaccerem, who repaired the dung gate of Jerusalem under Nehemiah (Neh. 3:14), B. C. 445.
8. The "goldsmith's son" who assisted in repairing the walls of Jerusalem (Neh. 3:31), B. C. about 445.
9. One of those who stood by Ezra when he read the book of the law to the people (Neh. 8:4), B. C. about 445.
10. One of the priests who subscribed the sacred covenant with Nehemiah (Neh. 10:3, A. V. "Milchijah"), B. C. 445.
11. One of the priests appointed, probably as singers, to assist in celebrating the completion of the walls of Jerusalem (Neh. 12:42, A. V. "Malchijah"), B. C. 445.

Mal'chiel (măl'kĭ-ĕl; *God is my king*), the younger son of Beriah, the son of Asher (Gen. 46:17), B. C. about 2000. His descendants were called Malchielites (Num. 26:45), and he himself was the "father" (founder) of Birzavith (I Chron. 7:31).

Mal'chielite (măl'kĭ-ĕl-īt), a descendant of *Malchiel* (Num. 26:45).

Malchi'ram (măl-kī'răm; *exalted is the king*, (God), the second son of King Jeconiah (Jehoiachin), born to him during his captivity (I Chron. 3:18), B. C. after 597. *See* II Kings 24:12.

Malchi-shu'a (măl-kī-shōō'à; *the king*, i. e., God, is *salvation*), one of the four sons of Saul, probably by Ahinoam (I Sam. 14:49; I Chron. 8:33; 9:39). He was slain, with his father, at the battle of Gilboa (I Sam. 31:2; I Chron. 10:2), B. C. c. 1004.

Mal'chus (măl'kŭs; Gr. *malchos*, from Heb. *mĕlĕk, king*), the servant of the high priest whose ear was cut off by Peter at the arrest of Jesus in the garden of Gethsemane (John 18:10). Caiaphas is doubtless the high priest intended, for John, who was personally acquainted with him (John 18:15), is the only evangelist who gives the name of Malchus.

Male (Heb. *zäkär, remembered*). This term was applied to male children as being the more worthy sex. The estimation in which such were held is shown by numerous passages in the Scriptures.

Malefactor, the rendering of two Greek words *kakopoios*, "*evil-doers*," John 18:30; *evil-doers* in I Pet. 2:12, 14; 3:16; 4:15; and *kakourgos*, "*evil-workers*," Luke 23:32, sq.; *evildoer* in II Tim. 2:9). By the term malefactor is not meant, strictly speaking, thieves or robbers, but rebels or insurgents. The persons mentioned in the Gospels were, no doubt, men who had taken up arms on a principle of resistance to Roman oppression, and especially to the payment of tribute money. Though professedly opposed to the Romans only, yet, when engaged in their unlawful courses, it made less difference between Romans and Jews than they at first set out with doing.

Male'leel (mà-lē'lê-ĕl) (Luke 3:37). *See* Mahalaleel.

Malice (Gr. *kakia, badness,* I Cor. 5:8; 14:20; Eph. 4:31; Col. 3:9; Tit. 3:3; I Pet. 2:1; *maliciousness,* Rom. 1:29; I Pet. 2:16; *malicious,* from Gr. *ponēros, hurtful,* III John 10). Of these two Greek words the former denotes rather the vicious disposition, and the latter the active exercise of the same. Another kindred word is *malignity* (Gr. *kakoētheia, bad character,* only in Rom. 1:29), given by Paul in his long list of Gentile sins. Aristotle defines it as "taking all things in the evil part" (*Rhet.*, ii, 13); and the Geneva version of the Scriptures so renders it. It is "that peculiar form of evil which manifests itself in a malignant interpretation of the actions of others, an attributing of them all to the worst motive" (Trench, *Gr. Syn.*, xi).

Malignity (Gr. *kakoēthaia,* bad character, depravity of heart) used in Rom. 1:29 for *malignant-subtlety, malicious craftiness.*

Mal'lothi (măl'lō-thī), one of the sons of Heman (I Chron. 25:4), and appointed by David head of the nineteenth division of temple musicians (25:26), B. C. before 960.

Mallows. *See* Vegetable Kingdom.

Mal'luch (măl'ŭk; *reigning,* or *counselor*).

1. A Levite of the family of Merari, and an ancestor of Ethan the musician (I Chron. 6: 44).

2. One of the descendants (or residents) of Bani, who divorced his Gentile wife after the return to Jerusalem (Ezra 10:29), B. C. 456.

3. A Jew of the family of Harim who put away his Gentile wife after the captivity (Ezra 10:32), B. C. 456.

4. One of the priests who sealed the covenant made by Nehemiah and the people to serve Jehovah (Neh. 10:4), B. C. 445. The associated names would seem to indicate that he is the same as one of those who returned with Zerubbabel from Babylon (Neh. 12:2), B. C. 536.

5. One of the "chief of the people" who subscribed the covenant made by Nehemiah (Neh. 10:27), B. C. 445.

Mam'mon (măm'ŭn; Gr. from Aram. *māmōna, wealth*), a term signifying *riches* (Luke 16:9, 11), but personified and spoken of as opposed to God (Matt. 6:24; Luke 16:13). The expression "make to yourselves friends of the mammon of unrighteousness," etc., is interpreted as follows by Godet (*Com.*, Luke 16: 13): "Instead of hoarding up or enjoying, hasten to make for yourselves, with the goods of another (God's), personal friends, who shall then be bound to you by gratitude, and share with you their well-being." According to Meyer and Ewald the "friends" are the angels, but Godet prefers to understand them as "men who have been succored by one on earth."

Mam're (măm'rē).

1. The Amorite who, with his brothers Aner and Eschol, was a confederate of Abraham (Gen. 14:13, 24), B. C. about 2065.

2. The name of Abraham's dwelling place, near Hebron (Gen. 23:17, 19; 35:27, R. V. "the oaks of Mamre"—marg. "terebinths"). Here Abraham entertained three angels, and was promised a son (Gen. 18:1, 10, 14). The cave of Machpelah lay "before, probably to the east of the grove of Mamre" (Gen. 23:17, 19; 25:9; 49:30, 50:13).

Man, Men, the rendering of fourteen Hebrew and seven Greek words. In some cases *man* is used in the sense of an *individual* without respect to sex. Thus it is the rendering of the Gr. *mēdeis, not one,* Matt. 16:20; 17:9; Luke 10:4, etc.; of *oudeis, none, nobody,* Matt. 11:27; Mark 3:27; Luke 8:51, etc.; of *some one* or *any,* Matt. 24:4; John 3:5; Acts 10:47, etc.); and in an inclusive sense *all,* Rom. 2:10).

1. **Names.** Several words are used with as much precision as terms of like import in other languages. (1) *Adam* (Heb. *'ädäm,* perhaps "red earth," occurring also in Ugaritic and Arabic presents man of the earth, earthy, Gen. 1:26). (*a*) The proper name of the first man (Luke 3:38; Rom. 5:14; I Tim. 2:13, 14; Jude, v. 14); see also the remarkable use of it in I Cor. 15:45, "the first man Adam." (*b*) The generic name of the human race as originally created; and afterward, like our *man,* person whether man or woman (Gen. 1:26, 27; 5:1; Deut. 8:3). (*c*) Man in opposition to woman (Gen. 3:12). (*d*) Very rarely for those who maintain the dignity of human nature (Eccles. 7:28), i. e., who manifest true uprightness. (*e*) The more degenerate and wicked portion of mankind (Gen. 6:2). (*f*) *Other* men, as distinguished from those named; as "both upon Israel and other men" (Jer. 32:30); men of inferior rank as opposed to those of higher rank (Isa. 2:9; 5:15; Psa. 62: 9). (2) *Man, as distinguished from a woman* (Heb. *'îsh,* Gr. *anēr*), presents him with immaterial and personal existence (I Sam. 21:4; Matt. 14:21); as a *husband* (Gen. 3:16; Hos. 2:16, marg.); and in reference to excellent mental qualities (Jer. 5:1, "Run ye to and fro through the streets of Jerusalem . . . and seek . . . if ye can find a *man*," etc.). (3) *Enosh* (Heb. *'ĕnōsh, mortal*), also occurring in Ugaritic describes man as transient, liable to sickness, etc., "Let not man (marg. 'mortal man') prevail against thee" (II Chron. 14:11). "To 'write with a man's pen' (Isa. 8:1) means to write in the vulgar, i. e., popular characters, that could be easily read" (Delitzsch, *Com.*, in loc.). (4) *Gever* (Heb. *gever*), connects man with human strength. It is applied to man, as distinguished from woman, e. g., "A man shall not put on a woman's garment" (Deut. 22:5); as distinguished from children (Exod. 12:37); to a male child in opposition to a female (Job 3:3), the birth of a male child being a matter of joy in the East, rather than that of a female. It is much used in poetry (Job 14:10; 22:2; Psa. 34:8; 40:4; Prov. 6:34, etc.). (5) *Methim* (Heb. *m^ethîm, men,* males). The singular is to be traced in the antediluvian proper names, Methusael and Methuselah. Perhaps it may be derived from the root *mûth,* "to die," in which case its use would be very appropriate in Isa. 41:14. If this conjecture be admitted, this word would correspond to *brotos,* and might be read "mortal." Other Hebrew words rendered *man* are *zäkär, remembered* (Lev. 12:2), as representing the sex worthy of distinction; *něphěsh,* a *breathing* creature (II Kings 12:4), an animate being; *bä'äl, master* or *husband*

(Prov. 22:24; 23:2; 29:22); *gŭlgōlĕth, skull* (Exod. 16:16), answering to our *poll*. The Greek words properly rendered *man* are: *Anthrōpos, man-faced,* and so a *human* being, and *'anēr,* a *male,* as distinguished from a woman.

It is noteworthy that the title Son of man, which Christ applied to himself, refers to man in this broadest and most comprehensive sense, and thus expresses the relationship he bears to every human being. For fuller presentation of terms and their force see Young's *Concordance,* also lexicons of Gesenius, Liddell and Scott, etc., etc. It is to be borne in mind, however, that while the precise force of these terms must be understood for accurate interpretation, the Bible doctrine concerning man is so presented that its most general and important features may be otherwise easily discovered.

2. **Origin.** Man is the most excellent of God's creatures upon earth. He came into existence not through the operation of natural causes, but by a distinct act of creation. He bore originally, and in an important sense still bears, the image and likeness of God. While with respect to his bodily organism he belongs to the animal world, he possesses a spiritual nature which gives him a most exalted rank above all animals. He alone of all creatures upon earth is truly a rational and moral and religious being, and is capable of communion with God. He alone is represented as sinful, yet the object of redemption. Before him is the certainty of future judgment and an immortal destiny (see Gen. 1:26-28; 9:6; Exod. 4:11; Job 35:10; Psa. 8:4-8; 94:9; Matt. 6:29-33; 12:12; 25:31-46; Rom. 5:12-21, and many other places). *See* Creation; Image of God; Immortality; Atonement; Judgment.

3. **Unity.** Man's original unity, or that the whole of mankind has descended from one human pair, is one of the obvious teachings of Scripture (see Gen. 1:27; 2:21-25; Matt. 19:4; Acts 17:26; Rom. 5:12; I Cor. 15:21, 47-49). While denied by certain natural philosophers, this doctrine is generally accepted not only by orthodox theologians, but by such distinguished scientists as Buffon, Linnaeus, Blumenbach, A. Von Humboldt, and many others. This doctrine is of religious and ethical importance inasmuch as it is related to man's noble origin, the reality of human brotherhood, the universality of sin and of redemption.

4. **Antiquity.** With respect to the antiquity of man, the Scripture chronology appears to date his origin to at least 6,000 years, probably, several thousand years earlier, since the geneologies of Genesis chapters 5 and 11 cannot legitimately be used for chronological purposes (*See* Genealogies, Genesis, Book of). To what extent our understanding of the Scriptures at this point is beset with difficulties, and how such difficulties should be treated, it is not practicable here to consider. It is to be noted, nevertheless, that natural science agrees with the Scriptures in regarding man as the most recent in origin of all creatures dwelling upon the earth.

Literature.—Van Oosterzee, *Christ. Dogm.,* vol. i, p. 359, sq.; Dorner, *Syst. Christ. Doct.,*

ii, 66-68, 92-95, 107, 219, 221; Hodge, *Syst. Theol.,* vol. ii, 2-130; J. Laidlaw, *The Bible Doctrine of Man;* Oehler, *Theologie der Alt. Test.,* 219, sq.; 225, sq.; the Duke of Argyll, *Primeval Man.*

The Man of Sin, (Gr. *ho anthrōpos tēs hamartias,* II Thess. 2:3). This is the devil-indwelt "man of lawlessness . . . the son of perdition" who "opposes and exalts himself against every so-called god or object of worship, so that he takes his seat in the temple of God (at Jerusalem), proclaiming himself to be God" (II Thess. 2: 3, 4, R. S. V.). Power will be "given him over all kindreds and tongues and nations" (Rev. 13:8). A world-wide reign of terror, blasphemy and murder will be inaugurated by him. "He shall speak words against the Most High and think to change times and laws" (Dan. 7:25). It will be his supreme attempt to be "like the Most High" (Isa. 14:14). "He shall stand up against the Prince (Christ)" (Dan. 8:25). His brief but horrible career will be brought to an end by the Second Coming of Christ (Rev. 19:11-17). He is the anti-Christ, the First Beast of Rev. 13:1-10. (J. A. Seiss, *The Apocalypse* II, pp. 388-412; Clarence Larkin, *The Book of Revelation,* pp. 103-126; *Dispensational Truth,* 115-123). Prophetic teaching has been thrown into considerable confusion by identifying the Second Beast of Rev. 13:11-18 with the anti-Christ. (W. Scott, *Exposition of Revelation,* p. 280; W. Kelly, *The Revelation Expounded,* pp. 159-164; A. C. Gabelein, *Annotated Bible* iv, pp. 242-243; C. I. Scofield, *Reference Bible,* p. 1342). But the First Beast and not the second is the anti-Christ of Scripture. This is well demonstrated by W. R. Newell (*The Book of Revelation,* pp. 195-201). Satan indwells this monstrous person and through him will strike his final furious blows at the Jewish remnant of the last days, who will be proclaiming "the Gospel of the Kingdom" (Matt. 24:14), and at the Gentiles, who will believe the good news of the imminent setting up of the millennial kingdom. As a man of lawlessness, the anti-Christ will be the consummation of human opposition to God's will and God's rule. *M. F. U.*

Man, Son of, (Gr. *ho huios tou anthrōpou*). This title, evidently taken from Dan. 7:13, where everlasting dominion is ascribed to Messiah, was assumed by Christ and occurs 61 times in the gospels only of Him. It is found once in the Acts (7:56), where Stephen sees heaven open and Christ, whom he calls "the Son of Man," standing at the right hand of God. In the light of the corresponding term, "the Son of God," which stresses Christ's Deity, the the term "Son of Man" emphasizes His Divine humanity. Whereas the Gospel of John presents Christ as the Son of God, the Gospel of Luke presents him as the Son of Man. The term "Son of Man" is Christ's racial name as a representative man (I Cor. 15:45-47). The term "Son of David" delineates His kingly Jewish name, as "Son of God," denotes His Divine Name. This term "Son of Man" was widely used by our Lord to demonstrate that His mission (Matt. 11:19; Luke 19:10), His death and glorious resurrection (Matt. 12:40; 20:18; 26:2) and His Second Coming in power (Matt. 24:37-44; Luke 12:40) went far beyond all mere Jewish limitations. Nathaniel in confessing Him as "King of Israel" receives the reply "Thou shalt see greater things . . . the angels of God ascending and descending upon the Son of Man" (John 1:50, 51). Under the name Son of Man, universal judgment is given to Christ (John 5:22-27). Under this designation is fulfilled in Christ the O. T. prophecies of blessing through the Seed of the woman and the coming God-Man (Gen. 1:26; 3:15; 12:3; Psa. 8:4; 80:17; Isa. 7:14; 9:6, 7; Zech. 13:7). The term "Son of Man" is used by the Lord 91 times in addressing Ezekiel the prophet. As a term in the case of our Lord, denoting His racial name, as a representative man, it implies transcendance, not mere blessing to the Jews. Somewhat of the same thought is involved in the use of the term referred to in Ezekiel. In Ezekiel's day Israel had forsaken her divine mission (Gen. 11:10; Ezek. 5:5-8). Although in exile, Jehovah will not forsake His people. On the other hand, he would have them to remember that they are but a small part of the entire race about whom He is concerned. There is therefore natural emphasis upon the word "man," as the cherubim which Ezekiel saw in his vision "had the likeness of a man," and when the prophet glimpsed the throne of God he saw "the likeness as the appearance of *a man* above upon it" (Ezek. 1:26). *M. F. U.*

Man'aen (măn'á-ĕn; Gr. form of Menahem), a Christian prophet or teacher who had been an associate *suntrophos* ("one brought up with") of Herod the tetrarch in his youth, and was one who assisted at Antioch in ordaining Paul and Barnabas (Acts 13:1).

Man'ahath (măn'á-hăth; *resting place*), the second of the five sons of Shobal, the son of Seir the Horite (Gen. 36:23; I Chron. 1:40), B. C. about 1850.

Mana'hethites (má-nā'hĕth-īts), A. V. marg. "Menuchoth," R. V. "Menuhoth;" I Chron. 2:54, R. V. "Manahathites," a term usually taken to mean inhabitants of Manahath, which is commonly identified with a town of that name in Judah. But in I Chron. 8:6, where only Manahath is mentioned, it is in connection with Benjamite genealogies. The expression "they removed them," however, may imply a removal beyond the circle of Benjamite towns; comp. v. 8, where the land of Moab is mentioned. The tribal lines were not always sharply drawn in the early ages, as we have seen under *Machirites*. And the hostility between Judah and Benjamin, included the other tribes as well as Judah, and must have been largely ignored from simple necessity, since Benjamin could not live alone and intermarriages with other tribes must have been frequent for a time. We incline, therefore, to the ordinary view, which is favored by Gesenius (*Heb. Lex.*, 12th edition). But the difference in the Hebrew printing is hard to explain, and some identify the town with the *Měnūhäh* of Judg. 20:43 (A. V. "with ease;" R. V. "at their resting place," marg. "at Menuhah"). It may be that I Chron. 2:52 and 54 refer to entirely different persons. In Gen. 36:23; I Chron. 1:40, Manahath is son of Shobal, son of Seir. The Manahathites in both verses are among the posterity of Caleb,

and this is interesting in connection with the possible Edomite descent of Caleb noticed under "Kenezite."—*W. H.* revised by *M. F. U.*

Manas'seh (má-năs'ĕ; *causing to forget*).

1. **The Patriarch.** The elder son of Joseph and his Egyptian wife Asenath (Gen. 41:51; 46:20), B. C. about 1860. Manasseh and his brother were both adopted by Jacob upon his deathbed, who however gave the first place and the birthright blessing to Ephraim (48:1, sq.). Nothing is known of Manasseh's personal history. His wife's name is not mentioned, nor is it certain that he had one. Machir, the son of an Aramitess concubine (I Chron. 7:14), was probably his only son and sole founder of his house. *See* Manassites.

2. Given in Judg. 18:30, as the father of Gershom, whose son Jonathan acted as priest to the Danites when they set up a graven image. It is generally thought that the reading is suspicious, and that it should be rendered "Moses," as in the Vulgate and many copies of the Septuagint.

3. **The Fourteenth King of Judah.** Manasseh was the son of King Hezekiah by his wife Hephzi-bah, and was born B. C. about 702, twelve years before his father's death (II Kings 21:2; II Chron. 33:1). Of Manasseh very few facts are given, although his was the longest reign in the annals of Judah. (1) **Sin.** Ascending the throne at the early age of twelve years, he yielded to the influence of the idolatrous or Ahaz party, and became in time a determined and even fanatical idolater; and as he grew up took delight in introducing into his kingdom the superstitions of every heathen country. The high places were restored, the groves replanted, the altars of Baal and Astarte rebuilt, and the sun, moon, and all the host of heaven were worshipped. The gods of Ammon, of Moab, and of Edom were zealously worshipped everywhere. Babylonian and Egyptian paganism was rife; incense and offerings rose on the roofs of the houses to the fabled deities of the heights; wizards practiced their enchantments, . . . and the valley of Hinnom was once more disgraced by the hideous statue of Moloch, to whom parents offered up their children as burnt sacrifices. In the very temple of the Lord stood an image of Astarte; and in the entrance of the court were placed white horses harnessed to a splendid chariot sacred to the sun. This apostasy did not go unrebuked by the prophets, whom the king endeavored to silence by the fiercest persecution recorded in the annals of Israel (II Kings 21:16; 24:3, sq.). Fuller particulars are preserved by Josephus, who says that executions took place every day (*Ant.*, x, 3, § 1). According to rabbinical tradition Isaiah was sawn asunder by order of Manasseh, and after his death the prophetic voice was no more heard till the reign of Josiah. (2) **Retribution.** The crimes of Manasseh were not long left unavenged. The Philistines, Moabites, and Ammonites, who had been tributary to Hezekiah, seem to have revolted during Manasseh's reign (Zeph. 2:4-9; Jer. chaps. 47-49). But the great blow was inflicted by Assyria, from whence an army came to Judea, and taking Manasseh prisoner,

conveyed him to Babylon (II Chron. 33:11). (3) **Archaeology.** In the Assyrian inscriptions of Esarhaddon there is a direct reference to Manasseh which illuminates the account of the wicked king's being carried away to Babylon, his repentance and subsequent restoration to the throne. According to II Chron. 33:10-13, Jehovah brought upon the idolatrous Manasseh and his people "the captain of the host of the king of Assyria, who took Manasseh with hooks and bound him with fetters and carried him to Babylon." There is no direct confirmation of this notation of the Chronicler in Assyrian literature, but Esarhaddon's inscriptions do relate the forced visit of Manasseh to the great Assyrian capital of Nineveh about the year 678 B. C. "At that time the older palace of Nineveh which the kings who went before, my fathers, had built . . . had come to seem too small to me, and the people of the lands my arms had despoiled I made to carry the basket and the hod . . . that small palace I tore down in its totality . . . and I commanded the kings of Syria and those across the sea—Baalu, king of Tyre; Manasseh, king of Judah; Kaushgabri, king of Edom; Mussurri, king of Moab . . . Milkiashapa, king of Gabail (Byblos), etc., etc. . . . twenty kings in all. I gave them their orders." (D. D. Luckenbill, *Ancient Records of Syria and Babylonia* ii, Sect. 690). It had been commonly supposed by critics that Manasseh's captivity in Babylon was a mistake for Nineveh. Assyrian cuneiform tablets, however, prove that Esarhaddon did in fact reconstruct the ancient city destroyed by his father Sennacherib. "At the beginning of my rule in the first year of my reign when I took my seat upon the royal throne in might there appeared favorable signs in the heaven and on earth. . . . Through the soothsayers' rites encouraging oracles were disclosed and for the rebuilding of Babylon and the restoration of Esagila (temple of the gods) they caused the command to be written down" (Luckenbill, Sect. 646). Esarhaddon gives the following description of his building of Babylon: "I summoned all my artisans and the people of Babylonia in their totality. I made them carry the basket and laid the head pad upon them. Babylon I built anew, I enlarged, I raised aloft, I made magnificent" (Sect. 647). It is very enlightening that with such a trophy of his reign that Esarhaddon would have allowed Manasseh and the more than a score of kings whom he compelled to come to Nineveh to return to their countries without seeing this evidence of his splendor. Moreover, on the Senjirli Stele of Esarhaddon Baalu, king of Tyre, appears lifting manacled hands in supplication to Esarhaddon, and beside him Tirhakah, king of Ethiopia, is shown with a hook through his lips and fastened by a rope to Esarhaddon's hand. (*See* S. Caiger, *Bible and Spade*, 1947, p. 164; cf. p. 163, Fig. 22). (4) **Reformation.** Manasseh was brought to repentance, and "humbled himself greatly before the God of his fathers." God heard his prayer, and restored him to his kingdom at Jerusalem. His captivity is supposed to have lasted about a year, and after his return Manasseh took measures to secure his kingdom, and especially the capital,

against hostile attacks. He removed the idols and the statues from the house of the Lord, and caused the idolatrous altars which he had built upon the temple hill and in Jerusalem to be cast forth from the city. He repaired the altar of Jehovah, and called upon the people to serve the Lord God of Israel. But the people still sacrificed on the high places, "yet unto the Lord their God only." The next Scripture mention of Manasseh is his death and burial in the garden of Uzzah (II Kings 21:18, 26; II Chron. 33:20), B. C. 641.

4. A descendant (or resident) of Pahath-moab, who put away his Gentile wife after the captivity (Ezra. 10:30), B. C. 456.

5. An Israelite of the family of Hashum, who did the same (Ezra 10:33), B. C. 456.

Manas'ses (mà-năs'ĕz; Gr. form of *Manasseh*).

1. The king of Judah (Matt. 1:10).

2. The son of Joseph (Rev. 7:6, in some editions).

Manas'sites (mà-năs'īts), descendants of Manasseh, the elder son of Joseph. The relation between Manasseh and Ephraim seems to have been a little like that between Jacob and Esau, the younger brother having priority o influence, while the elder retained the birthright of material prosperity. The great national leader, Joshua, was an Ephraimite. The territory of Ephraim was rich and well situated for traffic and communication, and, besides Joshua's inheritance, it contained Ebal, Gerizim, Shiloh, Shechem, and Samaria. Samuel, though a Levite, was a native of Ramah in Mount Ephraim, and Saul belonged to a tribe closely allied to the family of Joseph (*see* Machirites); so that during the priesthood of the former and the reign of the latter the supremacy of Ephraim may be said to have been practically maintained. And after the division of the kingdom Ephraim formed the essential part of the northern kingdom.

Manasseh's population was also great. In the first census at Sinai, Manasseh numbered 32,200 (Num. 1:10, 35; 2:20, 21; 7:54-59) and Ephraim 40,500. But fifty years later (Num. 26:34, 37) Manasseh takes its place in the catalogue as the eldest, and numbers 52,700 to Ephraim's 32,500. When David was crowned at Hebron, while Ephraim sent 20,800 men, western Manasseh alone sent 18,000, and eastern Manasseh with Reuben and Gad sent 120,000, "with all manner of instruments of war for the battle," out of a total muster of 336,000 for the whole country (I Chron. 12:23-28).

The tribe of Manasseh was divided, probably on account of difference of habit and occupation. One section was devoted to the pursuits of husbandry; they sought a quiet, peaceful region, with rich soil and genial clime, and they found these in the fertile vales and plains of central Palestine. Another, and apparently much larger, section was pastoral in its tendencies. It was also warlike—trained to arms and inured to fatigue. *Manasseh east*—The descendants of Machir, son of Manasseh, invaded northern Gilead and Bashan, ruled by King Og, drove out the Amorites, and occupied the whole kingdom (Num. 32:29-42;

Deut. 3:13-15). *Manasseh west*—This territory was small and not fully defined in the Bible. It lay on the north side of Ephraim, and included the northern section of the hills of Samaria, a region of great beauty and fertility.

The children of Manasseh, Machir (Josh. 17:1), Jair (Deut. 3:14), and probably Nobah (Num. 32:42), were mighty men of war, of whom it is nowhere hinted that they were unable to drive out the inhabitants of any land which they chose to attack. "The district which these ancient warriors, east of Jordan, conquered was among the most difficult, if not the most difficult, in the whole country. It embraced the hills of Gilead with their inaccessible heights and impassable ravines, and the almost impregnable tract of Argob, which derives its modern name of *Lejeah* from the secure 'asylum' it affords to those who have taken 'refuge' within its natural fortifications" (Smith, *Bib. Dict.*, s. v. "Manasseh").

In general it was Ephraim which mingled in public affairs; yet of fifteen judges Manasseh furnished four, Gideon, Abimelech, Jair, and Jephthah. Gideon has been thought the greatest of the judges; and he might have been a king and the founder of a dynasty if he had been willing (Judg. 8:8). But, being detached from the great body of Israel, they probably spread themselves like desert nomads over the wide regions whence they had expelled the Hagarites (I Chron. 5:19). Thus they fell into idolatry (v. 25). Whether their fall was more rapid or deeper than that of western Israel does not appear, for perhaps their exposed position might explain the fact that they were carried away in the first captivity (v. 26). The notices of Manasseh in the reforms of Asa (II Chron. 15:9), Hezekiah (30:1, 10, 11, 18; 31:1), and Josiah (34:6, 9) leave rather a favorable impression, but they seem to refer to west Manasseh only.—*W. H.*

Mandrake. *See* Vegetable Kingdom.

Ma'neh (mä'nĕ), the rendering in Ezek. 45:12 of the Heb. *mänĕh*, elsewhere translated "pound." *See* Metrology, IV.

Manger (Gr. *phatnē, crib*, Luke 2:7, 12; 13:15, "stall"). The Greek word means both stall and manger, from which cattle were fed. Probably it here refers to that portion of the inn which was used as a stable. In the East the cattle were shut up in an open yard inclosed by a rough fence of stones or other material. Poor travelers, or those excluded from the house through want of room, would share with their animals these humble quarters. Several of the Christian fathers assert that the stable itself was a cave. The identical manger in which the infant Jesus is traditionally stated to have lain is still shown; but probably it is only a superstition, resulting on the one hand from the common custom in the East of using caves for stables, and on the other from a mistaken application to the Messiah of Isa. 33:16, "He shall dwell in a lofty cave," quoted by Justin (Godet, *Com.*, on Luke).

Manna (Heb. *män, what?* Gr. *manna*), the name given by the Israelites to the miraculous food furnished them during their wanderings in the desert. When they saw it lying on the ground "they said one to another, what is it? for they knew not what it was" (Exod. 16:15).

The most important passages in the Old Testament on this topic are the following: Exod. 16:14-36; Num. 11:7-9; Deut. 8:3, 16; Josh. 5:12; Psa. 78:24, 25; Wisd. 16:20, 21. From these passages we learn that the manna came every morning, except the Sabbath, in the form of a small round seed resembling the hoar frost; that it must be gathered early, before the sun became so hot as to melt it; that it must be gathered every day, except the Sabbath; that the attempt to lay aside for a succeeding day, except on the day immediately preceding the Sabbath, failed by the substance becoming wormy and offensive; that it was prepared for food by grinding and baking; that its taste was like fresh oil, and like wafers made with honey, equally agreeable to all palates; that the whole nation subsisted upon it for forty years; that it suddenly ceased when they first got the new corn of the land of Canaan; and that it was always regarded as a miraculous gift directly from God, and not a product of nature.

The author of the Epistle to the Hebrews (9:4) includes a "golden pot that had manna" among the contents of the ark of the covenant for a memorial. It was a constant tradition of the Jews that the ark, the tables of stone, Aaron's rod, the holy anointing oil, and the pot of manna were hidden by Josiah when Jerusalem was taken by the Chaldeans; and that these shall be restored in the days of the Messiah. *See* Vegetable Kingdom.

Typical, Manna is often considered to be a type of Christ as "the bread of life," Who came down from heaven to die "for the life of the world" (John 6:35, 48-51). Christ is "the bread of life," upon whom a Christian feeds when he meditates upon Him (John 6:38-40; I Cor. 5:7, 8).

Figurative. Manna is the emblem or symbol of immortality; "I will give him to eat of the hidden manna" (Rev. 2:17; comp. John 6:3, sq.).

Mano'ah (má-nō'á; *rest, quiet*), the father of Samson, a Danite of Zorah. When his wife told him of the announcement that a son should be born to them, Manoah prayed to the Lord that he would send the messenger again to teach them how they should treat him. This prayer was granted; but when he knew that it was God's angel, Manoah feared that he and his wife would die, because they had "seen God." But his wife quieted his fears, assuring him of God's pleasure by his acceptance of their sacrifice (Judg. 13:2-23), B. C. before 1070. We hear of Manoah once again in connection with the marriage of Samson, when both parents remonstrated with their son on his choice of a wife, but to no purpose (14:2, 3). They accompanied him to Timnath, both at the bethrothal and the wedding (v. 5, 10), but are not named later. The probability is that Manoah did not survive Samson, who was buried "between Zorah and Eshtaol in the burying place of Manoah."

Manservant. *See* Service.

Manslayer, one who by accident strikes another so as to kill (Num. 35:6, 12; I Tim. 1:9). The cases of manslaughter mentioned appear to be a sufficient sample of the intention of the lawgiver: (1) Death by a blow in a sudden quarrel (Num. 35:22). (2) Death by a stone or missile thrown at random (vers. 22, 23). (3) By the blade of an ax flying from its handle (Deut. 19:5). (4) Whether the case of a person killed by falling from a roof unprovided with a parapet involved the guilt of manslaughter on the owner is not clear, but the law seems intended to prevent the imputation of malice in any such case by preventing as far as possible the occurrence of the fact itself (22:8). In all these and the like cases the manslayer was allowed to retire to a city of refuge (*q. v.*). Besides these the following may be mentioned as cases of homicide: (1) An animal not known to be vicious causing death to a human being was to be put to death and regarded as unclean. But if it was known to be vicious the owner also was liable to fine, or even death (Exod. 21:28, 31). (2) A thief overtaken at night in the act might lawfully be put to death, but if the sun had risen the act of killing him was to be regarded as murder (22:2, 3). *See* Murder.

Mantle. *See* Dress.

Manuscripts, Dead Sea. The remarkable manuscript finds from the Dead Sea area since 1947 have yielded a corpus of Biblical and intertestamental material of great historical and philological importance, which the most optimistic specialist could scarcely have imagined or dared hope for a decade ago. Today, as a result of a series of notable archaeological triumphs, scholars are in possession of a whole new body of material that is being scanned diligently and studied minutely and which is centering archaeological interest on Palestine as once it was centered on inscription-rich sites such as Boghaz-keui in Asia Minor in 1906; Nuzu (Yorgan Tepa, near Kirkuk), 1927-1931; Ras Shamra (Ugarit) in Syria, 1929-1937 and Mari (Tell el Hariri on the Middle Euphrates), 1933-1936.

1. **Evaluation of the Manuscripts.** Since W. F. Albright called the original discovery of the Dead Sea Scrolls in 1947 "the greatest manuscript discovery of modern times," (W. F. Albright, *Bib. Arch.*, xi, 3, Sept., 1948, p. 55), sentiment has not changed, but rather become more enthusiastic as larger numbers of manuscripts both Biblical and non-Biblical have poured in from the Dead Sea area. James Kelso says "the priceless MSS and fragments represent the greatest of all finds in the field of Biblical research" ("The Archaeology of Qumran" in *Jour. of Bib. Lit.* lxxiv, Sept., 1955, p. 146). In appraising this large body of material its value must be judged in the light of the textual criticism of the Old Testament and its paleogrpahic importance, as well as its affect upon the fields of history and archaeology.

2. **The Textual Value of the Manuscripts.** When the fact is remembered that before the great discoveries since 1947 there were no extant manuscripts of the Hebrew Old Testament prior to about the tenth century A. D., except a very short excerpt from Deuteronomy 6:4, called the Nash Papyrus, dating about 100 B. C., it is easy to see the bearing the new material will have in the field of textual criticism. Already the Isaiah Scroll is proving its value in this field of study. The variant readings of this document published in 1950 (*The*

Dead Sea Scrolls of St. Mark's Monastery, Vol. I, *The Isaiah Manuscript and the Habakkuk Commentary.* Edited for the Trustees by Millar Burrows with the assistance of John C. Trever and William Brownlee, Am. Schls. Orient. Research, 1950), are included in the critical apparatus of R. Kittel's *Biblia Hebraica* in the eighth edition, and are thus available to students of the original text of Isaiah. However, the great majority of the new manuscripts consist only of a single small fragment, or

282. John Allegro Working on Scroll Fragments
from Cave 4

group of fragments, and none will be complete or near complete, in contrast to the complete Isaiah Scroll. Nevertheless, these small samples will be of incalculable aid in the study of the Hebrew Text of the Old Testament. They have the distinct advantage of permitting samplings of text types and tend to give a cross section of the whole Old Testament. This sort of comparative study makes possible conclusions which are applicable by extrapolation to portions of the text that are missing, and are frequently of more value than complete manuscripts of isolated Biblical books. The new manuscript material may be expected to help directly in suggesting superior readings in cases of a doubtful text, or calling attention to a conflation, omission, misplacement, etc., as a result of transmission. Too long, for lack of ancient manuscript material, emendation of the Hebrew Text has been on the flimsy basis of human ingenuity and pure imagination. With a body of ancient manuscript evidence, now of hopeful proportions, with promise of continuing finds, a science of textual criticism comparable to that of the New Testament may at least be envisaged as a possibility for the Old Testament. Not only in direct textual emendation of the Hebrew Massoretic text, but also in appraising the textual value of the Septuagint readings on various portions of the Old Testament, the new manuscript evidence gives fair promise of great assistance to the critical student. Whereas there has been a trend in recent years to put less confidence in the Septuagint as a witness to the Hebrew text on the assumption that obvious divergences in the Greek rendering are the result of mistranslations, carelessness and other faults of the translators, it now seems evident from recovered fragments of the book of I Samuel, for instance, that there were Palestinian (not Alexandrian) texts of Samuel of precisely the type which the Greek translators had before them, and that their rendering was a literal and careful translation from the Hebrew text used. From this consideration, it is apparent that the voice of the Greek version must be seriously heard in future efforts in reconstructing the text of Samuel. This is not to suggest that the Septuagint readings generally preserve older and more accurate reading than the Massoretic Hebrew. But it does suggest that this may be the case in some instances inasmuch as the Septuagint of Samuel apparently represents an accurate attempt to render a Hebrew text current at the time. The vitally important question of the formation of the Hebrew Massoretic Text will be intimately affected by the new manuscript evidence from the Dead Sea Area. Such vexing questions as when the ancient Hebrew text was standardized and whether the exegetical methods of Rabbi Aqiba and the translating activity of Auila came toward the end of the process of establishing an official text or at the commencement of its struggle for realization, are promised an answer. The evidence is increasing to suggest that the minute textual methods of second-century rabbis took for granted a text that had already been well established, rather than the common contention that the literalistic methods gave the first impetus to textual standardization.

283. Cave 1 Area, Where Isaiah Manuscript Was Found

3. **The Paleographic Importance of the Manuscripts.** Students of ancient Biblical manuscripts are delighted with the paleographic importance of the Dead Sea manuscripts. The letters of the Qumran Scrolls being intermediate between the known script of the third century B. C. and the middle of the first century A. D., mark an important era in the development and formation of the letters. (See Frank M. Cross, "The Oldest Manuscripts from Qumran" in *Jour. of Bib. Lit.*, lxxiv, Sept., 1955, pp. 147-172). A sprinkling of archaic script from 200-150 B. C. also adds paleographic value. Fragments from some of the caves present a later script intermediate between the Qumran material and the earliest previously known fragments from the third and fourth centuries A. D. These fragments supply other missing links in the chain of the development of the script and give the paleographer new evidence for dating other finds.

4. **Critical and Historical Importance of the Manuscripts.** Besides their value in textual criticism of the Old Testament and in paleography, the manuscripts of the Dead Sea caves are having far-reaching effects in elucidating the origins and environment of early Christianity. Of special import in this field of research is the so-called Manual of Discipline found in the original cache of manuscripts in 1947. This extremely important document, containing the rules of the Jewish sect known as the Essenes, is calculated to play a major role in New Testament criticism. The Gospel of John and the Johannine Epistles are particularly affected. The new Essene materials from the last century and a half preceding Jesus' ministry have thoroughly discredited the rationalistic criticism of the nineteenth century which dated John's Gospel about 150 A. D. or later, or the twentieth century views that place it between 90 and 130 A. D., thus removing it from the authentic tradition of the Apostolic age and treating it as essentially an apocryphal book. (Cf. Lucette Mowrey, "The Sea Scrolls and the Background for the Gospel of John" in *Bib. Arch.*, xvii, Dec., 1954, pp. 78-97). Remarkably close parallels to the conceptual imagery of John's Gospel in the Essenic literature present incontrovertible evidence that the fourth Gospel reflects the true Jewish background of John the Baptist and Jesus and not that of a later second-century Gnostic environment. Now, on the basis of the new evidence, there is every reason to believe in the genuineness of John's Gospel, and "there is no reason to date the Gospel after 90 A. D; it may be earlier" (W. F. Albright, "The Bible After Twenty Years of Archaeology" in *Religion in Life*, xxi, 4, 152, p. 550). In addition to their value in literary and historical criticism the non-Biblical literature among the Dead Sea Scrolls (including the Commentary on Habakkuk as well as the Manual of Discipline) is greatly adding to our knowledge of the philosophy and religious thought of Judaism in the first two centuries B. C. The Jewish sect of the Essenes, which produced the Dead Sea Scrolls, has striking resemblances to the Damascene Covenanters, the Therapeutae of Egypt, the John the Baptist movement in the time of Jesus and primitive Christianity (William H. Brownlee, "A Comparison of the Covenanters of the Dead Sea Scrolls with Pre-Christian Jewish Sects" in the *Bib. Arch.*, xiii, 3, Sept. 1950, pp. 50-72). As a result, fresh historical light is being shed upon the intertestamental period, as well as upon such other sects as the Pharisees and the Sadducees (See R. Marcus, "Pharisees, Essenes and Gnostics," *Jour. Bib. Lit.*, lxxiii, 1954, pp. 157-161).

5. **Archaeological Importance of the Manuscripts.** Great impetus has been given Palestinian archaeology by the discovery of the Dead Sea Scrolls. Since 1947 the Dead Sea area has become alive with Bedouin and

scholars scrambling up and down cliffs and peering into every nook and corner in search of new caves and new manuscripts. This vast amount of enthusiasm and labor has been rewarded with new caves and new manuscripts, besides a great deal of valuable pottery, coins, and other items of archaeological significance and value. The dry climate of the area has remarkably preserved a large amount of cloth, leather, wood and basketry. Pottery and coins have aided dating. Of special ar-

284. Dining Room of Qumran Community, near Scrolls Caves

chaeological value is the excavation of Khirbet Qumran, the most prolific manuscript-bearing site of all, situated some seven miles south of Jericho on the marly plateau along the west shore of the Dead Sea. Here in 1951-1954 the Essene Community Center, which flourished from c. 110 B. C. to the time of Herod the Great (c. 37 B. C.) and again from 6 A. Ð. to 68 A. D., was excavated. The history of this community has been established and the archaeological facts brought to light are of the utmost importance in interpreting the rich manuscript finds from the caves in the surrounding area, which in turn are of such far-reaching import to Biblical studies. *See* Dead Sea Scrolls, Scripture—Manuscripts.
M. F. U.

Ma'och (mā'ŏk; perhaps, *oppression*), the father of Achish, the king of Gath, to whom David fled from Saul (I Sam. 27:2), B. C. about 1004.

Ma'on (mā'ŏn; *abode, dwelling*).

1. The son of Shammai, of the family of Caleb and tribe of Judah. He was the "father" (founder) of Beth-zur (I Chron. 2:45).

2. An elevated town in the tribe of Judah seven miles S. from Hebron, where David hid himself from Saul (I Sam. 23:24, 25), and near which Nebal's possessions were (25:2); probably now *Tell Main*, a small heap of ruins.

Ma'onites (mā'ŏn-īts; same form as Maon), oppressors of Israel, mentioned only in Judg. 10:12, where they are named in connection with the Egyptians, Amorites, children of Ammon, Philistines, Zidonians, and Amalekites. The name agrees well with the plural, *Mehunim* (*q. v.*), but no mention is made of any previous invasion of Israel by the Mehunim. And Midian, whose yoke had been so heavy and so lately borne, is not mentioned in the list. These facts have led some to receive the reading "Midian," which is given in both the great manuscripts of the LXX. If the reading "Maonites" be retained we may sup-

pose Maon in Judah to have been originally occupied by this people and to have taken its name from them. Maon was mentioned in connection with Ziph and Carmel. The modern *Maîn* is seven miles S. of Hebron.—W. H.

Ma'ra (mä'rå; *bitter*), the name chosen for herself by Naomi, as being more appropriate to her by reason of her afflictions than her former name, which signifies "my delight" (Ruth 1:20).

Ma'rah (mä'rå; *bitterness*), the sixth station of the desert wandering of Israel (Exod. 15:23, 24; Num. 33:8). Here the waters were miraculously sweetened by casting a tree into them, as directed by God. It is identified as '*Ain Hawârah*, forty-seven miles from '*Ayûn Mousa*.

Mar'alah (mǎr'á-lå; *trembling, earthquake*), a place four miles from Nazareth, on the southern boundary of Zebulun (Josh. 19:11), apparently within the bounds of Issachar, west of Sarid and east of Dabbasheth.

Maran-ath'a (mǎr-ǎn-ǎth'á; Gr. from Aram. *märänä*' '*athäh, our Lord cometh*), an expression used by Paul at the conclusion of his First Epistle to the Corinthians: "If any man love not the Lord Jesus Christ, let him be Anathema Maran-atha" (16:22). It is thought to have been used as a watchword, common to all believers in the first age. Coupled here with an anathema, or curse, it is the Christian's reminder as he waits the advent of the judge to excute the anathema.

Marble. *See* Mineral Kingdom.

Mar'cus (mär'kŭs; Col. 4:10; Philem., v. 24; I Pet. 5:13). *See* Mark.

Mare'shah (má-rē'shå; *summit, chief place*).

1. A person named as the "father" of Hebron, among the descendants of Judah. From the position his name occupies he is supposed to be the brother of Mesha, Caleb's firstborn (I Chron. 2:42), B. C. about 1380.

2. A son of, or, more probably, a city founded by, Laadah, of the family of Shelah (I Chron. 4:21).

3. A town of Judah mentioned with Keilah and Achzib (Josh. 15:44), rebuilt by Laadan (I Chron. 4:21) and fortified by Rehoboam (II Chron. 11:8). It was the native place of the prophet Eliezer (20:37), and near the valley of Zephathah, where the Ethiopians under Zerah were defeated (14:9-13). It was inhabited by Edomites in the Greek period and known as Marisa, where important tomb paintings have been found. It figured prominently in the Maccabean Wars (I Macc. 5: 66; II Macc. 12:35), being destroyed by the Parthians in 40 B. C.

Ma'ri (mä'rî), an ancient city on the Middle Euphrates, represented today by Tell Hariri, about six miles north of Abou Kemal. Since 1933 André Parrot has conducted excavations sponsored by the Musée du Louvre. These diggings have been most successful in revealing a brilliant civilization of this city in the third millennium B. C. Among the astonishing discoveries were a temple of Isthar and a ziggurat (temple tower). Most famous of all the buildings uncovered in Mari was the royal palace, a sprawling edifice covering more than fifteen acres. It consisted of royal apartments, administrative offices and even a school for

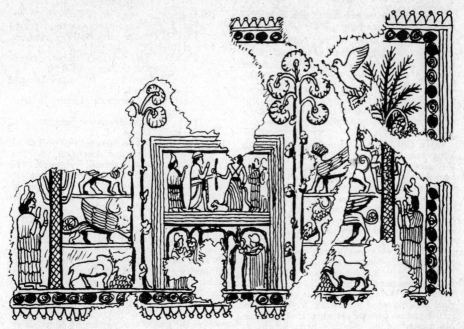

285. Mural from Palace of Mari Showing the Investiture of Zimri-Lim by the Goddess Ishtar

scribes. It was ornamented with great wall paintings, some of which were still preserved. From the palace archives over 20,000 tablets were recovered. Many of these cuneiform tablets record diplomatic correspondence by the last king of Mari, Zimri-lim, with the great Hammurabi of Babylon. The Mari Letters have helped to date Hammurabi (c. 1728-1626 B. C.), thus settling a very difficult point in Biblical chronology. In fact, the Mari documents have been a major discovery and have completely revised current knowledge of history, linguistics and historical background at a period around 1700 B. C. *See* Scripture MSS. O. T.; Scripture MSS. N. T., Dead Sea Scrolls.

M. F. U.

Mariner (Ezek. 27:9, 27, 29; to *shoot, row,* 27: 8), a sailor. *See* Ship.

Marishes, an old form of *Marsh* (*q. v.*).

Mark (Gr. *Markos,* Anglicized *Marcus* in Col. 4:10; Philem., v. 24; I Pet. 5:13), the evangelist, and probably the same as "John, whose surname was Mark" (Acts 12:12, 25), was the son of a certain Mary in Jerusalem (12:12), and was, therefore, presumably a native of that city. He was of Jewish parentage, his mother being a relative of Barnabas (Col. 4: 10). It was to her house that Peter went when released from prison by the angel (Acts 12:12). That apostle styles him his son (I Pet. 5:13), probably because he was converted under his ministry. He accompanied Paul and Barnabas on their first journey (Acts 12:25; 13:5), but left them at Perga and returned to Jerusalem (13:13). Whatever the reason for this act was it seems to have been sufficient in Paul's estimation to justify him in refusing to allow Mark to accompany him on his second journey. Barnabas was determined to take him, and thus Mark was the cause of a "sharp conten-

tion" between them and a separation (Acts 15:36-39). This did not completely estrange him from Paul, for we find Mark with the apostle in his first imprisonment at Rome (Col. 4:10; Philem., v. 24). Later he was at Babylon, and unites with Peter in sending salutations (I Pet. 5:13). He seems to have been with Timothy at Ephesus when Paul wrote to him during his second imprisonment, and urged him to bring Mark to Rome (II Tim. 4:11), A. D. 66. Tradition states that Mark was sent on a mission to Egypt by Peter, that he founded the Church of Alexandria, of which he became bishop, and suffered as a martyr in the eighth year of Nero. In the gospel of Mark his record is emphatically "the Gospel of Jesus Christ the Son of God" (Mark 1:1), living and working among men, and developing the mission more in acts than by words.

Mark. 1. "The Lord set a mark upon Cain" (Heb. *ōth,* Gen. 4:15) that no one might kill him. This was not a visible mark or brand upon his forehead, but some *sign* or *token* of assurance that his life should be preserved. What it was is impossible to determine.

2. In the sense of a *target* (Heb. *māṭṭārā',* watched,* I Sam. 20:20; Job 16:12; Lam. 3:12).

3. God commands the man with writing materials to "set a mark upon the foreheads" of all persons in Jerusalem, that they might be spared in the time of judgment (Ezek. 9:4, 6). The Hebrew letter *tau,* the last of the alphabet, was used as a mark (Job 31:35, marg. "my sign"), and in early times was written in the form of a cross. The mark (Gr. *charagma, stamp*) is to be stamped on the right hand or the forehead as the badge of the followers of Antichrist (Rev. 13:16, sq.; 14:9, 11; 16:2; 19:20; 20:4).

4. The *goal* or *end* one has in view, from the Greek *skopos*, something *watched* (Phil. 3:14).

5. In Lev. 19:28 we find two prohibitions of an unnatural disfigurement of the body: "Ye shall not make any cuttings in your flesh for the dead, nor print any *marks* upon you." The latter (Heb. *qăʻăqă, incision*) refers to tatooing, and has no reference to idolatrous usages, but was intended to inculcate upon the Israelites a proper reverence for God's creation (K. and D., *Com.*, in loc.).

6. In Gal. 6:17 Paul writes, "Henceforth let no man trouble me, for I bear in my body the marks of the Lord Jesus Christ," i. e., the brand of my master, Jesus Christ. The Greek *stigma* is the common word for the brand or mark with which masters marked their slaves. "From the very numerous records (on fragments of marble) of manumissions at Delphi and other shrines in Greece we have learned the legal process by which a slave gained his own liberty. He went to the temple of the god, and there paid his money to the priests; they then with his money bought the slave from his master, on the part of the god. He became for the rest of his life a slave to the god, which meant practically freedom, subject to certain periodical duties. If at any time his master or his master's heirs sought to reclaim him he had the record of the transaction in the temple.

"But on one point these documents are silent: If he traveled, if he were far away from home and were seized as a runaway slave, what security could he have? I believe St. Paul gives us the solution. When liberated at the temple, the priest, if he desired it, branded him with the 'stigmata' of his new master. Now St. Paul's words acquire a new and striking application. He had been the slave of sin; but he had been purchased by Christ, and his new liberty consisted in his being the slave of Christ. Henceforth, he says, let no man attempt to reclaim me; I have been marked on my body with the brand of my new master, Jesus Christ. Probably he referred to the many scars he bore of his persecutions" (Professor Mahaffy, in *Christian Work*).

Mark, Gospel of, the second gospel by order in the English Bible.

1. **Theme.** In all the gospels one unique Personality dominates. In Mark we have Christ as a Servant, as He appears as King in Matthew, Man in Luke and God in John. But Mark's Servant is also King, Man and God. In Mark, Jesus is seen as the Mighty Worker, rather than as the Great Teacher. It is preeminently the gospel of Jehovah's Servant, "The Branch" (Zech. 3:8). Chapter 10:45 describes the scope of the book, "For even the Son of Man came not to be ministered unto but to minister." No genealogy is included, for such is not important for a servant. In this gospel Christ appears as a lowly Servant Who emptied Himself "though in the form of God" "and was found in fashion like a man" (Phil. 2:6-8). This lowly Servant was nevertheless the Mighty Man (Isa. 9:6). In keeping with the servant character, the gospel is one of deeds rather than of words.

2. Outline.
   Part I. The Servant's Preparation, 1:1-13
   Part II. The Servant's Galilean Ministry, 1:14-7:23
   Part III. The Servant's Ministry North and East of Galilee, 7:24-9:50
   Part IV. The Servant's Ministry Enroute to Jerusalem, 10:1-52
   Part V. The Servant's Ministry in Jerusalem, 11-13
   Part VI. The Servant's Submission to Death, Chaps. 14, 15
   Part VII. The Servant's Triumphant Resurrection and Ascension, 16

3. **Attestation—External Evidence.** The gospel early circulated among Christians. By the middle of the second century it was included by Tatian in his Diatessaron or "Harmony of the Four Gospels" (c. 168 A. D.). It is quoted by Irenaeus in the last quarter of the second century as being Mark's. Others before him, such as Papias, assert that Mark was both Peter's disciple and interpreter. Mark's close association with Peter is corroborated by numerous details of internal evidence, suggesting an eye witness. But Mark evidently used other sources besides Peter. Quite a bit of material reveals Aramaic coloring. Rome is fixed by tradition as the place where the gospel was written by Mark. If so, it must be dated around 65-68 A. D., but if Luke's gospel was written before 63 A. D., Mark must be dated still earlier.

4. **Author.** Internal evidence agrees with the traditional Markan authorship. The writer is clearly a Christian Jew. He knows Jewish thought and life. He is acquainted with Aramaic. He writes with a thorough knowledge of Palestine.

5. **Sources.** Recent criticism accords this shortest and simplest of the four gospels a place of priority in time and primacy of importance. The reason for this is that it is now viewed as a basic source for Matthew and Luke, and especially underlies John. But in early traditional lists it appears in second, third and fourth places, never in the first. Until Lachmann's "discovery" of the priority of Mark in 1835 the gospel had little interest in critical circles. But this critical view is unsound and is not to be accepted without stern challenge. There is, however, a real sense in which Mark is dependent, not upon any canonical gospel, but upon Peter the Apostle. (*See* under 3. Attestation). M. F. U.

Market (Heb. *măʻărăb*), a mercantile term found only in Ezek., ch. 27 (rendered "merchandise," except in vers. 13, 17, 19, 25). It appears to have been used in several senses: (1) *Barter* (v. 9, 27); (2) *place* of trade (marg., v. 12, 13, 17, 19); (3) *gain* acquired by trade (v. 27, 34). In the New Testament the Greek word *'agora* is rendered *market* and *market place*, and denotes generally any place of public resort in towns or cities where trials are held (Acts 16:19), where citizens resort (17:17), and where commodities are exposed for sale (Mark 7:4). From this is derived *'agoraios*, "relating to the market place," and rendered "fellows of the baser sort" (literally, "loungers about the market," Acts 17:5). It is improperly rendered "law" in Acts 19:38, where it refers

286. The Agora (market place), Athens

to judicial days or assemblies (A. V., marg., *court days*). Markets in the East were held at or near the gates of cities, where goods were exposed either in tents or the open air (II Kings 7:18).

Ma′roth (mā′rŏth; *bitterness*), a town in the west of Judah, not far from Jerusalem, on the route of the invading Assyrian army from Lachish (Mic. 1:12).

Marriage, the rendering of several words and phrases in the Hebrew and Greek, meaning *to be master; to take*, i. e., a wife: *to magnify*, or *lift up* a woman; *to contract*; *to dwell together*; *to perform the duty of a brother; to become*, i. e., the wife of one. In all the Hebrew Scriptures there is no single word for the estate of marriage, or to express the abstract idea of *wedlock*.

1. **Origin**, etc. Marriage is a divine institution, designed to form a permanent union between man and woman that they might be helpful to one another (Gen. 2:18). Moses presents it as the deepest corporeal and spiritual unity of man and woman and monogamy as the form of marriage ordained by God (Gen. 2:24; comp. Matt. 19:5). Without the conjugal tie the inhabitants of this world would have been a mixed multitude. The family circle, family instruction, parental love and care would have been altogether unknown.

2. **Temporary reactions.** At an early period the original law, as made known to Adam, was violated through the degeneracy of his descendants, and concubinage and polygamy became common. The patriarchs themselves took more than one wife. Abraham, at the instigation of Sarah, took her maid as his subordinate wife. Jacob was inveigled, through the duplicity of Laban into taking Leah first, and then Rachel, to whom he had been betrothed; and afterward, through the rivalry of the sisters, he took both their handmaids. From these facts it has been inferred that polygamy was not wrong in ancient times, nor at all opposed to the divine law as revealed to the Jews. But this is an unwarrantable conclusion. It is true indeed, respect being had to the state of religious knowledge, the rude condition of society, and the views prevalent in the world, that the practice could not infer, in the case of individuals, the same amount of criminality as would necessarily adhere to it now, amid the clear light of Gospel times. But still all along it was a departure from the divine law.

For the reasons given above it was tolerated, but never with God's approval. Jesus told the Jews that "Moses because of the hardness of your hearts suffered you to put away your wives: but from the beginning it was not so" (Matt. 19:3-8). The Mosaic law aimed at mitigating, rather than removing evils which were inseparable from the state of society in that day. Its enactments were directed (1) to the discouragement of polygamy; (2) to obviate the injustice frequently consequent upon the exercise of the rights of a father or a master; (3) to bring divorce under some restriction; and (4) to enforce purity of life during the maintenance of the matrimonial bond.

3. **Laws of Intermarriage.** An important feature of the law of Moses is the restraint which it imposes upon marriage within certain degrees of relationship and affinity: (1) **Between an Israelite and a foreigner.** The only distinct prohibition in the Mosaic law refers to the Canaanites, with whom the Israelites were not to marry, on the ground that it would lead them to idolatry (Exod. 34:15; Deut. 7:3, 4). The legal disabilities resting upon the Ammonites and the Moabites (Deut. 23:3) totally forbade marriage between them and Israelite women, but permitted that of Israelites with Moabite women (Ruth 1:4). The prohibition against marriages with the Edomites and Egyptians was less stringent, as a male of those nations received the right of marriage on his admission to full citizenship in the third generation of proselytism (Deut. 23:7, 8). Thus the prohibition was *total* in regards to Canaanites on either side, *total* on the side of males in regard to the Ammonites and Moabites, and *temporary* on the side of males in regard of the Edomites and Egyptians. In the case of wives proselytism was not necessary, but it was so in the case of a husband. (2) **Between Israelites and Israelites.** The law began (Lev. 18:6-8) with the general prohibition against marriage between a man and the "flesh of his flesh." This was followed by special prohibitions against marriage with (1) a mother; (2) stepmother; (3) sister or half-sister; (4) granddaughter; (5) daughter of a stepmother; (6) aunt; (7) wife or uncle on the father's side; (8) daughter-in-law; (9) brother's wife, unless he died childless (*see* Marriage, Levirate); (10) a woman and her daughter, whether both together or in succession, or a woman and her granddaughter; (11) two sisters at the same time; (12) mother-in-law. The case of a daughter being taken in marriage is not mentioned, simply because it was regarded as very unlikely to occur; that of a full sister is included in No. 3, and of a mother-in-law in No. 10. Breaches of Nos. 1, 2, 3, 8, and 12 were to be followed by the death or extermination of the offender (Deut. 27:20, 22, 23), while the threat held out against 6, 7, and 9 was that the guilty parties should "bear their iniquity" and "die childless" (Lev. 12:12-18; 20:19-21). These prohibitions were based upon (1) moral propriety, (2) heathen practices, (3) social convenience.

In addition to the above, there were special prohibitions: (1) The high priest was forbidden to marry any one except a virgin selected from among his own people (Lev. 21:13, 14). (2) The priests were forbidden to marry prostitutes and divorced women (21:7). (3) Heiresses were prohibited from marrying outside of their own tribe (Num. 36:5-9; comp. Tob. vii, 10). (4) Persons defective in physical powers were not to intermarry with Israelites (Deut. 23:1). In the Christian Church we find the following prohibitions: (1) Bishops and deacons from having more than one wife, probably referring to second marriage of any kind. A similar prohibition applied to those entered upon the church records as widows (q. v.). They must have been the wife of one man, i, e., probably, not remarried. (2) A wife divorced by her husband and married to another man, if her second husband died or divorced her, could not revert to her first husband (Deut. 24:2-4). Such a marriage would lower the dignity of the woman, and make her appear too much like property. Such prohibition was also intended to prevent a frivolous severance of the marriage tie, and fortify the marital bond.

4. **Marriage Customs.** (1) **Age of marriage.** With regard to age, no restriction is pronounced in the Bible. Early marriage is spoken of with approval in several passages (Prov. 2: 17; 5:18; Isa. 62:5), and in reducing this general statement to the more definite one of years, we must take into account the very early age at which persons arrive at puberty in oriental countries. In modern Egypt marriage takes place in general before the bride has attained the age of sixteen, frequently when she is twelve or thirteen, and occasionally when she is only ten. The Talmudists forbade marriage in the case of a man under thirteen years and a day, and in the case of a woman under twelve years and a day. The usual age appears to have been higher, about eighteen years. (2) **Selection of bride.** Perhaps in imitation of the Father of the universe, who provided Adam with a wife, fathers from the beginning considered it their duty and prerogative to secure wives for their sons (Gen. 24:3; 38:6). In the absence of the father the selection devolved upon the mother (Gen. 21:21). In some cases the proposal was made by the father of the maid (Exod. 2:21). Occasionally the whole business of selecting the wife was committed to a friend. (3) **The betrothal.** The selection of the bride was followed by the espousal, which was not altogether like our "engagement," but was a formal prodeeding, undertaken by a friend or legal representative on the part of the bridegroom, and by the parents on the part of the bride; it was confirmed by oaths, and accompanied with presents to the bride. These presents were described by different terms, that to the bride by "a dowry" (Heb. *mōhăr*), and that to the relations by "a present" (Heb. *mättän*). Thus Shechem offers "never so much dowry and gift" (Gen. 34:12), the former for the bride, the latter for the relations. It has been supposed, indeed, that the *mohar* was a price paid down to the father for the sale of his daughter. Such a custom undoubtedly prevails in certain parts of the East at the present day, but it does not appear to have been the case with free women in patriarchal

times. It would undoubtedly be expected that the *mohar* should be proportioned to the position of the bride, and that a poor man could not on that account afford to marry a rich wife (I Sam. 18:23). A "settlement," in the modern sense of the term, i. e., a written document securing property to the wife, did not come into use until the post-Babylonian period: the only instance we have of one is in Tob. vii, 14, where it is described as an "instrument." The Talmudists styled it a *ketubah*, and have laid down minute directions as to the disposal of the sum secured, in a treatise of the Mishna expressly on that subject. The act of bethrothal was celebrated by a feast, and among the more modern Jews it is the custom in some parts for the bridegroom to place a ring on the bride's finger. Some writers have endeavored to prove that the rings noticed in the Old Testament (Exod. 35:22; Isa. 3:21) were nuptial rings, but there is not the slightest evidence of this. The ring was nevertheless regarded among the Hebrews as a token of fidelity (Gen. 41:42), and of adoption into a family (Luke 15:22). (4) **Marriage ceremonies.** Before the time of Moses, when the proposal was accepted, the marriage price paid, and the gifts distributed, the bridegroom was at liberty to remove at once the bride to his own home (Gen. 24:63-67). This was an unusual case, because of the bride being secured at a distance, while the bridegroom remained at home. Usually the marriage took place at the home of the bride's parents, and was celebrated by a feast, to which friends and neighbors were invited and which lasted seven days (Gen. 29:22, 27). The word "wedding" does not occur in the A. V. of the Old Testament; but it is probable that some ratification of the espousal with an oath took place (see Prov. 2:17; Ezek. 16:8; Mal. 2:14), and that a blessing was pronounced (Gen. 24:60; Ruth 4:11, 12). But the essence of the ceremony consisted in the removal of the bride from her father's house to that of the bridegroom or his father. There seems, indeed, to be a literal truth in the Hebrew expression "to take" a wife (Num. 12:1; I Chron. 2:21, marg.), for the ceremony appears to have mainly consisted in the taking. After putting on a festive dress, placing a handsome turban on his head (Isa. 61:10, A. V. "ornaments") and a nuptial crown (Cant. 3:11), the bridegroom set forth from his house, attended by his groomsmen (A. V. "companions," Judge. 14:11; "children of the bride-chamber," Matt. 9:15), preceded by a band of musicians or singers (Gen. 31:27; Jer. 7:34; 16:9; I Macc. 9:39), and accompanied by persons bearing flambeaus (II Esdr. 10:2; Matt. 25:7; comp. Jer. 25:10; Rev. 18:23, "the light of a candle"). Having reached the house of the bride, who with her maidens anxiously expected his arrival (Matt. 25:6), he conducted the whole party back to his own or his father's house, with every demonstration of gladness (Psa. 45:15). On their way back they were joined by a party of maidens, friends of the bride and bridegroom, who were in waiting to catch the procession as it passed (Matt. 25:6). The inhabitants of the place pressed out into the streets to watch the procession (Cant. 3:11). At the house a feast was prepared, to which all the friends and neighbors were invited (Gen. 29: 22; Matt. 22:1-10; Luke 14:8; John 2:2), and the festivities were protracted for seven, or even fourteen, days (Judg. 14:12; Tob. 8:19). The guests were provided by the host with fitting robes (Matt. 22:11), and the feast was enlivened with riddles (Judg. 14:12) and other amusements. The bridegroom now entered into direct communication with the bride, and the joy of the friend was "fulfilled" at hearing the voice of the bridegroom (John 3:29) conversing with her, which he regarded as a satisfactory testimony of the success of his share in the work. The last act in the ceremonial was the conducting of the bride to the bridal chamber, (Heb. *ḥĕdĕr*, Judg. 15:1; Joel 2:16), where a canopy, named *ḥŭppāh*, was prepared (Psa. 19:5; Joel 2:16). The bride was still completely veiled, so that the deception practiced on Jacob (Gen. 29:23) was very possible. A newly married man was exempt from military service, or from any public business which might draw him away from his home, for the space of a year (Deut. 24:5). A similar privilege was granted to him who was betrothed (Deut. 20:7).

5. **Marriage Relation.** In considering the social and domestic conditions of married life among the Hebrews, we must, in the first place, take into account the position assigned to women generally in their social scale. There is abundant evidence that women, whether married or unmarried, went about with their faces unveiled (Gen. 12:14; 24:16, 65; 29:11; I Sam. 1:13). Women not unfrequently held important offices. They took their part in matters of public interest (Exod. 15:20; I Sam. 18:6, 7); in short, they enjoyed as much freedom in ordinary life as the women of our own country. If such was her general position, it is certain that the wife must have exercised an important influence in her own home. She appears to have taken her part in family affairs, and even to have enjoyed a considerable amount of independence (II Kings 4:8; Judg. 4:18; I Sam. 25:14, etc.). (1) **Dependence of the wife.** And yet the dependence of the wife on her husband is shown by the Hebrew appellation for husband, (*bă'ăl*, Exod. 21:3, 22), literally, *lord, master;* and is seen in the conduct of Sarah, who speaks of her husband Abraham as *my lord* (Gen. 18:12). From this mastery of the husband over the wife arose the different standard of virtue which obtained in married life. The wife, subject to her husband as master, was obliged to regard the sanctity of the marriage relation, and any unchastity on her part was visited with death. The husband could take any unmarried woman he chose, and violate the laws of chastity, as we understand them, with impunity (Gen. 38:24). This absolute sanctity of marriage on the part of the wife was acknowledged by other nations of antiquity, as Egypt (Gen. 12:15-19) and Philistia (20:1-18; 26:9-11). Arising from the previously existing inequality of husband and wife, and the prevailing notion that the husband was lord over his wife, Moses could neither impose the same obligation of fidelity

nor confer the same right on both. This is evident from the following facts: (1) The husband in the case of the wife's infidelity could command her death as well as that of her paramour (Lev. 20:10; Deut. 22:22; Ezek. 16:38-40; John 8:3-5). (2) If he became suspicious of his wife he could bring her to the priest and have administered to her the water of jealousy (Num. 5:12-31). But if the husband was guilty of criminal intercourse with an unmarried woman, no statute enabled the wife to arraign him for a breach of marriage or infringement of her or their rights. Should he sin with a married woman, it was the injured husband that could demand the death of the seducer, not the wife of the criminal. (3) If the wife vowed anything to the Lord, or imposed upon herself voluntary obligations to Jehovah, her husband could nullify them (Num. 30:6-8). (4) The husband could divorce his wife if it so pleased him (Deut. 24:1-4). (2) **Protection by the wife.** The woman was protected by the following laws; (*a*) The daughter of an Israelite sold by her father as a maidservant (i. e., housekeeper and concubine), who did not please her master, was not to be treated as menservants, viz., be sent away free at the end of six years; but she was provided for as follows: She could be redeemed, i. e., another Israelite could buy her for a concubine, but she could not be sold to an alien (Exod. 21:7, 8). She might be given to her purchaser's son, in which case she was to be treated as a daughter. If he gives the son an additional wife, "her food, her raiment, and her duty of marriage, shall he not diminish" (vers. 9, 10). If these three things were not provided, then she was to "go out free, without money" (v. 11). (*b*) If her husband maliciously charges a newly married woman with lack of chastity, he is to be scourged, and loses his right of divorce (Deut. 22:13-19). (*c*) If she has children they must render equal obedience to her as to the father (Exod. 20:12; Deut. 27:16). (*d*) As has already been stated, the husband must not vex his wife by marrying her sister (Lev. 18: 18). (*e*) The husband was forbidden to transfer the primogeniture from the son of a less beloved wife to the child of his favorite wife. (*f*) If her husband dislikes her, he is not arbitrarily to dismiss her, but to give her a "bill of divorcement" (Deut. 24:1). (*g*) If divorced, or her husband dies, the woman is free and at liberty to marry another (Deut. 24:2).

6. **Social and Domestic Conditions.** In early times the Oriental woman appears to have enjoyed much freedom. She, whether married or single, went about with her face unveiled (Gen. 12:14; 24:16, 65; 29:11; I Sam. 1:13); she might meet and converse with men, even strangers, in a public place (Gen. 24:25, 45-47; 29:9-12; I Sam. 9:11); she might be found alone in the country without any reflection on her character (Deut. 22:25-27); or she might appear in a court of justice (Num. 27:1, sq.). If such was her general position, we can readily accord her a considerable amount of independence and influence at home. Thus we find her entertaining guests (II Kings 4:8) in the absence of her husband (Judg. 4:18), and even against

his wishes (I Sam. 25:14, sq.); she conferred with her husband respecting the marriage of her children (Gen. 27:46), and even sharply criticised the conduct of her husband (I Sam. 25:25; II Sam. 6:20). The ideal relations between husband and wife appear to have been those of tenderness and affection. Thus the husband is called the "friend" of his wife (Jer. 3:20, marg.; Hos. 3:1); while frequent notice is made of his love for her (Gen. 24:67; 29:18). The wife was the husband's consolation in bereavement (Gen. 24:67), and her grief at his loss presented a picture of the most abject woe (Joel 1:8). Polygamy, of course, produced jealousies and quarrels (Gen. 21:11; I Sam. 1:6), while purchase of wives and the small liberties allowed daughters in the choice of husbands must have resulted in many unhappy unions. In the New Testament the mutual relations of husband and wife are a subject of frequent exhortation (Eph. 5:22-33; Col. 3:18, 19; Tit. 2:4, 5; I Pet. 3:1-7).

7. **Duties.** In a Hebrew household the wife had general superintendence of the domestic arrangements, such as cooking (Gen. 18:6; II Sam. 13:8, 9), the distribution of food at the meals (Prov. 31:15), the manufacture of cloth and clothing (Prov. 31:13, 21, 22).

8. **Figurative.** Marriage is illustrative of Jehovah's relation with Israel (Isa. 54:5; 62:4; Jer. 3:14; Hos. 2:19-20). In the New Testament the image of the bridegroom is transferred from Jehovah to Christ (Matt. 9:15; John 3:29), and that of the bride to the Church (II Cor. 11:2; Eph. 5:23, 24, 32; Rev. 19:7; 21:2, 9; 22:17).

Marriage, Christian. Christianity confirms, simplifies, and vindicates from abuse the original and sacred ordinance of marriage. The stability and purity of the Church and State have been proportionate to the popular and legal stability of the marriage relationship. The original appointment of monogamy is confirmed (Matt. 19:6; Mark 10:6-8). The presence of Jesus at the wedding in Cana happily illustrates the feeling and teaching of Christianity respecting marriage. Christ taught the divine origin and sacredness of this institution. It is more than filial duty; it is unifying; the husband and wife become one through the purity and intensity of mutual love; common interests are necessitated by common affection (Matt. 19:5, 6; Eph. 5:31); only one single ground for divorce is lawful (Matt. 19:9). The utmost that may be inferred from the expression "which made themselves eunuchs for the kingdom of heaven's sake" (Matt. 19:12) is that marriage is not binding upon every member of the race; and that devotion or discretion may make it expedient to renounce or defer it. The example of Peter (Matt. 8:14; Mark 1:30; Luke 4:38), and the express teaching of New Testament writers (I Tim. 4:3; 5:14; Heb. 13:4), are in harmony with the conduct of Christ respecting the sanctity of the marriage relation. The counsel of St. Paul to the Corinthian Church (I Cor., ch. 7), evidently in reply to their request, is entirely consistent with the general doctrine of the New Testament. He guards marriage so carefully that even to those who are joined to unbelievers the advice

is given not to disturb their relationship except by mutual consent and for mutual good. "According to the principles thus laid down, marriage is not merely a civil contract; the Scriptures make it the most sacred relation of life; and nothing can be imagined more contrary to their spirit than the notion that a personal agreement, ratified in a human court, satisfies the obligation of this ordinance."

The Roman Catholic Church teaches that "marriage is a *sacrament* of the new law, and as such confers grace. Christians who are in mortal sin may contract a valid marriage, but they receive no grace, though they do receive the sacrament; and, therefore, have a claim and title to the sacramental grace when they have amended their lives by sincere repentance. Christians, on the other hand, who contract marriage with due dispositions, receive an increase of sanctifying grace, and, besides, special grace to live in mutual and enduring affection . . . and to bring up children, whom God may give them, in his fear and love" (*Cath. Dict.*, s. v.).

Matrimony was elevated to the dignity of the sacrament mainly on the ground of the apostle's words, "This is a great mystery; but I speak concerning Christ and the Church" (Eph. 5:32); in the Vulgate the Greek being rendered *sacramentum*. "It is not this that is conveyed by the passage, as indeed, in general, marriage 'has from Christ neither a sacramental *institution*, nor *form*, nor *substance*, nor *end*,' but it is rather the sacredly ideal and deeply moral character, which is forever assured to marriage by this typical significance in the Christian view" (Meyer, *Com.*, in loc.; Pope, *Christ. Theol.*, iii, pp. 237-243, 308).

Marriage, Levirate (from Lat. *levir*, a *brother-in-law*), the marriage of a man with his deceased brother's widow, in the event of his dying childless. The first instance of this custom occurs in the patriarchal period, where Onan is called upon to marry his brother Er's widow (Gen. 38:8). The Levirate marriage was not peculiar to the Jews; it has been found to exist in many Eastern countries, particularly in Arabia and among the tribes of the Caucasus. The Mosaic provision was as follows: If brothers (on the father's side) lived together, i. e., in the same place, and one of them died childless, the wife was not to go outside and marry a stranger; but the surviving brother was to take her to wife. The firstborn son by her took the name of the deceased, i. e., continued his name in the family register, that his name perished not out of Israel. In case the brother-in-law did not wish to marry the widow, she might cite him legally before the elders of the place. If, after conference with them, he still persisted in declaring his unwillingness, he was not compelled to do the duty of a brother-in-law. But he was obliged to submit to the humiliation of having his shoe plucked off by his sister-in-law in the presence of the elders, and of having his face spit upon; the one act denoting that he thus gave up all claim to his deceased brother's estate, the other an act expressive of contempt (Deut. 25:5-10). From Ruth 4:1-10, it would appear that in case of the refusal of the brother-in-law to take the widow, then the next male relative had the right to do so. The divine sanction which the Mosaic law gave to levirate marriage is not to be regarded as merely an accommodation to a popular prejudice. Such marriage was not strictly commanded, but it was considered a

287. Mars Hill. Athens

duty of love, the non-fulfillment of which brought reproach and ridicule on the man and his house. It did not abolish the general prohibition of marriage with a brother's wife, but proceeded from one and the same principle with it. By the *prohibition* the brother's house is preserved in its integrity; by this *command* it is raised to a permanent condition. In both cases the dead brother is honored, and fraternal love preserved as the moral foundation of his house. Based upon such a marriage as this was the ground for the question asked of our Lord by the Sadducees (Matt. 22:23, sq.). The rabbins taught that in the next world a widow who had been taken by her brother-in-law reverted to her first husband at the resurrection. Christ answered both parties by the declaration that "in the resurrection they neither marry, nor are given in marriage."

Marrow, the soft oleaginous substance contained in the hollow bones of animals. Heb. *mōăh,* Job 21:24; Gr. *muelos,* Heb. 4:12.

    Figurative. "Fat things full of marrow" (Isa. 52:6) is an expression symbolizing the full enjoyment of blessedness in the perfected kingdom of God. "Marrow" in Heb. 4:12 is used figuratively for the most secret thoughts of a person.

Mar′sena (mär′sĕ-nȧ; cf. Avestan, marshanā, *forgetful man*), perhaps *nobleman,* one of the "seven princes (satraps or viziers) of Persia

and Media" in the time of Ahasuerus (Esth. 1:14), B. C. about 479.

Mars′ Hill (Gr. *Aries Pagos, hill of Aries,* the Greek god of war, Roman Mars, Acts 17:22), another name for the *Areopagus* (*q. v.*).

Marsh (Heb. *gĕbĕ,* a *reservoir,* Ezek. 47:11), a swamp or wet piece of land. The place referred to by Ezekiel is the "Valley of Salt," near the Dead Sea; for there the Kidron, the course of which the prophet describes the holy waters as following, empties.

Mar′tha (mär′thȧ; Gr. from Aram. *lady, mistress*), the sister of Lazarus and Mary, who all resided in the same house at Bethany (Luke 10:38, 40, 41; John 11:1-39; 12:2). Martha appears to have been at the head of the household (Luke 10:38), and from that circumstance has been thought to have been a widow. This is, however, uncertain, and it is generally supposed that the two sisters (unmarried) managed the household for their brother. The incident narrated by Luke (10:38-42) shows that Jesus was intimate with the family and was at home in their house; and also brings out the contrary dispositions of the two sisters. Martha hastens to provide suitable entertainment for their friend and his followers, while Mary sits at his feet listening to his gracious discourse. The busy, anxious Martha, annoyed at the inactivity of Mary, complains impatiently to Jesus, "Lord, dost thou not care that my sister hath left me to serve alone? bid her therefore that she help me." This brought from the master the oft-quoted reply, "But one thing is needful; Mary hath chosen that good part, which shall not be taken away from her." At the death of Lazarus their respective characters are portrayed: Martha active, Mary meditative; Martha reproachful and objecting, Mary silent but immediately obedient to the summons of Jesus; Martha accepting Jesus as the Christ, and sharing in the belief of a resurrection, but not believing, as Mary did, in Jesus as "the Life." All that is recorded of Martha in addition is that at a supper given to Jesus and his disciples at Bethany, at which Lazarus was present, she, as usual, busied herself with serving.

Martyr (Gr. *martus,* so rendered only in Acts 22:20; Rev. 2:13 and 17:6), a witness (*q. v.*), and generally so given. The meaning of the word martyr, which has now become the most usual, is one who has proved the strength and genuineness of his faith in Christ by undergoing a violent death. *Stephen* (*q. v.*) in this sense was the first martyr, and the spiritual honors of his death tended in no small degree to raise to the most extravagant estimation, in the early Church, the value of the testimony of blood. Eventually a martyr's death was supposed, on the alleged authority of the following texts, to cancel the sins of the past life (Mark 10:39; Luke 12:50), to answer for baptism, and at once to secure admission into paradise (Matt. 5:10-12).

Marvel (Heb. *pälä′,* to *separate,* to *distinguish*), something great, unaccountable, a miracle; and so that which excites wonder (Exod. 34:10); "marvelous works" (I Chron. 16:12, 24; Job 5:9; 10:16; Psa. 9:1; 17:7, etc.). See Miracle.

Ma'ry (mā'rĭ; Gr. *Maria*, or *Mariam*; from Heb. *mĭr-yäm'*, *obstinacy, rebellion*).

1. The Mother of Jesus. Mary was the daughter of Heli, of the tribe of Judah and of the lineage of David, hence in the royal line. (1) **The annunciation.** In the summer of the year known as B. C. 5 Mary was living at Nazareth, a maiden, but betrothed to Joseph. At this time the angel Gabriel came to her with a message from God, and announced to her that she was to be the mother of the long-expected Messiah—that by the power of the Holy Spirit the everlasting Son of the Father should be born of her (Luke 1:26-35; comp. Rom. 1:3). (2) **Visit to Elizabeth.** Informed by the angel that her cousin Elizabeth was within three months of being delivered of a child, Mary set off to visit her, either at Hebron or Juttah. Immediately upon her entrance into the house she was saluted by Elizabeth as the mother of her Lord, and had evidence of the truth of the angel's saying with regard to her cousin. Mary abode with her cousin about three months, and returned to her own house (1:36-56). (3) **Married to Joseph.** In a few months Joseph found that Mary was with child, and determined to give her a bill of divorcement (see Deut. 24:1), instead of yielding her up to the law to suffer the penalty he supposed she had incurred (Deut. 22:23, 24); but being assured of the truth by an angel he took her to wife (Matt. 1:18-25). (4) **Mother of Jesus.** Soon after Joseph and Mary went to Bethlehem to be enrolled for the taxing, and while there Christ was born and laid in a manger (Luke 2:1, 7). On the eighth day Jesus was circumcised, and on the fortieth day after the nativity—until which time she could not leave the house (Lev. 12:2-4)—the Virgin presented herself with her babe for their purification in the temple. The poverty of Joseph and Mary is alluded to in the mention of their offering, "a pair of turtle-doves, or two young pigeons." There she met Simeon and the prophetess Anna, heard their thanksgiving and prophecy. Returning to Bethlehem, Mary and Joseph were warned of the purpose of Herod, and fled to Egypt. Returning the next year, they went to Nazareth (Matt. 2:11-23). At the age of twelve years Jesus accompanied his family to Jerusalem, and Mary was temporarily separated from him (Luke 2:42, sq.), A. D. 8. (5) **Subsequent mention of Mary.** Four times only, after our Lord's ministry commenced, is the veil removed, which, not surely without reason, is thrown over her. These four occasions are: *the marriage at Cana*, where Jesus solemnly withdraws himself from the authority of his earthly mother (John 2: 1-4); *at Capernaum*, where at a public gathering Mary desired to speak to Jesus, and he seems to refuse to admit any authority on the part of his relatives, or any privilege on account of their relationship (John 2:12; Matt. 12:46-50); *at the crucifixion*, where Christ with almost his last words commended his mother to the care of the disciple whom he loved, and from that hour St. John assures us that he took her to his abode (John 19:25-27); *after the ascension*, engaged in prayer in the upper room in Jerusalem, with other faithful fol-lowers of the Lord. The Scriptures leave Mary engaged in prayer (Acts 1:14). Tradition and speculation have conceived of her as kept from actual sin by the grace of God, the prevailing opinion of the twelfth century. In the thirteenth century it was maintained that, though conceived in sin, she was cleansed from it before her birth. Early in the fourteenth century Scotus threw out as a possibility the idea of an immaculate conception, which developed into the decree of December 8, 1854 (Smith). (6) **Character.** "Her faith and humility exhibit themselves in her immediate surrender of herself to the divine will, though ignorant how that was to be accomplished (Luke 1:38); her energy and earnestness in her journey from Nazareth to Hebron (v. 39); her happy thankfulness in her song of joy (v. 48); her silent, musing thoughtfulness in her pondering over the shepherds' visit (2:19), and in her keeping her Son's words in her heart (v. 51), though she could not fully understand their import. In a word, so far as Mary is portrayed to us in Scripture, she is, as we should have expected, the most tender, the most faithful, humble, patient, and loving of women, but a *woman* still" (Smith, *Dict.*).

NOTE—Was Mary the mother of any other children than Jesus? is a question that has caused almost endless controversy. Of course, the advocates of her perpetual virginity assert that she was not. From the accounts in Matt. 13:55; Mark 6:3, it would seem more than likely that she had a number of children. This presumption is increased by the fact that the persons named as the "brethren" of Jesus are mentioned in connection and in company with his *sisters* and *mother*. Indeed, the denial of the natural interpretation of these passages owes its origin, in all probability, to the tradition of perpetual virginity, the offspring of the false notion of the superior sanctity of celibacy.

2. Mary Magdale'ne (măg-dȧ-lē'nĕ, or commonly măg'dȧ-lĕn; *of Magdala*). (1) **Name.** Of this there are four explanations: *1.* The most natural is that she came from the town of Magdala (a *tower* or *fortress*) q. v., probably situated on the western shore of Lake Tiberias, and the same as that of the modern village of El-Mejdel. *2.* The Talmudists make mention of a *Miriam Megaddela:* "Miriam with the braided locks," which Lightfoot considers as identical with "the woman that was a sinner" (Luke 7:37). *3.* Jerome sees in her name and that of her town the old *Migdol* (*watch-tower*), and says that the name denotes the steadfastness of her faith. *4.* "Origen, looking to the more common meaning of *gădăl*, to *be great*), sees in her name a prophecy of her spiritual greatness as having ministered to her Lord and been the first witness of the resurrection." (2) **Personal history.** Mary Magdalene enters the Gospel narrative, with certain other women, as "ministering to Jesus of their substance" (Luke 8:2); all of them being moved by gratitude for their deliverance from "evil spirits and infirmities." Of Mary it is said that "seven demons (*daimonia*) went out of her" (v. 2; Mark 16:9). This life of ministration brought Mary Magdalene into companionship of the closest nature with Salome, the mother of James and John (Mark 15:40), and also with Mary, the mother of the Lord (John 19:25). They "stood afar off, beholding these things"

(Luke 23:49), during the closing hours of the agony on the cross. The same close association which drew them together there is seen afterward. She remained by the cross till all was over, and waited till the body was taken down and wrapped in the linen cloth and placed in the garden sepulcher of Joseph of Arimathea (Matt. 27:61; Mark 15:47; Luke 23:55). She, with *Salome* and Mary, the mother of James, "brought sweet spices that they might anoint" the body (Mark 16:1). The next morning, accordingly, in the earliest dawn (Matt. 28:1; Mark 16:2), they came to the sepulcher. Mary Magdalene had been to the tomb, had found it empty, and had seen the "vision of angels" (Matt. 28:5; Mark 16:5). She went with her cry of sorrow to Peter and John (Luke 24:10; John 20:1, 2), and, returning with them, tarried after they went back. Looking into the sepulcher, she saw the angels, and replied to their question as to her reason for weeping, "They have taken away my Lord, and I know not where they have laid him." Turning back, she saw Jesus, but did not at first recognize him. Recalled to consciousness by his utterance of her name, she exclaimed "Rabboni," and rushed forward to embrace his feet. But she must now learn that spiritual dependence upon Christ which can live without his visible presence. And that lesson is taught in the words, "Touch me not, for I am not yet ascended to my father." Mary then went to the disciples, and told them what she had seen and heard (John 20:11-18), and passes out of history.

NOTE—Mary Magdelene has long been in popular tradition equivalent to "Mary the sinner," and been identified with the penitent who anointed Jesus. There were probably two anointings recorded in the gospels, the acts of two different women: one in some city unnamed, during our Lord's Galilean ministry (Luke 7); the other at Bethany, before the last entry into Jerusalem (Matt. 26, Mark 14, John 12), by the sister of Lazarus. There is no reliable evidence to connect Mary Magdalene with either anointing. (1) When her name appears in Luke 8:2 there is not one word to connect it with the history that immediately precedes. (2) The belief that Mary of Bethany and Mary Magdalene are identical is yet more startling. The epithet Magdalene, whatever may be its meaning, seems chosen for the express purpose of distinguishing her from all other Marys. No one evangelist gives the slightest hint of identity. Nor is this lack of evidence in the New Testament itself compensated by any such weight of authority as would indicate a really trustworthy tradition (Smith, *Dict.*, s.v.).

3. **Mary, Sister of Lazarus.** The facts strictly personal to her are but few. She and her sister Martha appear in Luke 10:38, sq., as receiving Christ in their house. Mary sat listening eagerly for every word that fell from the Divine Teacher, and was commended by Jesus as having "chosen that good part," the "one thing needful," while "Martha was cumbered about much serving." The next mention of Mary is in connection with the raising of Lazarus. She sat still in the house until Martha came to her secretly and said, "The master is come, and calleth for thee," when she arose hastily to go and meet him. At first she gives way to complaint, "Lord, if thou hadst been here, my brother had not died;" but the great joy and love revived upon her brother's return to life, and found expression in the anointing at the last feast of Bethany (Matt. 26:6, sq.; Mark 14:3, sq.; John

11; 12:1-9). Matthew and Mark do not mention her by name. Of her subsequent history we know nothing, the ecclesiastical traditions about her being based on the unfounded hypothesis of her identity with Mary Magdalene.

4. **Mary, the Wife of Clopas** (Gr. *Maria hē tou Klōpa*, A. V. "of Cleophas"). In St. John's gospel we read that "there stood by the cross of Jesus his mother, and his mother's sister, Mary of Clopas, and Mary Magdalene" (John 19:25). The same group of women is described by St. Matthew as consisting of "Mary Magdalene, and Mary the mother of James and Joses, and the mother of Zebedee's children" (Matt. 27:56); and by St. Mark as "Mary Magdalene, and Mary the mother of James the Little and of Joses, and Salome" (Mark 15:40). From a comparison of these passages it appears that Mary of Clopas and Mary the mother of James the Little and of Joses are the same person, and that she was the sister of Mary the Virgin. In answer to the alleged improbability of two sisters having the same name, it may be said that Miriam, the sister of Moses, may have been the holy woman after whom Jewish mothers called their daughters. This is on the hypothesis that the two names are identical, but on a close examination of the Greek text we find that it is possible that this was not the case. Mary the Virgin is *Mariam;* her sister is *Maria.* Mary of Clopas was probably the elder sister of the Lord's mother. Mary is brought before us for the first time on the day of the crucifixion—in the parallel passages already quoted from St. Matthew, St. Mark, and St. John. In the evening of the same day we find her sitting desolately at the tomb with Mary Magdalene (Matt. 27:61; Mark 15:47), and at the dawn of Easter morning she was again there with sweet spices, which she had prepared on the Friday night (Matt. 28:1; Mark 16:1; Luke 23:56), and was one of those who had "a vision of angels, which said that He was alive" (Luke 24:23). It is probable that Clopas was dead, and that the two widowed sisters lived together in one house.

5. **Mary, Mother of Mark,** also sister to Barnabas (Col. 4:10). It would appear from Acts 4:37, 12:12, that while the brother disposed of his property for the benefit of the Church, the sister gave up her house as one of the places of meeting. The fact that Peter goes to that house on his release from prison indicates that there was some special intimacy (Acts 12:12) between them, and this is confirmed by the language which he uses toward Mark as being his "son" (I Pet. 5:13). "It has been surmised that filial anxiety about her welfare during the persecutions and the famine which harassed the Church at Jerusalem was the chief cause of Mark's withdrawal from the missionary labors of Paul and Barnabas."

6. A Christian woman at Rome to whom Paul sent greetings, as to one "who bestowed much labor on us" (Rom. 16:6).

Mas'chil (măs'kĭl), appears in the titles of Ps. 32, 42, 44, 45, 52-5, 74, 78, 88, 89, 142; meaning uncertain.

Mash (măsh), one of the sons of Aram, the son of Shem (Gen. 10:23). In I Chron. 1:17 the name appears as Meshech.

Ma'shal (mä'shăl), a Levitical town in Asher (I Chron. 6:74). It was assigned to the Gershonite Levites. Called Mishal in Josh. 21:30.

Mason. *See* Handicrafts.

Mas'rekah (măs'rê-ká; *vineyard*), a city in Idumaea, and the native place of Samlah, an Edomitish king (Gen. 36:36; I Chron. 1:47). Jebel el-Mushrak, 22 miles S. W. of Ma'an.

Mas'sa (măs'á; *burden*), a son of Ishmael (Gen. 25:14; I Chron. 1:30). His descendants were not improbably the *Masani*, who are placed by Ptolemy in the east of Arabia, near the borders of Babylonia. The Assyrian inscriptions name Massa with Tema and Nebaioth.

Mas'sah (măs'á; *trial, temptation*), a name given to the place where the Israelites murmured for want of water (Exod. 17:7; Deut. 6:16; 9: 22; 33:8); called also *Meribah* (*q. v.*).

Mast. *See* Ship.

Master.

1. A man who rules, governs or directs. A possessor, owner, (Heb. *'ädōn*), e. g., the owner of the hill of Samaria (I Kings 16:24); a master of servants (Gen. 24:14, 27; 39:2, 7; of kings, as lords of their subjects (Isa. 26:13); a husband as lord of a wife (Gen. 18:12) or a ruler to whom honor is due (Gen. 45:8); one to whom respect is due, as a father or brother (Gen. 31:35; Num. 12:11).

2. The Hebrew word *bă'ăl* commonly denotes a master of a house or husband (Gen. 20:3; Deut. 22:22, etc.); a land-owner or inhabitant (Judg. 9:2; I Sam. 23:11); or the owner of a house (Judg. 19:22). Without the article, the word is used to describe Baal, the great N. W. Semitic god of the storm, the principle deity of the Phoenicians.

3. Another Hebrew word translated master is *răb*, meaning *great or chief*, usually in combination, as in Dan. 1:3 "the master of the eunuchs."

4. Hebrew *săr* means a leader or commander (Gen. 21:22); of a city (I Kings 22:26), or a prison (39:21, 22). It means a prince in Exod. 2:14; Isa. 23:8.

5. "Master of the house," that is the head of the family, is denoted by the Greek *oikodespotēs* (Matt. 16:25; Luke 3:25; 14:21).

6. "Master" in the sense of an instructor or teacher is the rendering of the Greek *didaskalos* (Rom. 2:20, etc.). In the N. T. as an equivalent of rabbi (John 1:39).

7. The Greek word *kathēgētēs*, also used of a "master" in scholastic sense; that is, a teacher (Matt. 23:8, 10).

8. A superintendent or overseer in a general sense is rendered by the Greek *epistatēs*, *appointed over*. This expression is employed for *rabbi* (*q. v.*), by the disciples when addressing Jesus (Luke 5:5; 8:24, 25; 9:33, 49; 17:13).

9. A sailing master, rendered "ship master" in Rev. 18:17 is denoted by the Greek *kubernētēs* (Acts 27:11). *M. F. U.*

Mathu'sala (má-thū'sá-lá; Luke 3:37). *See* Methuselah.

Ma'tred (mä'trĕd), a daughter of Mezahab and mother of Mehetabel, who was wife of Hadar (or Hadad) of Pau, king of Edom (Gen. 36:39; I Chron. 1:50).

Ma'tri (mä'trī; *rainy*), a Benjamite, and head of the family to which Saul, the king of Israel,

belonged (I Sam. 10:21), B. C. considerably before 1020.

Matrimony. *See* Marriage.

Mat'tan (măt'ăn; a *gift*).

1. The priest of Baal slain before his altars in the idol temple at Jerusalem (II Kings 11: 18; II Chron. 23:17), B. C. 836. He probably accompanied Athaliah, the queen mother, from Samaria.

The father of Shephatiah, one of the princes who charged Jeremiah with treason and afterward cast him into prison (Jer. 38:1-6), B. C. before 588.

Mat'tanah (măt'á-ná; a *gift*), the fifty-third station of Israel, on the north side of Arnon (Num. 21:18, 19). Probably to be identified with Khirbet el-Medeiyineh.

Mattani'ah (măt-á-nī'á; *gift of Jehovah*).

1. The original name of *Zedekiah* (*q. v.*), king of Judah, which was changed when Nebuchadnezzar placed him on the throne instead of his nephew Jehoiachin (II Kings 24:17).

2. A Levite singer of the family of Asaph, resident at Jerusalem after the captivity (I Chron. 9:15), B. C. about 440. He is described as the son of Micah (Micha, Neh. 11: 17; Michaiah, 12:35), and after the return from Babylon lived in the villages of the Netophathites (I Chron. 9:16), or Netophathi (Neh. 12:28), which the singers had built in the neighborhood of Jerusalem (12:29). As leader of the temple choir after its restoration (11:17; 12:8) in the time of Nehemiah, he took part in the musical service which accompanied the dedication of the wall of Jerusalem (12:35). We find him among the Levites of the second rank, "keepers of the thresholds" (Neh. 12:25).

3. One of the fourteen sons of Heman, whose office it was to blow the horns in the temple service as appointed by David. He had charge of the ninth division of musicians (I Chron. 25:4, 16), B. C. about 975. He is possibly the same as the father of Jeiel, and descendant of Asaph, and ancestor of Jahaziel the Levite in the reign of Jehoshaphat (II Chron. 20:14).

4. A descendant of Asaph, the Levite minstrel, who assisted in the purification of the temple in the reign of Hezekiah (II Chron. 29:13), B. C. c. 715.

5. An Israelite "of the sons of Elam" who divorced his Gentile wife after the exile (Ezra 10:26), B. C. 456.

6-8. Three Israelites—one a descendant (or resident) of Zattu (Ezra 10:27); another, "of the sons" (i. e., inhabitants) of Pahath-maob (10:30); and still another, a descendant (or resident) of Bani (10:37)—who put away their Gentile wives after the captivity, B. C. 456.

9. A Levite, father of Zaccur and grandfather of Hanan, the under treasurer who had charge of the offerings for the Levites in the time of Nehemiah (Neh. 13:13), B. C. considerably before 444.

Mat'tatha (măt'á-thá; Luke 3:31). *See* Mattathah, 1.

Mat'tathah (măt'á-thá; *gift of Jehovah*).

1. (A. V. "Mattatha"). The son of Nathan and grandson of David, among the ancestry of our Lord (Luke 3:31).

2. An Israelite of the "sons" (inhabitants) of Hashum who put away his foreign wife in the time of Ezra (Ezra 10:33), B. C. 456.

Mattathi'as (măt-à-thī'ăs), Gr. form of Heb. Mattathiah (*gift of Jehovah*).

1. The son of Amos and father of Joseph, in the genealogy of our Lord (Luke 3:25).

2. The son of Semei in the same catalogue (Luke 3:26). "As no such name appears in the parallel passages of the Old Testament, and would here unduly protract the interval limited by other initimations of the generations, it is probably interpolated from No. 1" (Strong, *Harmony and Exposition of the Gospels*, p. 16).

Mattena'i (măt-tê-nā'ī; *liberal;* probably a contraction of *Mattaniah*).

1, 2. Israelites, one a son (or citizen) of Hashum (Ezra 10:33), and the other of Bani (10:37), who put away their heathen wives after the captivity, B. C. 456.

3. A priest of the family of Joiarib, who lived in the time of Joiakim, the son of Jeshua (Neh. 12:19), B. C. after 536.

Mat'than (măt'thăn), the son of Eleazar and father of Jacob, which last was father of Joseph, "the husband of Mary" (Matt. 1:15), B. C. considerably before 40.

Mat'that (măt'thăt; *gift* i. e., *of God*).

1. The son of Levi, and father of Heli, who was the father of the Virgin Mary (Luke 3:24), B. C. before 22.

2. The son of another Levi, and father of Jorim (Luke 3:29).

Mat'thew.—1. **Name and Family** (măth'ū; contraction of *Mattathias, a gift of Jehovah*). The son of a certain Alpheus, and surnamed Levi (Mark 2:14; Luke 5:27). It is not known whether his father was the same as the Alpheus named as the father of James the Less, but he was probably another.

2. **Personal History.** (1) **Residence and profession.** Matthew's residence was at Capernaum, and he was a publican. There was at that time a large population surrounding the Lake of Gennesaret; its fisheries supplied a source of livelihood, and its surface was alive with a busy navigation and traffic. A customhouse was established at Capernaum by the Romans, and Matthew was tax collector. The publicans proper were usually Romans of rank and wealth, who farmed or let out the business of collecting to resident deputies, who were called **portitors**. It was to this class that Matthew belonged. (2) **His call.** While Matthew was thus occupied, "sitting at the receipt of custom," Jesus said to him, "Follow me." He probably already knew Jesus, for he immediately "arose and followed him" (Matt. 9:9; Mark 2:14; Luke 5:27, 28). Shortly after Matthew made "a great feast in his own house" in honor of Jesus (Luke 5:29; Matt. 9:10; Mark 2:15), and perhaps as a farewell to his old associates, for "many publicans and sinners came and sat down" (Matt. 9:10). After this we find no mention of him save in the catalogues of the apostles (Luke 6:15), and his presence in the "upper room" in Jerusalem after our Lord's ascension (Acts 1:13). The gospel which bears his name was written by the apostle, according to the testimony of all antiquity. Tradition relates that Matthew

preached in Judea after the ascension for a number of years (twelve or fifteen), and then went to foreign nations.

Matthew, Gospel of, the first book of the N. T. It was undoubtedly placed first in the category of the four gospels because at an early date it was received as authentic and presented the life of Jesus Christ particularly as it affected Jews converted to Christianity.

288. Traditional Mount of Temptation

1. **The Theme.** The subject of the book is outlined in the first verse. The gospel of Matthew is "the book of the generation of Jesus Christ, the Son of David, the Son of Abraham" (Matt. 1:1). In this introduction our Lord is related to two of the most important O. T. covenants, the Davidic Covenant (II Sam. 7:8-16) and the Abrahamic Covenant (Gen. 15:18). Matthew, accordingly, describes Jesus Christ in this twofold character. In line with the scope indicated in verse 1 of chapter 1 he sets forth first the King, the Son of David, then the Son of Abraham in His obedience unto death. In this book the Covenant King of Israel, "David's Righteous Branch" (Jer. 23: 5; 33:15) is presented. The first 25 chapters deal with the King of the Davidic Covenant; His royal birth in Bethlehem, fulfilling Mic. 5:2; the ministry of John the Baptist, the King's forerunner, fulfilling Mal. 3:1, the ministry of the King Himself, His rejection by the nation Israel and His predictions of His Second Coming in power and great glory. Says S. Lewis Johnson, "The theme of Matthew, then, is the presentation of the King and His kingdom to the nation in fulfillment of the O. T. prophecy." (*Bibliothecra Sacra* 112, April, 1955, p. 144). Not until the closing part of the book (chaps. 26:28), does Matthew revert to the Abrahamic Covenant. He then records the propitiatory death of the Son of Abraham. To determine the "structure" and purpose of the gospel, one must take this division in 1:1 into consideration. The book is peculiarly the gospel for Israel, but as proceeding from the atonement of Christ, a gospel of world outreach.

2. **The Outline.**

Part I. The King, the Son of David, offered to Israel, 1:1-25:46

  a. The genealogy and birth of the King, 1:1-25

  b. The infancy and concealment of the King, 2:1-23

  c. The kingdom presented to Israel and rejected, 3:1-11:1

d. The revelation of the King's new program, 11:2-13:52
e. The ministry of the rejected King, 14:1-23:39
f. The rejected King's promise to return in power and glory, 24:1-25:46

Part II. The King, the Son of Abraham, put to death and raised again, 26:1-28:8
Part III. The King in resurrection ministry to His disciples, 28:9-20

3. **Author.** This gospel was incontestably written by the Apostle Matthew, whose original name was Levi. He was a Jew whose father's name was Alphaeus. As he was a tax collector under the Romans at Capernaum and thus a hated publican, it is unthinkable that his name would have been attached to the first gospel had he not been the actual writer of it. Moreover, seventeen independent witnesses of the first four centuries attest its genuineness.

4. **Original Language.** Despite the critical claim that Matthew originally wrote the gospel in Aramaic, this contention has never been proved. If there was an Aramaic original, it disappeared at a very early age. The Greek gospel, which is now the Church's heritage, was almost beyond doubt written in Matthew's lifetime. The Jewish historian Josephus furnishes an illustration of the fate of the Hebrew original of Matthew, if such ever existed. The celebrated historian himself tells us that he penned his great work, "The History of the Jews' Wars" originally in Aramaic, his native tongue, for the benefit of his own nation, and that he subsequently rendered it in Greek.

289. Traditional Mount of Beatitudes

4. **Date.** The Book of Matthew, like the other synoptics and the Book of Acts, does not report the fall of Jerusalem and the temple but describes these events as still future. These books have been written before this tragedy or a long time after it. It would be indeed audacious to put them long after 70 A. D. Therefore, they must have been penned before that date. Since Luke's gospel is earlier than Acts, and Matthew is certainly earlier than Luke, it seems entirely probable that if he wrote an Aramaic original he did so probably around 40-45 A. D. This would place the Greek Matthew around the middle of the first century A. D.

5. **The purpose.** Matthew seems definitely to have written to confirm persecuted Jewish believers in their faith and to reconcile them

in their thinking that the gospel was not a rejection of O. T. prophecies but rather an outworking of the great promises of the Abrahamic and Davidic Covenants. The Jews needed clear demonstration of the Messiah's Person and work and to have objections removed which hindered unbelieving Jews. The writer accomplishes this purpose by proving the kingship of the predicted divine-human Messiah; that He fulfilled O. T. predictions in His Person and work; that He produced the credentials of Israel's King and announced teachings of the kingdom; that His Person and work were rejected by the nation; that he announced a new program; His death, resurrection and Second Advent, and that after this present age of His building the Church, He will return to set up His kingdom. It is thus uniquely the gospel for the Jews. *M. F. U.*

Matthi'as (mà-thī'às; evidently a variant of Mattathias, *gift of Jehovah*). Of the family of Matthias no account is given, and of his life we have no account, excepting the incident narrated in Acts 1:15-26, viz., his being chosen an apostle. The one hundred and twenty were assembled at Jerusalem, waiting for the advent of the Holy Spirit; and, at the suggestion and under the supervision of Peter, proceeded to fill the place among the twelve left vacant by the defection and death of Judas Iscariot. Peter "laid down" the essential qualifications for the apostolic office—the having been one of the companions of Christ from his baptism by John till his ascension—and declared the object of the election "to be a witness with us of his resurrection" (5:21, 22). Two such men were chosen, but the ultimate decision was referred to God himself by the sacred trial of the lot, accompanied by prayer. The two were Joseph, called Barsabas, and surnamed the Just; and Matthias, upon the latter of whom the lot fell. He was straightway numbered among the apostles. Nothing reliable is recorded of his after life. He is not mentioned again in the New Testament. Eusebius and Epiphanius believed him to be one of the seventy disciples. One tradition says that he preached the Gospel in Judea, and was then stoned to death by the Jews. Others make him a martyr—by crucifixion—in Ethiopia or Colchis. An apocryphal gospel was published under his name, and Clement of Alexandria quotes from the Traditions of Matthias (Kitto, Smith).

The Lot. According to Grotius, this was taken by means of two urns. In one they placed two rolls of paper, with the names of Joseph and Matthias written within them, and in the other two rolls, one with the word "apostle" and the other blank; and one roll was drawn from each urn simultaneously. Clarke (*Com.*) thinks that the selection was by ballot, the Lord directing the mind of the majority to vote for Matthias. In the case of selection by lot there was no chance, for "the lot is cast into the lap (properly *urn*); but the whole disposing thereof is of the Lord" (Prov. 16:33).

Matthithi'ah (măt-ĭ-thī'à; *gift of Jehovah*).

1. A Levite, the eldest son of Shallum the Korahite, who had charge of the baked offerings, "things that were made in the pans" (I

Chron. 9:31), probably after the exile, B. C. about 445.

2. One of the sons of Jeduthun, a Levite appointed by David chief of the fourteenth division of the temple musicians (I Chron. 25:3, 21). He is probably the same as the one appointed to assist in the musical service at the removal of the ark to Jerusalem, and to act as doorkeeper (15:18, 21; 16:5), B. C. about 988.

3. An Israelite, or of the "sons" (residents) of Nebo, who put away his Gentile wife after the exile (Ezra 10:43), B. C. 456.

4. One of those who stood at the right hand of Ezra when he read the law to the people (Neh. 8:4), B. C. about 445.

Mattock, an agricultural implement like a pickax, with a wide point for grubbing up and digging out roots and stones (I Sam. 13:20, 21; II Chron. 34:6; Isa. 7:25). Until the time of Saul the Philistines had a monopoly on the smelting of iron, and Israelites had to take their tools to them for sharpening (I Sam. 13: 20, 21).

Maul, or **Mall** (Heb. *mēphîs*, a *breaker*), only in Prov. 25:18, "A man that beareth false witness against his neighbor is a maul." The language of Solomon suggests that he probably meant some weapon of war, in which case it might represent a mace or battleax. The R. S. V. renders "war-club." *See* Armor.

Maw (Heb. *qēbäh, hollow*), the rought, i. e., the fourth stomach of ruminating animals, in which the digestion of the food is completed. It was esteemed (like tripe) a great delicacy among the ancients. This, with the shoulder and the cheeks of a sacrificial animal, was given to the priest (Deut. 18:3). R. S. V. translates "stomach."

Maz'zaroth (măz'á-rŏth), only in Job 38:32, the twelve signs of the zodiac, which were imagined as *menazil*, i. e., lodging houses; or *burug*, strongholds, in which one after another the sun lodges as it describes the circle of the year. The question, "Canst thou bring forth Mazzaroth in his season?" means, Canst thou bring forth the zodiacal sign for each month, so that it becomes visible after sunset and is visible before sunset? To these priests offered incense; were abolished by Josiah (II Kings 23:5).

Me'ah (mē'á; a *hundred*), one of the towers on the wall of Jerusalem, rebuilt by Nehemiah (3:1; 12:39), near to the sheep gate. R. S. V. renders "Tower of the Hundred."

Meal. 1. (Heb. *qĕmäh, marrow*). The fatness of wheat, or barley, i. e., its ground substance (Num. 5:15; I Kings 4:22, etc.).

2. *Fine meal*, (Gen. 18:6, Matt. 13:33; Luke 13:21), the finest portion of flour (*q. v.*).

Meals, Meal Time. *See* Food, 5 (4).

Mea'rah (mē-ā'rá; a *cave*), a place between Tyre and Sidon (Josh. 13:4). Possibly only a cave, although extensive ruins are thought by Robinson possibly to be those of "Mearah of the Sidonians."

Measure. *See* Metrology.

Measuring Line. *See* Metrology, 1.

Meat. This word does not appear to be used in the Bible in the sense of animal food, which is denoted uniformly by "flesh." Perhaps the following may be exceptions: "Savory meat" (Gen. 27:4); "corn and bread and meat" (45:23). The only real and inconvenient ambiguity caused by the change which has taken place in the meaning of the word is in the case of the "meat offering," which consisted solely of flour and oil, sacrifices of flesh being confined to the other offerings. Several other words, distinct in the original, are rendered "meat;" but none of them presents any special interest except Heb. *țĕrĕph* (something *torn*). This word would be perhaps more accurately rendered "prey," or "booty." Its use in Psa. 111:5, especially when taken in connection with the word rendered "good understanding" in v. 10, which would rather be, as in the margin, "good success," throws a new and unexpected light over the familiar phrases of that beautiful psalm. In the New Testament the variety of the Greek words thus rendered is equally great. *See* Food.

Meat Offering (properly "meal offering"). *See* Sacrificial Offerings.

Mebun'nai (mê-bŭn'ī; *built, constructed*). In this form appears, in one passage only (II Sam. 23:27), the name of one of David's guard, who is elsewhere called *Sibbechai* (II Sam. 21:18; I Chron. 20:4), or *Sibbecai* (I Chron. 11:29; 27:11), in the A. V. The reading "Sibbechai" is evidently the true one.

Meche'rathite (mê-kē'răth-īt), a native or inhabitant of Mecherah (I Chron. 11:36); from II Sam. 23:34 it would appear to be a corruption for Maachathite.

Me'dad (mē'dăd; *beloved, friend*), one of the seventy elders chosen to assist Moses in the government of the people. He and Eldad remained behind in the camp, and were not among the rest of the seventy at the tabernacle. When the Spirit came upon these it descended also upon Medad and Eldad, so that they prophesied. A lad reported the matter to Moses, who did not forbid them, as requested by Joshua, but replied, "Would God that all the Lord's people were prophets," etc. (Num. 11:26, sq.), B. C. c. 1441.

Me'dan (mē'dăn), the third son of Abraham and Keturah (Gen. 25:2; I Chron. 1:32), B. C. after 2050.

Mede (mēd), an inhabitant of *Media* (*q. v.*), II Kings 17:6; Isa. 13:17; Dan. 5:28, 31.

Med'eba (mĕd'ê-bá; *water of quiet*), a city of great antiquity in Moab (Num. 21:30), belonging to Reuben (Josh. 13:16). It was a sanctuary of the Moabites in the days of Ahaz, and is named as one of the cities of Moab in the prophetic curse recorded in Isa. 15:2. When the Ammonites were defeated by Joab they found refuge in Medeba (I Chron. 19:1-15). The ruins, about eighteen miles E. of the Dead Sea, still remain, those of a large temple and extensive cisterns being important. Possibly the name is derived from these cisterns. Roads and streets can still be traced. Its name occurs on the Moabite Stone, 30.

Me'dia (mē'dĭ-á), an ancient Asiatic country situated S. of the Caspian Sea, N. of Elam, E. of the Zagros Mountains and W. of Parthia. It contains about 150,000 square miles, being about 600 miles in length and 250 miles in breadth. In the heyday of its power it stretched far beyond these confines. The country was noted for its horses. Its original inhabitants were subjugated by an Indo-European race, called in the Hebrew *mädai* (Gen. 10:2; I Chron. 1:5). The country is called Media (Esth. 1:3, 14, 18; 10:2; Isa. 21:2; Dan. 8:20). Darius is referred to in Dan. 5:31, as "the Median" (A. V.) or as "the Mede" (R. S. V.). Ezra 6:2 also refers to Media; elsewhere "the Medes" are alluded to. Media comes into historical perspective in the 9th century B. C., being encountered in the inscriptions of Shalmaneser III (c. 836 B. C.), who conducted a campaign against these peoples in the Zagros Mountain region. The "Amadai" (Medes) are listed among those who paid tribute to the Assyria Shamshi-Adad (825-812 B. C.), and Adad-Nirari III (812-782 B. C.) continued contact with these people. The mighty Tiglath-pileser III (745-727 B. C.) invaded Media and added districts of it to the Assyrian Empire. Sargon II, after capturing Samaria (721 B. C.), deported Israelites into the towns of the Medes (II Kings 17:6; 18:11). Sargon later around 710 B. C. more completely subdued the Median peoples and forced them to pay a tribute in the form of horses. Sargon's successor, Sennacherib, likewise put the Medes under heavy tribute.

In the succeeding years the Medes increased in power. About 614 B. C. they advanced down the Tigris and captured Asshur, ancient capital city of Assyria. In 612 B. C., Cyaxares in an alliance with the Chaldeans under Nabopolassar and the Scythian hordes captured Nineveh. This great event marked the crash of the Assyrian Empire. Cyaxares received as his part of the victor's spoil Assyria proper and the neighboring countries toward the N. and N. W. Nabopolassar's son Nebuchadnezzar married Cyaxares' daughter. This event strengthened the alliance between Media and Babylonia. Both countries were immeasurably strengthened in power. It was in the era of Nebuchadnezzar (c. 605-562 B. C.) that the Median kingdom reached the apogee of its power. In this period the empire included what is today part of Iraq, Iran, Anatolian Turkey and Armenia. It embraced Ecbatana, present-day Hamadan and Rhagae, modern Teheran.

Persia was dominated by Media until the rise of Cyrus II, the founder of the mighty Persian Empire. About 549 B. C. he subdued Media, establishing his capital in Pasargadae. Under the Persians, however, Media remained an important province and the dual name, Medes and Persians, long remained (Dan. 5:28; Esth. 1:19). The expression "the laws of the Medes and Persians" was reminiscent of the unchangeable character of Median law, which even a king could not alter without the consent of his government. Thus Medo-Persia became a dual nation which became a mighty empire lasting until the conquests of Alexander the Great (330 B. C.). After Alexander's decease, it became a part of Syria (I Macc. 6:56). Subsequently it constituted a part of the Persian Empire. The religion of the Medes became Zoroastrianism. This was a dualism with Ahuramazda, the Good, and Ahriman, the Bad. The great Persian emperors who were followers of Zoroaster, such as Darius I, were ardent Zoroastrians. They were remark-

able for their humaneness and high moral qualities. *M. F. U.*

Me'dian (mē'dĭ-ăn). Darius, "the son of Ahasuerus, of the seed of the Medes" (Dan. 9:1), or "the Mede" (11:1), is thus described in Dan. 5:31.

Mediation, a term, the proper use of which in theology refers to the work of Christ in establishing the Gospel dispensation, and in its continuance to the end.

1. **Scriptural Basis.** In several passages Christ is called the Mediator, "the Mediator of the New Testament," "the Mediator of the new covenant" (*mesitēs*, middleman, mediator) (see I Tim. 2:5; Heb. 8:6; 9:15; 12:24), also the general representations of the Scriptures concerning Christ present him as the one through whom is effected reconciliation between God and men, and through whom the moral and spiritual harmony of the world, broken by sin, shall ultimately be restored (e. g., II Cor. 5:18-20; Col. 1:21; Heb. 2:17; I Cor. 15:24-28).

2. **Theological.** The following features of doctrine are of chief importance: (1) The necessity for mediation arises from the holiness of God and the sinfulness of man. The reconciliation wrought by Christ, therefore, is represented as having two phases, that of God to man, and that of man to God (see II Cor. 5:18-20). It should always be borne in mind, however, that the whole provision of the mediatorial economy arises from the love of God (see John 3:16; Rom. 5:8). (2) Christ is the only mediator (in addition to Scriptures above cited see Acts 4:12; Gal. 2:12; 3:21). In his work of mediation his atoning death is central (see Matt. 20:28; 26:28; Rom. 5:6; I Cor. 1:18; 2:2; I Pet. 2:24; 3:18, and many other places). But more generally the whole work of Christ as prophet, priest, and king is embraced in his one work of mediation. The teachings of the Scriptures leave no room for the Roman Catholic view that priests and saints and angels, and especially the Virgin Mary, are mediators, which view is based upon a false doctrine of the prerogative of the priesthood, also a false conception of human merit. But still it is admissible and proper to recognize the real, though subordinate sense, in which all believers are members of "a royal priesthood" (I Pet. 2:9). The mediation of Christ, however, is supreme, and in its principal features stands entirely alone. (3) In Christ are found the necessary qualifications for this work. (*1*) He is the God-man. It was essential that the mediator should be divine; otherwise the sacrifices of himself could not have availed to take away sins; he could not be the perfect revelation of God to men, nor be the source of spiritual and eternal life to believers, nor control all events for the final consummation of his kingdom (see Heb. 9:14; Rom. 8:3; John 10:10; I Cor. 15:25). It was necessary that he should also be human; otherwise he could not have died to redeem us, nor stood as our representative before God's law, nor partaken in human experiences, nor be united with us in a common nature (see Heb. 2:11-16; 4:15; Rom. 8:3; Phil. 2:7). (*2*) He was without sin. As under the law the sacrifice laid upon the altar must be without blemish,

so the "Lamb of God that taketh away the sin of the world" must himself be free from sin, otherwise his sacrifice would not have been acceptable; he could not have access to God, nor be the source of holy life for his people (see Heb. 7:26; 4:15, 16; I Pet. 1:19; 2:22). *See* Atonement; Intercession, Jesus, Offices of; Kingdom of; Sinlessness of.

Mediator. *See* Atonement, Intercession.

Medicine. *See* Diseases, Treatment of.

Meditation, "a private devotional act, consisting in deliberate reflection upon some spiritual truth or mystery, accompanied by mental prayer and by acts of the affection and of the will, especially formation of resolutions as to future conduct" (*Cent. Dict.*, s. v.). Meditation is a duty which ought to be attended to by all who wish well to their spiritual interests. It should be *deliberate, close,* and *continuous* (Psa. 1:2; 119:97). The *subjects* which ought more especially to engage the Christian mind are: the works of creation (Psa. 19); the perfections of God (Deut. 32:4); the character, office, and work of Christ (Heb. 12:2, 3); the office and operations of the Holy Spirit (John, chaps. 15, 16); the dispensations of Providence (Psa. 97:1, 2); the precepts and promises of God's words (Psa. 119); the value, powers, and immortality of the soul (Mark 8:36); the depravity of our nature, and the grace of God in our salvation, etc.

Meekness (Hebrew from *'änäh, to be bowed down,* Gr. *praotēs, gentleness*). Meekness in the scriptural sense is an inwrought grace of the soul; and the exercises of it are first and chiefly toward God (Matt. 11:29; James 1:21). The Greek term "expresses that temper or spirit in which we accept his dealings with us without disputing and resisting; and it is closely linked with humility and follows close upon it (Eph. 4:2; Col. 3:13), because it is only the humble heart which is also the meek, and which, as such, does not fight against God, and more or less struggle and contend with him." "This meekness, however, which is first a meekness with respect to God, is also such in the face of men, even of evil men, out of the thought that these, with the insults and injuries which they may inflict, are permitted and used by him for the chastening and purifying of his people. This was the root of David's *humility* when, on occasion of his flight from Absalom, Shimei cursed and flung stones at him—the thought, viz., that the Lord had bidden him (II Sam. 16:11); that it was just for him to suffer these things, however unjust it might be for the other to inflict them; and out of like conviction all true humility must spring. He that is meek indeed will know himself a sinner among sinners; or, if in one case He could not know himself such, yet bearing a sinner's doom. And this will teach him to endure meekly the provocations with which they may provoke him, not to withdraw himself from the burdens which their sins may impose upon him (Gal. 6:1, II Tim. 2:25; Tit. 3:2)" (Trench, *Syn. of the N. T.*, i, 206, sq.).

Megid'do (mĕ-gĭd'ō, once Megiddon, Zech. 12:11; *place of troops*), one of the royal cities of the Canaanites (Josh. 12:21), first assigned to Issachar (Josh. 17:11), but afterward belong-

ing to Manasseh (Judg. 1:27). Megiddo did not become firmly occupied by the Israelites until the time of Solomon, who placed one of his twelve commissariats over "Taanach and Megiddo" (I Kings 4:12), and erected some costly works in the latter (9:15). The valley of Megiddo was a part of the plain of Esdraelon. It figured as a battlefield, and here *Barak* (*q. v.*) gained a notable victory over the king of Hazor, whose commanding general was Sisera (Judg. 4:15). To this place Ahaziah, king of Judah, fled, and there was mortally wounded by command of Jehu (II Kings 9:27). But the chief historical interest of Megiddo is concentrated in Josiah's death. He endeavored to stop Pharaoh-Necho, king of Egypt, while the Egyptian was passing through the glens of Carmel into the plain of Megiddo. He was defeated, and as he fled was shot by the Egyptian archers in his chariot, and died on the road to Jerusalem (II Kings 23:29, 30; II Chron. 35:20, sq.; Zech. 12:11). In the last passage the mourning mentioned is on account of Josiah's death.

290. Plain of Esdraelon

Megiddo is marked by the modern site, Tell el Mutesellim. It has been extensively excavated and forms one of the most important archaeological sites of Palestine. In 1903-5 its remarkable archaeological history began when G. Shumacher of the Deutsche Orientgesellschaft first began examining it. However, by far the greatest work on the site has been done by the Oriental Institute of the University of Chicago. Begun under the direction of Clarence S. Fisher in 1925, this work was continued in subsequent years by P. L. O. Guy and Gordon Loud. The site was occupied in the late Stone Age, long before 4500 B. C. Around 3500 B. C. the first city at this site, commanding the strategic Plain of Esdraelon, was built. This city was surrounded by a massive wall originally some thirteen feet thick and later buttressed to twice that thickness. A brick wall and gate of c. 1800 B. C. are known. The Canaanite city was apparently destroyed near the end of the twelfth century. Israel's occupation, represented by Level 5, began about a half century later. Thutmose III (c. 1468 B. C.) captured the then-existing city. The Canaanites held the important strategic center until dispossessed by the Israelites (c. 1100 B. C.). It is not known whether or not David erected any construction at Megiddo. Solomon, however,

291. Reconstruction of Gateway of Megiddo
(Solomonic period)

reconstructed the city as one of his chariot
towns; (I Kings 9:15; 10:26-29). He also
made it the center of one of his administrative districts. Solomon's Megiddo occupied
Stratum IV. Extensive stables of the Solomonic era were brought to light. Stone
pillars with holes in their corners served as
hitching posts. Stone mangers were in use and
the ground was paved with rough stones to
prevent the horses from slipping. It may be
that Ahab had something to do with these
constructions, but the concensus of opinion is
that they belong to Solomon (cf. W. F. Albright, *Am. Jour. Archeology*, 44, 1940, pp.
546-550. R. Engberg, *Bib. Archeologist*, iv,
Feb., 1941, p. 12f). Shishak (I Kings 14:25;
II Chron. 12:9) who over-ran Jerusalem and
Judea in the fifth year of Rehoboam, apparently took Megiddo c. 917 B. C. He left
evidence in an inscribed stela. Megiddo is a
large mound covering thirteen acres. Its
strategic layers rise 75 feet above the original
virgin rock. Immense amounts of money,
time and labor have been expended on the
excavation of this mound and the twenty cities
buried atop one another on the tell. A great
body of valuable Biblical material, however,
has been forthcoming and it has been one of
the most rewarding of Palestinian excavations.
M. F. U.

292. Decoration on Megiddo Ivory, (c. 1180 B. C.)

Megid′don (mê-gĭd′ŏn; Zech. 12:11). *See*
Megiddo.
Mehet′abeel (mê-hĕt′á-bêl; Neh. 6:10). *See*
Mehetabel, No. 2.
Mehet′abel (mê-hĕt′á-bĕl; *God benefits*).
1. The daughter of Matred and wife of

Hadad (or Hadar), the last-named king of
Edom (Gen. 36:39; I Chron. 1:50). *See* Hadad.
2. The father of Delaiah and grandfather of
Shemaiah, which latter had been hired by
Tobiah and Sanballat to intimidate Nehemiah
(Neh. 6:10), B. C. before 445.
Mehi′da (mê-hī′dá), a person whose descend-
ants (or place whose inhabitants) were among
the Nethinim who returned from Babylon
with Zerubbabel (Ezra 2:52; Neh. 7:54), B.
C. before 536.
Me′hir (mē′hẽr; *hire, price*), the son of Chelub
and father (founder?) of Eshton, of the family
of Judah (I Chron. 4:11).
Meho′lathite (mê-hō′lá-thīt), probably a
native of "Abel-meholah" (I Sam. 18:19; II
Sam. 21:8).
Mehu′jael (mê-hū′já-ĕl), the son of Irad
(grandson of Cain), and father of Methusael
(Gen. 4:18).
Mehu′man (mê-hū′mǎn; perhaps *faithful*), one
of the seven chamberlains (eunuchs) whom
Ahasuerus commanded to bring Queen Vashti
into the royal presence (Esth. 1:10), B. C.
about 478.
Mehu′nim (mê-hū′nǐm). *See* Meunim.
Me-jar′kon (mê-jär′kŏn; *waters of yellowish-
ness*), a town in the tribe of Dan (Josh. 19:46),
and probably receiving its name from a nearby
spring. From the clause which follows, "with
the border before (marg. 'over against')
Japho," it must have been in the neighborhood of Joppa.
Meko′nah (mê-kō′ná; *a base or foundation*), a
town situated near Ziklag, in the south of
Palestine, and inhabited by the men of Judah
after the captivity (Neh. 11:28).
Melati′ah (mêl-á-tī′á; *Jehovah has delivered*), a
Gibeonite who assisted in repairing the wall of
Jerusalem after the return from Babylon
(Neh. 3:7), B. C. 445.
Mel′chi (mĕl′kī; *my king*).
1. The son of Janna and father of Levi,
fourth in ascent from the Virgin Mary (Luke
3:24), B. C. much before 22.
2. The son of Addi, in the same genealogy
(Luke 3:28).
Melchi′ah (mĕl-kī′á; *Jehovah's king*), a priest,
the father of Pashur, which latter King Zedekiah sent to Jeremiah to inquire of the Lord
when Nebuchadnezzar made war against him
(Jer. 21:1); elsewhere called *Malchiah* (Jer.
38:1), *Malchijah* (I Chron. 9:12).
Melchis′edec (mĕl-kǐs′ĕ-dĕk; Heb. chaps. 5-7).
See Melchizedek.
Melchi-shu′a (mĕl-kī-shōō′á; I Sam. 14:49;
31:2). *See* Malchisua.
Melchiz′edek (mĕl-kǐz′ĕ-dĕk; *king of righteousness;* A. V. in New Testament, *Melchisedec*),
the king of Salem (i. e., Jerusalem), and
"priest of the most high God," who went out
to congratulate Abraham on his victory over
Chedorlaomer and his allies. He met him in
the "valley of Shaveh, which is the king's
dale." Melchizedek brought bread and wine
for the exhausted warriors, and bestowed his
blessing upon Abraham. In return the patriarch gave to the royal priest a tenth of all the
booty taken from the enemy (Gen. 14:18-20),
B. C. about 1970. Giving the tenth was a
practical acknowledgment of the divine priesthood of Melchizedek, for the tenth was, ac-

cording to the general custom, the offering presented to deity. Melchizedek is mentioned in Psa. 110:4, where it is foretold that the Messiah should be " a priest forever after the order of Melchizedek;" and in Heb. 5:7, where these two passages of the Old Testament are quoted and the typical relation of Melchizedek to our Lord is stated at great length. "After the order of Melchizedek" (Psa. 110:4) is explained by Gesenius and Rosenmüller to mean "manner," i. e., likeness in official dignity—a king and priest. The relation between Melchizedek and Christ as type and antitype is made in the Epistle to the Hebrews to consist in the following particulars: Each was a priest, (1) not of the Levitical tribe; (2) superior to Abraham; (3) whose beginning and end are unknown; (4) who is not only a priest, but also a king of righteousness and peace. "Without father," etc. (Heb. 7:3) refers to priestly genealogies. Melchizedek is not found on the register of the only line of legitimate priests; no record of his name is there; his father's name is not recorded, nor his mother's; no evidence points out his line of descent from Aaron. It is not affirmed that he had no father, that he was not born at any time, or died on any day; but that these facts were nowhere found on the register of the Levitical priesthood. Melchizedek offers an expressive type of Christ, the King-Priest, especially of Messiah's work in resurrection, inasmuch as the ancient character offers bread and wine, memorials of sacrifice (Gen. 14:18). The writer to the Hebrews beautifully describes the everlasting continuance and kingly authority of Christ's high priesthood by the phrase, "after the order of Melchisedek" (Heb. 6:20; 7:23, 24). The priesthood, as handed down through the line of Aaron, was often set aside by death. The Melchisedek aspect of Christ's priesthood portrays Christ in the perpetuity of His priestly office. "He ever lives to make intercession" (Heb. 7:25). Although the Aaronic priesthood could typify Christ's priestly work, it was limited in portraying the full scope of His priestly ministry. The Melchisedek type supplements the Aaronic type. As "King of Righteousness and King of Peace" (Isa. 11:4-9; Heb. 7:2) Christ will in the coming Kingdom Age assume both offices in His Person. The prophet Zechariah graphically sets this forth in the symbolic crowning of Joshua (Zech. 6:9-15). This significant event foreshadowed the millennial period when Messiah the Branch shall sit and rule "upon His throne; and he shall be a Priest upon His throne: and the counsel of peace shall be between them both" (vs. 13); that is, both offices, kingship and priesthood, will be united in One Person. Revised by *M. F. U.*

Mel'ea (měl'ĕ-à), the son of Menan, and father of Eliakim, among the maternal ancestry of Jesus (Luke 3:31).

Me'lech (mē'lĕk; *king*), the second son of Micah, the son of Merib-baal, or Mephibosheth (I Chron. 8:35; 9:41).

Mel'icu (mĕl'ĭ-kū; Neh. 12:14). *See* Malluch.

Mel'ita (mĕl'ĭ-tà), an island, the modern Malta. It is about seventeen miles long and nine wide, and about sixty in circumference. Here Paul's ship was wrecked (Acts 28:1, sq.).

The Phoenicians colonized it; the Greeks conquered it; the Carthagenians took it from the Greeks B. C. 528, and the Romans took it from them in B. C. 242. It is an English possession now.

Melody. *See* Music.

Melon. *See* Vegetable Kingdom.

Mel'zar (měl'zàr; Heb. *mělşâr*, from Akkad. maşşar, *watch, sentry*; marg. "steward"), the title of an officer in the Babylonian court, who had charge of the diet of the Hebrew youths in training for promotion as magi (Dan. 1:11, 16). "The *melzar* was subordinate to 'the master of the eunuchs;' and his office was to superintend the nurture and education of the young; he more nearly resembled our *tutor* than any other officer" (Smith, *Bib. Dict.*, s. v.). The R. S. V. renders "steward."

Mem (měm), the 13th letter of the Hebrew alphabet, corresponding to Greek *mu* (m), Latin and English *m*. In Psalm 119 it stands before the 18th section, in which each verse of the Hebrew begins with this letter.

Member (Gr. *melos*, a *limb*), a portion of the human body (Deut. 23:1; Job 17:7; Psa. 139:16; Rom. 6:13, 19, etc.).

Figurative. True believers are spoken of as being members of Christ's mystical body, viz., the Church (Eph. 4:25; 5:30).

Memorial, that by which the memory of any person or thing is preserved. Thus the feast of the Passover was a memorial of Jehovah sparing the firstborn of Israel in Egypt (Exod. 12:14); the heap of stones left in the bed of Jordan was a memorial of the Israelites crossing it (Josh. 4:7). The two engraved stones upon the shoulder braces of the high priest's ephod were "for a memorial" (Exod. 28:12); as were also the names engraved upon the jewels of his breastplate (v. 29). The sacrifice in the case of jealousy was called a memorial, because it brought iniquity to remembrance (Num. 5:15). A memorial was also a *record* (Exod. 17:14, "book of remembrance," Mal. 3:16). The act of Mary in anointing the feet of Jesus was to be spoken of as "a memorial of her," i. e., in her memory (Matt. 26:13; Mark 14:9; comp. Acts 10:4).

Mem'phis (měm'fĭs), an important ancient Egyptian capital situated on the Nile River some 10 miles N. of Cairo. The Hebrews were acquainted with Memphis under the name Noph (Isa. 19:13 A. V.) and Moph (Heb. text of Hosea 9:6). The city goes back to the time of Menes, founder of the First Dynasty (c. 2900 B. C.). Herodotus asserts that Menes built the city on a strip of land reclaimed from the Nile. Manetho considered Dynasties III-V and VII-VIII to be Memphite. King Djoser embellished the city and Imhotep, his renowned architect, constructed a step pyramid, a splendid monument in the Memphis acropolis at Saqqarah. This famous funerary structure is accounted the oldest extant stone structure in Egypt. Ptah was adored at this city. Memphis continued a famous metropolis even after the rise of Thebes, and did not lose its importance until overshadowed by Alexandria, Alexander the Great's brilliant city. Memphis existed down to the Middle Ages, but the ruins of its ancient buildings were carried away to build Cairo. Practically all

293. Sphinx and Pyramid of Cheops

that remains of importance now are a score of pyramids and the celebrated Sphinx, mute memorials of Memphis' ancient glory. Jeremiah refers to the city's outrages (2:16). The weeping prophet also predicted Nebuchadnezzar's Egyptian victories and that the people of Israel residing in Memphis would be carried away captive (46:14-19). The prophet Ezekiel also made predictions concerning the city (30:13, 16). M. F. U.

Memu'can (mē-mū'kăn), one of seven princes, or royal counselors, at the court of Ahasuerus, at whose suggestion Queen Vashti was divorced (Esth. 1:14, 16, 21), B. C. about 478.

Men'ahem (mĕn'a-hĕm; *comforter*), the seventeenth separate king of Israel. He was the son of Gadi, and probably one of the generals of King Zachariah. When he heard of the conspiracy of Shallum, his murder of the king, and his usurpation of the throne, he went up from Tirzah, where he then was, and slew the usurper in Samaria. Menahem in turn usurped the throne, and reduced Tiphsah because it refused to recognize him as king. He continued the calf worship of Jeroboam, and contributed to the ungodliness, demoralization, and feebleness of Israel, a melancholy picture of which has been left by the contemporary prophets, Hosea and Amos. During his reign the hostile force of Assyrians first appeared on the northeast frontier of Israel. Tiglath-pileser III (Pul) received from Menahem a gift of one thousand talents of silver, exacted from Israel by an assessment of fifty shekels a head, and became his ally. Menahem's reign lasted ten years, B. C. about 746-737. He left the throne to his son Pekahiah (II Kings 15:14-22).

Me'nan (mē'năn; meaning unknown), the son of Mattatha and father of Melea, in the ancestry of Jesus (Luke 3:31).

Me-ne, Me-ne, Te-kel, Uphar-sin, the words of an inscription supernaturally written upon the wall in Belshazzar's palace (Dan. 5:5-28). The words are Chaldee, and their meaning is given in the text; *mᵉnē, numbered*; *tᵉqăl, weighed*; *ūphărsîn*, from *pᵉrăs, divided*, i. e., *dissolved, destroyed*. "In all the three words there lies a double sense, which is brought out in the interpretation. . . . Daniel interprets mene: thus God has numbered thy kingdom, i. e., its duration, and has finished it, i. e., its duration is so counted out that it is full, that it now comes to an end. . . . The interpretation of

tekel presents this double meaning: Thou art weighed in the balances and found too light, i. e., deficient in moral worth. In upharsin, 'thy kingdom is divided,' the meaning is not that the kingdom was to be divided into two equal parts; but *peras* is to divided into pieces, to dissolve the kingdom" (Keil, *Com.*, in loc.).

It is recorded that the wise men could not "show the interpretation of the thing," and that it must have required a supernatural endowment on the part of Daniel—a conclusion confirmed by the exact coincidence of the event with the prediction.

Me'ni (mē'nĭ). *See* Gods, False.

Menstealer (Gr. *'andrapodistēs*), one who unjustly reduces free men to slavery, or steals and sells the slaves of others, and who was denounced by Paul (I Tim. 1:10). The stealing of a freeborn Israelite, either to treat him as a slave or sell him into slavery, was by the law of Moses punished by death (Exod. 21:16; Deut. 24:7).

Meon'enim (mē-ŏn'ē-nĭm; augurs). The Hebrew from *cănăn, to act covertly*, i. e., to practice *magic*). "The plain of Meonenim," (Judg. 9:37) is better rendered *the oak of Meonenim*, or *the augur's terebinth*. Some think that this was the oak "of Moreh," associated with events in the lives of Abraham (Gen. 12:6), of Jacob (35:4), Joshua (24:26), and Abimelech (Judg. 9:6), who was "made king by the plain—or oak—of the pillar that was in Shechem."

Meon'othai (mē-ŏn'ō-thī; *my dwellings*), apparently brother of Hathath, the son of Othniel (marg., "Hathath and Meonathai, who begat," etc.), and father of Ophrah (I Chron. 4:14), B. C. after 1440.

Meph'aath (mĕf'â-ăth; *illuminative*), a Levitical city (Josh 21:37; I Chron. 6:79) in the tribe of Reuben (Josh. 13:18). According to Eusebius, a garrison was stationed here as a defense against the inhabitants of the desert. It seems originally to have been a dependency of the Amorites (Num. 21:26), but afterward to have belonged to Moab (Jer. 48:21). Perhaps Tell Jawa, 6 miles S. of 'Amman.

Mephib'osheth (mĕ-fĭb'ō-shĕth; *exterminator of shame*, i. e., *idols*.

1. **The son of Saul** by his concubine Rizpah, the daughter of Aiah. He and his brother Armoni were among the seven victims who were surrendered by David to the Gibeonites, and by them crucified in sacrifice to Jehovah, to avert a famine from which the country was suffering (II Sam. 21:8, sq.), B. C. about 996.

2. **The son of Jonathan**, and grandson of Saul. (1) **Early life.** When his father and grandfather were slain at Gilboa, Mephibosheth was an infant of five years of age, living under the care of his nurse, probably at Gibeah. When the tidings of the disaster came to the royal household the nurse fled, carrying the child upon her shoulder. In her haste she let him fall, and Mephibosheth was crippled for life in both feet (II Sam. 4:4), B. C. about 1000. (2) **Befriended by David.** After the accident Mephibosheth seems to have found a refuge in the house of Machir, a Gadite sheik at Lo-debar, near Mahanaim, by whom he was brought up (Josephus, *Ant.*, vii, 5, 5).

He married and was living there, when David, having conquered his enemies, had leisure to make endeavors to fulfill his oath to Jonathan by the stone Ezel, that he would not "cut off his kindness from his house forever" (I Sam. 20:15). From Ziba he learned of the existence and whereabouts of Mephibosheth, and brought him and his son Micah (comp. I Chron. 9:40) to Jerusalem. The interview was characterized by fear and reverence on the part of Jonathan's son, and kindness and liberality on that of David. All the property of his grandfather was conveyed to Mephibosheth, and Zibah was commanded to cultivate the land in his interest. Mephibosheth took up his residence in Jerusalem, and was a daily guest at the royal table (II Sam., ch. 9), B. C. about 984. (3) **During Absalom's revolt.** The next mention of Mephibosheth respects his behavior upon the revolt of Absalom. Of this there are two accounts—his own (II Sam. 19:24-30) and that of Ziba (16:1-4)—and they naturally differ. Ziba, because of his loyalty and kindness, was rewarded with the possessions of his master. Mephibosheth met David a few days after and told his story, viz., that he had desired to fly with his benefactor, but was deceived by Ziba, so that he was obliged to remain behind. He had, however, done all that he could to evidence his sympathy with David, having gone into the deepest mourning for his aflicted friend. From the day the king left he had allowed his beard to grow ragged, his feet to be unwashed, and his linen unchanged. David doubtless believed his story, and revoked his judgment given to Ziba so much as to have the land divided between the two. Mephibosheth's answer was, "Yea, let him take all, forasmuch as my lord the king is come again in peace unto his own house," B. C. 967. We hear no more of Mephibosheth, except that the king did not suffer him to be included in the vengeance which the Gibeonites were allowed to execute upon the house of Saul (II Sam. 21:7).

Me′rab (mē′răb; *increase*), the eldest daughter of King Saul (I Sam. 14:49), whom, in accordance with the promise made before the death of Goliath (17:25), Saul had betrothed to David (18:17), B. C. about 1015. David's hesitation looks as if he did not much value the honor—at any rate, before the marriage Merab's younger sister, Michal, had displayed her attachment for David, and Merab was then married to Adriel the Meholathite, to whom she bore five sons (II Sam. 21:8), who were given up to the Gibeonites by David.

NOTE—In II Sam. 21:8, these children of Merab are said to be "the five sons of Michal, the daughter of Saul, whom she brought up for Adrial," etc. "The A. V. of this last passage is an accommodation. The Hebrew text has 'the five sons of Michal, daughter of Saul, which she bare to Adriel.' The most probable solution of the difficulty is that 'Michal' is the mistake of a transcriber for 'Merab.' But the error is one of very ancient date" (Smith, *Dict.*, s.v.).

Mera′iah (mē-rā′yá; *rebellion*), a chief priest contemporary with the high priest Joiakim (Neh. 12:12).

Mera′ioth (mē-rā′yŏth; *rebellious*).

1. The son of Zerahiah, a high priest of the line of Eleazar (I Chron. 6:6, 7, 52; Ezra 7:3). Lightfoot (*Temple Service*, iv, §1) thinks that he was the immediate predecessor of Eli in the office of high priest, and that at his death the high priesthood changed from the line of Eleazar to that of Ithamar. The same person is doubtless meant in I Chron. 9:11; Neh. 11:11, but placed by copyist's mistake between Zadok and Ahitub, instead of after the latter.

2. A chief priest whose house was represented in the time of Joiakim by Helkai (Neh. 12:15).

Mera′ri (mē-rā′rī; *bitter*, *sad*), the third named of the sons of Levi, probably born in Canaan (Gen. 46:11; Exod. 6:16; Num. 3:17; I Chron. 6:1, sq.), B. C. about 1890. All that is known of his personal history is the fact of his birth before the migration of Jacob to Egypt, and of his being one of the seventy persons who accompanied him thither (Gen. 46:8, sq.). He became the head of the third division of the Levites, that is, the Merarites.

Mera′rites (mē-rā′rīts). *See* Levites.

Meratha′im (mĕr-á-thā′ĭm; *twofold* or *double rebellion*, Jer. 50:21), the name given to Babylon. "The dual expresses intensity, without two rebillions of Babylon being supposed. The allusion is to rebellious defiance of the Lord (v. 24). The summons is addressed to the avenger described in v. 3" (Orelli, *Com.*, in loc.).

Merchandise, Merchant. *See* Commerce.

Mer′cury. *See* Gods, False.

Mercy (Heb. *ḥĕsĕd*, *kindness*; Gr. *'eleos*, *compassion*). "Mercy is a form of love determined by the state or condition of its objects. Their state is one of suffering and need, while they may be unworthy or ill-deserving. Mercy is at once the disposition of love respecting such, and the kindly ministry of love for their relief" (Miley, *Syst. Theol.*, i, 209, 210). The expression, "I will have mercy, and not sacrifice," indicates that God is pleased with the exercise of mercy rather than with the offering of sacrifices, though sin has made the latter necessary (I Sam. 15:22; Mic. 6:6-8). Mercy is a Christian grace, and is very strongly urged toward all men (Matt. 5:7; 23:23; James 3:17, etc.). *See* Grace, Love.

Mercy Seat. *See* Tabernacle.

Me′red (mē′rĕd; *rebellion*), the second son of Ezra, of the tribe of Judah (I Chron. 4:17, 18).

Mer′emoth (mĕr′ē-mŏth; *heights*, i. e., *exaltations*).

1. A priest, son of Uriah (Urijah), who was appointed to weigh and register the gold and silver vessels brought to Jerusalem (Ezra 8:33), B. C. about 457. He repaired two sections of the wall of Jerusalem under Nehemiah (Neh. 3:4, 21), B. C. 445.

2. A layman of the "sons" (inhabitants?) of Bani who divorced his Gentile wife after the captivity (Ezra 10:36), B. C. 456.

3. A priest, or more like a family of priests, who sealed the covenant with Nehemiah (Neh. 10:5). The latter supposition is more probable, as in Neh. 12:3 the name occurs among those who returned with Zerubbabel a century before.

Me′res (mē′rēz), one of the seven princes of

Persia and Media in the days of Ahasuerus (Esth. 1:14), B. C. about 478.

Mer′ibah (mĕr′ĭ-bȧ; *quarrel, strife*).

1. The latter of two names which Moses gave to a fountain, because of the complaints of the people of Israel. It was near Rephidim, in the Desert of Sin, probably in the wady Feiran, and on the western gulf of the Red Sea (Exod. 17:1-7), and called also "Masseh" (v. 7).

2. There is another Meribah near Kadesh (Num. 27:14, Meribah-Kadesh; Deut. 32:51), generally called by adding the word "waters" to distinguish it (Psa. 81:7; 106:32, A. V. "waters of strife;" "provocation," 95:8). It was at this place that Moses smote the rock, and offended God by his impatience (Num. 20:10-12); near the close of the desert wanderings (Deut. 32:51).

Mer′ibah-Ka′desh (mĕr′ĭ-bȧ-kā′dĕsh; Deut. 32:51). See Meribah, 2.

Mer′ib-ba′al (mĕr′ĭb-bā′ăl; *contender with Baal*), the son of Jonathan (I Chron. 8:34; 9:40), who in II Samuel is called *Mephibosheth* by substitution of Heb. *bōshĕth* ("shame") for the false god.

Mero′dach (mē-rō′dăk). See Gods, False.

Mero′dach-bal′adan (mē-rō′dăk-băl′ȧ-dăn; Akkad. *Marduk has given a son*), the name of a king of Babylon, contemporary with Hezekiah, king of Judah (Isa. 39:1). He is mentioned also with the name Berodach-baladan (II Kings 20:12), which form is due to a confusion of two Hebrew characters which are much alike in their old forms.

1. **Leader of the Chaldeans.** Merodach-baladan was by race a Chaldean, and though the Chaldeans were almost certainly Semites they were nevertheless quite a different people (*see* Chaldeans). The Chaldeans were divided into a number of small tribes settled, for the most part, about the head of the Persian Gulf. They all envied the Babylonians their superior position and their vastly greater wealth, and again and again made efforts to win ascendency and secure political control in the great valley. Had all these separate Chaldean tribes been united under one leader this might have been achieved long before the 8th century. The leadership was not secured until Merodach-baladan had made himself chief of the tribe of Bit Yakin, which had its seat in the marshes close by the head of the Persian Gulf. Even under so masterful a spirit as his the Chaldeans could hardly have united but for his success in winning power in Babylonia. The prize of power in Babylonia had long been so highly esteemed among the Chaldeans that whoever won it was sure of leadership in all the Chaldean tribes as well as in his own. If the chief of the tribe of Bit Yakin became lord of Babylon he was certain to be called lord of the tribes of Bit Dakkuri, Bit Amukkani, and of every other Chaldean clan. In the year 732 Ukinzir, prince of the tribe of Amukkani, made himself king of Babylon in defiance of the Assyrian king who had been the ruler of Babylonia. That made him a sort of leader of all the Chaldeans, though they were not yet united enough to support him to the bitter end when the Assyrians were ready

to attack him. When Tiglath-pileser III (*see* Tiglath-pileser) came into Babylonia to reconquer it the Chaldean states submitted one after another without a struggle. Of all these chiefs who thus sent presents and acknowledged themselves as subjects of the Assyrians there was none so important, none so significant as Merodach-baladan, who presented (B. C. 729) an immense gift of gold, precious stones, choice woods, embroidered robes, cattle, and sheep. It was the first time that he had ever made submission to the Assyrians. The submission was for a time only—he would soon be in the full tide of rebellion. During the short reign of Shalmaneser no attempt appears to have been made by Merodach-baladan or by any other Chaldean prince to gain ascendency in Babylonia, or even complete freedom from Assyrian overlordship. But so soon as he was dead, in 722, the opportunity came and was speedily embraced. The successor of Shalmaneser was Sargon II, who had tremendous difficulties to face in the far west, and would therefore presumably have but little time or energy to devote to Babylonia. 2. **King of Babylon.** Without any great difficulty Merodach-baladan took southern Babylonia, and then the city of Babylon itself. On New Year's Day 721 he was proclaimed the ruler of Babylon. That he dared this much is proof of the stuff of which he was made. Sargon, of course, had to meet the issue thus joined, and immediately entered Babylonia with his army. At Dur-ilu he met Merodach-baladan accompanied by Elamite allies. In the inscriptions written later Sargon claims a victory—that was the usual custom of writing royal documents—but it is perfectly clear from the sequel that it must have been a very small victory indeed. Merodach-baladan was left in possession of the city of Babylon, where he had enough wealth to satisfy him for the present, and enough difficulties with priests and people to tax his highest powers. He was not likely to attempt to conquer northern Babylonia under the conditions that now prevailed, and Sargon left him to his own will, while he went to meet continually recurring rebellions elsewhere.

Merodach-baladan was now practically king of Babylon, and naturally also head of all the Chaldean states. He had achieved much indeed, but he was left in a position of enormous difficulty—a position that would test his qualities of statesmanship, without which no king becomes really great. 3. **Reverses.** His statesmanship was not equal to his generalship, and he was soon in a turmoil. His Chaldean followers wanted plunder, so also did his Aramaean and Elamite allies, and all these were consumed with mutual jealousies. He doubtless desired to govern well, for by so doing it was possible to win cordial allegiance from the Babylonian people and a firm hold upon the throne. But some concession must be made to his hungry followers, and so he gradually ventured on a career of plunder. The chief property owners of Sippar, Nippur, Babylon, and Borsippa were removed into Chaldea, and their possessions handed over to his followers. This act lost for him the allegiance of the priesthood and of the wealthy classes, and these now turned longingly to Sargon as a possible deliverer from the rapacious Chaldean. An army was dispatched southward from Assyria, which soon cut off Merodach-baladan from his Elamite allies. He was powerless to meet this Assyrian army, and must therefore flee into the land from which he had come, after ruling Babylon for eleven years. Sargon pursued him into Chaldea, where he was wounded and fled into Elam. It would seem as though he must be undone by these reverses, but Merodach-baladan had patience and persistence, and would be heard from again. But he must wait a favorable opportunity, which did not come until Sargon was dead and Sennacherib was on his throne. 4. **Second Time King.** Then came a rebellion in Babylonia against him under the leadership of a certain Marduk-zakir-shumu, who is called the son of a slave. When he had reigned only one month Merodach-baladan appeared, and in 702 was again proclaimed king of Babylon. It was probably at just this time that Merodach-baladan sent his embassy to Hezekiah (II Kings 20:12-19; II Chron. 32:31; Isa. 39:1-8), though the date of it is obscure and doubtful. This embassy was sent nominally to congratulate Hezekiah upon his recovery from illness, but we shall probably not go far astray if we see in it an attempt to get Hezekiah to join in a rebellion in the west against the Assyrian king. Such a diversion as that would greatly help Merodach-baladan's position in Babylonia. The plan failed, for Sennacherib invaded Babylonia, and Merodach-baladan saved his life only by precipitate flight into his old home-land.

5. **Final Reverses.** Sennacherib then attacked the west, and while thus engaged a new rebellion began in Babylonia, in which, naturally enough, Merodach-baladan was ready to participate. It was, however, of very short duration, for Sennacherib entered the land again, and again Merodach-baladan must flee. He put his goods, his people, and his gods upon boats, and floated them down the Euphrates to the Persian Gulf, and settled on its eastern shores in a part of Elam, whither Sennacherib dared not follow. There in exile he soon died. His career is without a parallel among his people. It was filled with contradictions. No man before him of that race has held power so great for so long a time. He had failed ultimately, but his followers would in a later day succeed far beyond his dreams.—*R. W. R.,* revised by *M. F. U.*

Me′rom (mē′rŏm; *height, or upper waters*), a triangular shaped body of water, about four and one-half miles in length by three and one-half wide. It is two hundred and seventy feet below the Mediterranean Sea. The Jordan passes through it, and it was where Joshua won a great victory over the Canaanites (Josh. 11:5-7). It is in the upper part of Palestine, in a level plain at the foot of the hills of Naphtali which touch the roots of Hermon, itself ten thousand feet in height. Merom is, without doubt the Lake Semechonitis of Josephus (*Ant.,* v, 5, 1; *Wars,* iii, 10, 7). The only reference to it in Scripture (Josh. 11:5-9) gives it as the scene of the third

and last great victory gained by Joshua over the Canaanites. It is called now Lake of Huleh. Some scholars, however, identify Merom with present-day Meiron, located at the base of Jebal Jermak W. of Safed, where there is an important spring. Thutmose III (c. 1480

294. Waters of Merom

B. C.) refers to *Mrm.* Other scholars would locate Merom at Khirbet el-Bijar near Marun er-Ras where there is also abundance of spring water. Revised by *M. F. U.*

Meron′othite (mē-rŏn′ō-thīt), i. e., the native of a place called probably Meronoth, of which, however, no further traces have yet been discovered. Two Meronothites are named in the Bible: (1) Jehdeiah, who had the charge of the royal asses of King David (I Chron. 27:30); and (2) Jadon, one of those who assisted in the repair of the wall of Jerusalem after the return from the captivity (Neh. 3:7).

Me′roz (mē′rŏz), a place in northern Palestine, and referred to in Scripture in connection with a curse in the Song of Deborah (Judg. 5:23; comp. 21:8-10, I Sam. 11:7). It would seem as if its people might have helped in the campaign against Sisera, but failed to do so. It has been satisfactorily identified with Khirbet Mārūs some 7½ miles S. of Kadesh of Naphtali.

Me′sech (mē′sĕk, Psa. 120:5). See Meshech.

Me′sha (mē′shà).

1. A place in Arabia, the western limit of the children of Joktan (Gen. 10:30), and possibly identical with Massa and Mash. However that may be, there is frequent mention of the latter country in the cuneiform inscriptions. It corresponds roughly with the Arabia Petraea of the geographers. It was the desert district which stretched away westward and southward of Babylon.

2. King of Moab and tributary to Ahab. At the death of Ahab (c. 852) Mesha endeavored to shake off the yoke of Israel and free himself from the burdensome tribute of one hundred thousand lambs and one hundred thousand rams, with their wool. When Jehoram became king he secured the assistance of Jehoshaphat in reducing the Moabites to their former condition of tributaries. The two armies marched by a circuitous route around the Dead Sea, and were joined by the forces of the king of Edom. The Moabites were defeated and driven from their stronghold, from which the king and seven hundred fighting men made an attempt to break

through the besieging army. Beaten back, he withdrew to the wall of the city, upon which he offered up his firstborn son and heir to the kingdom as a burnt offering to Chemosh, the fire god of Moab. His bloody sacrifice had the effect of inducing the besiegers to retire to their own land with much spoil (II Kings 3:4-27), B. C. c. 851. The exploits of "Mesha, son (i. e., *votary*) of Chemosh, king of Moab," are recorded in the inscription on the Moabite Stone discovered by M. Ganneau at Dibon in Moab.

3. The eldest son of Caleb (brother of Jerahmeel, and son of Hezron), and "father" (founder) of Ziph (I Chron. 2:42), B. C. about 1390.

4. A son of the Banjamite Shaharaim by his wife Hodesh (I Chron. 8:9).

Me'shach (mē'shăk), the name given to Mishael, one of the companions of Daniel, by the chief eunuch of the Babylonian court. He, with Daniel and two other captive youths, was selected to be trained as personal attendants and advisers of the king (Dan. 1:7, etc.), B. C. about 604. *See* Shadrach.

Me'shech (mē'shĕk). 1. A Japhetic people alluded to in Gen. 10:2. Ezekiel refers to them as allied with Tubal and associated with Gog, the prince of Rosh, Meshech and Tubal (Ezek. 32:26; 38:2, 3; 39:1 R. V.). Ezekiel also mentions them as engaged in commerce in the emporia of Tyre, dealing in slaves and bronze vessels (Ezek. 27:13). In the records of Tiglath-pileser I (c. 1110 B. C.) and Shalmaneser III (860-825 B. C.) the land of *Musku* (Meshech) is mentioned and situated in the mountains on the northern boundary of Assyria and bordering on Tabal, Biblical Tubal, in the W. The Moschoi and Tibarenoi are referred to by Herodotus as living in the mountains S. E. of the Black Sea (III. 94, VII. 78). Both Strabo and Pliny refer to Moschoi.

2. Another name (I Chron. 1:17) for *Mash* (*q. v.*).　　　　　　　　　**M. F. U.**

Meshelemi'ah (mē-shĕl-ē-mī'á; *Jehovah remunerates*), a Levite of the family of Kore, who, with his seven sons and brethren, were gatekeepers of the tabernacle in the time of David (I Chron. 9:21; 26:1, 2, 9), B. C. before 975. They were all assigned to the east gate, except Zechariah (v. 14), who had the north gate.

Meshez'abeel (mē-shĕz'á-bēl; *God delivers*), R. V. and R. S. V. Meshez'abel (mē-shĕz'-á-bĕl), the grandfather of Meshullam, who assisted in repairing the wall of Jerusalem (Neh. 3:4), one of the "chief of the people" who sealed the covenant with Nehemiah (10:21), and father of Pethahiah the Zerahite of Judah (11:24), B. C. before 445. Probably the same person is referred to in all the passages.

Meshil'lemith (mē-shĭl'ē-mĭth; I Chron. 9:12). *See* Meshillemoth.

Meshil'lemoth (mē-shĭl'ē-mŏth; *deeds of recompense*).

1. A priest, the son of Immer and father of Meshullam (I Chron. 9:12, where he is called *Meshillemith*). He is said (Neh. 11:13) to be the son of Immer and father of Ahasai, B. C. before 440.

2. The father of Berechiah, one of the chiefs

of Ephraim who protested against the attempt of the Israelites to make slaves of their captive brethren of Judah (II Chron. 28:12), B. C. before 735.

Mesho'bab (mē-shō'băb; *returned, restored*), a chief of the tribe of Simeon, whose family so increased that he migrated to Gedor in the time of Hezekiah (I Chron. 4:34), B. C. about 719.

Meshul'lam (mē-shŭl'ăm; *repaid, rewarded*).

1. The grandfather of Shaphan, the scribe who was sent by King Josiah to take charge of the moneys collected for the repairs of the temple (II Kings 22:3), B. C. before 639.

2. The eldest named of the children of Zerubbabel (I Chron. 3:19), B. C. about 536.

3. A Gadite, and one of the chiefs of the tribe residing in Bashan, and whose genealogies were taken in the time of Jeroboam and of Jotham (I Chron. 5:13), B. C. 783-738.

4. A Benjamite, and one of the descendants of Elpaal resident at Jerusalem after the captivity (I Chron. 8:17).

5. A Benjamite, son of Hodaviah (I Chron. 9:7), or Joed (Neh. 11:7), and father of Sallu, who resided at Jerusalem after the captivity, B. C. before 445.

6. Another Benjamite (son of Shephathiah) who dwelt at Jerusalem after the exile (I Chron. 9:8), B. C. about 445.

7. A priest (son of Zadok) whose descendants dwelt in Jerusalem (I Chron. 9:11; Neh. 11:11), B. C. before 445. He is probably the same as *Shallum* (*q. v.*).

8. The son of Meshillemith, and ancestor of Maasiai (I Chron. 9:12), or Amashai (Neh. 11:13), B. C. long before 445.

9. A Levite of the family of Kohath, and one of the overseers of the temple repairs in the reign of Josiah (II Chron. 34:12), B. C. 639.

10. One of the "chief men" sent by Ezra to Iddo to gather together the Levites to join the caravan about to return to Jerusalem (Ezra 8:16), B. C. about 557.

11. A chief man in the time of Ezra, probably a Levite, who assisted Jonathan and Jahaziah in abolishing the marriages which some of the people had contracted with foreign wives (Ezra 10:15), B. C. 457. He is probably the temple porter mentioned in Neh. 12:25, which last is also called *Meshelemiah* (I Chron. 26:1), *Shelemiah* (v. 14), and *Shallum* (Neh. 7:45).

12. One of the "sons" (descendants) of Bani, who divorced his Gentile wife after the captivity (Ezra 10:29), B. C. 456.

13. The son of Berechiah who repaired a portion of the walls of Jerusalem after the captivity (Neh. 3:4, 30), B. C. 445. It was his daughter who married Johanan, the son of Tobiah the Ammonite (6:18).

14. The son of Besodeiah; he, with Jehoiada, repaired the old gate of Jerusalem (Neh. 3:6), B. C. 445.

15. One of the principal Israelites who stood at Ezra's left hand when he read the law to the people (Neh. 8:4), B. C. about 445. He is, perhaps, one of those who subscribed the sacred covenant (10:20).

16. One of the priests who signed the cove-

nant made by Nehemiah and the people to serve the Lord (Neh. 10:7).

17. A priest in the days of Joiakim, the son of Jeshua, and representative of the house of Ezra (Neh. 12:13), B. C. after 536.

18. A priest at the same time as the preceding, and a son of Ginnethon (Neh. 12:16).

Meshul'lemeth (mē-shŭl'ē-mĕth; f. of *Meshullam, q. v.*), the daughter of Haruz of Jotbah, wife of Manasseh, king of Judah, and mother of his successor, Amon (II Kings 21:19), B. C. about 690.

Meso'baite (mē-sō'bá-īt), a designation of Jasiel, the last named of David's heroes (I Chron. 11:47), probably meaning "from Zobah." *See* Mezobaite.

gation canals combed this region in antiquity and it was capable of supporting a dense population and a very high degree of civilization. Great kings like Rim-Sin of Larsa and Hammurabi of Babylon took pride in their great irrigation projects, as did many other of these early rulers. Today this region lies scorched and almost uninhabitable with blistering heat and fine wind-driven sand. This territory was over-run by Mohammedans in the seventh century A. D. and the Mongols in the thirteenth, and its vast irrigation culture vanished. It was under Turkish rule until 1917 when the British took Baghdad. Since then it has been succeeded by the Iraq government. Efforts are currently being made

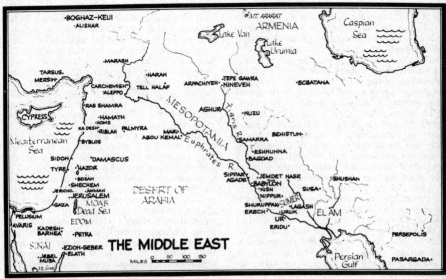

THE MIDDLE EAST

MILES 0   50   100   150

295.

Mesopota'mia (mĕs-ô-pô-tā'mǐ-á), *the country between the rivers*, the ordinary Greek rendering of the Hebrew Aram-Naharaim, meaning "Aram" or "Syria of the two rivers" (Gen. 24:10; Deut. 23:4; Judg. 3:8, 10) (See Roger T. O'Callaghan, *Aram-Naharaim*, Rome, 1948). Mesopotamia is now known as Iraq. The two great rivers of the region are the Tigris and Euphrates. The term Mesopotamia refers to the upper part of the valley of the two rivers known today by Arabs as Al Jazira or *"the island."* In modern usage the term Mesopotamia embraces also the lower part of the valley. The Tigris and the Euphrates were the life blood of this region in antiquity. These mighty rivers which cradled ancient civilization have their sources in the 10,000-ft. peaks of the Armenian Mountains. Here they gain sufficient water from melting snows to feed streams which flow through the desert. The silt-retaining waters of these great rivers have built the plain of Babylonia at the rate of about 72 feet a year or a mile-and-a-half a century. This region is of extreme fertility and, with irrigation, produces wheat, barley, figs, dates, pomegranates, corn and many other commodities. A network of irri-

to restore the irrigation network of ancient times.—*M. F. U.*

Mess (Heb. *măs'ēth*, a *raising*, as of the hands in prayer, Psa. 141:2; or of *flame*, Judg. 20:38, 40), a portion of food (Gen. 43:34; II Sam. 11:8).

Messi'ah (Heb. *māshîǎh, anointed;* rendered in the LXX by the Greek equivalent *Christos*). The word Christ is therefore almost invariably used instead of Messiah in the New Testament, as the official designation of our Lord. In two cases (John 1:41; 4:25) Messias is used—the Greek form of Messiah. In the Old Testament priests are referred to as the "anointed" (e. g., Lev. 4:3; 8:12; Psa. 105:15), also Kings (e. g., I Sam. 24:7-11; Psa. 2:2; Dan. 9:25, 26). We also read (I Kings 19:16) of anointing to the office of prophet. But along with these subordinate uses of the term, which undoubtedly foreshadowed the three great offices of Christ as prophet, priest, and king, there appeared its highest use in which it was employed to designate the One promised of God as the great Deliverer, and who was to be in a preeminent and altogether unique sense the Anointed, or the Messiah, of God. The subject is therefore very extensive, and offers to the student an immense field for investigation not only in the Old and New Testament Scriptures, but also in Jewish and Christian literature. We have space for only a brief presentation, as follows:

1. **The Messianic Idea.** (1) **The Old Testament Messianic revelation.** This appears not merely in particular predictions. The whole of the Old Testament is rather to be looked upon as bearing a prophetic character. The idea underlying the whole development of these Scriptures and the life dealt with therein is that of God's gracious manifestation of himself to men, and the establishment of his kingdom on the earth. This idea becomes more and more distinct and centralizes itself more and more fully in the person of the coming King, the Messiah. The creation and fall of man, the growing sinfulness of the race, make clear the need of deliverance. The preservation of a part of mankind from the flood, and the continuance of human history, has its great suggestion of promise. The call of Abraham, with the promise "in thy seed shall all the nations of the earth be blessed," revealed the divine purpose, which had been previously indicated, yet more distinctly (see Gen. 22:18; comp., 12:3; 9:26; 3:15). The founding of the Jewish nation, its theocratic character, its institutions, its ritual and history, all center about this one idea. The sinfulness of sin, the possibility and divinely appointed method of deliverance from sin, the realization of a kingdom of righteousness, lie at the very basis of the Jewish economy. Moreover, the chosen nation bore its peculiar character not merely for its own sake, but also for the sake of the world. Upon condition of fidelity to the covenant the promise was given, "Ye shall be unto me a kingdom of priests and a holy nation" (Exod. 19:6). The devout wish of Moses was significant also in the same direction, "Would God all the Lord's people were prophets" (Num. 11:29). But the highest glory of Israel was in the fact that from the nation one was to come in whom these noble relations to God and man, only to a large extent symbolized by the nation itself, should be perfectly fulfilled. The actual "Son" and "Servant" of God, the true Prophet, Priest, and King, was to be the Messiah. This is the key to the whole body of the Old Testament Scriptures. (2) **Designations.** That various designations were given to the Messiah was only natural, and to have been expected. Among them are the "Seed of Abraham," "Son of David," "Son of man," "My Son," "My Servant," "Mine Elect," "The Branch," "The Prince of Peace," "the Wonderful Counselor, the mighty God, the everlasting Father" (see Gen. 22:18; II Sam. 23:5; Psa. 2:7; Isa. 42:1; 9:6, 7; Zech. 3:8; 6:12; Dan. 7:13, 14; 10:16-18). (3) **Prophetic passages.** The number of passages in the Old Testament regarded by the Jews in pre-Christian times as prophetic of the Messiah is much larger than that of the special predictions to which Christians have commonly appealed. It is stated by Eldersheim to be upward of 456, of which 75 are from the Pentateuch, 243 from the prophets, and 138 from the Hagiographa. "But comparatively few of these," he adds,

"are what would be termed verbal predictions." This harmonizes, however, with what has already been said with regard to the general character of the Old Testament revelation. (For complete list of passages Messianically applied in the Rabbinic writings, see Edersheim's *Life and Times of Jesus*, Appendix IX). The predictions to which Christians as well as Jews have attached special importance embrace the following: Gen. 3:15 (the protoevangelium); 9:27; 12:3; 22:18; 49:8, 10; Deut. 18:18; II Sam. 7:11-16; 23:5; Psalms 2, 16, 22, 40, 110; Isa., chaps. 2, 7, 9, 11, 40, 42, 49, 53; Jer. 23:5, 6; Dan. 7:27; Zech. 12:10-14; Hag. 2:9; Mal. 3:1; 4:5, 6. For exposition of these and other passages, reference may profitably be made to the Old Testament commentaries, both Jewish and Christian. (4) **Jewish views of the Messiah.** What Messiah did the Jews expect, is one question and what should the Old Testament revelation have led them to expect, is another. The fact calls for explanation, that while Jewish expectation had been deepening, and in some respects becoming more definite and true during the centuries preceding the Christian era, so that at the time of our Lord's appearing it seemed to await its immediate fulfillment, the Jewish people were not prepared, as to the largest extent they have never been prepared, to recognize Jesus as the Christ. The reason is found in the rabbinical and popularly received ideas of the Messiah. The fatal mistake of the Jews was not in rejecting the Scriptures, but in giving to them a narrow and unspiritual interpretation. Jesus truly said, "Ye search the Scriptures, because ye think that in them ye have eternal life; and these are they which bear witness of me and ye will not come to me that ye may have life" (John 5:39, 40, R. V.). Their interpretation was far from being wholly false, as Edersheim shows with reference to the list of rabbinic interpretations above noted. It embraced "such doctrines as the premundane existence of the Messiah; his elevation above Moses, and even above the angels; his representative character; his cruel sufferings and derision; his violent death, and that for his people; his work in behalf of the living and of the dead; his redemption and restoration of Israel; the opposition of the Gentiles, their partial judgment and conversion; the prevalence of his law; the universal blessings of the latter days; and his kingdom." But this same interpretation left out certain elements of greatest and governing importance. The doctrines of original sin, and of the sinfulness of man's whole nature, were greatly reduced from their Scripture meaning, and practically omitted from the prevalent Jewish teaching. Consequently the deepest thought of the Messiahship, the salvation of the world from sin, was lacking. In keeping with this, the priestly office of the Messiah was also lost sight of. The prophetic office of the Messiah was also obscured. The all-absorbing ideas were those of kingship and deliverance. And these were chiefly of national significance. The restoration of national glory was the great hope of Israel. All else was subordinate to that. Of modern Jewish views our space permits only a few observations. While the denial has been constant that Jesus is the Christ, and while during many centuries the Jews almost universally continued to look for their national deliverer, and their hope was again and again stimulated and disappointed by the appearance of more than a score of false Messiahs, marked changes have taken place within recent years in Jewish opinions and belief upon this subject. (a) The relatively small and diminishing class known as Orthodox Jews adhere to the ancient expectation. (b) The Reformed Jews, embracing many of the most learned and influential, have laid this expectation aside. With this class the whole conception of the Messiah has become dim and confused. It is doubted as to whether the Messiah refers to a person or a time, also as to whether or not the person or time has arrived. (c) The main body of modern Jews still looks forward to the ingathering of the Jews and their restoration to national glory in the land of their forefathers, and along with this they expect an era of universal peace and harmony among men. But still there is great diversity of opinion as to the method and means by which these results are to be accomplished. The Messiah may mean a particular person born of the Jewish race, or the term may stand for a conjunction of events brought about by the Jewish people. A feature made prominent at present in Jewish denial of the Messiahship of our Lord is that, in their view, the Old Testament prophecies predict the full and blessed results of the Messianic reign as coming at once with the advent of the Messiah, and such results have not come; and they can find no prediction of a second advent. To us as Christians this objection has no force, in view of the comprehensiveness, and, at the same time, the gradual and incomplete development of Old Testament prophecy. The prophecies of the old dispensation do indeed look forward to the ripened results of Christ's reign. But the prophecies of the New Testament supplement those of the Old in unfolding the gradual methods by which these results are to be reached, and in predicting the final glorious coming of Christ.

2. **The Messianic Realization.** The question, is Jesus the Christ? is of greatest importance plainly, not to Jews only, but to all races of mankind. This question is answered affirmatively because Jesus distinctly claimed to be the Messiah, a claim reconcilable with his character only upon the supposition that his claim was valid. The conception of Messiahship which Jesus held and promulgated was unspeakably above the prevailing Jewish conception, and yet in reality that of Old Testament prophecy. The Gospel of Matthew gives important revelation concerning Messiah's kingdom. The phrase "Kingdom of Heaven," literally, "of the heavens," is peculiar to Matthew and denotes the Messianic rule on the earth of Christ as the Son of David. The designation is appropriate because it is the rule of the heavens over the earth (Matt. 6:10). The phrase is derived from the O. T. (Dan. 2:34-36:44; 7:23-27), and it is said that the "God of heaven" will set up this kingdom covenanted to David's

posterity (II Sam. 7:7-10) after the destruction of Gentile world powers by the returning Christ, "the Stone cut out without hands." This kingdom was confirmed to the Son of God through the Angel Gabriel (Luke 1:31-33). In Matthew's gospel the kingdom of heaven is described in three ways: 1. *At Hand.* From the beginning of John the Baptist's preaching (Matt. 3:2) to the rejection of the King and the announcement of His new message (Matt. 12:46-50). 2. *In the seven "mysteries of the kingdom of heaven"* now being consummated in this present age. 3. *The future prophetic aspect* when the kingdom will be established at the return of Christ in glory (Matt. chaps. 24, 25; Luke 9:12-19; Acts 15:14-17). Of this future Messianic glory our Lord had full consciousness in His earthly public ministry. See Prophecy; Christ; Son of Man.

Literature—Edersheim, *Life and Times of Jesus the Messiah;* Geikie, *Life and Words of Christ;* McCaul, *Messiahship of Jesus;* Fairbairn, *The Typology of Scripture;* Oehler, *Theologie der Alten Testaments;* Van Oosterzee, *Christ. Dogm.*, vol. ii, 526, sq.—E. McC. Revised by M. F. U.

Messi'as, the Greek form (*Messias,* John 1:41; 4:25) of the Hebrew title *Messiah* (q. v.), translated *Christ*.

Mete'yard (mēt'yârd; Heb. *mĭddäh, extension,* Lev. 19:35), a yard measure. Archaic expression for measuring-stick. *See* Metrology.

Me'theg-am'mah (mē'thĕg-ăm'á; *bridle of the mother*, i. e., *mother city*), the figurative term for a chief city of the Philistines, viz., Gath. To give up one's bridle to another is equivalent to submitting to him (II Sam. 8:1), and "bridle of the mother city" means the jurisdiction or power of the metropolis.

Methu'sael (mĕ-thū'sâ-ĕl; *man of God*), the son of Mehujael and father of Lamech, of the family of Cain (Gen. 4:18). R. S. V. renders Methu'shael.

Methu'selah (mĕ-thū'zĕ-là; *man of the dart*), the son of Enoch and grandfather of Noah. He, at the age of one hundred and eighty-seven years, became the father of Lamech, after whose birth he lived seven hundred and eighty-two years, and died at the advanced age of nine hundred and sixty-nine years (Gen. 5:21, 22, 25-27; I Chron. 1:3).

Metals. All the principal metals were familiar to the Hebrews and are mentioned in Scripture. (For Knowledge of Gold and Silver in the Ancient World see GOLDSMITH and METAL WORKERS under HANDICRAFTS).

1. Especially famous in antiquity was *copper*. This metal alloyed with tin has given its name to the Bronze-Stone or Chalcolithic Period, a now well-defined archaeological period extending from 4500 B. C. to 3000 B. C. Up until the Iron Age (1200-300 B. C.) copper was the most practical metal in the O. T. era. It was alloyed with tin and used for all kinds of utensils, weapons and knives (cf. Ex. 38:3; Num. 16:39; Jer. 52:18). The brass of the A. V. is taken by some scholars to mean copper; by others to denote bronze. Deut. 8:9 gives a graphic picture of the iron-copper-rich Arabah: "A land wherein thou

shalt eat bread without scarceness; thou shalt not lack anything in it. A land whose stones are iron and out of whose hills thou mayest dig brass." The reference here is obviously to copper. Nelson Glueck has uncovered copper smelting and mining centers in the Arabah region. Ezion-Geber, Solomon's seaport, was famous for the refining and exportation of raw copper. This site was explored from 1932 through the American Schools of Oriental Research and the Jordan Department of Antiquities. It is now known that King Solomon was a "copper king" and that Ezion-Geber was the Pittsburgh of his realm (I Kings 9: 26). Copper was also a well-known metal in Egypt, and Egyptians worked the copper mines of the Sinai Peninsula.

2. **Iron.** Iron after the time of Saul and David, when the Philistine iron-smelting monopoly was broken, introduced an economic revolution in Israel and became a factor in the development of the country. Iron is mentioned in Scripture in connection with Og's bed (Deut. 3:11), axe head (Deut. 19:5; cf. Num. 35:16). Tabernacle vessels (Josh. 6:19, 24), chariots (Josh. 17:16), military weapons (Rom. 17:7), chains for fetters (Psa. 107:10) and idols (Dan. 5:4). Before the dawn of the Iron Age (c. 1200 B. C.) iron was very scarce and valuable. Excavations of Sir Flinders Petrie at Gerar uncovered evidences of iron furnaces and various kinds of iron instruments, illustrating I Sam. 13:19-22. Previous to the Philistines the Hittites held the iron monopoly. The Phoenicians evidently got their secret from the Hittites. Archaeologists are of the opinion that the earliest iron in Bible lands was meteoric, containing a small amount of nickel. Both the Egyptian name of iron and the cuneiform ideogram suggest it was a "metal of heaven." This may be the explanation of the reference to iron among the descendants of Cain in Gen. 4:22. Moreover, excavations have shown that iron ores were occasionally smelted in Mesopotamia at an early date. At Tel Asmar (ancient Eshnunna), Henri Frankfort unearthed evidence of an iron blade from an occupational level belonging to c. 2700 B. C. (*Oriental Institute Commissions XVIII*, p. 59-61). A small steel axe has also been recovered from Ur (Millar Burrows, *What Mean These Stones?* New Haven, 1951, p. 158). However, for some inexplicable reason the discovery of iron was not pursued and did not come into general use on an industrial scale, as we have seen, until after 1200 B. C.—M. F. U.

Metrology, the science of weights and measures, whether these belong to money standards (coins) or to fixed quantities of capacity or extent. Metrology naturally divided itself into (1) Linear measures; (2) measures of capacity; (3) measures of weight; (4) measures of value, or money. For tables of various measures, see close of article.

I. LINEAR MEASURES. The names of the commonest smaller linear measures are taken from members of the human body, because, in nearly all nations, these were at first used to measure lengths. As men's bodies differed in size these measures varied. But the progress of art and commerce gradually brought them to a uniform standard. The linear measurements were:

(1) **Finger**, or **Digit** (Heb. *'ĕṣbă'*), the smallest measure among the Hebrews, and equal to the breadth of the human finger (about .75 inch). We find the thickness of the solid parts of Solomon's pillars measured by *fingers* (Jer. 52:21).

(2) **Handbreadth** (Heb. *ṭĕpăh*, between 3 and 4 inches, II Chron. 4:5; Psa. 39:5; *ṭōpăh*, Exod. 37:12), the width of four fingers closely pressed together. The handbreadth was in common use in early Hebrew times (Exod. 25:25; I Kings 7:26, etc.). It is used as an architectural term (I Kings 7:9, A. V. "coping"), and thought to mean the *corbels* upon which the roof beams rest.

(3) **Span** (Heb. zĕrĕth), the width from the end of the thumb to that of the little finger, when these were extended. This measure was in use among the Hebrews in very early times (Exod. 28:16; see 39:9; I Sam. 7:4). It was about 9 inches.

(4) **Cubit** (Latin *cubitum, elbow, cubit;* Heb. *'ămmăh;* Gr. *pēchus,* the *forearm*), an important and constant measure among the Hebrews (Exod 25:10, sq.; I Kings 7:24, sq.; Ezek. 40:5, etc.), and other ancient nations. It was commonly reckoned as the length of the arm from the point of the elbow to the end of the middle finger, about 18 inches. (1) *Egyptian cubit.* This was 6 handbreadths or palms, about 17.72 inches, but the royal Egyptian cubit was a palm longer (20.67 inches), evidence for this found in measuring sticks recovered from tombs. (2) *Babylonian cubit.* Herodotus states that the "royal" exceeded the "moderate" cubit by three digits. The majority of critics, however, think that Herodotus is speaking of the ordinary Greek cubit, though the opposite view is affirmed by Grote. Bockh estimates the Babylonian royal cubit at 20.806 inches. (3) *Hebrew cubit.* The Hebrews like the Egyptians and Babylonians had two cubits, the common and apparently older cubit (Deut. 3:11; II Chron. 3:3) and a cubit which was a handbreadth longer (Ezek. 40:5; 43:13). The common Hebrew cubit was 17.72 inches and the long cubit 20.67 inches, apparently the same as the the Egyptian royal cubit. The R. V. renders the passage "of six cubits to the joining."

(5) **Pace** (Heb. ṣă'ăd, II Sam. 6:13), a *step,* and so translated elsewhere. The above passage is the only one in which the term can be used as a measure of distance, and, if so, would answer to our yard.

(6) **Measuring reed** (Heb. *qănĕh, reed*), properly the calamus, or sweet cane, which, probably from its shape and length came to be used for a measure (Ezek. 40:3, 5; 42:15, sq.). Its length is given (40:5) as six times a cubit, plus six handbreadths, nearly 11 feet.

(7) **Furlong** (Gr. *stadion, established,* and so a distance, Luke 24:13; John 6:19; Rev. 14: 20), a Greek measure adopted by the Jews. Its length was six hundred Greek feet, or six hundred and twenty-five Roman feet, i. e., six hundred and six and three quarter English feet. This stade or furlong fell short of our furlong by fifty-three and one quarter feet. The term was also applied to a race course, as

those in most of large Greek cities were, like that at Olympia, six hundred Greek feet in length.

(8) **Mile** (Gr. *milion*, Matt. 5:41), equaled eight furlongs, or sixteen hundred and eighteen English yards, and was thus one hundred and forty-two yards less than the English statute mile. The *mile* was derived from the Roman system of measurement, and was in common use in our Lord's time.

(9) **Sabbath day's journey** (Gr. *sabbatou hodos*, Acts 1:12), a very limited distance, such as would naturally be regarded as the immediate vicinity of any locality. It is supposed to have been founded on the command, "Let no man go out of his place on the seventh day" (Exod. 16:29). This measure was fixed by the Jewish legislators at two thousand cubits; supposed to have been suggested by the space between the ark of God and the people (Josh. 3:4), or the extent of the suburbs of Levitical cities (Num. 35:5). The strict observance of the Sabbath day's journey, being called the "connection of boundaries." He who desired to go farther than two thousand cubits had only, before the beginning of the Sabbath, to deposit somewhere within this limit, and therefore perhaps at its end, food for two meals. He thus declared, as it were, that here would be his place of abode, and he might then, on the Sabbath, go not merely from his actual to his legal abode, but also two thousand cubits from the latter. Even such particular preparation was not necessary in all cases. If, for example, any one should be on the road when the Sabbath began, and see at a distance of two thousand cubits a tree or a wall, he might declare it to be his Sabbath home, and might then go not only two thousand cubits to the tree or wall, but two thousand cubits farther (Schurer, *Jewish People*, Div. II, ii, p. 121, 122).

(10) **A little way** (Heb. *kăbrăth hä'ărĕş*, Gen. 35:16; 48:7; II Kings 5:19), seems to indicate some definite distance, but it is impossible to state with precision what that distance was. The Septuagint renders it *a horse's race*, i. e., as the Arabians inform us, a *parasang* (thirty furlongs), about four English miles.

(11) **Day's journey** (Heb. *dĕrĕk yōm*), the most usual method of calculating distance in traveling in the East (Gen. 30:36; 31:23; Exod. 3:18; Num. 10:33, etc.; once in New Testament, Luke 2:44). Of course, it was not an exact measure, varying as the journey would according to the circumstances of the travelers, the country traveled, etc. The ordinary day's journey among the Jews was twenty to thirty miles, but when traveling in company only ten miles.

(12) **Mete'yard** (mēt'yârd; Heb. *mĭddäh*), a general term for measure, Archaic for measuring stick (Lev. 19:35).

II. MEASURES OF CAPACITY. It will be advisable to divide these measures into dry and liquid, remembering that some were used both ways.

1. **Dry Measures.** (1) **Handful** (Heb. *qō-mĕş*, Lev. 2:2; 5:12), probably never brought to any greater accuracy than the natural capacity of the human hand. It was also used as a liquid measure.

(2) **Cab** (Heb. *qăb, hollow*, II Kings 6:25), was, according to the rabbins, equal to one sixth seah (see below). It is equal to about 2 quarts.

(3) **Omer** (Heb. *'ōmĕr*, a *heap*, Exod. 16:16-36; "sheaf," Lev. 23:10), an ancient Hebrew measure. Its relative value was the one tenth ephah (Exod. 16:36), and it held about 5.1 pints. It contained the portion of manna assigned each individual for his daily food (Exod. 16:16-20).

(4) **Ephah** (Heb. *'ēphäh*), a measure of Egyptian origin, and in very common use among the Hebrews. It contained ten omers (Exod. 16:36), about three pecks and three pints, and was equivalent in capacity to the liquid measure, *bath*. According to Josephus (*Ant.*, viii, 2, 9), the ephah contained seventy-two sextarii.

(5) **Seah** (Heb. *sᵉʾäh, measure*; A. V. *measure*, Gen. 18:6; I Sam. 25:18; II Kings 7:16, 18; *ephah*, Judg. 6:19). It was a common household measure. According to the rabbins, it was equal to one third ephah, and was, perhaps, identical with A. V. "measure" *'shälîsh*, Isa. 40:12).

(6) **Homer** (Heb. *ḥōmĕr, heap*, Lev. 27:16; Num. 11:32; Ezek. 45:13; *kōr*, A. V. "measure;" *see* I Kings 4:22; 5:11; II Chron. 2:10; 27:5; Gr. *koros*, Luke 16:7). According to Fuerst, the *homer* was originally an ass load, and hence a measure of like capacity. It was supposed to have been called *kor* because of its being a circular measure. The homer contained ten ephahs (Ezek. 45:11), nearly eight bushels. The half-homer was known as *lĕthĕk* (Hos. 3:2).

2. **Liquid Measures.** (1) **Log** (Heb. *lōg, hollow*, Lev. 14:10, etc.), originally signified a *basin*. The rabbins reckoned it equal to six hen's eggs, their contents being measured by the amount of water they displaced, thus making it the one twelfth of a *hin*.

(2) **Hin** (Heb. *hîn*, of Egyptian origin, Exod. 29:40; 30:24; Num. 15:4, 7, 9; Ezek. 4:11, etc.), holding one sixth bath, nearly six pints.

(3) **Bath** (Heb. *băth, measured*), the largest of the liquid measures; first mentioned in I Kings 7:26; equal to the ephah, and so to the one tenth homer (Ezek. 45:11). Its capacity would thus be seven and a half gallons.

3. **Foreign Measures.** In the New Testament we find the following foreign measures:

(1) **Metretes** (Gr. *metrētēs, measure*; A. V. "firkin," John 2:6), known as *amphora*. It was used for measuring liquids, and contained seventy-two sextarii (see below), or somewhat less than nine English gallons.

(2) **Choenix** (Gr. *choinix*, only in Rev. 6:6, A. V. "measure"), a dry measure, containing two sextarii, or about one quart.

(3) **Sextarius** or **Xestes** (Gr. *chĕstēs*), a Greek measure with no Hebrew equivalent, holding about a pint (Josephus, *Ant.*, viii, 2, 9). Also any small vessel, as a cup or pitcher, whether a sextarius or not (Mark 7:8, A. V. "pot").

(4) **Modius** (Gr. *modius*), a dry measure holding sixteen sextarii, i. e., about one peck. It occurs three times in New Testament, and is rendered "bushel" (Matt. 5:15; Mark 4:21;

Luke 11:33). In each case it is accompanied by the Greek article, intimating that it was in use in every household.

(5) **Saton** (Gr. *saton*, Matt. 13:33; Luke 13:21, A. V. "measure"), a dry measure, supposed to be identical with the Hebrew seah, and to contain one peck.

(6) **Coros** (Gr. *koros*, Luke 16:7, A. V. "measure"), the same as the homer.

III. MEASURES OF WEIGHT. The Jewish rabbins estimated weights according to the number of grains of barley, taken from the middle of the ear, to which they were equivalent. In describing the weights used by the Hebrews we begin with the shekel, as it is the base of all the calculations of these weights.

(1) **Shekel** (Heb. *shĕqĕl*, *weight*), equal to twenty *gerahs* (Ezek. 45:12), or ten penny-weights English. Of all the Jewish weights none are so accurately marked as the shekel, from the fact that half a shekel was ordered by God to be paid by each Israelite as a ransom for his soul (Exod. 30:13). The circumstances of the captivity do not warrant the idea that the Hebrews lost their knowledge of their weights, least of all the shekel. The poorer classes were left in Canaan (II Kings 24:15, 16; 25:11, 12), and they would probably continue the use of the ancient weights and money; while the upper classes who were carried into captivity would likely retain some of them, especially the shekel. Then, too, we find the shekel in use in Jerusalem in the time of Zerubbabel. Although in very early times there may have been but one shekel (Gen. 23:15), it appears certain that from the period of Exodus there were at least two shekels—one used in all ordinary transactions (Exod. 38:29; Josh. 7:21; II Kings 7:1; Amos 8:5, etc.); the other used in the payment of vows, offerings, and other religious purposes (Exod. 30:13; Lev. 5:15; Num. 3:47), and called the "shekel of the sanctuary." It is a matter of much conjecture as to what, if any difference existed between these two shekels, and also "the shekel after the king's weight" (II Sam. 14:26). Jahn (*Arch.*, § 116) identifies the common and sacred shekels, and thinks that "the king's shekel" did not "amount to more than a fourth, perhaps not to more than the fifth or sixth part of the legal shekel." Keil (*Arch.*, ii, p. 231) thinks there was a common shekel, which was only the half of the holy one, or equal to the *bekah* (Exod. 38:26). He arrives at this conclusion by comparing I Kings 10:17 with II Chron. 9:16, "according to which three minas" (A. V. "pounds") equal three hundred common shekels; i. e., the mina contained one hundred shekels, whereas it contained only fifty holy or Mosaic shekels. He also identifies the "shekel after the king's weight" with the "shekel of the sanctuary." After the captivity, the probability is that only the holy shekel was in use. The passage (Ezek. 45:12) written when a considerable portion of the captivity was passed, directs that on the return home there should be but one uniform standard. That standard was to be the holy shekel, being composed of twenty gerahs (Exod. 30:13). Other evidence of this is furnished in the fact that while in

the earlier Scriptures reference was made to a difference of standard, no such distinction occurs after the captivity; the shekel coins of that period were all nearly of a weight.

(2) **Bekah** (Heb. *bĕqă'*, a *fraction*, only mentioned twice, Gen. 24:22; Exod. 38:26). In the latter passage it is said to equal one half a holy shekel. It was the weight in silver which was paid for each Israelite numbered (Exod. 38:26), and was equal to the tribute or didrachm (Matt. 17:24).

(3) **Gerah** (Heb. *gērāh*, *kernel*, a *bean* or *grain*), the smallest of the Hebrew weights, and the equivalent of the twentieth part of the holy shekel (Exod. 30:13; Lev. 27:25; Num. 3:47; 18:16; Ezek. 45:12).

(4) **Maneh** (Heb. *mānĕh*, a *portion*, the original of the Lat. *moneta* and our *money;* occurs only in I Kings 10:17; Ezra 2:69; Neh. 7:71, 72, rendered "pound;" Ezek. 45:12, A. V. *maneh*). From the latter passage it appears that there were sixty holy shekels in a maneh, whereas from the passages in Kings and Chronicles it is evident that a maneh was equivalent to one hundred shekels. These latter Keil thinks were the common shekels, a hundred of which would only make fifty holy (i. e., Mosaic) shekels. Sixty manehs formed a talent.

(5) **Talent** (Heb. *kĭkkār*, *circle;* Gr. *talanton*, a *balance*), the name given to this weight, perhaps, from its having been taken as "a round number" or sum total. It was the largest weight among the Hebrews, being used for metals, whether gold (I Kings 9:14; 10:10, etc.), silver (II Kings 5:22), lead (Zech. 5:7), bronze (Exod. 38:29), or iron (I Chron. 29:7). The talent was used by various nations, and differed considerably. It is perhaps impossible to determine whether the Hebrews had one talent only or several of different weights. From Exod. 38:24-29 we are led to infer that the talent of gold, silver, and brass was a talent of the same weight, and the evidence favors but one weight of that denomination, which contained three thousand shekels. Estimating a shekel at ten pennyweight, the talent would be equal to ninety-three pounds twelve ounces avoirdupois, or one hundred and twenty-five troy weight. A talent seems to have been a full weight for an able man to carry (II Kings 5:23). In the New Testament the talent occurs in a parable (Matt. 25:15) and as the estimate of a stone's weight (Rev. 16:21).

In addition to the above, which we can with certainty call Hebrew weights, both the Old Testament and New Testament refer to other weights, probably introduced from foreign nations. Of these we give the following brief account:

(6) **Dram** (Heb. *'ădārkōn*, I Chron. 29:7; Ezra 8:27, *dărkᵉmōn*, Ezra 2:69; Neh. 7:70, etc.), thought by some to be identical with each other and with the Persian *daric*. Others conclude from I Chron. 29:7 that the *'ădārkōn* was less than three tenths of a shekel.

(7) **Pound** (Gr. *mna*, Luke 19:13, 16, sq.), probably a Greek weight, used as a money of account, of which sixty went to the talent. It weighed one hundred drachmae, or fifteen ounces eighty-three and three quarter grains.

The "pound" in John 12:3; 19:39 is the rendering of the Gr. *litra*, a Roman pound of twelve ounces.

IV. MEASURES OF VALUE, OR MONEY. The necessity of some kind of money would arise in a very early state of civilization. The division of labor would require some measure of value; and commerce would take a more convenient, if more complicated form, by making this common measure to serve as a circulating medium. Men early decided that the precious metals formed by far the most convenient material for such a medium, although it is probable that they were first introduced in their gross and unpurified state. Money in ancient times was both uncoined and coined.

296. Ugaritic Bull Weight (One Mina)

1. **Uncoined Money.** It is well known that ancient nations that were without a coinage weighed the precious metals, a practice represented on the Egyptian monuments, on which gold and silver are shown to have been kept in the form of rings. It is uncertain whether any of these rings had a government stamp to denote their purity or value. Gold when brought as tribute was often in bags, which were deposited in the royal treasury. Though sealed and warranted to contain a certain quantity, they were weighed, unless intended as a present or when the honesty of a person was beyond suspicion. The Egyptians had also unstamped copper money, called "pieces of brass," which, like the gold and silver, continued to be taken by weight even in the time of the Ptolemies. Gradually the Greek coinage did away with the old system of weighing. The gold rings found in the Celtic countries have been held to have had the same use.

Bible notices. The pecuniary transactions recorded in the Bible were all, we can scarcely doubt, effected by bullion. Silver was weighed out by the patriarchs, who used it not only to buy grain from Egypt (Gen. 42:25, sq.; 43:15, sq.; 44:1, sq.), but land from the Canaanites (23:15, sq.). The narrative of the purchase of the burial place from Ephron gives us further insight into the use of money at that time (23:3, 9, 16). Here a currency is clearly indicated like that which the monuments of Egypt show to have been there used in a very remote age. A similar purchase is recorded of Jacob, who bought a parcel of a field at Shalem for a hundred kesitahs (33:18, 19). Throughout the history of Joseph we find evidences of the constant use of money in preference to barter (43:21; 47:13-16). Under the Mosaic law it was in silver shekels that

money was paid to the sanctuary for the ransom of male Israelites (30:13, sq.), compensations and fines (Exod. 21:22; Lev. 5:15; Deut. 22:19, 29), and the priestly valuations Lev. 27:3, 25, sq.; Num. 18:16), and all exchange and sales reckoned. Half shekels are mentioned (Exod. 30:13), which were called *bekahs* (38:26), as well as quarter shekels (I Sam. 9:8).

Very large sums were reckoned by the largest weights of the Israelites, the *talent*, a *round thing*, a name which indicates that there were lumps of silver in the form of thick round discs or rings, weighing three thousand shekels. We may thus sum up our results respecting the money mentioned in the books of Scripture written before the return from Babylon. From the time of Abraham silver money appears to have been in general use in Egypt and Canaan. This money was weighed when its value had to be determined, and we may therefore conclude that it was not of a settled system of weights. Since the money of Egypt and that of Canaan are spoken of together, we may reasonably suppose they were of the same kind. It is even probable that the form in both cases was similar or the same, since the ring money of Egypt resembles the ordinary ring money of the Celts, among whom it was probably the first introduced by the Phoenician traders.

2. **Coined Money.** Coined money was invented by the Lydians in Anatolia. Taking advantage of the abundance of gold and silver in their country, they turned out a great deal of coined currency. By the end of the seventh century B. C. coined money was plentiful in the Aegean world. Cyrus the Great, who conquered the fabulously opulent Croesus and his capital city of Sardis by 546 B. C., introduced coins into the mighty Persian Empire which he founded. Darius the Great (522-486 B. C.) made extensive use of this notable aid to commerce. He coined silver and gold and this, with many other commercial advantages, was the explanation of the might and grandeur of Persian power. The discovery of coinage was a great stride in commercial progress. It seems such a simple thing and doubtless Egyptians and Greeks, who came in contact with it through the Anatolian Lydians, must have wondered why they had not hit upon this brilliant idea earlier.

Revised by *M. F. U.*

Bible notices. The earliest coins mentioned in the Bible are the gold coins called *drams*, B. C. 538. It is thought by some that Jewish silver shekels and half shekels were introduced under Ezra (about B. C. 458); but it is most probable that they were issued under Simon Maccabaeus (*see* I Macc. 15:6), and copper coins were struck by the Asmonaean and Herodian family, B. C. 140. The following list embraces all the denominations of money mentioned in Old Testament and New Testament:

(1) **Bekah** (Heb. *bĕqăʿ, a half*), a Jewish weight of a half shekel's value (Exod. 38:26). As a coin it may have been issued at any time from Alexander until the earlier period of the Maccabees. *See* Shekel.

(2) **Brass** (*a*) (Heb. *nᵉhōshĕth, copper*, Ezek.

16:36, A. V. "filthiness"). In the expression, "Because thy filthiness is poured out," *neḥō-shēth* probably means brass or copper in the general sense of money. The only objection raised to this is that the Hebrews had no copper coin. But all that can be affirmed with certainty is that the use of copper or brass as money is not mentioned elsewhere in the Old Testament. But we cannot infer with certainty from this that it was not then in use. As soon as the Hebrews began to stamp coins, bronze or copper coins were stamped as well as the silver shekels, and specimens of these are still in existence from the time of the Maccabees. Judging from their size, these coins were in all probability worth a whole, a half, and a quarter gerah. (*b*) In Matt. 10:9 (Gr. *chalkos*, rendered "money" in Mark 6:8; 12:41) "brass" is used, apparently of a small Roman or Greek copper coin, of about the value of one half cent. The copper coins of Palestine are so minute, and so irregular in their weight, that their value, like that of the English copper coinage of the present day, was chiefly legal, or conventional, and did not represent the relative value of the two metals—silver and copper.

(3) **Denarius.** *See* Penny, below.

(4) **Didrachm.** *See* Tribute Money, below.

(5) **Dram** (Heb. *'ădărkōn*, I Chron. 29:7; Ezra 8:27; *dărkĕmōn*, Ezra 2:69; Neh. 7:70-72) is usually thought to mean the *daric* of the Persians, and seems to be etymologically connected with the Greek *drachma*. The dram is of interest as the earliest coined money which we can be sure was known to and used by the Jews. It must have been in circulation among the Jews during the captivity, and was extensively circulated in Greece. The coin was stamped on one side with the figure of a crowned archer, with one knee bent; on the other side a deep, irregular cleft. The darics in the British Meusum weigh 128.4 grains and 128.6 grains respectively, and are worth about $5.30. The *drachma*, as a silver coin ("piece of silver;" Luke 15:8, 9), was very common among the Greeks and Hebrews. It was a Greek coin, and at the time of Luke's writing was of about the same weight as the Roman *denarius* (or penny, *q. v.*), and was almost superseded by it. The author of the Chronicles uses the words used in his time to designate the current gold coins without intending to assume that darics were in use in the time of David. Probably the sum in darics is the amount contributed in gold pieces received as coins, while the talents represent the weight of the vessels and other articles brought as offerings.

(6) **Farthing.** Two names of coins in the New Testament are rendered in the A. V. by this word. (1) Gr. *kodrantēs*; Lat. *quadrans* (Matt. 5:26; Mark 12:42), a coin current in Palestine in the time of our Lord. It was equivalent to two lepta (A. V. "mites"). The name quadrans was originally given to the quarter of the Roman, *as*, or piece of three unciae, therefore also called teruncius. Its value was about 3.8 mills. (2) Gr. *'assarion* (Matt. 10:29; Luke 12:6), properly a small *as*, *assarium*, but in the time of our Lord used as the Greek equivalent of the Latin *as*. The

rendering of the Vulgate in Luke 12:6 makes it probable that a single coin is intended by two assaria. Its value is estimated at three fourths of a penny English money, or one and a half cents of ours.

(7) **Fourth part of a shekel** (Heb. *rĕbĕ', fourth*, I Sam. 9:8), the money which Saul's servant gave to Samuel as a present. It was the fourth of a shekel (*q. v.*).

(8) **Gerah** (Heb. *gērāh*, a *kernel*, Exod. 30: 31; Lev. 27:25; Num. 3:47; 18:16; Ezek. 45:12), the smallest weight and also the smallest piece of money among the Hebrews. It represented the twentieth part of a shekel, weighed thirteen and seven tenths Paris grains, and was worth about three cents.

(9) **Gold.** There is no positive mention of the use of *gold money* among the Hebrews, it being probably circulated by weight (I Chron. 21:25). The gold coinage current in Palestine in the New Testament period was the Roman imperial *aureus*, which passed for twenty-five denarii, about 22s. sterling or $3.30.

(10) **Half a shekel.** *See* Bekah.

(11) **Mite** (Gr. *lepton*, Mark 12:42; Luke 12:59; 21:2), a coin current in Palestine in the time of our Lord. It seems in Palestine to have been the smallest piece of money, being the half of the farthing (No. 1), and equal to 1.9 mills. From St. Mark's explanation, "two mites, which make a farthing" (v. 42), it may perhaps be inferred that the farthing was the commoner coin. In the Greco-Roman coinage of Palestine, the two smallest coins of which the assarion is the more common, seem to correspond to the farthing and the mite, the larger weighing about twice as much as the smaller.

(12) **Penny** (Gr. *dēnarion*, Matt. 18:28; 20:2, 9, 13; 22:19; Mark 6:37; 12:15; 14:5; Luke 7:41; 10:35; 20:24; John 6:7; 12:5; Rev. 6:6), a Roman silver coin, in the time of our Saviour and the apostles. It took its name from its being first equal to ten "asses," a number afterward increased to sixteen. The earliest specimens are of about the commencement of the 2d century B. C. From this time it was the principal silver coin of the commonwealth. In the time of Augustus eighty-four denarii were struck from the pound of silver, which would make the standard weight about sixty grains. This Nero reduced by striking ninety-six from the pound, which would give a standard weight of about fifty-two grains, results confirmed by the coins of the periods, which are, however, not exactly true to the standard. In Palestine, in the New Testament period, we learn from numismatic evidence that denarii must have mainly formed the silver currency. From the parable of the laborers in the vineyard it would seem that a denarius was then the ordinary pay for a day's labor (Matt. 20:2, 4, 7, 9, 10, 13), about fifteen cents.

(13) **Piece of gold.** This phrase occurs only in II Kings 5:5, where the word "*pieces*" is supplied by the translators. In several other passages of a similar kind in connection with gold, the A. V. supplies the word "shekels," which is probably correct.

(14) **Piece of money.** This expression represents two kinds of money in the Old Testa-

ment: (*a*) *Kesitah* (Gen. 33:18, 19). "The kesitah was a weighed piece of metal, and to judge from Gen. 23:16; Job 42:11, of considerably higher value than the shekel; not an unstamped piece of silver of the value of a lamb," as supposed by the old interpreters (Keil, *Arch.* ii, 24). These silver pieces, with their weight designated on them, are the *most ancient money* of which we have any information. It is clear that they circulated singly, from the fact that the worth of the article bought was given in the *number* of them. (*b*) The stater (*see* below).

(15) **Piece of silver.** Generally speaking, the word "pieces" has been supplied in the A. V. for a word understood in the Hebrew. The phrase is always "a thousand" or the like "of silver" (Gen. 20:16; 37:28; 45:22, etc.). In similar passages the word "shekels" occurs in the Hebrew, and there is little if any doubt that this is the word understood in all these cases. There are, however, two exceptional passages where a word equivalent to "piece" or "pieces" is found in the Hebrew. (*a*) The first occurs in I Sam. 2:36, where "piece" is the rendering of the Heb. *'ăgōräh*, something *gathered*. It may be the same as the gerah (*see* above). (*b*) The second is in Psa. 68:30, "till every one submit himself with pieces of silver." "Pieces" is here the translation of the Heb. *răṣ*, which occurs nowhere else in Scripture. Gesenius thinks pieces of uncoined silver is meant. Two words in the New Testament are rendered by "piece of silver." In Luke (15:8, 9) "pieces" is the rendering of the Gr. *drachmē* (*see* Dram, above); "pieces" is the rendering of the Gr. *'argurion* (Matt. 26:15; 27:3, 5, 6, 9), in the account of the betrayal of our Lord for "thirty pieces of silver." These are often taken to be denarii, but on insufficient ground. The parallel passage in Zechariah (11:12, 13) is rendered "thirty (pieces) of silver," but should doubtless be read "thirty shekels of silver." This was the sum payable as compensation for a slave that had been killed (Exod. 21:32), and also the price of a bond slave (Hos. 3:2). By paying thirty shekels they therefore gave him to understand that they did not estimate his services higher than the labor of a purchased slave. These shekels were probably tetradrachms of the Attic standard of the Greek cities of Syria and Phoenicia. These tetradrachms were common at the time of our Lord, and of them the *stater* was a specimen. The value put upon the conjuring books, doubtless by the conjurors themselves, was fifty thousand pieces of silver (Acts 19:19). The Vulgate has accurately rendered the phrase *denarii*, as there is no doubt that these coins are intended.

(16) **Pound** (Gr. *mna*, Luke 19:13-25), a value mentioned in the parable of the Ten Pounds, as is the talent in Matt. 25:14-30. The reference appears to be to a Greek pound, a weight used as a money of account, of which sixty went to the talent, the weight depending upon the weight of the talent. The *pound* contained one hundred drachmas, or from $16.50 to $17.60.

(17) **Shekel** (Heb. *shĕqĕl*, *weight*). The shekel was properly a certain *weight*, and the *shekel weight* of silver was the unit of value through

the whole age of Hebrew history down to the Babylonian captivity. It is now generally agreed that the oldest Jewish silver coins belong to the period of Simon Maccabaeus, B. C. 140. They are the *shekels* and *half shekels*, weighing two hundred and twenty and one hundred and ten grains, with several pieces in copper. The shekel presents on the obverse the legend SHEKEL OF ISRAEL; a cup or chalice, above which appears the date of Simon's government in which it was struck. Reverse, JERUSALEM THE HOLY; a triple lily or hyacinth. It is generally believed that the devices on this coin are intended to represent the pot that held manna and Aaron's rod that budded. The half shekel resembles the shekel, and they occur with the dates of the first, second, third, and fourth year of Simon. The value of the gold shekel is about five dollars and fifty cents; the silver about seventy-five cents. Of copper, we have parts of the copper shekel—the half, the quarter, the sixth.

(18) **Silverling** (Heb. *kĕsĕf*, i. e., *silver*, as elsewhere rendered), a word used only once in the A. V. (Isa. 7:23), for a piece of silver (*q. v.*).

(19) **Stater** (Gr. *statēr*, A. V. "a piece of money;" marg. "stater"). (1) The term stater is held to signify a coin of a certain weight, but perhaps means a standard coin. The gold staters were didrachms of the later Phoenician and the Attic talents, which, in this denomination, differ only about four grains troy. Of the former talent were the Daric staters or darics; of the latter, the stater of Athens. The electrum staters were coined by the Greek towns on the west coast of Asia Minor. They were three parts of gold to one of silver. Thus far the stater is always a didrachm. In silver the term is applied to the tetradrachm of Athens, which was of the weight of two gold staters of the same currency. There can therefore be no doubt that the name stater was applied to the standard denomination of both metals, and does not positively imply either a didrachm or a tetradrachm. (2) In the New Testament the stater is once mentioned (Matt. 17:24-27). The stater must here mean a silver tetradrachm; and the only tetradrachms then current in Palestine were of the same weight as the Hebrew shekel. And it is observable, in confirmation of the minute accuracy of the evangelist, that at this period the silver currency in Palestine consisted of Greek imperial tetradrachms, or staters, and Roman denarii of a quarter their value, didrachms having fallen into disuse (Smith. *Dict.*).

(20) **Talent** (Heb. *kĭkkär*, a *circle*; Gr. *talanton*, a *balance*), was the largest weight among the Hebrews, being used for metals, whether gold, silver, etc. A talent of gold was worth (Smith, *O. T. Hist.*, p. 395), in English money, £11,000, or about $30,000; of silver, £450, or $2,000. In the New Testament this word occurs (*a*) in the parable of the unmerciful servant (Matt. 18:23-25); (*b*) in the parable of the talents (Matt. 25:14-30). At this time the Attic talent obtained in Palestine; 60 *minae* and 6,000 *drachmae* went to the talent. It was consequently worth about £200, or about $560.

(21) **Third part of a shekel** (Num. 10:32), about tenpence halpenny English, or twenty-one cents.

(22) **Tribute money.** *See* Tribute.

Meu'nim (mē-ū'nĭm), plural of the gentilic adjective *me'ūnī* "from Maon," referring to the people of Maon. The word appears in the A. V. also as Mehunim. A people who lived in Mount Seir (II Chron. 20:1, 10), these people evidently had their capital at Ma'on, a dozen miles S. E. of Petra. The Simeonites near Gedar attacked them as foreigners (I Chron. 4:39-41). II Chron. 26:7 mentions them with the Philistines and the Arabians. After the captivity, some of their descendants served as Nethinim in the Jerusalem temple (Ezra 2:50; Neh. 7:52). They are identified by the Greek version with the Minaeans. If such an identification is correct, they formed probably the northernmost section of that S. Arabian people.—*M. F. U.*

Mez'ahab (mĕz'á-hăb; *water of gold*), the father of Matred and grandfather of Mehetabel, who was the wife of Hadar, or Hadad, the last-named king of Edom (Gen. 36:39; I Chron. 1:50).

Mezo'baite (mê-zō'bá-īt; an apparent gentilic adjective, I Chron. 11:47). R. V. and R. S. V. rendering.

Mi'amin (mī'á-mĭn; *from the right hand*).

1. A layman of Israel, of the family of Parosh, who divorced his Gentile wife after the captivity (Ezra 10:25), B. C. 456.

2. One of the priests who came to Jerusalem with Zerubbabel from Babylon (Neh. 12:5), B. C. about 536. He is probably the same person who is called Miniamin in Neh. 12:17.

Mib'har (mĭb'hár; *elite, choice*), the son of Haggeri, and one of David's heroes (I Chron. 11:38).

NOTE—"The verse in which it occurs appears to be corrupt, for in the corresponding catalogue of II Sam. 23:36 we find, instead of 'Mibhar the son of Haggeri,' 'of Zobah, Bani the Gadite.' It is easy to see, if the latter be the true reading, how *Bani haggadi* could be corrupted into *ben-haggeri*. But that 'Mibhar' is a corruption of *mittsobah*, 'of Zobah,' is not so clear, though not absolutely impossible. It would seem from the LXX of II Samuel that both readings originally coexisted" (Smith, *Bib. Dict.*, s. v.).

Mib'sam (mĭb'săm; *sweet odor, balsam*).

1. The fourth named of the sons of Ishmael (Gen. 25:13; I Chron. 1:29).

2. The son of Shallum and grandson of Shaul, the sixth son of Simeon (I Chron. 4:25).

Mib'zar (mĭb'zár; *fortress*), one of the "dukes" (phylarchs) of Edom descended from Esau (Gen. 36:42; I Chron. 1:53).

Mi'cah (mī'ká; a contraction of Micaiah, *who is like Jehovah?*).

1. A man of Mount Ephraim who lived, probably, in the time of the elders who survived Joshua, B. C. about 1360. He had stolen eleven hundred shekels of silver (about six hundred and seventy-five dollars) from his mother; but, impelled by the fear of her curse, had confessed and restored the money. Thereupon she put two hundred shekels into a goldsmith's hands to make an image (or images) for the semi-idolatrous establishment set up by Micah. At first Micah installed one of his sons as priest, but afterward appointed

a wandering Levite, named Jonathan, at a yearly stipend (Judg. 17:1, sq.). When the Danites were on their journey northward to settle in Laish they took away both the establishment and priest of Micah, who, upon overtaking the Danite army, found them too powerful for him to attack, and returned to his home (18:1-26).

2. The son of Shimei, father of Reaia, and one of the descendants of Joel, the Reubenite (I Chron. 5:5), B. C. before 782.

3. The son of Merib-baal (or Mephibosheth) and grandson of Jonathan (I Chron. 8:34, 35; 9:40, 41), B. C. after 1000.

4. (I Chron. 9:15). *See* Micha, 2.

5. The first in rank of the Kohathites of the family of Uzziel, as arranged by David (I Chron. 23:20), B. C. about 966. His son's name was Shamir, and a brother Isshiah is mentioned (I Chron. 24:24, 25).

6. The father of Abdon (II Chron. 34:20). *See* Michaiah, 1.

7. A prophet, styled "the Morasthite," as being a native of Moresheth of Gath (Mic. 1:1, 14, 15). He is thus distinguished from a former prophet, Micaiah (I Kings 22:8). The period during which Micah exercised the prophetical office is stated in the superscription to his prophecies (1:1) to have extended over the reigns of Jotham, Ahaz, and Hezekiah, kings of Judah, B. C. about 738-690. This would make him contemporary with Hosea, Amos, and Isaiah. One of his prophecies (Jer. 26:18) is distinctly assigned to the reign of Hezekiah, and was probably delivered before the great passover which inaugurated the reform in Judah. Very little is known of the circumstances of Micah's life. He was probably of the kingdom of Judah. For rebuking Jehoram for his impieties, Micah, according to Pseudo-Epiphanius, was thrown from a precipice and buried at Morathi, in his own country, near the cemetery of Enakim.

Micah, Book of, one of the books of the Minor Prophets named after the prophet, Micah, Hebrew *mîkāh*, an evident shortening of *Mikayahu*, signifying "Who is like Yahweh?" For the longer form of the name see Judg. 17:1, 4. The Septuagint renders Michaias and the Vulgate Michaeas.

1. **The Prophet.** Micah was a native, apparently, of Moresheth (Mic. 1:14), a Judaean town near Gath and at intervals a dependency of the Philistines. His prophetic ministry flourished in the reigns of Jotham (740-735), Ahaz (c. 735-715) and Hezekiah (c. 715-687). He was a simple villager but a prophet of social righteousness, defending the cause of the poverty-stricken masses like Amos, the herdsman. Like Hosea, Amos and Isaiah, Micah foretold the fall of the Northern Kingdom and the taking of Samaria (1:5-7). He warned of the coming desolation of Judah (1:9-16). His prophetic oracles have special reference to Judah, nevertheless he envisions all Israel (1:1, 5-7).

2. **The Outline.**

Part I. Prediction of Approaching Judgment, 1:1-2:13

  a. Upon Samaria, 1:2-8

  b. Upon Judah, 1:9-16

   c. Upon cruel oppressors, 2:1-11

   d. Upon a remnant, 2:12, 13

Part II. Prediction of the Messianic Kingdom, 3:1-5:15

   a. Preliminary Judgments, 3:1-12

   b. Description of the Kingdom, 4:1-5

   c. Establishment of the Kingdom, 4:6-13

   d. Rejection of the King at His First Coming, 5:1, 2

   e. Interval between the royal rejection and return, 5:3

   f. Messiah's Second Coming, 5:4-15

Part III. The Divine Controversy and Final Mercy, 6:1-7:20

   a. The people's ingratitude and sin, 6:1-7:6

   b. Prophetic intercession, 7:7-20

3. **Prophetic Style.** Micah writes in simple yet eloquent language. He is outspoken and fearless in denouncing iniquity (cf. 1:5; 2:1, 2). He is logical in his development but often abrupt in transition from one subject to another. He makes considerable use of metaphor (1:6; 3:2, 3, 6; 4:6-8, 13; 6:10, 11) and paronomasia, or play upon words (cf. chap 1) and is fond of rhetorical interrogation (cf. 1:5; 2:7; 4:9, etc.). He shows how God requires justice and loves mercy but requires these characteristics also in his followers.

4. **The Literary Composition.** Negative criticism has attacked the unity of Micah. Robert Pfeiffer is characteristic of the modern trend. According to this critic the first three chapters are authentic; however, section 4:1-5:15 is regarded as an interpolation, while 6:1-7:6 is said to be a later anonymous prophet's with its own editorial appendix (7:7-20). However, the expression "hear" (1:2; 3:1; 6:1) is an element of style suggesting unity of authorship. Moreover there are a number of parallels in chapters 4-7 with writings contemporary with Micah or written near his time (*See* Raven, *O. T. Intr.*, p. 230). Critics aver that the argument of the book is not closely knit. The fact that the book consists of various discussions delivered by the prophet over an extended period of time and under various circumstances is sufficient explanation of its lack of logical order. Critical views against Micah are vitiated by the unsound theory of the evolutionary development of religious concepts in Isaiah, Micah's contemporary. This view erroneously insists that certain theological ideas found in Micah did not come into developed form until a later date. This is purely supposition. There is no objective evidence to prove that such ideas, concerning salvation particularly, had not crystallized in Micah's day.—*M. F. U.*

Mica'iah (mī-kā′yȧ; *who is like Jehovah*), the son of Imlah, a prophet of Samaria, who, in the last year of the reign of Ahab, king of Israel, predicted his defeat and death, B. C. 853. Three years after the great battle with Benhadad, Ahab proposed to Jehoshaphat that they should jointly go up to battle against Ramoth-gilead. Jehoshaphat consented, but suggested that they should first "inquire at the word of the Lord." Ahab gathered together four hundred prophets in an open space at the gate of the city of Samaria, who gave the unanimous response,

"Go up; for the Lord shall deliver it into the hand of the king." Among them Zedekiah, the son of Chenaanah, made horns of iron as a symbol, and announced, from Jehovah, that with those horns Ahab would push the Assyrians till he consumed them. Jehoshaphat was dissatisfied with the answer, and asked if there was no other prophet of Jehovah at Samaria. Ahab replied that there was yet one—Micaiah, the son of Imlah; but he added, "I hate him, for he does not prophesy good concerning me, but evil." Micaiah, however, was sent for and urged to agree with the other prophets, "and speak that which is good." He at first expressed an ironical concurrence, and then openly foretold the defeat of Ahab's army and the death of Ahab himself. He declared that the other prophets had spoken under the influence of a lying spirit. Upon this Zedekiah smote Micaiah upon the cheek, and Ahab ordered him to be taken to prison and fed upon bread and water until his return (I Kings 22:1-28; II Chron. 18:7, sq.). We hear nothing further from the prophet in the sacred story, but Josephus narrates that Micaiah was already in prison when sent for to prophesy before Ahab and Jehoshaphat, and that it was Micaiah who had predicted death by a lion to the son of a prophet, under the circumstances mentioned in I Kings 20:35, 36; and had rebuked Ahab, after his brilliant victory over the Syrians, for not putting Benhadad to death.

NOTE—"The history of Micaiah is an exemplification in practice of contradictory predictions being made by different prophets. The only rule bearing on the judgment to be formed under such circumstances seems to have been a negative one. It is laid down in Deut. 18:21, 22, where the question is asked, How the children of Israel *were to know* the word which Jehovah had not spoken? And the solution is, that 'if *the thing follow not, nor come to pass, that is* the thing which Jehovah has not spoken'" (Smith, *Dict.*, s.v.).

Mi'cha (mī′kȧ; *who is like Jehovah?*). See Micah.

   1. A son of Mephibosheth (II Sam. 9:12), given in I Chron. 8:34, 35, as *Micah* (*q. v.*).

   2. The son of Zabdi and father of Mattaniah, of the family of the Levite Asaph (Neh. 11:17, 22), and probably the same that joined in the sacred covenant with Nehemiah (10:11), B. C. about 445.

Mi'chael (mī′kȧ-ĕl; *who is as* or *like God*).

   1. "One," or "the first of the chief princes" or archangels (Dan. 10:13; comp. Jude 9), described (Dan. 10:21) as the "prince" of Israel, and (12:1) as "the great prince which standeth" in time of conflict "for the children of thy people." As special guardian of the Jews, Michael will defend them in their terrific time of trouble (Jer. 30:5) during the Great Tribulation when the remnant will be delivered and established in the Millennial Kingdom. As Gabriel represents the ministration of the angels toward men, so Michael is the type and leader of their strife, in God's name and his strength, against the power of Satan. In the Old Testament, therefore, he is the guardian of the Jewish people in their antagonism to godless power and heathenism. In the New Testament (Rev. 12:7), he fights in heaven against the dragon—"that old serpent called the Devil and Satan, which

deceiveth *the whole world*," and so takes part in that struggle which is the work of the Church on earth. There remains still one passage (Jude 9; comp. II Pet. 2:11), in which we are told that "Michael the archangel, when contending with the devil . . . disputed about the body of Moses, durst not bring against him a railing accusation, but said, The Lord rebuke thee." The reference seems evidently to be to Moses appearance in glorified form on the Mount of Transfiguration (Matt. 17:1-8) as the representative of the redeemed who have passed through death into the Kingdom (Matt. 13:43; Luke 9: 30, 31).

2. The father of Sethur, which latter represented the tribe of Asher among the explorers of Canaan (Num. 13:13), B. C. 1440.

3. A chief man of the tribe of Gad, mentioned among those who settled in the land of Bashan (I Chron. 5:13).

4. Another Gadite and ancestor of Abihail (I Chron. 5:14). Perhaps the same as No. 3.

5. The son of Baaseiah and father of Shimea, and a Gershonite Levite among the ancestors of Asaph (I Chron. 6:40).

6. One of the four sons of Izraiah, a descendant of Issachar (I Chron. 7:3).

7. A Benjamite of the sons of Beriah (I Chron. 8:16).

8. A captain of the "thousands" of Manasseh who joined David at Ziklag (I Chron. 12:20).

9. The Father of Omri, whom David appointed ruler of the tribe of Issachar (I Chron. 27:18).

10. One of the sons of Jehoshaphat, king of Judah, whom he portioned before his death, and who were slain by their brother Jehoram upon his accession (II Chron. 21:2-4), B. C. 850.

11. A "son" (or descendant) of Shephatiah, whose son Zebadiah, with eighty-two males, came with Ezra from Babylon (Ezra 8:8), B. C. before 457.

Mi′chah (mī′kà; I Chron. 24:24, 25). *See* Micah, No. 6.

Micha′iah (mī-kā′yà), another form for *Micaiah*.

1. The father of Achbor, which latter was sent by Josiah to consult with the prophetess Huldah (II Kings 22:12). In the parallel passage (II Chron. 34:20) he is called *Micah* (*q. v.*).

2. The mother of King Abijah (II Chron. 13:2); elsewhere (II Chron. 11:20) called *Maachah* (*q. v.*).

3. One of the princes of Jehoshaphat, whom he sent to teach the law of Jehovah in the cities of Judah (II Chron. 17:7), B. C. about 870.

4. A priest of the family of Asaph, whose descendant, Zechariah, took part in the dedication of the walls of Jerusalem after the captivity (Neh. 12:35), B. C. before 445.

5. One of the priests who took part in the same ceremony (Neh. 12:41), B. C. 445.

6. The son of Gemariah, and the person who, having heard Baruch read the terrible predictions of Jeremiah, went and declared them to all the princes assembled in King Jehoiakim's house; and the princes forthwith

sent for Baruch to read the prophecies to them (Jer. 37:11-14), B. C. about 606.

Mi′chal (mī′kĕl; evidently a shortened form of *Michael, who is like God*?"), Saul's younger daughter (I Sam. 14:49), probably by Ahinoam (v. 50). After David had slain Goliath Saul proposed to bestow upon him his eldest daughter, Merab; but when the time arrived for the marriage, she was given to Adriel the Meholathite. The pretext under which Saul broke his promise is not given, but it appears to have been that Merab had no love for David. (1) **Marriage.** It was told Saul that his daughter Michal loved the young hero, and he seized the opportunity of exposing David to the risk of death. He asked no dowry of him save the slaughter of a hundred Philistines. Before the appointed time David doubled the tale of victims, and Michal became his wife (18:20-28), B. C. about 1010. (2) **Saves David's life.** Another great defeat inflicted by David upon the Philistines so excited the jealousy of Saul that he endeavored to slay him. Failing in the attempt, he sent watchers to David's house to put him to death in the morning. Michal aided his escape by letting him down through a window, and then dressed the bed as if still occupied by him. She took the teraphim (or household god), laid it upon the bed, its head enveloped with a goat's hair netting, as if to protect it from gnats, and the rest of the figure covered with the *beged* (or plaid). Saul's messengers forced their way to the room, despite Michal's declaration that David was sick, and discovered the deception. When Saul was informed thereof he was so enraged that Michal fabricated the story of David's threatening to kill her (19:11-17). (3) **Second Marriage.** Saul probably doubted Michal's story of David's escape, and when the rupture between the two men became incurable, Michal was married to Phalti (or Phaltiel) of Gallim (25:44; II Sam. 3:15). (4) **Restored to David.** When Abner revolted to David the king consented to make a league with him only on this condition, "But one thing I require of thee, that is, Thou shalt not see my face, except thou first bring Michal . . . when thou comest to see my face." Ishbosheth is requested to deliver up Michal, and, having done so, she is taken to the king by Abner, who ordered her weeping husband to return to his home (II Sam. 3:13-16). (5) **Rupture with David.** On the day of David's greatest triumph, viz., that of bringing the ark of the Lord to Jerusalem, the king appeared in the procession, dancing and leaping. When he returned to his own house, Michal, who had seen him from her window, met him with scornful words. She was offended that the king had let himself down to the level of the people; and availed herself of the shortness of the priest's shoulder dress to make a contemptuous remark concerning David's dancing. David's retort was a tremendous one, conveyed in words which once spoken could never be recalled. It gathered up all the differences between them which made sympathy no longer possible, and we do not need the assurance of the sacred writer that "Michal had no child unto the day of her death," to feel quite certain that all intercourse between her and David must have ceased from that date (II Sam. 6:16-23), B. C. 992. Her name appears only once more (21:8), as the mother of five sons, but the probable presumption is that Michal has been, by the mistake of the transcriber, substituted for Merab, who was the wife of Adriel.

Mich'mas (mĭk'măs) **Mich'mash** (mĭk'măsh; *something hidden*), Ezra 2:27; Neh. 7:31), a town of Benjamin, east of Beth-el, on the road to Jerusalem. Here Saul and the Philistines contended for the mastery, Saul taking his position with two thousand men, and placing the other one thousand at Gibeah with his son Jonathan. Jonathan smote the Philistine garrison that was at Geba, and the Philistines hastened to avenge the defeat. They collected an innumerable army of foot soldiers, besides thirty thousand chariots, six thousand horsemen, and encamped before Michmash. Saul retreated down the valley to Gilgal, near Jericho, to rally the Israelites (I Sam. 13:1, sq.). Jonathan resolved to attack the outpost of the Philistines at the pass of Michmash, and God gave him a great victory (14:1, sq.). Michmas is mentioned as the place whose inhabitants returned from captivity (Ezra 2:27; Neh. 7:31; 11:31). It is the present *Mukhmas*, a village in ruins upon the northern ridge of the Wady *Suweinit* (comp. Isa. 10:28).

Mich'methah (mĭk'mē-thȧ), a town on the border of Ephraim and Manasseh, west of Jordan (Josh. 16:6; 17:7), present Khirbet Juleijil.

Mich'ri (mĭk'rī), ancestor of Elah, one of the heads of the fathers of Benjamin (I Chron. 9:8) after the captivity, B. C. before 536.

Mich'tam (mĭk'tăm; a *writing*, especially a *psalm*). This word occurs in the titles of six psalms (16, 56-60), all of which are ascribed to David. Meaning uncertain.

Midday (Heb. *ṣōhẳr yōm*, *double light*, I Kings 18:29; *mằhẳṣîth hẳyyōm*, *half of the day*, Neh. 8:3; Gr. *hēmera mesos*, *middle day*, Acts 26:13). *See* Time.

Mid'din (mĭd'ĭn), a town west of the Dead Sea, mentioned only in Josh. 15:61. Its location is unknown.

Middle Wall, the *chel*, or sacred fence between the Court of the Gentiles and the interior sanctum of the temple (Eph. 2:14). This is an allusion to the ritual law of Moses, which was *intended* only to keep the Jews apart from the Gentiles, but which *produced* that mutual enmity to which the apostles refer.

Mid'ian (mĭd'ĭ-ăn; *strife*), the fourth named of the six sons of Abraham by Keturah (Gen. 25:2; I Chron. 1:32). Beyond the fact of his having four sons (Gen. 25:4; I Chron. 1:33), nothing is recorded respecting him.

Mid'ianites (mĭd'ĭ-ăn-īts), a race dwelling south and east of Palestine, in the desert north of the Arabian peninsula. There are no trustworthy accounts of Midian outside the Bible. In the Bible Midian appears in connection with (1) Abraham, (2) Joseph, (3) Moses, (4) Balaam, (5) Gideon.

1. In Gen. 25:1, 2, Midian is the fourth son of Abraham by Keturah, and evidently one of those who were sent away into the east country with gifts by Abraham during his lifetime

(v. 6). According to the Arab account (El, Makreezee, *Khitat*, "Medyen are the offspring of Shu'eyb, and are the offspring of Medyán (Midian), son of Abraham, and their mother was Kantoorà, the daughter of Yuktán (Joktan) the Canaanite." "Medyen is the city of the people of Shu'eyb," who is "generally supposed to be the same as Jethro, the father-in-law of Moses," though some deny it.

2. In the time of Joseph we find the Midianites associated with Ishmaelites so closely that it is hard to define their relationship; perhaps there was a company of Midianite merchantmen in an Ishmaelite caravan (Gen. 37:25, 27, 28, 36). In all likelihood the descendants of Ishmael and Midian, as well as of other exiled children of Abraham, had intermarried. In Judg. 8:24 the Midianites seem to be called Ishmaelites. But this latter term may have come to be applied generally to traders of that particular kind, as *Canaanite* (*q. v.*) came to mean merchant.

3. In the early life of Moses, in Exod. 2:15, sq., Moses, after killing the Egyptian, fled for refuge to the land of Midian. Here he married the daughter of Jethro, the priest of Midian, whose sheep he kept for forty years (Acts 7:30; Exod. 3:1). At the time of his call he was at Horeb, in the peninsula of Sinai (Exod. 3:1). As the Midianites were mostly nomads, this peninsula can have been only a temporary station for pasturage, unless, as is quite possible, it was then more fertile than now. But, according to the Arabians and Greeks, the city of Midian was on the Arabian side of the Arabian Gulf, where in all probability lay the true land of Midian.

4. In the time of Balaam, Moab, then ruled by Balak, son of Zippor, conferred with the elders of Midian in regard to Israel, and the resulting embassy to Balaam consisted of elders both of Moab and Midian. In the chapters which relate the prophecies of Balaam (Num., chaps. 23, 24) only Moab is mentioned. In 25:1 it is the daughters of Moab who entice Israel; but in 25:6-15 it is Midian, and in vers. 16-18; 31:1-16, vengeance is executed on Midian, and in 31:8, 9 it is among the Midianites that Balaam perishes. We may therefore conclude that Midian had a prominent part in the transaction (for connection of Moab with Midian, *see* Moabites).

5. **In the time of Gideon.** When Midian appears again (Judg. 6:1-8, 21) it is not as an organized army of warriors, nor as a nation powerful enough to bring the Israelites under its despotic sway. Israel by idolatry lost the divine protection and the national cohesion which would have protected the nation against such marauders. The Midianites united with the Amalekites and the children of the East, men, women, and children, as we suppose, with their belongings, certainly with their cattle (6:5), forming an innumerable horde of camel-riding nomads. They apparently were the first people to employ the domesticated camel on a large scale. This gave them greatly increased desert mobility c. 1150 B. C. They oppressed Israel, not by a strong military despotism, backed by chariots of iron, like Jabin and Sisera (4:2, 3), but by coming up when the harvest was ripe, "like

grasshoppers," and destroying "the increase of the earth." The story is best read in the inimitable language of the Bible itself. The whole account (6:1-8, 28), from the Midianite invasion at the beginning to the panic and route and final disappearance at the end, is the story of a mob, formidable from its numbers and its hunger. This ends the story of Midian. Henceforth it is hardly mentioned, except as a historical reminiscence (but see Isa. 60:6; Hab. 3:7). Certainly Midian is never again mentioned as a source of terror. It is probable that from the beginning they had intermarried with the Ishmaelites, and that in the end they were merged in the roving peoples of the northern part of the Arabian desert, under the general name of Arabs. Midian has been called the Judah of the Arabians.—W. H., revised by *M. F. U.*

Midnight. *See* Time.

Midwife, a woman assisting at childbirth. *See* Diseases, Treatment of.

Mig'dal-el (mĭg'dăl-ĕl; *tower of God*), a fortified city that fell to Naphtali (Josh. 19:38). A number of places are claimed as the original site. Doubtless Mujeidil about 12 miles N. W. of Kades (Kedesh) is the location.

Mig'dal-gad (mĭg'dăl-găd; *tower of fortune*), a town in the plain of Judah, between the hilly region and the territory held by the Philistines (Josh. 15:37). Its site is not positively known, but is in the Shephelah, perhaps near Lachish.

Mig'dol (mĭg'dŏl).

1. This was the encampment of Israel during the Exodus from Egypt. It was near the Red (Reed) Sea (cf. Exod. 15:4, 22; Deut. 11:4). It is also said to be before Pihahiroth and before Baal-sephon (Exod. 4:2; Num. 33:7). Since Migdol is the ordinary Canaanite word for "watch tower," this site may have been a military outpost enroute. The place is an example of Canaanite names in the Delta. An extended Semitic occupation of the N. E. Delta before the New Egyptian Empire (c. 1546-1085 B. C.) is indicated from other such Canaanite place names (cf. Succoth (Exod. 12:37); Baal-zephon (Exod. 14:2); Zilu (Tell Abu Seifah) and most likely Goshen itself (Exod. 8:22, 9:26). (W. F. Albright, *From the Stone Age to Christianity*, 1940, p. 184.)

2. A place referred to in Jer. 44:1; 46:14. Here Jews fled to Egypt and took up their residence after the destruction of Jerusalem by Nebuchadnezzar. The place was in the north of Egypt and is probably to be equated with the *Magdali* of the Tell el Armarna Tablets. It is modern Tell el Heir, almost a dozen miles S. of Pelusium. In Ezek. 29:10 and 30:6 the expression occurs "from Migdol to Syene, as far as the border of Ethiopia," evidently indicating extreme limits N. and S. in Egypt. —*M. F. U.*

Mighties (Heb. *gĭbbōr, powerful*, I Chron. 11: 12, 24), the titles given to the three great captains of David, elsewhere called "mighty men" (II Sam. 23:8), and meaning "a warrior," leader in war.

Mig'ron (mĭg'rŏn; *precipice*), a town of Benjamin, apparently on the route of the invading Assyrian army southward (Isa. 10:28). From Michmas a narrow valley extends northward out of and at right angles with what has been identified as the passage of *Michmas* (*q. v.*). Saul was stationed at the further side of Gibeah, "under a pomegranate tree which is by Migron" (I Sam. 14:2). Gibeah is at Tell el-Ful.

Mij'amin (mĭj'á-mĭn; *from the right hand*, i. e., side of good luck), the same as *Miniamin* (*q. v.*).

1. The head of the sixth division of priests in the time of David (I Chron. 24:9), B. C. before 960.

2. One of the priests who sealed the covenant made by Nehemiah and the people to serve Jehovah (Neh. 10:7), B. C. 445.

Mik'loth (mĭk'lŏth; *rods*).

1. One of the sons of Jehiel, "the father" (or prince) of Gibeon, and father of Shimeah (or Shimeam). He was one of the Benjamite residents of Jerusalem (I Chron. 8:32; 9:37, 38), B. C. about 536.

2. The principal officer of the second division of the army under Dodo, in the reign of David (I Chron. 27:4), B. C. after 1000.

Mikne'iah (mĭk-nē'yá; *possession of Jehovah*), a Levitical doorkeeper of the temple and harper, appointed by order of David (I Chron. 15:18, 21), B. C. about 966.

Milala'i (mĭl-á-lā'ī; *eloquent*), one of the "priests' sons" who took part in the dedication of the walls of Jerusalem (Neh. 12:36), B. C. about 536.

Mil'cah (mĭl'ká, *counsel, advice*).

1. The daughter of Haran and the wife of Nahor, by whom she had eight children, one of whom, Bethuel, was the father of Rebekah (Gen. 11:29; 22:20, 23; 24:15, 24, 47), B. C. about 1950.

2. The fourth named of the five daughters of Zelophehad of the tribe of Manasseh, to whom, as they had no brothers, an inheritance was given in the division of the land (Num. 26:33; 27:1; 36:11; Josh. 17:3), B. C. about 1375.

Mil'com (mĭl'kŏm). *See* Gods, False.

Mildew is properly a species of fungus or parasitic plant generated by moisture and corrosive of the surface to which it adheres. The mildew of grain is produced by a warm wind in Arabia, by which the green ears are turned yellow, so that they bear no grain (Deut. 28:22). *See* Vegetable Kingdom.

Mile'tum (mī-lē'tŭm; II Tim. 4:20). *See* Miletus.

Mile. *See* Metrology, I.

Mile'tus (mī-lē'tŭs), a town on the coast, thirty-six miles S. from Ephesus. It is some

297. Ruins of Miletus; View of Aqueduct and Byzantine Church

distance from the coast now as to site. It was the capital of Ionia. It was immoral. Its famous temple of Apollo is in visible ruins. Thales, Timotheus, Anaximander, Anaximenes, and Democritus were born here. Paul touched here on his journey and addressed the people (Acts 20:15-17). Some think the Miletus where Paul left Trophimus sick (II Tim. 4:20, A. V. "Miletum") to have been in Crete, but there seems to be no need for such a conclusion.

Milk is the rendering of two Hebrew words and one Greek word:

1. **Sweet milk** (Heb. *ḥälä, fat;* Gr. *gala*). This was in extensive use among the Hebrews, as well as other nations. They used not only the milk of cows, but also that of sheep (Deut. 32:14), of camels (Gen. 32:15), and goats (Prov. 27:27). It was not regarded as a mere adjunct in cooking, but as substantial food adapted to all ages and classes. The Scriptures frequently mention it in connection with honey as a delicacy (Exod. 3:8; 13:5; Josh. 5:6; Jer. 11:5).

2. **Curdled cheese** (Heb. *ḥĕm'äh,* frequently rendered in the A. V. "butter") seems to mean both butter and curdled milk. Curdled sour milk still forms, after bread, the chief food of the poorer classes in Arabia and Syria. Nor is it wanting on the tables of the well to do, and is brought to market in large quantities. It is carried by travelers, mixed with meat and dried, and then dissolved in water to make a refreshing drink. It was this curdled milk that Abraham set before the angels (Gen. 18:8) and Jael gave to Sisera (Judg. 4:19). If kept long enough in this state it acquired a slightly intoxicating property. It is rendered "butter" (Isa. 7:22), and its use in connection with honey is figurative of scarcity. Bread and wine would be unattainable, and so thickened milk and honey would be eaten *ad nauseam*. A very striking allusion to milk is that which forbids a kid to be seethed in its mother's milk (Exod. 23:19; 34:26; Deut. 14:21). *See* Kid.

Figurative. Milk occurs as a sign of abundance (Gen. 49:12; Ezek. 25:4; Joel 3:18, etc.), but more frequently with honey, "milk and honey" being a phrase which occurs about twenty times in Scripture. Milk is also illustrative of the blessings of the Gospel (Isa. 55:1; Joel 3:18), the first principles of God's word (I Cor. 3:2; Heb. 5:12; I Pet. 2:2), edifying discourse (Cant. 4:11), wealth of the Gentiles (Isa. 60:16).

Mill. The mill for grinding grain had not wholly superseded the mortar (*q. v.*) in the time of Moses (Num. 11:8); but fine meal, i. e., meal ground, or pounded fine, is mentioned so early as the time of Abraham (Gen. 18:6); hence mills and mortars must have been previously known. The mills of the ancient Hebrews probably differed but little from those at present in use in the East. These consist of two circular stones, about eighteen inches or two feet in diameter, the lower of which is fixed, and has its upper surface slightly convex, fitting into a corresponding concavity in the upper stone. The latter, called by the Hebrews *rekeb*, "chariot," and by the Arabs *rekkab*, "rider," has a hole in it

through which the grain passes, immediately above a pivot or shaft which rises from the center of the lower stone, and about which the upper stone is turned by means of an upright handle fixed near the edge. It is worked by women, sometimes singly and somtimes two together, who are usually seated on the bare ground (Isa. 47:1, 2), "facing each other; both have hold of the handle by which the upper is turned round on the 'nether' millstone. The one whose right hand is disengaged throws in the grain as occasion requires through the hole in the upper stone. The proverb of our Saviour (Matt. 24:41) is true to life, for *women* only grind. I cannot recall an instance in which men were at the mill" (Thomson, *The Land and the Book*, ch. 34). The labor is very hard, and the task of grinding in consequence performed only by the lowest servants (Exod. 11:5) and captives (Judg. 16:21; Job. 31:10; Isa. 47:1, 2: Lam. 5:13). So essential were millstones for daily domestic use that they were forbidden to be taken in pledge (Deut. 24:6; Josephus, *Ant.*, 8, § 26) in order that a man's family might not be deprived of the means of preparing their food. The handmills of the ancient Egyptians appear to have been of the same character as those of their descendants, and like them, were worked by women. They had also a large mill on a very similar principle, but the stones were of far greater power and dimensions, and this could only have been turned by cattle or asses, like those of the ancient Romans and of the modern Cairenes. It was the millstone of a mill of this kind, driven by an ass, which is alluded to in Matt. 18:6. With the movable upper millstone of the handmill the women of Thebez broke Abimelech's skull (Judg. 9:53).

Millennium, from Latin *mille*, thousand, *annum*, year; a theological term based upon Rev. 20, indicating the thousand-year period of Christ's future reign on the earth in connection with the establishment of the Kingdom over Israel (Acts 1:6). Basically, however, it is more accurate to employ the term "Kingdom," which has far-reaching roots in the O. T., rather than a term signifying merely a time during which the Kingdom continues.

1. **Schools of Thought.** Three common millennial views are held.

a. **Postmillennialism.** This interpretation maintains that present gospel agencies will root out evils until Christ should have a spiritual reign over the earth, which will continue for 1,000 years. Then the Second Advent of Christ would initiate the judgment and bring to an end the present order. This theory, largely disproved by the progress of history, is practically a dead issue. Postmillennialism was promulgated by the teaching in England of Daniel Whitby, 1638-1726.

b. **Amillennialism.** Advocates of this millennial view maintain that no millennium is to be looked for except that which, it is claimed, is in progress now in this gospel age. This theological interpretation spiritualizes or, rather, gives a mystical meaning to the vast Kingdom promises in the O. T. Zion is construed not to mean Zion but to refer to the Christian church. It makes no trenchant differentiation between Israel and the Church, a distinction which evidently underlies John the Baptist's prophecy of the baptism of the Spirit and Jesus' reference to this in Acts 1:5. This spiritual ministry formed the Church (Acts 2 cf. I Cor. 12:13). The Apostle Paul apparently makes clear distinction between Israel and the Church in I Cor. 10:32 and he also outlines a future for Israel in Romans 11. Amillennialism does not seem to take full account of these facts. Moreover, the view contends that Satan is at present bound, a position which premillennialists maintain is hardly justified by conditions in the present age.

c. **Premillennialism.** This interpretation teaches that the age will end in judgment at the Second Coming of Christ. The eternal state will not be ushered in. Rather Christ will restore the Kingdom to Israel and reign for at least 1,000 years. The criticism that such a view of the millennium is based on an obscure passage in Rev. 20 is not allowed by premillennialists since this reference, they say, embraces all the Kingdom promises of the O. T. as well as the Day of the Lord, which is very prominent in Scripture and connects with the Kingdom or millennium. Most of the opposition to premillennialism comes from the assumption that an earthly Kingdom with Israel at the head would involve a retrogression from the spirituality brought in by Christ through His death, resurrection and ascension. But premillennialists hold that the promise of the fulfilment of the covenants and promises to Israel in the O. T. demand such an earthly kingdom. The millennium will be the last of the ordered ages of time. Eternity will not dawn until the millennium is complete (Isa. 65:17; 66:22; II Pet. 3:13; Rev. 21:1). The millennium will be characterized by the binding of Satan and the severe limitation of sin. The perfect sinless state, however, will obtain in the eternal state after the millennium.—*M. F. U.*

Millet. *See* Vegetable Kingdom.

Millo (Heb. *the filling*), always with article, evidently a rampart consisting of two walls with a space between them filled in.

1. The name of the citadel of Shechem (Judg. 9:6, 20), the garrison of which joined in proclaiming Abimelech their king.

2. The Millo at Jerusalem (*q. v.*) was a similar kind of fortification, the definite article before the name indicating that it was a well known fortress, probably one that had been built by the Jebusites. "David built (that is, fortified) round about from Millo" (II Sam. 5:9; I Chron. 11:8), as did Solomon (I Kings 9:15; 11:27). It formed a prominent part of the fortifications by which Hezekiah prepared for the approach of the Assyrians (II Chron. 32:5). The same place is likely meant by the "House of Millo" where Joash was killed (II Kings 12:20, 21). Jebusite, Davidic and Solomonic Jerusalem has been explored. Masonry at the N. end of the city of David on Ophel apparently corresponds to Millo.—*M. F. U.*

Mina, the rendering in the margin (Luke 19: 13) of the Greek *mna*, but in the text as "pound." *See* Metrology, III.

Mincing (Heb. *ṭāpăp*, Isa. 3:16), to take short steps, just putting the heel of one foot against the toe of the other. The women whom the prophet rebuked could only take short steps, because of the chains by which the costly foot rings worn above the ankles were connected together. Tripping is a child's step. Although well versed in sin and old in years, the women of Jerusalem tried to maintain a youthful, childlike appearance. They therefore tripped along with short, childlike steps.

MINERAL KINGDOM

For the sake of continuous study we give the different objects in the mineral kingdom in alphabetical order. *See* also Metals, Precious Stones.

Adamant. *See* Diamond.

Agate (Gr. *'achatēs,* from the river of that name in Sicily). This name is applied to those varieties of semi-transparent quartz (chalcedony) which have the general character of being clouded, banded, or lined in several shades or colors. When the layers are even, and black and white, it is properly called *onyx;* and when red and white, *sardonyx,* though the terms are often used somewhat loosely. In these latter cases the cutting down from one layer to another gives the beautiful cameo effect of a raised device of one color upon a ground of another. All the agates were favorite stones with the ancients, and are abundant in collections of classical and oriental jewelry, being hard enough to take and retain a high polish, and not too hard to be cut and engraved readily be means of corundum points. In the Bible the word occurs in the A. V. four times, twice in the accounts of the breastplate (Exod., chaps. 28 and 39; Isa. 54:12; Ezek. 27:16). The first two are represented by the word *shᵉbū;* in the LXX, *achatēs,* and may be presumably taken as correct in the modern sense. In the other two cases the original is *kădkōd,* rendered by the LXX *iaspis,* in Isaiah; and *chorchor,* in Ezekiel. The former is very uncertain, but probably means some light-colored chalcedony (*see* Jasper, below), though this is a case of figurative use. The word in Ezekiel is obscure, by some connected with an Arabic root denoting redness, and hence thought to denote ruby, or some precious stone resembling it, but very vaguely (*see* further under Onyx and Sardonyx).

Alabaster (Gr. *'alabastron,* Matt. 26:7; Mark 14:3, and Luke 7:30) is pretty well identified with the substance now called oriental (or Egyptian) alabaster, also "onyx marble" and "Mexican onyx." This is a variety of carbonate of lime, usually stalagmitic in origin, with a layered structure due to its deposition from water, giving it a banded aspect of slightly varying shades and colors, often very delicate and beautiful. This banded character has led to its being called onyx frequently among the ancients, and onyx marble and Mexican onyx among ourselves, although it is very different from true onyx, which is a variety of agate and very hard. The name alabaster among the moderns, on the other hand, is applied to a still softer stone, the compact variety of gypsum, or sulphate of lime, used for small statuettes, paper weights, and little ornaments of no great value. The *alabastrites* of Theophrastus, Pliny, and the ancients generally was largely quarried and worked at Alabastron, a well-known locality near Thebes, and was the favorite material for the little flasks and vases for ointment and perfumery that are so abundant in Egyptian tombs and almost all ancient collections. Such articles were called '*alabastra*; but by a frequent change of usage the word was transferred to any perfume flask, or the like, without special regard to its material or to its source; as "a piece of delf" or "china" (originally Delft ware or China ware) now signifies any article of crockery. cf. the LXX of II Kings, 21:13. Horace, *Ode*, iv, 12, 17, uses *onyx* for a perfume flask; and other classical writers in the same way.

Amber (Heb. *hăshmă;* LXX *'ēlektron*, only in Ezek. 1:4, 27; 8:2, R. V. "electrum"). In all these cases it is used, in the attempted description of the visions of the divine glory, in close connection with "brightness" and "the appearance of fire." The Greek word had a twofold sense—the fossil resin known to us as amber, and an alloy of gold and silver, now called electrum by mineralogists. It is uncertain whether amber proper was known to the Hebrews; but the idea meant to be conveyed in these passages is plainly that of a brilliant glowing yellow, like amber, or like some highly polished metallic alloy, such as brass or electrum. The same idea is clearly brought out in Rev. 1:15, and suggested in Ezra 8:27 —"fine copper, precious as gold."

Amethyst (Heb. *'ăḥlāmäh;* Gr. *'amethustos*, the Greek name alluding to a notion that the amethyst prevented *intoxication;* used only in Exod. 28:19; 39:12; Rev. 21:20). This is one of the few cases in which there is little doubt as to the correctness of the rendering, the name having been used from Theophrastus's day to the present for the purple or violet-colored variety of quartz. It was a favorite stone among the ancients, often finely cut or carved in intaglio; and though not rare enough to be of great value, yet is still used in fine jewelry, from its rich and almost unique color, there being very few true purple gem-stones. The Greek name alludes to a notion that it prevented intoxication if worn at feasts, etc.; the Hebrew name signifies *dream-stone*, as though supposed to induce, or to interpret, dreams.

Asphalt, Bitumen (Heb. *hēmär, boiling up*, to be *red*, Gen. 11:3; 14:10; Exod. 2:3, A. V. "slime," *zĕphĕth, flowing*, or *fluid*, Isa. 34:9; while in Exod. 2:3 both words are used with some sense of difference implied). Much of the asphalt of ancient times came from the Dead Sea, which was called Lacus Asphaltites. The use of it as a cement for bricks at Babylon is described by Herodotus and other ancient writers, and may be seen in great ruins to this day, e. g., the so-called wall of Media, not far from Babylon. The chief modern source is the asphalt lake—over a mile in width—on the island of Trinidad, West Indies. Here it is liquid and boiling up in the central portion, and hard and solid around the shores; the black masses looking like dark rocks among the trees. Asphalt is a mixture of hydrocarbons, in part oxygenated, the softer kinds

graduating toward the mineral oils or petroleums. By exposure to the air it hardens, partly by evaporation and partly by oxidation. *See* Bitumen.

Bdellium (Heb. *bᵉdōlăḥ;* Gen. 2:12; Num. 11:7), a fragrant gum obtained from a tree in Arabia, Babylonia, Media and India. It is said to have had the same color as manna (Num. 11:7). In Gen. 2:12 it is listed with gold and onyx stone, or beryl, as products of the land of Havilah. The Septuagint renders it *anthrax*, (carbuncle or ruby) in Gen. 2:12 and *krystallos*, rock crystal, in Num. 11:7.
—*M. F. U.*

Beryl (Gr. *bērullos*, Rev. 21:20, for Heb. *tărshîsh*). The modern name designates the pale-colored varieties of silicate of glucina, the deep-green variety being emerald. In Rev. 21:20, beryl is no doubt correct, but in the Old Testament all is uncertain. The R. V. gives "beryl" in the margin for "onyx" in the text, in repeated instances; but in some of these, at least, this rendering cannot be correct. The passages in which *tărshîsh* occurs are: Exod. 28:20, in which there appears to be some confusion as to the places of the stones in the breastplate. In Cant. 5:14; Ezek. 1:16, and Dan. 10:6, it is rendered without translation by the LXX (Eng. "beryl"), the R. V. giving "topaz" in the margin in Canticles. In Ezek. 10:9 and 28:71, the LXX gives *lithos anthrakos* as *anthrax* (again Eng. "beryl"); here there is a strange confounding of this with a deep-red stone such as *anthrax* (or carbuncle), as appears also in regard to emerald (*q. v.*), indicating the uncertainty of the Greek translators as to the meaning of *tărshîsh;* as does also their merely transliterating the word in other cases, as noted above. But Jerome's rendering of Ezek. 1:16— *"quasi visio maris"* (Vulgate), almost establishes the impression of a green or blue-green stone like beryl, or, as Luther suggests, turquoise, rather than anything red or yellow. *See* Emerald.

Bitumen. *See* Asphalt and article on Bitumen.

Brass (Heb. *nᵉḥōshĕth;* Gr. *chalchos;* Lat. *aes*), should in the Scriptures be generally rendered bronze, or sometimes copper. Brass, the alloy of copper and zinc, is largely a modern material, while bronze (copper and tin) was used to an enormous extent in ancient times. It was the principal material for all manner of articles, both of ornament and use, as far back as the Chalcholithic Age (3500-3000 B.C.). Great interest attaches to the source of the tin so largely used in the manufacture of the ancient bronzes, as tin occurs in but few localities. Most of it is understood to have been brought from the great tin mines of the Cornwall peninsula and the Scilly Islands by the Phoenicians, who maintained for many centuries steady commerce thither by sea. The bronze articles then manufactured in the Punic cities and colonies were exported all over the world in exchange for the products of every region, to enhance the wealth of Tyre and Carthage. The bronze, however, varied a great deal in composition, and some contained an admixture of zinc, approaching more to brass. Such may have been the "fine copper, precious as gold" (Ezra 8:27; I Esdr.

8:57). The zinc mines at Laurium, in Greece, were extensively worked in ancient times; and it seems probable that various proportions of the three metals were employed, giving alloys all the way from bronze to brass; but the former is much the more ancient and frequent. *See* Tin.

Brass (bronze) was abundant among the Hebrews and their neighbors from very early times (Exod., chap. 38; II Sam. 8:8; I Chron. 18:8; 22:3, 14; 29:7). The last passage is interesting as showing that in David's time iron was yet more abundant, and that the "bronze age" was entirely past before 1000 B. C. so far as Palestine was concerned. The word occurs in both a literal and figurative sense. As applied to *mining*, it, of course, means copper (Deut. 8:9; Job 28:2, and probably, Gen. 4:22, R. V. marg.). As in Ezra 8:27, so in I Kings 7:45; II Chron. 4:16; Ezek. 1:7; Dan. 10:6, it seems probable that brass is meant. To the many other passages describing various objects, as *mirrors* (Exod. 38:8), *weapons*, and *armor* (I Sam. 17:5, 6, 38; II Sam. 8:8, 12; 21:16, etc.), the "brazen serpent" (Num. 21:9; II Kings 18:4), or the furnishings of the tabernacle (Exod. 26:11, 37), or of the temple (I Kings 7:14; II Chron. ch. 4; Jer. 52:17, 22), etc., the preceding remarks as to bronze and mixed alloys, or occasionally copper, will apply.

In the New Testament *chalchos* is used for money (Matt. 10:9; Mark 6:8; 12:41), and for a noisy musical instrument (I Cor. 13:1). The word *chalkolibanon* (Rev. 1:15; 2:18) is much disputed as to its meaning. There seems to be an evident reference to Dan. 10:6, or to Ezek. 1:7, 27, which renders the ordinary rendering probably very suitable; but the term itself is to us obscure, though doubtless familiar at the time. Very probably it was the name for some bright-colored alloy, *brass* or near to it, employed for handsome articles and highly esteemed. It may be a reference to *orichalcum*, the alloy of copper and gold; or to *electrum*, gold and silver, which is the LXX rendering of *ḥăshmăl* of Ezek. 1:4, 27; 8:2, A. V., "amber;" R. V. marg. "electrum." *See* Copper.

Figurative. In some cases the word is used, by metonymy, for a bond or fetter (Lam. 3:7; and in the dual, Judg. 16:21; II Sam. 3:34; II Kings 25:7)—much as we say "in irons." It also appears in many metaphors, as for a hot, rainless sky (Deut. 28:23), or a parched soil (Lev. 26:19); for baseness as contrasted with the precious metals (Isa. 60: 17; Jer. 6:28—here also with the opposite idea of value, as compared with wood); and constantly to express conceptions of physical strength, power, durability, etc. (Job. 6:12; 40:18; 41:27; Psa. 107:16; Isa. 45:2, *et saepe*); or of moral qualities, as firmness (Jer. 1:18), obstinacy (Isa. 48:4), and the like.

Brick. *See* article Brick.

Brimstone (Heb. *gŏphrîth*, from *găphăr*, to *cover;* whence *gŏphĕr*, Gen. 6:14, which Gesenius renders "pitch," such as the *pine*, etc.) is understood to mean not only pitch, but some other inflammable substances, specially sulphur. At first sight, if we think of black, tarry pitch, this view seems far fetched, as sulphur is different in appearance; but if *gŏphĕr* means resinous trees their inflammable yellow exudations may not inaptly be compared with sulphur. The trunks of our southern pitch-pines often show the resin where it has flowed out over the bark and hardened into opaque yellow masses not unlike sulphur. It is plain, however, that *gŏphrîth* is generally and properly rendered sulphur (brimstone); while pitch is denoted by two Hebrew words, *kŏphĕr* (Gen. 6:14) and *zĕphĕth* (Exod. 2:3; Isa. 34:9). Even among us the words tar, pitch, etc., are employed loosely in popular speech. The last passage cited shows clearly the use of *zepheth* for mineral pitch (asphalt), to depict a barren, desolate region, like the shores of the Dead Sea, associated also, as there, with *gŏphrîth*, *sulphur*, and by no means one of pine forests, where *kŏphĕr* might be obtained.

Sulphur (brimstone) in the Old Testament is repeatedly used to convey this idea of barrenness and desolation, evidently from its association with the Dead Sea; so, definitely, Deut. 29:23, also Isa. 34:9, and probably Job 18:15. Tristram, Lynch, and others describe its occurrence around the lake and in the valleys leading into it, and also on both sides of the Jordan Valley, where there are many hot sulphurous springs. These springs deposit sulphur, and pieces of it are scattered over the flats around portions of the lake. In some places it occurs with bitumen, for which the Dead Sea region is noted from very early times (Gen. 14:10)—an unusual association, but known also near Bologna, Italy. Some of the hot sulphur springs in Judea have been much esteemed for the treatment of rheumatic diseases, etc., and so are to this day; and some show ruins of Roman baths. Sulphur also occurs in connection (as frequently) with bands of gypsum (sulphate of lime) in the cliffs and terraces along the lower Jordan Valley, which go back to a former period of much greater height and extension of the Dead Sea. Sulphur is also referred to in the Old Testament in the combination "fire and brimstone" in connection with the violent storms (Gen. 19:24; Psa. 11:6; Ezek. 38:22). The idea here has, no doubt, been justly interpreted as referring to lightning—and so clearly, Isa. 30:33—perhaps from the popular idea, alluded to even by Pliny and Seneca, of a sulphurous odor (probably the ozone odor) after a discharge of lightning. The same combination (*pur kai theion*) recurs in the New Testament (Luke 17:29; Rev. 9:17; 14:10; 19:20; 20:10; 21:8), the translation of a familiar Hebrew phrase.

Bronze. *See* Brass.

Carbuncle is a name now only applied to certain bright red garnets when cut "en cabochon," i. e., convex and smooth; but the Lat. *carbunculus* and Greek *anthrax* (a small live coal), are used for a variety of deep red gems —garnets, rubies, spinels, etc. The Old Testament references are as indefinite as usual, carbuncle being used in the A. V. for several Hebrew words and with various marginal changes. *See* Isa. 54:12; Ezek. 27:16; 28:13. Cf. also Exod. 28:17; 39:10.

Chalced'ony (kăl-sĕd'ō-nĭ; Gr. *chalkedōn*, occurs only in Rev. 21:19. The modern chalcedony—light colored, non-crystalline quartz —probably was the ancient *iaspis* (*see* Jasper); King's *chalcedonius* was a blue-green stone, not readily identified by us; he speaks of it as resembling *callais*, i. e., turquoise, and as found at certain copper mines at Chalcedon; which points together suggest the modern chrysocolla—silicate of copper.

Chalkstones (Heb. *'ăbnē gîr, stones of boiling*, Isa. 27:9, literally *stones of lime*, i. e., limestone, from an obsolete root, *gîr*, to *boil, effervesce*, as lime in slacking). The making of lime by roasting limestone in kilns, and preparing mortar, cement, and whitewash therefrom, is one of great antiquity. Palestine is largely a country of limestone, chiefly cretaceous; and there are gypsum beds along portions of the Jordan Valley (*see* Brimstone); so that material for both lime and plaster was abundant. Tristram describes the extensive use of these substances in the East for lining cisterns, tombs, etc.—the former fairly honeycombing some portions of the country, especially among the hills, and fed by gutters, or channels of cement laid along the edges of the terraces, the material remaining hard and waterproof even after three thousand years. The "plaster" lining of sepulchers, used also as an outer coating for *adobe* houses (*see* Brick) and tombs (Matt. 23:27), probably means heavy whitewash, or a fine white mortar, in most cases. But in Dan 5:5 it may be plaster, as rendered, or stucco. The ancient limekiln was a pit or depression three or four feet deep, like a saucer in form, wherein were placed alternate layers of fuel (brushwood, etc.) and lime rock, broken up small by a wheel like that of an oilpress (alluded to in Isa. 27:9). The fuel was then kindled and the pit covered with sods, much as we do a charcoal heap, only leaving an aperture for draught.

Figurative (Isa. 27:9). The sense of the passage is given thus by Delitzsch—that Israel's repentance would be shown by the destruction of idolatrous altars, the stones of which would be broken to pieces, calcined, and slaked for mortar. In Amos 2:1 the burning of human bones into lime is denounced as an act of sacrilege on the part of Moab (comp. also the defiling of the idolatrous altars in this manner by Josiah, II Kings 23:16, 20; II Chron. 34:5, as predicted in I Kings 13:2). *See* Lime.

Chrys'olite (krĭs'ô-lĭt; *gold stone*) was plainly our topaz. The Greek name is definite as to color, and included not only yellow topazes, but other gems of similar tint, as the occasional yellow or "golden" beryls, some zircons, etc. The only distinct reference is Rev. 21:20; but the LXX employs the word for *tărshîsh* (Exod. 28:20; 39:13; indefinitely Ezek. 28:13). This word and *topazion* have exactly changed meanings between the Greek and the English, the ancient topaz being our chrysolite, and *vice versa*. The modern chrysolite—silicate of magnesia with some iron—is a rich yellow-green gem, called also olivine, and by jewelers peridot, but in nowise described as "golden."

Chrysop'rasus (krĭs-ŏp'rà-sŭs; Gr. *chrusoprasis, greenish-yellow*, only in Rev. 21:20), is again entirely uncertain. The modern chrysoprase, a light green chalcedony, probably was included in the ancient *iaspis* (*see* Jasper), and does not agree with the classical descriptions of the stone then so called. Pliny's account of *chrysoprasus*—bright green with gold spots— fails to correspond with any mineral that we know; and the attempt to identify this stone must be altogether conjectural.

Clay. This term is differently applied in scientific and in popular usage. In the former it denotes a definite compound, chiefly silicate of alumina, arising from the decomposition of certain feldspathic rocks, and forming whitish chalky looking beds. In this pure condition it is highly valuable for fine grades of pottery, etc. But it is generally much contaminated with other substances, all ordinary clays containing more or less oxide of iron, which causes pottery and bricks made from them to be yellow or red after burning. Most clays also contain silica and other foreign materials, and so graduate into common soil or earth. To all of these impure mixtures the term *clay* is applied, in distinction from sandy, gravelly, or calcareous soils. Two Hebrew words occur in the Old Testament for clay:

1. *Ṭîṭ*, usually rendered "mire" in A. V., like our common word *mud*, for the fine deposit left from the evaporation of water (Psa. 69:14; Jer. 38:6), or washed up on the shore (Isa. 57:20, A. V. "dirt"). It is used in the sense of clay for bricks or pottery (Isa. 41:25; Nah. 3:4).

2. *Ḥōmĕr* is properly clay for bricks or pottery (Isa. 29:16; 45:9; Jer. 18:4, etc.). In Job 4:19 *hōmĕr* seems to indicate a mud hut, from the idea of perishableness. The distinction seems usually to be in the thought of the material as wrought or unwrought, though this is not always borne out (*see* Job. 30:19; Isa. 10:6, where the word is used for mire), but its usual meaning is in connection with human arts or processes (Gen. 11:3, A. V. "mortar;" Job. 10:9; 38:14, and passages cited above).

3. *Pēlos* is the N. T. Gr. word used in all the meanings for clay (John 9:6, 11, 14, 15; Rom. 9:21). The passage, "But we have this treasure in earthen vessels" (II Cor. 4:7), is a striking allusion to the custom of keeping gold or silver in earthen jars, contrasting the precious contents with the humble receptacle.

Vessels and utensils of baked clay are, of course, often alluded to (II Sam. 17:28; Jer. 18:3, 4; 19:1), and fine pottery was made in Mesopotamia and Egypt from before 5,000 B. C. onward. Pottery remains in ancient excavated Biblical sites constitute the greatest ally of the scientific archaeologist for recognizing and dating ancient cultures.

Figuratively as a type of fragility (Psa. 2:9, etc.). The words usually employed are Heb. *kᵉlî yōṣēr*, A. V. "potter's vessel," or "earthen vessel."

Besides for making pottery and brick (*q. v.*), clay was much used in Palestine and throughout the East, and is still, for sealing doors, or earthen jars (Jer. 32:14), to secure them. Sepulchers were thus sealed, and probably our Lord's (Matt. 27:66). Another very important use of clay in the East, from remote antiquity, was for tablets and cylinders, for records (Ezek. 4:1), and even for ordinary correspondence. Quantities of these have been found in Assyria and Babylonia, and their cuneiform writings interpreted. The Chaldean traditions of the creation, the fall, and the deluge, have thus been recovered. Great discoveries of cuneiform literature inscribed on clay tablets include the Amarna Letters (1886), the Hittite monuments at Boghaz-Keui (1906), the Ras Shamra Tablets (1929-1937), the Mari Letters and the Lachish Ostraca (on pottery) 1935-1938.

Copper (Heb. $n^e h\bar{o}sh\breve{e}th$), this metal, though abundantly familiar to the Hebrews, is but seldom named in the A. V., the word being generally translated *brass* (i. e., bronze, properly), save in Ezra 8:27. It should clearly be rendered *copper* in Deut. 8:9, and Job 28:2. This metal was very early known and worked in the Orient, and for the most part alloyed with tin to form bronze, and probably later to some extent with zinc, to form brass, the favorite modern alloy. Its use preceded that of iron, as clearly shown in prehistoric archaeology, and asserted by Hesiod and Lucretius. Homer describes it in connection with the shield of Achilles (*Il.*, xviii, 474); and at ancient Troy Schliemann has found both copper and bronze objects, with the stone molds used in casting them. In the Near East copper was introduced c. 4500 B. C., with the Stone-Bronze Age c. 4500-3000 B. C., the Early Bronze Age 3000-2000 B. C.; Middle Bronze Age c. 2000-1500 B. C. and late Bronze Age 1500-1200 B. C. The Iron Age dates 1200-300 B. C.

It is impossible to determine the exact meaning of $n^e h\bar{o}sh\breve{e}th$ in its many Old Testament occurrences; the word was applied to copper and to its alloys, bronze and brass, so far as the latter was known. As to the abundance of it among the Hebrews, *see* Brass; also the interesting records of the source, use, and final disposal of the tabernacle "brass" (I Chron. 18:8; II Chron. 4:9-18; also I Kings 7:13-48, and II Kings 25:13). The sources of the great amount of copper used for the ancient bronzes, etc., are but vaguely known. The Egyptians obtained it from Arabia, in the Sinaitic peninsula. Modern travelers have described the vestiges still remaining of extensive and very ancient operations, especially at and near the place known as Wadi Maghâra: these include shafts in the sandstone rock, and ruins of reservoirs for water, of miners' settlements, of furnaces, with heaps of slag, etc., and hieroglyphic inscriptions going back as far as the fourth dynasty. By Homer's time, and doubtless long before, the copper mines of Cyprus identified with the very name of the island, were familiar and celebrated. In *Od.*, i, 181, Athéné appears in the disguise of a merchant, taking iron to Temese, in Cyprus, to exchange for copper. Many accounts in classical authors allude to the importance and value of the copper of Cyprus, and to the mines as a source of revenue to Cypriote kings and of gifts from them to other monarchs or to

temples, etc. They were worked down into Roman times, but have been long abandoned, though traces may still be seen. Eusebius refers to copper mines in Palestine, saying that under Diocletian's persecution the Christians were sentenced to labor in them (8:15, 17) at a place called Phreno, which Jerome locates in Idumea, between Petra and Zoar.

Figurative. This word is translated "filthiness" (Ezek. 16:36), as referring to the preceding verses (33, 34) for disgraceful pay or hire; somewhat like the more general idea of *aischrokerdēs* (I Tim. 3:3, 8), as applied to "unholy gain."

Coral (Heb. $r\ddot{a}'m\ddot{a}h$), something *high* in value (Job 28:18; Ezek. 27:16), is rather obscure, but the suggestion of something *high* (growing upward) is strongly suggestive of coral, and the familiar rendering in both the A. V. and R. V. may fairly stand. The red coral of the Mediterranean and the Red Sea has been gathered and valued from the earliest times, and is frequent in Egyptian jewelry. The small branches, polished, and beads made from it, have been used for ages, as they are today. Coral is, of course, not a precious stone, but the calcareous skeleton, or framework secreted (not "built"), by a connected community of small polyps, which inclose and conceal it entirely during life. The coral fishery is still an important industry of the eastern Mediterranean.

Crystal (Gr. *krustallos*, *ice*). This word, among the ancients, and even down to recent times, has been used simply to denote any hard material of great transparency and without marked color. Thus it was applied to glass, and to the clear colorless varieties of quartz, now designated as rock crystal. This latter substance was largely regarded by the ancients as a permanently solidified form of water, and was prized and admired for articles of ornament, as it is by the modern Europeans and Japanese, whose "crystal balls" and carved objects of *vertu* are so much valued in our art collections. The scientific application of the word is wholly different, modern, and technical, denoting the geometrical forms assumed by various substances in passing into the solid state, and with no reference to transparency. Of course the Scripture use of the word is entirely in the former sense, of some clear and brilliant substance, like ice or glass. Cf. Job 28:18; Ezek. 1:22 where the Hebrew words *gābîsh* and *qĕräh* both denote "ice" or "crystal."

Diamond, Adamant. With regard to these words there is little reason to think that the diamond was known to the Hebrews, or even to the ancient Greeks. The first definite reference to it is apparently found in the Latin poet Manilius, about A. D. 12; and Pliny describes it unmistakably in his great work on Natural History, which appeared some two years before his death, A. D. 79. The stone which the Greeks, and after them the Romans, called *adamas*, "the invincible," as being harder than anything else, was probably some of the forms of corundum, the next hardest of minerals. Diamond, or adamant, in the Old Testament is represented by two distinct Hebrew words, which divide themselves into two sets of three each; the first set relating to some stone of value and brilliancy, and the second to something very hard and having no connection with the second set. In the two descriptions of the breastplate (Exod. 28:18; 39:11), and in Ezekiel's account of the Tyrian treasures (28:13), the word is *yăhǎlōm* (*see* Jasper and Emerald). The other three passages represent the word *shāmîr*, a hard *point*. The reference in Jer. 17:1, "The sin of Judah is written with a pen of iron and with the point of a diamond" is of course a simple figurative expression, in which a stylus tipped with some hard mineral is contrasted with one of iron or steel. The substance employed for such engraving on stone was doubtless a small flake or pointed chip of corundum in some of its forms, which would easily cut or drill into any other mineral. This "adamantine claw," as the LXX gives it, was no doubt perfectly familiar to those for whom Jeremiah wrote. The passage, "As an adamant harder than flint have I made thy forehead" (Ezek. 3:9; LXX, "firmer than a rock;" comp. Isa. 50:7), is even more completely figurative. The third passage, "They made their hearts as an adamant stone" (Zech. 7:12) is not rendered by any noun in the LXX, "they adamantenized their hearts." In all these cases the allusion is undoubtedly to corundum as the hardest substance known to the ancients, and used for all purposes of drilling and engraving other stones; and it is of interest to notice the widespread use of a similar word in other languages for the same idea.

Dross. This general term includes, in the Old Testament, several distinct kinds of impurities present in metals, and necessary to be removed in order to obtain them in a useful and valuable state. The admixtures may be either: (1) Mechanical, of rocky or earthy material intermingled with the ore; (2) chemical, the substances united with the metal in the ore; and (3) other metallic elements present as alloys. Three words are employed in the Hebrew; of these the most frequent is *sîg* (Psa. 119:119; Prov. 25:4; Isa. 1:25; Ezek. 22:18, 19, etc.). In other cases *'ěrěṣ, earth* is employed, as in Psa. 12:6, where Gesenius well explains the phrase *lā'ārěṣ* in the sense of *from*, or *as to* earth, i. e., earthy mixture, a rendering much preferable to that of either the A. V. or R. V. This phrase could not be used for a clay crucible (A. V.), and the R. V. rendering is obscure and feeble. A third word is *bᵉdîl*, properly and usually *tin*, but employed in the sense (3) above, for a metallic admixture or alloy (Isa. 1:25), and there to be rendered, not *tin*, but *lead* (R. V. "alloy"), a common impurity in silver, and often removed by cupellation, of which there seems a hint in Jer. 6:29.

Emerald. With regard to this word the confusion seems absolutely hopeless. The stone itself was of course well known and highly valued, as it has been among almost all peoples from the remotest times. It is familiar in early Egyptian jewelry, and the ancient mines where it was procured have been rediscovered in Upper Egypt, at Mount Zabarah. The Hebrews, of course, must have known it in their Egyptian sojourn, and carried away emeralds with them, among the "spoil" of jewelry given them at their departure. But what word represents this gem in various Old Testament passages (Exod. 28:18; 39:11; Ezek. 28:13; *nōphĕk, shining*), is extremely doubtful. The Greek word *smaragdos* denotes our emerald, from the time that Theophrastus so fixed its use; but it also comprises other precious stones of similar color— e. g., the deeper varieties of beryl, which graduate into true emerald; also green tourmalines, peridots, malachite, etc. It is curiously confused in the LXX, however, with *'anthrax*, which like its Latin equivalent *carbunculus*, a glowing coal, denotes a red gem with deep fiery reflections. Both *'anthrax* and *carbunculus* included true ruby (so far as it was known), spinel ruby, several varieties of red garnet, and other gems of similar crimson color, such as occasional red tourmalines, zircons, etc. Theophrastus speaks of engraving upon *'anthrax*, which fact suggests garnet, which was a favorite engraved stone among the ancients. In the two passages (Rev. 4:3; 21:19), the original is *smaragdos*, and the English translation "emerald" is without question correct. The same is true for passages in the Apocrypha.

Flint. This term is often loosely applied to any very hard compact rock; in strictness it belongs only to the fine-grained and nearly opaque varieties of noncrystalline or cryptocrystalline quartz or silica, of dull color and luster, that occur, not as forming rock masses themselves, but in nodules and concretions in other rocks, especially limestone and chalk. But, as above stated, it is commonly used in a general sense, implying hardness and fine texture. In the Old Testament it is thus represented by the word *hăllāmîsh*, perhaps *hardness*, of rather obscure derivation, which appears in such passages as Deut. 8:15; 32:13; Psa. 114:8; and figuratively in Isa. 50:7. In Isa. 5:28; Ezek. 3:9, the word rendered "flint" in our A. V. is *ṣōr*, rock. Flint proper was the material almost everywhere employed in early prehistoric time for edge tools and weapons, prior to the use of metals. Its hardness, and the peculiar sharpness of its edges when broken or "flaked," rendered it all-important for such purposes to primitive man; and hence the science of prehistoric archaeology has dealt very largely with the study of flint implements, in their wide distribution, their varied forms, and their stages of evolution from ruder and more finished types. All this lies back of any Old Testament references; but a persistence in the use of stone implements for certain sacred purposes, long after metal tools were in common use, is alluded to by classical writers, and appears in the passages Exod. 4:25; and Josh. 5:2, 3 (R. V. "knives of flint"); *see* further on the subject in this introductory remarks upon Metals, *ad fin.*

Glass. *See* article on Glass.

Gold. A precious metal widely used in the ancient world and obtained in the O. T. from Havilah (Gen. 2:11); Sheba (I Kings 10:22); and Ophir (I Kings 9:28). Several Hebrew and Greek terms are employed to name it.

1. *Zāhāb* (*yellow, golden*), from partially used

roots, having the idea of shining, being bright (Gen. 2:11, 12). In Job 37:22 it is used figuratively for a brilliant sky, A. V. "fair weather;" R. V. "golden splendor;" perhaps as we say "northwest clear-off," with its brilliant golden sunset; or possibly there may be a reference to the aurora borealis, a rare phenomena in the latitude of Palestine, but one that might occasionally be seen, and produce a strong impression. In Zech. 4:12, A. V. "golden oil," it is applied to a clear yellow liquid. The root ideas are of luster and color.

2. *Bĕşĕr* (*clipping, dug out*), properly metal in a crude state, "golden ore." So Job 22:24; while in v. 25 the same word is rendered "defense" in A. V. The verb has the ideas successively to *cut, cut off, make difficult, fortify;* hence defense; but it seems more simple and more consonant with the ideas of the context to render it here as in R. V. "treasure;" the righteous man shall prosper temporally and acquire gold and silver in abundance, but his richest possession, his treasure (v. 25) and his delight (v. 26) shall be in God himself. In Job 28:19 it is again rendered *gold*. *Bĕşĕr* seems to stand in contrast with *päz* (3), as implying native gold, whether found in placer deposits, in grains and nuggets, or as occurring in rocks, to be smelted out; while the other word has the idea of gold that has been refined.

3. *Päz* (to *separate, purify*, as metals from the ore), this noun occurs in Psa. 19:10; 21:3; 119:127; Prov. 8:19; Cant. 5:11; Isa. 13:12; Lam. 4:2, and is usually rendered "fine gold," "most fine gold," etc. In Psa. 19:10 the familiar line of Watts, "gold that has the furnace passed," is probably very exact, although the LXX renders the word by Gr. *lithos timios* and *chrusion apuros* as though native gold, a signification that belongs more properly to the preceding noun.

4. *Sᵉgōr* (*closed, shut up,* i. e., a thing kept closed, a treasure, R. V. marg., Job 28:15), means treasured or precious gold (I Kings 6:20, 21; 7:49, 50; 10:21; II Chron. 4:20, 22; 9:20, "pure gold" in both versions).

The above four terms, therefore, present the idea of gold as (1) the bright yellow metal, which is (2) gathered from the soil or taken from the rock, in a condition in which it may be used to some extent as it is either hammered or melted, but is (3) purified and refined for choicer purposes, while in any of its forms it is (4) treasured with care. Two other words occur which are poetical in their use.

5. *Kĕthĕm* (*golden store*, or *hoard*), kindred in meaning to (4). This root idea appears in Job 31:24; but usually the word seems to have only the general sense of gold (Job. 28:16, 19; Psa. 45:9; Prov. 25:12; Lam. 4:1; Dan. 10:5, A. V. often "fine," or "pure" gold). In Cant. 5:11 it is joined with (3) above, in the phrase *kĕthĕm päz*, a store of gold, A. V. and R. V. "the most fine gold." In Isa. 13:12, A. V. "the golden wedge of Ophir," R. V. "pure gold of Ophir," and the same phrase in Job 28:16; Psa. 45:9, is given simply "gold of Ophir."

6. *Ḥārūş.* The word is frequent as a simple name for gold (Psa. 68:13, "yellow gold;"

Prov. 3:14; 8:10; 16:16; Zech. 9:3, rendered "choice," "fine," etc.).

7. *Chrusos* occurs in many New Testament passages.

Gold, from its color, its malleability, its durability, and its occurrence native in the metallic state, was doubtless the first metal to attract the attention of early man. In prehistoric archaeology, however, it does not appear much, or at all, until well into the Bronze Age. But once within the historic period, it assumes great prominence, both in early remains and later in the accounts of ancient writers, and seems to have been long used with an abundance unknown to the modern world. A large part of the gold now known exists in the form of coin or bullion, and is thus withdrawn from use in the arts; while anciently it was not so much employed as the "medium of exchange," but rather as an article of value and beauty. Gold coin, in our sense, is late. Egyptian representations show gold as weighed out in the form of rings (Gen. 43:21; I Chron. 21:25; 28:14; Ezra 8:25, 26), and many similar references to payment by weight, both in gold and silver. Gen. 13:2; 24:22, etc., give us early references to wealth in gold. In Exod. 12:35; 32:3, 4; 35:22; 37, passim; Num. 31:50-54, etc., we see great abundance of gold jewelry and other objects, at later periods; while in the time of David and Solomon the accounts are surprising (I Chron. 22:14, 16; I Kings 6:21, 22; ch. 10, passim; II Chron. 1:15; chaps 3 and 9, passim), but not more so than those given by classical authors, as to the enormous amounts of gold possessed by ancient monarchs and the lavish use of it for decorations and furniture in the temples and palaces. With the accounts of Solomon and the queen of Sheba may be compared, e. g., that of the funeral pile of Sardanapalus, as given by Athenaeus, which was made of perfumed woods, with enormous quantities of gold, and kept burning for fifteen days. Exploration is constantly bringing to light treasures of gold work throughout the ancient lands of the East, besides all that is already preserved in museums and collections, and all that has been captured, destroyed, and remelted, through centuries of war and pillage. *See* article on Goldsmiths under Handicrafts.

The gold of the ancient world must represent, in the first place, a great amount of "placer" deposits, accumulated during Tertiary and Quaternary time, from the erosion of rock sources, perhaps not very rich, but sufficient to yield considerable amounts at many points by this natural process of concentration long undisturbed. Most of these deposits must have been worked out at an early day; others lasted down to classical times, but have now long been exhausted. At present, the regions covered by the ancient civilizations, or in intercourse with them, yield but the merest fraction of the world's supply of gold, which comes chiefly from the Americas and Australia, and next from South Africa, the Urals and Siberia. These latter lands may have yielded, at times, portions of their gold to the ancient world; as Herodotus refers to it among the Scythians, an indefinite term for the peoples of northern and western Asia. The biblical sources—Sheba, Ophir, Uphaz, etc.—have been endlessly discussed; and though good arguments exist for both India and Arabia, there can be little doubt that Ophir was in the former, from the thoroughly East Indian character of the associated products mentioned as brought thence in I Kings 10:11, 22; and II Chron. 9:10, 21 (*almug* or *algum* being generally regarded as sandal wood), and from the length of the time occupied by the trips made, which suggests a much farther country than the neighboring Arabia. On the other hand, Sheba is S. W. Arabia, a region which yielded many rich products in ancient times. Both Diodorus and Strabo refer to Arabia as furnishing gold, though it is not found there now; the placers are doubtless exhausted, and their sources undiscovered or lost. Diodorus (iii, 12, 14) describes the gold mines at a place known as Eshuranib, in the Bisharee District, worked by captives and convicts, under strict military guard. Here the process was much the same as our quartz mining, but with very simple appliances; the rock was broken up small with hammers, then pounded in stone mills or troughs with iron pestles, then washed on inclined tables, and the gold thus separated was afterward refined in crucibles. The Old Testament has much to say of "beaten" gold, "hammered" gold, and "overlaying" with gold. The ancients knew the art of gilding, much like ours; but we find many articles of Assyrian and other work that are heavily plated with gold; and there are objects of later Indian manufacture now in England that show this same style, e. g., a life-size tiger's head, part of a support of a throne belonging to Tippoo Saib, made of wood and covered with thick, hammered gold, now in Windsor Castle (comp. Solomon's lion throne, I Kings 10:18-20; II Chron. 9:17-19). So the great image in the plain of Dura (Dan. 3:1) must evidently have been "golden" only in thin exterior plating, probably over wood. This idea was afterward taken up in Greece by Phidias and applied to his celebrated works. That such was the usual construction of smaller "golden" and "silver" idols also is implied in Isa. 41:7; 44:12, 13, and repeatedly stated in the "Epistle of Jeremiah" (Baruch, 6:39, 50, 57, 70), in the vivid account there given of the Chaldean images of the gods.

Hyacinth. *See* Jacinth.

Iron (Heb. *bärzěl*). This word is undisputed, and is, of course, frequent, both literally and in metaphors of strength, etc. In its first occurrence (Gen. 4:22) the reference is in all probability to meteoric iron. This seems an inescapable conclusion in the light of the immense priority of the use of copper and bronze to that of iron, as clearly shown in prehistoric archaeology. But the expression is simple enough in its general sense, describing Tubal-Cain as the pioneer in metallurgical arts, without implying his personal acquaintance with their later advances. Iron was apparently known and worked to a small extent long before it became frequent in the Iron Age, 1200-300 B. C. The readiness with which iron perishes by oxidation would obliterate the evidences of its earlier limited use. Iron was familiar to the civilized nations of the ancient world. Homer has many references to it, though with an association of value that indicates it as still somewhat rare and choice. It was freely used among the Etruscans, Egyptians, and Assyrians, as shown by explorations, and among the Canaanites, as seen in the Old Testament records. Layard found Assyrian articles of iron coated with bronze, which generally crumbled on exposure to the air. It would seem that its use was especially for tools and weapons of attack, while bronze and the copper alloys were for defensive armor and objects that did not need hardness and sharpness of edge and point. Thus Goliath was clad in bronze armor, like Homer's 'Achaioi Chalkochitōnes, but his spearhead was of iron (I Sam. 17:5-7). By the time of David's later years it was not only abundant (I Chron. 22:3; 29:2), but had come to be more so than bronze (29:7; Isa. 60:17). This was due to Saul and David's conquests over the Philistines who held the secret of smelting iron (I Sam. 13:19-22). The Philistines probably obtained the secret from the Hittites, whose monopoly on this important metal was not broken till about 1200 B. C. Sir Flinders Petrie found abundant confirmation of Philistine domination of iron smelting at *Gerar*, where iron furnaces and iron instruments were recovered. The industrial revolution of the Davidic-Solomonic era was due in large part to the "steel boom" in Israel. In Isa. 44:12, and more fully detailed in Eccles. 38:28, we find vivid and familiar pictures of the forge and the smith. The Old Testament references to iron are very varied; thus it appears in general among the spoils of war (Num. 31:22; II Sam. 8:8), for chariots—probably sheathed or plated with it (Josh. 17:16, 18; Judg. 1:19; 4:3, 13)—King Og's bedstead (Deut. 3:11), the huge spearhead of Goliath (I Sam. 17:7), for axes and axheads (Deut. 19:5; II Kings 6:5, 6; Isa. 10:34), for stonecutting tools (Deut. 27:5), saws, harrows, etc. (II Sam. 12:31); a stylus for engraving (Job 19:24; Jer. 17:1), and often for bonds or fetters (Psa. 105:18; 107:10; 149:8); also as a figure of strong dominion, an iron scepter or mace (2:9), etc. In these latter and other similar passages, as Deut. 28:48, the literal and figurative uses of the word blend into each other so as not always to be readily distinguished. Thus it is not clear whether the "iron furnace" (Deut. 4:20; I Kings 8:51; and Jer. 11:4) has an actual or metaphorical reference to the servitude in Egypt; the accounts in Exodus refer only to brickmaking, and in Psa. 81:6 to pottery; but other forms of hard labor may well have been involved.

Figurative. In clearly figurative uses it is often applied to ideas of physical strength, endurance, etc. (Deut. 33:25; Mic. 4:13; Job 40:18; Dan. 7:7, 19), and in mixed symbols (I Kings 22:11; II Chron. 18:10; and the striking similes of Dan. 2:32-45); and likewise to purely moral qualities, in either good or bad senses—firm, unyielding (Jer. 1:18; and Isa. 48:4); with the last compare the epithet so frequently applied to Israel, "a stiffnecked people" (Exod. 32:9; 33:3, 5; Deut. 9:6, 13: II Chron. 30:8, etc.). In Deut. 28:23 it is used with great vividness to depict the parched and hardened ground in a protracted drought; and so of a rainless sky (Lev. 26:19). In Ezek. 4:3 the "iron pan" to be used by the prophet as a sign against Jerusalem of the coming siege is compared with the portable screens for archers, etc., represented on Assyrian sculptures.

Jacinth (or **Hyacinth**). This name is now applied to the orange-red and red-brown varieties of zircon (silicate of zirconia); but the classical *huakinthos* (Rev. 21:20; *huakinthinos*, Rev. 9:17) appears rather to have been our blue sapphire. Yet there is some uncertainty regarding it, as Pliny speaks of it as golden colored; generally, however, the classical *hyacinthus* was blue. In Rev. 21:20 (Gr. *huakinthos*) it no doubt means sapphire; in R. V. it is used instead of "ligure" in the accounts of the breastplate (Exod. 28:19; and 39:12); and in these cases apparently a deep yellow gem is meant, possibly our zircon-hyacinth (*see* Ligure). Yet as the LXX uses *huakinthos* (for *t^ekēlĕth*) in all the descriptions of the tabernacle furnishings, where *blue* is employed in the English versions, and evidently meant; and as various ancient writers mention the *hyacinthus* as of some shade of blue there can be little question of its being our sapphire. *See* Ligure; Sapphire.

Jasper (Heb. *yāsh^ephēh;* Gr. *iaspis*). Great uncertainty hangs about the meaning of the word *iaspis* among the ancients. The name is now limited to the richly colored and strictly opaque varieties, many of which are fine ornamental stones, and were largely used for seals, cylinders, etc., by the ancients, but are totally remote from any idea of great preciousness or great brilliancy. As near as we can gather from Pliny's descriptions, the stone that he called *iaspis*—following Theophrastus —seems to have included several kinds of delicately colored translucent varieties of quartz (the chalcedonies); he especially mentions blue, green, and rosy tints. If so, what is now called chrysoprase would be included here. But these, also, however beautiful, are lacking in the elements of brilliancy and rarity. Probably some other minerals also were classed by Pliny as *iaspis*, perhaps the delicate green jades and other semitransparent stones of rich, light colors. Doubtless we should translate the phraseology of John in Rev. 21:11 (as in Exod. 24:10; and Rev. 21:18, elsewhere alluded to) not as a specific assertion of certain optical properties belonging to the stone named, but rather as an attempt to illustrate from various combined sources, conceptions too glorious for description. "Her light was like unto a stone most precious, even like a jasper stone, clear as crystal"—a light more beautiful than words can depict, with the rich sky-blue (or green or rosy or mingled opaline) hues of an *iaspis* and the transparency of crystal.

Lead (Heb. *'ōphĕrĕth*), very plainly indicated as this metal, from its heaviness (Exod. 15:10) and its ready dissipation by oxidizing at high temperatures (Jer. 6:29; comp. Eccles. 22:14 and 47:18); a very heavy metal, less valuable than tin. It was used for weights (Zech. 5:7, 8) and for filling in inscriptions cut in rock (Job 19:24; also Num. 31:22; Ezek. 22:18, 20; 27:12). The word translated "plumb line" (Amos 7:7, 8) is *'ănāk*, and like the English rendering implies a probable, though not necessary idea of lead as the material of the weight. In Zech. 4:10 the word "plummet" is *'ĕbĕn b^edîl*, a weight of tin, literally "stone of tin;" while in Zech. 5:8 the "weight of lead" is *'ĕbĕn hä'ōphĕrĕth*, "stone of lead." It is needless to seek specific details of composition in such references. Any heavy substance may thus be employed; but it is interesting to remember that the commonest ores of these two metals, cassiterite or tinstone (oxide of tin) and galena (sulphide of lead), are very heavy minerals, and a piece of either of them would serve well to suspend a plumb line. But the use of *'ĕbĕn* "stone," in the sense of a weight, is early and familiar in Hebrew; thus Isa. 34:11, "stones of emptiness" (A. V.) is "plummet of emptiness" in R. V., and better rendered by Gesenius "plummet of desolation," and so in various references. Other ancient uses of lead were for making solder (Isa. 41:7) for tablets for writing, and, in very early buildings, for fastening or filling in between rough stone work, so noted at Nineveh by Layard. Oxide of lead has been found also in the glaze upon both Egyptian and Assyrian pottery, as among the moderns. Lead is a metal of somewhat frequent occurrence, the only workable ore being the sulphide, galena. Lead mines at Jebel e' Rossas, near the Red Sea, between Kosseir and Berenice were well known.

Ligure (Heb. *lĕshĕm*, Exod. 28:19; 39:12). This is a very obscure and uncertain name. The English is a mere transliteration of the Greek of the LXX and Josephus; and the Vulgate is the same, *ligurium*. The word is generally identified with the *lugkourion* of Theophrastus, a stone which Pliny did not know. This appears to have been a deep-yellow gem, its name relating to the story that it was the solidified urine of the lynx. It has also been much confounded with amber, from which, however, Theophrastus clearly distinguishes it. He refers to its being a favorite stone for engraving for signets, etc., which fact agrees well with zircon (jacinth or hyacinth of modern jewelers), of which engraved specimens are familiar in collections of ancient gems, and to which it is most probably referred. He also states that it is electric, attracting light particles, etc.—which has led to the confusion with amber. This property, however, is possessed by various minerals in some degree, especially upon heating or rubbing. The latter is the case with zircon-hyacinth, and it was greatly used for intaglios by the Persians, Greeks, and Romans. The R. V. has "jacinth" for "ligure" in the passages above cited, and "amber" in the margin in the first.

Lime, is represented by the two Hebrew words *gîr* and *sîd*, discussed under the heads Chalkstones and Plaster (*q. v.*). The latter word is used in Isa. 33:12 and Amos 2:1; and the former in Isa. 27:9, and in Aramaic form *gîrä* (Dan. 5:5), the last being rendered plaster in our versions. The process of burning lime (*see* Chalkstones) was familiar; but it is not possible to say just what the Hebrew modes of using it were, or how far lime and plaster were discriminated. Our modern chemistry enables us to understand the nature and behavior of these substances, theoretically, far better than the ancients; but they certainly knew them practically and used them well. Carbonate of lime (limestone), when heated, loses its carbonic acid and passes to caustic or unslaked lime (calcium oxide); this, on contact with water, combines with it with great heat, forming calcium hydrate (slaked lime), which gradually takes up carbon dioxide again from the air and passes back to carbonate. If slaked lime be mixed with sand, we have mortar, which becomes in hardening an artificial stone consisting of grains of sand embedded in a mass of carbonate of lime—very hard and enduring. Sulphate of lime (gypsum, alabaster) contains a quantity of water held in the condition known as "water of crystallization;" by heating this water is driven off, and the anhydrous sulphate may then be pulverized, this being plaster; on contact with water the latter is again taken up, and the material suddenly solidifies or "sets." Various combinations and applications of these two great lime products have been used for ages and in many lands. Admixtures of clay with mortar yield certain forms of cement, and the hydraulic cement used for masonry under water is made from argillaceous limestones. Stucco consists essentially of a mixture of plaster with pulverized marble, and becomes hard and capable of polish far beyond simple plaster. White-wash is slaked lime (hydrate) mixed with a large quantity of water, so as to be spread thinly and evenly over walls, etc. Probably all these materials were known to the Hebrews; but it does not appear possible to distinguish any precise terms for them.

Marble (Heb. *shēsh, shǎyîsh, white;* Gr. *marmaros;* I Chron. 29:2; Cant. 5:15; Esth. 1:6; Rev. 18:12). In the New Testament the only reference is in Rev. 18:12. The term marble is loosely used in general for any fine-grained building or ornamental stone, not very hard, white or of delicate color, and taking a handsome polish. Strictly, it refers to crystalline limestones possessing these qualities, but other varieties are often included in the term, and even other stones. Palestine is a limestone country; and the word, as used in the Bible, has its ordinary meaning and requires no discussion. From I Kings 5:14, 18; 7:10, it would seem as though the material was the white or cream-colored Jurassic limestone of the Lebanon, of which the sun temple at Baalbec is constructed. In Herod's temple true white crystalline marble was largely employed. In the passage, Esth. 1:6, several other words are also used, which our translators refer to colored marbles, and the R. V. margin suggests porphyry and alabaster as included.

Mortar, or **Morter**, for building, to distinguish it from the apparatus for grinding (Heb. *hōmēr,* Gen. 11:3; Exod. 1:14, etc. The root *hämăr*) is properly to *boil* or *foam,* though it has some secondary meanings; but this primitive sense vividly suggests the slaking of lime in our ordinary making of mortar. In ancient buildings we find some without any fastening

material at all, the stones merely fitted together accurately; in some cases lead was used, and in others iron clamps; but most frequently we find either bitumen (Gen. 11:3, and many existing ruins in Mesopotamia), clay, or some form of cement or mortar prepared for the purpose, and often mixed with straw, as we use hair. Other references to the mixing or "treading" of mortar, in this case plainly not our lime mortar, are Isa. 41:25

298. Mortar

and Nah. 3:14; here *hōmēr* has apparently its frequent meaning of clay, simply, and the rendering "mortar" in our versions is not applicable. Another word, *'äphär,* properly dust or dry earth, is in some passages rendered "mortar," especially Lev. 14:42, 45—clay used for filling interstices, etc., in walls, or for coating them. In Ezek. 13:10-15; 22:28, the word mortar is supplied in our versions after "untempered," where either mortar or plaster may be meant, or perhaps some form of stucco or cement, used to protect *adobe* houses from the action of the weather. *See* Brick; Lime; Plaster.

Niter (Heb. *nĕthĕr;* Gr. *nitron*), a widely distributed name for native carbonate of soda, or natron, including also the closely-related minerals thermonatrite and trona. The name niter is now applied to an entirely different substance—saltpeter or nitrate of potash; and its use in Old Testament passages is inaccurate and confuses the sense. Natron occurs in nature only in solution; it contains ten molecules (over sixty per cent) of water, and is essentially the same material as that commonly known as "washing soda." By exposure to the air and by heat more or less of this water is lost, and several other sodium carbonates are thus produced, with varying proportions of water, and even the anhydrous salt. Thermonatrite and trona (abbreviated from natrona) are compounds of this kind, containing about fourteen and twenty per cent of water respectively, and occurring in the evaporated crusts and deposits from alkaline lakes in dry regions. The principal ancient source was at the "soda lakes" of Egypt, described by Pliny and Strabo, as well as by explorers. There are nine of these lakes, the largest being about five miles long and a mile and a half wide, others much smaller; they are situated some sixty miles N. W. of Cairo, in the desert of St. Macarius. Beneath the general surface of sand lies a heavy bed of dark clay impregnated with salt, gypsum, and carbonate of lime; the water leached from this clay is strongly charged with salt and with sulphates and carbonates of soda. In the dry season the smaller lakes evaporate to solid crusts, the larger concentrate and deposit beds of these salts, variously mixed in composition, but rich in sodium carbonates. The crusts are dug and broken with spades and poles, dried in the sun on the banks, taken to the Nile— some thirty miles—and there shipped on boats to Alexandria. Large amounts are sent to Crete for use in soap making, and the material is also widely employed in the East to "soften" the hard limestone waters for drinking. Similar deposits occur in other regions of the Old World, and largely in Nevada and California, especially Mono Lake and Owen's Lake, at the latter of which important soda works have been established.

The ancients employed these natural carbonates for washing, mixed with oil so as to form a true soap; and this primitive though effective method is still in use. They also made artificial vegetable alkalies of the same kind by burning plants and leaching the ashes with water; these were designated in Hebrew as *bōr* and *bōrîth*; so Mal. 3:2. The effect of pouring acid upon such a carbonate, producing violent effervescence, was evidently familiar, from Prov. 25:20, where the R. V. gives "soda" in the margin, correctly, for *nĕthĕr*—a vivid comparison for the revulsion of one in sorrow against untimely mirth. The two words *nĕthĕr* and *bōrîth* occur together in Jer. 2:22, where the latter is rendered "soap" in both versions, and the former "niter" in A. V. and "lye" in R. V.; and so also the R. V. margin gives "lye" for *bōrîth* in Job 9:30 and Isa. 1:25, for "never so clean" and "thoroughly" in the text; while in Mal. 3:2 both versions render it "soap." The reference in Isaiah seems to apply to the use of such an alkaline carbonate as a flux in the reduction and purification of metals.

Onyx (Gr. *'onux*, generally for Heb. *shōhăm*), probably in most cases the stone still so named (Gen. 2:12; Exod. 25:7, etc.). The term denotes the varieties of that stone that show somewhat even bands or layers of black or dark tints, and white. When cut parallel to the layers the semitransparent white bands show the darker bands through them, and suggest the finger nail, whence the name *'onux*. The same word has also been used, both anciently and among us, for other translucent banded stones, as "Mexican onyx," etc. (*see* Alabaster). The word *shōhăm* occurs quite often, and is very variously rendered by the LXX, indicating great uncertainty as to its meaning. References to the Arab. *sahum*, paleness, and *sachma*, blackness, made by various writers, give little aid, though strongly against any of the bright-colored stones above named. Josephus, however, states clearly that the stone on the breastplate was onyx, and the shoulder-pieces of the ephod sardonyx—the variety of onyx with bands of dark red (sardine or sardius). This testimony, from one personally familiar with the priestly vestments, is incontestible, and goes far to establish the same meaning for the other cases in

which *shōhăm* occurs. The R. V. gives "beryl" in the margin, in several instances, but there is no probability of this being meant; in the case of the engraved shoulder-pieces it is scarcely possible, even apart from the clear statement of Josephus. *See* Agate.

Pearls. These cannot strictly be classed among precious stones, yet they have always been associated with gems in connection with jewelry, and so may be treated of here. Pearls are formed by secretion in the bodies of many kinds of molluscan shellfish, and consist of the same material and possess the same color as the interior layers of the shell in which they occur. This material is partly mineral matter (carbonate of lime) and partly organic matter. Most of the pearls of commerce are yielded by the so-called "pearl oysters," which occur widely distributed along all the shores of the Indian and South Pacific Oceans. The scientific name of the chief pearl-yielding species is *Meleagrina margaritifera*. The ancient pearl fisheries were chiefly in the Red Sea and the Persian Gulf; the latter still retain great importance, but the former have ceased to be worked for a long time, while Ceylon and the north Australian coast now furnish large quantities.

The references to pearls in the Scriptures are rather curiously few, and in the Old Testament uncertain, although we know from ancient jewelry that pearls were familiar from very early times. Those in Egypt are presumably from the Red Sea, where they were sought and found as late as the Roman period. In the Red Sea occurs also the large delicate *pinna*, or "wing shell," which occasionally yields translucent pink pearls, greatly prized for their beauty and rarity. It seems probable, partly from the resemblance to the Arabic name and partly from the manner of expression, that the word Heb. *pᵉnînîm*, always plural, so variously rendered by Old Testament translators and in both our versions by *rubies* (*see* Precious Stones), refers to pearls (Job. 28:18; Prov. 3:15; 8:11; 20:15; 31:10; Lam. 4:7). This is the view of the rabbis and many commentators, yet the passage in Lamentations implies redness, and has perplexed the rendering. Gesenius would adopt *pearls* but for this, and inclines to the meaning *red coral*, deriving the word from *părăd*, to *divide* or separate, *q. s.* branching corals). Our revisers, in the margin, put *coral* in this passage and both *pearls* and *red coral* in the other passages. But the precious pink pearls yielded by the Red Sea pinnas, Gr. *pinna*, would seem to solve the apparent difficulty. The very name in the Greek is almost identical, and perhaps the derivation may be found in connection with *pᵉnîmăh*, and *pᵉnîmî*, *within, inner, q. s.* formed in and taken from the interior of a shellfish. It is possible, also, as the LXX and Vulgate rendering of the passages in Proverbs would suggest, that this word may have possessed an indefinite meaning, including pearls and strung jewels or beads, as of red coral, garnet, carnelian, etc. A feminine singular form, *pᵉnînäh*, occurs once as a proper name (I Sam. 1:2, 4), of the other wife of Elkanah, just as we use Pearl, and many European nations Marguerite, etc., now; and the same name is still met with among Arabic-speaking people, in almost the identical form of I Samuel.

The New Testament references (Matt. 13: 45; Rev. 21:21) are perfectly simple renderings of Gr. *margaritēs*, a *pearl*.

Pitch. *See* Asphalt, Bitumen.

Plaster. This rendering (in R. V. with the old form plaister retained) is given to the two words *tûăḥ* and *sîd;* these are derived respectively from *ṭûăḥ*, to spread upon or overlay with anything; and *sîd*, to cover with lime, to plaster, in a more definite sense. The noun *sîd* is plainly lime, from Isa. 33:12, and Amos 2:1; and hence, as used in Deut. 27:2, 4 (comp. Josh. 8:32) it would probably mean a fine white mortar. Plaster, made from gypsum, by heating it and mixing the dehydrated and powdered product with water, must indeed have been known to the Hebrews; as gypsum occurs in the terraces along the Jordan and Dead Sea valleys; but it is not quite clear whether this was included in *sîd*. The Egyptians seem to have used it freely, with colors, and overlaid with varnish, in their interior wall paintings. The other word, *ṭûăḥ*, seems more general; it is translated "the daubing" (Ezek. 13:12); "plaster" (Lev. 14: 42, 43, 48), and "overlay" of silver plating (I Chron. 29:4). In Dan. 5:5, the word is *gîră*, Aramaic form for ordinary Heb. *gîr*, properly lime, here probably stucco; gypsum slabs (alabaster) were much used for wall facings at Nineveh, but not so much at Babylon, where the scene referred to occurred. *See* Lime and Mortar.

Ruby (Heb. *pănîn; pănî*). These words, rendered "rubies" in A. V., are extremely uncertain, and were so to the seventy translators, who gave various renderings. The one in Lamentations is the only one which indicates *redness;* the others denote merely some beautiful and precious objects, are employed solely for comparison, and are in every case plural. From these facts, and from the resemblance to the Arabic name, the suggestion is strongly in favor of pearls as the meaning of *pᵉnînîm*. The R. V. gives "pearls" and "red coral" in the margin in Job and Proverbs, and "coral" in Lamentations. The rendering "red coral" is favored by Gesenius and others, and compared with the Arab. *panah*, a *branch;* but this is vague. An apt suggestion has been made in connection with the fact that pink pearls are occasionally obtained from the shell known to naturalists as *pinna*, in the Red Sea. These pink pearls are very highly prized and, doubtless, have been from remote antiquity. If these were meant in the passage cited, the various renderings would be greatly harmonized. Possibly, too, the name may have included not only pearls, but beads of coral, red carnelian, garnet, etc., or strung gems in general (*see* Pearls); *kădkôd, striking fire, sparkling* (Isa. 54:12; Ezek. 27:16), is rendered "agates" and "coral" in the A. V.; and "rubies" and "coral" in R. V. So far as the true ruby is concerned, it was known to the Hebrews, but more or less confounded, as among all the ancients, with spinel rubies, garnets, etc., under the names of anthrax and carbuncle (*q. v.*).

Salt (Heb. *mĕlăḥ*, powder; *hals*), the common substance—sodium chloride—familiar in various applications, in the Bible as with us. Beds of rock salt occur at many points around the Dead Sea, called the "Salt Sea" (Heb. *yăm hămmĕlăḥ*, Gen. 14:3; Num. 34:12; Deut. 3:17; Josh. 3:16; 12:3; 15:2, 5; 18:19), the Mediterranean being the "great sea" (Josh. 15:12) or the "sea." The flats at the southern end of the Dead Sea are coated with salt in the dry season; these or similar spots are alluded to (Deut. 29:23; Zeph. 2:9; and Jer. 17:6); and some locate here the "valley of salt" (II Sam. 8:13; II Kings 14:7; Psa. 60, title). The waters of the Dead Sea are intensely salt and bitter, from the large amount of magnesium salts that they contain, having the composition of "a half-exhausted mother-liquor" (Le Conte) from which most of the sodium salts have been deposited, as well as the lime salts, during a long and extreme concentration since the time when the lake extended over the greater part of the Jordan valley to hundreds of feet above its present level. The preserving properties of salt were well known; its use by the Phoenicians in curing fish is plain from Neh. 13:16; this salt they evidently made from Mediterranean water, as they had doubtless done for ages.

Figurative. In the East salt has long been regarded as possessing a certain sacred character, so that partaking of it together was regarded as a pledge of friendship and faithfulness (II Chron. 13:5); this idea appears in a strictly religious sense, as between God and men (Num. 18:19), and hence in the offering of all sacrifices salt was essential (Lev. 2:13; Ezra 6:9; Ezek. 43:24; and Mark 9:49, A. V.). In this last passage, where "and," introducing the second clause, has the comparative sense of "as," frequently implied in Hebrew parallelisms, the latter clause is omitted from the text in the R. V. and referred to the margin as perhaps a later scholium. The same practice was general in regard to sacrifices among the ancient nations.

In a figurative sense for purifying and preserving influences, it is spoken of in Matt. 5:13; Mark 9:50; Luke 14:34; Col. 4:6. In these references in the evangelists there is an allusion to a popular belief that salt can lose its virtue; Pliny seems to recognize this idea (xxxi, 39, 44) in speaking of *sal tabescens*. This belief might arise from the use of impure rock salt or mixed saline and earthy deposits from the Dead Sea flats, etc., from which the salt would dissolve out, leaving only a tasteless and useless residue.

In Judg. 9:45 is a reference to the custom of strewing salt over the ruins of a captured town, thus figuratively devoting it to desolation. In II Kings 2:20, the idea of purification is again seen in Elisha's "healing" of the spring. These two symbolic acts illustrate two contrasted associations connected with salt in the Eastern mind.

Sapphire (Heb. *săppîr;* Gr. *sappeiros*). The sapphiros of the ancients was not our sapphire, the transparent blue corundum, but usually the opaque stone known to us as lapis lazuli, varying from ultramarine to dark violet blue. With this were doubtless included some other blue stones, especially the rich blue chalcedony now called sapphirine quartz, and perhaps occasionally cyanite and even possibly some true sapphires. Lapis lazuli is frequent in ancient Egyptian and Babylonian jewelry, and was evidently familiar and highly prized. Sapphirine quartz was much employed for Babylonian cylinder seals. Both of these stones are good material for engraving upon; while true sapphire is too hard for any ordinary tools. The objection raised by some that the remarkable passage in Exod. 24:10—the vision of God as seen by Moses and the elders of Israel—implies transparency, does not apply to "a paved work of a sapphire stone, and as it were the body of heaven in clearness." They are plainly an attempt to describe an intense depth and beauty of color resembling, but surpassing, that of the sky. The word "and," moreover, distinguishes the two descriptions of color and of transparency; and there is no more implication from this comparison that the sapphire was a transparent stone than there is regarding gold, in the similar case in the Revelation, where John describes the heavenly city as "of pure gold as it were transparent glass."

As far as we can judge, the modern sapphire was the hyacinth (or jacinth) of the ancients. Greek mythology tells of Hyacinthus, who was transformed into a flower bearing his name. This was not our hyacinth, but apparently the blue flag; or, some have thought, the larkspur. The name was then transferred to a clear blue gem; and hence we may so understand the biblical hyacinth or jacinth—certainly at least in Rev. 21:20. The stone now so called is entirely different, comprising the orange-red and red-brown varieties of zircon. See Jacinth.

Sardine or **Sardius** (Heb. *'ōdĕm;* Gr. *sardios*). The name sard, derived from Sardis in Lydia, is applied to the deep red or brownish-red varieties of carnelian (i. e., Chalcedony, *q. v.*), which have always been favorite stones for engraving seals and like purposes, examples being abundant in collections of ancient gems. The *sardius* of Rev. 21:20, doubtless means this stone; the *lithos sardinos* of Rev. 4:3, is less certain. In the Old Testament, *sardion*, and *lithos sardiou* are used variously, but always implying red gems. In Exod. 25:7, and 35:9, where the LXX uses this word for *shōhăm* (A. V. onyx), it seems probable that sardonyx (*q. v.*) was included under *shōhăm* on the one hand and *sardiou* on the other. In Exod. 28:17; 39:10, and Ezek. 28:13, it is used for *'ōdĕm*, the R. V. giving "ruby" in the margin.

Sardonyx (Gr. *sardonux*), is the variety of onyx in which some of the layers are of red carnelian (sard). The name has long been used with little change; and the stone was a favorite among the ancients, as still, for the cameo effects produced by cutting designs in one layer with a background of another differently colored. In Rev. 21:20 this is doubtless the stone meant. In the Old Testament it is probable (as above suggested) that it is included in some of the references to both *onux* and *sardios*. Josephus says that the shoulder clasps of the ephod were sardonyxes, adding

that these are "needless to describe, as being known to everyone" (Exod. 28:9). As these were engraved with the names of the tribes (six upon each), they were doubtless large red and white sardonyx plates, perhaps of two inches long, with the names cut in intaglio in the contrasted colors. This particular account of the engraving, with Josephus' statement, disposes of the idea that *shōhăm* can mean beryl or emerald, which could rarely furnish pieces of such size, or be carved advantageously in such ways.

Silver. This precious metal was employed as a medium of commercial exchange from early antiquity (Gen. 23:16; 37:28). It was not coined until the time of Croesus of Lydia and the introduction of coinage into the Persian Empire by Cyrus the Great in the sixth century B. C. In early times it was weighed out in lumps (Job. 28:15; Isa. 46:6). It was used in patriarchal times for personal ornaments (Gen. 24:53 and later Exod. 3:22; Cant. 1:11). Royal crowns (Zech. 6:11), musical instruments, i. e., trumpets (Num. 10:2), drinking cups of the nobility (Gen. 44:2), were made of it. The metal was used extensively in the Tabernacle and Temple for sockets (Exod. 26:19), hooks, fillets of the pillars (Exod. 27:10; 38:19), platters and bowls (Num. 7:13). Idols were made of silver (Psa. 115:4; Acts 19:24). Silver was used in dim antiquity by the Sumerians in the third millennium B. C. The artisans of Ur fashioned many silver art objects and silver jewelry. Egyptians knew the metal in the Old Kingdom. Silver was especially prominent under the New Empire after 1450 B. C. Great quantities of silver jewelry and other objects from this period show the Egyptians evidently imported large quantities at this time. Centuries before this silver figures prominently in the Joseph narratives (cf. 44:2, 5, 12, 16; 45:22). The refining of silver is often referred to in the O. T. (Prov. 17:3; Isa. 48:10; Zech. 13:9; Mal. 3:3, etc.). An exquisite silver Persian bowl, now in the Metropolitan Museum of Art, comes from the reign of Artaxerxes I (464-424 B. C.).

Homer describes elegant articles of silver work, e. g., the *crater*, offered as a prize by Achilles at the funeral games of Patroclus (*Il.*, xxii, 704-745), "which was unrivaled on earth for beauty," wrought by Sidonians and brought by Phoenician merchants as a present to Thoas; and so a similar *crater*, given to Menelaus by a Sidonian king (*Od.*, iv, 615 sq.; xv, 115 sq.). From these and many other ancient references we learn of great use of silver for articles of value and elegance; but little has come down to us. Greek objects in silver are rare, and were so even in Roman times. Pliny and others give accounts of celebrated Greek silversmiths; but the few examples of their work then existing were of extreme value. Their favorite style was that of designs embossed on bands of silver, which were then soldered on the vase or patera itself. The work was so delicate and elaborate that it could not be molded for casts; and in his time, Pliny says, there were no artists capable of reproducing it. The designs were largely mythological or Homeric, and occasionally of domestic life. We have some fine specimens of Phoenician and Cypriote silver work of early date, such as those found among the Curium treasures in Cyprus (Metropolitan Museum of Art, New York—Cesnola collection), but all darkened and altered so as to possess none of their original beauty. The Phoenician work is widely distributed in the ancient world, and easily recognized by experts from its conventional and non-original character—Egyptian and Assyrian patterns and "motifs" being constantly and curiously mingled. The Phoenicians were great imitators, adapters, and traders, and possessed fine mechanical skill, but lacked originality. Their style of work was largely a combination of *repoussé* with chasing, the patterns being first hammered into relief from below, and then finished with a graver on the outer or upper side.

Among the many Old Testament references to silver a few distinctions only need be made; it is spoken of literally as:

(1) A precious metal for objects of beauty or value (*see* Joseph's Cup, Gen. 44:2): for royal or sacred vessels, especially in connection with the tabernacle or the temple, *see* Exod. 26:19-25; I Chron. 18:10; 28:14-17; 29:2, 5; II Chron. 24:14; Ezra 1:6, 11; 5:14; 8:26; Dan. 5:2; of bowls or "chargers" (*paterae*, Num., ch. 7); often as the material of idols, either cast or plated (*see* Gold; also Exod. 20:23; Judg. 17:3; Psa. 115:4; 135:15; Isa. 2:20; 31:7; Hos. 13:2; Jer. 10:9), imported in plates or sheets for overlaying images.

(2) *Smelted* or *wrought* (Job. 28:1; Psa. 12:6; Prov. 17:3; 25:4; Ezek. 22:18-22).

(3) *Money*, in payment of fines, tribute, gifts, etc., weighed out by shekels or talents (Gen. 23:15, 16; Lev. 27, passim; Deut. 22: 19, 29; Judg. 17:2, 4, 10; II Sam. 18:11, 12; I Kings 20:39; II Kings 5:22, 23; 15:20; Jer. 32:9, 10; Amos 2:6; 8:6).

The word *kĕsĕph* is simply rendered *money* in many passages, as, e. g., Gen. 42:25-35; 43: 12-23; Exod. 21:21, 34, 35; 22:7; 30:16; Lev. 25:37; Num. 3:48-51; Jer. 32:9, 25, 44; and so generally, also with frequent allusions to its estimation by weight. Coins were not known among the Jews until late (comp. I Macc. 15:6); the earlier forms must have been more like our bullion, small bars or flat pieces, or perhaps the ring money depicted upon some of the Egyptian remains, as weighed in scales.

The New Testament references are simple and need little comment. By that time coins were familiar (Matt. 26:15; 27:3-9—"pieces of silver," *'argurion*, a silver coin); the same rendering is given in Luke 15:8, both versions, to *drachmē*, perhaps an allusion to the almost universal custom among Eastern women of wearing coins as ornaments on head-dresses, bracelets, etc.—at times imitated among ourselves. In many cases *'argurion* is simply rendered *money* (Matt. 28:12; Mark 14:11; Luke 9:3; 22:5; Acts 8:20; here R. V. *silver,* but in A. V. identified with *chrēmata* in vers. 18 and 20, also rendered *money,* as likewise in Acts 24:26); while it is translated *silver* in Acts 20:33; I Pet. 1:18. Conversely,

'arguros, the general name for the metal or treasure consisting of it (so Acts 17:29; James 5:3; Rev. 18:12) is used for silver coins in Matt. 10:9.

The sources of ancient silver are but little known. Diodorus speaks (i, 33) of mines on the island of Meroe, together with gold, copper, and iron. An important source was Spain (comp. I Macc. 8:3); Strabo and others speak of it as yielding large amounts, chiefly from Tartessus and Carthago Nova. Jeremiah's statement (10:9) may have a like reference, if Tartessus be Tarshish, as has been often supposed.

Figurative. Silver is used figuratively: of God's words (Psa. 12:16); the tongue of the just (Prov. 10:20); of good rulers (Isa. 1:22, 23); of saints purified by affliction (Psa. 66: 10; Zech. 13:9); "reprobate silver," i. e., rejected as impure, is compared to wicked men (Jer. 6:30); as also the *dross* of silver (Isa. 1:22; Ezek. 22:18). Wisdom is declared to be more valuable than silver (Job 28:15; Prov. 3:14; 8:10, 19; 16:16).—Revised by *M. F. U.*

Slime. See Asphalt, Bitumen.

Steel. See Iron.

Sulphur. See Brimstone, Sodom, Gomorrah.

Tin (Heb. *bᵉdĩl;* Gr. *kassiteros.* This metal, though rare in its occurrence, was very early discovered and smelted, and played a most conspicuous part in the art and commerce of the ancient world. It is a remarkable fact that though its only ore, cassiterite or tinstone (the oxide), while very heavy, has no metallic aspect and occurs at but few and remote points, tin should have become known so early and its alloy with copper (bronze) become the great metal for all purposes of arts, arms, and ornaments during the entire extent of the Bronze Age of archaeology—(3500-1200 B. C.). The source of the main supply is judged to have been Cornwall, where the Phoenicians procured it through many centuries (*see* under Brass (bronze)), but its use was widespread, even in far earlier times. Stone molds are found at many points in Europe, showing that bronze articles were cast as well as procured by commerce. Either reduced tin, therefore, or the ore itself must have been a very early article of trade throughout prehistoric Europe. There are tin mines in both Saxony and Bohemia, and a little in the Iberian peninsula, but otherwise we know of no Old World sources between Cornwall and Malacca. To these extreme points, therefore, of the Eurasian continent, we must look for the main supply. There are evidences of important Phoenician tin traffic by sea with Cornwall, but the prehistoric use of bronze must probably go back to Indian sources, and to the earliest migrations from eastern and southern Asia, while Europe was yet in the Neolithic Age. Arrian found tin abundant in Arabia, but Smith has shown that at that period it came thither from Egypt and not from the East. After the time of Julius Caesar, British tin was brought overland via Marseilles.

The Old Testament references are Num. 31:22; Ezek. 22:18, 20; 27:12. In Isa. 1:25, as already noted, the rendering should be *lead,* frequent in connection with silver ores, as tin is not; and this passage, together with Zech. 4:10 (*see* under Lead), shows that the word *b⁰dîl* was used rather loosely. Eccles. 47:18 gives it a rank above lead in value; "Thou didst gather gold as tin, and multiply silver as lead."

Classical references are frequent, so Homer, in the shield of Achilles (*Il.*, 18, 474), and elsewhere in the Iliad and Hesiod. Pliny seems to have designated lead and tin respectively as *plumbum nigrum* and *plumbum candidum;* while his *stannum* was apparently an alloy of the two metals (Beckmann), a sort of hard pewter. It seems probable that tin and lead were not very clearly discriminated by the ancients, as indicated in the passages above cited from Isaiah and Zechariah.

Topaz (Gr. *topazion*, for Heb. *piṭdăh*, a *gem;* Exod. 28:17; 39:10; Job 28:19, and Ezek. 28:13). This word has exactly changed meanings with chrysolite in ancient and modern usage (*see* Chrysolite). The Gr. *topazion* was our chrysolite, apparently—the yellow-green gem called by jewelers peridot and by mineralogists olivine. Some of these are very rich olive greens, and have been even confounded with emeralds, though of a different shade; such are notable the reputed emeralds in the chapel of the Three Magi in the cathedral of Cologne. The history of these splendid peridots is not known, but they are thought to have been brought from the East at the time of the crusades. The "topaz" of Rev. 21:20 is probably a peridot, and the Old Testament references, though less certain, may be fairly taken as the same.

Turquoise. This stone is not named in the English versions, nor is it recognizable among the descriptions of Theophrastus, though plainly in Pliny, as *callais* and *callaina*. But as a peculiarly oriental gem from Khorassan and Turkestan and anciently from Arabia, and largely used in Egyptian jewelry from very early times, it must have been well known to the Hebrews; and there can hardly be any doubt that some of the obscure and disputed names of the Old Testament must refer to turquoise. Famous Egyptian turquoise mines were located at Serabit in the Sinai Peninsula, where this blue or blue-green mineral containing copper and iron was obtained. As early as the Third Dynasty and again during the strong Twelfth Dynasty, and particularly during the period of the New Empire (c. 1550-1319 B. C.) the Serabit mines yielded turquoise for jewelry, amulets, and sumptuous household furnishings. At Serabit El-Khadem Sir Flinders Petrie discovered important alphabetic inscriptions (1904-5).

Mines, Mining. Although the word "mine" does not occur in the A. V. of Scripture, it is evident from many allusions to it that mining was familiar to the Hebrews (*see* the remarkable description of ore mining in Job 28:1-11). Mining has been carried on from a very early date in the Sinaitic peninsula. The Monitu, who frequented this region from the dawn of history, discovered at an early period in the sides of the hills rich veins of metals and strata bearing precious stones. From these they learned to extract iron, oxides of copper, and manganese, and turquoises which they

exported to the Delta. (*See* Turquoise.) The fame of these riches excited the cupidity of the Pharaohs, who fitted out expeditions which established themselves by main force in the districts where the mines lay. In the Wady Magharah ("the Valley of the Cave") are still traces of the Egyptian colony of miners who settled there for the purpose of mining copper and left their hieroglyphic inscriptions upon the face of the rock. The ancient furnaces are still to be seen, and on the coast of the Red Sea are found the piers and wharves whence the miners shipped their metal in the harbor of Abu Zelimeh.

The copper mines of Phaeno in Idumea, according to Jerome, were between Zoar and Petra, in which during the persecution of Diocletian the Christians were condemned to work. There are traces or records of goldworking in Egypt. Those in the Bishâree desert have been discovered. Ruins of the miners' huts still remain at Serabit el-Khadem. Copper and iron were both native products of Palestine and were worked also in the island of Meroe, at the mouth of the Nile. The island of Cyprus is also mentioned as a source of copper.

Famous is Solomon's working of the copper mines of the Arabah and the imperial copper refinery discovered at Ezion-geber, modern Tell el-Kheleifeh excavated by Nelson Glueck. *See* Ezion-geber.

Mingled People (Heb. *'ěrěb, mixture*). This phrase is applied to the non-Egyptian settlers in the land, e. g., Phoenicians, especially Greek, Ionian, and Carian troops who had been settled there since the days of Psammetichus, father of Necho (Jer. 25:20; Ezek. 30:5).

The "mingled people" in the midst of Babylon (Jer. 50:37) were probably the foreign soldiers or mercenary troops, who lived among the native population, as the Targum takes it.

Min'iamin (mĭn'yà-mĭn; *from the right* hand).
1. One of the Levites who had charge of the distribution to his brethren of the sacred offerings in the time of Hezekiah (II Chron. 31: 15), B. C. 715.
2. One of the priests who came from Babylon with Zerubbabel (Neh. 12:17), and perhaps one of the trumpeters at the dedication of the wall of Jerusalem (12:41), B. C. 536-445. The name is elsewhere given as *Miamin* (12:5), or *Mijamin* (10:7). *See* Mijamin.

Minister. This term is used in the A. V. to describe various officials of a religious and civil character.
1. *M⁰shärēth*, which is applied (1) to an attendant upon a person of high rank (Exod. 24:13; Josh. 1:1; II Kings 4:43); (2) to the *attachés* of a royal court (I Kings 10:5; II Chron. 22:8; comp. Psa. 104:4), where, it may be observed, they are distinguished from the "servants" or officials of higher rank; (3) to the priests and Levites (Isa. 61:6; Ezek. 44:11; Joel 1:9, 13; Ezra 8:17; Neh. 10:36).
2. *Pělăḥ*, to serve, Ezra 7:24, a minister of religion.

In the New Testament we have three terms, each with its distinctive meaning:
3. *Leitourgos*, a *public servant*, answers most

nearly to the Hebrew *mᵉshārēth*, and is usually employed in the LXX as its equivalent. It betokens a subordinate public administrator (Rom. 13:6; 15:16; Heb. 8:2). In all these instances the original and special meaning of the word, as used by the Athenians of one who performs certain gratuitous public services, is preserved.

4. *Hupēretēs* differs from the two others in that it contains the idea of actual and personal attendance upon a superior. Thus it is used of the attendant in the synagogue, the *chazen* of the Talmudists (Luke 4:20), whose duty it was to open and close the building, to produce and replace the books employed in the service, and generally to wait on the officiating priest or teacher. The idea of *personal attendance* comes prominently forward in Luke 1:2; Acts 26:16. In all these cases the etymological sense of the words *hupo eretēs* (literally a *"sub-rower,"* one who rows under command of the steersman) comes out.

5. *Diakonos* is usually employed in relation to the ministry of the Gospel: its application is twofold, in a general sense to indicate ministers of any order, whether superior or inferior, and in a special sense to indicate an order of inferior ministers (*see* Deacon). Our Lord himself is called a minister, with reference to the holy service he had to perform as the great High Priest of his people's profession (Heb. 8:2).

Min′ni (mĭn′ī), a kingdom named (Jer. 51:27) along with Ararat and Ashkenaz, "the Minyai of Nicholas of Damascus (Josephus, *Ant.*, i, 3, 8); the Mannai of the inscriptions. Shalmaneser III of Assyria overran the country of the Minni in 830 B. C. In 715 the king of Minni revolted but was subdued to the Assyrian yoke. The Minni gave Ashurbanipal (669-626) a great deal of trouble, till they finally sided with the Medes and others to bring about the fall of Nineveh and the Assyrian Empire (612 B. C.). The territory of the Minni was in Armenia in the Lake Van and Lake Urmia region."

Min′nith (mĭn′ĭth), a town east of Jordan. An Ammonitish town, to which the terrible carnage of Jephthah reached (Judg. 11:33), and celebrated for the excellence of its wheat which was exported to the markets of Tyre (Ezek. 27:17). It was probably located about four Roman miles E. of Heshbon, now thought to be Mineh, where there are traces of terraces and walls.

Minstrel (Heb. *mᵉnăggēn*, one *striking* the lyre; Gr. *'aulētēs*). This word occurs but twice in the A. V. (II Kings 3:15; Matt. 9:23). In the former Elisha, in the presence of the confederate kings of Judah, exclaims, "But now bring me a minstrel," etc. It may be that through the music he expected "to collect his mind from the impressions of the outer world, and by subduing the self-life and life in the external world to become absorbed in the intuition of divine things" (Keil, *Com.*, in loc.). The word *minstrel* is used in Matt. 9:23, of the pipe-players, and the music is of the nature of a dirge or lament for the dead daughter of the ruler of the synagogue. Minstrels were common in royal courts at Babylon in Assyria, Egypt and Palestine.

Mint. *See* Vegetable Kingdom.

Miph′kad (mĭf′kăd; *appointment, census*), the name of a gate of Jerusalem, opposite the residence of the Nethinim and the bazaars, between the Horse Gate and the angle of the old wall near the Sheep Gate (Neh. 3:31); probably identical with the Prison Gate (12:39). Some identify it with the High Gate of Benjamin (Jer. 20:2), and locate it at the west end of the bridge; but that gate was probably situated elsewhere. In Ezek. 43:21 *miphkăd* is rendered "the appointed place" of the house, referring to the place set apart for burning the sin offering.

Miracles (Lat. *miraculum*, from *mirari*, to wonder), wonderful events; and yet to be distinguished from events that only seem to be, or merely are, wonderful. The term miracle is etymologically inadequate, and indicates only one, and that not the most important, feature of the proper conception. In general terms miracles may be defined as supernatural manifestations of divine power in the external world, in themselves special revelations of the presence and power of God; and in connection with other special revelations to which they are subservient, as aiding in their attestation, establishment, and preservation.

1. **Biblical Doctrine.** The Scripture representations of miraculous events in the Old and New Testaments furnish the primary grounds for their consideration.

(1) **Biblical names of miracles.** Of deepest significance among these are the words which literally mean "powers" and "signs" (e. g., Mark 9:39; Acts 2:22; 19:11, comp. Exod. 9:16; 15:6; Luke 23:8; John 2:11, comp. Num. 14:22; Deut. 11:3). Miracles are also called "wonders" (e. g., Exod. 15:11; Dan. 12:6). It is to be noted, however, that in the New Testament they are never referred to simply under that name, some other term, as "signs" or "powers," being used in connection to bring out the deeper meaning (e. g., John 4:48; Acts 4:30; II Cor. 12:12). As "wonders," miracles are out of the ordinary course of events. They produce astonishment as being outside the ordinary operations of cause and effect. Thus far the aspect is chiefly negative. But miracles are also "powers" (often translated "mighty works," "wonderful works," "miracles"). As such they are manifestations of the power of God. Whoever is the agent in their accomplishment the power is of God. They are wrought by "the spirit of God." In them is seen "the finger of God" (Luke 4:18; 11:20; Acts 3:12). As "signs" miracles point to something beyond themselves. They indicate the near presence of God. They reveal the connection of the one who works them with the spiritual world, and are thus seals attending his authority as a messenger from God (John 2:18, 23; 3:2; Matt. 12:38; Acts 14:3; II Cor. 12:12).

Another name of beautiful significance is that which St. John applies to the miracles of our Lord. He frequently uses simply the term "works," not indeed exclusively with reference to the miracles of Christ, and yet often with particular reference to them; as if miraculous works were only the natural and appropriate works of one who was himself miraculous (John 5:36; 7:21; 10:25, 32, 38; 14:11, 12). (For full discussion of this part of the subject see Trench, *Notes on the Miracles*, Preliminary Essay.)

(2) **Supernatural character of miracles.** The Bible recognizes a divinely established order in nature, but also a special series of facts brought about by the direct intervention of God; and such facts are miracles (Gen. 8: 22; James 5:7; I Kings 17:1; comp. Deut. 11:13-17). The Bible does not, however, represent nature, or natural law, as something independent or separate from God. The universe is not a vast mechanism which God has created and left to itself. The power which continually works therein is his power. What we call natural law, according to the biblical conception, is only the order of God's ordinary working in the natural world (Psa. 19: 1-3; 104; John 5:17; Heb. 1:3). A miracle, therefore, is a putting forth of the same power in the natural world in an extraordinary or supernatural manner. Thus we see why and in what sense miracles are "wonders." They are such not because the usual exhibitions of God's power in the natural world are in themselves less wonderful, but because of their unusual and supernatural character. In the biblical view the whole world is wonderful (Job, ch. 26, et al). To him who has eyes to see, nature everywhere is full of marvels. And therefore it is sometimes said that in the sense of being wonderful the whole system of things is miraculous, and accordingly we have no right to distinguish any fact or event as being in any special sense a miracle. And thus, to say everything is miraculous often becomes only another way of saying "nothing is miraculous." But a miracle is not only wonderful, but so in the sense of being "a new thing" (Num. 16:30), and therefore peculiarly fitted to awaken the feeling of wonder. And further, miracles are "powers" not in the sense of being greater, but different, manifestations of divine power than are usually exhibited. They are special acts of power, and therefore have special impressiveness. To produce a harvest implies power as great as to feed a multitude with a few loaves and fishes. But the manifestation is different. In the one case the power is often overlooked, in the other it is recognized (comp. Rom. 1:20; Acts 14:17; Luke 9:43; John 6:14). Likewise miracles are "signs" in the sense of being supernatural indications of the near presence and power of God. They declare the supremacy and perfect freedom of God even in the natural world. They are also "signs" of special grace from God because of their essential connection with that special revelation which centers in Jesus Christ, whose mission it is to release and restore the world from the disorder and dominion of sin.

It is not in place, nor is it practicable to discuss here philosophically the relation between the natural and supernatural and the meanings to be attached to these terms. But it should be said that to speak of miracles as contrary to nature is not to speak in harmony with the Scriptures. Nitzsch properly says "miracles belong to the higher order of things, which is a higher nature also." We may say

that they lie beyond or outside the ordinary method of God's working in the natural world to which our observation is confined; but still we must think of them as having their appropriate place in the one great plan and purpose of him whose will is law, and who fills the universe with his presence.

(3) **Purpose.** The end for which miracles are wrought has already in some measure been indicated. But further statement and illustration are requisite.

The miracles of the Bible serve the great end of God's gracious revelation. They are revelations in themselves, but are inwrought with the history of special revelation. Accordingly we find them confined to the great epochs or critical periods of that history.

The Theophanies of ante-Mosiac times were not strictly miracles; i. e., they are to be distinguished from miraculous works wrought by the instrumentality of man. They were divine manifestations, but not authentications of God's messengers. Moses appears in the Old Testament as the first great miracle-worker. And the reason for this is evident when we remember his unique position in the religious history of mankind, the greatness of his work, and the obstacles he encountered (Exod. 10:1, 2; 14:21-31; 20:1-19, et al.). One common purpose unites and explains all the miracles in connection with the deliverance of the chosen people from the land of bondage and their secure settlement in the land of promise; and that is the founding of a monotheistic religion, the worship of the true God in the midst of an idolatrous world. The next great displays of miraculous power were centuries later, and gathered about the persons of Elijah and Elisha when the cause of true religion was threatened with destruction. And again after a long interval came another, and, in some senses, remarkable, renewal of miracles with new messages from God to revive the sinking faith of the chosen nation during the captivity.

The coming of Christ marked the greatest of all epochs in religious history. The revelation he brought, which centered in himself, was that for which all preceding revelations were preparatory. Coming to offer such new matters for faith, and to ask from men such complete submission to his authority and such complete trust in his power and grace, it was necessary that he should exhibit the signs of his character and mission. All that was miraculous in his history and activity was subservient to the great purpose of his coming. And these signs of his heavenly nature were all the more essential because of the state of humiliation into which he had entered. The New Testament Scriptures, therefore, especially abound in miracles. Chief among them is the resurrection of our Lord. Space does not admit here of comparison between the miracles of Christ and the miracle workers of the Old Testament. But it should be noted that as a whole his were upon a grander scale, and, with a single exception, never works of judgment and destruction. The withering of the barren fig tree was the destruction of an insensate object, and the underlying purpose of even that act was merciful. The power to work miracles was given to the apostles, and was exercised by them for the purpose of carrying forward the work of establishing Christianity, committed to them by the ascended Lord (Rom. 15:18, 19; II Cor. 12:12).

Thus throughout the Bible record we find the same end in view. Miracles are to arrest the attention of men, and aid in winning their acceptance of revealed truth. And so far as the sacred record shows us they were wrought only when most needed—in the great crises of revealed religion.

(4) **Bible criteria of miracles.** The Scriptures are careful to note the distinction between true miracles and those that are false; also to furnish the tests by which judgment is to be formed. At many times in the past men have appeared who have professed to work miracles and have exhibited marvelous powers. Such was the case in the contest between Moses and the Egyptian magicians (Exod., chaps. 7, 8), Elymas and Simon Magus in the days of the apostles (Acts 13:6-12; 8:9-24), and, not to specify others of later date, Christ and the apostle Paul both left their predictions that deceivers of this kind would arise "with all power and signs and lying wonders" (II Thess., ch. 2; comp. Matt. 24:24); then "lying wonders" in many cases were, no doubt, mere tricks of expert jugglers. And yet in some instances it would accord with the view of the Scriptures to regard them as wrought by the aid of malign spiritual powers, Satan and his angels. Thus Trench regards the works wrought by the Egyptian magicians and others referred to in Acts 13:8; Matt. 24:24; II Thess. 2:9; Rev. 13:13; at all events it is a matter of large importance to distinguish between such acts of deception and actual miracles—i. e., works wrought by the power of God in connection with the history of revelation. *See* M. F. Unger, *Biblical Demonology* (1952) for the role of Satan and demons in miracle and deception.

The tests presented by the Scriptures are mainly two, viz., the character of the agent and the end for which the supernatural event is wrought. False prophets can work no true miracles, and the wonders they may work are to be tried also by the teaching they seek to establish (Deut. 13:1-3; Matt. 24:24; II Thess. 2:9). This is not, as may seem, if viewed superficially, reasoning in a circle. It simply takes cognizance of the fact that man is a moral being and has in him some measure of power at least intuitively to recognize truth. True miracles appeal not merely to the senses, but also to the heart and conscience. And besides this, there are some events—the resurrection of Christ, for example—which so far transcend the effects of all created power as to leave no proper occasion for doubt.

(5) **Importance of miracles.** The Scriptures would guard us at this point against two extremes. We are not to attach to miracles an exaggerated value or importance. They are not the highest evidence of truth. That is found rather in the truth itself. Miracles are not demonstrations of truth, certainly not in the sense of compelling those who behold them to accept the truth in connection with which they stand. Many who witnessed the divine

works of our Lord refused to believe in him. And he declared faith that was founded upon his words to be of higher value than that which was based upon his miracles (John 4:48; 14:11; 20:29). On the other hand we are not at liberty to underrate their importance. Christ did not work miracles needlessly. He appealed to them as among the evidences of his authority (Matt. 11:4, 5, 20-24; 12:28, 39, 40; John 5:36; 20:25, 37, 38; 14:11; 15:24). And many were led to faith by the aid of these means (e. g., John 11:45). Miracles are acts of condescension and special grace to unbelieving men. And though their ultimate effect depends upon the inner bent of those who behold them, still they are in this respect like the truth itself with which they stand connected. They are not only tests of character, but also divine means for awakening attention and reverent reflection and then leading those who are receptive to the recognition and acceptance of the truth (John 3:19, 21; 18:37, et al.).

The question quite often raised in these days—whether, on the whole, miracles are helps or hindrances to faith—here finds its answer. Much depends upon the person whose faith it is proposed to establish, and much, also, upon the kind of faith it is sought to establish. With the true faith of the Gospel miracles are bound up as an indispensable element, and are in thorough harmony with those supernatural measures and operations in man's spiritual life upon which the Gospel concentrates chief attention.

II. **Theological Considerations.** Under this head space permits only a few suggestions and references.

(1) **The possibility** of miracles is not a matter for question for one who believes in a personal God. The denial of such possibility is at bottom pantheistic or atheistic (e. g., Spinoza, Renan).

(2) **The credibility** of miracles has been subjected to frequent assaults from various standpoints, for compact history and refutation of which we refer to Trench in work above cited.

To appreciate rightly the truth in this matter we must not view miracles as isolated facts, but in their actual relationships. The Scriptural conception of God and of man, and of the purpose and work of God in redeeming and saving man, furnish the explanation which outweighs all theoretical objections. And, practically, whoever realizes in himself the proper effect of the Gospel, the renewing power of the Holy Spirit, has an inner witness to the power of God, and the reality of the divine revelations, which can leave no room for doubt as to those external acts of God with which the history of that revelation is interwoven. (Comp. Num. 16:30; II Cor. 5:17; Col. 3:10.)

(3) **The question of the continuance** of miracles beyond the apostolic age of the Church must be one of history. As conservative a theologian as Charles Hodge declares that "there is nothing in the New Testament inconsistent with the occurrence of miracles in the postapostolic age of the Church." At the same time, however, he discredits the mir-

acles claimed by the Roman Catholic Church to have been wrought by her saints, as well as the distinctive claim of that Church to power in that direction. Trench regards it as a strong presumption against the continuance of this power in the Christian Church that in the earlier history of God's dealings with his people miracles were only at great and critical periods.

The necessity no longer exists. And further, the professed miracles of later times will not bear the tests of genuineness. (For valuable discussion of this point and comparison of biblical with extra-biblical miracles we refer to Trench.) The passage in Mark 16:17, 18, which has been interpreted by some (e. g., Grotius, Lavater, Hess) in a wide sense and extending to all times has been taken in a restricted sense by others (e. g., Augustine and Protestant theologians generally).

The promise of miraculous power, it is held, was completely fulfilled in the early period of the Church when such power was needed for the establishment of Christianity.

It is proper to say that the portion of St. Mark's gospel in which this passage occurs (16:9-20) is regarded by some eminent Christian scholars (notably Meyer) as a later addition from some unknown source. The R. V. contains in the margin the note: "The two oldest Greek manuscripts and some other authorities omit from verse 9 to the end. Some other authorities have a different ending to the gospel."

It is proper also to remember that the craving for miracles manifest in some directions at the present day may spring not from faith, but the lack of it, and the failure to recognize the great spiritual works which God is constantly accomplishing (Matt. 16:14).

Literature—Works on Systematic Theology: Hodge, Dorner, Van Oosterzee; J. B. Mozley, *On Miracles;* Bampton Lectures, 1865; Bushnell, *Nature and the Supernatural;* Professor A. Hovey, *The Miracles of Christ;* Essay on Miracles by Professor H. L. Mansel, in *Aids to Faith;* F. Godet, *Die Wunderen des Heeren; Expositor,* First Series, articles in vols. v, viii, ix.—*E. McC.*

Mirage, an optical illusion common in the East, and directly referred to by Isaiah (Heb. *shäräb,* "parched ground," 35:7; "heat," 49: 10).

Mir'iam (mĭr'ĭ-ăm; *obstinacy, rebellion*).

1. The daughter of Amram and Jochebed, and sister of Moses and Aaron. She is probably (Josephus, *Ant.,* ii, 9, 4) the sister who was stationed near the river Nile to watch over her infant brother. (1) **At Red Sea.** The first mention of Miriam by name is when, after the passage of the Red Sea, she led the chorus of women who replied to the male chorus with timbrels and dancing. She is here called the "sister of Aaron," probably to point out the position she was to occupy in the congregation, as ranking, not with Moses, but with Aaron, and, like him, subordinate to Moses. She is the first personage of that household to whom prophetic gifts are ascribed. "Miriam the prophetess" is her acknowledged title (Exod. 15:20, 21), B. C. c. 1440. (2) **Rebels against Moses.** The ex-

alted position of Moses aroused a feeling of envy in the minds of his brother and sister, and they at length disputed the preeminence of his special calling. Miriam instigated the open rebellion, and was followed by Aaron. An occasion was found for their manifestation of discontent in the Cushite wife whom Moses had taken. "Hath Jehovah spoken only by Moses? hath he not spoken also by us?" Summoned to the tabernacle by Jehovah, a stern rebuke was administered to them, and Miriam, the instigator of the rebellion, was smitten with leprosy. When Aaron saw his sister thus smitten, he said to Moses, "Alas, my lord, . . . lay not the sin upon us." And Moses prayed unto Jehovah, "Heal her now, O God, I beseech thee." God heard his prayer, though not without inflicting deep humiliation upon Miriam. She was shut outside of the camp, excluded from the congregation for seven days, after which restoration and purification from her leprosy was promised. During her seclusion the people did not journey any farther (Num. 12:1-15), B. C. c. 1439. This stroke, and its removal, which took place at Hazeroth, form the last public event of Miriam's life. She died toward the close of the wanderings at Kadesh, and was buried there (Num. 20:1), B. C. about c. 1401. Her tomb was shown near Petra in the days of Jerome. According to Josephus she was married to the famous Hur, and, through him, was grandmother of the architect Bezaleel. In the Koran (ch. iii) she is confounded with the Virgin Mary; and hence the holy family is called the family of Amram, or Imram.

NOTE—The punishment of Miriam was severe, and yet just. "In her haughty exaggeration of the worth of her own prophetic gift she had placed herself on a par with Moses, the divinely appointed head of the whole nation, and exalted herself above the congregation of the Lord. For this she was afflicted with a disease which shut her out of the number of the members of the people of God. She could only be received back again after she had been healed, and by a formal purification" (K. and D., *Com.,* on Num. 12).

2. Probably the first named of the sons of Mered, of the family of Caleb, by Bithiah, the daughter of Pharaoh (I Chron. 4:17). *See* Mered.

Mir'ma (mĭr'mä; *deceit*), the last of the seven sons of Shaharaim by Hodesh; born in the land of Moab (I Chron. 8:10), B. C. after 1440.

Mirror. Two Hebrew words, (*mär'äh,* Exod. 38:8), and (*r*ᵉ*'i,* Job 37:18) are rendered in the A. V. "looking-glass," but from the context they evidently denote a mirror of polished metal. The Hebrew women on coming out of Egypt probably brought with them mirrors like those which were used by the Egyptians, and were made of a mixed metal, chiefly copper, wrought with such admirable skill, that they were susceptible of a luster, which has even been partially revived at the present day, in some of those discovered at Thebes, though buried in the earth for many centuries. The mirror itself was nearly round, inserted into a handle of wood, stone, or metal, whose form varied according to the taste of the owner. Some presented the figure of a female, a flower, a column, or a rod ornamented with the head of Hathor, a bird, or a fancy device;

and sometimes the face of a Typhonian monster was introduced to support the mirror, serving as a contrast to the features whose beauty was displayed within it. The metal of which the mirrors were composed, being li-

299. A Metal Mirror

able to rust and tarnish, required to be constantly kept bright (Wisd. 7:26; Ecclus. 12:11). This was done by means of pounded pumice-stone, rubbed on with a sponge, which was generally suspended from the mirror. The obscure image produced by a tarnished or imperfect mirror appears to be alluded to in I Cor. 13:12 (Smith, *Bib. Dict.*). See Glass.

Mis'gab (mĭs'găb; *height*), "the *high* fort," either simply appellative (Jer. 48:1) or, better, a surname of Kir Moab, the proud capital of Moab" (Isa. 15:1) (*see* Orelli, *Com.*, on Jer.). Others think it may be the Mizpeh of Moab (I Sam. 23:3), or a general name for the highlands of Moab (Isa. 25:12, A. V. "high fort").

Mish'ael (mĭsh'â-ĕl; *who is like God?*)

1. The first-named son of Uzziel (son of Kohath), the uncle of Aaron (Exod. 6:22). When Nadab and Abihu died Mishael and his brother Elzaphan, at the command of Moses, removed their bodies from the sanctuary (Lev. 10:4, 5), B. C. about 1439.

2. One of those who supported Ezra, on the left, when he read the law to the people after the captivity (Neh. 8:4), B. C. about 445.

3. One of the three Jewish youths trained with Daniel at the Babylonian court, and promoted to the rank of Magi (Dan. 1:6, 11, 19). His court name was Meshach (v. 7). They assisted Daniel in solving the dream of Nebuchadnezzar (2:17), and were "set over the affairs of the province of Babylon" (3:13). They were afterward cast into the fiery furnace for not worshipping the image set up by the king, but, being miraculously preserved, were promoted by royal decree (3:13-30), B. C. perhaps after 586.

Mi'shal (mī'shăl), a city of Asher (Josh. 19:26, A. V. "Misheal"), and assigned to the Gershom family of the Levites (21:30), called *Mashal* (I Chron. 6:74). Location uncertain.

Mi'sham (mī'shăm; *fleet, swift.* Arab. sa'ama, *to trot swiftly*, as a camel), a son of Elpaal, a Benjamite, and one of the builders of Ono, Lod, and their suburbs (I Chron. 8:12), B. C. after 1170.

Mi'sheal (mī'shē-ăl, Josh. 19:26). *See* Mishal.

Mish'ma (mĭsh'má; *hearing*).

1. The fifth son of Ishmael, and head of an Arabian tribe (Gen. 25:14; I Chron. 1:30), B. C. about 1800.

2. The son of Mibsam, of the tribe of Simeon, and father of Hamuel (I Chron. 4:25, 26), B. C. perhaps about 1300.

Mishman'nah (mĭsh-măn'á; *fatness*), one of the twelve Gadite warriors who joined David in the wilderness of Adullam (I Chron. 12:10), B. C. before 1000.

Mish'raites (mĭsh'rá-īts, only in I Chron. 2:53), the fourth of the four families of Kirjathjearim. It is usual to assume that Kirjathjearim, whose father was Shobal (v. 52), was the city of that name, and that the four families were its colonies. This is quite probable, but not certain. Sometimes the name of a person is the same as that of a place. Thus Ephrath in Gen. 35:16, 19, is the name of a place, while here in I Chron. 2:19 it is the name of Caleb's second wife. In I Chron. 2:42, 43 the familiar name Hebron is used as the name of a person, as also Haran in v. 46. With us in a host of cases a place takes the name of a person, as Washington, etc., etc. Sometimes the relation is less direct, as in Virginia and Florence. More rarely it is reversed, as in the name of Boston Corbett, the slayer of Booth. We have known America used as a Christian name.

"There is a Jewish tradition, embodied in the Targum of Rabbi Joseph, that the families of Kirjath-jearim were the sons of Moses whom Zipporah bare him, and that from them were descended the disciples of the prophets of Zorah and Eshtaol" (Smith, s. v. "Puhites"). But it is probable that the Mishraites, etc., were either colonies, or, as we incline to think, leading families of Kirjathjearim, and that Shobal was called its "father," as having founded or greatly improved it. This is the more probable since the statement is made of Shobal, as an entirely independent fact, that he "had sons" (I Chron. 2:52), and the name of Kirjath-jearim is not among them.—W. H.

Mispar. *See* Mispereth.

Mis'pereth (mĭs'pê-rĕth), one of those who returned with Zerubbabel from Babylon (Neh. 7:7), B. C. about 445. He is called Mizpar in Ezra 2:2. R. V. Mispar.

Mis'rephoth-ma'im (mĭs'rê-fŏth-mā'ĭm; *hot springs*, lit. *burning of waters*), understood by the Greek translators "as a proper name, though the rabbins and some Christian commentators render it in different ways, such as *salt pits*, *smelting huts*, or *glass huts*" (K. and D., *Com.*). It is mentioned (Josh. 11:8) as a place between Zidon and the valley of Mizpeh, whither Joshua pursued the allied Canaanites after the defeat of Jabin (comp. 13:6). It is now frequently identified with Khirbet el-Musheirifeh, 11 miles N. of Acre at the base of Ras en-Naqurah.

Mist, a rising vapor, fog, or cloud, which again distills upon the ground (Job. 36:27; Gen. 2:6, Heb. 'ēd.

Mite, a very small coin. *See* Metrology, IV.

Mith'cah (mǐth'kà) in R. V. Mith-ka (*sweetness*), the twenty-ninth station of the Israelites in the desert, mentioned between Tarah and Hashmonah (Num. 33:28, 29), perhaps Wadi Abu Takiyeh.

Mith'nite (mǐth'nīt), the designation of Joshaphat, one of David's guard in the catalogue of I Chron. 11:43.

Mith'redath (mǐth'rē-dǎth; *gift of Mithra,* a Persian god of the light between heaven and hell.

1. The treasurer of Cyrus, king of Persia, to whom the king gave the vessels of the temple, to be by him transferred to the hands of Sheshbazzar, the prince of Judah (Ezra 1:8), B. C. 536.

A Persian officer, stationed in Samaria, who joined in writing a letter to Artaxerxes in opposition to the Jews (Ezra 4:7), B. C. 522.

Miter, the rendering of two Hebrew words:

1. A *tiara* (Heb. *mǐṣněfĕth*), Exod. 28:4, 37, 39; 29:6, etc.), the turban or headdress of the high priest.

2. *A headdress* (Heb. *ṣănîf*, Zech. 3:5 only), elsewhere rendered "diadem" (Job 29:14), "hood" (Isa. 3:23). *See* Priest, Dress of.

300. Mitylene Harbor

Mityle'ne (mǐt-ȳ-lē'nē), the chief city on the island of Lesbos, in the Aegean Sea, between Chios and Assos, famous for riches and literary character, and had the privileges of a free city. Sappho, Alcaeus, Pittacus, and Theophrastus were natives of Mitylene. Paul touched there overnight (Acts 20:14, 15). The name was given to the entire island. It is now called Metelin. *See* Paul.

Mixed Marriages, i. e., between Jews and Gentiles, were strictly prohibited by the Mosiac law. *See* Marriage, 2 (1).

Mixed Multitude (Heb. *'ěrěb, mixture*). With the Israelites who journeyed from Rameses to Succoth, the first stage of the Exodus from Egypt, there went up (Exod. 12:38) "a mixed multitude," who have not hitherto been identified. During their residence in Egypt marriages were naturally contracted between the Israelites and the natives. This hybrid race is evidently alluded to by Rashi and Aben Ezra, and is most probably that to which reference is made in Exodus. That the "mixed multitude" is a general term, including all those who were not of pure Israelite blood, is evident; more than this cannot be positively asserted. In Exodus and Numbers it probably denoted the miscellaneous hangers-on of the Hebrew camp, whether they were the issue of spurious marriages with Egyptians, or were themselves Egyptians or belonging to other nations. The same happened on the return from Babylon, and in Neh. 13:3 (comp. 10: 28) a slight clew is given by which the meaning of the "mixed multitude" may be more definitely ascertained. According to Deut. 29:10 they seem to have occupied a very low position among the Israelites, and to have furnished them with hewers of wood and drawers of water. *See* Mingled People.

Miz'pah (mǐz'pà; *watch tower*), or **Miz'peh** (mǐz'pě), the name of several places.

1. The heap of stones raised by Jacob as a witness of the covenant made by him and Laban (Gen. 31:49). Laban called it, in the language of Aram, Jegarsahadutha, and Jacob called it Galeed, in the language of Canaan. Both names have the same meaning, "the cairn of testimony." Jacob and Laban made a covenant not to pass beyond Mizpah to the hurt of the other. The place was in Gilead, east of Jordan, and in later times was known from afar by its mizpah, or "watch tower," whose garrison kept watch upon the Aramaean tribes of the Hauran.

2. Another place east of Jordan, called Mizpah of Gilead (A. V. "Mizpeh"), where *Jephthah* (*q. v.*) lived (Judg. 11:34), and where the Israelites assembled under him against the Ammonites (10:17; 11:11). It is probably the same as the Ramath-Mizpeh of Gad (Josh. 13:26).

3. "The land of Mizpeh" (Josh. 11:3) was a district in Gilead inhabited by Hivites, "the country below *Hasbeya,* between *Nahr Hashbany* on the east, and *Merj Ayûn* on the west, with the village of *Mutelleh* or *Mtelleh,* at present inhabited by Druses, which stands upon a hill more than two hundred feet high, and from which there is a splendid prospect over the Huleh basin. It is from this that it has derived its name (*see* Robinson, *Bib. Tes.,* p. 272).

4. A city of Benjamin, named in the list of the allotment between Beeroth and Chephirah, and in apparent proximity to Ramah and Gibeon (Josh. 18:26, A. V. "Mizpeh"). Its connection with these two last-named places is also implied in the later history (I Kings 15: 22; II Chron. 16:6; Neh. 3:7). It was one of the places fortified by Asa against the incursions of the kings of northern Israel (I Kings 15:22; II Chron. 16:6; Jer. 41:9); and after the destruction of Jerusalem it became the residence of the superintendent appointed by the king of Babylon (Jer. 40:7, etc.), and was inhabited after the captivity (Neh. 3:7, 15, 19). Robinson (*Researches,* ii, p. 139, sq.) supposes it to be the present Neby Samwîl (i. e., prophet Samuel), 4½ miles N. W. of Jerusalem but it is more likely Tell en Naṣbeh about 8 miles N. of Jerusalem.

5. A city of Judah (Josh. 15:38), in the district of the Shefelah, or maritime lowland. Van de Velde suggests its identity with the present *Tell es-Sâfiyeh*—the Blanchegarde of the Crusaders.

6. A town of Moab to which David removed

his parents when threatened by Saul (I Sam. 22:3). It probably was a mountain fastness on the high land which bounded the Arboth-Moab, east of the Dead Sea, and which could be easily reached from Bethlehem by crossing the Jordan near its entrance into the Dead Sea.

Miz′par (mǐz′pȧr; *number*, Ezra 2:2). *See* Mispereth.

Miz′peh (mǐz′pě). *See* Mizpah.

Miz′raim (mǐz′râ-ǐm; Heb. *mǐṣrăyǐm*). In Gen. 10:6, 13, 14 and I Chron. 1:8, 11, 12, Mizraim is the second son of Ham and the father of "Ludim, and Anamim, and Lehabim, and Naphtuhim, and Pathrusim, and Casluhim (out of whom came Philistim), and Caphtorim." But elsewhere *mǐṣrăyǐm* is the standing name of Egypt, in which sense it occurs nearly eighty-seven times, the only exception being that in I Sam. 30:13 "a young man of Egypt" is, in Hebrew, "a young man an Egyptian."

It is very generally believed that Mizraim is a dual form, properly and originally signifying the two Egypts, upper and lower. *See* Egypt. In Isa. 11:11 the origin is left out of view, the name no doubt being mostly used for that part of Egypt which was nearest and most familiar, and Mizraim is lower Egypt in distinction from Pathros, which is upper Egypt. The same may be the case in Jer. 44:1, 15; Ezek. 29:14; 30:14; but in Jeremiah Egypt may possibly be the whole of which Pathros is a part, and in Ezekiel the use of the two names may be a poetic variation. So Robinson's Gesenius. Some, with Gesenius's 12th German edition, think the ending of Mizraim local instead of dual. The singular *măṣōr* is found only in II Kings 19:24; Isa. 19:6; 37:25; Mic. 7:6 A. V. "besieged," "defense."

The names of Mizraim and the descendants of Mizraim in Gen. 10:13, 14 and I Chron. 1:11, 12 appear to be all names of nations rather than of individuals, and they include far more than Egypt. "Mizraim, therefore, like Cush, and perhaps Ham, geographically represents a center whence colonies went forth in the remotest period of postdiluvian history." "We regard the distribution of the Mizraites as showing that their colonies were but a part of the great migration that gave the Cushites the command of the Indian Ocean, and which explains the affinity the Egyptian monuments show us between the pre-Hellenic Cretans and the Carians (the latter no doubt the Seleges of the Greek writers) and the Philistines" (Smith, "Mizraim").—*W. H.*—revised by *M. F. U.*

Miz′zah (mǐz′ȧ), the fourth and last of the sons of Reuel, the son of Esau by Bathshemath (Gen. 36:13; I Chron. 1:37), and a petty Edomite chieftain (Gen. 36:17).

Mna′son (nā′sŏn; perhaps *reminding*), a Christian with whom Paul lodged the last time he was in Jerusalem (Acts 21:16), A. D. 60. He was a native of Cyprus, and may have been acquainted with Barnabas, who was a Cyprian (4:36).

Mo′ab (mō′ăb; perhaps *from father*), the name of the son whom Lot's eldest daughter bore to him after the destruction of Sodom, and founder of the Moabites (Gen. 19:30-37), B. C. about 2055.

Mo′abite, Mo′abites (mō′ȧ-bīt), descendants of the elder of Lot's two surviving daughters, as Ammon of the younger. The starting point of both was in the vicinity of Zoar. Thence the roving Ammonites went to the northeast (*see* Ammonites), while the more peaceful Moabites remained near their ancestral home, displacing the Emim (Deut. 2:10, 11; comp. Gen. 14:5).

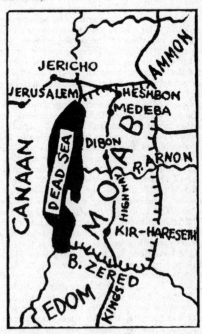

301. Moab

1. **Territory.** According to Smith (s. v. "Moab"), the territory of Moab at its greatest extent included three parts: (1) The "field of Moab" (Ruth 1:1, 2), a tract inclosed by natural fortifications; on the north by the chasm of the Arnon, on the west by the cliffs which rise almost perpendicularly from the shore of the Dead Sea, on the south and east by a semicircle of hills which opens only for the Arnon and another Dead Sea torrent. (2) The "land of Moab," the more open country from the Arnon north to the hills of Gilead. (3) The so-called "plains of Moab" (Num. 22:1), "the sunk" district in the tropical depths of the Jordan valley. Before the arrival of Israel, Sihon, king of the Amorites, had taken from "the former king of Moab," very possibly Zippor, the father of Balak (Num. 22:2), all the land "even unto Arnon" (Num. 21:26). Thus Moab was *penned up* in the closely fenced "field of Moab" above mentioned.

Coming up from Egypt the Israelites approached Moab through the desert "facing Moab," outside the bordering circle of hills on the southeast. They were forbidden to molest the Moabites in the enjoyment of the land which they had taken from the Emim

(Deut. 2:9-11). They therefore applied for permission to pass through the territory of Moab, and being refused, they went round its borders.

2. **Moab and Israel.** (1) **Refuses passage.** From Deut. 2:29 it would appear at first sight that both Moab and Edom granted the request of Israel to be allowed to pass through their territory, while Num. 20:18-21 and Deut. 23:4 seem to show that both Moab and Edom utterly refused. But more careful reading removes the difficulty and gives us a clear idea of the whole transaction. Israel's request in Num. 20:17 is to be allowed to *cross* the territory of Edom by the royal highway. This the martial Edomites refused, with a display of force, standing on their national dignity and declining to show any hospitality for relationship's sake. From Jephthah's statement in Judg. 11:17 it appears that the more timorous Moabites took the same course. But it nowhere appears that they showed any further signs of hostility. Indeed Jephthah (Judg. 11:25, 26) makes the special point that Moab did not fight against Israel while they were neighbors for three hundred years. Deut. 23:4, 7 makes no complaint of hostility on the part of either Edom or Moab, but only of want of hospitality on the part of Moab and Ammon, and the hiring of Balaam to curse Israel. There is not the slightest hint that either nation made any attempt to hinder the Israelites from passing along the edge of its territory, trading with the people as they are said to have done in Deut. 2:29. For in "Thou shalt not pass by me" in Num. 20:18, "by" must be taken in the sense of "by way of" ("via"). The Hebrew is *lō tăʿăbōr bī*, and the R. V. has "Thou shalt not pass through me." So far from being hostile, the Moabites were only too friendly, sending their daughters to cultivate friendly relations with the Israelites, and then to entice them to their idolatrous services. For in Num. 25:2 "they called" is feminine, referring to the daughters. Thus the conduct of Moab and Edom stood in strong contrast with the aggressive attitude assumed by Sihon, king of the Ammonites. Moses could, therefore, truthfully make use of the pacific conduct of those nations in his message to Sihon (Deut. 2:26-29); and so could Jephthah in his dealings with the children of Ammon (Judg. 11:15-27).

The peaceful character and rich possessions of Moab may account for the terror of Balak at the approach of the Israelites and for the special means which he took to guard against them. Instead of flying to arms, like Sihon, he first consults with the elders of Midian. Moab and Midian were kin by virtue of their common descent from Terah, thus (Gen. 11:27; 19:37; 25:2):

TERAH.
Keturah—Abraham.   Haran.
   Midian.   Lot.
                   Daughter.
                   Moab.

And perhaps the tradition in Targum (Pseudo-Jonathan on Num. 22:4) that up to this time Moab and Midian had been one nation, with kings alternately taken from Midian and Moab, and that Balak was a Midianite, may have at its foundation a real fact.

The result of the conference was that the two nations united in sending for Balaam. If we are right in understanding Mic. 6:5-7 as a quotation from Balaam it would almost seem that Balak in his desperation contemplated a sacrifice like that made by a later king of Moab (II Kings 3:26), and that he was restrained by Balaam in words of remarkable depth and truth which have been compared with those of our Lord (Matt. 9:13; 12:7; comp. Hos. 6:6).

"It is remarkable that Moses should have taken his view of the promised land from a Moabite sanctuary, and been buried in the land of Moab. It is singular, too, that his resting place is marked in the Hebrew records only by its proximity to the sanctuary of that deity to whom in his lifetime he had been such an enemy" (Smith). "He buried him in a valley of Moab over against Beth-Peor," i. e., the abode of Baal-Peor (Deut. 34:6; comp. Psa. 106:28).

(2) **Exclusion of Moab.** The exclusion of Moabites (and Ammonites) from the congregation of the Lord to the tenth generation was not on account of any active hostility, but, as is expressly said (Deut. 23:4), on account of their want of hospitality and of the hiring of Balaam, and we may well believe that the ingenuity which made the daughters of Moab the means of enticing the Israelites into drawing the curse upon themselves, made the exclusion of Moab more rigorous. The principal share in the transaction seems, however, to have belonged to *Midian* (*q. v.*). Indeed Moab is named in connection with the affair only in Num. 25:1. *See* Marriages, 2 (1).

The defeat of Midian in the field of Moab by the Edomite Hadad is sometimes understood to refer to a war between Moab and Midian; but it looks rather like a defeat of the allied Midianites and Moabites by Edom. This accords well with what is otherwise known of the martial character of Edom and the unwarlike disposition of Moab and Midian (see above, and also *Midian*, especially No. 5).

(3) **Time of judges.** After the conquest Moab once oppressed Israel for eighteen years; but as if recognizing the general unmilitary character of Moab, the text significantly says, "The Lord strengthened Eglon, the king of Moab, against Israel, . . . and he gathered unto him the children of Ammon and Amalek, and went out and smote Israel," etc. (Judg. 3:12, 13).

(4) **Time of the kingdom.** Of Saul we read simply that he fought against Moab (I Sam. 14:47). But the early relations of Moab and Israel seem on the whole to have been friendly as shown by the Book of Ruth. Ruth brought a Moabite element into the line of David, and hence, on the human side, into the ancestry of our Saviour. Thus David, when pressed by Saul, intrusted his father and mother to the

keeping of the king of Moab. But twenty years or more afterward, from some cause unknown to us, he treated the Moabites with great rigor (II Sam. 8:2), and their spoil, with that of other nations, went to swell the treasure amassed for the temple. The Moabites became tributary; and when we again hear of them they are acting for Solomon the same part which they had acted for the Israelites in Balaam's time, sending their daughters to lead him astray.

In the days of Ahab they still paid a tribute which shows both the severity of Israel's yoke and the resources of the country (II Kings 3:4, 5).

On the death of Ahab they revolted. According to the chronology of our English Bible (II Chron. 20:1, sq.), their first step was to collect an army of Moabites, Ammonites, and others, including Edomites (vers. 10, 23), and attack Judah, then ruled by Jehoshaphat. Judah met them with prayer and praise. By divine interposition, dissension broke out in the camp of the invaders, the Moabites and Ammonites first slaughtering the Edomites and then each other, so that nothing was left for Israel but to gather the spoil.

The consequence was a counter-invasion of Moab by Israel, eager to humble and perhaps regain a revolted province; Judah, ready to strike down a dangerous enemy, and Edom, mindful of the trap into which he had been led. This sequence of events shows how Edom came to act with Israel and Judah for once, and it explains the otherwise unaccountable and inexcusable severity with which Moab was treated when the victory was won. The story is told in II Kings 3:6-27.

Moab for a time must have been greatly reduced in power, so that nearly sixty years later we find predatory bands of Moabites as of Arabs (II Kings 13:20). But later, in the days of Isaiah, about the time of the death of Ahaz, "Moab has regained all and more than all of his former prosperity, and has besides extended himself over the district which he originally occupied in the youth of the nation, and which was left vacant by the removal of Reuben to Assyria" by Tiglath-pileser (II Kings 18:11; I Chron. 5:26).

3. **Prophecies.** Isaiah, in his "Burden of Moab" (chaps. 15, 16; comp. 25:10), predicts, in high-wrought poetic lamentation, the fall of Moab from his high estate, and his reduction to a small and feeble remnant (16: 14). Jeremiah, in his forty-eighth chapter, one hundred and forty years later (600 B. C.) echoes the lament of the older prophet, whose prophecy he had no doubt read, and gives Moab a gleam of hope at the last (Jer. 48:47). These prophecies refer naturally to injuries to be inflicted by Assyria and Babylon. But they are especially interesting from their allusions, which show clearly the condition of Moab. The nation appears in them as high-spirited, wealthy, populous, and even to a certain extent civilized, enjoying a wide reputation and popularity. . . . In his cities we discern a "great multitude of people," living in "glory," and in the enjoyment of great "treasure." . . . Outside the towns lie the "plentiful fields,"

luxuriant as the renowned Carmel—the vineyards and gardens of "summer fruits;" the harvest is being reaped and the "hay stored in abundance," . . . the land resounds with the clamor of the vintagers. These characteristics contrast very favorably with any traits recorded of Ammon, Edom, Midian, Amalek, the Philistines or the Canaanite tribes. Since the descriptions of Isaiah and Jeremiah agree, they seem to represent the nation as permanently flourishing.

In Josiah's time Zephaniah threatens Moab and Ammon with vengeance for their reviling words against Israel, but mentions no act of hostility. In II Kings 24:2 we find marauding bands of Moabites and Ammonites along with Syrians and Chaldees harassing Judah in the time of Jehoiakim.

Jeremiah (27:3) warned Edom, Moab, Ammon, Tyre, and Sidon as he warned Judah, not to resist Nebuchadnezzar into whose hand God had delivered those countries for the time, but to serve him and remain in their lands. It is to be presumed that they profited by his advice, since it appears from Jer. 40:11 that these countries had been a refuge to many of the Jews when the storm finally broke.

4. **After the Captivity.** Sanballat, who in Nehemiah's time was associated with Tobiah the Ammonite and Geshem the Arabian against the Jews (Neh. 2:10, 19, etc.), was a Horonite. If this name is derived from Horonaim, Sanballat was a Moabite, as he is quite often regarded. If from Beth-horon, he was probably a Samaritan. *See* Horonite.

In Judith, shortly after the captivity (4:3), Moab and Ammon occupy their ancient seats. The Maccabees do not mention Moab or any towns south of the Arnon. In the time of Josephus (*Ant.*, i, 11, § 5), the Moabites were "even still a great nation." The name remained to the time of Eusebius (A. D. about 380), and at the time of the Council of Jerusalem, A. D. 536, it formed the see of a bishop, under the name of Charak-Moba (Smith).

5. **Language and Worship.** The language of Moab was merely a dialect of Hebrew, differing from biblical Hebrew only in some comparatively trifling details.

The national deity of the Moabites was Chemosh (*q. v.*), mentioned only in Num. 21:29; Judg. 11:24; I Kings 11:7, 33; II Kings 23:13; Jer. 48:7, 13, 46.—*W. H.* revised by *M. F. U.*

Mo'abite Stone. One of the important memorials of alphabetic writing is the famous Moabite stone, erected by Mesha, king of Moab, in record of his successful revolt from Israel and in honor of his god *Chemosh* (*q. v.*), to whom his successes are ascribed. It was set up c. 850 B. C. The stone was discovered in 1868 by a German missionary, the Rev. F. Klein. He was on a visit to Moab, and was informed by an Arab sheik that close to where he then was a stone was lying, at Dhiban, the ancient Dibon, which was inscribed with old characters. On examining it he found that it was a stele of black basalt, rounded at the top and measuring nearly four feet in length and two in width. It was covered with thirty-four lines of an inscription in the letters of the

Phoenician alphabet. Mr. Klein had little idea of the importance of the discovery he had made, and contented himself with noting down a few words and compiling an alphabet out of the rest. On his return to Jerusalem he informed the Prussian consulate of the discovery, and measures were at once taken to secure the stone.

302. The Moabite Stone

In the spring of the following year. M. Clermont-Ganneau, the dragoman of the French consulate, heard that the stone was still lying at Dhiban with its inscribed face exposed to the weather, and he determined to get possession of it for France. Natives were accordingly sent to take squeezes of the inscription and to offer a large sum of money for the monument. The natives quarreled in the presence of the Arabs, and it was with some difficulty that a half-dried squeeze was carried off safely by Selim el-Oari, M. Clermont-Ganneau's agent, and delivered to the French consulate. It is upon this squeeze, which is now preserved in the Louvre, that we are largely dependent for our knowledge of the contents of the text. The largeness of the sums offered and the rival bidding of the two European consulates naturally aroused in the minds of both Moabite and Turkish officials an exaggerated idea of its mercantile value. The governor of Nablus accordingly demanded the splendid prize for himself, and the Arabs, rather than lose it for nothing, lighted a fire under it, poured cold water over it, and so shivered it into fragments. The pieces were distributed among different families and placed in their granaries, in order to act as charms in protecting the corn from blight. A considerable number of fragments have since been recovered, but without the squeeze which was taken while the stone was intact, it would have been impossible to fit many of them together, while for the missing portions of the text it is our only authority.

The work of restoration and interpretation was ably performed by Clermont-Ganneau, by way of amends for the overhasty zeal which brought about the destruction of the monument. The latest and best edition of the text, however, is that which was published in 1886 by the two German professors, Smend and Socin, after weeks of study of the squeeze preserved in the Louvre.

The inscription on this stone in a remarkable degree supplements and corroborates the history of King Mesha recorded in II Kings 3:4-27. It affords evidence of the knowledge of alphabetic writing in the lands of the Jordan. "The art of writing and reading can have been no new thing. As soon as Mesha has shaken off the yoke of the foreigner, he erects an inscribed monument in commemoration of his victories. . . . It is the first and most natural thing for him to do, and it is taken for granted that the record will have numerous readers. . . . Moreover, the forms of the letters as they appear on the Moabite Stone show that alphabetic writing must have been long practiced in the kingdom of Mesha. They are forms which presuppose a long acquaintance with the art of engraving inscriptions upon stones, and are far removed from the forms out of which they must have developed. Then, again, the language of the inscription is noteworthy. Between it and Hebrew the differences are few and slight. It is a proof that the Moabites were akin to the Israelites in language as well as in race, and that like their kinsfolk they had adopted the ancient 'language of Canaan.' The likeness between the languages of Moab and Israel extends beyond the mere idioms of grammar and syntax. It is a likeness which exists also in thought" (Sayce, *Higher Crit. and the Mon.*, p. 364, sq.).

Mo'abitess (mō'à-bī-tĕs; feminine of *Moabite*), a Moabitish woman (Ruth 1:22; 2:2, 21; 4:5, 19; II Chron. 24:26).

Moadi'ah (mô-à-dī'a; Neh. 12:17). *See* Maadiah.

Moderation (Gr. *'epieikēs, gentleness, fairness,* Phil. 4:5); rendered "patient" (I Tim. 3:3); "gentle" (Tit. 3:2; I Pet. 2:18).

Mol'adah (Heb. (*mŏl'à-dà, origin, birth*), a town in the southern part of Judah, probably about twenty miles S. of Hebron, named in connection with Kedesh and Beersheba (Josh. 15: 21-26). It was afterward assigned to Simeon (19:2; I Chron. 4:28), and was occupied after the exile (Neh. 11:26). Later it was called *Malada*, an Idumaean fortress (Josephus, *Ant.*, xviii, 6, 2), which Eusebius and Jerome located about twenty Roman miles S. of Hebron.

Mole. *See* Animal Kingdom.

Molech (mō'lĕk). *See* Gods, False.

Mo'lid (mō'lĭd; *begetter*), the son of Abishur by his wife Abihail, and descendant of Jerahmeel (I Chron. 2:29).

Moloch (mō'lŏk). *See* Gods, False.

Molten Image. *See* Calf, Image.

Molten Sea. *See* Laver.

Moment (Heb. *rĕgă', wink*, Num. 16:21, 45; Job. 20:5; Psa. 30:5, etc.; Gr. *'atomas, indivisible*, I Cor. 15:52; *stigmē,* a *point*, Luke 4:5), an instant, the smallest interval of time (*q. v.*).

Money. *See* Metrology, IV.

Money Changer (Gr. *kollubistes, a coin dealer; kermatistēs, money broker,* from *kerma,* a small coin).

1. Bankers who sat in the Court of the Gentiles (or in its porch), and for a fixed discount changed all foreign coins into those of the sanctuary. Every Israelite, rich or poor, who had reached the age of twenty, was obliged to pay into the sacred treasury, whenever the nation was numbered, a half shekel as an offering to Jehovah (Exod. 30:13-15). This tribute must in every case be paid in the exact Hebrew, half shekel. The money changers made a fixed charge of about one and a half pence, English money). This charge must have brought in a large revenue, since not only many native Palestinians might come without the statutory coin, but a vast number of foreign Jews presented themselves on such occasions in the temple. Some have estimated the bankers' profits at from forty thousand to forty-five thousand dollars. In addition to the tribute, money would be needed for other purposes. A great deal was bought within the temple area that was needful for the feast, in the way of sacrifices and their adjuncts, and for purification; and it would be better to get the right money from the authorized changers than have disputes with the dealers. Through their hands would pass the immense votive offerings of foreign Jews or of proselytes to the temple; indeed, they probably transacted all business matters connected with the sanctuary.

2. The Greek *trapezitēs* (Matt. 25:27, A. V. "exchangers") is a general term for a money changer, broker, banker; one who exchanges money for a fee and pays interest on deposits. The strong language and vigorous action of Jesus (Matt. 21:12; Mark 11:15) may be accounted for by the fact that avarice had taken up its abode in the temple to carry on its huckstering and money-changing.

Money, Love of (Gr. *philarguria,* I Tim. 6:10), avarice or covetousness (*q. v.*).

Money, Piece of (Gen. 33:19; Job. 42:11, etc.). *See* Metrology, IV.

Monsters (Heb. *tănîn*), supposed by some to mean the sea serpent or other large marine animal. Others believe it to be the jackal from its running with outstretched neck and body (Lam. 4:3, R. V. "jackal"). *See* Animal Kingdom.

Month. *See* Time.

Moon. The terms which were used to designate the moon contain no reference to its office or essential character; they simply describe it by the accidental quality of color—*yărēăh* signifying "pale," or "yellow," *lĕbänäh,* "white." The moon held an important place in the kingdom of nature, as known to the Hebrews. In the history of the creation (Gen. 1:14-16) it appears simultaneously with the sun, and is described in terms which imply its independence of that body so far as its light is concerned. Conjointly with the sun it was appointed "for signs and for seasons, and for days and years;" though in this respect it exercised a more important influence, if by the "seasons" we understand the great religious festivals of the Jews, as is particularly stated in Psa. 104:19, and more at length in

Ecclus. 43:6, 7. Besides this it had its special office in the distribution of light; it was appointed "to rule over the night," as the sun over the day, and thus the appearance of the two founts of light served "to divide between the day and between the night." The inferiority of its light is occasionally noticed, as in Gen. 1:16, in Cant. 6:10, and in Isa. 30:26. The worship of the moon was extensively practiced by the nations of the East and under a variety of aspects. Ur in lower Mesopotamia, Abraham's birthplace, was an important center of the worship of Sin, the moon-god, as well as Haran in Upper Mesopotamia whither Abram and Terah emigrated. In Egypt the moon was honored under the form of Isis, and was one of the only two deities which commanded the reverence of all the Egyptians. In Syria it was represented by that one of the Ashtaroth surnamed "Karnaim," from the horns of the crescent moon by which she was distinguished. There are indications of a very early introduction into the countries adjacent to Palestine of a species of worship distinct from any that we have hitherto noticed, viz., of the direct homage of the heavenly bodies—sun, moon, and stars—which is the characteristic of Sabianism. The first notice we have of this is in Job 31:26, 27, and it is observable that the warning of Moses (Deut. 4:19) is directed against this nature-worship rather than against the form of moon-worship which the Israelites must have witnessed in Egypt. At a later period, however, the worship of the moon in its grosser form of idol-worship was introduced from Syria, probably through Aramaic influence. In II Kings 23:5 we read that Josiah put down those "that burnt incense to Baal, to the sun, and to the moon," etc. Manasseh appears to have been the great patron of this form of idolatry, for "he worshipped all the hosts of heaven" (II Kings 21:3, 5). From his reign down to the captivity it continued to prevail among the Jews, with the exception of a brief period under Josiah. Jeremiah has several references to it (7:18; 8:2; 44:17). In one of these references the prophet gives us a little insight into the manner of worship accorded to the moon: "The children gather wood, and the fathers kindle the fire, and the women knead the dough, to make cakes to the queen of heaven" (7:18). These cakes were probably intended as gifts, in acknowledgment of a supposed influence exercised by the moon on the affairs of the world, or, more specially, on the products of the soil.

Figurative. In the figurative language of Scripture the moon is frequently noticed as presaging events of the greatest importance, such as the Second Coming of Christ, through the temporary or permanent withdrawal of its light (Isa. 13:10; Joel 2:31; Matt. 24:29; Mark 13:24). The moon becoming "as blood" (Rev. 6:12) points to approaching judgments.
—M. F. U.

Moon, New. *See* Festivals.

Mo'rasthite (mō'răs-thīt), one sprung from Moresheth-Gath, and applied to Micah the prophet (Jer. 26:18; Mic. 1:1), to distinguish him from the elder prophet Micah, the son of

Imlah (I Kings 22:8, sq.), as well as from others of the same name.

Mor'decai (môr'dĕ-kī; possibly from Akkad. *Marduk*, patron-god of Babylon).

1. **Esther's Cousin.** He was the son of Jair, a descendant of Kish the Benjamite, and resided at Shushan, the metropolis of Persia, at the time when Xerxes desired a successor to Queen Vashti, and had under his care his adopted daughter, Hadasseh (Esther). Among the fairest damsels of the land who were gathered at the palace was Esther, upon whom the king's choice fell. (1) **Service to the king.** Mordecai sat in the king's gate in those days (that is, probably, held some office in or about the palace), and became aware of the plot of two of the chamberlains against the life of the king, which, through Esther, was made known to the monarch. While the conspirators were punished no reward seems to have been bestowed upon Mordecai (Esth. 2:5, 23), B. C. about 478. (2) **Jews threatened.** Some years after the king promoted Haman. Mordecai alone refused to manifest the customary signs of homage to the royal favorite. Some think his refusal to bow before Haman arose from religious scruples, as if such salutation as was practiced in Persia were akin to idolatry; others, as seems far more probable, that he refused, from a stern unwillingness as a Jew, to bow before an Amalekite. Haman's indignation was aroused, and he determined upon revenge. Remembering the avowed enmity of the Israelites against his people, he resolved upon their extermination, and obtained from the king a decree for the slaughter of all the Jews in the empire. When Mordecai learned what had been done he "rent his clothes, and put on sackcloth with ashes, and went out into the midst of the city, and cried with a loud and bitter cry." Esther, having been informed of this through her servants, sent Hatach, one of the king's chamberlains, to learn the cause of Mordecai's grief. He sent word to the queen of the decree of extermination against the Jews, and an exhortation for her to interfere in behalf of herself and people. Esther was equal to the occasion, and, seizing a favorable opportunity, presented herself unbidden before Xerxes, and secured his consent to come with Haman to a banquet on the following day (3:1-5:8). (3) **Exaltation.** That night the monarch could not sleep and commanded the records to be read to him. Providentially that part of them was read which referred to the conspiracy frustrated by Mordecai. In answer to his question, "What honor and dignity hath been done to Mordecai for this?" the king's attendants replied, "Nothing." He then asked, "Who is in the court?" and they said, "Behold, Haman standeth in the court." The king said, "Let him come in," and then asked him, "What shall be done unto the man whom the king delighteth to honor?" Haman, supposing that he was the person alluded to, named the highest and most public honor he could conceive of, and received the astounding answer, "Do even so to Mordecai the Jew that sitteth at the king's gate." The next day Haman was hanged on the gallows that he had prepared for Mordecai (chaps. 6, 7). Mordecai was summoned into the royal pres-

ence, and was promoted to the position so recently held by Haman (8:1, 2, 15), "and his fame went out throughout all the provinces" (9:4). The first use he made of his power was, as far as possible, to counteract the decree obtained by Haman, which could not be recalled, as the kings of Persia had no power to rescind a decree once issued. The Jews were permitted to stand on their defense, and so were preserved from destruction. The feast of Purim (*see* Festivals, III) was instituted in memory of this deliverance, and is observed to this day (9:20, sq.). Mordecai is supposed to be the author of the Book of Esther, which contains the narrative.

2. A chief man among the Israelites who returned from Babylon to Jerusalem with Zerubbabel (Ezra 2:2; Neh. 7:7), B. C. 536. Perhaps the same as the above.

303. Hill of Moreh with Nain on Slope of Hill

Mo'reh (mō'rĕ; *teacher, teaching*).

1. The "plain of Moreh" (Gen. 12:6), to which Abraham came when he entered Canaan, where the Lord appeared to him, and where he built an altar. The proper rendering of "plain" is *oak* both in this passage and in Deut. 11:30, and is so rendered in the R. V. It is situated about one and a half miles from Shechem. It is thought by some that Moreh was an early Canaanite, and the plain (or "oaks") were named after him.

2. The "hill of Moreh," in the valley of Jezreel, on the north side of the well of Harod, near which the Midianites were encamped when attacked by Gideon (Judg. 7:1); probably the same as Little Hermon (Jebel Dahy) some 8 miles N. W. of Mt. Gilboa.

Mo'resheth-gath (mō'rĕsh-ĕth-găth; *possession of Gath*, i. e., *near by Gath*), apparently the birthplace or residence of the prophet Micah (Mic. 1:14), who was hence called Morasthite (1:1). Jerome (*Onomast*), places it a short distance east of Eleutheropolis, from which Dr. Robinson (*Researches*, ii, p. 423) concludes that it must have been near Mareshah. Commonly identified with Khirbet el-Başel, 1¼ miles from Eleutheropolis.

Mori'ah (mō-rī'à). "The land of Moriah" is named (Gen. 22:2) as the place whither *Abraham* (*q. v.*) went to offer up Isaac. It is thought to be the same with "Mount Moriah," one of the hills of Jerusalem on which Solomon built the temple, on the spot once occupied by the threshing floor of Ornan the Jebusite (II Chron. 3:1). The Jews themselves believe that the altar of burnt offerings in the temple stood upon the very site of the altar on which Abraham purposed to offer up his son.

Morning (Heb. *bōqĕr*, Gen. 1:5, etc.; Gr. *prōia*, Matt. 21:18), the early part of the day after sunrise. *See* Time.

Figurative. Morning is illustrative of a nearby time, as "the upright shall have dominion over them in the morning," i. e., speedily (Psa. 49:14); the glory of the Church (Cant. 6:10); the love of God is compared to the breaking of day, the morning (Isa. 58:8); Christ is called the "Morning Star" (Rev. 22:16), as he introduced the light of Gospel day; the reward of saints (2:28), stars being an emblem of lofty position; the morning cloud, as speedily disappearing before the sun, is figurative of the short-lived profession of hypocrites (Hos. 6:4); wings of the morning is figurative of rapid movements (Psa. 139:9). In the expression, "as the morning spread upon the mountains" (Joel 2:2), the prophet refers to the bright glimmer or splendor which is seen in the sky as a swarm of locusts approaches, from the reflection of the sun's rays from their wings (K. and D., *Com.*, in loc.).

Morning Sacrifice. *See* Sacrifice.

Morning Watch. *See* Watch.

Morsel (Heb. *păth, bit;* Gr. *brōsis, eating*), either the act or that which is eaten), a term answering to our *bit*, and usually referring to food (Judg. 19:5; Ruth 2:14; I Sam. 28:22; I Kings 17:11; Prov. 17:1, etc.; Heb. 12:16).

Mortal (Heb. *'ĕnōsh*), a term used for a human being (Job 4:17), as frequently with us. The Greek *thnētos* (*liable to die*), is applied to man's natural body in contrast with the body which shall be (Rom. 6:12; I Cor. 15:53, 54; II Cor. 4:11).

Mortality (Gr. *thnētos*, II Cor. 5:4), subjection to death. In the passage referred to Paul expresses the wish that what is mortal in us may be swallowed up (annihilated) by life, i. e., by the new, immortal power of life which is imparted to us in the moment of the change (Meyer, *Com.*, in loc.).

Mortar. 1. (Heb. *mᵉdōkäh*, Num. 11:8; *măktĕsh, hollow*, Judg. 15:19; Prov. 27:22), a hollow vessel of wood, stone, or metal, used to pulverize grain or other substances. The most ancient mention of its use is in the account of the manner in which the Israelites prepared the manna in the desert: "The people went about and gathered it, and ground it in mills, or ground it in a mortar" (Num. 11:8).

Figurative. "Though thou shouldest bray a fool in a mortar among wheat with a pestle, yet will not his foolishness depart from him" (Prov. 27:22). Grain may be separated from its husk and all its good properties preserved by such an operation. But the fool's folly is so essentially a part of himself that no such process can remove it from him.

2. The word descriptive of any cement used in building, and the rendering of two Hebrew words: (*hōmĕr, mire* or *clay*). Thus the builders of the tower of Babel "had brick for stone and slime," i. e., bitumen, "had they for mortar" (Gen. 11:3). *Mortar* in Exod. 1:14 is thought by some to mean *clay* from which the bricks were made; as also in Isa. 41:25, "He shall come upon princes as upon mortar;" and Nah. 3:13.

Another Hebrew word translated "mortar" is *'äphär*, (*powdered*, usually rendered *dust*). "Dust" and "mortar" are both used in the account of the treatment of a leprous house (Lev. 14:41-45). Here the mortar scraped from the walls is called "dust," while the fresh material placed upon the walls is called "mortar." (*See* Lime, Plaster.)

In Ezekiel (13:10, sq.) the figure is introduced of the people building a wall which the false prophets plastered (Heb. *täphēl*). The meaning of the figure is intelligible enough. The people build up false hopes, and the prophets not only paint these hopes for them in splendid colors, but even predict their fulfillment, instead of denouncing their folly. The plastering is therefore a figurative description of deceitful flattery or hypocrisy (*see* Matt. 23:27; Acts 23:3). The same word occurs in the sense of that which is unsavory (Job 6:6) or foolish (Lam. 2:14).

Mortgage (Heb. *'äräb, to give security*, Neh. 5:3), a lien upon real estate for debt (Gesenius reads the passage, "we must pawn our houses"). In I Sam. 17:18 it is rendered "pledge," and in Prov. 17:18 "surety."

Mortification (Gr. *thanatoō, to kill*, Rom. 8:13; *nekroō, to deaden*, Col. 3:5). Mortifying sin is based upon the believer's *position* "in Christ" by the Spirit's baptizing work. The believer *is* "dead indeed unto sin" and "alive unto God" in union with Christ (Rom. 6:11). This *position* becomes an *experiential possession* by "reckoning" (a word of faith). When the Christian *believes* he *is* what he is "in Christ," he begins to enjoy in his experience the benefits of that position.

The mortification of sin in believers is a duty enjoined in the word (Rom. 8:13; Col. 3:5). It consists in breaking the league with sin, declaration of open hostility against it, and strong resistance of it (Eph. 6:10; Gal. 5:24; Rom. 8:13). The chief agent in carrying on this mortification is the Holy Spirit (Rom. 8:13), with prayer, faith, and dependence upon God as the means. The *evidence* of mortification are not the cessation from one sin, for that may be only exchanged for another, or renounced because it is a gross sin, or there may not be an occasion to practice it. But if sin be mortified we shall not yield to temptation; our minds will be more spiritual; we shall find more happiness in spiritual services, and bring forth the fruits of the Spirit.

Mose′ra (mō-sē′rà; a *bond*), the thirty-ninth station of the Israelites in the desert, between Jaakan and Gudgodah (Deut. 10:6); evidently near Mount Hor, since Aaron is said to have died there (comp. Num. 33:37, 38). The exact location is uncertain.

Mose′roth (mō-sē′rŏth; *correction*), a station of the Israelites named between Hashmonah and Bene-jaaken (Num. 33:30, 31); probably the same as *Moserah* (A. V. Mosera).

Mo′ses (mō′zĕz), the deliverer, leader, lawgiver, and prophet of Israel.

1. **Name and Family.** The name in Hebrew is *mōshĕh* (*drawn out*), but the original is Egyptian *ms'*, a *child*, a *son*, reflecting that Pharaoh's daughter simply named him "child." Cf. Thutmose, Ahmose, etc., in which the same element appears frequently in Egyptian names.

Thutmose = "Son of Thoth," etc. Moses belonged to the tribe of Levi, and was the son of Amram by his wife Jochebed. The other members of the family were Aaron and Miriam, his elder brother and sister. His immediate pedigree is as follows:

which was almost identical with the Hebrew of the day (*see* Egypt, Babylonia). 3. *Avenges his countrymen.* When he was forty years old (7:23) Moses resolved to cast in his lot with his brethren (Heb. 11:24-26), and seeing an Israelite suffering the bastinado from an

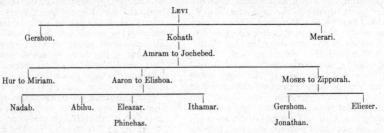

LEVI

Gershon. — Kohath — Merari.

Amram to Jochebed.

Hur to Miriam. — Aaron to Elishoa. — MOSES to Zipporah.

Nadab. — Abihu. — Eleazar. — Ithamar. — Gershom. — Eliezer.

Phinehas.

Jonathan.

2. **Personal History.** The life of Moses is divided into three equal portions of forty years each (Acts 7:23, 30, 36): His Life in Egypt, exile in Arabia, and government of Israel. (1) **Life in Egypt.** 1. *Birth, etc.* Moses was born B. C. about 1520, and, according to Manetho (Josephus, *Ap.*, i, 26; ii, 2), at Heliopolis; his birth, according to Josephus (*Ant.*, ii, 9, 2-4), having been foretold to Pharaoh by the Egyptian magicians, and to his father by a dream. At the time of Moses's birth the

304. **Infant Moses in Pharaoh's Palace (Bonifazio)**

decree (Exod. 1:10, 16) commanding the slaying of all male children was in force, but his mother was by some means able to conceal him, and hid him away for three months. When concealment was no longer possible she placed him in a small boat or basket of papyrus—perhaps from an Egyptian belief that the plant is a protection from crocodiles. She deposited him along the reeds of the Nile, and left his sister to watch the result. The daughter of Pharaoh, who may well have been the famous Queen Hatshepsut, and who herself a little later assumed the throne of Egypt, came to the river to bathe, saw the basket, and had it brought to her. It was opened, and the cry of the child moved the princess to compassion. She determined to rear it as her own. The sister was then at hand to recommend as Hebrew nurse the babe's mother, who was hired by the princess. 2. *Adoption.* The child was adopted by the king's daughter, and from this time for many years Moses must be considered as an Egyptian (2:1-10). In the Pentateuch this period is a blank, but in the New Testament he is represented as "educated in all the wisdom of the Egyptians," and "mighty in words and deeds" (Acts 7:22). The discovery of the tablets of Tel el-Amarna shows how extensive were the knowledge and use of writing throughout the East in the time of Moses and the young prince could write—doubtless in Egyptian hieroglyphics, Akkadian cuneiform, and in alphabetic cuneiform like Ugaritic,

Egyptian, and thinking that they were alone, he slew the Egyptian and buried the corpse in the sand. The next day he endeavored to act as peacemaker between two Hebrews, but his kindly offices were refused by them. It became evident to him that the time for the deliverance of his people had not yet arrived, and that safety was to be found only in flight (Exod. 2:11-15). (2) **Exile.** 1. *Marriage.* Moses fled, B. C. about 1480, at the beginning of the reign of the famous Thutmose III (if we follow the Massoretic chronology), into Midian, in or near the peninsula of Sinai, and rested himself by the well, where he chivalrously aided some maidens to water their sheep. By his help they returned to their homes earlier than usual, and upon telling their father, Jethro, the reason, he had Moses called in, and after a while gave him his daughter Zipporah to wife, Moses assuming charge of his father-in-law's flock (Exod. 2:15; 3:1). 2. *Call.* In the seclusion of this shepherd life Moses

305. **Obelisk of Hatshepsut, Possible Pharaoh's Daughter Who Adopted Moses**

received his call as a prophet. The traditional scene of this event is in the valley of Shoeib, on the north side of Jebel Musa, but we are unable to fix the spot with any certainty. It was at "the back" of the "wilderness" at Horeb (3:1); to which the Hebrew adds, while the LXX omits, "the mountain of God." Upon the mountain was the well-known acacia, the thorn tree of the desert, spreading out its tangled branches, thick set with white thorns, over the rocky ground. The angel of the Lord appeared to Moses in a flame of fire in the midst of the bush, the dry branches of which would naturally have burned in a moment, but which remained unconsumed. The twofold revelation was made to Moses (1) of the eternal self-existence of the one God; (2) of his mission to deliver his own people. Two signs attested to him his divine mission, viz., the crook turned into a serpent, and the hand of Moses made leprous and afterward cleansed. Should these be disbelieved by the people a third was promised, that the waters of the Nile thrown by Moses upon the land would be turned into blood. The objection of Moses, "Lord, I am not a man of words," etc., was answered by the promise of Jehovah's assistance. Moses's difficulties were now all exhausted and removed by the assurances of God, but, unwilling to undertake the mission, Aaron is to be his spokesman, and Moses consents. 3. *Return to Egypt.* He now returned to the home of his father-in-law, and received permission to visit his brethren. God appeared to him and assured him of the death of all those in Egypt who sought his life, B. C. c. 1440. Moses then set out upon his journey with his wife and sons. On the way Moses, threatened with death by Jehovah, was spared upon the circumcision of his son. It would seem to have been in consequence of this event, whatever it was, that the wife and her children were sent back to Jethro, and remained with him till Moses joined them at Rephidim (18:2-6). He once more received a token of the divine favor in the arrival of Aaron, who met him at the "Mount of God" and went with him to Egypt, and communicated to the people of Israel the words of Jehovah (ch. 4). (3) **Governor of Israel.** The history of Moses henceforth is the history of Israel for forty years, B. C. c. 1440-1400. He and Aaron appeared before Pharaoh to demand permission for the children of Israel to go to the wilderness and sacrifice to Jehovah. Then followed the contest between these two men and the king, and the plagues sent by Jehovah (Exod. chap. 5:12). 1. *Exodus.* On the night of the deliverance Moses took the decisive lead, and after that he is usually mentioned alone. Under the divine direction he did not lead the people by the nearest way to the promised land, i. e., through the country of the Philistines, lest, being opposed by this war-like people, the Israelites should turn back into Egypt. "But God let the people turn to the way of the wilderness of the Red Sea" (13:17, 18), through which the Israelites passed in safety while the hosts of Pharaoh perished in its waves. 2. *Journey to Sinai.* From the Red Sea Moses led Israel through Marah, where the bitter waters were sweetened (15:

23); Elim, where were twelve wells of water and seventy palm trees (15:27); the wilderness of Sin, where the people murmured for want of bread, and were supplied with quails and manna (ch. 16); Rephidim, at which place the smitten rock of Horeb gave forth water (17:1-7); the hands of Moses, upheld by Aaron and Hur, inspired the Israelites with courage, so that they defeated the Amalekites (17:8-16); and Jethro, Moses's father-in-law, brought to him his wife and two sons (ch. 18). 3. *At Sinai.* Arrived at Sinai, Moses responded to the call of Jehovah, and going up into the Mount of God received the message to the people to prepare for the divine communications (19:1-13); led the people to the nether part of the mount on the third day, where they received the decalogue (19:14; 20:17); conducted the ceremony of ratifying the covenant (24:3), reading all the "words of the Lord" (20:22-26) and "all the judgments" (chaps. 21-23); tarried forty days and nights in the mount (24:18), receiving details of the plan of the sanctuary and worship of God (chaps. 25-31), and the tables of stone (31:18). In ch. 32 we have a vivid description of the righteous indignation of Moses at the sin of Israel in the worship of the golden calf, which led him to destroy the tables of stone, and call for volunteers to slay the idolaters (vers. 1-29); and his no less earnest zeal in the capacity of mediator (32:30-33:16). The glory of Jehovah was revealed to him (vers. 17-23) and the tables of the law renewed (34:1-4); a covenant was made with Israel (vers. 10:27), and after a second stay of forty days upon the mount Moses returned to the people, his shining face covered with a veil (vers. 28-35). Moses then superintended the erection of the tabernacle and the preparation of the apparatus for worship (chaps. 35-40); received the "spiritual statute-book" of Israel as the congregation of Jehovah (Lev. chaps. 1-7), and consecrated Aaron and his sons for the priesthood (Lev., chaps. 8-9). Judgment was executed upon Nadab and Abihu (ch. 10) and further regulations promulgated (chaps. 11-27). After this Moses numbered the people, (Num. ch. 1), arranged the order of the tribes in the camp and on the march (ch. 2), numbered the Levites and arranged for their special calling (chaps. 3, 4), gave directions respecting unclean persons, trespass, Nazarites, etc. (chaps. 5, 6), received the dedicatory gifts from the princes of the tribes (ch. 7), consecrated the Levites (ch. 8), and prepared for the onward journey (chaps. 9-10:10). 4. *Journey.* On the twentieth day of the second month of the second year the cloud, lifted from the tabernacle, announced that the time to leave Sinai had come. Moses accordingly gave the order to march, and the people moved forward (Num. 10:11, sq.). Mention is made of Moses securing, by prayer, the quenching of the fire at Taberah (11:1-3); Moses's complaint of the burden of his charge and the appointment of seventy elders (11:10-30); the sedition of Miriam and Aaron (ch. 12); the sending out of the spies (chaps. 13, 14); the rebellion of Korah, Dathan, and Abiram (ch. 16); the death of Miriam and Aaron, and the smiting of the rock at Meribah (ch. 20); the plague of serpents (ch. 21); the appointment of Joshua by Moses as his successor (ch. 27); the assignment of their inheritance to the Reubenites and Gadites (ch. 32); the appointment of commissioners to divide the promised land (ch. 34); Moses's farewell address (Deut., chaps. 1-33). 5. *Death*. For forty years the

306. Michelangelo's "Moses"

care and burden of the Israelites had been upon the mind and heart of Moses. The people are encamped in Moab, awaiting the command to pass over Jordan into the land of promise. Moses had sinned at Meribah (Num. 20:12) in not sanctifying Jehovah in the eyes of the people, and had thereby forfeited the privilege of entering Canaan. At the command of God he blessed the people, and then ascended Nebo, a peak of Pisgah, from which a view was taken of the land promised to Abraham and Isaac and Jacob. After this favor had been granted him Moses died and was buried by Jehovah "in a valley in the land of Moab, over against Beth-peor," in an unknown sepulcher (Deut. 34:1-6), B. C. c. 1400.

3. **Character.** "Moses was in a sense peculiar to himself the founder and representative of his people. And in accordance with this complete identification of himself with his nation is the only strong personal trait which we are able to gather from his history (Num. 12:3). The word *meek* is hardly an adequate reading of the Hebrew *'anäyw*, which should rather be *much enduring*. It represents what we should now designate by the word *disinterested*. All that is told of him indicates a withdrawal of himself, a preference of the cause of his nation to his own interests, which makes him the most complete example of Jewish patriotism" (Smith, *Dict.*, s. v.). He joins his countrymen in their degrading servitude

(Exod. 2:11; 5:4), and forgets himself to avenge their wrongs (2:14). He desires that his brother should be leader instead of himself (4:13); and when Jehovah offers to destroy the people and make of him a great nation (32:10) he prays for their forgiveness —"If not, blot me, I pray thee, out of thy book which thou hast written" (v. 32).

4. **Moses and Archaeology.** The story of Moses being found in a papyrus ark among the flags by the riverside has many parallels in ancient lore. To the classical examples of Romulus and Remus, Bacchus and Perseus, must now be added account of the great Sargon I of Akkad (c. 2400 B. C.). The cuneiform legend of the 9th century B. C. thus speaks of Sargon: "My humble mother conceived me; she bore me in secret, placed me in an ark of bullrushes, made fast my door with pitch and gave me to the river which did not overwhelm me. The river lifted me up and carried me to Akki, the irrigator . . . Akki, the irrigator, hauled me out . . . took me to be his son and brought me up" (Hugo Gressmann, *Altorientalische Texte und Bilder zum Alten Testament*, 1909, Vol. I, p. 79). There is certainly no necessity to postulate a common origin for such simple, natural romances, but "if one must do so, the episode of Moses (sixteenth century B. C.) may have been the inspiration of them all (S. Caiger, *Bible and Spade*, Oxford, 1936, p. 68). Archae-

307. Moses and the Law (window of Abbey of Flairgny, Lorraine, 16th Century)

ology sheds light on Moses's name, which is apparently nothing more than Egyptian *mose*, pronounced *mose* after the twelfth century B. C., and meaning "the child." This Egyptian word is preserved in such composites as Ah-mose ("son of Ah," the god of light) and Thutmose ("son of Thot") (cf. Alan H. Gardner, *Jour. Egypt. Arch.*, V, 1918, p. 193). Pharoah's daughter, evidently, did not endow this unknown infant, a child of an alien race, with a special name. She simply contented herself to call him "the child." The sacred penman, however, as a result of an unusual coincidence of sound and circumstance, connects the name with the Hebrew root *masha*, "to draw out," because Pharoah's daughter "drew the infant out of" the water (Exod. 2:10). The presence of a Nubian element in Moses's family is another fact attested by his own name and those of his kinsmen. "And Miriam and Aaron spake against Moses because of the Cushite (Ethiopian or Nubian) woman he had married, for he had married a Cushite woman" (Num. 12:1). The name of Moses' brother Aaron's grandson, Phineas, means "Nubian" in Egyptian and "is interesting as providing an independent but an absolutely reliable confirmation" of the circumstance (W. F. Albright, *From the Stone Age to Christianity*, p. 193).

5. **Writings.** Although much controversy has been carried on respecting the extent of the authorship of Moses, it is probable that there should be attributed to him the Pentateuch (as far as Deut. 31:23), the song of Moses (Deut. 32:1-43), the blessing of Moses on the tribes (Deut. 33:1-29), and the ninetieth Psalm. The evidences of Moses being the author of the Pentateuch are thus summed up by Keil (*Introduction to the Old Testament*, p. 160, sq.): (1) In Exod. 17:14, after the victory over the Amalekites, Moses receives the divine command to write in *the* book (*băsēphĕr*), for a memorial, the will of God that Amalek should be utterly blotted out. According to Exod. 24:3, 4, Moses wrote the words of the covenant and the "rights" of Israel (20:2-17; chaps. 21:23) in "the Book of the Covenant." According to Num. 33:2, he wrote down the camping stations of the Israelites in the wilderness by the divine command. (2) According to Deut. 31:9-11, Moses wrote the law and gave it to the priests, with the command to read it before all Israel at the feast of tabernacles (vers. 24-26): "And it came to pass, when Moses had made an end of writing the words of this law in a book until they were finished, that Moses commanded the Levites, . . . Take this book of the law, and put it in the side of the ark of the covenant of the Lord your God, that it may be there for a witness against thee." To this double testimony we must add Deut. 17:18, that the future king who should be chosen was to write "a copy of this law" for himself, and was to read therein every day; ch. 27:1-8, where Moses commands the people to set up on Mount Ebal great stones overlaid with plaster, and to write upon these all the words of this law, which was actually done (Josh. 8:30-35); Deut. 28:58, 61; 29:19, 20, 26, where Moses threatens if they do not obey the

law *written in this book;* and 30:10, where he promises blessings if they "keep his commandments and his statutes which *are written in this book of the law.*"

308. St. Catherine's Monastery, Gebel Musa (Sinai)

6. **As a Lawgiver.** "It occurs at once as a striking thing that the uniform tradition is, that Moses gave laws and ordinances to Israel. . . . The *body* of laws that formed the constitution of Israel as a people is invariably referred to Moses. The persistence with which it is represented that law, moral and ceremonial, came from Moses, and the acceptance of the laws by the whole people as of Mosaic origin, proves at least that it was a deeply-seated belief in the nation that the great leader had given some formal legal constitution to his people," (Robertson, *Early Religion of Israel*, p. 335).

7. **Later Scripture Reference.** In the Old Testament the name of Moses does not occur so frequently, after the close of the Pentateuch, as might be expected. In Judges (18:30) the name is given as "Manasseh" in the Hebrew copies and A. V., in order to avoid the admission that the great lawgiver's grandson was the first idolatrous priest among them. In the Psalms and the Prophets, however, Moses is frequently named as the chief of the prophets. "In the New Testament he is referred to partly as the representative of the law, especially in the vision of the transfiguration, where he appears side by side with Elijah. As the author of the law he is contrasted with Christ, the Author of the Gospel: 'The law was given by Moses' (John 1:17). The ambiguity and transitory nature of his glory is set against the permanence and clearness of Christianity (II Cor. 3:13-18), and his mediatorial character against the unbroken communication of God in Christ (Gal. 3:19). His 'service' of God is contrasted with Christ's sonship (Heb. 3:5, 6). 1. Moses is, as it would seem, the only character of the Old Testament to whom Christ expressly likens himself— 'Moses wrote of me' (John 5:46). It suggests three main points of likeness: (*a*) Christ was, like Moses, the great prophet of the people— the last, as Moses was the first. (*b*) Christ, like

Moses, is a lawgiver: 'Him shall ye hear.' (*c*) Christ, like Moses, was a prophet out of the midst of the nation—'from their brethren.' As Moses was the entire representative of his people, feeling for them more than for himself, absorbed in their interests, hopes, and fears, so, with reverence be it said, was Christ. 2. In Heb. 3:1-19; 12:24-29; Acts 7:37, Christ is described, though more obscurely, as the Moses of the new dispensation—as the Apostle, or Messenger, or Mediator of God to the people—as the Controller and Leader of the flock or household of God. 3. The details of their lives are sometimes, though not often, compared (Acts 7:24-28, 35). In Jude 9 is an allusion to an altercation between Michael and Satan over the body of Moses. It probably refers to a lost apocryphal book, mentioned by Origen, called the 'Ascension, or Assumption, of Moses'" (Smith, *Bib. Dict.*, s. v.).

Moses, Books of. *See* Moses; Pentateuch.

Moses, Law of. *See* Law of Moses.

Most High (Heb. *'ĕlyōn, lofty*), a title applied to Jehovah as supreme (Gen. 14:18; Psa. 7:17; 9:2, etc.).

Most Holy. *See* Holy.

Mote (Gr. *karphros, dry twig,* or *straw*), any small, dry particle, as of chaff, wood, etc. (Matt. 7:3-5; Luke 6:41, 42), and figurative of some slight moral defect seen in another. These the self-righteous man is apt to see, while unconscious of greater evils in himself. The proverb was a familiar one with the Hebrews.

Moth. Figurative. The moth is a figure employed to represent destructive power. Apparently an insignificant figure, it is yet really a terrible one, inasmuch as it points to a power of destruction working imperceptibly and slowly, and yet effecting the destruction of the object selected with all the greater certainty (*see* Job. 4:19; 27:18; Isa. 50:9; 51:8; Hos. 5:12; Matt. 6:19, etc.). *See* Animal Kingdom.

Mother (Heb. *'ēm;* Gr. *mētēr*). The mother among the Israelites occupied a higher position in the family than was accorded to her by many other nations (*see* Family). When the father had more than one wife, the son appears to have confined the title "mother" to his real mother, by which he distinguished her from his father's other wives (Gen. 43:29). When precision was not required the stepmother was sometimes styled mother (37:10), where Jacob speaks of Leah as Joseph's mother. The stepmother was often distinguished from one's own mother by the name of "father's wife." "Mother," like brother, father, etc., was employed in a somewhat wider sense than is usual among us, as grandmother (I Kings 15:10); of any female ancestor (Gen. 3:20); of a benefactress (Judg. 5:7); of any intimate relationship (Job. 17:14).

Figurative. As in English so in Hebrew, a nation was considered as a mother, and individuals as her children (Isa. 50:1; Jer. 50:12; Ezek. 19:2; Hos. 2:14; 4:5). Large and important cities are called mothers (II Sam. 20:19; Josh. 15:45, etc.); a place where two ways part has the designation of mother

(Ezek. 21:21, A. V. marg., "mother of the way"), because out of it the two ways arise as daughters. In Job (1:21) the earth is represented as the common mother, to whose bosom all must return. The city, from its influence, is called mother, as "Babylon the great, the mother of harlots" (Rev. 17:5). The sentiment, at once so mild and tender, which is felt by a true mother for her child, is used to illustrate the love of God for his people (Isa. 44:1-8; 66:6-14; I Cor. 3:1, 2; I Thess. 2:7; II Cor. 11:2).

Motions (Gr. *pathēma*). This word, when spoken of an external state, signifies suffering, misfortune, calamity (Rom. 8:18; II Cor. 1:6; Col. 1:24, etc.); but when applied to the inward state it signifies an *affection, passion.* The "motions of sin" (Rom. 7:5) are the passions through which sins are brought about, of which the sins are the actual consequence.

Mouldy (Heb. *niqqŭd, crumbled,* Josh. 9:5, 12) refers to crumbs of bread; and the rendering had better be, "and all the bread of their provision was dry and crumbly."

Mount (Heb. *mŭṣṣāb,* a *station,* Isa. 29:3; *sōlᵉläh,* Jer. 6:6), an instrument of siege, the nature of which is a matter of conjecture, probably a rampart.

Mount E′phraim. *See* Ephraim.

309. Church on Mount of Beatitudes

Mount of Beatitudes, the name given to the mount mentioned in Matt. 5:1, probably the place known as the "Horns of Hattin," Kurun Hattîn, near Capernaum, and on the west of the Lake of Galilee. Hattin is the name of the village above which are the two elevations named in modern phrase "the horns." Its situation is central both to the peasants of the Galilean hills and the fishermen of the Galilean lake, between which it stands, and would therefore be a natural resort both to Jesus and his disciples when they retired from the shores of the sea for solitude, and also to the crowds who assembled from Galilee, from Decapolis, from Jerusalem, from Judea, and from beyond Jordan. None of the other mountains in the neighborhood could answer equally well to this description, inasmuch as they are merged into the uniform barrier of hills round the lake; whereas this stands separate, "the mountain" which alone could lay claim to a distinct name, with the exception of the one height of Tabor, which is too distant to answer the requirements.

Mount of Corruption. *See* Corruption, Mount of.

Mount of the Am′alekites, a place near Pirathon in Ephraim (Judg. 12:15). It is probable that it was known by that name because it had been formerly inhabited by Amalekites (comp. Judg. 5:14).

Mount of the Congregation. *See* Congregation, Mount of.

Mount of the Valley, a district east of Jordan, in the territory of Reuben, in which were a number of towns (Josh. 13:19). The valley appears to have been that of Jordan (v. 27); and the "mount" the hilly country at the northern end of the Dead Sea.

Mountain. Figurative. Mountain is used as symbolical of strength, stability. Thus when David says, "Lord, by thy favor thou hast made my mountain to stand strong" (Psa. 30:7), he means to express the stability of his kingdom. In like manner the kingdom of the Messiah is figured by a mountain (Isa. 2:2; Dan. 2:35), as also the Chaldean monarchy (Jer. 51:25; Zech. 4:7). Mountains are frequently used to signify places or sources of strength (Jer. 3:23); the righteousness of God (Psa. 36:6); persons in authority (Psa. 72:3); difficulties (Isa. 40:4; Zech. 4:7; Matt. 17:20); proud and haughty persons (Isa. 2:14); a burning mountain, of destroying enemies (Jer. 51:25); a threshed mountain, heavy judgments (Isa. 41:15); a mountain laid waste is figurative of desolation (42:15; Mal. 1:3); singing mountains, of great joy (Isa. 44:23; 55:12); of dropping new wine, of abundance (Amos 9:13).

Mountain of the Am′orites, the hill country (afterward that of Judah and Ephraim), between the Canaanites proper of the plains of Philistia and Sharon and Phoenicia on the west, and of the valley of the Jordan on the east. *See* Amorites.

Mount of Congregation, a mountain in the farthest north referred to in Isaiah 14:13 in connection with the fall of Satan (Lucifer). The reference is illustrated by a common concept among the Babylonians that the gods assembled on a mountain of the north.

Mourn, the rendering of quite a number of Hebrew and Greek words.

1. **Occasions.** Mourning is frequently referred to in Scripture as an expression of grief for the dead. Thus Abraham mourns for Sarah (Gen. 23:2), Jacob for Joseph, thinking him dead (37:34, 35), the Egyptians for Jacob (50:3, 10), the Israelites for Aaron (Num. 20:29), for Moses (Deut. 34:8), and for Samuel (I Sam. 25:1), David for Abner (II Sam. 3:31, 35), Mary and Martha for Lazarus (John 11:31); on account of calamities, either endured or impending, e. g., Job under his many afflictions (Job. 1:20, 21; 2:11), Israel under the threatening of divine displeasure (Exod. 33:4), the Ninevites in view of menaced destruction (Jonah 3:5), etc.; or in repentance of sin (3:5), the Israel-

ites on the day of atonement (Lev. 23:27; Acts 27:9; I Sam. 7:6; Zech. 12:10, 11).

2. **Modes.** The modes of expressing grief were numerous and varied. (1) **Weeping** was one of the chief of these, or as the general name for the expression of mourning. The tree under which Deborah, Rebekah's nurse, was buried, was called Allon-Bachuth, the "oak of weeping" (Gen. 35:8), on account of the lamentation made for her. The children of Israel wept every man in his tent door for flesh to eat (Num. 11:10). Tears are repeatedly referred to (Psa. 42:3; 56:8, etc.). In fact the orientals seem to have had tears at their command, and could weep at pleasure. (2) Another method was loud lamentation (Ruth 1:9; I Sam. 2:4; II Sam. 3:31; 13:36). Nor are orientals content with mere sobs; their excitableness appears in howls of grief, even amid the solemnities of worship (Joel 1:13; Mic. 1:8, etc.). The Egyptians were vociferous in their grief; "there was a great cry in Egypt at the death of the firstborn" (Exod. 12:30). Not only did the relatives of the deceased give utterance to loud cries, but hired mourners were often engaged to swell the lamentation with screams and noisy utterances (II Chron. 35:25; Eccles. 12:5) (*see* Dead, Burial of). (3) **Personal disfigurement** was doubtless resorted to that the public might be convinced of the greatness of the mourner's grief. Among the particular forms were: Rending the clothes (Gen. 37:29, 34; 44:13; II Chron. 34:27; Isa. 36:22; Jer. 36:24; Matt. 26:65; Mark 14:63, etc.); dressing in sackcloth (Gen. 36:34; II Sam. 3:31; 21:10; Psa. 35:13; Isa. 37:1; Joel 1:8, 13; Amos 8:10; Job 16:15, etc.); black or other somber-colored garments (II Sam. 14:2; Jer. 8:21; Psa. 38:6; 42:9; 43:2; Mal. 3:14, marg.); covering the face or head (Lev. 13:45; II Sam. 15:30; Jer. 14:4; Ezek. 24:17; sitting in, or sprinkling ashes or dust upon the person (II Sam. 13:19; 15:32; Josh. 7:6; Esth. 4:1, 3; Job. 2:12; 42:6; Isa. 61:3; Jer. 6:26; Rev. 18:19); removal of ornaments or neglect of person (Exod. 33:4; Deut. 21:12, 13; II Sam. 14:2; 19:24; Ezek. 26:16; Dan. 10:3; Matt. 6:16, 17); laying bare some part of the body (Isa. 20:2, 4; 47:2; 50:6; Jer. 13:22, 26; Nah. 3:5; Mic. 1:11; Amos 8:10); shaving the head, cutting the hair short, or plucking out the hair of the head or beard (Lev. 10:6; II Sam. 19:24; Ezra 9:3; Job 1:20; Jer. 7:29; 16:6); fasting (II Sam. 1:12; 3:35; 12:16, 22; Ezra 10:6; Ezek. 24:17, etc.); diminution in offerings to God, and prohibition to partake of sacrificial food (Lev. 7:20; Deut. 26:14; Hos. 9:4; Joel 1:9, 13, 16); sitting or lying in silence (Gen. 23:3; Judg. 20:26; II Sam. 12:16; Job 1:20; Ezra 9:3; Lam. 2:10); bowing the head (Lam. 2:10), and lifting up the hands (Psa. 141:2; Ezra 9:5; Lam. 1:17).

3. **Forbidden Modes.** Some of the expressions of mourning that were usual among the heathen were forbidden to the Israelites: cutting the flesh (Lev. 19:28), "making baldness between the eyes for the dead" (Deut. 14:1, i. e., shaving the eyebrows and eyelids, and the fore part of the head—an idolatrous custom). Priests were not to "defile themselves

for the dead" by any outward expression of mourning, except for near relatives (Lev. 21:1); and the high priest even for these (21:10, 11), under which restriction the Nazarites also came (Num. 6:7).

Mouse. *See* Animal Kingdom.

Mouth (Hebrew properly *pĕh;* Gr. *stoma*). In addition to its ordinary applications the Hebrews used the following idiomatic phrases: "Heavymouthed," i. e., slow of speech (Exod. 4:1;); "smooth mouth" (Psa. 55:21), i. e., a flattering mouth; "a mouth of deceit" (109:2).

Notice the following remarkable phrases: "To speak with one mouth to mouth," i. e., in person, without an interpreter or third party (Num. 12:8; comp. I Kings 8:15; Jer. 32:4); "with one mouth," i. e., with universal consent (Josh. 9:2, marg.; I Kings 22:13; II Chron. 18:12); "to put words into one's mouth," means, to suggest what one shall say (Exod. 4:15; Num. 22:38; 23:5, 12; II Sam. 14:19, etc.); "to be in one's mouth" is to be frequently spoken of (Exod. 13:9; comp. Psa. 34:1). "To lay the hand upon the mouth" is to be silent (Judg. 18:19; Job. 21:5; 40:4; Prov. 30:32), as silence is enjoined by our placing the finger upon the lip. "To write from the mouth of any one" is to do so from his dictation (Jer. 36:4, 27, 32; 45:1). "Baruch wrote from the mouth of Jeremiah" means from the prophet's dictation (36:4, 27, 32; 54:1). To "inquire at the mouth of the Lord" (Josh. 9:14) is to consult with him; while to "set the mouth against the heavens" (Psa. 73:9) is to speak arrogantly, blasphemously against God. God's word is called "the rod of his mouth" (Isa. 11:4). Mouth is sometimes used for that which one speaks, as well as for the speaker himself (Num. 3:16, marg.; Exod. 4:16; Jer. 15:19).

Mowing (Heb. *gēz*, literally *fleece*, something cut; rendered "mown grass" in Psa. 72:6) can scarcely be said to exist in Palestine, unless we understand thereby cutting with a sickle. The climate is too hot and dry to admit of grain growing sufficiently tall to need a scythe to cut it. The term "mower" (Heb. *gōṣĕr*, to *dock off*, Psa. 129:7) is usually rendered in the A. V. "reaper."

The "kings mowings" (Amos 7:1) may refer to some royal right of early pasturage, or tyrannical exaction from the people.

Mo'za (mō'zà; *going forth*).

1. The second son of Caleb by his concubine Ephah (I Chron. 2:46), B. C. about 1380.

2. Son of Zimri, and descendant of Saul (I Chron. 8:36, 37; 9:42, 43), B. C. perhaps about 850.

Mo'zah (mō'zà), a town of Benjamin connected with Mizpeh and Chephireh (Josh. 18:26). Its location is unknown, but it may be identified with Koloniyeh almost 5 miles N. W. of Jerusalem on the Jaffa Road.

Muffler (Heb. *răʿălāh*), long, fluttering veils, more expensive than the ordinary veils (Isa. 3:19).

Mulberry. *See* Vegetable Kingdom.

Mule. *See* Animal Kingdom.

Mup'pim (mŭp'ĭm), a Benjamite, and one of the fourteen descendants of Rachel who belonged to the original colony of the sons of Jacob in Egypt (Gen. 46:21). In Num. 26:39

the name is written Shupham; in I Chron. 7:12, 15 it is Shuppim; Shephupham (8:5).

Murder (Heb. *rāṣăḥ*, to *kill*) was, from the very beginning of human history, considered one of the greatest crimes. The principle on which the act of taking the life of a human being was regarded by the Almighty as a capital offense is stated on its highest ground as an outrage on the likeness of God in man, to be punished even when caused by an animal (Gen. 9:5, 6; see also John 8:44; I John 3:12, 15). Its secondary or social ground appears to be implied in the direction to replenish the earth which immediately follows (Gen. 9:7). The postdiluvian command was limited by the law of Moses, which, while it protected the accidental homicide, defined with additional strictness the crime of murder. It prohibited compensation or reprieve of the murderer, or his protection if he took refuge in the refuge city, or even at the altar of Jehovah (Exod. 21:12, 14; Lev. 24:17, 21; I Kings 2:5, 6, 31). Bloodshed, even in warfare, was held to involve pollution (Num. 35:33, 34; Deut. 21:1, 9; I Chron. 28:3). It is not certain whether a master who killed his slave was punished with death (Exod. 21:20). No punishment is mentioned for suicide attempted, nor does any special restriction appear to have attached to the property of the suicide (II Sam. 20:23). Striking a pregnant woman so as to cause her death was punishable with death (Exod. 17:23). If an animal known to be vicious caused the death of anyone, not only was the animal destroyed, but the owner, also, if he had taken no steps to restrain it, was held guilty of murder (21:29, 31). The duty of executing punishment on the murderer is in the law expressly laid on the "revenger of blood;" but the question of guilt was to be previously decided by the Levitical tribunal. In regal times the duty of execution of justice on a murderer seems to have been assumed to some extent by the sovereign as well as the privilege of pardon (II Sam. 13:39; 14:7, 11; I Kings 2:34). It was lawful to kill a burglar taken at night in the act, but unlawful to do so after sunrise (Exod. 22:2, 3).

Murrain. *See* Diseases.

Muse (Heb. *siăḥ, to ponder,* Psa. 143:5), to meditate, reflect; pertaining to delighting, as an old man, in memories. In Luke 3:15 the Greek term *dialogizomai* means to *reason, deliberate.*

Mu'shi (mū'shī), a son of Merari, son of Kohath (Exod. 6:19; Num. 3:20; I Chron. 6:19, 47; 23:21, 23; 24:26, 30). His offspring were called *Mushites* (Num. 3:33; 26:58).

Mu'shites. *See* Mushi.

Music was a prominent art in ancient Biblical times and plays a vital role both in Israel and adjacent lands.

1. **Vocal.** Hebrew music was primarily vocal. The lyre was a common instrument used to accompany the human voice. When singing first appears in the Bible, it is as a familiar part of merrymaking in connection with sending away guests and loved ones (Gen. 31:27). As a religious ceremony, vocal music first appears in Exod. 15:1, 20, in the antiphonal song led by Miriam in celebration

of the passage through the Red Sea. Another responsive song is probably found in Psa. 136 and I Sam. 18:7. The digging of the well ("Beer") was celebrated by a song (Num. 21: 17, 18). Moses taught Israel some of his last warnings in a song (Deut. 32:1-4). Deborah and Barak celebrated their triumph in song (Judg. 5:1-31). David was received by Israel's women after his victory over Goliath with song (I Sam. 18:6, 7). Barzillai mentioned "singing men and singing women" among social pleasures (II Sam. 19:35). Solomon was a song writer, composing songs "a thousand and five" (I Kings 4:32). Singing was very common in ancient Israel. David's trained choir numbered 288. The work continued under Solomon (II Chron. 5:12, 13; 9:11), Jehoshaphat (20:21, 23), Joash (23: 13, 18), Hezekiah (29:27-30), Josiah and after him (35:15, 25), Ezra (Ezra 2:41; 3:11; 7:24) and Nehemiah (Neh. 7:44; 10:28, etc.). The "songs of Zion" were famous (cf. Psa. 137).

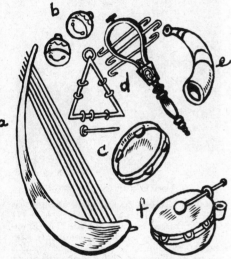

310. Musical Instruments: (a) Harp, (b) Bells, (c) Timbrel, (d) Sistrum, (e) Cornet, (f) drum

2. **Instrumental.** Instrumental music as well as vocal was common in ancient Israel. Saul was influenced thereby (I Sam. 10:5) and David's skill in playing upon the lyre had a profound effect upon the demonized Saul (I Sam. 16:23). David was not only a great warrior but a skilled musician and singer. Instrumental music certainly figured largely in Solomon's temple (I Chron. chap. 25). "Male and female musicians" are specifically mentioned as part of the tribute the Judean Hezekiah had to render to Sennacherib. These musicians were certainly not mediocre to be mentioned in connection with the Assyrian court. In Elisha's day a minstrel was easily procurable (II Kings 3:15). At the time of the exile, the Israelites are said to have hung their lyres on the trees and refused to sing the songs of Zion (Psa. 137). Instrumental music and singing were common in the post-exilic period (Ezra 3:10; Neh. 12: 27-36).

a. **The Hand Drum.** Miriam's timbrel (Heb. *tōph*) is translated nine times as "timbrel," eight times as "tabret." This has been sometimes rendered as tambourine. It was probably a drum. (*See* Sol. B. Finesinger, "Musical Instruments in the O. T.," *Hebrew Union College Annual* III, 1926, pp. 21-75; also Kurt Sachs, *A History of Musical Instruments*, N. Y., 1940). Sachs considers it to be made "of a wooden hoop and very probably two skins, without any jingling contrivance or sticks." The instrument was, therefore, like a tom-tom. It was evidently associated with merrymaking or praise (cf. Exod. 15:20; Judg. 11:34; I Sam. 18:6; Psa. 68:25). This instrument played an important part from patriarchal times through the period of the restoration.

b. **The Lyre.** The Hebrew word is *kĭnnōr*, which occurs 42 times and is translated "harp." But the lyre is not a harp. The Septuagint often translates *kinnor* by *kithara* (a kind of lyre) and quite a few times *kinura*, which is merely a reproduction of the Hebrew word. The Vulgate translates the Hebrew *kinnor chithara* 37 times and "lyre" twice. It is therefore quite certain that the *kinnor* was a species of lyre and was called *chithara* by both Greeks and Romans. The corresponding Hebrew word is manifestly a loan word from the Semitic *kinnor*. Several archaeological illustrations give a good idea of what the Israelite lyre was. On a Beni-hasan monument to be dated around 1900 B. C., one of the Semites entering Egypt is depicted performing on a lyre. Inasmuch as lyres were unknown in ancient Egypt in Old-Kingdom monuments, they were introduced by Asiatics coming from Palestine. The instrument consists of strings, according to the Rabbinic sources, made from the small intestines of sheep, and were stretched across a sounding board over a blank space attached to a cross bar. The performer apparently drew a plectrum across the strings with his right hand and deadened the strings with his left. Pictures on Assyrian monuments portray the lyre in similar fashion, as on the Black Obelisk of Shalmaneser III and the musicians appearing before Sennacherib at Lachish, although the players in this case seem to be drawing the index fingers over the strings instead of making use of a plectrum. David played with his hand before Saul (I Sam. 16:23).

c. **The Harp.** There is much confusion as to whether the Hebrews actually had the harp, but it seems almost unthinkable that this popular instrument was ignored by them. It is possible that the Hebrew word *nēbĕl* may refer to a harp. The word normally means "a skin bottle," but in 27 cases it refers to a musical instrument. The A. V. translates it by "psaltery" 23 times and "viol" four times. The Septuagint translates "psalterion" eight times and *nabla* fourteen times. The Vulgate translates *psalterium* seventeen times; *lyra* four times. Since the psaltery is plainly a harp, which has more and longer strings than the lyre, and since this instrument was common both in Egypt and Mesopotamia from very ancient times, the Hebrew instrument seems to be thus correctly identified. The Rabbinic tradition asserts that the harp was called *nēbĕl* because it was shaped like a skin bottle, the body being rounded out and covered with skin.

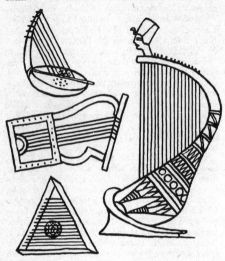

311. Egyptian Harps

c. **The Zither.** This instrument (Heb. *'āsēr*) means "ten" (Psa. 33:2; 92:3; 144:9). Sachs considers this instrument to be a zither of ten strings, but mostly it is considered to be a ten-stringed lyre. Phoenicians played this instrument, but it apparently was not used in Egypt or Mesopotamia.

d. **The Trumpet.** Trumpets consisted of the horn (*qĕrĕn*) of the ram or goat. The word *shōphär*, denoting "ram" or "ram's horn," is also another term for trumpet. The word *qĕrĕn*, referring to a musical instrument, is translated both cornet and horn, while *shōphär* is also translated "cornet" and also "trumpet." The *shōphär* was used for giving of signals for war, as in the case of Joshua, Ehud, Gideon and Joab. It announced the year of Jubilee, and also approaching danger (Jer. 4:5; Ezek. 33:3; Joel 2:1). It heralded the appearance of the new moon and full moon (Psa. 81:3). Another type of trumpet was of metal. Moses was instructed to prepare two trumpets of silver (Num. 10:12). These were called the *hătsōtsĕräh* and were in pairs, as Moses's two trumpets and the two trumpets on the Arch of Titus, as well as on Jewish coins. Doubtless two priests blew on the trumpets simultaneously.

d. **The Flute.** This instrument referred to in Nebuchadnezzar's band (Dan. 3:5, 7, 10, 15) means whistle (Heb. *măshrōqǐthä*) and could refer to any of the instruments of wood which were blown. It may be that the term *'ūgäb* (Gen. 4:21) was a kind of flute that was later used to describe woodwind instruments in general. Flutes occur in prehistoric, Old Kingdom and Middle Kingdom Egyptian drawings. It is inconceivable to think the flute was not known among the Israelites, being simply a reed indented with holes and blown. Flutes are still common in Palestine,

and were made of clay in Babylonia. Jubal in Gen. 4 is connected with the pipe, which is the simplest form of the flute.

e. **The Oboe.** The Hebrew word *ḥälîl*, usually rendered pipe, is commonly considered to be the flute. Sachs, however, considers it to be an oboe since at the time the instrument appears (the era of Saul), the double oboe was in common vogue. It is not impossible that the word *ḥälîl* is a general term for woodwind instruments.

312. Harp from Ur (ca. 2500 B. C.)

f. **The Sistrum.** In Egypt the sistrum was common. The Hebrew word is *mĕn'ăn'îm* (II Sam. 6:5) from the verb *to shake*. The Egyptian sistrum was connected commonly with Hathor worship. The head of the goddess was frequently shown above the handle above which was a metal loop with holes through which pieces of wire were placed and bent at the ends. Since the holes were larger than the wire, a jingling sound was given forth when shaken. The sistrum likewise appeared in early Babylonia. Sachs and Finesinger are both of the opinion that this instrument was the sistrum, certainly not "cornets" of the A. V. and scarcely castenets of the R. V. Excavations at Bethel in 1934 yielded a sistrum containing a Hathor carving.

8. **Cymbals.** The cymbals are seen on Assyrian reliefs and two types appear, that which is beaten horizontally and that which is beaten vertically. This instrument occurs first in the list of instruments upon which David played on the occasion of the bringing up of the ark (II Sam. 6:5; cf. Psa. 150:4). The original words referring to cymbals are onomatopoetic (Heb. *şĕlşĕlîm* and *mĕşǐltäyîm*).

h. **Other Musical Instruments.** The term *shălishîm* in I Sam. 18:6 is evidently some kind of musical instrument, but is enigmatic. "Stringed instruments" (Heb. *mǐnnîm*) refers to a family of instruments and not to any single instrument (Psa. 150:4). Dan. 3:5, 7, 10, 15 lists a number of instruments found in Babylon. These are rendered in the R. S. V. "horn, pipe, lyre, trigon, harp and big pipe, and every kind of music" (Dan. 3:5). In this list *karna* is Semitic and is the common word for horn and *măshrōqĭthä* (*see* Flute above) was probably a double oboe (Sachs). The other instruments are of Greek derivation. *Qaithros* is a cithara; *sabka'* is evidently a harp-shaped instrument; *pesanterin* is a psaltery; *sumphoneyah* (cf. our word symphony) is thought to be the bag-pipe. What sort of a scale the Hebrews used or how their music sounded is entirely unknown. Authorities such as Sachs think that the scale was pentatonic, but this is hypothetical.—*M. F. U.*

Mustard. *See* Vegetable Kingdom.

Mutter (Heb. *hägäh*, Isa. 8:19). Ancient wizards (*see* Magic) imitated the chirping of bats, which was supposed to proceed from the shades of hades, and uttered their magical formulas in a whispering tone.

Muzzle (Heb. *hăsăm;* Gr. *phimoō*, to stop the mouth). In the East the grain was threshed by oxen trampling upon it; and the command was not to muzzle the ox when threshing. This was not intended to apply merely to the ox employed in threshing, but to be understood in the general sense in which the apostle Paul used it (I Cor. 9:9; I Tim. 5:18), that a laborer was not to be deprived of his wages.

My'ra (mī'rà), one of the chief cities of Lycia in Asia Minor. It was situated about 2 miles from the sea, upon rising ground, at the foot of which flowed a navigable river with an excellent harbor. The town still stands, but in a dilapidated condition, called *Myra* by the Greeks, but *Dembre* by the Turks. It was at Myra that Paul, on his voyage to Rome, was transferred from the ship which had brought him from Cilicia to the ship from Alexandria (Acts 27:5).

Myrhh. *See* Vegetable Kingdom.

Myrtle. *See* Vegetable Kingdom.

Mys'ia (mĭsh'ĭ-à), a province in the northwest of Asia Minor, and separated from Europe only by the Propontis and Hellespont. Paul passed through this province, and embarked at its chief port, Troas, on his first voyage to Europe (Act 16:7, 8).

Mystery, (Gr. *mustērion*). The N. T. use of the term "mystery" has reference to some operation or plan of God hitherto unrevealed. It

313. Mysia

does not carry the idea of a secret to be withheld, but to be published (I Cor. 4:1). Paul uses the word 21 times. The term mystery, moreover, comprehends not only a previously hidden truth, presently divulged, but one that contains a supernatural element which still remains in spite of the revelation. The more important Biblical mysteries are the following:

1. The mysteries of the kingdom of heaven (Matt. 13:3-50).

2. The mystery of the translation of the living saints at the end of the Church age (I Cor. 15:51, 52; I Thess. 4:14, 17).

3. The mystery of the Church as the Body of Christ, composed of saved Jews and Gentiles of this age (Eph. 3:1-11; 6:19; Col. 4:3).

4. The mystery of the Church as the Bride of Christ (Eph. 5:28-32).

5. The mystery of "Christ in us the Hope of glory" (Gal. 2:20; Col. 1:26, 27).

6. The "mystery of God, even Christ" (Col. 2:2, 9; I Cor. 2:7). This involves Christ as the fullness of the Godhead in bodily form.

7. The mystery of iniquity (II Thess. 2:7; Matt. 13:33).

8. The mystery of the operation by which man is restored to godliness (I Tim. 3:16).

9. The mystery of Israel's blindness during the gospel age (Rom. 11:25).

10. The mystery of the seven stars (Rev. 1:20).

11. The mystery of Babylon, the harlot (Rev. 7:5, 7).   —*M. F. U.*

N

NAAM

Na'am (nā'ăm; *sweetness, pleasantness*), one of the sons of Caleb, the son of Jephunneh (I Chron. 4:15), B. C. about 1375.

Na'amah (nā'à-må; *sweetness, pleasantness*).

1. One of the four women whose names are preserved in the records of the world before the flood, all except Eve being Cainites. She was daughter of Lamech and Zillah and sister of Tubal-cain (Gen. 4:22).

2. Wife of Solomon and mother of King Rehoboam (I Kings 14:21, 31; II Chron. 12:13). On each occasion she is distinguished by the title "the (not 'an,' as in A. V.) Ammonite." She was, therefore, one of the foreign women whom Solomon took into his establishment (I Kings 11:1), B. C. after 960.

3. A city in the plain of Judah, mentioned between Beth-dagon and Makkedah (Josh. 15:41), not definitely located.

Na'aman (nā'à-màn; *pleasantness*).

1. One of the family of Benjamin who came down to Egypt with Jacob, as read in Gen. 46:21, or, more correctly, born in Egypt. According to the LXX version of that passage, he was the son of Bela, which is the parentage assigned to him in Num. 26:40, where, in the enumeration of the sons of Benjamin, he is said to be the son of Bela, and head of the family of the Naamites. He is also reckoned among the sons of Bela (I Chron. 8:3, 4), B. C. after 1876.

2. **"The Syrian"** was commander of the armies of Benhadad II (Josephus, *Ant.*, viii, 15, 5), king of Damascence Syria. He is described as "a great man with his master, and honorable,. . . . a mighty man of valor." He was, however, a leper; and when a little Hebrew captive girl spoke of a prophet in Samaria who could cure her master of leprosy, Benhadad furnished him with a letter to King Joram. But when the king read the letter to the effect that Naaman had been sent to him to be cured he rent his clothes, suspecting that the object was a quarrel. Elisha the prophet, hearing of this, sent for Naaman, who came to his house, not being permitted as a leper to enter. Elisha sent a messenger to him, saying, "Go and wash in Jordan seven times, and thy flesh shall come again to thee, and thou shalt be clean." Naaman was very

NAAMAN

indignant at the apparent incivility, and would doubtless have returned to Syria without a cure but for the entreaties of his servants. He bathed in the Jordan, and was cleansed of his leprosy. Returning to Elisha, he acknowl-

314. Cleansing of Naaman (Flemish tapestry, 15th Century)

edged that Jehovah was above all gods, and declared his intention of worshiping him alone. He asked permission to take home two mules' burden of earth, probably to set up in Damascus an altar to Jehovah. He desired to bestow valuable gifts upon Elisha, but the prophet refused to accept anything. His servant, Gehazi, coveting some of the riches proffered his master, hastened after Naaman and asked, in his master's name, for a portion. Naaman heard his request, and granted him more than he had asked (II Kings 5:1-23), B. C. about 848.

Character. "Naaman's appearance throughout the occurrence is most characteristic and consistent. He is every inch a soldier, ready at once to resent what he considers a slight cast either on himself or the natural glories of his country, and blazing out in a moment into sudden 'rage,' but calmed as speedily by a few good-humored and sensible words from his dependents, and after the cure has been effected evincing a thankful and simple heart, whose gratitude knows no bounds, and will listen to no refusal" (McC. and S., *Cyc.*, s. v.).

315. Abana River, Damascus (one of the Syrian rivers Naaman preferred to the Jordan)

NOTE—(1) *The expression* "Because that by him Jehovah had given deliverance to Syria" (v. 1) seems to point to services such as were incidentally to subserve the divine purposes toward Israel, and may on this account have been ascribed to Jehovah. (2). *Naaman's request* to be allowed to take away two mules' burden of earth is not easy to understand. The natural explanation is that, with a feeling akin to that which prompted the Pisan invaders to take away the earth of Aceldama for the Campo Santo at Pisa, the grateful convert to Jehovah wished to take away some of the earth of his country to form an altar. But in the narrative there is no mention of an altar.

Na′amathite (nā′a-ma-thīt), an epithet of Zophar, one of Job's friends, only found in Job 2:11; 11:1; 20:1; 42:9, and always in the phrase, "Zophar the Naamathite." There are several towns from which it might have been derived, as "Noam, a castle in the Yemen, and a place on the Euphrates; Niameh, a place belonging to the Arabs; and Noamee, a valley in Tihameh," not to mention the very common Naaman. The LXX calls Zophar the Minaean and the king of the Minaeans. But of the real meaning of the term nothing is known.—*W. H.*

Na′amite (nā′a-mīt), one of the family descended from Naaman (Num. 26:40), a Benjamite. The name is a contraction seldom occurring in Hebrew, and is rendered "the Naamanites" by the Samaritan codex.

Na′arah (nā′a-ra; *a girl*), the second named of the two wives of Ashur, of the tribe of Judah, and the mother by him of four sons (I Chron. 4:5, 6), B. C. about 1440.

Na′arai (nā′a-rī), the son of Ezbai, and one of David's heroes (I Chron. 11:37), B. C. about 1000. In II Sam. 23:35 he is called *Paarai*, probably through a scribal error.

Na′aran (nā′a-răn), a town in Ephraim, between Bethel and Jericho (I Chron. 7:28), and possibly the same as Naarath (Josh. 16:7). It is evidently Noorath mentioned by Eusebius, 5 Roman miles N. of Jericho, to be identified with 'Ain Duq.

Na′arath (nā′a-răth), a town named (Josh. 16:7) as one of the southern landmarks of Ephraim. It was in the Jordan valley and north of Jericho. Probably the same as *Naaran* (*q. v.*).

Na′ashon (nā′a-shŏn; Exod. 6:23). See Nahshon.

Na′asson (nā′a-sŏn), the Grecized form (Matt. 1:4; Luke 3:32) of the Heb. *Nahshon* (*q. v.*).

Na′bal (nā′băl; *foolish*), a descendant of Caleb, who dwelt in Maon (Tell Ma'in about 1½ miles S. of Carmel of Judah and 8½ miles S. of Hebron), when David, with his followers, was on the southern borders of Palestine (I Sam. 25:2, sq.), B. C. about 1004. He was a man of great wealth, having three thousand sheep and one thousand goats, which he pastured in Carmel (not the promontory of that name, but the present Kurmul, on the mountains of Judah). When David heard in the desert (v. 1) that Nabal was shearing his sheep, which was generally accompanied with festivities, he sent ten young men to Carmel to Nabal, and bade them wish him peace and prosperity, to remind him of David's friendly services, and solicit a present for himself and people. The services alluded to were doubtless protection afforded by David and his men to Nabal's shepherds and flocks against the Bedouin Arabs. Nabal refused the petitioners in a very churlish manner: "Who is David? and who is the son of Jesse? there be many servants nowadays that break away every man from his master. Shall I then take my bread, and my water, and my flesh that I have killed for my shearers, and give it unto men, whom I know not whence they be?" (vers. 10, 11). Thus, in order to justify his covetousness, he set down David as a worthless vagrant. David was greatly enraged at this reply, and started with four hundred men to take vengeance upon Nabal. In the meantime one of Nabal's servants told Abigail, his intelligent and godly wife, what had taken place. As quickly as possible she took a bountiful present of provisions (v. 18), and, sending it to David, followed herself to appease his wrath. They met, and Abigail, throwing herself at David's feet, besought his forgiveness. David's anger was appeased, and in his reply he praised Jehovah for having sent Abigail to meet him (v. 32), and congratulated her upon her understanding and acts, which had kept him from bloodshed (v. 33). He received her gifts, and dismissed her with the assurance that he had granted her request (v. 35). All this had occurred without the knowledge of Nabal, and when Abigail returned and found him in a drunken stupor she told him nothing until the next morning. Conscious of the danger that had threatened him, angry at the loss he had sustained, or vexed because his wife had humbled herself in such a manner, "his heart died within him, and he became as a stone" (v. 37). It was as if a stroke of apoplexy or paralysis had fallen upon him. He seems not to have changed in his nature by his affliction, for ten days later "the Lord smote Nabal, that he died" (v. 38). David not long after took Abigail for his wife (vers. 40-42).

Nabatae′ans (năb-à-tē′ănz). These remarkable
people were originally Arabians. Between the
sixth and fourth centuries B. C. they pushed
northward and seized the fortresses of Edom
and Moab. Gaining control of the great caravan routes of the Middle East, they developed a remarkable civilization. They came
into their greatest glory between 200 B. C.
and 100 A. D. In the year 106 A. D. they
were annexed to Rome as a province of
Arabia. The great fortress of Petra, sixty
miles S. of the Dead Sea, became their capital. This remarkable rose-colored city was
unknown to the West until 1812. Petra,
known in the O. T. as Sela (Isa. 16:1), contained notable "high places," or outdoor religious sanctuaries. Petra's great High Place
was discovered by G. L. Robinson in 1900.
The Conway High Place, found by Agnes
Conway Horsefield, flourished in the first
century B. C. The Nabataeans honored both
sun and moon. The chief deities were Dusa-
res, that is, Dionysus, and the female goddess
Alat. Numerous other deities are found in

317. Cistern and Altar at High Place, Petra

city by a basket let over the wall. The Nabataeans were very ingenious. They built dams,
reservoirs and aqueducts at the rock city of
Sela, N. W. of Buseirah, known in the Bible
as Bozrah (Isa. 63:1).—*M. F. U.*

Naboni′das (năb-ŏ-nī′dŭs), the last ruler of the
Neo-Babylonian Empire (556-539 B. C.). He
is called Nabunaid in the cuneiform records.
His son Belshazzar, who figures so prominently in Dan. 5, was associated with him
legally from his third regnal year to the capture of Babylon by Cyrus the Great, founder
of the Persian Empire (539 B. C.). He was
the last Babylonian ruler to repair the ziggurat of the moon god Sin at Ur. One of his
daughters was a devotee of the moon god
temple at Ur. No Babylonian document actually affirms that Nabunaid's son Belshazzar
was present at the fall of Babylon, yet there is
no positive evidence against his participation
in these events. Indeed, "of all known Babylonian records dealing with the situation at the
close of the Neo-Babylonian Empire, the fifth
chapter of Daniel ranks next to cuneiform
literature in accuracy so far as outstanding
events are concerned" (R. P. Dougherty,
Nabonidus and Belshazzar, New Haven, 1929,
p. 200). Joseph Free (*Archaeology and Bible
History*, 1950, p. 235) says: "The matter concerning Belshazzar, far from being an error
in the Scriptures, is one of the many striking
confirmations of the Word of God which have
been demonstrated by archaeology."
—*M. F. U.*

Nabopolas′sar (nă-bô-pô-lăs′àr), a Chaldean
who laid the foundations of the new Babylonian Empire by revolting against Assyria in
625 B. C. He was able to start reconstruction
of the city of Babylon. In 612 B. C., in alliance
with Cyaxares the Mede and the Scythians,
he took Nineveh, the Assyrian capital (cf.
Nahum 3:1-3). Nabopolassar was Nebuchadnezzar II's father, and the son succeeded to
the royal power after the battle of Carchemish
when Egypt was defeated (605 B. C.)
—*M. F. U.*

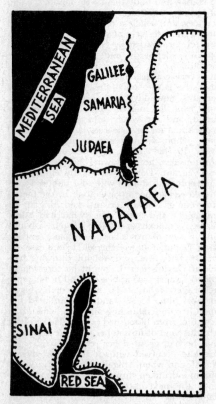

316. Nabataea

their pantheon. In the first century A. D.,
Nabataea was located S. of Idumaea, reaching to the Mediterranean Sea S. of Gaza.
It also extended through the Arabah almost
to Syrian Damascus. The Nabataean king
Aretas IV (9 B. C.-40 A. D.) appointed an
ethnarch of Damascus who plotted to apprehend Paul when the Apostle escaped from the

Na′both (nā′bŏth; (cf. Arab. *nabata*, to *sprout,
grow*, hence probably "a sprout"), was an Israelite of Jezreel, and the owner of a small
portion of ground (II Kings 9:25, 26) that lay
on the eastern slope of the hill of Jezreel. He
had also a vineyard, of which the situation is
not quite certain. The royal palace of Ahab
was close upon the city wall at Jezreel. According to both texts, it immediately adjoined
the vineyard, and it thus became an object of
desire to the king, who offered an equivalent

in money, or another vineyard in exchange for this. Naboth, in the independent spirit of a Jewish landholder, refused. "Jehovah forbid it me that I should give the inheritance of my fathers unto thee." Ahab was cowed by this reply; but the proud spirit of Jezebel was roused. She took the matter into her own hands; wrote letters in Ahab's name to the elders and nobles of Jezreel, directing them to proclaim a fast, and that Naboth should be placed at the head of the services. Two men of worthless character accused him of having "blasphemed God and the king," and he and his children (II Kings 9:26) were stoned to death. Jezebel then informed Ahab of the death of Naboth, whereupon he took possession. The perpetration of this crime brought upon Ahab and Jezebel the severest punishment (I Kings, ch. 21), B. C. about 854.

Na'chon (nā'kŏn; *prepared*), a name by which the threshing-floor was known near which Uzzah was slain (II Sam. 6:6). It is uncertain whether this is the name of the owner or merely an epithet applied to it, i. e., *the prepared floor*. In I Chron. 13:9 it is called the *floor of Chidon*, which is supposed by some to be another name of the owner. Eventually it was known by the name of Perez-uzzah (II Sam. 6:8). R. V. renders Nacon (nā'kŏn).

Na'chor (nā'kôr), a form of the name *Nahor* (*q. v.*).

1. The brother of Abraham (Josh. 24:2).
2. The grandfather of Abraham (Luke 3: 34).

Na'dab (nā'dăb; *spontaneous, liberal*).

1. The eldest son of Aaron and Elisheba (Exod. 6:23; Num. 3:2). He, his father and brother, and seventy old men of Israel were led out from the midst of the assembled people (Exod. 24:1), and were commanded to stay and worship God "afar off," below the lofty summit of Sinai, where Moses alone was to come near to the Lord, B. C. c. 1439. Nadab and his brothers Abihu, Eleazar, and Ithamar were anointed, with their father, to be priests of Jehovah (28:1). He and his brother, in offering incense, kindled it with "strange" fire, that is, fire not taken from that which burned perpetually (Lev. 6:13) on the altar, and for this offense were struck dead before the sanctuary by fire from the Lord (Lev. 10:1, 2; Num. 3:4; 26:61). On this occasion, as if to mark more decidedly the divine displeasure, Aaron and his surviving sons were forbidden to observe the usual mourning ceremonies for the dead. It seems likely from the injunction (Lev. 10:9, 10), that the brothers were in a state of intoxication when they committed the offense.

2. King Jeroboam's son, who succeeded to the throne of Israel B. C. about 913, and reigned two years (I Kings 15:25-31). He followed the idolatrous policy of his father (comp. 15:3 and 12:30). At the siege of Gibbethon a conspiracy broke out in the midst of the army, and the king was slain by Baasha, a man of Issachar.

3. A son of Shammai (I Chron. 2:28), of the tribe of Judah, and father of two sons (v. 30).

4. A son of Jehiel, the "father" (founder) of Gibeon (I Chron. 8:30; 9:36), of the tribe of Benjamin.

Nag'gai (năg'ī), A. V. **Nag'ge** (nă'gē; I Chron. 3:7), an ancestor of Jesus in the maternal line, the son of Maath, and father of Esli (Luke 3:25).

Na'halal (nā'há-lăl; *pasture*), a city in Zebulun on the border of Issachar (Josh. 19:15, A. V. "Nahallal"), but inhabited by Canaanites tributary to Israel (Judg. 1:30, A. V. "Nahalol"). It was given, with its suburbs, to the Merari family of Levites (Josh. 21:35). it is evidently modern Tell en-Nahl S. of Acre.

Naha'liel (nà-hā'lĭ-ĕl; *wadi* or *torrent, valley of God*), one of the encampments of Israel in the wilderness (Num. 21:19), between Mattanah and Bamoth. It was near Pisgah, north of Arnon. Its exact location is conjectural.

Na'hallal (nā'hăl-ăl; Josh. 19:15). See Nahalal.

Na'halol (nā'há-lŏl), another form (Judg. 1: 30) of *Nahalal* (*q. v.*).

Na'ham (nā'hăm; *solace, consolation*), a brother of Hodiah (or Jehudijah), the second, or Jewish, wife of Mered. He was the father of Keilah the Garmite and Eshtemoa (I Chron. 4:19). He is probably the same as Ishbah (v. 17).

Nahama'ni (nā-há-mā'nī; *compassionate*), a chief man among those who returned from Babylon with Zerubbabel (Neh. 7:7), B. C. about 445.

Na'harai (nā'há-rī; I Chron. 11:39). See Nahari.

Na'hari (nā'há-rī; *snorting*), the Beerothite, who was one of David's mighty men and the armor-bearer of Joab (I Chron. 11:39; II Sam. 23:37), B. C. about 975.

Na'hash (nā'hăsh; *serpent*).

1. "Nahash the Ammonite," king of Ammon at the foundation of the monarchy in Israel, B. C. c. 1020. He was directing an assault against Jabesh-gilead, and upon the inhabitants asking him to make a treaty with them he dictated that cruel alternative of the loss of their right eyes or slavery, which roused the swift wrath of Saul, and caused the destruction of the Ammonite force (I Sam. 11:1, 2-11). He is probably the same as Nahash, the father of Hanun, who had rendered David some special and valuable service, which David was anxious for an opportunity of requiting (II Sam. 10:2).

2. A person mentioned once only (II Sam. 17:25), in stating the parentage of Amasa, the commander in chief of Absalom's army. Amasa is there said to have been the son of a certain Ithra by Abigail, "daughter of Nahash and sister to Zeruiah." By the genealogy of I Chron. 2:16 it appears that Zeruiah and Abigail were sisters of David and the other children of Jesse. The question then arises, How could Abigail have been at the same time daughter of Nahash and sister to the children of Jesse? To this three answers may be given: 1. The universal tradition of the rabbis, that Nahash and Jesse were identical. 2. The explanation first put forth by Stanley, that Nahash was the king of the Ammonites, and that the same woman had first been his wife or concubine—in which capacity she had given birth to Abigail and Zeruiah—and afterward wife to Jesse, and the mother of his children. 3. A third possible explanation is, that Nahash was the name, not of Jesse, nor

of a former husband of his wife, but of his wife herself (Smith, *Bib. Dict.*, s. v.).

Na'hath (nā'hăth; *rest, quiet*).

1. One of the "dukes," or phylarchs, in the land of Edom, eldest son of Reuel, the son of Esau (Gen. 36:13, 17; I Chron. 1:37).

2. A Kohathite Levite, son of Zophai (I Chron. 6:26). He is the same as *Toah* (v. 34) and *Tohu* (I Sam. 1:1), and was an ancestor of Samuel.

3. A Levite in the reign of Hezekiah, and an overseer of the sacred offerings in the temple (II Chron. 31:13).

Nah'bi (nā'bī; *concealed, hidden*), the son of Vophsi, a Naphtalite, and one of the twelve spies (Num. 13:14), B. C. c. 1441.

Na'hor (nā'hôr; *snorting, snoring*).

1. The son of Serug, father of Terah, and Abraham's grandfather (Gen. 11:22-24; Luke 3:34; A. V. "Nachor"). He lived one hundred and forty-eight years, B. C. before 2200.

2. Grandson of the preceding, a son of Terah and brother of Abraham (Gen. 11:26; Josh. 24:2), B. C. about 2200. He married Micah, his brother Haran's daughter, by whom he had eight children (Gen. 11:29), and had as concubine Reumah, who bore him four children (22:23, 24). When Abraham and Lot migrated to Canaan Nahor remained in Haran, where his descendants were certainly living two generations later (24:10; 29:5). It was to the family descended from Nahor and Milcah that Abraham and Rebekah in turn had recourse for wives for their sons. The city of Nahor (Gen. 24:10) is frequently mentioned in the Mari Letters of the 18th century B. C., when it was ruled by an Amorite prince. It also is named in the Middle Assyrian documents. It was situated below Haran in the Balikh Valley of Upper Mesopotamia.

Nah'shon (nā'shŏn), the son of Amminadab, and prince of Judah when first numbered in the desert (Exod. 6:23; Num. 1:7; I Chron. 2:10, 11), B. C. 1439. His sister Elisheba was wife to Aaron (Exod. 6:23), and his son Salmon married Rahab after the taking of Jericho (Matt. 1:4). In the encampment (Num. 2:3), in the offering of the princes (7:12, 17), and in the order of the march (10:14), the first place is assigned to him as captain of Judah's host. We have no further particulars of his life, but we know that he died in the wilderness (26:64, 65). His name occurs in Matt. 1:4; Luke 3:32, in the genealogy of Christ, where his lineage is evidently copied from Ruth 4:18-20; I Chron. 2:10-12.

Na'hum (nā'hŭm; *compassionate*), the seventh of the minor prophets. Of himself little is known except from the title of the book, "The book of the vision of Nahum the Elkoshite" (ch. 1:1). The site of the village is disputed. According to Saint Jerome, it was in Galilee, and only insignificant ruins remained in his day. Toward the end of the 16th century the idea arose that Nahum was born at Alkosh, a town near Mosul, where also a modern tomb is pointed out as the place of his burial.

Nahum, Book of. One of the books of the Minor Prophets. Nahum was an accomplished poet who devoted his great talent to a moving description of the destruction of Nineveh, the mighty capital of the Assyrian Empire. He foresees in this a manifestation of God's punitive justice. The book stands seventh in the order of the Minor Prophets. Nahum's prophetic ministry occurred between the conquest of No-Amon (Thebes) in Egypt (3:8), regarded as a past event and which occurred in 661 B. C. under Ashurbanipal, and the destruction of Nineveh in 612 B. C. The prophet confines himself to one theme, the destruction of Nineveh, "the bloody city" (3:1).

1. **The Contents.**

Part I. An Ode to God's Majesty, 1:1-2:2

    a. Superscription, 1:1

    b. God's vengeance upon evil doers and his grace to His own, 1:2-11

    c. Judah's restoration, 1:12-2:2

Part II. An Ode on the Destruction of Nineveh, 2:3-3:19

    a. Prophecy of the seige and fall of the city, 2:3-13

    b. The cause of Nineveh's fall, 3:1-19

2. **The Subject.** Nahum's preview of Nineveh's destruction (chaps. 2, 3) previsions the crash of the Assyrian Empire. In 612 B. C. Cyaxares the Mede in league with Nabopolassar of Babylon commenced the siege of Nineveh. The terrifying aspect of Nineveh's fall is depicted as a just recompense of the powerful and cruel city. Nahum was a seventh-century prophet who lived at the same time as Zephaniah, Habakkuk and Jeremiah. In the destruction of Nineveh, Nahum sees the punishment of the horrible cruelty of the Assyrian world power.

3. **Authorship.** Since the latter part of the nineteenth century critics have customarily denied 1:2-2:2 in substance to Nahum. Chapter 1:2-10 is regarded as the remnant of a post-exilic acrostic poem which was later prefixed to Nahum's prophetic oracle concerning Nineveh. Robert Pfeiffer considers chapters 2:3-3:19 to be Nahum's triumphal ode and the intervening material (1:11-2:22) has in part redactional and partly an original section of the poem. The redactional portion was allegedly inserted about 300 B. C. In characteristic negative fashion, Pfeiffer denies the prophetic character of the book and avers that Nahum's poem on the fall of Nineveh was erroneously viewed as a prophecy and preserved as a result of this misapprehension. An example of critical subjectivity, Pfeiffer's view is to be rejected. If the introductory song was considered authored by a redactor, why could it not have been originally written by Nahum? The acrostic idea is based on violent emendations and upon the assumption that the redactor wrote it from a faulty memory. If the acrostic arrangement could be proved, the question still remains, why refuse to attribute it to Nahum. (*See* A. Holder, *Studies in the Book of Nahum*, Uppsala, 1946; W. R. Armed, "The Composition of Nahum 1:2-2:3" in *Zeitschrift fuer die altestamentliche Wissenschaft*, vol. 21, pp. 225-265.)—*M. F. U.*

Nail. 1. For fastening (Heb. *yāthēd*), usually a (wooden) peg, or nail of any material (Ezek. 15:3; Isa. 22:25). It is also a tent pin driven into the earth to fasten the tent rope to, one of which Jael drove into the temples of Sisera (Judg. 4:21, 22).

Figurative. A tent pin was a general designation for national rulers (Zech. 10:4), who stand in the same relation to the commonwealth as a tent pin to the tent, which it holds firmly and keeps upright (Isa. 22:23). The figure is changed, so that Eliakim, instead of being honored, is like to a nail (or peg) driven into the wall, and upon which his family hung. When the nail fell all that hung upon it (viz., his family) shared the same fate (v. 25).

2. (Heb. *măsmēr*), ordinary and ornamental nails. Those mentioned in I Chron. 22:3; II Chron. 3:9, were partly for pivots upon which the folding-doors turned, partly in the construction of the doors. Those used for fastening the gold plates upon the planks were also probably of gold.

Figurative. In the proverb "The words of the wise are as *nails* fastened by the master of assemblies" (Eccles. 12:11) we are taught that truth sinks deeply into the mind as a nail well pointed does when driven into the wall. The "master of assemblies" (literally *collections*) may be a person appointed by the king to see that the people get only that which is profitable to hear. In a collection of oriental proverbs, two hundred and six in number, made by Mrs. Lydia Einsler, and published in the *Journal of the German Palestine Society*, vol. xix, No. 2, is the following, "'She now has a house and nail in the wall,' referring to a woman who was of a low station socially, but had attained a higher. It was often used of a poor girl who had made a good marriage. The nail in the wall is typical of something firm and strong, able to support also heavy burdens; and in the light of these facts the peculiar statements of Ezra 9:8 and Isa. 22: 23-25, concerning 'the nail in the wall,' receive new side-light illustrations."

Nails are mentioned in the accounts of the crucifixion (John 20:25; Col. 2:14).

3. **Nail, of the finger** (Heb. *ṣippōrĕn*, Deut. 21:12), like cutting the hair, the paring of the nails—both signs of purification—was a symbol of a slave woman passing out of slavery and being received into fellowship with the covenant nation.

In Jer. 17:1 (marg.) "nail" is the rendering of the same Hebrew word, and means the "point" of a stylus or a metallic pin. In Dan. 4:33; 7:19 (Aramaic *ṭephăr*), occurs of the *claws* of a bird or beast.

Na′in (nā′ĭn; *pleasantness, beauty*), the city at the gate of which Jesus raised the widow's son to life (Luke 7:11, sq.). Josephus (*Wars*, iv, 9, 4) mentions a city of Nain, but that was east of Jordan. Robinson found a hamlet named Neïn, southwest of Capernaum, standing on a bleak, rocky slope of the northern declivity of Jebel ed-Duḥy (the "hill Moreh" of Scripture). In this locality Eusebius and Jerome place the city of Nain.

Na′ioth (nā′ŏth; *dwellings*), or, more fully, "Naioth in Ramah," was the place in which Samuel and David took refuge after the latter's escape from Saul (I Sam. 19:18, sq.). Thither Saul followed them, after having sent three companies of men to take David. When he came to Sechu, near Ramah, the Spirit of the Lord came upon him, so that he went along prophesying until he came to Naioth; and there he took off his clothes, and prophesied before Samuel, lying upon the ground all day and night (vers. 20-24). Keil and Delitzsch (*Com.*) think Naioth to be a proper name applied to the common dwelling of the pupils of the prophets, who had assembled round Samuel in the neighborhood of Ramah.

Naked (Heb. *'ĕrwāh, nudity*; Gr. *gumnos*), means absolute nakedness (Job 1:21; Eccles. 5:15; Amos 2:16; Mic. 1:8), but elsewhere in our sense of ragged, poorly clad (Isa. 58:7; Matt. 25:36; James 2:15). In John 21:7 the meaning is clad in the undergarment only (the outer garment being cast aside).

Figurative. "Naked" is used figuratively to signify *stripped of resources, disarmed;* thus "I have made Esau bare" (Jer. 49:10) signifies the destruction of Edom. The "nakedness of a land" (Gen. 42:9) signifies the weak and ruined parts of it where the country lies most open and exposed to danger. "Naked" is also put for discovered, made manifest (Job 26:6; Heb. 4:13). In such passages as Exod. 32:25; II Chron. 28:19; Ezek. 16:36-39, "naked" symbolizes the stripping from one of his righteousness through idolatry.

Names (Heb. *shēm;* Gr. *onoma*).

1. Names are designed to distinguish objects, and originally expressed the distinct impressions which objects made upon, or the special relations in which they stood to the person. Thus God brought the beasts to Adam, and from the impression they make upon him he assigns names to them (Gen. 2:19). Some names were given prophetically, as the name of Jesus, the Saviour (Matt. 1:21). Often the name of a natural object was given to a child as Jonah (dove); Tamar (palm tree); Tabitha (gazelle). Sometimes a name preserved the memory of a national event, as Ichabod (I Sam. 4:21). From a comparison of the roots of many names with the same roots in the cognate dialects it is evident the Hebrew was in early days much more closely allied to Arabic than when it became a literary tongue. Much use might be

318. Water Hole near Nain

made of the study of Hebrew proper names for the better understanding of the history of that people.

2. **Play on.** The Israelites were very fond of playing on names. The name to them was a *sign* of something quite sensous and outward.

Hence names rarely became hereditary in Hebrew; they still retained their significance, being proper personal names, very seldom passing into the unmeaning surname. They generally expressed some personal characteristic, some incident connected with the birth, some hope or wish or prayer of the parent; and henceforth the child embodied it, and for the parents' sake felt it like a personal vow, and made his life an effort to realize it. This tendency to play on names and find analogies or contrasts in them is seen throughout the Bible (see Ruth 1:20; I Sam. 25:3, 25; Rom. 9:6). So we have "Dan (judge) shall judge his people" (Gen. 49:16), and many other instances.

3. **Personal names.** These may be divided into two classes: those given at birth; those imposed in after life. (1) **Those given at birth.** At such times the slightest event was considered to be of importance—a chance word, a sly intimation by the gossip at the bedside, a pious or hopeful ejaculation by the mother; and, where names were sought for, any well-omened word was hastily seized and attached to the newcomer. Sometimes the name would express the time of birth, e. g., Shaharayim (the dawn), Hodesh (the new moon); sometimes the place, as Zerubbabel (born in Babylon). The condition of the mother is often indicated; thus Rachel dying in childbirth named her son Benoni (son of my pain), while Leah (exhausted) and Mahli (sick) are names that hint much weakness, if not death. Sometimes the name indicates a peculiarity of the child, as Esau (hairy), Edom (red), Korah (bald). Or the feeling of the parent found expression—Eve called her first born Cain (acquisition), but she came to know that a mother's feelings are made up more of sadness than of joy, and so she called her second son Abel (vanity). The strong affection of Hebrew women for their children is sometimes shown in the names they gave to their children, e. g., Adah (ornament), Peninnah (pearl), Rachel (dove), Susanna (lilies), etc. Religious names were frequently given, the most simple being expressive of thanks to God for the gift of a child, as Mahalaleel (praise to God); of wonder at God's liberality, Zabdiel (bountifully given), Zechariah (God has remembered). Again a name may express some great longing of the parent; so Rachel named her first son Joseph (adding, i. e., may God add to me another child); or resignation and trust, as Elioenai (toward Jehovah are my eyes). The name was generally given by the parents, but sometimes a number of their kinsmen and friends would agree in bestowing one (Ruth 4:17; Luke 1:59). (2) **Change of name.** Not seldom the name given at birth was changed for a new one, or at first added to the original name, and gradually took its place. Thus Abram's name was changed to Abraham (q. v.) when he renewed his covenant with Jehovah (Gen. 17:5); Jacob (the supplanter) became Israel (prince) after his successful struggle with the angel (Gen. 32:28). Princes often changed their names on their accession to the throne (II Kings 23:34; 24:17). This was also done in the case of private persons on entering upon public duties of importance (Num. 13:16;

comp. John 1:42; Acts 4:36). So the prophet Nathan, on assuming the charge of Solomon's education, gave him the name Jedidiah (II Sam. 12:25). Children frequently received names expressive of relationship, as Abimelech (father of the king); or some one of the several divine names is coupled in the same manner with another element, as Nathaneel, with the divine name El, or Jonathan, with the divine name Jehovah (contracted Jo) and the verb gave. The word El enters very early into the composition of names, while those compounded with the name Jehovah do not appear till the Mosaic era; and not till the time of Samuel are names compounded with this name of God common.

4. **Figurative.** The name in Hebrew is sometimes used to signify the collected attributes or characteristics of the object named. This is particularly the case with the divine name (Exod. 34:5). Our Lord says, "I have manifested thy name," etc. (John 17:6), where name embraces the whole divine nature revealed by the Son. The expression "name of God" indicates the entire administration of God, by which he reveals himself and his attributes to men; the glory and power of God displayed in nature (Psa. 8:1); God's revelation of himself to his people (Zech. 10:12); and when God announces his mighty presence it is said, "Thy name is near" (Psa. 75:1). In the New Testament the expression "the name of Christ" refers to all that Jesus is to men (Luke 24:47; Acts 9:15); "to believe in the name of Christ" (John 1:12), "saved by his name" (Acts 4:12), "to have life through his name" (John 20:31) all refer to the saving and life-giving power in Christ, which is communicated to the believer. The expression "Let everyone that nameth the name of Christ" (II Tim. 2:19) means everyone that acknowledges him to be what his name means, the Lord.

Nao'mi (nā-ō'mĭ; my pleasantness, delight), a woman of Bethlehem, in the days of the judges, whose history is interwoven with that of her daughter-in-law Ruth (Ruth, chaps 1-4), B. C. about 1322-1312. Her husband's name was Elimelech, and her two sons were Mahlon and Chilion. With them, because of a famine in her own country, she went to Moab, where they died. Returning to her native land, she was accompanied by Ruth, who became the wife of Boaz. Upon her return she replied to those asking her "Is this Naomi?" "Call me not Naomi, call me Mara: for the Almighty hath dealt very bitterly with me."

Na'phish (nā'fĭsh), the eleventh son of Ishmael (Gen. 25:15; I Chron. 1:31). The tribe descended from Nodab was subdued by the Reubenites, the Gadites, and the half of the tribe of Manasseh, when "they made war with the Hagarites, with Jetur, and Nephish, and Nodab" (I Chron. 5:19). The tribe is not again found in the sacred records, nor is it mentioned by later writers. It has not been identified.

Naph'tali (năf'tà-lī; my wrestling).
1. **The sixth son of Jacob,** and the second of Bilhah, Rachel's maid, and own brother to Dan. Of the personal history of Naphtali we know nothing, as up to the time of Jacob's

blessing the twelve patriarchs his name is only mentioned in the two public lists (Gen. 35: 25; 46:24).

2. **The Tribe of Naphtali.** (1) **Numbers.** When Israel went down into Egypt Naphtali had four sons (Gen. 46:24; I Chron. 7:13). While in Egypt Naphtali increased with wonderful rapidity, numbering at the first census fifty-three thousand four hundred (Num. 1: 43), ranking as *sixth*. The number decreased during the wilderness journey, for at the second census the adult males amounted to only forty-five thousand four hundred, ranking *eighth* (26:50). (2) **Position.** During the march through the wilderness Naphtali occupied a position on the north of the sacred tent with Dan and Asher (2:25-31). (3) **Territory.** In the apportionment of the land the lot of Naphtali was not drawn till the last one. Their portion lay at the northern angle of Palestine, and was inclosed on three sides by that of other tribes—Zebulun (south), Asher (west), trans-Jordanic Manasseh (east). (4) **Subsequent history.** Naphtali had its share in the incursions and molestations by the surrounding heathen. One of these, apparently the severest struggle of all, fell with special violence on the north of the country, and the leader by whom the invasion was repelled— Barak, of Kedesh-Naphtali—was the one great hero whom Naphtali is recorded to have produced (Judg. 4:6). Naphtali was also the first tribe captured by the Assyrians under Tiglath-pileser (II Kings 15:29). But though the history of the tribe ends here, yet, under the title of Galilee, the district which they formerly occupied became in every way far more important than it had ever been before.

3. **Mount Naphtali.** The mountainous district which formed the main part of the territory of Naphtali (Josh. 20:7), answering to "Mount Ephraim" and "Mount Judah."

Naph'tuhim (năf'tū-hĭm), a Mizraite nation or tribe, mentioned only as descendants of Noah (Gen. 10:13; I Chron. 1:11), and who probably settled at first, or when Gen., ch. 5, was written, either in Egypt or immediately west of it.

Napkin (Gr. *soudarion, sweat-cloth*), a handkerchief (so rendered, Acts 19:12), i. e., a cloth for wiping the perspiration from the face and for cleaning the nose (Luke 19:20; Acts 19: 12). It was also used for swathing the head of a corpse (John 11:44; 20:7).

Narcis'sus (nár-sĭs'ŭs; a well-known flower), a person at Rome to some of whose household (or friends) Paul sent salutation (Rom. 16: 11). He cannot be the celebrated favorite of the Emperor Claudius, as that person was put to death before the epistle was written.

Nard. *See* Spikenard.

Na'than (nā'thăn; *He*, i. e., God, *has given*).

1. **A Son of David;** one of the four who were born to him by Bathsheba (I Chron. 3:5; comp. 14:4 and II Sam. 5:14), B. C. about 977. Nathan appears to have taken no part in the events of his father's or his brother's reigns. To him are to be referred, probably, the words of Zech. 12:12. He appears as one of the forefathers of Mary in the genealogy of Luke (Luke 3:31).

2. **The Hebrew Prophet** who lived in the reigns of David and Solomon. (1) **First appearance.** The first mention of him is in a consultation with David, in which he advises him to build the temple (II Sam. 7:2, 3); but after a vision informed David that he was not to carry out his intention (vers. 4-17), B. C. about 984. (2) **Reproves David.** About a year after David's sin Nathan appears to reprove him. The reason for this delay seems to be set forth by David in Psa. 32, where he describes the state of his heart during this period, and the sufferings he endured while trying to conceal his crime. To insure success Nathan resorted to a parable of a rich man taking from a poor man his "little ewe lamb." The parable was so selected that David could not suspect that it had reference to him and his sin. With all the greater shock, therefore, did the prophet's words, "Thou art the man," come to the king (II Sam. 12:1-15), B. C. about 977. At the birth of Solomon Nathan came to David, according to Jehovah's instructions, and named the child Jedidiah, "because Jehovah loved him" (vers. 24, 25). (3) **Secures the kingdom for Solomon.** In the last years of David Nathan, with Bathsheba, secured the succession of Solomon (I Kings 1:8-30), and at the king's request assisted at his inauguration (vers. 32-38, 45), B. C. about 960. He assisted David by his advice when he reorganized the public worship (II Chron. 29:25). His son Zabud succeeded him as the "king's friend," and another son, Azariah, was "over the offices" in Solomon's time (I Kings 4:5). He left two works behind him —a Life of David (I Chron. 29:29), and a Life of Solomon (II Chron. 9:29). The last of these may have been incomplete, as we cannot be sure that he outlived Solomon. His grave is shown at Halhul, near Hebron.

3. An inhabitant of Zobah in Syria, and the father of Igal, one of David's chieftains (II Sam. 23:36), B. C. about 984. In I Chron. 11:38 it is given as Joel, the brother of Nathan.

4. A descendant of Judah, being the son of Attai and father of Zabad (I Chron. 2:36).

5. One of the chief Jews who were sent by Ezra from his encampment at the river Ahava to the Jews' colony at Casiphia, to obtain "ministers for the house of God" (Ezra 8:16, sq.), B. C. about 457. He is perhaps the same as the Nathan who put away his Gentile wife (10:39).

Nathan'ael (nà-thăn'â-ĕl; Gr. from Heb. *God has given*), a disciple of our Lord, of whose life we have no particulars save the references in John's gospel. It appears that after Jesus was proclaimed by John the Baptist to be the Lamb of God he was minded to go to Galilee. Having called Philip to follow him, the latter hasted to Nathanael to inform him that the Messiah had appeared. Nathanael expressed his distrust that any good could come from so small and inconsiderable a place as Nazareth. He accompanied Philip, however, and upon his approach was saluted by Jesus as "an Israelite indeed, in whom was no guile." This elicited the inquiry from Nathanael as to how he had become known to Jesus. The answer, "Before that Philip called thee, when thou was under the fig tree, I saw thee," satisfied him that Jesus was more than man, and "Nathanael answered and saith unto him, Rabbi, thou art the Son of God; thou art the King of Israel" (John 1:45-59), A. D. 25. We meet with the name of Nathanael only once more, and then simply as one of a small company of disciples at the Sea of Tiberias to whom Jesus showed himself after his resurrection (21:2). From this reference we learn that Nathanael was a native of Cana of Galilee. "It is very commonly believed that Nathanael and Bartholomew are the same person. The evidence for that belief is as follows: John, who twice mentions Nathanael, never introduces the name of Bartholomew at all. Matthew (10:3), Mark (3:18), and Luke (6:14) all speak of Bartholomew, but never of Nathanael. It may be, however, that Nathanael was the proper name and Bartholomew (son of Tholmai) the surname of the same disciple, just as Simon was called Bar-jona, and Joses, Barnabas. It was Philip who first brought Nathanael to Jesus, just as Andrew had brought his brother Simon; and Bartholomew is named by each of the first three evangelists immediately after Philip, while by Luke he is coupled with Philip precisely in the same way as Simon with his brother Andrew, and James with his brother John" (Smith, *Bib. Dict.*, s. v.).

Na′than-mel′ech (nā′thăn-měl′ĕk; *given of the king*), a chamberlain (i. e., eunuch) from before whose chamber at the temple entrance King Josiah removed the horses dedicated to the sun by the king of Judah (II Kings 23:11), B. C. 624.

Nativity of Christ. *See* Christmas, Jesus.

Natural. (1) (Heb. *lēăḥ, freshness*). It is recorded of Moses that at his death "his eye was not dim, nor his natural force abated" (Deut. 34:7). The meaning is his freshness, i. e., full vital energy, was preserved. (2) (Gr. *phusikos, produced by nature*), thus "the natural use" (Rom. 1:26, 27) means that which is agreeable to nature. "Natural branches" (11:21, 24) are those growing naturally as opposed to ingrafted branches. The phrase "as natural brute beasts" (II Pet. 2:12) means *governed by the instincts of nature* (R. V., "born mere animals"). The adverbial form is used in the passage, "but what they know naturally, as brute beasts" (Jude 10), i. e., under the guidance of nature. (3) (Gr. *psuchikos*), *having the nature and characteristics of the principle of animal life*, which men have in common with the brutes; thus the "natural body" (I Cor. 15:44, 46), and equivalent to "flesh and blood" (v. 50). In the expression "The natural man receiveth not the things of the Spirit" (2:14), the meaning is, the unregenerate man governed by his sensuous nature with its subjection to appetite and passion.

Natural History. In dealing with the natural history of the Bible we should be governed by principles similar to those which we use in determining the allusions to nature in other ancient and most modern books. Nothing like a scientific classification of animals and plants can be detected in the Bible any more than in Homer or Horace or Shakespeare or Wordsworth. Natural objects are grouped with reference to their more obvious characteristics.

Thus plants are divided into trees and herbs. Yet even in speaking of the knowledge of the vegetable kingdom which Solomon possessed, it is said that "he spake of trees, from the cedar tree that is in Lebanon even unto the hyssop that springeth out of the wall" (I Kings 4:33). All plants are here characterized as trees. Solomon seems to have divided the animal kingdom into four classes, corresponding to the modern classes of the vertebrates— "he spake also of beasts (mammalia), and of fowl (birds), and of creeping things, (reptiles, including amphibians), and of fishes" (4:33). The last class doubtless includes most or all of the aquatic creatures not included in the modern class of fishes. It is plain that in this classification of Solomon no notice is taken of insects, coelenterata, etc. Worms were probably included among *creeping things*. Moses seems to have recognized a somewhat similar division. In the ceremonial law a classification into clean and unclean was based on the correlation of certain organs and functions, as cleft hoofs and rumination, and, in the case of aquatic creatures the presence or absence of fins and scales. According to this, water mollusks, coelenterata, and scaleless fishes were in one class and other fishes in a second.—*G. E. Post.*

Nature. (Gr. *genesis;* elsewhere, as Rom. 1:26. *phusis, genus*). The following are the uses of these terms: (1) The law of the natural or moral world (Rom. 1:26; 2:14; 11:24); (2) birth, origin, natural descent, e. g., "Jews by nature" (Gal. 2:15; Rom. 2:27), "which by nature are no gods" (Gal. 4:8); (3) *genus, kind*: "For every kind (marg. 'nature') of beasts," etc., "is tamed, and hath been tamed of mankind" (marg. "nature of man," James 3:7).

Naughtiness (Heb. *rō‘ă, badness*, I Sam. 17:28, wickedness of heart); *ḥăwwäh* (Prov. 11:6), eagerly coveting, and so mischievous things; (Gr. *kakia*, James 1:21), malice, ill-will, vicious disposition.

Na′um (nā′ŭm), the son of Esli and father of Amos, in the maternal ancestry of Christ (Luke 3:25). He is probably the same as Johanan, the son of Elioenai (I Chron. 3:24).

Nave (Heb. *găb, hollow* or *curved*), the hub of a wheel, the central part into which the spokes are inserted (I Kings 7:33).

Navel (Heb. *shōr, twisted*, as a string), the umbilical connection of the fetus with the mother (Ezek. 16:4), hence abdomen where it is attached (Job. 40:16).

Figurative. The *bodice* or vestment of a woman (Cant. 7:2); so the passage is understood by some.

Navy (Heb. *’ŏnī, conveyance*, I Kings 9:26, etc.) is used in the sense of *fleet*. Solomon's "Tarshish fleet" *’ŏnī tarshish* were "smeltery ships" carrying raw smelted copper refined at Ezion-geber as a stock in trade for exchange for exotic wares. *See* Ezion-geber; Ship.

Naz′arene (năz′à-rēn), an inhabitant or native of Nazareth, as Matt. 21:11, etc., and rendered "of Nazareth." The term Nazarene (Gr. *Nazōraios*) occurs only in Matt. 2:23; Acts 24:5, and should have been rendered *Nazoraean* in English. At first it was applied to Jesus naturally and properly, as defining his residence. In process of time its population became impure (mixed with other peoples), its dialect rough, provincial, and strange, and its people seditious, so that they were held in little consideration. "The name of Nazarene was but another word for *despised one*. Hence, although no prophet has ever said anything of the word Nazarene, yet all those prophecies describing the Messiah as a *despised one* are fulfilled in his being a *Nazarene*. But we are convinced that something more than this is intended. The Hebrew word for Nazareth was Netzer, a *branch*, or rather *germ* . . . Nazareth is called a germ from its insignificance, yet it shall through Him, fill the earth with its importance" (Whedon, *Com.*, in loc.). The Christians were called "Nazarenes" (Acts 24:5), a contemptuous appellation, as the followers of Jesus, whose presumed descent from Nazareth stamped him as a false Messiah.

Naz′areth (năz′à-rĕth), the home of Joseph and Mary.

1. **Location.** Nazareth is situated on the most southern of the ranges of Lower Galilee, about ten miles from the plain of Esdraelon. "You cannot see from Nazareth the surrounding country, for Nazareth lies in a basin; but the moment you climb to the edge of this basin . . . what a view you have. Esdraelon lies before you, with its twenty battlefields— the scenes of Barak's and of Gideon's victories, of Saul's and Josiah's defeats, of the struggles for freedom in the glorious days of the Maccabees. There is Naboth's vineyard and the place of Jehu's revenge upon Jezebel; there Shunem and the house of Elisha; there Carmel and the place of Elijah's sacrifice. To the east the valley of Jordan, with the long range of Gilead; to the west the radiance of the Great Sea . . . You can see thirty miles in three directions" (Smith, *Hist. Geog.*, p. 432). Across the plain of Esdraelon emerged from the Samaritan hill the road from Jerusalem and Egypt. The name of the present village is *en-Nâzirah*, the same as of old, and is near Cana.

319. Nazareth

2. **Scripture Mention.** Nazareth is not mentioned in the Old Testament, or by Josephus; it was the home of Joseph and Mary (Luke 2:39); there the angel announced to Mary the birth of the Messiah (1:26-28), and thither Joseph brought Mary and Jesus after the sojourn in Egypt (Matt. 2:19-22); here Jesus grew up to manhood (Luke 4:16), and taught in the synagogue (Matt. 13:54; Luke

320. Mary's Well, Nazareth

4:16). His long and intimate association with this village made him known as "Jesus of Nazareth" (Luke 18:37; 24:19; John 1:45, etc.; Acts 2:22, etc.). The disrepute in which Nazareth stood (John 1:47) has generally been attributed to the Galileans' lack of culture and rude dialect; but Nathanael, who asked, "Can any good thing come out of Nazareth?" was himself a Galilean. It would seem probable that "good" must be taken in an ethical sense, and that the people of Nazareth had a bad name among their neighbors for irreligion or some laxity of morals.

3. **Present Condition.** Modern Nazareth is a better class Eastern village, with a population of about 10,000, composed of Moslems and Christians mainly.

Naz′arite, more properly **Naz′irite**, one of either sex who was bound by a vow of a peculiar kind to be set apart from others for the service of God. The obligation was either for life or for a defined time.

1. **Name** (Heb. *näzĕr*, and *nᵉzîr ᵉlōhîm*, *Nazarite of God*). The term comes from the verb *näzăr*, to *separate;* and denotes in general one who is separated from certain things and unto others, and so distinguished from other persons and consecrated unto God (Gen. 49: 26; Deut. 33:16). According to others, the word *nēzĕr*, *a diadem*, contains the original idea of *näzăr*, which will then radically signify *to crown*, and the hair is regarded as a crown to the person. In accordance with this view the Nazarite is a *crowned one*, because he has "the crown of God upon his head" (Num. 6: 7), evidently in allusion to the mass of uncut hair, which was considered an ornament (II Sam. 14:25, 26).

2. **Origin.** The origin of the custom is involved in obscurity. The prescriptions in Num. 6 presuppose it to have been an institution already in existence, and merely regulate it so as to bring it into harmony with the whole Mosaic legislation. There are no conclusive analogies tending to show that the custom was derived from a heathen source, especially from Egypt.

3. **The Nazarite Vow.** This vow consisted in the person consecrating his life to God for a fixed period. The Mosaic law speaks of such consecration as being limited to a particular time which was probably fixed by the one making the vow; yet instances occur of children being dedicated by their parents before their birth to be Nazarites all their lives,

e. g., Samson (Judg. 13:5, 14), Samuel (I Sam. 1:11), and John the Baptist (Luke 1:15). According to the Mishna the usual time was thirty days, but double vows for sixty days, and treble vows for a hundred days, were sometimes made. The vow of the apostle Paul seems also to have been a kind of Nazarite vow, in fulfillment of which he shaved his head at Cenchrea (Acts 18:18), although according to the law (Num. 6:9, 18) and the Talmud the shaving of the head was required to be done at the door of the temple.

4. **The Law of the Nazarite** (Num. 6:1-21). The Nazarite, during the term of his consecration, was bound to abstain from wine, grapes, with every production of the vine, and from every kind of intoxicating drink. He was forbidden to cut the hair of his head, or to approach any dead body, even that of his nearest relation. If a Nazarite incurred defilement by accidentally touching a dead body, he had to undergo certain rites of purification, and to recommence the full period of his consecration. There is nothing whatever said in the Old Testament of the duration of the period of the vow of the Nazarite of days. When the period of his vow was fulfilled he was released therefrom, and was required to offer a ewe lamb for a burnt offering, a ewe lamb for a sin offering, and a ram for a peace offering, with the usual accompaniments of peace offerings (Num. 6:13-20) and of the offering made at the consecration of priests (Exod. 29:2), "a basket of unleavened bread, cakes of fine flour mingled with oil, and wafers of unleavened bread anointed with oil" (Num. 6:15). He brought also a meat offering and a drink offering, which appear to have been presented by themselves as a distinct act of service (v. 17). He was to cut off the hair of "the head of his separation" (i. e., the hair which had grown during the period of his consecration) at the door of the tabernacle, and to put it into the fire under the sacrifice on the altar. The priest then placed upon his hands the sodden left shoulder of the ram, with one of the unleavened cakes and one of the wafers, and then took them again and waved them for a wave offering. These, as well as the breast and the heave, or right shoulder (to which he was entitled in the case of ordinary peace offerings, Lev. 7:32-34) were the perquisite of the priest. The Nazarite also gave him a present proportioned to his circumstances (Num. 6:21). From this the custom afterward grew up, that when poor persons took the Nazarite's vow upon them, those who were better off defrayed the expenses of the sacrifices (Acts 21:24). When all the service was concluded the late Nazarite was at liberty again to indulge in the use of wine (Num. 6:20).

5. **Meaning of the Vow.** As the name means, it was an act of consecrating oneself to Jehovah (Num. 6:2), and that negatively, "by renouncing the world with its pleasures—that are so unfavorable to sanctification—and all its defiling influences;" and positively, by giving a certain complexion to the life as being specially devoted to the Lord. Consequently, the Nazarite was "holy unto the Lord" (v. 8). Abstinence from the fruit of the vine was meant not merely to secure that sobriety which is necessary to qualify one for the service of the Lord, but to serve as a symbol of the renunciation of those delicacies of the flesh that tend to endanger a man's sanctification.

The long uncut hair of the Nazarite was the symbol of strength and abundant vitality (*see* II Sam. 14:25, 26), and was worn in honor of the Lord as a sign that he belonged to the Lord, and dedicated himself to his service with all his vital powers. Then, too, a luxurious growth of long hair was looked upon as imparting a somewhat handsome appearance, an ornament, and, in the case of the Nazarite, was the diadem of the head consecrated to God (Jer. 7:29).

Because the Nazarite was "holy to the Lord," and wore upon his head the diadem of his consecration, he was required, like the anointed priest, to avoid defiling himself by association or contact with the dead.

The time that the Nazarite vow lasted was not a lazy life, involving a withdrawal from the duties of citizenship, but was perfectly reconcilable with the performance of all domestic and social duties, the burial of the dead alone excepted. "The position of the Nazarite, as Philo, Maimonides, and others clearly saw, was a condition of life consecrated to the Lord, resembling the sanctified relation in which the priests stood to Jehovah, and differing from the priesthood solely in the fact that it involved no official service at the sanctuary and was not based upon a divine calling and institution, but was undertaken spontaneously for a certain time and through a special vow. The object was simply the realization of the idea of a priestly life, with its purity and freedom from all contamination from everything connected with death and corruption, a self-surrender to God stretching beyond the deepest earthly ties. In this respect the Nazarite's sanctification of life was a step toward the realization of the priestly character which had been set before the whole nation as its goal at the time of its first calling (Exod. 19:5); and although it was simply the performance of a vow, and therefore a work of perfect spontaneity, it was also a work of the Spirit of God which dwelt in the congregation of Israel, so that Amos could describe the raising up of Nazarites along with prophets as a special manifestation of divine grace" (K. and D., *Com.*, in loc.).

Ne'ah (nē'à), a town of Zebulun, on the southern border of Rimmon (Josh. 19:13). As it is stated to have been not far from Rimmon ("Methoar," i. e., "which pertains to" Neah) it lay perhaps at the modern site *Nimrin*, a little west of Kurn Hattin.

Neap'olis (Gr. nē-ăp'ŏ-lĭs, *new city*), a place in northern Greece and seaport town of Philippi, distant ten miles. Its remains are remarkable, and its aqueduct still indicates its importance, long since departed. A place where Paul first landed in Europe (Acts 16: 11), and the terminus of the great Egnatian Road. Its modern name is Kavalla.

Neari'ah (nē-à-rī'à; *servant of Jehovah*).

1. One of the six sons of Shemaiah in the line of the royal family of Judah after the

captivity (I Chron. 3:22, 23). Some identify him with *Nagge* (*q. v.*).

2. A son of Ishi, and one of the captains of the five hundred Simeonites who, in the days of Hezekiah, drove out the Amalekites from Mount Seir (I Chron. 4:42), B. C. about 715.

Ne′bai (nē′bī), in A. V. and margin of R. V. Nobai (nō′bī), in R. V. A family of the heads of the people who signed the covenant with Nehemiah (Neh. 10:19), B. C. 445.

Neba′ioth, or **Neba′joth** (nĕ-bā′yŏth) or (nĕ-bā′jŏth), the eldest son of Ishmael (Gen. 25:13; I Chron. 1:29) and father of a pastoral tribe named after him (Isa. 60:7; comp. Gen. 17:20). This Arabian clan was a neighbor to the people of Kedar and both the names occur in the records of Ashurbanipal (669-626 B. C.). They seem to be the forerunners of the later Nabataeans (*q. v.*).

Neba′joth (nĕ-bā′jŏth). *See* Nebaioth.

Nebal′lat (nĕ-băl′ăt), a place occupied by the Benjamites after the captivity (Neh. 11:34). Identified with *Beit Nabāla*, near Lydda.

321. Neapolis (Kavalla)

Ne′bat (nē′băt; *He*, i. e., God, *has regarded*), the father of Jeroboam, whose name is only preserved in connection with that of his distinguished son (I Kings 11:26; 12:2, 15, etc.), B. C. before 934. He is described as an Ephrathite, or Ephraimite, of Zereda.

Ne′bo (nē′bō), as a geographical name may signify an elevated place, answering to Arabic *naba'a* (*to be high*), or refer to a center of the worship of Nebo, a Babylonian deity.

1. A town east of Jordan, situated in the fertile country asked for by Reuben and Gad (Num. 32:3), taken possession of and rebuilt by Reuben (v. 38), although it does not occur in the catalogue of the towns of Reuben in the Book of Joshua (13:15-22), which may be because the Israelites gave it another name. Although rebuilt by the Reubenites (Num. 32:37, 38; 33:47; I Chron. 5:8), it reverted to Moab (*Moabite Stone*, 14, *see* Moabite Stone. Its modern site is on or near Mt. Nebo.

2. The mountain from which Moses saw the promised land (Deut. 32:49; 34:1), and in a ravine of which he was buried (32:50; 34:6). It was the head or summit of *Mount Pisgah* (*q. v.*), a portion of the general range of the "mountains of Abarim." Josephus says of Abarim (*Ant.*, iv, 8, 48) that it "is a very high mountain, situate over against Jericho, and one that affords a prospect of the greatest part

of the excellent land of Canaan." This is corroborated by Eusebius and Jerome. The mountains of *Abarim* are a mountain range forming the Moabitish tableland, which slope off into the steppes of Moab.

3. A man whose descendants, to the number of fifty-two, are mentioned among those of Judah and Benjamin who returned from Babylon with Zerubbabel (Ezra 2:29; 7:33). Seven of them put away their foreign wives (Neh. 10:43).

322. God Nebo

4. A Babylonian god (Isa. 46:1; 48:1). *See* Gods, False.

Nebuchadnez′zar (nĕb-û-kăd-nĕz′ẽr) and **Nebuchadrez′zar** (nĕb-û-kăd-rĕz′ẽr) (Akkad. *Nabu-kudduriuṣur*, Nebo, *defend the boundary*). The form of the name in *n* is due to dissimilation, and in Hebrew the name is more correctly represented in the form Nebuchadrezzar, than in the more common form Nebuchadnezzar. Nebuchadrezzar was the son of Nabopolassar, and was in all probability of Chaldean race, and not of pure Babylonian (*see* Babylonia). When the Assyrian power was tottering to its fall the Chaldeans, who lived in the south near the Persian Gulf, saw an opportunity of again seizing power in the much coveted city of Babylon. The signs of decay were evident in the reign of Asshurbanipal (*see* Assyria), though the collapse of the Assyrian commonwealth did not come until 607 B. C. The Chaldeans did not need to wait so long as that for their opportunity, but Nabopolassar seized the throne in 625 as soon as Asshurbanipal had ceased to reign in Assyria. But Nabopolassar was not accounted king at once by the Assyrians and numerous conflicts must have occurred during his reign between the successors of Asshurbanipal and the new Chaldean king in Babylon. Nabopolassar followed the ancient Babylonian custom of building temples and attending to the internal affairs of his splendid kingdom. His records have little to say of anything else.

1. **In the field.** His son Nebuchadnezzar was destined to be his successor and was his

representative in the field. He probably began his military service against the later Assyrian kings and soon achieved distinction. Toward the end of the reign of Nabopolassar the fall of Nineveh became imminent and the Babylonian king determined to gain not only his own complete independence of Assyria, but also as much as possible of the former Assyrian possessions. He allied his own family to that of the Manda, who were threatening to overthrow Assyria, by marrying his son Nebuchadrezzar to the daughter of Cyaxares. This alliance, as well as the vigilance and ability of Nebuchadrezzar as a warrior was completely successful. When the Manda delivered the final blow which ended forever the Assyrian commonwealth, they secured Nineveh and the northern and northwestern provinces of the Assyrian empire, while Nabopolassar secured all of southern Assyria and so much of the vast western provinces as were still in Assyrian control. All this territory, however, was but loosely held together during the latter part of the Assyrian control, and much of it was already lost to Egypt.

2. **Opposes Egypt.** It was quite natural that Egypt should early seek to profit by the weakening of Assyrian power. Palestine and Syria had belonged to Egypt by right of conquest during the reign of Thutmose III, and so late as the days of Amenophis III and Amenophis IV the governors of Syrian cities were wont to address the Egyptian kings as their lords and even as their gods. When Necho II succeeded his father, Psammetichus I, as king of upper and of lower Egypt, he promptly began the reconquest of Syria and Palestine. In 608 B. C. he left Egypt and marched up the seacoast, penetrating inland to the plain of Esdraelon at Megiddo. There Josiah, king of Judah, vainly opposed him and was killed. Necho was soon able to count himself master of the whole country. It was now his purpose to move eastward to the Euphrates and cross the great valley to seize what might fall to his share when the Assyrian empire met its end. He reached Carchemish, on the Euphrates, in 605, and there was confronted by Nebuchadnezzar at the head of his father's armies. The battle that ensued was one of the greatest in all history, judged simply by its immediate historic results. Necho was utterly and disastrously defeated, and fled in a rout homeward closely pursued by the victor. That one blow made Nebuchadnezzar the presumptive holder of all the valuable territory of Syria and Palestine. He pursued Necho to the very borders of Egypt.

3. **Becomes King.** At that critical moment, B. C. 604, his father died at Babylon, and he had to return post haste to take over the government. But for this he would probably have invaded Egypt. Had he dared so to do his success would have been almost certain, and he and his father would have made in twenty years an empire as vast as that achieved by the Assyrians after centuries of relentless conflict. The first years of the reign of Nebuchadnezzar were devoted to the establishing and ordering of his rule in Babylonia. The warlike enterprises which follow he has unfortunately not described for us. Following the example

of the earlier Babylonian kings Nebuchadnezzar has left to us almost exclusively records of his building operations and proofs of his zeal in the worship of the gods and of care in conserving their sanctuaries. From the Old Testament and from the classical historians we secure the necessary information for following his campaigns with reasonable fullness. The Egyptians had been defeated in their plan of securing by the sword possession of Syria and Palestine, but they had not given up the hope of attaining their desires in some other way. Apries, who is called Hophra (Egyptian *Mah-ab-Rē*) in the Old Testament, was now king of Egypt, and he set himself to arrange rebellions in Palestine which should culminate in the loss of this territory to Nebuchadnezzar.

323.

4. **Western Campaign.** Zedekiah unhappily foreswore himself, and Nebuchadnezzar promptly invaded his unhappy country and besieged Jerusalem for a year and a half. In 587 Jerusalem fell and numbers of its inhabitants were carried away captive to Babylonia, while Judah became a Chaldean province. In these acts of rebellion Edom, Moab, Tyre, Sidon, and Ammon had also joined, and these all were punished by Nebuchadnezzar. The punishment of Tyre was more difficult and less successful than that of the other partners. Nebuchadnezzar besieged it from 585 to 572 B. C., but was not able to take it. The city was so situated on its rocky island as not to be easily reduced from the mainland, and the Babylonians had no navy with which to cut off its supplies by sea and so reduce it by starvation. The city at last capitulated and resumed the payment of its former tribute, but was not otherwise punished. The punishment of Egypt for inciting the Palestinian states was undertaken and successfully carried through in 568. Nebuchadnezzar himself has left us no account of this very important campaign, but an Egyptian inscription proves that he marched the whole length of Egypt proper to Syene (the modern Aswân) as the direct result of this single campaign Egypt became subject to Babylonia during the reign of Amasis II, who had dethroned Hophra and succeeded him on the throne. To hold the

advantage thus gained Nebuchadnezzar had to invade Egypt again, and one of his own inscriptions mentions the sending of an expedition thither in the thirty-seventh year of his reign. Nebuchadnezzar also carried on a war (Jer. 49:28-33) against the Arabs of Kedar, but we have no other account of it than that preserved by the Old Testament. With this ends our knowledge of the warlike undertakings of Nebuchadnezzar. There is every reason to believe that he fought many a campaign of which we know nothing. He would not have been able to hold this great empire together without frequent recourse to the sword. By force he had achieved power and by force only could it be successfully maintained. It is curious and interesting to notice that on one occasion at least Nebuchadnezzar played the part of peacemaker. When the Manda who had overthrown Assyria pushed westward they came into conflict with the Lydians. On May 25, 585, during a fierce battle on the Halys an eclipse of the sun separated the combatants. Nebuchadnezzar interposed and made peace between them. A selfish desire to prevent too great success to his former allies doubtless contributed to this undertaking, but the deed may be accounted good, nevertheless.

5. **Works of Peace.** If we are to take Nebuchadnezzar's own estimate of his life and work we should arrive at the conclusion that he had but little interest in his campaigns and that his real concern was the glory of Babylon and its gods. The chief concern of Nebuchadnezzar was for the great temple of Bel-Marduk at Babylon known under the name of E-sagila. This he rebuilt and greatly adorned and beautified. To the Nebo temple of E-zida at Borsippa he also gave unstinted means and time. Besides these two temples he carried on works of repair and construction in bewildering number and variety at Ur, Larsa, Sippar, Erech, and Kutha. The city of Babylon also (*see* Babylon) he greatly beautified and strengthened. In it he built new streets, and its walls he greatly strengthened, so that the city was deemed impregnable. The worldwide glory of Babylon owed more to Nebuchadnezzar than to any other man. After a prosperous and eventful reign of forty-three years (604-562 B. C.) Nebuchadnezzar died and was succeeded by his son, Evil-Merodach (Amel-Marduk). Taking his reign as a whole it may safely be regarded as one of the strongest as it was clearly one of the most glorious in all the long history of Babylon as a world center. A man of great force and decision of character, not severe in his dealings beyond the custom of his age, a man who could plan and execute great and daring movements, he may surely be regarded as one of antiquity's greatest men.

6. **Nebuchadnezzar and Archaeology.** Nebuchadnezzar's Babylon was extensively excavated from 1899 to 1914 by Robert Koldewey and the *Deutsche Orientgesellschaft* (*see* Koldowey's, *Das wieder erstehende Babylon*, 4th ed., 1925). Among the tremendous complex ruins was the great Ishtar Gate, the huge structure piercing the double walled fortifications. It was adorned with a series of bulls and dragons in enameled colored brick (*see* R.

Koldowey, *Das Ischtar-Tor in Babylon*, 1918). This famous gate opened up to the city's procession street. Nebuchadnezzar's throne room was likewise done in enamel brick in exquisite geometric designs. Nebuchadnezzar's temple tower, or ziggurat, was in the temple area. Herodotus states that it rose to a height of eight stages. Only its ground plan remains. Nebuchadnezzar's hanging gardens were one of the seven wonders of the ancient world. Archaeology has shown the complete suitability of Nebuchadnezzar's words recorded in Dan. 4:30, "Is not this great Babylon which I have built for the royal dwelling-place by the might of my power and for the glory of my majesty?" (R. W. R., revised by M. F. U.

Nebuchadrez'zar (nĕb-û-kăd-rĕz'ĕr), another form of *Nebuchadnezzar* (*q. v.*).

Nebushas'ban (nĕb-û-shăs'băn; Akkad. *Nabū-shezibanni, Nebo, save me*), one of the officers of Nebuchadnezzar at the time of the capture of Jerusalem, to whose care Jeremiah was committed. He was Rab-saris, i. e., chief of the eunuchs (Jer. 39:13), as Nebuzaradan was Rab-tabbachim (chief of the bodyguard), and Nergal-sharezer, Rab-mag (chief of the magicians), the three being the most important officers then present, probably the highest dignitaries of the Babylonian court. Nebushasban's office and title were the same as those of Ashpenaz (Dan. 1:3), whom he probably succeeded.

Nebuzara'dan (nĕb-û-zàr-ā'dăn; *Nabū-zēr-iddina, Nebo has given offspring*), the Rab-tabbachim, i. e., chief of the slaughterers (A. V. Jer. 39:10, sq., "captain of the guard"), a high officer in the court of Nebuchadnezzar, apparently the next to the person of the monarch. He appears not to have been present during the siege of Jerusalem; probably he was occupied at the more important operations at Tyre, but as soon as the city was actually in the hands of the Babylonians he arrived, and from that moment everything was completely directed by him, B. C. 587. One act only is referred directly to Nebuchadnezzar, the appointment of the governor or superintendent of the conquered district. All this Nebuzaradan seems to have carried out with wisdom and moderation. He appears to have left Judea for this time when he took down the chief people of Jerusalem to his master at Riblah (II Kings 25:8-20). In four years he again appeared (Jer. 52:12). Nebuchadnezzar in his twenty-third year made a descent on the regions east of Jordan, including the Ammonites and the Moabites, who escaped when Jerusalem was destroyed. Thence he proceeded to Egypt, and, either on the way thither or on the return, Nebuzaradan again passed through the country and carried off seven hundred and forty-five more captives (52:30).

Ne'cho (nē'kô; II Chron. 35:20, 22; 36:4). An appellation applied to one of the *Pharaohs* (*q. v.*). R. V. Ne'co (Ne'coh).

Neck. This part of the human frame is used by the sacred writers with considerable variety and freedom in **figurative** expressions. Thus: "Thy neck is like the tower of David builded for an armory" (Cant. 4:4), and "like a tower of ivory" (7:4), with reference to the graceful ornament which the neck is, especially to the female figure. "To lay down the neck" (Rom. 16:4) is a strong expression for hazarding one's life. "Neck" is also used to represent that part of the building at which the roof or gable rests upon the wall (Hab. 3:13). "To put the foot upon the neck"

324. Placing Foot on Neck of Captive

(Josh. 10:24; II Sam. 22:41) is a usual expression in the East for triumphing over a fallen foe. A common reference was to a beast of burden, which bore upon his neck the yoke, and thus became an emblem of man in relation to a true or false service (Matt. 11:29). A stiff or hardened neck is a familiar expression for a rebellious spirit (Psa. 75:5; Prov. 29:1; Isa. 48:4, "thy neck is an iron sinew," i. e., inflexible; Acts 7:51). *See* Yoke.

Necklace (Heb. *răbîd, binding*), is a word not found in the A. V., but was in early times, as now, common in the East. Necklaces were sometimes made of silver or gold (Exod. 35:22), sometimes of jewels or pearls strung on a ribbon (Cant. 1:10), hanging to the breast or even to the girdle. To these were attached golden crescents (Isa. 3:18; Judg. 8:21) and amulets (Isa. 3:18). *See* Jewelry.

Necromancer (from Gr. *nekros, the dead*, and *manteia, divination*; Heb. *dōrēsh 'ĕl-hămmēthîm, one who inquires of the dead*). In many ancient nations there were those who pretended to be able by incantations to call up the dead, and consult with them on the mysteries of the present and future. The Mosaic law forbade consultation with the necromancer (Deut. 18:11). Another method of consulting the dead was by examining the viscera of one newly dead or slain, in order to draw out omens.

The most famous instance of necromancy in Scripture is Saul and the medium of Endor, recounted in I Sam. 28:1-25. It is an unequivocal divine condemnation of all traffic in occultism and a glaring expose of the fraudulency of spiritism. This practice of consulting the dead, so rife among the heathen nations, was strictly forbidden any Israelite. The reason is simple. It was a recourse to a medium who was under the control of a divining demon; in fact, the woman of Endor was identical with the modern spiritistic medium.

She is called "a woman who hath a familiar spirit," literally, "a woman controlled or mastered by a divining demon" (I Sam. 28:7, 8). In the episode, the spirit of Samuel was actually brought back from the spirit world, as the circumstances of the account indisputably prove. However, the seer's spirit was not brought back by the medium's power but by divine power, to pronounce doom upon Saul and to give a once-for-all Scriptural expose of the fraud of spiritism, its traffic in evil power, and its complete inconsistency with the worship of Israel's god. Neither ancient nor modern spiritism can recall or have communion with the spirits of the departed dead, as the medium's fear in the narrative of I Sam. 28 shows. What spiritistic mediums can do, however, is to impersonate the spirits of the departed dead and give superhuman knowledge by reason of their superior powers as evil spirit beings. For a full discussion see Merrill F. Unger, *Biblical Demonology*, 2nd ed., Chicago, 1953, pp. 143-164. M. F. U. *See* Magic.

Nedabi´ah (nĕd-á-bī´á; *Jehovah is generous*), the last named son of Jeconiah (I Chron. 3:18).

Needle (Gr. *hraphis*), occurs in Scripture only in the proverb, "It is easier for a camel to go through the eye of a needle," etc. (Matt. 19:24; Mark 10:25; Luke 18:25). *See* Camel.

Needlework (Heb. *rĭqmäh*, Judge 5:30; Psa. 45:14, *variegated work; rōqēm*, Exod. 26:36; 27:16; 28:39; 36:37; 38:18). It is best to understand this as *colored weaving*, i. e., stuff woven from yarn of different stripes or cubes; as distinguished from "cunning work," i. e., artistic weaving in which figures, flowers, and in some instances gold thread were woven (Exod. 26:1, 31; 28:6, etc.). *See* Embroidery.

Needy. *See* Poor.

Neesing, obsolete for sneezing (II Kings 4:35; Job 41:18).

Neginah (nĕ-gē´ná), **Neg´inoth** (nĕg´ĭ-nōth), appears in the titles of Psa. 4, 6, 54, 67, 76 and means *stringed instruments*.

Nehel´amite (nē-hĕl´á-mīt; *dreamed*, only in Jer. 29:24, 31, 32), a patronymic or patrial of unknown origin and signification, applied to the false prophet Shemaiah. No such name of person or place as Nehelam is known. The Targum gives the name as Helam. A place named Helam, between the Jordan and Euphrates, is mentioned in II Sam. 10:16, 17. This may be identical with Ptolemy's Alamatha, west of the Euphrates, and not far from Nicephorium and Thapsacus. Possibly the mention of "Nehelamite" contains a punning allusion to the dreams (*hălōmîm*) of the false prophets (*see* Jer. 23:25-28, 32, and other passages). Perhaps on this account, and because the radical letters of the two words are the same, *hlm*, the A. V. gives "dreamer" in the margin of Jer. 29:24.—W. H., revised by *M. F. U.*

Nehemi´ah (nē´hĕ-mī´á; *Jehovah consoles*).

1. The second named of "the children of the province . . . whom Nebuchadnezzar had carried away," and who returned with Zerubbabel from Babylon (Ezra 2:2; Neh. 7:7), B. C. 536.

2. The son of Azbuk, ruler of Beth-zur, in the mountains of Judah, and one who was

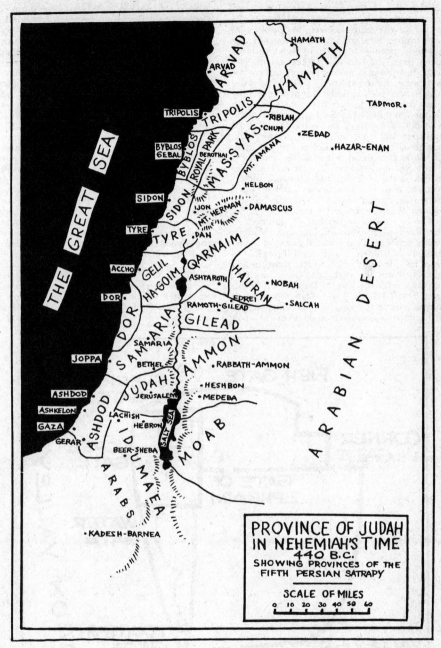

PROVINCE OF JUDAH
IN NEHEMIAH'S TIME
440 B.C.
SHOWING PROVINCES OF THE
FIFTH PERSIAN SATRAPY

SCALE OF MILES
0 10 20 30 40 50 60

325.

prominent in rebuilding the walls of Jerusalem (Neh. 3:16), B. C. 445.

3. **Governor of the Jews.** The genealogy of Nehemiah is unknown, except that he was the son of Hachaliah (Neh. 1:1), and brother of Hanani (7:2; comp. 1:2). All that we know certainly of Nehemiah is found in the book bearing his name. (1) **Cupbearer.** He first appears at Shushan as cupbearer to King Artaxerxes Longimanus (Neh. 2:1), B. C.

about 446. In that year he was informed of the deplorable condition of his countrymen in Judea, and determined to go to Jerusalem to endeavor to better their condition. (2) **Appointed governor.** Three or four months later he presented his request to the king to be allowed to go and rebuild Jerusalem. His royal master granted his request, and appointed him *Tirshathá, governor*. Accompanied by a troop of cavalry and letters from the king to the different satraps through whose provinces he was to pass, as well as to Asaph, the keeper of the king's forests, to supply him with timber, he started upon his journey, being under promise to return to Persia within a given time (2:1-10). (3) **At Jerusalem.** Nehemiah, without a moment's unnecessary delay, began the restoration of the city walls, which was accomplished in a wonderfully short time, viz., in fifty-two days (6:15). In this he was opposed by Sanballat and Tobiah, who not only poured out a torrent of abuse and contempt upon all engaged in the work, but actually made a conspiracy to fall upon the builders with an armed force, and put a stop to the undertaking. The project was defeated by the vigilance and prudence of Nehemiah. This armed attitude was continued from that day forward (ch. 4). He also reformed abuses, redressed grievances (ch. 5), introduced law and order (ch. 7), and revived the worship of God (ch. 8, sq.). Various stratagems were then resorted to to get Nehemiah away from Jerusalem, and if possible to take his life. But that which most nearly succeeded was the attempt to bring him into suspicion with the king of Persia, as if he intended to set himself up as an independent king as soon as the walls were completed. The artful letter of Sanballat so far wrought upon

Artaxerxes that he issued a decree stopping the work till further orders (Ezra 4:21). In these reforms Nehemiah enjoyed the cooperation of Ezra, who had preceded him to Jerusalem, and who is named as taking a prominent part in public affairs (8:1, 9, 13; 12:36). Nehemiah refused to receive his lawful allowance as governor during the whole term of his office because of the people's poverty, but entertained for twelve years, at his own cost, one hundred and fifty Jews, and welcomed any who returned from captivity (vers. 14-18). (4) **Return to Jerusalem.** Nehemiah, after twelve years' service, returned to Babylon (5:14; 13:6), B. C. 434. It is not known how long he remained there, but "after certain days" he obtained permission to again visit Jerusalem, where his services were needed because of new abuses that had crept in. When he arrived Nehemiah enforced the separation of the mixed multitude from Israel (13:1-3), expelled Tobiah the Ammonite from the temple chamber (vers. 4-9), made better arrangements for the support of the temple service (vers. 10-14) and for the observance of the Sabbath (vers. 15-22). His last recorded act was an effort to put an end to mixed marriages, which led him to "chase" away a son of Joiada, the high priest, because he was son-in-law to Sanballat the Horonite (v. 23,

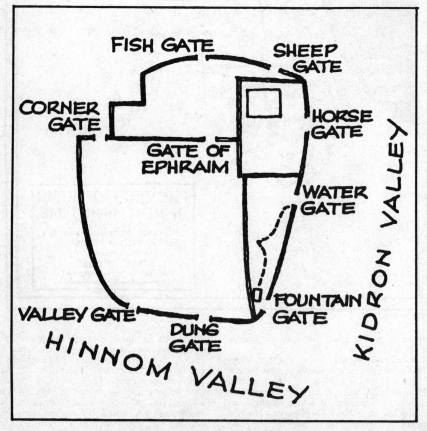

326. **Plan of Jerusalem at the Time of the Restoration of the Walls by Nehemiah (ca. 444 B. C.)**

sq.). It is supposed that Nehemiah remained in Jerusalem till about B. C. 405, toward the close of the reign of Darius Nothus, mentioned in 12:22. The time and place of his death is unknown. To Nehemiah is credited the authorship of the book that bears his name. (5) **Character.** Nehemiah's character seems almost without a blemish. He was a man of pure and disinterested patriotism, willing to leave a position of wealth, power, and influence in the first court of the world and share the sorrows of his countrymen. He was not only noble, high-minded, and of strict integrity, but he was also possessed of great humility, kindness, and princely hospitality. In nothing was he more remarkable than in his piety, walking before his God with singleness of eye, seeking the divine blessing and cooperation in prayer, and returning thanks to him for all his successes.

Nehemiah, Book of, a post-exilic book taking its name from its main character and traditional author, said to be "the words of Nehemiah, the son of Hachaliah" (Neh. 1:1). The book occurs in the third section of the Hebrew canon and constitutes one of the historical books of that group.

1. **Purpose.** It is closely linked with Ezra and together with that book shows God's faithfulness in the restoration of His exiled people to their own land. God's purpose is seen to work through great monarchs of the Persian Empire such as Cyrus, Darius I the Great and Artaxerxes. God is also seen to operate through the agency of His own anointed servants, such as Ezra, Nehemiah, Zerubbabel, Joshua, Haggai and Zechariah. The book narrates the rebuilding of the walls of Jerusalem and the establishment of civil authority under Nehemiah as governor. The Book of Nehemiah is more civil and secular than Ezra but it also contains a priestly slant.

2. **Date and Authority.** Nehemiah is commonly regarded as the work of the so-called chronicler. This priest-historian is supposed to have written I and II Chronicles and the book of Ezra-Nehemiah long after the time of these leaders. The date is customarily put at the beginning of the Greek period, around 330 B. C. These arguments, however, are unsound. It is much better to regard the book as belonging to the latter half of the fifth century B. C. Whether Ezra precedes Nehemiah or Nehemiah, Ezra is disputed by critics. Since Jewish tradition and the title of the book assign the authorship to Nehemiah, section 1:1-7:5 is to be looked upon as an excerpt from the author's memoirs, as the first person indicates. This material is inserted apparently without change. Other passages evidently taken from Nehemiah's memoirs are 11:1, 2; 12:27-43; 13:4-31. The work also consists of earlier documents which were incorporated into the author's work, such as 7:6-73a. The remainder of the book is based upon historical sources.

3. **The Outline.**
Part I. Nehemiah's Restoration of the Walls, 1:1-7:73
  a. Events making this possible, 1:1-2:20
  b. The actual construction, 3:1-6:19
  c. Watchmen set; census taken, 7:1-73

Part II. Ezra and Nehemiah's Religious Reformation, 8:1-13:31
  a. Covenant renewed, 8:1-10:39
  b. Princes, priests and Levites listed and dedication of walls, 11:1-13:13
  c. Nehemiah's second governorship and reforms, 13:4-31

(For critical study see C. C. Torrey, *The Composition and Historical Evaluation of Nehemiah*, Giessen, 1896; *Ezra Studies*, Chicago, 1910. For conservative treatment see J. O. Boyd, "The Composition of the Book of Ezra," *The Presbyterian Reformed Review*, XI, 1900, pp. 261-297; "The Documents of the Book of Ezra," *idem.*, 414-437; "The Historicity of the Book of Ezra," *idem.*, pp. 568-607). *M. F. U.*

Ne′hiloth (nē′hĭ-lŏth), title of Psa. 5, means *wind instruments.*

Ne′hum (nē′hŭm; *consoled*, i. e., by God), one of those who returned from Babylon with Zerubbabel (Neh. 7:7), B. C. about 445.

Nehush′ta (nḗ-hŭsh′tȧ; *bronze*), the daughter of Elnathan of Jerusalem, wife of Jehoiakim, and mother of Jehoiachin, kings of Judah (II Kings 24:8), B. C. about 616.

Nehush′tan (nḗ-hŭsh′tăn; a piece of *brass*, bronze), the name given by King Hezekiah to the "brazen serpent" (*q. v.*), when he broke it into pieces because the people had made it an object of worship (II Kings 18:4).

Nei′el (nḗ-ī′ĕl), a place mentioned as a landmark of Asher (Josh. 19:27), possibly *Neah* (v. 13). It has been associated with probability with Khirbet Ya'hîn, about 2 miles N. of Kabūl on the edge of the plain of Acre; at the south of the valley of Jiphtah-el.

Neigh (Heb. *ṣāhăl*, to *sound* clear, Jer. 8:16; 13:27; 50:11, A. V. "bellow as bulls;" marg. *neigh as steeds*; R. V. *neigh as strong horses*), the neighing of a horse, a sign of excessive wantonness; and used figuratively of man who with brutish heat "neighed after his neighbor's wife" (Jer. 5:8).

Neighbor (Heb. *rē'ă, associate;* Gr. *plēsion, near*), generally a person near, one connected by bonds of humanity, and whom natural regard would lead to treat with kindness and equity (Exod. 20:16, 17; Deut. 5:20). The construction placed upon "neighbor" (Lev. 19:18) was that of *friend* as opposed to enemy; and, therefore, it was held that to hate one's enemy was not forbidden by the law (Matt. 5:43). But Jesus, in the parable of the good Samaritan (Luke 10:29-37), taught that all the world were neighbors. Moreover, the Pharisees used the term neighbor in a very exclusive sense, viz., one who observed the law in the strictest manner. They called themselves neighbors; and, therefore, the question, "who is my neighbor?"

Ne′keb (nē′kĕb; *a hollow, narrow passage*), a town on the border of Naphtali (Josh. 19:33), half-way between Tiberias and Mount Tabor.

Neko′da (nḗ-kō′dȧ; *distinguished, speckled*).
1. One of the Nethinim whose descendants returned to Jerusalem after the captivity (Ezra 2:48; Neh. 7:50), B. C. 536.
2. The sons of Nekoda were among those who went up after the captivity from Telmelah, Tel-harsa, and other places, but were

unable to prove their descent from Israel (Ezra 2:60; Neh. 7:62).

Nem'uel (nĕm'ū-ĕl; or perhaps for *Jemuel, day of God*).

1. The first named son of Eliab, a Reubenite and brother of Dathan and Abiram (Num. 26:9), B. C. about 1438.

2. The eldest son of Simeon (I Chron. 4:24), from whom were descended the family of the Nemuelites (Num. 26:12). In Gen. 46:10 he is called *Jemuel* (*q. v.*).

Nem'uelites (nĕm'ū-ĕl-īts; Num. 26:12), descendants of *Nemuel*, 2 (*q. v.*), of the tribe of Simeon.

Ne'pheg (nē'fĕg).

1. One of the sons of Izhar, the son of Kohath (Exod. 6:21).

2. One of David's sons, born to him in Jerusalem (II Sam. 5:15; I Chron. 3:7; 14:6), B. C. after 1000.

Nephew is the rendering of Heb. *bēn*, normally "son" Judg. 12:14; *nĕkĕd, offspring*, Job 18:19; Isa. 14:22; Gr. *'ekyonon*, I Tim. 5:4; in the old English sense of *grandson*, or *descendant*.

Neph'ilim (nĕf'ĭ-lĭm; Gen. 6:4; Num. 13:33). *See* Giant. The Nephilim are considered by many as giant demigods, the unnatural offspring of the "daughters of men" (mortal women) in cohabitation with the "sons of God" (angels). This utterly unnatural union, violating God's created orders of being, was such a shocking abnormality as to necessitate the world-wide judgment of the Flood.

Ne'phish (nē'fĭsh; I Chron. 4:19). *See* Naphish.

Nephish'esim (nē-fĭsh'ê-sĭm; Neh. 7:52). *See* Nephusim.

Neph'thalim (nĕf'thà-lĭm; Matt. 4:13, 15; Rev. 7:6). *See* Naphtali.

Nephto'ah, The Water of (nĕf-tō'à; *an opening*), the spring or source of the water or (inaccurately) waters of Nephtoah, was one of the landmarks in the boundary line which separated Judah from Benjamin (Josh. 15:9; 18:15). It lay northwest of Jerusalem, in which direction it seems to have been satisfactorily identified in *Ain Lifta*, a spring situated a little distance above the village of the the same name. Nephtoah was formerly identified with various springs—the spring of St. Philip (*Ain Haniyeh*) in the *Wady el Werd;* the *Ain Yalo* in the same valley, but nearer Jerusalem; the *Ain Karim,* or Fountain of the Virgin of mediaeval times, and even the so-called Well of Job at the western end of the *Wady Aly.*

Nephu'sim (nē-fū'sĭm), the head of a family of Nethinim who returned with Zerubbabel from Babylon (Ezra 2:50), B. C. about 536. The parallel text (Neh. 7:52) has *Nephishesim.*

Ner (nûr; *light, lamp*), a Benjamite, father of Kish and Abner, and grandfather of King Saul (I Sam. 14:50; 26:5; II Sam. 2:8; I Chron. 8:33), B. C. about 1100. The statement in I Chron. 9:36, that Kish and Ner were both sons of Jehiel, is explained by the supposition of an elder Kish, uncle of Saul's father, or, rather, Ner's grandfather.

Ne'reus (nē'rê-ŭs; Lat. from Gr., the name of a sea god), a Christian at Rome saluted with his sister, by the apostle Paul (Rom. 16:15), A. D. 60 (55). A legendary account of him is given in *Acta Sanctorum,* from which may be gathered the tradition that he was beheaded at Terracina, probably in the reign of Nerva. His ashes are said to be deposited in the ancient church of *SS. Nereo et Archileo* at Rome.

Ner'gal (nûr'găl), one of the chief Assyrian dieties. *See* Gods, False.

Ner'gal-Share'zer (nûr'găl-shà-rē'zĕr; Akkad. *Nergal-shar-uṣur, Nergal, protect the king*), the name of two princes, the one Assyrian, the other Babylonian.

1. In the biblical description of the end of the reign of Sennacherib he is said to have been killed by his two sons, Adrammelech and Sharezer (II Kings 19:37; Isa. 37:38). There is little doubt that this name Sharezer is simply the latter part of the name Nergalsharezer. The name is given by Abydemus as Nergilos, so that the Old Testament has preserved the latter half of his name and the Greek historian the first half. Abbreviations of names in this manner are common among Assyrians and Babylonians. The Assyrian story of the death of Sennacherib is much more brief in its details, and does not mention the names of his murderers. It is as follows: "On the twentieth day of Tebet Sennacherib, king of Assyria, was killed by his son during an insurrection. . . . From the twentieth day of Tebet to the second day of Adar the insurrection continued, and on the eighteenth day of Sivan (of the following year) Esarhaddon ascended the throne." It will be observed that in this account the death of Sennacherib is ascribed to the act of one son, and not to two, as in the Old Testament. It is a probable conjecture that the death of the Assyrian king was due to the jealousy felt for his son Esarhaddon, who succeeded him.

2. The name of one of the Babylonian princes belonging to the retinue of Nebuchadnezzar (Jer. 39:3, 13). He held the office of *rab-mag* and is the Nergalsharuṣur, Greek Neriglissar, who married one of Nebuchadnezzar's daughters, murdered Evil-merodach (*q. v.*), his brother-in-law, and ascended the throne, reigning from 560-556.

Ne'ri (nē'rī), the son of Melchi, and father of Salathiel, in the genealogy of Christ (Luke 3:27).

Neri'ah (nē-rī'à; *lamp of Jehovah*), the son of Maaseiah and father of Baruch, the amanuensis of Jeremiah (Jer. 32:12, 16; 36:4, 8, 14, 32; 43:3, 6; 45:1; 51:59). He is probably the same as the preceding.

Ne'ro (nē'rō; II Tim., *subscription*), a Roman emperor, born at Antium, probably December 15, A. D. 37, was the son of Cneius Domitius Ahenobarbus by Agrippina, the sister of Caligula, his original name being Lucius Domitius Ahenobarbus. When he was twelve years old his mother married her uncle, the emperor Claudius, who four years afterward gave his daughter Octavia to Nero in marriage, having formally adopted him under the name of Nero Claudius Caesar Drusus Germanicus. He succeeded Claudius, A. D. 54, and for five years showed clemency and justice, though his private life was extremely licentious. Later he caused the death of Britannicus, the son and heir of Claudius. In A. D. 59 he procured from the Senate an order for the death of his mother to please his paramour, Poppaea, the wife of Otho. This was soon followed by the divorce of Octavia and Nero's marriage to Poppaea. In A. D. 64 a dreadful conflagration raged in Rome, said to have been started by Nero, who is reported to have watched the progress of the flames from the top of a high tower, chanting to his own lyre verses on the destruction of Troy. The truth of this story is doubtful, but it was believed at the time, and Nero sought to assign the odium of the conflagration to the Christians, many of whom were put to death. Having killed Poppaea by a kick when she was with child, Nero proposed to marry An-

327. Nero

tonia, his adopted sister, and on her refusal ordered her to be put to death. He then married Statilia Messalina, .whose husband Vestinus he had assassinated for marrying Messalina after the emperor had cohabited with her.

The jurist Longinus was exiled, and the most virtuous citizens were put to death. In the midst of these sad events Nero's ambition seemed to be to excel in circus games. He went to Greece to show his ability as musician and charioteer in the Olympian games returning to Rome in great pomp as victor. The formidable insurrection which broke out in Gaul alarmed Nero, and deserted by the pretorian guard and condemned to death by the Senate, he committed suicide.

It was during Nero's reign that the war commenced between the Jews and Romans which terminated in the destruction of Jerusalem by Titus. Nero was the emperor before whom Paul was brought on his first imprisonment at Rome; and in the persecution of the Christians by Nero Paul and Peter are supposed to have suffered martyrdom. The early Christians thought that Nero would return as Antichrist; and many modern writers find his name in the mystic number of the Apocalypse (Rev. 13:18).

Nest (Heb. *qēn*, from *qānǎn*, to *build;* Gr. *kataskēnōsis*, *encampment*, a *perch*). The following are Scripture references to the nests of birds: The law (Deut. 22:6, 7) directs that if anyone found a bird's nest by the road upon a tree or upon the ground, with young ones or eggs, and the mother sitting upon them, he was to let the mother go. The liking of the eagle for localities removed from man and command-

ing a wide view is referred to in Job 39:27, 28, "Doth not the eagle mount up at thy command, and make her nest on high?" etc. The loftiness of the eagle's nest was proverbial; it was "among the stars" (Obad. 4). The rock dove in Palestine often builds a nest on cliffs over abysses (Jer. 48:28).

Figurative. "*To die in one's nest*" (Job 29:18) seems to mean in the bosom of one's family, with children to succeed him. "To make his nest as high as the eagle" was a phrase by which the prophets reproved the pride and ambition of men (Jer. 49:16; Hab. 2:9). The figure of the partridge "gathering young which she hath not brought forth" (Jer. 17:11, marg.) is applied to one who gathers riches unlawfully; the robbing of a nest in the absence of the parent birds is symbolical of an easy victory (Isa. 10:14); the dominion exercised over the surrounding nations by Assyria is symbolized under the figure of a cedar of Lebanon, in whose boughs all the fowls of heaven made their nests (Ezek. 31:3-6; comp. Dan. 4:21).

Net, the rendering of several Hebrew and Greek words, and the frequency of images derived from them and show that nets were much used by the Hebrews for fishing, fowling, and hunting.

1. **Fishing Nets.** Of fish nets among the Hebrews we have no direct information, but it is likely that they were similar to those of the Egyptians. These used two kinds—the drag net, with floats on the upper edge and leads on the lower edge to keep it close to the bottom (Isa. 19:9). It was sometimes let down from a boat, while those who pulled it usually stood on the shore. In lake fishing the net is cast from and drawn into the boat, except in case of a large draught, when the fishermen dragged the net after their boats to the shore (John 21:6, 8). A smaller net was sometimes used for fishing in shallow water. It was furnished with a pole on either side; and the fisherman, holding a pole in each hand, thrust it below the surface of the water, awaiting the moment when the fish passed over it. This, or a smaller landing net, was used to land fish wounded with a spear or caught by a hook.

2. **Fowling Nets.** The Egyptians used the trap and the clap-net. "The trap was generally made of network, strained over a frame. It consisted of two semicircular sides or flaps of equal size, one or both moving on the common bar, or axis, upon which they rested. When the traps were set the two flaps were kept open by means of strings, probably of catgut, which, the moment the bait that stood in the center of the bar was touched, slipped aside, and allowed the two flaps to collapse, and thus secured the bird. Another kind, which was square, appears to have closed in the same manner; but its construction was different, the framework running across the center, and not, as in the others, round the edges of the trap. The clap-net was of different forms, though on the same general principle as the traps. It consisted of two sides, or frames, over which the network was strained; at one end was a short rope, which was fastened to a bush or a cluster of reeds, and

at the other was one of considerable length, which, as soon as the bird was seen feeding in the area of the net, was pulled by the fowlers, causing the two sides to collapse" (Wilkinson, *Anc. Egypt.*, ii, pp. 180, 182).

3. **Hunting Nets.** These were of universal use among the Hebrews, and were probably, like those of the Egyptians, of two kinds— one, a long net, furnished with several ropes, and supported on forked poles, varying in length to correspond with the inequalities of the ground over which it was extended. The other was smaller and used for stopping gaps, and is probably alluded to in Job 19:6; Psa. 140:5; Isa. 51:20.

4. **"Net"** (Heb. *sᵉbäk, twined*) is applied to network or latticework, especially round the capitals of columns ("network, wreathen work," etc., I Kings 7:18, 20, 41, 42; II Kings 25:17; II Chron. 4:12, 13; Jer. 52:22, 23), and also before a window or balcony ("lattice," II Kings 1:2).

Figurative. The spreading of the net is an appropriate image of the subtle devices of enemies (Psa. 9:15; 10:9; 25:15, etc.). "Fishes taken in an evil net" (Prov. 9:12) is figurative of men suddenly overtaken of evil, the unexpected suddenness of the capture being the point of comparison. "A wild bull (antelope) in a net" (Isa. 51:20) is the figure of one exhausted with ineffectual attempts to release himself. Being caught in a net represents the unavertable vengeance of God (Lam. 1:13; Ezek. 12:13; Hos. 7:12). In Hab. 1:14-16 "hooks" and "nets" are great and powerful armies by which the Chaldeans gained dominion over lands and peoples and brought home the spoil. To "sacrifice unto the net" (v. 16) is to attribute to the means which he has employed the honor due to God.

Nethan′eel (nē-thăn′ē-ĕl; *God gives*), in R. V. Nethanel (nē-thăn′ĕl).

1. The son of Zuar, and chief of the tribe of Issachar at the exodus (Num. 1:8; 2:5; 7:18, 23; 10:15), B. C. 1440.

2. The fourth son of Jesse, David's father (I Chron. 2:14), B. C. about 1026.

3. One of the priests who "blew the trumpets before the ark" when it was brought from the house of Obed-edom (I Chron. 15:24), B. C. about 989.

4. A Levite, and father of the scribe Shemaiah (I Chron. 24:6).

5. The fifth son of Obed-edom, and one of the porters of the temple appointed by David (I Chron. 26:4), B. C. before 960.

6. One of the princes commissioned by King Jehoshaphat to teach in the cities of Judah (II Chron. 17:7), B. C. about 870.

7. One of the chief Levites who made offerings when the observance of the passover was renewed by King Josiah (II Chron. 35:9), B. C. about 621.

8. A priest of the family of Pashur in the time of Ezra who had married a foreign wife (Ezra 10:22), B. C. 456.

9. The representative of the priestly family of Jedaiah in the time of Joiakim, the son of Jeshua (Neh. 12:21), B. C. before 445.

10. A Levite, of the sons of Asaph, who took part in the dedication of the wall of Jerusalem (Neh. 12:36).

Nethani′ah (nĕth-à-nī′à; *Jehovah bestows*).

1. The son of Elishama and father of Ishmael, who murdered Gedaliah (II Kings 25: 23, 25; Jer. 40:8, 14, 15; 41:1, sq.). He was of the royal family of Judah, B. C. before 586.

2. One of the four sons of Asaph the minstrel (I Chron. 25:2). He was chief of the fifth division of the temple musicians (v. 12), B. C. about 961.

3. One of the Levites appointed by Jehoshaphat to accompany the "princes" who were to teach the law in the cities of Judah (II Chron. 17:8), B. C. 869.

4. The father of Jehudi, which latter was sent by the princes to request Baruch to read the roll to them (Jer. 36:14), B. C. about 606.

Neth′inim (nĕth′ĭ-nĭm; those *given*, i. e., to the temple), the name applied to those who were set apart to do the menial work of the sanctuary.

1. **Origin and Duties.** As early as the time of Joshua the Gibeonites had been appointed to act as hewers of wood and drawers of water for the sanctuary (Josh. 9:21), and thus became the original Nethinim. As these Gibeonites were greatly decreased in numbers by the persecutions of Saul and in the massacre at Nob (I Sam. 22:1-19), and as the service as arranged by David required an increase of menial servants, "David and the princes gave the *Nethinim* for the service of the Levites" (Ezra 8:20). These were, probably, prisoners of war who had become proselytes, and are called Nethinim in post-exilian times (I Chron. 9:2; Ezra 2:43; 7:7; Neh. 7:46). Being given to the Levites, their duty was to relieve the latter of every menial and laborious work connected with the temple, such as drawing wood, carrying water, etc. No prescribed list of duties is given in the Scriptures, as these servants were entirely at the disposal of the Levites.

2. **Number, Revenue, Position, etc.** The first Nethinim, it must be remembered, were the Levites, who were *given* to Aaron and his sons (Num. 3:9; 8:19). These were, as already mentioned, relieved by the Gibeonites. For convenience they most probably lived near the temple, and were supported by contributions of the people. Only six hundred and twelve Nethinim returned from Babylon— three hundred and ninety-two with Zerubbabel (Ezra 2:58; Neh. 7:60), and two hundred and twenty with Ezra (Ezra 8:20), under the leadership of Ziha and Gispa (Neh. 11: 21), who, as their foreign names indicate, were of their own body. Some of the Nethinim lived in Ophel, which they helped to rebuild (3:26; 11:21), because of its proximity to the temple; while others, as before the exile, dwelt in the Levitical cities (Ezra 2:70). They were governed by a chief of their own body (Ezra 2:43; Neh. 7:46). Like the other sacred ministers they were exempted from taxation by the Persian satrap (Ezra 7:24), and were supported from the temple treasury and the second tithes. Though they conformed to the Jewish religion (Exod. 12:48; Deut. 29:11; Josh. 9:21; Neh. 10:28) they occupied a very low position, being reckoned below the *Mamzer*, or illegal offspring (Mishna, *Kiddushin*, iii, 12; iv, 1; *Jebamoth*, ii, 4). According to

Jewish authorities they were restricted to intermarriage among themselves, and if a Jew or Jewess married one of them, the issue shared in all the disqualifications of the Nethinim; and they were not exempted from military service when newly married. If a woman was suspected of being deflowered, or if she had an illegitimate child, it was ascribed to a *Nathin*, and offspring took the degraded position of the *Nathin*, unless the mother could bring proof as to other fatherhood. The decision of a court of justice was invalid if one of the members was a *Nathin*, as he was not to be considered to be a member of the congregation specified in Lev. 4:13; Num. 35:24. Eventually they appear to have been merged in the Jewish population, as no allusion to them occurs either in the Apocrypha or the New Testament.

Neto'phah (nē-tō'fà; *dripping, distillation*), a place in Judah, near Bethlehem, fifty-six of whose people returned with Zerubbabel from captivity (Ezra 2:22; Neh. 7:26). Mahari and Heleb (or Heldai), two of David's guard, were from Netophah (I Chron. 27:13, 15), as well as one of the captains who remained under arms near Jerusalem after its destruction by Nebuchadnezzar (9:16).

Neto'phathites (nē-tō'fà-thīts; *the Netophathite;* except Neh. 12:28, A. V. "Netophathi," R. V. "the Netophathites"), inhabitants of Netophah, which was near Bethlehem or connected with it (Neh. 7:26; comp. I Chron. 2:54), and seems to have belonged to Judah, since Maharai the Netophathite was a Zarhite (I Chron. 27:13; comp. Josh. 7:17), and Heldai the Netophathite was "of Othniel" (I Chron. 27:15; comp. Judg. 1:8-13). Netophah itself is mentioned only in Ezra 2:22; Neh. 7:26; but as two of David's men, Maharai and Heldai, just mentioned, were Netophathites, the town must have existed long before. The Jewish authors have a tradition "that the Netophathites slew the guards which had been placed by Jeroboam on the road leading to Jerusalem, to stop the passage of the first fruits from the country villages to the temple. . . . Jeroboam's obstruction, which is said to have remained in force till the reign of Hoshea. . . . was commemorated by a fast on the 23d Sivan," which is said to be still retained in the Jewish calendar. The Mishna mentions "oil of Netophah" and valley of "Beth Netophah." The site is now identified with Khirbet Bedd Faluḥ, about 3½ miles S. of Bethlehem.

Nettles. *See* Vegetable Kingdom.

Network. 1. The grate of the altar of burnt offering (Exod. 27:4; 38:4). (Heb. *rĕshĕth*.)

2. The plaited work around the two court pillars of the temple (I Kings 7:18, 20, 42), which, according to Keil (*Com.*, in loc.), was formed of seven cords plaited together in the form of festoons (comp. Jer. 52:22, 23). (Heb. *sᵉbäkäh*.)

3. "White works," the general name for cotton fabrics, or the different kinds of byssus that were woven in Egypt (Heb. *ḥōr, white*), Isa. 19:9 margin.

New Birth, the technical expression frequently used for regeneration (*q. v.*).

New Moon. *See* Festivals, I, 5.

Newness (Gr. *kainotēs*), a new state of spirit or life in which the Spirit places the believer (Rom. 6:4; 7:6).

New Testament. The New Testament or "New Covenant" is a term describing a portion of the Bible revealed in fulfillment of the O. T. and dealing with the nativity, ministry, life, death, resurrection and ascension of the predicted Messiah and the inauguration of the new dispensation of the Christian Church on the Day of Pentecost. The ministry of Christ is set forth in the four gospels. These gospels record selections from the events of Christ's life, Taken together they set forth a Personality, not a biography. The twenty-nine formative years of the Messiah are passed over silently. This silence is only once or twice broken. The gospels present not everything the Son of God did but they introduce in a wonderful way "The Doer." The gospels are elucidated by the O. T. The foreview of Christ, presenting and including His Person, work and kingdom are indispensable requisites to opening up the gospels. To understand the gospels one must not confuse the kingdom offered to Israel and the Church of Jesus Christ. The throne of David (Luke 1:32) must not be made identical with "My Father's throne" (Rev. 3:21), nor must the House of Jacob (Luke 1:33) be construed as the Church of Jesus Christ. It must also be remembered that the mission of the Messiah was primarily to the Jewish Nation (10:5, 6; 15:23, 25; John 1:11). He was "a minister of the circumcision" (Rom. 15:8). He fulfilled the law, died under the law, and set us free from the law (cf. Gal. 4:4). Therefore, to understand the gospels one must expect to be on legal ground up to the cross (Matt. 10:5, 6; 15:22-28; Mark 1:44). The Sermon on the Mount must be seen to be law, not grace. It demands perfect character which grace alone through divine power can produce. In understanding the N. T. it also must be borne in mind that the full-orbed revelation concerning grace is to be found in the epistles, not in the gospels and that Christ by His life, death and resurrection made possible the operation of divine grace. The gospels do not present the doctrine of the Church. Not until the Messiah was rejected as King and Savior by the Jews did He begin to announce a "mystery," until that moment "hid in God" (Eph. 3:3-10). His great new announcement was "I will build My Church" (Matt. 16:16-18). This Church was still future for it is based upon a wholly new operation of the Spirit, His baptizing work (Matt. 3:11; Mark 1:8; Luke 3:16, 17 cf. Acts 1:5 and 11:16). A study of these Scriptures reveals that the baptism of the Spirit occurred between Acts 1:5 and 11:16; that is, in the pivotal new beginning inaugurated on the day of Pentecost. On this day the Holy Spirit came to perform His baptizing work for the first time and consequently to give birth to the Christian Church. The rest of the N. T. deals with the great Pauline revelation governing this new Body and the rest of the N. T. books give practical teaching for this period. The Book of Revelation outlines the future and destiny of the Church (chaps. 2 and 3), as well as the destiny of Israel after her tribulation and establishment of the Kingdom (chaps. 4-20). The final two chapters present the eternal state. Since the dispensation of grace was not begun until the cross when "the veil of the temple was rent in twain from top to bottom" (Matt. 27:51), the term N. T. is rather a popular accommodation to describe the latter portion (less than one-third) of divine revelation rather than a strictly accurate usage. *M. F. U.* See Testament.

New Year, or **Feast of Trumpets.** *See* Festivals, I, 2.

Nezi'ah (nē-zī′à; *illustrious*), one of the Nethinim whose descendants accompanied Zerubbabel from Babylon (Ezra 2:54; Neh. 7:56), B. C. about 536.

Ne'zib (nē′zĭb; a *statue*, or *idol*), a town on the lowland of Judah, mentioned between Ashnah and Keilah (Josh. 15:43). It is to be located at Khirbet Beit Neṣib, about 2¼ miles S. of Khirbet Ḳila.

Nib'haz (nĭb′hăz), an Avite deity (II Kings 17:31). *See* Gods, False.

Nib'shan (nĭb′shăn), a town in the wilderness of Judah, on the shore of the Dead Sea, near Engedi (Josh. 15:62), but location not definite.

Nica'nor (nĭ-kā′nôr; Gr., *victorious*), a deacon of the church at Jerusalem (Acts 6:5).

Ni'cene Creed. *See* Creed.

Nicode'mus (nĭk-ô-dē′mŭs; Gr., *victor over the people*).

1. **Family.** His family is unknown, though some recognize him as Nicodemus Ben Gorion, the brother of Josephus the historian. This Nicodemus was a member of the Sanhedrin, and counted one of the three richest men of Jerusalem. But it was said that he afterward became poor; and his daughter was seen gathering barleycorns for food from under the horses' feet. Some have conjectured that this was the result of the persecutions he received for having embraced Christianity (Whedon, *Com.*, John 3:1).

2. **Personal History.** (1) **Interview with Jesus.** Nicodemus was a Pharisee and a member of the Sanhedrin. Being convinced by his miracles that Jesus was a "teacher come from God," he sought an interview with him; but fear of the Jews and a regard for his reputation, no doubt, influenced him to make the visit by night. He opened the conversation by an announcement of his belief in Christ's divine mission, and was answered by a declaration of the wonderful doctrine of the new birth (John 3:1-10). Jesus also maintained that this doctrine of regeneration should be accepted upon his own divine authority (vers. 10-13), and insisted upon the doctrine of responsibility for unbelief (vers. 18-21). (2) **Defends Jesus.** When, upon a later occasion, the officers sent to apprehend Christ returned without him, and were reproached by the rest of the Sanhedrin, Nicodemus said to them, "Doth our law judge any man before it hear him, and know what he doeth?" His timid word is answered by taunts, "Art thou also of Galilee?" and the old ignorant dogmatism, "Search and look: for out of Galilee ariseth no prophet" (7:45-52). (3) **At Christ's burial.** Perhaps encouraged by the example

of Joseph of Arimathea, Nicodemus assisted at the burial of Jesus. He brought a mixture of myrrh and aloes, about a hundred pounds' weight, to anoint the body, and assisted in its embalming and burial (19:39-42). Nothing further is known of Nicodemus from Scripture. Tradition adds that after he had thus publicly declared himself a follower of Jesus, and had been baptized by Peter, he was displaced from his office and expelled from Jerusalem.

3. **Character.** "A constitutional timidity is observable in all that the Gospel tells us about Nicodemus; a timidity which could not be wholly overcome even by his honest desire to befriend and acknowledge one whom he knew to be a prophet, even if he did not at once recognize in him the promised Messiah" (Farrar, *Life of Christ*, p. 92).

Nicola'itans (nĭk-ô-lā′ĭ-tănz), a sect or party which arose in the apostolic period of the Church, and is twice mentioned by name in the epistle to Ephesus and Pergamos (Rev. 2:6, 15). In the former passage it is said, to the credit of the church in Ephesus, that she shared in the feelings of the Lord concerning the Nicolaitans, and viewed them with the hatred which they deserved. In the epistle to Pergamos (v. 15) the charge is made that some of that church held to teachings of the Nicolaitans, who are compared to those who "hold the teaching of Balaam," etc. "The general voice of antiquity accuses them of holding the lawfulness of eating things offered to idols, and of mixing in and encouraging idolatrous worship; and as they are charged with denying God to be the creator of the world, and attributing its existence to other powers, they could unquestionably, on such grounds, permit themselves so to act, and thus far it is probable that the accusation is not ill-founded. The community of women was another doctrine which they are said to have adopted, and their conduct seems to have been in the highest degree licentious" (*Imp. Dict.*, s. v.). The real origin of the sect will perhaps never be ascertained with certainty. *See* Nicolaus.

Nicola'us (nĭk-ô-lā′ŭs, *conqueror of the people*), A. V. **Nic'olas** (nĭk′ô-làs; Gr., *victor over the ple*), a native of Antioch who had become a proselyte to the Jewish faith. He was afterward converted to Christianity, and was elected one of the first seven deacons (Acts 6:5). By some it has been believed that the sect of the Nicolaitans was founded by this Nicolas, but of this there is no positive evidence.

Nicop'olis (nĭ-kŏp′ô-lĭs; *city of victory*), a city to which Paul refers (Tit. 3:12), as the place where he intended to pass the following winter. Titus was at this time in Crete (1:5). There were several cities of this name, which leaves some doubt as to the one about which Paul wrote. Of the three, one was in Thrace, another in Cilicia, and a third in Epirus; the latter seems the most likely to have been meant. This was built by the Emperor Augustus Caesar in 30 B. C. in honor of a victory at Actium, which was only 4 miles distant.

Ni'ger (nī′jẽr; *black*), of Antioch (Acts 13:1). *See* Simeon, 5.

Night. *See* Time.

Figurative. The expression, "The morning cometh, and also the night" (Isa. 21:12), is thus interpreted by Delitzsch (*Com.*, in loc.), "even if the morning dawns, it will be swallowed up again directly by night. And the history was quite in accordance with such an answer. The Assyrian period of judgment was followed by the Chaldean, and the Chaldean by the Persian, the Persian by the Grecian, and the Grecian by the Roman." Thus night stands for a period of distress or trouble, and by a natural extension in the same line, so is *death* or the *grave* (John 9:4). "Children of the night" (I Thess. 5:5) are those who practice the deeds of depravity. "Night" is also used for a time of ignorance and helplessness (Mic. 3:6).

Night Hawk. *See* Animal Kingdom.

Night Marches. From Num. 9:21, "whether it was by day or by night that the cloud was taken up they journeyed," it is evident that the Israelites made *night marches*. Such marches might have been made either to escape heat or to avoid their many enemies—the Amalekites, Edomites, or Ammonites.

Night Monster (Heb. *lîlîth*, Isa. 34:14, marg.). The text has screech owl (*q. v.*), but the marginal reading is preferable. In Assyrian, Lilith was a "night demon," and the Biblical reference is apparently to a demonic creature; something seen in the night by special divine revelation. Respecting Dan. 2:19, "Then was the secret revealed unto Daniel in a night vision," Keil (*Com.*, in loc.) says: "A vision of the night is not necessarily to be identified with a dream. It is possible, indeed, that dreams may be, as the means of a divine revelation, dream visions, and as such may be called visions of the night, but in itself a vision of the night is a vision simply which anyone receives during the night while he is awake."

Night Watch. *See* Watch.

Nile, the one great river of Egypt navigable for larger craft for 2900 miles into the interior of Africa from the Mediterranean. Small craft can navigate it for 4000 miles. The name "Nile," from the Greek *Neilos*, Latin *Nilus*, probably means "dark blue," (cf. Arab., *En-nil*). The river is known to modern Egyptians as *El Bahr*, "the sea" (cf. Nahum 3:8). The Hebrew term is *Yeor*, which in the plural refers to the Nile River system (Isa. 7:18). The ancient Egyptians deified it as *Hapi*. Hecataeus of Miletus (5th century B. C.), accurately described Egypt as "the gift of the river." The geographer Ptolomey in the second century A. D. believed that the Nile River had its source in the heart of Africa at the base of "the Mountains of the Moon." Henry Stanley's discovery in 1888 proved the ancient geographer substantially correct. Stanley first caught sight of a cloud-wrapped mountain at the equator which he called "the Rain Maker." The Duke of Abruzzi in the early part of the twentieth century explored the 16,791-foot summit of the mountain and demonstrated that the Nile does rise in the Mountains of the Moon. Rains and melting snows from this mountain pour into the waters of Victoria, Albert and Edward Lakes, from which the Nile springs (James

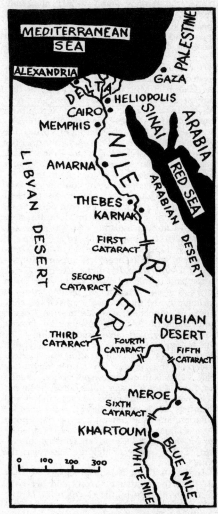

328. The Nile River

Ramsey Ullman, *High Conquest*, 1941, p. 152). The Nile is the second river of the world. The main part of the upper river is known as the White Nile (*el Bahr el Abyad*). The upper part of the Nile known as the White Nile is joined by the Blue Nile (*el Bahr el Azrak*) at Khartoum. The only other tributary is the Atbara flowing in from the S. E. The Nile is furnished a never-failing supply of water by almost daily equatorial rains.

The marvel of the Nile is its annual inundation. Occurring regularly, it over-flows its banks. At the beginning of June it commences its annual rise. Between July 15th and 20th it rises very rapidly. Toward the last part of September the water stops rising and remains constant for twenty to thirty days. In October it again rises, attaining its greatest height; then receding, the fields dry off in January, February and March, the soil becoming softened and fertilized, bearing splendid crops. Occasionally inundation failed to take place.

Under the famous Dynasty XII, a certain Egyptian official in the reign of Sesostris I speaks of unfruitful years when he did not collect arrears of the field due after short payment. In Joseph's time there was a serious seven-year famine (Gen. 41:54) due to failure of the inundation. There was likewise a recorded failure for seven years in the reign of the Caliph el-Mustansir. The famine at that time reached serious proportions in 1070 A. D. In pharaonic times the agricultural year consisted of three seasons: the inundation period—June to October; spring (or planting—October to February; summer (or harvest)—end of February to June. Today the great dam at Aswan gives Egypt a greater cultivatable area than in ancient times.

Between Khartoum at the confluence of the Blue and White Nile and Aswan (ancient Elephantine) there are six cataracts. From the first cataract at Aswan to Memphis, near modern Cairo, is a distance of 500 miles and was known as Upper Egypt. In the course of its last 100 miles from Memphis to the Mediterranean the Nile branches out into the so-called Delta, from its shape like the Greek letter, and is called Lower Egypt. The Delta forms a great triangle of fertile land cut through by the numerous mouths of the Nile, the most important of which are the Rosetta and Damietta. At the former the famous Rosetta Stone was uncovered, proving to be the key to the reading of ancient Egyptian hieroglyphics and inaugurating the modern science of Egyptology. In Upper Egypt the Nile Valley is mostly a narrow ribbon, usually not more than a dozen miles across, a thread of green wedged in between crags, shelves and relentless sands of the desert. The peculiar isolation and the advantages of the almost never-failing river gave Egypt an ideal locale for an early and very advanced stage of culture. Egypt in a very definite sense was the Nile.

In the O. T. the Nile is famous as the river in which the mother of Moses laid her babe in a papyrus boat by the river's brink (Exod. 2:3). The waters of the river were turned into blood at the time of the Exodus (Exod. 7:20f). The river of Egypt was famous for papyrus production (Isa. 19:7). Goshen was the N. E. area of the Delta nearest Palestine. In patriarchal times, evidently under the famous Twelfth Dynasty, Abraham migrated thither to escape dearth in the land of Canaan (Gen. 12:10-13:1). Joseph was sold into Egypt by his brothers and Jacob and his family settled there in a similar time of famine. (Gen. 46:3-50:26). Hebrews during their captivity built such store cities as Pithom and Raamses (Exod. 1:11). It was to Egypt that Joseph and Mary fled when endangered by the unscrupulous Herod (Matt. 2:13-21). Egypt was a site of great ancient cities whose monumental remains constitute great archaeological discoveries, such as Memphis, Amarna, Thebes, Heliopolis and others. *M. F. U.*

Nim'rah (nĭm'rà; *limpid*), a place mentioned, by this name, in Num. 32:3 only, among those who formed the districts of the "land of Jazer and the land of Gilead." It it is the same as *Beth-nimrah* (v. 36), which belonged to

329. Sailboat on the Nile

the tribe of Gad. It is located near the Wadi Sha'ib.

Nim'rim (nĭm'rĭm; *limpid waters* or [waters of] *the leopards*), a very fertile tract in Moab, southeast of the Dead Sea, probably in *Wady Nemeirah*. Springs existed near Beth-nimrah. These waters were cursed (Isa. 15:6; Jer. 48:34).

Nimrod (Heb. *rebel*), the son of Cush and founder of the kingdom of Babylon (Gen. 10:8, 9). In Micah 5:5, Babylon is designated as "the land of Nimrod." In the Bible Nimrod appears as a great personality in whom earthly imperial power first appears in human history. That this character is evil appears from several observations. 1. Earthly kingship initially comes into existence among the Hamitic peoples, upon one branch of which a prophetic curse was pronounced and in the entire family of which there is an absence of divine blessing (Gen. 9:25-27). 2. Nimrod is represented as the establisher of Babylon (Gen. 10:8, 9), which is invariably outlined in Scripture both in type and prophecy as a religiously and morally evil system (Isa. 21:9; Jer. 50:24; 51:64; Rev. 16:19; 17:5; 18:3). 3. Nimrod's name "no doubt suggested to the Israelites the idea of 'rebel' . . . against God" (A. Dillmann, *Genesis*, Edinburgh, 1897, Vol. 1, p. 350). The name Nimrod in the divine account is definitely meant to suggest the concept of rebellion as descriptive of the character of this first world empire-builder, despite the fact that the original name in Hamitic speech did not have this meaning. Nimrod has been explained plausibly as Sumerian (early non-Semetic Babylonian), *Nin-maradda*, "lord of Marad," a town S. W. of Kish (W. F. Albright, *O. T. Commentary*, Philadelphia, 1948, p. 138). If, however, Babylonian Cush is to be connected with the exceedingly ancient city kingdom of Kish founded c. 3200 B. C. from whence the Babylonian emperors of the third millennium B. C. took their titles of "kings of the world," archaeological light is thrown on the primeval imperial period preserved in the name of Nimrod. The dynasty of Kish consisting of twenty-three kings, is significantly enumerated first in the Mesopotamian dynasties which were established just after the Flood (cf. Jack Finegan, *Light From the Ancient Past*, 1946, p. 31; Thorkild Jacobsen, *The Sumerian King List, Assyriological Studies XI*, Chicago, 1939). Then, too, Nimrod is said to have been "a mighty hunter before Yahweh" (Gen.10:9). The simple meaning of this statement is that Nimrod was the exact opposite of the divine ideal of a king—that of a shepherd (cf. II Sam. 5:2; 7:7; Rev. 2:27; 19:15). Whereas a hunter gratifies himself at the expense of his victim, the shepherd expends himself for the good of the subjects of his care. Nimrod has been connected with the legendary name of Gilgamesh, the demi-god king of Uruk (Biblical Erech, Gen. 10:10), modern Warka, in S. W. Sumer. Although the beginning of Nimrod's kingdom is said to be "Babel and Erech and Akkad and Calneh in the land of Shinar," there is nothing to prove that Gilgamesh is a reflection of Nimrod. Others imagine that Nimrod is the Babylonian Merodach (Marduk) in human form. The existence in Mesopotamia of many cities preserving the name Nimrod is evidence of his widespread popularity in antiquity (cf. Birs Nimrud; Tell Nimrud, near Baghdad; the Mound of Nimrud (ancient Calah). Nimrod's designation as a "hunter" clearly connects him with the founding of the military state based on absolute force. However, Babylonian and Assyrian art picturing wild animals in hunting scenes may point to Nimrod also as a literal hunter, which in the Hebrew account is given a religious connotation. *M. F. U.*

Nimrud (*See* Calah).

Nim'shi (nĭm'shĭ), the grandfather of Jehu (II Kings 9:2, 14), but also briefly called his father (9:20; II Chron. 22:7).

Nin'eve (nĭn'ĕ-vĕ), the Grecized form (Luke 11:32) of *Nineveh* (*q. v.*).

Nin'eveh (nĭn'ĕ-vĕ), a famous and ancient city situated on the eastern bank of the Tigris River opposite the modern city of Mosul. The Bible names Nimrod as the founder of Nineveh (Gen. 10:8-10). In 612 B. C. the ancient splendid city and capital of the Assyrian Empire was so completely obliterated, according to its prophesied decimation by Hebrew prophets, that it became like a myth until its discovery by Sir Austen Layard and others in the 19th century. The site has now been extensively excavated. Its occupational levels reach back as far as prehistoric times. Excavated pottery indicates Sumerian origin. The actual walled city has been outlined to indicate an area three miles in length and less than a mile and a-half in breadth. The Hebrews, however, perhaps like other foreigners, were in the habit of embracing under the name Nineveh (Assyr. *Nuna* or *Ninua*), other cities. A modern comparison would be the complex of cities that constitute modern

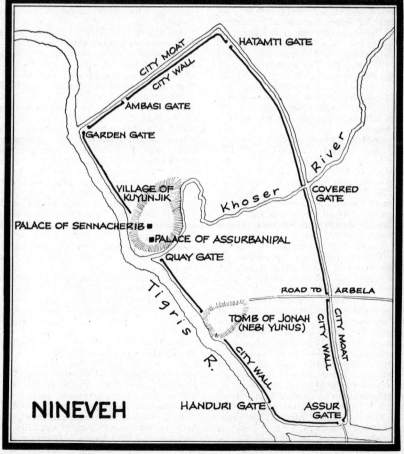

NINEVEH

330.

331. Relief from Palace of Sennacherib, Nineveh

New York. Such cities are Calah (*q. v.*), eighteen miles south; Resen, between Calah and Nineveh proper, and Rehoboth-Ir. The latter "must be Rebit-ninua, west of the capital, since the names are not only etymologically related but have the same meaning" (W. F. Albright in *O. T. Commentary*, Philadelphia, 1948, p. 138). The above-mentioned four places are catalogued in Gen. 10:11, 12 and Jon. 1:2; 3:2f; 4:11 as constituting "the great city." Other suburbs such as Tarbisu, Dursharrukin (or Sargonsburg) added to the aggregate size of "Nineveh" in the heyday of Assyrian empire.

Nineveh occurs early in cuneiform records under the reign of Gudea (21st century B. C.) and Hammurabi (c. 1700 B. C.). After the 12th century B. C. Nineveh became one of the royal residences of Assyria. Sargon II (722-702 B. C.) elevated it as the capital of the Assyrian Empire. Sennacherib (704-681 B. C.) greatly beautified and adorned the capital city. Splendid temples, palaces and fortifications made it the chief city of the empire (II Kings 19:36). Sennacherib built a massive wall forty to fifty feet high which extended for two and a-half miles along the Tigris and eight miles around the inner city. The defenses of the capital can still be traced. Sennacherib also built a water-system containing the oldest aqueduct in history at Jerwan, across the Gomer River. Austen Layard did the first successful digging in 1847, uncovering the splendid royal residence of Sennacherib in 1849-1851. He unearthed the 71-room palace with walls lined with sculptured slabs. The remains of Nineveh are a silent witness to the glory of Assyria under Sennacherib and his successors Esarhaddon (681-699 B. C.) and Ashurbanipal (669-626 B. C.). The Kuyunjik Mound not only yielded the vast palace of Sennacherib but also the royal residence and famous library of Ashurbanipal in which were housed 22,000 inscribed clay tablets. These are important for their accounts of the creation and flood and because they furnish scholars with invaluable background material for O. T. studies.

An alliance of Medes, Babylonians and Scythians destroyed Nineveh in August, 612 B. C., after a two-month siege. This great victory was due in part to the releasing of the city's water supply and the inundation of the Koser River, dissolving the sun-dried brick of which much of the city was built. Nahum prophesies the fall of the "bloody and cruel city" (Nah. 2:1-3:19; cf. Zeph. 2:13-15). Nineveh is a site so huge that perhaps it never will be completely excavated. A modern village covers one of the larger palaces. Cemeteries which cannot be disturbed cover other areas. Excavators have to bore through 30-45 feet of debris before Assyrian strata are reached. (For Nineveh's repentance see JONAH, BOOK OF). The nearby mound of Nebi Yunus, that is, "Mound of the Prophet Jonah," contains the palace of Esarhaddon. The popular tradition is that Jonah is buried beneath the mosque at Nebi Yunas. *M. F. U.*

Nin′evite (nĭn′ê-vīt; Luke 11:30), a "man of Nineveh" (Matt. 12:41).

Ni′san (nī′săn; Heb. *nisan*, from Akkad. *nisanu*, *beginning, opening*), the first month of the sacred year, called Abib in the Pentateuch, for which it is substituted only in the time of the captivity (Neh. 2:1; Esth. 3:7). *See* Calendar; Time.

Nis′roch (nĭs′rŏk; II Kings 19:37; Isa. 37:38), an Assyrian God. *See* Gods, False.

Niter. *See* Mineral Kingdom.

No or **No-A′mon** (nō-ă′mŏn; *the home of Amon, portion of Amon*), the name of the ancient Thebes, the chief seat of the worship of the god Ammon, denounced by Jeremiah (46:25). It was the metropolis of Upper Egypt, built on both sides of the Nile, and was a hundred and forty stadia in circuit, and celebrated for its hundred gates. Its ruins are the most notable on the Nile. It became celebrated in the eleventh dynasty, and suffered in the thirteenth because of the invasion of the Hyksos. In the 17th century B. C. Amosis liberated the country and it reached its height of magnificence. The splendor of the city departed with the removal of the residence of the Pharaohs to the Delta. In its ruins it is great. Its temple of Karnak is a marvel. Its architecture is a problem of mechanical skill. Its great hall contains one hundred and thirty-four columns, the loftiest seventy-five feet in height and twelve feet in diameter; the hall itself is one hundred and seventy-five feet wide by three hundred and twenty-nine feet long, every stone a book and every column a library in itself. The R. V. corrects some terms of reference to this place. In Jer. 46:25 "the multitude of No" is rendered "Amon of No;" in Nah. 3:8 the "populous No" is changed to "No-Amon."

Noadi′ah (nō-à-dī′à; *Jehovah convenes*).

1. One of the Levites who, with Meremoth, Eleazar, and others weighed the silver, gold, and vessels of the temple brought back from Babylon (Ezra 8:33), B. C. about 457.

2. A professed prophetess, who seems to have joined Tobiah and Sanballat in opposition to Nehemiah (Neh. 6:14), B. C. about 445.

No′ah (nō′à; *rest, quiet*).

1. The son of Lamech, and tenth in descent from Adam (Gen. 5:28, 29). Beyond the record of his birth the Scriptures tell us nothing of Noah till he was five hundred years old, when it mentions his three sons, Shem, Ham, and Japheth (5:32; 6:10). (1) **As preacher.** The wickedness of the human race had for a long time provoked the wrath of God. The cause of their unrighteousness was the intermarriage of the "sons of God" and the "daughters of men." Jehovah resolved to destroy the human race, but allowed a respite of one hundred and twenty years, during which Noah sought to bring them to repentance (Gen. 6:1-9; I Pet. 3:20; II Pet. 2:5). Thus he was "a preacher of righteousness," exercising faith in the testimony of God, and condemning the world by the contrasted excellence of his conduct. (2) **In the ark.** At length the cup of man's shocking iniquity, manifested in the breaking down of the divinely established orders of created beings (*see* Giants, Nephilim), was full, and the time of their destruction near at hand. Noah, because of his righteousness, was exempted from extermination, and was saved by means of the ark, constructed according to divine direction (Gen. 6:14-22). He entered the ark when he was six hundred years old, and the flood (*see* The Flood), commenced on the seventeenth day of the second month (7:6, 11), kept rising for forty days (vers. 12, 15), and only began to abate after one hundred and fifty days (8:3). On the seventeenth day of the seventh month the ark rested on Ararat, and after forty days Noah sent forth a raven, and at intervals of seven days (or a week) a dove. Finally, on the first day of the first month of his six hundred and first year, Noah removed the covering of the ark; and on the twenty-seventh day of the following month he returned again to dry land (8:4-19).

(3) **Noah's sacrifice.** The first thing that Noah did after leaving the ark was to build an altar and to offer sacrifice. He took his offerings from every clean beast and every clean fowl, such animals as were destined for man's food. God accepted the sacrifice, and promised no more to waste the earth with a plague of waters, but to continue without interruption the regular alternations of day and night, and of the seasons of the year (8:20-22). Jehovah blessed Noah and his sons, and pronounced his superiority over the inferior creation. All living creatures are given to man for food, with the prohibition against eating the blood. Provision is made for the security of human life against animals as well as men. To give Noah and his sons a firm assurance of the prosperous continuance of the human race, God established a covenant with them, and gave them as a sign the "bow in the cloud" (9:1-17). (4) **Intoxication.** After this Noah entered upon agricultural pursuits, and began to cultivate the vine. Whether in ignorance of its properties or not we do not know, but Noah drank of wine until intoxicated, and shamefully exposed himself in his tent. Ham saw the nakedness of his father displaying a lascivious bent of character, and told his brothers without, who reverently covered their father with a garment, walking backward that they might not see his nakedness. For this they received their father's blessing, whereas Ham reaped for his son Canaan a prophetic curse (9:20-27). (5) **Conclusion.** After this we hear no more of the patriarch but the sum of his years: "And Noah lived after the flood three hundred and fifty years. And all the days of Noah were nine hundred and fifty years; and he died" (9:28, 29). (6) **Character.** The character of Noah is given in a few words descriptive of him in Gen. 6:9: "Noah was a just man and perfect in his generations, and Noah walked with God;" i. e., he was *righteous* in his moral relations to God; *blameless* in his character and conduct. His righteousness and integrity were manifested in his walking with God. (7) **Noah and Archaeology.** In the Sumerian account of the Flood the flood hero appears under the name of Ziusudra and in the Babylonian version as Utnapishtim. The Babylonian account is contained in the eleventh chapter of the famous Gilgamesh Epic. Of all ancient traditions which bear upon the O. T., the Babylonian flood story, centering around Utnapishtim, manifests the most striking and detailed similarity to the Bible. Both Noah and his Babylonian counterpart are divinely warned of the flood, instructed to build a boat, pitch it with pitch and preserve human and animal life in it. Both accounts tell of the landing place of the boat and describe the sending out of birds. In both sacrifices are offered and with the idea of the gods or the One True God smelling the sacrifice. Both receive rewards after the flood. (For full account see Merrill F. Unger, *Archaeology and the Old Testament*, 1954, pp. 46-71; *The Epic of Gilgamesh in Ancient Near Eastern Texts*, edited by James R. Pritchard, Princeton, 1950; Alexander Heidel, *The Gilgamesh Epic and Old Testament Parallels*, Chicago, 1946.) *M. F. U.*

2. One of the five daughters of Zelophehad, of the tribe of Manasseh (Num. 26:33), B. C. c. 1435. As their father had died leaving no son, the daughters applied for an inheritance in the promised land in their father's right. Moses, under divine direction, granted their request (27:1, sq.), and this promise was redeemed by Joshua (Josh. 17:3).

Nob (nŏb), a sacerdotal city of Benjamin, situated on an eminence near Jerusalem. It would seem from Isa. 10:28-32, that it was on one of the roads leading from the north and within sight of the city. Here David applied to Ahimelech for bread, after he fled from Saul (I Sam. 21:1, sq.), from which it appears that the ark was then located there before being moved to Jerusalem (II Sam. 6:1, sq.). A company, of the Benjamites settled here after the return from the exile (Neh. 11:32). But the event for which Nob was most noted in the Scripture annals was a frightful massacre which occurred there in the reign of Saul (I Sam. 22:17-19). All trace of the name has disappeared from the country long ago. Jerome states that nothing remained in his time to indicate where it had been. Geographers are not agreed as to the precise spot with which we are to identify the ancient locality. Père Abel locates it on Scopus at Räs Umm et-Tala.

No'bah (nō'bà; a *barking*).

1. An Israelite, whose family is not named, but who probably belonged, like Jair, to one of the families of Machirites of the tribe of Manasseh. He took the town of Kenath and its villages (Heb. "daughters"), and gave it his own name, *Nobah* (Num. 32:42).

2. The name given by the above to the town of Kenath, after being taken by him (Num. 32:42).

No'bai (nō'bī). *See* Nebai.

Nobles. *See* Princes.

Nod (nŏd; *wandering, exile*). Its location is dependent upon that of Eden. The inhabitants of Bussorah and of Bushire claim that the land of Nod lay between these two cities on the northeast of the Persian Gulf. It was the retreat of Cain after the murder of Abel (Gen. 4:16). *See* Eden.

No'dab (nō'dăb; *nobility*), the name of a Bedouin tribe mentioned (I Chron. 5:19 only) in the account of the war of the Reubenites, Gadites, and the half tribe of Manasseh against the Hagarites. Nothing more is definitely known respecting them.

No'e (nō'ĕ), the Grecized form (Matt. 24:37, 38; Luke 3:36; 17:26, 27) of *Noah* (*q. v.*).

No'gah (nō'gà; *brilliance, lustre*), one of the sons of David who were born to him in Jerusalem by other wives than Bathsheba (I Chron. 3:7; 14:6), B. C. after 1000.

No'hah (nō'hà; *rest*), the fourth named of the sons of Benjamin, and the head of a family (I Chron. 8:2).

Non (nŏn), once (I Chron. 7:27) for *nun* (*nun*, "*fish*"), the father of Joshua.

Noon. *See* Time.

Noph (nŏf), the Hebrew name of the Egyptian city Memphis, the capital of lower Egypt. It was probably the seat of the Pharaohs in the time of Joseph, and raised by Psammeticus into the metropolis of the whole kingdom. Its

ruins are of great importance, including the colossal statue of Rameses. In Hos. 9:6 the Hebrew name is Moph, and translated *Memphis* (*q. v.*), which is its Greek and Latin form.

No'phah (nō'fà), one of the Moabite cities occupied by Amorites (Num. 21:30); probably the same as Nobah (Judg. 8:11), according to which passage it was near Jogbeha, not far from the eastern desert, and still existing in the ruined place called *Nowakis*, northwest of *Amman*.

North. 1. (Heb. *mᵉzärĕh, scatterer*, Job 37:9). The north wind, so called as dispersing clouds, and bringing clear, cold weather. Among the Hebrews the cardinal points of the heavens were considered with reference to the east. Thus to a man facing the east, the north would be at his left hand (Gen. 14:15; Job 23:9). Land lying to the north was considered as *higher*, and to the south as *lower;* hence to travel northward was to "go up" (Gen. 45: 25; Hos. 8:9; Acts 18:22; 19:1), while to travel southward was to "go down" (Gen. 12:10; 26:2; I Sam. 30:15, 16; 25:1; 26:2).

2. (Heb. *sàphōn, hidden*), the northern quarter of the heavens, called the "hidden," because the ancients regarded the north as the seat of gloom and darkness, in contrast to the bright and sunny south. Thus "Fair weather cometh out of the north" (Job 37:22); literally "gold cometh," which our version, with many excellent authorities, understands as meaning the golden splendor of the firmament, i. e., "fair weather." Delitzsch (*Com.,* in loc.) thinks that a contrast is made between the "gold" mined in the north and "the terrible majesty of Jehovah." The reason that Babylonia, Chaldea, Assyria, and Media were said to be north of Palestine (Zeph. 2:13; Jer. 1:14; 46:6, etc.; Ezek. 26:7) is that the kings of most of these countries, in order to avoid the deserts, invaded Palestine chiefly from the north side by way of Damascus and Syria; that is, via the so-called "Breasted's fertile crescent." By "the princes of the north" (Ezek. 32:30) some understand the Tyrians and their allies (26:16) joined with the Zidonians. "The families of the north" (Jer. 25:9) may mean kings who were dependent on Babylon; while "the king of the north" is the king of Syria, as opposed to the king of the south, viz., Egypt (Dan. 11:6-15, 40). The Hebrew word is applied to the north wind (Prov. 27:16; Cant. 4:16).

North Country. This name is applied to the countries lying north of Palestine, whence came invaders and foes (Isa. 41:25; Jer. 1:14, 15; Ezek. 26:7). *See* North.

Nose, Nostrils (Heb. *'àph;* dual *'àppàyïm*, properly *breathing place*, Num. 11:20). The same Hebrew word sometimes means *anger* (Prov. 22:24), as shown in the breathing.

Figurative. "I put my hook into thy nose" (II Kings 19:28; Job 41:2; Isa. 37:29) is a figurative expression taken from the custom of restraining wild animals, and means to control, humiliate. "Lo, they put the branch to their nose" (Ezek. 8:17) appears to be a proverbial expression variously interpreted. Some understand it as the barsom, which the Pharisees held in their hand while praying, or rather in front of the mouth as a magical mode of driving demons away. Two other explanations may be given—that it is a proverbial expression, "to apply the twig to anger," in the sense of adding fuel to the fire. The second, that of Hitzig, "They apply the sickle to their nose," i. e., by seeking to injure me they injure themselves (Keil, *Com.*, in loc.).

The words "they take away thy nose and ears" (Ezek. 23:25) are not to be interpreted, as the earlier expositors suppose, from the custom prevalent among the Egyptians and other nations of cutting off the nose of an adulteress, but depict the mutilation of prisoners.

Nose, Flat. *See* Diseases.

Nose Jewel. A ring worn in or on the nose as an adornment (Gen. 24:47 R. V.; Isa. 3:21; Ezek. 16:12). *See* Jewelry.

Novice (Gr. *neophutos, newly planted*), one lately converted, not yet matured in Christian experience (I Tim. 3:6). Later the term came to be applied to catechumens preparing for baptism.

Number, the rendering of several Hebrew and Greek words.

1. **Mode of Expressing Numbers.** Like most oriental nations, it is probable that the Hebrews in their written calculations made use of the letters of the alphabet. That they did so in post-Babylonian times we have conclusive evidence in the Maccabaean coins; and it is highly probable that this was the case also in earlier times. But, though, on the one hand, it is certain that in all existing manuscripts of the Hebrew text of the Old Testament the numerical expressions are written at length, yet, on the other, the variations in the several versions between themselves and from the Hebrew text, added to the evident inconsistencies in numerical statement between certain passages of that text itself, seem to prove that some shorter mode of writing was originally in vogue, liable to be misunderstood, and in fact misunderstood by copyists and translators. These variations appear to have proceeded from the alphabetic method of writing numbers.

2. **Arithmetic.** Although we know but little of the arithmetic of the Hebrews, they must have made considerable progress in the science. Thus we find *addition* (Num. 1:26), *subtraction* (Lev. 27:18), *overplus* (Lev. 25:27; Num. 3:46, 48), *multiplication* (Lev. 27:16), *division* (25:50), while *fractions* appear frequently (Gen. 47:24; Lev. 5:16; 6:5; Num. 15:4; Ezek. 4:11; 45:13). The proportions of the measurements of the temple in Ezekiel presuppose a considerable proficiency in mathematics.

3. **Scripture Numerics.** Many interpreters of Scripture are persuaded that numbers in the Bible have a symbolic meaning.

See F. W. Grant, *The Numerical Bible, The Pentateuch*, pp. 11-20 for interpretation of the spiritual meaning of Bible numbers.

Numbers, Book of. The fourth book of the Pentateuch continuing the redemptive history of Israel where Exodus leaves off. As Genesis is the book of origins, Exodus the book of redemption, Leviticus the book of worship and fellowship, Numbers is the book of the service and walk of God's redeemed people.

1. **The Name.** The Septuagint title *Arithmoi* (numbers) was rendered *Liber Numeri* in the Vulgate, which appears in English as the Book of Numbers or simply Numbers. The book is so designated because it makes a double reference to taking a census of the Jewish People—Chapters 1-3 and Chapter 26. As was usual, the Jews named the book from its opening word *wayyedabber*, ("and He [Jehovah] said"), or more often from the fifth word *bemidbar* ("in the wilderness").

2. **The Aim.** Numbers continues the journey commenced in the book of Exodus, beginning with the events of the second month of the second year (Num. 10:11) and ending with the eleventh month of the fortieth year (Deut. 1:3). The thirty-eight years of wandering deal with the failure of the redeemed people in the face of every divine provision for their welfare and success. The book is typically significant in warning against the dangers of unbelief. The people disobeyed at Kadesh Barnea (Num. 14) and suffered repeated defeat and eventual death in the desert (20:1-33:49).

3. **The Contents.**

Part I. *Departure from Sinai*, 1:1-10:10
  a. The numbering of the people, 1:1-54
  b. The arranging of the camp, 2:1-34
  c. Instructing priest and Levite, 3:1-4:49
  d. Protecting from defilement, 5:1-31
  e. Giving the Nazarite Law, 6:1-27
  f. Enumerating gifts of princes, 7:1-89
  g. Lighting of the Tabernacle lamps, 8:1-4
  h. Cleansing of the Levites, 8:5-26
  i. Observing the Passover, 9:1-14
  j. Guiding the camp, 9:15-23
  k. Signals for calling and removing the camp, 10:1-10

Part II. *From Sinai to Moab*, 10:11-21:35
  a. From Sinai to Kadesh Barnea, 10:11-14:45
  b. The Desert wandering, 15:1-9:22
  c. From Kadesh Barnea to Moab, 21-22:1

Part III. *Plains of Moab*, 22:2-36:13
  a. Balaam's oracles, 22:1-25:18
  b. Instructions, 26:1-31:54
  c. Territorial distribution in East Jordan, 32:1-42
  d. Itinerary from Egypt, 33:1-56
  e. Instruction before entering the land, 34:1-36:13

4. **The Critical Theory.** Critics who deny Mosaic authorship divide Numbers into P (Priestly Code) and JE (Jehovistic-Elohistic narrative). Chapters 1:1-10:28 are supposedly a long extract from P, while JE is interwoven in the book. This criticism of Numbers, of a piece with Pentateuchal higher criticism in general, is based upon the same erroneous philosophic, literary, and religious presuppositions. It is a product of rationalistic scepticism which attempted to reconcile prevailing modes of thinking of the nineteenth century with the testimony of the Mosaic books. *M. F. U.*

Nun (nŭn; a *fish*, as prolific), an Ephraimite, and father of Joshua (Exod. 33:11; Num. 11:28; 13:8, 16; 14:6, 30, 38; 26:65; 27:18; 32:12, 28, etc.). There is no account given of his life. Also the 14th letter of the Hebrew alphabet. Cf. Ps. 119:105-112.

Nurse, Nursing (Heb. *yänăq, to give milk;* once *'ämăn, to support, foster,* Ruth 4:16). It is clear, both from Scripture and from Greek and Roman writers, that in ancient times the position of the nurse, wherever one was maintained, was one of much honor and importance (*see* Gen. 24:59; 35:8; II Sam. 4:4; II Kings 11:2; III Macc. 1:20). The same term is applied to a foster father or mother, e. g., Num. 11:12; Ruth 4:16; Isa. 49:23. In great families male servants, probably eunuchs

in later times, were intrusted with the charge of the boys (II Kings 10:1, 5).

Nurture (Gr. *paideia,* Eph. 6:4). The whole training and education of children which relates to the cultivation of mind and morals, and employ for this purpose now commands and admonitions, now reproof and punishment. It includes also the care and training of the body. It also is a term describing God's dealing with his children under grace.

Nuts. *See* Vegetable Kingdom.

Nym′phas (nĭm′fås; *nymph-given*), a prominent Christian in Laodicea, whose house was used as a place of worship (Col. 4:15).

O

Oak. Worship of. Oak groves in early times were used as places of religious concourse; altars were set up in them (Josh. 24:26); Jacob buried idolatrous images under an oak (Gen. 35:4), probably because the oak was a consecrated tree, no one would presume to disturb them there. Idolatry was practiced under oaks (Isa. 1:29; 57:5; Ezek. 6:13); and idols were made of oaks (Isa. 44:14). *See* Vegetable Kingdom.

Figurative. The oak is a symbol of Israel (Isa. 6:13); of strong and powerful men (Amos 2:9); *fading oaks,* of the wicked under judgment (Isa. 1:30).

Oar. *See* Ship.

Oath. 1. **Bible Terms.** Two terms are employed in the Old Testament to express what we understand by *an oath, to take an oath, to swear,* in which sense it frequently occurs (Lev. 5:1; Num. 5:23; Isa. 24:6; Zech. 5:3, etc.). It also means *a sworn covenant* (Gen. 26:28; II Sam. 21:7); *an oath,* as an appeal· to God in attestation of the truth of a statement (Neh. 10:29; Exod. 22:11). 2. *shᵉbū‛äh,* from the Hebrew *shĕbă‛, seven,* the sacred number. To "sever one's self," or to do by sevens, was to act after the manner of God—to give what was done a peculiarly sacred character— hence to make oath or swear. Solemn agreements, or oaths, were often accompanied by a sevenfold action of some sort, e. g., the giving of seven ewe lambs by Abraham to Abimelech (Gen. 21:30).

2. **Nature of Oath.** Every oath contains two elements, viz., an affirmation or promise, and an appeal to God as omniscient, and the punisher of falsehoods. (1) The principle on which an oath is held to be binding is incidentally laid down in Heb. 6:16, viz., as an ultimate appeal to divine authority to ratify an assertion. There the Almighty is represented as promising or denouncing with an oath, i. e., doing so in the most positive and solemn manner. (2) On the same principle that oath has always been held most binding which appealed to the highest authority both as regards individuals and communities. (*a*) Thus believers in Jehovah appealed to him,

both judicially and extrajudicially. (*b*) Appeals of this kind to authorities recognized respectively by adjuring parties were regarded as bonds of international security, and their infraction as being not only grounds of international complaint, but also offenses against divine justice. (3) As a consequence of this principle, (*a*) appeals to God's name on the one hand, and to heathen deities on the other, are treated in Scripture as tests of allegiance (Exod. 23:13; 34:6; Deut. 29:12, etc.). (*b*) So also the soveriegn's name is sometimes used as a form of obligation (Gen. 42:15; II Sam. 11:11; 14:19). (4) Other forms of oath, serious or frivolous, are mentioned, some of which are condemned by our Lord (Matt. 5:33; 23:16-22; comp. James 5:12), yet he did not refuse the solemn adjuration of the high priest (Matt. 26:63, 64).

3. **Occasions.** The Hebrews used oaths under the following circumstances: (1) Agreement or stipulation for performances of certain acts (Gen. 14:22; 24:2, 8, 9, etc.). (2) Allegiance to a sovereign, or obedience from an inferior to a superior (Eccles. 8:2; II Chron. 36:13; I Kings 18:10). (3) Promissory oath of a ruler (Josh. 6:26; I Sam. 14:24, 28, etc.). Priests took no oath of office (Heb. 7:21). (4) Vow made in the form of an oath (Lev. 5:4). (5) Judicial oaths. Public or judicial oaths were required on the following occasions: (*a*) A man receiving a pledge from a neighbor was required, in case of injury happening to the pledge, to clear himself by oath of the blame of damage (Exod. 22:10, 11; I Kings 8:31; II Chron. 6:22). (*b*) A person suspected of having found, or otherwise come into possession of lost property, was to vindicate himself by an oath (Lev. 6:3). It appears that witnesses were examined on oath; a false witness, or one guilty of suppression of the truth, was to be severely punished (Lev. 5:1; Prov. 29:24; Deut. 19:16-19). (*c*) A wife suspected of incontinence was required to clear herself by oath (Num. 5:19-22). But this ordeal does not come under the civil administration of justice.

4. **Forms of Oaths.** As to the forms of oaths, the Jews appealed to God with or without an imprecation in such phrases as "God do so and more also if," etc. (I Sam. 14:44); "As the Lord liveth" (I Sam. 14:39; 19:6; II Sam.

15:21; I Kings 18:10); "As the Lord liveth, and as thy soul liveth" (I Sam. 20:3); "The Lord be between thee and me forever" (20:23); "The God of Abraham judge betwixt us" (Gen. 31:53). The Jews also swore "by heaven," "by the earth," "by the sun," "by Jerusalem," "by the temple" (Matt. 5:34; 23:16); "by the angels" (Josephus, *War*, ii, 16, 4); by the lives of distinguished persons (Gen. 42:15; I Sam. 1:26; 17:55; II Sam. 11:11; 14:19). The *external manner* of an oath was as follows: (1) Originally the oath of a covenant was taken by solemnly sacrificing *seven* animals, or it was attested by *seven* witnesses or pledges, consisting either of so many animals presented to the contracting party, or of memorials erected to testify to the act (Gen. 21:28-31). (2) Lifting up the hand. Witnesses laid their hands on the head of the accused (Gen. 14:22; Lev. 24:14; Deut. 33:40; Isa. 3:7). (3) Putting the hand under the thigh of the person to whom the promise was made. It has been explained (*a*) as having reference to the covenant of circumcision; (*b*) as containing a principle similar to that of phallic symbolism, i. e., the genital organ the symbol of the Creator; (*c*) as referring to the promised Messiah. (4) Oaths were sometimes taken before the altar, or, as some understand the passage, if the persons were not in Jerusalem, in a position looking toward the temple (I Kings 8:31; II Chron. 6:22). (5) Dividing a victim and passing between or distributing the pieces (Gen. 15:10, 17; Jer. 34:18). In every case the oath taken before a judgment seat seems to have consisted of an adjuration by the judge, and responded to by the persons sworn with an *amen* (Heb. *'āmēn, truly*, I Kings 22:16; Gr. *su 'eipas*, "thou hast said," Matt. 36:63, 64).

5. **Sanctity.** As the sanctity of oaths was carefully inculcated by the law, so the crime of perjury was strongly condemned; and to a false witness the same punishment was assigned which was due for the crime to which he testified (Exod. 20:7; Lev. 19:12; Deut. 19:16-19; Psa. 15:4; Jer. 5:2; 7:9; Ezek. 16:59; Hos. 10:4; Zech. 8:17).

6. **Christian.** The Christian practice in the matter of oaths was founded in great measure on the Jewish. Thus the oath on the gospels was an imitation of the Jewish practice of placing the hands on the book of the law. The meaning of our Lord's interdiction of swearing (Matt. 5:33, sq.) was that "Christianity should know no oath at all. To the consciousness of the Christian, God should always be so vividly present that, to him and others in the Christian community, his yea and nay are, in point of reliability, equivalent to an oath. His yea and nay are oath enough" (Meyer, *Com.*, in loc.). The prohibition of swearing does not refer to official oaths, but to private conduct, for none of the oaths referred to by our Lord are judicial oaths. The orientals were great swearers, and the secondary oaths forbidden by our Lord are just the ordinary profanities of their conversation. In these they avoided the use of God's name, and supposed that the breaking of these oaths did not constitute perjury.

Obadi'ah (ō-bà-dī'á; *servant of Jehovah*).

1. An officer of high rank in the court of Ahab, who is described as "over the house," i. e., apparently, lord high chamberlain, or mayor of the palace (I Kings 18:3), B. C. about 870-850. Notwithstanding his position he "feared the Lord greatly," and, during the persecution of the prophets by Jezebel, he concealed one hundred of them in a cave, supplying them with food. In the third year of the terrible famine that visited Samaria Ahab and Obadiah divided the land between them to search for pasture. While on his journey he unexpectedly met Elijah, who commanded him to tell the king of the prophet's appearance. Obadiah hesitated, fearing death at Ahab's hands, but when Elijah insisted he had no choice but to obey (18:5-16).

2. A man referred to in I Chron. 3:21, in an obscure manner. Keil (*Com.*, in loc.) and Smith (*Dict.*, s. v.) think the passage clearly corrupt. Strong (McC. and S., *Cycl.*, s. v.) considers that Obadiah was a son of Arnan, as the LXX, and Vulgate have, reading "his son" instead of "sons of;" and identifies him with Judah (Luke 3:26) and Abiud (Matt. 1:13) of Christ's genealogy.

3. According to the received text, one of the five sons of Izrahiah, a descendant of Issachar, and a chief man of his tribe (I Chron. 7:3).

4. One of the six sons of Azel, a descendant of Saul (I Chron. 8:38; 9:44).

5. A Levite, son of Shemaiah, who dwelt in one of the villages of the Netophathites, near Jerusalem (I Chron. 9:16). He is named as one of the temple porters (Neh. 12:25), B. C. about 445.

6. The second named of the eleven Gadite warriors of renown who joined David at Ziklag (I Chron. 12:9), B. C. before 1000.

7. The father of Ishmaiah, who was chief of the tribe of Zebulun in David's reign (I Chron. 27:19).

8. One of the princes whom Jehoshaphat employed to teach in the cities of Judah (II Chron. 17:7), B. C. about 870.

9. A Levite of the family of Merari, who was one of the overseers of temple repairs ordered by King Josiah (II Chron. 34:12), B. C. 622.

10. The son of Jehiel, of the sons of Joab, who came up with a company of two hundred and eighteen male kinsmen in the second caravan with Ezra (Ezra 8:9), B. C. about 457.

11. One of the priests who signed the covenant with Nehemiah (Neh. 10:5), B. C. 445.

12. The Prophet. As to the person and circumstances of Obadiah nothing certain is known; and the traditional accounts of him in the rabbins and fathers, some of whom identify him with Ahab's pious commander, others with the third captain sent by Ahaziah against Elisha (II Kings 1:13), are quite worthless and evidently false.

Obadiah, Book of, one of the Minor Prophets constituting the smallest book of the O. T. The name Obadiah, the prophet and traditional author of the oracle, means "the servant or worshiper of Jehovah."

1. **Subject.** The prophetic oracle is taken up wholly with the denunciation of Edom for

its unbrotherly conduct toward Judah, presenting a foreview of its complete decimation and Judah's deliverance in the Day of the Lord.

2. **Contents.**

Part I. Prophecy of Edom's Decimation, 1:1-9

   a. Fall of her impregnable fortifications, 1:2-4

   b. Edom's complete plundering, 1:5-9

Part II. Edom's Destruction Accounted For, 1:10-14

   a. Violence against Jacob, 1:10-14

Part III. Prophecy of the Day of Jehovah, 1:15-21

   a. Edom and all nations judged, 1:15, 16

   b. House of Jacob saved, 1:17-20

   c. The Millennial Kingdom established, 1:21

3. **The Date.** The prophecy is variously dated by critics. Oesterley and Robinson view the book as a group of oracles from "almost anytime between the end of the sixth and middle of the second centuries B. C." (*Introduction*, p. 370). Critics generally ascribe the prophecy to the Chaldean period after the destruction of Jerusalem in 587 B. C. and deny the unity of the book. Robert Pfeiffer is of the opinion that the original oracle against Edom is preserved in two editions, Obadiah 1:1-9 and Jeremiah 49:7-22. He dates Obadiah 1:1-15 about 460 B. C. and verses 16-21, which he regards as "apocalyptic fancy," even later. There is no genuine reason to deny the unity of the prophecy nor to refuse it a place in the reign of Jehoram (c. 848-841 B. C.). During Jehoram's reign the Philistines and Arabians over-ran Judah and plundered Jerusalem (II Chron. 21:16, 17; cf. Joel 3:3-6; and Amos 1:6). At that time the Edomites were particularly hostile to Judah (II Kings 8:20-22; II Chron. 21:8-20). All the requirements of the prophecy are satisfied in this historical context. In support of this view it may be said that the prophet Amos (c. 760) shows acquaintanceship with Obadiah (cf. Obad. 1:4 with Amos 9:2; Obad. 1:9, 10, 18 with Amos 1:11, 12; Obad. 1:14 with Amos 1:6, 9; Obad. 1:19 with Amos 9:12 and Obad. 1:20 with Amos 9:14). Jeremiah, too, doubtless used the prophecies (cf. Obad. 1:1-6 with Jer. 49:7-22). Moreover, the position of Obadiah in the Minor Prophets after Amos suggests a pre-exilic origin. (For critical literature *see* T. H. Robinson, "The Structure of the Book of Obadiah," *Jour. of Theol. Studies* 17, 1916, p. 402-408; G. W. Wade on *Obadiah* in the *Westminister Commentaries*, 1925). *M. F. U.*

O'bal (ō'băl), a son of Joktan, and founder of an Arabian tribe (Gen. 10:28). The locality (called Ebal in I Chron. 1:22) where they settled is unknown.

O'bed (ō'bĕd; *serving*).

1. The son of Boaz and Ruth, and father of Jesse, the father of David (Ruth 4:17; I Chron. 2:12), B. C. about 1070. The name of Obed occurs only in Ruth 4:17, and in the four genealogies (Ruth 4:21, 22; I Chron. 2:12; Matt. 1:5; Luke 3:32).

2. A descendant of Jarha, the Egyptian slave of Sheshan, in the line of Jerahmeel. He was grandson of Zabad, one of David's

mighty men (I Chron. 2:37, 38), B. C. after 1015.

3. One of David's mighty men (I Chron. 11:47), B. C. about 1000.

4. One of the gatekeepers of the temple, son of Shemaiah, the firstborn of Obed-edom (I Chron. 26:7), B. C. before 960.

5. Father of Azariah, one of the captains of hundreds who joined with Jehoiada in the revolution by which Athaliah fell (II Chron. 23:1), B. C. c. 842.

O'bed-e'dom (ō'bĕd-ē'dŏm; *servant of Edom*).

1. A Levite of the family of Korhites, and belonging to the class of doorkeepers (I Chron. 15:18, 24). He is called a *Gittite*, or *Gathite*, from his birthplace, the Levitical city of Gath-rimmon, in the tribe of Dan. After the death of Uzzah the ark, which was being conducted from the house of Abinadab in Gibeah to the city of David, was carried aside into the house of Obed-edom, where it continued three months, during which time Obed-edom was greatly prospered (13:14). It was brought thence by David (I Chron. 15:25; II Sam. 6:12), B. C. about 986. It was Obed-edom, the Gittite, who was appointed to sound "with harps on the Sheminith" (I Chron. 15:21; 16:5, 38). He is probably the same mentioned in I Chron. 26:4-8.

2. The son of Jeduthun, and one of the temple doorkeepers (I Chron. 16:38), B. C. before 960.

3. A person who had charge of the vessels of the sanctuary in the time of Amaziah, king of Judah (II Chron. 25:24), B. C. about 783.

Obedience, as a branch of Christian ethics, is to be viewed not only with respect to the relations existing between God and man and between man and society, but also with respect to the example of Christ and man's relation to him.

1. Perfect obedience to the commandments of God must be the object of our constant endeavors. The imperfect results of even our most strenuous efforts, however, reveal the necessity of God's grace in Christ. Nothing less than entire self-surrender to God and reverent trust can make this grace available (*see* I John 1:6-10; 2:1-6; Rom. 3:20; 5:1; 6:1, 2, et al). *See* Law; Atonement; Faith.

2. Christian obedience also includes that of children to their parents (*see* Luke 2:51; Eph. 6:1, 2); of the servants to their masters (*see* Tit. 2:9, 10; Col. 3:23; Eph. 6:6); proper respect to civil authority (*see* Matt. 22:21; Rom. 13:1-7); also proper recognition of the authority of the Church, or the obligations of Christian fellowship (Matt. 18:17; II Cor. 6:14-18). But *see*, further, Judgment, Right of Private.

Obedience of Christ. This embraces not only the holy life of our Lord, his complete conformity to the divine law to which he was subject as a man, but also his voluntary acceptance of his sacrificial sufferings and death as the Saviour of mankind (*see* John 8:46; 17:4-6; Matt. 3:15; Rom. 5:18; Gal. 4:4; Phil. 2:7, 8). The distinction between the active and passive obedience of Christ, however, has been too sharply drawn by many theologians and made the basis of artificial theorizing. Thus, while to the death of Christ is ascribed the blessing of pardon, to what is called his active obedience is referred the imputation of Christ's perfect righteousness to believers, in the stead of their imperfect righteousness (*see* Imputation). But, as Van Oosterzee observes, "the very doing of the Lord was to a certain extent a suffering; his suffering on the other hand, in some respects his highest form of action." The holy life of Christ is essentially connected with human salvation because: 1. While his atonement centers in his death, his whole life was sacrificial, and the offering of himself even in death could not have been acceptable without the spotless life which preceded (*see* I Pet. 1:18, 19). 2. Christ thus became in himself the perfect manifestation of truth and righteousness, and thus in his self-denial and love the perfect ideal of righteousness for mankind (*see* John 14:6-9; 13:14, 15; I Pet. 2:21; I Cor. 11:1; Phil. 2:4-12). 3. He is also thus fitted to be the "Second Adam," the source of spiritual life and strength to his people (*see* John 10:10; 15:4; Acts 3:15; I Cor. 15:45). 4. Thus also Christ achieved his exaltation to the throne of his mediatorial kingdom (*see* Phil. 2:9-11; Heb. 2:16-18).

O'bil (ō'bĭl), an Ishmaelite who was appointed keeper of the herds of camels in the reign of David (I Chron. 27:30).

Oblation (elsewhere rendered "offering").

1. *An offering presented* (Heb. *qōrbän; brought near*), usually of the meat offerings (Lev. 2:4, sq.; 7:14, 29).

2. *A heave-offering* (Heb. *tĕrūmäh, heave*), a portion *lifted* or taken by a person from his property, as an offering to God; consequently, everything that was offered by the Israelites, either voluntarily or in consequence of a command from the Lord, for the erection and maintenance of the sanctuary and its officials (Isa. 40:20; Ezek. 44:30; 45:1, etc.).

3. *A present* (Heb. *mĭnḥäh, a donation*), especially of a bloodless offering (Isa. 19:21; 66:3; Dan. 9:21, 27).

4. *A libation* (Heb. *mässēkäh, pouring*), in worship a *libation*, but is to be taken in Dan. 2:46 in the general sense of sacrifice. *See* First Fruits; Sacrificial Offerings.

O'both (ō'bŏth), the forty-sixth station of the Israelites in their journey from Egypt to Canaan, near Moab (Num. 21:10, 11; 33:43, 44), probably the oasis el-Weiba.

Obscurity. 1. *Darkness* (Heb. *'ōphĕl, dusk*). In Isa. 29:18 in the expression, "the blind shall see out of obscurity," the word "obscurity" means the gloom of blindness.

2. *Gloom* (Heb. *ḥōshĕk, darkness, destruction, ignorance*). In Isa. 58:10; 59:9, obscurity is synonymous with darkness.

Observation (Gr. *paratērēsis, that which may be seen; with outward show*). In the expression "The kingdom of God cometh not with observation" (Luke 17:20), the meaning is, "The coming of Messiah's kingdom is not so conditioned that this coming could be *observed* as a visible development; or that it could be said, in consequence of such observation, that here or there is the kingdom" (Meyer, *Com.*, in loc.).

Observer of Times. *See* Magic.

Och'ran (ŏk'răn), A. V., Ocran (ŏk'răn), the father of Pagiel, "the prince" of Asher, who assisted Moses in the numbering of the people (Num. 1:13; 2:27; 7:72, 77; 10:26), B. C. 1438.

O'ded (ō'dĕd; *reiteration*).

1. The father of Azariah the prophet who met Asa on his return from defeating the Ethiopians (II Chron. 15:1), B. C. before 905. The address is, in v. 8, ascribed to Oded, probably through a mistake of the copyists.

2. A prophet of the Lord in Samaria in the time of Pekah's invasion of Judah (B. C. about 735). He met the victorious army returning with their booty and prisoners (two hundred thousand), and pointed out to them their cruelty and guilt, exhorting them to turn away the anger of God by sending back their prisoners (II Chron. 28:9). His speech made a deep impression, and, according to the advice of some chiefs of Ephraim, the captives were fed, clothed, anointed, and returned to Jericho.

Odor. 1. *Sweet smell* (Heb. *niḥōäḥ, restful*, Lev. 26:31; Dan. 2:46, referring to incense (*q. v.*)).

2. In the general sense of *fragrance*, as from spices (*q. v.*); *see* II Chron. 16:14; Esth. 2:12; Jer. 34:5; John 12:3. In Phil. 4:18 is the expression, "an odor of a sweet smell," which seems to mean "a sweet smelling odor." The odors of the groves of Lebanon were anciently very famous (Hos. 14:7; Cant. 4:11); flowers, even exotics, were cultivated in pleasure gardens for this purpose (Cant. 1:12; 4:6, 14). Odorous extracts were used sometimes in the form of incense, sometimes as ointments (1:3; 4:10); sometimes in water, with which clothing, bed furniture, etc., was sprinkled (Prov. 7:17).

Offense. Three Hebrew words are rendered in the A. V. "offenses:"

1. An *obstacle*, or *enticement* (I Sam. 25:31; Isa. 8:14), Heb. *mĭkshōl*.

2. *Crime*, or *its penalty* (Eccles. 10:4), Heb. *hēt'*.

3. To acknowledge guilt (Hos. 5:15), Heb. *'äshäm*.

The Greek words rendered "offense" are: *paraptōma*, to *fall beside* or *near*, a *lapse*, or deviation from the truth; a *sin*, or *misdeed* (Rom. 5:15-20; 4:25; 16:17); *skandalon*, the *movable stick of a trap*, any impediment (Matt. 18:7; Rom. 9:23; Luke 17:1). "The offense of the cross" (Gal. 5:11) was the offense which the Jews took at Christianity, because faith in a crucified Saviour—faith without legal observances—was *alone* offered as the means of salvation. In Matt. 16:23 "offense" appears to mean that which displeases one; *ptaiō*, to *stumble in*, i. e., to sin against (James 2:10; 3:2).

Offering. *See* Sacrifice; Sacrificial Offerings.

Office, the rendering of several Hebrew and Greek words, with some variety of meaning: *position* (Gen. 41:13; I Chron. 23:28, marg. *station*); *visitation, custody* (Num. 4:16; II Chron. 24:11; Psa. 109:8); to *be a priest* (Luke 1:8); the *priestly fraternity* (Luke 1:9); Heb. 7:5); *function*, as of a member of the body, or of the Church (Rom. 12:4); *visitation, inspection* (I Tim. 3:1).

Officer. It is obvious that most, if not all, of the Hebrew words rendered "officer" are either of an indefinite character, or are synonymous terms for functionaries known under other and more specific names, as "scribe," "eunuch," etc.

1. *Eunuch* (Heb. *särîs*, to *castrate*, Gen. 37: 36; 39:1; 40:2), usually rendered eunuch (*q. v.*).

2. *Prefect* (Heb. *shōṭēr*, properly a *writer*), from the use of writing in judicial administration, a *magistrate;* the officers set over the Israelites in Egypt (Exod. 5:6-19), those appointed with the elders to administer public affairs among the Israelites (Num. 11:16; Deut. 20:5, 8, 9; 29:10; Josh. 1:10, etc.), magistrates in the cities and towns of Palestine (Deut. 16:18; I Chron. 23:4; 26:29, etc.), and apparently a military chief (II Chron. 26:11, A. V. "ruler," R. V. "officer").

3. *One appointed* (Heb. *niṣṣäb*, *fixed*, I Kings 4:5, 7; 5:16; 9:23, etc.), general receivers of taxes, or chief tax collectors, who levied the king's duties or taxes, which consisted in the East, for the most part, of natural productions or the produce of the land, and were delivered at the royal kitchen.

4. A *superintendent*, either civil, military, or ecclesiastical (Heb. *päqîd*, Gen. 41:34; Judg. 9:28; Esth. 2:3, etc.).

The two words so rendered in the New Testament each bear in ordinary Greek a special sense. In the case of *hupēretēs* (Matt. 5:25; John 7:32, sq.; 18:3, sq.; Acts 5:22, 26), this is of no very definite kind, but the word is used to denote an inferior officer of a court of justice, a messenger or bailiff, like the Roman viator or lictor. *Praktores* (Luke 12:58), at Athens, were officers whose duty it was to register and collect fines imposed by courts of justice; and "deliver to the officer" means, give in the name of the debtor to the officer of the court.

Offices of Christ, the threefold office of Christ as Prophet, Priest, and King.

1. **Biblical View.** This division of the saving work of Christ is derived from the Scriptures inferentially. The Old Testament term Messiah is generally, though not universally, held to have this threefold significance (*see* Messiah). Also the work ascribed by prophecy to Christ had this threefold character (*see* particularly Deut. 18:15; Isa. 49:7; ch. 53). Moreover, the divinely appointed economy of Judaism, with the three great offices of prophet, priest, and theocratic king, was typical of Christ. In the New Testament we find that Christ spoke of himself most distinctly as King. He referred to himself but indirectly as Prophet (e. g., Matt. 13:57), and never called himself Priest. His reserve may be explained by his words in John 16:12, 13. We find, however, from the gospels that his work in a large measure was actually that of a prophet; and as the time drew near for his great sacrifice he spoke of it in a way that clearly indicated his priestly character (*see* Matt. 26:26-28; John 10:11, 17, 18). This fullness of Christ's work, as might be expected, is more clearly set forth in the Acts of the Apostles and in the Epistles (*see* Acts 2:22, 33, 38;

4:12; 5:31; 7:37, 52; Heb. 1:2, 3; 2:9-11; 7:22-28, et al.).

Christ is Prophet because more than all others he has declared to men the truth and will of God. He is himself the revelation of God (*see* John 14:9; 17:25, 26; Heb. 1:1, 2, et. al.). He is Priest not only because of his holy character and mediatorial position, but also, and emphatically, because of his sacrificial work (*see*, besides Scriptures already cited, I John 2:1, 2; Rev. 5:9). *See* Atonement.

He is King not only by virtue of his divine nature, but also because as the God-man he is the divinely appointed head of the mediatorial kingdom, who in His second advent as "King of kings" (Rev. 19:16), will restore the kingdom to Israel (Acts 1:6), and fulfill the Davidic Covenant and the O. T. promises made to Israel (II Chron. 7; Isa. 60; Zech. 8, etc.). *See* Kingdom of Christ.

It is important in the highest degree that each and every one of these forms of the work of Christ should be duly recognized. Otherwise we fail to obtain the right conception of Christ, and of his relations to mankind.

2. **Historical.** The division of Christ's mediatorial work into three offices, based upon Scripture, was formally stated in the early Church, as indicated in the writings of Eusebius, Cyril of Jerusalem, and Augustine.

In the Middle Ages it was elaborated by Thomas Aquinas. It was introduced into the theology of the Lutheran and Calvinistic Churches. Through the influence of T. A. Ernesti, in 1773, and of others, this form of statement fell to a large extent into disuse. It was revived by Schleiermacher and others, who in this respect followed in his footsteps, and is now currently employed in the theology of the evangelical Churches of Europe and America.

Offscouring (Heb. *seḥî*, *refuse*, as *swept* off, Lam. 3:45; Gr. *peripsēma*, I Cor. 4:13, *brushed* off), a figurative term for something vile, worthless, as the apostles were looked upon by some in their day.

Og (ŏg), an Amorite, king of Bashan (Num. 21:33; 32:33; Deut. 4:47; 31:4), who ruled over sixty cities (Josh. 13:30), the chief of which were Ashtaroth and Edrie (v. 12) at the time of the occupation of Canaan, B. C. c. 1400. He was defeated by the Israelites at Edrei, and, with his children and people, were exterminated (Num. 21:33; Deut. 1:4; 3:1-13; 29:7; Josh. 2:10). His many walled cities were taken (Deut. 3:4-10) and his kingdom assigned to the trans-Jordanic tribes, especially the half tribe of Manasseh (Deut. 3:13; Josh. 9:10; 13:12, 30). He was a man of giant stature, and Moses speaks of his iron bedstead, nine cubits long by four broad, which was preserved as a memorial in Rabbath (Deut. 3:11). He was one of the last representatives of the giant race of Rephaim.

O'had (ō'hăd; *unity*), the third named of the sons of Simeon (Gen. 46:10), and head of a family in Israel (Exod. 6:15).

O'hel (ō'hĕl; *tent*), one of the children of Zerubbabel (I Chron. 3:20).

Oil. Name. The following original words are rendered "oil" in the A. V.: 1. Most generally oil is the rendering of the Heb. *shĕmĕn, grease,* sometimes in A. V. "ointment." 2. Heb. *yĭṣhär, shining, clear olive oil* (Num. 18:12; Deut. 7:13; 11:14; 12:17; II Kings 18:32, etc.). 3. Aram. *mᵉshăk,* an *unguent* (only in Ezra 6:9; 7:22). 4. Gr. *'elaion,* neuter of word meaning "olive."

Of the numerous substances, animal and vegetable, which were known to the ancients as yielding oil, the olive berry is the one of which most frequent mention is made in the Scriptures. The best oil is made from fruit gathered about November or December, when it has begun to change color, but before it has become black. The berry in the more advanced state yields more oil, but of an inferior quality.

1. **Harvesting.** In order not to injure either the crop or the tree great care is necessary in gathering, either by hand or shaking the fruit off carefully with a light stick. It is then carefully cleaned and carried to press, which is considered best; or, if necessary, laid on tables with hollow trays made sloping, so as to allow the first juice to flow into other receptacles beneath, care being taken not to heap the fruit too much, and so prevent the free escape of the juice, which is injurious to the oil though itself useful in other ways.

2. **Manufacture.** In order to make oil the fruit was either bruised in a mortar, crushed in a press loaded with wood or stones, ground in a mill, or trodden with the feet. The "beaten" oil of Exod. 27:20; 29:40; Lev. 24:2; Num. 28:5, was probably made by bruising in a mortar. The berries are bruised in a rude mill, consisting of a round stone, resembling a millstone, but very much larger, usually six to eight feet in diameter. This stone is laid flatwise on the ground. Its upper surface is depressed about three inches, except at its edge. The center of this stone is bored through and an upright pole is fastened in it, projecting about three feet above it. Another stone disk, five or six feet in diameter and a foot or eighteen inches thick, is set on edge in the depression on the top of the other. Through the center of this stone passes a long pole, one end of which has a ring attached to it, which fits over the end of the upright in the other disk, while the other end is attached to a whiffletree, by which a horse or mule draws it round and round the mill. The berries are placed in the cavity on the face of the horizontal stone, and the upright stone draws around the edge of the cavity, crushing the berries as it goes. A part of the oil thus expressed is drawn off by a hole in the elevated rim of the stone. The refuse is then transferred to baskets, which are piled on top of one another in the space between two grooved upright posts. A lever, weighted at its distal end with heavy stones, compresses these baskets, and expresses the crude oil. This is run into large stone reservoirs, in which it becomes clarified, and is kept for use or sale. From these the oil was drawn out for use in horns or other small vessels, which were stored in cellars or storehouses, of which special mention is made in the inventories of royal property and revenue (I Sam. 10:1; 16:1, 13; I Kings 1:39; 17:16; II Kings 4:2,

6; 9:1, 3; I Chron. 27:28; II Chron. 11:11; 32:28; Prov. 21:20). A supply of oil was always kept in the temple (Josephus, *Wars,* v, 13, 6), and an oil treasure was among the stores of the Jewish kings (II Kings 20:13; comp. II Chron. 32:28). Oil of Tekoa was reckoned the best. Trade in oil was carried on with the Tyrians, by whom it was probably often reexported to Egypt, whose olives do not, for the most part, produce good oil (II Chron. 2:10). Direct trade in oil was also carried on between Egypt and Palestine (Ezra 3:7; Isa. 30:6; 57:9; Ezek. 27:17; Hos. 12:1).

3. **Uses.** (1) **As food.** Oil is now, as formerly, in general use as food throughout western Asia, taking the place of butter and animal fat in various preparations (comp. Ezek. 16:13). Indeed, it would appear that the Hebrews considered oil one of the prime necessities of life (Sirach 39:31; comp. Jer. 31:12; 41:8; Luke 16:6, sq.). It is frequently mentioned with honey (Ezek. 16:13, 19; 27:17), and its abundance was a mark of prosperity (comp. Joel 2:19). (2) **Cosmetic.** As is the case generally in hot climates, oil was used by the Jews for anointing the body, e. g., after the bath, and giving to the skin and hair a smooth and comely appearance, e. g., before an entertainment. At Egyptian entertainments it was usual for a servant to anoint the head of each guest as he took his seat (Deut. 28:40; II Sam. 12:20; 14:2; Ruth 3:3). (3) **Funereal.** The bodies of the dead were anointed with oil by the Greeks and Romans, probably as a partial antiseptic, and a similar custom appears to have prevailed among the Jews. (4) **Medicinal.** As oil is in use in many cases in modern medicine, it is not surprising that it should have been much used among the Jews and other nations of antiquity for medicinal purposes. Celsus repeatedly speaks of the use of oil, especially old oil, applied externally with friction in fevers, and in many other cases. Josephus mentions that among the remedies employed in the case of Herod, he was put into a sort of oil-bath. The prophet Isaiah (1:6) alludes to the use of oil as ointment in medical treatment; and it thus furnished a fitting symbol, perhaps also an efficient remedy, when used by our Lord's disciples in the miraculous cures which they were enabled to perform (Mark 6:13). With a similar intention, no doubt, its use was enjoined by St. James (5:14). (5) **Light.** Oil was in general use for lamps, being still used in Egypt with cotton wicks twisted round straw, the receptacle being a glass vessel, into which water is first poured (Matt. 25:1-8; Luke 12:35). (6) **Ritual.** Oil was poured on or mixed with the flour used in offering (*see* Sacrificial Offerings), excepting the sin offering (Lev. 5:11) and the offering of jealousy (Num. 5:15). The use of oil in sacrifices was indicative of joy or gladness; the absence of oil denoted sorrow or humiliation (Isa. 61:3; Joel 2:19; Rev. 6:6). Kings, priests, and prophets were anointed with oil or ointment. Tithes of oil were also prescribed (Deut. 12:17; II Chron. 31:5; Neh. 10:37, 39; 13:12; Ezek. 45:14).

Figurative. Oil was a fitting symbol of the Spirit, or spiritual principle of life, by virtue of its power to sustain and fortify the vital energy; and the anointing oil, which was prepared according to divine instructions, was therefore a symbol of the Spirit of God, as the principle of spiritual life which proceeds from God and fills the natural being of the creature with the powers of divine life. The anointing with oil, therefore, was a symbol of endowment with the Spirit of God for the duties of the office to which a person was consecrated (Lev. 8:13; I Sam. 10:1, 6; 16:13, 14; Isa. 61:1). Oil was symbol of abundance (Deut. 8:8; Ezek. 16:13); lack of oil was a figure for want, poverty (Deut. 28:40; Joel 1:10); "to suck honey out of the rock, and oil out of the flinty rock" (Deut. 32:13) is a figure derived from the fact that Canaan abounds in wild bees, which make their hives in clefts of the rock and in olive trees which grow in a rocky soil, and suggests the most valuable productions out of the most unproductive places, since God so blessed the land that even the rocks and stones were productive; "the oil of joy" is a figure for the consolations of the Gospel (Isa. 61:3; Heb. 1:9); "excellent oil" (Psa. 141:5) is a figure for kind reproof. "His words were softer than oil" (55:21) are used to express the hypocritical pretense of a false friend (comp. Prov. 5:3). See Olive, in Vegetable Kingdom.

Oil, Holy, Anointing. The mode of preparing this oil is prescribed (Exod. 30:22-25). It was a compound consisting of one hin (about one gallon) of olive oil, five hundred shekels of pure myrrh, two hundred and fifty shekels of calamus, two hundred and fifty shekels of fragrant cinnamon, and five hundred shekels of cassia (the aromatic bark of a shrub that grows in Arabia). The proportions in which these ingredients were mixed compels us to assume that the cinnamon, calamus, and cassia were not mixed with the oil in their dry form, but as prepared spices, say in the shape of cinnamon-calamus and cassia ointment; or it may have been, as the rabiinical writers assure us, that the dry substances were steeped or boiled in water to extract the strength or virtue out of them, when to the liquid thus obtained the oil was added, when both were put upon the fire to boil till the whole of the watery element should evaporate. The preparing of the anointing oil was superintended by Bezaleel (Exod. 37:29).

Oil Tree (Isa. 41:19). See Vegetable Kingdom.

Ointment. 1. **Name.** Ointment is the rendering of the following words in the original: (1) Heb. *shĕmĕn* (II Kings 20:13; Psa. 133:2; Prov. 27:16; Eccles. 7:1; 9:8; 10:1; Isa. 1:6, etc.), probably *oil* (and so elsewhere rendered, except "olive," in I Kings 6:23, sq.; "pine," in Neh. 8:15; "fatness," in Psa. 109:24; "fat things," in Isa. 25:6; "fruitful," in Isa. 5:1). (2) Hebrew form *rōqăḥ*, an *aromatic* (Exod. 30:25), an odorous compound ("confection," Exod. 30:35; II Chron. 16:14; "pot of ointment," Job 41:31, etc.). (3) Gr. *muron, myrrh* (invariably rendered "ointment").

2. **Nature and Preparation.** The ointments and oils used by the Israelites were generally composed of various ingredients. Olive oil was combined with sundry aromatics, chiefly foreign (I Kings 10:10; Ezek.

27:22), particularly spices, myrrh, and nard. Being costly, these ointments were a much-prized luxury (Amos 6:6). The ingredients, and often the prepared oils and resins ready for use, were imported from Phoenicia in small alabaster boxes, in which the delicious aroma was best preserved. The preparation of these required peculiar skill, and formed a particular trade (see Apothecary); sometimes carried on by women (see Confectioners, I Sam. 8:13). The better kinds of ointments were so strong, and the different substances so perfectly amalgamated, that they have been known to retain their scent for centuries. One of the alabaster vases at Alnwick Castle contains some of the ancient Egyptian ointment, which has retained its odor for between two thousand and three thousand years.

3. **Uses.** The practice of producing agreeable odors by burning incense, anointing the person with aromatic oils and ointments, and of sprinkling the dress with fragrant waters, originated in, and is mostly confined to, warm climates. In such climates the perspiration is profuse, and much care is needful to prevent offensive results. It is in this necessity that we find a reason for the use of perfumes, particularly at feasts, weddings, and on visits of persons of rank. The following are the uses of ointments in Scripture: (1) **Cosmetic.** The Greek and Roman practice of anointing the head and clothes on festive occasions prevailed also among the Egyptians, and appears to have had place among the Jews (Ruth 3:3; Eccles. 7:1; 9:8; Prov. 27:9, 16, etc.). Oil of myrrh, for like purposes, is mentioned (Esth. 2:12). Egyptian paintings represent servants anointing guests on their arrival at their entertainer's house, and alabaster vases exist which retain the traces of the ointment which they were used to contain. (2) **Funereal.** Ointments as well as oil were used to anoint dead bodies and the clothes in which they were wrapped (Matt. 26:12; Mark 14:3, 8; Luke 23:56; John 12:3, 7; 19:40). (3) **Medicinal.** Ointment formed an important feature in ancient medical treatment (Isa. 1:6). The mention of balm of Gilead and of eye salve (*collyrium*) points to the same method (Isa. 1:6; John 9:6; Jer. 8:22; Rev. 3:18, etc.). (4) **Ritual.** Besides the oil used in many ceremonial observances, a special ointment was appointed to be used in consecration (Exod. 29:7; 30:23, 33; 37:29; 40:9, 15). Strict prohibition was issued against using this unguent for any secular purpose, or on the person of a foreigner, and against imitating it in any way whatsoever (30:32, 33). The weight of the oil in the mixture would be twelve pounds eight ounces English. A question arises: In what form were the other ingredients, and what degree of solidity did the whole attain? According to Maimonides, Moses, having reduced the solid ingredients to powder, steeped them in water till all the aromatic qualities were drawn forth. He then poured in the oil, and boiled the whole till the water was evaporated. The residuum thus obtained was preserved in a vessel for use. Another theory supposes all the ingredients to have been in the form of oil or ointment, and the measurement by weight of all, except

the oil, seems to imply that they were in some solid form, but whether in an unctuous state or in that of powder cannot be ascertained. A process of making ointment consisting, in part at least, in boiling, is alluded to (Job 41:31). See Anointing; Vegetable Kingdom.

Old. See Age; Elders.

Old Gate, a name (Neh. 3:6; 12:9) of a *Jerusalem* (*q. v.*) gate; probably the gate on the northeast corner.

Old Testament, the part of the Bible extending from Genesis to Malachi.

1. **Designation.** This portion of revealed Truth consists of 39 books, which make up about 8/13 of the content of the whole Bible. The 39 books of the Protestant canon are identical with the ancient Hebrew canon. Roman Catholics have a larger canon, consisting of eleven of the fourteen apocrypha, called deutero-canonical books. These books, however, have no legitimate place in the canon. The Old Testament bears a vital and inseparable relation to the N. T. It is fundamental and preparatory. The N. T. is enfolded in the Old and the Old is unfolded by the New. It is a mistake to separate the two testaments. In rejecting Christianity and the N. T. revelation Judaism makes this blunder. The terms Old and New Testament were popularized by the Latin fathers and did not come into vogue until the Christian Scriptures were complete. The term "O. T." was used as a device to distinguish the Christian Scriptures from the "Jewish Scriptures." In one sense of the word, the terms O. T. and N. T. are inaccurate, since the old or Mosaic covenant overlaps and was in force until the crucifixion of Christ and the veil of the temple was rent in twain from top to bottom. The new covenant is based upon the death, resurrection and ascension of Christ, and the Jew who would now enjoy salvation must come by "a new and living way" (Heb. 10:20), that is, Christ (John 14:6).

2. **Origin and Preservation.** The N. T. expressly declares the inspiration of the O. T. books (II Tim. 3:16; II Pet. 1:20, 21). Likewise, everywhere in the O. T. the Hebrew Scriptures are presented as the divinely revealed Word of God. God is everywhere set forth implicitly and explicitly as its principal Author. The sacred writers are represented as receiving or recording the divine message in its fullness and with divine accuracy. Internal evidence of its inspiration abounds everywhere. The sacred authors over and over prefix their messages with such commanding expressions as "Thus saith the Lord" (Exod. 4:22); "Hear the Word of the Lord" (Isa. 1:10). Prophets like Isaiah, Jeremiah and Daniel have had their predictions verified by time. Almost as unique as the inspiration of the O. T. is its preservation. Many other books besides Scripture existed (Eccles. 12:12). Echoes of ancient literary pieces survive in the Scripture references to the Book of Jasher (Josh. 10:13; II Sam. 1:18) and "the Book of the Wars of the Lord" (Num. 21:14). Human writings apparently contested with inspired documents. Divine intervention assured the giving, the reception and recording of Holy Scripture as well as its miraculously

meticulous and accurate preservation through the centuries—an almost incredible phenomenon when each manuscript had to be executed by hand.

3. **Position and Purpose in the Canon.** The O. T. comes before the New because it is introductory both historically, typically and redemptively to all that is enfolded there. The central unifying theme is the Person and work of Christ. From the proto-evangelium (Gen. 3:15) to Malachi's "Sun of righteousness," Christ is the interwoven and inseparable subject of all the O. T. The O. T. does not present the Church of the N. T. (except typically), which was a secret hidden in God (Eph. 3:1-9) and which was first revealed to the Apostle Paul. The O. T., however, fully presents the first advent of Christ, leaving the gap between the two comings filled in by the N. T. Church. The O. T., however, in amazing detail presents the coming of the Redeemer to work out man's salvation (cf. Isa. 53:1-12) and also with great elaboration sets forth the second coming of Christ and the establishment of the Millennial Kingdom, involving the restoration of Israel. The disciples' question in Acts 1:6, "Lord, wilt Thou at this time restore the Kingdom to Israel" finds the fullest elucidation in the O. T., not in connection with the Church, but in connection with the Great Tribulation and the cataclysmic second coming of Christ, as set forth in the Book of the Revelation (chaps. 4-19).

4. **Value of the O. T.** Although the O. T. Scriptures were given to one small nation, its message is omnitemporal and in no sense is it confined to Palestine or to the Jews, but because of its world outreach becomes vital to all peoples of every land and age. The target of relentless critical attack and stigmatized by unbelief, it continues with the N. T. to meet man's deepest needs and to lead the human race to the Fountain of salvation and dynamic inspiration for right living. *M. F. U.*

Olive. See Oil, Vegetable Kingdom.

Olive Yard (Heb. *zăyĭth*, Exod. 23:11; Josh. 24:13; I Sam. 8:14; II Kings 5:26; Neh. 5:11; 9:25), an orchard or grove of olive trees.

Olives, Mount of. The ridge of hills east of Jerusalem, and separated from it by the Jehoshaphat valley.

1. **Name.** Its descriptive appellation is "the Mount of Olives" (Heb. *hăr hăzzēthĭm*, only in Zech. 14:4; Gr. *to oros tōn 'elaiōv*, the mount on which the olives grew (Matt. 21:1; 24:3; 26:30; Mark 11:1; Luke 19:37; John 8:1). It is referred to (II Sam. 15:30) as "the ascent of *mount* Olivet;" "the hill that is before Jerusalem" (I Kings 11:7); "the mount of corruption" (II Kings 23:13), or "offense," from the heathen altars erected there by Solomon (comp. I Kings 11:7); "the mount" (Neh. 8:15). The hill has now two names, *Jebel et-Tûr*, i. e., "the Mount," and *Jebel et-Zeitûn*, "Mount of Olives."

2. **Physical Features.** The Mount of Olives is a limestone ridge, rather more than a mile in length, running in general direction north and south, covering the whole eastern side of the city of Jerusalem. At the north the ridge bends round to the west, inclosing the city on that side also. At the north about a mile inter-

venes between the city walls, while on the east the mount is only separated by the valley of Kidron. It is to the latter part that attention is called. At a distance its outline is almost horizontal, gradually sloping away at its southern end; but when seen from below the eastern wall of Jerusalem it divides itself into three, or perhaps four, independent summits or eminences. Beginning at the north they are: Galilee, or *Viri Galilaei*, from the address of the angel to the disciples (Acts 1:11); Mount of Ascension, now distinguished by the minaret and domes of the Church of the Ascension, in every way the most important; Mount of the Prophets, subordinate to the former; and Mount of Offense. Three paths lead from the valley to the summit. The first passes under the north wall of the inclosure of Gethsemane, and follows the line of the depression between the center and the northern hill. The second parts from the first about fifty years beyond Gethsemane, and, striking off to the right up the very breast of the hill, surmounts the projection on which is the traditional spot of the lamentation over Jerusalem, and thence proceeds directly upward to the village. The third leaves the other two at the northeast corner of Gethsemane, and, making a considerable detour to the south, visits the so-called "Tombs of the Prophets," and, following a very slight depression which occurs at that part of the mount, arrives in its turn at the village. Every consideration is in favor of the first path being that which David took when fleeing from Absalom, as well as that usually taken by our Lord and his disciples in their morning and evening walks between Jerusalem and Bethany, and that also by which the apostles returned to Jerusalem after the ascension. Tradition assigns many sacred sites to Mount of Ascension, Gethsemane, place of ascension, and of lamentation. The third of the traditional spots mentioned—that of the lamentation over Jerusalem (Luke 19:41-44)—has been shown to have been illy chosen, and that the road of our Lord's "triumphal entry" was not by the short and steep path over the summit, but the longer and easier route round the southern shoulder of the southern of the three divisions of the mount.

3. **Scripture Notices.** Olivet is mentioned in connection with the flight of David from Absalom (II Sam. 15:30); with the building there of high places by Solomon (II Kings 23:13); with the vision of the Lord's departure from Jerusalem (Ezek. 10:4, 19; 11:23), in which last passage the prophet said, "And the glory of the Lord went up from the midst of the city, and stood upon the mountain which is on the east side of the city." The command to "Go forth unto the mount and fetch olive branches," etc. (Neh. 8:15), indicates that the mount, and probably the valley at its base, abounded in various kinds of trees. In the time of Jesus the trees were still very numerous (Mark 11:8). The only other Old Testament mention of Olivet is in Zechariah's prophecy of the destruction of Jerusalem and the preservation of God's people in it (Zech. 14:4). The New Testament narrative makes Olivet the scene of four remarkable events in the history of Jesus: The triumphal entry—its scene the road which winds around the southern shoulder of the hill from Bethany to Jerusalem (Matt. 21:1, sq.; Mark 11:1, sq.; Luke 19:29, sq.); prediction of Jerusalem's overthrow (Mark 13:1); Gethsemane—after the institution of the Lord's Supper, "when they had sung a hymn" Jesus led his disciples "over the brook Cedron," "out into the Mount of Olives," to a garden called Gethsemane (John 18:1; Matt. 26:30, 36); the Ascension (*q. v.*).

Olivet. *See* Olives, Mount of.

Olym'pas (ô-lǐm'pǎs), a Christian at Rome, to whom Paul sent a salutation in his epistle to the church in that city (Rom. 16:15); perhaps of the household of Philologus.

O'mar (ō'mẽr), son of Eliphaz, the firstborn of Esau, and "duke" or phylarch of Edom (Gen. 36:11, 15; I Chron. 1:36). The name is supposed to survive in that of the tribe of *Amir* Arabs east of the Jordan.

Ome'ga (ô-mē'gà), the last letter of the Greek alphabet, as Alpha is the first.

Figurative. Omega is used metaphorically to denote the *end* of anything. "I am Alpha and Omega, the beginning and the ending . . . the first and the last" (Rev. 1:8, 11; comp. 21:6; 22:13; and Isa. 41:4; 44:6).

Omer, a Hebrew dry measure. *See* Metrology, II (3).

Omnipotence, exclusively an attribute of God, and essential to the perfection of his being. It is declared in such Scriptures as Gen. 17:1; Exod. 15:11, 12; Deut. 3:24; Psa. 62:11; 65:6; 147:5; Jer. 32:17; Matt. 6:13; 19:26; Eph. 3:20; Rev. 19:6. By ascribing to God absolute power, it is not meant that God is free from all the restraints of reason and morality, as some have taught, but that he is able to do everything that is in harmony with his wise and holy and perfect nature (*see* Matt. 23:19; Heb. 6:18). The infinite power of God is set before us in the Scriptures in connection with his work of creation (Gen. 1:1; Rom. 1:20), his work of upholding the world (Heb. 1:3), the redemption of mankind (Luke 1:35, 37; Eph. 1:19), the working of miracles (Luke 9:43), the conversion of sinners (I Cor. 2:5; II Cor. 4:7), and the complete accomplishment of the great purpose of his kingdom (Matt. 13:31, 32; I Pet. 1:5; Matt. 6:13; I Cor., ch. 15; Rev. 19:6). For fuller exposition see works of Systematic Theology, elsewhere referred to, Hodge, Dorner, Van Oosterzee.—*E. McC.*

Omnipresence, an attribute of God alone, by which is meant that God is free from the laws or limitations of space (*see* Psa. 139:7-10; Jer. 23:23, 24; Heb. 1:3; Acts 17:27, 28, et al.). It is essential to the right conception of God in this respect that we avoid all materialistic notions of his presence which confuse God with everything and thus lead to *Pantheism* (*q. v.*). God is a Spirit, and his infinite presence is to be regarded in the dynamical sense rather than in the sense of a substance infinitely extended. He is distinct from all his works while his power and intelligence and goodness embrace and penetrate them all. The ubiquity of God is also to be regarded as compatible with various manifestations of his presence according to the spheres of life in which he exists and operates. Thus in the most exalted sense he is "Our Father in heaven" (*see* Matt. 6:9, et al.).

Omniscience, the divine attribute of perfect knowledge. This is declared in Psa. 33:13-15; 139:11, 12; 147:5; Prov. 15:3; Isa. 40:14; 46:10; Acts 15:18; I John 3:20; Heb. 4:13, and in many other places. The perfect knowledge of God is exclusively his attribute. It relates to himself and to all beyond himself. It includes all things that are actual and all things that are possible. Its possession is incomprehensible to us, and yet it is necessary to our faith in the perfection of God's sovereignty. The revelation of this divine property like that of others is well calculated to fill us with profound reverence. It should alarm sinners and beget confidence in the hearts of God's children and deepen their consolation (*see* Job 23:10; Psa. 34:15, 16; 90:8; Jer. 17: 10; Hos. 7:2; I Pet. 3:12-14). The Scriptures unequivocally declare the divine prescience, and at the same time make their appeal to man, as a free and consequently responsible being.

Om'ri (ŏm'rĭ.)

1. The seventh king of Israel, originally commander of the armies of Elah, king of Israel, and engaged in the siege of Gibbethon when informed of the king's death and the usurpation of Zimri.

(a) **His kingship.** Proclaimed king by his army, Omri left Gibbethon and besieged Zimri in Tirzah, who in despair burned himself in his palace (I Kings 16:16), B. C. 886. Another competitor appeared in the person of Tibni, the son of Ginath. After a civil war of four years Omri was left undisputed master of the throne (vers. 21, 22), B. C. c. 876. Having resided six years in Tirzah, he removed to the mountain Shomron (Samaria), which he bought from Shemer for two talents of silver. He seems to have been a vigorous and unscrupulous ruler, anxious to strengthen his dynasty by intercourse and alliances with foreign states. He made a treaty with Benhadad I, of Damascus, surrendering to him some foreign cities (I Kings 20:34), among them, probably, Ramoth-gilead (22:3), and admitted into Samaria a resident Syrian embassy, which is described by the expression "he made streets in Samaria" for Benhadad. He united his son in marriage to the daughter of a principal Phoenician prince, which led to the introduction into Israel of Baal worship. Of Omri it is said: "Omri wrought evil in the eyes of the Lord, and did worse than all that were before him. For he walked in all the way of Jeroboam the son of Nebat, and in his sin wherewith he made Israel to sin, to provoke the Lord God of Israel to anger with their vanities" (20:25, 26). This wordly and irreligious policy is denounced by Micah (6:16) under the name of the "statues of Omri." He died B. C. c. 869, and was succeeded by his son Ahab. His daughter Athaliah was the mother of Ahaziah, king of Judah (II Kings 8:26).

(b) **Omri and archaeology.** The Moabite Stone attests the military prowess of Omri, mentioning his military successes over Moab,

lines 4-9. "Now Omri had taken possession of all the land of Medeba . . ." Years later Mesha, a wealthy sheep-owning king of Moab, was paying wool tribute to Israel (II Kings 3:4 f.). Assyrian records also attest the political and military importance of Omri. For a century after Omri's reign the Assyrians were still referring to Israel as "the land of the House of Omri." Jehu, a later Israelite usurper, is styled "Mar Humri" ("*son*," i. e., royal successor, of Omri). The Samaritan Ostraca unearthed at the "ostraca house" in Samaria, bear the names of both Yahweh and Baal, corroborating Omri's apostasy (II Kings 16:25 f.).

2. One of the sons of Becher, the son of Benjamin (I Chron. 7:8).

3. A descendant of Pharez, the son of Judah (I Chron. 9:4).

4. Son of Michael, and chief of the tribe of Issachar in the reign of David (I Chron. 27:18).

On (ŏn; *strength*).

1. The son of Peleth, and one of the chiefs of the tribe of Reuben, who took part with Korah, Dathan, and Abiram in their revolt against Moses (Num. 16:1). His name does not appear in the narrative of the conspiracy, nor is he alluded to when reference is made to the final catastrophe. There is a rabbinical tradition to the effect that he was prevailed upon by his wife to withdraw from his accomplices.

2. A city of Egypt, the residence of Potipherah, whose daughter Asenath became the wife of Joseph (Gen. 41:45, 50; 46:20). Jeremiah (43:13) calls it "Beth-shemesh, that is in the land of Egypt," to distinguish it from a city of the same name in Palestine (comp. Isa. 19:18). It was the same as *Heliopolis*, the city of the sun god *Ra*, and situated ten miles N. E. of Cairo. It was the chief city of Egyptian science. Herodotus speaks of it as one of the four great cities, noted for religious festivals in honor of the sun. Its magnificent ruins have become the richest adornments of other cities, like Rome and Constantinople. Two magnificent red Syene granite obelisks set up by the great Thutmose III (c. 1490-1450 B. C.) in front of the Temple of Re in Heliopolis now adorn the Thames Embankment in London and Central Park in New York. A single obelisk remains in Heliopolis, that set up by Senwosret I (c. 2000 B. C.) in honor of Re-Horus of the Horizon. This is a remnant of the glory of ancient Biblical On. Modern Heliopolis is Egypt's important airport. The ancient city was famous for the worship of the sun and many sun cults operated there. It was the religious capital of very early Egypt around 2900 B. C. The ancient city was about six miles from modern Cairo; nineteen miles N. of ancient Memphis. *M. F. U.*

O'nam (ō'năm; *strong, wealthy*).

1. One of the children of Shobal, the son of Seir the Horite (Gen. 36:23; I Chron. 1:40).

2. The son of Jerahmeel, of the tribe of Judah, by his wife Atarah (I Chron. 2:26). He was the father of Shammai and Jada (v. 28), B. C. about 1430.

O'nan (ō'năn; *strong*), the second son of Judah by the daughter of Shuah the Canaanite

(Gen. 38:4; 46:12; Num. 26:19; I Chron. 2:3), B. C. about 1925. When his brother Er, Judah's firstborn, was put to death by Jehovah on account of his wickedness, Onan refused, in defiance of the ancient custom, to become father by his widow, Tamar. For this he was punished by death (Gen. 38:8, sq.).

Ones'imus (ŏ-nĕs'ĭ-mŭs; Gr., *useful, profitable*), the servant (or slave) in whose behalf Paul wrote the Epistle to Philemon. He was a native, or certainly an inhabitant, of Colosse, since Paul, in writing to the Church there, speaks of him (Col. 4:9) as "one of you." Fleeing from his master Philemon to Rome, he was there led to embrace the Gospel through the instrumentality of the apostle (Philem., 10). After his conversion the most happy and friendly relations sprang up between the teacher and the disciple; and so useful had he made himself to Paul that he desired to have Onesimus remain with him. This, however, he forebore in view of the relations of Onesimus and his master's right to his services. Onesimus, accompanied by Tychicus, left Rome with not only this epistle, but with that to the Colossians (Col. 4:9, *subscription*), A. D. 60.

Onesiph'orus (ŏn-ê-sĭf'ô-rŭs; *benefit-bringing, profit-bearing*), a Christian of Ephesus who not only ministered to the apostle there (II Tim. 1:18), but who, being in Rome during Paul's second imprisonment, "was not ashamed of his chain," sought out Paul, and "often refreshed" him (1:16, 17), A. D. 60. In his epistle the apostle uttered his appreciation of the services rendered by Onesiphorus, and sent salutations to "the household of his friend" (4:19).

Onion. A bulbous-rooted plant popular in Egypt as an article of food (Num. 11:5; Herod. II:125). *See* Vegetable Kingdom.

Only Begotten (Gr. *monogenēs, single of its kind*), used of Christ (John 1:14, 18, etc.) to denote that in the sense in which he is the Son of God he has no brethren. *See* Sonship of Christ.

O'no (ō'nŏ; *strong*), a city of Benjamin built (or restored), apparently, by Shamed (I Chron. 8:12), some of the inhabitants of which returned after the captivity (Ezra 2:33; Neh. 7:37). The valley in which it was located was known as "the plain of Ono" (Neh. 6:2), probably the same as "the valley of craftsmen" (11:35), and in any case a part of the extension of the *Vale of Sharon* (*q. v.*). It is commonly identified with Kefr 'Ana, S. E. of Joppa.

On'ycha (ŏn'ĭ-kă), an ingredient of the holy incense (Exod. 30:34) used in the tabernacle ritual. It was likely obtained from a mollusk.

Onyx. *See* Mineral Kingdom.

O'phel (ō'fĕl; *mound,* or *tower*).

1. A fortified place or quarter of Jerusalem on the east side near the wall (II Chron. 27:3; 33:14), and occupied by the Nethinim after the rebuilding of the city (Neh. 3:26; 11:21). Josephus says (*Wars,* ii, 17, 9; 5:6, 1) that it adjoined the valley of the Kidron and the temple mount; and the wall of Ophel was doubtless part of the wall of the city in the time of Herod. Sir Charles Warren, after sinking a great number of shafts, has arrived

at the following facts: A great wall still exists, though buried in rubbish, joining the Haram wall at the southeast angle. It was evidently built for purposes of fortification, for it is fourteen feet thick. Some remains of a great wall were also found, leading apparently to the eastern jamb of the Triple Gate, which Sir Charles Warren thinks may have been a recess running from the Ophel wall.

2. The place in Central Palestine in which was the house where Gehazi deposited the presents which he took from Naaman (II Kings 5:24, A. V. "tower," R. V. "hill"). It was probably near the city of Samaria.

332. Area of Ophir

O'phir (ō'fêr). 1. One of the sons of Joktan, the son of Eber, a great-grandson of Shem (Gen. 10:26-29; I Chron. 1:23).

2. The famous gold-producing region prominent in the O. T. It is located in S. W. Arabia in what is now known as Yemen. It may have included a part of the adjacent African seaboard. Yemen was famous for its gold mines which are known to have still existed in the ninth century B. C. Ophir was visited by the trading fleet of Solomon and the Phoenicians. Solomon's navy was fitted out at Ezion-Geber (I Kings 9:26-28; 22:48; I Chron. 8:17, 18; 9:10), modern Tell el Keleifeh excavated by Nelson Glueck. Solomon used the copper of the Arabah, smelted at Ezion-Geber, as a stock-in-trade. His *tarshish* or "refinery" fleet sailed down the Red Sea and spent part of three years to make the trip, explainable by long hauls in excessively hot weather. In exchange for copper, Solomon's refinery fleet brought back not only the fine gold of Ophir but silver, apes, ivory and peacocks—better, "baboons" (I Kings 10:22). Gold of Ophir garnished Solomon's armor, throne, temple and House of the Forest of Lebanon (I Kings 10:14-19). *M. F. U.*

Oph'ni (ŏf'nī), a town in the northeast of Benjamin (Josh. 18:24), perhaps the Gophna of Josephus, and the Bethgufnin of the Talmud, which still survives in the modern *Jifna,* or *Jufna*, two and one-half miles N. W. of Beth-el.

Oph′rah (ŏf′rȧ; *fawn, hind*).

1. A city of Benjamin (Josh. 18:23; comp. I Sam. 13:17), probably the same as Ephrain (II Chron. 13:19), Ephraim (John 11:54), and Apherema (I Macc. 11:34).

2. A town of Manasseh, west of the Jordan and six miles S. W. of Shechem (Judg. 6:11, more fully Ophrah of the Abi-Ezrites, 8:27, 32). It was the native place of Gideon (Judg. 6:11), his residence after his ascension to power (9:5), and the place of his burial (8:32). Robinson has doubtless correct in locating it at et-Taiyibeh, 4 miles N. E. of Bethel. Because of the ephod having been deposited there it was a place of pilgrimage.

3. A Judaite, a son of Menothai (A. V Meonothai) (I Chron. 4:14), although it is more than likely that the word "begat" here means to found, and that Ophrah is the name of a village.

Oracle (Heb. *dᵉbîr*, from *dâbǎr*, to *speak;* Gr. *logion, utterance* of God), the divine communications given to the Hebrews. The manner of such utterances was various, God speaking sometimes face to face, as with Abraham and Moses; sometimes by dreams and visions, as with Joseph and Pharaoh; sometimes by signs and tokens, as with Gideon and Barak; sometimes by word of prophecy, and sometimes by a regularly organized system of communication, as with Urim and Thummim (*q. v.*). These last were distinctly Hebrew, and were always accessible, as in the case of David inquiring whether it would be safe for him to take refuge with the men of Keilah (I Sam. 23:9; comp. 30:7, 8). The earliest oracle on record, probably, is that given to Rebekah (Gen. 25:22), while the most complete is that of the child Samuel (I Sam. 3:1, sq.).

Heathen oracles are mentioned in Scripture, a celebrated case being that of Baalzebub, or Baalzebul, at Ekron, where inquiry was made respecting the recovery of King Ahaziah (II Kings 1:2). Other oracular means in Palestine were the teraphim, as that of Micah (Judg. 17:1, 5); the ephod of Gideon (8:27, etc.); the false gods of Samaria, with their false prophets, and consequently their oracles. Israel is reproached by Hosea with consulting wooden idols (4:12), and by Habakkuk (2:19).

Oration. *See* Orator.

Orator. 1. The rendering of Heb. *lāḥǎsh*, to *whisper* (Isa. 3:3). In the margin it is given as "skillful of speech," and in the R. V. "the skillful enchanter." It evidently refers to pretended skill in enchantment, and is the whispering or muttering of magical formulas.

2. *Professional advocate* (Gr. *hrētōr, speaker*), the title applied to Tertullus, who acted as the advocate of the Jewish persecutors of Paul before Felix (Acts 24:1). He was a forensic speaker, a class very common in Rome.

The *oration* (Gr. *dēmēgoria*), delivered by Herod (Acts 12:21), was a rhetorical effort addressed to the populace for the sake of popularity.

Orchard (Heb. *pǎrdēs, park*), a garden planted with trees (Eccles. 2:5; Cant. 4:13; rendered "forest" in Neh. 2:8).

Ordain, Ordained. These words are frequently used in the present sense of ordination (*q. v.*), of to *locate, establish* (Isa. 26:12), to *appoint* (II Kings 23:5). A peculiar use of the word is in the rendering of the Heb. *pä‘ǎl*, in the passage "he ordaineth his arrows against the persecutors" (Psa. 7:13), which Gesenius translates "he maketh his arrows burning," literally *into* or *for* burning, from a meaning of the Hebrew to *forge*.

Order, a word with many varieties of meaning, as it is the rendering of several Hebrew and Greek words. It is most frequently the rendering of the Heb. *‘ǎrǎk*, to set in a *row*, and is used in such phrases as the following: "He set the bread in order" (Exod. 40:23), "lay the wood in order upon the fire" (Lev. 1:7, etc.). The Greek term thus rendered is most often *taxis, arrangement*, from *tassō, set arrange*. Official dignity or office, e. g., the order of Melchisedec (Heb. 5:6, 10; 6:20, etc.), of Aaron (7:11).

Ordinances, Christian, or **of the Gospel.** These are institutions of divine authority relating to the worship of God; particularly Baptism (Matt. 28:19); the Lord's Supper (I Cor. 11:24, etc.). Besides these ordinances the following are sometimes classed in this category: public ministry, or preaching and reading the word (Rom. 10:15; Eph. 4:11, 13; Mark 16:15); hearing the word (Mark 4:24; Rom. 10:17); public prayer (Psa. 5:1, 7; Matt. 6:6; I Cor. 14:15, 19); singing of psalms (Eph. 5:19; Col. 3:16); fasting (Joel 2:12; Matt. 9:15; James 1:9); thanksgiving (Psa. 50:14; I Thess. 5:18).

Ordination. In the limited and technical sense ordination is the ceremony by which a person is set apart to an order or office; but in a broader, and in fact its only important sense, ordination signifies the appointment or designation of a person to a ministerial office, with or without attendant ceremonies.

1. **Bible Usage.** (1) **Old Testament ordination** was practiced early in Bible times. The Hebrew priests, Levites, prophets, and kings were solemnly ordained for their several offices (*see* under their several articles). Moses thus, i. e., by laying on of hands, appointed *Joshua* (*q. v.*) as his successor (Num. 27:18; Deut. 34:9). (2) **Example of Christ.** In the introduction of the Christian dispensation no exterior act of ordination was practiced by Christ. The calling, appointing, and commissioning of the twelve apostles was his personal act, unattended, so far as the record shows, with any symbolical act or ceremony. In the account (Mark 3:14) where "he ordained twelve, that they should be with him, and that he might send them forth to preach," the Greek word is *'epoiēse, he made*, i. e., he *appointed* them for the purposes named. The word rendered "ordained" (John 15:16; Gr. *'ethēka*) means "I have set, or placed." In no ordination of his disciples to their ministerial or apostolic office is it recorded that he *laid his hands upon them*. But just before his ascension, our Lord, in blessing his disciples, and breathing upon them the Holy Spirit, "lifted up his hands" (Luke 24:50; John 20:22). In so doing he illustrated the nature of the spiritual influence which was to come upon

them in its full manifestation at Pentecost. In this connection he uttered the words, so often and so grossly perverted, "Whosoever sins ye remit, they are remitted unto them; and whosoever sins ye retain, they are retained." A literal and materializing construction of this passage, with those relating to the keys, and the power of binding and loosing (Matt. 16:19; 18:18), became early in the history of the Church a great fountain of error in reference to the office and power of the clergy (see Peter). (3) **In the apostolic Church.** In the appointment of Matthias to the vacant apostleship, the principal interest appears to have centered in ascertaining whom the Lord had chosen (Acts 1:21-26); and in this case there is no evidence of the imposition of hands. *Deacons.*—The first ordination in the Christian Church was that of the seven deacons, in which case the apostles set them apart by prayer and the laying on of hands (Acts 5:5, 6). *Barnabas and Paul.*—Paul, although he had been called and set apart by Christ, submitted to the laying on of hands (Acts 13:1-3). "The simplest interpretation is that the Church as a whole held a special service for this solemn purpose. *Codex Bezae* makes all clear by inserting the nominative 'all.' . . . Further, there is no sign in 13:2, 3 that this 'consecration' by the Church was more efficacious than the original divine call; the ceremony merely blessed Barnabas and Saul for a special work, which was definitely completed in the next three years" (Ramsey, *St. Paul the Traveler*, pp. 66, 67). *Elders.*—It is recorded (14:23) that Paul and Barnabas "ordained them elders in every church." In this narrative the Greek word *cheirotoneō* is used for the first time. Unfortunately its meaning is by no means certain; "for, though originally it meant *to elect by popular vote*, yet it came to be used in the sense *to appoint* or *designate*. It must, certainly, be allowed that the votes and voice of each congregation were considered; and the term is obviously used in that way by Paul (II Cor. 8:19). As to the ceremonies used in these ordinations, only prayer, fasting, and commending the persons ordained to the Lord are mentioned.

In reviewing the scriptural instances of ordination we note the following: 1. Christ ordained in the sense of appointing his disciples to ministerial service by his own authority and without employing any ceremony. 2. In the election of Matthias to fill the place of Judas, it was deemed sufficient to learn by prayer and the lot whom the Lord had chosen, and without any exterior ceremony to number him with the eleven. 3. The laying on of hands as a ceremony of ministerial ordination was first practiced by the apostles in the case of the seven deacons. 4. It was also practiced in the case of Paul and Barnabas, and the elders of the New Testament Church. 5. We have no account of anyone having been ordained to the office of bishop in distinction from that of elder; still less is there any intimation that bishops were or were to become the only officers competent to ordain ministerial candidates; whereas elders were frequently, if not always, associated even with apostles in the act of ordination.

2. **Meaning of Ordination**, etc. Ordination in the early Church seems to have been regarded as a formal induction into the ministerial office, and as having more significance than a mere conferment of the authority of the Church. The clergy were at first elected by the people; and Clement of Rome speaks of them as having been appointed by other distinguished men, with the approbation of the whole Church. But the fact that the special ordination of the presbyters or the bishop was considered necessary, seems to imply that a special efficacy was associated with the rite. Augustine, however, distinctly exclaims, "What else is the imposition of hands than a prayer over a man?" With the growing importance of the episcopal office, and the sanctity associated with it and the clergy in general, the rite of ordination assumed the character of a sacramental act, in which a special grace was conferred, and which could only be performed by the bishop. The ordination of clergymen was as early as the 4th or 5th century admitted into the number of the sacraments. It is so held now by the Roman Catholic and Greek Churches. In the Church of England and the Episcopal Church of the United States ordination has not the significance of a sacrament; and the view of the English Reformers was not that the laying on of hands, as such, conferred any grace. Bishops only can ordain, and any other than episcopal ordination is invalid. The Lutheran and Reformed Churches have always acknowledged and practiced ordination; but their confessions and theologians have justly laid stress upon the necessity of the divine call or vocation to the ministry. The Moravians confine the right to ordain to their bishops, but recognize the validity of the ordination by other Protestants. The Disciples of Christ, Quakers, and Plymouth Brethren do not recognize any human rite of ordination. The Discipline of the Methodist Church provides for the ordination of deacons by the bishop (¶ 163), while an "elder is constituted by the election of the Annual Conferance, and by the laying on of hands of a bishop and some of the elders who are present" (Dis., ¶ 166). The following note in the Discipline (¶ 449) sets forth the Methodist view as to bishops: "This service is not to be understood as an ordination to a higher order in the Christian ministry, beyond and above that of elders or presbyters, but as a solemn and fitting consecration for the special and most sacred duties of superintendency in the Church."

O'reb (ō'rĕb; *a raven*), one of the chieftains of the Midianite host which invaded Israel, and was defeated and driven back by Gideon. He was killed, not by Gideon himself or the people under his immediate conduct, but by the men of Ephraim, who rose at his entreaty and intercepted the flying horde at the fords of the Jordan (Judg. 7:24, 25), B. C. about 1200. The terms in which Isaiah refers to it (10:26) are such as to imply that it was a truly awful slaughter. He places it in the same rank with the two most tremendous disasters recorded in the whole of the history of Israel—the destruction of the Egyptians in the Red Sea and of the army of Sennacherib (comp. Psa. 83:11).

O'reb, Rock of (ō'rĕb; the *raven's crag*), the place at which Gideon slew Oreb (Judg. 7:25; Isa. 10:26), thought by some to be east of Jordan. Keil and Delitzsch say (*Com.*, in loc.) that it was "west of Jordan, where the Ephraimites had taken possession of the waters of the Jordan in front of the Midianites."

O'ren (ō'rĕn), the third named of the sons of Jerahmeel, of the tribe of Judah (I Chron. 2:25), B. C. about 1190.

Organ. *See* Music.

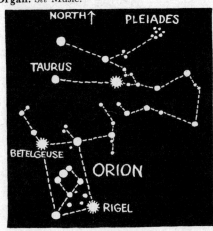

333. Orion

Ori'on (ō-rī'ŏn), the celestial constellation composed of myriads of stars, most of which are invisible without a telescope. It was early imagined to resemble the form of a hunter who, according to ancient legend, was put to death by Artemis after his pursuit of the Pleiades. Job attributed the creation of Orion, Arcturus and Pleiades to God (Job 9:9; 38: 31). This constellation is located S. of Taurus and Gemini. It includes the giants Betelgeuse and Rigel. *M. F. U.*

Ornament (Hebrew generally *'ădî, trapping*), the number, variety, and weight of the ornaments ordinarily worn upon the person, form one of the characteristic features of oriental costume, both in ancient and modern times. The monuments of ancient Egypt exhibit the wealthy ladies loaded with rings, earrings of very great size, anklets, armlets, bracelets of the most varied character, richly ornamented necklaces, and chains of various kinds. There is sufficient evidence in the Bible that the inhabitants of Palestine were equally devoted to finery. The Midianites appear to have been as prodigal as the Egyptians in the use of ornaments (Num. 31:50, 52; Judg. 8:26).

1. **Male.** From the most ancient times two ornaments pertained to men, a staff in the hand (Gen. 38:18), and a seal worn by a ribbon on the breast, or in a ring on the right hand (Gen. 41:42; Jer. 22:24; Esth. 3:10; 8:2). *Earrings*, which were worn by the Midianites (Judg. 8:24, sq.) and other orientals, seem not to have been worn by men among the Israelites (Exod. 32:2). Neither do gold necklaces appear as a male ornament among the Israelites, as they do among the Persians and Medes; nor does the custom of the Egyptians and Medo-Persians, whose kings adorned their highest ministers with gold chain as insignia of office or tokens of their favor (Gen. 41:42; Dan. 5:7).

2. **Female.** Much more varied were the ornaments and jewelry of Israelitish women. In the Old Testament Isaiah (3:18-23) supplies us with a detailed description of the articles with which the luxurious women of his day were decorated, and the picture is filled up by incidental notices in other places. The notices which occur in the early books of the Bible imply the weight and abundance of the ornaments worn at that period. *Earrings* were worn by Jacob's wives, apparently as charms, for they are mentioned in connection with idols: "They gave unto Jacob all the strange gods which were in their hand, and their earrings which were in their ears" (Gen. 35:4). *Nose rings* were worn in the right or left nostril, perhaps also in the division of the nose (Gen. 24:47; Isa. 3:21; Ezek. 16:12). *Necklaces*—These were made of metal, of jewels or pearls, strung on a ribbon (Cant. 1:10), hanging down to the breast or girdle. To these were attached golden *crescents* (Isa. 3:18; Judg. 8:21), perhaps also *amulets* (Isa. 3:20), *sunlets* (3:18), and *smelling bottles*. *Armlets* (Gen. 24:22; Num. 31:50, sq.); Isa. 3:19, worn also by men of rank (II Sam. 1:10), also in each passage rendered *bracelets*, *anklets* (Isa. 3:18), fastened with *chains* (3:20), which coquettes used to make a tinkling as they tripped along (3:16). These trinkets were made of gold in the case of women of rank; and, in addition, hand mirrors of metal (Exod. 38:8; Isa. 3:23), probably carried in the hand as ornaments. The poetical portions of the Old Testament contain numerous references to the ornaments worn by the Israelites in the time of their highest prosperity. The appearance of the bride is thus described in the Canticles (1:10, 11; 4:4, 9; 5:12; 7:1). In reference to the terms used in the Proverbs we need only explain that the "ornament" of the A. V. in 1:9; 4:9, is more specifically a *wreath* or *garland;* the "chains" of 1:9, the *drops* of which the necklace was formed; the "jewel of gold in a swine's snout" of 11:22, a *nose ring;* the "jewel" of 20:15, a *trinket*, and the "ornament" of 25:12, an *ear pendant. See* Dress; Jewelry.

Or'nan (ôr'năn), the form given (I Chron. 21:15, 18, 20-25, 28; II Chron. 3:1) to *Araunah* (q. v.).

Oron'tes (ō-rŏn'tēz), an historically famous river of Syria taking its source in the elevated Beka'a Valley. It runs N. through Syria and then W. into the Mediterranean Sea at the port of ancient Antioch on-the-Orontes, named Seleucia Pieria. Antioch was a famous N. T. center of early Christianity (Acts 11: 20-26; 13:1-3). Riblah appears prominently in II Kings and Jeremiah in connection with Zedekiah of Judah and Nebuchadnezzar (II Kings 25:20, 21; Jer. 39:5, 6; 52:9-11). Other important centers on the Orontes were Hamath, a Hittite stronghold, Kadesh, where Raamses II clashed with the Hittites, and

Homs (Emessa), a center of early Christianity. *M. F. U.*

Or'pah (ôr'på; *neck*), a Moabitess, and wife of Chilion, the son of Naomi. At first she was disposed to accompany her mother-in-law to Canaan, but afterward decided to remain among her own people. She gave Naomi the kiss of farewell, and returned "unto her people and unto her gods" (Ruth 1:4, 14).

Orphan (Heb. *yāthōm, lonely,* Lam. 5:3), one deprived of one or both parents. But the Hebrew word, as well as the Greek (*orphanos,* John 14:18), is used figuratively for one bereft of a teacher, guide, guardian. In this sense the Greek word *'aporphanizō* (I Thess. 2:17) is used, *bereft of your* intercourse and society.

O'see (ō'zê), a less correct mode (Rom. 9:25) of Anglicizing the name of the prophet *Hosea* (*q. v.*).

Oshe'a (ō-shē'á; *deliverer*), another form (Num. 13:8, 16, sometimes *Hoshea*) of the name of *Joshua* (*q. v.*)

Osnap'per (ŏs-năp'ẽr). *See* Ashurbanipal.

Ospray. *See* Animal Kingdom.

Ossifrage. *See* Animal Kingdom.

Os'tia (ŏs'tĭ-ă), a famous seaport of Rome at the mouth of the Tiber. The port connected with the city proper by the Ostian Way. Paul's ship landed at Puteoli (Acts 28:13), another port accommodating heavily-laden grain ships. Ostia was excavated 1914-1946. The town has given evidence of tremendous granaries and warehouses, a lavish theatre, several sanctuaries of the Mithra cult and other temples. The Ostian excavations have revealed a great deal about the wealth, commerce and religious sects in Rome at the time of Paul. *M. F. U.*

Ostrich. *See* Animal Kingdom.

    Figurative. In Lam. 4:3 the ostrich is used as a symbol of the unnatural cruelty of the Jews in their calamity; while in companionship the ostrich (Job 30:29, marg.) is a figure of extreme desolation; taken from the isolated life of that bird in the desert.

Oth'ni (ŏth'nĭ; apocopated from Othniel), one of the sons of Shemaiah, and a porter of the tabernacle (I Chron. 26:7).

Oth'niel (ŏth'nĭ-ĕl; *God is might*).

    1. "The son of Kenaz, Caleb's younger brother" (Judg. 3:9). The probability is that Kenaz was the head of the tribe (Judah), and that Othniel, as the son of Jephunneh, was one of the descendants of Kenaz. (1) **Captures Debir** (*q. v.*). The first mention of Othniel is on the occasion of the taking of Kirjath-sepher, or Debir, as it was afterward called. Caleb, to whom the city was assigned, offered as a reward to its captor Achsah, his daughter. Othniel won the prize (Josh. 15:16, 17; Judg. 1:12, 13), B. C. about c. 1380. (2) **Delivers Israel.** "Israel forgot the Lord their God, and served Baalim and the groves" (Ashtaroth). As a punishment for their idolatry the Lord delivered them into the hands of *Chushan-rishathaim* (*q. v.*), king of Mesopotamia, whom they were obliged to serve for eight years. In this oppression the Israelites cried unto the Lord, and he raised them up a deliverer in the person of Othniel the Kenizzite. "The Spirit of the Lord came upon him,

and he judged Israel, and went out to war." He prevailed against Chushan-rishathaim, "and the land had rest forty years; and Othniel the son of Kenaz died" (Judg. 3:7-11), B. C. about 1360.

    2. An Othniel is mentioned (I Chron. 27:15) as ancestor of Heldai, the head of a family of Netophathites, and probably the same person as above.

Ouch (ouch; pl. "ouches," Heb. *mĭshbĕṣäh, woven-together* in filigree fashion), an archaic term referring to the gold work, which not only served to fasten the stones upon the woven fabric of the ephod, but formed at the same time clasps or brooches, by which the two parts of the ephod were fastened together (Exod. 28:11, sq.; 39:6, sq.). *See* High Priest, Dress of.

Outcasts (Heb. *däḥäh, expell, drive out*). Israel is compared to an outcast, i. e., as a wife put away by her husband (Jer. 30:17; comp. Isa. 62:4). Because of the nation Israel's rejection of their Messiah, they have been driven out of the land of Palestine and scattered among the nations (Isa. 11:12). At the conversion of the remnant at the second advent of Christ they are to be restored in national blessing.

Outlandish (Heb. *nōkrî*, Neh. 13:26), "foreign," as the women of other nations which caused Solomon to sin.

Outrageous (Heb. *shätäph*, to *gush out*, Prov. 27:4), whence the metaphor, anger is an *outpouring*.

Oven (Heb. *ṭännūr, fire pot;* Gr. *klibanos, earthen pot*). Of ovens, or places for baking, there are in the East four kinds:

    1. The mere sand, heated by a fire, which was afterward removed. The raw dough was placed upon it, and in a little while turned; and then, to complete the process, covered with warm ashes and coals. Unless turned they were not thoroughly baked (Hos. 7:8).

    2. An excavation in the earth, lined with pottery. This is heated, the dough spread on the sides, and so baked.

    3. A large stone jar, about three feet high, open at the top, and widening toward the bottom, with a hole for the extraction of the ashes. Each household possessed such an article (Exod. 8:3); and it was only in times of extreme dearth that the same oven sufficed for several familes (Lev. 26:26). It was heated with dry twigs and grass (Matt. 6:30), and the loaves were placed both inside and outside of it.

    4. A plate of iron, placed upon three stones; the fire was kindled beneath it, and the raw cakes placed upon the upper surface. No doubt bakers had a special oven in ancient times (Hos. 7:4, 6), such as are now public in oriental cities.

    Figurative. "Ten women shall bake your bread in one oven" (Lev. 26:26) is a figurative expression for scarcity; for in ordinary times each woman would have enough baking for an oven of her own. "Thou shalt make them as a fiery oven" (Psa. 21:9) is a figure taken from the intense heat of an oven being prepared for baking; hence speedy destruction (comp. Hos. 7:4, 6, 7). "Our skin was black like an oven" (Lam. 5:10). As an oven is scorched and blackened with fire, so hunger dries up the pores till the skin becomes as if scorched by the sun.

Overlive (Josh. 24:31) is another form for *outlive*.

Overpass (Heb. *'ābăr,* to *cross* over,' Jer. 5:28), to excel, to go beyond, here in badness.

Overseer (Hebrew usually *pāqĭd,* a *visitor;* Gr. *episkopos,* a *bishop,* Acts 20:28); an officer having the superintendence of the household, as Joseph (Gen. 39:4, 5); a superintendent of workmen (II Chron. 2:18); of the Levites (31:13; 34:12); leader of singers (Neh. 12:42). *See* Bishop.

Overshadow (Gr. *episkiazō,* to *envelope in a shadow*). From a vaporous cloud that casts a shadow the word is transferred to a shining cloud surrounding and enveloping persons with brightness (Matt. 17:5; Luke 9:34).

Figurative. It is used of the Holy Spirit extending creative energy upon the womb of the Virgin Mary and impregnating it; a use of the word which seems to have been drawn from the familiar Old Testament idea of a cloud as symbolizing the immediate presence and power of God.

Owl. *See* Animal Kingdom.

Ox, a castrated male of the *Bos tauros* family valued in the O. T. period as a patient heavy draft animal. *See* Animal Kingdom.

Figurative. "As the ox licketh up the grass" (Num. 22:4) is a figure of easy victory. For an "ox to low over his fodder" (Job 6:5) is to complain without cause. "Ox led to slaughter," of a rash youth (Prov. 7:22), or of saints under persecution (Jer. 11:19). To "send forth the feet of the ox and the ass" (Isa. 32:20; literally, let the feet of the ox and the ass rove in freedom), is a figure of copious abundance, inasmuch as the cattle would not have to be watched lest they should stray into the grain fields. "A stalled ox" (Prov. 15:17) represents sumptuous living. Oxen not muzzled in treading corn (I Cor. 9:9, 10) is figurative of the minister's right to support.

Ox Goad. *See* Goad.

O'zem (ō'zĕm; probably *strength*).

1. The sixth son of Jesse, and next eldest above David (I Chron. 2:15), B. C. about 1060.

2. One of the sons of Jerahmeel (I Chron. 2:25), B. C. about 1190.

Ozi'as (ō-zī'ás), another form of the name of Uzziah, king of Judah (Matt. 1:8, 9).

Oz'ni (ŏz'nĭ; *cared,* i. e., *attentive*), the fourth son of Gad, and the founder of the family of Oznites (Num. 26:16).

Oz'nites (ŏz'nīts; *having* quick *ears*), the descendants of *Ozni* (*q. v.*), or Ezbon (Gen. 46:16), one of the families of the tribe of Gad (Num. 26:16).

P

Pa'arai (pā'á-rī), "the Arbite," one of David's valiant men (II Sam. 23:35), called in I Chron. 11:37 *Naarai* (*q. v.*).

Pace (Heb. *ṣă'ăd,* a *step,* as elsewhere rendered). This was not a formal measure, but taken in the general sense (II Sam. 6:13). *See* Metrology, I, 5.

Pa'dan (pā'dăn; Heb. *păddăn, plain, field*), R. V. and R. S. V. Paddan-Aram (*q. v.*) (Gen. 48:7).

Pa'dan-A'ram (pā'dăn-ā'răm; *plain* or *field of Aram,* i. e., Syria), R. V. and R. S. V. Paddan-Aram (păd'ăn-ā'răm), the name given to the country of Rebekah (Gen. 25:20), and the abode of Laban (28:2-7); called "the field of Aram" by Hosea (12:12, A. V. "country of Syria"). It was a district of *Mesopotamia* (*q. v.*), the large plain surrounded by mountains, in which the town of Haran was situated. Padan-aram was intimately associated with the history of the Hebrews. Abraham's family had settled there, and thither he sent his steward to secure a wife for Isaac (Gen. 24:10, sq.; 25:20); and later Jacob went there and married (28:2; 31:18, sq.).

Paddle (Heb. *yăthĕd, peg,* a *tent-pin,* Judg. 4:21). Outside the camp of Israel, in their journeying, was a space for the necessities of nature, and among their implements was this spade for digging a hole before they sat down, and afterward for filling it up. It was a tool for sticking in, or for digging (Deut. 23:13).

Pa'don (pā'dŏn; *redemption, ransom, deliverance*), the name of one of the Nethinim, whose descendants returned from Babylon (Ezra 2:44; Neh. 7:47), B. C. about 536.

Pa'giel (pā'gĭ-ĕl; *meeting* or *rendezvous* with God), the son of Ocran, and chief of the tribe of Asher at the time of the exodus (Num. 1:13; 2:27; 7:72; 10:26), B. C. c. 1440.

Pa'hath-Mo'ab (pā'hăth-mō'ăb; *governor of Moab*), the head of a leading family of Judah, whose descendants, to the number of two thousand eight hundred and twelve, returned to Jerusalem after the captivity (Ezra 2:6; Neh. 7:11, two thousand eight hundred and eighteen), and another company, of two hundred males, under Ezra (Ezra 8:4). Hashub the Pahath-moabite is named among the builders of the walls of Jerusalem (Neh. 3:11). In Ezra 10:30, eight of the "sons" of Pahath-moab are named as putting away their strange wives. That this family was of high rank in the tribe of Judah we learn from their appearing *fourth* in order in the two lists (Ezra 2:6; Neh. 7:11); and from their chief having signed *second,* among the lay princes (Neh. 10:14).

Pa'i (pā'ī; I Chron. 1:50). *See* Pau.

Painting, a form of art which played an important role in antiquity.

1. **Palestine.** Ancient painting as early as the fourth millennium B. C. showed remarkable vitality. The most popular type of work of this kind was done on cave walls or plastered surfaces. Very early paintings have been found at such sites as Megiddo and Jericho. Egyptian and Mesopotamian art of this type

also flourished. The wealth and ease afforded by these irrigation cultures fostered leisure and supplied the means for the cultivation of the arts. Famous in Palestine are the paintings on cave walls in the Hellenistic city of Marisa (Beit Jibrin) dating from the third century B. C.

2. **Egypt.** Egyptian belief in life after death manifested itself in bright coloring and cheerful painting adorning the walls of rock-cut tombs as at Thebes and Saqqarah. The Egyptians were skillful in designing objects of everyday life, the lotus with bud and leaf, the animals and birds of the Nile Valley, and lifelike people and events. In fine colors they portrayed on sarcophagi and mummy cases, festal meals and social pastimes, scenes from city life and farm life. The Egyptians ground their paints on stones worn smooth by constant use. These relics of an ancient art may be seen in many museums.

3. **Crete.** Knossos in Crete shows famous painted frescoes executed between 1900 and 1750 B. C. Minoan Crete, explored by Sir Arthur Evans, has given us much information of paintings in the House of the Frescoes and on sarcophagi. Such frescoes as the "Saffron Gatherer" and the "Toreodor and his horse" are notable for their artistic execution.

4. **Rome.** Fresco painting was widely popular in the time of Jesus and in the apostolic age. Excavations at Pompeii in the Villa of the Mysteries have yielded elaborate cultic rites executed in fresco paintings. Such paintings come from all parts of the Roman world. *M. F. U.*

Painting the Eyes. *See* Eyes, Painting of.

Palace, the dwelling of a king or important official. All over the Biblical world palaces figure prominently.

1. **In Israel.** Saul's austere palace-fortress has been excavated at Gibeah by W. F. Albright and displays stout masonry, cyclopean walls and rustic construction. David's first palace was at Hebron and must have been a crude edifice compared with his more lavish dwelling at Jebusite Jerusalem, which he captured. Hiram of Tyre sent him cedar trees, and carpenters and artisans to build him a house (II Sam. 5:11). David's palace must have been very simple, but nevertheless, evidently showed evidence of Phoenician artistry. Solomon's palace was much grander. This was indeed a lavish building, as we may gather from I Kings, but unfortunately, nothing survives of it. The vast wealth of Solomon and Phoenician skilled workers and material doubtless produced a fabulous structure. Herod the Great's palace in the first century B. C. was also grandly magnificent. At the city of Samaria Omri and his son Ahab in the first quarter of the ninth century B. C. built lavish palaces, as did also Jeroboam II in the following century. Herod also much later built grandly at Sebastieh.

2. **In Egypt.** All of the pharaohs of Egypt's thirty dynasties had ornate and expensive palaces. Knowledge of these has come down through tomb reliefs and other forms of art. Especially well known is the palace of Merenptah, the son of Raamses II, about 1230 B. C. This palace was destroyed by fire,

which left traces of painted frescoes; walls were brick, the roof of wood. The throne room opened at the end of a colonnaded court. The room was supported by six huge columns of white limestone, 25 feet high. The king's cartòuche appears on the bronze door fastenings. The palace of Amenhotep III at Thebes has also been excavated by the Metropolitan Museum of Art. (*See* its bulletins from 1916-1918). The palace of Amenhotep IV (c. 1385-1366 B. C.) is also very well known. It was built at Akhetaten at Amarna where the famous Amarna Letters were discovered. The king's palace was designated the "castle" of Aton. The palace was surrounded by a famous complex of buildings. A double wall (with fortified passages) ran around the palace. The queen, the famous Nofretete, had her own palace. The royal residence also had priestly quarters situated near the Chapel of Aton, as well as large servants' quarters and a place for craftsmen.

3. **In Mesopotamia.** Both Assyrians and the Babylonians had splendid palaces. The palaces of Sargon II (772-705 B. C.) and of his Son Sennacherib are well-known for their size and lavish decorations. Nebuchadnezzar's palace at Babylon in the sixth century B. C. is also famous. The throne room of Nebuchadnezzar II was adorned with enamel bricks done in artistic geometrical lines. Bulls and dragons in enameled, colored bricks were favorite decorative motifs in the Babylon of this era, which was world-famous for its many buildings, including temples, ziggurats, wide processional streets, hanging gardens and other architectural wonders. Nebuchadnezzar's palace fitted in with the splendor of its surroundings. A notable royal palace was uncovered at Mari on the Middle Euphrates. Dating from around 1700 B. C. This tremendous structure covers more than 15 acres, including not only royal apartments but administrative offices and even a school for scribes. It was adorned with great mural paintings, portions of which are still in a fair state of preservation, containing depictions of sacrifice and a scene in which the king of Mari receives from Ishtar, the goddess of propogation, the emblematic staff and ring symbolic of his royal power (Cf. A. Parrot in *Syria* 18, 1937, p. 325-354. Also copies of *Syria* from 1935-1939). The palaces of the great Persian monarchs at Persepolis are also noteworthy for their vastness and extravagance. The palaces of ancient Susa, which have been excavated by Jacque de Morgan, illustrate the story of Nehemiah, who refers to the time when he was "in Shushan, the palace" acting as cup-bearer to Artaxerxes, the king. It also reminds us of Dan. 8:2.

4. **In Crete.** The palaces excavated by Sir Arthur Evans reveal great labyrinths at Knossos and a whole series of chambers. These palaces constitute wonders of the ancient world and display the glory of Minoan culture. *M. F. U.*

Pa′lal (pā′lǎl; *He*, i. e., God, *judges*), the son of Uzai, and one of those who assisted in rebuilding the walls of Jerusalem (Neh. 3:25), B. C. 445.

Palesti′na (păl-ĕs-tī′nà; Exod. 15:14; Isa. 14: 29, 31), elsewhere *Palestine* (*q. v.*).

Palestine. Palestine, as the scene of ancient Biblical events, is the region of S. W. Asia extending S. and S. W. of the Lebanon

ranges, N. E. of Egypt and N. of the Sinai Peninsula. The River of Egypt (Gen. 17:18; II Chron. 7:8), the modern Wadi el-Arish, is its S. W. boundary. On the W. its boundary is the Mediterranean plain and on the E., the

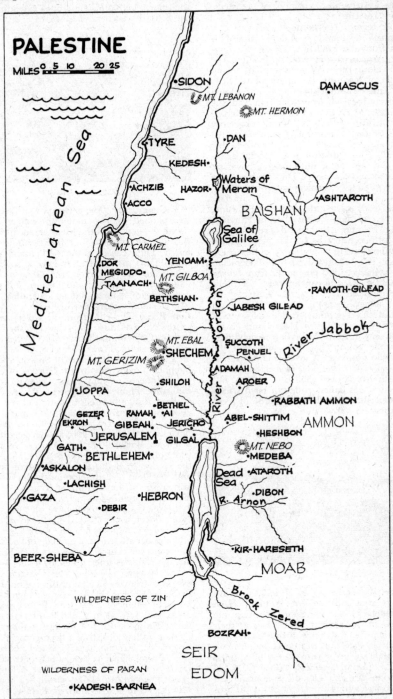

PALESTINE

MILES 0 5 10 20 25

Mediterranean Sea

SIDON
MT. LEBANON
DAMASCUS
MT. HERMON
TYRE
DAN
KEDESH
HAZOR
Waters of Merom
ACHZIB
ASHTAROTH
ACCO
BASHAN
MT. CARMEL
Sea of Galilee
DOR
YENOAM
MEGIDDO
MT. GILBOA
TAANACH
RAMOTH-GILEAD
BETHSHAN
JABESH GILEAD
River Jabbok
MT. EBAL
SUCCOTH
MT. GERIZIM
SHECHEM
PENUEL
ADAMAH
SHILOH
AROER
JOPPA
RABBATH AMMON
BETHEL
GEZER
RAMAH
AI
ABEL-SHITTIM
AMMON
EKRON
GIBEAH
JERICHO
HESHBON
JERUSALEM
GILGAL
GATH
MT. NEBO
BETHLEHEM
MEDEBA
ASKALON
Dead Sea
ATAROTH
LACHISH
DIBON
GAZA
HEBRON
R. Arnon
DEBIR
BEER-SHEBA
KIR-HARESETH
MOAB
WILDERNESS OF ZIN
Brook Zered
BOZRAH
SEIR
WILDERNESS OF PARAN
EDOM
KADESH-BARNEA

River Jordan

334.

Arabian Desert. It formed a tiny bridge between the ancient empires on the Tigris-Euphrates Rivers in Mesopotamia, on the Halys River in Asia Minor and the mighty civilization of Egypt on the Nile. It constitutes the westernmost extremity of Breasted's "Fertile Crescent."

1. **The Name.** The name of Palestine as a geographical distinction is of later origin. It is derived from the Philistines (*Peleste*), a non-Semitic Aegean strain, who settled in large numbers along the S. W. coastal plain during the reign of Raamses III of Egypt (c. 1190 B. C.). This area subsequently became known as Philistia (Joel 3:4) from which, in turn, the Greek name *hē Palaistinē* was derived. Herodotus in the fifth century B. C. was apparently the first to use *Palaistinē*. The Romans called it Palestina (cf. the A. V. of Exod. 15:14; Isa. 14:29, 31). Palestine as an official designation did not come into usage, however, until the second century A. D., first describing the S. W. plain of Phoenicia and subsequently applied to all Palestine W. of the Jordan. Canaan (*q. v.*) is the older name of Palestine, the former seemingly derived from Hurrian, meaning "belonging to the land of red purple." By the 14th century B. C. this geographical appellation came to be employed of the region in which the "Canaanites," or Phoenician traders exchanged red-purple die from murex shells on the Mediterranean coast for other commodities. In the Amarna Letters "the land of Canaan" is applied to the Phoenician coast and the Egyptians called all western Syria by this name. The "Holy Land" is referred to only in Zech. 2:10. This name differentiates the country as Jehovah's and the people who possessed it in covenant relation with Him. After the O. T. period in the Hellenistic-Roman era (333 B. C.-300 A. D.) the country was called Judea, a term which at first described only the region around Jerusalem after the Babylonian exile.

335. Jordan River

2. **Size.** It averages about 70 miles in width and its greatest width is some 90 miles. "Dan to Beersheba," an expression denoting the extremity of the ancient boundaries at their fullest extent, is a distance of only about 150 miles. O. T. Palestine was never much more than 10,000 sq. miles with barely 6000 miles W. of the Jordan and less than 4000 E. of the Jordan. In the Davidic-Solomonic era the boundaries roughly extended to the Euphrates and to the borders of Egypt, but this included tributary peoples, a population of about two million people or possibly over three million counting tributary peoples. In N. T. times Palestine consisted of Roman Judea, composed of Galilee, our Lord's home province in the N. W., Samaria, occupying the central highlands and Judea extending on the S. to the borders of Idumaea.

336. Nazareth

3. **Geography.** The geography of Palestine is explained by two mountain ranges separating the land from the Mediterranean to the Arabian Desert into four bands running N. and S. These consist of the level coastal Maritime Plain, the Central Range or southerly spur from Mt. Lebanon, the Ghor or deep valley of the Jordan, and Eastern Palestine, consisting of a long plateau extending from Mt. Hermon to Mr. Hor in Edom. (a) **Maritime Plain.** This runs from the River Leontes on the N., five miles N. of Tyre, to the desert beyond Gaza on the south. Mt. Carmel interrupts the valley. From Carmel S. to Joppa the area is known as the Plain of Sharon and the Shephelah from Joppa to the Brook of Gaza, the southern portion being known as the Philistine Plain. (b) **Central Range.** The Central Range as a continuation of the Lebanon Mts. consists of Galilee, Samaria and Judea. In Upper Galilee rise a number of hills, some to 2000 to 3000 feet in height and a few to almost 4000 feet. Lower Galilee is triangular, bounded by the Sea of Galilee and the Jordan to Bethshan on its eastern border and the Plain of Esdraelon on the S. W. side. It consists of ranges running E. and W. with elevation much less than Upper Galilee. Hills of Lower Galilee usually have an altitude of 400-600 feet, though Mt. Tabor reaches 1,843 feet and Mt. Gilboa has one peak 1,698 feet and another 1,648 feet. The Plain of Esdraelon intercepts the central region. South of Esdraelon the range is interrupted by many wadis. Mt. Ebal rises 3,077 feet and Gerizim 2,849 feet. Samaria was located in this region. From Bethel to Hebron, in Judea, the range has an average height of 2200 feet. Bethel reaches 2,930 feet, Jerusalem 2,598, Bethlehem 2,550 and Hebron 3,040. (c) **Jordan Valley.** The Jordan Valley consists of a deep gorge. At the foot of Mt. Hermon it is 1700 feet above sea level. From thence it descends rapidly to the Dead Sea where it is 1,290 feet below sea level. The bottom of the Dead Sea reaches 1300 feet still lower than its surface, recognized as the lowest point on the earth's surface and being a part of an amazing geological

fault running S. to the Red Sea and into East
Africa. (d) **Eastern Palestine** is a large, fertile
plateau, much of it more than 3000 feet above
sea level. It included ancient Bashan, Gilead
and Moab. This general territory is divided
naturally into four parts by four rivers. There
is the Yarmuk River with Bashan to the N.
and the Jabbok with Gilead to the N. and S.;
the Arnon, S. of which was Moab; and the
River Zered, with Edom located southward.
The Yarmuk and Jabbok are tributaries of
the Jordan. The Arnon and the Zered flow
into the Dead Sea. South of the Dead Sea lies
the deep copper-rich Arabah stretching to
Ezion-Geber at the head of the Red Sea.

4. **Climate.** Because of the diversity in elevation from Hermon's snowy 9,101 feet to
the Dead Sea's tropical 1,290 feet below sea
level, great variety of flora and fauna are accordingly found. In the hill country prevailing
W. winds create copious rains from October
to April. East winds from the desert bring
intense heat and discomfort (Job 1:19; Jer.
18:17; Ezek. 17:10). Two seasons characterize Palestine: winter—moist, rainy, mild,
from November to April; summer—hot and
rainless, May to October.

337. Sea of Galilee

5. **Biblical Archaeology.** Prehistoric archaeologists claim important finds in Palestine long before the Biblical period. In the
Chalcolithic Age (c. 4500-3000 B. C.) early
Palestinian cultures appear at Teleilat Ghas-
sul just N. of the Dead Sea, not far from
Jericho. At this early period mud brick houses
were adorned with amazing mural paintings.
Artistic frescoes survive. The Bronze Age
(c. 3000-2000 B. C.) is marked by the discovery of the earliest Canaanite sancturaies
at Megiddo, Jericho and Ai. The Middle
Bronze Age (c. 2000-1500 B. C.) is marked
at the beginning by Abraham's entrance into
Palestine which, in this period was thinly
settled in the highland regions, which were
heavily forested. Archaeology has fully corroborated the general background of the patriarchal period. The Middle Bronze Age
cities were stoutly fortified with high walls,
towers, moats and cyclopean masonry. In the
Late Bronze Age (1500-1200 B. C.) came the
Israelites. Their conquest of Palestine took
place around 1400 B. C. (Massoretic chronology). At this period City D of Jericho was
built upon three earlier predecessors. It was
this city that eventually fell to Joshua and

338. Ruins of Old Testament Jericho

the Israelites. During the period of Israelite
conquest Ai and Bethel figure prominently, as
well as Lachish. These cities have all been
excavated. The situation at Ai particularly
offers difficulty, because et-Tell, identified
as Ai, was unoccupied 2000-1050 B. C. But
there is growing question as to whether or
not this identification is correct. Other important sites excavated in Palestine and yielding much light on Biblical history are Beth-
shan, Taanach, Megiddo in the Plain of Esdraelon, Gezer on the lower slope above the
Maritime Plain, and Beth-shemesh, S. E. of
Gezer in the Shephelaḥ. Other important sites
excavated are Samaria, and in part Jerusalem,
Saul's fortress at Gibeah and Debir, or Tell
Beit Mirsim. Excavations at the large site of
Hazor are now in progress.

6. **History.** The first glimpse of the history
of Palestine is found in Genesis (ch. 10).
Canaan, the son of Ham, is the father of
Sidon, i. e., the Phoenician stock; Heth, i. e.,
the Hittites; the Jebusite, a local tribe in and
about Jerusalem; the Amorite, men of the
hills; the Girgashite, an unknown stock; the
Hivite, peasantry or fellahîn; the Arkite, citizens of Arka, in northern Phoenicia; the
Sinite, people from some locality near Arka;
The Arvadite, inhabitants of the island of
Arvad off Tartos; the Zemarite, inhabitants
of Sumra, and the Hamathite, the inhabitants
of Hamath. "And afterward were the inhabitants of the Canaanite spread abroad, and
the border of the Canaanite was from Sidon,

339. Ruins of New Testament Jericho: Tell 1
is to the right of the minaret; Tell 2 is near
the left edge of the picture

as thou goest toward Gerar unto Gaza; as
thou goest toward Sodom and Gomorrah and
Adama and Zeboim unto Lasha." These
boundaries are substantially those of Canaan,
and later those of Palestine. Some of the

primitive inhabitants of Canaan are called Rephaim—*giants* (Deut. 11:11, 20; 3:11; Num. 13:33). The Amorites appear to belong to this race, as also the Emim, the Zamzum-mims or Zuzims, Ammon or Ham, and the Anakim, who are described as redoubtable giants. They inhabited the hill contries, both east and west of the Jordan. The term is equivalent to "highlander." While Canaan is represented as the father of all Palestine, the Canaanites ("lowlanders") are one family or group of the seed of Canaan. They inhabited the Philistine plains and the Jordan valley. The Horites were the aborigines of Edom, and are the now well-known Hurrians of the cuneiform records. The Amalekites were a Bedouin stock, inhabiting the 'Arabah, the Tîh, and Sinai, where their descendants still live a more or less predatory life. The Hittites proceeded from the Taurus, who

340. The Brook Jabbok

extended their conquests southward to Hamath and Carchemish, and finally to southern Canaan. Some of them were in Hebron in Abraham's day. Ezekiel says (16:3) that the father of Jerusalem was an Amorite, and the mother a Hittite. During the eighteenth and nineteenth dynasties of Egypt the Egyptians vainly attempted to break the Hittite power. Rameses II finally made a treaty with them. It was not until the time of Sargon (B. C. 717) that they were finally expelled from Palestine and Mesopotamia and driven back into Asia Minor.

The earliest mention of Palestine in Babylonian records is its conquest by Naram-sin, son of Sargon of Akkad, about B. C. 2350. It was called then "the land of the Amorites." His conquests extended also to Cyprus. Other Babylonian records show that an extensive commerce existed between Babylonia and Palestine. The inference is almost inevitable that it depended upon the maintenance of the ancient suzerainty of Babylon. Babylonian science and writing existed in Palestine at that time, and relics of them have been found there and in Tel el-Amarna. Not until the reign of Thothmes III was Palestine finally conquered by Egypt, B. C. 1481, in a great battle near Megiddo. The Tel-el-Amarna tablets give many details of the Egyptian occupation of Palestine.

About B. C. 1400 the Hittites began to conquer large portions of Palestine, and the Amorites and Canaanites to regain their independence from Egypt. Edom had never sub-

mitted to the Egyptian yoke. Under Rameses II Palestine and Syria were temporarily reconquered.

During the sojourn of the patriarchs in Palestine they doubtless found both the Hebrew and Babylonian languages a medium of

341. Mount Gerizim (left), Mount Ebal (right), with Shechem between

polite intercourse, and the political affinities of the land a sure protection. When Jacob's sons went into Egypt the rulers were the Hyksos, Asiatic princes, with Babylonian culture, and friendly to Asiatics, so that it was no violence to national prejudice for Joseph to be made grand vizier. When the Israelites were oppressed it was by a king of African descent, who knew not Joseph and hated all that belonged to Babylonia. When the Israelites came to Canaan both Egyptian and Babylonian suzerainty were at an end, and the Hebrews had to contend not with mighty empires, but only with numerous discordant tribes of the natives, a circumstance which greatly facilitated their conquest. Canaan was an agricultural and commercial country, but not a center of conquering power. Its religion was of Babylonian origin.

The history of the Israelites from the Exodus, c. 1440 B. C. (Massoretic Chronology), to the captivity is given with so much detail in the Bible that it is unnecessary for us to present more than the leading outlines. After forty years in the wilderness the Israelites entered Canaan. In a few years they conquered most of eastern and western Palestine. They failed, however, to subdue part of the Philistine plain, all of Phoenicia, Lebanon, and Anti-Lebanon, and even part of the highlands of Judea, including Jerusalem, the future capital, and all of Edom and Moab. In the time of Saul and David the kingdom was

342. Street Scene in Tel Aviv

343. Jerash in the Decapolis

consolidated from the Mediterranean to the Euphrates, and from Phoenicia to the Red Sea. In the days of Rehoboam the kingdom was divided, and Judah and Benjamin, and sometimes Edom, formed the kingdom of Judah, and northern and eastern Palestine that of Israel, with ten tribes. Jeroboam tried to draw away the hearts of Israel from Jerusalem, as a religious center, by establishing a focus of idolatry at Beth-el, a few miles to the north. At first this effort was only partially successful. And even late into the history of the divided commonwealth the pious Israelites turned to the temple and worship at Jerusalem with an irrepressible yearning. So late as the time of Elijah seven thousand people in Israel had not as yet bowed the knee to Baal. At last, however, the whole people seems to have been corrupted, and in B. C. 721 Samaria was taken, and the ten tribes deported to Assyria and all traces of them henceforth lost. For a while longer some of the kings of Judah resisted the idolatry which had ruined Israel, but in B. C. 587, one hundred and thirty-three years after the fall of Samaria, Jerusalem was taken by Nebuchadnezzar, and the best of the people carried away captive to Babylon.

For seventy years Palestine remained a ruined country, the poor people who remained in it being subjected to the worst type of oriental despotism. In B. C. 536 the first installment of the Jews returned to Jerusalem under Zerubbabel, and a hundred years later, under Ezra and Nehemiah, others of the more enterprising of the exiles. The immense majority of the Hebrew people, however, remained in Assyria, Arabia, and other parts of

344. Amphitheater, Jerash in Decapolis

the East. Wherever they retained their national identity they were thoroughly cured of idolatry. To this day Judaism, although formal and Pharisaical, is in no part of the world idolatrous.

From the time of the restoration until the conquest of Alexander, B. C. 332, Palestine continued a province of Persia. During the period of the Seleucidae it was under the Greek yoke. In B. C. 167 Mattathias led a revolt which resulted in the independence of Judea under the Asmonean dynasty, which lasted until B. C. 63, when Pompey took Jerusalem and made Judea a vassal kingdom under Herod. In the time of Christ the Roman resident governed the vassal kings. This condition continued until the rapacity of Gessius Florus brought about a rebellion, which was finally ended by Vespasian and Titus, who destroyed Jerusalem and reduced Judea to a simple Roman province, A. D. 70. Hadrian rebuilt Jerusalem about A. D. 130, calling it Aelia Capitolina. Soon after the rebellion of Bar Cocheba broke out, but was put down with immense slaughter, A. D. 135. It was at this time that the Romans changed the name of Judea, which became hateful to them, to Syria Palestina. Jerusalem was made a heathen city, and Jews were forbidden to set foot in it on pain of death. Thenceforward Palestine had no history until, in the early part of the 7th century, it fell into Moslem hands. During the 11th and 12th centuries it was the scene of the crusades until, in A. D. 1187, it was conquered by Saladin. In A. D. 1517 it succumbed to the Turks who held it until 1917, when it was liberated and passed under British Protectorate. The State of Israel was established May 14, 1948 and has flourished. However, Israel-Arab tension continues. Revised by *M. F. U.*

Pal'lu (păl'ū; *distinguished*), the second named of the sons of Reuben (Gen. 46:9, *Phallu;* Exod. 6:14; Num. 26:5, 8; I Chron. 5:3), and founder of the Palluites (Num. 26:5), B. C. about 1900.

Pal'luite (păl'ū-īt), a descendant of *Pallu* (*q. v.*), of the tribe of Reuben (Num. 26:5).

Palm Tree. The palm tree is a beautiful and useful branchless tree crowned with a tuft of lovely fan-shaped leaves. Israel encountered seventy palm trees at Elim (Exod. 15:27; Num. 33:9). The palm was a welcome sight to weary travelers for it always signified rest, shade and refreshment. Where palms grew their long tap roots struck water. If properly

345. Palm Tree

cared for and watered, palms grow in Jerusalem. The date palm lives sometimes over two centuries and furnishes a prolific supply of edible dates. Other uses are wax, sugar, oil, tannin, dye stuffs, resin and even an intoxicating drink called arrak. Jericho was called the "city of palm trees." The palm tree was a common decorative motif in Solomon's temple (I Kings 6:29; 7:36; cf. also Ezekiel's temple, Ezek. 40:16; 41:18). Palms were among the "goodly trees" used in the celebration of the Feast of the Tabernacles (Lev. 23:40). They form a beautiful poetical figure to describe the prosperity of the righteous (Psa. 92:12). Revised by *M. F. U.*

Figurative. *Bible.*—The straightness and beauty of the palm would naturally suggest giving its name to women; and we have the comparison, "Thy stature is like to a palm tree" (Cant. 7:7). The palm is a figure of the righteous enjoying their deserved prosperity (Psa. 92:12), doubtless with reference to the greenness of its foliage, the symmetry of the tree, its fruit, etc. Palm branches are a symbol of victory (Rev. 7:9). *Christian.*—The primitive Church used the palm to express the triumph of the Christian over death through the resurrection; and on the tombs the palm is generally accompanied by the monogram of Christ, signifying that every

346. Palm Sunday Procession in the Kidron Valley, Jerusalem

victory of the Christian is due to this divine name and sign. The palm is especially the sign of martyrdom, as this was considered in the light of victory. *See* Vegetable Kindgom.

Palm Trees, City of. *See* Jericho.
Palmerworm. *See* Animal Kingdom.
Palsy. *See* Diseases.
Pal'ti (păl'tī; *delivered*), the son of Raphu, of the tribe of Benjamin, and appointed to represent that tribe among the twelve spies (Num. 13:9), B. C. c. 1440. Phalti (I Sam. 25:44).
Pal'tiel (păl'tĭ-ĕl; *God delivers*), the son of Azzan, and prince of the tribe of Issachar (Num. 34:26). He was one of the twelve appointed to divide the land of Canaan among the tribes, B. C. c. 1440.
Pal'tite (păl'tīt; i. e., sprung from *Beth-pelet*, in the south of Judah, Josh. 15:27). The same as *Palti* (*q. v.*), and the Gentile name of Helez, the chief of the seventh division of David's army (II Sam. 23:26), called the Pelonite in I Chron. 11:27; 27:10.

347. Pamphylia

Pamphyl'ia (păm-fĭl'ĭ-à; *of every race*), "one of the coast regions in the south of Asia Minor, having Cilicia on the east and Lycia on the west. In the Persian war, while Cilicia contributed one hundred ships and Lycia fifty, Pamphylia sent only thirty. The name probably then embraced little more than the crescent of comparatively level ground between Taurus and the sea. The Roman organization of the country, however, gave a wider range to the term Pamphylia. In St. Paul's time it was not only a regular province, but the Emperor Claudius had united Lycia with it, and probably also a good part of Pisidia. It was in Pamphylia that St. Paul first entered Asia Minor, after preaching the Gospel in Cyprus. He and Barnabas sailed up the river Cestrus to Perga (Acts 13:13). We may conclude, from Acts 2:10, that there were many Jews in the province; and possibly Perga had a synagogue. The two missionaries finally left Pamphylia by its chief seaport, Attalia. Many years afterward St. Paul sailed near the coast (27:5)" (Smith, *Bib. Dict.*, s. v.).
Pan. *See* Frying Pan.
Pan'nag (păn'ăg). In the account of the commerce of Tyre, it is stated (Ezek. 27:17), "Judah and the land of Israel, they were thy

merchants: they traded in thy market wheat of Minnith, and Pannag, and honey," etc. The meaning of *pannag* cannot be definitely ascertained. Some understand confectionery, sweetmeats made from honey. Some kind of sweetmeat is evidently intended. Cf. Akkad. *pannigu*, a variety of cake.

Pap (Heb. *shăd, bulging;* Gr. *mastos*), the breast, especially of a female (Ezek. 23:21; Luke 11:27; 23:29; Rev. 1:13).

Paper. *See* Writing, Papyrus, Gebal.

Pa′phos (pă′fŏs; *heated*), a city of Cyprus and its capital. It was famous for the worship of Venus, whose great temple was at "Old Paphos." Here Paul's convert, Sergius Paulus, was secured (Acts 13:7-13, see Conybeare and Howson's *Life of St. Paul*). Paphos is the modern *Baffa*.

348. The Nash Papyrus of the Ten Commandments and Deut. 6:4, Cambridge University Library

Papyrus. A plant growing along the Nile in Egypt during the Biblical period. No longer is it found in the Nile marshes of lower Egypt but grows in the Sudan. The region around Lake Huleh in Galilee and well-watered parts of the Plain of Sharon contain the plant. In the ancient world papyrus, Lat. *cyperus papyrus*, from which we get our word "paper," constituted a very common writing material. To prepare the writing product the outer covering of the stem of the plant was removed and the inner fibres were placed vertically. Superimposed upon these were soaked fibres laid horizontally. These two layers were stuck together with an adhesive substance, pressure applied, and the strips dried. The result was a yellowish piece of papyrus paper. Often the exterior was rubbed smooth to accommodate a finer type of writing with ink. Papyrus rolls were used in ancient Egypt during the Old Kingdom (c. 2800-2250 B. C.) and perhaps even earlier. Egyptian papyrus rolls are still in existence from the end of the third millennium B. C. According to the Story of Wenamon (II:41) about the twelfth century B. C. papyrus rolls were exported from Egypt to

Gebal in Phoenicia. Later for this reason the Greeks called this city "Byblus," meaning "papyrus," later "book." The largest ordinary papyrus roll in common use was about thirty feet long and some ten inches high, adequate for the non-vocalized Hebrew text of Isaiah. Egyptians upon occasion employed such huge rolls as the Papyrus Harris, 133 feet in length, and the Book of the Dead, 123 feet in length. Among the Jews the common use of the standard size papyrus rolls necessitated the division of some books like the Torah of Moses into five books. The books of Samuel, Kings and Chronicles and perhaps others were partitioned into two books when translated into Greek because Greek included the vowels, requiring more space than the consonatal Hebrew text. Evidently Baruch wrote on papyrus as Jeremiah dictated to him, using pen and ink. The reed or calamus made from the hollow stalk of course grass or rush was cut diagonally with a knife and split in the end like a modern pen, hence the term "pen knife" (Jer. 36:23). Ink was commonly made of soot or lamp black and gum mixed in water. Ancient Egyptians also employed papyrus for constructing boats (Isa. 18:2) (cf. Moses' "ark of bulrushes"). The A. S. V. has "papyrus" in the margin (Exod. 2:3). The papyrus was the symbol of Lower Egypt and the Egyptians made a notable discovery when they made use of this vegetable membrane as an excellent writing material. *M. F. U.*

Parable, a word derived from the Gr. verb *paraballō*, to *lay by the side of*, to *compare;* and so a *likeness, similitude*.

1. **Original Terms and their Meaning.** "Parable" is the rendering in the A. V. of the following Hebrew and Greek terms:

(1) Heb. *măshăl*, a *similitude* (Num. 23:7, 18; 24:3, 20, 21, 23). In this instance "parable" is thought by some to mean "a discourse expressed in figurative, poetical, or highly ornamented diction;" as also in the case of Job (27:1). In Psa. 49:4; 78:2 an obscure or enigmatical saying appears to be meant; while in other instances it signifies a fictitious narrative, invented for the purpose of conveying truth in a less offensive or more engaging form than that of direct assertion, as that by which Nathan reproved David (II Sam. 12:2, 3), that in which Jotham exposed the folly of the Shechemites (Judg. 9:7-15), and that addressed by Jehoash to Amaziah (II Kings 14:9, 10), although these latter two are more properly classified as "fables."

(2) Gr. *parabolē*, a *placing one thing beside another*, an example by which a doctrine or precept is illustrated (Luke 14:7); a pithy and instructive saying, involving some likeness or comparison, and have preceptive or admonitory force; an aphorism, a maxim (Luke 5:36; 6:39; Matt. 15:15); a proverb, and so rendered in Luke 4:23.

(3) Gr. *paroimia*, a saying out of the usual course; any dark saying which shadows forth some didactic truth, a symbolic or figurative saying (John 16:29, rendered "proverb"); an allegory, i. e., extended and elaborate metaphor (10:6).

2. **Definition and Distinctions.** In the New Testament the term "parable" is not confined

to those lengthened narratives to which alone we now usually apply it. Thus, "And he said unto them, Ye will surely say unto me this parable, Physician, heal thyself" (Luke 6:39); while the word is frequently used, either by the evangelists or by the disciples of Jesus, with reference to instructions of Christ, which we would call simply figurative, or metaphorical, or proverbial. In Luke 6:39 we read, "And he spake a parable unto them, Can the blind lead the blind? Shall they not both fall into the ditch?" (comp. Matt. 15:14, 15; Mark 7:17; Luke 14:7). In all these sayings of our Lord, however, it is obvious that the germ of a parable is contained. We have only to work upon the hint given us, and we have the perfect story.

Trench (*Notes on the Parables*, p. 9, sq.) says: "In the process of distinguishing it (the parable) from those forms of composition with which it is most nearly allied, and therefore most likely to be confounded, and justifying the distinction, its essential properties will come before us much more clearly than I could hope to bring them in any other way." In defining the difference between the parable and the *fable*, he writes: "The parable is constructed to set forth a truth spiritual and heavenly; this the *fable*, with all its value, is not; it is essentially of the earth, and never lifts itself above the earth. It never has a higher aim than to inculcate maxims of prudential morality, industry, caution, foresight; and these it will sometimes recommend even at the expense of the higher self-forgetting virtues. . . . Yet again there is another point of difference between the parable and the fable. While it can never be said that the fabulist is regardless of truth, since it is neither his intention to deceive, when he attributes language and discourse by reason to trees, and birds, and beasts, nor is anyone deceived by him; yet the severer reverence for truth, which is habitual to the higher moral teacher, will not allow him to indulge even in this sporting with the truth, this temporary suspension of its laws, though upon agreement, or, at least, with tacit understanding. . . . The great Teacher, by parables, therefore, allowed himself in no transgressions of the established laws of nature, in nothing marvelous or anomalous; he presents to us no speaking trees or reasoning beasts, and we should be at once conscious of an unfitness in his so doing."

He says that "The parable is different from the *myth*, inasmuch as in the *myth* the truth, and that which is only the vehicle of the truth, are wholly blended together. . . . The mythic narrative presents itself not merely as the vehicle of the truth, but as itself being the truth; while in the parable there is a perfect consciousness in all minds of the distinctness between form and essence, shell and kernel, precious vessel and yet more precious wine which it contains."

Again he says, "The parable is also clearly distinguishable from the *proverb*, though it is true that in a certain degree the words are used interchangeably in the New Testament, and as equivalent the one to the other. Thus, 'Physician, heal thyself' (Luke 4:23) is termed a parable, being more strictly a proverb. It is

not difficult to explain how this interchange of the two words should have come to pass. Partly from the fact of there being but one word in the Hebrew to signify both parable and proverb; which circumstance must have had considerable influence upon writers accustomed to think in that language, and itself arose from the parable and proverb being alike enigmatical and somewhat obscure forms of speech, 'dark sayings,' speaking a part of their meaning, and leaving the rest to be inferred."

The parable differs from the allegory "in form rather than in essence: there being in the allegory an interpenetration of the thing signifying and the thing signified, the qualities and properties of the first being attributed to the last, and the two thus blended together, instead of being kept quite distinct and placed side by side, as is the case in the parable. The allegory needs not, as the parable, an interpretation to be brought to it from without, since it contains its interpretation within itself, and, as the allegory proceeds, the interpretation proceeds hand in hand with it, or at least never falls far behind it." "I am the true vine," etc. (John 15:1-8) is an allegory, while John 10:1-16 contains two allegories.

3. **The Parable as a Means of Teaching.** Two characteristics of the parable render it eminently useful in teaching. It is illustrative, assisting to make truth intelligible, or, if intelligible before, to present it more vividly to the mind. It is an argument, and may be summoned as a witness, the world of nature being throughout a witness for the world of spirit (Rom. 1:20). The parable "does not indeed contain direct proof of the doctrine which it unfolds, but it associates with it all the force of that proof which is given by the exhibition of the universal prevalence of any principle. Growth, for example, we know to be a law of nature. Let us set out, therefore, with the conviction that the kingdom of grace corresponds with the kingdom of nature—the conviction, it is to be borne in mind, which constitutes the foundation of the parable; and, in a story calling our attention to that growth, we have not only an illustration, but a proof, that the same growth which appears in the natural must also appear in the spiritual world. The analogy convinces us that it must be so, and is therefore so far a proof" (Wm. Milligan, D.D., in *Imp. Dict.*, s. v.).

Again, "the mind takes a natural delight in this manner of teaching, appealing as it does not to the understanding only, but to the feelings, to the imagination, in short to the whole man, calling as it does the whole man, with all its powers and faculties, into pleasurable activity; and all things thus learned with delight are those longest remembered." The Scriptures are full also of *acted* parable, for every type is a *real* parable. The whole Levitical constitution, with its sacred precincts, its priesthood, its sacrifices, and all its ordinances, is a parable, and is so declared (Heb. 9:9). The wandering of Israel in the desert has ever been regarded as a parable of spiritual life.

Whedon (*Com.*, on Matt. 13:1, sq.) thus happily sums up the advantages of the parable as a means of teaching: "The sacred parable was a wonderful vehicle of truth to serve three distinct purposes, viz.: to *reveal*, to *conceal*, and to *perpetuate*. It *revealed* the sacred truth by the power of analogy and illustration. It *concealed* the truth from him who had not, by proper sympathy or previous instruction, the true key to its hidden meaning. To such a one it was a riddle or a tale. And so our Lord could give to his disciples in this method the deepest secrets of his kingdom for ages, while the caviler, who would have abused the truth, heard without understanding (v. 11). But the truth thus embodied in narrative was, as it were, materialized and made fit for *perpetuation*. It had a form and body to it by which it could be preserved in tangible shape for future ages."

4. **Interpretation of Parables.** It has been urged by some writers, by none with greater force or clearness than by Chrysostom, that there is a scope or purpose for each parable, and that our aim must be to discern this, not to find a special significance in each circumstance or incident. It may be questioned, however, whether this canon of interpretation is likely to lead us to the full meaning of this portion of our Lord's teaching. It must be remembered that in the great patterns of interpretation which he himself has given us there is more than this. Not only the sower and the seed and the several soils have their counterparts in the spiritual life, but the birds of the air, the thorns, the scorching heat have each of them a significance. It may be inferred from these two instances that we are, at least, justified in looking for a meaning even in the seeming accessories of a parable. The very form of the teaching makes it probable that there may be, in any case, more than one legitimate explanation. A parable may be at once ethical, and in the highest sense of the term prophetic. There is thus a wide field open to the discernment of the interpreter. There are also restraints upon the mere fertility of his imagination: (1) The analogies must be real, not arbitrary. (2) The parables are to be considered as parts of a whole, and the interpretation of one is not to override or encroach upon the lessons taught by others. (3) The direct teaching of Christ presents the standard to which all *our* interpretations are to be referred, and by which they are to be measured. (4) And, finally, the parable may not be made the first source of doctrine. Doctrines otherwise and already grounded may be illustrated, or indeed further confirmed by them, but it is not allowable to constitute doctrine first by their aid.

5. **Classification.** The following is a classification of the parables in the Scriptures:

PARABLES RECORDED IN THE OLD TESTAMENT.

Spoken by	Concerning	Spoken at	Recorded in
Balaam	The Moabites and Israelites	Mt. Pisgah	Num. 23:24.
Jotham	Trees making a king	Mt. Gerizim	Judg. 9:7-15.
Nathan	The poor man's ewe lamb	Jerusalem	II Sam. 12:1-4.
Woman of Tekoah	Two brothers striving	Jerusalem	II Sam. 14:5.
A young prophet	The escaped prisoner	Near Samaria	I Kings 20:35-49.
Jehoash	The thistle and the cedar	Jerusalem	II Kings 14:9.
Isaiah	The vineyard yielding wild grapes	Jerusalem	Isa. 5:1-7.
Ezekiel	The eagles and the vine	Babylon	Ezek. 17:3-10.
	The lion's whelps	Babylon	Ezek. 19:2-9.
	The boiling pot	Babylon	Ezek. 24:3-5.
	Israel, a vine planted by water	Babylon	Ezek. 24:10-14.

PARABLES RECORDED IN THE GOSPELS.

Parables	Import	Occasion	Recorded
1. The Sower	The relation between the preached truth and its hearers	Sermon on the seashore	Matt. 13:5-8; Mark 4:3-8; Luke 8:5-8.
2. The Tares	Present intermixture of good and bad	Sermon on the seashore	Matt. 13:24-30.
3. The Mustard Seed	The remarkable outward growth of the kingdom	Sermon on the seashore	Matt. 13:31, 32; Mark 4:31, 32; Luke 13:19.
4. The Leaven	The inward working of evil in the kingdom	Sermon on the seashore	Matt. 13:33; Luke 13:21.
5. The Hid Treasure	Israel's present condition in the kingdom	To the disciples alone	Matt. 13:44.
6. The Pearl of Great Price	The Church in the kingdom	To the disciples alone	Matt. 13:45, 46.
7. The Drag Net	The future separation of the good and bad	To the disciples alone	Matt. 13:47-50.
8. The Unmerciful Servant	The Gospel law of forgiveness illustrated	In answer to Peter's question, How oft shall I forgive, etc.?	Matt. 18:23-35.
9. The Laborers in the Vineyard	An answer to Peter's question, and a warning against the hireling spirit	Teaching the self-righteous	Matt. 20:1-16.
10. The Two Sons	Obedience better than profession	The chief priests demand his authority	Matt. 21:28-32.
11. The Wicked Husbandman	Guilt and rejection of Israel	The chief priests demand his authority	Matt. 21:33-46; Mark 12:1-12; Luke 20:9-19.

PARABLES RECORDED IN THE GOSPELS.—Continued.

PARABLES	IMPORT	OCCASION	RECORDED
12. Marriage of the King's Son.......	The long-suffering and goodness of God; the rejection of those despising it; and necessity of purity.....	In answer to remark of a self-righteous guest..............	Matt. 22:1-14.
13. The Ten Virgins................	Israel's preparation for the Lord's coming......................	In prophesying the Second Advent......................	Matt. 25:1-13.
14. The Talents...................	Duty of working while the day lasts.	At the house of Zaccheus........	Matt. 25:14-30.
15. The Seed Growing Secretly.......	The invisible energy of the Word....	Sermon on the seashore.........	Mark 4:26-29.
16. The Two Debtors..............	Love proportioned to grace received.	At Simon the Pharisee's self-righteous reflection..........	Luke 7:41-43
17. The Good Samaritan...........	Love is to know no limits, spare no pains......................	The lawyer's question, Who is my neighbor?..............	Luke 10:25-37
18. The Friend at Midnight.........	Perseverance in prayer............	Disciples ask a lesson in prayer..	Luke 11:5-8.
19. The Rich Fool.................	Vanity of riches without religion....	Brothers ask him to divide an inheritance..................	Luke 12:16-21.
20. The Barren Fig Tree...........	The longsuffering and severity of God regarding Israel............	Informed of the execution of the Galileans.................	Luke 13:6-9.
21. The Great Supper.............	Exclusion of those declining invitation......................	In answer to one dining with him.	Luke 14:16-24.
22. The Lost Sheep...............	Christ's peculiar love for sinners.....	Answer to Pharisees and scribes murmuring.................	Matt. 18:12-14; Luke 15:4-7.
23. The Lost Piece of Money........	Christ's peculiar love for sinners.....	Answer to Pharisees and scribes murmuring.................	Luke 15:8-10.
24. The Prodigal Son..............	Christ's peculiar love for sinners.....	Answer to Pharisees and scribes murmuring.................	Luke 15:11-32.
25. The Unjust Steward............	Christian prudence commended.....	To the disciples..............	Luke 16:1-9.
26. The Rich Man and Lazarus......	Unbelief punished, faith rewarded...	Rebuking the covetousness of Pharisees..................	Luke 16:19-31.
27. The Unprofitable Servants.......	Service without love not meritorious.	Teaching self-righteous ones....	Luke 17:7-10.
28. The Unjust Judge.............	Encouragement to constant prayer..	Teaching the disciples.........	Luke 18:1-8.
29. The Pharisee and the Publican....	Humility in prayer..............	Teaching the self-righteous.....	Luke 18:10-14.
30. The Pounds..................	Patient waiting and working for Christ......................	At the house of Zaccheus.......	Luke 19:12-27.

In addition to the parables tabulated above, we call attention to the allegories of (1) the vine and its branches (John 15:1-8), (2) the sheep and shepherd (10:1-16). We have also several sayings of our Lord which obviously contain the germ of a parable, as: The house on the rock and on the sand (Matt. 7:24-27; Luke 6:46-49); children in the market place (Matt. 11:16; Luke 7:32); the unclean spirit (Matt. 12:34-45; Luke 11:24-26); the city, and the candle (Matt. 5:14, 15; Mark 4:21; Luke 8:16); the householder (Matt. 13:52); the children of the bridechamber (Matt. 9: 15; Mark 2:19, 20; Luke 5:34, 35); the patched garment (Matt. 9:16; Mark 2:21; Luke 5:36); old and new bottles (Matt. 9:17; Mark 2:22; Luke 5:37); the harvest and lack of workmen (Matt. 9:37; Luke 10:2); the adversary (Matt. 5:25; Luke 12:58); the strait gate, etc. (Matt. 7:14; Luke 13:24); building a tower (Luke 14:28-30), and king going to war (Luke 14:31, 32); the fig tree (Matt. 24:32-35; Mark 13:28-31; Luke 21: 29-33); the watching servants (Mark 14:34, 35); the faithful and the unfaithful servants (Matt. 24:45-48); the watching householder (Matt. 24:43; Luke 12:39).

Paraclete (Gr. *paraklētos, summoned, called to one's side*), one who pleads another's cause before a judge, an advocate as in I John 2:1, where it is applied to Christ. When Jesus promised to his sorrowing disciples to send them the Holy Spirit as a paraclete ("comforter"), he takes the title to himself: "I will send you *another* paraclete" (John 14:16). If we take the term *paraclete* in the broad sense of helper we can readily apply it both to Jesus and the Spirit. He was eminently a helper to his disciples, teaching, guiding, strengthening, comforting them; and now that he has gone the Spirit is his substitute to carry on his work in them. In this present age it is, therefore, evident that the Holy Spirit is the believer's Paraclete on the earth, in-dwelling and helping him, while Christ is the Christian's Paraclete in heaven, interceding for Him at the Father's right hand. *See* Holy Spirit.

Paradise (Gr. *paradeisos, park*). This term has been applied to *Eden* (*q. v.*). In the later books of the Old Testament it appears in the sense of a *park* or *pleasure ground* (Heb. *pärdēs*, rendered "forest," Neh. 2:8; "orchard," Eccles. 2:5; Cant. 4:13). It first appears in Greek as coming straight from Persia. Greek lexicographers classify it as a Persian word. Modern philologists accept the same conclusion with hardly a dissentient voice. In Xenophon the word occurs frequently, and we get vivid pictures of the scene which it implied. A wide open park, inclosed against injury, yet with its natural beauty unspoiled, with stately forest trees, many of them bearing fruit, watered by clear streams, on whose banks roved large herds of antelopes or sheep—this was the scenery which connected itself in the mind of the Greek traveler with the word *paradeisos*, and for which his own language supplied no precise equivalent. Through the writings of Xenophon, and through the general admixture of orientalisms in the later Greek after the conquests of Alexander, the word gained a recognized place, and the LXX writers chose it for a new use which gave it a higher worth and secured for it a more perennial life. They used the same word whenever there was any allusion, however, remote, to the fair region which had been the first blissful home of man. It was natural, however, that this higher meaning should become the exclusive one, and be associated with new thoughts. Paradise, with no other word to qualify it, was the bright region which man had lost, which was guarded by the flaming sword. Paradise, or the Garden of Eden, became to the later Jews a common appellation for the state of bliss which awaits the just after death—by which they meant that delights like those of Eden are enjoyed by the departed—they are in a paradisaical state. With reference to this use of the term, but with a deeper insight into the spiritual relation of things, and the connection between the past and future, it is employed in the New Testament to indicate the destiny and experience of the redeemed (Luke 23:43; Rev. 22:2, 14). It is quite difficult to locate Paradise as mentioned by Paul (II Cor. 12:4). Whedon (*Com.*, in loc.) thinks it nearer to earth than the third heaven (v. 2). Meyer (*Com.*, in loc.) says, "The *paradise* is here not the *lower*, i. e., the place of *Sheol*, in which the spirits of the departed righteous are until the resurrection, but the *upper*, the paradise of God (Rev. 2:7) in heaven, where God's dwelling is."

Pa'rah (pā'rà; *young cow, heifer*), one of the towns of Benjamin (Josh. 18:23), identified as *Farah*, 5½ miles N. E. of Jerusalem.

Paralytic. See Diseases.

Paramour (Heb. *pîlĕgĕsh*, Ezek. 23:20), applied to the male lover in this passage, but elsewhere rendered concubine (*q. v.*).

Pa'ran (pā'răn), a wilderness region located in the E. central region of the Sinaitic Peninsula. This region bordered the Arabah and the Gulf of Aqabah on the east, and apparently comprised the Wilderness of Zin, Kadesh-barnea and Elath in its borders on the West.

Paran is first noticed in connection with the expedition of the eastern kings against Sodom (Gen. 14:6). We then learn that Ishmael dwelt in the wilderness of Paran (21:21); that after Israel left Sinai they camped in Paran (Num. 10:12; 12:16); that the spies were sent from Paran into Canaan (13:3), and returned "unto the wilderness of Paran, to Kadesh" (v. 26). Its mountainous nature and its rugged passes seem to have impressed the Israelites accustomed to the level country of Egypt (Deut. 1:19), and they feared to enter these passes until they were found to be open (v. 22). To Paran David repaired at the death of Samuel (I Sam. 25:1), probably because he could not find support for himself in the desert of Judah. Hadad the Edomite, when he revolted from Solomon, went to Egypt by the way of Paran (I Kings 11:18).

Par'bar (pär'bàr; *suburb*), a part of the city of Jerusalem connected with the temple (II Kings 23:11, "suburbs;" I Chron. 26:18). As to the meaning of the name, the rabbis generally agree in translating it "the outside place," while modern authorities take it as equivalent to the *parvârim* in II Kings 23:11 (A. V. "suburbs"). Accepting this interpretation, there is no difficulty in identifying the Parbar with the suburb mentioned by Josephus in describing Herod's temple, as lying in the deep valley which separated the west wall of the temple from the city opposite it; in other words, the southern end of the Tyropoeon. Parbar is possibly an ancient Jebusite name. Keil (*Com.*, I Chron. 26:18) thinks it to have been the name of an outbuilding on the west side, the back of the outer court of the temple by the door Shallecheth, which contained cells for storage of goods and furniture.

Parched Corn (Heb. *qâlî, roasted*), roasted ears or grains of wheat (Lev. 23:14; Ruth 2:14; I Sam. 17:17; 25:18). In II Sam. 17:28 the word occurs twice, which in the second place is understood by K. and D. (*Com.*, in loc.) to refer to parched pulse.

Parched Ground (Heb. *shäräb, a mirage*). The mirage, especially that appearance of water which is produced as if by magic in the dry, sandy desert (literally perhaps the "desert shine," just as we speak of the "alpine glow.") The sense in which it is here used is figuratively. "The *shäräb* ('parched ground') shall become a lake" (Isa. 35:7), i. e., the illusive appearance of a lake in the desert shall become a real lake of refreshing waters.

Parched Places (Heb. *ḥärēr, arid*, Jer. 17:6). Here parched is used in the usual sense of arid.

Parchment. See Writing.

Pardon. See Forgiveness; Justification.

Pare the Nails. See Nail.

Parent (Gr. *goneus*). The fifth commandment (Exod. 20:12; comp. Lev. 19:3; Deut. 5:16) enjoined filial piety to parents as a religious duty; and as the law was promulgated more fully the relation of children to parents was more accurately defined and more firmly established in society. A child who cursed (Exod. 21:17; Lev. 20:9; comp. Deut. 27:16; Prov. 20:20; Matt. 11:4) or struck his parents was punishable with death. Obstinate disobedience on the part of sons was, upon judicial investigation, punished with stoning (Deut. 21:18). But such crimes seem happily to have been almost unknown. According to the rabbinical ordinances a son was considered independent when he could gain his own living; and, although a daughter remained in the power of her father till marriage, she could not, after she was of age, be given away without her own express and full consent. A father might chastise his child, but only while young, and even then not to such an extent as to destroy self-respect. But to beat a grown-up son was forbidden on pain of excommunication; and the apostolic injunction, "Fathers, provoke not your children to wrath" (Eph. 6:4), finds an almost literal counterpart in the Talmud (Edersheim, *Jewish Social Life*, p. 99). According to the law a father married his sons (Gen., ch. 24; Exod. 21:9, sq.; Judg. 14:2, sq.) and daughters (Gen. 29:16, sq.; 34:12) at his pleasure; and he might sell the latter as concubines (Exod. 21:7). Much value was attached to the blessing of a parent, while the curse of one was accounted a great misfortune (Gen. 27:4, 12; 49:2, sq.).

Parlor, the now archaic rendering of the Heb. word for "chamber" or "apartment" (*ḥĕdĕr*), cf. I Chron. 28:11 where the expression refers to the inner rooms of the temple porch and holy place, generally rendered "chamber."

An upper *room of coolness* (Judg. 3:20-28),

was a room upon the flat roof of a house, which was open to currents of air, and so offered a cool retreat, such as are still met with in the East (Heb. '*ăliyäh, lofty*).

A corner cell or "chamber," as generally rendered, in a courtyard (I Sam. 9:22) was denoted by Heb. *lĭshkäh*.

Parmash'ta (pàr-măsh'tả; Old Persian, *the very first*), the seventh named of the sons of Haman (*q. v.*), slain by the Jews (Esth. 9:9).

Par'menas (pär'mē-năs), one of the seven deacons, "men of honest report, full of the Holy Ghost and wisdom" (Acts 6:5). There is a tradition that he suffered martyrdom at Philippi in the reign of Trajan, A. D. 33 (29). Hippolytus says that he was at one time bishop of Soli. He is commemorated in the calendar of the Byzantine Church on July 28.

Par'nach (pär'năk), father of Elizaphan, prince of the tribe of Zebulun at the close of the exodus (Num. 34:25), B. C. c. 1440.

Pa'rosh (pā'rŏsh; *a flea*), the descendants of Parosh, in number two thousand one hundred and seventy-two, returned from Babylon with Zerubbabel (Ezra 2:3; Neh. 7:8). Another detachment of one hundred and fifty males, with Zechariah at their head, accompanied Ezra (Ezra 8:3, A. V. "Pharaoh"). Seven of the family had married foreign wives (10:25). They assisted in the building of the wall of Jerusalem (Neh. 3:25), and signed the covenant with Nehemiah (10:14), B. C. before 536.

Parshanda'tha (pàr-shăn-dā'thả; Old Persian, *inquisitive, inquiring*), the eldest of Haman's ten sons who were slain by the Jews in Shushan (Esth. 9:7).

Par'thians (pär'thĭ-ăns), are mentioned as being present in Jerusalem on the day of Pentecost (Acts 2:9). They were a people of N. W. Persia (Iran), who lived in the general region S. E. of the Caspian Sea. The ancient Parthians are called a "Scythic" race, and probably belonged to the great Turanian family. Nothing is known of them till about the time of Darius Hystaspes, when they are found in the district which so long retained their name, and appear as faithful subjects of the Persian monarchs. Herodotus speaks of them as contained in the sixteenth satrapy of Darius. In the final struggle between the Greeks and Persians they remained faithful to the latter, serving at Arbela; but offering only a weak resistance to Alexander when, on his way to Bactria, he entered their country. In the division of Alexander's dominions they fell to the share of Eumenes, and Parthia for some while was counted among the territories of the Seleucidae. About B. C. 256, however, they ventured upon a revolt, and under Arsaces they succeeded in establishing their independence.

Parthia, in the mind of the writer of the Acts, would designate the great Empire the Parthians built up, which extended from India to the Tigris, and from the Chorassian desert to the shores of the Southern Ocean. Hence the prominent position of the name Parthians in the list of those present at Pentecost. Parthia was a power almost rivaling Rome—the only existing power which had tried its strength against Rome and not been worsted in the encounter. The Parthian dominion lasted for nearly five centuries, commencing in the 3d century before, and terminating in the 3d century after our era. The Parthians seized Jerusalem in 40 B. C. and Rome made Herod king of Judaea at that time to check the formidable westward push of the Parthian Empire.

Partiality, an inclination or bent of mind. (Gr. *prosklisis*, I Tim. 5:21). The exhortation of the apostle is that nothing should be done under undue inclination toward one or another party.

Partition, Middle Wall of, the expression used by Paul to designate the Mosaic law as the dividing line between the Jews and Gentiles (Eph. 2:14). The argument of the verse is as follows: Christ has procured peace. Then follows a statement of how Christ became our peace, "having made both one," not so, that one part assumed the nature of the other, but so that the separation of the two was done away with, and both were raised to a *new* unity. Then we have the statement in further explanation, "hath broken down the middle wall of partition," and thus removed the enmity which existed between the Jews and the Gentiles. As to any special wall or fence being alluded to, commentators are divided, some believing it to refer to the stone screen in the temple marking off the court of the Gentiles, while others think it meant the wall in large towns marking off the Jewish districts.

Partridge. *See* Animal Kingdom.

Paru'ah (pà-rōō'ả; *blossoming*, or *increase*), the father of Jehoshaphat, which latter was Solomon's purveyor in Issachar (I Kings 4:17), B. C. 960.

Parva'im (pàr-vā'ĭm), the name of a place rich in gold, from which it was brought to adorn Solomon's temple (II Chron. 3:6). The name does not occur elsewhere, and has never been satisfactorily explained. Gesenius and other authorities regard it as a general term signifying the East, and corresponding to our "Levant."

Pa'sach (pā'săk; to *divide*), the first named of the sons of Japhlet, of the tribe of Asher (I Chron. 7:33), B. C. about 1390.

Pas-dam'mim (păs-dăm'ĭm), a place mentioned (I Chron. 11:13; Ephes-dammim, I Sam. 17:1), as the scene of a fierce conflict with the Philistines. It was between Shochoh and Azekah. *See* Ephes-dammim.

Pase'ah (pà-sē'ả; *lame*).

1. One of the sons of Eshton, among the descendants of Judah, described as "the men of Rechah" (I Chron. 4:12).

2. The head of a family of Nethinim who returned with Zerubbabel (Ezra 2:49; Neh. 7:51). His "son" (or descendant), Jehoiada, assisted in restoring one of the gates of the city (Neh. 3:6), B. C. probably before 536. He is called Phaseah (7:51).

Pash'ur (păsh'ẽr), R. V. and R. S. V. **Pash'hur** (păsh'hẽr).

1. The son of Immer the priest. He was chief governor of the temple (Jer. 20:1), and when he heard the prophecies of Jeremiah he smote Jeremiah and put him in the stocks. The next day he released Jeremiah, who informed him that his name was changed to

Magor-missabib (i. e., *terror on every side*), and that he and all his house should be carried to Babylon and die there (20:2-6), B. C. about 605. Nothing more is known of him.

2. Another priest, the son of Malchiah, who in the reign of Zedekiah was one of the chief princes of the court (Jer. 38:1). He was sent, with others, by Zedekiah to Jeremiah at the time when Nebuchadnezzar was preparing his attack upon Jerusalem (ch. 21), B. C. about 589. Again, somewhat later, Pashur joins with others in petitioning the king to have Jeremiah put to death because of his denunciations. In the time of Nehemiah this family appears to have become a chief house, and its head the head of a course (I Chron. 9:12; Ezra 2:38; Neh. 7:41; 10:3; 11:12).

3. The father of Gedaliah, which latter took part with Jucal and the Pashur last named in the accusation and imprisonment of Jeremiah (Jer. 38:1), B. C. 589.

Passage (from Heb. *'ābăr*, to *cross*) has several meanings in the A. V.: To give passage (Num. 20:21); a *crossing* (Josh. 22:11; Jer. 22:20); a *transit*, either by water (Judg. 12:5, 6; Jer. 51:32), a *ford* (often so rendered), or a *pass* through mountains (I Sam. 13:23; Isa. 10:29).

Passenger (Prov. 9:15; Ezek. 39:11, 14, 15) is used in the A. V. in the sense of traveler.

Passion of Christ (Gr. *to pathein, suffering*), a term employed as in Acts 1:3, with reference to the crucifixion of our Lord. For the chief points of the history of the event, *see* Jesus Christ.

Passions, Like (Gr. *homoiopathēs*), used in the expressions "men of like passions with you" (Acts 14:15), and "a man subject to like passions as we are" (James 5:17), and meaning *suffering the like* with another, *of like feelings* or *affections*.

Passover, Feast of. *See* Festivals.

Pastor (Heb. *rō'eh, shepherd*, and usually so rendered). The rendering *pastor* is confined in the Old Testament to Jeremiah and to one portion of that book, viz., 2:8-23:2, and appears as follows: 2:8; 3:15; 10:21; 12:10; 17:16; 22:22; 23:1, 2. The Geneva Bible, which in all these passages both in the Old Testament and New Testament translates the Hebrew and Greek terms "shepherd," renders it in these very instances by "pastor;" and our A. V. has simply taken over the exceptional rendering. The Gr. *poimēn* (Eph. 4:11), a *shepherd*, as so elsewhere rendered.

Pastor, Christian (literally *shepherd*), may be considered the exact equivalent of the above Hebrew and Greek words. St. Paul's pastoral epistles contain the sum and substance of New Testament teaching on this subject. He lays down three functions: 1. The ministration in divine service includes the ordering of worship, administering the sacraments, and preaching the word. Here the pastor is appropriately termed minister. 2. The responsibility of the pastoral care springs out of the former. The feeding of the flock is the instruction of its members, but it is also the vigilant distributive attention to all its interests in the whole economy of life. The under shepherds must imitate the chief shepherd, who "calleth his own sheep by name." 3. This pastoral

relation passes naturally into what we have scriptural authority for calling the spiritual government of the Church. Its ministers are called *rulers* (Gr. *hēgoumenoi*), or *presidents* (Gr. *proestōtes*), and all its members are bidden to *obey them that have the rule*. The design of the Lord's gift of pastors and teachers, as supplementary to that of apostles and evangelists, is "the perfecting of the saints, for the work of the ministry, for the edifying of the body of Christ" (Eph. 4:12). Pastors are to be watchful (Heb. 13:17; II Tim. 4:5); gentle and affectionate (I Thess. 2:7, 8); should exhort, warn, and comfort (I Thess. 2:11; I Cor. 4:14, 15).

Pasture. *See* Shepherd.

Pat'ara (păt'à-rà), a seaport at which Paul exchanged ships during his third missionary journey (Acts 21:1, 2). It was on the coast of Lycia. It was a city of great magnificence and very populous in Paul's time, and its ruins are impressive, as, e. g., over one of the city's great gateways was the inscription, "Patara, the metropolis of the Lycians." Christianity had a footing in the city, and it was the residence of a bishop.

Path. Figurative. The dispensations of God are called his paths (Psa. 25:10; 65:11), as are also his precepts (17:5); the phenomena of nature are "paths of God" (Psa. 77:19; Isa. 43:16).

Path'ros (păth'rŏs; Egyptian, *Southland*), the name of upper Egypt as distinguished from Matsor, or lower Egypt (Isa. 11:11; Jer. 44:1, 15; Ezek. 30:14). It was the country which was called Thebais by the classic geographers and Paturissu in the cuneiform texts. Colonies of Jews were settled here.

Pathru'sim (păth-rōō'sĭm), the fifth in order of the sons (i. e., descended tribes) of Mizraim (Gen. 10:14; I Chron. 1:50), thought to have been inhabitants of Pathros, Egypt, and from it to have taken their name. *See* Pathros.

Patience. 1. Gr. makrothumia. Endurance, constancy, forbearance, long-suffering.

2. Gr. *Hupomonē* "a remaining under," steadfastness, constancy, a patient waiting for.

The difference between these two terms is thus given by Trench (*N. T. Syn.*, vol. ii, p. 14): "*Makrothumia* will be found to express patience in respect of persons, *hupomonē* in respect of things. . . . We should speak, therefore, of the *makrothumia* of David (II Sam. 16:10-13), the *hupomonē* of Job (James 5:11)." Patience is that calm and unruffled temper with which the good man bears the evils of life, whether they proceed from persons or things. It also manifests itself in a sweet submission to the providential appointments of God, and fortitude in the presence of the duties and conflicts of life. This grace saves one from discouragement in the face of evil (Luke 21:19); aids in the cultivation of godliness (II Pet. 1:6), the development of the entire Christian character (James 1:4), and, continued in till the end, will terminate in reward in the life to come (Rom. 2:7; James 5:7, 8).

Patience of God. Respecting the patience of God Trench says (vol. ii, p. 15), very appropriately: "While both graces (the two forms mentioned above, viz., with persons and with things) are possessed by men only the former is an attribute of God. Men may tempt and provoke him, and he does display patience in regard to them (Exod. 34:6; Rom. 2:4; I Pet. 3:20); there may be a resistance to God in *men*, because he respects the wills with which he created them, even when those wills are fighting against him. But there can be no resistance to God, nor burden upon him, the Almighty, from *things; therefore patience of things* is never ascribed to him." The "God of patience" (*hupomonē*) means that God is the author of patience in his servants (Rom. 15:5).

Pat'mos (păt'mŏs), a small, rocky island belonging to the group called "Sporades," in that part of the Aegean known as the Icarian Sea. On account of its rocky, barren, and desolate nature the Roman government used the island as a place of banishment for criminals. The prisoners were compelled to work the mines of the island. The Emperor Domitian banished the revelator St. John to this island (Rev. 1:9), A. D. 95. Patmos was the locale for the far-reaching apocalyptic visions of the Book of the Revelation. The 50-mile-square Aegean island has magnificent scenery and the white crags of the shore line and the beauty of the open ocean furnish an example of a geographical background which aids the Biblical interpreter to expound the events and experiences of the revelator who was banished to its shores. Revised by *M. F. U.*

Patriarch (Gr. *patriarchēs, patēr*, "father," *archēs*, "head"). The founder of a tribe, a progenitor. It is applied in the New Testament to Abraham (Heb. 7:4), to the sons of Jacob (Acts 7:8, 9), and to David (2:29). In common usage the title of patriarch is assigned especially to those whose lives are recorded in Scripture previous to the time of Moses.

Patriarchal Age, the. The period of Abraham, Isaac and Jacob. If one follows the Massoretic chronology and the general chronological scheme underlying the Hebrew Bible, Abraham was born c. 2161 B. C. and entered Canaan 2086 B. C. The patriarchal period would extend in this case from 2086-1871 B. C. and the Egyptian sojourn from 1871-1441 B. C. (cf. I Kings 6:1 with Exod. 12: 40-41). Scholars for the most part reject the numbers underlying the Biblical chronology and place Abraham's migration from Ur anywhere from 1900-1750 B. C. and the patriarchal period itself anywhere from 1750-1500 B. C. However, following the simple Biblical chronology, Abraham is placed, insofar as his early Mesopotamian connections are involved, under the new Sumero-Akkadian empire of Ur-Nammu, the founder of the famous third dynasty of Ur (c. 2080-1960 B. C.), who assumed the new title "kings of Sumer and Akkad." The mightiest work of this monarch was the erection of the great ziggurat at Ur, which is well preserved today. The patriarch thus left Ur just before it entered the hey-day of its power. On the other hand, the patriarchal age in Palestine would be coterminous with numerous smaller Elamite and Amorite states of Mesopotamia with strong city-states existing at Isin, Larsa and Eshnunna, whose princes took over the her-

itage of the third dynasty of Ur after its collapse. As far as Egypt is concerned the patriarchal age marked the strong Middle Kingdom under the Twelfth Dynasty (c. 2000-c. 1780 B. C.). Abraham went down to Egypt evidently in the early years of this Dynasty. Joseph became prime minister of and Jacob stood before one of the powerful pharoahs of this Dynasty, Amenemes I-IV or Senwosret I-III.

The Ur of Abraham's age has been excavated, showing a remarkably rich commercial emporium, the center of the important cult worshipping the moon god Sin. Archaeology has proved that Abraham, Isaac and Jacob were historical figures and not mere legendary creations, mythological heroes or personification of clans or tribes. (*See* R. P. DeVaux, *Review Biblique*, LIII, 1949, pp. 321-328). The old critical view of the unhistoricity of the patriarchal narratives has been almost completely exploded by recent archaeological discoveries at Nuzu between 1925 and 1941. The Nuzu Tablets furnish many illustrations of patriarchal customs such as adoption, marriage laws, rights of primogeniture and the teraphim. The Mari Letters from Tell Hariri since 1933 have added their weight of confirmation. Such names as Abraham, Isaac and Jacob occur extra-Biblically in the cuneiform tablets. Moreover, Abraham's sojourns at Haran (Gen. 11:31; 12:5), a town which is still in existence on the Balikh River sixty miles W. of Tell Halaf, has been astonishingly corroborated. Cuneiform sources of the nineteenth and eighteenth centuries B. C. mention Haran frequently. The name appears in Assyrian documents as Harranu (meaning "road"), likely describing the trade flowing through this city from Damascus, Carchemish and Nineveh. Haran, like Ur, was the center of the worship of the moon god Sin. The city of Nahor, Rebecca's home (Gen. 24:10), occurs frequently in the Mari Tablets discovered in 1935 and belonging to the eighteenth century B. C. Another clear indication of Abraham's residence in Aram-Naharaim is the names of Abraham's forefathers, Serug (Assyr. *Sarugi*), Nahor and Terah (*Til Turakhi*, "mount of Terah") in Assyrian times. Moreover, the general situation in Canaan at the time of Abraham's arrival in the Middle Bronze Age (2000-1500 B. C.) is thoroughly in agreement with the representations in Genesis. Archaeology has completely exploded the critical idea that the stories of the patriarchs are mostly retrogressions from the time of the dual monarchy (9th and 8th centuries B. C.). Places which are named in the patriarchal narratives, moreover, are not the towns and holy sites of later periods, such as Mizpeh and Gibeah, but are nearly all known from recent archaeological explorations to have existed in the patriarchal period. Examples are Dothan, Gerar, Jerusalem, Bethel, Shechem and Beer-sheba. Also the general historical background of the remarkable 14th chapter of Genesis has been essentially corroborated by modern archaeology. Archaeology has in the last twenty years performed a splendid service in vindicating the essential historicity of the patriarchal period of Genesis, besides marvelously illustrating its background. *M. F. U.*

Patrimony; the produce of the property which a *Levite* (*q. v.*) possessed according to his family descent (Deut. 18:8). Thus a Levite who went to the sanctuary might either let his property in the Levitical town and draw the yearly rent, or sell the house which belonged to him there.

Pat'robas (păt'rô-bàs; *life of his father*), one of the Christians at Rome to whom Paul sent salutations (Rom. 16:14).

Pa'u (pā'ů; *bleating*), a place in Idumaea (Gen. 36:39; Pai, I Chron. 1:50), the capital of Hadar, king of Edom. Its position is unknown.

Paul, *the great apostle* (Gr. *Paulos, little*; *Saulos*, perhaps from Heb. *shä'ül, asked*).

1. **Name.** The name *Paul*, which was applied for the first time by the historian in Acts 13:9, "Saul who also is called Paul" has given rise to much discussion. The usual theory is that the apostle had a Jewish name Saul and a Roman name Paul. Ramsay says (*Paul the Traveler*, etc., p. 81) "it was the fashion for every Syrian, Cilician, or Cappadocian who prided himself on his Greek education and his knowledge of the Greek language to bear a Greek name; but at the same time he had his other name in the native language by which he was known among his countrymen in general." But it is best to understand that Saul's name was changed as a matter of course *when he became a Christian . . .* that the word Paul means "little," and that Paul wanted to be known as the "Little One" in Christ's service; such changes in the cases of Abram, Gideon, Naomi, etc., are to be noted.

2. **Personal History.** Paul was a native of Tarsus, a city of Cilicia (Acts 21:39; 22:3), and was of pure Jewish descent, of the tribe of Benjamin (Phil. 3:5). Of his mother there is no mention, and the information respecting his father is very meager, viz.: that he was a Pharisee (Acts 23:6), and that from him Saul inherited the rights of Roman citizenship (22:28). "The character of a Roman citizen superseded all others before the law and in the general opinion of society, and placed him amid the aristocracy of any provisional town" (Ramsay, p. 31). It will help to a better understanding of the apostle's life and teaching to remember that he was (1) a Roman citizen; (2) a Tarsian, a citizen of no mean city (*see* Tarsus), (3) a Hebrew; and (4) a Pharisee. The date of his birth is unknown, though an ancient tradition gives it as the second year after Christ.

(1) **Previous to conversion.** It being the custom among the Jews that all boys should learn a trade, Paul learned that of "tent-making," "the material of which was haircloth supplied by the goats of his native province, and sold in the markets of the Levant by the well-known name of *cilicium*" (Coneybeare and Howson, *Life and Epistles of St. Paul*). At the proper age (probably about thirteen years) he went to Jerusalem to prosecute his studies in the learning of the Jews. Here he became a student of Gamaliel, a distinguished teacher of the law (Acts 22:3). Here Saul grew more and more familiar with the outward observances of the law, and gaining that experience of the "spirit of bondage" which should enable him to understand himself, and to teach others the blessing of the "spirit of adoption." Paul is first introduced to us in connection with the martyrdom of Stephen, and the persecution which followed, A. D. 36. "Stephen, full of faith and power, did great wonders and miracles among the people." The learned members of the foreign synagogues endeavored to refute his teachings by argument or by clamor. As the *Cilician* synagogue is mentioned among them, we can readily believe that Saul was one of the disputants. In this transaction he was, if not an assistant, something more than a mere spectator, for "the witnesses laid down their clothes at a young man's feet, whose name was Saul" (7:58). He is described as a young man (*neanias*), but was probably thirty years of age at least. After Stephen's burial Saul continued his persecution of the Church, as we are told again and again in St. Luke's narrative and in St. Paul's own speeches and epistles. He "made havoc of the Church," invading the sanctuaries of domestic life, "entering into every house" (8:3), and those whom he thus tore from their homes he "committed to prison." And not only did men thus suffer at his hands, but women also, a fact three times repeated as a great aggravation of his cruelty (8:3). These persecuted people were even "scourged in the synagogues" (26:11). Nor was Stephen the only one to suffer death, as we may infer from the apostle's own confession, "I persecuted this way unto the death, binding and delivering into prisons both men and women (22:4), and when they were put to death I gave my voice against them" (26:10). He even endeavored to cause them "to blaspheme" (26:11). His fame as an inquisitor was notorious far and wide. Even at Damascus Ananias had heard "how much evil he had done to Christ's saints at Jerusalem" (9:13). It was not without reason that in his later years he remembered how he had "persecuted the Church of God and wasted it" (Gal. 1:13).

(2) **Saul's conversion.** Owing to the persecution of the Church they were scattered abroad and went everywhere preaching the word. "And Saul breathing out threatenings and slaughter against the disciples of the Lord" determined to follow them. "Being exceedingly mad against them, he persecuted them even to strange cities" (Acts 26:11; comp. 8:3; Gal. 1:13; I Tim. 1:13). He went, therefore, to the high priest "and desired of him letters to Damascus," where he had reason to believe that Christians were to be found. While on his journey to that city his wonderful conversion took place, changing the proud and persecuting Saul into the loving, helpful Paul. We hesitate to enlarge upon the words of Scripture, and refer to the narrative of St. Luke (Acts 9:3-9; *see* Note). The conflict of Saul's feelings was so great and his remorse so piercing and deep, that during this time he neither ate nor drank. He could have had no intercourse with the Christians, for they had been terrified by the news of his approach; and the unconverted Jews could have no true sympathy with his present state

of mind. But he called upon God, and in his blindness a vision was granted him—a vision soon to be realized—of his being restored to sight by Ananias. After his restoration he was baptized, communed with the disciples, and "straightway preached Christ in the synagogues that he is the son of God," A. D. 37. Conscious of his divine mission, he never felt that it was necessary to consult "those who were apostles before him, but he went into Arabia" (Gal. 1:17). Of the time thus spent we learn further from himself (1:18) that it was three years, which may mean either three full years or one year with parts of two others. We are not told to what district he retired, or for what purpose—perhaps for seclusion, meditation, and prayer. Returning to Damascus (1:17) the Jews took counsel to slay him, but "the disciples took him by night, and let him down by the wall in a basket" (Acts 9:25). According to St. Paul (II Cor. 11:32) it was the ethnarch under Aretas the king, who watched for him, desiring to apprehend him.

(3) **First visit to Jerusalem.** Preserved from destruction at Damascus, Paul turned his steps toward Jerusalem. His motive for the journey, as he himself tells us, was "to see Peter" (Gal. 1:18). "He assayed to join himself to the disciples; but they were all afraid of him and believed not that he was a disciple." Barnabas became his sponsor to the apostles and Church, assuring them of the facts of Paul's conversion and subsequent behavior at Damascus. Barnabas's introduction quieted the fears of the apostles, and Paul "was with them coming in and going out at Jerusalem. And he spake boldly in the name of the Lord Jesus, and disputed against the Grecians." It is not strange that the former persecutor was singled out from the other believers as the object of a murderous hostility. He was therefore again urged to flee, and, by way of Caesarea,

betook himself to his native city, Tarsus. The length of his stay in Jerusalem was fifteen days (1:18), A. D. 39.

(4) **At Antioch.** While Paul was at Tarsus a movement was going on at Antioch which raised that city to an importance second only to that of Jerusalem in the early history of the Church. A large number believed there through the preaching of the disciples driven from Jerusalem, and when this was reported at Jerusalem, Barnabas was sent on a special mission to Antioch. Needing assistance, he went to Tarsus to seek Saul, A. D. 44. Ramsay thinks (p. 46) that Paul's stay in Tarsus was ten years. Returning with him to Antioch, they labored together for "a whole year." As new converts in vast numbers came in from the ranks of the Gentiles the Church began to lose its ancient appearance of a Jewish sect, and to stand as a self-existent community, and they were, therefore, first at Antioch distinguished as "Christians"—they that are connected with Christos. While Barnabas and Saul were evangelizing the Syrian capital, certain prophets came down from Jerusalem to Antioch, and one of them, named Agabus, announced that a time of famine was at hand (probably A. D. 46). No time was lost in preparing for the calamity. All the Antioch Christians, according to their ability, "determined to send relief unto the brethren which dwelt in Judea, which also they did, and sent it to the elders by the hands of Barnabas and Saul" (Acts 11:22-30). This was the occasion of Paul's *second visit* to Jerusalem. Having fulfilled their mission they returned to Antioch, bringing with them another helper, John, whose surname was Mark (12:25). While here the leaders of the Church "ministered to the Lord, and fasted, the Holy Ghost said, Separate me Barnabas and Saul for the work whereunto I have called them." Their breth-

349.

ren, after a season of fasting and praying, laid their hands on them; and so they departed (13:1-3).

(5) **First missionary journey.** The date of their departure is variously fixed between A. D. 45-50, probably 47-48, lasting perhaps 2 years. 1. *Cyprus.* Their first point of destination was the island of Cyprus, the native place of Barnabas. Reaching Salamis, "they preached the word of God in the synagogues of the Jews; and they had also John to minister." From Salamis they traveled to Paphos, at the other extremity of the island, the residence of the Roman governor, Sergius Paulus, who, hearing of the arrival of Barnabas and Saul, sent for them, "desiring to hear the word of God." Attached to the governor was a Jew named Bar-jesus, or Elymas, a false prophet and sorcerer, who, fearful of the influence of the apostles "withstood them, seeking to turn away the deputy from the faith." Paul rebuked Bar-jesus, denounced him in remarkable terms, declaring against him God's sentence of temporary blindness. The sight of Elymas began to waver, and presently a darkness settled on it so thick that he ceased to behold the sun's light. The proconsul, moved by the scene, and persuaded by the teaching of the apostle, became a believer. From this point of the apostolical history Paul appears as the great figure of every picture. He now enters on his work as the preacher to the Gentiles, and simultaneously his name is suddenly changed. Nothing is said to explain the change of name, though we find many conjectures among writers (*see* 1). 2. *Perga* and *Antioch.* From Paphos "Paul and his company" set sail for Perga in Pamphylia, where they remained but a short time. An event occurred there which was attended with painful feelings at the time, and involved the most serious consequences; "John departing from them returned to Jerusalem" (Acts 13:13). This abandonment of the expedition by John was doubtless due to a change of plan, and made a deep and lasting impression upon Paul (15:38). From Perga they traveled on to Antioch in Pisidia. Here "they went into the synagogue on the Sabbath day and sat down." Being invited, "after the reading of the law and the prophets," to speak, Paul stood up and addressed the people (13:16-41). The discourse made a deep and thrilling impression upon the audience, and the apostles were requested to repeat their message on the next Sabbath day. During the week so much interest was excited that on the Sabbath "almost the whole city came together to hear the word of God." Filled with envy because of the desire of the Gentiles to hear, the Jews "spake against those things which were spoken by Paul, contradicting and blaspheming." The apostles turned to the Gentiles and boldly proclaimed salvation to them. Opposition increasing, the apostles left Antioch (13:14-51) and came to Iconium. 3. *Iconium.* This city belonged at different times to Phrygia and Lycaonia. Ramsay, (*Paul the Traveler,* p. 109) thinks it was at this time in the former. Here they went first to the synagogue, and the effect of their discourses was such that great numbers, both of Jews and Greeks, believed

the Gospel. Persecution was raised by the unbelieving Jews, but the apostles persevered and lingered in the city some considerable time, encouraged by the miracles which God worked through their instrumentality. Learning the intention of the hostile Gentiles and their Jewish instigators to raise a riot and stone them, Paul and his company fled (13:51-14:6). 4. *Lystra* and *Derbe*, cities of Lycaonia, were now reached. Here their mission was attested by a miracle—the cure of a cripple. The simple natives ascribed the work to a present deity, and exclaimed, "The gods are come down to us in the likeness of men." They identified Paul with Mercury, and Barnabas with Jupiter, and were about to pay them divine honors. From this the apostles with difficulty dissuaded them. The people in general were disappointed at the repulse of the honors they had offered. The easy step from blind worship to rabid persecution was soon taken, at the instigation of certain Jews who came from Antioch and Iconium. Paul was stoned, and dragged out of the city for dead; but as the new disciples stood round him he revived and returned into the city, whence he and Barnabas departed the next day for Derbe, where they gained many disciples (14:7-21). 5. *Return.* We have now reached the limit of St. Paul's first missionary journey. He revisited Lystra, Iconium, and Antioch, "confirming the souls of the disciples, and exhorting them to continue in the faith." The apostles also ordained elders in every church for their teaching and guidance. They then passed through Pisidia and Perga (in Pamphylia) to Attalia, whence they embarked for Antioch in Syria, where they related the successes which had been granted to them, and especially "the opening of the door of faith to the Gentiles." And so ended the first missionary journey (14:21, sq.).

(6) **The council at Jerusalem** (Acts, ch. 15; Gal., ch. 2). While Paul and Barnabas were abiding at Antioch, certain men came down from Judea and taught the brethren that it was necessary for the Gentile converts to be circumcised. The older converts in Antioch all entered through the synagogue, and had necessarily accepted certain prohibitions as a rule of life. But in Galatia were many who became Christians without any connection with the synagogue. Paul does not seem to have imposed upon them any preliminary compliance; and even Peter had no scruple in associating freely with Antiochian Christians in general. It appears that Peter, having come to Antioch, fellowshiped with the Gentile converts until the arrival of some Jewish brethren, when he "withdrew, and separated himself" from them. Paul, seeing this, rebuked Peter "before all," and "withstood him to the face." This doctrine being vigorously opposed by the two apostles, it was determined to refer the question to the apostles and elders at Jerusalem. Paul and Barnabas themselves, and certain others, were selected for the mission. In Gal. 2:2, St. Paul says that he went up "by revelation." On their way to Jerusalem they announced to the brethren in Phoenicia and Samaria the conversion of the Gentiles. Arrived at Jerusalem,

Paul had private interviews with the more influential members of the Christian community (Gal. 2:2). The apostles and the Church in general, it appears, would have raised no difficulties; but certain believers, who had been Pharisees, thought fit to maintain the same doctrine which had caused the disturbance at Antioch. A formal decision became necessary. After considerable discussion Peter addressed the council, followed by Paul and Barnabas with a statement of facts. Then James gave his decision, which was adopted by the apostles, and elders, and brethren. They wrote to the Gentiles in Antioch, and Syria and Cilicia, disavowing the men who, they say, "going out from us, troubled you with words," and bearing emphatic testimony to Paul and Barnabas as the "beloved who have hazarded their lives for the name of our Lord Jesus Christ." Having been dismissed, the apostles returned to Antioch and read the epistle to the gathered multitude, who were greatly "rejoiced for the consolation." The apostles continued at Antioch preaching the word. Soon after Paul expressed a desire to revisit the cities where he had preached and founded churches. Barnabas determined to take John Mark with them, "and the contention was so sharp between them that they departed asunder one from the other" (Acts 15:36-39).

(7) **Second missionary journey.** Paul chose Silas for his companion, and the two went together through Syria and Cilicia, visiting the churches, and so came to Derbe and Lystra. At the latter place they found *Timothy* (*q. v.*), whom Paul desired to take with him, and therefore circumcised him because of the Jews. Paul then passed through the regions of Phrygia and Galatia, and avoiding, by direction of the Spirit, Asia and Bithynia, he came with his companions by way of Mysia to Troas, on the borders of the Hellespont (Acts 15:40; 16:8). 1. *Macedonia.* Paul saw in a vision a man of Macedonia, who besought him, saying, "Come over into Macedonia and help us!" The vision was understood to mean that "the Lord had called us to preach the Gospel unto them." They traveled north with the intention of entering Bithynia, but the Spirit of Jesus suffered them not, and they passed through Mysia without preaching in it (16:6-8). It is at this point that the historian, speaking of Paul's company (v.10), substitutes "we" for "they." He says nothing of himself. We can only infer that Luke, to whatever country he belonged, became a companion of Paul at Troas. The party immediately set sail from Troas, touched at Samothracia, passed on to Neapolis, and from thence journeyed to Philippi (16:9-12). 2. *At Philippi.* The first convert in Macedonia was Lydia, a woman of Thyatira, who already worshipped God. She made a profession of her faith in Jesus, and was baptized. So earnest was she in her invitation that Paul and his company made her house their home while at Philippi. A female slave, who brought gain to her masters by her powers of prediction when she was in the possessed state, beset Paul and his company. Some think that the young woman was a *ventriloquist*, appealing

to Plutarch, who tells us that in his time such persons were called *puthōnes*. Paul, in the name of Jesus, cast the spirit out of the girl, whereupon her masters, seeing their hope of gain was gone, dragged Paul and Silas before the magistrates. They yielded to the clamor of the multitude, and ordered the apostles to be beaten and cast into prison. This cruel wrong

350. Remains of Christian Churches at Philippi

was the occasion of the signal appearance of the God of righteousness and deliverance. The narrative tells of the earthquake, the jailer's terror, his conversion and baptism, also of the anxiety of the rulers when they learned that those whom they had beaten and imprisoned without trial were Roman citizens (16:13-40). 3: *At Thessalonica.* Leaving Philippi, Paul and Silas traveled through Amphipolis and Apollonia, and stopped at Thessalonica, where was a Jewish synagogue. For three Sabbaths Paul proclaimed Christ in the synagogue, and as a result some of the Jews, with many devout Greeks, "and of the chief women not a few," consorted with Paul and Silas. But the envy of the unbelieving Jews was excited, and, gathering a mob, they assaulted the house of Jason, with whom Paul and Silas were staying as guests. "And the brethren immediately sent away Paul and Silas by night" (17:1-10). How long they stayed in Thessalonica is uncertain, but the success of their work, and the language of I Thess., chaps. 1, 2, would indicate quite a length of time. 4. *Berea.* The next point reached was Berea, where the apostles found Jews more noble than those of Thessalonica had been. Accordingly they gained many converts, both Jews and Greeks. When the Thessalonian Jews heard of this they came hither and stirred up the people. A tumult was only avoided by Paul's departure for the coast, whence he set sail for Athens, leaving Silas and Timothy behind him (17:10-15). Some of "the brethren" went with Paul as far as Athens, where they left him, carrying back "a commandment unto Silas and Timotheus to come to him with all speed." 5. *At Athens.* And Paul was "left in Athens alone" (I Thess. 3:1), A. D., August, 51. As he looked about him "he saw the city wholly given to idolatry," and "his spirit was stirred in him." According to his custom, he sought out his brethren of the scattered race of Israel, declaring to them that the Messiah had come. He also began to discourse daily in the Agora (market place) to them that met with him, among whom were philosophers of the Epicureans and Stoics. His teachings were received, partly in pity, partly in contempt, and yet anyone with a novelty was welcome to his hearers, "for all the Athenians, and strangers which were there, spent their time in nothing else but either to tell or to hear some new thing." They, therefore, brought him to the Areopagus, that he might make to them a formal exposition of his doctrine. Here the apostle delivered that wonderful discourse reported in Acts 17:22-31. Beginning by complimenting them on their carefulness in religion, he, with exquisite tact and ability, exposed the folly of their superstitions, and unfolded the character and claims of the living and true God. But when Paul spoke of the resurrection the patience of his audience failed; some mocked him, and others thinking they had heard enough of his subject for the time, promised him another audience. "So Paul departed from among them." But some believed, among whom was Dionysius the Areopagite, and a woman named Damaris (32:34). We are not informed how long Paul remained in Athens, nor for what cause he left. 6. *At Corinth*. From Athens Paul proceeded to Corinth, where, as at Thessalonica, he chose to earn his own subsistence by working at his trade of tent-making. This brought him into an acquaintance with Aquila and Priscilla, with whom he made his home. "And he reasoned in the synagogue every Sabbath, and persuaded the Jews and the Greeks." While thus engaged Silas and Timothy came from Macedonia and joined him. The *First Epistle to the Thessalonians* was probably written at this time, drawn out from Paul by the report given him of the Church in Thessalonica (I Thess. 3:1, 2). Their coming greatly encouraged him, for he acknowledges himself to have been "in weakness, and in fear, and in much trembling" (I Cor. 2:3). This was doubtless that period of pressing want from which he was relieved by the arrival of "the brethren" (Silas and Timothy) from Macedonia with contributions (II Cor. 11:9). Rejected of the Jews, he turned to the Gentiles and worshipped in the house of a proselyte named Justus. Encouraged by the conversion of Crispus, the chief ruler of the synagogue, and by a vision of the Lord, he remained in Corinth, teaching the word, a year and six months. During this period he probably wrote the *Second Epistle to the Thessalonians*. The Jews then made an unsuccessful attempt against Paul, but were defeated by the calmness of Gallio, the deputy. 7. *Return*. After this long stay at Corinth he departed into Syria, taking with him Priscilla and Aquila (Acts 18:1-18). The apostle's destination was Jerusalem, desiring to be there on the day of Pentecost (20:16). He journeyed thither by the way of Ephesus, leaving his friends, Aquila and Priscilla, there. This visit seems to have been a brief one, the only record of it being, "And when he had landed at Caesarea, and gone up and saluted the Church (at Jerusalem), he went down to Antioch" (18:22). He thus completed his *Second Missionary Journey* in the early summer of A. D. 54 (Conybeare and Howson), or September, A. D. 53 (Lewin). Ramsay makes

it early in the spring of 53, as Passover in that year fell on March 22.

(8) **Third missionary journey.** After a considerable stay at Antioch "Paul departed, and went over all the country of Galatia and Phrygia in order, strengthening all the disciples" (Acts 18:23), also giving directions for the collection in behalf of the poor saints in Jerusalem (I Cor. 16:1, 2). 1. *At Ephesus*. He then came to Ephesus (probably October, A. D. 53), where he found about twelve disciples who had received the instructions of Apollos. Upon inquiry Paul found that they had only received John's baptism, and were ignorant of the Advent of the Spirit and all the ministries committed to Him in this age. He thereupon explained the mission of John as the teacher of repentance to prepare men's minds for Christ, who is the true object of faith. They believed, were baptized, having been introduced into the spiritual blessings of the new age. Entering upon his public ministry, for three months he spoke boldly in the synagogue, but being opposed he withdrew to the school of one Tyrannus, where he discoursed daily for two years. "And God wrought special miracles by the hands of Paul," so that many from among the exorcists became converts, and burned their books of magic to the value of about ten thousand dollars. At about this time (according to Conybeare and Howson) he paid a visit to Corinth, and, returning to Ephesus, wrote the *First Epistle to the Corinthians*. The religious change was becoming so great that the craftsmen who gained their living by making models of the statue of Diana became alarmed and raised an insurrection (*see* Demetrius, Diana). The danger increasing the apostle and his companion left the city (Acts 18-20:1), A. D., January, 56. 2. *At Troas and Macedonia*. On leaving Ephesus Paul went first to Troas, where he preached with great success, though much dejected by the nonarrival of Titus, who had been sent to Corinth (II Cor. 2:12, 13). The necessity of meeting Titus urging him forward, he sailed to Macedonia, and, landing at Neapolis, proceeded immediately to Philippi. Here he was "comforted by the coming of Titus" (7:6), and was probably here rejoined by Timothy (1:1). Titus was sent to Corinth with the *Second Epistle to the Corinthians*, and to finish the collection he had begun there (8:6, 16-18). Hearing that Judaizing teachers had been corrupting the Church of Galatia, Paul wrote the *Epistle to the Galatians*, powerfully refuting and remonstrating against the errors in question. Paul traveled through Macedonia, perhaps to the borders of Illyricum (Rom. 15:19), and then carried out the intention of which he had spoken so often, and arrived at Corinth, where he probably remained three months (Acts 20:2, 3). Here he wrote the *Epistle to the Romans*, about January, 57. Leaving Europe Paul now directed his course toward Jerusalem, accompanied by Luke. At Troas he restored Eutychus (*q. v.*) to life. Paul journeyed by land to Assos, where he took ship for Miletus. By invitation the elders of the Church at Ephesus met him here, and were bidden an affectionate farewell (20:3-38). The voyage was then

resumed, by the way of Coos, Rhodes, and Patara, to Tyre. Here Paul and his company remained seven days, and then sailed to Ptolemais, stopping one day, and reached Caesarea. In opposition to the entreaties of Philip (the evangelist) and others, as well as the prophetic intimations of danger from Agabus, Paul determined to go on to Jerusalem, which he probably did on horseback (21:1-17), probably May 20, 57.

(9) **Arrest at Jerusalem, etc.** This fifth visit of Paul to Jerusalem since his conversion is the last of which we have any certain record. He was gladly received by the brethren, and the following day had an interview with James and the elders, declaring "particularly what things God had wrought among the Gentiles by his ministry." The charge had been brought against him that "he taught *all the Jews among the Gentiles* to forsake Moses, saying that they ought not to circumcise their children, neither to walk after the customs." In order to dispel this impression he was asked to do publicly an act of homage to the law. They had four men who were under the Nazarite law, and Paul was requested to put himself under the vow with these, and to supply the cost of their offerings. When the seven days were almost ended some Jews from Asia stirred up the people against him on the charge of bringing Greeks into the temple to pollute it. The whole city was moved, the apostle was dragged out of the temple, and they were about to kill him. The appearance of soldiers and centurions sent by the tribune stayed their blows. The tribune ordered Paul to be chained, and, not able to learn who he was nor what he had done, sent him to the castle. He obtained leave to address the people (Acts 21:40; 22:1-21), and delivered what he himself called his "defense." At the mention of his mission to the Gentiles they shouted, "Away with such a fellow from the earth; for it is not fit that he should live." Seeing that a tumult was imminent, the tribune sent him within the castle, ordering him to be examined by scourging. From this outrage the apostle protected himself by mentioning his Roman citizenship. On the morrow he was taken before the Sanhedrin; no conclusion was arrived at; only a dissension between the Sadducees and Pharisees. The life of the apostle being in danger he was removed to the castle. That night he was cheered by a vision, in which he was told to "be of good cheer," for he must "bear witness of Jesus at Rome." The conspiracy of forty Jews to kill him was frustrated by tidings brought by Paul's sister's son, and it was determined to send him to Caesarea to Felix, the governor of Judea (22:21-23:24). 1. *Before Felix.* In charge of a strong guard of soldiers he was taken by night as far as Antipatris, the cavalry alone going with him to Caesarea. Felix simply asked Paul of what province he was, promising him a hearing when his accusers should come (23:23-35). Five days after the high priest Ananias and certain members of the Sanhedrin appeared, with Tertullus as their advocate. The charges made against Paul were denied by him, and Felix delayed proceedings until "Lysias, the chief captain, should come down," commanding that Paul should be treated with indulgence and his friends allowed to see him. "After certain days" Felix sent for Paul, influenced probably by the desire of Drusilla, his wife, to hear him, she being a Jewess. Felix trembled under his preaching, but was unrepentant, shutting his ears to conviction and neglecting his official duty, hoping that he might receive a bribe from Paul for his liberation. But not receiving this he retained Paul a prisoner without a hearing two years, until the arrival of Festus (chap. 24), A. D. 59. 2. *Before Festus.* As soon as the new governor, Festus, came to Jerusalem, he was requested to send for Paul. He replied that Paul should be kept at Caesarea, whither he ordered his accusers to accompany him. After ten days he returned, and on the next day Paul was brought before the tribunal. When asked if he was willing to be tried at Jerusalem the apostle, aware of his danger, replied that he stood at Caesar's judgment seat. He then uttered the words *"Caesarem appello"* ("I appeal unto Caesar"), which a Roman magistrate dared not resist. Festus conferred with his council and replied, "Hast thou appealed unto Caesar? unto Caesar shalt thou go" (25:1-12). 3. *Before Agrippa.* While waiting for an opportunity to send Paul to Rome Festus desired to prepare an account of the trial to be sent to the emperor. This was a matter of some difficulty, as the information elicited at the trial was so vague that he hardly knew what statement to insert; and it seemed "unreasonable to send a prisoner and not to signify the crime laid against him." About this time King Agrippa II, with his sister Berenice, came on a complimentary visit to the new governor. To him Festus recounted the case, confessing his own ignorance of Jewish theology, whereupon Agrippa expressed a desire to hear the prisoner. The next day Agrippa and Berenice came with great pomp, with suite of military officers and chief men of Caesarea. Paul was brought, and, permission having been given him to speak, he pronounced one of his greatest apologies for the Christian truth. When he spoke of the resurrection Festus exclaimed, "Paul, thou art beside thyself; much learning doth make thee mad." This Paul courteously denied, and, turning to the Jewish voluptuary, he made this appeal to him, "King Agrippa, believest though the prophets? I know that thou believest," to which the king ironically responded, "Thou wilt soon persuade me to be a Christian" (Conybeare and Howson, *trans.*). The reply of Paul concluded the interview, and it was decided that he had done nothing worthy of death, and might have been set at liberty but for his appeal to Caesar. There was no retreat, and nothing remained but to wait for a favorable opportunity of sending the prisoner to Rome (25:13-27 to 26:1-32).

(10) **Voyage to Rome.** At length (August, 59, Ramsay; A. D. 60, Conybeare and Howson) Paul, under the care of Julius, a centurion of the Augustan cohort who had charge of a convoy of prisoners, set sail in a coasting vessel belonging to Adramyttium. The next day they touched at Sidon, "and Julius cour-

teously entreated Paul and gave him liberty to go unto his friends and refresh himself." The next port reached was Myra, a city of Lycia, where they found a ship of Alexandria bound for Italy; and to this vessel Julius transferred his prisoners. Leaving behind the harbor of Cnidus and doubling Salmone, the headland of Crete, they beat up with difficulty under the lea of the island, as far as the fine harbor, near Lasaea, which still bears its ancient name of the *Fair Havens*. "The ship reached Fair Havens in the latter part of September, and was detained there by a continuance of unfavorable winds until after October 5" (Ramsay, p. 322). Contrary to the warning of the apostle that it would be perilous to continue the voyage at that season of the year, it was decided not to remain. The hope was to reach Phenice (*Phoenix*) and winter there. Overtaken by the *Euroclydon*, they were unable to bear up into the wind, and, letting the ship drive, were carried under the lee of a small island named *Clauda*. The storm raged with unabated fury, and the ship was drifting in the sea of *Adria*, when, on the fourteenth night after their departure from Clauda, they found themselves near land. In the morning they ran aground, and all escaped safely to the land, which they found to be Malta (*Melita*, Acts, ch. 27), about November. The people of the island treated them kindly, and were deeply impressed with Paul's shaking off the viper from his hand, believing him to be a god. The company remained three months on the island, Paul performing miracles of healing. They then departed from Malta in February, in the ship *Castor and Pollux*, and came, by the way of Syracuse and Rhegium, to Puteoli, in Italy. Here they found Christian brethren, with whom they tarried seven days: "and so went toward Rome," being met by brethren from that city at "*Appi Forum* and the *Three Taverns*" (28:11-15), spring, A. D. 60.

(11) **At Rome.** Upon his arrival in Rome the apostle was delivered to the prefect of the guard (pretorian), but was allowed to dwell in his own hired house (under the care of a soldier) and to receive visitors (Acts 28:16, 30). After three days he invited the chief men among the Jews to come to him, and explained his position. He had committed no offense against the holy nation; he came to Rome, not to accuse his countrymen, but compelled to appeal to Caesar by their conduct. "*For the hope of Israel*," he concluded, "*I am bound with this chain*." They replied that they had received no letters concerning him, and that none of the brethren coming from Jerusalem had spoken evil of him. They expressed also a desire to hear further concerning his religious sentiments. The day for the hearing was set. They came in large numbers, and to them "he expounded and testified the kingdom of God," endeavoring to persuade them by arguments from their own Scriptures, "from morning till evening." Some believed, and others did not, and, separating, they had "great reasoning among themselves" (vers. 17-29). He remained in his own hired house, under military custody, and yet receiving every indulgence which it was in the power of the prefect to grant. He was permitted to preach "the kingdom of God," and teach "those things concerning the Lord Jesus" (v. 31). This imprisonment lasted two years (v. 30), from A. D. 60, spring, to A. D. 62, spring. Here closes the account as given in the Book of Acts, but we gather from his epistles that during this time he wrote those to *Philemon, Colossians, Ephesians,* and *Philippians*.

(12) **Release and subsequent labors.** At the end of the two years it is the general opinion that Paul was granted a trial before Nero which resulted in his acquittal and liberation. He then probably fulfilled his intention, lately expressed (Philem. 22, and Phil. 2:24), of traveling eastward through Macedonia and on to Ephesus, and thence to Colossae and Laodicea. From Asia Minor he went to Spain (disputed by many), where he remained two years. Returning to Asia Minor and Macedonia, he wrote the *First Epistle to Timothy;* to Crete, *Epistle to Titus;* winters at Nicopolis; arrested there and forwarded to Rome for trial. This is the scheme as given by Conybeare and Howson. Lewin (*Life of St. Paul*) gives the following scheme: St. Paul sails for Jerusalem, and goes thence by Antioch and Asia Minor, visiting Colossae, to Ephesus—to Crete—to Macedonia and Corinth, wintering at Nicopolis—traditional journey to Spain—probably arrested at Ephesus and taken to Rome. Ramsay says (p. 360) that "the hints contained in the Pastoral Epistles hardly furnish an outline of his travels, which must have lasted three or four years, A. D. 62-65."

(13) **Second imprisonment and death.** This imprisonment was evidently more severe than the first one had been. Now he is not only chained, but treated "as a malefactor" (II Tim. 2:9). Most of his friends left him, many, perhaps, like Demas, "having loved this present world" (4:10), others from necessity, and we hear the lonely cry, "Only Luke is with me" (4:11). So perilous was it to show any public sympathy with him that no Christian ventured to stand by him in the court of justice. As the final stage of his trial approaches he looks forward to death as his final sentence (4:6-8). Probably no long time elapsed after Paul's arrival before his case came on for hearing. He seems to have successfully defended himself from the first (4:17) of the charges brought against him, and to have been delivered from immediate peril and from a painful death. He was now remanded to prison to wait for the second stage of the trial. He probably thought that this would not come on, or at least the final decision would not be given, until the following winter (4:21), whereas it actually took place about midsummer. We are not left to conjecture the feelings with which he awaited this consummation; for he has himself expressed them in that sublime strain of triumphant hope which is familiar to the memory of every Christian, and which has nerved the heart of a thousand martyrs: "I have fought a good fight, I have finished my course, I have kept the faith; henceforth there is laid up for me a crown of righteousness, which the Lord, the righteous judge, shall give me at that

day." The presence of Luke still consoled him, and Onesiphorus sought him out and visited him in his prison, undeterred by the fear of danger or of shame (1:16). He longed, however, for the presence of Timothy, to whom he wrote the *Second Epistle*, urging him "to come before winter" (4:21). We know not if Timothy was able to fulfill these last requests; it is doubtful whether he reached Rome in time to receive his parting commands and cheer his latest sufferings. The only intimation which seems to throw any light upon the question is the statement in the Epistle to the Hebrews (13:23) that Timothy had been liberated from imprisonment in Italy. We have no record of the final stage of the apostle's trial, and only know that it ended in martyrdom, A. D., summer, 68 (or 67). He died by decapitation, according to universal tradition, "weeping friends took up his corpse and carried it for burial to those subterranean labyrinths (Clem., *Rom.*, i, 5) where, through many ages of oppression, the persecuted Church found refuge for the living, and sepulchers for the dead."

3. **Character.** While we learn much concerning the character of Paul from his life and labors, his burning zeal, untiring industry, singleness of aim, patient suffering, sublime courage, it is in his letters that we must study his true life, for in them we learn "what is told of Paul by Paul himself" (Gregory Nazianzen). "It is not only that we there find models of the sublimest eloquence, when he is kindled by the visions of the glories to come, the perfect triumph of good over evil, the manifestation of the sons of God, and the transformation into God's likeness; but in his letters, besides all this which is divine, we trace every shade, even to the faintest, of his human character also. Here we see that fearless independence with which he 'withstood Peter to the face, because he was to be blamed' (Gal. 2:11); that impetuosity which breaks out in his apostrophe to the 'foolish Galatians' (3:1); that earnest indignation which bids his converts 'beware of dogs, beware of the concision' (Phil. 3:2), and pours itself forth in the emphatic 'God forbid' (Rom. 6:2; I Cor. 6:15), which meets every Antinomian suggestion; that fervid patriotism which makes him 'wish that he were himself accursed from Christ for his brethren, . . . who are Israelites' (Rom. 9:3); that generosity which looked for no other reward than 'to preach the glad tidings of Christ without charge' (I Cor. 9:18, 25), and made him feel that he would rather 'die than that any man should make this glorifying void;' that dread of officious interference which led him to shrink from 'building on another man's foundation' (Rom. 15:20); that delicacy which shows itself in his appeal to Philemon, whom he might have commanded, 'yet for love's sake rather beseeching him' (Philem., 9); that scrupulous fear of evil appearance which 'would not eat any man's bread for naught, but wrought with labor and travail night and day, that he might not be chargeable to any of them' (I Thess. 2:9); that refined courtesy which cannot bring itself to blame till it has first praised (comp. I Cor. 1:5-7; II Cor. 1:6,

7, with latter part of these epistles), and which makes him deem it needful almost to apologize for the freedom of giving advice to those who are not personally known to him (Rom. 15:14, 15); that self-denying love which 'will eat no flesh while the world standeth, lest he make his brother to offend' (I Cor. 8:13); that impatience of exclusive formalism with which he overwhelms the Judaizers of Galatia, joined with a forbearance so gentle for the innocent weakness of scrupulous consciences (I Cor. 8:12; Rom. 14:21); that grief for the sins of others which moved him to tears when he spoke of the enemies of the cross of Christ, 'of whom I tell you even weeping' (Phil. 3:18); that noble freedom from jealousy with which he speaks of those who, out of rivalry to himself, preach Christ even of envy and strife, supposing to add affliction to his bonds, 'What then? notwithstanding every way, whether in pretense or in truth, Christ is preached; and I therein do rejoice, yea, and will rejoice' (1:18); that tender friendship which watches over the health of Timothy, even with a mother's care (I Tim. 5:23); that intense sympathy in the joys and sorrows of his converts which could say, even to the rebellious Corinthians, 'Ye are in our hearts, to die and live with you' (II Cor. 7:3); that longing desire for the intercourse of affection, and that sense of loneliness when it was withheld, which perhaps is the most touching feature of all, because it approaches most nearly to a weakness" (Conybeare and Howson).

NOTE—(1) **Paul's citizenship.** It is a mistake to suppose that Paul's citizenship, which belonged to the members of the family, came from their being natives of Tarsus. Although it was a "free city" (*urbs libera*), enjoying the privileges of being governed by its own magistrates, and was exempted from the occupation of a Roman garrison, yet its citizens did not necessarily possess the *civitas* of Rome. The tribune (Acts 21:39; 22:24), knew that St. Paul was a Tarsian, without being aware that he was a citizen. This privilege had been granted, or descended to his father, as an individual right, perhaps for some services rendered to Caesar during the civil wars (Conybeare and Howson; Bloomfield, *New Testament*). (2) **Member of the Sanhedrin.** "There are strong grounds for believing that if Paul was not a member of the Sanhedrin at Stephen's death he was elected into that powerful senate soon after; possibly as a reward for the zeal he had shown against the heretic. He himself says that in Jerusalem he not only exercised the power of imprisonment by commission from the high priests, but also, when the Christians were put to death, *gave his vote* against them (Acts 26:10). From this expression it is natural to infer that he was a member of that supreme court of judicature. If this inference is well founded, and the qualification for members of the Sanhedrin was that they should be the fathers of children, Saul must have been a married man, and the father of a family. If so it is probable that his wife and children did not long survive; for otherwise some notice of them would have occurred in the subsequent narrative, or some allusion to them in the epistles" (Conybeare and Howson). (3) **Conversion.** Some regard the circumstances of the case as by no means miraculous, but as produced solely by certain terrific *natural phenomena*, which they suppose had such an effect on the high-wrought imagination, and so struck the alarmed conscience of Saul, as to make him regard as reality what was merely produced by fancy. "Paul, however ardent might be his temperament and vivid his imagination, *could not* so far deceive himself as to suppose that the *conversation* really took place if there had been no more than these commentators tell us. Besides he is so minute in his description as to say it was in the *Hebrew language*" (Bloomfield, *New Testament*). The seeming discrepancies found in the several accounts (Acts, chaps. 9, 22, 26) have been differently explained. "The Greek 'akouo,' like our word 'hear,' has two distinct meanings—*to perceive sound* and *to understand.* The men who were with Saul heard the sound, but did not understand what was said to him. As to the fact that one passage represents them as '*standing*,' the other as having 'fallen to the earth,' the word rendered 'stood' also means *to be fixed, rooted to the spot.* Hence the sense may be, not that they stood erect, but that they were rendered *motionless,* or *fixed to the spot,* by overpowering fear. Or, perhaps, when the light with such exceeding brilliancy burst upon them, they all 'fell to the earth,' but afterward rose and 'stood' upon their feet" (Haley, *Discrepancies of the Bible*). (4) **"Saul, who is also Paul"** (Acts 13:9). "The invariable use in the Acts of Saul up this point, and Paul afterward, and the distinct mention by St. Luke himself of the transition, is accounted for by the desire to mark the turning-point between Saul's activity among his own countrymen and his new labors as the apostle of the Gentiles" (Smith). "We are inclined to adopt the opinion that the Cilician apostle had this Roman name, as well as his other Hebrew name, in his earlier days, and even before he was a Christian . . . yet we cannot believe it accidental that the words which have led to this discussion occur at this point of the inspired narrative. The heathen name rises to the surface at the moment when St. Paul visibly enters on his office as the apostle to the heathen" (Conybeare and Howson, vol. i, pp. 152, 153). (5) **Journeys to Jerusalem.** In the Book of Acts we are informed of five distinct journeys made by the apostle to Jerusalem after the time of his conversion. In the Epistle to the Galatians St. Paul speaks of two journeys to Jerusalem—the first being "three years" after his conversion, the second "fourteen years" later (Gal. 1:18; 2:1). The question arises whether the second journey of the epistle must be identified with the second, third, or fourth of the Acts, or whether it is a separate journey, distinct from any of them. It is agreed by all that the fifth cannot possibly be intended. Paley and Schrader have resorted to the hypothesis that the *Galatian* visit is some supposed journey not recorded in the Acts at all. Conybeare and Howson (*Life and Epistles of St. Paul*) identify it with the third journey of Acts, ch. 15. (6) **"Ye are too superstitious"** (Acts 17:22). This translation (from the Vulg. *superstitiosiores*) cannot by any means be defended. Conybeare renders, "All things which I behold bear witness to your carefulness in religion," and adds, "The mistranslation of this verse in the A. V. is much to be regretted, because it entirely destroys the graceful courtesy of St. Paul's opening address, and represents him as beginning his speech by offending his audience" (*Life and Epistles*, vol. i, p. 378). Bloomfield (*New Testament*) translates "very religious," i. e., attentive to religion (as far as they understood it). *See* Superstitious. (7) **Vow at Cenchrea** (Acts 18:18). The impression on the reader's mind is that Paul himself shaved his head at Cenchrea. Eminent commentators hold the view that the ceremony was performed by Aquila; also that the vow was not one of *Nazarite,* but a *votum civile,* such as was taken during or after recovery from sickness, or deliverance from any peril, or on obtaining any unexpected good. In case of a Nazarite vow the cutting of the hair, which denoted that the legal time had expired, could only take place in the temple in Jerusalem, or at least in Judea (Conybeare and Howson; Bloomfield, *New Testament*). (8) **Reply to Ananias** (Acts 23:3-5). "God shall smite thee," etc. Some consider these words as an outburst of natural indignation, and excuse it on the ground of the provocation, as a righteous denouncing of an unjust ruler. Others think them a prophetic denunciation, terribly fulfilled when Ananias was murdered in the Jewish wars (Josephus, *Wars*, xi, 17, 9). "I wist not, brethren, that he was the high priest." These words are variously explained. "Some think that St. Paul meant to confess that he had been guilty of a want of due reflection; others that he spoke ironically, as refusing to recognize a man like Ananias as high priest; others have even thought that there was in the words an inspired reference to the abolition of the sacerdotal system of the Jews and the sole priesthood of Christ. Another class of interpreters regard St. Paul as ignorant of the fact that Ananias was high priest, or argue that Ananias was not really installed in office. And we know from Josephus that there was the greatest irregularity in the appointments about this time. Lastly, it has been suggested that the imperfection of St. Paul's vision was the

cause of his mistake" (Conybeare and Howson). (9) **Charge against St. Paul before Felix** (Acts 24:5, 6). St. Paul was accused of a threefold crime: First, with causing factious disturbances among all the Jews throughout the empire (which was an offense against the Roman government, and amounted to *lese majeste,* or treason against the emperor); secondly, with being a ringleader of the sect of the Nazarenes (which involved heresy against the law of Moses); and thirdly, with an attempt to profane the temple at Jerusalem (an offense not only against the Jewish, but also against the Roman law, which protected the Jews in the exercise of their worship) (Conybeare and Howson, vol. ii, p. 282). (10) **Thorn in the flesh** (II Cor. 12:7). "The best commentators are, with reason, agreed that the word skolops (thorn) must be taken in the natural sense, as denoting some very painful disorder or mortifying infirmity; *grievous afflictions* being, in all languages, expressed by metaphors taken from the piercing of the flesh by thorns or splinters. Various acute *disorders* have been supposed to be meant, as the headache" (Jerome, Tertullian), earache, impediment of speech (10:10), malady affecting the eyesight. "But it should rather seem that some *chronic* distemper or infirmity is meant, and probably such as was exceedingly mortifying as well as painful; otherwise the apostle would scarcely have felt such anxiety to have it removed. A most probable conjecture is that it was a *paralytic* and *hypochondriac affection,* which occasioned a distortion of countenance, and many other distressing effects, which would much tend to impair his usefulness" (Bloomfield, *New Testament*). Dr. Ramsay suggests (p. 94, sq.) that the malady was a species of chronic malarial fever, with its recurring regularity, weakness, producing sickness and trembling.

Pau'lus (pôl'ŭs). *See* Sergius Paulus.

Pavement (Heb. *rĭṣpäh,* hot *stone;* once, II Kings 16:17, *mărṣĕpĕth*). Originally a stone heated for baking purposes, hence a *tesselated pavement* (II Chron. 7:3; Esth. 1:6; Ezek. 40:17, 18). In John 19:13 "pavement" is the rendering of the Gr. *Lithostrōton,* and explained by the Hebrew equivalent *Gabbatha* (*q. v.*). In the account of Ahaz despoiling the temple, it is said that he "took down the sea from off the brazen oxen that were under it, and put in on a pavement of stones" (II Kings 16:17), probably a pedestal made of stones.

Figurative. The "paved work of a sapphire stone" (Exod. 24:10) is, probably, a reference to the splendid floors known in Egypt, and is used to indicate that God was enthroned above the heaven in superterrestrial glory.

Paw (Heb. *yäd*), only in Lev. 11:27 (comp. Job 39:21).

Figurative. To express *power.*

Pe (pä), the 17th letter of the Hebrew alphabet, heading the 17th section of Psalm 119, in which each verse of the original begins with this letter.

Peace (Heb. *shälōm, familiar;* Gr. *eirēnē, unity, concord*), a term used in different senses in the Scriptures. 1. Frequently with reference to outward conditions of tranquility and thus of individuals, of communities, of churches, and nations (e. g., Num. 6:26; I Sam. 7:14; I Kings 4:24; Acts 9:31, et al.). 2. Christian unity (e. g., Eph. 4:3; I Thess. 5:13). 3. In its deepest application, spiritual peace through restored relations of harmony with God (e. g., Isa. 9:6, 7; 26:3; 53:5; Psa. 119:165; Luke 2:14; John 14:27; ch. 16; Acts 10:36; Rom. 1:7; 5:1; Gal. 5:22, and many other places). *See* Atonement, Faith, Pardon, Adoption, Holy Spirit.

Peace Offering. *See* Sacrifices, Sacrificial Offerings.

Peacemakers (Gr. *eirēnopoios, worker of peace*). Some include in the meaning of this term the idea of *peaceful, peace-loving,* but it evidently goes further than the passive possession of peace and a love thereof. Meyer (*Com.,* Matt., 5:9) writes: "Not the *peaceful,* but the *founders of peace*" (comp. Col. 1:20), who as such minister to God's good pleasure, who is the God of peace (Rom. 16:20; II Cor. 13:11), as Christ himself was the highest founder of peace (Luke 2:14; John 16:33; Eph. 2:14 sq.).

Peacock. *See* Animal Kingdom.

Pearl (Gr. *margaritēs*), is mentioned in A. V. in Old Testament only once (Job. 28:18, *gäbîsh*). R. V. and R. S. V., with probability, translate it "crystal." Pearls are mentioned several times in the New Testament (Matt. 7:6; 13:45, 46; I Tim. 2:9; Rev. 17:4; Gr. *margarites.* The gates of pearl (Rev. 21:21) refer to mother of pearl. Both are depositions from the juice of the pearl oyster, *Avicula margaritifera,* L.

Figurative. In Matt. 7:6 *pearls* are a figure for the truths, privileges, and responsibilities of the Christian. "No sacred deposit, or responsibility, or even principle (symbolized by *pearls*) must be imparted to an unfit man. No doctrines or religious experiences must be brought before an incapable sensualist. In fine, in imparting the official trusts and the truths of the Gospel, we must *discern* men's moral qualities, and deal with them accordingly" (Whedon, *Com.,* on Matt., 7:6).

Peculiar (Heb. *sᵉgŭllāh, wealth;* Gr. *peripoiēsis,* I Pet. 2:9). In Exod. 19:5 we have the promise, "Now, therefore, if ye will obey my voice indeed, and keep my covenant, then ye shall be a *peculiar* treasure unto me above all people" (comp. Deut. 14:2; 26:18; Psa. 135:4, etc.). The Hebrew term does not signify property in general, but valuable property, which is laid by, or put aside, hence a treasure of gold or silver (I Chron. 29:3; Eccles. 2:8). "Jehovah had chosen Israel as his costly possession out of all the nations of the earth, because the whole earth was his possession, and all nations belonged to him as Creator and preserver. The reason assigned for the selection of Israel precludes the exclusiveness which would regard Jehovah merely as a national deity" (K. and D., *Com.*). In Tit. 2:14, *peculiar* is the rendering of the Gr. *periousios, special,* which means "that which is peculiarly one's own."

Ped'ahel (pĕd′ȧ-hĕl; *God delivers*), the son of Ammihud, and prince of the tribe of Naphtali. He was appointed by Moses one of the commissioners to divide Palestine (Num. 34:28), B. C. c. 1440.

Pedah'zur (pê-dä′zẽr; *the Rock,* i. e., God *ransoms*), the father of Gamaliel, a prince of Manasseh, and appointed with others to assist Moses in numbering the people (Num. 1:10; 2:20; 7:54, 59; 10:23), B. C. c. 1439.

Peda'iah (pê-dā′yȧ; *Jehovah ransoms*).

1. The father of Zebudah, who was the wife of Josiah and mother of Jehoiakim (II Kings 23:36), B. C. before 640.

2. The father of *Zerubbabel* (*q. v.*), by the widow of his brother Salathiel (I Chron. 3:18), in accordance with the Levirate law, B. C. before 536.

3. The father of Joel, which latter was the

"ruler" of the western half-tribe of Manasseh (I Chron. 27:20).

4. An Israelite, of the family of Parosh, who assisted in rebuilding the walls of Jerusalem (Neh. 3:25), B. C. 445.

5. Mentioned only in the genealogy of Sallu, as the son of Kolaiah and the father of Joed, of the tribe of Benjamin (Neh. 11:7), B. C. before 445.

6. A Levite whom Nehemiah appointed one of the treasurers, whose "office was to distribute unto their brethren" (Neh. 13:13), and probably one of those who stood on Ezra's left hand when he read the law (8:4), B. C. 445.

Pedigree (from Heb. *yălăd,* to *show lineage*). Before the departure of Israel from Sinai, Moses, on the first day of the second month of the second year after leaving Egypt, mustered the twelve tribes with the exception of Levi. They had the whole congregation gathered together by the heads of the tribes, and their names enrolled in genealogical registers. *See* Genealogy.

Peep (Heb. *şăphăph,* to *coo* or *chirp* as a *bird*) is applied to wizards who professed thus to imitate the voices of the *shades* or ghosts (Isa. 8:19). *See* Magic.

Pe'kah (pē′kȧ; God *has opened* the eyes), the eighteenth king of Israel. He is introduced into Scripture history as the son of Remaliah, and captain of King Pekahiah, whom he murdered and succeeded to the throne (II Kings 15:25), B. C. c. 734. From the fact that fifty Gileadites were with him in the conspiracy it has been conjectured that he was a native of Gilead. Under his predecessors Israel had been much weakened through the payment of enormous tribute to the Assyrians (*see* especially II Kings 15:20) and by internal wars and conspiracies. Pekah steadily applied himself to the restoration of its power. For this purpose he sought for the support of a foreign alliance, and fixed his mind on the plunder of the sister kingdom of Judah. He must have made the treaty by which he proposed to share its spoils with Rezin, king of Damascus, when Jotham was still on the throne of Jerusalem (15:37), but its execution was long delayed, probably in consequence of that prince's righteous and vigorous administration (II Chron. ch. 27). When, however, his weak son Ahaz succeeded to the crown of David, the allies no longer hesitated, and formed the siege of Jerusalem. The history of the war is found in II Kings, ch. 16 and II Chron. ch. 28. It is famous as the occasion of the great prophecies in Isa. chaps. 7-9. Pekah was despoiled of at least half of his kingdom, and fell into the position of an Assyrian vassal (II Kings 15:29), B. C. c. 724. About a year later Hoshea conspired against him and put him to death (v. 30). Of his character and reign it is recorded, "He did that which was evil in the sight of the Lord."

Pekahi'ah (pĕk-ȧ-hī′ȧ; *Jehovah has opened* (the eyes), *Jehovah has observed*), the seventeenth king of Israel, being the son and successor of Menahem. After a brief reign of scarcely two years, B. C. 735-734, a conspiracy was organized against him by Pekah, who, at the head of fifty Gileadites, attacked him in his palace, murdered him and his friends Argob and Arieh, and seized the throne (II Kings 15:23-26). His reign was an idolatrous one, he followed in the sinful practices of Jeroboam.

Pe'kod (pē'kŏd), a strong Aramaean tribe (the *Puqudu*) dwelling in the plain E. of the Tigris near its mouth. In Ezekiel's day they were a part of the Chaldean Empire (Jer. 50:21; Ezek. 23:23).

Pela'iah (pê-lā'yȧ; *Jehovah is wonderful*).

1. A son of Elioenai, of the royal line of Judah (I Chron. 3:24), B. C. after 400.

2. One of the Levites who assisted Ezra in expounding the law (Neh. 8:7), B. C. 445. He afterward sealed the covenant with Nehemiah (10:10).

Pelali'ah (pĕl-ȧ-lī'ȧ; *Jehovah has judged*), a priest, the son of Amzi and father of Jeroham (Neh. 11:12), B. C. before 445.

Pelati'ah (pĕl-ȧ-tī'ȧ; *Jehovah has delivered*).

1. A son of Hananiah, the descendant of Salathiel, of the family of David (I Chron. 3:21), B. C. after 536.

2. A son of Ishi, and captain of one of the marauding bands of Simeonites who, in the reign of Hezekiah, made an expedition to Mount Seir and smote the Amalekites (I Chron. 4:42), B. C. about 715.

3. One of the chief of the people who signed the covenant with Nehemiah (Neh. 10:22), B. C. 445.

4. Son of Benaiah, and one of the princes against whom Ezekiel was commanded to prophesy. The prophet saw him in a vision standing at the east gate of the temple; and the same vision revealed to him Pelatiah's sudden death (Ezek. 11:1, 13), B. C. about 592.

Pe'leg (pē'lĕg; *division*), the son of Eber, and fourth in descent from Shem. His brother's name was Joktan, and his son's Reu (Gen. 10:25; 11:16-19; I Chron. 1:25). His name is said to have been given him because "in his days was the earth divided" (Gen. 10:25; I Chron. 1:19). The "division" referred to is enigmatic and may point to the scattering of Noah's descendants (Gen. 11:8).

Pe'let (pē'lĕt; *deliverance*).

1. A son of Jahdai, who seems to have been of the family of Caleb the Hezronite (I Chron. 2:47), B. C. after 1400.

2. One of the sons of Azmaveth, one of David's Benjamite captains at Ziklag (I Chron. 12:3), B. C. about 1000.

Pe'leth (pē'lĕth; cf. Arab. *fulat, swift*).

1. A Reubenite, and father of On, who joined in the conspiracy of Korah, Dathan, and Abiram (Num. 16:1), B. C. c. 1430.

2. Son of Jonathan, and a descendant of Jerahmeel through Onan (I Chron. 2:33).

Pel'ethite (pĕl'ē-thīt; II Sam. 8:18; 15:18). The term is equivalent to *courier*, as one portion of the halberdiers had to convey the king's orders to distant places (II Chron. 30:6). Some believe the Pelethites and *Cherethites* (*q. v.*) to have been foreigners (Philistines, Ewald, *Hist. of Israel*, vol. i, p. 246, sq.; iii, p. 143); but the evidence is very meager.

Pelican. *See* Animal Kingdom.

Pel'onite (pĕl'ō-nīt). Two of David's mighty men, Helez and Ahijah, are called Pelonites

(I Chron. 11:27, 36). In I Chron. 27:10 it is stated that Helez was of the tribe of Ephraim. "Pelonite" would, therefore, be an appellation derived from his place of birth or residence. In II Sam. 23:26 he is called "Helez the Paltite," possibly a corruption of the text for Pelonite. And in the same list, instead of "Ahijah the Pelonite," we have "Eliam, the son of Ahithophel the Gilonite" (II Sam. 23:34).

Pen. *See* Writing.

Pence. *See* Metrology, IV, 4.

Peni'el (pê-nī'ĕl; Gen. 32:30). *See* Penuel.

Penin'nah (pê-nĭn'ȧ; *coral*), one of the wives of Elkanah, the father of Samuel. No mention is made of her save that she bore children and behaved provokingly toward Hannah, the other wife (I Sam. 1:2-7), B. C. about 1080.

Penknife (Heb. *tă'ăr*), a small knife which was used for sharpening the point of the writing reed (Jer. 36:23).

Penny. *See* Metrology, IV, 12.

Pentateuch, from Gr. *penta*, "five" *teuchos*, "a tool" or "implement;" a later Greek term applied to the five books of Moses, which in their ancient scroll form were kept in sheaths or cases for protection. The Greek term first appears in the second century A. D. and was later employed by Origen (J. E. Steinmueller, *Companion to Scripture Studies*, Vol. II, N. Y., 1942, p. 7).

1. **Contents.** The Pentateuch is the first of the three divisions of the ancient Hebrew canon, called earlier the Law or Torah. It catalogs the giving of those religious and civil institutions which form the basis of ancient Israel's theocratic national life. This section of the Hebrew Bible, introductory to the other two sections of the Prophets and the Writings, is composed of five books, Genesis, Exodus, Leviticus, Numbers and Deuteronomy. Moses is the traditional author. It is by no means impossible that the original five-volume arrangement was effected by Moses himself. These books, especially Genesis, Leviticus and Deuteronomy, are natural units in themselves. We may, therefore, conclude with Edward J. Young "that the five-volume division was the work of the original author of the Law, namely, Moses" (*Intr. to the O. T.*, Grand Rapids, 1949, p. 48.) If however, such five-volume division was not in effect from the beginning and the five books were originally one book, such a five-volume division was necessitated in later times for liturgical reasons to facilitate the reading of the Law in the synagogue services. The explanation of this is that ancient books were in the cumbersome form of rolls or scrolls. A scroll thirty feet long would ordinarily accommodate the Hebrew text of Genesis or Deuteronomy. If the length was longer than this, they became very difficult to handle. Hebrews were accustomed to employ the standard thirty-foot size. It is true that the Egyptians sometimes used extremely long rolls like the Papyrus Harris, 133 feet long, and the Book of the Dead, 123 feet long. But these were definitely exceptions and antiquarian relics, and intended not for everyday use. It can plainly be seen why the division of the Pentateuch would be necessitated. The five-volume divi-

sion of the Pentateuch is attested by both Philo and Josephus in the first century A. D., and its existence goes back to Septuagint times (third century B. C.), and probably to the time of Ezra-Nehemiah.

2. **Names.** In the O. T. the Pentateuch is variously designated by nomenclature descriptive of its contents. It is called the "Law" or "Torah" (Josh. 1:7), more fully "the Book of the Law" (Josh. 8:34); "the Book of the Law of Moses" (Josh. 8:31); "the Book of the Law of God" (Josh. 24:26); "the Law of Moses" (I Kings 2:3) and "the Book of the Law of the Lord" (II Chron. 17:9). The N. T. calls it "the Book of the Law" (Gal. 3:10); "the Law of the Lord" (Luke 2:23); "the Law of Moses" (Luke 2:22); or simply "the Law" (Matt. 5:17; Luke 10:26).

3. **Importance.** (1) **Religious Importance.** The Pentateuch is the foundation of all subsequent divine revelation. Both Christianity and Judaism rest on the inspired revelation of the Pentateuchal books. The Pentateuch describes the beginning of the cosmic universe, of man, of human sin, of human civilization, of the nations, of God's redemptive program in type (Gen. 3:21) and prophecy (Gen. 3:15). The three primary names of Deity—Jehovah, Elohim and Adonai—and five of the most important compound names occur in the opening book of the Pentateuch. This volume initiates the program of progressive self-revelation of God culminating in Christ. Christ is the central theme of the Pentateuch. This portion is honey-combed with the miraculous and with typical, symbolic and prophetic elements dealing with the Person and work of the coming Divine Redeemer (cf. I Cor. 10:11).

(2) **Historical Importance.** Most intimately is the Pentateuch bound up with history and archaeology. The Pentateuch is not history in the strict sense of the term, however, but a highly specialized history of redemption, or almost a philosophy of the history of redemption. It has an all-pervading purpose to include only such historical background as is essential for introducing and preparing the stage for the Redeemer. In other words, the Pentateuch is history but more than history; it is history wedded to prophecy, a Messiah-centered history combining with a Messiah-centered prophecy. To consummate the redemptive plan it initiates it has been called the philosophy of Israel's history (cf. Herbert C. Alleman, *O. T. Commentary*, Philadelphia, 1948, p. 171). In such a character, the Pentateuch catalogs the events concerning the origin of the Israelite people and their constitution as a theocratic nation. It interprets the old in the light of the nation's relationship to Jehovah and his redemptive purpose for the world. Archaeology has shed abundant light on the Pentateuch. Babylonian cuneiform tablets illustrate the creation and particularly the Flood, yielding amazing parallels of detail. The longevity of the patriarchs is illustrated by the Sumerian king list. The Table of the Nations (Gen. 10) is proved by archaeological discoveries to be an amazing document. The patriarchal age is set in the frame work of authentic history and the Egyptian sojourn, the Exodus and the Conquest are now much better understood as the result of the triumphs of scientific archaeology since 1800.

(3) **Cosmic Importance.** The Pentateuchal account of the Creation of the world and man stands unique in all ancient literature. All non-Biblical creation legends by their polytheistic crudity stand in striking contrast to Gen. 1:1 through 2:3. The unifying principle of the universe in one omnipresent and omniscient God is revealed in the majestic Genesis account through inspiration. Ancient Mesopotamian writers blindly groped after this principle. The Pentateuch is all the more striking against the background of a world grossly ignorant of the first principles of causation. The discovery of secondary causes and the explanation of the *how* of creation in its ongoing operation is the achievement of science. Revelation alone can sense the *why* of creation. The Bible alone discloses that the universe exists because God made it and has a definite redemptive purpose in it. Regarding its account of Creation as outlined in Gen. 1, the "sequence of created phases" which it stipulates is "so rational that modern science cannot improve on it, given the same language and the same range of ideas in which to state its conclusions. In fact, "modern scientific cosmogonies show such a disconcerting tendency to be short-lived that it may be seriously doubted if science has yet caught up with the Biblical story" (W. F. Albright, *O. T. Commentary*, Philadelphia, 1948, p. 135). In its account of the Flood the Pentateuch is also incomparably superior to the crudities and inconsistencies of the polytheistic account preserved in the eleventh book of the Assyrio-Babylonian classic, *The Epic of Gilgamesh.* M. F. U.

Pentecost (pĕn'tē-kŏst). *See* Festivals, II, 2. As to the leading events of *the* Pentecost, viz., that which followed the death of our Lord, *see* Tongues, Gift of.

Penu'el (pĕ-nū'ĕl; *face of God*).

1. The name of the place at which Jacob wrestled with God (Gen. 33:24-32; "Peniel," v. 30). The exact site is not known. It is placed not far from Succoth, east of the Jordan, and north of the Jabbok. The people of Penuel seem to have treated Gideon churlishly when he pursued the Midianites across the Jordan, for which he threatened to destroy their tower (probably castle, Judg. 8:8, 17), which was rebuilt by Jeroboam (I Kings 12:25).

2. A son of Hur, and grandson of Judah, and father (i. e., founder) of Gedor (I Chron. 4:4).

3. The last named of the eleven sons of Shashak, a chief man resident in Jerusalem (I Chron. 8:25).

Pe'or (pē'ôr; *opening, cleft*).

1. A mountain in Moab, to the top of which Balak led the prophet *Balaam* (q. v.), that he might see and curse the host of Israel (Num. 23:28), where it is written, "Peor, that looketh toward Jeshimon," i. e., "the wilderness on either side of the Dead Sea." Mount Peor was one peak of the northern part of the mountains of Abarim by the town of Beth-peor, and opposite to which Israel encamped

in the steppes of Moab (Deut. 3:29; 4:46, A. V. "Beth-peor").

2. In four passages (Num. 25:18, twice; 31:16; Josh. 22:17) Peor occurs as a contraction for Baal-peor.

3. The "Peor" referred to in Num. 25:18; 31:16 is the god Baal-peor. *See* Gods, False.

Per′azim, Mount (pĕr′ȧ-zĭm; *mount of breaches*), mentioned only in Isa. 28:21, unless it is identical with *Baal-perazim* (*q. v.*). Here David gained a victory over the Philistines (II Sam. 5:20). It is referred to by Isaiah, in warning the Israelites, as a remarkable instance of God's wrath.

Perdition (Gr. *'apōleia*). This word occurs only in the New Testament, and in that rarely. In the Greek it means a *perishing, destruction*, as "let thy money perish with thee" (Acts 8:20); with the included idea of misery (I Tim. 6:9). In particular it is *the destruction which consists in the loss of eternal life*, the lot of those excluded from the kingdom of God (John 17:12; II Thess. 2:3; Heb. 10:39; II Pet. 3:7; Rev. 17:8, 11). *See* Hell, Punishment.

Perdition, Son of (Gr. *huios tēs 'apoleia*). The Jews frequently expressed a man's destiny by calling him "the son" of the same; thus we read of the "children of disobedience, of the resurrection," etc.

1. Our Lord calls Judas Iscariot "the son of perdition," and refers to his end as the fulfillment of Scripture (John 17:12). The best commentary on this statement is made by St. Peter (Acts 1:20).

2. In II Thess. 2:3, "the man of sin" is also called the "son of perdition." *See* Sin, Man of.

Pe′res (pē′rĕs; Aram. *pᵉras*, to *split* up), one of the three words of the writing on the wall, and interpreted by Daniel (5:28), being the singular of the word rendered "Upharsin" (v. 26). The meaning of the verb is to *divide into pieces*, to *dissolve* the kingdom.

Pe′resh (pē′rĕsh; *distinction, separation, excrement*), a son of Machir, the Manassite, by his wife Maachah (I Chron. 7:16), B. C. about 1440.

Pe′rez (pē′rĕz; I Chron. 27:3; Neh. 11:4). *See* Pharez.

Pe′rez-uz′zah, or **Pe′rez Uzza** (*pē′rĕz-ŭz′a; the breach of Uzzah*), a place called also Nachon (II Sam. 6:6), and Chidon (I Chron. 13:9), the place where *Uzzah* (*q. v.*) died, as a result of touching the ark of God (II Sam. 6:6-8). About a mile and a half or two miles from the site of Kirjath-jearim, on the road to Jerusalem, is a small village still called *Khirbet el-Uz*, or "the ruins of Uzzah." This seems to be Perez-uzzah.

Perfection, Perfect, the rendering of several Hebrew and Greek words. The fundamental idea is that of completeness. Absolute perfection is an attribute of God alone. In the highest sense he alone is complete, or wanting nothing. His perfection is eternal, and admits of no possibility of defect. It is the ground and standard of all other perfection (*see* Job. 36:4; 37:16; Matt. 5:48). A relative perfection is also ascribed to God's works. It is also either ascribed to men or required of them. By this is meant complete conformity to those requirements as to character and conduct which

God has appointed. But this, it is constantly to be borne in mind, has reference to the gracious government of God which takes account of man's present debilitated condition (*see* Gen. 6:9; 17:1; Job 1:1, 8; 2:3; Matt. 5:48; Phil. 3:15; James 3:2; I Pet. 5:10, et al.). The term perfection as applied to man's present moral life has been a subject of much contention. The propriety of using the word as in any sense of actual description has even been denied. But fidelity to the Scriptures requires us to believe that, in some important sense, Christians may be perfect even in this life, though they still must wait for perfection in a larger sense in the life which is to come. This important sense in which the Bible presents man's present perfection relates to the believer's *position* in union with Christ by the Spirit's baptizing work (Rom. 6:3, 4; Gal. 3:27; Col. 2:10-12; I Cor. 12:13). Being placed "in Christ" the Christian acquires a perfect position, because the Father sees him in the Son's perfection. As far as his actual experience is concerned, however, the Christian realizes his *perfect position* only in proportion as he believes in ("reckons" upon) what he is "in Christ." He is what he is "in Christ" ("perfect" i. e., "complete," Col. 2, 9, 10), whether he reckons on it or not. The difference is that his *position of perfection* becomes *experiential* as he believes himself to be what he *is* "in Christ." (Rom. 6:11). For fuller discussion of this we refer to articles in this work. *See* Sanctification, Sin. *See* also Hodge, *Sys. Theol.*, vol. iii; Pope, *Comp. Christ. Theol.*, iii, 56, sq.; Wesley, *Plain Account of Christian Perfection;* Peck, *Christian Perfection;* Mahan, *Christian Perfection;* Fletcher, *Christian Perfection;* Foster, *Christian Purity.*— E. McC., revised by *M. F. U.*

Perfume. Such passages as the following: "Ointment and perfume rejoice the heart" (Prov. 27:9); "All thy garments smell of myrrh," etc. (Psa. 45:8); "Who is this that cometh out of the wilderness like pillars of smoke, perfumed with myrrh?" etc. (Cant. 3:6); "And thou wentest to the king with ointment, and didst increase thy perfumes" (Isa. 57:9), and others, give abundant and striking evidence of the use and love of perfume in the East. In hot climates the use of perfumes is a sanitary necessity. They not only mask bad smells, but correct them, and are wonderfully reviving to the spirits from the depression which they fall into in crowded places. There can be but little doubt, from what may be observed in the East, that the use of sweet odors in religious rites generally has originated in sanitary precautions. Being but little acquainted with soap, their chief substitutes for it were ointments and other preparations of gums, woods, etc. The Hebrews manufactured their perfumes chiefly from spices imported from Arabia, among which the following are mentioned in Scripture: *Algum* (II Chron. 2:8; 9:10, 11), or *almug* (I Kings 10:11, 12); *balm* (Gen. 37:25; 43:11; Jer. 8:22; 46:11, etc.); *bdellium* (Gen. 2:12; Num. 11:7); *frankincense* (Exod. 30: 34-36; Lev. 2:1, 2, 15; 24:7, etc.); *galbanum* (Exod. 30:34); *myrrh* (Exod. 30:23; Psa. 45:8; Prov. 7:17; Cant. 1:13; Matt. 2:11; John

19:39, etc.); *onycha* (Exod. 30:34); *saffron* (Cant. 4:14); *spikenard* (Cant. 1:12; 4:13, 14); *nardos* (Mark 14:3; John 12:3); and *stacte* (Exod. 30:34). These perfumes were generally in the form of ointments (*q. v.*), incense (*q. v.*), or extracted by some process of boiling, and then mixed with oil. Perfumes entered largely into the temple service, in the two forms of incense and ointment (Exod. 30:22-38). Nor were they less used in private life; not only were they applied to the person, but to garments (Psa. 45:8; Cant. 4:11), and to articles of furniture, such as beds (Prov. 7:17). On the arrival of a guest the same compliments were probably paid in ancient as in modern times (Dan. 2:46). When a royal personage went abroad in his litter attendants threw up "pillars of smoke" about his path (Cant. 3:6). The use of perfumes was omitted in times of mourning, whence the allusion in Isa. 3:24.

Per'ga (pûr'gȧ), the capital of Pamphylia, located on the river Cestrus, about seven miles from its mouth, was visited by Paul when on his first missionary journey (Acts 13:13, 14). The site is now called by the Turks *Eski-Kalesi*. It was celebrated for the worship of Artemis (Diana), whose temple stood on a hill outside the town. *See* Diana and Gods, False.

351. The Altar to Unknown Gods at Pergamos

Per'gamos (pûr'gȧ-mŏs), R. V. and R. S. V. **Per'gamum** (pûr'gȧ-mŭm), a city of Mysia in Asia Minor, about three miles N. of the river *Bakyrtchai* (the ancient Caicus), and about twenty miles from the sea. It had a vast library of two hundred thousand volumes, which was removed by Anthony to Egypt and presented to Cleopatra. In this town was first discovered the art of making parchment, which was called "pergamena" or parchment. The city was greatly addicted to idol-

atry, and its grove, which was one of the wonders of the place, was filled with statues and altars. Antipas met martyrdom here (Rev. 2:13), and here was one of the seven churches of Asia (ver. 12:17). The sumptuousness of the Attalic princes had raised Pergamos to the rank of the first city in Asia as regards splendor. It was a sort of union of a pagan cathedral city, a university town, and a royal residence, embellished during a succession of years by kings who all had a passion for expenditure and ample means of gratifying it. Under the Attalic kings Pergamos became a city of temples, devoted to a sensuous worship; and being in its origin, according to pagan notions, a sacred place, might not unnaturally be viewed by Jews and Jewish Christians as one "where was the throne of Satan" (v. 13). **Peri'da** (pē-rī'dȧ; Neh. 7:57). *See* Peruda.

Per'izzites (pĕr'ĭ-zīts; Hebrew always *hăpp*ᵉ*rizzî*), "the Perizzite," one of the nations whose land was given to Israel. They are not named in Gen., ch. 10, and their origin is not known. They first appear (Gen. 13:7) as dwelling in the land together with the Canaanites in Abram's day (34:30). In Judg. 1:4, 5 they dwell in the land given to Judah, in South Palestine, Bezek being apparently the stronghold of the Canaanites and Perizzites, though it may have been merely a rallying point. In Judg. 17:15-18 the Perizzites and *Rephaim* (*q. v.*) dwell in the "wood country" near Mount Ephraim, in the land of Ephraim and West Manasseh. They appear as late as the time of Solomon, who made them with other Canaanitish tribes tributary to Israel (I Kings 9:20; II Chron. 8:7). A late echo is in II Esd. 1:21, where "the Canaanites, the Perezites, and the Philistines" are named as the original inhabitants of the land. The "unwalled towns" (*'ärē hăpp*ᵉ*räzî*, Deut. 3:5) and the "country villages" (*kōphĕr hăpp*ᵉ*räzî*, I Sam. 6:18) are translated by the LXX as referring to the Perizzites, whence it has been suggested that Perizzite may mean "a dweller in an unwalled village," as does *pärūz* in the Mishna. We may compare the Arabic word meaning *low ground between hills* (where the unwalled villages would grow up). The LXX probably read *hăpp*ᵉ*rizî*.—W. H., revised by *M. F. U.*

Perjury. *See* Oath, 5.

Persecution (Gr. *diōgmos*, a *pursuing*), the active opposition with which Christians are beset by their enemies. Such a persecution is mentioned as arising on the day of Stephen's murder (Acts 8:1). This arose, doubtless, from the fact that Stephen, who was a Greek, had not only preached Jesus, but had declared that the city and temple would be destroyed, and the Gospel preached to all nations. The Pharisees, hitherto neutral, now made common cause with their rivals, the Sadducees, against the Christians; the prudent cautions of Gamaliel were ignored; the civil rulers did not interfere, the wild fury of fanatical bigotry rushed upon the witnesses of the truth and scattered them. There were ten persecutions waged by pagan authorities against the Christians: 1. Under Nero, A. D. 64; 2. Under Domitian, A. D. 95; 3. Under Trajan, A. D. 100; 4. Under Antoninus the philosopher in Gaul, 161-180; 5. Under Severus, A. D. 197; 6. Under Maximinus, A. D. 235; 7. Of great fierceness under Decius, A. D. 249; 8. Under Valerian, A. D. 257; 9. Under Aurelian, A. D. 274; and under Diocletian, A. D. 303.

Perseverance, a term used both in ethics and theology. In ethics it denotes the duty and privilege of a Christian to continue steadfastly in obedience and fidelity to Christ, this not in order to inherit eternal life, but to demonstrate love and gratitude to Christ for His great salvation (I Cor. 15:58; I Pet. 1:10; Rev. 3:2). Arminian views stipulate this faithfulness to inherit eternal life, but Calvinists hold that the N. T. teachings testify to the safety and security of the believer as a result of his faith in Christ and his resulting position in Christ (Rom. 8:28-39; Eph. 1:1-13; Eph. 2:8-10, etc.). The Christian's fidelity and obedience will be rewarded at the Judgment Seat of Christ. His salvation is not affected by lack of human faithfulness, but his rewards are. Calvinists teach that final perseverance is a result of the doctrine of unconditional election. Thus the Westminster Confession says, "This perseverance of the saints depends not upon their own free will but upon the immutability of the decree of election flowing from the free and unchangeable love of God the Father . . .". In other words, those who are real Christians cannot fall away or be eternally lost. Their position in Christ by the baptizing work of the Holy Spirit assures their eternal salvation. When men begin to interject human faithfulness and human works into the question of their eternal salvation, they take it off the Rock of Christ's finished work and place it upon a flimsy basis. If getting to heaven depended upon human merit or faithfulness in any degree, no human-being would ever get there or claim merit for entrance.

Christ will abundantly reward faithfulness in His redeemed children, but He can never accept their faithfulness as merit for salvation. Failure to distinguish between salvation and rewards has confused this subject in theological thinking and this is accordingly, a much disputed doctrine. *M. F. U.*

Persia, a world empire which flourished from 539-331 B. C.

1. **The Early History.** The original native name Parsa, or Persia, was descriptive of the homeland of the Persians in the western and larger part of the Iranian plateau which extended from the Indus on the E. to the Tigris on the W. Iran was another native designation of the land. This name was officially restored in 1935 by the Persian government and means "the (land) of the Aryans." It is descriptive of the people of Aryan language who came into the highland (c. 1500 B. C.). The Amadai or Medes and the inhabitants of the land of Parsua W. of Lake Urmia, or Persians, were the two Aryan tribes which were to come into the greatest prominence. The Medes occupied the N. W. portion of the territory. Their capital city was Hagmatana, later Ecbatana, modern Hamadan. Cyaxares, the Mede, was confederate with Nabopolassar in the fall of Nineveh in 612 B. C. Gradually the Persians migrated southward and settled in Anshan in a portion of country which they called Parsamash, in recollection of their old homeland of Parsua. Around 700 B. C. their leader was named Achaemenes. This name prevailed in the later Persian kings. About the middle of the seventh century B. C. the king of Parsamash was called Tiespes. He was a notable conqueror and increased the territories of the Persians E. of Anshan and N. of the Persian Gulf. This extended country became known as Parsa or Persian Land.

2. **Cyrus II**, **The Great.** The founder of the

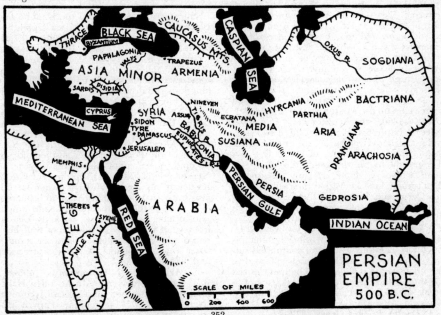

PERSIAN EMPIRE 500 B.C.

352.

mighty Persian empire ascended the throne of Anshan c. 559 B. C. Astyages, the Mede, was conquered by Cyrus who took Ecbatana. Henceforth Cyrus grew greater and greater with Parsa taking the lead, Media coming second and Elam third. The supremacy of the Persians was hereafter established, although the Medes continued to be held in high esteem. Reference is made in Scripture

This powerful ruler put down the rebellion, saved the empire and recorded his victory over his enemies on the famous Rock of Behistun visible from the old caravan road from Ecbatana to Babylon. This pivotal monument, with its trilingual inscriptions describing Darius' quelling of the insurrection, furnished the key to the decipherment of Akkadian cuneiform, as the Rosetta Stone opened

353. Tombs of Persian Kings, Naksk-i-Rustam

to "the Persians and the Medes" (Esth. 1:19), as well as "the Medes and the Persians" (Dan. 5:28). With lightning-like rapidity Cyrus extended his conquests, defeating Croesus of Lydia (c. 546 B. C.) and Babylon (539 B. C.), thus establishing the mighty Persian empire. Cyrus was a remarkably humane leader (cf. Isa. 45:1-4). It was he who issued the decree restoring the Jews to their homeland (II Chron. 36:22, 23; Ezra 1:2, 3). Archaeology has demonstrated that Cyrus' concession to the exiles was not an isolated account of generosity but a general policy of a remarkably beneficent leader of winning the favor of his new subjects by showing consideration to their religious beliefs. Cyrus' capital was Pasargadae in the Land of Parsa. On his ruined palace can still be read the repeated words, "I, Cyrus the king, the Achaemenid." Cyrus was killed in battle 530 B. C. Returned to Pasargadae, his body was buried in a tomb which is still extant. Plutarch (c. 46-120 A. D.), says the inscription on the tomb ran thus: "O man, whosoever thou art and whensoever thou comest, for I know that thou wilt come, I am Cyrus and I won for the Persians their empire. Do not, therefore, begrudge me this little earth which covers my body."

3. **Cambyses II** (530-522 B. C.) was Cyrus' son, who conquered Egypt. Shortly after his Egyptian triumphs Cambyses committed suicide. The Persian empire almost collapsed in the civil war that followed. Gaumata seized the throne and there was a general attempt to break away from Persian rule in Babylon, Armenia, Media and elsewhere.

4. **Darius I, The Great** (522-486 B. C.).

up the ancient language of the Nile River. Darius ruled a vast empire. The closing years of his reign saw the outbreak of the Graeco-Persian wars and the defeat of Persia at Marathon (491 B. C.), a precursor to the later defeat at Salamis (480 B. C.). The mighty empire over which Darius and his successors ruled extended from the Grecian Archipelago on the W. and the Danube and Black Sea, the Caucasus and the Caspian Sea on the N. to the Arabian and Nubian deserts on the S. (Esth. 1:1 and 10:1). This vast territory was nearly 3,000 miles long and 500-1,500 miles wide, comprising an area of some two million square miles. In this huge kingdom Judah was a tiny dependency practically lost in the vast stretch of empire.

5. **Xerxes** (486-465 B. C.) followed his father Darius on the Persian throne. This king, as well as his father, was devoted to Ahura-Mazda. Xerxes is evidently the Ahasuerus of the Book of Esther. Esther did not become queen until the seventh year of Xerxes' reign (478 B. C.) after his return from his defeat in Greece (480 B. C.) when Herodotus states that he paid attention to his harem (IX, 108). Although the queen at this time is said to have been Amestris, certainly Xerxes, from what we know of him, may well have had other wives, if Solomon, who was a much lesser monarch had "700 wives, princesses and 300 concubines . . .".

6. **Artaxerxes I Longimanus** (465-423 B. C.) succeeded Xerxes. In his reign Nehemiah was cup-bearer and visited Jerusalem (Neh. 2:1). The Elephantine Papyri, discovered in 1903 on the island of Elephantine

at the First Cataract of Egypt, shed important light on the Artaxerxes-Nehemiah era. Ezra 7:1-8 specifies that Ezra journeyed to Jerusalem in Artaxerxes' seventh year. This was 458 B. C., if Artaxerxes I is meant. In such a case Ezra precedes Nehemiah. However, some construe Artaxerxes to be Artaxerxes II, the seventh year of whose reign would be 398 B. C. (cf. Ezra 10:6).

7. **Later Kings.** Following Artaxerxes I the splendid Persian throne was occupied by Darius II (423-404 B. C.), Artaxerxes II Mnemon (404-359 B. C.), Artaxerxes III Ochus (359-338 B. C.), Arses (338-335 B. C.) and Darius III (335-331 B. C.), when the far-flung Persian empire fell to the conquests of Alexander the Great.

8. **Persia and Archaeology.** The great capital of the Persian empire was Persepolis, about 25 miles W. of Pasargadae, Cyrus' capital. Darius I transferred the main capital hither from Pasargadae, and it remained from that time forward the chief home of the Achaemenian dynasty. Excavations by the Oriental Institute of the University of Chicago under the direction of Ernst Herzfeld, 1931-1934, and Eric F. Schmidt in 1935-1939 have uncovered the splendors of this ancient Persian capital. The palace of Darius, known as the Tachara, the Tripylon, the Apadana, the Hall of the 100 Columns, the Gate of Xerxes, the harem of Darius and Xerxes, Xerxes' palace, known as Hadish, and the royal treasury tell of the long-buried splendor of the ancient Persian monarchs. Both Ecbatana and Susa were important cities in the Persian empire. Little remains today of the splendor of Ecbatana, but an inscription has been recovered in which Artaxerxes II Mnemon (404-359 B. C.) celebrated the building of a palace. This famous capital of Persia, a very early center of culture, appears as Shushan in the O. T. narratives (Neh. 1:1; Dan. 8:2; Esth. 1:2). Today it is called Shush. Persian Susa has yielded a magnificent royal palace commenced by Darius I and enlarged and embellished by later kings. Beautifully colored glazed bricks constituted the most notable part of the decoration of this palace. Winged bulls and griffins and the famous spearmen of the guard were executed in relief. The Persian empire was one of the largest and greatest kingdoms of antiquity, and it is intimately associated with the closing years of the captivity, the restoration and the period of the closing of the O. T. canon. *M. F. U.*

Per'sis (pûr'sĭs; Gr. *Persian*), a Christian woman at Rome to whom Paul sent salutations (Rom. 16:12).

Personality, in theology as in metaphysics, that which constitutes a person. Says Locke: "A person is a thinking, intelligent being that has reason and reflection, and can consider itself as itself, the same thinking thing in different times and places." In other words, the distinguishing marks of personality are self-consciousness and freedom.

1. According to the Scriptures, God is a person. He is not merely an eternal substance, but the one eternal free and self-conscious being. He says "I" and teaches men to say "thou." The Bible doctrine of God is there-fore not only opposed to atheism, which denies his existence, but also to pantheism, which merges his existence in that of the universe. It is objected, as by Mansel, e. g., that personality implies limitation, and therefore implies a contradiction in our thought of God, thus illustrating the limits of religious thought. This objection is ably answered by Hodge (*System. Theol.*, vol. i, chaps. 4, 5), where he shows that this objection is founded upon an arbitrary definition of the Absolute and Infinite. Also Mansel himself, a Christian theist, says upon this subject: "It is our duty to think of God as personal, and it is our duty to believe that he is infinite." Further, Hodge suggests, with respect to the objection that "Without a thou there can be no I," that according to the Scriptures and the faith of the Church, there are in the unity of the Godhead three distinct persons—the Father, the Son, and the Holy Spirit, "so that from eternity the Father can say I and the Son thou." The personality of God as a fact apprehended by our faith is essential to religion. "We do not worship a law, however simple and fruitful it may be; we do not worship a force if it is blind, however powerful, however universal it may be; nor an ideal, however pure, if it be an abstraction. We worship only a Being who is living perfection, perfection under the highest form—Thought, Love." *See* Trinity, Freedom.

2. Man is also a person. In this respect he is distinct from things and from animals. This is one of the features of his likeness to his Creator. Here is the basis of his moral obligation. *See* Image of God, Freedom.—E. McC.; revised by *M. F. U.*

Peru'da (pê-rōō'dä; *divided, separated;* in Neh. 7:57 the name is written *Pĕrîdä*), the name of one of "Solomon's servants," whose descendants returned with Zerubbabel from Babylon (Ezra 2:55), B. C. before 536.

Pestilence (Heb. *dĕbĕr;* Gr. *loimos*). The Hebrew term seems to have originally meant *destruction*, but is regularly applied to that common oriental epidemic, the *plague (q. v.)*. The prophets usually connect sword, pestilence, and famine (II Sam. 24:15).

Pestle (Heb. *'ĕlî, lifted*), the instrument used for triturating in a mortar (Prov. 27:22), probably used to separate the grain from the husk.

Pe'ter (pē'tēr). 1. **Name and Family.** (Gr. *Petros, a rock.*) Formerly Simon. Peter was the son of Jonas (John 1:42; 21:15, 16), and probably a native of Bethsaida in Galilee (John 1:44).

2. **Personal History.** (1) **Occupation.** Peter and his brother Andrew were fishermen on the Sea of Tiberias (Matt. 4:18; Mark 1:16), and partners of James and John (Luke 5:10). Although his occupation was a humble one, yet it was not incompatible with some degree of mental culture, and seems to have been quite remunerative. (2) **Meets Jesus.** With his brother Andrew, Peter was a disciple of John the Baptist; and when their teacher pointed out Jesus to Andrew as the Lamb of God, Andrew went to Peter and told him, "We have found the Messias." He brought him to Jesus, who looked upon him and said, "Thou art *Simon, the son of Jonas;* thou shalt be

called *Cephas*" (John 1:36-42). This interview resulted in no immediate change in Peter's external position. He returned to Capernaum and continued his usual vocation, waiting further instruction. (3) **Call.** This was received on the Sea of Galilee, where the four partners were engaged in fishing. The people were pressing upon Jesus to hear the word, and entering into Peter's boat, which at Christ's request was thrust out a little from the land, he discoursed to the multitude. After this he wrought the miracle of the great draught of fishes, foreshadowing the success of the apostles as fishers of men. Peter and Andrew immediately accepted the call, and, leaving all, were soon after joined by James and John, who also received a call to follow the Master (Matt. 4:18-22; Mark 1:16-20; Luke 5:1-11), A. D. 27. Immediately after this Jesus wrought the miracle of healing on Peter's wife's mother (Matt. 8:14, 15; Mark 1:29-31; Luke 4:38-40), and Peter for some time attended upon our Lord's ministry in Galilee, Decapolis, Petraea, and Judea, returning at intervals to his own city. During this period he was selected as one of the witnesses of the raising of Jairus's daughter (Mark 5:22, 37; Luke 8:41, 51). (4) **Apostle.** The special designation of Peter and his eleven fellow-disciples took place some time afterward, when they were set apart as our Lord's immediate attendants (Matt. 10:2-4; Mark 3:13-19; Luke 6:13). They appear then first to have received formally the name of apostles, and from that time Simon bore publicly, and as it would seem almost exclusively, the name Peter, which had hitherto been used rather as a characteristic appellation than as a proper name. (5) **Walks on the sea.** On one occasion the vessel, in which were a number of the disciples, was in the midst of the sea, tossed with waves. Jesus appeared, walking on the sea, much to the alarm of the disciples, who said, "It is a spirit." Hearing his words of encouragement, Peter put the Master to the test by saying, "Lord, if it be thou, bid me come unto thee on the water." Jesus replied, "Come," and Peter, obeying, walked for a while on the surface of the sea, but losing his confidence because of the tempest, began to sink, and uttered the cry, "Lord, save me." The Master took him by the hand, and accompanied him to the ship. When safe in the vessel Peter fell down at his feet, and declared, "Of a truth thou art the Son of God" (Matt. 14:25-33). (6) We find him asking the meaning of our Lord's parable of the blind leading the blind (15:15). (7) **Confession.** In a conversation with his disciples as to men's declarations concerning himself, Jesus asks, "But whom say ye that I am?" Peter promptly replied, "Thou art the Christ, the Son of the Living God." In his reply the Master made the declaration, so often commented upon, "Thou art Peter, and upon this rock I will build my church," etc. (Matt. 16:13-19; Mark 8:27-29; Luke 9:18-20). (8) **Rebukes Jesus.** Our Lord on one occasion began to inform his disciples of his coming sufferings and death, when "Peter took him and began to rebuke him, saying, Be it far from thee, Lord." But Jesus turned and said unto Peter,

"Get thee behind me, Satan," etc. (Matt. 16:21-23; Mark 8:31-33). Our Lord seems to call Peter Satan. Not quite so. But he recognizes Satan speaking in the words that Peter utters. (9) **Mount of Transfiguration.** Peter, with James and John, was a witness of our Lord's transfiguration, and in the ecstasy of the hour exclaimed, "Lord, it is good for us to be here: If thou wilt, let us make here three tabernacles; one for thee, and one for Moses, and one for Elias" (Matt. 17:1, sq.; Mark 9:2, sq.; Luke 9:28, sq.). (10) Mention is made of Peter's inquiry as to forgiveness (Matt. 18:21); declaration of having left all for Jesus' sake (Matt. 19:27; Mark 10:28; Luke 18:28); asking the meaning of the parable of the overturning of the temple (Mark 13:3) and of the servant watching for his lord (Luke 12:41); and calling the Master's attention to the withered fig tree (Mark 11:21). (11) **The last supper.** When Jesus would keep the Passover he commissioned Peter and John to make proper preparation (Luke 22:8). All being ready for the supper, Jesus began to wash the disciples' feet; but when he came to Peter, he, in his presumptuous humility, declared, "Thou shalt never wash my feet," but upon the Master replying, "If I wash thee not, thou hast no part with me," Peter consented, with the request that the washing might include both hands and head (John 13:2, sq.). When our Lord declared that one of them would betray him, Peter beckoned to John that he should ask of whom he spake (13:24). Still later he stoutly asserted that under no circumstances would he ever leave his Master, to which Jesus replied by saying, "Simon, Simon, behold Satan hath desired you, that he may sift you as wheat," and told him of his speedy denial (Matt. 26:33; Mark 14:29; Luke 22:31; John 13:36). (12) **At Gethsemane.** Peter and the two sons of Zebedee accompanied Jesus to Gethsemane (Matt. 26:37, sq.; Mark 14:32), and when Judas came, with his company, to apprehend the Lord, Peter drew his sword and cut off the right ear of Malchus, a servant of the high priest, for which he was promptly rebuked (Matt. 26:51; John 18:10). (13) **Denial.** When Jesus was apprehended Peter followed him at a distance to the palace of Caiaphas, "and went in (John speaking to the portress in his behalf), and sat with the servants to see the end." While in the court "a damsel (portress) came unto him, saying, Thou also wast with Jesus of Galilee." Peter "denied before them all, saying, I know not what thou sayest" (Mark. 26:58, 69, 70; Mark 14:66-68; Luke 22:55-57; John 18:15-17). Peter's *second* denial occurred in the porch, to which he had withdrawn. Another maid declared to those who were standing about, "This fellow was also with Jesus of Nazareth." Peter, with an oath, denied even an acquaintance with Jesus (Matt. 26:71, 72; Mark 14:69, 70; Luke 22:58, where the accuser was a man; John 18:25). His *third* denial was uttered after a while, Luke says *an hour*, and was in reply to some who charged him with being one of the disciples of Jesus, saying, "Thy speech betrayeth thee," Peter probably having made some remark in his Galilean dialect. He cursed and swore, and declared, "I know not the man." The crowing of the cock and the look of our Lord awakened Peter to a sense of his guilt, and he "went out and wept bitterly" (Matt. 26:73-75; Mark 14:70-72; Luke 22:59-62; John 18:26, 27). (14) **At the sepulcher.** On the morning of the resurrection the women, finding the stone removed from the door of the sepulcher, hastened to tell the disciples. Mary Magdalene outstripped the rest, and told Peter and John, who immediately ran toward the spot. John outran Peter, but did not enter the sepulcher. Peter, when he came up, went in and saw the linen clothes and the napkin laid carefully away, showing that there had been no violence or pillage. John now entered and believed that his Lord had risen, but Peter departed "wondering in himself at that which had come to pass" (Luke 24:10-12; John 20:1-8). (15) **Restoration.** "We are told by Luke (24:34) and by Paul that Christ appeared to him first among the apostles. It is observable, however, that on that occasion he is called by his original name, Simon, not Peter; the higher designation was not restored until he had been publicly reinstituted, so to speak, by his Master. That reinstitution took place at the Sea of Galilee (John, ch. 21), an event of the very highest import. Slower than John to recognize their Lord, Peter was the first to reach him: he brought the net to land. The thrice repeated question of Christ, referring doubtless to the three protestations and denials, was thrice met by answers full of love and faith. He then received the formal commission to feed Christ's sheep, rather as one who had forfeited his place, and could not resume it without such an authorization. Then followed the prediction of his martyrdom, in which he was to find the fulfillment of his request to be permitted to follow the Lord. With this event closes the first part of Peter's history" (Smith, *Bib. Dict.*, s. v.).

3. **History after Our Lord's Ascension.** After this Peter stands forth as the recognized leader of the apostles, although it is clear that he does not exercise or claim any authority apart from them, much less over them. It is he who points out to the disciples the necessity of filling the place of Judas and the qualifications of an apostle (Acts 1:15, sq.). (1) **Pentecost.** On the day of Pentecost Peter, as the spokesman of the apostles, preached that remarkable sermon which resulted in the conversion of about three thousand souls (2:14, sq.). (2) **First miracle.** Peter and John went up to the temple to pray, and as they were about to enter, a lame man, who was lying at the entrance of the gate called Beautiful, accosted them, asking alms. Peter said to him, "Look on us. . . . Silver and gold have I none; but such as I have I give thee: in the name of Jesus Christ of Nazareth rise up and walk." When the people ran together to Solomon's porch, Peter preached Jesus to them. For this the apostles were imprisoned, and the next day were brought before the Sanhedrin to answer the question "by what power or by what name they had done this?" Peter replied with boldness, and they were dismissed (3:1; 4:23). (3) **Ananias and Sapphira.** In this

miracle of judgment Peter acted simply as an instrument, not pronouncing the sentence, but denouncing the sin, and that in the name of his fellow-apostles and of the Holy Spirit (5:1-11). (4) **In prison.** Many miracles of healing being performed by the apostles, they were thrust into prison; "but the angel of the Lord by night opened the prison doors," and commanded them to go to the temple and preach the words of life. They were brought before the high priest and rebuked for their preaching, but Peter declared it to be their purpose "to obey God rather than men," and charged the rulers of the people with being guilty of the murder of Jesus. Angered at his words, they sought to slay the apostle, but were restrained by the wise counsel of Gamaliel (5:14, sq.). (5) **In Samaria.** After Philip had preached a while in Samaria, Peter and John were sent down to confirm the converts; and while there Peter rebuked Simon the sorcerer, and showed him that, though professedly a believer, he was still "in the gall of bitterness, and in the bonds of iniquity" (8:14-24). (6) **Meets Paul,** etc. About three years later (chap. 9:26, and Gal. 1:17, 18) we have two accounts of the first meeting of Peter and Paul. This interview was followed by other events marking Peter's position—a general apostolic tour of visitation to the churches hitherto established (Acts 9:32), in the course of which two great miracles were wrought on Eneas and Tabitha, and in connection with which the most signal transaction after the day of Pentecost is recorded, the *baptism of Cornelius* (10:1-48). His conduct gave great offense to his countrymen (11:2), and it needed all his authority, corroborated by a special manifestation of the Holy Spirit, to induce his fellow-apostles to recognize the propriety of this great act. (7) **Miraculous deliverance.** A few years later (A. D. 44), Herod, having found that the murder of

354. Roman Prisoner Chained to Guards

James pleased the Jews, arrested Peter and put him in prison. He was kept under the care of four quaternions (bands of four soldiers), who relieved one another on the watch. Two were stationed at the gate, while the other two were attached to Peter by chains. Notwithstanding these precautions, an angel delivered the apostle, who reported himself at the house of Mary, the mother of John Mark, where many of the Church were gathered praying for his safety (12:2-17). His miraculous deliverance marks the close of this second great period of his ministry. The special work assigned to him was completed. From that time we have no continuous history of him. It is quite clear that he retained his rank as the chief apostle; equally so, that he neither exercised nor claimed any right to control their proceedings. He left Jerusalem, but it is not said where he went. Certainly not to Rome, where there are no traces of his presence before the latter part of his life. Some years later (A. D. 51) we find him in Jerusalem at the convention of apostles and elders, assembled to consider the question whether converts should be circumcised. Peter took the lead in the discussion, contending that salvation came through grace, which was received through faith; and that all distinctions between believers were thereby removed (15:7, sq.). His argument was enforced by James, and the question was at once and finally settled. A painful collision occurred between Peter and Paul at Antioch. Peter had there eaten with Gentiles; but when certain from Jerusalem, sent by James, came, fearful of offending them (representing as they did the circumcision), he withdrew from all social intercourse with the Gentiles. Paul, apprehensive of disastrous consequences, and believing that Peter was infringing upon a great principle, says that he "withstood Peter to the face, because he was to be blamed" (Gal. 2:11-14). This controversy did not destroy their brotherly communion, which continued to the end of Peter's life (II Pet. 3:15, 16).

Peter was probably employed for the most part in building up and completing the organization of Christian communities in Palestine and the adjoining districts. There is, however, strong reason to believe that he visited Corinth at an early period. The name of Peter as founder, or joint founder, is not associated with any local church save those of Corinth, Antioch, or Rome, by early ecclesiastical tradition. From I Pet. 5:13, 14, it is probable that Peter either visited or resided for some time at Babylon, and that Mark was with him there when he wrote that epistle. It may be considered as a settled point that he did not visit Rome before the last year of his life. The evidence for his martyrdom there is complete, while there is a total absence of any contrary statement in the writings of the early fathers. Clement of Rome, writing before the end of the 1st century, speaks of it, but does not mention the *place*, that being, of course, well known to his readers. Ignatius, in the undoubtedly genuine epistle to the Romans (ch. 4), speaks of Peter in terms which imply a special connection with their church. In the 2d century Dionysius of Corinth, in the epistle to Soter, bishop of Rome (ap. Euseb., *H. E.*, ii, 25), states, as a fact universally known and accounting for the intimate relations between Corinth and Rome, that Peter and Paul both taught in Italy, and suffered martyrdom about the same time. In short, the churches most nearly connected with Rome and those least affected by its influence, which was as yet but inconsiderable in the East, concur in the statement that Peter was a joint founder of that church, and suffered death in that city. The time and manner of the apostle's

martyrdom are less certain. The early writers imply, or distinctly state, that he suffered at or about the same time with Paul, and in the Neronian persecution. All agree that he was crucified. Origen says that at his own request he was crucified with his head downward.

4. **Character.** Among the leading characteristics of Peter were: "Devotion to his Master's person (John 13:37), even leading him into extravagance (13:9), and an energetic disposition, which showed itself sometimes as boldness (Matt. 14:29) and temper (John 18:10). His temperament was choleric, and he easily passed from one extreme to another (13:8, 9)" (McC. and S., *Cyc.*, s. v.). "The contrast between Peter of the gospels—impulsive, unsteadfast, slow of heart to understand the mysteries of the kingdom—and the same apostle as he meets us in the Acts, firm and courageous, ready to go to prison and to death, the preacher of the faith, the interpreter of Scripture, is one of the most convincing proofs of the power of Christ's resurrection and the mighty working of the pentecostal gift" (E. H. Plumptre, *Bible Educator*, vol. iv, p. 129).

NOTE—(1) *Peter's prominence as an apostle.* By consulting Matt. 17:1; Mark 9:22; 14:33, we learn that Peter was among the most beloved of Christ's disciples. Sometimes he speaks in the name of the twelve (Matt. 19:27; Luke 12:41); sometimes he answers when questions are addressed to them all (Matt. 16:16; Mark 8:29); sometimes Jesus addresses him in place of them all (Matt. 26:40). His eminence among the apostles depended partly on the fact that he was chosen among the first, and partly on his own peculiar traits. This position became more decided after the ascension of Jesus, and perhaps in consequence of the saying in John 21:15, sq. The early Church regarded him as the representative of the apostolic body—a very distinct theory from that which makes him their head or governor in Christ's stead. *Primus inter pares*, Peter held no distinct office, and certainly never claimed any powers which did not belong equally to all of his fellow-apostles (McC. and S. *Cyc.*, s. v.). (2) *The rock.* "Thou art Peter, and upon this rock I will build my church," etc. "The expression *this rock* upon which *I will build my church*, has received very different interpretations . . . in various ages. The first is the construction given by the Church of Rome. . . . It affirms that the rock is Peter individually, that the commission constituted him supreme apostle, with authority, inherited from him by the bishops of Rome. But, 1. As may be shown, not Peter alone, but each apostle, was a *rock* and a recipient of the *keys*, and all were coequal in powers. 2. Were the authority conveyed to Peter alone and personally, it must still be shown that this personal prerogative was among the successional attributes conferred upon him. 3. That Peter was ever bishop of Rome is without historical foundation; and the pretense of a succession from him by the Romish bishop is a fable. It is to be clearly noted that Peter was not given the keys of the church but of "the kingdom of heaven" as a sphere of Christian profession (cf. Matt. 13). Since a key signifies power and authority (Isa. 22:22; Rev. 3:7), the Book of Acts gives the infallible commentary on Peter's use of this special prerogative. It was Peter who opened the door of Christian opportunity to Israel at Pentecost (Acts 2:38-40), to the Samaritans (Acts 8:14-17) and to the Gentiles in Cornelius' abode (Acts 10:34-46). After gospel opportunity was introduced to this age to Jew (Acts 2), Samaritan (Acts 8) and Gentile (Acts 10), there was no assumption whatever by Peter of any other authority (Acts 15:7-11). The power of binding and loosing (Matt. 18:18; John 20:23) was shared by the other disciples. It is preposterous to make this refer to human destiny, as Rev. 1:18 explains. Revised by *M. F. U.*

Peter, First Epistle of, one of the general or catholic epistles written by the Apostle Peter.

1. **Purpose and Message.** This is a letter of hope in the midst of suffering and testing.

Peter was writing to the "sojourners of the dispersion in Pontus, Galatia, Cappadocia and Bithynia" (1:1). The keynote of the book is suffering and glory. About seven words for suffering occur in it. The sufferings of Christ are used as an example (1:11; 2:21; 4:1, 2; 5:1). Suffering is to be looked for (4:12); it represents the will of God (4:19); it is to be borne patiently (2:23; 3:9); rejoicingly (4:13); others were suffering (5:9); suffering has value (1:6, 7; 2:19, 20:4:14). The practical note dominates the Epistle rather than the doctrinal.

2. **Occasion and Date.** The Epistle is probably to be dated around 65 A. D. and the Neronian persecutions apparently furnish its background. The provinces of Asia too mistreated the Christians in their borders. The Apostle shows acquaintance with early epistles such as James, I Thessalonians, Romans, Colossians, Ephesians and Philippians. Accordingly it was most probably written after the prison epistles. Many commentators consider the "Babylon" of 5:13 to have reference to the literal Babylon on the Euphrates (*see* Calvin, Alfred, Mayor, Moorehead). The majority of writers, however, make it a symbolic reference to Rome, but Alfred thinks "we are not to find an allegoric meaning in a proper name thus simply used in the midst of simple matter-of-fact sayings" (*Greek Testament* iv, p. 129).

3. **Authorship.** The early church presented almost unanimous agreement on the Petrine authorship. No other book has stronger attestation of authenticity than I Peter. II Peter 3:1 is the earliest acknowledgment of the First Epistle. The book seems to be alluded to in the Epistle of Barnabas and Clement's Epistle to the Corinthians. Polycarp quotes it in the Epistle to the Philippians. Irenaeus is the first to quote it by name. Internal evidence likewise agrees with the external. The writer calls himself Peter (1:1). He was a witness of the sufferings of Christ (5:1). The vocabulary reminds us of the Peter of the gospels and the Acts. There is a similarity between Peter's speeches in the Acts and his words in the Epistle (cf. Acts 10:34 with I Peter 1:17; Acts 2:32-36, Acts 10:40, 41 with I Pet. 1:21; Acts 4:10, 11 with I Pet. 2:7, 8).

4. **Outline.**

Salutation, 1:1, 2.

Part I. Suffering and the Certainty of Future Inheritance, 1:3-12

Part II. Suffering and Personal Life, 1:13-2:10

Part III. Suffering and Social and Domestic Life, 2:11-3:12

Part IV. Faith and Right Conduct and Suffering, 3:13-4:6

Part V. Right Conduct in the Light of the End, 4:7-19

Part VI. Suffering and Right Relationship Between Elders and the Congregation, 5:1-11

Conclusion, 5:12-14

Peter, Second Epistle of, a second general or catholic epistle, written by the Apostle Peter.

1. **Subject Matter.** Peter's Second Epistle may be viewed as a complement to the First Epistle. It deals with the Second Coming of Christ and the evils preceding this great event. The First Epistle also speaks of the Second Coming, but does not deal with the conditions prior to that prophetic event. Stern warning is given of coming apostasy, when monetary considerations would sway church leaders. As a result loose morality and general iniquity would abound. In chapter 1 Peter expounds certain precious promises of God's Word; in chapter 2 he inveighs against false teachers; in chapter 3 he deals with the certainty of the coming of the Lord and the prevailing skepticism of the end time.

2. **Authorship.** The writer of the Epistle strongly affirms himself to be Simon Peter (1:1). The book thus represents itself to be the genuine production of the Apostle Peter, who claims to have been present at the transfiguration of Christ (1:16-18) and to have been warned by our Lord of his impending death (1:14). Despite these clear claims, numerous modern critics consider the work written by a pseudonymous author in the post-Apostolic period. The writer is supposed to have assumed Peter's name a century or so after Peter's death. Supposed differences in style between First and Second Peter are alleged to indicate that the books were by different authors. While there are confessedly some differences in vocabulary, it has been shown by Zahn (*Intr. to the O. T.*, Vol. ii, p. 289f) that there are some striking likenesses. One may also ask whether a forger would run the risk of detection by failing to pay more attention to the style and language of First Peter. Second Peter, however, lacks any proved evidence of forgery. The autobiographical allusions are true to fact. No new material is added. There is nothing romantic or indisputably anachronistic about the Second Epistle. This is in striking contrast to the apocalyptic "Gospel of Peter" and the "Apocalypse of Peter." A claim is also made that the Epistle was penned at a period when the Pauline letters were made use of by heretics to promulgate their teachings (3:15, 16). This reference to Paul's letters, however, does not imply that they had been already collected or even that they had already all been written. The reference may merely refer to such as Peter had come to know. It cannot be shown that Peter deals with a more advanced stage of apostasy than Paul dealt with. Against the charge of spuriousness is the apostolic tone, the Christian earnestness, the genuineness of the autobiographical allusions and the absence of the fantastic. It ought, therefore, to be accepted as a genuine work of the Apostle Peter.

3. **Attestation.** While it is true that Peter's Second Epistle has less historical support of its genuineness than any other N. T. book, it bears points of resemblance to a number of writings during the period from A. D. 90-130. It is not mentioned in the Muratorian Fragment nor does it occur in the Old Syriac and Old Latin versions. All this is doubtless explainable on the basis of the brevity of the Epistle, its containing no striking new material and its not being addressed to any specific person or church. According to Zahn the Epistle of Jude gives an early attestation of it, and that we need no other.

4. Occasion and Date. Antinomian Gnosticism had begun to manifest itself. The false teachings spread with its immoral tendencies. The Apostle wrote to correct this evil and to forewarn of conditions at the end of the age. There is no decisive evidence that Second Peter was not written shortly after First Peter. It was penned probably in A. D. 66-67, which date would meet all requirements.

5. Purpose and Plan. The Epistle was the second in which the Apostle proposes to stir up the "pure minds" of his readers "by way of remembrance" (3:1). To this end he urges

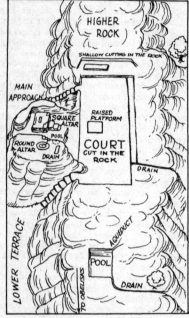

355. The Great High Place at Petra

upon them growth in Christian grace (1:5-15), warns against false teachers (chap. 2) and urges believers to patient expectation of the Lord's return (3:1-14).

6. Outline.

Introduction, 1:1-4

Part I. Exhortation to Christian growth, 1:5-11

Part II. Apostolic authority, 1:12-21

Part III. The peril of apostate teachers, 2:1-22

Part IV. Conduct in the light of the Lord's return, 3:1-18

— M. F. U.

Pethahi'ah (pĕth-à-hī'à; *Jehovah opens*), i. e., the womb.

1. A priest, head of the nineteenth course in the reign of David (I Chron. 24:16), B. C. about 970.

2. A Levite in the time of Ezra, who had married a foreign wife (Ezra 10:23). He is probably the same who is mentioned in Neh. 9:5, B. C. about 445.

3. The son of Meshezabeel and descendant of Zerah, who was counselor of King Artaxerxes in matters relating to the Jews (Neh. 11:24), B. C. 445.

Pe'thor (pē'thôr), a town in Mesopotamia where Balaam resided (Num. 22:5; Deut. 23:4). It was probably a noted seat of Babylonian magi, since these wise men were accustomed to congregate in particular localities. Shalmaneser II of Assyria captured this place from the Hittites, who called it Pitru. Still earlier, it appears in the lists of the great Egyptian conqueror Thutmose III (15th century B. C.). The town was located on the W. bank of the Euphrates a few miles S. of Carchemish.

Pethu'el (pē-thū'ĕl), the father of the prophet Joel (Joel 1:1), B. C. 8th century.

Petition. *See* Prayer.

Pe'tra (pē'trà), the capital of Edom and subsequently of Nabataea (*q. v.*). The name is from the Greek word *petra*, "rock," Heb. *sela*'. The rock-cut city of Petra was a noted pagan center, where there were many pillar cults. It was also a notable fortress and stronghold. This Transjordanian high place has been excavated. In 1934 the great "Conway High Place" at Petra was excavated by the Melchett Expedition in collaboration with W. F. Albright and others. George Robinson in his *Sarcophagus of Ancient Civilization* gives a description and study of the Petra High Place. In the O. T. Sela, the capital of Edom, between the Salt Sea and the Elamitic Gulf, is referred to (II Kings 14:7; Isa. 16:1). *M. F. U.*

Peul'ethai (pē-ŭl'ē-thī; *my wages*), the eighth-named son of Obed-edom, a Levite, and one of the porters of the tabernacle in the reign of David (I Chron. 26:5), B. C. after 1000.

Pha'lec (fā'lĕk), a Grecized form (Luke 3:35) of the Name of *Peleg* (*q. v.*).

Phal'lu (făl'ōō; Gen. 46:9). *See* Pallu.

Phal'ti (făl'tī; *delivered*), the son of Laish of Gallim, to whom Saul gave Michal in marriage after he had driven away David (I Sam. 25:44), B. C. before 1004. The only other reference to him is when Michal was restored to David, "And her husband went with her along weeping behind her to Bahurim. Then said Abner unto him, Go return. And he returned" (II Sam. 3:15, 16, where he is called Phaltiel), B. C. about 977.

Phal'tiel (făl'tĭ-ĕl), the son-in-law of Saul (II Sam. 3:15); elsewhere called *Phalti* (*q. v.*).

Phanu'el (fà-nū'ĕl; probably for *Penuel*, *face of God*), an Asherite, and father of Anna the prophetess (Luke 2:36), B. C. about 80.

Pha'raoh (fâr'ō), the title of Egyptian kings. It is the Hebrew form of the Egyptian title "the great house." During the early dynasties the expression was an honorific appellation

356. Valley of the Kings
(burial site of the Pharaohs)

for the chief Egyptian ruler, but from the powerful XVIII Dynasty when Egypt ruled the east (c. 1550-1320 B. C.), it was in common use as the official title of the kings of Egypt. (*See* Jack Finegan, *Light From the Ancient Past*, 1946, p. 88). Of the many pharaohs (30 dynasties in all), the following are among those alluded to in the Bible:

1. **The Pharaoh of the Patriarchs.** If one subscribes to the chronology embedded in the Massoretic Hebrew Text, Abraham was born 2161 B. C. and entered into Canaan 2086 B. C. This would make the patriarchal period in Palestine coeval with the strong Middle Kingdom in Egypt under the XII Dynasty (2000-1780 B. C.). Abraham visited one of the earlier kings of this dynasty and Joseph became prime minister of, and Jacob stood before, one of these powerful rulers (Amenemes I-IV) or Senwosret (I-III). Many scholars, however, make the pharaoh of Joseph one of the Hyksos kings (Dynasties XV-XVII) resident at Avaris-Tanis (c. 1720-1550 B. C.). This, however, is contrary to the Massoretic chronology.

357. Portrait of Tutankhamun

2. **The Pharaoh of the Oppression.** If the early date of the Exodus (c. 1441 B. C.) is subscribed to, Thutmose III (c. 1482-1450 B. C.) furnishes an ideal figure for the pharaoh of the oppression. According to the Bible, Moses waited for the death of the great oppressor before returning to Egypt from his refuge in Midian (Exod. 3:23). However, late-date theorists commonly identify Seti I (c. 1319-1301) as the pharaoh of the oppression, disregarding the Massoretic chronology.

3. **The Pharaoh of the Exodus.** Amenhotep II (c. 1450-1425 B. C.), son of the famous empire-builder Thutmose III, likely is the pharaoh of the Exodus. There are no references, of course, in the contemporary records of this pharaoh to such national disasters as the ten plagues or the destruction of the Egyptian army in the Red (Reed) Sea, much less to the escape of the Hebrews. This is not amazing, however, as Egyptians were loathe to catalog their disasters. If Amenhotep II was the pharaoh of the Exodus, his eldest son was slain in the tenth plague (Exod. 12:29).

358. Entrance to Tutankhamun's Tomb, Valley of the Kings

It is clear, as the records prove, that Thutmose IV (c. 1425-1412 B. C.) was not Amenhotep II's eldest son. He could therefore, have fitted into the historical situation. Many scholars make Raamses II (c. 1301-1234 B. C.) the pharaoh of the Exodus. This however is not proved.

4. **The Father-in-law of King Solomon** (c. 960-922 B. C.). Solomon married this Egyptian ruler's daughter. He was a firm ally of the Hebrew monarch (I Kings 3:1; 7:80).

5. **Pharaoh Shishak,** a member of the XXII or Libyan Dynasty, who appears on the Egyptian monuments as Sheshonk I and overran Judah and Jerusalem during the reign of Solomon's successor, Rehoboam (I Kings 14: 25) of Judah (c. 918 B. C.). Late in the reign of Solomon, Jeroboam, who was subsequently to become king of Israel, took refuge in the court of Shishak (I Kings 11:40).

6. **Zerah the Ethiopian,** evidently Osorkon I, Shishak's successor. This pharaoh was defeated in southern Palestine in Asa's reign (c. 913-873 B. C.) (cf. II Chron. 10:2; 14:9-15; 16:8).

7. **So** (c. 732-724 B. C.), whom Hoshea, king of Israel, tried to align against Assyria, was possibly a powerful general or *tartan* of Egypt rather than a pharaoh (II Kings 17:4).

8. **Tirhakah** of the XXV Dynasty conducted a military campaign against Sennach-

359. Mummy Head of Raamses II (often thought to be the Pharaoh of the Exodus)

erib of Assyria (II Kings 19:9). His name on the Egyptian monuments is rendered Taharka.

9. **Nechoh** of the XXVI Dynasty killed Josiah of Judah at Megiddo (II Kings 23:29, 30). Nechoh was conquered by Nebuchadnezzar, who built the Chaldean empire on defeated Egypt.

10. **Hophra**, called also *Apries* (c. 588-569 B. C.), ruled during the ministry of Jeremiah who with others, fled to Egypt. The prophet foretold that this pharaoh would be defeated by his enemies. The Bible refers to other unnamed pharaohs (I Kings 11:14-22; II Kings 18:21; I Chron. 4:18). *See* Egypt. *M. F. U.*

Pha′res (fā′rĕz; Matt. 1:3; Luke 3:33). *See* Pharez.

Pha′rez (fā′rĕz; *breach*), a twin son (with Zarah) of Judah by Tamar (his daughter-in-law (Gen. 38:29; I Chron. 2:4). Little is known of his personal history, although his family is often mentioned. He and his brethren were numbered among the sons of Judah (Gen. 46:12), and after the death of Er and Onan he is named as the second son (Num. 26:20). His family was very numerous, as is shown in Ruth 4:12: "Let thy house be like the house of Pharez, whom Tamar bare unto Judah." His descendants were notable in the time of David (I Chron. 11:11, etc.; 27:2, 3) and after the captivity (I Chron. 9:4; Neh. 11:4-6). In several of these passages he is called *Perez*.

Phar′isees (făr′ĭ-sēz; Gr. from Aram. *perīshā, separated*).

1. **Name.** The name *Separatists* is thought by some to have been derived from that separation which took place in the time of Zerubbabel, and then again in the time of Ezra, when Israel separated from the heathen dwelling in the land and from their uncleanness (Ezra 6:21; 9:1; 10:11; Neh. 9:2; 10:29). But this is correctly objected to on the ground that their name must have come to the Pharisees in consequence of their stricter view of the notion of uncleanness, not only from the uncleanness of the heathen, but from that with which they believed the great portion of Israel to have been affected. This seems to have been the sense in which they were called the *separated* or the *separating*, and they might have been so called from either praise or blame. It is not probable that they took the name themselves, but that their adversaries called them "the separatists." They called themselves *Ḥābĕrîm* (Aram. *hăbar, associate*), this term being in the language of the Mishna and of ancient rabbinical literature in general exactly identical with *Perushim*; a Haber in them meaning one who associates himself with the law in order to observe it strictly in opposition to the encroachments of Hellenism.

2. **Origin.** The *priests* and *scribes* determined the inner development of Israel after the captivity. Virtually identical in Ezra's time, they became more and more separated, until, in the Maccabaean period, two parties, sharply contrasted with each other, were developed from them. The *Sadducean* party came from the ranks of the priests, the party of the *Pharisees* from the Scribes. The characteristic feature of the Pharisees arises from their *legal tendency*,

that of the Sadducees from their *social position*. When once the accurate observance of the ceremonial law was regarded as the true essence of religious conduct, Pharisaism already existed, but not as a distinct sect or party. It appears that during the Greek period, the chief priests and rulers of the people took up an increasingly low attitude toward the law; they (the Pharisees) united themselves more closely into an association of such as made a duty of its punctilious observance. They appear in the time of John Hyrcanus under the name of "Pharisees," no longer indeed on the side of the Maccabees, but in hostile opposition to them. The reason for this was that the Maccabaeans' chief object was no longer the carrying out of the law, but the maintenance and extension of their political power. The stress laid upon religious interests by the Pharisees had won the bulk of the nation to their side, and Queen Alexandra, for the sake of peace with her people, abandoned the power to the Pharisees. Their victory was now complete; the whole conduct of internal affairs was in their hands. All the decrees of the Pharisees done away with by Hyrcanus were reintroduced, and they completely ruled the public life of the nation. This continued in all essentials even during subsequent ages. Amid all the changes of government under Romans and Herodians the Pharisees maintained their spiritual authority. Consistency with principle was on their side, and this consistency procured them the spiritual supremacy. Although the Sadducean high priests were at the head of the Sanhedrin, the decisive influence upon public affairs was in the hands of the Pharisees. "They had the bulk of the nation as their ally, and women especially were in their hands. They had the greatest influence upon the congregations, so that all acts of public worship, prayers, and sacrifices were performed according to their injunctions. Their sway over the masses was so absolute that they could obtain a hearing even when they said anything against the king or the high priest, consequently they were the most capable of counteracting the designs of the kings. Hence, too, the Sadducees, in their official acts, adhered to the demands of the Pharisees, because otherwise the multitude would not have tolerated them" (Schürer, *Jewish People*, div. ii, vol. ii, p. 28).

3. **Teachings.** Pharisaism thus represents the effect of Hellenism on normative Judaism, many of the differences between it and Sadducaism being due to their respective reaction toward Greek culture (cf. W. F. Albright, *From the Stone Age to Christianity*, 1941, pp. 272-273). (1) **Immortality.** The Pharisees teach "that every soul is imperishable, but that only those of the righteous pass into another body, while those of the wicked are, on the contrary, punished with eternal torment" (Josephus, *Wars*, ii, 8, 14); or "they hold the belief that an immortal strength belongs to souls, and that there are beneath the earth punishments and rewards for those who in life devoted themselves to virtue or vileness, and that eternal imprisonment is appointed for the latter, but the possibility of returning

to life for the former" (Josephus, *Ant.*, xviii, 1, 3). The above is merely the Jewish doctrine of retribution and resurrection (Dan. 12:2), and testified to by all subsequent Jewish literature, and also by the New Testament, as the common possession of genuine Judaism. (2) **Angels**, etc. The Pharisees also taught the existence of angels and spirits, while the Sadducees denied them (Acts 23:8), in this respect also representing the general standpoint of later Judaism. (3) **Providence, human freedom**, etc. The Pharisees "make everything depend on fate and on God, and teach that the doing of good is indeed chiefly the affair of man, but that fate also cooperates in every transaction" (Josephus, *Wars*, ii, 8, 14). "They assert that everything is accomplished by faith. They do not, however, deprive the human will of spontaneity, it having pleased God that there should be a mixture, and that to the will of fate should be added the human will with its virtue or baseness" (Josephus, *Ant.*, xviii, 1, 3). "If we strip off its Greek form, from what Josephus says, it is nothing more than this, that according to the Pharisees *everything* that happens takes place through God's providence, and that consequently in human actions also, whether good or bad, a cooperation of God is to be admitted. And this is a genuine Old Testament view" (Schürer, div. ii, vol. ii, p. 15). (4) **Political.** "In politics the standpoint of the Pharisees was the genuinely Jewish one of looking at political questions not from a political, but from a religious point of view. The Pharisees were by no means a 'political' party, at least not directly. Their aim, viz., the strict carrying out of the law, was not political, but religious. So far as no obstruction was cast in the way of this, they could be content with any government. It was only when the secular power prevented the practice of the law in that strict manner which the Pharisees demanded, that they gathered together to oppose it, and then really became in a certain sense a political party, opposing even external resistance to external force. To politics as such they were always comparatively indifferent." We must consider the Pharisee as acting under two different *religious* views: (1) The idea of the *Divine Providence* might be made the starting point. Thence would result the thought that the sway of the heathen over Israel was the will of God. Hence, first of all, this chastisement of God must be willingly submitted to; a heathen and, moreover, a harsh government must be willingly borne, if only the observance of the law was not thereby prevented. (2) *Israel's election* might be placed in the foreground. Then the rule of the heathen over the people of God would appear as an abnormity whose abolition was by all means to be striven for. Israel must acknowledge no other king than God alone and the ruler of the house of David, whom he anointed. The supremacy of the heathen was illegal and presumptuous. From this standpoint it was questionable, not merely whether obedience and payment of tribute to a heathen power was a duty, but whether it was lawful (Matt. 22:17, sq.; Mark 12:14, sq.; Luke 20:22, sq.).

4. **Practices.** As an Israelite avoided as far as possible all contact with a heathen, lest he should thereby be defiled, so did the Pharisee avoid as far as possible contact with the non-Pharisee, because the latter was to him included in the notion of the unclean Am-haarez (i. e., other Israelites than Pharisees). When, then, the gospels relate that the Pharisees found fault with the free intercourse of Jesus with "publicans and sinners," and with his entering into their houses (Mark 2:14-17; Matt. 9:9-13; Luke 5:27-32), this agrees exactly with the standpoint here described. The Pharisees, according to the Talmud, were of seven kinds: (1) *The Shechemite Pharisee*, who simply keeps the law for what he can profit thereby, as Shechem submitted to circumcision to obtain Dinah (Gen. 34:19). (2) *The Tumbling Pharisee*, who to appear humble always hangs down his head. (3) *The Bleeding Pharisee*, who in order not to see a woman walks with his eyes closed, and thus often meets with wounds. (4) *The Mortar Pharisee*, who wears a mortar-shaped cap to cover his eyes that he may not see any impurities or indecencies. (5) *The What-am-I-yet-to-do Pharisee*, who, not knowing much about the law, as soon as he has done one thing, asks, "What is my duty now? and I will do it" (comp. Mark 10:17-22). (6) *The Pharisee from fear*, who keeps the law because he is afraid of future judgment. (7) *The Pharisee from love*, who obeys the Lord because he loves him with all his heart (Delitzsch, *Jesus und Hillel*).

5. **Pharisaism and Christianity Compared.** (1) In relation to the Old Testament dispensation it was the Saviour's great effort to unfold the principles which had lain at the bottom of that dispensation, and carry them out to their legitimate conclusions, to "fulfill the law" (Matt. 5:17), to "fulfill," not to confirm, as too many suppose it to mean. The Pharisee taught such a servile adherence to the letter of the law that its remarkable character, as a pointing forward to something higher than its letter, was completely overlooked, and that its moral precepts, intended to elevate men, were made rather the instruments of contracting and debasing their ideas of morality. Thus, strictly adhering to the letter, "Thou shalt not kill," they regarded anger and all hasty passion as legitimate (5:21, 22). (2) While it was the aim of Jesus to call men to the law of God itself as the supreme guide of life, the Pharisees multiplied minute precepts and distinctions to such an extent, upon the pretence of maintaining it intact, that the whole life of Israel was hemmed in and burdened on every side by instructions so numerous and trifling that the law was almost, if not wholly, lost sight of (*see* Matt. 12:1-13; 23:23; Mark 3:1-6; 7:2-4; Luke 13:10-17; 18:12). (3) It was a leading aim of the Redeemer to teach men that true piety consisted not in forms, but in substance; not in outward observances, but in an inward spirit; not in small details, but in great rules of life. The whole system of Pharisaic piety led to exactly opposite conclusions. Under its influence "the weightier matters of the law, judgment, mercy, and faith" (Matt. 23:23; Luke 11:42) were undervalued and neglected; the idea of religion as that which should have

its seat in the heart disappeared (Luke 11:38-41); the most sacred obligations were evaded (Mark 7:11); vain and trifling questions took the place of serious inquiry into the great principles of duty (Matt. 19:3, etc.); and even the most solemn truths were handled as mere matters of curious speculation or means to entrap an adversary (Matt. 22:35, etc.; Luke 17:20, etc.). (4) The lowliness of piety was, according to the teaching of Jesus, an inseparable concomitant of its reality, but the Pharisees sought mainly to attract attention and excite the admiration of men (Matt. 6:2, 16; 23:5, 6; Luke 14:7; 18:11). (5) Christ inculcated compassion for the degraded, helpfulness to the friendless; liberality to the poor, holiness of heart, universal love, a mind open to the truth. The Pharisees regarded the degraded classes of society as classes to be shunned, not to be won over to the right (Luke 7:39; 15:2; 18:11), and pushed from them such as the Saviour would have gathered within his fold (John 7:47, 48). They made a prey of the friendless (Matt. 23:13); with all their pretence to piety they were in reality avaricious, sensual, and dissolute (Matt. 23:25; John 8:7), and devoted their energies to making converts to their own narrow views (Matt. 23:15). The exclusiveness of Pharisaism certainly justifies its being called a sect (Gr. *hairesis*, Acts 15:5; 26:6). Their number, which was comparatively small, was about six thousand.

Pha′rosh (fā′rŏsh; Ezra 8:3). *See* Parosh.

Phar′par (fär′pàr; *swift*, cf. Arab. *farfar*, *haste*), one of the two rivers of Damascus mentioned by Naaman, "Are not Abana and Pharpar, rivers of Damascus, better than all the waters of Israel?" (II Kings 5:12), the same as the "Awaj," a little south of Damascus. Its total length is forty miles, and it is but one-fourth the volume of the Barada, or Abana. It flows through the Wady el-Ajam, "the valley of the Persians."

Phar′zite (fär′zīt), the descendant of Pharez, son of Judah (Num. 26:20).

Phase′ah (fà-sē′à; Neh. 7:51). *See* Paseah.

Phe′be (fē′bê; *radiant*), a deaconess of the Church at Cenchrea, commended by Paul to the Church of Rome, who had been a recipient of her kindness (Rom. 16:1, 2). She seems to have been on the eve of setting out for Rome on some important business, the nature of which is unknown.

Phe′nice (fē′nĭs). *See* Phoenix.

Phenic′ia (fê-nĭsh′ĭ-à). *See* Phoenicia.

Phi-be′seth (fī-bē′sĕth), an Egyptian city (Bubastis). *See* Pi-beseth.

Phi′chol (fī′kŏl), chief captain of the army of Abimelech, the Philistine king of Gerar (Gen. 21:22, 32; 26:26), B. C. about 1980.

Philadel′phia (fĭl-à-dĕl′fĭ-à; *brotherly love*), a city in Lydia of Asia Minor, containing one of "the seven churches of Asia" (Rev. 1:11; 3:7). It was built by Attalus Philadelphus, whose name it bore. It was situated on the lower slopes of Tmolus, on the southern side of the valley of the *Ain-é-ghiul Sou*, a river which is probably the Cogamus of antiquity, and falls into the *Wadistchai* (the Hermus), in the neighborhood of *Sart-Kalesi* (Sardis), about 28 miles S. W. of the site of Philadelphia. Its

360. Philadelphia, Ruins of the Church of St. John (foreground)

elevation is nine hundred and fifty-two feet above the sea. A Roman town until 1392 A. D., it fell, after persistent resistance, into the hands of the Turk. It has been several times almost destroyed by earthquakes. Its name now is Ala-Sheher, "City of God."

Phile′mon (fĭ-lē′mŏn; *affectionate*), a member of the Church of Colossae, who owed his conversion to the apostle Paul, for such is the interpretation generally assigned to the words: "thou owest unto me thine own self besides" (Philem. 19). To him Paul addressed his epistle in behalf of Onesimus. His character, as given in that letter, was one of great nobility. The apostle commends his faith and love, his benevolence and hospitality, his docile, sympathizing, and forgiving spirit. His house at Colossae was shown in the time of Theodoret, and tradition represents him as bishop of that city, and as having suffered martyrdom.

Philemon, Epistle to, a brief epistle of Paul to Philemon, a Christian slave owner, whose slave Onesimus had run away from him.

1. **Object.** Onesimus had fled to Rome. He seems to have defrauded his master (vers. 18). At Rome he was converted under the ministry of Paul and was induced by the great Apostle to return to his master. The exquisite Epistle of Philemon recommends the converted runaway slave to Philemon's favorable reception. Paul urges that the new convert is no longer to be considered as a mere servant, but also as a brother in Christ. Paul also requests Philemon to prepare him a lodging, as he expected to visit Colossae shortly. Philemon is addressed to a certain "Apphia," perhaps Philemon's wife, and "Archippus," a minister in the Colossian church (Col. 4:17).

2. **Place of Writing.** Philemon is closely connected with Colossians. Onesimus carried both epistles. However Tychicus is joined with Onesimus in the Epistle to the Colossians (4:9). Paul and Timothy stand in the greetings of Paul. Paul is named as a prisoner in both (Philem. 1:9; Col. 4:18). In both Archippus is addressed (Philem. 1:2; Col. 4:17). It seems evident, therefore, that both epistles were written about the same time and place—at Rome during Paul's first imprisonment, A. D. 61 or 62.

3. **Authenticity.** Origen cites it as a Pauline letter addressed to Philemon concerning Onesimus. Tertullian refers to the brevity of this epistle as the "sole cause of its escaping the

falsifying hands of Marcion" (*Against Marcion*, 5:21). Eusebius refers to it as one of the "universally acknowledged Epistles of the canon" (*Ecc. History*, 3:25). Jerome and Ignatius also allude to it. It is quoted infrequently by the fathers evidently because of its brevity. Its coincidences with the Colossian Epistle attest its authenticity.

4. **Its Style.** This short epistle is a masterpiece of Christian tactfulness and politeness. In fact, it has been called "the polite epistle." Its politeness, however, has no trace of insencerity, often found in the urbanity of the world. As Luther noted, the Epistle exhibits "a right, noble, lovely example of Christian love." Verses 17 and 18 of the Epistle present a forceful illustration of imputation: "Receive him as myself," that is, reckon to him my merit; "if he hath wronged thee or oweth thee aught, put that on mine account," that is, reckon to me his demerit.

5. **Outline**
Salutation, 1:1-3
Part I. Appreciation of Philemon's character, 1:4-7
Part II. Pleading in behalf of Onesimus, 1:8-21
Part III. Paul's personal affairs, 1:22-24
Benediction, 1:25   *M. F. U.*

Phile′tus (fĭ-lē′tŭs; *beloved*), an apostate Christian named in connection with Hymenaeus (II Tim. 2:17) as holding false views regarding the resurrection. The apostle does not state their opinions, concerning which there have been many dissertations. Dean Ellicott (*Com.*, in loc.) says: "The false ascetism which is so often tacitly alluded to and condemned in these epistles led very probably to an undue contempt for the body, to false views of the nature of death, and thence to equally false views of the resurrection. Death and resurrection were terms which had with these false teachers only a *spiritual* meaning and application; they allegorized the doctrine, and turned all into figure and metaphor." The names of Philetus and Hymenaeus occur separately among those of Caesar's household whose relics have been found in the Columbaria at Rome.

Phil′ip (fĭl′ĭp). 1. **The Apostle** (Gr. *Philippos, lover of horses*) was of the city of Bethsaida, in Galilee (John 1:44; 12:21), but of his family we have no information. Little is recorded of Philip in the Scriptures. (1) **Call.** He had probably gone with Andrew and Peter to hear the preaching of John the Baptist. They had, without doubt, spoken to him of Jesus as the long-expected Saviour, for on the next day after Andrew brought his brother Simon to Jesus, Philip unhesitatingly complied with the Master's request to follow him (1:41-43). He was thus the fourth of the apostles who attached themselves to the person of Jesus. (2) **Invites Nathanael.** The first act of Philip was to invite Nathanael to "come and see" Jesus, saying, "We have found him, of whom Moses in the law and the prophets did write, Jesus of Nazareth, the son of Joseph" (1:45-47). His ready acceptance of Jesus, and what he said to Nathanael, seem to imply much acquaintance with the word. (3) **Ordained apostle.** When the twelve were specially set

apart for their office, Philip was numbered among them (Matt. 10:3; Mark 3:18; Luke 6:14). (4) **Other incidents.** When Jesus was about to feed the five thousand he asked Philip, "Whence shall we buy bread that these may eat?" And it is added, "This he said to prove him" (John 6:5-7). Bengel and others suppose that this was because the charge of providing food had been committed to Philip, while Chrysostom and Theodore of Mopsuestia rather suppose it was because this apostle was weak in faith. The answer of Philip agrees well enough with either supposition. Certain Greeks, desiring to see Jesus, made application to Philip for an introduction. Philip, uncertain at first whether to comply with their request or not, consulted with Andrew, who went with him, and mentioned the circumstance to Jesus (12:21, 22). The sacred history adds only the remark of Philip, "Lord, show us the Father, and it sufficeth us" (14:8), and refers to his presence at Jerusalem with the Church after the ascension (Acts 1:13). The later traditions concerning this apostle are vague and uncertain; but there is nothing improbable in the statement that he preached the gospel in Phrygia, and that he met his death at Hieropolis in Syria.

2. **The Evangelist.** Of his family antecedents nothing is known. (1) **As a deacon.** We first hear of Philip in his appointment as one of the seven deacons, his name following Stephen in the list (Acts 6:5). They were appointed to superintend the daily ministration of food and alms, and so remove all suspicion of partiality. The persecution that followed the death of Stephen stopped the "daily ministrations" of the Church. The teachers who had been most prominent were compelled to take flight, and Philip was among them. (2) **Encounters Simon Magus.** Philip found his way to the city of Samaria, where Simon Magus practiced sorcery. The latter was held in great reverence because of the wonders he wrought. Philip performed many substantial miracles, and thus drew away from the sorcerer the attention of the people, who listened gladly to the preaching of the Gospel. Simon himself seems to have regarded Philip as in league with some superhuman being, and looking upon baptism as the initiatory rite through which he might obtain the same powers; he solicited and obtained baptism from the evangelist (8:5-13). (3) **Teaches the eunuch.** After Peter and John had come to Samaria to complete the work begun by Philip, he was directed by the angel of the Lord to proceed to Gaza. On the way he met the treasurer of Candace, queen of Ethiopia, who had come to Jerusalem to worship. The eunuch was reading Isa. 53, when Philip drew near to his chariot and asked him if he understood that which he read. Upon invitation Philip took a seat and expounded the Scripture, preaching Jesus, the result of which was the conversion and baptism of the eunuch. Upon the return from the water in which the baptism occurred "the Spirit of the Lord caught away Philip, that the eunuch saw him no more." Philip continued his work as a preacher at Azotus (Ashdod) and among the other cities that had formerly belonged to the

Philistines, and, following the coast line, came to Caesarea (8:26-40). (4) **Later incidents.** For a number of years (estimated from fifteen to nineteen) we lose sight of the evangelist. The last glimpse we have of him in the New Testament is in the account of St. Paul's journey to Jerusalem. At his house the great apostle and his companions tarry for many days. The four daughters of Philip, "virgins which did prophesy," and Agabus, who prophesied of Paul's danger from the Jews, are mentioned in the narrative (21:8, sq.). The traditions concerning Philip are conflicting and uncertain. The Greek martyrologies make him to have been bishop of Tralles, in Lydia; but the Latins make him end his days in Caesarea.

Phil'ip (fĭl'ĭp), *Herod* (Matt. 14:3, etc.). *See* Herod, IV.

Phil'ip (fĭl'ĭp), the tetrarch (Luke 3:1). *See* Herod, IV.

361. Ruins of Christian Churches, Philippi

Philip'pi (fĭ-lĭp'ī; *lover of horses, warlike*), a town of Macedonia, anciently known as Krenides (Strabo, vii, 331), was situated about nine miles from the Aegean Sea, N. W. of the island of Thasos. King Philip took it from the Thracians and gave it his own name. The Philippi which St. Paul visited was a Roman colony founded by Augustus, and the remains which strew the ground are no doubt derived from that city. The establishment of Philip of Macedonia was probably not exactly on the same site. Philip, when he acquired possession of the site, found there a town named *Datus* or *Datum*, which was in all probability in its origin a factory of the Phoenicians, who were the first that worked the gold mines in the mountains here, as in the neighboring Thasos. The proximity of the gold mines was of course the origin of so large a city as Philippi, but the plain in which it lies is of extraordinary fertility. The position, too, was on the main road from Rome to Asia, the Via Egnatia, which from Thessalonica to Constantinople followed the same course as the existing post road. A battle was fought here between Octavius and Anthony on one side and Brutus and Cassius on the other, in which the former conquered, and the Roman republic was overthrown, B. C. 42. Paul and Silas were imprisoned here when on the second missionary journey (Acts 16:9-40; Thess. 2:2). The church at Philippi was generous (II Cor. 8:1-6; 11:9; Phil. 4:16). The First and Second Epistles to the Corin-

362. Neapolis (Kavalla), Port of Philippi

thians were written in this city (*see* Subscriptions). The first church in Europe was here. The place is a mass of ruins at the present time. French archaeologists conducted excavations at the site of ancient Philippi between 1914 and 1938, uncovering many sections of the city—particularly the market place and the foundations of a large arched gateway on the N. W. edge of the city (cf. Acts 16:13).

Philip'pians, Epistle to, a letter of the Apostle Paul addressed to the church at Philippi. It was the first city of the district called Macedonia Prima, correctly rendered "the leading city of the district of Macedonia, and a Roman colony" (Acts 16:12 R. S. V.). It was made a Roman colony by Augustus in honor of his celebrated victory over Brutus and Cassius. As a colony it was "a little Rome" itself, transplanted to the provinces. Its inhabitants were Roman citizens who had the privilege of voting and were governed by their own Senate and legislature.

1. **Purpose.** The Epistle is general, correcting no disorders, false doctrines or disturbances but exhorting the Philippians to consistency of Christian living. The immediate occasion was the expression of thanks for a contribution sent by Epaphroditus, who was now returning to take back the Apostle's letter. The only disturbance behind it was a lack of lowliness of mind among some with resulting disputing and friction between two women, Euodias and Syntyche.

2. **The Outline**

Salutation, 1:1, 2

Part. I. The Believer's Joy in Spite of Suffering, 1:3-30

Part II. The Believer's Example in Christ of Joyous and Loyal Service, 2:1-30
　a. Exhortation to unity and meekness, 1:1-3
　b. Christ's humiliation, 2:5-8
　c. Christ's exaltation, 2:9-11
　d. Manifestation of practical salvation, 2:12-16
　e. Paul's example, 2:17-30

Part III. Christ, the Source of the Believer's Joy, 3:1-21
　a. Warning against legalism, the enemy of joy, 3:1-6
　b. Trusting Christ, the Source of joy, 3:7-21

Part IV. Christ, the Believer's Joy, giving victory over worry, 4:1-23
　a. Exhortation to united joy, 4:1-4

b. The peace of God, the key to joy, 4:5-7
c. The presence of God in practical joy, 4:8-22
Benediction, 4:21-23

3. **Background and Date.** The Philippian church had been established by the Apostle Paul on his second missionary journey (Acts 16:9-40). The vision at Troas induced him to cross over into Europe and to visit the city of Philippi. There was apparently no synagogue in the city and the church began by the river-side. Lydia, a seller of purple from Thyatira, was converted. As a result of Paul's experience with a demon-possessed slave girl, he was cast into prison, miraculously delivered, and saw other converts in the Philippian jailor and his house. After this experience, he had to leave the city but Luke remained at Philippi. This is patent from the fact that from this point onward Luke uses the third person in speaking of the party. The small church established here was a nucleus of a real work of God. The church was loyal to Paul and twice sent a contribution while he was at Thessalonica (Phil. 4:15, 16) and the church also sent him a gift at Corinth (Acts 18:5; II Cor. 11:8, 9). To thank the Philippians and to send them instruction and comfort, Paul wrote the letter, since Epaphroditus was about to return to Philippi (Phil. 2:28). The Epistle was manifestly penned from Rome (cf. 1:13; 4:22) and very likely near the end of Paul's two years in Rome (Acts 28:30, 31). The general background would suggest that Philippians is the last of the four so-called Prison Epistles. The first three of these epistles were written about A. D. 60; therefore, Philippians must be dated at the close of the year A. D. 61. *M. F. U.*

Philis′tia (fĭl-ĭs′tĭ-á), the land of the *Philistines q. v.*), as it is usually styled in poetry (Psa. 60:8; 87:4; 108:9).

363. Philistia

Philistines, a powerful sea people that settled in the coastal strip in S. W. Palestine, extending along the Mediterranean from Joppa to S. of Gaza. Taking advantage of the fruitful, well-watered Maritime Plain about 50 miles long and 15 miles wide, they developed into a strong rival of the nation of Israel.

1. **Origin.** The Philistines are said to have come from Caphtor (Amos 9:7; Jer. 47:4;

cf. Deut. 2:23). For this reason the clause "hence went forth the Philistines" is commonly viewed as misplaced by a copyist and to belong after "Caphtorim" in Gen. 10:14. The monuments show that the Peleste, or Philistines, invaded Palestine with other "sea peoples" at the time of Raamses III (1195-1164 B. C.) of Egypt. This Egyptian monarch repulsed them in several battles, but some of the invaders survived in Syria and eventually reached S. E. Palestine. There they settled and in course of time gave their name to the country—Philistia (Joel 3:4). In turn, the Greek name, "Palestine," was derived from the name Philistia. The region around Gerar and Beersheba, however, was inhabited by Philistines as early as the patriarchal age (Gen. 21:32; 26:1) and before the Mosaic era settlers from Crete had destroyed the original inhabitants of the region of Gaza and settled there (Deut. 2:23). Biblical notices, which are commonly viewed as anachronistic by critics, place scattered groups of these people in S. W. Palestine centuries before the arrival of the main body in the first quarter of the twelfth century B. C. (e. g. John Garstang, *Joshua-Judges*, London, 1931, p. 287).

2. **Race.** The Philistines were a non-Semitic people. The fact that they were uncircumcised figures prominently in the O. T. They were apparently Aryans, viewed by some scholars as Indo-Europeans. Raamses III's temple at Medinet Habu contains reliefs depicting the Philistines. They appear as a tall, Hellenic-looking people.

3. **Government.** Their power and threat to Israel was due to a large extent to their political organization. It consisted of a league of five great cities. The famous Philistine pentapolis was composed of (1) Gaza, strategically located a few miles from the Mediterranean and controlling the Maritime Plain and caravan routes to Egypt and Arabia. (2) Ekron. This was a wealthy market in the Valley of Sorek, close to Danite territory. (3) Ashdod was on the main road to Joppa and lay E. of Lydda. (4) Ashkelon was a strong fort on the coast, controlling principal caravan routes. (5) Gath was N. E. of Gaza and bordered on the Shephelah. The effective political organization was headed by five Philistine lords, who are called in Hebrew, *seranim.* In numerous instances they are simply called *sarim,* the normal Hebrew word for "princes." Some scholars have connected *seranim* with a dialectal variation of *sar,* Hebrew "prince." It has also been connected with Greek *tyrant.* At the time of Joshua these five lords seem to have been joined in a confederacy. The Philistine cities are now better known as the result of excavation. The important mound of Tell Jemmeh, which appears to be ancient Gerar, has been partially examined and promises rich reward to future archaeological research. A number of tombs from the Philistine plain have been unearthed and may actually be the burying place of these Philistine rulers.

4. **Military Might.** Besides their warlike nature, effective political organization and economic power, as the result of the fertile farming section they inhabited, Philistine

364. Raamses III Battles the Philistines

militarism, which was a continual threat to Israel, was explainable by their early control of the iron monopoly. Iron came into use in Palestine around 1200 B. C. The Philistines knew the secret of smelting it, which they evidently got from the Hittites. They were able to import, smelt and forge iron and made use of various iron military weapons. By enforcing a rigid monopoly over Israel, the Philistines were able to make great strides in military encroachments upon Israelite territory. This Philistine iron monopoly is described in I Sam. 13:19-22: "Now there was no smith to be found throughout all the land of Israel; for the Philistines said, lest the Hebrews make themselves swords and spears; but every one of the Israelites went down to the Philistines to sharpen his plowshare, his mattock, his axe or his sickle. And the charge was a pim for the ploughshares and for the mattocks, and a third of a shekel for sharpening the axes and for setting the goads. So on the day of battle there was neither sword nor spear found in the hand of any of the people with Saul and Jonathan, but Saul and Jonathan his son had them." Sir Flinders Petrie at Tell Jemmeh, apparently ancient Gerar, found abundant evidence of iron manufacture. An iron smeltery and sword factory with furnaces and numerous iron weapons were discovered. Also iron-rimmed chariots were depicted on pottery.

5. **Religion.** The Philistines were intensely religious. They celebrated their victories in the "house of their idols" (I Sam. 31:9). They often carried their idol gods into battle (II Sam. 5:21). Dagon (Heb. *dāgōn*), a diminutive of *dāg*, "fish" was represented with the hands and face of a man and the tail of a fish (I Sam. 5:4). To his temple the captive ark was carried (5:2) and to him they offered thanksgiving when they had taken Samson (Judg. 16:23, 24). They also worshipped Ashtaroth (I Sam. 31:10). This is the ancient Assyrian goddess of propogation, Ishtar. At Ekron there was a sanctuary to Baal-zebub, "lord of habitation," who was sufficiently well known as the "god of Ekron" to attract the patronage of Ahaziah (II Kings 1:2f). His name in Greek became Beelzebub, "the prince of the demons" (Matt. 12:24).

6. **Philistine-Israelite Struggle.** In Judg. 3:3 the Philistines are left to prove Israel. Shamgar (Judg. 3:31) is said to have slain 600 Philistines with an ox goad. The tribe of Dan

had to remove to the N. E. because of the Philistine advance (Judg. 18:2). In Judg. 13:1, just previous to the time of Samson, Israel was overrun by the Philistines for forty years. Samson, the Israelite hero, wrought great victories over the Philistines but eventually met death in the Philistine temple of Dagon (chap. 13-16). About 1050 B. C., at the Battle of Ebenezer, the Philistines again overran the whole country, destroying Shiloh and carrying away the ark (I Sam. 4:4). The sacred relic of Israel, however, caused untold suffering to the Philistines, who returned it after seven months (I Sam. 5:6). About two decades later Israel recovered her territory under Samuel (I Sam. 7:1-14).

7. **Hebrew Domination.** Jonathan defeated the Philistines at Michmash (I Sam. chaps. 13 and 14). David won signal victories over them (I Sam., chaps. 17 and 18). During the Davidic era the Philistines were completely subjugated and were among tributary peoples under Solomon.

365. Philistine Pottery (c. 1100 B. C.)

8. **Under the Judahite Kings.** The divided monarchy caused some resurgence of Philistine power. Nadab, around 900 B. C., and other Judahite monarchs invaded Philistia (I Kings 15:27; 16:15). The Philistines paid

tribute to Jehoshaphat (c. 973-849 B. C.; II Chron. 17:11) but their power increased during the reigns of Jehoram (c. 849-842 B. C.) and Ahaz (c. 835 B. C.; II Chron. 21:16; 28:18). Uzziah and Hezekiah attacked them (II Chron. 26:6f). They suffered under Egyptian and Assyrian attacks in the eighth and seventh centuries B. C. because of their exposed position on the great highways between Egypt and the Euphrates. *M. F. U.*

Philol'ogus (fĭ-lŏl'ō-gŭs; *fond of talk*), a Christian at Rome to whom St. Paul sends his salutation (Rom. 16:15). Pseudo-Hippolytus makes him one of the seventy disciples, and bishop of Sinope. His name is found in the Columbarium "of freedmen of Livia Augusta" at Rome, which shows that there was a Philologus connected with the imperial household at the time when it included many Julias.

Philosophy (Gr. *philosophia*, "love of wisdom"). This term is used in Greek writings of either zeal for, or skill in, any art or science or other branch of knowledge. It occurs only once in the N. T. to describe the theology of certain Jewish Christian ascetics who busied themselves with refined and speculative inquiries into the nature and classes of angels and to the ritualism of the Mosaic legislature and the traditional Jewish regulations respecting practical living (*see* Col. 2:8). *M. F. U.*

Phin'ehas (fĭn'ē-ăs; Egyptian "the Nubian").

1. **Grandson of Aaron**, and son of Eleazar by his wife, "one of the daughters of Putiel" (Exod. 6:25). He first appears in Scripture history at the time of the licentious idolatry, where his zeal and action secured the cessation of the plague that was destroying the nation (Num. 25:7-11), B. C. c. 1435. For this he was rewarded by the special approbation of Jehovah, and by a promise that the priesthood should remain in his family forever (vers. 10-13). He was appointed to accompany as priest the expedition by which the Midianites were destroyed (31:6). Seven years later he also headed the party who were dispatched from Shiloh to remonstrate against the altar which the trans-Jordanic tribes were reported to have built near Jordan (Josh. 22: 13-32). In the partition of the country he received an allotment of his own—a hill on Mount Ephraim which bore his name—Gibeath-Pinehas. Here his father was buried (24:33). Phinehas appears to have been the chief of the Korahites, or Korhites (I Chron. 9:20). After the death of Eleazar he became high priest (the third of the series), in which capacity he is introduced as giving the oracle to the nation during the whole struggle with the Benjamites on the matter of Gibeah (Judg. 20:28). The verse which closes the Book of Joshua is ascribed to Phinehas, as the description of the death of Moses at the end of Deuteronomy is to Joshua. The tomb of Phinehas, a place of great resort to both Jews and Samaritans, is shown at *Awertah*, four miles S. E. of *Nablus*.

Character. The narrative of the Pentateuch presents Phinehas as an ardent and devoted priest, while in one of the Psalms (106:30, 31) he is commemorated in the identical phrase which is consecrated forever by its use in reference to the great act of faith of Abraham—"that was *counted to him for righteousness unto all generations for evermore*" (comp. Gen. 15:6; Rom. 4:3).

2. **Second son of Eli** (I Sam. 1:3; 2:34; 4:4, 11, 17, 19; 14:3). Phinehas was killed with his brother by the Philistines when the ark was captured, B. C. about 1050.

3. **A Levite** of Ezra's time (Ezra 8:33), unless the meaning be that Eleazar was of the family of the great Phinehas.

Phle'gon (flē'gŏn; *burning*), a Christian at Rome to whom Paul sent salutations (Rom. 16:14). Pseudo-Hippolytus states that he was one of the seventy disciples and bishop of Marathon.

Phoe'be (fē'bē). *See* Phebe.

Phoenic'ia (fē-nĭsh'ĭ-à), the narrow coast land stretching along the N. E. Mediterranean. It is bordered on the E. by the Lebanon Mountains and on the S. E. by the hills of Galilee. It is famous in history for such great commercial emporia as Tyre, Sidon, Byblos and Arvad. It was a part of O. T. Canaan. At present it consists of the Republic of Lebanon and S. Latakia. The boundary generally extended from Arvad southward over 120 miles to the Ladder of Tyre. At some periods the territory was included from Mt. Carmel to the Orontes River. In N. T. times Phoenicia extended as far S. as Dor, 16 miles S. of Tyre. It was thus a narrow ribbon of coast land at its greatest extent some 200 miles long. For references to Phoenicia see Acts 11:19; 15:3; 21:2.

Phoenicians, the inhabitants of Phoenicia.

1. **Name.** The name Phoenician is evidently derived from Greek *phoinos*, meaning *blood red*. Three possible explanations are available. (1) *Phoinos* refers to the reddish sun-burned skin of Phoenician seamen or, more likely, (2) to the reddish purple dye from the mollusks-murex widely exported by Phoenicians and widely used as a coloring material in antiquity. (3) However, it may be safest to derive the name Phoenician from *phoinix*, "the date palm." It would then signify the land of palms, like Palmyra.

2. **Race.** The Phoenicians were Semitic and were known as Canaanites as long as the Phoenician cities were important for their commercial activity. In the Table of Nations (Gen. 10:8-12), Canaan denotes the descendants of Ham, who settled in the land later known as Palestine and from whom the country took its original name. Thus originally Hamitic according to the Table of Nations, the Canaanites settled in a small country

366. Drawing of a Phoenician Battle Ship and Trading Vessel (copied from a representation on the wall of the Palace of Sennacherib at Nineveh, 700 B. C.)

that was like a bridge between Egypt and the great Semitic empires that flourished on the fertile Crescent. At a very early date they must have succumbed to the pressure of racial and linguistic intermixture with Semites with the loss of their own ethnic predominance. This is doubtless the explanation why anthropologically and ethnologically the evidence is that the Canaanites were predominantly Semetic rather than Hamitic. Such explanations as the nomenclature of Gen. 10 "expresses not race but empire or civilization" (J. A. Montgomery, *Record and Revelation*, Oxford, 1938, p. 2) or that Canaan is called a son of Ham "on account of the long domination of the land of Canaan by Egypt" (H. S. Gehman, the *Westminster Dictionary of the Bible*, Philadelphia, 1944, p. 89) are scarcely satisfactory, especially in view of the stress laid upon the Hamitic origin of Canaan (Gen. 9:22-27).

3. **Factors in Phoenician Commercialism.** Three outstanding reasons account for the world-famous commercial activities of the Phoenicians. (1) Their conquest by the Israelits around 1380 B. C. which deprived them of most of Palestine and crowded them on the narrow ribbon of coast land extending from Accho N. of Mt. Carmel to Ras Shamra-Ugarit more than 200 miles north. Shortly thereafter the Aramaeans took the hinterland of Syria E. of Mt. Lebanon. Thus hemmed in to the coast of northern Palestine and southern Syria, they took to the sea and became one of the most distinguished seafaring peoples of history, founding commercial colonies on the shores and islands of the Mediterranean as far west as Spain. In the ninth century they established Carthage. They also founded centers at Tartessus and at Gades in Spain. They seem to have gone past the Pillars of Hercules to secure tin from Cornwall, Britain. (2) The mountains which approach close to the narrow coastal strip further confined the Phoenicians and was a factor in their seafaring exploits. (3) Another circumstance was the plentiful yield of pine, cypress and cedar trees for shipbuilding. The men of Byblos (O. T. Gebal) were noted shipbuilders (Ezek. 27:9) and the Sidonians were expert in timber felling (I Kings 5:6). The two greatest ports were Tyre and Sidon, although Byblos, Arvad, Arka, Zarepath and Ugarit were famous.

4. **Religion.** Canaanite religion is now well known as the result of the recovery of the religious epic literature from ancient Ugarit. These priceless documents reveal the chief gods and goddesses of the numerous Canaanite cities in various periods. The important deities were El, the supreme Canaanite deity and his son, Baal, the reigning king of the gods who dominates the Canaanite pantheon. In Ugaritic literature, Baal is given the epithet of *Aliyan*, "the one who prevails." Both of these gods are utterly immoral in their actions as are the three goddesses, Anath, Astarte and Ashera. These three are patronesses of sex and war and reveal the barbarity and licentiousness of Canaanite cults. These Canaanite deities periodically exerted an extremely debilitating influence on Israel. Such degeneracy is illustrated in the Ahab-Jezebel apostasy (I Kings, chaps. 18 and 19). The gross

idolatrous lapse of Solomon (I Kings 11:5) is another example. Solomon suffered from the degenerating influence of the licentious cultic ritual of the Phoenician religion. The prophetic curse upon Canaan (Gen. 9:25-27) was principally religious and refers to the religious turpitude and moral degeneracy of Canaanite cults. This was a prime reason for their extermination by the conquering Israelites under divine orders.

367. The Mediterranean at Beirut

5. **Art.** From a very early period Canaanites played a conspicuous role in the cultural history of civilization. By the end of the fourth millennium important cities like Jericho, Gezer, Megiddo, Beth Shan, Byblos, Hamath, Jerusalem and Ai were already in existence. On the busy bridge between great civilizations, literature, music, religion, art and science developed. The Canaanites were in a position to absorb from other peoples, and it is hard to distinguish what they copied or assimilated from what they invented. The invention of the alphabet, which is attributed to the Canaanites, was adopted by the Greeks. In fact, the Greeks learned so much about writing and writing materials from the Canaanites that their word for book, *biblion*, hence "Bible," was connected with the Phoenician city Byblos. Phoenicians early knew the art of glassmaking, if they did not actually make the discovery themselves, although it seems as if the Egyptians made the actual discovery. The Phoenicians had great artistic ability in working fine metals for jewelry. The Canaanites also possessed literary skill, as the Ugaritic epic literature attests. Even though their religion degenerated morally it, nevertheless, had many artistic and aesthetic elements. In architecture the Phoenicians also excelled, as the account of Solomon's building activities, particularly of the temple in Jerusalem, attest (cf. I Kings, chaps. 5-10).

6. **History.** Phoenicia makes its debut in Egyptian history as early as the Hyksos Period. The great empire builder, Thutmose III, mentions conquests in Phoenicia and claimed this part of Canaan as a vassal dependency. The Tell el-Amarna Letters (c. 1400 B. C.) give a great deal of light concerning the Phoenician trading cities. During the period of the Judges in Israel Phoenicia was consolidating into a state. It was a powerful kingdom centered in Sidon and Tyre. Both David and Solomon maintained amiable relationships with the Tyrian rulers. Ahab of Israel by his intermarriage with Jezebel, the

daughter of the Tyrian king Ethbaal, introducted debilitating Canaanite cults into Israel. The apogee of Phoenician prestige extended from c. 1000 B. C. to 600 B. C. After this period the heritage of Phoenician civilization passed on to the Greek states in the Aegean and through them, as a result of Alexander the Great's conquests in the fourth century, became a world heritage. Excavations at the ancient Phoenician city of Gebal (Byblos) have shed light on the dawn of Phoenician history. The French archaeologists Montet and Denand have traced commercial and religious activities of this ancient Canaanite center back to c. 3000 B. C. Ancient Egypt imported fine woods for furniture and shipbuilding and mummy-case construction from Gebal. Papyrus was sent back and also gold, perfumes and other Egyptian luxuries. The Phoenician cities suffered under the relentless Assyrian conquerors. Ashurnasirpal II (872-850 B. C.) drained these commercial cities by heavy tribute. Shalmaneser III (c. 850-824 B. C.) did likewise. The great conqueror Tiglathpilesar III (c. 734 B. C.) exacted tribute from Arvad and controlled Byblos. At the time of Samaria's fall Assyria over-ran the Phoenician coasts. Sennacherib's invasion of the West land compelled Tyre and Sidon to form an alliance in the Chaldean period. Nebuchadnezzar III after destroying Jerusalem advanced against Tyre. His armies are said to have besieged the city for twelve years (585-573 B. C.), when the city surrendered apparently on favorable terms and the king was deported to Babylon. After the Babylonian period the Persians assumed control of Phoenicia. Alexander the Great conquered Tyre only after building a causeway to reach the insular city. After the city was destroyed by Alexander, it was rebuilt and again became important as a prosperous emporium in the Greek and Roman period. When a number of Roman emperors established colonies at Berytus, Accho, Tyre and Sidon, even after the loss of their political autonomy, Phoenician merchants cultivated extensive sea traffic (Zeph. 1:11; Neh. 13:16). The story of Phoenicia is one of an energetic and intrepid people who, shut out of their native land, took to the sea to carve out a world-famous destiny for themselves. *M. F. U.*

Phoe'nix (fē'nĭks), a harbor of Crete "looking northeast and southeast" (Acts 27:12 R. S. V.). The A. V. has "Phenice, a haven of Crete, and lieth toward the southwest and northwest." Paul and his fellow sojourners on the ship going to Addramyttium hoped to winter there. The harbor is in the southern part of the island. *M. F. U.*

Phryg'ia (frĭj'ĭ-à), a province of Asia Minor, inland. Once it seemed to include the greater part of the peninsula of Asia Minor, then it was divided into Phrygia Major and Minor, and the Romans again divided it into three parts, Phrygia Salutaris on the east, Phrygia Pacatiana on the west, and Phrygia Katakekaumene (*the burnt*) in the middle, for this part was volcanic. The country was fertile, and its rich pastures made it famous for its breeds of cattle. Paul crossed this province twice in the course of his missionary journeys.

368. Phrygia

It is the Greater Phrygia that is referred to in the New Testament. The town of Antioch in Pisidia (Acts 13:14), Colosse, Hierapolis, Iconium, and Laodicea were situated in it. In the passages (16:6; 18:23) Phrygia is mentioned in a manner not intended to be precise, the former referring to Paul's second missionary journey, and the latter to the third. Nor is Acts 2:10 inconsistent with this view. By Phrygia we must understand an extensive district, which contributed portions to several Roman provinces, and varying portions at different times.

Phu'rah (fū'rà), the servant of Gideon, who went with him by night when he visited the camp of the Midianites (Judg. 7:10, 11). See Pu'rah.

Phut (fŭt), the third name in the list of the sons of Ham (Gen. 10:6; I Chron. 1:8), elsewhere applied to an African country or people. In the list it follows Cush and Mizraim, and precedes Canaan. We cannot place the tract of Phut out of Africa, and it would thus seem that it was almost parallel to that of the Mizraites, as it could not be farther to the north; this position would well agree with Libya. The few mentions of Phut in the Bible clearly indicate a country or people of Africa, and it was, probably, not far from Egypt (Isa. 66:19, A. V. "Put;" Nah. 3:9; Jer. 46:9; Ezra 27:10; 30:5; 38:5). From these passages we cannot infer anything as to the exact position of this country or people; unless indeed in Nahum, Cush and Phut, Mizraim and Lubim, are respectively connected, which might indicate a position south of Egypt. Jeremiah (46:9) describes the Egyptian army as consisting of Ethiopians, of Phutites, and of Lydians; and Ezekiel (30:5) prophesies that Cush and Phut and Lud shall fall by the sword along with the Egyptians. See Put.

Phu'vah (fū'và), one of the sons of Issachar (Gen. 46:13). The name is given as "Pua" (Num. 26:23) and "Puah" (I Chron. 7:1). His descendants were called Punites (Num. 26:23). R. V., R. S. V. Pu'vah (*q. v.*).

Phygel'lus (fĭ-gĕl'ŭs; *a fugitive*) (II Tim. 1:15), a Christian connected with those in Asia of whom St. Paul speaks as turned away from himself. It is open to question whether their repudiation of the apostle was joined with a declension from the faith, and whether the open display of the feeling of Asia took place— at least so far as Phygellus and Hermogenes were concerned—at Rome. Phygellus may have forsaken (*see* II Tim. 4:16) the apostle at some critical time when his support was expected; or he may have been a leader of some party of nominal Christians at Rome, such as the apostle describes at an earlier period (Phil. 1:15, 16) opposing him there. R. V. and R. S. V. render Phygelus (fĭ-jē′lŭs).

Phylactery. 1. **Name.** (Gr. *safeguard, amulet,* so named because it was thought to ward off evil spirits and ill fortune). The name "phylactery" seems to be confined to the New Testament. Neither the Septuagint nor the other Greek versions have this term in their translations of the passages which enjoin this token. Even Josephus does not use the word "phylactery," though he mentions the custom. The Jews in Christ's time, and to this day, call phylacteries tᵉp̄ilin (Heb. for "prayer fillets").

2. **Form and Use.** Phylacteries were strips of parchment with four passages of Scripture written upon them in the following order: Deut. 11:13-22; Deut. 6:4-9; Exod. 13:11-16; Exod. 13:1-10. Each strip was rolled up, tied with the white hairs of a calf's or a cow's tail, and placed in one of the compartments of a small box. During prayer these phylacteries were worn by the male Israelites firmly attached with leathern straps to the forehead between the eyebrows, and on the left arm, so as to be near the heart. This practice— regarding the origin of which only this much is certain, that it was in existence in our Lord's time (Matt. 23:5; Josephus, *Ant.,* iv, 8, 13)—is founded upon a literal interpretation of Exod. 13:9, 16, where, with reference to the enactments as to the observance of the passover and the sanctifying of the first born, we read: "And it shall be for a sign unto thee upon thine hand, and for a memorial between thine eyes" (v. 9), and . . . "for frontlets between thy eyes" (v. 16); and Deut. 6:8; 11:18, where the injunction, so far as the latter part of it is concerned, is repeated, and that with reference to the whole of the commandments. Of course, the injunction was intended to be taken figuratively.

The box for the head phylactery and for the arm were ordinarily one and one-half inches square; the former having on the outside to the right the three-pronged letter *shin,* which is designed as an abbreviation of the divine name *Shaddai,* "the Almighty," while on the left side it had a four-pronged *shin,* the two constituting the sacred number seven.

3. **How Worn.** Through a flap in the box a very long leathern strap is passed. Before commencing his morning prayers the Israelite puts on first the phylactery for the arm. The strap, passed through the loop, makes a noose for the arm. Having put his naked arm through this in such a way that when it is bent it may touch the flesh and be near the heart to fulfil the precept, "Ye shall lay up these my words in your hearts" (Deut. 11:18),

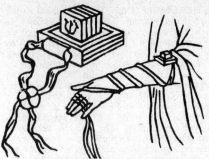

369. Phylactery on the Arm

he twists the strap three times close to the box in the form of the letter *shin,* and pronounces the following benediction: "Blessed art thou, O Lord our God, King of the universe, who hast santified us with the commandments and enjoined us to put on phylacteries." He then twists the strap seven times around the arm, forming two *shins,* one with three prongs and the other with four.

He next puts on the head phylactery, placing it exactly in the center between the eyes so as to touch the spot where the hair begins to grow (Deut. 11:18), and pronounces the following benediction before he finally secures it: "Blessed art thou, O Lord our God, King of the universe, who hast sanctified us with thy commandments, and enjoined upon us the command about phylacteries."

"To make broad their phylacteries" (Matt. 23:5) was to make the strips wider, requiring a larger box, thus making them more conspicuous. Some believe that this means having wider straps.

The real meaning of phylacteries is equivalent to amulets or charms. And as such the Rabbinists really regarded and treated them, however much they might otherwise have disclaimed all connection with heathen views and fear of demons.

Physician. "Physician, heal thyself" (Luke 4: 23), seems to mean that Jesus had been describing the various ills from which his hearers suffered and had applied the words of Isaiah to himself as the restorer of humanity. Jesus then added the proverb thus: "You are going even to turn into ridicule what you have just heard, and to say to me, Thou who pretendest to save humanity from its misery, begin by delivering thyself from thine own," viz., the want of esteem and consideration which attached to him.

"They that are whole need not a physician," etc. (5:31), was quoted to the scribes and Pharisees who objected to Jesus eating with Levi. So far as this concedes to the Pharisees that they were perfectly well, and therefore for them he, as a physician, was useless—so far it is irony. On the other hand it was calculated to excite serious doubts in their minds as to whether their point of view was correct (Godet, *Com.,* in loc.).

See Diseases, Treatment of.

Pi-be′seth (pī-bē′sĕth; Egyptian, *house of the goddess Bast*). The Greek rendering is *Boubastos;* the Egyptian *Pi-Pasht,* i. e., the place of *Pasht,* was so-called from the cat-headed

Bubastis or *Bast*, the Egyptian Diana, which was worshipped there in a splendid temple. It was situated on the royal canal leading to Suez, not far from its junction with the Pelusiac arm of the Nile. It was the chief seat of the *Nomas Bubastites*, was destroyed by the Persians, who demolished its walls (Diod. Sic., xvi, 51), and has entirely disappeared, with the exception of some ruins which still bear the name of Tell Basta. The prophet Ezekiel (30:17) declares that the young military men of Pi-beseth will fall by the sword, but the population of the city will go into exile.

Pictures. Strictly forbidden were images (Heb. *măskîth, figure*), idolatrous representations, either independent images, or more usually stones sculptured in low relief, or engraved and colored (Num. 33:52; comp. Ezek. 23:14, "portrayed"). Pictures, movable as with us, were probably unknown to the Jews; but colored sculpture and drawings on walls or wood, as mummy cases, must have been familiar to them in Egypt.

The "pictures of silver" (Prov. 25:11) were probably cornices with carvings, and the "apples of gold" representations of fruits or flowers, like Solomon's flowers and pomegranates (I Kings chaps. 6, 7).

Piece *of Gold, Money, Silver. See* Metrology **IV.**

Piety. Occurs in the A. V. only in the exhortation ("Let them learn first to show *piety* at home" (I Tim. 5:4; Gr. *'eusebeia*), better toward their own "household." Toward *God* the Greek word means reverence, toward *man* due and proper respect.

Pigeon. *See* Animal Kingdom, Sacrificial Offerings.

Pi-hahi′roth (pī-há-hī′rŏth), the place before, or at, which the Israelites encamped at the close of their third march from Rameses. It was "between Migdol and the sea, over against Baal-zephon" (Exod. 14:2, 9; Num. 33:7, 8, "Hahiroth"), and is not identified beyond dispute. But Père Abel places it in the swamps of Jeneffeh at the extremity of the pass between the mountain and the Bitter Lake.

Pi′late (pī′lát), the Roman procurator of Judea. A. D. 26-36.

1. **Name.** Pilate's family name, *Pontius* (pŏn′shŭs), indicates that he was connected, by descent or adoption, with the *gens* of Pontii. His cognomen, Pilatus, may have been derived from *pilatus*, armed with *pilum* (or javelin), or *pileatus*, the *pileus* (or cap) being the badge of manumitted slaves.

2. **Personal History.** (1) **Early History.** The early history of Pilate is unknown, save some unreliable traditions. A German legend relates that he was an illegitimate son of Tyrus, king of Mayence, who sent him to Rome as a hostage. There he committed a murder, and was sent to Pontus, where he subdued the barbarous tribes, receiving in consequence the name of Pontius, and was sent to Judea. (2) **Procurator.** Pilate was appointed governor of Judea by Tiberius (A. D. 26), and immediately offended the Jews by removing the headquarters of his army from Caesarea to Jerusalem. The soldiers, of course, took with them their standards, bearing the

image of the emperor, into the holy city. The sight of these standards planted within sight of the temple greatly enraged the people, who declared themselves ready rather to submit to death than to this idolatrous innovation. Pilate yielded to their demands, and ordered the standards to be returned to Caesarea (Josephus, *Ant.*, xviii, 3, 12; *War*, ii, 9, 2-4). On two other occasions Pilate nearly drove the Jews to insurrection; the *first*, when he hung up golden shields in his palace on Mount Zion, inscribed with the names of deities. These were only removed by an order from the emperor. The *second*, when he appropriated the revenue of the temple, arising from the redemption of vows, to the building of an aqueduct. To these acts must be added the slaughter of certain Galileans (Luke 13:1), who seem to have been slain while offering their sacrifices in the temple. (3) **His connection with Jesus.** It was the custom for the procurators to reside at Jerusalem, during the great feasts, to preserve order, and, accordingly, at the time of our Lord's last Passover Pilate was occupying his official residence in Herod's palace; and to the gates of this palace Jesus, condemned on the charge of blasphemy, was brought early in the morning by the chief priests and officers of the Sanhedrin, who were unable to enter the residence of a Gentile, lest they should be defiled and unfit to eat the Passover (John 18:28). Pilate, therefore, came out to learn their purpose, and demanded the nature of the charge. At first they seem to have expected that he would have carried out their wishes without further inquiry, and therefore merely described our Lord as a disturber of the public peace; but as a Roman procurator had too much respect for justice, or at least understood his business too well to consent to such a condemnation, they were obliged to devise a new charge, and therefore interpreted our Lord's claims in a political sense, accusing him of assuming the royal title, perverting the nation, and forbidding the payment of tribute to Rome (Luke 23:3— an account plainly presupposed in John 18:33). It is evident that from this moment Pilate was distracted between two conflicting feelings—a fear of offending the Jews and a conscious conviction that Jesus was innocent. Moreover, this last feeling was strengthened by his own hatred of the Jews, whose religious scruples had caused him frequent trouble, and by a growing respect for the calm dignity and meekness of the sufferer. First he examined our Lord privately, and asked him whether he was a king. At the close of the interview he came out to the Jews and declared the prisoner innocent. To this they replied that his teaching had stirred up all the people from Galilee to Jerusalem. The mention of Galilee suggested to Pilate a new way of escaping from his dilemma, by sending on the case to Herod Antipas; but Herod, though propitiated by this act of courtesy, declined to enter into the matter. So Pilate was compelled to come to a decision, and, first having assembled the chief priests and also the people, he announced to them that the accused had done nothing worthy of death; but, at the same time, in hopes of pacifying the Sanhedrin, he proposed to scourge him before he released him. But as the accusers were resolved to have his blood, they rejected this concession, and therefore Pilate had recourse to a fresh expedient. It was the custom for the Roman governor to grant every year, in honor of the Passover, pardon to one condemned criminal. Pilate therefore offered the people their choice between two—the murderer Barabbas and the prophet whom a few days before they had hailed as the Messiah. To receive their decision he ascended the *Bema*, a portable tribunal placed on the *Gabbatha*, a tessellated pavement in front of the palace. As soon as he was seated he received a message from his wife, who had "suffered many things in a dream," urging him not to condemn the Just One. But he had no alternative, as the rabble, urged by the

370. Coins of Pontius Pilate

priests, chose Barabbas for pardon, and clamored for the death of Jesus; insurrection seemed imminent, and Pilate yielded. Before issuing the fatal order he washed his hands before the multitude, as sign that he was innocent of the crime, in imitation, probably, of the ceremony enjoined in Deut., ch. 21. As it produced no effect, Pilate ordered his soldiers to inflict the scourging preparatory to execution; but the sight of unjust suffering so patiently borne seems again to have troubled his conscience, and prompted a new effort in favor of the victim. But the priests only renewed their clamors for his death, and, fearing that the political charge of treason might be considered insufficient, returned to their first accusation of blasphemy, and, quoting the law of Moses (Lev. 24:16), which punished blasphemy with stoning, declared that he must die, "because he made himself the Son of God." But this title augmented Pilate's superstitious fears, already aroused by his wife's dream (John 19:7); he feared that Jesus might be one of the heroes or demigods of his own mythology. He took him again into the palace and inquired anxiously into his descent ("Whence art thou?") and his claims. The result of this interview was one last effort to save Jesus by a fresh appeal to the multitude; but now arose the formidable cry, "If thou let this man go, thou art not Caesar's friend;" and Pilate, to whom political success was as the breath of life, again ascended the tribunal, and finally pronounced the desired condemnation. So ended Pilate's share in the greatest crime which has been committed since the world began. (4) **Later history.** Scripture gives us no further information concerning Pilate, but we learn from Josephus that his anxiety to avoid giving offense to Caesar did not save him from political disaster. The Samaritans were unquiet and rebellious. Pilate led his troops against them, and defeated them easily enough. The Samaritans complained to Vitellius, now president of Syria, and he sent Pilate to Rome to answer their accusations before the emperor. When he reached it he found Tiberius dead, and Caius (Caligula) on the throne, A. D. 36. Eusebius adds that soon afterward, "wearied with misfortunes," he killed himself. As to the scene of his death, there are various traditions. One is that he was banished to Vienna Allobrogum (Vienne on the Rhone), where a singular monument—a pyramid on a quadrangular base, fifty-two feet high—is called Pontius Pilate's tomb. Another is that he sought to hide his sorrows on the mountain by the Lake of Lucerne, now called Mount Pilatus; and there, after spending years in its recesses in remorse and despair, rather than penitence, plunged into the dismal lake which occupies its summit. We learn from Justin Martyr, Tertullian, Eusebius, and others that Pilate made an official report to Tiberius of our Lord's trial and condemnation; and in a homily ascribed to Chrysostom, though marked as spurious by his Benedictine editors (*Hom.*, viii, *in Pasch.*, vol. viii, p. 968, D), certain *hupomnēmata* (*Acta*, or *Commentarii Pilati*) are spoken of as well-known documents in common circulation. The *Acta Pilati*, now extant in Greek, and two Latin epistles from him to the emperor, are certainly spurious.

3. **Character.** Pilate seems to have been a representative of the rich and corrupt Romans of his age; a worldly-minded statesman, not insensible to justice and mercy, yet who lived exclusively in the life that now is. His desire was, doubtless, to save our Lord, but his own security and comfort would thereby have been interfered with. He was too selfish to suffer personal annoyance, and "the unrighteous condemnation of a good man was a trifle in comparison with the fear of the emperor's frown and the loss of place and power." Destitute of any fixed principles, and having no aim but office and influence, Pilate seems to have consulted the law of personal convenience, and to have done right only when it did not interfere with his selfish aims and purposes. Thus he yielded to the clamor of the Jews and acted contrary to his sense of justice, for fear that they would accuse him to the emperor of disloyalty, and thus secure his deposition.

Pil'dash (pĭl'dăsh; derivation uncertain), one of the eight sons of Nahor, Abraham's brother, by his wife and niece, Milcah (Gen. 22:22), B. C. about 2080.

Pil'eha (pĭl'ê-hà), the chief of the people who signed the covenant with Nehemiah (Neh. 10:24), B. C. 445.

Pilgrim (Gr. *parepidēmos*), one who comes from a foreign country to reside in a city or land; used

    Figuratively of the Christian whose native country is heaven (Heb. 11:13; I Pet. 2:11; comp. Gen. 47:9).

Pillar. The rendering of nine Hebrew words and one Greek word.

1. The essential notion of a pillar is of a shaft or isolated pile, either supporting or not supporting a roof. Pillars form an important feature in oriental architecture, partly, perhaps, as a reminiscence of the tent with its supporting poles, and partly also from the use of flat roofs, in consequence of which the

chambers were either narrower or divided into portions by columns. The general practice in oriental buildings of supporting flat roofs by pillars, or of covering open spaces by awnings stretched from pillars, led to an extensive use of them in construction. At Nineveh the pillars were probably of wood, and it is very likely that the same construction prevailed in the "house of the forest of Lebanon," with its hall and porch of pillars (I Kings 7:2, 6). The "chapiters" of the two pillars, Jachin and Boaz, resembled the tall capitals of the Persepolitan columns.

2. But perhaps the earliest application of the pillar was the votive or monumental. This in early times consisted of nothing but a single stone or pile of stones (Gen. 28:18; 31:46, etc.). The stone Ezel (I Sam. 20:19) was probably a terminal stone or a waymark. The "place" (*q. v.*) set up by Saul (15:12) is explained by St. Jerome to be a trophy. The word used is the same as that for Absalom's pillar. So also Jacob set up a pillar over Rachel's grave (Gen. 35:20). The monolithic tombs and obelisks of Petra are instances of similar usage. Absalom set up a pillar "to keep (his) name in remembrance" (II Sam. 18:18). But the word "pillar" (Heb. *măṣṣēbäh*), "pillar," is more often rendered "statue" or "image" (e. g., Deut. 7:5; 12:3; 16:22; Lev. 26:1, etc.).

Figurative. The figurative use of the term "pillar," in reference to the cloud and fire accompanying the Israelites on their march, or as in Cant. 3:6 and Rev. 10:1, is plainly derived from the notion of an isolated column not supporting a roof. In poetry we read of pillars on which earth and heaven rest (Job 9:6; 26:11; Psa. 75:3); and the comparison is made of a man, or his limbs, with pillars, for strength and firmness (Cant. 5:15; Jer. 1:18; Gal. 2:9; Rev. 3:12; 10:1). In I Tim. 3:15, we have the metaphorical expression, "the pillar and ground of the truth."

Pillar of Cloud and Fire. In Exod. 13:18, it is stated that "God led the people about, through the way of the wilderness;" in vers. 21, 22 (comp. 14:24; Num. 14:14; Neh. 9:12-19) it is said that "Jehovah went before them by day in a pillar of cloud, to lead them in the way, and by night in a pillar of fire to give them light; to go by day and night," etc.; that they might march at all hours. To this sign of the divine presence and guidance there was a natural similarity in the caravan fire, which consisted of small iron vessels or grates with wood fires burning in them, fastened at the end of long poles and carried as a guide in front of caravans, by which the direction of the road was indicated in the day time by the smoke and at night by the light of the fire. A still closer analogy is found in the custom of the ancient Persians of carrying fire, which they called "sacred and eternal," in silver altars in front of the army. The pillar of cloud and fire must not, however, be confounded with any such caravan or army fire, or set down as nothing more than a mythical conception, or a dressing up of this natural custom. The cloud was not the result of a caravan fire, nor a mere symbol of the divine presence;

it had a miraculous origin and supernatural character.

1. There was but one pillar of both cloud *and* fire (Exod. 14:24), for even when shining in the dark it is still called the pillar of cloud (14:19) or the cloud (Num. 9:21), so that it was a cloud covering the fire. By day it appeared as a cloud in contrast with the light of the sun, but by night as a fiery splendor, "a fire-look" (9:15, 16).

2. **Form.** When this cloud went before the army of Israel it assumed the form of a column; but when it stood still above the tabernacle or came down upon it, it most probably took the form of a round globe of cloud. When it separated the Israelites from the Egyptians at the Red Sea, we imagine it spreading out like a cloud bank, forming, as it were, a dividing wall.

3. **God's Presence.** In this cloud Jehovah, i. e., the visible representation of the invisible God under the Old Testament, was really present with Israel and spoke to them out of the cloud. In this, too, appeared "the glory of the Lord" (Exod. 16:10; 40:34; Num. 17:7). The fire in the pillar was the same as that in which the Lord revealed himself in the burning bush, and afterward descended upon Sinai amid thunder and lightning in a thick cloud (Exod. 19:16-18). It was a symbol of the "zeal of the Lord," and therefore was enveloped in a cloud which protected Israel by day from heat, sunstroke, and pestilence (Isa. 4:4, 5; 49:10; Psa. 91:5, 6; 121:6). At night it lighted up Israel's path by its splendor, and defended it from terror, calamity (Psa. 27:1, sq.; 91:5, 6). It also threatened destruction to those who murmured against God (Num. 17:10), sending out fire against the rebels and consuming them (Lev. 10:2; Num. 16:35).

Pillow.

In I Sam. 19:13, 16, it is recorded that Michal took an image (*teraphim*) and laid it in the bed and put a pillow of goats' hair for its bolster. This was probably, a piece of woven goats' hair folded up (Heb. *kᵉbîr; something plaited*).

A place for laying the head (Gen. 28:11,18, elsewhere "bolster") (Heb. *mᵉrăʾăshäh, a headpiece*).

A headpiece (Gr. *proskephalaion* Mark 4:38). Our Lord employed the rowers' bench or its cushion for a pillow.

Pilot (Heb. *ḥōbēl*, a *steersman*), is also rendered "ship-master" (Jonah 1:6), but in Ezek. 27:8 "pilots" seems to be used in a figurative sense for the chief men of Tyre. Keil (*Com.*, on Ezek.) thinks the meaning to be that the chief men in command of the ships (captains and pilots) were as a rule citizens of Tyre.

Pil′tai (pĭl′tī; *my deliverances*), the representative of the priestly house of Moadiah or Maadiah, in the time of Joiakim, the son of Jeshua, and apparently one of the priests who returned with Zerubbabel to Jerusalem (Neh. 12:17), B. C. 536.

Pim (pĭm), a weight equivalent to two-thirds of a shekel, examples of which have been recovered in Palestine. The expression occurs in I Sam. 13:21 in reference to the Philistine monopoly on iron when the Israelites went down to sharpen their plowshares, mattocks, axes and sickles: "And the charge was a pim for the plowshares and for the mattocks, and a third of a shekel for sharpening the axes and for setting the goads," (R. S. V.) The word "pim" is from Hebrew *payim*, dual of *peh* "mouth" i. e., "part," indicating *two-thirds*, or possibly from Akkadian *shinipu*, *two thirds*.

Pin (Heb. *yāthēd*, a *tent-pin*), the copper pegs driven into the ground to hold the cords of the tabernacle court (Exod. 27:19; 35:18; 38:20, 31, etc.), or for any other purpose or material (Judg. 16:14; Ezek. 15:3, rendered "nail" in Judg. 4:21, 22; 5:26; Ezra 9:8, etc.).

Pins and needles were also among the articles of the toilet, which have been occasionally found in the tombs. The former are frequently of considerable length with large gold heads, and some of a different form, tapering gradually to a point, merely bound with gold at the upper end, without any projecting head (seven or eight inches in length), appear to have been intended for arranging the plaits or curls of hair; like those used in England in the days of Elizabeth for nearly the same purpose.

Pine. *See* Vegetable Kingdom.

Pinnacle (Gr. *pterugion*, a *wing*, *any pointed extremity*, Matt. 4:5; Luke 4:9). It is impossible to decide definitely what portion of the temple is referred to as the pinnacle. The use of the definite article makes it plain that it was not *a* pinnacle, but *the* pinnacle. Much difference of opinion exists respecting it, but it may be that it was the *battlement* ordered by law to be added to every roof.

Pi'non (pī'nŏn), one of the "dukes" (i. e., head or founder of a tribe) of Edom (Gen. 36:41; I Chron. 1:52), B. C. about 1440.

Pipe. *See* Musical Instruments.

Pi'ram (pī'răm; perhaps wild ass), the Amorite king of Jarmuth who, with four confederate kings, made war against Gibeon, and were defeated by Joshua. They fled to the cave at Makkedah, from which they were brought at the close of the battle and pursuit and hanged. Their bodies were taken down and cast "into the cave wherein they had been hid" (Josh. 10:3-27), B. C. c. 1375.

Pir'athon (pĭr'à-thŏn; *height*, *summit*, cf. Arab. *far'*, top), is mentioned as the dwelling place of Abdon, who died after holding the office of judge for eight yeras, and was buried there (Judg. 12:13-15). It is also mentioned (II Sam. 23:30; I Chron. 11:31) as the home of Benaiah, the hero. It was in the land of Ephraim, on the mountains of the Amalekites. Fer'ata, on a height some 7½ miles W. by S. of Shechem is the plausible identification by Robinson.

Pir'athonite (pĭr'à-thŏn-īt), the native of, or dweller in, *Pirathon.* Two such are named in the Bible. 1. Abdon ben-Hillel (Judg. 12:13, 15). 2. From the same place came "Benaiah the Pirathonite of the children of Ephraim" (I Chron. 27:14).

Pis'gah (pĭs'gà). (Rashes-Siyâghah), occasionally called "the Pisgah" (cf. Num. 21:20; Deut. 3:27 A. V. margin). It is the headland of the rugged Abarim range in Jordan (ancient Moab), breaking through the ridge and skirting the N. E. end of the Dead Sea by Jericho (Deut. 34:1). Although Pisgah is often considered as identical to or a part of a neighboring peak, Mt. Nebo, it is actually slightly N. W. of Nebo.

From the top, or head, of the Pisgah Moses took his survey of the promised land, the particular peak upon which he stood being near Nebo (Num. 21:20; 23:14; Deut. 3:27; 34:1).

Upon Pisgah Balaam offered sacrifices, so that it was probably upon one of the ancient "high places" of Moab (Num. 23:14). The exact identification of Pisgah was long a problem, until the Duc de Luynes (1864) and Professor Paine, of the American Palestine Exploration Society (1873) independently identified it with Jebel Siyâghah, the extreme headland of the range of Abarim, of which the highest summit is Nebo. Respecting the view from this point Dr. Smith writes (*Hist. Geog.*, p. 563): "The whole of the Jordan valley is now open to you, from Engedi, beyond which the mists become impenetrable, to where, on the north, the hills of Gilead seem to meet those of Ephraim. The Jordan flows below. Jericho is visible beyond. Over Gilead, it is said, Hermon can be seen in clear weather, but the heat hid it from us. The view is almost that described as the last on which the eyes of Moses rested, the higher hills of West Palestine shutting out all possibility of a sight of the (Mediterranean) sea."

Pi'shon (pī'shŏn), one of the four rivers said to issue from Eden (Gen. 2:10-14). The Pishon and the Gihon were presumably canals (called "rivers" in Babylonia) which connected the Tigris and Euphrates as ancient river beds. Some scholars identify it with the Pallakottos Canal near the ancient Sumerian town of Eridu, not far from Abraham's city of Ur.
M. F. U.

Pisid'ia (pĭ-sĭd'ĭ-à), a mountainous district in Asia Minor, north of Pamphylia, twice visited by St. Paul, and in which he was probably "in peril of robbers" (Acts 13:14; 14:21-24; II Cor. 11:26). It was overrun with desperate bands of men who resisted the power of Rome. Antioch was in Pisidia, as distinguished from the more renowned Antioch in Syria.

Pi'son (pī'sŏn; *canal*), one of the four heads into which the stream was divided, which watered the Garden of Eden (Gen. 2:11). Numerous conjectures are made as to the identity of this stream, yet the matter is undetermined. (*See* Pishon.)

Pis'pa (pĭs'pà), the second named of the sons of Jether, of the tribe of Asher (I Chron. 7: 38). (A. V. Pispah.)

Pit, the rendering of several Hebrew and two Greek words, and used in the sense of a deep hole dug, in the first instance, for a well or cistern. When these were without water they were used as (1) *A place of burial* (Psa. 28:1; 30:3; Isa. 38:18); (2) *A prison* (Isa. 24:22; Jer. 37:16); (3) As a place of *destruction* (Zech. 9:11).

Figurative. To "go down into the pit" (Psa. 28:1; 30:3, 9, etc.), a phrase of frequent occurrence; is employed to denote dying without hope, but commonly a simple going to the place of the dead. "To dig a pit" (Psa. 7:15; 57:6; Prov. 26:27) is to plot mischief. The pit, as a place of great discomfort, and probable starvation, very naturally suggested a place of punishment (Rev. 9:1, sq.; 11:7; 17:8, etc.).

Pitch. *See* Mineral Kingdom.

Pitcher. A water jar, or pitcher, with one or two handles, used chiefly by women for carrying water, as in the story of Rebecca (Gen. 24:15-20). These pitchers were usually carried on the head or shoulder. The same word is used (A. V. "barrel," I Kings 17:12; 18:33) of the vessel in which the widow of Sarepta kept her meal, and the barrels of water used by Elijah on Mount Carmel; also of the pitchers employed by Gideon's three hundred men (Judg. 7:16). Heb. *kad*.

The Greek word (*keramion*) denotes an earthenware jar (Mark 14:13; Luke 22:10) and is rendered "jar" in the R. S. V.

Figurative. "The pitcher broken at the fountain" (Eccles. 12:6) is used figuratively for the cessation of life. "Earthen pitchers," as contrasted with "fine gold" (Lam. 4:2), is used to represent the real worth and the low valuation put upon good men.

Pi'thom (pī'thŏm), a store city of Egypt mentioned in Exod. 1:11 in connection with the bondage of the Children of Israel, who were said to have built it together with Raamses. It is located in the N. E. part of Egypt in the land referred to as Goshen. It was S. W. of Succoth and identified with Tell er-Retabah. The name seems to be derived from Egyptian Pi-Tum, signifying the "house or dwelling of Tum," the solar deity. Excavations at this site reveal constructions made of "bricks without straw" (cf. Exod. 1:14). Extensive brick work in the site constituted large storage spaces. Together with Raamses (Avaris-Tanis), Pithom was alleged to have been built by Raamses II (c. 1290-1224 B. C.), but in the light of Raamses II's notorious practice of taking credit for achievements wrought by his predecessors, these cities were evidently merely rebuilt or enlarged by him. Inasmuch as Tanis was called the house of Raamses only for a couple of centuries (c. 1300-1100 B. C.), the reference of Exod. 1:11 must be to the older city, Zoan-Avaris, where the oppressed Israelites labored centuries earlier. It is very probable, therefore, that the name Raamses is to be construed as a modernization of an archaic place name; namely Zoan-Avaris, once a flourishing city before the expulsion of the Hyksos (c. 1570 B. C.). If this is true, both Pithom and Raamses (Zoan-Avaris) were built by the enslaved Israelites long before the time of Raamses II. However, many scholars refer Exod. 1:11 to the reign of Seti I or Raamses II. *M. F. U.*

Pi'thon (pī'thŏn), the eldest son of Micah, the grandson of Jonathan, the son of Saul (I Chron. 8:35; 9:41), B. C. after 1000.

Pity. In many instances *pity* is the rendering of Hebrew words elsewhere translated "mercy." It is also the rendering of the Heb. *ḥâmal* (to *be gentle, clement*). In Exod. 2:6; I Sam. 23:21, it means to *have sympathy, compassion* with. Elsewhere it has the meaning of *to spare, to treat with pity* (I Sam. 15:3, 15; II Sam. 21:7; II Chron. 36:15, 17). It is written of God that "the Lord is very pitiful" (James 5:11), and that "like as a father pitieth his children, so the Lord pitieth them that fear him" (Psa.

103:13). The apostle Peter exhorts Christians to "love as brethren, be pitiful" (I Pet. 3:8). It will thus be seen that pity is both a divine characteristic and Christian grace.

Place (Heb. *yâd*, *hand*). "'He set him up a place' (I Sam. 15:12), literally 'hand,' or monument. This same word is used in II Sam. 18:18, and in Isa. 56:5, in the former of Absalom's column, or monument; in the latter, of the portion or 'memorial' promised to God's people within his house. This meaning is doubtless connected with the ancient custom of carving on the memorial pillar by a grave, a hand and arm. And the use of the hand as a memorial has not entirely ceased in the East. The dome of almost every Mohammedan mosque is surmounted by a carved crescent in wood or stone" (Rev. Wm. Ewing in *S. S. Times*).

Plague, a judgment or calamity which God sends upon men (Gen. 12:17; Exod. 11:1; Psa. 106:29, 30). This term is especially descriptive of the disease of leprosy (Lev. 13:3). The Hebrew word *něga'* means "a stroke" or "blow." Another common Hebrew word denoting calamities afflicted by God is *makkâh*, also meaning "a smiting" or "beating" (Lev. 26:21; Num. 11:33; Deut. 28:59; I Sam. 4:8; Jer. 19:8, etc.). Another original term denoting divine judgment, mostly of a final decision, is *negĕph*, also from a root "to smite," "to thrust," "punish" (Exod. 12:13; 30:12; Num. 8:19, etc.). A variation of this is the term *maggēphâh*, also referring to fatal disease, as a divine judgment (Exod. 9:14; I Sam. 6:4, etc.). The idea of plague is also expressed by the Hebrew word *dĕbĕr*, having the connotation of destruction (Hos. 13:14; Isa. 25:8). The Greek word *mastix* denotes "a whip" and is used figuratively of a disease (Matt. 5:29, 34; Mark 3:10; Luke 7:21). The term *plēgē* denotes "a stroke" and is a word used for public calamity and heavy affliction sent by God as a punishment (Rev. 9:18, 20; 11:6; 15:1; 16:9, etc.). *M. F. U.*

Plagues of E'gypt, the term usually employed in speaking of the divine visitations of wrath with which Jehovah punished the Egyptians, because they would not allow the Israelites to leave.

1. **History.** Moses, with Aaron as spokesman, appeared before Pharaoh to convey to him the divine command to allow the departure of the Israelites. In attestation of their authority Aaron cast down his rod before the king, and it became a serpent. This miracle, having been performed, or simulated by his magicians, Pharaoh hardened his heart against Jehovah, refused the desired permission, and thus produced the occasion for the ten plagues. Although it is distinctly stated that the plagues prevailed throughout Egypt, yet the descriptions seem principally to apply to that part of Egypt which lay nearest to Goshen, and more especially to "the field of Zoan," or the tract about that city, since it seems almost certain that Pharaoh dwelt in the Delta, and that territory is especially indicated in Psa. 78:43. The descriptions of the first and second plagues seem especially to refer to a land abounding in streams and lakes, and so rather to the lower than the upper country. Still we

must not forget that the plagues evidently prevailed throughout the land. There is nothing in the account of the plagues to fix the time occupied in their infliction. While some contend for the space of a year it seems to be that that time enables them to compare the plagues with certain natural phenomena occurring at fixed seasons of the year in Egypt. Each plague, according to the historian, lasted only a short time; and unless we suppose an interval of several weeks between each, a few months, or even weeks, would afford sufficient time for the happening of the whole.

2. **The Plagues.** (1) **That of blood** (Exod. 7:19-25). Pharaoh, having hardened his heart against the first sign, Moses and Aaron were empowered to enforce the release of Israel by a series of penal miracles. In the morning he met Pharaoh near the Nile, and made another demand for the people's release. Upon his refusal Aaron lifted up the rod over "the waters of Egypt," and they "were all turned to blood." "The changing of the water into blood is to be interpreted in the same sense as in Joel 2:31, where the moon is said to be turned into blood; that is to say, not as a chemical change into real blood, but as a change in the color, which caused it to assume the appearance of blood (II Kings 3:22). The reddening of the water is attributed by many to the red earth which the river brings down from Sennaar, but Ehrenberg came to the conclusion, after microscopical examinations, that it was caused by cryptogamic plants and infusoria. This natural phenomenon was here intensified into a miracle, not only by the fact that the change took place immediately in all branches of the river at Moses's word and through the smiting of the Nile, but even more by a chemical change in the water, which caused the fishes to die, the stream to stink, and what seems to indicate putrefaction, the water to become undrinkable" (K. and D., *Com.*, in loc.). The plague appears to have extended throughout Egypt, embracing the "streams," or different arms of the Nile; "the rivers," or Nile canals; "the ponds," or standing lakes formed by the Nile; and all the "pools of water," or the standing lakes left by the overflowings of the Nile. The "vessels of wood, and the vessels of stone," were those in which was kept the water for daily use, those of stone being the reservoirs in which fresh water was kept for the poor. "The Egyptians digged round about the river for water to drink," as it probably purified itself by filtering through the banks. The miracle was imitated by the magicians, but where they got water is not stated. On the supposition that the changing of the Nile water took place at the time when the river began to rise, and when the reddening generally occurs, many expositors fix upon the month of June or July for the time of this plague, in which case all the plagues would be confined to the space of about nine months. Perhaps a more likely date was September or October, that is to say, after the yearly overflow of the Nile. This plague was very humiliating, inasmuch as they were so dependent upon the Nile for water that it was worshiped as a god, as well as some of its fish. (2) **Plague of frogs** (Exod. 8:1-14). The second plague also proceeded from the Nile, and consisted in the unparalleled numbers in which the frogs appeared. These were the small Nile frog, called by the Egyptians *Dofda*. As foretold to Pharaoh, they not only penetrated into the houses and inner rooms ("bedchamber"), and crept into the domestic utensils, the beds, the ovens, and the kneading troughs, but even got upon the men themselves. This miracle was also imitated by the Egyptian magicians, who "brought up frogs upon the land of Egypt." Whether the Egyptian augurs really produced frogs by means of some evil occult power, or only simulated the miracle, is not stated. One thing is certain, that they could not remove the evil, for Pharaoh was obliged to send for Moses and Aaron to intercede with Jehovah to take them away. This request of Pharaoh, coupled with the promise to let the people go, was a sign that he regarded Jehovah as the author of the plague. Upon the morrow God removed the plague, the frogs died, and filled the land with the odor of their putrefaction. This plague must have been very aggravating to the Egyptians, for the frog was included among their sacred animals, in the second class of local objects of worship. It was sacred to the goddess Hekt, who is represented with the head of this animal. Then, too, the fertilizing water of Egypt had twice become a plague. (3) **Plague of lice** (Exod. 8:16-19). It seems that "lice" is not the correct word to be here used, but rather a small gnat or tick, so small as to be hardly visible to the eye, but with a sting causing a very painful irritation. They creep into the eyes and nose, and after the harvest they rise in great swarms from the inundated rice fields. The plague was caused by Aaron's smiting the dust of the ground with his staff, and all the dust throughout the land of Egypt was turned into gnats, which were upon man and beast. We are not able, nor is it necessary, to assert whether this miracle consisted in calling creatures into existence, or in a sudden creative generation and supernatural multiplication, for in either case we have a miracle. The failure of the magicians in this instance is thought to have been due to God's restraining the demoniacal powers, which the magicians had before made subservient to their purpose. Their declaration, "This is the finger of God," was not due to any purpose of glorifying God, but simply to protect their own honor, that Moses and Aaron might not be considered as superior to themselves in virtue or knowledge. It was merely equivalent to saying, It is not by Moses and Aaron that we are restrained, but by a *divine power*, possibly some god of Egypt. (4) **The plague of flies** (Exod. 8:20, sq.). The fourth plague was foretold to Pharaoh in the morning as he came forth to the water, doubtless for worship. It consisted of swarms of flies, probably dog flies. They are more numerous and annoying than gnats, and when enraged they fasten themselves upon the human body, especially the edges of the eyelids, and become a dreadful plague. As the Egyptian magicians only saw the work of some deity in the plague they could not imitate, a

distinction was made in the plagues which followed between the Israelites and the Egyptians. Jehovah placed a "division," i. e., a redemption, deliverance, between the two peoples. Thus Pharaoh was to be taught that Israel's God was the author of the plagues; that he had authority over Egypt; indeed, that he possessed supreme authority. Pharaoh called Moses, and told him to sacrifice to God in the land. This Moses declined to do, on the ground that by so doing the Israelites would be an abomination in the eyes of the Egyptians. This abomination would not have consisted in their sacrificing animals which the Egyptians considered holy, for the cow was the only animal offered in sacrifice which the Egyptians regarded as holy. The abomination would rather be that the Israelites would not observe the sacrificial *rites* of the Egyptians. The probability is that the Egyptians would look upon such sacrifice as an insult to their gods, and, enraged, would stone the Israelites. Pharaoh, therefore, promised to let the Israelites go if he were released from the plague, but hardened his heart as soon as the plague was taken away. (5) **Plague of murrain** (Exod. 9:1-7). This plague consisted of a severe *murrain*, which carried off the cattle of the Egyptians which were in the *field*, those of the Israelites being spared. A definite time was fixed for the plague, in order that, whereas murrains occasionally occur in Egypt, Pharaoh might see in this one the judgment of Jehovah. That the loss of cattle seems to have been confined to those in the *field* must be understood from v. 3 and from the fact that there were beasts to be killed by the hail (v. 25). The heart of Pharaoh still remained hardened. (6) **Boils.** The sixth plague was of boils breaking forth in blisters (Exod. 9:8-12). Moses and Aaron took soot or ashes from a smelting furnace or lime kiln, and threw it toward heaven. This flew like dust throughout the land, and became boils (*q. v.*). The magicians appear to have tried to protect the king by their secret arts, but were attacked themselves. The king's heart remained hardened, and he refused to let the people go. (7) **Plague of hail** (Exod. 9:17-35). In response to the continued hardness of Pharaoh, Jehovah determined to send such a hail as had not been known since Egypt became a nation (vers. 18, 24). A warning was sent out for all God-fearing Egyptians to house their servants and cattle, thus showing the mercy of Jehovah. The hail was accompanied by thunder and lightning, the latter coming down like burning torches, and multitudes of men and beasts were slain, trees and herbs destroyed. Terrified by the fierceness of the storm Pharaoh called for Moses and Aaron and said, " I have sinned this time: the Lord is righteous, and I and my people are wicked" (v. 27). Moses promised to pray to Jehovah in behalf of the Egyptians, that the storm should cease; but as soon as the storm ceased Pharaoh again hardened his heart and refused permission to Israel. "The account of the loss caused by the hail is introduced (vers. 31, 32) to show how much had been lost, and how much there was still to lose through continued refusal. According to Pliny the barley is reaped in the

sixth month after the sowing time, the wheat in the seventh. The barley is ripe about the end of February or beginning of March, the wheat at the end of March or beginning of April. The flax is in flower at the end of January. Consequently the plague of hail occurred at the end of January, or at the latest in the first half of February; so that there were at least eight weeks between the seventh and tenth plague" (K. and D., *Com.*, in loc.). The havoc caused by this plague was greater than any of the earlier ones; it destroyed men, which those others seem not to have done. (8) **Plague of locusts** (Exod. 10:1-20). Pharaoh still persisting in resisting the command of Jehovah, Moses was directed to announce another. He appeared before the king and put the question, "How long wilt thou refuse to humble thyself before me?" and added the command, "Let my people go, that they may serve me." A compromise was suggested, by which the men should be allowed to go and worship, but that the women should remain, knowing full well that in such a case the men would return. This compromise being rejected Moses and Aaron were driven from the king's presence. Moses lifted up his rod, and the Lord brought an east wind, which the next day brought locusts (*q. v.*). They came in such dreadful swarms as Egypt had never known before, nor has experienced since. "They covered the face of the whole earth, so that the land was darkened; and they did eat every herb of the land, and all the fruit of the trees which the hail had left; and there remained not any green thing in the trees or in the herbs of the field through all the land of Egypt." The fact that the wind blew a day and a night before bringing up the locusts showed that they came from a great distance, and therefore proved to the Egyptians that the omnipotence of God reached far beyond the borders of Egypt and ruled over every land. Another miraculous feature of the plague was its unparalleled extent, viz., over all Egypt, whereas ordinary swarms are confined to particular districts. In this respect the judgment had no equal either before or afterward (v. 14). In response to Pharaoh's entreaty "the Lord turned a mighty strong west wind, which took away the locusts and cast them into the Red Sea." Pharaoh's promise to allow the Israelites to depart was no more sincere than those which he had made before. (9) **Plague of darkness** (Exod. 10:21, sq.). As the king still continued defiant, a continuous darkness came over all Egypt, with the exception of Goshen (v. 23). It is described as the *darkness of obscurity*, i. e., the thickest darkness. The combination of two words or synonyms gives the greatest intensity to the thought. The darkness was so great that they could not see one another, and no man rose from his place. The Israelites alone "had light in their dwellings." This does not refer to their houses, and means that their part of the land was not visited by the plague. The cause of this plague is not given in the text, but most commentators agree that it was the *Chamsin*, a wind which generally blows in Egypt before and after the vernal equinox, and lasts two or three days. It rises suddenly, and fills the air with fine dust and coarse sand; the sun is obscured, and the darkness following is greater than the thickest fog. Men and animals hide themselves from this storm, and the inhabitants shut themselves up in the innermost rooms of their houses till it is over, for the dust penetrates even through well-closed windows. "The darkness which covered the Egyptians, and the light which shone upon the Israelites were types of the wrath and grace of God" (Hengstenberg). Pharaoh proposed another compromise, viz., that the Israelites, men, women, and children, should go, but that the flocks and herds should remain. But Moses insisted upon the cattle being taken for the purpose of sacrifices and burnt offerings, saying, "Not a hoof shall be left behind." This firmness of Moses he defended by saying, "We know not with what we shall serve the Lord until we come thither." At this Pharaoh was so enraged that he not only dismissed Moses, but threatened him with death if he should come into his presence again. Moses answered, "Thou hast spoken well," for as God had already told him that the last blow would be followed by the immediate release of the people, there was no further necessity for him to appear before Pharaoh. This announcement to Moses is recorded by the historian in chap. 11:1. (10) **Death of the firstborn** (Exod. 11-12:30). The brief answer of Moses (10:29) was followed by the address (11:4-8), in which he announces the coming of the last plague and declares that there should be "a great cry throughout all the land of Egypt, such as there was none like it, nor shall be like it any more;" and that the servants of Pharaoh would come to Moses and entreat him to go with all the Israelites. "And he went out from Pharaoh in a great anger." Then Moses commanded the Israelites to borrow (i. e., *ask*) from the Egyptians, and the latter readily assented. The Passover (*see* Festivals) was instituted, and the houses of the Israelites sprinkled with the blood of the victims. The firstborn of the Egyptians were smitten at midnight, as Moses had forewarned Pharaoh. The clearly miraculous nature of this plague, coming as it did without intervention on the part of Moses, taking only the firstborn, and sparing those of the Israelites, must have convinced Pharaoh that he had to deal with One who inflicted this punishment by his own omnipotence. That very night Pharaoh sent for Moses and Aaron, and gave them permission to depart with their people, their children, and their cattle, even urging haste. *See* Exodus.

3. **General Considerations.** (1) **Miraculous nature of the plagues.** Whether the plagues were exaggerations of natural evils or not, they were evidently of a miraculous character. They formed the chief part of the miraculous side of the great deliverance of the Israelites from Egyptian bondage. The historian obviously intends us to regard them as miraculous, and they are elsewhere spoken of as the "wonders" which God wrought in the land of Ham (Psa. 105:27), i. e., in Egypt (106:7), "tokens and wonders" which he sent into the midst of Egypt (135:9). Even if we admit them to have been of the same kind

as phenomena natural to the country, their miraculous character would be shown by the unparalleled degree to which the affliction reached; in their coming and going at the command of Moses as the agent of Jehovah; and in the exemption of the Israelites from the general calamity. In respect to the theory of natural explanations of these plagues the following is timely: "The *Christliche Welt*, of Leipzig, No. 45, contains an article entitled *Die Plagen Aegyptens*, in which the author, a physician and many years a resident of Cairo, gives the result of his observations of present facts as they illustrate the account given of the Egyptian plagues in the Book of Genesis. . . . Naturally this report aims, first of all, at a glorification of Jahweh; yet his account of the wondrous doings of Israel's God is grounded on the actual climatic conditions of the country. Modern research and observations enable us to understand intelligently the origin and progress of each plague as resulting from a state of affairs that actually exists in Egypt every year down to our own day. Indeed we can go further and say that if it ever should happen that *all* of these plagues should occur in the course of one winter—and only of this season can we think here—they would occur in exactly the order in which they are reported in Exodus" (*N. Y. Independent*, December 10, 1896). (2) **Design.** As we have already said, the plagues had for their ultimate object the liberation of Egypt; but there were probably other ends contemplated: 1. On Moses, tending to educate and discipline him for the great work on which he was about to enter; to give him confidence in Jehovah, and courage in obeying him. 2. Upon the Israelites, impressing them with God's care for them and his great power exercised in their behalf. 3. Upon the Egyptians, convincing them of the advantage of casting in their lot with Israel. 4. In demonstrating to Egypt, Israel, and other nations the vanity of Egypt's gods (Exod. 12:12). (3) **The Egyptian imitations.** The question arises whether these imitations were real miracles performed through the agency of evil spirits or tricks of legerdemain? It is certainly more conformable to scriptural modes of expression, and therefore more likely to be true, to consider these miracles real; and that the magicians were the instruments of supernatural powers of evil, which at any crisis in the history of redemption always condense their energies. On the other hand it may be said that the magicians did nothing more than the jugglers of India easily do today. It must be noted that they failed to perform a miracle on the instant, as in the case of the plague of the lice, when no time was allowed them. They were also unable to remove the infliction, or even exempt themselves therefrom. *See* Moses, Pharaoh.

Plain, a level stretch of land. Several Hebrew words are translated thus. The word plain in Judg. 11:33 answers more to our word "meadow," Heb. *'ābēl*. This term occurs widely in composition as *'abel meholah* (Judg. 7:22), *'abel shittim* (Num. 33:49, etc.). The Heb. *biqā'* denotes a wide expanse of level land, usually between mountain ranges, as the

Plain of Shinar (Gen. 11:2) and the Valley of Megiddo (II Chron. 35:22; Zech. 12:11). Sometimes it is rendered valley (cf. Neh. 6:2; Isa. 40:4). The Hebrew word *kĭkkät, circle* denotes the region "round about any place," as the southern part of the Dead Sea (Gen. 13:10-12) before the destruction of the cities of Sodom and Gommorah. The uniform word for plain is *mĭshŏr* (Deut. 3:10; Josh. 13:9; Zech. 4:7, etc.). **Figurative.** "My foot standeth in an even place" (Psa. 26:4); "lead me in a plain path" (27:11), that is, one free from obstacles over which one might stumble. It is used figuratively for righteousness as "Thou shalt judge the people with righteousness" (Psa. 67:4). *M. F. U.*

Plains of Palestine. *See* Palestine.

Plaiting. *See* Hair.

Plane (Heb. *măqṣū'äh*, a *scraper*), a carpenter's tool, perhaps a *chisel* or *carving* tool (Isa. 44: 13). *See* Handicraft.

Plane Tree, the rendering in the R. V. of the Hebrew ('*armān, naked*, Gen. 30:37; Ezek. 31:8). It is improperly rendered in the A. V. "chestnut" (*q. v.*). The plane tree is frequently found in Palestine, on the coast and in the north. Shedding its outward bark it came by its Hebrew name, *smooth* or *naked*. The Oriental plane trees (*Plantus orientalis*) grows to a height of some 85 feet and has palmately lobed leaves like the sycamore maple. The Oriental plane is found in S. Europe and W. Asia. It grows well on hillsides beside streams and is planted artificially in many places.

Plank (Heb. '*ēṣ*), something made of *wood*, as a plant (I Kings 6:15; Ezek. 41:25, 26).

Plant. *See* Agriculture, Garden, Vegetable Kingdom.

Plaster. The special uses of plaster mentioned in Scripture are:

1. When a house was infected with "leprosy," the priest was to take away the part of the wall infected, and, putting in other stones, to plaster the house with fresh mortar (Lev. 14:42, 48).

2. The words of the law were ordered to be engraved on Mount Ebal on stones which had been previously coated with plaster (Deut. 27:2, 4; Josh. 8:32). The process here mentioned was probably of a similar kind to that adopted in Egypt for receiving bas-reliefs. The wall was first made smooth, and its interstices, if necessary, filled up with plaster. When the figures had been drawn, and the stone adjacent cut away so as to leave them in relief, a coat of lime whitewash was laid on, and followed by one of varnish after the painting of the figures was complete.

3. It was probably a similar coating of cement on which the fatal letters were traced by the mystic hand "on the plaster of the wall" of Belshazzar's palace at Babylon (Dan. 5:5). *See* Lime, Mortar, Plaster in article Mineral Kingdom.

Plaster, Medicinal (Heb. *märäḥ*, to *soften* by rubbing), to anoint with healing salve or similar substance (Isa. 38:21).

Platter. Figurative. "To make clean the outside of the cup or *platter*," while it remained unclean within (Matt. 23:25, 26; Luke 11: 39), is a symbol of hypocrisy. *See* Dish.

Play. *See* Games, Music.

Pledge. *See* Hostages, Loan.

Ple'iades (plē'yà-dēz; *Kĭmäh, heap, cluster*, Job 9:9; 38:31; Amos 5:8, A. V. "seven stars"), a constellation of seven large and other smaller stars in the eastern sky, found in Taurus (the Bull), more particularly in the shoulder of the animal.

Plow, Plough. Egypt, probably with truth, claims the honor of inventing the plow. It was entirely of wood, of very simple form, as it is still in that country. It consisted of a share, two handles, and a pole or beam, the last being inserted into the lower end of the stilt, or the base of the handles, and was strengthened by a rope connecting it with the heel. It had no coulter, but was probably shod with metal. It was drawn by two oxen, guided and driven by the plowman with a long goad.

The plow now used in Palestine differs in some respects from that described above. It is lightly built, with the least possible skill or expense, consisting of two poles, which cross each other near the ground. The pole nearer the oxen is fastened to the yoke, while the other serves, the one end as the handle, the other as the plowshare. With these frail plows and tiny oxen, the farmer must wait until the ground is saturated and softened (Jer. 14:4), however late the season may be. Then they cannot sow and plow in more than half an acre per day, and few average so much (Thomson, *Land and Book*, i, p. 208). Thomson thinks that the twelve yoke of oxen (I Kings 19:19) were each yoked to a plow.

Figurative. Plowing was a symbol of: Repentance (Jer. 4:3); peace and prosperity (Isa. 2:4; Mic. 4:3); desolation (Jer. 26:18); of the labor of ministers (I Cor. 9:10); "the plowers *plow* upon my back" (Psa. 129:3) is a figure of scourging; keeping the hand upon the plow is a sign of constancy (Luke 9:62). "The *plowing* of the wicked is sin" (Prov. 21:4) is better rendered *the light of* the wicked, that in which they glory (the same Hebrew word (*nîr*), standing for plow and light.)

Plowman (Heb. '*ĭkkär*, Isa. 61:5) is not only a plowman, but a *farmer* in general. Among the Hebrews the rich and noble in the cultivation of the soil did not always put themselves upon a level with their servants; but it was not considered a degradation to put their hand to the plow, or otherwise occasionally join in agricultural labor (I Sam. 11:7; I Kings 19:19).

Plowshare (Heb. '*ēth*, Isa. 2:4; Joel 3:10; Mic. 4:3), the iron tip of the plow where it enters the earth. To beat a plowshare into a sword is symbolic of war; the reverse of peace.

Plumb Line (Heb. '*ănäk*, or **Plummet** (Heb. *mĭshqĕlĕth*), a line, to one end of which is attached a weight. Its use by masons was early known to the Egyptians, and is ascribed to their king Menes about 2900 B. C.

Figurative. A wall built with a plumb line is a perpendicular wall, a wall built with mechanical correctness and solidity. The wall built with a plumb line is a figurative representation of the kingdom of God in Israel, as a firm and well-constructed building. To hold a plumb line to a building may represent the act of construction; or it may be applied to a building in judgment as to the propriety of destroying it (II Kings 21:13; Amos 7:7, 8). The expression, "Judgment also will I lay to the line, and righteousness to the plummet" (Isa. 28:17), is a figure by which what Jehovah is about to do is depicted as a building which he is erecting, and which he will carry out, so far as his despisers are concerned, on no other plan than that of strict retribution. To carry a plummet in the hand (Zech. 4:10) is a sign of being engaged in the work of building or of superintending the erection of a building.

Poch′ereth (pŏk′ê-rĕth; *binder*). The "children" of Pochereth were among "Solomon's servants" who returned from the captivity with Zerubbabel (Ezra 2:57; Neh. 7: 9), B. C. before 536. The R. V. and R. S. V. render Pochereth-hazzebaim (pŏk-ĕ-rĕth-hă-zĕ-bā′ĭm; *binder of the gazelles*) translating Pochereth of Zebaim (A. V.) as Pochereth-hazzebaim.

Poet (Gr. *poiētēs*, a *performer*). This term occurs in Acts 17:28, in which Paul quotes from *Aratus* of Cilicia, in the 3d century, and *Cleanthes* of Mysia, "We are also his offspring." From this he argues the absurdity of worshiping idols.

Poetry, O. T. Modern scholarship has shown that large sections of the Hebrew Bible are poetic besides the three poetical books—Psalms, Proverbs and Job, recognized by the Massoretes. Many scholars have studied Hebrew versification in the past 200 years. These studies have been aided by extensive archaeological findings in Assyrian, Egyptian, Babylonian and Canaanite (Ugaritic) poetic literature. This considerable non-poetic literature has furnished an illuminating background for the study of Bible poetry and demonstrates that the poetry of the Hebrews shares many of the same forms and features of the poetry of neighboring peoples.

1. **Nature of Hebrew Poetry.** Hebrew verse is characterized by parallelism. This is a type of sense rhythm constituting thought arrangement rather than word arrangement. This basic phenomenon of Hebrew versification was first clearly set forth by Robert Lowth in 1753. (*See* Lowth's *De sacra poesi Hebraeorum praelectiones academicae*, English translation, 1847). Lowth distinguished three chief types of parallelism: a. *Synonymous parallelism*. This is a repetition of the same thought with equivalent expressions, the first line or stich reinforcing the second, giving a distich or couplet:

"He that sitteth in the heavens shall laugh;
The Lord will have them in derision" (Psa. 2:4).

b. *Antithetic parallelism* consists of the repetition of a contrasting thought in the second line to accentuate the thought of the first:

"The young lions do lack and suffer hunger:
But they that seek Jehovah shall not want any good thing." (Psa. 34:10).

c. *Synthetic parallelism* is a building up of thought, with each succeeding line adding to the first:

"And he shall be like a tree planted by the rivers of water,

That bringeth forth fruit in its season,
Whose leaf shall not wither
And whatsoever he doeth shall prosper" (Psa. 1:3).

This basic pattern of Hebrew poetry conveys thoughts pleasing to the mind and produces a musical cadence pleasing to the ear. There are numbers of variations in parallelism discovered since Lowth's day, such as *inverted parallelism* (Psa. 137:5, 6; Psa. 30:8-10). This occurs in a quatrain when the first line is parallel to the fourth instead of the second and the intervening lines are parallel. G. B. Gray in his *Forms of Hebrew Poetry*, 1915, made important advances in the study of parallelism. He distinguished many complete and incomplete parallelisms.

2. **Hebrew poetry is highly figurative.** The Hebrew language itself is resonant, rhythmic and musical, even in prose. Its vocabulary is vivid. It abounds in figures of speech such as alliteration, personification, hyperbole, metaphor, simile, metonymy and assonance. The difference between Hebrew prose and poetry is not always easy to define. In poetry the rhythms are confined within certain limits, whereas in prose they are absolutely free.

3. **Hebrew poetry is rhythmic.** Scholarly researches have shown that Hebrew versification is not qualitative; that is, it does not count syllables but depends upon a number of accents. Scholars have differentiated *lyric meter* to be two plus two as in Canticles; *epic* or *didactic*, three plus three, as in Job or Proverbs; *dirge* or *qinah*, three plus two, as in Lamentations. However, too often scholars have assumed that the ancient Hebrews had definite poetic laws and have superimposed such an artificial prosody on Hebrew poetry. This mistake has resulted in wholesale emendations. It must be concluded that Hebrew poetry is rhythmical, but not strictly metrical. Hebrew poets did not bind themselves by rigid rules. There is evidence also of stanzas or strophes but scholars need to beware of superimposing their own artificial divisions upon ancient Hebrew poetry. Research in this field promises to yield more light on Hebrew verse. M. F. U.

Poison, the burning venom of poisonous serpents (Deut. 32:24; Psa. 58:4; 140:3) is the Hebrew rendering of *hēmāh*, meaning "heat." The Greek word *ios* refers also to the serpent's poisonous venom (Rom. 3:13; Jas. 3:8).

Pole (Heb. *nēs*), in Num. 21:8, 9, is used of the pole upon which the brazen serpent was placed; elsewhere for the flag or standard itself, "sign," "banner," etc., as elsewhere.

Poll (Heb. *gŭlgōlĕth*, a *skull*, and so rendered in Judg. 9:53; II Kings 9:35), the *head* (Num. 3:47). Cutting the hair or shaving the head is rendered by the verb "to poll," from the Hebrew (*găzăz*, to *cut off; gălăh*, to *be bald;* and *kăsăh*, to *shear*).

Pollution (Gr. *'alisgēma, contamination*), a Hellenistic word (Acts 15:20). The pollution here referred to has reference to meat sacrificed to idols. After the sacrifice was concluded, a portion of the victim was given to the priests, the rest being eaten in honor of the gods, either in the temples or a private house. Some salted the flesh and laid it up for future use, while others sold it in the "shambles" (I Cor. 10:25, comp. 8:1, sq.). Of course this flesh, having been offered to idols, was an abomination to the Jews; and any use of it was thought to infect the user with idolatry. The Council of Jerusalem directed that converts decline invitations to such feasts, and refrain from the use of such meat, that no offense might be given (Acts 15:28, sq.).

Pol'lux (pŏl'ŭks). *See* Castor and Pollux under Gods, False.

Polygamy. *See* Marriage, 1.

Pomegranate. Representations of pomegranates, in blue, purple, and scarlet, ornamented the hem of the robe of the ephod (Exod. 28: 33, 34) (*see* High Priest, Dress of), and carved figures of the pomegranate adorned the tops of the pillars in Solomon's temple (*q. v.*). The "spiced wine of the juice of the pomegranate" (Cant. 8:2) is made at the present day in the East as it was in the days of Solomon.

    Figurative. The liquid ruby color of the pulp of this fruit is alluded to in the figurative description of the beautiful complexion of the bride (Cant. 4:3). *See* Vegetable Kingdom.

Pommel (Heb. *gŭlläh*, *round*), the ball, or round ornament, on the capital of a column (II Chron. 4:12, 13; "bowl" in I Kings 7:41, 42).

Pon'tius Pi'late (pŏn'shŭs pī'lat). *See* Pilate.

Pon'tus (pŏn'tŭs; the *sea*), a large district in the north of Asia Minor, extending along the coast of the Pontus Euxinus, from which circumstance the name was derived. It is three times mentioned in the New Testament (Acts 2:9, 10; 18:2; I Pet. 1:1). All these passages agree in showing that there were many Jewish residents in the district. As to the annals of Pontus, the one brilliant passage of its history is the life of the great Mithridates, a dynasty of kings which ruled from c. 337 to 63 B. C. Under Nero the whole region was made a Roman province, bearing the name of Pontus.

Pool.

    1. **Pond** (Heb. *'ăgăm*, Isa. 14:23; 35:7).

    2. **Pool** (Heb. *bᵉräkäh, benediction*, and so *prosperity*), a favor, or gift, sent from God. "Who passing through the valley of Baca (i. e., *weeping*) make it a well; the rain also filleth the pools" (Psa. 84:6). Through such valleys, by reason of their dry and barren condition, the worshippers often had to pass to Jerusalem. A kind providence might turn these valleys into pools by refreshing rains, so the grace of God refreshes and revives the hearts of his people, and instead of sorrows they have "rivers of delight" (36:8; 46:4).

    3. *Collection* of water, Exod. 7:19, a gathering of water, and so rendered in Gen. 1:10. (Heb. *mĭkwĕh*).

    4. A *diving place*, only in John 5:2, 4, 7; 9:7, 11. (Gr. *kolumbēthra*).

    The following are the principal pools (*reservoirs*) mentioned in Scripture:

    1. **Pool of Hezekiah** (II Kings 20:20). It was a basin opened by King Hezekiah in the city, and fed by a water course. In II Chron. 32:30 it is stated that "this same Hezekiah also stopped the upper water course of Gihon, and brought it straight down to the west side

of the city of David," i. e., by a subterranean channel into the city of David. This pool, called by the Arabs *Birket el-Hammâm*, is pointed out by tradition in the northwest part of the modern city, not far east of the Jaffa gate.

    2. **The Upper and Lower Pool.** The "upper" pool (Isa. 7:3; 36:2; II Kings 18:17) lying near the fuller's field, and on the road to it, outside the city. The lower pool is named in Isa. 22:9. They are generally known as the upper and lower pools of Gihon. It supports the identification of these with "the upper and lower pools" that there are no other similar or corresponding reservoirs in the neighborhood; and the western position of the upper pool suits well the circumstances mentioned in Scripture (Isa. 36:2). It may be added that a trustworthy tradition places the fuller's field westward of the city.

    3. **The Old Pool** (Isa. 22:11), not far from the double wall ("two walls"). This double wall was near the royal garden (II Kings 25:4; Jer. 39:4), which must be sought in the southeast of the city, near the fountain of Siloam (Neh. 3:15).

    4. **The Kings Pool** (Neh. 2:14) is thought to be found in the fountain of the Virgin Mary, on the east of Ophel (Robinson, ii, 102, 149), and is perhaps the same as the pool of Solomon. *See* Gibeon, Hebron, Samaria, Solomon, Bethesda, and Siloam for the pools under those names.

Poor. In the Hebrew and Greek, as in the English language, there were a number of words to express the condition of being in need. The Scriptures frequently mention the poor, and teach that no inconsiderable part of the duty required of believers under both Testaments has respect to the treatment accorded to the poor. No merit, however, is given to the assumption of poverty; and the Mosaic law takes every precaution to prevent poverty. Its extreme form of want and beggary was ever represented as the just recompense of profligacy and thriftlessness (Psa. 37:25; 109:20; Prov. 20:4; 24:34).

    Mosaic Enactments. It was contemplated from the first that there would be those among the covenant people who would be in circumstances calling for sympathy and aid (Deut. 15:11). Negatively, the poor man was to have no advantage over others on the ground of his poverty (Exod. 23:3); but neither, on the other hand, was his judgment on that account to be wrested (v. 6). Among the special enactments in his favor the following must be mentioned: (1) The right of gleaning (Lev. 19:9, 10; Deut. 24:19, 21). (2) From the produce of the land in sabbatical years the poor and the stranger was to have their portion (Exod. 23:11; Lev. 25:6). (3) Reentry upon land in the jubilee year, with the limitation as to town homes (Lev. 25:25-30). (4) Prohibition of usury, and of retention of pledges (Lev. 25:35, 37; Exod. 22:25-27, etc.). (5) Permanent bondage forbidden, and manumission of Hebrew bondmen or bondwomen enjoined in the sabbatical and jubilee years (Deut. 15:12-15; Lev. 25:39-42, 47-54). (6) Portions from the tithes to be shared by the poor after the Levites (Deut. 14:28; 26:12,

13). (7) The poor to partake in entertainments at the feasts of Weeks and Tabernacles (Deut. 16:11, 14; *see* Neh. 8:10). (8) Daily payment of wages (Lev. 19:13). Principles similar to those laid down by Moses are inculcated in the New Testament, as Luke 3:11; 14:13; Acts 6:1; Gal. 2:10; James 2:15. In later times mendicancy, which does not appear to have been contemplated by Moses, became frequent.

Poor in Sprit, the spiritually poor, i. e., those who feel, as a matter of consciousness, that they are in a miserable, unhappy condition; those *who feel within themselves the opposite of having enough, and of wanting nothing in a moral point of view* (Meyer, *Com.*, in loc.).

Poplar. *See* Vegetable Kingdom.

Por'atha (pôr'á-thá; Old Pers. *liberal, bounteous*), one of the ten sons of Haman slain by the Jews in the palace at Shushan (Esth. 9:8), B. C. about 509.

Porch.

1. **Vestibule, hall** (Heb. *'ūläm*, I Chron. 28: 11), the entrance hall of a building (Ezek. 40:7, 48), a pillar hall (I Kings 7:6), a throne hall (v. 7), and the veranda surrounding a court (Ezek. 41:15). It is especially applied to the vestibule of the temple (I Kings, chaps. 6 and 7; Joel 2:17). "The porch of the Lord" (II Chron. 15:8; 29:17) seems to stand for the temple itself.

2. **Veranda-chamber** (Heb. *mĭsdᵉrōn*, Judg. 3:23), strictly a vestibule, was probably a sort of veranda chamber in the works of Solomon, open in front and at the sides, but capable of being inclosed with awnings or curtains. It was perhaps a corridor or colonnade connecting the principal rooms of the house.

3. The porch (Matt. 26:71, Gr. *pulōn*), may have been the passage from the street into the first court of the house in which, in Eastern houses, is the *mustabah*, or stone bench, for the porter or persons waiting, and where also the master of the house often receives visitors.

4. **A colonnade or portico** (Gr. *stoa*) such as that of Bethesda, and that of the temple called Solomon's porch (John 5:2; 10:23; Acts 3:11; 5:12). Josephus described the porticoes, or cloisters, which surrounded the temple of Solomon, and also the royal portico.

Por'cius (pôr'shĭ-ŭs), (*Festus*). *See* Festus.

Porcupine, Porpoise. *See* Animal Kingdom.

Port (Heb. *shă'ăr*, Neh. 2:13), elsewhere rendered "gate" (*q. v.*).

Porter (Heb. *shō'ēr*, from *shă'ăr*, a *gate;* Gr. *thurōros*). As used in the A. V., *porter* has always the sense of door or gatekeeper. In the later books of the Old Testament, written after the building of the temple, the term is applied to those Levites who had charge of the various entrances (I Chron. 9:17; 15:18; II Chron. 23:19, etc.). In I Chron. 15:23, 24, we have the rendering "doorkeeper," and in John 18:16 "the damsel that kept the door." In II Sam. 18:26; II Kings 7:10, 11, we meet with the porter of the city gates (comp. Acts 12:13); and a porter seems to have been usually stationed at the doors of sheepfolds. The porters of the temple, who were *guards* as well, numbered four thousand in David's time (I Chron. 23:5), were divided into

courses (26:1-19), and had their posts assigned them by lot (v. 13). They entered upon their service on the Sabbath day, and remained a week (II Kings 11:5-7; those mentioned in vers. 4, 10, sq., are probably the king's bodyguard). *See* Watch.

Portion.

1. An allowance, as of food, clothing, etc. (Gen. 14:24; 47:22; Neh. 11:23; I Sam. 1:5; Psa. 17:14; Prov. 31:15; Isa. 53:12; Dan. 1:8, sq.). The command, "Go your way, eat the fat, and drink the sweet, and send portions unto them for whom nothing is prepared; for this day is holy unto our Lord" (Neh. 8:10) has reference to a custom, still existing in the East, of sending a portion of a feast to those who cannot well attend it, especially their relations, and those in mourning as well as in times of joy (II Sam. 11:8, 10; Esth. 9:19).

2. One's lot, destiny, etc. (Job 3:22; 20:29; 27:13; Psa. 11:6; Isa. 17:14); the result of effort (Eccles. 2:10).

3. Part of an estate, one's inheritance (*q. v.*). It may be that the expression, "The Lord is the portion of my inheritance" (Psa. 16:5; 119:57; Lam. 3:24) includes all the other meanings.

Possessed with Devils. *See* Demoniac.

Post. 1. (Heb. *räṣ*, a *runner*), primarily the person who conveyed any message with speed; and subsequently the means of regular communication. Reference to such communication in Scripture: Job declares, "My days are swifter than a post" (9:25, literally a *runner*), showing that at a very early time persons possessing swiftness of foot were so commonly employed by great men as couriers as to render such an allusion both intelligent and appropriate. Complete establishments of such formed a part of royal establishments (II Chron. 30:6, 10). Jeremiah shows that a regular postal service of this sort existed in his time (Jer. 51:31, "And one post shall run to meet another"), clearly implying that posts were wont to be maintained by relays of special messengers regularly organized for their work. The same sort of postal communication is referred to in Esth. 3:15; 8:13, 14.

2. Post, usually rendered "threshold" (Heb. *săph*) as in II Chron. 3:7; Ezek. 41:16; Amos 9:1. The word translated "post," however, usually refers to the upright timber at the side of a door (I Kings 6:33).

Pot, a term of very wide application, including

371. Painted Jar from the City of Lachish in Palestine

many sorts of vessels, the most common designation being Heb. *sîr*, a vessel of various sizes and shapes (Exod. 38:3; II Kings 4:38), and made of different materials, both earthenware and metal. An earthenware vessel for stewing or seething (Heb. *herês*) is mentioned (Psa. 22:15; Prov. 26:23) as well as a culinary vessel (Heb. *dûd*, Job 41:20; Psa. 81:6). In the N. T. a vessel for holding water of stone or hard earthenware is referred to in John 2:6 f; 4:8.

Potentate (Gr. *dunastês*, of *great authority*), the title applied to God (I Tim. 6:15, "the only potentate;" comp. Rom. 16:27), expressive of his transcendent power and authority.

Pot'iphar (pŏt'ĭ-fẽr; Egpyt., *whom Re*, i. e., the sun-god, *has given*, contraction of *Potipherah*, *q. v.*), an Egyptian and an officer ("captain of the guard") of Pharaoh. When Joseph was taken to Egypt Potiphar purchased him of the Midianite merchants. So favorably impressed did he become of the ability and fidelity of Joseph, that he made him overseer over his house, and committed all his possessions to his care. Upon the accusation of his wife Potiphar cast Joseph into prison (Gen. 39:1-20, B. C. c. 1890). After this we hear no more of Potiphar, unless, which is not likely, he was the chief of the executioners afterward mentioned.

Potiph'erah (pŏ-tĭf'ẽr-à), or **Potiphe'rah**, an Egyptian and priest of On (Heliopolis), whose daughter Asenath was married to Joseph (Gen. 41:45, 50; 46:20, B. C. about c. 1870). *See* Potiphar.

Potsherd (Heb. *hĕrês*), a fragment of an earthen vessel. Scraping the boil (*see* Job 2:8) with a potsherd will not only relieve the intolerable itching, but also remove the matter.

    Figurative. The potsherd is used as a figure of anything mean and contemptible (Isa. 45:9); also for that which is very dry (Psa. 22:15). Hypocritical professions of friendship are likened to "a potsherd covered with silver dross" (Prov. 26:23). It is worthless pretense.

Pottage (Heb. *nāzîd*, something *boiled*, Gen. 25:29, 34). The price paid Jacob by Esau in consideration of transferring his birthright. In v. 34 we read that it was made of lentils (*q. v.*).

Potter. *See* Handicrafts.

Potter's Field, a piece of ground which was purchased by the priests (Matt. 27:7) with the thirty pieces of silver rejected by Judas, and converted into a burial place for Jews not belonging to the city; Matthew adducing this (v. 9) as a fulfillment of an ancient prediction. According to Acts 1:18, the purchase is made by Judas himself, an idiom of Scripture by which an action is sometimes said to be *done* by a person who was the *occasion* of its being done. What that prediction was, and who made it, is not, however, at all clear. Matthew names Jeremiah; but there is no passage in the Book of Jeremiah, as we possess it, resembling that which he gives; and that in Zechariah (11:12) which is usually supposed to be alluded to, has only a very imperfect likeness to it. Four explanations suggest themselves: 1. That the evangelist unintentionally substituted the name of Jeremiah for that of Zechariah, at the same time altering the passage to suit his immediate object. 2. That this portion of the Book of Zechariah was in

the time of Matthew attributed to Jeremiah. 3. That the reference is to some passage of Jeremiah which has been lost from its place in his book, and exists only in the evangelist. Some support is afforded to this view by the fact that potters and the localities occupied by them are twice alluded to by Jeremiah. Its partial correspondence with Zech. 11:12, 13, is no argument against its having at one time formed a part of the prophecy of Jeremiah; for it is well known to every student of the Bible that similar correspondences are continually found in the prophets. *See*, for instance, Jer. 48:45; comp. with Num. 21:27, 28; 24:17; Jer. 49:27; comp. with Amos 1:4 (Smith, *Dict.*, s. v.). 4. "That it is to be regarded as a very old copyist's error, of a more ancient date than any of the critical helps that have come down to us" (Luther, *Com.*, on Zech., 1528).

    Meyer (*Com.*, on Matt. 27:9) says: "According to the historical sense of Zechariah, the prophet, acting in Jehovah's name, resigns his office of shepherd over Ephraim to Ephraim's own ruin; and having requested his wages, consisting of thirty pieces of silver, to be paid him, he casts the money, as being God's property, into the *treasury of the temple*." Accordingly Meyer thinks "into the treasury" ought to be read *'el* and not *'el hăyōṣēr* "to the potter." *See* Akeldama.

Potter's Gate, a gate of Jerusalem (Jer. 19:2) not mentioned elsewhere by this name. It is probably identical with the Valley Gate leading to the valley of *Hinnom* (*q. v.*), if not with the Dung Gate (Neh. 2:13; 3:13, sq.; 12:31), through which one went from the city southward. Potters' works seem to have been located in its vicinity. "The 'gate of potsherds' (A. V. "east gate"), so called from the many potsherds thrown down before it" (Orelli, *Com.*, in loc.).

Pound. *See* Metrology, IV, 2.

Poverty. *See* Poor.

Powders (Heb. *'ăbāqāh*, *dust*). Powdered spices, used for perfume and incense (Cant. 3:6).

Power, or the ability of performing, belongs essentially to God, who is All-powerful, the Omnipotent. Power has the sense of: *Ability*, *strength* (Gen. 31:6; Psa. 22:20; Isa. 37:27, etc.); *Right*, *privilege*, or *dignity* (John 1:12; Acts 5:4; I Cor. 7:37; 9:4, sq., Gr. *dunamis*); *absolute authority* (Matt. 28:18, same Greek as above) the *exertion* or *act* of power, as of the Holy Ghost (Eph. 1:19, Gr. *kratos*).

Praetorium (prē-tō'rĭ-ŭm). *See* Pretorium.

Praise, the rendering of a number of Hebrew and Greek words. Praise is an expression of approval or admiration; of gratitude and devotion for blessings received. When directed toward men, it should never descend to fulsome flattery; nor should the love of it become so great as to hush the voice of conscience and of duty. While without it there will be no sense of reproach, when it has gone beyond its proper place, instead of improving, it corrupts.

    Praise of God is the acknowledging of his perfections, works, and benefits. Praise and thanksgiving are generally considered as synonymous, yet some distinguish them thus: Praise properly terminates in God, on account of his natural excellencies and perfections, and is that act of devotion by which we confess and admire his several attributes; but *thanksgiving* is a more contracted duty, and imports only a grateful sense and acknowledgment of past mercies. We praise God for all his glorious acts of every kind, that regard either us or other men; . . . but we thank him, properly speaking, for the instances of his goodness alone, and for such only of these as we ourselves are some way concerned in.

Prayer. 1. **Scriptural Terms.** The following Hebrew terms are rendered *prayer* in the A. V.: 1. *T*ᵉ*fĭllăh*, in general, supplication to God (Psa. 65:2; 80:4; Isa. 1:15; Job 16:17, etc.); also intercession, supplication for another (II Kings 19:4; Isa. 37:4; Jer. 7:16; 11:14). 2. *Pălăl*, to *judge*, and then *to interpose as umpire, mediator* (Gen. 20:7; Deut. 9:20; I Sam. 7:5; Job 42:8), with the general sense of prayer (Psa. 5:2; I Sam. 1:26; II Sam. 7:27, etc.). 3. *Rib*, to *strive*, and so *to contend before a judge, to plead a cause* (Job 15:4; Psa. 55:17; Isa. 1:17, "plead for the widow;" Isa. 51:22, "God that pleadeth the cause of his people"). 4. *Athăr, to burn incense*, thence to *pray* to God (Job 33:26); the prayers of the righteous being likened to incense (Rev. 5:8). 5. *Hălăh*, to *caress*, to *stroke one's face*, to strive to please; spoken of one who entreats God's favor (Zech. 7:2; 8:21, 22). 6. *Lăhăsh*, to *whisper, prayer* uttered in a low voise (Isa. 26:16). *Lăhăsh* is a quiet whispering prayer (like the whispering forms of incantation in ch. 3:3); sorrow renders speechless in the long run; and a consciousness of sin crushes so completely that a man does not dare to address God aloud (29:4).

The following Greek terms are rendered prayer: 1. *Deēsis*, prayer for particular benefits. 2. *Proseuchē*, prayer in general, not restricted as respects its contents. 3. *Enteuxis* (I Tim. 4:5), confiding access to God. In combination, *deēsis* gives prominence to the expression of personal need, *proseuchē* to the element of devotion, *Enteuxis* to that of childlike confidence, by representing prayer as the heart's converse with God. 4. *Euchē*, which occurs only once in the New Testament in the sense of a prayer (James 5:15), but in this noun and its verb, the notion of the vow, of the dedicated thing is more commonly found than that of prayer. The two other occasions on which the word is found (Acts 18:18; 21:23), bear out this remark (Trench, *Syn.*, ii, p. 1). 5. *'Aitēma, petition* (Phil. 4:6, *requests;* I John 5:15, A. V. *petitions*).

2. **Scriptural History.** Prayer, constituting as it does the most direct expression of religious feeling and consciousness, has been, from the very first, the principal means by which men, created in the image of God, have evinced their attitude toward him; and from the earliest times, ever since in the days of Enoch men began to call upon the name of the Lord (Gen. 4:26), it has formed an integral part of the public worship of God. The patriarchs and pious Israelites in all ages have expressed the feelings and dispositions of their hearts by praise, thanksgiving, prayer, and intercession before God (Gen. 18:23, sq.; 20:17; 24:12; 25:21; 32:10, sq.; Exod. 32:11, sq.; I Sam. 1:10; 2-1, sq.; 8:6; 12:23; I

Kings 8:22, sq.; 17:20, sq.; II Kings 4:33; 19:15; Jonah 2:2; 4:2; Dan. 6:10, sq.; 9:3, sq., etc.). We find also that wherever the patriarchs erected an altar for worship, they did so with the view of calling upon the name of the Lord (Gen. 12:8; 13:4; 21:33).

The law did not prescribe any prayer for public worship, except the confession of sin on the great day of atonement (see Festivals, and Lev. 16:21), and the thanksgiving on the occasion of the offering of the firstlings and tithes (Deut. 26:3, sq.; ch. 13, sq.), yet it is certain that in Israel no act of worship was unaccompanied by prayer. It was not expressly mentioned in the law because it not only happened that prayer was a regular accompaniment of laying the hand on the victim in sacrifice, but also because it was usual for the congregation, or the Levites as representing it (I Chron. 23:30), to offer up prayer morning and evening while the incense was being burned (Luke 1:10). As early as David's time we hear of private prayer being offered three times a day (Psa. 55:17), which subsequently became an established practice (Dan. 6:11), the hours being at the time of the morning sacrifice, about the third hour (Acts 2:15), midday, about the sixth hour (10:9), and at the time of the evening sacrifice, about the ninth hour (Dan. 9:21; Acts 3:1).

Grace, before and after meals, was an ancient practice, although we find no explicit testimony regarding it earlier than in the New Testament (Matt. 15:36; John 6:11; Acts 27:35). How earnest and fervent the prayers of pious Israelites were may be seen from the Psalms and many other parts of the Old Testament. It degenerated into mere lip service at so early a period as to provoke the censure of the older prophets (Isa. 1:15; 29:13). Later, prayer seems to have degenerated into a mere performance, especially among the Pharisees (Matt. 6:5, 7). As a rule the Israelites prayed in a solitary room, especially the upper chamber (Dan. 6:11; Judith 8:5; Tobit 3:12; Acts 1:13), in elevated places and mountains with the view of being alone (I Kings 18:42; Matt. 14:23; Mark 6:46; Luke 6:12). If near the sanctuary, they offered their prayers in the court (I Sam. 2:1; Isa. 16:7; Luke 18:10; Acts 3:1), with faces turned toward the holy of holies (Psa. 5:3; I Kings 8:38); in which direction it was the practice to turn the face during prayer, even when at a distance from the temple (II Chron. 6:34; Dan. 6:11).

The posture. This was generally standing (I Sam. 1:26; Dan. 9:20; Matt. 6:5, etc.), but sometimes, as expressive of deeper devotion, in a kneeling attitude (I Kings 8:54; II Chron. 6:13; Ezra 9:5; Dan. 6:10; Luke 22:41, etc.), or with the head bowed down to the ground (Neh. 8:6). In both cases the hands were uplifted, and spread toward heaven or in the direction of the holy of holies (I Kings 8:22; Neh. 8:7; Lam. 2:19; 3:41; Psa. 28:2, etc.). In cases of deep, penitential prayer it was usual to smite the breast with the hand (Luke 18:13) and to bend the head toward the bosom (Psa. 35:13; comp. I Kings 18:42).

After the sacrificial worship was discontinued prayer came entirely to occupy the place of sacrifice. Very minute regulations regarding the order and the different sorts of prayer, as well as the outward posture, are given in the Talmud. The ancient rabbis and

372. Postures in Prayer

their followers regarded the wearing of phylacteries (*q. v.*) as essential to prayer.

3. **Christian Doctrine.** Prayer is the expression of man's dependence upon God for all things. What habitual reverence is to praise, the habitual sense of dependence is to prayer. "Prayer, or communion with God, is not reckoned among the means of grace technically so called. It is regarded rather as the concomitant of the others. But, while it is undeniably true that prayer is a condition of the efficacy of other means, it is itself and alone a means of grace" (Pope, *Syst. Theol.*, iii, 298). And it is a means of grace that has large value, for it affords the privilege of close communion with God, especially when one is alone with him in its supplications. While, on the one hand, there arises a deep sense of need, of helplessness, and unworthiness, there comes also an assurance of the divine fullness and love, which enlarges our petitions and brings confidence of answers to our prayers.

Requisites. Prayer requires sincerity, repentance or contrition, purpose of amendment and a good life, the spirit of consecration, faith, and submission to the will of God.

Elements of power. There are certain elements of power in prayer which have a clear and scriptural ground; fervency of mind (James 5:16). In such a prayer the mind is intensely active. The object for which we pray is grasped in all the vigor of thought and feeling. Another element of power lies in the help of the Holy Spirit. There are in Scripture clear promises of his help, and statements which mean the same thing (Zech. 12:10; Eph. 6:18). Then we have these explicit words: "likewise the Spirit also helpeth our infirmities," etc. (Rom. 8:26). . . . There are many ways in which he may thus help us. He may give us a deeper sense of our spiritual needs, clearer views of the fullness and free-

ness of the divine grace, and kindle the fervor of our supplication. We reach a deeper meaning in the words, "But the Spirit himself maketh intercession for us." He joins us in our prayers, pours his supplications into our own. Nothing less can be the meaning of these deep words. Here is the source of the glowing fervor and the effectual power of prayer. There are instances which cannot else be explained: such as the prayer of Jacob (Gen. 32:24-30), of Moses (Exod. 32:9-14), and of Elijah (James 5:17, 18). Another element of this power lies in the intercession of Christ. In his high-priestly office he presents our prayers with the incense of his own blood and the intercession of his own prayers (Rev. 8:3, 4).

4. **Objections.** The old question, "What profit should we have if we pray unto him?" (Job 21:15), is a question that continues to be asked. Those who deny the personality of God declare that it is vain to pray, for there is no God to hear our prayers. Such objectors set themselves against the common consciousness of all mankind, and may be dismissed with the question, "He that planteth the ear, shall he not hear?" (Psa. 94:9). Others admit the ability of God to hear, but they see no use in prayer, since God is so high, and his counsels far too firmly established to be ever moved by our poor petitions. We answer, God is "not far from every one of us" (Acts 17:27); and in giving man a strong instinct to pray God has virtually pledged himself to hear his prayer and to answer it (I John 5:14, 15).

Again it is urged that God is immutable, and "The idea of a supernatural providence, with answers to prayer, is the idea of a temporal agency of God above the order of nature. The objection is that such an agency is contradictory to the divine immutability. There is no issue respecting the truth of immutability. Is such an agency contradictory to this truth? An affirmative answer must reduce our Christian theism to the baldest deism. Only a false sense of immutability can require the same divine action towards nations and individuals, whatever the changes of moral conduct in them; the same toward Christian believers, whatever the changes of estate with them. A true sense of immutability requires changes of divine action in adjustment to such changes in men. It seems strange that any one who accepts the Scriptures can for a moment give place to this objection."

"Another objection is based on the divine omniscience. This objection is made specially against the efficacy of prayer. God foreknows all things, knows from eternity the state and need of every soul. Hence prayer is not necessary, nor can it have any influence upon the divine mind. These inferences are not warranted. If it were the office of prayer to give information of our wants, it is surely needless and must be useless. Prayer has no such office. It is required as the proper religious movement of a soul in its dependence and need, and thus becomes the means of God's blessings" (Miley, *Syst. Theol.*, i, p. 341, sq.).

Objection to the need of prayer on the ground of the wisdom and goodness of God— that being wise and good he will give what is good without asking, "admits but of one answer, viz., that it may be agreeable to perfect wisdom to grant that to our prayers which it would not have been agreeable to that same wisdom to have given us without praying for. A favor granted to prayer may be more apt, on that very account, to produce good effects upon the person obliged. It may be consistent with the wisdom of the Deity to withhold his favors till they are asked for, as an expedient to encourage devotion in his rational creation, in order thereby to keep up and circulate a knowledge and sense of their dependency upon him. Prayer has a natural tendency to amend the petitioner himself, and thus to bring him within the rules which the wisdom of the Deity has prescribed to the dispensation of his favors" (Paley, *Moral Philosophy*, book v, ch. 2.).

Prayer, Lord's. *See* Lord's Prayer.

Preacher, Preaching. By preaching is generally understood the delivering of a religious discourse based upon a text of Scripture.

1. **Scripture Terms.** The study of these is very interesting, showing as they do the various characteristics and purposes of preaching: (1) *To cheer with good tidings* (Heb. *bäsăr*, to *be cheerful, joyful*), as "I have preached righteousness in the great congregation" (Psa. 40:9); "to preach good tidings unto the meek," etc. (Isa. 61:1). (2) *To declare* (Heb. *qärä'*, to *call* out to), is used in the sense of proclaiming, as a herald, e. g., Sanballet accused Nehemiah of "appointing prophets to preach of thee at Jerusalem" (Neh. 6:7, announce him as king); and the same word is used (Neh. 8:8) of the Levites *reading* aloud the law and *teaching* the people (v. 9); and Jonah (3:2) was commanded to *preach* unto Nineveh, i. e., to proclaim judgment and mercy to its people. (3) *To address a public assembly* (Heb. cf. Heb. *gōhělěth*, an *assembler*). Thus Solomon is designated (Eccles. 1:2, etc.), "the only true signification of which seems to be that given the earliest versions, e. g., Vulgate and Septuagint, i. e., one addressing a public assembly and discoursing of human things; unless one chooses to derive the signification of preacher or orator from the primary notion of calling and speaking" (Gesenius, *Lex.*, s. v.). (4) *To Announce* (Gr. *'aggellō*), in several combinations, as: *'euaggelizō*, to announce good tidings, *evangelize* (Matt. 11:5; Luke 7:22; Heb. 4:2, 6), especially to instruct men concerning the things pertaining to Christian salvation (Luke 9:6; 20:1; Acts 1:37; Rom. 15:20; I Cor. 1:17; 9:16, 18, etc.); *katangelō*, to *proclaim publicly* (Acts 13:5; 15:36, etc.); *proeuangelizomai*, to announce or promise good tidings *beforehand*, i. e., before the event by which the promise is made good (Gal. 3:8). (5) *To discourse* (Gr. *dialegomai*, to *think different things with one's self*), to converse, discourse with anyone (Acts 20:9; comp. 18:4; 19:8, etc.). (6) *To speak* (Gr. *laleō*, to *talk*), to speak to one about a thing, i. e., to *teach* (Mark 2:2; Acts 8:25; 13:42; 14:25; 16:6, etc.). (7) *That which is heard* (Gr. *'akoē*, *hearing*), specially, the *preaching* of the Gospel (John 12:38; Rom. 10:16, A. V. "report;" Gal. 3:2, 5, A. V. "hearing"). (8) *To be a herald* (Gr. *kērussō*, to be *a herald*), to

officiate as a herald, used of the public promulgation of the Gospel and matters pertaining to it, by John the Baptist, Jesus, by the apostles and other Christian teachers (Matt. 11:1; Mark 1:4; 3:14; 16:20; Rom. 10:15, etc.). (9) *Freedom of utterance* (Gr. *parrēsia*, *boldness in speaking*, Acts 9:27; comp. II Cor. 3:12).

Thus it will be seen that to some extent preaching had been recognized in the old dispensation; Noah being "a preacher of righteousness" (II Pet. 2:5), the Psalmist and the prophets delivering their messages of truth in song, and accusation and rebuke, pleading and exhortation, prophecy and promise. The reading and exposition of Scripture was from the beginning the chief object of the synagogue service, and is frequently mentioned in the New Testament (Luke 4:16; Acts 13:15; 15:21). *See* Synagogue.

In the New Testament times our Lord and his apostles preached wherever the people could be gathered; in the synagogues, the mountain side, the shores of seas and rivers, the public street, the porch of the temple. The preaching of the word of God (the law and the Gospel) is the chief means ordained by Christ himself, and sufficient for all, by which the Holy Spirit brings about the commencement and continuance of saving faith in the heart of the sinner. So the apostle states (Rom. 10:17), "Faith cometh by hearing, and hearing by the word of God." The history of God's kingdom furnishes a number of instances showing that the operation of the Holy Ghost for conversion and sanctification is inseparably united to the preaching of the word, e. g., the day of Pentecost (Acts 2:37, sq.; 10:44, sq.); the many remarkable examples of the combined operation of the word and Spirit in the apostolic age (Acts 9:31; 16:14; Gal. 3:5, Eph. 1:13; James 1:18); see "what is written in praise of God's testimony under the old covenant (Psa. 19:8-11; 119; Jer. 23:29); and how the Lord himself spoke of the sufficiency of the testimony of Moses and the prophets (Luke 16:27-31); the testimony of Paul (Rom. 1:16) as to the power of God unto salvation; of Peter (I Pet. 1:23) as to the seed of regeneration; of the epistle to the Hebrews (4:12) as to the sharp and two-edged sword of the word—then compare all this with what experience tells us in varied forms of ourselves and others, and we shall no longer hesitate with the apostle to call the word of God, as nothing else on earth, 'the sword of the Spirit' (Eph. 6:17)" (Van Oosterzee, ii, p. 736).

Precious Stones. For discussion of these in detail, *see* Mineral Kingdom.

Predestination. *See* Election, Sovereignty of God.

Preparation (Gr. *paraskeuē*, a *making ready*); in the Jewish sense, the day of preparation (Matt. 27:62; Mark 15:42; Luke 23:54; John 19:31) was the day on which the Jews made the necessary preparation to celebrate a Sabbath (*q. v.*) or festival (*q. v.*).

Presbytery (Gr. *presbuterion*), the order or body of elders (I Tim. 4:14), mentioned in connection with the ordination of Timothy. *See* Elders, Ordination.

Presence (Heb. *pänĕh, face*). Jehovah's promise

to Moses was "My presence shall go with thee, and I will give thee rest" (Exod. 33:14). "The presence (*face*) of Jehovah is Jehovah in his own personal presence, and is identical with the 'angel' in whom the name of Jehovah was (23:20, 21), and who is therefore called in Isa. 63:9 'the angel of his presence' (*face*)" (K. and D., *Com.*).

Present. *See* Gift.

President (Aram. *särēk*, for the Heb. *shōṭēr*, and used only in Dan., ch. 6). According to Dan. 6:2, Darius not only appointed one hundred and twenty satraps for all the provinces and districts of his kingdom, but he also placed the whole body of satraps under a government consisting of three presidents, who should reckon with the individual satraps. This triumvirate, or higher authority of three, was also not newly instituted by Darius, but already existed in the Chaldean kingdom under Belshazzar (5:7), and was only continued by Darius. Daniel was one of the triumvirate.

Press. *See* Oil, 2; Wine Press.

Press is used (Mark 2:4; 5:27, 30; Luke 8:19, 45; 19:3) in the modern sense of *crowd*.

Press Fat (Heb. *yĕqĕb*, *trough*), the vat into which the juice flowed when pressed out of the grapes (Hag. 2:16). *See* Wine Press.

Presumptuous, Presumptuously. Presumption is the act of taking upon one's self more than good sense and propriety warrant; excessive boldness or overconfidence in thought and conduct. In Scripture we have several Hebrew words and one Greek word thus rendered:

1. *To act overboldly* (Heb. *zūd*, *to seethe*; figurative *to be insolent*), spoken mostly of those who knowingly and purposely violate the commands of God and commit sin (Exod. 21:14; Deut. 1:48; 17:13).

2. *Arrogance* (Heb. *zēd*, *arrogant; zādōn*), as presumptuous sins (Psa. 19:13); of resistance to priest or judge through pride. "Resistance to the priest took place when anyone was dissatisfied with his interpretation of the law; to the judge, when anyone was discontented with the sentence that was passed on the basis of the law. Such refractory conduct was to be punished with death, as rebellion against God."

3. In Num. 15:30 "presumptuously" is the synonym for "with a high hand," i.e., so that one who raised his hand, as it were, against Jehovah, or acted in open rebellion against him, blasphemed God and was to be cut off (comp. Gen. 17:14)—Heb. *yād*, *hand*.

4. *Insolence* (Gr. *tolmētēs*, *daring*, *bold*), spoken (II Pet. 2:10) of those who were self-willed, licentious, and despising authority.

Generally, *presumptuous* sins (Psa. 19:13) are those committed with knowledge (John 15:22), deliberation and contrivance (Prov. 6:14; Psa. 36:4), obstinacy (Jer. 44:16; Deut. 1:43) inattention to the remonstrances of conscience (Acts 7:51), opposition to the dispensations of Providence (II Chron. 28:22), and repeated commission of the same sin (Psa. 78:17).

Pretence (Gr. *prophasis*, *show*), under color as though they would, etc. (Matt. 23:14; Mark 12:40; Phil. 1:8). It is rendered *cloak* (I Thess. 2:5), where Paul says that he never "at any time used flattering words, . . . nor a cloak of covetousness;" the meaning being that he had never used his apostolic office in order to disguise or to hide avaricious designs.

Preto'rium (prĕ-tō'rĭ-ŭm; Gr. *praitōrion*, Mark 15:16). The word denotes: 1. The headquarters in a Roman camp, the tent of the commander-in-chief. 2. The palace in which the governor or procurator of a province resided. At Jerusalem it was the magnificent palace which Herod the Great built for himself, and which the Roman procurators seem to have occupied whenever they came from Caesarea to Jerusalem on public business. The same word is rendered in the A. V. "common hall" (Matt. 27:27); "palace" (Phil. 1:13); "hall of judgment" (John 18:28); "judgment hall" (John 18:28, 33; 19:9; Acts 23:35).

The pretorium in Rome (Phil. 1:13) was probably the quarters of the imperial body-guard, the *pretorian cohort*, which had been built for it by Tiberius. Ramsey (*St. Paul the Traveler*, p. 357) says: "The *pretorium* is the whole body of persons connected with sitting in judgment, the supreme imperial court, doubtless in this case the prefect or both prefects of the Pretorian Guard, representing the emperor in his capacity as the fountain of justice, together with the assessors and high officers of the court."

Prey. *See* Spoil.

Price. In addition to its usual meaning of *a stated sum* asked for anything *price* has the meaning of *wages* (Zech. 11:12).

Prick. (1) The rendering (Num. 33:55) of Heb. *sēk*, a briar or thorn; and so the expression "pricks in your eyes," etc., means to suffer the most painful injuries; and (2) of the Gr. *kentron*, a goad (*q. v.*).

Priest, Priesthood. The idea of a priesthood connects itself, in all its forms, pure or corrupted, with the consciousness, always more or less distinct, of sin. Men feel that they have broken a law. The power above them is holier than they are, and they dare not approach it. They crave for the intervention of some one whom they can think of as likely to be more acceptable than themselves. He must offer up their prayers, thanksgivings, sacrifices. He becomes their representative in "things pertaining unto God." He may become also (though this does not always follow) the representative of God to man. The functions of the priest and prophet may exist in the same person.

In pre-Mosaic times the office of priest was occupied by the father of a family (comp. Job 1:5), or the head of a tribe for his own family or tribe. Abraham, Isaac, and Jacob built altars, offered sacrifices, purified and consecrated themselves and their households (Gen. 12:7; 13:18; 26:25; 33:20; 35:1, 2). Melchizedek combined kingship and priesthood in his own person (14:18). Jethro is not merely the spiritual, but also the civil head of Midian (Exod. 2:16; 3:1).

In Egypt the Israelites came into contact with a priesthood of another kind, and that contact must have been for a time a very close one. The marriage of Joseph with the daughter of the priest of On—a priest, as we may infer by her name, of the goddess Neith (Gen. 41:45)—the special favor which he showed to the priestly caste in the years of famine (47:26), the training of Moses in the palace of the Pharoahs, probably in the colleges and temples of the priests (Acts 7:22)—all this must have impressed the constitution, the dress, the outward form of life upon the minds of the lawgiver and his contemporaries. There is scarcely any room for doubt that a connection of some kind existed between the Egyptian priesthood and that of Israel. The latter was not indeed an outgrowth or imitation of the former, for the one was "of the earth earthy," while the other was ethical and spiritual.

Priesthood, Hebrew. 1. **Name.** (Heb. *kōhēn*, one *officiating;* Gr. *hiereus.*) There is no consensus of opinion as to the etymology of the Heb. *kōhēn*, but the supposition of Bähr (*Symbolik,* ii, 15), in connecting it with an Arabic root which is equivalent to the Hebrew root *qäräb* (*to draw near*), answers most nearly to the received usage of the word. In the precise terminology of the law it is used of one who may "draw near" to the divine presence (Exod. 19:22; 30:20), while others remain afar off, and is usually applied to the sons of Aaron, It is, however, used in a wider sense when it is applied to Melchizedek (Gen. 14:18), Potipherah (41:45), Jethro (Exod. 2:16), and to the priests mentioned in Exod. 19:22, who exercised priestly functions before the appointment of Aaron and his sons. These last owed their position as priests to natural superiority of rank, either as firstborn or as elders.

In II Sam. 8:18 there is a case of great difficulty—the sons of David are described as priests (Heb. *kohanim,* A. V. "chief rulers," R. V. "priests"). This conjecture is offered (McClintock and Strong, *Cyc.,* s. v.): "David and his sons may have been admitted, not to distinctively priestly acts, such as burning incense (Num. 16:40; II Chron. 26:18), but to an honorary, titular priesthood. To wear the ephod in processions (II Sam. 6:14), at the time when this was the special badge of the order (I Sam. 22:18), to join the priests and Levites in their songs and dances, might have been conceded, with no deviation from the law, to the members of the royal house."

K. and D. (*Com.,* in loc.) explain as follows: "David's sons were *confidants,* not priests, domestic priests, court chaplains, or spiritual advisers, but as the title is explained in the corresponding text of the Chronicles (18:17), when the title had become obsolete, 'chief about the king' (marg. 'at the hand of the king'). The correctness of this explanation is placed beyond the reach of doubt by I Kings 4:5, where the *kohane* is called, by way of explanation, 'the king's friend.' These *kohanim,* therefore, were the king's confidential advisers."

2. **Essential Idea of Priesthood.** Moses furnishes us with the key to the idea of Old Testament priesthood in Num. 16:5, which consists of three elements—the being chosen or set apart for Jehovah as his own, the being holy, and the being allowed to come or bring near. The *first* expresses the fundamental condition, the *second* the qualification, the *third* the function of the priesthood. According to Exod. 19:5, sq., it is upon these three ele-

ments that the character of the whole covenant people is based. They were chosen to be God's peculiar people (Deut. 7:6), a kingdom of priests and a holy nation (see Exod. 19:4-6). Their sinfulness, however, prevented its realization; and when brought before Jehovah at Sinai they could not endure the immediate presence of God, and begged Moses to act as their mediator (20:18, sq.). In order to maintain fellowship between the holy God and the sinful nation; to have the people's gifts and sacrifices brought before God, on the one hand, and God's gifts, mercy, salvation, and blessing conveyed to the people on the other, the Aaronic priesthood was instituted. God, by an act of free favor, committed the priesthood to one particular family—that of Aaron (28:1), which priesthood they received as a gift (Num. 18:7). In like manner the whole tribe of Levi was assigned to the priests as their servants and assistants (see Levites). This divine preference was confirmed by the miracle of the budding rod (Num. 17:1, sq.), and the priesthood as a heritage to the descendants of Aaron. The *qualification,* viz., holiness, was represented in outward form by the act of consecration and the robes of office.

The *functions* were shown by the fellowship with Jehovah into which the priests were allowed to enter in the course of the various acts of worship. Holiness is essential to fellowship with God, and Aaron and his sons, no less than the people whom they were to represent before God, were stained by sin. As the sanctity imparted to them by their consecration, their official robes, and other legal requirements, which fitted them to serve at the altar, was only of an outward character, it follows that these could only have had a symbolical meaning. It was doubtless intended that they should symbolize, on the one hand, the sinless character of the human priesthood, and on the other serve as a type of the perfect priesthood of the true and eternal High Priest.

3. **Priests.** (1) **Selection.** God selected as priests the sons (descendants) of Aaron (Exod. 6:18, 20; 28:1), but two of his sons, Nadab and Abihu, died without issue, having been put to death for burning strange fire upon the altar (Lev. 10:1, sq.), the priesthood was invested in the descendants of Aaron's two other sons, Eleazar and Ithamar (10:6). The selection went still further, for among these all were disqualified who had any physical defect or infirmity—the blind, lame, flat-nosed (q. v.), limbs unduly long (unshapely), broken-handed, crooked-backed, lean and stunted, blemish of the eye, affected with scurvy, scab of any kind of eruption, stones broken. These, however, were supported, as the other priests (21:17-23); for no one whose legitimate birth entitled him to admission could be excluded.

In later times the Sanhedrin inquired into the genealogy of the candidate, sitting daily for this purpose in the "Hall of Polished Stones." If he failed to satisfy the court about his perfect legitimacy the candidate was dressed and veiled in black, and permanently removed. If his genealogy was satisfactory inquiry was next made as to any physical defects, of which Maimonides enumerates a hundred and forty that permanently and twenty-two which temporarily disqualified for the exercise of the priestly office. Those who stood the twofold test were dressed in white raiment, and their names properly inscribed. To this pointed allusion is made in Rev. 3:5.

The age for entering the priesthood is not mentioned, but it was probably from twenty-five years (Num. 8:24) to thirty years (4:3, 23, 30, 35, 47).

(2) **Support.** On their settlement in Canaan the priestly families had thirteen Levitical cities assigned to them, with "suburbs," or pasture grounds (Josh. 21:13-19). In addition the following were their chief sources of maintenance: 1. One tenth of the tithes paid to the Levites by the people (Lev. 23:10), partly in the raw state, as wheat, barley, grapes, fruits (Deut. 18:8), and partly as prepared for consumption, as wine, oil, flour, etc. (Lev. 23:17), and even to the first fruits of sheep shearing (Deut. 18:4). 2. A special tithe every third year (14:28; 26:12). 3. The redemption money of the firstborn, of which those of the human race were redeemed for five shekels (Num. 18:16); those of unclean beasts redeemed by a sum fixed by the priest with a fifth part of the value added (Lev. 27:27); those of clean beasts were not redeemed, but offered in sacrifice, the priest receiving the wave breast and the right shoulder (Num. 18:17, 18). 4. The redemption money paid for men or things specially dedicated to the Lord (Lev., ch. 27). 5. A percentage of the spoil (q. v.) of war (Num. 31:25-47). 6. The showbread, the flesh of the offerings (see Sacrifices, and Num. 18:8-14; Lev. 6:26, 29; 7:6-10). Their income, even under the most favorable circumstances must have been moderate, depended largely upon the varying religious state of the nation, since no law existed by which either payment of tithes or any other offering could be enforced. And yet the law obviously was intended to provide against the dangers of a caste of pauper priests.

(3) **Dress.** When not in actual service neither the priests, nor even the high priest, wore a distinctive dress; but when ministering in the sanctuary the priests were required to wear the following *official dress: Drawers*, i. e., short breeches (Exod. 28:42), reaching only from the loins to the thighs, and made of linen (39:28); a long *coat* with sleeves, made of fine diapered linen (ver. 27); a variegated *girdle*, woven of the same four colors as were in the veil hung before the holy place (ver. 29); a *cap* of linen, and probably resembling in shape the inverted calyx of a flower. They had nothing on their feet, as they were not allowed to tread the sanctuary without having their feet bare (see Exod. 3:5; Josh. 5:15). The additional dress of the high priest is given in Priest, the High.

(4) **Duties.** The functions of the priesthood were very clearly defined by the Mosaic law, and remained substantially the same, whatever changes might be brought about in their social position and organization. The duties prescribed in Exodus and Leviticus are the same as those recognized in Chronicles and Ezekiel. These functions could be entered upon the eighth day of the service of consecra-

tion (Lev. 9:1). They were such as pertained to "a coming nigh the vessels of the sanctuary and the altar" (Num. 18:3): 1. In the *holy place*, to burn incense on the golden altar, morning and evening; clean and trim lamps and light them every evening; put showbread on the table every Sabbath (Exod. 30:7, 8; 27:21; Lev. 24:5-8). 2. In the *court*, to keep the fire constantly burning on the altar of burnt offering (Lev. 6:9, 13), clear away ashes from the altar (vers. 10, 11), offer the morning and evening sacrifices (Exod. 29:38-44), bless the people after the daily sacrifice (Lev. 9:22; Num. 6:23-27), wave different portions of the sacrifice, sprinkle the blood, and put various parts of the victim upon the altar and see to their burning, to blow the silver trumpets (q. v.) and the jubilee horn at particular festival seasons. 3. Generally, to inspect unclean persons, especially lepers, and, when so warranted, to declare them clean (Num. 6:22, sq.; chaps, 13, 14); to administer the oath of purgation to the woman accused of adultery (5:15); to appraise things dedicated to the sanctuary (Lev. 27:2, sq.). 4. *Finally*, to instruct the people in the law, to act as a high court of appeals in any difficult case (Deut. 17:8, sq.; 19:17; 21:5), and in times of war to address the troops, if deemed necessary, before going into action (Deut. 20:2, sq.). The large number of offerings brought up to the sanctuary at the festival times taxed the strength and endurance of the priests to such an extent that the Levites had to be called in to help them (II Chron. 29:34; 35:14).

(5) **Consecration.** (Heb. *qădăsh to be holy*, with causative or intensive force, "to make clean".) The ceremony of the consecration of the high priest, as well as the ordinary priests, to their office is prescribed in Exod. 29:1-34 (comp. Exod. 40:12:15; Lev., ch. 8); and in the case of Aaron and his sons it was performed by Moses (Lev. 8:1-36). The candidate for consecration was conducted to the door of the tabernacle, and had his body washed with water; was invested with the official dress; was anointed with the holy oil (see Oil), which in the case of the high priest, was, according to tradition, poured upon the head; but in the case of the other priests it was merely smeared upon the forehead. In the consecration of Aaron and his sons the fact of anointing is not expressly mentioned, although it had been commanded (Exod. 28:41; 40:15), and the performance of it taken for granted (Lev. 7:36; 10:7; Num. 3:3).

A sacrificial service followed, with Moses officiating as priest. The sacrifice consisted of one young bullock for a *sin offering*, one ram for the *burnt offering*, the ram of *consecration*, a basket of unleavened bread, unleavened cakes kneaded in oil, and thinner unleavened cakes sprinkled with oil.

Those being consecrated (Exod. 29:1, sq.) they laid their hands upon the head of the bullock, which was then slaughtered, and its blood sprinkled upon the horns of the altar of burnt offering, the rest being poured upon the ground at its base. The fat of the viscera, caul of the liver, the two kidneys with their fat, were consumed upon the altar; while the skin, flesh, and dung were burned without the camp.

The ram for the burnt offering was then brought, and, after the hands of those being consecrated were laid upon its head, it was offered as in the case of other burnt offerings (see Sacrifice). Then came the offering of the ram of consecration. The hands of the consecrated were laid upon its head, it was slaughtered by Moses, who sprinkled some of its blood upon the tip of the right ear of Aaron and his sons, upon their right thumbs, and upon the great toe of their right feet, the rest being sprinkled upon the altar. Then he took the fat, the rump, the fat of the viscera, the caul of the liver, the two kidneys, with their fat, the right shoulder of this ram of consecration; and along with these an unleavened cake, a cake of oiled bread, a thin cake sprinkled with oil, and laid them upon the fat and the right shoulder. Placing these altogether on the hands of Aaron, he waved them before Jehovah. After this the whole was burned upon the altar.

The breast of the ram—the priest's portion —he now waved before Jehovah, afterward sprinkling some of the anointing oil and blood upon the priests and their garments. This concluded the ceremony. The remainder of the flesh was cooked by Aaron and his sons at the door of the tabernacle and eaten by them. Any portion remaining till the next day was burned. The consecration service lasted seven days (Exod. 29:35; Lev. 8:33, sq.), the sacrifice being repeated each day. Meantime those being consecrated were not allowed to leave the sanctuary (Lev. 8:35).

After the consecration services, the consecrated, whether high priest or ordinary priest, were required to offer a special meat offering of one tenth ephah of flour. This was kneaded with oil and baked in separate pieces—one half being offered in the morning and the other in the evening, wholly burned upon the altar (6:19-23). On the eighth day of consecration, the exercise of the priestly function was begun by the newly consecrated in the offering of a calf for a sin offering, and a ram for a burnt offering, for themselves. This was immediately followed by the offering of sacrifices for the people (9:1, sq.).

(6) **Regulations.** Above all Israel, the priests, whom Jehovah had chosen out of the whole nation to be the custodians of his sanctuary, and had sanctified to that end, were to prove themselves the consecrated servants of God in their domestic lives and sacred duties. They were not to defile themselves by touching the dead, excepting such as formed part of one's immediate family, as his mother, father, son, daughter, brother, or sister who was still living with him as a virgin (Lev. 21:1-6); by signs of mourning (vers. 10-12; the wife, though not mentioned, is probably included in the phrase, "his kin is near unto him);" by marriage with a public prostitute, a "profane" woman (a deflowered maid) or a divorced woman; i. e., any person of notoriously immoral life. Such marriage would be irreconcilable with the holiness of the priesthood (Lev. 21:7-9); but he might marry a virgin (ver. 14), or the widow of a priest (Ezek. 44:22). Licentious conduct on the part

of any of their own daughters was punished by the offenders being burned to death (Lev. 21:9). If they should happen, unwittingly or unavoidably, to have contracted Levitical uncleanness, they were required to abstain from the holy things until they had become legally purified (Lev. 22:2-7); and every transgression of the law of Levitical purity was regarded as a crime punishable by death (22:9).

Before entering the tabernacle the priests washed their hands and feet (Exod. 30:17-21; 40:30-32); and during the time of their administration they were to drink no wine or strong drink (Lev. 10:9; Ezek. 44:21); they were not to shave their heads.

The priesthood ministering in the temple were arranged into "ordinary" priests and various officials. Of the latter, besides the high priest were: The *Sagan*, or suffragan priest, who officiated for the high priest when he was incapacitated, and generally acted as his assistant, taking oversight of the priests, whence he is called "second priest" (II Kings 25:18; Jer. 52:24); two *Katholikin*, chief treasurers and overseers; seven *Ammarcalin*, subordinate to the *Katholikin*, and who had chief charge of the gates; and three *Gizbarim*, or undertreasurers. These fourteen officers, ranking in the order mentioned, formed the standing "council of the temple," which regulated everything connected with the affairs and services of the sanctuary. Next in rank were the "heads of each course" on duty for a week, and then the "heads of families" of every course. After them followed fifteen overseers; as overseer of gates, guards, lots, etc.

(7) **History.** The priests, at first, probably exercised their functions according to a definite principle of alternation, but when in the course of time their numbers greatly increased, David divided them into twenty-four classes or orders, sixteen of them consisting of the descendants of Eleazar and eight of the descendants of Ithamar, with a president to each class (II Chron. 36:14; Matt. 2:4; Josephus, *Ant.*, xx, 7, 8, etc.). Each main division was divided into subdivisions, ranging, according to the Talmud, from five to nine for each main division. Each main division and subdivision was ruled by a *head*. The order in which the classes took their turn was determined by lot, a new one being appointed each week to conduct the services during that week, beginning and ending on the Sabbath (II Kings 11:9; II Chron. 23:4). These classes are named in I Chron. 24. In like manner the various duties were assigned by lot (Luke 1:9), for which purpose there was a special *proefectus sortium* (director of lots) in the temple. According to rabbinical tradition four courses returned from captivity, from which twenty-four courses were chosen by lot.

At the disruption of the kingdom, the priests and Levites remained with the kingdom of Judah, and there alone exercised their functions, occupying themselves with matters of jurisprudence, and instructing the people in the law (II Chron. 17:7-9). King Jehoshaphat created a supreme court in Jerusalem (17:7-9), composed of princes, Levites, and priests; and so long and so far as king and people remained loyal to the law of Moses, the priests were highly esteemed and exercised a healthy influence upon the progress and development of the theocracy. Apostasy sank the priests into immorality, a departure from God, and into idol-worship (Hos. 6:9; Mic. 3:11; Zeph. 3:4; Jer. 5:31; 6:13; Ezek. 22:26; Mal., ch. 2). The officiating priests occupied rooms immediately adjoining the temple, while subsequent to the exile several priestly families took up their residence in private houses in Jerusalem (Neh. 11:10, sq.).

A few might enter more deeply into the divine life, and so receive, like Jeremiah, Zechariah, and Ezekiel, a special call to the office of a prophet; but others, doubtless, served Jehovah with a divided allegiance, acting also as priests of the high places, sharing in the worship of Baal (Jer. 2:8), of the sun and moon, and the host of heaven (8:1, 2). Some "ministered before their idols" in the very temple itself (Ezek. 44:12), and allowed others, "uncircumcised in heart and flesh" to join them (v. 7). They became sensual, covetous, tyrannical, drunkards, and adulterous (Isa. 28:7, 8; 56:10-12), and their corruption was shared by the prophets (Jer. 5:31; Lam. 4:13; Zeph. 3:4).

Although chastened by the captivity, many of the priests repudiating their heathen wives (Ezra 10:18, 19) and taking part in the instruction of the people (Ezra 3:2; Neh. 8:9-13), the root evils soon reappeared. The work of the priesthood was made the instrument of covetousness, every ministerial act being performed for a consideration (Mal. 1:10). They "corrupted the covenant of Levi" (2:8) and forgot the idea that the priest was the messenger of the Lord (2:7). They lost their influence and became "base and contemptible before all the people" (2:9). This, however, is not to be understood as implying that the priests had now lost all their influence. Politically and socially they still occupied the foremost place quite as much as ever they did; and by virtue of their political standing, in virtue of the powerful resources at their command, and, lastly and above all, in virtue of their sacred prerogative—the priests continued to have an extraordinary significance for the life of the nation.

4. Symbolical and Typical. The priestly prerogatives and qualifications had an undoubted symbolical and typical meaning, which ought to be recognized but not carried to extremes. The following brief summary is abridged from Keil, (*Arch.*, i, p. 227, sq.):

(1) **Symbolical.** 1. Selection. In their being chosen to be *Jehovah's peculiar possession*, the priests had no inheritance in Canaan, the Lord himself being their "part and inheritance" (Num. 18:20; Deut. 10:9, etc.). Jehovah, as the Lord of the whole earth and owner of Canaan, not only supplied sufficient dwellings for them, but also assigned an adequate allowance in tithes, first fruits, etc. Thus as belonging to Jehovah and provided for by him, they were taught to live by faith and to regard their whole good as centering in and coming from the Lord. They were also left free to devote themselves exclusively to the Lord's service, to the ministry of his word and law, and to their sacred duties.

2. Holiness. *Being holy* formed the indispensable condition of approach to God, the Holy One. Hence in the qualifications necessary for the priestly office—bodily defect or infirmity being regarded as the counterpart of spiritual defects and shortcomings—the bodily perfection of the priests was not intended merely to be a reflection in their persons of the sacredness of their functions and ministry, and of the place where they officiated, but rather to symbolize the priest's spiritual blamelessness and sanctification of heart. For the same reason every Levitical defilement was to be avoided, and home life and conjugal relations were to be such as would show consecration to God (Lev. 21:7, sq.).

3. Consecration. This was the outward sign of sanctification. The *washing of the body* symbolized the purifying of the soul from the pollution of sin. This *negative* preparation was succeeded by the positive impartment of the indispensable requisites for the holy office, viz., the dress and the anointing.

4. Dress.

Color. The predominating color of the dress was white, symbolical of glory and holiness (Dan. 12:6, 7; 10:5; Ezek. 9:3; 10:2, 7; Matt. 28:3; Rev. 7:9, etc.); and the priests wearing garments of that color appeared in the light of holy servants of God.

The *breeches*, intended to conceal the "flesh of nakedness," the parts having to do with secretions, symbolized the native side of holiness.

The *coat*, enveloping the whole body, woven in one piece without a seam and forming the principal article of dress, indicated spiritual integrity, the blamelessness and righteousness in which the idea of blessedness and life is realized, while the four-cornered form of the cloth of which the coat was made was for a sign that the one wearing it belonged to the kingdom of God.

Cap. This resembled in shape the calyx of a flower, and pointed to the blooming character, i. e., the fresh vigorous life of him who wore it. Hence the priest was forbidden to remove this headdress, but was to tie it on, lest it should fall off by accident; for, as the cap represented a flower, its falling off would have a significant resemblance to the falling of a flower (I Pet. 1:24; James 1:10; Psa. 103:15; Isa. 40:6-8).

Girdle. The girdle put on by an oriental when about to do anything in the shape of active work, was the priestly sign of service, and typical of the towel-girded Christ, who in washing the feet of the disciples proved that he "came not to be ministered unto but to minister" (Mark 10:45). Consequently it was of the same colors and wrought in the same style as the veils of the sanctuary, in order to show that the wearer was an office bearer and administrator in the kingdom of God.

5. High Priest.

Upper robe. Woven of blue yarn and in one piece, this article indicated entireness of spiritual integrity; blue pointing to the heavenly origin and character of the office. As every Israelite was to wear tassels of blue on the hem of his robe, to remind him of the law (Num. 15:38, sq.), we may infer that in the fringe of pomengranates and little bells there also lay some reference to the word and testimony of God; and that the tinkling of the bells were to be heard by the high priest to remind him that his calling was to be the representative, guardian, and promulgator of God's commandments.

The *pomegranates*, with their agreeable odor, sweet and refreshing juice and large quantities of delicious seeds, were meant to point to the divine law as a sweet and delicious spiritual food, invigorating the soul and refreshing the heart (comp. Psa. 19:8-11; 119:24, 43, 50, with Deut. 8:3; Prov. 9:8). Wearing the robe, to which this fringe was attached, the high priest appeared as the depository and organ of the word, and he could directly approach Jehovah only when clad in the robe of God's word, as the organ of that divine testimony on which covenant fellowship with the Lord was based.

Ephod (shoulder-piece) and breastplate. The two parts of which the ephod consisted were called shoulders. It was upon the shoulder that the burden of the office rested, upon it the *insignia* of office was worn (Isa. 22:22). The principal function of the high priest was to appear before God as the reconciling mediator on behalf of the people; and to show that this duty devolved upon him, he wore upon the shoulders of the ephod the names of the twelve tribes engraven upon two onyx stones . . . The *breastplate*, with the names of the twelve tribes engraven on precious stones, with the Urim and Thummim in its pocket, was the *breastplate of judgement*. By this the high priest was distinguished as the judicial representative of Israel, bearing the people upon his heart, i. e., not merely to keep them in mind, but being, as it were, blended together with them by a living sympathy, to intercede with them before Jehovah,

In the Urim and Thummim (*q. v.*), the high priest had a medium through which God would communicate to him, in every case in which the congregation needed divine light in order to know how to act, such a measure of illumination as would enable him to maintain or reestablish the rights of Israel when they were disputed or infringed (Num. 27:21).

Headdress. Its significance was not so much in its being a turban instead of the cap of the ordinary priests, as in the diadem with its description. The meaning of this diadem lies in its being designated a *crown* (Exod. 29:6; 39:30; Lev. 8:9; also the "king's crown," II Sam. 1:10; II Kings 11:12), indicating that its wearer was the crowned one among his brethren, the supreme spiritual head of the priesthood. This was a holy crown bearing the inscription, "Holiness to Jehovah," i. e., holy to the Lord. He who was thus crowned was consecrated to Jehovah (Psa. 106:10) and was required to wear the badge of his holiness upon his forehead. The high priest, in virtue of the holiness to the Lord conferred upon him, was to have the power to bear or take upon himself, and so put away the sin that adhered to the people's gifts in consequence of their impurity, in order that these gifts might be-

come acceptable to God, and they in turn enjoy his favor (Exod. 28:38).

Anointing. Being anointed with oil was symbolical of being endued with the Spirit of God (comp. I Sam. 10:1, 2; 16:13, sq.; Isa. 61); for the oil with its power of giving light, and of awakening and raising the animal spirits, furnished a significant symbol of the Spirit of God as the principle of spiritual light and life.

(2) **Typical**. "All the requirements necessary to qualify for the office of the priest had a typical meaning in the fact that they were insufficient duly to sanctify the priests and to constitute them mediators between the holy God and the sinful people. Freedom from outward defect, cleansing of the body, investing with the official robes, nor the anointing with oil, could be said to purify the inward nature, but only served to represent a state of outward purity, without, however, truly and permanently producing even this. Consequently, the Levitical priests were required to repeat the washing of hands and feet every day before entering upon service at the altar or going into the holy place. On the Day of Atonement the high priest had to offer a sin offering for himself and the rest of the priests before he could perform similar service for the congregation, and make atonement for them before God. If, therefore, a priest who was holy, blameless, undefiled, and separate from sinners was alone qualified to represent sinners before God, and make atonement for them, and if the priests of the Old Testament did not really possess these attributes, but could only be said to be invested with them in a symbolical form in virtue of certain divine prescriptions and promises, it followed that the various regulations as to the qualifications of the priests for the exercise of the functions intrusted to them could have been designed merely as a divine arrangement whereby to foreshadow the nature and character of Him who was to be the true priest and high priest. Accordingly they must have been intended to prepare the way for the realization of the insufficiency of the Levitical priesthood for adequately representing the sinful people before the holy God, and typically to point to the future appearing of the perfect Mediator, who would redeem the people of Israel from all sin, invest them with true sanctification, and make them a genuine kingdom of priests" (Keil, *Arch.*, ii, p. 240).

Priest, the High (Heb. *hăkkōhēn, the priest, hăkkōhēn hăggădōl, the great priest*). The high priest formed the culminating point in the Israelite hierarchy. The first to fill this high position was Aaron, who was succeeded by his eldest (surviving) son, Eleazar.

1. **Selection**. The high priest was required to satisfy all the necessary conditions of admission to the sacred office. See Priesthood, Hebrew, 3, 1.

2. **Support**. The source of the high priest's support was the same as that of the other priests; his proportion probably varying according to circumstances. See Priesthood, Hebrew 3.

3. **Dress**. As befitted the superior dignity of of his office, the high priest wore, in addition to the ordinary priest's attire (viz., the coat,

breeches, girdle, cap), an *official dress* entirely peculiar to himself, consisting of four parts:

373. The Breastplate

(1) **The breastplate** (Heb. *ḥōshěn*), called also "the breastplate of judgment" (Exod. 28:15; 29:30), a square piece of cloth made of the same material, and wrought in the same fashion as the ephod (see below). It was doubled so as to form a pocket one span broad. Upon this breastplate were twelve precious stones set in gold, and arranged in four rows, while on the stones were engraved the names of the twelve tribes of Israel. At each of the four corners was a ring of gold. By the two upper rings small chains of wreathed gold were attached, at the other ends of which chains were fastened for the purpose of fastening them to the ephod on the shoulders. To the two lower rings, again, blue cords (laces) were attached, the other ends of which were tied to rings that, for this purpose, were fastened to the bottom of the front part of the ephod immediately above the girdle. In this was the breastplate was securely bound to the ephod, and, at the same time, to the breast, both above and below, so that, held as it was by the chains and cords running obliquely in opposite directions, it could not possibly get displaced (Exod. 28:13-28; 39:8-21).

Into the breastplate were put the *Urim* and *Thummim* (Heb. *'urîm w^etŭmmîm* "*lights and perfections*"), in order that it might be upon Aaron's heart when he went in before the Lord (Exod. 28:30). Even such early writers as Josephus, Philo, and the Rabbins, are unable to furnish any precise information as to what the *Urim* and *Thummim* really were. The only Scripture account given of them is in Exod. 28:30; Lev. 8:8, from which it seems very evident that they were something of a material nature, which being put into the breastplate after the latter had been prepared and put on, formed the medium through which the high priest was enabled to ascertain the will of Jehovah in regard to any important matter affecting the theocracy (Num. 27:21). That the Urim and Thummim were placed in the pocket is made specially clear from Lev. 8:8, where, in the course of dressing himself, Aaron

puts on the breastplate, and then puts the Urim and Thummim inside of it, showing that the things thus put into the breastplate must be materially distinct from it. They were evidently some sort of small oracular objects. Some scholars connect them with the Babylonian tablets of destiny known as *Urtu* and *Tamitu* but this parallel is scarcely valid.

374. The Ephod of the Priest

(2) **The ephod** (Heb. *'ēphōd*) was woven of blue, purple, scarlet, and fine linen yarn, embroidered with figures of gold. It consisted of two pieces, the one covering the back, the other the breast and upper part of the body. The two parts were fastened together on the top of each shoulder by a golden clasp or fastening, an onyx set in gold, with the names of six tribes on each stone. Upon this ephod the breastplate was fastened (Exod. 28:6-12; 39:2-7). *See* Ephod.

The robe of the ephod was of blue color, woven without any seam. It was worn immediately under the ephod and was longer than it, reaching a little below the knees, so that the priest's coat could be seen under it. The blue robe had no sleeves, but only slits in the sides for the arms to come through. It had a hole for the head to pass through, with a border round it of woven work, to prevent its being rent. The skirt of this robe had a remarkable trimming of pomegranates in blue, red, and crimson, with a bell of gold between each pomegranate alternately.

(3) **The girdle** (Heb. *ḥēshěb*, a *belt*) was of the same material and manufacture as the ephod, and was used to bind the ephod firmly to the body (Exod. 28:8).

(4) **The miter** (Heb. *mǐṣněphěth, wound round*) was a kind of turban which, according to Josephus and Philo, consisted of an ordinary priest's cap with a turban of dark-blue color over it. On the front of this latter was a diadem of pure gold (i. e., a thin gold plate) on which was engraved, "Holy to Jehovah," and fastened with a dark-blue cord (Exod. 28:36-38; 39:30, sq.).

4. **Duties.** The functions peculiar to the high priest consisted partly in presenting the sin offering for himself (Lev. 4:3, sq.) and the congregation (v. 13, sq.), as occasion required, and the atoning sacrifice and the burnt offering on the great Day of Atonement (Lev., ch. 16). He also consulted the Lord by means of the Urim and Thummim, in regard to important matters affecting the theocracy, and informing the people thereon (Num. 27:21; I Sam. 30:7, sq.). The high priest had the supervision of the rest of the priests and

of the entire worship, and was at liberty to exercise all the other sacerdotal functions as well. According to Josephus (*Wars*, v, 5, 7), he officiated, as a rule, every Sabbath, and on new moons or other festivals in the course of the year. In addition to his strictly religious duties, the high priest was the supreme civil head of the people, the supreme head of the state, in so far, that is, as the state was not under the sway of foreign rulers. In the days of national independence the hereditary Asmonaean high priests were priests and kings at one and the same time; while, at a later period again, the high priests were—at least the presidents of the Sanhedrin, and even in all political matters—the supreme representatives of the people in their relations with the Romans.

5. **Consecration.** This has already been treated of in article Priesthood, Hebrew, 3 (5).

6. **Regulations.** The regulations were still more stringent in the case of the high priest than of the ordinary priests. He was not allowed to marry even a widow, but only a virgin of his own people; he was forbidden to approach a corpse or take part in funeral obsequies, the prohibition being absolute, while exceptions were made in the case of other priests; he was not to go out of the sanctuary to give way to his grief, nor to "profane the sanctuary of his God," i. e., by any defilement of his person which he could and ought to avoid; nor to contract a marriage not in keeping with the holiness of his rank (Lev. 21:10-15).

7. **History.** In history the high priests naturally arrange themselves into three groups:

(1) On the death of Aaron the *office* of high priest passed to his eldest son, Eleazar (Num. 20:28, sq.), and, according to divine promise (25:13) was vested in his descendants from Phineas downward (Judg. 20:28). Then, for reasons unknown, it passed in the person of Eli into the line of Ithamar, in which it continued till the deposition of Abiathar by Solomon, who, in appointing Zadok to the office, restored it once more to the exclusive possession of the house of Eleazar (I Kings 2:26, sq.; 35). In the group of high priests before David seven are named in Scripture, viz.: Aaron, Eleazar, Phineas, Eli, Ahitub (I Chron. 9:11; Neh. 11:11; I Sam. 14:3), Ahiah; while Josephus asserts that the father of Bukki—whom he calls Joseph, Abiezer, i.e., Abishua—was the last high priest of Phineas's line before Zadok.

(2) There were two high priests in the reign of David, apparently of nearly equal authority, viz., Zadok and Abiathar (I Chron. 15:11; II Sam. 8:17; 15:24, 35). It is not unlikely that after the death of Ahimelech and the secession of Abiathar to David, Saul may have made Zadok priest, and that David may have avoided the difficulty of deciding between the claims of his faithful friend Abiathar and his new and important ally Zadok by appointing them to a joint priesthood: the first place, with the ephod and Urim and Thummin, remaining with Abiathar, who was in actual possession of them. It appears that Abiathar had special charge of the ark and the services connected therewith, which

agrees exactly with the possession of the ephod by Abiathar and his previous position with David before he became king. Abiathar, however, forfeited his place by taking part with Adonijah against Solomon, and Zadok was made high priest in his place.

The first considerable difficulty that meets us in the historical survey of the high priests of the second group is to ascertain who was high priest at the dedication of Solomon's temple. Josephus says (*Ant.*, x, 8, 6) that Zadok was, and the *Seder Olam* makes him, the high priest in the reign of Solomon; but I Kings 4:2 distinctly asserts that Azariah, grandson of Zadok, was priest under Solomon, and I Chron. 6:10 tells us of an Azariah, grandson of the former, "He it is that executed the priest's office in the temple that Solomon built in Jerusalem," as if meaning at its first completion. We can hardly be wrong in saying that Azariah, the son of Ahimaaz, was the first high priest of Solomon's temple.

Smith thus presents the matter: "In constructing the list of the succession of priests of this group our method must be to compare the genealogical list in I Chron. 6:8-15 (A. V.) with the notices of high priests in the sacred history and with the list given by Josephus. Now, as regards the genealogy, it is seen at once that there is something defective; for, whereas from David to Jeconiah there are twenty kings, from Zadok to Jehozadak there are but thirteen priests. Then, again, while the pedigree in its six first generations from Zadok, inclusive, exactly suits the history, yet is there a great gap in the middle; for between Amariah, the high priest of Jehosphaphat's reign, and Shallum, the father of Hilkiah, the high priest in Josiah's reign—an interval of about two hundred and forty years —there are but two names, Ahitub and Zadok, and those liable to the utmost suspicion from their reproducing the same sequence which occurs in the earliest part of the same genealogy—Amariah, Ahitub, Zadok. Besides they are not mentioned by Josephus, at least not under the same names. This part, therefore, of the pedigree is useless for our purpose. But the historical books supply us with four or five names for this interval, viz., Jehoiada, Zechariah, Azariah, Urijah, and Azariah in the reign of Hezekiah. If, in the genealogy of I Chron. 6, Azariah and Hilkiah have been accidentally transposed, as is not impossible, then the Azariah who was high priest in Hezekiah's reign would be the Azariah of I Chron. 6:13, 14. Putting the additional historical names at four, and deducting the two suspicious names from the genealogy, we have fifteen high priests indicated in Scripture as contemporary with the twenty kings, with room, however, for one or two more in the history. The high priests of this series ended with Seraiah, who was taken prisoner by Nebuzar-adan and slain at Riblah by Nebuchadnezzar (II Kings 25:18)."

(3) An interval of about fifty-two years elapsed between the high priests of the second and third group, during which there was neither temple, altar, ark, nor priest. Jehozadak (or Josedech, Hag. 1:1, 14, etc.), who should have succeeded Seraiah, lived and died

a captive at Babylon. The pontifical office revived in his son, Jeshua (*q. v.*), and he stands at the head of this series, honorably distinguished for his zealous cooperation with Zerubbabel in rebuilding the temple and restoring the dilapidated commonwealth of Israel. His successors, so far as given in the Old Testament, were Joiakim, Eliashib, Joiada, Johanan, and Jaddua. Jaddua was high priest in the time of Alexander the Great. Jaddua was succeeded by Onias I, his son, and he again by Simon the Just, the last of the men of the great synagogue. Upon Simon's death, his son Onias being under age, Eleazar, Simon's brother, succeeded him. The high-priesthood of Eleazar is memorable as being that under which the LXX version of the Scriptures was made at Alexandria.

After the high-priesthood had been brought to the lowest degradation by the apostasy and crimes of the last Onias or Menelaus, and after a vacancy of seven years had followed the brief pontificate of Alcimus, his no less infamous successor, a new and glorious succession of high priests arose in the Asmonaean family. This family were of the course of Joiarib (I Chron. 24:7), whose return from captivity is recorded I Chron. 9:10; Neh. 11:10 and lasted from B. C. 153 till the family was destroyed by Herod the Great. Aristobulus, the last high priest of his line, was murdered by order of Herod, his brother-in-law, B.C. 35.

"There were no fewer than twenty-eight high priests from the reign of Herod to the destruction of the temple by Titus, a period of one hundred and seven years. The New Testament introduces us to some of these later and oft-changing high priests, viz., Annas, Caiaphas, and Ananias. Theophilus, the son of Ananus, was the high priest from whom Saul received letters to the synagogue at Damascus (Acts 9:1, 14). Phannias, the last high priest, was appointed by lot by the Zealots from the course of priests called by Josephus Eniachim (probably) a corrupt reading for Jachim") (Smith, *Dict.*, s. v. Schürer, *Jewish People in Time of Jesus Christ*, div. ii, v, i).

8. **Typology.** Aaron as high priest is a type of Christ. The functions, dress and ritual connected with the high priest's anointing are minutely instructive of the Person and work of Christ as a Priest. Although Christ is a Priest after the order of Melchisedek (Psa. 110:4; Heb. 5:6; 6:20; 7:21), He executes His priestly office after the *pattern* of Aaron. The order is expounded in Hebrews, chapter 7, the pattern, in Hebrews, chapter 9. Death often disrupted the Aaronic priesthood; therefore, Christ is a Priest after the order of Melchisedek as "King of Righteousness" and "King of Peace" and in the perpetuity of His priesthood. Melchisedek as a *Messianic* type was a king-priest, and the portrayal speaks of the royal authority and unending duration of Christ's High Priesthood (Heb. 7:23, 24). The Melchisedek type was needed in addition to the Aaronic type to present a full-orbed typical picture of Christ in His High Priestly work of sacrifice for sin and His present everliving, all-efficacious, intercessory ministry in behalf of His own (John 17:1-22; Heb. 7:24, 25). M. F. U.

Prince, Princess, the rendering of a large number of Hebrew and Greek words:

1. The fathers, who by right of birth stood at the head of tribes and portions of tribes, were called *princes* (Exod. 34:31; 35:27, A. V. "rulers") or *princes of Israel* (Num. 1:44; 7:42, etc.), and as representing the people, *princes of the congregation* (Num. 4:34; 31:13, etc.).

2. "Princes of provinces" (I Kings 20:14), who were probably local governors or magistrates. The different officials so designated are given in I Kings 4:1-6.

3. The "princes" mentioned in Dan. 6:1 (see Esth. 1:1) were the predecessors of the satraps of Darius Hystaspes.

Principalities (Gr. *'archē*, *first*, and so *rule*, *magistracy*), used by Paul of angels and demons who were *invested with power* (Rom. 8:38; I Cor. 15:24; Eph. 1:21; 3:10; 6:12; Col. 1:16; 2:10, 15; Tit. 3:1).

Principles, the elements, rudiments of any art, science, or discipline (Gr. *stoicheion*, Heb. 5:12). In Heb. 6:1 (Gr. *'archē*) the meaning of the passage is equivalent to the fundamentals of the doctrine of Christ, i. e., the instruction concerning Christ, such as it was at the very outset.

Print. 1. (Heb. *ḥāqāh*, to *carve*, *delineate*), used in the expression, "Thou settest a print upon the heels of my feet" (Job. 13:27), and variously understood. Perhaps this is most correct: "Thou makest to thyself furrows (or also lines) round the soles of my feet, so that they cannot move beyond the narrow boundaries marked out by thee," (Delitzsch, *Com.*, in loc.).

2. (Gr. *tupos*, a *mark*), a figure formed by a blow, a scar (John 20:25). *See* Mark.

Printed (Job 19:23), i. e., *recorded* in a book. *See* Writing.

Pris'ca (prĭs'kā; Lat. *old woman*, II Tim. 4:19). *See* Priscilla.

Priscil'la (prĭ-sĭl'à; Lat'. *little old woman*, diminutive of Prisca, *q. v.*), the wife of Aquila (*q. v.*), in connection with whom she is always mentioned (Acts 18:2, 18, 26; Rom. 16:3; I Cor. 16:19). She seems to have been in full accord with her husband in sustaining the "Church in their house" (I Cor. 16:19), in helping the apostle Paul (Acts 18:18), and in the theological teaching of Apollos (v. 26).

Prison. In Egypt it is plain both that special places were used as prisons, and that they were under the custody of a military officer (Gen. 40:3; 42:17). During the wandering in the desert we read on two occasions of confinement "in ward" (Lev. 24:12; Num. 15:34); but as imprisonment was not directed by the law, so we hear of none till the time of the kings, when the prison appears as an appendage to the palace, or a special part of it (I Kings 22:27). Later still it is distinctly described as being in the king's house (Jer. 32:2; 37:21; Neh. 3:25). This was the case also at Babylon (II Kings 25:27). But private houses were sometimes used as places of confinement (Jer. 37:15). Public prisons other than these, though in use by the Canaanitish nations (Judg. 16:21, 25), were unknown in Judea previous to the captivity. Under the

Herods we hear again of royal prisons attached to the palace, or in royal fortresses (Luke 3:20; Acts 12:4, 10). By the Romans Antonia was used as a prison at Jerusalem (Acts 23:10), and at Caesarea the pretorium of Herod (ver. 35). The most ancient prisons were simply water cisterns, out of which, since the sides came nearly together above, one could not easily escape unaided (Gen. 37:20, 22). *See* Punishment.

Figurative. Prison is used as a symbol of deep *affliction* (Psa. 142:7), of *hell* (Rev. 20:7), *bondage* to sin and Satan (Isa. 42:7; 49:9; 61:1).

Prisoner. *See* Punishment.

Privily, To Put Away (Matt. 1:19). *See* Divorce.

Prize (Gr. *brabeion, award*), a reward bestowed on victors (I Cor. 9:24; Phil. 3:14) in the public games (*q. v.*) of the Greeks.

Proch'orus (prŏk'ô-rŭs; Gr. *leader in a choric dance*), the third on the list of deacons following Stephen and Philip (Acts 6:5), A. D. 33 (30). This is the only mention of him made in the New Testament. There is a tradition that he was consecrated bishop of Nicomedia by St. Peter.

Proclamation, the rendering of several Hebrew words, denoting to *call, cry aloud,* etc., to express the publishing of the edict of a governing power in a formal manner. The laws of Moses, as well as the temporary edicts of Joshua, were communicated to the people by means of the genealogists, or "officers" (A. V.), but those of the kings were proclaimed publicly by criers (Jer. 34:8, 9; Jonah 3:5-7; comp. Dan. 3:4; 5:29, A. V. "herald").

Profane (Hebrew from *ḥālăl,* to *open, give access to;* Gr. *bebēloō, to desecrate*). To profane is to *make common,* to *defile,* since holy things were not open to the people, e. g., a sanctuary (Lev. 19:8; 21:9), the Sabbath (Exod. 31:14), the name of God (Exod. 19:22; Mal. 1:12), a father's bed by incest (Gen. 49:4). Esau, by despising his birthright, was called a "profane person" (Heb. 12:16). In Jer. 23:11 it is said "both prophet and priest are profane" (Heb. *hănēf, soiled*), a term implying the strongest opposite of holiness.

Prognosticator. *See* Magic.

Promise, a solemn asserveration, by which one pledges his veracity that he will perform, or cause to be performed, that which he mentions (I Kings 8:56; II Chron. 1:9; Psa. 77:8; 105:42). Promises differ from the commands of God, the former being significations of the divine will concerning a duty to be performed, while the latter relate to mercies to be received. Some promises are predictions, as the promise of the Messiah and the blessings of the Gospel (Rom. 4:13, 14; Gal. 3:14-29). Hence the Hebrews were called the "children of the promise" (Rom. 9:8), as all true believers in Christ are called "children" and "heirs of the promise" (Gal. 4:28; Heb. 6:12, 17). "There are four classes of promises mentioned in Scripture: (1) Relating to the Messiah; (2) relating to the Church; (3) the Gentiles; (4) Israel as a nation, now nationally set aside (Rom. 11:1-24), but yet to be restored (Ezek. 37:1-14; Zech. 8:1-12).

Property. *See* Law of Moses, 1 (2).

Prophecy. *See* Prophet.

Prophet, one who is divinely inspired to communicate God's will to his people, and to disclose the future to them.

1. **Names.** The general Hebrew word for prophet is *nābî'*, from verb *nābă'* cf. Akkad. năbū *to announce, call a declarer, announcer.* The primary idea of a prophet, therefore, is *a declarer, announcer,* one who utters a communication. The great majority of biblical critics prefer the active sense of *announcing, pouring forth the declarations of God.* Two other Hebrew words are used to designate the prophet *rō'ĕh* and *ḥōzĕh,* both meaning *one who sees,* and rendered in the A. V. by "seer." The three words occur in I Chron. 29:29, where they seem to be contrasted with each other: "Now the acts of David the king, first and last, behold, they are written in the book of Samuel the *seer* (*rōĕh*), and in the book of Nathan the *prophet* (*nābî'*), and in the book of Gad the *seer* (*ḥōzĕh*). *Rō'ĕh* occurs twelve times (I Sam. 9:11, 18, 19; II Sam. 15:27; I Chron. 9:22; 26:28; 29:29; II Chron. 16:7, 10; Isa. 30:10), and in seven of these it is applied to Samuel. It was superseded in general use by the word *nābî',* by which Samuel was designated as well as by *rō'ĕh* (I Sam. 3:20; II Chron. 35:18), and which seems to have been revived after a period of disuse (I Sam. 10:5, 10, 11, 12; 19:20, 24). *Hāzōn* is the word constantly used for the prophetical vision, and is found in Samuel, Chronicles, Psalms, Proverbs, and in most of the prophets. Whether there is any difference in the usage of these words, and, if any, what that difference is, has been much debated. On the whole, it would seem that the same persons are designated by the three words. Sometimes the prophets are called *watchmen* (Heb. *sōphĭ'ĭm,* Jer. 6:17; Ezek. 3:17; 33:2, 6, 7); *shōmēr,* a *watchman,* Isa. 21:11; 62:6; *rō'î, pastoral,* a shepherd (Zech. 11:5; 11:16). The word is uniformly translated in the LXX by *prophētēs,* and in the A. V. by "prophet." In classical Greek *prophētēs* signifies *one who speaks for another,* especially *one who speaks for a god* and so interprets his will to man. Hence its essential meaning is "an interpreter." The use of the word *prophētēs* in its modern sense is postclassical, and is derived from the LXX. From the medieval use of the word *prophēteia,* (*prophecy*) passed into the English language in the sense of *prediction,* and this sense it has retained as its popular meaning. The larger sense of *interpretation* has not, however, been lost. In fact the English word prophet, like the word inspiration, has always been used in a larger and in a closer sense.

2. **The Prophetical Order.** The prophetical institution was not a temporary expedient, but provision was made for it in the law. That the Israelites might not consult with false prophets, such as diviners, observers of times, enchanters, etc., Moses promised (Deut. 18:9, 15), "The Lord thy God shall raise up unto thee a prophet from the midst of thee, of thy brethren, like unto me; unto him shall ye hearken," etc. (comp. vers. 16-22). While this passage evidently refers to the Messiah, it does not exclude its reference to a succession of prophets, between Moses and Christ, run-

ning parallel with the kingdom of Israel. The Scriptures do not represent an unbroken series of prophets, each inducted into office by his predecessor, being silent on this point save in the cases of Joshua and Elisha, who were respectively inducted into office by Moses and Elijah. The prophets are described as deriving their prophetical office immediately from God, and not to have attached much importance to a series of incumbents, each receiving his commission from another, or from others.

From the days of Joshua to Eli "there was no open vision" (I Sam. 3:1), as during the time of the judges the priesthood, who were originally the instrument through which Israel was taught and governed in spiritual things, had sadly degenerated. The people were no longer affected by the acted lessons of the ceremonial service. They required less enigmatic warnings and exhortations. Under these circumstances a new moral power was evoked—the prophetic order. Samuel, himself a Levite, of the family of Kohath (I Chron. 6:28), and almost certainly a priest, was the instrument used at once for effecting a reform in the sacerdotal order (9:22), and for giving to the prophets a position of importance which they had never before held. Nevertheless, it is not to be supposed that Samuel created the prophetic order as a new thing before unknown. The germs both of the prophetic and regal order are found in the law as given to the Israelites by Moses (Deut. 13:1; 18:20; 17:18), but they were not yet developed, because there was not yet the demand for them.

(1) **Schools.** Samuel took measures to make his work of restoration permanent as well as effective for the moment. For this purpose he instituted companies, or colleges of prophets. One we find in his lifetime at Ramah (I Sam. 19:19, 20); others afterward at Beth-el (II Kings 2:3), Jericho (2:5), Gilgal (4:38), and elsewhere (6:1). Their constitution and object were similar to those of theological colleges. Into them were gathered promising students, and here they were trained for the office which they were afterward destined to fulfill. So successful were these institutions that from the time of Samuel to the closing of the canon of the Old Testament there seems never to have been wanting a due supply of men to keep up the line of official prophets. Their chief subject of study was, no doubt, the law and its interpretation; oral, as distinct from symbolical, teaching being henceforward tacitly transferred from the priestly to the prophetical order. Subsidiary subjects of instruction were music and sacred poetry, both of which had been connected with prophecy from the time of Moses (Exod. 15:20) and the judges (Judg. 4:4; 5:1).

(2) **Manner of Life.** The mode of life led by the prophets seems to have been subject to no uniform and rigid law, but, doubtless, changing according to circumstances. It must not be taken for granted that there was any peculiar dress adopted by them because of the instances of Elijah and John the Baptist wearing a hairy garment. Nor from their manner of living, are we to conclude that all adopted an ascetic mode of life. Sometimes, perhaps as an example, or because of persecution,

they lived in poverty (I Kings 14:3; II Kings 4:1, 38, 42; 6:5). It is probable that the writer of the Epistle to the Hebrews (11:37, 38) alludes to the sufferings and privation of the prophets, a vivid description of which is given in the accounts of Elijah, Elisha, and Jeremiah (ch. 20). Their persecution and consequent suffering did not arise from opposition to them as a distinct class, leading an unsociable, ascetic mode of life, but from opposition to their faithful ministry.

3. **Prophetic Function.** "The prophets had a practical office to discharge. It was part of their commission to show the people of God 'their transgressions and the house of Jacob their sins' (Isa. 58:1; Ezek. 22:2; 43:10; Mic. 3:8). They were, therefore, pastors and ministerial monitors of the people of God. It was their duty to admonish and reprove, to denounce prevailing sins, to threaten the people with the terrors of divine judgment, and to call them to repentance. They also brought the message of consolation and pardon (Isa. 40:1, 2). They were the watchmen set upon the walls of Zion to blow the trumpet, and timely warning of approaching danger (Ezek. 3:17; 33:7, 8, 9; Jer. 6:17; Isa. 62:6). Their function differed from that of the priests, the latter approaching God in behalf of men by means of sacrifice, the former coming to men as ambassadors from God, beseeching them to turn from their evil ways and live. The prophets do not seem to have had any official relation to the government, exerting an influence upon rulers and state affairs, not as officers of the state, but as special messengers from God. Nor must it be inferred that the prophetic and priestly classes were antagonistic. There were times when the priesthood settled down to formality and routine, or exercised their office for gain. At such time the prophetic voice was raised in scathing rebukes, whose terms almost lead one to conclude that in the prophetical estimation the whole priestly order, and all the ceremonies over which they presided, were in the essence wrong. Yet even in the midst of such rebukes there is a tone of respect for the law, and a recognition of the sacred function of the priest. So, also, when we come to any crisis in the history in which a positive advance is made, we perceive that it is not by a conquest of one party over the other, but by the hearty cooperation of both, that the movement of reform or advance succeeds. Moses, the forerunner of the prophets, has Aaron the priest beside him; and Joshua is still surrounded by priests in the carrying out of his work. Samuel is both priest and prophet; David and Solomon, in the same way, are served or admonished by both" (Robertson, *Early Religion of Israel*, p. 461).

In addition to the declaration of God's will, the denunciation of his judgments, the defense of truth and righteousness, and bearing testimony to the superiority of the moral to the ritual, prophecy had an intimate relation to God's gracious purpose toward Israel (Mic. 5:4; 7:20; Isa. 60:3; 65:25).

4. **Contents and Sphere.** The function of the prophet, as already seen, is not merely the disclosure of the future, but included the

exposition and application of the law, the declaration of God's will. It thus contained two elements—the *moral*, or *doctrinal*, and the *predictive*. The *doctrinal* element of prophecy teaches: "The existence of an eternal, self-conscious, intelligent, moral, and voluntary Being, who does all things according to the purpose of his will. It ascribes to him all the attributes of such a Being in infinite perfection. It is more or less a commentary upon the doctrine of divine providence, by representing the future even, which it brings to view, as a part of that system of things in which the Creator is present by the direction of his power and the counsels of his wisdom, appointing the issues of futurity, as well as foreseeing the acting with his 'mighty hand and outstretched arm,' seen or unseen, ruling in the kingdom of men, and ordering all things in heaven and earth" (Charles Elliott, *Old Testament Prophecy*, p. 44).

The prophets teach respecting man that he was created by God (Mal. 2:10), has a common origin (ib.), has the power of reason (Ezek. 12:2; Isa. 1:18), a capacity for holiness (ib.), for knowledge and progress (2:3-5); he is ruined and cannot save himself (Hos. 13:9; Jer. 2:22; 13:23); he is a subject of God's moral government, and owes entire obedience to his law (Dan. 4:34, 35; Ezek. 18:4, 5, 9; Isa. 1:19, 20; 23:11-16); worship and homage must be rendered by him to God (Isa. 60:6, 7; Mal. 1:11; 3:10). All duties arising out of human relations are also clearly stated and enforced. The prophets, moreover, inculcate, with remarkable clearness and decision, the doctrines of faith and repentance (Isa. 26:3, 4; 55:7; Ezek. 14:6; 18:30; 36:31).

By the *sphere* of prophecy are meant the parties to whom it was given and the objects which it more immediately contemplated. Its proper sphere, especially in its stricter sense of containing preintimations of good things to come, is the nation Israel in relation to the coming Messiah and the manner in which this relationship affects both the Jew and Gentile. The Church, born on the day of Pentecost (Acts 2) is not in view in the O. T. prophets but was a special mystery revealed to the Apostle Paul (Eph. 3:1-10; Rom. 16:25). Future Gentile salvation was clearly revealed, but not the "mysteries of the kingdom of heaven" (Matt. 13) which concern this present age. The bulk of O. T. prophecy concerns Israel's future national conversion and restoration in the coming millennial kingdom inaugurated at the Second advent of Christ (Isa. 35:1-10; Zech. 14:1-21, etc.).

Prophecy is not intended to open the future to idle curiosity, but for the higher purpose of furnishing light to those whose faith needs confirming. The revelation of future events may be needful in times of discouragement to awaken or sustain hope, to inspire confidence in the midst of general backsliding, and to warn of evil threatening the faithful. The predictions against Babylon, Tyre, Egypt, Nineveh, and other kingdoms, were delivered to the people of God to comfort them, by revealing to them the fate of their enemies. The prophecy of Jonah against Nineveh seems to be exceptional. He was sent to a heathen power to denounce the judgments of God against it. He did not, in his own land and among his own people, preach against Nineveh, but he entered the great city itself and delivered his message there. Thus his was a typical character, and his mission to Nineveh may have been typical of Israel to be "a light of the Gentiles," and intended to remind ancient Israel of the mission which it had neglected and forgotten.

5. **Prophetic Inspiration.** The Scriptures teach that the prophets received their communications by the agency of the Spirit of God. When the seventy elders were appointed the Lord said to Moses, "I will take of the spirit which is upon thee, and will put it upon them," etc. (Num. 11:17, 25). Samuel said to Saul, "And the Spirit of the Lord will come upon thee, and thou shalt prophesy with them, and shalt be turned into another man" (I Sam. 10:6). "And Saul sent messengers to take David: and when they saw the company of the prophets prophesying, and Samuel standing as appointed over them, the Spirit of God was upon the messengers of Saul, and they also prophesied" (19:20). According to Peter (II Pet. 1:21), "prophecy came not in old time by the will of man: but holy men of God spake as they were moved by the Holy Ghost."

The false prophets were those who "speak a vision of their own heart, and not out of the mouth of the Lord" (Jer. 23:16); "foolish prophets, that follow their own spirit, and have seen nothing" (Ezek. 13:3). The true prophet was God's spokesman to man, communicating what he had received from God (Exod. 4:16; 7:1).

The modes of communication between God and man are clearly stated on the occasion of the sedition of Aaron and Miriam: "And he said, Hear now my words: If there be a prophet among you, I the Lord will make myself known unto him in a vision, and will speak unto him in a dream. My servant Moses is not so, who is faithful in all my house. With him will I speak mouth to mouth, even apparently, and not in dark speeches; and the similitude of the Lord shall he behold" (Num. 12:6). Three modes are here given: (1) Vision; (2) dream; (3) direct communication and manifestation; the highest form being the last, and reserved for Moses. In this he resembled Christ, of whom he was a type. The other two were lower forms, whose comparative rank it is perhaps impossible to determine.

The state of the prophet, while under the influence of the Holy Spirit, has been a matter of considerable comment. Philo and the Alexandrine school held that the prophet was in a state of entire unconsciousness when under such influence. Athenagoras held that the prophets were entranced and deprived of their natural powers, "the Spirit using them as instruments, as a flute player might blow a flute." Montanus held the same theory: "The Almighty ruled alone in the prophet's soul, whose own self-consciousness retired back. God, therefore, spoke from the soul of the prophet, of which he took entire possession, as if in his own name." But such a theory identifies Jewish prophecy, in all essential points, with heathen divination. The diviners of the heathen world were supposed to be, when under the influence of inspiration, in a state of mind expressed by the Greek *ekstasis*, i. e., a *trance*, their being faculties held in complete abeyance. Such a state of mind was regarded as a natural and necessary sign of inspiration, the subject exhibiting the outward signs of violent excitement, resembling insanity.

The Hebrew prophets were not distinguished by such peculiarities. They were not subject to *amentia*, neither were they placed, as Montanus taught, in an altogether passive relation to the divine influence; but they were possessed of intelligent self-consciousness. They did not lose their self-possession, but spoke with a full apprehension of existing circumstances. At the same time the mind of the prophet seems to have been raised above its ordinary condition; and he sometimes adopted measures to prepare himself for prophesying (II Kings 3:15; I Sam. 10:5; I Chron. 25:1). The mind of the prophet was passive while receiving divine communications in visions and in dreams; but in the announcement of their visions and dreams the prophets were in full possession of intelligent self-consciousness. They were conscious that they had a divine commission, that they were sent by God to communicate his purposes; and, accordingly, they preface their prophetic utterances by the formulae, "The hand of the Lord was upon me" (Ezek. 1:3; 3:14; 33:22); "Isaiah saw" (Isa. 1:1); "Ezekiel saw" (Ezek. 1:1); "Thus saith the Lord" (Jer. 1:8, 19; 2:19; 30:11; Amos 2:11; 4:5; 7:3); "The word of the Lord came unto Jonah" (Jonah 1:1; Joel 1:1).

As to the question, Had the prophets a full knowledge of what they predicted? it would seem that their understandings were not so miraculously enlarged as to grasp the whole of the divine counsels which they were commissioned to enunciate. We have, as Oehler says, the testimony of the prophets themselves to this effect (Dan. 12:8; Zech, 4:5; I Pet. 1:10, 11).

6. Prophetic Style. A writer's characteristic manner of expression we call his *style*. The sacred writers form no exception; each one maintains his individuality; and it is therefore perfectly proper to speak of the style of Isaiah, Jeremiah, etc. But apart from the style which is the expression of the mental and moral idiosyncrasies of the prophets there is a style which characterizes them as prophets. This arises from the method of prophetic revelation. When inspired of God their intellectual and emotional nature was quickened. They knew by intuition, and their hearts glowed with seraphic ardor. They were in the region of spirit as contradistinguished from that of sense and time. At the same time they retained their personal characteristics and native susceptibilities. We find that prophecy made large use of the present and past condition of the nation, of the Levitical institutions and ceremonies, as symbols in presenting good things to come, e. g.: (1) The future is described in terms of the past (Hos. 8:13; 9:3; 11:5; comp. Rev. 2:14, 20);

(2) Prophecy made great use of the present, and especially of the standpoint and personal circumstances of the agent, to illustrate the future (Ezek. 48:35; comp. Rev. 21:22); (3) Frequently the prophetic style received its completion and coloring from the diversified circumstances of the parties addressed, as well as from the standpoint of the prophet (Dan., chaps. 8, 9); (4) The poetical element of prophecy arises from the ecstatical condition of the prophet; but, as it was the primary aim of the Hebrew religious teachers to influence the heart and conscience, the poetical element, though never entirely suppressed, was held in restraint to further the ends of spiritual instruction.

Prophecy, the oral or written message of a prophet.

1. **The Nature of Prophecy.** The *predictive* element was a frequent part of the content of the prophet's message. But this is not the only element. The prophets frequently appear in the role of social and political reformers, stirring preachers of righteousness and religious revivalists in addition to being predictors of judgment or blessing, as the occasion demanded. The prophet's message was ever religious and spiritual, announcing the will of God to men and calling for complete obedience. Often the prophetic element shone out in the prophet's preaching and writing. This element cannot be dispensed with as some modern critics would think. Neither can the opposite extreme of regarding the prophet's message as solely predictive be defended as tenable. Prophetic prognostication was not mere foretelling to appeal to idle curiosity nor even to maintain the integrity of the prophet, although this was occasionally the case (Cf. Deut. 18:22). The genius of prophecy was rather a prediction of the future arising from the conditions of the present and was inseparably connected with the profoundly religious and spiritual message the prophet was called to proclaim to his own generation. Besides being moral and spiritual in its purpose and frequently predictive in content, O. T. prophecy *was coeval with the beginning of redemptive history.* Critics commonly limit prophecy to the writing prophets and make it a comparatively late development in Israel, confining it to the eighth century or later. However, prophecy and written prophetical oracles go back to most ancient times and are coeval with the beginning of divine revelation (Cf. the first prophecy of a Divine Redeemer, Gen. 3:15, 16). Enoch, the seventh from Adam, was a prophet (Jude 1:14, 15). Noah uttered prophetic oracles (Gen. 9:25-27), Abraham was a prophet (Gen. 20:7). Moses was a prophet in a very special sense (Num. 12:6-8) and a type of Christ "The Prophet" par excellence (Deut. 18:18; John 6:15; 7:40). Prophecy occurred in the time of the judges (Judg. 4:4). There was a dearth of prophetic vision in the time of Samuel (I Sam. 3:1). Until the close of O. T. prophecy under Malachi, prophecy was continuously operative in Israel. It rose to great literary heights in Isaiah and Jeremiah. Moreover, prophecy was *of divine origin.* The various names of the prophet in the original language, such as

rō'ĕh (I Sam. 9:9), *ḥōzĕh* (II Sam. 24:11) and *nābhî'* (I Sam. 9:9) and the manner in which they received their message indisputably point to the divine authority and origin of their message.

2. **Biblical Concept of Prophecy.** Scripture plainly presents prediction as a manifestation of God's power glorifying His Person, exalting His redemptive work in Christ and setting forth the divine character of His revealed Word. The words of fulfilled prophecies with regard to the first advent of Christ speak of the wisdom and power of God in interposing for man's need. Scripture not only presents the prophetic word as a demonstration of God's power and wisdom but His response to man's need. Since man is ignorant of what a day may bring forth, the revelation of not only God's will for the present but the disclosure of His plans and purposes for the future are of inestimable benefit to the believer. In the light of these facts, widespread neglect of Biblical prophecy is not only tragic but inexcusable.

3. **Rules for Interpretation of Prophecy.** The prophetic portions of Scripture, constituting about one-fourth of its content, demand careful treatment to avoid excesses and abuses. (1) *Select a workable system of prophetic interpretation.* One ought to investigate thoroughly available systems such as premillennialism, amillennialism and postmillennialism. The student must not rest until he is thoroughly persuaded that the system he adopts is the correct one. (2) *Fix upon the background of the prophecies.* Many details of the historical background are necessary to see the prophecy in its full sweep and meaning. Neglect of simple matters of history and light from archaeology may result in serious deficiency in interpretation. (3) *Observe the context of prophecy.* Its immediate setting must be carefully scrutinized and no interpretation permitted that will violate the immediate context. Moreover, the remote text must be handled just as diligently. Each individual prophecy must be related in the widest context to the full sweep of God's purposes from eternity past to eternity future. (4) *Pursue normal literal interpretation rather than the mystical.* A good rule is as follows: "When the plain sense of Scripture makes common sense, seek no other sense; therefore, take every word at its primary, usual literal meaning unless it is patently a rhetorical figure, or unless the immediate context, studied in the light of related passages and axiomatic and fundamental truths clearly points otherwise." (5) *Determine the correct relationship between the form of prophecy and the ideas conveyed by it.* Satisfaction of one's thinking on this line will determine whether the interpreter is attracted to a premillennial, amillennial or postmillennial interpretation. Whatever system he adopts, he must satisfy himself that his system of interpretation resolves the difficulties and meets the requirements of the specific details and not merely of generalization. Inductive logic must take precedence over inductive reasoning in the interpretation of prophecy and Scripture in general. *M. F. U.*

Propitiation, the divine side of the work of Christ on the cross. Christ's atoning death for the world's sin altered the whole position of the human race in its relationship to God, for God recognizes what Christ accomplished in behalf of the world whether men enter into the blessings of it or not. The cross has rendered God propitious toward the unsaved as well as toward the erring saint (I John 2:2). The fact that Christ has borne all sin renders God propitious. The Greek words dealing with the doctrine of propitiation are *hilasmos*, signifying what our Lord became for the sinner (I John 2:2; 4:10); *hilastērion* denotes the place of propitiation (Rom. 3:25; Heb. 9:5), *hilaskomai* indicates that God has become gracious or propitious (Luke 18:13; Heb. 2:17). In this present age since the death of Christ God does not have to be asked to be propitious, because He has become so through the death of Christ. To ask Him thus to become propitious, in view of Christ's sacrifice, manifests unbelief. In the O. T. the mercy seat in the Holiest Place could be made a place of propitiation by sacrifice (Heb. 9:5). Now, however, the blood-sprinkled body of Christ on the cross became the mercy seat for sinners once and for all. The mercy seat was thus a continual throne of grace. What otherwise would be an awful judgment throne becomes an altar of infinite mercy. The prayer of the publican (Luke 18:13), "God be merciful to me a sinner," better translated "God, be Thou propitiated to me the sinner" was not a request for mercy as though God must be persuaded to be propitious. It was rather expressive of the relationship then existing between the O. T. covenant people of God on the ground of offered sacrifice when God was requested to be propitious on a special basis. Now the believer can rejoice that God is propitiated. To believe this is to enter into the benefits of it. *M. F. U.*

Proselyte (Gr. *prosēlutos*, a *newcomer*) is found only in the New Testament, the Heb. *gēr* being rendered *stranger*. From the time of the covenant between Jehovah and Abraham Israel had been a peculiar people, whose mission it was to proclaim among the nations that Jehovah alone was God. There were at all times strangers living in Israel to whom the Mosaic law did not grant the rights of citizenship, but to whom it did extend toleration and certain privileges, for which it obliged them to comply with certain of the religious enactments prescribed to Israel. They were required not to blaspheme the name of Jehovah (Lev. 24:16), not to indulge in idolatrous worship (20:2), not to commit acts of indecency (18:26), not to work on the Sabbath (Exod. 20:10), not to eat leavened bread during the celebration of the Passover (12:19), not to eat blood or the flesh of animals that had died a natural death or had been torn by wild beasts (Lev. 17:10, 15).

1. **Naturalization of.** Should such strangers wish to become citizens, the law sanctioned their admission on the condition of being circumcised. They thus bound themselves to observe the whole law, and were admitted to the full privileges and blessings of the people of the covenant (Exod. 12:48, 49; comp. Rom. 9:4). The exceptions to strangers thus freely admitted were the Ammonites

and Moabites, who were to be strictly excluded to the tenth generation (i. e., forever), and the Edomites, whose sons were not to be admitted till the third generation (Deut. 23:3, 8). The reason assigned for these exceptions was that these nations had shown unfriendliness to the Israelites when they left Egypt.

2. **In Canaan.** Among the proselytes at the time of the entrance into Canaan, the Kenites were the most conspicuous (Judg. 1:16). The presence of *strangers* was recognized in the solemn declaration of blessings and curses from Ebal and Gerizim (Josh. 8:33). The period after the conquest of Canaan was not favorable to the admission of proselytes, the people having no strong faith, no commanding position. The Gibeonites (9:16, sq.) furnish the only instance of conversion, and their position was rather that of slaves than of free proselytes.

3. **Under the Monarchy**, some foreigners rose to power and fortune, but they were generally treated by David and Solomon as a subject class brought under a system of compulsory labor from which others were exempted (I Chron. 22:2; II Chron. 2:17, 18). As some compensation for their sufferings they became the special objects of the care and sympathy of the prophets. In the time of the monarchy, when Israel developed into a powerful state, many foreigners were attracted for the sake of political and commercial relations. Still more did their numbers increase at a later period when Israel lost its independence and was subjected to the sway of heathen powers, whose yoke it was never able to shake off except for a somewhat limited period. In these circumstances, in which there was no longer any bond of national unity, the religious fellowship which the law, with its ceremonial regulations, had created among the people, developed into an inward bond of union that every day became only more firmly knit. Notwithstanding the stiff formalism of Pharisaic piety, still the spirit that had animated the law and the prophets was able not only to resist the corrupting influence of an effete heathenism, but also to attract a considerable number of Gentiles, and lead them to seek in the religion of the Jews that salvation which their own gods and idolatrous worship was unable to afford.

Consequently the Talmud and the rabbinical teachers distinguish two classes of proselytes—*proselytes of the gate,* i. e., Gentile strangers, who, while living among the Jews, had bound themselves to observe the seven Noachian precepts against (1) idolatry, (2) blasphemy, (3) bloodshed, (4) uncleanness, (5) theft, (6) eating flesh with the blood, and (7) of obedience; and the *proselytes of righteousness* (or proselytes of the covenant), who, having been formally admitted to participation in the theocratic covenant, professed their adherence to all the doctrines and precepts of the Mosaic law. The rabbins gave three essentials for admission of males as proselytes to Judaism—circumcision, baptism, and a sacrifice; for females, baptism and sacrifice. Baptism was probably an adaptation of ablution or bathing in water, such as we may well suppose would in every case accompany the

circumcision of a Gentile, the law forbidding the unclean to take part in any religious ceremony till they had bathed in water (Exod. 19:10).

"If the baptism of proselytes was of so late an origin, then it is, of course, impossible that the baptism of John and Christian baptism can have been borrowed from it. It is much more likely that the Jews, after the discontinuance of the temple worship, may have taken occasion from Christian baptism to transform the customary bathing with water that was required in order to purification, and which the person to be purified had to perform himself, into a formal act of baptism having the character of a rite of initiation" (Keil, *Arch.,* i, p. 427).

4. **After the Captivity.** The proselytism of this period was, for the most part, the conformity, not of a subject race, but of willing adherents. As early as the return from Babylon, we have traces of those who were drawn to a faith which they recognized as holier than their own. With the extension of the Roman empire, the Jews became more widely known and their power to proselytize increased. In most of the large cities of the empire there were men who had been rescued from idolatry and its attendant debasements, and brought under the power of a higher moral law. The converts who were thus attracted joined, with varying strictness, in the worship of the Jews. In Palestine even Roman centurions learned to love the conquered nation, built synagogues (Luke 7:5), feasted, prayed, and gave alms (Acts 10:2, 30), and became preachers of the new faith to their soldiers (v. 7).

Then to almost every Jewish community there was attached a following of "God-fearing" (A. V. *religious*) proselytes (Acts 13:43), Gentiles who adopted the Jewish mode of worship, attended the synagogues, but who in the observance of the ceremonial law restricted themselves to certain leading points, and so were regarded as outside the fellowship of the Jewish communities.

Proselytism had its dark side, the Jews of Palestine being eager to spread their faith by the same weapons as those with which they had defended it. The Idumaeans had the alternative of death, exile, or circumcision, while the Ithraeans were converted in the same way. Where force was not used, converts were sought by the most unscrupulous fraud; the vices of the Jew were engrafted on those of the heathen. Their position was pitiable; at Rome and other large cities they were the butt of popular scurrility, bound to make public confession and pay a special tax. Among the Jews they gained but little honor, being looked upon with suspicion, as converted Jews often are now. The better rabbis did their best to guard against these evils. Anxious to exclude all unworthy converts, they grouped them, according to their motives, with a somewhat quaint classification. 1. Love-proselytes, where they were drawn by the hope of gaining the beloved one. 2. Man-for-woman, or Woman-for-man proselytes, where the husband followed the religion of the wife, or conversely. 3. Esther-proselytes, where conformity was assumed to escape danger, as in the original Purim (Esth. 8:17). 4. King's-table-proselytes, who were led by the hope of court favor and promotion, like the converts under David and Solomon. 5. Lion-proselytes, where the conversion originated in a superstitious dread of a divine judgment, as with the Samaritans of II Kings 17:26. None of these were regarded as fit for admission within the covenant (Smith, *Bib. Dict.*; Schürer, *Jewish People*).

Provender (Heb. *mĭspŏ̄*, collected; Gen. 24:25, 32; 42:27; 43:24; Judg. 19:19, 21; Isa. 30:24). In the account of King Solomon's stables (I Kings 4:28) we read, "Barley also and straw for the horses and dromedaries brought they," etc. Barley seems to have been the ordinary food of cattle in Palestine and the southern lands, where oats are not cultivated. As they make but little hay in these countries, they are very careful of their straw, which they cut up very fine and mix with barley and beans. Balls made of bean and barley meal, or of pounded kernels of dates are fed. The "provender" mentioned in Isa. 30:24 was a mash (composed of barley and vetches, or things of that kind) made more savory with salt and sour vegetables. According to Wetzstein, it is ripe barley mixed with salt or salt vegetables.

Proverb (Heb. *mäshäl, to be like*). In the early stages of social intellectual growth, when men begin to observe and generalize on the facts of human life, they clothe the results of observation in the form of short and pithy sentences. Every race, not in savage condition, has its proverbs of this kind. The Hebrew word rendered "proverb" has a special significance. The proverb of the Israelites and other people of the East was primarily and essentially a "similitude." It was thus a condensed parable or fable, capable at any time of being expanded, sometimes presented with the lesson clearly taught, sometimes involved in greater or less obscurity, that its very difficulty might stimulate the desire to know, and so impress the lesson more deeply on the mind. The proverb might be a "dark saying," requiring an interpretation; e. g., "The fining-pot is for silver, and the furnace is for gold: but the Lord trieth the hearts" (Prov. 17:3), is a parable of which we find an expansion in Mal. 3:3, "He shall sit as a refiner of silver, and he shall purify the sons of Levi, and purge them as gold and silver." In Prov. 1:17, however, the proverb, "Surely in vain the net is spread in the sight of any bird," given as it is, without any interpretation, and capable of many, is a "dark saying," in which the teaching is deliberately involved in more or less obscurity.

Individual proverbs are quoted before we are brought into contact with any collection of them. The saying, "Wickedness proceedeth from the wicked," passed as a "proverb of the ancients" in the days of Saul (I Sam. 24:13). An individual instance of strange inconsistency was generalized as a type of all like anomalies, and the question, "Is Saul also among the prophets?" became a proverb in Israel (10:11; 19:24). The inclination to transfer to others the guilt which has brought suffering to one's

self is expressed in the proverb, "The fathers have eaten sour grapes, and the children's teeth are set on edge" (Jer. 31:29; Ezek. 18:2); in both instances being condemned as an error.

The book of Job is full of apothegms of the proverb type, one of which became the motto of the book of Proverbs; "the fear of the Lord, that is wisdom; and to depart from evil, that is understanding" (Job 28:28). When Solomon came into contact with "the children of the east country" (I Kings 4:30), whose wisdom clothed itself in this form, it was perfectly natural that he should express himself in, and become the patron of maxims, precepts, condensed parables in the shape of proverbs.

The Hebrew word *ḥĭdäh*, Hab. 2:6, has the meaning of a conundrum, something enigmatical. The passage is thus rendered by K. and D. (*Com.*): "Will not all these lift up a proverb upon him, and a song, and a riddle upon him?"

Our Lord employed proverbs in his teaching, as, "Physician, heal thyself" (Luke 4:23; comp. John 16:25, 29).

Proverbs, Book of, the proverbs of Solomon the son of David, king of Israel (1:1). The word proverb itself means "a sententious brief saying setting forth practical wisdom." In 'strictest sense it means a "repetition or comparison." The Septuagint has "Proverbs or Parables" of Solomon. The Vulgate has *Liber Proverbiorum*. The book is part of the so-called Wisdom Literature of the O. T.

1. **Contents.** The book consists not only of many sententious sayings of practical wisdom but didactic poems of longer length. Not mere human wisdom is treated but Divine Wisdom, or God in revelation as a Creator and Goal of all things, is treated as well (cf. chap. 8).

2. **Outline.**

Part I. Solomon's Proverbs, 1:1-9:18
   a. Wisdom's call, 1:1-33
   b. Wisdom's rewards, 2:1-7:27
   c. Wisdom's praise, 8:1-9:18
Part II. Solomon's Various Sayings, 10:1-22:16
Part III. The Words to the Wise, 22:17-24:34
Part IV. Solomon's Proverbs Set Down by Hezekiah's Scribes, 25:1-29:27
Part V. Agur's Words, 30:1-33
Part VI. Lemuel's Words, 31:1-9
Part VII. The Acrostic Poem of the Virtuous Wife, 31:10-31

3. **Connection With Other Literature.** The Proverbs of Amenemope of Egypt, who is dated variously between 1000-600 B. C., so closely resemble Prov. 22:17-25:22 usually considered non-Solomonic, that critics commonly see literary dependence of the latter. (cf. O. Eissfeldt, *Einleitung*, p. 525). W. F. Albright, for instance, is of the persuasion that the Egyptian Proverbs "were taken over, almost certainly through Phoenician intermediation" (*Arch. and the Religion of Israel*, 1942, p. 5). However, it may be said that both the author of this section of Proverbs and the Egyptian author may well have been influenced by a common third source. A much more probable and sounder view is that the Biblical work is older, since Proverbs Chaps.

1-24 assuredly was regarded as Solomonic in Hezekiah's time (8th century B. C.).

4. **Authorship and Date.** Critics commonly ascribe little or none of the book to Solomon. Eissfeldt does this on the basis of Aramaisms, but Aramaic elements may occur very early in Hebrew literature as well as very late. It is now known that the inscription of Zakir, King of Hamath, around 800 B. C. is written in a mixture of Hebrew and Aramaic. Two sections of the book of Proverbs are expressly attributed to Solomon (10:1-22:16; 25:1-29:27). Unless we view the introduction (1:1-6) as a later edition from the fifth or fourth century B. C., there is no reason for denying chapters 1-9 to Solomon. The third section (22:17-24:34) is similar to the first chapters (1-9). And this section does not seem to be intended as a separate division on the basis of authorship since the expression "words to the wise" is not a title to a new section. The fourth section is described as being copied out by Hezekiah's scribes, evidently from an old collection of Solomon's sayings. Certainly this section was not composed by them. Therefore strong Scriptural testimony exists that Solomon was the author of chapters 1-39; that is, of the entire book except chapters 30 by Agur and 31 by King Lemuel. I Kings 4:32 supports this. It attributes "3000 proverbs" to Solomon. It is also in line with Solomon's fame for wisdom (I Kings 3:5-48; 10:1). (See G. R. Berry, *The Book of Proverbs*, Phila., 1905; O. I. Eissfeldt, *Der Maschal im Alten Testament*, Giessen, 1913, and Gemser in Eissfeldt's *Handbuch*. M. F. U.

Providence (Lat. *providentia, foreseeing*), a term which in theology designates the continual care which God exercises over the universe which he has created. This includes the two facts of preservation and government.

1. The doctrine of providence is closely connected with that of creation. That God could create the world and then forsake it is inconceivable in view of the perfection of God. Accordingly, in the power and wisdom and goodness of the Creator, declared in the Scriptures, we have the pledge of constant divine care over all parts of his creation. This idea finds expression in various places in both the Old and New Testaments (e. g., Psa. 33:13, 15; Isa. 45:7; Acts 17:24-28). This sufficiently explains the absence of any mention of providence in the Apostles' Creed. The great truth is implied in the declaration of faith "in God the Father Almighty, Maker of heaven and earth." The faith of believers in revealed religion in all ages has been of the same character; and however often expressed it is still more frequently implied.

2. Belief in providence, while agreeable with, and supported by reason, has its strongest ground in the truth of special divine revelation. It is not surprising that enlightened heathen, as Cicero and Seneca, argued in its behalf. And that even among the opponents of Christianity there have been those who have adhered to this idea. For this is an idea not exclusively Christian, but a necessary feature of religion in general. And of the correctness of this idea human history as a whole, and the spectacle of the universe, furnish abundant illustrations. Facts irreconcilable by us with this belief, on account of the narrow limits of human understanding, exist in large number. And yet the overwhelming preponderance of the facts even within our observation is in the opposite direction. Broad observation and right reason preclude the idea of a government of the world by chance or blind force, and sustains the belief that "there is a power in the world that makes for righteousness." In addition the deep necessities of human nature and life are perpetually crying out "for the living God." That facts apparently opposed to faith at this point exist is what should be expected. For universal and perfect providence implies infinite knowledge; and "we know" only "in part." For every mind less than the infinite providence must have its mysteries. Our faith at this point, as at others, must therefore find its chief support and guidance from the word of God.

3. The Scriptures bearing upon this subject are very numerous and of great variety and force. Space does not admit here the attempt at reference. But aside from the large number of particular passages, the historical parts of the Bible are throughout illustrative of the great reality. In brief, it may be said that according to the Scriptures: 1. The providence of God is unlimited. It includes all things and all creatures; it has respect to all that takes place in the universe (see e. g., Psa. 145:9-17). The distinction between great things and small, often unreasonable in view of the dependence of the great upon the small, is rightly regarded by the care of the infinite God. Things seemingly of only slight importance or accidental are under his overruling power (see, e. g., I Kings 22:34; Esth. 6:1; Matt. 6:26; 27:19; Luke 12:6, 7; Acts 23:16). 2. The exercise of God's providence, nevertheless, has respect to the nature of different objects. All objects cannot be alike precious in his sight. And thus there is ground in Scriptures, as in reason, for the distinction between general and particular and special providence. Mankind holds a peculiar relation to God among all the works of his creation; and among mankind, the people of God, the faithful servants of his kingdom, are the objects of his special love and care (see Matt. 6:25-32; Psa. 91:11, 12; 147:19, 20; Acts 14:16, 17; Rom. 8:28-39). Thus Scripture clearly reveals God's special love and care of nationally elect Israel in the Old Testament (Mal. 1:2, 3) and of the Church, the Body of Christ, in the New Testament (Eph. 1:3-23), Moreover, God's unbroken love to Israel is declared in their future restoration after the period of Gentile visitation (Acts 15:14-16; Rom. 11:1-25). God's providential ways with Jew, Gentile and the Church of God (I Cor. 10:32) must always be clearly differentiated. 3. The constant and final aim of God's providence is the fulfillment of his purpose in creation. How broad and wonderful this is may defy our comprehension; but it is declared to be nothing less than the complete establishment of an all-embracing kingdom of God, under the rule of the Lord Jesus Christ (see Eph. 1:9-11; Col. 1:19, 20). 4. The particular

steps in this divine process are often unintelligible to us, but the purpose of God is independent and eternal, and is certain of its realization (see Psa. 97:2; Rom. 11:33; Eph. 1:4, 5; Rom. 11:34, 35, et al.). 5. Belief in the providence of God, according to the whole purport of Scriptures, is of the highest importance, because of its connection with a life of trust and gratitude and patience and hope.

4. Upon the various philosophical speculations as to method of God in providence, and his relation to natural causes, and to the free agency of man, we cannot here enter. For this we must refer the reader to works upon systematic theology, mentioned below (see Hodge, *Syst. Theol.*, vol. i, 575, sq.; Van Oosterzee, *Christ. Dogm.*, vol. i, 326, sq.; Dorner, *Syst. Christ. Doct.*, index; Pope, *Comp. Christ. Theol.*, vol. i, 437, sq.; Alford, *Meditations*). Chafer, Strong, Berkhof, etc.

Province (Heb. m⁰*dīnäh*, *district* ruled by a judge).

1. In the Old Testament this word appears in connection with the wars between Ahab and Benhadad (I Kings 20:14, 15, 19). The victory of the former is gained chiefly "by the young men of the princes of the provinces," i. e., probably, of the chiefs of tribes in the Gilead country.

2. More commonly the word is used of the divisions of the Chaldean (Dan. 2:49; 3:1, 30) and the Persian kingdoms (Ezra 2:1; Neh. 7:6; Esth. 1:1, 22; 2:3, etc.). The facts as to the administration of the Persian provinces which come within our view in these passages are chiefly these: Each province has its own governor, who communicates more or less regularly with the central authority for instructions (Ezra, chaps. 4 and 5). Each province has its own system of finance, subject to the king's direction (Herod, iii, 89). The total number of the provinces is given at one hundred and twenty-seven (Esth. 1:1, 8:9). Through the whole extent of the kingdom there is carried something like a postal system. The word is used, it must be remembered, of the smaller sections of a satrapy rather than of the satrapy itself.

3. (Gr. *'eparchia*, Acts 23:34; 25:1), the region subject to a prefect; a province of the Roman empire, either a larger province or an appendage to a larger one, as Palestine was to that of Syria. The classification given by Strabo (xvii, p. 840) of provinces supposed to need military control, and therefore placed under the immediate government of the Caesar, and those still belonging theoretically to the republic and administered by the Senate; and of the latter again into proconsular and pretorian, is recognized, more or less distinctly, in the gospels and the Acts. The right of any Roman citizen to appeal from a provincial governor to the emperor meets us as asserted by St. Paul (Acts 25:1). In the council of Acts 25:12 we recognize the assessors who were appointed to take part in the judicial functions of the governor.

Provocation, the rendering of four Hebrew words and one Greek word, with the meaning of *bitterness, anger, strife*. The word is generally used to designate the ungrateful, rebellious spirit and consequent conduct of the Israel-ites (Psa. 95:8; Neh. 9:18, 26; Heb. 3:8, 15). The expression (Job 17:2), "Doth not mine eye continue in their provocation?" means that on the part of his friends Job sees nothing but *disputings*. The prophet (Ezek. 20:38) complains of the people in the high place that "they presented the provocation of their offering," i. e., their gifts, which provoked irritation on the part of God, because they were offered to idols.

Prudence, Prudent, the rendering of several Hebrew and Greek words; in all of which there is the underlying meaning of *intelligence, understanding*, and in the good sense of the word when allied with wisdom (II Chron. 2:12; Prov. 8:12; Eph. 1:8).

Pruning Hook (Heb. *măzmērāh*, Isa. 2:4, 18:5; Joel 3:10; Mic. 4:3), a knife for pruning the vine.

Psalm. *See* Music.

Psalms, Israel's ancient collection of hymns of praise and worship, widely used in temple and synagogue worship. This part of the Hebrew Scriptures has been particularly cherished by God's people in every age. This collection of devotional material nearly always is found first in the third division of the Hebrew canon called The Writings (Cf. Luke 24:44, where it represents the entire third part of the Hebrew canon).

1. **The Name.** The ancient Hebrews called this collection *Tehillim*, that is, "songs of praise" or hymns. The fuller designation is *Sefer Tehillim*, that is, "the Book of Psalms." The expression psalms is from the Greek denoting "music on string instruments," or, more generally, "songs adapted to such music."

2. **Authorship.** There are 150 psalms arranged in five books according to an ancient pre-Septuagint scheme. The beginning of each book is marked by Psalm 1, 42, 73, 90 and 107. Seventy-three of these are ascribed to David in the Hebrew titles. This explains the designation, "the psalms of David." Although modern critics such as Otto Eissfeldt, Robert Pfeiffer, Julius Bewer and others customarily deny the Davidic authorship of the Psalms, there is ample internal evidence that David, the great poet and musician of Israel, was the principal author of the Psalter. This position, despite the contention of negative criticism, is indicated by the following reasons: (1) David's name is famous in the O. T. period for music and song and is closely associated with holy liturgy (II Sam. 6:5-15; I Chron. 16:4; II Chron. 7:6; 29:30). (2) David was especially endowed by the Holy Spirit (I Sam. 23:1, 2; Mark 12:36; Acts 2:25-31; 4:25, 26). (3) David's music and poetical gifts appear indelibly interwoven on the pages of O. T. history. He is called "the sweet psalmist of Israel" (II Sam. 23:1). He was a skilled performer on the lyre (I Sam. 16:16-18). He was the author of the masterful elegy written upon the death of Saul and Jonathan (II Sam. 1:19-27). He is referred to as a model poet-musician by the prophet Amos (Amos 6:5). (4) Much internal evidence in the psalms themselves point to David's authorship. Most of the songs attributed to him reflect some period of his life, such as Psa. 23, 51 and 57. In line with this evidence of Scripture, a

number of the psalms indicate Davidic authorship. The common expression *ledavid* is normally construed as indicating Davidic authorship. (5) Certain psalms are cited as Davidic in Scripture in general. Acts 4:25, 26 so cites Psalm 2. Acts 2:25-28 so cites Psalm 16. Romans 4:6-8 cites Psalm 32. Acts 1:16-20 thus refers to Psalm 69. Also, Rom. 11:9, 10. Cf. Acts 1:20 with Psalm 109; Matt. 22:44; Mark 12:36, 37; Luke 20:42-44; Acts 2:34 with Psalm 110. In addition to the Psalms ascribed to David, ancient tradition preserved in the superscription ascribes other psalms to Moses (Psa. 90), Solomon (Psa. 72 and 127); Heman (Psa. 88), Ethan (Psa. 89), Asaph (Psa. 50, 73-80), the sons of Korah (Psa. 42, 44-49, 84, 85 and 87). Forty-nine of the psalms are anonymous according to the Hebrew text.

3. **Composition and Date.** Close affinity of many of the psalms with the style, forms and expressions in the Ras Shamra epic poetry from ancient Ugarit, dating from the fourteenth century B. C., demonstrates the antiquity of many of these odes (cf. J. Patton, *Canannite Parallels in the Book of Psalms*, Baltimore, 1944). Unless one's thinking is distorted by the unsound presuppositions of the Wellhausen school, it is reasonable to view the bulk of the psalms as pre-exilic, some dating even from before the Davidic-Solomonic era. Even if one did concede that the Book of Psalms in the precise form in which it has come down to us is a post-exilic collection, there is not the slightest historical or archaeological reason to suppose with Pfeiffer that the great mass of the Psalms were written between 400 and 100 B. C. or that "the real question with regard to the Psalter is not that it contains Maccabaean psalms of the second century, but rather whether any psalms are pre-exilic psalms" (*Intro.*, p. 629). Fortunately archaeology is silencing such radical, unbelieving criticism. Archaisms, ancient literary forms and expressions, closely parallel ancient Canaanite poetic literature and speak out eloquently for a pre-exilic date.

4. **Contents.** Although the Psalter is largely composed of devotional hymns, heartfelt praise and personal testimonies of praise and thanksgiving to the Lord, yet many of these poetic gems give far-reaching predictions and are prophetic as well as devotionally didactic. Psalm 2 is a magnificent prophetic panorama of Messiah's redemptive career and His return as King of Kings. Psalm 22 is an amazing detailed prophecy of the suffering and death of Christ in His first advent. Psalm 110 is a far-reaching prophecy of Christ as a perpetual Priest. Psalm 16 heralds His future resurrection; Psalm 72 envisions the coming millennial kingdom. Psalm 45 brings into view a vast prophetic perspective. In all the O. T. there is no more practical, instructive, beautiful or popular book than the Psalms.—*M. F. U.*

Psalmody. *See* Music.

Psaltery. *See* Music.

Ptolema'is (tŏl-ē-mā'ĭs), a city called Accho originally, and located in Galilee (Acts 21:7). It was named after Ptolemy when he was in possession of Coele-Syria. Paul was there for one day on his return from his third missionary journey (21:7). *See* Accho (Acco).

Pu'a (pū'á), another form (Num. 26:23) of Phuvah (q. v.) (Puvah).

Pu'ah (pū'á), the name in the A. V. of two men and one woman.

1. Heb. *păwwāh*, I Chron. 7:1. *See* Phuvah.

2. Heb. *pū'äh*, one of the two midwives to whom Pharaoh gave instructions to kill the Hebrew male children at their birth (Exod. 1:15). The two, Shiphrah and Puah, are supposed to have been the chief and representatives of their profession.

3. Heb. *pū'äh*, the father of Tola, who was of the tribe of Issachar and a judge of Israel (Judg. 10:1).

Publican (Gr. *telōnēs*, a collector of the Roman revenue. The Roman senate had found it convenient, at a period as early as—if not earlier than—the second Punic war, to farm the *vectigalia* (direct taxes) and the *portoria* (customs) to capitalists, who undertook to pay a given sum into the treasury (*in publicum*), and so received the name of *publicani*. Contracts of this kind fell naturally into the hands of the *equites*, as the richest class of Romans. Not infrequently they went beyond the means of any individual capitalist, and a joint-stock company (*societas*) was formed, with one of the partners, or an agent appointed by them, acting as managing director (*magister*). Under this officer, who resided commonly at Rome, transacting the business of the company, paying profits to the partners and the like, were the *submagistri*, living in the provinces. Under them, in like manner, were the *portitores*, the actual customhouse officers, who examined each bale of goods exported or imported, assessed its value more or less arbitrarily, wrote out the ticket, and enforced payment. The latter were commonly natives of the province in which they were stationed, as being brought daily into contact with all classes of the population. It is this class (*portitores*) to which the term publican refers exclusively in the New Testament. These publicans were encouraged by their superior in vexatious and even fraudulent exactions, and remedy was almost impossible. They overcharged (Luke 3:13), brought false charges of smuggling in the hope of extorting hush-money (19:8). The strong feeling of many Jews as to the unlawfulness of paying tribute made matters worse. The Scribes (Matt. 22:15) for the most part answered in the negative. The publicans were also regarded as traitors and apostates, defiled by their frequent intercourse with the heathen, and willing tools of the oppressor. Practically excommunicated, this class furnished some of the earliest disciples of John the Baptist and Jesus. The position of Zacchaeus as a "chief among the publicans" (Luke 19:2, Gr. *architelōnēs*) implies a gradation of some kind among the publicans; perhaps he was one of the *submagistri*.

"The Talmud distinguishes two classes of publicans—the tax-gatherer in general (*Gabbai*) and the *Mokhes* or *Mokhsa*, who was specially the *douanier* or customhouse official. Although both classes fell under the rabbinic ban, the *douanier*—such as Matthew was—was the object of chief execration. And this because his exactions were more vexatious, and gave more scope to rapacity. The *Gabbai*, or tax-gatherer, collected the regular dues, which consisted of ground, income, and poll tax . . . If this offered many opportunities for vexatious exactions and rapacious injustice, the *Mokhes* might inflict much greater hardship upon the poor people. There was a tax and duty upon all imports and exports; on all that was bought and sold; bridge money, road money, harbor dues, town dues, etc. The classical reader knows the ingenuity which could invent a tax and find a name for every kind of exaction, such as on axles, wheels, pack animals, pedestrians, roads, highways; on admission to markets; on carriers, bridges, ships, and quays; on crossing rivers, on dams, on licenses—in short, on such a variety of objects that even the research of modern scholars has not been able to identify all the names. But even this was as nothing compared to the vexation of being constantly stopped on the journey, having to unload all one's pack animals, when every bale and package was opened, and the contents tumbled about, private letters opened, and the *Mokhes* ruled supreme in his insolence and rapacity" (Edersheim, *Life and Times of Jesus*, i, p. 515, sq.). *See* Taxes.

Pub′lius (pŭb′lĭ-ŭs), the "chief man," and probably governor of Melita (Malta), who received and lodged Paul and his companions after their shipwreck. The apostle miraculously healed the father of Publius of a fever, and cured others who were brought to him (Acts 28:7, 8), A. D. 62 (59). The Roman martyrologies assert that he was the first bishop of the island, and afterward succeeded Dionysius as bishop of Athens. Jerome records a tradition that he was crowned with martyrdom.

Pu′dens (pū′dĕnz; Gr. from Lat. *modest, bashful*), a Christian at Rome who united with others in sending salutations to their friend Timothy (II Tim. 4:21). This is the only mention of him in Scripture. He is commemorated in the Byzantine Church on April 14 and in the Roman Church on May 19. Modern researchers among the Columbaria at Rome, appropriated to members of the imperial household, have brought to light an inscription in which the name of Pudens occurs as that of a servant of Tiberius or Claudius. Although the identity of Paul's Pudens with any legendary or heathen namesake is not proved, yet it is probable that these facts add something to our knowledge of the friend of Paul and Timothy.

Pu′hite (pū′hīt). According to I Chron. 2:53, the "Puhites" were of the "families of Kirjath-jearim," descended from Shobel.

Pul (pŭl), the name of an Assyrian king mentioned in the Old Testament in several passages (II Kings 15:19; I Chron. 5:26). According to these passages Pul received from Menahem, king of Samaria, a tribute of one thousand talents of silver, in return for which he was, on his part, not to interfere with the exercise of royal authority by Menahem. These passages in Kings and Chronicles have given great trouble to the student of the Old Testament. When the Assyrian inscriptions

were first discovered, almost immediately were found in them the names of Sennacherib, Shalmaneser, Tiglath-pileser, and other Assyrian kings, but the name of Pul was found in no inscription. Furthermore, when the Assyrian lists of kings and of eponyms were found, the name of Pul did not appear in them, and at the period to which this king is assigned by the Old Testament there was no gap in any of the lists in which the name of a king (Pul) could be inserted. To add to the difficulty, a king by the name of Phulus is mentioned by Alexander Polyhistor and by Eusebius, both of whom call him king of the Chaldeans, whereas the Old Testament makes him out to be an Assyrian king. Numerous efforts on the part of various biblical and Assyrian scholars were made to reconcile the difficulties, but in vain, until the suggestion of Sir Henry Rawlinson, R. Lepsius, and Schrader, that Pul was none other than the well-known Assyrian king, Tiglath-pileser III.

375. Tiglath-pileser III Besieging a Fort, Impaled Victims in background, Battering Ram in foreground

The theory was that Tiglath-pileser did not belong to the ancient royal house of Assyria; that his name in reality was Pu-lu; that he came, perhaps, from Babylonia into Assyria, and when he had seized the throne called himself by the historical name Tiglath-pileser, a name made famous, about B. C. 1110, by one of the earliest Assyrian conquerors. This theory was supported by Schrader with a masterly array of facts and arguments. At last the Babylonian chronicle was found by Pinches in the British Museum, and on this Babylonian chronicle, at the year 728, stands the name Pul, written Pu-lu; whereas, on the other king lists of the Babylonians at that same year stands the name of Tiglath-pileser. All Assyriologists are now agreed that the Babylonian chronicle has settled the question, and that Tiglath-pileser and Pul are one and the same person. It is not, however, certainly known whether the name Pul was the original name of the monarch, or whether it was a name assumed by him when he had become king of Babylon. (For particulars concerning his reign see article Tiglath-pileser.)—R. W. R.

2. A place difficult of location, mentioned once (Isa. 66:19). The balance of evidence is in favor of identification with the African Phut or Put (Heb. *pūt*, Gen. 10:6; Jer. 46:9, marg.; Ezek. 27:10).

Pulpit (Heb. *mĭgdāl, tower, rostrum*). The only mention of pulpit in Scripture is Neh. 8:4, where it is stated that "Ezra the scribe stood upon a pulpit of wood . . . and opened the book in the sight of the people." It was a raised platform, broad enough to accommodate fourteen persons.

Pulse. See Vegetable Kingdom.

Punishment. The rendering of a considerable variety of Hebrew and Greek words in the Scripture. The principal meanings expressed by these terms are reproof, chastisement, restraint, penalty, full justice, vengeance. The specific meaning in each case must be determined by the terms employed and the connection.

1. **Biblical View.** (1) **In the Old Testament** the punishments most frequently mentioned, and upon which chief stress is laid, are temporal. They were inflicted directly by God, or divinely prescribed to be inflicted by persons duly authorized. Instances of the former are found in Gen. 3:16-24; 4:10-13; 6:12, 13; 19:24; Num. 16:28-33, and many other places. In early times we find punishment authorized to be inflicted by the hand of man (Gen. 9:5, 6), but more and more plainly it appears that this is to be done in accordance with divinely appointed and developed social order. The penalties prescribed under the Jewish economy were of great variety, and related to every kind of crime and breach of civil and ecclesiastical regulations. Among capital offenses were blasphemy, Sabbath breaking, witchcraft, adultery, rape, incest, manstealing, idolatry (Lev. 24:14, 16, 23; Num. 15:32, 33; Exod. 22:18; Lev. 20:10; Deut. 22:25; Lev., ch. 22; Exod. 21:16; Lev. 20:2). See further Exod. 21:15, 17; Deut. 22: 21-23; Lev. 21:9; Exod. 22:25; Deut. 19:16, 19.

The ordinary mode of capital punishment was stoning, though other forms, as hanging and burning, are also mentioned. It is believed, however, that these latter were preceded by death in the ordinary way of execution (Exod. 19:13; Num. 25:4; Lev. 21:9; Josh. 7:25).

The meaning of the phrase "cut off from his people," as descriptive of punishment, is disputed. It is used many times in the Old Testament, sometimes with reference to crimes the penalty for which is death but frequently also with reference to offenses the penalties for which are not so clear (Exod. 12:15-19; 30:32-35, 38; Lev. 7:25; 17:9; 19:8). Among minor forms of punishment were exemplified the principles of retaliation (Exod. 21:24, 25; Lev. 24:19-22) and of compensation (Exod. 21:18-36; 22:2-4, 6, 7; Lev. 6:4, 5; 24:8-21; Deut. 19:21; 22-18, 19). Stripes, stocks, and imprisonment also appear among penalties prescribed or employed (Deut. 25:3; Lev. 26:12; Jer. 20:2).

The severity of the Old Testament dispensation in this respect has often been made a subject of unfavorable criticism. But the character of the people, and the condition of the times, and the necessity for impressing the importance of morality and religion, and of developing the right national life furnish the sufficient explanation. It is not to be forgotten, moreover, that the doctrine of a future life, as a state of reward and punishment, was not as strongly emphasized in those times as afterward. See Immortality.

(2) **In the New Testament** we find a relaxing of the severity of the Old Testament with respect to temporal penalties; but in connection with this the bringing into prominence of the motives and influences of the Gospel revelation (Matt. 5:19-48; Luke 7:37-50; John 8:3-11).

That capital punishment is discountenanced by the New Testament is, however, an unwarranted opinion. The sanctity of human life still has around it its ancient safeguard (comp. Gen. 9:6 with Rom. 13:1-6; Matt. 26:52; Rev. 13:10). The retribution, however, upon which the New Testament lays chief stress is that of the future. Of the fact of future punishment and of the eternal duration in some form the teachings of Christ and the apostles leave no room for doubt (Matt. 12:32; ch. 25; 26:24; Mark 3:29; 9:43; Rev. 14:11; 20:10). See also Judgment, the Final; Hell.

2. **Theological and Ethical.** The primary ground for the infliction of punishment is not the reformation of offenders. In the divine administration a distinction is clearly made between chastisement and punishments properly so called. And in the administration of human government the object of reformation often has a proper recognition, though the reason and warrant for the penal sanctions of law are still deeper than that. The chief end is not the discouragement or prevention of crime or wrong doing. This is often an important effect, and a proper though still subordinate object. The underlying idea—that most deeply fundamental—is justice.

Punishment. Mosaic Law. The law of retribution seems to underly punishment in all ages. It is found in the form of *blood revenge* among many ancient peoples as a primitive (Gen. 27:45) custom, going back for its final basis to Gen. 9:5, sq. (*see* Redeemer). Very naturally, in acting as redeemer the person would be tempted to inflict greater injury than that which he avenged. According to the Mosaic code, punishment was made to correspond to the heinousness of the offense, that there should fall upon the culprit what he had done to his neighbor, no more, thus giving no authority for personal revenge. It also limited the punishment to the guilty party without extending it to his children (Deut. 24:16). In the case of property, punishment was required only in order to restoration; and by way of restitution, if the guilty man had invaded his neighbor's property or violated the integrity of his house. What is said (19:19, sq.) in regard to the false witness holds good of all the penal enactments of the Mosaic law: "Do unto him as he had thought to do unto his brother, and put away the evil from the midst of thee." Thus we see, at the root of all the enactments of the Mosaic penal code there lies the principle of strict but righteous retribution, and its intention is to extirpate evil and produce reverence for the righteousness of the holy God in the heart of the people.

1. **Capital Punishment.** That death was regarded as a fit punishment for murder appears plain from the remark of Lamech (Gen. 4:24). In the postdiluvian code, if we may so call it, retribution by the hand of man, even

in the case of an offending animal, for bloodshed, is clearly laid down (9:5, 6). In the Mosaic law we find the sentence of capital punishment, in the case of murder, clearly laid down. The murderer was to be put to death, even if he should have taken refuge at God's altar or in a city of refuge, and the same principle was to be carried out even in the case of animals (Exod. 21:12, 14, 28, 36; Lev. 24:17, 21; Num. 35:31; Deut. 19:11, etc.). The wide range of crimes punishable by death according to the Mosaic law may be accounted for by the peculiar conditions of the Israelites. A nation of newly-emancipated slaves, they were probably intractable; and their wanderings and isolation did not permit of penal settlements or remedial punishments. They were placed under immediate divine government and surveillance. Willful offenses, under such circumstances, evinced an incorrigibleness which rendered death the only means of ridding the community of such transgressors, and this was ultimately resorted to in regard to all individuals above a certain age, in order that a better class might enter into Canaan (Num. 14:29, 32, 35).

(1) **Capital crimes.** (*a*) Absolute: 1. Striking or reviling a parent (Exod. 21:15, 17). 2. Blasphemy (Lev. 24:14, 16, 23). 3. Sabbath-breaking (Num. 15:32-36; Exod. 31:14; 35:2). 4. Witchcraft, and false pretension to prophecy (Exod. 22:18; Lev. 20:27; Deut. 13:5; 18:20). 5. Adultery (Lev. 20:10; Deut. 22:22). 6. Unchastity (Deut. 22:21, 23; Lev. 21:9). 7. Rape (Deut. 22:25). 8. Incestuous and unnatural connections (Lev. 20:11, 14, 15; Exod. 22:19). 9. Man-stealing (Exod. 21:16; Deut. 24:7). 10. Idolatry, actual or implied, in any shape (Lev. 20:2; Deut. 13:6, 10, 15; 17:2-7; *see* Josh., ch. 7, 22:20; Num. 25:1-8). 11. False witness, in certain cases (Deut. 19:16, 19).

(*b*) Relative. There are some thirty-six or thirty-seven cases in the Pentateuch named as involving the penalty of "cutting off from the people." On the meaning of this expression some controversy has arisen (see 2, 7, below). 1. *Breach of morals:* willful sin in general (Num. 15:30, 31); fifteen cases of incestuous or unclean connection (Lev. 18:29; 20:9-21). 2. *Breach of covenant:* uncircumcision (Gen. 17:14; Exod. 4:24); neglect of Passover (Num. 9:13); Sabbath-breaking (Exod. 31:14); neglect of Atonement Day (Lev. 23:29); or work done on that day (v. 30); offering children to Molech (20:3); witchcraft (20:6); anointing a stranger with holy oil (Exod. 30:33). 3. *Breach of ritual:* eating leavened bread during Passover (12:15, 19); eating fat of sacrifices (Lev. 7:25); eating blood (7:27; 17:14); eating sacrifice in an unclean condition (7:20, 21; 22:3, 4, 9); eating of sacrifice on third day after offering (19:7, 8); making holy ointment for private use (Exod. 30:32, 33); making incense for private use (30:34-38); neglect of purification in general (Num. 19:13-20); offering a sacrifice elsewhere than at a tabernacle (Lev. 17:9); slaying an animal elsewhere than at the tabernacle door (17:3, 4); touching holy things illegally (Num. 4:15, 18, 20; comp. II Sam. 6:7; II Chron. 26:21).

(2) **Penalties, capital.** (*a*) The following,

properly Hebrew, were prescribed by the law:
1. Crucifixion (*q. v.*).
2. Stoning. This was the ordinary mode of execution (Exod. 17:4; Luke 20:6; John 10:31; Acts 14:5). "So far as can be learned from the Pentateuch *stoning* is enjoined for those cases in which sentence of death was to be executed on individuals judicially; when, on the contrary, either the avenger of blood carried out the punishment, or where many were to be executed, the sword was used, the spear (Num. 25:7), or arrow (Exod. 19:13), to kill from a distance. Thus stoning is enjoined (Lev. 20:27, sq.; Deut. 17:3, sq.) to punish the individual who practiced idolatry and seduced others; on the contrary (13:16), for the punishment of a whole city which was given over to idolatry, it is commanded, 'Thou shalt slay the inhabitants of that city with the sword.' Accordingly it is no doubt stoning which is meant when the law merely uses the formulas, 'He shall be put to death,' or 'his blood shall be upon him' " (Keil, *Arch.*, ii, 357, 358). If the crime had been proven by testimony, the witnesses were to cast the first stones at the condemned (Deut. 17:7; John 8:7; Acts 7:58). It was customary to add the raising of a heap of stones over the body or its ashes (Josh. 7:25; 8:29; II Sam. 18:17).

3. Hanging. This among the Jews is generally spoken of as following death by some other means (Num. 25:4; Deut. 21:22; II Sam. 21:6, 9), as a means of aggravating capital punishment. The law provided that persons hanged should not be allowed to remain suspended overnight, but be buried the same day, lest—he that was hanged being accursed of God—Jehovah's land should be defiled (Deut. 21:23).

4. Death by the sword or spear was the mode adopted when either the avenger of blood carried out the punishment, or where many were to be executed (Exod. 32:27; Num. 25:7), or the *arrow* to kill at a distance (Exod. 19:13). *Beheading*, practiced in Egypt from most ancient times (Gen. 40:19), first appears among the Jews in the Roman period (Matt. 14:10, sq.).

5. Burning was, in pre-Mosaic times, the punishment for unchastity (Gen. 38:24). The Mosaic law enjoined burning for unchastity only in the case of a priest's daughter (Lev. 21:9), or of carnal intercourse with a mother or daughter (20:14). Burning is mentioned as following death by other means (Josh. 7:25), and some have thought that it was never used excepting after death. Certainly this was not the case among other nations (Dan., ch. 3).

6. Strangling is said by the rabbis to have been regarded as the most common but least severe of the capital punishments, and to have been performed by immersing the convict in clay or mud, and then strangling him by a cloth twisted round the neck.

7. "Cutting off" has been variously understood, some thinking that it meant death in all cases, others that in some cases only excommunication (*q. v.*) must be understood. Jahn (*Arch.*, 258) says, "When God is introduced as saying in respect to any person, 'I

will cut him off from the people,' the expression means some event in divine providence which shall eventually terminate the life of that person's family" (see I Kings 14:10; 21:21; II Kings 9:8). Saalschütz explains it to be premature death by God's hand. Knobel Corn, and Ewald think death punishment absolutely is meant. Keil says (Arch., ii, p. 358): "From Lev. 20:2-6, so much only appears, that God himself will cut off the transgressor if the earthly magistrate shuts his eyes to the crime of idolatry and does not cut off the idolater. Certainly in Lev., ch. 20, all the abominations of which it holds in the comprehensive formula (18:29), 'Whosoever shall do any of these abominations, even the souls that do them shall be cut off from among their people,' have not the punishment of death attached to them. For some of the forbidden marriages only childlessness is threatened (20:20, sq.). But from this it merely follows that for certain cases God reserved the cutting off to be otherwise executed; and in these cases the civil magistrate was not to intervene. But in connection with all other offenses, for which the law prescribes cutting off without any such reserve, the civil magistrate was obliged to carry out sentence of death as soon as the guilt was judicially established; even for transgressions of the laws of purification and other matters of ritual, if the sin was proved to have been committed 'with a high hand,' i. e., in presumptuous rebellion against Jehovah, and not merely in thoughtlessness and haste."

We may, perhaps, conclude that the primary meaning of "cutting off" is a sentence of death to be executed in some cases without remission, but in others avoidable: (1) By immediate atonement on the offender's part; (2) by direct interposition of the Almighty, i. e., a sentence of death always "recorded," but not always executed.

(b) Capital punishments coming from other lands were:

1. Beheading was known and practiced among the Egyptians (Gen. 40:17-19), and by the Hebrews in the time of the early kings (II Sam. 4:8; 20:21, 22; II Kings 10:6-8). Herod and his descendants ordered decapitation (Matt. 14:8-12; Acts 12:2).

2. Dichotomy, cutting in pieces (I Sam. 15:33), common among the Babylonians, Egyptians, and Persians.

3. Burning alive in a furnace (Dan. 3:20, sq.); roasting in the fire (Jer. 29:22; II Macc. 7-5); putting to death in hot ashes (II Macc. 13:5, sq.); casting into the lion's den (Dan. 6:8, 13, sq.); beating to death on the tumpanon (II Macc. 6:19), probably a circular instrument of torture, on which prisoners were stretched and tortured or beaten to death. In war we find: sawing in pieces captives (II Sam. 12:31; I Chron. 20:3; comp. Heb. 11:37); hurling from precipices (II Chron. 25:12); comp. Psa. 141:6; Luke 4:29) —the latter a frequent punishment among the Romans; the cutting open of the bodies of pregnant women (II Kings 8:12; 15:16, etc.), and the dashing of children against walls, when hostile cities were taken (Isa. 13:16, 18; Hos. 13:16, etc.). In the New Testament are

incidentally mentioned drowning (Matt. 18:6; Mark 9:42) and fighting with wild beasts (I Cor. 15:32).

2. **Secondary Punishments.** (1) **Retaliation**, "eye for eye," etc. (Exod. 21:24, 25), which is, probably, the most natural of all kinds of punishment, and would be the most just of all, if it could be instantaneously and universally inflicted; but when delayed, it is apt to degenerate into revenge. Of course it was early seen that such a law could not always be enforced with strict justice, for the same member might be worth more to one man than to another, thus the right arm of a sculptor could not be so well spared as that of a singer. Moses accordingly adopted the principle, but lodged the application of it in the judge. "If a man blemish his neighbor, as he hath done, so shall it be done to him. Life for life, eye for eye, tooth for tooth," etc. (Lev. 24:19-22). This law applied also to the beasts.

But the law of retaliation applied to the free Israelite only, not to slaves. In the case of the latter, if the master struck out an eye and destroyed it, i. e., blinded him with the blow, or struck out a tooth, he was to let him go free, as a compensation for the loss of the member. The willful murder of a slave was followed by capital punishment.

(2) **Compensation.** If identical, then it was retaliation (see above); but it was also analogous, thus—payment for loss of time or power (Exod. 21:18-36; Lev. 24:18-21; Deut. 19:21). A stolen sheep (killed or sold) was to be compensated for by four others, a stolen ox by five others (Exod. 22:1). The thief caught in the act in a dwelling might be killed or sold; if a stolen animal were found alive in his possession, he might be compelled to restore double (22:2-4). Damage done by an animal was to be fully compensated (v. 5); as was damage caused to a neighbor's grain (v. 6). A stolen pledge found in the thief's possession was to be compensated double (v. 7); a pledge lost or damaged was to be compensated (vers. 12, 13); while a pledge withheld was to be restored with twenty per cent of the value (Lev. 6:4, 5). All trespass was to pay double (Exod. 22:9). Slander against the woman by her newly married husband was to be compensated for by the payment of one hundred shekels, and the man further punished with stripes (Deut. 22:18, 19).

(3) **Corporal.** Stripes, consisting of forty blows with a rod (Deut. 25:2, sq.); whence the Jews took care not to exceed thirty-nine (II Cor. 11:24; Josephus, Ant., iv, 8, 21). If a man smote his servant with a rod so that he or she died, he was punishable (Exod. 21:20).

Scourging with thorns is mentioned (Judg. 8:16), and with "scorpions," i. e., whips with barbed points like the point of a scorpion's sting (I Kings 12:11). In addition, we find mention of the stocks (Jer. 20:2); passing through fire (II Sam. 12:31); mutilation (Judg. 1:6; II Macc. 7:4); plucking out hair (Isa. 50:6; Neh. 13:25); and later, imprisonment, confiscation, or exile (Ezra 7:26; Jer. 37:15; 38:6; Acts 4:3; 5:18; 12:4; Rev. 1:9).

The Scriptures mention the following punishments inflicted by other nations. Putting out the eyes of captives, flaying them alive, tearing out the tongue, etc. Exposure to wild beasts is mentioned by the apostle Paul (I

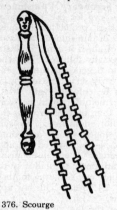

376. Scourge

Cor. 15:32; II Tim. 4:17), but without any particulars.

(4) **Imprisonment**, though not unknown to the Israelites from their acquaintance with Egypt (Gen. 39:20, sq.; 40:3, sq.; 41:10; 42:19) is not recognized in the Mosaic law as a mode of punishment. "They put him in ward" (Lev. 24:12) means that the offender was secured till a decision had been arrived at. Imprisonment is wholly superfluous where bodily punishments prevail, and where fines in the case of those without means must be paid by servitude. Not till the time of the kings is imprisonment introduced, especially to punish too outspoken prophets (II Chron. 16:10; Jer. 20:2; 32:2, sq., etc.). After the exile it was quite a common punishment along with others, in cases of debt (Ezra 7:26; Matt. 11:2; 18:30). Prisoners were bound with chains (Judg. 16:21; II Sam. 3:34; Jer. 40:1); and when the punishment would be made severer, they were placed in stocks (Jer. 20:2). The Roman *custodia militaris* (military imprisonment) consisted in chaining the prisoner by one or both hands to the soldier who watched him (Acts 12:4; 21:33), or in prison putting his feet in the stocks (16:24).

Pu'nites (pū'nīts), the descendants of Phuvah or Pua, of the tribe of Issachar (Num. 26:33).

Pu'non (pū'nŏn), a station of the Israelites in their journey to Canaan (Num. 33:42), east of the mountains of Edom, a tribe seat of the Edomitish phylarch (Gen. 36:41). It lay next beyond Zalmonah, between it and Oboth. According to Jerome it was "a little village in the desert, where copper was dug up by condemned criminals, between Petra and Zoar." Identified with present-day Feinan.

Pur (pŭr; *lot*) is only mentioned (Esth. 3:7; 9:24, 26) in connection with Haman's consulting the astrologers to decide upon the auspicious day for destroying the Hebrews. *See* Festivals, Lot.

Pu'ra (pū'rà), Gideon's servant. A. V. Phurah (*q. v.*).

Purely (Heb. *bŏr*, Isa. 1:25). The Hebrew term may mean *pureness*, and we then have the margin rendering "according to pureness,"

i. e., *thoroughly purge;* or an *alkali* made from plants, which was employed to hasten smelting.

Pureness is from the same Greek root as purity (II Cor. 6:6), and with about the same meaning.

Purge. *See* Uncleanness.

Purification. *See* Uncleanness.

Purifier, of Silver. *See* Silver.

Pu'rim (pū'rĭm), an annual festival of the Jews (Esth. 9:26) in commemoration of the wonderful deliverance of the Israelites in Persia. *See* Festivals.

Purity (Gr. *hagneia, cleanness*). Freedom from foreign mixture, but more particularly the temper directly opposite to criminal sensualities, or the ascendency of irregular passions, chastity (I Tim. 4:12; 5:2).

Purloining (Gr. *nosphizō, to set apart, divide*), the secretly appropriating and setting apart for one's self the property of another, as of a servant thus misusing the property of his master (Tit. 2:10). The same Greek term is used of the act of Ananias, in ostensibly giving all his property to the Church, and then appropriating part of the purchase money to his own use (Acts 5:2, 3).

Purple, a brilliant red-blue color prized by the ancients for dying garments (Prov. 31:22; Jer. 10:9). The chief source of the famous Tyrian purple was the tiny mollusk (murex) found along the coast of Phoenicia and adjacent lands. It was exported far and wide as a staple commodity of Phoenician commerce (Ezek. 27:7, 16). Murex shells were found at the seaport of ancient Ugarit (modern Ras Shamra) demonstrating that purple was manufactured there about 1400 B. C. Great labor was required to extract the purple dye and hence only royalty and the wealthy could afford the resulting richly colored garments (Esth. 8:15; Dan. 5:7; I Macc. 10:20, 62, 64; II Macc. 4:38; Luke 16:19; Rev. 17:4). Such a robe was placed on Jesus as a jest, making mockery of his claims to kingship. Purple prefiguring Christ's kingship was largely used in the Mosaic Tabernacle (Exod. 25:4; 26:21, 31, 36) and in the high priest's dress (Exod. 28:5, 6, 15; 39:29).—*M. F. U.*

Purposes of God. *See* Election, Pre-destination.

Purse (Heb. *kîs;* Gr. *balantion*, Luke 1:04; *zōnē*, Mark 6:8, a girdle, and so a *pocket*). The Hebrews in journeying were provided with a bag in which they carried their money (Gen. 42:35; Prov. 1:14; 7:20; Isa. 46:6). Ladies wore ornamental purses (Isa. 3:22, A. V. "crisping pins;" II Kings 5:23, "bags"), the name given to them by Isaiah is supposed to refer to the long, round form of the purse. The girdle (*q. v.*) was also used as a purse (Matt. 10:9; Mark 6:8).

Purtenance (Heb. *qĕrĕb*, the *nearest part*, i. e., the *center*). This word stands in one passage of the A. V. (Exod. 12:6) for the viscera, or "inwards" (as elsewhere rendered) of a sacrificial victim.

Put (pŭt) A. V. Phut (*q. v.*). Latest views of the identification of Put are with Punt, South of African Cush where it is commonly connected with the coast of Somaliland. (I Chron. 1:8; Nah. 3:9). *See* Phut.

Pute'oli (pū-tē'ô-lī; *little wells*), a famous watering place of the Romans, located in a sheltered part of the Bay of Naples. Its Greek name was Dicaearchia. It was the most accessible harbor near to Rome. So Paul was brought to this port with other prisoners (Acts 28:13). Vespasian conferred great privileges upon the city. Cicero had a villa here, and Hadrian a tomb. Portions of its famous baths remain to this day, and a part of the pier at which St. Paul must have landed on his way to Rome. The present name is Pozzuoli.

Pu′tiel (pū′tĭ-ĕl; perhaps, *afflicted of God*), the father of the wife of Eleazar the priest, and mother of Phinehas (Exod. 6:25), B. C. before 1210.

Pu′vah. *See* Phu′vah.

Pygarg (pī′gärg), a variety of antelope. *See* Animal Kingdom.

Qoph (kōf), the nineteenth letter of the Hebrew alphabet, corresponding to our English "q". Psalm 119 in its nineteenth section is headed by this letter, in which each verse of the original Hebrew begins with *qoph*.

Quail. *See* Animal Kingdom.

Quarries (Heb. *p^esîl, carved*), in the account of Ehud's exploit (Judg. 3:19, 26), may mean *images* (see Deut. 7:25; Isa. 42:8; Jer. 8:19; 51:52, etc.), probably of false gods. Keil and Delitzsch (*Com.*, in loc.) are of the opinion that "stone quarries" is the correct rendering, and locate this Gilgal in the vicinity of Mount Ephraim. That the ancient Canaanites had extensive quarries is shown by the immense blocks in the foundation of the temple at Baalbek.

Quar′tus (kwôr′tŭs; *a fourth*), a Christian of Corinth whose salutations Paul sent to the Church at Rome (Rom. 16:23). There is the usual tradition that he was one of the seventy disciples; and it is also said that he ultimately became bishop of Berytus.

Quaternion (Gr. *tetradion*). "A quaternion of soldiers" was a guard consisting of four soldiers, this being the usual number of the guard to which the custody of captives and prisoners was intrusted, two soldiers being confined with the prisoner and two keeping guard outside. In the account (Acts 12:4) the four quaternions mentioned were on guard one at a time during each of the four watches.

Queen. The Hebrews had no equivalent for our word *queen*, in the sense of a female sovereign, neither did the wives of the king have the dignity which the word queen now denotes.

· 1. *Queen regnant or queen consort* (Heb. *mălkäh*, the feminine of *mĕlĕk*, king). It is applied in the sense of queen *regnant* to the queen of Sheba (I Kings 10:1). It is also applied to the queen *consort*, the chief wife, as distinguished from all other females in the royal harem (Esth. 1:9, sq.; 7:1, sq.).

2. A wife of the first rank (Heb. *shēgäl*) as distinguished from mere concubines; it is applied to Solomon's bride or, perhaps, mother (Psa. 45:9), and to the wives of the first rank in the harems of the Chaldean and Persian monarchs (Dan. 5:2, 3; Neh. 2:6).

3. *Mistress* (Heb. *g^ebîräh*) is expressive of authority and dominion. *Gebir* (*masculine, lord*) is the word which occurs twice with reference to Isaac's blessing of Jacob: "Be *lord* over thy brethren;" and "I have made him thy *lord*" (Gen. 27:29, 37). It would therefore be applied to the female who exercised the highest authority, and this, in an oriental household, is not the wife, but the mother, of the master.

This is one of the inevitable results of polygamy—the number of wives, their social position before marriage, and their precarious hold upon their husband's affections, combine to annihilate their influence. This is transferred to the mother, as being the only female who occupies a fixed and dignified position. The extent of the queen-mother's influence is well illustrated in the interview between Solomon and Bathsheba (I Kings 2:19, sq.). The term *g^ebîräh* is only applied twice with reference to the wife of a king—the wife of an Egyptian king (11:19), where the position of royal consort was more queenly than in Palestine; and Jezebel (II Kings 10:13), who as the daughter of a powerful king appears to have enjoyed peculiar privileges after marriage.

Where women can never become the head of state there can never be a queen regnant; and where polygamy is allowed or practiced there can be no queen consort. By queen, then, we understand the *chief wife* of the king's harem. This rank may be obtained by being the *first* wife of the king, or the *first after accession*, especially if she was of high birth and became mother of the firstborn son; otherwise she may be superseded by a woman of higher birth and connections subsequently married, or by the one who gave birth to the heir apparent. The king, however, often acted according to his own pleasure, promoting or removing as he willed.

Queen of Heaven (Heb. *m^elĕkĕth hăshshäm-ăyîn*, Jer. 7:19; 44:17, 18, 19, 25). Astarte, an ancient Semitic deity, identical with Babylonian Ishtar (Venus), (*see* Gods, False). The epithet "of heaven" alludes to her astral character. Special cakes were baked to this goddess (comp. the grape cakes, Hos. 3:1, with which there may be some connection), which were symbolic representations of the goddess. Her worship belonged chiefly to the women (Jer. 44:17), Astarte representing the female principle of fertility. She was a "mother goddess."

Quick, Quicken (from Heb. *ḥäyäh, to live*). In the Psalms (71:20; 80:18; 119:25, 37, 40, 88; 143:11, etc.) the causative form of the word is used, signifying to *make alive*, to *comfort, refresh*. In the Greek we have *zōopoieō*, to *make alive* (Rom. 8:11; I Cor. 15:36; I Tim. 6:13; I Pet. 3:18, etc.). When the priest examined one with the leprosy it was commanded that if he saw "*quick* raw flesh in the rising" then the priest was to pronounce him unclean (Lev. 13:10, 24). The meaning evidently was that the flesh showed life, i. e., the skin growing and forming anew. The Greek *zōntes* signifies the *living* as opposed to the *dead*, as "the Judge of the quick and the dead" (Acts 10:42; II Tim. 4:1; Heb. 4:12; I Pet. 4:5).

Quicksands, the (Gr. *surtis, shoal*), a great sandbank in the Mediterranean Sea, especially on the north coast of Africa. Of these the "Syrtis major" was near Cyrenaica, now called the *Gulf of Sidra;* and the "Syrtis minor," near Byzacene, now the *Gulf of Cabes.* The ship in which the apostle Paul was sailing was nearer to the former. The ship was caught in a northeasterly gale on the south coast of Crete, and was driven to the island of Clauda (Acts 27:17). This line of drift continued would reach the greater Syrtis, whence the natural fear of the sailors.

Quirin′ius (kwĭ-rĭn′ĭ-ŭs). *See* Cyrenius.

Quiver. *See* Armor, 1 (4).

R

Ra′amah (rā′á-má), the fourth-named son (descendant) of Cush and grandson of Ham (Gen. 10:7; I Chron. 1:9). The tribe of Raamah became afterward renowned as traders (Ezek. 27:22). Raamah occurs in the inscriptions of Sheba as a place in S. W. Arabia near Mä′în, referred to as Regma in the Septuagint and the Vulgate.

Raami′ah (rá-á-mī′á; *Jehovah has thundered*), one of the leaders of the Jews who returned from captivity with Zerubbabel (Neh. 7:7), B. C. about 445. In Ezra 2:2 he is called Reelaiah (*q. v.*).

Raam′ses (răm′sēz; Exod. 1:11). *See* Rameses.

Rab′bah (răb′á; *great*, i. e. city), the name of several places:

1. A very strong place on the east of the Jordan, which when its name is first introduced in the sacred records was the chief city of the Ammonites. In five passages (Deut. 3:11; II Sam. 12:26; 17:27; Jer. 49:2; Ezek. 21:20) it is styled at length Rabbath of the Ammonites, or children of Ammon; but elsewhere (Josh. 13:25; II Sam. 11:1; 12:27, 29; I Chron. 20:1; Jer. 49:3; Ezek. 25:5; Amos 1:14) simply Rabbath. It appears in the sacred records as the single city of the Ammonites. When first named it is in the hands of the Ammonites, and is mentioned as containing the bed or sarcophagus of the giant Og (Deut. 3:11). It was not included in the territory of the tribes east of Jordan; the border of Gad stops at "Aroer, which faces Rabbah" (Josh. 13:25). It was, probably, to Rabbah that Abishai led his forces while holding the Ammonites in check (II Sam. 10:10, 14), while the main army, under Joab, rested at Medeba (I Chron. 19:7). The next year Rabbah was made the main point of attack, Joab in command (II Sam. 11:1); and after a siege, of probably two years, it was taken (II Sam. 12:26, sq.; I Chron. 20:1). We are not told whether the city was demolished, or whether David was satisfied with the slaughter of its inmates. In the time of Amos, two centuries and a half later, it had again a "wall" and "palaces," and was still the sanctuary of Molech—"the king" (Amos 1:14). So it was also at the date of the invasion of Nebuchadnezzar (Jer. 49:2, 3), when its dependent towns are mentioned, and when it is named in such terms as imply that it was of equal importance with Jerusalem (Ezek. 21:20). At Rabbah, no doubt, Baalis, king of the Bene-Ammon (Jer. 40:14), held such court as he could muster; and within its walls was plotted the attack of Ishmael, which cost Gedaliah his life and drove Jeremiah into Egypt. It received the name of Philadelphia from Ptolemy Philadelphus (B. C. 285-247), its ancient name, however, still adhering to it. It was once the seat of a bishopric and very prosperous, till conquered by the Saracens. Its modern name is Amman, about twenty-two miles from the Jordan, in a valley which is a branch, or perhaps the main course, of the *Wady Zerka*, usually identified with the Jabbok. *See* Rabbath.

2. A city of Judah, named with Kirjath-jearim (Josh. 15:60 only), but location entirely unknown. It apparently is mentioned in the Tell el Amarna Letters as Rubute.

3. In Josh. 11:8, only, Zidon is mentioned with the affix *Rabbah* (see A. V. margin), but rendered in the text "great Zidon."

Rab′bath of the Children of Ammon is the full appellation (Deut. 3:11; Ezek. 21:20) of Rabbah, 1 (*q. v.*).

Rabbi, Heb. *rabbi*, Gr. *hrabbi, my teacher*, a respectful term applied by the Jews to their teachers and spiritual instructors (Matt. 23:7, 8; John 1:39, 49; 3:26; 6:25). The terms *rabbi* and *rabboni* both mean simply "master" (John 1:38; 20:16). The use of the title of *rabbi* cannot be substantiated before the time of Christ. Later Jewish schools had three grades of honor: *rab*, "master," the lowest; *rabbi*, "my master," the second; and *rabboni*, "my lord, my master," the most elevated. *M. F. U.*

Rab′bith (răb′ĭth; *multitude*), a city in the tribe of Issachar (Josh. 19:20), supposed by Knobel to be *Araboneh*, northeast of Arâneh, at the southern foot of Gilboa. Conder equates it with Râba 8 miles S. of Mt. Gilboa.

Rabboni. *See* Rabbi.

Rab′mag (răb′măg; *chief magician*, or *priest*), a title ascribed (Jer. 39:3, 13) to Nergal-sharezer (*q. v.*), which title he, with certain other important personages, bears in the Babylonian inscriptions. It probably corresponds to Akkadian *rab mugi* (*great prince*).

Rab′saris (răb′sá-rĭs; Heb. *rab-saris*, Assy. *rabu-sha-reshi*, originally "first eunuch," a title of a high Assyrian official and not a personal name at all.

1. The title is mentioned in the narrative of Sennacherib's campaign against Judah in the days of Hezekiah (II Kings 18:17; Isa. 36:2). In the English translation the Assyrian monarch is represented as sending to Jeru-

salem "Tartan and Rabsaris and Rabshekeh from Lachish." It is now known from the Assyrian monuments that *tartan* (Assy. *turtannu*, "second in rank"), *rabshakeh* (Assy. *rabshaqu*, "chief officer") and *rabsaris* were all titles of high Assyrian officials; in fact, they are Assyrian words taken over into Hebrew (*See* W. F. Albright, *O. T. Commentary*, Phila., 1948, p. 161f; Millar Burrows, *What Mean These Stones?* New Haven, 1941, p. 43f).

2. The same title is met with in Jer. 39:3 to designate one of the Babylonian princes present at the capture of Jerusalem. The other reference is Jer. 39:13f, where the rabsaris was of the group who set free the prophet Jeremiah from the prison court when he was placed under the custody of Gedaliah.

M. F. U.

Rab'shakeh (răb'shá-kê), Assy. *rab-shaqu*, "chief officer," one of the high Assyrian officials mentioned several times in the narrative of Sennacherib's campaign against Judah during Hezekiah's reign (II Kings 18:17; Isa. 36:2). (*See* Tartan and Rabsaris.) The title is one of high rank, for in the inscriptions of Tiglath-pilesar III an army is mentioned as being sent against Tyre under the command of a *rabshekeh.* M. F. U.

Raca' (rá-kä'; Gr. from Aram. *rēqā*, *empty*, *worthless*, *good-for-nothing*), a very common term of opprobrium in the time of Christ (Matt. 5:22), denoting a certain looseness of life and manners. It differs from "fool," which follows in that the latter conveys the idea of *impious*, *godless*, because such a one neglects and despises what relates to salvation. Thus there would be a greater criminality in calling a man a "fool," since foolishness in Scripture is the opposite of spiritual wisdom.

Race. 1. (Heb. *'ōraḥ*, Psa. 19:5), is a poetic word signifying a *way*, *path*, and is used to illustrate the going forth of the sun, as a "strong man to make a journey."

2. One of the contests in the Grecian games (*q. v.*).

Ra'chab (rā'kăb; Matt. 1:5). *See* Rahab.

Ra'chal (rā'kăl), a town in the tribe of Judah which David made a depository for spoil taken from the Amalekites (I Sam. 30:29).

Ra'chel (rā'chĕl; *ewe*), the younger daughter of Laban, and one of Jacob's wives.

1. **Meeting with Jacob.** When Jacob came to Haran he met some shepherds, who told him, in answer to his inquiries, that they knew Laban, and that Rachel was already coming to the well near by to water her father's sheep. He rolled the stone from the well's mouth, watered the sheep, greeted her with a kiss, and told Rachel who he was. Rachel then hastened to her father with the tidings of what had happened (Gen. 29:1-12), B. C. about 2095.

2. **Jacob's Wife.** Laban received Jacob as his relative, and, after a month's service, an agreement was entered into between them that Jacob should serve Laban seven years for his daughter Rachel. The motive on the part of Jacob was, doubtless, that his relations with Esau made a protracted stay with Laban advisable; while Laban was probably influenced by his avarice. At the expiration of the period of service Jacob claimed his

reward, but was deceived by Laban, who led his elder daughter, Leah, into the bridechamber. Complaining of the deception, he was told to let Leah's marriage week pass over and then he should have Rachel, which promise was fulfilled (Gen. 29:13-30). Mention is made of her jealousy toward her sister on account of Leah having children while she herself was childless; of her removing and secreting the teraphim, or household gods of her father. This incident indicates that she was not altogether free from the superstition and idolatry which prevailed in the land. She at length became the mother of children, Joseph (30:24) and Benjamin, dying shortly after the latter's birth (35:18, 19). She "was buried on the way to Ephrath, which is Bethlehem." The site of her tomb is about two miles S. of Jerusalem and one mile N. of Bethlehem.

377. Rachel's Tomb

Character. "From what is related to us concerning her character there does not seem much to claim any high degree of admiration and esteem. The discontent and fretful impatience shown in her grief at being for a time childless, moved even her fond husband to anger (Gen. 30:1, 2). She appears, moreover, to have shared all the duplicity and falsehood of her family. See, for instance, Rachel's stealing her father's images, and the ready dexterity and presence of mind with which she concealed her theft" (ch. 31). In Jer. 31:15, 16, the prophet refers to the exile of the ten tribes under Shalmaneser, king of Assyria, and the sorrow caused by their dispersion (II Kings 17:20), under the symbol of Rachel, the maternal ancestor of the tribes of Ephraim and Manasseh, bewailing the fate of her children, which lamentation was a type or symbol of that which was fulfilled in Bethlehem when the infants were slaughtered by order of Herod (Matt. 2:16-18).

Rad'dai (răd'á-ī; *treading down*), the fifth son of Jesse, and brother of King David (I Chron. 2:14), B. C. about 1025.

Ra'gau (rā'gô), son of Phalec, and one of the ancestors of our Lord (Luke 3:35). He is the same person as Reu, son of Peleg, the difference in the names arising from our translators having followed the Greek form, in which the Hebrew *ayin* was frequently expressed by *gamma*.

Ragu'el (rá-gū'ĕl; *friend of God*), the name given (Num. 10:29) to Jethro, the father-in-law of Moses. It has been supposed that one of the names represented an official title, but which one is uncertain.

Ra′hab (rā′hăb; *broad, wide*). 1. A woman of Jericho at time of Israel's entrance into Canaan.

(1) **Entertains Spies.** Just before crossing the Jordan Joshua sent two men to spy out the land of Canaan as far as Jericho. In this city dwelt Rahab, "a harlot," in a house of her own, although she had a father, a mother, brothers, and sisters living in Jericho. From the presence of the flax upon the roof and a stock of scarlet (or crimson) thread in the house, it has been supposed that she was engaged in the manufacture of linen and the art of dyeing. She had heard of the wonderful progress of Israel, the passage of the Red Sea, and the overthrow of their enemies, and was convinced that Jehovah purposed to give the land of Canaan to the Israelites. The spies found in her one who was ready to befriend them. Fearful of their being discovered, she hid them among the flax stocks on the roof, and informed the officers sent in search of the spies that they had departed from her house before the closing of the city gates. The officers started in pursuit, and when it was night Rahab informed the spies of what had happened, and secured from them a pledge to spare her life and the lives of her kindred, on the condition that she should hang out a scarlet line at the window from which they had escaped, and that her family should remain under her roof. She then assisted them to escape by letting them down by a cord from her window, which overlooked the city wall. (Josh. 2:1-21), B. C. 1440.

(2) **Rahab Spared.** At the taking of Jericho the spies, under the command of Joshua, took Rahab and her relatives out of her house, and removed them to a place of safety outside the camp of Israel (Josh. 6:22, 23), and thus made good their oath. The narrator adds, "And she dwelleth in Israel unto this day," not necessarily implying that she was alive at the time he wrote, but that the family of strangers, of which she was reckoned the head, continued to dwell among the children of Israel. As regards Rahab herself, we learn from Matt. 1:5 that she became the wife of Salmon, the son of Naason, and the mother of Boaz, Jesse's grandfather. The suspicion naturally arises that Salmon may have been one of the spies whose life she saved, and that gratitude for so great a benefit led in his case to a more tender passion, and obliterated the memory of any past disgrace attaching to her name. But however this may be, it is certain, on the authority of Matthew, that Rahab became the mother of the line from which sprung David, and eventually Christ; for that the Rachab mentioned by Matthew is Rahab the harlot is as certain as that David in the genealogy is the same person as David in the books of Samuel.

(3) **Character.** Both Jewish and Christian writers, for very obvious reasons, have been unwilling to admit the disreputable character of Rahab when introduced into Scripture history, and have chosen to interpret the word *zōnäh, harlot*, "hostess," as if from *zun*, "to nourish." "Dismissing, as inconsistent with

truth, the attempt to clear her character of stain by saying that she was only an innkeeper, and not a harlot, we may yet notice that it is very possible that to a woman of her country and religion such a calling may have implied a far less deviation from the standard of morality than it does with us, and, moreover, that with a purer faith she seems to have entered upon a pure life. As a case of casuistry, her conduct in deceiving the king of Jericho's messengers with a false tale, and, above all, in taking part against her own countrymen, has been much discussed. With regard to the first, strict truth either in Jew or heathen, was a virtue so utterly unknown before the promulgation of the Gospel that, as far as Rahab is concerned, the discussion is quite superfluous. With regard to her taking part against her own countrymen, it can only be justified, but is fully justified, by the circumstance that fidelity to her country would in her case have been infidelity to God, and that the higher duty to her Maker eclipsed the lower duty to her native land" (Smith, *Dict.*, s. v.). Her faith is commended in the Epistle to the Hebrews (11:31) and by James (2:25).

2. (Heb. *răhăb, insolence, pride, violence*.) A symbolical or poetical name applied to Egypt. It suggests the character of the "sea monster" (Psa. 68:31; 74:13; 87:4; 89:10; Isa. 51:9, 10.; Ezek. 29:3; 32:2).

Ra′ham (rā′hăm; *compassion, pity*), among the descendants of Caleb, the son of Hezron, Raham is mentioned (I Chron. 2:44) as the son of Shema and father of Jorkoam. By some Jorkoam is regarded as a place of which Raham was the founder.

Ra′hel (rā′hĕl), a form in the A. V. (edition of 1611) for the name *Rachel*, but now omitted everywhere excepting in Jer. 31:15, where it is probably retained through the oversight of the editors.

Rail. To upbraid, reproach (II Chron. 32:17), calumniate (Mark 15:29; Luke 23:39). *To reproach*, abuse (I Cor. 5:11; I Tim. 6:4).

Raiment. *See* Dress.

Raiment, Changes of. Handsome garments, of fur, byssus, and purple embroidered with gold (Ezek. 16:10, 13; Eccles. 9:8), were often made by Israelitish women (Prov. 31:22), and also imported (Zeph. 1:8). Because they were often changed during marriages and other festive occasions, they were called *garments of change*. Kings and men of rank had always a large wardrobe of these, partly for their own use (Prov. 31:21; Job 27:16; Luke 15:22), partly to give away as presents (Gen. 45:22; I Sam. 18:4; II Kings 5:5; 10:22; Esth. 4:4; 6:8, 11).

Rain. The Hebrew term for rain generically is *mäṭăr*; a burst of rain or shower is *gĕshĕm*; a poetical word is *rᵉbîbîm*, i. e., "many," from the multitude of drops (rendered in the A. V. "showers," Deut. 32:2; Jer. 3:3; 14:22; Mic. 5:7, etc.); *zĕrĕm* expresses violent rainstorm, tempest, accompanied with hail (Job 24:8). Dr. George Adam Smith (*Hist. Geog.* p. 63, sq.) says: "The ruling feature of the climate of Syria is the division of the year into a rainy and a dry season. Toward the end of October heavy rains begin to fall, at intervals, for a day or several days at a time. These are what the Bible calls the *early* or *former* rain (Heb. *yōrĕh*) literally the *pourer*. It opens the agricultural year. The soil, hardened and cracked by the long summer, is loosened, and the farmer begins plowing. Till the end of November the average rainfall is not large, but it increases through December, January, and February, begins to abate in March, and is practically over by the middle of April. *The latter rains* (Heb. *mălqōsh*), of Scripture are the heavy showers of March and April. Coming as they do before the harvest and the long summer drought, they are of far more importance to the country than all the rains of the winter months, and that is why these are passed over in Scripture, and emphasis is laid alone on the *early and the latter rains*. This has given most people to believe that there are only two intervals of rain in the Syrian year, at the vernal and autumnal equinox; but the whole of the winter is the rainy season, as indeed we are told in the well-known lines of the Song of Songs:

> 'Lo, the winter is past,
> The rain is over and gone.'

Hail is common, and is often mingled with rain and with thunderstorms, which happen at intervals through the winter, and are frequent in spring. In May showers are very rare, and from then till October not only is there no rain, but a cloud seldom passes over the sky, and a thunderstorm is a miracle." *See* Dews, Palestine.

Figurative. Rain frequently furnishes the writers of the Old Testament with forcible and appropriate metaphors: 1. Of the word of God (Isa. 55:10); as *rain* and snow return as vapor to the sky, but not without having first of all accomplished the purpose of their descent, so the word of God shall not return to Him without fulfilling its purpose. 2. The wise and refreshing doctrine of faithful ministers (Deut. 32:2; Job 29:23). 3. Of Christ in the communications of his grace (II Sam. 23:4; Psa. 72:6; 84:6; Ezek. 34:26; Hos. 6:3). 4. Destructive, God's judgments (Job 20:23; Psa. 11:6; Ezek. 38:22), of a poor man oppressing the poor (Prov. 28:3).

Rainbow (Heb. *qĕshĕth*, "bow in the cloud," Gen. 9:13-16; Ezek. 1:28; Gr. *iris*, Rev. 4:3; 10:1), the token of the covenant which God made with Noah when he came forth from the ark, that the waters should no more become a flood to destroy all flesh. The right interpretation of Gen. 9:13 seems to be that God did not merely take the rainbow, which had hitherto been but a beautiful object shining in the heavens when the sun's rays fell on falling rain, and consecrate it as the sign of his love and the witness of his promise (Eccles. 43:11). Although this is the conclusion of some interpreters, we agree with Keil and Delitzsch (*Com.* on Gen. 9:13f.) that "The establishment of the rainbow as a covenant sign of the promise that there should be no flood again, presupposes that it appears then for the first time in the vault and clouds of heaven. From this it may be inferred, not that it did not rain before the flood (see 2:5, 6), but that the atmosphere was differently constituted." Revised by *M. F. U.*

Figurative. Springing as it does from the effect of the sun upon the dark mass of the clouds, it typifies the readiness of the heavenly to pervade the earthly; spread out as it is between heaven and earth, it proclaims peace between God and man; and while spanning the whole horizon, it teaches the all-embracing universality of the Noahic covenant. In the wondrous vision shown to St. John in the Apocalypse (Rev. 4:3), it is said that "there was a rainbow round about the throne, in sight like unto an emerald:" amid the awful vision of surpassing glory is seen the symbol of Hope, the bright emblem of Mercy and of Love, looking forward from the awful judgments of the Great Tribulation to the establishment of the Millennial Kingdom and finally to the sinless eternal state.

Raisins, dried grapes, or rather cakes made of them, such as the Italians still call *simmaki* (Num. 6:3; I Sam. 25:18; II Sam. 16:1, etc.). *See* Vine.

Ra'kem (rā'kĕm; *variegated*), the pausal form in Hebrew of Rekem.

Rak'kath (răk'ăth; Aram. *bank, shore*), a "fenced," i. e., fortified city in the tribe of Naphtali (Josh. 19:35 only). From its relation to Hammath and Chinnereth, it would seem to have been located on the western shore of the Sea of Galilee, not far distant from the warm baths of Tiberias, which is on the site of ancient Hammath.

Rak'kon (răk'ŏn; probably, *shore*), one of the towns belonging to Dan (Josh. 19:46), apparently near Joppa. Location unknown, but Conder suggests Tell er-Reqqeit, 6 miles N. of Joppa.

Ram. 1. (Heb. *räm, high*).

(1) The son of Hezron, a descendant of Pharez, of the tribe of Judah, born in Egypt after Jacob's migration, as his name does not appear in Gen. 46:12. He is mentioned first in Ruth (4:19), and appears in the genealogy in I Chron. 2:9, 10, B. C. after 1875. He is called Aram in the ancestral lists of the New Testament (Matt. 1:3, 4; Luke 3:33).

(2) The firstborn of Jerahmeel, and nephew of the preceding (I Chron. 2:25, 27). The names of his sons were Maaz, Janim, and Eker.

(3) A son of Barachel the Buzite is described as "of the kindred of Ram" (Job 32:2). Ewald identifies Ram with Aram, mentioned in Gen. 22:21, in connection with Huz and Buz, but Aram and Ram are differentiated in Hebrew and Aram was not descended from Buz.

2. *A stag*, (Heb. *'ăyyĭd*). *See* Sheep in Animal Kingdom, Sacrificial Offerings.

Ram, Battering. *See* Armor, 1 (6).

Ra'ma (rā'mà; Matt. 2:18), the Greek form of Ramah (*q. v.*).

Ra'mah (rā'mà; a *height;* comp. Ezek. 16:24). Many ancient cities and towns of Palestine were located on the tops of hills for the purpose of safety, and those which were specially conspicuous came to be called *the Height;* and this in time came to be used as a proper name. Several places in Palestine were called by this name. In the A. V. we have several forms of the word—*Ramath* (Josh. 13:26), *Ramoth*

(21:38; I Sam. 30:27), and *Ramathaim* (I Sam. 1:1).

1. **Ramah of Asher**, a town only mentioned (Josh. 19:29) in the description of the boundaries of Asher. It was, evidently, near the seacost. Robinson (*Bibl. Res.*, p. 63) supposes that Ramah is to be found in the village of *Rameh*, on the southeast of Tyre, where several sarcophagi are to be seen. Smith (*Bib. Dict.*) prefers a place of the same name about three miles E. of Tyre.

2. **Ramah of Benjamin**, one of the cities allotted to the tribe of Benjamin, mentioned with Gibeon and Beeroth, and in the same group with Jerusalem (Josh. 18:25). The next reference to it is in Judg. 4:5, where it is said that Deborah dwelt between Ramah and Beth-el. Its position is clearly indicated in the story of the Levite (Judg. 19:1, sq.). In the account of his return from Bethlehem to Mount Ephraim (v. 13) Ramah is mentioned with Gibeah as lying on the north of Jerusalem. Ramah and Gibeah were near the road on the right, and about two miles apart. When Israel was divided Ramah, lying between the rival kingdoms, appears to have been destroyed, for we read of Baasha, king of Israel, going up and *building* Ramah (I Kings 15:17). His object was to guard the approach from the north to Jerusalem, and thus prevent any of his subjects from going there to worship and so fall away to the king of Judah. The latter was alarmed at the erection of a fortress so near his capital, and stopped the work by bribing the Syrians to invade northern Palestine (vers. 18-21), and then carried off all the building material (v. 22). The position of Ramah is specifically given in the catalogue of places (Isa. 10:28-32) disturbed by the gradual approach of the king of Assyria. At Michmash he crosses the ravine; and then successfully dislodges or alarms Geba, Ramah, and Gibeah of Saul. Each of these may be recognized with almost absolute certainty at the present day. Geba is *Jeba*, on the south brink of the great valley; and a mile and a half beyond it, directly between it and the main road to the city, is *er-Râm* (its name the exact equivalent of ha-Râmah) on the elevation which its ancient name implies. Its distance from the city is two hours, i. e., five English or six Roman miles. Nebuchadnezzar established his headquarters on the plain of Hamath, at Riblah (Jer. 39:5), and from thence sent his generals, who took Jerusalem. It was here that the Jewish captives were assembled in chains, among whom was Jeremiah himself (40:1; 39:8-12). Here were, probably, slaughtered such as, from weakness, age, or poverty, it was not thought worth while to transport to Babylon, thus fulfilling part of the prophecy, "A voice was heard in Ramah, lamentation and bitter weeping; Rachel weeping for her children," etc. (Jer. 31:15 comp. Matt. 2:18). Ramah was rebuilt and reoccupied by the descendants of its former inhabitants after the captivity (Ezra 2:26; Neh. 7:30). The Ramah in Neh. 11:33 is thought by some to occupy a different position in the list, and may be a distinct place farther west, nearer the plain.

3. **Ramah of Gilead** (II Kings 8:29; II Chron. 22:6), elsewhere Ramoth-gilead (*q. v.*).

4. **Ramah of Naphtali**, one of the "fenced" cities of Naphtali (Josh. 19:36), named between Adamah and Hazor. It would appear, if the order of the list may be accepted, to have been in the mountainous country northwest of the Sea of Galilee. It is the present *Rameh*, a large, well-built village, inhabited by Christians and Druses, surrounded by extensive olive plantations, and provided with an excellent well. It stands upon the slope of a mountain in a beautiful plain southwest of Safed, but without any relics of antiquity.

5. **Ramah of Samuel**, the birthplace and home of that prophet (I Sam. 1:19; 2:11, etc.), elsewhere called Ramathaim-zophim (*q. v.*).

6. **Ramah of the South.** *See* Ramath-negeb.

7. A place occupied by the Benjamites after their return from captivity (Neh. 11:33), which may be the Ramah of Benjamin (see above), or the Ramah of Samuel; but its position in the list (remote from Geba, Michmash, Beth-el, v. 31; comp. Ezra 2:26, 28) seems to remove it farther west, to the neighborhood of Lod, Hadid, and Ono. The situation of the modern *Ramleh* agrees very well with this, a town too important and too well placed not to have existed in the ancient times.

Ramatha'im-Zo'phim (rā'mȧ-thā'ĭm-zō'fĭm; the *double height, watchers*), the birthplace of the prophet Samuel (I Sam. 1:1), his permanent and official residence (7:17; 8:4), and the place of his burial (25:1). The name in its full form occurs only in I Sam. 1:1, everywhere else in the A. V. it is called Ramah. Some locate this place near Gibeah of Saul (I Sam. 10:26; 14:16; 22:6; 26:1); while K. and D. (*Com.*, on I Sam. 1:1) say, "It is identical with Ramah of Benjamin, and was situated upon the site of the present village of er-Ram, two hours N. W. of Jerusalem."

Ra'mathite (rā'mȧ-thīt; *inhabitant of Ramah*), an epithet of Shimmei, who was over the vineyards of David (I Chron. 27:27).

Ra'math-Le'hi (rā'mȧth-lē'hī; *lifting up of the jawbone*), mentioned in Judg. 15:15-17, as the place where Samson slew a thousand Philistines with the jawbone of an ass. Then he threw away the jawbone, and as a memorial of the event, and by a characteristic play upon the old name, he called the place *Ramoth-lehi*, i. e., the lifting (or wielding) of the jawbone.

Ra'math-Miz'peh (rā'mȧth-mĭz'pě; the *height of the watch tower*), one of the northern landmarks of the territory of Gad (Josh. 13:26). It was probably the same place with that early sanctuary at which Jacob and Laban set up their cairn of stones (Gen. 31:48, 49), and which received the names of Mizpeh, Galeed, and Jegar-sahadutha: and it seems very probable that all these are identical with Ramoth-gilead, so notorious in the later history of the nation.

Ra'math-ne'geb (rā'mȧth-ně'gěb). 1. **Ramath of the South**, a place on the southern border of Simeon (Josh. 19:8), simply called Baal (I Chron. 4:33), and is probably the same as *Bealoth* (Josh. 15:24). It cannot be positively identified, though by some the supposition of

Van de Velde (*Memoir*, p. 342) appears probable, that it is identical with Ramath-lehi.

2. **South Ramoth** (I Sam. 30:27) is mentioned as one of the cities to which David sent portions of the spoils of the Amalekites. It is doubtless the same as Ramath-negeb.

Ram'eses or **Raam'ses** (răm'ê-sēz), or (răm'sēz), a N. E. Egyptian city of Goshen, first mentioned in Gen. 47:11, where it is related that a possession was given to Jacob and his sons "in the land of Raamses" which was in "the land of Goshen." The name next occurs in Exod. 1:11 as one of the two store cities built together with Pithom by the enslaved Hebrews. Archaeology has fixed Pithom at Tell er-Retabeh and Raamses at Tanis, Hyksos Avaris, and indicates that these cities were (allegedly, at least) built by the famous Raamses II (cf. 1290-1224 B. C.). But it seems as if these towns were merely rebuilt or enlarged by the great pharaoh. Tanis was called Per-re'emasese, that is, "the House of Raamses" only during the period of 1300-1100 B. C. The reference in Exod. 1:11 must be to the older city Zoan-Avaris, where the oppressed Israelites labored centuries earlier. Accordingly Exod. 1:11 does not conflict with I Kings 6:1, which places the Exodus about 1441 B.C., and the name Raamses is to be construed as a modernization of an archaic place name like Dan for Laish in Gen. 14:14. Since Zoan-Avaris was a flourishing city during the Hyksos Period (before 1570 B. C.), there was ample time for the enslaved Israelites

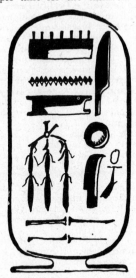

378. Cartouche of Raamses II (Raamses-Meriamon, "Raamses, the beloved of Amon"), the Great Egyptian Conqueror of the 13th Century, B.C.

to have built the earlier city for, according to the early date of the Exodus, they entered Egypt (c. 1870 B. C.). However, many scholars employ this verse and archaeological data to substantiate a 1280 B. C. date for the Exodus, or even later, and do not recognize Raamses as a modernization for Zoan-Avaris.

M. F. U.

Rami'ah (rá-mī'á; Jehovah is lifted up), an Israelite of the sons of Parosh, who put away his Gentile wife after the captivity (Ezra 10:25), B. C. 456.

379. Heavy-Armed Sherdeu of Rameses II's Mercenary Bodyguard

Ra'moth (rā'mŏth; *heights*).

1. An Israelite, of the sons of Bani, who divorced his Gentile wife after the captivity (Ezra 10:29), B. C. 456.

2. One of the four Levitical cities of Issachar (I Chron. 6:73), although Jarmuth appears (Josh. 21:28, 29) in place of Ramoth.

3. A city in the tribe of Gad (Deut. 4:43; Josh. 20:8; 21:38; I Chron. 6:80), elsewhere called Ramoth-gilead (*q. v.*).

4. A city in the tribe of Simeon ("South Ramoth," I Sam. 30:27). See Ramath-negeb.

Ra'moth-gil'ead (rā'mŏth-gĭl'ê-ăd; *heights of Gilead;* "Ramoth in Gilead," Josh. 20:8; 21:38; I Kings 22:3, etc.; "Ramah" simply, II Kings 8:29; II Chron. 22:6), one of the chief cities of Gad, on the east of Jordan. It was allotted to the Levites, and appointed a city of refuge (Deut. 4:43; Josh. 20:8), which would indicate that it was a place of importance even at the period of the conquest. In the time of Solomon it was the residence of one of his twelve purveyors, and was the center of a district which comprised the towns of Jair and the entire region of Argob (I Kings 4:13). Later it fell into the hands of Benhadad, king of Syria, and proved the occasion of Ahab's death, who with Jehoshaphat, king of Judah, endeavored to retake it (I Kings 22:3, sq.; II Chron. 18:3, sq.). It appears to have been won back by Israel, for it was in holding it against Hazael that Joram received the wounds which obliged him to return to Jezreel (II Kings 8:28; 9:14); and it was while Jehu was maintaining possession of Ramoth that he was anointed king of Israel, and sallied forth at the head of the army to slay his master (9:1, sq.). It has been identified by Nelson Glueck with Tell Ramith in N. Transjordan, after previous incorrect identifications with Jerash (Gerasa) and es-Salt by former scholars.

Rams' Horns. See Music.

Rams' Skins dyed red formed part of the offering made by the Israelites to the tabernacle (*q. v.*).

Range. 1. *A cooking* (Heb. *kîr*, Lev. 11:35), perhaps of pottery, or of stones, upon which pots were placed.

2. *A rank* or row of soldiers (Heb. *s⁽e⁾dērāh*) drawn up in cordon (II Kings 11:8, 15; II Chron. 23:14); timbers of chambers in a building (I Kings 6:9).

Ransom (Hebrew from *pädäh*, *release*; *kōphĕr*, *forgiveness*; or *gä'ăl*, a price paid to recover a person or thing from one detaining the same, as prisoners of war (I Cor. 6:19, 20). A ransom is that which is substituted for the party (Exod. 21:30). The people of Jehovah are redeemed by wonderful miracles (Isa. 35:10). *See* Redemption, Redeemer.

Ra′pha, or **Ra′phah** (rä′fà; *He*, i. e. God, *has healed*).

1. The last named of the sons of Benjamin, son of Jacob (I Chron. 8:2, "Rapha"). B. C. after 1900.

2. The son of Binea and father of Eleasah, the eighth in descent from Jonathan, the son of Saul (I Chron. 8:37, "Raphah;" *Rephaiah* in I Chron. 9:43), B. C. after 1000.

Ra′phu (rä′fū; *healed*, *cured*), the father of Palti, which latter represented the tribe of Benjamin among those sent to spy out the promised land (Num. 13:9), B. C. 1440.

Ras Sham′ra (räs shäm′rä), present-day Minet el-Beida, an important archaeological site excavated 1929-1937, located on the N. Syrian coast about eight miles N. of Latakia and opposite the pointed peninsula of Cyprus. The French under C. F. A. Schaeffer have excavated this mound and uncovered an extremely important corpus of Canaanite religious epic poetry inscribed on clay tablets in alphabetic cuneiform. The dialect at Ras Shamra is closely allied to the Hebrew of the Mosaic era. The cuneiform material is to be dated in the early fourteenth century B. C. The language is called "Ugaritic," after the ancient city which was known as Ugarit. The great value of these cuneiform texts lies in the remarkable light they shed on the character of Caanite religion. We now know the Canaanite picture very well. El and Baal were the two great gods. Anath, Astarte and Asherah were the three goddesses which were patronesses of sex and war. The Ugaritic literature has shown the moral depravity and effeteness of Canaanite cultures and demonstrates that the divine command to extirpate Canaanite cults and their devotees was really

381. Artist's Drawing of the Scene of a Lion Attacking a Gazelle Engraved on a Golden Cup from Ras Shamra—Ugarit

justified (cf. Gen. 15:16). Canaanite religion with its orgiastic nature worship, the cult of fertility in the form of serpent symbols, sensuous nudity and gross mythology are revealed in their stark reality in these texts. No longer can critics accuse the God of Israel of injustice in ordering the extermination of these debilitating cults. It was a question of Israel's destroying or being destroyed. Ugaritic epic literature is of first-rate importance in understanding O. T. religion; and these religious texts themselves have shed abundant light on O. T. poetry, vocabulary and Hebrew etymology and syntax. The discovery at Ras Shamra-Ugarit constitutes one of the major archaeological triumphs of the first half of the twentieth century.

Rasor, Razor. *See* Hair.

Raven. *See* Animal Kingdom.

Ravin occurs twice in the A. V., once (Gen. 49:27, "Benjamin shall *ravin* as a wolf") meaning to tear in pieces; and in Nah. 2:12, where it is said that "the lion . . . filled his holes with prey, and his dens with *ravin*," i. e., *spoil*. The Hebrew is elsewhere (Psa. 22:13; Ezek. 22:25, 27) rendered "ravening."

Razor. *See* Barber, Hair.

Rea′ia (rĕ-ā′yà), a Reubenite, son of Micah, and apparently prince of his tribe (I Chron. 5:5), B. C. before 720. The name is identical with Reaiah (*q. v.*).

Rea′iah (rē-ā′yà; *Jehovah has seen*).

1. A descendant of Shubal, the son of Judah (I Chron. 4:2). In ch. 2:52 he is called (apparently) *Haroeh* (härō′ĕh, *the seer*).

2. The children of Reaiah were a family of of Nethimim who returned from Babylon with Zerubbabel (Ezra 2:47; Neh. 7:50), B. C. before 536.

Reaping. Figurative. The relation between *reaping* and *sowing* has been recognized among all people, and suggested many illustrations. In the Scripture reaping is frequently used in

380. Ras Shamra and the Phoenician Coast

the figurative sense: (1) The reward of wickedness (Job 4:8; Prov. 22:8; Hos. 8:7; 10:13; Gal. 6:8). (2) The reward of righteousness (Hos. 10:12; Gal. 6:8, 9); ministers receiving temporal support for spiritual labors (I Cor. 9:11). (3) The final judgment (Matt. 13:30, 39-43; Rev. 14:14-16). (4) "The plowman shall overtake the reaper" (Amos 9:13) is another form of "And your threshing shall reach unto the vintage" (Lev. 26:5), the meaning of which is that while one is plowing the land another shall be cutting the ripe grain, so abundant and continuous shall be the harvests. *See* Agriculture.

Re'ba (rē'bȧ; *fourth*), one of the five Midianite kings slain by the Israelites in Moab (Num. 31:8; Josh 13:21), B. C. about 1200.

Rebec'ca (rĕ-bĕk'ȧ), the Grecized form (Rom. 9:10) of the name Rebekah (*q. v.*).

Rebek'ah (rĕ-bĕk'ȧ; a *rope, noose*, as of a maiden who ensnares by her beauty), the daughter of Bethuel, Abraham's brother (Gen. 22:23).

1. **Marriage.** In arranging for the marriage of his son Isaac, Abraham intrusted the commission to his trusty servant (generally supposed to be Eliezer), and made him swear not to take a wife for him from the daughters of the Canaanites, but to bring one from his (Abraham's) native country and his kindred. He went, therefore, to the city of Nahor, and came to a halt by the well without the city at the time when the women came out to draw water. He then prayed to Jehovah, fixing upon a sign by the occurrence of which he might decide upon the maiden whom Jehovah had chosen to be the wife of Isaac. Rebekah did just what had been fixed upon as a token, and Abraham's servant pressed his suit so earnestly that she and her family consented to her marriage, and she started for her future home the following day. Arriving in Canaan, she was received by Isaac and became his wife (Gen. 24:1-67).

2. **Mother.** For nineteen years after marriage Rebekah remained childless; then, after the prayers of Isaac and her journey to inquire of the Lord, Esau and Jacob were born (Gen. 25:21-26). Jacob was the favorite of his mother (25:28), while Esau was a source of grief both to her and Isaac (26:35).

3. **In Philistia.** Driven by famine into the country of the Philistines, Isaac was fearful lest the beauty of his wife should be a source of danger to him, and therefore declared that she was his sister. Before long the deception was discovered, and Abimelech, the king, commanded that no one should molest her, on pain of death (Gen. 26:1-11).

4. **Suggests Deception.** Some time after this Rebakah suggested the deceit that Jacob practiced upon his father, assisted him in carrying it out, and prevented the consequences of Esau's anger by sending Jacob away to her own kindred (Gen. 27:5-46).

5. **Death and Burial.** The Scriptures do not state when nor where the death of Rebekah took place, but it has been conjectured that it occurred while Jacob was absent in Padan-aram, B. C. probably before 1950. The place of her burial, incidentally mentioned by Jacob on his deathbed (Gen. 49:31), was in the field of Machpelah. Paul (Rom. 9:10-12) refers to Rebekah as being made acquainted with the purpose of God regarding her children before they were born.

Receipt of Customs (Gr. *telōnion, place of toll*), the place in which the taxgatherer sat to receive taxes (Matt. 9:9, etc.).

Receiver (Heb. *shāqăl*, to *weigh*), one who tested the weight of gold and silver (Isa. 33:18). The meaning of the whole passage appears to be that the dreadful past is forced out of mind by the glorious present.

Re'chab (rē'kăb; *charioteer, horseman, rider*).

1. One of the two "sons of Rimmon the Beerothite" who slew Ish-bosheth, the son of Saul, in the hope of obtaining favor with David. But when the king heard of their crime he was so filled with abhorrence thereat that he caused them to be put to death (II Sam. 4:2-12), B. C. about 992.

2. The father of Jehonadab (or Jonadab), who assisted Jehu in destroying the worshipers of Baal (II Kings 10:15-28), B. C. before 842. He was the ancestor of the Rechabites (Jer. 35:6, 8, 14, 16, 19).

3. The father of Malchiah, which latter was ruler of part of Beth-haccerem, and repaired the "dung gate" of Jerusalem after the captivity (Neh. 8:14), B. C. 445.

Rech'abites (rĕk'ȧ-bīts), descendants (assuming "father," Jer. 35:8, to be taken literally) of Jonadab, the son of Rechab. They appear in sacred history but once, as is fully told in Jer., ch. 35, their mode of life being described in vers. 6-11. Their ancestor Jonadab (vers. 6, 10, 19), or Jehonadab (vers. 8, 14, 16, 18), son of Rechab, is presumably the same as the Jehonadab, son of Rechab (II Kings 10:15, 23). This is all that we know of him, though John of Jerusalem says he was a disciple of Elisha.

In I Chron. 2:55 "the house of Rechab" is connected in kinship with the Kenites. Jehonadab's connection with Jehu shows that Jehonadab was at that time in the land of Israel, but the two facts are not definite enough to conflict.

The Rechabite movement, like that of the Nazarites of Amos 2:11, seems to have been the result of an attempt to stem the tide of luxury and license which threatened to sap the strength of the people and the state. A return to the simplicity of nomadic life was required of the Rechabites, and was enforced from generation to generation, though the invasion of Nebuchadnezzar drove them to seek other shelter in Jerusalem. It was here that they were tested by Jeremiah under divine command, and for their fidelity received the blessing, "Jonadab, the son of Rechab, shall not want a man to stand before me forever." This is sometimes understood in a liturgical sense of ministering before the Lord (Deut. 10:8; 18:5, 7; comp. Gen. 18:22; Judg. 20:28), and is held, not unreasonably to imply that the Rechabites were adopted into Israel and incorporated with the Levites. R. Judah is cited as having mentioned a Jewish tradition that their daughters married Levites, and that their children ministered in the temple.

The LXX in the title of Psa. 71 mentions

the sons of Jonadab. In Neh. 8:14 Malchiah, son of Rechab, repairs a gate of the city. In I Chron. 2:55, the "Kenites that came of Hemath, the father of the house of Rechab," are scribes. According to Hegesippus, "one of the priests of the sons of Rechab, the son of Rechabim, who are mentioned by Jeremiah the prophet," cried out protesting against the slaying of James the Just. Followers of the sect still are to be found in Mesopotamia and Yemen.

A parallel has been sought in the Wahabys, followers of Asd-ul-Nahab, during the last and present century. Zealous to protect his countrymen from the vices of Turkish civilization, he proscribed opium and tobacco as Mohammed did wine. They have been called the Puritans of Islam; and their rapid and formidable development has been thought to present a strong analogy to the political influence and tenacious vitality of Jehonadab and his descendants.—W. H. Revised by *M. F. U.*

Re'chah (rē′kà). In I Chron. 4:12, Bethrapha, Paseah, and Tehinnah the father, or founder, of Ir-nahash, are said to have been "the men of Rechah." It is an unidentified place in Judah.

Reconciliation is the restoration to friendship and fellowship after estrangement. O. T. reconciliation contains the idea of an atonement or covering for sin (Lev. 6:30; 16:20; Ezek. 45:20). In the N. T. it possesses the idea "to change thoroughly" (Gr. *katalassō*, II Cor. 5:18, 19), "to change thoroughly from one position to another" (*apokatalatto*, Eph. 2:16; Col. 1:20, 21). Reconciliation, therefore, means that someone or something is completely altered and adjusted to a required standard (cf. Rom. 5:6-11). By the death of Christ the world is changed in its relationship to God. Man is reconciled to God, but God is not said to be reconciled to man. By this change lost humanity is rendered savable. As a result of the changed position of the world through the death of Christ the divine attitude toward the human family can no longer be the same. God is enabled to deal with lost souls in the light of what Christ has accomplished. Although this seems to be a change in God, it is not a reconciliation; it is rather a "propitiation." God places full efficacy in the finished work of Christ and accepts it. Through His acceptance of it He remains righteous and the justifier of any sinner who believes in Jesus as his reconciliation. When an individual heart sees and trusts in the value of Christ's atoning death, he becomes reconciled to God, hostility is removed, friendship and fellowship eventuate.—*M. F. U.*

Recorder (Heb. *măzkîr, rememberer*), a state officer of high rank among the Jews. Among the several new posts created by David when he ascended the throne, was the "recorder" (II Sam. 8:16; 20:24; I Kings 4:3; II Kings 18:18, 37; II Chron. 34:8; Isa. 36:3, 22). The recorder had to keep the annals of the kingdom; and his office was a different one from that of the "chancellor" (*q. v.*). The latter (A. V. "scribe") had to draw up the public documents; the recorder had to keep them, and incorporate them in the connected history of the nation. Both of these offices are

met with throughout the East, and David apparently followed Egyptian models in instituting this office.

Red. *See* Color.

Red Heifer. *See* Sacrifices, Uncleanness.

Red Sea (Heb. *yăm sūph, sea of reeds*). The Reed or Papyrus Sea which the Israelites miraculously crossed "may reasonably be supposed to be the Papyrus Lake or Papyrus Marsh, known from the Egyptian documents from the thirteenth century, to be located near Tanis" (W. F. Albright, *O. T. Commentary*, Phila., 1948, p. 142). The topography of this region has been altered to some degree since the digging of the Suez Canal. Lake Ballah has disappeared. In the fifteenth century B. C. (taking the early date of the Exodus) the vicinity of Lake Timsah between Lake Ballah and the Bitter Lakes may well have been more marshy than it is at the present day. Israel's crossing of the "Reed Sea" was undoubtedly in the vicinity of Lake Timsah or just north of it (cf. G. E. Wright and F. Filson, *The Westminster Historical Atlas to the Bible*, Phila., 1945, p. 38). The Red Sea is a 1350-mile long body of water extending from the Indian Ocean to the Suez Gulf. It is over 7200 feet deep, and over 100 miles wide. The Arabian Peninsula borders on its E. coast. Egypt, Cush and Punt of ancient times border on the W. It has two arms, one the Gulf of Suez and the other the Gulf of Akabah. Akabah figures prominently in the O. T. (cf. I Kings 22:49f; II Chron. 9:21). The University of California African Expedition in 1947 discovered the Red Sea embarkation harbor for the turquoise miners who came from Egypt to mine at Serabit el-Khadem. The very nature of the topography of the surrounding land, the long distances and the nature of the Red Sea almost preclude the possibility of Israel's crossing the Red Sea to the extreme south but rather crossing the Sea of Reeds in the north.—*M. F. U.*

Red Sea, Passage of. *See* Exodus.

Redeem. *See* Redeemer, Redemption.

Redeemed. The children of Israel are called "the redeemed of the Lord" (Isa. 35:9; 51:11; 62:12), as being emancipated from Babylonian captivity, and with further reference to spiritual deliverance from the bondage of sin. *See* Redeemer; Redemption.

Redeemer (Heb. *gō'ēl, the nearest kinsman*). According to the custom of retribution, it fell to the nearest kinsman to avenge the blood of a slain relative; to protect the life and property of a relative. This obligation was called by the Israelites *redeeming*, and the man who was bound to fulfill it *a redeemer*. The law and duty of the *redeemer* is assumed by Moses as a matter of tradition, and brought under theocratic principle. As redeemers are reckoned full brothers, next to them the father's brothers, then full cousins, finally the other blood relatives of the clan (Lev. 25:48, sq.). The Hebrews being an agricultural people, the chief function of the redeemer (*gō'ēl*) was to "redeem" the land that had been sold by a brother in distress. When the nation came into bondage it needed a redeemer through the "redemption" of the lands to be secured, and they looked to Jehovah to become their *gō'ēl*.

Thus the exile gave a force and a meaning to the term more striking than it could have had before. Of thirty-three passages in the Old Testament in which *gō'ēl* is applied to God, nineteen occur in Isaiah, and in that part of the complication which deals with conditions existing in the Babylonian exile (Isa. 48:20; 52:9; 62:12; Psa. 107:2). In spiritualizing the term *gō'ēl*, Isaiah (49:26; comp. Psa. 19:14) places it on a par with "saviour." *See* Kinsman; Redemption.

Redemption (Heb. *pädäh*, to *deliver*, to *sever*). The thoughts constantly impressed upon the Israelites were, that they were a people belonging to Jehovah, that he had redeemed (i. e., severed them from bondage), and that Canaan, with all it might produce, was the gift of God, the Israelites using it as a bounty from Jehovah. Therefore all Israel owed service to God, and were, in spirit at least, to be priests unto the Most High. But Levi and his descendants being set apart for the service of the sanctuary, all others were to be redeemed in the person of the firstborn both of man and beast. The firstborn sons, so far as the mothers were concerned, were presented, on the fortieth day after their birth, to the Lord, and redeemed for five shekels (Num. 18:16; comp. Exod. 13:15; Luke 2:27). The firstlings of oxen, sheep, and goats were to be brought to the sanctuary within a year, dating from the eighth day after birth, and sacrificed (Num. 18:17, sq.; *see* Sacrifices). The firstborn of an ass, an unclean animal, was required by the original prescription (Exod. 13:12, sq.; 34:20) to be redeemed with a lamb, and if not redeemed, put to death; later, the law provided that it was to be redeemed with money, the amount being according to the priest's valuation, with a fifth part added (Lev. 27:27; Num. 18:15). With regard to the products of the soil, the best of the firstlings were sacred to Jehovah, as the Lord of the soil (Exod. 23:19), and were given to the priest to present to Jehovah. In addition to individual offerings, the congregation as a body were required annually to offer to the Lord, by way of thanksgiving for the blessing of the harvest, a firstling sheaf at the Passover (*q. v.*). These were not to be burned, but given to the priests for their use, with the proviso that only those who were ceremonially clean could eat thereof. The amount of offerings of this kind was not specified by the law, but it was left to each individual's discretion. *See* Tithes.

Redemption (Gr. *'apolutrōsis*, a *loosing* away; *lutrōsis*, a *loosing*, particularly by paying a price; for other terms, see Strong's *Concordance*), a comprehensive term employed in theology with reference to the special intervention of God for the salvation of mankind. Its meaning centers in the atoning work of Christ as the price paid for human redemption, and on account of which Christ is called the Redeemer. But along with this are other conceptions relating to the necessity for redemption, also the various stages and measures in the redemptive economy and the effects of God's gracious work.

1. Christ is man's Redeemer; but as such he is divinely appointed. The redemption he wrought manifests not only the love of the Son, but also that of the Father. The Holy Spirit is also active in the administration of redemption. The Trinity is a redemptional Trinity (see Rom. 5:8; John 3:16; Matt. 28:19). Still, for the reason above named, the Son of God is the Redeemer of mankind (see Rom. 3:24; Gal. 3:13; Eph. 1:7; I Pet. 1:18, 19; I Cor. 1:30; comp. Matt. 20:28; I Tim. 2:6).

2. Redemption implies antecedent bondage. Thus the word refers primarily to man's subjection to the dominion and curse of sin (see Gal. 3:13; I Cor. 15:56). Also in a secondary sense to the bondage of Satan as the head of the kingdom of darkness, and to the bondage of death as the penalty of sin (see Acts 26:18; Heb. 2:14, 15). Redemption from this bondage, it is important to observe, is represented in the Scriptures as both universal and limited. It is universal in the sense that its advantages are freely offered to all. It is limited in the sense that it is effectual only with respect to those who meet the conditions of salvation announced in the Gospel. For such it is effectual in that they receive forgiveness of sins, the power to lead a new and holy life. Satan is no longer their captor, and death has lost its sting and terror. They look forward "to the redemption of the body" (see Heb. 2:9; Acts 3:19; Eph. 1:7; Acts 26:18; II Tim. 2:26; I Cor. 15:55-57; Rom. 8:15-23). *See* Incarnation, Atonement, Resurrection.— E. McC.

Reed. Figurative. "A reed shaken by the wind" (Matt. 11:7; Luke 7:24) is a symbol of a fickle person; "A bruised reed and a smoking wick" (flax; Isa. 42:3; Matt. 12:20) represent those who are *spiritually miserable and helpless*. A forceful figure is used by the prophet Ahijah (I Kings 14:15), "the Lord shall smite Israel, as a reed is shaken in the water," meaning that as the reeds are swept by the raging current, so shall Israel be helpless before the judgments of God. "A broken reed" (Isa. 36:6), or "a staff of reed" (Ezek. 29:6), represents an uncertain support, since it is liable to break when one leans on it, and its jagged edges pierce the shoulder of the man who grasps it. *See* Vegetable Kingdom.

Reed, a measure of length. *See* Metrology, I (6).

Reela'iah (rē-ĕl-ā'yȧ; *Jehovah has caused to tremble*), one of the "children of the province" who returned from Babylon with Zerubbabel (Ezra 2:2), B. C. about 536. In Neh. 7:7 his name is given as *Raamiah*.

Refine, Refiner. Refining in Scripture was of liquids and metals, and the processes were quite different. In respect to liquids the primary idea was that of straining or filtering, the word for which was *zäqáq;* but in respect to metals it was that of melting, and for this the word was *şäräph*. But the first word also, in course of time, came to be used of gold or other metals to denote their refined or pure state (I Chron. 28:18; 29:4). The refiner's art was essential to the working of the precious metals. It consisted in the separation of the dross from the pure ore, which was effected by reducing the metal to a fluid state by the application of heat and by the aid of solvents, such as alkali (Isa. 1:25) or lead (Jer. 6:29), which, amalgamating with the dross, permitted the extraction of the unadulterated metal. The instruments required by the refiner were a crucible or furnace and a bellows or blow pipe. The workman sat at his work (Mal. 3:3); he was thus better enabled to watch the process and let the metal run off at the proper moment. The Egyptians carried the working of metals to an extraordinary degree of perfection; and there is no doubt that the Hebrews derived their knowledge of these arts from this source, though there is evidence that the art of working in copper and iron was known before the flood (Gen. 4:22).

Figurative. The Bible notices of refining are chiefly of a figurative nature: Of the corrective judgments of God (Isa. 1:25; 48:10; Jer. 9:7; Zech. 13:9; Mal. 3:2, 3); the purity of God's word (Psa. 18:30, A. V. "tried;" 119:140); failure of means to effect an end is graphically depicted in Jer. 6:29, "The bellows are burned, the lead is consumed of the fire; the founder melteth in vain: for the wicked are not plucked away."

Reformation (Gr. *diorthōsis*, "a setting right," "a making straight" Heb. 9:10) refers to the times of perfecting things, by a change of external forms into vital and spiritual worship referring to the times of the Messiah and the salvation He brought.

Refuge, Cities of. These were six in number (Num., ch. 35): Kadesh, in Naphtali; Shechem, in Mount Ephraim; Hebron, in Judah —these were west of Jordan. Golan, in Bashan; Ramoth-gilead, in Gad; Bezer, in Reuben—east of Jordan.

Refuge, City of. *See* Cities of Refuge.

Refuse. 1. The refuse of cattle, etc. (I Sam. 15:9; Heb. *māsăs*, to *waste*), were those that were diseased, or otherwise undesirable.

2. "The refuse of the wheat" (Amos 8:6, Heb. *măppä*) was the waste, the chaff, which was sold to the poor by their rich oppressors.

Re'gem (rē'gĕm; perhaps from Arab. *ragm, a friend*), the first named of the sons of Jahdai, who appears to have been of the family of Caleb (I Chron. 2:47), B. C. after 1440.

Re'gem-me'lech (rē'gĕm-mē'lĕk; *friend of the king*), the name of a person sent with Sharezer to the house of God to pray before the Lord (Zech. 7:2), B. C. 518. It is thought, however, that the "house of God" (Bethel) should be the subject of the sentence, which would then read, "Then Beth-el (i. e., the inhabitants of that place) sent Sharezer and Regem-melech and his men to entreat the face of Jehovah" (Keil and Delitzsch, *Com.*, in loc.).

Regeneration (Gr. *paliggenesia, a being born again*), the spiritual change wrought in man by the Holy Spirit, by which he becomes the possessor of a new life. It is to be distinguished from justification, because justification is a change in our relationship to God, while regeneration is a change in our moral and spiritual nature. The necessity, in the one case, is in the fact of guilt; in the other, depravity. They coincide in point of time and are alike instantaneous, and thus are both covered by the general term conversion, as that term is popularly and loosely applied (*see* Conversion). Still they are distinct in that the one is the removal of guilt by divine forgiveness, and the other is the change from the state of depravity, or spiritual death, to that of spiritual life. Regeneration is also to be distinguished from sanctification, inasmuch as the latter is the work of God in developing the new life and bringing it to perfection, while the former is the beginning of that life. *See* Sanctification.

Regeneration is represented in the Scriptures principally by such terms as "born again," "born of God," "born of the Spirit" (see John 3:3-13; I John 3:9; 4:7; 5:1; I Pet. 1:23). There are also other forms of expression of deep significance with reference to the same great fact (see Ezek. 36:25, 26; Eph. 4:22-24; II Cor. 5:17; Col. 3:9, 10).

The work of regeneration is specially ascribed in the Scriptures to the Holy Spirit (see John 3:5-8; Tit. 3:5). This is in full accord with the whole tenor of special revelation in representing the agency of the Spirit in the economy of salvation. *See* Holy Spirit.

Regeneration by baptism, or baptismal regeneration, has been a widely prevalent error. This is due in part to an improper use of the term. A proselyte from heathenism to the Jewish religion was said to be "born again." A corresponding use of the term crept into the early Christian Church. Those who received baptism, the initiatory rite of church membership, were said to be regenerated; but this was probably without any intention of denying the deeper work of the Holy Spirit. It was only a loose and improper way of indicating the change in a man's external relationship. And it is proper to say that some of the advocates of the baptismal regeneration in the Church of England still use the term in this sense, and make a distinction between regeneration as effected by baptism and the great work of spiritual renewal. But the error has its broader basis in an unscriptural idea of the character and efficiency of the sacraments. And thus it is held not only by Roman Catholics, but also by many Lutherans and many in the Church of England. *See* Sacraments.

Region Round About, The (Gr. *perichōros, lying round about*). In the Old Testament it is used by the LXX as the equivalent of the singular Hebrew word *hăkkĭkkär* (literally "the round"), which seems, in its earliest occurrence, to denote the *circle* or oasis of cultivation in which stood Sodom and Gomorrah and the rest of the five "cities of the *Kikkar*" (Gen. 13:10-12; 19:17, 25, 28, 29; Deut. 34:3). In Matt. 3:5, and Luke 3:3, it denotes the populous and flourishing region which contained the towns of Jericho and its dependencies in the Jordan valley, inclosed in an amphitheater of the hills of Quarantana, a densely populated region, and important enough to be reckoned as a distinct section of Palestine. It is also applied to the district of Gennesaret, which has similarities to that of Jericho, being inclosed in the amphitheater of the hills of Hattin, bounded in front by the lake, as the others were by the Jordan, and also thickly populated (Matt. 14:35; Mark 6:55; Luke 6:37; 7:17).

Register. *See* Genealogy.

Rehabi'ah (rē-há-bī'á; *Jehovah is enlarged*), the only son of Eliezer, the son of Moses (I Chron. 23:17; 24:21; 26:25), B. C. after 1400.

Re'hob (rē'hŏb; *wide street, open space*).

1. The father of Hadadezar, king of Zobah, whom David smote at the Euphrates (II Sam. 8:3, 12), B. C. before 986.

2. A Levite who sealed the covenant with Nehemiah (Neh. 10:11), B. C. 445.

3. A city on the northern border of Palestine, marking the limit of the exploration of the spies in that direction (Num. 13:21; "Beth-Rehob" in II Sam. 10:6, 8). It was probably in the tribe of Naphtali, the modern Tell el-Kadhy (Judg. 18:28).

4. A town allotted to Asher (Josh. 19:28), close to Sidon.

5. Another town in Asher (Josh. 19:30). One of these two towns was assigned to the Gershonite Levites (Josh. 21:30; II Chron. 6:75), and was not possessed by the Israelites (Judg. 1:31).

Rehobo'am (rē-hô-bō'ăm; *enlarger of the people*).

1. **Family.** The son of Solomon by the Ammonite princess, Naamah (I Kings 14:21, 31). He was born B. C. about 975.

2. **Personal History.** (1) **Accession.** Rehoboam selected Shechem as the place of his coronation, probably as an act of concession to the Ephraimites, who were always dissatisfied with their inferior position in the confederation of the tribes (I Kings 12:1; II Chron. 10:1), B. C. about 934. (2) **Insurrection.** The people demanded a remission of the severe burdens imposed by Solomon, and Rehoboam promised them an answer in three days, during which time he consulted first his father's counselors, and then the young men "that were grown up with him, and which stood before him." Rejecting the advice of his elders to conciliate the people at the beginning of his reign, he returned as his reply the frantic bravado of his contemporaries. Thereupon rose the formidable song of insurrection, heard once before when the tribes quarreled after David's return from the war with Absalom. Rehoboam sent Adoram to reduce the rebels to reason, but he was stoned to death by them; whereupon the king and his attendants fled to Jerusalem. On Rehoboam's return to Jerusalem he assembled an army of one hundred and eighty thousand men from the two faithful tribes of Judah and Benjamin, in the hope of reconquering Israel. The expedition, however, was forbidden by the prophet Shemaiah (I Kings 12:1-24); still during Rehoboam's lifetime peaceful relations between Israel and Judah were never restored (II Chron. 12:15; I Kings 14:30). (3) **Reign.** Rehoboam now occupied himself in strengthening the territories which remained to him by building a number of fortresses (II Chron. 11:6-10). The pure worship of God was maintained in Judah. But Rehoboam did not check the introduction of heathen abominations into his capital; the lascivious worship of Astoreth was allowed to exist, "images" were set up, and the worst immoralities were tolerated (I Kings 14:22-24; II Chron. 12:1). (4) **Egyptian invasion.** In the fifth year of Rehoboam's reign the country was invaded by Egyptians and other

African nations, under Shishak (Sheshonk I), numbering twelve hundred chariots, sixty thousand horse, and a vast multitude of infantry. The fortresses about Jerusalem and that city itself were taken, and Rehoboam purchased a peace by delivering up the temple treasures. After this great humiliation the moral condition of Judah seems to have improved (II Chron. 12:12), and the rest of Rehoboam's life to have been unmarked by any events of importance. He died B. C. 918, after a reign of seventeen years, having ascended the throne B. C. 934, at the age of forty-one (I Kings 14:21; II Chron. 12:13). He had eighteen wives, sixty concubines, twenty-eight sons, and sixty daughters. Of all his wives Maachah was his favorite, and to her son Abijah he bequeathed his kingdom (II Chron. 11:18-22).

Reho'both (rē-hō'bŏth; *broad places*), one of the four cities founded by Asshur (Gen. 10:11, 12), the others being Nineveh, Caleh, and Resen. Rehoboth was evidently a part of the great city of Nineveh.

1. **The City.** Probably the words "rehoboth ir" are to be translated as it is in the Vulgate and in the margin of the A. V., "the streets of the city," i. e., of Nineveh. Rehoboth-ir is best regarded as a suburb of greater Nineveh, which in course of time came to be included in the city's vast market places.

2. **The Well.** The third of the series of wells dug by Isaac (Gen. 26:22). A *Wady Ruhaibeh*, containing the ruins of a town of the same name, with a large well, is crossed by the road from *Khan en-Nukhl* to Hebron, by which Palestine is entered on the South. It lies about 19 miles S. W. of Beersheba.

3. **By the River.** The city of a certain Saul, or Shaul, one of the early Edomite kings (Gen. 36:37; I Chron. 1:48). Its location is uncertain.

Re'hum (rē'hŭm; *compassionate*).

1. One of the "children of the province" who returned from the captivity with Zerubbabel (Ezra 2:2), B. C. about 536. In Neh. 7:7 he is called *Nehum*.

2. An officer of the king of Persia, perhaps lieutenant governor of the province of Samaria, who united with Shimshai in writing a letter to Artaxerxes which influenced him against the Jews (Ezra 4:8, 9, 17, 23), B. C. 465.

3. A Levite, son of Bani, who repaired part of the wall of Jerusalem under Nehemiah (Neh. 3:17), B. C. 445.

4. One of the "chief of the people" who signed with Nehemiah the covenant to serve Jehovah (Neh. 10:25), B. C. 445.

5. One of the priests who accompanied Zerubbabel at the same time as the preceding (Neh. 12:3).

Re'i (rē'ī; *friendly, sociable*), one of David's friends who refused to espouse the cause of Adonijah (I Kings 1:8), B. C. 960.

Reins. 1. "Reins" is once (Isa. 11:5) the rendering of the Heb. *ḥălăṣ*, *strength*, elsewhere "loins" (*q. v.*).

2. A name for the *kidneys* (*q. v.*), when they are used figuratively.

Re'kem (rē'kĕm; *variegation*).

1. One of the five Midianite kings slain by

the Israelites along with Balaam (Num. 31:8; Josh. 13:21), B. C. c. 1380.

2. One of the sons of Hebron, and father of Shammai of the tribe of Judah (I Chron. 2:43, 44), B. C. after 1380.

3. A descendant of Machir, the son of Manasseh by his wife Maachah (I Chron. 7:16). The name is sometimes given as *Rakem*.

Release (Heb. *shămăṭ*, to *let alone*; Gr. *'apoluō*, to *release*).

1. The Sabbatic year (*see* Festivals) was also called "the year of release" (Deut. 31:10), because Moses commanded that during that year the poor were not to be oppressed. The specific command was: "Every creditor that lendeth ought unto his neighbor shall release it; he shall not exact it of his neighbor, or of his brother, because it is called the Lord's release" (15:1, 2, 3, 9). The Hebrew term does not signify a remission of the debt, the relinquishing of all claim for payment, but simply the lengthening of the term, not pressing for payment. In Exod. 23:11 it is said of the land, "But the seventh year thou shalt let it rest (Heb. *shămăṭ*), and lie still," etc. This does not mean an entire renunciation of the field or possession; so in the case of debt it does not imply an absolute relinquishment of what has been lent, but simply *leaving* it, i. e., not pressing for it during this year.

2. It is related (Esth. 2:18) that when Ahasuerus took Esther to wife that he "made a release (Heb. *hănăhăh*, *quiet*) to the provinces." The exact nature of this quiet is not known, but the LXX and Aramaic understand it as immunity from taxes.

3. A custom which prevailed of allowing some prominent criminal to go free at the Passover (Matt. 27:15; Luke 23:17; John 18:39). The origin of the custom is unknown, but it is probable that it prevailed among the Jews before they were subject to the Romans, for Pilate said, "Ye have a custom." Perhaps it was memorial of the great national deliverance which was celebrated at the feast of the Passover. The Romans, who prided themselves in respecting the usages of conquered people, had fallen in with the custom.

Religion, a term, when viewed etymologically, of uncertain derivation. Cicero refers it to *religare*, to read over again, to consider, and thus regards it as meaning attention to divine things. Lactantius and Augustine derive the word from *religare*, to bind back, and thus representing religion as the ground of obligation. The word thus translated in the New Testament, where it occurs but three times, is *thrēskeia*, and it means outward religious service (see Acts 26:5; James 1:26, 27). In philosophical, as well as in common use, the word has a variety of meanings, e. g., Schleiermacher defines religion as "the feeling of absolute dependence;" Kant, "the observance of moral law as a divine institution;" Fichte, "Faith in the moral order of the universe." In general it refers to any system of faith and worship, as the religion of the Jews or of pagan nations, or of Christians. In the popular language of believers in Christianity it means especially and almost exclusively the Christian religion. The term calls attention to the all-important fact that man is a religious

being. There is that in his nature which prompts him to some sort of faith and worship. With or without special revelation from God, he requires the satisfaction and consolation and guidance which comes from faith in the unseen and the eternal. The limits of this article do not admit of representations of the various forms of religion which have appeared in the history of the race. For these see articles under their appropriate heads. Scientific research and comparative study in this direction, began in the nineteenth century. The distinction between natural and revealed religion, their relative value and importance, the inadequacy of the one and the completeness of the other properly falls under the head of theology. *See* Theology—E. McC.

Religious Proselytes. *See* Proselytes.

Remali'ah (rĕm-á-lī'á; perhaps, *Jehovah adorns*), the father of Pekah, king of Israel (II Kings 15:25, 27, 30, 32, 37; 16:1, 5; II Chron. 28:6; Isa. 7:1, 4, 5, 9; 8:6), B. C. before 735.

Re'meth (rē'mĕth; *height*), a city of Issachar (Josh. 19:21), called in I Chron. 6:73 Ramoth. *See* Ramoth, 2.

Rem'mon (rĕm'ŏn; Josh. 19:7). *See* Rimmon.

Rem'mon-meth'oar (rĕm'ŏn-mĕth'ô-är; Josh. 19:13). *See* Rimmon.

Rem'phan (rĕm'făn), better Rephan. *See* Gods, False.

Rend, Rent (Heb. *qärä'*). This Hebrew term is the only one which calls for special notice.

1. The rending of one's clothes (*q. v.*) as a sign of grief, and its figurative use; thus, "Rend your hearts and not your garment" (Joel 2:13) signifies contrition of heart, and not mere outward signs of grief.

2. The prophet in denouncing the people said (4:30), "Though thou rentest thy face (marg. *eyes*) with painting, in vain shalt thou make thyself fair." Allusion is made to the Eastern practice of painting the eyes (*q. v.*).

Repentance (Gr. *metanoia*, a *change* of mind), in the theological and ethical sense a fundamental and thorough change in the hearts of men from sin and toward God. Although faith alone is the condition for salvation (Eph. 2:8-10; Acts 16:31), repentance is bound up with faith and inseparable from it, since without some measure of faith no one can truly repent, and repentance never attains to its deepest character till the sinner realizes through saving faith how great is the grace of God against whom he has sinned. On the other hand there can be no saving faith without true repentance. Repentance contains as essential elements (1) a genuine sorrow toward God on account of sin (II Cor. 7:9, 10; Matt. 5:3, 4; Psa. 51). (2) An inward repugnance to sin necessarily followed by the actual forsaking of it (Matt. 3:8; Acts 26:20; Heb. 6:1). (3) Humble self-surrender to the will and service of God (see Acts 9:6, as well as Scriptures above referred to). Repentance, it should be observed, has different stages of development. (1) In its lowest and most imperfect form it may arise from fear of the consequences or penalty of sin. If it goes no farther than this it is simply remorse, and must end in despair. (2) It deepens in character with the recognition of the baseness of sin itself. But here again it is merely a burden of soul from which man may seek to free himself in vain till he recognizes the great hope set before him in the Gospel. (3) It becomes most complete and powerful in those who have experienced the saving grace of God, and thus realize more fully than ever the enormity of sin and the depths of the divine compassion which has been operative in their salvation.

Repentance, it is thus to be seen, is the gift of God (Acts 5:31; 11:18; Rom. 2:4). It is so because God has given his word with its revelations concerning sin and salvation; also the Holy Spirit to impress the truth and awaken the consciences of men and lead them to repentance. But as with faith so with repentance it is left with men to make for themselves the great decision.—E. McC. revised by M. F. U.

Repetition (*battologeō*, to *stutter, prate*). Our Lord, in his sermon on the Mount (Matt. 6:7) cautions us against *using vain repetitions in* prayer. This injunction is not directed against simple repetitions, which may often arise in the fervency of earnest prayer, but against such repetitions on the ground of supposed merit. The Gentile nations were accustomed to attach merit to much speaking in their prayers. The Jews adopted this bad practice to such an extent that it was one of their maxims that, "He that multiplieth prayer shall be heard."

Re'phael (rē'fā-ĕl; *God heals*), a son of the Levite Shemaiah of the house of Obed-edom, and appointed one of the doorkeepers of the house of God by David (I Chron. 26:7), B. C. about 960.

Re'phah (rē'fā; *wealth, opulence*), a son of Beriah of the tribe of Ephraim (I Chron. 7:25).

Repha'iah (rĕ-fā'yà; *Jehovah heals*).

1. The sons of Rephaiah, the sons of Arnon, etc. (I Chron. 3:21), were, it is supposed, branches of the family of David whose descent or connection with Zerubbabel is for us unascertainable. Rephaiah is probably the same as Rhesa (*q. v.*), mentioned in Luke 3:27.

2. A son of Ishi, and one of the chiefs of Simeon in the time of Hezekiah, who led the expedition of five hundred men against the Amalekites of Mount Seir (I Chron. 4:42), B. C. about 715.

3. One of the six sons of Tola, and head of a family in Issachar (I Chron. 7:2), B. C. before 1440.

4. The son of Binea, and eighth in descent from Jonathan, the son of Saul (I Chron. 9:43), B. C. long after 1000. He is called *Rapha* in 8:37.

5. The son of Hur, and the "ruler of the half part of Jerusalem." He repaired part of the wall of the city (Neh. 3:9), B. C. 445.

Reph'aim (rĕf'ā-ĭm; *spirits of the deceased, giant aborigines*), a race first mentioned in Gen. 14:5 as dwelling in Ashteroth Karnaim (quite probably not the same as Ashtaroth, the residence of Og, Deut. 1:4, et al.), and being smitten by Chedorlaomer and his allies. In Gen. 15:20 they appear among the nations to be dispossessed by Israel. As they are not mentioned in Gen. 10:15-18, they were probably not Canaanites, but an older, perhaps aboriginal race. Their few recorded names

"have, as Ewald remarks, a Semitic aspect," though, to be sure, they may have been Semitized. They are mentioned (A. V. "giants") in Deut. 2:11, 20; 3:11, 13; Josh. 12:4; 13:12; 17:15, with the Perizzites (Gen. 15:20).

Rephaim is also used of the dead in Job 26:5; Psa. 88:10; Prov. 2:18; 9:18; 21:16; Isa. 14:9; 26:14, 19. This usage also is found in the Ras Shamra epic literature from ancient Ugarit. *See* Giants.

Reph'aim, Valley of (*valley of the giants*) is first mentioned in Joshua's description of the northern border of Judah (Josh. 15:8). It was the scene of several conflicts between the Philistines and David (II Sam. 5:17-22; 23:15-17; I Chron. 14:9, sq.). From I Chron. 11:15, 16, it seems clear that Rephaim was not very distant from Bethlehem. The valley was proverbial for its crops of grain (Isa. 17:5). It apparently is to be identified with the valley about 3 miles in length lying S. W. of Jerusalem and extending half way to Bethleham, called *Baqa'*.

Reph'idim (rĕf'ĭ-dĭm), one of Israel's camping sites on their journey from the Wilderness of Sin to Mount Sinai. At this now-unknown site the episode of the murmuring of the Children of Israel occurred because of a lack of water. Accordingly Moses struck the rock in Horeb and obtained an abundance of water (Exod. 17:1-7; 19:2). Moses named the place "Meribah" or strife. At Rephidim also occurred the clash between the Israelites and the Bedouin Amelekites. During this celebrated encounter Aaron and Hur supported Moses' hands in prayer while Joshua secured a great victory (Exod. 17:8-16).—M. F. U.

Reproach (Hebrew usually *ḥĕrpäh;* Gr. *oneidos*), a severe expression of censure or blame, "mine enemies reproach me" (Psa. 42:10; see Job 19:3, etc.). It is sometime directed against God, and is then often equivalent to blasphemy (II Kings 19:4, 16; Isa. 37:4, 17, etc.). It also is the *object* of contempt, scorn, derision, as "let us build up the wall of Jerusalem, that we be no more a reproach" (Neh. 2:17; comp. Psa. 22:6; 79:4; Jer. 6:10; 24:9, etc.).

Reprobate. 1. Used only once in the Old Testament: "Reprobate silver shall men call them, because the Lord hath rejected them." (Jer. 6:30, Heb. *mä'ăs,* to reject, spurn).

2. In the New Testament "reprobate" is the rendering of the Gr. *'adokimo* (*not standing the test*). In Rom. 1:28 the apostle says of the Gentiles that, "even as they did not like to retain God in their knowledge, God gave them over to a *reprobate* mind," etc. The meaning of reprobate here depends upon whether it is taken in the active sense, when it means a blinded mind, one no longer capable of judging; if in the passive sense, then reprobate conveys the meaning of rejected. The former is its more probable sense. "Reprobate" in II Cor. 13:5, 6, 7; II Tim. 3:8, is to be taken in the sense of *unapproved*. In Tit. 1:16 the margin is "void of judgment."

Reputation. 1. This word occurs in Eccles. 10:1, as the rendering of the Heb. *yāqän* (*valuable, costly*), and means "held in high esteem." Similar in meaning is the Gr. *timios, of great* price, Acts. 5:34, "Gamaliel, had in reputation among the people."

2. "Them which were of reputation" (Gr. dokountes, Gal. 2:2) are those thought of, i. e., those highly esteemed, looked up to, and so of influence.

3. "He made himself of no reputation" (Phil. 2:7) is the rendering of the Gr. kenoō, to empty one's self. See Kenosis.

4. "Hold such in reputation" (Phil. 2:29, Gr. entimos, valuable) is more properly rendered in the R. V. "Hold such in honor."

Re′sen (rē′sĕn). An ancient city of Assyria (Gen. 10:12), one of a number of towns forming the composite city called Nineveh (q. v.). Resen stood midway between Nineveh and Calah.

Resh (rĕsh), the twentieth letter of the Hebrew alphabet, corresponding to English "r." It stands at the beginning of the twentieth section of Psalm 119, in which portion each verse in the Hebrew begins with this letter.— M. F. U.

Re′sheph (rē′shĕf; flame), a son of Beriah, of the tribe of Ephraim (I Chron. 7:25).

Respect of Persons (Heb. nākǎr; Gr. prosōpolēpteo). The Hebrew verb means to scrutinize, and hence care for, or reject; the Greek verb is derived from two others meaning to accept the face; and both have the idea of partiality. This is contrary to the word, for God commanded that the judges should pronounce judgment without respect of persons (Lev. 19:15; Deut. 1:17; 16:19). God is declared to have no respect of persons, i. e., he is impartial (Acts 10:34; Rom. 2:11; Eph. 6:9; Col. 3:25); and Christians are warned against the same (James 2:1, 3, 9; comp. Prov. 24:23; 28:21).

Restitution. See Punishment, Mosaic Law, 2.

Resurrection of Christ, the return of Christ to bodily life on the earth on the third day after his death.

1. **Scripture Doctrine.** Only within recent years have rationalistic interpretations of the Scriptures ventured to assert that the phrase "raised from the dead" does not mean an actual bodily resurrection, and that it simply declares that Christ as a Spirit did not remain in hades, but was raised to heaven. That this is a most irrational interpretation is seen from the explicit declaration and the whole tenor of the Scriptures upon this point. Likewise the "vision hypothesis," that Christ after his death only appeared to his disciples in a way purely subjective, is contrary to the Scriptures, neither can it be, as we shall see, sustained upon grounds of reason. The resurrection of our Lord is set before us in the New Testament as the miraculous restoration of his physical life, the reunion of his spirit with his body, and yet in such a way that the material limitations, in which he had previously confined his life, were set aside. The resurrection was the beginning of the glorification. It occurred on the morning of the third day after his death, counting according to custom, for days parts of days (comp. Matt. 16:21; Luke 24:1).

The body in which the disciples saw the risen Lord was real, that in which they had seen him living, and that which had died (see Luke 24:39; John 20:24-29). And yet, as is manifest from the Gospel accounts of his appearances during the forty days and of his visible ascension, his body was undergoing the mysterious change of that glorification of which the resurrection was the beginning and the ascension into heaven the end (see John 20:4, 14, 26; 21:4; Luke 24:37). What the change was that adapted the Lord's body to its destined heavenly environment is a question of profitless speculation. But it is evident from the Scriptures that in the resurrection Christ's glorification only began, also that Christ now dwells in heaven in a glorified body (Phil. 3:21; Col. 3:4). The resurrection of Christ is represented in the Scriptures as wrought by the power of God. Its miraculous power is strongly proclaimed (see Acts 13:30; Rom. 1:4; I Cor. 15:15). And thus it presents no difficulty for faith to one who really believes in God. Indeed, the Scriptures represent it as in the deepest sense not unnatural, but natural that Christ should be raised from the dead (see Acts 2:24).

The testimony of the Scriptures as to the reality of the resurrection is most ample and without a note of discord as to the essential fact itself. The witnesses were not few, but many (see, in addition to accounts in the gospels, I Cor. 15:1-8). The declaration of St. Paul that he had "seen the Lord" (I Cor. 9:1) properly places him among the witnesses to the great reality.

The proclamation of the resurrection lies at the basis of apostolic teaching (see Acts 1:22; 4:2, 33; 17:18; 23:6; I Cor. 15:14, et al.). It ranks first among the miracles which bear witness to Christ's divine character (Rom. 1:4). It is the divine seal of approval upon Christ's atoning work, and thus is in close connection with the justification of sinners (4:25; 5:10; 8:34). It is connected with our spiritual renewal as the new life of believers comes from the risen Christ (Col. 3:1-3). It is the pledge of the resurrection and glorification of the true followers of Christ (Rom. 8:11; I Cor. 15:20-22; Phil. 3:21; I Thess. 4:14).

2. **Theological.** The denial of this great fact has always come from the enemies of Christianity. This is but natural, as Christianity must stand or fall with the resurrection. Christ "rose from the dead" has always been a cardinal article of faith in the Christian Church. The historic proofs of this fact are most weighty when the relation of the fact to the whole body of saving truth is duly considered. They may fail to convince unbelievers who have no appreciation of the great realities of sin and salvation. But still they are of great value for the defense of the faith and for the comfort of believers. The matter resolves itself mainly into two considerations, viz., the credibility of the witnesses and the difficulties of denial as greater than those of belief. As to the credibility of the witnesses, account is to be taken not only of their number and variety, but also of the essential harmony of their reports, the absence of all motive to falsehood, and their self-sacrificing devotion to the Gospel which based itself upon the resurrection. The difficulties which beset denial are found (a) in the

impossibility of explaining the empty grave except upon the ground that the resurrection actually took place; (*b*) the attitude of the enemies of Christ after the resurrection, revealing as it did their helpless confusion; (*c*) the belief of the disciples, their sudden transition from hopelessness to triumphant faith, which would be inexplicable except upon the actuality of the resurrection; (*d*) the founding of Christianity in the world, which can be rationally accounted for only in view of the fact that Christ actually rose from the dead. —E. McC.

Resurrection of the Body (Gr. *'anastasis, to make to stand,* or *rise up*), the reunion of the bodies and souls of men which have been separated by death. This is rightly held to be an important article of Christian belief, though it is left by the revelations of Scripture as to many details in impenetrable obscurity.

1. **Spiritual.** The Old Testament in the earlier parts does not speak explicitly upon this subject. Christ, however, declares the doctrine to be generally presupposed in the old economy (see Luke 20:37, 38). Allusions to it are to be found in (Gen. 22:5, cf. Heb. 11:19; Psa. 16:10, 11) Psa. 49:14, 15; Isa. 26:19, 20.; Isa. 53:10; Ezek. ch. 37. A clear reference appears in Dan. 12:3. It is plainly taught also in the Apocryphal books of the Old Testament (Wisd. 3:1; 4:15; II Macc. 7:14, 23, 29). It was a belief held commonly among the Jews in the time of Christ (see Matt. 22:30; Luke 20:39; John 11:24; Acts 23:6, 8). The Sadducees were the exceptions in their denial of the doctrine. Christ appeared and confirmed this belief, though careful to guard against erroneous sensuous conceptions held by some in connection with it, as appears in some of the passages to which reference has been made. Naturally it was a marked feature of apostolic doctrine (see Acts 4:2; 26:3; I Cor., ch. 15; I Thess. 4:14; Phil. 3:20, 21; Rev. 20:6-14, et al.). The teaching of the Scriptures sums up as follows: 1. The body shall rise again. The integrity of man's being, a creature of soul and body, shall be restored. 2. In some sense the identity of the body shall be preserved. 3. The body is to be so changed and refined as to fit it for the new surroundings of the future life. For the saints it is to be a "glorified body." 4. The resurrection of the righteous will take place at the coming of Christ (I Thess. 4:13-18; I Cor. 15:53), of the unsaved at the Great White Throne Judgment after the Kingdom Age (Rev. 20:11-15). 5. The power is of God in Christ, who said, "I am the resurrection and the life."

2. **Theological.** The article in the Apostles' Creed containing this doctrine was doubtless intended to express the faith of the early Church in the teaching of Christ and the apostles. It was also intended to meet the Manichean heresy that there is an essential antagonism between matter and spirit, that matter is by nature evil, and accordingly the soul of man is degraded by union with the body. That this simple but great statement of the dignity of the human body, a dignity as real as that of the human spirit, and that both soul and body are destined to immortality, has been overlaid by many crude speculations, is what might have been expected, and in no measure detracts from the great truth of revelation to which the statement points. As to the sense in which the resurrection body shall be identical with the body laid aside in death, that is a matter upon which the Scriptures open the way to no definite conclusion. It may be remarked, however, that the continued identity of the body even in this present life does not depend upon its possession continuously of the same substance; nor is it identity of size or form or appearance. It is identity of relationship and functions. The substance of which the body is composed is constantly changing. Likewise there are changes in respect to other material features. Still the body remains as the vestiture, and in some degree the expression of the Spirit in union with it. The coarse representation of bodily resurrection, in which many have indulged, based upon the idea of the literal return of the same fleshly parts laid aside in death is therefore without warrant in reason. And this is not required nor warranted by Scripture. A careful study of St. Paul's great chapter upon the subject (I Cor., ch. 15) must show this. The most that can be affirmed is that God will reinvest the souls of men with bodies, and that these bodies, while changed, shall have in some important sense identity with the bodies which have experienced death and dissolution. It is not strange that this doctrine has been denied by rationalists, and materialists, and skeptics generally. But it is logically held by Christians because of their faith in Christ and in the teachings which bear his authority. It has great religious and ethical value, inasmuch as it recognizes the dignity of the body and its true relation to the soul in union with it, and opens to us the hope of complete glorification.—E. McC., revised by *M. F. U.*

Retribution. *See* Punishment, Future.

Re'u (rē'ū; *friend*), the son of Peleg and father of Serug, in the ancestry of Abraham (Gen. 11:18-21; I Chron. 1:25). He lived two hundred and thirty-nine years. He is called *Ragau* in Luke 3:35.

Reu'ben (rōō'bĕn; *see a son*). 1. **Name and Family.** The firstborn son of Jacob and Leah (Gen. 29:32), B. C. about 1900.

2. **Personal History.** (1) **His crime.** When Jacob dwelt in Edar, Reuben committed an offense (Gen. 35:22) which was too great for Jacob ever to forget, and of which he spoke with abhorrence even upon his dying bed (2) **Befriends Joseph.** When his brethren were planning for the destruction of Joseph in Dothan, Reuben, as the eldest son, interfered in his behalf. By his advice Joseph's life was spared—he was stripped of his distinguished garment and cast into a pit. In Reuben's absence Joseph was sold to the Ishmaelites. When Reuben returned, with the intention of rescuing his brother, he found that he had gone, and manifested great grief threat (37:21, 22, 29). (3) **In Egypt.** Reuben accompanied his brethren into Egypt in search of food, and accepted Joseph's harsh treatment of himself and brethren as a proper

judgment upon them because of their sin (42:22). He delivered Joseph's message to Jacob demanding Benjamin's presence in Egypt, and offered his two sons as pledges for his brother's safe return (v. 37). Upon the removal of Jacob into Egypt, B. C. c. 1876, Reuben had four sons—Hanoch, Phallu, Hezron and Carmi (46:9).

3. **Character.** Reuben seems to have been of an ardent, impetuous, unbalanced, but not of an ungenerous nature; not crafty and cruel, as were Simeon and Levi, but rather, to use the metaphor of the dying patriarch, boiling up like a vessel of water over the rapid wood fire of the nomad tent, and as quickly subsiding into apathy when the fuel was withdrawn.

4. **The Tribe of Reuben.** (1) **Numbers.** At the time of the migration into Egypt Reuben's sons were four, and from them sprang the chief families of the tribe. The census of Mount Sinai (Num. 1:20, 21; 2:11) shows that the numbers of this tribe at the exodus was forty-six thousand five hundred men above twenty years of age, and fit for active warlike service, ranking seventh in population. At the later census, taken thirty-eight years after, and just before entering Canaan, its numbers had decreased to forty-three thousand seven hundred and thirty, which made it rank as ninth (26:7). (2) **Position.** During the journey through the wilderness the position of Reuben was on the south side of the tabernacle. The "camp" which went under his name was formed of his own tribe, that of Simeon and of Gad. (3) **Inheritance.** The country allotted to this tribe was east of Jordan, extending on the south to the river Arnon, on the east to the desert of Arabia; on the west were the Dead Sea and the Jordan, and the northern border was probably marked by a line running eastward from the Jordan through *Wady Heshbân* (Josh. 13:17-21; Num. 32:37, 38).

Reu′benite, (rōō′bĕn-īt), a descendant of Reuben (Num. 26:7, etc.).

Reu′el (rōō′ĕl; *friend of God's*, or *God is a friend*).

1. The son of Esau by his wife Bashemath (Gen. 36:4, 10, 35). His four sons (Gen. 36:13; I Chron. 1:37) were chiefs ("dukes") of the Edomites (Gen. 36:17).

2. A priest of Midian and herdsman, who gave a hospitable reception to Moses when he fled from Egypt, and whose daughter Zipporah became the wife of Moses (Exod. 2:18). Reuel is undoubtedly the same person as Jethro (*q. v.*), the first being probably his proper name, and the latter a title or surname, indicating his rank.

3. The father of Eliasaph, the captain of the host of Gad at the time of the census at Sinai (Num. 2:14), B. C. c. 1439. The parallel passages (1:14; 7:42, 47; 10:20) give the name as *Deuel*.

4. The son of Ibnijah and father of Shephathiah, of the tribe of Benjamin (I Chron. 9:8).

Reu′mah (rōō′mà; *exalted, elevated*), Nahor's concubine, and by him mother of Tebah and others (Gen. 22:24).

Revelation (Gr. *'apokalupsis*, an *uncovering* or *unveiling*), a term expressive of the fact that God has made known to men truths and realities which men could not discover for themselves.

An important distinction commonly recognized is between general and special revelation.

By general revelation is meant that which is given to all men, in nature and history, and in the nature of man himself. The reality and validity of revelation in this sense is declared in such scriptures as Psa. 19:1; Isa. 40:26; Rom. 1:19, 20; Exod. 9:16; Acts 14:15-17; 17:15; Rom. 2:14, 15; Matt. 6:22-34. But the actual power of this revelation over men has, in numberless cases, been reduced or nullified by sin (see Rom. 4:24-28). And, besides, the coming of sin into the world, the establishment of the economy of redemption, has necessitated the making known of truths not made known by general revelation. Therefore God has given the special revelation brought to us in the Holy Scriptures. The Scriptures reiterate the truths proclaimed in nature, in history, and in man himself; and, in addition thereto, declare the salvation which God has provided for mankind in Jesus Christ.

It is true that the Scriptures contain many things not in the nature of revelation—matters of fact, the knowledge of which lay within the reach of unaided human powers. But these are only the framework of the great revelation in connection with them. It is to be observed further that revelation is not to be confounded with inspiration. Revelation refers to the truths or facts which God has made known; inspiration to the process by which the knowledge has come. The proofs of revelation and of inspiration, however, closely related, and in some measure interwoven, are therefore not identical. *See* Inspiration.

The reality of special revelation is proved by evidence both external and internal. The external proof is found in miracles and prophecy. *See* Miracles, Prophecy.

The internal proofs are the contents of the revelation itself. The greatness of the truths, their adaptation to the necessities of human life, their practical effects when accepted, and above all the personal character of Jesus Christ, who is the center of the whole revelation and the supreme medium thereof, form sufficient proof that the revelation of the Scriptures has come from God. Thus the revelation is to be recognized as the sun is known, by its own shining. True, it will not be recognized by those who ignore the reality of sin and the necessity for salvation. But to everyone who truly feels this sad reality, not only will the special revelation of salvation seem possible, but also real and indispensable.

And they who seek and find the salvation proclaimed by the Scriptures find a peculiar personal evidence of the divine authority of the Scriptures. *See* Assurance.

The term "continuous revelation" has come somewhat prominently into use in recent years. By this it is commonly meant that special revelation did not cease with the closing of the Scripture canon; that revelations as authoritative as those of the Scriptures are still being made. We have not space for adequate discussion of this view. It should be noted, nevertheless, that it is a denial of

382. The Roman Empire in John's Day

the sufficiency of the revelations already given, and opens the way for fanaticism and grave errors. Properly enough, however, we may recognize the progress which has been exhibited throughout the whole history of revelation; and, besides that, the deeper and larger understanding of divine truth to which the Christian world is continually attaining, whether that truth comes through revelation general or special.

Revelation, Book of the, the last book of the N. T. and the consummation of Biblical prophecy disclosing the future of the Jew, the Gentile and the Church of Christ. This great prophetic unfolding deals mainly with the events preceding the second coming of Christ, the establishment of the Millennial Kingdom and, finally, the eternal state.

1. **The Name.** The name of the book comes from Latin *revelatio, an unveiling*, Gr. *apokalypsis, the removing of a veil*. It is thus a book written to be understood. The book is not correctly called the Revelation of Saint John. It is precisely "the Revelation of Jesus Christ" (1:1). That is, it is an unveiling of His future plan for the earth and for His redeemed saints both for time and eternity. It is necessary to view the book as in no sense sealed (Rev. 22:10 cf. Dan. 12:9). A distinct blessing is vouchsafed to the person that reads and to those who hear the words of this prophecy (Rev. 1:3). It is mere pious prating to say that God does not intend this book to be understood or that the symbolism and figures of the prophecy are incomprehensible. The figures and symbols of the book, which furnish the basis of its interpretation, are found elsewhere in divine revelation and can only be understood in the light of a coherent and connected comparative study of all other lines of prophecy and prophetic type and symbolism as they converge upon the Book of the Revelation. Interpretation of the book demands a

thorough acquaintance with all the other great prophecies which merge in this book, which is "like a great Union Station where the trunk lines of prophecy come in from other portions of Scripture" (J. Vernon McGee, *Briefing the Bible*, 1949, p. 122).

2. **Great Themes.** About a dozen great prophetic themes find their consummation in the Book of the Revelation: (1) The Lord Jesus Christ (Gen. 3:15), Whose present session (Rev. 3:21), future triumph over evil, redemption of the earth, destruction of the ungodly, establishment of His earthly kingdom are consummated at His second advent (4:1-19:16). Christ's Kingdom rule and his ministry in the eternal state (chaps. 21, 22) constitute the grand fulfillment of all prophecy. (2) The Church, the Body of Christ (Matt. 16:18; I Cor. 12:13; Rev. chaps. 2, 3). (3) The resurrection and translation of saints (4:1, 2). (4) The Great Tribulation (Deut. 4:29, 30; Jer. 30:5-8; Rev. chaps. 4-19). (5) Satan and demon power (Isa. 14:12-14; Ezek. 28:11-18; Rev. 12:7-12; 16:13; 20:1, etc.). (6) The man of sin (II Thess. 2:1-8; Rev. 13:1-10). (7) The false prophet (Rev. 13:11-18). (8) Destruction of Gentile world power (Dan. 2:31-45; Rev. chaps. 5-19). (9) The redemption of the earth (Rev. 5) with the loosing of the seals, trumpets and vials (chaps. 6-19). (10) The second advent of Christ (Rev. 19:1-10). (11) The judgment of Sinners (Rev. 20:11-15). (12) The first resurrection and the kingdom age (Rev. chaps. 20:4-6). (13) The new heavens and the new earth (Rev. chap. 21). (14) The eternal state (chap. 22).

3. **Methods of Interpretation.** Various interpretations of the book prevail. (1) **The Preterist Interpretation.** This views the book as referring chiefly to events contemporary to that day, to comfort the then-persecuted church, written in symbols in a general sense

intelligible to the saints of that period. (2) **Continuous Historical Interpretation.** This considers the book as forecasting the entire period of church history from the revelator's time to the present, in which the chief phases of the church's struggle to final victory are set forth. This has been a very commonly accepted view. (3) **The Spiritualist Interpretation.** This separates the symbolism of the book from any historical revelation and regards the book as a pictorial representation of the great principles of divine government for an omni-temporal application. (4) **The Futuristic Interpretation.** This construes the bulk of the book as future in John's day. It

383. Philadelphia, Site of One of the Seven
Churches of Revelation 2-3

accepts the divinely-given key of interpretation in Rev. 1:19 and interprets the "things which thou hast seen" as embracing chaps. 1:1-18 and the "things which are," chaps. 2, 3 referring to the church period and the "things which shall be after these things" as referring to the yet future period after the glorification of the church and its removal from the earthly scene, with chaps. 4 to the end concerning chiefly Israel and the Gentile nations in the still-future period preceding the second coming of Christ.

4. **Background and Destination.** The author is John the beloved (1:1). The beloved apostle came to Ephesus around A. D. 70. He seems to have been a circuit minister at Ephesus, Pergamos, Symrna, Thyatira, Sardis, Philadelphia and Laodicea. He was put in prison on the Patmos Isle in the Aegean in the fifteenth year of Domitian, according to Eusebius (*Ecclesiastical History* III, 18). The Apocalypse was doubtless intended especially for the seven churches of Asia (cf. 1:4 and 10 and 11 and chaps. 2 and 3). The book was also evidently intended for other churches in Asia Minor.

5. **Occasion and Date.** John wrote by express command of Christ (1:10-13). The "angels" of the seven churches of chaps. 2 and 3 are apparently the "ministers" of those churches and the apostle wrote to comfort them and their congregations. Quite a few scholars date the book about 68 or 69 A. D. (Wescott, Lightfoot, Hort and Salmon). The reasons for this, though, are not convincing. The best date seems to be 95 or 96 A. D. (cf. Swete, Milligan, Moffatt and Zahn). This date accords with evidence from Irenaeus, Clement of Alexandria and Eusebius to the effect that the banishment to Patmos was in

the later reign of Domitian, 81-96 A. D. This view is in agreement with the fact that the Domitian persecution, unlike the Neronic, was the result of the Christians' refusal to worship the emperor (cf. 1:9; 13:9, 10, 12).

6. **Authenticity.** External witness to the book is sufficiently strong. Traces of the book are found in literature immediately after the apostolic age. Justin Martyr, Irenaeus, Tertullian, Hippolytus, Clement of Alexandria, Origen, the Muratorian Fragment, etc., lend their support to its genuineness. The internal evidence is also adequate. The writer calls himself John four times (1:1, 4, 9; 22:8). He calls himself "servant" of Christ (1:1) and "brother and partaker with you in the tribulation and kingdom and patience which are in Jesus" (1:9). The fact that he does not call himself an apostle has been urged against authorship by John the Apostle, but this argument is invalid to one who believes that the apostle is the author of the fourth gospel where the author's humility is reflected. The early church accepted the fact that it was John who was in exile and the witness to the fact by Clement of Alexandria, Eusebius and Irenaeus give this claim good support. The claim that grammatical irregularities of the Apocalypse rule out Johannine authorship are not sustained. Many factors, including the apocalytic and highly figurative and symbolic meaning of the book offer sufficient explanation of this phenomenon.

384. Sardis, Site of One of the Seven
Churches of Revelation 2-3

6. **Outline.**

Introduction and Salutation, 1:1-8

Part I. "The Things Which Thou Hast Seen"—The Glorified Christ, 1:9-20

Part II "The Things Which Are"—The Seven Churches, chaps. 2-3

1. The Apostolic Church—Ephesus, 2:1-7
2. The Persecuted Church—Symrna, 2:8-11 (Apostolic period to Constantine)
3. The Wordly Church—Pergamus, 2:12-17 (Constantine 316 A. D. to 500 A. D.)
4. The Pagan Church—Thyatira, 2:18-29 (especially from 500-1500 A. D. on to the end)
5. The Protestant Church—Sardis, 3:1-6 (from sixteenth century on to the end)
6. The Missionary Church—Philadelphia, 3:7-13 (from 1750 A. D. to the end)
7. The Apostate Church—Laodicea, 3:14-22 (from c. 1900 A. D. to the end)

385. Nazareth with the Valley of Jezreel (Armageddon) background

Part III. "The Things Which Shall Be After These Things"—The Great Tribulation and the Second Coming of Christ, chaps. 4-22
1. The Church in heaven with Christ, chap. 4
   a. Loosing of 7-sealed book, chap. 5
2. The Great Tribulation, 6:1-11:19
   a. The seven seals, 6:1-8:1
   b. The seven trumpets, 8:2-11:19
3. The Seven Performers during the Great Tribulation, chaps. 12, 13
   a. The Woman—Israel 12:1-2
   b. The Red Dragon—Satan, 12:3-4
   c. The Male Child—Christ, 12:5-6
   d. Michael, the Archangel, wars with the dragon, 12:7-12
   e. Satan's persecution of the Woman, Israel, 12:13-16
   f. The remnant of Israel, 12:17
   g. The Beast out of the sea—political power and a person, 13:1-10
   h. The Beast out of the earth—Anti-Christ, 13:11-18
4. The Latter Part of the Great Tribulation, chap. 14
5. The Seven Vials, chaps. 15, 16
6. Judgment of Ecclesiastical and Commercial Babylon, chaps. 17, 18
7. Christ's Second Advent, chap. 19
8. The Millennium, chap. 20
9. Eternity Unveiled, chaps. 21, 22
   a. The New Earth, 21:1
   b. The New Jerusalem, 21:2-27
   c. The New River, 22:1-7
Epilogue, Final Instructions and Invitation, 22:8-21.—M. F. U.

Reveling (Gr. *kōmos*, a *carousel*), in the Greek writings, was a nocturnal and riotous procession of half-drunken and frolicsome fellows, who after supper parade through the streets with torches and music in honor of Bacchus or some other deity, and sing and play before the houses of their male and female friends; hence used generally of *feasts and drinking parties that are protracted till late at night, and indulge in revelry* (Rom. 13:13, A. V. "rioting;" Gal. 5:21; I Pet. 4:3).

Revenge, Revenger. These words are often used in the sense of to avenge a wrong, or the one who brings punishment (*see* Avenger). This is the meaning in Num. 35:19-27; II Sam. 14:11; Psa. 79:10; Jer. 15:15. The civil magistrate is called by Paul "the minister of God, a revenger to execute wrath upon him that doeth evil" (Rom. 13:4); while in II Cor. 7:11 the apostle recognizes as a prominent virtue of the church in Corinth its zeal and vengeance, i. e., *disciplinary zeal* against the incestuous person. He writes the church (II Cor. 10:6) that he has "a readiness to revenge all disobedience, when your obedience is fulfilled." *How* he intends to execute this vengeance he does not tell; he might do it by excommunication, by giving the intruders over to the power of Satan (I Cor. 5:5), or by the exercise of his miraculous apostolic power. Revenge, or vengeance, is attributed to God in two very remarkable passages (Deut. 32:41-43; Nah. 1:2), in which Jehovah is represented as bringing certain punishment upon the wicked. The ordinary understanding of *revenge* is quite different from the above, and implies a vindictive feeling against the offender. It differs from *resentment*, which rises up in the mind immediately upon being injured; for revenge may wait years after the offense is committed. In this vindictive sense we have scriptural instances (Jer. 20:10; Ezek. 25:15). This sort of revenge is forbidden by the command to love our enemies and to return good for evil.

Revenue. *See* King.

Reverence. 1. In the sense of paying respect to some distinguished person, reverence is mentioned in II Sam. 9:6; I Kings 1:31; Esth. 3:2, 5; in the parable of the vineyard (Matt. 21:37; Mark 12:6; Luke 20:13); and of the respect given to fathers (Heb. 12:9) and husbands (Eph. 5:33).

2. We are taught to reverence God (Psa. 89:7; 111:9), his sanctuary (Lev. 19:30; 26:2). *See* Worship.

Revile, Reviler, Reviling (Heb. *qālăl*, to *make light of*, Exod. 22:28), "Thou shalt not revile the gods." *Elohim* does not mean either the gods of other nations, or rulers, but simply God, whose majesty was despised in every breach of the commandments of Jehovah. Another Hebrew term is *gǐddūph* (*vilification*) and is used by Isaiah (51:7) and Zephaniah (2:8). Kindred to *gǐddūph* is the Gr. *loidoreo*, which means to villify, heap reproach upon, and is used to represent the treatment of our Lord by his enemies (John 9:28; I Pet. 2:23), of the question put by Paul to the high priest (Acts 23:4), as also "revilers" in the catalogue of evildoers (I Cor. 6:10). In the expression, "They that passed by reviled him" (Matt. 27:39) the evangelist uses the Gr. *blasphēmeō*, a very strong term, signifying to *rail at*, *calumniate*, showing an utter want of reverence for the divine Sufferer. In Mark 15:32 it is recorded, "And they that were crucified with him reviled him" (Gr. *'oneidizō*), meaning that they unjustly reproached him.

Rewards (Gr. *misthos*, meaning *hire*, *wage*, *reward*, Matt. 5:12; 5:46; 6:1; 10:41; Mark 9:41; Acts 1:18; Rom. 4:4; I Cor. 3:8, etc.; *apodidomi*, *to give away* or *to give back*, Matt. 6:4, 18; 16:27; II Tim. 4:14; Rev. 18:6). Rewards are offered by God to a believer on the basis of faithful service rendered after salvation. It is clear from Scripture that God offers to the *lost* salvation and for the faithful service of the *saved*, rewards. Often in theological thinking salvation and rewards are confused. However, these two terms must be carefully distinguished. Salvation is a free gift (John 4:10; Rom. 6:23; Eph. 2:8, 9), while rewards are earned by works (Matt. 10:42; Luke 19:17; I Cor. 9:24, 25; II Tim. 4:7, 8). Then, too, salvation is a present possession (Luke 7:50; John 5:24). On the other hand, rewards are future attainment to be dispensed at the second coming of Christ for His Own (Matt. 16:27; II Tim. 4:8). Rewards will be dispensed at the Judgment Seat of Christ (II Cor. 5:10; Rom. 14:10). The doctrine of rewards is inseparably connected with God's grace. A soul being saved on the basis of divine grace, there is no room for the build'ng up of merit on the part of the believer. Yet God recognizes an obligation on His part to reward His saved ones for their service to Him. Nothing can be done to merit salvation

but what the believer has achieved for God's glory, God recognizes in His great faithfulness with rewards at the Judgment Seat of Christ. For the central passages on rewards see I Cor. 3:9-15 and 9:16-27; II Cor. 5:10. A principal point of contention between the Roman Catholics and Protestants concerns the basis of reward. Roman Catholics hold that reward is based on the actual merit of the good works of believers, while Protestants regard rewards as wholly of grace.—M. F. U.

Re'zeph (rē'zĕf; *glowing stone or coal*), a stronghold near Haran, taken by the Assyrians (II Kings 19:12; Isa. 37:12). There were nine cities of this name. This was probably located west of the Euphrates, called now *Rusafah*, on the route to Palmyra.

Rezi'a (rê-zī'á; *delight*), one of the sons of Ulla, of the tribe of Asher (I Chron. 7:39).

Rez'in (r z'ĭn)

1. A k ng of Damascus, who was contemporary wi h Pe .ah in Israel and with Jotham and Ahaz in Judah. Allying himself with Israel, he carried on constant war against Judah, attacking Jotham toward the close of his reign (II Kings 15:37), B. C. 742. His chief war was with Ahaz, whose territories he invaded in company with Pekah, B. C. about 741. The combined army laid seige to Jerusalem, where Ahaz was, but "could not prevail against it" (Isa. 7:1; II Kings 16:5). Rezin, however, "recovered Elath to Syria" (II Kings 16:6). Soon after this he was attacked, defeated, and slain by Tiglath-pileser III, king of Assyria (16:9). Compare Tiglath-pileser's own inscriptions, where the defeat of Rezin and the destruction of Damascus are distinctly mentioned.

2. One of the families of the Nethimim (Ezra 2:48; Neh. 7:50).

Re'zon (rē'zŏn; *prince*), the son of Eliadah, a Syrian in the service of Hadadezer, king of Zobah. When David defeated Hadadezer (II Sam. 8:3) Rezon forsook his lord, and gathering a band about him, established himself as king of Damascus (I Kings 11:23-25). The settlement of Rezon at Damascus could not have been till some time after the disastrous battle in which the power of Hadadezer was broken, for we are told that David at the same time defeated the army of Damascene Syrians who came to the relief of Hadadezer, and put garrisons in Damascus, B. C. about 984. From his position at Damascus Rezon harassed the kingdom of Solomon during the latter part of his reign.

Rhe'gium (rē'jĭ-ŭm; *broken off*, alluding to the abrupt character of the coast), a town on the southwest coast of Italy, at the southern entrance of the Strait of Messina, mentioned incidentally (Acts 28:13) in the account of Paul's voyage from Syracuse to Puteoli. It is now called *Reggio*, a town of about ten thousand inhabitants.

Rhe'sa (rē'sà), a name given in the genealogy of Christ (Luke 3:27) as the son of Zorobabel and father of Joanna. He is probably the same as Rephaim (*q. v.*).

Rho'da (rō'dà; *rose bush*), the maiden who announced the arrival of Peter at the door of Mary's house after his release from the prison by the angel (Acts 12:13, 14). A. D. 44.

386. St. Paul's Harbor, Rhodes

Rhodes (rōdz; *a rose*), an island in the Mediterranean Sea, near the coast of Asia Minor. Its capital was also called Rhodes and was a very ancient center of commerce, literature, and art. It was built in the 5th century B. C. The Colossus, one of the wonders of the world, was erected at its harbor; it is about eighteen miles broad and forty-six miles long. In the Middle Ages the island was famous as the home of the Knights of St. John. Its population now is about twenty thousand. Paul touched here (Acts 21:1) on his return voyage to Syria from his third missionary journey, but it is not stated whether or not he landed.

Ri'bai (rī'bī; *my contention*), a Benjamite of Gibeah, whose son Ittai was one of David's mighty men (II Sam. 23:29; I Chron. 11:31), B. C. 1000.

Riband (Heb. *päthil, twisted*), rather the thread by which the tassels were fastened to garments (Num. 15:38).

Rib'lah (rĭb'là; *fertility*, cf. Arab. *rabala, to increase, multiply*).

1. A landmark on the eastern boundary of Israel, as given by Moses (Num. 34:11), the position being given with much precision. It was between Shepham and the sea of Chinnereth, to the east of Ain (i. e., *the fountain*). This shows that it was different from Riblah of Hamath.

2. **Riblah of Hamath** (II Kings 23:33, etc.), the camping ground of the kings of Babylon, from which they directed operations against Palestine and Phoenicia. Hither Pharoah-Nechoh brought King Jehoahaz (*q. v.*) in chains (see II Kings 25:6, 20, 21; Jer. 39:5, 52). Riblah is preserved in the miserable village of *Rible*, from ten to twelve hours S. S. W. of Hums (Emesa), by the river el-Ahsy (Orontes).

Riches. This term is frequently used in a figurative sense to represent the gifts and graces of God's Holy Spirit, as "Despisest thou the riches of his goodness," etc. (Rom. 2:4; comp. 9:23; Eph. 1:7, 18; 2:7; 3:8; Phil. 4:19).

Riddance (Heb. *käläh, to end, complete*). "And when ye reap the harvest of your land, thou shalt not make a clean riddance of the corners of thy field" (Lev. 23:22), is another form of the command: "Thou shalt not wholly reap the corners" (19:9). The word is also used in Zeph. 1:18, in the sense of ridding the land of inhabitants.

Riddle (Heb. *ḥîdäh, tied* in a knot, *twisted*), elsewhere "dark sentence," "hard question," "dark saying," etc. The Hebrew word is derived from an Arabic root meaning "to bend off," "to twist," and is used for artifice (Dan. 8:23), a proverb (Prov. 1:6), a song (Psa. 49:4; 78:2), an oracle (Num. 12:8), a parable (Ezek. 17:2), and in general any wise or intricate sentence (Psa. 94:4; Hab. 2:6, etc.), as well as a riddle in our sense of the word (Judg. 14:12-19). Riddles were generally proposed in verse, like the celebrated riddle of Samson, which, however, was properly no riddle at all, because the Philistines did not possess the only clew on which the solution *could* depend. The riddles which the queen of Sheba came to ask of Solomon (I Kings 10:1; II Chron. 9:1) were rather "hard questions" referring to profound inquiries. Keil (*Com.*, I Kings 10:1) says that a riddle is "a pointed saying which merely hints at a deeper truth, and leaves it to be guessed." According to Josephus (*Ant.*, viii, 5, 3), Solomon was very fond of the riddle. They were also known to the Egyptians, and were used at banquets by Greeks and Romans. "Riddle" is used once in the New Testament (I Cor. 13:12, marg.); being in the text "darkly" (Gr. *'ainugma*, an *obscure saying*). The Gospel revelation is an enigma, "Inasmuch as it affords to us no full clearness of light upon God's decrees, ways of salvation, etc., but keeps its contents sometimes in a greater, sometimes in a less degree (Rom. 11:33, sq.; I Cor. 2:9) concealed, bound up in images, similitudes, types, and the like forms of human limitation and human speech, and, consequently, is for us of a mysterious and *enigmatic nature*, standing in need of future light, and vouchsafing *faith*, indeed, but not the external figure" (Meyer, *Com.*, in loc.).

Rider (Heb. *rōkĕb*). It would seem natural that horses should have been used for riding as early as for draught; and the book of Job clearly indicates such use in the description of the chase of the ostrich, "She scorneth the horse and his rider" (Job 39:18). The horse and chariot were introduced into the land of the Nile by the Hyksos invaders c. 1750. Camels were widely domesticated by the time of Gideon (Judg. 6:5) about 1200 B. C., greatly facilitating desert mobility. By the Egyptians, Babylonians, and early Greeks, war chariots were used instead of cavalry, the drivers of the chariot horses being called "riders" (Exod. 15:1, 21). The Persians discovered the value of cavalry, in which the Hebrews were always deficient. White asses were ridden in the time of the judges, and the mules in the age of the kings, horses being generally reserved for chariots. *See* Army, Horses, Chariot.

Righteousness (Heb. *ṣĕdĕq*; Gr. *dikia*), purity of heart and rectitude of life; the being and doing right. The righteousness or justice (*q. v.*) of God is the divine holiness applied in moral government and the domain of law. As an attribute of God it is united with his holiness as being essential in his nature; it is legislative or rectoral, as he is the righteous governor of all creatures; and is administrative or judicial, as he is a just dispenser of rewards and punishments. The righteousness of Christ denotes not only his absolute perfection, but is taken for his perfect obedience to the law, and suffering the penalty thereof in our stead. It is frequently used to designate his holiness, justice, and faithfulness (Gen. 18:25; Deut. 6:25; Psa. 31:1; 119:137, 142; Isa. 45:23; 46:13; 51:5-8; 66:1). The righteousness of the law is that obedience which the law requires (Rom. 3:10, 20; 8:4). The righteousness of faith is the justification (q. v.) which is received by faith (Rom. 3:21-28; 4:3-25; 5:1-11; 10:6-11; II Cor. 5:21; Gal. 2:21). The perfect righteousness of Christ is imputed to the believer, when he accepts Christ as his Savior (I Cor. 1:30; II Cor. 5:20, 21).

Rim'mon (rĭm'ŏn; *pomegranate*).

1. A Benjamite of Beeroth, whose sons, Baanah and Rechab, murdered Ish-bosheth (II Sam. 4:2-9), B. C. before 988.

2. A Syrian deity Akkad. *a thunderer* (II Kings 5:18), worshipped in Damascus. See Gods, False.

3. A town in the south of Judah (Josh. 15:32), allotted to Simeon (19:7, A. V. incorrectly "Remmon;" I Chron. 4:32); in each passage the name Rimmon follows that of Ain, also one of the cities of Judah and Simeon. The two are joined in Neh. 11:29, and are given in the A. V. as En-Rimmon (q. v.). The only other notice in the Bible is in Zech. 14:10. It is identified with the village Umm er-Rumāmīn ("mother of pomegranates"), about 9 miles N. of Beersheba.

4. A city of Zebulun assigned to the Merarite Levites (I Chron. 6:77); by some thought to be identical with Rimmon-methoar (q. v.); while others think that Dimnah (Josh. 21:35) may have been originally Rimmon, as the D and R in Hebrew are very easily confounded.

Rim'mon-meth'oar (rĭm'ŏn-mĕth'ō-ȧr; *the one marked off*), one of the landmarks of the eastern boundary of Zebulun (Josh. 19:13, A. V. "Remmon." Methoar is not a proper name, but the participle of *tä'ȧr, bounded off*, or *stretched;* and is better rendered in the R. V. "which is stretched unto Neah." It was probably identical with Rimmon, 4.

Rim'mon-pe'rez (rĭm'ŏn-pē'rĕz; *pomegranate of the breach*), one of the seventeen camping grounds (Num. 33:19) of the Israelites during their thirty-seven years of wandering about in the desert after leaving Kadesh (14:25). Of these seventeen places, Ezion-geber is the only one that can be pointed out with certainty. A. V. Rimmon-parez.

Rim'mon, the Rock of, the cliff or mountain pass to which the Benjamites fled when pursued after the slaughter at Gibeah. Six hundred reached it and maintained themselves there for four months, until released by the rest of the tribes (Judg. 20:45, 47; 21:13). It is mentioned as being in the wilderness, i. e., no doubt the desert which rises from Jericho to the mountains of Beth-el (Josh. 16:1). Rimmon has been preserved in the village of Rammūn, about fifteen miles N. of Jerusalem, which stands upon and around the summit of a conical limestone mountain, and is visible in all directions.

Ring. The ring was at a very ancient date a symbol of authority and dignity. That it was so among the ancient Egyptians is evident from the fact that Pharaoh gave his ring to Joseph (Gen. 41:42), as a token that he transferred to him the exercise of the royal authority. Such a transfer is twice related of Ahasuerus, once in favor of Haman, and again in favor of Mordecai (Esth. 3:8-10; 8:2). These were probably signet rings. A very early instance of a signet ring is to be found in the history of Judah (Gen. 38:18, A. V. "signet" merely); but *ḥāthăm* signifies a signet ring worn on the hand, or suspended by a cord from the neck (Jer. 22:24). In the New Testament the ring is a symbol of honor and dignity, though no longer of power and authority (Luke 15:22). A "gold-ringed man" (James 2:2, A. V. "with a gold ring;" Gr. *chrusodaktulios, gold-ringed*) was a man of wealth. The ring was generally worn on the fourth finger of the left hand, under the belief that a vein ran from that finger direct to the heart. The wearing of rings on the right hand was a mark of effeminacy, but they were frequently worn in considerable numbers on the left. See Jewelry, Tabernacle.

Ringstreaked, or **Straked** (Heb. 'āqōd, *striped*), a term applied to the parti-colored rams of Jacob's flock (Gen. 30:35, etc.).

Rin'nah (rĭn'ȧ; *a shout*), a son of Simeon, of the tribe of Judah (I Chron. 4:20).

Riot (Gr. 'asōtia) the character of an abandoned man; denotes dissolute life, profligacy (Tit. 1:6; I Pet. 4:4; rendered "excess" in Eph. 5:18). The adverbial form is given in the parable of the prodigal, "He wasted his substance in riotous living" (Luke 15:13). In II Pet. 2:13 the apostle says of some that "They count it pleasure to riot in the day time" (Gr. *truphē, soft living*); effeminacy, understood by some as sexual indulgence, which was considered by the ancients, when indulged in during the day, as sottishness. In Luke 7:25 it is rendered "live delicately."

The sense of riotous in the expression, "riotous eaters of flesh" (Prov. 23:20) and "a companion of riotous men" (28:7), is *gluttonous* (A. V. "glutton," 23:21; Heb. *zälăl*, to *squander*, in the sense of squandering one's own body).

Ri'phath (rī'făth), the second son of Gomer, and grandson of Japheth (Gen. 10:3; I Chron. 1:6, in which latter passage the name is given *Diphath* by a clerical error).

Ris'sah (rĭs'ȧ; *a ruin*), one of the stations of Israel in the wilderness (Num. 33:21, 22), thought to be identical with Rasa, thirty-two Roman miles from Ailah (Elah); but no site has been identified with it.

Rith'mah (rĭth'mȧ; *broom plant*), an encampment of Israel (Num. 33:18, 19), probably northeast of Hazeroth.

River, the rendering of seven Hebrew words. In the case of some of them other terms are employed, as *stream, channel, flood*, but in certain passages the word *river* stands as an equivalent for every one of them.

1. **A flowing stream** (Heb. 'ūbāl from yābăl) to *flow*), used only in Dan. 8:2, 3, 6.

2. **Water channel** (Heb. 'āphíq) is applied to streams or rivers, with a primary respect to the channels, often in Palestine deep rock walls or ravines, that contain or bound them; and so *channel* comes usually to be a quite suitable rendering for it (II Sam. 22:16),

though K. and D. render it *beds* of the sea (Psa. 18:15; Isa. 8:7). Perhaps "channels" would be better than "rivers" in Ezek. 32:6; Joel 1:20; 3:18).

3. **A river** (Heb. *yᵉʾōr*), a word of Egyptian origin, and frequently used of the Nile, and appears to have been the common designation for it in Egypt (Gen. 41:1, 2; Exod. 1:22; 2:3, 5). Subsequent writers, when speaking of the river of Egypt, generally borrow the same word, sometimes using it in the plural, the Nile and its branches (Isa. 7:18; 19:6; Jer. 46:7; Ezek. 29:3). The word is sometimes used of rivers generally (Job 18:10; II Kings 19:24; Isa. 37:5; Dan. 12:5, 6).

4. **A flowing stream** (Heb. *yūbăl*), found only in Jer. 17:8, is radically identical with No. 1.

5. **A stream** (Heb. *nähär*), in a great number of passages, stands for river in the strict and proper sense, being often applied to the Jordan, the Nile, and other rivers. As the Euphrates was the river by way of eminence in the East, it was often known simply as *hăn-nähär* ("the river"). Wherever the expression, "the river," stands thus absolutely it is to be understood of the Euphrates (Gen. 31:21; Josh. 1:4; II Sam. 10:16; Isa. 7:20; 8:7, etc.). It is unfortunately rendered "flood" (Josh. 24:2, 14, 15).

6. **A wadi** (Heb. *năḥăl, flowing*). It comes nearer to our *torrent* than to the deeper and steadier volume of water which properly bears the name of river; and was applicable to the many temporary currents in Palestine and surrounding regions, which sometimes flow with great force after heavy rains, but soon become dry channels. The word thus came to mean both a stream and its channel, or *valley;* and sometimes it is applied to a valley or glen, apart altogether from the idea of a stream (Gen. 26:17). In Lev. 11:9, 10, it is applied to the stream itself; while we have the "valley," the "brook," and the "river" Zered (Num. 21:12; Deut. 2:13; Amos 6:14), the "brook" and the "river" of Jabbok (Gen. 32:23; Deut. 2:37), or of Kishon (Judg. 4:7; I Kings 18:40). In Num. 13:23 "the *brook* Eshcol" should be "the *valley;*" and in Deut. 3:16 the same word is rendered—"unto *the river* Arnon half *the valley*" (comp. Josh. 12:2). "The city that is in the midst of the *river*" (Josh. 13:9) should read "in the midst of the *valley.*"

7. **A gushing fountain stream** (Heb. *pĕlĕg*, to *gush*, or *flow over*) is used for streams, without respect, apparently, to their size, but to the distribution of their waters through the land. It is used ten times in the Scripture, always in the poetical or prophetical books (Psa. 65:9; 119:136; Job 20:17; 29:6; Prov. 5:16; Isa. 30:25, etc.).

8. **A word commonly rendered "conduit"** (II Kings 18:17; 20:20; Isa. 7:3; 36:2); once a "watercourse" (Job 28:25) is rendered "little rivers" (Ezek. 31:4). It is *tᵉʾäläh*, and means simply a *channel*, or conduit, for conveying water.

9. The Greek word *potamos, running water*, corresponds to Nos. 3 and 5.

Figurative. "Rivers" and "waters" are frequently used in Scripture to symbolize abundance, as of grace of God (Psa. 36:8; 46:4; Isa. 32:2; 41:18; John 1:16; 7:38, 39), of peace (Isa. 66:12), of good things of life (Job 20:17; 29:6), of God's providence (Isa. 43:19, 20), affliction (Psa. 69:2; Isa. 43:2). The *fruitfulness of trees* planted by rivers is figurative of the permanent prosperity of the righteous (Psa. 1:3; Jer. 17:8). *Drying up* of rivers represents God's judgments (Isa. 19:1-8; Jer. 51:36; Nah. 1:4; Zech. 10:11), as does also their overflowing (Isa. 8:7, 8; 28:2, 18; Jer. 47:2).

River of Egypt (ē'jĭpt).

1. The Nile (Gen. 15:18). In the R. V. the word "brook" is used, while in the A. V. the word "river" is found, referring especially to the E. channel or Pelusiac branch.

2. The great wadi (Heb. *năḥăl*, called in the R. V. "the brook of Egypt." The Hebrew word *năḥăl* signifies a stream which flows rapidly in winter, or in the rainy season. This is a desert wadi, called now Wady el-ʿArish (Num. 34:5; Josh. 15:4, 47; I Kings 24:7; Isa. 7:18; Ezek. 47:19).

Riz'pah (rĭz'pȧ, *a live coal*), a concubine of King Saul. Rizpah was a foreigner, the daughter (or descendant) of Aiah, a Hivite. She is first mentioned as the subject of an accusation leveled against Abner (II Sam. 3:7), B. C. 997. We next hear of her in the tragic story narrated in II Sam. 21:8-11, the particulars of which are as follows: A famine, which lasted three successive years, induced David to seek the face of Jehovah, and to ask the cause of the judgment resting upon the land. The Lord replied, "Because of Saul, and because of his bloody house, because he hath slain the Gibeonites." David, therefore, sent for the Gibeonites to inquire of them as to the wrong which had been done them by Saul, and as to how he should make atonement therefor. They asked for the crucifixion at Gibeah of seven men of Saul's sons. David granted the request, because, according to the law (Num. 35:33), blood-guiltiness, when resting upon the land, could only be expiated by the blood of the criminal, and gave up to the Gibeonites two sons of Rizpah, and five sons of Merab, the daughter of Saul. The victims were sacrificed "at the beginning of the barley harvest," about the middle of Nisan (our April), and hung in the full blaze of the summer sun till the fall of the periodical rain in October. During all this time, without any tent to protect her, and only a garment of sackcloth to rest upon, Rizpah watched the bodies, and "suffered neither the birds of the air to rest on them by day, nor the beasts of the field by night," B. C. c. 970.

Road. 1. (Heb. *päshăṭ*, to *spread out*). Occurs in the A. V. only in I Sam. 27:10, "And Achish said, Whither have ye made a road to-day?" A better rendering is, "Ye have not made an invasion to-day, have ye?" It is used in our modern sense of a *raid*, and is rendered *invaded* (v. 8; 23:27; 30:1; "invasion," v. 14).

2. As a means of communication. Not only the trade, but the migrations of races from the most ancient times, prove that journeys of great extent were made in early antiquity. Commerce and military expeditions necessitated the making of *roads* and paths, of which

the earliest trace is perhaps to be found in the *king's way* (Num. 20:17; 21:22). At first roads were mere tracks formed by caravans passing from one point to another; afterward regular paths were made by laying earth and stones. These were required by law, especially for the approaches to the cities of refuge (Deut. 19:3). In earlier times the roads between different cities were in a miserable condition, hardly passable in winter or in the rainy season, though the hard, rocky ground in the mountainous parts of Palestine made it easy to construct good roads. The "king's way," mentioned above, was the public high road—probably constructed at the royal cost, and kept up for the king and his armies to travel upon, and perhaps also toll was taken for the king from the trading caravans. Regular military roads were first constructed in Palestine by the Romans, and provided with milestones. Jacob and his family traveled a well-known road from Beersheba to Egypt—the middle, or "Shur road," portions of which have been found. The Hebrews probably became acquainted with road-making in Egypt, where, in the Delta especially, the nature of the country would require roads and highways to be thrown up and maintained.

Five roads in Palestine are worthy of mention: (1) That which ran from Ptolemais, on the coast of the Mediterranean, to Damascus, which remains to this day. (2) The one passing along the Mediterranean coast southward to Egypt. Beginning at Ptolemais, it ran first to Caesarea, thence to Disopolis, then through Ascalon and Gaza down into Egypt, with a branch through Disopolis to Jerusalem. Down this branch Paul was sent on his way to Felix (Acts 23:23, 26). (3) The third connected Galilee with Judea, running through the intervening Samaria (Luke 17:11; John 4:4). This journey took three days. (4) Three chief roads running from Jerusalem: (*a*) One in the northeast direction over the Mount of Olives, by Bethany, through openings in hills and winding ways on to Jericho (Matt. 20:29; 21:1; Luke 10:30, sq.; 19:1, 28, sq.), crossing the Jordan into Perea. This was the road taken by the Galilean Jews in coming and returning from Jerusalem in order to avoid the unfriendly Samaritans. It was the one over which the Israelites came into Canaan, and by which the Syrian and Assyrian armies advanced on Israel (II Kings 8:28; 9:14; 10:32, sq.; I Chron. 5:26). (*b*) From Jerusalem southward to Hebron, between mountains, through pleasant valleys, whence travelers went through the wilderness of Judea to Aila, as the remains of a Roman road still show; or took a westerly direction on to Gaza, a way still pursued, which is of two days' duration. (*c*) The third road went to the Mediterranean at Joppa (Jaffa), which has been used, since the time of the crusades, by pilgrims from Europe and Egypt to the holy city.

The *highway* (Heb. *meṣillāh, an embanked highway, a thoroughfare*) was frequently prepared for temporary purposes, such as the visit of royalty (Isa., ch. 45; 62:10); and also for permanent use (Num. 20:19; Judg. 20:31; I Sam. 6:12, etc.). Roads were commanded to be made to the cities of refuge (Deut. 19:3).

Roast. *See* Food.

Rob, Robber, Robbery. These words are each the rendering of a number of Hebrew and Greek words. Theft and plunder, systematically organized, have ever been principal employments of the nomad tribes of the East since Ishmael the Bedouin became a "wild man" and a robber by trade (Gen. 16:12), and robbery has been considered in the highest degree creditable. In the singular history of Abimelech we are told that "the men of Shechem set liers in wait for him in the top of the mountains, and they robbed all that came along that way by them" (Judg. 9:25). Job suffered serious loss from a predatory incursion of the Chaldeans (Job. 1:17), as did the people of Keilah, a lowland Judean town, from the Philistines (I Sam. 23:1). Other instances are recorded of invasions of spoilers (Judg. 2:14; 6:3, 4; I Sam., chaps. 11 and 15; II Sam., chaps. 8 and 10; II Kings 5:2; I Chron. 5:10, 18-22, etc.).

The Mosaic law strictly forbade robbery, as other wrongs against others (Lev. 19:13; *see* Law), and it was denounced in the Proverbs (22:22) and by the prophets (Isa. 10:2; 17:14; Ezek. 22:29; 33:15); while Hosea (6:9) compares the apostate priests to "troops of robbers that wait for a man."

In New Testament times, civilization and Roman power had done much to subdue these predatory hordes; but even then we learn from the parable of the good Samaritan what was to be expected by travelers; and the road from Jerusalem to Jericho was as dangerous a few years ago as in the time of our Lord. St. Paul mentions "perils of robbers" (II Cor. 11:26), and it would appear that he was especially subject to dangers of this kind while passing through Pisidia. These were *plunderers*, *brigands* (Gr. *lēstēs*), and are not to be confounded with *thief* (Gr. *kleptēs*), one who takes property by stealth (John 10:8, where both are mentioned).

Luke, in describing the uproar in Ephesus (Acts 19:23-41), says that the clerk of the city, in endeavoring to appease the multitude, told them that Paul and his companions were neither "robbers of churches, nor yet blasphemers of your goddess." The Greek term used for "robbers of churches" is *hierosulos* (*temple despoiler*), used in its verbal form, "dost thou commit sacrilege" (Rom. 2:22), where the meaning is, "thou who abhorrest idols and their contamination, dost yet not hesitate to plunder their shrines." The plundering of heathen temples was indirectly forbidden to the Jews (Deut. 7:25).

The apostle, speaking of Christ Jesus (Phil. 2:6), says, "Who, being in the form of God, thought it not robbery to be equal with God" (Gr. *harpagmos*, the act of *seizing*, with the secondary sense of *a thing to be seized*). Grimm (*Greek-Eng. Lex.*, word *morphē*) thus explains the sentence: "*Who, although* (formerly, when he was the eternal Word) *he bore the form* (in which he appeared to the inhabitants of heaven) *of God* (the sovereign as opposed to the form of a servant), *yet did he not think that this equality with God was to be eagerly clung to or retained*," etc.

Robe. *See* Dress; High Priest, Dress of.

Robo'am (rô-bō'ăm), the Greek form (Matt. 1:7) of King Rehoboam (*q. v.*).

Rock.

Figurative. A rock is illustrative of God, as the Creator of his people (Deut. 32:18); as the strength of his people (Deut. 32:4; II Sam. 22:2, 3; Psa. 18:1, 2; 62:7; Isa. 17:10); as their defense and refuge (Psa. 31:2, 3; 94:22, etc.), and salvation (Deut. 32:15; Psa. 89:26; 95:1).

Christ the Rock. As a Rock, Christ is portrayed as smitten that the Spirit of life may flow from Him to all who will drink (Exod. 17:6; John 4:13, 14; 7:37-39; I Cor. 10:4). To the Church, Christ as the Rock is the foundation (Matt. 16:18) and the chief Cornerstone (Eph. 2:20). To the Jews at the first advent Christ the Rock was a "Stumbling Stone" (Psa. 118:22; Rom. 9:32; I Cor. 1:23). To Israel at the second advent, Christ will be the "head Stone of the corner" (Zech. 4:7). To the Gentile world governments, Christ the Rock will be the "Stone cut out without hands" (Dan. 2:34). As the Rock, Christ will be the Stone which will fill the whole earth in the kingdom Age after the destruction of the Gentile world power. To unbelievers, Christ the Rock is a crushing Stone of judgment (Matt. 21:44).—*M. F. U.*

Rod, the rendering of several Hebrew words and one Greek term:

1. Heb. *shēbĕṭ*. A stick for punishment (Lev. 21:20; II Sam. 7:14; Job 9:34, etc.; Prov. 10:13, etc.; Isa. 11:4, etc.; Jer. 10:16; 51:19), and, in a few instances, a shepherd's staff (Ezek. 20:37; Mic. 7:14).

Figurative. "He that spareth his rod hateth his son" (Prov. 13:24), and "the rod and reproof giveth wisdom" (29:15), are proverbs in which *rod* is used as a figure for *punishment.* "I will cause you to pass under the rod" (Ezek. 20:37) refers to a custom among shepherds, who let the sheep pass under their shepherd's rod for the purpose of counting them and seeing whether they are in good condition or not. The figure is here applied to God, who will cause his flock, the Israelites, to pass through under the rod, i. e., take them into his special care. "Feed thy people with thy rod" (Mic. 7:14) is to feed them under his guidance, the rod being a symbol of leading, protection. Rod is used for tribe (Psa. 74:2; Jer. 10:16); as a symbol of power and authority (Psa. 2:9; 120:2; 125:3; Jer. 48:17, etc.); of afflictions, as the means by which God disciplines his people (Job 9:34; Heb. 12:6, 7).

2. *A walking staff* (Heb. *mǎṭṭĕh*, *branch*; Exod. 4:2; 7:9; I Sam. 14:27, 43). In the case of Moses and Aaron the rod was a shepherd's staff, belonging to Moses, but sometimes employed by Aaron in performing miracles. It was also called "the rod of God" (Exod. 4:20; 17:9), probably because through it Jehovah wrought such wonders. Aaron's priesthood was confirmed by a miracle calculated to silence the murmurings of the people. God commanded Moses to take twelve rods of the tribe princes of Israel and to write upon each the name of the tribe. As only twelve rods were taken for all the tribes of Israel, and Levi was included among them,

Ephraim and Manasseh must have been reckoned as the one tribe of Joseph (see Deut. 17:12). These rods were to be laid in the tabernacle before the ark of the covenant; and there the rod of the man whom Jehovah chose, i. e., intrusted with the priesthood (Num. 16:5), would put forth shoots. On the following morning "the rod of Aaron for the house of Levi was budded, and brought forth buds, and bloomed blossoms, and yielded almonds" (Num. 17:1-9; comp. Heb. 9:4).

3. Paul, in recounting his afflictions, writes (II Cor. 11:25), "Thrice was I beaten with rods" (Gr. *hrabdizō, to strike with a stick*), i. e., bastinadoed.

Rods as a means of divination was a common heathen practice. *See* Rhabdomancy, under Magic.

Roe, Roebuck. *See* Animal Kingdom.

Ro'gelim (rō'gê-lĭm; *treaders*, i. e., *fullers*), a town in Gilead, the residence of Barzillai (II Sam. 17:27; 19:31). Nothing farther is known respecting it.

Roh'gah (rō'gà), the second son of Shamer, of the tribe of Asher, and fifth in descent from that patriarch (I Chron. 7:34), B. C. about 1440.

Roll. A book in ancient times consisted of a single long strip of papyrus or parchment, which was usually kept rolled up on a stick, and was unrolled when a person wished to read it. Hence arose the term *megĭlläh* from *gälăl*, "to roll," strictly answering to the Lat. *volumen*, whence comes our *volume*. The use of the term *megĭlläh* implies, of course, the existence of a soft and pliant material, perhaps parchment. The roll was usually written on one side only, and hence the particular notice of one that was "written within and without" (Ezek. 2:10). The writing was arranged in columns. We may here add that the term in Isa. 8:1, rendered in the A. V. "roll," more correctly means *tablet* (*gĭlläyōn*). "The house of the rolls" (Ezra 6:1) was evidently the royal library, and was made up of clay tablets.

Roller (Heb. *hĭttūl, swathed*), a bandage, so called from being wrapped around a broken limb, for the purpose of healing it. In surgery, a roller is a long strip of muslin or other webbing, rolled up for convenience, and unrolled in using. "I have broken the arm of Pharoah, king of Egypt; and, lo! it shall not be bound up to be healed, to put a roller to bind it," etc. (Ezek. 30:21). The arm is a figurative expression here for military power, as it wields the sword. God broke the arm of Pharoah by the defeat at the hands of the Chaldeans. And that it should remain unbandaged means that his power was not to be restored.

Romam'ti-e'zer (rô-măm'tĭ-ē'zĕr; *I have raised a help*), one of the sons of Heman the seer. In the arrangement of the temple service by David, Romamti-ezer was appointed chief of the twenty-fourth section, consisting of twelve persons of his family (I Chron. 25:4, 31), B. C. a little before 960.

Ro'man. (1) A citizen of the Roman empire (Acts 22:25, sq.; 23:27). *See* Citizenship, 2. (2) Inhabitants of Rome (Acts 2:10). (3) Those who represent the Roman government (John 11:48; Acts 28:17).

Ro′man Empire, the government of the Romans under the emperors, beginning with Augustus. The following is mostly taken from Smith's *Bible Dictionary:*

1. **Its Inauguration.** By the victory of Actium, Octavianus became the undisputed master of the Roman world; but he shrank from taking the name of king or dictator, which were odious to the Roman people. But he long before had taken the title of Caesar, and now allowed himself to be called Augustus, retaining the old official title of imperator. He was in theory simply the first citizen of the republic, intrusted with temporary powers to settle the disorders of the state. The empire was nominally elective, but practically it passed by adoption, and till Nero's time a sort of hereditary right seemed to be recognized.

2. **Extent.** Before the conquests of Pompey and Caesar the Roman empire was confined to a narrow strip encircling the Mediterranean Sea. Pompey added Asia Minor and Syria; Caesar added Gaul. The generals of Augustus overran the northwestern portion of Spain and the country between the Alps and the Danube. The boundaries were now the Atlantic on the west, the Euphrates on the east, the deserts of Africa, the cataracts of the Nile, and the Arabian deserts on the south, the British Channel, the Rhine, the Danube, and the Black Sea on the north. The only subsequent conquests of importance were those of Britain by Claudius and Dacia by Trajan. The population of the empire at the time of Augustus has been calculated at eighty-five million.

3. **The Provinces.** The usual fate of a country conquered by Rome was to become a subject province, governed directly from Rome by officers sent out for that purpose. Sometimes, however, petty sovereigns were left in possession of a nominal independence on the borders, or within the natural limits, of the province. There were differences, too, in the political condition of cities within the provinces. Some were free cities, i. e., were governed by their own magistrates, and were exempted from occupation by a Roman garrison. Other cities were "colonies," i. e., communities of Roman citizens transplanted, like garrisons of the imperial city, into a foreign land. Augustus divided the provinces into two classes: (1) Imperial, (2) Senatorial; retaining in his own hands, for obvious reasons, those provinces where the presence of a large military force was necessary, and committing the peaceful and unarmed provinces to the Senate. The imperial provinces at first were: Gaul, Lusitania, Syria, Phoenicia, Cilicia, Cyprus, and Egypt. The senatorial provinces were: Africa, Numidia, Asia, Achaia and Epirus, Dalmatia, Macedonia, Sicily, Crete and Cyrene, Bithynia and Pontus, Sardinia, Baetica. Cyprus and Gallia Narbonensis were subsequently given up by Augustus, who in turn received Dalmatia from the Senate. Many other changes were made afterward. The New Testament writers invariably designate the governors of senatorial provinces by the correct title of '*anthupatoi*, proconsuls (Acts 13:7; 18:12; 19:38). For the governor of an imperial province, properly styled "Legatus Caesaris," the word *hēgemōn* (Governor) is used in the New Testament. The provinces were heavily taxed for the benefit of Rome and her citizens. They are said to have been better governed under the empire than under the

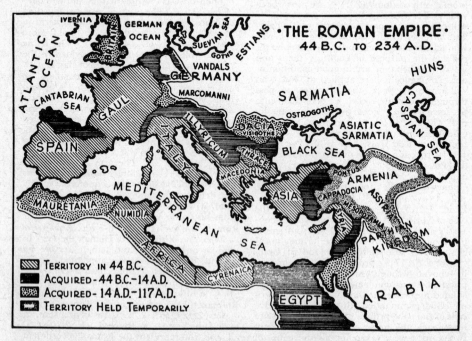

387. Map of the Roman Empire, 44 B.C. to A.D. 234

commonwealth, and those of the emperor better than those of the Senate. Two important changes were introduced under the empire. The governors received a fixed pay, and the term of their command was prolonged. The condition of the Roman empire at the time when Christianity appeared has often been dealt upon, as affording obvious illus-

SPREAD OF CHRISTIANITY
IN THE ROMAN EMPIRE
X 45 A.D.
325 A.D. (EMPEROR CONSTANTINE)

388.

trations of St. Paul's expression that the "fullness of time had come" (Gal. 4:4). The general peace within the limits of the empire, the formation of military roads, the suppression of piracy, the march of the legions, the voyages of the corn fleets, the general increase of traffic, the spread of the Latin language in the West as Greek had already spread in the East, the external unity of the empire, offered facilities hitherto unknown for the spread of world-wide religion. The tendency, too, of a despotism like that of the Roman empire to reduce all its subjects to a dead level, was a powerful instrument in breaking down the pride of privileged races and national religions, and familiarizing men with the truth that "God hath made of one blood all nations on the face of the earth" (Acts 17:24, 26). But still more striking than this outward preparation for the diffusion of the Gospel was the appearance of a deep and widespread corruption which seemed to defy any human remedy. The chief prophetic notices of the Roman empire are found in the Book of Daniel.

Romans, Epistle to, the greatest of Paul's epistles, and considered by many as the greatest book in the N. T. Galatians has been called the "Magna Charta" of Christian liberty and the Roman epistle has been called the "constitution" of Christianity. Its subject material, its logical reasoning, its vigor of style, and its relevance to human need give it a foremost place in Biblical revelation. It is a book, in one sense, simple and clear, but in another sense so grand in its sweep as to baffle complete fathoming.

1. **Occasion.** The Epistle appears to have been occasioned by the Apostle's interest in the church at Rome. He tells us that he intended to pay a visit in the near future (Acts 19:21; Rom. 1:13; 15:22-29). The fact that Phoebe, a deaconess of the church at Cenchraea, was going to Rome presented an opportunity to send the epistle to the Christians in that city (Rom. 16:1-2). Paul was all the more compelled to write to this church, inas-

much as it had come into existence apparently without authoritative leadership, and needed thorough instruction in the great fundamentals of salvation.

2. **Date.** The letter was written in Corinth during Paul's three months' visit in Greece (Acts 20:2, 3). This fact is made evident by reference to the Apostle's journey to Jerusalem with a collection for the poor at the time of writing (Rom. 15:25-27). Since this collection was emphasized in the earlier letter to Corinth (I Cor. 16:1-4; II Cor. chaps. 8, 9), it is quite evident that these letters were written about the same time. It clearly appears from these considerations that Romans is later than II Corinthinians because the Apostle is about to leave for Jerusalem (Rom. 15:25). The Second Corinthian epistle was written from Macedonia, and from Macedonia Paul went to Greece. Numerous instances in the Corinthinian epistles point to the fact that the Epistle to the Romans was written from Corinth not long after Paul penned II Corinthians, that is, A. D. 56.

3. **The Genuineness.** The external evidence comes from quotations and reminiscences of this epistle in Clement of Rome, Ignatius, Justin Martyr, Polycarp, Hippolytus, Marcion, the Muratorian Canon and the Old Latin and Syriac Versions. From the time of Irenaeus onward the Epistle was universally recognized as Pauline and canonical. The internal evidence of genuineness is also strong. The writer claims to be Paul (1:1) and makes personal references that can only be identified with the great Apostle (cf. 11:13; 15:15-20). Style, argument, theology and many other factors point to Pauline authenticity. At the beginning of the modern critical period a few Dutch, Swiss and English scholars contested the authenticity of the book on the ground that the Apostle was acquainted with so many individuals by name in a city where he had never been (see chap. 16). But this argument has been repeatedly shown to be very weak because travel was extensive in Paul's day, and he may well have met these individuals elsewhere in the empire before they went to Rome to live.

4. **Background.** The origin of Christianity in Rome must be traced to converts scattered through the empire who came to visit or live in the imperial city. That Peter was the founder of the church is indefensible since it would be unthinkable that Paul would omit his name if he had been bishop in the city. It is possible that the sojourners at Jerusalem on the Day of Pentecost (Acts 2:10) may also have been instrumental in the founding of the Roman church. Some critics have denied the authenticity of chapters 15 and 16, but there is no valid internal evidence supporting this, neither is there support for it in the ancient manuscripts.

5. **Contents.** After introductory matters, the Apostle demonstrates the universal sinfulness of the human race and the need for divine righteousness (1:18-3:20). He then sets forth the justifying righteousness which God has provided for every believer through the redemptive work of Christ (3:21-5:11). Three objections against God's way of salvation

through the work of Christ on the basis of faith alone are refuted. *Objection No. 1. Men may be saved and yet continue in sin.* This is shown to be untrue because of the believer's union with Christ into a new moral life (6:1-14). *Objection No. 2. Deliverance from the law releases men from moral obligation.* But this is impossible since the believer undertakes a new and higher obligation, devoting himself to the law of God (6:15-7:6). *Objection No. 3. The law of God is made an evil thing by justifying grace.* But this is not so because the law's inability to save is not that it is evil but that man is sinfully incapable of keeping it (7:7-25). In Chapter 8 the Apostle Paul deals with the triumphs of the redeemed life, and the believer's assurance not only of justification but of glorification and full conformity to Christ. The believer is to rejoice in full security. Chapters 9-11 deal with the great truths of salvation in dispensational relation to the Jew: his past (chap. 9), his present, chapter 10; his future, chapter 11. The rest of the epistle consists of exhortations to Christian living, chapter 12; to the doing of civil and social duties, chapter 13; living according to Christian love and unity, chapter 14:1-15:13, ending with personal salutations, chapter 15:14-16:27.

6. **Outline.**

Introduction, 1:1-15

Part I. Doctrinal Exposition, 1:16-8:39
1. The theme, 1:16, 17
2. Justification expounded, 1:18-5:11
3. Sanctification expounded, 5:12-8:39

Part II. Dispensational Harmonization, chaps. 9-11
1. Israel's present rejection, 9:1-15
2. Israel's rejection justified, 9:6-29
3. Israel's rejection explained, 9:30-10:21
4. Israel's rejection in its extent, 11:1-10
5. Israel's rejection terminated, 11:11-32
6. Exultation and praise, 11:33-36

Part III. Practical Exhortation, 12:1-15:13
1. The Christian's relation to consecration, 12:1, 2
2. The Christian's relation to God's gifts, 12:3-8
3. The Christian's relation to fellow Christians, 12:9-16
4. The Christian's relation to mankind in general, 12:17-21
5. The Christian's relation to civil government, 13:1-14
6. The Christian's relation to a weak brother, 14:1-15:13

Conclusion, 15:14-16:27

Rome (Lat. *Roma*), one of the most famous cities of the world. Its history touches every community of men, and is immensely fabulous and traditional as well as substantial. It has reached the extremes of civilization and of moral corruption, and has been preeminent in art and science as well as in spiritual tyranny. Its name was once a synonym for political power and territorial expansion.

1. **The Founding.** The origin of the city is mythological rather than historical. Romulus, its founder and first king, was the traditiona

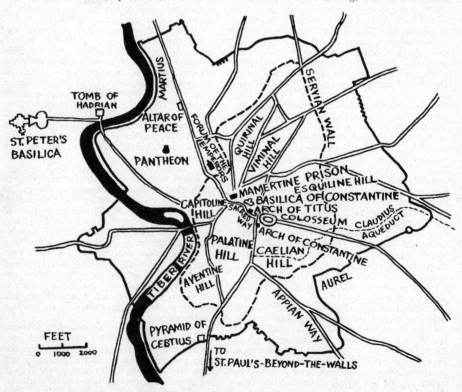

389. Hills and Sites of Rome

son of Mars, and was preserved, when outcast by his cruel relatives, through the kind attention of a wolf and a shepherd's wife.

The foundation of Rome dates from 753 B. C. It takes its name, according to Cicero, from the name of its founder, Romulus. It was located upon marshy ground by the river Tiber, in Italy, and about seventeen miles from the Mediterranean Sea, into which the Tiber flows. The Tiber itself, which flows within the walls to the distance of three miles, is navigable only for small provision boats, and after heavy rains it rises twenty feet, inundating the low part of the city.

Originally the settlement of Rome was confined to the Palatine hill, but before the reign of the founder, Romulus, ended, the Capitoline and the Quirinal mounts were added. The Caelian hill was added by Tullus Hostilius, and the Aventine by Ancus Martius, and the Esquiline and the Viminal were added by Servius Tullius, who inclosed the whole seven hills with a stone wall. Hence it has been called *Urbs Septicollis*, "the city of the seven hills."

The original wall of Rome was so insignificant that it was ridiculed by Remus, the brother of Romulus. For this he was killed. The people whom Romulus induced at the first to live within the wall of Rome were fugitives, criminals, and foreigners. As an asylum for outlaws it was shunned by the neighboring inhabitants. Matrimonial proffers were declined by respectable people. Wives were secured by strategy. They were captured by force from a great company of the Sabines, who had come to witness a show. By a compromise the Sabines afterward came to Rome and became joint occupants of the city.

After a reign of thirty-nine years, in 714 B. C., Romulus, who suddenly disappeared, was reported to have been taken up to heaven. Divine honors were paid to him under the name of Quirinus. He was ranked by the Romans among the twelve great deities. A temple was erected in his honor, and a priest, called Flamen Quirinalis, was appointed to offer him sacrifices.

2. **Monarchy.** The monarchical government existed under seven princes, in the following order: Romulus, B. C. 753; after one year's interregnum, Numa, 715; Tullus Hostilius, 672; Ancus Martius, 640; Tarquin Priscus, 616; Servius Tullius, 578; and Tarquin the Proud, 534, expelled twenty-five years later, B. C. 509. This has been called the period of the infancy of the Roman empire.

Each ruler left his impress. One was employed in regulating the forms of worship, another in enforcing discipline in the army and increasing the importance of the soldiers, while another devoted himself to enlarging and beautifying the public buildings and fortifying the defenses.

3. **The Republic.** The final abolition of the kingly office and the rule of alien princes was followed by a period of government under the consuls. Two consuls were elected annually from the patrician families—until B. C. 367, when L. Sextius was created first plebeian consul—and together possessed full kingly authority. The candidate for the consulship was required to be forty-three years of age, and he must have discharged beforehand the inferior functions of questor, edile, and pretor. In the case of Scipio, Martius, Pompey, and Augustus, these rules were disregarded. A consul presided over the Senate and convened or dismissed it at pleasure. The authority of the consuls was equal. They appeared alternately in public invested with the symbols of authority, and preceded by the lictors. The Romans reckoned their years by the names of their consuls, until the consular office was (541 A. D.) abolished by Justinian, for it had become a mere title without dignity or authority. The consular period was characterized by party struggles between the Patricians and the Plebeians. Step by step the common people gained privileges, until the plebeian legionaries, just returned from a victorious campaign, instead of obeying orders to march against the Volsci and Aequi, intrenched themselves at Mons Sacer, three miles from the city, and defied the Patricians. Compromise resulted in the office of the tribune, chosen from the Plebeians; at first two, then five, and then, by the year B. C. 449, ten. The power of the tribune became formidable enough to lead the senators to repent of the concession when too late. The office remained till Augustus, to meet the case, conferred the power of tribune upon himself, whence he was called *tribunitia potestate donatus*. His successors followed his example until the power of the tribune, as an offset to imperialism, was lost. Under Constantine the office was formally abolished.

390. Ionic Temple near the Tiber, Rome

4. **Empire.** With the battle of Actium Octavianus was invested with the title of Augustus, to which was added the title "Imperator," or emperor. This brings Rome into relations with the sacred history of the world. In the reign of Augustus Christ was born in Bethlehem of Judea, and in the reign of his successor, Tiberius, Christ was crucified on Calvary. The successive emperors were among the worst of mankind. One after another they miserably perished in the midst of conspiracy and shame, or died by their own hands. The history of Rome, politically and morally, from Tiberius, in 37 A. D., to the reign of Constantine, in 313 A. D., when the edict in favor of the Christian religion was issued, was lamentably bad.

391. The Arch of Titus and Part of the Forum, Rome

5. Religion. The religion of Rome was pagan, and immensely superstitious. The altars and temples were erected not only to the deities whom they supposed presided over their own city, but they built temples in honor of the gods of the people whom they conquered in their many wars. There were no less than four hundred and twenty temples dedicated to idolatry in Rome.

6. Scripture Notice. "Rome is not mentioned in the Bible except in the books of Maccabees and in three books of the New Testament, viz., the Acts, the Epistle to the Romans, and the Second Epistle to Timothy. The conquests of Pompey seem to have given rise to the first settlement of Jews at Rome. The Jewish king Aristobulus and his son formed part of Pompey's triumph, and many Jewish captives and emigrants were brought to Rome at that time. Many of these Jews were made freedmen. Julius Caesar showed them some kindness. They were favored also by Augustus. Claudius 'commanded all Jews to depart from Rome' (Acts 18:2), on account of tumults connected, possibly, with the preaching of Christianity at Rome. This banishment cannot have been of long duration, for we find Jews residing at Rome apparently in considerable numbers at the time of St. Paul's visit (28:17). It is chiefly in connection with St. Paul's history that Rome comes before us in the Bible. The localities in and about Rome especially connected with the life of St. Paul, are: 1. The Appian way, by which he approached the city (28:15). 2. 'The palace,' or 'Caesar's court' (Phil. 1:13).

392. The Forum, Rome

This may mean either the great camp of the pretorian guards which Tiberius established outside the walls on the northeast of the city, or as seems more probable, a barrack attached to the imperial residence on the Palatine. The connection of other localities at Rome with St. Paul's name rests only on traditions of more or less probability. We may mention especially: 1. The Mamertine prison, or Tullianum, built by Ancus Martius, near the forum. It still exists beneath the church of *S. Giuseppe dei Falegnami.* Here it is said that St. Peter and St. Paul were fellow-prisoners for nine months. The story, however, of the imprisonment in the Mamertine prison seems inconsistent with II Tim., especially 4:11. 2. The chapel on the Ostian road which marks the spot where the two apostles are said to have separated on their way to martyrdom. 3. The supposed scene of St. Paul's martyrdom, viz., the church of *St. Paolo alle tre fontane*, on the Ostian road. To these may be added, 4. The supposed scene of St. Peter's martyrdom, viz., the church of *St. Pietro in Montorio*, on the Janiculum. 5. The chapel '*Domine quo Vadis*,' on the Appian road, the scene of the beautiful legend of our Lord's appearance to St. Peter as he was escaping from martyrdom. 6. The places where the bodies of the two apostles, after having been deposited first in the catacombs, are supposed to have been finally buried—that of Paul by the Ostian road, that of Peter beneath the dome of the famous basilica which bears his name" (Smith, *Bib. Dict.*, s. v.).

One of the chief matters of interest to the Bible reader is the relation of the Roman government to the world at the time of Christ. It was supreme. Judea was a Roman province. The Jewish people were under the authority of Rome. As Christianity spread, it attracted the attention of the emperors, some of whom were more favorable toward it than others. Diocletian, A. D. 284, persecuted the Church. But Constantine, A. D. 323, being sole ruler of the empire, protected the Christian religion, declaring it to be the state religion, and selected Byzantium as the state capital. Julian apostatized from Christianity in 361. As emperor he attempted to restore the pagan religion of Rome. As the residence of the popes, Rome has been a center of interest. Between two and three hundred of them have ruled the Church. The temporal authority which they held over the Papal States was taken from them in 1871, when Italy was united under Victor Emmanuel, and Rome was made the political capital of the nation. The Pope still occupies the Vatican as his residence, but there is more real religious freedom in Rome now than in many countries remote from the Vatican.

Roof. *See* House.

Figurative. To receive one under the shelter of the roof represents hospitality; in the case of Lot so greatly estimated that he was willing to sacrifice his duty as a father to maintain it (Gen. 19:8); and by the centurion considered too great an honor for him to receive the Lord as a guest (Matt. 8:8).

Room, as an apartment (*see* House). It is frequently used in the present sense of *place* or *stead* (I Kings 2:35; 8:20; II Kings 15:25; 23:34, etc.); of *space*, abundant room (Psa. 31:8; 80:9); and also *entrance, opportunity*, as "A man's gift maketh room for him" (Prov. 18:16).

"The highest room," as at a wedding (Luke 14:8) is the rendering of the Gr. *prōtoklisia* (the *first reclining place*), the chief place at the table. The relative rank of the several places at table varied among Persians, Greeks, and Romans. What arrangement was current among the Jews in Christ's day is thus set forth by Edersheim (*Jesus the Messiah*, ii, p. 207, sq.): "In regard to the position of the guests, we know that the uppermost seats were occupied by the rabbis. The Talmud formulates it in this manner: That the worthiest lies down first, on his left side, with his

393. The Great Altar Inside St. Peter's, Rome

feet stretching back. If there are two 'cushions' (divans) the next worthiest reclines above him, at his left hand; if there are three cushions the third worthiest lies below him who had laid down first (at his right), so that the chief person is in the middle."

Root (Heb. *shōrĕsh*; Gr. *hriza*, a common figure often referred to in Scripture.

Figurative. From the important relation which the root bears to the plant we have in Scripture many beautiful and forceful illustrations taken therefrom. Thus:

1. The root of a family is the progenitor from whom the race derives its name; thus, "Out of the serpent's root shall come forth a cockatrice" (Isa. 14:29), meaning that though the Davidic kingdom was broken down by the Syro-Ephraimitish war, another would arise to be a scourge to Israel's oppressors. Messiah is called "a root of Jesse" (11:10), as containing its sap and strength in his divine capacity (comp. Rev. 5:5; and 22:16, as "the root and the offspring of David," referring to both his divine and human nature). The progenitor of a race is also called its root (Prov. 12:3).

2. Root means the essential cause of anything, as "the love of money is the root of all evil" (I Tim. 6:10; comp. Heb. 12:15, "lest any root of bitterness spring up").

3. "Rooted" means firmly established, "being rooted and grounded in love" (Eph. 3:17; comp. Col. 2:7); also "to take root" (Job 5:3; Psa. 80:9, "to take deep root;" Isa. 27:6; 37:31; 40:24).

4. Opposed to this is "to root up," or "out," which has the sense of to destroy, remove (I Kings 14:15; Job 31:12; Psa. 52:5; Jer. 1:10; Luke 17:6, "pluck up by the root").

5. The roots of a plant being near water is symbolic of prosperity; "my root was spread out by the waters" (Job 29:19); literally "open to water," and so never lacking. Ezekiel

(31:7) says of Assyria, "His root was by great great waters," which accounted for "the length of his branches." The opposite figure is of a "root dried up" (Hos. 9:16).

6. "A root waxed old in the earth" (Job 14:8) denotes loss of vitality; while of sinners it is said, "Their root shall be as rottenness, and their blossom shall go up as dust" (Isa. 5:24).

7. Of our Lord in his humiliation, it was said, "He shall grow up as a tender plant, and as a root out of dry ground" (Isa. 53:2), "both figures depicting the lowly and unattractive character of the small though vigorous beginning, the miserable character of the external circumstances in the midst of which the birth and growth of the servant had taken place" (Delitzsch, *Com.*, in loc.).

Rope, Ropemakers. *See* Handicaps.

Rosh (rŏsh; *the head*). In the genealogy of Gen. 46:21, Rosh is reckoned among the sons of Benjamin, but the name does not occur elsewhere, and it is probable that "Ehi and Rosh" ('*ĕhî w^erōsh*) is a corruption of "Ahiram" (comp. Num. 26:38). It is also possible that Rosh is the correct reading, but like Er and Onan of Judah he died childless.

Rot, Rotten, Rottenness, the rendering of several Hebrew words, used mostly figuratively. Job says (13:28) that "he, as a *rotten* thing, consumeth;" i. e., that which is *worm-eaten*, droppeth to pieces, a symbol of gradual decay. Brass and "rotten wood" are contrasted together (Job 41:27), as representing strength and weakness. "The name of the wicked shall rot" (Prov. 10:7) is illustrative of the speedy oblivion into which they go. "Rottenness in the bones" (Prov. 12:4; 14:30; Hab. 3:16), in the Proverbs means an incurable disease, robbing one of power; in Habakkuk great terror.

Row, Rowers. *See* Ship.

Rubies. *See* Mineral Kingdom; Precious Stones.

Rudder. *See* Ship.

Ruddy (Heb. '*ădăm*, from '*ădmônî, to be red*). Applied to David (I Sam. 16:12; 17:42), and understood by many to mean *red-haired*. It seems rather to refer to the complexion. This view is confirmed by the application of kindred words, as "Her Nazarites were purer than snow, they were whiter than milk, they were more ruddy in body than rubies" (Lam. 4:7); and "My beloved is white and ruddy" (Cant. 5:10), who is immediately described as black-haired (v. 11).

Rude. Paul, in II Cor. 11:6, writes, "But though I be *rude in speech*, yet not in knowledge." The Greek term *idiōtēs* means properly a *private person*, as opposed to a magistrate. In the New Testament it means *an unlearned, illiterate*, as opposed to the learned, the educated (Acts 4:13, rendered "unlearned"). "Rude in speech," i. e., in respect to speech, means untrained in the art.

Rudiments (Gr. *stoicheion, any first thing*), letters of the alphabet, the "elements" (II Pet. 3:10), from which all things have come; primary principles"; in Col. 2:8 the ceremonial requirements, especially of Jewish tradition.

Rue. *See* Vegetable Kingdom.

Ru'fus (rōō'fŭs; *red*), brother of Alexander, and son of Simon the Cyrenian, whom the Jews compelled to bear the cross of Jesus when on his way to the crucifixion (Mark 15:21). Rufus is included by the apostle Paul (Rom. 16:13) among those in Rome to whom he sends salutations. It is generally supposed that this Rufus is identical with the one mentioned by Mark, and yet, as this was a common name, they may be different individuals.

Ruha'mah (rōō-hä'mà; *she has received mercy*), a figurative title applied to the daughter of the prophet Hosea, signifying that God would restore Israel to favor (Hos. 2:1), on condition of their repenting and returning to him. Both Peter (I Pet. 2:10) and Paul (Rom. 9:25, 26) quote this prophecy with evident application to the Gentiles, as well as Jews. Through its apostasy from God, Israel has become like the Gentiles, and has fallen from the covenants of promise consequently the readoption of the Israelites as the children of God will be a practical proof that "the gifts and calling" of God (Rom. 11:29) with respect to Israel are "without repentance."

Ruin, the rendering of very expressive Hebrew terms:

Derivatives from Heb. *năphăl* (to *fall*), the ruin of a city by dilapidation, separating all its stones (Isa. 25:2, "Thou hast made of a fenced city a ruin;" 17:1); of a country (Isa. 23:13; Ezek. 31:13; comp. 27:27). Other terms occur in the original, and numerous mounds of ruined cities (*tells*) dot the ancient Biblical world. Excavation of the various strata of occupational history of these tells has made possible the modern science of Biblical archaeology and immeasurably increased the knowledge of Bible backgrounds.

Figurative. Ruin is a fall or stumbling because of sin or temptation to sin. "They" (the gods of Damascus) "were the ruin of him," etc. (II Chron. 28:23; comp. Ezek. 18:30; 21:15).

Ruler, the rendering of several Hebrew and Greek words, and used to designate a large number of officials, as: *King* (I Sam. 25:30; II Sam. 6:21); "rulers of the people," or "princes" (*q. v.*); prime minister, as Joseph (Gen. 41:43); Daniel (Dan. 2:48; 5:7); town prefect (Judg. 9:30; II Chron. 29:20; Neh. 3:9); chief adviser (II Sam. 20:26; 8:18); house steward (Matt. 24:45, 47; Luke 12:42); superintendent of workmen, as chief herdsman (Gen. 47:6), mechanics (I Kings 11:28; I Chron. 27:31; 29:6); "ruler," or "governor of the feast" (*see* Feast, Governor of); "ruler of the synagogue" (*see* Synagogue); "ruler of the treasures," i. e., chief treasurer (I Chron. 26:24); the high priest was the "ruler of the house of God" (I Chron. 9:11; II Chron. 35:8), as was sometimes his assistant (Neh. 11:11). *See* Law, Administration of.

Ru'mah (rū'mà; *elevation*), a city named as the home of Pedaiah, the father of Zebudah, Jehoiakim's mother (II Kings 23:36). It is probably the same as *Arumah* (Judg. 9:41), in the neighborhood of Shechem.

Rump (Heb. '*ălyăh*), or rather *tail*. Moses prescribed that in certain sacrifices the tail of the victim should be burned upon the altar, viz., the ram of consecration (Exod. 29:22), the lamb of the peace offering (Lev. 3:9), and of the trespass offering (7:3). The rump was esteemed the most delicate portion of the animal, being the fattest. The fat tails of the sheep in Northern Africa, Egypt, Arabia, and Syria often weigh fifteen pounds or more, and small carriages on wheels are sometimes placed under them to bear their weight. The broad part of the tail is an excrescence of fat, from which the true tail hangs.

Run, Running. *See* Footman, Games.

Rush. *See* Reed.

Rust (Gr. *brōsis, eating; 'ios*). The first of these Greek terms is rendered "rust" (Matt. 6:19, sq.) in the wider sense of *corrosion*. It is, however, generally used, as almost everywhere in Greek writers, of that which is eaten, food (Heb. 12:16; II Cor. 9:10). The second term means *poison*, and is so rendered (Rom. 3:13; James 3:8); but in James 5:3 seems to mean rather the "tarnish" which overspreads silver than "rust," by which we now understand "oxide of iron."

Ruth (rōŏth, *a female friend*), a Moabitess, first the wife of Mahlon, and then of Boaz, and an ancestress of David and of Christ.

Personal History. (1) **Wife of Mahlon.** In the time of the Judges Elimelech, an inhabitant of Bethlehem in Judah, emigrated into the land of Moab with his wife Naomi and his two sons, Mahlon and Chilion, because of a famine in the land (Ruth 1:1, 2). There he died, and his two sons married Moabite women, named Orpah and Ruth, the latter becoming the wife of Mahlon (4:10), B. C. before 1100. (2) **Return to Bethlehem.** After the death of her two sons Naomi resolved to return to her own country and kindred, and Ruth determined to accompany her, notwithstanding her mother-in-law's entreaty that she should follow her sister-in-law and return to her own people and her god. Ruth answered her in beautiful and earnest words: "Entreat me not to leave thee, or to return from following after thee: for whither thou goest, I will go; and where thou lodgest, I will lodge: thy people shall be my people, and thy God my God: where thou diest, will I die, and there will I be buried: the Lord do so to me, and more also, if aught but death part thee and me" (1:16, 17). They arrived at Bethlehem just at the beginning of the barley harvest. (3) **Marries Boaz.** Ruth went out to glean for the purpose of procuring support for herself and mother-in-law, and in gleaning came by chance upon Boaz, a relative of Naomi. When he heard that she had come with Naomi from Moab, Boaz spoke kindly to her, and gave her permission not only to glean in the field and even among the sheaves, but to appease her hunger and thirst with the food and drink of his reapers (2:1-16). His kindness to her induced Naomi to counsel Ruth to seek an opportunity for intimating to Boaz the claim she had upon him as the nearest kinsman of her deceased husband. Ruth followed this advice, and Boaz promised to fulfill her request provided the nearer redeemer, who was still living, would not perform his duty (3:1-13). As he was indisposed to do so, Boaz obtained from him a release, redeemed himself the patrimony of Elimelech, and took Ruth to be his wife (4:1-13). In process of time she became the mother of Obed, the father of Jesse and grandfather of David (vers. 13, 17; Matt. 1:5).

The artifice that Naomi suggested and Ruth adopted to induce Boaz to act as her redeemer (chap. 3:1, sq.) appears, according to our customs, to be objectionable from a moral point of view; judged, however, by the customs of that time it is not. Boaz, who was an honorable man, praised Ruth for having taken refuge with him instead of looking for a husband among younger men, and took no offense at the manner in which she had approached him and proposed to become his wife. The anxiety manifested by Ruth is explained by the desire to continue the family name, and to have the possessions of her father-in-law redeemed and restored to the family.

S

Sabach'thani (sȧ-băk'thȧ-nī), or **Sabachtha'ni** (sȧ-băk-thā'nī; Gr. for Aram. *shăbăqtănī, thou hast left me*), quoted by our Lord upon the cross from Psa. 22 (Matt. 27:46; Mark 15:34). *See* Jesus.

Sabae'ans (sȧ-bē'ănz). *See* Sabeans.

Sab'aoth (Gr. *sabaōth*, for Heb. *sᵉbä'ōth, armies*, Rom. 9:29; James 5:4). In the Old Testament it frequently occurs in the epithet, "Jehovah, God of hosts," or simply "Jehovah of hosts." This epithet, "Jehovah, God of hosts,' designates him as the supreme head and commander of all the heavenly forces; so that the host of Jehovah and the host of heaven are the same (I Kings 22:19), viz., the angels, who are the Lord's agents, ever ready to execute his will. It is never applied to God with reference to the army of Israel, though once the companies composing it are called "the hosts of the Lord" (Exod. 12:41), because they were under his guidance and were to fight for his cause.

Sabbath (Heb. *shăbbäth, repose*, i. e., *cessation* from exertion; Gr. *sabbaton*). The name *Sabbath* is applied to divers great festivals, but principally and usually to the seventh day of the week, the strict observance of which is enforced not merely in the general Mosaic code, but in the Decalogue itself.

1. **Origin.** The account of the creation states that God "rested on the seventh day," etc. (Gen. 2:2). The Sabbath rest was a Babylonian as well as a Hebrew institution. Its origin went back to pre-Semitic days, and the name Sabbath was of Babylonian origin. In the cuneiform tablets the *Sabattu* is described as "a day of rest for the soul." In Accadian (i. e., early Babylonian) times the Sabbath was known as *dies nefastus*, a day on which certain work was forbidden; and an old list

of Babylonian festivals and fast days tells us that on the seventh, fourteenth, nineteenth, twenty-first, and twenty-eighth days of each month the Sabbath day had to be observed. The king on that day "must not eat flesh that has been cooked over the coals or in the smoke, he must not change the garments of his body, white robes he must not wear, sacrifices he may not offer, in a chariot he may not ride." Even the prophet or soothsayer was not allowed to practice his art. We find traces of the week of seven days, with the rest day, or Sabbath, which fell upon the seventh, in Babylonia.

2. **Jewish Sabbath.** (1) **Origin.** The Sabbath was of divine institution, and is so declared in passages where ceasing to create is called "resting" (Gen. 2:3; Exod. 20:11; 31:17). The blessing and sanctifying of the seventh day has regard, no doubt, to the Sabbath, which Israel, as the people of God, was afterward to keep; but we are not to suppose that the theocratic (Jewish) Sabbath was thus early instituted. The Sabbath was instituted by Moses. It is in Exod. 16:23-29 that we find the first incontrovertible institution of the day, as one given to and to be kept by the children of Israel. Shortly afterward it was reenacted in the fourth commandment. Many of the rabbis date its first institution from the incident recorded in Exod. 15:25. This, however, seems to want foundation of any sort. We are not on sure ground till we come to the unmistakable institution in ch. 16, in connection with the gathering of manna. The opinion of Grotius is probably correct, that the day was already known, and in some measure observed as holy, but that the rule of abstinence from work was first given then, and shortly afterward more explicitly imposed in the fourth commandment.

(2) **Purpose.** The Hebrew Sabbath differed from the Babylonian in that it had no connection with Babylonian astronomy and the polytheistic worship with which it was bound up. It was not dependent upon changes of the moon; the festival of the new moon and the weekly Sabbath were separated from each other. Instead of a Sabbath which occurred on each seventh day of lunar months, with an unexplained Sabbath on the nineteenth, the Old Testament recognizes only a Sabbath which recurs at regular intervals of seven days, irrespective of the beginning and ending of the month. The Sabbath is divested of its heathen associations, and is transformed into a means of binding together more closely the chosen people and keeping them apart from the rest of mankind. In place of astronomical reasons, which preside over the Babylonian Sabbath, two reasons are given for its observance in Israel—God's resting on the seventh day of creation (Exod. 20:8-11; 31:16, 17), and that Israel had been a "servant in the land of Egypt," and had been brought out "thence through a mighty hand and by a stretched-out arm" (Deut. 5:15). "These are not the subjects of Sabbath celebration; indeed, the Sabbath has no one event as the subject of its observance, but is only the day which Israel is called to sanctify to the Lord its God, because God blessed and hal-

lowed the day at the creation by resting on it. The completion of creation, the rest of God, is his blessedness in the contemplation of the finished work, the satisfaction of God in his work, which overflows in blessing upon his creatures. This blessedness was lost to the world through the fall, but not forever, for, through redemption, divine mercy will restore it. The rest of God is the goal which the whole creation is destined to reach. To guide to this goal the Sabbath was enjoined by way of compensation for the losses which accrue to man under the curse of sin, from that heavy, oppressive labor which draws him from God. Thus the Sabbath was hallowed, i. e., separated from other days of the week to be a holy day for man, by putting the blessing of his rest on the rest of this day. The return of this blessed and hallowed day is to be to him a perpetual reminder and enjoyment of the divine rest. This significance of the Sabbath explains why its keeping through all future generations of Israel is called a perpetual covenant and a sign between Jehovah and the children of Israel forever (Exod. 31:17)" (Keil, *Arch.*, ii, p. 2, sq.).

(3) **Observance.** According to Mosaic law the Sabbath was observed: 1. By cessation from labor (Exod. 20:10). The idea of work is not more precisely defined in the law, except that the kindling of fire for cooking is expressly forbidden (35:3), and the gathering of wood is treated as a transgression (Num. 15:32, sq.); whence it is evident that work, in its widest sense, was to cease. "Accordingly, it was quite in keeping with the law when not only labor, such as burden-bearing (Jer. 17:21, sq.), but traveling, as forbidden by Exod. 16:29, and trading (Amos 8:5, sq.) were to cease on the Sabbath, and when Nehemiah, to prevent marketing on this day, ordered the closing of the gates" (Neh. 10:31; 13:15, 19). 2. By a holy assembly, the doubling of the daily offering by two lambs of the first year, with the corresponding meat and drink offerings (Num. 28:9, sq.; Sacrificial Offerings, iii, 4), and the providing of new showbread in the holy place (Lev. 24:8). Thus the Sabbath was to Israel "a day of gladness" (Num. 10:10; comp. Hos. 2:11), "a delight, the holy of the Lord, honorable" (Isa. 58:13). From such passages as Isa. 58:13, sq., it will appear that the essence of Sabbath observance is placed in the most unconditional and all-embracing self-denial, the renunciation of the whole natural being and natural desires, the most unconditional dedication to God (see Isa. 56:2; Ezek. 20:12, 21). The object of this cessation from labor and coming together in holy convocation was to give man an opportunity to engage in such mental and spiritual exercises as would tend to the quickening of soul and spirit and the strengthening of spiritual life. In this higher sense it is evident that our Lord meant that "the Sabbath was made for man" (Mark 2:27).

(4) **Reward**, etc. According to Ezekiel (20:12, 20) the Sabbath was to be a sign between Jehovah and Israel, "that they might know that I am the Lord that sanctify them." That is, "that Jehovah was sanctifying them —viz., by the Sabbath rest—as a refreshing

and elevation of the mind, in which Israel was to have a foretaste of that blessed resting from all works to which the people of God was ultimately to attain" (Keil, *Com.*, in loc.). The penalty of defiling the Sabbath was death (Exod. 31:15; 25:2; comp. Num. 15:32, sq.). But if the law of the Sabbath was broken through ignorance or mistake, pardon was extended after the presentation of a sin offering. At times the Jews dispensed with the extreme severity of the law (Isa. 56:2; Ezek. 20:16; 22:8; Lam. 2:6; Neh. 13:16); indeed, the legal observance of the Sabbath seems never to have been rigorously enforced until after the exile. *See* Lord's Day, Sunday, Synagogue.

(5) **Typology.** The Sabbath commemorates God's creation rest. It marks a finished creation. After Sinai it was a day of legal obligation. The Sabbath is mentioned often in the Book of Acts in connection with the Jews. In the rest of the N. T. it occurs but twice (Col. 2:16; Heb. 4:4). In these passages the Sabbath is set forth not as a day to be observed, but as typical of the present rest into which the believer enters when "he also ceases from his own rest" and trusts Christ.

(6) **Contrast to the First Day of the Week.** As the Sabbath commemorates God's creation rest, the first day speaks of Christ's resurrection. The seventh day marks God's creative rest. On the first day Christ was unceasingly active. The seventh day commemorates a finished creation, the first day, a finished redemption. In the present dispensation of grace Sunday perpetuates the truth that one-seventh of one's time belongs to God. In every other particular there is contrast.—M. F. U.

Sabbath, Covert for the (Heb. *mēsăk hăshshăbbăth*, II Kings 16:18). This was, no doubt, a covered place, stand, or hall in the court of the temple used by the king whenever he visited the temple with his retinue on the Sabbath or feast days. In what the removal of it consisted it is impossible to determine from the lack of information as to its original character. Some think it means to change the name, others believe it to have been a taking down thereof. The motive may have been fear of the king of Assyria or his own idolatry (comp. II Chron. 28:24).

Sabbath, Morrow after the (Heb. *măhărăth hăshshăbbăth*), a term of disputed meaning (Lev. 23:11, 15), occurring in connection with the feast of the Passover. The Sabbath referred to is not the weekly Sabbath, but the day of rest, the first day of holy convocation of the Passover, the fifteenth Abib (*Nisan*). As a day of rest, on which no laborious work was to be performed (v. 8), the first day of the feast is called "Sabbath," irrespectively of the day of the week upon which it fell. Thus "the morrow after the Sabbath" is equivalent to "the morrow after the Passover" (Josh. 5:11).

Sabbath, Second after the First (Gr. *sabbaton deuteroprōton, Sabbath second-first*, Luke 6:1). This expression has given rise to much discussion, and many views of its meaning are given. Of these we mention only a few. Bleek supposes an interpolation. Wetstein and Storr say that the first Sabbath of the first, second,

and third months of the year were called first, second, and third; the second-first Sabbath would thus be the *first* Sabbath of the *second* month. Louis Cappel suggests the following: The civil year of the Israelites commenced in autumn, in the month Tizri, and the ecclesiastical year in the month Nisan (about mid-March to mid-April), and there were thus every year two first Sabbaths—one at the commencement of the civil year, of which the name would have been *first-first;* the other at the beginning of the ecclesiastical year, which would be called *second-first.* Edersheim (*Life of Jesus,* ii, 54, sq.), and Strong (*Concordance,* s. v.) advocate the very probable view that the "second-first Sabbath" was the one following immediately after the Paschal week, the 22d Nisan.

Sabbath Day's Journey. *See* Metrology, I, 9.

Sabbatical Year. *See* Festivals, I, 3.

Sabe′ans (sá-bē′ănz), the inhabitants of a kingdom in S. W. Arabia, S. of Ma'in, north of the kingdom of Qataban in the Yeman-Hadhramaut region of S. Arabia. This general region was explored in 1950-51 by the Arabian Expedition of the American Foundation for the Study of Man organized by Wendell Phillips (*see Qataban and Sheba,* 1955). The excavations in S. Arabia have helped to outline its general history. The kingdoms of Ma'in, Saba, Qataban, Ausan and Hadhramaut are now much better known. Before 1200 B. C. there was a southward migration of Sheba and allied tribes. About 1000 B. C. to 700 B. C. there was a great expansion of Sabean influence. From about the ninth century to the middle of the fifth century B. C. priest-kings of Sheba are known. From c. 400-25 B. C. the kingdom of the Minaeans and the kingdom of Qataban flourished. The ruins of Mariaba (Mareb) are a mute evidence of the splendor that the Sabaean monarchs possessed. About 950 B. C. the Biblically famous Queen of Sheba (Saba) set out on a 1200-mile desert trek to visit the rich and powerful king of Israel in the north, taking with her lavish gifts (I Kings 10:1-13). This great queen, accustomed to wealth and splendor herself, was so overwhelmed by Solomon's majesty that "there was no more spirit in her" (II Chron. 9:4). In Matt. 12:42; Luke 11:31 this ruler is designated as a queen from "the south." The queen's strenuous journey to Jerusalem over inhospitable terrain was almost certainly dictated by commercial reasons. Her conference with Solomon must have involved delimitation of commercial interests and arrangement of trade treaties which regulated the equitable exchange of the products of Arabia, including the lucrative incense trade and Palestinian products and particularly the raw copper of the Wadi Arabah. Although the Queen of Sheba of Solomon's day has not been attested as yet in S. Arabian inscriptions, there is not the slightest reason for denying either her or her visit to the Israelite monarch. The account is very definitely not a "romantic tale" as generally used to be supposed (cf. James A. Montgomery, *Arabia and the Bible,* 1934, p. 180). Although queens played little part in the later history of S. Arabia, they ruled large tribal confederacies in northern Arabia from the ninth to the seventh centuries B. C., as the cuneiform inscriptions relate. W. F. Albright's researches in S. Arabia and the vast quantity of material being studied promise to shed important light on S. Arabian history and on the Sabaeans. Much is now known of Sabaean religion from excavated tablets. It was of the astral type, their chief deity being Attar, the male counterpart of the goddess of procreation, the Babylonian Ishtar.—*M. F. U.*

Sab′ta (săb′tà; meaning unknown), the third son of Cush and grandson of Ham (Gen. 10:7; I Chron. 1:9).

Sab′tah (săb′tà; Gen. 10:7). *See* Sabta.

Sab′techa (săb′tĕ-kà), the fifth-named son of Cush, the son of Ham (Gen. 10:7; I Chron. 1:9).

Sa′car (sā′kàr; *wages*).

1. A Hararite and father of Ahiam, one of David's mighty men (I Chron. 11:35). In II Sam. 23:33 he is called *Sharar*.

2. The fourth son of Obed-edom (I Chron. 26:4).

Sackbut. *See* Music.

Sackcloth (Heb. *săq;* Gr. *sakkos, a mesh,* i. e., coarse loose cloth), a coarse texture of a dark color, made of goat's hair (Isa. 50:3; Rev. 6:12), and resembling the *cilicium* of the Romans. It was used (1) for making sacks (Gen. 42:25; Lev. 11:32; Josh. 9:4), and (2) for making the rough garments used by mourners (Gen. 37:34; Esth. 4:1-4), which were in extreme cases worn next the skin (I Kings 21:27; II Kings 6:30; Job 16:15; Isa. 32:11), and this even by females (Joel 1:8; II Macc. 3:19), but at other times were worn over the coat (Jonah 3:6) in lieu of the outer garment.

Figurative. *Girding with sackcloth* is a figure for heavy afflictions (Psa. 35:13; 69:11; Isa. 3:24; 15:3; 22:12; 32:11). *Putting off,* of joy and gladness (Psa. 30:11; Isa. 20:2). *Covering the heavens,* of severe judgments (Isa. 50:3; Rev. 6:12). Prophets and ascetics wore it over the underclothing, to signify the sincerity of their calling (Isa. 20:2; comp. Matt. 3:4).

Sacrament (Lat. *sacramentum,* a military *oath* of enlistment) is the term applied to baptism and the Lord's Supper, which are generally believed to have been instituted for the perpetual observance of the Christian Church and placed among its means of grace. As signs they represent in action and by symbols the great blessings of the covenant; as seals they are standing pledges of the divine fidelity in bestowing them on certain conditions, being the Spirit's instrument in aiding and strengthening the faith which they require, and in assuring to that faith the present bestowment of its object.

The Roman Catholic Church holds to seven sacraments, viz., baptism, confirmation, the eucharist, penance, extreme unction, orders, and matrimony. It teaches that a sacrament is "a visible sign of invisible grace instituted for our justification" (*The Rom. Catechism,* p. ii, ch. 1, No. 4). The *Catholic Dictionary* (art. "Sacraments") has the following: "Just as Christ appeared in flesh, just as virtue went forth from that body which he took, just as he saved us by that blood which he willingly shed in love for us, so he continues to make

sensible things the channel of that grace by which our lives are elevated and sanctified. In baptism we are born again; in confirmation we grow up to perfect men in Christ," etc.

Sacrifice. 1. Scripture Terms. The following terms are used to express the sacrificial act:

(1) Something *given;* a *gift* (Gen. 33:13, 18, 20, 21; 43:11, etc.); *tribute* (II Sam. 8:2, 6; I Kings 5:1; II Kings 17:4); an *offering* to God (I Chron. 16:29; Isa. 1:13), spoken especially of a bloodless offering (Heb. *mĭnḥâh; see* Meat Offering, below).

(2) Something *brought near,* an offering as a symbol of communion or covenant between man and God. (Heb. *qōrbän.*)

(3) A *bloody* sacrifice (Heb. *zĕbăḥ* from *zäbăḥ, to slay*), in which the shedding of blood is the essential idea. Thus it is opposed to *mĭnḥâh* (Psa. 40:6) and to *'ōläh,* the whole burnt offering (Exod. 10:25; 18:12, etc.).

(4) *Whole burnt offering* (Heb. *'ōläh*) that which is completely immolated as a holocaust (Lev. 1:3).

(5) Gr. *thusia,* is used both of the victim offered and the act of immolation, whether literal or figurative; *prosphora, present;* in the New Testament a *sacrifice* (A. V. "offering," Acts 21:26; 24:17; Eph. 5:2; Heb. 10:5, etc.); *holokautōma, wholly consumed* (Lat. *holocaustum*), a whole burnt offering, i. e., a victim the whole of which is burned (Mark 12:33; Heb. 10:6, 8), same as (4).

2. Origin. The beginnings of sacrifice are found in the primitive ages of man and among all the nations of antiquity. Cain and Abel offered sacrifices to God (Gen. 4:3, 4)—Cain "of the fruit of the ground," and Abel "of the firstlings of his flock and the fat thereof." Noah expressed his gratitude for deliverance from the flood by presenting burnt offerings unto the Lord (8:20, sq.). The patriarchs were in the habit of building altars and offering sacrifices thereon, calling upon God at the places where he had revealed himself to them (12:7; 13:4; 26:25; 31:54; 33:20; 35:7; 46:1). "Indeed, *to sacrifice* seems as natural to man as to pray; the one indicates what he feels about himself, the other what he feels about God. The one means a felt need of *propitiation,* the other a felt sense of *dependence*" (Edersheim, *The Temple,* p. 81).

3. Fundamental Idea. The fundamental idea of sacrifices may be gathered partly from their designation, partly from their nature. Sacrifices do not appear to have been instituted at first by divine command; though they must not, on that account, be looked upon as human inventions. They are the spontaneous expressions, so natural to man as the offspring of God, of reverance and gratitude which he feels toward him. But we must not fail to note that with gratitude and reverence there was also the thought of securing a continuance of God's favor and mercy. Nor must we lose sight of their expressing the idea of propitiation and substitution. Nor can we afford to forget that in all ages blood has been the symbol of life, and its shedding the symbol of the offering of one's life. Abundant testimony is given of this in *The Blood Covenant,* by Rev. H. C. Trumbull. He says that in the earliest recorded sacrifice, "the narrative shows Abel lovingly and trustfully reaching out toward God with *substitute* blood, in order to be in covenant oneness with God; while Cain merely proffers a gift from his earthly possessions. Abel so trusts God that he gives *himself* to him. Cain defers to God sufficiently to make a *present* to him. The one shows unbounded faith; the other shows a measure of affectionate reverence" (p. 211).

Again in the sacrifice of Noah we have an expression not only of gratitude and reverence, but of a desire for further communications of divine grace. This seems to be implied in the answer given by the Lord to Noah, "I will not again curse the ground for man's sake" (Gen. 8:21). In the presentation of the best of his possessions the worshipper symbolized the giving of himself, his life, his aims, to God. "The most direct surrender of himself that a man can make to God is realized in prayer, an act in which the soul merges itself in Him from whom it came, in which the spirit unites itself with its God. Now that which corresponds to this inward surrender, as being an outward, visible, tangible verification of it, is sacrifice, which, on this account, has been called 'embodied prayer.' " In the "burnt offerings' of Job for his children (Job 1:5) and for his three friends (42:8), the idea of expiation is distinctly set forth; for in the first instance the influencing thought with Job was, "It may be that my sons have sinned;" and in the latter God said to Job's friends, "My servant Job shall pray for you; for him will I accept."

In the Pentateuch the fundamental idea of sacrifice is that of *substitution*, which again seems to imply everything else. In the Levitical sacrifices the first fruits go for the whole products; the firstlings of the flock, the redemption money for that which cannot be offered, and the life of the sacrifice, which is in its blood, for the life of the sacrificer.

4. Mosaic Sacrifices. We have seen that in the time of the patriarchs sacrifices were the spontaneous outward expression of grateful reverence and faithfulness toward God. Under the Mosaic law the offering of sacrifices was enjoined as a covenant duty; the material of the sacrifices and the rites to be observed in offering them were minutely described; and the sacrifices thus offered acquired the character of *means of grace*.

The *ground* on which the legal offering of sacrifices is based is the commandment, "None shall appear before me empty" (Exod. 23:15), or "Appear not before the face of Jehovah" (Deut. 16:16), i. e., "Every man shall give as he is able, according to the blessing of the Lord thy God which he hath given thee" (v. 17). These gifts were not in the nature of tribute, which they were to present to Jehovah as the King of Canaan, but in recognition of their deliverance by him from Egypt, and of their adoption by him as his peculiar people. Through these gifts, as such expression, they were to enjoy the benefits and blessings of the covenant, forgiveness of sins, sanctification, and true happiness. These gifts were to be accompanied by the consecration of the offerers; and the assurance of God's acceptance of such gifts was to the pious Israelite a divine promise that he would obtain the blessings he sought.

"They thus possessed a *sacramental* virtue and efficacy; and in the Old Testament worship no religious act was regarded as complete unless accompanied by sacrifice. The sacrificial system was framed with the view of awakening a consciousness of sin and uncleanness; of impressing upon the worshipper the possibility of obtaining the forgiveness of sin, and of becoming righteous before God" (Keil, *Arch.*, i, p. 252).

At the very threshold of the Mosaic dispensation is the sacrifice of the Paschal lamb, a *substitute* for Israel's firstborn, and resulting in Israel's redemption. This was commanded to be renewed yearly at the Feast of Passover.

But there was one sacrifice which even under the Old Testament required no renewal; offered when Jehovah entered into covenant relationship with Israel, and they became the people of God (*see* Sacrificial Offering, 7). An altar was built at the foot of Sinai, indicating the presence of Jehovah; with twelve boundary stones, or pillars, representing the twelve tribes. These were most likely round the altar, and at some distance from it, preparing the soil upon which Jehovah was to enter into communion with Israel (Exod., ch. 24). The blood of the oxen was divided into two parts, one half being sprinkled upon the altar, signifying that "the natural life of the people was given up to God, as a life that had passed through death, to be pervaded by his grace; and then through the sprinkling upon the people it was restored to them again, as a life renewed by the grace of God." This covenant was made "upon all the words" which Jehovah had spoken, and the people had promised to observe. Consequently it had for its foundation the divine law and right, as the rule of life for Israel. On the ground of this covenant-sacrifice all others rested.

5. Symbolical Meaning. The presenting to God as a gift a portion of the results of one's toil implied a surrender of the person of the offerer himself. That God did not require the death of the man, but the surrender of his heart, the Israelites could not fail to learn in the case of Abraham when called upon to offer up Isaac. The presenting of sacrifices under the impression that they embodied the fact of man's surrender of himself to God, is insisted upon by Mosaic law as a covenant obligation. But from his being unholy and sinful, man is unable to surrender himself to the holy God. This view was impressed upon the Israelites, and they were reminded of the fundamental principle of the covenant "to be holy as Jehovah is holy," by the commandment that the animal offered be free from physical defects.

Leaning the hand upon the head of the animal was a symbol of the transference to the victim of the disposition animating the offerer in approaching the altar, and to devote it to the object which the sacrifice was intended to secure. It thus took the place of the offerer, and becoming his substitute, its further treatment and disposal were supposed to be fraught with benefit to him. The slaughtering of the animal, as a preliminary to its being offered upon the altar, pointed to the necessity of death in the case of the man inwardly alienated from God by sin, if he ever expected to attain to life in the enjoyment of loving fellowship with him.

When the blood, in which the soul resides, flowed from the animal on its being slaughtered, the soul was understood to be at the same time separated from the body, and it was not till the blood was sprinkled that, in virtue of the divine promise (Lev. 17:11), the soul of the offerer of the victim was brought within the range and under the influence of the divine favor.

Then, when the flesh of his victim came to be burned upon the altar, the man's own body was understood to be at the same time surrendered to the purifying fire of divine love, so that in this way he was symbolically covered in body and soul from the divine wrath, and brought within the sphere of the justifying, sanctifying, and saving grace of God.

6. **Typical Meaning.** There is a power ascribed (Lev. 17:11) to the blood of the victim, when sprinkled upon the altar, of covering the unholy man from the divine wrath, because the soul was supposed to be in the blood. But that power the blood could not be said to possess, either on account of its being shed for the man or in virtue of its being shed on the altar. Sacrifices, merely as such, had no virtue to procure for the offerer forgiveness of sin, justification, sanctification, and felicity; all of which the Israelites not only looked for through their sacrifices, but which so far as the Old Testament dispensation admitted of it, they actually received.

The domestic animals reared by man, and the fruits of the field for which he toiled, were suited, as being the products of his divinely appointed earthly calling, to shadow forth the fruit of his mental and spiritual labors in the kingdom of God. Yet between the animal and man there always would remain such a difference of nature and essence as must necessarily disqualify the former from taking the place of the latter as a true and adequate substitute. The animal has no will of its own, whereas the man is a being endowed with freedom; a being that by virtue of his innate freedom of will, choice, and action stands in a moral relation to God, so that his life and conduct are subject to the laws that regulate the moral and spiritual order of the world.

The object of the sacrifice is to establish a moral relation between the man as a personal being and God the absolute Spirit, to heal the rupture between God and man that had been caused by sin. Now, as free personality is the soil out of which sin has sprung, so must the atonement be a work rooted in free personality as well. Being outside the sphere of moral freedom, the animal may be regarded as innocent and sinless; but for the same reason it cannot possess innocence in the true sense of the word, and so have a righteousness such as could form an adequate satisfaction for the sin and guilt of man.

But even a perfect human being, if such could be found among the sons of Adam, would be unable by laying down his life to offer a sacrifice of such atoning efficacy as would reconcile another to God. The truth is that, in relation to God, everyone must answer for *his own soul*, and not for another as well (comp. Psa. 49:7, sq.). Much less could such a result be effected by means of animal sacrifices and meat offerings; these could not possibly take away sin (Heb. 10:4, 11). If, then, God did invest the animal sacrifice with such a significance as is here in question, he can only have done so in view of the true and perfect sacrifice, which in the fullness of the times was to be offered through the eternal Spirit (9:14) by Christ, the Son of God and Son of man.

Although there was no express mention of the typical character thus attaching to the sacrifices prescribed in the law, it was hinted at in the special regulations with regard to the mode of offering them; while in the course of time it came to be revealed through prophecy, although it was not till Christ voluntarily offered himself as a sacrifice upon Golgotha that it was completely unveiled. For detailed Typology *see* Sacrificial Offerings.

Sacrifice, Human. As a supreme test of Abraham's loyalty to Jehovah, he was asked to offer up his son Isaac. From this it has been argued that human sacrifice was customary among the early Israelites. But of this there is no proof. Such sacrifice was in harmony with the fierce ritual of Syria. "The belief in the efficacy of the sacrifice of the firstborn was deeply inrooted in the minds of the people of Canaan. In time of distress and necessity they offered to the gods their best and dearest, "the fruit of their body for the sin of their soul" (Mic. 6:7). Phoenician mythology related how when war and pestilence afflicted the land, Krones offered up his son Yeoud as a sacrifice, and human sacrifices were prevalent late into historical times. The Old Testament tells us that Ahaz "made his son to pass through the fire," a euphemistic expression for those offerings of the firstborn which made the valley of Tophet an abomination" (Jer. 7:31).

The king of Moab, when he saw that "the battle was too sore for him," "took his eldest son that should have reigned in his stead, and offered him for a burnt offering upon the wall" (II Kings 3:26, 27).

But there is nothing in Scripture to show that the Israelites practiced human sacrifice, or that it was enjoined by Jehovah. The case is thus put by Professor Robertson (*The Early Religion of Israel*, p. 254): "To Abraham, not unfamiliar with various ways in which among his heathen ancestors the deity was propitiated, the testing question comes, 'Art thou prepared to obey thy God as fully as the people about thee obey their gods?' and in the putting forth of his faith in the act of obedience, he learns that the nature of his God is different. Instead, therefore, of saying that the narrative gives proof of the existence of human sacrifice as an early custom in Israel, it is more reasonable to regard it as giving an explanation why it was that, from early time, this had been a prime distinction of Israel that human sacrifice *was not practiced* as among the heathen."

Sacrifices, Mosaic. 1. Classification of. The sacrifices prescribed by the Mosaic law are included under two classes:

1. Those offered *for the sake of* communion with Jehovah; and, 2. those offered *in* communion, and may be tabulated as follows: (1) *For* communion, or propitiatory, including sin offerings and trespass offerings. (2) *In* communion, (*a*) burnt offerings; (*b*) peace offerings, including thank offerings, votive offerings, and freewill offerings; (*c*) meat and drink offerings.

The propitiatory offerings were intended to lead to the worshipper's being pardoned and brought into communion with God. The others were offered after being admitted to this state of grace. Each of these sacrifices is considered in detail below. It should be carefully borne in mind that, when several sacrifices were offered on the same occasion, those of a propitiatory nature took precedence of the burnt offerings, the latter being followed by the peace offering. The meat and drink offerings were presented alike with the burnt and thank offerings, or simply by themselves.

2. **Material.** In this respect the sacrifices were divided into two classes: the *bloody*, those which were slaughtered; and the *bloodless*, i. e., the meat and drink offerings.

The material for altar sacrifices were:

(1) **Animal**, including oxen, sheep, goats, and fowls (i. e., turtledoves and young pigeons). The pigeons were intended for those who could not afford more costly offerings (Lev. 5:7; 12:8) and to serve as sin offerings of an inferior order. Male and female cattle (both large and small) might be offered (3:1, 6), though among sheep special prominence was given to the ram (Num. 15:5, sq.; 28:11, sq.) and to the male of goats (7:16, sq., 22, sq.).

The animal intended for sacrifice was required to be (*a*) of a certain age, eight days at least (Lev. 22:27; Exod. 22:30), although sheep and goats were usually offered when a year old (Exod. 29:38; Lev. 9:3, etc.), oxen when they reached their third year; (*b*) they must be absolutely free from blemish (Lev. 22:20-24).

(2) **Vegetable materials.** These were grain, olive oil, and wine; the incense, partly vegetable and partly mineral; and salt.

The grain was offered (*a*) roasted in the ear (Lev. 2:14), (*b*) as *fine flour* (2:1), to both of which incense and oil were added (2:1, 15, sq.); or (*c*) as *unleavened bread* or biscuits. This last was of three kinds—bread baked in the oven, bread baked in a pan, bread fried in oil. In each case the flour was mixed with oil (2:1, sq.).

Every meat offering had to be salted (2:13), as well as the animal sacrifices (Ezek. 43:24; Mark 9:49). Leaven and honey were not allowed in any offering to Jehovah made by fire (Lev. 2:13).

3. **Principle Underlying Selection.** The animals, etc., selected for sacrifice were from the ordinary articles of diet among the Hebrews, thus expressing gratitude to God for blessings bestowed, and prayer for continuance of his goodness. Further, as these offerings were the fruit of their life and labors, pre-

senting them symbolized a consecration to God of their life with all its energies and endowments.

4. **Presentation of Offerings.** The manner of presentation was regulated by the sacficial ritual, and in the case of animal sacrifices was generally as follows:

The victim was brought to the door of the tabernacle, near which the altar was placed; the person bringing the sacrifice leaned with his hand upon the animal's head, and then slaughtered it at the north side of the altar (Lev. 1:4, 5, 11; 3:2, 8; 6:25; 7:2). In the case of sacrifices connected with the regular services of the sanctuary, those offered on festival occasions and in behalf of the whole people, the victims were slaughtered, flayed, and cut up by the priests.

The victim slain, the priest caught the flowing blood in a vessel, and, according to the nature of the sacrifice, sprinkled some of it either on the side of the altar, its horns, or on the horns of the altar of incense, or upon (i. e., in the direction of) the ark, emptying what remained at the foot of the great altar (Exod. 29:12; Lev. 4:17, 18, etc.).

The animal was then flayed by the offerer and cut into pieces (Lev. 1:6; 8:20), and either burnt entirely upon the altar or the fat burned up on the altar, while the remainder of the flesh was burned without the camp. It was then eaten by the priests, or partly by the priests and partly by the one bringing the sacrifice.

If the sacrifice consisted of pigeons the priest wrung off the pigeon's head and allowed the blood to flow upon the side of the altar. He then took away the viscera and flung it upon the ash heap beside the altar. The head and body were then burnt upon the altar (1:15).

In regard to vegetable offerings, if connected with burnt offerings, part of the flour and oil, some of the ears of corn and the cakes, with the incense, were burned upon the altar, the remainder falling to the priests, who must consume it in the court of the tabernacle without leaven (2:2, sq.; 6:9-11; 7:9, sq.; 10:12, sq.). If, in connection with a thank offering, one cake was presented as a wave offering to Jehovah, which cake fell to the priest who sprinkled the blood (7:14), the remainder of the offering was to be eaten by those who presented it.

Sacrificial Offerings. 1. Sin Offering. (1) **Name.** (Heb. *ḥaṭṭā'th*, an *offense*) A penalty, or an offering for sin, first directly enjoined in Lev. ch., 4. The Hebrew word is not applied to any sacrifice in ante-Mosaic times, and it is therefore peculiarly a sacrifice of the law.

(2) **Meaning.** In Lev. 4:2 we read that, "if a soul shall sin through ignorance against any of the commandments of the Lord concerning things which ought not to be done, and shall do against any of them," that conduct would furnish reason for a sin offering. The meaning is that of sinning "in error." This does not mean merely sinning through ignorance, hurry, want of consideration, or carelessness (comp. Lev. 5:1, 4, 15), but also sinning unintentionally (Num. 35:11, 15, 22, 23); hence such sins as spring from weakness

of flesh and blood, as distinguished from those committed with a "high hand," i. e., in haughty, defiant rebellion against God and his commandments. The one sinning "presumptuously" was to be cut off from among his people (15:30).

The object and effect of the sin offering

394. Turtledove Used in Sacrificial Offerings

were declared to be the forgiveness of sin (Lev. 4:20, 26, 31, 35; 5:10) and cleansing (ceremonial purgation) from the pollution of sin (12:8; 14:20; 16:19, etc.). It was thus the offering among the Hebrews in which the ideas of propitiation and of atonement for sin were most distinctly marked. Its presentation presupposed the consciousness of sin on the part of the person presenting it (comp. 4:14, 23, 28; 5:5). The laying on of the hands of the offerer was understood to typify the fact that the sin for which pardon and cleansing were being sought was transferred to the victim, which thereby became sin (4:4, 14). The soul of the offerer, being represented by the blood, was, through the sprinkling of the latter, brought into the fellowship with or within the sphere of operation of the divine grace. The blood of the sin offering being sprinkled upon the *horns* of the altar, which were symbolic of power and might, the soul was thereby symbolically brought within the full force and efficacy of that divine grace in which it was required to participate in order that its sin might be duly atoned for.

The burning of the fat of the victim upon the altar as an offering made by fire for a sweet savour unto Jehovah (Lev. 4:31) was symbolical of the handing over of the better part of the man, the part that is susceptible of renewal, to the purifying fire of the divine holiness and love, in order that the inward man might be renewed from day to day by the Spirit of the Lord, and at length be changed into the glory of the children of God.

(3) **Material.** The material for the sin offering was regulated partly by the position of the one in whose behalf it was offered, and partly by the nature of the offense for which an atonement was to be made.

1. *A Young Bullock.* Consecration of priests

and Levites to their office (Exod. 29:10, 14, 35; Num. 8:8). For the high priest on the Day of Atonement (Lev. 16:3). Sin of high priest (4:3), or sin of the whole congregation (4:13).

2. *A He-goat.* New moon and annual festivals (Num. 28:15, 22, 30; 29:5, 11, 16, 19, etc.). Dedication of the tabernacle and temple (Num. 7:16, 22; Ezra 6:17; comp. 8:35). Sin of a prince (Lev. 4:23).

3. *A She-goat.* Sin by one of the common people (Lev. 4:28, 32; 5:6).

4. *A She-lamb,* of a year old. Nazarite released from vow (Num. 6:14). Cleansing of a leper (Lev. 14:10, 19).

5. *A Turtledove or Young Pigeon,* for purifying of a woman after childbirth (Lev. 12:6); a man in his issues (15:14); a woman who had protracted issue of blood (15:29); a Nazarite defiled by contact with a dead body (Num. 6:10). A turtledove or young pigeon, as a substitute for the lamb in case of poverty, on occasion of ordinary offense (Lev. 5:7); for purification of the leper (14:22).

6. *Tenth of an ephah of flour,* as a substitute for the pigeon, when poverty prevented the latter, and on occasion of any ordinary offense (5:11).

(4) **Occasions.** The sin offerings were:

1. *Regular,* offered upon the following occasions: (1) For the whole people, at the New Moon, Passover, Pentecost, Feast of Trumpets, Feast of Tabernacles (Num. 28:15-29:38), and the Day of Atonement (Lev., ch. 6). (2) Consecration of priests and Levites (Exod. 29:10-14, 36). (3) The sacrifice of the red heifer, from the ashes of which was made the "water of separation" (Num. 19:1-10).

2. *Special,* offered on the following occasions: (1) For any *sin of ignorance* against the commandment of the Lord, on the part of priest, prince, people, or individual (Lev. 4:1, sq.). (2) For ceremonial defilement (5:2, 3); such as, of women (12:6-8), leprosy (14:9, 31), issues in men and women (15:15, 30), defilement of a Nazarite, or at expiration of his vow (Num. 6:6-11, 16).

(5) **Ritual,** or mode of presenting the sin offering. After the animal had been brought forward, and the hand duly laid upon it, it was slaughtered. If the victim was a bullock offered in behalf of the high priest or of the whole congregation, its blood was taken into the holy place and there sprinkled seven times toward the inner veil, then upon the horns of the altar of incense; after which the remainder was poured out at the foot of the altar of burnt offering (Lev. 4:5, sq.; 16, sq.).

If the victim was a ram, a she-goat, or a lamb, the blood was merely put upon the horns of the altar of burnt offering, the remainder being poured out at the foot of the altar (4:25. 30, 34). Upon the Day of Atonement the high priest took the blood of the sin offering (the bullock) for himself, and the blood of the goat offered in behalf of the people, into the most holy place, and sprinkled it upon and before the mercy seat (16: 14, 15).

The next step was, in all cases (except pigeons), to separate the fatty portions from the animal, viz., the fat covering the intestines and such as was upon them, the kidneys and their fat, the fat on the flanks, the caul, and, in the case of a certain kind of sheep, the fat of the tail, and then burn them upon the altar (4:8-10, 19, 26, 31, 35).

In those cases in which the blood was sprinkled in the holy place, or the holy of holies (and in the case of the bullock sacrifice as a sin offering at the consecration of the priests, Exod. 29:14), the flesh, along with the skin, head, bones, intestines, and dung, was carried without the camp (afterward the city) to a clean place where the ashes of sacrifice were usually emptied, and there consumed by fire (Lev. 4:11, sq., 20, sq.; 6:23; 16:27). In the case of the other sin offerings, the blood of which was not applied as above, the flesh was eaten by the priests in the holy place (Lev. 6:26; Num. 18:9, 10). The skin probably went, as in the trespass offering, to the officiating priest.

The additional regulations respecting the sin offering were: "Whatsoever shall touch the flesh thereof shall be holy" (Lev. 6:18, 27), i. e., every layman touching the flesh became holy as the priest, and was obliged to guard against defilement in the same manner (comp. 21:1-8); the vessel, in which it was boiled for the priests to eat, was broken if of earthenware, and scoured if of copper; garments upon which its blood had been sprinkled were to be washed (Lev. 6:27, 28).

(6) **Typology.** The sin offering as nonsweet savor presents Christ atoning for the guilt of sin (Heb. 13:11, 12). It portrays our Lord as actually burdened with the believer's sin, standing in the sinner's place and stead. It is in contrast to the sweet-savor offering which presents Christ's own perfections. The sin offering tells forth our Lord's death as presented in Isa. 53, Psa. 22 and I Pet. 2:24. This offering, however, carefully guards the infinite holiness of Him "Who was made sin for us" (I Cor. 5:11; cf. the law of this offering, Lev. 6:24-30). The sin offerings were efficacious and substitutionary (Lev. 4:12) and in their expiatory aspect vindicate the law through substitutionary sacrifice.—*M. F. U.*

2. **Trespass Offering** (Heb. *'āshām, fault*).

(1) **Meaning.** While the trespass offering was propitiatory in its character, it differed from the sin offering in that the latter made atonement for the *person* of the offender, while the former only atoned for one special offense, "In fact, the trespass offering may be regarded as representing ransom for a special wrong, while the sin offering symbolized general redemption" (Edersheim, *Temple*, p. 100, sq.).

(2) **Material.** The trespass offering consisted of a ram, which was valued by a priest according to the shekel of the sanctuary (Lev. 5:15, 18; 6:6; 19:21). The only exception was in the case of a leper and a Nazarite, when the offering consisted of a lamb, without any mention of valuation (Lev. 14:11, sq.; Num. 6:12).

(3) **Occasions.** The trespass offerings, being prescribed for special sins, are not included in the general festal sacrifices. They were offered for the following offenses: 1. "If a soul commit a trespass, and sin through ignorance

in the holy things of the Lord" (Lev. 5:15), i. e., to inadvertently take away from Jehovah that which belonged to him, of sacrifice, first fruits, tithes, etc. The ram for sacrifice was to be accompanied by compensation for the harm done and the gift of a fifth part of the value to the priest. 2. Ignorant transgression of any definite prohibition of the law (v. 17). 3. Fraud, suppression of the truth, or perjury against a neighbor; with compensation and with the addition of a fifth part of property in question to the person wronged (6:1, sq.). 4. Rape of a betrothed slave (19:20-22). 5. At the purification of a leper (14:12), and the polluted Nazarite (Num. 6:12).

(4) **Ritual.** The victim was slaughtered on the north side of the altar, its blood sprinkled upon the latter, the fat burned upon it, and the flesh eaten by the priests in the holy place (as in the sin offering), the skin also belonging to the officiating priest. With reference to the accompanying meat offering, everything baked in the oven, and everything prepared in a pan or pot, was to belong to the priest officiating; while such portions as were mixed with oil or were dry were to belong to "all the sons of Aaron," i. e., divided among all the priests.

(5) **Typology.** This ritual prefigures Christ's atoning for the damage of sin. It is a nonsweet savor offering. It has in view not so much the guilt of sin, which is the aspect in the sin offering, but rather the injury. Psa. 51:4 expresses this aspect of the offering "against Thee, Thee only have I sinned, and done this evil in Thy sight; that Thou mightest be justified when Thou speakest and be clear when Thou judgest." In other words, that which is due God's rights as an infinitely Holy Being in every sinner is typically signified.—*M. F. U.*

3. **Burnt Offering.** (1) **Name** (Heb. *'ōlāh, ascending* as smoke, the name given to this sacrifice because it was to be wholly consumed and to *rise* in smoke toward heaven). There is also in use the poetical term *kālīl, complete,* (Deut. 33:10; I Sam. 7:9; Psa. 51:19; Gr. *holokautōma*; Mark 12:33; Heb. 10:6), alluding to the fact that, with the exception of the skin, it was *wholly* and *entirely* consumed. The victims in the other sacrifices were only partially consumed upon the altar.

(2) **Meaning.** The burnt offering symbolized the entire surrender to God of the individual or of the congregation, God's acceptance thereof, with a view to the renewal and sanctification of the entire man and consecration to a course of life pleasing to God. The law of sacrifice does not teach that the burnt offering had any reference to atonement or forgiveness of sins, provision being made therefor by the atoning sacrifices (sin and trespass offerings). The burnt offering was based solely on the assumption that Israel had been admitted into a covenant of grace with Jehovah, and so it could only be offered by those Israelites who retained their standing in the covenant. Strangers were permitted, if not guilty of any notorious offense, to offer burnt and thank offerings to Jehovah without being fully (i. e., by circumcision) admitted into covenant with the God of Israel.

Anyone forfeiting his covenant rights by sin or transgression was required to be again reconciled to God by means of a sin offering before he could venture to present a burnt offering. If there was any atoning element in the burnt offering it was only to a limited extent. And yet, inasmuch as sin adheres to all, even in a state of grace, it was necessary that in the burnt offering there should be so much of the element in question as would cover any defects and imperfections.

Expressing as it did the inward religious disposition expected of every true Israelite the burnt offering was required to be presented on the morning and evening of every day, the Sabbath, the new moons, and festival occasions. At the new moons and festivals the burnt offerings had to be preceded by a sin offering, it being necessary in this way to make atonement for those sins which had been committed in the interval between one festival and another.

(3) **Material.** The animals prescribed for this sacrifice by the law were a young bullock, a ram or he-lamb, and a he-goat—always a male. In case of poverty turtledoves or young pigeons might be offered, irrespective of sex (Lev. 1:3, 10, 14). The male was commanded, probably, to teach that the act of surrender was to be of an active, energetic character.

(4) **Occasions.** 1. *Regular* burnt offerings were offered as follows: (1) Every morning and evening (Exod. 29:38-42; Num. 28:3-8). (2) Each Sabbath, double that of the daily offering (Num. 28:9, 10). (3) At the new moon, the three great festivals, the Day of Atonement, and Feast of Trumpets (see Num. 28:11-29:39).

2. *Special* burnt offerings: (1) At the consecration of priests (Exod. 29:15; Lev. 8:18; 9:12). (2) At the purification of women (Lev. 12:6, 8). (3) At the cleansing of lepers (14:19). (4) Removal of other ceremonial uncleanness (15:15, 30). (5) On any accidental breach of the Nazarite vow, or its conclusion (Num. 6:11, 14).

3. *Freewill* burnt offerings on any solemn occasion, e. g., dedication of the tabernacle (Num., ch. 7) and of the temple (I Kings 8:64).

The burnt offering was the only sacrifice that non-Israelites were allowed to bring. The emperor Augustus had a daily burnt offering brought for him of two lambs and a bullock; and ever afterward this sacrifice was regarded as indicating that the Jews recognized him as their ruler. Hence, at the commencement of the Jewish war, Eleazar carried its rejection, which was considered as a mark of rebellion.

(5) **Ritual.** The victim was led to the altar by the person offering it, duly consecrated by the laying on of hands, and then slain by the offerer. The priest then took the blood and sprinkled it round about upon the altar. The animal was flayed, the skin falling to the officiating priest as a perquisite (Lev. 7:8); the flesh was next cut up, the intestines and hind legs washed, and then the several parts, including the head and fat, were laid upon the burning wood, the whole being consumed.

In case the offering was a pigeon the priest wrung off its head and allowed the blood to flow beside the altar; he then took the increments and flung them on the ash heap beside the altar. He made an incision at the wings and placed the bird upon the altar fire, and there burned it (1:14-17). When the burnt offering consisted of a bullock or smaller cattle, the law required it to be followed by a meat and drink offering varying in quantity according to the kind of victim offered—a regulation, however, which did not apply in the case of pigeons.

(5) **Typology.** This ritual sets forth Christ offering Himself without spot to God in performing the divine will with joy, even to the point of death. In the offering the note of penalty is not conspicuous (Heb. 9:11-14; 10:5-7). The offering is sweet savor. These offerings are so-called because they deal with Christ in His own perfections and in His perfect devotion to the Father's will. They are in contrast to the non-sweet savor offerings which typify Christ as carrying the sinner's demerit. The whole burnt offering is both atoning and substitutionary, Christ dies in the believer's stead. The sacrificial animals, the bullock, the sheep, the goat and turtledove or pigeon all symbolize Christ in some aspect of His redeeming character. The young ox, His patient endurance as a Saviour (I Cor. 9:9, 10; Isa. 52:13-15; Phil. 2:5-8). The sheep or ram portrays Christ in unresisting abandonment to death (Isa. 53:7). The goat typifies a sinner and, when used of Christ, as He Who was "numbered with the transgressors." The turtledove or pigeon symbolizes mourning innocence (Isa. 38:14; Heb. 7:26). It also portrays poverty (Lev. 5:7). It shows forth Him Who became poor that we might become rich (II Cor. 8:9; Phil. 2:6-8).—*M. F. U.*

4. **Peace Offering** (Heb. *zĕbăḥ shᵉlämim, sacrifice of peace*), another sacrifice offered *in communion* with God. It was divided into three kinds: the *thank offering* (*zĕbăḥ hătōdäh, sacrifice of thanks*, Lev. 7:12; 22:29); the *votive offering* (*zĕbăḥ nĕdĕr, sacrifice of a vow*, Num. 6:14; 15:3, 8); the *freewill offering* (*zĕbăḥ nᵉdäbäh*, Lev. 7:16; 22:18, 21). It always followed all the other sacrifices.

(1) **Meaning.** The peace offerings have their root in the state of grace with its fellowship with God, and find their culminating point in the sacrificial feast. They served to establish the Hebrew more firmly in the fellowship of the divine grace; to be mindful of God when in possession and enjoyment of the divine mercies; and when adversity threatened to obscure his feeling and consciousness of God's nearness and mercy, he might be enabled, through the peace offering, to maintain this feeling and consciousness, and quicken them afresh.

In times of prosperity and success he would naturally feel thankful to God and embody his act by means of sacrifice; hence *thank offering*. In case anyone desired to secure a blessing which had not yet fallen to his lot, he would naturally endeavor by means of a vow to prevail upon God to bestow it; hence the *votive offering*. The motive impelling to the *freewill offering* seems to have centered in the desire to thank God for the enjoyment of his bounties and to be assured of their continuance (*see* Ritual (4), below).

(2) **Material.** The victims prescribed for these sacrifices were unblemished oxen or smaller cattle of either sex (Lev. 3:1, 6; 9:4, 18, etc.), though deformed animals were allowable in freewill offerings (22:23). These sacrifices were always accompanied by a meat and drink offering (7:11, etc.). No mention is found of pigeons being used in the peace offerings.

(3) **Occasions.** *Public* peace offerings were customary on occasions of festive inauguration (Exod. 24:5; II Sam. 6:17, sq.; I Kings 8:63); the election of kings (I Sam. 11:15); and upon the fortunate issue of important enterprises (Deut. 27:7; Josh. 8:31). They were expressly prescribed for the Feast of Pentecost (Lev. 23:19). The festivals were observed with peace offerings (Num. 10:10; II Chron. 30:22); and Solomon arranged three times a year a sacrificial festival of burnt and peace offerings (I Kings 9:25).

Private peace offerings were the result of free impulse, or in fulfillment of a vow (Lev. 7:16; 22:21; Num. 15:8), in recognition of a special favor from Jehovah (Lev. 7:12; 22:29), and regularly at the expiration of a Nazarite vow (Num. 6:14).

(4) **Ritual.** The offerer led the victim to the altar, laid his hand upon its head, and slew it. The priest caught the blood and sprinkled it upon the altar. At this stage the fat of the intestines—the same parts as in the case of the sin offering—was taken from the animal and burned upon the altar on the burnt offering (Lev. 3:3-5, 9-11, 14-16; 9:18, sq.). The breast and the right shoulder were then separated from each other, the shoulder being heaved—laid aside—as the portion of the officiating priest, directly from the offerer; while the breast was waved, i. e., symbolically presented to the Lord, from whom the priests received it for their use. The priest's part might be eaten by him, either boiled or roasted, in some clean place (7:30, sq.; 10:13, sq.). All the flesh of public peace offering (not burned upon the altar) belonged to the priests (23:20).

The rest of the flesh belonged to the offerer, furnishing material for the sacrificial feast. In the case of the thank offering it must be eaten the same day, in other cases at farthest the second day. Whatever was not eaten within the prescribed time had to be burned, but not on the altar (7:15-17; 22:30).

One cake of each of the three kinds making up the meat offering was the portion of the officiating priest (7:14).

The *meaning* of the sacrificial proceedings in the case of peace offering is worthy of study. As stated above, the fat of the peace offering was to be consumed on the top of the burnt offering, "which is upon the wood that is on the fire," as an "offering made by fire, of a sweet savour unto the Lord" (3:5). Thus the peace offering presupposed the previous reconciliation of the offerer with God, and the sanctification of his life as the basis of admission into fellowship with God, which was realized in the sacrificial feast. As he partook of this meal the material food was trans-

formed into a symbol of his being spiritually fed with the mercies of God, of his being satisfied with fullness of joy in the presence of the Lord (Psa. 16:11).

The *sacrificial feast.* "In consequence of the consecrated character imparted to the whole victim by assigning the choicest portions of the flesh to the Lord and the officiating priest, the sacrificial feast was transformed into a covenant feast, a feast of love and joy, which symbolized the privilege of dwelling in the house and family of the Lord, and so shadowed forth the rejoicing of his people before him (Deut. 12:12, 18) and the blessedness of eating and drinking in the kingdom of God" (Luke 14:15; 22:30) (Keil, *Arch.*, i, 330, sq.).

(5) **Typology.** As a sweet savor offering this ritual portrays Christ as our Peace (Eph. 2:14-18). Christ made Peace (Col. 1:20); proclaimed peace (Eph. 2:17); He is our Peace (Eph. 2:14). The offering sets forth God as propitiated and the sinner reconciled; God and the sinner brought together in peace, both satisfied with the finished work of Christ. Closely associated with peace is fellowship. With this idea in mind the peace offering affords food for the priests (Lev. 7:31-34).— *M. F. U.*

5. **Meal and Drink Offerings.** (1) **Name.** "Meat" offering is more properly given in the R. V. as "meal offering," and is the rendering of the Heb. *mĭnḥāh, offering,* while drink offering is the rendering of Heb. *nĕsĕk, libation*.

(2) **Meaning.** One meaning of these offerings, which is analogous to that of the offering of the tithes (first fruits and the showbread), appears to be expressed in the words of David: "All that is in the heaven and in the earth is thine . . . All things come of thee, and *of thine own have we given thee*" (I Chron. 29:10-14). It recognized the sovereignty of Jehovah and his bounty in the bestowal of earthly blessings by dedicating to him the best of his gifts— flour, as the main support of life; oil, the symbol of richness; wine, as the symbol of vigor and refreshment (see Psa. 104:15).

Another meaning is ascribed to these offerings, viz., a symbol of the spiritual food which Israel strove after as the fruit of its spiritual labor, or those good works in which true sanctification must necessarily embody itself.

(3) **Material.** The material of the meal offering consisted either of grain—offered partly unground, in the shape of roasted ears and partly fine flour, in both instances oil being poured on and incense added—or of cakes, prepared in three different ways with oil, but without any leaven (*see* Sacrifices, Classification of, 2). Both kinds of meal offerings required to be seasoned with salt (Lev. 2:13).

The *drink offering* consisted in every instance of wine.

(4) **Occasion.** Meal offerings were either *public* or *private*, and were either brought in conjunction with burnt or peace offerings (never with sin or trespass offerings) or by themselves.

The three public meal offerings were the twelve loaves of showbread; the omer, or sheaf of wheat, on the second day of Passover (*q. v.*); and the two wave loaves at Pentecost.

Four private meal offerings were prescribed by law, viz : (1) The daily meal offering of the high priest, according to the Jewish interpretation of Lev. 6:14, sq.; (2) that at the consecration of priests (6:20); (3) that in substitution for a sin offering, in case of poverty (5:11, 12); and that of jealousy (Num. 5:15).

The following were voluntary, viz., that of fine flour with oil, unbaken (Lev. 2:1); that "baken in a pan," "in a frying pan," "in the oven," and the "wafers" (2:4-7).

(5) **Ritual.** In all baked meat offerings an "omer" was always made into ten cakes—except the high priest's daily meal offering, of which twelve cakes were baked as representative of Israel. In presenting a meal offering the priest first brought it in the golden or silver dish in which it had been prepared, and then transferred it to a holy vessel, putting oil and frankincense upon it. Standing at the southeast corner of the altar, he took the "handful" that was to be burned, put it in another vessel, laid some of the frankincense on it, carried it to the top of the altar, salted it, and then placed it on the fire.

The rest of the offering belonged to the priests (Lev. 6:16, sq.), except in the meal offering of the high priest and at the consecration of the priests (6:20-23), when it was entirely burned, and none allowed to be eaten.

Every meal offering was accompanied by a drink offering of wine; but the law contains no regulation as to the mode in which it was to be presented or how the wine was to be disposed of.

(6) **Typology.** This offering exhibits Christ in His human perfections tested by suffering. The fine flour represents the sinless humanity of our Lord. The fire is testing by suffering even unto death. Frankincense symbolizes the aroma of His life toward the Father (Exod. 30:34). The absence of leaven, a type of evil, shows forth His character as "The Truth." The oil mingled with the offering speaks of his conception by the Spirit (Matt. 1:18-23). Oil poured upon the offering speaks of his enduement with the Spirit (John 1:32, 6:27). —M. F. U.

6. **Heave and Wave Offering**, so called from a special ceremony connected with their presentation.

(1) **Heave offering** (Heb. *t'rūmäh, lifted up raised*). Everything which the Israelites voluntarily (Exod. 25:2, sq.; 35:24; 36:3), or in compliance with a legal prescription (Exod. 30:15; Lev. 7:14; Num. 15:19, sq.; 18:27, sq.; 31:29, sq.), took and separated from what belonged to them, and presented (Exod. 29:28; Num. 18:8, sq.; 5:9) to Jehovah, not as a sacrifice, but as an offering (Isa. 40:20) by way of contribution for religious purposes, such as the erection and upholding of the sanctuary (Exod. 25:2, sq.; 30:13, sq.; 35:5, 21, 24; 36:3, 6; Ezra 8:25, etc.), or for the maintenance of the priests.

Those portions of the offerings which were waved were also regarded as gifts to Jehovah, which he was understood to hand over to the priests; every heave offering could likewise be regarded as a wave offering. The heave offerings could only be used by the priests and their children (Num. 18:19; Lev. 22:10).

(2) **Wave offerings** (Heb. *t'nūphäh, undulation*). These offerings were so called because of the manner of their presentation. The offering was placed upon the hands of the offerer, and, after putting his hands under those of the offerer, the priest moved the whole backward and forward, constituting a horizontal movement. The rabbinical suggestion, that there was a distinct rite of "heaving," besides that of "waving," seems to rest on a misunderstanding of such passages as Lev. 2:2, 9; 7:32; 10:15, etc. Some think that "heaving" applies to an upward movement, as well as the horizontal, but there is little ground for this opinion.

The following were the offerings to be *waved* before the Lord—the *breast* of a private thank offering (Lev. 7:30); the fat, breast, and shoulder of the thank offerings at the consecration of the priests, the so-called consecration of offerings (Exod. 29:22-26; Lev. 8:25-29); the firstling sheaf offered on the second day of the passover (Lev. 23:11); the two lambs as a thank offering at the Feast of Pentecost (23:20); the lamb and the log of oil as a trespass offering for the purification of the leper (14:12); the thank offering of the Nazarite (Num. 6:20); the jealousy offering (Num. 5:25).

7. **Heifer, The Red.** The medium appointed for the purification of such as might be rendered unclean by contact with the dead was composed of running water and the ashes of the "red heifer" (Num. 19:1, sq.). The ashes were prepared as follows: A heifer, without blemish, and which had never been yoked, was slaughtered outside the camp, Eleazer (the son and successor of the high priest) dipping his finger in the blood and sprinkling it seven times toward the sanctuary. Then the heifer, along with the skin, flesh, blood, and dung, was burned in the presence of the priest, who at the same time took the cedar wood, hyssop, and scarlet wood, and cast them into the flames. A man free from defilement gathered the ashes, and carried them to a clean place outside the camp, where they were stored for use as occasion might require. All persons connected with the ceremony were rendered unclean till evening.

The purifying medium was applied as follows: A man, who was himself free from defilement, took some of the ashes, put them in a vessel, and poured some fresh running water over them. Dipping a bunch of hyssop into the mixture, he sprinkled it upon the person to be purified on the third and seventh day. In like manner the tent in which the corpse had lain and the furniture were all sprinkled with the same water.

The red heifer is called a sin offering (Num. 19:9, 17); and as death is the result of sin, it followed that the removal of the defilement of death would naturally call for a sin offering. The color, condition, and sex of the victim represent a full, fresh, and vigorous life; and possessing this, the animal, as a sin offering, was perfectly adapted to the purpose of bearing the guilt of the sins of the congregation that were imputed to it, as well as of vicariously suffering death as the wages of sin. The heifer was burned outside the camp by way of exhibiting the necessary fruit and consequence of sin.

(7) **Typology.** The red heifer portrays the sacrifice of Christ as the medium of the believer's cleansing from the pollution contracted in his walk as a pilgrim through the world. The order of cleansing is: (1) The slaying of the sacrifice. (2) The sevenfold sprinkling of the blood, showing forth the completed putting away of the believer's sins before God (Heb. 9:12-14). (3) The burning of the sacrifice to ashes and their preservation as a memorial of the sacrifice. (4) The cleansing by sprinkling with the ashes mingled with water. The water is typical of the Holy Spirit and the Word (John 7:37-39; Eph. 5:26). The whole ritual portrays the fact that the Holy Spirit employs the Word of God to convict the believer of sin allowed in the life. Thus convicted, the believer is made conscious of the fact that the guilt of sin has been borne in the sacrifice of Christ. Instead of losing hope the convicted believer confesses the unworthy act and is forgiven and cleansed (John 13:3-10; I John 1:7-10).—*M. F. U.*

OFFERINGS PRESCRIBED BY THE MOSAIC RITUAL

Having treated of Sacrifice in its general sense, of the Mosaic Sacrifices, and the general Sacrificial Offerings—with their meaning, material, occasion, and ritual—we now proceed to group the materials of the sacrificial offerings, which were prescribed by the law for regular occasions. Thus one will be able to see at a glance what offerings were presented daily, on the Sabbath, and at various festivals.

Daily (Num. 28:3-8).

The daily sacrifice was offered morning and evening, each consisting of a yearling lamb, for a burnt offering; a tenth deal of flour, for a meal offering; one fourth hin wine, for a drink offering.

Sabbath (Num. 28:9, 10; Lev. 24:8).

The daily offerings (see above); and two yearling lambs, for a burnt offering; two tenth deals of flour, mingled with oil, for a meal offering; one half hin wine, for a drink offering; twelve fresh loaves of showbread.

New Moon (Num. 28:11-15).

The daily offerings; and two young bullocks, one ram, seven lambs, for burnt offering; flour mingled with oil, three tenth deals for each bullock, two tenth deals for the ram, one tenth deal for each lamb; drink offering

Feast of Trumpets, or seventh New Moon (Num. 29:1-6).

The daily and new moon offerings; and one bullock, one ram, seven yearling lambs, for burnt offering; flour mingled with oil; three tenth deals for the bullock, two tenth deals for the ram, one tenth deal for each lamb, for meal offering; one kid of the goats, for sin offering; drink offerings.

Passover (Exod. 12:1, sq.).

The daily offerings; and a kid (lamb or goat, Exod. 12:5) was selected on the tenth of Abib, slain on the fourteenth, and its blood sprinkled on the doorposts and lintels.

Unleavened Bread (Num. 28:17-24).

The daily offerings; and one goat, for sin offering; two young bullocks, one ram, and seven yearling lambs, burnt offering; flour mingled with oil, three tenth deals for each bullock, two tenth deals for the ram, one tenth deal for each lamb, meal offering. The above offerings were for each day of the feast (fifteenth to twenty-first Abib). On the second day of the feast (sixteenth Abib) the first sheaf of the new harvest (barley) was offered by waving, not burning. With this sheaf was offered a male yearling lamb, for a burnt offering; two tenth deals flour and oil, for meal offering; one fourth hin wine, for drink offering.

Pentecost (Feast of Weeks) (Num. 28:27-31; Lev. 23:16-20).

The daily offerings; and a kid of the goats for a sin offering; two young bullocks, one ram, seven yearling lambs, for burnt offering; three tenth deals flour and oil for each bullock, two tenth deals for the ram, one tenth deal for each lamb, meal offering; one half hin of wine for the bullock, one third hin of wine for the ram, one fourth hin of wine for each lamb, drink offering. After the above was presented the new meal offering, viz., "two wave loaves," made of two tenth deals wheat flour, baked with leaven. With these were offered seven yearling lambs, one young bullock, and two rams, for burnt offering, with the prescribed meal and drink offerings; a he-goat, for a sin offering; two yearling lambs, for a peace offering.

Day of Atonement (Lev. 16:3; Num. 29:7-11).

The daily offerings; and a bullock for a sin offering, and a ram for a burnt offering, for the priesthood; two goats for a sin offering, and a ram for a burnt offering, for the people; followed by one young bullock, one ram, seven lambs, for burnt offering; flour mingled with oil, three tenth deals for bullock, two tenth deals for ram, and one tenth deal for each lamb, meal offering; one half hin wine for bullock, one third hin wine for ram, and one quarter hin wine for each lamb, drink offering.

Feast of Tabernacles (Num. 29:13, sq.).

The daily offerings; and,

DAY	Bullocks	Rams	Lambs	Goats
First	13	2	14	1
Second	12	2	14	1
Third	11	2	14	1
Fourth	10	2	14	1
Fifth	9	2	14	1
Sixth	8	2	14	1
Seventh	7	2	14	1
Total seven days	70	14	98	7
Eighth day	1	1	7	1

The bullocks, rams, and lambs together made the burnt offerings, while the ram was for a sin offering. Each bullock, ram, and lamb was accompanied by its prescribed meal and drink offering, the formula for which was:

Meal offering. Three tenth deals flour for a bullock, two tenth deals for a ram, one tenth deal for a lamb; the flour in each case to be mingled with oil.

Drink Offering. One half hin wine for a bullock, one third hin wine for a ram, one fourth hin wine for a lamb.

Sacrilege (Gr. *hierosuleō*), the robbing of a temple. In Rom. 2:22, "Thou that abhorrest idols, dost thou commit sacrilege?" R. V. "rob temples." The meaning is, "thou who abhorrest idols and their contamination dost yet not hesitate to plunder their shrines." In Acts 19:37 we have the noun form, "robbers of churches." The crime under the term "profane" (*q. v.*) is frequently alluded to.

Saddle. 1. *A mount* (Heb. *mĕrkăb, covering*, Lev. 15:9), a saddle, or, more correctly, a *seat*, as in a palanquin.

2. "To saddle," (Heb. *hăbăsh*, to *wrap firmly*), to *gird* about, i. e., to tighten the girths of an animal (Gen. 22:3; Num. 22:21; Judg. 19:10; II Sam. 16:1, etc.).

The saddle in principle, i. e., some covering to protect the animal's back from being chafed, was doubtless of early invention; but the saddle, properly so called, was in all probability invented by the Persians.

Sad′ducee (săd′û-sē), a member of one of the religious parties which existed among the Jews in the days of our Lord, the others being the Essenes and the Pharisees.

1. **Name.** The Hebrew word by which they were called is *şăddûqêm; Gr. Saddoukaios* (Matt. 3:7; 16:1, 6, 11, 12; 22:23, 34; Mark 12:18; Luke 20:27; Acts 4:1; 5:17; 23:6-8). The ordinary Jewish statement is that the Sadducees were named from a certain Zadok, a disciple of Antigonus of Socho, who is mentioned in the Mishna as having received the oral law from Simon the Just. Epiphanius states that the Sadducees called themselves such from Heb. *şĕdĕq, righteousness*, and that there was anciently a Zadok among the priests, but that they did not continue in the doctrines of their chief. Edersheim suggests (*Life of Jesus*, i, 324) "that the linguistic difficulty in the change of the sound *i* into *u—Tsaddiqim* into *Tsadduqim*, may have resulted, not grammatically, but by popular witticism. Some wit may have suggested: Read not *Tsaddiqim*, the 'righteous,' but *Tsadduqim* (from *Tsad-u*), 'desolation,' 'destruction.' Whether or not this suggestion approves itself to critics, the derivation of Sadducees from *Tsaddiqim* is certainly that which offers most probability."

2. **Aristocratic.** We gain but a distorted image of the Sadducees if we only look at the points of differences between them and the Pharisees. Still, each party had its strong characteristic, that of the Pharisees being a *rigid realism*, while the Sadducees were *aristocratic*. Josephus repeatedly designates them as such: "They only gain the well-to-do; they have not the people on their side" (*Ant.*, xiii, 10, 6). "This doctrine has reached few individuals, but these are of *the first consideration*" (*Ant.*, xviii, 1, 4). What Josephus really means is that the Sadducees were the aristocrats, the wealthy *euporoi*, the persons of rank (*prōtoi tois axiōmasin*), i. e., from the *priesthood*. The New Testament (Acts 5:17) and Josephus (*Ant.*, xx, 9, 1) testify that the high-priestly families belonged to the Sadducean party. The Saddu-

ceans were not, however, merely the priestly party, but aristocratic priests.

3. **Tenets.** (1) **The law.** The Sadducees acknowledged only the written law as binding and rejected the entire traditionary interpretation and further development of the law during the centuries by the scribes. Thus Josephus writes (*Ant.*, xiii, 10, 6): "The Sadducees say, only what is written is to be esteemed as legal . . . what has come down from tradition of the fathers need not be observed." While they rejected the tradition of the elders, they did not, as some of the fathers supposed, reject the prophets.

(2) In *legal* matters the Sadducees were, according to Josephus (*Ant.*, xx, 9, 1): "very rigid in judging offenders above all the rest of the Jews," while the Pharisees were much milder and more merciful. This may be connected with the fact that the Sadducees strictly adhered to the letter of the law, while the Pharisees sought to mitigate its severity by interpretation, although the latter in some instances were the more severe. "They saw in the tradition of the elders an excess of legal strictness which they refused to have imposed upon them, while the advanced religious views were, on the one hand, superfluous to their worldy-mindedness, and on the other, inadmissible by their higher culture and enlightenment" (Schürer, *Jewish People*, div. ii, vol. i, p. 41). Respecting *legal* matters, the Sadducees held: (*a*) That the *levirate law* was obligatory only when marriage was not consummated, i. e., when a woman's betrothed husband died without cohabitating with her, then his surviving brother could perform the duty of *levir* without committing incest, as she was still a virgin. This restriction of the levirate law on the part of the Sadducees imparts additional force to the incident recorded in Matt. 22:23, etc.; Mark 12:18; Luke 20:27, etc. According to the understanding of the Sadducees, the marriage would have been consummated only between the woman and the seventh brother; while the Pharisees would have made them all cohabit with the woman. The Sadducees would say, only the last brother could be her husband, but according to the Pharisaic practice, she would have been the real wife of them all. (*b*) The ceremony of *taking off the shoe* (Deut. 25:9) was understood literally by the Sadducees, who insisted that the rejected widow should spit into the man's face, while the Pharisees held that spitting *before his face* met all the requirements of the case. (*c*) The *right of retaliation*. With the same conservatism and rigor the Sadducees insisted upon the literal carrying out of the law, "eye for eye," etc. (Exod. 21:23, etc.), while the Pharisees, with a due regard for the interests of the people, maintained that pecuniary compensation was sufficient. (*d*) The Sadducees insisted that false witnesses should be put to death only when the accused had been executed in consequence of their false testimony (Deut. 19:19-21), while the Pharisees required that this should take place so soon as sentence had been passed. In this case the Pharisees were the more severe. (*e*) The Sadducees required compensation, not only if an ox or an ass (Exod. 21:32, 35, sq.), but

also if a manservant or a maidservant had injured anyone, arguing that the master is far more answerable for him than his cattle, as he is to watch over his moral conduct. The Pharisees denied this, submitting that the slave was a responsible creature, and that, if the master be held responsible for his conduct, a dissatisfied slave might, out of spite, commit ravages in order to make his master pay. (*f*) The *law of inheritance* formed another distinctive feature of the Sadducees. They maintained that when a son, being heir presumptive, and having sisters, died, leaving a daughter, that the daughter is not to receive all the property but that the sisters of the deceased are to have an equal share with the daughter, urging that the daughter is only second degree, while the sisters are the first degree. The Pharisees, on the contrary, maintained that the deceased brother's daughter is the rightful and sole heir, inasmuch as she is the descendant of the male heir, whose simple existence disinherited his sisters.

(3) **Ritual.** Respecting questions of *ritual*, a difference can only so far be spoken of that the Sadducees did not regard as binding Pharisaic decrees with respect, e. g., to clean and unclean. They derided their Pharisaic opponents on account of the oddities and inconsistencies into which their laws of cleanness brought them. But they did not renounce the principle of Levitical uncleanness in itself, for they demanded a higher degree of cleanness for the priest who burned the red heifer (*q. v.*) than did the Pharisees. They differed somewhat from the Pharisees regarding the festival laws, but the only difference of importance is that the Sadducees did not acknowledge as binding the confused mass of Pharisaic enactments.

In short, "the difference in principle between the two parties is confined, on the whole, to this general rejection of Pharisaic tradition by the Sadducees. All other differences were such as would naturally result from the one party not accepting the other's exegetical tradition. The Sadducee theoretically agreed with Pharisaic tradition in some, perhaps many, particulars—he only denied its *obligation*, and reserved the right of private opinion" (Schürer, div. ii, vol. ii, p. 38).

(4) **Doctrinal.** (*a*) The Sadducees refused to believe in a resurrection of the body and retribution in a future life, or in any personal continuity of the individual (Matt. 22:23; Mark 12:18; Luke 20:27; Josephus, *Wars*, i i 18, 14). The Jews "would not consider themselves bound to accept any doctrine as an article of faith, unless it had been proclaimed by Moses, their great lawgiver;" "and it is certain that in the written law of the Pentateuch there is a total absence of any assertion by Moses of the resurrection of the dead. This fact is presented to Christians in a striking manner by the well-known words of the Pentateuch which are quoted by Christ in argument with the Sadducees on this subject (Exod. 3:6; Mark 12:26, 27; Matt. 22:31, 32; Luke 20:37). It cannot be doubted that in such a case Christ would quote to his powerful adversaries the most cogent text in the law; and yet the text actually quoted does not do

more than suggest an *inference* on this great doctrine. It is true that in other parts of the Old Testament there are individual passages which express a belief in a resurrection, such as in Isa. 26:19; Dan. 12:2; Job 19:26; and in some of the Psalms; and it may at first sight be a subject of surprise that the Sadducees were not convinced by the authority of those passages. But although the Sadducees regarded the books which contained these passages as sacred, it is more than doubtful whether any of the Jews regarded them as sacred in precisely the same sense as the written law. Hence, scarcely any Jew would have felt under the necessity of believing man's resurrection, "unless the doctrine had been proclaimed by Moses; and as the Sadducees disbelieved the transmission of any oral law by Moses, the striking absence of that doctrine from the written law freed them from the necessity of accepting the doctrine as divine" (Smith, *Bib. Dict.*, s. v.).

(*b*) According to Acts 23:8, the Sadducees denied that there was "angel or spirit," i. e., independent spiritual realities besides God. To this category of spirits, denied by them, belonged also the spirits of the departed; for they held the soul to be a refined matter, which perished with the body (Josephus, *Ant.*, xviii, 1, 4; *Wars*, ii, 8, 14). The two principal explanations which have been suggested as to the belief of the Sadducees upon this point are, either they regarded the angels of the Old Testament as transitory unsubstantial representations of Jehovah, or that they disbelieved merely the angelical system which was developed among the Jews after the captivity.

(*c*) Free will and predestination. If we may believe Josephus, the Sadducees, in dissenting from the fantastic, imaginary development of Judaism, came to lay great stress upon human freedom. With a strong insistence upon personal liberty there came a decrease of the religious motive. They insisted that man was placed at his own disposal, and rejected the thought that a divine cooperation takes place in human actions as such. The real difference between the Pharisees and the Sadducees seems to have amounted to this—that the former accentuated God's preordination, the latter man's free will; and that, while the Pharisees admitted only a partial influence of the human element on what happened, or the cooperation of the human with the divine, the Sadducees denied all absolute preordination, and made man's choice of evil or good to depend entirely on the exercise of free will and self-determination.

The Pharisees accentuated the divine to the verge of fatalism, and insisted upon absolute and unalterable preordination of every event in its minutest detail. We can well understand how the Sadducees would oppose notions like these, and all such coarse expressions of fatalism. Neither the New Testament nor rabbinic writings bring the charge of the denial of God's prevision against the Sadducees.

4. **History.** Dr. Milligan (*Imp. Bib. Dict.*) says of the party of Sadducees: "Its origin, like that of the Pharisees, is in all probability

to be sought in that remarkable period of Jewish history which is embraced between the restoration of Israel to its own land, or rather between the cessation of prophecy after that event, and the Christian era. No traces of Sadduceeism are to be found in Israel previous to the captivity . . . In the presence of the divinely inspired prophet of Jehovah, the representative of the theocracy in its noblest form and most glorious anticipations, no tendency like that of the Sadducees, so denationalized, so cold, so skeptical, and so worldly, could have taken root. The very nature of the case, therefore, requires us to seek its origin at a more recent date, and naturally carries us to that strange period, of both outward and inward confusion through which, after the death of Alexander the Great, Palestine had to pass." In this Greek period, political interests were combined with Greek culture; and to effect anything in the political world one must of necessity have stood on a more or less friendly footing with Hellenism. In the higher ranks of the priesthood Hellenism gained ground, while, in the same proportion, it was alienated from the Jewish religious interest. This tendency received a check in the rising of the Maccabees, while the religious life was revived and strengthened. It was then that the rigidly legal party of the "Chasidees" gained more and more influence. And therewith their pretensions also increased. Those only were to be acknowledged as true Israelites who observed the law according to the full strictness of the interpretations given to it by the scribes. This made the *aristocratic* party the more strenuous in their opposition, and there resulted a firmer consolidation of parties, the "Chasidees" becoming "Pharisees," and the aristocratic party being called "Sadducees" by their opponents.

Under the earlier Maccabees (Judas, Jonathan, and Simon) this 'Zadokite' aristocracy was necessarily in the background. The ancient, high-priestly family, which, at least in some of its members, represented the extreme philo-Hellenistic standpoint, was supplanted. The high priestly office remained for a time unoccupied. In the year 152 Jonathan was appointed high priest, and thus was founded the new high-priestly dynasty of the Asmonaeans, whose whole past compelled them at first to support the rigidly legal party. Nevertheless there was not in the times of the first Asmonaeans (Jonathan, Simon) an entire withdrawal of the Sadducees from the scene. The Asmonaeans had to come to some kind of understanding with it, and to yield to it at least a portion of seats in the 'Gerusia.' Things remained in this position till the time of John Hyrcanus, when the Sadducees again became the really ruling party, John Hyrcanus, Aristobulus I, and Alexander Jamaeus becoming their followers. The reaction under Alexandra brought the Pharisees back to power. Their *political* supremacy was, however, of no long duration. Greatly as the spiritual power of the Pharisees had increased, the Sadducean aristocracy was able to keep at the helm in politics. The price at which the Sadducees had to secure themselves power at

this later period was indeed a high one, for they were obliged in their official actions actually to accommodate themselves to Pharisaic views. With the fall of the Jewish state the Sadducees altogether disappear from history. Their strong point was politics. When deprived of this their last hour had struck. While the Pharisaic party only gained more strength, only obtained more absolute rule over the Jewish people in consequence of the collapse of political affairs, the very ground on which they stood was cut away from the Sadducees. Hence it is not to be wondered that Jewish scholars soon no longer knew who the Sadducees really were.

Sa'doc (sā'dŏk; *just, righteous*), an ancestor of Jesus (Matt. 1:14; Hebrew form Zadok).

Saffron. *See* Vegetable Kingdom.

Sail, the incorrect rendering of the Heb. *nēs* (Isa. 33:23; Ezek. 27:7), usually a *standard*, or *flagstaff;* and in the passages cited a *flag* of a ship. In Acts 27:17 it represents the Gr. *skeuos*, and seems to be used specially and collectively of the sails and ropes of a ship (*q. v.*).

Sailor. *See* Ship.

Saint. Positionally every N. T. believer; experientially—a person eminent for piety and virtue: a consecrated person.

1. *Godly* (Heb. *ḥāsîd, pious, just*), used of pious Israelies, and so of the godly in general (I Sam. 2:9; II Chron. 6:41; Psa. 30:4; 31:23; 37:28; 50:5; 52:9; 79:2; 85:8; 97:10; 116:15; 132:9, 16; 145:10; 148:14; 149:1, 5, 9).

2. *A holy person* (Heb. *qādōsh;* Gr. *hagios, pure, clean*). Applied to persons *consecrated* to God's service: (*a*) The priests (Psa. 106:16; comp. Exod. 28:41; 29:1; Lev. 21:6; I Sam. 7:1; I Pet. 2:5); (*b*) the firstborn (Exod. 13:2, A. V. "sanctify;" I Pet. 2:5, "holy"); (*c*) the *pious* Israelites (Psa. 16:3; 34:9; 89:5, 7), (*d*) Angels (Deut. 33:2, 3). (*e*) N. T. believers, members of the Body of Christ, the Church of God. *All* the saved of the N. T. era are saints (*hagioi*) by virtue of their *position* "in Christ" (I Cor. 1:2; Rom. 6:3, 4; 8:1; Eph. 1:3, etc.). The N. T. refutes the idea of a special class of "saints." While it is true that *in experience* some believers are more "holy" than others, yet in their position before God, all believers are "sanctified," i. e., saints by virtue of what they are "in Christ." The Christian's perfect *position* (Rom. 6:1-10) is made a comfortable *experience* of Christ by faith (Rom. 6:11); "Reckoning" (i. e., believing themselves to be what they are in their position before God), they become such in their everyday experience. The more one's experience conforms to one's position, the more practical holiness is manifested in the child of God (saint).—M. F. U.

Sa'la (sā'là; Greek from of Salah), the patriarch Salah, the father of Eber (Luke 3:35).

Sa'lah (sā'là; *missile, javelin*), one of the patriarchs, and only named son of Arphaxad (Gen. 10:24; 11:12-15; I Chron. 1:18, 24). In the last two references he is called *Shelah*. At thirty years of age he became the father of Ebet, and lived to be four hundred and thirty-three years old. *See* Shelah.

Sal'amis (săl'à-mĭs), a city at the east extremity of the island of Cyprus, and the first place visited by Paul and Barnabas after leaving the mainland at Selucia (Acts 13:5). From the use of "synagogues" in the plural it may be inferred that there were many Jews in the city. And it is very probable from them came some of those early Cypriote Christians mentioned in Acts 11:19, 20.

Sala'thiel (sá-lā'thǐ-ĕl; I have *asked God*), son of Jechonias, king of Judah, and father of Zorobabel, according to Matt. 1:12; but son of Neri and father of Zorobabel, according to Luke 3:27; while the genealogy in I Chron. 3:17-19 leaves it doubtful whether he is the son of Assir or Jechonias. Upon the incontrovertible principle that no genealogy would assign to the true son and heir of a king any inferior and private parentage, whereas, on the contrary, the son of a private person would naturally be placed in the royal pedigree on his becoming the rightful heir to the throne, we may assert, with the utmost confidence, that St. Luke gives us the true state of the case when he informs us that Salathiel was the son of Neri, and a descendant of Nathan, the son of David. And from his insertion in the royal pedigree, both in I Chronicles and St. Matthew's gospel, after the childless Jechonias, we infer, with no less confidence, that, on the failure of Solomon's line, he was next heir to the throne of David. Keil (*Com.*, in loc.) supposes that Assir may have left only a daughter, who married a man belonging to a family of her paternal tribe, viz., Neri, and that from this marriage sprang Salathiel. Coming into the inheritance of his maternal grandfather, he would be legally regarded as his legitimate son. The A. V. has Salathiel in I Chron. 3:17, but everywhere else in the Old Testament Shealtiel (*q. v.*).

Sal'cah (săl'ká), a city of Bashan, named in the early records of Israel (Deut. 3:10; 13:11), and apparently one of the capitals of Og's kingdom (12:5). From I Chron. 5:11 it would seem that Salcah was upon the eastern confines of both Manasseh and Gad. Salcah is the modern Salkhad, a town on the N. E. border of the mountainous kingdom of Bashan, E. of the River Jordan.

Sal'chah (săl'ká; Deut. 3:10). *See* Salcah.

Sa'lem (sā'lĕm *peaceful*), the name of a place, mentioned in connection with Melchizedek as its king (Gen. 14:18; Heb. 7:1, 2). It is doubtless the name of Jerusalem (Psa. 76:2). The name appears as Uru-salim ("City of Peace") in the Amarna Letters and is incontrovertibly Jerusalem (*q. v.*).

Sa'lim (sā'lĭm; peaceful), the place west of the Jordan where John was baptising (John 3:23), probably the Shalem mentioned in Gen. 33:18, and about seven miles south of Aenon.

Sal'lai (săl'á-ī).

1. A leading Benjamite who, with nine hundred and twenty-eight of his tribesmen, settled in Jerusalem on the return from the captivity (Neh. 11:8), B. C. 445.

2. One of the chiefs of the priests who returned to Jerusalem with Zerubbabel (Neh. 12:20), B. C. about 536. In v. 7 he is called Sallu.

Sal'lu (săl'û), the name of two Hebrews, spelled differently in the original.

1. A son of Meshullam, a Benjamite dwell-

ing in Jerusalem after the captivity (Neh. 11:7; I Chron. 9:7), B. C. about 445.

2. Another form (Neh. 12:7) of the name Sallai, No. 2 (*q. v.*).

Sal'ma (săl'má).

1. Another form (I Chron. 2:11) for Salmon (*q. v.*).

2. The second named of the sons of Caleb, and father (founder) of Bethlehem (I Chron. 2:51), and of the Netophathites (v. 54), B. C. probably about 1400.

Sal'mon (săl'mŏn), the son of Nashon, and ancestor of Boaz (Ruth 4:20:21; I Chron. 2:11, *Salma;* Matt. 1:4, 5; Luke 3:32), B. C. before 1150.

Salmo'ne (săl-mō'nê), a promontory of E. Crete (Acts 27:7) present-day Cape Sidero.

Salo'me (sá-lō'mě; feminine of Solomon).

1. The daughter of Herodias by her first husband, Herod Philip (Josephus, *Ant.*, xviii, 5, 4). She is the "daughter of Herodias," mentioned in Matt. 14:6, as dancing before Herod Antipas, and securing, at her mother's instigation, the death of John the Baptist. To do honor to the day and to the company Salome broke through the rule of strict seclusion from the other sex, and condescended, though a princess and the daughter of kings, to dance before Antipas and his guests. "The dancing then in vogue both in Rome and the provinces, from its popularity under Augustus, was very like that of our modern ballet. The dancer did not speak, but acted some story by gestures, movements, and attitudes, to the sound of music. Masks were used in all cases to conceal the features, but all other parts of the body, especially the hands and arms, were called into action, and a skillful pantomimist could express feelings, passions, and acts with surprising effect. The dress of the performer was planned to show the beauty of the figure to the greatest advantage, though it varied with the characters represented" (Geikie, *Life of Christ*, p. 300). Salome was married in the first place to Philip, tetrarch of Trachonitis, her paternal uncle, who died childless; and, secondly, to her cousin Aristobulus, son of Herod, king of Chalcis, by whom she had three sons.

2. The wife of Zebedee, as appears by a comparison of Matt. 27:56, with Mark 15:40 Many modern critics are of the opinion that she was the sister of Mary, the mother of Jesus, alluded to in John 19:25. Others make the expression "his mother's sister" refer to "Mary the wife of Cleophas," immediately following. We can hardly regard the point as settled, though the weight of modern criticism is decidedly in favor of the former view. The only events recorded of Salome are that she preferred a request on behalf of her two sons for seats of honor in the kingdom of heaven (Matt. 20:20), that she attended at the crucifixion of Jesus (Mark 15:40), and that she visited his sepulcher (16:1). She is mentioned by name only on the two later occasions.

Salt.—Uses. Not only did the Hebrews make general use of salt in the food both of man (Job 6:6) and beast (Isa. 30:24), but they used it in their religious services as an accompaniment to the various offerings presented on the altar (Lev. 2:13, "every oblation of thy meat offering shalt thou season with salt"). The salt of the sacrifice is called "the salt of the covenant of thy God," because in common life salt was the symbol of covenant. The meaning which the salt, with its power to strengthen food and preserve it from putrefaction and corruption, imparted to the sacrifice was the unbending truthfulness of that self-surrender to the Lord embodied in the sacrifice, by which all impurity and hypocrisy were repelled. In addition to the uses of salt already specified, the inferior sorts were applied as a manure to the soil, or to hasten the decomposition of dung (Matt. 5:13; Luke 14:35). Too large an admixture, however, was held to produce sterility; and hence also arose the custom of sowing with salt the foundations of a destroyed city (Judg. 9:45), as a token of its irretrievable ruin. See Mineral Kingdom.

Figurative. As one of the most essential articles of food, salt symbolized hospitality (*see* Covenant of Salt). Of the ministry of good men, as opposing the spiritual corruption of sinners (Matt. 5:13); of grace in the heart (Mark 9:50); of wisdom or good sense in speech (Col. 4:6); graceless professors as salt without savor (Matt. 5:13; Mark 9:50); from the belief that salt would, by exposure to the air, lose its virtue; pits of salt was a figure of desolation (Zeph. 2:9); "salted with fire" (Mark 9:49); refers to the purification of the good, and punishment of sinners.

Salt, City of, a city in the wilderness of Judah (Josh. 15:62), probably at the southwestern extremity of the Dead Sea, where some of the hills are of pure salt, hence its name. Dr. Robinson (*Bib. Res.*, ii, 109) thinks that it lay near the plain at the south end of the Dead Sea, which he would identify with the Salt, Valley of (*q. v.*).

Saltwort. *See* Vegetable Kingdom.

Salt, Covenant of. *See* Covenant of Salt.

Salt Sea. *See* Dead Sea.

Salt, Valley of, a name employed five times in Scripture. The ravine is on the border between Judah and Edom, south of the Dead Sea. It was the scene of several battles (II Sam. 8:13; II Kings 14:7; I Chron. 18:12; II Chron. 25:11).

Sa'lu (sā'lū), the father of Zimri, which latter was slain by Phinehas for bringing a Midianitish woman into the camp of Israel (Num. 25:14), B. C. about 1400.

Salutation (Heb. *bārăk*, in some forms "to bless"; *shālōm, well, happy,* to be *friendly;* Gr. *'aspasmos,* a *greeting*), the friendly greeting which in ancient, as in modern times, has been wont to take place when meeting or parting. Salutations may be classed under two heads:

1. **Conversational.** (1) The salutation at meeting consisted in early times of various expressions of blessing, such as "God be gracious unto thee" (Gen. 43:29); "Blessed be thou of the Lord" (Ruth 3:10; I Sam. 15:13); "The Lord be with you," "The Lord bless thee" (Ruth 2:4); "The blessing of the Lord be upon you; we bless you in the name of the Lord" (Psa. 129:8). Hence the term "bless" received the secondary sense of "salute." The

Hebrew term used in these instances (*shālōm*) has no special reference to "peace," as stated in the marginal translation, but to general well-being, and strictly answers to our "welfare." (2) The salutation at parting consisted originally of a simple blessing (Gen. 24:60; 28:1; 47:10; Josh. 22:6), but in later times the term *shālōm* was introduced here also in the form "Go in peace," or rather, "Farewell" (I Sam. 1:17; 20:42; II Sam. 15:9). In modern times the ordinary mode of address current in the East resembles the Hebrews: *Es-selám aleykum,* "Peace be on you," and the term "salam" has been introduced into our own language to describe the oriental salutation. Eastern salutations were often complicated and tedious, taking up much of one's time. Our Lord's injunction "salute no man by the way" (Luke 10:4) seems to mean that the apostles were to travel like men absorbed in one supreme interest, which would not permit them to lose times in idle ceremonies.

2. **Epistolary.** The epistolary salutations in the period subsequent to the Old Testament were framed on the model of the Latin style; the addition of the term "peace" may, however, be regarded as a vestige of the old Hebrew form (II Macc. 1:1). The writer placed his own name first, and then that of the person whom he saluted; it was only in special cases that this order was reversed (II Macc. 1:1; 9:19; I Esdr. 6:7). A combination of the first and third persons in the terms of the salutation was not unfrequent (Gal. 1:1, 2; Philem. 1; II Pet. 1:1). A form of prayer for spiritual mercies was also used. The concluding salutation consisted occasionally of a translation of the Lat. *valete* (Acts 15:29; 23:30), but more generally of the term *'aspazomac,* "I salute," or the cognate substantive, accompanied by a prayer for peace or grace.

Salvation, a term which stands for several Hebrew and Greek words, the general idea being safety, deliverance, ease, soundness. In the Old Testament the term refers to various forms of deliverance, both temporal and spiritual. God delivers his people from their enemies and from the snares of the wicked (see Psa. 37:40; 59:2; 106:4). He also saves by granting forgiveness of sins, answers to prayer, joy, and peace (79:9; 69:13; 51:12, et al.). The Old Testament prophecies center upon One who was to come as the bringer of salvation (*see* Messiah).

In the New Testament salvation is regarded almost exclusively as from the power and dominion of sin. And of this Jesus Christ is the author (see Matt. 1:21; Acts 4:12; Heb. 2:10; 5:9, et al.). It is freely offered to all men, but is conditioned upon repentance and faith in Christ (see John 3:16; Heb. 2:3, et al). Salvation proceeds from the love of God, is based upon the atonement wrought by Christ, is realized in forgiveness, regeneration, sanctification, and culminates in the resurrection and glorification of all true believers. See Atonement; Forgiveness; Regeneration; Sanctification; Resurrection.—E. McC.

Sama'ria, City of (sȧ-mā'rĭ-ȧ; *watch* mountain), an important place in central Palestine, noted as the capital of the northern kingdom, as giving name to the region about, and later to a schismatic sect.

1. Geography. Samaria stood upon a hill about three hundred feet high, in a wide basin formed by the valley which runs from Shechem to the coast—the present Wady esh-Sha'ir, or Barley Vale—and an incoming glen. Surrounded by mountains on three sides, Samaria has a great view to the west. The broad vale is visible for eight miles, then a low range of hills, and over them the sea, about twenty-three miles away. The mountains surrounding Samaria are terraced to the top, and planted with olives and figs, and sown in grain, in the midst of which appear a number of attractive villages.

395. General View of the Ruins of Samaria

2. History. Samaria was purchased from its owner, Shemer, for two talents of silver, by Omri, king of Israel, who "built a city on the hill, and called the name of the city which he built after the name of the owner of the hill, Samaria" (I Kings 16:24). From that time until the captivity of the ten tribes—about two hundred years—it continued to be the capital.

During all this time it was the seat of idolatry (Isa. 9:9; Jer. 23:13, 14; Ezek. 16:46-55; Amos 6:1; Mic. 1:1). There Ahab built a temple to Baal (I Kings 16:32, 33; comp. II Kings 10:35). On the other hand, it was the scene of the ministry of the prophets Elijah and Elisha (q. v.). Jehu broke down the temple of Baal, but does not appear to have otherwise injured the city (II Kings 10:18-28). The city was twice besieged by the Syrians, about B. C. 863 (I Kings 20:1) and about B. C. 850 (II Kings 6:24-7:20); but on both occasions the siege was ineffectual, the latter time relief coming miraculously. It was taken in B. C. 721 by Shalmaneser's successor, Sargon, king of Assyria (18:9, 10), and the kingdom of the ten tribes destroyed. In 331 it yielded to Alexander the Great, who visited it on his way back from Egypt in order to punish the Samaritan murderers of the governor he had appointed over Coele-Syria. Ptolemy Lagos deemed it dangerous enough to have it dismantled before he gave over Coele-Syria to Antigonus; and, being rebuilt, it was again destroyed fifteen years later. It withstood a year's siege by John Hyrcanus, the Maccabee, before being taken by him. It was rebuilt by Gabinius, the successor of Pompey, Augustus gave Samaria to Herod, who fortified and embellished it, and named it Sebaste, the Greek for Augusta.

In the New Testament it is recorded (Acts 8:5) that Philip the deacon "went down to *the* city of Samaria," which more literally means "into a city of the Samaritans." Still it is likely that the evangelist would resort to the capital city. Thus ends the Bible history of Samaria.

(3) **Archaeology.** From 1908 to 1910 the site of Samaria was excavated by Harvard University under the direction of G. A. Reisner, D. G. Lyon and C. S. Fisher (cf. *Harvard Excavations at Samaria*, 1908-1910, 2 vols., 1924). From 1931 to 1933 excavation was continued by Harvard University, the Hebrew University of Jerusalem, the British Academy, the British School of Archaeology in Jerusalem and the Palestine Exploration Fund under J. W. Crowfoot's direction. Further work was done in 1935 (cf. J. W. Crowfoot, Kathleen M. Kenyon and E. L. Sukenik, *The Buildings at Samaria*, 1942). These various excavations have revealed the following periods: 1. The Omri-Ahab Era, Periods I and II. 2. The Jehu Era, Period III. 3. The eighth century when the city reached its acme of prosperity, Periods IV-VI. Stout walls from the Omri-Ahab Period and other fortifications reveal how Samaria could have held out against the Syrians (II Kings 6:24-30), and against the powerful Assyrians (II Kings 17:5). Large numbers of cisterns were also discovered, compensating for the lack of natural water supply. The famous Samaritan ostraca are usually placed in the reign of Jeroboam II in the eighth century. These inscribed pieces of pottery were recovered in one of the palace storehouses. They are accounts of royal revenue received in the form of oil and wine. Numerous stewards are mentioned recalling Biblical names such as Nimshi, Ahinoam and

396. Herodian Ruins, Samaria

Gomar (Gomer). Names of women found in the Bible occur. Many of the names contain Yahu as an element, indicating that theophorous names were used at this time. Also numerous ivories in the form of plaques or furniture inlays were recovered. Portrayed on the ivories are papyrus reeds, lotus, lions, bulls, sphinxes and Egyptian gods such as Isis and Horus. The high artistic quality and the Egyptian gods indicate strong foreign influence at this period. These ivories recall the "beds of ivory" and "houses of ivory" denounced by Amos (Amos 6:4; cf. I Kings 22:39).—*M. F. U.*

Sama′ria, Region of (Greek usually *Samareia*). This term includes all the tribes over which Jeroboam made himself king, whether east or west of Jordan. The expression "cities of Samaria" (I Kings 13:32) is used for the kingdom of the ten tribes, which did not receive this name till after the building of the city of Samaria as the capital of the kingdom and the residence of the kings of Israel (16:24). It is used elsewhere in the same sense; thus, by "Ephraim and the inhabitants of Samaria" is meant Israel (Isa. 9:9-12). Israel, Ephraim, and Samaria are equivalent terms in Hosea, who also calls the calf of Bethel "thy calf, O Samaria" (Hos. 8:5). In Amos 3:9 the "mountains of Samaria" are spoken of; and we find the expression in Ezekiel (16:53), the "captivity of Samaria and her daughter."

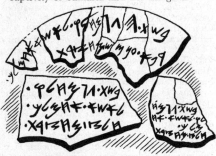

397. Hebrew Ostraca from Samaria (early eighth century B.C.)

Samar′itans (sȧ-măr′ĭ-tănz; Heb. *shōmrōnim*), a name found in the Old Testament only in II Kings 17:29. It is customary to refer "Samaritans" in this passage to the colonists brought by the king of Assyria in place of the deported Israelites; but the text seems rather to mean that these colonists put their gods into the houses of the high places which the "Samaritans," i. e., the former inhabitants of Samaria, had made for their own religious use. But the Samaritans of subsequent history and of the New Testament are the descendants of the colonists brought in by the king of Assyria.

1. **The Captor and the Captivity.** It was Shalmaneser V, who reigned five years, beginning with 727, who laid siege to Samaria; but it was taken by his successor, Sargon II, B. C. 721. At least it was under Sargon's supervision, for very soon after Shalmaneser's death his attention was claimed by Merodach-baladan, who had established himself as king at Babylon. Sargon carried off 27,290 inhabitants as he himself recounts. He took fifty chariots as "the portion of his royalty," and contented himself with the same tribute as "the former king." Thus it is plain that he neither desolated nor depopulated the land. But he put an end to its independence, and set over it an Assyrian governor. In 720 we find Samaria, with Arpad, Simyra, and Damascus, joining in the revolt headed by Hamath.

2. **Extent of the Captivity.** It must have been confined to Samaria and a small sur-

rounding region. In Hezekiah's time (II Chron. 30:11), in Josiah's (34:9), and even in Jeremiah's (Jer. 41:5) there were Israelites in the northern kingdom who clung to the worship of God at Jerusalem. The 27,290 captives taken away by Sargon may, indeed, have been increased by himself afterward or by other monarchs. But all the indications are that the depopulation was not thorough, and was limited to the city of Samaria and its vicinity. This would account for the fact that the Galilee of our Lord's day was a Jewish region. The Samaria of Josephus, indeed, embraced what was formerly the territory of Ephraim, but the Cuthaean Samaritans "possessed only a few towns and villages of this large area" and western Manasseh.

3. **Repeopling.** This work was not done all at once. In settling the affairs of that unquiet region more than one band of colonists was brought in. Heathen colonists were introduced by Sargon in 722 and again in B. C. 715 (II Kings 17:24), by Esarhaddon, B. C. 680 (Ezra 4:2), and finally by Asnapper (Osnapper), i. e., Ashurbanipal, the last great Assyrian emperor (669-626 B. C.) who added people from Elam, etc., to the population.

4. **Resultant Population.** The Samaritans were a mixed race with a heathen core (Ezra 4:2). Their blood would become more and more Hebraized by the addition of renegade Jews and by the intermarriage with surrounding Israelites, who would find among them the familiar worship of former times.

398. A Sunken Courtyard at Samaria

5. **Worship.** Since the priest who was sent to "teach them the manner of the God of the land" was of the Samaritan captivity, and not from Jerusalem (II Kings 17:27), their worship must have descended from that of Jeroboam. The schism headed by Jeroboam was not religious, but political (12:4, 16), and his object was to separate Israel not from God, but from Jerusalem (v. 27). His golden calves were designed as images of the God who brought them up out of the land of Egypt. The notion of plurality is not so clearly marked in Hebrew as in English (*hĭnnēh, lo!*), being an interjection ("Behold, thy gods!"). There is no sign of plurality, except the verb *hĕ′ĕlū.* But *′ĕlōhîm,* even when it refers to the one God, sometimes has a plural verb, and that in cases where we should not expect it (Gen. 20:13; 35:7; II Sam. 7:23, in reference to this very deliverance from Egypt; Psa. 58:12, a participle; see Gesenius,, *Heb.-Gr.,*

399. Mount Gerizim, Samaria

§ 146, 2, n. 2; Green, § 275, 3a). Thus, Jeroboam's sin may have been a violation not so much of the first commandment as of the second. Indeed, archaeological research suggests that the two golden calves served not as idols, but as supports for the invisible presence of Yahweh. This is indicated by popular contemporary Near Eastern iconography, where the gods of the heathen, such as Baal, are pictured enthroned on the back of a bull or some other animal. With all the Jewish horror of Jeroboam's worship, the charge is not usually that he introduced other gods (perhaps only in I Kings 14:9, where the reference is possibly to images; and II Chron. 11:15), but that it was schismatic (II Chron. 13:9) and irregular (I Kings 12:31-33). Now, while he decisively separated the people from Jerusalem, it would be altogether for his interest to conciliate them by making the new worship as much like the old as possible (in I Kings 12:32 note the phrase "like unto the feast that is in Judah"). For a few needful changes he might plausibly argue that David and Solomon had taken great liberties; that the temple with its burdensome cost was far enough from the simple tabernacle, for whose construction God himself had given minute directions; that Jerusalem had no special divine sanction; and finally that he himself had just as good a divine call as David and better than Solomon or Rehoboam. Putting all these things together, with what is said, under the next head, of the probability that copies of the Pentateuch would be preserved in the northern kingdom, we may be reasonably sure that Jeroboam's ritual would not be very far from that handed down from Moses. This would act as a purge on the imported polytheism of the transplanted peoples, but would result in little more than a dual worship—a mixture of paganism and Judaism.

6. **Samaritan Pentateuch.** Whether the northern kingdom would be likely, in separating from the Levitical worship, to carry the Pentateuch with it is a question which, in the lack of positive evidence, everyone must answer according to his own judgment. The tabernacle was most of the time in the territory which afterward belonged to the kingdom of Israel. It was in Shiloh till the time of Eli, B. C. about 1051 (I Sam. 4:3). Shiloh was long remembered as its resting place (Psa. 78:60; Jer. 7:12, 14; 26:6). At the close of David's reign, B. C. 960, it was no farther south than Gibeon (I Chron. 21:29), a little south of the border. The focus of the old worship thus having been in the northern kingdom, of course there would be copies of the ceremonial law there, and it is hardly conceivable that there should not be copies of the whole Pentateuch, if not more of the Bible, at least in the Levitical cities. It is therefor not impossible that the Samaritan Pentateuch came into the hands of the Samaritans as an inheritance from the ten tribes whom they succeeded. However, it is much more probable to conclude that it was introduced by Manasseh (comp. Josephus, *Ant.*, xi, 8, §§ 2, 4) at the time of the foundation of the Samaritan sanctuary on Mount Gerizim.

7. **First Discord Between Jews and Samaritans.** All that we know is told in Ezra, ch. 4. That the Samaritans who wished to join with the Jews are called "adversaries," may mean either that they were then seen to be adversaries in disguise, or that they were adversaries when the account was written. Perhaps the latter; for in the refusal no charge of hypocrisy was made against them. It was only that the right to build belonged to others, and that they could have no part in it. The genealogies were carefully kept (Ezra, ch. 8), and it is probable that considerations of birth were so prominent that there was no need of inquiry into anything else.

Were the Jews right? It is not for us to sit in judgment on the case. We can only inquire for our own instruction. We must believe that they knew their own business best, and presume that they were right. Yet there are some facts which cannot escape our notice. Their course in regard to aliens and children of mixed marriages, as shown in Ezra 10:3, and indicated in Neh. 13:1, 3 (comp. "forever," of v. 1, with "to the tenth generation" of Deut. 23:3), though natural and probably justifiable under the circumstances, was yet, so far as we know, somewhat in advance of what God had required. Aliens and slaves were allowed to eat the passover if they were circumcised (Exod. 12:44, 48, 49; *see* Moabites).

8. **Subsequent History.** (1) **Ancient.** The relation between Jew and Samaritan was one of hostility. The expulsion of Manasseh by Nehemiah for an unlawful marriage, and his building of the Samaritan temple on Mount Gerizim by permission of Darius Nothus, took place about 409 B. C. The inhospitality (Luke 9:52, 53) and hostility of the Samaritans induced many pilgrims from the north to Jerusalem to go on the east of the Jordan. The Samaritans sometimes, by rival flames, perplexed the watchers for the signal fires which announced the rising of the paschal moon from Mount Olivet to the Euphrates. They rejected all the Old Testament except the Pentateuch, of which they claimed to have an older copy than the Jews, and to observe the precepts better. The Jews repaid hate with hate. They cast suspicion on the Samaritan copy of the law, and disallowed the steadfast claim of the Samaritans to Jewish birth (John 4:12). Social and commercial relations, though they could not be broken off (4:8), were reduced to the lowest possible figure.

"The Samaritan was publicly cursed in their synagogues—could not be adduced as a witness in the Jewish courts—could not be admitted to any sort of proselytism, and was thus, so far as the Jew could affect his position, excluded from eternal life." It ought to be said, however, that the rabbinic regulations for the intercourse of Jews and Samaritans varied greatly at different times, and that the older Talmudical authorities incline to

400. Samaritan Pentateuch Used on Mount Gerizim

treat the Samaritans more like Jews. In 332 the Samaritans desired Alexander the Great to exempt them from tribute in the Sabbatical year, on the ground that, as Israelites, they did not cultivate the land during that year. Becoming satisfied of "the hollowness of their pretensions," he deferred granting their request (Josephus, *Ant.*, xi, 8, § 6, comp. ix, 14, § 3), and on account of their conduct besieged and destroyed Samaria. John Hyrcanus took "Shechem and Gerizim, and the nation of the Cuthaeans, who dwelt at that temple which resembled the temple which was at Jerusalem, and which Alexander permitted Sanballat, the general of his army, to build for the sake of Manasseh, who was son-in-law to Jaddua the high priest, as we have formerly related, which temple was now deserted two hundred years after it was built" (Jos., *Ant.*, ix, 13, §1; as for Manasseh, comp. *Ant.*, xi, 7, §§ 1, 2). The temple on Gerizim was "deserted," B. C. 130. This gives about 330 for the date of its building. The "Sanballat the Horonite" (*see* Horonite) of the Bible was contemporary with Nehemiah, 445 B. C., and was father-in-law of one of the sons of Joiada, the son of Eliashib, the high priest (Neh. 13:28). But the Sanballat of Josephus was a Cuthaean, of the same race as the Samaritans, and was sent to Samaria by Darius Codomanus, the last king of

Persia (d. 330). He was father-in-law to Manasseh, the brother of the high priest Jaddua, who was the son of John, the son of Judas, the son of Eliashib (Jos., *Ant.*, xi, 7 §§ 1, 2). There must, therefore, have been two Sanballats, unless Josephus has confused the account. In the persecution under Antiochus, 170 B. C., the Samaritans disowned their relation to the Jews, and consecrated their temple on Mount Gerizim to Jupiter. (2) **Later history.** After the destruction of Samaria by Alexander the Great, Shechem became more prominent, and there, after the conquest by John Hyrcanus, already alluded to, they built a second temple. With lapse of time they reacted from their polytheism into an "ultra Mosaism." In our Lord's time they still preserved their identity after seven centuries; and "though their limits had been gradually contracted, and the rallying place of their religion on Mount Gerizim had been destroyed one hundred and sixty years before by John Hyrcanus (130 B. C.) and though Samaria (the city) had been again and again destroyed, and though their territory had been the battlefield of Syria and Egypt, still preserved their nationality, still worshipped from Shechem and their other impoverished settlements toward their sacred hill; still retained their nationality, and could not coalesce with the Jews." In the 1st century the Samaritans were numerous enough to excite the fears of Pilate, whose severity toward them cost him his office (Jos., *Ant.*, xviii, 4, § 1), and of Vespasian, under whom over ten thousand were slaughtered after refusing to surrender (B. J., iii, 7, § 32). They greatly increased in numbers, particularly under Dositheus, about the time of Simon Magus. In the 4th century they were among the chief adversaries of Christianity. They were severely chastised by the emperor Zeno, and thence were hardly noticed till the latter half of the 16th century, when correspondence was opened with them by Joseph Scaliger. Two of their letters to him and one to Job Sudolf are still extant, and are full of interest. Shechem is represented by the modern *Nâblus*, corresponding to Neapolis, which was built by Vespasian, a little west of the old town. Here has been a settlement of about two hundred, who have observed the law and kept the Passover on Mount Gerizim "with an exactness of minute ceremonial which the Jews have long since intermitted." —W. H., revised by *M. F. U.*

401. Samaritan Priests Celebrate
Passover, 1956

Sa'mekh (sä'měk), 15th letter of the Hebrew alphabet, heading the 15th section of Psalm 119.

Sam'gar-ne'bo (săm'gár-nē'bô; apparently from Akk. *Shumgir-nabū, Nebo, be gracious*), one of the officers of Nebuchadnezzar's army present at the taking of Jerusalem (Jer. 39:3), B. C. 587. As in v. 13, the chief of the eunuchs is called *Nebu-shasban*, it has been supposed that Nebu-sarsechim is only another name of the same person, and that Samgar is merely the name of his office.

Sam'lah (săm'lá; *a garment*), one of the kings of Edom before the establishment of the Israelitish monarchy (Gen. 36:36, 37; I Chron. 1:47, 48). He was the successor of Hadad (Hadar), and was of the city of Masrekah.

Sa'mos (sā'mŏs), a noted island in the Aegean Sea, near the coast of Lydia, in Asia Minor, separated by a narrow strait, in its narrowest part not quite a mile wide. When Paul touched there on his voyage from Greece to Syria (Acts 20:15) it was a free city in the province of Asia. It was the seat of the worship of Juno, and her temple, called the Heraeon, was enriched by some of the finest works of art known in Greece. Its chief manufacture was pottery, of fine red clay, the Samian ware being celebrated all over the civilized world. Its wine ("Levantine") ranks high.

Sam'son (săm'sŏn), the renowned judge and deliverer of Israel.

1. **Name and Family**. (Heb. *shĭmshōn, little sun*). Samson was the son of Manoah, of Zorah, in the tribe of Dan, whose birth was foretold to his parents by an angel of the Lord, accompanied with the announcement that he was to be a Nazarite from his nativity (Judg. 13:2-5, 24).

2. **Personal History**. Samson grew up under special influences of the Spirit of God, and at last was impelled to commence the conflict with the Philistines, which only terminated with his death. (1) **Marries a Philistine.** When he was about twenty years old Samson saw at Timnath a daughter of the Philistines who pleased him, and on his return asked his parents to take her for him as a wife. They were averse to such a marriage, but Samson persisted, being convinced that it would in some way aid him in visiting vengeance upon the Philistines. On his first visit to his future bride he slew a lion with his hands, and when he went to espouse her he found the skeleton occupied by a swarm of bees. At the wedding feast he proposed a riddle, conforming to the oriental custom of furnishing entertainment to the guests. Unable to solve it, they urged his wife to secure the answer from him and inform them. He yielded, but, seized with indignation, went to Ashkelon, slew thirty Philistines, and gave the changes of garments to those who had solved the riddle. He returned to his father's house, and his wife was given to his companion (Judg. 14:1-20). (2) **His revenge.** Samson soon after visited his wife, but was refused admission to her by her father. He interpreted the treatment which he had received from his father-in-law as the effect of the disposition generally of the Philistines toward the Israelites, and resolved to avenge his wrong upon the whole nation. He

secured three hundred foxes (jackals), and, by tying firebrands to their tails, set fire to the grain fields, vineyards, and olive yards of his enemies (15:1-5). The Philistines retorted by burning Samson's wife and father-in-law; and this provocation so aroused Samson that he smote them "hip and thigh" (i. e., with a cruel and unsparing slaughter), after which he went down and dwelt in the cleft of the rock Etam (15:6-8). (3) **Delivered up to the Philistines.** The Philistines came to avenge themselves, and encamped in Judah, and the Judeans, instead of recognizing Samson as a deliverer, went to Etam, to the number of three thousand, for the purpose of binding him and handing him over to their enemies. He consented on condition that they themselves would not kill him. They bound him with two new cords, and brought him to Lehi (*lĕhî, a jaw*), and in this apparently helpless condition delivered him to the Philistines. When he heard their shout of joy his preternatural strength suddenly put itself forth, and, snapping the cords asunder, he seized upon a fresh jawbone of an ass, and smote therewith a thousand men. Casting away his weapon, he called the name of the place Ramath-lehi (*the jawbone height*). Weary and athirst, Samson, conscious that he was fighting for the cause of Jehovah, prayed unto the Lord, who caused a stream to flow from the rock, which Samson called En-hakkore (i. e., the *well of him that prayed*). Samson drank and was revived again (15:9-20). (4) **At Gaza.** After this Samson went to the city of Gaza, and became intimate with a woman of loose character residing there. His presence being made known, the Gazites fastened the city gates, intending to kill him in the morning, when, as they supposed, he would leave the house. But at midnight Samson arose, and, breaking away bolts, bars, and hinges, carried the gates to the top of a neighboring hill looking toward Hebron (16:1-3), B. C. about 1070. (5) **Delilah.** After this Samson became infatuated with a woman of Sorek, named Delilah, through whom the Philistine princes determined to get possession of his person. They supposed that his supernatural strength arose from an amulet that he wore, and offered to Delilah a tempting bribe if she would discover to them his secret. She entered into the agreement, and used all her arts and blandishments to persuade Samson to reveal it to her. He deceived her three times by false statements, but at last, teased into compliance, "he told her all his heart," and said, "If I be shaven, then my strength will go from me, and I shall become weak, and be like any other man." Delilah, satisfied that Samson had spoken the truth this time, sent word to the Philistines, who came, bringing the promised reward. Then she made him sleep, his head upon her lap, cut off his hair, and gave the preconcerted signal, "Philistines be upon thee, Samson." Forsaken by Jehovah, he fell an easy prey to his enemies. (6) **Imprisonment and death.** The Philistines put out Samson's eyes, and led him, bound with fetters of brass, to Gaza, where he was made to grind grain in the prison. As this was an employment which in the East usually devolved on women, to assign it to such a man as Samson was virtually to reduce him to the lowest state of degradation and shame. After a time the unshorn locks of Samson recovered their growth, the Philistines for some reason being inattentive thereto, and with it such a profound repentance seems to have wrought in

402. Philistine Prisoners Being Led into the Presence of Raamses III

his heart as virtually reinvested him with the character and powers he had lost. His captivity was regarded by the Philistines as a great victory, and he seems to have been kept by them, like a wild beast, for show and insult. On the occasion of a sacrificial festival to Dagon, to whom they ascribed the capture of their enemy, they brought Samson from the prison that he might make sport for them. Determined to use his recovered strength against his enemies, a large number of whom crowded the building, Samson persuaded the attendant to place him between the pillars upon which the roof rested. After a brief prayer he grasped the pillars, and, leaning forward with resistless force, brought down the building, causing his own death and that of three thousand Philistines. His relatives came to Gaza, took away his body, and placed it in the burying place of his father, between Zorah and Eshtaol (16:21-30). He judged Israel B. C. about 1070. Though a mournful victory, it was still a victory, and a pledge to Israel that their temporary backslidings and defeats, if sincerely repented of and improved, would lead to ultimate triumph.

3. **Character.** The mention of Samson's name in the list (Heb. 11:32) of ancient worthies "who had by faith obtained an excellent repute," warrants us in a favorable estimate of his character as a whole. And yet the inspired narrative records infirmities that must forever mar the luster of his heroic deeds. In Samson the Nazarite we see a man towering in supernatural strength through his firm faith in, and confident reliance upon, the gift

of God committed to him. On the other hand we see in Samson an adventurous, foolhardy, passionate, and willful man, dishonoring and frittering away the God-given power by making it subservient to his own lusts.

NOTE—*Samson's strength.* The superhuman strength of Samson did not really lie in his hair, but in the fact of his *relation* to God as a Nazarite, of which his unshorn hair was the *mark* or *sign.* As soon as he broke away from his Nazariteship by sacrificing his hair, which he wore in honor of the Lord, Jehovah departed from him, and with Jehovah went his strength. *Overthrow of Dagon's temple.* "So far as the fact itself is concerned, there is no ground for questioning the possibility of Samson's bringing down the whole building by pulling down two middle columns. . . . In all probability we have to picture this temple of Dagon as resembling the modern Turkish kiosks, viz., as consisting of a spacious hall, the roof of which rested in front upon four columns, two of them standing at the ends, and two close together in the center. Under this hall the leading men of the Philistines celebrated a sacrificial meal, while the people were assembled upon the top of the roof, which was surrounded by a balustrade'" (K. and D., *Com.,* in loc.).

Sam′uel.—1. **Name and Family.** (săm′ū-ĕl; *asked* or *heard of God*). The son of Elkanah (*q. v.*), a Levite (I Chron. 6:1-28; 33-38) of Ramathaim-zophim, on the mountains of Ephraim, and Hannah, to whom he was born in response to her earnest prayer (I Sam. 1:1-20), B. C. probably 1080.

2. **Personal History.** (1) **As a child.** When Hannah prayed for a son she vowed to dedicate him to the Lord as a Nazarite (I Sam. 1:11), and as soon as he was weaned brought him to Shiloh and gave him over to Eli (1:24-28). Thus Samuel served as a boy before the Lord, clothed with an ephod, and receiving every year from his mother a mantle reaching down to his feet, such as was worn only by high personages, or women, over the other dress (2:11, 18, 19). (2) **Call.** At the time when Samuel served the Lord before Eli, both as a boy and as a young man, "the word of the Lord was precious; there was no open vision." A revelation from God presupposing susceptibility on the part of men, the unbelief and disobedience of the people might restrain the fulfillment of this and all similar promises, and God might even withdraw his word to punish the idolatrous nation. The word of the Lord was then issued to Samuel for the first time. While sleeping in his place, probably in the court of the tabernacle, where cells were built for the priests and Levites, Samuel heard his name called. Supposing it was Eli who had called him, he hastened to receive his commands, but Eli told him to lie down again, as he had not called him. When, however, this was repeated a second and a third time, Eli perceived that the Lord had called Samuel, and instructed him how to act should he hear the voice again. The Lord revealed to Samuel the doom of Eli's house, which he reluctantly made known the next morning to the aged priest. Other revelations followed, and their exact fulfillment secured to Samuel a reputation for trustworthiness that made Shiloh an oracle (3:1-21). (3) **Judge.** After the disastrous defeat of the Israelites by the Philistines (4:1, sq.) Samuel does not appear again in history for a period of twenty years. During the most of this time the ark of the Lord had rested in Kirjath-jearim, and all the house of Israel lamented after the Lord (7:1,

2). Samuel, who had learned that loyalty to Jehovah was necessary to secure to Israel deliverance from its foes, issued a proclamation exposing the sin of idolatry, and urging religious amendment. He summoned the tribes to assemble at Mizpeh, to spend a day in penitence and prayer. At this assembly Samuel seems to have been elected, or in some way recognized, as judge (7:3-6), B. C. 1050. (4) **Eben-ezer.** When the Philistines heard of the gathering at Mizpeh they made war upon the Israelites, who in their fear entreated Samuel not to cease to pray for their deliverance. The Philistines advanced while Samuel was engaged in sacrifice and prayer, but were thrown into confusion by a terrific thunderstorm sent by Jehovah. This was an unprecedented phenomenon in that climate at that season of the year. The enemies of Israel were defeated, and pursued to a place called Beth-car. As a memorial of the victory, Samuel placed a stone between Mizpeh and Shen, and named the place Eben-ezer (*stone of help*) (7:7-12). (5) **Judicial labors.** Samuel had now the entire government of the nation, and visited, in the discharge of his official duties, Beth-el, Gilgal, and Mizpeh. His own residence was in his native city, Ramah (or Ramathaim), where he judged Israel, and also built an altar to conduct the religious affairs of the nation. This was contrary to the letter of the law, but the prophets seem to have had power to dispense with ordinary usage; and, moreover, the tabernacle at Shiloh had lost what was most essential to it as a sanctuary since it had been despoiled of the ark by the Philistines (7:15-17). (6) **The monarchy.** Samuel had appointed his sons as judges in his old age, and as they had perverted justice the elders of Israel entreated him to appoint them a king to judge them after the manner of all the nations (8:1-5). The proposed change of government displeased Samuel; nevertheless he laid the matter before Jehovah in prayer, and was instructed to accede to their request, though not without setting before them the perils and tyranny of a monarchical government (8:6-19). The people were sent to their homes, and Samuel proceeded to the election of a sovereign. Saul was pointed out by Jehovah as the man whom he was to set apart as king of Israel, and was anointed and saluted as monarch (8:19-10:8). After Samuel had privately anointed Saul king, he made provision for his recognition as such by the people. He summoned the people to Mizpeh, but before proceeding to the election itself charged the people with their sin in rejecting God by their demand for a king. He then caused the sacred lot to be taken, and the lot fell upon Saul, who was formally introduced to the people (10:17-25). (7) **Renewal of the monarchy.** There were certain worthless people ("children of Belial") who were opposed to Saul's elevation to the throne, but the victory of the Ammonites so influenced the people in his favor that Samuel convened the people at Gilgal "to renew the kingdom." This consisted, probably, of a ratification of the new constitution and the installation of the sovereign. This solemn service was concluded by

the farewell address of Samuel, in which he handed over the office of judge to the king. The address was confirmed by the miraculous sign of a thunderstorm in answer to the prayer of Samuel. It was then wheat harvest, which occurs in Palestine between the middle of May and the middle of June, during which time it scarcely ever rains (11:14-12:25). (8) **Reproves Saul.** Although Saul had begun his reign, Samuel continued to exercise his functions as prophet and judge. He judged Israel "all the days of his life" (7:15), and from time to time crossed the path of the king. Saul was engaged in war against the Philistines, and having mustered his forces at Gilgal awaited the coming of Samuel to sacrifice unto Jehovah. As Samuel did not appear at the time appointed, Saul, in his anxiety lest the people should lose heart and desert him, resolved to offer the sacrifice himself—a fearful violation of the national law. The offering of the sacrifice was hardly finished, when Samuel arrived, and, rebuking Saul for his presumption, made known to him the short continuance of his kingdom. He then left him and went unto Gibeah of Benjamin (13:1-15). (9) **Parts with Saul.** Later we find Samuel charging Saul with the extirpation of the Amalekites, who had attacked, in a most treacherous manner, the Israelites on their journey from Egypt to Sinai. Saul was instructed to smite man and beast with the ban (i. e., to put all to death); but he not only left Agag, the king, alive, but spared the best of the cattle, and merely executed the ban upon such as were worthless. Samuel announced to him that his disobedience had secured for him his rejection by Jehovah. Saul entreated Samuel to remain and worship with him, but the latter refused, and turned to depart. Saul endeavored to retain the prophet by force, and in the struggle the mantle of Samuel was torn, in which Samuel saw the omen of the rending away of the kingdom from Saul. Samuel yielded to the renewed entreaty of Saul that he would honor him by his presence before the elders and the people, and remained while Saul worshipped. After Saul had prayed, Samuel directed him to bring Agag, king of the Amalekites, whom he slew before the altar of Jehovah, and then returned to his own home at Ramah. From that time they met no more, although Samuel did not cease to grieve for Saul (15:1-35). (10) **Anoints David.** Since Saul had been rejected by God, and the government was not to remain in his family, it was necessary, in order to prevent strife and confusion, that his successor should be appointed before the death of the king. Samuel was therefore instructed by the Lord to go to Bethlehem, and anoint David, the youngest son of Jesse, as the chosen one. The sacrificial meal over, Samuel returned to Ramah (16:1-13). (11) **Befriends David.** When Saul, in his insane rage, endeavored to slay David, the latter fled to Samuel, and they two went and dwelt in Naioth. The king pursued David, but when he came to Naioth and saw Samuel and the prophets, the Spirit of the Lord came upon him also, and he was obliged to relinquish the attempt to seize him (19:18-24). (12) **Death.** In 25:1 we have a very brief account of the death of Samuel, and the great mourning made for him by the Israelites, who buried him in his own house (B. C. about 1017). The expression "his house" means the house in which he lived, with the court belonging to it, where Samuel was placed in a tomb erected especially for him. The place long pointed out as his tomb is the height, most conspicuous of all in the neighborhood of Jerusalem, immediately above the town of Gibeon, known to the Crusaders as "Montjoye," as the spot from whence they first saw Jerusalem, now called *Neby Samwil*, "the prophet Samuel."

3. **Character.** In studying the character of Samuel it is impossible not to be impressed with his *piety*. Dedicated to the service of God by his mother, that service never became an irksome routine. God was the center around which he, as well as heaven, turned. In all his difficulties he repaired to God for counsel. In all his acts and decisions he was guided by the word of Jehovah. His advice to the Israelites was the motto of his own life, "Turn not aside from following the Lord, but serve the Lord with all your heart." Nor was his *patriotism* less apparent. His object was not the possession of power, but the welfare of his people. Place, honor, and power were not sought by him, but he by them. And when the people, without respect to his gray hairs and long service, called upon him to resign his office there was no feeble cry for pity, nor peevish reproach for their ingratitude. He challenges inspection of his character and official life; remonstrates with Israel on their choice as being an act of disloyalty not against himself, but Jehovah; and warns them of the evils which would result from the establishment of a monarchy. And when Saul was selected as his successor, rising above the weaknesses of our nature, Samuel received him with the utmost courtesy, and treated him with even paternal kindness. There is no more magnanimous thing in history.

NOTE—(1) *Samuel's artifice*, I Sam. 16:2. The fear of Samuel on this occasion can only be explained on the supposition that Saul was already given up to the power of the evil spirit, so that the very worst might be dreaded if he discovered that Samuel had anointed another king. As to the artifice employed, "there was no untruth in this, for Samuel was really about to conduct a sacrificial festival, and was to invite Jesse's family to it, and then anoint the one whom Jehovah should point out to him as the chosen one. It was simply a concealment of the principal object of his mission from any who might make inquiry about it, because they themselves had not been invited" (Keil, *Com.*, in loc.). (2) *Samuel's ghost (see* Art. SAUL). (3) Acts 3:24, "All the prophets from Samuel, and those that follow after." Peter, doubtless, thus spoke because Samuel was the first of the regular succession of prophets. Moses, Miriam, and Deborah, perhaps Ehud, had been prophets, but it was only from Samuel that the continuous succession was unbroken.

Samuel, Books of. The name of these two books can only find a logical explanation in the fact that Samuel was the principal character in the first part and anointed the other two principal characters. I and II Samuel were originally a single book. The Septuagint translators divided them into two books called I and II Kings. The other books of Kings, which deal with the later historical period, were called III and IV Kings. This designation was carried over into the Old Latin and the Vulgate. The same division was transferred to the Hebrew Bible in 1448, but with the difference that each book retained the title which it possessed in the Hebrew manuscript, and I-IV Kings became I and II Samuel and I and II Kings.

1. **Purposes.** These two historical books carry on Israelite history from the closing years of the era of the Judges to the establishment of David's kingdom. They also delineate Samuel's personal history. The moral failure of the priesthood and judgeship is recorded in the death of Eli and his sons. The rise of the prophetic office alongside the kingly office is set forth. Samuel, the prophet-judge, is portrayed as the founder of both, as well as of the schools of the prophets (I Sam. 19:20; II Kings 2:3-5). Samuel anointed both Saul and David. The book recounts David's accession to the kingship at Hebron and later at Jerusalem after its conquest (II Sam. 5:6-12). The great Davidic covenant (II Sam. 7:8-17) is set forth and forms a basis of all subsequent kingdom truth.

2. **Outline.**
Part I. Samuel as Judge, I Sam. chaps. 1-7
   a. His birth and boyhood, 1:1-2:10
   b. Eli's rejection and Samuel's call, 2:11-3:21
   c. Philistine domination, 4:1-7:1
   d. Samuel as judge, 7:2-7
Part II. Saul as King, I Sam. chap. 8-II Sam. chap. 1
   a. Demand for a king, 8:1-22
   b. Choice of Saul, 9:1-11:15
   c. Samuel's farewell address, 12:1-25
   d. Saul's Philistine war, 13:1-14:52
   e. His disobedience and rejection, 15:1-35
   f. David's anointing and call to Saul's court, 16:1-23
   g. David and Goliath, 17:1-58
   h. David's flight from Saul's court, 18:1-20:43
   i. David's wanderings, 21:1-30:31
   j. Saul's death, 31:1-13
   k. David's lament, II Sam. 1:1-27
Part III. David as King, II Sam. chaps. 2-24
   a. His coronation over Judah, 2:1-7
   b. He establishes national religious unity, 2:8-6:23
   c. The Davidic Covenant, 7:1-29
   d. David's wars, 8:1-10:19
   e. David's sin and repentance, 11:1-12:31
   f. The crimes of Amnon and Absalom, 13:1-14:33
   g. Absalom's rebellion, 15:1-19:8
   h. David's restoration, 19:9-20:26
   i. The famine, 21:1-14
   j. Roster of heroes, 21:15-22
   k. David's last words, 22:1-23:7
   l. His heroes, 23:8-39
   m. His census and punishment, 24:1-25

3. **Authorship.** The book is anonymous. In all probability the author was a prophet in the monarchial period who employed earlier sources left by Samuel, Gad, Nathan (I Chron. 29:29) and possibly others. This is suggested by the fact that the work possesses unity as well as plan and purpose and is thus to be regarded as the production of a single

author or compiler. The date of its composition is very likely to be placed not later than David's reign. That the book ends just previous to David's decease suggests that it was written at that period. The reference to Judah and Israel (I Sam. 27:6) need not rule out this date since such a distinction prevailed as early as the Davidic period before the consolidation of the monarchy (I Sam. 18:6; II Sam. 2:10; 24:1).

4. Composition and Date. Otto Eissfeldt, *Einleitung*, p. 306, 307; *Die Komposition der Samuelisbeucher*, (1931) disconnects the text into three sources, L, J and E, which are regarded as continuations of the sources of the heptateuch. This theory has not been widely received. It is commonly held that the books of Samuel consist of at least two principal sources, J, the earlier, about the tenth century B. C. and E, the latter, about the eighth century B. C. (R. Pfeiffer, *Intr.*, pp. 341-365). The relationship of these documents is claimed to be similar to J and E in the Pentateuch and the Judges, if not a continuation of these documents, as K. Budde maintained. It is claimed that in the seventh century these two sources were united and allegedly contain contradictions, conflations, differences in style, etc. Later a deuteronomic editor of the sixth century deleted certain portions contrary to his religious convictions, but these were supposedly subsequently restored. The critical theory is to be rejected because it is at variance with the unity of the books, because it makes out the compiler or editor to be a mere blunderer. It is unsound in insisting that differences of viewpoint are evidences of variety of authorship. The critical argument that style and diction indicate composite authorship is weak and inconclusive. (For discussion see Merrill F. Unger, *Introductory Guide to the O. T.*, 1951, pp. 294-297; E. J. Young, *Intr.*, 1949, pp. 173-183).— *M. F. U.*

Sanbal′lat (săn-băl′ăt; cf. Akk. *Sin;* the moongod; *has given life*). He is called "Sanballat the Horonite" (Neh. 2:10, 19; 13:28). This scarcely means that he was from Horonaim in Moab, but more likely that he was a resident of Beth-horon in Samaria. All that we know of him from Scripture is that he had apparently some civil or military command in Samaria, in the service of Artaxerxes (4:2), and that, from the moment of Nehemiah's arrival in Judea, he set himself to oppose every measure for the welfare of Jerusalem and was a constant adversary to the Tirshatha, the official title of the Persian governor of Judah, borne by Nehemiah (Neh. 8:9; 10:1). His companions in this hostility were Tobiah the Ammonite and Geshem the Arabian (2:19; 4:7), B. C. 445. The only other incident in his life is his alliance with the high priest's family by the marriage of his daughter with one of the grandsons of Eliashib (13:28), which, by the similar connection formed by Tobiah the Ammonite (13:4), appears to have been part of a settled policy concerted between Eliashib and the Samaritan faction. The expulsion from the priesthood of the guilty son of Joiada by Nehemiah must have still further widened the breach between him

and Sanballat, and between the two parties in the Jewish state. Here, however, the scriptural narrative ends—owing, probably, to Nehemiah's return to Persia—and with it likewise our knowledge of Sanballat.

Sanctification (Gr. *hagiasmos*, *separation, a setting apart*). The Hebrew term *qādăsh*, rendered sanctify, has a corresponding meaning. The dominant idea of sanctification, therefore, is separation from the secular and sinful, and setting apart for a sacred purpose. As the holiness of God means his separation from all evil (*see* Holiness of God), so sanctification, in the various Scripture applications of the term, has a kindred lofty significance.

In the Old Testament economy, things, places, times, as well as persons, were sanctified, i. e., consecrated to holy purposes (see Gen. 2:3; Exod. 13:2; 40:10-13, etc.). Connected with this were the Mosaic rites of purification (see, e. g. Num. 6:11; Lev. 22:16, 32; Heb. 9:13). These rites, however, when applied to persons in a ceremonial and legal sense, were efficacious only in a ceremonial and legal sense, and did not extend to the purifying of the moral and spiritual nature. They were symbolical, and thus were intended not only to remind the Jew of the necessity of spiritual cleansing, but also of the gracious purpose of God to actually accomplish the work. So David prayed not only "Purge me with hyssop, and I shall be clean," but also "Create in me a clean heart, O God, and renew a right spirit within me" (Psa. 51:7-10).

While in the Old Testament, as well as the New, men are sometimes called upon to sanctify themselves, i. e., to consecrate themselves truly to God (see Exod. 19:22; Lev. 11:44; 20:7, 8; I Pet. 3:15), the thought everywhere prevails that inward cleansing is the work of God. *See* Holy Spirit.

Sanctification, Entire. Is it the privilege of believers to be wholly sanctified in this life? The doctrine of the Roman Catholic Church is that baptism, rightly administered, washes away not only guilt, but also depravity of every kind; and thus, in its own peculiar way, that Church answers the question in the affirmative (*see* Baptism). Among Protestant theologians there is wide difference of belief; and there are undoubtedly greater differences of statement, because of confusion in the use of terms. We have space only to indicate in a most general way the two leading views, and to add a few suggestions for guidance.

(1) **The Calvinistic view** is that sanctification is imperfect in this life. Corruption of nature remains even in the regenerate so that during this life no man is able to live without sin. For formal expression of this doctrine the reader is referred to the Westminster Confession and to the Larger Catechism of the Presbyterian Church.

(2) **The Methodist view**, on the other hand, despite various shades of opinion and form of statement, is that entire sanctification in a true and scriptural sense is attainable in this life; and accordingly Christians may arrive at a state of spiritual purity in which they are able to remain free from condemnation. This view is in agreement with the Calvinistic in regarding sanctification as distinct from re-

generation (*see* Regeneration). But it is in strongest contrast thereto in regarding the work of spiritual purification as one that may be wrought instantaneously, and in the present life. It should be said that the essential features of Methodist doctrine are held by many other denominations.

(3) **Summary N. T. Statement.** The N. T. presents the doctrine of sanctification in three aspects: *positional, experiential* and *ultimate. Positional* sanctification is the possession of everyone "in Christ." The great doctrinal epistles of the N. T. first present the marvels of saving grace manifested in the believer's position and then close with an appeal for life consonant with this divinely wrought position (Rom. 12:1; Eph. 4:1; Col. 3:1). *Positional* sanctification is just as complete for the weakest and youngest believer as it is for the strongest and oldest. It depends only upon one's union with and position "in Christ." All believers are "saints" and are "sanctified" (Acts 20:32; I Cor. 1:2; I Cor. 6:11; Heb. 10:10, 14; Jude 1:1). First Corinthians presents proof that imperfect believers are nevertheless positionally sanctified and therefore "saints." The Corinthian Christians were carnal in life (I Cor. 5:1, 2; 6:1-8) but they are twice said to have been "sanctified" (I Cor. 1:2 and 6:11). Thus this positional aspect of sanctification is absolutely essential if the doctrine as a whole is to be clearly understood.

Experiential. The basis of *experiential* sanctification, or actual holiness of life, is positional sanctification or what one is in Christ. Only those "in Christ," that is, regenerate and thus concomitantly sanctified, are candidates for experiential sanctifications. This phase of sanctification is effected by faith which reckons upon one's position in Christ (Rom. 6:1-10). One's position is true whether or not he reckons or counts it as true. But it becomes *experientially real* only in proportion as one reckons it to be true (Rom. 6:11).

Ultimate. This is glorification or complete conformity to Christ at His coming (I John 3:1-3; Rom. 8:29, 30; Jude 1:24, 25).— E. McCC., revised by *M. F. U.*

Sanctuary, a sacred place of resort and worship. Israel's early sanctuary was at Shiloh, which was the center of the nation's religious institutions after the conquest. About this central shrine the twelve tribes were grouped. The close parallel between this institution and the amphictyonies which were found in other Mediterranean lands a few centuries later has been set forth by Martin Noth, *Das System der Zwoelf Staemme Israels*, 1930, pp. 39-60. Classical writers report numerous amphictyonies of which a number are explicitly stated to have had twelve tribes. The best known is the famous Delphic amphictyony traceable back at least to the eighth century B. C. Characteristic of these systems was a central sanctuary which formed a bond by which the political structure was cemented together. The Danish excavations at Shiloh have revealed evidences of the destruction of Israel's sanctuary by the Philistines c. 1050 B. C. Shiloh was recognized by the Israelites as their inter-tribal focus from about 1375 B. C. (cf. Judg. 20:26-28; I Sam. 1:3f). Other ancient Near Eastern countries

had their great central sanctuary to which pilgrimages were made. Nineveh in Assyria and Nippur in Babylonia were such places of religious resort during the third quarter of the second millennium. The temple of Sin in Harran and Belit-ekalli in Qatna were popular in the eighteenth century B. C., as shown by the Mari Tablets. The temple of Baaltis in Byblus received votive offerings from Egypt for many centuries. Other shrines in early Israel were at Gibeon, Bethel, Gilgal, Dan and presumably at Beersheba. Possibly every Israelite town had at least one place where sacrifice might conveniently be offered to the Lord. Such a meeting-place was called a *bamah*, a Canaanite word meaning "back" or "ridge." The Conway High Place at Petra, excavated by W. F. Albright in 1934, belongs to the circular processional type and is to be compared to pre-Islamic sanctuaries. The Great High Place of Petra, discovered by George L. Robinson in 1900, and numerous other sites, were clearly intended for sacrificial feasts in the open air. Several of them possess rock-cut dining rooms with couches. Rustic *bamoth* were customarily built on hills or under trees, ostensibly for the purpose of catching the cool west wind and obtaining shelter from the sun. At these places of religious resort were held festal gatherings on new moons, Sabbaths and other occasions. Sacrifices of sheep, goats and other cattle were made as well as offerings of grain, wine, oil, flax, wool, figs and raisin cakes. Gifts were dispensed to the priests and Levites who had charge of the place or consumed in picnic fashion by the worshippers. (cf. W. F. Albright, *Archaeology and the Religion of Israel*, 1942, pp. 102-107) When the temple was constructed at Jerusalem by Solomon it became the religious mecca of all the Israelites.—*M. F. U.*

See Holy Place; Tabernacle; Temple.

Sand (Heb. *ḥōl, whirling*). Small loose bits of disintegrating rocks, found abundantly along the southern shores of the Mediterranean and conspicuous in the shifting dunes of the wilderness and desert regions of Arabia, Egypt and Palestine.

Figurative. The aggregate sand of the seashore is often used to express a very great multitude; thus God promised Abraham and Jacob to multiply their posterity as the stars of heaven and the sand of the sea (Gen. 22:17; 32:12). Job (6:3) compares the weight of his misfortunes to that of the sand of the sea; and Solomon says (Prov. 27:3), "A stone is heavy, and the sand weighty; but a fool's wrath is heavier than them both." The omnipotence of God is expressed by his placing the sand for the bound of the sea (Jer. 5:22). The shifting sand is used as symbolic of instability (Matt. 7:26).

Sandal (Gr. *sandalion*, representing the Heb. *nă'ăl*, rendered *shoe* in the A. V.). The sandal, apparently the article used by the Hebrews for protecting the feet, consisted simply of a sole attached to the foot by thongs. The Gr. *hupodēma* properly applies to the sandal exclusively, as it means what is bound *under* the foot.

1. **Material,** etc. We learn from the Talmudists that the materials employed in the

construction of the sole were either leather, felt, cloth, or wood, and that it was occasionally shod with iron. In Egypt various fibrous substances, such as palm leaves and papyrus stalks, were used in addition to leather, while in Assyria wood or leather were employed. In Egypt the sandals were usually turned up at the toe like our skates, though other forms, rounded and pointed, are also exhibited. Royal Egyptian sandals from the 18th dynasty (The New Kingdom) exist (from about 1546-1319 B. C.). In Assyria the heel and the side of the foot were encased, and sometimes the sandal consisted of little less than this. Sandals were worn by all classes of society in Palestine, even by the very poor (Amos 8:6), and both the sandal and the thong, or shoe latchet, were so cheap and common that they passed into a proverb for the most insignificant thing (Gen. 14:23; Eccles. 46:19).

403. Sandals (top to bottom), Egyptian 1200 B.C., Babylonian, Greek *pediba*, Roman *crepeda*

2. **Use.** They were not, however, worn at all periods; they were dispensed with indoors, and were only put on by persons about to undertake some business away from their homes, such as a military expedition (Isa. 5:27; Eph. 6:15), or a journey (Exod. 12:11; Josh. 9:5, 13; Acts 12:8). On such occasions persons carried an extra pair. During mealtimes the feet were undoubtedly uncovered, as implied in Luke 7:38; John 13:5, 6.

Figurative. It was a mark of reverence to cast off the shoes in approaching a place or person of eminent sanctity (Exod. 3:5; Josh. 5:15). It was also an indication of violent emotion or of mourning if a person appeared

barefoot in public (II Sam. 15:30; Isa. 20:2; Ezek. 24:17, 23). To carry or to unloose a person's sandal was a menial office betokening great inferiority on the part of the person performing it (Matt. 3:1; Mark 1:7; John 1:27; Acts 13:25). A sandal thong (or lace), or even sandals themselves (Gen. 14:23; Amos 2:6; 8:6) are put for anything of little value; this is easily understood when one sees a pair of sandals shaped in a few minutes out of a piece of hide, and which would be dear at a few cents.

San'hedrin (săn′hē-drĭn; Aramaized form of Gr. *sunedrion*, a *council, assembly session*).

1. **History.** The rise of this great council of the Hebrews took place in the time of Greek supremacy, though the Rabbins endeavor to trace its origin to the college of seventy elders named by Moses. The first occasion on which it is mentioned, and that under the designation of *gerousia* (Gr., the *eldership*), is in the time of Antiochus the Great, B. C. 223-187. From its designation, *gerousia*, it is evident that it was an *aristocratic* body, with the *hereditary high priest* at its head. It continued to exist and exercise its functions under the Asmonaean princes and high priests (II Macc. 1:10; 4:44; 11:27). When the Roman order of affairs was introduced by Pompey the high priest still retained the position of "governor of the nation" (Josephus, *Ant.*, xx, 10), thus making it likely that the gerousia still remained. Gabinius, B. C. 57-55, divided the whole Jewish territory into five "conventions" (Josephus, *Wars*, i, 8, 5), or "councils" (Josephus, xiv, 5, 4). As things now stood the council of Jerusalem no longer exercised sole jurisdiction. After ten years Caesar reappointed Hyrcanus II to his former position of *ethnarch*, and the jurisdiction of the council of Jerusalem once more extended to Galilee (Josephus, *Ant.*, xiv, 9, 3-5). Here for the first time the council of Jerusalem was designated by the term *Sanhedrin*. Herod The Great inaugurated his reign by ordering the whole of the Sanhedrin to be put to death (Josephus, *Ant.*, xiv, 9, 4), and evidently formed a Sanhedrin of those who were disposed to be tractable. After Herod's death Archelaus obtained only a portion of his father's kingdom—Judea and Samaria—and in consequence the jurisdiction was probably restricted to Judea proper. Under the procurators (*q. v.*) the internal government of the country was to a greater extent in the hands of the Sanhedrin than during the reigns of Herod and Archelaus. In the time of Christ and the apostles the Sanhedrin is frequently mentioned as being the supreme Jewish court of justice (Matt. 5:22; 26:59; Mark 14:55; 15:1; Luke 22:66; John 11:47; Acts 4:15, 21, sq.; 6:12, sq.; 22:30; 23:1, sq.; 24:20). Sometimes the terms *presbuterion* (Luke 22:66; Acts 22:5) and *gerousia* (Acts 5:21) are substituted for Sanhedrin. The Sanhedrin was undoubtedly abolished, so far as its existing form was concerned, after the destruction of Jerusalem, A. D. 70.

2. **Composition.** This great council was formed (Matt. 26:3, 57, 59; Mark 14:53; 15:1; Luke 22:66; Acts 4:5, sq.; 521; 22:30) of high priests (i. e., the acting high priest, those who had been high priests, and mem-

bers of the privileged families from which the high priests were taken), elders (i. e., tribal and family heads of the people and priesthood), and scribes (i. e., legal assessors), Pharisees, and Sadducees alike (comp. Acts 4:1, sq.; 5:17, 34). According to the Mishna the number of members was seventy, with a president, a vice president, and servants of the court (John 18:22; Mark 14:65, etc.). Josephus and the New Testament state that the acting high priest, as such, was always head and president. Wherever names are mentioned we find that it is the high priest for the time being that officiates as president —Caiaphas, in the time of Christ (Matt. 26:3, 57), and Ananias, in the time of Paul (Acts 23:2; 24:1). It is thought that membership was for life, and that new members were appointed either by the existing members or by the supreme political authorities. We may well assume that the *one* requirement of legal Judaism, that none but Israelites of pure blood should be eligible for the office of judge in a criminal court, would also be insisted upon in the case of the supreme Sanhedrin. New members were admitted through the ceremony of laying on of hands.

3. **Jurisdiction.** The jurisdiction of the Sanhedrin was restricted in the time of Christ to the eleven toparchies of Judea proper; hence it had no judicial authority over Jesus, so long as he remained in Galilee, but only when he entered Judea. "In a certain sense, no doubt, the Sanhedrin exercised such jurisdiction over *every* Jewish community in the world, and in that sense over Galilee as well. Its orders were regarded as binding throughout the entire dominion of orthodox Judaism. It had power to issue warrants to the congregations (synagogues) in Damascus for the apprehension of Christians in that quarter (Acts 9:2; 22:5; 26:12). At the same time, however, the extent to which the Jewish communities were willing to yield obedience to the orders of the Sanhedrin always depended upon how far they were favorably disposed toward it. It was only within the limits of Judea proper that it exercised any direct authority." It would not be proper to say that the Sanhedrin was the *spiritual* or *theological* in contradistinction to the civil judicatories of the Romans. It was rather that *supreme native* court which here, as almost everywhere else, Rome continued to allow, only imposing certain restrictions with regard to competency. "To this tribunal then belonged all those judicial matters and all those measures of an administrative character which either could not be competently dealt with by the inferior local courts, or which the Roman procurator had not specially reserved for himself. The Sanhedrin was, above all, the final court of appeal for questions connected with the Mosaic law, but not in the sense that it was open to anyone to appeal to it against the decisions of the inferior courts, but rather in so far as it was called upon to intervene in every case in which the lower courts could not agree as to their judgment. And when once it had given a decision in any case the judges of the local court were, on pain of death, bound to acquiesce in it" (Schürer, div. ii, vol. 1, 185, sq.). From the New Testament, we

learn that Jesus appeared before the Sanhedrin on a charge of blasphemy (Matt. 26:65; John 19:7), Peter and John charged with being false prophets and deceivers of the people (Acts, chaps. 4 and 5), Stephen with being a blasphemer (6:13, sq.), and Paul with being guilty of transgressing the Mosaic law (ch. 23). The Sanhedrin enjoyed a considerable amount of criminal jurisdiction. It had the right of ordering arrests to be made by its own officers (Matt. 26:47; Mark 14:43; Acts 4:3; 5:17, 18); of finally disposing of such cases as did not involve sentence of death (Acts 4:5-23; 5:21-40). When it pronounced sentence of death it required to be ratified by the procurator (John 18:31). Such instances as the stoning of Stephen must be regarded as an excess of jurisdiction or an act of irregular mob justice. Thus we see that the Sanhedrin had a tolerably extensive jurisdiction, the serious restriction being that the Roman authorities could at any time take the initiative, and proceed independently, as, for example, when Paul was arrested. Further, the procurator, or even the tribune of the cohorts stationed at Jerusalem, might call the Sanhedrin together for the purpose of submitting to it any matter requiring to be investigated from the standpoint of Jewish law (Acts 20:30; comp. 23:15, 20, 28).

404. Tiberias. It became a center of Rabbinic learning after the fall of Jerusalem. It was a seat of the great Sanhedrin and the place of publication of the Mishnah (collection of ancient Hebrew traditional law) in the third century A.D.

4. **Time and Place of Meeting.** The local courts usually sat on the second and fifth days of the week (Monday and Thursday); but whether this was the practice of the Sanhedrin we have no means of knowing. There were no courts held on festival (*q. v.*) days, much less on the Sabbath. The *place* in which the Sanhedrin usually met was situated, according to Josephus (*Wars*, v, 4, 2), close to the socalled Xystos, on its east side toward the temple mount. In cases which did not admit of delay it assembled in the high priest's house (Matt. 26:3, 57; Mark 14:53).

5. **Judicial Procedure.** According to the Mishna this was as follows: The members sat in a semi-circle, that they might be able to see one another. In front stood the two clerks of the court, one on the right hand and the other on the left, whose duty it was to record the votes of those who were in favor of acquittal on the one hand, and of those who were in favor of condemnation on the other. There also sat in front of them three rows of disciples

of the learned men, each of whom had a special seat. The prisoner was required to appear in a humble attitude, dressed in mourning. The following order was observed in *capital* cases: Arguments first in favor of *acquittal,* then those in favor of *conviction;* if anyone had spoken in favor of the accused he could not afterward say anything unfavorable, though the converse was allowed; student disciples might speak in favor, but not against the accused, although, if the case did not involve a capital sentence, they could speak for or against the accused; sentence of acquittal might be pronounced on the day of trial, but one of condemnation not until the day following. The voting, each member standing, began with the youngest members of the court, although on some occasions it began with the most distinguished member. For acquittal a simple majority was sufficient; for condemnation a majority of two was required. If twelve of the twenty-three judges necessary to form a quorum voted for acquittal and eleven for conviction the prisoner was discharged; but if twelve were for conviction and eleven for acquittal, then the number of the judges had to be increased by adding two, which was repeated if necessary until either an acquittal was secured or the majority requisite for a conviction was obtained. But, of course, they had to restrict themselves to the maximum number of seventy-one (Keil, *Arch.,* i, 350, sq.; Schürer, *Jewish People,* div. ii, vol. i, 163, sq.).

Sansan'nah (săn-săn'á; *palm branch*), a city in Judah (Josh. 15:31), identified with Khirbet esh-Shamsäniyät about 10 miles N. E. of Beersheba.

Saph (săf; *a threshold* or *dish*), a Philistine giant, of the race of Rapha, slain by Sibbechai the Hushathite (II Sam. 21:18; "Sippai," I Chron. 20:4).

Sa'phir (sā'fêr; *beautiful*), one of the towns in Judah addressed by the prophet Micah (1:11), possibly identified with es-Suafir, southeast of Ashdod. Robinson found several villages of this name in the vicinity. A. S. V. and A. S. V. Shaphir.

Sapphi'ra (să-fī'rá; Gr. from Aram., *beautiful*), the wife of Ananias, and accomplice in the sin for which he died. About three hours after the death of her husband she entered the place, unconscious of what had taken place. Questioned by Peter as to the price obtained for the land they had sold, she repeated the lie of her husband, and exposed herself to the fate of Ananias. Peter replied to her: "How is it that ye have agreed together to tempt the Spirit of the Lord? Behold, the feet of them which have buried thy husband are at the door, and shall carry thee out." On hearing these words she fell dead at his feet (Acts 5:7-10).

NOTE—*Severity of punishment.* The offense of Ananias and Sapphira, according to the average standard of human morality, was not a very heinous one. They had devoted a large sum to charity, they had defrauded no one, but had simply retained their own and then denied the fact. The following considerations are offered in explanation by Whedon (*Com.,* in loc.): "1. The divine Spirit being present with unparalleled power in the Church, the sin, as Peter says (vers. 3, 4), is *directly against him.* 2. The reason for this selection was to present and record at this *beginning* of the Christian Church a repre-

sentative and memorial instance of the just doom of the *hypocrite.* This couple were deliberate, positive, conceited, and intentionally *permanent hypocrites.* Their death was God's declaration to all future ages of the true deserts of all deliberate *hypocrites* in the Church of Christ." 3. In addition it may be added that this was evidently a "sin unto death" (i. e. "physical" death), cf. I John 5:16. Similar cases occur in I Cor. 5:1-5; 11:30. The death of Samson and Saul give typical illustrations of a believer's "sin unto (physical) death" in the O. T.

Sapphire. *See* Mineral Kingdom.

Sa'ra (sā'rá), a Grecized form (Heb. 11:11; I Pet. 3:6) of Sarah.

Sa'rah (sā'rá; *a princess*), the wife of the patriarch Abraham.

1. **Name and Family.** The original name of Sarah was Sarai (*q. v.*), and was changed at the same time that Abram's name was changed to Abraham, viz., on the establishment of the covenant of circumcision. The Hebrew name of Sarah is *säräh* (*princess*). Of her birth and parentage we have no certain account in Scripture. In Gen. 20:12 Abraham speaks of her as "my sister, the daughter of my father, but not the daughter of my mother," which would make her his half-sister; but the statement of Abraham is held by many to mean no more than that Haran, her father, was his half brother, for the colloquial usage of the Hebrews in this matter makes it easy to understand that he might call a niece a sister. In that case Abraham was really her uncle as well as husband.

2. **Personal History.** As his wife, the history of Sarah is substantially that of Abraham. She came with him from Ur to Haran (Gen. 11:31), from Haran to Canaan (12:5), and accompanied him in all his wanderings. (1) **Taken by Pharoah.** When Abraham went down into Egypt apparently under the powerful and splendid 12th dynasty of the Middle Kingdom (c. 2000-1775), he arranged with Sarah that she should announce herself as his sister, fearing for his life on account of her beauty. Although she was then sixty-five years of age, so beautiful did she appear to the Egyptians that she was taken by Pharoah; but, plagued by Jehovah, he returned her to Abraham with a reproof for his untruthfulness (12:10-20). (2) **Hagar.** Having no children of her own, Sarah gave to Abraham her Egyptian handmaid, Hagar, who became the mother of Ishmael (16:1-16). Later she demanded that Hagar and Ishmael should be cast out from all rivalry with herself and Isaac (21:9, sq.), a demand symbolically applied (Gal. 4:22-31) to the displacement of the old covenant by the new. (3) **Abimelech.** After the destruction of Sodom Abraham removed to the south country, and remained for some time in Gerar. Here Abimelech, the Philistine king, took Sarah, whom Abraham had again announced to be his sister, into his harem, probably to ally himself with Abraham, the rich nomad prince. Warned by God in a dream, Abimelech restored Sarah to her husband (Gen. 20:1-18). (4) **Birth of Isaac.** Jehovah fulfilled his promise to Sarah, and at the appointed time she gave birth to Isaac (21:1-3). This was recognized at the time, and later by Paul (Rom. 4:19), as a miracle, both Sarah and Abraham being advanced in years. (5) **Death.** Thirty-seven years after the

birth of Isaac, and when she had reached the age of one hundred and twenty-seven, Sarah died at Hebron, and was buried in the cave of Machpelah (Gen. 23:1-3), B. C. c. 1980. Isaiah is the only prophet who names Sarah (51:2). Paul alludes to her hope of becoming a mother (Rom. 4:19), and afterward cites the promise which she received (9:9), and Peter eulogizes her submission to her husband (I Pet. 3:6).

Sa′rai (sā′rī; perhaps *contentious*), the original name of Sarah, and always used in the history from Gen. 11:29 to 17:15.

Sa′raph (sā′răf; *burning* or *serpent*), one of the descendants of Shelah, the son of Judah (I Chron. 4:22), who seems to have lived about the time of the entrance of Israel into Canaan, as he is said to have had dominion in Moab (B. C. about 1400).

Sardine. *See* Mineral Kingdom.

Sar′dis (sär′dĭs), a city of W. Asia Minor about fifty miles E. of Symrna, which was the fifth named of the seven churches addressed by John (Rev. 1:11; 3:1, 4). This important city was founded probably as early as the beginning of the Iron Age and located on important commercial routes running E. and W. through the rich kingdom of Lydia, of which it was the capital. It was also made wealthy by textile manufacturing and jewelry making. Here are said to have been minted the first coins under the opulent Croesus. Cyrus the Great overcame the city in 546 B. C. Antiochus the Great did the same in 218 B. C. Wealthy Sardis citizens took up with mystery cults, notably with that of Sybele. Among the ruins of the city Artemis' magnificent temple of the fourth century B. C., survives in part as well as an adjacent Christian church from the fourth century A. D.—*M. F. U.*

405. General View of Sardis

Sar′dite (sär′dīt), a descendant of Sered, the son of Zebulun (Num. 26:26).

Sardius, Sardonyx. *See* Mineral Kingdom.

Sarep′ta (sả-rĕp′tả), the Greek form (Luke 4:26) of Zarephath (*q. v.*).

Sar′gon (sär′gŏn), the name of an Assyrian king mentioned only once in the Bible (Isa. 20:1), and then merely to give the date to an important prophecy of Isaiah. The Assyrian form of the name is Sharrukin. Sargon was the successor of Shalmaneser V (*see* Shalmaneser) and the father of Sennacherib (*see* Sennacherib), and ruled in Assyria B. C. 722-705. Abundant historical materials concerning his reign have come down to us. Remains of the walls which he built, colossal carved bulls

covered with inscriptions, tools, palace utensils, and beautifully inscribed prisms have all been found in different parts of Assyria, and all bear their witness to his glory and success.

406. Bull in Glazed Brick from the Palace of Sargon II (722-705 B.C.)

1. **His lineage.** Sargon began to reign in Assyria in the same month in which Shalmaneser V died. This would seem to indicate that there was no doubt or difficulty about the succession. Yet it is clear that he was not the son of Shalmaneser, nor apparently any relative of his predecessor. Indeed, he never alludes in any of his known inscriptions to his ancestors. It is therefore, with justice, believed that he was not of royal origin at all. In the reign of his grandson Esar-haddon a genealogical table was made out, by which Sargon's ancestry was traced back to Bel-bani, an early ruler in Assyria. This was evidently only an attempt to gain the honor of noble lineage. Whatever his origin—and it was probably humble, since nothing is said of it— Sargon seems to have been accepted as king without question. He may, therefore, have been adopted by Shalmaneser and designated as his successor.

2. **His exploits.** Sargon was one of the greatest soldiers ever produced in Assyria, and his coming upon the scene of action was at the very time when he was sorely needed by a weakened empire. The reign of Shalmaneser had been brief. His death left the state in confusion. Babylonia was overrun by the Chaldeans, and under the leadership of Merodach-baladan was in open revolt. There was a siege in progress at Samaria at the end of Shalmaneser's reign, and the king of Egypt was threatening and ill-tempered. The northern boundary of Assyria was dangerously beset by the tribes of Armenia, and northern Syria must again be reduced to subjection. A weak man upon the throne of Assyria, and all would have been lost that Tiglath-pileser III had gained, and perhaps the empire's very life would have been in jeopardy. The occasion was great, and Sargon was equal to it.

The first event in the reign of Sargon, according to his own inscription, was the fall of Samaria. He speaks of it in these words: "The city Samaria I besieged, and twenty-seven thousand two hundred and ninety people, inhabitants of it, I took away captive. Fifty chariots in it I seized, but the rest I allowed to retain their possessions. I appointed my governor over them, and the tribute of the late king I imposed upon them." We do not know whether Sargon was actually present at Samaria or not. The city may have been taken by one of his generals, though he says that *he* took it. We know from other clear instances that the Assyrian kings were not careful to distinguish their own from the successes of their generals in the field. Whether he or his representative was the real conqueror, Sargon was proud of the achievement. In his Cylinder Inscription he calls himself "subjugator of the broad land of Beth-Omri," and again elsewhere "the conqueror of the city of Samaria and the whole land of Beth-Omri." In the treatment of Israel Sargon followed the plans first matured by Tiglath-pileser; he "carried Israel away unto Assyria, and placed them in Halah, and in Habor, on the river Gozan, and in the cities of the Medes" (II Kings 17:6), and to fill the place thus vacated he brought men from Babylon, and from Cutha, and from Avva, and from Hamath and Sepharvaim, and placed them in the cities of Samaria instead of Israel (17:24). This colonization as begun by Tiglath-pileser and extended by Sargon, was handed on from people to people till it found its fullest extension in the Roman empire.

After the downfall of Samaria Sargon was speedily confronted by another confederation. A leader in Hamath, by name Ilu-bi'di, had formed a coalition to throw off the Assyrian supremacy. He was aided by several provinces nearby, among them Arpad and Damascus, and was supported by Hanno, king of Gaza. Sargon made haste from Assyria in order to attack Ilu-bi'di before his allies could join him. He met Ilu-bi'di at Qarqar (or Karkar), and completely overcame him. He then moved southward and found that Hanno was supported by Seveh of Egypt. A battle was fought at Rapichi (modern Refah), and again

407. Winged Bull from the Palace of Sargon II (now in the Oriental Institute of the University of Chicago)

was Sargon victorious. Seveh and his troops fled in confusion to Egypt, and Hanno was taken prisoner and carried off to Assyria. These victories brought enforced peace in Palestine, and Sargon was free to undertake conquest and pacification elsewhere. In 719 he was carrying on war in the north as far as Lake Urumiah; in the next year he was collecting tribute in Cappadocia. In the year 718 Sargon crossed the Euphrates and attacked

Carchemish. The ancient Hittite empire had fallen piece by piece into the hands of the Assyrians. Carchemish and its provinces alone remained. They were now reduced, and the territory completely absorbed into Assyria. So ended a great culture state of the ancient world. The following years were full of abundant labors in the putting down of insurrections in Armenia, Que (eastern Cilicia), and in Arabia, and another attack upon an Egyptian king finds mention. In every case peace was achieved for a season by force, but new disturbances were ever breaking forth elsewhere.

408. Assyrian Plow in Glazed Brick from the Wall of the Palace of Sargon II

In 711 difficulties again attracted Sargon's attention in Syria. Azuri, king of Ashdod, thought that the time was ripe for refusing to pay the Assyrian tribute. Sargon hastily dispatched a Tartan against him (Isa. 20:1), who removed Azuri from the throne and put in his place his brother Achimit, who was an Assyrian sympathizer. The people of Ashdod would not endure a man of such sentiments, and deposed him by force. Suddenly Sargon appeared, took Ashdod and Gath, which had joined in the rebellion, carried away the chief inhabitants to Assyria, and supplied their places by colonists from the east. This ended the troubles for the present, and Sargon could now turn his attention to Babylonia. The state of this land might well cause alarm. The whole country was in open revolt, under the leadership of Merodach-baladan, who had formed also a confederacy with Elam (*see* Merodach-baladan). Sargon realized that this must be a severe struggle. His plans were carefully laid. He attacked the confederate forces separately, won victories, and soon was in possession of Babylon. In 709 he was again acknowledged as king in Babylon, and the rebellion that had begun with the beginning of his reign was over. The years 709-707 were brilliant indeed. Tribute was sent to him from the island of Dilnum, in the Persian Gulf, from Cyprus, in the far-away Mediterranean. He was at the zenith of his power, and the world did him obeisance.

3. **Last years.** For the last few years of his reign we have no Assyrian documents. Only brief hints show that his armies were engaged till the very last in subduing insurrections here

and there over his vast empire. It was indeed impossible that peoples so widely separated and so diverse in all their thoughts and emotions should be so speedily welded into a unified and symmetrical empire. Conquests might be made quickly; concourse of feeling must be of slow growth. Sargon died in 705. The broken fragments of the Eponym list seem to say that he was murdered, but they are too badly mutilated to make us perfectly sure. So ended the career of the greatest conqueror who ever ruled in Assyria. He was not so great as a pacificator as Esar-haddon, nor were his works of peace so magnificent as those of Ashurbanipal, but in war he surpassed all who preceded or followed him upon that throne.

4. **His royal city.** But he was not only a warror; he has left at least one magnificent evidence of his skill in the arts of peace. When he began his reign the Assyrian capital was Calah. He determined to erect a new city, and place within it a palace which should surpass in magnificence all that had preceded it. The site selected was at the foot of Mount Musri, north of Nineveh. The city built there he named after himself, Dur-Sharrukin (Sargonsburg), and the palace within its square of walls was the first Assyrian ruin explored by moderns. It was excavated in the years 1842-1845 by Botta, and was surprising for its magnificence even in ruins. In 707 the city and palace were ready for occupation. And the ruins have been excavated by the Oriental Institute of the University of Chicago. Sargon also began the collection of thousands of cuneiform tablets continued by his great grandson Ashurbanipal. These were recovered in the famous library at Nineveh. But Sargon did not long enjoy his own magnificence. The man of war was not to rest in the results of peace.

409. Tree in Glazed Brick from the Palace of Sargon II

Sa'rid (sā'rĭd; *survivor*), a place at the center, probably, of the southern boundary of Zebulun (Josh. 19:10), from which the line is traced in a westerly direction (v. 11), and in an easterly direction (v. 12). It is now identified with Tell Shadua S. W. of Nazareth and N. of the Plain of Esdraelon.

410. Crow in Glazed Brick from the Palace of Sargon II

Sa'ron (sā'rŏn; *the Sharon*), the district in which Lydda stood (Acts 9:35). *See* Sharon.

Sar'sechim (sär'sē-kĭm), one of the generals of Nebuchadnezzar's army at the taking of Jerusalem (Jer. 39:3), B. C. 587.

Sa'ruch (sā'rŭk), the Greek form (Luke 3:35) of the name of the patriarch Serug (*q. v.*).

Sa'tan (sā'tăn; Heb. *sätän*, Gr. *Satanas*, an *adversary*, *opponent*), the chief of fallen spirits.

1. **Scripture Names and Titles.** Satan is also called the Devil, the Dragon, the Evil One, the Angel of the Bottomless Pit, the Prince of this World, the Prince of the Power of the Air, the God of this World, Apollyon, Abaddon, Belial, Beelzebub. But Satan and the Devil are the names most frequently given. The term Satan is used in its generic sense in I Kings 11:14, "The Lord stirred up an adversary (*sätän*) unto Solomon, Hadad the Edomite." It is used in the same sense (I Kings 11:23; I Sam. 29:4; Num. 22:22; comp. II Sam. 19:22; I Kings 5:4; 11:25; Psa. 109:6).

2. **Scripture Doctrine.** Satan is mentioned first in the Book of Job (1:6-12; 2:1, sq.). He mixes with the sons of God (angels), among whom he no longer has any essential belonging; he arbitrarily roams about and seeks his own, but is still used as a servant by God, on whom he remains dependent. His independent activity is in this passage mainly that of the spy of evil, of the accuser of man to God, especially the accuser of the pious, and he maintains the assertion that even their fear of God is interested. Job is delivered into the hands of Satan for testing. Satan's intention was to lead Job into apostasy and ruin; but the conduct of Job proves that disinterested fear of God may be a truth. The luster of a fidelity and love which in the loss of all external goods regards God as the highest good is revealed by Job as a triumph over Satan.

We find mention of Satan as a personality in Zech 3:1, where after the exile he would hinder the reinstitution of divine worship, asserting that Israel is rejected by the just judgment of God, and is not worthy of the renewal of the priesthood. But the filthy garments are stripped off the high priest, and he receives festal garments instead, with the declaration that his sins are taken away. The vision expresses that the restoration of the priesthood after the exile is a victory of the gracious God over Satan, who maintains strict right. It also adumbrates the restoration of the nation Israel as a high priestly nation in the future Kingdom Age. Still in the Old Testament Satan never appears openly as the enemy of God himself. "Though he has his special purposes and aims, he is yet the servant of God for punishment or trial, the asserter or executor of the negative side of the divine justice" (Dorner, *Christ. Doct.*, iii, p. 79).

In the New Testament mention is made of a plurality of evil spirits, with Satan as their head (Matt. 8:28; 9:34; 12:26; Luke 11:8, 19). They were endowed with high talents, power, and knowledge (Matt. 8:29; Mark 1:24). Although Satan is used in the New Testament in a figurative sense (Matt. 16:23), yet Jesus said the enemy is the devil (Matt. 13:19, 39; Mark 4:15), and the history of the temptation is no misunderstood parable (Matt. 4:10; comp. Luke 22:31). It is declared that Satan was a murderer from the beginning (John 8:44), the enemy and falsifier of God's word (Matt. 13:19, 39); that he aroused hatred to Jesus and put treason into the heart of Judas (John 13:27, comp. 6:70; Luke 22:53); that the prince of this world is already judged by Christ, or, as Luke puts it, Satan is hurled from heaven (Luke 10:18), i. e., is inwardly and fundamentally vanquished. "The whole history of the world subsequent to Christ is a struggle against the empire of Satan. Thus the Apocalypse especially depicts the history of Satan, particularly in the future as he affects the Church (Rev. 2:9, 13, 24), the Jew and the Gentiles (Rev. chaps. 4-19).

Sa'tan, Synagogue of (Rev. 2:9, 13; 3:9), i. e., Satan's assembly; probably of Jews who persecuted the Christians, because of their misguided zeal for the law of Moses; who, professing to worship God, really serve Satan (Rev. 2:9, 13).

Sa'tan, the Depths of, the false teachings developed in the church of Thyatira (the Roman Church of the Dark Ages), preceding the Protestant Reformation (Rev. 2:24). They included every kind of worldliness and demon-inspired corruption of the truth (I Tim. 4:1-4). These doctrines were called by their advocates "the deep things of God," but the Lord styles them "the deep things of *Satan*."

Satisfaction. *See* Atonement, Propitiation.

Satyr. *See* Gods, False; Animal Kingdom.

Saul (sôl; *asked for*).

1. **An Early King of the Edomites**, successor of Samlah at "Rehoboth by the river" (Gen. 36:37, 38). In I Chron. 1:48 he is called *Shaul*.

2. **The First King of Israel.** Saul was the son of Kish, of the tribe of Benjamin, a powerful and wealthy chief, although the family to which he belonged was of little importance (I Sam. 9:1, 21). The time and place of Saul's birth are not given. The Israelites had been since Joshua under the rule of judges raised up by God to meet emergencies that arose through the defection and idolatry of the people. "In those days there was no king in

Israel: every man did that which was right in his own eyes" (Judg. 21:25). The corrupt administration of Samuel's sons furnished the Hebrews an occasion for rejecting the theocracy (I Sam., ch. 8). This, together with an invasion of the Ammonites and a love of novelty, conspired in prompting the demand for a king. Samuel, instructed by God, granted it, but told the people the evils that would follow. They still persisted in their demand, and Saul was introduced into history. The reign of Saul may be divided into two periods: 1. The establishment and vigorous development of his regal supremacy (chaps. 8-15). 2. The decline and overthrow of his monarchy (chaps. 16-31).

I. The Establishment of a Monarchy is introduced by the negotiations of the elders of Israel with Samuel concerning the appointment of a king (I Sam., chap. 8). This was followed by (1) **Meeting of Saul with Samuel.** Having been sent by his father after some strayed asses, Saul went with his servant through the mountains of Ephraim, then through Shalisha and Shalim, and after that through the land of Benjamin, without finding the asses. Arrived at Zuph, he determined to return home, because he was afraid that his father would trouble himself about them (Saul and the servant). But his servant proposed that they should go and consult the man of God who was in the city near at hand, and learn from him what they should do. Samuel, having been forewarned by God, met Saul at the gate of the city, told him he was the one for whom he looked, and invited him to the feast, assuring him that the asses were found. He awakened the expectation of Saul by the question, "And on whom is the desire of all Israel? Is it not on thee and on all thy father's house?" (9:20). (2) **Saul anointed.** Early the next day they arose, and, the servant being sent on before, "Samuel took a vial of oil and poured it upon Saul's head, and kissed him, and said, Is it not because the Lord hath anointed thee to be captain over his inheritance?" (9:27; 10:1). To confirm the consecration Samuel gave him three signs which should occur on his journey home—*first*, two men at the tomb of Rachel should meet him, and tell him of the finding of the asses and the anxiety of Saul's father for him; *second*, three men should be met in the plain of Tabor, going with sacrifices to Beth-el, and they should give Saul two loaves from their offerings; *third*, at Gibeah he should meet a company of prophets, and he himself should prophesy (10:2-13). (3) **Chosen king.** The mysterious interview with Samuel did not seem to suffice for the full acknowledgment of Saul as king. Samuel, therefore, called a national assembly at Mizpeh, and here instructed the tribes to choose a king by lot. The result of the lot being regarded as a divine decision, Saul was accredited by this act in the sight of the whole nation as the king appointed by the Lord, and he himself more fully assured of the certainty of his own election on the part of God. Saul was hiding away, but was found, brought before the people, and introduced to them by Samuel, and received by them with the cry, "God save the king!" He returned to his home in Gibeah, followed by a band of men "whose heart God had touched." But he already began to taste the bitterness of royalty, for there were some who said, "How shall this man save us?" (10:13-27), B. C. c. 1025. (4) **Victory over the Ammonites.** Nahash, the king of the Ammonites, laid siege to Jabesh in Gilead, and only consented to save its inhabitants on the condition that he should put out their right eyes. They asked for seven days in which to send among their brethren for help. They dispatched messengers to Gibeah, and, probably unaware of the election of Saul, stated their case to the people. Returning from the field, Saul learned the tidings from Jabesh, and the Spirit of the Lord came upon him. Deeply angered, he hewed in pieces a yoke of oxen and sent them through all Israel, calling the people to rally about him for the defense of their countrymen. They came together at Bezek to the number of three hundred thousand. The next day Saul arranged the army into three divisions, who forced their way into the camp of the foe from three different sides, and routed them completely (11:1-11). (5) **Renewal of the monarchy.** After the victory the people were so enthusiastic in favor of Saul that they demanded the death of those who had spoken against him as king. Saul refused to grant them their request, saying, "There shall not a man be put to death this day: for to-day the Lord hath wrought salvation in Israel." Samuel called the people to Gilgal, where the election of Saul was confirmed (11:12-15). (6) **Saul's first transgression.** In the second year of his reign Saul set to work systematically to deliver Israel from their enemies. He gathered three thousand select men (the beginning of a standing army), two thousand being with himself and the other one thousand with Jonathan. Jonathan smote the garrison of the Philistines in Geba, which became the signal of war, Saul summoning the people to assemble in Gilgal. The Philistines gathered a great army—thirty thousand chariots, six thousand horsemen, and foot soldiers as the sand by the seashore —and encamped in Michmash. Saul waited seven days for Samuel's coming, but as he did not come the people began to disperse and leave Saul, who then resolved that he would offer the sacrifices without the presence of the prophet. Scarcely was the ceremony over when Samuel arrived and asked Saul what he had done. Saul pleaded the danger he was in, and his desire to secure the favor of heaven; but the prophet rebuked him, and told him that his kingdom should not continue, i. e., to his descendants (13:1-14). (7) **Saul deserted.** Saul did not even accomplish the object of his unreasonable sacrifice, viz., to prevent the dispersion of the people. When he mustered the people still with him there were only six hundred men (13:15). The Philistines overran the country, and the Israelites could not offer a successful resistance, for the Philistines possessed the secret of smelting iron (*see* Iron), and "there was no smith found throughout all the land of Israel: for the Philistines said, Lest the Hebrews make them swords or spears" (v. 19). (8) **Saul's oath.**

Jonathan, with a few faithful followers, made an assault upon the Philistine garrison at Michmash, which resulted in a panic in the camp, so that they slew one another. The spies of Saul at Gibeah saw the engagement,

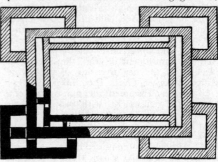

411. Saul's Fortress at Gibeah (c. 1000 B.C.) restored

and the king called for the ark and high priest to consult as to what he should do. The tumult in the camp of the Philistines increasing, he rushed to the pursuit, driving the foe down the pass of Beth-aven as far as Aijalon. But by a rash denunciation he (*a*) impeded his success (14:30), (*b*) involved the people in a violation of the law (vers. 32, 33), and (*c*) unless prevented by the people, would have put Jonathan to death for tasting innocently of food. Saul returned from the pursuit of the Philistines (14:1-46). (9) **Other wars.** By this victory over the Philistines Saul first really secured the regal authority over the Israelites. He afterward gained victories over Moab, the Ammonites, Edom, the kings of Zobah, the Philistines again, and the Amalekites (14:47, 48). Mention is now made of his family and of his commander in chief, Abner (vers. 49, 50), B. C. c. 1022. (10) **Disobedience and rejection.** Samuel, by divine commission, commanded Saul, as the king anointed by Jehovah through him, to destroy Amalek. He was to smite and ban everything belonging to it, man and beast (15:3). Saul mustered the people at Telaim, two hundred thousand foot and ten thousand men of Judah. "And Saul smote the Amalekites from Havilah until thou comest to Shur, that is over against Egypt." But he disobeyed the divine injunction by taking Agag, the king, alive, and sparing all the best of the cattle and all that was valuable, destroying only that which was vile and refuse. Instead of pursuing the campaign and finishing the destruction of the fugitives, he returned to Gilgal. Samuel, informed by God of the king's disobedience, went to Saul, who informed him that he had fulfilled the divine command; but the bleating of the sheep and the lowing of the oxen revealed his crime. Saul pleaded that the people wished to offer sacrifice to the Lord in Gilgal. Samuel then reminded the king of the low estate from which God had brought him, of the superiority of *obedience* to sacrifice, and, although Saul acknowledged his sin, reiterated the sentence of rejection. As he turned to depart Saul seized the prophet's mantle with such despairing energy that it was rent,

whereupon Samuel said that even so had Jehovah rent his kingdom from him and given
it to another. Samuel then sent for Agag and
hewed him in pieces before the Lord, and
departed in grief from Saul to see him no
more (ch. 15).

II. Saul's Decline and Overthrow. Saul was
not immediately deposed, but the consequences of his rejection were speedily brought
to light. (1) **David's introduction to Saul.**
"The Spirit of the Lord departed from Saul,
and an evil spirit from the Lord troubled
him." When his attendants perceived the condition of the king, they advised him to have
the evil spirit charmed away by music, and
upon Saul's consenting they recommended
David, who was still residing with his father,
although he had been anointed king by Samuel. David was sent for, and played upon his
harp. "So Saul was refreshed, and was well,
and the evil spirit departed from him" (I Sam.
16:14-23). (2) **Saul's conduct to David.** The
overthrow of the Philistine giant (Goliath)
by David, and his conduct when brought before Saul, won for him the love of Jonathan.
The wisdom of his subsequent conduct made
him acceptable to the men of war and the
people, and secured for him the praise of the
women who celebrated the overthrow of the
Philistines. This aroused the jealousy and rage
of Saul, who commenced a series of murderous attempts upon the life of David, whom he
seems to have regarded as a rival. He twice
attempted to assassinate him with his own
hand (18:10, 11; 19:10); he sent him on
dangerous military expeditions (18:13-17;);
he gave him Michal, his daughter, to wife,
hoping that the dowry demanded (a hundred
foreskins of the Philistines) would endanger
David's life (18:22-27). He seems to have been
willing to make any sacrifice in order to
effect his purpose against David, sending men
even to Samuel at Ramah, whither David
had fled (19:18, sq.), attempting, as the text
(20:33) would seem to indicate, the life of his
son Jonathan; slaying Ahimelech, the priest
(22:11-19), under pretense of his being a partisan of David, and eighty-five other priests
of the house of Eli, to whom nothing could
be imputed, as well as the whole population
of Nob. This crime of Saul put David in possession of the sacred lot, which Abiathar, the
only surviving member of Eli's priestly family, brought with him, and by which he was
enabled to obtain divine direction in his critical affairs (22:20, 23; 23:1, 2). Having compelled David to assume the position of an
outlaw, Saul then took measures to apprehend
and destroy him (23:9, sq.), and, although
spared by David when in the latter's power
at En-gedi (ch. 24), took Michal and gave
her to Phalti for wife (25:44). After David
had again shown his respect for the Lord's
anointed by sparing the king while asleep in
his camp upon the hill of Hachilah, Saul acknowledged his fault and said to David,
"Blessed be thou, my son David: thou shalt
both do great things, and also shalt still prevail." And he followed after David no more
(ch. 26). (3) **Saul with "the witch" at Endor.** Another invasion of Israel by the Philistines drove King Saul to despair, so that, in

utter helplessness, he had recourse to ungodly means of inquiring into the future. He
had "put away those that had familiar spirits,
and the wizards, out of the land" (28:3). But
now Samuel was dead, and, receiving no
oracle from God, Saul, desperate and infatuated, commanded his servants (v. 7) to
seek for a woman that had a familiar spirit.
They directed him to the woman of En-dor.
Assured by Saul that no evil should happen to
her, she asked, "Whom shall I bring up unto
thee?" And he said, "Bring me up Samuel."
The woman began her conjuring arts, and
"when she saw Samuel, she cried aloud, 'Why
hast thou deceived me? for thou art Saul.'"
The king quieted her fear, and then asked her
what she had seen. From her description Saul
immediately recognized Samuel. Then followed a conversation in which Saul tells of
his deep distress because of the Philistines, and
Samuel replies that Jehovah had torn the
kingdom out of his hand and given it to
David, because he had disobeyed him in
sparing the Amalekites. He foretold his defeat
by the Philistines, and added that on the
morrow Saul and his sons should be with him
among the dead. Saul fell prostrate to the
earth, faint with terror and exhaustion, for
he had fasted all the day and night. Urged
by the woman and his servants, he partook of
food and returned to his camp (28:7-25).
(4) **Death and burial.** The two armies arrayed against each other soon came to an
engagement in the plain of Jezreel (29:1);
but the Israelites, being obliged to yield, fled
up the mountains of Gilboa, and were pursued and slain there (31:1). The hottest pursuit was made after Saul and those who kept
around him. His three sons, Jonathan, Abinadab, and Melchi-shua, were slain, and he
himself was mortally wounded. He begged
his armor-bearer to slay him, that he might
not fall into the hands of the uncircumcised.
On his refusal Saul fell upon his own sword

412. Saul's Last Battle

and died. The day following, when the Philistines stripped the dead, they found Saul and his three sons, and, having cut off their heads, sent them as trophies into their own land. They also fastened their bodies to the wall of Beth-shan; but the men of Jabesh-gilead came, took down the bodies, burned them, and buried them under a tree in Jabesh (ch. 31), B. C. about 1000. The news of Saul's death was speedily brought to David at Ziklag, who mourned deeply because of it, and slew the Amalekite who claimed to have killed the king (II Sam. 1:1, sq.). Besides the children already mentioned Saul left another son, Ish-bosheth, who was shortly afterward proclaimed king by Abner, and two sons, Armoni and Mephibosheth, by his concubine Rizpah (21:8).

Character. There is not in sacred history a character more melancholy to contemplate than that of Saul. He was naturally humble and modest, though of strong passions. His natural rashness was controlled neither by a powerful understanding, nor a scrupulous conscience, and the obligations of duty and ties of gratitude, always felt by him too slightly, were totally disregarded when ambition, envy, and jealousy had taken possession of his mind. He seems never to have accepted God unconditionally and trusted him implicitly, but, as the names of his children would indicate, wavered between the worship of God and the old heathenish superstition. Now he would be under the influence of prophetic inspiration, again the slave of his common pursuits; at one time pleading with the prophet to reveal to him the will of Jehovah, at another disobeying his commands; now driving out of the land all having familiar spirits, only to consult afterward the witch of En-dor. In him, also, is seen that moral anomaly or contradiction, which would be incredible did we not so often witness it, of an individual pursuing habitually a course which his better nature pronounces not only sinful but insane (I Sam. 24:16-22).

3. Saul and Archaeology. Saul's capital at Gibeah has been explored and his citadel on the summit of Tell el-Ful, three miles N. of Jerusalem, has been excavated. Long ago this was identified with Saul's fortress by the brilliant pioneer Palestinian explorer Edward Robinson, and was excavated by W. F. Albright in 1922 and 1933. (See *Annual of the Am. Schools* IV, 1922, 1923, *Bulletin* LII, 1933, pp. 6-12, *Archaeology of Palestine*, 1949, p. 120f). Gibeah yielded at the bottom of the mound fortress No. 1 which showed traces of destruction by fire and is probably referred to in Judg. 20:40. Directly above this were the remnants of a second, identified as Saul's stronghold. The structure measuring 170 x 155 feet had separately bonded corner towers and casemated walls. The principal building at Gibeah with massive stone construction and deep walls "was like a dungeon rather than a royal residence in comparison with the Canaanite masonry with which Solomon graced Jerusalem" (Madeleine S. and J. Lane Miller, *Ency. of Bible Life*, 1944, p. 176). W. F. Albright says, "Saul was only a rustic chieftain as far as architecture and the amenities of life

were concerned" (*From the Stone Age to Christianity*, p. 224). What was true of Saul was in a general sense culturally true of all Israel up to the dawn of the Davidic-Solomonic era. Palestine excavations have fully demonstrated Israel's rusticity of life and poverty in the premonarchial period.

4. The Hebrew Name of the Apostle Paul. Why he changed his name is not mentioned, but perhaps the most probable reason was "that the name Paul was given to the apostle as a memorial of the conversion of Sergius Paulus, effected by him" (Meyer, *Com.*, Acts 13:7).

Saviour, a term applied in Scripture, in its highest sense, to Jesus Christ, but in a subordinate manner to human deliverers.

1. Names. In the Old Testament Saviour is usually some derivative of the verb *yāshă'*, to *save*. Beyond this ordinary sense, this term expresses *assistance* and *protection* of every kind —assistance aggressively, "to fight for you against your enemies, to save you" (Deut. 20:4); of *protection* against attack, "Salvation will God appoint for walls and bulwarks" (Isa. 26:1); of *victory*, "The Lord preserved David" (i. e., gave him victory, II Sam. 8:6); of *prosperity*, "Thou shalt call thy walls Salvation" (Isa. 60:18). No better instance of this last sense can be adduced than the exclamation "Hosannah!" meaning "save, I beseech thee," which was uttered as a prayer for God's blessing on any joyous occasion (Psa. 118:25).

The Greek representative of the above is *sōtēr*. The LXX has *sōtēr* where the A. V. has "salvation"; and thus the word "Saviour" was more familiar to the ear of the reader of the Old Testament in our Lord's age than to us.

2. Person. The title "Saviour" is applied to Jehovah in the Old Testament (II Sam. 22:3; Psa. 106:21; Isa. 43:3, 11; 45:15, 21; 49:26; 60:16; 63:8; Jer. 14:8). The judges were called "saviours," as having rescued their country from oppressors (Judg. 3:9, 15, A. V. "deliverer"). Jeroboam II is styled a *saviour* in delivering Israel from the Syrians (II Kings 13:5). *See* Atonement; Redeemer; Salvation.

Savor, Savors (Heb. *rêăḥ*, *odor*), a term used in the Old Testament almost entirely to denote the pleasing effect upon Jehovah of the sacrifices offered him by the Jews (Exod. 29:18; Lev. 1:9, 13, 17, etc.). In Joel 2:20, "And his ill savor shall come up," we have a rendering of Heb. *ṣăḥănăh*, *putrefaction*.

Figurative. In the sense of to *be minded* (Gr. *phroneō*, to *think*, *feel*, Matt. 16:23; Mark 8:33); of *taste or flavor*, as of salt which has lost its savor (Matt. 5:13; Luke 14:34), the rendering of Gr. *mōrainō*, to *make flat* or *tasteless;* in II Cor. 2:14, 16 (Gr. *'osmē*, "the knowledge of God is symbolized as an odor which God everywhere makes manifest through the apostolic working, inasmuch as he by that means brings it to pass that the knowledge of Christ everywhere exhibits and communicates its nature and its efficacy" (Meyer, *Com.*, in loc.). Acceptableness to God of the apostolic working is symbolized by "sweet savor" (v. 15, Gr. *euōdia*, *fragrance*, comp. Eph. 5:2).

Savory Meat (Heb. *măţ'ăm*, *delicacy*, "dainties," Prov. 23:3, "dainty meats," v. 6), a term applied to the food prepared for Isaac (Gen. 27:3, 9, etc.). It was probably so called from being cooked with different sorts of vegetables, being made specially tasty.

Saw (Heb. *m*ᵉ*gēräh*, II Sam. 12:31; I Kings 7:9; I Chron. 20:3; *măssōr*, Isa. 10:15). Egyptian saws, so far as has yet been discovered, were single-handed, though St. Jerome has been thought to allude to circular saws. As is the case in modern oriental saws, the teeth usually incline toward the handle, instead of away from it, like ours. They have, in most cases, bronze blades, apparently attached to the handles by leather thongs, but some of those in the British Museum have their blades let into them like our knives. A double-handed iron saw has been found at Nimrud. No evidence exists of the use of the saw applied to stone in Egypt, nor without the double-handed saw does it seem likely that this should be the case; but we read of sawn stones used in the temple (I Kings 7:9). The expression, "put them under saws" (II Sam. 12:31), has been understood to mean hard labor (see margin), but "cut them with saws" (I Chron. 20:3) can hardly be other than torture.

Scab. *See* Diseases.

Scabbard (Heb. *tă‘ăr*, Jer. 47:6), elsewhere "sheath." *See* Sword.

Scaffold (Heb. *kĭyyōr*, II Chron. 6:13), a platform built by Solomon for the dedicatory services of the temple, upon which he stood to pray.

Scale. 1. (Heb. *qăsqĕsĕth*): (*a*) Of fishes (Lev. 11:9, 10, 12; Deut. 14:9, 10; Ezek. 29:4); (*b*) Of the laminae of a coat of mail (I Sam. 17:5); similarly the Gr. *lepis*, a *flake*, incrustation from the eyes (Acts 9:18).

2. *Strong ones of shields* (Job. 41:15), of the scaly armor of the "leviathan," i. e., crocodile.

3. Of *balances* (Heb. *pĕlĕs*, Isa. 40:12), or rather a *steelyard*. *See* Balances.

4. *To scale* the walls of a city, Prov. 21:22 (Heb. *‘äläh*).

Scall. *See* Diseases.

Scalp (Heb. *qŏqŏd*, the *crown* of the head, Psa. 68:21, as elsewhere rendered), so called from the *parting* of the head at that spot.

Scapegoat. *See* Azazel; Festivals; Day of Atonement.

Scarlet, a brilliant crimson, the coloring substance for which was obtained from an insect (*Coccus ilicis*) called *qirmiz* in Arabic, whence the English word "crimson." The color-producing insect is found on the holm oak. The female alone produces the coloring matter, feeding on the leaves of the tree and yielding eggs containing a red substance. The Greeks called the insect *kokkos*, meaning "berry," because being pea-like, it resembles a berry. The Hebrews called the color *shänî*, "brilliance," "crimson," *shĕnî’tōlă‘ăth*, "brightness of (produced by) the worm," *tōlă‘ăth shänî*, "worm of brightness," " crimson-producing worm," or simply *tōlä*, "worm." In Greek *kokkinos* was an adjective meaning "pertaining to the coccus worm." The Oriental worm is akin to the cochineal insect of Mexico (*Coccus cacti*), but has been supplanted commercially by its new-world rival, which yields a much more valuable dye. Crimson was used in the vestments of the high priest and the hangings of the tabernacle, in the purification of the leper (Lev. 14:4) and in the water of separation (Num. 19:6; Heb. 9:19). *M. F. U.*

Scent. 1. (Heb. *rēăḥ, odor*), that which anything exhaled, as by *water* (Job 14:9), or by *wine* (Jer. 48:11). In the latter passage Moab is likened to wine, which has never been poured out or drawn, and hence preserved its original taste and flavor.

2. (Heb. *zēkĕr, memento*, Hos. 14:7), where it is said figuratively of those who sit under the shadow of Israel, that they shall "grow as the vine, the *scent* (remembrance, i. e., renown) as the wine of Lebanon."

Scepter (Heb. *shēbĕṭ, rod;* Gr. *hrados*, Heb. 1:8), a staff borne by a ruler as the badge of his authority. Sceptres are depicted on many bas-reliefs of Assyrian and Persian kings. Sometimes scepters were short like a mace, sometimes long, and garnished with royal insignia. We know that in some cases the scepter was a strong rod (Ezek. 19:11, 14), about the height of a man, which ancient kings and chiefs bore as insignia of honor. It is thought that it originated in the shepherd's staff, since the first kings were mostly nomad princes (Lev. 27:32; Mic. 7:14). Diodorus Siculus (iii, 3) informs us that the scepter of the Egyptian kings bore the shape of a plow; of Osiris was a flail and crook; while that of the queens, besides the crown, was two loose feathers on the head.

413. Hittite King Bearing Spear and Scepter

Figurative. The allusions to it are all of a metaphorical character, and describe it simply as one of the insignia of supreme power (Gen. 49:10; Num. 24:17; Psa. 45:6; Isa. 14:5; Amos 1:5; Zech. 10:11). The use of the

414. An Egyptian King's Scepter

staff as a symbol of authority was not confined to kings; it might be used by any leader, as instanced in Judg. 5:14, where for "pen of the writer," as in the A. V., we should read "scepter of the leader."

Sce'va (sē'vá), a Jew of Ephesus, described as a "high priest" (Acts 19:14-16), either as having exercised the office at Jerusalem, or as being chief of one of the twenty-four classes. His seven sons attempted to exorcise spirits by using the name of Jesus, and on one occasion severe injury was inflicted by the demoniac on two of them (as implied in the term *'amphoterōn, both*, the true reading in v. 16).

Schism. *See* Heresy, 2.

School (Gr. *scholē*, Acts 19:9), a place where there is *leisure*, a place of tuition. *See* Tyrannus.

Schoolmaster (Gr. *paidagōgos*), a guide and guardian for boys. Among the Greeks and Romans the name was applied to trustworthy slaves, who were charged with the duty of supervising the life and morals of boys of the better class. The name carries with it the idea of severity (as of a stern censor and enforcer of morals) in I Cor. 4:15, where the father is distinguished from the tutor as one whose discipline is usually milder. In Gal. 3:24, sq., the Mosaic law is likened to a tutor because it arouses the consciousness of sin, and is called *paidagōgos* (A. V. "schoolmaster unto Christ"), i. e., preparing the soul for Christ, because those who have learned by experience with the law that they are not and cannot be commended to God by their works, welcome the more eagerly the hope of salvation offered them through the death and resurrection of Christ, the Son of God.

Schools, Hebrew. 1. **Elementary.** We have no account of education specifically before the time of Moses. This much is certain that the mother looked to the training of the children in their earliest years (Prov. 31:1; II Tim. 3:15), while the boys were trained by their fathers, or in well-to-do families by tutors (Num. 11:12; Isa. 49:23). This instruction was chiefly in reading and writing, but especially in the law. That reading and writing must have formed part of education from the very settlement of Palestine is evident from the fact that the Israelites were commanded to write the precepts of the law upon the door-

posts and gates of their houses (Deut. 6:9; 11:20); and upon their passage over Jordan, to write the law upon great stones (27:2-8), so as to be easily read by every Israelite. These admonitions unquestionably presuppose that the people could read plain writing (*q. v.*). Arithmetic must have been taught, as the days of the week, the months, the festivals, etc., were not designated by proper names, but by numerals. In fact, every art or science which occurs or is alluded to in the Old Testament, and upon the understanding of which depended the understanding of the Scriptures, must have to some extent formed a part of the strictly religious Jewish education. There is, however, no trace of schools for the instruction of youth or of the people in pre-exilic times. Only in a single instance (II Chron. 17:7-9) have we any information as to how far and in what way the priests fulfilled their calling to teach the people all the ordinances which God gave by Moses (Lev. 10:11). While there were no national or elementary schools before the exile, there were cases in which professional teachers were resorted to—when the position or official duties of the parent rendered his teaching impossible; when the parents were incapacitated, or the child's attainments surpassed the parent's abilities; or the son was preparing himself for a different vocation from that of his father.

In postexilic times. We possess minute information of the schools after the captivity and at the time of Christ. The regular instruction of the child began with the fifth or sixth year, when every child was sent to school. Tradition ascribes to Joshua, the son of Gamalia, the introduction of schools in every town, and the compulsory education in them of all children above the age of six . . . It was even deemed unlawful to live in a place where there was no school. Such a city deserved to be either destroyed or excommunicated. Joshua arranged that in every province and in every town schoolmasters be appointed, who should take charge of all boys from six or seven years of age. A school or teacher was required for every twenty-five children. When there were only forty children in a community, they were allowed to have one master and an assistant. The father himself, as a rule, saw to it that the child should be in the class at the proper time. *Course of study.*—"The grand object of the teacher was moral as well as intellectual training. To keep children from all intercourse with the vicious; to suppress all feelings of bitterness, even though wrong had been done to one's parents; to punish all real wrongdoing; not to prefer one child to another; rather to show sin in its repulsiveness than to predict what punishment would follow, either in this or the next world, so as not to 'discourage' the child—such are some of the rules laid down" (Edersheim, *Sketches of Jewish Life*, pp. 135, 136). The teacher was to strictly fulfill all promises made to the child, to avoid bringing up disagreeable or indelicate thoughts, be patient, punish without excessive severity—with a strap, but never with a rod. At ten the child began to study the Mishna; at fifteen he must be ready for the Talmud. In the study of the Scriptures the pupil was to proceed from Leviticus to the rest of the Pentateuch, thence to the Prophets, and lastly to the Hagiographa. Instruction was imparted in questions and answers, or in a catechetical form. After the master had delivered his dicta or theme, the pupils asked questions (Luke 2:46), which he frequently answered by parables or counter questions (Matt. 16:13, etc.; 22:17-22; Luke 10:25, etc.). Sometimes the teacher introduced the subject by asking a question, the replies of the pupils constituting the discussion, which was concluded by the master pointing out the most appropriate answer. This mode of instruction is strikingly illustrated by the questions put by our Saviour to his disciples (Mark 8:27-30).

2. **Theological Schools.** The schools of the prophets (q. v.), called into life by Samuel (I Sam. 10:5; 19:20), and more firmly organized under Elijah and Elisha in the kingdom of the ten tribes (II Kings 2:3, 5; 4:38; 6:1), were not theological schools. Not till after the exile, when prophecy began to fail, did the study of the law become a matter of scholastic learning; and the priest Ezra is mentioned as the first who set his heart to search and do the law of Jehovah, and *to teach ordinances and judgments* in Israel (Ezra 7:10). He is described as "a ready scribe in the law of Moses" (7:6; comp. vers. 12, 21); he must have made the study of the law his chief business. From Ezra onward notable scribes or lawyers are mentioned, who not only applied themselves to the faithful observing and handing down the letter of the law and of the Scriptures, but made the contents of Scripture their special study, especially applying the law of Moses to the practical duties of life, but also gave decisions in doubtful cases (Matt. 2:4; Luke 2:46). Thus a complete system of casuistry, founded on the law, was gradually formed for all the relations of life. This was orally transmitted by the scribes (q. v.) and their associates; and as the *tradition of the elders* (Mark 7:5) was ranked on an equality with, and eventually above, the written law of Moses. On the institution of these schools we lack more exact information for the period from the exile to the dissolution of the Jewish state. Students seeking a deeper knowledge of the law turned to eminent scribes for instruction. This was given by the teachers, partly at their homes, partly in the synagogues, partly in the porticoes of the temple, in the form of conversations or disputations. Instruction was gratuitous, the scribes earning their livelihood by following a trade, unless having means of their own or acquired by marriage. The teachers sat while instructing, the scholars at first standing, but afterward sitting at the feet of their teachers (Acts 22:3).

3. **Schools of the Prophets.** From I Sam. 19:20 we learn that there was a company of prophets at Ramah, under the superintendency of Samuel, whose members lived in a common building. The origin and history of these schools are involved in obscurity, but would seem to have been called into existence by Samuel. We have no direct evidence that there were other such unions besides the one at Ramah, but it is probable that there was one at Gibeah (I Sam. 10:5, 10). The next mention of them is in the times of Elijah and Elisha, as "sons of the prophets" (I Kings 20:35), living in considerable numbers at Gilgal, Beth-el, and Jericho (see II Kings 4:38; 2:3, 5, 7, 15; 4:1; 9:1). About one hundred sons of the prophets sat down before Elisha at meals, in Gilgal (II Kings 4:38, 42, 43). The number at Jericho may have been as great, for fifty of the sons of the prophets went with Elijah and Elisha to the Jordan (comp. 2:7 with vers. 16, 17). From these passages we feel warranted in the belief that the sons of the prophets lived in a common house (see also 6:1). Those who were married most likely lived in their own houses (4:1). We must not conclude, from their living together and performing certain duties in common, that these prophets were an Old Testament order of monks. The prophets did not wish to withdraw from active life for the purpose of carrying on a contemplative life of holiness, but their unions were formed for the purpose of mental and spiritual training that they might exert a more powerful influence upon their contemporaries. The name "schools of the prophets" expresses most fully the character of these unions; only we must not think of them as merely educational institutions, in which the pupils of the prophets received instruction in prophesying or in theological studies.

"Prophesying could neither be taught nor communicated by instruction, but was a gift of God which he communicated to whomsoever he would. But the communication of this divine gift was by no means an arbitrary thing, but presupposed such a mental and spiritual disposition on the part of the recipient as fitted him to receive it; while the exercise of the gift required a thorough acquaintance with the law and the earlier revelations of God, which the schools of the prophets were well adapted to promote. It is therefore justly and generally assumed that the study of the law and of the history of the divine guidance of Israel formed a leading feature in the occupations of the pupils of the prophets, which also included the cultivation of sacred poetry and music and united exercises for the promotion of the prophetic inspiration" (K. and D., *Com.*, I Sam. 19:18-24). Thus we find that from the time of Samuel the writing of sacred history formed an essential part of the prophet's labor.

The cultivation of sacred music and poetry may be inferred partly from the fact that, according to I Sam. 10:5, musicians walked in front of the prophesying prophets, playing as they went along, and partly from the fact that sacred music not only received a fresh impulse from David, who stood in close relation to the association of prophets at Ramah, but was also raised by him into an integral part of public worship. Music was by no means cultivated merely that the sons of the prophets might employ it in connection with their discourses, but also as a means of awakening holy susceptibilities and emotions in the soul, of lifting up the spirit to God, and so preparing it for the reception of divine revelations (see II Kings 3:15). Occasion of forming such schools is to be found in the decline of the priesthood under Eli and his sons, and the utter absence of the sanctuary in the times of Elijah and Elisha, thus furnishing the faithful with places and means of edification; and in the advantages which would naturally arise from association, in bringing the young men under the influence of their elders, who were under the powerful influence of the Holy Spirit, thus uniting them with their spiritual fathers in fighting for the honor of Jehovah.

Science (Heb. *măddäs'*, Dan. 1:4; Gr. *gnōsis*, I Tim. 6:20). In these two passages the terms are rendered "science," but elsewhere knowledge. In the passage, Dan. 1:4, the expression "cunning in knowledge" may well be rendered "skillful in understanding or knowledge." The Greek term is used about thirty times in the New Testament, and except in the above passage is rendered "knowledge." It should be so rendered here, and the passage would read "oppositions (or contradictions) of falsely named knowledge," i. e., the higher knowledge of Christian and divine things which false teachers boast of.

Scoff (Heb. *qālăs*, to *disparage*, Hab. 1:10), to ridicule, make light of, as a fortification, enemy.

Scoffer (Gr. *empaiktēs*), one who *trifles*, and so *derides* (II Pet. 3:3).

Scorn, Scorner. 1. In Esth. 3:6 (comp. Job 12:4) it is recorded of Haman that "he thought *scorn* to lay hands on Mordecai alone," the rendering of Heb. *bāzäh*, to *tread under foot*, to *despise*, and so rendered in Esth. 1:17; Prov. 19:16; Psa. 73:20; Isa. 53:3.

2. A frivolous and impudent person, who sets at naught and scoffs at the most sacred precepts and duties of religion, piety, and morals (Psa. 1:1; Prov. 9:7, 8; 13:1; 14:6; 15:12; 19:25; 22:10; 24:9; Isa. 29:20, etc.). (Heb. *lûṣ*, to *make mouths*, *deride*).

3. To *laugh*, *scorn* (Heb. *sāḥăq*), spoken of the wild ass, having contempt for civilization (Job. 39:7); of the ostrich, in her swiftness, despising the pursuit of the horse (Job 39:18).

4. To *despise*, *refuse* (Heb. *qālăs*). Spoken of Jerusalem refusing payment for her adulteries, as would an ordinary prostitute (Ezek. 16:31).

5. To *stammer*, *imitate* in derision. (Heb. *lā'ăg*). "Scorning" (Job 34:7) is *blasphemy*, and "to drink scorn like water" is to give oneself up to mockery with delight, and to find satisfaction in it (comp. 15:16). It is used of the treatment accorded to the godly by their enemies (Psa. 44:13; 79:4; 123:4).

6. To *laugh down*, to *deride* (Matt. 9:24; Mark 5:40; Luke 8:53), *katagelaō*.

Scorpion, an instrument of scourging, a whip with barbed points like the point of a scorpion's sting. *See* Animal Kingdom.

Figurative. This instrument was used figuratively by Rehoboam, king of Judea, to represent the harsher measures with which he would deal with the people than had his father (I Kings 12:11). *See* Scourge.

Scourge. Hebrew generally *shūṭ*, to *whip;* noun *shōṭ*, a *whip* (Job 9:23; Isa. 10:26; 28:15, 18); *bĭqqōrĕth*, properly to *examine* (Lev. 19:20); Gr. *mastigoō*, *flog* (Matt. 10:17; 20:19; 23:34;

Luke 18:33; John 19:1; Acts 22:24); *phraggelloō*, to *lash*, as a public punishment (Matt. 27:26; Mark 15:15), and its derivative, a *whip* (John 2:15). A common punishment in the East. The instrument of punishment in ancient Egypt, as it is also in modern times generally in the East, was usually the stick, applied to the soles of the feet—bastinado. Under the Roman method the culprit was stripped, stretched with cords or thongs on a frame, and beaten with rods. The punishment of scourging was prescribed by the law in the case of a betrothed bondwoman guilty of unchastity (Lev. 19:20), and in the case of both the guilty persons, as appears from the ex-

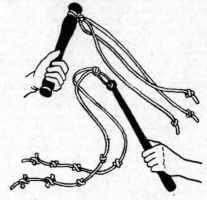

415. Scourges

pression "they shall not be put to death." In case a man was sentenced to stripes the judge was to confine the number to forty, i. e., to forty at most, lest "thy brother should seem vile unto thee" (Deut. 25:1-3). There were two ways of scourging—one with thongs or whips made of rope ends or straps of leather, the other with rods or twigs. Scourging is frequently mentioned in the New Testament (Matt. 10:17; 23:34; Acts 5:40), and thirty-nine stripes as the maximum (II Cor. 11:24). The "scorpion" (*q. v.*) was probably a severer instrument.

Figurative. "The scourge of the tongue" (Job 5:21) is symbolical of wordy strife (see Psa. 31:20). In Heb. 12:6 "scourgeth" is used of the chastisement sent upon men by God.

Screech Owl. *See* Animal Kingdom.

Scribe (Heb. *sāphēr*; Gr. *grammateus*.) The *grammateus* of a Greek state was not the mere writer, but the keeper and registrar of public documents (Thucydides, iv, 118; vii, 10; so in Acts 19:35). The name of Kirjath-sepher (Josh. 15:15; Judg. 1:12) may possibly connect itself with some early use of the title. In the song of Deborah (Judg. 5:14) the word appears to point to military functions of some kind. The "pen of the writer" of the A. V. is probably the rod or scepter of the commander numbering or marshaling his troops, i. e., the *musterer-general*, whose duty it was to levy and muster the troops (R. V. "marshal's staff"). Three men are mentioned as successively filling the office of scribe under David and Solomon (II Sam. 8:17; 20:25; I Kings 4:3). We may think of them as the king's secretaries, writing his letters, drawing up his decrees, managing his finances (comp. II Kings 12:10). At a later period the word again connects itself with the act of numbering the military forces of the country (Jer. 52:25, and probably Isa. 33:18). Other associations, however, began to gather round it about the same period. The zeal of Hezekiah led him to foster the growth of a body of men whose work it was to transcribe old records, or to put in writing what had been handed down orally (Prov. 25:1). To this period, accordingly, belongs the new significance of the title. It no longer designates only an officer of the king's court, but a class, students and interpreters of the law, boasting of their wisdom (Jer. 8:8). *See* Scribes, Writing.

Scribes, Jewish. 1. Name. Hebrew and Greek as above; also Gr. *nomikos*, "learned in the law," "jurists" (Matt. 22:35; Luke 7:30; 10:25; 11:45, 52; 14:3); *nomodidaskalos*, "teacher of the law" (Luke 5:17; Acts 5:34).

2. **Institution.** The period of the Sopherim, *scribes*, began with the return of the Jews from captivity. The law read by Ezra (Neh., chaps. 8-10) was the Pentateuch in essentially the same form as we have it now; and from that time was acknowledged by Israel as the binding rule of life, i. e.:

(1) **Canonical.** Obedience to it was the condition of membership among the chosen people and a share in the promises given to them. The entire Pentateuch came to be regarded as dictated by God, even to the last eight verses, containing the account of Moses's death. From insisting upon divine dictation the next step was to declare that the law had been handed to Moses by God, the only question being whether it was all delivered at once or in volumes. As an addition to the law the writing of the prophets and pre-exilic history of Israel attained to similar authority. At a still later period there was added to this body of the "prophets" *a third collection* of writings, which gradually entered into the same category of canonical Scriptures. In proportion as the law became comprehensive and complicated there arose the necessity of its scientific study and of a professional acquaintance with it. Its many details and the application of its several enactments to everyday life necessarily involved patient study. In the time of Ezra and long after this was chiefly the concern of *priests*, Ezra himself being both *priest and scribe*. This was naturally the case, as the Pentateuch related largely to priestly functions and privileges. The higher the law rose in the estimation of the people, the more did its study and exposition become an independent business; and an independent class of "biblical scholars or scribes," i. e., of men who made acquaintance with the law a profession, was formed, besides the priests. When under Greek influence the priests, at least those of the higher strata, often applied themselves to heathen culture and more or less neglected the law, the scribes appeared as the zealous guardians of the law. From this time on they were the *real teachers* of the people, over whose life they bore complete sway. In the New Testament times the scribes formed a finely compacted class, holding undisputed

supremacy over the people. Everywhere he appears as the mouth piece and representative of the people; he pushes to the front, the crowd respectfully giving way and eagerly hanging on his utterances as those of a recognized authority. The great respect paid them is expressed by the title of honor bestowed upon them, "my master" (Heb. *răbbī;* Gr. *hrabbi,* Matt. 23:7, etc.). From this respectful *address* the *title* Rabbi was gradually formed; but its use cannot be proved before the time of Christ.

(2) **Respect.** The rabbis required from their pupils the most absolute reverence, surpassing even the honor felt for parents. Thus it was taught that "respect for a teacher should exceed respect for a father, for both father and son owe respect to a teacher" (*Kerithoth,* vi, 9, fin.). The practical application of this principle was: "If a man's father and teacher have lost anything, the teacher's loss should have the precedence—i. e., he must first be assisted in recovering it—the burden of a teacher is to be born in preference to that of a father, a teacher must be ransomed from captivity before one's own father." The rabbis in general everywhere claimed the first rank (Matt. 23:6, 7; Mark 12:38, 39; Luke 11:43; 20:46).

3. **Employment.** This referred, if not exclusively, yet first and chiefly, to the law and the administration of justice.

(1) **As jurists.** As such the task of the scribe was threefold: *The theoretic development of the law.* The scribes developed with careful casuistry the general precepts of the law; and where the written law made no direct provision they created a compensation, either by establishing a precedent or by inference from other valid legal decisions. In this way, during the last centuries before Christ, Jewish law became gradually an extensive and complicated science. This law being unwritten, and propagated by oral tradition, very assiduous study was necessary to obtain even a general acquaintance with it. Added to an acquaintance with the law, the scribes assumed that it was their special province to develop what was already binding into more and more subtle casuistic details. In order to settle a system of law binding upon all, it was necessary to come as near as possible to a general consensus of opinion. Hence the whole process of systematizing the law was carried on by oral discussion, the acknowledged authorities instructing their pupils in the law and debating legal questions with each other. This made it necessary that the heads at least of the body should dwell in certain central localities, though many would be scattered about the country to give instruction and render legal decisions. The central point till A. D. 70 was Jerusalem; after that at other places, as Jamnia and Tiberias. Gradually the theories of the scribes became *valid law;* hence, the maxims developed by the scribes were recognized in practice so soon as the schools were agreed about them. The scribes were, in fact, though not by formal appointment, *legislators,* especially after the destruction of the temple; for there being no longer a *civil* court of justice like the Sanhedrin, the judgment of the rabbinical scribes *determined what was valid law.* In

case of doubt the matter was brought "before the learned," who pronounced an authoritative decision.

(2) **Teaching the law.** This was the second chief task of the scribes. The idea of legal Judaism was that every Israelite should have a professional acquaintance with the law; if this was impracticable, then the greatest possible number. As a consequence the famous rabbins gathered about them large numbers of pupils. The oral law being never committed to writing, constant repetition was necessary in order to fix it in the minds of the students. Thus, in rabbinic diction, "to repeat" means exactly the same as "to teach." Questions were propounded to pupils for their decision, while pupils asked questions of the teachers. All knowledge of the law being strictly traditional, a pupil had only two duties—to keep everything faithfully in memory and to teach only what had been delivered to him. For such instruction there were special localities, called "houses of teaching," often mentioned in connection with synagogues as places, which in legal respects enjoyed certain privileges. In Jerusalem the catechetical lectures were held "in the temple" (Matt. 21:23; 26:55; Mark 14:49; Luke 2:46; 20:37; John 18:20), i. e., in the colonnades, or some other space of the outer court.

(3) **Judicial.** A third duty of the scribes was *passing sentence* in the court of justice; for so far as men were learned in the law they would be called to the office of judge. With respect to the great Sanhedrin it is expressly stated in the New Testament that *scribes* were among its members. After the fall of the Jewish state, A. D. 70, the scribes, being recognized as independent *legislators*, were also regarded as independent *judges*. Their sentences were voluntarily acquiesced in, whether they gave judgment collectively or as individuals. Being learned in the law and the elaboration of the historical and didactic portions of Scripture, the scribes were specially qualified for *delivering lectures* and *exhortations* in the synagogues. They also had the *care of the text of Scripture* as such.

4. Literature. 1. In the developing and establishment of the law there was evolved a *law of custom*, besides the written Torah (law), called the *Halachah* (Heb. *hǎlākäh, that which is current and customary*). 2. The manipulation of the historical and didactic portions of the Holy Scriptures produced an abundant variety of the historical and didactic notions, usually comprised under the name of the *Haggadah*, Heb. *hǎggädäh* (*narrative, legend*).

(1) **The Halachah** contained "either simply the laws laid down in Scripture, or else derived from or traced to it by some ingenious and artificial method of exegesis; or added to it, by way of amplification and for safety's sake; or, finally, legalized customs. They provided for every possible and impossible case, entered into every detail of private, family, and public life; and with iron logic, unbending rigor, and most minute analysis pursued and dominated man, turn whither he might, laying on him a yoke which was truly unbearable. The return which it offered was the pleasure and distinction of knowledge, the acquisition of righteousness and the final attainment of rewards" (Edersheim, *Life and Times of Jesus*, vol. i, p. 98).

(2) **The Haggadah** "is an amplification and remodeling of what was originally given, according to the views and necessities of later times. It is true that here also the given text forms the point of departure, and that a similar treatment to that employed in passages from the law takes place in the first instance. The history is worked up by combining the different statements in the text with each other, completing one by another, settling the chronology, etc. Or the religious and ethical parts are manipulated by formulating dogmatic propositions from isolated prophetic utterances, by bringing these into relation to each other, and thus obtaining a kind of dogmatic system. A canonical book of the Old Testament (Book of Chronicles) furnishes a very instructive example of the *historical* Midrash (i. e., exposition, exegesis). A comparison of its narrative with the parallel portions of the older historical books (Kings and Samuel) will strike even the cursory observer with the fact that the chronicler has enlarged the history of the Jewish kings by a whole class of narratives, of which the older documents have as good as nothing" (Schürer, *Jewish People*, div. ii, vol. i, 339, sq.).

5. History. This is properly divided into five periods, indicated by the appellations given to the scribes in successive times:

(1) **The Sopherim** (see above), or "scribes," properly so called, lasting from the return from Babylon, and ending with the death of Simon the Just, B. C about 458-300, about one hundred and sixty years.

(2) **The Tanaim** (*repeaters*, i. e., *teachers* of the law), in New Testament times, "teachers of the law" (Luke 5:17; Acts 5:34).

(3) **The Amoraim**, or later doctors of the law (Heb., to *expound*), "wise men" and "doctors of the law," who alone constituted the authorized recorders and expositors of the Halachah (A. D. 220—completion of the Babylonian Talmud, about A. D. 500).

(4) **The Saboraim**, or teachers of the law after the conclusion of the Talmud (Heb. to *think, discern*), who determined the law from a careful examination of all the pros and cons urged by the Amoraim in their controversies on divine, legal, and ritual questions contained in the Talmud, A. D. 500-657.

(5) **The Gaonim**, the last doctors of the law in the rabbinic succession. The period of the Gaonim extends from A. D. 657 to 1034 in Sora, and to 1038 in Pumbaditha (Schürer, *Jewish People;* Edersheim, *Life and Times of Jesus;* McC. and S., *Cyc.*, s. v.).

416. A Scrip

Scrip (Heb. *yălkŭṭ*, only in I Sam. 17:40; Gr. *pēra*), the bag in which the shepherds of Palestine carried their food or other necessaries. In the marginal reading of the A. V. "scrip" appears in II Kings 4:42 for the Heb. *ṣĭktōn* (to *wind*, and so a *sack tied* at the mouth), which in the text of the A. V. is translated *husk*. The scrip of the Galilean peasants was of leather, used especially to carry their food on a journey, and slung over their shoulders. When Christ sent forth his apostles he forbade them to provide themselves with these satchels (Matt. 10:10; Mark 6:9; Luke 9:3; 10:4; 22:35, 36), teaching them to depend upon Providence while executing their missions. The new rule given in Luke 22:35, 36, perhaps also the facts that Judas was the bearer of the bag (John 12:6), and that when the disciples were without bread they were ashamed of their forgetfulness (Mark 8:14-16), show that the command was not intended to be permanent.

Scripture (Heb. *käthäb*, *written;* Gr. *graphē*, *document*). It is not till the return from the captivity that the word meets us with any distinctive force. In the earlier books we read of the law, the book of the law. In Exod. 32:16 the commandments written on the tables of testimony are said to be "the writing of God," but there is no special sense in the word taken by itself. In the passage from Dan. 10:21, where the A. V. has "the scripture of truth," the words do not probably mean more than "a true writing." The thought of *the* Scripture as a whole is hardly to be found in them. This first appears in II Chron. 30:5, 18 ("as it was written," A. V.). In the singular it is applied chiefly to this or that passage quoted from the Old Testament (Mark 12:10; John 7:38; 13:18; 19:37; Luke 4:21; Rom. 9:17; Gal. 3:8, etc.). In two difficult passages some have seen the wider, some the narrower sense. (1) *Pasa graphē theopneustos* (II Tim. 3:16) has been translated in the A. V., "All Scripture is given by inspiration of God." Others render "Every Scripture being inspired, is also profitable . . ." The R. V. renders "Every Scripture inspired of God is also profitable for teaching," etc. (2) The meaning of the genitive in *pasa prophēteia graphēs* (II Pet. 1:20) seems at first sight distinctly collective: "Every prophecy of [i. e., contained in] the Old Testament Scripture." A closer examination of the passage will perhaps lead to a different conclusion. (3) In the plural, as might be expected, the collective meaning is prominent. In II Pet. 3:16 we find an extension of the term to the Epistles of St. Paul; but it remains uncertain whether "the other Scriptures" are the Scriptures of the Old Testament exclusively, or include other writings, then extant, dealing with the same topics. (4) In one passage *ta hiera grammata* (II Tim. 3:15) answers to "the holy Scriptures" of the A. V. *See* Bible; Canon.

Scripture Manuscripts—Old Testament. The word Scripture is derived from the Lat. *scriptum*, or *scriptura*, and has for its Greek equivalent *graphē*, and Heb. *mĭqrä'* (Neh. 8:8). In its English use in the Bible it means "the writings," as in Exod. 32:16; Dan. 10:21.

The New Testament employs the plural *graphai*, *writings*. The precise writing referred to by the word Scripture is not always clear. The word is found thirty-two times in the King James Version, and the plural, Scriptures, twenty-one times, all the passages except one being in the New Testament. In the singular the word refers to passages in the Old Testament, which are quoted or alluded to in the New. In the plural the reference is to books or collections of books of the Old Testament. The epithet "holy" is applied to the Scriptures in Rom. 1:2 and II Tim. 3:15. Their inspiration is distinctly attested in II Tim. 3:16, "All Scripture is given by inspiration of God." Other translations, "every Scripture being inspired," or "every Scripture is inspired," do not modify the clear declaration of the inspiration of the Old Testament Scriptures. Every separate portion of the Holy Book is inspired, and forms a living portion of a living and organic whole. While this expression does not exclude such verbal errors which are the result of transmission of the text over many centuries, it still does certainly assure us that these writings, as we have seen them, are individually pervaded by God's Spirit, and warrants our belief that they are (in the words of Clement of Rome, ad Cor. i, 45) the true utterances of the Holy Spirit and an assertion of the *full* inspiration of the Bible. *See* Canon, Inspiration.

1. Manuscripts of the Hebrew Scriptures. The sacred writings have been preserved to us down to the time of the invention of printing by the process of transcription. Hence there arose at an early period a class of scholars known as scribes (Heb. *sōphĕrîm*), meaning writers. Their business was to copy the Scriptures (Jer. 8:8). In the reign of Artaxerxes, king of Persia, Ezra was well known as a scribe, and went up from Babylon to Jerusalem, "and he was a ready scribe in the law of Moses" (Ezra 7:6). The scribes became teachers and expounders of the law. In the time of our Lord they were generally hostile to his claims as the Messiah, and were among his most bitter persecutors. Through a succession of scribes the Holy Scriptures were transmitted from generation to generation. The ancient Hebrew differed in its written character from the Hebrew current in our modern Hebrew Bibles. It was written in the old Phoenician letters, of which one of the most ancient specimens is found on the Moabite stone discovered in 1868, in Dibon, in Moab and dating about 850 B. C. and also in the Gezer Calender dating from about 925 B. C. Gradually this early character was displaced, and in the time of Christ the present Hebrew characters were in use. It is said in Matt. 5:18, "one jot or one tittle shall in no wise pass from the law." Jot, or its Hebrew equivalent, *yodh*, is the smallest letter in the Hebrew alphabet, but the equivalent letter in the early Phoenician character was not small, showing that the old character had given place at this time to the later Hebrew. The word *manuscript*, abbreviated MS. for singular and MSS. for plural, is from the Latin *cordices manuscripti*, i. e., cordices written by hand. The word *codex*, from the Latin *codex*, or *candex*, the stock of a tree, board covered with wax for writing; hence, book, plural codices, books.

Hebrew manuscripts were originally without accents, vowels, or marks of punctuation. The Hebrew vowel points were not introduced until about the 6th century of the Christian era, by a body of learned men called the Massoretes, who studied the Hebrew Scriptures with great minuteness, and made a collection of writings called "the Massora, or the Traditions." By means of their system of vowel points they established the pronunciation and meaning of the original Hebrew on a firm foundation.

Until the modern sensational MSS. finds in the Dead Sea area from 1947-1956, Hebrew MSS. of the O. T. were not earlier than the 10th century B. C. Now the Isaiah Manuscript of the Dead Sea Scrolls dating about 150 B. C. together with other fragmentary finds of various O. T. books, pushes the date of O. T. MSS. back about a millennium. But the work of the Massoretes is nevertheless of immense importance, despite recent MSS. discoveries. *See* Dead Sea Scrolls; Manuscripts, Dead Sea.

417. John C. Trever and Archbishop Athanasius Y. Samuel examine the Isaiah Scroll from the Dead Sea Collection

The proper task of the Massora was the guarding of the Bible manuscripts against degeneration through carelessness and willfulness on the part of transcribers, and, in consequence, the most painful and minute supervision was exercised upon them; but just in this way the Massora affords a glimpse into the form of the text transmitted from early times, which cannot be too highly valued.

There are two words in our Hebrew Bible that served the purpose of modern textual emendations; they are *keri*, "read," and *kethib*, "written." When a word was found in the text which was believed incorrect, instead of substituting the true word, placing it in the text, the Massoretes wrote the correct word in the margin and left the incorrect word in the text, with the vowels of the correct word. The word in the text would be thus shown to be wrong, and by placing these vowels with the word in the margin the true text would be clear. This fear to remove the incorrect word from the text showed a reverence amounting to superstition for the exact wording of their sacred writings. The Hebrew manuscripts which have been preserved except the MSS. finds since 1947, are not nearly so ancient as many of those of the Greek New Testament, nor are complete manuscripts so numerous.

The total number of Hebrew manuscripts is two thousand, but the greater part contains only fragments or portions of the Old Testament.

The oldest Hebrew Codex in existence is a Babylonian manuscript dated A. D. 916. It is a manuscript of the prophets. Of the whole Old Testament the oldest manuscript is dated A. D. 1010 (Buhl, *Canon and Text of the Old Testament*).

The Codex Laudianus is also of the 11th century. It is in the Bodleian Library in Oxford, England. It agrees quite closely with the Samaritan Pentateuch.

Codex Carlsruhensis is at Carlsruhe, and is the oldest that has a certain date—A. D. 1106. It contains the Prophets with the Targum.

The Codex Caesenoe is in the Malatesta Library in Bologna, and is assigned to the end of the 11th century. It contains the Pentateuch sections of the Prophets, Canticles, Ruth, Lamentations, Ecclesiastes, and Esther.

The Codex Parisiensis is in the National Library in Paris, and is assigned to the 12th century. It contains the Old Testament entire.

Codex 634 of De Rossi contains a small part of the law—Lev. 21:19-Num. 1:50. It belongs to the 8th century.

Codex Norimbergensis, in Nuremberg, contains the Prophets and Hagiographa. It is assigned to the 12th century.

The remarkable thing about the Hebrew text is the agreement of the old manuscripts that have come down to us. The Hebrew text of the Old Testament has been rendered into the Greek of the Septuagint Version, which many regard as a witness to the true text, even when it varies from our present Hebrew text. The exact value of the Septuagint in determining the original Hebrew is yet undetermined, but the question is being illuminated by the Dead Sea MSS. finds.

That our Hebrew text has been carefully preserved is evident from the great care taken by Jewish scholars in its preservation. The care of the Massoretes and other scholars in preserving the text indicates care also in ascertaining the true text, and serves to assure us of the genuineness of our present Hebrew Scriptures.

418. The Isaiah Manuscript from Qumran

Scripture Manuscripts—New Testament. The text of the New Testament is attested by manuscript testimony more voluminous in quantity and more reliable than that of any of the writings of the same period. Indeed there are no ancient writings whose evidence of a correct text is stronger than the New Testament.

1. **Reliability of the Text of the New**

Testament. Over 200 uncial manuscripts and fragments, about 170 papyrus manuscripts and fragments, and more than 2400 minuscule manuscripts of the N. T. text exist today (Sir Frederick Kenyon, *Our Bible and the Ancient Manuscripts*, pp. 105-107). This testimony to the New Testament text is not only remarkable for its bulk but also for its substantial agreement. While numerous textual variations occur, they are of a relatively minor nature. Substantial variations affect only about a thousandth part of the entire text, according to the estimation of careful students (cf. Gregory, *Canon and Text of the N. T.*, p. 528). Also amazing is the close relationship in point of time, between the oldest N. T. manuscripts and the original texts. Not more than a century and a half intervenes between the oldest copies of the Pauline letters preserved in the Chester Beatty papyri and their original composition, and scarcely three centuries come between the Codex Vaticanus and the Codex Sinaiticus and the period of the composition of the New Testament. When it is remembered that knowledge of classical authors depends on mss. between the ninth and eleventh centuries A. D., or a thousand years removed from their originals, as used to be the case also with the O. T., until the discovery of the Dead Sea Mss. (1947-1955), it can be comprehended why the certainty with which the N. T. text is established surpasses any other book of antiquity.

419. Chester Beatty Papyrus of Genesis 25:1-11

2. The Greek Manuscripts. These are the most important materials for textual criticism because the N. T. books were originally written in Greek. Although the theory that various books of the N. T. were penned in Aramaic and that the respective books of the Greek N. T. are merely translations from this original is held by some scholars, notably C. C. Torrey (all the gospels and the first half of Acts), the discovery of large numbers of papyri has done much to undermine this theory. Supposed mistranslations in the gospels appear in regular idiom in the Greek papyri of the general period. Manuscripts written in Greek, therefore, incontestably con-

stitute the most important materials for textual criticism. These are made up of papyri, uncial manuscripts and minuscules or cursive manuscripts.

(a) **The Papyri.** These are written on papyrus (*q. v.*). Since a number of these contain portions of the N. T. from a century to a century and a half earlier than our oldest uncial manuscripts, the importance of these documents for the study of the N. T. is inestimable. When Sir Frederic Kenyon first published *Our Bible and the Ancient Manuscripts* in 1895, there existed but one or two

420. Codex Sinaiticus, Psalm 23 (Aleph)

papyri that contained a portion of Scripture, but by 1931 the number had increased to fifty-three important ones, with other specimens running the total up to 170. But by far the most important mss. of this class are the Chester Beatty Papyri. These first became known in 1931 and consist of portions of codices of various books of the Old Testament and the New Testament. Mr. Chester Beatty of London purchased the collection containing portions of seven manuscripts of the O. T., and three of the N. T., besides some extracanonical books. The material is dated by U. Wilcken c. A. D. 200 (*Archiv fuer Papyrusforschung* 11, 1935, p. 112), and gives a text 125 to 150 years earlier than that of the Codex Vaticanus. P45 Chester Beatty Papyrus I, originally contained all the Gospels and Acts, but is extant only in about one-seventh of its original content. P46 Chester Beatty Papyrus II contains most of the Pauline Epistles in an aggregate of eighty-six leaves out of a total of 104, Philemon and the pastoral Epistles not being included. P47 Chester Beatty Papyrus III contains a considerable portion of the book of Revelation (9:10-17:2). (b) *Uncial Manuscripts*. These are written in separated half-capital characters and are early. They are distinguished from the cursives in which the letters are bound together by ligatures. Uncial script looks like letters printed with pen or pencil in contrast to letters written in regular script. Over 212 uncials are known. The most important of these textually are the *Codex Vaticanus* (B), *Codex Sinaiticus* (Aleph), *Codex Alexandrinus* (A), *Codex Ephraemi Rescriptus* (C), *Codex Bezae* (D) and *Codex Washingtonianus* (W). *Codex Vaticanus* has been in the Vatican Library at Rome since 1481. It dates around 350 A. D. The complete codex contains 759 leaves, 142 belonging to the N. T. *Codex Sinaiticus* (Aleph) was discovered in St.

421. Codex Alexandrinus, Facsimile Table of Contents (A)

Catherine's Monastery by Constantin Tischendorf in 1844 and 1859 and apparently belongs to the latter part of the fourth century A. D. It contains all the N. T. and a large part of the O. T. *Codex Alexandrinus* (A) is in the British Museum. It is called Alexandrinus because it was thought to come from Alexandria, Egypt, and "A" because it was the first important uncial to be used by Biblical textual critics. It contains 733 leaves of the original 822, and dates c. 400 A. D. or a little later. *Codex Ephraemi Rescriptus* (C) is in the National Library in Paris. It is a palimpsest and belongs to the fifth century. *Codex Bezae* (D) is bilingual—being written in Greek and Latin. Stephanus used some of the readings in the margin of his Greek Testament in 1550, and Beza employed it in the later editions of his Greek Testament. *Codex Washingtonianus* (W) has 187 leaves containing only the four Gospels and dates evidently c. 400 A. D. It was purchased in Egypt in 1906 by Mr. C. L. Freer of Detroit and is in the Freer Collection of the Library at Washington. Other important uncial manuscripts may be mentioned. *Codex Claromontanus* (D²) dates from the sixth century and constitutes a leading Western authority for the text of the Epistles of Paul. Discovered at Clermont, France, it was taken to Paris in 1656. It is bilingual, containing both Greek and Latin texts. At one time it belonged to Beza. *Codex Basiliensis* (E) contains the Four Gospels with some lacunae. It dates from the eighth century and is in Basle, Switzerland. *Codex Laudianus* (E²) is in the Bodleian Library at Oxford and is a seventh-century copy of the Book of Acts in Greek and Latin. The *Codex Regius* (L) contains the Gospels and is placed in the eighth century. It is now in the National Library in Paris. *Codex Borgianus* contains an Alexandrian text of 179 verses of Luke and John, and dates probably from the fifth century. It is now in Rome. *Codex Koridethianus* (Theta) belonged to a monastery at Koridethi and is now in the Library of Tiflis. It contains only the Gospels and dates from the eighth century. The manuscript was published in 1913 and its discovery is ranked in importance to that of *Aleph.* (c)

423. Codex of Ephraem (C)

The Minuscule Manuscripts. These are written in the cursive or flowing style of script to which the formal and cumbersome uncial style gave way from the eighth century on. The word "minuscule" is taken from the Latin, *minusculus,* "somewhat small," and refers to the small cursive letters, connected in script, as differentiated from the capital or uncial, which were written separately. Thousands of cursives exist. Sir Frederic Kenyon listed 2429 in 1941 (*Our Bible and the Ancient Manuscripts,* p. 153) and the number has been constantly increasing. The importance of the minuscule manuscripts is normally less than the uncials, since they are for the most part later. But there are exceptions and textual critics often rank certain minuscules higher than certain uncials. The minuscules sometimes run in groups or families and can be traced back to the same uncial. Of the individual minuscules Number 33, from the ninth century, containing the Gospels, Acts, and the Epistles is one of the best. Other important cursives are minuscule 81, 157 and 565. Minuscule 1582 was discovered more recently in the Vatopedi Monastery on Mt. Athos and is of primary importance. It is placed in the tenth century. (d) *Lectionaries.* These are reading lessons employed in public worship services. Those selected from the Gospels are known as *Evangeliaria* or *Evangelistaria.* Those

422. Codex Alexandrinus, Page 1 of Manuscript (A)

selected from the Acts of the Apostles or the Epistles are called *Apostoli* or *Praxapostoli* and are found from the sixth century onward. More than 1600 of these are in existence and are more and more being valued for textual criticism.—*M. F. U.*

Scroll (Heb. *sēphĕr;* Gr. *bibliov,* Isa. 34:6), the form of an ancient book (*q. v.*). In Rev. 6:14 the heaven is said to depart as a scroll is rolled up.

Scull. *See* Skull.

Scum (Heb. *ḥĕl'āh, rust*), in Ezek. 24:6, 11, 12, Jerusalem is likened to a pot with spots of rust upon it, that cannot be removed. The uncleanness of the pot is this rust, which is to be burned away by the heat.

Scurvy. *See* Diseases.

Scyth'ian (sĭth'ĭ-ăn), one of a nomad race, or collection of races, dwelling mostly on the north of the Black Sea and the Caspian, stretching thence indefinitely into inner Asia. They called themselves Scoloti, and the native traditions traced their origin to Targetaus, son of Zeus, or perhaps son of their corresponding god Papaeus (Hd., iv, 59), and a daughter of the river Borysthenes (*ibid.*, iv, 5, 6). In the name *Targ*etaus some have seen the origin of the name Turk.

The Scoloti were fierce barbarians, who "scalped their enemies, and used their skulls as drinking cups (*ibid.*, iv, 64, 65), and offered human sacrifices" (Smith). Their "justice," so highly praised by the earlier poets, was probably a rough and ready impartiality, which is very easy when there is no regard for human life or suffering. In the only place where Scythians are mentioned (Col. 3:11) they are evidently taken as representatives of the barbarian world. It has been inferred, however, and is by no means impossible, that there were Scythians in the early Church.

In the time of Psammetichus, king of Egypt, the contemporary of Josiah, the Scythians invaded Palestine and plundered the temple of Venus Urania in Askalon; and they were only prevented from entering Egypt by prayers and presents (Hd., i, 105). Some suppose that their possession of Bethshean gave it its name, Scythopolis (LXX, *Skuthōnpolis,* Judg. 1:27; comp. Judith 3:10; II Macc. 12:29; and I Macc. 5:52; Josephus, *Skuthopolis*). They took Sardis, B. C. 629; defeated Cyaxares of Media, 624; occupied "Asia" for twenty-eight years, till they were expelled, B. C. 596.

Most moderns, following Josephus (*Ant.*, i, 6, § 1) and Jerome, identify the Magog of Ezek. 38:2; 39:1, 6, the land of which Gog was prince, with the land of the Scythians, who in Ezekiel's time inhabited the region between the Caspian and Euxine. The Scythians of the time of Herodotus and Ezekiel are quite probably believed to have been a Japhetic race. They were backward in civilization so that their name became proverbial for wildness or barbarity much as the Greeks used the epithet "Barbarian" (cf. Col. 3:11). —*W. H., revised by M. F. U.*

Sea (Heb. *yām, roaring;* Gr. *thalassa,* probably *salty*) is sometimes given in the A. V. as the "deep." *Yām* is used in Scripture in the following senses:

1. The "gathering of the waters," i. e., the ocean (Deut. 30:13; I Kings 10:22; Psa. 24:2; Job 26:8, 12; 38:8).

2. With the article, of some part of the great circumambient water, viz.: (*a*) Of the Mediterranean Sea, called the "hinder," the

424. The Mediterranean from Mount Carmel and Haifa

"western," and the "utmost" sea (Deut. 11:24; 34:2; Joel 2:20); "sea of the Philistines" (Exod. 23:31); "the great sea" (Num. 34:6, 7; Josh. 15:47); "the sea" (Gen. 49:13; Psa. 80:11; 107:23; I Kings 4:20, etc.). (*b*) Of the Red Sea (Exod. 15:4; Josh. 24:6), or of one of its gulfs (Num. 11:31; Isa. 11:15), and perhaps the sea (I Kings 10:22) traversed by Solomon's fleet. The place "where two seas met" (Acts 27:41) is understood by Smith, and approved by Ramsay, to be "a neck of land projecting toward the island of Salmonetta, which shelters St. Paul's Bay on the northwest."

3. The term is also applied to the great lakes of Palestine, whether fresh or salt; e. g., (*a*) The Sea of Chinnereth (Num. 34:11) called in the New Testament "the Sea of Galilee" (Matt. 4:18), the "Sea of Tiberias" (John 21:1), and the Sea (or Lake) of Gennesareth (Mark 14:34; Luke 5:1). *See* Galilee, Sea of. (*b*) The Dead Sea, called also the Salt Sea (Gen. 14:3), the Sea of the Plain, or the Arabah (Deut. 4:49), and the Eastern Sea (Joel 2:20; Ezek. 47:18; Zech. 14:8). It is neither named nor alluded to in the New Testament. (*c*) The Lake Merom is only named in Josh. 11:5, 7, A. V. "waters of Merom."

4. *Yām* is also applied to great rivers, as the Nile (Isa. 19:5; Amos 8:8, A. V. "flood;" Nah. 3:8; Ezek. 32:2), and the Euphrates (Jer. 51:36).

Figurative. To "shut up the sea with doors" (Job 38:8) is a symbolical expression for restraining, fixing a bound thereto: "The sea hath spoken" (Isa. 23:4) is figurative for the rock island upon which new Tyre stood, and made her lamentation; the noise of hostile armies is likened to the "roaring of the sea" (Isa. 5:30; Jer. 6:23); *"waves of the sea"* represent righteousness (Isa. 48:18), a devastating army (Ezek. 26:3, 4), and in their restlessness the wicked (Isa. 57:20), and the unsteady (James 1:6); the diffusion of spiritual truth over the earth is symbolized by the covering waters of the sea (Isa. 11:9; Hab. 2:14); "Raging waves of the sea, foaming out their own shame" (Jude 13), is a figurative description of false teachers who threw out their obscene teachings like wrecks upon the shore. "The abundance of the sea" (Isa. 60:5) is everything of value that is possessed by islands and coast lands; "The princes of the sea" (Ezek. 26:16) is a figurative term for the merchants of Tyre; "From sea to sea" (Amos 8:12; Mic. 7:12) stands for "from one end of the world to the other."

Sea, Brazen (I Kings 7:23-44; Jer. 52:17), molten (II Kings 25:13; II Chron. 4:2), the great laver (*q. v.*) in Solomon's temple. This immense copper bowl was placed on twelve bulls, and orientated toward the four points of the compass. It was a new feature of the sanctuary court (I Kings 7:23-26). It took the place of the laver of the tabernacle, was ornately decorated with bunches of flowers and high relief and was for the purpose of ceremonial washings. In the name given to it by Solomon ("sea"), and in its construction, it demonstrates Syro-Phoenician influence as well as cosmic significance. The sea in the ancient Near East was widely recognized as possessing cosmic import (I. Benzinger, *Hebraeische Archaeologie*, 1927, p. 329). Solomon's "molten sea" can hardly be thought of as completely unconnected with the Mesopotamian "sea" (*apsu*), a term used both as a designation of the subterranean fresh water ocean, the source of life and fertility, and of a basin of holy water set up in the temple (W. F. Albright, *Archaeology and the Religion of Israel*, p. 148f; p. 217, note 67; G. E. Wright, *The Biblical Archaeologist* VII, 1944, p. 74). Moreover, these various cosmic sources of water were pictured in mythological imagery as dragons, both in Akkadian (Apsu and Tiamat), Canaanite ("sea") *yammu*, and "river," *naharu*, and in Biblical Hebrew ("sea") *yam* "rivers," *neharoth* (Isa. 51:10; Psa. 74:3) for "sea" and for "rivers" (Psa. 74:15; Hab. 3:8, 9). In Mesopotamia the term "sea" denoted the supposed subterranean source of the great life-giving rivers of that land. Among the Phoenicians and Syrians this expression was used of the Mediterranean as the main source of Canaanite livelihood. The relation of the sea to the portable lavers that Solomon made (I Kings 7:38), which correspond to Phoenician portable lavers discovered at Cyprus, was similar to that between the "sea" (*apsu*) and "the portable basins of water" (*egubbe*) in Babylonian temples (W. F. Albright, *Archaeology and the Religion of Israel*, p. 149).—M. F. U.

Sea Monster. *See* Dragon, Whale, in article Animal Kingdom.

Sea of Glass (Gr. *thalassa hualinē, glassy sea*, Rev. 4:6; 15:2). The "glass sea" recalls the typology of the O. T., which enters richly into the structure of the apocalypse. The allusion is evidently to the tabernacle laver (Exod. 30:18-21) and possibly more directly to the molten sea in the Solomonic temple (I Kings 7:23-37), both being used for priestly ablutions. However, the "sea of glass" points to a fixed state of holiness, both inward and outward, and its being "before the throne" would indicate that the purity is in keeping with the holy character of the throne itself. The "glass sea" is said to be "like crystal." The crystal denotes the splendor and beauty of that scene of holiness spread out before the throne. The two symbols, glass and crystal, are closely

425. Replica of Solomon's Copper "Sea" (Temple Laver), Holding About 10,000 Gallons of Water (from the Howland-Garber model)

allied but are not quite the same. The former is a manufactured article; the latter a native substance. The sea of glass is expressive of smoothness, and this heavenly sea is of crystal, demonstrating that the peace of heaven is not like earthly seas, disturbed by winds, but is crystallized into an eternal peace.—M. F. U.

Sea of Ja′zer (Jer. 48:32), a lake, now represented by some ponds in the high valley in which the city of Jaazer (*q. v.*) is situated.

Seah. See Metrology, ii, 1, 5.

Seal, Sealskin. See Animal Kingdom.

Seal, Signet (Heb. *hōthäm;* Gr. *sphragis*), a portable instrument used to stamp a document or other article, instead of or with the sign manual. The impression made therewith had the same legal validity as an actual signature, as is still the case in the East. Indeed, the importance attached to this method is so great that, without a seal, no document is considered authentic. In a similar manner coffers, doors of houses and tombs, were sealed.

1. **Egyptian.** The most familiar form of Egyptian jewelry is that of the so-called scaraboid seals; in these an elliptical piece of stone was carved on its upper convex surface into the likeness of a scarabeus, the sacred beetle of the Egyptians; and on the lower flat side bore inscriptions in intaglio. Examples of these seals are known as far back as the 4th dynasty, B. C. c. 2550. Sometimes they were made of blue pottery or porcelain, and in many cases consisted of a lump of clay, impressed with a seal and attached to the document by strings.

2. **Mesopotamian.** At Uruk, Biblical Erech (Gen. 10:10), modern Warka, c. 3200 B. C. the cylinder seal and script were introduced. In the White Temple two small square tablets of gypsum plaster were uncovered which contained impressions of cylinder seals. Such early seals were made in the form of a small engraved cylinder which left its impression by being rolled across soft wet clay. A jar or package was sealed with moist clay, and the cylinder seal was rolled over it. From their origin somewhere in the fourth millennium B. C. cylinder seals constantly were used until they gave way to the stamp seals of Persian times. They thus have a demonstrable history of more than three millennia. From Mesopotamia their manufacture and employment spread to peripheral regions as widely distant as India and Egypt. The adornment of the seals shows Mesopotamia's original contribution to art. The Uruk seals display amazing vitality and excellence. Henri A. Frankfort, formerly research professor of Oriental Archaeology at the Oriental Institute of the University of Chicago and now at the University of London, has made monumental studies in the development of the cylinder seal from the pre-historic period to the dynasties of ancient Sumer and Babylon down to the Persian period. See Frankfort's *Cylinder Seals* supplemented by *Cylinder Seals from the Diyala Region.* Professor Frankfort deals with almost 1000 stratified seals discovered during the course of his inspection of work for seven years in Iraq. Leon Legrain of the University of Pennsylvania has also published two volumes in the field of cylinder seals. Of special interest

is the lapis lazuli seal of Queen Shubad uncovered by Woolley at Ur. Cylinder seals were incised on various hard surfaces including gold, silver, rock crystal, blue chalcedony, carnelian, marble, ivory, jasper, glazed pottery and simple baked clay. The well-known seal of Darius the Great displays the king in his two-wheeled chariot between two date palms. Often seals contain both pictures and written material. Jar-handle seals were also common from c. 2500 B. C. These were used not only in signing Babylonian clay documents but in safekeeping jars containing valuable papers or commodities for shipment to distant lands. A cloth was placed over the neck of the container, soft clay smeared on top of the binding cord and the cylinder rolled over the wet clay. If the seal was undisturbed at its destination, the merchandise was safe. —M. F. U.

3. **Hebrew.** The use of clay in sealing is noticed in the book of Job (38:14), and the signet ring as an ordinary part of a man's equipment in the case of Judah (Gen. 38:18), who probably, like many modern Arabs, wore it suspended by a string from his neck or arm (Cant. 8:6). The ring or the seal, as an emblem of authority both in Egypt, in Persia, and elsewhere, is mentioned in the cases of Pharoah with Joseph (Gen. 41:42), of Ahab (I Kings 21:8), of Ahasuerus (Esth. 3:10, 12; 8:2), of Darius (Dan. 6:17; also I Macc. 6:15), and as an evidence of a covenant in Jer. 32:10, 14; Neh. 9:38; 10:1; Hag. 2:23. Engraved signets were in use among the Hebrews in early times, as is evident in the description of the high priest's breastplate (Exod. 28:11, 36; 39:6); and the work of the engraver is mentioned as a distinct occupation (Ecclus. 38:27).

Figurative. "It is turned as clay to the seal," i. e., "it changeth like the clay of a signet ring" (Delitzsch, *Com.*, in loc.), is an allusion to a cylinder seal, revolving like day and night (Job 38:14). In Cant. 8:6 is the prayer, "Set me as a seal upon thine heart, as a seal upon thine arm," implying approaching absence of the bridegroom, and that she wished that her impression may be graven on his arm and heart, i. e., his *love* and *power*. The meaning of the figurative expression, "I will make thee—Zerubbabel—as a signet" (seal ring, Hag. 2:23), is evident from the importance of the signet ring in the eyes of an oriental, who is accustomed to carry it continually with him, and to take care of it as a very valuable possession; also in the same sense when Jehovah says, "Though Coniah [i. e., Jehoiakim] were the signet upon my right hand, yet would I pluck thee hence" (Jer. 22:24). The term *sealed* is used for that which is *permanent* (Isa. 8:16), *confirmed* (John 6:21; Rom. 4:11), that which is to be *kept secret* (Dan. 8:26; 12:4, 9), *impenetrable* to men, but known to Christ (Rev. 5:2-8), *approval* (John 3:33); to "seal up the stars" (Job 9:7) means to cover them with clouds, so that their light is excluded from men, while to "seal up the hand of every man" (37:7) is to prevent men from working by reason of the cold. The "seal of the living God," on which is supposed to be engraven the name of Jehovah, impressed upon the foreheads of the faithful, symbolizes safety and deliverance from judgment (Rev. 7:2-8). A seal also denotes the indwelling of the Holy Spirit (Eph. 1:13; 4:30; II Cor. 1:22; see Mark). The seals upon the "foundation of God" (II Tim. 2:19) are inscriptions upon this mystical building, proper to be impressed upon the minds of all professing Christians, both for encouragement and for warning.

Seam. Our Lord's inner garment, for which the soldiers cast lots (John 19:23), was "without seam," i. e., it was woven entire, from the neck down.

Sea Mew, Sea Monster. See Animal Kingdom.

Sear (Gr. kautēriazō, to brand). The term is used (I Tim. 4:2) figuratively of the conscience. Those of whom the apostle speaks were branded with the marks of sin, i. e., carry about with them the perpetual consciousness of sin. But the meaning seems more precisely to be that their conscience, like cauterized flesh, was deprived of sensation.

Season. See Time.

Seat, as furniture. See House.

Seat. 1. A throne, as usually rendered, but also any seat occupied by a king (Judg. 3:20), or other distinguished person, as the high priest (I Sam. 1:9; 4:13, 18), the king's mother (I Kings 2:19), prime minister (Esth. 3:1). (Heb. kĭssē'). In the New Testament we have Gr. bēma, of the "judgment seat" (Matt. 27:19; John 19:13; Acts 18:12, 16, 17; 25:6, 10, 17); of Christ (Rom. 14:10; II Cor. 5:10); kathedra, in the usual sense of place (Matt. 21:12; Mark 11:15); but generally of the exalted seat occupied by men of eminent rank or influence, as teachers and judges; thus "the Pharisees sit in Moses' seat," i. e., consider themselves as Moses' successors in explaining and defending the law (Matt. 23:2).

2. **An abode** (Heb. môshäb, a seat; I Sam. 20:18, 25; Job 29:7); a sitting, i. e., assembly of persons sitting together (Psa. 1:1); the site of an image (Ezek. 8:3).

Figurative. "I sit in the seat of God" (Ezek. 28:2), the language ascribed to the prince of Tyre is that of pride. "The Tyrian state was the production and seat of its gods. He, the prince of Tyre, presided over this divine creation and divine seat; therefore, he the prince, was himself a god, a manifestation of the deity, having its work and home in the state of Tyre" (Kliefoth). The prophetic meaning sets forth Satan in his connection with the government of this world system (Dan. 10:13, 20; Eph. 6:10).

3. *A place, dwelling* (Job 23:3). Heb. tᵉkūnäh.

4. **Throne** (Gr. thronos), used figuratively for kingly power (Luke 1:52); of Satan (Rev. 2:13; 13:2; 16:10); of the elders (q. v.) (4:4; 11:16).

5. "The uppermost seats" (Luke 11:43), "highest" (20:46), is the rendering of Gr. prōtokathedria, the first or principal seats, and means preeminent in council.

Se'ba (sē'bá).

1. The oldest son of Cush, and hence a country and people among the Cushites (Gen. 10:7; I Chron. 1:9).

2. The name of a people (Psa. 72:10; Isa. 43:3). See Sabeans.

Se'bat (sē'bǎt) or **She'bat** (shē'bǎt), the fifth month of the Hebrew civil year. See Calendar; Time.

Seca'cah (sē-kā'ká; thicket, enclosure), a town in the wilderness of Judah, near the Dead Sea (Josh. 15:61). Noted for its "great cistern," identified by some with Sikkeh, but position uncertain.

Se'chu (sē'kū) or **Se'cu** (sē'kū; a lookout place), site of a "great well," probably lying on the route between Saul's residence, Gibeah, and that of Samuel, Ramathaim-zophim (I Sam. 19:22). The modern Suweikeh, immediately south of Beeroth, is suggested as its site.

Second Coming of Christ, the great event which will wind up this present age. Premillennialists believe that Christ will come to establish a visible earthly kingdom for at least 1000 years over Israel. Amillennialists hold that the second coming of Christ will initiate the eternal state. The amillennialist rejects the future earthly program for Israel and mysticalizes the great O. T. prophecies concerning Zion and Jerusalem, etc., to refer to the Christian church. The postmillenialist believes that Christ will return to the earth after the millennium. Premillennialists believe that the return of Christ consists of two events or stages. Pretribulation premillennialists hold that Christ will return for his Church (I Cor. 15:51f; I Thess. 4:13-18), glorify it and take it to heaven before a seven-year period known as the Great Tribulation (Jer. 30:5; Dan. 9:27, etc.). At the end of this cataclysmic seven-year period Christ will return in power and glory to judge the nations and set up his millennial kingdom. Mid-tribulationists believe that Christ will return in the middle of Daniel's seventieth week. Post-tribulationists reject the idea of a separate appearance of Christ for the Church, and have the church going through the entire tribulation. Exhaustive inductive study of Scripture seems to favor the pretribulation-rapture view.—M. F. U.

Second Sabbath after the first (Luke 6:1). See Sabbath, Second.

Secret. See Mystery.

Sect (Gr. hairesis, a choice), a religious party, as Sadducees (Acts 5:17); Pharisees (15:5); Nazarenes (24:5; comp. 26:5; 28:22).

Secun'dus (sē-kŭn'dŭs, second), a Thessalonian Christian, and one of the party who went with the apostle Paul from Corinth as far as Asia, probably to Troas or Miletus, on his return from his third missionary visit (Acts 20:4).

Security is the doctrine that maintains the continuation of salvation for those who are saved. It must be distinguished from the doctrine of assurance (q. v.). It must also be clearly remembered that it concerns only the regenerate. The doctrine of security is based upon twelve undertakings of God for His people, four related to the Father, four to the Son, and four to the Holy Spirit. 1. **The Father's Undertakings.** (1) The efficacy of the perpetual prayer of the Son upon the Father (John 17:9-12, 15, 20). (2) Infinite divine power made available to save and keep (John 10:29; Rom. 4:21; 8:31-39; Eph. 1:19-

21). (3) God's infinite love (Eph. 1:4; Rom. 5:7-10). (4) God's sovereign purpose or covenant which is unconditional (John 3:16; 5:24; 6:37).

2. **The Son's Undertakings.** (1) His intercession (John 17:1-26; Rom. 8:34; Heb. 7:23-25). (2) His advocacy (Rom. 8:34; Heb. 9:24; I John 2:1, 2). (3) His substitutionary death (Rom. 8:1; I John 2:2). (4) His glorious resurrection (John 3:16; 10:28; Eph. 2:6).

3. **The Spirit's Undertakings.** (1) Regeneration or quickening into eternal life is the partaking of the divine nature and an entrance into that which cannot be removed (John 1:13; 3:3-6; Titus 3:4-6; I John 3:9). (2) Baptism, by which the believer is united to Christ so as to partake eternally in the new creation glory and blessing (I Cor. 6:17; 12:13; Gal. 3:27). (3) Sealing, by which the Holy Spirit stamps and thus secures the Christian as God's son (Eph. 1:13, 14; 4:30). (4) Indwelling, by which the Spirit inhabits the redeemed body forever (John 7:37-39; Rom. 5:5; 8:9; I Cor. 6:19; I John 2:27).

The N. T. clearly teaches that God offers no salvation at the present time which is not eternal. Although this doctrine has been greatly misunderstood and abused, when rightly understood, it offers a powerful boon to a holy life (cf. I John 2:1). Arminian doctrines reject security, employing experience as a proof. However, the following Scriptures commonly so employed, when clearly classified, do not favor insecurity. (2) Passages concerning false teachers of the last days of the Church (I Tim. 4:1-3; II Pet. 2:1-22; Jude 1:17-19) which concern apostates or those who were never saved. (2) Passages comprehending no more than moral reform. For example, Luke 11:24-26. (3) Passages dispensationally misapplied (Ezek. 21:1-48; 33:7-8; Matt. 18:23-35; 24:13; 25:1-13). (4) Passages relating to loss of rewards and chastisement (John 15:2; I Cor. 3:15; 9:27; 11:27-32; Col. 1:21-23; I John 1:5-9; 5:16). (5) Passages relating to falling from grace, that is, leaving the grace-way of life for the legal-way of life (Gal. 5:4). (6) Passages containing various admonitions (Heb. 6:4-9; 10:26-31).

The doctrine of security has suffered much confusion and misuse. It is rejected by many theologians and subscribed to by others, but abused by antinomian teaching and living. It is nevertheless a clear teaching of Scripture, and when properly understood and faithfully believed, it is a doctrine of immense spiritual benefit and blessing.—M. F. U.

Sedition (Gr. *stasis*, a *standing*), used generally in the sense of *rebellion* (Ezra 4:15, 19), insurrection (Luke 23:19, 25; Acts 24:5), "discussion" (Acts 15:2); Gr. *dichostasia*, a *standing apart* (Gal. 5:20).

Seducer (Gr. *goēs*, lit. a *howler*), a deceiver, an impostor (II Tim. 3:13), as a false teacher. These went from bad to worse under the influence of self-deception, as well as that of deceiving others.

Seed. *See* Agriculture.

    Figurative. As the prolific principle of future life, seed in Scripture is taken for posterity of man (Gen. 3:15; 4:25; 13:15, etc.), of beasts (Jer. 31:27), trees (Gen. 1:11, 12,

29, etc.). The seed of Abraham denotes not only those who descend from him by natural issue, but those who imitate his character, independent of natural descent (Rom. 4:16). Seed is figurative of God's word (Luke 8:5, 11; I Pet. 1:23), and its preaching is called "sowing" (Luke 8:5; Matt. 13:32; I Cor. 9:11). *Sowing* seed is symbolical of scattering or dispersing a people (Zech. 10:9), of dispensing liberally (Eccles. 11:6; II Cor. 9:6), of working evil (Job 4:8), righteousness (Hos. 10:12), or deeds in general (Gal. 6:8). Christ compares his death to the sowing of seed with its results (John 12:24); Paul likens the burial of the body to the sowing of seed (I Cor. 15:36-38).

Seedtime. *See* Agriculture.

Seer. *See* Prophet.

Seethe (Heb. *bāshăl, boil*), seething pot (Heb. *nāphăḥ*, to *blow* hard). Food (*q. v.*) was often prepared by boiling (Exod. 16:23; 23:19, etc.). The pot in which it was boiled took its name, "a *pot blown*," i. e., with a fanned fire under it, a kettle violently boiling (Job 41:20); Jer. 1:13).

Se'gub (sē'gŭb; *elevated*).

1. The youngest son of Hiel the Bethelite and rebuilder of Jericho. Segub died for his father's sin (I Kings 16:34), according to Joshua's prediction, "Cursed be the man before the Lord, that riseth up and buildeth this city Jericho: he shall lay the foundation thereof in his firstborn, and in his youngest son shall he set up the gates of it" (Josh. 6:26), B. C. between 875 and 854.

2. The son of Hezron (grandson of Judah) by the daughter of Machir, the "father" of Gilead. He was himself the father of Jair (I Chron. 2:21, 22), B. C. perhaps about 1900.

Se'ir (sē'ĭr; *rough, hairy*), a chief of the Horites (*q. v.*), the former inhabitants of the country afterward possessed by the Edomites (Gen. 36:20, 21; I Chron. 1:38). Whether he gave the name to the country or took it from it is uncertain.

Se'ir, Land of. The mountainous territory of Edom (Gen. 32:3; 36:30). *See* Mount Seir.

Se'ir, Mount (mownt sē'ĭr; Gen. 14:6, sq.).

1. **Mount Seir** is the range of mountains running southward from the Dead Sea, east of the valley of Arabah, to the Elanitic Gulf. The earliest mention of Mount Seir is in the Bible account of Chedorlaomer's campaign, in the days of Abraham. This was long before the birth of Esau; and it is said that the Horites (*q. v.*) were then its inhabitants. They are the Hurrians now known so well from the cuneiform tablets from ancient Nuzu and other sites, who between about 1780 and 1600 invaded N. Mesopotamia and gradually spread over Palestine and Syria. The Israelites were forbidden to enter this region, as Jehovah had given it to Esau for a possession (Deut. 2:5). The mention of Esau's removal to Mount Seir follows immediately on the mention of Isaac's death and burial (Gen. 35:27-29; 36:1-8). At the base of this chain of mountains are low hills of limestone or argillaceous rocks; then lofty masses of porphyry, which constitute the body of the mountain; above these is sandstone broken into irregular ridges and grotesque groups of cliffs;

and again, farther back and higher than all, are long elevated ridges of limestone without precipices. Beyond all these stretches off indefinitely the high plateau of the great eastern desert. The height of the porphyry cliffs is estimated by Robinson at about two thousand feet above the Arabah (the great valley between the Dead Sea and Elanitic Gulf), while the limestone ridges farther back do not fall short of three thousand feet. The whole breadth of the mountainous tract between the Arabah and the eastern desert above does not exceed more than fifteen or twenty miles. These mountains are quite different in character from those which front them on the west side of the Arabah. The latter seem to be not more than two thirds as high; while those on the east appear to enjoy a sufficiency of rain, and are covered with tufts of herbs and occasional trees. The general appearance of the soil is not unlike that around Hebron, though the face of the country is very different. It is, indeed, the region of which Isaac said to his son Esau, "Behold, thy dwelling shall be (far) from the fatness of the earth, and the dew of heaven from above" (27:39).

2. **The Land of Seir** is located to the south and east of Beer-sheba. Esau married and had children long before he permanently left his old home near Beer-sheba, and that region over which Esau extended his patriarchal stretch came to be known as "the land of Seir" (or Esau), and the "country (or field) of Edom" (Gen. 32:3). Here Esau was living when Jacob came back from Padan-aram, for Isaac was not yet dead, and it was not until after his death that Esau removed to Mount Seir (35:27-29; 36:1-8). When the brothers had met, Jacob spoke of himself as journeying by easy stages toward the home of Esau, in Seir—Esau's present "Seir," not Esau's prospective "Mount Seir" (comp. 33:13-20; 35:27). Then it was—and even until the very day of Jacob's return—that Esau was a dweller in "the land of Seir, the country of Edom" (32:1-3), not the Mount Seir, or the Edom which was the equivalent of Mount Seir. This designation of the land of Esau's occupancy in southern Canaan by the name of "Seir," which existed at the time of Jacob's return from Padan-aram, was never lost to it. It was found there when the Israelites made their unauthorized raid northward from Kadesh-barnea (Deut. 1:44). To the present time there remain traces of the old name of "Seir" in the region southeast from Beer-sheba, and yet north of the natural southern boundary line of the land of Canaan. The extensive plain "Es Seer" is there, corresponding with the name and location of "Seir" (1:44) at which, or unto which, the Israelites were chased by the Amorites when they went up in foolhardiness from their Kadesh-barnea.

3. **Another Mount Seir** formed one of the landmarks on the north boundary of Judah (Josh. 15:10 only). It was to the west of Kirjath-jearim and between it and Beth-shemesh. It is a ridge of rock to the southwest of *Kureyet el Enab*, a lofty ridge composed of rugged peaks, with a wild and desolate appearance, upon which *Saris* and *Mishir* are situated (Robinson, *Bib. Res.*, p. 155).

Sei′rah A. V. **Se′irath** (sĕ-ī′răth; *woody district, shaggy*), a place in the mountains of Ephraim, bordering on Benjamin, to which Ehud went for refuge after killing Eglon at Jericho (Judg. 3:26, 27).

426. Mount Selah, Petra

Se′la, Se′lah (sē′lȧ; *rock*), and so rendered in A. V. (Judg. 1:36; II Chron. 25:12; Obad. 3) was probably the capital city of the Edomites, later known as Petra. It took its name from its situation and the mode in which it was built, since it was erected in a valley surrounded by rocks, and in such a manner that the houses were partly hewn in the natural rock. It was still flourishing in the first centuries of the Christian era, and splendid ruins still exist. The excavations are remarkable, consisting of what appear to be the facades of great temples and immense theaters, hewn in rock of variegated colors. The place seems to have been the very center of interest and trade from time immemorial. It was taken by Amaziah, king of Judah, and called by him Joktheel (II Kings 14:7; II Chron. 25:11, 12). About 300 B. C. Sela (Gr. Petra, *rock*) passed from the Edomites to the Nabataean Arabs, whose remarkable kingdom lasted till A. D. 105, when Arabia Petraea became a province of the Roman Empire.

Se′lah (sē′lȧ). *See* Music.

Se′la-Hammah′lekoth (sē′lȧ-hă-mä′lê-kŏth; *cliff of divisions*), a rock in the wilderness of Maon, and the scene of one of David's most remarkable escapes from Saul (I Sam. 23:28). Not identified certainly.

Se′led (sē′lĕd; *exultation*), a descendant of Jerahmeel, of the tribe of Judah. He was the elder of two sons of Nadab and died childless (I Chron. 2:30).

Seleu′cia (sē-lū′shĭ-ȧ), a town near the mouth of the Orontes and the seaport of *Antioch* (*q. v.*), from which Paul sailed forth on his first missionary journey (Acts 13:4), and it is almost certain that he landed there on his return from it (14:26). It was built by Seleucus Nicator, who built so many other cities of the same name that this one was called *Seleucia Pieria*, being near Mount Pierus, and also *Seleucia ad Mare*, being nearer the sea. It retained its importance in Roman times, and was a free city in the days of Paul. Now called el-Kalusi.

Self-will (Heb. *räşōn, pleasure*, and, in a wicked sense, *wantonness*, Gen. 49:6). In the New

Testament, self-willed is the rendering of Gr. *'authadēs*, *self-pleasing*, *arrogant* (Tit. 1:7; II Pet. 2:10).

Selvedge (Heb. *qāṣäh*, *termination*), the edge of a piece of cloth (Exod. 26:4; 36:11).

Sem (sĕm), the Grecized form (Luke 3:36) of the name of Shem (*q. v.*).

Semachi'ah (sĕm-à-kī'à; *Jehovah has sustained*), the last named of the six sons of Shemaiah, the son of Obed-edom (I Chron. 26:7).

Sem'ein (sĕm'ĕ-ĭn) in A. V. **Sem'ei** (sĕm'ĕ-ī), the son of Joseph, and father of Mattathias, in our Lord's genealogy (Luke 3:26) probably *Shemaiah* (*q. v.*).

Sena'ah (sē-nā'à). The "children of Senaah" are enumerated among the "people of Israel" who returned from the captivity with Zerubbabel (Ezra 2:35; Neh. 7:38). In Neh. 3:3 the name is given with the article, has-Senaah. *See* Hassenaah. The names in these lists are mostly those of towns; but Senaah does not occur elsewhere in the Bible as attached to a town. The Magdal-Senna, or "great Senna," of Eusebius and Jerome, seven miles north of Jericho ("Senna"), however, is not inappropriate in position.

Senate (Gr. *gerousia*, *eldership*), a deliberative body, and in the New Testament (Acts 5:21) of not only those elders of the people who were members of the Sanhedrin, but *the whole body of elders* generally, the whole council of the representatives of the people (Meyer, *Com.*, in loc.).

Senators (Heb. *zäqēn*, *old*), chief men, magistrates (Psa. 105:22). The Hebrew word is elsewhere rendered elder (*q. v.*)

Se'neh (sē'nĕ; *thorn-bush*), the name of one of the two isolated rocks which stood in the "passage of Michmash," climbed by Jonathan, and his armor-bearer, when he went to examine the Philistine camp (I Sam. 14:4). It was the southern one of the two (14:5), and the nearest to Geba. The name in Hebrew means a "thorn," or thorn-bush. Josephus mentions that the last encampment of Titus's army was at a spot "which in the Jews' tongue is called the valley," or perhaps the plain "of thorns, near to a village called Gabath-saoulé," i. e., Gibeath of Saul.

Se'nir (sē'nĭr). The Amorite name of Hermon (Deut. 3:9; Song 4:8; Ezek. 27:5). *See* Shenir.

Sennach'erib (sē-năk'ĕr-ĭb; Akkad. *Sin*, i. e., the moon-god, *has multiplied the brothers*). Sennacherib, one of the kings of Assyria, son of Sargon, ascended the throne on the twelfth day of Ab (July-August), B. C. 705. His father, Sargon, had been a usurper, and having gained his position by the sword, he also lost his life by it at the hands of a murderous soldier. There seems to have been no opposition to Sennacherib's accession, as so often happened in the history of Assyria. He inherited a vast empire from his father, with abundant opportunities for its further extension. He had, however, not inherited his father's boldness or daring, nor his resources. All the powers of his mind were employed in holding together that which he had received. It is indeed doubtful whether he left his empire as strong as he had received it.

The records of Sennacherib's reign have not come down to us in as complete a form as those of his predecessor or successor. Of the later years of his reign we have no Assyrian accounts. The earlier years are, however, well covered by the beautiful and well-preserved prism called the Taylor Cylinder, now in the British Museum. Of all Assyrian documents which have come down to us not one is in better preservation than this. It was found by Colonel Taylor in 1830. It is fourteen and one half inches high, and is covered on all of its six sides with fine Assyrian script, which sets forth the annals of the king. Complete translations of the records of Sennacherib can be found in Daniel D. Luckenbill, *Ancient Records of Assyria And Babylonia*, Vol. II and in James Pritchard's, *Ancient N. E. Texts* (Princeton, 1950).

1. Campaign Against Babylon. Sargon had left a powerful empire, but not all sources of possible difficulty had been blotted out, nor all peoples within the great territory reduced to complete submission. Sennacherib was sure to meet with troubles in Babylonia. The people of Babylon had been brought into the Assyrian empire by force. They could not be expected to forget that they had a magnificent history behind them, while yet the people of Assyria were but laying the foundations of their state. It was hard for a city with so grand a history as Babylon to yield submission to the upstart power of Assyria. In the confusions that followed the close of Sargon's reign the Babylonians saw the opportunity for another rebellion. The leader of this uprising was Merodach-baladan, who came from the lowland country far south of Babylon, near the Persian Gulf, called, in the texts of that period, the land of Kardunyash. It was probably a national uprising which Merodach-baladan led (*see* Merodach-baladan), but he had allies from the mountain land of Elam, and with their help he had himself crowned king in Babylon. Once more was there in his person national rule in Babylonia, and the Assyrian supremacy was, temporarily at least, overthrown. For nine months Merodach-baladan reigned undisputedly. Then Sennacherib invaded Babylonia with an army which Merodach-baladan could not resist. The contest was fought at Kish, and the rout of the Babylonians was complete. Merodach-baladan fled alone and escaped with his life. The victorious Sennacherib· entered Babylon and plundered everything which had belonged to his unfortunate adversary, but seems not to have disturbed the possessions of the citizens. He then marched south into the land of Kaldi, whence the rebels had drawn their supplies. The overthrow was complete in every particular. Seventy-five cities and four hundred smaller towns and hamlets were taken and despoiled. This invasion was not carried out without heartless cruelty, as the description of the taking of one city testifies. Says Sennacherib: "The men of the city Khirimme, a rebellious enemy, I cast down with arms; I left not one alive; their corpses I bound on stakes and placed them around the city." Over the reduced country an Assyrian named Bel-ibni was made king, subject to Sennacherib. But this was not the end of Sennacherib's difficulties with Babylonia.

2. **Against the Kassites.** The next campaign directed against the people called the Kassi, together with the Medes and other races living along and beyond the upper waters of the Tigris, and even among the mountains northeast of Assyria, is boasted of by Sennacherib, but there seems to have been little result from it. He claims to have "widened his territory," but we can find no evidence that Assyrian supremacy was actually carried much farther. The chief result of the campaign was probably "a heavy tribute" and the intimidating of some peoples who otherwise might have been troublesome until campaigns against the West were undertaken.

3. **Against Palestine-Syria.** The third campaign of Sennacherib was directed against the land of the Hittites, 701 B. C. At this period this term did not mean the same as it did before the days of Sargon. The empire of the Hittites had been destroyed, and land of the Hittites now meant only the land of Phoenicia and Palestine. This western country had often before been invaded from Babylonia and Assyria (*see* articles Assyria, Sargon, Shalmaneser, Tiglath-pileser, and Chedorlaomer), but though conquests had been made, there were still more to be made. Rebellions were frequent. It would be yet a long time before autonomy should die out among the commercial Phoenicians and the patriotic and religious Hebrews. Sennacherib seems to have come suddenly into the west, and his success at first was probably due to the unpreparedness of the native kings and princes. Elulaeus, king of Sidon, offered no resistance, but fled from the invader. His cities of Sidon, Sarepta, Acco (now Acre), Ekdippa, and others were quickly subdued and plundered. Ethobal was made king over them, and a heavy annual tribute assessed upon the inhabitants. The news of this great Assyrian victory spread southward, and many petty kings sent presents and acknowledged Sennacherib as their suzerain, hoping thereby to save their cities from destruction and their lands from plunder. Among those who thus yielded without a blow for freedom were the rulers of Arvad, Byblos, Moab, and Edom. The king of Ashkelon, Tsidqa by name, had not sent, and his land was therefore next attacked. The resistance seems to have been slight, and Ashkelon was soon taken. The king and all his family were deported to Assyria as captives, and his cities of Beth-dagon, Joppa, Beniberak (Josh. 19:45), and Azuru were plundered. The people of Ekron had also refused to submit to Sennacherib. Their ruler, Padi, who had been set over them by the Assyrians, they cast in chains and delivered over to Hezekiah, king of Judah. This move on their part probably signifies their allegiance to the league of Judah and Egypt, which proposed to resist Sennacherib. When Sennacherib was ready to attack the city of Ekron the Egyptian army appeared, accompanied by its allies from Melukhkha, a battle took place at Eltekeh (19:44; 21:23), and once more Sennacherib claims a victory. Of the fight he says little, save that a few captives were made. He did not, however, follow up the Egyptians, and it is therefore probable that he respected

their prowess and was desirous of avoiding the risk of a second and desperate conflict. He was content rather with taking Eltekeh and Timnath (Gen. 38:12; Josh. 15:10, etc.; modern *Tibneh*), and then fell back to punish Ekron. His own words describe his own deeds: "To the city of Ekron I went; the governors (and) princes, who had committed a transgression, I killed and bound their corpses on poles around the city. The inhabitants of the city who had committed sin and evil I counted as spoil; to the rest of them who had committed no sin and wrong, who had no guilt, I spoke peace. Padi, their king, I brought forth from the city of Jerusalem; upon the throne of lordship over them I placed him. The tribute of my lordship I laid upon him."

4. **Invasion of Judah.** Immediately upon this victory over Ekron comes Sennacherib's invasion of the kingdom of Judah. This was known to us from the biblical account in II Kings 18:13-19:36. It fills a large space in Israel's history, and it was a moment of thrilling interest when Sennacherib's own version of the invasion was found. His story is so important for the student of the Bible that it may well be here translated entire: "As for Hezekiah the Jew, who did not submit to my yoke, forty-six of his strong walled cities, as well as the small cities in their neighborhood, which were without number—by constructing a rampart out of trampled earth and by bringing up battering rams, by the attack of infantry, by tunnels, breaches and (the use of axes), I besieged and took. Two hundred thousand one hundred and fifty men, young (and) old, male and female, horses, mules, asses, camels, oxen and sheep without number I brought out from them, I counted as spoil. (Hezekiah) himself I shut up like a caged bird in Jerusalem, his royal city; the walls I fortified against him, (and) whosoever came out of the gates of the city, I turned back. His cities, which I had plundered, I divided from his land and gave them to Mitinti, king of Ashdod, to Padi, king of Ekron, and to Sillibel, king of Gaza, and (thus) diminished his territory. To the former tribute, paid yearly, I added the tribute of alliance of my lordship and laid that upon him. Hezekiah himself was overwhelmed by the fear of the brightness of my lordship; the Arabians and his other faithful warriors whom, as a defense for Jerusalem his royal city he had brought in, fell into fear. With thirty talents of gold (and) eight hundred talents of silver, precious stones, rouge dakkasi, lapis lazuli, couches of ivory, thrones of ivory, ivory, *ushu* wood, *ukarinnu* wood, various objects, a heavy treasure, and his daughters, his women of the palace, male and female musicians, to Nineveh, the city of my lordship, I caused to be brought after me; and he sent his ambassadors to give tribute and to pay homage." Sennacherib does not name the place where he received this great tribute from Hezekiah. From the Bible we learn that it was Lachish (II Kings 18:14). From Sennacherib himself we also learn that he had besieged and taken the same city of Lachish, present-day Tell ed-Duweir, now well known as a result of ar-

chaeological excavation. A splendid wall relief has come down to us, upon which Sennacherib is represented seated upon a throne receiving men bearing presents. In front of the king's head are these words: "Sennacherib, the king of the world, the king of Assyria, sat on his throne, and the spoil of the city of Lachish marched before him." With the words, given above, of tribute and embassies of homage Sennacherib concludes his account of his campaigns to the west. The biblical account adds one detail more in these words: "And it came to pass that night, that the angel of the Lord went forth, and smote in the camp of the Assyrians an hundred fourscore and five thousand; and when men arose early in the morning, behold, they were all dead corpses" (II Kings 19:35). Of this great destruction there is no word or hint in Sennacherib's inscriptions. It was indeed not to be expected that such a record would be made under any circumstances. The Assyrians report only victories. At any rate Sennacherib never invaded Palestine again. The chronological data of the Assyrians locate this famous Judean campaign in the year 701 B. C.

5. **Later Campaigns.** After the Judaean campaign Sennacherib found opposed to him a powerful coalition of Elamites, Babylonians, Aramaeans, and Medians, with whom he fought at Chalule in the year 691 B. C. The result was a doubtful victory for the Assyrian army. It seems indeed that Sennacherib did little more than ward off destruction and postpone for a time the inevitable ruin of the empire.

Again and again was there trouble and rebellion in Babylonia. Now it is the once-defeated Merodach-baladan, again it is Suzub, the Chaldean. Indeed so numerous were the uprisings in Babylonia that it is now almost impossible to distinguish them and understand their significance. After several invasions and fruitless peacemakings, Sennacherib took Babylon, and actually broke down its walls, and practically ruined the city. This was in 689 B. C. In this year came thus to an end for a time the glory of this once invincible city. The destruction can only be regarded as an act of revengeful folly. It did not quell the turbulent sprits of the Babylonians, who could not be brought into subjection by such means, and it only left a legacy of trouble to Sennacherib's son and successor. Sennacherib's own opinion of the people of Babylonia was expressed in the phrase "evil devils." He could not understand them, and their patriotic love of the city by the Euphrates was not a sentiment to be admired, but passion to be destroyed.

The results of all these wars can only be found, as we look back upon them, in the retention of what Sargon had won. Of real expansion, there was none.

In spite of wars and dissensions Sennacherib was able also to give attention to the arts of peace. In Nineveh he constructed two magnificent palaces, and the city walls and gates he rebuilt or restored. By constructing the huge so-called Aqueduct of Jerwan, Sennacherib made Nineveh a garden city. This, the first Mesopotamian aqueduct known, brought water from some 30 miles distant. He also introduced the *shadûf* or well sweep from Egypt.

The inscriptions give no hint concerning the manner of Sennacherib's death in the year 681 B. C. The Bible, however, supplies the missing detail by showing that he died at the hands of his two sons, Adrammelech and Sharezer, while he was engaged in worship (II Kings 19:37). These statements agree well with the known facts that Sennacherib had preferred Esarhaddon above his brothers, and that there was jealousy among the other members of the family.

Sense. 1. (Heb. *sĕkĕl, intelligence.*) Thus it is said that Ezra and others "read in the book, in the law of God, distinctly, and gave the sense" (Neh. 8:8), i. e., caused the people to understand.

2. Gr. *aisthētērion, faculty of the mind* for perceiving, understanding, judging (Heb. 5:14).

Sensual (Gr. *psuchikos,* A. V. *natural*), having the nature and characteristics of the *psuchē*, i. e., *of the principle of animal life,* which men have in common with the brutes (I Cor. 15:44), similar to "flesh and blood" (v. 50). It has also the meaning of *governed by the psuchē*, i. e., the sensuous nature with its subjection to appetite and passion (Jude 19; comp. I Cor. 2:14). So in James 3:15, sensual wisdom is that which is in harmony with the corrupt desires and affections, and springing from them. The regenerate receive a new nature, but the old is not eradicated, but exists alongside the new. The believer is given a new position "in Christ" (Rom. 6:1-10) upon which he is to "reckon" (Rom. 6:11), and thus by the Spirit's power to overcome the lusts of the old nature (Gal. 5:16; Rom. 8:1-28).

Sentences. Riddles, enigmas (Dan. 5:12); understanding mysteries, i. e., using dissimulation, artifice (8:23), as shown in v. 25.

Senu′ah (sē-nū′á; Neh. 11:9). *See* Hasenuah.

Separation. The Levitical law provided that persons contaminated by certain defilements should be excluded for a longer or shorter period from the fellowship of the sanctuary, and sometimes even from intercourse with their fellow-countrymen. These defilements comprised the uncleanness of a woman in consequence of child-bearing (Lev., ch. 12), leprosy (chaps. 13, 14), and both natural and diseased secretions from the sexual organs of either male or female (ch. 15), and from a human corpse (Num. 19:11-22). *See* Uncleanness.

Se′phar (sē′fär; *numbering*), "a mountain of the east," mentioned in connection with the Joktanite boundaries (Gen. 10:30). The immigration of the Joktanites was probably from west to east, and they occupied the southwestern portion of the peninsula. There is quite a general agreement that Sephar is preserved in the very ancient city of *Zhafar*—now pronounced *Isfôr*—in the province of Hadramaut, of South Arabia, not far from the seaport Mirbat.

Sepha′rad (sē-fä′rǎd). In Obadiah (v. 20) it is said that the captives of Jerusalem were "in Sepharad." Sepharad may possibly be Sardis in W. Asia minor or a part of Media S. W. of the Caspian Sea. The name occurs in Assyrian inscription, and may have connection with Shaparda mentioned by Sargon as a district of S. W. Media. Cf. II Kings 17:6.

Sepharva'im (sĕ-fär-vä'yĭm), the name of a city under Assyrian rule, from which people were transported and settled in Samaria, in the reign of Sargon, along with other people from Cutha, Babylon, Avva, and Hamath (II Kings 17:24). It appears from other Biblical allusions that Sepharvaim was in a country which had but a short time before this been conquered by the Assyrians; it was not in a land which formed an integral portion of the Assyrian empire (II Kings 18:34; 19:13; Isa. 36:19; 37:13). It has been identified commonly with the city *Sippar*, the ruins of which were found by Hormuzd Rassam, at Abu Habba, southwest of Bagdad, and near the Euphrates. This identification is, however, fraught with great difficulty, and may indeed be regarded as practically impossible. Sepharvaim has a different form from *Sippar*; it is mentioned always in connection with Hamath, as though it were located in the vicinity; it was recently conquered by the Assyrians while Sippar was an ancient city in Babylonian territory. For these and other reasons scholars have with practical unanimity ceased to connect Sepharvaim with the ancient Babylonian city of Sippar. Instead of this the identification proposed by Halevy has received common acceptance, viz., that Sepharvaim is the same as the city Sibraim (Ezek. 47:16), and that this is the city mentioned in the Babylonian chronicle under the name of Saberim, which lies in the Hamath district, and was conquered by Shalmaneser V in 727 B. C. In these particulars it exactly suits the requirements of the biblical Sepharvaim. The proof is, however, not positive, though the case is at least plausible.— R. W. R., revised by *M. F. U.*

Se'pharvite (sē'fär-vīt), a native of *Sepharvaim* (*q. v.*) (II Kings 17:31).

Sep'tuagint. *See* Scripture, Versions of.

Sepulcher. *See* Tomb.

Se'rah (sē'rà; written Sarah in Num. 26:46), the daughter of Asher, the son of Jacob (Gen. 46:17; Num. 26:46; I Chron. 7:30). The mention of her name in a list of this kind, in which no others of her sex are named, and contrary to the usual practice of the Jews, seems to indicate something extraordinary in connection with her history or circumstances. The Jews have a tradition that she was very remarkable for piety and virtue, and was therefore privileged to be the first person to tell Jacob that his son Joseph was still living; on which account she was translated to paradise, where, according to the ancient book Zohar, are four mansions, each presided over by an illustrious woman, viz., Sarah, daughter of Asher; the daughter of Pharaoh, who brought up Moses; Jochebed, the mother of Moses; and Deborah, the prophetess.

Sera'iah (sĕ-rā'yà; *Jehovah has prevailed*).

1. The scribe (or secretary) of David (II Sam. 8:17), B. C. 986. In other places the name is ocrrupted into "Sheva" (20:25),

"Shisha" (I Kings 4:3), and "Shavsha" (I Chron. 18:16).

2. The son of Azariah, and high priest in the reign of Zedekiah (II Kings 25:18; I Chron. 6:14; Ezra 7:1). When Jerusalem was captured by the Chaldeans, B. C. 587, he was sent as prisoner to Nebuchadnezzar at Riblah, and there put to death (Jer. 52:24-27).

3. An Israelite, the son of Tanhumeth, the Netophathite, and one of those to whom Gedaliah advised submission to the Chaldeans (II Kings 25:23; Jer. 40:8), B. C. 588.

4. The second son of Kenaz, and father of a Joab who was a head of a family of the tribe of Judah, in the valley of Charashim (I Chron. 4:13, 14).

5. Son of Asiel, and father of Josibiah, of the tribe of Simeon (I Chron. 4:35).

6. A priest who returned from the captivity (Ezra 2:2; Neh. 12:1, 12), B. C. 536. He is, perhaps, the same who is mentioned (Neh. 10:2) as sealing the covenant with Nehemiah as "ruler of the house of God" (11:11).

7. The son of Azriel, and one of the persons commanded by King Jehoiakim to apprehend Jeremiah and Baruch (Jer. 36:26), B. C. about 606.

8. The son of Neriah, and brother of Baruch (Jer. 51:59, 61). He went with Zedekiah to Babylon in the fourth year of his reign, and is described as *sar mĕnûchâh* (literally "prince of rest;" A. V. "a quiet prince;" marg. "prince of Menuchah, or chief chamberlain"); R. V. "quartermaster" a title which is interpreted by Kimchi as that of the office of chamberlain. Perhaps he was an officer who took charge of the royal caravan on its march, and fixed the place where it should halt. Seraiah was sent on an embassy to Babylon, about four years before the fall of Jerusalem, and was commissioned by the prophet Jeremiah to take with him on his journey the roll in which he had written the doom of Babylon, and sink it in the midst of the Euphrates, as a token that Babylon would sink, never to rise again (Jer. 51:60-64), B. C. 595.

Seraphim. 1. **Name.** (Heb. perhaps *säräph, burning, fiery.*) The meaning of the word "seraph" is extremely doubtful; the only word which resembles it in the current Hebrew is *säräph*, "to burn," whence the idea of *brilliancy* has been extracted; but it is objected that the Hebrew term never bears this secondary sense. Gesenius connects it with an Arabic term (*sharafa*) signifying *high* or *exalted;* and this may be regarded as the generally received etymology.

2. **Nature.** An order of celestial beings, whom Isaiah beheld in vision standing above Jehovah as he sat upon his throne (Isa. 6:2, 6). They are described as having each of them three pairs of wings, with one of which they covered their faces (a token of humility); with the second they covered their feet (a token of respect); while with the third they flew. They seem to have borne a general resemblance to the human figure, for they are represented as having a face, a voice, feet, and hands (v. 6).

3. **Occupation.** The seraphim which Isaiah saw hovered above on both sides of Him that sat upon the throne, forming two opposite choirs, and presenting antiphonal worship.

Their occupation was twofold—to celebrate the praises of Jehovah's holiness and power (v. 3), and to act as the medium of communication between heaven and earth (v. 6). They are beings expressive of the divine holiness and demand that the saint shall be cleansed before serving (Isa. 6:6-8). From their antiphonal chant ("one cried unto another") we may conceive them to have been ranged in opposite rows on each side of the throne. See Cherubim.

Se′red (sē′rĕd; cf. Syriac s⁰rad, to be affrighted), the firstborn of Zebulun (Gen. 46:14), and head of the family of the Sardites (Num. 26:26).

Sergeant (Gr. hrabdoukos), a rod holder, i. e., a Roman lictor, a public servant who bore a bundle of rods before the magistrates of cities and colonies as insignia of their office, and who executed the sentences which they pronounced (Acts 16:35).

Ser′gius Paul′us (sûr′jĭ-ŭs-pô′lŭs), the Roman proconsul of Cyprus at the time when Paul with Barnabas visited that island on his first missionary tour. He is described as an intelligent ("prudent") man, and hence entertained Elymas, desiring to learn the truth. On becoming acquainted with Barnabas and Paul he was convinced of the truth, and accepted the Gospel (Acts 13:7-12).

Sermon on the Mount. 1. The name usually given to a discourse delivered by Jesus to his disciples and a multitude on a mountain near Capernaum, A. D., perhaps 28 (Matt., chaps. 5-7; Luke 6:20, sq.). The time, however, is no more distinctly given than is the place. Meyer (Com., in loc.) thinks that it was after Jesus had chosen his first four apostles, and that "his disciples," in addition to these four, were his disciples generally. Edersheim (Life and Times of Jesus, i, 524) locates it immediately after the choice of the twelve, grouping together Luke 6:12, 13, 17-19; comp. with Mark 3:13-15, and Matt. 5:1, 2.

2. **The Discourse Itself.** "It is the same as that found in Luke 6:20-49; for, although differing in respect of its contents, style, and arrangement from that of Matthew, yet, judging from its characteristic introduction and close, its manifold and essential identity as regards the subject-matter, as well as from its mentioning the circumstance that, immediately after, Jesus cured the sick servant in Capernaum (Luke 7:1, sq.), it is clear that Matthew and Luke do not record two different discourses" (Meyer, Com.).

The plan, according to Gess, is as follows: The happiness of those who are fit for the kingdom (Matt. 5:3-12); the lofty vocation of Jesus's disciples (5:13-16); the righteousness, superior to that of the Pharisees, after which they must strive who would enter the kingdom (5:17-6:34); the rocks on which they run the risk of striking, and the help against such dangers (7:1-27).

3. **Application.** This remarkable discourse of Jesus has first of all an omnitemporal moral application, and hence its principles are applicable to the Christian. It is a perennial truth that the pure in spirit, rather than the proud, are blessed and that those who mourn because of their sins, who are meek and

hunger and thirst after righteousness are filled. The merciful are always blessed and the pure in heart "see God." However, in the Jewish slant of Matthew, presenting Christ as King, premillennialists frequently hold the application is literally to the establishment of the future Davidic kingdom. This discourse gives the divine constitution for the righteous government of the earth. It will be the fulfillment of "righteousness" as used by the prophets in describing this kingdom which is to be restored to Israel (cf. Isa. 11:4, 5; Isa. 32:1; Dan. 9:24). In the time of our Lord the Jews rejected the kingdom because they had made "righteousness" to mean mere ceremonialism and had missed its deeper meaning as a matter of motive and of the heart. The Jews were never rebuked for expecting a visible Messianic kingdom. Had they heeded the prophets, however, they would have plainly seen that only the poor in spirit, the meek and the pure in heart would have a share in it (Isa. 11:4; Psa. 72). Careful exegesis of the Sermon on the Mount must not confuse it with the era of grace initiated by the death, resurrection and ascension of Christ. The Sermon, however, is very commonly construed by expositors as applicable solely to the Christian church. This interpretation, however, can scarcely be reconciled with its scope and purpose, particularly in the Gospel of Matthew. M. F. U.

Serpent. See Animal Kingdom; Temptation.

Figurative. The malice of the wicked is compared to the "poison of the serpent" (Psa. 58:4; comp. 140:3); the poisonous bite of the serpent is a figure of the baneful influence of wine (Prov. 23:31, 32); unexpected evil is like the bite of a serpent lurking in a wall (Eccles. 10:8), and a "babbler" like an uncharmed serpent, which bites (10:11); enemies who harass and destroy are compared to serpents (Isa. 14:29; Jer. 8:17), while the voice of discomfited Egypt is likened to serpents roused from their lair by the woodman (Jer. 46:22). The serpent is a figure for hypocrites (Matt. 23:33), those who are prudent (10:16); and the handling of serpents (Mark 16:18) is mentioned as a proof of supernatural protection (comp. Acts 28:5). See Brazen Serpent, Satan.

Serpent, Brazen. See Brazen Serpent.

Serpent, Fiery (Heb. säräph, burning, Num. 21:6; Deut. 8:15). As the Israelites traveled round the land of Edom they found food and water scarce and rebelled against Jehovah. In consequence they were afflicted by a plague of fiery serpents (literally "burning snakes"), so called from their burning, i. e., inflammatory bite, which filled the victim with heat and poison. The punishment brought the people to reflection and confession of sin. They were pardoned through faith, which they manifested by looking to the brazen serpent (q. v.). The fiery flying serpents (Isa. 30:6) may be so called because of rapid movement, which appears like a flight, or it may refer to a species of serpent, the Naja tripudians, which dilates its hood into a kind of shining wing on each side of the neck and is very poisonous.

Serpent Charming, the art of taming serpents (Heb. lăḥăsh, a whisper, Jer. 8:17; Eccles. 10: 11), while those who practiced the art were known as $m^e n\check{a}h\check{a}sh\hat{i}m$. There can be no question at all of the remarkable power which, from time immemorial, has been exercised by certain people in the East over poisonous serpents. The art is most distinctly mentioned in the Bible, and probably alluded to by James (3:7). The usual species operated upon, both in Africa and in India, are the hooded snakes (*Naja tripudians* and *Naja haje*) and the horned *Cerastes*. That the charmers frequently, and perhaps generally, take the precaution of extracting the poison fangs before the snakes are subjected to their skill, there is much probability for believing; but that this operation is not always attended to is clear from the testimony of Bruce and numerous other writers. Some have supposed that the practice of taking out or breaking off the poison fangs is alluded to in Psa. 58:3 "Break their teeth, O God, in their mouth." The serpent charmer's usual instrument is a flute.

Se'rug (sē'rŭg; *shoot, tendril*), the son of Reu, father of Nahor, the grandfather of Abraham (Gen. 11:20; I Chron. 1:26). When thirty years of age he begat Nahor, and lived two hundred years afterward, B. C. before 2300. In Luke 3:35, the name is Grecized into *Saruch* (*q. v.*). A city by this name in Mesopotamia near Haran attests the presence of the Hebrew patriarchs in this region.

Servant. *See* Service.

Servant of Jeho'vah, "my servant," etc., a term used figuratively in several senses:

1. A *worshipper* of God (Neh. 1:10), and Daniel in particular (Dan. 6:20); to pious persons, as Abraham (Psa. 105:6, 42), Joshua (Josh. 24:29; Judg. 2:8), and many others.

2. A *minister* or ambassador of God on some special service (Isa. 49:6), e. g., Nebuchadnezzar, whom God used to chastise his people (Jer. 27:6; 43:10); but usually some favorite servant, as the *angels* (Job 4:18), *prophets* (Ezra 9:11; Jer. 7:25; Dan. 9:6; Amos 3:7); and especially *Moses* (Deut. 34:5; Josh. 1:1, 13, 15; Psa. 105:26). Paul and other apostles call themselves the "servants of Jesus Christ" and "of God" (Rom. 1:1; Col. 4:12; Tit. 1:1; James 1:1; II Pet. 1:1; Jude 1; Rev. 1:1).

3. The *Messiah* is typified as the servant of the Lord for accomplishing the work of redemption (Isa. 42:1; 52:13; comp. Matt. 12:18).

4. The term "servant" is also applied to the relation of men to others occupying high positions: as Eliezer, who had a position in Abraham's household something similar to that of a prime minister at court (Gen. 15:2; 24:2); Joshua, in relation to Moses (Exod. 33:11); Gehazi, in relation to Elisha (II Kings 4:12), etc. *See* Service.

Service, the rendering of several Hebrew and Greek words: Heb. *'ābăd*, to *serve, work*; *shărăth*, to *attend*; Gr. *diakonia, attendance; leitourgia, public function*, as of a priest; *douleuō*, to *be a slave; latreuō*, to *minister*.

While there were persons employed for wages (*see* Hireling), the servants of the Israelites, as of other ancient peoples, consisted chiefly of slaves—men and maid servants—held as property. These were bought from neighboring nations or from foreign residents in Canaan, captives taken in war, or children of slaves born in the house of the master. In so far as anything like slavery existed, it was a mild and merciful system, as compared to that of other nations. It cannot be said to be a Mosaic institution at all, but being found by the Jewish lawgiver, it was regulated by statute with the purpose and tendency of mitigating its evils and of restricting its duration. One source of slavery was branded with utter reprobation by Moses, the punishment of death being made the penalty of stealing or making merchandise of a human being, whether an Israelite (Deut. 24:7) or foreigner (Exod. 21:16). With regard to the kind of service which might be exacted by Hebrew masters from their servants, a distinction was made between those who were of their own brethren and foreigners.

1. **Hebrew.** Because the Israelites were the servants of God they were not to be treated, when they became servants to their brethren, as bond servants, but as hired servants and sojourners, and their masters were to rule over them with kindness (Lev. 25:39). In several ways a Hebrew might become the servant of his brethren:

(1) When he, through poverty, became unable to maintain himself as an independent citizen, in which case he might pass by sale under the power of another (Exod. 21:2, sq.). "The passage which lays down the law in such a case (Lev. 25:39) does not imply that the sale was compulsory, but is understood by Rosenmüller, Gesenius, Knobel, and others, as meaning that the individual sold himself, or rather the right to his labor, to some one of his brethren, that he might obtain the means of subsistence for himself and family" (Lindsay, in *Imp. Dict.*).

(2) By the commission of a theft. The law required restitution to the extent at least of double the value of the amount stolen, and in some cases even five times more. If the thief could not make the required restitution, then he was to be sold for his theft (Exod. 22:3), and so by his labor make the restitution.

(3) The children of a Hebrew servant became by the condition of their *birth* servants of the master (Exod. 21:4).

(4) Although it is not clearly stated in the law that a man might be claimed personally, and with his children sold by his creditors, in fact, the person and children of a debtor were claimed (II Kings 4:1; Neh. 5:5; comp. Isa. 50:1; Job 24:9). From Lev. 25:39, 47, it may be understood that while the impoverished man might sell himself it was only to work off his debt till the jubilee year.

(5) Every Israelite, male or maid, who had become a slave might be redeemed at any time by relatives. If not thus redeemed he was bound to receive his freedom without payment after six years' service, with a present of cattle and fruits (Exod. 21:2; Deut. 15:12-15). If he brought a wife with him into service, she received her freedom with him; if he received a wife from his master, then she and her children remained in bondage (Exod. 21:3; Jer. 34:8, sq.).

(6) Respecting an Israelite maid sold to another Israelite as housekeeper and concubine, these conditions prevailed: (*a*) She

could not "go out as the menservants do," i. e., she could not leave at the termination of six years, or in the year of jubilee, if her master was willing to fulfill the object for which he had purchased her (Exod. 21:7). (b) If she did not please her lord she was to be immediately redeemed, not sold to a strange people (v. 8). (c) If he betrothed her to his son, he was bound to make such provision for her as he would for one of his own daughters (v. 9). (d) If either he or his son, having married her, took a second wife, it should not be to the prejudice of the first, either in respect to support, clothing, or cohabitation (v. 10). (e) In failure of these, she was freed without money (v. 11).

(7) If a Hebrew servant, from love for master or wife and children, preferred not to accept freedom in the seventh year, but wished to remain in his master's house, he was brought before the elders and had his ear bored against door or post with an awl in token of lifelong servitude (Exod. 21:6; Deut. 15:17). The boring of the ear is found among many Eastern people as a token of servitude, not only in case of slaves, but also of dervishes and others devoted to a deity. This act was not prescribed in the law as symbolizing anything shameful or despicable; for Moses seeks in every way to protect and restore personal freedom, and could not therefore approve of anyone voluntarily devoting himself to perpetual slavery. It was allowed because love and the allegiance of love was prized more highly than loveless personal freedom (Keil, *Bib. Arch.*). The custom of reducing Hebrews to servitude appears to have fallen into disuse subsequently to the Babylonian captivity. Vast numbers of Hebrews were reduced to slavery as war captives at different periods by the Phoenicians (Joel 3:6), the Philistines (Amos 1:6), the Syrians (I Macc. 3:41; II Macc. 8:11); the Egyptians (Josephus, *Ant.*, xii, 2, §3), and, above all, by the Romans.

2. **Hebrew Slave and Foreign Master.** Should a Hebrew become the servant of a "stranger," meaning a non-Hebrew, the servitude could be terminated only in two ways, viz., by the arrival of the year of jubilee or by the repayment to the master of the purchase money paid for the servant, after deducting the value of the services already rendered. The estimate was based upon the pay of a hired laborer (Lev. 25:47-55).

3. **Non-Hebrew Slaves.** (1) **Source.** The majority of non-Hebrew slaves were war captives, either of the Canaanites who had survived the general extermination of their race under Joshua, or such as were conquered from the other surrounding nations (Num. 31:26, sq.). Besides these, many were obtained by purchase from foreign slave dealers (Lev. 25:44, 45); and others may have been resident foreigners who were reduced to this state either by poverty or crime. The children of slaves remained slaves, being the class described as "born in the house" (Gen. 14:14; 17:12; Eccles. 2:7), and hence the number was likely to increase as time went on. The average value of a slave appears to have been thirty shekels (Exod. 21:32).

(2) **How considered.** The slave is de-scribed as the "possession" of his master, apparently with a special reference to the power which the latter had of disposing of him to his heirs as he would any other article of personal property (Lev. 25:45, 46); the slave is also described as his master's "money" (Exod. 21:21), i. e., as representing a certain money value. Such expressions show that he was regarded very much in the light of a *mancipium* or chattel.

(3) **Freeing.** That the slave might be manumitted appears from Exod. 21:26, 27; Lev. 19:20. As to the methods by which this might be effected we are told nothing in the Bible; but the Rabbinists specify the following four methods: *1.* redemption by a money payment, *2.* a bill or ticket of freedom, *3.* testamentary disposition, or *4.* any act that implied manumission, such as making a slave one's heir.

4. **Protection.** Both respecting the Israelite and the stranger provision was made for the protection of his person (Lev. 24:17, 22; Exod. 21:20). A minor personal injury, such as the loss of an eye or a tooth, was to be recompensed by giving the servant his liberty (Exod. 21:26, 27). The position of the slave in regard to religious privileges was favorable. He was to be circumcised (Gen. 17:12), and hence was entitled to partake of the paschal sacrifice (Exod. 12:44), as well as of the other religious festivals (Deut. 12:12, 18; 16:11, 14), and enjoy the rest of the Sabbath (Exod. 20:11; Deut. 5:14, sq.). The occupations of slaves were of a menial character, as implied in Lev. 25:39, consisting partly in the work of the house and partly in personal attendance.

Servitor (Heb. *mᵉshārēth*, an *attendant*), but not in a menial capacity (II Kings 4:43).

Servitude. See Service.

Seth (sĕth). The third son of Adam, and father of Enos when he was one hundred and five years old. He died at the age of nine hundred and twelve (Gen. 4:25, 26; 5:3-8; I Chron. 1:1; Luke 3:38). The significance of his name is "appointed" or "put" in the place of the murdered Abel; but Ewald thinks that another signification, which he prefers, is indicated in the text, viz., "seedling," or "germ."

Se'thur (sē'thŭr; *hidden*), son of Michael, the representative of the tribe of Asher among the twelve spies sent by Moses to view the promised land (Num. 13:13), B. C. c. 1440.

Seve'neh (sĕ-vē'nĕ). This is the Hebrew rendering of an Egyptian town name, known to its inhabitants as Syene, the modern Aswan, situated at the First Cataract of the Nile on the Ethiopian side. It was a stronghold opposite the island of Elephantine where the famous Elephantine Papyri written in Aramaic were found in 1903. At this place Jews during the Persian Empire had a temple to Jehovah, where they celebrated the religious rites of Judaism. The prophet Ezekiel utters doom upon Egypt which will extend "from Migdal to Syene" (29:10; 30:6). The A. S. V. renders Syene as Seveneh. See Syene. M. F. U.

Seventy Disciples of Our Lord (Luke 10:1, 17). These were, doubtless, other persons than the "twelve," whom our Lord seems to have kept by his side. Considerable speculation has arisen owing to the number seventy, some thinking that Jesus had in view the ancient Hebrew analogue of the seventy—originally seventy-two—*elders of the people* (Num. 11:16-25). Godet (*Com.*, on Luke) says: "There is another explanation of the number which seems to us more natural. The Jews held, agreeably to Gen. 10, that the human race was made up of seventy (or seventy-two) peoples—fourteen descended from Japhet, thirty from Ham, and twenty-six from Shem.

Seventy Weeks. These are seventy weeks of years referred to in Daniel's prophecy (Dan. 9:20-27). During these seventy weeks of seven years each Daniel prophesied that Israel's national chastisement would be terminated and the nation reestablished in "everlasting righteousness" (vs. 24). In Daniel's vision the weeks are divided into three parts, seven weeks equaling forty-nine years; sixty-two weeks, totaling 434 years; one week equaling seven years (Dan. 9:25-27). In the seven weeks or forty-nine years Jerusalem was to be reconstructed in "troubled times." This was brought to pass as recorded in the books of Ezra-Nehemiah. In the sixty-two weeks or 434 years Messiah was to come at His first advent (v. 25), fulfilled in Messiah's birth and his being "cut off but not for Himself" at the crucifixion. The date of Christ's crucifixion is evidently not specified except that it is to be after the "three score and two weeks." The city was to be destroyed by "the people of the prince that shall come." This was fulfilled by the Romans under Titus in A. D. 70. Verse 27, by many commentators, is connected immediately with the events of the first advent. However, many premillennialists place it in the end time and between verse 26 and 27. In this extended period they place the church age as an era unrevealed in O. T. prophecy (Matt. 13:11-17; Eph. 3:1-10). During this time it is maintained that the mysteries of the kingdom of heaven (Matt. 13:1-50) and the outcalling of the church are consummated. According to this view, the church-age will terminate at an unspecified moment and will usher in Daniel's seventieth week. The personage of verse 27 thus, under this interpretation, is identical with the little horn of Daniel 7, who will make a covenant with the Jews to restore their Judaic ritual for one week—seven years. In the middle of the week he will break the covenant and fulfill Dan. 12:11 and II Thess. 2:3-11. This interpretation views v. 27 as dealing with the last three and one-half years of the Great Tribulation (Matt. 24:15-28). This era is connected with the "time of trouble" spoken of by Daniel (Dan. 12:1), with the "abomination of desolation" (Matt. 24:15) and with the "hour of trial" (Rev. 3:10). It is thus apparent that Dan. 9:27 is a battleground between the various millennial schools of eschatological thought.—*M. F. U. See* Daniel, Book of; Weeks.

Shaalab'bin (shā-à-lăb'ĭn; Josh. 19:42), or **Shaal'bim** (shā-ăl'bĭm; Judg. 1:35; I Kings 4:9), a town in Dan named between Ir-shemesh and Ajalon (Josh. 19:42). It is frequently mentioned in the history of David and Solomon under the latter form. It may possibly be the present *Selbit*, 3 miles N. W. of Aijalon.

Shaal'bonite (shā-ăl'bō-nīt). Eliahba the Shaalbonite was one of David's thirty-seven heroes (II Sam. 23:32; I Chron. 11:33). He was the native of a place named Shaalbon, which is not mentioned elsewhere, unless it is identical with Shaalbim or Shaalabbin, of the tribe of Dan.

Sha'aph (shā'ăf; Aram. *balsam*).
1. The last named of the sons of Jahdai of the tribe of Judah (I Chron. 2:47).
2. Third named of the four sons of Caleb by Maachah, his concubine. He was the "father" (i. e., founder) of Madmannah (I Chron. 2:49), B. C. after 1380.

Shaara'im (shā-à-rā'ĭm; *two gates*).
1. A city called also Sharaim (Josh. 15:36), near Azekah, in Judah (I Sam. 17:52).
2. A town in Simeon (I Chron. 4:31), evidently identical with Sharuhen (*q. v.*), between Gaza and Beer-sheba.

Shaash'gaz (shā-ăsh'găz), the eunuch who had charge of the concubines in the court of Xerxes (Esth. 2:14), B. C. c. 478.

Shab'bethai (shăb'ê-thī; perhaps *sabbath-born*), a Levite who assisted in taking account of those who had married Gentile wives (Ezra 10:15), B. C. 457. He is probably the same as the one mentioned (Neh. 8:7) as assisting in the instruction of the people in the law, and as one of the "chief of the Levites who had the oversight of the outward business of the house of God" (11:16).

Shachi'a (shà-kī'à), the sixth named of the seven sons of Shaharaim by his wife Hodesh (I Chron. 8:10).

Shad'dai (shăd'ī), an adjunct used with the Canaanite-Hebrew name for God, El. El Shaddai denotes the particular character in which God revealed Himself to the patriarchs (Gen. 17:1; 28:3; 35:11; 43:14; 48:3). Exodus 6:2, 3 specifically states that God appeared "unto Abraham, unto Isaac and unto Jacob by the name of God Almighty (El Shaddai)" and that He was not known to them by the name Jehovah, that is revealed to them under the meaning of that name. Some present-day critics insist that El Shaddai means "God of mountain(s)" and that the Genesis passages inaccurately are translated "God Almighty." This view, however, is unacceptable and Shaddai is best taken from the root *shādād*, "to be strong or powerful," as in Arabic. Thus Shaddai would be an epithet intensifying the thought of power or strength inherent in the word El (cf. the Vulgate and the Septuagint "Omnipotens." The word "el" is a generic name for god in N. W. Semitic (Hebrew and Ugaritic) and was almost certainly an adjectival formation from the root *'wl*, "to be strong, powerful" and so meaning "the strong or powerful one." In the Ugaritic tablets El is the head of the pantheon, and this is the name by which God is called in the O. T. (Gen. 33:20). In prose El occurs more often with the adjunct El Elyon, "The Most High God" (Gen. 14:18), El Hai, "The Living God" (Josh. 3:10) as well as "El Shaddai." In Hebrew poetry El is much more frequent, where it often stands without an adjunct (Psa. 18:31, 33, 48; Psa. 68:21; Job 8:3).—*M. F. U.*

Shadow (Heb. *ṣēl;* Gr. *skia*).

Figurative. 1. "Shadow of death" (Heb. *ṣalmāwĕth*), is taken from the shadow representing darkness, gloom, etc., and so is figurative of the grave (Job 10:21; 12:22; 16:16; Isa. 9:2; Jer. 2:6); also severe trial (Psa. 23:4); state of ignorance (Matt. 4:16).

2. A shadow, swiftly moving, is symbolic of the fleetness of human life (I Chron. 29:15; Job 8:9; 14:2; Psa. 102:11).

3. Covering and protection from heat; thus the Messiah "is as the shadow of a great rock in a weary land" (Isa. 32:2; 49:2; Cant. 2:3; Psa. 17:8; 63:7; 91:1).

4. An image cast by an object and representing the form of that object, as opposed to the "body" or thing itself (Col. 2:17); hence *a sketch, outline,* as the Jewish economy (Heb. 8:5; 10:1).

The second Greek term means "a shadow caused by revolution" (James 1:17), the thought being that "with the Father of light there is neither parallax nor tropical shadow." As the sun *appears to us* to have changes, whence come summer and winter, day and night, but in reality the changes we experience are from ourselves; so God, the source of all good, does not change, though he may appear to do so.

Sha'drach (shā'drăk; apparently Akk. *Shudur, command of,* and Sumerian *Aku,* the moon-god). The name, however, may be simply a corruption of Marduk, the city-god of Babylon, the Babylonian name given to Hananiah, the chief of the three Hebrew children.

1. **Captive.** He was one of the Jewish captives carried to Babylon by Nebuchadnezzar, B. C. about c. 605. Being of goodly person and of superior understanding, he was selected, with his three companions, for the king's service, and was placed under tuition in the language and learning of the Chaldeans as taught in the college of the magicians. Like Daniel he lived on pulse, i. e., leguminous plants such as peas and beans, which are very nourishing, and water. When the time of his probation was over, he and his three companions, being found superior to all the other magicians, were advanced to stand before the king (Dan. 1:7, sq.).

2. **Promotion.** When Nebuchadnezzar determined upon the slaughter of the magicians because they could not tell him his forgotten dream, Shadrach united with his companions in prayer to God to reveal the dream to Daniel (Dan. 2:17, 18); and Daniel, being successful, Shadrach shared in the promotion, being appointed to a high civil office (v. 49).

3. **Fiery Furnace.** At the instigation of certain envious Chaldeans an ordinance was published that all persons should worship the golden image to be set up in the plain of Dura, the exact site of which is uncertain as there are several places called Duru in Babylonia. For example, there is a river Dura with Tulūl Dūra nearby. For refusing to comply, Shadrach, with Meshach and Abed-nego, were cast into the fiery furnace; but their faith remained firm, and they escaped unhurt. The king acknowledged Jehovah to be God and promoted his faithful servants (Dan. 3:1-30). After their deliverance from the furnace we hear no more of Shadrach, Meshach,

and Abed-nego in the Old Testament; neither are they spoken of in the New Testament, except in the pointed allusion to them in the Epistle to the Hebrews, as having "through faith quenched the violence of fire" (Heb. 11:34). But there are repeated allusions to them in the later apocryphal books, and the martyrs of the Maccabean period seem to have been much encouraged by their example (I Macc. 2:59, 60; III Macc. 6:6; IV Macc. 13:9; 16:3, 21; 18:12).

Shaft. 1. (Heb. *yārēk,* a *thigh*), the *shank* of the golden candlestick (Exod. 25:31).

2. (Heb. *ḥēs,* a *dart*), and used figuratively of one who is used to preach the word (Isa. 49:2).

Sha'gee (shä'gē; *wandering, erring;* A. V. Shage), father of Jonathan the Hararite, one of David's guard (I Chron. 11:34). *See* Shammah, 5.

Shahara'im (shā-hȧ-rā'ĭm; *double dawn,* i. e., morning and evening twilight), a Benjamite who became the father of several children in the land of Moab (I Chron. 8:8).

Shahazu'mah (shȧ-hȧ-zōō'mȧ), in A. V. Shahazi'mah (shȧ-hȧ-zī'mȧ, *toward the heights*), a place in the tribe of Issachar, between Tabor and the Jordan (Josh. 19:22). Identical with Tell el Mekarkash in the Tabor-Jordan region.

Sha'lem (shā'lĕm; *peaceful, secure*), named in the A. V. as a place near Jacob's well (Gen. 33:18, 20). It is probable that Shalem is not a proper name. The R. V. renders "Jacob came in *peace* to the city of Shechem."

Sha'lim, Land of (shā'lĭm), R. V. Sha'alim (shā'ȧ-lĭm; *foxes*), the region through which Saul passed in looking for the asses of Kish, which were lost (I Sam. 9:4). Possibly *Shual,* near Ophrah (13:17).

Shali'shah (shȧ-lī'shȧ; *triangular;* A. V. Shalisha), a district adjoining on Mount Ephraim (I Sam. 9:4), north of Lydda. Unquestionably the country round Baal-shalisha (II Kings 4:42). It is mentioned in connection with Saul's search after the asses of his father.

Shal'lecheth, The Gate of (shăl'ē-kĕth; a *casting down*), one of the gates of the temple through which the refuse was thrown, by the causeway going up out of the Tyropoeon valley (I Chron. 26:16). This fate fell to the lot of Hosah, to act as porter.

Shal'lum (shăl'ŭm; *recompense, retribution*).

1. **The Sixteenth King of Israel.** His father's name was Jabesh. Shallum conspired against Zechariah, son of Jeroboam II, killed him, and thus brought the dynasty of Jehu to a close, as was predicted (II Kings 10:30), B. C. 742. He reigned only a month, being in turn dethroned and slain by Menahem (15: 10-15).

2. **The Son of Tikvah** and husband of the prophetess Huldah (II Kings 22:14; II Chron. 34:22), B. C. 626. He was custodian of the priestly wardrobe, and was probably the same as Jeremiah's uncle (Jer. 32:7).

3. **Son of Sisamai** and father of Jekamiah, and a descendant of Shesham of Judah (I Chron. 2:40, 41).

4. **The Third Son of Josiah,** king of Judah, known in the books of Kings and Chroni-

cles as Jehoahaz (I Chron. 3:15; Jer. 22:11). *See* Jehoahaz.

5. **Son of Shaul**, the son of Simeon (I Chron. 4:25).

6. **A High Priest**, son of Zadok and father of Hilkiah (I Chron. 6:12, 13), and an ancestor of Ezra (Ezra 7:2), B. C. after 950. He is the Meshullam of I Chron. 9:11; Neh. 11:11.

7. **The Youngest Son of Naphtali** (I Chron. 7:13), called *Shillem* (Gen. 46:24), B. C. about 1925.

8. **A Descendant of Kore**, and chief of the porters of the sanctuary in the time of David (I Chron. 9:17, 19, 31), B. C. about 980. He seems to have been the same Shallum whose descendants returned from the exile (Ezra 2:42; 10:24; Neh. 7:45). With this Shallum we may identify Meshelemiah and Shelemiah (I Chron. 26:1, 2, 9, 14), and is perhaps the "father" of Maaseiah (Jer. 35:4).

9. **The Father of Jehizkiah**, which latter was one of the chieftains of Ephraim who took part in returning the prisoners carried away from Judah (II Chron. 28:12), B. C. before 741.

10. **A Jew** of the descendants of Bani, who put away his idolatrous wife (Ezra 10:42), B. C. 456.

11. **A Levitical Porter** who did the same (Ezra 10:24), B. C. 456.

12. **The Son of Halohesh**, the "ruler of the half part of Jerusalem," who with his daughters assisted in building its walls (Neh. 3:12), B. C. 445.

Shal′lun (shăl′ŭn; another form of Shallum, *retribution*), "the son of Colhozeh, the ruler of part of Mizpah; he built it, and covered it, and set up the doors thereof, the locks thereof, and the bars thereof, and the wall of the pool of Siloah by the king's garden, and unto the stairs that go down from the city of David" (Neh. 3:15), B. C. 445.

Shal′mai (shăl′mī). The children of Shalmai (or *Shamlai*, as in the margin of Ezra 2:46) were among the Nethinim who returned with Zerubbabel (Ezra 2:46; Neh. 7:48), B. C. about 536. R. V. Sal′mai.

Shal′man, an abbreviated form of Shalmaneser, king of Assyria (Hos. 10:14), although some scholars connect the name with a Moabite monarch Salamanu, occurring in an inscription of Tiglath-pileser III (745-727) and alive in Hosea's day.

Shalmane′ser (shăl-măn-ē′zĕr; Assyr., "the god Shulman is chief"). The Assyrian inscriptions have made known to us five kings of the name Shalmaneser. Of these only one is mentioned by name in the Old Testament, and he is Shalmaneser V, of Assyrian history. But though Shalmaneser III is not named in the Old Testament, the evidence is there of his influence and his work. Without some knowledge of him it is impossible to understand the reign of Ahab, king of Israel, with whom he was contemporary.

1. **Shalmaneser III.** The reign of Ashurnasirpal (884-860 B. C.) was one of the most brilliant and daring of all Assyrian history. In him the spirit of the mighty Tiglath-pileser I (about 1110 B. C.) seemed to live again. The boundaries of the Assyrian empire were carried far beyond their previous limits, and

Assyrian influence began to be counted a force far and near. Under his leadership the Assyrians invaded Armenia and ravaged the country south of Lake Van. With the sword went also Assyrian commerce and culture. The Assyrian system of cuneiform writing was introduced into the land where later the kingdom of Van held sway, and so a center of influence was located. To the westward also marched Ashurnasirpal victoriously, reaching even the Mediterranean, and receiving tribute from Tyre and Sidon. But there his work ceased. Would his successor be able to retain what he won; would he be able to increase it? He was succeeded by his son Shalmaneser II, whose glorious reign (859-824 B. C.) surpassed even his father's.

Of the reign of Shalmaneser III we possess several well-preserved original monuments. The most beautiful of them is the famous Black Obelisk, now in the British Museum. A solid block of basalt, over six feet high, is covered on all four sides with inscriptions cut into the stone, and accompanying these are well-executed pictures of the objects which the king had received as gifts, or in payment of tribute. A second important text is the Monolith Inscription, a large slab, with a portrait, nearly life-size, of the king, and this covered over with two columns of writing. Besides these, several colossal bulls, covered with inscriptions, have also been found. From these original sources of information we can now reconstruct the king's reign.

At the beginning of his reign Shalmaneser set himself to strengthen the kingdom of his father in Mesopotamia and in Armenia. Five years were devoted to this task. His land was now strong, and he could turn his attention to the outside. In the sixth year of his reign (854 B. C.) he turned westward to take up the work of conquest where his father had left it. Ashurnasirpal II had not disturbed Israel; that was reserved for his son. The fame of the exploits of Shalmaneser had passed through Syria and into Palestine. It was evident to the peoples of all that country that no single nation could successfully oppose so great a warrior as he. The only hope was in a coalition. A union for the general defense was composed of the peoples of Damascus, Hamath, Israel, Phoenicia, Que (eastern Cilicia), and Musri (western Cappadocia). These combined forces Shalmaneser III met in battle at Qarqar (sometimes written Karkar), in 853 B. C., and thus tells the story of the battle: "From *Argana* I departed; to *Qarqar* I approached. *Qarqar*, his royal city, I wasted, destroyed, burned with fire; 1,200 chariots, 1,200 horses, 20,000 men of Adadidri, of Damascus; 700 chariots, 700 horses, 10,000 men of Ithuleni, the Hamathite; 2,000 chariots, 10,000 men of Ahab, the Israelite . . . ." Shalmaneser listed eleven kings with their forces and continues thus:—These 12 [there must be a mistake here, for only 11 have been mentioned] kings he took to his assistance; to make battle and war against me they came. With the exalted power which Ashur, the lord, gave me, with the powerful arms which Nergal, who goes before me, had granted me, I fought with them, from *Qarqar* to *Gilzan*. I accomplished their defeat; 14,000 of their warriors I slew with arms; like Ramman I rained a deluge upon them, I strewed hither and yon their bodies." This is a bold claim of an overwhelming victory. It was a victory for the Assyrians beyond a doubt, but it does not appear at this distance that the victory was won without great sacrifices. It is clear, at any rate, that Shalmaneser did not feel it sufficiently great to justify him in attempting to seize Hamath or Damascus.

In the year 849 Shalmaneser III again invaded the west land, and again his inscriptions record victory. He was, however, in this campaign not endeavoring to attack Israel, and hence his deeds do not interest students of the Bible. Another expedition followed in 845, and this also was without effect upon Israel; the king was beating down Syria by successive blows, and this time he seems to have dealt a severe blow to the northern confederation, for Damascus is left to stand alone. In 842 Shalmaneser, upon a new invasion, found new rulers to oppose him. Ben-hadad (*q. v.*) no longer lived, and Hazael was ruler in Damascus. In this campaign, he again excites the interest of biblical students. Jehu was now king of Israel, a man daring enough to usurp a throne, but not courageous enough to face the Assyrians. Jehu attempts to buy off the Assyrians by sending costly presents to

427. Jehu, King of Israel, Paying Tribute to Shalmaneser III, (from the Black Obelisk of Shalmaneser)

Shalmaneser. On the Black Obelisk Shalmaneser has left a picture of Jehu's ambassadors stooping to kiss his feet, and bringing to him presents. Accompanying the picture are the words, "The tribute of Jehu, son of Omri: silver, gold, etc." Jehu was not the son of Omri, but would be so called by the Assyrians, who long spoke of Israel as the "land of Omri." In 839 Shalmaneser received the tribute of Tyre, Sidon, and Byblos, and this was his last expedition to the west. Thereafter he was occupied near at home with a rebellion in 827. In 825 he died, and Shamshi-Ramman II, his son, ruled in his stead.

2. **Shalmaneser V**, a king of Assyria, who reigned 727-722. He was the successor of Tiglath-pileser III (*see* Tiglath-pileser), and ascended the throne in the very month in which his predecessor died. Few historical inscriptions of this king have yet been found. A weight containing his name, and a boundary stone dated in his reign, are the monuments of his date which have come into our possession. Our knowledge of his reign begins with the eponym lists. These are lists of the names of Assyrian kings, accompanied in some cases with a brief note mentioning the campaigns conducted by the monarch. In the eponym list for the year 727 B. C. is the record that Shalmaneser ascended the throne. Under the same year is the record of a campaign against a city, the name of which is unhappily broken off. As this record stands before the words recording the king's accession, it may be that the campaign was begun by his predecessor and continued by him. The Babylonian chronicle sets down in this same accession year, during the last three months, the destruction of the city of Shamara'in, or Shabara'in. This city was once thought by some to be the city of Samaria. This view is improbable on philological grounds. With more probability it is now by many supposed to be the biblical Sepharvaim (II Kings 17:24), but even this view is uncertain. In the year 726 the eponym list says that there was no campaign. For the remaining three years of the king's reign there were campaigns, but the lands against which they were directed are unknown, for the eponym list is broken at this point. It is now known, however, that Shalmaneser V warred against Phoenicia, capturing the mainland of Tyre and taking Sidon and Acre. The next definite information of the events in the reign of Shalmaneser V is found in the Old Testament. Hoshea was king of Israel in Samaria at the time that Shalmaneser was reigning in Assyria. He had paid tribute to the Assyrians, but decided to make a bold attempt to throw off the yoke. He therefore sought aid from the Egyptian king So (or Seveh), and this was naturally construed as rebellion by the Assyrians (17:4). Shalmaneser invaded Palestine and laid siege to Samaria. The siege continued for three years, and at its conclusion many of the inhabitants of Samaria were carried into captivity. Samaria fell in 722 B. C., and that was the year of Shalmaneser's death. The inscriptions of his successor, Sargon, claim that the city was taken by him and not by Shalmaneser (*see* Sargon). This may have been the case. If so, Samaria fell at the beginning of 721 B. C., or it may be merely a boast of Sargon. In any case the historical character of the book of Kings is not impugned.—R. W. R., revised by M. F. U.

Sha′ma (shā′mȧ; *He*, i. e., God, *has heard*), the eldest son of Hothan, and, with his brother Jehiel, a member of David's guard (I Chron. 11:44), B. C. about 1000.

Shamari′ah (shăm-a-rī′ȧ; II Chron. 11:19). *See* Shemariah, 2.

Shambles (Gr. *makellon*, a *meat market*). Such markets seem to have been introduced into Palestine by the Romans, and the Jews were forbidden to deal with them because they offered the flesh of unclean animals for sale. When Paul urged the Corinthians to buy whatever was offered "in the shambles, asking no questions for conscience' sake" (I Cor. 10:25), he meant that they should not stop to inquire whether it had or had not been sacrificial flesh. The flesh offered for sale was to be *flesh* to them, and nothing more. *See* Market.

Shame, Shamefacedness. The Greek term *'aischunē*, *shame*, is subjective, making reference to one's self and one's actions, having a tendency to restrain a bad act; while *'aidōs*, *shamefacedness* (I Tim. 2:9; Heb. 12:28, "reverence"), is objective, having reference to others, precedes and prevents a bad act.

Sha'med (shä'mĕd), properly **She'mer** (shē-mēr; *preserved*), the third-named son of Elpaal, and builder of Ono and Lod. He was a Benjamite (I Chron. 8:12), B. C. 1380.

Sha'mer (shä'mēr; *preserved*).

1. The son of Mahli, and father of Bani, of the tribe of Levi (I Chron. 6:46), B. C. perhaps about 1440.

2. The second son of Heber, an Asherite (I Chron. 7:32, where he is called *Shomer*), and father of Ahi and others (v. 34), B. C. perhaps before 1440.

Sham'gar (shăm'gär; apparently a Hurrian name, *Shimigar*, i. e., a god, *gave*), the third judge of Israel (Judg. 5:16). Nothing is recorded about the descent of Shamgar, save that he was the son of Anath. He may have been of the tribe of Naphtali, since Beth-anath is in that tribe (Judg. 1:33). In the days of Shamgar Israel was in a most depressed condition, and the whole nation was cowed. At this conjuncture Shamgar was raised up to be a deliverer. With no arms in his hand but an oxgoad he made a desperate assault upon the Philistines, and slew six hundred of them (Judg. 3:31; comp. I Sam. 13:21), B. C. probably before 1150. He does not seem to have secured for the Israelites any permanent victory over the Philistines, nor is an account given of the length of his services. Moreover, he is not called a judge, but is probably so reckoned because he answered the description as given in Judg. 2:16.

Sham'huth (shăm'hŭth; *desolation*), the fifth captain for the fifth month in David's arrangement of his army (I Chron. 27:8), B. C. about 1000. From a comparison of the lists in I Chron., chaps. 11 and 27, it would seem that Shamhuth is the same as *Shammoth* the Harorite.

Sha'mir (shä'mĭr; *a flint, thorn*).

1. A town among the mountains of Judah (Josh. 15:48). It is to be sought in the ruin Sōmerah, 13 miles S. W. of Hebron or at nearby El-Birch.

2. A town upon the mountains of Ephraim, the residence and burial place of judge Tola (Judg. 10:1, 2). Its situation is still unknown.

3. A Kohathite Levite, son of Michah, and appointed by David to the service of the sanctuary (I Chron. 24:24).

Sham'ma (shăm'á; *desolation*), the eighth named of the eleven sons of Zophah, an Asherite (I Chron. 7:37), B. C. after 1440.

Sham'mah (shăm'á; *desolation*).

1. The third named of the sons of Reuel, the son of Esau (Gen. 36:13; I Chron. 1:37), and head of one of the families (Gen. 36:17).

2. The third son of Jesse, David's father, and one of the brothers not chosen by Jehovah to be anointed king (I Sam. 16:9), B. C. before 1000. With his two elder brothers he joined the Hebrew army (17:13). He is elsewhere, by a slight change in the name,

called *Shimea* (I Chron. 20:7), *Shimeah* (II Sam. 13:3, 32), *Shimma* (I Chron. 2:13).

3. The son of Agee the Hararite, and one of the three captains of David's champions, B. C. 992. The exploit by which he obtained this high distinction was the invaluable assistance he rendered to David against the Philistines. By a comparison of the two accounts (II Sam. 23:11, 12; I Chron. 11:13, 14) it seems that David had joined battle with the Philistines at Pas-dammim. Shammah took his stand in the middle of a cultivated field, where the Philistines were in great numbers, and wrested it from the foe. Shammah may also have shared in the dangers of forcing a way through the Philistine host to gratify David's thirst for the waters of Bethlehem (II Sam. 23:13-17); but Keil and Delitzsch (*Com.*, in loc.) think that this deed was performed by three of the thirty heroes whose names are not given.

NOTE—*Lentil and barley field*. The scene of Shammah's exploit is said in Samuel to be a field of lentils and in I Chron. a field of barley. It is more likely that it was a field of barley, and that by a very slight change and transposition of letters in the original words one word was substituted for the other. The reason that Shammah is not mentioned in I Chron. is that "three lines have dropped out from the text" in consequence of a copyist's error. (K. and D., *Com.*, in loc.).

4. "Shammah the Harodite" was another of David's mighty men (II Sam. 23:25). He is called "*Shammoth* the Harorite" (I Chron. 11:27) and "*Shamhuth* the Izrahite" (27:8). In the latter passage he is mentioned as the leader of the fifth division of David's army.

5. In the list of mighty men (II Sam. 23:32, 33) we find "Jonathan, Shammah the Hararite;" while in I Chron. 11:34, it is "Jonathan, the son of Shage the Hararite." Combining the two, Kennicott proposes to read "Jonathan, the son of Shamha, the Hararite" (Smith *Bib. Dict.*).

Sham'mai (shăm'â-ī).

1. The elder son of Onam, of the tribe of Judah (I Chron. 2:28), B. C. about 1350.

2. The son of Rekem, and father of Maon, of the tribe of Judah (I Chron. 2:44, 45), B. C. after 1370.

3. Named, apparently, as the sixth child of Ezra, of the tribe of Judah (I Chron. 4:17), B. C. after 1190. Bertheau suggests, however, that the last clause of v. 18 be inserted in v. 17 after the name Jalon. If this suggestion is accepted, then Shammai would be the son of Mered by his Egyptian wife, Bilhiah.

Sham'moth (shăm'ŏth; *desolation, ruins*), "the Harorite," one of David's guard (I Chron. 11:27); apparently the same as "Shammah the Harodite" (II Sam. 23:25), and "Shamhuth" (I Chron. 27:8).

Shammu'a (shă-mū'á; *renowned, heard-about*).

1. The son of Zaccur, and the man who represented the tribe of Reuben among the twelve spies (Num. 13:4), B. C. c. 1440.

2. One of the sons of David (by his wife Bathsheba, I Chron. 3:5), born in Jerusalem (14:4), B. C. about 989. In the A. V., II Sam. 5:14, the same Hebrew name is Anglicized, "Shammuah," and in II Chron. 3:5 he is called *Shimea*.

3. A Levite, the father of Abda (Neh.

11:17), B. C. before 445. The same as *Shemaiah*, the father of Obadiah (I Chron. 9:16).

4. The representative of the priestly family of Bilgah, or Bilgai, in the days of Joiakim (Neh. 12:18), B. C. about 500.

Shammu'ah (shă-mū'á), son of David (II Sam. 5:14), elsewhere called *Shamua* and *Shimea. See* Shammua.

Sham'sherai (shăm'shĕ-rī), or **Shamshera'i** (shăm-shĕ-rā'ī), the first named of the six sons of Jeroham, resident at Jerusalem (I Chron. 8:26), B. C. about 1120.

Sha'pham (shā'făm), the chief second in authority among the Gadites in the days of Jotham (I Chron. 5:12), B. C. about 750.

Sha'phan (shā'făn; *hyrax, rock badger*), the scribe or secretary of King Josiah.

1. **Family.** He was the son of Azaliah (II Kings 22:3; II Chron. 34:8), father of Ahikam (II Kings 22:12; II Chron. 34:20), Elasah (Jer. 29:3), and Gemariah (36:10-12), and grandfather of Gedaliah (39:14; 40:5, 9, 11; 41:2; 43:6), Michaiah (36:11), and probably of Jaazaniah (Ezek. 8:11). There seems to be no sufficient reason for supposing that Shaphan, the father of Ahikam, and Shaphan the scribe, were different persons.

2. **Personal History.** The history of Shaphan brings out some points with regard to the office of scribe which he held. He appears on an equality with the governor of the city and the royal recorder, with whom he was sent by the king to Hilkiah to take an account of the money which had been collected by the Levites for the repair of the temple and to pay the workmen (II Kings 22:4; II Chron. 34:9; comp. II Kings 12:10), B. C. about 659. Ewald calls him minister of finance (*Gesch.*, iii, 697). It was on this occasion that Hilkiah communicated his discovery of a copy of the law, which he had probably found while making preparations for the repair of the temple. Shaphan was intrusted to deliver it to the king, who was so deeply moved upon hearing it read that he sent Shaphan, with the high priest and others, to consult Huldah the prophetess. Shaphan was then apparently an old man, for his son Ahikam must have been in a position of importance, and his grandson Gedaliah was already born. Be this as it may, Shaphan disappears from the scene, and probably died before the fifth year of Jehoiakim, eighteen years later, when we find Elishama was scribe (Jer. 36:12).

Sha'phat (shā'făt; *He*, i. e., *God, judges*).

1. The son of Hori, and the spy chosen from the tribe of Simeon to assist in exploring the promised land (Num. 13:5), B. C. c. 1440.

2. The father of the prophet Elisha (I Kings 19:16, 19; II Kings 3:11; 6:31), B. C. before 865.

3. One of the six sons of Shemaiah in the royal line of Judah, after the captivity (I Chron. 3:22), B. C. perhaps about 350.

4. One of the chiefs of the Gadites in Bashan in the time of Jotham (I Chron. 5:12), B. C. about 738.

5. The son of Adlai, who was over David's oxen in the valleys (I Chron. 27:29), B. C. after 1000.

Sha'pher (shā'fĕr; Heb. *Shepher, brightness*), a mountain at which the Israelites encamped during their wilderness journeyings, situated between Kehelathah and Haradah (Num. 33:23). Its identification is doubtful.

Sha'phir (shā'fĕr). *See* Saphir.

Sha'rai (shā'rā-ī), one of the "sons" of Bani, who put away his Gentile wife (Ezra 10:40), B. C. 456.

Shara'im (shá-rā'ĭm; Josh. 15:36). *See* Shaaram, 1.

Sha'rar (shā'rár; Aram. *firm*), the father of Ahiam the Hararite (II Sam. 23:33), B. C. before 990. In I Chron. 11:35 he is called *Sacar*, which Kennicott thinks the true reading.

Share (Heb. *măhărĕshĕth*), an agricultural instrument, probably a small garden hoe or spade (I Sam. 13:20).

Share'zer (shá-rē'zĕr; Akkad. *protect the king*).

1. A son of Sennacherib (*q. v.*), who, with his brother Adrammelech, murdered their father while he was worshipping in the temple of the god Nisroch (II Kings 19:37; Isa. 37:38), B. C. 681.

2. In Zech. 7:2, Anglicized Sherezer (*q. v.*).

Shar'on (shăr'ŭn; a *plain*), a part of the coastal plain of Palestine extending from Joppa to Mount Carmel, proverbially fertile and noted for its flowery beauty (Isa. 35:2; Cant. 2:1). It has a width from about six to twelve miles. The plain was well watered and was a garden spot (I Chron. 27:29). In modern Palestine it is dotted with citrus farms and numerous settlements. In antiquity it was a favorite caravan route along the sea, connecting Asia Minor, Egypt and Mesopotamia.* The plain furnished a home for very early man, as discovery of cave burial places have indicated. Dor, Lydda, Joppa, Caesarea, Rakkon and Antipatris were well-known Biblical cities located in this plain.—*M. F. U.*

Shar'onite (shăr'ō-nīt), the designation (I Chron. 27:29) of Shitrai, David's chief herdsman in the plain of Sharon.

Sharu'hen (shá-rōō'hĕn), a town originally in Judah, but afterward allocated to Simeon (Josh. 19:6), hence in the Negeb, or "south country." It is called *Shilhim* (15:32) and *Shaaraim* (I Chron. 4:31). Its present location is Tell el-Far'ah, a short distance S. W. of Lachish (Tell ed-Duweir) on the main ancient road between Palestine and Egypt. The site reveals impressive evidence of Hyksos, Egyptian and Roman fortifications. It rises 150 feet above the surrounding desert terrain and was of immense strategic importance in antiquity. It is N. W. of Beersheba.

Sha'shai (shā'shī; *whitish*, or *noble*), one of the "sons" of Bani, who put away his Gentile wife after the exile (Ezra 10:40), B. C. 456.

Sha'shak (shā'shăk), son of Beriah, a Benjamite (I Chron. 8:14). He was the father of Ishpan and others (vers. 22-25), B. C. after 1360.

Sha'ul (shā'ŭl; *asked*, i. e., *of God*).

1. The son of Simeon by a Canaanitish woman (Gen. 46:10; Exod. 6:15; Num. 26:13; I Chron. 4:24), B. C. c. 1900.

2. I Chron. 1:48, 49. In Gen. 36:37 he is less accurately called Saul (*q. v.*).

3. Son of Uzziah, a Kohathite (I Chron. 6:24).

Sha′ulites (shā′ŭ-līts), the family founded by Shaul, 1 (Num. 26:13).

Sha′veh, Valley of (shā′vĕ; *valley of the plain*), a valley called also the "king's dale," or Kidron, on the north of Jerusalem (Gen. 14:17; II Sam. 18:18). Here Absalom had erected a monument to himself, whether in the form of a column, an obelisk, or a monolith cannot be determined. It was situated about two stadia (one fourth of a mile) east of Jerusalem.

Sha′veh-kiriatha′im (shā′vĕ-kĭr-yà-thā′ĭm; *plain of Kirjathaim*), a plain near the city of Kirjathaim of Moab (Gen. 14:5). It belonged afterward to Reuben (Num. 32:37; Josh. 13:19). Chedorlaomer defeated the Emim here. "It is probably still to be seen in the ruins of *el Teym*, or *et Tueme*, about a mile to the west of Medabah" (K. and D., *Com.*, on Gen.).

Shaving. *See* Hair.

Shav′sha (shăv′shà), the secretary of King David (I Chron. 18:16), and apparently the same as Seraiah (*q. v.*).

Sheaf, the rendering of three Hebrew words:
1. *Bundle of grain* (Heb. *'ălŭmmäh, bound*); "sheaf" in Gen. 37:7; Psa. 126:6; 129:7.
2. *Bunch* (Heb. *'ämîr, handful*, as rendered in Jer. 9:22) hence a *sheaf* (Amos 2:13; Mic. 4:12; Zech. 12:6).
3. *A heap* (Heb. *'ōmer*).

The Mosaic law contains the following prescriptions respecting sheaves: 1. One accidentally dropped or left upon the field was not to be taken up, but remained for the benefit of the poor (Deut. 24:19). *See* Glean. 2. The day after the Feast of the Passover the Hebrews brought into the temple a sheaf of barley, with accompanying ceremonies (Lev. 23:10-12). *See* Festivals.

She′al (shē′ăl; *asking*), one of the "sons" of Bani, who put away his foreign wife (Ezra 10:29), B. C. 456.

Sheal′tiel (shē-ăl′tĭ-ĕl; *I have asked God*), father of Zerubbabel (Ezra 3:2, 8; 5:2; Neh. 12:1; Hag. 1:1, 12, 13; 2:2, 23). *See* Salathiel.

Sheari′ah (shē-à-rī′à; *Jehovah esteems*), the fourth of Azel's six sons, and one of the descendants of Saul (I Chron. 8:38; 9:44), B. C. long after 1000.

Shearing House, a place on the road between Jezreel and Samaria, at which Jehu, on his way to the latter, encountered forty-two members of the royal family of Judah, whom he slaughtered at the well or pit attached to the place (II Kings 10:12, 14). The translators of our version have given in the margin the literal meaning of the name—"house of binding of the shepherds." It is probable that the original meaning has escaped. It is commonly identified with Beit Kad, about 16 miles N. E. of Samaria.

She′ar-ja′shub (shē′är-jä′shŭb; *a remnant shall return*), the son of Isaiah, who accompanied his father when he went to deliver to King Ahaz the prophecy contained in Isa. 7:3, B. C. about 735. The name, like that of Maher-shalal-hash-baz, had a prophetic significance.

She′ba (shē′bà).
1. A son of Ramah, son of Cush (Gen. 10:7; I Chron. 1:9). He is supposed to have settled somewhere on the shores of the Persian Gulf.

2. A son of Joktan, son of the patriarch Eber (Gen. 10:28; I Chron. 1:22). The Joktanites were among the early colonists of southern Arabia, and the kingdom which they there founded was, for many centuries, called the kingdom of Sheba, after one of the sons of Joktan.

3. The elder son of Jokshan, son of Keturah (Gen. 25:3; I Chron. 1:32), B. C. probably after 2000. He evidently settled somewhere in Arabia, probably on the eastern shore of the Arabian Gulf, where his posterity appear to have become incorporated with the earlier Sabeans (*q. v.*) of the Joktanic branch.

4. The son of Bichri, a Benjamite from the mountains of Ephraim (II Sam. 20:1-22), the last chief of the Absalom insurrection. He is described as a "man of Belial," i. e., "a worthless wretch." But he must have been a person of some consequence from the immense effect produced by his appearance. It was, in fact, all but an anticipation of the revolt of Jeroboam. The occasion seized by Sheba was the emulation between the northern and southern tribes on David's return (20:1, 2). The king might well say, "Sheba, the son of Bichri, shall do us more harm than did Absalom" (v. 6). Sheba traversed the whole of Palestine, apparently rousing the population, Joab following in full pursuit. It seems to have been his intention to establish himself in the fortress of Abel-Beth-maachah, famous for the prudence of its inhabitants (v. 18). That prudence was put to the test on the present occasion. Joab's terms were—the head of the insurgent chief. A woman of the place undertook the mission to her city, and proposed the execution to her fellow-citizens. The head of Sheba was thrown over the wall, and the insurrection ended, B. C. about 967.

5. One of the Gadite chieftains resident in Bashan in the reign of Jeroboam II (I Chron. 5:13), B. C. about 784.

6. The kingdom of Sheba. The kingdom of the Sabeans (*q. v.*), which, according to some, embraced the greater part of the Yemen, or Arabia Felix. When the fame of Solomon came to the ears of the Queen of Sheba (Saba), she undertook a journey to Jerusalem to convince herself of the truth of the report which had reached her. She proposed to test his wisdom by enigmas (I Kings 10:1-13; II Chron. 9:1-12). A large number of inscriptions have been found in southwestern Arabia written in the so-called Sabaean characters. They show, among other things, that, besides the famous kingdom of Sheba, there was another monarchy called Ma'in, hence the classical and now current term "Minean." The Sabeans were governed by priest-kings (Psa. 72:10). The ruins of their capital city, Mariaba (Mareb), reveal the advancement of their culture. Solomon was able to answer all the Queen of Sheba's riddles; and this demonstration of his wisdom, with the wonders of his retinue, his table, and palace, filled her with amazement. She then said with astonishment to Solomon, that of what her eyes now saw she had not heard the half. After an exchange of valuable presents, she returned

to her own country. Jesus spoke of her as the "queen of the south" (Matt. 12:42). Reference is made to the commerce that took the road from Sheba along the western borders of Arabia (Job 6:19; Isa. 60:6; Jer. 6:20; Ezek. 27:22, 23).

7. One of the towns allotted to Simeon (Josh. 19:2), mentioned between Beer-sheba and Moladah. Sheba is lacking in the Chronicles, probably omitted through a copyist's error, as *Shema* answers to it in 15:26, where it stands before *Moladah*, just as Sheba does here.

She′bah (shē′bà; *seven, an oath*), the famous well which gave its name to the city of Beer-sheba (Gen. 26:33). According to this version of the occurrence, Shebah, or, more accurately, *Shibah*, was the fourth of the series of wells dug by Isaac's people, and received its name from him, apparently in allusion to the oaths which had passed between himself and the Philistine chieftains the day before. It should not be overlooked that, according to the narrative of an earlier chapter, the well owed its existence and its name to Isaac's father (21:32). Some commentators, as Kalisch (*Com.*, on Gen. 26:33), looking to the fact that there are two large wells at *Bir es Seba*, propose to consider the two transactions as distinct, and as belonging the one to the one well, the other to the other. Others see in the two narratives merely two versions of the circumstances under which this renowned well was first dug.

She′bam (shē′băm), one of the towns in the pastoral district on the east of Jordan—demanded by, and finally ceded to the tribes of Reuben and Gad (Num. 32:3 only). It is probably the same which appears in the altered forms of Shibmah and Sibmah.

Shebani′ah (shĕb-à-nī′à; (perhaps, *Jehovah has brought back* or *returned*).

1. One of the priests who blew the trumpet before the ark of the Lord when it was removed from the house of Obed-edom to Jerusalem (I Chron. 15:24), B. C. about 986.

2. One of the Levites who stood upon the "stairs" and offered the prayer of confession and thanksgiving (Neh. 9:4, 5), and joined in the sacred covenant with Nehemiah (10: 10), B. C. 445.

3. Another Levite who signed the covenant (Neh. 10:12).

4. A priest who also sealed the covenant (Neh. 10:4). His son is prominently mentioned in 12:14, and he is probably the same as *Shechaniah* (v. 3).

Sheb′arim (shĕb′à-rĭm; *breaches, ruins*), apparently the name of a place (Josh. 7:5), but probably stone "quarries" (R. V.), near the slope east of Ai. Not identified.

She′bat. *See* Sebat.

She′ber (shē′bēr; cf. Arab. *sabr, lion*), a son of Caleb by his concubine Maachah (I Chron. 2:48), B. C. about 1365.

Sheb′na (shĕb′nà), a person occupying a high position in Hezekiah's court, officially described as "over the house." The office he held was that of minister of the household, and included the superintendence of all the domestic affairs of the sovereign (Isa. 22:15), B. C. about 719. He subsequently held the subordinate position of secretary (Isa. 36:3; 37:2; II Kings 19:2), his former post having been given to Eliakim. In his post of eminence Shebna had helped to support a spirit of self-security and forgetfulness of God; and Isaiah was sent to pronounce against him the prophecy of his fall (Isa. 22:15, sq.).

Shebu′el (shĕ-bū′ĕl; perhaps *Return, O God* or *captive of God*).

1. A descendant of Gershom (I Chron. 23:16; 26:24), who was ruler of the treasures of the house of God; called also *Shubael* (24:20), B. C. before 960. He is the last descendant of Moses of whom there is any trace.

2. One of the fourteen sons of Heman the minstrel (I Chron. 25:4), called also *Shubael* (25:20), B. C. before 960.

Shecani′ah (shĕk-à-nī′à; I Chron. 24:11; II Chron. 31:15), another form for *Shechaniah*. See Nos. 2 and 5.

Shechani′ah (shĕk-à-nī′à; *Jehovah has dwelt*).

1. Apparently the son of Obadiah, and presumably a descendant of David (I Chron. 3:21, 22). Keil (*Com.*, in loc.) thinks that the list from v. 21 to the end of the chapter is a genealogical fragment inserted into the text at some later time.

2. The tenth in order of the priests who were appointed by lot in the reign of David (I Chron. 24:11, "Shecaniah"), B. C. about 960.

3. One of the priests appointed by Hezekiah to distribute tithes among their brethren (II Chron. 31:15), B. C. 719. The name is given in the A. V. "Shecaniah."

4. One of the "sons" of Pharosh, and ancestor of the Zechariah who, with one hundred and fifty males, accompanied Ezra from the exile (Ezra 8:3), B. C. before 457.

5. Another Israelite, and progenitor of Jahaziel, who with three hundred males went up with Ezra from Babylon to Jerusalem (Ezra 8:5), B. C. before 457.

6. The son of Jehiel, of the "sons of Elam," and one of the Jews who proposed to Ezra the repudiation of the Gentile wives (Ezra 10:2), B. C. 457.

7. The father of Shemaiah, who was "keeper of the east gate," and assisted in repairing the wall of Jerusalem under Nehemiah (Neh. 3:29), B. C. before 445.

8. The son of Arah, and father-in-law of Tobiah, the Ammonite who opposed Nehemiah (Neh. 6:18), B. C. 445.

9. One of the "priests and Levites" (probably the former), who returned with Zerubbabel from Babylon (Neh. 12:3), B. C. about 536.

She′chem (shē′kĕm; a *shoulder, ridge*).

1. The son of Hamor, the Hivite prince at Shechem (Gen. 33:19). Charmed with the beauty of Dinah, Jacob's daughter, Shechem took her with him and seduced her. This wrong was terribly avenged by the girl's brothers, Simeon and Levi (Gen. 34:1-31; Judg. 9:28; Acts 7:16, A. V. *Sychem*).

2. A man of Manasseh, of the family of Gilead, and head of the family of Shechemites (Num. 26:31). His family is mentioned in Josh. 17:2.

3. A son of Shemidah, a Gileadite (I Chron. 7:19).

428. Mount Gerizim (left), Mount Ebal (right)
with Shechem between

4. An ancient and important city of Palestine, called also Sichem (Gen. 12:6), Sychar (John 4:5), and Sychem (Acts 7:16).

(1) **Name.** It is not known whether the city was named after Shechem (Gen. 33:18, sq.), or he received his name from it. The etymology of the Hebrew word *shekem* indicates that the place was situated on some mountain or hillside; and that presumption agrees with Josh. 20:7, which places it on Mount Ephraim (see also I Kings 12:25), and with Judg. 9:6, which represents it as under the summit of Gerizim, which belonged to the Ephraim range.

(2) **Location.** After Vespasian destroyed the Samaritan temple on Mt. Gerizim, he built his new city ("Neapolis") farther up the valley, leaving the ancient Shechem in ruins. Archaeology has shown that Shechem was Tell Balâtah, not the site of the later Roman city Neapolis or Nablūs, which was considered for a long time to be Shechem, but is N. W. of it (*See* W. F. Albright, *The Archaeology of Palestine*).

(3) **Archaeology.** Excavations at Tell Balâtah by the Germans between 1913-1934 show that the ancient city of Shechem was a prosperous place between 2000-1800 B. C. and later between 1400 and 1200 B. C. Important Bronze Age fortifications were discovered at the site. The ruins include a wall thirty feet high, dated from the 17th-16th centuries. A fourteenth century B. C. temple was also found. Walls evidently dating from the middle of the 11th century and attributable to the era of Abimelech (Judg. chap. 9) also came to light. Clay tablets inscribed in Akkadian writing were also dug up at the site. A Drew University-McCormick Theological Seminary team began a new excavation at Shechem in 1956, working there again in 1957.

(4) **Bible allusions.** Abraham, on his first migration to the land of promise, pitched his tent and built an altar under the oak (or terebinth) of Moreh, at Shechem. "The Canaanite was then in the land;" and it is evident that the region, if not the city, was already in possession of the aboriginal race (see Gen. 12:6). At the time of Jacob's arrival here, after his sojourn in Mesopotamia (33:18; ch. 34), Shechem was a Hivite city, of which Hamor, the father of Shechem, was the headman. It was at this time that the patriarch purchased from that chieftain "the parcel of the field," which he subsequently

bequeathed as a special patrimony to his son Joseph (Gen. 33:19; Josh. 24:32; John 4:5). The field lay undoubtedly on the rich plain of the *Mukhna*, and its value was the greater on account of the well which Jacob had dug there, so as not to be dependent on his neighbors for a supply of water. The defilement of Dinah, Jacob's daughter, and the capture of Shechem and massacre of all the male inhabitants by Simeon and Levi, are events that belong to this period (Gen. 34:1, sq.). In the distribution of the land, Shechem fell to Ephraim (Josh. 20:7), but was assigned to the Levites, and became a city of refuge (21:20, 21). It was the scene of the promulgation of the law, when its blessings were heard from Gerizim and its curses from Ebal (Deut. 27:11; Josh. 8:33-35); and here Joshua assembled the people shortly before his death, and delivered to them his last counsels (24:1, 25); After the death of Gideon, Abimelech, his illegitimate son, induced the Shechemites to revolt and make him king (Judg., ch. 9). After a reign of three years he was expelled from the city, and in revenge destroyed the place, and, as an emblem of the fate to which he would consign it, sowed it with salt (vers. 25-45). It was soon restored, however, for we are told in I Kings, ch. 12, that all Israel assembled at Shechem, and Rehoboam, Solomon's successor, went thither to be inaugurated as king. Here, at this same place, the ten tribes renounced the house of David, and

429. German Excavations at Shechem

transferred their allegiance to Jeroboam (I Kings 12:16), under whom Shechem became for a time the capital of his kingdom. The most of the people of Shechem were carried into captivity (II Kings 17:5, 6; 18:9, sq.), but Shalmaneser sent colonies from Babylon to occupy the place of the exiles (17:24). Another influx of strangers came under Esarhaddon (Ezra 4:2). From the time of the origin of the Samaritans the history of Shechem blends itself with that of this people and of their sacred mount, Gerizim. It was to the Samaritans that Shechem owed the revival of its claims to be considered the religious center of the land; but this was in the interest of a narrow and exclusive sectarianism (John 4:5, sq.).

She′chemites (shē′kê-mīts), a family designation of the descendants of Shechem, 3 (Num. 26:31).

Shechi′nah (shē-kī′nà; Aram. and late Heb. *shᵉkīnāh, residence*, i. e., of God), a word not in

Scripture, but used by later Jews and by Christians to express the visible divine Presence, especially when resting between the cherubim over the mercy seat. *See* Ark, under Tabernacle.

Shed′eur (shĕd′ē-ēr; *Shaddai is light*), the father of Elizur, chief of the tribe of Reuben at the time of the Exodus (Num. 1:5; 2:10; 7:30, 35; 10:18), B. C. c. 1440.

Sheep, the rendering of several words in the original (*see* also Animal Kingdom):

1. A ram just old enough to *butt* (Exod. 12:5; Job 31:20). Heb. *kĕbĕs.*

2. A *young* sheep, a lamb (Gen. 30:32, 33, 35; Lev. 1:10, etc.; Num. 18:17), Heb. *kĕsĕb.*

3. A *flock* of sheep (Gen. 4:2; 29:10; 31:19; 38:13, etc.), the most frequent word thus rendered, Heb. *'ṣōn.*

4. *One* of a flock, a single sheep (Gen. 22:7, 8, A. V. "lamb;" Exod. 12:5, etc.), though sometimes used collectively (Jer. 50:17), Heb. *sĕh.*

5. Any four-footed tame animal accustomed to graze, but always a sheep in New Testament (Matt. 7:15; 10:16; 12:11, sq.). (Gr. *probaton*). Sheep were an important part of the possessions of the ancient Hebrews and of Eastern nations generally. The first mention of sheep occurs in Gen. 4:2. They were used in the sacrificial offerings, both the adult animal (Exod. 20:24; I Kings 8:63; II Chron. 29:33), and the lamb, i. e., "a male from one to three years old," but young lambs of the first year were more generally used in the offerings (see Exod. 29:38; Lev. 9:3; 12:6; Num. 28:9, etc.). No lamb under eight days old was allowed to be killed (Lev. 22:27). A very young lamb was called *tâleh* (see I Sam. 7:9; Isa. 65:25). Sheep and lambs formed an important article of food (I Sam. 25:18; I Kings 1:19; 4:23; Psa. 44:11, etc.). The wool was used as clothing (Lev. 13:47; Deut. 22:11; Prov. 31:13; Job 31:20, etc.). "Rams' skins dyed red" were used as a covering for the tabernacle (Exod. 25:5). Sheep and lambs were sometimes paid as tribute (II Kings 3:4). It is very striking to notice the immense numbers of sheep that were reared in Palestine in biblical times. Sheep-shearing is alluded to in Gen. 31:19; 38:13; Deut. 15:19; I Sam. 25:4; Isa. 53:7, etc. Sheep dogs were employed in biblical times, as is evident from Job 30:1, "the dogs of my flock." Shepherds in Palestine and the East generally go before their flocks, which they induce to follow by calling to them (comp. John 10:4; Psa. 77:20; 80:1), though they also drove them (Gen. 33:13).

Figurative. The nature of sheep and their relation to man have given rise to many beautiful figures. Jehovah was the Shepherd of Israel, and they were his flock (Psa. 23:1; 74:1; 78:52; 79:13; 80:1; Isa. 40:11; Jer. 23:1, 2, etc.); apostasy of sinners from God is likened to the straying of a lost sheep (Psa. 119:176; Isa. 53:6; Jer. 50:6); Jesus came to earth as the good Shepherd (Luke 15:4-6; John 10:8, 11). As the sheep is an emblem of meekness, patience, and submission, it is expressly mentioned as typifying these qualities in the person of our blessed Lord (Isa. 53:7; Acts 8:32, etc.).

Sheepcote, or **Sheepfold,** the rendering of the following Hebrew and Greek terms:

1. *Sheepcote* (Heb. *näwĕh, habitation;* II Sam. 7:8; I Chron. 17:7; "fold," Isa. 65:10; Jer. 23:3; Ezek. 34:14; "stable," 25:5), in a general sense is a place where flocks repose and feed.

2. *Enclosure* (Heb. *gᵉdērāh,* "cote," I Sam. 24:3; "fold," Num. 32:16, 24, 36; Zeph. 2:6), a built pen, such as joins buildings, and used for cattle as well as sheep.

3. *Fold* (Heb. *mĭklāh, pen,* "sheepfold," Psa. 78:70; "folds," 50:9; Hab. 3:17), is probably what we understand by *stalls.*

4. *Cote* (Gr. *aulē, court,* John 10:1), the roofless inclosure in the open country in which flocks were herded at night.

When sheep are exposed to the depredations of robbers, it is customary in the East to shelter them in well-built inclosures, which are impregnable when once the flock is within them. When no danger from this source is feared the flocks are folded only when they are to be shorn.

Sheep Gate (*shă′ăr,* "gate," *hăṣṣ′ōn,* "flock," i. e., "gate of the flock"), one of the gates of Jerusalem rebuilt by Nehemiah (Neh. 3:1, 32; 12:39). It was located between the tower of Meah and the chamber of the corner (3:1, 32), or gate of the guardhouse (12:39, A. V. "prison gate"). It is probably the same as inaccurately rendered in A. V. "sheep market" (John 5:2).

Sheep Market (Gr. *probatikē, relating to sheep,* John 5:2). The word "market" is an interpolation of our translators, perhaps after Luther's *schafhaus* (sheep house). It should probably be rendered "sheep gate" (*q. v.*).

Sheepmaster (Heb. *nōqēd, marker,* II Kings 3:4), a term signifying both a shepherd (Amos 1:1) and also a possessor of flocks. In Arabic it is properly the possessor of a superior kind of sheep or goats.

Sheep-Shearer (Hebrew from *gāzăz, to shear*). What the harvest was to an agricultural, that the sheep-shearing was to a pastoral people: celebrated by a festival corresponding to our harvest-home, marked often by the same revelry and merrymaking (Gen. 31:19; I Sam. 25:4, 8, 36; II Sam. 13:23-28, etc.). Sheepshearers are mentioned in Gen. 38:12; II Sam. 13:23, 24.

Shee′rah (shē′rȧ). *See* Sherah.

Sheepskins (Gr. *mēlōtē,* a simple garment made of the sheep's pelt (*see* Dress, 1), and used figuratively (Heb. 11:37) to represent a condition of extreme poverty.

Sheet. 1. This is rendered "fine linen" (Prov. 31:24; Isa. 3:23), and means, probably, a shirt (Judg. 14:12, Heb. *sädin.*)

2. *A sail* (Gr. *'othonē,* Acts 10:11; 11:5).

Shehari′ah (shē-hȧ-rī′áh; *sought by Jehovah*), the second of the six sons of Jeroham, Benjamites residing in Jerusalem at the captivity (I Chron. 8:26), B. C. 588.

Shekel. *See* Metrology, iv.

Sheki′nah (shē-kī′nȧ), another spelling of Shechinah (*q. v.*).

She′lah (shē′lȧ).

1. The youngest son of Judah by the daughter of Shuah (Gen. 38:5, 11, 14, 26; 46:12;

Num. 26:20; I Chron. 2:3; 4:21), B. C. after 1925. His descendants (I Chron. 4:21-23) were called *Shelanites*.

2. The son of Arphaxad (I Chron. 1:18). *See* Salah.

She'lanite (shē'là-nīt), a descendant of Shelah (*q. v.*), son of Judah (Num. 26:20).

Shelemi'ah (shĕl-ê-mī'à; *Jehovah repays*).

1. The porter of the east entrance to the tabernacle, his son Zechariah having the northern gate (I Chron. 26:14), B. C. about 960. He is called *Meshelemiah* (9:21; 26:1, 2), *Meshullam* (Neh. 12:25), and *Shallum* (I Chron. 9:17, 31).

2. One of the "sons" of Bani in the time of Ezra (Ezra 10:39), B. C. 456.

3. Another of the "sons" of Bani in the time of Ezra (Ezra 10:41), B. C. 456.

4. The father of Hananiah, which latter repaired part of the walls of Jerusalem (Neh. 3:30), B. C. 445. He is probably an apothecary, or manufacturer of incense (v. 8).

5. A priest appointed by Nehemiah to serve as a treasurer of the Levitical tithes (Neh. 13:13), B. C. 445.

6. The grandfather of Jehudi, who was sent by the princes to invite Baruch to read Jeremiah's roll to them (Jer. 36:14), B. C. about 606.

7. Son of Abdeel, one of those who received the orders of Jehoiakim to take Baruch and Jeremiah (Jer. 36:26).

8. The father of Jehucal, or Jucal, in the time of Jedekiah (Jer. 37:3), B. C. about 597.

9. The father of Irijah, the captain of the ward who arrested Jeremiah (Jer. 37:13; 38:1), B. C. before 586.

She'leph (shē'lĕf; Heb. *a drawing forth*, but cf. Arab. *salafa*, *to cultivate*), the second of the thirteen sons of Joktan (Gen. 10:26; I Chron. 1:20). The tribe which sprang from him has been satisfactorily identified, and is found in the district of *Sulaf*.

She'lesh (shē'lĕsh; *triplet*, *triad*, but cf. Arab. *salis*, *meek*, *obedient*), a son of Helem, and great-grandson of Asher (I Chron. 7:35), B. C. perhaps about 1290.

Shelo'mi (shē-lō'mĭ; *at peace*), the father of Ahihud, which latter represented the tribe of Asher among the commissioners appointed to divide the promised land (Num. 34:27), B. C. 1171.

Shel'omith (shĕl'ô-mĭth; fem. of Shelomi, *peaceful*).

1. The daughter of Dibri, of the tribe of Dan, and mother of the man who was stoned for blasphemy (Lev. 24:11), B. C. c. 1439.

2. The daughter of Zerubbabel (I Chron. 3:19), B. C. perhaps after 536.

3. First named of the three sons of Shimei, chief of the Gershonites in the time of David (I Chron. 23:9), B. C. about 950. In v. 10 his name should probably take that of "Shimei."

4. A Levite, chief of the Izharites in the time of David (I Chron. 23:18), B. C. before 960. In 24:22 he is called *Shelomoth*.

5. A Levite, and descendant of Eliezer, the son of Moses, who in the reign of David was one of the temple treasurers (I Chron. 26:25, 26, 28), B. C. before 960.

6. The last child of Rehoboam by his wife Maachah (II Chron. 11:20), B. C. about 934.

7. According to the present text the sons of Shelomith, with the son of Josiphiah at their head, returned from Babylon with Ezra (Ezra 8:10). There appears, however, to be an omission, and the true reading is probably "Of the sons of Bani, Shelomith the son of Josiphiah."

Shel'omoth (shĕl'ô-mŏth; I Chron. 24:22). *See* Shelomith, 4.

Shelu'miel (shē-lū'mĭ-ĕl; *peace of God*), the son of Zurishaddai, and prince of the tribe of Simeon at the time of the Exodus (Num. 1:6; 2:12; 7:36, 41; 10:19), B. C. c. 1440.

Shem (shĕm; *name*), one of the three sons of Noah, born when his father was five hundred years of age (Gen. 5:32), B. C. perhaps before 5000. At the age of ninety-eight years he entered the ark, being married but childless (7:7), and two years after the flood (i. e., the beginning of the flood) he became the father of Arphazad, other children being born still later (11:10, 11; 10:22). He assisted Japheth in covering the nakedness of his father when it was made known by Ham. In the prophecy of Noah which is connected with this incident (9:23-37) the first blessing falls on Shem. His death at the age of six hundred years is recorded in 11:11. The portion of the earth occupied by the descendants of Shem (10:21-31) intersects the portions of Japheth and Ham, and stretches in an uninterrupted line from the Mediterranean Sea to the Indian Ocean. It includes Syria (Aram), Chaldea (Arphaxad), parts of Assyria (Ashur), of Persia (Elam), and of the Arabian peninsula (Joktan). The servitude of Canaan under Shem, predicted by Noah (9:26), was fulfilled primarily in the subjugation of the people of Palestine (Josh. 23:4; II Chron. 8:7, 8). The eminent spiritual blessings of Shem are fulfilled in Messiah, who came from the line of Shem (cf. Rom. 9:3-5).

NOTE—The expression, "Unto Shem . . . the brother of Japheth the elder," etc. (Gen. 10:21), has caused much discussion as to the relative ages of Japheth and Shem. Many prominent authorities support the seniority of Shem, while a large number argue in favor of Japheth.

She'ma (shē'mà; *report, rumor, fame*).

1. The last-named son of Hebron and father of Raham, of the tribe of Judah (I Chron. 2:43, 44).

2. The son of Joel and father of Azaz, of the tribe of Reuben (I Chron. 5:8). He is probably the same as Shemaiah of v. 4.

3. One of the sons of the Benjamite Elpaal, and one of those who drove out the inhabitants of Gath (I Chron. 8:13), B. C. after 1170.

4. One of those who stood at Ezra's right hand when he read the law to the people (Neh. 8:4), B. C. about 445.

5. A town in south Judah, named between Amam and Moladah (Josh. 15:26). In the parallel list of towns set off from Judah to Simeon (Josh. 19:2) it is given as Sheba, which is perhaps the more nearly correct.

Shema'ah (shē-mā'à; *report, fame*), a Benjamite of Gibeah, and father of Ahiezer and Joash, who joined David at Ziklag (I Chron. 12:3), B. C. about 1002.

Shema'iah (shē-mā'yà; *Jehovah has heard*).

1. A prophet in the reign of Rehoboam. When the king had assembled one hundred and eighty thousand men of Benjamin and

Judah to reconquer the northern kingdom after its revolt, Shemaiah was commissioned to charge them to return to their homes and not to war against their brethren (I Kings 12:22; II Chron. 11:2), B. C. after 934. His second and last appearance was upon the occasion of the invasion of Judah and siege of Jerusalem by Shishak, king of Egypt (II Chron. 12:5, 7). He wrote a chronicle containing the events of Rehoboam's reign (v. 15).

2. The son of Shechaniah, among the descendants of Zerubbabel (I Chron. 3:22). He was keeper of the east gate of the city, and assisted Nehemiah in restoring the wall (Neh. 3:29), B. C. 445. He is probably the same as Semei (Luke 3:26).

3. Father of Shimri and ancestor of Ziza, a prince of the tribe of Simeon (I Chron. 4:37), B. C. before 726. Perhaps the same as Shimei (vers. 26, 27).

4. The son of Joel, a Reubenite, and father of Gog (I Chron. 5:4). He is probably the same as Shema (v. 8).

5. Son of Hasshub, a Merarite Levite who lived in Jerusalem after the captivity (I Chron. 9:14). He was one of those who had "the oversight of the outward business of the house of God" (Neh. 11:15), B. C. 445.

6. The son of Galal and father of the Levite Obadiah (or Abda), who "dwelt in the villages of the Netophatites" after the captivity (I Chron. 9:16), B. C. before 445. In Neh. 11:17 he is called Shammua.

7. Son of Elizaphan, and chief of his house of two hundred men in the reign of David. He took part in the removal of the ark from Obededom (I Chron. 15:8, 11), B. C. about 988.

8. A son of Nethaneel, and a Levite scribe who, in the time of David, registered the division of the priests into twenty-four orders (I Chron. 24:6), B. C. about 960.

9. The eldest son of Obed-edom, the Gittite, and a gate keeper of the temple (I Chron. 26:4, 6, 7), B. C. before 960.

10. One of the Levites sent by Jehoshaphat, in his third year, to teach the people of the cities of Judah (II Chron. 17:8), B. C. 872.

11. A descendant of Jeduthun the singer, who assisted in the purification of the temple in the reign of Hezekiah (II Chron. 29:14), B. C. 719. He is perhaps the same as the Shemiah who distributed tithes among his brethren (31:15).

12. A Levite in the reign of Josiah, who, with others, made large contributions of sacrifices for the passover (II Chron. 35:9), B. C. 621.

13. One of the sons of Adonikam, who, with his two brothers, brought sixty males from Babylon with Ezra (Ezra 8:13), B. C. about 457.

14. One of the "heads" whom Ezra sent for to his camp by the river of Ahava, for the purpose of obtaining Levites and ministers for the temple from "the place Casiphia" (Ezra 8:16), B. C. about 457.

15. A priest of the family of Harim, who put away his foreign wife at Ezra's bidding (Ezra 10:21), B. C. 456.

16. A layman of Israel, son of another

Harim, who also had married a foreigner (Ezra 10:31), B. C. 456.

17. Son of Delaiah, the son of Mehetabeel, a prophet in the time of Nehemiah, who, bribed by Tobiah and Sanballat, pretended fear, and proposed to Nehemiah that they should seek safety in the temple (Neh. 6:10, sq.), B. C. 445.

18. A head of a priestly house who returned with Zerubbabel from Babylon (Neh. 12:6, 18), B. C. 536. If the same, he lived to sign the covenant with Nehemiah (10:8), B. C. 445. The Shemaiah, son of Mattaniah and father of Jonathan, mentioned in 12:35, is perhaps the same.

19. One of the princes of Judah at the time of the dedication of the wall of Jerusalem (Neh. 12:34), B. C. 445.

20. One of the musicians who took part in the dedication of the new wall of Jerusalem (Neh. 12:36), B. C. 445.

21. One of the priestly trumpeters on the same occasion (Neh. 12:42).

22. The father of the prophet Urijah (*q. v.*), of Kirjath-jearim (Jer. 26:20), B. C. before 609.

23. Shemaiah the Nehelamite, a false prophet in the time of Jeremiah (Jer. 29:24-32).

24. The father of Delaiah, one of the princes who heard Baruch's roll (Jer. 36:12), B. C. before 607.

Shemari'ah (shĕm-à-rī'á; *Jehovah keeps or preserves*).

1. One of the Benjamite warriors who came to David at Ziklag (I Chron. 12:5), B. C. about 1002.

2. The second son of Rehoboam by his wife Abihail (II Chron. 11:19; A. V. "Shamariah"), B. C. about 934.

3. One of the family of Harim, a layman of Israel, who put away his foreign wife in the time of Ezra (Ezra 10:32), B. C. 456.

4. Another of the family of Bani under the same circumstances (Ezra 10:41).

Sheme'ber (shĕm-ē'bēr), king of Zeboiim, and ally of the king of Sodom when he was attacked by the northeastern invaders under Chedorlaomer (Gen. 14:2), B. C. about 2065.

She'mer (shē'mēr; *kept*), the owner of the hill on which the city of Samaria was built (I Kings 16:24). King Omri bought it for two talents of silver, and named it Shomeron, after Shemer (I Kings 16:24), B. C. about 886. *See* Sha'mer.

Shemi'da (shē-mī'dá; *the name*, i. e., descendants, *has known*), one of the six sons of Gilead and founder of the family Shemidaites, of the tribe of Manasseh (Num. 26:32; Josh. 17:2). His three sons are mentioned in I Chron. 7:19, where the name is given as "Shemidah."

Shemi'dah (shē-mī'dá; I Chron. 7:19). *See* Shemida.

Shemi'daites (shē-mī'dá-īts) descendants (Num. 26:32) of Shemida, who obtained their inheritance among the male posterity of Manasseh (Josh. 17:2, A. V. "children of Shemida").

Shem'inith (shĕm'ĭ-nĭth), a musical term (I Chron. 15:21; Psa. 6, title; 12, title), perhaps referring to eight strings or octaves.

Shemir'amoth (shē-mĭr'à-mŏth; possibly *name of the heights* or *name most high*).

1. A Levite musician of the second degree in the choir founded by David (I Chron. 15:18), playing "with psalteries on Alamoth" (v. 20; comp. 16:5), B. C. about 986.

2. One of the Levites sent by Jehoshaphat to teach the law to the inhabitants of Judah (II Chron. 17:8), B. C. after 875.

Shemu'el (shē-mū'ĕl; *heard of God*). The same Hebrew word commonly translated Samuel (*q. v.*).

1. Son of Ammihud, appointed from the tribe of Simeon to divide the land of Canaan (Num. 34:20), B. C. c. 1400.

2. Another form of Samuel the prophet (I Chron. 6:33).

3. A descendant of Tola, and one of the chiefs of the tribe of Issachar (I Chron. 7:2).

Shen (shĕn; Hebrew with article *hăshshēn, the tooth*), a place (I Sam. 7:12) between which and Mizpeh Samuel set up the stone Ebenezer, to commemorate the rout of the Philistines. The name may indicate a projecting point of rock (I Sam. 14:4), or a place situated upon such a point. Its exact locality is unknown.

Shenaz'ar (shē-năz'àr; Akkad., *O Sin*, i. e., moon-god, *protect*), one of the sons of Jeconiah and brother of Salathiel (I Chron. 3:18), B. C. after 606.

She'nir (shē'nĕr; Deut. 3:9; Cant. 4:8). **Se'nir** (sē'nĕr; I Chron. 5:23; Ezek. 27:5, *pointed,* and so *peak*), the name given by the Amorites to Mount Hermon (*q. v.*). The Sidonians called it Sirion, and in Psa. 29:6 Sirion is used poetically for Hermon.

She'ol (shē'ŏl; *Hades,* or the world of the dead), a word usually derived from *shā'ăl,* "to ask or seek," perhaps with the signification expressed in English, "the insatiable sepulcher." We have no clew to the origin of the word, and must seek for its meaning in the several passages in which it occurs. In Gen. 37:35, "And Jacob said, I will go down *into the grave* (Heb. *to Sheol*) unto my son mourning," the meaning is obvious. In Num. 16:30 Moses declares that Korah shall go down alive into the *pit,* viz., the interior of the earth (v. 33). In II Sam. 22:6 the A. V. has, "The sorrows of hell compassed me about." The English word *hell* does not here mean a place of torment, for it will be seen that the sorrows (Heb. "snares") of *Sheol* are equivalent to the nets of death. In Job 11:8 there seems to be an allusion to the belief that there is a dark and deep abyss beneath the center of the earth, tenanted by departed spirits, but not necessarily a place of torment. "Hell from beneath is moved for thee," etc. (Isa. 14:9), is thus rendered by Delitzsch (*Com.,* in loc.), "The kingdom of the dead below is all in uproar on account of thee;" and its meaning thus interpreted, "All Hades is overwhelmed with excitement and wonder, now that the king of Babel . . . is actually approaching."

In the great majority of cases *Sheol,* in the Old Testament, is used to signify the grave; and it can have no other meaning in Gen. 37:35; 42:38; I Sam. 2:6; I Kings 2:6; Job 14:13; 17:13, 16, and in many passages in the writings of David, Solomon, and the prophets. The darkness and gloom of the grave was such that the word denoting it came to be applied to the abiding place of the miserable. When this was supposed to be the case our translators rendered the word "hell." Some passages are doubtful, but concerning others scarcely a question can be entertained (e. g., Job 11:8; Psa. 139:8; Amos 9:3), in which the word denotes the opposite of heaven. Still more decisive are Psa. 9:17; Prov. 23:14; in which *Sheol* can only mean the abode of the wicked, as distinguished from and opposed to the righteous.

In the New Testament the Gr *hadēs* is used in much the same sense as *sheol* in the Old, except that in a less proportion of cases can it be construed to signify "the grave." In this sense it occurs in Acts 2:31; I Cor. 15:55; but in general the Hades of New Testament appears to be the world of future punishment (e. g., Matt. 11:23; 16:18; Luke 16:23). *See* Hades, Hell, Gehenna, Lake of Fire, Tartarus.

She'pham (shē'făm), a place mentioned by Moses in his specification of the eastern boundary of the promised land (Num. 34:10, 11). Location on N. E. near Riblah.

Shephathi'ah (shĕf-à-thī'à; I Chron. 9:8), more properly Shephatiah, 2.

Shephati'ah (shĕf-à-tī'à; *Jehovah judges*).

1. The fifth of the six sons born to David in Hebron. His mother's name was Abital (II Sam. 3:4; I Chron. 3:3), B. C. about 994.

2. Son of Reuel, and father of Meshullam, a Benjamite chieftain dwelling in Jerusalem after the captivity (I Chron. 9:8), B. C. before 536.

3. The Haruphite, or Hariphite, one of the Benjamite warriors who joined David in his retreat at Ziklag (I Chron. 12:5), B. C. about 1002.

4. Son of Maachah, and prince of the Simeonites in the time of David (I Chron. 27:16), B. C. before 960.

5. The last named of the six sons of Jehoshaphat, king of Judah, all of whom were richly endowed by their father (II Chron. 21:2, 3), B. C. after 875.

6. The family of Shephatiah, three hundred and seventy-two in number, returned with Zerubbabel (Ezra 2:4; Neh. 7:9). A second detachment of eighty, with Zebadiah at their head, came up with Ezra (Ezra 8:8), B. C. before 536.

7. The family of another Shephatiah were among the children of Solomon's servants who came up with Zerubbabel (Ezra 2:57; Neh. 7:59), B. C. before 536.

8. A descendant of Perez, or Pharez, the son of Judah and ancestor of Athaiah (Neh. 11:4), B. C. long before 536.

9. The son of Mattan, one of the princes of Judah, who counseled Zedekiah to put Jeremiah in the dungeon (Jer. 38:1), B. C. 589.

Shephe'lah, The (shē-fē'là; *the low,* i. e., *land*), the name given to the southern division of the low-lying district between the central highlands of Palestine (*q. v.*) and the Mediterranean. Though the name may originally have been used to include the maritime plain, yet the Shephelah proper was the region of low hills between that plain and the high central range. It contained the strategic defense cities of Lachish, Debir, Libnah, and Beth-shemesh.

She′pher (shē′fēr), in A. V. Shapher (q. v.).

Shepherd (from Heb. rō′ĕh, one who tends, to tend; Gr. poimēn).

1. **Duties.** The routine of the shepherd's duties appears to have been as follows: In the morning he led forth his flock from the fold (John 10:4), which he did by going before them and calling to them, as is still usual in the East; arrived at the pasturage, he watched the flock with the assistance of dogs (Job 30:1), and, should any sheep stray, he had to search for it until he found it (Ezek. 34:12; Luke 15:4); he supplied them with water, either at a running stream or at troughs attached to wells (Gen. 29:7; 30:38; Exod. 2:16; Psa. 23:2); at evening he brought them back to the fold, and reckoned them to see that none was missing, by passing them "under the rod" as they entered the door of the inclosure (Lev. 27:32; Ezek. 20:37), checking each sheep as it passed, by a motion of the hand (Jer. 33:13); and, finally, he watched the entrance of the fold throughout the night, acting as porter (John 10:3). The shepherd's office thus required great watchfulness, particularly by night (Luke 2:8; comp. Nah. 3:18). It also required tenderness toward the young and feeble (Isa. 40:11), particularly in driving them to and from the pasturage (Gen. 33:13). In large establishments there were various grades of shepherds, the highest being styled "rulers" (Gen. 47:6), or "chief shepherds" (I Pet. 5:4); in a royal household the title of abbir, "mighty," was bestowed on the person who held the post (I Sam. 21:7). Shepherds in Bible lands were of two varieties—those who were nomadic, and migrated to new pastures and sources of water. Those who resided in towns and tended flocks in nearby meadows.

2. **Life.** The office of the Eastern shepherd, as described in the Bible, was attended with much hardship, and even danger. He was exposed to the extremes of heat and cold (Gen. 31:40); his food frequently consisted of the precarious supplies afforded by nature, such as the fruit of the "sycamore," or Egyptian fig (Amos 7:14), the "husks" of the carob tree (Luke 15:16), and perchance the locusts and wild honey which supported John the Baptist (Matt. 3:4); he had to encounter the attacks of wild beasts, occasionally of the larger species, such as lions, wolves, panthers, and bears (I Sam. 17:34; Isa. 31:4; Jer. 5:6; Amos 3:12); nor was he free from the risk of robbers or predatory hordes (Gen. 31:39). To meet these various foes the shepherd's equipment consisted of the following articles: A mantle, made probably of sheepskin, with the fleece on, which he turned inside out in cold weather, as implied in the comparison in Jer. 43:12 (comp. Juv., xiv, 187); a scrip or wallet, containing a small amount of food (I Sam. 17:40); a sling, which is still the favorite weapon of the Bedouin shepherd (17:40); and, lastly, a staff, which served the double purpose of a weapon against foes, and a crook for the management of the flock (I Sam. 17:40; Psa. 23:4; Zech. 11:7). If the shepherd was at a distance from his home, he was provided with a light tent (Cant. 1:8; Jer. 35:7), the

removal of which was easily effected (Isa. 38:12). In certain localities, moreover, towers were erected for the double purpose of spying an enemy at a distance, and protecting the flock: such towers were erected by Uzziah and Jotham (II Chron. 26:10; 27:4), while their existence in earlier times is testified by the name Migdal-Eder (Gen. 35:21, A. V. "tower of Edar;" Mic. 4:8, A. V. "tower of the flock"). Shepherds found shelter in caves such as those near Bethlehem or at 'Ain Feshka, where the Dead Sea Scrolls were uncovered, or the Cave of Pan at Banias. Often the shepherd simply slept under the stars or in a light easily transported tent. (Song 1:8).

The hatred of the Egyptians toward shepherds (Gen. 46:34) may have been mainly due to their contempt for the sheep itself, which appears to have been valued neither for food nor generally for sacrifice, the only district where they were offered being about the Natron lakes.

Figurative. The shepherd is used frequently in Scripture as illustrative:

1. Of God as the Leader of Israel (Psa. 77:20; 80:1).

2. Of Christ as the good Shepherd (Ezek. 34:23; Zech. 13:7; Isa. 40:11; John 10:14; Heb. 13:20).

3. Of kings as leaders of the people (Isa. 44:28; Jer. 6:3; 49:19).

4. Of ministers (Jer. 23:4), foolish shepherds as bad ministers (Isa. 56:11; Jer. 50:6; Ezek. 34:2, 10; Zech. 11:8, 15-17).

She′phi (shē′fī; bareness), the fourth of the five sons of Shobal, the son of Seir of Edom (I Chron. 1:40), called in the parallel passage (Gen. 36:23) Shepho.

She′pho (shē′fō; Gen. 36:23). See Shephi.

Shephu′phan (shē-fū′făn), one of the sons of Bela, the firstborn of Benjamin (I Chron. 8:5). His name is also written Shephuphum (A. V. "Shupham," Num. 26:39) and Muppim (Gen. 46:21).

She′rah (shē′rà; kinswoman), daughter of Ephraim (I Chron. 7:24), and foundress of the two Beth-horons, and of Uzzen-Sherah, B. C. probably about 1169. This Ephraim was probably a descendant of the patriarch, and lived after Israel took possession of Canaan. (R. V. Sheerah.)

Sherd, a piece of broken pottery. The numerous potsherds found in ancient Biblical and near-Biblical sites are of inestimable value to the archaeologist in dating occupational strata and in determining density of population in any era. Pottery chronology is now a precise science. Perhaps more than any one factor it has lifted modern archaeology out of the category of a treasure hunt and placed it on a solid scientific basis. Sir Flinders Petrie in 1890 worked out sequence dating by types of pottery found in different strata. Petrie's initial methods have been greatly refined. Two basic principles underlying scientific archaeology are (1) stratigraphy or the examination of the kinds of pottery found in occupational levels and (2) typology, the study of the relation of the forms of pottery found at a given level. At Ras Shamra in N. Syria pottery excavated shows influences as far distant as Turkistan, Susa and Nineveh. Palestinian pottery gives evidence of great artistic ability, showing Israel's creative skill.—*M. F. U. See* Potsherd.

Sherebi'ah (shĕr-ē-bī'à; *Jehovah has sent scorching heat*), a Levite of the family of Mahli, the son of Merari, who, with eighteen of his brethren, joined Ezra at the river Ahava (Ezra 8:18, 24). When Ezra read the law to the people Sherebiah was among the Levites who assisted him (Neh. 8:7); B. C. about 445. He took part in the psalm of confession and thanksgiving which was sung at the solemn fast after the Feast of Tabernacles (9:4, 5), and signed the covenant with Nehemiah (10:12). He is again mentioned as among the chief of the Levites who belonged to the choir (12:8, 24).

She'resh (shē'rĕsh; *root*), son of Machir, the Manassite, by his wife Maachah (I Chron. 7:16).

Shere'zer (shĕr-ē'zēr; for derivation see Sharezer), a messenger sent, with Regem-melech, in the fourth year of Darius, to inquire at the temple regarding a day of humiliation in the fifth month (Zech. 7:2), B. C. 518.

Sheriff (Aram. *tiphtai*, a *lawyer*), a court official at Babylon (Dan. 3:2, 3), "a judge in the the narrower sense of the word" (Keil, *Com.*).

She'shach (shē'shăk). This is supposed to be a symbolical name for Babel—Babylon—(Jer. 25:26; 51:41). It is thought by some critics to be a cabalistic plan, called "Athbash," making the word Sheshach represent Babel. The letters of the alphabet were numbered both in their regular and reverse order. When the cypher of a name was devised, its consonants were replaced by the identical numbers in the reverse numbering. Since "B" is letter 2 of the Hebrew alphabet and "S" or "Sh" the second from the end, and "L" the 12th from the beginning and K number 12 from the end, the cypher for Babel became Sheshak.

She'shai (shē'shī; *whitish*), one of the three sons of Anak, who dwelt in Hebron (Num. 13:22), and were driven thence and slain by Caleb at the head of the children of Judah (Josh. 15:14; Judg. 1:10), B. C. c. 1364.

She'shan (shē'shăn), a son of Ishi, in the posterity of Jerahmeel, of the tribe of Judah. Having no sons, he gave his daughter, probably Ahlai, to his Egyptian slave, Jarha, through which union the line was perpetuated (I Chron. 2:31, 34, 35), B. C. about 1190.

Sheshbaz'zar (shĕsh-băz'ĕr; Akkad., apparently *Sun-god, guard the lord or son*), apparently the Chaldean name given, apparently, to Zerubbabel (Ezra 1:8, 11; 5:14, 16). That Sheshbazzar means Zerubbabel is evident from (1) his being called the "prince (*hănnäst'*) of Judah," a term marking him as head of the tribe in the Jewish sense. (2) His being characterized as "governor" *pĕhäh*, appointed by Cyrus, both which Zerubbabel was; and yet more distinctly by the assertion (5:16) that "Sheshbazzar laid the foundation of the house of God which is in Jerusalem," compared with the promise to Zerubbabel (Zech. 4:9), "The hands of Zerubbabel have laid the foundation of this house; his hands shall also finish it."

Sheth (shĕth; *a placing, compensation*).
1. The patriarch Seth (I Chron. 1:1).
2. In the A. V. of Num. 24:17 the Heb.

Sheth is rendered as a proper name, but there is reason to regard it as an appellative, and to translate, instead of "the sons of Sheth," "the sons of tumult," or *confusion*, the wild warriors of Moab (comp. Jer. 48:45).

She'thar (shē'thär; foreign derivation), one of the seven princes of Persia and Media, who had access to the king's presence, and were the first men in the kingdom in the third year of Xerxes (Esth. 1:14).

She'thar-boz'enai (shē'thär-bŏz'ē-nī) A. V. **She'thar-boz'nai** (shē'thär-bŏz'nī), a Persian officer of rank, having a command in the province "on this side the river," under Tatnai, the satrap, in the reign of Darius Hystappis (Ezra 5:3, 6; 6:6, 13). He joined with Tatnai and the Apharsachites in trying to obstruct the progress of the temple in the time of Zerubbabel, and in writing a letter to Darius, of which a copy is preserved in Ezra, ch. 5. As regards the name Shethar-boznai, it seems to be certainly Persian. The first element of it appears as the name Shethar, one of the seven Persian princes in Esth. 1:14 (Smith).

She'va (shē'và; *vanity*).
1. The scribe or royal secretary of David (II Sam. 20:25). He is called elsewhere *Seraiah* (8:17), *Shisha* (I Kings 4:3), and *Shavsha* (I Chron. 18:16).
2. Son of Caleb ben-Hezron by his concubine Maachah (I Chron. 2:49).

Shewbread. *See* Showbread.

Shib'boleth (shĭb'bō-lĕth; a *stream*, as *flowing*; or an *ear* of grain, as *growing out*). This word came into notice in the Old Testament history merely with respect to its proper pronunciation. After the defeat of the Ephraimites by Jephthah and the Gileadites on the farther side of Jordan, the latter seized the fords of the river, with the view of cutting off the return of the Ephraimites. To test whether those who approached the river were really Ephraimites, they asked them to pronounce the word *shibboleth*. If any one pronounced it *sibboleth*—the way the Ephraimites did—doing away with the aspirate, he was adjudged an Ephraimite, and put to death. Thus forty-two thousand Ephraimites fell (Judg., ch. 12).

Shib'mah (shĭb'mà; Num. 32:38). *See* Sibmah.

Shic'ron (shĭk'rŏn; *drunkenness*), a town near the western end of the northern boundary of Judah, named between Ekrah and Mount Baalah (Josh. 15:11). As it is not named among the cities of Judah (vers. 21-63), it would seem to have been in Dan. It is, perhaps, the present ruined village *Beit Shit*, about halfway between Ekron and Ashdod.

Shield. *See* Armor, 2, (1).

Shigga'ion (shĭg-gā'yŏn), used in the title of Psa. 7, meaning not certain.

Shigio'noth (shĭ-gĭ-ō'nŏth). Shigionoth, pl. of Shiggaion (Hab. 3:1).

Shi'hon (shī'hŏn; *overturning, a ruin*), a city in Issachar (Josh. 19:19), named between Haphraim and Anaharath. A name resembling it at present in that neighborhood is 'Ayun esh-Sh'ian, 3 miles W. N. W. of Mount Tabor. R. V. renders Shion.

Shi'hor (shī'hŏr; I Chron. 13:5). *See* Sihor.

Shi'hor-lib'nath (shī'hŏr-lĭb'năth; *turbid* or *muddy stream of Libnath*). It is generally believed to be a river south of Carmel, on the borders of Asher, probably the modern *Nahr-Zerka*, or crocodile brook (Josh. 19:26). Crocodiles are still found in the Zerka.

Shik'keron (shĭk'ē-rŏn), a Judean town (Josh. 15:11). *See* Shic'ron.

Shil'hi (shĭl'hī; perhaps, *He*, i. e., Jehovah, *has sent*), the father of Azubah, the mother of King Jehoshaphat (I Kings 22:42; II Chron. 20:31), B. C. before 875.

Shil'him (shĭl'hĭm; *missiles*), a place in the south of Judah (Josh. 15:32). It is called also Sharuhen (Josh. 19:6), and Shaarim (I Chron. 4:31). *See* Sharuhen.

Shil'lem (shĭl'ĕm; *recompense*), a son of Naphtali (Gen. 46:24; Num. 26:49), elsewhere (I Chron. 7:13) called Shallum (*q. v.*).

Shil'lemite (shĭl'ē-mīt), a descendant of Shillem (*q. v.*).

Shilo'ah (shĭ-lō'á; Isa. 8:6). *See* Siloam.

Shi'loh (shī'lō), the name, apparently, of a person.

A title of the Messiah (Gen. 49:10), Heb. *shīlōh*. While there has been much discussion as to the grammatical interpretation of the word, the entire Jewish synagogue and the whole Christian Church agree as to the fact that the patriarch is here proclaiming the coming of the Messiah. "The objection that the expectation of a personal Messiah was foreign to the patriarchal age, and must have been foreign to the nature of that age" (Kurtz), is not valid. For the expectation of a personal Saviour did not arise for the first time with Moses, Joshua, and David, but was contained in the germ of the promise of the seed of the woman and in the blessing of Noah upon Shem, and still further expanded in the promises of God to the patriarchs. When Jacob had before him the founders of the twelve-tribed nation the question naturally arose, from which of the twelve tribes would the promised Saviour proceed? Reuben (*q. v.*) had forfeited the right of primogeniture by his incest, and it could not pass over to either Simeon or Levi on account of their crime against the Shechemites. Consequently the dying patriarch transferred, both by his blessing and prophecy, the chieftainship and promise to his fourth son, Judah. Judah was to bear the scepter with victorious, lionlike courage, until in the future *Shiloh* was to descend from Judah.

The gradual advance of Messianic prophecy places the personal meaning of Shiloh beyond all possible doubt. Balaam's prophecy transfers Jacob's proclamation of the lion nature of Judah to Israel as a nation (Num. 23:24; 24:9), and introduces the figure of the scepter from Gen. 49:9, 10. As champion, even after the death of Joshua, Judah by divine direction opened the attack upon the Canaanites (Judg. 1:1, sq.), and also the war against Benjamin (20:18). From Judah was raised up the first judge in the person of Othniel (3:9, sq.). The election of David raised Judah to the rank of ruling tribe, and it received the scepter over all the rest (I Chron. 28:4). The authority of Zerubbabel as "governor of Judah" (Hag. 2:2) would seem to have rested upon a recognition of this traditional supremacy.

Solomon sang of the King's Son who should have dominion from sea to sea and from the river to the ends of the earth (Psa. 72); and the prophets after Solomon prophesied of the Prince of Peace, who should increase government and peace without end upon the throne of David, and of the sprout out of the rod of Jesse, whom the nations should seek (Isa. 9:5, 6; 11:1-10; comp. Ezek. 21:27). "Thus did the kingdom of Judah arise from its temporary overthrow to a new and imperishable glory in Jesus Christ (Heb. 7:14), who conquers all foes as the Lion of the tribe of Judah (Rev. 5:5), and reigns as the true Prince of Peace, as 'our peace' (Eph. 2:14), forever and ever" (K. and D., *Com.*, on Gen.).

Shi'loh (shī'lō), the site of Israel's early sanctuary in the time of the Judges, was located E. of the main road from Jerusalem to Bethel at Shechem. It was situated about nine miles N. of Bethel. Considering all factors, Shiloh was a good choice of a sanctuary from the point of view of a central location. It was the focal point of Israel's amphictyonic organization before the establishment of the kingdom. Such a central religious institution of a common shrine around which were grouped the twelve tribes has close parallels in Mediterranean lands (cf. Martin Noth, *Das System der Zwoelf Staemme Israels*, 1930, pp. 39-60). Numerous amphityonies such as the Delphic in the eighth century B. C. and the Etruscan, centering around the temple of the goddess Voltumna, are illustrations. Israel, moreover, was not the only country in the ancient Near East which had its central sanctuary to which pilgrimages were made. Nippur in Babylonia and Nineveh in Assyria in the early second millennium B. C. were such places, as is known from contemporary documents. Other examples are the temple of Sin at Haran and the shrine of Belit-ekalli at Qatna. The sanctuary of Baaltis at Byblos performed a similar function. Excavations by the Danish Expedition have uncovered pottery and other evidence demonstrating that Shiloh was destroyed c. 1050 B. C., presumably at the hands of the Philistines when the ark was carried away (I Sam. 4). Jeremiah takes this destruction for granted (Jer. 7:12-15; 26:6, 7), and findings at the site offer an interesting instance of archaeology's ability to supplement information contained in the Biblical account. When the Philistines brought back the ark to Israel it was not set up again at Shiloh (I Sam. 6:21-7:2). Archaeology has made it obvious that the site was destroyed by Philistines. (For an account of the excavations at Shiloh see H. Kjaer, *Jour. of Pal.-Orient. Soc.*, 1930, pp. 87-114).—*M. F. U.*

Shilo'ni (shī-lō'nī; a Shilonite). This word, occurring only in Neh. 11:5, A. V., should be rendered—as in other cases—"the Shilonite," being preceded by the definite article.

Shi'lonite (shī'lō-nīt).

1. The native or resident of Shiloh—a title ascribed only to Ahijah (I Kings 11:29; 12:15; 15:29; II Chron. 9:29; 10:15).

2. The Shilonites are mentioned among the descendants of Judah dwelling in Jerusalem at a date difficult to fix (I Chron. 9:5). They are doubtless the members of the house of

Shelah, who in the Pentateuch are more accurately designated Shelanites.

Shil'shah (shĭl'shà; *triad*), son of Zophah, of the tribe of Asher (I Chron. 7:37), B. C. before 960.

Shim'ea (shĭm'ē-à; *report, rumor, fame*).

1. Son of David by Bath-sheba (I Chron. 3:5), called in II Sam. 5:14; I Chron. 14:4, Shammua (*q. v.*).

2. A Merarite Levite, son of Uzza and father of Haggiah (I Chron. 6:30), B. C. before 987.

3. A Gershonite Levite, ancestor of Asaph the minstrel (I Chron. 6:39).

4. The brother of David (I Chron. 20:7), elsewhere called Shammah, Shimma, and Shimeah.

Shim'eah (shĭm'ē-à).

1. Brother of David and father of Jonathan and Jonadab (II Sam. 21:21); called also Shammah (I Sam. 16:9), Shimea (I Chron. 20:7), and Shimma (2:13).

2. A descendant of Jehiel, the father or founder of Gibeon (I Chron. 8:32), B. C. perhaps 536. He is called (9:38) Shimeam.

Shim'eam (shĭm'ē-ăm; *their fame*), the descendant of Jehiel (I Chron. 9:38), called (8:32) Shimeah (*q. v.*).

Shim'eath (shĭm'ē-ăth; feminine of *Shimeah*), an Ammonitess, mother of Jozachar or Zabad, one of the murderers of King Joash (II Kings 12:21; II Chron. 24:26), B. C. before 797.

Shim'eathites (shĭm'ē-à-thīts), one of the families of "scribes" resident at Jabez, in the tribe of Judah (I Chron. 2:55); descendants, apparently, of a Shimea not of the Kenites, possibly the brother of David (II Sam. 21:21).

Shin'ei (shĭm'ē-ī; perhaps, *a renowned one*).

1. Son of Gershon, the son of Levi (Num. 3:18; I Chron. 6:17, 29; 23:7, 9, 10; Zech. 12:13; *Shimi*, Exod. 6:17). In I Chron. 6:29, according to the present text, he is called the son of Libni, and both are reckoned as sons of Merari; but there is reason to suppose that there is something omitted in this verse, as he is everywhere else represented to be Libni's *brother*. Strong (*Cyclopoedia*) conjectures that Shelomith should be read instead of Shimei in I Chron. 23:10. Keil (*Com.*, in loc.) thinks the Shimei of vers. 7 and 10 to be another than the one in v. 9.

2. The son of Gera, a Benjamite of the house of Saul, and resident, during David's reign, of Bahurim, on the other side of the Mount of Olives (II Sam. 16:5). (1) **Curses David.** When David, in his flight from Absalom, had come to Bahurim, Shimei ran out of the place cursing the king and pelting him and his servants with stones. Abishai wanted to put an end to this cursing, and requested permission to "take off his head," but was forbidden by the king, who said, "It may be that the Lord will look on mine affliction, and that the Lord will requite me good for his cursing this day." The royal party passed on, Shimei following them and casting stones and dirt as long as they were in sight (II Sam. 16:5-13), B. C. about 967. (2) **Spared.** The next we learn of Shimei is his suing for pardon at the hands of the king. Just as David was crossing the Jordan in the ferryboat (II Sam. 19:18), the first person to welcome him was

Shimei, who may have seen him approaching from the heights above. He threw himself at David's feet in abject penitence, and, notwithstanding the desire of Abishai that he should be put to death, his life was spared (19:16-23). (3) **Executed.** But the king's suspicions were not set at rest by this submission, and on his deathbed he recalls the whole scene to the recollection of his son Solomon. Solomon gave Shimei notice that from henceforth he must consider himself confined to the walls of Jerusalem on pain of death. He was to build a house in Jerusalem (I Kings 2:36, 37). For three years the engagement was kept. At the end of that time, for the purpose of capturing two slaves who had escaped to Gath, he went out on his ass and made his journey successfully. On his return the king took him at his word, and he was slain by Benaiah (vers. 30-46), B. C. around 955.

3. An adherent of Solomon at the time of Adonijah's usurpation (I Kings 1:8), B. C. 958. Unless he is the same as Shimei, the son of Elah (4:18), Solomon's commissariat officer, or with Shimeah, or Shammah, David's brother, it is impossible to identify him.

4. Son of Elah, and Solomon's commissariat officer in Benjamin (I Kings 4:18), B. C. 954.

5. Son of Pedaiah and brother of Zerubbabel (I Chron. 3:19), B. C. 536.

6. A Simeonite, son of Zacchur. Special mention is made of his numerous family (I Chron. 4:26, 27), B. C. perhaps before 1210.

7. A Reubenite, son of Gog and father of Micah (I Chron. 5:4).

8. A Gershonite Levite, son of Jahath (I Chron. 6:42).

9. Son of Jeduthun, and chief of the tenth division of the singers in David's reign (I Chron. 25:17), B. C. before 960.

10. The Ramathite who was over David's vineyards (I Chron. 27:27), B. C. before 960.

11. A Levite of the sons of Heman, who took part in the purification of the temple under Hezekiah (II Chron. 29:14), B. C. c. 720.

12. The Levite who, with his brother Cononiah, had charge of the offerings in the reign of Hezekiah (II Chron. 31:12, 13), B. C. 719. Perhaps the same as the preceding.

13. A Levite in the time of Ezra who had married a foreign wife (Ezra 10:23), B. C. 456.

14. One of the family of Hashum who put away his foreign wife at Ezra's command (Ezra 10:33).

15. A son of Bani, who had also married a foreign wife and put her away (Ezra 10:38).

16. Son of Kish, a Benjamite and ancestor of Mordecai (Esth. 2:5), B. C. before 518.

Shim'eon (shĭm'ē-ŏn; *a hearing*, i. e., in prayer), a layman of Israel, of the family of Harim, who had married a foreign wife, and divorced her in the time of Ezra (Ezra 10:31).

Shim'hi (shĭm'hī), a Benjamite, apparently the same as Shema, the son of Elpaal (I Chron. 8:21).

Shim'i (shĭm'ī; Exod. 6:17). *See* Shimei, 1.

Shim'ite (shĭm'īt), a descendant (Num. 3:21; comp. Zech. 12:13) of Shimei (1), the son of Gershon.

Shim'ma (shĭm'à; I Chron. 2:13). *See* Shimeah, 1.

Shi'mon (shī'mŏn). The four sons of Shimon are enumerated in an obscure genealogy of the tribe of Judah (I Chron. 4:20).

Shim'rath (shĭm'răth; *a guarding, watching*), a Benjamitè, the ninth named of the sons of Shimhi (I Chron. 8:21).

Shim'ri (shĭm'rī; *vigilant, watchful*).

1. Son of Shemaiah, and head of a Simeon-ite family (I Chron. 4:37), B. C. probably after 1170.

2. The father of Jediael, one of David's guard (I Chron. 11:45), B. C. before 982.

3. The son of Elizaphan, and one of the Levites who aided in the purification of the temple under Hezekiah (II Chron. 29:13), B. C. c. 720.

Shim'rith (shĭm'rĭth; feminine of *Shimri*), a Moabitess, mother of Jehozabad, one of the assassins of King Joash (II Chron. 24:26; in II Kings 12:21, Shomer).

Shim'rom (shĭm'rŏm; I Chron. 7:1). *See* Shimron.

Shim'ron (shĭm'rŏn; *guardianship*).

1. The fourth son of Issachar, according to the lists of Genesis (46:13) and Numbers (26:24), and the head of the family of the *Shimronites*, B. C. about 1910. In I Chron. 7:1 later editions give "Shimrom."

2. A town of Zebulun (Josh. 19:15), one of those which joined the confederacy under Jabin against Joshua (11:1-5), the same more fully called Shimron-meron (12:20).

Shim'ronite (shĭm'rṓ-nīt), a descendant (Num. 26:24) of Shimron, the son of Issachar.

Shim'ron-me'ron (shĭm'rŏn-mē'rŏn), a town conquered by Joshua (Josh. 12:20), and prob-ably the same as elsewhere (11:1) called sim-ply Shimron (*q. v.*).

Shim'shai (shĭm'shī; *sunny*), the scribe or sec-retary of Rehum, who was a kind of satrap of the conquered province of Judea and of the colony of Samaria, supported by the Per-sian court (Ezra 4:8, 9, 17, 23). He was ap-parently an Aramean, for the letter which he wrote to Artaxerxes was in Aramaic (4:7), and the form of his name is in favor of this supposition.

Shin (shĭn), 21st letter of the Hebrew alphabet (English "s" or "sh"). *See* Psalm 119 (21st section).

Shi'nab (shī'năb), the king of Admah in the time of Abraham (Gen. 14:2), B. C. c. 1965.

430. Plain of Shinar

Shi'nar (shī'nȧr), the name of a country (Gen. 10:10; 11:2, ff.). In the biblical story Shinar is the name of the land in which were located the cities of Babylon, Erech, Accad, and Cal-neh. It was, therefore, a part of the land of Babylonia, and may be roughly spoken of as southern Babylonia, though some of these cities, perhaps, would more strictly be in-cluded in northern Babylonia. Very little light from the Babylonian inscriptions has come upon this word Shinar. It is probable that it is connected with the Babylonian Sumer, which occurs so constantly upon the Baby-

431. Victory Stela of Naram-Sin, King of Sumer and Accad

lonian inscriptions. Its most common usage is in the political expression, "king of Sumer and Accad," but the meaning of this phrase is still a subject of controversy among As-syriologists. We find some of the earliest kings of Babylonia bearing this title, and it con-tinued irregularly in use down to a very late period in the history of Assyria. It appears to have been a political rather than a geo-graphical expression, and its limits must have varied in different periods of history. The land to which it is applied in the Old Testament is altogether alluvial, and was celebrated in the ancient world not only by the Babylonians, but also by the Greeks and Romans as a land of prodigious fertility. Modern travelers do not speak in such high terms of it, and part of its fertility, at least, must have been ascribed to the wonderful care with which it was tilled and to the elaborate systems of irrigation by which it was watered. In its cities the earliest kingdoms known to us in the history of the human race were founded.

Before the fourth millennium B. C., a non-Semitic people known as the Sumerians entered this fertile region and developed a high degree of civilization and a pictograph cuneiform writing that was the precursor of Semitic cuneiform. Isaiah named Shinar as one of the places from which the Jews would be regathered at the end time (Isa. 11:11). Zech. 5:11 mentions Shinar in connection with the woman and the ephah, symbolizing the spirit of godless commercialism as originating in Babylon. Nebuchadnezzar carried away temple treasures taken from Jerusalem to the Shinar area (Dan. 1:2).—*M. F. U.*

Shi'on (shī'ŏn). *See* Shihon.

Ships (Heb. *'ŏnîyyāh,* "conveyance;" *sĕphînāh,* "a boat;" Gr. *ploion*).

1. **Navigation.** Shipbuilding and navigation were important both in Egypt and Mesopotamia. Very early in history the Egyptians made boats. Besides the small vessels used for fishing in the Nile, immense barges transported building stones from Upper Egypt. Funeral barges as well as passenger boats of wood propelled by oars were a common sight in ancient Egyptian times. Egyptians also ventured out into the Mediterranean in larger, more sea-worthy vessels. The ancient story of Wen-amon tells of the purchase of cedar for the construction of Egyptian sacred barges. Babylonians built boats that plied the Tigris-Euphrates as well as larger ones that sailed into the Persian Gulf on extended commercial voyages. The Phoenicians were famous boat builders and sailors from very early times. Byblos seamen ran a close second to the Egyptians. The famous "Byblos travelers" carried on trade with the Egyptians. This name was given to these vessels because they transported from Phoenicia to Egypt cargoes of wine, papyrus pith, oils, cedar, mummy cases, masts and flagpoles. In exchange the Phoenicians carried back jewelry, perfumes, gold, metal work and luxury wares. By the time of Solomon, Phoenician trading vessels on the Mediterranean went as far as Spain. Skilled Phoenician craftsmen built Solomon's *tarshish* or copper refining fleet at Ezion-geber, and Tyrian sailors manned them.

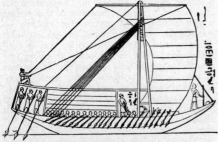

432. Egyptian Ship

2. **Ancient ships.** (1) **Egyptian.** Long before the time of Menes (c. 2900 B. C.), Egyptians employed ships on the Nile. By the end of the fifth millennium B. C. evidence of ships is found. Amratian vases depict large galleys.

Predynastic ships had sharply upturned prows and looked like the gondolas of Venice. During many centuries the Egyptian navy was very strong. "Celestial barks" carried deceased pharoahs to their final resting place. James Breasted refers to some of these being 770 cubits long. (2) **Mesopotamian.** Round reed basket-like barks were calked with bitumen for Mesopotamian river traffic. These common boats were the precursors of later Assyrian craft made of skin and timber rafts supported on inflated skins. Even to the present day the round *guffahs* are still to be seen on the Euphrates. Seafaring vessels came up the Persian Gulf transporting luxury wares to the Tigris-Euphrates region. The Gulf of Suez was also a very common water route in antiquity. Caravans picked up the cargoes and followed regular desert routes. (3) **Phoenician.** Phoenician ships were not large but were skilfully manned and made. They had masts of cedar, oars of oak and were often lavishly adorned with ivory benches inlaid with boxwood. They furnished a picturesque sight with vari-colored sails. Happily the Phoenicians had plenty of wood in the forests of Lebanon at their back door. Their famous ships, often no larger than a good-sized coastal fishing boat of the present day, made a brilliant record in ancient history. (4) **Cretan.** As early as the sixteenth century B. C., the island of Crete became famous as a seafaring locality. The Minoan sea-kings because of their great commercial wealth were able to build the famous Minoan culture. From Heracleion near Knossos, Cretan vessels plied trade with such distant places as Troy, Athens and cities of Asia Minor. Cretan vessels went as far as Ugarit in N. Syria. Phaestos on the southern coast of Crete carried on extensive trade with N. Africa and Egypt. (5) **Greek.** By the seventh century B. C. the Greeks became conspicuous in sea traffic. They improved upon Phoenician boats. The famous Corinthian war ships had two decks, one for rowers and one for fighters. The Greeks increased the size of their ships and had to resort to anchors. They also employed slave labor. Corinth was a famous trading center, being situated on a strategic isthmus. Small vessels could be carted across the isthmus, making the city a great trading emporium. (6) **Roman.** In antiquity the difference between the long, narrow ship of war and the short-prowed merchant vessel was pronounced (cf. *odyssey* V, 250; IX, 323). Merchant vessels were mostly sailing vessels. War ships were customarily propelled by oars. Early Roman vessels had from one to three banks of oars. Later vessels were constructed with four, five, or more banks of oars. The rowers were crowded together and faced the stern. The number of rowers in an ancient trireme, that is with three banks of oars, was 170; that of a Roman quinquereme, five banked, in the Punic wars was 300. Some ships were much larger than this. One eight-banked vessel is said to have had a crew of 1600. Oars were long and rhythm was maintained by a stroke of a hammer or the music of a flute.

3. **Bible Reference.** The following allusions to seafaring are found in the Old Testa-

ment: The prophecy concerning Zebulun (Gen. 49:13); in Balaam's prophecy (Num. 24:24); in one of the warnings of Moses (Deut. 28:68); in Deborah's song (Judg. 5:17); the illustrations and descriptions in Job (9:26), the Psalms (48:7; 104:26; 107:23), Proverbs (23:34; 30:19; 31:14). We have already referred to Solomon's ships (I Kings 9:26; II Chron. 8:18; 9:21), and the disastrous expedition of Jehoshaphat's ships from the same port of Ezion-geber (I Kings 22:48, 49; II Chron. 20:36, 37). Tyre is depicted allegorically as a splendid ship (Ezek., ch. 27), while Isaiah speaks of the "ships of Tarshish" (2:16; 23:1, 14). In the narrative of Jonah (1:3-16) several nautical terms are introduced; and Daniel (11:40) speaks of ships of war.

Frequent mention is made in the New Testament of vessels on the Sea of Galilee. There Jesus addressed the multitude from on board a vessel (Matt., Gr. ploion), i. e., a small fishing vessel; and frequent mention is made of his sailing up and down the lake (Matt. 8:23; 9:1; 14:13; John 6:17). Some of his earliest followers were owners of barks which sailed on this inland sea (Matt. 4:21; Luke 5:3; John 21:3). Josephus calls these vessels skaphē, a skiff (comp. Acts 27:16, 30, 32); probably like our modern fishing smack, generally propelled by oars, but also employing sails.

4. **Construction and Equipment.** (1) **The hull** of ancient vessels presents no special peculiarities; the bow and stern were similar in shape; merchant ships had no hold, the cargo being stowed away upon the deck, the sides of which were protected by an open rail, the stempost and the sternpost rising in a curve, most frequently terminating in an ornament representing a waterfowl bent backward. On the stern projections we sometimes see an awning represented, and on the bow the anchors were stowed. Capstans were evidently used to raise anchors. The personification of ships led to the painting of an eye on each side of the bow, a custom still prevalent in the Mediterranean. Indeed our own sailors speak of the "eyes" of a ship, and it is said in Acts 27:15 that the ship "could not bear up into the wind," literally "look the wind in face." A badge, sign, or emblem was also placed at the prow (28:11).

(2) **Masts, rigging, etc.** These, in distinction from the hull or vessel itself, were called skevē, gear (Acts 27:19, "tackling," A. V.). Its principal feature was a large mast with one large, square sail fastened to a yard of great length. Other masts were sometimes used, arranged as the mainmast. The sail that was hoisted when the ship of Paul was run aground was a "foresail," or a small sail substituted for the larger sail in stormy weather (Gr. 'artemōn, A. V. "mainsail"). The mast is mentioned (Isa. 33:23), and from Ezekiel (27:5) we learn that Lebanon cedar was sometimes used to make them of; "the oak of Bashan" for the oars (v. 6) and cypress of Senir (Antilibanus) for the sheathing of the hull. Ropes and sails were made of byssus linen, the latter being woven in party colors.

(3) **Anchors.** Although ships rigged and constructed like those of the ancients might, under favorable circumstances, be able to work to windward, it must have been "slowly and with difficulty;" and in the event of a ship being caught in a gale, on a lee shore, the only mode of escape was to anchor. No better proof could be given of the superiority in this branch of seamanship than the successful manner in which Paul's ship was brought to anchor in the face of a lee shore in a gale of wind, and finally run ashore, when it could be done in safety to the lives of all on board (Imp. Dict., s. v.). The anchors were much like those of modern make, except that in place of the palms, or iron plates attached to the extremities of the arms, the arms themselves were beaten flat, as in the Dutch anchors.

(4) **Undergirders** (Gr. hupozōmata, Acts 27:17). The imperfection of the build, and the tendency to strain the seams, led to taking on board "helps" (Gr. boētheia), cables or chains, which in case of necessity could be passed around the hull, at right angles to its length and made tight—a process called in the English navy frapping.

(5) **Steering.** Ancient ships were steered by means of two paddle rudders, one on each quarter, acting in a rowlock or through a porthole, as the vessel was large or small. The same thing is true not only of the Mediterranean, but of the early ships of the Northmen. There is nothing out of harmony with this early system of steering in James 3:4, where Gr. pēdalion, helm, occurs in the singular; for "the governor" or steersman (Gr. euthunōn), would only use one paddle rudder at a time.

5. **Officers and Crew.** Luke mentions (Acts 27:11; comp. Jonah 1:6; Rev. 18:17) two principal officers of the ship: the master (Gr. kubernētes, literally pilot), undoubtedly equivalent to our captain; the owner (Gr. nauklēros), a shipowner or master of a trading vessel, who took passengers and freight for hire. The "governor" (James 3:4, Gr. euthunōn), is merely the man at the helm. The "shipmen" (Gr. nautai) were common sailors.

Figurative. An industrious housewife is likened to a merchant ship, bringing "her food from afar" (Prov. 31:14). "Shipwreck" is symbolical of one departing from the faith (I Tim. 1:19). Revised by M. F. U.

Shi'phi (shī'fī; abounding, abundant), a Simeonite, father of Ziza, a prince of the tribe in the time of Hezekiah (I Chron. 4:37), B. C. before 719.

Shiph'mite (shǐf'mīt), an epithet of Zabdi, officer over David's stores of wine (I Chron. 27:27); probably as a native of Shepham (q. v.) or perhaps Siphmoth (I Chron. 27:27).

Shiph'rah (shǐf'rà; splendor, beauty), the name of one of the two midwives of the Hebrews who disobeyed the command of Pharaoh to kill the male children (Exod. 1:15-21).

Shiph'tan (shǐf'tăn; judicial), father of Kemuel, a prince of the tribe of Ephraim, and one of the commissioners to divide Canaan (Num. 34:24), B. C. after 1400.

Shipmaster. See Ship, 5.

Shi'sha (shī'shà), father of Elihoreph and Ahiah, the royal secretaries in the reign of Solomon (I Kings 4:3), B. C. before 960. He is apparently the same as Shavsha, who held the same position under David. *See* Shavsha.

Shi'shak (shī'shăk). Egyptian Sheshonk I (Sheshonq I) was founder of the XXII Libyan Dynasty. Shishak is usually dated c. 935-914 B. C. He is the first pharaoh referred to specifically by name in the Bible. He is famous for his plundering expedition in the fifth year of Rehoboam (I Kings 14:25-28) when he seized Solomon's golden shields and other temple and royal treasures. Egyptian records do not give the date of Shishak's expedition. The uncertain chronology of the early kings of the Davidic line does not enable scholars to come to agreement on the precise date. Albright sets the accession of Rehoboam c. 922 B. C. Accordingly his fifth regnal year would be c. 917 B. C. (*Bull. Am. Schools of Orient. Research*, 87, 1942, p. 28; 130, April, 1953, p. 7). The gold masked body of Shishak was uncovered intact in his burial chamber at Tanis (1938-39). At Karnak (ancient Thebes) his triumphal inscription is recorded. It enumerates his conquests which include towns in all parts of Judah and extend up the coastal plain and cross Esdraelon into Gilead. The evidence from this monument shows that he invaded the Northern Kingdom as well as the Southern Kingdom, in spite of his previous friendship for Jeroboam (I Kings 11:40; cf. W. F. Albright, *O. T. Commentary*, 1948, p. 151). A part of a stela of Shishak has been dug up at Megiddo. This indicates that he actually did capture and occupy this important fortress city as recounted in the Karnak inscription. A triumphal Karnak relief displays captives of Shishak taken in his incursions into Palestine. *M. F. U.*

Shit'rai (shĭt'rī), the Sharonite who had charge of David's herds that fed in Sharon (I Chron. 27:29), B. C. before 970.

Shit'tah Tree (shĭt-à); (Isa. 41:19). *See* Vegetable Kingdom.

Shit'tim (shĭt'ĭm; *acacias*).

1. Israel's last camping place east of Jordan before entering Palestine (Num. 25:1; Josh. 3:1; Mic. 6:5); an abbreviation of Abelshittim (Num. 33:49). It was the place from which Joshua sent forth spies into Canaan (Josh. 2:1). *See* Abel-shittim.

2. The barren valley of the Jordan above the Dead Sea, and was chosen by the prophet Joel (3:18) to denote a very dry valley, as the acacia grows in a dry soil. It was probably west of the Jordan. In the prophecy the spring which waters this valley, and proceeds from the house of Jehovah, the physical as well as spiritual blessings, which will come to Palestine and its inhabitants in the Kingdom Age, are portrayed (cf. Zech. 14:8; Ezek. 47:1-12).

Shittim Wood. *See* Vegetable Kingdom.

Shi'za (shī'zà), the father of Adina, one of David's Reubenite warriors (I Chron. 11:42), B. C. before 1000.

Sho'a (shō'à), a people listed with the Babylonians, Chaldeans and Assyrians (Ezek. 23:23). They may be the Sutu mentioned in the Amarna Letters, who were Syrian nomads who invaded the E. Tigris country, and joining with Aramaean peoples, were never conquered by the Assyrians.

Sho'bab (shō'băb; *backsliding, rebellious*).

1. Second named of the sons born to David in Jerusalem (II Sam. 5:14; I Chron. 3:5; 14:4), B. C. about 1000.

2. Apparently the son of Caleb, the son of Hezron, by his wife Azubah (I Chron. 2:18), B. C. about 1390.

Sho'bach (shō'băk), the general of Hadarezer, king of the Syrians of Zoba, who was defeated by David in person at Helam. Shobach was wounded, and died on the field (II Sam. 10: 15-18). In I Chron. 19:16, 18, he is called *Shophach*, B. C. c. 1001.

Sho'bai (shō'bī; possibly, *one who takes prisoner*). The children of Shobai were a family of the doorkeepers of the temple who returned with Zerubbabel (Ezra 2:42; Neh. 7:45), B. C. before 536.

Sho'bal (shō'băl).

1. The second son of Seir the Horite (Gen. 36:30; I Chron. 1:38), and one of the "dukes," or phylarchs, of the Horites (Gen. 36:29), B. C. about 1840.

2. One of the three sons of Hur, the son of Caleb (I Chron. 2:50). He became the founder ("father") of Kirjath-jearim, B. C. about 1390. The passage should probably be rendered, "These are the sons (i. e., descendants) of Caleb, through his son Hur," etc. In I Chron. 4:1, 2, Shobal appears with Hura among the sons of Judah. He is possibly the same as the preceding.

Sho'bek (shō'běk; cf. Arab. *sabiq, victor, one who goes before*), one of the heads of the people who sealed the covenant with Nehemiah (Neh. 10:24), B. C. 445.

Sho'bi (shō'bī; possibly, *one who takes captive*), son of Nahash, of Rabbah, of the children of Ammon. He was one of the first to meet David at Mahanaim, on his flight from Absalom, and supply him with bedding, cooking utensils, and food (II Sam. 17:27), B. C. about 970.

Sho'cho (shō'kô; II Chron. 28:18), **Sho'choh** (I Sam. 17:1). *See* Sochoh.

Shock of Corn (Heb. *gädish*, a *heap;* hence "a tomb," Job 21:32), a "stack" (Exod. 22:6) of grain reaped (Judg. 15:5; Job 5:26).

Sho'co (shō'kô; II Chron. 11:7). *See* Sochoh.

Shoe. Ancient shoes were actually sandals. These are still made in Oriental lands by taking pieces of leather the size of a person's feet and attaching straps to secure them to the ankles. Sandals were commonly carried on a journey to conserve them. Our Lord's feet were shod with sandals, evidently laced up with thongs, according to Roman style. This explains John the Baptist's allusion that he was not worthy to loose "the latchet (thong) of His shoes." Sandals were used in Egypt very early. Royal sandals survive from the splendid XVIII Dynasty. *M. F. U.*

Figurative. To take off one's shoes or sandals was a token of reverence or respect (Exod. 3:5; Josh. 5:15). In Ruth 4:7 (comp. Deut 25:9, 10) it is recorded, "Now this was the manner in former time in Israel redeeming and concerning changing, for to confirm all things; a man plucked off his shoe, and gave it to his neighbor." From the expression *"formerly,"* and from the description of the custom, we infer that it had largely gone out of use when the book was written. The custom itself, which existed among the Indians and ancient Germans, arose from the fact that fixed property was taken possession of by treading upon the soil; and hence taking off the shoe and handing it to another was a symbol of the transfer of possession or right of ownership. From this thought we have the expression, "Over Edom will I cast out my shoe" (Psa. 60:8; 108:9), i. e., claim it as my own. The declaration (Matt. 3:11), "whose shoes I am not worthy to bear," is explained by Egyptian paintings representing a servant bearing on his arm the shoes of his master, a mark of servile condition. Shoes were removed in mourning and replaced on occasion of joy (Cant. 7:1). Shoes with blood on them is figurative of being engaged in war (I Kings 2:5). See Sandal, Dress.

Shoe Latchet. See Latchet, Shoe.

Sho'ham (shō'hăm; *beryl, onyx*), a Merarite Levite, son of Jaaziah, employed about the ark by David (I Chron. 24:27), B. C. about 983.

Sho'mer (shō'mēr; *guard, keeper*).

1. Second named of the three sons of Heber, an Asherite (I Chron. 7:32), called in v. 34 *Shamer* (*q. v.*).

2. The father of Jehozabad, who slew King Joash (II Kings 12:21). In the parallel passage in II Chron. 24:26, the name is converted into the feminine form Shimrith, who is further described as a Moabitess. This variation may have originated in the dubious gender of the preceding name Shimeath, which is also made feminine by the chronicler. Others suppose that in Kings the father is named and in Chronicles the mother.

Sho'phach (shō'făk), the general of Hadarezer (I Chron. 19:16, 18), called in II Sam. 10:16, *Shobach* (*q. v.*).

Sho'phan (shō-făn), given in A. V. as a town of Gad (Num. 32:35), but it is thought that the word is simply a suffix to the preceding word Atroth (R. V. "Atroth-shophan").

Shore. 1. *Seashore* (Heb. *hōph, chafed* by waves, Gesenius, or *inclosed*, Fuerst; comp. Eng. *cove*), a roadstead (Judg. 5:17; Jer. 47:7; "coast" in Josh. 9:1; Ezek. 25:10; "haven" in Gen. 49:13; "seaside" in Deut. 1:7).

2. *Extremity* of the land (Josh. 15:2; elsewhere "brine" or "brink"), Heb. *qāṣēh* (*extremity, end*).

3. *Lip*, used in our sense of seashore (Gen. 22:17; Exod. 14:30, etc.), Heb. *sāphāh*, (*lip*).

4. The *beach*, on which the waves *dash* (Matt. 13:2, 48; John 21:4; Acts 21:5; 27:39, 40) Gr. *aigialos*.

5. *Lip*, usually rendered the "lip" (Matt. 15:8; Mark 7:6; Rom. 3:13, etc.), once "shore" (Heb. 11:12), as the place upon or from which the waves pour (Gr. *cheilos*, the lip.

Shoshan'nim (shō-shăn'ĭm; lilies), **Shoshan'nim-E'duth** (shō-shăn'ĭm-ē'dŭth; lilies testimony), Psa. 60 title.

Shoulder, the *neck*, as the place to receive a burden (Gen. 21:14; 24:14, 45, etc.). Twice (Num. 6:19; Deut. 18:3) it represents Heb. word for *arm*, the foreshoulder offered in sacrifice. cf. The right, or "heave" shoulder (Exod. 29:22, 27; Lev. 7:32-34, etc.). The

shoulder properly so called, is the spot from which garments are suspended (Exod. 28:12; 39:7), especially of the "shoulder pieces" of the high priest (*q. v.*). In Isa. 11:14 it is the peculiar name of Philistia's coast land (Josh. 15:11), used figuratively of the shoulder of the nation. The Gr. term *ōmas* (Matt. 23:4; Luke 15:5) is the common word for shoulder.

Figurative. To *withdraw one's shoulder* (Neh. 9:29), i. e., to refuse an appointed burden, is figurative of disobedience, rebellion; while to "remove one's shoulder from his burden" (Psa. 81:6) is to deliver him from bondage. Job, in assurance of innocence, exclaims, "Oh . . . that mine adversary had written a book," i. e., an *indictment* made out in legal form, and adds, "Surely I would take (carry) it upon my shoulder" (Job 31:35, 36). The meaning doubtless is that he would wear it upon his shoulder as a mark of his dignity. "The staff of the shoulder" (Isa. 9:4) is the staff which strikes the shoulder; or the wood, like a yoke, on the neck of slaves, the badge of servitude. "The government shall be on his shoulder" (9:6), like the expression, "And the key of the house of David will I lay upon his shoulder" (22:22) refers to the custom of wearing the ensign of office upon the *shoulder*, in token of *sustaining* the government. The same idea is expressed by the epaulets worn in the army and navy. To "lay burdens on men's shoulders," etc. (Matt. 23:4) is selfishly to burden men with obligations which the scribes and Pharisees would not concern themselves with.

Shoulder Blade (Heb. *shĭkmāh*, only in Job 31:22), where it means the socket or bone to which the arm is attached.

Shoulder Piece (Heb. *kāthēph, clothed*), the side pieces on the upper part of the high priest's ephod, which came over the shoulder, where the front and back flaps were fastened (Exod. 28:7, 25; 39:4; simple "shoulders," 28:12; 39:7; or "sides," 28:27; 39:20). See Priest, High.

Shovel, the implement used for removing ashes from the altar (Exod. 27:3, etc.). See Tabernacle. It is also the rendering of Heb. *rāḥath* (Isa. 30:24), a winnowing fork.

Showbread. See Tabernacle.

Shower. See Rain.

Shrine (Gr. *naos*, a *temple*, Acts 19:24), a miniature representation of the splendid temple of Diana, with a statue of the goddess.

Shroud (Heb. *hōrĕsh, thicket*), the rendering in the A. V. of Ezek. 31:3, but "forest" (II Chron. 27:4); "bough" (Isa. 17:9); probably a shadowing thicket.

Shrub (Heb. *sĭaḥ*, Gen. 21:15), a *bush*, as rendered in Job 30:4, 7; "plant" in Gen. 2:5. See Vegetable Kingdom.

Shu'a (shōō'à). 1. (I Chron. 2:3), a Canaanite of Adullam, whose daughter was the wife of Judah and the mother of his first three children (Gen. 38:2, 12); in both passages the A. V. has incorrectly "Shuah."

2. The daughter of Heber, the grandson of Asher (I Chron. 7:32).

Shu'ah (shōō'à). 1. The last named of the six sons of Abraham by Keturah (Gen. 25:2; I Chron. 1:32).

2. The father of Judah's Canaanitish wife (I Chron. 2:3). See Shua, 1.

3. A brother (some manuscripts have *son*) of Chelub, among the descendants of Judah (I Chron. 4:11).

Shu'al (shōō'ăl; *fox, jackal*).

1. The third named of the eleven sons of Zophah (I Chron. 7:36).

2. The "land of Shual" (I Sam. 13:17) is named as invaded by one of the marauding companies of Philistines; probably five or six miles N. E. from Beth-el in Benjamin. It has not been identified.

Shu'bael (shōō'bā-ĕl), two Levites (I Chron. 24:20; 25:20); called elsewhere *Shebuel* (q. v.).

Shu'ham (shōō'hăm), the son of Dan (Num. 26:42); elsewhere (Gen. 46:23), called *Hushim* (q. v.).

Shu'hamite (shōō'hăm-it). The descendants of Shuham numbered four thousand four hundred and sixty when Israel entered Canaan (Num. 26:42, 48).

Shu'hite (shōō'hit), a term only used as an epithet of Bildad in Job 2:11; 18:1; 25:1; 42:9. It is quite probably a patronymic from Shuah, son of Abraham of Keturah (Gen. 25:2; I Chron. 1:32). His descendants formed accordingly, an Arab tribe, doubtless the Shuhites who resided near the land of Uz (Job 2:11). Assyrian Suhu, on the W. of the Euphrates near the mouths of the Balikh and Habur is a likely identification. In this case the Shuhites would be in the extreme north, toward the Euphrates. This identification would favor a northeast or Aramaic location for the land of Uz rather than a southern, i. e., an Edomite or Arabian one.—W. H., revised by *M. F. U.*

Shu'lamite (shōō'lăm-it; *peaceful*), the title applied (Cant. 6:13) to the young woman in the Song of Solomon. The more correct form is Shulammite (R. V. cf. R. S. V.). Since the LXX translates the term *Sounamitis*, i. e., Shunammite, it is evidently derived from the town of Shunam near Mt. Gilboa. The form Shulammite may have been adopted because of its assonance with Solomon (Heb. *Sh°lōmōh*), and, indeed, as a kind of title (not a proper name), it may actually be the feminine of Solomon.

Shu'mathites (shōō'măth-its). One of the principal familes of Kirjath-jearim (I Chron. 2: 53).

Shu'nammite (shōō'năm-mit), a native of *Shunem, q. v.*), as is evident from II Kings 4:8, 12, where it is applied to the hostess of Elisha. It was also applied to the beautiful Abishag, the nurse of David in his old age (I Kings 1:3; 2:17, 21, 22).

Shu'nem (shōō'nĕm), a place belonging to Issachar. Here the Philistines encamped befour Saul's last battle (Josh. 19:18; I Sam. 28:4). It was the home of Abishag (I Kings 1:3), also the residence of the woman whose son Elisha restored to life (II Kings 4:8-37). Identified with Solem (*Sūlam*) at the southwest foot of Little Hermon, three miles N. of Jezreel, and in the midst of a rich country.

Shu'ni (shōō'nī), son of Gad, and founder of the family of the Shunites (Gen. 46:16; Num. 26:15), B. C. c. 1910.

Shu'nite (shōō'nit), the patronymic given to a descendant of *Shuni* (q. v.), the son of Gad (Num. 26:15).

Shu'pham (shōō'făm), given in Num. 26:39 as a "son" of Benjamin and head of the family of Shuphamites. He is doubtless the same person elsewhere (I Chron. 8:5) called *Shephuphan* (q. v.). He was, if the same person, a son of Bela, the son of Benjamin, and was reckoned among Benjamin's sons because, like them, he founded an independent family (K. and D., *Com.*, in loc.).

Shu'phamite (shōō'făm-it), the designation of a descendant of "Shupham" (Num. 26:39), or Shephuphan (I Chron. 8:5).

Shup'pim (shŭp'ĭm).

1. In the genealogy of Benjamin "Shuppim and Huppim, the children of Ir," are reckoned (I Chron. 7:12; comp. 5:15). Ir is the same as Iri, the son of Bela, the son of Benjamin, so that Shuppim was the greatgrandson of Benjamin.

2. A Levite who, together with Hosah, had charge of the temple gate Shallecheth (I Chron. 26:16), B. C. about 960. Keil (*Com.*, in loc.) thinks that the word has come into the text by a repetition of the last two syllables of the preceding word.

Shur (shōōr; *wall fortification*) is referred to as "before Egypt, as thou goest toward Assyria" (Gen. 25:18); and as "even unto the land of Egypt" (I Sam. 27:8); and as "over against Egypt" (15:7). From its meaning "a wall," as well as from various references to it in the text, it would seem that Shur was a barrier of some kind across the great northeastern highways out of Egypt, near the eastern boundary line of Egypt. This barrier was the great defensive wall built across the eastern frontier —a wall hardly less prominent in the history of ancient Egypt than the Great Wall of China. This fortified barrier is mentioned in records from the Twelfth Dynasty c. 2000-1775 B. C.

"With the Great Wall standing there across the entrance of Lower Egypt as a barrier and a landmark between the delta and the desert, it follows almost as a matter of course that the region on either side of the wall should bear the *name* of the wall: on the western side was the Land of Mazor, the Land Walled in; on the eastern side was the Wilderness of Shur, the Wilderness Walled out. Hence it comes to pass that the desert country eastward of Lower Egypt is known in the Bible as the Wilderness of Shur" (Trumbull, *Kadesh-Barnea*, p. 44, sq.).

Shur is first mentioned in the narrative of Hagar's flight from Sarah (Gen. 16:7). Abraham afterward "dwelled between Kadesh and Shur, and sojourned in Gerar" (20:1). The first clear indication of its position occurs in the account of Ishmael's posterity. "And they dwelt from Havilah unto Shur, that [is] before thou goest toward Assyria" (25:18; comp. I Sam. 15:7; 27:8). The wilderness of Shur was entered by the Israelites after they had crossed the Red Sea (Exod. 15:22, 23). It was called the Wilderness of Etham (Num. 33:8).

Shushan (shōō'shăn). The Hebrew word means "lily" and the Greek form is Susa. It took its name from the great abundance of lilies which grew in its neighborhood. The famous mound has been excavated and its early occupational levels go back to c. 4000

B. C., its latest levels to 1200 A. D. It was explored by a French expedition in 1884-86, and the Code of Hammurabi was uncovered there by Jacques de Morgan, 1901. The ancient site lies on the Karkheh about 150 miles N. of the Persian Gulf. It is famous in the Bible as one of the capitals of the Persian Empire maintained by Darius the Great (cf. Neh. 1:1; Esth. 2:8; 3:15, etc.). The city was a winter residence of the great Persian kings. It was also the place of Daniel's vision (Dan. 8:2) under Belshazzar. Shushan colonists were transported to Samaria by Ashurbanipal, that is, "Asnapper," referred to in Ezek. 4:9, 10. Its present day name is Shush. Susa became a part of the Achaemenid Empire when Cyrus took Babylon and its provinces. The most splendid monument of Persian Susa is the royal palace, begun by Darius I and enlarged and adorned by later kings (cf. R. de Mecquenem, "A Survey of Persian Art," Art. I, pp. 321-326). The outline of Darius' splendid palace which he built of cedar wood from Lebanon, silver from Egypt, gold from Bactria and ivory from India can still be traced by some rows of bricks and remains of the pavements. Panels of artistically colored glazed bricks constituted the most remarkable feature in the palace decorations. Many of the designs were executed in relief and show winged bulls and griffins and include the famous "spearmen of the guard."— M. F. U.

Shu'shan-e'duth (shoō'shăn-ē'dŭth; Psa. 60, title), a musical term (*q. v.*).

Shu'thalhite (shoō'thăl-hīt), a designation of a descendant of Shuthelah (*q. v.*), the son of Ephraim (Num. 26:35).

Shu'thelah (shoō'thē-lȧ).

1. First named of the three sons of Ephraim (Num. 26:35, 36), B. C. perhaps about 1850. His descendants to a second Shuthelah are given in I Chron. 7:20, 21.

2. The sixth in descent from the preceding, being the son of Zabad and father of Ezer and Elead (I Chron. 7:21).

Shuttle (Heb. 'ĕrĕg, a *weaving*), is used in Job 7:6 as a figure of the swiftness of life. His days pass as swiftly by as the little shuttle moves backward and forward in the warp.

Si'a (sī-ȧ; *assembly, congregation*), one of the chief of the Nethinims, whose "children" returned with Zerubbabel (Neh. 7:47), B. C. before 536. In Ezra 2:44 the name is given as Siaha.

Si'aha (sī'ȧ-hȧ; *congregation*), a chief Nethinim (Ezra 2:44). In Neh. 7:47 he is called Sia (*q. v.*).

Sib'becai or **Sib'bechai** (sĭb'ē-kī), "the Hushathite," probably so called from his birthplace (I Chron. 11:29). He belonged to the prominent family of Judah, the Zarhites, and was captain of the twenty-four thousand men of David's army serving in the eighth month. Sibbecai's great exploit, which gave him a place among the mighty men of David's army, was his combat with Saph, or Sippia, the Philistine giant, in the battle of Gezer, or Gob (II Sam. 21:18; I Chron. 20:4), B. C. about 970.

Sib'boleth (sĭb'ō-lĕth), another form (Judg. 12:6) of Shibboleth (*q. v.*).

Sib'mah (sĭb'mȧ; *coolness*, cf. Arab. *shabima, to be cold*), a town east of Jordan, which was taken possession of and rebuilt by the tribe of Reuben (Josh. 13:19; A. V. "Shibmah," Num. 32:38). It was probably the same as *Shebam* (v. 3); and belonged originally to that portion of Moab which was captured by the Amorites under Sihon (21:26). It is mentioned by Isaiah (16:8, 9) and Jeremiah (48:32), both making reference to its vintage. The wine of Sibmah was so good that it was placed upon the table of monarchs, and so strong that it smote down, i. e., inevitably intoxicated, even those who were accustomed to good wine. Not positively identified. Jerome placed it near Heshbon.

Sibra'im (sĭb-rā'ĭm; *double hope*), a landmark on the northern boundary of Palestine, between Berothah and Hazar-hatticon (Ezek. 47:16), perhaps identical with *Ziphron* (Num. 34:9).

Si'chem (sī'kĕm), another form (Gen. 12:6), of Shechem (*q. v.*).

Sick, Sickness. See Diseases, Treatment of.

Sickle, the rendering of two Hebrew words and one Greek word:

1. Heb. *hĕrmĕsh*, a *reaping hook* (Deut. 16:9; 23:25).

2. Heb. *măggăl*, with the same meaning (Jer. 50:16; Joel 3:4, 13).

3. The instrument generally used for cutting grain. (Gr. *drepanon.*) See Agriculture, 4. The Israelites might pluck and eat the standing grain of a neighbor, but were forbidden to "move a sickle," i. e., reap it (Deut. 23:25).

Figurative. "To thrust in the sickle" is a figurative expression for gathering a harvest (Mark 4:29; Rev. 14:14-19).

Sid'dim, Vale of (sĭd'ĭm; *the valley of the fields;* perhaps so called from the high cultivation in which it was kept before the destruction of Sodom and the other cities), the scene of the battle between Chedorlaomer, and his allies, and the five confederate kings (Gen. 14:3). However, it is possible that Siddim may designate "salt flats" from Hittite *siyanta*, "salt." In any case the term denotes the territory S. of the peninsula of "The Tongue," which projects into the Dead Sea from the E. shore. This region underwent a violent cataclysm about the middle of the 20th century B. C. when its cities were destroyed and its area became submerged under the waters of the Dead Sea (Gen. 19).

Some writers unwarrantedly contend for the location of Siddim at the N. end of the Dead Sea. But archaeological evidence now disfavors this view. The region was full of "slime [bitumen] pits" (v. 10), and here the Egyptians got the bitumen with which they embalmed their dead; and even to this day "pits" exist.

Si'don (sī'dŏn), sometimes Zidon (*q. v.*), as in the A. V. This ancient Phoenician city was built on a promontory and small island, which was connected to the mainland by a bridge. The town was some twenty miles N. of Tyre and is called Saida at the present day and is now located in the Republic of Lebanon. It is situated between mountains to its back and the sea to its front. Its people very early took to seafaring commerce. As the oldest capital of the Phoenicians, its antiquity is attested by Gen. 10:15. The city is referred to around 1400 B. C. in the Amarna Letters. It figures prominently in the division of the land after the Hebrew conquest (Josh. 19:28). The Phoenicians were called Sidonians from the

433. A View of Sidon from the Fortress

eleventh to the eighth centuries B. C. Its early preeminence is attested by Homer, who often mentions Sidon but never Tyre, and who employs the name as synonymous with Phoenicia and Phoenicians. Later, however, it was outclassed by Tyre, but Phoenicians generally continued to be known as Sidonians (I Kings 5:6; 16:31), as if in recollection of Sidon's ancient preeminence. Solomon was influenced by Sidonian cults (I Kings 11:5-7) and hired expert Sidonian timber cutters. Sidonians worshipped Baal and Ashtoreth. Jezebel of infamy was daughter of Ethbaal. Her introduction of the licentious worship of Canaanite cults into Israel brought internal misery (I Kings 16:31-33, etc.). The Sidonians were skillful in philosophy, art and astronomy, as is indicated by Strabo, the Greek historian of the first century, B. C. Biblical references include Isa. 23:12; Jer. 27:3, 6; Ezek. 28:21-24; Joel 3:4-6. Shalmaneser of Assyria captured the city in 725 B. C. It was invaded by Sennacherib, dominated by Esarhaddon, overrun by the Babylonians after the fall of Assyria and made a province by the Persians. It was conquered by Alexander the Great (330 B. C.). It enjoyed importance under the Romans, and Herod embellished it. Our Lord visited the general territory (Mark 7:24, 31) and made reference to the iniquity of its inhabitants (Matt. 11:21-24). Paul visited the place on his way to Rome (Acts 27:3). It figures in early church history at the time of the Crusades and finally under Moslem rule. —M. F. U.

Sido'nians (sĭ-dō'nĭ-ăns). See Zidonians.

Siege. See Warfare.

Sieve (Heb. *keˇbäräh*, *netted*, Amos 9:9; *näphäh*, Isa. 30:28). The ancient Egyptians often made sieves of string, and those for coarser work were constructed of small rushes or reeds.

Figurative. "The sieve of vanity" (literally nothingness, Isa. 30:28) is a sieve in which everything that does not remain in it as good grain is given up to annihilation. To sift a nation (Amos 9:9) or person (Luke 22:31) means to prove, test them.

Sign, the rendering of several Hebrew and Greek words, which usually denote a miraculous, or, at least, divine or extraordinary token

of some (generally) future event. Thus the rainbow was given to Noah as a sign of his covenant (Gen. 9:12, 13), and for the same purpose circumcision was appointed to Abraham (17:11; comp. Exod. 3:12; Judg. 6:17). Signs and wonders sometimes denote those proofs or demonstrations of power and authority furnished by miracles and other tokens of the divine presence (Matt. 12:38; John 4:48; Acts 2:22). The word is used for a miraculous appearance, which would attest the divine authority of a prophet or teacher (see Matt. 16:1; 24:30).

Signet. See Seal.

Si'hon (sī'hŏn), a king of the Amorites, with capital at Heshbon, near Medeba, in the E. Jordanic country, not far from Mt. Nebo, who refused to the Israelites permission to pass through his territory when nearing the promised land. Shortly before the time of Israel's arrival he had dispossessed the Moabites of a splendid territory, driving them south of the natural bulwark of the Arnon (Num. 21:26-29). When the Israelite host appears he does not hesitate or temporize like Balak, but at once gathers his people together and attacks them (v. 21). But the battle was his last. He and all his host were destroyed, and their district from Arnon to Jabbok became at once the possession of the conqueror, B. C. c. 1401. The kingdom of Sihon is mentioned in Josh. 13:21, 27, and his dukes, i. e., vassals.

Si'hor (sī'hôr), or, correctly, **Shi'hor** (shī'hôr), one of the names given to the Nile in Scripture (Isa. 23:3; Jer. 2:18). The Heb. *Shihôr* means *black, dark, turbid,* suggested by Egyptian *Shi-hrw, lake* or *pool of Horus.* Opinions vary as to the identity of Sihor (Josh. 13:3) and Shihor (I Chron 13:5). Keil (*Com.*) thinks them to be the brook of Egypt, the modern *Wady el Arish.*

Si'las (sī'lås; apparently Gr. from Aram. *Sheˇīlā* (Saul), which in turn is evidently a contracted form of *Silvanus* (*sylvan*), a prominent member of the church in Jerusalem (Acts 15:22). Of his immediate family no account is given, but his name, derived from the Latin *silva,* "wood," betokens him a Hellenistic Jew, and he appears to have been a Roman citizen (16:37). He is probably the same as *Sylvanus,* mentioned in Paul's epistles.

1. **Mission to Antioch.** Upon the return of Paul and Barnabas to Jerusalem from their missionary tour, a discussion arose respecting circumcision, and the council decided adversely to the extreme Judaizing party. Silas was appointed a delegate to accompany Paul and Barnabas on their return to Antioch with the decree of the Council of Jerusalem (Acts 15:22, 32), A. D. about 50. After accomplishing this mission he remained in Antioch, although granted permission to return (vers. 33, 34). The qualification of Silas for speaking to a congregation is stated (v. 32).

2. **Paul's Companion.** Upon the separation of Paul and Barnabas Silas was selected by Paul as the companion of his second missionary journey (Acts 15:40). "The choice of Silas was, of course, due to his special fitness for the work, which had been recognized during his ministration in Antioch. Doubtless he had shown tact and sympathy in managing

the questions arising from the relations of the Gentile Christians to the Jews" (Ramsay, *St. Paul*, p. 176). His double character, Hebrew and Roman, was also a qualification for a coadjutor of Paul. In further notices of him we learn that he was scourged and imprisoned with Paul at Philippi. At Berea he was left behind with Timothy, while Paul proceeded to Athens (Acts 17:14), and we hear nothing more of his movements until he rejoined the apostle at Corinth (18:5). His presence at Corinth is several times noticed (II Cor. 1:19; I Thess. 1:1; II Thess. 1:1). He probably returned to Jerusalem with Paul, where he remained, ceasing any longer to be his companion. Whether he was the Sylvanus who conveyed Peter's first epistle to Asia Minor (I Pet. 5:12) is uncertain; the probabilities are in favor of the identity. A tradition of very slight authority represents Silas to have become bishop of Corinth.

Silence. 1. *Stillness, quietness* (Heb. *d^emāmāh*) is used poetically by hendiadys (Job. 4:16), *I hear stillness and a voice*, i. e., a still voice, a light whisper. The verb is used (19:21), "and kept silence at my counsel," to indicate respectful attention.

2. *The state of being dumb* (Heb. *ḥārāsh*), which often depends upon deafness, and is joined with it. Spoken of God as not listening to and answering the prayers of men (Psa. 28:1; 35:33; 50:3, 21); of men as listening to God without interrupting him (Isa. 41:1).

3. The act of *not speaking* (Gr. *sigaō*), of one wishing to speak in a tongue ("unknown"), in which case he is not to speak unless an interpreter is present (I Cor. 14:28); of women in the churches (v. 34), "an appendix to the regulative section regarding the gifts of the Spirit, vers. 26, 33" (Meyer, Alford, Westcott). Others think that Paul makes an appeal in support of his instruction to the authority or experience of the Church.

Silk. This luxurious material doubtless was introduced into Bible lands from its home in China via India. Phoenician cities imported raw silk, as did Persia and S. Europe. Tyre and Berytus were renowned for weaving it. It was a prize material among Medes and Persians, and Greeks knew it by the name "Median garments." In early Christian times silk robes of gorgeous patterns were common in Dura-Europas. Ezekiel refers to silk (16:10, 13), and was so understood by the rabbis (Heb. *mĕshi, drawn*), referring to the fine texture.

The only *undoubted* notice of silk in the Bible occurs in Rev. 18:12, where it is mentioned among the treasures of the typical Babylon (Gr. *sērikos*, from *Sēr*, an Indian tribe from whom silk was procured). It is, however, in the highest degree probable that the texture was known to the Hebrews from the time that their commercial relations were extended by Solomon. The value set upon silk by the Romans, as implied in Rev. 18:12, is noticed by Josephus, as well as by classical writers.

Sil'la (sĭl'á), is named in II Kings 12:20, "the house of Millo, which goeth down to Silla." Silla is regarded by many as an abbreviation of *mĕsĭllāh*, "which goes down by the road," and Thenius supposes that the reference is to

the road which ran diagonally from the Joppa gate to the Haramarea, corresponding to the present David's road. Some think it a place in the valley below.

Silo'ah (sĭ-lō'á), or **Shilo'ah** (shī-lō'á).

1. **"The Waters of Shiloah"** is used (Isa. 8:6) "as a symbol of Davidic monarchy enthroned upon Zion, which had the promise of God, who was enthroned upon Moriah, in contrast with the imperial or world kingdom, which is compared to the overflowing waters of the Euphrates" (Delitzsch, *Com.*, in loc.). There is no reason to doubt that the "waters" are the same as No. 3.

2. **"The Pool of Siloah"** "by the king's garden" (Neh. 3:15), was near the gate of the fountain, and was doubtless the same as No. 3.

3. **"The Pool of Siloam"** "which is by interpretation, Sent," John 9:7) is found three times in Scripture—Neh. 3:15; Isa. 8:6; John 9:7. If we compare Neh. 3:15 with 12:37, we shall find that the pool of Shiloah, the stairs that go down from the city of David (southern portion of the temple mount), and the king's garden were in close proximity. Josephus frequently mentions Siloam, placing it at the termination of the Valley of the Cheesemongers or the Tyropoeon (*Wars*, v. 4, 1)—but outside the city wall (*Wars*, v. 9, 4)—where the old wall bent eastward (*Wars*, v. 6, 1), and facing the hill upon which was the rock Peristereon, to the east (*Wars*, v, 12,2). From these descriptions it is quite evident that Josephus speaks of the same place as the present *Birket Silwân*, on the other side of the Kidron.

Further, the evangelist's account (John 9:7) of the blind man sent by Jesus to wash *at* the pool of Siloam seems to indicate that it was near the temple. It was from Siloam that water was brought in a golden vessel to the temple during the Feast of Tabernacles (see p. 364, col. 2); to which our Lord probably pointed when he stood in the temple and cried, "If any man thirst, let him come unto me, and drink."

The pool of Siloam is fed by a conduit which is cut for a distance of seventeen hundred and eighty feet through the solid rock, and which takes its start from the so-called Virgin's Spring (*see* En-rogel). The object with which it was cut is unmistakable. The Virgin's Spring is the only spring of fresh water in the immediate neighborhood of Jerusalem, and in time of siege it was important that while the enemy should be deprived of access to it, its waters should be made available for those who were within the city. But the spring rose outside the walls, on the sloping cliff which overlooks the valley of Kidron. Accordingly a long passage was excavated in the rock, by means of which the overflow of the spring was brought into Jerusalem, the spring itself being covered with masonry, so that it could be 'sealed' in case of war. That it was so sealed we know from II Chron. 32:3, 4. The following account of the channel and its inscription is from Major C. R. Conder (*Palestine*, p. 27, sq.). "The course of the channel is serpentine, and the farther end near the pool of Siloam enlarges into a passage of considerable height. Down this channel the waters of the spring rush to the pool whenever the sudden flow takes place. In autumn there is an interval of several days; in winter the sudden flow takes place sometimes twice a day. A natural siphon from an underground basin accounts for this flow, as also for that of the 'Sabbatic river' in North Syria. When it occurs the narrow parts of the passage are filled to the roof with water.

"This passage was explored by Dr. Robinson, Sir Charles Wilson, Sir Charles Warren, and others; but the inscription on the rock close to the mouth of the tunnel was not seen, being then under water. When it was found in 1880 by a boy who entered from the Siloam end of the passage, it was almost obliterated by the deposit of lime crystals on the letters. Professor Sayce, then in Palestine, made a copy, and was able to find out the general meaning of the letters. In 1881 Dr. Guthe

familiar to his hearers and did not need to be more particularly mentioned. But we are without the means that might enable us more exactly to define either. Some think it to be the village now called *Silwân*, east of the valley of Kidron, and to the northeast of the pool. It stands on the west slope of the Mount of Olives. Edersheim (*Life of Jesus*, p. 222) locates the tower at the Siloam Pool, which "had fallen on eighteen persons and killed them," perhaps in connection with that construction of an aqueduct into Jerusalem by Pilate, which called forth, on the part of the Jews, the violent opposition which the Romans so terribly avenged.

Silva'nus (sĭl-vā'nŭs; *sylvan*), a companion of the apostle Paul in his journey through Asia Minor and Greece (II Cor. 1:19; I Thess. 1:1; II Thes. 1:1; I Pet. 5:12), given in the Book of Acts as Silas (*q. v.*).

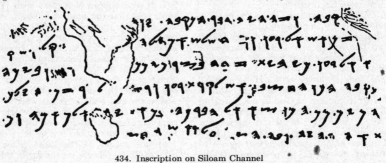

434. Inscription on Siloam Channel

cleaned the text with a weak acid solution, and I was then able, with the aid of Lieutenant Mentell, R.E., to take a proper 'squeeze.' It was a work of labor and requiring patience, for on two occasions we sat for three or four hours cramped up in the water in order to obtain a perfect copy of every letter, and afterward to verify the copies by examining each letter with the candle so placed as to throw the light from right, left, top, bottom. We were rewarded by sending home the first accurate copy published in Europe, and were able to settle many disputed points raised by the imperfect copy of the text before it was cleaned."

The inscription records only the making of the tunnel; that it began at both ends; that the workmen heard the sound of the picks of the other party, and thus guided they advanced, and when they broke through were only a few feet apart. The character of the letters seem to indicate that the scribes of Judah had been accustomed for a long time to write upon papyrus or parchment.

The pool itself is an oblong tank, partly hewn out of the rock and partly built with masonry, about fifty-three feet long, eighteen feet wide, and nineteen feet deep. The water has a peculiar taste—somewhat brackish—but not disagreeable, though becoming more so with the advance of the hot season.

"Silo'am, Tower In." Reference is made by our Lord (Luke 13:4) to this tower as having recently fallen upon and killed eighteen persons. The circumstance itself, and the locality in which it took place, were doubtless quite

Silver. *See* Mineral Kingdom.

Silverling (Isa. 7:23), a silver coin. *See* Metrology, iv.

Silversmith (Acts 19:24). *See* Handicrafts; Metals.

Sim'eon (sĭm'ē-ŭn; *hearing*).

1. The second son of Jacob by Leah (Gen. 29:33), B. C. probably before 1925. In connection with Levi Simeon undertook to avenge the seduction of their sister Dinah (*q. v.*), but performed such acts of wanton cruelty and injustice upon the Shechemites that Jacob was fearful of the surrounding people. In obedience, therefore, to his father's command, he removed southward to Beth-el (ch. 34; 35:1). He was selected as hostage for the appearance of Benjamin (42:24, 36), but was subsequently released (43:23). Judging from Jacob's dying words (49:5-7) and from Jewish traditions, he was artful, fierce, and cruel.

The Tribe of Simeon. At the migration into Egypt Simeon had six sons. At the Exodus the tribe numbered fifty-nine thousand three hundred warriors (Num. 1:23), ranking third. When the second census was taken the numbers had decreased to twenty-two thousand two hundred, and ranked lowest of the tribes (26:14). The assignment of Simeon in the promised land was "within the inheritance of the children of Judah" (Josh. 19:1-9; I Chron. 4:28-33). This territory, which contained eighteen or nineteen cities, with their villages spread around the venerable well of Beersheba, was possessed by the help of Judah (Judg. 1:3, 17).

2. An Israelite who divorced his Gentile wife (Ezra 10:31). *See* Shimeon.

3. A just and devout Israelite, endowed with the gift of prophecy, and who, having received divine intimation that his death would not take place till he had seen the Messiah, entered the temple, and there recognizing the Holy Child, took him in his arms and gave thanks for the privilege of seeing Jesus (Luke 2:25-35), B. C. 4. All attempts to identify him with other Simeons have failed.

4. The son of Judah and father of Levi in the genealogy of our Lord (Luke 3:30). He is perhaps the same as Masseiah, the son of Adaiah (II Chron. 23:1).

5. The proper name of Niger, one of the teachers and prophets in the church at Antioch (Acts 13:1), in which passage only he is mentioned. This name shows that he was a Jew by birth, taking that of Niger as more convenient in his intercourse with foreigners.

6. A form (Acts 15:14) of the name of *Simon* Peter.

Sim'eonite (sĭm'ê-ŏn-īt), a patronymic designation of a descendant of Simeon, 1 (see Num. 25:14; 26:14; I Chron. 27:16).

Similitude. 1. An *appearance, shape, likeness* (Heb. *t*e*mūnäh*). Jehovah, upon the sedition of Aaron and Miriam, made this distinction between a prophet, as usually known, and Moses: "If there be a prophet among you, I the Lord will make myself known unto him in a vision . . . My servant Moses is not so, who is faithful in all mine house. With him will I speak mouth to mouth, even apparently, and not in dark speeches; and the *similitude* of the Lord shall he behold" (Num. 12:6-8; comp. Deut. 4:12, 15, 16). "The *form* [A. V. 'similitude'] of Jehovah" was not the essential nature of God, his unveiled glory—for this no mortal man can see (Exod. 33:18, sq.)—but a form which manifested the invisible God in a clearly discernible mode, differing from the vision of God in the form of a man (Ezek. 1:26; Dan. 7:9, 13), or of the angel of Jehovah. "God talked with Moses without figure, in the clear distinctness of a spiritual communication, whereas to the prophets he only revealed himself through the medium of ecstasy or dream" (K. and D., *Com.* on Num. 12:6-8).

2. A *model*, a *pattern* (A. V. II Kings 16:10) of an altar; an *image;* something cast, as of oxen (II Chron. 4:3); a *likeness* (A. V. Gen. 1:26, "after our likeness"); appearance (A. V. Ezek. 1:16) as of the wheels, of a man (Dan. 10:6). (Heb. *d*e*mūth*). The verb *dämäh* (to *liken, compare*) is used (Hos. 12:10) in the sense of employing parables (*q. v.*).

3. *Structure, model*, a resemblance, as "they changed their glory [i. e., God] into the similitude of an ox" (Psa. 106:20; comp. 144:12). Heb. *tăbnîth*.

4. The word in the New Testament is from the Gr. *homoios* (*similar*), and means that which is like, or similar (Rom. 5:14; Heb. 7:15), *likeness* as of man to God (James 3:9; see *d*e*mūth* above.

Si'mon (sī'mŏn; Gr. *Simōn*), perhaps a contraction of the Hebrew *Shimeon*—Simeon).

1. One of the apostles, usually called Simon Peter (*q. v.*).

2. "Simon the Canaanite," one of the twelve apostles (Matt. 10:4; Mark 3:18), otherwise described as Simon Zelotes (Luke 6:15; Acts 1:13). The latter term (Gr. *Zē-lōtēs*), which is peculiar to Luke, is the Greek equivalent for the Aramaic term *Qănn*e*'ān*, preserved by Matthew and Mark. Each of these equally points out Simon as belonging to the faction of the zealots, who were conspicuous for their fierce advocacy of the Mosaic ritual. He is not to be identified with Simon the brother of Jesus.

3. A brother of James and Jude, and a kinsman of Jesus (Matt. 13:55; Mark 6:3). He is by many thought to be the same as Simon the Canaanite, but for this there is no evidence. The prevailing opinion is that he is identical with the Simeon who became bishop of Jerusalem after the death of James, but Eusebius makes them two persons.

4. "Simon the Leper." A resident at Bethany, distinguished as "the leper." It is not improbable that he had been miraculously cured by Jesus. In his house Mary anointed Jesus preparatory to his death and burial (Matt. 26:6, etc.; Mark 14:3, etc.; John 12:1, etc.).

5. "Simon of Cyrene." A Hellenistic Jew, born at Cyrene, on the north coast of Africa, who was present at Jerusalem at the time of the crucifixion of Jesus, either as an attendant at the feast (Acts 2:10) or as one of the numerous settlers at Jerusalem from that place (6:9). Meeting the procession that conducted Jesus to Golgotha, as he was returning from the country, he was pressed into the service to bear the cross (Matt. 27:32; Mark 15:21; Luke 23:26) when Jesus himself was unable to bear it any longer. Mark describes him as the father of Alexander and Rufus, perhaps because this was the Rufus known to the Roman Christians (Rom. 16:13), for whom he more specially wrote. The Basilidian Gnostics believed that Simon suffered in lieu of Jesus.

6. The Pharisee in whose house a penitent woman washed the feet of Jesus with her tears, and anointed them with ointment (Luke 7:40, 43, 44).

7. The father of Judas Iscariot (John 6:71; 12:4; 13:2, 26).

8. The Samaritan magician living in the age of the apostles, and usually designated in later history as Simon Magus. According to Justin Martyr (*Apol.*, i, 26) he was born at Gitton, a village of Samaria, identified with the modern *Kuryet Jît*, near *Nablus*. He was probably educated at Alexandria, and there became acquainted with the eclectic tenets of the Gnostic school. Either then or subsequently he was a pupil of Dositheus, who preceded him as a teacher of Gnosticism in Samaria, and whom he supplanted with the aid of Cleobius. He is first introduced to us in the Bible as practicing magical arts in a city of Samaria, perhaps Sychar (Acts 8:5; comp. John 4:5), and with such success that he was pronounced to be "that power of God which is called Great" (Acts 8:10). The preaching and miracles of Philip having excited his observation, he became one of his disciples, and received baptism at his hands. Subse-

quently he witnessed the effect produced by the imposition of hands, as practiced by the apostles Peter and John, and, being desirous of acquiring a similar power, he offered a sum of money for it. His object evidently was to apply the power to the prosecution of magical arts. The motive and the means were equally to be reprobated; and his proposition met with a severe denunciation from Peter, followed by a petition on the part of Simon, the tenor of which bespeaks terror, but not penitence (v. 24). From his endeavor to obtain spiritual functions by a bribe is derived the word *simony*. There are many stories concerning his subsequent career which are, without doubt, fabulous.

9. The Tanner, a Christian convert with whom Peter lodged while at Joppa. His house was by the seaside, as the trade of a tanner was considered unclean by the Jews, and not allowed to be carried on inside their towns (Acts 9:43; 10:6, 17, 32).

Simplicity (Heb. *tōm*, *innocence*, *integrity*) is predicated of the two hundred followers of Absalom in his conspiracy (II Sam. 15:11), who "knew not anything," i. e., of their leader's intention. In Prov. 1:22 *simplicity* is the rendering of *päthäh* (intransitive), to let oneself be enticed, seduced. In the New Testament *simplicity* stands for Gr. *haplotēs*, free from pretense and dissimilation; thus in Rom. 12:8 the apostle exhorts to an openness of heart which manifests itself by liberality, without self-seeking; and in II Cor. 1:12 declares his own simplicity, i. e., sincerity. The "simplicity that is in Christ" (11:3) is that single-hearted faith in Christ which is opposed to false wisdom in matters pertaining to Christianity.

Sim′ri (sĭm′rī; *vigilant*), son of the Merarite Levite Hosah. He was not the firstborn, but for some reason his father made him "chief among his brethren." He was appointed by David doorkeeper of the ark (I Chron. 26:10), B. C. before 960.

Sin (Heb. *ḥăṭā′äh;* Gr. *hamartia*, a falling away from or missing the right path). Also numerous other Heb. words.

1. **General.** The underlying idea of sin is that of law and of a lawgiver. The lawgiver is God. Hence sin is everything in the disposition and purpose and conduct of God's moral creatures that is contrary to the expressed will of God (Rom. 3:20; 4:15; 7:7; James 4:12, 17).

The sinfulness of sin lies in the fact that it is against God, even when the wrong we do is to others or ourselves (Gen. 39:9; Psa. 51:4).

The being and law of God are perfectly harmonious, "God is love." The sum of all the commandments likewise is love; sin thus in its nature is egotism, selfishness. Self is put in the place of God (Rom. 15:3; I Cor. 13:5; II Tim. 3:1, 2; II Thess. 2:3, 4). Selfishness (not pure self-love, nor the exaggeration of it, but really in opposition to it) is at the bottom of all disobedience, and it becomes hostility to God when it comes into collision with his law.

All sin thus has a positive character, and the distinction between sins of commission and those of omission is only upon the surface.

In both cases is actual disobedience (see Matt. 23:23).

2. **Original.** A term used to denote the effect of Adam's sin upon the moral life of his descendants. It is formally defined as "that whereby man is very far gone from original righteousness, and is of his own nature inclined to evil" (*see* Fall). The fact of sin in this sense is plainly declared in the Scriptures (Rom. 5:12, 19; comp. Gen. 3:4; Eph. 2:1-3; II Tim. 2:26; I John 3:4). In accord with this is the further fact of the universality of sin, also proclaimed in Scripture (Matt. 7:11; 15:19; Rom. 3:9, 23; I John 1:19; James 3:2; comp. I Kings 8:46; Job 14:4; Prov. 20:9), and borne witness to by history and human self-consciousness.

The nature of the connection between the sin of Adam and the moral condition of his descendants is, however, a matter upon which opinions have greatly differed.

The chief forms of doctrine have been as follows:

(1) **By Calvinists** it has been held that the sin of Adam was immediately imputed to the whole human family, so that not only is the entire race depraved, but also actually guilty on account of the first transgression. To sustain this opinion it is argued that Adam was not only the natural, but also the representative or federal head of the human race. His fall involved the whole race in guilt (*see* Imputation).

(2) **Arminian.** The view more generally held is that the effect of Adam's sin upon the moral state of mankind is in accordance with and by virtue of the natural law of heredity. The race inherited proneness to sin. But this proneness to sin does not imply guilt, inasmuch as punishment can justly be inflicted only on account of actual sin, which consists in voluntary transgression. This view is held by many Presbyterians, Congregationalists, Episcopalians, and universally by Methodists.

(3) **Pelagianism.** The doctrine known as Pelagianism (*q. v.*) denies any necessary connection between the sin of Adam and the character and actions of his descendants. Every human being is by nature as pure as was Adam before his sin. The prevalence of sin is to be accounted for upon the ground of evil example and surroundings. Accordingly it is possible for men to lead lives of such complete freedom from sin that they may stand in no need of redemption or of regenerating grace. This doctrine is repudiated by all evangelical Churches.

The recognition of the reality of sin, not only in the sense of actual disobedience, but also in the sense of innate sinfulness, is essential. For only thus can be seen the necessity for a special revelation, and only thus are men prepared to accept the Gospel of salvation in Christ.

3. **Forgiveness of Sin.** *See* Justification; Repentance.

4. **The Unpardonable Sin** (Matt. 12:31, 32; Luke 12:10; Heb. 10:26; I John 5:16). The passages referred to undoubtedly point to one particular sin, and that is unpardonable. What this sin is has been a matter of much

discussion. The view held by Wesley and others is that it is "the ascribing those miracles to the power of the devil which Christ wrought by the power of the Holy Spirit." This view is by some held to be inadequate. Lange expresses the convictions of some when he says: "We have here to understand fully conscious and stubborn hatred against God and that which is divine as it exists in its highest development." And proponents of this view hold that this sin is unpardonable not because the grace of God is not sufficient for its forgiveness, but because it springs from a state of the soul in which there is left no disposition for repentance and faith in Jesus Christ. Thus they who are in anxiety lest they have committed this sin show in this very fact that such anxiety is groundless. Nevertheless, they who persist in sinning against religious life have great reason to fear lest they become thus fearfully guilty. But in the above-mentioned Scriptures, it is very questionable that Heb. 10:26 and I John 5:16 refer to the unpardonable sin. The "sin unto death" is not spiritual but physical death, resulting from sin in a *believer's* life and consequent chastisement. It has nothing to do with what Jesus called the "unpardonable sin." This is apparently what Wesley described it to be, as above-mentioned, and was possible only during the earthly public ministry of our Lord in the flesh. *See* Holy Spirit, Sin Against.—E. McC., revised by M. F. U.

Sin (sĭn). 1. (Heb. *Sîn*), a city of Egypt, called by the Greeks Pelusium. It lay on the eastern arm of the Nile, about three miles from the sea. This strategic fort had to be captured before any army could penetrate Egypt. Sennacherib failed to take it, but Esarhaddon did in 671 B. C. and overran Egypt. Ezekiel (30:15, 16) calls it "the strength" (i. e., "fortress" or "bulwark") of Egypt.

2. **Wilderness of Sin**, a tract or plain lying along the eastern shore of the Red Sea. It is thought to be the present plain of El-Kaa, which commences at the mouth of Wady Taiyibeh, and extends along the whole southwestern side of the peninsula. It was the scene of the murmurings and the miracle of the quails and manna (Exod. 16:1; 17:1; Num. 33:11, 12). It is connected also with the Plain el-Markhah on the coast.

Sin Offering. *See* Sacrificial Offerings.

Si'na (sī'nà), the Greek form (Judith 5:14; Acts 7:30, 38) of Sinai (*q. v.*).

Si'nai (sī'nī), the mountain district reached by the Israelites in the third month after leaving Egypt.

1. **Name.** The name is a very ancient one, and its meaning not definitely fixed. If Semitic it, perhaps, means *thorny* (i. e., cleft with ravines, from Heb. *seneh*, "thorn bush"). It may, however, take its name from the moongod Sin, whose cult had made its way into Arabia.

2. **Bible Notices.** When the Israelites left Elim they came to the wilderness of Sin, and then to Rephidim, where they encamped (Exod. 16:1, sq.; 17:1), and in the third month after the Exodus arrived at the "Wilderness of Sinai" (19:1). Moses went up into the Mount and received a preliminary mes-

age from Jehovah, declaring his past assistance and promise of future guidance and protection, on the condition of obedience (vers. 3-6). The people were commanded to prepare themselves for a direct message from Jehovah, a boundary line was set around the mountain to prevent any of the people from approaching rashly or inadvertently to "touch the mount" (v. 12). The "top of the mount" was in full view from the camp; so that when the Lord "came down" upon it the thick cloud in which his glory was shrouded was "in sight of all the people" (vers. 11, 16). The people were brought out of their camp "to meet with God; and they stood at the nether part of the mount" (v. 17); for they "saw the thunderings, and the lightnings, and the noise of the trumpet, and the mountain smoking: and when the people saw it, they removed, and stood afar off" (20:18).

Moses received the tables of the law twice (*see* Moses), and was made acquainted with the details of the rites and ceremonies recorded in the Pentateuch (31:18; ch. 34; Lev. 7:36, etc.). On the first day of the second month after leaving Egypt the census was taken (Num. 1:1-46); the position assigned to the various tribes when in camp and on the march (1:47-2:34); the firstborn were redeemed (3:40-51); the office and duties of the Levites enumerated (4:1-49); the tabernacle was reared and covered with the cloud (9:15, sq.), and, finally, on the twentieth day of the second month, in the second year, "the children of Israel took their journeys out of the wilderness of Sinai" (10:11, sq.; comp. 33:15, 16).

3. **Horeb and Sinai.** Concerning these names there has been much difference of opinion. Ewald (*Geschichte*, ii, 57) pronounces Sinai the older name, and Horeb the name used by the author of Deuteronomy (except 33:2), which book he assigns to a later writer. Hengstenberg (*Pent.*, ii, 325-327) agrees with Gesenius that the one name is more general than the other, but differs in this respect, that he makes Horeb the mountain ridge and Sinai the individual summit from which the ten commandments were given. The following are his reasons: 1. The name Sinai is used at the time that the Israelites were upon the very spot of the legislation (see from Exod. 19:11 to Num. 3:1); whereas Horeb is always used in the recapitulation in Deuteronomy (except 33:2). 2. The name Horeb occurs in the earlier books thrice, all in Exodus, but it is in circumstances which best suit the general or comprehensive meaning which we attach to it (see Exod. 3:1; 17:6; 19:2; comp. 33:6). 3. An argument may be drawn from the use of the preposition connected with these two names. Thus in Exod. 17:6 we find the Lord saying, "Behold, I will stand *upon* the rock *in* Horeb," i. e., *upon* the particular spot, but *in* the district. The preposition *in* (in the A. V. needlessly varied into "at" once or twice), which is used with Horeb, not only here, but almost always where the name occurs in Deuteronomy, perhaps·always, except "from" (1:2, 9). The same is true of all the passages in which Horeb is mentioned in later Scripture (I Kings 8:9; II Chron. 5:10; Psa. 106:19; Mal.

4:4), except I Kings 19:8, A. V. "unto Horeb the mount of God." With Sinai, on the other hand, there are connected several prepositions "in" and "from," as in the case of Horeb: also "to," but especially "upon" (Exod. 19:11, 18, 20; 24-16), which describes the descent of the Lord, or the resting of the symbol of his presence, upon that individual peak from which the law was given; whereas we have no reason to think that it rested upon the whole mass of mountains which are clustered together.

435. St. Catherine's Monastery at the Foot of Mount Sinai

"Understanding Horeb to be the more general name, there might still be differences of opinion how wide a circuit should be included under it, though the common opinion seems to be that there is no necessity for taking it wider than that range (some three miles long from north to south) which is called by the modern Arabs *Jebel Tûr* or *Jebel et-Tûr*, sometimes with the addition of Sina, though Robinson says extremely rarely" (McC. and S., *Cyc.*, s. v.).

4. **Identification of Sinai.** Tradition offers the following sites:

(1) Mount Serbal, on Wadi Feiran. This goes back to the time of Eusebius. The main objection to this identification, however, is that there is no plain or wadi of sufficient size in the neighborhood to offer camping ground for so large a host.

(2) Jebel Musa (Mountain of Moses) is the Sinai of later ecclesiastical tradition. Jebel Musa is part of a short ridge extending about two miles. The ridge has two peaks, one Ras es-Safsaf, with an altitude of 6,540 feet and Jebel Musa, 7,363 feet. St. Catherine's Monastery, a monastery of Greek monks, is located at the foot of Jebel Musa.

(3) Some scholars reject Jebel Musa because it is near the Serabit copper and turquoise mines, where there were Egyptian soldiers. They select Jebel Hellal, a 2000-foot elevation thirty miles S. of El-'Arish.

(4) Many Jewish scholars identify Mount Sinai with volcanic Mount Seir in southern Palestine, a region near enough to Midian for Moses to have led his flocks (Exod. 3:1). Says George Ernest Wright (*The 20th Century Ency. of Rel. Knowledge*, 1955, p. 1023): "A number of scholars today hold that Mount Sinai is to be located in Midian S. E. of Edom. The chief evidence for this view is a belief that Exodus 19 reflects volcanic activity and that the sacred mountain must be located in a volcanic region." But Prof. Wright shows

that in a theophany volcanic phenomena are not necessary. Wright thus summarizes the latest evidence: "Consequently, we are left with the traditional location of Mount Sinai as still the most probable."—*M. F. U.*

Sincerity (Heb. *tāmîm, without blemish*), the acting or speaking without hypocrisy (Josh. 24:14; Judg. 9:16, 19). The Gr. *'adolos*, means unadulterated, as "the sincere [pure] milk of the word" (I Pet. 2:2). Paul desires the Philistines (1:10) to be pure, their behavior innocent, etc., that thus they may "be *sincere* (Gr. *hagnōs*) and without offense till the day of Christ." Sincerity in Eph. 6:24 and Tit. 2:7 is the rendering of the Gr. *'aphtharsia;* the meaning of the first passage being to "love our Lord Jesus Christ with never-diminishing (undecaying) love" (A. V. "love in uncorruptness"); while in Tit. 2:7 the A. V. renders "in thy doctrine *showing* uncorruptness, gravity." "The sincerity of your love" (II Cor. 8:8) may properly be rendered that "your love is legitimate" (Gr. *gnēsios;* while *eilikrineia*) means *found pure* when tested by the sunlight, and so *pure, unsullied* (Phil. 1:10; I Cor. 5:8; II Cor. 1:12; 2:17).

Sinew, the rendering of the Hebrew term *gîd hānnāshĕh* denoting "the sinew that shrank" (Gen. 32:32), i. e., the *nervous ischiadicus*, the principal nerve in the neighborhood of the hip, which is easily injured by any violent strain in wrestling. Because of the dislocation of the thigh of Jacob the Israelites avoid eating this nerve.

Singing. *See* Music.

Figurative. Singing is symbolic of joy (Neh. 12:27; Isa. 35:2; 44:23; 51:11), and so the absence of it is expressed by the cessation of song (Isa. 16:10).

Single Eye is the rendering in the A. V. of *'ophthalmos haplous* (Matt. 6:22; Luke 11:34). *Haplous* means simple, that in which there is nothing complicated or confused; and thus in our sense of *sound, healthy*, which can focus with clarity and without distraction on the object in view.

Si'nim (sî'nĭm; Isa. 49:12), the name of a remote people, from whose land men should come to the light of Israel and of the Gentiles. It is, of course, not quite impossible that it may refer to the Lebanon Sinites (*q. v.*), or with the tribe Sina in the Hindu-Kush (Lacouperie in *Babylonian and Oriental Record*). The LXX. gives *Persai*, but the early interpreters looked to the south as to Sin (Pelusium) or Syene.

Si'nites (sī'nīts; Gen. 10:17; I Chron. 1:15), a tribe mentioned only in the phrase "and the Sinites," and in the connection, "And Canaan begat Sidon, his firstborn, and Heth, and the Jebusite, and the Amorite, and the Girgashite, and the Hivite, and the Arkite, and the Sinite, and the Arvadite, and the Zemarite, and the Hamathite." From its position in the list it is inferred that it lay toward the north, perhaps in the northern part of the Lebanon district. In that region were "*Sinna*, a mountain fortress mentioned by Strabo . . . *Sinum*, or *Sini*, the ruins of which existed in the time of Jerome," and others with somewhat similar names. The Targums of Onkelos and Jonathan give Orthosia, a maritime town northeasterly from Tripolis. It was a place of importance, as commanding the only road "betwixt Phoenice and the maritime parts of Syria." Delitzsch mentions the cuneiform *Sianu*, which is mentioned with *Semar* and *Arka*.—W. H.

Sinlessness of Christ, the perfect freedom of Christ, not only from all outward acts of sin, but also from all inward inclination to sin.

1. **Scripture Statement.** The Old Testament prophecies relating to Christ, whether symbolically expressed or uttered in words, point to his perfect purity (see Isa. 9:6, 7; ch. 53). The New Testament bears most emphatic testimony to the same fact (see Matt. 11:29, 30; John 4:34; 6:38; 8:29, 46; 15:10; 17:4; Acts 3:14; Rom. 8:3; II Cor. 5:21; Heb. 4:15; 7:26, 27; I Pet. 1:19; 2:22; I John 2:2; 3:5). It is distinctly stated that Christ was tempted, and if so we must admit the abstract possibility of his sinning. Yet his temptations were in no case such as spring from a sinful nature, and the fact remains that he was absolutely without sin (*see* Temptation of Christ).

2. **Theological Suggestions.** (1) The sinlessness of Christ is to be looked at with reference to his human nature, and is to be distinguished from the holiness which he possessed as an attribute of his divine nature.

(2) The fact of his sinlessness is morally demonstrated, aside from the testimony of the Scriptures, as follows: 1. Christ certainly made upon those around him the impression that he was a person of at least unusual moral excellence. 2. It is a fact which has the force of a law that the higher imperfect beings rise in moral attainments the more keenly conscious they become of remaining moral defects. 3. Christ manifested no consciousness of moral defect, but the opposite. He taught men to confess their sins, but he made no such confession; he taught men to pray for forgiveness, but uttered no such prayer for himself; he declared the necessity of the new birth by the work of the Holy Spirit, but it was for others. He recognized in himself no such necessity. And thus it follows that in Christ we find a reversal of the law which prevails with respect to all limited measure of human excellence, or he was supremely excellent, absolutely without sin.

(3) The objections of infidels are too trivial or too abstruse to be entered upon here with any fullness. However, it may be said that the blighting of the barren fig tree by the wayside cannot be shown to be an interference with the rights of private property. And, moreover, Christ had the right to use this insensate object for the purpose of symbolically impressing his solemn lesson. The destruction of the swine at Gadara is to be viewed with reference to the deliverance of a human soul as of infinitely higher importance than the loss of the lives of many animals. And, besides, it cannot be shown that Christ really willed or directly caused the destruction. We may dismiss this part of the subject in recalling the fact that the unbelieving world has in reality but little to say against the moral perfection of Jesus.

(4) The sinlessness of Christ is a fact of many-sided importance. 1. Christ, because he was sinless, is one of the highest, may we not say, the highest of the credentials of Christianity. He is a moral miracle, and is himself greater than all his miracles. 2. The fact has important relation to the authority of his teaching (see Matt. 17:5; John 8:46). 3. Christ in his sinlessness exhibits to us the highest good. He was not free from poverty, and persecution, and hatred, and loneliness, and death, but he was free from sin. 4. His sinlessness is importantly related to the value of his atoning sacrifice. His offering of himself was of unspeakable value because he was spotless (see I Pet. 1:19; comp. John 1:29). 5. Likewise the efficacy of his intercession is based upon the same fact (I John 2:1; Heb. 4:14-16). 6. This fact also throws light upon his proffer of new life to men. He is at the same time our perfect example, and the one through whom we receive power to follow in his steps (John 10:10; I Pet. 2:21).

The doctrine of Christ's unsullied purity is therefore one which has been steadfastly held as of greatest moment by the Church in all ages.—E. McC.

Si′on, Mount (sī′ŭn). 1. (Heb. *hăr si′ōn; elevated, lofty*), one of the various names of Mount Hermon, which are fortunately preserved, all not improbably more ancient than "Hermon" itself (Deut. 4:48 only).

2. The Greek (*Siōn*) of the Hebrew name Zion, the famous mount of the temple (1 Macc. 4:37, 60; 5:54; 6:48, 62; 7:33; 10:11; 14:27; Heb. 12:22; Rev. 14:1). *See* Zion.

Siph′moth (sĭf′mŏth), one of the places in the south of Judah which David frequented during his freebooting life (I Sam. 30:28). No one appears yet to have even suggested an identification of it, but may be referred to in I Chron. 27:27, where Zabdi is called the *Shiphmite*.

Sip′pai (sĭp′ī), one of the sons of "the giants" slain by Sibbechai at Gezer (I Chron. 20:4), called in the parallel passage (II Sam. 21:18) by the equivalent name of Saph (*q. v.*).

Si′rah (sī′rä), a well about a mile north of Hebron. Abner was recalled here by Joab (II Sam. 3:26), and treacherously slain. The well is probably the '*Ain Sārah* of today.

Sir′ion (sĭr′ĭ-ŏn; *cuirass, coat of mail*), one of the various names of Mount Hermon, that by which it was known to the Zidonians (Deut. 3:9). The name in Psa. 29:6 is slightly altered in the original (Heb. *shĭryōn*).

Sis′mai (sĭs′mī), A. V. **Sis′amai** (sĭs′á-mī), son of Eleasah, and father of Shallum, descendants of Sheshan, in the line of Jerahmeel (I Chron. 2:40).

Sis′era (sĭs′ĕr-à; uncertain derivation).

1. The "captain" of the army of Jabin, king of Canaan. He dwelt in Harosheth of the Gentiles (present-day Tell 'Amar on the N. bank of the Kishon where the stream enters the plain of Acre, about 16 miles N. N. W. of Megiddo), and for twenty years oppressed the Israelites with a force of nine hundred chariots of iron (Judg. 4:2, 3). When Sisera received tidings of the march of Barak to Mount Tabor, he mustered his army at the Kishon, where it was thrown into confusion and utterly routed (vers. 10-16). Sisera, to save himself, sprang from his chariot and fled on foot.

He took refuge in the tent of Jael, the wife of Heber the Kenite. She received the fugitive in the usual form of oriental hospitality, but when he had fallen asleep Jael took a tent stake and drove it into his temples, so that he died (vers. 17-22). B. C. about 1120. *See* Jael.

2. The name reappears in the lists of the Nethinim, who returned from the captivity with Zerubbabel (Ezra 2:53; Neh. 7:55). It doubtless tells of Canaanite captives devoted to the lowest offices of the temple.

Sis'mai (sĭs'mī), a man of Judah (I Chron. 2:40). *See* Sisamai.

Sister (Heb. *'āḥōth;* Gr. *'adelphē*), a term used by the Hebrews with equal latitude as *brother* (*q. v.*). It may denote a relation by the same father and mother, by the same father only, by the same mother only, or merely a near relative (Matt. 13:56; Mark 6:3). Sarah was called the sister of Abraham (Gen. 12:13; 20:12), though only his niece according to some, or, according to others, sister by the father's side. Respecting marrying such relatives, *see* Marriage.

Sit, Sitting (Heb. *yāshăb;* Gr. *kathezomai*), the favorite position of the orientals, who, in the absence of chairs, sit upon the floor with their feet crossed under them. "In Palestine people *sit* at all kinds of work; the carpenter saws, planes, and hews with his hand-adze sitting upon the ground or upon the plank he is planing. The washerwoman sits by the tub; and, in a word, no one stands where it is possible to sit" (Thomson, *Land and Book*, i, 191).

Figurative. Of *judges* who *sit* in judgment (Isa. 28:6; Joel 3:12; Mal. 3:3, "sit as a refiner of silver"); hence the *seat of violence*, i. e., of unjust judgment (Amos 6:3); mourners, who *sit* upon the ground (Isa. 3:26; 47:1; Job 2:13) or solitary (Lam. 1:1; 3:28); of an army which *sits down* in a place, i. e., holds it (I Sam. 13:16); of those who *sit still*, who remain quiet, as opposed to those who go to war (Jer. 8:14).

Sit'nah (sĭt'nà; *strife, contention, opposition*, same root as in Satan), the second of the two wells dug by Isaac, where a contest was had with the Philistines (Gen. 26:21). The modern *Shutneh.*

Sivan' (sē-vän'; Heb. *sīwān* from Akkad. *sīmānu*), the third month of the Hebrew *sacred* year, and ninth of the *civil* year (Esth. 8, 9). *See* Calendar; Time.

Skin. 1. The rendering generally of the Heb. *'ōr* (*naked*), and meaning the skin of a man, the skin or hide of animals (Lev. 4:11; 7:8, etc.); also as prepared, i. e., *leather* (Lev. 11: 32; 13:48; Num. 31:20).

2. *Flesh* (Heb. *bāsār,* so generally rendered) is *only* rendered *skin* in Psa. 102:5, "My bones cleave to my skin" (flesh).

3. The human skin as smooth and naked (Job 16:15), Heb. *gělěd, smooth, polished*, where Job says, "I have sewed sackcloth upon my skin." This is to be attributed doubtless to the hideous distortion of his body by elephantiasis, which will not admit of the use of the ordinary form of clothes.

4. *Leathern* (Gr. *dermatinos*), that which is made of skin, *leathern*, as a girdle (Mark 1:6). *See* Bottle; Dress.

436. Ancient Slings

Figurative. "Skin for skin" (Job 2:4) seems to mean "one gives up one's skin to preserve one's skin; one endures pain on a sickly part of the skin, for the sake of saving the whole skin; one holds up the arm to avert the fatal blow from the head." "The skin of my teeth" (19: 20) is supposed to be that which surrounds the teeth in the jaw, viz., the periosteum. The disease has destroyed the gums and wasted them away from the teeth, leaving only the periosteum. "Can the Ethiopian change his skin?" (Jer. 13:23) is symbolical of the inability of one to get rid of an evil character which has become second nature.

Skirt (Heb. *shūl*), the flowing *train* of a robe or female dress (Jer. 13:22, 26; Lam. 1:9; Nah. 3:5); more vaguely (*kānāph,* literally a *wing*) the flap of a robe (Deut. 22:30; 27:20; Ruth 3:9, etc.).

Figurative. To raise the skirts of a woman's garment is put for a symbol of insult and disgrace (Jer. 13:22, 26; Nah. 3:5); whereas to cover her with one's skirt was a token of matrimony (Ruth 3:9).

Skull. *See* Golgotha.

Sky (Heb. *shăḥăq, vapor,* Deut. 33:26; II Sam. 22:12; Job. 37:18, etc.) may mean the clouds or the firmament. "His excellency is in the sky" (Deut. 33:26) is a figurative expression to denote omnipotence.

Slander (Heb. *dĭbbār*), a defaming, evil report (Num. 14:36; Psa. 31:13; Prov. 10:18). In the apostolic Church the wife of a deacon are forbidden (I Tim. 3:6) to be a *slanderer* (Gr. *diabolos*), i. e., a calumniator, false accuser.

Slave, Slavery. *See* Service.

Sleep, the rendering of several Hebrew and Greek words, used in the general sense of sleep or repose for the body (Psa. 4:8; 121:4; Jonah 1:5, 6). The manner of sleeping in warm Eastern climates is very different from that in colder countries. Their beds are generally hard, feather beds being unknown. The poor often sleep on mats, or wrapped in their outer garment, for which reason the latter was not allowed to be retained in pledge overnight (Gen. 9:21, 23; Exod. 22:26, 27; Deut. 24:12, 13). The wealthy sleep on mattresses stuffed with wool or cotton, being often only a thick quilt, used singly or piled upon each other. In winter a similar quilt of finer material forms the coverlet, while a thin blanket suffices in summer; unless, indeed, the convenient outer garment is used (I Sam. 19:13). *See* Bed.

Figurative. Sleep is employed as a symbol of *death* (Deut. 31:16; II Sam. 7:12; Job 7:21; Dan. 12:2; John 11:11, etc.); of *supineness,* indolence, or stupid inactivity of the wicked Rom. 13:11, 12; Eph. 5:14; I Cor. 11:30).

Slime. *See* Asphalt; Bitumen, in Mineral Kingdom.

Slime Pits. *See* Siddim.

Sling. *See* Armor.

 Figurative. The proverb, "As he that bindeth a stone in a sling," etc. (Prov. 26:8), is probably better rendered by Gesenius "As a bag of gems in a heap of stones," the Heb. (*mărgēmäh,* A. V. "sling") meaning a "heap of stones" (comp. Matt. 7:6).

Slip (Heb. *zᵉmōräh, pruned*), is the layer of a vine. To set "strange slips" (Isa. 17:10) is thought to be figurative for making foreign alliances, e. g., with the king of Damascus.

Slothful. In Prov. 12:24, "the slothful shall be under tribute," the Heb. *rᵉmîyäh* means *remiss, treacherous;* and the meaning seems to be, "The deceitful man will come to dependence." In v. 27 we have an expression which means that such a man does not improve his opportunities. The Heb. *'āṣăl,* has the usual meaning of *to be slack, indolent,* and is most generally used in the Old Testament.

Slow. 1. *Heavy* (Heb. *kābēd*), as when Moses said, "I am not eloquent (literally, a man of words), but *heavy* in mouth and in tongue" (Exod. 4:10); a difficulty in speaking, though not exactly stammering.

 2. *Extended* (Heb. *'ärēk, to make long*) is used in the frequent expression, "slow to anger" (Neh. 9:17; Psa. 103:8; Prov. 16:32, etc.), and expresses the same state of mind as the term "long-suffering."

 3. A very peculiar expression is found in Tit. 1:12, "slow bellies" (Gr. *gasteres 'argai*), to describe the Cretians. The one word is used to indicate their sensuality, the other their sloth (R. V. "idle gluttons").

Sluggard, another rendering in the A. V. of the Hebrew, rendered Slothful (*q. v.*).

Smith. *See* Handicraft; Metals.

437. Harbor at Smyrna

Smyr'na (smûr'nà; *myrrh*), a rich, prosperous, and dissolute city of Ionia, forty miles N. of Ephesus, at the mouth of a small river, Meles. Anciently it was one of the finest cities of Asia, and was called "the lovely—the crown of Ionia—the ornament of Asia." It is now the chief city of Anatolia, with a mixed population of two hundred thousand people, one third of whom are Christians. It is referred to in Rev. 2:8-11 as the seat of one of the seven churches. It was largely inhabited by Jews bitterly opposed to Christ and Christianity; and the church of Smyrna becomes the type of a suffering Church. It will be observed that

at Smyrna the Church is still faithful, and that against her no word of reproach is uttered. It was Polycarp's field of Christian usefulness, and here he suffered martyrdom, A. D. around 169.

Snail. *See* Animal Kingdom.

Snare (usually the rendering of some form of (Heb. *yäqäsh,* to *ensnare;* frequently of *păḥ,* a *spring net;* Gr. *brochos, noose; pagis, trap*), a net or trap, especially of the fowler (Isa. 8:14; Amos 3:5); also such as seizes man and beast (Job 18:10; Jer. 18:22). Snares were set in the path or hidden in the ground (Psa. 140:5; 119:10; Prov. 7:23; 22:5; Jer. 18:22). The snare (Heb. *păḥ*) was formed of two parts which, when set, were spread out upon the ground, and slightly fastened with a trap-stick; so that as soon as a bird or beast touched the stick the parts flew up and inclosed the bird in the net or caught the foot of the animal (Job 18:9).

 Figurative. Snare is used for anything that may be the cause of *injury* or *destruction,* e. g., the nations about Israel (Josh. 23:13); false gods (Judg. 2:3; I Kings 11:4; Psa. 106:36); false prophets (Hos. 9:8); riches, love of (I Tim. 6:9); death, as a hunter (II Sam. 22:6; Psa. 18:5; comp. 91:3).

Snout (Heb. *'ăph, nostril,* hence, *face*) is only mentioned in Prov. 11:22, "as a jewel of gold in a swine's snout, so is a fair woman without discretion." Clark (*Com.*) thus comments: "Beauty in a woman destitute of good breeding and modest carriage is as becoming as a gold ring on the snout of a swine."

Snow (Heb. *shĕlĕg, white;* Gr. *chiōn*). In the historical books of Scripture snow is twice mentioned as actually falling (II Sam. 23:20; I Chron. 11:22; comp. I Macc. 13:22). In the poetical books the allusions are so frequent as to make it probable that snow was an ordinary occurrence in Palestine. "During most winters both hail and snow fall on the hills. On the Central Range snow has been known to reach a depth of nearly two feet, and to lie for five days, or even more. . . . This explains the feat of Benaiah, who *went down and slew a lion in the midst of a cistern in the day of the snow* (II Sam. 23:20)" (Smith, *Hist. Geog.*, p. 64, sq.). The snow lies deep in the ravines of the highest ridge of Lebanon until the summer is far advanced, and, indeed, never wholly disappears; the summit of Hermon also perpetually glistens with frozen snow. From these sources, probably, the Jews obtained their supplies of ice for the purpose of cooling their beverages in summer (Prov. 25:13).

 Figurative. The color of snow is given as an image of brilliancy (Dan. 7:9; Matt. 28:3; Rev. 1:14); of purity (Isa. 1:18; Lam. 4:7, referring to the white robes of princes); of the blanching effects of leprosy (Exod. 4:6; Num. 12:10; II Kings 5:27); of cleansing power (Job 9:30); "snow waters," i. e., melted snow, easily dried up in the burning sand (24:19), is used to express the swift and utter destruction of the godless; snow, fertilizing the earth before it again returns as vapor to the sky, pictures the effective power of God's word (Isa. 55:10). "Will a man leave the snow of Lebanon?" (Jer. 18:14) is thus rendered by Orelli (*Com.*), "Does the snow of

Lebanon disappoint on the rock of the fields?" i. e., the Lebanon snow feeds without ceasing, the water flowing therefrom. Phenomena of nature, stable and trustworthy, are contrasted with the fickleness of Israel.

Snuff (Heb. *shä'ăph*), to inhale eagerly, as Jer. 14:6, where the wild asses tormented by burning thirst, pant for wind like jackals (comp. 2:24). "Snuff" (Heb. *năphăḥ*, to *blow at*), means to express contempt, as of God's altar (Mal. 1:13).

Snuff-Dish, Snuffer, articles used in the *Tabernacle* (*q. v.*).

So (Heb. *Sŏ'*), a king of Egypt. Hoshea, the last king of Israel, evidently intending to become the vassal of Egypt, sent messengers to So, and made no present, as had been the yearly custom to the king of Assyria (II Kings 17:4), B. C. 725. The consequence of this step was the imprisonment of Hoshea, the taking of Samaria, and the carrying captive of the ten tribes (18:10, 11).

Identification. As the Hebrew Consonants may be rendered Sewe, he is frequently and undoubtedly correctly identified with Sib'e, tartan of Egypt, who, in alliance with king Hanun of Gaza, collided in battle with Sargon of Assyria at Raphia on the Mediterranean, about 20 miles south of Gaza (B. C. 720). The allies here discomfited, Hanun captured, Sib'e fled, and was later put under tribute to Assyria. Sib'e is scarcely Shabako.

Soap (Heb. *bŏrîth*). The Hebrew *bŏrîth* is a general term for any substance of *cleansing* qualities. As, however, it appears in Jer. 2:22, in contradistinction to *nether* (Heb. *nĕthĕr,* A. V. "nitre"), which undoubtedly means "natron," or mineral alkali, it is fair to infer that *bŏrîth* refers to vegetable alkali, or some kind of potash, which forms one of the usual ingredients in our soap. It occurs in Mal. 3:2, but there is nothing to tell us whether it was obtained from the vegetable or mineral kingdom. But *bŏr* (Job 9:30) denotes a vegetable alkali used for washing. Numerous plants, capable of yielding alkalies, exist in Palestine and the surrounding countries; we may notice one named *Hubeibeh* (the *Salsola Kali* of botanists) found near the Dead Sea, the ashes of which are called *el-Kuli,* from their strong alkaline properties, the *Ajram,* found near Sinai, which, when pounded, serves as a substitute for soap. Modern travelers have also noticed the *Saponaria officinalis* and the *Mesembryanthemum nodiflorum,* both possessing alkaline properties, as growing in Palestine.

Sober, Soberly, etc. 1. (Gr. *nēphō* and derivatives), calm and collected in spirit, temperate, dispassionate (I Thess. 5:6, 8; II Tim. 4:5, A. V. "watch;" I Pet. 1:13).

2. Gr. *sōphroneō,* and derivatives, the being of a sound mind, as of one who has ceased to be under the power of an evil one (Mark 5:15; Luke 8:35); the opposite of *'ekstēnai,* to be beside one's self (II Cor. 5:13); the exercise of self-control, so as to (*a*) place a moderate estimate upon one's self (Rom. 12:3), (*b*) to curb one's passion (Tit. 2:6).

So'cho (sō'kô; *thorn-hedge;* I Chron. 4:18), variously called Sochoh (I Kings 4:10), Shochoh (I Sam. 17:1), Shoco (II Chron. 11:7), choh

Shocho (28:18). It was in the low country of Judah (Josh. 15:35), and was settled by the sons of Ezra, of the tribe of Judah. It was one of the cities fortified by Rehoboam after the revolt of the northern tribes (II Chron. 11:7). Here Goliath was slain, and it was also one of Solomon's commissariat districts. It lay on the north side of Wady es-Sunt, and is identified with modern *Khirbet Shuweikeh,* fourteen miles S. W. of Jerusalem.

So'choch (sō'kô; I Kings 4:10). *See* Socho.

Socket. *See* Tabernacle.

So'coh (sō'kô). 1. A city in the low country of Judah (Josh. 15:35). *See* Socho.

2. Another city of Judah, in the mountain district (Josh. 15:48), one of a group of eleven towns. Robinson located it in the Wady el-Khalîl, about ten miles S. W. of Hebron; bearing, like the other Socho, the name of *Shuweikeh.*

So'di (sō'dī; *my secret council,* i. e., is Jehovah), father of Gaddiel, the spy appointed to represent the tribe of Zebulun (Num. 13:10), B. C. c. 1440.

Sodom, a town of the patriarchal age located in the plain or "circle of the Jordan" (Gen. 13:12) together with its sister cities Gomorrah, Admah, Zeboiim and Zoar. The Biblical notices that the district of the Jordan, where these cities were located, was exceedingly fertile and well peopled (c. 2065 B. C.), but that not long afterwards was abandoned, are in full accord with archaeological evidence (cf. W. F. Albright, *The Archaeology of Palestine and the Bible,* p. 133f). Scholars used to place these cities north of the Dead Sea, but it is now generally agreed that they were situated in "the Vale of Siddim," together with its sister cities (Gen. 14:3), and that this was the area at the southern end of the Dead Sea, now covered with water. Sometime around the middle of the twenty-first century B. C., this region with its cities was overwhelmed by

438. Jebel Usdum (Mound of Salt) at South End of the Dead Sea

a great conflagration (Gen. 19:23-28). The area is said to have been "full of slime (that is, asphalt pits)" (Gen. 14:10). Bitumen deposits are still to be found in this locality. The entire valley is on the long fault line which forms the Jordan Valley, the Dead Sea and the Arabah. An earthquake-ridden region throughout its history, geological activity was doubtless an accompanying factor in the destruction of the cities, although the Bible account records only the miraculous elements.

The salt and free sulphur of this area, now a burned out region of oil and asphalt, were apparently mingled by an earthquake, causing a violent explosion. Carried up into the air red-hot, the exploding salt and sulphur literally caused a rain of fire and brimstone over the whole plain (Gen. 19:24, 28). The account of Lot's wife being turned into a pillar of salt is frequently connected with the great salt mass in the valley called by the Arabs *Jebel Usdum*, that is, "Mountain of Sodom." This is a hill some five miles long stretching N. and S. at the S. W. end of the Dead Sea. Somewhere under the slowly rising waters of the southern part of the lake in this

439. The Destruction of Sodom (Carat)

general locality the "cities of the plain" are probably to be found. In classical and N. T. times their ruins were still visible, not yet being covered with water (Tacitus *History* V:7; Josephus *Wars* IV:4). Jesus refers to the destruction of Sodom and Gomorrah (Matt. 10:15). Sodom's wickedness and moral depravity became proverbial (Rom. 9:29; Rev. 11:18). Fresh water irrigation at the southern end of the Dead Sea was sufficient to maintain the cities of the Jordan pentapolis and furnishes another evidence of the location of Sodom in this region.—*M. F. U. See* Gomorrah.

Sod'oma (sŏd'ô-má; Rom. 9:29), the Greek form of Sodom (*q. v.*).

Sod'omite (Heb. *qādēsh, consecrated, devoted*). The sodomites were not inhabitants of Sodom, nor their descendants, but men *consecrated* to the unnatural vice of Sodom (Gen. 19:5; comp. Rom. 1:27) as a religious rite. This dreadful "consecration," or, rather, desecration, was spread in different forms over Phoenicia, Syria; Phrygia, Assyria, Babylonia. Ashtaroth, the Greek Astarte, was its chief object. The term was especially applied to the emasculated priests of Cybele, called Galli, perhaps from the river Gallus in Bithynia, which was said to make those who drank it mad. In Deut. 23:17, the toleration of a sodomite was expressly forbidden, and the pay received by a sodomite was not to be put into the temple treasury (v. 18). "The price of a dog" is a figurative expression used to denote the gains of a *qādēsh* (sodomite), who was called *kinaidos*, by the Greeks, from the doglike manner in which he debased himself (see Rev. 22:15, where the unclean are called "dogs").

Solder (Heb. *děbĕq, joint*), welding of metal (Isa. 41:7), a metallic substance or mixture used in melted form to hold metals together, as a metal idol.

Soldier. *See* Army.

Sol'omon. 1. **Name and Family.** Solomon's name (Heb. *Shĕlōmōh*) means "peaceable." He was also called Jedidiah, meaning "beloved of Jehovah." He was a son of King David by Bathsheba (II Sam. 12:24; I Chron. 3:5). He succeeded King David to the throne and ruled from c. 965-925 B. C.

2. **His Empire.** The tendency of scholars in the past has been to give scant credence to the Biblical notices of Solomon's power and glory as related in I Kings chaps. 3-11 (cf. Matt. 6:29; 12:42; Luke 11:31). The German scholars, Hugo Winckler and Hermann Guthe restricted the Davidic empire, which Solomon inherited, narrowly to Palestine, excluding even Damascus. Zobah, Hadadezer's kingdom conquered by David, was customarily located south of Damascus in Hauran, Biblical Bashan. Analysis of the Assyrian provincial organization, which was constructed on older foundations, however, shows that Zobah, Assyrian *Subatu*, lay north of Damascus and not south of it (Emil Forrer, *Die Provinzeinteilung des Assyrischen Reiches*, 1921, pp. 62, 69). Egyptian lists and the Amarna Letters also prove that Hadadezer's chief cities, Tibhath and Chun, which David conquered (I Chron. 18:8), were just S. of Hums. Thus archaeology has vindicated the wide extent of the Davidic-Solomonic Empire as delineated in Kings. The general historical background of the Davidic-Solomonic period has also been authenticated. Solomon's glory used to be commonly dismissed as "Semitic exaggeration" or a romantic tale. It was contended that such a sprawling realm could not have existed between great empires like Egypt, the Hittites, Assyria and Babylonia. The monuments, however, have shown that during the period from 1100-900 B. C. the great empires surrounding Israel were either in eclipse or abeyance, so that Solomon could rule with the splendor attributed to him in the Bible. After 1150 B. C., the Twentieth Egyptian Dynasty was very weak, with a succession of feeble Ramessides. Not until Shishak (Egyptian Sheshonq I, c. 940-920 B. C.) did Egyptian power revive. The Hittite Empire had collapsed c. 1200 B. C. and only small Hittite city-states such as Senjirli, Carchemish and Hamath existed. The latter Solomon had to conquer and made it a store city (II Chon. 8:3, 4). Assyria had no strong emperor from Tiglathpileser I (c. 1110 B. C.) to the rise of Ashurnasirpal II (c. 880 B. C.). Archaeology has thus authenticated the historical background of the Davidic-Solomonic era.

3. **Solomon's Remarkable Prosperity.** Solomon is known as "the first great commercial king of Israel" (Theodore H. Robinson, *The History of Israel*, Vol. I, p. 256). He took full advantage of peculiarly favorable conditions both by land and by sea for trade expansion. The widespread domestication of the Arabian camel from the twelfth century B. C. onward, as Albrght has noted (*From The Stone Age to Christianity*, 1940, p. 120f), effected a remarkable increase in nomadic mobility. It was now possible for desert caravans to venture two or three days' journey from a water supply. Ample archaeological

evidence shows that there was extensive caravan trade between the Fertile Crescent and S. Arabia in the Solomonic era. Solomon monopolized the entire caravan trade between Arabia and Mesopotamia and from the Red Sea to Palmyra ("Tadmor," II Chron. 8:4), an oasis 140 miles N. E. of Damascus, which he built (I Kings 9:18). Exercising control over the trade routes both to the E. and W. of the Jordan, the Israelite monarch was enabled to collect enormous revenue from merchants seeking passage through his territories (I Kings 10:15). Solomon also exploited the incipient iron industry, as a result of David's breaking the Philistine monopoly on iron (I Sam. 13:19, 20).

4. **Copper Mining and Refining.** Archaeology has shown that Phoenician technicians built the seaport of Ezion-geber for Solomon. In 1938-40 Nelson Glueck discovered an important copper smeltery there. It was clearly the work of Phoenician craftsmen who were widely experienced in the art of setting up copper furnaces and refineries at similar smelting settlements in Sardinia and Spain. Such a station, from which raw copper ore was exported, was called a *tarshish*, and the ships especially equipped for transporting such cargoes were called "tarshish ships" (cf. F. Thieberger, *King Solomon*, 1947, p. 206). Discovery of the copper refinery at Ezion-geber, modern Tell el-Kheleifeh, indicates another source of Solomon's proverbial wealth. It was Solomon "who was the first one who placed the mining industry in the Wadi Arabah upon a really national scale" (Nelson Glueck, *The Other Side of the Jordan*, 1941, p. 98). As the result, copper became the king's chief export. The royal fleet set out from Ezion-geber laden with raw ore, and brought back valuable goods obtainable in Arabian and nearby African ports.

440. War Chariot from Egypt (cf I. Kings 10:29)

5. **Trade in Horses and Chariots.** This lucrative business involved Solomon as a middleman in the trading of horses from Egypt and Asia Minor. "And Solomon's import of horses was from Egypt and Kue, and the King's traders received them from Kue at a price" (I Kings 10:28, A. R. V.). Assyrian records prove that Kue is Cilicia, the country between the Taurus Mountains and the Mediterranean Sea in Asia Minor. According to Herodotus, this region was famous in the Persian period for fine horses (III:90). "A chariot could be imported from Egypt for 600 shekels of silver and a horse for 150" (I Kings 10:29).

Thus, at the rate of four horses to one chariot, Solomon conducted this lucrative business.

6. **His Army.** Solomon used the horse and chariot trade not only for commercial reasons, but to build up a powerful standing army of chariotry (I Kings 4:26). This army was stationed in a number of chariot cities such as Gezer, Megiddo, Hazor and Jerusalem (I Kings 9:15-19). The Israelite monarch is said to have had 1400 chariots and 1200 horsemen which "he bestowed in the chariot cities and with the king at Jerusalem" (I Kings 10:26). Excavations at Megiddo, Hazor and Gezer have confirmed Solomon's building operations there. At Megiddo a group of stables capable of housing 450 horses and about 150 chariots has been uncovered. Similar groups of stables from Hazor and Tell el Hesi add evidence of Solomon's military might.

7. **Domestic Economy.** Solomon divided his realm into twelve districts which ignored old tribal boundaries and was a nucleus of a highly efficient organization (I Kings 4:7-20). Solomon resorted to heavy direct taxation, free donations of labor (I Kings 9:20, 21) as well as special levies (I Kings 5:13-18).

8. **Foreign Policy.** As a skillful diplomat, Solomon made ties of amity with the important maritime kingdom of Tyre, which was ruled by Hiram I (969-936 B. C.). Hiram, a common Phoenician royal name attested by royal sarcophagus discovered at Byblos (Gebal) 1924-25, was called "king of the Sidonians." Besides, Solomon cultivated royal marriages. He married a princess of Egypt (I Kings 3:1, 2) and royal women of surrounding smaller kingdoms. The ancient practice of such regal marriages is well illustrated by the Amarna Letters, in which Egyptian pharoahs marry Hittite women and Mitannian princesses.

9. **Voyages to Ophir.** Phoenician seamen not only built Solomon's copper port at Eziongeber but his navy as well (I Kings 9:26-28). "Once every three years came the navy of tarshish bringing gold, silver, ivory, apes and peacocks" (I Kings 10:22). The word "peacocks" is better rendered as "a kind of monkey." Ophir was the region of S. W. Arabia, modern Yemen, on the Red Sea adjacent to Sheba and Havilah (Gen. 10:29). Since the voyage took three years, portions of the African coast must also be meant. The time denoted by "three years" simply means a full year with portions of two others. The navy, accordingly, set sail in November or September of the first year, returning in early spring of the third. Babylonians more than a millennium earlier allowed three years for a voyage to Melukka, approximately in the same general region.

10. **Visit of the Queen of Sheba.** Solomon's far-reaching commerce by land and sea must have brought him in competition with the famous Queen of Sheba. The account of the visit of this monarch to Jerusalem (I Kings, chap. 10), traversing over 1200 miles, used to be dismissed as a "romantic tale." Archaeology has shown the essential historicity of the account in which the queen must have come seeking delimitations of spheres of commercial interest. Although the Queen of

Sheba had not been attested epigraphically, recent researches in S. Arabia by the American Foundation for the Study of Man, 1950-51, have shown the historical reasonableness of the account. This expedition, conducted by Wendell Philips and under the archaeological supervision of W. F. Albright, examined the ruins of four once-flourishing S. Arabian monarchies: Ma'in, Saba (Sheba), Qataban and Hadhramaut. The famous spice route skirted this region and the taxes from this trade sup-

441. Solomon's Pool

ported three kingdoms. Large numbers of inscriptions, pottery and other archaeological finds are now in process of study, and the historical background of the Queen of Sheba gives favorable promise of complete illumination.

11. Solomon's Temple. Solomon's magnificent temple and the royal buildings at Jerusalem were in striking contrast to Saul's rusticity, exhibited by the excavations of Albright at Gibeah (Tell el Ful). Solomon was greatly indebted to Phoenician architectural ability. The plan of Solomon's temple was typically Phoenician, as is shown by the discovery of a similar temple at Tell Tainat in N. Syria in 1936 by the University of Chicago. Similar ground plans of sanctuaries from the general period of 1200-900 B. C. show that the specifications of the Solomonic structure are pre-Greek and authentic and are not anachronistically Hellenic. Like Solomon's Temple, the shrine at Tell Tainat was rectangular with three rooms, a portico with two columns and a cella or shrine with a raised platform. The decorations of the Temple, such as palmettes, cherubim and lilies were characteristically Syro-Phoenician. The cherubim (winged lions with human heads) were inherited from the Tabernacle. Three hybrid animals appear in the iconography hundreds of times between 1800 and 600 B. C. Many representations are found with a deity or king seated on a cherub-supported throne (cf. I Sam. 4:4).

Like the N. Syrian shrine at Tell Tainat, Solomon's Temple had two columns which stood at the portico. These had dynastically significant names, as is now known. Jachin (Heb., "He will establish," that is, "Yahweh will establish thy throne forever"); Boaz (Heb., "In Him is strength," that is, "In Yahweh is the king's strength," or something similar). These pillars have been thought of as stylized trees or sacred obelisks. W. Robertson Smith explained them as gigantic cressets or fire altars, which identification is followed by Albright (*Archaeology and the Religion of Israel*, pp. 144-148), and is suggested by the painted tombs of Marisa in southern Palestine, where such incense burners appear, and by the fact that the two pillars are clearly said to be crowned with a *gullah* or oil basin or a lamp stand (I Kings 7:41). Thus Solomon was highly indebted to Syro-Phoenician art.

12. Apostasy and Death. By intermarriage with many foreign women, Solomon courted spiritual declension and gross idolatry. Of the numerous deities to which his foreign wives turned his heart, perhaps the best known in the ancient world was Ashtoreth, called "the abomination of the Sidonians" (I Kings 11:5, 33), since her cult was early established among the Phoenicians. This fertility goddess, known as Astarte among the Greeks and as Ishtar in Babylonia, was the protagonist of sexual love and war in Babylonia and Assyria. Her degraded moral character is revealed by the Ugaritic literature from Ras Shamra. She is pictured on a seal found at Bethel where her name is given in hieroglyphic characters. Solomon thus courted disaster by this means. He died disillusioned and spiritually insensible, the breakup of the monarchy soon to follow as a result of the folly of his son, Rehoboam.—*M. F. U.*

Sol'omon, Song of. See Canticles.

Sol'omon's Porch. 1. "The porch of judgment" attached to the palace (I Kings 7:7). See Palace. 2. The portico (Gr. *stoa Solomōnos*), the outer corridor of the temple (John 10:23; Acts 3:11; 5:12). See Temple.

Sol'omon's Servants. (Ezra 2:58; Neh. 7:57, 60), the descendants ("sons") of persons thus named returned from captivity. Following as they do in the lists, the priests, Levites, and the Nethinim, they would seem to have some connection with the temple service. Smith (*Bib. Dict.*, s. v.) suggests: 1. The name as well as the order implies inferiority even to the Nethinim. They are descendants of the *slaves* of Solomon. The servitude of the Nethinim, "*given* to the Lord," was softened by the idea of dedication. 2. The starting point of their history is probably found in I Kings 5:13, 14; 9:20, 21; II Chron. 8:7, 8. Canaanites, who had been living till then with a certain measure of freedom, were reduced by Solomon to the Helot state, and compelled to labor in the king's stone quarries, and in building his palaces and cities. To some extent, indeed, the change had been effected under David, but it appears to have been then connected especially with the temple, and the servitude under his successor was at once harder and more extended (I Chron. 22:2). 3. The last passage throws some light on their special office. The Nethinim, as in the case of the Gibeonites, were appointed to be hewers of *wood* (Josh. 9:23), and this was enough for the services of the tabernacle. For the construction and repairs of the temple another kind of labor was required, and the new slaves were set to the work of hewing and squaring *stones* (I Kings 5:17, 18). Their descendants appear to have formed a distinct order, inheriting, probably, the same functions and the same skill.

Sol'omon's Song. *See* Canticles.

Son (Heb. *bēn;* Gr. *huios;* the Child. *bar, son,* occurs in the Old Testament, and appears in the New Testament in such words as Barnabas). "Son" is used in a great variety of meanings in both the Old and New Testaments; (1) the immediate offspring; (2) grandson, as Laban is called son of Nahor (Gen. 29:5), though he was his grandson (24:29); so Mephibosheth is called the son of Saul, though he was the son of Jonathan, Saul's son (II Sam. 19:24); (3) remote descendants (Num. 2:14, 18); (4) son by adoption, as Ephraim and Manasseh to Jacob (Gen., ch. 48); (5) son by nation, as sons of the East (I Kings 4:30; Job 1:3); (6) son by education, i. e., a disciple, as Eli called Samuel his son (I Sam. 3:6). Solomon calls his disciple his son in the Proverbs often, and we read of the "sons of the prophets" (I Kings 20:35, etc.), i. e., those under training for service; similarly a Christian convert (I Tim. 1:2; Tit. 1:4; Philem. 10; I Cor. 4:15, 17; I Pet. 5:13); (7) son by disposition and conduct, as sons of Belial (Judg. 19:22; I Sam. 2:12), sons of the mighty, i. e., heroes (Psa. 29:1); sons of the band (II Chron. 25:13, A. V. "soldiers of the army"), sons of the sorceress, i. e., those who practice sorcery (Isa. 57:3); (8) son in reference to age, as the "son of one year" (Exod. 12:5), i. e., a year old; (9) a production or offspring of any parent, as sparks are called "sons of the burning coal" (Job 5:7, marg.), an arrow is "son of the bow" (41:28), because the arrow flies from the bow; also "son of the quiver" (Lam. 3:13); "son of the floor," i. e., thrashed grain (Isa. 21:10); "sons of oil," i. e., branches of the olive (Zech. 4:14, marg.); expressive of deserving, as son of beating, i. e., deserving beating (Deut. 25:3), so son of perdition (John 17:12); (11) Son of God, by excellence above all, viz., Jesus (Mark 1:1; Luke 1:35; John 1:34; Rom. 1:4; Heb. 4:14); (12) sons of God, i. e., angels (Job 1:6; 38:7), perhaps so called as possessing power delegated from God, his deputies, vicegerents; (13) believers are sons of God (John 1:12; Phil. 2:15, etc.); (14) sons of the world (Luke 16:8), i. e., worldly-minded persons; sons of disobedience, those who are unrestrained in evil; sons of hell (Matt. 23:15); sons of the devil, i. e., under his power (Acts 13:10); sons of the bridechamber (Matt. 9:15; Mark 2:19), the youthful companions of the bridegroom, as in the instance of Samson. Offspring, especially sons, were highly valued among all Eastern nations, and barrenness was regarded as one of the severest afflictions (see Gen. 16:2; 29:31; 30:1, 14, etc.). *See* Children; Family.

Son of God. *See* Sonship of Christ.

Son of Man, Gr. *huios tou anthrōpou.* This is a term, like "the Son of God," which is now theologically chiefly associated with Christ and is used in both the Old and New Testaments. Christ employed this expression to designate Himself some eighty times. It portrays Him as the Representative Man. It designates Him as the "last Adam" in distinction to the "first man Adam" (I Cor. 15:45). It sets Him forth as "the Second Man . . . the Lord from heaven" as over against "the first man . . . of

the earth" (I Cor. 15:47). "The Son of Man" is thus our Lord's racial name, as the "Son of David" is distinctly his Jewish name and "the Son of God" His Divine Name. This term is uniformly used of Christ in connection with His mission (cf. Luke 19:10), His death and resurrection (cf. Matt. 12:40; 20:18; 26:2) and His second advent (cf. Matt. 24:37-44; Luke 12:40). It transcends purely Jewish limitations and has application to the salvation of the entire race. Thus, when Nathaniel owns Christ as "King of Israel" our Lord's reply is, "thou shalt see greater things; the angels of God ascending and descending upon the Son of Man." It is, for example, in this name that universal judgment is committed to our Lord (John 5:22, 27). The term also implies that in Him the O. T. prophetic blessings centering in the coming Man are to find their fulfillment (Gen. 3:15; Psa. 8:4; Isa. 7:14; 9:6, 7; Zech. 13:7). The term "Son of Man" occurs conspicuously in the Book of Ezekiel, being used ninety-two times in addressing the prophet. The thought of going beyond the confines of Judaism is also involved in the phrase when applied to Ezekiel. When Israel was in her captivity, being oblivious of her special mission (Jer. 11:10; Ezek. 5:5-8), the Lord reminds her by this term of address to Ezekiel that He will not forsake her but that nevertheless she is only a small portion of the race for whom He is concerned. As used of Ezekiel, the expression "the son of man" suggests what the prophet is to God, not what he is to himself. As "the son of man" the prophet is chosen, spiritually endowed and delegated by God. These factors are also true of the Messiah as the Representative Man, the new Head of regenerated humanity.— *M. F. U.*

Song (Heb. *shîr;* Gr. *ōdē*). Songs were used on occasions of thanksgiving and triumph, as the song of Moses at the deliverance from Pharoah (Exod. 15:1); the song of Israel at the well of Beer (Num. 21:17); the song of Moses in Deuteronomy (ch. 32); of Deborah (Judg. 5:12); of David on bringing the ark to Jerusalem (I Chron. 13:8); of Hannah (I Sam., ch. 2); of the Virgin Mary (Luke 1:46); the songs in heaven (Rev. 5:9, sq.; 14:3; 15:3, sq.; 19:4, sq.).

Figurative. Songs (*see* Singing) were indicative of joy, and their absence of sorrow. "Ye shall have a song, as in the night" (Isa. 30:29), is a figurative allusion to the joyful singing of the Israelites on the festal night before the passover. "And, lo, thou art unto them as a very lovely song," etc. (Ezek. 33:32), is more correctly rendered, "Thou art unto them like a pleasant singer," etc., i. e., the prophet was like the singer of pleasant songs, to which they listened for pleasure, but without obedience.

Song of Solomon. *See* Canticles.

Sonship of Believers. *See* Adoption.

Sonship of Christ, a matter of doctrine with reference to the divine nature of Christ. It is inwrought with the doctrine of the Trinity (*q. v.*), and in the very nature of the case points to a relationship which in its deepest essence cannot be comprehended by the human understanding (see Matt. 11:27). And yet the Scriptures throw some rays of light on the subject.

1. **Scriptural.** The term Son of God is used in the Scriptures in various senses. In the Old Testament it is sometimes applied to Israel (e. g., Exod. 4:22), also figuratively to heavenly beings (Job 1:6; 38:7). In the New Testament it is also employed in different applications (Luke 3:38; Matt. 5:9, 45). It is in one instance (Luke 1:35) applied to Christ on account of his miraculous conception. And yet it is plain beyond all question that the Scriptures apply this title to Christ in a sense far deeper than all these. Both Christ himself and his apostles speak of his Sonship in a way which cannot be employed with reference to any, even the highest, of God's creatures (see John 3:13, 16; 5:17-31; 6:62; 8:58; 10:30; 14:1, 11; Rom. 1:3, 4; 9:5; Col. 2:9; Tit. 2:13). *See* Kenosis; Word.

2. **Theological.** The doctrine of the Scriptures, universally held by the Christian Church, includes the following features:

(1) The Sonship of Christ involves an antemundane and eternal distinction of personality between the Son and the Father. He is the eternal Son even as the Father is the eternal Father. Thus both Christ and the apostles speak of his preexistent state (John 8:58; 17:5; Rom. 8:3; II Cor. 8:9; Phil. 2:5-8). And thus while he teaches men to pray, saying "Our Father," for himself he simply says "Father," or "My Father" (see John 15:8, and many other places).

(2) The Sonship of Christ implies also that he as the Son "has the ground of his existence in the Father, and as the Father has not in the Son" (see Van Oosterzee, vol. 1, p. 276). Christ is the "only begotten of the Father" (John 1:15, 18), the "only begotten Son" (3:16), "his own Son" (Rom. 8:3). Upon these and similar Scripture expressions is based the doctrine of the eternal generation. This theological term, however, it is rightly held, is one which is liable to abuse, and should never have associated with it anthropomorphistic conceptions, and should exclude all idea of time. The idea to be reverently held is that the Son of God has the ground of his existence eternally in the Father.

(3) The Son is in the most complete sense partaker in the same nature with the Father. He possesses the same attributes (John 5:21; 21:17; Luke 11:49), performs the same works (Matt. 9:2, sq.; John 5:24-29), and claims equal honor with the Father (John 5:23; 14:1; 28:19). As the Son, having the ground of his existence in the Father, he is in this sense subordinate. Also in his incarnate state he became subordinate in a still deeper sense (*see* Kenosis). And yet before his incarnation he "thought it not robbery to be equal with God;" and in his glorified state "in him dwelleth all the fullness of the Godhead bodily."

The doctrine of the eternal Sonship of Christ has been the ground of many hard-fought battles (see particularly Arianism and Sabellianism in works on theology), but the Christian Church steadfastly holds to the teachings of the Scriptures. And the truth at this point is most important; for only in the light of this truth can we recognize in Christ the perfect revelation of God, and realize the efficacy of his saving ministry.—E. McC.

Soothsayer, Soothsaying. *See* Magic, (15).

Sop (Gr. *psōmion, fragment*), a piece of bread dipped into the sauce (John 13:26-30). In the East the animal food is so thoroughly cooked as to be easily separated by the fingers. When, however, the food is in a semifluid state, or so soft that the fingers cannot conveniently hold it, it is conveyed to the mouth by means of a thin piece of bread. It is customary for the host to honor a guest by thus passing to him any dainty morsel. The handing of the "sop" to Judas would indicate that his place at the table must have been near to our Lord.

So'pater (sō'pà-tẽr; *saviour of* his *father*), a disciple of Berea, who accompanied Paul from Greece into Asia, on his return from his third missionary journey (Acts 20:4). In the *Codex Sinaiticus*, and several other manuscripts, his father's name is given as Pyrrhus. It is a question whether or not he is the same with Sosipater (*q. v.*).

Sophe'reth (sŏ-fē'rĕth; *secretariat*, probably denoting an official position). "The children of Sophereth" were a family who returned from Babylon with Zerubbabel, among the descendants of Solomon's servants (Ezra 2:55; Neh. 7:57), B. C. about 536.

Sorcerer, Sorcery. The term sorcerer, from the Latin *sors*, "a lot," "one who throws or declares a lot" would assign it initially the more circumscribed sphere of augural prognostication. But the term, as commonly employed, includes one who practices in the whole field of divinatory occultism. As such, it comprehends a necromancer, who may be classified as a certain type of sorcerer. The appellation "witch," a term which in reality has no proper place in our English Bible, inasmuch as the superstitious ideas popularly associated with this expression involve medieval extravagances, actually refers to a sorcerer. The term "witch" occurs twice in the A. V., and in both cases has been rendered by "sorcerer" and "sorceress" by the Revisers of 1884 (Exod. 22:18; Deut. 18:10). The Hebrew participles, in each case, denote "one who practices magic by using oracular formulas, incantations and mystic mutterings." The term "sorcerer" is, therefore, a better translation of the Hebrew words because it avoids the superstition time has attached to the designation "witch," and is manifestly sufficiently elastic in scope to comprehend the broader range of demonological phenomena categorized under it. The term "witch of Endor" occurs widely in literature and particularly in common parlance, but is not found in the Bible. The epithet has come from the misleading heading and summary of the A. V. This character is defined in I Sam. 28:7 as "a woman who is mistress of a divining spirit." She was, therefore, a sorceress; more precisely, a spiritistic medium or necromancer, not a "witch." Sorcery is thus the practice of the occult arts under the power of evil spirits or demons and has been common in all ages of the world's history. (For a full discussion see Merrill F. Unger, *Biblical Demonology*, 2nd ed., 1953, pp. 143-164).— M. F. U. *See* Magic, (16).

Sore. *See* Diseases.

So′rek (sō′rĕk; *a choice* or *excellent vine*), a valley in which was the home of Delilah (Judg. 16:4). Smith (*Hist. Geog.*, p. 218) identifies it with the present *Wady es Surar*, through which runs the railroad from Joppa to Jerusalem. It is the way the Philistines used to come up in the days of the judges and of David; there is no shorter road into Judea from Ekron, Jamnia, and, perhaps, Ashdod. Just before the Wady es Surar approaches the Judean range its width is increased by the entrance of the Wady en Najil from the south. It was by the level road up the Sorek valley that the ark was taken to Bethshemesh (I Sam. 6:10, sq.). The territory which the Book of Joshua assigns to Dan lies down the two parallel valleys that lead through the Shephelah to the sea, Ajalon and Sorek. The head of the vale of Sorek has usually been regarded as the scene of the battle in which the Philistines took the ark (ch. 4):

Sorrow, the rendering of a number of Hebrew and Greek words, representing mental pain or grief, arising from the privation of some good we actually possessed. It is the opposite of joy; contracts the heart, sinks the spirit, and injures the health. Scripture cautions against it (II Sam. 12:20; Ecclus. 30:24, 25; I Thess. 4:13, etc.). Paul distinguishes two sorts of sorrow: "Godly sorrow worketh repentance to salvation not to be repented of: but the sorrow of the *world* worketh death" (II Cor. 7:10). The one is that sorrow for sin wrought by God which leads to repentance, while the other is a sorrow about worldly objects which, when separated from the fear of God, tends to death, temporal and eternal. Sorrow, in the expression, "The sorrows of hell compassed me about" (Psa. 18:5), may be rendered "the *cords* of the grave," etc.

Sosip′ater (sō-sĭp′ȧ-tẽr; *saver* of his *father*), a kinsman of Paul, mentioned in the salutations of the Epistle to the Romans (16:21) as being with the apostle. He is perhaps the same as Sopater.

Sos′thenes (sŏs′thē-nēz; *of safe strength*).

1. The ruler of the synagogue at Corinth, who was beaten by the Greeks in the presence of Gallio when the latter refused to entertain the charge made to him against Paul (Acts 18:17). Some have thought that he was a Christian, and was maltreated thus by his own countrymen, because he was known as a special friend of Paul. A better view is that Sosthenes was one of the bigoted Jews; and that "the crowd" were Greeks who, taking advantage of the indifference of Gallio, and ever ready to show their contempt of the Jews, turned their indignation against Sosthenes. In this case he must have been the successor of Crispus (v. 8).

2. Paul wrote the First Epistle to the Corinthians jointly in his own name and that of a certain Sosthenes, whom he terms "the brother" (I Cor. 1:1). Some have held that he was identical with the Sosthenes mentioned in the Acts. If this be so, he must have been converted at a later period, and have been at Ephesus, and not at Corinth, when Paul wrote to the Corinthians. The name was a common one, and but little stress can be laid

on that coincidence. Ramsay (*St. Paul*, p. 259) says: "Probably two persons at Corinth named Sosthenes were brought into relations with Paul, one a Jew, the other a prominent Christian; or, perhaps, the Jew was converted at a later date."

So′tai (sō′tī). The "children" of Sotai were a family of the descendants of Solomon's servants who returned with Zerubbabel (Ezra 2:55; Neh. 7:57), B. C. before 536.

Soul (generally the rendering of Heb. *nĕphĕsh*, a *breathing* creature; Gr. *psuchē*, breath, etc., the equivalent of *nĕphĕsh*). The Hebrew term may indicate not only the entire inner nature of man, but also his entire personality, i. e., all that pertains to the person of man; in the sense of person; somebody, everybody (Deut. 26:16; Josh. 10:39; 11:11, 14); and numbers are reckoned, as well in the New Testament as in the Old, by souls (I Pet. 3:20). It would thence be wrongly concluded that the soul is what constitutes the person of man; for the brute is also called *nĕphĕsh*. In *nĕphĕsh*, in itself is not involved the conception of the personal living, but only of the self-living (the individual). In such cases *nĕphĕsh* indicates the person of the man, but not the man as a person. The beast is *nĕphĕsh*, as a self-living nature by the power of the spirit that proceeds from God and pervades the entire nature, the individual constitution of which spirit is the soul of the brute; but man is *nĕphĕsh* "as a self-living nature by the power of the Spirit that proceeds from God, and is in the form of God, and is therefore personal, the operation of which spirit is his endowment with soul" (Delitzsch, *Bib. Psych.*, pp. 181, 182).

The Greek term *psuchē*, has the simple meaning of *life* (Matt. 6:25; Luke 12:22); that in which there is life, a *living being* (I Cor. 15:45); every soul, i. e., *every one* (Acts 2:43; 3:23; Rom. 13:1). It also has the meaning of the seat of the feelings, desires, affections, aversions (our *soul, heart*, etc.; R. V. almost uniformly *soul*); the human soul, in so far as it is so constituted that, by the right use of aids offered it by God, it can attain its highest end and secure eternal blessedness; the soul regarded as a moral being designed for everlasting life (III John 2; Heb. 13:17; James 1:21; 5:20; I Pet. 1:9). Another meaning of *psuchē* is the soul as an essence which differs from the body, and is not dissolved by death (Matt. 10:28); the soul freed from the body, a disembodied soul (Acts 2:27, 31; Rev. 16:3; 20:4). *See* Spirit.

Sour (Heb. *bōsĕr*, *immature*). The proverb, quoted in Jer. 31:29, 30, and Ezek. 18:2, "The fathers have eaten sour grapes, and the children's teeth are set on edge," is easily understood. The sour grapes which the fathers eat are the sins which they commit; the setting of the children's teeth on edge is the consequence thereof, i. e., the suffering which the children have to endure. The teaching of the proverb is that children would have to atone for their fathers' sin, without any culpability of their own. This fatal error is condemned by both Jeremiah and Ezekiel. Jehovah declares with an oath that this proverb shall not be used any more, for their iniquity shall be made manifest; and announces that all souls are his, and he will mete out to each his deserts. In Hosea it is declared of Israel, "their drink is sour" (4:18), i. e., *deteriorated* (Heb. *sūr*), and their rulers (lit. *shields*) love shame, viz., the things that bring shame.

South, the country or quarter of the heavens which the Shemite, standing with his face to the east, supposes to be on his right hand.

1. *Negeb* (Heb. *něgěb*), rendered in A. V. "the south," means literally the *dry* or *parched* land; and probably took its name from the hot, drying winds, which annually blow into Syria from Africa and Arabia. Thus our Lord said (Luke 12:55), "And when ye see the south wind blow, ye say, There will be heat." The word is occasionally applied to a dry tract of land. Caleb's daughter says to her father, "Thou hast given me a south land [i. e., *dry* land]; give me also springs of water" (Judg. 1:15). It is also used in the geographical sense in Num. 34:3; Josh. 15:2; I Chron. 9:24; II Chron. 4:4; Ezek. 40:2; 46:9, etc.

A very important use of the word (Negeb) is as the designation of the regions lying south of Judea, consisting of the deserts of Shur, Zin, and Paran, the mountainous country of Edom or Idumea, and part of Arabia Patrea. The Negeb at present is a part of the Israeli State. It consists of an area about sixty miles square S. of Hebron, extending from N. of Beersheba to S. of Kadesh-barnea. It drops from the Judean highlands to the Arabian desert, its ridges criss-crossing in an E. and W. direction making it throughout the centuries a barrier against trade routes and marching armies. It formed a natural bulwark against southern Judea. Thus, Israel could not enter the Prom-

442. Kur Nub Reservoir in the Negeb

ised Land from the S. because of this formidable obstacle (Deut. 1:42-46). In this rugged terrain David roved as an outlaw (I Sam. 27:5-10). The Amalekites and the Kenites are especially associated with this part of the country (Num. 13:29; I Sam. 27:10). This section later comprised Idumaea or "New Edom." The Negeb was suitable for grazing in patriarchal times (Gen. 20:14). Efforts to occupy and cultivate the Negeb were successful between the fourth and seventh centuries

A. D. Under aggressive control by the Israeli State, the region promises to be developed and "blossom as the rose."—*M. F. U.*

2. A bright, sunny region, hence *the south,* the southern quarter (Ezek. 40:24, sq.; 42:12, sq.; Eccles. 1:6); poetically for the *south wind* (Job 37:17), Heb. *dārōn.*

3. *Teman* (Heb. *tēmän,* what is on the *right* hand), the *south,* the southern quarter (Josh. 12:3; 13:4; Job 9:9; Isa. 43:6); and, perhaps, meaning Egypt (Zech. 6:6). It is used poetically for the *south wind* (Psa. 78:26; Cant. 4:16).

4. *Right* (Heb. *yämin,* the *right* side), the *south,* as "Thou hast made the north and the south" (Psa. 89:12). The word is evidently here used in its widest sense, comprehending not only all the countries lying south, but also the Indian Ocean, etc., the whole hemisphere. In some passages where our translation renders the word *right,* the meaning would have been clearer had it been rendered *south* (II Sam. 24:5; Job 23:9; comp. I Sam. 23:19, 24).

5. *Desert* (Heb. *mīdbār,* "promotion cometh not from the south" (Psa. 75:6), literally "wilderness," as this lay in the South.

6. The Greek words are: (1) *lips* (bringing *moisture*), the quarter of the heavens from which the southwest wind blows (Acts 27:12); (2) *mesēmbria (noon),* but, with respect to locality, *the south* (8:26); (3) *notos,* the southern quarter or wind (Matt. 12:42; Luke 11:31; 13:29; Rev. 21:13).

Sovereignty of God, a term by which is expressed the supreme rulership of God. This is rightly held to be not an attribute of God, but a prerogative based upon the perfections of the divine Being.

The possession of the most complete sovereignty is a necessary part of the proper conception of God, and is abundantly declared in the Scriptures (e. g., Psa. 50:1; 66:7; 93:1; Isa. 40:15, 17; I Tim. 6:15; Rev. 11:17). The method of the divine rulership is, however, to be judged in the light of special revelation. The term absolute sovereignty, as used in Calvinism, means the sovereign election of a certain number to salvation, and the sovereign reprobation of others. There is a sense, indeed, in which the sovereignty of God is absolute. He is under no external restraint whatsoever. He is the Supreme Dispenser of all events. All forms of existence are within the scope of his dominion. And yet this is not to be viewed in any such way as to abridge the reality of the moral freedom of God's responsible creatures, or to make men anything else than the arbiters of their own eternal destinies. God has seen fit to create beings with the power of choice between good and evil. He rules over them in justice and wisdom and grace.

This is the whole tenor of the Scriptures, and the plain declaration of many passages (e. g., Deut. 10:17; Job 36:5; Acts 10:34, 35; Rom. 2:6; Col. 3:25; I Pet. 1:17).

Thus understood the sovereignty of God is the great ground of confidence for his people, and the proper basis upon which to urge sinners to repentance. *See* Election.

For Calvinistic statement, see Hodge, *Syst. Theol.;* for Calvinistic view greatly modified, see Van Oosterzee, *Dogmatics;* for Arminian, see Pope, *Comp. Christ. Doc.;* Miley, *Syst. Theol.;* Watson, *Theol. Inst.*—E. McC.

Sower, Sowing. *See* Agriculture.

Spain (Gr. *Spania*), the name anciently applied to the peninsula which now comprises Spain and Portugal, the usual Greek name being *Iberia*, and the natives were called Iberians. The Carthaginians, during the flourishing times of their republic, established many settlements upon the Spanish coast, such as Carthage (now Cartagena), and Malacca, the royal city (now Malaga). Under the management of Hamilcar Barca and Hannibal a considerable part of Spain became a Carthaginian colony, and gradually passed under the Roman power. The Hebrews were acquainted with the position and mineral wealth of Spain from the time of Solomon.

Paul, in his epistle to the Romans (15:24), tells them of his purpose of visiting Rome whenever he should take his journey into Spain. "Such an intention implies in the plainest way an idea already existent in Paul's mind of Christianity as the religion of the Roman empire." "From" Rome, "the center of the Roman world, Paul would go on to the chief seat of Roman civilization in the west, and would thus complete a first survey" (Ramsay, *St. Paul*, p. 255). Whether the journey was ever made is an open question. *See* Paul.

Span. *See* Metrology.

Spark. In Job 18:5 it is predicated that his light "shall be put out, and the *spark* (Heb. *shābîb, flame*) of his fire shall not shine." *Spark* here probably refers to the lamp hanging in the tent that has gone out (comp. 21:17; 29:3). When misfortune breaks in upon the Arab, he says, "Fate has put out my lamp." The declaration of Eliphaz (Job 5:7) means that "Misfortune does not grow out of the ground like weeds; it is rather established in the divine order of the world, as it is established in the order of nature that sparks of fire should ascend."

In describing the leviathan, it is said (Job 41:19), "Out of his mouth go burning lamps, and sparks of fire leap out." Bartram has observed of the alligator, that as it comes on the land a thick smoke issues from his distended nostrils. This would seem to give the impression of a fire existing beneath, and bursting forth. The Hebrew word is *kîdôd, struck* off. "Sparks" (Isa. 50:11) is the rendering of Heb. *ziqāh* (to *spring*, to *let fly*), and may be understood as *burning arrows*. These are figurative for the blasphemies and anathemas cast at the servant of Jehovah.

Sparrow. *See* Animal Kingdom.

Figurative. "I watch, and am as a sparrow alone upon the house top" (Psa. 102:7) is a figure of loneliness, while our Lord's allusion to God's care for the comparatively worthless sparrow (Matt. 10:29, 31; Luke 12:6, 7) is an incentive for man to trust divine Providence.

Spear. *See* Armor.

Speckled. 1. (Heb. *nāqōd, marked*), spotted, as black goats or sheep, with white spots, or *vice versa* (Gen. 30:32, 33, 35, 39; 31:8, 10, 12). Jacob, in order to increase his wages, resorted to the following plan: "In the first place (30:37-39) he took fresh rods of storax,

maple, and walnut trees, all of which have a dazzling white wood under their dark outside, and peeled white strips upon them. These partially peeled and, therefore, mottled rods he placed in the drinking troughs; . . . in order that if copulation took place at the drinking time, it might occur near the mottled sticks, and the young be speckled and mottled in consequence" (K. and D., *Com.*).

2. (Heb. *ṣābū'ă, dyed*), colored, mottled (Jer. 12:9), elsewhere in modern Hebrew, the *hyena*, but in the above passage a *many-colored bird of prey*.

3. (Heb. *sārŭq*), *red* in color, as the horses (Zech. 1:8). *See* Color.

Spectacle (Gr. *theatron*), one to be gazed at and made sport of (I Cor. 4:9).

Spelt, an inferior kind of wheat (Exod. 9:32; Isa. 28:25). *See* Vegetable Kingdom.

Spice. The spices mentioned as being used by Nicodemus for the preparation of our Lord's body (John 19:39, 40) are "myrrh and aloes," by which latter word must be understood, not the aloes of medicine (*Aloe*), but the highly-scented wood of the *Aquilaria agallochum*. The evangelist John computes the amount at one hundred litres (A. V. "pounds"), referring doubtless to the Roman pound of about twelve ounces. This would make seventy-five pounds avoirdupois. The amount mentioned may seem large, but Josephus (*Ant.*, 17, 8, 3) tells us that there were five hundred spice-bearers at Herod's funeral; and in the Talmud it is said that eighty pounds of opobalsamum were employed at the funeral of a certain rabbi. It must also be remembered that Nicodemus was a rich man. The ancient Bible world enjoyed an extensive trade in spices. Caravan routes by which aromatic vegetable substances were transported from one country to another, particularly across Arabia, became highways for the spread of culture. Spice trade rivalled the modern perfume and cosmetic industry. *See* Vegetable Kingdom.

Spider. *See* Animal Kingdom.

Figurative. Bildad compares the trust of the ungodly and secretly wicked (Heb. *hānēph*, A. V. "hypocrite") to a spider's web (Job 8:14); as easily as a spider's web is cut through, by the lightest touch or a breath of wind, so that on which the evil man depends and trusts is cut asunder. In Prov. 30:28 the spider is introduced as one of the instances of instinctive sagacity and providence; tolerated, even in palaces, to destroy flies. To "take hold with her hands" means to use with activity the limbs provided for taking prey. In the declaration of Isaiah (59:5), they "weave the spider's web," we have a figure to represent the worthlessness and deceptive character of the works of the wicked.

Spikenard. *See* Vegetable Kingdom.

Spin (Heb. *ṭāwäh;* Gr. *nēthō*, Exod. 35:25, 26; Matt. 6:28; Prov. 31:19). The latter passage implies (according to the A. V.) the use of the same instruments which have been in vogue for hand spinning down to the present day, viz., the distaff and spindle. The distaff, however, appears to have been dispensed with, and the term so rendered means the spindle itself, while that rendered "spindle" represents the *whirl* of the spindle, a button of circular rim which was affixed to it, and gave steadiness to its circular motion. The "whirl" of the Syrian women was made of amber in the time of Pliny. The spindle was held perpendicularly in the one hand, while the other was employed in drawing out the thread.

Spindle (Heb. *kishôr, director*), the *twirl* or lower part of the instrument used in giving motion to the whole (Prov. 31:19). In the East it is held in the hand, often perpendicularly, and is twirled with one hand, while the other draws out the thread. The spindle and distaff are the most *ancient* of all the instruments used for *spinning*, or making thread.

Spirit (Heb. *rûaḥ, breath, wind;* Gr. *pneuma, wind, breath,* the *vital principle,* etc.), a term used in the Scriptures generally to denote purely spiritual beings, also the spiritual, immortal part in man. Other terms *nĕphĕsh; psuchē*) refer to the animal soul or life of man, though it seems evident that these words are also used frequently in a broader and deeper sense with reference to man's spiritual nature (e. g., Gen. 2:7; Psa. 42:2; Matt. 10:28; 11:29). *See* Soul. There are, however, passages (as I Thess. 5:23; Heb. 4:12) which emphasizes a distinction between soul and spirit.

The term soul specifies that in the immaterial part of man which concerns life, action and emotion. Spirit is that part related to worship and divine communion. The two terms are often used interchangeably, the same functions being ascribed to each (cf. John 12:27; I Cor. 16:18; II Cor. 7:13 with Matt. 11:29; II Cor. 7:1 with I Pet. 2:11; Jas. 5:20 with I Cor. 5:5; I Pet. 4:5). The deceased are mentioned both as soul and sometimes as spirit (Gen. 25:18; I Kings 17:21; John 10:17; Acts 2:27; Rev. 24 with Matt. 27:50; John 19:30; Acts 5:5; Heb. 12:23). However, *soul* and *spirit* as synonymous terms are not always employed interchangeably. The soul is said to be lost, for example, but not the spirit. When no technical distinctions are set forth, the Bible is *dichotomous,* but otherwise it is *trichotomous.* (cf. Matt. 10:28; Acts 2:31; Rom. 8:10; Eph. 4:4; Jas. 2:26; I Pet. 2:11). Theologians have poured over these distinctions ceaselessly. The origin of man's immaterial nature is subject to three theories: (1) The *creational,* maintaining that *soul and spirit* are created at birth. (2) *Traducian. Soul and spirit* are generated the same as the body. (3) The soul is pre-existent, embracing the idea of transmigration of souls.— *M. F. U.*

Spirit, The Holy. *See* Spirit, The Holy.

Spirits, Discerning of. *See* Discerning of Spirits.

Spiritual Gifts (Gr. *ta pneumatika,* the spiritual supply; *charismata, gifts*), a phrase to denote the endowments bestowed by the Holy Spirit in the primitive Church (I Cor. 12:1), and the same as "gifts" (v. 4). A *spiritual gift* "means any extraordinary faculty, which operated for the furtherance of the welfare of the Christian community, and which was itself wrought by the grace of God, through the power of the Holy Spirit, in special individuals, in accordance, respectively, with the measure of their individual capacities, whether it were that the Spirit infused entirely new powers, or stimulated those already

existing to higher power and activity (Rom. 12:6, sq.)" (Meyer, *Com.,* I Cor. 12:1). These gifts included *word of wisdom, knowledge; faith; healing; working of miracles; prophecy; discerning of spirits; tongues* and their *interpretation* (vers. 8-10). See under various heads.

Spirituality, the quality of being spiritual, as opposed to material. Thus theology predicates spirituality of God (*see* Spirit). The spirituality of man refers to the immaterial part of his nature. The term is also used with reference to the disposition or internal condition of men when in such a state as prepares them to recognize and properly appreciate spiritual realities. True spirituality in the last sense is the result of the inworking of the Holy Spirit (see I Cor. 2:14, 15; 3:1, 16, et al.). In an ecclesiastical sense the term is used in the Church of England to denote the whole body of the clergy, with reference to the nature of their office.

Spit, Spittle (Heb. from *râqaq; yâraq,* Num. 12:14; Deut. 25:9; Gr. *ptusma*), a source of legal defilement; e. g., the spittle of a person having an issue defiled the one upon whom it fell (Lev. 15:8). To spit in one's face was regarded as the grossest insult (Num. 12:14; Deut. 25:9; Isa. 50:6; Matt. 26:67; 27:30); indeed it was a great indignity to spit toward anyone, so that an oriental never allows himself to spit in the presence of one whom he respects. Spittle was employed by our Lord in the cure of the blind man (John 9:6), and the rabbins cite it as a remedy in like cases, especially the spittle of persons who were fasting.

Spoil, the rendering of a number of Hebrew and Greek words, consisted of captives of both sexes, cattle, and whatever a captured city might contain, especially metallic treasures. Within the limits of Canaan no captives were to be made (Deut. 20:14, 16); beyond those limits, in case of warlike resistance, all the women and children were to be made captives, and the men put to death. The law of booty was that it should be divided equally between the army who won it and the people of Israel, but of the former half one head in every five hundred was reserved to God and appropriated to the priests, and of the latter one in every fifty was similarly reserved and appropriated to the Levites (Num. 31:26-47; comp. II Sam. 8:10, sq.; I Chron. 26:27, sq.). A portion of the spoil was assigned to the oppressed, the aged, widows, and orphans (II Macc. 8:28, 30). As regarded the army, David added a regulation that the baggage guard should share equally with the troops engaged (I Sam. 30:24, 25). The division of the spoil was a joyous feast for the people (Isa. 9:2).

Spoke, an incorrect rendering of Heb. *ḥĭshshûr,* which rather means the *hub,* where the spokes unite (I Kings 7:33).

Sponge. *See* Animal Kingdom.

Spoon. *See* Tabernacle.

Sport. The expression, "Against whom do ye sport yourselves?" (Isa. 57:4) may well be rendered "Over whom do ye make yourselves merry?" *See* Games.

Spot. 1. A *blemish* (Heb. *mûm*), and usually so rendered, either *physical* (Lev. 21:17, sq.; 22:20; 24:19, 20, etc.; II Sam. 14:25; Cant.

4:7); or *moral* (Deut. 32:5; Job 11:15; 31:7; Prov. 9:7).

2. A *whitish* spot on the skin, the "bright spot" of incipient leprosy (Lev. 13:2-39; 14:56). Heb. *bōḥĕrĕth*.

3. (Heb. *bōḥăq*, to be *pale*), the "freckled spot" of pronounced leprosy (Lev. 13:39).

4. The mark upon the panther, (Heb. *ḥăbărbūrāh, a streak*), or, according to Gesenius, the stripes of the tiger (Jer. 13:23), used as an illustration of the inability of men to rid themselves of evil character.

5. (Heb. *tālā', to cover with *pieces*), spotted, variegated; as "sheep or goats" (Gen. 30:32-39; Ezek. 16:16, A. V. "divers colors").

6. In Heb. 9:14 Jesus is said to have "through the eternal Spirit, offered himself without spot to God" (Gr. *'amōmos*), i. e., in an ethical sense, without blemish, fault. The Gr. (*spilos, spot*) has also a moral sense of *fault* (Eph. 5:27); and its negative form (*'aspilos*) means *spotless*, free from *censure* (I Tim. 6:14), from *vice*, and so *unsullied* (II Pet. 3:14).

Spouse. *See* Marriage.

Spreadings (Heb. *mĭphräs*, an *expansion*). "Also can any understand the spreading of the clouds?" (Job 36:29). Here *spreading* does not mean bursting, but spreadings (comp. Ezek. 27:7). "It is the growth of the storm clouds, which collect often from a beginning 'small as a man's hand' (I Kings 18:44), that is intended."

Sprinkling. Instances of sprinkling are given in the Scriptures, viz., with *blood* (Exod. 29:16, 20, 21; Lev. 1:5, 11, etc.); *see* Sacrifice; with *water* (Lev. 14:51; Num. 8:7; 19:13, 20, etc.); with *oil* (Lev. 14:16). *See* Anointing.

Figurative. "So shall he sprinkle many nations" (Isa. 52:15) would seem to be a figure setting forth the expiation and purifying of many nations; and then the antithesis would be: *Many* were astonished; so *many* (not merely men, but) *nations* shall be sprinkled. They were amazed that such an abject person claimed to be the Messiah; yet it is He that shall justify and cleanse. Many commentators understand the phrase as meaning "He shall cause many nations to leap with astonishment." "The figurative expression, 'to sprinkle with clean water' (Ezek. 36:25), is taken from the lustrations prescribed by the law, more particularly the purifying from defilement by the dead by sprinkling with the water prepared from the ashes of a red heifer" (Num. 19:17-19; comp. Psa. 51:9). "Having our hearts cleansed from an evil conscience" (Heb. 10:22) stands over by contrast with mere physical cleansing (Heb. 9:13, 19; comp. Exod. 24:8; Lev. 8:11). As the Old Testament covenant people were sprinkled with the (cleansing) blood of the sacrifice, so are Christians *sprinkled* by the blood of Christ, and their consciences delivered from the sense of guilt.

Sta'chys (stā'kĭs; an *ear*, i. e., of grain), a Christian at Rome to whom Paul sent salutations, calling him "my beloved" (Rom. 16:9). According to an old tradition recorded by Niceporus Callistus, he was bishop of Byzantium. He is said by Hippolytus and Dorotheus to have been one of the seventy disciples.

Stacte. *See* Vegetable Kingdom.

Staff (Heb. *măṭṭĕh, măqqēl, shēbĕṭ;* Gr. *hrabdos;* all meaning a *stick*). Rods and staffs were employed for different purposes by the ancients, as with us. Men and women were goaded with them (Exod. 21:20; Num. 22:27; I Sam. 17:43, etc.); grain was sometimes beaten with them (Judg. 6:11; Ruth 2:17; Isa. 28:27); they were used by old and infirm persons for support or defense (Exod. 21:19; Zech. 8:4), also by travelers (Gen. 32:10; Exod. 12:11; II Kings 4:29; Matt. 10:10). A staff, like a *seal*, was a sign of rank (Gen. 38:18, 25), sometimes inscribed with the owner's name; also a badge of office (Exod. 4:2, sq.; Num. 20:8, etc.). The staff of the shepherd was used to aid in climbing hills, beating bushes and low brush in which the flock strayed, and where snakes and reptiles abounded.

Stair (Hebrew usually *mă'ălĕh*, or *mă'ălāh*, an *ascent;* once *mădrēgäh*, Cant. 2:14, a *precipice*, "steep place," Ezek. 38:20; *lūl*, a winding stair, I Kings 6:8). The stairs probably ran around the inside of the quadrangle of the house, as they do still, e. g., in the ruin called "the house of Zaccheus" at Jericho. Respecting the meaning of II Kings 9:13, *see* Jehu.

Stake (Heb. *yăthēd*, a *peg*), a peg or nail, and often so rendered; especially a *tent pin* (Isa. 33:20; 54:2). In the former passage the idea of continuance and permanency is figured by a tent that is not moved, nor its pegs drawn. The enlargement and strengthening of Zion is illustrated by a tent, the inside space of which is widened, and the tent pins driven deeper into the ground.

Stall, the rendering of Hebrew and Greek words signifying a *stable* or cattle (Amos 6:4 ; Mal. 4:2). A "stalled ox" (Prov. 15:17) is one that is fattened. "Stalls" is used in the sense of *pairs*, as of horses (I Kings 4:26; II Chron. 9:25; 38:28). The expression, "There shall be no herds in the stall" (Hab. 3:17) is used to denote calamity, disaster. Stables containing stalls for horses have been excavated, particularly those for Solomon's horses at Megiddo.

Stammerer (Heb. *'llēg*, a *stutterer*, Isa. 32:4; *lä'ăg*, properly, to *speak unintelligibly*, Isa. 28:11; 33:19), hence to *mock* or deride.

Standard. *See* Ensign.

Star (Heb. *kōkäb, round* or *shining;* Gr. *'astēr*).

1. Under the term stars the Hebrews included constellations, planets, indeed all the heavenly bodies except the sun and moon. In fact the ancient Hebrews knew very little of the starry heavens, and no indications are given in Scripture of scientific astronomy (*q. v.*). We find there only the ordinary observations of landsmen (Amos 5:8), especially hepherds (Psa. 8:3).

Figurative. The patriarchs observed the stars (Gen. 37:9); and metaphors drawn from the starry world, either with reference to the countless number of the stars (Gen. 22:17; Exod. 32:13; Nah. 3:16, etc.) or to their brightness (Num. 24:17; Isa. 14:12; Rev. 22:16) came into frequent and early use. The Psalmist, to exalt the power and omniscience of Jehovah, represents him as taking a survey of the stars, as a king reviewing his army (Psa. 147:4). Stars were frequently employed as symbols of persons in exalted stations; e. g., "the star out of Jacob" designates King David (Num. 24:17), applied by some to the Messiah. The patriarchs were called "stars" (Gen. 37:9), and "stars" denote the princes, rulers, and nobles of the earth (Dan. 8:10; Rev. 6: 13; 8:10-12; 9:1; 12:4). Christ is called the "Morning Star," as he introduced the light of Gospel day, revealing more fully the truths of God than the ancient prophets. The study of the stars led to their worship (*see* Idolatry), and to calculations of human affairs (*see* Astrology).

2. Star in the East (Matt. 2:2), seen by the wise men (Magi) on their journey to Jerusalem, and as they approached Bethlehem. After ascertaining at what time they first observed the star, Herod sent them to Bethlehem, with the request to inform him when they found the child. As they left Jerusalem the star which had attracted their attention at its "rising" (Gr. *'anatolē*), and which, it would appear, they had not seen of late, once more appeared. In ancient times such guidance by a star was a matter of belief and expectancy; and "they rejoiced with exceeding great joy."

This phenomenon has been generally understood to be some supernatural light resembling a star, that appeared in some country far to the east of Jerusalem, to men who were versed in the study of celestial phenomena; and that it conveyed to their minds an impulse to travel to Jerusalem to find a newborn king. However, by some scholars the star has been removed from the category of supernatural events, and has been referred to the ordinary astronomical phenomenon of a conjunction of the planets Jupiter and Saturn.

Star Gazer (Isa. 47:13). *See* Magic.

Stately (Heb. *kᵉbŭddāh, magnificent*). In speaking of the ungodly alliance between Judah and Chaldea, the former sent ambassadors to Chaldea, and, for the purpose of receiving the Chaldeans, adorned herself as a woman would do for the reception of her paramours. She seated herself upon "a stately bed" (Ezek. 23:41), i. e., a *splendid divan*, and in front of this there was a table spread, upon which stood the incense and the oil that she ought to have offered to Jehovah.

Stature (Gr. *hēlikos*, literally *how much?*).

1. "Which of you by taking thought can add one cubit unto his stature?" (Matt. 6:27). "Stature" here is usually taken in the sense of the height of one's body, but others think it refers to the *life* itself; according to this view the duration of life determined by God is set forth under the figure of a definite lineal measure. This is more appropriate, it is claimed, for the admonition is directed against excessive anxiety about food and clothing, which, though necessary to the preservation of life, have nothing in common with stature.

2. "Stature" in Eph. 4:13 is the *age suitable* for anything; figuratively of an attained state of mind fit for a thing, and so the age in which we are fitted to receive the fullness of Christ.

Staves. *See* Staff; Tabernacle.

Stay, in the A. V. of Isa. 19:13, "even they that are the stay of the tribes thereof," is the rendering of the Heb. *pĭnnäh*, an *angle;* and the passage may be rendered "the princes of Zoan . . . the corner stones of the castes" of Egypt. Instead of supporting and defending their people, they now only led them astray. In Isa. 31:1, "stay" is used in the sense of *rely* (comp. 48:2). In the description of Solomon's throne (I Kings 10:19; II Chron. 9:18), "stays" is the rendering of the Heb. *yäd* (*hand*), i. e., arms on both sides of the seat.

Steadfastness. 1. Gr. *stereōma*. That upon which a thing can rest; in Col. 2:5, "steadfastness of faith," the term is used figuratively in a military sense, *solid front*.

2. *Stērigmos* (II Pet. 3:17), in the usual sense of *stability*.

Steel. *See* Metals; Mineral Kingdom.

Steph'anas (stĕf'á-năs; *crown*), a Corinthian disciple whose household Paul baptized (I Cor. 1:16), being the first converted to Christianity in Achaia, and one of those who "addicted themselves to the ministry of the saints" (16:15). Just the form that this ministry took we have no precise information. He appears to have been with Paul when he wrote his first letter to the Corinthians (16: 17).

Ste'phen (stē'fĕn). 1. **Name** (Gr. *Stephanos*, a *crown*).

2. **Personal History.** Stephen, as his Greek name seems to indicate, was probably of Hellenistic origin. Where or when born, however, we have no means of ascertaining. (1) **As deacon.** The first authentic account we have of Stephen is in Acts 6:5. In the distribution of the common fund that was intrusted to the apostles for the support of the poorer brethren, the Hellenists complained that a partiality was shown to the natives of Palestine, and their widows were neglected. The apostles, hearing of the complaint, took measures immediately to remove the cause of it. Unwilling themselves to be taken from the work of the ministry, they advised the church to select seven men of honest report, full of the Holy Spirit and wisdom, for this business (v. 3). The brethren proceeded immediately to select the prescribed number, among whom Stephen is first mentioned. The newly elected deacons were brought to the apostles, who ordained them to their work (v. 6). From the first Stephen occupied a prominent position. He is described as "a man full of faith and of the Holy Ghost" (v. 5), "full of faith and power" (v. 8), and of irresistible "wisdom and spirit" (v. 10). He attracted attention by the "great wonders and miracles" which he did among the people. (2) **His teaching.** From his foreign descent and education he was naturally led to address himself to the Hellenistic Jews. In these disputations he probably took more advanced grounds than the apostles had respecting the discontinuance and abrogation of the Mosaic system, contending that already it had, as a ritual system, lost all force and binding obligation by its complete fulfillment in Christ. Certain adherents of several synagogues were leaders in the disputation with Stephen. (3) **Arrest.** Unable to withstand his reasoning, they caused his arrest, appearing against him before the Sanhedrin with false witnesses. The charge against him was *blasphemy*, in speaking "against this

holy place and the law" (v. 13). Stephen doubtless saw that he was to be the victim of the blind and malignant spirit which had been exhibited by the Jews in every period of their history. Yet he stood serene, collected, and undismayed. "And all that sat in the council . . . saw his face as it had been the face of an angel" (v. 15), from which we may not unreasonably conclude that it pleased God to manifest his approbation of his servant by investing his countenance with a supernatural and angelic brightness, such as that with which the face of Moses shone when he had been speaking with the Lord. (4) **His defense.** The high priest that presided asked the judicial question, "Are these things so?" To this Stephen replied in a speech which has every appearance of being faithfully reported. He began with the call of Abraham, and traveled historically in his argument through all the stages of their national existence, evidently designing to prove that the presence and favor of God had not been confined to the holy land or the temple of Jerusalem. He also showed that there was a tendency from the earliest times toward the same ungrateful and narrow spirit that had appeared in this last stage of their political existence. He then suddenly broke away from his narrative and denounced them as "stiff-necked and uncircumcised in heart and ears," and as "always resisting the Holy Ghost." The effect upon his hearers was terrible; "they were cut to the heart, and gnashed on him with their teeth." On the other hand Stephen, filled with the Holy Spirit, was granted a vision of the glory of God, and Jesus at his right hand, risen to meet and welcome his spirit as it should escape his mangled body, and to introduce him into the presence of his Father, and to a crown of unfading glory. (5) **His martyrdom.** Enraptured, he exclaimed, "Behold, I see the heavens opened, and the Son of man standing on the right hand of God!" The fate of Stephen was settled, for his judges broke into a loud yell, stopped their ears, ran upon him with one accord, dragged him out of the city to the place of execution. Saul was present and consented to his death. In striking contrast to the fearful rage of his enemies was the spirit shown by Stephen. First offering a petition for himself, he then prays, "Lay not this sin to their charge," and, in the beautiful language of Scripture, *"fell asleep"* (7:60). "Devout men carried Stephen to his burial, and made great lamentation over him" (8:2), A. D. 34.

NOTE.—1. *The trial.* The trial of Stephen appears to have been irregular, and the judicial act was not completed. There are, indeed, the witnesses, and part of the prisoner's defense; and here the legal action stops. The high priest does not, as in our Lord's trial, ask the opinion of the council, and then deliver sentence in accordance with their views. The whole proceedings broke up with a tumult at what they deemed the blasphemy of Stephen. 2. *Saul consenting.* The witnesses against Stephen acted as his executioners (Deut. 17:7; John 8:7), and laid their outer garments for safety at the feet of Saul. One of the prominent leaders in the transaction was deputed by custom to signify his assent to the act by taking the clothes into his custody.

Steward (usually Heb. *săr, head* person; Gr. *epitropos, manager; oikonomos, overseer*), a manager or superintendent of another's household,

as Eliezer over the house of Abraham (Gen. 15:2). We read also of Joseph's steward (43: 19; 44:1, 4); "stewards over all the substance and possession of the king," David (I Chron. 28:1); of Tirzah (I Kings 16:9); and of Herod (Luke 8:3). As great confidence was reposed in these officials, Paul describes Christian ministers as the stewards of God over his Church (Tit. 1:7; comp. I Cor. 4:1, 2). Believers are also said to be stewards of God, of God's gifts and graces (I Pet. 4:10).

Stock. The rendering of several Hebrew and Greek words, meaning: the *trunk* of a tree (Isa. 44:19; Job 40:20, A. V. "food"); the *stump* (Job 14:8; 40:24, A. V. "stock"), or *trunk* (Isa. 11:1, A. V. "stem"); a *tree* or piece of *wood* (Jer. 2:27; 10:8); a plant *transplanted* (Acts 13:26; Phil. 3:5), race or *kindred;* a *gazingstock* (Nah. 3:6).

Stocks. 1. (Heb. *măhpĕkĕth, wrench;* Jer. 20:2, 3; II Chron. 16:10, A. V. "prison," literally *the house of the stocks*), a wooden frame in which the feet, hands, and neck of a person were so fastened that his body was held in a bent position.

2. The block or log of wood in which the feet of a criminal are fastened, and which he must drag about with him when he moves (Job 13:27; 33:11), Heb. *săd.*

3. An ankle band. The rendering of Prov. 7:22 may be "as one bound in fetters (goeth) to the punishment of the fool" (Heb. *'ĕkĕs, fetter*).

4. A *prison;* or, better, *stocks* proper, or some other confinement for the feet (Jer. 29:26), Heb. *ṣinōq.* Orelli (*Com.,* in loc.) thinks that the *ṣinōq* was a kind of *neck iron* (comp. Arab. *zinak,* neck chain).

5. Gr. *xulon, wood,* a log with holes in which the feet, hands, and neck of prisoners were inserted and fastened with thongs (Acts 16:24); probably similar to *Sad,* 2.

Stocks has an altogether different meaning in Hos. 4:12, "My people ask counsel at their stocks" (Heb. *'ēṣ*). The stocks here referred to were idols made of wood (comp. Jer. 10:3; Hab. 2:19).

Sto'ics (stō'ĭks). The Stoics and Epicureans, who are mentioned together in Acts 17:18, represent the two opposite schools of practical philosophy which survived the fall of higher speculation in Greece. The Stoic school was founded by Zeno of Citium (about B. C. 280), and derived its name from the painted "portico" (*stoa*) in which he taught. Zeno was followed by Cleanthes (about B. C. 260), Cleanthes by Chrysippus (about B. C. 240), who was regarded as the intellectual founder of the Stoic system. Stoicism soon found an entrance at Rome, and under the empire Stoicism was not unnaturally connected with republican virtue. The ethical system of the Stoics has been commonly supposed to have a close connection with Christian morality. But the morality of Stoicism is essentially based on pride, that of Christianity on humility; the one upholds individual independence, the other absolute faith in another; the one looks for consolation in the issue of fate, the other in Providence; the one is limited by periods of cosmical ruin, the other is consummated in a personal resurrection (Acts 17:18). (Smith, *Dict.*).

Stomacher (Heb. *p⁽e⁾thîgîl*), an article (Isa. 3:24) of female dress (*q. v.*).

Stone (usually Heb. *'ĕbĕn;* Gr. *lithos*).

1. **Kinds.** The ordinary stones mentioned as found in *Palestine* (*q. v.*) are chiefly lime-stone (Isa. 27:9), especially marble and sand-stone; basalt (Josephus, *Ant.*, viii, 7, 4); flint and firestone (II Macc. 10:3).

2. **Uses.** Stones were applied in ancient Palestine to many uses:

(1) They were used for the ordinary purposes of building, and in this respect the most noticeable point is the very large size to which they occasionally run (Mark 13:1). Robinson gives the dimensions of one as twenty-four feet long by six feet broad and three feet high. For most public edifices hewn stones were used; an exception was made in regard to altars (Exod. 20:25; Deut. 27:5; Josh. 8:31). The Phoenicians were particularly famous for their skill in hewing stone (II Sam. 5:11; I Kings 5:18). Stones were selected of certain colors in order to form ornamental string-courses (I Chron. 29:2). They were also employed for pavements (II Kings 16:17; comp. Esth. 1:6).

(2) Large stones were used for closing the entrances of caves (Josh. 10:18; Dan. 6:17), sepulchers (Matt. 27:60; John 11:38; 20:1), and springs (Gen. 29:2).

(3) Flint stones (Heb. *ṣūr*, or *ṣōr*), occasionally served the purpose of a knife, particularly for circumcision and similar objects (Exod. 4:25; Josh. 5:2, 3).

(4) Stones were further used as a munition of war for slings (I Sam. 17:40, 49), catapults (II Chron. 26:14), and bows (Wisd. 5:22; comp. I Macc. 6:51); as boundary marks (Deut. 19:14; 27:17; Job 24:2; Prov. 22:28; 23:10); such were probably the stone of Bohan (Josh. 15:6; 18:17), of Abel (I Sam. 6:15, 18), the stone Ezel (20:19), the great stone by Gibeon (II Sam. 20:8), and the stone Zoheleth (I Kings 1:9); also as weights for scales (Deut. 25:13; Prov. 16:11), and for mills (II Sam. 11:21).

(5) Large stones were set up to commemorate any remarkable event (Gen. 28:18; 31:45; 35:14; Josh. 4:9; I Sam. 7:12). Such stones were occasionally consecrated by anointing (Gen. 28:18). A similar practice existed in heathen countries, and by a singular coincidence these stones were described in Phoenicia by a name very similar to Beth-el, viz., *baetylia*. The only point of resemblance between the two consists in the custom of anointing.

(6) That the worship of stones prevailed among the heathen nations surrounding Palestine, and was from them borrowed by apostate Israelites, appears from Isa. 57:6 (comp. Lev. 26:1). "The smooth stones of the stream" are those which the stream has washed smooth with time, and rounded into a pleasing shape. "In Carthage such stones were called *abbadires;* and among the ancient Arabs the *asnâm*, or idols, consisted for the most part of rude blocks of stone of this description . . . Stone worship of this kind had been practiced by the Israelites before the captivity, and their

heathenish practices had been transmitted to the exiles in Babylon" (Delitzsch, *Com.* in loc.).

(7) Heaps of stones were piled up on various occasions; the making of a treaty (Gen. 31:46); over the grave of a notorious offender (Josh. 7:26; 8:29; II Sam. 18:17); such heaps often attaining a great size from the custom of each passer-by adding a stone.

(8) Stones were used for tablets (Exod. 24:12; Josh. 8:32) and guide stones to the cities of refuge (*q. v.*).

(9) "A time to cast away stones, and a time to gather stones" (Eccles. 3:5) seems to refer to the custom of spoiling an enemy's field by throwing stones upon it (II Kings 3:19, 25); and the clearing a field of stones preparatory to its cultivation (Isa. 5:2).

Figurative. Stones are used figuratively to denote *hardness* or *insensibility* (I Sam. 25:37; Ezek. 11:19; 36:26), or *firmness*, *strength* (Gen. 49:24), where "the stone of Israel" is equivalent to "the rock of Israel" (II Sam. 23:3; Isa. 30:29). Christians are called "living stones," i. e., not like the inanimate *things* of the material temple, but *living men* built up on Christ, the living and chief corner stone. "I will make Jerusalem a burdensome stone for all people" (Zech. 12:3) may be a figure founded upon the labor connected with building, the heavy stones of which hurt those who attempt to carry them away. The "white stone" (Rev. 2:17) has been understood as referring to the pebble of acquittal used in the Greek courts; to the lot cast in elections in Greece; to the white stone given to the victors at the Grecian games; and to the stones of hospitality usual in ancient times, a "sort of *carte blanche*, entitling the person who showed it to ask for and receive what he might want." Precious stones (*q. v.*) are used in Scripture in a figurative sense to signify value, beauty, durability, etc., in those objects with which they are compared (see Cant. 5:14; Isa. 54:11, 12; Lam. 4:7; Rev. 4:3; 21:11, 21). *See* Stone.

Stoning. *See* Punishment.

Stool (Heb. *'ōbnăyim*, a *pair of stones*, as a *potter's wheel*, is used of a low stool, so called from its resemblance to a potter's wheel). A chair of peculiar form upon which a Hebrew woman sat during childbirth (Exod. 1:16).

Storax. *See* Vegetable Kingdom.

Store City (I Kings 9:19; II Chron. 8:4, 6; 16:4; 17:12; "treasure city," Exod. 1:11; storehouse, II Chron. 32:28), a place of deposit for merchandise and provisions.

Storehouse, the rendering of several original terms, meaning a *treasury* (I Chron. 27:25; Psa. 38:7; Mal. 3:10, as elsewhere rendered); a *receptacle* for provisions (Deut. 38:8; "barn" in Prov. 3:10), usually underground in the East; a *granary* (Jer. 50:26; comp. Exod. 1:11; Luke 12:24). The Egyptians had storehouses for stuffs and jewels, gold, preserved fruits, grain, liquors, armour, provisions, etc. Their grain storehouses had only two openings, one top for pouring in the grain, another on the ground level for drawing it out. For the security and management of these there were employed troops of porters, storekeepers, accountants, "primates," who superintended the works, record keepers, and directors. Great nobles coveted the administration of the storehouses, and even the sons of kings did not think it derogatory to their dignity to be entitled "directors of the granaries" or "directors of the armory." ●

Stork. *See* Animal Kingdom.

Straight Street, one of the ancient thoroughfares of Damascus, on which was located the house of Judas, where Paul was visited by Ananias (Acts 9:11). It still retains the same name in an Arabic form (*Derb el-Mustakim*), running westward from the Bab es-Shurky, or East Gate. Its length was about one English mile, and its breadth about one hundred feet. It is not *quite* straight now, nor is its architecture imposing.

Strain. *See* Gnat, in Animal Kingdom.

Stranger. *See* Foreigner.

Strangle (Heb. *ḥănăq,* to *choke;* Gr. *pnigō*). It was forbidden by Moses, and also by the primitive Christians, to eat animals put to death by strangulation, not having the blood properly removed (Gen. 9:4; Acts 15:20).

Straw (Heb. *tĕbĕn;* "chaff" in Jer. 33:28; "stubble" in Job 21:18). Both wheat and barley straw were used by the ancient Hebrews chiefly as fodder for their horses, cattle, and camels (Gen. 24:25; I Kings 4:28; Isa. 11:7; 65:25). There is no intimation that straw was used for litter. It was employed by the Egyptians for making bricks (Exod. 5:7, 16), being chopped up and mixed with the clay to make them more compact and to prevent their cracking. This is abundantly illustrated by archaeology. The ancient Egyptians reaped their corn close to the ear, and afterward cut the straw close to the ground and laid it by. This Pharoah refused to give to the Israelites. *See* Vegetable Kingdom.

Stream of Egypt occurs once in the A. V. instead of "the river of Egypt" (Isa. 27:12). *See* River of Egypt.

Striker (Gr. *plēktēs*), a pugnacious, contentious, quarrelsome fellow (I Tim. 3:3; Tit. 1:7).

Stringed Instruments. *See* Music.

Stripes. *See* Punishment.

Strong Drink. *See* Drink, Strong.

Stubble. 1. The dry portion of grain; left standing in the fields (Exod. 5:12), and then burned over (Exod. 15:7; Isa. 5:24; Joel 2:5, etc.); or broken up by threshing and separated from the grain (Job 13:25; 41:20; Psa. 83:13; Isa. 40:24, etc.). Heb. *qăsh. See* Vegetable Kingdom.

2. Job 21:18. *Straw,* as used for provender, Heb. *tĕbĕn.* Gr. *kalamē* (I Cor. 3:12). The stalk of grain after the ears are removed. *See* Agriculture.

Stumbling, Stumbling-block or **Stone.** 1. (Heb. *mĭkshōl, obstacle*) is used as any object over which a person may trip the foot, and hence the cause of ruin or disgust (Isa. 57:14; Jer. 6:21; Ezek. 7:19, etc.), or an *idol* (Zeph. 1:3), i.e., an incitement to apostasy.

2. (Heb. *nĕgĕph, tripping*), a cause of stumbling (Isa. 8:14). Notice the heaping together of synonyms, especially in v. 15.

3. Gr. *proskomma,* an obstacle against which, if one strike his foot, he necessarily falls; figuratively, that over which the soul stumbles into sin (I Cor. 8:9). To put a stumbling-block in

another's way is, figuratively, to furnish an occasion for sinning (Rom. 14:13). "Stone of stumbling" is used figuratively of Jesus Christ, with regard to whom it especially annoyed and offended the Jews that his words and deeds, and particularly his ignominious death, failed to correspond to their preconceptions respecting the Messiah (Rom. 9:32, 33; I Pet. 2:8).

Stump (Heb. *'ĭqqär*) of a tree cut down, but able to sprout again (Dan. 4:15, 23, 26). In I Sam. 5:4 it is recorded that the image of Dagon was miraculously overthrown, his hands and his head cut off, and only the stump left. This was to prove to the Philistines the utter helplessness of their god.

Su'ah (sū'à; *sweepings*), the first mentioned of eleven sons or descendants of Zophah, one of the "heads" of the house of Asher (I Chron. 7:36).

Suburbs (Heb. *mĭgräsh*), a place where cattle are driven to graze, a *pasture;* especially the open country set apart for pasture round the Levitical cities (Num. 35:2; Josh. 21:11; I Chron. 6:55). It also meant an open place, area, round a city or building (Ezek. 27:28; 45:2; 48:17).

Suc'coth (sŭk'ŏth; *booths*).

1. An ancient town in Palestine, and the place where Jacob built booths for his cattle and a house for himself after separating from Esau (Gen. 33:17; Josh. 13:27). The bronze foundries for making the fine work for the temple were built here (I Kings 7:46; II Chron. 4:17). There Gideon met with opposition when pursuing the Midianites (Judg. 8:5, 8, 14-16). The place is referred to in Psa. 60:6; 108:7. The site is now located at Tell Ahṣaṣ, about a mile or more N. of the Jabbok (Nahr ez-Zerḳa), about 9 miles N. E. of Damiyeh.

2. The first encampment of Israel after leaving Rameses (Exod. 12:37). It was the name of a district or region, and not a city. "It is not necessary to suppose that all the Israelites reached Succoth on the day of their hurried start from their homes in Rameses-Goshen . . . Brugsch argues strongly for the correspondence of the Egyptian Thuku with the Hebrew Succoth. As to the location of the Egyptian Thuku, it is shown by the monuments that Pi-tum (the House of [the god] Tum), the Pithom of the Bible text, was the chief city of the district of Thuku. However, more recently Succoth has been identified with Tell el-Maskhutah.

Suc'coth-be'noth (sŭc'ŏth bē'nŏth). *See* Gods, False.

Su'chathite (sū'kăth-īt), a descendant probably of an unknown Israelite by the name of Suchah, and the last named of the families of scribes living at Jabez (I Chron. 2:55).

Suk'kiim (sŭk'ĭ-ĭm), a race mentioned only in II Chron. 12:3 as associated with the Lubim (*q. v.*) and the Cushim ("Ethiopians") in the army with which Shishak invaded Judah in the days of Rehoboam.

Gesenius, connecting the name with *sŭkkäh* (a booth or tent), thought them "dwellers in tents," in which case they might be an Arab tribe, like the Scenitae.

According to the LXX. they were Troglodytes. This name, from *trōglē,* a hole, and *duo,* to enter, corresponds fairly well with our "cave dwellers." It was given to various races, especially to a race inhabiting both shores of the Red Sea, their territory on the eastern side being southeast of Syene and northeast of Meroe. Their dwellings have been compared with the catacombs of Naples. Some of these Troglodytes were serpent eaters, but most were herdsmen. Their language seemed to the Greeks a "shriek or whistle" rather than an articulate speech. Their food was principally animal; their drink was a mixture of blood and milk. They were so fleet of foot as to be able to run down the animals which they hunted. They served as light-armed soldiers in the army of Xerxes, B. C. 480. Aristotle "describes the Troglodytae as pygmies who, mounted on their horses, waged incessant war with the cranes in the Ethiopian marshes." The *Ababdeh* of the Troglodytic region, and the *Barnagas* on the Abyssinian frontier, are said to resemble the Troglodytes in manners and customs.

It is said that no hieroglyphic name has been found resembling the name Sukkiim. This would favor the Arabian theory.—W. H. revised by *M. F. U.*

Sulphur. *See* Brimstone, in Mineral Kingdom.

Sumer. *See* Shinar.

Summer (Heb. *qăyĭṣ, harvest* of fruits, II Sam. 16:1, 2, etc.). *See* Agriculture; Palestine.

Sun (Heb. *shĕmĕsh*), called in the history of the creation the "greater light" in contradistinction to the moon or "lesser light," in conjunction with which it was to serve "for signs, and for seasons, and for days, and for years," while its special office was "to rule the day" (Gen. 1:14-16). The "signs" referred to were probably such extraordinary phenomena as eclipses, which were regarded as conveying premonitions of coming events (Jer. 10:2; Matt. 24:29, with Luke 21:25).

Sunrise and sunset are the only defined points of time in the absence of artificial contrivances for telling the hour of the day. Between these two points the Jews recognized three periods, viz., when the sun became hot, about 9 a. m. (I Sam. 11:9; Neh. 7:3); the double light or noon (Gen. 43:16; II Sam. 4:5), and "the cool of the day," shortly before sunset (Gen. 3:8). The sun also served to fix the quarters of the hemisphere, east, west, north, and south, which were represented respectively by the rising sun, the setting sun (Isa. 45:6; Psa. 50:1), the dark quarter (Gen. 13:14; Joel 2:20), and the brilliant quarter (Deut. 33:23; Job 37:17; Ezek. 40:24); or otherwise by their position relative to a person facing the rising sun—before, behind, on the left hand, and on the right hand (Job 23:8, 9).

The apparent motion of the sun is frequently referred to in terms that would imply its reality (Josh. 10:13; II Kings 20:11; Psa. 19:6; Eccles. 1:5; Hab. 3:11).

Figurative. Of God's favor (Psa. 84:11); of the law of God (19:7); Christ's coming (Mal. 4:2); of the glory of Christ (Matt. 17:2; Rev. 1:16; 10:1); of supreme rulers (Gen. 37:9; Isa. 13:10); (its clearness) of the purity of the Church (Cant. 6:10); (its brightness) of the future glory of saints (Dan. 12:3, with Matt.

13:43); (its power) of the triumph of saints (Judg. 5:31); (darkened) of severe calamities (Ezek. 32:7; Joel 2:10, 31; Matt. 24:29; Rev. 9:2); (going down at noon) of premature destruction (Jer. 15:9; Amos 8:9); (no more going down) of perpetual blessedness (Isa. 60:20); (before or in sight of) of public ignominy (II Sam. 12:11, 12; Jer. 8:2); of the person of the Saviour (John 1:9; Mal. 4:2), and of the glory and purity of heavenly beings (Rev. 1:16; 10:1; 12:1).

443. The Life-giving Rays of the Sun-god Aton Are Imparted to Akhnaton and Nofretete

Sun, Worship of. The worship of the sun, as the most prominent and powerful agent in the kingdom of nature, was widely diffused throughout the countries adjacent to Palestine. The Arabians appear to have paid direct worship to it, without the intervention of any statue or symbol (Job 31:26, 27), and this simple style of worship was probably familiar to the ancestors of the Jews in Chaldea and Mesopotamia. The Hebrews must have been well acquainted with the idolatrous worship of the sun during the captivity in Egypt, both from the contiguity of On, the chief seat of the worship of the sun as implied in the name itself (On=the Hebrew Beth-shemesh, 'house of the sun,' Jer. 43:13), and also from the connection between Joseph and Poti-pherah ('he who belongs to Re'), the priest of On (Gen. 41:45). After their removal to Canaan the Hebrews came in contact with various forms of idolatry, which originated in the worship of the sun; such as the Baal of the Phoenicians, the Molech or Milcom of the Ammonites, and the Hadad of the Syrians. It does not follow that the object symbolized by them was known to the Jews themselves. Hebrews at times became contaminated with the worship of sun images (Lev. 26:30; Isa. 17:8). The great sun god of the ancient Middle East was Shamash. Pharoah Ikhnaton (c. 1380 B. C.) of the Eighteenth Dynasty abolished all images and pictured Aton, the world-creator and universal ruler, as the sun disc whose rays converged in small hands, dispensing blessings. Ezekiel mentions among many abominations "the greatest abomination" (Ezek. 8:15, 16). This was the worship of the sun in the portico of the temple which faced eastward. Says Albright, "It may have been precisely Ezekiel's zeal for pure monotheism which led him to consider this practice as relatively worse than the others."—*M. F. U.*

Sun'day, or **Lord's Day**. 1. **Name and Change of the Day.** Sunday is the first day of the week, adopted by the first Christians from the Roman calendar (Lat. *Dies Solis, Day of the Sun*), because it was dedicated to the worship of the sun. The Christians reinterpreted the heathen name as implying the Sun of Righteousness, with reference to this "rising" (Mal. 4:2). It was also called *Dies Panis* (*Day of Bread*), because it was an early custom to break bread on that day. In *The Teaching of the Twelve* it is called the "Lord's Day of the Lord" (*Kuriakēn de Kuriou*).

Jewish Christians at first continued to frequent the temple and synagogue services, but at a very early date "the first day of the week" took the place of the Jewish Sabbath as the chief time of public worship (Acts 20:7; I Cor. 16:2) in many of the churches of Jewish Christians. It was the day of the resurrection of Christ, of most of his appearances to the disciples after the resurrection, and on this day the Holy Spirit was poured out at Pentecost. For these reasons, and especially after the destruction of the sacred city had rendered the sacrificial service of the temple impossible, Sunday became the recognized day of assembly for fellowship and for the celebration of the Lord's Supper. The Jewish Christians at first observed both the seventh and the first day of the week, but the Gentile Christians kept the "Lord's Day" from the beginning. The relation of the seventh to the first, as understood by the Jewish Christians, may not be easy to determine, yet there seem to be indications that the seventh was regarded as a day of preparation for the first. The idea of Christian worship would attach mainly to the one; the obligation of rest would continue attached to the other; although a certain interchange of characteristics would grow up, as worship necessitated rest, and rest naturally suggested worship.

In his letter to the Magnesians Ignatius evidently addressed a church of mixed character, since he speaks of some "who were brought up in the ancient order of things," who "have come to the possession of a new hope, no longer observing the Sabbath, but living in the observance of the Lord's Day," etc.

"There is neither in this writer nor in the Barnabas epistle an intimation that Sunday was regarded as in any way a substitute for the Jewish Sabbath, nor yet a continuation of it; rather it was a new institution. It is, however, impossible to determine the time of its beginning; no impressive enactment, like that in the case of the Decalogue, was needed . . . Not until the 4th century do we find a statement intimating that the Jewish Sabbath, with its sanctions and duties, was transferred to the first, or the Lord's Day . . . The observance of the Jewish Sabbath in the churches of the Jewish Christians continued for the first five centuries. In the East both days were celebrated with rejoicing; in the West the Jewish Sabbath was observed as a fast.

"The reign of Constantine marks a change in the relations of the people to the Lord's Day. The rescript of the emperor, commanding the observance of Sunday, seems to have had little regard for its sanctity as a Christian institution; but the day of the sun is to be generally regarded with veneration . . . Later enactments made plain the duties of civil and ecclesiastical officers respecting the observance of Sunday, until it takes its place as an institution to be guarded and regulated by the government."

2. **Sanctity and Ground of Observance.** "The resurrection of Christ was the one all-sufficient fact which accounts for the rise and growth of the Christian Church. 'Jesus and the resurrection' was the burden of the apostolic preaching. Hence the recollection of the day of the resurrection was so indelibly impressed upon the hearts of the first disciples that on its return they came together to pray and to recall the memory of the Lord by breaking of bread and the celebration of the eucharist. It was the dictate of the glowing love for Christ, whose followers they delighted to be reckoned . . . We fail to find the slightest trace of a law or apostolic edict instituting the observance of the 'day of the Lord;' nor is there in the Scriptures an intimation of a substitution of this for the Jewish Sabbath. The primal idea of the Jewish Sabbath was cessation of labor, rest; the transference of this idea to the first day of the week does not appear in the teachings of Christ nor of his apostles. Nor in the Council of Jerusalem, when the most important decisions are reached relative to the ground of union of Jewish and Gentile Christians, is one word found respecting the observance of the Sabbath. Contrariwise, Paul distinctly warns against the imposition of burdens upon the Church respecting days, but declares for a conscientious freedom in these observances. 'Let every man be fully persuaded in his own mind' (Rom. 14:5, 6). Still more strongly does he upbraid the Galatian church for putting itself again in bondage to the weak and beggarly elements, as days, months, times, and years; while in his letter to the Colossians (2:16, 17) he speaks of the entire abolition of the Jewish Sabbath."

Justin Martyr, in his dialogue with the Jew Tryphon, who taunts the Christians with having no festivals nor Sabbaths, clearly claims that Sunday is to them a new Sabbath, and that the entire Mosaic law has been abrogated (*Cum Tryph.*, cc. 10, 11). The new law binding upon Christians regards every day as a Sabbath, instead of passing one day in rest or absolute idleness.

"With respect to the strictness with which the first day of the week was observed during the first three centuries, the following facts are important to notice: Between the death of the apostles and the edict of Milan, the Lord's Day was sanctified by a Church unrecognized by the State and exposed to opposition and sometimes to bitter persecution. The motive for its observance was, therefore, purely moral and religious. The social position of the early Church, drawing its members for the most part from the poorer artisans, traders, and slaves, forbade the strict and general keeping of the Lord's Day, much more of both the Sabbath and Sunday. Thus the universal hallowing of the day of the resurrection was impossible" (Bennett, *Christ. Arch.*, p. 444, sq.).

3. **Legal Observance**. In the midst of the corrupt influence of heathenism and the growing indifference of the Church, it was thought necessary to bring some stress of authority upon the Christian conscience to hold it to the faithful observance of the first day, as the Jews had known the power of a positive enactment in keeping them steadfast in the hallowing of their Sabbath. "The constant temptation of the Christians to attend upon the heathen spectacles and festivities could, in the case of such whose piety was low, no longer, as at first, be broken by considerations of the high privileges of Christian worship and of the commemoration of the resurrection of Christ, but the restraints coming from a quasi legal enactment were found to be more and more necessary" (ibid., p. 450).

"The obligation to observe the day does not come from the fourth commandment, but from the apostolic institution of the Lord's Day. Nevertheless, from the time of the attempts of the emperors to adjust the civil conditions to the recognition of Sunday as the chief religious holiday, the sense of obligation to keep sacred the first day of the week, coming from legal enactment, more and more supplanted the consideration of the high and holy privilege which had animated the Christian Church during the first years of its activity. From the last part of the 6th century the strict legalistic view becomes more and more prominent, and the rulers in State and Church incline to strengthen the civil and conciliatory enactments respecting the Lord's Day by divine authority, as contained in the fourth commandment" (ibid., p. 451).

Superfluous (Heb. *sără*, to *prolong*), the having any member too long or large, and so *deformed*. Any person so afflicted was not allowed to officiate in the tabernacle or temple service (Lev. 21:18), nor was any such animal permitted as a sacrifice (22:23).

Superscription (Gr. *'epigraphē, written upon*), an inscription, title; in the New Testament of an inscription in black letters upon a whitened tablet, such as Pilate wrote and caused to be placed on the cross (Luke 23:38; John 19:19); also an inscription upon a coin (Matt. 22:20; Mark 12:16; Luke 20:24).

Superstition (Gr. *deisidaimonia, reverence for the gods*), a word which Festus, in the presence of Agrippa, the Jewish king, employs ambiguously and cautiously (Acts 25:19, A. V. 'religion'), so as to leave his own judgment concerning its truth in suspense.

Superstitious (Gr. *deisidaimōn, reverencing the gods*), in a good sense, *godly;* in a bad sense, superstitious. Paul, in the opening of his address to the Athenians (Acts 17:22) calls them, with kindly ambiguity, *divinity-fearing*, devout, without the knowledge of the true God.

Suph (sōōf; *reeds*), a word in the R. V. marg. (Deut. 1:1), referred to as meaning the Red Sea; most probably an abbreviation of *Yamsuph*, or the Red (Reed) Sea.

Su'phah (sōō'fä; Num. 21:14, A. V. marg.; R. V. text), also instead of the Red Sea.

Supper. *See* Banquet; Food; Lord's Supper.

Supplication. 1. Heb. *t*ᵉ*ḥinnäh* has the meaning of favor, mercy (Josh. 11:20; Ezra 9:8); also prayer, i. e., a cry for mercy (I Kings 8:28, etc.; II Chron. 6:19, 24, 29, 35; Psa. 6:9; 55:1; Dan. 9:20).

2. Heb. *ḥănăn*, to *incline*, to *be favorably disposed;* and then to implore favor, to entreat (I Kings 8:33; Esth. 4:8; Job 8:5; Psa. 30:8, etc.).

3. *Petition* (Gr. *deēsis, asking*), in the New Testament, requests addressed by men to God (James 5:16; I Pet. 3:12, A. V. "pray" and "prayers"); joined with *proseuchē, prayer*, i. e., any pious address to God (Acts 1:14; Eph. 6:8; Phil. 4:6; I Tim. 2:1; 5:5). *Deēsis* is the asking of favor in some special necessity; *proseuchē* is exercised in all presentation of desires and wishes to God. Trench (*Syn. N. T.* second series, p. 3) makes this important point of distinction, viz., "that *proseuchē* is *res sacra*, a word restricted to sacred uses; it is always prayer to God; *deēsis* has no such restriction."

Surety (from Heb. *'ärăb*, to *braid, intermix*), to deposit a pledge, either in money, goods, or in part payment, as security for a bargain (Gr. *'egguos*). The earliest form of surety mentioned in Scripture is the pledging of person for person, as when Judah undertook with his father to be surety for Benjamin (Gen. 43:9); and when circumstances seemed to call for a fulfillment of the obligation, he actually offered himself in the room of Benjamin. In this sense the Psalmist asks God to be surety for him (Psa. 119:122), as did, also, in his great distress, Hezekiah (Isa. 38:14).

The more common kind of surety spoken of is financial. The Mosaic regulations respecting debts were such that, except in rare cases, the creditor was not likely to suffer any considerable loss; and it may be that this was the reason why the Mosaic law contains no statute on *suretyship*. In later times they were very common, as we learn from Proverbs, where foresight is taught (Prov. 6:1, sq.; 11:15; 17:18), by pointing to the fact that the surety has to stand for the debtor, and could not expect any milder treatment than he (Prov. 20:16; 22:26, sq.; comp. Siriach 8:16; 29:20, 24).

Figurative. In the highest sense the term is applied to Christ, who, in his character as mediator, is represented as "the surety (*'egguos*) of a better covenant" (Heb. 7:22), having made himself responsible for all that in this covenant was required to be accomplished for the salvation of those who were to share in its provisions.

Surfeiting (Gr. *kraipalē*), the giddiness and headache caused by drinking wine to excess (Luke 21:34 only). Fulsomeness, in the early sense of that word, would express it very well, with only the drawback that by fulsomeness might be indicated the disgust and loathing from overfulness of meat as well as wine, while surfeiting expresses only the latter (Trench, *Gr. Syn.*, 2d series, p. 51).

Surname. (Gr. *'epikaleomai*, to *invoke*, to *put a name upon;* to surname; Matt. 10:3; Luke 22:3; Acts 1:23, etc.). The expression (Acts

15:17) "all the Gentiles upon whom my name is called," means those who were declared to be dedicated to him (comp. James 2:7, A. V. "worthy name").

Su'sa (soō'sȧ; Esth. 11:3; 16:18; Apochrypha). *See* Shushan.

Su'sanchites (soō'sǎn-kīts; Heb. *Shūshǎnî*, i. e., *Shushanchites*, Ezra 4:9 only), one of the nations settled in Samaria by the Assyrians, and still remaining in the days of Artaxerxes. It is supposed that they were the inhabitants either of the province Susiana or of its capital Susa (Shushan); probably the latter, as Dan. 8:2 seems to make Shushan the capital of Elam, and in Ezra 4:9 Elamites are mentioned separately—W. H. revised by *M. F. U.*

Susan'na (sŭ-zǎn'nȧ; Gr. from Heb. "a lily"), one of the women who followed our Lord and "ministered unto him of their substance" (Luke 8:3), A. D. 28. No particulars of her life are known. The name, apparently of common occurrence, is of the same origin and meaning as Sheshan (I Chron. 2:31, 34, 35). The Susanna who figures prominently in the symbolism of the ancient Church is the heroine of the apocryphal story of the judgment of Daniel.

Su'si (sū'sī; a *horseman*), the father of Gaddi, who was the representative of the tribe of Manasseh in the first commission sent by Moses to "spy out the land" of Canaan (Num. 13:11), B. C. before 1440.

Swaddle (Heb. *ṭāphǎḥ*, to *bear upon the palm*); in English, to carry in the arms (Lam. 2:22); elsewhere (Ezek. 16:4) the rendering of *ḥāthǎl*, to wrap in bandages, to *swaddle* (comp. Luke 2:17).

    Figurative. The thick mist (A. V. "darkness") is called (Job 38:9) the swaddling clothes of the sea.

Swaddling Band. A cloth in which new-born babes were wrapped (Job 38:9; Ezek. 16:4; Luke 2:7, 12). The infant was placed diagonally on a square piece of cloth. Two corners were turned across its body one across the feet, the other under its head. The whole was fastened by bands wound around the exterior.

Swallow. *See* Animal Kingdom.

Swan. *See* Animal Kingdom.

Swear. *See* Oath.

Sweat (Heb. *yĕzǎ', perspiration*). In setting forth the requisites, obligations, and privileges of the priest's office, Ezekiel (44:18) designates linen as the material for their clothing, assigning as the reason that the priest is not to cause himself to sweat by wearing woolen clothing. Sweat produces uncleanness; and the priest, by keeping his body clean, is to show even outwardly that he is clean and blameless.

Sweat, Bloody. *See* Bloody Sweat.

Swelling. 1. The "swelling of Jordan" is a phrase (Jer. 12:5; 49:19; 50:44, A. V.) which should be rendered "*pride* of Jordan," as in Zech. 11:3. Orelli renders it "jungles of Jordan," where lions lurk. Heb. *gä'ōn*, pride.

    2. (Gr. *huperochē*, to *be above*), superior in rank (authority, I Tim. 2:2); R. V. "those who are in high place."

    3. (Gr. *huperogkos*, a *swelling*), immoderate, extravagant; expressive of arrogance, as "great swelling words" (II Pet. 2:18; Jude 16).

4. (Gr. *phusiōsis*, a puffing up of soul, loftiness, pride (II Cor. 12:20).

Swine. Figurative. "A fair woman without discretion" (Prov. 11:22), "Neither cast ye your pearls before swine" (Matt. 7:6), are proverbs which are easily understood. "As if he offered swine's blood" (Isa. 66:3) is used of those who, without reflection, and merely as an external act, offer sacrifices to God. Even though they offer sacrifices which are prescribed, their state of mind is no more acceptable than if they offered that which was unclean. *See* Animal Kingdom.

Sword. *See* Armor.

Sycamine, Sycamore, Sycomore. *See* Vegetable Kingdom.

Sy'char (sī'kȧr). Sychar used to be identified with Shechem. It is now located at the site of the village of 'Askar, on the eastern slope of Ebal, almost 2 miles E. N. E. from Nablus, about a half mile N. of Jacob's well, and a short distance S. E. of Shechem.

    For this the first evidence we get is at the beginning of the 4th century, when two visitors to the land, Eusebius and the Bordeaux Pilgrim (the latter about A. D. 333), both mention a Sychar, distinct from Shechem, lying, says the former, before Neapolis, the present Nablus, and the latter adds that it was a Roman mile from Shechem. In mediaeval times the abbot Daniel (1106, 1107) speaks of "the hamlet of Jacob called Sichar. Jacob's well is there. Near this place, at half a verst away, is the town of Samaria . . . at present called Neapolis." Fetellus (1130) says: "A mile from Sichem is the town of Sychar; in it is the fountain of Jacob, which, however, is a well." Other travelers mention both Sichem and Sychar and all this time, in spite of ecclesiastical tradition, the name Sychar should have continued to exist in the neighborhood, and solely among the natives, is a strong proof of its originality, of its having been from the first a native and not an artificial name. *See* Shechem.

Sy'chem (sī'kĕm; Acts 7:16). *See* Shechem.

Sye'ne (sī-ē'nē; Heb. *Seveneh*), a town of Egypt on the frontier of Cush, or Ethiopia. Ezekiel speaks (29:10) of the desolation of Egypt "from Migdol (A. V. 'tower') to Syene, even unto the border of Ethiopia," and of its people being slain "from Migdol to Syene" (30:6). Its ancient Egyptian name is *Sun*, preserved in the Coptic *Souan*, *Senon*, and the Arabic *Aswan*. It was separated by an arm of the Nile, ninety yards wide, from Elephantine, forming a suburb of that important city. *See* Seveneh.

Synagogue (Hellenistic Gr., *sunagōgē*, "gathering *of people*," "a congregation," "a place of prayer," Acts 16:13)

    1. **Object.** As only a small proportion of the people could become proficient in the study of the law under the scribes, and as it was desirable that all should have at least an elementary acquaintance therewith, the custom grew up in post-exilic times of reading the Scriptures in the synagogue on the Sabbath day. It must be understood that the main object of these Sabbath day assemblages in the synagogues was not public worship in its stricter sense, but religious instruction, which to an

Israelite was above all *instruction in the law.* Thus Josephus says (*Apion*, ii, 7), "Not once or twice or more frequently did our lawgiver command us to hear the law, but to come together weekly, with the cessation of other work, to hear the law and to learn it accurately." Philo called the synagogues "houses of instruction," in which "the native philosophy" was studied, and every kind of virtue taught. In the New Testament, too, the teaching (Gr. *didaskein*) always figures as the chief function of the synagogue.

2. **Origin.** The origin of these Sabbath day meetings in buildings erected for the purpose must be sought for in the post-exilic period. The first traces of them are "the synagogues of God" (Psa. 74:8), but their commencement may well be as far back as the time of Ezra. R. H. Pfeiffer and other scholars are of the opinion that the synagogue may have originated in Ezekiel's addresses to the Babylonian exiles (*Hist. of N. T. Times*, p. 50). Such gatherings in the prophet's house (Ezek. 8:1; 20:1-3) may well be the forerunners of the synagogue gatherings. In the time of Christ "teaching in the synagogue on the Sabbath day" was already an established institution (Mark 1:21; 6:2; Luke 4:16, 31; 6:6; 13:10; Acts 13:14, 27, 42, 44; 15:21; 16:13; 17:2; 18:4). According to Acts 15:21, "Moses of old time hath in every city them that preach him, being read in the synagogues every Sabbath day." Josephus, Philo, and, later, Judaism generally, trace back the whole system to Moses, but there is no evidence of a pre-exilian origin.

3. **Religious Community.** The system presupposes a *religious community.* This was an independent organization in towns in which Jews might be excluded from civic rights, or Jews and others had equal rights. In such cases the Jews would be thrown back upon self-organization as a religious community; for whether they cooperated or not in civil affairs, the necessity of independent organization for religious matters was the same. Where Jews only had civic rights, and the local authorities were Jewish, matters relating to the synagogue were probably under their jurisdiction and direction. In the Mishna, for example, it is presumed as quite self-evident that the synagogue, the sacred ark, and the sacred books were quite as much the property of the town as the roads and baths.

4. **Conduct of Synagogues.** The general direction of affairs was committed to elders, while special officers were appointed for special purposes. But the peculiarity here is that just for the acts proper to public worship— the reading of the Scriptures, preaching and prayer—no special officials were appointed. These acts were, on the contrary, in the time of Christ still freely performed in turn by members of the congregation.

5. **Officials.** (1) **The ruler of the synagogue** (Gr. *'archisunagōgos*) had the care of external order in public worship, and the supervision of the concerns of the synagogue in general. This officer was found in the entire sphere of Judaism, not only in Palestine, but also in Egypt, Asia Minor, Greece, Italy, and the Roman empire in general. The Hebrew title *rō'sh hăkkᵉnēsĕth*, "the minister of the synagogue") was undoubtedly synonymous with the Greek term. This office differed from that of an elder of the congregation, although the same person could fill the offices of both. The ruler of the synagogue was so called, not as head of the community, but as conductor of their assembly for public worship. Among his functions is specially mentioned that of appointing who should read the Scriptures and the prayer, and summoning fit persons to preach; to see that nothing improper took place in the synagogue (Luke 12:14), and to take charge of the synagogue building. Although it was customary to have but one ruler for each synagogue, yet sometimes more are mentioned (Acts 13:15).

(2) **Receiver of alms** (Heb. *găbbā'ē ṣᵉdäqäh*). This official had nothing to do with public worship as such, and is, therefore, where the civil and religious communities were not separated, to be regarded rather as a civil official. According to the Mishna the collection was to be made by two, the distribution by three persons. Not only was money collected, but also natural products.

(3) **The minister** (Heb. *hăzzän hăkkᵉnēsĕth;* Gr. *huperetēs;* Luke 4:20). His office was to bring forth the Holy Scriptures at public worship and to put them away again. He was in every respect the servant of the congregation, having, for example, to execute the punisment of scourging and also to instruct the children in reading.

The person (Heb. *shᵉliăh ṣĭbbūr*) who pronounced the prayer in the name of the congregation is also generally regarded as one of the officers of the synagogue. There were also "ten unemployed men," whose business it was, especially in the post-Talmudic period, to be always present for a fee in the synagogue at public worship, for the purpose of making up the number of ten members required for a religious assembly; but they are hardly to be regarded as officials.

6. **Building** (Heb. *bēth hăkkᵉnēsĕth, house of assembly;* Gr. *sunagōgē*). Synagogues were built by preference outside the towns and near

444. The Capernaum Synagogue

rivers, or on the seashore, for the sake of giving everyone a convenient opportunity for performing such Levitical purification as might be necessary before attending public worship. The size and architecture of course varied. Archaeological research has shown that in many towns the synagogue was a very important building. This is attested by the gorgeous white limestone structure dating c. 200 A. D. uncovered at Capernaum, apparently built on the site of the one where Jesus ministered. Decorational motifs include garland-carrying boys, lions, eagles, stars, vines and palms. Synagogues also have been uncovered at Chorazin near Capernaum, at Beth Alpha in the Valley of Jezreel, at Bethsaida Julius and at Kepher Bir'im. At Caesarea, Beth-shan, Lydda and elsewhere inscriptional allusions to synagogues have been found. At Corinth an inscription has been recovered reading: "Synagogue of the Jews." This was found on a stone apparently separated from its place in a structure which has disappeared. The synagogue in which Paul preached (Acts 18:4) may have contained this very stone and may have stood on the famous Lechaeum Road. Almost all these synagogues lie north and south, so that the entrance is at the south. As a rule they appear to have had one chief entrance and two smaller side doors.

The fittings of synagogues in New Testament times were very simple. The chief was the *closet* (Heb. *tēbāh*) in which were kept the rolls of the law and the other sacred books. These were wrapped in linen cloths and lay in a case. A representation of an old silver case for the Pentateuch among the modern Samaritans exists as well as other types of cases. An elevated place (Gr. *bēma, tribune*), upon which stood the reading desk, was erected at least in post-Talmudic times, for the person who read the Scriptures or preached. Lamps were also used; and trombones and trumpets were indispensable instruments in public worship. The former were blown especially on the first day of the year, the latter on the feast days.

The large synagogue at Alexandria is said to have had the form of a basilica. It is possible that they were sometimes built like theaters, without a roof, but this is only really testified concerning those of the Samaritans. —M. F. U.

7. **Where Located.** The value attached to these Sabbath day assemblies leads us to assume that there was in every town of Palestine, and even in smaller places, at least *one* synagogue. In the post-Talmudic period it was required that a synagogue should be built wherever *ten* Israelites were dwelling together. In the larger towns there was a considerable number of synagogues, e. g., in Jerusalem, Alexandria, and Rome. The different synagogues in the same town seem to have been distinguished from each other by special emblems, as a "synagogue of the vine" in Sepphoris, "of the olive tree" in Rome.

8. **Worship.** The order of worship in New Testament times was tolerably developed and established. The congregation sat in an appointed order, the most distinguished in the front seats, the younger behind; men and women probably apart (see Matt. 23:6; Mark 12:39; Luke 11:43; 20:46). In the great synagogue in Alexandria the men are said to have been set apart according to their respective trades. A special division was prepared for the leper. The chief parts of the service were, according to the Mishna, the recitation of the *Shema*, prayer, the reading of the Torah, the reading of the prophets, the blessing of the priest, followed by the *translation* of the Scripture that had been read, and the *discourse*. The Shema, so called from its commencing words, *sh*e*mā' Yĭsrā'ēl*, "Hear, O Israel," consists of Deut. 6:4-9; 11:13-21; Num. 15:37-41, together with benediction before and after. It is rather a confession of faith than a prayer. The custom of praying the first three and last three benedictions of the Shemoneh Esreh at Sabbath and festival worship reaches back to the age of the Mishna. The Shemoneh Esreh was the chief prayer which every Israelite, even women, slaves, and children, had to repeat three times a day—morning, afternoon, and evening. It was the custom to pray standing and with the face turned toward the holy of holies, i. e., toward Jerusalem. The prayer was offered by some one named by the ruler of the synagogue, the congregation making only certain responses, especially the amen. He who uttered the prayer stood in front of the chest in which lay the rolls of the law. Every adult member of the congregation was competent to do this; and might also recite the Shema, read the lesson from the prophets, and, if a priest, pronounce the blessing.

The Scripture lessons, from both the law and the prophets, could be read by any member of the congregation, even by minors, the latter being only excluded from reading the Book of Esther at the feast of Purim. If priests and Levites were present, they took precedence in reading the lesson. The reader usually stood (Luke 4:16), but both sitting and standing were allowed at the reading of the Book of Esther, and the king was allowed to sit when he read his portion of Scripture at the Feast of Tabernacles in the Sabbatic year. The lesson from the Torah was so arranged that the whole Pentateuch was completed in a cycle of three years, for which purpose it was divided into one hundred and fifty-four sections.

On Sabbaths several members of the congregation, at the least seven, who were summoned for the purpose by some official, originally, indeed, by the ruler of the synagogue, took part in the reading; each (at the reading of the Torah) to read at least *three* verses, but not to repeat them by heart. The reading of the law was already followed in New Testament times by a *paragraph from the prophets* (see Luke 4:17; Acts 13:15). The prophets not being read in course, a choice of them was open, and they were always read by one person, and that on the chief services of the Sabbath. The second language of Scripture not being familiar to the bulk of the people, its reading was followed by *translation* into the Aramaic dialect. The reading of the Scripture was followed by a lecture or sermon, explaining and applying the portion read (Matt. 4:23; Mark 1:21; Luke 4:15; 6:6; 13:10;

John 6:59; 18:20); the preacher *sitting* (Luke 4:20) on an elevated place. The position of preacher was open to any competent member of the congregation.

The service closed with the blessing pronounced by a priestly member of the congregation, to which the whole congregation responded Amen. If no priest or Levite was present the blessing was not pronounced, but was made into a prayer.

Syn′tiche (sĭn′tĭ-chē; *fortunate*), a Christian woman of Philippi, who seems to have been at variance with another female member named Euodias or Euodia (Phil. 4:2, 3), A. D. 57. Paul pathetically entreats them to live in mutual harmony, and mentions their names with a respect bordering on fondness, as fellow-laborers in the Gospel, whose names were written in the book of life. It has been surmised that they were deaconesses, in which case their good fellowship would be of almost vital importance to the infant Church.

Syr′acuse (sĭr′á-kŭs), a town on the eastern coast of the island of Sicily, once connected with the mainland by a causeway, a fact curiously recorded upon the coinage, which represents dolphins swimming round the head of Arthusa while the island remained, but meeting at the nose of the figure when it was no longer an island. The city was founded about 735 B. C. and was very prosperous. It defeated an Athenian fleet of 200 vessels in 413 B. C. In 212 B. C. it was conquered by the Romans. It was a place of great splendor, the birthplace of Archimedes, and here Saint Paul remained three days when on his way to Rome (Acts 28:12). Called now Syracusa, having a small population.

2. **Territory.** Ancient geographers are not agreed as to the extent of Syria, confounding, with Herodotus, Syria and Assyria. The Hebrew Aram seems to commence on the northern frontier of Palestine, and to extend thence northward to the skirts of Taurus, westward to the Mediterranean, and eastward probably to the Habur River. It was subdivided into five principalities:

(1) Aram-Dammesek, or "Syria of Damascus" (II Sam. 8:5, 6). This was the rich country about Damascus, lying between Antilibanus and the desert, and the last with the district about Harran and Orfah, the flat country stretching out from the western extremity of Mons Masius toward the true source of the Habur, at *Ras-el-Ain*. Aramnaharaim seems to be a term including this last tract and extending beyond it, though how far beyond is doubtful. See Roger O'Callaghan *Aram-naharaim*, Rome, Pontifical Biblical Institute. (2) Aram-Zobah, or "Syria of Zobah" (10:6), seems to be the tract between the Euphrates and Coele-Syria. The other divisions were: (3) Aram-Maachah (10:6, 8); (4) Aram-Beth-rehob (10:6, 8); and (5) Aram-Naharaim (Gen. 24:10), or "Mesopotamia." The exact location of the last three is difficult to determine. Probably they were portions of the tract intervening between Antilibanus and the desert.

The Greek writers used the term Syria still more vaguely than the Hebrews did Aram. On the one hand they extended it to the Euxine; on the other they carried it to the borders of Egypt. Still they seem always to have had a feeling that Syria proper was a narrower region. The LXX. and New Testa-

445. The Seleucid (Syrian) Kingdom, 300 B. C.

Syr′ia (sĭr′ĭ-á; Heb. *'ărăm;* Gr. *Suria*).

1. **Name.** In Gen. 10:22 *Aram*, the youngest son of Shem, is mentioned as the founder of the Aramaean nation, and thus the country is rightly called "Aram" (Num. 23:7); but the same Hebrew word is rendered "Mesopotamia" (Judg. 3:10) and "Syria" (10:6). The designation Syria is an abbreviated form of Assyria and came into common use after the conquests of Alexander the Great.

ment writers distinguish Syria from Phoenicia on the one hand, and from Samaria, Judea, Idumea, etc., on the other. In the present article it seems best to take the word in this narrow sense, and to regard Syria as bounded by Amanus and Taurus on the north, by the Euphrates and the Arabian Desert on the east, by Palestine on the south, by the Mediterranean near the mouth of the Orontes, and then by Phoenicia upon the west. The tract thus circumscribed is about three hundred miles long from north to south, and from fifty to one hundred and fifty miles broad. It contains an area of about thirty thousand square miles.

3. **Physical Features.** (1) **Mountains.** The general character of the tract is mountainous, as the Hebrew name Aram (apparently from a root signifying "height") implies. On the west two longitudinal chains, running parallel with the coast at no great distance from one another, extend along two thirds of the length of Syria, from the latitude of Tyre to that of Antioch. In the latitude of Antioch the longitudinal chains are met by the chain of Amanus, an outlying barrier of Taurus, having the direction of that range, which in this part is from southwest to northeast. The most fertile and valuable tract of Syria is the long valley intervening between Libanus and Antilibanus. The northern mountain region is also fairly productive; but the soil of the plains about Aleppo is poor, and the eastern flank of the Antilibanus, except in one place, is pecu-

446. The Lebanon Mountains

liarly sterile. The mountain ranges are: (a) Lebanon, extending from the mouth of the Litany to *Arka*, a distance of nearly one hundred miles, and is composed chiefly of Jura limestone, but varied with sandstone and basalt. (*See* Lebanon.) (b) Antilibanus. This range, as the name implies, stands over against Lebanon, running in the same direction, i. e., nearly north and south, and extending the same length. (c) Bargylus. Mount Bargylus, called now *Jebel Nosairi* toward the south, and toward the north *Jebel Kraad*, extends from the mouth of the *Nahr-el-Kebir* (Eleutherus), nearly opposite Homs, to the vicinity of Antioch, a distance of rather more than one hundred miles. One of the western spurs terminates in a remarkable headland, known to the ancients as Mount Casius, and now called *Jebel-el-Akra*, or the "Bald Mountain." (d) Amanus. North of the mouth of the Orontes, between its course and the eastern shore of the Gulf of Issus (*Iskanderun*), lies the range of Amanus, which divides Syria from Cilicia. Its average elevation is five thousand feet, and it terminates abruptly at *Ras-el-Khanzir*, in a high cliff overhanging the sea.

(2) **Rivers.** 1. The Orontes is the largest river in Syria, and has its source about fifteen miles from that of the Litany. Its modern name is the *Nahr-el-'Asi*, or "Rebel Stream," an appellation given to it on account of its violence and impetuosity in many parts of its course. It is also called el-Maklûb ("The Inverted"), from the fact of its running, as is thought, in a wrong direction. It runs northwest across the plain to the foot of Lebanon, where its volume is more than trebled by the great fountain of Ain el-'Asy. Hence it winds along the plain of Hamath, passing Riblah, Homs, Hamath and Armea. At Antioch it sweeps round to the west, and falls into the Mediterranean at Seleucia. 2. The *Litany* is the next largest river, having its source in a small lake situated in the middle of the Coele-Syrian valley, about six miles to the S. W. of Baalbek. It enters the sea about five miles N. of Tyre. The other Syrian streams of some consequence, besides the Litany and the Orontes, are the *Barada*, or river of Damascus; the *Koweik*, or river of Aleppo; and the *Sajur*, a tributary of the Euphrates.

(3) **The lakes.** The principal lakes of Syria are the *Agh-Dengiz*, or Lake of Antioch; the *Sabakhah*, or Salt Lake, between Aleppo and Balis; the *Bahr-el-Kades*, on the upper Orontes; and the *Bahr-el-Merj*, or Lake of Damascus.

(4) **The great valley.** By far the most important part of Syria, and on the whole its most striking feature, is the great valley which reaches from the plain of *Umk*, near Antioch, to the narrow gorge on which the Litany enters about latitude 33° 30'. This valley, which runs nearly parallel with the Syrian coast, extends the length of two hundred and thirty miles, and has a width varying from six or eight to fifteen or twenty miles. The more southern portion of it was known to the ancients as Coele-Syria, or "the Hollow Syria."

(5) **The eastern desert.** East of the inner mountain chain, and south of the cultivable ground about Aleppo, is the great Syrian Desert, an elevated, dry upland, for the most part of gypsum and marls, producing nothing but a few spare bushes of wormwood and the usual aromatic plants of the wilderness. The region is traversed with difficulty, and has never been accurately surveyed. The most remarkable oasis is at Palmyra, where there are several small streams and abundant palm trees.

(6) **Principal towns.** These may be arranged, as nearly as possible, in the order of their importance: 1. Antioch; 2. Damascus; 3. Apamea; 4. Seleucia; 5. Tadmor, or Palmyra; 6. Laodicea; 7. Ephiphania (Hamath); 8. Samosata; 9. Hierapolis (Mabug); 10. Chalybon; 11. Emesa; 12. Heliopolis; 13. Laodicea ad Libanum; 14. Cyrrhus; 15. Chalcis; 16. Poseideium; 17. Heraclea; 18. Gindarus; 19. Zeugma; 20. Thapsacus. Of these, Samosata, Zeugma, Thapsacus, are on the Euphrates; Seleucia, Laodicea, Poseideium, and Heraclea, on the seashore; Antioch, Apamea, Epiphania, and Emesa (*Hems*), on the Orontes; Heliopolis and Laodicea ad Libanum, in Coele-Syria; Hierapolis, Chalybon, Cyrrhus, Chalcis, and Gindarus, in the northern highlands; Damascus on the skirts, and Palmyra in the center of the eastern desert.

4. **History.** (1) The first occupants of Syria

appear to have been of Hamitic descent. The Canaanitish races, the Hittites, Jebusites, Amorites, etc., are connected in Scripture with Egypt and Ethiopia, Cush and Mizraim (Gen. 10:6, 15-18). These tribes occupied not Palestine only, but also lower Syria, in very early times, as we may gather from the fact that Hamath is assigned to them in Genesis (10:18). Afterward they seem to have become possessed of upper Syria also. After a while the first comers, who were still to, a great extent nomads, received a Semitic infusion, which most probably came to them from the southeast. The only Syrian town whose existence we find distinctly marked at this time is Damascus (14:15; 15:2), which appears to have been already a place of some importance. Next to Damascus must be placed Hamath (Num. 13:21; 34:8). Syria at this time, and for many centuries afterward, seems to have been broken up among a number of petty kingdoms.

(2) **Testimony of the monuments.** The Egyptian records show that under the powerful 18th and 19th Egyptian dynasties, when Egypt ruled the East, from the 16th to the 13th century B. C., Syria as well as Palestine was made a dependency of Egypt; that she was forced to relax her hold in consequence of local uprisings; finally she fully retrieved her position under the 19th dynasty, and that then she was met by the Hittites, and compelled to call a halt upon the Syrian border. (Cf. The Amarna Letters, and the Hittite Monuments from Boghaz-keui.)

(3) **Syria and Israel.** The Jews first come into hostile contact with the Syrians, *under that name*, in the time of David. Claiming the frontier of the Euphrates, which God had promised to Abraham (Gen. 15:18), David made war on Hadadezer, king of Zobah (II Sam. 8:3, 4, 13). The Damascus Syrians were likewise defeated with great loss (v. 5). Zobah, however, was far from being subdued as yet. When, a few years later, the Ammonites determined on engaging in a war with David, and applied to the Syrians for aid, Zobah, together with Beth-rehob, sent them twenty thousand footmen, and two other Syrian kingdoms furnished thirteen thousand (II Sam. 10:6). This army being completely defeated by Joab, Hadadezer obtained aid from Mesopotamia (v. 16), and tried the chance of a third battle, which likewise went against him, and produced the general submission of Syria to the Jewish monarch. The submission thus begun continued under the reign of Solomon (I Kings 4:21). The only part of Syria which Solomon lost seems to have been Damascus, where an independent kingdom was set up by Rezon, a native of Zobah (11:23-25). On the separation of the ten tribes from Rehoboam, Syria was ripe for revolt. Rezon disappears from the scene, and Ben-hadad, in the reign of Asa, king of Judah, is king of Aram, with Damascus as its capital. *See* Damascus; Ben-hadad. He forms an alliance with Asa, and subdues the northern part of the kingdom of the ten tribes (15:18-20). Later Ben-hadad lays siege to Samaria, the capital of Ahab, but is defeated; meeting with a still greater disaster the following year. In an endeavor to re-

cover Ramoth-gilead Ahab was defeated and slain. Samaria was again besieged in the days of Jehoram, son of Ahab; but in consequence of a panic it was delivered. *See* Ahab. War continued to be waged between the Syrian kings (Hazael, Ben-hadad II, Rezin) and kings of Israel (Jehoram, Jehu, Jehoahaz, Joash, Jeroboam II).

In the latter days of Jotham, king of Judah, we find Rezin, king of Aram, and Pekah, king of Israel, confederate with Israel. They invade the country, threaten the capital, and recover Elath to Aram, in the reign of Ahaz, who, to protect himself, became a vassal of Tiglathpileser, king of Assyria. The latter accordingly "went up against Damascus, and took it, and carried the people of it captive to Kir, and slew Rezin" (II Kings 16:9). It was probably at the same time that he "took Ijon and Abelbeth-maachah, and Janoah," etc., and carried them captive to Assyria (15:29).

(4) **Relations with Assyria, Babylonia, etc.** Syria became attached to the great Assyrian empire, from which it passed to the Babylonians, and from them to the Persians. In B. C. 333 it submitted to Alexander without a struggle. Upon the death of Alexander Syria became, for the first time, the head of a great kingdom. On the division of the provinces among his generals, B. C. 321, Seleucus Nicator received Mesopotamia and Syria. Antioch was begun in B. C. 300, and, being finished in a few years, was made the capital of Seleucus's kingdom. The country grew rich with the wealth which now flowed into it on all sides. The most flourishing period was the reign of the founder, Nicator. The empire was then almost as large as that of the Achemenian Persians, for it at one time included Asia Minor, and thus reached from the Aegean to India. The reign of Nicator's son, Antiochus I, called Soter, was the beginning of the decline, which was progressive from his date. It passed under the power of Tigranes, king of Armenia, in B. C. 83, and was not made a province of the Roman empire till after Pompey's complete defeat of Mithridates and his ally Tigranes, B. C. 64.

(5) **Under the Romans.** As Syria holds an important place in the New Testament as well as in the Old, some account of its condition under the Romans is in order. That condition was somewhat peculiar. While the country generally was formed into a Roman province, under governors who were at first propretors or questors, then proconsuls, and finally legates, there were exempted from the direct rule of the governor, in the first place, a number of "free cities," which retained the administration of their own affairs, subject to a tribute levied according to the Roman principles of taxation; and secondly, a number of tracts, which were assigned to petty princes, commonly natives, to be ruled at their pleasure, subject to the same obligations as the free cities as to taxation. The free cities were Antioch, Seleucia, Apamea, Epiphania, Tripolis, Sidon, and Tyre; the principalities, Comagêné, Chalcis ad Belum (near *Baalbek*), Arethusa, Abila or Abilêné, Palmyra, and Damascus. The principalities were sometimes called kingdoms, sometimes tetrarchies. They

were established where it was thought that
the natives were so inveterately wedded to
their own customs, and so well disposed for
revolt, that it was necessary to consult their
feelings, to flatter the national vanity, and to
give them the semblance without the substance of freedom.

447. Syrian Tribute Bearer

Although previously overrun by the Romans, Syria was not made tributary and governors appointed, until B. C. 64. Down to the
battle of Pharsalia the country was fairly
tranquil, the only trouble being with the
Arabs, who occasionally attacked the eastern
frontier. The Roman governors, particularly
Gabinius, took great pains to restore the
ruined cities. After Pharsalia (B. C. 46) the
troubles of Syria were renewed. Julius Caesar
gave the province to his relative, Sextus (B. C.
47), but Pompey's party was still so strong in
the East that the next year one of his adherents, Caecilius Bassus, put Sextus to death,
and established himself in the government so
firmly that he was able to resist for three
years three proconsuls appointed by the Senate to dispossess him, and only finally yielded
upon terms which he himself offered to his
antagonists. Bassus had but just made his submission when, upon the assassination of Caesar, Syria was disputed between Cassius and
Dolabella (B. C. 43). The next year Cassius
left his province and went to Philippi, where

he committed suicide. Syria then fell to Antony, who appointed as his legate L. Decidius
Saxa (B. C. 41). Pacorus, the crown prince
of Parthia, overran Syria and Asia Minor,
defeating Antony's generals and threatening
Rome with the loss of all her Asiatic possessions (B. C. 40-39). Ventidius, however, in
B. C. 38, defeated the Parthians, slew Pacorus,
and recovered for Rome her former boundary.
A quiet time followed. In B. C. 27 a special
procurator was therefore appointed to rule it,
who was subordinate to the governor of Syria,
but within his own province had the power
of a legatus. Syria continued without serious
disturbance from the expulsion of the Parthians (B. C. 38) to the breaking out of the
Jewish war (A. D. 66). In B. C. 19 it was
visited by Augustus, and in A. D. 18-19 by
Germanicus, who died at Antioch in the last
named year. In A. D. 44-47 it was the scene
of a severe famine.

(6) **Syria and Christianity.** A little earlier
than A. D. 47 Christianity had begun to
spread into Syria, partly by means of those
scattered at the time of Stephen's persecution
(Acts 11:19), and partly by the exertions of
Paul (Gal. 1:21). Antioch, the capital, became as early probably as A. D. 44 the see of a
bishop, and was soon recognized as a patri-
archate.

Syr′ia Ma′achah (sĭr′ĭ-á mā′á-ká). See Maachah, 3.

Syr′iac (sĭr′ĭ-ăk) (Dan. 2:4), **Syr′ian** (sĭr′ĭ-ăn)
Tongue (Ezra 4:7) or **Language** (II Kings
18:26; Isa. 36:11), is the rendering in the
A. V. of Heb. ′ărămîth in the Aramaic (language). Aramaic was a Semitic language, the
tongue of the merchant Aramaeans.

Syr′ian (sĭr′ĭ-ăn), (Heb. an Aramaean), an inhabitant either of western Syria (q. v.), i. e., on
the Mediterranean (II Kings 5:20), or of
eastern, i. e., Mesopotamia.

Syrophoeni′cian (sī-rô-fê-nĭ′shăn), a general
name (Mark 7:26) of a female inhabitant of
the northern portion of Phoenicia, popularly
called Syrophoenicia, by reason of its proximity
to Syria and its absorption by conquest into
that kingdom. The woman of Syrophoenicia
applied to Jesus to heal her afflicted daughter,
who was possessed with a demon. When she
came near to him and worshipped, saying,
"Lord, help me," he replied, "It is not meet
to take the children's bread, and to cast it to
dogs." Whether this was to try her faith, or to
show that at that time his work and mission
were among Israel, is hard to determine. Her
faith, however, was great and met its merited
reward in the cure of her daughter. Matthew
(15:22) calls her a "woman of Canaan," being in respect to her nationality, in common
with the Phoenicians, a descendant of Canaan.

Syr′tis (sûr′tĭs), banks of quicksands off the
African coast dreaded by Mediterranean sailors (Acts 27:17). See Quicksand.

T

Ta'anach (tā'à-năk), a royal city of the Canaanites, whose king was among the thirty-one conquered by Joshua (Josh. 12:21). It was apportioned to the western half tribe of Manasseh (Josh. 17:11; 21:25; I Chron. 7:29), and became a city of the Kohathite Levites (Josh. 21:25). In the great struggle of the Canaanites under Sisera against Deborah and Barak it appears to have been the headquarters of their army (Judg. 5:19). They seem to have still occupied the town, but to have been compelled to pay tribute (Josh. 17:13; Juds. 1:28). Taanach is generally named with Megiddo, and they were evidently the chief cities of that fine, rich district in the western portion of the plain of Esdraelon. Taanach is located some five miles S. E. of Megiddo, being generally named with Megiddo as an important city of the rich plain of Esdraelon. It is at present a large mound marking the site of an ancient fortress in the militarily strategic Plain of Armageddon. It was periodically occupied by Egyptians and Babylonians. The place was excavated by the Germans and Austrians in 1901-04. These researches yielded a dozen cuneiform tablets from about the fifteenth century B. C. Although these excavations were not accurate stratigraphically, they yielded a great deal of information concerning the Late Bronze Age (c. 1500-1200 B. C.). *M.F.U.*

Ta'anath-Shi'loh (tā'à-năth-shī'lō; *approach to Shiloh*), a place mentioned as on the northern boundary of Ephraim (Josh. 16:6), at its eastern end between the Jordan and Janohah. It is Khirbet Ta'na, a heap of ruins southeast of Nablus, where there are large cisterns to be found.

Tab'baoth (tăb'à-ŏth; *rings*, or *spots*), one of the Nethinim whose descendants returned from Babylon with Zerubbabel (Ezra 2:43; Neh. 7:46), B. C. before 536.

Tab'bath (tăb'ăth), a place mentioned in connection with the flight of the Midianite host (Judg. 7:22). It is identified with *Rās Abū Ṭabat.*

Ta'beel (tā'bê-ĕl; Aram. *God is good*), probably the original pronunciation of Tabeal (tā-bē-ăl; "good-not"), evidently a scornful alteration of Tabeel.

1. The father of the man whom Rezin, king of Syria, and Pekah, king of Israel, proposed to seat on the throne of Judah instead of Ahaz (Isa. 7:6), B. C. c. 735. In the A. V. the name is spelled *Tabeal*. It has been conjectured that "the son of Tabeal" was identical with Zichri, the "mighty man of Ephraim," whose sanguinary deeds are recorded in II Chron. 28:7, and who may have thus promoted the war in hope of receiving the crown. Because of the Aramaic form of the name, however, others have supposed him to have been a Syrian warrior, who, in the event of success, might hold the Judaic kingdom in fealty to

Rezin, as suzerain. The Targum of Jonathan turns the name into a mere appellative, and makes the passage read: "We will make king in the midst of it whoso seems good to us."

2. A Persian official in Samaria, who, together with Bishlam, Mithredath, and others, wrote to King Artaxerxes a letter of bitter hostility to the rebuilders of Jerusalem (Ezra 4:7, A. V. "Tabeel"), B. C. 522. The letter was written in the "Syrian," i. e., Aramaic "tongue," and it has been argued thence, as well as from the form of his name, that he and his companions were Aramaeans.

Tab'erah (tăb'ê-rà; *burning*), a place in the wilderness of Paran, so called from the fact that the fire of the Lord consumed the discontented of the children of Israel (Num. 11:3; Deut. 9:22).

Tabering (Heb. *tāphăph*, to *drum*), used for the smiting of timbrels (Psa. 68:25), but in Nah. 2:7 for smiting upon the breast, as an expression of violent agony in deep mourning (comp. Luke 18:13; 23:27).

Tabernacle. 1. (Heb. *'ōhĕl, tent*) and (*mĭshkän, residence*) are both used of the Jewish tabernacle (*q. v.*), but the terms are found to be carefully discriminated. *'Ohĕl* denotes the cloth roof, while *mĭshkän* is used for the wooden walls of the structure.

2. Heb. *sŭccäh*, from *säkäk*, to *entwine*, is used to denote a hut, booth (Lev. 23:34; Psa. 76:2; Job 36:29; Isa. 4:6; Amos 9:11; Zech. 14:16).

3. Heb. *sĭccŭth* is used to denote an *idolatrous* booth which the worshippers of idols constructed in their honor, like the tabernacle of the covenant in honor of Jehovah (Amos 5:26).

4. The Greek words rendered "tabernacle" are: (1) Any habitation made of green boughs, skin, cloth, etc. (Matt. 17:4; Mark 9:5; Luke 9:33; John 7:2; Heb. 11:9, etc.). (Gr. *skēnē*.) The "tabernacle of Molech" (Acts 7:43; comp. Amos 5:26) was a portable shrine, in which the image of the god was carried. (2) *Skēnōma*, used of the tabernacle, etc.

Figurative. "The light shall be dark in his tabernacle" (Job 18:6), is a symbol of misfortune. When Job says, "The secret of God was upon my tabernacle" (29:4), he means that the blessed fellowship of God, confiding, unreserved intercourse, ruled over his tent. "Who shall abide in thy tabernacle?" (Psa. 15:1; comp. 27:5), is to be on terms of peaceful communion with God, i. e., in the Church.

The term *tabernacle* is transferred to heaven, as the true dwelling place of God (Heb. 9:11; Rev. 13:6); used figuratively for the *human body* in which the soul dwells as in a tent, and which is taken down at death (II Cor. 5:4). To spread one's tabernacle over others (Rev. 7:15, *skēnōsei 'ep' autous*, A. V. "dwell among") is to afford shelter and protection. The "tabernacle" (*hut*) of David seems to be employed in comtempt of *his house*, i. e., family, reduced to decay and obscurity (Acts 15:16).

Tabernacle of Is′rael. 1. **Sources of Information.** The fullest, most definite, as well as most reliable source of information respecting the tabernacle is the Bible, especially the passages in Exodus. Chapters 25-28 minutely prescribe the construction of the edifice and its furniture, while the parallel passage (chaps. 35-40) describes the execution of the task. We are also aided by the specifications of the temple of Solomon (I Kings, ch. 6; II Chron., chaps. 3, 4), including that seen in vision by Ezekiel (chaps. 40-43), both of which temples were modeled, in all essential features, after the plan of the tabernacle. Outside the Scriptures the principal authority is Josephus, who, in his description of the earliest sacred buildings of the Jews (*Ant.*, III, vi, 2-vii, 7), repeats substantially the statements of Scripture. The rabbinical writings of the Jews give us little information which could aid us in reconstructing the tabernacle.

2. **Names and Synonyms.** (1) *Dwelling* (Heb. *mǐshkän*, from *shäkän*, to *lie down*), a *dwelling*. It connects itself with the Jewish, though not scriptural word Shechinah, as describing the dwelling place of the divine glory. It is not applied in prose to the common dwellings of men, but seems to belong rather to the speech of poetry (Psa. 76:2; Cant. 1:8). In its application to the tabernacle it denotes (*a*) the ten tricolored curtains; (*b*) the forty-eight planks supporting them; (*c*) the whole building, including the roof.

(2) *A tent* (Heb. *′ōhěl*) is more connected with the common life of men as the *tent* of the patriarchs (Gen. 9:21, etc.). For the most part, as needing something to raise it, it is used, when applied to the sacred tent, with some distinguishing epithet. In one passage only (I Kings 1:39) does it appear with this meaning by itself. In its application to the tabernacle the term *′ohěl* means (*a*) the tent roof of goat's hair; (*b*) the whole building.

(3) *House* (Heb. *bäyǐth*) is applied to the tabernacle (Exod. 23:19; 34:26; Josh. 6:24; 9:23; Judg. 18:31; 20:18), as it had been, apparently, to the tents of the patriarchs (Gen. 33:17). So far as it differs from the two preceding words it conveys the idea of a fixed settled habitation; and was, therefore, more fitted to the tabernacle after the people were settled in Canaan than during their wanderings. Its chief interest to us lies in its having descended from the first word ever applied in the Old Testament to a local sanctuary, Beth-el, "*the house of God*" (Gen. 28:17), keeping its place, side by side, with other words— tent, tabernacle, palace, temple, synagogue— and at last outliving them all; rising in the Christian *Ecclesia* to yet higher uses (I Tim. 3:15).

(4) *Place of Sanctity* (Heb. *mǐqdäsh*, Gr. *hagiasma*, etc.), the *holy*, consecrated place (Exod. 25:8, A. V. "sanctuary;" Lev. 12:4); applied, according to the consecrated scale of holiness of which the tabernacle bore witness, sometimes to the whole structure (Lev. 4:6; Num. 3:38; 4:12, A. V. "sanctuary"), sometimes to the innermost sanctuary, the Holy of Holies (Lev. 16:2).

(5) *Temple* (Heb. *hēkäl*), as meaning the stately building or palace of Jehovah (I Chron. 29:1, 19), is applied more commonly to the temple (II Kings 24:13, etc.); but also used of the tabernacle at Shiloh (I Sam. 1:9; 3:3) and Jerusalem (Psa. 5:7).

(6) Two compound phrases are used in Scripture: (*a*) "The tabernacle of the congregation" (Exod. 29:42, 44), the A. V. rendering of *′ōhěl mō′ēd*, literally the tabernacle of *meeting*, "where I will *meet* with thee" (v. 42; comp. 30:6, 36; Num. 17:4). (*b*) Heb. *′ōhěl hä′ēdūth*, A. V. "the tent of testimony," Num. 9:15; "the tabernacle of witness," 17:7; 18:2). In this case the tent derives its name from that which is the center of its holiness, i. e., the two tables of stone within the ark, which are emphatically *the* testimony (Exod. 25:16, 21; 31:18).

3. **History.** We find mention in the Old Testament of three tabernacles:

(1) The *provisional* tabernacle, which was established after the sin of the golden calf.

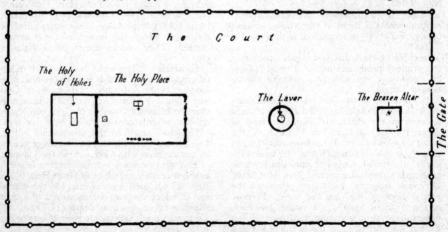

448. The Plan of the Tabernacle

There followed a transitional period, the whole future depending upon the penitence of the people. In this period a tent is pitched, probably that of Moses himself, outside the camp, and called the "tabernacle of the congregation," or "of meeting." Of this provisional tabernacle there was no ritual and no priesthood. The people went out to it as to an oracle (Exod. 33:7).

(2) The *Sinaitic* tabernacle, which was erected in accordance with directions given to Moses by Jehovah (see below).

(3) The *Davidic* tabernacle, erected by David in Jerusalem for the reception of the ark (II Sam. 6:12); while the old tabernacle remained till the days of Solomon at Gibeon, together with the brazen altar, as the place where sacrifices were offered (I Chron. 16:39; II Chron. 1:3).

Upon the intercession of Moses, Jehovah renewed his covenant with Israel, gave them another copy of the law, and invited them to make their offerings of material for the construction of the tabernacle. This they did in excess of what was wanted (Exod. 36:5, 6), and the work proceeded under the direction of Bezaleel and Aholiab (35:30; 36:2). The tabernacle was completed on the first day of the first month (Nisan) of the second year after the Exodus, and the ritual appointed for it begun (40:2). Instead of being placed without the camp, like the provisional tabernacle, it stood in its very center. The priests on the east, the other three families of the Levites on the other sides, were closest in attendance, the "bodyguard" of Israel's theocratic King. In the wider square Judah, Zebulum, Issachar, were on the east; Ephraim, Manasseh, Benjamin, on the west; the less conspicuous tribes, Dan, Asher, Naphtali, on the north; Reuben, Simeon, Gad, on the south side. When the army put himself in order of march the position of the tabernacle, carried by the Levites, was still central, the tribes of the east and south in front, those of the north and west in the rear (Num., ch. 2).

In all special facts connected with the tabernacle the original thought reappears. It is the place where man *meets* with God.

As long as Canaan remained unconquered, and the people were still therefore an army, the tabernacle was moved from place to place, wherever the host of Israel was for the time encamped; and finally was placed at Shiloh (Josh. 9:27; 18:1). The reasons of the choice are not given. Partly, perhaps, its central position, partly its belonging to the powerful tribe of Ephraim, may have determined the preference.

It remained in Shiloh during the whole period of the Judges, the ark being taken from the building in the time of Eli (I Sam. 4:4), and never returned. Excavations by the Danish Expedition at Shiloh indicate that Israel's central sanctuary was destroyed about 1050 B. C., evidently at the hands of the Philistines at the battle of Ebenezer.

Under Samuel's administration worship was transferred to Mizpeh (I Sam. 7:6) and elsewhere (I Sam. 9:12; 10:3; 20:6; Psa. 132:6). In David's day the showbread was kept at Nob (I Sam. 21:1-6), implying the existence there of at least part of the sacred furniture of the tabernacle; and at the close of his reign "the high place that was at Gibeon" possessed some fragments of the original tabernacle, with its altar of burnt offering (I Chron. 16:39; 21:39; comp. I Kings 3:4; II Chron. 1:3-6). This is the last mention of the edifice itself. Meanwhile David had set up a *tent* on Mount Zion, to which he finally transported the ark (I Chron. 15:1; 16:1; II Sam. 6:17, A. V. "tabernacle"); which in turn was superseded by the temple (*q. v.*).

A striking Hebrew tradition exists as to the ark of the covenant: That it was taken by Jeremiah and secreted in a cavern (II Macc. 2:4-8), at the time of the Babylonian capture of the city; and that its hiding place has never been found, and never will be, until Messiah shall set up his kingdom and restore the glory of Israel. There are other rabbinical tales of similar character, but not deserving of attention.

4. **Structure.** In Exodus (25:10-27:19) we have the prescribed order for the building of the tabernacle, beginning with the ark and proceeding outward, while in 36:8-38:31 we have a *description* of its construction, pursuing the reverse order; which order will be followed in this article. It is proper to state here that the cubit used in this article is the Egyptian royal cubit equal to approximately 20.625 inches. The common estimate for the cubit is eighteen inches.

(1) **The court** was an inclosed space about the tabernacle one hundred cubits long by fifty cubits wide, or, in round numbers, one hundred and seventy-two feet by eighty-six feet. Inclosing this space was a peculiarly constructed fence. Its framework consisted of pillars of "shittim" (acacia) wood, five cubits, i. e., a little over eight and one half feet high (Exod. 27:18). They were, doubtless, round and of the same thickness throughout, probably about five inches. The bottom was held in place by a "socket," or plate of bronze (A. V. "brass"), evidently laid flat upon the ground. The socket had a mortise, or hole, to receive the tenon which was in the bottom end of the pillar.

The pillars were kept upright by cords (Exod. 35:18) fastened to pins of copper (27:19) driven into the ground, both on the inside and the outside. The "fillets" were curtain rods hung upon hooks near the upper end of the pillars, and served as the top rail of a fence, to keep the pillars at a proper distance apart. The fillets were of shittim wood, covered with silver, while the hooks and the caps which protected the tops of the pillars were of the same metal (38:17, 19). Hooks were also placed at the bottom of the pillars, by which the lower edge of the curtain was fastened. The pillars, when set up and braced by the fillets and stay ropes, formed the complete framework of a fence. Upon this was hung sheets of "fine twined linen," probably like our *duck*, sewed endwise together so as to form a continuous screen from the doorway all round the corners to the doorway again. This was five cubits wide, the same as the height of the pillars, but as the pillars rested upon sockets, the curtain would be kept off from the ground.

The hanging for "the gate of the court" was in the middle of the eastern end, and was "needlework, of blue, and purple, and scarlet, and fine twined linen" (Exod. 38:18), i. e., the warp was of bleached linen threads and the woof of alternate bars of wool dyed blue, purple, and scarlet. Its size was five cubits high by twenty cubits long. Entrance into the court was only effected by lifting this curtain at the bottom. In this court was the altar of burnt offering, which probably stood in the center of the front half of the space, about halfway between the entrance and the tabernacle. Midway between the altar and the tabernacle (30:18) stood the laver (*q. v.*). The tabernacle itself was situated at the front edge of the rear half of the inclosure, and being thirty cubits long and ten cubits wide, it would leave equal spaces (viz., ten cubits) behind it and on either side.

(2) **The tabernacle.** This was composed of two parts, the tabernacle proper (Heb. *mĭshkän*) and the tent (*'ōhĕl*, A. V. "a covering upon the tabernacle," Exod. 26:7). The tabernacle proper consisted of planks (A. V. "boards") of the acacia (A. V. "shittim") wood, each ten cubits long by one and a half broad (26:16); their entire surface being plated with sheets of gold. Twenty of these formed each side wall (vers. 18, 20), each plank having two tenons at its foot to enter the socket. There were eight rear planks (v. 25), six of which were of the same dimensions as those on the side, thus making nine cubits. As the width of the tabernacle was probably the same as its height, viz., ten cubits, thus making of the Holy of Holies a perfect cube, this would leave one cubit of space to be filled by the two corner boards. There is nothing in the Hebrew to indicate the breadth of these two boards, and we assume that they were only one half cubit wide. If, now, the rear planks are placed within the side planks, so as to be flush with the end, each corner plank will rest on two sockets, and we have the sixteen sockets demanded. This will oblige us to count the rear socket of the sides, as is done with the posts of the courts. The meaning seems to be that as you look at each side forty sockets are seen, while if you look at the rear, sixteen are in view.

In order to keep the planks in line, three series of bars were provided, made of acacia wood overlaid with gold, to pass through rings of gold on the outside of the planks (Exod. 26:26-29; 36:31-34). Of these five were on each side and five on the rear, the middle bar reaching from end to end, while the upper and lower ones were divided, their ends being fastened (as Josephus suggests) with dowels. They were probably of different lengths, to prevent the break being in the center.

The whole structure was, doubtless, stayed with cords, one end fastened to the copper knobs to which the tent cloth was attached, and the other end to copper pins driven into the ground. The planks were covered on the outside with a double blanket of skins, probably suspended from the knobs above mentioned, thus keeping the wind and dust from

entering between the planks, and also protecting the gold sheeting. The inner blanket was of "badger skins" (Exod. 26:14; 36:19, R. V. "seals"), but may have been of the Angora goat. This was probably hung with the hair turned inward toward the planks, while the other blanket (of ram skins dyed red) was hung with the hair on the outside, to shed the rain.

(*a*) The roof (Heb. *'ōhĕl, tent*) was made of goats'-hair canvas, i. e., camlet, such as is still used by the Arabs, being generally of a foxy black or brownish color (Cant. 1:5). It consisted of an inner covering and a fly. The material was woven in eleven pieces, each thirty cubits long by four wide (Exod. 26:7, sq.; 36:14, sq.), five of these pieces being joined so as to make the inner tent, and six forming the fly. This sixth breadth, being thirty cubits long, would allow itself to be double across the front and single across the rear of the tabernacle (26:9, 13). The lower edge of each sheet was buttoned over curtain knobs on the planks by means of fifty loops attached to their selvedge. The tent extended one cubit over the sides (vers. 10-13). The roof was sustained by posts, one of them being an extension of the central front doorpost, their heads probably rounded so as not to tear the roof canvas.

(*b*) The door of the tent. The entrance to the tabernacle was closed with a screen like that of the court, supported by five pillars, covered with gold; their hooks were of gold, and their "fillets" (curtain rods) were covered with gold; while their sockets were of bronze (Exod. 26:36, 37; 36:37, 38). If these pillars are arranged so as to leave six spaces, each space will be a little over thirty-four inches wide. Evidently the curtain rods had rings in their ends, which slipped down over hooks in the tops of the posts and on the planks.

(*c*) The wall drapery. Each of these consisted of five pieces of cloth woven of the same material as the door screen, four cubits wide and twenty cubits long. These pieces were sewed together at the ends, and hung by "loops" of blue cord to the gold knobs on the inside of the planks (Exod. 26:1-6; 36:8-13). An especial dignity was given to these side curtains, over that of the door screen, by their embroidery of "cherubim of cunning work" (26:1; 36:8), instead of the simple tracery on the latter. As will be seen, the hangings were each twice as long as the entire circuit of the walls, therefore they must have been gathered into some manner of festoons.

(*d*) The veil (Heb. *pōrĕkĕth*, a *separation*), particularly described in Exod. 26:31-33; 36:35, 36, was the screen between the Holy Place and the Holy of Holies. It was of the same material as the door screens, but was embroidered with cherubim. Of these it is thought that there were two, their extended wings touching each other. The veil, like the other hangings, was suspended upon pillars, and, probably, "fillets" (curtain rods), though these latter are not mentioned. These pillars (and fillets) were covered with gold, the hooks were of gold, and the sockets of silver. For the veil four pillars were used, and as no one of them ran up to the peak, it did not, therefore, need to be in the center. The upper corners of the veil were fastened to the gold hooks in the planks. If we follow the proportions of the Holy Place and the Most Holy Place in the temple, we must suppose the latter in the tabernacle to have been square, and the former to have been twice as long as broad. This will fix the dividing line between the two rooms at two thirds of the width of the seventh plank from the rear, the presumption being that the pillars were wholly within the Most Holy Place.

5. **Furniture.** 1. The altar of burnt offering (Heb. *mǐzbăḥ hāʻōlāh*, Exod. 30:28; *brazen altar, mǐzbăḥ hănnᵉḥōshĕth*, Exod. 39:39; *table of the Lord*, Mal. 1:7, 12) was placed in the court, between the entrance and the tabernacle. It was made strong and light for convenient transportation; a hollow box of acacia ("shittim") wood, five cubits square and three cubits high (Exod. 27:1-8), overlaid with sheets of copper (A. V. "brass"). At each corner was a "horn," apparently a triangular extension of the sides at their junction. The altar had a grate (Heb. *măkbăr*, a *netting*) placed halfway between the top and bottom (v. 5). At each corner of the grate was a ring, through which were passed the copper-covered poles by which the altar was carried when on the march, like a handbarrow. Of course it was lined both inside and outside with copper to protect it from the heat. At the end of twenty years two hundred and fifty censers were flattened out and nailed on its sides, telling their awful story (Num. 16:17, 36-40) to the coming generations. The common censer in Egypt was a small, shallow, platelike vessel, about half a cubit in diameter. As the priests were not allowed to go up the altar by steps (Exod. 20:26), and as it would be too high to reach from the ground, the earth was, probably, raised about the altar so as to approach it by an incline.

The utensils for the altar (Exod. 27:3) made of copper were: *ash pans; shovels* for cleaning the altar; *basins* for receiving the blood to be sprinkled on the altar; *flesh hooks*, i. e., large *forks*, to handle the pieces of flesh; *fire pans* (Exod. 38:3; A. V. "censers," Num. 16:17); *snuff dishes* (Exod. 25:38). According to Lev. 6:13, the fire on this altar was never allowed to go out.

2. The laver (Heb. *kǐyyōr*, rounded, a *basin*) stood about midway between the altar and the tabernacle. It was the basin used by the officiating priests, and was made from the bronze mirrors of the women (Exod. 30:18; 38:8). It was probably round, of considerable size, with another and shallower basin beneath it, into which the water ran after being used, and in which the priests washed their feet. We have no Scripture information as to its size or shape. As no mention is made of a vessel in which was washed the parts of the victims offered in sacrifice, the laver was likely used for this purpose also. As washing in the East was always in running water, the laver was, doubtless, supplied with faucets from which the water would flow upon the object to be cleansed, whether the hands or feet of the priests or the parts of the sacrifice (*see* Laver). In the sacred structure itself there were four articles of furniture, three in the Holy Place and one in the Holy of Holies.

3. The table of showbread (Heb. *shūlhän lĕhĕm pänîm, table of the face*, i. e., of Jehovah). This was placed on the north or right side, and facing the candlestick (Exod. 40:22). It was made of acacia wood, two cubits long, one broad, and one and one half high. This proportion between the length and the height is accurately maintained in the sculptural form on the Arch of Titus. The surface, or top of the table, rested on a frame, a handbreadth deep, while round it ran a "crown" or molding of gold, projecting above the top, to keep articles from slipping off the table. The legs were apparently mortised into the sides (as usual nowadays), with rings near each corner for the carrying staves (25:23-30; 37:10-16).

The bread placed upon the table (Heb. "*face-bread*") was made of fine wheat flour (unleavened), baked in twelve loaves (cakes), each containing one fifth of an ephah of flour. These, according to Jewish tradition, as well as the dimensions of the table, would seem to have been placed upon plates in two piles of six each. They were renewed every Sabbath to be eaten by the priests exclusively (and that in the sanctuary only), and were then replaced by fresh loaves (I Sam. 21:6), which had been prepared overnight by the Levites (I Chron. 9:32). To each pile of loaves incense was added, probably placed in bowls beside the bread, "for a memorial, even an offering made by fire unto the Lord" (Lev. 24:5-9).

The *utensils* belonging to the table were: the *dishes* for the showbread; *bowls* (A. V. "spoons") for the incense; *jugs* (A. V. "covers"), which, as they were used for making libations with (A. V. "to cover withal") were doubtless for wine, with a spout for pouring; and *cups*, all being of pure gold.

4. The golden candlestick (Heb. *mᵉnōräh*) stood on the south or left side of the Holy Place, directly opposite the table of showbread (Exod. 40:24), the construction of which, except as to size, is minutely described (25:31-40; 37:17-24). The material of which it was made was pure gold, of which an entire talent was used for the candlestick and its vessels. The different parts were of "beaten work" *mǐqshäh*, hammered out of sheets. It consisted of a pedestal (*yārēq*), elsewhere meaning the *leg*, or, rather, the part of the body from which the legs and feet spring; and the shaft (*qäneh*, *reed* or *stalk*), from which, probably, at equal distances from one another, there projected three branches on each side, and rising as high as the central shaft. The central shaft and the six branches terminated in sockets, into which the seven lamps were placed. The ornamentation of the candlestick, a very beautiful design, consisted of a "bowl" (Heb. *gᵉbîʻă*), which was almond-shaped (i. e., the nut), tapering from a head. Above this was the "knop" (Heb. *kăphtōr*, *chaplet* or *chapter*), like the capital of a column, and under the intersection of the branches (25:35). Surmounting all was the "flower" (Heb. *pĕräḥ*, literally "blossom"), like a bud just ready to burst into bloom. There were four of these ornamental groupings on the main stem, one being placed at intervals at each of the three points where the branches diverged, the fourth being probably at the upper end, just under the lamp

which was placed upon it. There were three of these groups on each branch, one under the lamp, and the two others, probably, placed equidistant from each other. This is evidently the form of the candlestick, which is known to us chiefly by the passages in Exod. 25:31-40; 37:17-24, the light thrown thereon by the Jewish writers, and by the representation on the Arch of Titus at Rome.

Dimensions. The size of the candlestick is not given in the Bible description of it, and we are therefore left to conjecture. Jewish tradition assigns it a height of about five feet and a breadth of about three and one half feet. On the Arch of Titus it measures two feet nine inches high by two feet broad; but the figures there delineated are not life-size, and the proportion with the table of showbread on the same sculpture, as well as with the men there exhibited, yields a size about the same as the above tradition. We may therefore fix the entire height, including the base, at about three cubits, and the entire breadth at about two cubits. Taking the estimate of a cubit at 20.67 inches, the dimensions would be about 62 x 41 inches.

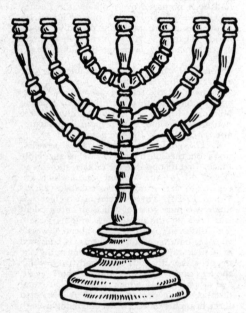

449. The Golden Candlestick

Finally came the lamps themselves (Heb. singular *nēr*), which were of the kind generally used in the East, but here of gold. These were placed, of course, upon the top of the main shaft, and the branches in sockets. Opinion generally places them on a horizontal line, although the instructions given in Exodus afford no information. The lamps were supplied with olive oil, *pure* (i. e., "prepared from olives which had been cleansed from leaves, twigs, dust, etc., before they were crushed"), *beaten* (i. e., "obtained not by crushing in oil presses, but by beating, when the oil which flows out by itself is of the finest quality and a white color") (K. and D., *Com.,* on Exod. 27:20).

It is likely that the plane of the lamps ran from east to west—thus the better lighting up of the Holy Place. The lamps were lighted at the time of the evening sacrifice (Exod. 30:8), and extinguished, trimmed, and filled at the time of the morning sacrifice (Exod. 30:7; I Sam. 3:3). They are traditionally believed to have held half a "log," i. e., a little more than a half pint.

The utensils belonging to the candlestick were the "tongs" and the snuff dishes (Exod. 25:38), made of the same gold as the candlestick itself. The "tongs" were used to pull up the wick and to hold the coal while blowing it to light the lamp. The "snuff dishes" were *coal pans* (Exod. 27:3; Lev. 16:12), used for bringing the live coals from the great altar.

450. The Golden Altar or Altar of Incense

5. The altar of incense (Heb. *mǐzbēăḥ mǐqṭăr qᵉtŏrĕth*) occupied the middle space near to and in front of the inner veil (Exod. 30:1-6; 37:25-28; 40:5; Lev. 16:18). It was, however, reckoned as belonging to the Most Holy Place (I Kings 6:22; Heb. 9:4), apparently on account of its great sanctity. In construction it was a simple box of acacia wood, two cubits high, one cubit wide, and one cubit broad, with a top, and horns like the large altar, the whole being covered with gold. It had no grate, because the fire did not come directly in contact with it. It had a molding around the edge and rings to carry it, and staves. No utensils belonged especially to it. Upon this altar neither burnt offerings nor meat offerings were allowed to be offered, nor drink offerings to be poured, but it was used exclusively to burn incense upon morning and evening.

6. The ark. (*a*) *Names.* It was called the *ark of the covenant* (Heb. *'ărōn bᵉrîth,* Num. 10:33), or *ark of the testimony* (Heb. *'ărōn hā‘ēdūth,* Exod. 25:22, etc.), from the law which was kept therein. (*b*) *Construction, contents,* etc. The ark was made of acacia wood ("shittim") two and one half cubits long, one and one half cubits broad, and one and one half cubits high (external dimensions), and plated inside and out with pure gold. Running round each side was a gold border (A. V. "crown"), extending above the top of the ark, so as to keep the lid from moving.

This lid was called the "mercy seat" (Exod. 25:20, 22; Heb. *kăppŏrĕth,* a *covering*), of the same size as the ark itself, and made of acacia wood covered with gold. The ark was transported by means of two gold-covered poles, run through two gold rings on each side, from which they were not to be drawn (25:15) unless it might be necessary to remove them in order to cover the ark when the tabernacle was removed (Num. 4:6).

Upon the lid, or mercy seat, or at the ends of the ark, as in the Temple (*q. v.*), were placed the Cherubim (*q. v.*), probably figures beaten out of gold as was the candlestick. In shape they were probably human, with the exception of their wings, though some authorities think they were of the same complex form as the cherubim mentioned by Ezekiel (1:5-14). They were no doubt the normal or full height of a man, and are always spoken of as maintaining an upright position (II Chron. 3:13). They stood facing each other, looking down upon the mercy seat, with their wings forward in a brooding attitude (Exod. 25:20; comp. Deut. 32:11). The golden censer, with which the high priest once a year entered the Most Holy Place, was doubtless set upon this lid.

Between the cherubim was the *Shechinah* (Heb. *sh*e*kināh, residence*), the cloud in which Jehovah appeared above the mercy seat (Exod. 25:22; comp. Lev. 16:2). It was not the cloud of incense (Lev. 16:13), but the manifest appearance of the divine glory. Because Jehovah manifested his essential presence in this cloud, not only could no unclean and sinful man go before the mercy seat, i. e., approach the holiness of the all-holy God, but even the anointed high priest, if he went before it at his own pleasure, or without the expiatory blood of sacrifice, would expose himself to certain death.

The *contents* of the ark were: the two tables of stone, on which Jehovah wrote the Ten Commandments, or rather those prepared by Moses from the original, broken by him when he heard of Israel's idolatry (Exod. 31:18-34:29; Deut. 9:10-10:4); the autograph copy of the law, written by Moses (Deut. 31:26), presumed to be the Pentateuch in full, and thought to be the same as was afterward discovered in the time of Josiah (II Kings 22:8), but which must, in the meanwhile, have been removed, together with all the contents, for in the days of Solomon the ark contained the two tables only (I Kings 8:9). The other contents of the ark were a golden pot of miraculously preserved manna (Exod. 16:33, 34), and "Aaron's rod that budded" (Heb. 9:4; comp. Num. 17:10).

6. Care of the Tabernacle. The following are the directions for the care of the tabernacle and its furniture (Num. 4:4-33; 7:3-9; 10:17, 21): "The service" (v. 4) signifies military service, and is used here with special reference to the service of the Levites as the sacred militia of Jehovah. The following were the duties of the Kohathite Levites: When the tabernacle was to be taken down for removal the priests took down the veil and covered the ark of testimony with it; over this they put a covering of "badgers' skins," and finally a "cloth wholly of blue." Removing the dishes from the table of showbread, they spread over it a cloth of blue, then replaced the dishes and spread upon them a cloth of scarlet, and finally a covering of "badgers' skins." The candlestick, with its lamps, snuffers, and extinguishers, was then covered with a cloth of blue,

over which was placed a covering of badgers' skins. The altar of incense was covered with a cloth of blue and badgers' skins, and then all other "instruments of ministry" in the sanctuary were wrapped in blue and badgers' skins and placed upon a "bar," i. e., a bier made of two poles with crosspieces. After this the great altar was cleansed from the ashes, covered with a purple cloth, the altar utensils packed in it, and then covered with badgers' skins. When all this preparation was completed the Kohathites came forward to bear the furniture away. The only thing not mentioned as prepared by the priests was the laver, probably because it was carried without any covering.

To the care and carrying by the Gershonites were assigned the tapestry of the tabernacle, viz., the inner covering, the tent of goats' hair, the two outside coverings of the planks, the entrance curtain, the veil, the hangings of the court and its entrance curtain, with all the cords and the various implements used in said work. Thus their office was to perform whatever was usually done with these portions of the sanctuary, especially in setting up or taking down the tabernacle (Num. 3:25-4:33).

The charge of the Merarites was: the planks of the tabernacle with the bars, the pillars and their sockets (both of the sacred building and its court), and their pins and cords. That is, they were to take them down, carry them on the march, and to fix them when the tabernacle was set up again (Num. 3:36, 37; 4:31, 32). *See* Levites.

7. Typology of the Tabernacle and Furniture. (1) **Design.** The design of the tabernacle is thus stated: "Let them make me a sanctuary that I may dwell among them" (Exod. 25:8). This sanctuary was styled *the tent of meeting* (Heb. *'ōhĕl mō'ēd*) between Jehovah and His people. The Lord said, "I will meet with you to speak with you there" (Exod. 29:42); "and I will dwell among the Children of Israel and will be their God" (vs. 45). Thus the tabernacle and all that pertained to it was typical of the presence of God with His people. In accordance with this promise, the glory of Jehovah filled the tabernacle, but the Presence was manifested to the people in the pillar of cloud and fire above the sacred structure (Exod. 40:34-38; Num. 9:15-23). The fiery cloud by day moved at God's direction, and thus prefigured His guidance. The entire divine institution portrayed the approach of God's redeemed people to His Presence. Following is a discussion of the tabernacle typology as presented by many Bible teachers. (2) **General Typology.** The tabernacle in comprehensive terms is set forth in the N. T. as typical in three ways: (a) Of the Church, as "a habitation of God through the Spirit" (Exod. 25:9; Eph. 2:19-22). (b) Of the believer who is "a temple of the Holy Spirit" (I Cor. 6:19; II Cor. 6:16). (c) As a portrayal of heavenly reality (Heb. 9:23-24). In its minute details the tabernacle speaks of Christ. This is true of the high priest, the furniture, the ritual and the worship. (3) **As a Type of Christ.** (a) **The Brazen Altar** (Exod. 27:1-8) is a type of Christ's cross, on which our Lord as a whole burnt offering offered Himself without spot unto God. (b) **Laver.** The laver, in which the priests washed before entering the holy place or approaching the ăltar to minister, is a type of Christ cleansing the believer from the defilement of sin (John 13:2-10) and from "every spot or wrinkle or any such thing" (Eph. 5:25-27). (c) **The Golden Candlestick.** The Candlestick typifies Christ as our Light, bringing to us the full radiance of divine life. It is noteworthy that natural light was shut out from the tabernacle. Only the Spirit of God can show us the things of Christ (I Cor. 2:14, 15). The divine Spirit always takes the things of Christ and reveals them unto us, as Jesus announced in His Upper Room Discourse (John 16:14, 15). (d) **The Table of Shew Bread.** The Table of Shew Bread is a type of Christ as the Bread of Life, the Sustainer of each individual believer-priest (I Pet. 2:9; Rev. 1:6). The manna portrays the life-giving Christ; the Shew Bread the life-sustaining Christ. Christ is the Bread which came down from heaven (John 6:33-58). As the Shew Bread prefigures the "grain of wheat" (John 12:24) pulverized in the mill of suffering (John 12:27) and subjected to the fire of divine judgment for sin (John 12:31-33). (e) **The Altar of Incense.** (Exod. 30:1-10) portrays Christ our Intercessor (John 17:1-26; Heb. 7:25) through Whom our prayers and petitions ascend to God (Heb. 13:15; Rev. 8:3, 4). It also speaks of the Christian as a Believer-Priest offering the sacrifice of praise and worship (Heb. 13:15). (f) **The Veil.** The Veil (Exod. 26:31-35) was a type of Christ's human body (Matt. 26:26; 27:50; Heb. 10:20). Accordingly, it was supernaturally torn in two when Christ died (Matt. 27:51), granting instant access to God to everyone who approaches on the ground of faith in him. The death of Christ portrayed by the Veil also marked the termination of all legality. The unobstructed way to God was now open. The officiating priesthood at the death of Christ must have repaired the Veil that had been definitely rent. Antitypically this was a picture of attempting to put the believer or sinner back under law. (g) **The Ark of the Covenant.** (Exod. 25:10-22). In its materials, acacia wood and gold, it is a type of the humanity and deity of Christ. Acacia wood grows in the desert and fittingly portrays Christ's humanity in its lowliness as a "root out of a dry ground" (Isa. 53:2). The fact that it was overlaid with pure gold (Exod. 25:11) suggests deity in manifestation as setting forth the divine glory. In its contents the Ark typifies Christ as having God's law in His heart (Exod. 25:16; 25:21). The Ark portrays Christ in resurrection inasmuch as it contained Aaron's rod that budded (Num. 17:10). The employment of the Ark, particularly the Mercy Seat, typifies the divine throne. It was transformed from a throne of judgment to a throne of grace as far as the erring Israelite was concerned by the blood of atonement which was sprinkled upon it. The cherubim with outstretched wings guarded the holiness of the Mercy Seat. The Ark was the commencement of everything in the tabernacle symbolism. It was placed in the Holy of

Holies, showing that God begins from Himself in His outreach toward man in revelation. On the other hand, in the human approach the worship begins from without, moving toward God in the very center of the holiest place. Man begins at the Brazen Altar, that is, at the cross, where atonement is made in the light of the fire of God's judgment.—*M. F. U.*

Tabernacles, Feast of. *See* Festivals.

Tab'itha (tăb'ĭ-thá; Gr. from Aram *t͜ebĭthá, gazelle*), a benevolent Christian widow of Joppa whom Peter restored to life (Acts 9:36-42). She was probably a Hellenistic Jewess, known to the Greeks by the name Dorcas (*q. v.*), and to the Hebrews by the Aramaic equivalent. It is not certain, however, that Tabitha bore both names; Luke may have translated the name for the benefit of his Gentile readers, and used its definition thereafter for their convenience. The Greeks used Dorcas, i. e., "female gazelle," as a term of endearment for their women. Soon after Peter had miraculously cured the palsied Aeneas in Lydda the church at Joppa was bereaved by the death of Tabitha. They at once sent for the apostle, whether merely to receive his Christian consolation or in the hope that he could restore their friend to life, does not appear. A touching picture is given of the widows who stood "weeping, and showing the coats and garments which Dorcas had made." Peter "put them all forth," prayed, and commanded the lifeless woman to arise. She opened her eyes, arose, and by the apostle was presented to her friends. The facts, which became widely known, produced a profound impression in Joppa, and occasioned many conversions (9:42).

Table. 1. A *divan*, i. e., a company of persons seated round about a room (Cant. 1:12, A. V. "at table") (Heb. *mēsăb*).

2. A table as spread with food, viands (Judg. 1:7; I Sam. 20:29, 34; I Kings 2:7, etc.). Heb. *shŭlḥān, spread out, extended.* As to the form of tables among the Hebrews little is known; but, as among other orientals, they were probably not high. They were doubtless, among the ancient Israelites, similar to those of modern Arabs, a piece of skin or leather, a mat, or a linen cloth spread upon the ground. Hence the fitness of the name *something spread*, and the figurative expression, "Let their table become a snare before them" (Psa. 69:22),

451. Roman Triclinium

i. e., let their feet become entangled in it, as it is spread on the ground.

3. Gr. *'anakeimai*, to lie at table (John 13:28) on the divan.

4. A couch to recline on at meals (Mark 7:4) (Gr. *klinē*, *bed*.)

5. A table on which food is placed (Matt. 15:27; Mark 7:28; Luke 16:21; 22:21, 30); the table of showbread (Heb. 9:2); the table or stand of a money changer, where he sits, exchanging different kinds of money for a fee, and paying back with interest loans or deposits (Matt. 21:12; Mark 11:15; John 2:15). (Gr. *trapeza*.)

Figurative. "The table of the Lord is contemptible" (Mal. 1:7; comp. v. 12), is what the prophets charge the priests with representing. The table of Jehovah is the altar, and they made it contemptible by offering upon it bad, blemished animals, which were unfit for sacrifices. "They shall speak lies at one table" (Dan. 11:27), is a figure of feigned friendship. Eating, especially in the presence of enemies (Psa. 23:5; comp. Isa. 21:5), denotes a sense of security. In I Cor. 10:21, "Ye cannot be partakers of the Lord's table, and of the table of devils," brings into sharp contrast the holy communion and the sacrifices offered to heathen deities. Paul makes the real existences answering to the heathen conception of these gods to be *demons*.

6. **Tablet** (Heb. *lūăḥ*, *glistening*), whether of *polished* stone or wood (Exod. 27:8, etc.; A. V. "board"), or for writing on (Isa. 30:8; Hab. 2:2; Prov. 3:3).

7. Gr. *pinakidion* (Luke 1:63) and Gr. *plax*, *flat*, the former a small writing tablet, the latter meaning the same as No. 1 (II Cor. 3:3).

Table of Showbread. *See* Tabernacle.

Table of The Lord is a phrase used to designate the table of the Christian Church, and evidently taken from I Cor. 10:21. In the Old Testament the words table (*q. v.*) and altar appear to have been applied indifferently to the same thing (Ezek. 41:22).

Tables of The Law (Heb. *lūḥōth 'ĕbĕn*, *stone tablets*, Exod. 24:12; 31:18), also called "tables of the covenant" (Deut. 9:9, 15), or "of the testimony" (Exod. 31:18) were given to Moses on Mount Sinai, having the Ten Commandments written by the finger of God.

Tablet, the inaccurate rendering in the A. V. of:

1. Heb. *kūmăz*, (*jewel*), probably gold *drops* like beads worn around the neck or arm by

452. General View of Mount Tabor, Palestine

the Israelites in the desert (Exod. 35:22; Num. 31:50).

2. Heb. *Băttē hănnĕphĕsh* (*houses of the breath*, i. e., perfume bottles, Isa. 3:20).

Ta'bor (tā'bẽr). 1. **Mount**, now called Jebel et Tur; a conical and quite symmetrical mound of limestone, on the northeastern part of the plain of Esdraelon. It is about six miles east of Nazareth. The northern slope is covered with oak trees and syringa. It rises to the height of one thousand three hundred and fifty feet above the plain, which itself is four hundred feet above the Mediterranean Sea. The ascent is usually made on the west side, near the little village of Debûrieh, probably

453. Franciscan Convent, Mount Tabor

the ancient Daberath (Josh. 19:12). Tabor is named (19:22) as a boundary between Issachar and Zebulun. Barak, at the command of Deborah, gathered his forces on Tabor, and descended thence with "ten thousand men" into the plain, conquering Sisera on the banks of the Kishon (Judg. 4:6-15). Here the brothers of Gideon were slain by Zebah and Zalmunna (8:18, 19); and some think Tabor is intended when it is said (Deut. 33:19) of Issachar and Zebulun that "they shall call the people unto *the mountains:* there they shall offer the sacrifices of righteousness." Dr. Robinson says the prospect from it is the finest in Palestine. Lord Nugent says he cannot recollect ever to have seen from any natural height a more splendid sight. In the time of Christ the summit is said to have been crowned by a fortified town, the ruins of which are present there now (I Chron. 6:77). It is difficult to see how such a scene as that of Christ's transfiguration could have taken place there, and the New Testament clearly points to some part of Hermon as the place.

2. **The City.** Tabor is mentioned in the lists of I Chron., ch. 6, as a city of the Merarite Levites, in the tribe of Zebulun (v. 77). The list of the towns of Zebulun (Josh., ch. 10) contains the name of Chisloth-tabor (v. 12). It is therefore possible either that Chisloth-tabor is abbreviated into Tabor by the chronicler, or that by the time these later lists were compiled the Merarites had established themselves on the sacred mountain, and that Tabor is Mount Tabor.

3. **The Oak or Terebinth** (not "plain" as in A. V.), is mentioned (I Sam. 10:3) as one of the points in the homeward journey of Saul after his anointing by Samuel. The place is nowhere else mentioned, and nothing further can be determined concerning it than that it

stood by the road leading from Rachel's tomb to Gibeah.

Tabret. *See* Music.

Tab'rimmon (tăb'rĭm-ŏn), in A. V., **Tab'rimon** (Aram. "Rimmon is good," Rimmon being the god of thunder, a weather-god, of Damascus, Akkad. "thunderer"), the father of Ben-hadad I, king of Syria in the reign of Asa (I Kings 15:18), B. C. before 900.

Tache, one of the knobs upon which were hung the curtains of the tabernacle (*q. v.*).

Tach'monite, The (tăk'mō-nīt), "the Tachmonite that sat in the seat," chief among David's captains (II Sam. 23:8), is in I Chron. 11:11 called "Jashobeam, an Hachmonite," or, as the margin gives it, "son of Hachmoni." Kennicott has shown that the words translated "he that sat in the seat" are a corruption of Jashobeam, and that "the Tachmonite" is a corruption of the "son of Hachmoni," which was the family or local name of Jashobeam. Therefore he concludes "Jashobeam the Hachmonite" to have been the true reading.

Tackling (Heb. *ḥĕbĕl*, Isa. 33:23; Gr. *skeuē*, Acts 27:19) represents the spars, ropes, chains, etc., of a ship (*q. v.*).

454. Air View of the Ruins of the Temple, Palmyra

Tad'mor (tăd'môr; cf. Heb. *tamar, a palm tree*), a city built by Solomon in the wilderness (II Chron. 8:4; R. A. "Tamar"), and the parallel passage (I Kings 9:18) adds "in the land," indicating the land on the southern border of Palestine (Ezek. 47:19; 48:28). The Greeks and Romans call the city Palmyra. It was one hundred and seventy-six miles from Damascus, and the center of vast commercial traffic as well as a military station. Its grandeur is attested by its magnificent ruins. Presuming that Tadmor is the same as Palmyra, the following facts may properly be mentioned. The first author of antiquity who mentions Palmyra is Pliny the Elder. Later, Appian writes of it in connection with a design of Mark Anthony to allow his cavalry to plunder it. In the 2d century A. D. it seems to have been beautified by the emperor Hadrian. It became a Roman colony under Caracalla (211-217 A. D.), and received the *jus Italicum*. In the reign of Gallienus the Roman Senate invested Odenathus, a senator of Palmyra, with the regal dignity, on account of his services in defeating Sapor, king of Persia. Upon his assassination his widow, Zenobia, wished to make of Palmyra an independent monarchy, and for a while successfully resisted the Roman arms; but was defeated and taken pris-

oner by the emperor Aurelian (A. D. 273), who left a Roman garrison in Palmyra. This garrison was massacred in a revolt, for which Aurelian punished the city so severely that it never recovered from the blow. Today a living town named Tudmur is an important station on the Iraq-Tripoli oil pipe line about ½ mile from the ruins of ancient Palmyra.

Ta'han (tā'hăn).

1. The head of one of the families of the tribe of Ephraim at the end of the Exodus (Num. 26:35), B. C. c. 1440.

2. Apparently the son of Telah and the father of Laadan, in the genealogy of Ephraim (I Chron. 7:25), B. C. after 1440.

Ta'hanites (tā'hȧ-nīts), the descendants (Num. 26:35) of Tahan, 1 (*q. v.*).

Tahap'anes (tȧ-hăp'ȧ-nēz). *See* Tahpanhes.

Ta'hath (tā'hăth; *that which is beneath*).

1. A Kohathite Levite, son of Assir and father of Uriel, or Zephaniah, in the ancestry of Samuel and Heman (I Chron. 6:24, 37).

2. An Ephraimite, son of Bered and father of Eladah (I Chron. 7:20). Perhaps identical with Tahan, 1 (*q. v.*).

3. Apparently the grandson of the foregoing, being registered as son of Eladah and father of Zabad (I Chron. 7:20).

4. The name of a desert station between Makbeloth and Tarah (Num. 33:26); not identified.

Tah'panhes (tä'păn-hēz; Jer. 2:16, marg.; 43:7, 8, 9; 44:1; 46:14), **Tahap'anes** (tȧ-hăp'ȧ-nēz; Jer. 2:16), or **Tehaph'nehes** (tē-hăf'nē-hēz; Ezek. 30:18), an important city in the time of Jeremiah and Ezekiel. Jeremiah (ch. 39) and Josephus (*Ant.*, x, 9, 1) tells us that Nebuchadnezzar had taken Jerusalem, made Zedekiah captive, burned the city, and carried away most of the inhabitants to Babylon. A feeble remnant of Judah gathered under Johanan and fled to Tahpanhes, in Egypt. In this party were "the king's daughters," Jeremiah the prophet, and Baruch, his amanuensis (compare other passages above). Here stood a house of Pharaoh, respecting which the command came to Jeremiah, "Take great stones in thine hand, and hide them in the clay in the brickkiln, which is at the entry of Pharaoh's house in Tahpanhes, in the sight of the men of Judah; and say unto them, Thus saith the Lord of hosts, the God of Israel; Behold, I will send and take Nebuchadrezzar the king of Babylon, my servant, and will set his throne upon these stones that I have hid; and he shall spread his royal pavillion over them," etc. (Jer. 43:8-10). That this prediction became history, and that the Babylonian king did twice invade Egypt and conquered it, is no longer doubted.

The site of Tahpanhes was found by Sir Flinders Petrie and identified with modern Tell Defenneh, an Egyptian frontier town at the easternmost mouth of the Nile River in the Delta.

Ta'hash (tā'hăsh; *dugong*), a son of Nahor (Gen. 22:24). *See* Tha'hash.

Tah'penes (tä'pē-nēz), an Egyptian wife of the Pharaoh who received Hadad, the Edomite prince, when he fled from his father's desolated capital (I Kings 11:18-20), B. C. about 940. The sister of Tahpenes was given to

Hadad in marriage, and their son, Genubath, was "weaned" by the queen herself, and brought up "in Pharaoh's household among the sons of Pharaoh." At that time Egypt was divided into perhaps three monarchies. Psusennes, of the Tanitic line, has been conjectured to have been the husband of this Tahpenes, brother-in-law of Hadad and father-in-law of Solomon; but there has been no name found among those of that period bearing any resemblance to Tahpenes.

Ta'hrea (tä'rē-à), a great-grandson of Jonathan, and one of the four sons of Micah (I Chron. 9:41), B. C. after 1037. In the parallel passage (8:35) he is called Taria (*q. v.*).

Tah'tim-hod'shi (tä'tĭm-hŏd'shī), one of the places visited by Joab during his census of the land of Israel. It occurs between Gilead and Dan-jaan (II Sam. 24:6). The name has puzzled all the interpreters, but is thought by some to mean "the Hittites of Kadesh." *See* Kadesh.

Talent, the greatest weight of the Hebrews. *See* Metrology.

Tal'itha Cu'mi (tăl'ĭ-thà kōō'mĭ), two Aramaic words (Mark 5:41), signifying "Damsel, arise."

Tal'mai (tăl'mi; *pertaining to furrows, plowman,* but cf. Hurrian, talma, *big*).

1. One of the gigantic sons of Anak who dwelt in Hebron (Num. 13:22). They were expelled from their stronghold by Caleb (Josh. 15:14) and killed by the men of Judah (Judg. 1:10), B. C. about 1380. There is a tall race, of light complexion, figured on the Egyptian monuments, and called in the hieroglyphic inscriptions *Tanmahu,* who have been supposed to represent the descendants of this man. The interchange of the liquid *l* for *n,* so constant in all languages," makes plausible the conjecture that this is the Egyptian rendering of Talmai.

2. The son of Ammihud, and king of Geshur, a small Aramaean kingdom in the northeast of Bashan (II Sam. 3:3; 13:37; I Chron. 3:2). His daughter, Maacah, was one of David's wives and mother of Absalom, B. C. before 1000.

Tal'mon (tăl'mŏn), the head of a family of doorkeepers in the temple, "the porters for the camps of the sons of Levi" (I Chron. 9:17; Neh. 11:19). Some of his descendants returned with Zerubbabel (Ezra 2:42; Neh. 7:45), and were employed in their hereditary office in the days of Nehemiah and Ezra (Neh. 12:25).

Ta'mah (tä'mà). The children of Tamah were among the Nethinim who returned with Zerubbabel (Neh. 7:55), B. C. before 536. In Ezra (2:53) the name is Anglicized *Thamah. See* Te'mah.

Ta'mar (tä'mēr; *a palm tree,* sometimes *Thamar*).

1. The wife of Er, the son of Judah, and, after his death, of his brother Onan. The sudden death of his two sons so soon after their marriage with Tamar made Judah hesitate to give her the third also, thinking, very likely, according to a superstition (Tobit 2:7, sq.), that either she herself or marriage with her had been the cause of their deaths. He therefore sent her to her father, with the promise

that he would give her his youngest son as soon as he was grown up, though he never intended to do so. Desirous of retaining the family inheritance and name through children, Tamar waited until satisfied that Shelah was not to be given to her as a husband, and then determined to procure children from Judah himself, who had become a widower. She ensnared him by pretending to be one of those women who were consecrated to the impure rites of Canaanitish worship. He gave her pledges, which she produced some three months after, when she was accused of unchastity and sentenced to death by Judah. He acknowledged his own guilt, and the provocation he had furnished her to do wrong. Tamar's life was spared, and she became the mother of the twins Pharez and Zarah (Gen. 38:6-30; Thamar, Matt. 1:3), B. C. about 1925.

2. A daughter of David by Maachah, as is evident from her being the full sister of Absalom (II Sam. 13:1; comp. 3:3). Ammon, the eldest son of David by Ahinoam (3:2), conceived a passion for Tamar because of her beauty, and, being unable to gratify his desire, he quite pined away. Jonadab noticed his condition, and, learning its cause, suggested to him the means of accomplishing his wicked purpose. He feigned illness, and begged his father, who visited him, to allow his sister to come to his house and prepare food for which he had a fancy. She came and prepared some cakes, probably in an outer room; but Amnon refused to eat, and, ordering all his attendants to retire, he called her into his chamber, and there accomplished his infamous purpose. Amnon's love gave way to brutal hatred, and he ordered her to leave his apartments. Tamar remonstrated, telling him that this wrong would be greater than that already done her. The meaning of this seems to be that by being thus sent away it would inevitably be supposed that she had been guilty of some shameful conduct herself. Her brother would not listen to her, but ordered one of the attendants to put her out and bolt the door after her. Notwithstanding she wore the dress of a princess, a garment with sleeves (A. V. "of divers colors"), Amnon's servant treated her as a common woman, and turned her out of the house. Then Tamar put ashes upon her head, rent her royal dress, laid her hand upon her head, and ran crying through the streets. She shortly encountered Absalom, who took her to his house, where she remained in a state of widowhood. David failed to punish the crime of his firstborn, but she was avenged two years afterward by Absalom (II Sam. 13:1-32; I Chron. 3:9), B. C. about 980.

3. Daughter of Absalom (II Sam. 14:27). She ultimately, by her marriage with Uriel of Gibeah, became the mother of Maachah, the future queen of Judah, or wife of Abijah (I Kings 15:2).

4. A place in the southern border of Palestine, supposed to be *Thamara,* on the road from Hebron to Elath (Ezek. 47:19; 48:28).

Tamarisk. *See* Vegetable Kingdom.

Tam'muz (tăm'ŭz). Ezekiel refers to the worship of this god in 8:14, where he describes women mourning for this deceased deity at the north gate of the Jerusalem temple. Tammuz was an ancient Akkadian deity whose worship spread throughout the Semitic world. He was the husband and brother of Ishtar, the Babylonian goddess of procreation. In Babylonian legends Tammuz supposedly died early in the fall when vegetation dried up. He departed to the nether world, being recovered by the wailing Ishtar. Bursting buds of springtime marked his return to the upper world. The Greek counterpart of Tammuz was Adonis and the Egyptian, Osiris. Tammuz cults are thought to be referred to in Jer. 22:19; Amos 8:10; Zech. 12:10. The fourth Babylonian month, corresponding to July, was named in honor of this god which, in post-Biblical times, became the name of the fourth month to the Jews. Byblos, the Biblical Gebal, was a very prominent center of Adonis cults, very much like that of Tammuz. Tammuz worship was connected with licentious festivals. In Babylon the cult included the annual marriage of the king to the fertility goddess in the form of a priestess. This symbolized the regeneration of nature. The Tammuz-Ishtar cult was degrading and thoroughly inconsonant with the chaste worship of Yahweh.—*M. F. U.*

Ta'nach (tā'năk; Josh. 21:25), a slight variation of Taanach (*q. v.*).

Tanhu'meth (tăn-hū'mĕth; *consolation*), the father of Seraiah (*q. v.*), in the time of Gedaliah (II Kings 25:23), B. C. 588. In this passage he appears as a Netophathite by the clerical omission of another name, as is evident from the parallel passage (Jer. 40:8).

Tanner, a dresser of hides (Acts 9:43). The art of treating skins of animals was widely cultivated in antiquity. It was known by the Hebrews (Exod. 25:5). The Egyptians were adept at it. Ancient Egyptian literature gives an insight into the process of tanning. A three-day treatment with salt and flour cleansed the skins from foreign matter. Lime was used to remove the hair. The acrid juices of desert plants or oak bark were also used. The skin was dried for several days and treated with acid barks and leaves, like sumac. Hebrews and Egyptians and other ancient peoples used leather for various purposes—for tent coverings (Exod. 26:14), containers for water (Gen. 21:14), for milk (Judg. 4:19) and wine (Matt. 9:17f), oil and other liquids. It was also used for shields, the leather being oiled to keep it soft and pliable (II Sam. 1:21; Isa. 21:5). Various articles of clothing were also made of leather. Elijah and John the Baptist wore leather garments (II Kings 1:8; Matt. 3:4). Sandals, shields and helmets were also prepared. Another common use was leather finely treated for writing parchments. The art of tanning, although very necessary, was a malodorous task and one that was regarded as unclean by many who recognized certain animals as unclean. Thus, under Judaism, tanners had to live outside the city, often near the water, like Simon the tanner who lived by the seashore at Joppa (Acts 10:6). It is highly significant in the context of Acts 9:43 and 10:9f, that Peter lodged with Simon the tanner. This is an element in the narrative showing the divine dealing with the Apostle of the circumcision in over-coming the Judaistic horror of the ceremonially unclean. The entire Acts narrative displays God's working with Peter to break down his prejudices against the Gentiles and to prepare him for the scene and sermon in Cornelius' house when the gospel was opened to the Gentiles.—*M. F. U.* See Leather, Workers in.

Ta'phath (tā'făth), the daughter of Solomon, who married Ben-abinadab, who was commissary for the region of Dor (I Kings 4:11), B. C. after 960.

Tappu'ah (tăp-pū'à; an *apple*).

1. The second named of the four sons of Hebron, of the lineage of Caleb (I Chron. 2:43), B. C. before 1370.

2. A city of Judah, in the Shephelah, or lowland (Josh. 15:34), probably Beit-Nettif (Beth-letepha, a corruption of Beth-el-Taphua).

3. A town in the tribe of Ephraim (Josh. 16:8), near Manasseh, in which latter territory probably lay the "land of Tappuah" (17:8). It probably contained a fine spring, and hence called En-tappuah (*q. v.*), and is commonly identified with Sheik Abu Zarad, near present-day Jāsûf, about 8 miles S. of Shechem.

Ta'rah (tā'rà; cf. Akkad. *turahu, ibex*), one of the halting places of Israel, between Tahath and Mithcah (Num. 33:27, 28). *See* Terah.

Tar'alah (tăr'à-là), a town in the western section of the territory of Benjamin (Josh. 18:27), perhaps identical with the modern village of *Beit-Tirza* in Wady Ahmed, north of Beit-Jala.

Ta'rea (tā'rē-à), son of Micah, in the lineage of King Saul (I Chron. 8:35; "Tahrea" in 9:41).

Tares. *See* Vegetable Kingdom.

Target (Heb. *kîdōn*), a spear (I Sam. 17:6), as usually rendered; *sinnäh* (I Kings 10:16; II Chron. 9:15; 14:8), a large *shield*, as usually rendered.

Tar'pelites (tär'pĕl-īts; only Ezra 4:9), one of the peoples settled in the cities of Samaria, and remaining there in the days of Artaxerxes. Some have compared the Median Tapuri of Ptolemy, the Tapyri of Strabo; others the Tarpetes of Strabo, who dwelt near the Palus Maeotis, or Sea of Azof. This latter location seems too far off. The *Speaker's Commentary* proposes Tubal, the classic Tibareni, on the coast of Pontus, which is also at some distance. Some have conjectured that the word has no ethnic connotation at all, but is a special title of Persian officials at Samaria. In reality nothing is known.—W. H. revised by *M. F. U.*

Tar'shish (tär'shĭsh). 1. This is a Phoenician word from the Akkadian meaning smelting plant or refinery. Four times in the A. V. it occurs *tharshish* (I Kings 10:22; 22:48; I Chron. 7:10). The term *tarshish* is employed quite a few times in the O. T. in connection with ships, merchants and trade. The "navy" or "fleet of Tarshish" (Heb. *'ŏnî tărshîsh*) which Solomon's ally Hiram I of Tyre built for the Hebrew monarch at Ezion-geber on the Persian Gulf, has been illuminated from ancient Oriental sources. A better rendering of Solomon's merchant marine in the light of increased knowledge of early Phoenician trading activities in the Mediterranean would be "smeltery" or "refining fleet," which brought smelted metal home from the colonial mines. Phoenician boats used to ply the sea regularly, transporting smelted ores from the mining towns in Sardinia and Spain. A Phoenician inscription from Nora in Sardinia from the ninth century B. C. refers to a *tarshish* or smelting site in this island. Smeltery fleets or *tarshish* ships hauled material from this and other mining stations in the western Mediterranean. Solomon's fleet, on the other hand, transported the raw copper mined in the Arabah and smelted at Ezion-geber (*q. v.*), to distant ports in southern Arabia and N. Africa in exchange for gold, silver, ivory, apes and baboons (I Kings 10:22 cf. I Kings 9:26, 28). Solomon's "little Pittsburgh" was excavated at the site of modern Tell el Kheleifeh, 1938-40. This important copper smeltery seems evidently the work of Phoenician craftsmen who were widely experienced in the art of setting up copper furnaces and refineries at smelting settlements in Sardinia and in Spain (the later Tartessus), which were called *tarshish*, after which the ships, particularly fitted for carrying such ore, were called "tarshish ships" (cf. Frederic Thieberger, *King Solomon*, London, 1947; p. 206). Ships of *tarshish* were built by Jehoshaphat in imitation of Solomon. His venture, however, came to grief (I Kings 22:49f; II Chron. 20:36f). Tarshish ships developed from the original idea of material carrying boats to all ships of first-rate magnitude to whatever place the voyage may have taken them (Psa. 48:7; Isa. 23:1; 60:9; Ezek. 27:25).

2. Second son of Javon, the grandson of Japheth (Gen. 10:4; I Chron. 1:7).

3. A man, the son of Bilhan, the Benjaminite (I Chron. 7:10).

4. A high Persian official at Susa (Biblical Shushan) (Esth. 1:14).—*M. F. U.*

Tar'sus (tär'sŭs), the capital of Cilicia, and the birthplace and early residence of the apostle Paul (Acts 9:11; 21:39; 22:3). The passages 9:30 and 11:25 give the limits of his residence in his native town, which succeeded the first visit to Jerusalem and preceded his active ministry at Antioch and elsewhere (comp. Acts 22:21; Gal. 1:21). It was during this period, probably, that he planted the Gospel there, and it has never since entirely died out. It would seem that Paul was there also at the beginning of his second and third missionary journeys (Acts 15:41; 18:23).

Tarsus was situated in a wide and fertile plain on the banks of the Cydnus, which flowed through it; hence it is sometimes called *Tarsoi* in the plural. The founding of Tarsus is legendary. The Assyrians entered Cilicia c. 850 B. C. and Shalmaneser III's Black Obelisk mentions the taking of the city. It appears in history in Xenophon's time, when it was a city of considerable importance. It was occupied by Cyrus and his troops for twenty days, and given over to plunder.

After Alexander's conquests had swept this way, and the Seleucid kingdom was established at Antioch, Tarsus usually belonged to that kingdom, though for a time it was under

455. Tarsus of Cilicia

the Ptolemies. In the civil wars of Rome it took Caesar's side, and on the occasion of a visit from him had its name changed to Juliopolis. Augustus made it a "free city." It was renowned as a place of education under the early Roman emperors. Strabo compares it in this respect to Athens and Alexandria. Tarsus also was a place of much commerce.

"It is probable, but not certain, that Paul's family had been planted in Tarsus with full rights as part of a colony settled there by one of the Seleucid kings in order to strengthen their hold on the city . . . The Seleucid kings seem to have had a preference for Jewish colonists in their foundations in Asia Minor" (Ramsay, *Paul the Traveler*, p. 32). Both land and sea highways made Tarsus a famed ancient emporium. The famous Cilician Gates, one of antiquity's most famous mountain passes, is not far distant, and access by water to the Mediterranean made Tarsus a famous trading center.

Tar'tak. *See* Gods, False.

456. Sargon II with His Tartan (from a Khorsabad relief)

Tar'tan (tär'tăn; Assyrian *tartanu* and *turtanu*), the title or official designation of the commander-in-chief of the Assyrian army (II Kings 18:17; Isa. 20:1). Archaeology has shown conclusively that the expression "tartan" is not a proper name.—*M. F. U.*

Taskmasters (Heb. *sārē mĭssîm, masters of burdens,* Exod. 1:11; *nāgăs,* to *drive,* 3:7; 5:6-14), persons appointed by order of Pharoah to see that the Hebrews were assigned hard, wearing toil. It was his hope, by such oppression, to break down the physical strength of Israel and thus lessen its increase; and also to crush their spirit so as to banish the very wish for liberty. So Israel was compelled to build provision or magazine cities, i. e., cities for storing the harvests.

Tat′tenai (tăt′ĕn-ī) A. V. **Tat′nai** (tăt′nī), a Persian governor of Samaria when Zerubbabel began to rebuild Jerusalem. He seems to have been appealed to by the Samaritans to oppose that undertaking, and, accompanied by another high official, Shethar-boznai, went to Jerusalem. They sent a fair and temperate report of what they saw and heard to the supreme government, suggesting that search be instituted to learn whether the building was going on in accordance with a royal decree (Ezra 5:3, 6). The statement of the Jews being verified by the discovery of the original decree of Cyrus, Tattenai and his colleagues applied themselves with vigor to the execution of the royal commands (6:6, 13), B. C. 536-519.

Tattler (Gr. *phluaros,* from *phluō,* to *throw up bubbles,* I Tim. 5:13), a person uttering or doing silly things, garrulous, babbling.

Tau (tŏ, tou) written tav in the A. R. V., the twenty-second and last letter of the Hebrew alphabet, pronounced "t" or "th" when followed by a vowel. This letter (Heb. *taw*) heads the twenty-second section of Psa. 119, in which portion every verse of the original Hebrew commences with this letter.—*M. F. U.*

Tavern. *See* Inn.

or, rather, such voluntary contributions were received as the exigencies of the time required. Only when the nation became settled in Palestine did taxation assume a regular and organized form.

2. **Under the Judges.** Under the theocratic government, provided for by the law, the only payments obligatory upon the people as of permanent obligation were: the tithes (*q. v.*), the first fruits (*q. v.*), the redemption money of the firstborn (*q. v.*), and such other offerings as belonged to special occasions.

3. **Under the Monarchy.** The kingdom, with its centralized government and greater magnificence, involved, of course, a larger expenditure, and, therefore, a heavier taxation. The chief burdens appear to have been: (1) A tithe of the produce both of the soil and of live stock (I Sam. 8:15, 17); (2) forced military service for a month every year (I Sam. 8:12; I Kings 9:22; I Chron. 27:1); (3) gifts to the king (I Sam. 10:27; 16:20; 17:18); (4) import duties (I Kings 10:15); (5) the monopoly of certain branches of commerce (I Kings 9:28; 22:48; 10:28, 29); (6) the appropriation to the king's use of the early crop of hay (Amos 7:1). At times, too, in the history of both the kingdoms there were special burdens. A tribute of fifty shekels a head had to be paid by Menahem to the Assyrian king (II Kings 15:20), and under his successor, Hoshea, this assumed the form of an annual tribute (17:4).

4. **Under the Persians.** The financial system of Darius Hystaspis provided for the payment by each satrap of a fixed sum as the tribute due from his province. In Judea, as in other provinces, the inhabitants had to

457. A Pharaoh of the Empire Receiving Asiatic Tribute Bearers

Tax′es.

1. **In Early Times.** From the very beginning of the Mosaic polity provision was made for a national income. Taxes, like all other things in that polity, had a religious origin and import. While Israel was in the migratory state, only such incidental taxes were levied,

provide in kind for the maintenance of the governor's household, besides a money payment of forty shekels a day (Neh. 5:14, 15). A formal enumeration is given in Ezra 4:13; 7:24, of the three great branches of the revenue: (*a*) The fixed, *measured* payments (Heb. *mĭddäh*), probably direct taxation; (*b*) The excise or *octroi*, on articles of consumption (Heb. *b*ᵉ*lō*); (*c*) Probably toll payable at bridges, forts, or certain stations on the highroad. Heb. *hǎläk*. The influence of Ezra secured for the whole ecclesiastical order, from the priests down to the Nethinim, an immunity from all three (Ezra 7:24); but the burden pressed heavily upon the great body of the people.

5. **Under Egypt and Syria** the taxes imposed upon the Jews became still heavier, the "farming" system of finance being adopted in the worst form. The taxes were put up at auction; and the contract sum for those of Phoenicia, Judea, and Samaria has been estimated at about eight thousand talents. A man would bid double that sum, and would then force from the province a handsome profit for himself.

6. **Roman Taxation.** "The Roman taxation, which bore upon Israel with such crushing weight, was systematic, cruel, relentless, and utterly regardless. In general, the provinces of the Roman empire, and what of Palestine belonged to them, were subject to two great taxes—poll tax (or, rather, income tax) and ground tax. All property and income that fell not under the ground tax was subject to poll tax, which amounted for Syria and Cilicia to one per cent. The poll tax was really twofold, consisting of income tax and head money, the latter, of course, the same in all cases, and levied on all persons (bond or free) up to the age of sixty-five—women being liable from the age of twelve, and men from that of fourteen. Landed property was subject to a tax of one tenth of all grain and one fifth of the wine and fruit grown, partly in product and partly commuted into money. Besides these, there was tax and duty on all imports and exports, levied on the great public highways and in the seaports. Then there was bridge money and road money, and duty on all that was bought and sold in the towns . . . The Romans had a peculiar way of levying these taxes—not directly, but indirectly— which kept the treasury quite safe, whatever harm it might inflict upon the taxpayer, while at the same time it threw upon him the whole cost of the collection. Senators and magistrates were prohibited from engaging in business or trade; but the highest order, the equestrian, was largely composed of great capitalists. These Roman knights formed joint stock companies which bought at public auction the revenues of a province at a fixed price, generally for five years. The board had its chairman, or *magister*, and its offices at Rome. These were the real publicans (*q. v.*), who underlet certain of the taxes" (Edersheim, *Social Life*, p. 53, sq.).

Taxing (Gr. *'apographē*, Luke 2:2; Acts 5:37), an enrollment (or registration) in the public records of persons, together with their property and income, as the basis of an *'apotimēsis*, *census*, or valuation, i. e., that it might appear how much tax should be levied upon each one. Another form of the same Greek verb (*'apographesthai*), is used in Heb. 12:23, "To the general assembly and church of the first-born, which are *written*" (R. V. "enrolled"). The English word conveys to us more distinctly the notion of a tax or tribute actually

levied, but it appears to have been used in the 16th century for the simple assessment of a subsidy upon the property of a given county, or the registration of the people for the purpose of a poll tax. The word *'apographē* by itself leaves the question, whether the returns made were of population or property, undetermined. In either case "census" would have seemed the most natural Latin equivalent. Two distinct registrations, or taxings, are mentioned in the New Testament, both of them by St. Luke. The first is said to have been the result of an edict of the emperor Augustus, that "all the world [i. e., the Roman empire] should be taxed" (Luke 2:1), and is connected by the evangelist with the name of Cyrenius, or Quirinius (*q. v.*). The second, and more important (Acts 5:37), is distinctly associated, in point of time, with the revolt of Judas of Galilee. The account of Josephus brings together the two names which St. Luke keeps distinct, with an interval of several years between them.

Teach (Heb. properly *lämǎd*, but many other words also; Gr. *didaskō*, and other terms). Inasmuch as men are delivered from the bonds age of sin, and builded up in righteousnes-through the agency of the truth, teaching becomes essential. Moses and Aaron were teachers of Israel in the statutes of Jehovah (Exod. 18:20; Lev. 10:11; 14:57), having been first taught of God (Exod. 4:12). Moses commanded fathers to teach their children the commandments of God with persistency and care (Deut. 4:9, 10, 14; 11:19). The priests were to continue to instruct the people, especially by reading the law to them at the Feast of Tabernacles, in the seventh year (24:8; 31:9-13). It is frequently recorded of Jesus that he "taught" the people (Matt. 5:2; Mark 1:21; 4:2; Luke 4:15, 31, etc.).

Teaching is an important branch of the commission which Christ gave to his apostles before his ascension. "Go," said he, "teach all nations;" as recorded by another evangelist, "Preach the Gospel to every creature." In this way they were to make disciples, as the Gr. *mathēteusate* imports. It is one of the precious promises of the new covenant that all its subjects shall be "taught of the Lord" (Isa. 54:13; quoted by Jesus, John 6:45).

"Teachers" are mentioned as among divine gifts (Eph. 4:11), i. e., those who undertook in the religious assemblies of Christians to teach, with the special assistance of the Holy Spirit (comp. I Cor. 13:28, sq.; Acts 13:1; James 3:1). If anyone was accepted as a teacher in this sense, he was the more dangerous, as he would seem to be inspired in his utterances (2:1).

Tears. *See* Mourn.

Te'bah (tē'bȧ; *slaughter*), the first named of the four sons of Nahor by his concubine Reumah (Gen. 22:24).

Tebali'ah (tĕb-à-lī'ȧ; *Jehovah has immersed*, i. e., *dipped* or *immersed*), the third named of the sons of Hosah, "of the children of Merari" (I Chron. 26:11).

Te'beth (tē'bĕth; Akkad. *ṭebetu, the month of sinking in*, i. e., wet, muddy, month), the tenth month of the second year of the Hebrews

(Esth. 2:16), corresponding in the main to *January*.

Tehaph′nehes (tĕ-hăf′nĕ-hĕz; Ezek. 30:18). *See* Tahpanhes.

Tehin′nah (tĕ-hĭn′nȧ; *graciousness*), a name occurring in the genealogy of the men of Rechah, of the tribe of Judah. He is mentioned as a son of Eshton, and founder of the city of Nahash (I Chron. 4:12).

Teil Tree (Isa. 6:13). *See* Vegetable Kingdom.

Te′kel (tĕ′kĕl; Aram. *t°kal, weighed*), the second word in the sentence of the Babylonian king (Dan. 5:25, 27). The interpretation presents the double meaning, "Thou art weighed in the balances, and art found too light," i. e., deficient in moral worth.

Teko′a, Teko′ah (tĕ-kō′ȧ; perhaps *trumpet clang*), a town in Judah, about six miles S. of Bethlehem, and on the range of hills which rise near Hebron and stretch toward the Dead Sea. By the "wilderness of Tekoa" (II Chron. 20:20) must be understood the adjacent region east of the town. Tekoa is now called *Ta′ḵūa*, and is a ruined site, showing many Hebrew traces. We first meet with Tekoah in the account (II Sam. 14:2, sq.) of Joab employing a "wise woman" residing there to effect a reconciliation between David and Absalom. Here, also, Ira, the son of Ikkesh, one of David's thirty "mighty men," was born, and was called on that account "the Tekoite" (23:26). Tekoa was one of the places fortified by Rehoboam at the beginning of his reign, to prevent an invasion from the south (II Chron. 11:6). People from Tekoa took part in building the walls of Jerusalem after the captivity (Neh. 3:5, 27). Jeremiah exclaims (6:1), "Blow the trumpet in Tekoa, and set up a sign in Beth-haccerem," both signals of warning of an enemy's approach. Tekoa was also the birthplace of Amos (Amos 1:1), and he was here called to be a prophet of God.

Teko′ite (tĕ-kō′īt), an inhabitant of Tekoah (*q. v.*).

Tel-a′bib (tĕl-ā′bĭb; *mound or hill of ears of grain*), the residence of Ezekiel on the river Chebar (Ezek. 3:15). The Chebar was a great canal (called a river, *Nāru* in Babylonia) S. E. of Babylon. Tel-abib doubtless derives its name from the fertility of the valley, rich in grain, by which it was surrounded.

Te′lah (tē′lȧ; *fracture, breach, break*), son of Rephah (or Resheph), and father of Tahan, in the lineage between Ephraim and Joshua (I Chron. 7:25), B. C. before 1440.

Tela′im (tĕ-lā′ĭm; *young lambs*), probably the same as Telem (*q. v.*), the place where Saul gathered his army to fight Amalek (I Sam. 15:4).

Telas′sar (tĕ-lăs′ĕr; *the hill of Asshur*), a city which lay in the hill country of the upper Mesopotamian plain identified by some as Tel Afer. It is mentioned in II Kings 19:12 (A. V. "Thelasar") and in Isa. 37:12 as a city inhabited by "the children of Eden," which had been conquered and was held in the time of Sennacherib by the Assyrians. It was apparently a city of Bit Adini, a small kingdom on the upper Euphrates.

Te′lem (tē′lĕm).

1. One of the temple porters who put away his Gentile wife (Ezra 10:24), B. C. 456.

2. A town in the southern border of Judah (Josh. 15:24), where it is mentioned between Ziph and Bealoth. It is very probably the same as Telaim (*q. v.*).

Tel-har′esha (tĕl-här′ê-shȧ; Neh. 7:61). *See* Tel-harsa.

Tel-har′sa (tĕl-här′sȧ; *mound of workmanship*), one of the Babylonian towns from which some Jews, who "could not show their father's house, nor their seed, whether they were of Israel," returned to Judea with Zerubbabel (Ezra 2:59; Neh. 7:61, A. V. "Tel-haresha"). It was probably in the low country near the sea, in the neighborhood of Tel-melah and Cherub.

Tell, an Arabic word denoting a truncated artificial mound built up by successive layers of ancient civilization. The word occurs in Hebrew in Josh. 11:13: "But as for the cities that stood on their mounts (Heb. *'al tillam*), Israel burned none of them save Hazor only; that did Joshua burn." The word tell is now very widely used in place names in Arabic countries in the Near Middle East and in Egypt and, as correctly translated in the Biblical passage, denotes a mound. Examples of place names incorporating *tell* are very numerous in Palestine: Tell en Nasbeh, Tell el Ful (Gibeah), Tell Jezer (Gezer), Tell ed-Duweir (Lachish), etc. In Egypt the well-known Tell el Amarna is found. In Mesopotamia exam-

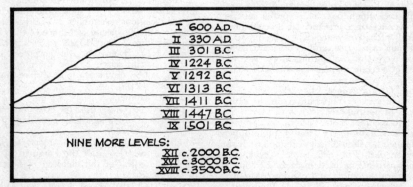

458. Illustration of the Occupational Levels (strata) of a mound (tell). This is Tell Beisan, ancient fortress city of Bethshan (I Sam. 31:10), which guarded the eastern approaches to the Valley of Esdraelon.

ples are Tell Abib, Tell Melah and many others. When a site had been occupied for many centuries, the occupational levels formed one upon another "in such a way as to suggest a giant layer cake" (Millar Burrows, *What Mean These Stones?* 1941, p. 12). Digging in such a way as to keep the superimposed occupational levels distinct is the modern scientific means of excavation. The remains found in each layer, particularly pottery, may be carefully studied and clearly dated as the result of the now-developed science of stratigraphy. When a city was destroyed by a catastrophe such as war, fire or

Cairo were found the famous Amarna Letters in 1887. This important corpus of inscriptions consisted of over 300 clay tablets in Akkadianized *lingua franca* of the fifteenth and fourteenth centuries B. C. These constitute diplomatic correspondence between the pharaoh of Egypt and his vassal governors and princes in Syria-Palestine. According to the chronology preserved in the Massoretic Hebrew Bible, these documents reflect conditions existing at the time of the conquest of Palestine under Joshua. Many scholars, however, place the Exodus and the conquest considerably later and view these letters as giving

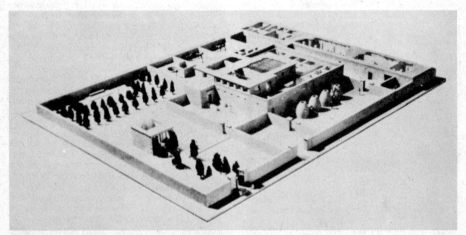

459. Reconstruction of a Dwelling at Amarna

earthquake, new settlers simply leveled the ruins and built upon them. Thus the ground level of the new city was raised several feet higher than the old one and the remnants of the old lay on the new. This process kept repeating as time went on until the occupational site rose higher and higher. When the site was finally abandoned at its highest level, the winds and rains of many years leveled off the top and eroded the side, except where the process was arrested by a city wall. This is the explanation of the flat tops of the mounds. The fact that ancient Oriental cities followed this pattern has been one of the greatest boons to modern scientific archaeology and the precise dating of ancient cultures. Tell Beisan, the ancient fortress city of Beth-shan (I Sam 31:10), which guarded the eastern approaches of the Valley of Esdraelon, has been excavated and shows eighteen levels from the top, running from 600 A. D. (Level 1) to c. 3500 B. C. (Level 18). When the archaeologist strikes virgin soil, he knows he has reached the time when the site was first occupied.—M. F. U.

Tell el-amar′na (tĕl ĕl-à-mär′nà), the modern name of the ancient Akhetaton, the capital city of Amenhotep IV (Akhnaton) who reigned (c. 1387-1366 B. C.). At this place, located some 160 miles above the Delta at

conditions a century or a century and a half before that event.—*M. F. U.*

Tel-me′lah (tĕl-mē′là; *hill of salt*, called in I Esdr. 5:36 "Thermeleth"), a place probably near the Persian Gulf, and from which the Jews returned (Ezra 2:59; Neh. 7:61).

Te′ma (tē′mà), the ninth son of Ishmael (Gen. 25:15; I Chron. 1:30); whence the tribe called after him, mentioned in Job 6:19; Jer. 25:23; and also the land occupied by this tribe (Isa. 21:14.) It denotes Taima in Arabia midway between Damascus and Mecca.

Te′mah (tē′mà, in A. V. Tamah and Tha′mah). *See* Tamah.

Te′man (tē′măn; the *south*, or *right*).

1. The eldest son of Eliphaz, the son of Esau (Gen. 36:11; I Chron. 1:36). He was a duke (or prince) of the Edomites (Gen. 36:15, 42; I Chron. 1:36, 53), and gave his name to the region in which the tribe he founded settled (Gen. 36:34), B. C. after 1900.

2. The country of the Temanites, the southern portion of Idumaea. In after ages it was the chief stronghold of Idumaea; hence when the Lord, by the prophet Ezekiel, pronounced the doom of Edom, he said, "I will make it desolate from Teman" (25:13). The Temanites were celebrated for their courage and wisdom (Jer. 49:7); hence the force and point of Obadiah's judgment, "Thy mighty men,

O Teman, shall be dismayed!" (v. 9). In Hab. 3:3 Teman is used for Idumaea generally.

Tem′ani (tĕm′á-nī; Gen. 36:34), or **Te′manite** (tē′măn-īt), a descendant of Teman (*q. v.*) or an inhabitant of that land (I Chron. 1:45; Job 2:11, sq.).

Tem′eni (tĕm′ĕ-nī), the third son of Ashur, "father" (founder) of Tekoa, by his wife Naarah (I Chron. 4:6), B. C. about 1360.

Temperance. 1. (Gr. *'egkrateia*), self-control; the virtue of one who masters his desires and passions, especially his sensual appetites (Acts 24:25; Gal. 5:23; II Pet. 1:6, where it is named as one of the Christian graces). In I Cor. 9:25 the verbal form is used, and is rendered "is temperate," i. e., *exhibits self-government*.

2. (Gr. *sōphrōn*, Tit. 2:2) has the meaning of *sound mind* (R. V. "*sober-minded*").

460. The Parthenon at Athens

Temple, a building set apart for the worship of a deity. In this article attention is specially called to the three buildings at Jerusalem which successively bore the name of temple. As these were all built upon the same site, and after the same general pattern, they were in nature and design the same, viz., that of the one built by Solomon. This latter was, in its essential features, a reproduction of the tabernacle, in more lasting material, and the necessary adjuncts of a permanent building.

1. **Name.** The usual and appropriate Hebrew term for temple is *hēkäl*, an old Akkadian word signifying *palace*, a *large building*, frequently joined with *Jehovah*, and denoting "the palace of deity." Occasionally it is also qualified by *qōdĕsh* (*sanctuary*), to designate its sacredness. Sometimes the simpler phrase, *house of Jehovah*, is used. (Heb. *bēth yhwh*).

The Greek terms employed are *naos* (*shrine*), and *hieron* (a *sacred* place).

2. **The Temple of Solomon.** (1) **The inception.** The idea that the tabernacle, a temporary building, should be supplanted by a permanent one of stone, seems to have been suggested to David by the Spirit (I Chron. 28:12, 19), especially after he had secured peace by conquest of his enemies (II Sam. 7:1-12; I Chron. 17:1-14; 28:1, sq.); but he was forbidden to build for the reason which he stated to Solomon, "The word of the Lord came to me, saying, Thou hast shed blood abundantly, and hast made great wars: thou shalt not built an house unto my name, because thou hast shed much blood upon the earth in my sight" (I Chron. 22:8). He, how-

ever, collected much material for the building and made arrangements to have the task completed by his son Solomon. The latter was a man of peace, and his reign a period of prosperity and peace (II Sam. 7:9-13; I Kings 5:3, 4; I Chron. 22:7-10).

(2) **Preparation.** Solomon, as soon as he found himself securely seated upon the throne, made arrangements for beginning to build the temple (I Chron., chaps. 22, 28, 29). He entered into a treaty with Hiram, king of Tyre, stipulating that this monarch should permit him to get cedar and cypress wood and blocks of stone from Lebanon; and that he would allow workmen sent by Solomon to fell the wood and quarry and hew the stones, under the direction of skilled workmen, subjects of Hiram. In return Solomon was to send supplies of wheat, oil, and wine. It was also arranged that Solomon was to have the services of a skillful artist by the name of Huram, to take charge of the castings and of the manufacture of the more valuable furnishings of the temple (I Kings 5:15, sq.; II Chron., ch. 2). So, in the fourth year of his reign, c. 960 B. C., Solomon began the erection of the sacred edifice, which was built on Mount Moriah to the east of Zion, an eminence which David himself selected for the purpose when he built an altar upon it after the plague had ceased (I Chron. 21:18, sq.; 22:1). To secure an adequate site for the temple and its courts, an area of at least four hundred cubits by two hundred being required, the summit of the hill had to be leveled and the superficies enlarged by means of substructions built on the sides. The edifice was completed in the eleventh year of Solomon's reign, i. e., in seven and a half years (B. C. c. 949).

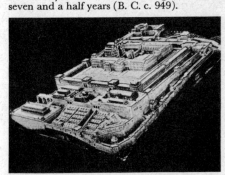

461. Schick Reconstruction of Solomon's Temple

(3) **The structure.** The temple proper was a building formed of hewn stones, sixty cubits long, twenty wide, and thirty in height (measuring from the inside), and covered with a flat roof composed of rafters and boards of cedar, overlaid with marble. Josephus (*Ant.*, viii, 3, 2) says, "The temple was sixty cubits high and sixty cubits in length, and the breadth was twenty cubits; above this was another story of equal dimensions, so that the height of the whole structure was one hundred and twenty cubits." Josephus probably gave the external dimensions, while in the Book of Kings the internal measurements are given. In the inside the building was divided by means of a partition of cedar wood into the Holy Place

and the Most Holy Place, so that the former was forty cubits long, twenty wide, and thirty high; while the latter was a cube measuring twenty cubits in each direction, the other ten cubits going to form "upper chambers" (II Chron. 3:9). On the inside the walls were lined with wood, so as to cover the stones; the walls and roof being covered with cedar, and the floor with planks of "fir" (cypress wood). The side walls were covered over with carved work, representing cherubim, palms, garlands, and opening flowers (I Kings 6:18; II Chron. 3:5), overlaying them all with thin plates of gold. The floor as well as the walls and ceilings were covered with gold (I Kings 6:30).

The entrance to the Holy of Holies consisted of a folding door in the partition wall, four cubits wide, made of olive wood, and ornamented with overlaid carvings of cherubim, palms, and opening flowers. These doors, as well as those at the entrance of the Holy Place, were hung on hinges of gold (I Kings 7:50). These doors stood open, but a veil was hung over it, similar in material and ornamentation to that in the tabernacle. The entrance to the Holy Place consisted of a folding door of cypress wood with doorposts of olive, each one being divided into an upper and lower section (like the Dutch doors), and ornamented in the same manner as the door of the Holy of Holies.

In the front of the building was a porch twenty cubits wide and ten cubits deep (I Kings 6:3; II Chron. 3:4). There would seem to be an error in the text (II Chron. 3:4) as to the height of the "porch;" for a front one hundred and twenty cubits high to a house only thirty cubits high could not be called 'ūlām (a porch); it would only have been a migdāl (a tower). Two bronze (A. V. "brass") pillars, Jachin and Boaz (see below), stood at the entrance of the Temple. On the sides and rear of the building wings were added, each three stories high, containing rooms for storing furniture and stores required for the temple service. These wings were so constructed that the rafters of the different stories rested upon

projections on the outside of the walls of the main building, so as to avoid inserting them in the walls themselves (I Kings 6:5, sq.). Each story was five cubits high, and five, six, and seven cubits wide, respectively, and they were communicated with by means of passages and stairs (6:8).

(4) **The courts.** There was an **inner** court (I Kings 6:36) running round the temple and reserved exclusively for the priests. It was formed by an outer or boundary wall, composed of three layers of hewn stone and a "row of cedar beams," probably laid upon the stones to protect the masonry. Outside of this was the "great court" (II Chron. 4:9), intended for the use of the people, and probably inclosed with masonry. Access to it was by doors of bronze (A. V. "brass"). From the fact that the court of the priests (inner) is called "the *higher* court" (Jer. 36:10), it is likely that it was on a higher level than the outer court; and it is not unlikely that the temple itself was higher than the inner court, so that the whole would have a terracelike aspect. So far as can be gathered from subsequent statements of an incidental nature (II Kings 23:11; Jer. 35:4; 36:10; Ezek., ch. 8, etc.), it would appear that there were vestibules and porticoes at the gates of the outer court, and that, if we may judge from the pattern of the temple (I Chron. 18:12) at all the four sides, probably in the corners and on both sides of the gate, as the temple of Ezekiel's vision would seem to show. The measurement of the courts is not given, but following the analogy of the tabernacle (comp. Ezek. 40:27) we may venture to assume that the court of the priests was one hundred cubits, and the same in breadth, measuring it on the east or front side of the temple; thus making the entire measurement one hundred cubits wide by two hundred in length. We will then have for the outer court an area of at least four hundred cubits long and two hundred cubits wide.

(5) **The furniture.** In the Holy of Holies was placed the ark, with its mercy seat, which was taken from the tabernacle. It stood between two cherubim, which were ten cubits

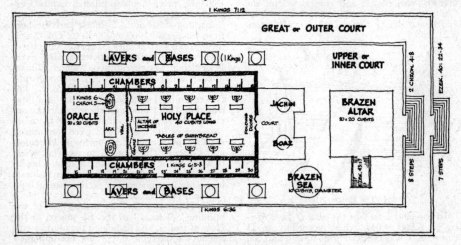

462. The Plan of Solomon's Temple

high, made of olive wood and overlaid with gold. Their wings were outstretched, about five cubits long, touching each other over the ark, while the outer wings touched the side walls of the apartment (I Kings 6:23-28; II Chron. 3:10-13). They stood upon their feet and faced "inward," i. e., toward the Holy Place (II Chron. 3:13).

one in the tabernacle. The following utensils for this altar are mentioned: pots, shovels, basins, and forks (I Kings 7:40, 45; II Chron. 4:11, 16). *See* Altar. A little to the south, but between the altar and the porch, stood the *brazen* or *molten sea*, a huge round basin, described in article Laver. There were also on each side of the altar, at the right and left

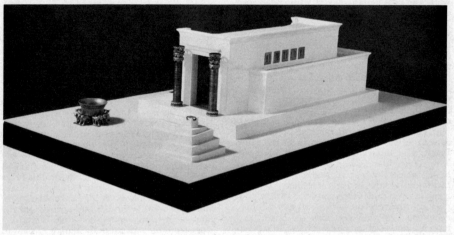

463. The Howland-Garber Model of Solomon's Temple

In the *Holy Place* were the *altar of incense*, or "golden altar" (I Kings 7:48; comp. 6:22; II Chron. 4:19), made of cedar wood and overlaid with gold; ten golden *candlesticks* with seven lamps to each, and placed in front of the Holy of Holies, five of them being on the right side and five on the left side (I Kings 7:49; II Chron. 4:7); and ten *tables for the showbread*, five being on each side (II Chron. 4:8). The form and construction of these objects have not been minutely described, as they were clearly modeled after those in the tabernacle, only made on a larger scale to correspond with the greater dimensions of the temple apartments. Of course the several articles of furniture were accompanied with their utensils, viz., *snuffers* and *extinguishers* for the candlesticks; for the tables, the *bowls*, *basins*, and *dishes*, etc. (I Kings 7:49, 50; II Chron. 4:21, etc.).

464. The Brazen Altar

In the *inner court* was the *altar of burnt offering* (I Kings 8:64), which according to II Chron. 4:1 was twenty cubits square and ten cubits high, and made after the pattern of the

wing of the temple, ten brazen *lesser lavers* on wheels (I Kings 7:27-39; II Chron. 4:6). *See* Laver.

3. **Archaeology.** Archaeology has shown that the plan of Solomon's temple was characteristically Phoenician, as would be expected, since it was constructed by a Tyrian architect (I Kings 7:13-15). Similar plans of sanctuaries of the general period, 1200-900 B. C. have been excavated in Northern Syria. The temple at Tell Tainat, excavated in 1936 by the University of Chicago, is smaller but similar to Solomon's structure. At Tell Tainat the shrine gives evidence that Solomon's temple is pre-Greek and authentic as I Kings 6-7 would indicate. Archaeology has also shown that the proto-Aeolian pilaster capital, extensively used in Solomon's temple, has been illustrated at Megiddo, Samaria and Shechem from the period 1000 to 700 B. C. The temple decorations such as lilies, palmettes and cherubim were likewise characteristically Syro-Phoenician. The cherubim or winged sphinxes appear hundreds of times in the iconography of western Asia between 1800-600 B. C. The two columns, Jachin and Boaz, are also illustrated at Tell Tainat and elsewhere in the ancient Near East. Such pillars flanked the main entrance of the temple and were common in the first millennium B. C. in Syria, Phoenicia and Cyprus. They spread to Assyria, where they are found in Sargon's temple at Khorsabad and eastward to the Phoenician colonies in the Mediterranean. For archaeological light *see* Jachin and Boaz.

(7) **History.** After the completion of the building Solomon had the ark placed in the Holy of Holies, and dedicated the temple with solemn thanksgiving and prayer, accompanied with liberal thank offering. This service, par-

ticipated in by the heads of the tribes as well as men from all parts of Israel, lasted seven days. So large was the number of victims offered that it was necessary for a time to convert the inner court in front of the porch into a place of sacrifice, as the altar of burnt offering was not capable of holding the multitude of sacrifices (I Kings 8:1, sq.; II Chron. chaps. 5, 6; 7:7). Immediately after the consecration prayer, in offering up which Solomon knelt upon the brazen platform that was erected in the inner court and in front of the altar (II Chron. 6:13), fire fell from heaven and consumed the burnt offering (7:1).

At the disruption of the kingdom the temple ceased to be the sanctuary of the *whole* people, Jeroboam having erected special places of worship at Beth-el and Dan for the use of the revolting ten tribes; but the temple continued to be the authorized center of worship for the kingdom of Judah. As early as the days of Rehoboam the treasures of the temple were plundered by Shishak, king of Egypt (I Kings 14:26), and gold and silver therefrom were subsequently sent to Ben-hadad, king of Syria, to purchase an alliance against Baasha, king of Israel (15:18, sq.).

Under Jehoshaphat the outer court was renewed (II Chron. 20:5), while under Jehoash considerable repairs were made upon the temple itself (II Kings 12:5, sq.), which repairs had been made necessary by the havoc wrought by the wicked Athaliah (II Chron.

other hand, had the altar of burnt offering taken away and another put in its place, made after one he had seen in Damascus; he also had the decorations removed from the laver stands, the basins themselves taken out, and the oxen removed from under the brazen sea, and the latter placed upon a "pavement of stones" (II Kings 16:10-17). This was done to secure for the king of Assyria those artistic objects, as he had already given him silver and gold from the temple and palace (v. 8). King Hezekiah was also compelled to pay tribute to Sennacherib, which he did by taking silver from the temple, and stripping the gold from the temple doors and posts (18:15, sq.). Worst of all was the desecration of the temple by Manasseh, who caused altars for the whole host of heaven to be erected in both courts, an image of Astarte to be set up in the sanctuary (21:4, 5, 7), and "houses of the sodomites" (23:7), probably tents or huts, erected in the temple court for the paramours to dwell in, and in which there were also women who wove tent-temples for Asherah; and kept horses consecrated to the sun in a place set apart for them in the inner court toward the back of the temple (v. 11). Josiah purged the sacred place of these abominations (v. 4, sq.); but soon after Nebuchadnezzar captured Jerusalem, and gathered together all the treasures of the temple, including all the golden utensils, and carried them off (24:13). Eleven years later Jerusalem was

465. Interior View of Solomon's Temple (Howland-Garber model)

24:7). During the reign of Amaziah all the gold and silver (as well as the utensils which had gold or silver about them) that were in the temple, were plundered by Jehoash, king of Israel (II Kings 14:14). After this Jotham "built the higher gate" of the temple (II Kings 15:35; II Chron. 27:3), probably at the entrance to the inner court. Ahaz, on the

destroyed by the Chaldeans, who burned the temple to the ground after pillaging it of its valuables, which they took to Babylon (II Kings 25:9, 13, 17; Jer. 52:13, 17-23).

4. **The Temple of Zerubbabel.** "We have very few particulars regarding the temple which the Jews erected after their return from the captivity (about 520 B. C.), and no de-

scription that would enable us to realize its appearance. But there are some dimensions given in the Bible and elsewhere which are extremely interesting as affording points of comparison between it and the temples which preceded it, or were erected after it. The first and most authentic are those given in the Book of Ezra (6:3), when quoting the decree of Cyrus, wherein it is said, 'Let the house be builded, the place where they offered sacrifices, and let the foundations thereof be

466. One of the Smaller Lavers from
Solomon's Temple

strongly laid; the height thereof threescore cubits; and the breadth thereof threescore cubits; with three rows of great stones, and a row of new timber.' Josephus quotes this passage almost literally, but in doing so enables us with certainty to translate the word here called *row* as 'story'—as indeed the sense would lead us to infer. The other dimension of sixty cubits in breadth is twenty cubits in excess of that of Solomon's temple, but there is no reason to doubt its correctness, for we find both from Josephus and the Talmud that it was the dimension adopted for the temple when rebuilt, or, rather, repaired, by Herod. We are left, therefore, with the alternative of assuming that the porch and the chambers all around were twenty cubits in width, including the thickness of the walls, instead of ten cubits, as in the earlier building. This alteration in the width of the pteromata made the temple one hundred cubits in length by sixty in breadth, with a height, it is said, of sixty cubits, including the upper room, or Talar, though we cannot help suspecting that this last dimension is somewhat in excess of the truth. The only other description of this temple is found in Hecataeus the Abderite, who wrote shortly after the death of Alexander the Great. As quoted by Josephus, he says, that 'in Jerusalem, toward the middle of the city, is a stone-walled inclosure about five hundred feet in length, and one hundred cubits in width, with double gates,' in which he describes the temple as being situated. Hecataeus also mentions that the altar was twenty cubits square and ten high. And although he mentions the temple itself, he unfortunately does

not supply us with any dimensions. From these dimensions we gather that if 'the priests and Levites and elders of families were disconsolate at seeing how much more sumptuous the old temple was than the one which on account of their poverty they had just been able to erect' (Ezra 3:12), it certainly was not because it was smaller, as almost every dimension had been increased one third" (Smith *Bib. Dict.*).

According to the Talmud this temple lacked five things that were in Solomon's temple, viz., the ark, the sacred fire, the Shekinah, the Holy Spirit, and the Urim and Thummim. The Holy of Holies was empty, and on the spot where the ark should have stood, a stone was set upon which the high priest placed the censer on the great day of atonement. In the Holy Place there was only one golden candlestick, one table of showbread, and the altar of incense (I Macc. 1:21, sq.; 4:49); while in the court was an altar of burnt offering built of stone (4:45).

History. This temple was plundered by Antiochus Epiphanes, who also defiled it with idolatrous worship (I Macc. 1:21, sq.; 46, sq.; 4:38; II Macc. 6:2, sq.), but was restored by Judas Maccabeus (I Macc. 4:36, sq.). He also fortified the outside against future attacks (6:7). It was taken by Pompey on the day of atonement after a three months' siege, and later by Herod the Great (Josephus, *Ant.*, xiv, 4, 2, sq.; xvi, 2).

5. **Ezekiel's Temple.** The vision of a temple which the prophet Ezekiel saw while residing on the banks of the Chebar in Babylonia in the twenty-fifth year of the captivity, does not add much to our knowledge of the subject. It is not a description of a temple that ever was built but of one which is to be built in Jerusalem during the ideal spiritual and political conditions to prevail during the Kingdom Age (cf. Isa. 11:1-16; 35:1-10; 60:1:22; Zech. 14:8-20). The temple itself is quite similar to that built by Solomon (*q. v.*). There can be little doubt but that the arrangements of Herod's temple were in a great measure influenced by the description here given (see Ezek. 41:1-43:17).

6. **Herod's Temple.** The temple as it existed after the captivity was not such as would satisfy a man as vain and fond of display as Herod the Great; and he accordingly undertook the task of rebuilding it on a grander scale. Although the reconstruction was practically equivalent to an entire rebuilding, still this temple cannot be spoken of as a third one, for Herod himself said, in so many words, that it was only intended to be regarded as an enlarging and further beautifying of that of Zerubbabel. After the necessary preparation the work of building was begun in the eighteenth year of Herod's reign (20 or 21 B. C.), and the temple proper, on which priests and Levites were employed, was finished in a year and a half, and the courts in the course of eight years. Subsidiary buildings were gradually erected, added to through the reigns of his successors, so that the entire undertaking was not completed till the time of Agrippa II and the procurator Albinus (A. D. 64).

For our knowledge of the last and greatest

of the Jewish temples we are indebted almost wholly to the works of Josephus, with an occasional hint from the Talmud. The Bible unfortunately contains nothing to assist the researches of the antiquary in this respect.

The temple and its courts occupied an area of one stadium (Josephus), or five hundred cubits (Talmud). They were arranged in terrace form, one court being higher than another, and the temple highest of all, so as to be easily seen from any part of the city or vicinity, and thus presenting a very imposing appearance (Mark 13:2, 3).

467. Temple of Baachus, Baalbek

(1) **The outer court** was surrounded with a high wall, with several gates on its west side, and had porticoes running all round it, those on three of the sides having double, and that on the south side having triple piazzas. These porticoes were covered with roofs of cedar supported on marble pillars, twenty-five cubits high, and were paved with mosaic work. This outer court, which could be frequented by Gentiles and unclean persons, had on its inner side and extending all round a rampart surrounded with a stone parapet, i. e., a mound ten cubits broad, the top of which was reached by a flight of fourteen steps. This constituted the outer boundary of the *inner temple area* (*to deuteron hieron*, Josephus). Some distance back from the rampart we come to the wall by which the temple and its inner courts were surrounded. On the outside this was forty cubits high, while on the inside it was only twenty-five, the level of the inner space being so much higher.

(2) **Women's court.** Entering by the east gate we come to the *court of the women*, a square of one hundred and thirty-five cubits, separated from the *court of the Israelites* by a wall on the west side, and having gates on the north and south sides for the women to enter by. These gates, as well as those on the east and west wides of this court, had rooms built over them to a height of forty cubits, each room being ornamented with two pillars twelve cubits in circumference, and provided with double doors thirty cubits high and forty wide, and overlaid with gold and silver. According to *Middoth*, ii, 3, the gates, with the exception of the eastern one, were only twenty cubits high and ten wide.

The eastern gate, called in the Talmud *Nicanor's*, or the *great* gate, was made of Corinthian brass, and was regarded as the principal gate on account of its greater height (being fifty cubits) and width (forty cubits), and

from its being more richly decorated with precious metals. It is undoubtedly the "gate of the temple which is called "Beautiful" (Acts 3:2). Round the walls of the court, except the west side, ran porticoes (porches), the roof of which rested on lofty and highly finished pillars. In each corner was a room, used, respectively, for storing the wood deemed unfit to be burned on the altar; for those affected with leprosy to wash themselves; for storing sacrificial wine and oil; and that one in which the Nazarites shaved their hair and cooked the flesh of the consecration sacrifices. According to Josephus (*Wars*, v, 5, 2) it was in some of the pillars of this court that the thirteen alms boxes were placed.

(3) **The inner court.** The entrance to the court of the Israelites was the western gate of the outer court, and was reached by a stair of fifteen steps. This inner court measured one hundred and eighty-seven cubits long (from east to west), and one hundred and thirty-five wide (from south to north), and surrounded the temple. Against its walls were chambers for storing the utensils required for the services, while it had three gates on both the south and north sides, making seven entrances in all. Eleven cubits of the eastern end was partitioned off by a stone balustrade one cubit high, for the men (the *court of the Israelites*), separating it from the rest of the space which went to form the court of the priests. In this latter stood the *altar of burnt offering*, made of unwrought stone, thirty cubits in length and breadth, and fifteen high. West of this was the temple, and between it and the altar stood the laver.

(4) **The temple proper.** The temple stood so much higher than the court of the priests that it was approached by a flight of twelve steps. It stood in the western end of the inner court and on the northwest part of the temple mount, and was built, according to Josephus (*Ant.*, xv, 11, 3), upon new foundations of massive blocks of white marble, richly ornamented with gold both inside and out. Some of these stones were forty-five cubits long, six broad, and five high. Its length and height,

468. **Mosque of Omar Built by Caliph Omar over Site of Solomon's Temple in the 7th Century**

including the porch, was one hundred cubits, while on each side of the vestibule there was a wing twenty cubits wide, making the total width of this part of the building one hundred cubits. The porch was ten cubits deep, measuring from east to west, fifty wide, ninety in height, and had an open gateway seventy cubits high and twenty-five in width.

The interior of the temple was divided into the *Holy Place* and the *Holy of Holies.* "The temple had doors also at the entrance, and lintels over them of the same height as the temple itself. They were adorned with embroidered veils, with their flowers of purple, and pillars interwoven; and over these, but under the crown work, was spread out a golden vine, with its branches hanging down from a great height" (Josephus, *Ant.*, xv, 11, 3). The holy place was forty cubits long, twenty wide, and sixty in height, and contained one golden candlestick, a single table of showbread, and one altar of incense. Separated from it by a wooden partition was the Holy of Holies, twenty cubits long and sixty high, which was empty. The rabbinical writers maintain that there were two veils over its entrance. It was this veil that was rent on the occasion of our Lord's crucifixion. As in the case of Solomon's temple, side rooms three stories high were built on the sides of the main structure.

Tempt (Heb. *bäthăn;* Gr. *peirazō*, both meaning to *test* or *try*) is used in different senses; not always involving an evil purpose, as an inducement to sin.

1. "God did tempt Abraham" (Gen. 22:1) in commanding him to offer up his son Isaac, intending to prove his obedience and faith, to confirm and strengthen him by this trial, and to furnish in him an example of perfect obedience for all succeeding ages. When it is recorded that God proved his people, whether they would walk in his way or not (Exod. 16:4), and that he permitted false prophets to arise among them, who prophesied vain things to try them whether they would seek the Lord with their whole hearts, we should interpret these expressions by that of James 1:13, 14, "Let no man say when he is tempted, I am tempted of God: for God cannot be tempted with evil, neither tempteth he any man: but every man is tempted, when he is drawn away by his own lust, and enticed."

2. Satan tempts us to every kind of evil, and lays snares for us, even in our best actions. He lays inducements before our minds to solicit us to sin (I Cor. 7:5; I Thess. 3:5; James 1:13, 14). Hence Satan is called that old serpent, the devil, and "the tempter" (Rev. 12:9; Matt. 4:3). He tempted our first parents (*see* Temptation); our Saviour (*see* Temptation of Christ); he tempted Ananias and Sapphira to lie to the Holy Spirit (Acts 5:3).

3. Men are said to tempt God when they unreasonably require proofs of the divine presence, power, or goodness. It is proper for us to seek divine assistance, and to pray him to give us what we need, but we are not to tempt him, or expose ourselves to dangers from which we cannot escape without miraculous interposition. God is not obliged to work miracles in our favor; he requires of us only such actions as are within the ordinary measure of our strength. The Israelites frequently tempted God in the desert, as if they had reason to doubt his presence, his goodness, or his power, after all his appearances in their behalf (Exod. 16:2, 7, 17; Num. 20:12; Psa. 78:18, 41, etc.).

4. Men tempt or try one another when they would know whether things or men are really what they seem or are desired; also when they wish them to depart from the right. The queen of Sheba came to prove the wisdom of Solomon by giving him riddles to explain (I Kings 10:1; II Chron. 9:1). Daniel desired of the eunuch to prove them for some days whether abstinence from food of certain kinds would make them leaner (Dan. 1:12, 14). The scribes and Pharisees often tempted our Lord and endeavored to catch him in their snares (Matt. 16:1; 19:3; 22:18).

Temptation (Heb. *mӑssäh;* Gr. *peirasmos*, a *testing*) is generally understood as the enticement of a person to commit sin by offering some seeming advantage. The sources of temptation are Satan, the world, and the flesh. We are exposed to them in every state, in every place, and in every time. The nearest approach to a definition of the process of temptation from within is given us by James, "Every man is tempted, when he is drawn away of his own lust, and enticed" (James 1:14). "Temptation proper in the case of a fallen creature is, strictly speaking, within. It craves the gratification that is offered from without: 'then when it hath conceived, it bringeth forth sin' (1:15). The contest in the regenerate man is this lust of the flesh opposing the Spirit of the new nature; and the Spirit continually moving the renewed spirit to oppose its desires. In this sense our first parents were not tempted, though in their case the temptation from without assailed a will capable of falling, and was the means of engendering the concupiscence that then engendered all sin. In this sense the glorified in heaven, after a probation ended, will be incapable of temptation. In this sense our sinless Redeemer was absolutely untemptable and impeccable. 'He was in all points tempted like as we are, yet without sin' (Heb. 4:15) . . . He had no mother lust which could conceive and bring forth sin . . . But there is another aspect of temptation which brings him still nearer to us, and that is, the trial of the spirit from without. This he underwent to the utmost; indeed, as much beyond the possibility of his servants' temptation as their internal temptation was impossible to him" (Pope, *Christ. Theol.*, iii, 205). *See* Tempt; Temptation of Christ.

Temptation of Christ. An experience in the life of our Lord recorded in Matt. 4:1-11; Mark 1:12, 13; Luke 4:1-13. That Christ was tempted on other occasions in other ways than here indicated would seem evident from Luke 22:28 and Heb. 4:15. This, however, through which he passed immediately after his baptism and before his entrance upon his ministry, was an event of so much importance as to be regarded as preeminently his temptation. And to this commonly exclusive reference is made.

1. **Character of the Narration.** Much labor and ingenuity are often expended in seeking to determine to what extent the narrative of the gospels is to be taken literally. How much of it is to be understood as descriptive of actual outward occurrences, and how much was internal, subjective? Did Satan actually bear Christ away to a "pinnacle of the temple" at Jerusalem? Did he also take our Lord to "an exceeding high mountain" from the summit of which he showed him "all the kingdoms of the world?" Did such changes in the scene of the temptation actually take place in an outward, material sense, or did they simply take place in the mind of Jesus? Is the gospel narrative in these respects marked by the figurative manner common among orientals? Upon these questions the opinions of commentators are greatly divided. There has been no end of discussion, and with little profit. The popular interpretation has been literal. And not a few scholars have attempted to defend this interpretation. But, on the other hand, even as orthodox a scholar as Calvin has held the account to be that of a vision or allegory. But it should be observed that whichever view is taken the reality of the temptation is in no measure lessened, nor is the fact disguised that the real agent of the temptation was Satan.

2. **The Temptation as Related to the Character of Christ.** How could he, the sinless One, be tempted? Did the temptation imply in any sense the possibility of his falling into sin? As to the first question it should be remembered that temptation does not necessarily imply a sinful nature on the part of the one tempted. The first man Adam, though created "in the image and after the likeness" of God, was tempted and fell into sin. And does not the passage Heb. 4:15 teach that not only did Jesus successfully resist temptation, but also that his temptation was not such as springs up within a sinful nature? Christ was "without sin" in both these senses. His temptation was wholly from without, from the evil one, though appealing to desires within him that were wholly innocent. As to the possibility of his yielding to temptation these views have been held: (1) The Calvinistic view, that Christ had no volitional power to yield to temptation. Edwards strongly advocated this view in his work on the Will. (2) The Arminian view, that the man Jesus had such volitional power. (3) The view that "the eternal Logos had the volitional power to sin, having concentrated and reduced himself to finite and human conditions." Van Oosterzee appropriately says, "The sinlessness of the Lord is to be regarded as an attribute of his true humanity, and thus to be clearly distinguished from the absolute holiness of him who cannot even be tempted of evil. The moral purity of the Lord did not in itself exclude even the least possibility of sinning. Had such possibility been absolutely wanting, the former would, even in the Son of man, have lost all moral worth. The great thing here is precisely this, that he who was exposed to the severest temptation, ever so maintained the dominion over himself that it could be said of him, he was able not to sin, "*potuit non peccare.*" As the result of a sustained conflict, he so perfectly vanquished the power of evil that sinning became for him morally an absolute impossibility; in other words, the "*potuit non pecare*" was evermore raised to a "*non potuit pecare.*" He could not sin. And yet discussion upon this theme, as Edersheim says, "sounds, after all, like the stammering of divine words by a babe." It is a subject for reverent faith rather than exact dogmatizing.

469. Mount of Temptation

3. **The Nature of the Threefold Temptation.** According to Mark, the temptation was protracted throughout the "forty days." The temptations described by Matthew and Luke are therefore regarded as the culminating features of the long struggle. The order of the temptations vary in the two gospels named, a matter of little or no consequence. The long fast, once a favorite matter for infidel objections, no longer presents any difficulty whatever. The significance of the separate assaults of evil have been variously interpreted; a fact due in considerable measure to the comprehensiveness of the whole great event. Says Smith: "The three temptations are addressed to the three forms in which the disease of sin makes its appearance in the soul—to the solace of sense, and the love of praise and the desire of gain (I John 2:16). But there is one element common to them all, they are attempts to call up a willful and wayward spirit in contrast to a patient and self-denying one." The subject, however, can hardly be summed up thus briefly.

1. The temptation to change the stones into bread by a miracle was an appeal to Christ to step out of his divinely appointed path for the sake of satisfying his hunger. He had accepted the conditions of a human life, and it was for him to do his duty and trust in God for sustenance. His power to work miracles was not for himself but for others (*see* Kenosis). Had he obeyed the temptation he would have become unlike men who must put their trust in divine Providence. "He would have become his own providence."

2. The second temptation was to prove his Sonship, to exhibit his faith in his Sonship, by casting himself down from a pinnacle of the temple. This temptation was at the opposite extreme from the preceding. The first was a temptation to distrust, the second that of extravagant, unwarranted confidence, or presumption. Again was the call to step out of the path divinely appointed, but by presumptuously plunging himself into needless perils. The Scripture quoted by the adversary was

quoted in a mutilated form. "He shall give his angels charge concerning thee." "To keep thee in all *thy ways*" was left out. As in the former instance all temptation to give unlawful prominence to temporal, material, good, is illustrated, so in the present instance all attempts to build up Christ's kingdom by means of display, rather than by the patient, divinely appointed processes, find their rebuke; likewise all forms of fanatical presumption.

3. The temptation to win power by an act of homage to the devil.

Inconceivable as this may seem at first, nevertheless this was the bold form in which was embodied the idea of winning power for good and holy ends by a compromise with evil at the outset. It was an appeal to holy ambition, but upon the ground of doing evil that good might come. The kingdom was to be won, but in the way suggested it would have been at the expense of ruining the King. At this point also the great temptation of Christ has its most practical lessons.

The manner and complete success of Christ's resistance appear upon the surface of the narrative and call here for no comment.— E. McC.

Ten. *See* Number.

Ten Commandments. *See* Decalogue.

Tender-hearted. 1. Heb. *răk lēbâb*, literally *tender of heart*, i. e., fainthearted, timid, as spoken of Solomon's son Rehoboam in his youth (II Chron. 13:7).

2. Gr. *eusplagchos, having strong bowels*, in biblical and ecclesiastical language, compassionate, tender-hearted (Eph. 4:32; I Pet. 3:8, A. V. "pitiful;" R. V. "tender-hearted").

Tenons (Exod. 26:17, 19; 36:22, 24), probably dowel pins at the end of the planks of the Tabernacle (*q. v.*).

Tent (Heb. usually *'ōhĕl;* Gr. *skēnē*), a movable habitation, made of curtains extended upon poles. The patriarchs of the Israelites, whose fathers and kindred already possessed fixed houses in Mesopotamia, dwelt in tents because they lived in Canaan only as pilgrims. The Israelites did not dwell in houses until their return from Egypt. Their tents, in material, form, and furniture, no doubt resem-

470. Bedouin Tent

bled the tents of the present Bedouins, consisting sometimes of plaited mats, but generally of cloth coverings, either coarser, of goat hair (black, Cant. 1:5), or finer, woven from yarn. The goat-hair cloth is sufficient to resist the heaviest rain. The tent poles, called *amud*,

or columns, are usually nine in number, placed in three groups, but many tents have only one pole, others two or three. The ropes which hold the tent in its place are fastened not to the tent cover itself, but to loops consisting of a leathern thong tied to the ends of a stick, round which is twisted a piece of old cloth, which is itself sewed to the tent cover. The ends of the tent ropes are fastened to short sticks or pins, called *wed* or *aoutad*, which are driven into the ground with a mallet (Judg. 4:21). Round the back and sides of the tent runs a piece of stuff removable at pleasure to admit air. The tent is divided into two apartments, separated by a carpet partition drawn across the middle of the tent and fastened to the three middle posts. The furniture deemed necessary was a carpet, cushions, a low table (sometimes replaced by a round skin), eating and cooking utensils, and a lamp. When the pasture near an encampment is exhausted, the tents are taken down, packed on camels and removed (Isa. 38:12; Gen. 26:17, 22, 25). The larger tents of the well-to-do are divided into three rooms; the first, at the entrance, in the case of common people, is reserved for the young and tender of the flock or herd, the second for the men, and the innermost for the women. The manufacture of tents formed a regular trade, at which Paul occasionally labored, especially in connection with Aquila (Acts 18:3).

Figurative. So prominent a feature of oriental life could hardly fail to suggest many striking metaphors. Thus the heavens are compared to a tent (Isa. 40:22). The prosperity of Israel restored is referred to as an enlargement of a tent (54:2; see also 33:20). The setting up of a tent, especially a large one, was a work needing the help of others, and one bereft of friends is referred to as having no helpers in erecting his tent (Jer. 10:20). The tent being rapidly taken down and removed became a symbol of the frailty of life (Isa. 38:12; II Cor. 5:1).

Tenth Deal (a *tenth*), a dry measure, specially for grain and meal (Exod. 29:40; Lev. 14:10, 21; Num. 15:4, 6, 9, etc.); more fully the tenth of an ephah. *See* Metrology, II.

Te'rah (tē'rá; cf. Akkad. *turahu, ibex*). 1. The son of Nahor born in Ur of the Chaldees; the father of Abram, Nahor, and Haran, and through them the ancestor of the great families of the Israelites, Ishmaelites, Midianites, Moabites, and Ammonites (Gen. 11:24-32). We learn from the Scripture that Terah was an idolater (Josh. 24:2), that he took part in the family migration toward Canaan, and that he died in Haran at the age of two hundred and five years, B. C. c. 2100. 2. A camping place of Israel in the desert. *See* Tarah.

Teraphim. The teraphim were figurines or images in human form. Rachel's theft of Laban's teraphim (Gen. 31:34) is much better understood in the light of the documents from Nuzu, not far from modern Kirkuk, excavated 1925-1934. The possession of these household gods apparently implied leadership of the family and, in the case of a married daughter, assured her husband the right to the property of her father (Cyrus H. Gordon, *Revue Biblique* XLIV, 1945, p. 35f). Since Laban evidently had sons of his own when Jacob left for Canaan, they alone had the right to their father's gods, and the theft of these household idols by Rachel was a serious offense (Gen. 31:19, 30, 35) aimed at preserving for her husband the first title to her father's estate. (See H. H. Rowley, "Recent Discoveries in the Patriarchal Age" in the *Bull. of the John Rylands Library*, Manchester, 32, 1949, p. 76).

471. Assyrian Teraphim

Albright construes the teraphim as meaning "vile things," but the images were not necessarily cultic or lewd, as frequently the depictions of Astarte were. Micah's teraphim (Judg. 17:15) were used for purposes of securing an oracle (cf. I Sam. 15:23; Hos. 3:4; Zech. 10:2). Babylonian kings oracularly consulted the teraphim (Ezek. 21:21). Josiah abolished the teraphim (II Kings 23:24), but these images had a strange hold on the Hebrew people even until after the Exilic Period. —M. F. U.

Te′resh (tē′rĕsh; cf. Avestan *tarshav*, *firm*, *solid*), one of the two eunuchs whose plot to assassinate Ahasuerus was discovered by Mordecai (Esth. 2:21; 6:2). He was hanged B. C. about 478.

Terrace (Heb. *mᵉsĭlläh*, *thoroughfare*), a staircase, constructed out of algum trees, for Solomon's palace (II Chron. 9:11).

Terror, the rendering of several Hebrew words and one Greek word denoting great fear, that which agitates both body and mind. Some of these words have as their primary meaning the *cause* of fear, others the *result*. Thus *'ēmäh* (Josh. 2:9; Job 20:25; Psa. 33:18; 55:4; 88:15) is that which inspires dread, as a king (Job 33:7), a bugbear; idols (Jer. 50:38), from the fear with which they fill their worshippers; *mᵉḥĭttäh* (Isa. 54:14) is a breaking in pieces, and so consternation, from *ḥäthäth*, to *be broken*, *confounded* (Gen. 35:5; Ezek. 26:17; 32:23-32); *bäläh* denotes the falling away of a person in sickness, a garment through age, etc., and so the mind consumed with anxiety and care. Other words simply express fear, as the Greek word *phobos*. Death is called the "king of terrors" (Job 18:14; comp. 24:17), in distinction from the terrible disease which is called its "firstborn" (18:13). Death is also personified elsewhere (Psa. 49:15; Isa. 28:15).

Ter′tius (tûr′shĭ-ŭs, from Lat. *tertius*, *third*), probably a Roman, was the amanuensis of Paul in writing the Epistle to the Romans (Rom. 16:22). Some have proposed without reason to identify him with Silas. Nothing certain is known of him.

Tertul′lus (tĕr-tŭl′ŭs, diminutive form of Tertius), "a certain orator" retained by the high priest and Sanhedrin to accuse the apostle Paul at Caesarea before the procurator, Felix (Acts 24:1, 2). He evidently belonged to the class of professional orators, multitudes of whom were to be found not only in Rome, but in other parts of the empire, where they went with the expectation of finding occupation at the tribunals of the provincial magistrates. We may infer that Tertullus was of Roman, or, at all events, of Italian origin; while the Sanhedrin would naturally desire his services on account of their own ignorance of the Latin language and of the ordinary procedure of a Roman law court. The historian probably only gave an abstract of the speech, giving, however, in full the most salient points, and those which had the most forcibly impressed themselves upon him, such as the exordium and the character ascribed to Paul (v. 5).

Testament, the frequent rendering of Gr. *diathēkē*, *a will*, *disposition*, *covenant*).

1. A disposition, arrangement of any sort, which one wishes to be valid (Gal. 3:15), especially the *last disposal* which one makes of his earthly possessions after his death, a *testament* or *will*.

2. A covenant, a compact, very often used in Scripture. The word *covenant* is used to denote the close relationship which God entered into: with Noah (Gen. 6:18; 9:9, sq.); with Abraham, Isaac, and Jacob, and their posterity (Lev. 26:42); and afterward, through Moses, with the people of Israel (Exod., ch. 24; Deut. 5:2; 28:69). By this last covenant the Israelites are bound to obey God's will as expressed and solemnly promulgated in the Mosaic law; and he promises them his almighty protection and blessings of every kind in this world, but threatens transgressors with the severest punishments. Hence in the New Testament we find mention of *the ark of the covenant*, or *law*, in which the tables were deposited (Heb. 9:4; Rev. 11:19, A. V. "the ark of his testament"); of the *covenant of circumcision* (Heb. 9:20; comp. Acts 7:8).

The new and more satisfactory bond of friendship which God in the Messiah's time would enter into with the people of Israel is called *kainē diathēkē*, the *new testament*—which divine promise Christ has made good (Heb. 8:8-10; 10:16). Thus we find two testaments (covenants) spoken of, the Mosaic and the Christian (Gal. 4:24); with the former of which (Heb. 9:15, 18; comp. 8:9) the latter is contrasted (Matt. 26:28; Mark 14:24; Luke 22:20; I Cor. 11:25; Heb. 13:20), of which Christ is the Mediator (8:6).

Old and New Testaments. When the books written by Christ's apostles, or by apostolic men, came to be placed alongside the sacred books of the Hebrews, as comprising the entire scriptural canon, it became necessary to distinguish the two divisions by appropriate designations. A usage which already prevailed furnished the designations required. The gracious engagements into which God was pleased to enter with individuals and communities bear in the Old Testament the name of *berîth*, or *covenant* (*q. v.*), and to this corresponds the Gr. *diathēkē* in the LXX. and the New Testament. Of these covenants two stand out from all the rest as of preeminent importance—God's covenant with Israel mediated by Moses, and that covenant which he promised to establish through the Messiah. This latter is called by Jeremiah (31:31) "a new covenant," and familiarly used by the apostles (II Cor. 3:6; Heb. 9:15, etc.), would naturally suggest the application of the phrase "the first testament" to the former (Heb. 9:15). In the Latin Church the usage prevailed of calling these two covenants *Vetus et Novum Testamentum*, i. e., the Old and New Testament; and *Testament* has naturally passed into the title of the two divisions of the Scriptures in the English and most of the European versions.

Teth (tāth), the 9th letter of the Hebrew alphabet. It stands at the beginning of the 9th section of Psalm 119, in which section each verse begins with that letter.

Tetrarch (Gr. *tetrarchēs*), properly the sovereign or governor of the fourth part of a country. 1. Herod Antipas (Matt. 14:1; Luke 3:1, 19; 9:7; Acts 13:1), who is commonly distinguished as "Herod the tetrarch," although the title of "king" is also assigned to him both by Matthew (14:9) and by Mark (6:14, 22, sq.). 2. Herod Philip, who is said by Luke (3:1) to have been "tetrarch of Ituraea and of the region of Trachonitis." 3. Lysanias, who is said (Luke 3:1) to have been "tetrarch of Abilene." The title of tetrarch was at this time probably applied to petty tributary princes without any such determinate meaning. But it appears from Josephus that the Tetrarchies of Antipas and Philip were regarded as constituting each a fourth part of their father's kingdom. We conclude that in these two cases, at least, the title was used in its strict and literal sense.

Thaddae′us (thå-dē′ŭs), a name in Mark's catalogue of the twelve apostles (Mark 3:18) in the great majority of manuscripts. In Matthew's catalogue (Matt. 10:3) Lebbaeus is probably the original reading. From a comparison with the catalogue of Luke (Luke 6:16; Acts 1:13) it seems scarcely possible to doubt that the three names of Judas, Lebbaeus, and Thaddaeus, were borne by one and the same person. Edersheim (*Life of Jesus*, i, 522) derives the term Thaddaeus from *thodah*, praise, and adds, "In that case both Lebbaeus and Thaddaeus would point to the heartiness and thanksgiving of the apostle, and hence his character." His real name seems to have been Judas Labbaeus, and his surname Thaddaeus.

Tha′hash (thā′hăsh; *dugong*), the third son of Nahor by his concubine Reumah (Gen. 22:24). *See* Tahash.

Tha′mah (thā′má; Ezra 2:53). *See* Tamah.

Tha′mar (thā′mår; Matt. 1:3). *See* Tamar, 1.

Thank Offering. *See* Sacrificial Offerings.

Thanksgiving (Heb. *tōdäh;* Gr. *eucharistia*), is a duty of which gratitude is the grace. This obligation of godliness is acknowledged by the universal sentiment of mankind; but as a Christian grace it has some blessed peculiarities. It is gratitude, as for all the benefits of divine Providence, so especially for the general and personal gifts of redemption. The very term most in use shows this; it is *charis*, which is the grace of God in Christ, operating in the soul of the believer as a principle, and going back to him in gratitude: "Thanks be unto God for his unspeakable gift." The ethical gratitude of Christianity connects every good gift and every perfect gift with the gift of Christ. Moreover, it is a thanksgiving which in the Christian economy, and in it alone, redounds to God for all things: *in everything give thanks*. This characteristic flows from the former. The rejoicing which we have in the Lord, and the everlasting consolation we possess in him, makes every possible variety of divine dispensation a token for good. The Christian privilege is to find reason for gratitude in all things: "for this is the will of God in Christ Jesus concerning you."

Thankworthy is the rendering of the Gr. *charis*, grace), in the declaration (I Pet. 2:19), "For this is thankworthy, if a man for conscience toward God endure grief, suffering wrongfully." The meaning is, this wins for us (God's) favor (R. V. "is acceptable").

Tha′ra (thā′rà; Luke 3:34). *See* Terah.

Thar′shish (thär′shĭsh), a less correct form for Tarshish (*q. v.*).

Theater (Gr. *theatron, place for seeing*).

1. A place in which games and dramatic spectacles are exhibited and public assemblies held, for the Greeks use the theater also as a forum (Acts 19:29, 31).

2. A public show, and, figuratively, a man who is exhibited to be gazed at and made sport of (I Cor. 4:9, A. V. and R. V. "a spectacle"). The writer of the Epistle to the Hebrews speaks (12:1) of "so great a cloud of witnesses," having in mind, no doubt, the agonistic scene, in which Christians are viewed as running a race, and not the theater or stage, where the eyes of the spectators are fixed on them.

(1) **The Greek theater** was originally intended for the performance of dithyrambic choruses at the feast of Dionysus. The hymn celebrated the sufferings and actions of the god in a style corresponding to the passionate character of his worship; and it was sung to the accompaniment of a flute and a dance round the altar. "From the first it consisted of two principal parts: (*a*) the circular dancing place (*orchestra*), with the altar of the god in the center, and (*b*) the place for the spectators, or the theater (*thĕātron*) proper. The *thĕātron* was in the form of a segment of a circle, with the seats rising above one another in concentric tiers. The seats were almost always cut in the slope of a hill. When the dithyrambic choruses had developed into the drama, a structure called the *skēnē* (Lat. *scena*) was added, with a stage for dramatic representations. It was erected on the side of the *orchestra* away from the spectators, and at such a

height and distance as to allow of the stage being in full view from every part of the theater. The first stone theater was that built at Athens, the home of the Greek drama; and the theaters in every part of the Hellenic world were constructed on the same general principles. It is estimated that the theater in Athens had room for twenty-seven thousand five hundred persons . . . The tickets of admission discovered in Attica are of two kinds: (*a*) ordinary leaden tokens about the size of either a florin or a six-penny bit, or (*b*) counters of bone or ivory about the size of a half crown."

(2) **The Roman theater.** "In Rome, where dramatic representations, in the strict sense of the term, were not given until 240 B. C., a wooden stage was erected in the circus for each performance, and taken down again . . . Those who wanted seats had to bring their own chairs; sometimes, by order of the senate, sitting was forbidden. In 154 B. C. an attempt was made to build a permanent theater with fixed seats, but it had to be pulled down by order of the senate. In 145 B. C., on the conquest of Greece, theaters were provided with seats after the Greek models were erected; these, however, were only of wood, and served for one representation alone. The first stone theater was built by Pompey in 55 B. C., a second one by Cornelius Balbus (13 B. C.), and in the same year the one dedicated by Augustus to his nephew Marcellus, and was called by his name, the ruins of which still exist. Besides these there were no other stone theaters in Rome. The Roman theater differed from the Greek. In the first place the *auditorium* formed a semicircle only, with the front wall of the stage building as its diameter, while in the Greek it was larger than a semicircle. Again a covered colonnade ran round the highest story of the Roman theater, the roof of which was of the same height as the highest part of the stage. The orchestra, moreover, which was inclosed by the *căvĕa*, contained places for spectators; these were, at the first, reserved exclusively for the senators; foreign ambassadors whom it was wished to honor were afterward admitted to them . . . Places of dignity were also assigned to magistrates and priests, probably on the *podium*, or the space in front of the lowest row of seats, where there was room for a few rows of chairs. The first fourteen rows of the ordinary seats were (68 B. C.) appropriated to the *equites;* after them came the general body of citizens,

who were probably arranged in the order of their tribes; in the upper part of the *căvĕa* were the women, who sat apart, in accordance with a decree of Augustus; the lowest class were relegated to the highest tier. Even children were admitted, only slaves being excluded. Admission was free, as was the case with all entertainments intended for the people. The tickets of admission did not indicate any particular seat, but only the block of seats and the row in which it would be found" (Seyffert, *Dict. of Class. Antiq.*, s. v.). At Athens, Corinth, Antioch, Amman, Jerash, Pompeii and Italian Ostia can be seen the ruins of theaters which were in use during the Biblical period. Amphitheaters for gladiatorial and athletic contests were as popular as theaters (cf. I Cor. 9:24-27; II Tim. 4:7).

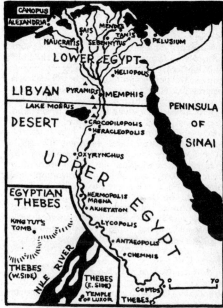

473. Thebes, Upper and Lower Egypt

Thebes (thēbz), the Greek name of a city of Egypt, and its capital during the brilliant 18th dynasty; called in the A. V. "No-Amon," R. V. "Noamon," or simply No (Jer. 46:25); R. V. "Amon of No" (Ezek. 30:14-16) (see No). Thebes is referred to by classical writers as being very ancient. The city spreads itself on both banks of the Nile, just as London and Paris extend over both banks of the Thames and Seine. On the right bank are the temples of *Karnak* and of *Luxor*. On the left bank, going from north to south, are the temple of *Goornah*, of *Deir-el-Bahri*, the *Rameseum*, the Colossi, the temple of *Deir-el-Medineh*, and of *Medinet-Abou*. Of these the most wonderful was Karnak, whose ruins are today the most picturesque of all Egypt. Thebes declined after attacks by the Assyrians under Esarhaddon and Asshurbanipal in the seventh century B. C. It was crushed by Rome 30-29 B. C.

In October, 1899, nine columns of the great hall of the temple of Karnak collapsed. Their

472. Luxor Temples

474. Valley of the Tombs of the Kings, near Thebes

fall, as indeed the general decay of the temple, is perhaps due to the infiltration of the Nile, whose water, saturated as it is with nitre, eats away the sandstone.

The'bez (thē'bĕz), the scene of the death of the usurper Abimelech (Judg. 9:50). He had suffocated a thousand Shechemites in the hold of Baal-berith by the smoke of green wood, and then besieged and took Thebez. This town possessed a strong tower, to which the men, women, and children betook themselves. When Abimelech advanced to the tower, and drew near to set the door on fire, a woman threw a millstone down upon him from the roof of the tower, and smashed his skull. Whereupon he called to his armor-bearer to give him a death-blow with his sword, that men might not say of him, "A woman slew him." Thebez is preserved in the large village of *Tubâs*, northeast of Shechem, a still important town. It is situated on the slopes and summit of a hill, whose sides are pierced with numerous cisterns, some in use. Hundreds of people even now live underground, in caves cut in the rock.

Theft. *See* Law.

Thela'sar (thē-lā'sĕr; II Kings 19:12). *See* Telassar.

Theocracy (Gr. *theokratia*, *rule of God*), the form of government among the early Israelites, in which Jehovah was recognized as their supreme civil ruler, and his laws were taken as the statute book of the kingdom. Moses, Joshua, and the Judges were the appointees and agents of Jehovah. The kings were each specifically anointed in his name and the prophets were commissioned to inform them of his will, and did not hesitate to rebuke and even veto their actions if contrary to the divine will. The later history of Israel is a rehearsal of the conflict and intercourse between the great head of the kingdom and the refractory functionaries.

According to the amillennial view, the theocratic idea passed over in its spiritual import, to the Messiah as the heir of David's perpetual dynasty, Christ becoming the ruler of His Church in the hearts of its members. According to premillennial escatology, Christ was rejected as King by the Jews. His death, burial and resurrection brought in an entirely new entity, the Church, begun at Pentecost (Acts 2) and completed at the coming of Christ for His own (I Thess. 4:13-18; I Cor. 15:53f). According to pretribulation rapturists, the Church will be removed preceding Daniel's seventieth week when the Lord will again take up with Israel (Dan. 9:27). After the apocalyptic judgments of this seven-year period and the destruction of godless Gentiles and wicked Jews, the remnant of Israel will be the nucleus of the theocratic kingdom established over Israel at the second coming of Christ (cf. Acts 1:6). This mediatorial Davidic kingdom, in which the Jew will be reinstated to full divine favor as head over the nations, will last at least 1000 years (Rev. 20), after which there will be a Satanic revolt and judgment. After this the eternal state will be brought in (Rev. 21, 22). Thus, amillennialists and premillennialists differ as to the state of Israel and the nation's theocratic future.— M. F. U.

Theoph'ilus (thē-ŏf'ĭ-lŭs; *friend of God*), the person to whom Luke inscribes his gospel and the Acts of the Apostles (Luke 1:3; Acts 1:1). We meet with a considerable number and variety of theories concerning him. The traditional connection of Luke with Antioch has disposed some to look upon Antioch as the abode of Theophilus, and possibly as the seat of his government. We may safely reject the Patristic notion that Theophilus was either a fictitious person or a mere personification of Christian love. The epithet *kratiste* ("most excellent") is a sufficient evidence of his historical existence. It does not, indeed, prove that he was a governor, but it makes it most probable that he was a person of high rank. All that can be conjectured with any degree of safety concerning him comes to this, that he was a Gentile of rank and consideration who came under the influence of Luke or under that of Paul at Rome, and was converted to the Christian faith.

"The only traditional information we possess about this person is that found in the 'Clementine Recognitions' (x, 71), about the middle of the 2d century: 'So that Theophilus, who was at the head of all the men in power at the city (of Antioch), consecrated, under the name of a church, the great basilica (the palace) in which he resided.' According to this, Theophilus was a great lord residing in the capital of Syria" (Godet, *Com.*, on Luke).

Thessalo'nian (thĕs-á-lō'nĭ-ăn), the designation (Acts 20:4; I Thess. 1:1; II Thess. 2:1); "of Thessalonica," (27:2) of an inhabitant of Thessalonica (*q. v.*).

Thessalonians, First Epistle to. This, perhaps the earliest Pauline Epistle, was written by the Apostle in conjunction with Silvanus (Silas) and Timothy.

1. Occasion. Paul had established the Thessalonian church on his second missionary journey and was expelled from Thessalonica. From this city he went to Berea and to Athens. The Epistle alludes to Paul's life at Thessalonica (chap. 2). At Athens he had sent Timothy back to Thessalonica to help the Christians amid their persecutions (chap. 3:1-3). Acts 18:5 records that Silas and Timothy rejoined the Apostle at Corinth. It is clear, therefore, that the Epistle was written from that city in A. D. 52 or 53. Three special needs existed among the Thessalonians calling for apostolic instruction. (a) They were careless about their daily work, evidently under the impression that the second advent would very shortly take place. (b) A concern among them lest their Christian friends who died would suffer loss at the coming of Christ for His own. (c) Friction between church officers and those who possessed miraculous spiritual endowments.

475. Ancient Walls of Thessalonica

2. **Purpose.** The letter was written to urge the Thessalonians to worthwhile conduct and work in the light of the return of Christ; to comfort them concerning those who had died in the Lord; and to instruct them in the elementary truths of the Christian gospel.

3. **Outline.**

Salutation, 1:1
Part I. The Exemplary Church, 1:1-10
  a. Gratitude for the Thessalonians, 1:2-4
  b. Operation of the gospel among them, 1:5-10
Part II. The Exemplary Minister, 2:1-20
  a. Paul's ministry at Thessalonica, 2:1-12
  b. The Thessalonians' response, 2:13-16
  c. The Apostle's subsequent relations with the Thessalonians, 2:17-19
Part III. The Exemplary Brother, 3:1-13
  a. Apostolic concern and their welfare, 3:1-8
  b. The Apostolic intercession, 3:9-13
Part IV. Exemplary Walk, 4:1-18
  a. The Walk Described, 4:1-12
  b. The coming of Christ, the Dynamic of a holy walk, 4:13-18
Part V. Exemplary Watchfulness and the Day of the Lord, 5:1-24
  a. The Day of the Lord and the need for watchfulness, 5:1-11
  b. The duties of church and private life, 5:12-22
  c. Prayer for santification, 5:23, 24
Conclusion, 5:25-28

4. **Attestation and Authorship.** The Epistle claims to be written by Paul (1:1 and 2:18). Paul's character shines out from this Epistle. Note his anxiety for their welfare (3:1, 2), his earnest desire for their spiritual edification (3:8-11), his compassion toward them (2:7) and his sympathy with those in distress (4:13, 18). External evidence is found in Marcion, who accepted it into his canon. It is found also in the Old Syriac and the Old Latin Versions. The Muratorian Canon catalogs it sixth in the list of Pauline epistles. Irenaeus first refers to it by name in *Against*

Heresies, V, 6, 1. Tertullian also quotes it as "written by the Apostle." Clement of Alexandria seems to be the first to ascribe it to Paul in *Instructor* I, 5. Thenceforth references to it are numerous.—*M. F. U.*

Thessalonians, II Epistle to. The second epistle of Paul to the Thessalonians was written to correct the erroneous notion among the Christians at Thessalonica that the persecutions from which they were suffering were those of "the great and terrible Day of the Lord" from which they had been taught to expect deliverance by "the coming of our Lord Jesus Christ and by our gathering together unto Him." The theme of this Epistle has been obscured by the mistranslation of the A. V. in chap. 2:2 where "the Day of Christ is at hand" should be rendered, "Day of the Lord is now present."

1. **Purpose.** Second Thessalonians was written to instruct the Thessalonians concerning the Day of Christ "and our gathering together unto him" (Thess. 1:4, 14-17) and to settle them in their conviction that in the Day of Christ the Lord would appear to translate the living saints and to raise the deceased ones, so that actually the Apostle Paul in II Thess. 2:1 is arguing for a pretribulation out-taking of the Church as the Body of Christ. In chap. 2:1-12 he outlines the events of the Day of the Lord which will occur after the out-taking of the Church.

2. **Purpose and Plan.** (a) The Apostle comforts the Thessalonians in their sufferings (1:4-10). He argues for the imminency of the coming of Christ for His own (2:1). (b) He stresses the fact that the Day of the Lord, so voluminously prophesied in the O. T., will not arrive until *the apostasy* has set in and the "man of lawlessness" has been made manifest (2:2-10). (c) He urges the Thessalonians to faithfulness in view of the coming of Christ for His own (2:13-3:5). (d) He warns the idle and the disorderly to be properly adjusted to the doctrine taught (3:6-15). (e) He shows them how to distinguish his epistles from those of forgers (3:17).

476. A View of Today's Thessalonica

3. **Outline.**

Salutation, 1:1-4
Part I. Comfort in their sufferings, 1:5-12
Part II. The Day of the Lord and the man of sin, 2:1-12
  a. Argument for pretribulation rapture, 2:1, 2
  b. Signs of the Day of the Lord, 2:3-12

Part III. Exhortations and Instructions, 2: 13-3:15
  a. Exhortations to steadfastness and faithfulness, 2:13-3:5
  b. Admonition against disorderliness and idleness, 3:6-15
Benediction, 3:16-18

4. Attestation and Authorship. The essential evidence for this Epistle is earlier and more extensive than that of the first Epistle. Justin Martyr refers to chap. 2:3, 4 in his *Dialogue with Trypho*, chap. CX. Irenaeus mentions it by name, ascribing it to Paul. Tertullian quotes it as by the "apostle," manifestly Paul, as seen by the context. Clement of Alexandria makes reference to chap. 3:1, 2 in *Stromata* (V, III). The Muratorian Canon, Old Syriac, Old Latin and Marcion's Canon include it. The Epistle is of immense importance eschatologically.—*M. F. U.*

477. "Panagia of Halkeon" Church in Thessalonica
(one of the most representative
Byzantine churches)

Thessalonica (thĕs-á-lô-nī′ká), called anciently Therma. It was named after the wife of Cassander, who rebuilt the city. Under the Romans it was one of four divisions of Macedonia. Paul and Silas organized a church there (Acts 17:1-4; I Thess. 1:9). In Acts 20:1-3 Paul's visit is named; see also Phil. 4:16; II Tim. 4:10. In Acts 17:6, 8, the rulers of the city are called, in the original, *politarchai*. The modern city Salonika is a strategic Balkan metropolis having a population in excess of 200,000. Because of its position it played a vital role in the First and Second World Wars. Placed on the great road (*Via Egnatia*), which connected Rome with the whole region north of the Aegean Sea, Thessalonica was an invaluable center for the spread of the Gospel. In fact it was nearly, if not quite, on a level with Corinth and Ephesus in its share of the commerce of the Levant. The circumstance noted in Acts 17:1, that here was the synagogue of the Jews in this part of Macedonia, had evidently much to do with the apostle's plans, and also doubtless with his success. The first scene of the apostle's work at Thessalonica was the synagogue (17:2, 3). Today a large part of the Jewish segment of the population is Sephardic (Spanish-Portuguese).

Theu′das (thū′dás), an insurgent mentioned by Gamaliel in his speech before the Sanhedrin, at the time of the arraignment of the apostles (Acts 5:35-39). He seems to have been a religious impostor, and to have had about four hundred adherents, who were all slain or scattered. Josephus (*Ant.*, xx, 5, 1) informs us "that a certain magician, whose name was Theudas, persuaded a great part of the people to take their effects with them and follow him to the river Jordan; for he told them he was a prophet, and that he would, by his own command, divide the river, and afford them an easy passage over it; and many were deluded by his words. Fadus . . . sent a troop of horsemen out against them; who, falling upon them unexpectedly, slew many of them, and took many of them alive. They also took Theudas alive, and cut off his head, and carried it to Jerusalem."

Thief. *See* Law.

Thieves. The prophet Isaiah (1:23) says of the Israelitish rulers that they were "companions of thieves," meaning thereby that they allowed themselves to be bribed by presents of stolen goods to acts of injustice toward those who had been robbed. The men who under this name appear in the history of the crucifixion were robbers rather than thieves, belonging to the lawless bands by which Palestine was at that time and afterward infested. Against these brigands every Roman procurator had to wage continual war. It was necessary to use an armed police to encounter them (Luke 22:52). Of the previous history of the two who suffered on Golgotha we know nothing. They had been tried and condemned, and were waiting their execution before our Lord was accused. It is probable enough, as the death of Barabbas was clearly expected at the same time, that they had taken part in his insurrection. At first the thieves reviled our Lord, but afterward one of them in penitence prayed to be remembered when Jesus should come to his kingdom (Matt. 27:38, 44; Mark 15:27).

Thigh (Heb. *yärēk;* Gr. *mēros*), the part of the body from the legs to the trunk.

1. In taking an oath it was an ancient custom to put the hand under the thigh. Abraham required it of his servant, when he made him swear that he would take a wife for Isaac of the daughters of the Canaanites (Gen. 24:2-9). Jacob required it of Joseph when he bound him by oath to bury him in Canaan (47:29-31). This custom, the so-called bodily oath, was, no doubt, connected with the significance of the hip as the part from which the posterity issued (46:26, margin) and the seat of vital power. The early Jewish commentators supposed it to be especially connected with the rite of circumcision.

2. It is stated (Gen. 32:25-32) that the angel touched the hollow of Jacob's thigh and put it out of joint. By the dislocation of his hip the carnal nature of his previous wrestling was declared to be powerless and wrong. By his wrestling with God Jacob entered upon a new stage in his life. Because of the dislocation of Jacob's thigh the custom grew up among his descendants of refraining from eating the *nervus ischiadicus*, the principal nerve in the neighborhood of the hip, which is easily injured by any violent strain in wrestling.

3. If the wife, accused by her husband of infidelity, was guilty, a part of the curse pronounced upon her was that her thigh should rot (Num. 5:21). Precisely the nature of this disease it is impossible to determine. Michae-

lis supposes it to have been dropsy of the ovary.

Figurative. The phrase "hip and thigh" (Heb. *shōq*, Judg. 15:8) occurs in the account of Samson's slaughter of the Philistines, and is a proverbial expression for a cruel, unsparing slaughter. *To uncover the thigh* (Isa. 47:2) was to lay aside all feminine modesty, as to "grind at the mill" was to take a servant's place. *Striking the thigh* was the sign of the deepest shame (Jer. 31:19) or of sorrow (Ezek. 21:12). In Rev. 19:16 it is written, "And he hath on his vesture and on his thigh a name written," etc. The name may have been written upon the sword, which hung upon the thigh. Montfaucon gives an account of several images of warriors having inscriptions *upon the thighs.*

Thim′nathah (thĭm′nȧ-thä; Josh. 19:43). *See* Timnah.

Thirst (Heb. *ṣämä′;* Gr. *dipsos*), a painful sensation occasioned by the absence of liquids from the stomach. This sensation is sometimes accompanied by vehement desire, and the term is therefore used figuratively in the Scripture, in the moral sense of a longing after God (Psa. 42:2; 63:1; 143:6, etc.). A longing after criminal indulgence is also called thirst (Jer. 2:25). A state of continued satisfaction is expressed by the phrase, "They shall hunger no more, neither *thirst* any more" (Rev. 7:16).

Thistle. *See* Vegetable Kingdom.

Thom′as (tŏm′ȧs; from Aram. *t°′ōmä, twin*), also called *Didymus*, its Greek equivalent.

1. **Name and Family.** Out of this name has grown the tradition that he had a twin sister, Lydia, or that he was a twin brother of our Lord; which last, again, would confirm his identification with Judas (Matt. 13:55). He is said to have been born in Antioch, but is also considered by some a native of Galilee, like most of the other apostles (John 21:2).

2. **Personal History.** In the first three gospels we have an account of his call to the apostleship (Matt. 10:3; Mark 3:18; Luke 6:15). The rest that we know of him is derived from the gospel of John. When Jesus declared his intention of going to Bethany, Lazarus being dead, Thomas, apprehensive of danger, said to the other disciples, "Let us also go, that we may die with him" (John 11:16). At the last supper, when Jesus was speaking of his departure, Thomas said unto him, "Lord, we know not whither thou goest; and how can we know the way?" (14:5). When Jesus appeared to the first assembly after his resurrection, Thomas, for some reason, was absent. The others told him, "We have seen the Lord." Thomas broke forth into an exclamation which conveys to us at once the vehemence of his doubt, and the vivid picture that his mind retained of his Master's form as he had last seen him lifeless on the cross (20:25). "And after eight days again his disciples were within, and Thomas with them: then came Jesus, the doors being shut, and stood in the midst, and said, Peace be unto you." Turning to Thomas, he uttered the words which convey as strongly the sense of condemnation and tender reproof as those of Thomas had shown the sense of hesitation and

doubt. "Then saith he to Thomas, Reach hither thy finger, and behold my hands; and reach hither thy hand, and thrust it into my side: and be not faithless, but believing." The effect upon Thomas is immediate. Doubt is removed, and faith asserts itself strongly. The words in which he expresses his belief contain a high assertion of his Master's divine nature: "And Thomas answered and said unto him, My Lord and my God." The answer of our Lord sums up the moral of the whole narrative: "Thomas, because thou hast seen me, thou hast believed: blessed are they that have not seen, and yet have believed" (20:26-29). From this incident came the title of "Doubting Thomas," and he has been characterized as "slow to believe, subject to despondency, seeing all the difficulties of a case, viewing things on the darker side." It may be that he was of a critical tendency of mind, in which he did not recognize the statement of eye-witnesses as a sufficient ground of faith. In the New Testament we hear of Thomas only twice again, once on the Sea of Galilee, with six other disciples (21:2), and again in the assembly of the apostles after the ascension (Acts 1:13). The earlier traditions, as believed in the fourth century, represent him as preaching in Parthia, or Persia, and as finally buried in Edessa. The later traditions carry him farther east. His martyrdom is said to have been occasioned by a lance.

Thorn, the rendering of several Hebrew and Greek words; indeed there are no less than twenty-two words rendered in the A. V. "thorn," "thistle," "brier," etc. (*see* Vegetable Kingdom). In the passage "Canst thou put a hook into his [the *leviathan*] nose? or bore his jaw through with a thorn?" (Job 41:2; comp. II Chron. 33:11; Heb. *ḥōăḥ*) *thorn* was a hook or ring put through the nostrils of large fishes in order to let them down again alive into the water and retain them as captives.

Figurative. "A grieving thorn" (Ezek. 28:24) should be rendered a smarting sting, figurative of the hurts of heathenism. "The most upright is sharper than a thorn hedge" (Mic. 7:4) refers to the corruption of the nation, which was so great that even the most upright injured all who came in contact with him. In Job 5:5, "taketh it even out of the thorns," means that even a thorny hedge does not prevent them from taking the food of the orphan. From want of energy "the way of the slothful man is as an hedge of thorns" (Prov. 15:19), i. e., full of almost insurmountable obstacles (comp. 22:5). To be overgrown with thorns is a figure of desolation (24:31). "The crackling of thorns under a pot" (Eccles. 7:6) is that to which the laughter of fools is compared. The wicked are often compared to thorns (II Sam. 23:6; Nah. 1:10). Dried cow dung was the common fuel in Palestine; its slowness in burning makes the quickness of a fire of thorns the most graphic as an image of the sudden end of fools (comp. Psa. 118:12). Thorns and thistles are symbolic of false prophets (Matt. 7:16).

Thorn in the Flesh. *See* Paul.

Three. *See* Numbers.

Three Taverns. *See* Appii Forum.

Threshing. *See* Agriculture.

Figurative. Threshing is used in Scripture as a figure of providential chastisement (Isa. 21:10); crushing oppression (Isa. 41:15; Mic. 4:12, 13); judicial visitation (Jer. 51:33); the labors of ministers (I Cor. 9:9, 10). Dust made by threshing is a figure of complete destruction (II Kings 13:7).

478. Threshing Floor

Threshing Floor (Heb. *gōrĕn, even*), a level and hard-beaten plot in the open air (Judg. 6:37; II Sam. 6:6), on which sheaves of grain were threshed (Isa. 21:10; Jer. 51:33; Mic. 4:12; Matt. 3:12). The top of a rock was a favorite spot for this purpose; on this the sheaves were spread out, and sometimes beaten with flails —a method practiced especially with the lighter grains, such as fitches or cummin (Isa. 28:27)—but more commonly by oxen. The oxen were either yoked side by side and driven round over the grain, or yoked to a machine (Lat. *tribulum* or *trahea*), consisting of a board or a block of wood, with stones or pieces of iron fastened to the lower surface to make it rough. This was dragged over the grain, beating out the kernels.

The threshing floors were watched all night to guard against theft of the grain (Ruth 3:4, 6, 14); they were often of considerable value, and frequently named in connection with the winepress (Deut. 16:13; II Kings 6:27; Hos. 9:2; Joel 2:24), since grain, wine, and oil were the more important products of the soil. They were sometimes given particular names, as that of Nachon (II Sam. 6:6) or Chidon (I Chron. 13:9), Atad (Gen. 50:10), Ornan or Araunah (II Sam. 24:18, 20; I Chron. 21:15).

479. Winnowing on Threshing floor

Threshold, the rendering in A. V. of:

1. A sill or bottom of a doorway (Judg. 19:27; I Kings 14:17; Ezek. 40:6, 7; Zeph. 2:14). Heb. *săph*.

2. Heb. *mĭphtän*, a *stretcher*, probably the bottom beam or sill of a door (I Sam. 5:4, 5; Ezek. 9:3; 10:4, 18; 46:2; 47:1).

Throne (Heb. *kĭssē'*; Gr. *thronos; bēma*). The Hebrew term *kĭssē'* applies to any elevated seat occupied by a person in authority, whether a high priest (I Sam. 1:9), a judge (Psa. 122:5), or a military chief (Jer. 1:15). The use of a chair in a country where the usual postures were squatting and reclining, was at all times regarded as a symbol of dignity (II Kings 4:10; Prov. 9:14). In order to specify a throne in our sense of the term it was necessary to add to *kĭssē'* the notion of royalty; hence the frequent occurrence of such expressions as "the throne of the kingdom" (Deut. 17:18; I Kings 1:46; II Chron. 7:18). The

480. Ancient Throne

characteristic feature in the royal throne was its elevation: Solomon's throne was approached by six steps (I Kings 10:19; II Chron. 9:18); and Jehovah's throne is described as "high and lifted up" (Isa. 6:1). The materials and workmanship were costly. It was furnished with arms or "stays." The steps were also lined with pairs of lions. As to the form of the chair, we are only informed in I Kings 10:19 that "the top was round behind." The king sat on his throne on state occasions. At such times he appeared in his royal robes.

Figurative. The throne was the symbol of supreme power and dignity (Gen. 41:40). "To sit upon the throne" implied the exercise of regal power (Deut. 17:18; I Kings 16:11); to "sit upon the throne of another" (I Kings 1:13) meant to succeed him as king. "Thrones" also designates earthly potentates and celestial beings, archangels (Col. 1:16).

Thum'mim (thŭm'ĭm). *See* Urim and Thummim.

Thunder (Heb. *qōl*, a *voice*, i. e., of Jehovah; *rā'ăm*, a *peal;* Gr. *brontē*). In a physical point of view the most noticeable feature in connection with thunder is the extreme rarity of its occurrence during the summer months in Palestine and the adjacent countries. From the middle of April to the middle of September it is hardly ever heard. Hence it was selected by Samuel as a striking expression of the divine displeasure toward the Israelites (I Sam. 12:17). Rain in harvest was deemed as extraordinary as snow in summer (Prov. 26:1), and Jerome asserts that he had never witnessed it in the latter part of June or in July (*Com.*, on Amos 4:7). The plague of hail in Egypt is naturally represented as accompanied with "mighty thunderings" (Exod. 9:22-29, 33, 34). It accompanied the lightnings at the giving of the law (19:16; 20:18). It is referred to as a natural phenomenon subject to laws of the Creator (Job 28:26; 38:25).

In John 12:28 it is related that there "came a voice from heaven" in response to the prayer of Jesus. "It is a voice which came miraculously from God; yet, as regards its intelligibility conditioned by the subjective disposition and receptivity of the hearers, which sounded with a *tone as of thunder*, so that the definite words which resounded in this form of sound remained unintelligible to the unsusceptible, who simply heard that majestic kind of sound, but not its contents, and said, *brountēn gegonenai* ('It is thunder')" (Meyer, *Com.*, in loc.). Mark (3:17) tells us that our Lord surnamed James and John "Boanerges, which is, The sons of thunder." Some have thought that this applied to them because of their eloquence; others to their courage and energy. It seems more likely that it referred to their impetuous, ardent temperament.

Figurative. In the imaginative philosophy of the Hebrews thunder was regarded as the voice of Jehovah (Job 37:2, 4, 5; 40:9; Psa. 18:13, 29:3-9; Isa. 30:30, 31), who dwelt behind the thundercloud (Psa. 81:7). Thunder was, to the mind of the Jew, the symbol of divine power (29:3, etc.) and vengeance (I Sam. 2:10; II Sam. 22:14).

481. Waterfront at Tiberias

Thunderbolt (Heb. *rĕshĕph*, a live *coal*, an *arrow*). In accordance with the popular notion "hot thunderbolts" (Psa. 78:48) meant lightnings, with reference, doubtless, to the manner in which lightning strikes the earth.

Thyati'ra (thī-á-tī'rá), a city in Asia Minor, the seat of one of the seven Apocalyptic churches (Rev. 1:11; 2:18). It was situated on the confines of Mysia and Ionia, a little south of the river Hyllus, and at the northern extremity of the valley between Mount Tmolus and the southern ridge of Temnus. It was one of the many Macedonian colonies established in Asia Minor, in the sequel of the destruction of the Persian empire by Alexander. The waters of Thyatira are said to be so well adapted for dyeing that in no place can the scarlet cloth, out of which fezes are made, be so brilliantly or so permanently dyed as here. So in the Acts (16:14) Lydia, the first convert of Paul at Philippi, is mentioned as a seller of purple from Thyatira. The principal deity of the city was Apollo, worshipped as the sun-god under the surname Tyrimnas. He was no doubt introduced by the Macedonian colonists, for the name is Macedonian. A priestess of Artemis is also mentioned in the inscriptions. The modern city of Akhisar marks the site of the ancient city in the territory which is now Anatolian Turkey.

Thyine Wood, a prized ornamental fragrant wood of the cypress family enumerated as luxury product of Babylon (Rev. 18:12). *See* Vegetable Kingdom.

482. Tiberias

Tibe'rias (tī-bē'rĭ-ás), a city in the time of Christ, on the Sea of Galilee; first mentioned in the New Testament (John 6:1, 23; 21:1), and then by Josephus, who states that it was built by Herod Antipas, and was named by him in honor of the emperor Tiberius, A. D. 14-37. It was one of nine towns round the sea, each one having not less than fifteen thousand inhabitants. Because Tiberias was situated on the edge of the ancient walled town Rakkath (Josh. 19:35) or Hammath, whose cemetery lies beneath it, in Jesus' time it was avoided by strict Jews. Our Lord apparently did not visit the city, noted for its laxness as a hot-water bath resort. Tiberias was the capital of Galilee from the time of its origin until the reign of Herod Agrippa II, who changed the seat of power back again to Sepphoris, where it had been before the founding of the new city. Many of the inhabitants were Greeks and Romans, and foreign custom prevailed there to such an extent as to give offense to the stricter Jews. After the destruction of Jerusalem in A. D. 70, Tiberias became a Jewish metropolis and center of Rabbinic learning. After 150 A. D., it was well known as the seat of the Sanhedrin and the rabbinical schools from which came the Talmud and the Masorah. The city lies about 12 miles S. of the entrance of the Jordan into the Lake of Galilee and 6 miles N. of the river's exit from the sea. The vicinity is rich in archaeological possibilities, especially the area between the city and the famous hot springs. Masonry of various dates survives, including a synagogue.

Tibe′rias, The Sea of, another name (John 21:1 only) for the Sea of Galilee (comp. 6:1). It is thought that the evangelist used this name as being more familiar to nonresidents in Palestine than the indigenous name of the "Sea of Galilee" (*q. v.*) or "Sea of Gennesaret."

483. Coin of Tiberius

Tibe′rius (tī-bē′rĭ-ŭs; *pertaining to the Tiber;* in full, Tiberius Claudius Nero Caesar), the second Roman emperor, successor of Augustus, who began to reign A. D. 14, and reigned until A. D. 37. He was the son of Tiberius Claudius Nero and Livia, and hence a stepson of Augustus. He was born at Rome on the 16th of November, B. C. 42. He became emperor in his fifty-fifth year, after having distinguished himself as a commander in various wars, and having evinced talents of a high order as an orator and an administrator of civil affairs. He even gained the reputation of possessing the sterner virtues of the Roman character, and was regarded as entirely worthy of the imperial honors to which his birth and supposed personal merits at length opened the way. Yet, on being raised to the supreme power, he suddenly became, or showed himself to be, a very different man. His subsequent life was one of inactivity, sloth, and self-indulgence. He was despotic in his government, cruel and vindictive in his disposition. Tiberius died at the age of seventy-eight, after a reign of twenty-three years. He is mentioned in Scripture only in Luke 3:1, where he is termed Tiberius Caesar. John the Baptist, it is there said, began his ministry in the fifteenth year of his reign, an important chronological statement, helping to determine the year of Christ's birth and entrance on his public life.

Tib′hath (tĭb′hăth; *slaughter*), a city of Hadadezer, king of Zobah (I Chron. 18:8), called Betah (*q. v.*) in II Sam. 8:8, probably an accidental transposition of the first two letters.

Tib′ni (tĭb′nī; *straw*), the sixth king of Israel, and son of Ginath. After the tragic death of Zimri there was a division among the people, "half followed Tibni . . . and half followed Omri." After a struggle lasting four years Omri's party prevailed, and, according to the brief account of the historian, "Tibni died, and Omri reigned" (I Kings 16:21, 22), B. C. about 886.

Ti′dal (tī′dăl), the name of a king who accompanied Chedorlaomer in his raid into Palestine about 1960 B. C. Of the personality of this king nothing else is known. The country ruled by Tidal was Goiim, often translated "nations or Gentiles." It is not yet certainly located. Hommel believes it to be Goi, in northeastern Babylonia. *See* articles on Chedorlaomer, Arioch, and Amraphel.

Tig′lath-pile′ser (tĭg′lăth-pĭ-lē′zẽr), the name of an Assyrian king (*see* also Pul). The name of Tiglath-pileser fills a large place in the history of the Hebrew people before the fall of Samaria. It was in the reign of Tiglath-pileser III, known also to us under the name of Pul, that they first sensibly felt the menace of complete overthrow by the Assyrians. (1) **Name and origin.** The name Tiglath-pileser appears in Assyrian under the form of *Tukulti-apil-esharra*, meaning "my trust is the son of Esharra," i. e., the god Ninib, but this was abbreviated even by the Assyrians themselves. It was a famous name in the annals of Assyria, for one of the greatest Assyrian conquerors, Tiglath-pileser I (about 1120 B. C.), had borne it. Tiglath-pileser III was, however, a far greater man than his earlier namesake. He was not of royal origin. Of his origin, indeed, nothing is known. It is probable that he was an Assyrian general. He may have been also an administrator or governor of one of the vast provinces of the Assyrian empire. He appears suddenly upon the scene of historical action. He says nothing in his inscriptions of his father or of his mother. His inscriptions were mutilated long after his death by Esarhaddon, an indignity offered to no other king, and these facts lead irresistibly to the conclusions that he was not a member of the royal family. The king who preceded him upon the throne was Asshur-nirari III, who reigned weakly from 754 to 745 B. C. In the year 746 there was a rebellion against his rule. Whether Tiglath-pileser, then perhaps a general, set this rebellion on foot, participated in it, or merely reaped its results, we have no means of knowing, but immediately upon the death of Asshur-nirari III he was acknowledged king of Assyria. (2) **Reign.** The very first years of his reign showed him a masterful man. In other instances in Assyrian history such an usurpation would have been followed by petty wars and insurrections all over the kingdom, but no audible murmur was heard at the beginning of his reign. He was evidently known everywhere as a man with whom it would be dangerous to trifle. His reign was not long (745-727 B. C.), and he may have come to the throne comparatively late in life. Whatever his name was, he assumed at once the royal style of Tiglath-pileser, adopting as his own a famous name. Were it not for the abuse of his inscriptions, suffered at the hands of Esarhaddon, we should know all the events of his reign in great detail. He had restored the palace of Shalmaneser in Kalchi. Upon the walls of its great rooms he placed stone slabs with beautifully engraved inscriptions recounting the campaigns of his reign. Besides these he left inscriptions written upon clay, giving accounts of his campaigns grouped in geographical order; and supplemented these by other inscriptions on clay containing lists of the countries conquered, but without any details of the campaigns. The first matter that claimed the attention of the new king was an invasion of Babylonia, rendered necessary to drive out nomadic Aramaeans who had invaded and settled in the country, and threatened to destroy its civilization. The march of the new Assyrian king southward was a triumphal progress. He was heralded as a deliverer, and soon reestablished an orderly government in the kingdom of Babylonia. After this he turned into the northwest and into the east, where he collected heavy tribute from peoples who had refused it during the weak reign of his predecessor. At the very beginning he introduced an entirely new method of dealing with conquered peoples. Before his reign the Assyrian kings had for the most part contented themselves with predatory raids by which they enormously increased the wealth of Assyria, but contributed little to the upbuilding of stable government in the conquered lands. Peoples thus conquered paid tribute while the conqueror was at hand, and refused when they thought he was far enough away to place them out of danger. Some of the previous kings had tried in a very slight fashion colonization and deportation, but without conspicuous success. These were made by Tiglath-pileser III his chief methods. He

already Assyrian tributaries, but Assyrian influence had been little felt for a long time. If it had been possible to unite all the petty kingdoms of Syria, Palestine, and their neighboring countries into one great confederation for mutual defense it would probably have been possible to prevent the reconquest of the west by the Assyrians, even under so great a master as Tiglath-pileser III. But the weakness of the west lay in its utter inability to put aside selfish and petty concerns to work for united interests. Some of these states determined again, about 739 B. C., to throw off the Assyrian yoke. At the head of the coalition thus formed Azariah, or Uzziah, king of Judah, took his stand. To support him Hamath, Damascus, Tyre, Que, Melid, Samaria, and others, to the number of nineteen, had banded together. It was indeed a promising confederation. If these nineteen states should put their full quota of men into the field under competent military direction they would, no doubt, be able to resist the Assyrians, and to prevent, and, at least, postpone the engulfing of Syria into the now rapidly growing Assyrian empire. But before any combination of their forces could be brought about Tiglath-pileser came west and entered Palestine, apparently determined to attack the ringleader, Uzziah, in his own territory, before his allies could come to his aid. As soon

484. Final Assault on Damascus

first conquered a people and then deported the best of them to another part of his dominions, bringing from that place enough people to colonize the land thus vacated. For many peoples this was punishment worse than death. From his point of view it contributed to stability by making successful rebellion almost an impossibility. He further set Assyrian governors over conquered provinces, and endeavored not only to collect tribute annually, but also to administer all the affairs of the land as a part of the Assyrian empire which he was building. Campaign followed campaign, north, east, and south, with lesser invasions also in the west. All these things affected the Hebrew people but little. They were, however, a threat of what might be when once he was free to set about to the conquest of Palestine. (3) **Relation with Israel.** Nominally some of the states of Syria and Palestine were

as he entered the northern kingdom Menahem threw down his arms and paid the Assyrians one thousand talents of silver as a token of subjection. Here was practically an end of the entire confederation. Tiglath-pileser was apparently satisfied with this collapse, and as the others were willing to pay tribute, he did not pursue the advantage which he had gained, but went back to Assyria laden with a heavy booty, to which Rezon of Damascus and Hiram of Tyre had also contributed. In 734 B. C. we find him again on the Mediterranean coast. In this year he seems to have crossed the plain of Syria, near Damascus, and to have gone straight to the coast, which he followed toward the south. He had no fear of Tyre nor of Sidon, for they were busy with commerce, and he needed to strike but a few light blows before Gaza was reached. Here, if ever, Egypt and Syria and all the West ought to have made a stand against the Assyrians, but no stand was made, and Gaza was overwhelmed. In the reign of Ahaz, king of Judah, with him Pekah of Samaria and Rezon of Damascus, was another opportunity for coalition against Assyria, but Pekah and Rezon thought they saw in the youth of Ahaz a chance for the enrichment of their own kingdoms. They united forces and invaded Judah. So began the Syro-Ephraimitic war. Ahaz was likely to be overwhelmed. To whom should he turn for help? No help was to be had in Egypt, and in the madness of the hour he sent an embassy to meet Tiglath-pileser and sue for help against Damascus and Samaria. Tiglath-pileser accepted a bribe from Ahaz, for it suited his own future purposes so to do, and at once threatened Damascus. This drew off from Judah the armies of Damascus and Samaria. Tiglath-pileser then passed by Damascus, came down the sea coast past his tributary states of Tyre and Sidon, and turned into the plain of Esdraelon above Carmel. His own accounts fail us at this point, but the biblical narrative fills the gap by stating that he took a number of cities and overran the land (II Kings 15:29). He might then have attacked Samaria itself, but the party of assassins made that unnecessary, for they slew the king, and in his place Tiglath-pileser set up Hoshea as the nominal king of Samaria, but as his personal representative (15:30). Damascus was next besieged, captured (732 B. C.), and the entire country about it given over to desolation. Tiglath-pileser boasts that he destroyed at this time five hundred and ninety-one cities, whose inhabitants were carried away with all their possessions to Assyria. Ahaz of Judah came to pay honor in Damascus to this foreign conqueror, who was now practically master over the whole country. He it was who had prepared the way for the destruction of Samaria by Shalmaneser V and Sargon II (722-721 B. C.). His later career has but little bearing upon the Old Testament story. In 728 B. C., upon New Year's Day, he was solemnly anointed king of Babylon, and in 727 he died. Upon any basis of estimate whatever he ranks as one of the greatest conquerors and one of the greatest executives among all the lines of great rulers who made Assyria a dreaded name in Asia. He made the Assyrian empire out of a kingdom and a few dependencies. He made it a world power, binding province to province, and transforming local centers into general centers by deportation and colonization.— R. W. R. revised by *M. F. U.*

Ti'gris (tī'grĭs), is used in the Septuagint as the equivalent of the Heb *Hĭddĕķĕl* (A. V. Hiddekel, Gen. 2:14), one of the rivers of Eden. The name of Hiddekel, or Tigris, was also Akkadian. In the old language of Babylonia it was termed *Idiglat, Digla,* "the encircling." From *Idiglat* the Persians derived their Tigra with a play upon a word in their own language which signified an 'arrow.' The Hiddekel, we are told, flowed 'to the east of Asshur.' But the Asshur meant is not the land of Assyria, as the A. V. supposes, but the city of Assur, the primitive capital of the country,

now represented by the mound of Kalah Sherghat. The land of Assyria lay to the east as well as to the west of the Tigris. Daniel (10:4) calls it "the great river, which is Hiddekel." It rises in the mountains of Armenia, about thirty miles northwest of Diarbekir, at no great distance from the sources of the Euphrates, and pursues a meandering course of upward of one thousand one hundred miles, when they at last unite and flow as one stream into the Persian Gulf. *See* Hiddekel.

Tik'vah (tĭk'vá; *hope, expectation*).

1. The son of Harhas, and father of Shallum, the husband of Huldah the prophetess (II Kings 22:14), B. C. before 624. He is called in II Chron. 34:22, Tikvath.

2. The father of Jahaziah, which latter was one of the rulers appointed by Ezra to superintend the divorcement of the Gentile wives after the captivity (Ezra 10:15), B. C. before 437.

Tik'vath (tĭk'văth), the father of Shallum (II Chron. 34:32). *See* Tikvah 1. (II Kings 22:14).

Til'gath-pilne'ser (tĭl'găth-pĭl-nē'zĕr), a variation (I Chron. 5:6, 26; II Chron. 28:20) of Tiglath-pileser (*q. v.*).

Tile (Heb. *lᵉbēnäh* from *läbēn, to be white,* so called from the *whitish* clay), a brick (Ezek. 4:1) used to write upon. When the clay was in a soft, moist state, in its hold or frame, the characters were inscribed upon it, and then the clay was baked. Such was the perfection of the manufacture that some of them are in a state of fine preservation after three thousand years. *See* Writing.

Tiling (Gr. *keramos, pottery ware*). The rendering of the A. V., Luke 5:19, "through the tiling" (*dia tōn keramōn*), has been the cause of considerable difficulty. Some have understood by the tiling the layer of sticks, brush, and hard-rolled clay which constitutes the ordinary flat roof of an oriental house. Of course, the breaking up of this might be readily repaired, but would cause an intolerable dust at the time. Dr. Edersheim (*Life of Jesus,* i, 503) says: "The roof itself, which had hard-beaten earth or rubble underneath it, was paved with brick, stone, or any other hard substance, and surrounded by a balustrade which, according to Jewish law, was at least three feet high. It is scarcely possible to imagine that the bearers of the paralytic would have attempted to dig through this into a room below, not to speak of the interruption and inconvenience caused to those below by such an operation. But no such objection attaches if we regard it not as the main roof of the house, but as that of the covered gallery under which we are supposing the Lord to have stood . . . In such case it would have been comparatively easy to 'unroof' the covering of 'tiles,' and then 'having dug out' an opening through the lighter framework which supported the tiles, to let down their burden 'into the midst before Jesus.' "

Tillage. 1. *To break up with a plow.* (Heb. *nîr*; Prov. 13:23; comp. Jer. 4:3; Hos. 10:12).

2. *Servile labor* (Heb. *'ăbōdäh, work*), i. e., *servile* labor (Lev. 25:39); *work, business* (I Chron. 9:19). Specifically, *work* of the field, agriculture (I Chron. 27:26; Neh. 10:37).

Ti'lon (tī'lŏn), the last named of the four "sons" of Shimon, of the tribe of Judah (I Chron. 4:20).

Time'us, more correctly **Timae'us** (tĭ-mē'ŭs), father of the blind beggar cured by Christ (Mark 10:46), the son being thence called Bartimeus (*q. v.*).

Timbrel. *See* Music.

Time, the rendering of several Hebrew and Greek terms, of which the following are most important:

1. *Day* (Heb. *yōm*), used both in the particular sense of a natural day (see below), and in the general sense of a set time or period of time.

2. *An appointed time* (Heb. *zᵉmän*); thus "To everything there is a season" (Eccles. 3:1), i. e., everything remains but for a time; all things are frail and fleeting. In Dan. 2:16 it is an appointed season.

3. *Set time* (Heb. *mō'ēd*, an *appointment*), a space of time, appointed and definite (Exod. 34:18; I Sam. 13:8; Isa. 14:31, etc.).

4. *Time to come* (Heb. *mäḥär*, *to-morrow*) (Exod. 13:14; Josh. 4:6, 21; comp. I Sam. 20:12).

5. *A set time* (Aram. *'iddän*), is used in the Book of Daniel in a sense that has been much disputed. In Dan. 4:16, 23, 25, 32, the prophet writes of Nebuchadnezzar, "Let his heart be changed from man's, and let a beast's heart be given unto him; and let seven times pass over him." Gesenius (*Lexicon*) gives its meaning as prophetic language for a year. "Following the example of the LXX. and of Josephus, many ancient and recent interpreters understood by the word *'iddänin*, *years*, because the *times* in 7:25; 12:7 are also years, and because in 4:29 mention is made of twelve months, and thereby the *time* is defined as one year. But from 4:29 the duration of the *'iddänin* cannot at all be concluded, and in 7:25 and 12:7 the *times* are not years. *'Iddän* designates generally a definite period of time, whose length or duration may be very different" (Keil, *Com.*, on Dan. 4:16).

6. Heb. *'ēth* is a general term for *time*; e. g., the *time of evening* (Josh. 8:29, A. V. "eventide"); *time of bearing* (Job 39:1, 2); *at* or *about* a time (Dan. 9:21); *time* or *season* of love (Ezek. 16:8), i. e., of young women at marriageable age, etc.

7. Heb. *pä'äm*, a *stroke*, a tread of the foot, step (Psa. 119:126); one time (Gen. 18:32, A. V. "this once;" Exod. 9:27; Prov. 7:12, A. V. "now").

8. *Hidden time*, i. e., obscure and long, of which the beginning or end is indefinite, *duration*, *everlasting*, *eternity* (Josh. 24:2; Deut. 32:7, A. V. "days of old;" Prov. 8:23, "everlasting") (Heb. *'ōläm*, *concealed*).

9. An *occasion*, *set* time (Gr. *kairos*). A *space* of time, opportunity, etc. Gr. *chronos*.

Time, Divisions of. The following are mentioned in Scripture:

1. **Year** (Heb. *shänäh*, as a *revolution* of time), so called from the *change* of the seasons. The years of the Hebrews in the preexilic period were *lunar*, of 354 days 8 hours 38 seconds, and consisted of twelve unequal lunar months. As this falls short of the true year (an astronomical month having 29 days 12 hours

44 minutes 2.84 seconds), they were compelled, in order to preserve the regularity of harvest and vintage (Exod. 23:16), to add a month occasionally, thus making it, on the average, to coincide with the solar year (containing 365 days 5 hours 48 minutes 45 seconds). The method of doing this among the very ancient Hebrews is unknown. Among the later Jews an intercalary month was inserted after Adar and was called Ve-dar, or second Adar. The intercalation was regularly decreed by the Sanhedrin, which observed the rule never to add a month to the sabbatical year.

The Hebrew year began, as the usual enumeration of the months shows (Lev. 23:34; 25:9; Num. 9:11; II Kings 25:8; Jer. 39:2; comp. I Macc. 4:52; 10:21), with Abib or Nisan (Esth. 3:7), subsequent to and in accordance with the Mosaic arrangement. As we constantly find this arrangement spoken of as a *festal* calendar, most rabbinical and many Christian scholars understand that the *civil* year began, as with the modern Jews, with Tisri (October), but the *ecclesiastical* year with Nisan.

A well-defined and universal era was unknown among the ancient Hebrews. National events were sometimes dated from the exodus from Egypt (Exod. 19:1; Num. 33:38; I Kings 6:1), usually from the accession of the kings (as in Kings, Chronicles, and Jeremiah), or the erection of Solomon's temple (I Kings 8:1; 9:10), later from the beginning of the exile (Ezek. 33:21; 40:1), but in Ezek. 1:1 otherwise. For special purposes, such as the tithing of cattle and the planting of trees, the Jewish year began at distinct times. The regnal year began with Nisan. The first year of each king's reign began on the first day of Nisan after his accession, the preceding days being counted to his predecessor. This accounts for the precise specification of the time of three months, as exceptional, in the case of the reigns of Jehoahaz and Jeconiah. The post-exilian books date according to the reigning years of the Persian masters of Palestine (Ezra 4:24; 6:15; 7:7, sq.; Neh. 2:1; 13:6; Hag. 2:1, 2, etc.).

As Syrian vassals the Jews adopted the Greek (I Macc. 1:10) or Seleucid era, which dated from the overthrow of Babylon by Seleucus Nicator I. Still another national reckoning is given (I Macc. 13:41, sq.), viz., from the year of the deliverance of the Jews from the Syrian yoke, i. e., seventeen of the Seleucian era, or from the autumn of B. C. 143.

2. **Month** (Heb. *ḥōdĕsh*, the *new* moon). The Hebrew months were lunar, and began from the new moon as ocularly observed; at least this is the case from the post-exilian period. In this period the length of the lunar month depended upon the day when the appearance of the new moon was announced by the Sanhedrin, which thus made the month either twenty-nine days or thirty days, according as the day was included in the following or the preceding month. The general rule was that in one year not less than four nor more than eight full months should occur. The final adjustment of the lunar to the solar year was by

intercalation, so that whenever in the last month, Adar, it became evident that the passover, which must be held in the following month, Nisan, would occur before harvest, i. e., not at the time when the sun would be in Aries, an entire month was interjected between Adar and Nisan, constituting an intercalary year. This, however, according to the Gemara, did not take place in a sabbatic year, but always in that which preceded it; nor in two successive years, nor yet more than three years apart.

Before the exile the individual months were usually designated by numbers (the twelfth month occurs in II Kings 25:27; Jer. 52:31; Ezek. 29:1); yet we find also the following names: *Ear month* (Heb. *ḥŏdĕsh hä'äbîb*; Exod. 13:4; 23:15; Deut. 16:1), corresponding to the later Nisan; *Bloom month* (*ḥŏdĕsh zîw*; I Kings 6:1, 37), the second month; *Rain month* (*yĕrăḥ bûl*; 6:38), the eighth month; *Freshet month* (*yĕrăḥ hä'äthänîm*; 8:2), the seventh month; all of which seem to be mere appelatives. Occasionally the months were newly numbered after the post-exilian period.

After the exile the months received the following names: (1) *Nisan* (Neh. 2:1; Esth. 3:7), the first month, in which the passover was held and in which the vernal equinox fell; (2) *Iyâr* (Targum on II Chron. 30:2); (3) *Sivân* (Esth. 8:9); (4) *Tammûz*; (5) *Ab*; (6) *Elûl* (Neh. 6:15), the last month of the civil year in the post-exilian age; (7) *Tishrî*, in which the festivals of atonement and tabernacles fell; (8) *Marchesvân* (Josephus, *Ant.*, i, 3,3); (9) *Chislêu* (Neh. 1:1; Zech. 7:1); (10) *Tebêth* (Esth. 2:16); (11) *Shebât* (Zech. 1:7); (12) *Adâr* (Esth. 3:7; 8:12).

3. **Week** (Heb. *shäbū'ă, sevened;* Gr. *sabbaton, rest,* by extension *sennight,* i. e., the interval between two sabbaths). The division of time into weeks is met with as early as Gen. 2:2, 3; and in the narrative of the deluge more than one allusion occurs to this mode of computing time (7:4, 10; 8:10, 12). Later, weeks appear to have been known among the Syrians of Mesopotamia (29:27, 28), while still later they attached a certain sacredness to the number *seven,* if we may judge from the procedure of Balaam (Deut. 23:4; Num. 23:1, 4, 14, 29). Weeks appear to have been known in Egypt in the time of Joseph (Gen. 50:10, 11). The septenary (weekly) institutions constituted a very prominent feature of the Mosaic law (Num. 19:11; 28:17; Exod. 13:6, 7; 34:18; Lev. 14:38; 23:42; Deut. 16:8, 13). Ordinarily, however, days rather than weeks (as among the Greeks and Romans) constituted the conventional mode of computing time (see Lev. 12:5; Dan. 10:2, sq.).

In the post-exilic period the reckoning by weeks became more customary, and at length special names for particular week days came into use (Mark 16:2, 9; Luke 24:1; Acts 20:7; I Cor. 16:2). The astronomical derivation of the week naturally grows out of the obvious fact that the moon changes about every seven —properly, seven and three eighths—days, so that the lunar month divides itself into four quarters. The days of the week were named long before the Christian era on regular astronomical principles from the seven planets,

which was an Egyptian invention. They began with Saturn's day (Saturday), inasmuch as Saturn was the outermost planet; but among the Jews this day (the Sabbath) was the last of the week, and so the Jewish and Christian week commences with Sunday. These heathen names were never in general use among the Jews. Weeks (or heptads) of years belong, among the Jews, to prophetical poetry, but in one instance they occur in a literal sense in prose (Dan. 9:24-27).

4. **Day** (Heb. *yŏm;* Gr. *hēmera*), one of the commonest and most ancient of the divisions of time. As used in Gen. 1:5, etc., day marks an entire revolution of time, as of natural day and night; not day as distinguished from night, but day and night together. "If the days of creation are regulated by the recurring interchange of light and darkness, they must be regarded not as periods of time of incalculable duration, of years or thousands of years, but as simple earthly days. It is true the morning and evening of the first three days were not produced by the rising and setting of the sun, since the sun was not yet created; but the constantly recurring interchange of light and darkness, which produced day and night upon the earth, cannot for a moment be understood as denoting that the light called forth from the darkness of chaos returned to that darkness again, and thus periodically burst forth and disappeared. The only way in which we can represent it to ourselves is by supposing that the light called forth by the creative mandate was separated from the dark mass of the earth, and concentrated outside or above the globe, so that the interchange of light and darkness took place as soon as the dark chaotic mass began to rotate, and to assume in the process of creation the form of a spherical body. The time occupied in the first rotations of the earth upon its axis cannot, indeed, be measured by our hourglass; but even if they were slower at first, and did not attain their present velocity till the completion of our solar system, this would make no essential difference between the first three days and the last three, which were regulated by the rising and setting of the sun" (K. and D., *Com.,* on Gen. 1:5).

From a very early period the time of reckoning the day was from sunset to sunset, and this became the Jewish method (Lev. 23:32; comp. Exod. 12:18). The Phoenicians, Numidians, and other nations of the East are said to have followed the same custom, if it was not indeed the custom generally followed in remote antiquity. "The ancient Germans (Tacitus, ch. xi) compute not the number of days, but of nights; the night appears to draw on the day." And Caesar says (*Bell. Gal.*, vi, 18) of the Gauls, "They measure time not by the number of days, but of nights; and accordingly observe their birthdays, and the beginning, of months and years, so as to make the day follow the night." Of this custom we have a memorial in our "sennight," "fortnight," to express the period of seven and fourteen days respectively.

Figurative. Day is often used by sacred writers, in a general sense, for a definite period of time—an era or season, when something remarkable has taken place, or is destined to do so (Gen. 2:4; Isa. 22:5; Joel 2:2, etc.). And it accorded with Hebrew usage to designate by the term day or night what probably formed only a part of these; thus by three days and three nights might be understood only a portion of three (Matt. 12:40; 27:63, 64; comp. with I Kings 12:5, 12). As it is also by day that the more active portion of man's life is spent, so day is used to express the whole term of life considered as a season of active labor (John 9:4).

5. **Hour** (Aram. *shā'āh*, properly a *look;* Gr. *hōra*). The mention of hours first occurs in Scripture at the time of the Babylonian captivity (Dan. 3:6; 5:5). It would appear that the Babylonians were among the first to adopt the division of twelve equal parts for the day, as Herodotus testifies (ii, 109) that the Greeks derived this custom from the Babylonians. The Hebrews also adopted it; and in the New Testament we read of the third, sixth, the ninth hours of the day, which were the more marked divisions of the twelve. The night was divided into the same number of parts. From the variations in sunrise and sunset this division, which had these natural phenomena for its two terminations, could never attain to exactness, and was therefore unsuited to nations that had reached a high degree of civilization. Such nations accordingly fell upon the plan of adopting midnight as the fixed point from which the whole diurnal revolution might be reckoned, divided into twice twelve, or twenty-four hours.

The following table gives the Jewish divisions of the day, according to natural phenomena and religious observances:

of Lotan, and daughter of Seir the Horite (Gen. 36:22; I Chron. 1:39).

2. A duke (or shiek) of Edom (Gen. 36:40; I Chron. 1:51, A. V. "Timnah").

Tim'nah (tĭm'nȧ; Heb. *tĭmnäh, an allotted portion*), a name which occurs, simple and compounded, and with slight variations of form, several times, in the topography of the Holy Land.

1. A place which formed one of the landmarks on the north boundary of the allotment of Judah (Josh. 15:10). It is probably identical with the Thimnathah which belonged to Dan (19:43), and that again with the Timnath, or, more accurately, Timnathah, of Samson (Judg. 14:1, 5), and the Thamnatha of the Maccabees. The modern representative of all these various forms of the same name is probably *Tibnah*, a village about two miles west of *Ain Shems* (Beth-shemesh), among the broken undulating country by which the central mountains of this part of Palestine descend to the maritime plain. In the later history of the Jews Timnah must have been a conspicuous place. It was fortified by Bacchides as one of the most important military posts of Judea (I Macc. 9:50), and it became the head of a district or toparchy.

2. A town in the mountain district of Judah (Josh. 15:57). It was the place near which Tamar entrapped Judah into intercourse with her (Gen. 38:12-14, A. V. "Timnath"). A distinct place from No. 1.

3. The name of a person. *See* Timna, 2.

Tim'nath (tĭm'năth; *portion*). *See* Timnah.

Tim'nath-he'res (tĭm'năth-hē'rĕz; *portion of the sun*; Judg. 2:9). *See* Timnath-Serah.

Tim'nath-se'rah (tĭm'năth-sē'rȧ; *double portion*,

ENGLISH HOUR	JEWISH	SCRIPTURE	NAME IN TALMUD
6:00 p. m.	Sunset.	Gen. 28:1; Exod. 17:12; Josh. 8:29, etc.	Twilight (Arab. 'Ahra).
6:20 "	Stars appear.		Evening Shema, or prayer.
10:00 "	First watch ends	Lam. 2:19.	The ass brays.
12:00 "	Midnight.	Exod. 11:4; Ruth 3:8; Psa. 119:62; Matt. 25:6; Luke 11:5.	
2:00 a. m.	Second watch ends.	Judg. 7:19.	The dog barks.
3:00 "	Cock crow.	Mark 13:35; Matt. 26:75.	
4:30 "	Second cock crow.	Matt. 26:75; Mark 14:30.	
5:40 "	Column of dawn.		Twilight (Arab. Subah).
6:00 "	Sunrise (third watch ends).	Exod. 14:24; Num. 21:11; Deut. 4:41; Josh. 1:15; I Sam. 11:11.	Three blasts of trumpet (Arab. Doher). Morning sacrifice.
9:00 "	First hour of prayer.	Acts 2:15.	
12:00 m.	Noon.	Gen. 43:16; I Kings 18:26; Job 5:14.	
1:30 p. m.	Great vesper.		First Mincha.
3:30 "	Small vesper.		Second Mincha (Arab. 'Aser). Arab. Mogoreb, before sunset.
5:40 "			Evening sacrifice at northeast of altar. Nine blasts of trumpet.
6:00 "	Sunset.	Gen. 15:12; Exod. 17:12; Luke 4:40, etc.	Six blasts of trumpet, on eve of Sabbath.

Times, Observer of (Deut. 18:10, 14; Lev. 19:26; II Kings 21:6; II Chron. 33:6). *See* "Astrologer," "Prognosticator," "Stargazer," in article Magic.

Tim'na (tĭm'nȧ; Heb. *tĭmnä'*, cf. the same name in S. Arab., the capital of Qataban, some 50 miles S. E. of Marib).

1. A concubine of Eliphaz, son of Esau, and mother of Amalek (Gen. 36:12). In I Chron. 1:36 she is named (by an ellipsis) as a *son* of Eliphaz. She is probably the same as the sister

Josh. 19:50; 24:30), the name of the city which was presented to Joshua after the partition of the country (19:50); and in "the border" of which he was buried (24:30). It is specified as "in Mount Ephraim, on the north side of Mount Gaash." In Judg. 2:9, the name is altered to Timnath-heres. The latter form is that adopted by the Jewish writers. Accordingly, they identify the place with *Kefar Cheres*, which is said by Rabbi Jacob, hap-Parchi, and other Jewish travelers, to be about five miles south ("nine miles." G. A. Smith) of Shechem (*Nablûs*). No place with that name appears on the maps. Another and more promising identification is Tibnah, 12 miles N. E. of Lydda and 8½ miles S. W. of Kefr Haris, where the Samaritans locate the sepulchres of Joshua and Caleb. "Heres" is probably "Serah" inadvertently written backwards.

Tim'nite (tĭm'nīt), a designation of Samson's father-in-law, from his residence in Timnah (Judg. 15:6).

Ti'mon (tī'mŏn; Gr. *reckoning, worthy*), the fifth named of the seven "deacons," appointed to serve as almoners on the occasion of complaints of partiality being made by the Hellenistic Jews at Jerusalem (Acts 6:5). Nothing further of him is known.

Timo'theus (tĭ-mō'thē-ŭs), the Greek form of Timothy (*q. v.*).

Tim'othy (tĭm'ō-thĭ; *venerating God*), the convert and friend of Paul.

1. **Family.** Timothy was the son of one of those mixed marriages which, though unlawful, were quite frequent in the later periods of Jewish history. His mother was a Jewess, while his father (name unknown) was a Greek (Acts 16:1-3).

2. **History.** (1) **Early life.** The picture of Timothy's early life, as drawn by the apostle Paul, represents a mother and grandmother, full of tenderness and faith, piously instructing him in the Scriptures, and training him to hope for the Messiah of Israel (II Tim. 1:5; 3:15). Thus, though far removed from the larger colonies of Israelitish families, he was brought up in a thoroughly Jewish atmosphere; although he could hardly be called a Jewish boy, having never been admitted by circumcision within the pale of God's ancient covenant. (2) **Conversion.** Timothy was probably living at Lystra when Paul made his first visit to that city (Acts 16:1), and appears to have been converted at that time (Acts 14:6; comp. II Tim. 1:5). No mention is made of Timothy until the time of Paul's second visit, but it is safe to assume that his spiritual life and education were under the care of the elders of the church (Acts 14:23). (3) **Circumcision.** Those who had the deepest insight into character, and spoke with a prophetic utterance, pointed to Timothy (I Tim. 1:18; 4:14) as specially fit for missionary work; and Paul desired to have him as a companion. The apostle circumcised him (Acts 16:3), and Timothy was set apart as an evangelist by the laying on of hands (I Tim. 4:14; II Tim. 4:5). (4) **Paul's companion.** Henceforth Timothy was one of Paul's most constant companions. They and Silvanus, and probably Luke also, journeyed to Philippi (Acts 16:12), and there already the young evangelist was conspicuous at once for his filial devotion and his zeal (Phil. 2:22). He seems to have been left behind at Philippi to watch over the infant church. He appears at Berea, where he remained with Silas after Paul's departure (Acts 17:14), joining Paul at Athens. From Athens he is sent back to Thessalonica (I Thess. 3:2), as having special gifts for comforting and teaching. He returns from Thessalonica, not to Athens, but to Corinth, and

his name appears united with Paul's in the opening words of both the letters written from that city to the Thessalonians (I Thess. 1:1; II Thess. 1:1). Of the five following years of his life we have no record. When we meet next with him it is as being sent on in advance when the apostle was contemplating the long journey which was to include Macedonia, Achaia, Jerusalem, and Rome (Acts 19:22). It is probable that he returned by the same route and met Paul according to a previous arrangement (I Cor. 16:10), and was thus with him when the second epistle was written to the church of Corinth (II Cor. 1:1). He returns with the apostle to that city, and join in messages of greeting to the disciples whom he had known personally at Corinth, and who had since found their way to Rome (Rom. 16:21). He forms one of the company of friends who go with Paul to Philippi and then sail by themselves, waiting for his arrival by a different ship (Acts 20:3-6). We have no mention of him until he joins the apostle, probably soon after his arrival in Rome. He was with Paul when the Epistles to the Philippians, to the Colossians, and to Philemon were written (Phil. 1:1; 2:19; Col. 1:1; Philem. 1). It follows from I Tim. 1:3 that he and Paul, after the release of the latter from his imprisonment, revisited the proconsular Asia, that the apostle then continued his journey to Macedonia, while the disciple remained, half reluctantly, even weeping at the separation (II Tim. 1:4), at Ephesus, to check, if possible, the outgrowth of heresy and licentiousness which had sprung up there. He had to exercise rule over presbyters, some older than himself (I Tim. 4:12), to render judgments (5:1, 19, 20), to regulate the almsgiving and sisterhood of the church (vers. 3-10), and ordain presbyters and deacons (3:1-13). These duties, together with the danger of being entangled in the disputes of rival sects, made Paul very anxious for the steadfastness of his disciple. Among his last recorded words Paul expresses his desire to see him again (II Tim. 4:9, 21). It is uncertain whether Timothy was able to fulfill these last requests of the apostle, or that he reached Rome before his death, although some have seen in Heb. 13:23 an indication that he shared Paul's imprisonment. (5) **Legends.** According to an old tradition, Timothy continued to act as bishop of Ephesus, and suffered martyrdom under Domitian or Nerva.

Note—"He took and circumcised Timotheus" (Acts 16:1, 3). Paul's conduct in circumcising Timotheus has been considered inconsistent with his principle and conduct in refusing to circumcise Titus (Gal. 2:3, 4). "The two cases are, however, entirely different. In the latter there was an attempt to enforce circumcision as necessary to salvation; in the former it was performed as a voluntary act, and simply on prudential grounds" (Haley, *Discrepancies*, p. 260).

Timothy, First Epistle, is the first of three pastoral letters written by Paul to two of his young converts (I Tim. 1:2; Titus 1:4) who had accompanied him on many of his missionary journeys. They had been established as pastors of churches and these epistles were directed to them to give them instructions for the orderly management of the organized congregations. These letters thus have a special message to youthful ministers. Although the messages are directed to young pastors and not to churches, their messages are peculiarly applicable to the churches.

1. **The Date.** Apparently Paul was released from prison at Rome between 63 and 67 A. D. If this is true, it was during this interval that he composed this Epistle. He also sent Titus an epistle at this time. If Paul endured one Roman imprisonment, I Timothy was written just before Paul's last visit to Jerusalem.

2. **Theme.** The golden text of the Epistle may be said to be 3:15, "that thou mayest know how thou oughtest to conduct thyself in the house of God, which is the church of the living God, the pillar and ground of the truth." The approaching end of the apostolic period witnessed the increase of the number of the local churches and the consequent need of definite revelation concerning questions of order, creed and discipline. At first these problems had been directed by the apostles themselves. But now definite instructions applicable to all occasions and periods were necessary.

3. **Purpose.** The Apostle had four main goals in penning this letter to Timothy: (1) To encourage him to oppose false teaching (1:3-7, 18-20; 6:3-5, 20, 21). (2) To furnish Timothy with written credentials authorized by himself (1:3, 4). (3) To instruct him in the management of ecclesiastical affairs (3:14, 15). (4) To exhort him to diligence in the performance of his pastoral duties (4:6-6:2).

4. **Outline.**

Salutation, 1:1, 2
Part I. Defense of the church's faith, 1:3-20
Part II. Regulations for church conduct, 2:1-3:16
  a. Concerning prayer, 2:1-8
  b. Place of women, 2:9-15
  c. Qualifications of elders and deacons, 3:1-16
Part III. Warning against apostasy and false doctrine, 4:1-5
Part IV. Prescriptions for ministerial conduct, private and public, 4:6-6:2
Part V. False and true teachers contrasted, 6:3-19
Part VI. Closing appeal to faithfulness, 6:20-21

5. **Attestation and authenticity.** Three classifications of objections have been commonly urged against the pastoral epistles—I and II Timothy and Titus. (1) Chronological. (2) Linguistic. (3) Ecclesiastical. Some assume Paul was in prison in Rome only once and that the pastorals cannot be fitted into the events of his ministry. But the third group of Paul's epistles distinctly favors the idea that Paul was released after two years (Acts 28:30, 31). The linguistic peculiarities hinge on the numerous *hapax legomena* in the pastorals—ninety-six in I Timothy; sixty in II Timothy; forty-three in Titus, this being about twice as many as in the other Pauline epistles. This argument, however, has never been conclusive, since Paul is writing on a distinct subject that required a different vocabulary. Ecclesiastical objection maintains that the pastorals imply too finished a stage

of church organization for so early a period as the Pauline age. This, however, is hardly a tenable objection since the Apostle had already ordained elders in every city on his first missionary journey and the churches which he addressed, as at Philippi (Phil. 1:1) were well organized "with bishops and deacons." There is no evidence in these epistles of "a second-century sacerdotalism." All the pastorals are to be taken as genuinely Pauline since their internal evidence manifestly reflects the character and temperament of the great Apostle.—*M. F. U.*

Timothy, Second Epistle. This pastoral letter has been called the "swan song" of Paul. It is the final message of the Apostle. There is a deep solemnity in the Epistle bordering almost on a note of sadness. But above it there is an over-tone of triumph. "I have fought a good fight, I have finished my course, I have kept the faith" (4:6-8).

1. **The Date.** The following is a probable calendar of Paul's life during the closing years of his career: 58 A. D. he is arrested in Jerusalem; 61 A. D. he arrives in Rome; 61-63 A. D. mark his first Roman imprisonment; 64-67 A. D. he is released, during which interval he writes I Timothy and Titus from Macedonia; 67 A. D., II Timothy is penned from Rome; 67-68 A. D., Paul is arrested and put to death.

2. **Purpose.** Second Timothy, like II Peter, Jude and II and III John, concerns the personal walk and testimony of a true servant-soldier of Christ in a day of apostasy. After the salutation (1:1-3), Paul (1) appeals for loyalty to the gospel message (1:3-18) and for soldierly endurance in Timothy's ministry, 2:1-13. (2) He gives important direction concerning Timothy's ministerial conduct, 2:14-26. (3) He warns against perilous times that are to come, 3:1-9. (4) He urges Timothy to follow his example, 3:10-13. (5) He alludes to Timothy's early training as a basis for his present faithfulness, 3:14-17. (6) He urges faithful proclamation of the Word of Truth in view of approaching apostasy and his own martyrdom, 4:1-8. (7) He expresses longing for fellowship, 4:9-18. He dispatches greetings, 4:19-22.

3. **Outline.**

Salutation, 1:1-3
Part I. Appeal to faithfulness and endurance, 1:4-18
Part II. Appeal to activity in service, 2:1-26
  a. As a good soldier, 2:1-14
  b. As a good student, 2:15-26
Part III. Warning of apostasy, 3:1-4:5
  a. Prophetic foreview of the last days, 3:1-9
  b. Authority of the Scriptures in the last days, 3:10-17
  c. Instructions for the last day, 4:1-5
Part IV. Allegiance to the Lord, 4:6-22
  a. Paul's final testimony, 4:6-8
  b. His last words, 4:9-22

—*M. F. U.*

Tin. *See* Mineral Kingdom.

Tinkling (Heb. *'ākăs*), mentioned as a characteristic of the manner in which the Jewish women carried themselves (Isa. 3:16). They could only take short steps because of the chains by which the costly foot rings worn above their ankles were joined together. These chains were probably ornamented with bells, as is sometimes the case now in the East, which tinkled as they walked. The Gr. *'alalazō* (I Cor. 13:1), refers to the clanging sound which comes from cymbals when beaten together.

Tiph′sah (tĭf′sà; *a ford, passage*), the limit of Solomon's dominion toward the Euphrates (I Kings 4:24), and said to have been attacked by Menahem, king of Israel (II Kings 15:16). It is generally admitted that this town is the same as the one known to Greeks and Romans as Thapsacus, a strong fortress on the western bank of the Euphrates above the confluence of the Balikh. Situated at the termination of the great trade road from Egypt, Phoenicia, and Syria, to Mesopotamia and the kingdoms of inner Asia, its possession was of great importance.

Ti′ras (tī′răs), the youngest son of Japheth, the son of Noah (Gen. 10:2; I Chron. 1:5). Several efforts have been made to identify his descendants, ancient authorities generally fixing on the Thracians. But the matter is still enveloped in obscurity. Probably best equated with the Tyrsenoi, an ancient Pelasgic people of the Aegean Coastland.

Ti′rathite (tī′rà-thīt), the designation of one of the three families of scribes residing at Jabez (I Chron. 2:55), the others being the Shimeathites and Suchathites.

Tire, an old English word used in the A. V. exclusively for dressing the head.

1. To make *comely, adorn* the head as did Jezebel (II Kings 9:30; Heb. *yāṭăb*).

2. A *headdress, turban* (Ezek. 24:17; Heb. *p°′ēr*).

3. A pendent disk worn by women on the head or neck (Isa. 3:18; Heb. *săhărōn*).

Tir′hakah (tĭr′hà-kà) was an Ethiopian prince mentioned in II Kings 19:9 as coming against Sennacherib in the Assyrian invasion of Judah (701 B. C.). His name appears as Taharka in the Egyptian records. At the time an Ethiopian dynasty was ruling Egypt in the person of Shabaka, not Tirhakah, who did not ascend the throne until c. 691 B. C., some dozen years later. The explanation is that Tirhakah, mentioned as king (II Kings 19:9; Isa. 37:9) actually opposed Sennacherib in 701 B. C. as a high military commander under his uncle, Shabaka, who was the ruling pharoah. Whether the nephew had the status of a regent at the time or whether the Judaean analyst wrote proleptically, is not known. Tirhakah became the third king in the Twenty-fifth Egyptian Dynasty. Against Esarhaddon he was initially victorious but three years later (670 B. C.), he was defeated, expelled from Memphis and never returned. He maintained himself in Upper Egypt until his decease in 663 B. C., when the Twenty-sixth Dynasty took over under Psamtik I.—*M. F. U.*

Tir′hanah (tĭr′hà-nà; derivation uncertain). the second son of Caleb the Hezronite by his concubine Maachah (I Chron. 2:48).

Tir′ia (tĭr′ĭ-à; *fear*), the third named of the four sons of Jehaleleel of the tribe of Judah (I Chron. 4:16).

Tirsha′tha (tûr-shā′thà; Heb. from Pers.; cf. Avestan *tarshta, feared, revered*), the title of the governor of Judea under the Persians (Ezra 2:63; Neh. 7:65, 70). and added as a title after the name of Nehemiah (8:9; 10:1). In the margin of the A. V. it is rendered "governor;" an explanation justified by Neh. 12:26, where "Nehemiah the governor" occurs, instead of the more usual expression "Nehemiah, the Tirshatha." According to Gesenius, it denotes the prefect or governor of a province of less extent than a satrapy. It is used of officers and governors under the Assyrian (II Kings 18:24; Isa. 36:9), Babylonian (Jer. 51:57; Ezek. 23:6, 23), Median (Jer. 51:28), and Persian (Esth. 8:9; 9:3) monarchies.

Tir′zah (tûr′zà; *delightfulness, pleasantness*).

1. The youngest of the five daughters of Zelophehad (Num. 26:33; 27:1; 36:11; Josh. 17:3), B. C. c. 1370. This was the case that gave rise to the Levirate provision, that in the event of a man dying without male children his property should pass to his daughters.

2. An ancient Canaanitish city, whose king was among the thirty-one overcome by Joshua on the west of Jordan (Josh. 12:24). It was the capital of the kings of Israel down to the time of Omri (I Kings 14:17; 15:21, 33; 16:6, sq.), who besieged Zimri there, and the latter perished in the flames of his palace (16:18). Once, and once only, does Tirzah reappear, as the seat of the conspiracy of Menahem (son of Gadi) against Shallum (II Kings 15:14, 16). Its beauty was well known (Cant. 6:4).

Tell el-Far′ah, "mound of the elevated ridge" was identified by W. F. Albright in 1931 as Tirzah. This is a spacious mound located some eleven miles N. W. of Nablus. Its excavation has been begun by Pere Roland de Vaux. Occupation at the site goes back to the middle of the fourth millennium. It ceased in the ninth century B. C. Tirzah is, however, identified by some with Jemma′in, S. of Shechem. Continuing excavations at Tell el-Far′ah gives fair promise of clarifying obscurities.—*M. F. U.*

Tishbite, a term applied in the O. T. to Elijah (I Kings 17:1; 21:17; II Kings 1:3, 8; 9:36). The term Tishbite refers to a native of a certain town by the name of Tishbeh, or something similar. Since a site of this name is unknown (although a Thisbe is mentioned as being on the right of Kydios (Kadesh) of Naphtali in Galilee above Asher), scholars such as Nelson Glueck render I Kings 17:1 as "Elijah, the Jabeshite, from Jabesh-Gilead." Jabesh-Gilead was a few miles W. of Abel-Meholah. Under this view the brook Cherith, where Elijah sojourned, would be a small branch of the Jabesh which empties into the Jordan.—*M. F. U.*

Tithe (Heb. *mă′ăsēr*; Gr. *dekatē*, a *tenth*). The use of tithes is frequently referred to in both profane and biblical history.

1. **In early times** the two prominent instances are: (1) Abram presenting the tenth of all his property, or rather of the spoils of his victory, to Melchizedek (Gen. 14:20; Heb. 7:2, 6). (2) Jacob, after his vision at Luz, devoting a tenth of all his property to God in

case he should return home in safety (Gen. 28:22).

2. **Mosaic Law.** The tenth of all produce, flocks, and cattle was declared to be sacred to Jehovah by way, so to speak, of feu-duty or rent to him who was, strictly speaking, the owner of the land, and in return for the produce of the ground; though, if so disposed, a man was at liberty to redeem the tithes of the fruits of his field and his trees by paying the value of them with a fifth part added (Lev. 27:30, sq.). The law did not specify the various fruits of the field and of the trees that were to be tithed. The Mishna (*Maaseroth*, i, 1) includes everything eatable, everything that was stored up or that grew out of the earth. The Pharisees, as early as the time of Jesus, made the law to include the minutest kitchen herbs, such as mint and cummin (Matt. 23:23; Luke 11:42). With regard to animal tithes, the law prescribes that every tenth beast that passes under the staff, i. e., under which the shepherd makes them pass when he counts his flock, was to be sacred to the Lord, good and bad alike. It forbids any attempt to substitute one beast for another on pain of both animals—the tenth as well as the one exchanged for it—being required to be redeemed (Lev. 27:32, sq.). This tenth, called *Terumoth*, is ordered to be assigned to the Levites as the reward of their service, and it is ordered further that they are themselves to dedicate to the Lord a tenth of these receipts, which is to be devoted to the maintenance of the high priest (Num. 18:21-28).

This legislation is modified or extended in the Book of Deuteronomy, i. e., from thirty-eight to forty years later. Commands are given to the people: 1. To bring their tithes, together with their votive and other offerings and first fruits to the chosen center of worship, the metropolis, there to be eaten in festive celebration in company with their children, their servants, and the Levites (Deut. 12:5-18). 2. All the produce of the soil was to be tithed every year, and these tithes with the firstlings of the flock and herd were to be eaten in the metropolis. 3. But in case of distance permission is given to convert the produce into money, which is to be taken to the appointed place, and there laid out in the purchase of food for a festal celebration, in which the Levite is, by special command, to be included (14:22-27). 4. Then follows the direction that at the end of three years all the tithe of that year is to be gathered and laid up "within the gates," and that a festival is to be held, in which the stranger, the fatherless, and the widow, together with the Levite, are to partake (vers. 28, 29). 5. Lastly, it is ordered that after taking the tithe in each third year, "which is the year of tithing," an exculpatory declaration is to be made by every Israelite that he has done his best to fulfill the divine command (26:12-14).

From all this we gather: 1. That one tenth of the whole produce of the soil was to be assigned for the maintenance of the Levites. 2. That out of this the Levites were to dedicate a tenth to God for the use of the high priest. 3. That a tithe, in all probability a *second* tithe, was to be applied to festival pur-

poses. 4. That in every third year either this festival tithe or a *third* tenth was to be eaten in company with the poor and the Levites. The question arises, Were there *three* tithes taken in this third year; or is the third tithe only the second under a different description? It must be allowed that the *third* tithe is not without support. Josephus distinctly says that one tenth was to be given to the priests and Levites, one tenth was to be applied to feasts in the metropolis, and that a tenth besides these was every third year to be given to the poor (comp. Tob. 1:7, 8). On the other hand Maimonides says the third and sixth years' *second* tithe was shared between the poor and the Levites, i. e., that there was no third tithe. Of these opinions that which maintains three separate and complete tithings seems improbable. It is plain that under the kings the tithe system partook of the general neglect into which the observance of the law declined, and that Hezekiah, among his other reforms, took effectual means to revive its use (II Chron. 31:5, 12, 19). Similar measures were taken after the captivity by Nehemiah (Neh. 12:44), and in both these cases special officers were appointed to take charge of the stores and storehouses for the purpose. Yet, notwithstanding partial evasion or omission, the system itself was continued to a late period in Jewish history (Heb. 7:5-8; Matt. 23:23; Luke 18:12).

The firstborn, the firstlings, and of the tenth of the flocks and herds and produce of the soil were offered to Jehovah as being sacred to him. Tithes and offerings, along with the firstborn, were intended, therefore, to be the representatives of the entire produce of the land and of the whole of property generally, and, being paid over as they were to Jehovah, they constituted a practical confession and acknowledgment that the whole land, that all possessions in general, belonged to him, and that it was he alone who conferred them upon those who enjoyed them.

Tittle (Gr. *keraia*, a *little horn*, *extremity*, *point*), used by Greek grammarians of the accents and diacritical points. In Matt. 5:18; Luke 16:17, it means the little lines or projections by which the Hebrew letters, in other respects similar, differ from each other, as ה and ה , ד and ר , כ and כ . The meaning is that not even the minutest part of the law shall perish.

Ti'tus (tī'tŭs; a common Latin name, Grecized *Titos*), a fellow-laborer of Paul. We find no mention of Titus in the Acts, and must draw materials for a biography of him from Second Corinthians, Galatians, and Titus, combined with Second Timothy. If, as seems probable, the journey mentioned in Gal. 2:1, 3, is the same as that recorded in Acts 15, then Titus was closely associated with Paul at Antioch, and accompanied him and Barnabas thence to Jerusalem. At Troas the apostle was disappointed in not meeting Titus (II Cor. 2:13), who had been sent on a mission to Corinth; but in Macedonia Titus joined him (7:6, 7, 13-15). He was sent back to Corinth, in company with two other trustworthy Christians, bearing the second epistle to the Corinthians, and with the earnest request that he would attend to the collection being taken for the poor Christians of Judea (8:6, 17). The "brethren" who took the first epistle to Corinth (I Cor. 16:11, 12) were doubtless Titus and his companion, whoever he may have been. In the interval between the first and second imprisonment of Paul at Rome he and Titus visited Crete (Tit. 1:5). Here Titus remained and received a letter written to him by the apostle. From this letter we learn that Titus was originally converted through Paul's instrumentality (v. 4). Next we learn the various particulars of the responsible duties which he had to discharge in Crete. He is to complete what Paul had been obliged to leave unfinished (v. 5), and to organize the Church throughout the island by appointing presbyters in every city. Next he is to control and bridle (v. 11) the restless and mischievous Judaizers, and he is to be peremptory in so doing (v. 13). He is to urge the duties of a decorous and Christian life upon the women (2:3-5), some of whom, possibly, had something of an official character (vers. 3, 4). The notices which remain are more strictly personal. Titus is to look for the arrival in Crete of Artemas and Tychicus (3:12), and then he is to hasten to join Paul at Nicopolis, where the apostle is proposing to pass the winter. Zenas and Apollos are in Crete, or expected there; for Titus is to send them on their journey, and supply them with whatever they need for it (v. 13). Whether Titus did join the apostle at Nicopolis we cannot tell. But we naturally connect the mention of this place with what Paul wrote at no great interval of time afterward (II Tim. 4:10); for Dalmatia lay to the north of Nicopolis, at no great distance from it. From the form of the whole sentence it seems probable that this disciple had been with Paul in Rome during his final imprisonment.

Tradition. The traditional connection of Titus with Crete is much more specific and constant, though here again we cannot be certain of the facts. He is said to have been permanent bishop in the island, and to have died there at an advanced age. The modern capital, *Candia*, appears to claim the honor of being his burial place. In the fragment by the lawyer Zenas, Titus is called bishop of Gortyna. Lastly, the name of Titus was the watchword of the Cretans when they were invaded by the Venetians (Smith, *Dict.*, s. v.).
Titus, an epistle of Paul written to his trusted companion Titus, who had been left as superintendent of the churches on the island of Crete. Like the First Epistle to Timothy, this letter had as its purpose to give the young pastor instructions to aid him in his work.

1. **Occasion and Date.** Paul was led to pen this Epistle because of the condition of Christian work on the island of Crete, Titus' need for help, and the fact that Zenos and Apollos were going to the island. The Apostle himself had begun to organize the work in this field, but had to leave before the task was finished. The entrance of false teaching in the form of legalism necessitated a strong stand for the truth. In his task Titus needed clear instruction as well as encouragement. When Zenos and Apollos planned a journey through

Crete, Paul sent Titus this letter to help and encourage him (Tit. 3:13). The thought and style of this Epistle resemble I Timothy more than II Timothy. The date of its composition was, therefore, around A. D. 65.

2. **The Purpose.** (1) After an extended greeting, 1:1-4, Paul urges Titus to complete the organization of the work in Crete, 1:5. (2) Paul reviews the requirements of elders, 1:6-9. (3) He urges a strong position against false teachers, 1:10-16. (4) He gives instruction concerning the various classes in home relations, 2:1-10. (5) He elucidates how a holy and godly life is made possible, 2:11-15. (6) He enjoins good citizenship, 3:1, 2. (7) He reviews the reasons for godly living, 3:3-8. (8) He issues a warning against false teaching, 3:9-11. (9) He outlines his future plans, 3:12-14. (10) He dispatches greetings, 3:15.

3. **Outline.**
Salutation, 1:1-4
Part I. The problems of the church as an organization, 1:5-16
   a. Qualifications of elders, 1:5-9
   b. Necessity for a strong stand against false teachers, 1:12-16
Part II. The problems of pastoral teaching and preaching, 2:1-3:11
   a. Inculcating duties and domestic relations, 2:1-10
   b. Motivating true Christian living, 2:11-15
   c. Teaching concerning Christian citizenship, 3:1, 2
   d. Inspiring godly living, 3:3-8; dealing with heretics, 3:9-11
Conclusion, 3:12-15

—*M. F. U.*

Ti′zite (tī′zīt), the designation of Joha (*q. v.*), the brother of Jediael and son of Shimri, a hero in David's army (I Chron. 11:45).

To′ah (tō′á; cf. Akkad. *tahu, child*), son of Zuph and father of Eliel, ancestor of Samuel and Heman (I Chron. 6:34), called *Tohu* (I Sam. 1:1) and *Nahath* (I Chron. 6:26).

Tob (tŏb; *good*). "The land of Tob" was, according to II Sam. 10:6, 8, a district in the northeast of Perea, on the border of Syria, or between Syria and Ammonitis, called *Tōbion* (I Macc. 5:13), or more correctly *Toubin* (II Macc. 12:17). There Jephthah took refuge when expelled from home by his halfbrother (Judg. 11:3), and there he remained, at the head of a band of freebooters, till he was brought back by the sheiks of Gilead (v. 5). It is undoubtedly mentioned again in II Sam. 10:6, 8, as Ish-tob, i. e., Man of Tob, meaning, according to a common Hebrew idiom, the "men of Tob." After a long interval it appears again, in the Maccabean history (I Macc. 5:13), in the names Tobie and Tubieni (II Macc. 12:17). G. A. Smith (*Hist. Geog.*, p. 587) says: "The name of the land of Tob, which was north of Mizpeh, may survive in that of the wady and village of Taiyibeh, east of Pella."

Tob-adoni′jah (tŏb-ăd-ô-nī′já; *good is the Lord Jehovah*), one of the Levites sent by Jehoshaphat through the cities of Judah to teach the law to the people (II Chron. 17:8), B. C. after 875.

Tobi'ah (tô-bī'à; *Good is Jehovah*).

1. "The children of Tobiah" were one of the families returning with Zerubbabel who were unable to prove their kinship with Israel (Ezra 2:60; Neh. 7:62), B. C. before 536.

2. One of the leading opponents to the rebuilding of Jerusalem under Nehemiah. Tobiah was formerly a slave at the Persian court, and had probably, as a favorite, been appointed governor of the Ammonites (Neh. 2:10, 19). Tobiah, though a slave and an Ammonite, found means to ally himself with a priestly family, and his son Johanan married the daughter of Meshullam, the son of Berechiah, while he himself was the son-in-law of Shechaniah, the son of Arah (6:18), and these family relations created for him a strong faction among the Jews. He and Sanballat (*q. v.*), on receiving news of the expected arrival of Nehemiah, were greatly exasperated and endeavored to terrify him by asking whether he intended to rebel against the king. Nehemiah replied that they had no authority of any kind in Jerusalem, and did not allow himself to be intimidated (2:19, 20). When he heard that the building of the walls had been actually commenced, Tobiah, in unmingled scorn, declared, "Even that which they build, if a fox go up, he shall even break down their stone wall" (4:3). Then followed the league against the Jews entered into by Sanballat and Tobiah with the surrounding nations (v. 7, sq.). After that an unsuccessful attempt was made to inveigle Nehemiah into a conference in the valley of Ono (6:1, sq.). Still later we find Tobiah carrying on a secret correspondence with the Jewish nobles hostile to Nehemiah (vers. 17-19). During Nehemiah's absence from Jerusalem Eliashib, the high priest, installed Tobiah in "a great chamber," i. e., one of the very large buildings in the forecourts of the temple, from which he was ejected by Nehemiah upon his return (13:4-9).

Tobi'jah (tô-bī'jà; Hebrew same as Tobiah [*q. v.*]).

1. One of the Levites sent by Jehoshaphat to teach the law in the cities of Judah (II Chron. 17:8), B. C. after 875.

2. One of the captivity in the time of Zechariah, in whose presence the prophet was commanded to take crowns of silver and gold and put them on the head of Joshua the high priest (Zech. 6:10, 14), B. C. 519.

To'chen (tō'kĕn; *a weight, measure*), one of the towns of Simeon (I Chron. 4:32); probably the same as Telem (Josh. 15:24) or Telaim (I Sam. 15:4).

Togar'mah (tô-gär'mà), a son of Gomer, and brother of Ashkenaz and Riphath (Gen. 10:3; I Chron. 1:6). The descendants of Togarmah are mentioned among the merchants who trafficked with Tyre in "horses, horsemen, and mules" (Ezek. 27:14); and are also named with Persia, Ethiopia, and Libya, as followers of Gog, the chief prince of Meshech and Tubal (38:5, 6). The name may be preserved in the E. Cappodocian city of Til-garimmu, listed in the Assyrian records.

To'hu (tō'hŭ; cf. Akkad. *tahu, child*; I Sam. 1:1), the same as Toah (I Chron. 6:34), or Nahath (v. 26).

To'i (tō'ĕ), the king of Hamath on the Orontes, in the time of David. When the latter defeated the Syrian king, Hadadezer, Toi's powerful enemy, Toi sent his son Joram (or Hadoram) to congratulate him upon his victory, and to make presents of gold, silver, and brass (II Sam. 8:9, 10), B. C. about 984. The name is apparently Hittite.

Token (Heb. *'ôth*, a *sign*). "And the blood shall be to you for a *token*" (Exod. 12:13), i. e., a pledge that God would spare the Israelites upon whose doorposts was the blood. A *sign* of something past, a *memorial* (Exod. 13:9, A. V. "sign," 16; Isa. 55:13; Ezek. 14:8, "sign"). A sign of something *future*, a *portent, omen* (Isa. 8:18, A. V. "signs"). A sign or token of anything in itself not visible; e. g., the token of a covenant, circumcision (Gen. 17:11), the Sabbath (Exod. 31:13, A. V. "sign"). Hence, an *argument, proof* (Job 21:29). The prophetic sign of the truth of a prophecy (Exod. 3:12).

To'la (tō'là; *a worm*).

1. The eldest son of Issachar (Gen. 46:13; I Chron. 7:1). His six sons (I Chron. 7:2) became progenitors of the Tolaites (Num. 26:23), which numbered in David's time twenty-two thousand six hundred fighting men (I Chron. 7:2).

2. A judge of Israel. He was the son of Puah, of the tribe of Issachar. He succeeded Abimelech in the judgeship, and ruled Israel twenty-three years in Shamir, Mount Ephraim, where he died and was buried (Judg. 10:1, 2). The date is uncertain, as Tola doubtless ruled contemporaneously with some other judge.

To'lad (tō'lăd; *posterity*), a town in Simeon in David's time (I Chron. 4:29); given in the fuller form El-tolad (Josh. 15:30). Possibly Khirbet Erka Sakra, 13 miles S. E. of Beersheba.

To'laites (tō'là-īts), the general name of the descendants of Tola (*q. v.*), the son of Issachar (Num. 26:23).

Toll. *See* Tax; Tribute; Publican.

485. Tombs in the Valley of Kidron

Tomb (Heb. *gădîsh, heaped* up, a *tumulus*; Gr. *mnēmeion*, a *remembrance*), a natural cave enlarged and adapted by excavation, or an artificial imitation of one, was the standard type of sepulcher. This was what the structure of the Jewish soil supplied or suggested.

"The caves, or rock-hewn sepulchers, consisted of an antechamber in which the bier was deposited, and an inner or rather lower cave in which the bodies were deposited, in a recumbent position, in niches. According to

486. Unsealed Tomb   Sealed Tomb

the Talmud these abodes of the dead were usually six feet long, nine feet wide, and ten feet high. Here there were niches for eight bodies—three on each side of the entrance and two opposite. Larger sepulchers held thirteen bodies. The entrance to the sepulcher was guarded by a large stone or by a door (Matt. 27:65; Mark 15:46; John 11:38, 39). This

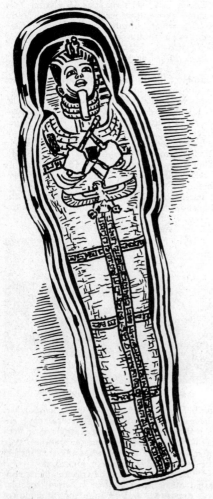

487. The Mummy of King Tutankhamen

structure of the tombs will explain some of the particulars connected with the burial of our Lord, how the women coming early to the grave had been astonished in finding the 'very great stone' 'rolled away from the door of the sepulcher,' and then, when they entered the outer cave, were affrighted to see what seemed 'a young man sitting on the right side, clothed in a long white garment' (Mark 16:4, 5) (Edersheim, *Jewish Social Life*, p. 171).

Of the twenty-two kings of Judah who reigned at Jerusalem from c. 1000 to 590 B. C., eleven, or exactly one half, were buried in one hypogeum in the "city of David." Of all these it is merely said that they were buried in "the sepulchers of their fathers" or "of the kings" in the city of David, except of two—Asa and Hezekiah. Two more of these kings (Jehoram and Joash) were buried also in the city of David, "but not in the sepulchers of the kings." The passage in Neh. 3:16, and in Ezek. 43:7, 9, together with the reiterated assertion of the books of Kings and Chronicles, that these sepulchers were situated in the city of David, leave no doubt but that they were on Zion, or the Eastern Hill, and in the immediate proximity of the temple. They were in fact certainly within that inclosure now known as the "Haram Area;" but those royal tombs have evidently not survived to modern times. *See* Dead; Grave.

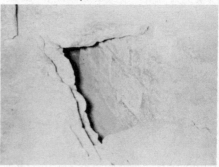

488. Lazarus' Tomb, Bethany

Tongs. 1. (Heb. *mĕlqāḥ,* I Kings 7:49; II Chron. 4:21; Isa. 6:6), or (*mălqāḥ,* Exod. 25:38; 37:23, A. V. "snuffers;" Num. 4:9), pincers either for holding coals or for trimming a lamp, from Heb. *lăqăḥ, to take.*

Tongue (Heb. *lāshōn;* Gr. *glōssa*) is variously used in Scripture.

1. **Literally** for the human tongue (Judg. 7:5; Job 27:4; Psa. 35:28; Prov. 15:2; Zech.

14:12; Mark 7:33, 35, etc.); the tongue of the dog (Psa. 68:23); the viper (Job 20:16).

2. **A particular language** or dialect spoken by any particular people, e. g., "Everyone after his tongue" (Gen. 10:5, 20, 31; comp. Deut. 28:49; Esth. 1:22; Dan. 1:4; John 5:2; Acts 1:19; 2:4, 8, 11; I Cor. 12:10, etc.).

3. **For the people** speaking a language (Isa. 66:18; Dan. 3:4, 7; Rev. 5:9; 7:9; 10:11, etc.).

4. **Personified.** "Unto me shall every tongue [i. e., man] swear" (Isa. 45:23; comp. Rom. 14:11; Phil. 2:11; Isa. 54:17). Such expressions as the following are used: the tongue is said to meditate (Psa. 52:2), to hate (Prov. 26:28), to rejoice (Acts 2:26), to be bridled (James 1:26), to be tamed (3:8).

5. **Figurative.** For speech generally. "Let us not love in tongue only" (I John 3:18); "a soft tongue," i. e., *soothing language* (Prov. 25:15). "Rage of the tongue" (Hos. 7:16)— i. e., verbal abuse—"strife of tongues" (Psa. 31:20), and "scourge of tongue" (Job 5:21) mean contention and execration. "They bend their tongues like their bow for lies" (Jer. 9:3) is to tell determined and malicious falsehoods. To "sharpen the tongue" (Psa. 140:3) is to prepare cutting speeches (comp. 57:4); "to smooth the tongue" (Jer. 23:31) is to employ flattery; while "to smite with the tongue" (18:18) is to traduce. To mock is figuratively expressed by "to stick out the tongue" (Isa. 57:4). "To hide under the tongue" (Job 20:12) is to enjoy wickedness; while "honey and milk under the tongue" is figurative for delicious language. "To divide the tongues of the wicked" is to bring about dissension among them (Psa. 55:9; comp. II Sam. 15:34; 17:14, 15). "The cleaving of the tongue to the palate" may mean profound attention (Job 29:10), excessive thirst (Lam. 4:4; comp. Psa. 22:15), or dumbness (Ezek. 3:26; Psa. 137:6). To gnaw one's tongue is a sign of fury, despair, or torment (Rev. 16:10).

6. *Vicious* uses of the tongue are expressed by the following phrases: flattery (Psa. 5:9; Prov. 28:33), backbiting (Psa. 15:3, literally "run about with the tongue," Prov. 25:23), deceit (Psa. 50:19), unrestrained speech (73:9), lying (109:2), etc. *Virtuous* uses are specified: "keeping the tongue" (Psa. 34:13; I Pet. 3:10; Prov. 21:23), "ruling the tongue" James 1:26), etc.

Tongues, Confusion of (Gen. 11:1-9). The biblical account of this event begins with the statement, "And the whole earth was of one language, and of one speech" (v. 1). The author of the Book of Genesis conceived the unity of the human race to be of the most rigid nature—not simply a generic unity, nor again simply a specific unity, but a specific based upon a numerical unity, the species being nothing else than the enlargement of the individual. Unity of language is assumed by the sacred historian apparently as a corollary of the unity of race. No explanation is given of the origin of speech, but its exercise is evidently regarded as coeval with the creation of man. Speech, being inherent in man as a reflecting being, was regarded as handed down from father to son by the same process of imitation by which it is still perpetuated.

The original unit of speech was restored in Noah. Disturbing causes were, however, early at work to dissolve this twofold union of community and speech. The human family endeavored to check the tendency to separation by the establishment of a great central edifice, and a city which should serve as a metropolis of the whole world (vers. 3, 4). The project was defeated by the interposition of Jehovah, who determined to "confound their language, so that they might not understand one another's speech" (vers. 5-7). *See* Babel, Tower of.

The desire for renown and the purpose to thus maintain their unity were thus manifested, revealing pride and the loss of spiritual unity and brotherly love. "Consequently the undertaking, dictated by pride, to preserve and consolidate by outward means the unity which was inwardly lost, could not be successful, but could only bring down the judgment of dispersion" (K. and D., *Com.*). By the firm establishment of an ungodly unity the wickedness and audacity of men would have led to fearful enterprise. Therefore God determined, by confusing their language, to prevent the heightening of sin through ungodly association, and to frustrate their design.

The nature of the confusion of tongues has been variously understood. It is unnecessary to assume that the judgment inflicted on the builders of Babel amounted to a loss, or even a suspension, of articulate speech. The desired object would be equally attained by a miraculous forestallment of those dialectical differences of language which are constantly in process of production. The elements of the one original language may have remained, but so disguised by variations of pronunciation, and by the introduction of new combinations, as to be practically obliterated.

"When it is stated, first of all, that God had resolved to destroy the unity of lips and words by a confusion of the lips, and then that he scattered the men abroad, this act of divine judgment cannot be understood in any other way than that God deprived them of the ability to comprehend one another, and thus effected their dispersion. The event itself cannot have consisted merely in a change of the organs of speech produced by the omnipotence of God, whereby speakers were turned into stammerers who were unintelligible to one another" (K. and D., *Com.*, in loc.).

Tongues, Gift of. 1. **Promise of.** The promise of a new power coming from the Divine Spirit, giving not only comfort and insight into truth, but fresh powers of utterance of some kind, appears once and again in our Lord's teaching. The disciples are to take no thought what they shall speak, for the Spirit of their Father shall speak in them (Matt. 10:19, 20; Mark 13:11). The lips of Galilean peasants are to speak freely and boldly before kings. In Mark 16:17 we have a more definite term employed: "They shall speak with new tongues." It can hardly be questioned that the obvious meaning of the promise is that the disciples should speak in new languages which they had not learned as other men learn them.

2. Fulfillment. After our Lord's ascension, while the disciples were gathered together in one place, "suddenly there came a sound from heaven as of a rushing mighty wind, and it filled all the house where they were sitting. And there appeared unto them cloven tongues, like as of fire, and it sat upon each of them" (Acts 2:2, 3). After this *external* phenomenon there now ensued the *internal* filling of all who were assembled with the Holy Spirit. The *immediate result* was that they began to speak with other tongues. For the sure determination of what Luke meant by this, it is decisive that *heterais glossais* "other tongues," on the part of the speakers was, in point of fact, the same thing which the congregated Parthians, Medes, Elamites, etc., designated as "our own tongue," comp. v. 8. The "other tongues," therefore, are, according to the text, to be considered as absolutely nothing else than *languages, which were different from the native language of the speakers.* "They, the Galileans, spoke, one Parthian, another Median, etc., consequently languages of *another sort,* i. e., *foreign* (I Cor. 14:21); and these indeed—the point wherein precisely appeared the *miraculous* operation of the Spirit—*not acquired by study* (Mark 16:17)" (Meyer, *Com.,* in loc.). When the event is admitted to be distinctly miraculous, and the power a special gift of God, it need not be considered either impossible or inconceivable; and incapacity of conceiving the *modus operandi* should not lead to a refusal of the credibility and certainty of the fact.

In the list of spiritual endowments mentioned in I Cor. 12:8-10 are "divers kinds of tongues," and "the interpretation of tongues" (comp. vers. 28-30; 14:4, 5, 13, 14). By many the speaking with tongues is a miraculous gift by which a person is able to speak a foreign tongue without learning it. On the other hand there are those who, with Meyer understand by *glossais lalein* such an outburst of prayer in petition, praise, and thanksgiving, as was "so ecstatic that in connection with it the speaker's own conscious intellectual activity was suspended, while the tongue did not serve as the instrument of the utterance of self-active reflection, but, independently of it, was involuntarily set in motion by the Holy Spirit, by whom the man in his deepest nature was seized and borne away" (*Com.,* in loc.). The spiritual gifts are classified and compared, arranged, apparently, according to their worth, placed under regulation. The facts which may be gathered are briefly these: (1) The phenomena of the gift of tongues were not confined to one church or section of a church. (2) The comparison of gifts, in both the lists given by St. Paul (I Cor. 12:8-10, 28-30), places that of tongues, and the interpretation of tongues, lowest in the scale. (3) The main characteristic of the "tongue" is that it is unintelligible. The man "speaks mysteries," prays, blesses, gives thanks, in the tongue (14:15, 16), but no one understands him. He can hardly be said, indeed, to understand himself. (4) The peculiar nature of the gift leads the apostle into what appears at first a contradiction. "Tongues are for a sign," not to believers, but to those who do not believe; yet the effect on unbelievers is not that of attracting but repelling. They involve of necessity a disturbance of the equilibrium between the understanding and the feelings. Therefore it is that, for those who believe already, prophecy is the greater gift.

Tongues of Fire. In the account of the descent of the Holy Spirit upon the disciples at Pentecost it is said (Acts 2:3): "And there appeared unto them cloven tongues, like as of fire (Gr. *glōssai hōsei puros*), and it sat upon each of them." The words mean: There appeared to them, i. e., were seen by them, tongues which appeared like little flames of fire, luminous, but not burning; not really consisting of fire, but only "as of fire." As only *similar* to fire, they bore an analogy to *electric* phenomena; their tongue-shape referred as a sign to that miraculous speaking which ensued immediately after, and the *fire*like form to the *divine* presence (comp. Exod. 3:2), which was here operative in a manner so entirely peculiar. The whole phenomenon is to be understood as a miraculous operation of God manifesting himself in the Spirit, by which, as by the preceding sound from heaven, the effusion of the Spirit was made known as *divine,* and his efficacy on the minds of those who were to receive him was enhanced (Meyer, *Com.,* in loc.).

Tooth (Heb. *shēn; lehî,* in Psa. 58:6; Prov. 30:14; Joel 1:6; Gr. *'odous*).

1. Literal Use. In this sense the term is used with reference to the loss of the member by violence, in illustration of the law of retaliation (Exod. 21:24; Lev. 24:20; Deut. 19:21). Such loss admitted of a pecuniary compensation, and under private arrangement, unless the injured party became exorbitant in his demand, when the case was referred to a judge. Our Lord's comment upon the law (Matt. 5:38) prohibits private revenge. *Lehî* is used for the human jawbone (Psa. 3:7), for that of an ass (Judg. 15:15-17), and for that of a leviathan (Job 41:14). Although *shinnáyim* is the general word for teeth, yet the Hebrews had a distinct term for molars or jaw teeth, especially of the larger animals; thus *methálle'ōth* (Job 29:17; Psa. 57:4; Prov. 30:14; Joel 1:6), and, by transposition, Heb. *mállet'e'ōth* (Psa. 58:6).

2. Figurative. "His teeth shall be white with milk" (Gen. 49:12) seems to denote a super-abundance of milk, as "his eyes shall be red with wine" denotes plenty thereof. "I will send upon them the teeth of beasts" (Deut. 32:24) expresses devastation by wild animals. "The teeth of lions" (Job 4:10) is a symbol of the cruelty and rapacity of the wicked. "To take one's flesh into one's teeth" (Job 13:14) is thought by some to mean to gnaw it with anguish (comp. Rev. 16:10), while others interpret it "to be intent upon the maintenance of life, as a wild beast upon the preservation of his prey, by holding it between its teeth and carrying it away" (Delitzsch, *Com.,* in loc.). *Gnashing of teeth* means, properly, grinding the teeth with rage or despair (Job 16:9; Psa. 35:16; 37:12; 112:10; Lam. 2:16; Matt. 8:12, etc.). By "the skin of my teeth" (Job 19:20) is generally understood the gums; Delitzsch, however, thinks it be the periosteum, a skin in the jaw. Job's disease was such that the gums especially were destroyed and wasted away about the teeth, only the periosteum round about the teeth being still left to him, and single remnants of the covering of his loose and projecting teeth. "To smite upon the jawbone" and "to break the teeth" mean to disgrace and disable (Psa. 3:7; comp. Mic. 6:13; I Kings 20:35; Lam. 3:30). The teeth of calumniators, etc., are compared to "spears and arrows" (Psa. 57:4; comp. I Sam. 24:9); and to "break the teeth" of such persons is to disable them (Psa. 58:6). To "escape from the teeth" of one's enemies is to avoid their malice Psa. 124:6; Zech. 9:7). Oppression is compared to "jaw teeth like swords and grinders like knives" (Prov. 30:14). Beautiful teeth are compared (Cant. 4:2; 6:6) to sheep newly shorn and washed; but the remaining part of the comparison, "whereof every one bear twins and there is not one barren among them," is much better rendered by Le Clerc, "all of them twins, and none hath lost his fellow." "To break the teeth with gravel stones." A very forcible figure is in "He hath also broken my teeth with gravel stones" (Lam. 3:16; comp. Prov. 20:17), referring to the grit that often mixes with bread baked in ashes, as is the custom in the East, and figurative of harsh disappointment. "Iron teeth" (Dan. 7:1, 19) are the symbol of destructive power. Hypocritical and greedy prophets are represented as those who "bite with their teeth and cry, Peace" (Mic. 3:5). "I will take away his blood out of his mouth, and his abominations from between his teeth" (Zech. 9:7), refers to idolaters keeping a feast, which is interrupted by Jehovah, and idolatry abolished. "Cleanness of teeth" (Amos 4:6) is the figure of hunger, famine. "To cast in the teeth" is an old English phrase, for the Hebrew has no such idiom, signifying to reproach. The Greek *oneidizon auton*, "they upbraided him" (Matt. 27:44). The action of acid is referred to in Ezek. 18:2; comp. 10:26.

Topaz. *See* Mineral Kingdom.

To'phel (tō'fĕl), apparently a boundary of the great Sinaitic desert of Paran (Deut. 1:1). It is supposed by Hengstenberg and Robinson, and many of the more modern writers, to be the large village of *Täfilĕh*, the chief place in *Jebal*, west of the Edomitish mountains. The suggestion of Schultz that Tophel may have been the place where the Israelites purchased food and drink of the Edomites (2:28, 29) has much to be said in its favor; for the situation of Tophel warrants the supposition that it was here that they passed for the first time from the wilderness to an inhabited land. Its identification remains uncertain.

To'phet (tō'fĕt), or **To'pheth** (tō'fĕth). 1. **Name.** Tophet is commonly supposed to be derived from *tôph*, or drum, from the drums used to drown the cries of children who were made to pass through the fire to Moloch. Gesenius connects the root idea with *tûth, to spit*, and rendered place to be *spit* upon, *be abhorred* (Job 17:6). Others regard Tophet as from *tôphtĕh* (*contempt*), *the place of burning dead bodies.*

2. **Location**, etc. Tophet lay somewhere east or southeast of Jerusalem, for Jeremiah went out by the Sun Gate, or east gate, to go to it (Jer. 19:2). It was in "the Valley of the Son of Hinnom" (7:31), which is "by the entry of the east gate" (19:2). Thus it was not identical with Hinnom. It was in Hinnom and was, perhaps, one of its chief groves or gardens, and watered by Siloam, perhaps a little to the south of the present *Birket el-Hamra*. The name Tophet occurs only in the Old Testament (II Kings 23:10, "Topheth;" Isa. 30:33; Jer. 7:31, 32; 19:6, 11-14). The New Testament does not refer to it, nor the Apocrypha.

In Tophet the deity (Baal, Jer. 19:5; Moloch, 32:35) was worshipped by sacrifices in heathen fashion, first by the ancient Canaanites, and afterward by apostate Israelites (comp. Psa. 106:38; Jer. 7:31). This was done first by Ahaz (II Kings 16:3), then especially by Manasseh (21:6). Thus it became the place of abomination, the very gate or pit of hell. The pious kings defiled it (23:10), and threw down its altars and high places, pouring into it all the filth of the city, till it became the "abhorrence" of Jerusalem. Every vestige of Tophet, name and grove, is gone, and we can only guess at the spot.

Torah (Heb. *instruction, law*) is the name of the first of the three divisions of the Hebrew canon—Torah (Law), Nebiim (Prophets) and Kethubim (Writings). The Torah or Law comprises the five books of Moses, which were the mainstay of Judaism. The Torah, however, came to have a wider meaning among Jews and embraced the whole body of religious literature of Judaism inherited from their prophets, priests and wise men. In addition to the written Torah the Pharisees and rabbis recognized an oral Torah, which comprised specific applications of the general principles of the written Torah. In the time of our Lord the oral traditions had become so minute and devoid of spiritual meaning as to set aside the law of God and in some cases completely nullify it (cf. Matt. 15:2; Mark 7:9, 18; Col. 2:8). In the period of the rise of the synagogue (c. 400 B. C.-168 B. C.), the Law was divided into sections for systematic public reading. The Pentateuch came to be divided into 290 "open" and 379 "closed" *parashiyoth*. The "open" marked by a *pe* (p) are paragraphs beginning a new line. The "closed" are shorter and are marked by a *samekh* (s) and preceded by a blank space in the line. The Mishnah (c. 200 A. D.) mentions these divisions, which existed earlier. The Talmud (c. 500 A. D.) distinguishes between the *open* and *closed parashiyoth*. By the time of Christ, the Prophets had been added to the Torah lessons for weekly public reading (Luke 4:16-21).—M. F. U.

Torch. The Heb. (*lăppîd*, Zech. 12:6), and the Gr. (*lampas*, John 18:3), usually signify, and are translated, a *lamp*. In Nah. 2:3 "torch" stands for Heb. (*pelädäh, steel*); "the chariots shall be with flaming torches," i. e., with polished scythes or armature.

Figurative. A flaming torch is used by the prophet (Zech. 12:6) as a symbol of great anger and destruction.

Tor'mah (tôr'må; *fraud, deceit*), occurs only in the margin of Judg. 9:31. By a few commentators it has been conjectured that the word was originally the same as Arumah (v. 41). The Septuagint and Aramaic take the word as an appellative — *en kruphē, secretly;* so also do Rashi and most of the earlier commentators, while R. Kimchi, the elder, has decided in favor of the second rendering as a proper name. As the word only occurs here it is impossible to determine in favor of either view.

Tormentor (Gr. *basanistēs*, Matt. 18:34), one who elicits the truth by means of the rack, an inquisitor; used in this passage of a jailor, probably because the business of torturing was assigned to him. Torture was usually employed to extort confession or evidence, as when Claudius Lysias, the chief captain, commanded Paul to be brought into the castle and "examined by scourging" (Acts 22:24).

Tortoise. *See* Animal Kingdom.

Tou (tō'ōō; I Chron. 18:9, 10). *See* Toi.

Tow (tō). 1. The coarse and broken part of flax hemp or jute, separated by the hatchel or swingle and ready for spinning. (Heb. *nᵉʿōrĕth*, Judg. 16:9; Isa. 1:31). It is extremely inflammable.

2. Heb. *pĭshtäh* (Isa. 43:17), *flax,* as elsewhere rendered.

Towel (Gr. *lention*), a linen cloth or apron, which servants put on when about to work (John 13:4, 5). Girding one's self with a towel was the common mark of a slave, by whom the service of footwashing was ordinarily performed.

Tower. 1. A siege tower (Isa. 23:13; Heb. *'ŏrnän, strong*).

2. *Mĭgdōl* is from a root meaning "to become great." *See* Migdol.

3. *Pĭnnōth,* the corners and battlements of the walls of the fortifications (Zeph. 1:16; 3:6; II Chron. 26:15).

4. *'Ophĕl, hill,* II Kings 5:24. *See* Ophel.

5. *Mäşōr,* a *fortress,* only in Hab. 2:1.

6. *Mĭşpĕh. See* Mizpeh.

7. Gr. *Purgos,* a *tower,* a fortified structure rising to a considerable height, to repel a hostile attack, or to enable a watchman to see in every direction. The "tower of Siloam" seems to designate a tower in the walls of Jerusalem, near the fountain of Siloam (Luke 13:4). Watchtowers or fortified posts in frontier or exposed situations are mentioned in Scripture, as the tower of Edar (Gen. 35:21; Mic. 4:8; Isa. 21:5, 8, 11, etc.), the tower of Lebanon (Cant. 7:4). Remains of such fortifications may still be seen, which probably have succeeded to more ancient structures built in the same places for like purposes. Besides these military structures, we read in Scripture of towers built in vineyards as an almost necessary appendage to them (Isa. 5:2; Matt. 21:33; Mark 12:1). Such towers are still in use in Palestine in vineyards, especially near Hebron, and are used as lodges for the keepers of the vineyards.

Town is not carefully distinguished from city in the A. V., and is sometimes the rendering of Heb. *'îr,* a place guarded by watchmen; generally rendered "city;" *qîr* or *qîräh, wall.* In the Greek we have *kōmē, hamlet.* Neither in the Old nor in the New Testament is the distinction between cities and towns carefully

observed. "Palestine had at all times a far larger number of towns and villages than might have been expected from its size, or from the general agricultural pursuits of its inhabitants. Even at the time of its first occupation under Joshua we find somewhere about six hundred towns . . . with probably an average population of from two to three thousand. But the number of towns and villages, as well as their populousness, greatly increased in later times . . . Alike the New Testament, Josephus, and the rabbis give us three names, which may be rendered villages, township, or towns—the latter being surrounded by walls, and again distinguished into those fortified already at the time of Joshua, and those of later date. A township might be either 'great,' if it had its synagogue, or small if it wanted such; this being dependent on the residence of at least ten men (*see* Synagogue). The villages had no synagogue; but their inhabitants were supposed to go to the nearest township for market on the Monday and Thursday of every week, when service was held for them, and the local Sanhedrin also sat (*Megill.,* i, 1-3). . . . Approaching one of the ancient fortified towns, one would come to a low wall that protected a ditch. Crossing this moat, one would be at the city wall proper, and enter through a massive gate, often covered with iron, and secured by strong bars and bolts. Above the gate rose the watchtower. 'Within the gate' was the shady or sheltered retreat where 'the elders' sat . . . The gates opened upon large squares, on which the various streets converged . . . These streets are all named, mostly after the trades or guilds which have there their bazaars. In these bazaars many of the workmen sat outside their shops, and in the interval of labor exchanged greetings or banter with the passers-by . . . The rule of these towns and villages was exceedingly strict. The representatives of Rome were chiefly either military men or else fiscal or political agents. Then every town had its Sanhedrin, consisting of twenty-three members if the place numbered at least one hundred and twenty men, or of three members if the population were smaller . . . Of course all ecclesiastical and, so to speak, strictly Jewish causes, and all religious questions, were within their special cognizance. Lastly, there were also in every place what may be called municipal authorities, under the presidency of a mayor—the representative of the elders—an institution so frequently mentioned in Scripture, and deeply rooted in Jewish society. Perhaps these may be referred to (Luke 7:3) as sent by the centurion of Capernaum to intercede for him with the Lord.

"What may be called the police and sanitary regulations were of the strictest character. Of Caesarea, e. g., we know that there was a regular system of drainage into the sea. . . . (Josephus, *Ant.,* xv, 9, 6). But in every town and village sanitary rules were strictly attended to. Cemeteries, tanneries, and whatever also might be prejudicial to health, had to be removed at least fifty cubits outside a town. Bakers' and dyers' shops, or stables, were not allowed under the dwelling of another person. Again, in building, the line of each street had to be strictly kept, nor was even a projection beyond it allowed. In general the streets were wider than those of modern Eastern cities. The nature of the soil, and the circumstance that so many towns were built on hills (at least in Judea), would, of course, be advantageous in a sanitary point of view. It would also render the paving of the streets less requisite. But we know that certain towns *were* paved—Jerusalem with white stones (Josephus, *Ant.*, xx, 9, 7). To obviate occasions of dispute, neighbors were not allowed to have windows looking into the courts or rooms of others, nor might the principal entrance to a shop be through a court common to two or three dwellings" (Edersheim, *Sketches of Jewish Social Life*, pp. 87-93).

Town Clerk (Gr. *grammateus*), the city secretary, recorder, to whose office belonged the superintendence of the archives, the drawing up of official decrees, and the reading of them in public assemblies of the people. This official appeased the mob in Ephesus, when Demetrius and his fellow-craftsmen raised a tumult (Acts 19:35). The speech delivered by him may be analyzed thus: He argues that such excitement as the Ephesians evinced was undignified, inasmuch as they stood above all suspicion in religious matters (vers. 35, 36); that it is unjustifiable, since they could establish nothing against the men whom they accused (v. 37); that it was unnecessary, since other means of redress were open to them (vers. 38, 39); and, finally, if neither pride nor a sense of justice availed anything, fear of the Roman power should restrain them from such illegal proceedings (v. 40).

Trachoni'tis (trăk-ô-nī'tĭs; Gr. *rough* or *hilly region*, only in Luke 3:1). "Trachonitis was the territory which contained the Trachon or Trachons. These are described by Strabo (xvi, 2, 20) as 'the two so-called Trachones' lying 'behind Damascus,' The name . . . corresponds exactly to the two great stretches of lava, 'the tempests in stone,' which lie to the southeast of Damascus—the Lejá and the Safá. Each of these is called by the Arabs a *wa'ar*, a word meaning rough, stony tract, and thus equivalent to Trachon. The latter, beyond the reach of civilization, was little regarded, and the Lejá became known as the Trachon *par excellence*, as is proved by the two inscriptions at either end of it—in Musmireh, the ancient Phaenä, and the Bereke, each of which is called a chief town of the Trachon . . . Now the Trachonitis was obviously the Trachon *plus* some territory round it. In the north it extended westward from the borders of the Lejá to the districts of Ulatha and Paneas in the northern Jaulan; and in the south it bordered with Batanea, but also touched Mons Alsadamus, the present Jebel Hauran. Philo uses the name Trachonitis for the whole territory of Philip" (Smith, *Hist. Geog.*, p. 543).

The portion of Philip's tetrarchy most difficult to define is the Ituraean; and it is uncertain whether it covered or overlapped Trachonitis. Luke's reference is ambiguous, and we have no modern echo of the name to guide us.

Trade. 1. In the sense of occupation, as when Joseph told Pharoah, "The men are shepherds, for their trade hath been to feed sheep" (Heb. *'ănshē mĭqnĕh, men of cattle*, Gen. 46:32, 34). "Trading" (Luke 19:15) is the rendering of the Greek *diapragmateuomai*, to undertake a business earnestly, for the sake of gain.

2. In the sense of traffic, commerce (*năthăn*, to *give*, i. e., to pay), something as an equivalent for the sale (Ezek. 27:12-14); (*săhăr*, to *go about, travel*), to traverse the country as a merchant, to trade, traffic (Gen. 34:10); Gr. *'ergazomai*, to *work*, to make gains by trading, our "do business" (Matt. 25:16), and especially as seamen (Rev. 18:17).

Traffic is the rendering of Heb. *kĕnă'ăn* (literally *Canaan*). The expression, "land of trading" (Ezek. 17:4), should read "a land of Canaan" (comp. 16:29); the sentence will then read, "He plucked off the top of his young twigs, and carried it into a land of Canaan," an epithet applied to Babylonia as being a land whose trading spirit had turned it into a Canaan. In Gen. 42:34 "traffic" is the rendering of *săhăr* (see 2), while in I Kings 10:15 the Hebrew is *mĭshăr*, from the same root, signifying to travel about for the purpose of trade. Similar in meaning is the Hebrew word in Ezek. 28:5, 18. "Traffickers" (Isa. 23:8) is from the Hebrew signifying Canaanite.

Tradition (Gr. *paradosis*, a *giving over*), a giving over either by *word of mouth* or in *writing;* objectively, *what is delivered*, as Paul's teaching (II Thess. 3:6; comp. 2:15; I Cor. 11:2, A. V. "ordinances"). It is also used of the body of precepts, especially ritual, which, in the opinion of the later Jews, were orally delivered by Moses, and orally transmitted in unbroken succession to subsequent generations, which precepts, both illustrating and expanding the written law, as they did, were to be obeyed with equal reverence (Matt. 15:2, sq.; Mark 7:3, 5, 9, 13; Col. 2:8). "The traditions of my fathers" (Gal. 1:14) are precepts received from the fathers, whether handed down in the Old Testament books or orally. Meyer, in his *Com.* on Matt. 15:2, says: "The Jews, founding upon Deut. 4:14; 17:10, for the most part attached greater importance to this tradition than to the written law. They laid special stress upon the traditional precept, founded on Lev. 15:11, which required that the hands should be washed before every meal. Jesus and his disciples ignored this tradition as such, which had been handed down from the men of olden time."

Train. 1. *Wealth* (Heb. *hăyĭl, strength*), the term used respecting the queen of Sheba; "she came to Jerusalem with a very great train" (I Kings 10:2), i. e., a retinue of men, and camels laden with riches.

2. "Train up a child," etc. (Prov. 22:6), has the sense in Hebrew *hănăk* of "to imbue one with anything," to initiate; and so to train up a child according to his way, according to his disposition and habits.

3. Isaiah (6:1) says that the Lord's train (Heb. *shūl*) filled the temple. "The heavenly temple is that superterrestrial place, which Jehovah transforms into heaven and a temple, by manifesting himself there to angels and

saints. But while he manifests his glory there he is obliged also to veil it, because created beings are unable to bear it. But that which veils his glory is no less splendid than that portion of it which is revealed. And this was the truth embodied for Isaiah in the long robe and train. He saw the Lord, and what more he saw was the all-filling robe of the indescribable One" (Delitzsch, *Com.*, in loc.).

Trance. 1. In the only passage (Num. 24:4, 16) in which this word occurs in the English of the Old Testament, there is, as the Italics show, no corresponding word in Hebrew.

2. In the New Testament the word occurs three times (Acts 10:10; 11:5; 22:17, Gr. *'ekstasis*, The word may be defined as throwing of the mind out of its normal state, of the man who by some sudden emotion is transported out of himself, so that in his rapt condition, although he is awake, his mind is so drawn off from all surrounding objects and wholly fixed on things divine that he sees nothing but the forms and images lying within, and perceives with his bodily eyes and ears realities shown him by God."

Transfiguration (Gr. *metamorphoō*, to *change into another form*). It is recorded (Matt. 17:2; Mark 9:2) that our Lord "was transfigured" before his disciples, Peter, James, and John; and this is explained (Luke 9:29), "And as he prayed, the fashion of his countenance was altered, and his raiment was white and glistening." Each of the evangelists represent it as taking place about eight days after the first distinct intimation our Lord made to them of his approaching sufferings, death, and resurrection. The location is merely given as a high mountain, which is traditionally thought to have been Mount Tabor; but as Jesus was at this time sojourning in the neighborhood of Caesarea Philippi, it seems likely that it was one of the ridges of Hermon. While our Lord was praying he was "transfigured," i. e., his external aspect was changed, his face gleaming like the sun, and his raiment being so white that it shone like light. The cause of this appearance was that his divine glory shone out through his human form, and not, as in the case of Moses, caused by God having appeared to him.

The disciples seem to have been in a slumber when this divine radiance began to shine forth; but when they woke up they were filled with wonder and fear, beholding also two men, Moses and Elias, in glory, conversing with him. Peter, recovering himself, in the rapture of the moment, suggested that three tents should be pitched to secure the continued presence and fellowship of such glorious company. He had scarcely given expression to his thought when a bright cloud overshadowed them, out of which came a voice saying, "This is my beloved Son, hear ye him." The theme of conversation is not given by Matthew or Mark, but Luke records that they spake concerning his death.

Premillennialists see in the transfiguration scene all the essential features of the future millennial kingdom in manifestation: (1) The Lord appears, not in humiliation, but in glory (Matt. 17:2). (2) Moses is present in a glorified state, representative of the re-

deemed who have passed via death into the kingdom (Matt. 13:43; Luke 9:30, 31). (3) Elijah is also seen glorified, representative of the redeemed who have come into the kingdom by translation (I Thess. 4:13-18; I Cor. 15:50-53). (4) The unglorified disciples, Peter, James and John, represent in the vision and for the time being, Israel in the flesh in the future kingdom (Acts 1:6; Ezek. 37:21-27). (5) The crowd at the foot of the mountain (Matt. 17:14) represent the nations who are to enter the kingdom after it is established over Israel (Isa. 11:10-12). The scene as a whole represents the second coming of Christ in glory to establish his kingdom, or in the words interpreting the scene: "the Son of Man coming in His kingdom" (Matt. 16:28). Agreeable with this interpretation of the transfiguration episode is Peter's comment in II Pet. 1:16-18. As the preaching of the kingdom was fast approaching its end in the rejection and imminent death of the King, it became necessary to encourage the disciples in the expectation of that Messianic kingdom in fullfilment of the covenants and promises made to Israel in the O. T. The transfiguration bore out this assurance.—*M. F. U.*

Transformed (Gr. *metamorphoō*), used of the change of the moral character for the better (Rom. 12:2), through the *renewal of the thinking power*. "The apostle considers it as a peculiar operation of the Christian faith, that believers are seriously concerned to prove in everything what is the will of God (Eph. 5:10); whereas man, in his natural state, looks even to the point of how he may please men" (Tholuck, *Com.*). The apostle (II Cor. 3:18) speaks of the Christian being "changed into the same image from glory to glory," etc. In this passage the Gospel is spoken of as a *mirror*, in which the glory of Christ gives itself to be seen; the Christian, studying the Gospel, becomes so transformed that the same image which he sees in the "mirror" —the image of the glory of Christ—presents itself on him, i. e., he is so transformed that he becomes like the glorified Christ.

In II Cor. 11:13, sq., the apostle, characterizing false prophets, says of them that they are "deceitful workers, transforming themselves into the apostles of Christ. And no marvel; for Satan himself is transformed into an angel of light" (see vers. 14, 15). The Greek is *metaschēmatizō*, and means to *assume the appearance of another*. The persons of whom Paul speaks were servants of Satan, but in working against the apostle in doctrine and act they hypocritically assumed the mask of an apostle, though they were the opposite of a true apostle.

Transgression (Heb. mostly *pĕshă'*, *revolt*; Gr. *parabasis*, *violation*), sometimes used synonymously with sin, but sometimes used in a distinctive sense, as indicating a violation of the law through ignorance, e. g., Exod. 34:7; Rom. 4:15. All sin is transgression, but all transgression is not sin in the sense of incurring guilt. *See* Sin.

Translate, in both its Hebrew and Greek originals, has the sense of removal of a person or thing from one state or condition to another (II Sam. 3:10), where it has reference to transferring a kingdom from Saul to David.

In the case of Enoch, the patriarch "walked with God: and . . . was not; for God took him" (Gen. 5:24), that is, he was translated or changed without seeing death, from an unglorified state to one of glory and immortality. By faith Enoch was translated (*metatethē*, "placed over into another sphere") that he should "not see death;" and he was not found, "because God had translated him" (Heb. 11:5). Similarly Elijah was translated (II Kings 2:11), and the saints living at the return of the Lord (John 14:3) for His own, will be gloriously changed or glorified (I Thess. 4:13-18; I Cor. 15:50-53; I John 3:1-3). In like fashion, the Christian is said to be "translated" that is, "put over" (Gr. *methistēmi*), "into the kingdom of the Son of God's love" (Col. 1:13) when he believes on Christ. This involves a complete change in position from darkness to light, from the kingdom of Satan to God's kingdom, out of "Adam" and into "Christ," from "death to life." It is thus apparent that the term "translate" may apply both to the change in position effected by regeneration or that involved in glorification at the coming of the Lord.—*M. F. U.*

Translations, English Bible.

1. **Early Versions.** There were portions of the Bible, and possibly the entire work, rendered into the English vernacular very early in the history of the language. Gildas states that "When the English martyrs gave up their lives in the 4th century all the copies of the Holy Scriptures which could be found were burned in the streets." Cranmer, Thomas More, and Foxe, with many others, bear testimony to the existence of "divers copies of the Holy Bible in the English tongue." The following are fragments of translations which are clearly traced: Caedmon's versifications of an English translation (689); St. Cuthbert's *Evangelistarium*, which is a Latin translation with an interlinear English (689); St. Aldhelm's translation; Eadfurth's translation (720); King Alfred's (901); Aelfric's (995). These, however, were all made from the Latin, and not from the original Hebrew. After the Conquest the language underwent a great change; the old English Bibles fell into disuse, until they were practically unknown, only a few fragments remaining.

2. **Wyclif's Version.** In the 14th century there was a growing demand for an English version. This need was met by two translations, made respectively by John Wyclif and Richard Purvey. Each carried on his work without the knowledge of the other. Wyclif's was completed in 1384 and Purvey's in 1388. The latter, however, was thought to be only a correction of the former and at one time was even published in the name of Wyclif. The Wyclif version is characterized by (1) The everyday speech of the common people. In many instances the word *children* is rendered "brat;" *father* is "dad;" *chariot* is "cart." (2) The exact rendering of the English idiom for the ancient. Thus, *raca* is "Fy" or "Pugh;" *mammon* is "richesse." (3) The literalness of the translation. The following is a specimen: "The disciplis scien to hym, Maister now the Jewis soughten for to stoone thee, and est goist thou thidir? Jheus answered whether ther ben not twelue ouris of the dai? If ony man wandre in the night he stomblish, for light is not in him. He seith these thingis and aftir these thingis he seith to hem Lazarus oure freend slepith but Y go to reise hym fro sleep Therfor hise disciplis seiden: Lord if he slepith he schal be saaf."

3. **Tyndale's Version.** In 1526 William Tyndale made a translation of the New Testament from the original Greek. He afterward made a translation of the Pentateuch and other portions of the Old Testament. The whole was printed in Germany and imported into England. Tyndale's introduction and comments awakened intense opposition; and many copies of the work were publicly burned by the order of the Bishop of London. As in Wyclif's version, the language was the common speech of the people. Many of his words have lost their old-time meaning, as is seen in the following rendering of Tit. 1:1: "Paul, the rascal of God and the villein of Jesus Christ." The aim of the translator was to render the simple sense of the original uninfluenced by theological thought. Thus, instead of "grace" he used the word "favor," "love" instead of "charity," "acknowledging" instead of "confessing," "elders" instead of "priests," "repentance" instead of "penance," "congregation" instead of "church."

4. **Coverdale's Version.** In 1535 Miles Coverdale completed and printed an English translation of the entire Bible. It was probably done under the influence of Cromwell and with the aid of many assistants. It was not with Coverdale, as it was with Tyndale, a work of love. He undertook it as a task imposed upon him and did it perfunctorily and mechanically. Nor was it a translation from the original, but mainly from the German and Latin. It shows a strong royal and ecclesiastical influence. It uses a variety of English equivalents for the same original. It bears the marks of haste and carelessness.

5. **Matthew's Bible.** This is the first "Authorized Version" of the Holy Bible in English. It is a fusion of the Tyndale and the Coverdale versions, and was printed in London by the king's license in 1737, by the publishers Grafton and Whitchurch. It bears the name of Thomas Matthew, which is undoubtedly a pseudonym. The real editor is John Rogers, the protomartyr. His notes and comments were far in advance of his time, and soon evoked a strong ecclesiastical opposition to this version.

6. **Travener's Version.** This version appeared in 1539, and was made necessary by the ecclesiastical opposition to the Matthew's Bible. It, however, is but an expurgated edition of this version.

7. **Cranmer's Version** was printed in 1539 with the sanction of Cranmer's name. The translation was made by a corps of scholars under the direction of the archbishop and his coadjutors. It was a large folio and illustrated with a picture supposed to be the work of Holbein. It had the license of the king, and was called "The Great Bible."

8. **The Geneva Bible.** This was a popular revision of "The Great Bible" made by Hebrew and Greek scholars who were refugees in

489. Title Page, Geneva Bible

Geneva. The cost of the other (about $30) made it inaccessible to the people. The purpose of the Geneva version was to give to England a household edition of the word of God. It was a small quarto with marginal notes, and was divided into chapters and verses. It at once became popular, and there were over two hundred editions of it.

9. **The Bishop's Bible** appeared in 1568, and was made on the suggestion of Archbishop Parker. He was assisted in his work by eight of his bishops and some of the scholars of the Church. It was elegantly printed, profusely illustrated, and ornamented with elaborate initial letters. From one of these, introducing the Epistle to the Hebrews, this version was popularly called "The Leda Bible." It never received the approval of the scholars, and its cost kept it from the possession of the people.

10. **The Rheims and Douay Version.** A translation was made by Martin, Allen, and Bristow, who were refugees in Rheims, where in 1582 they published the New Testament. The work was completed by the publication in 1609 of the Old Testament. This was done in Douay, which fact gives the name to the version. Altogether aside from its Romish viewpoint, it is the poorest rendering into English of any of the versions. The following are given as fair specimens of its literary style: "Purge the old leaven that you may be a new paste, as you are asymes." "You are evacuated from Christ." In Gal. 5:19 this version substitutes for "drunkenness," "ebrieties," for "revelings," "comessations;" and for "long-suffering," "longanimity." In Heb. 9:23, for

"the patterns of things in the heavens," the Douay has "the exemplars of the celestials." In Heb. 13:16, "to do good and to communicate forget not, for with such sacrifices God is well pleased," the Douay reads, "Beneficence and communication do not forget, for with such hosts God is promerited."

11. **The Authorized Version.** It is also known as the King James Bible, from James I, by whose authority and support it was undertaken and completed. It was begun in 1604 and finished in seven years. Forty-seven of the ablest scholars were selected to do the work, each taking a portion and finally reviewing the whole. It was to correspond with the Bishop's Bible, excepting where the original Hebrew and Greek made it impossible. The excellence of the work done is attested by the simple fact that this version has held the heart of the English-speaking world for nearly three centuries, and that no subsequent version has been able to supplant it.

490. Title Page, The Bishop's Bible

12. **The Revised Version.** There has been a number of attempts at revision of the A. V., but nothing of importance was done until 1870 when the convocation of Canterbury formally originated an inquiry which resulted in a new version completed in 1885. This version was felt to be needed because of the change which two centuries had made in the meaning of many English words; because of the fuller knowledge of the Hebrew and the Greek text now possessed; because of the confessed inaccuracy of many of the renderings in the A. V.; and because of the obscurities occasioned by the form of the English text where there is no distinction made between

prose and poetry, and where the divisions into chapters and verses make unnatural and abrupt breaks in the inspired thought. The aim of the translators was to introduce as few alterations into the text of the A. V. as faithfulness to the truth would allow; and to make the language of such alterations conform to that of the rest of the book. The New Version has not won the heart of the English-speaking world, but is accepted as an able commentary on the text which since 1611 has been a sacred classic.

13. **The American Standard Version.** The R. V. with such alterations as were recommended by the American branch of revisers, and which was not published until 1901.

14. **The Polychrome Version.** An entirely new translation made from the original text, under the direction of Professor Haupt, of Johns Hopkins University, and which aims to give the rendering on the basis of the most recent school of Higher Criticism. This translation has had only slight acceptance.

15. **Revised Standard Version.** An authorized revision of the American Standard Version of 1901. The O. T. section, copyright 1952; N. T. section, copyright 1946. This translation of the entire Bible was launched with great fanfare and at great expense. Its reception, however, has been mixed. Hailed by liberals, it has been unfavorably received by many conservatives. Its translators were almost completely of the liberal school. Although possessing the results of the latest scholarship, it has departed from the A. V., R. V., and A. S. V. in their high veneration for the Hebrew Massoretic Text of the O. T., and in many instances contains renderings of pivotal passages that are doctrinally weak and unreliable. It appears it will not supplant the A. V., R. V., or A. S. V., at least among conservative Christians.

Trap, the rendering of several Hebrew and one Greek word, and used figuratively of fatal dangers, of destructive sins (Job 18:10; Prov. 13:14), also of a person or thing as *a cause of ruin* (Exod. 10:7; I Sam. 18:21; Rom. 11:9).

Tread, Treaders. *See* Winepress.

Treasure (Hebrew mostly from *'āsăr,* to *hoard;* Gr. *thēsauros*), anything collected in storehouses, e. g., treasures of grain, wine, oil; brass, silver, gold; coined money. So winds, rain, hail, snow, etc., are in the treasures of God (Psa. 135:7; Jer. 51:16). Pharoah compelled the Hebrews to build him treasure cities, or magazines (Exod. 1:11), and the kings of Judah had keepers of their treasures, both in city and country (I Chron. 27:25; II Chron. 32:27, etc.), and these places were called treasure cities. The temple treasury (Mark 12:41; John 8:20) was that portion of the Court of the Women in which were thirteen chests to receive the offerings of worshippers, either for the temple service or for the poor. These chests were narrow at the mouth and wide at the bottom, and shaped like trumpets, whence their name.

Figurative. "Ye shall be a peculiar treasure unto me," etc. (Exod. 19:5; comp. Psa. 135:4), means more than property in general, for in this sense all peoples are the Lord's. The meaning is that Israel were a costly, valued possession as compared to other people, because they were a covenanted people and recognized Jehovah alone as God. "The fear of the Lord is his treasure" (Isa. 33:6) means that piety is the wealth of a nation. The word treasures is often used to denote great abundance, as: "In Jesus Christ are hidden all the treasures of wisdom and knowledge" (Col. 2:3); and the "treasures of wickedness" (Prov. 10:2; Mic. 6:10) are those things which are accumulated through wrong (comp. Luke 16:9); "the treasures of darkness" (Isa. 45:3) refer to the carefully stored riches of Babylon and the Lydian Sardes, which Cyrus acquired by conquest; Amos (3:10) says of the rich in Samaria, "They know not to do right . . . who store up violence and robbery in their palaces," i. e., they heap up injustice and violence in their palace like treasures (comp. Rom. 2:5); "this treasure in earthen vessels" (II Cor. 4:7) "is referred either, in accordance with v. 6, to *the light kindled by God in the heart,* or to the *ministry of the Gospel*" (Calvin, Bengel, etc.). In Matt. 12:35; Luke 6:45, the heart of a good man is compared to a treasure of good things, while the depraved man has his treasury of evil. "Treasure hid in a field" (Matt. 13:44) refers to the custom of burying money, jewels, and other valuables, that they may remain free from molestation or suspicion. Thomson (*Land and Book,* i, p. 194) refers to the finding of several copper pots which contained a large quantity of ancient copper coins, all of issues of Alexander and his father Philip, and adds: "I suspect it was the royal treasure, which one of Alexander's officers concealed when he heard of his unexpected death in Babylon, intending to appropriate it to himself; but being apprehended, slain, or driven away by some of the revolutions which followed that event, the coin remained where he had hid it." Such a fact illustrates the above text. A man discovers the place where the treasure is hid, keeps the discovery to himself, buys the field, and the treasure is his own. Job represents (3:21) the man weary of life as seeking the grave with the eagerness of one digging for hid treasure; and Solomon (Prov. 2:4) compares wisdom to "hid treasures."

Treasurer (Heb. *gizbär,* Ezra 1:8; 7:21; Aram. *gĭdbär,* Dan. 3:2, 3), an important officer in all oriental courts. In Isa. 22:15 Shebna is not a "treasurer" as rendered in the A. V., but *associate* (Heb. *sōkēn*), and is officially described as "over the house." This name was given to an office of state of great importance, in fact the highest of all, and one so vastly superior to all others (36:3; 37:2) that it was sometimes filled by the heir to the throne (II Chron. 26:21).

Treasury. *See* Treasure.

Treaty. *See* Alliance, Covenant.

Tree (Heb. *'ēṣ;* Gr. *dendron*). Trees in Palestine, as elsewhere were objects of beauty and utility (Psa. 1:3).

Mosaic Regulations. When the Israelites planted fruit trees in Palestine they were to treat the fruit of every tree as uncircumcised, i. e., not to eat it. "The reason for this command is not to be sought for in the fact that in the first three years fruit trees bear only a little fruit, and that somewhat insipid, and that if the blossom or fruit is broken off the first year the trees will bear all the more plentifully afterward, though this end would no doubt be thereby attained; but it rests rather upon ethical grounds. Israel was to treat the fruits of horticulture with the most careful regard as a gift of God, and sanctify the enjoyment of them by a thank offering. In the fourth year the whole of the fruit was to be a holiness of praise for Jehovah, i. e., to be offered to the Lord as a holy sacrificial gift, in praise and thanksgiving for the blessing which he had bestowed upon the fruit trees" (K. and D., *Com.*). The Hebrews were forbidden to destroy the fruit trees of their enemies in time of war, "for the tree of the field is man's life" (Deut. 20:19, 20).

Noted Trees. There are in Scripture many memorable trees, e. g., Allon-bachuth (Gen. 35:8), the tamarisk in Gibeah (I Sam. 22:6), the terebinth in Shechem (Josh. 24:26), under which the law was set up; the palm tree of Deborah (Judg. 4:5), the terebinth of enchantments (9:37), the terebinth of wanderers (4:11), and others (I Sam. 14:2; 10:3; sometimes "plain" in A. V.). This observation of particular trees was among the heathen extended to a regular worship of them. *See* Vegetable Kingdom.

Worship of Trees. Among the Canaanites and other Eastern peoples worship was carried on in holy groves (*q. v.*). In the absence of groves they chose green trees with thick foliage (Ezek. 6:13; 20:28), such as the vigorous oak, the evergreen terebinth (Isa. 1:29, 30; 57:5), and the poplar or osier, which remains green even in the heat of summer (Hos. 4:13). To explain how this worship came about, Stade (*Geschicte*, i, p. 451) says that at such places were graves of patriarchs or other heroes—as Hebron, the burying place of Abraham, etc.; but Robertson (*Early Religion of Israel*, p. 248) says: "I believe the prophet, who reproved the worship under green trees, came nearer to a true explanation of the origin of the worship in the hint, 'because the shadow thereof is good' (Hos. 4:13), than modern critics, with their learned disquisition as to the tree suggesting life and being the abode of 'a spirit or a divinity.' "

Tree of Knowledge, and **Of Life.** These were planted by God in the garden of Eden; "the one to train man's spirit through the exercise of obedience to the word of God, the other to transform his earthly nature into the spiritual essence of eternal life. These trees received their names from their relations to man, that is to say, from the effect which the eating of their fruit was destined to produce upon human life and its development. The fruit of the tree of life conferred the power of eternal, immortal life; and the tree of knowledge was planted to lead men to the knowledge of good and evil. The tree of life was to impart the power of transformation into eternal life. The tree of knowledge was to lead man to the knowledge of good and evil; and, according to the divine intention, this was to be attained through his not eating of the fruit. This end was to be accomplished, not only by his discerning, in the limit imposed by the prohibi-

tion, the difference between that which accorded with the will of God and that which opposed it, but also by his coming eventually, through obedience to the prohibition, to recognize the fact that all that is opposed to the will of God is an evil to be avoided, and, through voluntary resistance to such evil, to the full development of the freedom of choice originally imparted to him into the actual freedom of a deliberate and self-conscious choice of good" (K. and D., *Com.*, Gen. 2:17). But by yielding to the temptation to eat of its fruit our first parents came to know good from evil by a sad, bitter experience, and by receiving the evil into their own soul became the victims of the threatened death. The various references to the "tree of life" evidently consider it to have been the divinely appointed medium for securing in some way the immortality of our first parents (Prov. 3:18; 11:30; Ezek. 47:12; Rev. 2:7; 22:2, 14).

Trench. 1. *A channel* (Heb. *te'ālāh*), a conduit (I Kings 18:32, 35, 38, as elsewhere rendered), a kind of ditch cut for the purpose of receiving and draining water from adjacent parts. Something of this kind Elijah probably had dug round the altar on Carmel (v. 32).

2. A *pale* or *stake* (Gr. *charax, pale* or *stake*), a palisade or rampart, i. e., pales between which earth, stones, trees, and timbers are heaped and packed together (Luke 19:43).

Trespass. 1. *Rebellion* (Heb. *pěshă', revolt*), the breaking away from an allegiance, covenant (Exod. 22:9; I Sam. 25:28).

2. Heb. *mā'ăl* (to *cover* up), to act covertly, and so treacherously, as an adulterous woman against her husband (Lev. 26:40); or to take away by stealth, to steal (Josh. 7:1).

3. An offense committed, a hurt or wrong done a neighbor. The Hebrew (*'āshäm*) means a *side slip*, and the Greek (*paraptōma*), a *lapse* or *deviation* from truth and uprightness. They both convey the meaning of an error or slip rather than a deliberate or gross sin (Lev. 5:6, etc.; Matt. 6:14, 15, etc.).

Trespass Offering. *See* Sacrificial Offerings.

Trial. *See* Law, Administration of; Temptation.

Tribe. *See* Israel, Constitution of.

Tribulation (Heb. *şär*, or *şăr, narrow;* Gr. *thlipsis*, a *pressure*) has in the A. V. much the same meaning as *trouble,* or *trial*, i. e., afflictive dispensations to which a person is subjected either by way of punishment (Judg. 10:14; Matt. 24:21, 29; Rom. 2:9; II Thess. 1:6) or by way of trial (John 16:33; Rom. 5:3; II Thess. 1:4).

Tribulation, the Great. This is the period of unparalleled suffering which, according to premillennial eschatology, will precede the establishment of the future kingdom of Israel (Acts 1:6). The trouble will embrace the entire earth (Rev. 3:10). Yet in a very distinctive sense it will center upon Jerusalem and Palestine, being called by Jeremiah specifically "the time of Jacob's trouble" (Jer. 30:7). It will involve the Jewish people who will have gone back to Palestine in unbelief. It will also be connected with catastrophic judgments upon the Gentile nations because of their wickedness and anti-Semitism. The colossal scenes of the Revelation, beginning with chapter 5, with the opening of the seven-sealed book, through chapter 10, form a prelude to world-wide commotion prior to the Great Tribulation itself described in Rev. 11-18. The Great Tribulation is made identical with the last three and one-half years of Daniel's Seventieth Week of years (Dan. 9:24-27; Rev. 11:2, 3). The gigantic wars, cataclysms, pestilences, etc., that befall the earth are actually the manifestation of the risen, victorious Christ taking an open hand to claim His redeemed rights to the earth in preparation for the divine program involving His people on the earth. Psalm 2 in giving the order of the establishment of the kingdom in the ousting of Christ's enemies, closely interweaves the first advent and Messiah's death in shame with His second advent in glory to receive the rewards of His conquest over sin and death. The Tribulation will see the nations raging (Psa. 2:1), with the derision of Jehovah (v. 4) that men should vainly imagine to set aside His covenant (II Sam. 7:8-17) and His plan for the earth (Psa. 89:34-37). The Great Tribulation adumbrated in Psa. 2 is described in Matt. 24:15-51. It eventuates in the establishment of the rejected King in Zion (Psa. 2:6) and the subjugation of the earth to the king's millennial rule (vs. 7-9), with a present appeal to Gentile world powers to be warned by the certainty of the establishment of Christ's kingdom (vs. 10-12). According to Rev. chaps. 13-19 there will be the cruel reign of the "beast out of the sea" (Rev. 13:1) who, breaking his covenant with the Jews (II Thess. 2:4) will demand divine worship. This earth ruler, the Beast, is empowered by Satan, and the entire terrific episode of fighting God is made possible by the unprecedented activity of demons (Rev. 9:1-11; Rev. 16:13-16). The terrific bowl judg-

491. Babylonian Tribute Bearer

ments of Rev. 16 are the "Lamb's" final demonstration of power. He destroys His enemies and frees His redeemed earth from the domination of wicked men at His visible glorious return setting up the kingdom. Those who are not premillennialists hold that the tribulation of Revelation was fulfilled in the Roman persecutions of the Church or in great catastrophes occurring over the last nineteen centuries.—*M. F. U.*

Tributary (Heb. *măs*, commonly derived from *māsăs*, to *pine away*, because tribute is a consuming of strength), one who becomes subject to tribute service (Deut. 20:11; Judg. 1:30, 33, 35; Lam. 1:1). *See* Tribute.

492. Syrians Bringing Tribute to Egypt
(15th Century B.C.)

Tribute. 1. (Heb. *măs*, a *consuming*), spoken mostly of tribute to be paid in *service*, fully "tribute of one serving" (I Kings 9:21), a condition of serfdom (Josh. 16:10; 17:13; Judg. 1:28). Thus we see that Adoram was appointed overseer over the tributary service in the time of Solomon (II Sam. 20:24; I Kings 4:6).

2. A portion paid to the Lord (Num. 31:28, sq.). (Heb. *měkěs*).

3. Something *measured* out (II Kings 23:33; Ezra 4:20). (Heb. *mǐddāh*).

4. *Something consumed*, a tax on things consumed, *excise* (Ezra 4:13; 7:24). (Aram. *bᵉlō*).

5. A fine imposed (Ezra 6:8; Neh. 5:4). (Heb. *'ōněsh*).

6. That which an Israelite gave to the Lord, according to his ability (Deut. 16:10). (Heb. *mǐssāh, number*).

7. A temple tax levied upon all Jews (Gr. *didrachon*, a double drachma; Matt. 17:24); and *kēnsos*, a register and valuation of property in accordance with which taxes were paid, the tax or tribute levied on individuals, and to be paid yearly (Matt. 17:25; 22:17; Mark 12:14). "Tribute money" (Matt. 22:19) was the coin with which the tax was paid. *For'os* (Gr. *phoros*, a *burden*) was the annual tax upon houses, lands, and persons (Luke 20:22, 23:2).

Figurative. Of Issachar, Jacob said "Issachar is a strong ass couching down between two burdens; . . . and became a servant unto tribute" (Gen. 49:14, 15). The simile of a strong ass, etc., pointed to the fact that this tribe would content itself with material good, and not strive after political power and rule. Like an idle beast of burden, he would rather submit to the yoke and be forced to do the work of a slave than risk his possessions and his peace in the struggle for liberty. *See* Tax.

Trinity, the term by which is expressed the unity of three persons in the one God. The Christian doctrine is: 1. That there is only one God, one divine nature and being. 2. This one divine being is tripersonal, involving the distinctions of the Father, the Son, and the Holy Spirit. 3. These three are joint partakers of the same nature and majesty of God. This doctrine is preeminently one of revelation. And while it brings before us one of the great mysteries of revelation, and transcends the finite comprehension, it is essential to the understanding of the Scriptures; and, as we shall see, has its great value and uses.

1. **Scripture Doctrine.** Although the doctrine of the Trinity is implicit rather than explicit in the Old Testament, at the same time, it is properly held that with the accompanying light of the New Testament this truth can be found in the Old (e. g., Num. 6:24-26; Isa. 6:3; 63:9, 10, the sanctity of the symbolical number three—the plural form of Elohim, also places in which the deity is spoken of as conversing with himself). This is in accord with the gradual development of revealed truth in other particulars. The religion of the Old Testament is emphatically monotheistic. The almost exclusive proclamation of the unity of God was essential as a safeguard against polytheism.

The New Testament teaching upon this subject is not given in the way of formal statement. The formal statement, however, is legitimately and necessarily deduced from the Scriptures of the New Testament, and these, as has been suggested, cast a light backward upon the intimations of the Old. Reliance, it is held by many competent critics, is not to be placed upon the passages in Acts 20:28 and I Tim. 3:16; and I John 5:7 is commonly regarded as spurious. Aside from these, however, it is plain that both Christ and the apostles ascribe distinct personality to the Father, the Son, and the Holy Spirit (*see* articles, Father, God the; Sonship of Christ; Holy Spirit, The). And these utterances are such as to admit legitimately of no other conception than that of the unity of these three persons in the ontological oneness of the whole divine nature (see, e. g., Matt. 28:19; John 14:16, 17; I Cor. 12:4-6; II Cor. 13:13; Eph. 4:4-6; I Pet. 1:2; Rev. 1:4-6). The same worship is paid, the same works are ascribed to each of these three persons, and in such a way as to indicate that these three are united in the fullness of the one living God. The Monotheism of the Old Testament is maintained, while glimpses are nevertheless, afforded into the tripersonal mode of the divine existence.

2. **Theological Suggestions.** (1) The Christian faith at this period does not ground itself upon philosophy, for it here extends to a matter far above the reach of philosophical reflection. Also but little stress, if any, is to be laid upon apparent resemblances between pagan religions and Christianity at this point—resemblances more apparent than real. The doctrine is to be accepted by faith in the divine revelation; and while it is above reason, and cannot be comprehended in its depth and

fullness, it does not follow, nor can it be shown, that it is opposed to reason.

(2) The question whether the Trinity is merely one of manifestation or that of essential nature has been raised again and again in the history of the Church (*see* Sabellianism in works of Doctrine). Undoubtedly the history of revelation shows a progress in the unfolding of truth concerning God. And in that sense the Trinity is dispensational. But it is also emphatically to be borne in mind that if God reveals himself, he must reveal himself as he is, and the Trinity of revelation must therefore rest upon a Trinity of nature. The attempt to remove difficulty by any sort of Sabellian interpretation only raises difficulty of a deeper character. Can God on the whole reveal himself other than he actually is?

(3) On the other hand Christianity has reason to guard itself, as it has generally sought to do, against tritheistic conceptions. Both the unity and the tripersonal nature of God are to be maintained. And thus the proper baptismal formula is not, "In the name of God the Father, God the Son, and God the Holy Spirit," but the words as our Lord gave them (Matt. 28:19).

(4) It is admitted by all who thoughtfully deal with this subject that the Scripture revelation here leads us into the presence of a deep mystery; and that all human attempts at expression are of necessity imperfect. The word person, it may be, is inadequate, and is doubtless used often in a way that is misleading, "That God is alike one Person, and in the same sense three Persons, is what Christianity has never professed" (Van Oosterzee). Said Augustine, "Three persons, if they are to be so called, for the unspeakable exaltedness of the object cannot be set forth by this term." And yet the long standing and prevailing doctrine of the Church expresses more nearly than any other the truth concerning God as it comes to us in the Holy Scriptures. And it is further to be borne in mind that this teaching of the Church has been called forth for the purpose of combating various forms of error. It has not been held as a complete or perfect expression of the truth concerning the unfathomable being of God, but rather as a protest against the denials of the personality and supreme deity of the Son and of the Holy Spirit.

(5) Accordingly the doctrine has a large measure of importance. It has been called "a bulwark for Christian theism." Unitarianism is very apt to degenerate into deism or pantheism. Also this doctrine affords us a glimpse into the wonderful being of God, while at the same time it constantly proclaims the impossibility of comprehending God. Thus while it is a stumbling-block to rationalism, it is for those who accept it a safeguard against all tendency to rationalism or intellectual pride. And, further, in the Trinity we should behold not only a God who is exalted far above us, but also Christ with us, and the Holy Spirit who will dwell in us. Thus in a proper way is harmonized the divine transcendence with the divine immanence.

The glory of the Gospel depends upon this truth; for Christ is most clearly seen to be

God's unspeakable gift, the bringer of the most perfect revelation, and the author of eternal salvation, when we recognize his essential oneness with the Father. Likewise the Holy Spirit is thus seen to be, in his relation to a sinful world, and to the Church, as well as to individual believers, the infinite source of hope and new and holy life.

3. **Historical.** Briefly it may be said that the faith of the primitive Christians at this point, as many others, was without attempt at scientific form. The elements of the doctrine, however, were embraced by their simple reliance upon the teaching of Christ and his apostles. It was only gradually, and after a considerable period, in its conflict with Judaism and paganism, that the thought of the Church arrived at something of formal statement. The word Trinity (*Trinitas*) was first employed by Tertullian (2d century), though his word was only the Latin translation of the Greek *trias*, employed by Theophilus of Antioch. The word Person was also first employed by Tertullian, though he used it in the inadmissible sense of individual.

The Council of Nicaea (A. D. 325) was an epoch in Christian history. The heresy of Sabellius and Paul of Samosata, which refused to recognize the Father as in any personal sense distinct from the Son and the Holy Spirit, had been previously condemned. But Arius, who began with the Sabellian idea that the Trinity is only one of manifestation, changed his position and declared that there were three persons in God, but that these three were unequal in glory. In short, the Son and the Holy Spirit owed their existence to the divine will, and, accordingly, were creatures of God (*see* Arianism in books on Doctrine). The Council of Nice, in opposition to Arianism and various other theories, adopted the formal statement of the consubstantiality of the Father, the Son, and the Holy Spirit, while maintaining the distinction of personality. The doctrine of the Nicene Council was reaffirmed at various succeeding councils, and is the generally recognized doctrine of the Christian Church. E. McC. revised by *M. F. U.*

Triumph (Heb. *'ālăz*, to *exult;* *'ălăş*, to *jump* for joy; Gr. *thriambeuō*, a *noisy song*). The nations of antiquity generally celebrated success in war by a triumph, which usually included a splendid procession, a display of captives and spoil, and a solemn thanksgiving to the gods.

1. **The Egyptians.** The return of a king in triumph from war was a grand solemnity celebrated with all the pomp which the wealth of the nation could command. The inhabitants flocked to meet him, and with welcome acclamations greeted his arrival and the success of his arms. The priests and chief people of each place advanced with garlands and bouquets of flowers; the principal person present addressed him in an appropriate speech; and as the troops filed through the streets or passed without the walls the people followed with acclamations, uttering earnest thanksgiving to the gods, the protectors of Egypt, and praying them forever to continue the same marks of favor to their monarch and

their nation. The Assyrian sculptures abound with similar representations.

2. **The Romans.** Among them the highest honor which could be bestowed on a citizen or magistrate was the triumph or solemn procession, in which a victorious general passed from the gate of the city to the capitol. He set out from the Campus Martius along the Via Triumphalis, and from thence through the most public places of the city. The streets were strewn with flowers and the altars smoked with incense. The procession was formed as follows: First, a numerous band of music, singing and playing triumphal songs; the oxen to be sacrificed, their horns gilded and heads adorned with fillets and garlands; the spoils, and captives in chains; the lictors, having their fasces adorned with laurel; a great company of musicians and dancers; a long train of persons carrying perfumes; the general dressed in purple embroidered with gold, wearing a crown of laurel, in his right hand a laurel branch and a scepter in his left, his face painted with vermilion, and a golden ball suspended from his neck. He stood erect in his chariot, with a public slave by his side to remind him of the vicissitudes of fortune and of his mortality. Behind him came the consuls, senators, and other magistrates, on foot; the whole procession closing with the victorious army.

3. **The Hebrews** celebrated their victories by triumphal processions, the women and children dancing to the accompaniment of musical instruments (Judg. 11:34-47), and singing hymns of triumph to Jehovah; of which hymns that sung by Miriam (Exod. 15:1-21) and Deborah (Judg. 5:1-31) are notable examples. Triumphal songs were uttered for the living (I Sam. 18:6-8; II Chron. 20:21-28), and elegies for the dead (II Sam. 1:17-27; II Chron. 35:25). Great demonstrations of joy were made, and the shout of victory resounded from mountain to mountain (Isa. 42:11; 52:7, 8; 63:1-4; Jer. 50:2; Ezek. 7:7; Nah. 1:15). Monuments in honor of victory were erected, and the arms of the enemy were hung up as trophies in the temples (I Sam. 21:9; 31:10; II Sam. 8:11, 12; II Kings 11:10).

Indignities to prisoners formed a leading feature among ancient nations; such as maiming, blinding, and killing. Many representations appear upon the monuments of putting the foot upon the head or neck of a conquered foe (Josh. 10:24), and it forms the ground of many figurative representations in the Scriptures (Psa. 110:1; Isa. 60:14; I Cor. 15:26).

Tro'as (trō'ăz; Gr. the Troad, region about Troy), a city on the coast of Mysia, opposite the southeast extremity of the island of Tenedos, and near Troy. It was formerly called *Antigonia Troas*, having been built by Antigonus; but was embellished by Lysimachus, and named *Alexandria Troas* in honor of Alexander the Great. It flourished under the Romans, and, with its environs, was raised by Augustus to be a *colonia* with the *Jus Italicum.* It was while in Troas that Paul received the divine intimation that he was to carry the Gospel into Europe (Acts 16:8-11); where he rested for a short time on the northward road from Ephesus (during the next missionary journey), in the expectation of meeting Titus (II Cor. 2:12, 13); where on his return southward he met those who had preceded him from Philippi (Acts 20:5, 6), and remained a week; and where, years after, he left a cloak, some books and parchments in the house of Carpus (II Tim. 4:13).

Trogyl'lium (trô-jǐl'ǐ-ŭm), a town and promontory on the Ionian coast, directly opposite Samos, the channel here being about one mile in width. Paul sailed through this channel on his way to Jerusalem at the close of his third missionary journey, spending a night at Trogyllium (Acts 20:15). "St. Paul's Port" is the name still given to the harbor there.

Troop. 1. Heb. *gäd* (*fortune*) is an improper rendering (Isa. 65:11) for Gad, the God of fortune. *See* "Gad" in article Gods, False.

2. A marauding party in the forays for which Palestine has always been notorious, especially beyond Jordan (Gen. 49:19; II Sam. 3:22; 22:30; Job. 19:12; Psa. 18:29, etc.), sometimes in the A. V. "bands," (Heb. *gᵉdūd*)

Troph'imus (trŏf'ǐ-mŭs; Gr. *nourishing*), a companion of the apostle Paul. He was a native of Ephesus in Asia Minor, and, together with Tychicus, accompanied Paul in his third missionary journey when returning from Macedonia toward Syria (Acts 20:4). Trophimus went to Jerusalem, where he was the innocent cause of the tumult in which the apostle was apprehended. Certain Jews from the district of Asia saw the two missionaries together, and *supposed* that Paul had taken Trophimus into the temple (Acts 21:27-29). In II Tim. 4:20 Paul writes that he had left Trophimus in ill health at Miletus.

Trough (Heb. *shōqēth*, *drinking*), a vessel of wood or stone for watering animals (Gen. 24:20; 30:38; Exod. 2:16, Heb. *răhăt;* Gen. 30:38, 41, A. V. "gutter"). *See* Kneading Trough.

Trow (an archaic rendering into English of Greek *dokeō*, Luke 17:9), to be of opinion, to think; so used that the object is easily understood from the context.

Truce Breaker (Gr. *'aspondos, without a treaty*), one who cannot be persuaded to enter into a covenant, implacable (II Tim. 3:3; Rom. 1:31, A. V. "covenant breaker").

Trump, Trumpet. *See* Music.

Trumpets, Feast of. *See* Festivals.

Tryphe'na (trī-fē'nà; *delicate, luxurious, dainty*), a Christian woman of Rome to whom, in connection with Tryphosa, Paul sent a special salutation (Rom. 16:12). What other relation they sustained is not known, but it is more than likely that they were fellow-deaconesses.

Trypho'sa (trī-fō'sà; Gr. *delicate, luxurious*). *See* Tryphena.

Tsadhe' (tsà-dā'), the eighteenth letter of the Hebrew alphabet, corresponding to no single letter in English. It is anglicized by *ts* or *tz*. It heads the eighteenth section of Psalm 119, in which section each verse of the Hebrew commences with this letter. *M. F. U.*

Tu'bal (tū'băl; meaning uncertain), one of the seven sons of Japheth (Gen. 10:2; I Chron. 1:5). He is thought to have been the founder of the Tiberani, said by the scholiasts to have been a Scythian tribe. Tubal and Meshech,

the Tabali and Mushki of the Assyrian monuments, were the representatives of eastern Asia Minor. Their territory originally extended far to the south. In the time of Sargon and Sennacherib that of the Tabali adjoined Cilicia, while the Mushki inhabited the highlands to the east of them, where they were in contact with the Hittites. In later days, however, Meschech had retreated to the north, and the classical geographers place the Tibarêni and the Mushki at no great distance from the Black Sea.

Tu'bal-Cain (tŭ'băl-kān; (*Tubal, the smith*), the son of Lamech by his wife Zillah, who is described (Gen. 4:22) as "hammering all kinds of cutting things in brass and iron"— the inventor of edge tools.

Turban. *See* Dress.

Turtle, Turtledove. *See* Animal Kingdom.

Twelve. *See* Number.

Twilight. *See* Time.

Twinkling. The apostle Paul, in speaking of those who shall be alive when Christ comes in judgment, says (I Cor. 15:52), "We shall all be changed in a *moment*" (Gr. *en atomō, that which cannot be divided*), "in the *twinkling of an eye*" (*en hripē 'ophthalmou, the jerk* of the eyelash). Both these were common expressions to denote the shortest conceivable time.

Tych'icus (tǐk'ǐ-kŭs; *fortuitous*), one of Paul's fellow-laborers. We first meet him as a companion of the apostle during a portion of his return journey from the third missionary tour (Acts 20:4). He is there expressly called (with Trophimus) a native of Asia Minor; but while Trophimus went with Paul to Jerusalem (21:29), Tychicus was left behind in Asia, probably at Miletus (20:15, 38). In Paul's first imprisonment he was with the apostle again (Col. 4:7, 8; Eph. 6:21, 22). The next reference to him is in Tit. 3:12. Here Paul (writing possibly from Ephesus) says that it is probable he may send Tychicus to Crete, about the time when he himself goes to Nicopolis. In II Tim. 4:12 (written at Rome during the second imprisonment), he says, "I am herewith sending Tychicus to Ephesus." There is much probability in the conjecture that Tychicus was one of the two "brethren" (Trophimus being the other) who were associated with Titus (II Cor. 8:16-24) in conducting the business of the collection for the poor Christians in Judea.

Tyran'nus (tī-răn'ŭs; Lat. from Gr. *a tyrant, an absolute sovereign*), the man in whose school Paul taught for two years during his sojourn at Ephesus (Acts 19:9). The fact that he taught in his school after quitting the synagogue favors the opinion that he was a Greek, but whether he was a convert is uncertain. Paul taught every day in the lecture room of Tyrannus. "Public life in the Ionian cities ended regularly at the fifth hour (11 a. m.); . . . thus Paul himself would be free, and the lecture room would be disengaged after the fifth hour; and the time, which was devoted generally to home life and rest, was applied by him to mission work" (Ramsay, *St. Paul*, p. 271).

Tyre (tīr; Heb. *şōr, a rock;* Gr. *Turos*), an ancient Phoenician city, located on the shore of the Mediterranean Sea, twenty miles from

Sidon and twenty-three miles from Acre. It once consisted of two parts—a rocky coast defense of great strength on the mainland, and a city upon a small but well-protected island, about half a mile from the shore. Tyre was already a city on an island in the sea in the 14th century B. C., as we learn from an Egyptian papyrus of that date. At the time that Alexander the Great besieged Tyre for seven months, the configuration of the locality was changed, and a causeway being built, the island no longer existed. The city was spoken of as "a crowning city, whose merchants are princes, whose traffickers are the honorable of the earth" (Isa. 23:8). The Tyrian mer-

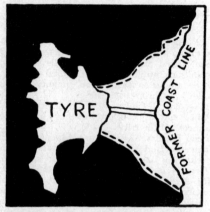

493. Alexander the Great's 650 Foot Causeway to Tyre

chants sailed to all ports and colonized almost everywhere. David early formed an alliance with them for trading purposes (II Sam. 5:11; I Kings 5:1; II Chron. 2:3). *See* Hiram; Solomon; Tarshish, Ezion-geber.

These friendly relations survived for a time the disastrous secession of the ten tribes, and a century later Ahab married a daughter of Ethbaal, the king of the Zidonians (I Kings 16: 31), who, according to Menander, was daughter of Ithobal, king of Tyre. When mercantile cupidity induced the Tyrians and the neighboring Phoenicians to buy Hebrew captives from their enemies, and to sell them as slaves to the Greeks and Edomites, there commenced denunciations and, at first, threats of retaliation (Joel 3:4-8; Amos 1:9, 10). But the likelihood of the denunciations being fulfilled first arose from the progressive conquests of the Assyrian monarchs.

Our knowledge of its condition thenceforward until the siege by Nebuchadnezzar depends entirely on various notices of it by the Hebrew prophets, who denounced the idolatry and wickedness of the city (Isa. 23:1; Jer. 25:22; Ezek., chaps. 26, 27, 28; Amos 1:9, 10; Zech. 9:2, 4). Some of these notices are singularly full, and especially the twenty-seventh chapter of Ezekiel furnishes us on some points with details such as have scarcely come down to us respecting any one city of antiquity, excepting Rome and Athens. One point especially arrests the attention, that Tyre, like its splendid daughter Carthage,

employed mercenary soldiers (Ezek. 27:10, 11). Independently, however, of this fact respecting Tyrian mercenary soldiers, Ezekiel gives interesting details respecting the trade of Tyre. It appears that its gold came from Arabia by the Persian Gulf (v. 22), just as in the time of Solomon it came from Arabia by the Red Sea.

Only thirty-four years before the destruction of Jerusalem commenced the celebrated reformation of Josiah (B. C. 622). This momentous religious revolution (II Kings, chaps. 22, 23) fully explains the exultation and malevolence of the Tyrians. In that reformation Josiah had heaped insults on the gods who were the objects of Tyrian veneration and love. Indeed, he seemed to have endeavored to exterminate their religion (23:20). These acts must have been regarded by the Tyrians as a series of sacrilegious and abominable outrages; and we can scarcely doubt that the death in battle of Josiah at Megiddo, and the subsequent destruction of the city and temple of Jerusalem were hailed by them with triumphant joy as instances of divine retribution in human affairs. This joy, however, must soon have given way to other feelings, when Nebuchadnezzar invaded Phoenicia, and laid siege to Tyre. That siege lasted thirteen years, and it is still a disputed point whether Tyre was actually taken by Nebuchadnezzar on this occasion. Alexander the Great took the island city of Tyre in 332 B. C., after a seven-month siege. Victory came only after he built a half-mile causeway out to the island. At the time our Lord visited Tyre (Matt. 15:21; Mark 7:24) it was perhaps more populous than Jerusalem. Paul spent seven days there (Acts 21:3-7). Tyre suffered violent destruction in the thirteenth century when the Moslems took it from the Crusaders. The town is in ruins now, consisting of miserable huts and people, about five thousand "impoverished Metawileh, or Persian schismatics, and Arab Christians." After the death of Stephen the Martyr, a church was formed here, and here Paul spent some time (Acts 21:3, 4), and it was early the seat of a Christian bishopric (Smith, *Bib. Dict.*).

As a great maritime trading port, the most celebrated product of Tyre, and a source of very great wealth, was the famous purple dye made from mollusks (*murex*) found on the nearby shores. Sidon was the older city (cf. Gen. 10:15; Isa. 23:12). In later centuries, however, Tyre far outstripped Sidon. Canaan-

494. General View Showing the Harbor of Tyre

ite cults, which we now know from the Ras Shamra literature of the fourteenth century B. C. to be effete and morally debasing, helped to make Tyre a profligate, self-centered, opulent and worldly-wise city. The cult of Melcarth was firmly established for many

centuries. Ezekiel denounced judgments upon the wicked city (Ezek. 28:1-19).

Ty'rus, the Greek form (*Turos*) of *Tyre* (Jer. 25:22; 27:3; 47:4; Ezek. 26:2-4, 7, 15; 27:2, 3, 8, 32; Hos. 9:13; Amos 1:9, 10; Zech. 9:2, 3).

U

U'cal (ū'kăl; *I am strong* or possibly, *consumed*), a word which occurs as a proper name in the received version of Prov. 30:1: "The man spake unto Ithiel, even unto Ithiel and Ucal." Most authorities endorse this translation, and regard these two persons as disciples of "Agur the son of Jakeh," a Hebrew teacher, whose authorship of this unique chapter has rescued his name from obscurity; but the passage is very obscure. By slightly varying the punctuation it has been translated, "I have labored for God, and have obtained" (Cocceius); "I have wearied myself for God, and have given up the investigation" (J. D. Michaelis); "I have wearied myself for God, and have fainted" (Bertheau); "I have wearied myself for God, and I became dull" (Hitzig), etc. If either of these views be correct, the repetition of the first clause of the sentence is merely for poetical effect. Bunsen, however, supposes the speaker to have given himself a symbolical name, somewhat in the manner of the English Puritans, and translates, "The saying of the man 'I-have-wearied-myself-for-God:' I have wearied myself for God, and have fainted away." Davidson, with greater accuracy, reads: "I am weary, O God, I am weary, O God, and am become weak." Ewald combines the two names into one, which he renders, "God-be-with-me-and-I-am-strong," and bestows it upon a character whom he supposes to engage in a dialogue with Agur. Keil follows Ewald's translation of the names, but disjoins them, and regards the first as typifying the reverential believers in God among Agur's disciples, and the second the self-righteous freethinkers "who thought themselves superior to the revealed law, and in practical atheism indulged the lusts of the flesh."

U'el (ū'ĕl; *will of God*), one of the sons of Bani. He is mentioned in Ezra 10:34 as one of those who "gave their hands that they would put away" their Gentile wives after the captivity, B. C. 456.

Uk'naz (ŭk'năz; the marginal reading of "even Kenaz," I Chron. 4:15), grandson of Caleb the son of Jephunneh. *See* Kenza.

U'lam (ū'lăm; perhaps, *leader, first,* cf. Arab. '*awwal, first*).

1. A son of Sheresh, and father of Bedan, of the tribe of Manasseh. Mentioned only in the genealogical record (I Chron. 7:16, 17).

2. The firstborn of Eshek, a direct descendant from Mephibosheth, the grandson of King Saul; lived about B. C. 588. His sons and grandsons, numbering one hundred and fifty, were famous as archers and "mighty men of valor" (I Chron. 8:39, 40).

Ul'la (ŭl'ȧ; I Chron. 7:39), a descendant of Asher, and father of three of the "chief of the princes" of the tribe.

Uncial Letters. *See* Scripture, Manuscripts of.

Uncircumcised (Heb. '*ārēl, exposed;* Gr. '*akrobustia*) is used figuratively, for a *heathen* (Gen. 34:14; Judg. 14:3; 15:18; I Sam. 14:6; Jer. 9:26; Rom. 4:9; I Cor. 7:18, etc.); "of uncircumcised lips" (Exod. 6:12, 30) means one whose lips are, as it were, covered with a foreskin, so that he cannot easily bring out his words, "slow of speech" (4:10); "of uncircumcised ears" (Jer. 6:10; Acts 7:51) are those whose ears are closed with a foreskin, i. e., closed to the prophet's testimony by their impure heart; "uncircumcised in heart" (Lev. 26:41; Ezek. 44:9; Acts 7:51; comp. James 1:21; Col. 2:13) are those who are in an impure, God-offending state of nature (Jer. 4:4, "take away the foreskins of your hearts"). The "uncircumcised tree" was the one under three years of age, whose fruit by the law was treated as unclean (Lev. 19:23).

Unclean, Uncleanness. Although sin has its origin and its proper seat in the soul, it pervades the whole body as the soul's organ, bringing about the body's dissolution in death and decomposition. Its effects have spread from man to the whole of the earthly creation, because, as having dominion over nature, he has brought nature with him into the service of sin. God has also made the irrational creature subject to "vanity" and "corruption" on account of man's sin (Rom. 8:20, 21). "It is in this penetration of sin into the material creation that we may find the explanation of the fact that from the very earliest times men have neither used every kind of herb nor every kind of animal as food; but that, while they have, as it were, instinctively avoided certain plants as injurious to health or destructive to life, they have also had a *horror naturalis* (i. e., an inexplicable disgust) at many of the animals, and have avoided their flesh as unclean. A similar horror must have been produced upon man from the very first, before his heart was altogether hardened by death as the wages of sin, or rather by the effects of death, viz., the decomposition of the body; and different diseases and states of the body, that were connected with symptoms of corruption and decomposition, may also have been regarded as rendering unclean. Hence, in all nations and all the religion of antiquity, we find that contrast between clean and unclean, which was developed in a dualistic form, it is true, in many of the religious systems, but had its primary root in the corruption that had entered the world through sin" (K. and D., *Com.*, on Lev., ch. 11).

This contrast between *clean* and *unclean* was limited by Moses to three particulars: (1) Food; (2) contact with dead bodies, human and animal; (3) bodily conditions and diseases. The law pointed out most minutely the unclean objects and various defilements within these spheres, and prescribed the means for avoiding or removing them. In this article the subject will be treated as follows: (1) Causes of uncleanness; (2) disabilities of uncleanness; (3) purification from uncleanness.

1. Causes of Uncleanness. (1) **Food.** Certain articles of diet were prohibited as conducing to uncleanness. These were things strangled or dead of themselves, or through beasts or birds of prey; whatever beast did not both part the hoof and chew the cud; and certain other smaller animals rated as "creeping things;" certain classes of birds mentioned in Lev., ch. 11, and Deut., ch. 14, twenty or twenty-one in all; whatever in the waters had not both fins and scales; whatever winged insect had not besides four legs, the two hind legs for leaping; besides things offered in sacrifice to idols; and all blood, or whatever contained it (save, perhaps, the blood of fish, as would appear from that only of beast and bird being forbidden, Lev. 7:26), and, therefore, flesh cut from the live animal; as also all fat, at any rate that disposed in masses among the intestines, and probably wherever discernible and separable among the flesh (3:13-17; 7: 23). The eating of blood was prohibited even to "the stranger that sojourneth among you" (17:10, 12:14). Besides these, we find the prohibition against "seething a kid in its mother's milk" (Exod. 23:19; 34:26; Deut. 14:21). Thus it will be seen that all animals are unclean which bear the image of sin, of death, and corruption, e. g., all larger land animals, all ravenous beasts which lie in wait for life or tear and devour the living; all winged creatures, not only birds of prey, but also marsh birds and others, which live on worms, carrion, and all sorts of impurities; all serpentlike fishes and slimy shellfish, and small creeping things, except some kinds of locusts, "because, partly, they recall the old serpent, partly they seek their food in all sorts of impurities, partly they crawl in the dust and represent corruption in the slimy character of their bodies" (Keil, *Bib. Arch.*, ii, 117, 118).

(2) **Defilement by death.** The dead body of a human being, no matter whether he had been killed (Num. 19:16, 18; 31:19) or had died a natural death, had the effect of rendering unclean for seven days the tent (or house) in which the man had died, and any open

vessels that were in it, as well as the persons who lived in it or happened to enter it. It was equally defiling to touch the body of anyone who had died in the open air, or even to touch a dead man's bones or a grave. When thus defiled the uncleanness was not confined to himself, but extended to everything he touched, and everyone that touched him, and such were unclean till evening (19:22).

The carcass of any animal, clean or unclean, defiled everyone who touched, carried, or ate it, until the evening, so that he was required to bathe himself in water and wash his clothes before he became clean again (Lev. 11:24-28, 31, 36, 39, 40; 17:15). But it was no more defiling to touch clean animals slaughtered by men, and unclean animals that had been killed by them, than it was to touch unclean animals while still alive. Eight kinds of the smaller animals (Heb. *sĕhrĕs*, a *swarm*), viz., the weasel, mouse, and six of the lizard species, that communicated their defiling influence to inanimate objects, such as pots for cooking, if they or any part of their carcasses happened to fall upon them, such earthen vessels as any of them dropped into, and, lastly, food in the preparation of which water had been used that had been thus contaminated, or seed that had been wet with such polluted water (11:32-37).

(3) **Defilement by bodily conditions and diseases.** (*a*) Leprosy (*q. v.*), either in connection with persons, dwellings, or fabrics (Lev., chaps. 13, 14). (*b*) The discharge of seminal fluid, whether of an involuntary character (as during sleep or in dreams), or such as occurred during sexual intercourse. Both alike constituted the man, and, in the latter case, the woman also unclean till evening (15:16-18). (*c*) The flux; whether the catamenial discharge of the woman, the morbid issue of blood in a woman, or the flux in men, i. e., the discharge of mucus from the urethra (Num. 5:2). (*d*) Childbirth. Contact with persons in the above states, or even with clothing or furniture that had been used by them while in those states, involved uncleanness in a minor degree (Lev. 15:5-11, 21-24).

2. Disabilities of Uncleanness. Defilement by contact with a dead human body rendered the person or object unclean for seven days. Defilement from the carcass of an animal made the person or object unclean until evening. The leper was required to rend his clothes, to bare his head, and put a covering upon his upper lip, and then to cry to everyone he met, "Unclean; unclean;" and, besides this, he had to isolate himself by living outside the camp (or city) (Lev. 13:45, sq.; Num. 5:2; 12:10, 14, sq.). Houses affected with leprosy were examined by the priest, who, before entering, had all the contents of the house removed in order to prevent everything within from becoming unclean. If symptoms of leprosy were discovered the house was closed for seven days. After seven days the house was again examined, and if indications of leprosy were evident, the affected stones were removed, with the scrapings of the walls, and carefully replastered. If the evil broke out anew, the house was pronounced unclean, pulled down, and removed to an unclean place outside the city. Leprosy in clothes or fabrics made of linen, wool, or leather, required that the article should be shut up for seven days, and if still affected it was burned (Lev. 13:47-59). Persons or objects defiled by the discharge of seminal fluid were unclean until evening; persons defiled by a flux were removed from the camp (Num. 5:2); the menstruous woman was considered unclean for seven days, as well as the man who might have intercourse with her at this time; everything on which she lay or sat was unclean until evening (Lev. 15:19-24). A man or woman with an issue was unclean as long as the disorder lasted, and also rendered unclean anything upon which they sat or laid, or the person whom they might touch, and in the case of the man anyone upon whom his spittle might come (15:25-29); the woman at childbirth became unclean just as at the time of her courses, and that for seven days at the birth of a boy, and fourteen if it was a girl, besides being obliged to remain at home in the blood of her purifying for thirty-three days more in the former case and sixty-six in the latter, and was debarred from touching anything holy and from coming to the sanctuary (12:2-8).

3. **Purification from Uncleanness.** The regulations with respect to defilements and their corresponding purifications were not prescriptions framed with a view to the cultivation of cleanliness, tidiness, and decency—not merely sanitary regulations—but they were of a religious nature, having as their object the cultivation of holiness and spiritual life. It was owing to the well-understood connection between defilements on the one hand and sin and its consequence, *death*, on the other, that the Levitical purification ranked side by side with the sacrifices; and that they formed, quite as much as these latter, an integral part of the Mosaic ritual. The term "purification," in its legal and technical sense, is applied to the ritual observances whereby an Israelite was formally absolved from the taint of uncleanness, whether evidenced by any overt act or state, or whether connected with man's natural depravity.

The following regulations respecting purification are given in the law:

(1) **Of those defiled by contact with the dead.** The medium appointed in such cases was a kind of sprinkling water, composed of running water and the ashes of a sin offering specially suited to the occasion (Num., ch. 19). A heifer, without blemish, and which had never been yoked, was slaughtered without the camp, Eleazar dipping his finger in the blood and sprinkling it seven times toward the sanctuary. The heifer, entire, was then burned in the presence of the priest, who cast cedar wood, hyssop, and the scarlet wool into the flames. The ashes were then carried by a man free from defilement to a clean place outside the camp, where they were stored for use as occasion might require. A man free from defilement took some of these ashes, put them into a vessel, and then poured some fresh running water over them. Dipping a bunch of hyssop into the mixture, he sprinkled it upon the person to be purified, both on the third and the seventh day. On the latter day, after

atonement had been made, the person being purified was required to wash his clothes and bathe himself in water, after which he became clean on the evening of that day. The tent in which the corpse had lain, as well as the furniture that it contained, were all sprinkled with this same water and were thus purified (vers. 12, 17-19).

(2) **Of those recovered from leprosy.** The ceremonial for the purifications is based upon the idea that this malady is the bodily symbol not so much of sin as of death. "As being a decomposing of the juices of the body, as a putrefying and dropping off of its members, as being the presence of corruption in the living body, leprosy forms the counterpart of death. . . . Consequently the person affected with this disease was required to display the tokens of his intimate association with death in the kind of dress he wore, in his shaved head, and in his rent garments; and hence it was, too, that he was excluded not merely from the pale of the sanctuary, but was even debarred from all intercourse whatever with the covenant people, called as it was to be a holy nation" (Keil, *Bib. Arch.*, i, 393).

The rites are described in Lev. 14:4-32. The two stages of the proceedings indicated—the first, which took place outside the camp, the readmission of the leper to the community of men; the second, before the sanctuary, his readmission to communion with God. In the first stage the slaughter of the one bird and the dismissal of the other symbolized the punishment of death deserved and fully remitted. In the second, the use of oil and its application to the same parts of the body, as in the consecration of priests (8:23, 24), symbolized the rededication of the leper to the service of Jehovah. The ceremonies to be observed in the purification of a house or a garment infected with leprosy were identical with the first stage of the proceedings used for the leper (14:33-53).

(3) **Of those defiled by sexual discharges.** Such purification was, in every instance, effected by bathing the body and washing the objects defiled in running water, the purifying medium of nature's own providing. If, however, the state of defilement lasted longer than seven days, as in the case of those suffering from an issue of blood, a discharge of mucus from the urethra, or childbirth, then a sin offering and a burnt offering were added to the washing with water. These were offered at a certain period after the healing and the washing—those suffering from an issue of blood or a mucus discharge, and the leper after his first cleansing, at seven days; while in the case of childbirth it was thirty-three or sixty-six days. In those cases where the defilement lasted over a week communion with the Lord could only be secured by the offering of a sin offering (of a pigeon) and a burnt offering (a lamb).

The necessity of purification was extended in the post-Babylonian period to a variety of unauthorized cases. Cups and pots, brazen vessels and couches were washed as a matter of ritual observance (Mark 7:4). The washing of the hands before meals was conducted in a formal manner (v. 3), and minute regulations are laid down on this subject in a treatise of the Mishna entitled *Yadaim*. What may have been the specific causes of uncleanness in those who came up to purify themselves before the passover (John 11:55), or in those who had taken upon themselves the Nazarite's vow (Acts 21:24, 26), we are not informed; in either case it may have been contact with a corpse, though in the latter it would rather appear to have been a general purification preparatory to the accomplishment of the vow. In conclusion it may be observed that the distinctive feature in the Mosaic rites of purification is their expiatory character. The idea of uncleanness was not peculiar to the Jew. But with all other nations simple ablution sufficed—no sacrifices were demanded. The Jew alone was taught, by the use of expiatory offerings, to discern, to its full extent the connection, between the outward sign and the inward fount of impurity.

Unction (Gr. *chrisma*, ointment, anointing), the gift of the Holy Spirit as an efficient aid in getting a knowledge of the truth (I John 2: 20). Not that the work of Jesus was imperfect, but the Spirit helps us to understand the truth he taught, and thus to glorify him (John 16:14), in whom the full revelation of God had been given (v. 15).

Undefiled (Heb. *tăm*, complete), one who is sound in a moral sense, as the pious man (Psa. 119:1); or, as in Cant. 5:2; 6:9, of a bride who is innocent of connection with another than her spouse. In the New Testament "undefiled" is the rendering of the Greek *'amiantos, not defiled*, i. e., free from that by which the nature of a thing is deformed or its force and vigor impaired. Thus Jesus was undefiled (Heb. 7:26), i. e., pure from sin. "The bed undefiled" (13:4) is one free from adultery. A religion that is sincere and clean (James 1:27), and the inheritance provided for the just (I Pet. 1:4), are "undefiled."

Undergirding. See Ship.

Undersetters (Heb. *käthēp*, a shoulder, usually so rendered) were parts of the laver (*q. v.*) in Solomon's temple, probably props running up from the body of the vehicle and holding the basin between them.

Unicorn. See Animal Kingdom.

Unity (Heb. *yăhăd*, adverb *unitedly*) is used to signify a oneness of sentiment, affection, or behavior, such as should exist among the people of God (Psa. 133:1). The "unity of the faith" (Eph. 4:13, Gr. *henotēs*, oneness) is the unanimity of belief in the same great truths of God, and the possession of the grace of faith in a similar form and degree.

Unknown God (Gr. *'agnōstos theos*, unknown god), the inscription observed by Paul upon an altar in Athens (Acts 17:23), which he ingeniously adduces in his speech before the people as an instance of their religiousness. This was not addressed to the philosophers; they did not dedicate altars to an unknown god, but regarded all such proceedings as the mere superstition of the vulgar. Pausanius (i, 1, 4) and Philostratus (*Vit. Appolon.*, vi, 2) both mention "unknown gods," and it is evident from both passages that at Athens there were *several* altars so inscribed. "It is related

that Epimenides put an end to a plague in Athens by causing black and white sheep, which he had let loose on the Areopagus, to be sacrificed on the spots where they lay down, *to the god concerned*, yet not known by name, viz., who was the author of the plague; and that therefore one may find in Athens *altars without the designation of a god by name*. From this particular instance the general view may be derived, *that on important occasions, when the reference to a god known by name was wanting, as in public calamities of which no definite god could be assigned as the author, in order to honor or propitiate the god concerned by sacrifice, without lighting upon a wrong one, altars were erected which were destined and designated 'agnōsto theō* (unknown god)" (Meyer, *Com.*).

Unknown Tongue (I Cor. 14:2, 4, 13, 14, 19, 27) is a gloss of the A. V., for the Greek has simply *glōssa* (a *tongue*), and obviously a different language from that usually employed by the speaker (Mark 16:17; Acts 2:4).

Unlearned (Gr. *'agrammatos, unlettered*), illiterate, without learning (Acts 4:13), while elsewhere "unlearned" is the rendering of *'amathēs* (II Pet. 3:16), *without knowledge; 'apaideutos* (II Tim. 2:23), *without instruction, rude, uneducated; idiōtēs*, (I Cor. 14:16, 23, 24), a *private* person, i. e., an *unlearned, illiterate* man as opposed to the learned.

Unleavened Bread (Heb. *măṣṣăh, sweet;* Gr. *'azumos*), bread baked from unfermented dough (Gen. 19:3; Judg. 6:19; I Sam. 28:24). This was formally presented for the paschal cakes (Exod. 12:8, 15, 20; 13:3, 6, sq.), and thus become a symbol of the festival popularly called "the feast of unleavened bread" *q. v.*). See Leaven.

Un'ni (ŭ'nī; *afflicted* or perhaps, *answered*).

1. A relative of Heman the singer, who with other Levites was appointed, by order of King David, to perform on the psaltery in the tabernacle service (I Chron. 15:18, 20), B. C. about 986.

2. A Levite employed in the musical service of the temple after the return from captivity (Neh. 12:9), B. C. 535. This name should be written Unno.

Untempered Mortar (Heb. *tăphēl*, the plaster coating or cement of a wall, probably from the primary meaning of *tăphăl*, to *stick* or *plaster* over, from which has sprung the secondary meaning of *weak, insipid*. The meaning of the figure "to daub with untempered mortar" (Ezek. 13:10, 11, 14, 15; 22:28) is, "the people build up foolish hopes, and the prophets not only paint these hopes for them in splendid colors, but even predict their fulfillment, instead of denouncing their folly . . . The plastering is therefore a figurative desdription of deceitful flattery or hypocrisy" (Keil, *Com.*).

Uphar'sin (û-fär'sĭn). See Mene.

U'phaz (ū'făz), the name of a famous gold region (Jer. 10:9; Dan. 10:5), is thought by many to be a corruption of Ophir (*q. v.*); but Orelli (*Com.*, on Jer. 10:9) says: "It is inconceivable that the word arose by error from this well-known name. Assyria and Babylon might have other gold mines. Still the views respecting the site of this Uphaz remain mere conjectures."

Upper Chamber or **Room** (Heb. *'ăliyäh, lofty;* II Kings 1:2; 23:12; I Chron. 28:11; II Chron. 3:9; "summer parlor," Judg. 3:23; "loft," I Kings 19:17, 23; "chamber over the gate," II Sam 18:23; Gr. *'anōgeon,* Mark 14:15; Luke 22:12; *huperōon, upper,* Acts 1:13; 9:37, 39; 20:8), a room in the upper part of the house, used to receive company, hold feasts, to retire for meditation and prayer (Mark 14:15; Luke 22:12). Among the Hebrews it seems to have been on or connected with the flat roofs of their dwellings; in Greek houses it occupied the upper story (I Kings 17:19, sq.; II Kings 4:10; Acts 1:13; 9:37, 39; 10:9; 20:8). Rich, luxurious men were charged with sinfully multiplying chambers of this sort (Jer. 22:13, 14). They were used as "summer houses for their coolness" (Judg. 3:20; II Kings 1:2; 23:12). In Scripture the lower portion was the winter house, the upper room was the summer house; or, if on the same story, the outer apartment is the summer house, the inner is the winter house.

Ur of the Chaldees, Abraham's native city in southern Babylonia, not very far from the ancient city of Uruk to the N. E. and Eridu to the S. W. Modern excavation of the city began in 1854 with J. E. Taylor. The city was then only a ruined site named the Mound of Bitumen (Arabic *al muqayyar*). In 1918 H. R. Hall resumed excavations. Sir Leonard Woolley conducted excavations in 1922f. The famous royal cemeteries, dating c. 2500 B. C., yielded jewelry and art treasures of unbelievable beauty, particularly gorgeous head attire, personal jewels and a golden tumbler and cup of Queen Shubad. The Hebrew Bible is quite clear in its statements that Abraham's home was originally in Lower Mesopotamia in the city of Ur and that he emigrated to Haran and Upper Mesopotamia on his way to Canaan (Gen. 11:28-31; 12:1-4;

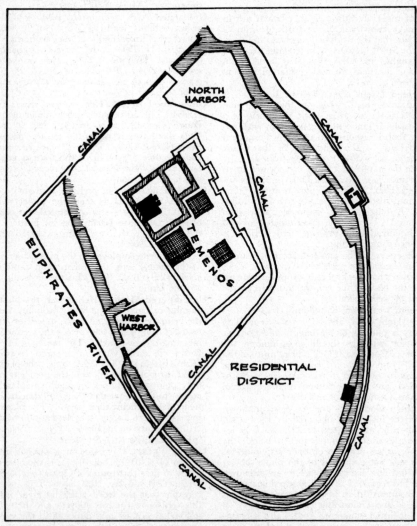

495. Ur in the Abrahamic Age, Showing Temenos Area and Harbors of the Busy Emporium on the Euphrates River

15:7; Neh. 9:7). Interestingly enough, Ur in connection with Abraham is referred to as "Ur of the Chaldees" (Chaldeans). The qualifying phrase "of the Chaldeans" is not an anachronism, as many critics contend (cf.

496. Gold Vessels from Queen Shubad's Tomb, ca. 2500 B.C.

Jack Finegan, *Light From the Ancient East*, p. 57, note 28). It is rather an instance of numerous archaic place names being defined by a later scribal gloss to make clear to a subsequent age where and what these places were, when their history and locality had been forgotten. The Chaldeans came into southern Babylonia after 1000 B. C. It was, of course, quite natural for the Hebrew scribe to define the then incomprehensible foreign name by a term intelligible to his own day. As a result of archaeological excavation, the city of Ur is now one of the best-known sites of southern Babylonia. Woolley in his *Abraham: Recent Discoveries and Hebrew Origins*, (London, 1936, pp. 72-117) gives us a description of the worship of the city god of Ur, the moon god, Nannar, and his consort Ningal. Woolley describes in minute detail the sacred *temenos* of

497. Pottery from Tell el-Obeid near Abraham's City of Ur in Lower Mesopotamia

the city in which were the famous ziggurat and the various buildings erected to the moon god and his consort, with a description of the moon god ritual. It is now possible to have a far clearer idea of Abraham's surroundings when "the God of glory" appeared unto him when he was yet in Ur before he dwelt in Haran (Acts 7:2). "The God of glory appeared unto our father Abraham when he was in Mesopotamia, before he dwelt in Haran."

498. Marduk, Identified as the Sun-god, in Tramat and Before Ea, the Water-god (from Ur)

Archaeology has revealed that in Abraham's day Ur was a great and prosperous city. The Biblical chronology as preserved in the Massoretic Text, would place the life of Abraham at least in part, under the new Sumero-Akkadian Empire of Ur-Nammu, the founder of the strong Third Dynasty of Ur (c. 2070-1960 B. C.) (*See* Abraham). These famous kings took the new title "king of Sumer and Akkad." The greatest work of Ur-Nammu was the erection of the great ziggurat at Ur, upon which Abraham gazed as did Joseph upon the pyramids in Egypt. Happily, the ziggurat at Ur is the best preserved type of this characteristic architectural feature of early Babylonia. The resurrection of Ur offers a fine example of archaeology's increasing ability to illustrate ancient Biblical history.—*M. F. U.*

Ur (*ūr; light*), mentioned in I Chron. 11:35, as the father of Eliphal, one of David's "valiant men," B. C. before 1000. There is evident confusion at this point in the genealogical list, both here and in the parallel passage (II Sam. 23:34). Hepher must either be regarded as another name for Ur, or else omitted as an error in copying. The phrase "the son of" should be erased from II Sam. 23:34, and Ahasbai and Ur might then be identified.

499. A Goddess of Abraham's Day

Ur'bane (ûr'bān; *urbane, polite, of the city;* Gr. from Lat. Urbanus, ûr-bä'nŭs), a Christian at Rome to whom Paul sent salutations, as having been his associate in labor, "our helper in Christ" (Rom. 16:9).

U'ri (ū'rī; an abbreviation of Urijah) (*q. v.*).

1. The father of Bezaleel, one of the architects of the tabernacle. He was of the tribe of Judah, and son of Hur (Exod. 31:2; 35:30; 38:22; I Chron. 2:20; II Chron. 1:5), B. C. before 1440.

2. The father of Geber, Solomon's purveying officer in Gilead (I Kings 4:19), B. C. before 960.

3. One of the temple porters who put away his Gentile wife after the exile (Ezra 10:24), B. C. 456.

Uri'ah (û-rī'à; *Jehovah is light*).

1. One of David's heroes (I Chron. 11:41; II Sam. 23:39), and husband of Bath-sheba. He was a Hittite. His name, however, and his manner of speech (II Sam. 11:11) indicate that he had adopted the Jewish religion. He married Bath-sheba, a woman of extraordinary beauty, the daughter of Eliam. The time of the illicit intercourse between David and his wife, Uriah was in camp with Joab; but when the king was informed by Bath-sheba that she was with child by him, he ordered Uriah to come to Jerusalem, on the pretext of asking news of the war—really in the hope that his return to his wife might cover the shame of his own crime. The king met with an unexpected obstacle in the austere, soldier-like spirit which guided all Uriah's conduct, and which gives us a high notion of the character and discipline of David's officers. On the morning of the third day David sent him back to the camp with a letter containing the command to Joab to cause his destruction in the battle. The device of Joab was to observe the part of the wall of Rabbath-Ammon where the greatest force of the besieged was congregated, and thither, as a kind of forlorn hope, to send Uriah. A sally took place. Uriah and the officers with him advanced as far as the gate of the city, and were there shot down by the archers on the wall. Just as Joab had forewarned the messenger, the king broke into a furious passion on hearing of the loss. The messenger, as instructed by Joab, calmly continued, and ended the story with the words: "Thy servant Uriah the Hittite is dead also." (II Sam. 11:24), B. C. about 980.

2. A priest in the reign of Ahaz, who is introduced in Scripture history as a witness to Isaiah's prophecy concerning Maher-shalal-hashbaz (Isa. 8:2), B. C. about 735. He is perhaps the same as Urijah, the priest who built the idolatrous altar for King Ahaz (II Kings 16:10, sq., "Urijah"). He was probably high priest at the time, succeeding to Azariah, who was high priest in the reign of Uzziah, and was succeeded by that Azariah who was high priest in the reign of Hezekiah. Hence it is likely that he was son of the former and father of the latter.

3. A priest of the family of Hakkoz (A. V., "Koz"), who supported Ezra while reading the law to the people ("Urijah," Neh. 8:4), B. C. 457. He is probably the same as the father of Meremoth (Ezra 8:33; Neh. 3:4, 21).

Uri'as (ū-rī'às), the Greek form of *Uriah*, the husband of Bath-sheba (Matt. 1:6).

U'riel (ū'rĭ-ĕl; *God is light*).

1. A Levite of the family of Kohath. His father's name was Uzziah (I Chron. 6:24).

2. Chief of the Kohathites, who assisted, with one hundred and twenty of his brethren, in bringing the ark from the house of Obed-edom (I Chron. 15:5, 11), B. C. about 992.

3. Uriel of Gibeah was the father of Maachah, or Michaiah, wife of Rehoboam, and mother of Abijah (II Chron. 13:2), B. C. before 930. In 11:20 she is called the daughter (granddaughter) of Absalom.

Uri'jah (û-rī'jà). 1. (II Kings 16:10, sq.) *See* Uriah, 2.

2. Neh. 3:4, 21. *See* Uriah, 3.

3. The son of Shemaiah of Kirjath-jearim, who prophesied in the days of Jehoiakim. When the king sought his death he fled to Egypt, but his retreat was soon discovered. Elnathan brought him to Jehoiakim, who put him to death, and cast his body among the graves of the common people (Jer. 26:20-23), B. C. about 609.

U'rim (ū'rĭm) **and Thum'mim** (thŭm'ĭm; *lights* and *perfections*). Into the breastplate of the high priest (*q. v.*) were placed "the Urim and the Thummim; and they shall be upon Aaron's heart, when he goeth before the Lord" (Exod. 28:30). These formed the medium through which the high priest ascertained the will of Jehovah in regard to any important matter affecting the theocracy (Num. 27:21). Even such early writers as Josephus, Philo, and the Rabbins are unable to furnish any precise information as to what the Urim and Thummim really were. On every side we meet with confessions of ignorance.

1. **Meaning of the Words.** In *Urim* Hebrew scholars, with hardly an exception, have seen the plural of *ur* (light or fire). The LXX. translators, however, appear to have had reasons which led them to another rendering. The literal English equivalent would of course be "lights;" but the renderings in the LXX. and Vulg. indicate, at least, a traditional belief among the Jews that the plural form did not involve numerical plurality. *Thummim.* Here also there is almost a consensus as to the derivation from *tôm* (perfection, completeness). What has been said as to the plural of Urim applies here also. "Light and Perfection" would probably be the best English equivalent. The mere phrase, as such, leaves it therefore uncertain whether each word by itself denoted many things of a given kind, or whether the two taken together might be referred to two distinct objects, or to one and the same object. In Deut. 33:8 we have separately, "Thy Thummim and thy Urim," the first order being inverted. Urim is found alone in Num. 27:21; I Sam. 28:6; Thummim never by itself, unless we find it in Psa. 16:5.

2. **Scripture References.** The first reference (Exod. 28:30) to these objects would seem to indicate that they needed no explanation. Inside the breastplate, as the tables of the covenant were placed inside the ark (25:16; 28:30), are to be placed "the Urim and the Thummim," the Light and the Perfection; and they, too, are to be on Aaron's

heart when he goes in before the Lord (28: 15-30). Not a word describes them. They are mentioned as things already familiar both to Moses and the people, connected naturally with the functions of the high priest, as mediating between Jehovah and his people. The command is fulfilled (Lev. 8:8). They pass from Aaron to Eleazar with the sacred ephod and other *pontificalia* (Num. 20:28). They are mentioned again (Num. 27:21; Deut. 33:8, 9). Once, and once only, are they mentioned by name in the history of the Judges and the monarchy (I Sam. 28:6). There is no longer a priest with Urim and Thummim (Ezra 2:63; Neh. 7:65) to answer hard questions.

3. **Theories.** Some think the Urim and Thummim to have been identical with the twelve stones on the breastplate. Josephus (*Ant.*, iii, 7, 5) identifies them with the sardonyxes on the shoulders of the ephod, and says that they were bright before a victory, or when the sacrifice was acceptable, dark when any disaster was impending. "Another theory is that in the middle of the ephod, or within its folds, there was a stone or plate of gold, on which was engraved the sacred name of Jehovah; and that by virtue of this, fixing his gaze on it, or reading an invocation which was also engraved with the name, or standing in his ephod before the mercy seat, or at least before the veil of the sanctuary, he became capable of prophesying, hearing the divine voice within, or listening to it as it proceeded in articulate sounds from the glory of the Shekinah."

Michaelis (*Laws of Moses*, v, 52) gives his own opinion that the Urim and Thummim were three stones, on one of which was written Yes, on another No, while the third was left neutral or blank. These were used as lots, and the high priest decided according as the one or the other was drawn out. Kalisch (on Exod. 28:31) identifies the Urim and the Thummim with the twelve tribal gems, looks on the name as one to be explained by an hendiadys (light and perfection — perfect illumination), and believes the high priest, by concentrating his thoughts on the attributes they represented, to have divested himself of all selfishness and prejudice, and so to have passed into a true prophetic state. The process of consulting Jehovah by Urim and Thummim is not given in Scripture.

Usury (Heb. *nĕshĕk*, a *biting*, i. e., *extortion;* Gr. *tokos*, a *yield*) is used in the A. V. in the sense of *interest* for money, and does not necessarily imply the demand for exorbitant increase. According to the Mosaic law the Israelites were forbidden to take usury from their brethren upon the loan of money, food, or anything else, i. e., they were not upon the return of the loan to demand anything more (Lev. 25:36, 37; Deut. 23:19, 20, etc.); although interest might be taken from foreigners (ver. 20). The Israelites not being a commercial people, money was not often loaned for the purpose of business, but rather to aid the struggling poor. This last is the only kind of usury forbidden in the law, and the avoiding of this is sometimes given among the characteristics of the godly man (Psa. 15:5; Jer. 15:10; comp. Prov. 28:8).

The practice of mortgaging lands, sometimes at exorbitant interest, grew up among the Jews during the captivity, in direct violation of the law (Lev. 25:36; Ezek. 18:8, 13, 17); and Nehemiah exacted an oath to insure its discontinuance (Neh. 5:3-13). Jesus denounced all extortion, and promulgated a new law of love and forbearance (Luke 6:30, 35). The taking of usury in the sense of a reasonable rate of interest for the use of money employed in trade is different, and is nowhere forbidden; and is referred to in the New Testament as a perfectly understood and allowable practice (Matt. 25:27; Luke 19:23).

U'thai (ū'thī).

1. The son of Ammihud, of the children of Pharez, the son of Judah. He resided at Jerusalem after the return from Babylon (I Chron. 9:4).

2. One of the sons of Bigvai, who returned with seventy males in the second caravan with Ezra (Ezra 8:14), B. C. about 457.

Uz (ŭz) once Huz (Gen. 22:21).

1. A son of Aram (Gen. 10:23; I Chron. 1:17), and a grandson of Shem.

2. A son of Nahor, by Milcah (Gen. 22:21, A. V., *Huz*).

3. A son of Dishan, and grandson of Seir (Gen. 36:28).

4. The land of Uz was the country in which Job lived (Job 1:1). The LXX. renders *en chōra rē 'Aisitidi*; and Ptolemy (v, 19, 2) says that the Aisitai, i. e., the Uzzites, dwelt in the Arabian desert, west from Babylon, under the Caucabenes, and adjacent to the Edomites of Mount Seir, who at one period occupied Uz, probably as conquerors (Lam. 4:21). The position of the country may further be deduced from the native lands of Job's friends —Eliphaz, the Temanite, being an Idumaean; Elihu, the Buzite, probably a neighbor of the Chaldeans; and Bildad, the Shuhite, being one of the Bene-Kedem. "The land of Uz" is mentioned in only two other passages of Scripture; grouped by Jeremiah (25:20) with Egypt, Philistia, Edom, and Moab, but in Lam. 4:21 identifying it with a portion of Edom, or affirming that some of the Edomites in his day inhabited Uz.

U'zai (ū'zī), the father of Palal, one of those who assisted in rebuilding the walls of Jerusalem (Neh. 3:25), B. C. before 447.

U'zal (ū'zăl; derivation uncertain), the sixth of the thirteen sons of Joktan, a descendant of Shem (Gen. 10:27; I Chron. 1:21). Authorities quite generally agree that Sanaa, the metropolis of Yemen, is the modern name of the Uzal founded by this person.

Uz'za (ŭz'à; *strength*).

1. The proprietor, apparently, of (or the person after whom was named) the garden in which Manasseh and Amon were buried (II Kings 21:18, 26), B. C. before 643.

2. I Chron. 6:29. See Uzzah, 2.

3. The older of the two sons of Ehud the Benjamite, born to him after the removal of his former children (I Chron. 8:7).

4. The "children of Uzza" were a family of Nethinim who returned with Zerubbabel (Ezra 2:49; Neh. 7:51), B. C. before 536.

Uz'zah (ŭz'á; *strength*).

1. One of the sons of Abinadab of Kirjath-jearim. He, with his brother Ahio, accompanied the ark when David sought to remove it to Jerusalem. When the procession had reached the threshing floor of Nachon the oxen drawing the cart upon which the ark was placed stumbled. Uzzah, who was walking beside it, put out his hand to prevent its falling. He died immediately, being smitten by God on account of his offense. The event produced a profound sensation, and David, fearing to carry the ark any farther, had it placed in the house of Obed-edom (II Sam. 6:3-10; I Chron. 13:7, 9, 11), B. C. about 988.

NOTE—Why was Uzzah so severely punished? is a question variously answered. We think the following answer correct: "According to Num., ch. 4, the ark was not only to be moved by none but Levites, but it was to be carried on the shoulders; and in v. 15 even the Levites were expressly forbidden to touch it on pain of death. But instead of taking these instructions as their rule, they had followed the example of the Philistines when they sent back the ark (I Sam. 6:7, sq.), and had placed it upon a new cart and directed Uzzah to drive it, while, as his conduct on the occasion clearly shows, he had no idea of the unapproachable holiness of the ark of God, and had to expiate his offense with his life, as a warning to all the Israelites" (K. and D., *Com.*, in loc.).

2. A Levite of the sons of Merari, the son of Shimei, and father of Shimea (I Chron. 6:29).

Uz'zen-she'rah (ŭz'ĕn-shē'rá), a place near Beth-horon, founded or rebuilt by Sherah, an Ephraimitess (I Chron. 7:24), and probably an heiress who had received these places as her inheritance. The place Uzzen-Sherah, is not elsewhere referred to. R. V. Uzzen-she'erah.

Uz'zi (ŭz'ī; *strong*).

1. Son of Bukki, and father of Zerahiah, in the line of the high priests (I Chron. 6:5, 51; Ezra 7:4). Josephus (*Ant.*, v, 11, 5) relates that after Ozi (Uzzi), of the family of Eleazar, Eli, of the family of Ithamar, received the high priesthood. But the circumstances that led to the transfer of this honor are unknown.

2. Son of Tola, the son of Issachar (I Chron. 7:2, 3).

3. Son of Bela, of the tribe of Benjamin (I Chron. 7:7).

4. The son of Michri and father of Elah, among the ancestors of a Benjamite house which settled at Jerusalem after the return from captivity (I Chron. 9:8), B. C. before 536.

5. A Levite, son of Bani, and overseer of the Levites dwelling at Jerusalem in the time of Nehemiah (Neh. 11:22), B. C. 536.

6. A priest, chief of the course of Jedaiah, in the time of Joiakim the high priest (Neh. 12:19). He is probably the same as one of the priests who assisted Ezra in the dedication of the wall of Jerusalem (12:42), B. C. about 500.

Uzzi'a (ŭ-zī'á; probably for *Uzziah*), the "Ashterathite" (i. e., from Ashtaroth, beyond Jordan), who was one of David's warriors (I Chron. 11:44), B. C. after 1000.

Uzzi'ah (ŭ-zī'á; *Jehovah is strength*).

1. The tenth king of Judah.

(1) **Name and family.** In some passages his name appears in the lengthened form Azariah, which Gesenius attributes to an error of the copyists. This is possible, but there are other instances of the princes of Judah changing their names on succeeding to the throne. His father was Amaziah, who was slain by conspirators.

(2) **History.** 1. *Chosen king.* After the murder of Amaziah, his son Uzziah was chosen by the people to occupy the vacant throne at the age of sixteen (II Kings 14:21), B. C. 783. 2. *Wars.* He began his reign by a successful expedition against his father's enemies, the Edomites, who had revolted from Judah in Jehoram's time, eighty years before, and penetrated as far as the head of the Gulf of Akaba, where he took the important place of Elath (II Kings 14:22; II Chron. 26:1, etc.). Uzziah waged other victorious wars in the south, especially against the Mehunim, or people of Maân, and the Arabs of Gurbaal. Toward the west Uzziah fought with equal success against the Philistines, leveled to the ground the walls of Gath, Jabneh, and Ashdod, and founded new fortified cities in the Philistine territory. 3. *Reign.* Uzziah strengthened the walls of Jerusalem, and was a great patron of agriculture. He never deserted the worship of the true God, and was much influenced by Zechariah, a prophet who is only mentioned in connection with him (II Chron. 26:5). So the southern kingdom was raised to a condition of prosperity which it had not known since the death of Solomon. During his reign an earthquake occurred which was apparently very serious in its consequences, for it is alluded to as a chronological epoch by Amos (Amos 1:1; comp. Zech. 14:5) as a convulsion from which the people "fled." 4. *Sin and death.* The end of Uzziah was less prosperous than his beginning. Elated with his splendid career, he determined to burn incense on the altar of God, but was opposed by the high priest Azariah and eighty others (see Exod. 30:7, 8; Num. 16:40; 18:7). The king was enraged at their resistance, and, as he pressed forward with his censer, was suddenly smitten with leprosy. Uzziah was "buried with his fathers," yet apparently not actually in the royal sepulchers (II Chron. 26:23), B. C. about 742.

(3) **Uzziah and Archaeology.** The great Assyrian conqueror, Tiglath-pileser's westward advance in 743 B. C. called for a new Syrian-Palestinian coalition to resist the Assyrian danger. The natural leader of such an alliance was Judah under Uzziah (Azariah). This king headed by far the strongest and most influential state in Syria-Palestine at the time (II Kings 14:21, 22; II Chron. chap, 26). (Stanley Cook, *The Cambridge Ancient History* III, p. 378). He was far more powerful than Menahem of Israel and Rezin of Damascus, both of whom evidently had to pay tribute to the Assyrians. It is not surprising, therefore, that Tiglath-pileser should make clear reference in his annals to *Azriyau* of *Yaudu* in connection with what is obviously a reference to an anti-Syrian coalition (D. D. Luckenbill, *Ancient Records of Assyria and Babylonia*, Vol. I, Sect. 7, 70; Edwin R. Thiele, *The Mysterious Numbers of the Hebrew Kings*, Chicago, 1951, p. 78). Azariah's disappearance from the Assyrian records with no hint of his fate except that the far-reaching coali-

tion he headed was broken up by the military power of Tiglath-pileser III would point to the conclusion that shortly thereafter he died, probably not later than 742 B. C., in any case before the Assyrians could take punitive action against him—*M. F. U.*

2. A Kohathite Levite, and ancestor of Samuel (I Chron. 6:24), B. C. perhaps 1300.

3. Father of Jehonathan, one of David's overseers (I Chron. 27:25), B. C. before 1000.

4. Father of Athaiah, or Uthai, resident in Jerusalem after the exile (Neh. 11:4), B. C. before 536.

5. A priest of the sons of Harim, who had taken a foreign wife in the days of Ezra (Ezra 10:21), B. C. 456. Revised *M. F. U.*

Uzzi′el (ŭ-zī′ĕl; *God is strength*).

1. Fourth son of Kohath, father of Mishael, Elzaphan, or Elizaphan, and Zithri, and uncle to Aaron (Exod. 6:18, 22; Lev. 10:4), B. C. before 1440.

2. A Simeonite captain, son of Ishi, in the days of Hezekiah (I Chron. 4:42), B. C. about 712.

3. Head of a Benjamite house, of the sons of Bela (I Chron. 7:7).

4. A musician of the sons of Heman, in David's reign (I Chron. 25:4).

5. A Levite, of the sons of Jeduthun, who took an active part in purifying the temple in the days of Hezekiah (II Chron. 29:14-19), B. C. 719.

6. Son of Harhaiah, probably a priest in the days of Nehemiah, who took part in repairing the wall (Neh. 3:8). He is described as "of the goldsmiths," i. e., of those priests whose hereditary office it was to repair or make the sacred vessels, B. C. about 445.

Uzzi′elite (ŭ-zī′ê-līt), a descendant of Uzziel the Levite. In David's time the Uzzielites numbered one hundred and twelve adult males (Num. 3:27; I Chron. 26:23; 15:10).

V

Vagabond (Heb. *nūd*, Gen. 4:12, 14; *nū̆ʽă*, Psa. 109:10) has the sense of *wandering* in both of the original terms. Perhaps a good render- of "a fugitive and vagabond" is "an aimless wanderer". The "vagabond Jews" mentioned in Acts 19:13 were itinerating Jewish demon-exorcisers—sorcerers, who, for the healing of demoniacs, used secret arts and charms.

Vail. *See* Veil, Dress.

Vainglory (Gr. *kenodoxia*) glorying without reason, self-esteem, empty pride (Phil. 2:3).

Vajez′atha (vå-jĕz′å-thå; R. V. **Vaiza′tha** (vī-zä′thå; from Old Persian, *son of the atmosphere*), one of the ten sons of Haman, whom the Jews slew in Shushan (Esth. 9:9), B. C. after 480.

Valiantness, valor, bravery.

Valley, the rendering in the A. V. of the following Hebrew and Greek words:

1. Rather a plain than a valley, wider than the latter, but, like it, surrounded by mountains (Heb. *bĭqäh, a split*). It denotes a wide alluvial bottom, and its levelness is referred to in Isa. 40:4; usually rendered "valley" (Deut. 8:7; 11:11; 34:3; Josh. 11:8, 17; 12:7; II Chron. 35:22; Psa. 104:8, etc.), but "plain" (Gen. 11:2; Neh. 6:2; Isa. 40:4; Ezek. 3:22, 23; 8:4; Amos 1:5). This Hebrew term is applied to the following places: The *valley of Shinar* (Gen. 11:2); *valley of Jericho* (Deut. 34:3); *valley of Lebanon* (Josh. 11:17); *valley of Megiddo* (II Chron. 35:22; Zech. 12:11); *valley of Mizpeh* (Josh. 11:8); *valley of Ono* (Neh. 6:2); *valley of Aven* (Amos 1:5).

2. A long broad sweep between parallel ranges of hills of less extent than No. 1, answering quite closely to our idea in general of a valley in its proper sense. (Heb. *ʽēmĕq, a deep place*). It is applied to the following localities: *Valley of Achor* (Josh. 7:24, 26; 15:7; Isa. 65:10; Hos. 2:15); *valley of Ajalon* (Josh. 10:12); *valley of Hebron* (Gen. 37:14); *valley of Jehoshaphat* (Joel 3:2, 12), called (v. 14), figuratively, *the valley of decision; valley of Jezreel* (Josh. 17:16; Judg. 6:33; Hos. 1:5);

valley of Keziz (Josh. 18:21). This term is sometimes used as an appellative for certain well-known localities, e. g., *the valley of weeping* (Psa. 84:6, A. V. "valley of Baca"); *the valley of blessing* (II Chron. 20:26, A. V. "valley of Berachah"); *valley of the oak* (I Sam. 17:2, 19; 21:9, A. V. "valley of Elah"); *valley of giants* (Josh. 15:8; 18:16; "valley of Rephaim," II Sam. 5:18, 22, etc.); *valley of Shaveh* (Gen. 14:17), or *of the king* ("dale," Gen. 14:17; II Sam. 18:18); *valley of the slime pits* (Gen. 14:3, 8, 10, A. V. "of Siddim"); *the valley of booths* (Psa. 60:6; 108:7, A. V. "of Succoth"), etc.

3. A deep, narrow *ravine* with a stream in the bottom, either between hills or through an open plain. (Heb. *găy*, or *gă′*, *a gorge*). In the A. V. it is invariably rendered "valley," and is applied to the following localities: *The valley of Hinnom* (Josh. 15:8; 18:16; Neh. 11:30), or *of the son of Hinnom* (Josh. 15:8; 18:16; II Kings 23:10, etc.), the ravine on the southwestern side of Jerusalem, whence the term Gehenna; *the valley of Jiphthah-el*, a ravine between Zebulun and Asher (Josh. 19:14, 27); *the valley of Zephathah*, a ravine in the tribe of Simeon (II Chron. 14:10); *the valley of Gedor*, another ravine in Simeon (I Chron. 4:39); *the valley of Hamon-gog* (Ezek. 39:11, 15), or *of the passengers* (v. 11), a ravine on the east of the Sea of Galilee; *the valley of the craftsmen* (I Chron. 4:14), a ravine in Judah; *the valley of the mountains* (Zech. 14:5), a ravine near Jerusalem; *the valley of salt* (II Sam. 8:13; II Kings 14:7; I Chron. 18:12; II Chron. 25:11; Psa. 60, title), a ravine on the southwestern shore of the Dead Sea; *the valley of the hyenas* (I Sam. 13:18), in the tribe of Benjamin. Others, such as *the valley of vision* (Isa. 22:1, 5), *of slaughter* (Jer. 7:32; 19:6), are fanciful names; and still more poetical is *the valley of the shadow of death* (Psa. 23:4).

4. *Wady* (Heb. *năḥăl, receiving;* A. V. often "brook," "river," "stream"). *Wady* expresses as no English word can the bed of a stream

(often wide and shelving, and like a "valley" in character, which in the rainy season may be nearly filled by a foaming torrent, though for the greater part of the year dry), and the stream itself which after the subsidence of the rains has shrunk to insignificant dimensions. Many of the wadies of Syria, owing to the demolition of the wood which formerly shaded the country and prevented too rapid evaporation after rain, are now entirely and constantly dry. As Palestine is emphatically a land of wadies, so this Hebrew term is of very frequent occurrence in the Bible. Stanley enumerated fifteen of these water courses or torrent beds—those of Gerar, of Eshcol, of Zered, of Arnon, of Jabbok, of Kanah, of Kishon, of Besor, of Sorek, of Kidron, of Gaash, of Cherith, of Gad. This last could not be distinguished by a mere English reader from the "river of Egypt," viz., the Nile, although in the original an entirely different word is used.

5. Heb. *hăshshᵉphēlāh* is the only case in which the employment of the term "valley" is unfortunate. This district (*see* Shephelah) has no resemblance to a valley, but is a broad swelling tract of many hundred miles in area, which sweeps gently down from the mountains of Judah toward the Mediterranean. It is rendered "vale" (Deut. 1:7; Josh. 10:40; I Kings 10:27; II Chron. 1:15; Jer. 33:13), and "the valley," or "valleys" (Josh. 9:1; 11:2, 16; 12:8; 15:33; Judg. 1:9; Jer. 32:44).

6. In the New Testament we read of our Lord standing in "the plain" (Gr. *topos pedinos,* Luke 6:17), a *level place;* and "valley" (Gr. *pharagx,* 3:5), *ravine.*

Valley Gate (Heb. *shăᵃ̆r hăggăy'*), an entrance at the northwestern end of Jerusalem (Neh. 2:13; 3:13; comp. II Chron. 26:9; 33:14), probably corresponding to the present Jaffa gate.

Vani′ah (vȧ-nī′ȧ), one of the sons of Bani, and an Israelite who divorced his Gentile wife after the captivity (Ezra 10:36), B. C. 456.

Vanity.

1. Nothingness, a vain and empty thing (Isa. 41:29; Zech. 10:2), specially of the nothingness of idols and of everything pertaining to idolatry (I Sam. 15:23), and so put for *an idol* (Isa. 66:3); (Heb. *'āwĕn, a panting*). Hence in Hosea the city (*house of God, bēth'ēl*) is scornfully called the *house of idols* (*bēth 'āwĕn,* Hos. 4:15; 10:5); it has the meaning of *nothingness* as to worth; *naughtiness,* i. e., wickedness, iniquity (Num. 23:21; Job 36:21; Isa. 1:13); also of *toil, trouble* (Psa. 55:3, A. V. "iniquity;" Prov. 22:8, A. V. "vanity").

2. Something vain, empty, fruitless (Job 9:29; 21:34; 35:16; Jer. 10:3, 8; Lam. 4:17). (Heb. *hĕbĕl, a breath*); specifically of *idols* (II Kings 17:15; Psa. 31:6; Jer. 2:5; Jonah 2:8).

3. Heb. *shāw'* has the meaning of *desolation;* so "months of vanity" (Job 7:3) are those of calamity. Evil and calamity are both implied in 15:31, "Let him not trust in vanity [evil], deceiving himself: for vanity [*calamity*] shall be his recompense." To "speak vanity" (Psa. 41:6) is to utter falsehood. This term is also applied to idols (31:6).

4. Heb. *tōhū* (to *lie waste*), a desert (Deut. 32:10; 11:24, "wilderness") also a *worthless*

thing (Isa. 41:29), as an *idol* (44:9; comp. 59:4).

5. Gr. *mataiotēs* corresponds to *shāw'* and means that which is devoid of truth and appropriateness (II Pet. 2:18); that which is perverse or depraved (Eph. 4:17); frailty, want of vigor (Rom. 8:20).

Vav (väv), the Hebrew letter *waw,* sixth in the alphabet. It stands at the beginning of each verse in the original of Psalm 119:41-48.

VEGETABLE KINGDOM

The flora of Syria and Palestine is very rich. The phaenogamous plants and higher cryptogams are distributed through one hundred and twenty-four orders, eight hundred and fifty genera, and about three thousand five hundred species, with many well-characterized varieties. Only one hundred names of plants are given in the Bible. Of these thirty-six cannot be determined with certainty. Of the sixty-four which are determinable thirty-five are cultivated. Of the identity of most of these, as *wheat, barley, flax, olives, vines, figs,* etc., there can be no doubt. In one case, *rye* (A. V. Exod. 9:32; Isa. 28:25, R. V. "spelt"), the name is a mistranslation. Of the wild plants mentioned, some, as *algum, lign aloes,* etc., are exotics, of which it is impossible to determine with certainty the species. Others, as *anise, ash, bay tree, chestnut, heath, juniper, hemlock, mulberry, poplar, rose of Sharon,* are mistranslations. Others, as *flag, reed, thistle, thorn,* refer to plants agreeing in mode of growth rather than ordinal or generic relationships, and are the equivalent of a number of Hebrew words, the generic or specific signification of which has been lost. Others still, as the *lily,* are ordinal for all plants of a given type. The effort, therefore, to construct a scriptural flora, accurate and precise in its details, must be abandoned, and each name of a plant treated on its own merits.

Al′gum (ăl′gŭm) or **Almug Trees**. There is no reason to doubt the identity of the *algum* and the *almug,* as is proven by a comparison of I Kings 10:11 and II Chron. 9:10. As to the algum trees "out of Lebanon" (II Chron. 2:8), they may have been the same as those that were imported from Ophir. In this case they may have then been indigenous, or cultivated, and have since become extinct; or they may have been another sort of tree called by the same name, as in the case with many other trees. There is no necessity for supposing an interpolation, nor even for inferring, as some have done, that "out of Lebanon" refers to "cedar trees and fir trees" only, and not to *algums.* We have no means of determining certainly what tree was intended. The weight of authority is in favor of the *red sandalwood,* but not a particle of evidence. As now seen in commerce it is not suitable either for *terraces* (marg. *highways,* or *stairs,* II Chron. 9:11), more properly *staircases,* or for *pillars* (marg. *a prop,* or *rails,* I Kings 10:12), more properly *balustrades,* or for *harps* and *psalteries.* Since Josephus says algum wood resembles the wood of the fig tree, but is whiter and has a brighter sheen, it may be the *Sabtalum album,* a native of India, and used in India and China as an odiferous substance to perfume temples and houses of Sanskrit *valgu, valgam.*

Al'mond (ăl'mŏnd; Heb. *shaqēd, the awakening one*, probably from its early blossoming), a tree very much resembling in form and blossom the peach; and is only another species of the same genus. Its flowers appear as early as February, or even January. The almond is diffused by culture from China to Spain, on both sides of the Mediterranean, in the south of England, and in southern portions of the United States. There is no region, however, where it thrives better than in Syria.

The almond tree blossoms toward the end of January, or the beginning of February, before the coming of the leaves, so that the appearance of a tree in full bloom is very striking. Although the blossoms are tinged with pink, the general effect is white. The fruit is eaten in two stages, the first the tender, acidulous, unripe, crisp pod, and the other the ripe almonds, so familiar everywhere. There are four species of wild almonds in the Bible lands. The Hebrew name of the almond is the *waker*, in allusion to its being the first of the fruit trees to awake in the winter and put forth its luxuriant blossoms. This tree is referred to by Jacob when he tells his sons to take into Egypt "of the best fruits in the land . . . and almonds" (Gen. 43:11). In Eccles. (12:5), "The almond tree shall flourish," doubtless refers to the profuse flowering and white appearance of the tree when in full bloom and before the leaves appear (Jer. 1:11, 12). In Num. 17:8 the rod of Aaron is described as having "budded, and brought forth buds, and bloomed blossoms, and yielded almonds." With its oblong-oval sharpened at one end and rounded at the other, the shape of the almond nut is remarkably graceful. This naturally led to its selection for ornamental carved work; and it was the pattern selected for the bowls of the golden candlestick (Exod. 25:33, 34; 37:19), "symbolizing the speedy and powerful result of light" (Keil, *Arch.*, i, 146).

Figurative. In Jer. 1:11, 12, there is an allusion to another of the meanings of the Hebrew root, which is to *hasten*. In the first of the two verses the almond tree is mentioned by its name *shäqēd*, and in the second it is said "for I will hasten my word," *hasten* being from the same root as *almond*. The almond was chosen to symbolize God's haste in fulfilling his promises.

There can be no reasonable doubt that the allusion in Eccles. 12:5 is to the white hair of the aged.

Al'oes, Lign Aloes (ăl'ōs; Heb. *'ăhālîm;* Gr. *'aloē*). This is doubtless the *lignum aloes* of the ancients, the product of *Aquilaria Agallocha*, Roxb., and other trees of the same genus, growing in India and China. It was well known to the Greeks and also to the Arabians. The species grows in Sylhet, in the E. of Bengal, being a large tree with lanceolate leaves, the wood containing a resin, and an essential oil, constituting the perfume prized in antiquity. It is mentioned in four places in the Old Testament and once in the New Testament (Num. 24:6; Psa. 45:8; Prov. 7:17; Cant. 4:14; John 19:39). A question has been raised as to the identity of the tree mentioned in Num. 24:6

with the other trees of the same name. This question may safely be answered in the affirmative. Although the lign aloes is a native of India and China it is easy to suppose that it was cultivated in the tropical valley of the Jordan, which is well known to have produced trees in ancient times all traces of which have now disappeared. But even if it were to be supposed that it was not cultivated in Palestine, it might have been alluded to as a well-known tree of foreign growth, of which the luxuriance was proverbial, in this respect resembling the *cedar*, in the same passage, which, if it indicated the *cedar of Lebanon*, was to the Israelites of that day also a foreign tree, mentioned as an emblem of prosperity.

Amo'mum (à-mō'mŭm; Gr. *'amōmum*). This word occurs only in Rev. 18:13, and is rendered in the A. V. "odors." Amomum is a fragrant plant of India. It belongs to a genus of plants, natural order *Scitamineoe*, belonging to tropical regions of the Old World, and allied to the ginger plant. They are herbaceous, with creeping rootstocks and large sheathing leaves, and are remarkable for the pungency and aromatic properties of their seeds. Several specimens yield the cardamoms and grains of paradise of commerce. The one mentioned in Revelation had seeds like grapes, from which an ointment was made.

An'ise (ăn'ĭs; Gr. *'anēthon*). The marginal rendering *dill* is undoubtedly the true one. The Gr. *'anēthon* is the exact equivalent of the Lat. *anethum*, which is the *dill*, and not the *anise*. It is the aromatic, carminative seed of *Anethum graveolens*, L., an umbellifera, cultivated widely in the East, and used both in cookery and domestic medicine. It was subject to tithe among the Hebrews (Matt. 23:23).

Apple. The Hebrew word *tăppŭäh* for apple is nearly the same as the Arabic *tuffâh*, and wherever the name of the tree has been preserved in that of a place, as in *Beth Tappuah*, the Arabic has preserved it in the modified form, in this *tuffâh*, showing that the reference to the familiar fruit is recognized. The apple is a favorite fruit with the natives of this land, and although they do not now possess any very fine varieties, they are particularly fond of the smell of an apple (Cant. 7:8). They habitually smell an apple to revive themselves when faint (2:5). Most of the apples cultivated here are sweet (v. 6). The allusions to the size of the apple tree in 2:3, 8:5, are borne out by the facts of the case. There is no occasion, then, to seek for any other tree, as some have done, to meet the Scripture requirements.

Ash (Heb. *'ōrēn*). This word occurs but once in the A. V. (Isa. 44:14). It is impossible to say with certainty what tree the original *'ōrēn* meant. It is, however, wholly improbable that it was an *ash*. The LXX. and Vulg. have *pine*. There are three kinds of pines common in Syria and Palestine, but only one of these is planted. This is the familiar *stone pine* or *maritime pine, Pinus Pinea*, L. It is one of the most extensively cultivated trees of the country, with wood hard enough to be carved into an image, and never sown in irrigated districts, but nourished only by the rain. Large forests of this tree have been planted along the sandy coast to resist the encroachment of the drifted sand, and also still more extensive forests in the mountains, for the sake of its valuable timber.

Aspala′thus (ăs-pá-lā′thŭs). The name of one or more aromatic substances mentioned only once (Ecclus. 24:15). The substance and plant producing it are indeterminable.

Balm (Heb. *ṣŏri*), an aromatic gum, or resin (Gen. 37:25), probably produced in Gilead, or a prime article of commerce there (Jer. 8:22; 46:11; 51:8), well known to Jacob (Gen. 43:11), and dealt in by Judah and Israel in the latter days of their monarchies (Ezek. 27:17). No tree now growing in Gilead produces the traditional balm, now known as *Mecca balsam.* This substance is the gum of *Balsamodendron Gileadense* and *B. opobalsamum,* which grow in southern Arabia. But there can be no doubt that in Roman times these trees were cultivated in the lower Jordan valley. This would bring a part of its area of cultivation within the limits of Gilead. In any case it was to such an extent an article of commerce in .that district that it went by the name of *balm of Gilead.* Dioscorides erroneously says that the tree grew "only in the country of the Jews, which is Palestine, in the Ghor." Balm of Gilead was once an important element in the *materia medica,* but it has now fallen into disuse. Some have supposed that *mastich* is the balm of Gilead. Avicenna, however, clearly distinguishes it from that well-known gum. The so-called balm of Gilead, prepared by the monks of Jericho, from the fruits of the *zaqqûm, Balanites Aegyptiaca,* Del., has no claim except their authority. It is said, however, to have healing properties.

Barley (Heb. *sᵉʽŏräh;* Gr. *krithinos*), a well-known grain, cultivated from the remotest antiquity, and frequently mentioned in the Bible. A wild species, found in Galilee, and northeastward to the Syrian desert, *Hordeum Ithaburense,* Boiss. (*H. spontaneum,* Koch), may be the original stock from which the cultivated varieties were derived. It is conspicuous by its very long awns, which are sometimes a foot in length. Barley is the universal provender for horses, mules, and, to a certain extent, for asses (I Kings 4:28), taking the place of oats with us. It is still used for bread among the very poor (II Kings 4:42). It was sometimes mixed with other cheap grains, for making bread (Ezek. 4:9). From its cheapness it was the jealousy offering (Num. 5:15); part of the price of an adulteress (Hos. 3:2) and of lewd women (Ezek. 13:19); a barley cake expressed the low rank and poverty of Gideon (Judg. 7:13).

The barley harvest is earlier than the wheat harvest (Exod. 9:31, 32), and begins in April, in the Jordan valley, and continues to be later as the altitude increases, until, at a height of six thousand feet above the sea, it takes place in July and August. Barley is sown in October and November, after the "early rain." It is never sown in the spring, for the simple reason that it would not have rain, and so could not mature any grain, even if there were moisture enough in the soil to cause it to germinate. That which is sown on the higher levels be-

haves like winter wheat in cold climates, dying down under the snow, and sprouting again in the spring.

Bay Tree (Heb. *'ezräh, springing up*). The translation of the A. V., "like a green bay tree" (Psa. 37:35), is well amended by the R. V., to "like a green tree in its native soil."

Beans (Heb. *pôl, thick, plump*). Beans are mentioned twice, once as part of a mixture of cheap cereals, used for making a coarse kind of bread (Ezek. 4:9), and once as part of the provisions of David at Mahanaim (II Sam. 17:28). The vegetable alluded to in each case is the *horse bean, Faba vulgaris,* L., which is extensively cultivated, both as human food and for fodder. As human food it is either cooked unripe in the green pod, like string beans, or the ripe seeds are boiled like our white beans.

Bitter Herbs (Heb. *mᵉrōr, bitter*). The Hebrews were commanded to eat the passover lamb with *bitter herbs* (Exod. 12:8; Num. 9:11). There are many such, wild and cultivated, which are habitually used by the natives of the East in salads; among them are *lettuce, water cress, pepper grass,* and *endive.* The object of the ordinance was both to remind the Israelites of their "bitter bondage" (Exod. 1:14), and of the *haste* with which they made their exit from Egypt. Unleavened bread, a roast lamb, and a few bitter herbs constituted a meal the elements of which were always at hand and could be got together with the least possible delay. So far from these herbs however being distasteful to them, the orientals are very fond of them.

Box Tree (Heb. *tᵉʽăsshûr*). We have no reliable data to enable us to determine the tree intended by the Hebrew original of this word. It is mentioned in two passages (Isa. 41:19; 60:13) in connection with the *cedar, shittah, myrtle, fir,* and *pine.* It seems rather unlikely that a shrub, known only in far northern Syria, should be associated with these familiar trees. The Syrian box, *Buxus longifolia,* Boiss., is only two to three feet in height, and must have been unfamiliar to the readers of the Bible in the time of Isaiah. The old Arabic version gives *sherbîn,* which is either the *wild cypress* or the *lizzâb, Juniperus excelsa,* M. B. It might be better to transliterate the Hebrew, as is done in the case of algum, and call the tree *teashshûr.*

Bramble. *See* Thistles, Thorns.

Briers. *see* Thistles, Thorns.

Bulrush. *See* Reed.

Burning Bush (Heb. *sᵉnĕh, bramble,* Exod. 3:2-5; Deut. 33:16), one of the many thorny shrubs growing in Sinai. The monks of the Convent of St. Catherine point out a *blackberry bush* (*Rubus tomentosus,* Borck, var. *collinus,* Boiss.), growing behind the chapel of the convent, as the bush in question. This is improbable, as Rubus is not indigenous there. The burning bush might be one of the *seyal* trees, *Acacia tortilis,* Hayne, or *A. Seyal,* Del., or the *nebk, Zizyphus Spina Christi,* L., or some other thorn bush.

Calamus. *See* Reed.

Camphire (Heb. *kōphĕr* from Malay *kapur*). This is the *henna* plant, *Lawsonia alba,* L. It is cultivated everywhere in the Holy Land. Its clusters of cream-colored flowers are much admired by the orientals, and form a part of almost every nosegay during the flowering season. The scriptural allusions (Cant. 1:14; 4:13, 13) show that it was equally esteemed in ancient times. Its leaves are also used for dyeing finger- and toe-nails a reddish-orange color. There is, however, no allusion to this use of the plant in the Scripture.

Cane. *See* Reed.

Caperberry (R. V. Eccles. 12:5; A. V. "desire;" Heb. *'ăbîyōnäh, provocative of desire),* the immature fruit of *Capparis spinosa,* L., a plant growing everywhere in clefts of rocks and walls. It is stimulant, and supposed to be aphrodisiac. If *caperberry* be the correct rendering of *'ăbîyōnäh* the meaning of the passage is that even the caperberry shall fail to excite desire, a meaning in effect similar to that of A. V.

Cas′sia (kăsh′ĭ-à; Heb. *qĭddäh,* Exod. 30:24; Ezek. 27:19; *q⁰sʸ'äh, peeled,* Psa. 45:8). Probably *Cassia lignea* of commerce, which consists of strips of the bark of *Cinnamomum Cassia,* Blume, a plant growing in China and Malaysia. *Cassia buds* are the immature flowers of the same. Both have the flavor and aroma of cinnamon.

500. Cedars of Lebanon

Cedar (Heb. *'ĕrĕz).* By far the greater number of references to the cedar in the Scriptures are to be understood of the famous "cedar of Lebanon." This is a tree of very wide distribution, and fulfills well the conditions demanded, with the following exceptions: 1. The *cedar wood used in purification,* in connection with scarlet and hyssop. This would seem to have been a tree found in the Sinaitic desert, and in use long before the Israelites could have easily obtained the cedar of Lebanon. It might well have been *Juniperus Phoenicia,* L., which is found in Mount Hor and its neighborhood, and could also have grown on the mountains of Sinai. 2. The "cedars in the garden of God" (Ezek. 31:8). The comparison of the Assyrian, who is called "a cedar of Lebanon" (v. 5), with these trees would seem to indicate some other tree. We have no means of determining what it was. 3. The "cedars by the waters" (Num. 24:6) can hardly be cedars of Lebanon, because this tree never grows in such a location. True, in poetry, even in the Scriptures, it is not to be expected that all the congruities of time and place shall be rigidly observed. But unless we suppose such poetic license, we must infer that the trees here referred to were some water-loving species then known as *cedars,* now no longer determinable.

It is likely that the subalpine regions of Lebanon and Antilebanon were clothed with these trees. At Bsherreh in the Republic of Lebanon about 100 miles N. of Beirut exists a fine group of the ancient cedars of Lebanon. These noble trees display the characteristics of the ancient trees. They have reddish-brown bark and sturdy trunks as much as forty feet in girth. They have a very wide branch spread and bear cones some five inches long, and have bright green needles about one-half inch long. A fine prize for architectural uses, they grow very slowly. *M. F. U.*

They are abundant in Amanus and the Taurus. Their range is from the Himalayas to the Atlas, and from central Asia Minor to Lebanon. They also existed in Cyprus. It is a tall tree (Isa. 2:13, etc.), "with fair branches and with a shadowing shroud" (Ezek. 31:3); suitable for masts of ships (27:5), and for beams, pillars, and boards (I Kings 6:9; 7:2), and for carved work (Isa. 44:14). Of this noble tree much of the temple was built, as well as Solomon's house and other important public edifices in Jerusalem. It was used for roofing the temple of Diana at Ephesus and that of Apollo at Utica, and other famous buildings. Its claim to be the "king of trees" is not to be considered with reference to the whole forest world, but only in comparison with the trees found in Bible lands. This claim was never disputed in the period of the Hebrew nationality in this land, and the sacred grove at Besherri, on Lebanon, still bears the ancient name of "the cedars of the Lord."

Chaff, the husks which surround the seeds of the cereals. A. V. incorrectly renders by *chaff ḥäshäsh,* which should be *cut grass,* and *tĕbĕn,* which should be *cut straw. Chaff* is the correct rendering for the Hebrew *mōṣ (winnowed). Chaff,* after the threshing is over, is mingled with the *cut* and *split straw (tĕbĕn).* Winnowing separates the product of threshing into four heaps—*grain, cut straw, chaff,* and finally the *dust,* caused by the comminution of a part of the straw and chaff and its commingling with the dust of the earthen floor. This, which is *'ûr* in Hebrew, is also erroneously translated (Dan. 2:35) "chaff."

Chestnut Tree (Heb. *'ărmōn).* As this tree is not found in the Holy Land, some other must be sought that will fill the conditions required. The R. V. very properly follows the LXX. and the Vulg., and gives *plane tree.* A scratch in the bark of this tree would at once show a *white streak* (Gen. 30:37). The plane tree is also of a stature and imposing appearance sufficient to make it suitable for comparison in the group with which the cedar of Lebanon is compared (Ezek. 31:8). This tree often attains a height of a hundred feet and a diameter at its base of from six to ten feet. It is abundant along all water courses in Syria and Mesopotamia.

Cinnamon (Heb. *qĭnnämōn).* No one can doubt the substance intended, as the Hebrew name is the same as the English. It was used by that race as a perfume for the holy oil (Exod. 30: 23) and for beds (Prov. 7:17). It seems to have been cultivated by Solomon (Cant. 4:14). It is a part of the wares of Babylon the Great (Rev. 18:13).

Cockle (Heb. *bŏ'shäh*, cf. *to be bad*, in Heb. *to have a stench* in Aram.). The word rendered cockle (Job 31:40) should be, as in the margin of the A. V., *stinking weeds*, or of R. V. *noisome weeds*. There are multitudes of these in the fields of Palestine and Syria, as the *goose weeds*, *stink weeds*, *arums*, *henbane*, and *mandrake*.

Corian'der (cô-rĭ-ăn'dẽr, the aromatic seed of *Coriandrum sativum*, L. It is somewhat larger than a hemp seed, and only spoken of to illustrate the size and color of the grains of manna (Exod. 16:31; Num. 11:7).

501. Egyptian Corn

Corn, the generic name for the cereal grains. Those cultivated in Bible lands are *wheat*, *barley*, *vetch*, *fitches* (*Nigella sativa*, L.), *millet*, *beans*, *pulse* (edible seeds in general), *lentils*, and *maize* (not mentioned in Scripture, as it is a grain of modern introduction). *Rye* (Exod. 9:32; Isa. 28:25) is an erroneous translation for *vetch*. See Harvest, Fan, Threshing Floor, Agriculture.

Cotton, Heb. *karpas*, from Sanskrit *karpāsa* (cotton). Indian cotton was cultivated in Persia, and the fine cotton draperies in the royal palace at Shushan (Esth. 1:6), correctly are rendered by this term. We have no evidence, however, that the ancient Hebrews knew cotton, although it has been cultivated from time immemorial in India and other parts of the East.

Crown of Thorns. *See* Thistles, Thorns.

Cucumber. There are two kinds of cucumbers cultivated in the East, both of which were probably known to the ancient Egyptians and the Hebrews. One is identical with our ordinary kind, but more delicate in flavor and more wholesome. The other is tougher, more dry, and less delicate in flavor. The former kind grows only in irrigated ground, while the latter flourishes during the hot, rainless months of summer, without a drop of water, except what it can extract from the parched soil or absorb from the atmosphere during the night. It was doubtless the custom in Egypt to water both kinds, and hence the succulent character of the vegetable so keenly regretted by the Israelites during their thirsty journey in the wilderness (Num. 11:5; Heb. *qĭshshŭ'*, hard).

The garden of cucumbers (Isa. 1:8; Heb. *mĭqshäh*) is still a feature of oriental landscapes, some of these being on rolling ground, exposed to the blazing sun of August, without water, and others being among the irrigated orchards of orange and other fruit trees, but all supplied with a *lodge*, where the watchman keeps guard over the tempting vegetable, none of which would reach its lawful owner but for this precaution. This lodge is a frail structure of poles and leaves, adapted only to protect the watchman from the sun by day and the dew by night, during the rainless summer of Syria and Palestine. As soon as the last of the cucumbers is gathered the lodge is "left," a useless reminder of past plenty and prosperity.

Cum'min (kŭm'ĭn; Heb. *kămmōn, preserving;* Gr. *kuminon*), one of the aromatic seeds, subject to tithe by the Jewish law (Matt. 23:23). It is still known by its ancient name (*kammûn*) throughout the Arabic world. It is an aromatic and carminative, used in cooking and in domestic medicine. It is still threshed with a rod (Isa. 28:25, 27). It has been superseded in modern times by caraway seeds, more nutritious and tasty.

Cypress (R. V. **Holm Oak**). It is impossible to determine what tree is meant by the Hebrew (*tĭrzäh*, Isa. 44:14) original of the word translated as above. The Vulgate renders it by Ilex, the evergreen oak (*quercus ilex*). See Holm Tree.

Dill. *See* Anise.

Ebony (Heb. *hōbĕn*), the hard, close-grained, black heart wood of *Diospyros Ebenum*, L., which grows in the East Indies. It has been an article of commerce from ancient times, having been brought to Palestine from Dedan, on the Persian Gulf (Ezek. 27:15). It is used for cabinet work, rulers, etc. An ebony was brought in ancient times from Ethiopia, but we have no certainty as to the tree which produced it. Virgil (*Georg.*, ii, 116) says that "India also produces the black ebony."

Elm (Hos. 4:13) should be *terebinth*, as in R. V.

Fig (Heb. *t^e ēnäh;* Gr. *sukon*), the fruit of the well-known tree. It is one of the favorite articles of food in the East, and, in the dried state, a considerable article of commerce. The failure of the fig trees was a national calamity. Their productiveness was a token of peace and the divine favor. They are associated with the *vine*, the *palm*, the *pomegranate*. The *fig tree* differs from most other fruit trees in that its fruit is green and inconspicuous, concealed among leaves until near the time of ripening. If the promise given from a distance by the leaves be not fulfilled on approaching (Mark 11:13), the tree is a *hypocrite*. Such a one our Saviour cursed.

Fir (Heb. *b^erōsh*), probably the *cypress*, *Cupressus sempevirens*, L. This tree fulfills all the conditions of the various passages in which *fir* occurs (I Kings 6:15, 34; II Chron. 3:5; Ezek. 27:5). The tall trunk of this tree is well adapted for masts. Other possible candidates which have been suggested are *Pinus Halpensis*, Mill., and *Juniperus excelsa*, M. B. The R. V. margin, in the first three of the above passages, favors "cypress."

Fitch is a plant sometimes incorrectly identified with black cummin, whose seeds are used for seasoning. The fitch is apparently properly an herb cultivated for forage and regarded as a tare (Isa. 28:25, Heb. *qĕṣăḥ*). *M. F. U.*

Flag (Heb. *'āḥū*), a generic word for such plants as have a more or less grasslike or sedgy form, and grow in swamps or by river banks (Job 8:11). The Hebrew original, *'āḥū*, is rendered (Gen. 41:2, 18) A. V. "meadow," R. V. "reed grass." It would be better to render it in all the passages *fens*. Another word *sūph* (Exod. 2:3, 5), is well translated "flags."

Flax (Heb. *pĭshtāh*), a well-known plant, *Linum sativum*, L. The fibers of the bark, when separated, twisted, bleached, and woven, are *linen*. In the raw state they are "tow" (Judg. 16:9; Isa. 1:31). Somewhat twisted, tow constitutes a "wick" (R. V. marg. Isa. 42:3; 43:17).

Flowers. The flowers of the Holy Land are renowned for their beauty. The most showy and widely diffused are the *scarlet* and *blue anemones*, the *scarlet ranunculi* and *poppies*, the numerous *silenes*, the purple *pea blossom*, a number of showy *roses*, the scarlet *pomegranate*, a host of *composites*, the *styrax*, a number of *crocuses, colchicums, irises, tulips*, and *ixiolirions*, etc. In many places they are so abundant as to impart a rich and varied coloring to the landscape.

Forest (Heb. *yă'ăr*, a *thicket*). While the Holy Land has never been a wooded country in historic times, it was doubtless more so at the time of the Hebrew conquest than it has been ever since. Numerous woods and forests are mentioned by name. According to Albright, in the Middle Bronze Age (2000-1500 B. C.) the mountains of Palestine were heavily forested on the watershed ridge and the western slope so that there was little arable land (cf. Albright, *Archaeology of Palestine and the Bible*, pp. 130-133). Since the cistern had not come into use, the general situation favors the Biblical representation of the patriarchs being free to roam over wide areas of sparsely populated central highland range and to be free to feed flocks on the lower ranges. In the last decade or so millions of cedar, pine and spruce seeds have been planted in the Lebanon regions from U. S. Army airplanes in cooperation with the Lebanese government. Also, the Israeli State is reforesting many areas in Palestine. *M. F. U.*

Frankincense (Heb. *lĕbōnäh*). *See* Galbanum, below.

Fruit. The Holy Land is not only a land of *flowers*, but also of *fruits*. Owing to the great diversity of level, from the tropical valley of the Jordan, one thousand three hundred feet below the sea, to subalpine Lebanon, the fruits of the country present a cosmopolitan variety. The most characteristic are the *banana, orange*, and its congeners, *dates*, most of the *rosaceous fruits, persimmon, jujube, grapes, figs, olives*, and *pomegranates*. The orange is in season for six months, the grape nearly as long. Figs ripen during four months. Almost all *garden vegetables* thrive, and many of them are in season for months.

Gal'banum (găl'bà-nŭm; Heb. *lĕbōnäh, whiteness*), a gum resin with a pungent balsamic odor (Exod. 30:34). It was one of the constitu-

502. Frankincense

ents of the sacred incense. Two ferulas, *F. galbaniflua*, Boiss, et Buhse, and *F. rubricaulis*, Boiss., both growing in Persia, are believed to be the sources of the gum. It is used in medicine as an *antispasmodic*. It is a greasy, sticky granulated resin, presenting a whitish appearance at first, but afterward changing to yellow, and having a pungent odor and taste, and which, when mixed with fragrant substances, has the effect of increasing the odor and fixing it longer.

Gall. While some of the references to *gall* clearly point to *bile*, or *gall bladder* (Job 16:13; 20:14, 25, 'Heb. *mĕrōräh*), others as clearly point to a *plant* (Deut. 29:18; Lam. 3:19, etc., Heb. *rō'sh*). It is probable that the *poppy* is the plant intended. The "gall" which was offered to Christ on the cross (Matt. 27:34) was doubtless *myrrh* (Mar. 15:23).

Garden, a term used in Scripture with a far wider signification than in ordinary literature. It includes *park, orchard, vegetable*, and *flower gardens*. The *garden of Eden* was a vast farm, including all the above. A peculiar feature of most oriental cities is that, while the houses are crowded together, and few gardens are found among them, the environs are mostly composed of fruit and vegetable gardens, and trees of various sorts, planted for utilitarian purposes. The effect of these gardens, surrounding the towns, as in the case of Jaffa, Sidon, Beirut, Damascus, and Homs, is extremely beautiful.

Garlic (Heb. *shūm*), a well-known vegetable, more agreeable to oriental than to most European palates. It is mentioned but once (Num. 11:5).

Gopher Wood (Heb. *gōphĕr*), an unknown wood, used in the construction of the ark (Gen. 6:14).

Gourd, a swift-growing plant designated by the Heb. *qīqäyōn* (Jon. 4:6-10). The Septuagint renders the Hebrew by the Greek *kolokynthē*, meaning the pumpkin *Cucurbita pepo*, which is in reality a type of the gourd family. This is a native of the Caspian Sea country and is very rapidly growing and may well have been introduced into Assyria by Jonah's time. On the other hand, the Heb. *qīqäyōn* is very similar to Graeco-Egyptian *kiki*, designating the castor oil plant. This is sometimes called Palma Christi, that is, Christ's palm, the marginal reading of the R. V. in Jon. 4:6-10. This plant attains a height from eight to ten feet, sometimes growing very rapidly. If this was the plant which shaded Jonah, its rapid growth was still miraculous. *M. F. U.*

503. Carob Leaves and Beans

Gourds, Wild (Heb. *păqqŭ'äh*, *splitting* open, II Kings 4:39), were probably *colocynths*, which grew abundantly in the locality alluded to, and suit the requirements of the passage.

Grapes. *See* Vine.

Grass, a term used in Scripture in an indefinite sense, referring to *green herbage* in general. All the four Hebrew words, *yĕrĕk, hāzîr, dĕshĕh,* and *'ēsĕb,* translated "grass," have this wide meaning. The idea conveyed to us by the term *grasses,* as plants with hollow colms, strap-shaped leaves, and an inflorescence of glumes and pales, is a strictly modern creation of descriptive botany.

Green Herbs, Green Grass, Green Thing. *See* Grass.

Hay. Hay is never, and probably never has been, made in the Holy Land. The grasses from which it is prepared are not cultivated. In the three passages where it occurs in A. V. (Prov. 27:25; Isa. 15:6; I Cor. 3:12) it would better be rendered *herbage* or *grass,* understood in the most generic sense.

Hazel (Gen. 30:37) should be *almond,* as in R. V. (Heb. *lūz*).

Heath (Heb. *'ărō'ēr*). There is one species of *heath, Erica verticillata,* Forsk., which grows in Lebanon. Perhaps this is the plant intended (Jer. 17:6; 48:6). It is in no way likely that it is "tamarisk," as in R. V. marg. in the above passages.

Hedge. Hedges are more commonly used to separate gardens and orchards in the East than are walls. Many thorny plants are set out for this purpose. Also some of the giant grasses, as *Arundo Donax,* L., and *Saccharum Aegyptiacum,* L.

Hemlock, an unfortunate translation of the Heb. *rō'sh* (A. V. Hos. 10:4) (*see* Gall), and of

lă'ănäh (Amos 6:12), which should be, as in R. V., "wormwood."

Henna. R. V. for A. V. "camphire," marg. "cypress" (Cant. 1:14; 4:13). *See* Camphire.

Herb. *See* Grass.

Holm Tree (R. V. Isa. 44:14, A. V. "cypress," Sus. 58). The *holm oak* is *Quercus coccifera,* L., one of the finest trees of Bible lands. It is widely diffused, and usually planted near solitary tombs. *See* Cypress (R. V. Holm Oak).

Husks (Gr. *keration, horned,* Luke 16:15), the pods of *Ceratonia Siliqua,* L., the *carob tree.* This tree is an evergreen, cultivated everywhere in the Holy Land. The pods are still often fed to swine, and are eaten by the people. An inspissated decoction of them is known as *dibs kharrûb,* i. e., *carob honey.*

Hyssop (Heb. *'ēzōb;* Gr. *hussōpos*), a labiate plant, probably *Origanum Mary,* L. It was used in sprinkling (Exod. 12:22; Lev., ch. 14; Heb. 9:19), and in quenching the thirst of a victim on the cross (John 19:29). It grew out of walls (I Kings 4:33), probably the walls of terraces. There is no reason to believe that the "reed" (Matt. 27:48; Mark 15:36), on which the sponge soaked in vinegar was raised to Christ's mouth, was the same as the "hyssop" upon which the sponge was put (John 19:29). Even were it so the stem of the *caper plant,* which has been proposed as the *hyssop,* would not suit the requirements of the term "reed," which suggests a *straight,* not a *zigzag* stem.

Ivy (II Macc. 6:7) grows everywhere over rocky walls in the Holy Land.

Juniper (Heb. *rōthĕm,* I Kings 19:4, R. V. marg. "broom;" Job 30:4, R. V. text "broom"). The plant intended is doubtless the *retem* of the Arabs, *Retama roetam,* L., a desert, almost leafless, shrub, furnishing a very poor refuge from the sun's rays. Its roots make good fuel and charcoal (Psa. 120:4). The Juniper of the Bible is not the coniferous tree of the genus *Juniperus,* of which several species exist in Lebanon, Bashan and Galilee.

Leeks (Heb. *hāṣîr*), a kind of onion, *Allium Porrum,* L., cultivated extensively in the East. It is mentioned once with onions and garlic (Num. 11:5).

Lentils (Heb. *'ädäsh,* Gen. 25:34; II Sam. 17:28; 23:11; Ezek. 4:9). The seed of *Ervum Lens,* L., a cereal everywhere cultivated in the East. A pottage made of it is as much used now as food as it was in Jacob's time.

Lign Aloes. *See* Aloes.

Lily (Heb. *shūshän*), while in a special sense the word for *iris,* is as broad in its application as its rendering in our versions, *lily.* The expression "lily of the valleys" (Cant. 2:1) does not refer to the flower understood by this designation in ordinary speech, as it is not found in Palestine. The lily of other passages in Canticles was evidently a garden flower (2:16; 4:5; 6:3). The allusion (5:13) may be to rosy color, or fragrance, or both. From earliest times the lily has been imitated in stone and bronze, as an architectural ornament (I Kings 7:19; II Chron. 4:5). The expression "lilies of the field" (*ta krina tou agrou,* Matt. 6:28-30) is well translated. Fortunately we have only to go to the grain fields of Palestine to find precisely what fulfills the conditions of the allusion. They are as follows: A plant which would naturally be called a *lily* (not a *ranunculus*, nor an *anemone*, nor a *poppy*, plants having names of their own in both Greek and English, and never confounded with lilies in either ancient or modern speech), growing among the wheat, adorned

504. A Lily of Palestine

with regal colors, and having stems, which, when dried, would answer as fuel for the oriental oven. There are three species of the *sword lily*, *Gladiolus segetum*, Gawl, *G. Illyricus*, Koch, and *G. atroviolaceus*, Boiss., with pink to purple and blackish-violet flowers, which grow everywhere among standing corn, and have stems suitable for light fuel. As they are the only plants which fulfill all the conditions, we cannot but believe that they were the very plants to which our Saviour pointed to illustrate the heavenly Father's care of his children.

Mallows (Heb. *mălūăḥ*, *salt plant*), a term used only once in the Bible (Job 30:4, R. V. "saltwort"). The Arabic equivalent of the Hebrew *mălūăḥ* refers to the *sea orache*, *Atriplex Halimus*, L., a plant growing in just such regions as the one referred to by Job. Dioscorides says that they were cooked as vegetables. The leaves are sour, and furnish little nourishment.

Mandrake (Heb. *dūdāï*, Gen. 30:14; Cant. 7:13, R. V. marg. in both "love apples"), a narcotic plant of the order *Solanaceae*, *Mandragora officinarum*, L., esteemed by the ancients as a love philter, and evidently so referred to in both the above-cited passages. taken in considerable quantities, it is an acrid narcotic poison. It is not used in modern medicine.

Manna (Heb.. *män*, *what?*). Many have sought to identify manna with some substance naturally produced in the desert, answering to the conditions of the food rained down on the Israelites in the wilderness, during a period of forty years. There is a substance called *mann* by the Arabs, and having some nutrient properties, which exudes from *Tamarix mannifera*, Ehr., and certain oaks, and *Alhagi Maurorum*, D. C., and *A. Camelorum*, Fisch. But this substance corresponds in no way with the properties of the scriptural *manna*. The latter was clearly a miraculous production, and ceased as soon as the necessity for it passed away (Exod. 16:14, 31; Num. 11:7, 8; Josh. 5:12). Among its most remarkable characteristics was the double supply on Friday, and the total lack on the Sabbath.

Mas'tich (măs'tĭk), a fragrant, terebinthine gum, exuding from *Pistacia Lentiscus*, L., a small tree, growing abundantly in Palestine and Syria, mentioned only in the Apocrypha

(Sus. 54). It is the universal chewing gum of the East. A preserve is also made of it.

Melons (Heb. *'ăbăttĭăḥ*, Num. 11:5), doubtless generic for *watermelons* and *cantaloupes*, of which there are several luscious varieties in the Holy Land. Being very cheap, and serving to quench the thirst engendered by the hot climate of Bible lands, it would naturally be lamented by the Israelites in the desert.

Mildew (Heb. *yērägön*, *paleness*). Various sorts of parasitic fungi, on plants, the growth of which is favored by moisture. It is the opposite of *blasting* (*shĭddäphōn*, which is the drying up of plants by the hot sirocco, or khamsîn winds (see Deut. 28:22; I Kings 8:37, etc.).

Millet (Heb. *dōḥăn*, Ezek. 4:9), the seed of *Panicum miliaceum*, L., and of *Setaria Italica*, Kth. It is about as large as a mustard seed. In the single passage where it occurs it formed part of the basis of a very complex bread. Some have supposed that *Sorghum vulgare*, L., is the plant intended by the Hebrew original *dōḥăn*.

Mint, a tithable herb. The most common species of mint is *Mentha sativa*, L., which is universally cultivated and used as a flavoring in salads and in cookery. *Hdusma* (Matt. 23:23; Luke 11:42) was probably generic for other kinds of mint, as well as the above.

Mulberry Tree (Heb. *bäkä'*, II Sam. 5:23, 24; I Chron. 14:14, 15), a tree, to the identification of which we have no clue. It would be better to transliterate the Hebrew term, which is from the same root as Baca (Psa. 84:6), which signifies *weeping*, *distilling*. The expression would then read *trees b'käïm*. They were certainly not *mulberries*. The *mulberry* is mentioned, however, in the Apocrypha (I Macc. 6:34). The *sycamine* (Luke 17:6) is the *black mulberry* (*see* Sycamine).

Mustard (Gr. *sinapi*), a well-known plant, of which two species, *Sinapis arvensis*, L., and *S. alba*, L., flourish in the Holy Land. Beside

ACTUAL SIZE SEEDS

APPROXIMATELY 2/3 SIZE

505. Mustard

these *S. nigra*, L., the *black mustard*, is cultivated as a condiment. All produce minute seeds (Matt. 17:20; Luke 17:6). All, in favorable soil in this warm climate, attain a size quite sufficient for the exigencies of the passages (Matt. 13:31, 32; Mark 4:32; Luke 13:19). The birds, in the latter passage, it will be observed, *lodge*, not *nest*, in the branches. The term "great tree" is to be taken only as an exaggerated contrast with the minute seed, and to be explained by the parallel "greatest

506. Mustard Tree

among herbs" (Matt. 13:32). There seems to us to be no evidence whatever that *Salvadora Persica*, Garcin, is the plant intended by *sinapi*.

Myrrh (Heb. *mōr, distilling;* Arabic *murr;* Gr. *smyrna, myrrha*), is the well-known gum resin extracted from the Arabian *Balsamodendron Myrrha*, Nees. It was used as a perfume, for embalming, and as an ingredient of the holy anointing oil. It was one of the gifts of the Magi. Another Hebrew word, *lōṭ*, is translated *myrrh* (Gen. 37:25; 43:11). It should be translated *ladanum* (R. V. Gen. 37:25, marg.). This is a gummy exudation from *Cistus villosus*, L., a plant growing in great abundance in the Holy Land.

507. Myrrh

Myrtle, a well-known and beautiful evergreen shrub, *Myrtus communis*, L., with white flowers, berries which are at first white, and then turn bluish black. They are edible, though rather too astringent for Western palates. The Hebrew name of Esther, *Hadasseh*, is derived from the name of this plant (Heb. *hădăs*). The translation "myrtle trees" (Zech. 1:8, 10, 11) is an error, as the original has only *hădăsîm*,

508. Myrtle

myrtles, with no hint as to whether they were *trees* or *shrubs*.

Nettle. The Hebrew *ḥārūl*, which occurs thrice (Job. 30:7; Prov. 24:31; Zeph. 2:9), and is translated "nettle," R. V. marg. "wild vetches," probably signifies *thorn, scrub,* or *brush.* The Holy Land is preeminently a land of such scrubs, and the sense of the above passages is well met by the term. The Hebrew word *qimmōsh (qîmōsh)* (Isa. 34:13; Hos. 9:6), from a root signifying *to sting*, doubtless refers to the true *nettles*, of the genera *Urtica* and *Forskahlea*, of the order *Urticaceae*, of which there are a number of species in this land. This rendering perfectly suits the passages cited.

Nuts. The nuts of Gen. 43:11 (Heb. *bōṭĕn*), are without doubt *pistachios*, as in R. V. marg. They are, and always have been, luxuries in the East. The nuts of Cant. 6:11 (*'ĕgōz*), are *walnuts*. They are universally cultivated and greatly esteemed in Bible lands.

Oak. Several kinds of oak are found in Palestine and adjoining countries. *Quercus sessili-flora* flourishes on lofty Lebanon slopes and in the Hauran. The prickly evergreen oak is found in four varieties. These varieties of oak are found in Carmel, Bashan and Gilead and often attain considerable size. The deciduous Valonia oak is found in Galilee and Gilead. Five Hebrew words are rendered oak. The Hebrew word *'allōn* is apparently the correct Hebrew term, for it was a characteristic tree of Bashan (Gen. 35:8; Isa. 2:13; Ezek. 27:6; Zech. 11:2). Another Hebrew term for oak is *'ēlāh.* In two passages it is associated with *'allōn* and is translated "terebinth" in the R. V. (Isa. 6:13; Hos. 4:13). It is commonly rendered "terebinth" in the margin of the R. V. The Hebrew term *'ēlōn* is translated oak in the text of nine passages of the R. V., terebinth being put in the margin. The A. V., under the influence of the Targum and the Vulgate, renders *'ēlōn* by "plane tree" but in the margin of Judg. 9:6 it has oak. Isa. 1:29 renders the Hebrew word *'ēl* as oak. M. F. U.

Oil Tree. The Hebrew expression '*ēṣ shĕmĕn* is of uncertain meaning. It occurs only in three connections (I Kings 6:23, 31-33, "olive;" Neh. 8:15, A. V. "pine," R. V. "wild olive;" Isa. 41:19, "oil tree," R. V. marg. "oleaster"). It evidently, from its name denotes some tree rich in oleaginous or resinous matter, the presence of which is a sign of fertility. It is of a size and hardness sufficient to furnish material for a carved image ten cubits high. It grows in the mountains and has foliage suited for booths, and is not the olive, which is mentioned by name in the same connection (Neh. 8:15); some *fatwood* tree, for example any of the *pines* (as in A. V., Neh. 8:15, not "wild olive" as in R. V.). It is useless to seek to identify it. Better call it "oil tree."

509. Olives

Olive (Heb. *zăyĭth;* Gr. from '*elaia*), a tree, with leaves of the characteristic dull green at their upper surface and a silvery sheen at their lower, universally cultivated in Bible countries. It is alluded to many times in the Bible, often as an emblem of peace, prosperity, and wealth. Much is said of its beauty, fruitfulness, and usefulness to mankind. Its berries and oil are now, as always, leading articles of commerce. Disasters to olive trees are national afflictions, and the failure of the crop is a cause of ruin and a sign of the divine wrath. The olive berry (Isa. 17:6; James 3:12) is a small drupe, of an oblong ovoid shape, green when young, becoming dark purple, then black, and containing a large amount of oil and a bitter principle. The bitter, appetizing taste and the nutritive properties of the berry cause it to be a prime article of diet in all Eastern lands. It is eaten after pickling in brine, or preserved in olive oil.

510. Olive Press

Only the fully ripe berries are preserved in the latter way. But the chief value of the olive tree consists in the rich and abundant oil which is expressed from the berry. Large groves of olive trees exist in the neighborhood of most of the cities of the coast of Syria and Palestine, and throughout Lebanon and the hill country of Palestine. The oil produced from them is one of the chief articles of commerce in this land. Oil forms a large element in the diet of the people, being used for salads, which are an accompaniment of most of their meals, and for frying, in place of butter, especially during the fasts of the various Christian sects. It is also much used in the manufacture of soap. It is boiled with crude carbonate of soda; and makes a very excellent grade of hard soap, of which considerable quantities are exported to Europe, and the remainder consumed in the country.

Onions (Heb. *bĕṣĕl*). Much as the onion is cultivated and used as an article of food and commerce, it is only mentioned once in the Bible, in connection with the longing of the Israelites in the desert for the good things of Egypt (Num. 11:5). Those familiar with the delicately flavored onions of the East prefer them to the ranker product of the West.

Palm Tree (Heb. *tämär;* Gr. *phoinix*). The palm tree in Scripture very commonly designates the date palm. *Phoenix dactylifera.* This lovely single-stocked tree climbs often to eighty feet in height. Its stem ends in a picturesque bunch of leaves. It is highly ornamental as well as useful. Its sap yields sugar from which a strong drink called *arrack* is made. Its fruit is highly edible and nourishing and is widely used as an article of food. Even the seeds are ground and yield food for camels. The leaves serve to cover roofs and for fences, baskets, mats and other household articles. In the Bible the palms are characterized as "goodly trees" (Lev. 23:40). In Hebrew-Phoenician art they formed a characteristic motif for the Solomonic temple (I Kings 6:29; II Chron. 3:5). Palms were used to celebrate the Feast of Tabernacles (Lev. 23:40). The beauty and utility of the palm furnished a lovely figure for the psalmist of the prosperity of the godly (Psa. 92:12). By Christian times the palm came to denote victory (Rev. 7:9). The finest and best palm trees were found around Jericho, Engedi and along the banks of the Jordan. They live normally a century and a half to two centuries. The palm tree has a

511. Papyrus Harvest in Early Egypt

long tap root that goes down to sources of water. The fact that it grows in perennial freshness in almost desert-like conditions makes it a fitting symbol of constancy, patience, uprightness and prosperity. *M. F. U.*

Pan'nag (Heb. *pănnăg*, Ezek. 27:17), a substance, perhaps the one known by the Arabs as *halâwa*. It is made of a decoction of soapwort root, to which is added syrup of dibs and sesame oil. The mixture is stirred over the fire until the elements are fully incorporated, and set aside to crystallize. *Pannag* was, as *halâwa* is now, an article of internal commerce in Palestine and Syria, and of export to other lands. In Akkadian *pannigu* is a kind of cake.

Papyrus. The papyrus was a water plant which grew luxuriantly in Egypt in ancient times and in certain sections of Palestine. To the present day it is found in the swamps around Lake Huleh in Galilee. Ancient paper was made from the fibres of the papyrus plant. The paper manufactured was pale yellow. Papyrus rolls were from ten to thirty feet long and about nine and one-half inches high. Egyptians sometimes had huge papyrus rolls, such as the 123-foot long Papyrus Harris. Use of papyrus for writing materials goes back to the Old Kingdom in Egypt, probably before 2700 B. C. The dry Egyptian climate was favorable to the preservation of papyri and some extant copies go back to the third millennium. In antiquity Egypt was a source of supply for ancient paper. Gebal on the Mediterranean coast received papyrus from Egypt and this center of the paper trade was later called Byblos, meaning "papyrus" or "book" by the Greeks. Our modern word Bible through Greek and Latin goes back to this source. Leather was used very early, and parchment also came into later use. Papyrus reeds tied together to form boats were used in ancient Egypt. Isaiah refers to Ethiopians dispatching "ambassadors by the sea, even in vessels of papyrus" (chap. 18:2). In Egyptian art the papyrus growing in the marshes of the Delta symbolized Lower Egypt. The lotus, on the other hand, stood for Upper Egypt. *M. F. U.*

513. Egyptian Noble Hunting Fowl in Papyrus Marches

Pine Tree. We have already seen under *Oil Tree* that (Heb. *ēṣ shĕmĕn*, Neh. 8:15) is probably, as in A. V., "pine," or *fat wood*, not, as in R. V., "wild olive." Another word (Heb. *tĭdhär*) is rendered in the only place in which it occurs "pine" (Isa. 41:19, R. V. marg. "plane"). There is, however, no etymological basis for this rendering, nor for R. V. marg. "plane," for which there is another Hebrew word, *'ărmōn* (*see* Chestnut), nor for Gesenius's rendering "oak." We prefer to transliterate it *tĭdhär*. Under *Ash* we have given our reasons for the opinion that (Heb. *'ōrĕn*), probably refers to the *stone pine, Pinus Pinea,* L. On the whole it must be admitted, however, that it is not absolutely certain that any of these words signifies *pine.*

Plane Tree. *See* Chestnut.

Pome'granate (pŏm'grăn'ĭt), a well-known tree, *Punica Granatum,* L., cultivated everywhere in the East. The fruit is spherical, often

512. The Papyrus Plant of Egypt (see Gebal)

four inches or more in diameter, green when young, turning red in ripening, with a woody, astringent rind, inclosing a large number of luscious pulpy seeds of a pinkish color. The pomegranate is frequently mentioned in company with the vine, fig, and palm. The rind contains much tannin, and a decoction of it is a remedy against the tape worm (see I Sam. 14:2; Cant. 4:13, etc.).

514. Pomegranate

Poplar, the translation of Heb. (*lǐbněh*), Arabic *lubna*, *white tree* (Gen. 30:37, R. V. marg. "storax;" Hos. 4:13). There can be little doubt that *storax* is the correct rendering. *Storav officinale*, L., although usually a shrub, often attains a height of twenty feet, which would answer the requirements of the passage in Hosea. The lower surface of its leaves·is white, and it bears a wealth of large white blossoms, which well entitle it to the name of the *white tree*. Its effect in the landscape is similar to that of *Cornus florida*, L., the *flowering dogwood* of the northern woods in the United States.

Pottage. *See* Lentils.

Pulse (Dan. 1:12, 16), a word of far more restricted meaning than the Hebrew *zērō'ă*, or *zērä'on*, something *sown*, which signifies primarily *vegetables* in general, and more particularly *edible seeds which are cooked*, as *lentils*, *horse beans*, *beans*, *chick peas*, and the like. Daniel and his companions were pleading for a simple vegetable diet in place of the rich, unwholesome dishes of the king's table.

Purslane. *See* Egg.

Raisin. *See* Vine.

Reed Grass. *See* Flag.

Reeds, Rushes. Six Hebrew words are used for marsh plants. Two, *'ähū*, and *soof* (Heb. *sūph*), are frequently but not always rendered "flag" (*see* Flag). Of the remaining four:

1. *'ăgmōn* is rendered "reed," "marsh," "hook," "rope," "caldron," "burning rushes," "rush," and "bulrush." It doubtless refers in a general way to swamp plants of the orders *Cyperaceae* and *Gramineae*, and the like.

2. *gōměh* probably includes the *papyrus*, *bulrushes*, *club rushes*, and *twig rush*, i. e. plants of the orders *Juncaceae* and *Cyperaceae*.

3. *qānĕh*, which is cognate with *cane*, may be considered as the equivalent of the English *reed*, taken as that term is in a broad sense. It includes the tall grasses with woody stems, such as *Arundo Donax*, L., the *Persian reed*, *Saccharum Aegyptiacum*, Willd., the Arabic

ghazzâr (both of which may be considered as included under the expression "reed shaken with the wind," Matt. 11:7), *Phragmites communis*, L., the *true reed*. Qānĕh is variously translated "reed," "stalk," "bone," "beam" of a balance, "branches" of a lampstand, "cane," "calamus."

4. *'ărōth*, translated "paper reeds" (A. V. Isa. 19:7), should be, as in R. V., "meadows."

Rose (Heb. *ḥăbăṣĕlĕth*). The word occurs in A. V. twice (Cant. 2:1; Isa. 35:1), in both of which R. V. marg. has "autumn crocus." It is probable that *narcissus* is the correct rendering. Two species, *Narcissus Tazetta*, L., and *N. serotinas*, L., grow in the Holy Land. The rose is mentioned in the Apocrypha (Ecclus. 24:14; 39:13). There are seven species of rose which grow in the Holy Land. The most widely distributed of these is *Rosa Phoenicia*, Boiss., which grows on the coast and in the mountains. A pink rose, with very fragrant petals, is cultivated in Damascus for the sake of its essential oil, the famous *attar of roses*. *Rose water* and *syrup of rose leaves* are also extensively manufactured throughout the country.

Rue (Gr. *pēganon*), a plant with a penetrating, to most persons disagreeable, odor. It was tithable (Luke 11:42). The officinal species, *Ruta graveolens*, L., is cultivated. The allied wild species, *R. Chalepensis*, L., is widely diffused throughout the country.

Rush. *See* Reed.

Rye, the A. V. rendering (Exod. 9:32; Isa. 28:25) of the Heb. *kŭssĕmĕth* (A. V. "fitches," Ezek. 4:9). The R. V. renders it in all three passages "spelt." We believe it to be the *kirsenneh*, which is the cognate Arabic for the leguminous plant *Vicia Ervilia*, L., a cereal universally cultivated in the East. Rye is unknown in these lands, and spelt (*q. v.*), is not commonly cultivated. The Vulgate renders the word *vicia*. Fitches is a corruption of this Latin word, but it is elsewhere used for the seeds of *Nigella sativa* (*see* Fitches). It is not a happy choice here. It would be better to translate *kŭssĕmĕth* by *vetch*, with a marginal note, "the kirsenneh of the Arabs."

Saffron (Heb. *kărkōm*, Cant. 4:14), an aromatic, composed of the styles of several species of crocus, principally *C. cancellatus*, Herb. Bot. They are of an orange color, and are principally used to impart an agreeable odor and flavor to boiled rice. The flowerets of *Carthamus tinctorius*, L., known as *safflower*, or *bastard saffron*, are used for a similar purpose.

Saltwort. *See* Mallows.

Shit′tah Tree, Shit′tim Wood (Heb. *shĭṭṭäh*; *shĭṭṭīm*), a tree, of which two species, *Acacia Seyal*, Del., and *A. Tortilis*, Hayne, grow in the deserts of Sinai and et-Tih, and around the Dead Sea. The wood is hard, very heavy, indestructible by insects, of a fine and beautiful grain, and thus suitable in every way for the construction of the framework and furniture of the tabernacle. It also yields the officinal gum arabic. Shittim, Abel-Shittim, and the Valley of Shittim were named from this tree. Shitta Tree, shittim wood, or acacia (*sayal*) is remarkably luxuriant in dry places, sometimes attaining a height of twenty feet. It is adorned with lovely yellow flowers. Its

515. Acacia (Shittim) Foliage, Flower and Fruit

insect-resisting wood was used also for tanning leather, for fuel and for parts of mummy cases. *M. F. U.*

Spelt, an inferior kind of wheat, the chaff clinging to the grain. The Egyptians used it for bread (Herodotus II. 36). In Egypt it came up after barley. The word is the revised rendering of Heb. *kŭssĕmĕth* (Exod. 9:32; Isa. 28:25). It is translated rye. In Ezek. 4:9 the A. V. renders fitches. *M. F. U.*

Spice, Spicery. Two generic Hebrew words for aromatics occur in the Old Testament, *săm* and *băsăm.* Several of the individual aromatics included under these words are given, as *frankincense, stacte, onycha, galbanum, myrrh, cinnamon, calamus,* and *cassia* (Exod. 30:23, 34). These and numerous other aromatics, among them *spikenard* and *lign aloes,* were used as perfumes, anointing oils, and incense, and for embalming bodies. *Nᵉkŏth* (Gen. 37:25) has been supposed by some to be *gum traga-canth.* We are inclined, however, to regard it as also a generic term, which is not badly expressed by "spicery," better by *aromatics.*

Spike′nard (spīk′nård; Heb. *nĕrd,* Gr. *nardos*), an aromatic oil extracted from an East Indian plant, *Nardostachys Jatamansi,* D. C. (Cant. 1:12; 4:13, 14; Mark 14:3; John 12:3).

Stac′te (stăk′tē; Heb. *năṭăph,* Exod. 30:34), an aromatic; R. V. marg. "opobalsamum" is not probable; nor is it likely that it is *storax,* which we believe to be a product of the plant designated as *libneh* (*see* Poplar). Stacte is in fact *myrrh,* and its Hebrew original in the above passage, *năṭăph,* signifying *drops,* probably refers to *myrrh in tears.* The same word (Job 36:27) is used for *drops of water.*

Storax. *See* Myrrh, Poplar, Stacte.

Straw. During the process of oriental threshing the straw is cut into bits half an inch to two in length, and more or less crushed and shredded, and pulverized, and mixed with the chaff. This product is known in Arabic as *tibn,* the cognate of the Hebrew *tĕbĕn,* which is usually translated *straw,* sometimes incorrectly *chaff* and *stubble.* As hay is unknown, this cut straw is its substitute.

Stubble (Heb. *qăsh, dry; tĕbĕn,* Job 21:18; Gr. *kalamē,* I Cor. 3:12). As grain is, for the most part, pulled up by the roots in oriental harvesting, there is very little true *stubble* in an Eastern field. But there is an abundance of dry sticks and fallen straws, with weeds and thorny plants growing among them. On this *stubble* the herds and flocks subsist in summer, and it astonishes occidentals to see what large numbers of animals get a living from land that to their eyes seems blasted and desert. Such dry sticks and straws are readily lighted, and the flames spread like prairie fire.

Sweet Cane. *See* Reed.

Sycamine. The Gr. *sukaminos* meant also the *sycamore,* but the English term has come to mean only the *black mulberry, Morus nigra,* L. The fruit of it resembles in shape and external appearance the larger sorts of blackberries, but it has a decidedly different, though pleasant acid flavor. It is mentioned but once, in the New Testament (Luke 17:6). Wherever *sukaminos* occurs in the LXX, it refers to the *sycomore.*

Sycamore, a fig tree; the rendering in the Old Testament of *shăqăm* and *shĭqmăh* in the Hebrew, and *sukaminos* in the LXX. It is a spreading tree, *Ficus Sysomorus,* L., of the order *Urticaceae,* often planted by roadsides, where it affords a favorable point of view for sightseers. It also grows wild and reaches a very large size. Its wood is light but durable, and much used for house carpentry and fuel. It was once abundant in the Holy Land (I Kings 10:27, etc.) and in Egypt (Psa. 78:47). Its fruit is a small edible fig.

Tamarisk. The tamarisk is a bush tree, highly ornamental, which yields pink and white flowers in Spring. A number of species occur in Palestine. It is the correct rendering of Heb. *'ĕshĕl* (Gen. 21:33; I Sam. 22:6; 31:13). *M. F. U.*

516. Tare

Tares (Gr. *zizanion*), R. V. *darnel.* Tares are very numerous in the grain fields, along with a large number of other species of plants not suitable for human food. They are left until the stalks are well grown together, and then, not long before the harvest (Matt. 13:30), women and children, and sometimes men, go carefully among the grain and pull up all but the wheat and barley. Nowadays these weeds are not burned, but fed to cattle. If any tares remain unnoticed until the grain is harvested and threshed out, the seeds are separated from the wheat and barley and set aside for poultry. There are four kinds of tares in the Holy Land, far the most common of which in the grain fields is *Lolium temulentum*, L., or the bearded darnel, a poisonous grass, almost indistinguishable from wheat while the two are growing into blade. But when they come into ear, they can be separated without difficulty.

Teil Tree (Isa. 6:13) should be *terebinth*, as in R. V.

Terebinth. *See* Turpentine, Oak, Teil Tree.

Thicket. *See* Forest.

517. Thistle

Thistles, Thorns (including *Bramble, Brier*). Seventeen Hebrew words are used for plants with prickles and thorns. Probably most of them once referred to definite species, which we have now no means of fixing. It is clear that translators, both ancient and modern, have given up in despair all hope of unraveling the intricacies of the tangle, and have translated these numerous terms to suit their conviction of the needs of the context of the various passages in which they occur. One of them, *sǎrpǎd* (Isa. 55:13), is probably no thorn, but the *elecampane*, which is placed in the above passage in parallelism with the *myrtle*. The number of names for thorny plants, though so large, is small in comparison with the number of such plants. At least fifty genera, and more than two hundred species, in the Holy Land, are armed with prickles or thorns, and many more with stinging hairs. If the weary traveler sits confidingly on a grassy bank by the wayside, he is sure to rise more quickly than he sat down, happy if he is able to extract the thorns which are often broken off in his flesh. It is often difficult to force

horses through fields overrun with *Eryngiums, Cirsiums, Onopordons*, and the like. They will swerve from side to side, and attempt to leap over their tormentors, and sometimes become almost frantic from the pain. Many herbs have heads several inches in diameter, bristling with spines two to six inches long. Such are sometimes dragged out on the threshing floors and broken to pieces, as food for asses and camels. With such, perhaps, Gideon "taught [threshed] the men of Succoth" (Judg. 8:16). The number of intricate thorn bushes suitable for hedges is large (Job 5:5).

The *"crown of thorns"* which was platted for our Saviour's head (Mark 15:17, etc.); Gr. *'akanthinos* may have been composed of *Calycotome villosa*, L., or *Poterium spinosum*, L. *Zizyphus Spina-Christi*, L., the traditional Christ thorn, would not have been easy to procure in Jerusalem.

Thyine, a prize ornamental wood obtained from a large tree of the cyprus family (*Collistris Quadrivalvis*). This luxury commodity was marketed in the emporia of mystic Babylon (Rev. 11:12). The wood was reddish-brown, extremely hard and fragrant. The Romans greatly prized it, and it was very expensive.— *M. F. U.*

Tow. *See* Flax.

Trees. Trees are valued in this land, mainly as yielding fruit or timber. Systematic planting of shade trees is almost unknown, except in cemeteries and around the tombs of saints. The forests have been greatly reduced in number and contain few large trees (*see* Forest). Some efforts have been made from time to time to acclimatize foreign trees. Solomon appears to have had botanical gardens, and such are mentioned by Josephus in his days. Pliny mentions the palm groves of Jericho. Trees have important symbolical meanings in Scripture. Man fell from eating the fruit of the "tree of knowledge of good and evil," and was driven off in the attempt to attain the "tree of life." This tree, in restored Paradise, supplies food and medicine for all.

Turpentine. This tree is only mentioned in the Apocrypha (Ecclus. 24:16). It is the *terebinth* (*butm* of the Arabs), *Pistacia Terebinthus*, L., and its variety Palaestina (*P. Palaestina*, Boiss.). It is generally diffused, the trees being usually solitary, seldom in groves or forests. Another species, *Pistacia mutica*, Fisch et Meyer, is more common east of the Jordan and in Jebel Bil'âs, of the Syrian Desert. Several of the words translated "oak" in A. V. may refer to this tree. *See* Oak.

Vine, a plant mentioned early and very frequently in Scripture. It was and is one of the most important sources of livelihood and wealth to the people of the East. It is associated with the *fig, palm*, and *pomegranate* in the enumeration of the products of the land. *Gĕphĕn* is generic for *vine*, *sōrēq* (Jer. 2:21), a *choice vine*, and *näzîr* (*unpruned vine*).

Vine of Sodom (Deut. 32:32). It is impossible to identify any plant growing near the site of Sodom which corresponds with this poetical allusion. Various plants have been suggested, but none of them fulfills the necessary conditions. The *colocynth* is a vine, but does not produce clusters nor grapelike fruit. The *'ushr*,

518. Vine Leaf and Flower

Calotropis procera, Willd., also bears neither clusters nor grapes. *Solanum nigrum*, L., and its allied species, called in Arabic *'inab-edh-dhîb*, *wolf's grapes*, have fruits too small to be called grapes, are not vines, and are not peculiar to this region. *Solanum coagulans*, Forsk., is not a vine, and bears fruits like small tomatoes, not grapes. *Cucumis prophetarum*, L., produces no clusters nor grapes. In our view it is better to regard the *vine of Sodom* as a poetic creation, similar to the wine in the same passage. The poet, filled with the idea of bitterness suggested by the waters of the Dead Sea, pictures an ideal vine, nourished by this bitter sea, producing bitter clusters, grapes of gall, the wine of which is dragon's poison and the cruel venom of asps. Such imagery is in strict accord with Hebrew poetical license.

Vinegar of excellent quality is made from the light wines of the country. It is uncertain whether the vinegar presented to our Saviour on the cross was acid wine or true vinegar.

Vineyards are often hedged about, but as often not. They are provided with towers or booths for watchmen. The vines must be regularly pruned. *Grapes* are of many kinds in the Holy Land and of superior excellence. The *vintage* takes place in September and October, and is a season of great rejoicing. The grapes are either eaten as such, or dried into raisins, or the juice expressed in the wine vat and fermented into wine, or boiled down in great caldrons into dibs, i. e., grape honey. Neither the unfermented juice (*mistâr*) of the grapes nor the inspissated syrup is known as wine. The latter is never diluted as a beverage.

519. Wheat Fields in Palestine

Weeds (Heb. *sūph*, Jonah 2:5) are *sea weeds* (Gr. *chortos*, Ecclus. 40:16), *worthless land plants*.

Wheat was cultivated in Palestine and adjacent lands at a very early period. Palestinian wheat was sown in November or December after the early rains. The harvest was in April, May or June. Wheat flour constituted the ordinary ingredient of the bread of the Hebrews (Exod. 29:2). The grains were also roasted and eaten. The fertile, well-watered Nile Valley was the granary of the ancient world, particularly in times of dearth (Gen. 41:22). Grains of wheat have been found in Egyptian tombs and elsewhere.

520. Threshing, Jordan

Willow. Several species of willows are found in the Holy Land. There are two Hebrew words for willow—*ṣâph ṣâphâh*, the equivalent of the Arabic *sifsâf*, and *'ärâb*. Tradition says that the willow on which the Israelites hung their harps was the *weeping willow*, called from that circumstance *Salix Babylonica*, L. Many places mentioned in Scripture are named from willows.

Wormwood (Heb. *lǎ'ǎ nâh;* Gr. *'apsinthos*), bitter plants growing in waste, usually desert places. They are an emblem of calamity and injustice. They belong to the genus *Artemisia*, of which there are five species in the tablelands and deserts of Palestine and Syria.— G. F. Post.

Veil (Heb. *pärōkĕth*), the screen separating the Holy and Most Holy Places in the tabernacle (*q. v.*) and temple (*q. v.*). It was this piece of tapestry that was rent by the earthquake at Christ's crucifixion (Matt. 27:51, etc.).

Vein (Heb. *môṣâh*, a *source*), signifies the issuing place, i. e., the place from which anything naturally comes forth (Job 38:27), or whence it is obtained (I Kings 10:28); the place where a mineral is found, the *mine* (Job 28:19), the place where the gold comes forth, therefore a gold mine.

Vengeance. Punishment inflicted in return for an injury or offense suffered; retribution; often passionate or unrestrained revenge. 1. (Heb. *nâqǎm*, to *grudge*) is to punish. In a bad sense, as of an injured person, it is to take vengeance, to avenge oneself (Judg. 15:7; I Sam. 18:25; Ezek. 25:15), and is the manifestation of *vindictiveness* (Lam. 3:60). When vengeance is predicted of the Lord it must be taken in the better sense of righteous punishment (Psa. 94:1; Jer. 11:20; 20:12, etc.).

2. Gr. *dikē 'ekdikesis* (*punishment*). Both these words express the idea of executing righteous judgment (Acts 28:4), vindicating one from wrongs (Luke 18:7, sq.; 21:22), avenging an injured person (Acts 7:24).

3. Gr. *'orgē* (*impulse, desire*), as attributed to God in the New Testament, is that in God which stands opposed to man's disobedience, and passes over into the notion of retribution, punishment (Rom. 3:5). *See* Wrath.

Venison (Heb. *ṣăyid*, the *chase; ṣēdäh*, Gen. 27:3), *game* taken in hunting (25:28; 27:5-33).

Versions of the Scriptures, a general name for translations of the Scriptures into other languages than the original. After the Hebrew tongue became a dead language in the 2d century before Christ, and still more after the spread of Christianity, translations of the Hebrew Scriptures into the prevailing languages became a necessity. Accordingly, almost every language then current had at least one version, which received ecclesiastical authority, and was used instead of the original Hebrew text.

In the case of the New Testament, there did not for a long time exist any occasion for a translation, as the Greek language, in which it was written, was universally prevalent in the civilized world at the time of the promulgation of the Gospel. In certain provinces of the Roman empire, however, the Latin soon came into common use, especially in North Africa, and hence the old Latin and afterward the Vulgate arose. Still later the Syriac version was made for the use of the oriental Christians, to whom that language was vernacular.

In this article the several versions are arranged into two general groups, ancient and modern.

1. **Ancient.** (1) **Arabic.** (1) Versions of the Old Testament. (*a*) Made from the Hebrew text. Saadia Gaon, the Hebrew commentator of the 10th century, translated portions (some think the whole) of the Old Testament into Arabic. His version of the Pentateuch was printed at Constantinople in 1546. The version of Isaiah by Saadia was printed by Paulus at Jena at 1791, from a Bodleian manuscript; the same library contains a manuscript of his version of Hosea. The Book of Joshua in the Paris and Walton's Polyglots is also from the Hebrew; and this Rodiger states to be the fact in the case of the polyglot text of I Kings, ch. 12; II Kings 12:16; Neh. 1-9: 27. (*b*) Made from the Peshito Syriac. This is the base of the Arabic text contained in the polyglots of Judges, Ruth, Samuel, Kings, and Nehemiah. (*c*) Made from the LXX. The version in the polyglots of the books not specified above. Another text of the Psalter in *Justiniani Psalterium Octuplum*, Genoa, 1516. (2) Versions of the New Testament. (*a*) The Roman edition of the four Gospels, 1590-91. (*b*) The Erpenian Arabic. The whole New Testament, edited by Erpenius, 1616, at Leyden, from a manuscript of the 13th or 14th century. (*c*) The Arabic of the Paris Polyglot, 1645. In the Gospels this follows mostly the Roman text; in the Epistles a manuscript from Aleppo was used. (*d*) The *Carshuni* Ara-

bic text (i. e., in Syriac letters), the Syriac and Arabic New Testament, published in Rome, 1703.

(2) **Armenian.** This translation was undertaken by Mesrob (Miesrob), A. D. 410, aided by his pupils Joannes Eccelensis and Josephus Palnensis. Their work was begun with translating Proverbs, ending with the completion of the whole Old Testament. In the New Testament they used the Syriac as their basis, from their inability to obtain any Greek books. In 431 Joseph and Eznak returned from the Council of Ephesus, bringing with them a copy of the Scriptures; and Isaac, the Armenian patriarch, and Mesrob began a new version from the Greek. Hindered by their lack of a competent knowledge of the Greek, Eznak and Joseph were sent, with Moses Chorenensis, to Alexandria to study that language. There they made what Moses called a *third* translation. The first printed edition of the Old and New Testaments in Armenian appeared at Amsterdam, 1666, under the care of Oscan (or Uscan), described as an Armenian bishop. Zohrab, in 1789, published at Venice an improved text of the Armenian New Testament; and in 1805 he and his coadjutors completed an edition of the entire Armenian Scriptures based upon a manuscript written in the 14th century. Charles Rieu, of the British Museum, undertook the task of collating the Venice text of 1805 for Tregelles, thus supplying him with a valuable portion of the materials for his critical edition of the New Testament.

(3) **Aramaic** (Targums).

(4) **Egyptian.** The conversion to Christianity of native Egyptians unfamiliar with Greek, beginning with the third century, resulted in the formation of a Coptic or "Egyptian" church and created a need for translation of the Bible into Coptic dialects. The earliest version, completed about 350 A. D., is in *Sahidic*, the dialect of Upper Egypt. Translations were also made into *Akhmimic* (also Upper Egypt), *Fayumic* (Middle Egypt) and *Bohairic* (around Alexandria). All of these were made from fourth century Septuagint texts but contain occasional earlier readings (cf. H. S. Gehman, *Jour. Bib. Lit.* 46, 1927, pp. 279-330). *M. F. U.*

(5) **Gothic.** The Moeso-Goths were a German tribe which settled on the borders of the Greek empire, and their language is essentially a German dialect. Their version of the Bible was made by Ulphilas, a bishop born 318 A. D., after Greek manuscripts in the New Testament, and after the Septuagint in the Old Testament. In the latter part of the 16th century the existence of a manuscript of this version was known through Morillon having mentioned that he had observed one in the library of the monastery of Werden on the Ruhr, in Westphalia. In 1648, almost at the conclusion of the Thirty Years' War, among the spoils from Prague was sent to Stockholm a copy of the Gothic Gospels, known as the *Codex Argenteus*. It is now preserved in the library of the University of Upsal. "The manuscript is written on vellum that was once purple, in silver letters, except those at the beginning of sections, which are golden. The

Gospels have many lacunae. It is calculated that when entire it consisted of three hundred and twenty folios; there are now but one hundred and eighty-eight. It is pretty certain that this beautiful and elaborate manuscript must have been written in the 6th century, probably in upper Italy, when under the Gothic sovereignty. Knittel, in 1762, edited from a Wolfenbuttel palimpsest some portions of the Epistle to the Romans in Gothic, in which the Latin stood by the side of the version of Ulphilas. New light dawned on Ulphilas and his version in 1817. While the late Cardinal Mai was engaged in the examination of palimpsests in the Ambrosian Library at Milan, of which he was at that time a librarian, he noticed traces of some *Gothic* writing under that of one of the codices. This was found to be part of the Books of Ezra and Nehemiah. In making further examination, four other palimpsests were found which contained portions of the Gothic version. Mai deciphered these manuscripts in conjunction with Count Carlo Ottavio Castiglione, and their labors resulted in the recovery, besides a few portions of the Old Testament, of almost the whole of the thirteen Epistles of St. Paul and some parts of the Gospels. The edition of Gabelentz and Loebe (1836-45) contains all that has been discovered of the Gothic version, with a Latin translation, notes, and a Gothic dictionary and grammar."

(6) **Greek Versions of the Old Testament.** Of these there are six.

(1) Septuagint. The most complete version of the Old Testament was that made into Greek in Egypt, called the Septuagint. It was probably begun in the time of the first Ptolemy, about 280 B. C., and completed in the course of the next thirty or forty years. All agree that Alexandria was the birthplace of this version. That which led to the making of this version was, doubtless, the fact that a very large number of Jews had settled in Egypt. Isaiah speaks of their presence not only in lower Egypt, but in Pathros (i. e., Upper Egypt), and even in Cush (i. e., the Sudan and Abyssinia) (Isa. 11:11). He foresaw the time when whole cities there would speak the Aramaean tongue (19:18), and condemned the policy which caused so many Israelites to migrate thither (30:2). They naturally adopted the language of commerce, which was Greek. When the Greek empire of Alexander was divided among his generals, and the Ptolemys took Egypt, and fostered the Jews, they, with increased numbers and wealth, naturally wished to have their law and other Scriptures in the language of their daily life.

A fabulous account of this version is given in a letter of Aristeas, narrating how King Ptolemy sent an embassy to the high priest at Jerusalem, with large sums in silver and gold; and how the high priest selected six men of each tribe, who, after a magnificent reception, were shut up in cells on the seacoast, and completed the translation in seventy-two days. The internal evidence proves that it was made gradually, and by men deficient in the knowledge handed down in the schools in Palestine. They often divide sentences wrongly, mistake the meaning of rare words, and not infre-

quently confess their ignorance by transcribing Hebrew words in Greek characters. But the story was so generally current that the version was called the Septuagint, as being made by seventy [and two] men.

The letter of Aristeas was received as genuine and true for many centuries. The general belief of scholars now is that it was the work of some Alexandrian Jew, whether with the object of enhancing the dignity of his law or the credit of the Greek version, or for the meaner purpose of gain.

This translation holds a very important place in Church history for the following reasons:

First, for many ages it was the sole means by which the Old Testament was known to Christians. The Hebrew Scriptures were absolutely unknown in the West, and only partially known in the East; and thus the Church was unable to distinguish between what was genuine and what apocryphal. The old Latin version (*Vetus Itala*) was made from the Septuagint.

An equally important service which it rendered was that it prepared the Gentile world for the reception of Christ. Those devout men and women of whom we read so much in St. Paul's missionary tours were Gentiles whose hearts had been reached by the revelation in the Old Testament of the unity, holiness, omnipresence, and almighty power of God; and it was the Septuagint which had given them this knowledge. Without this preparation, going on for nearly three centuries, the Gentile world would not have been fit to receive doctrines so pure and refined as those of Christianity.

A third most important use is that the Septuagint bears witness to the substantial accuracy of the Hebrew text. Made in Egypt at a distance from the Palestinian schools, and by men evidently untrained in the vast traditional knowledge of the scribes, it has preserved for us a text long current in Egypt, and made from manuscripts some of which may possibly have been carried thither in the times of Isaiah and Jeremiah. Of course there are considerable differences of reading, and these often are of great value. But the wonder is that this text, which branched off from the main stem three centuries before Christ, agrees so generally, and often even minutely, with the ordinary Hebrew text as given by the Massoretes in the 9th and 10th centuries after Christ.

(2) Aquila. In the 2d century there were three versions executed of the Old Testament Scriptures into Greek. The first of these was made by Aquila, a native of Sinope in Pontus, who had become a proselyte to Judaism. The Jerusalem Talmud describes him as a disciple of Rabbi Akiba, which would place him some time in the reign of the emperor Hadrian (A. D. 117-138). It is supposed that this object was to aid the Jews in their controversies with the Christians.

(3) Theodotion. The second version, of which we have information as executed in the 2d century, is that of Theodotion. He is said to have been an Ephesian, and most generally described as an Ebionite. His work was rather

a revision of the Septuagint, with the Hebrew text, than a *translation*.

(4) Symmachus is stated by Eusebius and Jerome to have been an Ebionite; while Epiphanius and others style him a Samaritan. It may be that as a Samaritan he made this version for some of that people who used the Greek, and who had learned to receive more than the Pentateuch. Epiphanius says that he lived under the emperor Severus. The translation which he produced was undeniably better than the others as to sense and general phraseology.

(5) The Fifth, Sixth, and Seventh Versions. Besides the translations of Aquila, Symmachus, and Theodotion, the great critical work of Origen, comprised as to portions of the Old Testament three other versions, placed for comparison with the LXX., which, from their being anonymous, are only known as the fifth, sixth, and seventh; designations taken from the places which they respectively occupied in Origen's columnar arrangement. Eusebius says that two of these versions were found, the one at Jericho and the other at Nicopolis, on the Gulf of Actium. Epiphanius says that the fifth was found at Jericho, and the sixth at Nicopolis; while Jerome speaks of the fifth as having been found at the latter place. The contents of the *fifth version* appear to have been the Pentateuch, Psalms, Canticles, and the minor prophets. The existing fragments prove that the Hebrew translator used the Hebrew original; but it is quite certain that he was aided by the work of former translators. The *sixth version* seems to have been just the same in its contents as the fifth (except II Kings). Of the *seventh version* very few fragments remain. It seems to have contained the Psalms and the minor prophets; and the translator was probably a Jew. The existing fragments of these varied versions are mostly to be found in the editions of Origen's *Hexapla*, by Montfaucon and by Bardht.

(6) The Veneto-Grecian Version. A manuscript of the 14th century, in the library of St. Mark, at Venice, contains a peculiar version of the Pentateuch, Proverbs, Ecclesiastes, Canticles, Ruth, Lamentations, and Daniel. All of these books except the Pentateuch were published by Villoison at Strasburg in 1784; the Pentateuch was edited by Ammon at Erlangen (1790-91). It may be said briefly that the translation was made from the Hebrew, although the present punctuation and accentuation is often not followed; and the translator was no doubt acquainted with some other Greek versions.

(7) **Latin Versions.** *See* Vulgate.

(8) **Samaritan Versions.** The Samaritan Pentateuch. A recension of the commonly received Hebrew text of the Mosaic law, in use with the Samaritans, and written in the ancient Hebrew, or so-called Samaritan character.

(*a*) *History.* This recension is found vaguely quoted by some of the early fathers of the Church, under the name of "the old Hebrew according to the Samaritans." Eusebius of Caesarea observes that the LXX. and the Samaritan Pentateuch agree against the received text in the number of years from the deluge to Abraham. Cyril of Alexandria speaks of certain words (Gen. 4:8) wanting in the Hebrew, but found in the Samaritan. The Talmud, on the other hand, mentions the Samaritan Pentateuch distinctly and contemptuously as a clumsily forged record. Down to within the last two hundred and fifty years, however, no copy of this divergent code of laws had reached Europe, and it began to be pronounced a fiction, and the plain words of the Church fathers—the better known authorities—who quoted it, were subjected to subtle interpretations. Suddenly, in 1616, Pietro della Valle, one of the first discoverers also of the cuneiform inscriptions, acquired a complete codex from the Samaritans in Damascus. In 1623 it was presented by Achille Harley de Saucy to the Library of the Oratory in Paris, and in 1628 there appeared a brief description of it by J. Morinus in his preface to the Roman text of the LXX. It was published in the Paris Polyglot, whence it was copied, with few emendations from other codices, by Walton. The number of manuscripts in Europe gradually grew to sixteen. During the present century another but very fragmentary copy was acquired by the Gotha Library. A copy of the entire (?) Pentateuch, with Targum (? Samaritan Version) in parallel columns, 4to, on parchment, was brought from Nâblus by Mr. Grove, in 1861, for the Comte de Paris, in whose library it is.

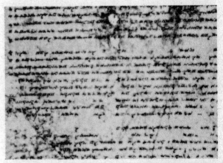

521. Samaritan Pentateuch

(*b*) *Description.* Respecting the external condition of these manuscripts, it may be observed that their sizes vary from 12mo to folio, and that no scroll, such as the Jews and the Samaritans use in their synagogues, is to be found among them. Their material is vellum, or cotton paper; the ink used is black in all cases, save the scroll used by the Samaritans at Nâblus, the letters of which are in gold. There are neither vowels, accents, nor diacritical points. The individual words are separated from each other by a dot. Greater or smaller divisions of the text are marked by two dots placed one above the other, and by an asterisk. A small line above a consonant indicates a peculiar meaning of the word, an unusual form, a passive, and the like; it is, in fact, a contrivance to bespeak attention. The whole Pentateuch is divided into nine hundred and sixty-four paragraphs, or *Kazzin*, the termination of which is indicated by these figures, =, ∴, or < . To none of the manuscripts which have as yet reached Europe can be assigned a higher date than the tenth Christian century. The scroll used in Nâblus is said by the Samaritans to have been written by Abishua, the son of Phinehas. Its true date is not known.

(*c*) *Critical character.* A controversy was maintained respecting the claims of the Samaritan Pentateuch for genuineness above the received text, until 1815, when Gesenius (*De Pent. Sam. Origine, Indole, et Auctoritate*) abolished the remnant of the authority of the Samaritan Pentateuch. There are many variations in the Samaritan Pentateuch, some mere blunders arising from an imperfect knowledge of the first elements of grammar and exegesis; others, from the studied purpose of conforming certain passages to the Samaritan mode of thought, speech, and faith; still others, to a tendency toward removing, as well as linguistic shortcomings would allow, all that seemed obscure or in any way doubtful, and toward filling up all apparent imperfections either by repetitions or by means of newly invented and badly fitting words and phrases. These variations have been arranged by Gesenius as follows: 1. The *first* class, consists of readings by which emendations of a grammatical nature have been attempted. 2. The *second* class of variants consists of glosses and interpretations received into the text. 3. The *third* class exhibits conjectural emendations of real or imaginary difficulties in the Massoretic text. 4. The *fourth* class exhibits readings in which apparent deficiencies have been corrected or supplied from parallel passages in the common text. 5. The *fifth* class is an extension of the one immediately preceding, and comprises larger phrases, additions, and repetitions from parallel passages. 6. To the *sixth* class belong those "emendations" of passages and words of the Hebrew text which contain something objectionable in the eyes of the Samaritans, on account either of historical improbability or apparent want of dignity in the terms applied to the Creator. 7. The *seventh* class comprises what we might briefly call Samaritanisms, i. e., certain Hebrew forms, translated into the idiomatic Samaritan. 8. The *eighth* and last class contains alterations made in favor or on behalf of Samaritan theology, hermeneutics, and domestic worship. Thus the word *Elohim*, four times construed with the plural verb in the Hebrew Pentateuch, is in the Samaritan Pentateuch joined to the singular verb (Gen. 20:13; 31:53; 35:7; Exod. 22:9).

(*d*) *Origin and age.* Respecting these questions opinions have been much divided: that the Samaritan Pentateuch came into the hands of the Samaritans as an inheritance from the ten tribes, whom they succeeded, which is the popular opinion; that it was introduced by Manasseh at the time of the foundation of the Samaritan sanctuary on Mount Gerizim. Other, but very isolated, notions are those of Morin, Le Clerc, Poncet, etc., that the Israelitish priest sent by the king of Assyria to instruct the new inhabitants in the religion of the country brought the Pentateuch with him. Further, that the Samaritan Pentateuch was the production of an impos-

tor, Dositheus, who lived during the time of the apostles, and who falsified the sacred records in order to prove that he was the Messiah (Ussher). Against which there is only this to be observed, that there is not the slightest alteration of such a nature to be found. Finally, that it is a very late and faulty recension, made after the Massoretic text (6th century after Christ), into which glosses from the LXX. had been received (Frankel).

(*e*) *Versions.* According to the Samaritans themselves, a Samaritan version of the Samaritan Pentateuch was made by the high priest Nathaniel, who died about B. C. 20. It would seem to have been composed before the destruction of the second temple; and being intended, like the Targums, for the use of the people exclusively, it was written in the popular Samaritan idiom, a mixture of Hebrew, Aramaic, and Syriac. In this version the original has been followed, with a very few exceptions, in a slavish and sometimes perfectly childish manner, the sense evidently being of minor consideration. In other cases, where no Samaritan equivalent could be found for the Hebrew word, the translator, instead of paraphrasing it, simply transposes its letters, so as to make it *look* Samaritan. On the whole it may be considered a very valuable aid toward the study of the Samaritan text, on account of its very close verbal adherence.

(9) **Slavonic version.** In the year 862 there was a desire expressed, or an inquiry made, for Christian teachers in Moravia, and in the following year the labors of missionaries began among them. They were Cyrillus and Methodius, two brothers from Thessalonica. To the former is ascribed the invention of the Slavonic alphabet and the commencement of translating the Scriptures. He appears to have died in Rome, while Methodius continued for many years to be the bishop of Slavonians. He is said to have continued his brother's translation, although *how much* they themselves actually executed is quite uncertain. The Old Testament is, as might be supposed, a version of the LXX., but what measure of revision it may since have received appears by no means certain. As the oldest known manuscript of the whole Bible is of A. D. 1499, it may reasonably be questioned whether this version may not in large portion be comparatively modern. The oldest manuscript of any part of this version is an Evangeliarium in Cyrillic characters (A. D. 1056). The first printed portion was an edition of the Gospels in Wallachia (1512); in 1575 the same portion was printed at Wilna; and in 1581 the whole Bible was printed at Ostrog in Volhynia. The general text is such as would have been expected in the 9th century; so some readings from the Latin have, it appears, been introduced in places.

(10) **Syriac versions.** (1) Of the Old Testament. 1. *From the Hebrew.* In the early times of Syrian Christianity there was executed a version from the Old Testament of the original Hebrew, the use of which must have been widely extended among those professing the Christian religion among that people.

(a) *Name.* Ephraem the Syrian, in the latter half of the 4th century, gives abundant proof of its use in general by his countrymen. When he calls it *our version* it does not appear to be in opposition to any other Syriac translation, but in contrast to the original Hebrew text, or to those in other languages. At a later period this Syriac translation was designated *Peshito* (*Simple*). It is probable that this name was applied to the version after another had been formed from the Hexaplar Greek text.

(b) *Date.* This translation from the Hebrew has always been the ecclesiastical version of the Syrians. Its existence and use prior to the divisions of the Syrian churches is sufficiently proved by Ephraem alone. It is highly improbable that any part of the Syriac version is older than the advent of our Lord; those who placed it under Abgarus, king of Edessa, seem to have argued on the account that the Syrian people then received Christianity. All that the account shows clearly is, that it was believed to belong to the earliest period of the Christian faith among them. Ephraem, in the 4th century, not only shows that it was then current, but also gives the impression that this had even then been *long* the case. For in his commentaries he gives explanations of terms which were even then obscure. This might have been from age; if so, the version was made comparatively long before his days; or it might be from its having been in a dialect different from that to which he was accustomed at Edessa. In this case, then, the translation was made in some other part of Syria. Probably the origin of the old Syriac version is to be compared with that of the old Latin; and that it differed as much from the polished language of Edessa as did the old Latin, made in the African province from the contemporary writers of Rome. The old Syriac has the peculiar value of being the first version from the Hebrew original made for Christian use.

(c) *Origin and history.* The proof that this version was made from the Hebrew is twofold; we have the direct statements of Ephraem, and we find the same thing as evident from the internal examination of the version itself. The first printed edition of this version was that which appeared in the Paris Polyglot of Le Jay in 1645; it is said that the editor, Gabriel Sionita, a Maronite, had only an imperfect manuscript. In Walton's Polyglot, 1657, the Paris text is reprinted, but with the addition of the Apocryphal books which had been wanting. In the punctuation given in the polyglots a system was introduced which was in part a peculiarity of Gabriel Sionita himself. Dr. Lee collated for the text which he edited for the Bible Society six Syriac manuscripts of the Old Testament in general, and a very ancient copy of the Pentateuch; he also used in part the commentaries of Ephraem and of Bar-Hebraeus. From these various sources he constructed his text, with the aid of that found already in the polyglots. But we now have in the manuscript treasures brought from the Nitrian valleys, the means of far more accurately editing this version. It has been much discussed whether this translation were a Jewish or a Christian work. There need be no reasonable objection made to the opinion that it is a Christian work.

(d) *Relation to other texts.* It may be said that the Syriac *in general* supports the Hebrew text that we have. A resemblance has been pointed out between the Syriac and the reading of some of the Aramaic Targums. If the Targum is the older, it is not unlikely that the Syriac translator examined the Targums in difficult passages. If existing Targums are more recent than the Syriac, it may happen that their coincidences arise from the use of a common source—an earlier Targum. But there is another point of inquiry of more importance; it is, how far has this version been affected by the LXX.? and to what are we to attribute this influence? It is possible that the influence of the LXX. is partly to be ascribed to copyists and revisers; while in part this belonged to the version as originally made. When the extensive use of the LXX. is remembered, and how soon it was superstitiously imagined to have been made by direct inspiration, so that it was deemed canonically authoritative, we cannot feel wonder that readings from the LXX. should have been from time to time introduced. Some comparison with the Greek is probable even before the time of Ephraem; for, as to the Apocryphal books, while he cites some of them (though not as Scripture), the Apocryphal additions to Daniel and the Books of Maccabees were not yet found in Syriac. Whoever translated any of these books from the Greek may easily have also compared with it in some place the books previously translated from the Hebrew.

(e) *Recensions.* In the Book of Psalms this version exhibits many peculiarities. Either the translation of the Psalter must be a work independent of the Peshito in general, or else it has been strangely revised and altered, not only from the Greek, but also from liturgical use. It is stated that, after the divisions of the Syrian Church, there were revisions of this one version by the Monophysites and by the Nestorians. The *Karkaphensian* recension mentioned by Bar-Hebraeus was only known by name prior to the investigations of Wiseman. It is found in two manuscripts in the Vatican, and was formed for the use of Monophysites.

2. *The Syriac version from the Hexaplar Greek text.* The only Syriac version of the Old Testament up to the 6th century was apparently the Peshito. Moses Aghelaeus, who lived in the middle of the 6th century, speaks of the versions of the New Testament and the Psalter, "which Polycarp (rest his soul!), the chorepiscopus, made in Syriac for the faithful Xenaias, the teacher of Mabug, worthy of the memory of the good." It is said that the Nestorian patriarch, Marabba, A. D. 552, made a version from the Greek. The version by Paul of Tela, a Monophysite, was made in the beginning of the 7th century; for its basis he used the Hexaplar Greek text—i. e., the LXX., with the corrections of Origen, the asterisks, obeli, etc., and with the references to the other Greek versions. The Syro-Hexaplar version was made on the principle of following the Greek, word for word, as exactly as possible. It contains the marks introduced by Origen; and the references to the versions

of Aquila, Symmachus, Theodotion, etc. In fact, it is from this Syriac version that we obtain our most accurate acquaintance with the results of the critical labors of Origen. It is from a manuscript in the Ambrosian library at Milan that we possess accurate means of knowing this Syriac version. This manuscript contains the Psalms, Job, Proverbs, Ecclesiastes, Canticles, Wisdom, Ecclesiasticus, minor prophets, Jeremiah, Baruch, Daniel, Ezekiel, and Isaiah.

(2) Syriac New Testament versions. (a) The Peshito Syriac. It may stand as an admitted fact that a version of the New Testament in Syriac existed in the 2d century; and it seems equally certain that in the 4th century such a version was as well known of the New Testament as of the Old. To the translation in common use among the Syrians—orthodox, Monophysite, or Nestorian—from the 5th century and onward, the name of Peshito has been as commonly applied in the New Testament as the Old. There seem to be but few notices of the old Syriac version in the early writers. In 1552 Moses of Mardin came to Rome to Pope Julius III, commissioned by Ignatius the Jacobite (Monophysite) patriarch, to state his religious opinions, to effect (it is said) a union with the Romish Church, and *to get the Syriac New Testament printed*.

In this last object he failed both at Rome and Venice, but was successful at Vienna. Widmanstadt, chancellor of Ferdinand I, had studied Syriac many years before, and through his influence the emperor undertook the charge of an edition, which appeared in 1555, through the joint labors of Widmanstadt, Moses, and Postell. The lexicon which accompanies this edition is of great value. Later editions are those of Professor Lee (1816); Mr. William Greenfield (1828), published by Messrs. Bagster. It appears probable that the New Testament of the Peshito is not from the same hand as the Old.

This Syriac version has been variously estimated. Some have thought that in it they had a genuine and unaltered monument of the 2d or perhaps even of the 1st century. They naturally upheld it as almost coordinate in authority with the Greek text, and as being of a period anterior to any Greek copy extant. Others, finding in it indubitable marks of a later age, were inclined to deny that it had any claim to a very remote antiquity. It appears probable that the New Testament of the Peshito is not from the same hand as the Old. Not only may Michaelis be right in supposing a peculiar translator of the Epistle to the Hebrews, but also other parts may be from different hands; this opinion will become more general the more the version is studied.

(b) The Curetonian Syriac gospels. Among the manuscripts brought from the Nitrian monasteries in 1842, Dr. Cureton noticed a copy of the gospels differing greatly from the common text; and to this the name of Curetonian Syriac has been rightly applied. Every criterion which proves the common Peshito not to exhibit a text of extreme antiquity equally proves the early origin of this. Dr. Cureton considers that the manuscript of the gospels

is of the 5th century, in which competent judges are agreed. The manuscript contains Matt. 1-8:22; 10:31-23:25; Mark (the last four verses only); Luke 2:48-3:16; 7:33-15:21; 17:24-24:41; John 1:1-42; 3:6-7:37; 14:11-29.

In examining the Curetonian text with the common printed Peshito we often find such identity of phrase and rendering as to show that they were not wholly independent translations. Then again we meet with such variety in the forms of words, etc., as seem to indicate that in the Peshito the phraseology had been revised and refined. But the great (it might be said characteristic) difference between the Curetonian and the Peshito gospels is in their readings; for while the latter cannot in its present state be deemed an unchanged production of the 2d century, the former bears all the marks of extreme antiquity, even though in places it may have suffered from the introduction of readings current in very early times.

(c) The Philoxenian Syriac version, and its revision by Thomas of Harkel. Philoxenus, or Xenaias, a Monophysite, Bishop of Hierapolis or Mabug at the beginning of the 6th century, caused Polycarp, his chorepiscopus, to make a new translation of the New Testament into Syriac This was executed in A. D. 508, and it is generally termed Philoxenian from its promoter. This version has not been transmitted to us in the form in which it was first made; we only possess a revision of it, executed by Thomas of Harkel in the following century (The Gospels, A. D. 616). From the subscriptions we learn that the text was revised by Thomas with *three* (some copies say *two*) Greek manuscripts. In describing this version as it has come down to us, the *text* is the first thing to be considered. This is characterized by extreme literality: the Syriac idiom is constantly bent to suit the Greek, and everything is in some manner expressed in the Greek phrase and order. As to the kind of Greek text that it represents, it is just what might have been expected in the 6th century.

(d) Syriac versions of portions wanting in the Peshito. These are the Second Epistle of Peter, Second and Third of John, Jude, the Apocalypse, John 8:1-11.

(e) The Jerusalem Syriac Lectionary. The manuscript in the Vatican containing this version was written in A. D. 1031 in peculiar Syriac writing; the portions are of course those for the different festivals; the dialect is not common Syriac.

(11) **Targum** (Heb. *tărgūm*, a *translation, interpretation*), the name given to an *Aramaic* version of the Old Testament, of which there are several extant.

Moses commanded that at the end of every seven years, in the Feast of Tabernacles, the law should be read in the hearing of all Israel (Deut. 31:10-13). How far the ordinance was observed in early times we have no means of judging. It would appear that such readings did take place in the days of Jeremiah. After the exile Ezra commanded that the law should be read "before the congregation, both men and women" (Neh. 8:2, 8), with the addition of an *oral* paraphrase in the Aramaic dialect.

This ecclesiastical usage, rendered necessary by the change of language consequent on the captivity, was undoubtedly continued in after-times. The office of interpreter thus became one of the most important, and the canon of the Talmud, that as the law was given by a mediator, so it can be read and expounded only by a mediator, became paramount. Both translation and explanation were designated by the term *Targum*. In the course of time there sprang up a guild, whose special office it was to act as *interpreters*, while formerly the learned alone volunteered their services. These interpreters were subjected to certain bonds and regulations as to the form and substance of their renderings.

Again, certain passages liable to give offense to the multitude are specified, which may be read in the synagogue and translated; others, which may be read but not translated; others, again, which may be neither read nor translated. Altogether these interpreters (*Meturgemanim*) do not seem to have been held generally in very high respect, one of the reasons being probably that they were paid, and thus made the Torah "a spade to dig with it." The same causes which, after many centuries of oral transmission of the whole body of the traditional law, engendered also, and about the same period, as it would appear, written Targums—for certain portions of the Bible, at least. The fear of the adulterations and mutilations which the divine word, amid the troubles within and without the commonwealth, must undergo at the hands of incompetent or impious exponents, broke through the rule that the Targum should only be *oral*, lest it might acquire undue authority. The gradual growth of the code of the written Targum, such as now embraces almost the whole of the Old Testament, is shrouded in deep obscurity. The Targums now extant are:

(1) The Targum of Onkelos on the Pentateuch. (*a*) *Authorship, etc.* Onkelos is the same name as Aquila, the Greek translator of the Old Testament; and the Targum was so called because the new Aramaic version was started under the name which had become expressive of the type and ideal of a Bible translation; so that, in fact, it was a Targum done in the manner of Aquila—*Aquila-Targum*. Still others dissent, and identify Onkelos and Aquila as the same person. With regard to the date, the Targum was begun to be committed to writing about the end of the 2d century A. D. So far, however, from its superseding the oral Targum at once, it was, on the contrary, strictly forbidden to read it in public. Nor was there any uniformity in the version. Down to the middle of the 2d century we find the masters most materially differing from each other with respect to the Targum of certain passages, and translations quoted were not to be found in any of our Targums. We shall not be far wrong in placing the work of collecting the different fragments with their variants, and reducing them into one—finally authorized version—about the end of the 3d or the beginning of the 4th century, and in assigning Babylon to it as the birthplace.

(*b*) *Style, etc.* We now turn to the Targum itself. Its language is Aramaic, closely approaching in purity of idiom to that of Ezra and Daniel. It follows a sober and clear, though not a slavish exegesis, and keeps as closely and minutely to the text as is at all consistent with its purpose, viz., to be chiefly, and above all, a version for the people. Its explanations of difficult and obscure passages bear ample witness to the competence of those who gave it its final shape and infused into it a rare unity. It avoids the legendary character with which all the later Targums entwine the biblical word as far as ever circumstances would allow. Only in the poetical passages it was compelled to yield—though reluctantly—to the popular craving for Haggadah; but even here it chooses and selects with rare taste and tact. In spite of its many and important discrepancies, the Targum never for one moment forgets its aim of being a clear though free translation *for the people*, and nothing more. Wherever it deviates from the literalness of the text, such a course, in its case, is fully justified—nay, necessitated—either by the obscurity of the passage or the wrong construction that naturally would be put upon its wording by the multitude. The explanations given agree either with the real sense, or develop the current traditions supposed to underlie it. As to the Bible text from which the Targum was prepared, we have no certainty whatever on this head, owing to the extraordinary corrupt state of our Targum texts.

(2) Targum on the Prophets—viz., Joshua, Judges, Samuel, Kings, Isaiah, Jeremiah, Ezekiel, and the twelve minor prophets—called Targum of Jonathan ben Uzziel. We shall probably not be far wrong in placing *this* Targum some time, although not long, after Onkelos, or about the middle of the 4th century, the latter years of R. Joseph, who, it is said, occupied himself chiefly with the Targum when he had become blind. This Targum may fairly be described as holding, in point of interpretation and enlargement of the text, the middle place between Onkelos, who only in extreme cases deviates into paraphrase, and the subsequent Targums, whose connection with their texts is frequently of the most flighty character.

(3 and 4) Targum of Jonathan-ben-Uzziel and Jerushalmi-Targum on the Pentateuch. Onkelos and Jonathan on the Pentateuch and Prophets, whatever be their exact date, place, authorship, and editorship, are the oldest of existing Targums, and belong, in their present shape, to Babylon and the Babylonian academies flourishing between the 3d and 4th centuries A. D. The one which extends from the first verse of Genesis to the last of Deuteronomy is known under the name of Targum Jonathan (ben Uzziel), or Pseudo-Jonathan, on the Pentateuch. The other, interpreting single verses, often single words only, is extant in the following proportions: a third on Genesis, a fourth on Deuteronomy, a fifth on Numbers, three twentieths on Exodus, and about one fourteenth on Leviticus. The latter is generally called *Targum Jerushalmi*, or, down to the 11th century (Hai Gaon, Chananel), *Targum Erets Israel*, Targum of Jerusalem, or of the Land of Israel. Not before the first half

of this century did the fact become fully and incontestably established that both Targums were in reality one—that both were known down to the 14th century under no other name than Targum Jerushalmi—and that some forgetful scribe, about that time, must have taken the abbreviation "y," "t" (T. J.) over one of the two documents, and, instead of dissolving it into Targum-Jerushalmi, dissolved it erroneously into what he must till then have been engaged in copying, viz., Targum-Jonathan, scribe ben Uzziel (on the Prophets).

(5) Targums of Joseph the Blind on the Hagiographa. These Targums on the Hagiographa which we now possess have been attributed vaguely to different authors, it being assumed in the first instance that they were the work of one man. Popular belief fastened upon Joseph the Blind. Yet, if ever he did translate the Hagiographa, certain it is that those which we possess are not by his or his disciples' hands, i. e., of the time of the 4th century. Between him and our hagiographical Targums, many centuries must have elapsed.

(6) Targum on the Book of Chronicles. This Targum was unknown up to a very recent period. In 1680 it was edited for the first time from an Erfurt manuscript by M. F. Beck, and in 1715 from a more complete as well as correct manuscript at Cambridge, by D. Wilkins. The name of Hungary occurring in it, and its frequent use of the Jerusalem-Targum to the Pentateuch, amounting sometimes to simple copying, show sufficiently that its author is neither "Jonathan b. Uzziel" nor "Joseph the Blind," as has been suggested. But the language, style, and the Haggadah, with which it abounds, point to a late period and to Palestine as the place where it was written. Its use must be limited to philological, historical, and geographical studies.

(7) The Targum to Daniel. Munk found it, not indeed in the original Aramaic, but in what appears to him to be an extract of it written in Persian.

(8) There is also an Aramaic translation extant of the Apocryphal pieces of Esther.

(12) **Vulgate.** The popular name given to the common Latin version of the Bible, usually attributed to Jerome. This version should have a deep interest for all the Western churches. For many centuries it was the only Bible generally used; and, directly or indirectly, it is the real parent of all the vernacular versions of western Europe. The Gothic version of Ulphilas alone is independent of it. In the age of the Reformation the Vulgate was rather the guide than the source of the popular versions. That of Luther (N. T., in 1523) was the most important, and in this the Vulgate had great weight. From Luther the influence of the Latin passed to our own Authorized Version. But the claims of the Vulgate to the attention of scholars rest on wider grounds. It is not only the source of our current theological terminology, but it is, in one shape or other, the most important early witness to the text and interpretation of the whole Bible.

(1) Name. The name *Vulgate,* which is equivalent to *Vulgata editio* (the *current* text of Holy Scripture), has necessarily been used differently in various ages of the Church. There can be no doubt that the phrase originally answered to the *koinē ekdosis* of the Greek Scriptures. In this sense it is used constantly by Jerome in his Commentaries. In some places Jerome distinctly quotes the Greek text; but generally he regards the old Latin, which was rendered from the LXX., as substantially identical with it, and thus introduces Latin quotations under the name of the LXX. or *Vulgata editio.* In this way the transference of the name from the current Greek text to the current Latin text became easy and natural. Yet more: as the phrase *koinē ekdosis* came to signify an uncorrected (and so corrupt) text, the same secondary meaning was attached to *Vulgata editio.* Thus in some places the *Vulgata editio* stands in contrast with the true Hexaplaric text of the LXX. This use of the text *Vulgata editio* to describe the LXX. (and the Latin version of the LXX.) was continued to later times. As a general rule the Latin fathers speak of Jerome's version as "our" version (*nostra editio, nostri codices*).

(2) The old Latin versions. (a) Origin. The history of the earliest Latin version of the Bible is lost in complete obscurity. All that can be affirmed with certainty is that it was made in Africa. During the first two centuries the Church of Rome was essentially Greek. The same remark holds true of Gaul; but the Church of North Africa seems to have been Latin-speaking from the first. At what date this Church was founded is uncertain. It is from Tertullian that we must seek the earliest testimony to the existence and character of the *Old Latin (Vetus Latina).* On the first point the evidence of Tertullian, if candidly examined, is decisive. He distinctly recognizes the general currency of a Latin version of the New Testament, though not necessarily of every book at present included in the canon. This was characterized by a "rudeness" and "simplicity" which seems to point to the nature of its origin. The version of the New Testament appears to have arisen from individual and successive efforts; and the work of private hands would necessarily be subject to revision for ecclesiastical use. The separate books would be united in a volume, and thus a standard text of the whole collection would be established. With regard to the Old Testament the case is less clear. It is probable that the Jews who were settled in North Africa were confined to the Greek towns; otherwise it might be supposed that the Latin version of the Old Testament is in part anterior to the Christian era, and that (as in the case of Greek) a preparation for a Christian Latin dialect was already made when the Gospel was introduced into Africa. However this may have been, the substantial similarity of the different parts of the Old and New Testaments establishes a real connection between them, and justifies the belief that there was one popular Latin version of the Bible current in Africa in the last quarter of the 2d century.

(b) Canon. With regard to the African canon of the New Testament the old version offers important evidence. From considerations of style and language it seems certain that the Epistle to the Hebrews, James, and Second Peter did not form part of the original African version. In the Old Testament, on the other hand, the Old Latin erred by excess and not by defect.

(c) *Revision*. After the translation once received a definite shape in Africa, which could not have been long after the middle of the 2d century, it was not publicly revised. The old text was jealously guarded by ecclesiastical use, and was retained there at a time when Jerome's version was elsewhere almost universally received. In the Old Testament the version was made from the unrevised edition of the LXX. But while the earliest Latin version was preserved generally unchanged in North Africa, it fared differently in Italy. There the provincial rudeness of the version was necessarily more offensive. In the 4th century a definite ecclesiastical recension (of the gospels at least) appears to have been made in North Italy by reference to the Greek, which was distinguished by the name of *Itala*. The *Itala* appears to have been made in some degree with authority: other revisions were made for private use, in which such changes were introduced as suited the taste of scribe or critic. The next stage in the deterioration of the text was the intermixture of these various revisions.

(d) *The labors of Jerome*. At the close of the 4th century the Latin texts of the Bible current in the Western Church had fallen into the greatest corruption. The evil was yet greater in prospect than at the time; for the separation of the East and West was growing imminent. But in the crisis of danger the great scholar was raised up which probably alone, for fifteen hundred years, possessed the qualifications necessary for producing an original version of the Scriptures for the use of the Latin churches. Jerome (Eusebius Hieronymus) was born, A. D. 329, at Stridon, in Dalmatia, and died at Bethlehem A. D. 420. After long and self-denying studies in the East and West, Jerome went to Rome A. D. 382, probably at the request of Damasus, the pope, to assist in an important synod. His active biblical labors date from this epoch, and in examing them it will be convenient to follow the order of time, noticing (1) the revision of the old Latin version of the New Testament; (2) the revision of the old Latin version (from the Greek) of the Old Testament; (3) the new version of the Old Testament from the Hebrew.

Jerome had not been long in Rome (A. D. 383), when Damasus applied to him for a revision of the current Latin version of the New Testament by the help of the Greek original. "There were," he says, "almost as many forms of text as copies." The gospels had naturally suffered most. Jerome therefore applied himself to these first. But his aim was to revise the old Latin, and not to make a new version. Yet, although he proposed to himself this limited object, the various forms of corruption which had been introduced were, as he describes, so numerous that the difference of the old and revised (Hieronymian) text is throughout clear and striking. Some of the changes which Jerome introduced were made purely on linguistic grounds, but it is impossible to ascertain on what principle he proceeded in this respect. Others involved questions of interpretation. But the greater number consisted in the removal of the interpolations by which the synoptic gospels especially were disfigured. This revision, however, was hasty.

Jerome next undertook the revision of the Old Testament from the LXX. About the same time (about A. D. 383) at which he was engaged on the revision of the New Testament, Jerome undertook also a first revision of the Psalter. This he made by the help of the Greek, but the work was not very complete or careful. This revision obtained the name of the *Roman* Psalter, probably because it was made for the use of the Roman Church at the request of Damasus. In a short time "the old error prevailed over the new correction," and at the urgent request of Paula and Eustochium Jerome commenced a new and more thorough revision (*Gallican* Psalter). The exact date at which this was made is not known, but it may be fixed with great probability very shortly after A. D. 387, when he retired to Bethlehem, and certainly before 391, when he had begun his new translations from the Hebrew. In the new revision Jerome attempted to represent as far as possible, by the help of the Greek version, the real reading of the Hebrew. This new edition soon obtained a wide popularity. Gregory of Tours is said to have introduced it from Rome into the public services in France, and from this it obtained the name of the *Gallican* Psalter. Numerous manuscripts remain which contain the Latin Psalter in two or more forms. From the second (Gallican) revision of the Psalms Jerome appears to have proceeded to a revision of the other books of the Old Testament, restoring all, by the help of the Greek, to a general conformity with the Hebrew. The revised texts of the Psalter and Job have alone been preserved; but there is no reason to doubt that Jerome carried out his design of revising all the "canonical Scriptures." He speaks of this work as a whole in several places, and distinctly represents it as a Latin version of Origen's Hexaplar text, if, indeed, the reference is not to be confined to the Psalter, which was the immediate subject of discussion. But though it seems certain that the revision was made, there is very great difficulty in tracing its history.

The next work of Jerome was the translation of the Old Testament from the Hebrew. This version was not undertaken with any ecclesiastical sanction, as the revision of the gospels was, but at the urgent request of private friends, or from his own sense of the imperious necessity of the work. Its history is told in the main in the prefaces to the several installments which were successively published. The Books of Samuel and Kings were issued first, and to these he prefixed the famous *Prologus galeatus*, addressed to Paula and Eustochium, in which he gives an account of the Hebrew canon. At the time when this was published (about A. D. 391-392) other books seem to have been already translated; and in 393 the sixteen prophets were in circulation, and Job had lately been put into the hands of his most intimate friends. Indeed, it would appear that already in 392 he had in some sense completed a version of the Old Testament; but many books were not completed and published till some years afterward. The next books which he put into circulation, yet with the provision that they should be confined to friends, were Ezra and Nehemiah, which he translated at the request of Dominica and Rogatianus, who had urged him to the task for three years. This was probably in the year 394, for in the preface he alludes to his intention of discussing a question which he treats in *Ep.* lvii, written in 395. In the preface to the Chronicles he alludes to the same epistle as "lately written," and these books may therefore be set down for that year. The three books of Solomon followed (A. D. 398), having been "the work of three days," when he had just recovered from the effects of a severe illness. The *Octateuch* (i. e., Pentateuch, Joshua, Judges, Ruth, and Esther) was probably issued after A. D. 400. The remaining books were completed at the request of Eustochius, shortly after the death of Paula (A. D. 404).

Thus the present Vulgate contains elements which belong to every period and form of the Latin version: (1) *Unrevised old Latin:* Wisdom, Ecclus., I and II Macc., Baruch. (2) *Old Latin revised from the LXX.:* Psalter. (3) *Jerome's free translation from the original text:* Judith, Tobit. (4) *Jerome's translation from the original:* Old Testament except Psalter. (5) *Old Latin revised from manuscripts:* Gospels. (6) *Old Latin cursorily revised:* the remainder of New Testament.

(*e*) *Revision of Alcuin.* Meanwhile the text of the different parts of the Latin Bible were rapidly deteriorating, the simultaneous use of the old and new versions necessarily leading to great corruptions of both texts. Mixed texts were formed according to the taste or judgment of scribes, and the confusion was further increased by changes introduced by those having some knowledge of the Greek. The growing corruption, which could not be checked by private labor, attracted the attention of Charlemagne, who intrusted to Alcuin (about A. D. 802) the task of revising the Latin text for public use. This Alcuin appears to have done simply by the use of manuscripts of the Vulgate, and not by reference to the original texts. Alcuin's revision probably contributed much toward preserving a good Vulgate text. The best manuscripts of his recension do not differ widely from the pure Hieronymian text, and his authority must have done much to check the spread of the interpolations which reappear afterward, and which were derived from the intermixture of the old and new versions. But the new revision was gradually deformed, though later attempts at correction were made by Lanfranc of Canterbury (A. D. 1089), Cardinal Nicolaus (A. D. 1150), and the Cistercian abbot Stephanus (about A. D. 1150).

History of the Printed Text. Early editions. It was a noble omen for the future of printing that the first book which issued from the press

was the Bible; and the splendid pages of the *Mazarin Vulgate* (Mainz: Gutenburg and Fust) stand yet unsurpassed by the latest efforts of typography. This work is referred to about the year 1455, and presents the common text of the 15th century. Other editions followed in rapid succession. The first collection of various readings appears in a Paris edition of 1504, and others followed at Venice and Lyons in 1511, 1513; but Cardinal Ximenes (1502-17) was the first who seriously revised the Latin text, to which he assigned the middle place of honor in his polyglot between the Hebrew and Greek texts. This was followed in 1528 (2d edition, 1532) by an edition of R. Stephens. About the same time various attempts were made to correct the Latin from the original texts (Erasmus, 1516; Pagninus, 1518-28; Cardinal Cajetanus; Steuchius, 1529; Clarius, 1542), or even to make a new Latin version (Jo. Campensis, 1533). A more important edition of R. Stephens followed in 1540, in which he made use of twenty manuscripts, and introduced considerable alterations into his former text. In 1541 another edition was published by Jo. Benedictus at Paris, which was based on the collation of manuscripts and editions, and was often reprinted afterward. Vercellone speaks much more highly of the *Biblia Ordinaria*, with glosses, etc., published at Lyons, 1545, as giving readings in accordance with the oldest manuscripts, though the sources from which they are derived are not given.

(*f*) *The Sixtine and Clementine Vulgates.* The first session of the Council of Trent was held on December 13, 1545. After some preliminary arrangements the Nicene Creed was formally promulgated as the foundation of the Christian faith on February 4, 1546, and then the council proceeded to the question of the authority, text, and interpretation of Holy Scripture. A committee was appointed to report upon the subject, which held private meetings from February 20 to March 17. Considerable varieties of opinion existed as to the relative value of the original and Latin texts, and the final decree was intended to serve as a compromise. In affirming the authority of the "old Vulgate" it contains no estimate of the value of the original texts. A papal board was engaged upon the work of revision, but it was currently reported that the difficulties of publishing an authoritative edition were insuperable. Nothing further was done toward the revision of the Vulgate under Gregory XIII, but preparations were made for an edition of the LXX. This appeared in 1587, in the second year of the pontificate of Sixtus V, who had been one of the chief promoters of the work. After the publication of the LXX, Sixtus immediately devoted himself to the production of an edition of the Vulgate. He himself revised the text, and when the work was printed he examined the sheets with the utmost care, and corrected the errors with his own hand. The edition appeared in 1590, with the famous constitution *Aeternus ille* (dated March 1, 1589) prefixed, in which Sixtus affirmed with characteristic decision the plenary authority of the edition for all future time. He further forbade expressly the publication of various readings in copies of the Vulgate. Upon the accession of Gregory XIV, a commission was appointed to revise the Sixtine text, under the presidency of the Cardinal Colonna (Columna). At first the commissioners made but slow progress, and it seemed likely that a year would elapse before the revision was completed. The mode of proceeding was therefore changed, and the commission moved to Zagorolo, the country seat of Colonna; and, if we may believe the inscription which still commemorates the event, and the current report of the time, the work was completed in *nineteen days*. The task was hardly finished when Gregory died (October, 1591), and the publication of the revised text was again delayed. His successor, Innocent IX, died within the same year, and at the beginning of 1592 Clement VIII was raised to the papacy. Clement intrusted the final revision of the text to Toletus, and the whole was printed by Aldus Manutius (the grandson) before the end of 1592.

2. **Modern Versions.** *See* Translations, English Bible.

Vestry (Heb. *meltāḥāh*, apparently from an old root *to spread* out), the *wardrobe* of the temple of Baal (II Kings 10:22). The priests of Baal, like those of almost all religions, had their sacred dresses (A. V. "vestments"), which were worn at the time of worship, and were kept in a wardrobe in the temple.

Vial. 1. A bottle or *flask*, as of oil (I Sam. 10:1; "box" in II Kings 9:1, 3). (Heb. *păk*.)

2. Gr. *phialē* (Rev. 5:8, etc.), a *bowl.*

Victual. The rendering of several Hebrew and Greek words. *See* Banquet; Food, etc.

Village, a collection of houses less regular and important than a town (*q. v.*) or city (*q. v.*). "Village," in the A. V., is the rendering of several Hebrew and Greek words.

1. Heb. *kāphār* (*protected,* I Chron. 27:25; Cant. 7:11) is the proper term for village. It appears also in the forms *kephîr* (*covered* as by walls, Neh. 6:2), and *kōphĕr* (I Sam. 6:18), and is represented by the Arabic *kefr,* still so much used. In the Hebrew the prefix *kāphār* implied a regular village, as Capernaum, which had in later times, however, outgrown the limits implied by its original designation.

2. Heb. *ḥāṣēr, inclosed,* is properly an *inclosure,* as of farm buildings inclosing a court (Josh. 13:23, 28), the encampment of nomads (Gen. 25:16; Deut. 2:23, A. V. "Hazerim"), and of hamlets near towns (Josh. 15:32, sq.; I Chron. 4:33; Neh. 11:25), especially unwalled suburbs of walled towns (Lev. 25:31; comp. v. 34).

3. Gr. *kome* is applied to Bethpage (Matt. 21:2), Bethany (Luke 10:38; John 11:1), Emmaus (Luke 24:13), Bethlehem (John 7:42). A distinction between city or town (*polis*) and village (*kōmē*) is pointed out in Luke 8:1.

Villainy (Heb. *nebālāh, foolishness*). In Isa. 32:6 "the vile person will speak villainy" may better be rendered "the fool speaks folly." In Jer. 29:23 "villainy" is wickedness in the practice of adultery.

Vine. 1. **Names.** The following Hebrew and Greek names denote the vine:

(1) *Gĕphĕn* (*twining*), or more definitely, *gĕphĕn hăyyăyĭn,* "the vine of the wine" (Gen. 40:9 and fifty-two other places).

(2) *Sōrēk* is a term denoting some choice kind of wine (Jer. 2:21; Isa. 5:2; Gen. 49:11), thought to be the same as that now called in Morocco *serki,* and in Persia *kishmish,* with small round dark berries and soft stones.

(3) *Nāzîr* (*unpruned*) is an "undressed vine" (A. V., Lev. 25:5, 11), i. e., one which every seventh and every fiftieth year was *not pruned.*

(4) Gr. *'ampelos,* a generic word for vine.

2. **Culture.** The grapevine (*Vitus vinifera*) is supposed to be a native of the shores of the Caspian. Its culture extends from about the twenty-first to the fiftieth degree of north latitude, and reaches from Portugal on the west to the confines of India on the east. It is, however, only along the center of this zone that the finest wines are made. Although Egypt is not now noted for its grapes, we find it mentioned early in Scripture (Gen. 40:9-11; Num. 20:5; Psa. 78:47) and the monuments amply confirm the culture of grapes in ancient Egypt.

Palestine, even before Israel took possession of it, was a land of vineyards (Deut. 6:11; 28:30; Num. 13:23); and Moses enacted rules and regulations for the culture of the vine, while their prospective owners still wandered in the desert (Exod. 22:5; 23:11; Lev. 25:5, 11; Num. 6:3; Deut. 22:9; 23:24; 24:21). For this culture the portion of Judah was especially adapted, and in obtaining for his inheritance the hilly slopes of the south, the prophecy of his ancestor was fulfilled, "He washed his garments in wine, and his clothes in the blood of grapes" (Gen. 49:11). Here, more than elsewhere, are to be seen on the sides of the hills the vineyards, marked by their watchtowers (*see* Towers) and walls, seated on their ancient terraces—the earliest and latest symbol of Judah. The elevation of the hills and table-lands of Judah is the true climate of the vine, and at Hebron, according to the Jewish tradition, was its primeval seat. It was from the Judean valley of Eshcol—"the torrent of the cluster"—that the spies cut down the gigantic cluster of grapes. Although from many of its most famous haunts the vine has disappeared—e. g., from En-gedi—both in southern Palestine and on the slopes of Lebanon there are specimens sufficient to vindicate the old renown of this "land of vineyards." The grapes of Hebron are still considered the finest in the Holy Land. Bunches weighing from six to seven pounds are said to be by no means uncommon.

3. **Vineyard** (Heb. *kĕrĕm, garden;* Gr. *'ampelōn*). The preparation of a vineyard is the most costly and onerous of all the operations of that primitive husbandry in Eastern lands, the methods of which have remained unchanged and unimproved from the earliest times of which we possess any records. It is, in fact, the only branch of agriculture, as there practiced, which demands any considerable outlay. In the first place, the vineyard must be carefully inclosed by a permanent fence, which is required for no other crop. The pasture lands outside the villages are all unfenced, and the boundaries only marked

by well-known stones or landmarks. The grainfields are equally open, or only protected by thorn branches strewn on the ground, while the olive yards nearer the town or village are equally unprotected. When the vineyard has been thus hedged, the next operation is to gather out the stones, not the small stones which strew all the hillsides, and are indispensable for the retention of moisture in the soil, but the larger boulders, which are heaped in long rows like a ruined stone wall. On these rows the vines are trailed, to preserve the fruit from damp. Next, there must be a wine press (*q. v.*) when out of the native rock; for the grapes are always pressed on the spot, lest they should be bruised and injured by conveyance to a distance. These wine presses, or vats, are the most imperishable records of the past in the deserted land. They are simply two parallel troughs, one above the other, with a perforated conduit between them. The bunches of grapes are thrown into the upper vat, where they are trodden, and the juice flows into the lower one. These "wine fats," found in abundance through the whole land, and even far into the southern desert, are silent witnesses to its former fertility. Then, unless the vineyard adjoins the village, there must be a temporary lodge, or booth, erected on poles; but, more generally, a permanent tower, of which many traces may still be seen, for the watchman, during the season, to guard the vintage from thieves or jackals. (Cf. Isa. 5:1-7).

4. **Mosaic Regulations.** It was contrary to the law to eat the fruit of a vineyard during the first three years after its planting. The fourth year all the fruit was holy to the Lord, " to praise the Lord withal." Only in the fifth year did the produce of the vines fall entirely to the owner's disposal (Lev. 19:23-25; comp. Mark 12:2). In later times, however, while it was still held wrong to eat during the first three years, the rule was greatly relaxed regarding the fourth year. Various markings were adopted whereby the passer-by might distinguish the three years' from the four years' vineyard, and so escape the peril of eating from the former. The proper "season" for claiming produce would therefore not come until the fifth year.

The vine in the Mosaic ritual was subject to the usual restrictions of the "seventh year" (Exod. 23:11), and the jubilee of the fiftieth year (Lev. 25:11). The gleanings were to be left for the poor and the stranger (Jer. 49:9; Deut. 24:21). The vineyard was not to be sown "with divers seed" (Deut. 22:9), but fig trees were sometimes planted in vineyards (Luke 13:6; comp. I Kings 4:25: "Every man under his vine and under his fig tree"). Persons passing through a vineyard were allowed to eat grapes therein, but not to carry any away (Deut. 23:24).

5. **Vintage** (Heb. *bâsîr, clipped*). The vintage began in September, and was a time of general festivity. The towns were deserted, and the people lived in the vineyards—in lodges and tents (Judg. 9:27; Jer. 25:30; Isa. 16:10). The grapes were gathered with shouts of joy by the "grape gatherers" (Jer. 25:30),

and put into baskets (6:9), and then carried to the wine press.

In Palestine the finest grapes, even today, are dried as raisins, and the juice of the remainder, after having been trodden and pressed, is boiled down to a syrup, which, under the name of *dibs* (Heb. *debăsh*), is much used by all classes, wherever vineyards are found, as a condiment with their food. Even the leaves and the stocks of the vine are useful. The cuttings of the vine and the leaves are much used for manure to the vineyards. The leaves are also used as a vegetable, chopped meat and rice being rolled up together in single leaves, and boiled for the table, making a very agreeable dish. The leaves are also used for fodder, while the wood serves as fuel (Ezek. 15:3, 4; comp. John 15:6).

6. **Figurative.** The vine is a symbol of the nation Israel; thus Israel was a vine brought from Egypt (Psa. 80:8; comp. Isa. 5:2, sq.). To dwell under one's vine and fig tree is an emblem of domestic happiness and peace (I Kings 4:25; Psa. 128:3; Mic. 4:4) and a prophetic figure of future millennial blessing. The rebellious people of Israel are compared to "wild grapes," "an empty vine," "the degenerate plant of a strange vine" (Isa. 5:2, 4; Jer. 2:21; Hos. 10:1). By the vine our Lord symbolizes the spiritual union existing between himself and believers (John 15:1-6), unfruitful branches being mere professors. The quick growth of the vine is a symbol of the growth of saints in grace (Hos. 14:7); its rich clusters, of the graces of the saints (Cant. 7:8); the worthlessness of its wood, of the unprofitableness of the wicked (Ezek. 15:2, 3, 6); a vine setting fruit, but not bringing it to maturity, is representative of Israel not answering the rightful expectations of Jehovah (Hos. 10:1). The vineyard is used as a figure of Israel's chastisement for her sin (Isa. 5:7; 27:2; Jer. 12:10; comp. Matt. 21:33); while the failure of the vineyard is a symbol of severe calamities (Isa. 32:10); to plant vineyards and eat the fruit thereof is a figure of peaceful prosperity (Neh. 9:25; Isa. 65:21; Ezek. 28:26). See Vegetable Kingdom.

Vine of Sodom. See Vegetable Kingdom.

Vinegar. See Wine.

Vineyard. See Vine.

Vineyards, Plain of the (Heb. *'ăbēl kerămîm*), a place E. of the Jordan to which Jephthah pursued the Ammonites (Judg. 11:33), and possibly now represented by a ruin bearing the name of *Beit el-Kerm*—"house of the vine" —to the north of Kerak. Its situation cannot be definitely determined.

Vintage. See Vine.

Viol. See Music.

Violence. Vehement, forcible or destructive action, often involving infringement, outrage or assault. The rendering of two Hebrew and three Greek words:

1. Heb. *ḥāmās* has the sense of using violence, especially with evil intent (Gen. 6:11, 13; 49:5, A. V. "cruelty;" Psa. 18:48, A. V. "violent man").

2. Heb. *gāzăl* (to *strip off*) has the meaning of to *rob* (Lev. 6:2; Job 20:19; 24:2), in which passages the sense is that of seizing another's property by fraud or injustice, especially of

the rich and powerful who seize upon the possessions of the poor by fraud and force (Eccles. 5:8; Jer. 22:3; Ezek. 18:7, 12, 16, 18).

3. Gr. *bia* (*vital, activity*), strength in violent action, force (Acts 5:26; 24:7). In Matt. 11:12, "The kingdom of heaven suffereth violence" (*biazetai*), carried by storm, i. e., a share in the heavenly kingdom is sought for with the most ardent zeal and the intensest exertion.

4. Gr. *dunamis* (*strength, ability*) is used in the expression, "Quenched the violence of fire" (Heb. 11:34).

5. Gr. *diaseiō*, Luke 3:14, "do violence to no man," means to extort money, or other property, from one by intimidation.

Viper. *See* Animal Kingdom.

Virgin, the rendering of two Hebrew words and one Greek word:

1. Heb. *bᵉthūlāh* (*separately*) properly denotes a *virgin, maiden* (Gen. 24:16; Lev. 21:13; Deut. 22:14, 23, 28; Judg. 11:37; I Kings 1:2); the passage Joel 1:8 is not an exception, as it refers to the loss of one betrothed, not married.

2. Heb. *'almāh* (*veiled*), a young woman of marriageable age (Gen. 24:43; Exod. 2:8; Psa. 68:25, A. V. "damsel"; Prov. 30:19; Cant. 1:3; 6:8); a virgin, Isa. 7:14. Although the primary idea of this word is not unspotted virginity, for which the Hebrews had a special word, *bᵉthūlāh*, "virgin" is, nevertheless, the proper rendering in Isa. 7:14 of *'almāh*, which may not only take this meaning (Gen. 24:43), but in the light of Matt. 11:23 *must* take this meaning. The Holy Spirit through Isaiah did not use *bᵉthūlāh*, because both the ideas of virginity and marriageable age had to be combined in one word to meet the immediate historical situation and the prophetic aspect centering in a virgin-born Messiah.

3. Gr. *parthenos*, a virgin (Matt. 1:23; 25:1, 7, 11; Luke 1:27; Acts 21:9; I Cor. 7:25, 28, 33), i. e., either a marriageable maiden or a young married woman, a pure virgin (II Cor. 11:2). In Rev. 14:4 it is used in the sense of a man who has abstained from all uncleanness and whoredom attendant upon idolatry, and so has kept his chastity.

Respecting the virginity of Mary, the mother of our Lord, *see* Mary.

Virtue (Gr. *'aretē, manliness; dunamis, power, strength*). The first of these terms denotes a virtuous course of thought, feeling, and action, moral goodness (II Pet. 1:5), any *particular* moral excellence, as modesty, purity (Phil. 4:8). The latter term indicates *power, ability*, and is often so rendered. In Mark 5:30; Luke 6:19; 8:46, it indicates the power of Christ to heal disease.

Vision (some derivative of Heb. *ḥāzāh*, to *perceive;* Gr. *haraō;* or of *rā'āh*, to *see; optomai*), a supernatural presentation of certain scenery or circumstances to the mind of a person while awake (Num. 12:6-8). Balaam speaks of himself as having seen "the vision of the Almighty" (24:16). In the time of Eli it is said, "And the word of the Lord was precious in those days; there was no open vision" (I Sam. 3:1), i. e., there was no public and recognized revelation of the divine will (comp.

Prov. 29:18, "Where there is no vision the people perish"). *See* Dream.

Visitation (Heb. *pᵉqūdāh;* Gr *.episkopē*), inspection, is sometimes taken for a visit of mercy from God (Gen. 50:24; Exod. 13:19; Luke 1:68), but oftener for a visit of rigor and vengeance, or at least of close inspection (Exod. 32:34; Isa. 23:17; I Pet. 2:12).

Vocation (Gr. *klēsis*, an *invitation*), a theological term signifying calling (Rom. 11:29; I Cor. 1:26; Eph. 1:18; 4:4; Phil. 3:14; II Thess. 1:11; II Tim. 1:9; Heb. 3:1; II Pet. 1:10).

The dominant idea is that God in his grace calls men to forsake a sinful life and to enter into the kingdom and service of the Lord Jesus Christ.

The long-standing point of controversy between Calvinistic and Arminian theologians relates to the character of this call, the former holding that there is an "external call" to all men, addressed indiscriminately to all men, while the "effectual call" is given only to those who by the divine decree are predestined to everlasting life, the latter refusing to recognize any such distinction.

Methodists and Arminians generally regard the divine call, under whatever external conditions it is made, as in every case one of thoroughly gracious reality, and so efficacious that if it is heeded the man is certain of salvation.

See Election; Atonement; Holy Spirit.

Voph'si (vŏf-sī), the father of Nahbi, one of the explorers of Canaan (Num. 13:14).

Vow (Heb. from *nādǎr*, to *promise;* Gr. *euchē*, a *prayer*), defined as a religious undertaking, either, positive, to do something, or, negative, to abstain from doing a certain thing. Under the old covenant the principle of vowing was recognized as in itself a suitable expression of the religious sentiment, and as such was placed under certain regulations. It was not, except in a few special cases, imposed as an obligation on the individual conscience. The Lord never said, Thou shalt vow so and so; but, If thou shouldst make a vow, or when thou dost so, then let such and such conditions be observed. The conditions specified in the law related almost exclusively to the faithful performance of what had been freely undertaken by the worshipper—what he had pledged himself before God to render in active service or dedicated gifts. He was on no account to draw back from his plighted word, but conscientiously to carry it into effect, since otherwise a slight would manifestly be put upon God and a stain left upon the conscience of the worshipper (Deut. 23:21-23; Eccles. 5:5; Psa. 50:14; Nah. 1:15).

Mosaic Regulations. 1. A man could not devote to sacred uses the firstborn of man or beast, which was devoted already (Lev. 27:26); if he vowed land, he might redeem it or not (vers. 16, 20) (*see* Redemption). 2. Animals fit for sacrifice, if devoted, were not to be redeemed or changed, and if a man attempted to do so he was required to bring both the devotee and the changling (27:9, 10, 33). They were to be free from blemish (Mal. 1:14). An animal unfit for sacrifice might be redeemed, with the addition to the priest's valuation of a fifth, or it became the

property of the priests (Lev. 27:12, 13).
3. The case of *persons* stood thus: A man might devote either himself, his child (not the firstborn), or his slave. If no redemption took place, the devoted person became a slave of the sanctuary (II Sam. 15:8) (*see* Nazarite). Otherwise he might be redeemed at a valuation according to age and sex (Lev. 27:1-7).
4. **General regulations.** Vows were entirely voluntary, but once made were regarded as compulsory, and evasion of performance of them was held to be contrary to true religion (Num. 30:2; Deut. 23:21; Eccles. 5:4). If persons in a dependent condition made vows —as an unmarried daughter living in her

father's house, or a wife, even if she afterward became a widow—the vow, if in the first case her father, or in the second her husband, heard and disallowed it, was void; but if they heard without disallowance, it was to remain good (Num. 30:3-16). Votive offerings arising from the profit on any impure traffic were wholly forbidden (Deut. 23:18).

Vows in general and their binding force as a test of religion are mentioned (Job 22:27; Psa. 22:25; 50:14; 66:13; 116:14; Prov. 7:14; Isa. 19:21; Nah. 1:15). *See* Oath.

Vulgate. *See* Versions.

Vulture. *See* Animal Kingdom.

W

Wages. 1. Usually some form of Heb. *säkăr* (Gen. 31:8; Exod. 2:9; Ezek. 29:18, 19); elsewhere "hire," "reward," etc.

2. Heb. *măskĕrĕth* (Gen. 29:15; 31:41; Ruth 2:12, "reward").

3. Heb. *pe'ŭläh* (Lev. 19:13; Psa. 109:20, "reward").

4. Two Greek words are thus rendered: *misthos*, John 4:36, elsewhere "reward," or "hire;" *opsōnion*, Luke 3:14; II Cor. 11:8; Luke 6:23, "reward".

Wages, according to the earliest usages of mankind, are a return for something of value, specifically for work performed. Thus labor is recognized as property, and wages as the price paid or obtained in exchange for such property. The earliest mention of wages is of a recompense not in money, but in kind. This was given to Jacob by Laban (Gen. 29:15, 20; 31:7, 8, 41). Such payment was natural among a pastoral and changing population like that of the tent-dwellers of Syria. In Egypt money payments by way of wages were in use, but the terms cannot now be ascertained.

Among the Hebrews wages in general, whether of soldiers or laborers, are mentioned (Hag. 1:6; Ezek. 29:18, 19; John 4:36). The *rate* of wages is only mentioned in the parable of the householder and vineyard (Matt. 20:2), where the laborer's wages are given as one denarius per day (about sixteen cents), a rate which agrees with Tob. 5:14, where a drachma is mentioned as the rate per day, a sum which may be taken as fairly equivalent to the denarius, and to the usual pay of a soldier in the latter days of the Roman republic. In earlier times it is probable that the rate was lower. But it is likely that laborers, and also soldiers, were supplied with provisions. The Mosaic law was very strict in requiring daily payment of wages (Lev. 19:13; Deut. 25:14, 15). The employer who refused to give his laborers sufficient provisions was censured (Job. 24:11), and the iniquity of withholding wages is denounced (Jer. 22:13; Mal. 3:5; James 5:4). *See* Service.

Wagon (Heb. *'ăgäläh*, that which *rolls* or *turns* round, Gen. 45:19, 21, 27; 46:5; Num. 7:3, 6-8; *rĕkĕb*, Ezek. 23:24, elsewhere "chariot"). The oriental wagon, or *'ăgäläh*, is a vehicle composed of two or three planks, fixed on two solid circular blocks of wood, from two to five feet in diameter, which serve as wheels. To the floor are sometimes attached wings, which splay outward like the sides of a wheelbarrow. For the conveyance of passengers mattresses or clothes are laid in the bottom, and the vehicle is drawn by bullocks or oxen. The covered wagons for conveying the materials for the tabernacle were probably constructed on Egyptian models. Others of a lighter description, and more nearly approaching the modern cart, occur in the Assyrian monuments. Some of these have eight, others as many as twelve spokes in their wheels.

Wail. *See* Mourning.

Walk. Figurative. *Walk* is often used in Scripture for conduct in life, general demeanor, and deportment. Thus it is said that Enoch and Noah "walked with God," i. e., they maintained a course of action conformed to God's will and acceptable in his sight. In the Old and New Testaments we find God promising to walk with his people; and his people, on the other hand, desiring the influence of the Holy Spirit, that they may walk in his statutes. "To walk in darkness" (I John 1:6, 7) is to be involved in unbelief and misled by error; "to walk in the light" (v. 7) is to be well informed, holy, and happy; "to walk by faith" (II Cor. 5:7) may be rendered "through faith we walk," i. e., faith is the sphere through which we walk. "To walk after the flesh" (Rom. 8:1, 4; II Pet. 2:10) is to gratify the carnal desires, to yield to fleshly appetites, and to be obedient to the lusts of the flesh; while "to walk after the Spirit" (Gal. 5:16) is to be guided and aided by the Holy Spirit, the active and animating principle of the Christian life.

Wall (Heb. properly *qîr*, as a *defense*; or *hōmäh*, as a *barrier*; sometimes *shūr*, perhaps from its *rocky* character; Gr. *teichos*). In ancient times the walls of cities and houses were usually built of earth, or of bricks (*q. v.*) of clay, mixed with reeds and hardened in the sun. When any breach took place in such a mass of earth, by heavy rains or a defect in the foundation, the consequences were serious (Gen. 49:6; Psa. 62:3; Isa. 30:13); and we can easily understand how such walls could be readily destroyed by fire (Amos 1:7, 10, 14). The extensive mounds on the plains of Mesopotamia and Assyria, marking the sites of ancient cities, show that the walls were principally constructed of earth or clay. The wall surrounding the palace of Khorsabad is fixed by Botta at forty-eight feet nine inches; probably about the same as that of Nineveh, upon which three chariots could be driven abreast. The wall of Babylon was eighty-seven feet broad, and six chariots could be driven together upon it. Not infrequently stone walls, with towers and a fosse, surrounded fortified cities (Isa. 2:15; 9:10; Neh. 4:3; Zeph. 1:16).

522. Walls of Jerusalem

Figurative. In Scripture language a wall is a symbol of *salvation* (Isa. 26:1; 60:18); of *protection*—of God (Zech. 2:5), of those who afford protection (I Sam. 25:16; Isa. 2:15; 5:5); of the *wealth of the rich* in his own conceit (Prov. 18:11). A "brazen wall" is symbolical of prophets in their testimony against the wicked (Jer. 15:20); the "wall of partition" (Eph. 2:14), of the separation of Jews and Gentiles; "whited walls" (Acts 23:3), of hypocrites.

Wandering in the Wilderness. *See* Wilderness of Wandering.

War. Warfare and bloodshed are described realistically in the Bible from the entrance of sin into the human race (Gen. 3). The first great Messianic prophecy (Gen. 3:15) announces hostility between the "Seed of the woman" and "the seed of the serpent." The great drama is consummated by "the Seed of the woman" conquering "the seed of the serpent," ousting his control of the earth (Rev. chap. 6-19) and ruling as King of Kings and Lord of Lords at His second advent. Throughout the millennial earth peace is supreme, but the peace of eternity will only eventuate as the final revolt of Satan is put down and he and all his followers are placed in the eternal lake of fire (Rev. 20:1-3 and 7-10). In the light of this Biblical description of the struggle of good against evil, Christ against anti-Christ, it is not surprising that war should be prominent in Bible history not only among the Israelites but among surrounding nations.

1. **Sumerians.** The Sumerians, the pre-Semitic inhabitants of the fertile plains of the Euphrates in southern Babylonia before 3000 B. C., excelled in the arts of war. They employed the four-wheeled war chariot, the battle bow and developed military equipment. A striking example is a solid gold helmet fashioned before 2500 B. C. of incredible workmanship. This superb piece of armor was

523. Gold Helmet and Dagger from Ur, c. 2500 B.C.

unearthed by Sir Leonard Woolley. Extant from this early period also is a gold sheath dagger with lapis lazuli handle, flint arrows, electrum double axe heads and copper spear heads. The Standard of Ur portrays infantrymen with copper helmets and heavy cloaks. These soldiers carry short spears or axes and charioteers are armed with spears and javelins. The Sumerian armies used chariots and phalanxes before 3000 B. C.

2. **Egyptians.** Egyptians were not especially militarily minded. They preferred to hire the warlike black Nubians to man their foreign expeditions. In the Old Kingdom the common Egyptian soldier was equipped with a leather shield, a long bow with arrows of flint, a mace, a long spear, a curved dagger and occasionally a battle axe. He wore a simple uniform. The New Empire from 1550 B. C. on used the horse and the chariot and the composite bow. These formidable weapons enabled Egypt to conquer and rule the East. During this period fine javelins, spears, daggers and arrows with points of ivory, glass or wood were employed. The collection of Tutankhamun in the Cairo Museum illustrates the high development of New Kingdom weapons. Egyptians excelled in fort building, erected along the cataracts of Upper Egypt to restrain the invasion of the war-loving Nubians. A series of similar forts guarded the Delta area from Asiatic invaders, especially on the N. E. The famous turquoise and copper mines of the Sinai Peninsula were also protected by well-manned fortresses. Only occasionally would Egypt build up any considerable navy, being protected by her isolated inland position. However, at certain periods the Egyptians conducted successful naval engagements. One striking example is Raamses III who used his fleet against a Lybian confederacy in the twelfth century B. C.

3. **Assyrian.** The Assyrians were the "giant of the Semites" at the beginning of the ninth century B. C. under Ashurnasirpal II. Shal-

524. A Company of Egyptian Soldiers

maneser III and later under great militarists and conquerors like Tiglath-pilesar III, Sargon II, Sennacherib and Esarhaddon. The cruel and relentless Assyrian armies made Israel and surrounding countries tremble. With powerful bows and arrows shot from chariots, their irresistible cavalry attacks and their employment of all of the weapons of their Sumerian and Babylonian precursors, they were a terrifying scourge.

4. **Chaldean.** Even more fearful than the Assyrians were the superb Chaldean fighters and horsemen. They employed all the military art and weapons of the Assyrians. Habakkuk outlines the terror the Chaldeans struck to the Hebrews (Hab. 1:6-9). Ezekiel enumerates the military equipment of the common Chaldean soldier. He speaks of "warriors clothed in full armor, horsemen riding on horses, all of them young men." He speaks of "chariots . . . wagons and a host of peoples; they shall set themselves against you on every side with buckler, shield and helmet . . ." Ezek. 23:24).

5. **The Hebrews.** (1) **Preliminary.** Before entering on an aggressive warfare the Hebrews sought for the divine sanction by consulting either the Urim and Thummim (Judg. 1:1; 20:2, 27, 28; I Sam. 14:37; 23:3; 28:6; 30:8) or some acknowledged prophet (I Kings 22:6; II Chron. 18:5). Divine aid was further sought in actual warfare by bringing into the field the ark of the covenant, which was the symbol of Jehovah himself (I Sam. 4:4, 18; 14:18). Formal proclamations of war were not interchanged between the belligerents. Before entering the enemy's district spies were sent to ascertain the character of the country and the preparations of its inhabitants for resistance (Num. 13:17; Josh. 2:1; Judg. 7:10; I Sam. 26:4).

(2) **Actual warfare.** When an engagement was imminent a sacrifice was offered (I Sam. 7:9; 13:9), and an inspiriting address delivered either by the commander (II Chron. 20:20) or by a priest (Deut. 20:2). Then followed the battle signal (I Sam. 17:52; Isa. 42:13; Jer. 50:42; Ezek. 21:22; Amos 1:14). The combat assumed the form of a number of hand-to-hand contests. Hence the high value attached to the fleetness of foot and strength of arm (II Sam. 1:23; 2:18; I Chron. 12:8). At the same time various strategic devices were practiced, such as the ambuscade (Josh. 8:2, 12; Judg. 20:36), surprise (Judg. 7:16), or circumvention (II Sam. 5:23). Another mode of settling the dispute was by the selection of champions (I Sam., ch. 17; II Sam. 2:14), who were spurred on to exertion by the offer of high reward (I Sam. 17:25; 18:25; II Sam. 18:11; I Chron. 11:6). The contest having been decided, the conquerors were recalled from the pursuit by the sound of a trumpet (II Sam. 2:28; 18:16; 20:22).

(3) **Siege of a town.** The siege of a town or fortress was conducted in the following manner: A line of circumvallation was drawn round the place (Ezek. 4:2; Mic. 5:1), constructed out of the trees found in the neighborhood (Deut. 20:20), together with earth and any other materials at hand. This line not only cut off the besieged from the surrounding country, but also served as a base of operations for the besiegers. The next step was to throw out from this line one or more "mounds," or "banks," in the direction of the city (II Sam. 20:15; II Kings 19:32; Isa. 37:33), which were gradually increased in height until they were about half as high as the city wall. On these mounds or banks towers were erected (II Kings 25:1; Jer. 52:4; Ezek. 4:2; 17:17; 21:22; 26:8), whence the slingers and archers might attack with effect. Battering-rams (Ezek. 4:2; 21:22) were brought up to the walls by means of the bank, and scaling ladders might also be placed on it.

(4) **Treatment of conquered, etc.** The treatment of the conquered was extremely severe in ancient times. The bodies of the soldiers killed in action were plundered (I Sam. 31:8; II Macc. 8:27); the survivors were either killed in some savage manner

525. Return of Seti I from a Syrian Campaign

(Judg. 9:45; II Sam. 12:31; II Chron. 25: 12), mutilated (Judg. 1:6; I Sam. 11:2), or carried into captivity (Num. 31:26; Deut. 20:14). Sometimes the bulk of the population of the conquered country was removed to a distant locality. The Mosaic law mitigated to a certain extent the severity of the ancient usages toward the conquered. The conquerors celebrated their success by the erection of monumental stones (I Sam. 7:12; II Sam. 8:13), by hanging up trophies in their public buildings (I Sam. 21:9; 31:10; II Kings 11: 10), and by triumphal songs and dances in which the whole population took part (Exod. 15:1-21; Judg., ch. 5; I Sam. 18:6-8; II Sam., ch. 22; Judith 16:2-17; I Macc. 4:24).

6. **Roman.** Roman armor was unequaled in the ancient world. A superb example of this is shown in the Hadrian marble torso in the Athenian agora. Our Lord came in intimate contact with Roman legions and Roman military might. The long Roman sword appears in the prophecy of Calvary uttered by Simeon to Mary, the mother of Jesus "A sword shall pierce through thine own soul" (Luke 2:35). Jesus refers to the sword (Matt. 26:55) and his side was transfixed by the long Roman spear, while the soldiers gambled at the foot of the cross. Very widely traveled, the Apostle Paul on numerous occasions came into close contact with Roman military power. In all the cities in which he preached Roman soldiers or Roman legions were present. When he was ordered by Claudius Lycias to go to Caesarea for a governmental trial, 200 soldiers, 200 spearmen and seventy horsemen formed his personal escort. Paul's graphic description of the panoplied Roman warrior in Eph. 6:10-20 is thus perfectly natural. In this remarkable illustration of the Spirit-filled believer's conflict in prayer are outlined the main items in the equipment of a Roman warrior.

7. **Figurative.** War is a figure of our contest with death (Eccles. 8:8). In the song of Moses, Jehovah is declared to be "a man of war" (Exod. 15:3), one who knows how to make war, and possesses the power to destroy his foes. War illustrates the malignity of the wicked (Psa. 55:21), the contest of saints with the enemies of their salvation (Rom. 7:23; II Cor. 10:3; Eph. 6:12; I Tim. 1:18), and between antichrist and the Saint (Rev. 11:7; 13:4, 7). *M. F. U.*

Washing. *See* Ablution.

Watch. 1. The rendering of some form of the Heb. *shämär* (to *protect*), and may mean day or night watch; thus there was a guard (A. V. "watch") of the king's house (II Kings 11:5-7), and in Jerusalem under Nehemiah (Neh. 4:9; 7:3). The Jews, like the Greeks and Romans, divided the night into military watches instead of hours, each watch representing the period for which sentinels or pickets remained on duty. Thus we read of "a watch in the night" (Psa. 90:4). The proper Jewish reckoning recognized only three such watches, entitled the first or "beginning of the watches" (Lam. 2:19), the middle watch (Judg. 7:19), and the morning watch (Exod. 14:24; I Sam. 11:11). These would last respectively from sunset to 10 p.m.; from 10

p.m. to 2 a.m.; and from 2 a.m. to sunrise. Subsequently to the establishment of the Roman supremacy, the number of watches was increased to four, which were described either according to their numerical order, as in the case of the "fourth watch" (Matt. 14: 25, Gr. *phulakē*), or by the terms "even," "midnight," "cockcrowing," and "morning" (Mark 13:35). These terminated respectively at 9 p.m., midnight, 3 a.m. and 6 a.m.

2. Heb. *shäqäd* (to *be alert*) is to be wakeful, and so watchful, either for good (Jer. 31:28; 51:12) or evil (Isa. 29:20).

3. A Roman sentry, one of the soldiers who guarded the tomb of our Lord (Matt. 27:65, 66). Gr. *koustōdia*.

4. Gr. *grēgoreō* means to *keep awake*, to *watch*, and so to take heed lest through remissness and indolence some destructive calamity suddenly overtake one (Matt. 24:42; 25:13; Mark 13:35; Rev. 16:15), or lest one be led to forsake Christ (Matt. 26:41; Mark 14:38), or fall into sin (I Thess. 5:6; I Cor. 16:13; I Pet. 5:8; Rev. 3:2, sq.). To "watch" (Col. 4:2) is to employ the most punctilious care.

5. Gr. *nēphō* (to *abstain from wine, be sober*), is used in the New Testament figuratively, *to be calm and collected in spirit; to be temperate, dispassionate, circumspect* (I Thess. 5:6, 8; II Tim. 4:5; I Pet. 1:13; 5:8).

Watchtower. *See* Tower.

Water (Heb. *mäyïm;* Gr. *hudōr*) is frequently mentioned in Scripture both as an element in fertility and as a drink.

1. **Supply.** The long rainy season in Palestine means a considerable rainfall, and while it lasts the land gets a thorough soaking. But the land is limestone and very porous. The heavy rains are quickly drained away, the wadies are left dry, the lakes become marshes or dwindle to dirty ponds, and on the west of Jordan there remain only a few short perennial streams, of which but one or two, and these mere rills, are found in the hill country. Hence the water of running streams and fountains, as opposed to that of stagnant cisterns, pools, or marshes, is called *living water* (Gen. 26:19; Zech. 14:8; John 4:10, 11; 7:38; Rev. 7:17). In the hot countries of the East the assuaging of thirst is one of the most delightful sensations that can be experienced (Psa. 143: 6; Prov. 25:25), and every attention which humanity and hospitality can suggest is paid to furnish travelers with water. Public reservoirs or pools are opened in several parts of Egypt and Arabia (Matt. 10:42). Sometimes water is so scarce as to be paid for (Num. 20: 17, 19; Lam. 5:4).

2. **Peculiar Usages.** Among the optical illusions which the deserts of the East have furnished is the *mirage*. This phenomenon of "waters that fail," was called by the Hebrews *shäräb*, i. e., *heat*, and is rendered "the parched ground" (Isa. 35:7); properly, "And the mirage shall become a pool," i. e., the desert which presents the appearance of a lake shall be changed into real water.

3. **Figurative.** Water occasionally is used for *tears* (Jer. 9:1, 7); hence, figuratively, *trouble* (Psa. 66:1) and *misfortune* (Lam. 3:54; Psa. 69:1; 119:136; 124:4, 5); *persecution* (Psa. 88:17); *hostile* armies (Isa. 8:7; 17:13). Water

is put for *children* or *posterity* (Num. 24:7; Isa. 48:1); for *clouds* (Psa. 104:3); for the refreshing power of the Holy Spirit (Isa. 12:3; 35:6, 7; 55:1; John 7:37, 38); divine *support* (Isa. 8:6); the gifts and graces of the Holy Spirit (Isa. 41:17, 18; 44:3; Ezek. 36:25); water *poured out*, the *wrath of God* (Hos. 5:10) and of *faintness* by terror (Psa. 22:14). *Deep* water is used of the counsel in the heart (Prov. 20:5) and of the words of the wise (18:4). Water "spilled on the ground" is a figure of death (II Sam. 14:14); while its *instability* figures a wavering disposition (Gen. 49:4). "*Stolen* waters" (Prov. 9:17) denote unlawful pleasures with strange women. The difficulty of stopping water (17:14) is a symbol of strife and contention, while its rapid flowing away represents the career of the wicked (Job. 24:18; Psa. 58:7). *See* Fountain; Well.

Water of Jealousy. *See* Jealousy Offering.

526. A Waterpot

Waterpot (Gr. *hudria*), a large vessel of stone in which water was kept standing (John 2:6, 7) for the sake of *cleansing*, which the Jews practiced before and after meals. The "firkin" (Gr. *metrētēs*) was a measure containing about eight and seven eighths gallons. The "waterpot" mentioned in 4:28 was a jar of earthenware in which water was carried.

Waterspout (Heb. *ṣinnūr*, *hollow*) was a cataract, waterspout (Psa. 42:7; rendered in the A. V. of II Sam. 5:8, "gutter;" R. V. "water course").

Wave Offering. *See* Sacrificial Offerings.

Waymarks (Heb. *ṣĕyūn*, *conspicuous*), pillars to mark the road for the returning exiles (Jer. 31:21). Caravans set up *pillars* or pointed *heaps* of stone to mark the way through the desert against their return.

Wean, Weaning. *See* Children.

Weapon. *See* Armor.

Weasel. *See* Animal Kingdom.

Weaving. Weaving was common in almost every home in Palestine in Bible times. Families wove their own textiles from common articles of dress to coarse tent cloth. Woolen looms and dyeing vats were uncovered in excavation at Lachish in southern Judea, and other places. The Canaanites long before the arrival of the Hebrews wove and dyed their own fabrics. Evidence of the weaver and dyer's art come from Tell Beit Mirsim, Ugarit and Byblos, which was particularly famous for its woven materials, and many other places. Samson's "thirty linen garments and thirty changes of raiment" (Judg. 13:14) indicate the activity of the weaving arts in the time of the Judges. Carpet looming was also common (Prov. 7:15). *M. F. U.*

Web. *See* Spider; Weaving.

Wedding. *See* Marriage.

Wedge. In early Bible times bars or wedges of metal stamped with private markings such as an ox, gazelle or some other figure of Babylonians or Egyptians were employed by Palestinian merchants. Cf. the "wedge of gold" stolen by Achan at the time of the Conquests c. 1400 B. C. (Josh. 7:21).

Weeds. *See* Vegetable Kingdom.

Week, a measure of time (*q. v.*).

Weeks, Feast of. *See* Festivals.

Weeping. *See* Mourning.

Weight. 1. A *stone*. A weight of balance, even when not made of stone, since anciently, as at the present day, the orientals often made use of stones for weights (Lev. 19:36; Deut. 25:15, etc.). (Heb. *'ĕbĕn*).

2. Heb. *mishqāl* or *mishqōl* may mean either the *weight* numerically estimated (Gen. 24:22; Lev. 19:35; Num. 7:13, etc.), or the act of *weighing* (Ezra 8:34).

3. Heb. *pĕlĕs* (Prov. 16:11; "balance," Isa. 40:12), a *steelyard*.

4. In the New Testament "weight" is mentioned only once in its literal sense, and is the rendering of Gr. *talantiaios*, *talentlike* in weight (Rev. 16:21). The Israelites were commanded to have "just weights" (Lev. 19:36; Deut. 25:15; Prov. 20:10, 23), and the prophet Micah (6:11) denounces "the bag of deceitful weights," referring to the stone weights which were carried in a bag.

5. **Figuratively.** Job, in speaking of the fixed laws ordained by Jehovah for the duration of the world, particularizes by examples: "He appointed the *weight* for the winds" (28:25) i. e., the measure of its force or feebleness. To "eat bread by weight" (Ezek. 4:10, 16) denotes extreme poverty or scarcity of food. The "weight of glory" (II Cor. 4:17) is a figurative expression to denote the intensity of the celestial splendor, especially as contrasted with the transitoriness of our present afflictions. The writer of the Hebrews (12:1) urges his readers to "lay aside every weight" (Gr. *ogkos*). This word means anything *prominent*, an *encumbrance;* it is used figuratively for whatever disposition (as sensuality and worldlymindedness) bows the soul down to earth, and consequently impedes it in running its spiritual race.

Well. 1. **Names.** The rendering of the following Hebrew and Greek words:

(1) Heb. *bĕ'ēr* (a *pit*), something *dug*, and having the meaning of our word *cistern* (Gen. 16:14; 21:19, sq.; 26:19, sq.: II Sam. 17:18, etc.).

(2) Heb. *bōr* (from No. 1) is found in I Sam. 19:22; II Sam. 3:26; 23:15, 16; I Chron. 11:17, 18.

(3) Heb. *mā'yān* (from No. 4), a *spring*, as in Psa. 84:6.

(4) Heb. *'ayin* (an *eye*), a fountain; whether so called from its resemblance to the eye, or, *vice versa*, the eye, from its resemblance to a

fountain, may be doubtful (Gen. 24:13, 16; 49:22; Neh. 2:13); a living *spring*.

(5) Gr. *pēgē* (*gushing*), a fountain spread by a spring (John 4:6, 14; II Pet. 2:17).

(6) Gr. *phrear* (*hole*, John 4:11, 12), a pit *dug*, and thus distinguished from a living spring.

2. Importance. The heat and the large flocks and herds have made a special necessity of a supply of water (Judg. 1:15) in a hot climate; it has always involved among Eastern nations questions of property of the highest importance, and sometimes given rise to serious contention. Thus the well Beer-sheba was opened, and its possession attested with special formality by Abraham (Gen. 21:30, 31). The Koran notices abandoned wells as signs of desertion (Sur. 22). To acquire wells which they had not themselves dug was one of the marks of favor foretold to the Hebrews on their entrance into Canaan (Deut. 6:11). To possess one is noticed as a mark of independence (Prov. 5:15), and to abstain from the use of wells belonging to others, a disclaimer of interference with their property (Num. 20:17, 19; 21:22). Similar rights of possession, actual and hereditary, exist among the Arabs of the present day.

3. Construction. Wells in Palestine are usually excavated from the solid limestone rock, sometimes with steps to descend into them (Gen. 24:16). The brims are furnished with a curb or low wall of stone, bearing marks of high antiquity in the furrows worn by the ropes used in drawing water. It was on a curb of this sort that our Lord sat when he conversed with the woman of Samaria (John 4:6), and it was this, the usual stone cover, which the woman placed on the mouth of the well at Bahurim (II Sam. 17:19), which was dry at times.

527. Egyptian Shaduf

4. Raising the Water. The usual methods for raising water are the following: (1) The rope and bucket, or water-skin (Gen. 24:14-20; John 4:11). (2) The *sakiyeh*, or Persian wheel. This consists of a vertical wheel furnished with a set of buckets or earthen jars, attached to a cord passing over the wheel, which descend empty and return full as the wheel revolves. (3) A modification of the last method, by which a man, sitting opposite to a wheel furnished with buckets, turns it by drawing with his hands one set of spokes prolonged beyond its circumference, and pushing another set from him with his feet. (4) A method very common, both in ancient and modern Egypt, is the *shaduf*, a simple contrivance consisting of a lever moving on a pivot, which is loaded at one end with a lump of clay or some other weight, and has at the other a bowl or bucket. Wells are usually furnished with troughs of wood or stone, into which the water is emptied for the use of persons or animals coming to the wells. Unless machinery is used, which is commonly worked by men, women are usually the water carriers.

5. Figurative. Wells are figurative of: God as the source of salvation (Isa. 12:3; comp. Jer. 2:13; John 4:10; Cant. 4:15); mouth of the righteous (Prov. 10:11); widsom and understanding in a man (16:22; 18:4); "drinking from one's own," domestic happiness (5:15); "wells without water," of hypocrites (II Pet. 2:17).

Wen. *See* Diseases.

West. The oriental, in speaking of the quarters of the heavens, supposes his face turned to the east. So the east is *before* him, the west *behind*, the south at his *right* hand, and the north at his *left*. The "going down of the sun (*bō' hǎshshǎmēsh*) also denoted the west, as did the "sea" (*yǎm*) which was westward from Palestine.

Whale. *See* Animal Kingdom.

Wheat. *See* Vegetable Kingdom.

Figurative. On account of its excellence as a food, wheat is a figure of good men, as tares are of evil (Matt. 3:12; 13-25, 29, 30; Luke 3:17).

Wheel. Wheels were well-known in the ancient Biblical world. Water buckets were manipulated by ropes pulled over wheels set up at wells and cisterns (Eccles. 12:6). The Potter's wheel referred to in Jer. 18:3, and other places, was very ancient. Solomon's temple was equipped with wheeled lavers (I Kings 7:30-33). Nahum refers to the noise of the chariot wheels of the Assyrians (Nah. 3:1). Ezekiel saw wheels in his apocalyptic vision (Ezek. 1:15-21). Canaanite chariot wheels are referred to in Judg. 5:28. Chariot wheels go back to about 3000 B. C. or earlier and were wooden discs manufactured of two half-circle pieces fastened with metal around a central core. Sumerian chariots were four- or two-wheeled. Common Egyptian chariots had wheels of six spokes which, however, were larger than the eight-spoked wheels of Etruscan chariots. *M. F. U.*

Whelp (Heb. *bēn*, *son* or *offspring*, Job 4:11; 28:8; elsewhere *gǔr*, or *gōre*, Gen. 49:9; Deut. 33:22; Jer. 51:38; Ezek. 19:2, 3, 5; Nah. 2:13), the cub of a lion, or of a jackal (Lam. 4:3); the cubs of a bear (II Sam. 17:8; Prov. 17:12; Hos. 13:8) are not designated by the Hebrew word.

Whip (Heb. *shōṭ*, *lash*; sometimes rendered "scourge," Job. 5:21; 9:23; Isa. 10:26; 28:15). In all slaveholding countries the whip has been used upon human beings as a means of coercion and punishment. The system of administering personal chastisement has been universal throughout the East. For this purpose, however, the rod was oftener used. Whips were made of various materials, from the simple scourge (*q. v.*) to the cruel scorpion (*q. v.*).

Whirlwind. The three common Hebrew words rendered in A. V. "whirlwind," all refer, not to a wind revolving with great rapidity upon its own axis, but to a wind blowing with fury and producing blight and destruction; hence *tempest* or *storm*, rather than *whirlwind*, would have been the proper term.

The two in most frequent use are *sûphäh*, from a root meaning to *snatch away*, and signifying a sweeping desolating blast (Job 21:18; 37:9; Isa. 21:1; Hos. 8:7, etc.); and *să'ăr*, from a root, to *toss*, indicating the same thing, but more with reference to its vehement agitating motion (II Kings 2:1, 11; Job 40:6; Isa. 40:24, etc.). The other *rûăḥ* (Ezek. 1:4), should be rendered simply *wind*. The Greek equivalent of *rûăḥ* is *pneuma* (John 3:8, etc.).

Figurative. In a large proportion of the passages the terms are used in a figurative sense, as with reference to the resistless and sweeping destruction sure to overtake the wicked (Psa. 58:9; Prov. 1:27; 10:25; Isa. 41:16, etc.).

Widow (Heb. *'ălmänäh, bereaved;* Gr. *chēra, deficient,* as of a husband).

1. **Mosaic Regulations.** In the Mosaic legislation special regard was paid to widows. It is true that no legal provision was made for their maintenance; but they were left dependent partly on the affection of relations, more especially of the eldest son, whose birthright, or extra share of the property, imposed such a duty upon him, and partly on the privileges accorded to other distressed classes, such as a participation in the triennial third tithe (Deut. 14:29; 26:12), in leasing (24:19-21), and in religious feasts (16:11, 14). God himself claimed a special interest in the widows, even calling himself their husband (Psa. 68:5; 146:9); and uttered the severest denunciations against such as defraud and oppress them (Psa. 94:6; Ezek. 22:7; Mal. 3:5). With regard to the remarriage of widows, the only restriction imposed by the Mosaic law had reference to the contingency of one being left childless, in which case the brother of the deceased husband had a right to marry the widow (Deut. 25:5, 6; Matt. 22:23-30). *See* Marriage; Levirate.

2. **New Testament Usage.** In the apostolic Church the widows were sustained at the public expense, the relief being daily administered in kind, under the superintendence of officers appointed for this special purpose (Acts 6:1-6). Particular directions are given by St. Paul as to the class of persons entitled to such public maintenance (I Tim. 5:3-16). Out of the body of such widows a certain number were to be enrolled, the qualifications for such enrollment being (1) that they were not under sixty years of age; (2) that they had been "the wife of one man," probably meaning *but once married,* and (3) that they had led useful and charitable lives (vers. 9, 10). Some have thought this implies a re-

ceiving of the more elderly and approved widows into a kind of ecclesiastical order (v. 9), either of deaconesses or of a sort of overseers for those of their own sex; but the language is certainly vague and indefinite.

Wife. *See* Marriage.

Wild Beats. *See* Animal Kingdom.

Wild Vine or **Grape.** *See* Vegetable Kingdom.

Wilderness. A wild uninhabited region suitable only for pasturage (Heb. *mĭdbär*) or sparse human occupation. A sterile tract of country not supporting human life, *'ărăbäh* (Job 24:5; Isa. 33:9; Jer. 51:43), or conspicuously an arid desert *ṣiyyäh* (Job 30:3; Psa. 78:17) and hence a place of desolation (Heb. *yᵉshimōn,* Deut. 32:10; Psa. 68:17; Heb. *tōhū,* Job 12:24; Psa. 107:40). The Greek term is *'erēmia, solitude,* used in the N. T.

Wilderness of Wandering, the land in which the Israelites sojourned and wandered for forty years on their way from Egypt to Canaan. It lay within the peninsula of Sinai, or that peninsula extended, i. e., within the angle or fork formed by the two branches of the Red Sea—the Gulf of Suez and the Gulf of Akabah—or the lines of these branches produced, having the Holy Land to the north of it. It is that portion of Arabia called Arabia Petraea (or rocky Arabia), from its rocky and rugged character. It consisted of several districts: (1) The wilderness of Shur, or Etham, i. e., the great wall of Egypt, extending from Suez to the Mediterranean; (2) the wilderness of Paran, occupying the center of the peninsula; (3) the wilderness of Sin, in the lower part of the peninsula; (4) the wilderness of Zin to the northeast. It was in the plain or wilderness of Paran (Gen. 14:6; 21:21; Num. 13:26), still called the Wilderness of Wandering, and in the neighboring mountains, that the children of Israel chiefly wandered after their retreat from Kadesh. But their wandering was not altogether confined to this region, for it seems to have extended to the region of Sinai, or the district of the *Tawarah* Arabs, and then toward the close of the thirty-eight years to the plain of the Arabah and to the wilderness of Zin. All of this region was deficient in water. Hence the occasion for the miraculous stream of water which followed the Israelites for so many years. It was deficient also in food for *man,* but apparently not in food for *cattle.* There is little doubt that the wilderness once afforded greater resources than at present; although there seems to have been no city nor village (Psa. 107:4). The *wandering* of Israel, properly speaking, commenced on their retreat from Kadesh (Num. 14:33; 32:13), for up to that time their journey had been direct, first to Sinai and then to Kadesh.

1. **The Direct Journey.** The first part, viz., to Sinai, has been given in article on Exodus (*q. v.*). Having rested there for about one year, the Israelites moved northward to the wilderness of Paran (Num. 10:12); Taberah (Num. 11:3; Deut. 9:22); Kibroth-hattaavah (Num. 11:34; 33:16); Hazeroth (11:35; 33:17); desert of Arabah by the way of Mount Seir (Deut. 1:1, 2, 19); Rithmah (Num. 33:18); Kadesh in the desert of Paran (Num. 12:16; 13:26; Deut. 1:2, 19).

2. **Wanderings.** In consequence of unbelief and rebellion, the Lord swore that they should *wander* in the wilderness until all that were above twenty years old should perish (Num. 14:33). Their *wandering*, therefore, began on their retreat from Kadesh. The following stations were encamped in until their return to Kadesh: Rimmon-parez (33:19); Libnah (v. 20); Rissah (v. 21); Kehelathah (v. 22); Mount Shapher (v. 23); Haradah (v. 24); Makheloth (v. 25); Tahath (v. 26); Tarah (v. 27); Mithcah (v. 28); Hashmonah (v. 29); Moseroth (v. 30); Bene-jaakan (v. 31); Horhagidgad (v. 32); Jotbathah (v. 33); Ebronah (v. 34); Ezion-geber (v. 35), by the way of the Red Sea (Deut. 2:1); Kadesh, in the desert of Zin (Num. 20:1), by the way of Mount Seir (Deut. 2:1).

3. **From Kadesh to Jordan.** To Beeroth Bene-jaakan (Deut. 10:6); Mount Hor (Num. 20:22; 33:37), or Mosera (Deut. 10:6), where Aaron died; Gudgodah (v. 7); Jotbath (v. 7); by way of the Red Sea (Num. 21:4); by Eziongeber (Deut. 2:8); Elath (v. 8); Zalmonah (Num. 33:41); Punon (v. 42); Oboth (21:10; 33:43); Ije-abarim (21:11), or Iim (33:44, 45); the brook Zered (21:12; Deut. 2:13, 14); brook Arnon (Num. 21:13; Deut. 2:24); Dibongad (Num. 33:45); Almon-diblathaim (v. 46); Beer (well) in the desert (21:16, 18); Mattanah (21:18); Nahaliel (v. 19); Bamoth (v. 19); Pisgah (v. 20), or mountains of Abarim, near Nebo (33:47); by way of Bashan to the plains of Moab by Jordan (21:33; 22:1; 33:48).

Willow. *See* Vegetable Kingdom.

Willows, The Brook of the, a stream mentioned by Isaiah (15:7) in his dirge over Moab. His language implies that it is one of the boundaries of the country. It is best identified with the lower course of the Wadi-el-Hesä at the juncture of the upper course of the Seil el-Kerahi, in the vicinity of a plain covered with willow trees.

See Vegetable Kingdom.

Wills. Under a system of close inheritance like that of the Jews, the scope for bequest in respect of land was limited by the right of redemption and general reentry in the jubilee year. Keil says (*Bib. Arch.*, pp. 309, 311, note 5), "of wills there is not a trace to be found in the Mosaic law or throughout the whole of the Old Testament . . . Neither the expression 'command his house' (put his house in order), II Sam. 17:23; II Kings 20:1; Isa. 38:1, nor the writing mentioned in Tob. 7:14, indicates a testamentary disposition. Not till the time of the later Jews do testaments occur; comp. Gal. 3:15; Heb. 9:17, and among princely families (Josephus, *Ant.*, xiii, 16, 1; xvii, 3, 2; *War*, ii, 2, 3), as well as in Talmudic law, after the Greek and Roman fashion."

Wimple. *See* Dress.

Window. *See* House.

Winds. That the Hebrews recognized the existence of four prevailing winds as issuing, broadly speaking, from the four cardinal points—north, south, east, and west—may be inferred from their custom of using the expression "four winds" as equivalent to the

"four quarters" of the hemisphere (Ezek. 37:9; Dan. 8:8; Zech. 2:6; Matt. 24:31).

1. The north wind, or, as it was usually called "the north," was naturally the coldest of the four (Ecclus. 43:20), and its presence is hence invoked as favorable to vegetation in Cant. 4:16. It blows chiefly in October, and brings dry cold (Job 37:9). It is described in Prov. 25:23 as bringing rain; in this case we must understand the northwest wind. The northwest wind prevails from the autumnal equinox to the beginning of November, and the north wind from June to the equinox.

2. The east wind crosses the sandy wastes of Arabia Deserta before reaching Palestine, and was hence termed "the wind of the wilderness" (Job 1:19; Jer. 13:24). It blows with violence, and is hence supposed to be used generally for any violent wind (Job 27:21; 38:24; Psa. 48:7; Isa. 27:8; Ezek. 27:26). It is probably in this sense that it is used in Exod. 14:21. In Palestine the east wind prevails from February to June.

3. The name "sherkiyeh," our *sirocco* (literally "the east"), is used of all winds blowing in from the desert, east, southeast, south, and even south-southwest. They are hot winds. "When ye see the south wind blow, ye say, There will be heat; and it cometh to pass" (Luke 12:55; comp. Job 37:17; Jer. 4:11; Ezek. 17:10; 19:12; Hos. 13:15). They blow chiefly in the spring, and for a day at a time; and they readily pass over into rain by a slight change in the direction, from southwest to full southwest.

4. The west and southwest winds reach Palestine loaded with moisture gathered from the Mediterranean, and are hence expressively termed by the Arabs "the fathers of the rain." Westerly winds prevail in Palestine from November to February, and, damp from the sea, drop their moisture and cause the winter rains. "In summer the winds blow chiefly out of the drier northwest, and, meeting only warmth, do not cause showers, but greatly mitigate the daily heat. This latter function is fulfilled morning by morning with almost perfect punctuality . . . He strikes the coast soon after sunrise; in Hauran, in June and July, he used to reach us between ten and twelve o'clock, and blew so well that the hours previous to that were generally the hottest of our day. The peasants do all their winnowing against this steady wind" (Smith, *Hist. Geog.*, pp. 66, 67).

In addition to the four regular winds, we have notice in the Bible of the local squalls (Mark 4:37; Luke 8:23), to which the Sea of Genessaret was liable. In the narrative of St. Paul's voyage we meet with the Greek term *lips* to describe the southwest wind; the Latin *carus* or *caurus* (*chōros*), the northwest wind (Acts 27:12); and *euroclydon*, a wind of a very violent character coming from east-northeast (v. 14).

Wine. 1. **Bible Terms.** The product of the wine press was described in Hebrew by a variety of terms, indicative either of the quality or of the use of the liquid.

(1) Heb. *yăyĭn* (*effervescing*) is rendered invariably in the A. V. "wine," excepting Judg. 13:14, "vine"; Cant. 2:4, "banqueting." This

term corresponds to the Gr. *oinos,* and our *wine.* In most of the passages in the Bible where *yăyĭn* is used (eighty-three out of one hundred and thirty-eight), it certainly means *fermented grape juice,* and in the remainder it may fairly be presumed to do so. In four only (Isa. 16:10; Jer. 40:10-12; Lam. 2:12) is it really doubtful. In no passage can it be positively shown to have any other meaning. The intoxicating character of *yăyĭn* in general is plain from Scripture. To it are attributed the "darkly flashing eye" (Gen. 49:12; A. V. "red"), the unbridled tongue (Prov. 20:1; Isa. 28:7), the excitement of the spirit (Prov.

528. Gathering Grapes in the Vineyard

31:6; Isa. 5:11; Zech. 9:15; 10:7), the enchained affections of its votaries (Hos. 4:11), the perverted judgment (Prov. 31:5; Isa. 28:7), the indecent exposure (Hab. 2:15, 16), and the sickness resulting from the *heat* (*ḥēmäh,* A. V. "bottles") of wine (Hos. 7:5).

So in actual instances: Noah planted a vineyard, and drank of the *yăyĭn* and was *drunken* (Gen. 9:21); Nabal drank *yăyĭn* and was *very drunken* (I Sam. 25:36, 37); the "drunkards of Ephraim" were "overcome with *yăyĭn* (Isa. 28:1). Jeremiah says, "I am like a drunken man, and like a man whom *yăyĭn* hath overcome" (Jer. 23:9). The intoxicating quality of *yăyĭn* is confirmed by rabbinical testimony. The Mishna, in the treatise on the Passover, informs us that four cups of wine were poured out and blessed, and drunk by each of the company at the eating of the paschal lamb, and that water was also mixed with wine, because it was considered too strong to be drunk alone. The Gemara adds, "The cup of blessing is not to be blessed, *until it is mixed* with water." To meet the objection, How can intoxication be hindered? the rabbins replied, "Because wine between eating does not intoxicate a man." But although usually intoxicating, yet it was not only permitted to be drunk, but was also used for sacred purposes, and is spoken of as a blessing (Gen. 49:12; Deut. 14:24-26; Exod. 29:40; Lev. 23:13; Num. 15:5; Amos 4:9). Some, indeed, have argued from these passages that *yăyĭn* could not always have been alcoholic. But this is begging the question, and that in defiance of the facts. Although invariably fer-

mented, it was not always inebriating, and in most instances, doubtless, was but slightly alcoholic, like the *vin ordinaire* of France.

(2) Heb. *tírōsh,* properly signifies *must,* the freshly pressed juice of the grape (the *gleuchos* of the Greeks, or sweet wine); rendered "new wine" in Neh. 10:39; 13:5, 12; Prov. 3:10; Isa. 24:7; 65:8; Hos. 4:11; 9:2; Joel 1:10; Hag. 1:11; Zech. 9:17; "sweet wine" in Mic. 6:15. In this last passage it seems to be used for that from which wine is made. The question whether either of the above terms ordinarily signified a solid substance, would be at once settled by a reference to the manner in which they were consumed. With regard to *yăyĭn* we are not aware of a single passage which couples it with the act of *eating.* In the only passage where the act of consuming *tírōsh* alone is noticed (Isa. 62:8, 9), the verb is *shäthäh,* which constantly indicates the act of *drinking.* There are, moreover, passages which seem to imply the actual manufacture of *tírōsh* by the same process by which wine was ordinarily made (Mic. 6:15; Prov. 3:10; Joel 2:24). As to the intoxicating character of this drink, the allusions to its effects are confined to a single passage, "Whoredom and wine [*yăyĭn*] and new wine [*tírōsh*] take away the heart," where *tírōsh* appears as the climax of engrossing influences, in immediate connection with *yăyĭn.*

(3) Heb. *shēkär* (an *intoxicant*), an inebriating drink, whether wine prepared or distilled from barley, honey, or dates, *yăyĭn* referring more especially to wine made from grapes. *Shēkär* is rendered in the A. V. "strong drink" twenty-one times, and once "strong wine" (Num. 28:7; Psa. 69:12, "drinkers of strong drink"). The liquors included under *shēkär* might therefore be pomegranate wine, palm wine, apple wine, honey wine, perhaps even beer, for some have identified it with the liquor obtained from barley by the Egyptians. The word is employed in the following passages in such a manner as to show decisively that it denotes an intoxicating drink; Lev. 10:9, where the priests are forbidden to drink wine, or *shēkär,* when they go into the tabernacle; I Sam. 1:15, where Hannah, charged with drunkenness by Eli, replies it is not so— "I have drunk neither wine nor *shēkär;*" Psa. 69:12, where the psalmist complains, "I was the song of the drinkers of *shēkär*" (A. V. "drunkards"); Prov. 31:4, 5, "It is not for kings to drink wine; nor for princes *shēkär:* lest they drink, and forget the law;" Isa. 5:22, "Woe unto them that are mighty to drink wine, and men of strength to mingle *shēkär*" (comp. 28:7; 29:9).

(4) Heb. *'äsîs* (Cant. 8:2; Isa. 49:26; Joel 1:5; 3:18; Amos 9:13) is derived from a word signifying "to tread," and therefore refers to the method by which the juice was expressed from the fruit. It would very properly refer to *new* wine as being recently trodden out, but not necessarily to unfermented wine.

(5) Heb. *Sōbe, potation,* occurs only three times (Isa. 1:22, "wine;" Hos. 4:18, "drink;" Nah. 1:10 "drunken"), but the verb and participle often—the latter to denote drunk, a drunkard, a toper.

(6) Heb. *mēsĕk,* a *mixture,* is wine mixed

with water or aromatics (Psa. 75:8, A. V. "mixture"). But the noun appears to have been restricted in usage to a bad sense, to denote wine mingled with stupefying or exciting drugs, so that the wine might produce more powerful effects than was possible otherwise, at a time when distillation had not been discovered.

(7) In the New Testament we have the following Greek words: '*oinos*, comprehending every sort of wine. *Gleuchos* (*must*), sweet or "new wine," which seems to have been of an intoxicating nature (Acts 2:13), where the charge is made, "These men are full of new wine;" to which Peter replies (v. 15), "These men are not drunken as ye suppose." If the wine was not intoxicating the accusation could only have been ironical. From the explanations of the ancient lexicographers we may infer that the luscious qualities of this wine were due not to its being recently made, but to its being produced from the purest juice of the grape. *Genēma tēs ampelou*, fruit of the vine (Luke 22:18). *Oinos 'akratos*, pure wine (Rev. 14:10). *Oxos*, sour wine or vinegar (Matt. 27:48; Mark 15:36, etc.). *Sikera* (Luke 1:15, A. V. "strong drink"), an intoxicating beverage made of a mixture of sweet ingredients, whether derived from grain or vegetables, or from the juice of fruits, or a decoction of honey. It corresponds to No. 4.

2. Biblical History of Wine. Wine is first mentioned in the case of Noah, who "planted a vineyard, and did drink of the wine [*yăyĭn*] and was drunken" (Gen. 9:20, 21). The second notice is in Gen. 19:32, etc., where it is said that the daughters of Lot made their father drink wine [*yăyĭn*] so that he became stupidly intoxicated. It is mentioned in the blessing pronounced by Isaac upon Jacob (27:28); in connection with Egypt (40:11), when the chief butler says, "I took the grapes, and pressed them into Pharaoh's cup." With regard to the uses of wine in private life there is little to remark. It was produced on occasions of ordinary hospitality (14:18), and at festivals, such as marriages (John 2:3). The monuments of ancient Egypt furnish abundant evidence that the people of that country, both male and female, indulged liberally in the use of wine. Under the Mosaic law wine formed the usual drink offering that accompanied the daily sacrifice (Exod. 29:40), the presentation of the first fruits (Lev. 23:13), and other offerings (Num. 15:5). Tithe was to be paid of wine as of other products. The priest was also to receive first fruits of wine, as of other articles (Deut. 18:4; comp. Exod. 22:29). The use of wine at the paschal feast was not enjoined by the law, but did become an established custom, at all events in the post-Babylonian period. The wine was mixed with warm water on these occasions, as implied in the notice of the warming kettle. Hence in the early Christian Church it was usual to mix the sacramental wine with water.

Figurative. Wine is figurative of the blood of Christ (Matt. 26:27-29); of the blessings of the Gospel (Prov. 9:2, 5; Isa. 25:6; 55:1); of the exhilarating effect of the Holy Spirit's fullness (Eph. 5:18); of the wrath and judgments of God (Psa. 60:3; 75:8; Jer. 13:12-14;

25:15-18); of the abominations of the apostasy (Rev. 17:2; 18:3); of violence and rapine (Prov. 4:17).

Wine Press. Each vineyard had its wine press, the practice being to extract the juice from the grape in the field. These presses were generally hewn out of the solid rock, and a large number of them remain at the present day. From the scanty notices contained in the Bible we gather that the wine presses of the Jews consisted of two receptacles or vats placed at different elevations, in the upper one of which the grapes were trodden, while the lower one received the expressed juice. The two vats are mentioned together only in Joel 3:13: "The press [*gath*] is full; the vats [*troughs, yĕkĕb*] overflow"—the upper vat being full of fruit, the lower one overflowing with the must. *Gath* is also strictly applied to the upper vat in Neh. 13:15; Lam. 1:15, and Isa. 63:2, with Heb. *pūrāh*, *crushing*, in a parallel sense in the following verse. The term *pūrāh*, as used in Hag. 2:16, probably refers to the contents of a wine vat rather than to the press or vat itself. The two vats were usually dug or hewn out of the solid rock (Isa. 5:2, marg.; Matt. 21:33). Ancient wine presses, so constructed, are still to be seen in Palestine.

529. An Egyptian Wine Press

Figurative. The very forceful use of the wine press as a figure is found in Isa. 63:3-6, where Jehovah is represented as taking vengeance upon the ungodly nations. The nations are the grapes, which are cut off and put into the wine press (Joel 3:12); and the red upon his garments is the life blood of these nations. This work of wrath had been executed by Jehovah, because he had in his heart a day of vengeance, which could not be delayed, and because the year of his promised redemption had arrived. The New Testament counterpart of this passage is the destruction of antichrist and his army (Rev. 19:11, sq.). He who effects this destruction is the Faithful and True, the Logos of God. The vision of John is evidently based upon that of Isaiah. Merciless oppression is forcibly illustrated in Job 24:9-12, where serfs are said to "tread wine presses and suffer thirst."

Wing (Heb. generally *kănăph*, *extremity*; Gr. *pterux, feather*). The Hebrew word conveys the meaning not only of the wings of birds, but also the lappet, skirt, or flap of a garment (Ruth 3:9; Jer. 2:34), the extremity of a country (Job 38:13; Isa. 24:16, marg.).

Figurative. God says that he has borne his people on eagles' wings (Exod. 19:4; Deut. 32:11), i. e., he had brought them out of

Egypt with strong and loving care. The eagle watches over its young in the most careful manner, flying under them when it leads them from the nest, lest they should fall upon the rocks and be destroyed. "To mount up with wings as eagles" (Isa. 40:31), i. e., their course of life, which has Jehovah for its object, is, as it were, possessed of wings. The *wings* of the sun (Mal. 4:2) are the rays by which it is surrounded. As the rays of the sun spread light and warmth over the earth, for the benefit of plants and living creatures, so will the Sun of righteousness bring healing for all the hurts inflicted by sin. "The wings of the wind" (II Sam. 22:11; Psa. 18:10), and "of the morning" (Psa. 139:9) are expressive of the swiftness with which the winds and the morning move onward. The idea of protection, defense, is given by such expressions as "Hide me under the shadow of thy wings" (Psa. 17:8; comp. 36:7; 57:1; 61:4; 63:7; 91:4; Matt. 23:37; Luke 13:34).

Winnow. *See* Agriculture.

Winter (Heb. usually *ḥōrĕph*, strictly *autumn;* Gr. *cheimōn*, the *rainy* season). In Palestine winter includes part of autumn and the seasons of seedtime and cold, extending from the beginning of September to the beginning of March (Gen. 8:22; Psa. 74:17; Zech. 14:8; Matt. 24:20). The cold of winter is not usually very severe, though the north winds are very penetrating from the middle of December to the middle of February. Snow and hail during most winters fall on the hills. On the central range snow has been known to reach a depth of nearly two feet, and to lie for five days or even more, and the pools at Jerusalem have sometimes been covered with ice. But this is rare. On the central range the ground seldom freezes, and the snow usually disappears in a day. On the plateaus east of Jordan snow lies regularly for some days every winter, and on the top of Hermon there are fields of it during the summer. *See* Calendar.

Winterhouse (Heb. *ḥōrĕph*). In Scripture the lower portion of the house was called the "winterhouse," as was also the inner apartment, while the outer and upper ones were called the "summerhouse" (Jer. 36:22).

Wisdom. 1. Heb. *ḥŏkmäh*, has the special meaning of *dexterity, skill* in an art (Exod. 28:3; 31:6; 36:1, 2). It has also and more generally the meaning of intelligent, sensible, judicious, endued with reason and using it (Deut. 4:6; 34:9; Prov. 10:1, etc.); skillful to judge (I Kings 2:9); thus the wisdom of Solomon is manifested in his acute judgment (3:26; 10:1, sq.), in the verses and sentences he composed or retained in his memory (I Kings 5:12; Prov. 1:2). Wisdom includes skill in civil matters (Isa. 19:11), the faculty of interpreting dreams and prophesying (Dan. 5:11), as well as the art of enchantment and magic (Exod. 7:11). A higher and more enlightened wisdom is ascribed to angels (II Sam. 14:20), to God (Job 9:4; 28:23).

2. Heb. *säkäl* (to *be prudent, circumspect,* I Sam. 18:30; Job 22:2; Psa. 2:10; 94:8, etc.).

3. Heb. *tūshĭyäh* (properly *uprightness*), counsel, understanding (Job 11:6; 12:16; 26:3; Prov. 3:21, etc.).

4. Heb. *bīnäh* (*understanding*), the faculty of insight, intelligence (Prov. 4:7, "understanding," v. 5; 39:26).

5. The Greek terms are: *sophia,* broad and full intelligence; used of knowledge of very diverse matters, so that the shade of meaning in which the word is taken must be discovered from the context in every particular case; *phronēsis,* understanding, specially knowledge and holy love of the will of God (Luke 1:17; Eph. 1:8).

Occasional Uses. (1) Wisdom is put for ingenuity, mechanical dexterity (Exod. 28:3; 31:3); (2) craftiness, sublety, whether good or bad (Exod. 1:10; II Sam. 13:3; Prov. 14:8); (3) the skill or arts of magicians, etc. (Gen. 41:8; Exod. 7:11; Eccles. 9:17); (4) sagacity, learning, experience (Job 12:2, 12; 38:37; Psa. 105:22); (5) the current pagan philosophy of the apostolic age (I Cor. 1:20; 2:5; 3:19; II Cor. 1:12).

The Dominant Uses. (1) An attribute of God, intimately related to the divine knowledge, but manifesting itself in the selection of proper ends and the proper means for their accomplishment. Thus not only the world of nature, but especially the economy of redemption, is a manifestation of divine wisdom (see Psa. 104:24; Rom. 11:33; I Cor. 1:24; Rev. 7:12). Thus the Old Testament appeal of wisdom to men is the appeal of the "Only Wise God" (see Proverbs and Psalms). (2) In men wisdom is not only practical understanding of matters relating to this life (I Kings 3:12), but in the highest sense it is the theoretical and practical acceptance of divine revelation. Wisdom is in the deepest sense a divine gift (see Acts 6:10; I Cor. 2:6; 12:8; Eph. 1:17; Col. 1:9; 3:16; James 1:5; 3:15-17).

Witch. *See* Magic; Saul; Sorcery.

Withered. *See* Diseases.

Witness (Heb. *'ēd;* Gr. *martureō,* to *testify*).

1. **A Memorial.** Among people with whom writing is not common, the evidence of a transaction is given by some tangible memorial or significant ceremony. Abraham gave seven ewe lambs to Abimelech as an evidence of his property in the well of Beer-sheba. Jacob raised a heap of stones, "the heap of witness," as a boundary mark between himself and Laban (Gen. 21:30; 31:47, 52). The tribes of Reuben and Gad raised an "altar" as a witness to the covenant between themselves and the rest of the nation; Joshua set up a stone as an evidence of the allegiance promised by Israel to God (Josh. 22:10, 26, 34; 24:26, 27).

2. **Legal Usages.** Thus also symbolical usages, in ratification of contracts or completed arrangements, as the ceremony of shoe-loosing (Deut. 25:9, 10; Ruth 4:7, 8), the ordeal prescribed in the case of a suspected wife (Num. 5:17-31), with which may be compared the ordeal of the Styx. But written evidence was by no means unknown to the Jews. Divorce was to be proved by a written document (Deut. 24:1, 3). In civil contracts, at least in later times, documentary evidence was required and carefully preserved (Isa. 8:16; Jer. 32:10-16).

3. **Evidence in Law.** On the whole the law was very careful to provide and enforce evi-

dence for all its infractions and all transactions bearing upon them. Among special provisions with respect to evidence are the following: 1. Two witnesses at least are required to establish any charge (Num. 35:30; Deut. 17:6; John 8:17; II Cor. 13:1; comp. I Tim. 5:19). 2. In the case of the suspected wife, evidence besides the husband's was desired (Num. 5:13). 3. The witness who withheld the truth was censured (Lev. 5:1). 4. False witness was punished with the punishment due to the offense which it sought to establish. 5. Slanderous reports and officious witness are discouraged (Exod. 20:16; 23:1; Lev. 19:16, 18, etc.). 6. The witnesses were the first executioners (Deut. 13:9; Acts 7:58). 7. In case of an animal left in charge and torn by wild beasts, the keeper was to bring the carcass in proof of the fact and disproof of his own criminality (Exod. 22:13). 8. According to Josephus, women and slaves were not admitted to bear testimony (*Ant.*, iv, 8, 15).

4. **New Testament Use of Word.** In the New Testament the original notion of a witness is exhibited in the special form of one who attests his belief in the Gospel by personal suffering. Hence it is that the use of the ecclesiastical term "martyr" has arisen.

Witness of the Spirit, the direct testimony of the Holy Spirit to true believers as to their acceptance with God and their adoption into the divine household.

1. **Scriptural.** The two classic passages upon which this doctrine is especially based are Rom. 8:16; Gal. 4:6. It is, however, argued that just as Christ in his visible ministry not only forgave sins, but also announced to penitent sinners their forgiveness, so it is one of the offices of the Holy Spirit still to proclaim directly to those who are pardoned the fact of their pardon. Also this view is confirmed by other representations than those named in the Scriptures of the presence and activity of the Holy Spirit (see Rom. 8:1, 2; II Cor. 1:22; Eph. 1:13; 4:30). The Holy Spirit is "the Spirit of Adoption." It is because he speaks within us that we are able to cry, "Abba, Father;" are consciously free from condemnation, and are "sealed with that Holy Spirit of promise."

2. **Theological Suggestions.** 1. The fact to which the witness of the Spirit particularly relates is that of the gracious change in relation of the pardoned sinner to God. He is no longer guilty, and "an alien," but forgiven, and by adoption a child of God. The one point upon which the Scriptures lay emphasis is that the Spirit's witness is to the fact of adoption, connected, of course, with justification and regeneration. 2. The witness of our own spirit is to be distinguished from the witness of the Holy Spirit. In Rom. 8:16 the word used is *summartureō*, which means two or more witnesses jointly, yet distinctly, giving testimony to the same fact. And two witnesses here are mentioned, the spirit of the man himself and the Spirit of God. The witness of our own spirit is indirect in the sense that it is based upon a comparison of the facts of our spiritual life and experiences with the representations and requirements of the Scriptures. We know whether or not we have truly repented and

believed in Christ, and whether we have peace and joy and love and the spirit of obedience (see Rom. 5:1; 8:1-14; I John 2:29; 3:14, 19, 21; 4:7). But the witness of the Spirit is beyond this, though associated with it. As Wesley says, "The testimony of the Spirit is an inward impression on the souls of believers, whereby the Spirit of God directly testifies to their spirit that they are 'children of God,'" and, further, "there is in every believer both the testimony of God's Spirit and the testimony of his own that he is a child of God." This direct and distinct witness of the Spirit is frequently merged into and confused with the witness of our own spirit, as notably by Chalmers (*Lectures on Rom.*, p. 202), where he reduces the work of the Spirit to the graving upon us the lineaments of a living epistle of Jesus Christ, and tells us in the epistle of a written revelation what these lineaments are." But this is in opposition to a fair exegesis of Rom. 8:16, where the idea of two joint yet distinct testimonies appear. 3. The witness of the Spirit is to be regarded as a sequence or reward of saving faith, and not the basis of such faith or a necessary element therein. Wesleyan writers, and Wesley himself, have not always been sufficiently clear upon this point. At times Wesley distinguishes most clearly between "justifying faith and a sense of pardon," and adds, "How can a sense of pardon be the condition of our receiving it?" (*Works*, xii, 109, 110). But elsewhere (*Sermons*, x, 8, 9) he argues that "we cannot love God till we know he loves us; and we cannot know his pardoning love to us till his Spirit witnesses to our spirit." He is seeking to prove here that the witness of the Spirit must precede the witness of our own spirit; but in seeking this he goes too far, and makes the witness of the Spirit the basis of our faith and an essential element therein. It is of the largest importance that it should be understood that saving faith is simply complete reliance of the penitent soul upon the grace of God in Jesus Christ, as offered in his word, and that the witness of the Spirit comes in God's own time and way to those who do thus truly repent and believe. While the Spirit's witness is a great boon proffered to all believers, and none should rest without it, yet there are ways of directly seeking it which involve not faith, but unbelief, and disparagement of the sure promises of God as contained in his Holy Word.

Wizard. The wizard (Heb. *yĭd 'ōnî*) is properly the "knowing or wise one" as the English word connotes, as well as the Septuagint "gnostes." Like the "familiar spirit" (Heb. *'ob*), it means in the first instance the alleged "spirit of a deceased person" (actually the divining demon). Then it came to mean him or her who divines by such a spirit or demon. Thus both terms mean (1) the divining spirit (2) the medium through whom the demon divines. The two concepts, "the divining spirit" and "the divining medium" are frequently so closely identified as to be thought of as one, as in Lev. 19:31; 20:6. In the Hebrew "unto them that have familiar spirits" is simply "unto the familiar spirits." The same is true of the term "wizard." Implicit in its meaning is the thought of the wise and knowing demon, and the clever and cunning medium, who is skillful in oracular science because the intelligent spirit is in him. It is a super-human knowledge of the spirit inhabiting the human body that makes a spiritistic medium a wizard. *See* Magic, Sorcery, Witch Necromancer.—M. F. U.

Wolf. The following allusions are made to the wolf in the Scriptures: Its ferocity is mentioned in Gen. 49:27; Ezek. 22:27; Hab. 1:8; Matt. 7:15; its nocturnal habits in Jer. 5:6; Zeph. 3:3; Hab. 1:8; its attacking sheep in Ecclus. 13:17; John 10:12; Matt. 10:16; Luke 10:3.

 Figurative. Of the wicked (Matt. 10:16; Luke 10:3); of wicked rulers (Ezek. 22:27; Zeph. 3:3); of false teachers (Matt. 7:15; Acts 20:29); of the devil (John 10:12); of the tribe of Benjamin (Gen. 49:27); of fierce enemies (Jer. 5:6; Hab. 1:8); of the peaceful reign of the Messiah, under the metaphor of a wolf dwelling with a lamb (Isa. 11:6; 65:25). *See* Animal Kingdom.

Wood. *See* Vegetable Kingdom.

Wood Carrying, Festival of. *See* Festivals, 4.

Wool. *See* Dress, 1.

Worm. *See* Animal Kingdom.

Wormwood. *See* Vegetable Kingdom.

Worship. The act of paying divine honors to a deity; religious reverence and homage. The rendering in the A. V. of the following Hebrew and Greek words:

 1. Heb. *shâḥâh* (to *bow down*), to prostrate oneself before another in order to do him honor and reverence (Gen. 22:5, etc.). This mode of salutation consisted in falling upon the knees and then touching the forehead to the ground (Gen. 19:1; 42:6; 48:12; I Sam. 25:41, etc., often rendered "bowed"). It is, however, used specifically to bow down before God, spoken of worship rendered to God, and also to false gods (Gen. 22:5; Exod. 24:1; 33:10; Judg. 7:15; Job 1:20; Psa. 22:27; 86:9).

 2. Aram. *sᵉgîd* (to *fall down*), spoken of in connection with idol worship; to fall down in adoration of idols (Dan. 3:5, 6; 10-12, 14, 15, 28); in honor of a man, as of Daniel (2:46).

 3. Heb. *'âṣâb* (to *carve, labor*), to *serve* an idol, as in Jer. 44:19; or according to others, to *fashion her*, i. e., the image (see Orelli, *Com.*, in loc.).

 4. The Greek words thus rendered are: *proskuneō*, properly to *kiss the hand to* (*toward*) *one*, in token of reverence, also by kneeling or prostration to do homage—the word most frequently used in the New Testament. *Sebomai*, to *revere* a deity (Matt. 15:9; Mark 7:7; Acts 18:13; 19:27). "Proselytes of the gate" are called "men that worship God" (*sebomenē tōn theon*, Acts 16:14; 18:7), or simply "devout persons" (*tois sebomenois*, Acts 17:17). *Latreuō* (to *serve*) is used in the New Testament to render religious service or honor, and in the *strict* sense to perform sacred services, to offer gifts, to worship God in the observance of the rites instituted for his worship (Heb. 10:2; "service," 9:9). *Ethelothrēskeia* (*voluntary worship*), i. e., worship which one devises and prescribes for himself, contrary to the contents and nature of the faith which ought to be directed to

Christ; said of the misdirected zeal and practices of ascetics (Col. 2:23). *Therapeuō*, to *do service*, as in Acts 17:25.

 General Observations. It is as natural to worship as it is to live. The feeling and expression of high adoration, reverence, trust, love, loyalty, and dependence upon a higher power, human or divine, is a necessity to man. To these sentiments, to a greater or less degree, in every man, something or somebody, real or imaginary, appeals. And that something secures his worship. "Worship is as old as humanity. It has its root in a necessity of the human soul as native to it as the consciousness of God itself, which impels it to testify by word and act its love and gratitude to the Author of life and the Giver of all good" (Keil, *Bib. Arch.*, p. 55).

 Primitive Worship. We are not informed as to the nature of the worship rendered by our first parents; but we learn from earliest records that their sons were moved to present a portion of the product of their labor in sacrifice to God. Men as early as Enos, the grandson of Adam (Gen. 4:26), called upon the name of the Lord; or, in other words, the regular and solemn worship of God as Jehovah (i. e., as the God of salvation) was celebrated in word and act—with prayer and sacrifice. Max Müller (in his essay) says: "That feeling of sonship which distinguishes man from every other creature, and not only exalts him above the brute, but completely secures him against sinking into a purely physical state of being, that original intuition of God, and that consciousness of his being dependent upon a higher power, can only be the result of a primitive revelation in the most literal sense of the word." This view is entertained by Schelling. The other view is that worship cannot be traced to a divine source; that the original condition of the human family was of an extremely rude and imperfect character; and that fetichism, as being the lowest, was also the earliest form of religion, and that for this reason we ought to regard religion, even in its most advanced forms, as springing originally from a barbarous fetichism. But the grounds upon which this opinion is based are weak in the extreme. "It would be nearer the truth to say that they are as divine as they are human in their origin, seeing that they are based upon the relation of man to God involved in his creation, and are evoked by a sense of the divine training and guidance under which he finds himself after his creation" (Keil, *Bib. Arch.*, p. 56).

 In primitive times that form of worship which Enos introduced was still maintained, for Enoch "walked with God" (Gen. 5:24); Noah was righteous before him, and expressed his gratitude by presenting burnt offerings (6:9; 7:20).

 In a subsequent age God chose for himself a faithful servant in the person of Abraham, made him the depository of his revelation, and the father and founder of that people, which was destined to preserve the knowledge and worship of his name till the time when the Saviour should issue from its midst. While other nations multiplied their modes of worship according to the political constitution which they adopted, and to suit the number and variety of their duties, they devised a corresponding variety of ritual, with a numerous priesthood and a multitude of sacred observance. But Abraham, and the posterity born to him, preserved a simple form of worship as became shepherds, while it was at the same time duly in keeping with the revelation imparted to them. Wherever they pitched their tents for any length of time they built *altars*, that, in compliance with ancient usage, they might call upon the name of the Lord (Gen. 12:7, 8; 13:4, 18, etc.). Those altars, were, doubtless, simple mounds (Heb. *bä-mōth*) composed of earth and stone, while the victim sacrificed upon them consisted of animals of an edible nature (i. e., clean) taken from the fold.

We have no information regarding the particular ceremonies observed in connection with these sacrifices; but it is probable that prayer was offered by the patriarchs in person, who were in the habit of discharging the priestly functions. The offerings were for the most part burnt offerings, i. e., offerings that were entirely consumed upon the altar; although instances are given of a portion of the sacrifice being reserved for use in the sacrificial feasts (Gen. 3:54; 46:1). In the selection of animals for sacrifices the patriarchs were probably guided by the directions given to Abraham (15:9); while the way in which the sacrifice of Isaac terminated (22:12, 13) must have shown that the animal victim was to be regarded merely as a symbol of the heart's devotion to God. Whether these sacrifices were offered at regular intervals or on special occasions (see Job 1:5), we cannot say.

Besides altars, *memorial stones* (Heb. *măṣṣē-bōth*) were erected by the patriarchs on spots where God had favored them with special revelations, drink offerings being poured upon them (Gen. 28:18, sq.; 35:14, sq.). The narrative of Jacob's vow (28:20, sq.) tells of his promise that if God would watch over him, supply his wants, and bring him back in safety, that he would acknowledge Jehovah as his God, that he would consecrate the pillar he had set up and make it a house of God, and render to Jehovah the tenth of all his income. We read (35:1, sq.) of his exclusion of strange gods from his house and, after due preparation on the part of his household, his building of an altar at Beth-el.

In the above-mentioned forms of worship the rite of circumcision was added. In obedience to a divine order, and as a token of the covenant which Jehovah made with him, Abraham performed this rite upon himself and the male members of his household, enjoining it upon his posterity as an inviolable obligation (17:1, sq.). Nothing further is known regarding the forms of worship which obtained among the patriarchs.

Mosaic. When Israel became a nation with an organized civil government, in order to fulfill its divine mission, it was necessary that its religious affairs should also be remodeled, and that the character and style of its worship should be fixed and regulated by positive divine enactments. This did not necessitate an entirely new system of worship, since they

were to serve and honor the God of their fathers. Therefore the worship introduced by Moses was grafted on that of Israel's ancestors, improved and perfected only as the circumstances of the Israelites as a confederacy of tribes or a monarchy seemed to require with such forms and ceremonies as would further Israel's divinely appointed mission. This object was further secured by the Mosaic ritual, inasmuch as it embraced all the essential elements of a complete system of worship, giving precise directions as to the *place* of worship, with its structure and arrangements, instituting a distinct order of sacred functions, prescribing the religious ceremonies, fixing the sacred seasons and the manner in which they were to be observed.

This system bore the stamp of genuine worship, being framed by Moses in accordance with revelation, and recognizing Jehovah as the true God. Nor is it a vital objection to its being true worship that it had a material and sensuous character, and that many of its forms and ceremonies were such as belonged to the ritual of pagan religions. These facts have been variously misconstrued, and have been taken advantage of for the purpose of disparaging the origin and character of the Mosaic worship. It is true that the Mosaic worship embodies itself, for the most part, in outward forms and ceremonies, for one can only give expression to his relation to his Creator through *corporeal media*. Religious thought and feeling can only express themselves in word and act; and therefore forms are necessary in every kind of worship. And being copies or impressions of religious ideas, they must have an allegorical or symbolical character.

Further, the religion of the Old Testament is monotheism, in contradiction to the polytheism of heathen nations. Jehovah is represented not only as the only true God; not merely as the almighty Creator, Preserver, and Governor of the world and every creature; not simply as the eternal, absolute Spirit, the good and merciful One who has destined man to enjoy the felicity of life which springs from personal fellowship with himself; as the omnipresent and near One watching over all his creatures, to keep the weak and distressed; who seeks to conduct those who have wandered from him back to the fountain of life; who selected for himself, from degenerate humanity, a race to be in a special sense his people, and to whom he, in a special sense, would be God, with the purpose of saving the world. This is accompanied with such directions for the regulations of their life, that, if accepted and complied with, Israel would become to Jehovah "a peculiar treasure above all people" (Exod. 19:5, sq.), "a kingdom of priests and a holy nation."

Christian. The Church of Christ is not only his representative body on earth, it is also the temple of divine service, continuing and perfecting the worship of the past. This service includes offerings presented to God, and blessings received from him. The former embraces the entire ordinance of worship, with its nature, reasons, and observances; the latter embraces the means of grace, common prayer, the word, and the sacraments. These, however, are really one, and their relations to each other as one are of great importance. Both require for their realization the institution of the evangelical ministry. The worship of the Christian Church may be regarded in its di-

wrinkle" (Gr. *hrutis*). The former is any blemish on the person, the latter probably means the tokens of approaching age. If so, it reminds us of the continued youth and attractiveness of the Church.

From " Syria ", vol. v (Librairie Orientaliste Paul Geuthner, Paris)

530. The Ahiram Inscription of Byblus, c. 1000 B.C. The inscription reads: "The coffin which [It]tobal, son of Ahirma, king of Byblus, made for his father as his abode in eternity. And if any king or any governor or any army commander attacks Byblus and exposes this coffin, let his judicial sceptre be broken, let his royal throne be overthrown and let peace flee from Byblus; and as for him let a vagabond [?] efface his inscription!"—*Journal, American Oriental Society,* vol. 67 (1947), pp. 155-6.

vine principles and in its human arrangements. As to the former, its object is the revealed Trinity; its form is mediatorial, through the Son incarnate, by the Holy Spirit; its attributes are spirituality, simplicity, purity, and reverent decorum; its seasons are the Lord's day preeminently, and all times of holy assembly. As to the latter, it is left to the congregation itself to determine the minor details, according to the pattern shown in the Scripture.

As an institute of worship the Church of Christ has its ordinary channels for the communication of the influences of the Holy Ghost to the souls of men, viz., the means of grace; the supreme means being the word and prayer. Special attention is also called to the sacraments (*q. v.*), baptism, and the Lord's Supper.

Wounds. *See* Diseases.

Wrath (Gr. *thumos, passion*). In the list of probable evils to be avoided (II Cor. 12:20) is "wrath." *Thumos* and *orgē* (Gr. *orgē*) are found several times together in the New Testament (Rom. 2:8; Eph. 4:31; Col. 3:8; Rev. 19:15). The general opinion of scholars is that *thumos* is the more turbulent commotion, the "boiling agitation of the feelings, either presently to subside and disappear, or else to settle down into *orgē*, wherein is more of an abiding and settled habit of the mind ('*ira inveterata*'), with the purpose of revenge" (Trench, i, pp. 178, 179).

Wrinkle. Job in his complaint (16:8) says, "Thou hast filled me with wrinkles" (Heb. *qāmăt*), a figurative expression, meaning to be shriveled up. Paul speaks (Eph. 5:27) of the Church as a bride "not having a spot or

Writing, the art of reducing human thought to a permanent form in readable characters or signs upon an impressionable substance or material.

1. **Antiquity.** About 3200 B. C. writing enters the arena of history. The Sumerians used a pictograph script employing innumerable small pictures to stand for words. This was the oldest written language. At Uruk in southern Babylonia, where the first cylinder seals were discovered, writing emerged. In the Red Temple at Uruk a number of flat clay tablets were done in a crude pictograph script. This gave way to Sumerian cuneiform (from the Latin *cuneus,* meaning "wedge," and referring to the wedge-shaped form of the letters made with the imprint of a stylus upon wet clay). The Semitic Babylonians, who came into Lower Babylonia and inherited the culture of the Sumerians, adopt-

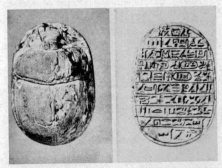

531. Egyptian Hieroglyphics on a Scarab of Amenhotep III Announcing His Marriage to Tiy

ed cuneiform writing. This type of script spread to Assyria, and the mounds of Mesopotamia have yielded innumerable clay tablets inscribed in this style of writing. The Amarna Letters (c. 1400-1350 B. C.), consisting of some 300 clay tablets written in an Akkadianized *lingua franca*, illustrate the wide use of cuneiform writing even in the foreign office in Egypt. Of special importance in the history of writing was the discovery of the Ras Shamra epic religious literature at Ugarit in North Syria (1929-1937). Although this was written in cuneiform, it turned out to be the simple alphabetic, easily read variety, closely allied to alphabetic Hebrew. It offers innumerable parallels to O. T. vocabulary, syntax and poetic style. Since 1923, a number of important Canaanite inscriptions have been unearthed at the ancient city of Byblos, Biblical Gebal, including that written on the sarcophagus of Ahiram, belonging probably to the eleventh century B. C. Phoenician in-

Semitic and non-Semitic, have been derived. The origin of the proto-Semitic alphabet is still obscure. Sir Flinders Petrie uncovered early samples of this script at Serabit el Khadem in the Sinaitic Peninsula (1904-5). This discovery pushed alphabetic writing back before the time of Moses. Albright has precisely dated these documents in the early fifteenth century B. C. (*Bull. Am. Schools* 110, April, 1958, p. 22). It is of unusual significance that this early "Sinai-Hebrew script" was found in the very region where Moses was instructed to write (Exod. 17:8-14). Earlier samples of alphabetic script have been found in the Syro-Palestine area; these date 1800-1500 B. C. In Egypt writing on papyrus goes back at least to the Old Kingdom (c. 2800-2500 B. C.). At Boghaz-keui, an important Hittite capital, large numbers of tablets written in cuneiform characters in the Hittite language and one-half dozen other languages were found in 1906 and following.

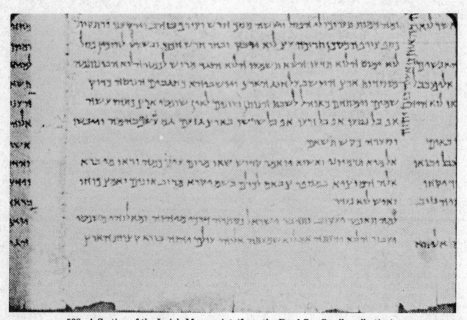

532. A Section of the Isaiah Manuscript (from the Dead Sea Scrolls collection)

scriptions from Cyprus, Sardinia, Carthage and other colonies in the western Mediterranean date after 900 B. C. The Gezer Calendar, written in perfect classical Hebrew, dates about 925 B. C., the Moabite Stone, c. 850 B. C. The Samaritan Ostraca date from the reign of Jeroboam II, c. 776 B. C.; the Siloam Inscription, 701 B. C.; and the Lachish Letters, 589 B. C. As far as the O. T. is concerned, the important thing is that a simple alphabetic language was divinely prepared to record the history of redemption instead of the unwieldy and cumbersome syllabic cuneiform scripts of Babylonia-Assyria, or the complex hieroglyphic writing of Egypt. Hebrew takes its origin from the old Phoenician alphabet, from which all alphabets in current use,

2. **Scripture Mention.** Writing is first distinctly mentioned in Exod. 17:14, and the connection clearly implies that it was not then employed for the first time, but was so familiar as to be used for historic records. Moses is commanded to preserve the memory of Amalek's onslaught in the desert by committing it to writing. The tables of the testimony are said to be "written by the finger of God" (Exod. 31:18) on both sides, and "the writing was the writing of God, graven upon the tables (32:15). The engraving of the gems of the high priest's breastplate with the names of the children of Israel (28:11), and the inscription upon the miter (39:30) have to do more with the art of the engraver than of the writer, but both imply the existence of alpha-

betic characters. The curses against the adulteress were written by the priest "in *the* book," and blotted out with water (Num. 5:23). This proceeding, though principally distinguished by its symbolical character, involves the use of some kind of ink, and of a material on which the curses were written which would not be destroyed by water. Hitherto, however, nothing has been said of the application of writing to the purposes of ordinary life, or of

"cradle of civilization." (2) **Skins of animals** were used at an early date in Egypt, at least by the time of the Fourth Dynasty (2550-2450 B. C.) and their use was widespread. Carefully prepared skins of sheep or goats were sewed together to make rolls which varied from a foot or two to perhaps 100 feet, according to the number of books written on one roll. The skin was either wound in a single roll with a stick or wound around two sticks,

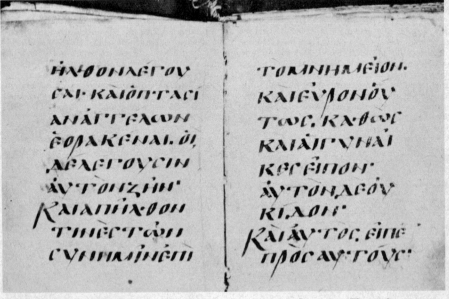

533. The Oldest Greek Text in the Sinai Library, a Seventh-century Lectionary. The parchment was taken from an earlier book whose erased text is as yet unidentified. This opening shows Luke 24:23-25.

the knowledge of the art among the common people. Up to this point such knowledge is only attributed to Moses and the priests. From Deut. 24:1, 3, however, it would appear that it was extended to others. It is not absolutely necessary to infer from this that the art of writing was an accomplishment possessed by every Hebrew citizen, though there is no mention of a third party; and it is more than probable these "bills of divorcement," though apparently informal, were the work of professional scribes. It was enjoined as one of the duties of the king (Deut. 17:18) that he should transcribe the book of the law for his own private study. If we examine the instances in which writing is mentioned in connection with individuals, we shall find that in all cases the writers were men of superior position. In Isa. 29:11, 12, there is clearly a distinction drawn between the man who was able to read and the man who was not, and it seems a natural inference that the accomplishments of reading and writing were not widely spread among the people, when we find that they are universally attributed to those of high rank or education—kings, priests, prophets, and professional scribes.

3. **Materials.** (*a*) **Clay Tablets.** Writing on soft wet clay with a stylus and cuneiform script was the oldest medium of inscription in the Tigris-Euphrates Valley, the so-called

one at each end. Not until the second or third century A. D. did the roll give way to the codex, or book form with leaves sewed together. (3) **Papyrus rolls** were prepared for writing in Egypt during the Old Kingdom (c. 2800 B. C.), perhaps earlier. Egyptian papyrus rolls are still in existence from the end of the third millennium B. C. The story of Wen-Amon tells of the exportation of papyrus rolls from Egypt to Gebal in Phoenicia. Ordinary papyrus rolls were about thirty feet long, but sometimes, as in the case of Papyrus Harris and the Book of the Dead, 123 to 133 feet in length. But among the Jews the common use of the standard-size papyrus rolls necessitated the splitting up of certain books like the Torah of Moses into five books. Jeremiah 36 gives us an example of one of the first editions of Scripture. Baruch evidently wrote Jeremiah's prophecies on a papyrus roll, likely writing on leather and using pen and ink. The reed, or calamus, made from the hollow stem of coarse grass or rush was cut diagonally with a knife to form a flexible point. To keep the pen point in good writing order the scribe carried a knife with him, hence the term "pen knife" (Jer. 36:23). Ink was made of soot and lamp black and gum diluted with water. *See* Ink, Inkhorn, Pen, Roll.—*M. F. U.*

Writing Table. *See* Tablet.

X Y Z

Xer′xes (zūrk′sēz), the Greek name of Ahasuerus (*q. v.*), husband of Esther. He ruled the Persian Empire from B. C. 486-465.

Yarn (*See* Linen). "Linen yarn" is the inaccurate translation of Hebrew *mĭqwēh*, found in I Kings 10:28 and *mĭqwē'*, found in II Chron. 1:16. Archaeology has revealed that these passages have nothing to do with "yarn." Correctly translated by the R. S. V. they are: "And Solomon's import of horses was from Egypt and Kue and the king's treasury received them from Kue at a price." II Chron. 1:16: "And Solomon's import of horses was from Egypt and from Kue and the king's treasurers received them from Kue at a price." In Assyrian records Kue is Cilicia, the country between the Taurus Mountains and the Mediterranean Sea in Asia Minor, according to Herodotus, famous in the Persian Period for fine horses. *See* Solomon, 5.—*M. F. U.*

Year. *See* Time.

Yodh (yōd), in A. R. V.; in A. V. (jōd), the tenth letter of the Hebrew alphabet, standing at the head of the tenth section of Psalm 119, in which section each verse begins with this letter.—*M. F. U.*

534. Oxen and Yoke

Yoke. A bar or frame of wood by which two draft animals, especially oxen, are joined at the necks or heads for working together, as for drawing a load or pulling a plow. The rendering of the following Hebrew and Greek words:

1. Heb. *ṣĕmĕd* (I Sam. 11:7; I Kings 19:19; 21; Job 1:3; 42:12; Jer. 51:23) has the same meaning as our "yoke of oxen," viz., two. It also means so much land as two oxen will plow in a day.

2. Heb. *mōṭāh* (Isa. 58:6, 9; Jer. 27:2; 28:10, 12, 13; Ezek. 30:18), the bars of the yoke, i. e., the oxbows of the same form as now.

3. Heb. *'ōl* (Jer. 2:20; 5:5), the curved piece of wood upon the neck of draught animals, by which they are fastened to the pole or beam. This is the Hebrew term most frequently rendered "yoke."

4. The Greek terms are *zugos* (Matt. 11:29,

30; Acts 15:10; Gal. 5:1; I Tim. 6:1), which has the usual meaning of *yoke;* and *zeugos* (Luke 14:19), meaning two draught cattle (horses, mules, or oxen) yoked together.

Figurative. Yoke is frequently used as a symbol of servitude to others (Gen. 27:40; Lev. 26:13; Deut. 28:48; I Tim. 6:1); to one's own sins (Lam. 1:14); God's *disciplinary* teaching (Lam. 3:27; comp. Psa. 90:12; 119:71); troublesome laws imposed on one, especially of the Mosaic law (Acts 15:10; Gal. 5:1); hence the name is so transferred to the commands of Christ as to contrast them with the commands of the Pharisees, which was a veritable "yoke;" yet even Christ's commands must be submitted to, though easier to be kept (Matt. 11:29).

Zaana′im (zà-á-nā′ĭm), a "plain," or, more accurately, "the oak by Zaanaim"—probably a sacred tree—marking the spot near which Heber the Kenite was encamped when Sisera took refuge in his tent (Judg. 4:11), and said to be near Kedesh, on the northwest of Lake Huleh. It is probably the same as Zaanannim (Josh. 19:33), (*q. v.*). It is to be identified with Khan et-Tujjar, about 3 miles N. E. of Mt. Tabor.

Za′anan (zā′à-năn), a place named by Micah (1:11) in his address to the towns of the Shephelah. Keil objects to its identification with Zenan, "as Zenan was in the plain, and Zaanan was most probably to the north of Jerusalem."

Zaanan′nim (zā-à-năn′ĭm), only in Josh. 19: 33; Judg. 4:11, marg., and probably the same as *Zaanaim* (*q. v.*).

Za′avan (zā′à-văn; *unquiet*), the second named of the three sons of Ezer and a Horite chief (Gen. 36:27; I Chron. 1:42; "Zavan").

Za′bad (zā′băd; S. Arab. *He*, i. e., God, *has given*).

1. Son of Nathan, son of Attai, son of Ahlai, Sheshan's daughter (I Chron. 2:31-37), and hence called son of Ahlai (11:41), B. C. about 992. He was one of David's mighty men, but none of his deeds has been recorded.

2. An Ephraimite, son of Tahath, and father of Shuthelah, 2 (I Chron. 7:21).

3. Son of Shimeath, an Ammonitess; an assassin who, with Jehozabad, slew King Joash (II Chron. 24:26), B. C. 797. The assassins were both put to death by Amaziah, but their children were spared (25:3, 4), in obedience to the law of Moses (Deut. 24:16). In II Kings 12:21 his name is written, probably more correctly, Jozachar.

4, 5, 6. Three Israelites, "sons" respectively of Zattu (Ezra 10:27), Hashum (10:33), and Nebo (10:43), who divorced their Gentile wives after the captivity, B. C. 456.

Zab′bai (zăb′â-ī).

1. One of the "sons" of Bebai, who divorced his Gentile wife (Ezra 10:28), B. C. 456.

2. Father of the Baruch who assisted in repairing the walls of Jerusalem after the exile Neh. 3:20), B. C. 445.

Zab'bud (zăb'ŭd; *given*), a "son" of Bigvai, who returned from Babylon with Ezra (8:14), B. C. 459.

Zab'di (zăb'dī; *giving*).

1. The son of Zerah and grandfather of Achan, of the tribe of Judah (Josh. 7:1, 17, 18), B. C. before 1395.

2. The third of the nine sons of Shimhi the Benjamite (I Chron. 8:19).

3. The Shiphmite (i. e., inhabitant of Shepham), and David's custodian of wine cellars (I Chron. 27:27), B. C. about 960.

4. Son of Asaph, the minstrel, and grandfather of Mattaniah, a prominent Levite in the time of Nehemiah (11:17), B. C. 445.

Zab'diel (zăb'dĭ-ĕl; cf. S. Arab. *El has given*).

1. The father of Jashobeam, which latter was commander of the first division of David's army (I Chron. 27:2), B. C. about 960.

2. The "son of Haggedolim" (i. e., "mighty men of valor"), who was overseer of one hundred and twenty-eight of the captives returned from the captivity (Neh. 11:14), B. C. 445.

Za'bud (zā'bŭd; *given*), the son of Natnan (I Kings 4:5). He is described as a priest (A. V. "principal officer"), and as holding at the court of Solomon the confidential post of "king's friend," which had been occupied by Hushai the Archite during the reign of David (II Sam. 15:37; 16:16; I Chron. 27:33).

Zab'ulon (zăb'ū-lŏn), the Greek form of the name *Zebulun* (Matt. 4:13, 15; Rev. 7:8).

Zac'cai (zăk'ā-ī; probably shortened form of Zechariah). The sons of Zaccai to the number of seven hundred and sixty returned with Zerubbabel (Ezra 2:9; Neh. 7:14), B. C. before 536.

Zacche'us (ză-kē'ŭs), more properly **Zacchaeus** (Gr. for Heb. *Zaccai*), a chief publican (*architelōnēs*) residing at Jericho, who, being short of stature, climbed up into a sycamore tree in order that he might see Jesus as he passed through that town. When Jesus came to the tree he paused, looked up, and calling Zaccheus by name, bade him hasten and come down, because he intended to be a guest at his house. With undisguised joy Zaccheus hastened down and welcomed the Master. The people murmured, saying, "That he was gone to be a guest with a man that is a sinner." Zaccheus was especially odious as being a Jew and occupying an official rank among the taxgatherers, which would indicate unusual activity in the service of the Roman oppressors. He seems to have been deeply moved by the consideration shown him by Jesus, and, before all the people, made the vow which attested his penitence, "Behold, half of my goods, Lord, I hereby give to the poor; and whatever fraudulent gain I ever made from any one, I now restore fourfold," greater restitution than the law required (Num. 5:7). Jesus thereupon made the declaration, "This day is salvation come to this house, forasmuch as he also is (in the true spiritual sense) a son of Abraham" (Luke 19:1-10).

Zac'chur (zăk'ûr; I Chron. 4:26), *see* Zaccur, 2.

Zac'cur (zăk'ûr; *remembered*).

1. The father of Shammua, the Reubenite spy (Num. 13:4), B. C. before 1440.

2. Son of Hamuel, and father of Shimei (I Chron. 4:26; A. V. "Zacchur").

3. A Levite, and third named of the four "sons of Merari by Jaaziah" (I Chron. 24:27).

4. Son of Asaph the singer, and leader of the third course of Levitical musicians (I Chron. 25:2, 10; Neh. 12:35).

5. The son of Imri, who assisted Nehemiah in rebuilding the city wall (Neh. 3:2), B. C. 445.

6. A Levite, or family of Levites, who signed the covenant with Nehemiah (10:12), B. C. 445.

7. A Levite whose son or descendant, Hanan, was one of the treasurers over the treasuries (marg. "storehouses") appointed by Nehemiah (13:13), B. C. 434.

Zachari'ah (zăk-à-rī'á; another form of *Zechariah*), the son of Jeroboam II, the last of the house of Jehu, and fourteenth king of Israel. He ascended the throne upon the death of his father (II Kings 14:29), B. C. about 742. He reigned only six months, being slain by Shallum (15:8-10).

Zachari'as (zăk-à-rī'ás), Greek form of Heb. *Zechariah*).

1. Son of Barachias, who, our Lord says, was slain by the Jews between the altar and the temple (Matt. 23:35; Luke 11:51). There has been much dispute who this Zacharias was. Many of the Greek fathers have maintained that the father of John the Baptist is the person to whom our Lord alludes; but there can be little or no doubt that the allusion is to Zechariah, the son of Jehoiada (II Chron. 24:20, 21).

2. Father of John the Baptist (Luke 1:5, sq.).

Za'cher (zā'kĕr; *memorial*), one of the sons of Jehiel, the father or founder of Gibeon, by his wife Maachah (I Chron. 8:31; 9:37, "Zechariah").

Za'dok (zā'dŏk; *just righteous*).

1. Son of Ahitub, and, with Abiathar, high priest in the time of David. He was of the house of Eleazar, the son of Aaron (I Chron. 24:3), and eleventh in descent from Aaron. (1) **Joins David.** In I Chron. 12:28 we are told that he joined David at Hebron, after Saul's death, with twenty-two captains of his father's house, and, apparently, with nine hundred men (4,600—3,700, vers. 26, 27), B. C. 1000. (2) **Fidelity to David.** From this time Zadok was unwavering in his loyalty to David. When Absalom revolted and David fled from Jerusalem, Zadok and all the Levites bearing the ark accompanied him, and it was only at the king's express command that they returned to Jerusalem, and became the medium of communication between the king and Hushai the Archite (II Sam., ch. 15; 17:15). After Absalom's death Zadok and Abiathar were the persons who persuaded the elders of Judah to invite David to return (19:11). When Adonijah, in David's old age, set up for king, and had persuaded Joab and Abiathar the priest to join his party, Zadok

was unmoved, and was employed by David to anoint Solomon to be king in his room (I Kings, ch. 1). (3) **Reward.** For this fidelity he was rewarded by Solomon, who "thrust out Abiathar from being priest unto the Lord," and "put in Zadok the priest" in his room (2:27, 35). From this time, however, we hear little of him. It is said in general terms in the enumeration of Solomon's officers of state that Zadok was the priest (I Kings 4:4; I Chron. 29:22), but no single act of his is mentioned. Zadok and Abiathar were *kōhănîm*, i. e., officiating high priests (II Sam. 15:35; 36, 19: 11). The duties of the office were divided. Zadok ministered before the tabernacle at Gibeon (I Chron. 16:39); Abiathar had the care of the ark at Jerusalem; not, however, exclusively (I Chron. 15:11; II Sam. 15:24, 25, 29).

2. In the genealogy of the high priests in I Chron. 6:12, there is a second Zadok, son of a second Ahitub, and father of Shallum. It is supposed by some that the name was inserted by error of a copyist, while others identify him with *Odeas*, mentioned by Josephus (*Ant.*, x, 8, 6). He is perhaps the same person as the one mentioned in I Chron. 9:11; Neh. 11:11.

3. Father of Jerusha, the wife of Uzziah, and mother of King Jotham (II Kings 15:33; II Chron. 27:1), B. C. before 738.

4. Son of Baana, who repaired a portion of the wall in the time of Nehemiah (3:4). He is probably the same who is in the list of those that sealed the covenant in Neh. 10:21, as in both cases his name follows that of Meshezabeel (B. C. 445).

5. Son of Immer, a priest who repaired a portion of the wall opposite his house (Neh. 3:29), B. C. 445.

6. The scribe whom Nehemiah appointed one of the three principal treasurers of the temple (Neh. 13:13), B. C. 445.

Za'ham (zā'hăm; *loathsome fool*), the last of the three sons of Rehoboam by Abihail (II Chron. 11:19), B. C. about 930. Keil (*Com.*, in loc.) holds that Mahalath is the wife of Rehoboam, and that Abihail, the daughter of Eliab, was Mahalath's mother.

Za'in. See Zayin.

Za'ir (zā'ĭr; *little*), a place east of the Dead Sea, in Idumea, where Israel discomfited the Edomites (II Kings 8:21). Its identification is not positive, though Sa'ir, a village 5 miles N. E. of Hebron is probable.

Za'laph (zā'lăf; perhaps *caper-plant*), the father of Hanun, who assisted in repairing the wall of Jerusalem after the captivity (Neh. 3:30), B. C. 445.

Zal'mon (zăl'mŏn; *dark*, cf. *Arab. zalima* and Ethiopic *ṣalma to be dark*).

1. An Ahohite (i. e., sprung from the Benjamite family of Ahoah), and one of David's warriors (II Sam. 23:28). In the parallel passage (I Chron. 11:29), he is called *Ilai* (*q. v.*).

2. A wood near Shechem (Judg. 9:48), a kind of "black forest," as rendered by Luther. David (Psa. 68:14, "white as snow in Salmon") uses language symbolical of the presence of light in darkness, or brightness in calamity.

Zalmo'nah (zăl-mō'nà; *dark, shades*. cf. *Zalmyn*), a station of Israel in the wilderness (Num. 33:41, 42). It lay southeast of Edom, perhaps in the *Wady el-Amrân*, which runs into into the *Wady Ithm*, close to where Elath anciently stood.

Zalmun'na (zăl-mŭn'à; *probably, shade denied*, i. e., *deprived of protection*), one of the two kings of Midian who were captured and slain by Gideon (Judg. 8:5-21; Psa. 83:11), B. C. about 1100. See Zebah.

Zamzum'mim (zăm-zŭm'ĭm; *noise-makers, murmerers*, cf. Arab. *zamzama, to mumble, to hum*), only in Deut. 2:20, the name given by the Ammonites to the people called by others *Rephaim* (*q. v.*). They were "a people great, many, and tall." "From a slight similarity between the two names, and from the mention of both in connection with the Emim, it is usually assumed that the Zamzummims were identical with the Zuzims" (*q. v.*).— W. H. revised by *M. F. U.*

Zano'ah (zà-nō'à).

1. A town in the low country of Judah (Josh. 15:34). It was inhabited by Judeans after the captivity (Neh. 11:30), who also assisted in repairing the walls of Jerusalem (3:13). The site is marked now by Khirbet Zanū' or *Zanuḥ* in the Wady Ismail, some ten miles west of Jerusalem.

2. A town in the hill country of Judah, ten miles southwest of Hebron (Josh. 15:56). In I Chron. 4:18 Jekuthiel is said to have been the father (i. e., founder or rebuilder) of Zanoah.

Zaph'enath-pane'ah (zăf'ĕ-năth-pà-nē'à; Egyptian, "*sustenance of the land is the living one*"). This was Joseph's name given to him by the reigning pharaoh (Gen. 41:45). Some modern Egyptologists maintain that this designation represents Egyptian "jed-pa-Neter-ef-'onekh", which could be construed: "says the god: He will live," "he" referring to the new born child having the name. The name, apparently, however, refers to Joseph as sustainer of life with reference to his divine call as a savior during famine. *M. F. U.*

Za'phon (zā'fŏn; *north*), a place mentioned, in connection with Beth-aram, Beth-nimrah, and Succoth, as part of the inheritance of Gad (Josh. 13:27). It was in "the valley" (i. e., of Jordan), and probably not far from the southern extremity of the Sea of Galilee. Located by Nelson Glueck at Tell el Kos.

Za'ra (zā'rà), the Greek form (Matt. 1:3) of the Hebrew name *Zerah* 2 (*q. v.*).

Za'rah (zā'rà; Gen. 38:30; 46:12). See Zerah, 2.

Za'reah (zā'rê-à; Neh. 11:29). See Zorah.

Za'reathite (zā'rê-à-thīt; I Chron. 2:53). See Zorathite.

Za'red (zā'rĕd; Num. 21:12). See Zered.

Zar'ephath (zăr'ĕ-făth), a town which derives its claim to notice from having been the residence of the prophet Elijah during the latter part of the drought (I Kings 17:9, 10). Beyond stating that it was near to, or dependent on, Zidon, the Bible gives no clue to its position. Josephus (*Ant.*, viii, 13, 2) says that it was "not far from Sidon and Tyre, for it lies between them." It is on the seashore, north of Tyre. And to this Jerome adds

(*Onom.*, "Sarefta") that it "lay on the public road," i. e., the coast road. Both these conditions are implied in the mention of it in the itinerary of Paula by Jerome, and both are fulfilled in the situation of the modern village of *Sarafend*. Of the old town considerable indications remain. One group of foundations is on a headland called *Ain el-Kantarah;* but the chief remains are south of this, and extend for a mile or more, with many fragments of columns, slabs, and other architectural features. In the New Testament Zarephath appears under the Greek form of Sarepta (Luke 4:26).

Zar'ethan (zär'ĕ-thăn), in A. V. Zar'etan, a place named in the account of the passage of Jordan by the Israelites, "That the waters which came down from above stood and rose up upon an heap very far from the city Adam, that is beside Zaretan" (Josh. 3:16; R. V. "rose up in one heap, a great way off, at Adam, the city that is beside Zarethan"). "Near Beisan is an unusually large mound called Tell es Sârem. A good deal of clay is found here, and a mile to the south is a stream the Arabic of which means 'red river.' . . . It has been suggested that the waters of the Jordan were suddenly dammed up by a landslip or similar convulsion. The appearance of the banks, and the curious bends of the river near this place, would seem to support the idea. . . . It is clear from the Bible statement that the waters were arrested a long way off, above Jericho" (Harper, *Bib. and Mod. Disc.*, p. 148). Kurn Sartabeh is a little more than fifteen miles above Jericho, which tallies well with the expression "very far." Nelson Glueck, however, identifies Zarethan as Tell es-Sa'idiyeh, 12 miles N. N. E. of the Jordan and overlooking the Wadi Kufringi on the N. *See* Zarthan.

Za'reth-sha'har (zā'rĕth-shā'har; *the splendor of dawn*), a city in Reuben "in the mount of a valley" (Josh. 13:19), and near the eastern shore of the Dead Sea. Identified with the ruins of Zara, in Wady Zurka Main.

Zar'hites, The (zär'hĭts), a branch of the tribe of Judah; descended from Zerah, the son of Judah (Num. 26:13, 20; Josh. 7:17; I Chron. 27:11, 13).

Zar'tanah (zär'tà-nà), a place named (I Kings 4:12) to define the position of Bethshan. It is possibly identical with *Zarthan* (*q. v.*).

Zar'than (zär'thăn).

1. A place in the "circle" of Jordan, mentioned in connection with Succoth (I Kings 7:46), between which and Zarthan the bronze (or copper) vessels for the temple were cast. It is given in II Chron. 4:17 as Zeredathah.

2. It is also named in the account of the passage of the Jordan by the Israelites (Josh. 3:16, A. V. "Zaretan") as defining the position of the city Adam.

Zat'thu (zăt'thū; Neh. 10:14). *See* Zattu.

Zat'tu (zăt'ū), an Israelite whose "children," to the number of nine hundred and forty-five (Ezra 2:8) or eight hundred and forty-five (Neh. 7:13), returned with Zerubbabel (B. C. before 536). Several of his descendants renounced their Gentile wives (Ezra 10:27), and a person (or family) was among those

who sealed the covenant made by Nehemiah (Neh. 10:14, "Zatthu").

Za'van (zā'văn; I Chron. 1:42). *See* Zaavan.

Za'yin (zä'yĭn), the 7th letter of the Hebrew alphabet. Cf. Psalm 119, section 7.

Za'za (zā'zà), the second son of Jonathan, a descendant of Jerahmeel, of the tribe of Judah (I Chron. 2:33).

Zebadi'ah (zĕb-à-dī'à; *Jehovah has given*).

1. A Benjamite, of the sons of Beriah (I Chron. 8:15).

2. A Benjamite, of the sons of Elpaal (I Chron. 8:17).

3. One of the two sons of Jeroham of Gedor, who joined David at Ziklag (I Chron. 12:7), B. C. before 1000.

4. Third son of Meshelemiah the Korhite (I Chron. 26:2).

5. Son of Asahel, the brother of Joab, of the fourth division of David's army (I Chron. 27:7), B. C. before 960.

6. A Levite in the reign of Jehoshaphat, sent to teach the law in the cities of Judah (II Chron. 17:8), B. C. 872.

7. The son of Ishmael, and prince of the house of Judah in the reign of Jehoshaphat (II Chron. 19:11), B. C. about 853.

8. Son of Michael, of the "sons" of Shephatiah, who returned with Ezra from captivity with eighty males (Ezra 8:8), B. C. about 457.

9. A priest of the sons of Immer, who had married a foreign wife after the return from Babylon (Ezra 10:20), B. C. 456.

Ze'bah (zē'bà; *sacrifice*), one of the two Midianitish kings overthrown by Gideon. He is mentioned in Judg. 8:5-21; Psa. 83:11, and always in connection with Zalmunna. They seem to have commanded the invasion of Palestine, leading their hordes with the cry, "Seize these goodly pastures" (v. 12). While Oreb and Zeeb, two of the inferior leaders of the incursion, had been slain, with a vast number of their people, by the Ephraimites, at the central fords of the Jordan, the two kings had succeeded in making their escape by a passage farther to the north (probably the ford near Beth-shean), and thence by the *Wady Yabïs*, through Gilead, to Karkor, a place which is not fixed, but which lay doubtless high up on the Hauran. Here they were reposing with fifteen thousand men, a mere remnant of their huge horde, when Gideon overtook them. The name of Gideon was still full of terror; and the Bedouins were entirely unprepared for his attack—they fled in dismay, and the two kings were taken. They were brought to Ophrah, the native village of their captor, and then Gideon asked them, "What manner of men were they which ye slew at Tabor?" Up to this time the sheikhs may have believed that they were reserved for ransom; but these words once spoken, there can have been no doubt what their fate was to be. They met it like noble children of the desert, simply requesting that the blow should be struck by their captor himself; "and Gideon arose and slew them."

Zeba'im (zĕ-bā'ĭm; *the gazelles*), apparently the name of the native place of the "sons of Pochereth," who are mentioned in the catalogue of "Solomon's slaves" as having returned with Zerubbabel (Ezra 2:57; Neh. 7:59).

Zeb′edee (zĕb′ĕ-dē; the Greek form, probably, of *Zabdi* or *Zebediah*), the father of James the Great and John (Matt. 4:21), and the husband of Salome (Matt. 27:56; Mark 15:40). He was a Galilean fisherman, living probably either at or near Bethsaida. From the mention of his "hired servants" (Mark 1:20), and the acquaintance between John and Annas the high priest, it has been inferred that the family were in good circumstances. He appears only once in the gospel narrative, viz., in Matt. 4:21, 22; Mark 1:19, 20, where he is seen in his boat with his two sons, mending their nets.

Zebi′na (zē-bī′nà; Aram. *bought, purchased*), one of the "sons" of Nebo, who put away his Gentile wife after the captivity (Ezra 10:43), B. C. 456.

Zeboi′im (zē-boi′ĭm; Gen. 14:2, 8). *See* Zeboim.

Zebo′im (zē-bō′ĭm), the rendering of 1. Heb. *ṣᵉbō′îm* (*gazelles*), one of the five cities in the vale of Siddim, destroyed by Jehovah (Gen. 10:19; Deut. 29:23; Hos. 11:8). It was ruled over by a separate king, Shemeber (Gen. 14:2, 8). *See* Sodom.

2. Heb. *ṣᵉbō′îm* (*hyenas*), the name of a valley, i. e., the ravine or gorge, apparently east of Michmash (I Sam. 13:18), near to which one of the flying columns of the Philistines came. "The wilderness" is no doubt the district of uncultivated mountain tops and sides lying between the central portion of Benjamin and the Jordan valley. In that very district there is a wild gorge known as *Shuk ed-Duba*, "ravine of the hyena."

Zebu′dah (zē-bū′dà; *given*), a daughter of Pedaiah, of Rumah, wife of Josiah, and mother of King Jehoiakim (II Kings 23:36), B. C. before 608.

Ze′bul (zē′bŭl; *habitation, dwelling*), ruler of the city of Shechem under Abimelech. He advised Abimelech of the defection of the Shechemites, and counseled him to advance upon the city. He closed the gates of the city against Gaal and his men that went out to fight against Abimelech, and thus assisted in their overthrow (Judg. 9:28-41), B. C. about 1100.

Zeb′ulonite (zĕb′û-lŭn-īt), a member of the tribe of Zebulun (Judg. 12:11, 12; Num. 26:27, A. V. "Zebulunite").

Zeb′ulun (zĕb′û-lŭn; *dwelling, habitation*).
1. The tenth son of Jacob, and the sixth and last of Leah (Gen. 30:19, 20). We have nothing recorded concerning Zebulun personally. In the genealogical list (ch. 46) he is mentioned as having, at the time of the migration into Egypt, three sons, founders of the chief families of the tribe (comp. Num. 26:26).

Tribe. During the desert journey Zebulun, with Judah and Issachar, formed the first camp. The tribe then numbered fifty-seven thousand four hundred (1:31). The head of the tribe at Sinai was Eliab, son of Helon (7:24), and at Shiloh, Elizaphan, son of Parnach (34:25). Its representative among the spies was Gaddiel, son of Sodi (13:10). The territory of Zebulun in Canaan lay between the Sea of Galilee and the Mediterranean Sea. Nazareth and Cana were in it; and it embraced a section of the shore of the former

sea, where Christ performed so many of his miracles. Then was fulfilled the prophecy of Isaiah (Isa. 9:1, 2; comp. Matt. 4:12-16). In the visions of Ezekiel (48:26-33) and of John (Rev. 7:8) this tribe finds due mention.

2. A place on the eastern border of the tribe of Asher, between Beth-dagon and the valley of Jiphthah-el (Josh. 19:27).

Zeb′ulunite (zĕb′û-lŭn-īt; Num. 27:27). *See* Zebulonite.

Zechari′ah (zĕk-à-rī′à; *Jehovah remembers*).
1. A chief of the Reubenites at the time of the captivity by Tiglath-pileser (I Chron. 5:7), B. C. about 740.

2. Son of Meshelemiah, or Shelemiah, a Korhite and keeper of the north gate of the tabernacle of the congregation (I Chron. 9:21). In 26:2, 14, he is described as "one counseling with understanding."

3. One of the sons of Jehiel (I Chron. 9:37).

4. A Levite of the second order in the temple band as arranged by David, appointed to play "with psalteries on Alamoth" (I Chron. 15:18, 20; 16:5), B. C. about 975.

5. One of the priests who, with trumpets, accompanied the ark from the house of Obed-edom (I Chron. 15:24), B. C. about 988.

6. Son of Isshiah, or Jesiah, a Kohathite Levite, descended from Uzziel (I Chron. 24:25).

7. Fourth son of Hosah, of the children of Merari (I Chron. 26:11).

8. The father of Iddo, who was chief of his tribe, Manasseh in Gilead, in the reign of David (I Chron. 27:21), B. C. about 1000.

9. One of the princes of Judah sent to teach the people the law in the reign of Jehoshaphat (II Chron. 17:7), B. C. c. 885.

10. The son of Benaiah and father of Jahaziel, which latter was the Gershonite Levite who encouraged the army of Jehoshaphat against the Moabites (II Chron. 20:14), B. C. before 875.

11. One of the sons of King Jehoshaphat (II Chron. 21:2), c. 880.

12. Son of the high priest Jehoiada in the reign of Joash, king of Judah (II Chron. 24:20), and therefore the king's cousin. After the death of Jehoiada, Zechariah probably succeeded to his office, and in attempting to check the reaction in favor of idolatry which immediately followed, he fell a victim to a conspiracy formed against him by the king, and was stoned in the court of the temple, B. C. 836. It is probable that "Zacharias, son of Barachias," who was slain between the temple and the altar (Matt. 23:35), is the same as Zechariah, the son of Jehoiada, and that the name of Barachias as his father crept into the text from a marginal gloss, the writer confusing this Zechariah either with Zechariah the prophet, who was the son of Berechiah, or with another Zechariah, the son of Jeberechiah (Isa. 8:2).

13. A prophet in the reign of Uzziah, who appears to have acted as the king's counselor, but of whom nothing is known (II Chron. 26:5), B. C. after 780.

14. The father of Abijah, or Abi, Hezekiah's mother (II Chron. 29:1), B. C. before 719.

15. A Levite who, in the reign of Hezekiah,

assisted in the purification of the temple (II Chron. 29:13), B. C. 719.

16. A Kohathite Levite and an overseer of the temple restoration in the reign of Josiah (II Chron. 34:12), B. C. 621.

17. One of the rulers of the temple in the reign of Josiah (II Chron. 35:8), B. C. about 621.

18. The leader of the "sons" of Pharosh, who, to the number of one hundred and fifty, returned with Ezra (8:3), B. C. about 457.

ing Maher-shalal-hash-baz (Isa. 8:2), B. C. about 742.

28. The eleventh of the twelve minor prophets. Zechariah was of priestly descent, a son of Berechiah and grandson of Iddo (Zech. 1:1, 7), the chief of one of the priestly families that returned from exile along with Zerubbabel (Neh. 12:4). His mention in Ezra 5:1; 6:14, as the son of Iddo is explained by the hypothesis that owing to some unexplained cause—perhaps the death of his father

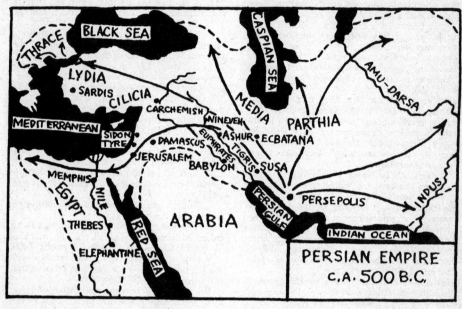

535. Persian Empire in Zechariah's Day

19. The leader of the twenty-eight "sons" of Bebai, who returned from captivity with Ezra (8:11), B. C. 457.

20. One of the chiefs of the people whom Ezra summoned in council at the river Ahava (Ezra 8:16). He stood at Ezra's left hand when he expounded the law to the people (Neh. 8:4), B. C. 457.

21. One of the family of Elam who divorced a foreign wife after the captivity (Ezra 10:26), B. C. 456.

22. One of the ancestors of Athaiah, of the tribe of Judah (Neh. 11:4), B. C. before 536.

23. The son of Shiloni and father of Joiarib, of the family of Perez (Neh. 11:5).

24. A priest and ancestor of Adaiah, which latter was prominent in Jerusalem after the captivity (Neh. 11:12), B. C. before 445.

25. The representative of the priestly family of Iddo in the days of Joiakim, son of Jeshua (Neh. 12:16). Probably the same as Zechariah the prophet, the son of Iddo, B. C. about 536.

26. One of the priests, son of Jonathan, who blew with the trumpets at the dedication of the city wall by Ezra and Nehemiah (Neh. 12:35, 41), B. C. 445.

27. The son of Jeberechiah, who was taken by the prophet Isaiah as one of the "faithful witnesses to record," when he wrote concern-

—Zechariah followed his grandfather in the priestly office, and so the historian dropped the father's name. Zechariah commenced his prophetic labors in the eighth month of the second year of Darius, B. C. 520. In the fourth year of Darius a deputation of Jews came to the temple to inquire whether the day on which Jerusalem and the temple were reduced to ashes by the Chaldeans was still to be kept as a day of mourning and fasting. Zechariah replied to them declaring that, in the sight of Jehovah, obedience is better than fasting. Two other oracles delivered by Zechariah are recorded in his book of prophecies (chaps. 9-11 and 12-14).

Zechariah, Book of, one of the post-exilic books of the Minor Prophets. The prophet's name means in Hebrew, "Yahweh remembers." He was a "son of Berechiah, the son of Iddo . . ." (Zech. 1:1; Ezra 5:1; 6:14; Neh. 12:16). The prophet commenced his ministry two months after his contemporary Haggai, in October-November, 520 B. C. The combined prophecies or preaching of the two eventuated in the finished temple in the latter part of 516 B. C. The total prophetic ministry of Zechariah (at this period) lasted about two years in contrast to Haggai, whose total recorded ministry occupied only four months. Zechariah's last dated prophecy was marked

November-December, 518 B. C. Chapters 9-14, constituting the last part of Zechariah's prophecy, is undated and must be put much later, probably after 480 B. C., in the light of the allusion to Javan, or Greece. No serious impediment exists for denying a half-century ministry to the prophet. He, doubtless, outlived Darius I the Great (522-486 B. C.), whose exploits in saving the Persian Empire are recorded on the famous Rock of Behistun, which proved the key to unlocking Babylonnian-Assyrian cuneiform toward the end of the first half of the nineteenth century. Zechariah prophesied during the high priesthood of Joshua and the governorship of Zerubbabel.

1. **Character of the Book.** George L. Robinson aptly terms the book, "The most Messianic, the most truly apocalyptic and eschatological of all the writings of the O. T." (*Int'l. Stand. Bible Ency.*, p. 3136). Zechariah contains more allusions to the coming Messiah both in His first and second advents and future millennial glory than all the other minor prophets combined. His series of eight nightly visions extending from 1:7-6:8 give a remarkable detailed depiction of the future Messianic kingdom over Israel. Even more striking is the symbolical crowning of the high priest (6:9-15). This portrays the union of the kingly and priestly office in Messiah during the Kingdom Age. Chap. 8 gives one of the clearest descriptions of the future restoration of Jerusalem (vs. 1-5), and the return of Israel to the land (vs. 6-8), with a remarkable setting forth of the future prosperity of the land and people Israel during the reign of Christ subsequent to His second advent in glory (vs. 9-23). In the last section of the prophecies (chap. 9-14) two prophetic burdens, or oracles, are given, outlining the great Messianic future of Israel. The first prophetic burden presents Christ in His first advent when rejected (9:1-11:17). This constitutes one of the most amazing and detailed prophecies of Christ's rejection and crucifixion. The second prophetic burden delineates the second advent in glory and the acceptance of Messiah-King by a delivered remnant which will form the nucleus of the nation in the Kingdom Age (12:1-14:21). Chaps. 12 and 13 describe the future deliverance and national conversion of Israel (cf. Rom. 11:25, 26). Chap. 14 portrays the second coming of Christ in glory to set up his earthly kingdom (14:1-21; cf. Rev. 19:11-16).

3. **Messianic Designations.** Important Messianic predictions in Zechariah include The Branch (chaps. 3 and 6; cf. Isa. 4:2; Jer. 23:5); Christ as King-Priest (6:13); Christ's triumphal entry into Jerusalem and coming glory (9:9, 10); Christ portrayed as Shepherd (11:12, 13); Christ crucified (12:10); the sufferings of Christ (13:7); the second coming of Christ (chap. 14).

4. **Outline.** Call to Repentance, 1:1-6
Part I. Foregleams of the future Messianic Kingdom, 1:7-8:23
 1. A series of eight night visions, 1:7-6:8
  (a) The man among the myrtle trees, 1:7-17
  (b) The four horns and carpenters, 1:18-21

  (c) The man with the measuring rod, 2:1-13
  (d) The cleansing of the high priest, 3:1-10
  (e) The candlestick and the two olive trees, 4:1-14
  (f) The flying roll, 5:1-4
  (g) The woman and the ephah, 5:5-11
  (h) The four chariots, 6:1-8
 2. The symbolical crowning of the high priest, 6:9-15
 3. The answer to the question of the feasts, 7:1-8:23
  (a) The question and divine reply, 7:1-14
  (b) Future restoration of Jerusalem, 8:1-5
  (c) Future return to Palestine, 8:6-8
  (d) Kingdom prosperity of land and people, 8:9-23
Part II. Two prophetic burdens—Israel's great Messianic future, 9:1-14:21
 1. The first burden—the first advent and rejection of Messiah-King, 9:1-11:17
  (a) The advent, 9:1-10:12
  (b) The rejection, 11:1-17
 2. The second burden—second advent and acceptance of Messiah-King, 12:1-14:21
  (a) Future deliverance and national conversion of Israel, 12:1-13:9
  (b) Messiah-King's return in glory, 14:1-21

5. **Authorship.** The Zecharian authenticity of chaps. 1-8 is practically uncontested. Chaps. 9-14, however, are commonly denied Zecharian authorship. But great confusion exists among scholars who deny the Zecharian authorship of the second part. Some scholars make all of chaps. 9-14 pre-exilic; others assert a post-exilic authorship; others confidently assign chaps. 9-11 to one or more pre-exilic authors, and chaps. 12-14 to one or more post-exilic authors. Zecharian authorship is favored by the voice of tradition which was practically uncontested until Joseph Mede in 1653 denied that chaps. 9-11 were the work of Zechariah. The external point of view of chaps. 9-14 is post-exilic. No reigning king of Judah or Israel is mentioned. The kingship of Messiah alone is recognized. The reference to "the sons of Greece" (9:13) is post-exilic but not necessarily post-Zecharian. Similar rare expressions are found in both sections of the book (cf. 7:14 and 9:8 for the expression "from passing through and returning"). The expression "saith the Lord" appears prominently in both parts, some fourteen times in chaps. 1-8 and in 10:12; 12:1, 4; 13:2, 7, 8 in the later section. "Lord of hosts" appears characteristically in both sections. The poetic style of 9-14 in contrast to the prosaic form of chaps. 1-8 does not necessitate a different author. Undoubtedly Zechariah penned chaps. 9-14 considerably later than 1-8, probably when he was an aged man. *M. F. U.*

Ze'dad (ze'dăd), a city on the northern boundary of Palestine, as promised by Moses (Num. 34:8), and as restored by Ezekiel (Ezek. 47:15). It is identified with Sadad,

S. E. of Homs on the road from Riblah to Palmyra.

Zedeki'ah (zĕd-ê-kī'à; *Jehovah is just or righteous*).

1. **Son of Chanaanah,** and the person who acted as spokesman of the prophets when consulted by Ahab as to the result of his proposed expedition to Ramoth-gilead (B. C. 875). Preparing himself with a pair of iron horns (the horns of the *reëm*, or wild buffalo, being the recognized emblem of the tribe of Ephraim), Zedekiah illustrated the manner in which Ahab should drive the Syrians before him. When Micaiah delivered his prophecy Zedekiah came near and smote him upon the cheek. For this he was threatened by Micaiah in terms that evidently alluded to some personal danger. The probability that Zedekiah and his followers were false prophets is strengthened by the question of the king, "Is there not here besides a prophet of *Jehovah*, that we may inquire of *him*?" (I Kings 22:11; II Chron. 18:10).

2. **The Last King of Judah.** (1) **Family.** Zedekiah was the son of Josiah by his wife Ḥamutal, and therefore own brother to Jehoahaz (II Kings 24:18; comp. 23:31; I Chron. 3:15). His original name had been *Mattaniah*, which was changed to Zedekiah by Nebuchadnezzar, when he carried off his nephew Jehoiachin to Babylon, and left him on the throne of Jerusalem. (2) **Reign.** Zedekiah was twenty-one years of age when he was made king (II Kings 24:17, 18; II Chron. 36:11), B. C. 597. The earlier portion of Zedekiah's reign was marked by an agitation throughout the whole of Syria against the Babylonian yoke. In this movement Jerusalem seems to have taken the lead, since in the fourth year of Zedekiah's reign we find ambassadors from all the neighboring kingdoms —Tyre, Sidon, Edom, and Moab—at his court, to consult as to the steps to be taken. This happened either during the king's absence or immediately after his return from Babylon, whither he went, perhaps, to blind the eyes of Nebuchadnezzar to his contemplated revolt (Jer. 51:59). The first act of overt rebellion of which any record survives was the formation of an alliance with Egypt, of itself equivalent to a declaration of enmity with Babylon. As a natural consequence it brought on Jerusalem an immediate invasion of the Chaldeans. The mention of this event in the Bible, though sure, is extremely slight, and occurs only in Jer. 37:5-11; 34:21, and Ezek. 17:15-20; but Josephus (x, 7, 3) relates it more fully, and gives the date of its occurrence, viz., the eighth year of Zedekiah. Nebuchadnezzar, aware of Zedekiah's defection, sent an army and reduced the whole country of Judea, excepting Jerusalem, Lachish, and Azekah (Jer. 34:7). Pharaoh having marched to the assistance of Zedekiah, the Chaldeans at once raised the siege and advanced to meet him. The nobles seized this opportunity of reenslaving those whom they had so recently manumitted (ch. 34). Shortly after this Jeremiah was put in prison, and would probably have lost his life but for the interference of Zedekiah (37:15-21). On the tenth day of the tenth month of Zedekiah's ninth year the Chaldeans were again before the walls (52:4). From this time forward the siege progressed slowly but surely to its consummation, with the accompaniment of both famine and pestilence. Zedekiah again interfered to preserve the life of Jeremiah from the vengeance of the princes (38:7-13). While the king was hesitating the end was rapidly coming nearer. The city was indeed reduced to the last extremity. The fire of the besiegers had throughout been very destructive, but it was now aided by a severe famine. The bread had long since been consumed (38:9), and all the terrible expedients had been tried to which the wretched inhabitants of a besieged town are forced to resort in such cases. At last, after sixteen dreadful months, the catastrophe arrived. It was on the ninth day of the fourth month, about the middle of July, at midnight, as Josephus with careful minuteness informs us, that the breach in those stout and venerable walls was effected. Passing in through the breach, they made their way, as their custom was, to the center of the city, and for the first time the temple was entered by a hostile force. Zedekiah fled, but was betrayed by some Jews who had deserted to the enemy. After his capture he and his sons were sent to Nebuchadnezzar at Riblah, while his daughters were kept at Jerusalem. Nebuchadnezzar reproached Zedekiah for breaking his oath of allegiance, ordered his sons to be slain before him, and then his own eyes to be thrust out. He was loaded with chains and taken to Babylon, where he died.

NOTE—At first sight there seems a discrepancy between Jer. 34:3; II Kings 25:7; Ezek. 12:13. The first passage, however, does not assert that he should see the king and go thither. The above facts verify the predictions. Zedekiah saw the *king* of Babylon, but not the *city* itself, having lost his sight before being taken there.

3. A son of Jeconiah and grandson of Jehoiakim, king of Judah (I Chron. 3:16), B. C. 598 or later. Some identify him with the person mentioned in v. 15, but Keil (*Com.*, in loc.) conjectures that he was a literal son, and not simply a successor of Jeconiah, and that he died before the exile.

4. The son of Maaseiah and a false prophet among the captives in Babylon. He was denounced by Jeremiah· (29:21) for having, with Ahab, uttered false prophecies, and for flagitious conduct. Their names were to become a byword, and their terrible fate—death by burning—a warning, B. C. about 586.

5. The son of Hananiah, and one of the princes of Judah who received the announcement that Baruch had delivered the words of Jeremiah to the people (Jer. 36:12), B. C. 607.

Ze'eb (zē'ĕb; *a wolf*), one of the princes of Midian who were defeated by Gideon, probably near the Jordan. Zeeb was slain in a wine press, which in later times bore his name (Judg. 7:24, 25; 8:3; Psa. 83:11).

Ze'lah (zē'là; *slope, side*), a town in Benjamin, which was the family burying place of Kish, the father of Saul (II Sam. 21:14; comp. Josh. 18:28), probably the native place of Saul, the first king of Israel. It has not been identified. Probably Khirbet Ṣalaḥ, N. W. of Jerusalem.

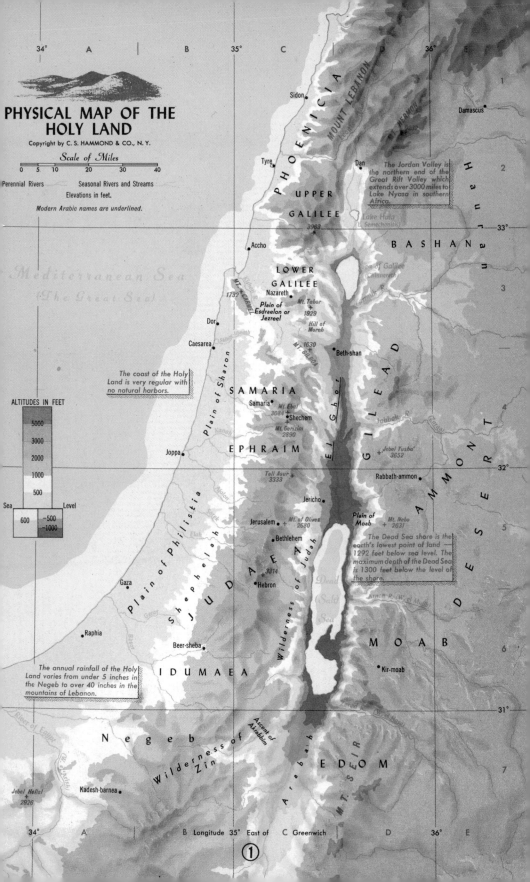

PHYSICAL MAP OF THE HOLY LAND

Copyright by C. S. HAMMOND & CO., N. Y.

Scale of Miles

0 5 10 20 30 40

Perennial Rivers
Seasonal Rivers and Streams
Elevations in feet.

Modern Arabic names are underlined.

ALTITUDES IN FEET

5000	
3000	
2000	
1000	
500	
Sea	Level
600	−500
	−1000

Mediterranean Sea
(The Great Sea)

The Jordan Valley is the northern end of the Great Rift Valley which extends over 3000 miles to Lake Nyasa in southern Africa.

The coast of the Holy Land is very regular with no natural harbors.

The Dead Sea shore is the earth's lowest point of land — 1292 feet below sea level. The maximum depth of the Dead Sea is 1300 feet below the level of the shore.

The annual rainfall of the Holy Land varies from under 5 inches in the Negeb to over 40 inches in the mountains of Lebanon.

PHOENICIA
MOUNT LEBANON
Sidon
Damascus
Tyre
Dan
Hauran
UPPER
GALILEE
BASHAN
Accho
Lake Hula
(L. Semechonitis)
3963
Sea of Galilee
(Chinnereth)
LOWER
GALILEE
Nazareth
Mt. Tabor
1929
MT. CARMEL
1732
Plain of Esdraelon or Jezreel
Hill of Moreh
Dor
MT. GILBOA
1630
Caesarea
Beth-shan
El Ghor
GILEAD
Plain of Sharon
SAMARIA
Samaria
Mt. Ebal
3084
Shechem
Mt. Gerizim
2890
Rabbath R.
Joppa
EPHRAIM
Jebel Yusha'
3652
Tell Asur
3333
AMMON
Rabbath-ammon
Jericho
Jerusalem
Mt. of Olives
2680
Plain of Moab
Mt. Nebo
2631
Bethlehem
Gaza
DESERT
Shephelah
Plain of Philistia
3314
Hebron
JUDAEA
Wilderness of Judah
Dead (Salt) Sea
Raphia
Beer-sheba
MOAB
Kir-moab
IDUMAEA
Arnon R. (Wadi Mujib)
Negeb
Wilderness of Zin
Ascent of Akrabbim
EDOM
Arabah
MT. SEIR
Jebel Helal
2926
Kadesh-barnea
River of Egypt

Longitude 35° East of Greenwich

①

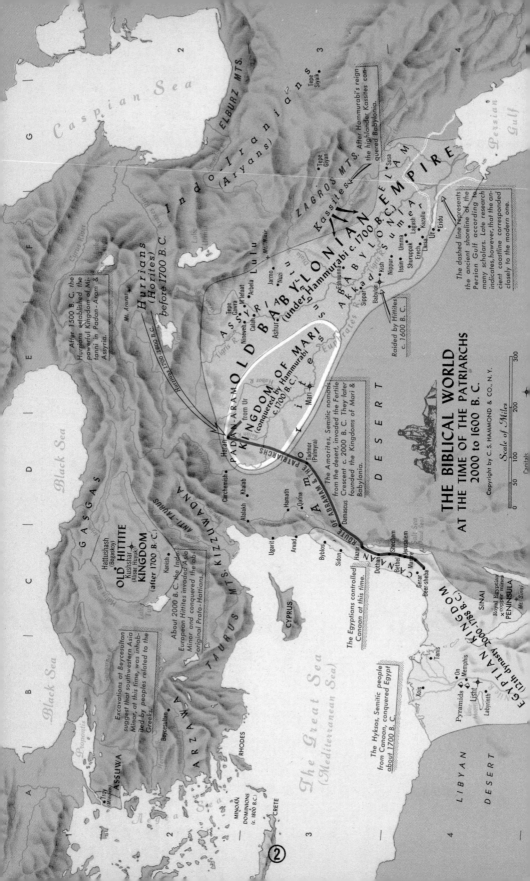

THE BIBLICAL WORLD
AT THE TIME OF THE PATRIARCHS
2000 to 1600 B.C.

Copyright by C. S. HAMMOND & CO., N.Y.

Scale of Miles

0   50   100   200   300

Capitals

Caspian Sea

Black Sea

Black Sea

The Great Sea
(Mediterranean Sea)

Persian Gulf

Propontis

ELBURZ MTS.

I n d o - I r a n i a n s
(Aryans)

ZAGROS MTS.

Hurrians
(Horites)

before 1700 B.C.

After 1500 B.C. the
Hurrians established the
powerful Kingdom of Mi-
tanni in Padan-Aram &
Assyria.

After Hammurabi's reign
the highlander Kassites conquered Babylonia.

The dashed line represents
the ancient shoreline of the
Persian Gulf according to
many scholars. Late research
indicates, however, that the ancient coastline corresponded
closely to the modern one.

OLD BABYLONIAN EMPIRE
(under Hammurabi c. 1700 B.C.)

S U M E R
A K K A D

E L A M

A S S Y R I A

PADAN-ARAM

KINGDOM OF MARI
(conquered by Hammurabi,
c. 1700 B.C.)

Raided by Hittites,
c. 1600 B.C.

Kassites

A m o r i t e s

A m o r i t e s

D E S E R T

D E S E R T

Tepe
Siyalk

Tepe
Giyan

Susa

Eridu

Ur
Kazallu
Larsa
Lagash
Umma
Erech
Shuruppak
Nippur
Issin

Babylon
Sippar
Kish

Abu-Shahrein
Mari
Tadmor
(Palmyra)
Tadmor
(Palmyra)

Haran
from Ur

Harran

Carchemish
Khalab
Alalakh
Hamath
Qatna

Arvad

Ugarit

Byblos
Sidon
Damascus

ROUTE OF ABRAHAM & THE PATRIARCHS

GASGAS

ANTI-TAURUS MTS.

TAURUS MTS.

KIZZUWADNA

ASSUWA

ARZAWA

OLD HITTITE KINGDOM
(after 1700 B.C.)

Hattushash
(Bogazköy)

Kushshar
(Alisar Huyuk)

Kanish

Beycesultan

Excavations at Beycesultan
suggest that southwestern Asia
Minor, at this time, was inhabited by peoples related to the
Greeks.

About 2000 B.C. the Indo-
European Hittites invaded Asia
Minor and conquered the ab-
original Proto-Hattians.

Mt. Ararat

Nineveh
Calah
Ashur
Arbela
Nuzi
Jarmo
Mefaat

Tepe
Gawra

Lulu
Lullu
Mt. Musir

Troy
(Mycenae)

MINOAN
DOMINIONS
(c. 1800 B.C.)

CRETE

RHODES

CYPRUS

CANAAN

Hazor
Dothan
Shechem
Bethel
Jericho
Jerusalem
Mamre
Gerar
Beer-sheba

Dead Sea
(Salt Sea)

Tanis

SINAI
PENINSULA

Royal Egyptian
copper mines

Mt. Sinai

WOODDOM KINGDOM
2000-1788 B.C.

The Egyptians controlled
Canaan at this time.

The Hyksos, Semitic people
from Canaan, conquered Egypt
about 1700 B.C.

EGYPTIAN KINGDOM
(12th dynasty 2000-1788 B.C.)

On
Memphis
Lisht
Labyrinth
Pyramids
Xois

LIBYAN
DESERT

LIBYAN
DESERT

The Amorites, Semitic nomads
from the desert, invaded the Fertile
Crescent c. 2000 B.C. They later
founded the Kingdoms of Mari &
Babylonia.

Hittites 1700-1600 B.C.

2

CANAAN BEFORE THE CONQUEST

Copyright by C. S. HAMMOND & CO., N.Y.

Scale of Miles

0 5 10 20 30 40

Perennial Rivers — — —

Seasonal Rivers & Streams

Capitals ....✦

HITTITE EMPIRE Ubi

Damascus

Phoenicians from the cities of Sidon and Tyre traded throughout the Mediterranean.

Sidon
Zarephath
Tyre
Kanah
Misrephoth-maim
Achzib
Accho
Achshaph
Chinnereth
Madon
Shimron
Jokneam
Dor
Megiddo
Taanach
Ibleam
Dothan
Sochoh
Tirzah
Shechem
Jacob's Well
Aphek
Ono
Lod
Joppa
Gezer
Ekron
Chephirah
Kirjath-jearim
Ashdod
Beth-shemesh
Makkedah
Libnah
Ashkelon
Gath
Eglon
Lachish
Gaza (Azzah)
Gerar
Kirjath-sepher (Debir)
Raphia
Sharuhen
Bethel
Ai
Beeroth
Gibeon
Jericho
Gilgal
Jerusalem (Jebus, Salem)
Bethlehem
Jarmuth
Adullam
Mamre
Kirjath-arba (Hebron)
Hazeon-tamar (En-gedi)
Beer-sheba
Arad
Hormah
Rehoboth
Kadesh-barnea (En-mishpat)

MT. HERMON

Laish (Dan)
Kedesh
Hazor
Merom

BASHAN (KINGDOM OF OG)

Karnaim
Ashtaroth
Edrei
Ramoth-gilead
Ham
Beth-shan
Pella
Jabesh-gilead
Mahanaim
Succoth
Penuel (Peniel)
Adam
Jazer
Rabbath-ammon

The 13th and 12th century kingdoms of Bashan, Ammon, Moab and Edom displaced the Rephaim, Zuzim, Emim and Horites respectively.

Heshbon
Mt. Nebo (Pisgah)
Medeba
Jahaz
Kiriathaim
Dibon
Aroer

AMMON

KINGDOM OF SIHON

Plains of Moab

The Great Sea
(Mediterranean Sea)

Canaanites

Canaan at this time was an Egyptian province organized on a city-state system. The local kings were only required to pay tribute and to furnish labor for Egyptian royal projects.

Hittites
Jebusites
Hittites
Kenites

Mt. Tabor
Mt. Ebal
Mt. Gerizim

Plain of Sharon

Amalekites

Ascent of Akrabbim

Wilderness of Zin

Salt Sea (Dead Sea)

Kir-moab (Kir-hareseth)
Ar

MOAB

The destroyed cities of Sodom and Gomorrah are believed to be beneath the shallow waters of the Dead Sea which now cover the Vale of Siddim (shaded portion).

Zoar

Bozrah

EDOM

Oboth
Punon

MTS. SEIR

Arabah

River of Egypt

Sea of Chinnereth

Yarmuk R.
River Jordan
Jabbok R.
Arnon R.
Besor
Gerar

③

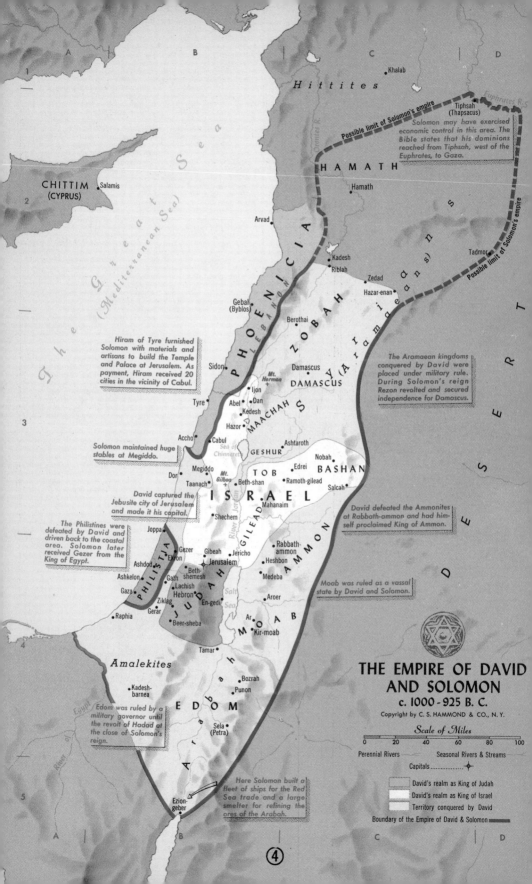

The Empire of David and Solomon, c. 1000–925 B.C.

A1 · B1 · C1 · D1
A2 · B2 · C2 · D2
A3 · B3 · C3 · D3
A4 · B4 · C4 · D4
A5 · B5 · C5 · D5

•Khalab

Hittites

Possible limit of Solomon's empire

Tiphsah
(Thapsacus)

Euphrates R.

Solomon may have exercised
economic control in this area. The
Bible states that his dominions
reached from Tiphsah, west of the
Euphrates, to Gaza.

CHITTIM
(CYPRUS)

•Salamis

HAMATH

•Hamath

•Arvad

Possible limit of Solomon's empire

Tadmor•

The Great Sea (Mediterranean Sea)

•Kadesh
•Riblah

Zedad•

Hazar-enan•

ZOBAH

SYRIA (Aramaeans)

Gebal
(Byblos)

PHOENICIA

Berothai•

The Aramaean kingdoms
conquered by David were
placed under military rule.
During Solomon's reign
Rezon revolted and secured
independence for Damascus.

Hiram of Tyre furnished
Solomon with materials and
artisans to build the Temple
and Palace at Jerusalem. As
payment, Hiram received 20
cities in the vicinity of Cabul.

Sidon•

•Damascus

DAMASCUS

Mt.
Hermon+

LEBANON

•Ijon

Tyre•

Abel• •Dan
•Kedesh

MAACHAH

Hazor•

Ashtaroth•

GESHUR

•Nobah

Accho•
•Cabul

Sea of
Chinnereth

Solomon maintained huge
stables at Megiddo.

Dor•

Megiddo•

Mt.
Gilboa+

Taanach•

Beth-shan•

TOB

Edrei•

BASHAN

•Ramoth-gilead

Salcah•

David captured the
Jebusite city of Jerusalem
and made it his capital.

•Shechem

ISRAEL

Mahanaim•

GILEAD

David defeated the Ammonites
at Rabbath-ammon and had himself proclaimed King of Ammon.

The Philistines were
defeated by David and
driven back to the coastal
area. Solomon later
received Gezer from the
King of Egypt.

Joppa•

Gezer•

•Gibeah

•Jericho

•Rabbath-
ammon

AMMON

Ekron•
Ashdod•

Beth-
shemesh

•Jerusalem

Heshbon•

Ashkelon•

Gath•

•Lachish

Hebron•

Medeba•

Moab was ruled as a vassal
state by David and Solomon.

Gaza•

PHILISTIA

Ziklag•

•En-gedi

Aroer•

Gerar•

JUDAH

Salt
Sea

•Raphia

•Beer-sheba

Ar•

MOAB

•Kir-moab

River of Egypt

•Tamar

Amalekites

•Kadesh-
barnea

•Bozrah

•Punon

EDOM

THE EMPIRE OF DAVID
AND SOLOMON
c. 1000 - 925 B.C.

Copyright by C. S. HAMMOND & CO., N. Y.

Edom was ruled by a
military governor until
the revolt of Hadad at
the close of Solomon's
reign.

•Sela
(Petra)

Arabah

Scale of Miles

0 · 20 · 40 · 60 · 80 · 100

Perennial Rivers   Seasonal Rivers & Streams

Capitals

Ezion-
geber

Here Solomon built a
fleet of ships for the Red
Sea trade and a large
smelter for refining the
ores of the Arabah.

David's realm as King of Judah

David's realm as King of Israel

Territory conquered by David

Boundary of the Empire of David & Solomon

④

DESERT

JUDAH AFTER THE FALL OF ISRAEL
c. 700 B.C.

Copyright by C. S. HAMMOND & CO., N. Y.

Scale of Miles

0 5 10 20 30

Perennial Rivers ....
Seasonal Rivers & Streams ....
Capitals ....

The Great Sea

(Mediterranean Sea)

Sennacherib conquered Phoenicia, with the exception of Tyre, in 701 B.C.

After Samaria fell, Sargon II exiled most of the influential people. The Ten Tribes were moved to various parts of Mesopotamia and disappeared forever from the pages of history.

With the conquest of Samaria in 721 B.C. by Sargon II, the Kingdom of Israel came to an end.

In 701 B.C. Sennacherib captured 46 cities of Judah as he pushed down toward the Egyptians, defeating them at Eltekeh.

In 701 B.C. Jerusalem was besieged, though not taken, by Sennacherib.

Ammon, Moab and Edom fell to the Assyrian Esarhaddon in 690 B.C., but they were never held long enough to be organized as regular provinces of the empire.

Raphia Here Sargon II defeated the Egyptian army in 720 B.C.

Judah was never a province of Assyria. Throughout Assyrian domination, it preserved a nominal independence under its own king, though paying tribute regularly and homage when it was required.

Sidon
Zarephath
Damascus
MOUNT LEBANON
PHOENICIA
Leontes R.
Ijon
MT. HERMON
DAMASCUS
Tyre
Abel-beth-maachah
Dan
Kedesh
Achzib
Hazor
QARNINI
Accho
Ramah
GALILEE
Chinnereth
Sea of Galilee
B a s h a n
Karnaim
Jotbah
Ashtaroth
MT. CARMEL
Gath-hepher
Hammath
Aphek
HAURAN
Jokneam
Plain of MEGIDDO
Jezreel
Mt. Tabor
Edrei
Dor
Megiddo
Shunem
Taanach
Jezreel
Ramoth-gilead
Plain of Sharon
Dothan
Beth-shan
Pella
GILEAD
Du-Ru
Mahanaim
Samaria
Mt. Ebal
Shechem
Mt. Gerizim
Jabbok R.
Aphek
Shiloh
AMMON
Joppa
Rabbath-ammon
Lod
Bethel
Ai
Michmash
Jericho
Jabneh (Jabneel)
Mizpeh
Gibeon
Geba
Gilgal
Ekron
Gezer
Beth-horon
Ramah
Anathoth
Heshbon
Elealeh
Gederoth
Gibbethon
Ajalon
Gibeah
Nob
Mt. Nebo
Medeba
Eltekeh
Jerusalem
Ashdod
Beth-shemesh
Timnah
Jahaz
Saphir
Libnah
Adullam
Tekoa
Ashkelon
Gath
Moresheth-gath
En-gedi
Dibon
Mareshah
Aroer
Gaza
Lachish
Hebron
Arnon R.
Adoraim
Gerar
Debir
Dumah
M O A B
Ar
Salt Sea (Dead Sea)
Beer-sheba
Kir-moab (Kir-haresheth)
J U D A H
Zoar
EGYPTIAN KINGDOM
E D O M
PHILISTIA
SAMARIA

⑤

GREAT EMPIRES OF THE SIXTH CENTURY B.C.

Copyright by C. S. HAMMOND & CO., N.Y.

Scale of Miles
0   100   200   300   400   500

Capitals
Limits of the Persian Empire c. 500 B.C.
Persian Royal Road

MEDIA
(625–550 B.C.)

NEW BABYLONIAN EMPIRE
(625–539 B.C.)

KINGDOM OF LYDIA
(670–546 B.C.)

KINGDOM OF EGYPT
(26th DYNASTY)
663–525 B.C.

ELAM

ARACHOSIA

GEDROSIA
(MAKA)

CARMANIA

PERSIS

SOGDIANA

BACTRIA

MARGIANA

PARTHIA

ARIA

DRANGIANA

CHORASMIA

Massagetae (Scythians)

Saka (Scythians)

INDIA

ARMENIA

CAPPADOCIA

PAPHLAGONIA

PHRYGIA

LYCIA

CILICIA

ASSYRIA

ARABIA

JUDAH

CYPRUS

CRETE

RHODES

GREECE

MACEDONIA

THRACE

EPIRUS

ILLYRIA

Scythians

Albania

ETHIOPIA
(CUSH)

Libyans

PISIDIA

COLCHIS

SUSIANA

Caspian Sea
(Mare Hyrcanium)

Black Sea
(Pontus Euxinus)

Mediterranean Sea

Arabian Sea

Persian Gulf

Red Sea

Present shoreline

Taxila
Pattala
Gandara
Maracanda (Samarkand)
Bagae
Bactra
Dahae
Rhagae
Ecbatana (Achmetha)
Behistun
Aspadana
Pasargadae
Persepolis
Susa (Shushan)
Uruk
Nippur
Babylon
Sippar
Opis
Arbela
Haran
Thapsacus
Tadmor
Carchemish
Damascus
Byblos
Sidon
Tyre
Arvad
Megiddo
Jerusalem
Gaza
Elath
Pelusium
Tahpanhes
Syene (Elephantine I.)
Thebes (No)
Pathros
Memphis (Noph)
Sais
Naucratis
Ob (Noph)
Ammonium
Cyrene
Barca
Pteria
Ancyra
Sardis
Miletus
Ephesus
Marathon
Athens
Sparta
Thermopylae
Salamis
Chalcedon
Byzantium
Apollonia
Sinope
Trapezus
Phasis
Panticapaeum
Chersonesus
Olbia

The Persians under Cyrus the Great overthrew the Medes, conquered Lydia and Babylonia to fulfill the prophecy of Daniel.

Darius I extended the Persian empire into Europe. Attempts to subjugate Greece by Darius and Xerxes I failed as the Greeks won at Marathon and Salamis.

The rise of the New Babylonian (Chaldean) Empire brought an end to the Kingdom of Judah and exile of her people.

The Edict of Cyrus (538 B.C.) allowed the Jews to return to their homeland.

Pharaoh Necho defeated Josiah of Judah but was later driven out of Palestine after being defeated at Carchemish (605 B.C.) by Nebuchadnezzar.

Egypt came under Persian rule after Cambyses defeated Psamtik III at Pelusium in 525 B.C.

⑥

PALESTINE IN THE TIME OF CHRIST

Copyright by C. S. HAMMOND & CO., N.Y.

Scale of Miles

0 5 10   20   30   40

Perennial Rivers ....
Seasonal Rivers & Streams ....
Capitals ....
Roads & Trade Routes ____

Tetrarchy of Lysanias
Tetrarchy of Philip
Tetrarchy of Herod Antipas
Territory under Roman procurator
Cities of the Decapolis ....□

Areas tributary to Salome
Decapolis *
Independent *
Roman province of Syria

* The Decapolis and Ascalon retained their independence under the Roman governor of the province of Syria.

Archelaus, upon Herod's death, came ruler of Judaea, Samaria and Idumaea. His reign lasted until 6 A.D. when he was removed and exiled. His territory then was placed under a Roman procurator.

Salome, Herod's sister, was given Jamnia, Azotus and Phasaelis. They, in turn, passed to Livia, wife of Augustus and then to Emperor Tiberius.

The Great Sea

(Mediterranean Sea)

PHOENICIA

ABILENE
Abila
Damascus
Sidon
Sarepta (Zarephath)
MOUNT LEBANON
MT. HERMON
Tyre
PANIAS
Dan Caesarea Philippi
ULATHA
Lake Semechonitis
ITURAEA
TRACHONITIS
Ladder of Tyre
Cadasa (Kedesh)
Gischala
GAULANITIS
BATANAEA
BASHAN
Raphana
Seleucia
Horns of Hattin (Kurûn Hattin) is a possible site of the Sermon on the Mount.
Chorazin
Bethsaida (Julias)
Ptolemais (Accho)
Jotapata
Cana
Magdala (Dalmanutha)
Tabigha
Capernaum
Sea of Galilee
Gergesa
Gamala
AURANITIS
Dion
GALILEE
Sepphoris
Nazareth
Tiberias
Philoteria
Hippos
Abila
MT. CARMEL
Mt. Tabor
Gadara
Capitolias
Edrei
Plain of Esdraelon
Nain
Dora
Bethabara
G I L E A D
DECAPOLIS
Pella
Caesarea
Residence of Roman procurators.
En-gannim (Ginaea)
Scythopolis (Beth-shan)
SAMARIA
Gerasa
Plain of Sharon
Samaria (Sebaste)
Mt. Ebal
Shechem Sychar
Mt. Gerizim Jacob's Well
Amathus
Jabbok R.
Apollonia
Antipatris
Arimathaea (Ramathaim)
Gophna
Phasaelis
PERAEA
Joppa
Lydda (Diospolis)
Bethel
Archelais
Ephraim
Beth-nimrah
Philadelphia (Rabbath-ammon)
Gezer (Gazara)
Ramah
Jericho
Jamnia
Ekron
Nicopolis (Emmaus)
Emmaus
Mt. of Olives
Jerusalem
Bethany
Khirbet Qumran
Julias (Livias, Beth-haram)
Heshbon
Azotus (Ashdod)
Bethlehem
Herodium
The Dead Sea Scrolls were found in a cave here; also the ruins of an Essene monastery.
Ascalon
JUDAEA
Mareshah (Marisa)
Hebron
Wilderness of Judah
Callirhoe
Machaerus
Here John the Baptist was imprisoned and beheaded by order of Herod Antipas.
Gaza
Ziph
En-gedi
Dibon
Gerar
Juttah
Carmel
Salt or Dead Sea (L. Asphaltitis)
Raphia
Masada
Rabbath Moab (Areopolis, Rabba)
Beersheba
IDUMAEA
Kir-moab (Kir-haresheth)
A R A B I A
A M M O N
N A B A T A E A N S

(7)

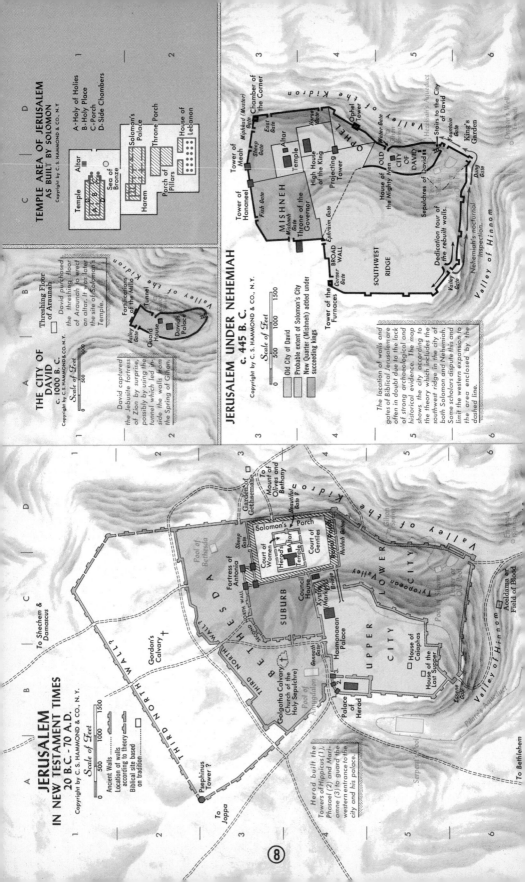

Ze'lek (zē'lĕk; *cleft, fissure*), an Ammonite and one of David's valiant men (II Sam. 23:37; I Chron. 11:39).

Zelo'phehad (zē-lō'fē-hăd; *shadow of the fear*, i. e., *protection against fear*), the son of Hepher and descendant of Manasseh through Gilead (Josh. 17:3), B. C. before 1170. He died without male heirs, and his five daughters claimed his inheritance. The claim was admitted by divine direction, and a law was promulgated, to be of general application, that if a man died without sons his inheritance should pass to his daughters (Num. 26:33; 27:1-11). A still further enactment (ch. 36) provided that such heiresses should not marry out of their own tribes—a regulation which the five daughters of Zelophehad complied with, all being married to Manassites.

Zelo'tes (zē-lō'tēz; Gr. *a zealous one*), Greek for Aramaic Cananaean; a member of a Jewish patriotic party, the surname of the apostle Simon (Luke 6:15; Acts 1:13), to distinguish him from Simon Peter. In the parallel lists (Matt. 10:4, Mark 3:18) he is called Simon *the Canaanite*, this being thought by some to be a transliteration of the Heb *qăn'än*, *zeal*. Meyer (*Com.*, on Matt. 10:4) says: "*Zealots* were a class of men who, like Phineas (Num. 25:7), were fanatical defenders of the theocracy; and who, while taking vengeance on those who wronged it, were themselves guilty of great excesses. But the *hō Kananaios* is not to be explained in this way, inasmuch as this form of the epithet is derived from the name of some *place* or other."

Zel'zah (zĕl'zá), a place in the border of Benjamin, mentioned by Samuel when taking leave of Saul at Ramah (I Sam. 10:2). Among the signs which the prophet said would confirm his anointing of Saul was the latter's meeting with two men at Rachel's sepulcher. This was on the way from Bethel to Bethlehem, and to the west in full view is the village of *Beit Jala*, which may be identical with Zelzah.

Zemara'im (zĕm-á-rā'ĭm; *double fleece*).
    1. One of the ancient towns assigned to Benjamin (Josh. 18:22), in the eastern section of its territory, and grouped with Beth-arabah and Beth-el. It is probably to be identified with the ruins of Khirbet es-Samrah, on the road from Jerusalem to Jericho.
    2. The mountain from which Abijah, king of Judah, addressed Jeroboam and the army of Israel (II Chron. 13:4). It is described as being "in Mount Ephraim," i. e., within the general highland district of that tribe.

Zem'arites (zĕm'á-rīts; "the Zemarite," only found Gen. 10:18 and I Chron. 1:16), the name of a people reckoned among the sons of Canaan, "the Arvadite, and the Zemarite, and the Hamathite," whence it is naturally assumed that the Zemarites lived between Arvad and Hamath. The old interpreters, as the Jerusalem Targum, the Arabic version, etc., locate them at Emessa, the modern *Hums*. Michaelis placed them at *Sumra*, the classical Simyra. It is possible that the names Zemaraim (Josh. 18:22) and Mount Zemaraim (II Chron. 13:4) represent southern migrations of Zemarites; or, as the list in Gen. 10:15-18 is not altogether in strict geo-

graphical order, the Zemarites as a whole may have lived in the vicinity of Zemaraim and Mount Zemaraim.—W. H., revised by *M. F. U.*

Zemi'ra (zē-mī'rá; *music*), one of the nine sons of Becher, the son of Benjamin (I Chron. 7:8).

Ze'nan (zē'năn; *point*, or perhaps, *place of flocks*), a town in the lowland district of Judah (Josh. 15:37), and supposed to be the same as Zaanan (Mic. 1:11).

Ze'nas (zē'năs; shortened from Zenadorus, *gift of Zeus*), a Christian lawyer of Crete mentioned in Tit. 3:13, in connection with Apollos. It is impossible to determine whether Zenas was a Roman jurisconsult or a Jewish doctor. Grotius thinks that he was a Greek who had studied Roman law. The New Testament usage of *nomikos*, "*lawyer*," leads rather to the other inference.

Zephani'ah (zĕf-á-ni'á; *Jehovah conceals* or *treasures*).
    1. A Kohathite Levite, ancestor of Samuel and Heman (I Chron. 6:36).
    2. The son of Maaseiah (Jer. 21:1), and *sagan*, or second priest, in the reign of Zedekiah. He succeeded Jehoiada (29:25, 26) and was probably a ruler of the temple, whose office it was among others to punish pretenders to the gift of prophecy. In this capacity he was appealed to by Shemaiah the Nehelamite to punish Jeremiah (29:27). Twice was he sent from Zedekiah to inquire of Jeremiah the issue of the siege of the city by the Chaldeans (21:1), and to implore him to intercede for the people (37:3). On the capture of Jerusalem he was taken and slain at Riblah (52:24, 27; II Kings 25:18, 21), B. C. about 587.
    3. The prophet, son of Cushi, who prophesied against Judah and Jerusalem in the days of King Josiah (Zeph. 1:1), B. C. about 630.
    4. Father of Josiah (Zech. 6:10) and of Hen, according to the reading of the received text of Zech. 6:14, B. C. 520.

Zephaniah, Book of, one of the Minor Prophets, whose name in Hebrew means "Jehovah hides, or protects." He was likely a great-grandson of Hezekiah (chap. 1:1). The allusion of the epithet "the king" has caused some critics, such as Aage Bentzen (*Intr.* II, 1949, p. 154) to deny this. If he was not related to Hezekiah, however, there is no adequate explanation of the prophet's abandonment of the usual custom of referring only to the father in the superscription.

2. **The Date.** The prophet exercised his ministry in the early reign of Josiah (640-608 B. C.), doubtless prior to the great reformation of 621 B. C. This is confirmed by the allusion to the presence of foreign cults (1:4) and to Assyria (2:13). It is certainly possible that Zephaniah had access to the court and perhaps, like Nahum and Jeremiah, his contemporaries, exerted much influence in bringing about the revival under Hezekiah. Zephaniah deals with the coming invasion of Nebuchadnezzar as a figure of the Day of the Lord (1:1-2:3). He utters stern predictions of judgment on certain peoples (2:4-15). He outlines the moral state of Israel for which the captivity was to come as a punishment (3:1-7). He prophesies that the judgment of the

nations is to be followed by kingdom blessing under Messiah (3:8-20).

3. **Contents.**

Part I. The Day of the Lord Prefigured, 1:1-3:7
  (a) In judgment upon Judah and Jerusalem, 1:1-2:3
  (b) In judgment upon surrounding nations, 2:4-15
  (c) In Jehovah's manifestation to sinful Jerusalem, 3:1-7

Part II. The Kingdom Prophesied, 3:8-20
  (a) The judgment of the nations, 3:8-13
  (b) Messiah revealed as King, 3:14-20

4. **Composition.** On subjective and insufficient grounds the authenticity of various parts of chapters 2 and 3 have been contested by such critics as Stade, Kuenen, Wellhausen, Budde and Eissfeldt. Oesterley and Robinson acknowledge that the general authenticity of the book has not been seriously doubted although they note that different editors have discovered reason to support considerable interpolations (*Intr.*, London, 1934). However, from a strictly objective view, there is no valid reason to deny any of the prophecies to Zephaniah. *M. F. U.*

Ze′phath (zē′făth; *beacon, watchtower*), the earlier name (Judg. 1:17) of a Canaanitish town, destroyed by Judah and Simeon, and renamed Hormah. Two identifications have been proposed for Zephath: that of Robinson with the well-known pass *es-Sufâ;* and that of other scholars with a site 3 miles E. of Beersheba called Tell es-Saba‘.

Zeph′athah (zĕf′à-thà; *watchtower*), a valley near Mareshah (II Chron. 14:10), where Asa joined battle with Zerah the Ethiopian. A deep valley is found near the site of Mareshah, running down to Beit Jibrin (Eleutheropolis), and thence into the plain of Philistia. This may be the valley of Zephathah.

Ze′phi (zē′fī; I Chron. 1:36). *See* Zepho.

Ze′pho (zē′fō), or **Ze′phi** (zē′fī; *watch*), a son of Eliphaz, son of Esau (Gen. 36:11), and one of the "dukes" of the Edomites (v. 15). In I Chron. 1:36 he is called *Zephi.*

Ze′phon (zē′fŏn; *watching, expectation*), the first of the seven sons of Gad (Num. 26:15) and progenitor of the *Zephonites.*

Zeph′onites (zĕf′ō-nīts; Num. 26:15). *See* Zephon.

Zer (zŭr), a fortified town in the territory assigned to Naphtali (Josh. 19:35). It has not been identified.

Ze′rah (zē′rà; *dawning, rising, shining*).

1. Son of Reuel, son of Esau (Gen. 36:13; I Chron. 1:37), and one of the "dukes," or phylarchs, of the Edomites (Gen. 36:17). Jobab, an early king of Edom, perhaps belonged to his family (Gen. 36:33; I Chron. 1:44).

2. Less properly, *Zarah.* Twin son with his brother Pharez of Judah and Tamar (Gen. 38:30; I Chron. 2:6; Matt. 1:3). His descendants were called Zarhites, Ezrahites, and Izrahites (Num. 26:20; I Kings 4:31; I Chron. 27:8, 11).

3. Sons of Simeon (I Chron. 4:24; "Zohar," Gen. 46:10).

4. A Gershonite Levite, son of Iddo, or Adaiah (I Chron. 6:21, 41).

5. The Ethiopian (or Cushite) king defeated by Asa. After a period of ten years' peace Asa's reign was disturbed by war. Zerah, with a million men and three hundred chariots, invaded the kingdom and pressed forward to Mareshah. Thither Asa marched to meet him, and drew up his army in battle array in the valley of Zephathah. After commending his cause to Jehovah, Asa made the attack, which was eminently successful. Asa pursued the fleeing Ethiopians as far as Gerar, crippling them so that they could not recover themselves and again make a stand (II Chron. 14:9-13). Some scholars identify Zerah with one of the Osorkons of the Twenty-second or Bubastite Dynasty, particularly with Osorkon I (924-895 B. C.), successor of Shishak. However, the reference may simply be to an Arabian invasion, since the name Zerah occurs in S. Arabic inscriptions.

Zerahi′ah (zĕr-à-hī′à; *Jehovah has risen*).

1. A priest, son of Uzzi and ancestor of Ezra the scribe (I Chron. 6:6, 51; Ezra 7:4), B. C. about 457.

2. Father of Elihoenai, of the sons of Pahath Moab (Ezra 8:4), B. C. about 457.

Ze′red (zē′rĕd), or **Za′red** (zā′rĕd); a valley separating Moab from Edom (Deut. 2:13, 14), and where the Israelites encamped before crossing the Arnon (Num. 21:12). It seems to be the same as the Wâdi el-Hesā, a water-course entering the Dead Sea at the southeast corner, forming one of the last obstacles overcome by Israel on their way from Egypt to the Promised Land (Deut. 2:13 f.).

Zer′eda (zĕr′ē-dà), a town in Mount Ephraim given as the birthplace of Jeroboam, the son of Nebat the Ephrathite, and servant (i. e., officer) of Solomon (I Kings 11:26). By some it is identified with *Zarthan* (q. v.); others, because of its connection with Mount Ephraim, think that it cannot be the same. Conder identifies it with *Surdah*, a village a little more than a mile south of Jufua. 'Ain Şeredah, the fountain of Khirbet Balâtah in Mt. Ephraim 15 miles S. W. of Shechem, at the bend of the Wadi Deir Ballut offers an exact equivalent of name (Albright).

Zered-a′thah (zĕr-ē-dā′thà), same as *Zereda*, another name (II Chron. 4:17) for *Zarthan* (q. v.), the place of Solomon's brass foundry.

Zer′erath (zĕr′ē-răth), a place mentioned (Judg. 7:22) in describing the route of the Midianites before Gideon. Keil and Delitzsch (*Com.*) identify it with *Zarthan* (q. v.).

Ze′resh (zē′rĕsh; evidently from Avestan root *zarsh, the joyful one*), the wife of Haman the Agagite, who advised the hanging of Mordecai (Esth. 5:10, 14; 6:13), B. C. about 478.

Ze′reth (zē′rĕth; perhaps, *splendor*), son of Ashur, the founder of Tekoa, by his wife Helah (I Chron. 4:7), B. C. perhaps 1370.

Ze′ri (zē′rī), one of the sons of Jeduthun, and a Levitical harper in the reign of David (I Chron. 25:3). He is probably the Izri mentioned in v. 11.

Ze′ror (zē′rŏr; a *particle*), a Benjamite ancestor of Kish, the father of Saul (I Sam. 9:1), B. C. before 1095.

Zeru′ah (zē-rōō′à; *smitten, leprous*), the mother of Jeroboam, the son of Nebat (I Kings 11:26), B. C. before 934.

Zerub'babel (zĕ-rŭb'á-bĕl; Heb. from Akkad. *zēru Bābili, seed (progeny) of Babylon*), the head of the tribe of Judah at the time of the return from Babylonian captivity.

1. **Family.** Zerubbabel is called the son of Shealtiel (Ezra 3:2, 8; 5:2; Neh. 12:1; Hag. 1:1, 12, 14; 2:2), and in the genealogies ("Zorobabel," Matt. 1:12; Luke 3:27). In I Chron. 3:19 he is given as the son of Pedaiah, the brother of Shealtiel (see note below). Josephus (*Ant.*, xi, 3, 10) speaks of him as "the son of Salathiel, of the posterity of David and of the tribe of Judah."

2. **History.** In the first year of Cyrus, Zerubbabel was living in Babylon, and was recognized as prince of Judah in the captivity. He was probably in the king's service, as he had received an Aramaic name (*Sheshbazzar*) and had been intrusted by Cyrus with the office of governor of Judea. (1) **Goes to Jerusalem.** Zerubbabel led the first colony of captives to Jerusalem, accompanied by Jeshua the high priest, a considerable number of priests, Levites, and heads of houses of Judah and Benjamin. Arrived at Jerusalem, their first care was the building of the altar on its old site and to restore the daily sacrifice (Ezra, ch. 2; 3:1-3), B. C. about 536. (2) **Rebuilding the temple.** The great work of Zerubbabel was the rebuilding of the temple. Aided by a grant of material and money, Zerubbabel was enabled to lay the foundation in the second month of the second year of their return. This was done with the utmost solemnity, amid the trumpet blasts of the priests, the music of the Levites, and the loud songs of thanksgiving of the people (vers. 8-13). (3) **Hindrances.** The work had not advanced far before the mixed settlers in Samaria put in a claim to take part in it; and when Zerubbabel and his companions declined the offer, they endeavored to hinder its completion. They "troubled them in building," and hired counselors to misrepresent them at the court. The result was that no further progress was made during the remaining years of the reign of Cyrus and the eight years of Cambyses and Smerdis (4:1-24). Nor does Zerubbabel appear quite blameless for this long delay. The difficulties in the way of building the temple were not such as need have stopped the work; and during this long suspension of sixteen years Zerubbabel and the rest of the people had been busy in building costly houses for themselves (Hag. 1:2-4). (4) **Building resumed.** Moved by the exhortations of the prophets Haggai and Zechariah, Zerubbabel threw himself heartily into the work, and was zealously seconded by Jeshua and all the people. This was in the second year of the reign of Darius Hystaspes (B. C. 520), who enjoined Tatnai and Shetharboznai to assist the Jews with whatsoever they had need of at the king's expense. The work advanced so rapidly that on the third day of the month Adar, in the sixth year of Darius, the temple was finishĕd, and was forthwith dedicated with much pomp and rejoicing (Ezra 5:1 to 6:22), B. C. 516. The only other works of Zerubbabel which we learn from Scripture history are the restoration of the courses of priests and Levites, and of the provision for

their maintenance, according to the institution of David (Ezra 6:18; Neh. 12:47); the registering the returned captives according to their genealogies (Neh. 7:5), and the keeping of a passover in the seventh year of Darius. In the genealogies of Jesus (Matt. 1:12; Luke 3:27), he is represented as son of Salathiel, though the Book of Chronicles tells us he was the son of Pedaiah and nephew of Salathiel. It is of more moment to remark that while Matthew deduces his line from Jechonias and Solomon, Luke deduces it through Neri and Nathan. Zerubbabel was the legal successor and heir of Jeconiah's royal estate, the grandson of Neri, and the lineal descendant of Nathan, the son of David. In the New Testament the name appears in the Greek form of *Zorobabel*.

NOTE—The discrepancy between I Chron. 3:19 and other passages as to the parentage of Zerubbabel is explained by Keil (*Com.*, in loc.) by the supposition that "Shealtiel died without any male descendants, leaving his wife a widow. . . . After Shealtiel's death his second brother, Pedaiah, fulfilled the Levirate duty, and begat, in his marriage with his sister-in-law, Zerubbabel, who was now regarded, in all that related to laws of heritage, as Shealtiel's son."

Zerui'ah (zĕr-û-ī'á), the mother of David's three great generals, Abishai, Joab, and Asahel. She and Abigail are specified (I Chron. 2:16) as "sisters of the son of Jesse," while it is stated in II Sam. 17:25, that Abigail was the daughter of Nahash. Some early commentators have concluded that Abigail and Zeruiah were only stepsisters of David, i. e., daughters of his mother by Nahash, and not by Jesse. Of Zeruiah's husband there is no mention in the Bible.

Ze'tham (zē'thăm; *olive tree*), the son of Laadan, a Gershonite Levite (I Chron. 23:8), and, with his brother, a keeper of the temple treasury (26:22), B. C. about 960.

Ze'than (zē'thăn; *olive tree*), a Benjamite, of the sons of Bilhan (I Chron. 7, 10), B. C. probably about 960.

Ze'thar (zē'thår; Old Pers., Avestan, *jantar, smiter, slayer*), one of the seven eunuchs of Ahasuerus (Esth. 1, 10), B. C. about 480.

Zi'a (zī'á; *trembling motion*), one of the Gadites who dwelt in Bashan (I Chron. 5:13).

Zi'ba (zī'bá; probably from Aram. *branch, twig*), a former servant of Saul of whom David made the inquiry, "Is there not yet any of the house of Saul, that I may show the kindness of God unto?" Mephibosheth was in consequence found, and Ziba was commanded to cultivate the land which was restored to the king's son (II Sam. 9:2-12). At this first mention of Ziba he had fifteen sons and twenty servants (v. 10). When David, in his flight from Jerusalem, had gone a little over the height (Mount of Olives) Ziba met him with a present of asses, food, and wine. To the king's inquiry, "Where is thy master's son?" Ziba replied, "Behold, he abideth at Jerusalem: for he said, Today shall the house of Israel restore me the kingdom of my father." This improbable calumny was believed by David in the excited state in which he then was, and he gave to Ziba all the property of Mephibosheth (16:1, sq.). On David's return Mephibosheth accused Ziba of having slandered him, and David gave command that the land should be divided between them (19:29).

Zib'eon (zĭb'ē-ŭn), father of Anah, whose daughter Aholibamah was Esau's wife (Gen. 36:2). Although called a Hivite, he is probably the same as Zibeon, the son of Seir, the Horite (Gen. 36:20, 24, 29; I Chron. 1:38, 40).

Zib'ia (zĭb'ĭ-à; *gazelle*), A Benjamite, the son of Shaharaim by his wife Hodesh (I Chron. 8:9).

Zib'iah (zĭb'ĭ-à; *gazelle*), a native of Beer-sheba and mother of King Jehoash (II Kings 12:1; II Chron. 24:1).

Zich'ri (zĭk'rī; *mindful*).

1. Son of Izhar, the son of Kohath (Exod. 6:21).

2. A Benjamite, of the sons of Shimhi (I Chron. 8:19).

3. A Benjamite, of the sons of Shashak (I Chron. 8:23).

4. A Benjamite, of the sons of Jeroham (I Chron. 8:27).

5. Son of Asaph (I Chron. 9:15); elsewhere called *Zabdi* (Neh. 11:17) and *Zaccur* (12:35).

6. A descendant of Eliezer, the son of Moses and father of the treasurer Shelomith (I Chron. 26:25), B. C. before 960.

7. The father of Eliezer, the chief of the Reubenites in the reign of David (I Chron. 27:16).

8. Of the tribe of Judah, father of Amasiah, which latter volunteered at the head of two hundred thousand men in Jehoshaphat's army (II Chron. 17:16), B. C. after 875.

9. Father of Elishaphat, one of the conspirators with Jehoiada to make Joash king (II Chron. 23:1), B. C. about 799.

10. A mighty man of Ephraim who slew Maaseiah the son of King Ahaz, the governor of the palace, and the prime minister (II Chron. 28:7), B. C. about 735.

11. The father of Joel, which latter was overseer of the Benjamites after their return to Jerusalem from captivity (Neh. 11:9), B. C. before 536.

12. A priest of the family of Abijah in the days of Joiakim (Neh. 12:17), B. C. about 445.

Zid'dim (zĭd'ĭm; *sides*), a place in Naphtali (Josh. 19:35). Evidently Kefar *Haṭṭya*, mentioned in the Talmud, less than a mile north of the well known Horns of Hattin.

Zidki'jah (zĭd-kī'jà) (Neh. 10:1). See Zedekiah.

Zi'don (zī'dŏn; *fishery*).

1. The eldest son of Canaan (Gen. 10:15, "Sidon;" I Chron. 1:13).

2. A very ancient and wealthy city, on the Mediterranean, about twenty-five miles north of Tyre. The modern Saidā in the Republic of Lebanon. It is situated on a small promontory in the narrow plain between the Lebanon and the sea. It had a very commodious harbor, now nearly choked up with sand. It was distant one day's journey from the fountains of Jordan. Although it was assigned to Asher (Judg. 1:31) it was never conquered; but, on the contrary, was sometimes a formidable enemy (10:12). Even in Joshua's time it was called Tsidon-rabba, or Great Zidon (Josh.

11:8; 19:28), or Zidon the metropolis, i. e., of Zidonia. The city is mentioned in the Amarna Letters c. 1400-1370 B. C.

Zidon claimed to be the mother city of which Tyre was a colony; and correctly, though the weight of ancient authority is pretty evenly divided. Zidon, in Gen. 49:13, is the firstborn of Canaan. Tyre first appears in the Bible at the time of the invasion of Palestine by the Israelites (Josh. 19:29). Both cities were of great antiquity. According to the researches of Herodotus, who visited Tyre for the very purpose of investigating this question (Herodotus, ii, 43, 44), Tyre was founded two thousand three hundred years before his own time, hence 2750 B. C.

From the time of Solomon to the invasion of Nebuchadnezzar Zidon is not often directly mentioned in the Bible, and was outstripped by its "daughter" city Tyre (Isa. 23:20). It was threatened by the prophet Joel (3:4) and Jeremiah (27:3). During the Persian domination Zidon seems to have attained its highest point of prosperity, excelling at the close of this period all other Phoenician cities in wealth and importance. This prosperity was suddenly cut short by an unsuccessful revolt against Persia; for upon the approach of the Persian troops the inhabitants shut themselves up with their families, and each man set fire to his own house. Forty thousand persons are said to have thus perished, B. C. 351. It gradually recovered, and cooperated with Alexander against Tyre, but from that time ceased to play any important political part in history.

Zidon is mentioned in the New Testament. Jesus went once to the coasts of Tyre and Zidon (Matt. 15:21); Sarepta, a city of Zidon, is referred to (Luke 4:26); and Paul touched at Zidon on his voyage from Caesarea to Rome (Acts 27:3). *See* Sidon; Zidonians.

Zido'nians (zī-dō'nĭ-ănz), the inhabitants of Zidon. In Gen. 10:19 Zidon and Gaza are two of the extreme points of Canaan. In 49:13 Jacob makes Zidon the limit of Zebulun. This, perhaps, means that the territory of Zidon, though afterward limited by that of Tyre, originally "extended southward to the tribe of Zebulun and Mount Carmel." In Josh. 19:28, 29, Great Zidon and Tyre are on the border of Asher.

The Zidonians were not dispossessed (Judg. 3:3), and were among the early oppressors of Israel (10:12). In Josh. 13:6 the R. V. reads "even all the Zidonians." This would make the inhabitants of the hill country Zidonians, indicating that the Zidonian population had "spread up into the hill country;" and this idea is favored still more by their skill in cutting timber (I Kings 5:6). So in Judg. 18:7 we find them described as living "quiet and secure," devoted, no doubt, to the cultivation of their lands, and not engaged in trade, having "no business with any man." The language of the text indicates this "careless," "quiet and secure" life was the usual "manner of the Zidonians." The Zidonians adored, as tutelary god and goddess, Baal (whence the name of the king Ethbaal, I Kings 16:31) and Ashtoreth (I Kings 11:5, 33; II Kings 23:13).

Jezebel, the wife of Ahab, was the daughter of the king of the Zidonians (I Kings 16:31), but the example of taking Zidonian women had been set by Solomon (11:1).

In Homer, also, the Sidonians are praised for their skillful workmanship, but never as traders, except as they may have passed under the general name Phoenician (*Iliad*, vi, 289-295; *Od.*, iv, 614-618; xv, 425); and the two are distinguished in *Iliad*, xxiii, 743, 744, where Phoenicians convey Sidonian work. The Homeric poems do not mention Tyre, but they mention both Sidon (*Od.*, xv, 425) the Sidonians (*Iliad.*, vi, 289, 290; see also *Od.*, iv, 84 and 618; xv, 118; *Iliad.*, xxiii, 743; and their country Sidonia, *Iliad.*, vi, 291; *Od.*, xiii, 285). Strabo the Greek historian (63 B. C.) observes that while the poets glorified Sidon, the Phoenician colonists in Africa gave "more honor" to Tyre.—W. H. revised by M. F. U.

Zif (zĭf; *bloom, splendor*), the early name (I Kings 6:1, 37) of the second Hebrew month, Iyar. *See* Calendar, ziv.

Zi'ha (zī'hà).

1. One of the Nethinim whose descendants returned from the captivity (Ezra 2:43; Neh. 7:46), B. C. before 536.

2. A ruler of the Nethinim after the return from Babylon (Neh. 11:21), B. C. 536.

Zik'lag (zĭk'lăg), a town in the Negeb, or south country of Judah (Josh. 15:31). The next mention is of its assignment, with other places in Judah, to Simeon (19:5). It was made David's residence for a year and four months by the appointment of Achish, king of Gath (I Sam. 27:6). It was destroyed once by the Amalekites, who in turn were routed utterly by David (30:1, 2). It was at Ziklag that David received the news of Saul's death (II Sam. 1:1; 4:10). It was inhabited in the post-captivity period (Neh. 11:28). It is probably to be identified with Tell el-Khuweilfeh, S. E. of Gaza, between Debir and Beersheba.

Zil'lah (zĭl'à; *shadow*, i. e., protection), one of the two wives of Lamech, the Cainite, to whom he addressed his song (Gen. 4:19, 22, 23). She was the mother of Tubal-cain and Naamah.

Zil'pah (zĭl'pà; cf. Arab. *zulfah, dignity*), the female servant given by Laban to his daughter Leah as an attendant (Gen. 29:24), and by Leah to Jacob as a concubine. She was the mother of Gad and Asher (30:9-13; 35:26; 37:2; 46:18), B. C. about 1925.

Zil'thai (zĭl'thī; A. S. V. Zillethai; *shadow, protection*).

1. A Benjamite, of the sons of Shimhi (I Chron. 8:20), B. C. after 1170.

2. One of the captains of thousands of Manasseh who deserted to David at Ziklag (I Chron. 12:20), B. C. about 1000.

Zim'mah (zĭm'à; *purpose*).

1 A Gershonite Levite, son of Jahath, the grandson of Gershon (I Chron. 6:20), B. C. after 1210. He is probably the same as the son of Shimei in v. 42.

2. Father or ancestor of Joah, a Gershonite in the reign of Hezekiah (II Chron. 29:12), B. C. before 726. At a much earlier period we find Zimmah and Joah as father and son (I

Chron. 6:20), for in the various families the same name often repeats itself.

Zim'ran (zĭm'răn; probably *antelope*), the eldest son of Keturah and Abraham (Gen. 25:2; I Chron. 1:32). His descendants have not been positively identified.

Zim'ri (zĭm'rī; *pertaining to an antelope*).

1. The son of Salu, a Simeonite chieftain, slain by Phinehas with the Midianitish princess Cozbi (Num. 25:14), B. C. c. 1400. When the Israelites at Shittim were suffering for their impure worship of Baal-peor, Zimri brought this woman into his tent to commit adultery with her. This shameless wickedness so inflamed the zeal of Phinehas, the high priest, that he seized a spear and pierced both of them through in the very act.

2. The fifth king of Israel, who reigned only seven days. He is first mentioned as captain of half the chariots of the royal army and as chief conspirator against King Elah, who was murdered while indulging in a drunken revel in the house of his steward in Tirzah. His first act as king was the slaying of all the house of Baasha. But the army, which at that time was besieging the Philistine town of Gibbethon, when they heard of Elah's murder, proclaimed their general Omri king. He immediately marched against Tirzah and took the city. Zimri retreated into the innermost part of the late king's palace, set it on fire, and perished in the ruins (I Kings 16:9-20), B. C. about 887.

3. The eldest of the five sons of Zerah, the son of Judah (I Chron. 2:6).

4. Son of Jehoadah and descendant of Saul (I Chron. 8:36; 9:42).

Zin (zĭn), a wilderness or open, uncultivated region lying south of Palestine (Num. 13:21; 20:1; 27:14; 33:36; 34:3; Deut. 32:51; Josh. 15:1). By some it is supposed to be a portion of the desert tract between the Dead Sea and the Gulf of 'Aqabah. But it must have been to the west of this tract (called 'Arabah), as is clearly indicated in Num. 34:4. Directly west of the 'Arabah is a wild mountain region, rising in successive slopes or terraces from the 'Arabah in one direction, and from the Desert et-Tîh in another. It now bears the name of the Arabs who inhabit it, and is commonly known as the Azâzimeh mountains, or the Azâzimat. This is a distinct and well-defined local wilderness, full meeting the conditions of the various references to the wilderness of Zin in the Bible. It may fairly be identified as that wilderness, and again as a portion of the wilderness of Paran in its larger sense. Yet its northeastern portion was probably in Edom, and it is possible that only the remainder was known as Zin. The wilderness of Zin is not to be confused with the Wilderness of Sin (*q. v.*), the original words being quite different.

Zi'na (zī'nà; I Chron. 23:10). *See* Zizah.

Zion, originally the rock escarpment on the ridge between the Kidron and the Tyropeoean Valleys of Jerusalem. Subsequently the term was widened to include the entire western ridge of early Jerusalem. Centuries later the term was applied to the entire city (Psa. 126:1; Isa. 1:26, 27). By the fourth century the name of Zion was adapted to the southern portion of the western hill.

1. **Archaeological Location.** Zion constituted a formidable natural fortress which the Jebusites inhabited before Jerusalem was taken by David (II Sam. 5:7). The Gihon Spring, or the Virgin Fountain, below the eastern rock escarpment, and En-rogel or Job's Well, at the junction of the Kidron and

536. Zion and the Valley of Hinnon

Hinnom Valleys, were factors in the early choice of the site. Jerusalem's water system has been explored, showing that the inhabitants of Jerusalem (c. 2000 B. C.) had made a rock-cut passage similar to the one at Gezer and Megiddo (Chester C. McCown, *The Ladder of Progress in Palestine*, N. Y., 1943, p. 230). Evidence brought to light as the result of excavations of Sir Charles Warren, Clermont-Ganneau, Hermann Guthe, Frederick Bliss, Captain Raymond Weill, John Garstang and J. W. Crowfoot show that the city which David captured was like a huge human footprint about 1250 feet long by 400 feet wide. This became the City of David, or Zion. In Zion David constructed his palace (II Sam. 5:11). David acquired the threshing floor of Araunah farther up the ridge. There he erected an altar (II Sam. 24:18f) and there Solomon built his palatial temple.

2. **Theological Use.** Zion has a threefold significance in the Bible apart from its original historical significance. (*a*) **David's City.** In the O. T. Zion refers to Jerusalem, the city that David conquered and made a capital of the United Kingdom of Israel (I Chron. 11:5; Psa. 2:6; Isa. 2:3). (2) **The Millennial City.** In a prophetic sense, Zion has reference to Jerusalem as the future capital city of the nation Israel in the Kingdom Age (Isa. 1:27; 2:3; 4:1-6; Joel 3:16; Zech. 1:16, 17; 8:3-8; Rom. 11:26). Amillennial theologians deny this equation and spiritualize, rather "mysticalize," the term to mean the Christian Church of this age. (3) **The Heavenly City.** The N. T. also refers Zion to the New Jerusalem (Heb. 12:22-24), the eternal city into which the Church will be received (cf. Rev. chaps. 21, 22).—*M. F. U.*

Zi'or (zī'ôr; *smallness*), a town in the mountain district of Judah (Josh. 15:54), where it is mentioned in the group around Hebron to the south. It has been identified with Ṣaʿir (Ṣiʿīr), 5 miles N. N. E. of Hebron.

Ziph (zĭf).

1. The eldest son of the four sons of Jehaleleel (I Chron. 4:16).

2. A town apparently in the south or Simeonite part of Judah (Josh. 15:24), mentioned with Ithnan and Telem. Identified with ez-Zeifeh, S. W. of Kurnūb.

3. A town in the desert (A. V. "wilderness") of Ziph, to which David fled from Saul (I Sam. 23:14, sq.; 26:2, 3); and was fortified by Rehoboam (II Chron. 11:8), having been originally built by Mesha, the son of Caleb (I Chron. 2:42). It has been preserved in the ruins of Tell Zîf, 4 miles S. E. of Hebron. The "wilderness of Ziph" was that portion of the desert of Judah which was near to and surrounded the town of Ziph.

Zi'phah (zī'fà; feminine of *Ziph*), the second son of Jehaleleel, and brother of the preceding (I Chron. 4:16).

Ziph'ims (zĭf'ĭms) (Psa. 54, *title*). See Ziphites.

Ziph'ion (zĭf'ĭ-ŏn) (Gen. 46:16). See Zephon.

Ziph'ites (zĭf'īts) (R. V. always "*Ziphites;*" I Sam. 23:19; 26:1; Psa. 54, *title*), inhabitants of Ziph, who twice revealed to Saul the hiding of David in their vicinity. The interesting events which happened at that place, the farewell interview between David and Jonathan, the sparing of Saul's life by David, and temporary relenting of Saul, belong rather to the geography or to the biographies of Saul and David. This Ziph was "in the highland district" in Judah; it is named between Carmel and Juttah (Josh. 15:55). The Ziph of v. 24 is a different place.—*W. H.* revised by *M. F. U.*

Ziph'ron (zĭf'rŏn), a place on the northern boundary of the Promised Land, and, consequently, of Naphtali (Num. 34:9), where it is mentioned between Zedad and Hazarenan. It is thought by Knobel and Wetstein to be preserved in the ruins of *Zifran*, northeast of Damascus, near the road from Palmyra. In the parallel passage (Ezek. 47:16) Hazarhatticon occurs in a similar connection.

Zip'por (zĭp'ôr; *bird, sparrow*), father of Balak, king of Moab. His name occurs only in the expression "son of Zippor" (Num. 22:2, 4, 10, 16; 23:18; Josh. 24:9; Judg. 11:25), B. C. c. 1400. Whether he was the "former king of Moab," alluded to in Num. 21:26, we are not told, nor do we know that he himself ever reigned.

Zippo'rah (zĭ-pō'rà; feminine of *Zippor, sparrow*), daughter of Reuel or Jethro, the priest of Midian, wife of Moses and mother of his two sons Gershom and Eliezer (Exod. 2:21; 4:25; 18:2; comp. v. 6), B. C. c. 1440. The only incident recorded in her life is that of the circumcision of Gershom (4:24-26). *See* Moses.

Zith'ri (zĭth'rī; *protective*), the son of Uzziel, and grandson of Kohath, of the tribe of Levi (Exod. 6:22). This is the only mention made of him in Scripture.

Ziv (zĭv), the second Jewish month approximating our May (A. V. Zif) (*q. v.*).

Ziz (zĭz; *a flower, a bright shining thing*), an ascent or cleft leading up from the Dead Sea toward Tekoa (II Chron. 20:16; comp. v. 20), by which the band of Moabites, Ammonites, and Mehunim, who attacked Jehoshaphat, made their way. There can be very little doubt that the pass was that of *Ain Jidy;* "the very same route which is taken by the Arabs in their marauding expeditions at the present day; along the shore as far as to *Ain Jidy*, and then up the pass, and so northward below Tekûa" (Robinson, *Bib. Res.*, i, 508, 530). The name, "ascent, or height of Hazziz," has perhaps remained attached to the *Wady el Haṣaṣah*, which leads from the W. shore of the Dead Sea N. of Engedi to the tableland of Judea.

Zi'za (zī'zả).

1. Son of Shiphi, a chief of the Simeonites in the reign of Hezekiah (I Chron. 4:37), B. C. about 719.

2. Son of Rehoboam by Maachah, the granddaughter of Absalom (II Chron. 11:20), B. C. after 934.

Zi'zah (zī'zả), a Gershonite Levite, second son of Shimei (I Chron. 23:11; called *Zina* in v. 10).

Zo'an (zō'ăn), a Delta city located on the eastern bank of the Tanitic branch of the Nile (Psa. 78:12, 43). This important royal store-city was built seven years after Hebron in Palestine (Num. 13:22). The name of this town under the Hyksos was Avaris. Raamses II later rebuilt the location and called it Raamses. The oppressed Israelites built the earlier site before it was named Raamses, according to the date of the Exodus, as preserved in the Massoretic Text (*See* Raamses). It is, therefore, clear that Zoan, Avaris and Tanis are names referring to the same site, or one contiguous. Zoan continued in importance until the time of Alexander the Great, whose brilliant city Alexandria stripped Tanis of its commercial importance. The modern village of San marks the ancient site. Excavations by Pierre Montet since 1930 have uncovered extensive buildings evidently erected by Hebrew slave labor. (*See* Exodus).—*M. F. U.*

Bible Notices. From the Bible we learn that Zoan was one of the oldest cities in Egypt, having been built seven years after Hebron, which already existed in the time of Abraham (Num. 13:22; comp. Gen. 22:2), B. C. about 2000; that it was one of the principal capitals of the Pharaohs (Isa. 19:11, 13); and that "the field of Zoan" was the scene of the marvelous works which God wrought at the hand of Moses (Psa. 78:12, 33). To Tanis came ambassadors either of Hoshea or Ahaz, or else possibly of Hezekiah: "For his princes were at Zoan, and his ambassadors came to Hanes" (Isa. 30:4). As mentioned with the frontier town Tahpanhes, Tanis is not necessarily the capital. But the same prophet, perhaps, more distinctly points to a Tanite line (19:13). The doom of Zoan is foretold by Ezekiel, "I will set fire in Zoan" (Ezek. 30:14), where it occurs among the cities to be taken by Nebuchadnezzar.

Zo'ar (zō'ẽr; *littleness, smallness*), one of the five cities which lay on the floor of the Jordan valley, after the name of which they were called *Cities of the Kikkar, or Circle*. It was one of the most ancient cities of the land of Canaan. Its original name was Bela (Gen. 14:2, 8). In the general destruction of the cities of the plain Zoar was spared to afford shelter to Lot (19:22, 23, 30). It is mentioned in the account of the death of Moses as one of the landmarks which bounded his view from Pis-

gah (Deut. 34:3), and it appears to have been known in the time both of Isaiah (15:5) and Jeremiah (48:34). These are all the notices of Zoar contained in the Bible. It was situated in the same district with the four cities already mentioned, viz., in the "plain" or "circle" "of the Jordan," and the narrative of Gen. 19 evidently implies that it was very near to Sodom (vers. 15, 23, 27). The position of Sodom is now known almost certainly to be at the S. extremity of the Dead Sea, and the 5 cities of the plain are doubtless under the waters of the shallow S. part of the Salt lake. *See* Sodom, Gomorrah.

Zo'bah (zō'bả), a portion of northern Syria lying between Hamath and the Euphrates, and so closely connected with Hamath that the great city was sometimes called Hamath-Zobah. Solomon, David, and Saul all had trouble with the people of Zobah (I Sam. 14:47; I Kings 11:23-25; II Sam. 8:3, 5, 12; 23:36; I Chron. 18:3, 5, 9; 19:6; II Chron. 8:3; Psa. 60).

Zoba. Archaeological location of Zoba to the N. of Damascus instead of S. of it has been an element in authenticating the historicity of I Kings, chaps. 3-11, which delineate Solomon's great power and glory. German scholars such as Hugo Winckler and Hermann Guthe showed a tendency to restrict the Davidic-Solomonic empire to Palestine proper, locating Hadadezer's conquered kingdom in Hauran, Biblical Bashan. Analysis of the Assyrian provincial organization, however, which was constucted on older foundations shows that Zoba (Assyrian *Subatu*) lay north, not south of Damascus. (E. Forrer, *Die Provinzeinteilung des Assyrischen Reiches*, 1921, pp. 62, 69). Egyptian lists and the Amarna Letters prove also that Hadadezer's chief cities, Tibhath and Khun, which David took in this region (I Chron. 18:18), were in this territory S. of Hums. Scientific research has thus substantiated the sprawling extent of Davidic-Solomonic territorial control and illustrated the reasonableness of the Biblical representations of Solomon's prosperity and splendor.— *M. F. U.*

Zobe'bah (zô-bē'bả), the second child (probably daughter, as the word is feminine) of Coz (Hakkoz) of the tribe of Judah (I Chron. 4:8).

Zo'har (zō'hảr; *whiteness*).

1. A Hittite, and father of Ephron, from which latter person Ephraim bought the grave of Machpelah (Gen. 23:8; 25:9).

2. Fifth named of the six sons of Simeon (Gen. 46:10; Exod. 6:15); elsewhere (I Chron. 4:24) called *Zerah*.

Zo'heleth (zō'hě-lěth; *serpent, slippery*), a rocky and dangerous ledge or plateau "by En-rogel" upon which Adonijah slew oxen and sheep (I Kings 1:9). It overhangs the Kidron valley. This has been most satisfactorily identified by M. Clermont Ganneau for the present Arab name *Zahweilah*, a cliff on which the village of Silwân or Silvam stands. To this the women of the village resort to draw water at the "Virgin's Fount."

Zo'heth (zō'hěth), son of Ishi, of the tribe of Judah (I Chron. 4:20).

Zo'phah (zō'fà; *bellied jug*, cf. Arab. *ṣuffaḥa, to make wide*), son of Helem, or Hotham, the son of Heber, an Asherite (I Chron. 7:35, 36).

Zo'phai (zō'fī), a Kohathite Levite, son of Elkanah and ancestor of Samuel (I Chron. 6:26), B. C. before 1050. In v. 35 he is called *Zuph.*

Zo'phar (zō'fĕr; perhaps *chirper*. Cf. Arab. *ṣafara, to whistle*), one of the three friends of Job (Job 2:11; 11:1; 20:1; 42:9). He is called a Naamathite, or inhabitant of Naamah, whose location is probably in N. Arabia. In the LXX. Zophar, the friend of Job, is called "king of the Minaeans."

Zo'phim (zō'fĭm; *watchers, field of watchers*). The "field of Zophim" was on the top of Pisgah (Num. 23:14), one of the high places to which Balak brought Balaam, that he might see Israel. It is the modern Tail'at eṣ Ṣufa.

Zo'rah (zō'rà; *stroke, scourge, hornet*), a town of Dan, but really within the limits of Judah (Josh. 19:41; Judg. 18:2). It was both the birthplace and burial place of Samson (Judg. 13:2, 25; 16:31), and afterward fortified by Rehoboam (II Chron. 11:10). It was on the hillside overlooking Sorek.

Zo'rathites (zō'rà-thīts), people of Zorah, a town in the lowland of Judah (Josh. 15:33, A. V. "Zoreah," R. V. "Zorah"), but assigned to Dan (19:41). In I Chron. 4:1, 2 the "families of the Zorathites" are descended from Ahumai and Lahad, sons of Jahath, the son of Reaiah, the son of Shobal, the son of Judah. The Hebrew word rendered in the A. V. mostly Zorah, but in Neh. 11:29 Zareah and in Josh. 15:33 Zoreah, is the same—ṣŏr'äh, R. V. always Zorah. So the Zorathites of I Chron. 4:2 and the Zareathites of I Chron. 2:53 are alike, "the Zorathite" (comp. "the Amalekite," etc.), R. V. "the Zorathites." If, as is likely, they refer to one people, it is better to read I Chron. 2:50 with the R. V., "These were the sons of Caleb; the son of Hur, the firstborn of Ephrathah, Shobal the father of Kirjath-jearim." The list of Judah's "sons" (I Chron. 4:1) will then be successive descendants. The "Zorites" of I Chron. 2:54 will belong to a separate branch.—W. H. revised by *M. F. U.*

Zo'reah (zō'rê-à) (Josh. 15:33). *See* Zorah.

Zo'rites, The (zō'rīts), are named in the genealogies of Judah (I Chron. 2:54) apparently among the descendants of Salma, and near connections of Joab. They are hence classed with the "Zareathites and the Eshtaulites (v. 53).

Zorob'abel (zō-rŏb'à-bĕl) (Matt. 1:12; Luke 3:27). *See* Zerubbabel.

Zu'ar (zū'ẽr; *small, little*), the father of Nethaneel, of the tribe of Issachar. Nethaneel was chief of his tribe at the time of the Exodus (Num. 1:8; 2:5; 7:18, 23; 10:15), B. C. before 1440.

Zuph (zŭf; *honeycomb*).

1. A Levite of the family of Kohath, and father of Tohu, in the ancestry of Samuel (I Sam. 1:1; I Chron. 6:35; "Zophai," v. 26).

2. A district at which Saul and his servant arrived after passing through those of Shalisha, of Shalim, and of the Benjamites (I Sam. 9:5 only). It evidently contained the city in which they encountered Samuel (v. 6), and that again was certainly not far from the "tomb of Rachel." The district apparently lay south of Benjamin. It has not been identified with certainty.

Zur (zûr; *a rock*).

1. Father of Cozbi (Num. 25:15), and one of the five princes of Midian who were slain by the Israelites when Balaam fell (31:8; Josh. 13:21), B. C. about 1380.

2. Son of Jehiel, the founder of Gibeon (I Chron. 8:30; 9:36).

Zu'riel (zū'rĭ-ĕl; *my rock is God*), son of Abihail, and chief of the Merarite Levites at the time of the Exodus (Num. 3:35), B. C. 1440.

Zurishad'dai (zū-rĭ-shăd'ī; *my rock is the Almighty*), father of Shelumiel, the chief of the tribe of Simeon at the time of the Exodus (Num. 1:6; 2:12; 7:36, 41; 10:19), B. C. 1440.

Zu'zim (zū'zĭm; only Gen. 14:5), the name of an ancient people dwelling in Ham, who were smitten by Chedorlaomer. The LXX. both manuscripts) has *'ethnē ischura*; the Targum of Onkelos and the Samaritan version also translate the name "strong people." This rendering depends upon some different Hebrew reading, possibly '*azzuzim*. Sayce thinks it originated in a transcription of a cuneiform rendering of Zamzummim. It is quite generally suspected to be an abridgement of Zamzummim (*q. v.*).—W. H. revised by *M. F. U.*